CW00402200

SOCIAL SECURITY LEGISLATION 2009/10

VOLUME III: ADMINISTRATION, ADJUDICATION AND THE EUROPEAN DIMENSION

SOCIAL SECURITY LEGISLATION 2009/10

General Editor
David Bonner, LL.B, LL.M

VOLUME III:
ADMINISTRATION,
ADJUDICATION AND THE
EUROPEAN DIMENSION

Commentary By

Mark Rowland, LL.B.
Judge of the Upper Tribunal

Robin White, M.A., LL.M.
Professor of Law, University of Leicester
Deputy Judge of the Upper Tribunal

Consultant Editor
Child Poverty Action Group

SWEET & MAXWELL

THOMSON REUTERS

Published in 2009 by
Thomson Reuters (Legal) Limited (Registered in England and Wales,
Company No 1679046. Registered office and address for service:
100 Avenue Road, Swiss Cottage,
London NW3 3PF, trading as Sweet & Maxwell)

For further information on our products and services, visit
http://www.sweetandmaxwell.co.uk

Typeset by Servis Filmsetting Ltd, Stockport, Cheshire
Printed and bound in Great Britain
by Ashford Colour Press, Gosport, Hants

ISBN 978-0-414-04118-9

No natural forests were destroyed to make this product;
only farmed timber was used and replanted.

A CIP catalogue record for this book is
available from the British Library

All rights reserved. Crown Copyright Legislation is reproduced under the
terms of Crown Copyright Policy Guidance issued by HMSO.

No part of this publication may be reproduced or transmitted in any form
or by any means, or stored in any retrieval system of any nature without
prior written permission, except for permitted fair dealing under the
Copyright, Designs and Patents Act 1988, or in accordance with the terms
of a licence issued by the Copyright Licensing Agency in respect of photo-
copying and/or reprographic reproduction. Application for permission for
other use of copyright material including permission to reproduce extracts
in other published works shall be made to the publishers. Full acknowledgment of author, publisher and source must be given.

Application for permission for other use of copyright material controlled
by the publisher shall be made to the publishers. Material is contained in
this publication for which publishing permission has been sought, and for
which copyright is acknowledged. Permission to reproduce such material
cannot be granted by the publishers and application must be made to the
copyright holder.

Thomson Reuters and the Thomson Reuters logo are trademarks of
Thomson Reuters. Sweet & Maxwell® is a registered trademark of
Thomson Reuters (Legal) Limited.

Commentators have asserted their moral rights under the Copyright,
Designs and Patents Act 1988 to be identified as the authors of the
commentary in this Volume.

© 2009 Thomson Reuters (Legal) Limited

CHILD POVERTY ACTION GROUP

The Child Poverty Action Group (CPAG) is a charity, founded in 1965, which campaigns for the relief of poverty in the United Kingdom. It has a particular reputation in the field of welfare benefits law derived from its legal work, publications, training and parliamentary and policy work, and is widely recognised as the leading organisation for taking test cases on social security law.

CPAG is therefore ideally placed to act as Consultant Editor to this 4-volume work—**Social Security Legislation 2009/10**. CPAG is not responsible for the detail of what is contained in each volume, and the authors' views are not necessarily those of CPAG. The Consultant Editor's role is to act in an advisory capacity on the overall structure, focus and direction of the work.

For more information about CPAG, its rights and policy publications or training courses, its address is 94 White Lion Street, London, N1 9PF (telephone: 020 7837 7979—website: *http://www.cpag.org.uk*).

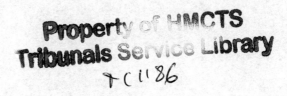
Property of HMCTS
Tribunals Service Library
TC 1186

FOREWORD

I am especially pleased to be invited to write a Foreword to this work, because I am in a position to offer my personal endorsement of its immense worth, having been an appreciative reader since John Mesher's first edition in 1984.

The statute-derived law of social security is extensive, dynamic and notoriously complex. The case-law is profuse. The European dimension adds a further layer of difficulty. A practitioner's guide which not only assembles the diverse law but also supplies a detailed, lucid and balanced commentary from a widely-respected team of authors is indispensable.

This work is a staple resource for our tribunals. I commend it to all who need a serious understanding of the law of social security.

HHJ Robert Martin
President of the Social Entitlement Chamber
First-tier Tribunal

PREFACE

Administration, Adjudication and the European Dimension is Volume III of the four volume series, Social Security Legislation 2009/10. The companion volumes are *Volume I: Non Means Tested Benefits and Employment and Support Allowance; Volume II: Income Support, Jobseeker's Allowance, State Pension Credit and the Social Fund; and Volume IV: Tax Credits and HMRC-administered Social Security Benefits.* The "year" in the title of the works now relates to a tax/contribution year, which better conveys the period the books (and the *Supplement*) are designed to cover.

Each of the volumes in the series provides a legislative text, clearly showing the form and date of amendments and up to date to April 13, 2009. The commentary in this volume includes references to some later case law.

Tribunal reform, heralded in Part V of last year's edition, has led to the absorption of what were the appeal tribunals and the Social Security Commissioners into the First-tier Tribunal and the Upper Tribunal. The creation of those new tribunals has in turn led to more legislation and, in particular, Tribunal Procedure Rules. Although not specifically social security legislation, those provisions concerned with the powers of tribunals and their procedures and practice have been included in this volume in an expanded Part V. Such provisions are obviously important to those concerned with social security adjudication, but the opportunity has been taken to omit general provisions relating to judicial appointments, the administration of tribunals and most of the mechanics of the transfer of functions from the old tribunals.

Provisions specific to social security administration or adjudication have been retained as far as possible in this volume, in Parts I and II, but where a separate scheme exists for particular types of payments, it has sometimes been more practical to retain some procedural provisions alongside the substantive provisions in Vol.I (see, for example, the procedural provisions relating to vaccine damage payments and the new mesothelioma scheme).

This year's edition incorporates all the consequential changes to the legislation in Parts I and II required by the introduction of the mesothelioma scheme and, more importantly, employment and support allowance. In addition, there is much new case law which has been reflected in revisions to the commentary on a wide range of topics. The maturity of some of the case law on the European side has resulted in a complete re-write of some of the commentary in Parts III and IV, concerning European Union Law and Human Rights Law.

As always, revising and updating the legislative text and commentary has required considerable flexibility on the part of the publisher and a great deal of help from a number of sources, including CPAG as advisory editor to the series, for which we express sincere thanks. Particular mention must be made here of the debt owed by all of us to John Mesher, who began the provision of annotated legislation for tribunals, has given wise advice on the development of this series, and who happily remains on call as consultant in respect of Vol.II.

To maximise space for explanatory commentary we have provided lists of definitions only where the commentary to the provision is substantial, or where reference to definitions is essential for a proper understanding. Users of this book should always check whether particular words or phrases they are called on to apply have a particular meaning ascribed to them in legislation. Generally the first or second regulation in each set of regulations contains definitions of key terms (check the "Arrangement of Regulations" at the beginning of each set for an indication of the subject matter covered by each regulation or Schedule). There are also definition or "interpretation" sections in each of the Acts (check the "Arrangement of Sections" at the beginning of each Act for an indication of the subject matter covered by each section or Schedule).

Users of the series, and its predecessor works, have over the years provided valuable comments which have invariably been helpful to the editors in ensuring that the selection of legislative material for inclusion and the commentary upon it reflect the sorts of difficulties encountered in practice. In doing so, readers have thus helped to shape the content of each of the volumes in the current series. We hope that readers will maintain that tradition. Please write to the General Editor of the series, David Bonner, School of Law, University of Leicester, University Road, Leicester, LE1 7RH, who will pass on any comments received to the appropriate commentator.

Our gratitude must also go to the new President of the Social Entitlement Chamber of the First-tier Tribunal and his staff for continuing the tradition of help and encouragement.

Mark Rowland
Robin White

CONTENTS

Contents

USING THIS BOOK: AN INTRODUCTION TO
LEGISLATION AND CASE LAW

Introduction

This book is not a general introduction to, or general textbook on, the law relating to social security but it is nonetheless concerned with both of the principal sources of social security law – *legislation* (both primary and secondary) and *case law*. It sets out the text of the most important legislation, as currently in force, and then there is added commentary that refers to the relevant case law. Lawyers will be familiar with this style of publication, which inevitably follows the structure of the legislation.

This note is designed primarily to assist readers who are not lawyers to find their way around the legislation and to understand the references to case law, but information it contains about how to find social security case law is intended to be of assistance to lawyers too.

Primary legislation

Primary legislation of the United Kingdom Parliament consists of *Acts of Parliament* (also known as *Statutes*). They will have been introduced to Parliament as *Bills*. There are opportunities for Members of Parliament and peers to debate individual clauses and to vote on amendments before a Bill is passed and becomes an Act (at which point the clauses become sections). No tribunal or court has the power to disapply, or hold to be invalid, an Act of Parliament unless it is inconsistent with European Community law.

An Act is known by its "short title", which incorporates the year in which it was passed (e.g. the Social Security Contributions and Benefits Act 1992), and is given a chapter number (abbreviated as, for instance, "c.4" indicating that the Act was the fourth passed in that year). It is seldom necessary to refer to the chapter number but it appears in the running heads in this book.

Each *section* (abbreviated as "s." or, in the plural, "ss.") of an Act is numbered and may be divided into *subsections* (abbreviated as "subs." and represented by a number in brackets), which in turn may be divided into *paragraphs* (abbreviated as "para." and represented by a lower case letter in brackets) and *subparagraphs* (abbreviated as "subpara." and represented by a small roman numeral in brackets). Subparagraph (ii) of para.(a) of subs. (1) of s.72 will usually be referred to simply as "s.72(1)(a)(ii)". Upper case letters may be used where additional sections or subsections are inserted by amendment and additional lower case letters may be used where new paragraphs and subparagraphs are inserted. This accounts for the rather ungainly s.171ZS of the Social Security Contributions and Benefits Act 1992 (in Vol.IV).

Sections of a large Act may be grouped into a numbered *Part*, which may even be divided into *Chapters*. It is not usual to refer to a Part or a Chapter unless referring to the whole Part or Chapter.

Where a section would otherwise become unwieldy because it is neces-sary to include a list or complicated technical provisions, the section may simply refer to a *Schedule* at the end of the Act. A Schedule (abbreviated as "Sch.") may be divided into paragraphs and subparagraphs and further divided into heads and subheads. Again, it is usual to refer simply to, say, "para.23(3)(b)(ii) of Schedule 3". Whereas it is conventional to speak of a section *of* an Act, it is usual to speak of a Schedule *to* an Act.

When Parliament wishes to change the law, it may do so by passing a new Act that amends a previous Act or it may do so by passing a freestanding Act, although even then consequential amendments to other legislation are usually required. Thus, for instance, when incapacity benefit was intro-duced by the Social Security (Incapacity for Work) Act 1994, the changes were largely made by inserting sections 30A to 30E and Part XIIA into the Social Security Contributions and Benefits Act 1992 and repealing the provisions in that Act dealing with sickness and invalidity benefit. In contrast, when jobseeker's allowance was introduced by the Jobseekers Act 1995, it was decided that the main provisions relating to the new benefit would be found in the 1995 Act itself and the 1992 Act was amended only so as to repeal, or amend, the provisions dealing with, or referring to, unemployment benefit.

When there has been a proliferation of Acts or Acts have been very sub-stantially amended, the legislation may be consolidated in a new Act, for which there is a fast track procedure in Parliament. Only limited amend-ments may be made by a consolidation Act but such an Act reorganises and tidies up the legislation. Because social security law is so frequently amended, it tends to be consolidated every decade or two. The last consoli-dation Acts relevant to this book were the Social Security Contributions and Benefits Act 1992 (in Vols I and II) and the Social Security Administration Act 1992 (in this volume).

Secondary legislation

Secondary legislation (also known as *subordinate legislation* or *delegated legisla-tion*) is made by *statutory instrument* in the form of a set of *Regulations* or a set of *Rules* or an *Order*. The power to make such legislation is conferred on ministers and other persons or bodies by Acts of Parliament. To the extent that a statutory instrument is made beyond the powers (in Latin, *ultra vires*) conferred by primary legislation, it may be held by a tribunal or court to be invalid and ineffective. Secondary legislation must be laid before Parliament. However, most secondary legislation is not debated in Parliament and, even when it is, it cannot be amended although an entire statutory instrument may be rejected.

A set of Regulations or Rules or an Order has a name indicating its scope and the year it was made and also a number, as in the Social Security (Disability Living Allowance) Regulations 1991 (SI 1991/2890) (the 2890th statutory instrument issued in 1991). Because there are over 3,000 statu-tory instruments each year, the number of a particular statutory instrument is important as a means of identification and it should usually be cited the first time reference is made to that statutory instrument.

Sets of Regulations or Rules are made up of individual *regulations* (abbre-viated as "reg.") or *rules* (abbreviated as "r." or, in the plural, "rr."). An Order is made up of *articles* (abbreviated as "art."). Regulations, rules and articles may be divided into paragraphs, subparagraphs and heads. As in Acts, a set of Regulations or Rules or an Order may have one or more Schedules attached to it. The style of numbering used in statutory instruments is the same as in sections of, and Schedules to, Acts of Parliament. As in Acts, a large statutory instrument may have regulations or rules grouped into Parts and, occasionally, Chapters. Statutory instruments may be amended in the same sort of way as Acts.

Northern Ireland legislation

Most of the legislation set out in this book applies only in Great Britain, social security not generally being an excepted or reserved matter in relation to Northern Ireland. However, Orders in Council, which are statutory instruments but have the effect of primary legislation in Northern Ireland, largely replicate the primary legislation in Great Britain and enable subordinate legislation to be made that, again, largely replicates the subordinate legislation in Great Britain. Much of the commentary in this book will therefore be relevant to the equivalent provision in Northern Ireland legislation.

European Community legislation

The United Kingdom being a Member State of the European Union, European Community legislation has effect within the United Kingdom. The primary legislation is in the form of the *Treaties* agreed by the Member States. Relevant subordinate legislation is in the form of *Regulations*, adopted to give effect to provisions of the Treaties, and *Directives*, addressed to Member States and requiring them to incorporate certain provisions into their domestic laws. Directives are relevant because, where a citizen brings proceedings against an organ of the state, as is invariably the case where social security is concerned, the citizen may rely on the Directive as having direct effect if the Member State has failed to comply with it. European Community Treaties, Regulations and Directives are divided into *Articles* (abbreviated as "Art."). United Kingdom legislation that is inconsistent with European Community legislation may be disapplied. The most relevant provisions of European Community legislation are set out in Part III of this volume.

Finding legislation in this book

If you know the name of the piece of legislation for which you are looking, use the list of contents at the beginning of each volume of this book which lists the pieces of legislation contained in the volume. That will give you the paragraph reference to enable you to find the beginning of the piece of legislation. Then, it is easy to find the relevant section, regulation, rule, article or Schedule by using the running heads on the right hand pages. If you do not know the name of the piece of legislation, you will probably need to use the index at the end of the volume in order to find the relevant paragraph number but will then be taken straight to a particular provision.

The legislation is set out as amended, the amendments being indicated by numbered sets of square brackets. The numbers refer to the numbered entries under the heading "AMENDMENTS" at the end of the relevant section, regulation, rule, article or Schedule, which identify the amending statute or statutory instrument. Where an Act has been consolidated, there is a list of "DERIVATIONS" identifying the provisions of earlier legislation from which the section or Schedule has been derived.

Finding other legislation

Legislation in its unamended form may be found on *http://www.opsi.gov.uk/ legislation/*. Obscure provisions of Great Britain social security legislation not included in this book may be found, as amended, but without commentary, at *http://www.dwp.gov.uk/publications/specialist-guides/law-volumes/*. Northern Ireland social security legislation may be found at *http://www.dsdni.gov.uk/ law_relating_to_social_security*. European Community legislation may be found at *http://eur-lex.europa.eu/en/index.htm*.

Interpreting legislation

Legislation is written in English and generally means what it says. However, more than one interpretation is often possible. Most legislation itself contains definitions. Sometimes these are in the particular provision in which a word occurs but, where a word is used in more than one place, any definition will appear with others. In an Act, an interpretation section is usually to be found towards the end of the Act or of the relevant Part of the Act. In a statutory instrument, an interpretation provision usually appears near the beginning of the statutory instrument or the relevant Part of it. In the more important pieces of legislation in this book, there is included after every section, regulation, rule, article or Schedule a list of "DEFINITIONS", showing where definitions of words used in the provision are to be found.

However, not all words are statutorily defined and there is in any event more to interpreting legislation than merely defining its terms. Decision-makers and tribunals need to know how to apply the law in different types of situations. That is where case law comes in.

Case law and the commentary in this book

In deciding individual cases, courts and tribunals interpret the relevant law and incidentally establish legal principles. Decisions on questions of legal principle of the superior courts and appellate tribunals are said to be binding on decision-makers and the First-tier Tribunal, which means that decision-makers and the First-tier Tribunal must apply those principles. Thus the judicial decisions of the superior courts and appellate tribunals form part of the law. The commentary to the legislation in this book, under the heading "GENERAL NOTE" after a section, regulation, rule, article or Schedule, refers to this *case law*.

The commentary itself in this book is not binding on any decision-maker or tribunal because it is merely the opinion of the author. It is what is actually said in the legislation or in the judicial decision that is important. The legislation is set out in this book, but it will generally be necessary to look elsewhere for the precise words used in judicial decisions. The commentary refers to decisions in a way that enables that to be done.

The largest part of the case law regarding social security benefits is still in the form of decisions of the former Social Security Commissioners and former Child Support Commissioners, who heard appeals from decisions of appeal tribunals. However, on November 3, 2008, when the functions of appeal tribunals were transferred to the First-tier Tribunal, the functions of the Social Security Commissioners and Child Support Commissioners in Great Britain were transferred to the Upper Tribunal and allocated to the Administrative Appeals Chamber of that tribunal. In Northern Ireland, which has a largely separate judiciary and tribunal system, there continue to be Commissioners.

The reporting of decisions of the Upper Tribunal and Commissioners

About 50 of the most important social entitlement decisions of the Administrative Appeals Chamber of the Upper Tribunal are selected to be "reported" each year, using the same criteria as were formerly used for reporting Commissioners' decisions in Great Britain. The selection is made by an editorial board of judges and decisions are selected for reporting only if they are of general importance and command the assent of at least a majority of the relevant judges (i.e. currently, the former Commissioners). The term "reported" simply means that they are published in printed form and on the internet (see *Finding case law*, below) with headnotes (i.e. summaries) and an index, but there are two other important consequences of a decision being reported. Reported decisions are available in all tribunal venues and can be consulted in local social security offices and some main libraries. They also have a greater precedential status than ordinary decisions (see *Judicial precedent* below).

A handful of Northern Ireland Commissioners' decisions are also selected for reporting each year, the selection being made by the Chief Social Security Commissioner in Northern Ireland.

Citing case law

Unreported decisions of the Commissioners in Great Britain were known simply by their file number, which began with a "C", as in *CIS/2287/2008*. The letters following the "C" indicated the type of benefit in issue in the case (e.g. "IS" is income support, "P" is retirement pension, and so on). Scottish and, at one time, Welsh cases were indicated by a "S" or "W" immediately after the "C", as in *CSIS/467/2007*. The last four digits indicated the calendar year in which the case was registered, rather than the year it was decided. A similar system still operates in Northern Ireland, save that the letters indicating the type of benefit appear in brackets after the numbers and, in recent years, the financial year, rather the calendar year, has been identified, as in *C 10/06-07 (IS)*.

Reported decisions of Commissioners were then given a different number, beginning with an "R". The type of benefit in issue was indicated by letters in brackets and the year in which the decision was selected for reporting or, since 2000, the year in which it was published as a reported decision, was indicated just by two digits, as in *R(IS) 2/08*. Scottish and Welsh reported decisions were not distinguished in any way. Again, in Northern Ireland there is a similar system, save that the type of benefit is identified by letters in brackets after the number, as in *R 1/07 (DLA)*.

When they are first registered, Upper Tribunal social security cases are given the same sort of file number as Commissioners' cases were but, once a case is decided, it ceases to be known by that number. Instead, the case is known by the names of the appellant and respondent (or one of each if there was more than one), with the names of individuals anonymised through the use of letters, and it is given a *neutral citation number*, indicating the year and the tribunal that made the decision. "UKUT" stands for the Upper Tribunal and "(AAC)" stands for the Administrative Appeals

Chamber. In this book, the names of official bodies are also abbreviated (e.g. SSWP (for Secretary of State for Work and Pensions), HMRC (for Her Majesty's Revenue and Customs) and CMEC (for the Child Maintenance and Enforcement Commission). Thus, one case is *SSWP v JJ* [2009] UKUT 2 (AAC). For the 2009 volume of reported decisions, the same style of number is used for Upper Tribunal decisions as was used for Commissioners' decisions and, when a reported decision is being cited, this should be added after the neutral citation number. *NT v SSWP* [2009] UKUT 37 (AAC); R(DLA) 1/09 is one example.

Decisions of courts are also known by the parties' names (not usually anonymised) and, since 2001, a neutral citation number ("EWCA Civ" for the Civil Division of the Court of Appeal in England and Wales, "NICA" for the Court of Appeal in Northern Ireland, "CSIH" for the Inner House of the Court of Session (in Scotland), "UKHL" for the House of Lords, and so on). If the case is reported, a reference to the relevant set of law reports usually follows. Conventionally, this includes either the year the case was decided (in round brackets) or the year in which it was reported (in square brackets), followed by the volume number (if any), the name of the series of reports (in abbreviated form, so see the Table of Abbreviations at the beginning of each volume of this book) and the page number. *Abdirahman v Secretary of State for Work and Pensions* [2007] EWCA Civ 657; [2008] 1 W.L.R. 254 (also reported as *R(IS) 8/07*) was a Court of Appeal decision, decided in 2007 but reported in 2008 in volume 1 of the Weekly Law Reports at page 254 (and also in the 2007 volume of reported Commissioners' decisions).

It is only necessary to include the neutral citation number or a reference to a series of reports the first time a decision is cited. After that, the name of the case is usually sufficient.

All decisions on the Tribunals Service website have neutral citation numbers. If you wish to refer a tribunal or decision-maker to a decision of the Upper Tribunal that does not have a neutral citation number, contact the office of the Administrative Appeals Chamber (*adminappeals@tribunals.gsi.gov.uk*) who will provide a number and add the decision to the website.

Decision-makers and claimants are entitled to assume that judges and other members of both the First-tier Tribunal and the Upper Tribunal have immediate access to reported decisions of Commissioners or the Upper Tribunal and they need not provide copies, although it may sometimes be helpful to do so. However, where either a decision-maker or a claimant intends to rely on an unreported decision, it will be necessary to provide a copy of the decision to the judge and any other members of the tribunal. A copy of the decision should also be provided to the other party before the hearing because otherwise it may be necessary for there to be an adjournment to enable that party to take advice on the significance of the decision.

Finding case law

The extensive references described above are used so as to enable people easily to find the full text of a decision. Most decisions of any significance since the late 1990s can be found on the internet.

Decisions of the Commissioners in Great Britain and of the Upper Tribunal may be found on the Tribunals Service website at *http://www.*

administrativeappeals.tribunals.gov.uk/Decisions/decisions.htm. This includes reported decisions since 1991 and other decisions considered likely to be of interest to tribunals and tribunal users since about 2000. Decisions of Commissioners in Northern Ireland may be found on *http://www.dsdni.gov. uk/index/law_and_legislation.htm*.

In addition, reported decisions of Commissioners in Great Britain were published in bound volumes by The Stationery Office and in loose-leaf form by Corporate Document Services, 7 Eastgate, Leeds LS2 7LY (CDS Orderline: tel 0113 3994040) on behalf of the Department for Work and Pensions. The Department reproduce the looseleaf version on the internet (*http://www.dwp.gov.uk/publications/specialist-guides/decisions-of-the-commissioners/*), so reported decisions may be found both there and on the Tribunals Service website. Decisions of the Upper Tribunal are being included in the 2009 bound and looseleaf volumes.

Reported decisions of the Northern Ireland Commissioners are published by The Stationery Office, in the same bound volumes as Great Britain decisions since 2000 and in separate volumes before then. The Stationery Office also publishes individual Northern Ireland decisions in looseleaf form.

Copies of decisions of Commissioners or of the Administrative Appeals Chamber of the Upper Tribunal that are otherwise unavailable may be obtained from the offices of the Upper Tribunal (Administrative Appeals Chamber) or, in Northern Ireland, from the Office of the Social Security and Child Support Commissioners.

Decisions of courts in the United Kingdom may be found on, or through links from, the free website of the British and Irish Legal Information Institute, *http://www.bailii.org/*, which also carries several Northern Ireland Commissioners' decisions. It provides fairly comprehensive coverage of decisions of the House of Lords (through a link to *http://www.publications. parliament.uk/pa/ld/ldjudgmt.htm*) and most of the higher courts in England and Wales since about 1996, decisions of the Court of Session since 1998 and decisions of the Court of Appeal in Northern Ireland since 2000 (although some earlier decisions have been included, so it is always worth looking).

Decisions of the European Court of Justice (concerned with the law of the European Community) are all to be found on *http://www.curia. europa.eu*.

Decisions of the European Court of Human Rights are available at *http:// www.echr.coe.int*, using the HUDOC database.

Most decisions of the courts in social security cases, including decisions of the European Court of Justice on cases referred by United Kingdom courts and tribunals, are reported with the decisions of the Commissioners and Upper Tribunal and may therefore be found on the same websites and in the same printed series of reported decisions. So, for example, *R(I) 1/00* contains Commissioner's decisions *CSI/12/1998*, the decision of the Court of Session upholding the Commissioner's decision and the decision of the House of Lords in *Chief Adjudication Officer v Faulds* reversing the decision of the Court of Session. The most important decisions of the courts can also be found in the various series of law reports familiar to lawyers (in particular, in the *Law Reports*, the *Weekly Law Reports*, the *All England Law Reports*, the *Public and Third Sector Law Reports*, the *Industrial Cases Reports* and the *Family Law Reports*) but these are not widely available outside academic or other law libraries, although the *All England Law Reports* are occasionally to be found in the larger public libraries. See the Table of Cases at the beginning of each volume of this book for all the places where a decision mentioned in that volume is reported.

If you know the name or number of a decision and wish to know where in a volume of this book there is a reference to it, use the Table of Cases, the Table of Upper Tribunal Decisions or the Table of Social Security Commissioners' Decisions at the beginning of the relevant volume to find the paragraph(s) where the decision is mentioned.

Judicial precedent

As already mentioned, decisions of the Upper Tribunal, the Commissioners and the higher courts in Great Britain become *case law* because they set binding precedents and which must be followed by decision-makers and the First-tier Tribunal in Great Britain. This means that, where the Upper Tribunal, Commissioner or court has decided a point of legal principle, decision-makers and appeal tribunals must make their decisions in conformity with the decision of the Upper Tribunal, Commissioner or court, applying the same principle and accepting the interpretation of the law contained in the decision. So a decision of the Upper Tribunal, a Commissioner or a superior court explaining what a term in a particular regulation means, lays down the definition of that term in much the same way as if the term had been defined in the regulations themselves. The decision may also help in deciding what the same term means when it is used in a different set of regulations, provided that the term appears to have been used in a similar context.

Only decisions on points of law set precedents that are binding and, strictly speaking, only decisions on points of law that were necessary to the overall conclusion reached by the Upper Tribunal, Commissioner or court are binding. Other parts of a decision (which used to be known as *obiter dicta*) may be regarded as helpful guidance but need not be followed if a decision-maker or the First-tier Tribunal is persuaded that there is a better approach. It is particularly important to bear this in mind in relation to older decisions of Social Security Commissioners because, until 1987, the right of appeal to a Commissioner was not confined to points of law.

Where there is a conflict between precedents, a decision-maker or the First-tier Tribunal is generally free to choose between decisions of equal status. For these purposes, most decisions of the Upper Tribunal and decisions of Commissioners are of equal status. However, a decision-maker or First-tier Tribunal should generally prefer a reported decision to an unreported one unless the unreported decision was the later decision and the Commissioner or Upper Tribunal expressly decided not to follow the earlier reported decision. This is simply because the fact that a decision has been reported shows that at least half of the relevant judges of the Upper Tribunal or the Commissioners agreed with it at the time. A decision of a Tribunal of Commissioners (i.e. three Commissioners sitting together) or a decision of a three-judge panel of the Upper Tribunal must be preferred to a decision of a single Commissioner or a single judge of the Upper Tribunal.

A single judge of the Upper Tribunal will normally follow a decision of a single Commissioner or another judge of the Upper Tribunal, but is not bound to do so. A three-judge panel of the Upper Tribunal will generally follow a decision of another such panel or of a Tribunal of Commissioners, but similarly is not bound to do so, whereas a single judge of the Upper Tribunal will always follow such a decision.

Strictly speaking, the Northern Ireland Commissioners do not set binding precedent that must be followed in Great Britain but their decisions are relevant, due to the similarity of the legislation in Northern Ireland, and are usually regarded as highly persuasive with the result that, in practice, they are generally given as much weight as decisions of the Great Britain Commissioners. The same approach is taken in Northern Ireland to decisions of the Upper Tribunal on social security matters and to decisions of the Great Britain Commissioners.

Decisions of the superior courts in Great Britain and Northern Ireland on questions of legal principle are almost invariably followed by decision-makers, tribunals and the Upper Tribunal, even when they are not strictly binding because the relevant court was in a different part of the United Kingdom or exercised a parallel – but not superior – jurisdiction.

Decisions of the European Court of Justice come in two parts: the Opinion of the Advocate General and the decision of the Court. It is the decision of the Court which is binding. The Court is assisted by hearing the Opinion of the Advocate General before itself coming to a conclusion on the issue before it. The Court does not always follow its Advocate General. Where it does, the Opinion of the Advocate General often elaborates the arguments in greater detail than the single collegiate judgment of the Court. Decision-makers, tribunals and Commissioners must apply decisions of the European Court of Justice, where relevant to cases before them, in preference to other authorities binding on them.

The European Court of Human Rights in Strasbourg is quite separate from the European Court of Justice in Luxembourg and serves a different purpose: interpreting and applying the European Convention on Human Rights, which is incorporated into United Kingdom law by the Human Rights Act 1998. Since October 2, 2000, public authorities in the United Kingdom, including courts, Commissioners, tribunals and decision-makers have been required to act in accordance with the incorporated provisions of the Convention, unless statute prevents this. They must take into account the Strasbourg case law and are required to interpret domestic legislation, so far as it is possible to do so, to give effect to the incorporated Convention rights. Any court or tribunal may declare secondary legislation incompatible with those rights and, in certain circumstances, invalidate it. Only the higher courts can declare a provision of primary legislation to be incompatible with those rights, but no court, tribunal or Upper Tribunal can invalidate primary legislation. The work of the Strasbourg Court and the impact of the Human Rights Act 1998 on social security are discussed in the commentary in Part IV of this volume.

See the note to s.3(2) of the Tribunals, Courts and Enforcement Act 2007 in Part V of this volume for a more detailed and technical consideration of the rules of precedent.

Other sources of information and commentary on social security law

For a comprehensive overview of the social security system in Great Britain, CPAG's *Welfare Benefits and Tax Credits Handbook*, published annually each spring, is unrivalled as a practical introduction from the claimant's viewpoint.

From a different perspective, the Department for Work and Pensions publishes a number of guides to the law and to the way it applies the law, available at *http://www.dwp.gov.uk/publications/specialist-guides/*, the most important of which is the fourteen-volume *Decision Makers' Guide*. Similarly, Her Majesty's Revenue and Customs publish manuals relating to tax credits, child benefit and guardian's allowance, which they administer, see *http://www.hmrc.gov.uk/thelibrary/manuals-subjectarea.htm*. (Note that the *Child Benefit Technical Manual* (also dealing with guardian's allowance) is found under the heading "personal taxation".) These guides and manuals are extremely useful but their interpretation of the law is not binding on tribunals and the courts, being merely internal guidance for the use of decision-makers.

There are a number of other sources of valuable information or commentary on social security case law: see in particular publications such as the *Journal of Social Security Law*, CPAG's *Welfare Rights Bulletin, Legal Action* and the *Adviser*. As far as online resources go there is little to beat *Rightsnet* (*http://www.rightsnet.org.uk*). This site contains a wealth of resources for people working in the welfare benefits field but of special relevance in this context are Commissioners'/Upper Tribunal Decisions section of the "Toolkit" area and also the "Briefcase" area which contains summaries of the decisions (with links to the full decisions). Sweet and Maxwell's online subscription service *Westlaw* is another valuable source (*http://www.westlaw. co.uk*), as is the Merrill Corporation's *Casetrack* (*http://www.casetrack.com/ ct/casetrack.nsf/index?openframeset*) and LexisNexis *Lexis* (*http://www.lexis. com*).

Conclusion

The internet provides a vast resource but a search needs to be focused. Social security schemes are essentially statutory and so in Great Britain the legislation which is set out in this book forms the basic structure of social security law. However, the case law shows how the legislation should be interpreted and applied. The commentary in this book should point the way to the case law relevant to each provision and the Internet can then be used to find it where that is necessary.

CHANGE OF NAME FROM DEPARTMENT OF SOCIAL SECURITY TO DEPARTMENT FOR WORK AND PENSIONS

The Secretaries of State for Education and Skills and for Work and Pensions Order 2002 (SI 2002/1397) makes provision for the change of name from the Department of Social Security to Department for Work and Pensions. Article 9(5) provides:

"(5) Subject to article 12 [which makes specific amendments], any enactment or instrument passed or made before the coming into force of this Order shall have effect, so far as may be necessary for the purposes of or in consequence of the entrusting to the Secretary of State for Work and Pensions of the social security functions, as if any reference to the Secretary of State for Social Security, to the Department of Social Security or to an officer of the Secretary of State for Social Security (including any reference which is to be construed as such as reference) were a reference to the Secretary of State for Work and Pensions, to the Department for Work and Pensions or, as the case may be, to an officer of the Secretary of State for Work and Pensions."

TABLE OF CASES

Table of Cases

Table of Cases

Table of Cases

Table of Cases

TABLE OF UPPER TRIBUNAL DECISIONS

TABLE OF SOCIAL SECURITY COMMISSIONERS' DECISIONS

TABLE OF ABBREVIATIONS USED IN THIS SERIES

(No.2) Regulations	Statutory Paternity Pay (Adoption) and Statutory Adoption Pay (Adoptions from Overseas) (No.2) Regulations 2003
1978 Act	Employment Protection (Consolidation) Act 1978
1998 Act	Social Security Act 1998
2002 Act	Tax Credits Act 2002
2004 Act	Child Trust Funds Act 2004
AA	Attendance Allowance
AAC	Administrative Appeal Chamber
AA 1992	Attendance Allowance Act 1992
AA Regulations	Social Security (Attendance Allowance) Regulations 1991
A.C.	Law Reports Appeal Cases
A.C.D.	Administrative Court Digest
ADHD	Attention Deficit Hyperactivity Disorder
Adjudication Regs	Social Security (Adjudication) Regulations 1986
Admin L.R.	Administrative Law Reports
Administration Act	Social Security Administration Act 1992
AIDS	Acquired Immune Deficiency Syndrome
All E.R.	All England Reports
All E.R. (E.C.)	All England Reports (European Cases)
AMA	Adjudicating Medical Authority
AO	Adjudication Officer
AOG	*Adjudication Officers' Guide*
ASPP	Additional Statutory Paternity Pay
A.T.C.	Annotated Tax Cases
Attendance Allowance Regulations	Social Security (Attendance Allowance) Regulations 1991
BAMS	Benefits Agency Medical Service
Benefits Act	Social Security Contributions and Benefits Act 1992
B.H.R.C.	Butterworths Human Rights Cases
B.L.G.R.	Butterworths Local Government Reports
Blue Books	*The Law Relating to Social Security*, Vols 1–11
B.M.L.R.	Butterworths Medico Legal Reports
B.P.I.R.	Bankruptcy and Personal Insolvency Reports

B.T.C.	British Tax Cases
B.W.C.C.	Butterworths Workmen's Compensation Cases
C	Commissioner's decision
C&BA 1992	Social Security Contributions and Benefits Act 1992
CAA 2001	Capital Allowance Act 2001
CAB	Citizens Advice Bureau
CAO	Chief Adjudication Officer
CBJSA	Contribution-Based Jobseeker's Allowance
C.C.L. Rep.	Community Care Law Reports
CCM	Claimant Compliance Manual
CCN	New Tax Credits Claimant Compliance Manual
C.E.C.	European Community Cases
CERA	Cortical Evoked Response Audiogram
CESA	Contributory Employment and Support Allowance
Ch.	Chancery Division Law Reports
Child Benefit Regulations	Child Benefit (General) Regulations 2006
Claims and Payments Regulations	Social Security (Claims and Payments) Regulations 1987
Claims and Payments Regulations 1979	Social Security (Claims and Payments) Regulations 1979
C.M.L.R.	Common Market Law Reports
C.O.D.	Crown Office Digest
Com. L.R.	Commercial Law Reports
Commissioners Procedure Regulations	Social Security Commissioners (Procedure) Regulations 1999
Computation of Earnings Regulations	Social Security Benefit (Computation of Earnings) Regulations 1978
Computation of Earnings Regulations 1999	Social Security Benefit (Computation of Earnings) Regulations 1996
Const. L.J.	Construction Law Journal
Contributions and Benefits Act	Social Security Contributions and Benefits Act 1992
Convention	Human Rights Convention
Council Tax Benefit Regulations	Council Tax Benefit (General) Regulations 1992 (SI 1992/1814)
CP	Carer Premium
CP	Chamber President
CPAG	Child Poverty Action Group
C.P.L.R.	Civil Practice Law Reports
CPR	Civil Procedure Rules
C.P. Rep.	Civil Procedure Reports
Cr. App. R.	Criminal Appeal Reports
Cr. App. R. (S.)	Criminal Appeal Reports (Sentencing)

CRCA 2005	Commissioners for Revenue and Customs Act 2005
Credits Regulations 1974	Social Security (Credits) Regulations 1974
Credits Regulations 1975	Social Security (Credits) Regulations 1975
Crim. L.R.	Criminal Law Review
CRU	Compensation Recovery Unit
CSA 1995	Child Support Act 1995
CS(NI)O	Child Support (Northern Ireland) Order 1995
CSO	Child Support Officer Act 2000
CSPSSA 2000	Child Support, Pensions and Social Security Act 2000
CTC	Child Tax Credit
DAT	Disability Appeal Tribunal
DCP	Disabled Child Premium
Decisions and Appeals Regulations 1999	Social Security Contributions (Decisions and Appeals) Regulations 1999
Dependency Regulations	Social Security Benefit (Dependency) Regulations 1977
DLA	Disability Living Allowance
DLA Regulations	Social Security (Disability Living Allowance) Regulations 1991
DLAAB	Disability Living Allowance Advisory Board
DLAAB Regs	Disability Living Allowance Advisory Board Regulations (SI 1991/1746)
DLADWAA 1991	Disability Living Allowance and Disability Working Allowance Act 1991
DM	Decision Maker
DMA	Decision-making and Appeals
DMG	Decision Makers Guide
DMP	Delegated Medical Practitioner
DPTC	Disabled Person's Tax Credit
DSDNI	Department for Social Development, Northern Ireland
DSS	Department of Social Security
DTI	Department of Trade and Industry
DWA	Disability Working Allowance
DWP	Department of Work and Pensions
DWPMS	Department of Work and Pensions Medical Services
EAA	Extrinsic Allergic Alveolitis
EAT	Employment Appeal Tribunal
ECHR	European Convention on Human Rights
ECHR rights	European Convention on Human Rights rights
EctHR	European Court of Human Rights
ECJ	European Court of Justice
E.C.R.	European Court Report

Table of Abbreviations used in this Series

ECSMA Agreement	European Convention on Social and Medical Assistance
EC Treaty	European Community Treaty
EEA	European Economic Area
E.H.R.R.	European Human Rights Reports
E.L.R.	Education Law Reports
EMA	Education Maintenance Allowance
EMO	Examining Medical Officer
EMP	Examining Medical Practitioner
ERA	Evoked Response Audiometry
ERA 1996	Employment Rights Act 1996
ER(NI)O	Employers Rights (Northern Ireland) Order 1996
ESA	Employment and Support Allowance
ESA Regulations	Employment and Support Allowance Regulations 2008
ESA WCAt	Employment and Support Allowance Work Capability Assessment
Eu.L.R.	European Law Reports
FA 1990	Finance Act 1990
FA 1996	Finance Act 1996
FA 2000	Finance Act 2000
FA 2004	Finance Act 2004
F(No.2) A 2005	Finance (No.2) Act 2005
Family Credit Regulations	Family Credit (General) Regulations 1987
Fam. Law	Family Law
F.C.R.	Family Court Reporter
FIS	Family Income Supplement
Fixing and Adjustment of Rates Regulations 1976	Child Benefit and Social Security (Fixing and Adjustment of Rates) Regulations 1976
F.L.R.	Family Law Report
FTT	First-tier Tribunal
GA	Guardians Allowance
GA Regulations	Social Security (Guardian's Allowance) Regulations 1975
General Benefit Regulations 1982	Social Security (General Benefit) Regulations 1982
General Regulations	Statutory Maternity Pay (General) Regulations 1986
GMP	Guaranteed Minimum Pension
G.P.	General Practitioner
GRA	Gender Recognition Act
GRB	Graduated Retirement Benefit
GRP	Graduated Retirement Pension
G.W.D.	Greens Weekly Digest

Table of Abbreviations used in this Series

HASSASSA	Health and Social Services and Social Security Adjudication Act 1983
HCD	House of Commons Debates
HCV	Hepatitis C Virus
HCWA	House of Commons Written Answer
HESC	Health, Education and Social Care
H.L.R.	Housing Law Reports
HMIT	Her Majesty's Inspector of Taxes
HMRC	Her Majesty's Revenue & Customs
HNCIP	(Housewives') Non-Contributory Invalidity Pension
Hospital In-Patients Regulations 1975	Social Security (Hospital In-Patients) Regulations 1975
Housing Benefit Regulations	Housing Benefit (General) Regulations 1987 (SI 1987/1971)
HPP	Higher Pensioner Premium
HRA 1998	Human Rights Act 1998
H.R.L.R.	Human Rights Law Reports–UK Cases
HSE	Health and Safety Executive
IB	Incapacity Benefit
IB/IS/SDA	Incapacity Benefits' Regime
IBJSA	Income based Jobseekers Allowance
IB PCA	Incapacity Benefit Person Capability Assessment
IB Regs	Social Security (Incapacity Benefit) Regulations 1994
IB Regulations	Social Security (Incapacity Benefit) Regulations 1994
IBS	Irritable Bowel Syndrome
ICA	Invalid Care Allowance
ICA Regulations	Social Security (Invalid Care Allowance) Regulations 1976
ICA Unit	Invalid Care Allowance Unit
I.C.R.	Industrial Cases Reports
ICTA 1988	Income and Corporation Taxes Act 1988
IFW Regs	Incapacity for Work (General) Regulations 1995
IIAC	Industrial Injuries Advisory Council
Imm. A.R.	Immigration Appeal Reports
Incapacity for Work Regulations	Social Security (Incapacity for Work) (General) Regulations 1995
Income Support General Regulations	Income Support (General) Regulations 1987
Increases for Dependants Regulations	Social Security Benefit (Dependency) Regulations 1977
IND	Immigration and Nationality Directorate of the Home Office
I.N.L.R.	Immigration and Nationality Law Reports

Table of Abbreviations used in this Series

IO	Information Officer
I.O.	Insurance Officer
IPPR	Institute of Public Policy Research
IRESA	Income Related Employment and Support Allowance
I.R.L.R.	Industrial Relations Law Reports
IS	Income Support
ISAs	Individual Savings Accounts
IS Regs	Income Support Regulations
ITA 2007	Income Tax Act 2007
ITEPA	Income Tax (Earnings and Pensions) Act
ITEPA 2003	Income Tax (Earnings and Pensions) Act 2003
I.T.L. Rep.	International Tax Law Reports
ITS	Independent Tribunal Service
ITTOIA	Income Tax (Trading and Other Income) Act 2005
IVB	Invalidity Benefit
IWA 1994	Social Security (Incapacity for Work) Act 1994
IW (Dependants) Regs	Social Security (Incapacity for Work) (Dependants) Regulations
IW (General) Regs	Social Security (Incapacity for Work) (General) Regulations 1995
IW (Transitional) Regs	Incapacity for Work (Transitional) Regulations
JHRC	Joint Human Rights Committee
Jobseeker's Regulations 1996	Jobseekers Allowance Regulations 1996
J.P.	Justice of the Peace Reports
JSA	Jobseekers Allowance
JSA 1995	Jobseekers Allowance Act 1995
JSA Regs 1996	Jobseekers Allowance Regulations 1996
JSA Regulations	Jobseekers Allowance Regulations
JSA (Transitional) Regulations	Jobseeker's Allowance (Transitional) Regulations 1996
JS(NI)O 1995	Jobseekers (Northern Ireland) Order 1995
J.S.S.L.	Journal of Social Security Law
J.S.W.F.L.	Journal of Social Welfare and Family Law
J.S.W.L.	Journal of Social Welfare Law
K.I.R.	Knight's Industrial Law Reports
L. & T.R.	Landlord and Tenant Reports
LCWA	Limited Capability for Work Assessment
LEL	Lower Earnings Limit
Lewis	R. Lewis, *Compensation for Industrial Injury* (1987)
L.G.R.	Local Government Law Reports
Ll.L.Rep	Lloyd's List Law Report

Lloyd's Rep.	Lloyd's Law Reports
L.S.G.	Law Society Gazette
LTAHAW	Living Together as Husband and Wife
Luxembourg Court	Court of Justice of the European Communities (also referred to as ECJ)
MA	Maternity Allowance
MAF	Medical Assessment Framework
MAT	Medical Appeal Tribunal
Maternity Allowance Regulations	Social Security (Maternity Allowance) Regulations 1987
Maternity Benefit Regulations	Social Security (Maternity Benefit) Regulations 1975
Medical Evidence Regulations	Social Security (Medical Evidence) Regulations 1976
MS	Medical Services
NCIP	Non-Contributory Invalidity Pension
NDPD	Notes on the Diagnosis of Prescribed Diseases
NI	National Insurance
N.I..	Northern Ireland Law Reports
NICs	National Insurance Contributions
NIRS 2	National Insurance Recording System
N.L.J.	New Law Journal
N.P.C.	New Property Cases
OCD	Obsessive compulsive disorder
Ogus, Barendt and Wikeley	A. Ogus, E. Barendt and N. Wikeley, *The Law of Social Security* (4th ed., Butterworths, 1995)
OPA	Overseas Pensions Act 1973
OPB	One Parent Benefit
OPSSAT	Office of the President of Social Security Appeal Tribunals
Overlapping Benefits Regulations	Social Security (Overlapping Benefits) Regulations 1979
Overpayments Regulations	Social Security (Payments on account, Overpayments and Recovery) Regulations
P.	Probate, Divorce and Admiralty Law Reports
P. & C.R.	Property and Compensation Reports
PAYE	Pay As You Earn
PCA	Personal Capability Assessment
PD	Prescribed Diseases
P.D.	Practice Direction
Pens. L.R.	Pensions Law Reports
Persons Abroad Regulations	Social Security Benefit (Persons Abroad) Regulations 1975
Persons Residing Together Regulations	Social Security Benefit (Persons Residing Together) Regulations 1977
PIE	Period of Interruption of Employment

PILON	Pay In Lieu of Notice
PIW	Period of Incapacity for Work
P.I.W.R.	Personal Injury and Quantum Reports
P.L.R.	Estates Gazette Planning Law Reports
Polygamous Marriages Regulations	Social Security and Family Allowances (Polygamous Marriages) Regulations 1975
PPF	Pension Protection Fund
Prescribed Diseases Regulations	Social Security (Industrial Injuries) (Prescribed Diseases) Regulations 1985
PSCS	DWP's Pension Service Computer System
PTA	Pure Tone Audiometry
PTSR	Public and Third Sector Law Reports
PVS	Private of Voluntary Sectors
Q.B.	Queens Bench Law Reports
R	Reported Decision
RC	Rules of the Court of Session
REA	Reduced Earnings Allowance
Recoupment Regulations	Social Security (Recoupment) Regulations 1990
RIPA	Regulation of Investigatory Powers Act 2000
RMO	Regional Medical Officer
RSI	Repetitive Strain Injury
R.T.R.	Road Traffic Reports
S	Scottish Decision
SAP	Statutory Adoption Pay
SAYE	Save As You Earn
SB	Supplementary Benefit
SBC	Supplementary Benefits Commission
S.C.	Session Cases
S.C. (H.L.)	Session Cases (House of Lords)
S.C. (P.C.)	Session Cases (Privy Council)
S.C.C.R.	Scottish Criminal Case Reports
S.C.L.R.	Scottish Civil Law Reports
SDA	Severe Disablement Allowance
SDP	Severe Disability Premium
SEC	Social Entitlement Chamber
SERPS	State Earnings Related Pension Scheme
Severe Disablement Allowance Regulations	Social Security (Severe Disablement Regulations Allowance) Regulations 1984
S.J.	Solicitors Journal
S.J.L.B.	Solicitors Journal Law Brief
S.L.T.	Scots Law Times
SMP	Statutory Maternity Pay
SMP (General) Regulations	Statutory Maternity Pay (General) Regulations

SMP (General) Regulations 1986	Statutory Maternity Pay (General) Regulations 1986
SP	Senior President
SPC	State Pension Credit
SPCA	State Pension Credit Act 2002
SPCA(NI)	State Pension Credit Act (Northern Ireland) 2002
SPP	Statutory Paternity Pay
SPP and SAP (Administration) Regs 2002	Statutory Paternity Pay and Statutory Adoption Pay (Administration) Regulations 2002
SPP and SAP (General) Regulations 2002	Statutory Paternity Pay and Statutory Adoption Pay (General) Regulations 2002
SPP and SAP (National Health Service)	Statutory Paternity Pay and Statutory Adoption Pay (National Health Service Employees) Regulations 2002
SPP and SAP (Weekly Rates) Regulations	Statutory Paternity Pay and Statutory Adoption Pay (Weekly Rates) Regulations 2002
SSA	Social Security Agency
SSA 1975	Social Security Act 1975
SSA 1978	Social Security Act 1978
SSA 1979	Social Security Act 1979
SSA 1981	Social Security Act 1981
SSA 1986	Social Security Act 1986
SSA 1989	Social Security Act 1989
SSA 1990	Social Security Act 1990
SSA 1992	Social Security Act 1992
SSA 1998	Social Security Act 1998
SSAA 1992	Social Security Administration Act 1992*
SSAC	Social Security Advisory Committee
SSAT	Social Security Appeal Tribunal
SSCBA 1992	Social Security Contributions and Benefits Act 1992*
SSCB(NI) Act 1992	Social Security Contributions (Northern Ireland) Act 1992
SS(CP)A	Social Security (Consequential Provisions) Act 1992
SSHBA 1982	Social Security and Housing Benefits Act 1982
SS(MP) A 1977	Social Security (Miscellaneous Provisions) Act 1977
SS (No.2) A 1980	Social Security (No.2) Act 1980
SSP	Statutory Sick Pay
SSPA 1975	Social Security Pensions Act 1975
SSP (Gen.) Regulations	Statutory Sick Pay (General) Regulations 1982
SSP (General) Regulations 1982	Statutory Sick Pay (General) Regulations 1982

* Where the context makes it seem more appropriate, these could also be referred to as Contributions and Benefits Act 1992, Administration Act 1992.

SSPA 1975	Social Security Pensions Act 1975
SSWP	Secretary of State for Work and Pensions
State Pension Credit Regulations	State Pension Credit Regulations 2002
S.T.C.	Simon's Tax Cases
S.T.C. (S.C.D.)	Simon's Tax Cases: Special Commissioners Decisions
S.T.I.	Simon's Tax Intelligence
STIB	Short-Term Incapacity Benefit
Strasbourg Court	European Court of Human Rights
T	Tribunal of Commissioners' Decision
Taxes Act	Income and Corporation Taxes Act 1988
T.C.	Tax Cases
TCA 1999	Tax Credits Act 1999
TCA 2002	Tax Credits Act 2002
TC (Claims and Notifications) Regs 2002	Tax Credits (Claims and Notifications) Regulations 2002
TCGA	Taxation of Chargeable Gains Act 1992
TCTM	Tax Credits Technical Manual
TEU	Treaty on European Union
TMA 1970	Taxes Management Act 1970
T.R.	Taxation Reports
Transfer of Functions Act	Social Security Contributions (Transfer of Functions etc.) Act 1999
Treaty	Rome Treaty
U	Unemployment Benefit
U.K.H.R.R.	United Kingdom Human Rights Reports
UKUT	United Kingdom Upper Tribunal
Unemployment, Sickness and Invalidity Benefit Regs	Social Security (Unemployment, Sickness and Invalidity Benefit) Regulations 1983
USI Regs	Social Security (Unemployment, Sickness and Invalidity Benefit) Regulations 1983
UT	Upper Tribunal
VAMS	Veterans Agency Medical Service
VCM	Vinyl Chloride Monomer-Related
VERA 1992	Vehicle Excise and Registration Act 1992
VWF	Vibration White Finger
W	Welsh Decision
WCA	Work Capability Assessment
WCAt	First Element of Limited Work Capability Assessment
WFHRAt	Work Focused Health Related Assessment
WFTC	Working Families Tax Credit
Widow's Benefit and Retirement Pensions Regs	Social Security (Widow's Benefit and Retirement Pensions) Regulations 1979
Wikeley, Annotations	N. Wikeley, "Annotations to Jobseekers Act 1995

	(c.18)" in *Current Law Statutes Annotated* (1995)
Wikeley, Ogus and Barendt	Wikeley, Ogus and Barendt, *The Law of Social Security* (5th ed., Butterworths, 2002)
W.L.R.	Weekly Law Reports
Workmen's Compensation Acts	Workmen's Compensation Acts 1925 to 1945
WRA 2007	Welfare Reform Act
WRAAt	Work Related Activity Assessment
WRPA 1999	Welfare Reform and Pensions Act 1999
WRP(NI)O 1999	Welfare Reform and Pensions (Northern Ireland) Order
WTC	Working Tax Credit
WTC (Entitlement and Maximum Rate) Regulations 2002	Working Tax Credit (Entitlement and Maximum Rate) Regulations 2002
W.T.L.R.	Wills & Trusts Law Reports

PART I

STATUTES

Forfeiture Act 1982

(1982 c.34)

ARRANGEMENT OF SECTIONS

1. The "forfeiture rule"   **1.1**
2. Omitted.
3. Omitted.
4. Upper Tribunal to decide whether rule applies to social security benefits
5. Exclusion of murder
6. Omitted.
7. Omitted.

An Act to provide for relief for persons guilty of unlawful killing from forfeiture of inheritance and other rights; to enable such persons to apply for financial provision out of the deceased's estate; to provide for the question whether pension and social security benefits have been forfeited to be determined by the Social Security Commissioners; and for connected purposes.

[13th July 1982]

1.—(1) In this Act, the "forfeiture rule" means the rule of public policy   **1.2**
which in certain circumstances precludes a person who has unlawfully killed another from acquiring a benefit in consequence of the killing.

(2) References in this Act to a person who has unlawfully killed another include a reference to a person who has unlawfully aided, abetted, counselled or procured the death of that other and references in this Act to unlawful killing shall be interpreted accordingly.

GENERAL NOTE

There is a general rule of English law that a person should not benefit from his or   **1.3**
her wrongdoing. More specifically, the forfeiture rule has the effect that, in certain circumstances, a person who has unlawfully killed another forfeits his or her right to any benefit that might otherwise have been acquired as a result of the death, e.g. an inheritance under a will or an indemnity under an insurance policy. In *R. v National Insurance Commissioner, Ex p. Connor* [1981] Q.B. 758 (also reported as an appendix to *R(G) 2/79*), the forfeiture rule was applied to prevent a woman convicted of the manslaughter of her husband from obtaining entitlement to widow's benefit. A Tribunal of Commissioners subsequently held that it also applied to entitlement to a Category B retirement pension based on a victim's contribution record (*R(P) 1/88*). The same rule applies in Scotland (*Burns v Secretary of State for Social Services* [1985] S.L.T. 351 (also reported as an appendix to *R(G) 1/83*)).

There is an "unlawful killing" where death is the direct consequence of "criminal conduct", including aiding and abetting suicide, which is a crime under the Suicide Act 1961 even though suicide itself is not (*Dunbar v Plant* [1998] Ch. 412). It follows that the forfeiture rule applies in any case of manslaughter, including manslaughter on the ground of diminished responsibility (*R(FP) 1/05*, in which it was held that *R(G) 3/84* must now be regarded as wrongly decided, and *In re Land, decd.* [2006] EWHC 2069 (Ch); [2007] 1 W.L.R. 1009), and presumably also applies to causing death by dangerous driving. It also follows that the forfeiture rule applies if the killing was abroad, provided that the death was the direct consequence of what would have been a crime in Great Britain (*R(G) 1/88*). Subs.(2) recognises that acting as an accessory to a crime may be enough to cause the forfeiture rule to apply and, in *R(FG) 1/04*, it was held that a person convicted under s.4 of the Offences against the Person Act 1861 of soliciting to murder was likely to have "counselled . . . the death of [the victim]" for the purposes of the subsection. The forfeiture rule does not apply where a person is of unsound mind to the extent of being incapable of committing a crime (*Re Houghton, Houghton v Houghton* [1915] 2 Ch. 173).

It is not necessary that the claimant have been convicted of any crime, provided that the Upper Tribunal is satisfied that he or she committed one (*Gray v Barr* [1970] 2 Q.B. 626, where a shotgun with which the victim was being threatened went off accidentally and the perpetrator was acquitted of manslaughter after a summing up that was "remarkable for failing to draw the jury's attention to the formidable evidence against [him]"). However, the Upper Tribunal would be slow to go behind an acquittal and it has been held that the criminal standard of proof should be applied in such a case (*R(G) 2/90*). It would probably be even slower to go behind a conviction but, in *R(FP) 1/05*, there was left open the possibility of finding in another case that a conviction of manslaughter on the grounds of diminished responsibility had been inappropriate and that a verdict of not guilty by reason of insanity would have been the correct one.

Section 4 of this Act permits the Upper Tribunal to modify the forfeiture rule so that it does not apply with its full force, but s.5 provides that it cannot be modified in a case of murder.

1.4   **2.** *Omitted.*
1.5   **3.** *Omitted.*

[⁶Upper Tribunal] to decide whether rule applies to social security benefits

1.6   **4.**—(1) Where a question arises as to whether, if a person were otherwise entitled to or eligible for any benefit or advantage under a relevant enactment, he would be precluded by virtue of the forfeiture rule from receiving the whole or part of the benefit or advantage, that question shall (notwithstanding anything in any relevant enactment) be determined by [⁶the Upper Tribunal].

[¹(1A) Where [⁶the Upper Tribunal] determines that the forfeiture rule has precluded a person (in this section referred to as "the offender") who has unlawfully killed another from receiving the whole or part of any such benefit or advantage, [⁶the Upper Tribunal] may make a decision under this subsection modifying the effect of that rule and may do so whether the unlawful killing occurred before or after the coming into force of this subsection.

(1B) [⁶The Upper Tribunal] shall not make a decision under subsection (1A) above modifying the effect of the forfeiture rule in any case unless [⁶it] is satisfied that having regard to the conduct of the offender and of the deceased and to such other circumstances as appear to [⁶the Upper Tribunal] to be material, the justice of the case requires the effect of the rule to be so modified in that case.

(1C) Subject to subsection (1D) below, a decision under subsection (1A) above may modify the effect of the forfeiture rule in either or both of the following ways—

(a) so that it applies only in respect of a specified proportion of the benefit or advantage;

(b) so that it applies in respect of the benefit or advantage only for a specified period of time.

(1D) Such a decision may not modify the effect of the forfeiture rule so as to allow any person to receive the whole or any part of a benefit or advantage in respect of any period before the commencement of this subsection.

(1E) If [⁶the Upper Tribunal] thinks it expedient to do so, [⁶the Upper Tribunal may direct that its] decision shall apply to any future claim for a benefit or advantage under a relevant enactment, on which a question such as is mentioned in subsection (1) above arises by reason of the same unlawful killing.

(1F) It is immaterial for the purposes of subsection (1E) above whether the claim is in respect of the same or a different benefit or advantage.

(1G) For the purposes of obtaining a decision whether the forfeiture rule should be modified the Secretary of State may refer to [⁶the Upper Tribunal] for review any determination of a question such as is mentioned in subsection (1) above that was made before the commencement of subsections (1A) to (1F) above (whether by [⁶the Upper Tribunal] or not) and shall do so if the offender requests him to refer such a determination.

(1H) Subsections (1A) to (1F) above shall have effect on a reference under subsection (1G) above as if in subsection (1A) the words "it has been determined" were substituted for the words "[⁶the Upper Tribunal] determines".]

(2) [⁶Tribunal Procedure Rules may make provision] for carrying this section into effect; and (without prejudice to the generality of that) the rules may, in relation to the question mentioned in subsection (1) above or any determination under that subsection [² or any decision under subsection (1A) above]—

(a) apply any provision of any relevant enactment, with or without modifications, or exclude or contain provisions corresponding to any such provisions; [⁶. . .]

(b) [⁶. . .]

(3) [⁶. . .]

(4) [⁶. . .]

(5) In this section—

[⁶. . .]; and

"relevant enactment" means any provision of the following and any instrument made by virtue of such a provision:

the Personal Injuries (Emergency Provisions) Act 1939,

the Pensions (Navy, Army, Air Force and Mercantile Marine) Act 1939,

the Polish Resettlement Act 1947,

[³ . . .],

[² the Social Security Acts 1975 to 1991],

[³ the Social Security Contributions and Benefits Act 1992],

[⁵ section 1 of the Armed Forces (Pensions and Compensation) Act 2004,]

[⁴ the Pension Schemes Act 1993]

and any other enactment relating to pensions or social security prescribed by regulations under this section.

AMENDMENTS

1. Social Security Act 1986, s.76 (July 25, 1986).
2. Statutory Sick Pay Act 1991, s.3(1)(c) (February 12, 1991).

3. Social Security (Consequential Provisions) Act 1992, ss.3 and 4 and Sch.2, para.63.

4. Pension Schemes Act 1993, Sch.8, para.15 (February 7, 1994).

5. Armed Forces (Pensions and Compensation) Act 2004, s.7(1) (April 6, 2005).

6. Transfer of Tribunal Functions Order 2008 (SI 2008/2833), Sch.3 para.38 (November 3, 2008).

DEFINITIONS

"forfeiture rule"—see s.1(1).
"offender"—see subs.(1A).
"relevant enactment—see subs.(5).

GENERAL NOTE

Subss. (1) to (1H)

1.7   Until November 3, 2008, the powers provided for in this section were exercised by Social Security Commissioners.

1.8   Subss.(1A) to (1H) were added after a Tribunal of Commissioners held that subs. (1) gave Commissioners power only to decide whether the forfeiture rule applied and did not give them any power to modify it (*R(G) 1/84, R(G) 2/84, R(P) 1/84*). Whenever a claimant's entitlement to a social security benefit under a "relevant enactment" (see subs.(5)) arises at least partly in consequence of the death of someone the claimant has killed, there is likely to arise the question whether the killing was unlawful and the forfeiture rule applies. The Secretary of State or other authority responsible for determining entitlement to benefit is then bound to refer the case to the Upper Tribunal so that it can decide under subs.(1) whether the forfeiture rule does apply (see the note to s.1) and, if so, whether it should be modified under subs.(1A).

The forfeiture rule cannot be modified in a case of murder (see s.5). However, the Act recognises that in other cases the forfeiture rule is capable of being unduly harsh and so the Upper Tribunal may modify the effect of the rule. The paramount consideration when considering modification is the culpability of the claimant (*Dunbar v Plant* [1998] Ch. 412). The Upper Tribunal has a broad discretion and may even decide that the forfeiture rule should have no effect at all, although that will be rare (*R(G) 1/98*, holding *R(G) 3/90* to have been implicitly overruled). Equally, though, the Upper Tribunal may decline to modify the effect of the forfeiture rule. In *R(G) 1/91*, a Commissioner refused to modify the rule where the Court of Appeal had quashed a conviction for murder and substituted a verdict of manslaughter on the ground of diminished responsibility because the trial judge had failed adequately to address the jury in relation to two written medical reports put to a defence witness in cross-examination when the prosecution had failed to call the authors of the reports to give evidence. The Commissioner, who was not bound by the same rules of evidence, held that the weight of evidence was against a finding of diminished responsibility and pointed to a finding of murder, although he acknowledged that s.5 did not apply because the claimant did not actually stand convicted of murder. In *R(FP) 1/05*, where the claimant's plea of guilty to manslaughter on the ground of diminished responsibility had been accepted, a Commissioner considered the claimant's culpability to be low but he still refused to modify the forfeiture rule because only 47p pw was at stake and he considered that the effect of the forfeiture rule was not harsh but was just.

Modification is usually in the form of an order directing that the forfeiture rule will have effect only for a certain period or that it will have effect only to reduce benefit by a certain proportion or both (subs.(1C)).

Subs. (2)

See the Tribunal Procedure (Upper Tribunal) Rules and, in particular, rr. 26 and 47.   **1.9**

Subs. (4)

By reg.14(1) of the Forfeiture Regulations 1999 (SI 1999/1495), the Social   **1.10**
Security Act 1998 is made a prescribed enactment. Those Regulations started life as
the Social Security Commissioners (Procedure) Regulations 1999 but, with effect
from November 3, 2008, paras 130 to 136 of Sch.1 to the Tribunals, Courts and
Enforcement Act 2007 (Transitional and Consequential Provisions) Order 2008 (SI
2008/2683) renamed them, amended regs 1 and 4(1) and deleted all the rest of the
regulations except regulation 14(1), subject to a saving in respect of Scotland (see
the note to ss.5 to 7 of the Social Security Act 1998). What is left reads—

1. These Regulations may be cited as the Forfeiture Regulations 1999 and shall
   come into force on June 1, 1999.

4.—(1) In these Regulations, unless the context otherwise requires—"the 1998
   Act" means the Social Security Act 1998.

14.—(1) For the purposes of section 4(5) of the Forfeiture Act 1982, the 1998
   Act shall be prescribed as a relevant enactment.

This appears to be an unnecessary provision but arguably reg.14(1) could not be
deleted as an amendment consequential on the coming into force of the Tribunals,
Courts and Enforcement Act 2007. Presumably the 1998 Act was originally prescribed with subs.(2)(a) in mind rather than any other part of s.4 because, unlike the
Acts mentioned in subs.(5) itself, the 1998 Act is entirely procedural.

Exclusion of murderers

5.—Nothing in this Act or in any order made under section 2 or referred   **1.11**
to in section 3(1) of the Act [¹ or in any decision made under section 4(1A)
of this Act] shall affect the application of the forfeiture rule in the case of a
person who stands convicted of murder.

AMENDMENT

1. Social Security Act 1986, s.76(4) (July 25, 1986).

DEFINITION

"forfeiture rule"—see s.1(1).

GENERAL NOTE

This section was applied in *R(G) 1/90*. Note that it applies only if the claimant has   **1.12**
actually been convicted of murder, although if the Upper Tribunal is satisfied that
the actions of the claimant amounted to murder notwithstanding the lack of a conviction, it would be likely to refuse to exercise the power of modification conferred
by s.4(1A) anyway (see, for instance, *R(G) 1/91*). In *R(G) 1/88*, the claimant was
convicted of homicide in Germany where the killing took place and a Commissioner
held that it was necessary to consider whether the claimant's actions would have
amounted to murder had the killing taken place in Great Britain. A conviction for
soliciting to murder, contrary to s.4 of the Offences against the Person Act 1861,
does not amount to a conviction for murder, even though it may be tantamount to
finding the claimant was an accessory to murder which, in many cases, would mean
that he or she could in fact have been convicted of murder *(R(FG) 1/04)*.

6. *Omitted.*   **1.13**

7. *Omitted.*   **1.14**

Social Security Administration Act 1992

(1992 c.5)

ARRANGEMENT OF SECTIONS

PART I

CLAIMS FOR AND PAYMENTS AND GENERAL ADMINISTRATION OF BENEFIT
SECTION

Necessity of Claim

†Unreliable heading. (Council tax benefit replaced community charge benefits w.e.f. 1.4.93.)

PART II

ADJUDICATION

PART III

OVERPAYMENTS AND ADJUSTMENTS OF BENEFIT

Adjustments of benefits

Housing benefit

Community charge benefits†

†Unreliable heading. (Council tax benefit replaced community charge benefits w.e.f. 1.4.93.)

Social fund awards

Northern Ireland payments

Adjustment of child benefit

PART IV

RECOVERY FROM COMPENSATION PAYMENTS

PART V

INCOME SUPPORT AND THE DUTY TO MAINTAIN

PART VI

ENFORCEMENT

110.–121.   *Omitted.*

PART VII

PROVISION OF INFORMATION

Inland Revenue

122.   *Omitted.*

Persons employed or formerly employed in social security administration or adjudication

123.   *Omitted.*

The Registration Service

124.   Provisions relating to age, death and marriage.
125.   Regulations as to notification of deaths.

Personal representatives—income support and supplementary benefit

126.   Personal representatives to give information about the estate of a deceased person who was in receipt of income support or supplementary benefit.
126A.   *Omitted.*

Housing benefit

127.   *Repealed.*

Community charge benefits

128.   *Repealed.*

Expedited claims for housing and council tax benefit

128A.   *Repealed.*

Statutory sick pay and other benefits

129.   Disclosure by Secretary of State for purpose of determination of period of entitlement to statutory sick pay.
130.   Duties of employers—statutory sick pay and claims for other benefits.

Statutory maternity pay and other benefits

PART VIII

ARRANGEMENTS FOR HOUSING BENEFIT AND COMMUNITY CHARGE BENEFITS† AND RELATED SUBSIDIES

PART IX

ALTERATION OF CONTRIBUTIONS ETC.

PART X

REVIEW AND ALTERATION OF BENEFITS

PART XI

COMPUTATION OF BENEFITS

PART XII

FINANCE

PART XIII

ADVISORY BODIES AND CONSULTATION

The Social Security Advisory Committee and the Industrial Injuries Advisory Council

PART XIV

SOCIAL SECURITY SYSTEMS OUTSIDE GREAT BRITAIN

Co-ordination

Reciprocity

PART XV

MISCELLANEOUS

Travelling expenses

PART XVI

GENERAL

Subordinate legislation

14

SCHEDULES:

1. Claims for benefit made or treated as made before 1st October 1990.
2.–9. *Omitted.*
10. Supplementary benefit etc.

PART I

CLAIMS FOR AND PAYMENTS AND GENERAL ADMINISTRATION OF BENEFIT

Necessity of claim

Entitlement to benefit dependent on claim

1.—(1) Except in such cases as may be prescribed, and subject to the fol-   **1.16**
lowing provisions of this section and to section 3 below, no person shall be
entitled to any benefit unless, in addition to any other conditions relating to
that benefit being satisfied—

  (a) he makes a claim for it in the manner, and within the time, prescribed in relation to that benefit by regulations under this Part of
this Act; or

  (b) he is treated by virtue of such regulations as making a claim for it.

[²(1A) No person whose entitlement to any benefit depends on his
making a claim shall be entitled to the benefit unless subsection (1B) below
is satisfied in relation both to the person making the claim and to any other
person in respect of whom he is claiming benefit.

(1B) This subsection is satisfied in relation to a person if—

  (a) the claim is accompanied by—

    (i) a statement of the person's national insurance number and
information or evidence establishing that that number has been
allocated to the person; or

    (ii) information or evidence enabling the national insurance number
that has been allocated to the person to be ascertained; or

  (b) the person makes an application for a national insurance number
to be allocated to him which is accompanied by information or evidence enabling such a number to be so allocated.

(1C) Regulations may make provision disapplying subsection (1A) above
in the case of—

  (a) prescribed benefits;

  (b) prescribed descriptions of persons making claims; or

  (c) prescribed descriptions of persons in respect of whom benefit is
claimed,

or in other prescribed circumstances.]

(2) Where under subsection (1) above a person is required to make a
claim or to be treated as making a claim for a benefit in order to be entitled
to it—

  (a) if the benefit is a [³ . . .] [³bereavement payment, the person] shall
not be entitled to it in respect of a death occurring more than 12
months before the date on which the claim is made or treated as
made; and

(b) if the benefit is any other benefit except disablement benefit or reduced earnings allowance, the person shall not be entitled to it in respect of any period more than 12 months before that date,
except as provided by section 3 below.

(3) Where a person purports to make a claim on behalf of another—

(a) for an attendance allowance by virtue of section 66(1) of the Contributions and Benefits Act; or

(b) for a disability living allowance by virtue of section 72(5) or 73(12) of that Act,

that other shall be regarded for the purposes of this section as making the claim, notwithstanding that it is made without his knowledge or authority.

(4) In this section and in section 2 below "benefit" means—

(a) benefit as defined in section 122 of the Contributions and Benefits Act;

[¹(aa) a jobseeker's allowance;] and

[⁴(ab) state pension credit;] and

[⁵ (ac) an employment and support allowance;]

(b) any income-related benefit.

(5) This section (which corresponds to section 165A of the 1975 Act, as it had effect immediately before this Act came into force) applies to claims made on or after 1st October 1990 or treated by virtue of regulations under that section or this section as having been made on or after that date.

(6) Schedule 1 to this Act shall have effect in relation to other claims.

AMENDMENTS

1. Jobseekers Act 1995, Sch.2, para.38 (October 7, 1996).
2. Social Security Administration (Fraud) Act 1997, s.19 (December 1, 1997).
3. Welfare Reform and Pensions Act 1999, Sch.8, para.16 (April 24, 2000).
4. State Pension Credit Act 2002, s.11 and Sch.1, paras 1–2 (April 7, 2003).
5. Welfare Reform Act 2007, s.28 and sch.3, para.10 (October 27, 2008).

DERIVATION

1.17   Social Security Act 1975, s.165A.

DEFINITIONS

"the 1975 Act"—see s.191.
"claim"—*ibid.*
"disablement benefit"—*ibid.*
"the Contributions and Benefits Act"—*ibid.*
"income-related benefit"—*ibid.*
"prescribe"—*ibid.*

GENERAL NOTE

Subs. (1)

1.18   The general rule is that there cannot be entitlement to benefit unless a claim is made for it. But note that this is a general rule, not a universal one. The general rule is subject to special cases for which special provision is made, and to the provisions of this section. "Benefit" for the purposes of this section is defined in para.(4). Section 1 applies to claims made on or after October 1, 1990. Schedule 1 deals with earlier claims.

The introduction of the predecessor of s.1 was precipitated by the decision of the House of Lords in *Insurance Officer v McCaffrey* [1984] 1 W.L.R. 1353 that (subject to an express provision to the contrary) a person was entitled to benefit if he met the conditions of entitlement even though he had not made a claim for that benefit. Claiming went to payability, not entitlement. This was contrary to the long-standing assumption of the Department and was corrected with effect from September 2, 1985.

Section 3, which is excluded from the operation of s.1, deals with late claims for bereavement benefit where the death of the spouse is difficult to establish.

Secretary of State for Work and Pensions v Nelligan, R(P) 2/03 [2003] EWCA Civ 555, Judgment of April 15, 2003, is the Court of Appeal's decision on the appeal against the Commissioner's decision in *CP/3643/2001*. The Commissioner had concluded that s.43(5) of the Contributions and Benefits Act 1992 contained an exception to the general rule that there must always be a claim for benefit. He decided that a married woman does not need to claim *both* a Category A *and* a Category B pension in order to obtain payment of the latter. The Court of Appeal allowed the appeal. It concluded that s.43(5) only applied where there had been a claim for *both* a Category A *and* a Category B retirement pension. There was no derogation from the general principle in s.1 of the Administration Act 1992. The Court of Appeal considered that s.43 was about making a choice between two competing entitlements rather than about establishing entitlement to benefit.

Subss. (1A)–(1C)

These provisions were inserted by s.19 of the Social Security Administration (Fraud) Act 1997 and came into force on December 1, 1997. The effect of subss. (1A) and (1B) is to impose an additional condition of entitlement to benefit where subs.(1)(a) applies (i.e. in the normal case). Claimants will not be entitled to benefit unless when making a claim they provide a national insurance (NI) number, together with information or evidence to show that it is theirs, or provide evidence or information to enable their NI number to be traced, or apply for a NI number and provided sufficient information or evidence for one to be allocated to them. This requirement for an NI number applies to both claimants and any person for whom they are claiming, except in prescribed circumstances (subs.(1C)). See reg.2A of the Income Support Regulations, and the Jobseeker's Allowance Regulations, for who is exempt and note the different dates from which this requirement bites for these benefits.

In *CH/4085/2007*, the Commissioner described subs.(1B) as "a most unsatisfactory provision in a number of respects" (para.17). The Commissioner notes that there are no regulations governing the issue of national insurance numbers, and regards *CIS/345/2003* as wrong in taking the view that reg.9 of the Crediting and Treatment of Contributions, and National Insurance Numbers Regulations 2001 governed this. But the primary legislation was not, in the view of the Commissioner so incomplete as to be unworkable in the case before him. He counsels that regulations should be made in case the primary legislation does prove unworkable in a different factual situation. The case before him concerned an application which had been made by post by a local authority on behalf of a claimant for housing benefit. The Commissioner explains:

> 25. More important is the issue at the heart of this appeal: what is meant by "information or evidence enabling [a national insurance] number to be so allocated". The problem, which appears not to have been anticipated by the draftsman, is that it is not possible for a claimant to satisfy the Secretary of State that a national insurance number should be allocated by way of a postal application. What the Secretary of State actually requires in order to allocate a national insurance number is sufficient evidence to show that the applicant does not already have a national insurance number (*i.e.*, the evidence that would be required under section 1(1B)(a)(ii) so as to enable a national insurance number to be

1.19

found if one had been allocated), information that a claim for a benefit requiring an application for a national insurance number has been, or is to be, made and information as to identity so that the Secretary of State can be satisfied that the claimant is genuine. It is the information as to identity that is the difficulty. A local authority should satisfy itself as to the identity of those in respect of whom benefit is claimed but the Secretary of State does not rely on the local authority doing so. Instead, the person concerned is called to "an evidence of identity interview" at a jobcentre and is told what evidence to bring, it being made plain that photocopies are not accepted. The interview enables the person's face to be compared with a photograph in a passport, makes it unnecessary for valuable original documents as to identity to be sent by post and enables a person to be questioned to test his or her statements. However, it has not been the understanding of the parties that the application is only "made" at the interview.

30. Against this background, the phrase "information or evidence enabling [a national insurance] number to be so allocated" cannot, in my judgment, extend to information and evidence provided at an interview. This is clear from the fact that the application must be "accompanied" by the information and evidence and, in any event, if Parliament had intended to include the information that is provided at interview, it would in my view simply have made entitlement conditional on a national insurance number being allocated, which it has deliberately not done so as not to delay the award of benefit. Moreover, the legislation does not specify what information or evidence must be sent with the application because regulation 9(1A) of the 2001 Regulations does not apply. A person can be expected to send only what he or she has been told to send and the source of that information is likely to be those administering the benefit being claimed. The jobcentre will presumably ask for information that could have been sent in advance and has been omitted such as, for instance, information as to the applicant's place of birth, which was not included with the information originally sent by the local authority on behalf of the claimant's husband in this case. It cannot be right that a claimant should be penalised because a local authority acting on her husband's behalf neglects to include information that can perfectly well be provided subsequently. In my judgment, the information and evidence mentioned in the legislation is only that information and evidence that the person concerned could reasonably have been expected to send when the application was made. ... .

31. However, that is not to say that a failure to attend an interview or to supply all the information required will not be relevant to entitlement to benefit. If a person does not take all the steps necessary to obtain a national insurance number after supplying the initial information and evidence, an adjudicating authority may be entitled to infer that the application for a national insurance number was not genuine, or has ceased to be genuine, and therefore not sufficient to satisfy the statutory condition of entitlement. That could justify revision or supersession of an award. Thus, while I agree ... that the tribunal should have found that the claimant had supplied sufficient information and evidence to satisfy section 1(1B)(b), I accept that [counsel for the local authority] is entitled to draw attention to the failure to attend the interview.

32. On the other hand, evidence of a failure to attend an interview is insufficient to show that an application was not, or has ceased to be, genuine. Regard must at least be had to the cause of the failure but even a lack of good cause may not indicate a lack of intention to pursue an application. Social security legislation makes specific provision for cases where a person has failed to attend a jobcentre to "sign on" or has failed to attend a medical examination. Here, no specific provision is made but adjudicating authorities must act fairly. Some enquiry must be made as to why the person failed to attend the interview and as to whether the person will attend another one. If no reply is received, it may be appropriate to infer that there was never any intention of obtaining a national insurance number, but that was not the position here.

Subs. (2)

This provision imposes an overall limit of 12 months to the entitlement to benefit before the date of claim. Not all benefits are caught by subs.(1) and there is a further exclusion in para.(b). Regulation 19 of and Sch.4 to the Claims and Payments Regulations impose the ordinary time-limits for claiming and since April 1997 allow the limits in the cases of income support, JSA, family credit and disability working allowance (and their successor benefits) to be extended for a maximum of three months only in tightly defined circumstances. The test of good cause has been abandoned. Where there is such an extension, the claim is then treated as made on the first day of the period for which the claim is allowed to relate (reg.6(3)). Although the drafting is not at all clear, the reference in subs.(2) to the 12-month limit from the date on which the claim is made or is treated as made seems to make the limit start from the date fixed by reg.6(3). However, reg.19(4) prevents an extension of the time-limit for the benefits covered by reg.6(3) leading to entitlement earlier than three months before the actual date of claim. But the restriction seems to stem from that regulation and not from s.1(2), or the earlier forms set out in Sch.1.

1.20

Note that from April 1997 the time limit for claiming social fund maternity and funeral payments is three months (Claims and Payments Regulations, reg.19(1) and Sch.4, paras 8 and 9) and there is no longer any provision allowing claims for these payments to be made outside this time limit.

Subs. (3)

Subsection (3) deals with a particular situation which may arise in connection with claims to attendance allowance and disability living allowance. In general, there is no objection to claims being made by someone on behalf of another person, though the Department will require a clear indication that the agent is acting with the express authority of the person claiming.

1.21

Subs. (4)

This subsection contains the definition of "benefit" for the purposes of the section.

1.22

The starting point is the definition of benefit in s.122 of the Contributions and Benefits Act, which (so far as current benefits are concerned) refers to benefits under Pts II to V of the Contributions and Benefits Act. Specific provisions of para.(4) add jobseeker's allowance, an employment and support allowance, State pension credit, and any income-related benefit.

Though fairly comprehensive, this list does not include child benefit and winter fuel payments. On the latter see *CIS/2337/2004*, para.9. This does not mean that claims are not required for those benefits (indeed provision is made for claims elsewhere in the social security legislation), but it does mean that s.1 does not apply in relation to entitlement to benefit being dependent upon a claim.

It can be argued that the form of decision will differ depending upon whether a claim is a condition of entitlement. It is at least arguable that, if a claim is not a condition of entitlement and no claim has been made but a person claims to be entitled to the benefit, any decision should be in the form that there is a nil award. By contrast, if an adverse decision is made because no claim has been made where a claim is a condition of entitlement, then the form of the decision should be that there is no entitlement. This fine distinction is unlikely to impress those seeking a benefit, but may assist in drawing a distinction between the majority of cases where s.1 makes a claim a condition of entitlement, and the much smaller class of cases where s.1 does not apply.

Subs. (5)

There were a number of different versions of the section from which this section is derived and subs.(5) indicates that this section is limited to claims made on or after October 1, 1990. Schedule 1 sets out the earlier variations of the section. In

1.23

many cases concerning claims to benefit care will need to be taken to apply the law as at the date of the claim. There is a particular risk of error where appeals are being reheard after the considerable delays inherent in successful appeals. Obviously, as time goes by this risk will diminish and eventually disappear.

Retrospective effect of provisions making entitlement to benefit dependent on claim

1.24
    2.—(1) This section applies where a claim for benefit is made or treated as made at any time on or after 2nd September 1985 (the date on which section 165A of the 1975 Act (general provision as to necessity of claim for entitlement to benefit), as originally enacted, came into force) in respect of a period the whole or any part of which falls on or after that date.

(2) Where this section applies, any question arising as to—

(a) whether the claimant is or was at any time (whether before, on or after 2nd September 1985) entitled to the benefit in question, or to any other benefit on which his entitlement to that benefit depends; or

(b) in a case where the claimant's entitlement to the benefit depends on the entitlement of another person to a benefit, whether that other person is or was so entitled,

shall be determined as if the relevant claim enactment and any regulations made under or referred to in that enactment had also been in force, with any necessary modifications, at all times relevant for the purpose of determining the entitlement of the claimant, and, where applicable, of the other person, to the benefit or benefits in question (including the entitlement of any person to any benefit on which that entitlement depends, and so on).

(3) In this section "the relevant claim enactment" means section 1 above as it has effect in relation to the claim referred to in subsection (1) above.

(4) In any case where—

(a) a claim for benefit was made or treated as made (whether before, on or after 2nd September 1985, and whether by the same claimant as the claim referred to in subsection (1) above or not), and benefit was awarded on that claim, in respect of a period falling wholly or partly before that date; but

(b) that award would not have been made had the current requirements applied in relation to claims for benefit, whenever made, in respect of periods before that date; and

(c) entitlement to the benefit claimed as mentioned in subsection (1) above depends on whether the claimant or some other person was previously entitled or treated as entitled to that or some other benefit,

then, in determining whether the conditions of entitlement to the benefit so claimed are satisfied, the person to whom benefit was awarded as mentioned in paragraphs (a) and (b) above shall be taken to have been entitled to the benefit so awarded, notwithstanding anything in subsection (2) above.

(5) In subsection (4) above "the current requirements" means—

(a) the relevant claim enactment, and any regulations made or treated as made under that enactment, or referred to in it, as in force at the time of the claim referred to in subsection (1) above, with any necessary modifications; and

(b) subsection (1) (with the omission of the words following "at any time") and subsections (2) and (3) above.

DERIVATION

Social Security Act 1975, s.165B.   1.25

DEFINITIONS

"the 1975 Act"—s.191.
"benefit"—see s.1(1).
"claim"—see s.191.
"claimant"—*ibid*.

GENERAL NOTE

There are a number of benefits where entitlement can depend on whether a   1.26
person was entitled to a benefit at some earlier date (e.g. on reaching pensionable
age). While the predecessor of s.1 clearly governed such questions from September
2, 1985, onwards, it was arguable that in relation to earlier dates the *McCaffrey*
principle (see note to s.1(1) above) had to be applied. *R(S) 2/91* decided that that
argument was correct. The predecessor of s.2 was inserted by the Social Security
Act 1990 to reverse the effect of that decision and to do so retrospectively back to
September 2, 1985.

The form of s.2 is complex and the retrospective effects are difficult to work out.
It only applies to claims made or treated as made on or after September 2, 1985
(subs.(1)). Thus very late appeals or very long good causes for late claim might not
be affected. Then on any such claim if a question of entitlement at any other date
arises (including dates before September 2, 1985) that question is to be decided
according to the principle of s.1 as it was in force at the relevant time (subs.(2)). The
only exception to this is that if for any period benefit has been awarded following
a claim, that beneficiary is to be treated as entitled to that benefit even though under
the current requirements he would not be (subs.(4)).

[¹ Claim or full entitlement to certain benefits conditional on work-focused interview.

2A.—(1) Regulations may make provision for or in connection with—   1.27
  (a) imposing, as a condition falling to be satisfied by a person who—
        (i) makes a claim for a benefit to which this section applies, and
        (ii) is under the age of 60 at the time of making the claim,
      a requirement to take part in a work-focused interview;
  (b) imposing, at a time when—
        (i) a person under that age and entitled to such a benefit, and
        (ii) any prescribed circumstances exist,
      a requirement to take part in such an interview as a condition of that
      person continuing to be entitled to the full amount which is payable
      to him in respect of the benefit apart from the regulations.
  (2) The benefits to which this section applies are—
  (a) income support;
  (b) housing benefit;
  (c) council tax benefit;
  (d) widow's and bereavement benefits falling within section 20(1)(e)
      and (ea) of the Contributions and Benefits Act (other than a bereave-
      ment payment);
  (e) incapacity benefit;
  (f) severe disablement allowance; and
  (g) [² carer's allowance].
  (3) Regulations under this section may, in particular, make provision—

21

(a) for securing, where a person would otherwise be required to take
   part in interviews relating to two or more benefits—
   (i) that he is only required to take part in one interview, and
   (ii) that any such interview is capable of counting for the purposes
       of all those benefits;
(b) for determining the person by whom interviews are to be
   conducted;
(c) conferring power on such persons or the designated authority to
   determine when and where interviews are to take place (including
   power in prescribed circumstances to determine that they are to take
   place in the homes of those being interviewed);
(d) prescribing the circumstances in which persons attending interviews
   are to be regarded as having or not having taken part in them;
(e) for securing that the appropriate consequences mentioned in subsection (4)(a) or (b) below ensue if a person who has been notified that
   he is required to take part in an interview—
   (i) fails to take part in the interview, and
   (ii) does not show, within the prescribed period, that he had good
       cause for that failure;
(f) prescribing—
   (i) matters which are or are not to be taken into account in deter-
       mining whether a person does or does not have good cause for
       any failure to comply with the regulations, or
   (ii) circumstances in which a person is or is not to be regarded as
       having or not having good cause for any such failure.

(4) For the purposes of subsection (3)(e) above the appropriate consequence of a failure falling within that provision are—
(a) where the requirement to take part in an interview applied by virtue of
   subsection (1)(a) above, that as regards any relevant benefit either—
   (i) the person in question is to be regarded as not having made a
       claim for the benefit, or
   (ii) if (in the cases of an interview postponed in accordance
       with subsection (7)) that person has already been awarded the
       benefit, his entitlement to the benefit is to terminate immedi-
       ately;
(b) where the requirement to take part in an interview applied by virtue
   of subsection (1)(b) above, that the amount payable to the person
   in question in respect of any relevant benefit is to be reduced by the
   specified amount until the specified time.

(5) Regulations under this section may, in relation to any such reduction,
provide—
(a) for the amount of the reduction to be calculated in the first instance
   by reference to such amount as may be prescribed;
(b) for the amount as so calculated to be restricted, in prescribed
   circumstances, to the prescribed extent;
(c) where the person in question is entitled to two or more relevant
   benefits, for determining the extent, and the order, in which those
   benefits are to be reduced in order to give effect to the reduction
   required in his case.

(6) Regulations under this section may provide that any requirement to
take part in an interview that would otherwise apply to a person by virtue
of such regulations—

(a) is, in any prescribed circumstances, either not to apply or not to apply until such time as is specified;

(b) is not to apply if the designated authority determines that an interview—
    (i) would not be of assistance to that person, or
    (ii) would not be appropriate in the circumstances,

(c) is not to apply until such time as the designated authority determines, if that authority determines that an interview—
    (i) would not be of assistance to that person, or
    (ii) would not be appropriate in the circumstances,
    until that time;

and the regulations may make provision for treating a person in relation to whom any such requirement does not apply, or does not apply until a particular time, as having complied with that requirement to such extent and for such purposes as are specified.

(7) Where—

(a) a person is required to take part in an interview by virtue of subsection (1)(a), and

(b) the interview is postponed by or under regulations made in pursuance of subsection (6)(a) or (c),

the time to which it is postponed may be a time falling after an award of the relevant benefit to that person.

(8) In this section—

"the designated authority" means such of the following as may be specified, namely—

(a) the Secretary of State,

(b) a person providing services to the Secretary of State,

(c) a local authority,

[³ (ca) subject to subsection (9), a county council in England,]

(d) [³ subject to subsection (9),] a person providing services to, or authorised to exercise any function of, [³ any authority mentioned in paragraph (c) or (ca)];

"interview" (in subsections (3) to (7)) means a work-focused interview;

"relevant benefit", in relation to any person required to take part in a work-focused interview, means any benefit in relation to which that requirement applied by virtue of subsection (1)(a) or (b) above;

"specified" means prescribed by or determined in accordance with regulations;

"work-focused interview", in relation to a person, means an interview conducted for such purposes connected with employment or training in the case of that person as may be specified;

and the purposes which may be specified include purposes connected with a person's existing or future employment or training prospects or needs, and (in particular) assisting or encouraging a person to enhance his employment prospects.]

[³ (9) A county council in England or a person providing services to, or authorised to exercise any function of, such a council may be specified as the designated authority only in relation to interviews with persons to whom the council is required to make support services available under section 68(1) of the Education and Skills Act 2008 (support services: provisions by local education authorities).]

AMENDMENTS

1. This section was added by the Welfare Reform and Pensions Act 1999, ss.57–58 with effect from November 11, 1999.

2. The Regulatory Reform (Carer's Allowance) Order 2002 (SI 2002/1457), art.1 (September 1, 2002 for the purpose of making regulations; April 1, 2003 for all other purposes).

3. Education and Skills Act 2008, Sch.1, para.45 (January 26, 2009).

[¹ Full entitlement to certain benefits conditional on work-focused interview for partner

1.28   **2AA.**—(1) Regulations may make provision for or in connection with imposing, at a time when—

(a) a person ("the claimant") who—

    (i) is under the age of 60, and

    (ii) has a partner who is also under that age,

is entitled to a benefit to which this section applies at a higher rate referable to his partner, and

(b) prescribed circumstances exist,

a requirement for the partner to take part in a work-focused interview as a condition of the benefit continuing to be payable to the claimant at that rate.

(2) The benefits to which this section applies are—

(a) income support;

(b) an income-based jobseeker's allowance other than a joint-claim job-seeker's allowance;

(c) incapacity benefit;

(d) severe disablement allowance; and

(e) [³ carer's allowance].

[⁴ (f) an employment and support allowance;]

(3) For the purposes of this section a benefit is payable to a person at a higher rate referable to his partner if the amount that is payable in his case—

(a) is more than it would be if the person concerned was not a member of a couple; or

(b) includes an increase of benefit for his partner as an adult dependant of his.

(4) Regulations under this section may, in particular, make provision—

(a) for securing, where the partner of the claimant would otherwise be required to take part in work-focused interviews relating to two or more benefits—

    (i) that the partner is required instead to take part in only one such interview; and

    (ii) that the interview is capable of counting for the purposes of all those benefits;

(b) in a case where the claimant has more than one partner, for determining which of those partners is required to take part in the work-focused interview or requiring each of them to take part in such an interview;

(c) for determining the persons by whom work-focused interviews are to be conducted;

(d) conferring power on such persons or the designated authority to determine when and where work-focused interviews are to take place (including power in prescribed circumstances to determine that they are to take place in the homes of those being interviewed);

(e) prescribing the circumstances in which partners attending work-focused interviews are to be regarded as having or not having taken part in them;

(f) for securing that if—

(i) a partner who has been notified of a requirement to take part in a work-focused interview fails to take part in it, and

(ii) it is not shown (by him or by the claimant), within the prescribed period, that he had good cause for that failure,

the amount payable to the claimant in respect of the benefit in relation to which the requirement applied is to be reduced by the specified amount until the specified time;

(g) prescribing—

(i) matters which are or are not to be taken into account in determining whether a partner does or does not have good cause for any failure to comply with the regulations; or

(ii) circumstances in which a partner is or is not to be regarded as having or not having good cause for any such failure.

(5) Regulations under this section may, in relation to a reduction under subsection (4)(f), provide—

(a) for the amount of the reduction to be calculated in the first instance by reference to such amount as may be prescribed;

(b) for the amount as so calculated to be restricted, in prescribed circumstances, to the prescribed extent;

(c) where the claimant is entitled to two or more benefits in relation to each of which a requirement to take part in a work-focused interview applied, for determining the extent to, and the order in, which those benefits are to be reduced in order to give effect to the reduction required in his case.

(6) Regulations under this section may provide that any requirement to take part in a work-focused interview that would otherwise apply to a partner by virtue of the regulations—

(a) is, in any prescribed circumstances, either not to apply or not to apply until the specified time;

(b) is not to apply if the designated authority determines that such an interview would not be of assistance to him or appropriate in the circumstances;

(c) is not to apply until such time as the designated authority determines (if that authority determines that such an interview would not be of assistance to him or appropriate in the circumstances until that time);

and the regulations may make provision for treating a partner to whom any such requirement does not apply, or does not apply until a particular time, as having complied with that requirement to such extent and for such purposes as are specified.

(7) In this section—

[² "couple" has the meaning given by s.137(1) of the Contributions and Benefits Act;]

"designated authority" means such of the following as may be specified, namely—

    (a) the Secretary of State,
    (b) a person providing services to the Secretary of State,
    (c) a local authority, and
[⁵ (ca) subject to subsection (8), a county council in England, and]
    (d) [⁵ subject to subsection (8),] a person providing services to, or authorised to exercise any function of, [⁵ any authority mentioned in paragraph (c) or (ca)];
"partner" means a person who is a member of the same couple as the claimant;
"specified" means prescribed by or determined in accordance with regulations;
and
"work-focused interview" has the same meaning as in section 2A above.]

[⁵ (8) A county council in England or a person providing services to, or authorised to exercise any function of, such a council may be specified as the designated authority only in relation to interviews with persons to whom the council is required to make support services available under section 68(1) of the Education and Skills Act 2008 (support services: provisions by local education authorities).]

AMENDMENTS

    1.Inserted by the Employment Act 2002, s.49 (July 5, 2003).
    2.Civil Partnership Act 2004, s.254 and Sch.24, para.55 (December 5, 2005).
    3. Welfare Reform Act 2007, Sch.7(3) (July 3, 2007).
    4. Welfare Reform Act 2007, s.28 and Sch.3, para.10 (October 27, 2008)
    5. Education and Skills Act 2008, Sch.1, para.46 (January 26, 2009).

[¹ Supplementary provisions relating to work-focused interviews

1.29   **2B.**—(1) Chapter II of Part I of the Social Security Act 1998 (social security decisions and appeals) shall have effect in relation to relevant decisions subject to and in accordance with subsections (3) to (8) below (and in those subsections "the 1998 Act" means that Act).

(2) For the purposes of this section a "relevant decision" is a decision made under regulations under section 2A above that a person—
    (a) has failed to comply with a requirement to take part in an interview which applied to him by virtue of the regulations, or
    (b) has not shown, within the prescribed period mentioned in section 2A(3)(e)(ii) above, that he had good cause for such a failure.

[³ (2A) For the purposes of this section a "relevant decision", in relation to regulations under section 2AA above, is a decision that—
    (a) the partner of a person entitled to a benefit has failed to comply with a requirement to take part in an interview which applied to the partner by virtue of the regulations, or
    (b) it has not been shown within the prescribed period mentioned in section 2AA(4)(f)(ii) above that the partner had good cause for such a failure.]

(3) Section 8(1)(c) of the 1998 Act (decisions falling to be made under or by virtue of certain enactments are to be made by the Secretary of State) shall have effect subject to any provisions of regulations under section 2A [⁴ or 2AA] above by virtue of which relevant decisions fall to be made otherwise than by the Secretary of State.

(4) For the purposes of each of sections 9 and 10 of the 1998 Act (revision and supersession of decisions of Secretary of State) any relevant decision made otherwise than by the Secretary of State shall be treated as if it were such a decision made by the Secretary of State (and accordingly may be revised by him under section 9 or superseded by a decision made by him under section 10).

(5) Subject to any provisions of regulations under either section 9 or 10 of the 1998 Act, any relevant decision made, or (by virtue of subsection (4) above) treated as made, by the Secretary of State may be—
  (a) revised under section 9 by a person or authority exercising functions under regulations under section 2A [4 or 2AA] above other than the Secretary of State, or
  (b) superseded under section 10 by a decision made by such a person or authority,
as if that person or authority were the Secretary of State.

(6) Regulations shall make provision for conferring (except in any prescribed circumstances) a right of appeal under section 12 of the 1998 Act (appeal to [5First-tier Tribunal]) against—
  (a) any relevant decision, and
  (b) any decision under section 10 of that Act superseding any such decision,
whether made by the Secretary of State or otherwise.

(7) Subsections (4) to (6) above apply whether—
  (a) the relevant decision, or
  (b) (in the case of subsection (6)(b)) the decision under section 10 of the 1998 Act,
is as originally made or has been revised (by the Secretary of State or otherwise) under section 9 of that Act; and regulations under subsection (6) above may make provision for treating, for the purposes of section 12 of that Act, any decision made or revised otherwise than by the Secretary of State as if it were a decision made or revised by him.

(8) Section 12 of the 1998 Act shall not apply to any decision falling within subsection (6) above except in accordance with regulations under that subsection.

(9) In [2. . .]
  (b) section 72(6) of the Welfare Reform and Pensions Act 1999 (supply of information),
any reference to information relating to social security includes any information supplied by a person for the purposes of an interview which he is required to take part in by virtue of section 2A [4 or 2AA] above.

(10) In this section "interview" means a work-focused interview within the meaning of section 2A above.]

AMENDMENTS

1. Welfare Reform and Pensions Act 1999, s.57 (November 11, 1999).
2. Employment Act 2002 (2002 c.22) s.54 and Sch.8 (November 24, 2002).
3. Employment Act 2002 (2002 c.22) s.54 and Sch.7 (July 5, 2003).
4. Employment Act 2002 (2002 c.22) s.53 and Sch.7 (July 5, 2003).
5. The Transfer of Tribunal Functions Order 2008 (SI 2008/2833), art.102 (November 3, 2008).

[1 Optional work-focused interviews

2C.—(1) Regulations may make provision for conferring on local authorities functions in connection with conducting work-focused interviews in

1.30

cases where such interviews are requested or consented to by persons to whom this section applies.

(2) This section applies to[³ . . .] [³ —

(a) persons making claims for or entitled to any of the benefits listed in section 2A(2) above or any prescribed benefit; and

(b) partners of persons entitled to any of the benefits listed in section 2AA(2) above or any prescribed benefit;]

and it so applies regardless of whether such persons have, in accordance with regulations under section 2A [³ or 2AA] above, already taken part in interviews conducted under such regulations.

(3) The function which may be conferred on a local authority [⁴ or on a county council in England] by regulations under this section include functions relating to—

(a) the obtaining and receiving of information for the purposes of work-focused interviews conducted under the regulations;

(b) the recording and forwarding of information supplied at, or for the purposes of, such interviews;

(c) the taking of steps to identify potential employment or training opportunities for persons taking part in such interviews.

[⁴(3A) Regulations under this section may confer functions on a county council in England only in relation to interviews with persons to whom the council is required to make support services available under section 68(1) of the Education and Skills Act 2008 (support services: provision by local education authorities).]

(4) Regulations under this section may make different provision for different areas or different authorities.

(5) In this section "work-focused interviews", in relation to a person to whom this section applies, means an interview conducted for such purposes connected with employment or training in the case of such a person as may be prescribed; and the purposes which may be so prescribed include—

(a) purposes connected with the existing or future employment prospects or needs of such a person, and

(b) (in particular) assisting or encouraging such a person to enhance his employment prospects.]

AMENDMENTS

1. This section was added by the Welfare Reform and Pensions Act 1999, ss.57–58 with effect from November 11, 1999.

2. Employment Act 2002, s.54 and Sch.8 (November 24, 2002).

3. Employment Act 2002, s.53 and Sch.7 (July 5, 2003).

4. Education and Skills Act 2008, Sch.1, para.47 (January 26, 2009).

[¹*Bereavement benefits*

Late claims for bereavement benefit where death is difficult to establish

1.31   **3.**—(1) This section applies were a person's spouse [³ or civil partner] has died or may be presumed to have died on or after the appointed day and the circumstances are such that—

(a) more than 12 months have elapsed since the date of death; and
(b) either—
  (i) the spouse's [³ or civil partner] body has not been discovered or identified or, if it has been discovered and identified, the surviving spouse [³ or civil partner] does not know that fact; or
  (ii) less than 12 months have elapsed since the surviving spouse [³ or civil partner] first knew of the discovery and identification of the body.

(2) Where this section applies, notwithstanding that any time prescribed for making a claim for a bereavement benefit in respect of the death has elapsed, then—
(a) in any case falling within paragraph (b)(i) of subsection (1) above where it has been decided under section 8 of the Social Security Act 1998 that the spouse [³ or civil partner] has died or is presumed to have died, or
(b) in any case falling within paragraph (b)(ii) of subsection (1) above where the identification was made not more than 12 months before the surviving spouse [³ or civil partner] first knew of the discovery and identification of the body,

such a claim may be made or treated as made at any time before the expiration of the period of 12 months beginning with the date on which that decision was made or, as the case may be, the date on which the surviving spouse [³ or civil partner] first knew of the discovery and identification.

(3) If, in a case where a claim for a bereavement benefit is made or treated as made by virtue of this section, the claimant would, apart from subsection (2) of section 1 above, be entitled to—
(a) a bereavement payment in respect of the spouse's [³ or civil partner's] death more than 12 months before the date on which the claim is made or treated as made; or
(b) any other bereavement benefit in respect of his or her death for a period more than 12 months before that date,

then, notwithstanding anything in that section, the surviving spouse [³ or civil partner] shall be entitled to that payment or, as the case may be, to that other benefit [² . . .].

(4) In subsection (1) above "the appointed day" means the day appointed for the coming into force of sections 54 to 56 of the Welfare Reform and Pensions Act 1999.]

AMENDMENTS

1. This section was added by the Welfare Reform and Pensions Act 1999, ss.57–58 with effect from November 11, 1999.
2. Tax Credits Act 2002, s.60 and Sch.6 (April 6, 2003).
3. Civil Partnership Act 2004, s.254 and Sch.24, para.56 (December 5, 2005).

SAVING

Article 3 of The Tax Credits Act 2002 (Commencement No.3 and Transitional Provisions and Savings) Order 2003 (SI 2003/938) provides: 1.32

"Saving provision

3.—(1) Notwithstanding the coming into force of the specified provisions, the Contributions and Benefits Act and the Administration Act shall,   1.33

in cases to which paragraph (2) applies, subject to paragraph (3), continue to have effect from the commencement date as if those provisions had not come into force.

(2) This paragraph applies where a person—

(a) is entitled to a relevant increase on the day before the commencement date; or

(b) claims a relevant increase on or after the commencement date and it is subsequently determined that he is entitled to a relevant increase in respect of a period which includes the day before the commencement date.

(3) The provisions saved by paragraph (1) shall continue to have effect until—

(a) subject to sub-paragraph(c), where a relevant increase ceases to be payable to a person to whom paragraph (2) applies for a period greater than 58 days beginning with the day on which it was last payable, on the day 59 days after the day on which it was last payable; or

(b) in any other case, subject to sub-paragraph (c), on the date on which entitlement to a relevant increase ceases;

(c) where regulation 6(19) or (23) of the Social Security (Claims and Payments) Regulations 1987 applies to a further claim for a relevant increase, on the date on which entitlement to that relevant increase ceases.

(4) In this article—

'the commencement date' means 6th April 2003;

'a relevant increase' means an increase under section 80 or 90 of the Contributions and Benefits Act;

'the specified provisions' means the provisions of the 2002 Act which are brought into force by article 2."

GENERAL NOTE

Subs. (4)

1.34   The appointed day referred to in this subsection is April 24, 2000.

Treatment of payments of benefit to certain widows

1.35   **4.** In any case where—

(a) a claim for widow's pension or a widowed mother's allowance is made, or treated as made, before 13th July 1990 (the date of the passing of the Social Security Act 1990); and

(b) the Secretary of State has made a payment to or for the claimant on the ground that if the claim had been received immediately after the passing of that Act she would have been entitled to that pension or allowance, or entitled to it at a higher rate, for the period in respect of which the payment is made,

the payment so made shall be treated as a payment of that pension or allowance, and, if and to the extent that an award of the pension or allowance, or an award at a higher rate, is made for the period in respect of which the payment was made, the payment shall be treated as made in accordance with that award.

DERIVATION

1.36   SSA 1990, s.21(1) and Sch.6, para.27(2).

Claims and payments regulations

Regulations about claims for and payments of benefit

5.—(1) Regulations may provide—   1.37

(a) for requiring a claim for a benefit to which this section applies to be made by such person, in such manner and within such time as may be prescribed;

(b) for treating such a claim made in such circumstances as may be prescribed as having been made at such date earlier or later than that at which it is made as may be prescribed;

(c) for permitting such a claim to be made, or treated as if made, for a period wholly or partly after the date on which it is made;

(d) for permitting an award on such a claim to be made for such a period subject to the condition that the claimant satisfies the requirements for entitlement when benefit becomes payable under the award;

(e) [³ for any such award to be revised under section 9 of the Social Security Act 1998, or superseded under section 10 of that Act, if any of those requirements are found not to have been satisfied;]

(f) for the disallowance on any ground of a person's claim for a benefit to which this section applies to be treated as a disallowance of any further claim by that person for that benefit until the grounds of the original disallowance have ceased to exist;

(g) for enabling one person to act for another in relation to a claim for a benefit to which this section applies and for enabling such a claim to be made and proceeded within the name of a person who has died;

(h) for requiring any information or evidence needed for the determination of such a claim or of any question arising in connection with such a claim to be furnished by such person as may be prescribed in accordance withthe regulations;

[⁵ (hh) for requiring such persons as may be prescribed to furnish any information or evidence needed for a determination whether a decision on an award of benefit to which this section applies—

(i) should be revised under section 9 of the Social Security Act 1998; or

(ii) should be superseded under section 10 of that Act;]

(i) for the person to whom, time when and manner in which a benefit to which this section applies is to be paid and for the information and evidence to be furnished in connection with the payment of such a benefit;

(j) for notice to be given of any change of circumstances affecting the continuance of entitlement to such a benefit or payment of such a benefit;

(k) for the day on which entitlement to such a benefit is to begin or end;

(l) for calculating the amounts of such a benefit according to a prescribed scale or otherwise adjusting them so as to avoid fractional amounts or facilitate computation;

(m) for extinguishing the right to payment of such a benefit if payment is not obtained within such period, not being less than 12 months, as may be prescribed from the date on which the right is treated under the regulations as having arisen;

(n) [³...]

(nn) [²...]

(o) [³...]

(p) for the circumstances and manner in which payments of such a benefit may be made to another person on behalf of the beneficiary for any purpose, which may be to discharge, in whole or in part, an obligation of the beneficiary or any other person;

(q) for the payment or distribution of such a benefit to or among persons claiming to be entitled on the death of any person and for dispensing withstrict proof of their title;

(r) for the making of a payment on account of such a benefit—

(i) where no claim has been made and it is impracticable for one to be made immediately;

(ii) where a claim has been made and it is impracticable for the claim or an appeal, reference, review or application relating to it to be immediately determined;

(iii) where an award has been made but it is impracticable to pay the whole immediately.

(2) This section applies to the following benefits—

(a) benefits as defined in section 122 of the Contributions and Benefits Act;

[¹(aa) a jobseeker's allowance;]

[⁶(ab) state pension credit;]

[¹¹(ac) an employment and support allowance;]

(b) income support;

(c) [⁹...];

(d) [⁹...];

(e) housing benefit;

(f) any social fund payments such as are mentioned in section 138(1)(a) or (2) of the Contributions and Benefits Act;

[¹³(fa) health in pregnancy grant;]

(g) child benefit; and

(h) Christmas bonus.

[¹⁰...]

[¹² (2A) The regulations may also require such persons as are prescribed to provide a rent officer with information or evidence of such decriptions as is prescribed.

(2B) For the purposes of subsection (2A), the Secretary of State may prescribe any description of information or evidence which he thinks is necessary or expedient to enable rent officers to carry out their functions under section 122 of the Housing Act 1996.

(2C) Information or evidence required to be provided by virtue of subsection (2A) may relate to an individual claim or award or to any description of claims or awards.]

[⁷ (3A) The references in paragraphs (h) and (hh) of subsection (1) above to information or evidence needed for the determination of a claim or of any question arising in connection with a claim or (as the case may be) for a determination whether a decision on an award should be revised or should be superseded, includes, in the case of state pension credit, a reference to information or evidence as to the likelihood of future changes in a person's circumstances which is needed for determining—

(a) whether a period should be specified as an assessed income period under section 6 of the State Pension Credit Act 2002 in relation to any decision; and

(b) if so, the length of the period to be so specified.]

(4) Subsection (1)(n) above shall have effect in relation to housing benefit as if the reference to the Secretary of State were a reference to the authority paying the benefit.

(5) Subsection (1)(g), (i), (l), (p) and (q) above shall have effect as if statutory sick pay [8,] statutory maternity pay [8, statutory paternity pay and statutory adoption pay] were benefits to which this section applies.

[5(6) As it has effect in relation to housing benefit subsection (1)(p) above authorises provision requiring the making of payments of benefit to another person, on behalf of the beneficiary, in such circumstances as may be prescribed.]

AMENDMENTS

1. Jobseekers Act 1995, Sch.2, para.39 (October 7, 1996).

2. Social Security Act 1998, Sch.6, para.5(1) (May 21, 1998). This amendment applies from May 21, 1998 until s.21(2)(d) of the 1998 Act comes into force.

3. Social Security Act 1998, Sch.8 (July 5, 1999).

4. Social Security Act 1998, s.74 (March 4, 1999).

5. Housing Act 1996, s.120 (with unlimited retrospective effect, so with effect from July 1, 1992).

6. State Pension Credit Act 2002, s.11 and Sch.1 (July 2, 2002 for the purpose of making regulations only).

7. State Pension Credit Act 2002, s.11 and Sch.1 (July 2, 2002 for the purpose of making regulations only).

8. Employment Act 2002, s.53 and Sch.7 (December 8, 2002).

9. Tax Credits Act 2002, s.60 and Sch.6 (April 8, 2003).

10. Welfare Reform Act 2007, s.67 and Sch.8 (April 7, 2008).

11. Welfare Reform Act 2007, s.28 and Sch.3 para.10 (October 27, 2008).

12. Welfare Reform Act 2007, s.35 (April 7, 2008).

13. Health and Social Care Act 2008, s.132(1) (July 21, 2008 in relation to enabling the exercise on or after July 21, 2008 of any power to make orders or regulations and defining expressions relevant to the exercise of any such power; January 1, 2009 in relation to England and Wales; not yet in force otherwise).

DERIVATION

Subss.(1) and (2): Social Security Act 1986, s.51(1) and (2). **1.38**

DEFINITIONS

"the Contributions and Benefits Act"—see s.191.
"prescribed"—*ibid.*

GENERAL NOTE

An argument was put in *R(DLA) 4/05* concerning the relationship of reg.13C **1.39** of the Claims and Payments Regulations (further claim for and award of disability living allowance—the provision which permits a continuation claim for a disability living allowance to be made during the last six months of the current award) with s.5. The Tribunal of Commissioners responded:

"Although at first sight regulation 13C(2)(b) may appear to provide a power to make an award, that is not so. Regulation 13C can best be understood by looking at the enabling provisions in section 5 of the 1992 Act. Section 5(1)(c) authorises the making of a regulation that permits a claim to be made in advance. Section 5(1)(d) authorises the making of a regulation that permits an award on such a claim to be made subject to a condition. It does not authorise the making of a regulation that permits an award to be made in advance because it is unnecessary to do so. The power to make an award follows from the duty to determine a claim, imposed on the Secretary of State by sections 1 and 8(1) of the 1998 Act. One can see that regulation 13C(1) is made under section 5(1)(c), regulation 13C(2)(a) is made under section 5(1)(b), regulation 13C(2)(b) is made under section 5(1)(d) and regulation 13C(3) is made under section 5(1)(e). Thus, what regulation 13C(2)(b) permits is not the making of an award in the light of the prospective claim but the imposition of a condition on the award that is required to be made by the 1998 Act. The word 'accordingly' [in reg.13C(2)(b)] therefore means no more than 'on that claim' and its only significance is that it links paragraph (2)(b) with paragraphs (1) and (2)(a) so that, in conformity with the enabling provision (giving effect to the word "such" in both places where it occurs in section 5(1)(d)), the condition may be imposed only on an award made on a renewal claim made in advance and treated as made on the renewal date." (para.16.)

1.40   **6.** *Omitted.*

Community charge benefits, etc.

Relationship between community charge benefits and other benefits

1.41   **7.**—(1) Regulations may provide for a claim for one relevant benefit to be treated, either in the alternative or in addition, as a claim for any other relevant benefit that may be prescribed.

(2) Regulations may provide for treating a payment made or right conferred by virtue of regulations—

(a) under section 5(1)(r) above; or

(b) under section 6(1)(r) to (t) above,

as made or conferred on account of any relevant benefit that is subsequently awarded or paid.

(3) For the purposes of subsections (1) and (2) above relevant benefits are—

(a) any benefit to which section 5 above applies; and

(b) [¹council tax benefit].

AMENDMENT

1. Local Government Finance Act 1992, Sch.9, para.13 (April 1, 1993).

DERIVATION

1.42   Social Security Act 1986, s.51B.

DEFINITIONS

"claim"—see s.191.
"prescribed"—*ibid.*

GENERAL NOTE

Subs. (1)

See Claims and Payments Regulations, Sch.1.   **1.43**

Subs. (2)

See the Social Security (Payments on account, Overpayments and Recovery)   **1.44**
Regulations, regs 5–8.

[¹ Sharing of functions as regards certain claims and information

7A.—(1)Regulations may, for the purpose of supplementing the persons   **1.45**
or bodies to whom claims for relevant benefits may be made, make provision—
  (a) as regards housing benefit or council tax benefit, for claims for that
      benefit to be made to—
        (i) a Minister of the Crown, or
        (ii) a person providing services to a Minister of the Crown;
  (b) as regards any other relevant benefit for claims for that benefit to be
      made to—
        (i) a local authority,
        (ii) a person providing services to a local authority, or
        (iii) a person authorised to exercise any function of a local authority
              relating to housing benefit or council tax benefit.
[⁴ (c) as regards any relevant benefit, for claims for that benefit to be made
      to—
        (i) a county council in England,
        (ii) a person providing services to a county council in England, or
        (iii) a person authorised to exercise any function a county council in
              England has under this section.]
  (2) Regulations may make provision for or in connection with—
  (a) the forwarding by a relevant authority of—
        (i) claims received by virtue of any provision authorised by subsec-
            tion (1) above, and
        (ii) information or evidence supplied in connection with making
             such claims (whether supplied by persons making the claims or
             by other persons);
  (b) the receiving and forwarding by a relevant authority of information
      or evidence relating to social security [³ or work] matters supplied
      by, or the obtaining by a relevant authority of such information or
      evidence from—
        (i) persons making, or who have made, claims for a relevant
            benefit, or
        (ii) other persons in connection with such claims, including informa-
             tion or evidence not relating to the claim or benefit in question;
  (c) the recording by a relevant authority of information or evidence
      relating to social security matters supplied to, or obtained by, the
      authority and the holding by the authority of such information or
      evidence (whether as supplied or obtained or recorded);
  (d) the giving of information or advice with respect to social security
      matters by a relevant authority to persons making, or who have
      made, claims for a relevant benefit.
[⁴ (e) the verification by a relevant authority of information or evidence

35

supplied to or obtained by the authority in connection with a claim for or an award of a relevant benefit.]

(3) In paragraphs (b) and [⁴ (d) and (e)] of subsection (2) above—

(a) references to claims for as relevant benefit are to such claims whether made as mentioned in subsection [⁴ (1)(a) (b) or (c)] above or not; and

(b) references to persons who have made such claims include persons to who awards of benefit have been made on the claims.

(4) Regulations under this section may make different provision for different areas.

(5) Regulations under any other enactment may make such different provision for different areas as appears to the Secretary of State expedient on connection with any exercise by regulations under this section of the power conferred by subsection (4) above.

(6) In this section—

(a) "benefit" includes child support or a war pension (any reference to a claim being read, in relation to child support, as a reference to an application [² (or an application treated as having been made)] under the Child Support Act 1991 for a maintenance assessment [2 maintenance assessment]);

(b) "local authority" means an authority administering housing benefit or council tax benefit;

[⁴ "(c) "relevant authority" means—

   (i) a Minister of the Crown;

   (ii) a local authority;

   (iii) a county council in England;

   (iv) a person providing services to a person mentioned in sub-paragraphs (i) to (iii);

   (v) a person authorised to exercise any function of a local authority relating to housing benefit or council tax benefit;

   (vi) a person authorised to exercise any function a county council in England has under this section;]

(d) "relevant benefit" means housing benefit, council tax benefit or any other benefit prescribed for the purposes of this section;

[³ (e) "social security or work matters" means matters relating to—

   (i) social security, child support or war pensions, or

   (ii) employment or training;]

and in this subsection "war pension" means a war pension within the meaning of section 25 of the Social Security Act 1989 (establishment and functions of war pensions committees).]

AMENDMENTS

1. Welfare Reform and Pensions Act 1999, s.71 (November 11, 1999).

2. Child Support, Pensions and Social Security Act 2000, s.26 and Sch.3, para.12 (March 3, 2003 for certain purposes only: see SI 2003/192).

3. Employment Act 2002, s.53 and Sch.7 (November 24, 2002).

4. Welfare Reform Act 2007, s.41 (July 3, 2007).

[¹ 7B Use of social security information

1.46   (1) A relevant authority may use for a relevant purpose any social security information which it holds.

(2) Regulations may make provision as to the procedure to be followed

by a relevant authority for the purposes of any function it has relating to the administration of a specified benefit if the authority holds social security information which—

(a) is relevant for the purposes of anything which may or must be done by the authority in connection with a claim for or an award of the benefit, and

(b) was used by another relevant authority in connection with a claim for or an award of a different specified benefit or was verified by that other authority in accordance with regulations under section 7A(2) (e) above.

(3) A relevant purpose is anything which is done in relation to a claim which is made or which could be made for a specified benefit if it is done for the purpose of—

(a) identifying persons who may be entitled to such a benefit;

(b) encouraging or assisting a person to make such a claim;

(c) advising a person in relation to such a claim.

(4) Social security information means—

(a) information relating to social security, child support or war pensions;

(b) evidence obtained in connection with a claim for or an award of a specified benefit.

(5) A specified benefit is a benefit which is specified in regulations for the purposes of this section.

(6) Expressions used in this section and in section 7A have the same meaning in this section as in that section.

(7) This section does not affect any power which exists apart from this section to use for one purpose social security information obtained in connection with another purpose.]

AMENDMENT

1. Welfare Reform Act 2007, s.41 (October 1, 2007).

Industrial injuries benefit

Notification of accidents, etc.

8. Regulations may provide—　　　　　　　　　　　　　　　　　　　　　1.47

(a) for requiring the prescribed notice of an accident in respect of which industrial injuries benefit may be payable to be given within the prescribed time by the employed earner to the earner's employer or other prescribed person;

(b) for requiring employers—

　(i) to make reports, to such person and in such form and within such time as may be prescribed, of accidents in respect of which industrial injuries benefit may be payable;

　(ii) to furnish to the prescribed person any information required for the determination of claims, or of questions arising in connection with claims or awards;

　(iii) to take such other steps as may be prescribed to facilitate the giving notice of accidents, the making of claims and the determination of claims and of questions so arising.

DERIVATION

1.48   SSA 1975, s.88.

GENERAL NOTE

1.49   The regulations made under this section are the Claims and Payment Regulations 1979, regs 24 and 25. The provisions of the regulations are, of course, significant in trying to ensure that the adjudicating authorities have access to a record of the circumstances surrounding an industrial accident, and the opportunity to put questions to the employer. Entries in the accident book are not always illuminating, but it is in the interests of the employees that they give the fullest possible contemporaneous account of the accident, particularly where its effects may be slow to emerge (as, sometimes, in head or back injuries).

Medical examination and treatment of claimants

1.50   **9.**—(1) Regulations may provide for requiring claimants for disablement benefit—

(a) to submit themselves from time to time to medical examination for the purpose of determining the effect of the relevant accident, or the treatment appropriate to the relevant injury or loss of faculty;

(b) to submit themselves from time to time to appropriate medical treatment for the injury or loss of faculty.

(2) Regulations under subsection (1) above requiring persons to submit themselves to medical examination or treatment may—

(a) require those persons to attend at such places and at such times as may be required; and

(b) with the consent of the Treasury provide for the payment by the Secretary of State to those persons of travelling and other allowances (including compensation for loss of remunerative time).

DERIVATION

1.51   SSA 1975, s.89.

DEFINITION

"medical examinations," "medical treatment"—see s.191.

GENERAL NOTE

1.52   The regulations referred to are the Claims and Payments Regulations 1979, reg.26.

Obligations of claimants

1.53   **10.**—(1) Subject to subsection (3) below, regulations may provide for disqualifying a claimant for the receipt of industrial injuries benefit—

(a) for failure without good cause to comply with any requirement of regulations to which this subsection applies (including in the case of a claim for industrial death benefit, a failure on the part of some other person to give the prescribed notice of the relevant accident);

(b) for wilful obstruction of, or other misconduct in connection with, any examination or treatment to which he is required under regulations to which this subsection applies to submit himself, or in proceedings under this Act for the determination of his right to benefit or to its receipt,

or for suspending proceedings on the claim or payment of benefit as the case may be, in the case of any such failure, obstruction or misconduct.

(2) The regulations to which subsection (1) above applies are—

(a) any regulations made by virtue of section 5(1)(h), (i) or (l) above, so far as relating to industrial injuries benefit; and

(b) regulations made by virtue of section 8 or 9 above.

(3) Regulations under subsection (1) above providing for disqualification of the receipt of benefit for any of the following matters, that is to say—

(a) for failure to comply withthe requirements of regulations under section 9(1) or (2) above;

(b) for obstruction of, or misconduct in connection with, medical examination or treatment, shall not be made so as to disentitle a claimant to benefit for a period exceeding 6 weeks on any disqualification.

DERIVATION

SSA 1975, s.90(2)–(4) as amended.   **1.54**

GENERAL NOTE

In *R(S)9/51* it was held that a deeply held personal conviction that a claimant's religious beliefs require him or her to refuse to have a medical examination amounted to good cause for refusal to do so. Mere prejudice or distaste for the process will not alone suffice. But the decision did go on to point out the possible consequential difficulties of meeting the burden of proof for entitlement to benefit if the refusal to submit to a medical examination resulted in their being no, or little, medical evidence available. Much would depend on the cogency of the other evidence available which might be sufficient to establish incapacity without full medical evidence. See also *CSIS/065/1991* discussed in the annotations to reg.2 of the Medical Evidence Regulations.   **1.55**

[¹Disabled person's tax credit]

Initial claims and repeat claims

[² . . .]   **1.56**

AMENDMENTS

1. Tax Credits Act 1999, Sch.1 (October 5, 1999).
2. Repealed by Tax Credits Act 2002, s.60 and Sch.6 (April 8, 2003).

DERIVATION

Social Security Act 1986, s.27B(1)–(3).   **1.57**

Necessity of application for certain payments

1.58   **12.**—(1) A social fund payment such as is mentioned in section 138(1)(b) of the Contributions and Benefits Act may be awarded to a person only if an application for such a payment has been made by him or on his behalf in such form and manner as may be prescribed.

(2) The Secretary of State may by regulations—

(a) make provision with respect to the time at which an application for such a social fund payment is to be treated as made;

(b) prescribe conditions that must be satisfied before any determination in connection with such an application may be made or any award of such a payment may be paid;

(c) prescribe circumstances in which such an award becomes extinguished.

DERIVATION

1.59   Social Security Act 1986, s.33(1) and (13).

DEFINITIONS

"the Contributions and Benefits Act"—see s.191.
"prescribed"—ibid.

GENERAL NOTE

Subs. (1)
1.60   This provision applies to the "ordinary" social fund, not to funeral or maternity payments or cold weather payments. See the Social Fund (Applications) Regulations.

Subs. (2)
1.61   See the Social Fund (Miscellaneous Provisions) Regulations.

[¹ Health in pregnancy grant

12A Necessity of application for health in pregnancy grant

1.62   (1) No person is entitled to health in pregnancy grant unless she claims it in the manner, and within the time, prescribed in relation to health in pregnancy grant by regulations under section 5.

(2) No person is entitled to health in pregnancy grant unless subsection (3) or (4) is satisfied in relation to her.

(3) This subsection is satisfied in relation to a person if her claim for health in pregnancy grant is accompanied by—

(a) a statement of her national insurance number and information or evidence establishing that that number has been allocated to her; or

(b) information or evidence enabling the national insurance number that has been allocated to her to be ascertained.

(4) This subsection is satisfied in relation to a person if she makes an application for a national insurance number to be allocated to her which is accompanied by information or evidence enabling a national insurance number to be allocated to her.

(5) The Commissioners for Her Majesty's Revenue and Customs may by regulations make provision disapplying subsection (2) in the case of prescribed descriptions of persons making a claim.]

AMENDMENTS

1. Added by Health and Social Care Act 2008, s.132(3) (July 21, 2008 in relation to enabling the exercise on or after July 21, 2008 of any power to make orders or regulations and defining expressions relevant to the exercise of any such power; January 1, 2009 in relation to England and Wales; not yet in force otherwise).

Child benefit

Necessity of application for child benefit

13.—(1) Subject to the provisions of this Act, no person shall be enti- 1.63
tled to child benefit unless he claims it in the manner, and within the time, prescribed in relation to child benefit by regulations under section 5 above.

[¹ (1A) No person shall be entitled to child benefit unless subsection (1B) below is satisfied in relation to him.

(1B) This subsection is satisfied in relation to a person if—
(a) his claim for child benefit is accompanied by—
    (i) a statement of his national insurance number and information or evidence establishing that that number has been allocated to him; or
    (ii) information or evidence enabling the national insurance number that has been allocated to him to be ascertained; or
(b) he make an application for a national insurance number to be allocated to him which is accompanied by information or evidence enabling such a number to be so allocated.

(1C) Regulations may make provision disapplying subsection (1A) above in the case of—
(a) prescribed descriptions of persons making claims, or
(b) prescribed descriptions of children [² or qualifying young persons] in respect of whom child benefit is claimed,
or in other prescribed circumstances.]

(2) Except where regulations otherwise provide, no person shall be entitled to child benefit for any week on a claim made by him after that week if child benefit in respect of the same child [² or qualifying young person] has already been paid for that week to another person, whether or not that other person was entitled to it.

AMENDMENTS

1. Welfare Reform and Pensions Act 1999, s.69 (May 15, 2000).
2. Child Benefit Act 2005, Sch.1, Pt 1, para.20 (April 10, 2006).

DERIVATION

1.64   CBA 1975, s.6.

GENERAL NOTE

1.65   There is a general bar on receiving child benefit if it has already been paid to someone else in respect of the same child even though that other person was not entitled to it.

The rules relating to claims for and payments of child benefit are now to be found in the Claims and Payments Regulations 1987.

See reg.38 of the Child Benefit (General) Regulations 2006 in Volume 1 for an escape route from the application of the rule in subs.(2).

Statutory sick pay

Duties of employees etc. in relation to statutory sick pay

1.66   **14.**—(1) Any employee who claims to be entitled to statutory sick pay from his employer shall, if so required by his employer, provide such information as may reasonably be required for the purpose of determining the duration of the period of entitlement in question or whether a period of entitlement exists as between them.

(2) The Secretary of State may by regulations [¹ made with the concurrence of the Inland Revenue] direct—

(a) that medical information required under subsection (1) above shall, in such cases as may be prescribed, be provided in a prescribed form;

(b) that an employee shall not be required under subsection (1) above to provide medical information in respect of such days as may be prescribed in a period of incapacity for work.

(3) Where an employee asks an employer of his to provide him with a written statement, in respect of a period before the request is made, of one or more of the following—

(a) the days within that period which the employer regards as days in respect of which he is liable to pay statutory sick pay to that employee;

(b) the reasons why the employer does not so regard the other days in that period;

(c) the employer's opinion as to the amount of statutory sick pay to which the employee is entitled in respect of each of those days,

the employer shall, to the extent to which the request was reasonable, comply with it within a reasonable time.

AMENDMENT

1. Transfer of Functions Act 1999, Sch.3 (April 1, 1999).

DERIVATION

1.67   SSA 1981, s.17(2)–(3).

Statutory maternity pay

Duties of women, etc., in relation to statutory maternity pay

15.—(1) A woman shall provide the person who is liable to pay her stat-   1.68
utory maternity pay—
(a) with evidence as to her pregnancy and the expected date of confinement in such form and at such time as may be prescribed; and
(b) where she commences work after her confinement but within the
maternity pay period, with such additional information as may be
prescribed.
[¹(1A) Any regulations for the purposes of subsection (1) above must be
made with the concurrence of the Inland Revenue.]
(2) Where a woman asks an employer or former employer of hers to
provide her with a written statement, in respect of a period before the
request is made, of one or more of the following—
(a) the weeks within that period which he regards as weeks in respect of
which he is liable to pay statutory maternity pay to the woman,
(b) the reasons why he does not so regard the other weeks in that period,
and
(c) his opinion as to the amount of statutory maternity pay to which the
woman is entitled in respect of each of the weeks in respect of which
he regards himself as liable to make a payment,
the employer or former employer shall, to the extent to which the request
was reasonable, comply with it within a reasonable time.

AMENDMENT

1. Transfer of Functions Act 1999, Sch.3 (April 1, 1999).

DERIVATION

SSA 1986, s.49 and Sch.4, paras 6 and 7.   1.69

[¹*Payments in respect of mortgage interest etc.*]

Payment out of benefit of sums in respect of mortgage interest etc.

15A.—(1) This section applies in relation to cases where—   1.70
(a) mortgage interest is payable to a qualifying lender by a person   1.71
("the borrower") who is entitled, or whose partner, former partner
or qualifying associate is entitled, to income support [² ...] [⁸ an
income-based jobseeker's allowance or an income-related employment and support allowance]; and
(b) a sum in respect of that mortgage interest is or was brought into
account in determining the applicable amount for the purposes of
income support [² ...] [⁸ an income-based jobseeker's allowance or
an income-related employment and support allowance] in the case of
the borrower or the partner, former partner or qualifying associate;
and any reference in this section to "the relevant beneficiary" is a reference
to the person whose applicable amount for the purposes of income support

or[² ...] [⁸ an income-based jobseeker's allowance or an income-related employment and support allowance] is or was determined as mentioned in paragraph (b) above.

[³ (1A) This section also applies in relation to cases where—

(c) mortgage interest is payable to a qualifying lender by a person (also referred to as "the borrower") who is, or whose partner, or former partner or qualifying associate is, entitled to state pension credit; and

(d) a sum in respect of that mortgage interest is or was brought into account in determining the appropriate minimum guarantee for the purposes of state pension credit in the case of the borrower or the partner, former partner or qualifying associate;

and any reference in this section to "the relevant beneficiary" includes a reference to the person whose appropriate minimum guarantee for the purposes of state pension credit is or was determined as mentioned in paragraph (b) above.]

(2) Without prejudice to paragraphs (i) and (p) of section 5(1) above, regulations may, in relation to cases where this section applies, make provision—

(a) requiring that, in prescribed circumstances, a prescribed part of any relevant benefits [³ (other than state pension credit)] to which the relevant beneficiary is entitled shall be paid by the Secretary of State directly to the qualifying lender and applied by that lender towards the discharge of the liability in respect of the mortgage interest;

[³ (aa) authorising or requiring that, in prescribed circumstances, a prescribed part of any state pension credit to which the relevant beneficiary is entitled may (or, as the case may be, shall) be paid by the Secretary of State directly to the qualifying lender and shall be applied by that lender towards the discharge of the liability in respect of the mortgage interest;]

(b) for the expenses of the Secretary of State in administering the making of payments under the regulations to be defrayed, in whole or in part, at the expense of qualifying lenders, whether by requiring them to pay prescribed fees or by deducting and retaining a prescribed part of the payments that would otherwise be made to them under the regulations or by such other method as may be prescribed;

(c) for requiring a qualifying lender, in a case where by virtue of paragraph (b) above the amount of the payment made to him under the regulations is less than it would otherwise have been, to credit against the liability in respect of the mortgage interest (in addition to the payment actually made) an amount equal to the difference between—

(i) the payment that would have been so made, apart from paragraph (b) above; and

(ii) the payment actually made;

and, in any such case, for treating the amount so credited as properly paid on account of benefit due to the relevant beneficiary;

(d) for enabling a body which, or person who, would otherwise be a qualifying lender to elect not to be regarded as such for the purposes of this section, other than this paragraph;

(e) for the recovery from any body or person—

    (i) of any sums paid to that body or person by way of payment under the regulations that ought not to have been so paid; or

    (ii) of any fees or other sums due from that body or person by virtue of paragraph(b) above;

(f) for cases where the same person is the borrower in relation to mortgage interest payable in respect of two or more different loans; and

(g) for any person of a prescribed class or description who would otherwise be regarded for the purposes of this section as the borrower in relation to any mortgage interest not to be so regarded, except for the purposes of this paragraph;

but the Secretary of State shall not make any regulations under paragraph (b) above unless he has consulted with such organisations representing qualifying lenders likely to be affected by the regulations as he considers appropriate.

(3) The bodies and persons who are "qualifying lenders" for the purposes of this section are—

[⁴ (a) a deposit taker;]

  (b) [⁴ . . .]

[⁴ (c) an insurer;]

  (d) any county council, [⁵ county borough council,] district council . . . or London Borough Council,

  (e) the Common Council of the City of London,

[⁶ (ee) any council constituted under section 2 of the Local Government etc (Scotland) Act 1994]

  (f) the Council of the Isles of Scilly,

  (g) any new town corporation, and such bodies or persons not falling within the above paragraphs as may be prescribed.

(4) In this section—

[³ "appropriate minimum guarantee" has the meaning given by section 2(3) of the State Pension Credit Act 2002;]

[⁴ "deposit taker" means—

(a) a person who has permission under Part 4 of the Financial Services and Markets Act 2000 to accept deposits, or

(b) an EEA firm of the kind mentioned in paragraph 5(b) of Schedule 3 to that Act which has permission under paragraph 15 of that Schedule (as a result of qualifying for authorisation under paragraph 12 of that Schedule) to accept deposits;

"insurer" means—

(a) a person who has permission under Part 4 of the Financial Services and Markets Act 2000 to effect and carry out contracts of insurance, or

(b) an EEA firm of the kind mentioned in [paragraph 5(d)] of Schedule 3 to that Act which has permission under paragraph 15 of that Schedule (as a result of qualifying for authorisation under paragraph 12 of that Schedule) to effect and carry out contracts of insurance;]

"mortgage interest" means interest on a loan which is secured by a mortgage of or charge over land, or (in Scotland) by a heritable security, and which has been taken out to defray money applied for any of the following purposes, that is to say—

    (a) acquiring any residential land which was intended, at the time of the acquisition, for occupation by the borrower as his home;

    (b) carrying out repairs or improvements to any residential land which was intended, at the time of taking out the loan, for occupation by the borrower as his home;

    (c) paying off another loan; or

    (d) any prescribed purpose not falling within paragraphs (a) to (c) above;

but interest shall be regarded as mortgage interest by virtue of paragraph (c) above only to the extent that interest on that other loan would have been regarded as mortgage interest for the purposes of this section had the loan not been paid off;

"partner" means—

    (a) any person [7 who is married to, or a civil partner of, the borrower] and who is a member of the same household as the borrower; or

    (b) any person [7 who is neither married to, nor a civil partner of, the borrower but who lives together with the borrower as husband and wife or as if they were civil partners], otherwise than in prescribed circumstances;

and "former partner" means a person who has at some time been, but no longer is, the borrower's partner;

"qualifying associate", in relation to the borrower, means a person who, for the purposes of income support, [3 or an income-based jobseeker's allowance], [8state pension credit or an income-related employment and support allowance], falls to be treated by regulations under Part VII of the Contributions and Benefits Act [8 , the State Pension Credit Act 2002 or Part 1 of the Welfare Reform Act 2007], as responsible for so much of that expenditure which relates to housing costs (within the meaning of those regulations) as consists of any of the mortgage interest payable by the borrower, and who falls to be so treated because—

    (a) the borrower is not meeting those costs, so that the person has to meet them if he is to continue to live in the dwelling occupied as his home; and

    (b) the person is one whom it is reasonable, in the circumstances, to treat as liable to meet those costs;

"relevant benefits" means such of the following benefits as may be prescribed, namely—

    (a) benefits, as defined in section 122 of the Contributions and Benefits Act;

[2 (aa) a jobseeker's allowance;]

    (b) income support;

[3 (c) state pension credit;]

[8 (d) an employment and support allowance;]

"residential land" means any land which consists of or includes a dwelling.

[4 (4A) The definitions of "deposit taker" and "insurer" in subsection (4) must be read with—

    (a) section 22 of the Financial Services and Markets Act 2000;

    (b) any relevant order under that section; and

    (c) Schedule 2 to that Act.]

[⁷ (4B) For the purposes of this section, two people of the same sex are to be regarded living together as if they were civil partners if, but only if, they would be regarded together as husband and wife were they instead two people of the opposite sex.]

(5) For the purposes of this section, regulations may make provision—

(a) as to circumstances in which residential land is or is not to be treated as intended for occupation by the borrower as his home; or

(b) as to circumstances in which persons are to be treated as being or not being members of the same household.]

AMENDMENTS

1. Social Security (Mortgage Interest Payments) Act 1992, s.1 and Sch., para.1 (July 1, 1992; the equivalent amendment to the Social Security Act 1986 came into force on March 16, 1992).

2. Jobseekers Act 1995, Sch.2, para.40 (October 7, 1996).

3. State Pension Credit Act 2002, s.14 and Sch.2 (July 2, 2002 for the purpose only of making regulation; fully in force October 6, 2003).

4. The Financial Services and Markets Act 2000 (Consequential Amendments and Repeals) Order 2001 (SI 2001/3649) (October 6, 2003).

5. Local Government (Wales) Act 1994, Sch.8, para.11 (April 1, 1996).

6. Local Government etc. (Scotland) Act 1994, Sch.13, para.175 (April 1, 1996).

7. Civil Partnership Act 2004, s.254 and Sch.24, para.57 (December 5, 2005).

8. Welfare Reform Act 2007, s.28 and Sch.3, para.10 (October 27, 2008).

DEFINITION

"Contributions and Benefits Act"—see s.191.

GENERAL NOTE

Section 15A authorises the regulations which set out the meat of the scheme for direct payment to lenders of the element of housing costs in relation to income-based benefits to cover mortgage interest and supplies some basic definitions. The main provisions are in Sch.9A to the Claims and Payments Regulations.

1.72

Emergency payments

Emergency payments by local authorities and other bodies

16.—(1) The Secretary of State may make arrangements—

(a) with a local authority to which this section applies; or

(b) with any other body,

for the making on his behalf by members of the staff of any such authority or body of payments on account of benefits to which section 5 above applies in circumstances corresponding to those in which the Secretary of State himself has the power to make such payments under subsection (1)(r) of that section; and a local authority to which this section applies shall have power to enter into any such arrangements.

1.73

(2) A payment under any such arrangements shall be treated for the

purposes of any Act of Parliament or instrument made under an Act of Parliament as if it had been made by the Secretary of State.

(3) The Secretary of State shall repay a local authority or other body such amount as he determines to be the reasonable administrative expenses incurred by the authority or body in making payments in accordance with arrangements under this subsection.

(4) The local authorities to which this section applies are—

(a) a local authority as defined in section 270(1) of the Local Government Act 1972, other than a parish or community council;

(b) the Common Council of the City of London; and

(c) a local authority as defined in section 235(1) of the Local Government (Scotland) Act 1973.

DERIVATION

1.74   Social Security Act 1988, s.8.

PART II

ADJUDICATION

1.75   *Repealed.*

PART III

OVERPAYMENTS AND ADJUSTMENTS OF BENEFIT

Misrepresentation etc.

Overpayments—general

1.76   **71.**—(1) Where it is determined that, whether fraudulently or otherwise, any person has misrepresented, or failed to disclose, any material fact and in consequence of the misrepresentation or failure—

(a) a payment has been made in respect of a benefit to which this section applies; or

(b) any sum recoverable by or on behalf of the Secretary of State in connection with any such payment has not been recovered,

the Secretary of State shall be entitled to recover the amount of any payment which he would not have made or any sum which he would have received but for the misrepresentation or failure to disclose.

[[1](2) Where any such determination as is referred to in subsection (1) above is made, the person making the determination shall [[2] in the case of the Secretary of State or a [[14] First-tier Tribunal], and may in the case of [[14] the Upper Tribunal] or court]—

(a) determine whether any, and if so what, amount is recoverable under that subsection by the Secretary of State, and

48

(b) specify the period during which that amount was paid to the person concerned.]

(3) An amount recoverable under subsection (1)(above is in all cases recoverable from the person who misrepresented the fact or failed to disclose it.

(4) In relation to cases where payments of benefit to which this section applies have been credited to a bank account or other account under arrangements made with the agreement of the beneficiary or a person acting for him, circumstances may be prescribed in which the Secretary of State is to be entitled to recover any amount paid in excess of entitlement; but any such regulations shall not apply in relation to any payment unless before he agreed to the arrangements such notice of the effect of the regulations as may be prescribed was given in such manner as may be prescribed to the beneficiary or to a person acting for him.

(5)[[12] . . .]

[[4] (5A) Except where regulations otherwise provide, an amount shall not be recoverable [[12] under subsection (1) or under regulations under subsection (4) above unless the determination in pursuance of which it was paid has been reversed or varied on an appeal or [[2] has been revised under section 9 or superseded under section 10 of the Social Security Act 1998]]].

(6) Regulations may provide—

(a) that amounts recoverable under subsection (1) above or regulations under subsection (4) above shall be calculated or estimated in such manner and on such basis as may be prescribed;

(b) for treating any amount paid to any person under an award which is subsequently determined was not payable—

(i) as properly paid; or

(ii) as paid on account of a payment which it is determined should be or should have been made, and for reducing or withholding any arrears payable by virtue of the subsequent determination;

(c) for treating any amount paid to one person in respect of another as properly paid for any period for which it is not payable in cases where in consequence of the subsequent determination—

(i) the other person is himself entitled to a payment for that period; or

(ii) a third person is entitled in priority to the payee to a payment for that period in respect of the other person, and for reducing or withholding any arrears payable for that period by virtue of the subsequent determination.

(7) Circumstances may be prescribed in which a payment on account by virtue of section 5(1)(r) above may be recovered to the extent that it exceeds entitlement.

(8) Where any amount paid [[8], other than an amount paid in respect of child benefit or guardian's allowance,] is recoverable under—

(a) subsection (1) above;

(b) regulations under subsection (4) or (7) above; or

(c) section 74 below,

it may, without prejudice to any other method of recovery, be recovered by deduction from prescribed benefits.

(9) Where any amount paid in respect of a [[11] couple] is recoverable as mentioned in subsection (8) above, it may, without prejudice to any other method of recovery, be recovered, in such circumstances as may

be prescribed, by deduction from prescribed benefits payable to either of them.

(10) Any amount recoverable under the provisions mentioned in subsection (8) above—

(a) if the person from whom it is recoverable resides in England and Wales and the county court so orders, shall be recoverable by execution issued from the county court or otherwise as if it were payable under an order of that court; and

(b) if he resides in Scotland, shall be enforced in like manner as an extract registered decree arbitral bearing a warrant for execution issued by the sheriff court of any sheriffdom in Scotland.

[⁵(10A) Where—

(a) a jobseeker's allowance is payable to a person from whom any amount is recoverable as mentioned in subsection (8) above; and

(b) that person is subject to a bankruptcy order,

a sum deducted from that benefit under that subsection shall not be treated as income of his for the purposes of the Insolvency Act 1986.

(10B) Where—

(a) a jobseeker's allowance is payable to a person from whom any amount is recoverable as mentioned in subsection (8) above; and

(b) the estate of that person is sequestrated,

a sum deducted from that benefit under that subsection shall not be treated as income of his for the purposes of the Bankruptcy (Scotland) Act 1985.]

(11) This section applies to the following benefits—

(a) benefits as defined in section 122 of the Contributions and Benefits Act;

[⁶(aa) subject to section 71A below, a jobseeker's allowance;]

[⁹(ab) state pension credit;]

[¹³(ac) an employment and support allowance;]

(b) [⁷ . . .] income support;

(c) [¹⁰ . . .]

(d) [¹⁰ . . .]

(e) any social fund payments such as are mentioned in section 138(1)(a) or (2) of the Contributions and Benefits Act; and

[¹⁵ (ea) health in pregnancy grant; and]

(f) child benefit."

[¹¹ (12) In this section, "couple" has the meaning given by section 137(1) of the Contributions and Benefits Act.]

AMENDMENTS

1. Social Security (Overpayments) Act 1996, s.1(2) (for determination made after July 24, 1996).

2. Social Security Act 1998, Sch.7 (July 5, 1999).

3. Social Security (Overpayments) Act 1996, s.1(3) (for determinations made after July 24, 1996).

4. Social Security (Overpayments) Act 1996, s.1(4) (for determinations made after July 24, 1996).

5. Jobseekers Act 1995, s.32(1) (October 7, 1996).

6. Jobseekers Act 1995, Sch.2 (October 7, 1996).

7. Jobseekers Act 1995, Sch.3 (October 7, 1996).

8. Tax Credits Act 2002, s.51 and Sch.4 (February 26, 2003 for the purpose of making regulations only; April 1, 2003 for the purpose of transfer of functions only; for remaining purposes date to be appointed).

9. State Pension Credit Act 2002, s.14 and Sch.2 (July 2, 2002 for the purposes of making regulations only; fully in force October 6, 2003).

10. Tax Credits Act 2002, s.60 and Sch.6 (April 8, 2003).

11. Civil Partnership Act 2004, s.254 and Sch.24, para.58 (December 5, 2005).

12. Welfare Reform Act 2007, s.44 (July 3, 2007).

13. Welfare Reform Act 2007, s.28 and Sch.3, para.10 (October 27, 2008).

14. The Transfer of Tribunal Functions Order 2008 (SI 2008/2833), art.103 (November 3, 2008).

15. Health and Social Care Act 2008, s.132(4) (January 1, 2009 in relation to England and Wales; not yet in force otherwise).

DERIVATION

Social Security Act 1986, s.53. **1.77**

GENERAL NOTE

This general note is structured under the following headings: **1.78**
Regulations: para.**1.79**
Limitation periods: para.**1.80**
Recovery of overpayments and bankruptcy: para **1.81**
Recovery at common law: para **1.82**
The requirement for revision or supersession as a precondition for recovery: para.**1.83**
The Secretary of State must present all the evidence: para **1.84**
The test to be applied: para.**1.85**
Any person: para.**1.86**
Appointees: para.**1.87**
The common law of agency: para.**1.88**
Overpayments involving spouses: para.**1.89**
Recoverability decisions against a claimant's estate where there are no duly constituted personal representatives: para.**1.90**
Whether fraudulently or otherwise: para.**1.91**
Misrepresents: para.**1.92**
Fails to disclose: para.**1.93**
Mental capacity: para.**1.96**
Material fact: para.**1.97**
Missing documents: para.**1.98**
Causation: para.**1.99**
The amount of the overpayment which is recoverable: para.**1.100**
Automated credit transfers: para.**1.101**
Tax credits: substitution of subs.(8)–(9): para.**1.102**
Welfare Reform and Pensions Act 1999: para.**1.103**
A useful book: para.**1.104**

Regulations
The regulations referred to in this section are the Social Security (Payments on **1.79**
Account, Overpayments and Recovery) Regulations 1988, para. 2.684 below.

Limitation periods
Arguments that overpayments are not recoverable because of the application of **1.80**
the limitation periods applicable to the recovery of debts in actions before the courts
are destined to fail. In *R(SB)5/91* the Commissioner said,

"The plain fact is that section 9(1) of the Limitation Act 1980 simply has no
application to proceedings before the adjudicating authorities. But when the
amount of the overpayment has been *finally* determined by them, as in this case it
is by my decision (unless it is proposed to take the matter on appeal to the Court

51

of Appeal) then, and then only, for the purposes of recovery of the overpayment by action in the Courts, time begins to run." (para.7.)

In *CIS/026/1994* the claimant sought a review of the overpayment decision on the grounds that the Secretary of State was no longer able to seek recovery of the overpaid benefit because more than six years had passed and any action in a court would be barred by the operation of s.9(1) of the Limitation Act 1980, and that this constituted a relevant change of circumstances. The overpayment was at the time of the application being recovered at the rate of £5 per week from the claimant's retirement pension. The Commissioner regarded the applications as wholly misconceived (as had the tribunal). The Commissioner confirmed that, so far as relevant to social security payments, "the Limitation Acts take away only the remedy by action or by set-off and that they leave the right otherwise untouched. The social security adjudicating authorities are not concerned with and have no jurisdiction in respect of remedies by action or set-off." (para.5.)

Recovery of overpayments and bankruptcy

1.81   A number of cases have considered the interrelationship between s.71 and the bankruptcy provisions of the Insolvency Act 1986. It seems that the timing of determinations under s.71 will be relevant in deciding whether a discharged bankrupt is freed from liability for deductions from benefit in repayment of an overpayment of benefit.

R. *(Steele) v Birmingham City Council and another*, [2005] EWCA Civ 1824 concerned an overpayment of jobseeker's allowance. The claimant was awarded the benefit in December 1999. In September 2001, he was adjudged bankrupt on his own petition. In March 2002 an overpayment decision was made by the Secretary of State. Recovery of the overpayment was by means of deductions from benefit. The deductions were suspended during the period of bankruptcy, but were started again when the claimant was discharged from his bankruptcy. The claimant argued that the payments were a contingent liability within the meaning of the Insolvency Act 1986 and therefore he was released from this debt following his discharge from bankruptcy. In judicial review proceedings at first instance, the claimant was successful. But the decision was successfully appealed by the Secretary of State. The Court of Appeal ruled that the claimant was under no obligation or liability to repay the overpaid benefit until a determination was made under s.71. No such determination had been made before the date of his bankruptcy. It followed that the overpaid amount was not a bankruptcy debt for the purposes of a release on discharge from bankruptcy under s.281(1) of the Insolvency Act 1986.

Different timings applied in R. *(Balding) v Secretary of State for Work and Pensions*, [2007] EWCA Civ 1327. The claimant was in receipt of income support. An overpayment determination was made in July 1994. In June 1995 the claimant, on his own petition, was adjudged to be bankrupt. The claimant was discharged from bankruptcy in June 1998. The Secretary of State sought to recover the overpayment by deductions from the claimant's benefit, arguing that such deductions were outside the scope of the bankruptcy legislation. The Court of Appeal upheld the decision of the Administrative Court: [2007] EWCA 759 (Admin) and praised the judgment of Davis J. in the court below for its depth of analysis of the issues involved. Regardless of the method of recovery chosen by the Secretary of State (deductions from benefit, or recovery in debt proceedings in the courts), there was a liability to repay money under an enactment. Discharge from bankruptcy wiped out the liability to repay the sum under the insolvency legislation.

Recovery at common law

1.82   The issue of recovery of overpaid benefit at common law is raised in obiter comments in R. *(Steele) v Birmingham City Council and another*, [2005] EWCA Civ 1824. Counsel for the claimant had argued in the alternative that the claimant was under a common law obligation to make repayment by way of restitution as soon as it was paid. Nourse L.J. said that this submission was based on a misunderstanding of something which had been said by himself and Millett L.J. in *Chief Adjudication Officer v Sheriff*, Court of Appeal, May 4, 1995, which referred to recovery on ordinary principles of restitution. In commenting on what had been said in the earlier case, Nourse L.J. noted:

> "It is clear that our observations were directed simply to the case where the benefit is paid without a claim having been made. Once a claim is made, the machinery of section 71 is invoked and there is no room for recovery at common law, whether by way of restitution or otherwise."

Accordingly, Nourse L.J. rejected this submission (para.16). However, Arden L.J. did not consider it necessary in this appeal to express a view on the question whether section 71 supersedes any remedy at common law (para.28).

It therefore remains unclear whether there is any separate power of recovery under common law, but it may be fair to say that the odds are stacked against such a liability arising under principles of restitution save in the most exceptional cases (such as payment without a claim which was what had been envisaged in the remarks made in the *Sheriff* case).

The judicial review brought by the Child Poverty Action Group to test the proposition that recovery of overpaid benefit other than through the mechanism in s.71 is unlawful has now been decided: *R. (on the application of the Child Poverty Action Group) v Secretary of State for Work and Pensions,* [2009] EWHC 341 (Admin). The decision is that s.71 "neither expressly nor by necessary implication removes the Defendant's power to claim repayment at common law of money paid by mistake." (para.31). The mistake may arise as one of fact or law (para.33). The judge expresses the hope that the Secretary of State will consider "the wording of the letter and any accompanying document sent to recipients of benefit". It seems that the current letter and documents do not make clear that recovery at common law is available only where there has been a mistake of fact or law. The decision of the Administrative Court is under appeal to the Court of Appeal.

The requirement for revision or supersession as a precondition for recovery

For a person to be paid benefit, a decision maker will have made a decision awarding the benefit. If it later turns out that benefit has been paid to which the claimant was not entitled, that decision must be changed before the benefit is recoverable. The decision which changes the entitlement to benefit for a past period through the process of revision or supersession is generally referred to as the *entitlement decision.* The entitlement decision must be clear as to what the entitlement should have been for the period or periods in issue.

1.83

A second decision will be made, based on the entitlement decision, calculating the amount of the overpayment and deciding that it is recoverable from the claimant because the claimant failed to disclose or misrepresented a material fact which caused the overpayment of benefit to be made. This decision is generally referred to as the *recoverability decision*. It can be made at the same time as the entitlement decision, or at a later date. Section 71(5A) of the Administration Act 1992 provides (subject to the rule found in reg.12 of the Overpayments Regulations discussed below) that no amount is recoverable unless there has been an entitlement decision.

If the two decisions are made at different times, an appeal against a recoverability decision does not also constitute an appeal against the underlying entitlement decision.

CIS/3512/2007 addressed an important point in relation to entitlement decisions and overpayment decisions which are separated in time. In this case, a decision maker in November 2004 determined that the appellant and partner were living together as husband and wife with the consequence that the appellant ceased to be entitled to income support. That decision was upheld on appeal to a tribunal in May 2005. In February 2005 a revised overpayment decision was made that a large overpayment was recoverable from the appellant. On appeal to a tribunal against that decision, a tribunal considered that the appellant and partner were not at the material time living together as husband and wife. On the Secretary of State's appeal to the Commissioner, the question of whether the second tribunal could revisit the decision on cohabitation addressed by the first tribunal was raised. The Secretary of State's representative submitted that the second tribunal was not precluded from revisiting the factual issue because of the wording of s.17 of the Social Security Act 1998 on finality of decisions. The consequence was that "while, ... the determination of the fact [of cohabitation] was conclusive for the purposes of entitlement, it was not so in relation to the issue of disclosure of a material fact [for the purposes of the overpayment decision]" (para.8). The Commissioner accepts the correctness of this proposition with some reluctance, although he commented that it appeared "absurd that the same issue of fact should be capable of being determined by two separate tribunals in a manner which is contradictory." (para.8).

R(IS) 1/09 involved a set of circumstances with some similarity to those which arose in *CIS/3512/2007*. The issue here related to the beneficial ownership of a house. The entitlement decision was to the effect that the appellant had no entitlement to income support because he had capital in excess of the prescribed limits. The appellant appealed against this decision, but was unsuccessful. Subsequently an overpayment decision was made. The appeal against this was heard by the same chairman who had heard the appeal against the entitlement decision. In that appeal, there was a full reconsideration of the issues underlying the entitlement decision, even though the chairman considered that he was bound by his earlier decision on entitlement. He had proceeded to full consideration of the factual issue in case he was wrong on the proposition that he was bound by his earlier decision. On appeal to the Commissioner, the question of apparent bias was canvassed on the initiative of the Commissioner. The ultimate conclusion was that there was nothing in this case which would lead a fair-minded and informed observed to doubt the chairman's impartiality. There was, accordingly, nothing to taint the tribunal's decision.

There is considerable case law on the extent to which tribunals and Commissioners can correct defects in the entitlement decision which must precede or accompany the recoverability decision. This is discussed below.

A common ground on which appeals to the Commissioner have succeeded is whether there have been proper entitlement and recoverability decisions: see R (IS)7/91. In a number of unreported decisions (*CSSB/621/1988, CSSB/316/1989, CSSB/517/1989* and *CSIS/118/1990)* Commissioners have exhorted tribunal to remember that revision or supersession evidenced by an entitlement decision is a prerequisite to recovery under s.71. Where the overpayments span a number of years, every decision over that period must be identified and revised before the overpayment is recoverable: see para.6 of *CSIS/45/1990*, and *CPC/3743/2006*

In *R(IS) 13/05* the Commissioner confirmed that a decision that a couple is living together as husband and wife is not a decision which meets the requirements of s.71(5A), and a decision that an overpayment is recoverable cannot be based on such a determination. Such a decision is commonly only the first step in revising or superseding a person's entitlement to benefit. It is the ensuing decisions on which an overpayment decision must be founded.

In *CIS/1055/1997* the Commissioner holds that the determination referred to is a recovery determination (and not an entitlement determination). The new provisions apply to recovery determinations made after July 24, 1996 regardless of the date of any entitlement determination (including the entitlement determination which resulted in there having been an overpayment of benefit). In *CSIS/174/1996* the Commissioner indicated that in his view the determination must be that of an adjudication officer and could not be a decision of a tribunal correcting an earlier omission. The Commissioner considers that best practice is for the review decision itself to be put before the tribunal and not simply a summary of it in the written submission to the tribunal. This is considered essential where the claimant puts in issue any of its terms.

In *CSB/1272/1989* the Commissioner considers whether a tribunal could use its powers to determine questions first arising in the course of the appeal to correct a failure by an adjudication officer to review the award of benefit as required by what was then s.53(4) of the Social Security Act 1986. That decision attracted some cautionary comments in *CSB/1093/1989*. The issue is now largely academic since the power to determine questions first arising in the course of the appeal has not been re-enacted in the Social Security Act 1998. There will be little alternative but to set aside any decision where there has not been a review as required by the section.

The nature of the evidence which an adjudication officer was expected to produce to demonstrate that there has been a review was considered in *R(IS)2/96*. The Commissioner holds that a computer print-out is not sufficient by itself to establish that a review has taken place (though it might, if the output is intelligible and records that a proper determination had taken place), since there must be some human interaction with the computer to convert computer-based information into a review decision. The Commissioner notes that the computer print-out in issue in the case was, by itself, unintelligible. However, verbal evidence to interpret the print-out, or submission of a copy of a letter informing the claimant of the decision which contained sufficient detail might suffice to show that there had been a review and revision of entitlement. Failure to provide such evidence would mean that the adjudication officer had failed to meet the burden of proof in overpayment cases.

In *CIS/362/2002* the Commissioner re-affirms that recovery is conditional on a valid revision or supersession of the decision awarding benefit. Defects of form might be correctable by tribunals and Commissioners, but not defects of substance. In this case, the relevant decision "was so defective in substance as to be invalid as a supersession in relation to the relevant period.": (para.12). In *CIS/764/2002* the same Commissioner clarified his views on this issue as follows:

"In a supersession case not involving overpayment recoverability an appeal tribunal may, if the relevant evidence is available, conduct or perfect a defective decision taken by the Secretary of State, providing that the defects in the Secretary of State's decision are not so great that it must be said that the decision is invalid, rather than merely defective. In my judgment that is the line to be drawn, not a line between defects of substance and defects of form. That is what I said recently in paragraph 12 of decision *CIS/362/2002* [and] was consistent with the Tribunal of Commissioners' decision *R(IS) 2/97*. I did not say there, as Mr Miller suggested in his written submission dated 20 August 2002, that no defects of substance could be corrected. I referred to 'defects of substance which rendered the purported review invalid' and to a decision being 'so defective in substance as to be invalid as a supersession'. Defects merely of form may always be corrected by an appeal tribunal. Defects of substance may be corrected, providing that they are not so great as to render the decision invalid. In a case where the decision under appeal combines an overpayment recoverability decision with a supersession decision, that general approach is not displaced, for the reasons given in paragraph 41 of decision *CSIS/399/2001* and *CSIS/400/2001*. It may be different if the overpayment recoverability decision is taken separately from the supersession decision and is appealed on its own." (para.11.)

R(IB) 2/04 considered the scope of the general power to make review and supersession decisions under ss.9 and 10 of the 1998 Act, and concluded that tribunals had powers to remedy defects in decisions save where they were so serious as to render the decision in issue wholly incoherent. In general a Secretary of State's decision which altered the original decision with effect from the date of the original decision should be treated as a review under s.9 and a Secretary of State's decision which altered the decision from a later date should be treated as a supersession under s.10. This broad interpretation of a tribunal's powers has not removed all the difficulties in relation to the procedural requirements in relation to overpayments decisions. In *CIS/362/2003*, the Commissioner had noted that the test for remedying defects in overpayments cases may be stricter than in other cases.

This issue is further explored in *CIS/3228/2003*. The case concerned a decision that there had been a £6,018.53 overpayment of income support, which had arisen when the claimant had failed to disclose the receipt of a residence order allowance. After an adjournment before the tribunal, the Secretary of State had produced a certificate indicating that on December 11, 2001 a decision had been made superseding the award of income support from January 4, 1996 but purporting to revise the claimant's entitlement arising from a decision of January 4, 1996. However, the submission to the tribunal stated that all decisions awarding income support from January 4, 1996 were superseded, whereas the certified decision related only to the first decision awarding benefit.

There was no dispute that the proper process for complying with s.71(5) required a decision *revising* all the decisions awarding benefit; these would take effect from the date of the decisions which were revised. But a supersession decision on the grounds of ignorance of fact could only take effect from the date of the supersession decision. The Secretary of State's representative conceded that the certified decision was defective in that it certified a supersession decision rather than a revision decision.

The Commissioner concludes that a certified record of a decision is conclusive evidence of the decision (para.13). However, in the light of the decision of the Tribunal of Commissioners in *R(IB) 2/04* it was open to a tribunal to regard the decision as a revision rather than a supersession:

16. In my judgment, a tribunal's power to overlook mere defects of form in decisions made under section 9 or section 10 of the 1998 Act is not limited to cases where a supersession decision or a decision which has been revised under section 9 is under appeal to the tribunal. In *CIS/764/2002* Mr Commissioner Mesher held that defects of substance in a decision which were not so great as to affect its validity could be corrected by a tribunal if the supersession decision and the overpayment recoverability decision were both under appeal. Although the Commissioner reserved the position in relation to such cases where an overpayment recoverability decision is taken separately from the supersession decision and is appealed on its own, he did not suggest that it was necessary for the supersession decision to be under appeal in order for the tribunal to have power to ignore errors which did not affect the substance of the decision.

17. If the decision in this case recorded in the certified record is taken at face value, it changed the decision awarding income support as from the date on which the awarding decision took effect, and could therefore only have been a revision decision under section 9 of the 1998 Act. The record of the decision gave a valid ground for the making of such a decision, namely that the decision awarding benefit was made in ignorance of a material fact. The tribunal was not called on to exercise any jurisdiction over the decision altering entitlement to benefit, other than to determine whether a valid decision had been made which complied with the requirements of section 71(5A) of the Administration Act. On the basis that the certified record of the decision taken on 11 December 2001 was correct in recording a decision which removed benefit from the date of the award, I do not consider that the erroneous description of the decision as a supersession decision prevented the tribunal from regarding it as a valid revision decision.

However, although the tribunal could have treated the supersession decision as a revision decision, there remained defects which rendered the overpayment not recoverable in that the decision did not alter all the decisions awarding benefit (only the first decision), and the decision failed to specify the amounts of the revised entitlement. On the latter point the Commissioner says:

20. . . . . . I consider that a decision awarding a claimant benefit of a stated amount can only be effectively revised if it is replaced by a new decision which also specifies the amount of benefit (if any) to which the claimant is entitled, in the light of

the fact which was not taken into account when the original decision was made. A revision decision to the effect that an earlier decision awarding benefit of a specified amount has been "revised", but which does not state the amount of the revised entitlement is, in my judgment inchoate. If a revision (or supersession) decision resulting in an overpayment is made separately from a recovery decision, it will therefore be necessary for the claimant's revised benefit entitlement to be calculated as part of the revision decision before a valid overpayment recoverability decision can be made under section 71(1).

In this case, the Secretary of State appears to have been hoist with his own petard in certifying a decision. That is conclusive and cannot be revisited. Although it could be treated as a valid revision decision, if it remained defective for not referring to all relevant decisions awarding benefit, and if it failed to specify the amount of the revised entitlement, it could not ground recovery of overpaid benefit.

In *CIS/0170/2003* a different Commissioner took the same view, noting further that there could not be a supersession decision based upon change of circumstances where the claimant's circumstances had not changed. It is not a change of circumstances where something new which has been in existence for a long time comes to the notice of the Secretary of State. In this decision, the Commissioner warns tribunals against being too ready to substitute revision decisions for faulty supersession decisions. In many cases, there will be insufficient evidence (especially where one or both parties is not present) and the tribunal must take care not simply to "construct a narrative" to borrow a phrase from *CIS/3228/2003*. Furthermore, where computer printouts are provided under the Generalised Matching Service, these must be accompanied by full explanations of the significance of the various codes used. Otherwise there is a real risk of making findings of fact which no reasonable tribunal could make.

The outcome is that there will remain scope for arguments to be put before tribunals that the procedural requirements for recovery of overpaid benefit have not been met.

CIS/3605/2005 was concerned with the application of s.71(5A) in a case in which the amount of income support to which the claimant was entitled had reduced following the cessation of child benefit. Complications arose when that entitlement had been resurrected for a number of periods. The claimant argued that the revision decision had been made in ignorance of the true position on the dates for which child benefit had been awarded and so was invalid. The Commissioner concluded:

> "10. It seems to me that the claimant's argument confuses the concepts of correctness and validity. The Secretary of State had statutory power to make the decision of 14th August 2002, even if it was based on an inaccurate understanding of the facts. It was subject to supersession, revision, and appeal, but until one of those events took place it was, in law, a valid decision, and satisfied the requirements of section 71(5A) for the purposes of a recoverability decision.
>
> 11. This approach is consistent with the jurisprudence of the House of Lords in administrative law. Thus, a decision which might traditionally have been regarded as void is nevertheless to be treated as having legal effect until a court has decided that it is void (*Re Racal Communications Ltd* [1980] 2 All ER 634) and an order may be void for one purpose and valid for another (*Calvin v Carr* [1980] AC 574; *R v Wicks* [1998] AC 92)."

CIS/764/2002 and *CIS/3228/2003*, on the need for revision or supersession of all decisions authorising payment of benefit during a period of alleged overpayment, have been followed in *CIS/203/2002* (a post-*Hinchy* decision of August 24, 2006).

CIB/2762/2007 provides guidance for tribunals on the proper approach in a case in which there are separate entitlement and overpayment decisions, where the appellant has appealed only against the overpayment decision, and where it transpires that the entitlement decision contains an error of law. In the case before him the error of law in the entitlement decision completely undermined the overpayment decision. In such circumstances the tribunal is precluded from making any change to the entitlement decision, but that does not mean that it is powerless to address the issue. The proper course of action in such cases is to adjourn the appeal with directions for the Secretary of State to revise the entitlement decision, and then in consequence of that revision to revise the overpayment decision. This is rather complex and so it may be helpful to reproduce the Commissioner's decision on the appeal:

> "27. For the reason given above, the decision of the appeal tribunal of 19 March 2007 must be set aside as erroneous in point. It is expedient for me to substitute the decision that the appeal tribunal should have given on the claimant's appeal against the decision of 8 May 2006 on its findings of fact. However, for the same reasons as given above, justice requires that I should defer giving a decision until the Secretary of State has had an opportunity to consider the revision of the decisions of 6 March 2006 and 8 May 2006. I refer the case to the Secretary of State for that consideration to be given as soon as possible. I direct the representative of the Secretary of State, as well as informing the claimant of the outcome of that consideration, to inform me of the outcome and to say whether or not it is submitted that the claimant's appeal against the decision of 8 May 2006 has lapsed. I shall then either give a ruling that that appeal has lapsed and that my present decision is the final one or give a decision on that appeal. If for any reason the Secretary of State is not able to comply with that direction within one month of the date on which this decision is sent to him, an explanation in writing is to be sent to the Commissioners' office."

The Secretary of State must present all the evidence

1.84 Generally in overpayment cases, the burden is on the Secretary of State to establish all the facts which justify a conclusion that an overpayment is recoverable. The absence of a representative of the Secretary of State in tribunals can present difficulties, and tribunals will need to consider whether it is fair to both parties to adjourn with directions for the submission of further evidence where the evidence presented in the papers on behalf of the Secretary of State is incomplete.

In *C1/06-07(IS)*, a Commissioner in Northern Ireland stresses the importance of the Department's presenting documentary evidence in support of key matters on which the decision to recover overpaid benefit is based. In this case, it was two forms through which the Department claimed to have notified the claimant that he had been found capable of work. Had the claimant disclosed the content of these decisions the overpayment of income support in issue could not have occurred. The Commissioner said,

> "26. . . . In general terms I consider that the Department should supply copies or pro formas of relevant notifications in recoverability cases. In cases where notification is an issue the tribunal should ask to see at least pro formas of these documents if they have not been furnished."

A similar point on the need for the Secretary of State to present all the evidence to the tribunal was made by the Commissioner in *CIS/1462/2006*, a case in which there was a possible trust which meant that the claimant had no beneficial interest in certain resources. The Commissioner also criticises (in paras 18–20) in strong terms the failure of the Secretary of State to ensure representation in cases, such as this, which are of some complexity. He also noted that the burden of proof rests with the Secretary of State.

The test to be applied

1.85 The test laid down in subs.(1) requires a number of conditions to be satisfied. Where:

(a) any person

(b) whether fraudulently or otherwise

(c) misrepresents, or

(d) fails to disclose

(e) a material fact

(f) and this results in an overpayment of benefit for any period

the amount of the overpayment is recoverable from the person misrepresenting or failing to disclose that material fact.

It is for the Department to prove on the balance of probabilities the facts which justify the recovery of the overpayment: *R(SB)43/83*. Appeals involving overpayments require fastidious attention to the facts which are often hotly disputed. In such disputes having regard to where the burden of proof lies is particularly important.

Any person

The person making the misrepresentation or failing to disclose need not be the claimant. It can be anyone. In *R(SB)21/82* recovery was sought from the claimant's wife; and in *R(SB)23/83* it was the claimant's personal representative. It had been made clear in *Secretary of State for Social Services v Solly* [1974] 3 All E.R. 922 that recovery from the estate of a deceased person was possible. However, tribunals are not the place in which which objections to liability by the executor on the grounds, for example, that the estate has already been distributed are to be resolved. Those are matters concerning a decision to pursue recovery (which were reserved under the old adjudication system for the Secretary of State) rather than liability for the overpayment, and may need adjudication in court: *R(SB)1/96*.

Non-disclosure by someone other than the claimant requires some clear evidence of responsibility on that person to disclose information. In *R(SB)21/82* the Commissioner said that the non-disclosure must have occurred "in circumstances in which, at least, disclosure by the person was reasonably to be expected." Following the decision of the Court of Appeal in *B v Secretary of State* (see below at para.1.93), it is eminently arguable that the source of the obligation is much higher than this, namely that recovery from a third party can only succeed where a legal obligation to disclose can be established.

In *CG/065/1989* the adjudication officer had sought recovery (in addition to recovery from the claimant) from two solicitors who had acted for the claimant. The Commissioner advises that where recovery is sought from more than one party, a tribunal should deal with the recoverability of the overpayment from each of the parties covered by the adjudication officer's decision. It will not be enough to decide only that the overpayment is recoverable from the claimant.

Appointees

Special considerations can arise where recovery is sought from an appointee.

In *CG/065/1989*, a case concerning recovery from solicitor appointees, the Commissioner contemplated recovery being available from both the claimant and any appointee. In *CIS/734/1992* the Commissioner held that there could be no recovery from the claimant by reason of the appointee's misrepresentation or failure to disclose, but there could be recovery from the appointee. In *CIS/332/1993* the acts of the appointee, when acting as such, are treated as acts of the claimant and so recovery is only available from the claimant (or the claimant's estate) and not the appointee (paras 22–24). Reliance is placed, in part, on an analogy with the situation in *R(SB)34/83*, which concerned a failure to disclose material facts by a receiver appointed by the Court of Protection, and where the resulting overpayment was recoverable from the claimant's estate rather than from the receiver personally.

1.86

1.87

The Commissioner notes that the decision in *CIS/734/1992*, which was predicated on the claimant's lack of capacity because of his mental state, meant that it would be inappropriate to impute to him any failure to disclose or misrepresentation of the appointee. But it is, of course, of the essence of an appointment that the claimant is for some reason unable to act. Are distinctions based on physical and mental capacity appropriate when reg.33 of the Claims and Payments Regulations under which such appointments are made speaks of the appointee exercising any right to which the claimant may be entitled? The Commissioner acknowledges that the matter is one of extreme difficulty.

In *R(IS)5/00* a different Commissioner describes the distinction between a person in their capacity as appointee and in their personal capacity as "puzzling and metaphysical". In upholding the decision of a tribunal that an overpayment was recoverable from an appointee who was the mother of the claimant and had failed to disclose increases in the claimant's savings, the Commissioner appears to differ from the view that the capacity in which a person acts affects the person from whom the overpayment is recoverable.

There is logic in both positions. The first Commissioner is making the point that an appointee's acts are those of the claimant who is unable to act for himself or herself. If a person is acting as appointee, then the recovery should be from the claimant. The second Commissioner reflects the realities of daily life by noting that a person in the position of appointee will almost certainly not make clear distinctions in the capacity in which they are dealing with the Department. If they should have disclosed something such as an increase in savings, then recovery can be sought from them as well as from the claimant.

The decision of the Tribunal of Commissioners in *R(IS)5/03* was handed down on October 28, 2002. The principal point in issue related to the liability of appointees for overpayments of benefit under s.71(3) of the Social Security Administration Act 1992. The appeal had been referred to a Tribunal of Commissioners in order to resolve the conflict between *CIS/332/1993* and *R(IS) 5/00*.

The overpayment had arisen when income support continued in payment at the previous rate when the costs of the claimant's accommodation in a nursing home was met wholly by the health authority. The claimant's mother was her appointee under an appointment made by the Secretary of State for all benefit purposes. The appointee had failed to inform the Department that the costs of her daughter's accommodation in a nursing home were fully met by the health authority.

The Tribunal of Commissioners draws on the common law relating to agency, but recognises that the social security context requires certain modification to the common law rules applicable in a contractual situation. This is justified, in particular, because normal agency principles come into play where the principal has delegated authority to an agent. In the social security context, no such delegation exists, since it is the payer (the Secretary of State) who authorises another to act on behalf of persons unable to act for themselves. The benefit recipient, where reg.33 of the Claims and Payments Regulations applies, is not a party to the delegation of powers. It had been argued by the appellant and CPAG that to render the appointee personally liable would produce a situation in which, for example, social workers might be unwilling to undertake responsibilities as appointees to the disadvantage of benefit recipients. The Tribunal of Commissioners in preferring the principles set out in *R(IS) 5/00*, and concluding that *CIS/332/1993* is wrongly decided, mollified the impact of their decision by finding that there are exceptions to the liability of an appointee. Generally, both the claimant and the appointee will be liable for over-payments resulting from misrepresentations or failure to disclose. There are two exceptions to this rule. The first is that only the appointee will be liable for the overpayment if the appointee has retained the benefit instead of paying it to or applying it for the benefit of the claimant. The second exception is that the appointee will not be liable if the appointee has acted with "due care and diligence". This will avoid an appointee becoming personally liable where the appointee makes a wholly innocent representation, because some change in the claimant's affairs has not been made known to the appointee, and the appointee has not failed to exercise the powers of appointee in such a manner that the appointee could be held to be at fault.

The resurrection of a due care and diligence test in relation to certain overpayments where appointees have been appointed (failure to take due care and diligence to avoid overpayment used to be the test for recovery of non-means tested benefits under repealed s.119 of the Social Security Act 1975) would seem likely to generate a new line of case law which may draw on the old authorities, and might not be as straightforward as the Tribunal thinks. The Tribunal refers (in para.61) to the use of due care and diligence in making a representation, and this is more limited than the old notion of due care and diligence to avoid an overpayment.

Despite the inevitable intricacies which always seem to arise in the manifold scenarios in which overpayments of benefits arise, this decision now makes it clear that the starting point is that both the claimant and any appointee are liable for overpayments of benefit subject to the two qualifications set out in the tribunal's decision.

The issue has also been considered in some detail in the context of a disability living allowance claim by a Deputy Commissioner in Scotland in *CSDLA/1282/2001*. In this case an overpayment of a disability living allowance arose as a result of the failure to disclose that the claimant had been admitted to hospital. At the material time the claimant's son held a Power of Attorney in respect of his mother's affairs, but had not been made an appointee by the Secretary of State under reg.33 of the Claims and Payments Regulations. There had been disclosure to the local office in relation to the claimant's entitlement to income support and retirement pension, and the child benefit she was receiving for her grand-daughter, but there had been no notification to the DLA Unit. In remitting the case for a rehearing, the Deputy Commissioner concludes, (1) following *CA/1014/1999*, that a person holding a power of attorney is not an appointee for the purposes of reg.33 of the Claims and Payments Regulations; (2) that benefit was not receivable by the son and so he was under no duty to inform the Benefits Agency of changes of circumstances under reg.32 of the Claims and Payments Regulations; and (3) that it was not open to the decision-maker to seek recovery from the son where he held a Power of Attorney but had not been made an appointee by the Secretary of State. *CA/1014/1999* has been followed and discussed in *CSDLA/1282/2001* and *CIS/242/2003*.

A useful article on the appointee system can be found at Lowery, R and Lundy, L, "The Social Security Appointee System" [1994] J.S.W.F.L. 313.

The common law of agency

One issue raised in *Tkachuk v Secretary of State for Work and Pensions*, reported as *R(IS) 3/07*, was the interaction of social security codes with the common law of agency. The decision of the Commissioner and that of the Court of Appeal upholding it are reported at *R(IS) 3/07*. It had been argued before the Commissioner that the enactment of certain provisions indicated that rules in the social security legislation had "replaced the common law of agency with their own specific limited provisions for the operation of a form of agency." (para.25 of the Commissioner's decision). The Commissioner, however, ruled:

1.88

26. I do not draw the same inference from the fact of the enactment of those provisions. Where people act through agents there is room for genuine misunderstandings in some cases and a lack of good faith in others. It is for that reason that the common law has rules such as the rule that notice to an agent constitutes notice to the principal. That particular rule is a common law protection for people who have to transact with the agents of others. They are protected from the consequences of any deliberate or inadvertent lack of communication between principal and agent. Similarly, those devising statutory codes avoid confusion and argument by, in some cases, ruling out agency. In other cases they supplement the common law by enacting as part of a statutory code an existing common law rule

as it is or in some more specific form. The requirements of section 1 of the Social Security Administration Act 1992 and the Claims and Payments Regulations that claims for benefits are to be made on a form prescribed by the Secretary of State, the main requirement being the claimant's signature on the form, rule out the signing of claims by agents except in cases to which regulation 33 applies. Regulation 4(2) of the 2000 Immigration etc Notices Regulations, regulation 4 of the Immigration (Notices) Regulations 2003 (SI 2003/658) and regulation 33 of the Claims and Payments Regulations are examples of statutory provisions which either supplement or modify the common law rules of agency to take account of the circumstances in which the legislation will be operated. Regulation 4 of the 2000 Regulations as read with the rest of those regulations makes it clear that time for appealing an appealable Secretary of State's decision starts running when the agent receives notice of the decision. Regulation 4 of the 2003 regulations provides that notice of immigration appeal tribunal decisions will be sent to both agent and principal. That guards against any attempt to deny that the appellant had knowledge of the decision. Regulation 33 of the Claims and Payments Regulations enables an agent to be appointed quickly for an incapacitated claimant for social security benefit without the delays which would be involved in an application to the Court of Protection or the drawing up of a Power of Attorney (when the claimant still has the capacity to grant such a power). I am satisfied that the concept of agency underlies both the immigration control and the social security statutory codes even though some of the common law rules have either been modified or supplemented.

That conclusion was upheld by the Court of Appeal. The issue also arose in *VB v SSWP* [2008] UKUT 15 (AAC) in the context of an overpayment appeal in which there was a financial adviser *who at the material time was not the appointee for the claimant* but whose knowledge was, it was argued, attributable to the claimant. The Judge observed:

> 79. In my view it would be a quite unwarranted extension of the scope of section 71 to hold that where a claimant's advisor is aware of a material fact, the claimant herself is necessarily fixed with knowledge of that same fact by means of importing the common law rules of agency. Such an interpretation would not be consistent with the purpose of agency identified by Mr Commissioner Angus. It would also be inconsistent with the approach of the Tribunal of Commissioners in R(SB) 9/84. There the Tribunal of Commissioners held, in the context of showing good cause for a late claim, that failure or delay by a duly appointed appointee would be imputed to a claimant. However, "responsibility should not be imputed to a claimant for delay or failure to act by an unappointed person who lodges on a claimant's behalf a claim which is refused" (at paragraph 9).

Overpayments involving spouses

1.89   In *CIS/619/1997* the Commissioner follows *CIS/13742/1996* in holding that s.71 requires a review of the claims of both husband and wife before reg.13 of the Overpayments Regulations can be used to offset benefit payable to one spouse against an overpayment that is recoverable from the other spouse. Tribunals faced with such cases should have regard to these two decisions in dealing with an appeal before them. The Commissioner also questions the propriety of inclusion in papers relating to the wife's appeal of details concerning the husband where she had maintained throughout that she was living separately from her husband. He suggests that there might be breach of confidentiality in relation to the husband's affairs, and appears to urge that such cases may be ones in which consideration would need to be given to disclosure of the husband's affairs to the tribunal as distinct from disclosure to the claimant. He recognises that this in turn gives rise to issues touching on the requirement to provide a fair hearing from the claimant and of natural justice.

Recoverability decisions against a claimant's estate where there are no duly constituted
  personal representatives

In *CJSA/1423/1999* the Commissioner held that the Secretary of State has no   **1.90**
power under s.71 to seek recovery from the estate of a deceased claimant where
there are no duly constituted personal representatives. The Secretary of State is not,
however, without any powers in such circumstances, since "he could have made
application to the High Court for a limited grant of administration under section
116 of the Supreme Court Act 1981. The court can apparently make a limited grant
of that kind for a variety of purposes." (para.38.)

Whether fraudulently or otherwise

The wording makes clear that there is no need to prove any fraudulent intent.   **1.91**
Wholly innocent mistakes by claimants can result in recoverable overpayments:
R(SB)28/83; *R(SB)9/85*; and *R(SB)18/85*. Innocent misrepresentations are easy to
imagine. But it may be better to think of non-fraudulent failures to disclose rather
than innocent failures, since non-disclosures involve some breach of a duty to disclose. In *R(SB)28/83* it was suggested that the duty to disclose extends to matters
relevant to the claim to benefit which a person with reasonable diligence would have
been aware.

This interpretation of the section is confirmed by the Court of Appeal in *Page and
Davis v Chief Adjudication Officer*, published as a supplement to *R(SB)2/92*, where
Dillon LJ said:

> "The whole burden of the phrase 'whether fraudulently or otherwise' must be
> . . . that it is to apply even if the misrepresentation is not fraudulent, in other
> words, if it is innocent. No other construction makes any sense, in my view, of
> this particular subsection."

Misrepresents

Misrepresentation is founded on positive and deliberate action: *R(SB)9/85*, and   **1.92**
may be oral or in writing, or even in some cases arise from conduct such as the
cashing of a giro-cheque. As noted above the reason why the statement represented
to the Department is incorrect is irrelevant. If a statement has been made, whether
written or oral (*R(SB)18/85*) which is untrue, it is a misrepresentation whatever
the explanation for the incorrect information proffered. A misrepresentation in a
written document may be qualified by an oral statement; it is often asserted by
claimants that the form does not accurately reflect everything that was said. While
generally claimants bear responsibility for the contents of forms, if it is accepted that
an oral qualification has not been properly noted, this may preclude the written representation from being a misrepresentation: *R(SB)18/85*.

Questions can arise as to whom the misrepresentation is addressed. Most representations will be made to the Department, but it is sometimes argued that the
misrepresentation was made, for example, to the Post Office. Does this constitute a
misrepresentation for the purposes of s.71?

A written misrepresentation may also be qualified or modified when that written
communication is read in conjunction with other written communications which
should be before the decision-maker in making the decision which resulted in the
overpayment of benefit: *R(SB)2/91*, paras 10–13. In such cases, it goes without
saying that careful findings of fact are vital. Tribunals should call for originals (or
clear copies) of statements signed by persons which are claimed to be the misrepresentation on which an overpayment decision is founded.

Rather more complex than cases where a claimant argues that they have qualified
the contents of a misrepresentation in some way in completing the form on which the
claim is based are those cases where the claimant argues that they have qualified
the contents of a current claim by information contained in an earlier claim. These
situations are much less likely to lead to the overpayment not being recoverable. So in
CSB/108/1992 a claimant, who misrepresented that he did not have an army pension

believing that it was not relevant to a claim to supplementary benefit and who sought to rely on statements which appear to have been made by him in connection with claims for unemployment benefit and sickness benefit, did not succeed in escaping a liability to repay overpaid supplementary benefit. The Commissioner indicated that the contemporaneity of the oral qualifications was crucial.

In *R(SB)3/90* the Commissioner holds that there can still be a misrepresentation of a material fact even where there has been an earlier disclosure of that fact (para.11). Although disclosure prevents any recovery of an overpayment based on the failure to disclose head, a misrepresentation by declaration on a claim form that a claimant had no money coming in when superannuation payments from a former employer were in payment, receipt of which had previously been disclosed, overrides that disclosure. The Commissioner specifically states that the Department is entitled to rely on statements in the current claim form and is under no duty to check back to see whether those statements are consistent withearlier disclosures. So it remains incumbent on claimants to be meticulous in their completion of claim forms even after a course of dealing with the Department. The reasoning of the Commissioner in *R(SB) 3/90* is implicitly approved by the Court of Appeal in *Morrell v Secretary of State for Work and Pensions* [2003] EWCA Civ 526, *R(IS)6/03*, at paras 38–48.

CSU/03/1991 adds a gloss to *R(SB)3/90*. *CSU/03/1991* was a case in which two forms had been submitted by the claimant containing conflicting information about the claimant's pension position. When he initially claimed unemployment benefit, he disclosed on Form UB461 the correct amount of his pension expressed as a weekly amount, but a few days later he erred in recording on Form UB81(PEN) the pension as £293.75 per *year* rather than per *month*. The claimant's argument was that in considering his claim the adjudication officer should have had both documents before him or her, that this would have indicated the error and no overpayment would have resulted. The adjudication officer sought to argue that he or she was not required to check back to see whether any inconsistent information was given in earlier documents. The Commissioner held that something had clearly gone wrong in the Department; both documents should have been before the adjudication officer in determining this claim and the adjudication officer could not rely on *R(SB)3/90* as the basis for recovering the overpayment of benefit which resulted from the adjudication officer's reliance on the incorrect figure on the Form UB81(PEN).

In *CIS/5140/2001* the Commissioner applied the principle established in *R(SB)3/90* to a variant of the facts of that case. The claimant had received money from her mother each month to help her with her payments of rent to her landlord. The Department sought recovery of an overpayment of benefit arising because that income (and the Commissioner concludes that it was properly categorised as income in the circumstances of the case) was not taken into account in determining the amount of income support payable. There were two periods in issue, separated by a period during which the Department could not seek recovery because it knew of the true facts. The recovery for the second period was sought because the claimant had repeated the misrepresentation about her income in completing a review form. The Commissioner concludes that the Department was entitled to rely on the statements about income in the review form to ground recovery based upon a misrepresentation of fact despite their prior knowledge of the true position.

In *CIS/5117/1998*, the Commissioner addresses the question of the extent to which silence can constitute a misrepresentation. The claim form for income support had been completed by an officer of the Department, and read back to him. The form indicated that the claimant was married and living with his wife. None of the questions about his wife, and in particular about her earnings or other income, had been answered. The tribunal found as a fact that the claimant had not been asked questions about his wife's earnings or other income by the Department's officer. An overpayment decision went on appeal to the tribunal which found that there had been no misrepresentation or failure to disclose in the circumstances of this case. The adjudication officer appealed. The Commissioner upheld the tribunal; the only substantial issue was whether or not the claimant made a misrepresentation by his silence when he made the claim on which the award of income support was based.

The Commissioner concludes that *R(SB)18/85* applied to this case. The claimant answered all the questions put to him by the officer of the Department, and the form was not read over to the claimant in its entirety. In these circumstances, says the Commissioner, the claimant's "misrepresentation" that the information on the form was complete "was qualified by the fact that he had supplied all the information for which he had been asked" in circumstances where the officer had given him no opportunity to answer the relevant questions about his wife's earnings, gave no indication that such matters might be material to benefit entitlement, and did not read back the entries on the claim form to confirm their correctness.

The facts of this case are unusual, and appear to represent a failure by the Department to follow its own recommended procedures. But, where such unusual circumstances are established, the claimant's silence does not amount to a misrepresentation. In so far as *CIS/645/1993* suggests that silence as to material facts known to the claimant amounts to a misrepresentation, that decision must be read as referring to a deliberate decision to say nothing on a matter known to be material.

EL v SSWP [2008] UKUT 4 (AAC) concerned a recoverability decision based upon misrepresentation in which the Secretary of State sought argue that a claimant had misrepresented his circumstances by not providing a response to the question, "Please use this space to tell anything else you think we might need to know" on the claim form. The claimant was a Mexican national who had been given limited leave to remain in the United Kingdom on the condition that he have no recourse to public funds. His employment had come to an end and he had claimed and been awarded income-based jobseeker's allowance. The Judge concludes that failure to respond to so open-ended a question cannot constitute a misrepresentation. Failure to reply to a specific question would generally constitute a misrepresentation, but failure to respond to a question couched in such general terms would not. The claimant had been asked no question about his immigration status. The overpayment was accordingly not recoverable.

In *Hinchy v Secretary of State for Work and Pensions* [2003] EWCA Civ 138 (February 20, 2003), the Court of Appeal touched on but did not resolve the question of whether misrepresentation provided a separate basis for seeking to recover an overpayment where the claimant signed a declaration in an order book in circumstances where the Secretary of State and his officials are to be treated as knowing a material fact. The Court did suggest that it would be odd if a representation to the Post Office "would amount to a misrepresentation causing the payment" (Aldous LJ at para.33) Carnwath LJ expressed his reservations more clearly, "I would need some persuasion that the signing of the declaration, without more, is sufficient to found a claim under section 71, in any case where it turns out for some reason the entitlement had not arisen or had changed." (para.47)

There is no comment on this aspect of the case in the decision of the House of Lords in this case, which is discussed below.

In *CTC/4025/2003*, the Commissioner considered an appeal by a claimant against whom a decision seeking to recover overpaid tax credits had been made. The claimant had responded to a question on the claim form "Do you have a partner with whom you normally live?" in the negative. At the time a marriage of very short duration was in difficulties and the claimant and her husband were living apart. However, the effect of reg.9(1) of the Family Credit (General) Regulations was that the husband and wife were to be treated as members of the same household for the purposes of claims to Working Families Tax Credit. The Commissioner rejects the argument originally put to the tribunal (and which the Secretary of State conceded in the submission to the Commissioner involved "quite a leap") that because the regulations treated the claimant and her husband as members of the same household, she must have misrepresented the facts by saying that she was not living with a partner. The overpayments were not recoverable from her.

The appeal in *CFC/2766/2003* concerned entitlement to working families tax credit. Shortly before the claim was made, the claimant disposed of significant amounts of capital. When the claim was made, the claimant correctly reported capital of no more than £2,500. When the capital disposal came to light, the Department sought recovery of an overpayment of the tax credit on the grounds that the claimant had misrepresented the position in relation to their capital. But the claimant had not done so. There was no question asking about capital they once had but no longer have.

CSIS/0345/2004 concerned a claimant who had misrepresented her income. When the claimant claimed income support, she had not disclosed sick pay received from her employer under income protection insurance offered by the employer. She claimed not to have done so on the basis of advice from an officer of the Department to the effect that such income was not relevant to entitlement to income support. The Commissioner notes that, where recovery of overpayments is sought on the grounds of misrepresentation, the reason for the misrepresentation is irrelevant. The sole issue was, accordingly, whether (assuming that the tribunal accepted that there had been the course of dealing put forward by the claimant) the representation on the claim form could be regarded as qualified by the earlier disclosure of receipt of the sick pay when the enquiry was made. The Commissioner said,

" . . ., even if . . . the disclosure was clearly made in terms of 'sick pay', the connection between such a prior general enquiry and the later determination made on the claim once the form was actually submitted, was much too remote for there to be any reasonable expectation that a link would be made and the disclosure taken into account. The concept of a prior disclosure qualifying a later written representation, so that the latter is no longer to be regarded as an incorrect one, must be restricted to very special circumstances; otherwise, the rationale behind recoverability based even on *innocent* misrepresentation, that it was positive and deliberate action upon which a decision maker must be entitled to rely, would be subverted." (para.29).

Fails to disclose

1.93   The notion of a failure to disclose is more open ended than that of a misrepresentation. The case law is complicated and can be confusing. The interpretation of s.71 in this context may be in a state of flux at the moment, and some long-established principles have recently been questioned by the Commissioners and the courts.

The discussion will accordingly be discussed under three headings:
  (a) The nature of the duty to disclose
  (b) Disclosure to whom and the continuing duty to disclose
  (c) Disclosure at an office displaying the **one** logo

(a) the nature of the duty to disclose

The starting point is that the legislation uses the term "fails to disclose", which is not the same as "does not disclose". One of the most quoted extracts from a Commissioner's decision is that in *R(SB) 21/82* that a failure to disclose "necessarily imports the concept of some breach of obligation, moral or legal—i.e. that non-disclosure must have occurred in circumstances in which . . . disclosure by the person in question was reasonably to be expected" (para.4(2)). It should, however, be remembered that this decision involved recovery from someone other than the claimant. Both Commissioners and judges in the courts have taken the view that the duty to disclose will, in most cases, be a legal one rather than a moral one: see *Hinchy v Secretary of State for Work and Pensions* [2005] UKHL 16, para.39 (dissenting opinion of Lord Scott); para 53 (opinion of Baroness Hale) and the Tribunal of Commissioners in *CIS/4348/2003*, paras 16–17 (though this is without prejudice to arguments on a moral duty to disclose).

The emerging consensus appears to be that the duty to disclose is either inherent in the recoverability scheme established by s.71, or can be found, in particular, in reg.32 of the Claims and Payments Regulations: see *Hinchy v Secretary of State for Work and Pensions* [2005] UKHL 16, paras 19 to 22 (opinion of Lord Hoffmann); para.40 (dissenting opinion of Lord Scott); and para.54 (opinion of Baroness Hale); and the Tribunal of Commissioners in *CIS/4348/2003*, paras 22–32.

For a case which discusses the duty to disclose under reg.32(1A) in the context of an overpayment of carer's allowance arising by reason of an increase in a pension, see *PG v SSWP* [2009] UKUT 77 (AAC). What is significant about the case is the discussion of the application of the judgment in *Hinchy* in the context of two centrally administered benefits.

Regulation 32 of the Claims and Payments Regulations contains two duties. The first duty is for benefit recipients to provide such certificates, documents and information affecting the right to benefit as the Secretary of State or the Board of Inland Revenue may require. The second duty is to notify the Secretary of State or the Board of any change of circumstances which benefit recipients might "reasonably be expected to know might affect the right to benefit, or to its receipt, as soon as reasonably practicable after its occurrence, by giving notice in writing . . . of any such change to the appropriate office."

Note that the duty to provide information required by the Secretary of State or the Board of Inland Revenue under the first head of reg.32 is an unqualified duty, whereas the duty to notify changes of circumstances is qualified by the requirement that the claimant might reasonably be expected to know that the change of circumstances is relevant to continuing benefit entitlement.

The decision of the Tribunal of Commissioners in *CIS/4348/2003* of October 12, 2004 affirmed on appeal to the Court of Appeal as *B v Secretary of State for Work and Pensions*, judgment of July 20, 2005 [2005] EWCA Civ 929 reported as *R(IS) 9/06* (leave to appeal to the House of Lords was refused—the claimant has now made an application to the European Courts of Human Rights alleging a violation of human rights), overturns some leading authorities of long standing in ruling, in essence, that there is no over-riding requirement applying in every case that disclosure must be reasonably expected of the claimant before an overpayment of benefit can be recovered on the grounds of the failure to disclose. However, the detail is rather more complex than this simple statement suggests.

The facts in the appeal before the Tribunal of Commissioners can be simply stated. The claimant has a learning disability. She was a lone parent in receipt of income support and received an allowance for her children. When they were taken into care, she did not disclose this fact despite clear indications in documentation she received from the Department that this was a specific change of circumstances that required disclosure. The tribunal had accepted that she would not have understood the meaning of what was written in the order book, and presumably also in other written communications from the Department. The issue was whether the mental capacity of the claimant was such as to prevent the Secretary of State from seeking recovery of the overpayment of income support (para.8).

The Tribunal of Commissioners begins by examining the relevant principles before considering the conflicting Commissioners' decisions. The following matters were accepted as common ground:

  (i)   There can be a wholly innocent failure to disclose, exemplified by those who do not disclose some material fact because they do not appreciate that it is a material fact.

 (ii)   Persons cannot fail to disclose for the purposes of s.71 a matter unless it is known to them. Whether a matter is known to someone is determined by applying a subjective test.

(iii)   A material fact for the purposes of s.71 is a fact which is objectively material to the decision to award benefit.

(iv)   Failure to disclose is not the same as mere non-disclosure. "It imports a breach of some obligation to disclose" (para.13).

Where the obligation to disclose comes from was more contentious. The Tribunal of Commissioners reject the importing of insurance law obligations; these flow from a common law duty, whereas in the social security context, there are "specific duties of disclosure set out in a statutory scheme in respect of benefits." (para.15). The Tribunal of Commissioners expresses some difficulty with the concept of breach of a "moral" obligation to disclose (to which reference is made in *R(SB) 21/82*) and could not envisage a case where it would be necessary to rely on a moral duty as distinct from a legal duty to disclose. However, the appeal before them turned on the nature of the legal duty to disclose and the Tribunal of Commissioners does not consider the issue further.

The duty to disclose is not found in s.71; that section presupposes a duty but does not impose it (para.20). The duty is to be found in reg.32 of the Claims and Payments Regulations. The Tribunal of Commissioners was concerned with the version of this regulation in force prior to its amendment by SI 2003/1050, but does not regard the amendment made by the 2003 amending regulations as affecting the substance of the provisions. The reasoning adopted is expressly stated to apply to the current version of the reg.32.

Reg.32 contains two duties. The first duty required a claimant to furnish information on request material to any decision relating to entitlement to or payment of benefit (this is contained in reg.32(1) and (1A) of the current version). The second duty required a claimant to notify a change of circumstances affecting the continuance of entitlement to benefit (this is contained in reg.32(1B) of the current version). The two duties are "entirely distinct" (para.30).

For further discussion of the nature of the duties under reg.32(1A) and (1B), see *CDLA/2328/2006* discussed in the General Note to reg.32 of the Claims and Payments Regulations.

The first duty is not qualified in any way, but the second duty is. It requires notification of changes of circumstances as soon as reasonably practicable which claimants might reasonably be expected to know might affect the continuance of entitlement to benefit or the payment of benefit. The Tribunal of Commissioners expressly reject the argument that the words qualifying the second duty also inform the first duty.

Some of the s.71 case law is relevant to the proper construction of reg.32. First, one cannot fail to furnish information or notify a change of circumstances unless the information or change of circumstances is known (para.32(a)). Secondly, where information is requested by the Secretary of State under the first duty, any view the claimant might have as to the relevance of the information to benefit entitlement does not arise.

In the context of meeting the obligation set out in the first duty, no question arises concerning the mental capacity of the person required to furnish the information. It is not open to claimants to argue that they were unable to respond to an unambiguous request because, as a result of mental incapacity, they did not understand the request (para.34). The consequences of failing to disclose information in breach of the first duty in reg.32 are to be found in s.71:

"That provides simply that, where there was a breach of the obligation to disclose any material fact under regulation 32(1), whether fraudulent or innocent, then the Secretary of State shall be entitled to recover any overpayment that results." (para.36).

The Tribunal of Commissioners then considers whether, on basic principles, s.71 can be said to import a notion that disclosure is only required where it can reasonably be expected of the claimant:

". . . even had we been persuaded that the duty to disclose sufficient to enable recovery of overpayments arose from section 71 itself, we would not have been persuaded that the duty was restricted to circumstances in which the claimant could reasonably have been expected to disclose it. That construction is simply impermissible in context. We would have held that in respect of any duty arising under section 71—as with the duty actually arising under regulation 32(1)—the subjective opinion or appreciation of the claimant as to materiality has no part to play in the scope of the duty." (para.42).

The Tribunal of Commissioners then turns to the well-established line of authority which had adopted the approach that the test did involve consideration of whether disclosure was reasonably to be expected of the claimant. The leading authority is, of course, *R(SB) 21/82*, which has been cited in many Commissioners' decisions including three decisions of Tribunals of Commissioners: *R(SB) 15/87; CG/4494/1999;* and *R(IS) 5/03*. The Tribunal of Commissioners concludes that successive decisions of Commissioners have been misled by the importation into s.71 of qualifying words from the then-equivalent of the second duty in reg.32 in *R(SB) 21/82*. The Tribunal of Commissioners says that, "On the most generous view, the words do not represent a possible construction of s.71." (para.52). The Tribunal of Commissioners further concludes that the issue has "never been the subject of any analysis or full argument" (para.58). The Tribunal of Commissioners concludes,

> "59. We do not resile from the fact that, in adopting the proper construction of the relevant statutory provisions, we are changing the direction of the law by abandoning a supposed but erroneous requirement in respect of recovery cases to which regular reference has been made over the years. However, having the law properly applied cannot of itself be unfairly prejudicial, even if that law is adverse to the interests of a particular person. We do not see any way in which claimants could be unfairly prejudiced by the benefit system adopting the proper construction of these statutory provisions now. They cannot for example possibly have organised their affairs on the basis that R(SB) 21/82 is good law, with the result that they would suffer a detriment if the position were changed now. There seems to us to be no reason to perpetuate error now by slavish adherence to previous decisions.
>
> 60. For these reasons, insofar as previous decisions of Commissioners (including Tribunals of Commissioners) are inconsistent with the reasoning of this decision, they must be treated as wrongly decided."

The Tribunal of Commissioner refer specifically to *R(A) 1/95*. The Tribunal agrees that mental capacity is relevant as to whether the claimant knew of the matter not disclosed, and that mental capacity is not relevant to the issue of whether there was a failure to disclose. However, they disapprove of the reasoning in paragraph 6 of this decision, partly because they cannot deduce any proper explanation of the passage from *R(SB) 21/82* to which the Commissioner makes reference, and partly because it relies upon an insurance analogy which the Tribunal of Commissioners does not consider to be helpful in this context of recovery of overpayments.

The Tribunal of Commissioners goes on to consider what protection there is for claimants whose capacity may affect their ability to handle their affairs. Two protections are identified. First, there is the possibility that an appointee is appointed to act on their behalf. The Tribunal of Commissioners notes that, where no appointment has been made, "the higher courts have in the past taken a fairly robust approach to submission based on a lack of capacity" (para.64). Secondly, there is the possibility that the Secretary of State will exercise the discretion not to recover the overpayment in the particular circumstances of any given case, though the Tribunal comments that it is not "aware of any published guidelines on the exercise of this discretion." (para.65).

The decision is bound to reverberate through the system for some time. It is certain to generate appeals to the Commissioner on its application in the variety of circumstances in which overpayments of benefit arise. The following points should be borne in mind in applying the decision:

   (1) This decision should be the starting point in any overpayment case involving a failure to disclose.

(2) The decision does not equate the words "failed to disclose" with "did not disclose". There must still be some breach of duty.

(3) It remains the case that there can be no failure to disclose some fact or matter which is not known to the person (though there can, of course, be a misrepresentation in relation to such a matter: see, for example, *CIS/2042/2004*).

(4) The legal duty can be found in reg.32 of the Claims and Payments Regulations.

(5) Where the first duty in reg.32 is in issue, it follows that the adjudicating authorities will need to identify with some clarity where the requirement to furnish information came from. In the case before the Commissioners, this was straightforward. The information provided to the claimant in connection with her claim required her to notify the Secretary of State if her children ceased to live with her or were taken into care. It is submitted that it will not be enough to convert the first duty into some general duty to furnish information to the Secretary of State. There are bound to be cases where the requirement to furnish information is rather less clear cut, and will need to be explored with some care.

(6) If the case falls within the second duty, then there is a requirement that the change of circumstances is one which claimants might reasonably be expected to know might affect the continuance of entitlement or the payment of benefit. There will also be a temporal question to consider: whether the claimant notified the Secretary of State of the change as soon as reasonably practicable.

The *Hinchy* judgment in the House of Lords (see below) expressly states that it is concerned with a different question from that raised in the decision of the Tribunal of Commissioners.

CFC/2766/2003 was decided after *CIS/4348/2003*, and concerned a situation where it was alleged that the claimant had failed to disclose spending of capital prior to her first claim for benefit. As noted above in the section on misrepresentation, her answers on the claim form did not constitute misrepresentations as she was only asked what her current level of capital was. Moreover, on the face of it neither of the duties under regulation 32(1) discussed in *CIS/4348/2003* would apply as the loss of the capital was not a change in circumstances since the claim had been made nor had the claimant been asked by the Secretary of State to provide information about changes in her capital prior to the date of claim. This may have provided the basis for Commissioner Howell distinguishing *CIS/4348/2003*, but his comments perhaps suggest a deeper unease with the correctness of that decision. On failure to disclose he directed the tribunal to whom he referred the case back that:

> ". . . it is not of course necessary for the Board to prove that the failure of disclosure was other than innocent, and I further direct the tribunal that, as is well settled law, the principal question is whether disclosure was reasonably to be expected of the claimant in all the circumstances. That long established principle was laid down and confirmed by two Commissioners of unquestionable learning and experience, Mr I Edwards-Jones QC and Mr J S Watson QC, in the (reported) cases *R(SB) 21/82* and *R(SB) 28/83*, has since been followed and applied as good law and practical sense on countless occasions by Commissioners and tribunals over the last 20 years and more, and should at least for the present continue to be applied in the context of facts such as these, notwithstanding the doubts voiced in quite a different context by a recent tribunal of Commissioners in case CIS/4348/2003."

A different Commissioner has also commented on the ambit of *CIS/4348/2003* in *CDLA/1823/2004*. The Commissioner indicates that the Tribunal of Commissioners was dealing with cases where disclosure had not been made despite being required by clear and unambiguous instructions. In many cases, the situation will not be as clear cut. In such cases, the Commissioner considers that whether there has been a failure to disclose "must inevitably be determined by considering whether the Secretary of State could reasonably have expected the claimant to disclose or notify that fact." (para.9.) A tribunal would need to consider how a reasonable claimant would have construed any instruction to report changes in circumstances or some other instruction. In the case before him, there was no evidence as to the instructions given to the claimant.

In *R (IB) 4/05* the Commissioner follows the decision in *CIB/3925/2003* to the effect that the advice given to recipients of incapacity benefit about exempt work are couched in terms which do not *require* notification to the Department before undertaking such work, though it was accepted that undertaking the work without giving the required notice had the result that entitlement to incapacity benefit ceased. The advice to benefit recipients could not be said to be "unambiguous" such that non-disclosure of undertaking such work could ground recovery of any overpayment of incapacity benefit.

This approach is confirmed in the decision of the Court of Appeal in *Hooper v Secretary of State for Work and Pensions* [2007] EWCA Civ 495, reported as *R(IB) 4/07*, which concerned an overpayment that had arisen when a recipient of incapacity benefit had started work without notifying the Secretary of State. The Commissioner had taken the view that a direction in a factsheet given to the claimant that "you should tell the office . . . before you start work" constituted a requirement because it was a "polite way of wording an instruction". The Court of Appeal disagreed. There was no reason why the language used could not be clearer in indicating a formal requirement to notify by using the word "must" rather than "should". Dyson LJ said, "The context is not one which demanded politeness at the expense of clarity." (para. 57). In the course of his judgment, Dyson J expressly approves the reasoning of Commissioners Mesher and Howell in *CIB/3925/2003* and *R(IB) 4/05*.

In *CIS/1887/2002*, the Commissioner ruled that there can be no failure to disclose where both benefits in question were being handled by the same local office, even where the benefits were being handled by different sections of that local office. The claimant submitted a claim for both income support and incapacity benefit to the same office. Income support was awarded, and an award of incapacity benefit was subsequently made. The claimant did not tell the local office of this award, and his income support continued to be paid resulting in a substantial overpayment of that benefit.

The Commissioner, following *CSB/0677/1986* concluded:

"21. It is also in my judgment a principle established beyond question that for the purposes of section 71 there is no 'failure to disclose' where the material fact in question is already known to the person or office to whom, under the principle laid down by the House of Lords in *Hinchy*, notification would otherwise have to be made. This too I take to be axiomatic and not called in question by anything said in the recent decision of their Lordships. It may be the kind of point Lord Hoffmann had in mind when he said 'a disclosure which would be thought necessary only by a literal-minded pedant . . . need not be made', though perhaps a true pedant would be the least likely to think disclosure necessary in such circumstances, taking the (accurate) view that there can be no question of 'disclosure' to a person or entity of something that he or it knows already.

"22. In my judgment the question of liability under section 71 is concluded in favour of the claimant, and against the Department's view as accepted by the tribunal, by the fact that all questions affecting both of the interconnected benefits involved in this case were being dealt with by the single local benefits office at the same address; and there was nothing in any of the correspondence, literature or other evidence put before the tribunal to show that the staff from time to time dealing with the relevant incapacity benefit and income support questions were separately identified to the claimant or any else as different 'offices'; or that the

71

need to track down and notify any separate individual or section of individuals within that same office at the same address was either reasonably to be expected mf the claimant or in any way brought to his attention. On the contrary, all the material before the tribunal pointed to the opposite conclusion, and that has been reinforced by the further submissions and explanations of the system in such an office provided for me for the purposes of this appeal."

For a case discussing the application of *B v SSWP,* and *CIS/1887/2002* in the context of an overpayment of income support (connected to the carers premium because there was an underlying entitlement to a carer's allowance) following the admission of the person for whom the claimant cared (his mother) to hospital, see *GK v SSWP* [2009] UKUT 98 (AAC).

In *CIS/4422/2002* the Commissioner has followed the approach adopted in *CIS/1887/2002* in ruling that, in situations where a claimant's benefit is being dealt with inside the same local office, this "does not mean that the claimant has gratuitously to notify it of the actions of its own staff." (para. 1). In this case ". . . there was no evidence of any requirement on [the claimant] to send any separate notification to any separately identified section of staff working within what was otherwise presented to him as a single local office of the Department for Work and Pensions . . ." (para.10). The overpayment was accordingly not recoverable.

In *CIS/1960/2007*, the Commissioner ruled that income support and state pension credit are not inter-connected benefits, so that an appellant was not assisted by a disclosure of a relevant fact in connection with his claim for state pension credit whose non-disclosure in relation to his claim for income support resulted in an over-payment of income support.

In *CIS/1996/2006* and *CIS/2125/2006* the Commissioner alludes to the negative consequences of the decision in *B v Secretary of State* in noting that there can be no obligation on a claimant's partner to disclose, and so, if the partner was the only person who knew the material fact, there can be no failure to disclose. The pertinent paragraph of the decision reads:

"As the submissions . . . on behalf of the Secretary of State in each of these appeals are right to concede, the tribunal's findings of facts and reasons were insufficient to show how the duty of disclosure it placed on the appellant arose. Moreover in my judgment the tribunal misdirected itself in holding that the facts could bring him within regulation 32(1B) of the Claims and Payments regulations at all. That provision, as the decision rightly said, imposes a duty; but a person in this appellant's position is not one of the people on whom that duty is expressed to be imposed. An income support claimant's partner, whose details have to be included in the claim, does not thereby become another claimant; is not a 'benefi-ciary' (an expression which is undefined, but in this context must mean a person with some entitlement to the relevant benefit); or a person 'by whom' the benefit awarded, not to the partner but to the claimant in his or her own right, is receiv-able. Nor is the income support under such an award receivable by the claimant in any sense as agent for or 'on behalf of' a partner merely because that partner's existence and resources are disclosed in the claim and taken into account in cal-culating the applicable amount, and thus the net overall level of benefit, appropri-ate to the *claimant* on the claim and any resulting award." (para.14).

VB v SSWP [2008] UKUT 15 (AAC) illustrates the importance of careful analysis of the nature of the material fact which it is argued causes the overpayment and who may be regarded as in breach of the duty to disclose. The tribunal was dealing with an appeal against overpayment decisions which had arisen when an elderly woman in a residential care home had moved from being self-funded to funded, at least in part, by the local authority. She was being assisted by a financial adviser, who was not at the initial stages her appointee, though he did later become her appointee.

The adviser disclosed to the Disability Benefits Unit that attendance allowance would cease to be in payment. State pension credit was put in payment. However, no disclosure was made to the Pension Service that the basis of funding of the care home had changed. The Judge concluded that the basis of the decision under appeal was poorly drafted; it had referred to a failure by the claimant to disclose a move to a care home. The real issue was the effect of the change in the funding of that care. Before the Upper Tribunal, it was conceded that there was no absolute duty under reg.32(1) or (1A) of the Claims and Payments Regulations to disclose. The duty under reg.32(1B) was qualified; it concerned matters the claimant might reasonably be expected to know would affect the benefit in payment. The Judge observes that the claimant could not reasonably have been expected to realise the possible materiality of the change in the funding arrangement to her state pension credit award. He doubted that this was a material fact.

In *R(A) 2/06*, the Commissioner considered the extent to which oral representations by an officer of the Department can have an impact on the statutory duty to disclose. The case concerned a claimant with an appointee who was in a care home. When the local authority took over the payment of the care home fees, no disclosure was made and attendance allowance continued to be paid resulting in an overpayment of that benefit. In the run-up to the change of legislation which resulted in the local authority payment of the care home fees, the daughter (who was the appointee) was visited by a Customer Liaison Manager. In evidence, the appointee said that the Customer Liaison Manager "told me that the visit . . . would initiate any action required with regard to my mother's benefit changes when council funding started and there was no need for me to take any further action." (para.6 of the Decision.)

The Commissioner concludes that *R(IS) 5/03* has survived the Court of Appeal's decision in *B v Secretary of State*. He also accepts that a particular duty to provide information is capable of being modified by an oral representation made by an officer of the Department, though it will be vital that careful findings of fact are made about such representations and their context. Finally, the Secretary of State must present evidence to show any duty to disclose; such a duty will not be implied and any assumption made by the Secretary of State that there is a duty to disclose is likely to be challenged in overpayment cases.

In *CIS/1867/2006* the claimant sought to rely on telephone advice that the capital limit for income support purposes was £8,000. The claimant, in fact, had capital in excess of £3,000 but below £8,000. As a result of its non-disclosure there was an overpayment of income support. The Commissioner concludes in deciding the case himself that the telephone advice was not given in response to disclosure of possession of capital, and did not relieve the claimant of the obligation to read the disclosure requirements in the back of her payment book. In the course of his decision, the Commissioner indicates that the Secretary of State must, in such cases, provide a copy of the instructions as to disclosure given to a claimant, and must indicate that the diminishing capital rule has been applied (paras 7 and 8 of the decision).

(b) disclosure to whom and the continuing duty to disclose

Compliance with the duty to disclose, and the continuing duty to disclose, have proved to be contentious issues, which have required a decision of the House of Lords to resolve. That decision has reversed the decision of the Court of Appeal and re-affirmed the long-standing authorities of the Commissioners in *R(SB) 54/83* and *R(SB) 15/87*, reaffirmed by a Tribunal of Commissioners in *CG/449/1999*. It will be helpful to set out the decision of the House of Lords in *Hinchy* v *Secretary of State for Work and Pensions* [2005] UKHL 16, reported as *R(IS) 7/05*, before setting out some of the detail of the circumstances claimants may face.

1.94

The facts were straightforward. The claimant had been in receipt of disability living allowance (awarded for a fixed period of five years) which had passported her to entitlement to a severe disability premium as part of her income support. Her claim for renewal of the disability living allowance was unsuccessful. The claimant did not disclose to the Department that her disability living allowance had ended. Though she ceased to be entitled to the severe disability premium, it continued in payment for some time. The Department sought recovery of the overpaid income support on the grounds that the claimant had failed to disclose the termination of the award of her disability living allowance. There was a clear instruction (though quite how clear this was is questioned by two of their Lordships: Lord Scott in his dissent and Baroness Hale in her opinion allowing the appeal) in the documentation given to the claimant requiring her to notify the Department if there was any change in her overall benefit entitlement. It transpired at the appellate stages of the case that there was a postcard notification system in operation between the disability living allowance centre and the local office administering the income support, and that the local office had received notice of the fixed term award at its outset, which had triggered the award of the severe disability premium.

The claimant challenged the recoverability claim on two grounds. Both were subsequently determined on the facts (and so could not ground an appeal), but the appeal before the Commissioner raised the question of whether a person could fail to disclose (within the meaning given to that phrase in s.71) some fact which was already known to the Secretary of State for Work and Pensions. After reviewing the duty of disclosure in s.71 and reg.32 of the Claims and Payments Regulations, Lord Hoffmann, giving the lead opinion in the House of Lords, considered that the line of authority established in the Commissioners' decisions reflected the realities of benefit administration, and went on to say:

> "32. . . . The claimant is not concerned or entitled to make any assumptions about the internal administrative arrangements of the department. In particular, she is not entitled to assume the existence of infallible channels of communication between one office and another. Her duty is to comply with what the Tribunal called the 'simple instruction' in the order book. . . . For my part, I would approve the principles stated by the Commissioners in *R(SB) 15/87* and *CG/4494/99*. The duty of the claimant is the duty imposed by regulation 32 or implied by section 71 to make disclosure to the person or office identified to the claimant as the decision maker. The latter is not deemed to know anything which he did not actually know."

Baroness Hale agreed, noting that there was nothing intrinsically wrong in requiring disclosure from the claimant of information known to one part of the Department which may or may not be known to another part of the Department. Baroness Hale has some reservations about whether the requirement to disclose the termination of the disability living allowance was made sufficiently clear in this case, but concedes that this goes to findings of fact rather than a question of law.

Lord Scott dissented essentially on the ground that the instructions the claimant had received did not impose on her an obligation to inform the local office that her disability living allowance award had come to an end. He also appears to accept that the local office had actual knowledge (as distinct from deemed knowledge) of the duration of the award of disability living allowance by reason of its receipt of the notification of its award at its outset.

Accordingly the existing authorities remain determinative of when and how disclosure must be made, and would suggest the following propositions:

(i) A personal disclosure to an officer in the local office administering the award of benefit is complete disclosure and absolves the person from further disclosure even if it is not acted on by the department and the claimant continues to receive benefit or suffers no reduction in benefit: *R(SB)15/87*. Subsequent statements when signing for benefit are not misrepresentations because the representation made is that there has been no change subsequent to the disclosure. This proposition is approved by the Commissioner in *CIS/14025/1996*, para.6. The words of the Commissioners in *R(SB)15/87* spell out exactly who the officer should be to whom the disclosure is made:

"We accept that a claimant cannot be expected to identify the precise person or persons who have the handling of the claim. His duty is best fulfilled by disclosure to the local office where his claim is being handled whether in the claim form or otherwise in terms that make sufficient reference to his claim to enable the matter disclosed to be referred to the proper person. If he does this, it is difficult . . . to visualise any circumstances in which a further duty to disclose the same matter can arise. In the case of a [supplementary benefit or income support] claimant required to be available for employment who is directed . . . to deliver or send his claim to the relevant unemployment benefit office for onward transmission to the department, disclosure on the claim form submitted must also be regard as fulfilling the duty."

But disclosure to the Post Office where benefit is collected will not amount to disclosure to the Department: *CSS/33/1990*, para.6.

(ii) A continuing obligation to disclose will exist where a claimant (or someone acting on the claimant's behalf) has disclosed to an officer of the Department either not in the local office or not in the section of that office administering the benefit. Such disclosure will initially be good disclosure provided that the claimant acted reasonably in thinking that the information would be brought to the attention of the relevant officer. But if subsequent events suggest that the information has not reached that officer, then it might well be considered reasonable to expect a claimant to disclose again in a way more certain to ensure that the information is known to the relevant benefit section. How long it will be before a subsequent disclosure is required will vary depending on the particular facts of each case.

The above paragraph is approved by the Commissioner in *CIS/14025/1996*, para.6. He notes that in such circumstances it is the practice of the Department to expect a further disclosure after the second payment following the first disclosure, and says he would "not cavil with such an approach", though each case must be considered on its own facts. The stronger the claimant's belief that the information would be passed to the adjudication officer (or now decision-maker), the longer it is reasonable to wait before a second disclosure is made.

(iii) The disclosure need not be in writing though it will normally be reduced to written form in the Department and signed by the person making the disclosure: see reg.32 of the Claims and Payments Regulations. Nor need it be made by the claimant in person. Where the information is proffered by someone acting on behalf of the claimant, it must be reasonable for that person to act as the claimant's delegate (this should be presumed if the claimant has asked to delegate to act) and it must be made clear that the delegate is acting on behalf of the claimant and in connection with the claimant's claim to benefit. Note that there are suggestions in para.29 of *R(SB)15/87* that the disclosure may well be complete even if the information was given in the course of some entirely separate transaction if (1) the information was given to the relevant benefit office, (2) the claimant knew the information had been given, and (3) it was reasonable for the claimant to believe it was unnecessary for him to take any action himself. Casual or incidental disclosure is not good enough. Careful findings of fact will be needed because it seems quite common for the delegate to be also at the office in connection with his or her own claim to benefit. What remains unclear is whether such delegated disclosure removes the continuing obligation to disclose. The matter may depend on findings of fact about the delegated disclosure. The clearest evidence that the information has been disclosed in full and in connection with the claimant's claim to benefit at the relevant local office would certainly justify a conclusion that the disclosure was complete and would relieve the claimant of any continuing obligation to disclose just as if the disclosure had been made personally.

In *CIS/14025/1996*, para.7, the Commissioner comments as follows on this proposition:

"Finally Bonner implies that it might be different in certain circumstances, depending on the dicta in para 29 . . . of *R(SB)15/87*. That paragraph however concerns the disclosure *on behalf of* another person. Thus disclosure may be made *on behalf of* the claimant:

(a) if the information was given to the relevant office;
(b) the claimant knew that the information had been given and;
(c) it was reasonable for the claimant to believe that it was unnecessary for him to take any action himself.

That does not, in my view, go to the adequacy of the disclosure made; it only goes to whether disclosure by one person can be said to have been disclosure on behalf of another. In this context disclosure, as it were, by chance of 'casual or incidental' is not disclosure on behalf of a claimant. While I have relied on the general principles set out in Bonner above, I dissent from the particular view expressed concerning para 29 of *R(SB)15/87*."

(iv) There appears to be a difficulty over written disclosures posted to the Department. Can the claimant rely on something akin to the presumption that a posted letter arrives in the ordinary course of post contained in s.7 of the Interpretation Act 1978 unless the contrary is proved. This is probably a case where the continuing obligation to disclose exists because subsequent events may indicate that the postal disclosure has not been effective. The difficulty relates to issues of evidence and proof: must the Department rebut the presumption that the letter was delivered or can they simply say that they have no record of receipt and that it is for the claimant to ensure that his or her disclosure arrives? The former will probably be more difficult than the latter since it would be proper to inquire as to the incidence of letters going stray after arriving at the Department.

In *CIS/5848/1999* the Commissioner addresses the issue of when *separate* notifications of circumstances to the Secretary of State are required. The scenario is a familiar one. A claimant, with children, claimed income support for herself and her children; unusually she was not in receipt of child benefit when she claimed income support but she also claimed that benefit. When she claimed that benefit she disclosed that she was also an income support claimant. Income support was paid without deduction of child benefit. The overpayment which resulted from this came to light about six months later; the Commissioner says, "the probable explanation is either a belated putting-together of information already in the possession of the Secretary of State in different places in the department's records, or a belated realisation, on the part of those responsible for calculating her income support, of the significance of the information they already had." The appeal tribunal upheld an overpayment decision. The adjudication officer's case was based upon a failure to disclose receipt of payments of child benefit. The claimant argued, and the Commissioner found on the balance of probabilities, that the claimant's child benefit award was duly communicated by the child benefit centre to the officials concerned with calculating her income support entitlement. That says the Commissioner was sufficient to dispose of the appeal in favour of the claimant; their failure to recalculate the benefit was not caused by the claimant's lack of a separate notification of the same piece of information. The issues of when a beneficiary is fixed with knowledge of a change which must be reported to the Department, and of whether notification is required when the Department holds the information continue to prove troublesome.

In *CDLA/6336/1999* the claimant, who was in receipt of a disability living allowance and income support, was admitted to hospital having taken an overdose of medication. That part of the Department dealing with her income support award was notified by means of an in-patient certificate issued by the admitting hospital. The information later found its way to the DLA Unit, which reviewed and revised the claimant's award of a disability living allowance and raised a recoverable overpayment. The Commissioner concluded that, although delivery of the information to the office handling the income support did not, of itself, constitute good disclosure, it was necessary to consider the rules on disclosure on behalf of the claimant. There was some evidence that the claimant had told the hospital that the Benefits Agency needed to be told of her admission to hospital and that this had been done. There needed to be a careful consideration of whether (a) the information was given to the relevant officer; (b) the claimant knew that the information had been given; and (c) it was reasonable for the claimant to believe that it was unnecessary to take action himself or herself in all the circumstances of the case. The Commissioner indicates that condition (a) would be met if the notification to the local office was made in circumstances where it was reasonable to assume that it would be passed to the DLA Unit; that would be met if the notification contained an implied or express request that the DLA Unit be notified and if there was some general practice of the local office passing on the information in the circumstances presented by the claimant. Much would turn on the facts of the particular case. The Commissioner rejected an argument that recovery could be based on misrepresentation, since, if the disclosure had been made in accordance with the tests set out above, there would, in the particular circumstances of the case, be no continuing duty to disclose and any representation that any material facts had been reported would be factually true and not a misrepresentation.

In *CG/160/1999* a Commissioner considered the question of knowledge in the context of an overpayment which had arisen when an entitlement to an invalid care allowance had ceased because the person being cared for ceased to be entitled to the requisite rate of the care component of a disability living allowance. The Commissioner concludes that it did not help the claimant that the reduction of the care component from the middle rate to the lowest rate was within the knowledge of the Department as a whole, since the tribunal had found that the claimant was aware of the need to report any reduction in the rate of disability living allowance to which her mother (for whom she was caring) was entitled.

Before the Commissioner, it was argued that the tribunal had made no finding of fact as to whether the claimant actually knew of the reduction in her mother's benefit. The decision contains a helpful discussion of the concept of "constructive knowledge". This was not an issue which arose in the Court of Appeal decisions in *Sharples*, which concerned knowledge of assets of another person, or in *Franklin*, which concerned a change in the mortgage interest rate. The Commissioner accepted that having the theoretical means of knowledge is not enough to fix a person with constructive knowledge (para.10); rather the test is "whether it is reasonable to expect a claimant to have made enquiries, or to have kept making enquiries, about material facts" (para.10). The Commissioner remitted the case for a fresh hearing because the tribunal had made no finding of fact on whether the claimant did or did not know of the change in her mother's disability living allowance award. He was also critical of the tribunal's allowing a case such as this to proceed as a "paper" hearing.

In *CIS/5131/1998* and *CIS/1148/1999* a Commissioner considered whether the ability of the Department to check by data matching what benefits a claimant was receiving could preclude the recovery of an overpayment of benefit which had resulted from a failure to disclose a benefit by the claimant; he did so in the light of the Commissioners' decisions in *CIS/2498/1997* and *CIS/5848/1999*. The Commissioner declined to draw quite such sweeping conclusions on the impact of easier means of communication within the Department than the Commissioners in the cases cited. In any event, it was not part of the claimant's case that the Department should have known about his benefit position; he had argued that there was an oral qualification to the written form, but the tribunal had not accepted his evidence in that regard.

A number of these issues was addressed by a Tribunal of Commissioners in two cases: *CG/4494/1999* and *CG/5631/1999*. The main decision is *CG/4494/1999*; the purpose of the calling a Tribunal of Commissioners was to determine whether *CIS/2498/1997* and *CIS/5848/1999* were rightly decided.

CG/4494/1999 concerned an overpayment of invalid care allowance which had arisen when entitlement to that benefit had ceased because the person being cared for ceased to be entitled to an attendance allowance. It was argued that the overpayment was recoverable because the claimant to the invalid care allowance had failed to disclose the termination of entitlement to the attendance allowance. The tribunal had found that the amount was recoverable but on the basis that the claimant had misrepresented, rather than failed to disclose, a material fact. The claimant did not speak, read or write English.

The key issue was that the Department knew of the cessation of attendance allowance; it was argued for the claimant that if the Secretary of State knew the relevant fact, then any overpayment would not be causally linked to the misrepresentation. It was further argued that "if anybody of any authority in the Department knew about the cessation of attendance allowance the the Minister had the appropriate knowledge." (para.11.) This argument was rejected by the tribunal, as was a similar argument based on the wording of regs 20 and 32 of the Claims and Payments Regulations. What was key was knowledge by that part of the Department responsible for administering the particular benefit.

The Tribunal of Commissioners then comments on *CIS/2498/1997* and determines that it should not be followed. A similar conclusion is drawn in respect of the *obiter* remarks of the Commissioner in *CIS/5848/1999*, though in para.20 of their decision, the Commissioners note,

" . . . we were favoured by Mr Drabble [counsel for the Department] with an account of the steps taken and being taken by the Department to relate internally decisions by one benefit team to the work of another. We do not think it is likely to be helpful to record what those steps are since they are not matters which affect the law or our interpretation of it. . . . All that we would say is that we are heartened to hear that what Mr Commissioner Howell Q.C. hoped might happen has begun to occur."

The tribunal also spends some time considering the plea of *non est factum* having regard to the claimant's inability to read, speak or write English. The Tribunal of Commissioners affirms that there are three conditions for a plea of *non est factum* to succeed:

1. The claimant was under a disability (which might include illiteracy).

2. The document signed was fundamentally, radically or totally different from that which the person thought they were signing.

3. The person signing the document was not careless in doing so, and took such precautions as ought to have been taken in all the circumstances to ascertain the content and significance of the document.

The case was remitted for consideration by a fresh tribunal on this issue, though the Tribunal of Commissioners expresses its agreement with the proposition that if the claimant had the capacity to make the claim, then she had the capacity to make a representation about it.

The other decision of the Tribunal of Commissioners is *CG/5631/1999*. In addition to certain issues which were identical with those raised in *CG/4494/1999*, a further issue arose in this appeal which required a separate decision; the decision is an exception to the general principle laid down in *CG/4494/1999*. Indeed in *CG/2888/2000* it is described as an "important exception". The Commissioner in this case notes that the principle established in *CG/4494/1999* "does not apply where an automatic computer interface exists between two parts of the Department." (para.9). The Commissioner indicates that the decision in *CG/5361/ 1999* is not limited only to the interface in relation to (1) disability living allowance or attendance allowance, and (2) invalid care allowance. The Commissioner continues,

> "It must apply between any two parts of the Department if the two conditions behind that decision are met. First, the need to link the information about the two benefits or allowances arises where the receipt of one benefit or of a specific amount of that benefit is conditional in law upon the receipt (or non-receipt) of another benefit (or of a specific amount of the second benefit). Second, the two parts of the Department dealing with the two benefits have in place an automatic computer interface between their systems so that a change in one benefit by one part of the Department is notified in the ordinary course of events by the computer interface to the other part of the Department." (para.10.)

It appears to have been established in this case that there is an automatic computer link between the Child Benefit Centre and those responsible for survivor's benefits. There will remain problematic evidential issues (and responses to enquiries may be more likely to be forthcoming at Commissioner level than at tribunal level), since it seems that the computer systems within the Department for sharing and passing information are many and various, and change from time to time. The position is further complicated by frequent restructuring of the Department.

So, where does *CG/4494/1999* leave the authorities in relation to recoverability of overpayments? The answer would appear to be: much as before. The advent of computerised data systems with easy national access has not yet reached the point where the possibility of data matching within the Department will provide much protection for claimants where overpayments arise because of the inter-relationship of conditions of entitlement to different benefits. It remains safest to disclose information to the office handling the particular benefit, preferably in writing rather than relying upon an officer of the Department to reduce the disclosure to writing. It would probably be overly optimistic to conclude that the decision breathes new life into the plea of *non est factum* in the social security context. In cases of lack of knowledge of English, this will, in virtually all cases, be known to the claimant and will trigger the requirement of care (for example, appropriate use of interpretation or explanation in the first language) under the third condition identified by the Commissioners. This is likely to ensure that the claimant will not be able to argue that the document signed was fundamentally different from what claimants think they are deciding.

There may be special considerations which arise where claims are made by those aged 60 or more (the current "qualifying age" under the State Pension Credit Act 2002) by virtue of reg.4(6C) and 4(6CC) of the Claims and Payments Regulations. Where these paragraphs apply, disclosure to the local authority or other authority referred to in reg.4(6B) may well be good disclosure.

(c) Disclosure at an office displaying the **one** *logo*

1.95

CIS/4848/2002 raises a point which may be of very practical significance in overpayments cases. The claimant had made disclosure that he and his partner were living together as husband and wife when they attended what they described as a "One Stop Shop." Only when the appeal came before the Commissioner was it established that the claimant had not attended a One Stop Shop but an office of the Department displaying the **one** logo. The distinction proved to be crucial. One Stop Shops or One Stop Offices are run by local councils, and are concerned with all matters for which council have responsibility. There is no requirement for such offices to pass on information relating to social security entitlements. By contrast, offices displaying the **one** logo are a form of one stop shop where there is a mandatory requirement that an office of a participating local authority *shall* pass on information relating to social security benefits administered by the Department except where it relates solely to benefits administered by the local authority. Clearly disclosure that two people are living together as husband and wife relates to a number of social security benefits administered by the Department. It followed that disclosure to the office displaying the **one** logo was good disclosure to the Department. There was accordingly no recoverable overpayment. Some of these principles may be relevant if a claimant discloses information to a place where a claim can be made other than at the office which will handle the benefit. See, in relation to the making of a claim, reg. 4 and following of the Claims and Payments Regulations. The general principles will also be relevant where disclosure is made to Contact Centres, and Benefit Delivery Centres.

Mental capacity

1.96   As noted above, questions of mental capacity have been raised both in relation to misrepresentations and failures to disclose. The issue is not without difficulty even though some basic guidance is contained in the case law reported above.

CSB/1093/1989 explores in some detail issues concerning mental capacity in overpayments cases. The particular question addressed was the extent to which claimants are entitled to escape the normal consequences of material misrepresentations by contending that they were mentally incapacitated at the time when they signed the relevant document.

The case concerned an overpayment of supplementary benefit which had arisen when, over a period of six months, the claimant misrepresented that her son was still a member of the family for benefit purposes when he had left school and had undertaken a Youth Training Scheme. It was argued on behalf of the claimant that her mental condition, combined with effects of anti-depressant drugs, was such that she could not be held responsible for putting her signature to the declarations in connection with the benefit claim. There is a discussion of the possibility of pleading *non est factum* (that the mind did not go with the pen with the result that the signature is to be treated as not having been made). The Commissioner stresses the narrow nature of the defence of *non est factum* and the difficulty of applying the doctrine to the realities of a modern social security system. The Commissioner indicates at paras 17 and 18 that he believes that the case of *Re Beaney, deceased* [1978] 1 W.L.R. 770, which was not concerned with social security at all, might be of assistance to tribunals. Mrs Beaney was an old lady whose health had been deteriorating for some time. She executed a transfer of a house to her eldest daughter in circumstances where all parties present at the signing of the document, including a solicitor who was an old friend of Mrs Beaney's late husband, thought that she understood what she was doing. Medical evidence, however, was that she had advanced senile dementia and her mental state was such that she could not have understood what she was doing. The two younger children sought a declaration that the transfer was void for want of capacity. The judge stated in his judgment that the degree or extent of understanding required in respect of any instrument is relative to the particular transaction which it is to effect. The more trivial the transaction, the lower the requisite degree of understanding. The Commissioner indicates that regard must be had to this test and that the key question is whether a claimant at the time of signing realised that he or she was signing a document in connection with a claim to benefit which could result in the payment of benefit. If the answer is negative, then s.71 cannot be applied to that claimant.

In difficult cases all the evidence will need to be considered over the period under review. So lucid letters written by the claimant about benefit in the relevant period will be relevant evidence of capacity. The most important evidence will be that of expert medical witnesses, whose views are to be preferred, as in *Re Beaney*, to the views of witnesses who are without medical qualifications.

In *Chief Adjudication Officer v Sheriff*, Court of Appeal, May 4, 1995, *The Times*, May 10, 1995 was reported as *R(IS)14/96*. The Court of Appeal concluded that, even where a receiver has been appointed by the Court of Protection, a claimant who signs a claim form for benefit is capable of making a misrepresentation as to the facts upon which payment of benefit is based. Nor can such a person defeat a claim to repayment of overpaid benefit by arguing that he or she lacked capacity to make a representation. Nourse L.J. said:

"If the representor need not know of the material fact misrepresented, I cannot see why it should make any difference if she does not know that she is making a representation. That no doubt would make the misrepresentation more innocent. But it would not take it outside s.53(1) [now s.71(1)]. So that can be no ground for saying that the misrepresentation was not made by the claimant."

Millett L.J. put it even more bluntly:

". . . it does not avail a recipient of benefit from whom the Secretary of State seeks repayment of benefit on the ground that he misrepresented a material fact to deny that he had mental capacity to make the representation."

The discussion on the extent to which mental incapacity will enable a person to escape the consequences of a failure to disclose must now be read in the light of the decision in *B v Secretary of State* [2005] EWCA Civ 929, where the Court of Appeal ruled that "the statutory meaning of 'failed to disclose' admits of no qualification in favour of claimants who do not appreciate that they have an obligation to disclose something once they are aware of it . . ." (para. 44).

R(IS) 4/06 is authority for four propositions. First, even if the doctrine of *non est factum* applied to social security, which was doubtful, there was no evidence that the form was fundamentally different from the form the claimant thought he was signing and he could reasonably have taken precautions to ascertain its contents and significance (*Lloyds Bank Plc v Waterhouse* [1993] 2 FLR 97 followed) (paras 9 to 23). Secondly, there is a difference between acting deliberately and acting dishonestly or fraudulently and it is possible for a claimant to make an innocent misrepresentation by omission (paras 30 and 31). Thirdly, the language of the declaration signed by the claimant could not be read other than as a guarantee that the form had been completed in a way that accurately set out all details that might affect entitlement to the benefit claimed and hence as a misrepresentation and not a failure to disclose (*Chief Adjudication Officer v Sherriff* (reported as *R(IS) 14/96*) followed) (para. 39). Finally, in the present case there was no ambiguity or contradiction in the information in the claim form as there was in *CIS/222/1991*, but simply an incompleteness which did not require further investigation by the adjudication officer before deciding the claim and (following *Duggan v Chief Adjudication Officer* (reported as the Appendix to *R(SB) 13/89*)) any failure to investigate by the decision-maker did not relieve the claimant of responsibility for the overpayment (paras 42 to 47).

Material fact

The fact misrepresented or not disclosed must be "material". This will usually be determined by consideration of issues of causation (see below). But it seems right that a representation by a claimant that he or she is entitled to benefit, being a question of law, should only be treated as a material fact in so far as it amounts to a representation that the circumstances justifying the award of the benefit have not changed: see *CIS/156/1990* discussed below. However, if a claimant who made a representation that they were entitled to benefit when they *knew* they were not, such a representation would become a misrepresentation of fact since the claimant knew the representation of entitlement to be untrue.

In *R(SB)3/90* the Commissioner holds that there can still be a misrepresentation of a material fact even though there has been an earlier disclosure of that fact (para.11) (discussed above).

However, where the misrepresentation in issue is the result of the signing of a declaration to the effect that the claimant has reported any fact affecting payment, great care will need to be taken by tribunals in considering whether there are good grounds for recovery. In *CSB/790/1988* the Commissioner held that the declaration made, for example, each time a person receives payment from a payment book is

1.97

simply a declaration that the claimant had reported facts she understood should be reported as a result of reading the instructions in the order book. The declaration was held merely to guard against failure to disclose material facts and was of no assistance on the issue of misrepresentation. The key passage in the Commissioner's decision reads:

"The declaration on the order books . . . is as follows:
'I declare that I have read and *understand* all the instructions in this order book, that I have *correctly* reported any fact which could affect the amount of my payment and that I am entitled to the above sum.' (my emphasis).
What was the representation made in that declaration? It seems to me that it was no more than that the claimant had reported any fact she understood should be reported, as a result of reading the instructions, and imports the claimant's belief as to whether or not she had already informed 'the issuing office' of her child benefit. It was a representation as to what she believed. . . The point turns on what was actually represented and not whether the representation was innocent or otherwise." (para.10.)

Two cases from Northern Ireland (where the requirements for recovery of overpayments are the same), *C1/89(WB)* and *C2/89(CB)*, concerned the receipt of child benefit for a child who had left school in circumstances where the claimant was not aware of this. Recovery was sought in reliance on a misrepresentation alleged to have been made when the claimant signed the order book to the effect that her circumstances had not changed. The Commissioner in Northern Ireland refused to accept that such a declaration could be converted into a misrepresentation of material fact. The Commissioner says that "a misrepresentation of material fact must be just that". So it will be important for tribunals to ask themselves what material fact has been misrepresented by the signing of a particular statement. These decisions get perilously close to saying that declarations made to the best of a person's knowledge and belief do not amount to misrepresentations. Again tribunals will need to take considerable care not to jump to the conclusion that the circumstances in which a misrepresentation is made are not relevant to the issue of recovery under s.71. Decisions should also be clear as to the exact nature of the material fact the subject of the misrepresentation.

In *CSB/329/1990* the Commissioner was faced with a situation in which an elderly Asian who spoke little English continued to sign orders to the effect that there had been no change in his circumstances when two non-dependants had moved into his home. The Commissioner noted that he was in no way bound by the Northern Ireland decisions and was not disposed to follow them since they could not be reconciled with well-known decisions of the Commissioners in Great Britain (at para.5).

Perhaps the starting point today is the decisions of the Court of Appeal on July 1, 1993, in *Jones v Chief Adjudication Officer* and *Sharples v Chief Adjudication Officer*, reported at *R(IS) 7/94*.

On the same day, Jones had claimed unemployment benefit from the Department of Employment and income support from the Department of Health and Social Security. Unemployment benefit was put in payment first, from December 13, 1988. Jones received regular giro cheques. Income support was subsequently put in payment without taking into account the payment of unemployment benefit, and so there was an overpayment of income support. Jones had signed a declaration to the effect that he had reported any fact to the Department of Health and Social Security which would affect the amount of his payment and that he was entitled to the sum in the order. He did not report the award of unemployment benefit to the Department of Health and Social Security. On appeal to the Commissioner, the Commissioner held that the overpayment was recoverable because Jones had misrepresented a material fact in signing the declaration in the order book. Jones appealed to the Court of Appeal on the grounds that a representation that material facts had been correctly reported was not itself a representation of a material fact and that a representation that he was entitled to the benefit was a representation of law and not of fact.

Sharples claimed supplementary benefit. On the claim form he had indicated that neither he nor his partner had any life insurance or endowment policies, and had confirmed that as far as he was aware, the information on the form was true and complete. Sharples had made this statement unaware that his partner had such assets. Supplementary benefit was in fact overpaid. The Commissioner held that there was a recoverable overpayment in that Sharples had misrepresented a material fact in completing the forms. Sharples appealed on the grounds that he had only represented the facts to the best of his knowledge and that he was unaware of the policies held by his partner when he completed the form.

By a majority of 2–1, Jones lost his appeal. The reasoning of the judges in the majority differs. Stuart Smith L.J. held that, by signing the order book, Jones had represented that he had correctly reported any facts of which he knew which could affect his benefit entitlement. That was a representation of a material fact "since unless the statement is true the claimant is not entitled to the amount of benefit claimed." Stuart Smith L.J. also considered that Jones had failed to disclose a material fact, since he knew he was in receipt of unemployment benefit and must have known that the payment of unemployment benefit had an effect on the amount of income support payable. Dillon L.J. considered that the claimant was not entitled to qualify the representation by the addition of a qualification that he was reporting facts "in so far as disclosure could reasonably be expected of me". Evans L.J. dissented holding that a declaration of entitlement to the sum paid was a representation of law. It was only a representation of fact in so far as the claimant was confirming that he or she was the person entitled to receive the payable order.

In *Sharples*, the Court of Appeal was unanimous in concluding that the terms of the declaration which was qualified by the words indicating that the information given was to the best of the claimant's knowledge were such that there was no misrepresentation since Sharples did not know of the policies owned by his partners.

CTC/5401/2002 concerned an overpayment of tax credit. The claimant had responded to questions on the claim form concerning whether or not he had a job by indicating that he did not. He was a supply teacher, and, although he did not work on the day he completed the claim form, he was under contract at the time to provide sessional teaching for the education authority. The terms of the declaration he had signed were 'to the best of my knowledge and belief'. The Commissioner concludes that the proper question to ask is not merely whether the claimant believed that his answers were true, but also to consider whether he believed that (in this case) the Inland Revenue would take the same view. The Commissioner says:

> "The Inland Revenue are entitled to ask in a claim form broad questions in a non-technical form with a view to determining later whether the technical criteria for entitlement to a tax credit are satisfied. A person who provides a narrower answer because he believes that is all that is technically relevant does so at his own peril. Of course, if he is correct, there is no question of an overpayment arising. Further, if the answers on the form are qualified in the way they were on this form, he may avoid having to repay and overpayment caused by an answer that is wrong because it is based on too narrow a construction of the question, provided he genuinely believed that the narrow construction given by him to the question is not the one intended by the Inland Revenue and he knows that the answer is also not a correct and complete answer to the broad question being asked, he must repay any overpayment arising because the answer is too narrow." (para.9.)

The terms of declarations are not the same in all circumstances, and it will be absolutely essential to make precise findings of fact as to the terms of any declaration signed by claimants. The qualification in the declaration signed by Sharples is no longer used. But even where there are no qualifying words, it may be appropriate to read them in. In *Franklin v Chief Adjudication Officer*, reported as *R(IS) 16/96*, the Court of Appeal ruled on December 13, 1995 that a declaration in the terms, "I declare that I have read and understood all the instructions in the order book, that I have correctly reported any facts which could affect the amount of any payment and I am entitled to the above sum", should be construed as a declaration that the claimant had reported all material facts known to her. She had been unaware of a reduction in the mortgage interest applicable to her, which had resulted in there being an overpayment of housing costs as part of her income support.

In *CIS/102/1993* the Commissioner supports the view both that a representation that a claimant is entitled to a payment of benefit is a representation of law and not of fact, and that there can be a representation of material fact by conduct where a person continues to cash orders in an order book knowing that their entitlement to benefit has been reviewed and revised so as to withdraw the entitlement. In a Northern Ireland decision, *R6/94(IS)*, the Commissioner holds at para.9 that any person who signs an order book declaration of entitlement knowing full well that there is no entitlement to the benefit payable misrepresents a material fact.

In *CSB/18/1992* and *CIS/674/1994* the Commissioner followed the *Jones* and *Franklin* approach. In the latter case the Commissioner draws a helpful distinction between responses to specific questions, where ignorance of the true facts does not prevent recovery on the grounds of a misrepresentation of a material fact, and responses to non-specific questions where knowledge of the true facts is a prerequisite to the making of the representation. In other words, it will be essential in every case to articulate what it is that the claimant has misrepresented.

A further limitation on the ambit of the representation made by signing the declaration on a payable order is suggested, obiter, by the Commissioner in *CG/662/1998*, *CG/1567/1998* and *CG/2112/1998*. In these cases, an indefinite award of invalid care allowance had been made to the claimant in respect of care for a person who had been awarded a disability living allowance for a fixed period. Contrary to the instruction at the back of the order book, the claimant had not reported the non-renewal of the award of the disability living allowance and an overpayment of invalid care allowance occurred. The Commissioner decides on the basis of the majority decision in *Jones* that by signing the order book declaration, the claimant had misrepresented that he had correctly reported any fact that could affect the amount of benefit payable. The relevant fact was the end of the award of the disability living allowance and its non-renewal. However, he went on to suggest that the representation made by signing the declaration was limited not only to facts known to the claimant, as in *Jones*, but also to facts that had not already been reported on the signatory's behalf or otherwise. But this is subject to the conditions set out in para.29 of *R(SB)15/87*, namely:

> "(a) the information was given to the relevant benefit office;
> (b) the claimant was aware that the information had been so given; and
> (c) in the circumstances it was reasonable for the claimant to believe that it was unnecessary for him to take action himself."

In his view these conditions had to be strictly applied. Thus, on the facts of these cases, while the existence of *accurate* information in the computer system might be enough to satisfy (a) (it was accepted that the ICA Unit both knew that disability living allowance had been awarded for a fixed period and had the means of knowing—through the Benefits Agency's computer records—that a renewal claim had not been successful to the required extent), (b) was not satisfied because the claimant could not have known, at the time he signed the order book, whether or not the information was accurate. In addition (c) was not met because the Benefits Agency was perfectly entitled to ask the claimant to report facts as a means of checking the accuracy of information held on computer and the fact that the Agency apparently did not use the computer at all in these circumstances did not make it reasonable for the claimant not to follow the instruction in the order book.

The view expressed by the Commissioner is *obiter* and did not assist the claimant in this case but might apply on other facts. For example, if the claimant could show that he knew that the appropriate benefit office had the correct information, it might well be reasonable for him to take no further action, depending on the particular circumstances of the case.

Missing documents

Arguments concerning missing documents are often raised in appeals concerning overpayments. *R(IS)11/92* now provides detailed guidance on the principles to be applied in such cases. In this case the Commissioner confronts what he describes as "a certain mythology" building up around the old prize case *The Ophelia* [1915] P. 129 and [1916] 2 A.C. 206. *The Ophelia* concerned the practice of "spoliation of documents" that is the deliberate destruction of documents and the presumption that the contents of the documents destroyed by their holder are contrary to their claims. The case has been relied upon before a number of tribunals to found an argument that where the Department has destroyed documents they hold, the contents of those documents are to be presumed to be helpful to the claims made by claimants.

The Commissioner at para.23 reviews the evidence before him concerning the "weeding" of files. The information in that paragraph is no more than the Commissioner's findings of fact in the case on the evidence given to him and should not be taken as reflecting universal practice. In every case, it will be important for tribunals to hear some evidence on what the practices adopted in the particular office having the conduct of the claim. What does seem clear, however, is that there is a general practice of weeding files after 18 months of documents which appear no longer to have relevance to any current claim.

The Commissioner then turns his attention to the implications of the doctrine of spoliation in *The Ophelia* for tribunals and states a number of important propositions:

- The case seems to have passed out of current thinking (para.28). *The Ophelia* is not a binding authority, but is only of persuasive authority. It is, however, not to be lightly disregarded if the principle it enshrines accords with common sense in the social security jurisdiction (para.29).

- The assertion that *The Ophelia* supports the proposition that documents which have been destroyed by the Department must be presumed to support the claimant's case is mythology. Spoliation had a technical meaning and is not the same as simple destruction. The key distinction is between deliberate destruction of documents *with the intention of destroying evidence,* and the deliberate destruction of documents *where there is no such intention.* Adverse presumptions come into place only in the former context (para.30).

- There is no such thing as "The Ophelia principle"; it is merely a case illustrating the application of a principle of evidence applicable in the prize jurisdiction. The underlying principle, however, remains good law. Reliance on the rule that destroyed documents must be construed against the destroyer of those documents depends on the establishment of some reprehensible act or omission by the destroyer (paras 31 and 32).

The Commissioner goes on to note that that where documents have been destroyed, then a tribunal will need to rely on secondary evidence concerning the contents of the destroyed documents; such evidence might be oral or written. Tribunals can, of course, admit any evidence which they regard as relevant and helpful.

The Commissioner summarised his conclusion on *The Ophelia* in Appendix III of the decision; paras (3) and (4) bear quotation:

"(3) The strong presumptions which are to be drawn against a party who destroys documents *only* fall to be drawn where the documents were destroyed with the intention of destroying evidence. (The intention to destroy evidence will, of course, be almost impossible to establish where the destroying party is aware

1.98

of copies of the destroyed documents.) Where there is no such intention, the only detriment to which the destroying party lays himself open is the loss of the corroboration which the documents might have afforded him.

(4) Accordingly, in the social security jurisdiction *no* presumptions fall to be drawn where the Department of Social Security has destroyed documents withthe intention of clearing storage space or simply because no point can be seen in retaining such documents."

For a case concerning missing documents and proof of an amount owed in a different context, see *Post Office Counters Ltd v Mahida* [2003] EWCA Civ 1583, where the Court of Appeal indicated that a party which had destroyed documents which they knew were vital to a claim they were making and which they had reason to believe were in contention, might well find themselves unable to rely upon secondary evidence to prove their claim. The circumstances in issue concerned irregularities in the accounting by a sub-postmistress in relation to benefit payments, which the Post Office was seeking to recover. Part of the evidence was material from the Department of Social Security in Northern Ireland. Original documents had been destroyed in accordance with standard "weeding" policy.

Tribunals should have regard to where the burden of proof lies in cases with a history. In overpayments cases, it is for the decision-maker to show that the grounds for recovering any overpayment exist. This in turn generally required the decision maker to show that there is evidence which will ground a revision on review.

CG/3049/2002 conerned a substantial overpayment of widow's benefit which was claimed on the basis that the claimant had failed to disclose that she was living with a man as husband and wife. Her argument was that she had informed the Department of her situation when she applied for widow's benefit. She argued that if the claim form had asked about her living arrangements, she would have disclosed the factual situation accurately. The form could not be found. In remitting the case for a rehearing, the Commissioner indicated that the responsibilities of tribunals following the decision in *R(IS) 11/92* is to seek to reconstruct the claim form. The Commissioner directs the new tribunal in the following terms:

"As the whole case then depends on what the claim form did or did not say, the tribunal should do its best, following *R(IS) 11/92* to reconstruct the form. That might, for example, involve taking evidence on oath or affirmation from the claimant about the full circumstances of the claim, and also seeing and putting to her a copy of the claim form that would have been used in 1997. And the tribunal must also bear in mind that if there is no evidence, it should not guess. The critical question is: are the submission and assertions of either party just guesswork, or are they something more than that? In weighing the evidence and the lack of it, the tribunal must have the principle of equality of arms in mind (under article 6 of the European Convention on Human Rights). It should not make assumptions that the Department is less likely to have made a mistake than the claimant unless it has evidence for that. If the tribunal cannot establish what was in the claim form then, to repeat the words of Commissioner Mitchell, it should leave the tree lying where it fell." (para.14.)

Causation

1.99   Under s.71 the overpayment must be "in consequence of the misrepresentation or failure to disclose" and so there must be a clear causal connection between the misrepresentation or failure to disclose and the overpayment: *R(SB)3/81*, *R(SB)21/82* and *R(SB)15/87*. So, for example, if a clear finding of fact could be made that an overpayment was the result of an administrative error by the Department unconnected with any misrepresentation or failure to disclose, there would be no causal link between the misrepresentation or failure to disclose and the overpayment, which would not be recoverable. But it seems that failure of an administrative procedure for notification between benefit sections will not break the chain of causation: *CSB/64/1986*. Arguments that a breakdown of internal communication between parts of the Department have caused the overpayment, have been met with the consistent arguments that the test of causation is whether, if the claimant had disclosed or not misrepresented a material fact, the Secretary of State would have made payment of the benefit. If the answer is that he would not, then the necessary causal connection is made: *R(SB)3/90* and *Duggan v Chief Adjudication Officer*, appendix to *R(SB)13/89*. But if it can be shown that the inter-office communication system did operate (that is, that there was actual rather than deemed knowledge) but was not then used to initiate any reviews, there would be a break in the chain of causation: *R(SB)15/87* and *CIS/159/1990* and *CSIS/7/1994*. See also *CIS/5899/1999* discussed in relation to the obligation to disclose material facts.

The scope of *Duggan* where there has been an error or neglect by an adjudication officer is discussed in *CIS/2447/1997*. The claimant stated on her income support claim form in November 1993 that her partner was not working. In October 1995 it came to light that he had always been in full-time work. The claimant's income support award had been reviewed in March 1994 following the birth of her son. It was argued that any overpayment after that review resulted not from the misrepresentation on the claim form but from the adjudication officer's negligence. This was because the adjudication officer had failed to identify any basis for the claimant's continued entitlement to income support after that time. She was no longer exempted from the condition of being available for work on the ground of pregnancy and she was not a single parent. The tribunal rejected this argument, holding that the circumstances were not distinguishable from those in *Duggan*. The Court of Appeal's decision in that case was closely related to its particular facts. It had not laid down a general rule that, whatever the extent or nature of the error by an adjudication officer, it did not remove the causative effect of some earlier failure to disclose or misrepresentation by a claimant. All the circumstances of the case had to be looked at. For example, if in the present case, the claimant had later told the income support office that she had won £10,000 and the adjudication officer had mistakenly determined that that did not affect entitlement to income support, the continued payment of benefit could not be said to have as even one of its causes the initial misrepresentation that her partner was not in full-time work. However, the actual facts of this case did not fall into that category. The information that her baby had been born would not on its own have inevitably led to to the conclusion that entitlement to income support would cease. Even though the claimant might have become a person required to be available for work, her entitlement to income support would only have ceased if she had, for example, refused to make herself available for work. The adjudication officer's failure to investigate such issues was an *additional*, but not the *sole*, cause of the overpayment and, as such, did not break the chain of causation between the initial misrepresentation and the overpayment. As had been noted in *R(F)2/99* adjudicating bodies have no jurisdiction to apportion responsibility for overpayments between a number of parties on the basis of a number of causes of the overpayment. This is, however, something the Secretary of State might take into account in determining whether to seek recovery of all or part of a recoverable overpayment.

An example of an error by the adjudication officer which did exonerate the claimant can be found in *CIS/222/1991*. The Commissioner holds that if the claimant's answers on the claim form were plainly inconsistent and ambiguous, this put the adjudication officer on notice to investigate the position. If this was not done, any overpayment was not recoverable as it was due to error on the part of the Department rather than a misrepresentation by the claimant. Here the information *on the claim form* should have triggered investigation by the adjudication officer, but the adjudication officer chose not to resolve those conflicts before awarding benefit.

In *R(IS) 4/06* the overpayment arose because the appellant's wife's pension was not taken into account in relation to a claim for income support. The appellant himself was illiterate and the form was completed on his behalf by his wife. The appellant signed the form, and this was said to constitute a misrepresentation on his part. Some questions on the claim form were unanswered. It was argued that this was a case of a failure by the Department to investigate the claim fully, and this had caused the overpayment. The Commissioner rejected that argument on the grounds that the claim form was incomplete rather than ambiguous and contained sufficient information to enable a decision to be made. He distinguished *CIS/222/1991* as a case in which a proper decision could not be made without further investigations. Even if the decision maker in *R(IS) 4/06* was partly responsible for the incorrect decision, the appellant was also to blame for not giving correct answer's about his wife's pension. See also *CIS/1960/2007*.

A variant of these circumstances arose in *CDLA/2203/2007*. A claim for a disability living allowance was made in which the claims in the claim pack were seriously exaggerated (described by the appellant herself as 'ridiculous'). Nevertheless a tribunal in dealing with a large overpayment appeal concluded that the chain of causation was broken because a proper decision on the original claim would have been time limited to one year. The failure to so limit the award broke the chain of causation and this rendered the overpayment recoverable only for the first year for which recovery was sought. The Deputy Commissioner set aside the tribunal's decision on the grounds that the decision which produced the overpayment was one which a decision maker could reasonably have made on the information available at the time. It was an error of law for a tribunal to proceed on the basis that the question of whether the appellant's misrepresentations (about her difficulties) caused the overpayment was to be answered by reference to a hypothetical correct decision different from the decision actually made. There was no break in the chain of causation which limited the amount of the overpayment.

Note that if income support is paid while a claimant is waiting for a decision on entitlement for another benefit and arrears of the other benefit are paid for this period, any excess income support cannot be recovered under this section, since it does not result from a failure to disclose. But s.74 and the Overpayments Regulations will operate to allow the excess to be deducted from the arrears of the other benefit or recovered from the recipient.

The situation dealt with in *CIS/13742/1996* is a particular illustration of the fact that the overpayment has to result from the misrepresentation or failure to disclose. The claimant and her partner (who were now separated) had each claimed benefit as single people while they were living together as husband and wife (and had thus been paid more benefit in total than that to which they would have been entitled had they claimed as a couple). The adjudication officer decided that the total amount of the overpayment was recoverable from the claimant. However the Commissioner holds that this was incorrect. Any overpayment to the partner was not due to any action or failure to act on the part of the claimant but due to the fact that he had held himself out as a single person. Thus the claimant was not the cause of the overpayment to the partner and as a result recovery of any such overpayment could not be sought from her. But had the claimant herself been overpaid benefit? From November 21, 1983 the claimant could have claimed benefit in respect of herself and her family (up to November 21, 1983 the claim could only have been made by her partner). Thus if the claimant could show that such a claim would have been successful, there would be no question of an overpayment because she would have received less benefit than she was entitled to. If, however, she could not have qualified as the claimant for the family, she would be liable to repay *all* the benefit that she had received in the relevant period. The Commissioner did, however, comment that in his view it would be inequitable for the Secretary of State to require her to repay more than the amount of the actual excess benefit paid.

The question of recovery of an overpayment from one member of a couple where both had been claiming income support separately was also considered in *CIS/619/1997*. The Commissioner agrees with *CIS/13742/1996* that unless there had been a review of the decision awarding benefit to the other member of the couple (in this case the husband), the overpayment, and any offset against it under the Overpayments Regulations could only be considered in connection with the claimant's own claim. It was therefore incumbent on the tribunal to ascertain the position on the husband's claim (which they had not done). See now also *CG/4494/1999* discussed above in para.1.94.

The amount of the overpayment which is recoverable

It is for the Secretary of State to determine the amount of the overpayment and this must be checked by tribunals.

In *CS/366/1993* the Commissioner gives advice on the level of proof of payment of a benefit recovery of which is being sought. This is an issue which can come up in overpayment appeals, when a claimant either directly or indirectly puts in issue whether they have ever received the money which the adjudication officer, or now decision-maker, says is recoverable. The Commissioner reminds tribunals that the burden of proof is on the balance of probabilities. Where there is evidence of entitlement to and payment of benefit, that may be sufficient to show that the benefit was paid. It certainly is in the absence of any challenge by the claimant. Equally, no higher burden will lie with the adjudication officer if the claimant does not adduce evidence that he or she did not receive the benefit, but simply asked the adjudication officer to prove that the benefit was paid.

A schedule showing how the overpayment is calculated is normally included in the appeal papers, but great care must be taken in simply adopting these, especially if there is any variation of the decision under appeal. The tribunal may, for example, find that an overpayment is recoverable for a different period. This will affect the amount recoverable. The need for tribunals to state expressly the sum which is recoverable and how it is calculated was stressed in *R(SB)9/85*. This advice was repeated in *R(SB)11/86* where the Commissioner helpfully approves the practice of leaving a difficult recalculation to the adjudication officer *provided that* it is made clear that the claimant or the adjudication officer may refer the matter back to the tribunal in the event of any particular difficulty or disagreement arising. The approach tribunals should adopt is to recalculate benefit in the light of the facts as found by them to determine the amount of the overpayment: *R(SB)20/84* and *R(SB)10/85(T)*. In *R(SB)11/86* it was held that underpayments of benefit during the relevant period could be taken into account, but this may need to be qualified in the light of reg.13 of the Overpayments Regulations.

A controversial question under the pre-April 1987 law was how far it was possible to take account of underpayments of benefit against the overpayment. Regulation 13(b) of the Overpayments Regulations provides that from the gross amount of the overpayment is to be deducted any additional amount of income support which should have been awarded on the basis of the claim as originally presented or with the addition of the facts misrepresented or not disclosed. This allows a somewhat more extensive set-off than under the old law. *R(IS)9/96* holds that reg.13 makes it mandatory for an adjudication officer to consider the question of a possible underpayment of benefit of income support when calculating the overpayment. A tribunal must also consider the question of any offset before it reaches a decision on the recoverability of the overpayment; it cannot merely decide that an overpayment is recoverable and then refer the question of any offset back to the adjudication officer: *CSG/357/1997*.

R(IS)5/92 confirms that the reg.13(b) deduction from the amount of the overpayment is not limited to the period after the beginning of the overpayment but can go back to the date of claim. In addition, *CSIS/8/1995* points out that the overpayment may relate to an entirely different benefit. Again, there need be no connection between the respective periods. But the examination of the additional amount which would have been payable must be based on the claim as originally presented, or with the addition of the material facts misrepresented or not disclosed. In *R(IS)5/92* the Commissioner construes "claim as presented" in reg.13(b) as including facts that would be discovered by "any reasonable enquiry . . . prompted by the claim form." This is applied in *CIS/136/1992* to require the adjudication officer to consider an award of income support on hardship grounds. *CIS/137/1992* points out that reg.13 is concerned with deductions from an overpayment and so only comes into play after the overpayment had been calculated. The review which results in a decision as

1.100

to the amount of benefit that ought to have been paid is therefore to be carried out without any fetter being imposed by reg.13.

Another problem now dealt with by regulations arises when the misrepresentation or failure to disclose is of capital resources. If it emerged that a claimant who had been in receipt of income support or family credit for a few years throughout had capital of £1 over the limit, it would be most unfair to require repayment of the whole amount of benefit. If the capital had been properly taken into account, so that benefit was not initially awarded, the capital would immediately have been reduced below the limit in order to provide for living expenses. So the Commissioner applied the "diminishing capital" principle: *CSB/53/1981, Chief Supplementary Benefit Officer v Leary*, appendix to *R(SB)6/85* and *R(SB)15/85*. The position is now governed by reg.14 of the Overpayments Regulations. This provides for the reduction of the figure of capital resources at quarterly intervals from the beginning of the period of the overpayment period by the amount overpaid in income support, income-based jobseeker's allowance, working families tax credit, disabled person's tax credit or state pension credit in the previous quarter. No other reduction of the actual amount of capital resources is allowed: reg.14(2). Under the Commissioners' approach the notional reduction had to be made week by week. It will be considerably easier to make the calculation at 13-week intervals, but the tendency will be for smaller reductions of the overpayment to be produced.

It is for the decision-maker to prove the existence of the amount of capital taken into account in calculating an overpayment: *R(SB)21/82*. Here, sums had suddenly appeared in building society accounts and there was no evidence where they had come from. The Commissioner commends the adoption of a lower figure of overpayment rather than a higher one based on the assumption that the capital assets had not been possessed before any evidence existed about them. The Commissioner in *R(SB)43/83* agrees strongly on the burden of proof, but points out that if the person concerned was alive and failed to give any proper explanation of the origin of such sums, adverse inferences could be drawn against them, enabling the adjudication officer to discharge the burden of proof. He goes on to hold that the estate of a deceased person should be in the same position. Therefore, a heavy responsibility devolved on the executor to make every reasonable enquiry as to the origin of the money. But if after such efforts there was no evidence where the money came from the burden of proof on the adjudication officer would not have been discharged.

Care needs to be taken by tribunals in the way in which matters relating to the amount of the overpayment are handled. As noted above, *R(SB)11/86* helpfully approved the practice of giving directions for the recalculation of the overpayment, while making it clear that either party is free to return to the tribunal for a determination by the tribunal of any disputed issue. *CSB/083/1991* illustrates how things can go wrong. A tribunal concluded that there had been a recoverable overpayment but went on to say, "The amount of overpayment is therefore recoverable. Actual amount to be rechecked, and this matter is therefore adjourned."

The claimant took issue with the decision on recoverability and appealed to the Commissioner who held that the determination of the tribunal did not constitute a decision and consequently the Commissioner was without jurisdiction. It is unclear whether a decision which followed more closely the guidance in *R(SB)11/86* would constitute a decision. On the one hand, all the ingredients to convert the directions into a decision would be present, but on the other, the possibility of the parties returning to the tribunal suggests that there is not yet a final determination of all the relevant issues before the tribunal. A claimant who continued to dispute the recoverability of any overpayment is not in a good position to agree a recalculation of the overpayment. Those receiving applications for leave to appeal in such cases may need to consider carefully whether there is a full decision of the tribunal which will attract a right of appeal.

In *CIS/442/1992* the Commissioner reminds tribunals of the proper procedure to follow when the calculation of the amount of the overpayment is initially left for determination by the parties. Where reference back to the tribunal is necessary, then that reference should be to the same tribunal which dealt with the issue of liability (para.5). Should it prove necessary to refer the case back to a differently constituted tribunal, then both the issue of liability and the issue of calculation will need to be considered at the adjourned hearing (para.7). A different tribunal should only hear the case if satisfied that it is not practicable to reconvene the original tribunal (para.7).

An argument was raised that s.53(1A) of the SSA 1986 (now s.71(2) of the Administration Act) outlawed the practice of remitting the calculation of the amount of the overpayment in the manner set out in *R(SB)11/86*. The Commissioner concludes that this argument is misplaced and that the new subsection did nothing to disturb "the existing practice of remitting matters of quantification" (para.8).

In *CIS/764/2002* the Commissioner says,

"I conclude in the present case (although the issue may need eventually to be argued out in some other case) that when there has been an abatement under section 74(2) of the Social Security Administration Act 1992, the relevant amount of income support is to be treated as if had not been paid as income support. Therefore it cannot be touched by a subsequent decision about the recoverability of an overpayment of income support under section 71. I rest that on the overall context of sections 71 and 74, if the conclusion is not required by regulations 5 and 13(a) of the Payments Regulations." (para.22.)

The Commissioner had concluded that the requirements of regs 5 and 13(a) of the Payments on Account Regulations required the same result: see para.20 of the decision.

In *R. v Secretary of State for Social Security, Ex p. Britnell* [1991] 1 W.L.R. 198, the House of Lords held that the power in reg.20 of the Overpayments Regulations to apply the recovery provisions of s.71 to any amount recoverable under any enactment repealed by the Social Security Act 1986 as if it was an amount recoverable under s.71 was valid and wide enough to encompass recovery of overpaid unemployment benefit in 1973–74 from a subsequent entitlement to supplementary benefit.

Note that in certain circumstances duplicated benefit may be recovered from a benefit due in another Member State of the European Union: *R(SB)1/91* and *R(SB)3/91*.

For a case concerned with the off-setting of working families tax credit to which the claimant is entitled against an overpayment of income support, see *Larusai v Secretary of State for Work and Pensions* [2003] EWHC 371 (Admin) which is discussed in the annotations to reg.13 of the Payments on account etc Regulations.

Automated credit transfers

Subsection (4) provides an independent ground for recovering overpayments resulting from the use of payments to a bank account or other similar account. Recovery will only be available if the claimant received, before agreeing to such method of payment, notice in the form specified in reg.11 of the Overpayments Regulations. These overpayments arise most often in cases of child benefit.

1.101

Tax credits: substitution of subss. (8)–(9)

Section 71(8)–(9) is, with effect from October 5, 1999, by virtue of s.2 and Pt IV, para.10 of Sch.2 to the Tax Credits Act 1999 to be read as follows in any case where the overpayment was made in respect of tax credits:

1.102

"(8) An amount recoverable under subsection (1) above in any year of assessment—

(a) shall be treated for the purposes of Part VI of the Taxes Management Act 1970 (collection and recovery) as if it were tax charged in an assessment and due and payable;

(b) shall be treated for the purposes of section 203(2)(a) of the Income and Corporation Taxes Act 1988 (PAYE) as if it were an underpayment of tax for a previous year of assessment.

(8A) Where—

(a) an amount paid in respect of a claim is recoverable under subsection (1) above; and

(b) a penalty has been imposed under section 9(1) of the Tax Credits Act 1999 (penalties for fraud etc.) on the ground that a person fraudulently or negligently made an incorrect statement or declaration in connection withthat claim,

the amount shall carry interest at the rate applicable from the date on which it becomes recoverable until payment.

(9) The rate applicable for the purposes of subsection (8A) above shall be the rate from time to time prescribed under section 178 of the Finance Act 1989 for those purposes."

See *Larusai v Secretary of State for Work and Pensions* [2003] EWHC 371 (Admin) discussed in the annotations to reg.13 of the Payments on account, etc. Regulations for the relationship between working families tax credit and benefits administered by the Department in relation to recovery of overpayments of benefits administrated by the Department.

Welfare Reform and Pensions Act 1999

1.103   Note that s.68 of the Welfare Reform and Pensions Act 1999 provides that certain overpayments of benefit are not to be recoverable. In dealing with overpayments the provisions of that section should be checked to determine whether they exclude recovery.

A useful book

1.104   A detailed, but now somewhat dated, guide on overpayments is P. Stagg, *Overpayments and Recovery of Social Security Benefits* (Legal Action Group, 1996), ISBN 0 905 09973 7.

[¹ Overpayments out of social fund

1.105   **71ZA.**—(1) Subject to subsection (2) below, section 71 above shall apply in relation to social fund payments to which this section applies as it applies in relation to payments made in respect of benefits to which that section applies.

[²(2) Section 71 above as it so applies shall have effect as if the following provisions were omitted, namely—

(a) in [³ . . .] subsection (5A), the words "reversed or varied on an appeal or";

(b) [³ . . .]

(c) subsections (7), (10A) and (10B).]

(3) This section applies to social fund payments such as are mentioned in section 138(1)(b) of the Contributions and Benefits Act.]

AMENDMENTS

1. Social Security Act 1998, s.75(1) (October 5, 1998).
2. Note that until ss.9, 10 and 38 of the 1998 Act come into force, subs.(2) is substituted by para.8 of Sch.6 to the Act.
3. Welfare Reform Act 2007, Sch.8 (July 3, 2007).

GENERAL NOTE

Section 75(2) of the Social Security Act 1998 provides that s.71ZA applies to social fund overpayment decisions made on or after October 5, 1998.

1.106

Recovery of jobseeker's allowance: severe hardship cases

71A.—(1) Where—

1.107

(a) a severe hardship direction is revoked; and

(b) it is determined by [² the Secretary of State] that—

  (i) whether fraudulently or otherwise, any person has misrepresented, or failed to disclose, any material fact; and

  (ii) in consequence of the failure or misrepresentation, payment of a jobseeker's allowance has been made during the relevant period to the person to whom the direction related,

[² the Secretary of State] may determine that [² he] is entitled to recover the amount of the payment.

(2) In this section—

"severe hardship direction" means a direction given under section 16 of the Jobseekers Act 1995; and

"the relevant period" means—

(a) if the revocation is under section 16(3)(a) of that Act, the period beginning with the date of the change of circumstances and ending with the date of the revocation; and

(b) if the revocation is under section 16(3)(b) or (c) of that Act, the period during which the direction was in force.

(3) Where a severe hardship direction is revoked, the Secretary of State may certify whether there has been misrepresentation of a material fact or failure to disclose a material fact.

(4) If the Secretary of State certifies that there has been such misrepresentation or failure to disclose, he may certify—

(a) who made the misrepresentation or failed to make the disclosure; and

(b) whether or not a payment of jobseeker's allowance has been made in consequence of the misrepresentation or failure.

(5) If the Secretary of State certifies that a payment has been made, he may certify the period during which a jobseeker's allowance would not have been paid but for the misrepresentation or failure to disclose.

(6) A certificate under this section shall be conclusive as to any matter certified.

(7) Subsections (3) and (6) to (10) of section 71 above apply to a jobseeker's allowance recoverable under subsection (1) above as they apply to a jobseeker's allowance recoverable under section 71(1) above.

(8) The other provisions of section 71 above do not apply to a jobseeker's allowance recoverable under subsection (1) above.]

AMENDMENTS

1. Jobseekers Act 1995, s.18 (October 7, 1996).
2. Social Security Act 1998, Sch.7, para.82 (October 18, 1999).

GENERAL NOTE

Section 16 of the Jobseekers Act 1995 enables the Secretary of State to direct that a person under the age of 18 is to qualify for JSA in order to avoid severe hardship.

1.108

The direction may be revoked on the ground of change of circumstances (s.16(3) (a)) or on the ground that the young person has failed to pursue an opportunity, or rejected an offer, of training without good cause (s.16(3)(b)) or on the ground that mistake as to or ignorance of a material fact led to the determination that severe hardship would result if JSA was not paid (s.16(3)(c)). A special provision is needed for recovery in cases of misrepresentation or failure to disclose because the revocation of the direction is not a review which can found action under s.71 and it appears that it does not enable the decision on entitlement to JSA to be reviewed for any period before the date of the revocation. Note that the Secretary of State's certificate is conclusive on almost every issue (subs.(3)–(6)). The provisions of s.71 about the mechanics of recovery apply.

Special provision as to recovery of income support

1.109   **72.** [¹. . .]

AMENDMENT

1. Repealed by Jobseekers Act 1995, Sch.3 (October 7, 1996).

Overlapping benefits—general

1.110   **73.**—(1) Regulations may provide for adjusting benefit as defined in section 122 of the Contributions and Benefits Act [¹, or a contribution-based jobseeker's allowance] [⁶ or a conyributiry employment and support allowance] which is payable to or in respect of any person, or the conditions for [² receipt of that benefit] where—
   (a) there is payable in his case any such pension or allowance as is described in subsection (2) below; or
   (b) the person is, or is treated under the regulations as, undergoing medical or other treatment as an in-patient in a hospital or similar institution.

(2) Subsection (1)(a) above applies to any pension, allowance or benefit payable out of public funds (including any other benefit as so defined, whether it is of the same or a different description) which is payable to or in respect of—
   (a) the person referred to in subsection (1);
   (b) that person's [⁴ wife, husband or civil partner];
   (c) any [⁵ . . .] dependent of that person; or
   (d) the [⁴ wife, husband or civil partner] of any adult dependant of that person.

(3) Where but for regulations made by virtue of subsection (1)(a) above two persons would both be entitled to an increase of benefit in respect of a third person, regulations may make provision as to their priority.

[³(4) Regulations may provide for adjusting—
   (a) benefit as defined in section 122 of the Contributions and Benefits Act;
   (b) a contribution-based jobseeker's allowance, or
   [⁶(c) a contributory employment and support allowance,]
payable to or in respect of any person where there is payable in his case any such benefit as is described in subsection (5) below.]

(5) Subsection (4) above applies to any benefit payable under the legislation of any member State other than the United Kingdom which is payable to or in respect of—

(a) the person referred to in that subsection;
(b) that person's [⁴ wife, husband or civil partner];
(c) any [⁴ . . .] dependent of that person; or
(d) the [⁴ wife, husband or civil partners] of any adult dependant of that person.

AMENDMENTS

1. Jobseekers Act 1995, Sch.2, para.49(2)(a) (June 11, 1996).
2. Jobseekers Act 1995, Sch.2, para.49(2)(b) (June 11, 1996).
3. Jobseekers Act 1995, Sch.2, para.49(3) (June 11, 1996).
4. Civil Partnership Act 2004, s.254 and Sch.24, para.59 (December 5, 2005).
5. Child Benefit Act 2005, Sch.1, Pt 1, para.21 (April 10, 2006).
6. Welfare Reform Act 2007, s.28 and Sch.3, para.10 (October 27, 2008).

DERIVATION

SSA 1975, s.85 as amended.   1.111

GENERAL NOTE

See the Hospital In-Patients Regulations and Overlapping Benefits   1.112
Regulations.

Income support and other payments

74.—(1) Where—   1.113
(a) a payment by way of prescribed income is made after the date which is the prescribed date in relation to the payment; and
(b) it is determined that an amount which has been paid by way of income support [² . . .] [², an income-based jobseeker's allowance [³ state pension credit or an income-related employment and support allowance]] would not have been paid if the payment had been made on the prescribed date,
the Secretary of State shall be entitled to recover that amount from the person to whom it was paid.
(2) Where—
(a) a prescribed payment which apart from this subsection falls to be made from public funds in the United Kingdom or under the law of any other member State is not made on or before the date which is the prescribed date in relation to the payment; and
(b) it is determined that an amount ("the relevant amount") has been paid by way of income support [² . . .] [², an income-based jobseeker's allowance [³, state pension credit or an income-related employment and support allowance]] that would not have been paid if the payment mentioned in paragraph (a) above had been made on the prescribed date,
then—
     (i) in the case of a payment from public funds in the United Kingdom, the authority responsible for making it may abate it by the relevant amount; and
    (ii) in the case of any other payment, the Secretary of State shall be entitled to receive the relevant amount out of the payment.

(3) Where—

(a) a person (in this subsection referred to as A) is entitled to any prescribed benefit for any period in respect of another person (in this subsection referred to as B); and

(b) either—

   (i) B has received income support [[1]or an income-based jobseeker's allowance] for that period; or

   (ii) B was, during that period, a member of the same family as some person other than A who received income support [[1] or an income-based jobseeker's allowance] for that period; and

(c) the amount of the income support [[4] an income-based jobseeker's allowance or an income-based employment and support allowance] has been determined on the basis that A has not made payments for the maintenance of B at a rate equal to or exceeding the amount of the prescribed benefit,

the amount of the prescribed benefit may, at the discretion of the authority administering it, be abated by the amount by which the amounts paid by way of income support . . . [[4], an income-based jobseeker's allowance or an income-related employment and support allowance] exceed what it is determined that they would have been had A, at the time the amount of the income support [[1]or an income-based jobseeker's allowance] was determined, been making payments for the maintenance of B at a rate equal to the amount of the prescribed benefit.

(4) Where an amount could have been recovered by abatement by virtue of subsection (2) or (3) above but has not been so recovered, the Secretary of State may recover it otherwise than by way of abatement—

(a) in the case of an amount which could have been recovered by virtue of subsection (2) above, from the person to whom it was paid; and

(b) in the case of an amount which could have been recovered by virtue of subsection (3) above, from the person to whom the prescribed benefit in question was paid.

(5) Where a payment is made in a currency other than sterling, its value in sterling shall be determined for the purposes of this section in accordance with regulations.

AMENDMENTS

1. Jobseekers Act 1995, Sch.2, para.50 (October 7, 1996).

2. State Pension Credit Act 2002, s.14 and Sch.2 (July 2, 2002 for the purposes of making regulations only; fully in force October 6, 2003).

3. Welfare Reform Act 2007, s.28 and Sch.3, para.10 (October 27, 2008).

4. The Employment and Support Allowance (Miscellaneous Amendments) Regulations 2008, (SI 2008/2428), reg.23 (October 27, 2008).

DERIVATION

1.114   Social Security Act 1986, s.27.

DEFINITION

"prescribed"—see s.191.

GENERAL NOTE

1.115   Most of this section was originally, in substance, s.12 of the Supplementary Benefits Act 1976. There are changes in form from the old s.12, but the overall aim is the same, to prevent a claimant from getting a double payment when other sources of income are not paid on time. This is an important provision, which is often overlooked. In *R(IS) 14/04* the Commissioner confirms that there is an appeal against a determination that there is a recoverable overpayment under this section to an appeal tribunal under the Social Security Act 1998 in the following terms:

". . . a determination made by the Secretary of State under section 74(1) that a particular amount of income support has been paid to the claim but would not have been so paid had he received his prescribed income payments at the prescribed date, and in consequence is legally recoverable from him under the terms of section 74(1), is an appealable decision within the jurisdiction of the tribunal under section 12 Social Security Act 1998. The appeal does not however extend to any subsequent question of whether or how to enforce any liability so established, which is an administrative or discretionary matter for the Secretary of State." (para.21.)

The determination of appeals under s.74 will be a much more technical matter than appeals under s.71. The question which arises under this section is whether there has been a payment of a prescribed benefit which would not have been made had prescribed income been paid to the claimant on the prescribed date.

In *CIS/0155/2001* the Commissioner was called upon to consider whether a tribunal had any jurisdiction to control the way the Secretary of State exercises the jurisdiction to seek recovery of an overpayment arising under s.74. The Commissioner concludes that the appropriate way in which to challenge the way in which the discretion to recover had been exercised in this case was by application for judicial review, and that any consideration of such questions was outside the jurisdiction of the tribunal (and indeed the Commissioner). The decision is expressed to be without prejudice to the position after November 29, 1999 when certain provisions of the Administration Act 1992 were replaced by new provisions in the Social Security Act 1998.

CIS/5048/2002 illustrates the limitations of this section. The claimant had been receiving income support for herself and her husband. The claimant's husband had applied for, and was awarded, incapacity benefit for himself which he had not disclosed to his wife. The result was an overpayment of income support, which the Secretary of State sought to recover under s.74. The Commissioner ruled on the appeal:

"10. Two subsections of section 74 were invoked in the submission to the tribunal, subsections (2) and (4). Subsection (2) allows, on the facts of this case, an abatement of the incapacity benefit paid to the husband. It does not authorise any deduction from the claimant. There is nothing in the subsection that allows recovery from 'the other' member of a married or unmarried couple (other than joint claimants). For the record, I indicated in a direction that I do not see how section 74(3) could be applied here either, and the secretary of state's representative has not disputed this. As I noted in those directions, there is in any event no mention of subsection (3) anywhere in the papers. Subsection (4) applies where an abatement could have been made under subsection (2) or subsection (3) but has not been made. As applied here with subsection (2) it allows recovery from the person from whom the abatement could have been retained the husband, not the claimant. So neither of the preconditions for subsection (4) to be applicable to the claimant are present. The decision of the tribunal therefore cannot stand. Equally, neither can the decision of the Secretary of State.

11. I have not considered whether section 74(1) could apply to the claimant because it has not been put in issue. The secretary of state's representative makes the suggestion, which I agree is the best way forward in this case, that the appropriate action is for me to set aside the decision of the Secretary of State and refer the matter back to the Secretary of State. That I do. The Secretary of State can make further decisions about overpayment if he so decides, and those decisions

will have their own rights of appeal. He will note the comments of the solicitors about the inapplicability of section 71 to the claimant."

Subs. (1)

1.116   Prescribed income is defined in reg.7(1) of the Social Security (Payments on account, Overpayments and Recovery) Regulations 1988 ("the Overpayments Regulations") as any income which is to be taken into account under Pt V of the Income Support (General) Regulations or Pt VIII of the Jobseeker's Allowance Regulations. The prescribed date under reg.7(2) is, in general, the first day of the period to which that income relates. If as a result of that income being paid after the prescribed date, more income support or income-based JSA is paid than would have been paid if the income had been paid on the prescribed date, the excess may be recovered. Note that the right to recover is absolute and does not depend on lack of care on the claimant's part, or on the effect of this section having been pointed out. That approach is confirmed in *CIS/625/1991*, where the Commissioner rejected the argument that there had to be an investigation of what an adjudication officer would in practice have done if the income had been paid on time. An example would be where a claimant has not been paid part-time earnings when they were due and as a result has been paid income support on the basis of having no earnings. Once the arrears of wages are received, the excess benefit would be recoverable. Late payment of most social security benefits is covered in subss.(2) and (4), but can also come within subs.(1). For instance, if a claim is made for child benefit and while a decision is awaited income support is paid without any deduction for the amount of the expected child benefit, then if arrears of child benefit are eventually paid in full (i.e. the abatement procedure of subs.(2) does not work) the "excess" income support for the period covered by the arrears is recoverable under subs.(1) or (4).

It is essential that the dates on which prescribed income was due to be paid and on what dates due payments would have affected income support entitlement should be determined: *R(SB) 28/85* and *CIS/625/1991*.

Subs. (2)

1.117   Prescribed payments are listed in reg.8(1) of the Overpayments Regulations and include most social security benefits, training allowances and social security benefits from other E.C. countries. As under the excess income support or JSA, if the abatement mechanism breaks down, the Secretary of State may recover the excess under subs.(4). Under s.71(8)(c), amounts may be recovered by deduction from most benefits.

In *CIS/12082/1996* and *CIS/4316/1999* the same Commissioner ruled that Article 111 of E.C. Reg.574/72 does not preclude the application of s.74(2). *CIS/4316/1999* illustrates the application of s.74(2) in the context of the complex rules for determining entitlement to retirement pension where contributions have been made in more than one Member State of the European Union.

In *CIS/764/2002* the Commissioner says,

"I conclude in the present case (although the issue may need eventually to be argued out in some other case) that when there has been an abatement under section 74(2) of the Social Security Administration Act 1992, the relevant amount of income support is to be treated as if had not been paid as income support. Therefore it cannot be touched by a subsequent decision about the recoverability of an overpayment of income support under section 71. I rest that on the overall context of sections 71 and 74, if the conclusion is not required by regulations 5 and 13(a) of the Payments Regulations." (para.22.)

The Commissioner had concluded that the requirements of regs.5 and 13(a) of the Payments on Account Regulations required the same result: see para.20 of the decision.

Subs. (4)
See notes to subss. (2) and (3). 1.118

Subs. (5)
R(SB) 28/85 had revealed problems in valuing a payment of arrears in a foreign 1.119
currency which might cover quite a long period during which exchange rates varied.
This provision authorises regulations to be made to deal with the conversion. See
reg.10 of the Payments Regulations, which appears to require the actual net amount
received to be taken into account, reversing the effect of *R(SB) 28/85*.

[¹ Payment of benefit where maintenance payments collected by Secretary of State

74A.—(1) This section applies where— 1.120

(a) a person ("the claimant") is entitled to a benefit to which this section
applies;

(b) the Secretary of State is collecting periodical payments of child or
spousal maintenance made in respect of the claimant or a member of
the claimant's family; and

(c) the inclusion of any such periodical payment in the claimant's relevant
income would, apart from this section, have the effect of reducing the
amount of the benefit to which the claimant is entitled.

(2) The Secretary of State may, to such extent as he considers appropriate, treat any such periodical payment as not being relevant income for
the purposes of calculating the amount of benefit to which the claimant is
entitled.

(3) The Secretary of State may, to the extent that any periodical payment
collected by him is treated as not being relevant income for those purposes,
retain the whole or any part of that payment.

(4) Any sum retained by the Secretary of State under subsection (3) shall
be paid by him into the Consolidated Fund.

(5) In this section—

"child" means a person under the age of 16;

"child maintenance", "spousal maintenance" and "relevant income"
have such meaning as may be prescribed;

[² "couple" has the meaning given by section 137(1) of the Contributions
and Benefits Act;]

"family" means—

(a) [² couple];

(b) a [² couple] and a member of the same household for whom one of
them is, or both are, responsible and who is a child or a person of a
prescribed description;

(c) except in prescribed circumstances, a person who is not a member
of a [² couple] and a member of the same household for whom that
person is responsible and who is a child or a person of a prescribed
description;

[² . . .]

(6) For the purposes of this section, the Secretary of State may by regulations make provision as to the circumstances in which—

(a) persons are to be treated as being or not being members of the same
household;

(b) one person is to be treated as responsible or not responsible for
another.

(7) The benefits to which this section applies are income support, an income-based jobseeker's allowance [³, an income-related employment and support allowance] and such other benefits (if any) as may be prescribed.]

AMENDMENTS

1. Child Support Act 1995, s.25 (October 1, 1995).
2. Civil Partnership Act 2004, s.254 and Sch.24, para.60 (December 5, 2005).
3. Welfare Reform Act 2007, s.28 and Sch.3, para.10 (October 27, 2008).

GENERAL NOTE

1.121   See reg.2 of the Social Security Benefits (Maintenance Payments and Consequential Amendments) Regulations 1996 for definitions of "child maintenance", "spousal maintenance" and "relevant income" and regs 3–5 for other points of interpretation.

Where maintenance payments are being collected on behalf of an income support or income-based JSA claimant or any member of the family, s.74A provides for part or the whole of those payments to be retained by the Secretary of State, in which case they will be disregarded for the purpose of calculating the claimant's benefit. See regs 55A and 60E of the Income Support Regulations and regs 119 and 127 of the Jobseeker's Allowance Regulations.

1.122   **75.–77.** *Omitted.*

Social fund awards

Recovery of social fund awards

1.123   **78.**—(1) A social fund award which is repayable shall be recoverable by the Secretary of State.

(2) Without prejudice to any other method of recovery, the Secretary of State may recover an award by deduction from prescribed benefits.

(3) The Secretary of State may recover an award—

(a) from the person to or for the benefit of whom it was made;
(b) where that person is a member of a [³ couple], from the other member of the couple;
(c) from a person who is liable to maintain the person by or on behalf of whom the application for the award was made or any person in relation to whose needs the award was made.

[¹(3A) Where—

(a) a jobseeker's allowance is payable to a person from whom an award is recoverable under subsection (3) above; and
(b) that person is subject to a bankruptcy order,

a sum deducted from that benefit under subsection (2) above shall not be treated as income of his for the purposes of the Insolvency Act 1986.

(3B) Where—

(a) a jobseeker's allowance is payable to a person from whom an award is recoverable under subsection (3) above; and
(b) the estate of that person is sequestrated,

a sum deducted from that benefit under subsection (2) above shall not be treated as income of his for the purposes of the Bankruptcy (Scotland) Act 1985.]

(4) Payments to meet funeral expenses may in all cases be recovered, as if they were funeral expenses, out of the estate of the deceased, and (subject to section 71 above) by no other means.

[³ (5) In this section "couple" has the meaning given by section 137(1) of the Contributions and Benefits Act.]

(6) For the purposes of this section—

(a) a man shall be liable to maintain his wife [³ or civil partner] and any children of whom he is the father; and

(b) a woman shall be liable to maintain her husband [³ or civil partner] and any children of whom she is the mother;

(c) a person shall be liable to maintain another person throughout any period in respect of which the first-mentioned person has, on or after 23rd May 1980 (the date of the passing of the Social Security Act 1980) and either alone or jointly with a further person, given an undertaking in writing in pursuance of immigration rules within the meaning of the Immigration Act 1971 to be responsible for the maintenance and accommodation of the other person; and

(d) "child" includes a person who has attained the age of 16 but not the age of 19 and in respect of whom either parent, or some person acting in place of either parent, is receiving income support [² or an income-based jobseeker's allowance].

(7) Any reference in subsection (6) above to children of whom the man or the woman is the father or mother shall be construed in accordance with section 1 of the Family Law Reform Act 1987.

(8) Subsection (7) above does not apply in Scotland, and in the application of subsection (6) above to Scotland any reference to children of whom the man or the woman is the father or the mother shall be construed as a reference to any such children whether or not their parents have ever been married to one another.

(9) A document bearing a certificate which—

(a) is signed by a person authorised in that behalf by the Secretary of State; and

(b) states that the document apart from the certificate is, or is a copy of, such an undertaking as is mentioned in subsection (6)(c) above,

shall be conclusive of the undertaking in question for the purposes of this section; and a certificate purporting to be so signed shall be deemed to be so signed until the contrary is proved.

AMENDMENTS

1. Jobseekers Act 1995, s.32(2) (October 7, 1996).
2. Jobseekers Act 1995, Sch.2, para.51 (October 7, 1996).
3. Civil Partnership Act 2004, s.254 and Sch.24, para.61 (December 5, 2005).

DERIVATIONS

Subss.(1)–(3): Social Security Act 1986, s.33(5)–(7).   **1.124**
Subs.(4): 1986 Act, s.32(4).
Subs.(5): 1986 Act, s.33(12).
Subss.(6)–(9): 1986 Act, ss.26(3)–(6) and 33(8).

DEFINITION

"prescribed"—see s.191.

GENERAL NOTE

Subs. (1)–(3)

1.125   These provisions give the framework for recovery of social fund loans. See the Social Fund (Recovery by Deductions from Benefits) Regulations 1988.

Income support and JSA are prescribed benefits for the purposes of subs.(2) (reg.3(a) and (c) of the Social Fund (Recovery by Deductions from Benefits) Regulations). In *Mulvey v Secretary of State for Social Security, The Times*, March 20, 1997, the House of Lords on March 13, 1997 held that where deductions were being made from benefit under subs.(2) when the claimant was sequestrated (the Scottish equivalent of a declaration of bankruptcy), the Secretary of State was entitled to continue to make the deductions. If that were not so, the gross benefit would become payable to the claimant, who would thus gain an immediate financial advantage from sequestration, a result which Parliament could not have intended.

> "Prior to sequestration the [claimant] had no right to receive by way of income support more than her gross entitlement under deduction of such sum as had been notified to her by the [Secretary of State] prior to payment of the award by the [Secretary of State]. This was the result of the statutory scheme and she could not have demanded more. The [Secretary of State's] continued exercise of a statutory power of deduction after sequestration was unrelated thereto and was not calculated to obtain a benefit for him at the expense of other creditors. The only person who had any realistic interest in the deductions was the [claimant] from which it follows that the [Secretary of State] was not seeking to exercise any right against the permanent trustee." (Lord Jauncey)

The view of the Inner House of the Court of Session was thus approved. See the notes in the 1996 edition for the earlier decisions in *Mulvey*.

English bankruptcy law is not the same as Scottish sequestration law. However, in *R. v Secretary of State for Social Security, Ex p. Taylor and Chapman, The Times*, February 5, 1996, Keene J. reached the same conclusion as the Inner House in *Mulvey* in relation to the effect of s.285(3) of the Insolvency Act 1986 in these circumstances. The deductions in *Chapman* were not being made under subs.(2) but from the claimant's retirement pension under s.71(8) in order to recover an overpayment of income support, but it was accepted that the position was the same in both cases. Keene J. rejected a submission by the Secretary of State that the operation of s.285(3) was precluded in this situation, but held that it did not prevent the deductions under subs.(2) and s.71(8) being made. The Secretary of State was not seeking to go against "the property of the bankrupt" within the terms of s.285(3) as the claimants' entitlement under the 1992 Act was to the net amount of benefit. In *Mulvey* (above) Lord Jauncey said this about the contrary argument:

> "Even more bizarre would be the situation where overpayments obtained by fraud were being recovered by deduction from benefits. On sequestration the fraudster would immediately receive the gross benefit. It is difficult to believe that Parliament can have intended such a result."

Note that s.32 of the Jobseekers Act 1995 amends both ss.78 and 71 to provide that amounts deducted under subs.(2) or s.71(8) from JSA payable to a bankrupt person are not to be treated as income for the purposes of the Insolvency Act 1986 and the Bankruptcy (Scotland) Act 1985 (in effect giving preference to the DSS over other creditors, although the House of Lords in *Mulvey* rejected such a comparison).

Subs. (4)

1.126   Subsection (4) contains an important provision for the recovery of any payment for funeral expenses out of the estate of the deceased. Regulation 8 of the Social Fund Maternity and Funeral Expenses (General) Regulations lists sums to be deducted in calculating the amount of a funeral payment. These include assets of the deceased which are available before probate or letters of administration have been granted. The old reg.8(3)(a) of the Single Payments Regulations required the deduction of the value of the deceased's estate, but since it might take some time for the estate to become available, the provision in subs.(4) is preferable.

The funeral payment is to be recovered as if it was funeral expenses. Funeral expenses are a first charge on the estate, in priority to anything else (see *R(SB) 18/84*, paras 8 and 10, for the law in England and Scotland). *CIS/616/1990* decides that the right to recover is given to the Secretary of State. The adjudication officer (and the tribunal) has no role in subs.(4).

The only other method of recovery is under s.71, which applies generally where there has been misrepresentation or a failure to disclose and does depend on a review of entitlement by an adjudication officer followed by a determination of an overpayment.

Subss. (6)–(9)
See the notes to s.105.

1.127

Northern Ireland payments

Recovery of Northern Ireland payments

79. Without prejudice to any other method of recovery—
  (a) amounts recoverable under any enactment or instrument having effect in Northern Ireland and corresponding to an enactment or instrument mentioned in section 71(8) above shall be recoverable by deduction from benefits prescribed under that subsection;
  (b) amounts recoverable under any enactment having effect in Northern Ireland and corresponding to section 75 above shall be recoverable by deduction from benefits prescribed under subsection (4) of that section; and
  (c) awards recoverable under Part III of the Northern Ireland Administration Act shall be recoverable by deduction from benefits prescribed under subsection (2) of section 78 above and subsection (3) of that section shall have effect in relation to such awards as it has effect in relation to such awards out of the social fund under this Act.

1.128

DERIVATIONS

Paragraph (a): Social Security Act 1986, s.53(7A).
Paragraph (b): 1986 Act, s.29(8).
Paragraph (c): 1986 Act, s.33(8A).

1.129

DEFINITIONS

"the Northern Ireland Administration Act"—see s.191.
"prescribed"—*ibid.*

Child benefit—overlap with benefits under legislation of other member States

80. Regulations may provide for adjusting child benefit payable in respect of any child [¹ or qualifying young person] in respect of whom any benefit is payable under the legislation of any member State other than the United Kingdom.

1.130

DERIVATION

1.131   CBA 1975, s.4A.

AMENDMENT

1. Child Benefit Act 2005, Sch.1, Pt 1, para.22 (April 10, 2006).

PART IV

RECOVERY FROM COMPENSATION PAYMENTS

1.132   *Repealed.*

PART V

INCOME SUPPORT AND THE DUTY TO MAINTAIN

Failure to maintain—general

1.133   **105.**—(1) If—

(a) any person persistently refuses or neglects to maintain himself or any person whom he is liable to maintain; and

(b) in consequence of his refusal or neglect income support [¹ ...] [³ , an income-based jobseeker's allowance or an income-related employment and support allowance] is paid to or in respect of him or such a person,

he shall be guilty of an offence and liable on summary conviction to imprisonment for a term not exceeding 3 months or to a fine of an amount not exceeding level 4 on the standard scale or to both.

(2) For the purposes of subsection (1) above a person shall not be taken to refuse or neglect to maintain himself or any other person by reason only of anything done or omitted in furtherance of a trade dispute.

[⁴ (3) Subject to subsection (4), for the purposes of this Part, a person shall be liable to maintain another person if that other person is—

(a) his or her spouse or civil partner, or

(b) a person whom he or she would be liable to maintain if sections 78(6)(c) and (9) had effect for the purposes of this Part.]

[¹ (4) For the purposes of this section, in its application to an income-based jobseeker's allowance [³ or an income-related employment and support allowance], a person is liable to maintain another if that other person is his or her spouse [² or civil partner].]

AMENDMENTS

1. Jobseekers Act 1995, Sch.2, para.53 (October 7, 1996).
2. Civil Partnership Act 2004, s.254 and Sch.24, para.62 (December 5, 2005).
3. Welfare Reform Act 1007, s.28 and Sch. 3, para.10 (October 27, 2008).
4. Child Maintenance and Other Payments Act 2008, s.45(1) (July 14, 2008).

DERIVATION

1.134   Social Security Act 1986, s.26.

GENERAL NOTE

Subs. (1)

The criminal offence created by subs.(1) of refusing or neglecting to main-   **1.135**
tain oneself is at first sight rather extraordinary, but it is only committed if as a
consequence income support or income-based JSA is paid. Prosecution is very
much a last resort after the ordinary sanctions against voluntary unemployment
have been used. In 1984–85 there were none (NACRO, *Enforcement of the Law
Relating to Social Security*, para.8.6). Prosecution of those who refuse or neglect to
maintain others is more common.

Liability to maintain

Under subs.(3), liability to maintain another person for the purposes of Pt V is   **1.136**
tested, except in relation to income-based JSA, according to s.78(6)–(9). Both men
and women are liable to maintain their spouses and children. This liability remains
in force despite the enactment of the Child Support Act 1991, with the result that
the Department retains its power to enforce that liability under ss.106–108. But
although this power remains, in practice the Department does not enforce the
liability to maintain children now that the Child Support Agency has acquired this
role. Note also that since April 5, 1993, the courts have not had power to make
new orders for maintenance for children (s.8(3), Child Support Act 1991). Under
subs.(4) the only liability to maintain which is relevant to s.105 for the purposes of
income-based JSA is the liability of one spouse to maintain the other.

The definition of child goes beyond the usual meaning in s.137 of the
Contributions and Benefits Act of a person under 16 to include those under 19 who
count as a dependant in someone else's income support entitlement (s.78(6)(d)).
The effect of the reference in s.78(4) to s.1 of the Family Law Reform Act 1987 is
that in determining whether a person is the father or mother of a child it is irrelevant
whether the person was married to the other parent at the time of the birth or not.
If a married couple divorce, their liability to maintain each other ceases for the purposes of Pt V, but the obligation to maintain their children remains. This then is the
remnant of the old family means-test that used to extend much wider until the Poor
Law was finally "abolished" by the National Assistance Act 1948. For the enforcement of this liability, see ss.106–108, and for a criminal offence, subs.(1).

Section 78(6)(c) was new in 1980. In *R. v W. London SBAT, Ex p. Clarke* [1975]
1 W.L.R. 1396, the court had held that the sponsor of an immigrant was under no
obligation to maintain the immigrant for supplementary benefit purposes. This
position is now reversed, and s.78(9) provides for conclusive certificates of an
undertaking to maintain to be produced. The liability to maintain is enforced under
s.106. The SBC policy struck down in *Clarke*'s case had deemed the immigrant to
be receiving the support from his sponsor even where it was not forthcoming. This
is not now the case. It is only a resource when actually received.

Recovery of expenditure on benefit from person liable for maintenance

106.—(1) Subject to the following provisions of this section, if income   **1.137**
support is claimed by or in respect of a person whom another person is
liable to maintain or paid to or in respect of such a person, the Secretary of
State may make a complaint against the liable person to a magistrates' court
for an order under this section.

(2) On the hearing of a complaint under this section the court shall have
regard to all the circumstances and, in particular, to the income of the liable
person, and may order him to pay such sum, weekly or otherwise, as it may
consider appropriate, except that in a case falling within section 78(6)(c)
above that sum shall not include any amount which is not attributable to
income support (whether paid before or after the making of the order).

(3) In determining whether to order any payments to be made in respect of income support for any period before the complaint was made, or the amount of any such payments, the court shall disregard any amount by which the liable person's income exceeds the income which was his during that period.

(4) Any payments ordered to be made under this section shall be made—

(a) to the Secretary of State in so far as they are attributable to any income support (whether paid before or after the making of the order);

(b) to the person claiming income support or (if different) the dependant; or

(c) to such other person as appears to the court expedient in the interests of the dependant.

(5) An order under this section shall be enforceable as a magistrates' court maintenance order within the meaning of section 150(1) of the Magistrates' Court Act 1980.

(6) In the application of this section to Scotland, subsection (5) above shall be omitted and for the references to a complaint and to a magistrates' court there shall be substituted respectively references to an application and to the sheriff.

(7) [¹ . . .]

DERIVATION

1.138   Social Security Act 1986, s.24.

AMENDMENT

1. Child Maintenance and Other Payments Act 2008, Sch.8 para.1 (July 14, 2008).

DEFINITION

"child"—see ss.105(3) and 78(b).

GENERAL NOTE

1.139   This section gives the Department an independent right to enforce the liability to maintain in s.78(6), which now covers both spouses and children, by an order in the magistrates' court, providing that income support has been claimed or paid for the person sought to be maintained.

Recovery of expenditure on income support: additional amounts and transfer of orders

1.140   **107.**[¹ . . .]

AMENDMENT

1. Repealed by Child Maintenance and Other Payments Act 2008, Sch.8 para.1 (October 27, 2008).

Reduction of expenditure on income support: certain maintenance orders to be enforceable by the Secretary of State

1.141   **108.**—(1) This section applies where—

(a) a person ("the claimant") who is the parent of one or more children is in receipt of income support either in respect of those children or in respect of both himself and those children; and

(b) there is in force a maintenance order made against the other parent ("the liable person")—

    (i) in favour of the claimant or one or more of the children, or

    (ii) in favour of some other person for the benefit of the claimant or one or more of the children,

and in this section "the primary recipient" means the person in whose favour that maintenance order was made.

(2) If, in a case where this section applies, the liable person fails to comply with any of the terms of the maintenance order—

(a) the Secretary of State may bring any proceedings or take any other steps to enforce the order that could have been brought or taken by or on behalf of the primary recipient; and

(b) any court before which proceedings are brought by the Secretary of State by virtue of paragraph (a) above shall have the same powers in connection with those proceedings as it would have had if they had been brought by the primary recipient.

(3) The Secretary of State's powers under this section are exercisable at his discretion and whether or not the primary recipient or any other person consents to their exercise; but any sums recovered by virtue of this section shall be payable to or for the primary recipient, as if the proceedings or steps in question had been brought or taken by him or on his behalf.

(4) The powers conferred on the Secretary of State by subsection (2)(a) above include power—

(a) to apply for the registration of the maintenance order under—

    (i) section 17 of the Maintenance Orders Act 1950;

    (ii) section 2 of the Maintenance Orders Act 1958; or

    (iii) the Civil Jurisdiction and Judgments Act 1982; [² or

    (iv) Council Regulation (EC) No 44/2001 of 22nd December 2000 on jurisdiction and the recognition and enforcement of judgments in civil and commercial matters; and]

(b) to make an application under section 2 of the Maintenance Orders (Reciprocal Enforcement) Act 1972 (application for enforcement in reciprocating country).

(5) Where this section applies, the prescribed person shall in prescribed circumstances give the Secretary of State notice of any application—

(a) to alter, vary, suspend, discharge, revoke, revive, or enforce the maintenance order in question; or

(b) to remit arrears under that maintenance order;

and the Secretary of State shall be entitled to appear and be heard on the application.

(6) Where, by virtue of this section, the Secretary of State commences any proceedings to enforce a maintenance order, he shall, in relation to those proceedings, be treated for the purposes of any enactment or instrument relating to maintenance orders as if he were a person entitled to payment under the maintenance order in question (but shall not thereby become entitled to any such payment).

(7) Where, in any proceedings under this section in England and Wales, the court makes an order for the whole or any part of the arrears due under the maintenance order in question to be paid as a lump sum, the Secretary

of State shall inform [¹ the Legal Services Commission] of the amount of
that lump sum if he knows—
    (a) that the primary recipient either—
            (i)   received legal aid under the Legal Aid Act 1974 in connec-
                  tion with the proceedings in which the maintenance order was
                  made, or
            (ii) was an assisted party, within the meaning of the Legal Aid Act
                  1988, in those proceedings, or
        [¹(iii) received services funded by the Legal Services Commission as
                  part of the Community Legal Service; and]
    (b) that a sum remains unpaid on account of the contribution required
         of the primary recipient—
            (i)   under section 9 of the Legal Aid Act 1974 in respect of those
                  proceedings, or
            (ii) under section 16 of the Legal Aid Act 1988 in respect of the
                  costs of his being represented under Part IV of that Act in those
                  proceedings, [¹ or
            (iii) by virtue of section 10 of the Access to Justice Act 1999 in
                  respect of services funded by the Legal Services Commission as
                  part of the Community Legal Service.]
    [³ (8) In this section "maintenance order"—
    (a) in England and Wales, means—
            (i)   any order for the making of periodical payments which is, or has
                  at any time been, a maintenance order within the meaning of
                  the Attachment of Earnings Act 1971;
            (ii) any order under Part 3 of the Matrimonial and Family
                  Proceedings Act 1984 (overseas divorce) for the making of peri-
                  odical payments;
            (iii) any order under Schedule 7 to the Civil Partnership Act 2004
                  for the making of periodical payments;
    (b) in Scotland, means any order, except an order for the payment of a
         lump sum, falling within the definition of "maintenance order" in
         section 106 of the Debtors (Scotland) Act 1987, but disregarding
         paragraph (h) (alimentary bond or agreement).]

AMENDMENTS

    1. Access to Justice Act 1999, Sch.4, para.48 (April 1, 2000)
    2. The Civil Jurisdiction and Judgments Order 2001 (SI 2001/3929), art.5 and
Sch.3 (March 1, 2002).
    3. Child Maintenance and Other Payments Act 2008 Sch.7 para.2(2) (October
27, 2008).

DERIVATION

1.142   Social Security Act 1986, s.24B.

GENERAL NOTE

1.143   Section 108 enables the Department to enforce certain private maintenance
orders in favour of lone parent claimants of income support. Only lone parents are
covered by subs.(1)(a), and not mere separated or divorced spouses, but the maintenance order may be in favour either of the parent or the child(ren) or both. The
Secretary of State may at his discretion and without the consent of the lone parent
take steps (including those specified in subs.(5)) to enforce the order as if he were

the person entitled to payment under the order (subss.(2), (3) and (6)). But any sums recovered are payable to the primary recipient under the order (subss.(3) and (6)). Under subs.(5) regulations may specify who has to inform the Department of applications to vary, suspend etc. the private order or to remit arrears. Regulation 3 of the Income Support (Liable Relatives) Regulations specifies various court officials. The Secretary of State is given the right to be heard on any such application, but has no power to make such an application, e.g. to increase the amount of an order. This is because subs.(2) only operates when there is a failure to comply with the terms (i.e. the existing terms) of the order.

Subsection (7) requires the Secretary of State to inform the Legal Aid Commission when a lump sum of arrears is to be paid when the Commission might be able to recover a contribution out of the lump sum.

Overall s.108 is a powerful weapon for the Department to enforce the payment of maintenance orders. If the lone parent has her own order, which is not being paid, income support will make up the shortfall. There is thus no great incentive for the lone parent to go through all the hassle of enforcement, and there may be other circumstances making her reluctant to take action. The Department will have no such inhibitions.

The Secretary of State predicted that the amount of maintenance recovered by the Department in respect of lone parents on income support would rise to about £260 million in 1990–91, having gone up from £155 million in 1988–89 to £180 million in 1989–90 (HC *Hansard*, March 28, 1990, Vol.170, col. 571). The predicted increase was partly based on the provisions now contained in ss.107 and 108 and partly on giving greater priority and resources to such work, with changes in the administrative guidance. These changes are to point up the need to stress to lone parents on benefits the advantages of reflecting the absent parent's proper responsibilities in the maintenance arrangements from the outset and also to indicate that the "normal expectation" should be that a lone parent will co-operate in establishing where responsibility lies. It is, however, recognised that there may be circumstances in which lone parents will not wish to name the father of a child. The White Paper, *Children Come First*, proposed reductions in the lone parent's benefit if she declines without good cause to take maintenance proceedings. The Child Support Act 1991 imposes such an obligation only in relation to applications under the Act.

Diversion of arrested earnings to Secretary of State—Scotland

109.—(1) Where in Scotland a creditor who is enforcing a maintenance order or alimentary bond or agreement by a current maintenance arrestment or a conjoined arrestment order is in receipt of income support [1 or an income-related employment and support allowance] the creditor may in writing authorise the Secretary of State to receive any sums payable under the arrestment or order until the creditor ceases to be in receipt of income support [1 or an income-related employment and support allowance] or in writing withdraws the authorisation, whichever occurs first.

(2) On the intimation by the Secretary of State—

(a) to the employer operating the current maintenance arrestment; or

(b) to the sheriff clerk operating the conjoined arrestment order;

of an authorisation under subsection (1) above, the employer or sheriff clerk shall, until notified by the Secretary of State that the authorisation has ceased to have effect, pay to the Secretary of State any sums which would otherwise be payable under the arrestment or order to the creditor.

1.144

AMENDMENT

1. Welfare Reform Act 1007, s.28 and Sch.3 para.10 (October 27, 2008).

DERIVATION

1.145   Social Security Act 1986, s.25A.

1.146   **Part VI**. *Omitted.*

GENERAL NOTE

1.147   Note that s.67 and Sch.6 to the Child Support, Pensions and Social Security Act 2000 make substantial amendments to Pt VI of this Act with effect from April 2, 2001.

1.148   **121E.–123.** *Omitted.*

PART VII

INFORMATION

The Registration Service

Provisions relating to age, death and marriage

1.149   **124.**—(1) Regulations made by the Registrar General under section 20 of the Registration Service Act 1953 or section 54 of the Registration of Births, Deaths and Marriages (Scotland) Act 1965 may provide for the furnishing by superintendent registrars and registrars, subject to the payment of such fee as may be prescribed by the regulations, of such information for the purposes—

(a) of the provisions of the Contributions and Benefits Act to which this section applies;

[[1](aa) of the provisions of Parts I and II of the Jobseekers Act 1995;]

[[3](ab) of the provisions of the State Pension Credit Act 2002; and]

[[6] (ac) of the provisions of Part 1 of the Welfare Reform Act 2007;]

(b) of the provisions of this Act so far as they have effect in relation to matters arising under those provisions,

including copies or extracts from the registers in their custody, as may be so prescribed.

(2) This section applies to the following provisions of the Contributions and Benefits Act—

(a) Parts I to VI except section 108;

(b) Part VII, so far as it relates to income support and [[5] . . .];

(c) Part VIII, so far as it relates to any social fund payment such as is mentioned in section 138(1)(a) or (2);

(d) Part IX;

(e) Part XI; and

(f) Part XII.

(3) Where the age, marriage or death of a person is required to be ascertained or proved for the purposes mentioned in subsection (1) above, any person—

(a) on presenting to the custodian of the register under the enactments relating to the registration of births, marriages and deaths, in which particulars of the birth, marriage or death (as the case may be) of the first-mentioned person are entered, a duly completed requisition in writing in that behalf; and

(b) on payment of a fee of [² £3.50] in England and Wales and [⁴ £9.00] in Scotland,

shall be entitled to obtain a copy, certified under the hand of the custodian, of the entry of those particulars.

(4) Requisitions for the purposes of subsection (3) above shall be in such form and contain such particulars as may from time to time be specified by the Registrar General, and suitable forms of requisition shall, on request, be supplied without charge by superintendent registrars and registrars.

(5) In this section—

(a) as it applies to England and Wales—

"Registrar General" means the Registrar General for England and Wales; and

"superintendent registrar" and "registrar" mean a superintendent registrar or, as the case may be, registrar for the purposes of the enactments relating to the registration of births, deaths and marriages; and

(b) as it applies to Scotland—

"Registrar General" means the Registrar General of Births, Deaths and Marriages for Scotland;

"registrar" means a district registrar, senior registrar or assistant registrar for the purposes of the enactment relating to the registration of births, deaths and marriages in Scotland.

AMENDMENTS

1. Jobseekers Act 1995, Sch.2, para.59 (October 7, 1996).
2. The Registration of Births, Deaths and Marriages (Fees) Order 2002 (SI 2002/3076), art.1 (April 1, 2003; this Order specifies a fee of £7 where the certificate is issued by a superintendent registrar or any other custodian of the register).
3. State Pension Credit Act 2002, s.14 and Sch.2 (July 2, 2002 for the purpose of making regulations only; fully in force October 6, 2003).
4. The Registration of Births, Deaths and Marriages (Fees) (Scotland) Order 2009 (SSI 2009/65) (April 1, 2009).
5. Tax Credits Act 2002, s.60 and Sch.6 (April 8, 2003).
6. Welfare Reform Act 1007, s.28 and Sch.3 para.10 (October 27, 2008).

DERIVATION

Social Security Act 1975, s.160.   1.150

DEFINITIONS

"the Contributions and Benefits Act"—see s.191.
"prescribed"—*ibid.*

[¹ **Provisions relating to civil partnership: England and Wales**

124A.—(1) Regulations made by the Registrar General under section 36   1.151
of the Civil Partnership Act 2004 may provide for the furnishing by registration authorities, subject to the payment of the prescribed fee, of such information for the purposes mentioned in section 124(1) above as may be so prescribed.

(2) Where the civil partnership of a person is required to be ascertained

or proved for those purposes, any person—

    (a) on presenting to the registration authority for the area in which the civil partnership was formed a request in the prescribed manner in that behalf, and

    (b) on payment of the prescribed fee,

shall be entitled to obtain a certified copy of such entries in the register as are prescribed by regulations made under section 36 of the 2004 Act.

    (3) "The prescribed fee" means any fee prescribed under section 34(1) of the 2004 Act.

    (4) "The prescribed manner" means—

    (a) in accordance with any regulations made under section 36 of the 2004 Act, and

    (b) in such form as is approved by the Registrar General for England and Wales,

and forms for making a request under subsection (2) shall, on request, be supplied without charge by registration authorities.]

AMENDMENT

    1. Civil Partnership Act 2004 (Overseas Relationships and Consequential etc. Amendments) Order 2005 (SI 2005/3129), Sch.1, para.4 (December 5, 2005).

[¹ Provisions relating to civil partnership: Scotland

1.152   **124B.**—(1) Where the civil partnership of a person is required to be ascertained or proved for the purposes mentioned in section 124(1) above, any person, on presenting to a district registrar a request in the approved manner in that behalf, [² and on payment of the sum of [³ £9.00]] shall be entitled to obtain a copy, certified by the registrar, of the entry in the civil partnership register of the particulars of the civil partnership.

    (2) "The approved manner" means in such form and containing such particulars as may be approved by the Registrar General for Scotland.

    (3) Forms for making a request under subsection (1) shall, on request, be supplied without charge by district registrars.

    (4) "Civil partnership register" has the same meaning as in Part 3 of the Civil Partnership Act 2004.]

AMENDMENT

    1. Civil Partnership Act 2004 (Overseas Relationships and Consequential etc. Amendments) Order 2005 (SI 2005/3129), Sch.1, para.4 (December 5, 2005).

    2. Local Electoral Administration and Registration Services (Scotland) Act 2006 asp 14 (Scottish Act) Pt 2 s.53(2) (October 1, 2006).

    3. Registration of Births, Deaths and Marriages (Fees) (Scotland) Order 2009/65 (Scottish SI) Sch.1 para.1 (April 1, 2009).

Regulations as to notifications of deaths

1.153   **125.**—(1) Regulations [³made with the concurrence of the Inland Revenue] may provide that it shall be the duty of any of the following persons—

    (a) the Registrar General for England and Wales;

    (b) the Registrar General of Births, Deaths and Marriages for Scotland;

    (c) each registrar of births and deaths,

to furnish the Secretary of State, [³or the Inland Revenue, for the purposes of their respective functions] under the Contributions and Benefits Act [¹, the Jobseekers Act 1995] [²the Social Security (Recovery of Benefits) Act 1997] [⁴, the Social Security Act 1998] [⁵, the State Pension Credit Act 2002] [⁶ , Part 1 of the Welfare Reform Act 2007] and this Act and the functions of the Northern Ireland Department under any Northern Ireland legislation corresponding to [¹any of those Acts], with the prescribed particulars of such deaths as may be prescribed.

(2) The regulations may make provision as to the manner in which and the times at which the particulars are to be furnished.

AMENDMENTS

1. Jobseekers Act 1995, Sch.2, para.60 (October 7, 1996).
2. Social Security (Recovery of Benefits) Act 1997, s.33 and Sch.3, para.5 (October 6, 1997).
3. Social Security Contributions (Transfer of Functions, etc.) Act 1999, s.1(1) and Sch.1, para.25 (April 1, 1999).
4. Social Security Act 1998, s.86 and Sch.7 (dates as for implementation of SSA 1998 for various benefits as set out on para.1.88 of this volume).
5. State Pension Credit Act 2002, s.14 and Sch.2 (July 2, 2002 for the purpose of making regulations only; fully in force October 6, 2003).
6. Welfare Reform Act 1007, s.28 and Sch.3, para.10 (October 27, 2008).

DERIVATION

Social Security Act 1986, s.60.   1.154

DEFINITIONS

"the Contributions and Benefits Act"—see s.191.
"the Northern Ireland Department"—*ibid.*
"prescribed"—*ibid.*

Personal representatives—income support and supplementary benefit

Personal representatives to give information about the estate of a deceased person who was in receipt of income support or supplementary benefit

126.—(1) The personal representatives of a person who was in receipt of   1.155
income support [¹, an income-based jobseeker's allowance] [², state pension credit] [³, an income-related employment and support allowance] or supplementary benefit at any time before his death shall provide the Secretary of State with such information as he may require relating to the assets and liabilities of that person's estate.

(2) If the personal representatives fail to supply any information within 28 days of being required to do so under subsection (1) above, then—

(a) the appropriate court may, on the application of the Secretary of State, make an order directing them to supply that information within such time as may be specified in the order; and

(b) any such order may provide that all costs (or, in Scotland, expenses) of and incidental to the application shall be borne personally by any of the personal representatives.

(3) In this section "the appropriate court" means—

(a) in England and Wales, a county court;
(b) in Scotland, the sheriff;
and any application to the sheriff under this section shall be made by summary application.

AMENDMENTS

1. Jobseekers Act 1995, Sch.2, para.61 (October 7, 1996).
2. State Pension Credit Act 2002, s.14 and Sch.2 (July 2, 2002 for the purpose of making regulations only; fully in force October 6, 2003).
3. Welfare Reform Act 2007, s.28 and Sch.3, para.10 (October 27, 2008).

DERIVATION

1.156   Social Security Act 1986, s.27A.

GENERAL NOTE

1.157   Under s.71(3) an overpayment which would have been recoverable from a person may be recoverable from that person's estate (*Secretary of State for Social Services v Solly* [1974] 3 All E.R. 922, *CSSB 6/1995*). Section 126 provides a specific obligation for the estate to provide information about the assets in it. However, s.126 only applies to the estates of income support, income-based JSA or supplementary benefit claimants. It does not apply to all benefits. Nor does it apply to anyone other than a recipient of income support, JSA or supplementary benefit. Sometimes a person other than a recipient may become liable to recovery by making a misrepresentation or failing to disclose a material fact: *R(SB) 21/82* and *R(SB) 28/83*. See the note to s.71(3).

1.158   **126A.** *Omitted.*

1.159   **127.–128A.** *Repealed by Sch.2 to the Social Security Administration (Fraud) Act 1997 (July 1, 1997).*

Statutory sick pay and other benefits

Disclosure by Secretary of State for purpose of determination of period of entitlement to statutory sick pay

1.160   **129.** Where the Secretary of State considers that it is reasonable for information held by him to be disclosed to an employer, for the purpose of enabling that employer to determine the duration of a period of entitlement under Part XI of the Contributions and Benefits Act in respect of an employee, or whether such a period exists, he may disclose the information to that employer.

DERIVATION

1.161   SSHBA 1982, s.17(1).

Duties of employers—statutory sick pay and claims for other benefits

1.162   **130.**—(1) Regulations may make provision requiring an employer, in a case falling within subsection (3) below to furnish information in connection with the making, by a person who is, or has been, an employee of that

employer, of a claim for—
 (a) [¹ short-term incapacity benefit];
 (b) a maternity allowance;
 (c) [¹ long-term incapacity benefit];
 (d) industrial injuries benefit; or
 (e) [³ . . .]
 [⁵ (f) an employment and support allowance.]
 (2) Regulations under this section shall prescribe—
 (a) the kind of information to be furnished in accordance with the regulations;
 (b) the person to whom information of the prescribed kind is to be furnished; and
 (c) the manner in which, and period within which, it is to be furnished.
 (3) The cases are—
 (a) where, by virtue of paragraph 2 of Schedule 11 to the Contributions and Benefits Act or of regulations made under paragraph 1 of that Schedule, a period of entitlement does not arise in relation to a period of incapacity for work;
 (b) where a period of entitlement has come to an end but the period of incapacity for work which was running immediately before the period of entitlement came to an end continues; and
 (c) where a period of entitlement has not come to an end but, on the assumption that—
   (i) the period of incapacity for work in question continues to run for a prescribed period; and
   (ii) there is no material change in circumstances, the period of entitlement will have ended on or before the end of the prescribed period.
 (4) Regulations [² made with the concurrence of the Inland Revenue] —
 (a) may require employers to maintain such records in connection with statutory sick pay as may be prescribed;
 (b) may provide for—
   (i) any person claiming to be entitled to statutory sick pay; or
   (ii) any other person who is a party to proceedings arising under Part XI of the Contributions and Benefits Act,
   to furnish to the Secretary of State [²or the Inland Revenue (as the regulations may require)] within a prescribed period, any information required for the determination of any question arising in connection therewith; and
 (c) may require employers who have made payments of statutory sick pay to furnish to the Secretary of State [²or the Inland Revenue (as the regulations may require)] such documents and information, at such times, as may be prescribed.
 [⁴ (5) Regulations made with the concurrence of the Inland Revenue may require employers to produce wages sheets and other documents and records to officers of the Inland Revenue, within a prescribed period, for the purpose of enabling them to satisfy themselves that statutory sick pay has been paid, and is being paid, in accordance with regulations under section 5 above, to employees or former employees who are entitled to it.]

AMENDMENTS

1. Social Security (Incapacity for Work) Act 1994, Sch.1 (April 13, 1995).
2. Transfer of Functions Act 1999, Sch.1 (April 1, 1999).
3. Welfare Reform and Pensions Act 1999, Sch.1, para.39 (November 3, 2000).
4. National Insurance Contributions and Statutory Payments Act 2004, s.9(2) (January 1, 2005)
5. Welfare Reform Act 2007, s.28 and Sch.3, para.10 (October 27, 2008).

DERIVATION

1.163   SSHBA 1982, ss.9, 17 and 18.

Disclosure by Secretary of State for purpose of determination of period of entitlement to statutory maternity pay

1.164   **131.** Where the Secretary of State considers that it is reasonable for information held by him to be disclosed to a person liable to make payments of statutory maternity pay for the purpose of enabling that person to determine—

(a) whether a maternity pay period exists in relation to a woman who is or has been an employee of his; and

(b) if it does, the date of its commencement and the weeks in it in respect of which he may be liable to pay statutory maternity pay, he may disclose the information to that person.

DERIVATION

1.165   SSA 1986, s.49.

Duties of employers—statutory maternity pay and claims for other benefits

1.166   **132.**—(1) Regulations may make provision requiring an employer in prescribed circumstances to furnish information in connection with the making of a claim by a woman who is or has been his employee for—

(a) a maternity allowance;

[5 (aa) an employment and support allowance;]

(b) [1 short-term incapacity benefit];

(c) [1 long-term incapacity benefit under section 30A], 40 and 41 of the Contributions and Benefits Act; or

(d) [3 . . .].

(2) Regulations under this section shall prescribe—

(a) the kind of information to be furnished in accordance with the regulations;

(b) the person to whom information of the prescribed kind is to be furnished; and

(c) the manner in which, and period within which, it is to be furnished.

(3) Regulations [2 made with the concurrence of the Inland Revenue]

(a) may require employers to maintain such records in connection with statutory maternity pay as may be prescribed;

(b) may provide for—

(i) any woman claiming to be entitled to statutory maternity pay; or

    (ii) any other person who is a party to proceedings arising under Part XII of the Contributions and Benefits Act,
to furnish to the Secretary of State [² or the Inland Revenue (as the regulations may require)], within a prescribed period, any information required for the determination of any question arising in connection therewith; and

  (c) may require persons who have made payments of statutory maternity pay to furnish to the Secretary of State [² or the Inland Revenue (as the regulations may require)] such documents and information, at such time, as may be prescribed.

[⁴ (4) Regulations made with the concurrence of the Inland Revenue may require employers to produce wages sheets and other documents and records to officers of the Inland Revenue, within a prescribed period, for the purpose of enabling them to satisfy themselves that statutory maternity pay has been paid, and is being paid, in accordance with regulations under section 5 above, to employees or former employees who are entitled to it.]

AMENDMENTS

  1. Social Security (Incapacity for Work) Act 1994, Sch.1 (April 13, 1995).
  2. Transfer of Functions Act 1999, Sch.1 (April 1, 1999).
  3. Welfare Reform and Pensions Act 1999, Sch.13, Pt IV (November 3, 2000).
  4. National Insurance Contributions and Statutory Payments Act 2004, s.9(3) (January 1, 2005);
  5. Welfare Reform Act 2007, s.28 and Sch.3, para.10 (October 27, 2008).

DERIVATION

  SSHBA, 1982, s.49.   **1.167**

Maintenance proceedings

Furnishing of addresses for maintenance proceedings, etc.

  133. The Secretary of State may incur expenses for the purpose of fur-   **1.168**
nishing the address at which a [¹person] is recorded by him as residing, where the address is required for the purpose of taking or carrying on legal proceedings to obtain or enforce an order for the making by the [¹person] of payments—

  (a) for the maintenance of the [¹ person's spouse, former spouse, civil partner or former civil partner]; or

[¹ (b) for the maintenance or education of any child of the person, or of any child of the person's spouse, former spouse, civil partner or former civil partner.]

DERIVATION

  SSA 1975, s.161.   **1.169**

AMENDMENT

  1. Civil Partnership (Pensions and Benefit Payments) (Consequential, etc. Provisions) Order 2005, (SI 2005/2053), Sch.1(2), para.6(2) (December 5, 2005).

1.170   **134.–154.** *Omitted.*

PART XI

COMPUTATION OF BENEFITS

Effect of alteration of rates of benefit under Parts II to V of Contributions and Benefits Act

1.171   **155.**—(1) This section has effect where the rate of any benefit to which this section applies is altered—

(a) by an Act subsequent to this Act;

(b) by an order under [⁴ section 150,150A or 152] above; or

(c) in consequence of any such Act or order altering any maximum rate of benefit;

and in this section "the commencing date" means the date fixed for payment of benefit at an altered rate to commence.

(2) This section applies to benefit under Part II, III, IV or V of the Contributions and Benefits Act.

(3) Subject to such exceptions or conditions as may be prescribed, where—

(a) the weekly rate of a benefit to which this section applies is altered to a fixed amount higher or lower than the previous amount; and

(b) before the commencing date an award of that benefit has been made (whether before or after the passing of the relevant Act or the making of the relevant order),

except as respects any period falling before the commencing date, the benefit shall become payable at the altered rate without any claim being made for it in the case of an increase in the rate of benefit or any review of the award in the case of a decrease, and the award shall have effect accordingly.

(4) Where—

(a) the weekly rate of a benefit to which this section applies is altered; and

(b) before the commencing date (but after that date is fixed) an award is made of the benefit,

the award either may provide for the benefit to be paid as from the commencing date at the altered rate or may be expressed in terms of the rate appropriate at the date of the award.

(5) Where in consequence of the passing of an Act, or the making of an order, altering the rate of disablement pension, regulations are made varying the scale of disablement gratuities, the regulations may provide that the scale as varied shall apply only in cases where the period taken into account by the assessment of the extent of the disablement in respect of which the gratuity is awarded begins or began after such day as may be prescribed.

(6) Subject to such exceptions or conditions as may be prescribed, where—

(a) for any purpose of any Act or regulations the weekly rate at which a person contributes to the cost of providing for a child [² or qualifying young person], or to the maintenance of an adult dependant, is to be

118

calculated for a period beginning on or after the commencing date for an increase in the weekly rate of benefit; but

(b) account is to be taken of amounts referable to the period before the commencing date,

those amounts shall be treated as increased in proportion to the increase in the weekly rate of benefit.

(7) So long as sections 36 and 37 of the National Insurance Act 1965 (graduated retirement benefit) continue in force by virtue of regulations made under Schedule 3 of the Social Security (Consequential Provisions) Act 1975 or under Schedule 3 to the Consequential Provisions Act, regulation may make provision for applying the provisions of this section—

[¹(a) to the amount of graduate retirement benefit payable for each unit of graduated contributions,

(b) To increased of such benefit under any provisions made by virtue of section 24(1)(b) of the Social Security Pensions Act 1975 or section 62(1)(a) of the Contributions and Benefits Act, and

(c) to any addition under section 37(1) of the National Insurance Act 1965 (addition to weekly rate of retirement pension for [³ widows, widowers and surviving civil partners]) to the amount of such benefit].

AMENDMENTS

1. Pensions Act 1995, s.131(3) (July 19, 1995).
2. Child Benefit Act 2005, Sch.1, Pt 1, para.23 (April 10, 2006).
3. Civil Partnership (Pensions and Benefit Payments) (Consequential, etc. Provisions) Order 2005, (SI 2005/2053), Sch.1(2), para.9 (December 5, 2005).
4. Pensions Act 2007, Sch.1(5), para.23 (July 26, 2007: insertion has effect as specified in 2007 c.22 s.5(3) and (7)).

DERIVATION

SSA 1986, s.64.   1.172

[¹Power to anticipate pensions up-rating order

155A.—(1) This section applies where a statement is made in the   1.173
House of Commons by or on behalf of the Secretary of State which specifies—

(a) the amounts by which he proposes, by an order under [⁴ section 150 or 150A above (as the case may be)] above, to increase—

   (i) the weekly sums that are payable by way of retirement pension [² or shared additional pension]; or

   (ii) the amount of graduated retirement benefit payable for each unit of graduated contributions; and

(b) the date of which he proposes to bring the increases into force ("the commencing date").

(2) Where before the commencing date and after the date on which the statement is made, an award is made of a retirement pension [³, a shared additional pension] or a graduated retirement benefit, the award may provide for the pension or benefit to be paid as from the commencing date at the increased rate or may be expressed in terms of the rate appropriate at the date of the award.]

AMENDMENTS

1. Social Security Act 1998, s.76 (November 16, 1998).
2. Welfare Reform and Pensions Act 1999, Sch.12, para.25(3) (December 1, 2000).
3. Welfare Reform and Pensions Act 1999, Sch.12, para.25(3) (December 1, 2000).
4. Pensions Act 2007, Sch.1(5), para.24 (July 26, 2007: substitution has effect as specified in 2007 c.22 s.5(3) and (7)).

Up-rating under sections 150 above of pensions increased under section 52(3) of the Contributions and Benefits Act.

1.174

[[1]156.—(1) This section applies in any case where a person is entitled to a Category A retirement pension with an increase, under section 52(3) of the Contributions and Benefits Act, in the additional pension on account of the contributions of a spouse [[2] or civil partner] who had died.

(2) Where in the case of any up-rating order under section 150 above—
(a) The spouse's [[2] or civil partner's] final relevant year is the tax year preceding the tax year in which the up-rating order comes into force, but
(b) The person's final relevant year was an earlier tax year,

then the up-rating order shall not have effect in relation to that part of the additional pension which is attributable to the spouse's [[2] or civil partner] contributions.

(3) Where in the case of any up-rating order under section 150 above—
(a) The person's final relevant year is the tax year preceding the tax year in which the up-rating order comes into force, but
(b) The spouse's [[2] or civil partner's] final relevant year was an earlier tax year,

Then the up-rating order shall not have effect in relation to that part of the additional pension which is attributable to the person's contributions.]

AMENDMENTS

1. Pensions Act 1995, s.130(1) (July 19, 1995).
2. Civil Partnership Act 2004, s.254 and Sch.24, para.66 (December 5, 2005).

DERIVATION

1.175

SSPA 1975, s.23(2A).

Effect of alteration of rates of child benefit

1.176

157.—(1) Subsections (3) and (4) of section 155 above shall have effect where there is an increase in the rate or any of the rates of child benefit as they have effect in relation to the rate of benefit to which that section applies.

(2) Where in connection with child benefit—
(a) any question arises in respect of a period after the date fixed for the commencement of payment of child benefit at an increased rate—
(i) as to the weekly rate at which a person is contributing to the cost of providing for a child [[1] or qualifying young person]; or
(ii) as to the expenditure that a person is incurring in respect of a child [[1] or qualifying young person]; and

(b) in determining that question account falls to be taken of contributions made or expenditure incurred for a period before that date,
the contributions made or expenditure incurred before that date shall be treated as increased in proportion to the increase in the rate of benefit.

DERIVATION

CBA 1975, s.5(6).   1.177

AMENDMENT

1. Child Benefit Act 2005, Sch.1, Pt 1, para.24 (April 10, 2006).

Treatment of excess benefit as paid on account of child benefit

158.—(1) In any case where—   1.178
(a) any benefit as defined in section 122 of the Contributions and Benefits Act or any increase of such benefit ("the relevant benefit or increase") has been paid to a person for a period in respect of a child [¹ or qualifying young person]; and
(b) subsequently child benefit for that period in respect of the child [¹ or qualifying young person] becomes payable at a rate which is such that, had the relevant benefit or increase been awarded after the child benefit became payable, the rate of the relevant benefit or increase would have been reduced,
then, except in so far as regulations otherwise provide, the excess shall be treated as paid on account of child benefit for that period in respect of the child [¹ or qualifying young person].
(2) In subsection (1) above "the excess" means so much of the relevant benefit or increase as is equal to the difference between—
(a) the amount of it which was paid for the period referred to in that subsection; and
(b) the amount of it which would have been paid for that period if it had been paid at the reduced rate referred to in paragraph (b) of that subsection.

DERIVATION

SS(MP)A 1977, s.17(4).   1.179

AMENDMENT

1. Child Benefit Act 2005, Sch.1, Pt 1, para.25 (April 10, 2006).

GENERAL NOTE

This provision avoids increases of benefits overlapping with, in particular, increase   1.180
of child benefit. See also paras (4) and (5) of reg.2 of the Fixing and Adjustment of
Rates Regulations.

Effect of alteration in the component rates of income support

159.—(1) Subject to such exceptions and conditions as may be prescribed, where—   1.181
(a) an award of income support is in force in favour of any person ("the recipient"); and

   (b) there is an alteration in any of the relevant amounts, that is to say—
        (i) any of the component rates of income support;
       (ii) any of the other sums specified in regulations under Part VII of the Contributions and Benefits Act; or
      (iii) the recipient's benefit income; and
   (c) the alteration affects the computation of the amount of income support to which the recipient is entitled,
then subsection (2) or (3) below (as the case may be) shall have effect.

(2) Where, in consequence of the alteration in question, the recipient becomes entitled to an increased or reduced amount of income support ("the new amount"), then, as from the commencing date, the amount of income support payable to or for the recipient under the award shall be the new amount, without any further decision of [¹the Secretary of State], and the award shall have effect accordingly.

(3) Where, notwithstanding the alteration in question, the recipient continues on and after the commencing date to be entitled to the same amount of income support as before, the award shall continue in force accordingly.

(4) In any case where—
   (a) there is an alteration in any of the relevant amounts; and
   (b) before the commencing date (but after that date is fixed) an award of income support is made in favour of a person,
the award either may provide for income support to be paid as from the commencing date, in which case the amount shall be determined by reference to the relevant amounts which will be in force on that date, or may provide for an amount determined by reference to the amounts in force at the date of the award.

(5) In this section—
"alteration" means—
   (a) in relation to—
       (i) the component rates of income support; or
      (ii) any other sums specified in regulations under Part VII of the Contributions and Benefits Act,
   their alteration by or under any enactment whether or not contained in that Part; and
   (b) in relation to a person's benefit income, the alteration of any of the sums referred to in section 150 [², 150A] above—
       (i) by any enactment; or
      (ii) by an order under [² section 150, 150A or 152] above,
to the extent that any such alteration affects the amount of his benefit income;
"benefit income", in relation to any person, means so much of his income as consists of—
   (a) benefit under the Contributions and Benefits Act, other than income support; or
   (b) a war disablement pension or war widow's pension;
"the commencing date" in relation to an alteration, means the date on which the alteration comes into force in the case of the person in question;
"component rate", in relation to income support, means the amount of—
   (a) the sum referred to in section 126(5)(b)(i) and (ii) of the Contributions and Benefits Act; or

(b) any of the sums specified in regulations under section 135(1) of that Act; and

"relevant amounts" has the meaning given by subsection (1)(b) above.

AMENDMENTS

1. Social Security Act 1998, Sch.7, para.95 (November 29, 1999 for purposes specified in SI 1999/3178 art.2(1) and Sch.1; not yet in force otherwise).
2. Pensions Act 2007, Sch.1(5), para.25 (July 26, 2007: insertion has effect as specified in 2007 c.22 s.5(3) and (7)).

DERIVATION

Social Security Act 1986, s.64A.   1.182

DEFINITIONS

"the Contributions and Benefits Act"—see s.191.
"war disablement pension"—*ibid.*
"war widow's pension"—*ibid.*

GENERAL NOTE

The general rule under s.159 is that if there is an alteration in the prescribed   1.183
figures for personal allowances, premiums, the relevant sum (i.e. assumed "strike
pay" in trade dispute cases), or any social security benefits which count as income
for income support purposes (subss.(1) and (5)), then any consequent change in
the amount of income support which is payable takes effect automatically without
the need for a decision by an adjudication officer (subs.(2)). Thus no right of appeal
arises against the change in the amount, although the claimant can always request a
review of the decision awarding benefit, as altered under s.159.

[¹ Effect of alteration of rates of a jobseeker's allowance

159A.—(1) This section applies where—   1.184
(a) an award of a jobseeker's allowance is in force in favour of any person
("the recipient"); and
(b) an alteration—
(i) in any component of the allowance, or
(ii) in the recipient's benefit income,
affects the amount of the jobseeker's allowance to which he is entitled.

(2) Subsection (3) applies where, as a result of the alteration, the amount
of the jobseeker's allowance to which the recipient is entitled is increased
or reduced.

(3) As from the commencing date, the amount of the jobseeker's allowance payable to or for the recipient under the award shall be the increased
or reduced amount, without any further decision of [² the Secretary of
State]; and the award shall have effect accordingly.

(4) In any case where—
(a) there is an alteration of a kind mentioned in subsection (1)(b); and
(b) before the commencing date (but after that date is fixed) an award of
a jobseeker's allowance is made in favour of a person,
the award may provide for the jobseeker's allowance to be paid as from the
commencing date, in which case the amount of the jobseeker's allowance
shall be determined by reference to the components applicable on that date,
or may provide for an amount determined by reference to the components
applicable at the date of the award.

(5) In this section—

"alteration" means—

  (a) in relation to any component of a jobseeker's allowance, its alteration by or under any enactment; and

  (b) in relation to a person's benefit income, the alteration of any of the sums referred to in [³ section 150 or 150A] above by any enactment or by an order under section 150 [³ or 150A] above, to the extent that any such alteration affects the amount of the recipient's benefit income;

"benefit income", in relation to a recipient, means so much of his income as consists of—

  (a) benefit under the Contributions and Benefits Act; or

  (b) a war disablement pension or war widow's pension;

"the commencing date" in relation to an alteration, means the date on which the alteration comes into force in relation to the recipient;

"component", in relation to a jobseeker's allowance, means any of the sums specified in regulations under the Jobseekers Act 1995 which are relevant in calculating the amount payable by way of a jobseeker's allowance.]

AMENDMENTS

1. Jobseekers Act 1995, s.24 (October 7, 1996).
2. Social Security Act 1998, Sch.7, para.96 (October 18, 1999).
3. Pensions Act 2007, Sch.1(5) para.26 (July 26, 2007: insertion has effect as specified in 2007 c.22 s.5(3) and (7)).

DEFINITIONS

"the Contributions and Benefit Act"—see s.191.
"war disablement pension"—*ibid.*
"war widow's pension—*ibid.*

GENERAL NOTE

1.185   This section has the same effect for income-based JSA as s.159 does for income support.

[¹ Effect of alterations affecting state pension credit]

1.186   **159B.**—(1) Subject to such exceptions and conditions as may be prescribed, subsection (2) or (3) below shall have effect where—

  (a) an award of state pension credit is in force in favour of any person ("the recipient"); and

  (b) an alteration—

     (i) in any component of state pension credit,

     (ii) in the recipient's benefit income,

     (iii) in any component of a contribution-based jobseeker's allowance,

     [³ (iiia) in any component of a contributory employment and support allowance,] or

     (iv) in the recipient's war disablement pension or war widow's or widower's pension, affects the computation of the amount of state pension credit to which he is entitled.

(2) Where, as a result of the alteration, the amount of state pension credit to which the recipient is entitled is increased or reduced, then, as from the

commencing date, the amount of state pension credit payable in the case of the recipient under the award shall be the increased or reduced amount, without any further decision of the Secretary of State; and the award shall have effect accordingly.

(3) Where, notwithstanding the alteration, the recipient continues on and after the commencing date to be entitled to the same amount of state pension credit as before, the award shall continue in force accordingly.

(4) Subsection (5) below applies where a statement is made in the House of Commons by or on behalf of the Secretary of State which specifies—

(a) in relation to any of the items referred to in subsection (1)(b)(i) to (iv) above, the amount of the alteration which he proposes to make by an order under [⁴ section 150,150A or 152] above or by or under any other enactment; and

(b) the date on which he proposes to bring the alteration into force ("the proposed commencing date").

(5) If, in a case where this subsection applies, an award of state pension credit is made in favour of a person before the proposed commencing date and after the date on which the statement is made, the award—

(a) may provide for state pension credit to be paid as from the proposed commencing date at a rate determined by reference to the amounts of the items specified in subsection (1)(b)(i) to (iv) above which will be in force on that date; or

(b) may be expressed in terms of the amounts of those items in force at the date of the award.

(6) In this section—

"alteration" means—

(a) in relation to any component of state pension credit, its alteration by or under any enactment;

(b) in relation to a person's benefit income, the alteration of any of the sums referred to in section 150 [⁴, 150A] above by any enactment or by an order under section 150 or 152 above to the extent that any such alteration affects the amount of his benefit income;

(c) in relation to any component of a contribution-based jobseeker's allowance, its alteration by or under any enactment; and

(d) in relation to a person's war disablement pension or war widow's or widower's pension, its alteration by or under any enactment;

"benefit income", in relation to a person, means so much of his income as consists of benefit under the Contributions and Benefits Act;

"the commencing date", in relation to an alteration, means the date on which the alteration comes into force in relation to the recipient;

"component"—

(a) in relation to contribution-based jobseeker's allowance, means any of the sums specified in regulations under the Jobseekers Act 1995 (c 18) which are relevant in calculating the amount payable by way of a jobseeker's allowance;

(b) in relation to state pension credit, means any of the sums specified in regulations under section 2, 3 or 12 of the State Pension Credit Act 2002;

[³ (c) in relation to a contributory employment and support allowance, means any of the sums specified in regulations under Part 1 of the Welfare Reform Act 2007 which are relevant in calculating the amount payable by way of a contributory employment and support allowance;]

"war disablement pension" means—

  (a) any retired pay, pension or allowance granted in respect of disablement under powers conferred by or under—

    (i) the Air Force (Constitution) Act 1917 (c 51);

    (ii) the Personal Injuries (Emergency Provisions) Act 1939 (c 82);

    (iii) the Pensions (Navy, Army, Air Force and Mercantile Marine) Act 1939 (c 83);

    (iv) the Polish Resettlement Act 1947 (c 19); or

    (v) Part 7 or section 151 of the Reserve Forces Act 1980 (c 9); or

  (b) without prejudice to paragraph (a), any retired pay or pension to which [2 any of paragraphs (a) to (f) of that section 641(1) of the Income Tax (Earnings and Pensions) Act 2003] applies;

"war widow's or widower's pension" means—

  (a) [5 any widow's widower's or surviving civil partner's] pension or allowance granted in respect of a death due to service or war injury and payable by virtue of any enactment mentioned in paragraph (a) of the definition of "war disablement pension"; or

  (b) a pension or allowance for a [5 widow, widower or surviving civil partner] granted under any scheme mentioned in [2 section 641(1) (e) or (f) of the Income Tax (Earnings and Pensions) Act 2003.]

AMENDMENTS

1. Inserted by State Pensions Credit Act 2002, s.14 and Sch.2 (July 2, 2002 for the purpose of making regulations only; fully in force October 6, 2003).

2. Income Tax (Earnings and Pensions) Act 2003, s.722, Sch.6, Pt 2, paras 186, 188(1), (3). (Income Tax (Earnings and Pensions) Act 2003, s.722, Sch.6, Pt.2, paras 186, 188(1), (3).

3. Welfare Reform Act 1007, s.28 and Sch.3, para.10 (October 27, 2008).

4. Pensions Act 2007, Sch.1(5) para.27 (July 26, 2007: insertion has effect as specified in 2007 c.22 s.5(3) and (7)).

5. Civil Partnership (Pensions and Benefit Payments) (Consequential, etc. Provisions) Order 2005 (SI 2005/2053), Sch.1(2) para.10 (December 5, 2005)

[1 159C Effect of alteration of rates of an employment and support allowance

1.187   (1) Subject to such exceptions and conditions as may be prescribed, subsection (2) or (3) shall have effect where—

  (a) an award of an employment and support allowance is in force in favour of any person ("the recipient"), and

  (b) an alteration—

    (i) in any component of the allowance,

    (ii) in the recipient's benefit income, or

    (iii) in the recipient's war disablement or war widow's or widower's pension,

affects the computation of the amount of the employment and support allowance to which he is entitled.

(2) Where, as a result of the alteration, the amount of the employment and support allowance to which the recipient is entitled is increased or

reduced, then, as from the commencing date, the amount of the employment and support allowance payable in the case of the recipient under the award shall be the increased or reduced amount, without any further decision of the Secretary of State; and the award shall have effect accordingly.

(3) Where, notwithstanding the alteration, the recipient continues on and after the commencing date to be entitled to the same amount by way of an employment and support allowance as before, the award shall continue in force accordingly.

(4) Subsection (5) applies where a statement is made in the House of Commons by or on behalf of the Secretary of State which specifies—

(a) in relation to any of the items referred to in subsection (1)(b)(i) to (iii), the amount of the alteration which he proposes to make by an order under [² section 150, 150A or 152] or by or under any other enactment, and

(b) the date on which he proposes to bring the alteration into force ("the proposed commencing date"").

(5) If, in a case where this subsection applies, an award of an employment and support allowance is made in favour of a person before the proposed commencing date and after the date on which the statement is made, the award—

(a) may provide for the employment and support allowance to be paid as from the proposed commencing date at a rate determined by reference to the amounts of the items referred to in subsection (1)(b)(i) to (iii) which will be in force on that date, or

(b) may be expressed in terms of the amounts of those items in force at the date of the award.

(6) In this section—

"alteration" means—

(a) in relation to any component of an employment and support allowance, its alteration by or under any enactment;

(b) in relation to a person's benefit income, the alteration of any of the sums referred to in [² section 150 or 150A] by any enactment or by an order under [² section 150, 150A or 152] to the extent that any such alteration affects the amount of his benefit income;

(c) in relation to a person's war disablement pension or war widow's or widower's pension, its alteration by or under any enactment;

"benefit income", in relation to a person, means so much of his income as consists of benefit under the Contributions and Benefits Act;

"the commencing date", in relation to an alteration, means the date on which the alteration comes into force in relation to the recipient;

"component", in relation to an employment and support allowance, means any of the sums specified in regulations under Part 1 of the Welfare Reform Act 2007 which are relevant in calculating the amount payable by way of an employment and support allowance;

"war disablement pension" and "war widow's or widower's pension" have the same meaning as in section 159B.]

AMENDMENT

1. Welfare Reform Act 2007, s.28 and Sch.3, para.10 (October 27, 2008).

2. Pensions Act 2007, Sch.1(5), para.28 (October 27, 2008: insertions came into force on July 26, 2007 but could not take effect until the commencement of the

Welfare Reform Act 2007 Sch.3, para.10(23) on October 27, 2008 and has effect as specified in 2007 c.22 s.5(3) and (7)).

Implementation of increases in income support due to attainment of particular ages

1.188   **160.**—(1) This section applies where—

(a) an award of income support is in force in favour of a person ("the recipient"); and

(b) there is a component which becomes applicable, or applicable at a particular rate, in his case if he or some other person attains a particular age.

(2) If, in a case where this section applies, the recipient or other person attains the particular age referred to in paragraph (b) of subsection (1) above and, in consequence—

(a) the component in question becomes applicable, or applicable at a particular rate, in the recipient's case (whether or not some other component ceases, for the same reason, to be applicable, or applicable at a particular rate, in his case; and

(b) after taking account of any such cessation, the recipient becomes entitled to an increased amount of income support,

then, except as provided by subsection (3) below, as from the day on which he becomes so entitled, the amount of income support payable to or for him under the award shall be that increased amount, without any further decision of [¹ the Secretary of State], and the award shall have effect accordingly.

(3) Subsection (2) above does not apply in any case where, in consequence of the recipient or other person attaining the age in question, some question arises in relation to the recipient's entitlement to any benefit under the Contributions and Benefits Act, other than—

(a) the question whether the component concerned, or any other component, becomes or ceases to be applicable, or applicable at a particular rate, in his case; and

(b) the question whether, in consequence, the amount of his income support falls to be varied.

(4) In this section "component", in relation to a person and his income support, means any of the sums specified in regulations under section 135(1) of the Contributions and Benefits Act.

AMENDMENT

1. SI 1999/3178, Sch.1 (November 29, 1999).

DERIVATION

1.189   Social Security Act 1986, s.64B.

DEFINITION

"the Contributions and Benefits Act"—see s.191.

GENERAL NOTE

1.190   Section 160 extends the process begun by s.159 of taking routine adjustments in the amount of income support out of the ordinary mechanism of review.

[¹Implementation of increases in income-based jobseeker's allowance due to attainment of particular ages

160A.—(1) This section applies where—

(a) an award of an income-based jobseeker's allowance is in force in favour of a person ("the recipient"); and

(b) a component has become applicable, or applicable at a particular rate, because he or some other person has reached a particular age ("the qualifying age")

(2) If, as a result of the recipient or other person reaching the qualifying age, the recipient becomes entitled to an income-based jobseeker's allowance of an increased amount, the amount payable to or for him under the award shall, as from the day on which he becomes so entitled, be that increased amount, without any further decision of [² the Secretary of State]; and the award shall have effect accordingly.

(3) Subsection (2) above does not apply where, in consequence of the recipient or other person reaching the qualifying age, a question arises in relation to the recipient's entitlement to—

(a) a benefit under the Contributions and Benefits Act; or

(b) a jobseeker's allowance.

(4) Subsection (3)(b) above does not apply to the question—

(a) whether the component concerned, or any other component, becomes or ceases to be applicable, or applicable at a particular rate, in the recipient's case; and

(b) whether, in consequence, the amount of his income-based jobseeker's allowance falls to be varied.

(5) In this section "component", in relation to a recipient and his jobseeker's allowance, means any of the amounts determined in accordance with regulations made under section 4(5) of the Jobseekers Act 1995.]

1.191

AMENDMENTS

1. Jobseekers Act 1995, s.25 (October 7, 1996).
2. Social Security Act 1998, Sch.7, para.98 (October 18, 1999).

DEFINITION

"the Contributions and Benefits Act"—see s.191.

GENERAL NOTE

See s.160.

1.192

[¹ 160B Implementation of increases in employment and support allowance due to attainment of particular ages

(1) This section applies where—

(a) an award of an employment and support allowance is in force in favour of a person ("the recipient"), and

(b) a component has become applicable, or applicable at a particular rate, because he or some other person has reached a particular age ("the qualifying age").

(2) If, as a result of the recipient or other person reaching the qualifying age, the recipient becomes entitled to an employment and support allowance of an increased amount, the amount payable to or for him under the award shall, as from the day on which he becomes so entitled, be that

1.193

129

increased amount, without any further decision of the Secretary of State; and the award shall have effect accordingly.

(3) Subsection (2) does not apply where, in consequence of the recipient or other person reaching the qualifying age, a question arises in relation to the recipient's entitlement to a benefit under the Contributions and Benefits Act.

(4) Subsection (2) does not apply where, in consequence of the recipient or other person reaching the qualifying age, a question arises in relation to the recipient's entitlement to an employment and support allowance, other than—

(a) the question whether the component concerned, or any other component, becomes or ceases to be applicable, or applicable at a particular rate, in the recipient's case, and

(b) the question whether, in consequence, the amount of his employment and support allowance falls to be varied.

(5) In this section, "component", in relation to a recipient and his employment and support allowance, means any of the amounts determined in accordance with regulations made under section 2(1)(a) or 4(2)(a) of the Welfare Reform Act 2007.]

AMENDMENT

1. Welfare Reform Act 2007, s.28 and Sch.3, para.10 (October 27, 2008).

PART XII

FINANCE

1.194   **161.–166.** *Omitted.*

The social fund

1.195   **167.**—(1) The fund known as the social fund shall continue in being by that name.

(2) The social fund shall continue to be maintained under the control and management of the Secretary of State and payments out of it shall be made by him.

(3) The Secretary of State shall make payments into the social fund of such amounts, at such times and in such manner as he may with the approval of the Treasury determine.

(4) Accounts of the social fund shall be prepared in such form, and in such manner and at such times, as the Treasury may direct, and the Comptroller and Auditor General shall examine and certify every such account and shall lay copies of it, together with his report, before Parliament.

(5) The Secretary of State shall prepare an annual report on the social fund.

(6) A copy of every such report shall be laid before each House of Parliament.

DERIVATIONS

1.196   Subs.(1): Social Security Act 1986, s.32(1).
Subss.(2)–(6): 1986 Act, s.32(5)–(7B).

Allocations from social fund

168.—(1) The Secretary of State shall allocate amounts for payments   1.197
from the social fund such as are mentioned in section 138(1)(b) of the
Contributions and Benefits Act in a financial year.

(2) The Secretary of State may specify the amounts either as sums of
money or by reference to money falling into the social fund on repayment
or partial repayment of loans, or partly in the former and partly in the latter
manner.

(3) Allocations—

(a) may be for payments by [¹ a particular appropriate officer or group
of appropriate fund officers],

(b) may be for different amounts for different purposes;

(c) may be made at such time or times as the Secretary of State considers appropriate; and

(d) may be in addition to any other allocation [² . . .]

(4) The Secretary of State may at any time re-allocate amounts previously
allocated, and subsections (2) and (3) above shall have effect in relation to
a re-allocation as they have effect in relation to an allocation.

(5) The Secretary of State may give general directions to [¹ appropriate
officers] or groups of [¹ appropriate officers], or to any class of [¹ appropriate officers], with respect to the control and management by [¹ appropriate
officers] or groups of [¹ appropriate officers] of [² any amounts allocated to
them] under this section.

[¹(6) In this section "appropriate officer" means an officer of the
Secretary of State who, acting under his authority, is exercising functions of
the Secretary of State in relation to [² section 138(1)(b) payments]

AMENDMENT

1. Social Security Act 1998, Sch.7, para.103 (November 29, 1999).
2. Welfare Reform Act 2007, Sch.8 (July 3, 2007).

DERIVATION

Social Security Act 1986, s.32(8A)–(8E).   1.198

DEFINITION

"the Contributions and Benefits Act"—see s.191.

Adjustments between social fund and other sources of finance

169.—(1) There shall be made—   1.199

(a) out of the social fund into the Consolidated Fund or the National
Insurance Fund;

(b) into the social fund out of money provided by Parliament or the
National Insurance Fund,

such payments by way of adjustment as the Secretary of State determines
(in accordance with any directions of the Treasury) to be appropriate in
consequence of any enactment or regulations relating to the repayment
or offsetting of a benefit or other payment under the Contributions and
Benefits Act [¹ or the State Pension Credit Act 2002].

(2) Where in any other circumstances payments fall to be made by way
of adjustment—

(a) out of the social fund into the Consolidated Fund or the National Insurance Fund; or

(b) into the social fund out of money provided by Parliament or the National Insurance Fund,

then, in such cases or classes of cases as may be specified by the Secretary of State by order, the amount of the payments to be made shall be taken to be such, and payments on account of it shall be be made at such times and in such manner, as may be determined by the Secretary of State in accordance with any direction given by the Treasury.

AMENDMENT

1. State Pension Credit Act 2002, s.14 and Sch.2 (July 2, 2002 for the purpose of making regulations only; fully in force October 6, 2003).

DERIVATION

1.200   Social Security Act 1986, s.85(11) and (12).

DEFINITION

"the Contributions and Benefits Act"—see s.191.

PART XIII

ADVISORY BODIES AND CONSULTATION

The Social Security Advisory Committee and the Industrial Injuries Advisory Council

The Social Security Advisory Committee

1.201   **170.**—(1) The Social Security Advisory Committee (in this Act referred to as "the Committee") constituted under section 9 of the Social Security Act 1980 shall continue in being by that name—

(a) to give (whether in pursuance of a reference under this Act or otherwise) advice and assistance to the Secretary of State in connection with the discharge of his functions under the relevant enactments;

(b) to give (whether in pursuance of a reference under this Act or otherwise) advice and assistance to the Northern Ireland Department in connection with the discharge of its functions under the relevant Northern Ireland enactments; and

(c) to perform such other duties as may be assigned to the Committee under any enactment.

(2) Schedule 5 to this Act shall have effect with respect to the constitution of the Committee and the other matters there mentioned.

(3) The Secretary of State may from time to time refer to the Committee for consideration and advice such questions relating to the operation of any of the relevant enactments as he thinks fit (including questions as to the advisability of amending any of them).

(4) The Secretary of State shall furnish the Committee with such

information as the Committee may reasonably require for the proper discharge of its functions.

(5) In this Act—

"the relevant enactments" means—

    (a) the provisions of the Contributions and Benefits Act [¹, this Act and the Social Security (Incapacity for Work) Act 1994], except as they apply to industrial injuries benefit and Old Cases payments;

[² (aa) the provisions of the Jobseekers Act 1995;] and

[³ (ab) section 10 of the Child Support Act 1995;]

[⁴ (ac) the provisions of the Social Security (Recovery of Benefits) Act 1997; and]

[⁵ (ad) the provisions of Chapter II of Part I of the Social Security Act 1998 and section 72 of that Act;]

[⁶ (ae) sections 60, 72 and 79 of the Welfare Reform and Pensions Act 1999;]

 [⁷ (af) section 42, sections 62 to 65 and sections 68 to 70 of the Child Support Pensions and Social Security Act 2000 and Schedule 7 to that Act;]

[⁸ (ag) sections 7 to 11 of the Social Security Fraud Act 2001;]

[⁹ (ah) the provisions of the State Pension Credit Act 2002;]

[¹¹ (ai) section 7 of the Age-Related Payments Act 2004;]

[¹² (aia) the provisions of Part 1 of the Welfare Reform Act 2007;]

[¹³ (aj) sections 32 and 33 of the Welfare Reform Act 2007;]

    (b) the provisions of Part II of Schedule 3 to the Consequential Provisions Act, except as they apply to industrial injuries benefit; and

"the relevant Northern Ireland enactments" means—

    (a) the provisions of the Northern Ireland Contributions and Benefits Act and the Northern Ireland Administration Act, except as they apply to Northern Ireland industrial injuries benefit and payments under Part I of Schedule 8 to the Northern Ireland Contributions and Benefits Act; and

[² (aa) any provisions in Northern Ireland which correspond to provisions of the Jobseekers Act 1995; and]

[³ (ab) any enactment corresponding to section 10 of the Child Support Act 1995 having effect with respect to Northern Ireland; and]

[⁴ (ac) any provisions in Northern Ireland which correspond to provisions of the Social Security (Recovery of Benefits) Act 1997; and]

[⁵ (ad) any provisions in Northern Ireland which correspond to provisions of Chapter II of Part I of the Social Security Act 1998 and section 72 of that Act;]

[⁶ (ae) any provisions in Northern Ireland which correspond to sections 60, 72 and 79 of the Welfare Reform and Pensions Act 1999;]

 [⁷ (af) any provisions in Northern Ireland which correspond to section 42, any of sections 62 to 65, 68 to 70 of the Child Support, Pensions and Social Security Act 2000 or Schedule 7 to that Act; and]

[⁸ (ag) any provisions in Northern Ireland which correspond to sections 7 to 11 of the Social Security Fraud Act 2001, and]

[⁹ (ah) any provisions in Northern Ireland which correspond to provisions of the State Pension Credit Act 2002; and]

[¹² (aia) any provisions in Northern Ireland which correspond to Part 1 of the Welfare Reform Act 2007;]

[¹³ (aj) any provisions in Northern Ireland which correspond to sections 32 and 33 of the Welfare Reform Act 2007;]
   (b) the provisions of Part II of Schedule 3 to the Social Security (Consequential Provisions) (Northern Ireland) Act 1992, except as they apply to Northern Ireland industrial injuries benefit; and
[¹⁰ (c) section 32(6) of the Pension Schemes (Northern Ireland) Act 1993;]
and in this definition—
   (i) "Northern Ireland Contributions and Benefits Act" means the Social Security Contributions and Benefits (Northern Ireland) Act 1992;
   (ii) "Northern Ireland industrial injuries benefit" means benefit under Part V of the Northern Ireland Contributions and Benefits Act other than under Schedule 8 to that Act.

AMENDMENTS

1. Social Security (Incapacity for Work) Act 1994, Sch.1, para.51 (April 13, 1995).
2. Jobseekers Act 1995, Sch.2, para.67 (April 22, 1996).
3. Child Support Act 1995, Sch.3, para.20 (October 6, 1997).
4. Social Security (Recovery of Benefits) Act 1997, Sch.3, para.8 (October 6, 1997).
5. Social Security Act 1998, Sch.7, para.104 (March 4, 1999).
6. Welfare Reform and Pensions Act 1999, Sch.12, para.81 (November 11, 1999).
7. Child Support, Pensions and Social Security Act 2000, s.73 (December 1, 2000).
8. Social Security Fraud Act 2001, s.12 (April 1, 2002).
9. State Pension Credit Act 2002, Sch.2, para.20 (July 2, 2002 for the purpose of making regulations only; fully in force October 6, 2003).
10. Pension Schemes (Northern Ireland) Act 1993, Sch.7, para.26 (February 7, 1994).
11. Age-Related Payments Act 2004, s.7(5) (July 8, 2004).
12. Welfare Reform Act 2007, s.28 and Sch.3, para.10 (October 27, 2008).
13. Welfare Reform Act 2007, s.33(7)(a) (October 6, 2008).

GENERAL NOTE

1.202   In *Howker v Secretary of State for Work and Pensions* [2002] EWCA Civ. 1623, *R(IB)3/03* the Court of Appeal (hearing the appeal against the decision in *CIB/4563/1998*, confirmed the jurisdiction of Commissioners (and presumably also tribunals) to invalidate subordinate legislation. The circumstances of this case involved the Secretary of State through his official misleading the Social Security Advisory Committee by presenting information which was obviously incorrect which resulted in the securing of the agreement of the Committee to the proposed changes. The Court of Appeal concluded that it was manifest that the procedure intended by Parliament for the making of regulations had not been observed and so the regulations as made were invalid for failure to comply with the requirements of s.172. See annotation to reg.27(b) of the Incapacity for Work General Regulations in Vol. I for the substance of the Court's decision.

The Industrial Injuries Advisory Council

1.203   **171.**—(1) The Industrial Injuries Advisory Council (in this Act referred to as "the Council") constituted under section 62 of the National Insurance (Industrial Injuries) Act 1965 shall continue in being by that name.

(2) Schedule 6 to this Act shall have effect with respect to the constitution of the Council and the other matters there mentioned.

(3) The Secretary of State may from time to time refer to the Council for consideration and advice such questions as he thinks fit relating to industrial injuries benefit or its administration.

(4) The Council may also give advice to the Secretary of State on any other matter relating to such benefit or its administration.

Functions of Committee and Council in relation to regulations

172.—(1) Subject—   1.204
(a) to subsection (3) below; and
(b) to section 173 below,
 where the Secretary of State proposes to make regulations under any of the relevant enactments, he shall refer the proposals, in the form of draft regulations or otherwise, to the Committee.

(2) Subject—
(a) to subsection (4) below; and
(b) to section 173 below, where the Secretary of State proposes to make regulations relating only to industrial injuries benefit or its administration, he shall refer the proposals, in the form of draft regulations or otherwise, to the Council for consideration and advice.

(3) Subsection (1) above does not apply to the regulations specified in Part I of Schedule 7 to this Act.

(4) Subsection (2) above does not apply to the regulations specified in Part II of that Schedule.

(5) In relation to regulations required or authorised to be made by the Secretary of State in conjunction with the Treasury, the reference in subsection (1) above to the Secretary of State shall be construed as a reference to the Secretary of State and the Treasury.

Cases in which consultation is not required

173.—(1) Nothing in any enactment shall require any proposals in 1.205
respect of regulations to be referred to the Committee or the Council if—
(a) it appears to the Secretary of State that by reason of the urgency of the matter it is inexpedient so to refer them; or
(b) the relevant advisory body have agreed that they shall not be referred.

(2) Where by virtue only of subsection (1)(a) above the Secretary of State makes regulations without proposals in respect of them having been referred, then, unless the relevant advisory body agrees that this subsection shall not apply, he shall refer the regulations to that body as soon as practicable after making them.

(3) Where the Secretary of State has referred proposals to the Committee or the Council, he may make the proposed regulations before the Committee have made their report or, as the case may be the Council have given their advice, only if after the reference it appears to him that by reason of the urgency of the matter it is expedient to do so.

(4) Where by virtue of this section regulations are made before a report of the Committee has been made, the Committee shall consider them and make a report to the Secretary of State containing such recommendations

with regard to the regulations as the Committee thinks appropriate; and a copy of any report made to the Secretary of State on the regulations shall be laid by him before each House of Parliament together, if the report contains recommendations, with a statement—

    (a) of the extent (if any) to which the Secretary of State proposes to give effect to the recommendations; and

    (b) in so far as he does not propose to give effect to them, of his reasons why not.

(5) Except to the extent that this subsection is excluded by an enactment passed after 25th July 1986, nothing in any enactment shall require the reference to the Committee or the Council of any regulations contained in either—

    (a) a statutory instrument made before the end of the period of 6 months beginning with the coming into force of the enactment under which those regulations are made; or

    (b) a statutory instrument—

        (i) which states that it contains only regulations made by virtue of, or consequential upon, a specified enactment; and

        (ii) which is made before the end of the period of 6 months beginning with the coming into force of that specified enactment.

(6) In relation to regulations required or authorised to be made by the Secretary of State in conjunction with the Treasury, any reference in this section to the Secretary of State shall be construed as a reference to the Secretary of State and the Treasury.

(7) In this section "regulations" means regulations under any enactment, whenever passed.

1.206   **174.–176.** *Omitted.*

PART XIV

SOCIAL SECURITY SYSTEMS OUTSIDE GREAT BRITAIN

Co-ordination

1.207   **Section 177:** *repealed by the Northern Ireland Act 1998, Sch.15 (December 2, 1999).*

1.208   **Section 178:** *repealed by the Northern Ireland Act 1998, Sch.15 (December 2, 1999).*

Reciprocal agreements with countries outside the United Kingdom

1.209   **179.**—(1) For the purpose of giving effect—

    (a) to any agreement with the government of a country outside the United Kingdom providing for reciprocity in matters relating to payments for purposes similar or comparable to the purposes of legislation to which this section applies, or

(b) to any such agreement as it would be if it were altered in accordance with proposals to alter it which, in consequence of any change in the law of Great Britain, the government of the United Kingdom has made to the other government in question,

Her Majesty may by Order in Council make provision for modifying or adapting such legislation in its application to cases affected by the agreement or proposed alterations.

(2) An Order made by virtue of subsection (1) above may, instead of or in addition to making specific modifications or adaptions, provide generally that legislation to which this section applies shall be modified to such extent as may be required to give effect to the provisions contained in the agreement or, as the case may be, alterations in question.

(3) The modifications which may be made by virtue of subsection (1) above include provisions—

(a) for securing that acts, omissions and events having any effect for the purposes of the law of the country in respect of which the agreement is made have a corresponding effect for the purposes of this Act, [1 the Jobseeker's Act 1995], [2 Chapter II of Part I of the Social Security Act 1998] [3 Part II of the Social Security Contributions (Transfer of Functions, etc.) Act 1999] [5, Part III of the Social Security Contributions (Transfer of Functions etc.) (Northern Ireland) Order 1999] [6, the State Pension Credit Act 2002] [7, Part 1 of the Welfare Reform Act 2007] and the Contributions and Benefits Act (but not so as to confer a right to double benefit);

(b) for determining, in cases where rights accrue under such legislation and under the law of that country, which of those rights is to be available to the person concerned;

(c) for making any necessary financial adjustments.

(4) This section applies—

(a) to the Contributions and Benefits Act;

(aa) [1 to the Jobseeker's Act 1995];

(ab) [2 to Chapter II of Part I of the Social Security Act 1998];

(ac) [3 to Part II of the Social Security Contributions (Transfers of Functions, etc.) Act 1999]; and

[4(ad) to Part III of the Social Security Contributions (Transfer of Functions etc.) (Northern Ireland) Order 1999;]

[5(ae) to the State Pension Credit Act 2002; and]

[7(af) to part 1 of the Welfare Reform Act 2007;]

(b) to this Act,

except in relation to the following benefits—

(i) community charge benefits;

(ii) payments out of the social fund;

(iii) Christmas bonus;

(iv) statutory sick pay; and

(v) statutory maternity pay.

(5) The power conferred by subsection (1) above shall also be exercisable in relation to regulations made under the Contributions and Benefits Act or this Act and concerning—

(a) income support;

[1(aa) jobseeker's allowance];

[5(ab) state pension credit];

[7(ac) employment and support allowance;]]

    (b) [6 . . .];
    (c) [6 . . .];
    (d) housing benefit; or
    (e) child benefit.

AMENDMENTS

    1. Jobseekers Act 1995, Sch.2 (April 22, 1996).
    2. Social Security Act 1998, Sch.7 (July 5, 1999).
    3. Transfer of Functions Act 1999, Sch.7 (April 1, 1999).
    4. Social Security Contributions (Transfer of Functions etc.) (Northern Ireland) Order 1999 (April 1, 1999).
    5. State Pension Credit Act 2002, s.14 and Sch.2 (July 2, 2002 for the purpose of making regulations only; fully in force October 6, 2003).
    6. Tax Credits Act 2002, s.60 and Sch.6 (April 8, 2003).
    7. Welfare Reform Act 2007, s.28 and Sch.3, para.10 (October 27, 2008).

DERIVATION

1.210   SSA 1975, s.143 as amended and CBA 1975, s.15 as amended.

GENERAL NOTE

1.211   For details of current reciprocal arrangements, see annotations to s.113, of the Contributions and Benefits Act 1992.

    For a discussion on how s.179 acts to modify other social security provisions, see *Compbell v Secretary of State for Work and Pensions* [2005] EWCA Civ 989.

[1 Exchange of information with overseas authorities]

1.212   **179A.**—(1) This section applies where it appears to the Secretary of State—

    (a) that there are arrangements in force for the exchange of relevant information between him and any authorities in a country outside the United Kingdom ("the overseas country"); and

    (b) that the arrangements and the law in force in the overseas country are such as to ensure that there are adequate safeguards in place against any improper use of information disclosed by the Secretary of State under this section.

    (2) For the purpose of facilitating the carrying out by authorities in the overseas country of any function relating to anything corresponding to, or in the nature of, a social security benefit, the Secretary of State may make any such disclosure of relevant information to authorities in the overseas country as he considers necessary to give effect to the arrangements.

    (3) It shall be the duty of the Secretary of State to take all such steps as may be reasonable for securing that relevant information disclosed to him in accordance with the arrangements is not used for any purpose for which its use is not expressly or impliedly authorised by or under the arrangements.

    (4) This section does not apply where provision is in force under section 179 above for giving effect to the arrangements in question.

    (5) The purposes for which information may be required to be disclosed to the Secretary of State under section 122D above or section 116D of the Northern Ireland Administration Act (information required from authorities administering housing benefit or council tax benefit) shall be deemed

to include the further disclosure of that information in accordance withthis section.

(6) In this section "relevant information" means any information held by the Secretary of State or any authorities in a country outside the United Kingdom for the purposes of any functions relating to, or to anything corresponding to or in the nature of, a social security benefit.]

AMENDMENT

1. Inserted by the Social Security Fraud Act 2001, ss.1 and 5 (February 14, 2003).

PART XV

MISCELLANEOUS

180.–182B. *Omitted.*   1.213

National insurance numbers

[¹ Requirement to apply for national insurance number

182C.—(1) Regulations may make provision requiring a person to apply   1.214
for a national insurance number to be allocated to him.

[²(1A) Regulations under subsection (1) above may require the application to be made to the Secretary of State or to the Inland Revenue.]

(2) An application required by regulations under subsection (1) above shall be accompanied by information or evidence enabling such a number to be allocated.]

AMENDMENTS

1. Social Security Administration (Fraud) Act 1997, Sch.1, para.9 (July 1, 1997).
2. Social Security Contributions (Transfer of Functions, etc.) Act 1999, s.1(1) and Sch.1, para.31 (April 1, 1999).

GENERAL NOTE

See subss.(1A)–(1C) of s.1, inserted by s.19 of the Social Security Administration   1.215
(Fraud) Act, which make having, or applying for, a national insurance number a
condition of entitlement to benefit in most cases.

                                                                                   1.216
183. *Omitted.*

Control of pneumoconiosis

184. As respects pneumoconiosis, regulations may provide—   1.217
  (a) for requiring persons to be medically examined before, or within a prescribed period after, becoming employed in any occupation in relation to which pneumoconiosis is prescribed, and to be medically examined periodically while so employed, and to furnish information required for the purposes of any such examination;
  (b) for suspending from employment in any such occupation, and in

such other occupations as may be prescribed, persons found on such an examination—
    (i) to be suffering from pneumoconiosis or tuberculosis, or
    (ii) o be unsuitable for such employment, having regard to the risk of pneumoconiosis and such other matters affecting their susceptibility to pneumoconiosis as may be prescribed;
  (c) for the disqualification for the receipt of benefit as defined in section 122 of the Contributions and Benefits Act in respect of pneumoconiosis of any person who fails without good cause to submit himself to any such examination or to furnish information required by the regulations or who engages in any employment from which he has been suspended as mentioned in paragraph (b) above;
  (d) for requiring employers—
    (i) to provide facilities for such examinations,
    (ii) not to employ in any occupation a person who has been suspended as mentioned in paragraph (b) above from employment in that occupation or who has failed without good cause to submit himself to such an examination,
    (iii) to give to such officer as may be prescribed the prescribed notice of the commencement of any prescribed industry or process;
  (e) for the recovery on summary conviction of monetary penalties in respect of any contravention of or failure to comply with any such requirement as is mentioned in paragraph (d) above, so, however, that such penalties shall not exceed £5.00 for every day on which the contravention or failure occurs or continues;
  (f) for such matters as appear to the Secretary of State to be incidental to or consequential on provisions included in the regulations by virtue of paragraphs (a) to (d) above or section 110(1) of the Contributions and Benefits Act.

1.218   **185.** *Omitted.*

Supplementary benefit etc.

Applications of provisions of Act to supplementary benefit etc.

1.219   **186.** Schedule 10 to this Act shall have effect for the purposes of making provision in relation to the benefits there mentioned.

Miscellaneous

Certain benefit to be inalienable

1.220   **187.**—(1) Subject to the provisions of this Act, every assignment of or charge on—
  (a) benefit as defined in section 122 of the Contributions and Benefits Act;
[¹(aa) a jobseeker's allowance;]
[²(ab) state pension credit;]
[³(ac) an employment and support allowance;]
  (b) any income-related benefit; or
  (c) child benefit,

and every agreement to assign or charge such benefit shall be void; and, on the bankruptcy of a beneficiary, such benefit shall not pass to any trustee or other person acting on behalf of his creditors.

(2) In the application of subsection (1) above to Scotland—

(a) the reference to assignment of benefit shall be read as a reference to assignation, "assign" being construed accordingly;

(b) the reference to a beneficiary's bankruptcy shall be read as a reference to the sequestration of his estate or the appointment on his estate of a judicial factor under section 41 of the Solicitors (Scotland) Act 1980.

(3) In calculating for the purposes of section 5 of the Debtors Act 1869 or section 4 of the Civil Imprisonment (Scotland) Act 1882 the means of any beneficiary, no account shall be taken of any increase of disablement benefit in respect of a child or of industrial death benefit.

AMENDMENTS

1. Jobseekers Act 1995, Sch.2, para.72 (October 7, 1996).
2. State Pension Credit Act 2002, s.14 and Sch.2 (July 2, 2002 for the purposes of making regulations only; fully in force October 6, 2003).
3. Welfare Reform Act 2007, s.28 and Sch.3, para.10 (October 27, 2008).

1.221

DERIVATIONS

Social Security Act 1975, s.87.
"the Contributions and Benefits Act"—see s.191.
"income-related benefit"—*ibid.*

1.222

GENERAL NOTE

The House of Lords in *Mulvey v Secretary of State for Social Security, The Times,* March 20, 1997 dealt with the part of s.187(1) providing that, on bankruptcy or sequestration of a beneficiary, benefit does not pass to the trustee in bankruptcy. It held that the purpose was "to make clear beyond peradventure that the permanent trustee [the Scottish equivalent of the trustee in bankruptcy] could have no interest in any entitlement of a debtor to receive any of the social security benefits to which it applied" (Lord Jauncey). The Secretary of State's obligation to make payment of benefit is owed to the beneficiary and cannot be owed to the trustee in bankruptcy or permanent trustee. See the notes to s.78(2) for the situation where deductions are being made from benefit for the repayment of social fund loans or the recovery of overpayments.

1.223

188. *Omitted.*

1.224

PART XVI

GENERAL

Subordinate legislation

189.—(1) Subject to [. . .¹] [²any provision proving for an order or regulations to be made by the Treasury or the Inland Revenue and to] any [⁸ . . .]

1.225

express provision of this Act, regulations and orders under this Act shall be made by the Secretary of State.

(2) [. . .[1]]

(3) Powers under this Act to make regulations or orders are exercisable by statutory instrument.

(4) Except in the case of regulations under section [. . .[1]] 175 above and in so far as this Act otherwise provides, any power conferred by this Act to make an Order in Council, regulations or an order may be exercised—

(a) either in relation to all cases to which the power extends, or in relation to those cases subject to specified exceptions, or in relation to any specified cases or classes of case;

(b) so as to make, as respects the cases in relation to which it is exercised—

   (i) the full provision to which the power extends or any less provision (whether by way of exception or otherwise);

   (ii) the same provision for all cases in relation to which the power is exercised, or different provision for different cases or different classes of case or different provision as respects the same case or class of case for different purposes of this Act;

   (iii) any such provision either unconditionally or subject to any specified condition;

and where such a power is expressed to be exercisable for alternative purposes it may be exercised in relation to the same case for any or all of those purposes; and powers to make an Order in Council, regulations or an order for the purposes of any one provision of this Act are without prejudice to powers to make regulations or an order for the purposes of any other provision.

(5) Without prejudice to any specific provision in this Act, a power conferred by this Act to make an Order in Council, regulations or an order [. . .[1]] includes power to make thereby such incidental, supplementary, consequential or transitional provision as appears to Her Majesty, or the authority making the regulations or order, as the case may be, to be expedient for the purposes of the Order in Council, regulations or order.

(6) Without prejudice to any specific provisions in this Act, a power conferred by any provision of this Act, except section 14, [. . .[1]], 130 and 175, to make an Order in Council, regulations or an order includes power to provide for a person to exercise a discretion in dealing with any matter.

(7) Any power conferred by this Act to make orders or regulations relating to housing benefit or [[3] council tax benefit] shall include power to make different provision for different areas [[4] or different authorities].

[[7] (7A) Without prejudice to the generality of any the preceding provisions of this section, regulations under any of sections 2A to 2C and 7A above may provide for all or any of the provisions of the regulations to apply only in relation to any area or areas specified in the regulations.]

(8) An order under [[9] section140B, 140C, 150, 150A, 152, 165(4)(a) or 169] above [. . .[7]] shall not be made [[8] by the Secretary of State] without the consent of the Treasury.

(9) Any powers of the Secretary of State under any provision of this Act, except under [sections 80, 154 and 175] to make any regulations or order, where the power is not expressed to be exercisable with the consent of the Treasury, shall if the Treasury so direct be exercisable only in conjunction with them.

(10) Where the Lord Chancellor proposes to make regulations under this Act, other than under section 24 above, it shall be his duty to consult the Secretary of State with respect to the proposal.

(11) A power under any of section 179 above to make provision by regulations or Order in Council for modifications or adaptations of the Contributions and Benefits Act or this Act shall be exercisable in relation to any enactment passed after this Act which is directed to be construed as one withthem, except in so far as any such enactment relates to a benefit in relation to which the power is not exercisable; but this subsection applies only so far as a contrary intention is not expressed in the enactment so passed, and is without prejudice to the generality of any such direction.

(12) Any reference in this section or section 190 below to an Order in Council, or an order or regulations, under this Act includes a reference to an Order in Council, an order or regulations made under any provision of an enactment passed after this Act and directed to be construed as one with this Act; but this subsection applies only so far as a contrary intention is not expressed in the enactment so passed, and without prejudice to the generality of any such direction.

AMENDMENTS

1. Social Security Act 1998, Sch.7 (September 6, 1999).   1.226
2. Transfer of Functions Act 1999, Sch.3 (April 1, 1999).
3. Local Government Finance Act 1992, Sch.9 (April 1, 1993).
4. Social Security Administration (Fraud) Act 1997, Sch.1 (July 1, 1997).
5. Housing Act 1996, Sch.13 (April 1, 1997).
6. Social Security (Recovery of Benefits) Act 1997, Sch.3 (October 6, 1997).
7. Welfare Reform and Pensions Act 1999, Sch.12, paras 79 and 82 (November 11, 1999).
8. Tax Credits Act 2002, s.60 and Sch.6 (February 26, 2003 for the purpose of making regulations in relation to child benefit and guardian's allowance; April 1, 2003 for remaining purposes).
9. Pensions Act 2007, Sch.1(5) para.29 (July 26, 2007: insertion has effect as specified in 2007 c.22 s.5(3) and (7)).

GENERAL NOTE

In accordance with s.2(1) of the Tax Credits Act 1999, this section is to be read,   1.227
in relation to tax credit, as if references to the Secretary of State were references to the Treasury or, as the case may be, the Board.

DERIVATIONS

SSA 1975, ss.113, 133, 166 and 168 as amended.
Parliamentary control of orders and regulations.

190.—(1) Subject to the provision of this section, a statutory instrument   1.228
containing (whether alone or with other provisions)—
   (a) an order under [¹⁰ section 141, 143, 145, 150, 150A, or 162(7)] above; or
[⁷(aza) any order containing provision adding any person to the list of persons falling within section 109B(2A) above; or]
[⁸(aa) the first regulations to be made under section 2A;]
[⁹ (ab) the first regulations to be made under section 2AA;]
   (b) regulations under [³section 154] above,

shall not be made unless a draft of the instrument has been laid before Parliament and been approved by a resolution of each House of Parliament.

(2) Subsection (1) above does not apply to a statutory instrument by reason only that it contains regulations under section 154 above which are to be made for the purpose of consolidating regulations to be revoked in the instrument.

(3) A statutory instrument—

    (a) which contains (whether alone or with other provisions) orders or regulations made under this Act by the Secretary of State [5, the Treasury or the Inland Revenue]; and

    (b) which is not subject to any requirement that a draft of the instrument be laid before and approved by a resolution of each House of Parliament,

shall be subject to annulment in pursuance of a resolution of either House of Parliament.

(4) [1 . . .]

1.229   AMENDMENTS

    1. Social Security Act 1998, Sch.7 (November 29, 1998).
    2. Social Security Act 1998, Sch.7 (April 6, 1999).
    3. Social Security (Recovery of Benefits) Act 1997, Sch.3 (October 6, 1997).
    4. Social Security Administration (Fraud) Act 1997, Sch.1 (July 1, 1997).
    5. Transfer of Functions Act 1999, Sch.3 (April 1, 1999).
    6. Welfare Reform and Pensions Act 1999, Sch.13 (April 6, 2000).
    7. Social Security Fraud Act 2001, s.20 (February 26, 2002).
    8. Welfare Reform and Pensions Act 1999, Sch.12, paras 79 and 83 (November 11, 1999).
    9. Employment Act 2002, s.53 and Sch.7 (July 5, 2003).
    10. Pensions Act 2007, Sch.1(5) para.30 (July 26, 2007: insertion has effect as specified in 2007 c.22 s.5(3) and (7)).

GENERAL NOTE

1.230   In accordance with s.2(1) of the Tax Credits Act 1999, this section is to be read, in relation to tax credit, as if references to the Secretary of State were references to the Treasury or, as the case may be, the Board.

DERIVATION

1.231   SSA 1975, s.167 as amended and CBA 1975, s.22.

Supplementary

Interpretation—general

1.232   **191.** In this Act, unless the context otherwise requires—

    "the 1975 Act" means the Social Security Act 1975;

    "the 1986 Act" means the Social Security Act 1986;

    "benefit" means benefit under the Contributions and Benefits Act [1and includes a jobseeker's allowance] [19 . . .]; [21 , state pension credit and an employment and support allowance];

    [2"billing authority" has the same meaning as in Part I of the Local Government Finance Act 1992;]

"Christmas bonus" means a payment under Part X of the Contributions and Benefits Act;

"claim" is to be construed in accordance with"claimant";

"claimant" (in relation to contributions under Part I and to benefit under Parts II to IV of the Contributions and Benefits Act) means—

(a) a person whose right to be excepted from liability to pay, or to have his liability deferred for, or to be credited with, a contribution, is in question;

(b) a person who has claimed benefit;

and includes, in relation to an award or decision a beneficiary under the award or affected by the decision;

"claimant" (in relation to industrial injuries benefit) means a person who has claimed such a benefit and includes—

(a) an applicant for a declaration under [³ section 29 of the Social Security Act 1998] that an accident was or was not an industrial accident; and

(b) in relation to an award or decision, a beneficiary under the award or affected by the decision;

[. . .]

[. . .⁴]

"the Consequential Provisions Act" means the Social Security (Consequential Provisions) Act 1992;

[⁵"contribution" means a contribution under Part I of the Contributions and Benefit Act;]

[⁶"contribution-based jobseeker's allowance" has the same meaning as in the Jobseekers Act 1995;]

"contributions card" has the meaning assigned to it by section 114(6) above;

"the Contributions and Benefits Act" means the Social Security Contributions and Benefits Act 1992;

[²¹ "contributory employment and support allowance" means a contributory allowance under Part 1 of the Welfare Reform Act 2007 (employment and support allowance);]

[⁷"council tax benefit Scheme" shall be construed in accordance with section 139(1) above;]

"disablement benefit" is to be construed in accordance with section 94(2)(a) of the Contributions and Benefits Act;

"the disablement questions" is to be construed in accordance with section 45 above;

"dwelling" means any residential accommodation, whether or not consisting of the whole or part of a building and whether or not comprising separate and self-contained premises;

[⁹"financial year" has the same meaning as in the Local Government Finance Act 1992;]

"5 year general qualification" is to be construed in accordance with section 71 of the Courts and Legal Services Act 1990;

"housing authority" means a local authority, a new town corporation

"house benefit scheme" is to be construed in accordance with section 134(1) above;

[¹"income-based jobseeker's allowance" has the same meaning as in the Jobseekers Act 1995;]

"income-related benefit" means—

(a) income support;

(b) [⁸ working families tax credit]

(c) [⁸ disabled person's tax credit]

(d) housing benefit; and

[²(e) council tax benefit];

[²¹ "income-related employment and support allowance" means an income-related allowance under Part 1 of the Welfare Reform Act 2007 (employment and support allowance);]

"industrial injuries benefit" means benefit under Part V of the Contributions and Benefits Act, other than under Schedule 8;

[¹⁰"Inland Revenue" means the Commissioners of Inland Revenue]

. . .¹⁰;

. . .¹¹;

"local authority" means—

(a) in relation to England . . .¹², the council of a district or London borough, the Common Council of the City of London or the Council of the Isles of Scilly;

[¹¹(aa) in relation to Wales, the council of a county or county borough;] and

(b) in relation to Scotland [¹²a council constituted under section 2 of the Local Government etc. (Scotland) Act 1994];

"medical examination" includes bacteriological and radiographical tests and similar investigations, and "medically examined" has a corresponding meaning;

"medical practitioner" means—

(a) a registered medical practitioner; or

(b) a person outside the United Kingdom who is not a registered medical practitioner, but has qualifications corresponding (in the Secretary of State's opinion) to those of a registered medical practitioner;

"medical treatment" means medical, surgical or rehabilitative treatment (including any course of diet or other regimen), and references to a person receiving or submitting himself to medical treatment are to be construed accordingly;

[¹⁵ "money purchase contracted-out scheme" has the same meaning as in section 8(1)(a)(ii) of the Pensions Act;]

"new town corporation" means—

[²² (a) in relation to England—

(i) a development corporation established under the New Towns Act 1981; or

(ii) the Homes and Communities Agency so far as exercising functions in relation to anything transferred (or to be transferred) to it as mentioned in section 52(1)(A) to (d) of the Housing and Regeneration Act 2008;

(ab) in relation to Wales—

(i) a development corporation established under the New Towns Act 1981; and

(ii) the Welsh Ministers so far as exercising functions in relation to anything transferred (or to be transferred) to them as mentioned in section 36(1)(A)(i) to (iii) of that Act; and]

(b) in relation to Scotland, a development corporation established under the New Towns (Scotland) Act 1968;]

[20 "the Northern Ireland Department" means the Department for Social Development but—
  (a) in section 122 and sections 122B to 122E also includes the Department of Finance and Personnel; and
  (b) in sections 121E, 121F, 122, 122ZA, 122C and 122D also includes the Department for Employment and Learning;]

"the Northern Ireland Administration Act" means the Social Security (Northern Ireland) Administration Act 1992;

"occupational pension scheme" has the same meaning as in [15section 1] of the Pensions Act;

"the Old Cases Act" means the Industrial Injuries and Diseases (Old Cases) Act 1975;

"Old Cases payments" means payments under Part I of Schedule 8 to the Contributions and Benefits Act;

[17"pensionable age" has the meaning given by the rules in paragraph 1 of Schedule 4 to the Pensions Act 1995];

"the Pensions Act" means the [15Pension Schemes Act 1993];

"personal pension scheme" has the meaning assigned to it by [15section 1 of the Pensions Act] [15and "appropriate", in relation to such a scheme, shall be construed in accordance with section 7(4) of that Act]

"prescribe" means prescribe by regulations; [23 and "prescribed" must be construed accordingly;]

"President" means the President of social security appeal tribunals; disability appeal tribunals and medical appeal tribunals;

"rent rebate", [. . .18] and "rent allowance" shall be construed in accordance with section 134 above;

[. . .18]

[19 "state pension credit" means state pension credit under the State Pension Credit Act 2002;]

"tax year" means the 12 months beginning with 6th April in any year;

"10 year general qualification" is to be construed in accordance with section 71 of the Courts and Legal Services Act 1990; and

"widows benefit" has the meaning assigned to it by section 20(1)(e) of the Contributions and Benefits Act.

AMENDMENTS

1. Jobseekers Act 1995, Sch.2 (April 22, 1996).
2. Local Government Finance Act 1992, Sch.9 (March 6, 1992).
3. Social Security Act 1998, Sch.7 (July 7, 1999).
4. Social Security (Recovery of Benefits) Act 1997, Sch.3 (October 6, 1997).
5. Social Security Administration (Fraud) Act 1997, Sch.1 (July 1, 1997).
6. Jobseekers Act 1995, Sch.2 (April 22, 1996).
7. Housing Benefit Act 1996, Sch.13 (April 1, 1997).
8. Tax Credits Act 1999, Sch.1 (October 5, 1999).
9. Local Government Finance Act 1992, Sch.9 (March 6, 1992).
10. Transfer of Functions Act 1999, Sch.1 (April 1, 1999).
11. Social Security (Incapacity for Work) Act 1994, Sch.1 (April 13, 1995).
12. Local Government etc. (Scotland) Act 1994, Sch.14 (April 1, 1996)
13. Local Government (Wales) Act 1994, Sch.16 (April 1, 1996).
14. Local Government etc. (Scotland) Act 1994, Sch.13 (April 1, 1996)
15. Pension Schemes Act 1993, Sch.8 (February 7, 1994).
16. Social Security Administration (Fraud) Act, Sch.1 (July 1, 1997).
17. Pensions Act 1995, Sch.4 (July 19, 1995).

18. Housing Act 1996, Sch.13 (April 1, 1997).
19. State Pension Credit Act 2002, s.14 and Sch.2 (July 2, 2002 for the purpose of making regulations only; fully in force October 6, 2003).
20. Employment Act 2002, s.53 and Sch.7 (September 9, 2002).
21. Welfare Reform Act 2007, s.28 and Sch.3, para.10 (October 27, 2008).
22. Housing and Regeneration Act 2008, Sch.8 para.61 (December 1, 2008).
23. Welfare Reform Act 2007, Sch.5 para.10 (July 3, 2007).

DERIVATIONS

1.233

SSA 1975, s.168 and Sch.20.
Short title, commencement and extent.

1.234

192.—(1) This Act may be cited as the Social Security Administration Act 1992.

(2) This Act is to be read, where appropriate, with the Contributions and Benefits Act and the Consequential Provisions Act.

(3) The enactments consolidated by this Act are repealed, in consequence of the consolidation, by the Consequential Provisions Act.

(4) Except as provided in Schedule 4 to the Consequential Provisions Act, this Act shall come into force on 1st July 1992.

(5) The following provisions extend to Northern Ireland—
[. . .¹];
[²]
section 170 (with Schedule 5);
[³ section 171(with schedule 6);]
[section 177 (with Schedule 8);]
and this section.

(6) Except as provided by this section, this Act does not extend to Northern Ireland.

AMENDMENTS

1. Social Security Act 1998, Sch.7 (October 5, 1999).
2. Social Security (Recovery of Benefits) Act 1997, Sch.3 (October 6, 1997).
3. Northern Ireland Act 1998, Pt VIII s.89(9) (December 2, 1999).

SCHEDULES

SCHEDULE 1

1.235

CLAIMS FOR BENEFIT MADE OR TREATED AS MADE BEFORE 1ST OCTOBER 1990

Claims made or treated as made on or after 2nd September 1985 and before 1st October 1986

1. Section 1 above shall have effect in relation to a claim made or treated as made on or after 2nd September 1985 and before 1st October 1986 as if the following subsections were substituted for subsections (1) to (3)—
"(1) Except in such cases as may be prescribed, no person shall be entitled to any benefit unless, in addition to any other conditions relating to that benefit being satisfied—
  (a) he makes a claim for it—
    (i) in the prescribed manner; and
    (ii) subject to subsection (2) below, within the prescribed time; or
  (b) by virtue of a provision of Chapter VI of Part II of the 1975 Act or of regulations made under such a provision he would have been treated as making a claim for it."
"(2) Regulations shall provide for extending, subject to any prescribed conditions, the time within which a claim may be made in cases where it is not made within the prescribed time but good cause is shown for the delay.

(3) Notwithstanding any regulations made under this section, no person shall be entitled to any benefit (except disablement benefit or industrial death benefit) in respect of any period more than 12 months before the date on which the claim is made."

Claims made or treated as made on or after 1st October 1986 and before 6th April 1987

2. Section 1 above shall have effect in relation to a claim made or treated as made on or after 1986 and before 6th April 1987 as if the subsections set out in paragraph 1 above were substituted for subsections (1) to (3) but with the insertion in subsection (3) of the words "reduced earnings allowance" after the words "disablement benefit".

Claims made or treated as made on or after 6th April 1987 and before 21st July 1989

3. Section 1 above shall have effect in relation to a claim made or treated as made on or after 6th April 1987 and before 21st July 1989, as if—

  (a) the following subsection were substituted for subsection (1)—

"(1) Except in such cases as may be prescribed, no person shall be entitled to any benefit unless, in addition to any other conditions relating to that benefit being satisfied—

  (a) he makes a claim for it in the prescribed manner and within the prescribed time; or
  (b) by virtue of regulations made under section 51 of the 1986 Act he would have been treated as making a claim for it."; and
  (c) there were omitted—
      (i) from subsection (2), the words "except as provided by section 3 below"; and
      (ii) subsection (3).

Claims made or treated as made on or after 21st July 1989 and before 13th July 1990

4. Section 1 above shall have effect in relation to a claim made or treated as made on or after 21st July 1989 and before 13th July 1990 as if there were omitted—

  (a) from subsection (1), the words "and subject to the following provisions of this section and to section 3 below";
  (b) from subsection (2), the words "except as provided by section 3 below"; and
  (c) subsection (3).

Claims made or treated as made on or after 13th July 1990 and before 1st October 1990

5. Section 1 above shall have effect in relation to a claim made or treated as made on or after 13th July 1990 and before 1st October 1990 as if there were omitted—

  (a) from subsection (1), the words "the following provisions of this section and to"; and
  (b) subsection (3)

GENERAL NOTE

See annotations to s.1

              1.236

Pension Schemes Act 1993

(1993 C.48)

ARRANGEMENT OF SECTIONS

170.   Decisions and appeals

An Act to consolidate certain enactments relating to pension schemes with-amendments to give effect to recommendations of the Law Commission and the Scottish Law Commission

[5th November 1993]

          1.237

[¹ Decisions and appeals

1.238   **170.**—(1) Section 2 (use of computers) of the Social Security Act 1998 ("the 1998 Act") applies as if, for the purposes of subsection (1) of that section, this Act were a relevant enactment.

[²(2) It shall be for an officer of the Inland Revenue—

  (a) to make any decision that falls to be made under or by virtue of Part III of this Act, other than a decision which under or by virtue of that Part falls to be made by the Secretary of State;

  (b) to decide any issue arising in connection with payments under section 7 of the Social Security Act 1986 (occupational pension schemes becoming contracted out between 1986 and 1993); and

  (c) to decide any issue arising by virtue of regulations made under paragraph 15 of Schedule 3 to the Social Security (Consequential Provisions) Act 1992 (continuing in force of certain enactments repealed by the Social Security Act 1973).

(3) In the following provisions of this section a "relevant decision" means any decision which under subsection (2) falls to be made by an officer of the Inland Revenue, other than a decision under section 53 or section 54.

(4) Sections 9 and 10 of the 1998 Act (revisions of decisions and decisions superseding earlier decisions) apply as if—

  (a) any reference in those sections to a decision of the Secretary of State under section 8 of that Act included a reference to a relevant decision; and

  (b) any other reference in those sections to the Secretary of State were, in relation to a relevant decision, a reference to an officer of the Inland Revenue.

(5) Regulations may make provision—

[³(a) generally with respect to the making of relevant decisions;

  (b) with respect to the procedure to be adopted on any application made under section 9 or 10 of the 1998 Act by virtue of subsection (4); and

  (c) generally withrespect to such applications, revisions under section 9 and decisions under section 10;]

but may not prevent such a revision or decision being made without such an application.

(6) Section 12 of the 1998 Act (appeal to [⁴First-tier Tribunal] applies as if, for the purposes of subsection (1)(b) of that section, a relevant decision were a decision of the Secretary of State falling within Schedule 3 to the 1998 Act.

(7) The following provisions of the 1998 Act (which relate to decisions and appeals)—

sections 13 to 18,

sections 25 and 26,

section 28, and

Schedules 4 and 5,

shall apply in relation to any appeal under section 12 of the 1998 Act by virtue of subsection (6) above as if any reference to the Secretary of State were a reference to an officer of the Inland Revenue.]]

AMENDMENTS

1. Social Security Act 1998, s.86(1) and Sch.7, para.131 (March 4, 1999).
2. Social Security Contributions (Transfer of Functions, etc.) Act 1999, s.16 (April 1, 1999).
3. Welfare Reform and Pensions Act 1999, Sch.11, para.22.
4. Transfer of Tribunal Functions Order 2008 (SI 2008/2833), Sch.3, paras 111 and 112 (November 3, 2008).

GENERAL NOTE

A former employee may be entitled to both a state pension and one or more **1.239** private pensions. The Social Security Contributions and Benefits Act 1992 provides for a Category A retirement pension, the state pension, consisting of a basic pension and an additional pension under either the former State Earnings-Related Pension Scheme or, from 2002, the new "second state pension" scheme. However, employees have been able to "contract out" of the liability to make contributions for an additional pension provided they were making contributions to an approved occupational or personal pension scheme. The Pensions Schemes Act 1993, provides for guaranteed minimum pensions from contracted-out occupational pension schemes. See Vol.1 of this work for both Acts.

Over a working life, a person may have contributed both to an additional pension under one or both of the state schemes and to one or more occupational or personal pension schemes. Where a guaranteed minimum pension is payable under an occupational scheme to a person entitled to an additional pension under the State Earnings-Related Pension Scheme, overlap is avoided by s.46 of the 1993 Act which provides for an adjustment to the Category A retirement pension. This involves the determination of a number of questions, some of which are to be determined by the Secretary of State and some of which are allocated to the Her Majesty's Revenue and Customs (to whom the functions of the Commissioners for Inland Revenue have been transferred by the Commissioners for Revenue and Customs Act 2005, s.5(2)) by this section. In *R(P) 1/04*, the Commissioner held that it was for the Secretary of State to determine entitlement to a Category A retirement pension and to identify the occupational pension schemes relevant to that entitlement, for the Inland Revenue to determine entitlement to a guaranteed minimum pension in respect of each occupational pension scheme and for the Secretary of State to aggregate the guaranteed minimum pensions and decide on the amount of any reduction of the Category A retirement pension under s.46 of the 1993 Act.

Section 170(6) and (7) provides for appeals against decisions of Her Majesty's Revenue and Customs relating to guaranteed minimum pensions to be heard by the First-tier Tribunal as though it were a social security case rather than a tax case. However, it was pointed out in *R(P) 1/04* that there can be no appeal until a formal decision is issued and that the Inland Revenue did not always issue a formal decision unless a calculation was disputed. In those circumstances, as any dispute was likely to be raised first in a challenge to the final decision issued by the Secretary of State, it was suggested that it might be necessary for the Secretary of State or an appeal tribunal to refer a question to the Inland Revenue for formal determination even though regs 11A and 38A of the Social Security and Child Support (Decisions and Appeals) Regulations 1999 did not strictly apply.

Perhaps surprisingly, an appeal against a refusal to issue a contracting-out or appropriate scheme certificate is one type of case that falls, by virtue of this section, to be treated as a social security case. However, where a question arises as to whether a particular claimant was in contracted-in or contracted-out employment for the purpose of ascertaining his entitlement to a pension, it arises as part of a question as to his liability to pay contributions or as to what contributions have been paid and so is a question falling within the jurisdiction of the tax authorities by virtue of s.8(1)(c) or (e) of the Social Security Contributions (Transfer of Functions, etc.) Act 1999 (*CP/3833/2003*).

Employment Tribunals Act 1996

(1996 c.17)

An Act to consolidate enactments relating to industrial tribunals and the Employment Appeal Tribunal.

[22nd May 1996]

GENERAL NOTE

1.241   This Act started life as the Industrial Tribunals Act 1996 but was given its new short title by s.1(2) of the Employment Rights (Dispute Resolution) Act 1998, which also renamed the tribunals themselves, with effect from August 1, 1998.

Power to provide for recoupment of benefits

1.242   **16.**—(1) This section applies to payments which are the subject of proceedings before [¹ employment tribunals] and which are—

(a) payments of wages or compensation for loss of wages,

(b) payments by employers to employees under sections 146 to 151, sections 168 to 173 or section 192 of the Trade Union and Labour Relations (Consolidation) Act 1992,

(c) payments by employers to employees under —

(i) Part III, V, VI or VII,

(ii) section 93, or

(iii) Part X,

of the Employment Rights Act 1996, or

(d) payments by employers to employees of a nature similar to, or for a purpose corresponding to the purpose of, payments within paragraph (b) or (c),

and to payments of remuneration under a protective award under section 189 of the Trade Union and Labour Relations (Consolidation) Act 1992.

(2) The Secretary of State may by regulations make with respect to payments to which this section applies provision for any or all of the purposes specified in subsection (3).

(3) The purposes referred to in subsection (2) are—

(a) enabling the Secretary of State to recover from an employer, by way of total or partial recoupment of jobseeker's allowance or income support—

(i) a sum not exceeding the amount of the prescribed element of the monetary award, or

(ii) in the case of a protective award, the amount of the remuneration,

(b) requiring or authorising an [¹employment tribunal] to order the payment of such a sum, by way of total or partial recoupment of either benefit, to the Secretary of State instead of to an employee, and

(c) requiring an [¹employment tribunal] to order the payment to an employee of only the excess of the prescribed element of the monetary award over the amount of any jobseeker's allowance or income support shown to the tribunal to have been paid to the employee and enabling the Secretary of State to recover from the employer, by way of total or partial recoupment of the benefit, a sum not exceeding that amount.

(4) Regulations under this section may be framed—

(a) so as to apply to all payments to which this section applies or to one or more classes of those payments, and

(b) so as to apply to both jobseeker's allowance and income support, or to only jobseeker's allowance or income support.

(5) Regulations under this section may—

(a) confer powers and impose duties on [¹ employment tribunals] or [² . . .] other persons,

(b) impose on an employer to whom a monetary award or protective award relates a duty—

   (i) to furnish particulars connected with the award, and

   (ii) to suspend payments in pursuance of the award during any period prescribed by the regulations,

(c) provide for an employer who pays a sum to the Secretary of State in pursuance of this section to be relieved from any liability to pay the sum to another person,

[² (cc) provide for the determination by the Secretary of State of any issue arising as to the total or partial recoupment in pursuance of the regulations of a jobseeker's allowance, unemployment benefit or income support,

(d) confer on an employee a right of appeal to [³the First-tier Tribunal] against any decision of the Secretary of State on any such issue, and]

(e) provide for the proof in proceedings before [¹ employment tribunals] (whether by certificate or in any other manner) of any amount of jobseeker's allowance or income support paid to an employee.

(6) Regulations under this section may make different provision for different cases.

AMENDMENTS

1. Employment Rights (Dispute Resolution) Act 1998, s.1(2) (August 1, 1998).

2. Social Security Act 1998, Sch.7, para.147 (October 18, 1999).

3. Transfer of Tribunal Functions Order 2008 (SI 2008/2833), Sch.3 para.137 (November 3, 2008).

DEFINITIONS

"income-based jobseeker's allowance"—see s.17(4).
"monetary award"—see s.17(3).
"the prescribed element"—*ibid*.

GENERAL NOTE

See the Employment Protection (Recoupment of Jobseeker's Allowance and Income Support) Regulations 1996.   **1.243**

Recoupment: further provisions

1.244   **17.**—(1) Where in pursuance of any regulations under section 16 a sum has been recovered by or paid to the Secretary of State by way of total or partial recoupment of jobseeker's allowance or income support—

(a) no sum shall be recoverable under Part III or V of the Social Security Administration Act 1992, and

(b) no abatement, payment or reduction shall be made by reference to the jobseeker's allowance or income support recouped.

(2) Any amount found to have been duly recovered by or paid to the Secretary of State in pursuance of regulations under section 16 by way of total or partial recoupment of jobseeker's allowance shall be paid into the National Insurance Fund.

(3) In section 16—

"monetary award" means the amount which is awarded, or ordered to be paid, to the employee by the tribunal or would be so awarded or ordered apart from any provision of regulations under that section, and

"the prescribed element", in relation to any monetary award, means so much of that award as is attributable to such matters as may be prescribed by regulations under that section.

(4) In section 16 "income-based jobseeker's allowance" has the same meaning as in the Jobseekers Act 1995.

Social Security (Recovery of Benefits) Act 1997

(1997 c.27)

ARRANGEMENT OF SECTIONS

Introductory

Reviews and appeals

Courts

Reduction of compensation: complex cases

Miscellaneous

Provisions relating to Northern Ireland

General

An Act to re-state, with amendments, Part IV of the Social Security Administration Act 1992.

[19th March 1997]

GENERAL NOTE

1.246   This Act provides for the recovery from those who cause personal injury or disease of benefits paid to those who are injured or made ill. As the long title says, the Act is to "re-state, with amendments," Pt IV of the Social Security Act 1992, which was a true consolidation measure and re-enacted s.22 of, and Sch.4 to, the Social Security Act 1989 which first introduced a scheme like this for recovering benefits. This Act is not a consolidation measure because, while a number of the provisions are the same as under the old schemes, the amendments make some fundamental changes.

The Compensation Recovery Unit of the Department for Work and Pensions is at Durham House, Washington, Tyne and Wear NE38 7SF (*www.dwp.gov.uk/cru*) publish a free guide to the procedure. A person making a compensation payment in consequence of an accident injury or disease (whether voluntarily or pursuant to a court order or agreement or otherwise—see s.1(3)—unless the payment is exempt—see s.1(2) and Sch.1) *must* apply under s.4 to the Compensation Recovery Unit for a "certificate of recoverable benefits" *before* making the payment. Under s.5, that certificate should specify the amount of relevant benefits (listed in col.2 of Sch.2) paid, or expected to be paid within the "relevant period" (which will end when the compensation payment is made if the maximum period of five years has not already elapsed—see s.3), *in respect of* the accident, injury or disease (see the definition of "recoverable benefit" in s.1(4)(c) which refers back to s.1(1)(b)). The compensator must then pay to the Secretary of State a sum equal to the total amount of those recoverable benefits (s.6) and pay to the victim the compensation payment. Certain parts of the compensation payment may be reduced to reflect the benefits received by the victim during the "relevant period" (s.8), but benefits paid after that period must be ignored in the assessment of damages (s.17).

Sections 10–14 provide for reviews of, and appeals against, certificates of recoverable benefits.

Introductory

Cases in which this Act applies

1.247   **1.**—(1) This Act applies in cases where—
  (a) a person makes a payment (whether on his own behalf or not) to or in respect of any other person in consequence of any accident, injury or disease suffered by the other, and
  (b) any listed benefits have been, or are likely to be, paid to or for the other during the relevant period in respect of the accident, injury or disease.

(2) The reference above to a payment in consequence of any accident, injury or disease is to a payment made—
  (a) by or on behalf of a person who is, or is alleged to be, liable to any extent in respect of the accident, injury or disease, or
  (b) in pursuance of a compensation scheme for motor accidents;
but does not include a payment mentioned in Part I of Schedule 1.

(3) Subsection (1)(a) applies to a payment made—
  (a) voluntarily, or in pursuance of a court order or an agreement, or otherwise, and
  (b) in the United Kingdom or elsewhere.

(4) In a case where this Act applies—
  (a) the "injured person" is the person who suffered the accident, injury or disease,
  (b) the "compensation payment" is the payment within subsection (1)(a), and

(c) "recoverable benefit" is listed benefit which has been or is likely to be paid as mentioned in the subsection (1)(b).

DEFINITIONS

"compensation scheme for motor accidents"—see s.29.
"listed benefit"—*ibid.*
"payment"—*ibid.*
"the relevant period"—see s.3.

GENERAL NOTE

In *Rand v East Dorset Health Authority* [2001] P.I.Q.R. Q1, this Act was held not to **1.248** apply where parents of a child were awarded damages in respect of the defendants' negligence in failing to inform them before the child's birth that the child would be suffering from Down's Syndrome. It had been claimed that the child would have been aborted had the parents received the information and the damages had been awarded purely for economic loss resulting from negligent mis-statement and so were not awarded "in consequence of any accident, injury or disease suffered by the [parents]". That decision was distinguished in *R(CR) 4/03*, which was also a case of medical negligence. There, a doctor was alleged to have failed to recognise symptoms of diabetes in a woman in an advanced stage of pregnancy. It was claimed that, had the symptoms been detected, the condition would have been confirmed and an emergency Caesarean section could have been performed with a high chance of the child being born alive. As it was, the child died *in utero* and labour had to be induced and the mother suffered a major depressive episode. Compensation was claimed not only under the Fatal Accidents Act 1976 (which compensation is exempt under reg.2 of the Social Security (Recovery of Benefits) Regulations 1997) but also for the mother's psychiatric injury. The case was settled. The Commissioner held that compensation was paid in consequence of an accident, injury or disease suffered by the mother. It is therefore slightly odd that, in July 2009, the guidance published on the Compensation Recovery Unit's website (*www.dwp.gov.uk/cru*) says: "Form CRU1 need not be submitted for a compensation claim arising from alleged professional negligence. CRU does not pursue this type of case and cannot issue a Certificate." The Commissioner also commented that the phrase "accident, injury or disease" was an "odd one" because it was not clear how benefits might be paid in respect of an accident if there was neither injury nor disease. He suggested that there might be little difference between an "accident" and an "injury" in this context.

The crucial question in most cases arising under this Act is whether listed benefits have been paid "in respect of" the accident, injury or disease within the meaning that phrase has in subs.(1)(b), so as to fall within the scope of the term "recoverable benefit" as defined in subs.(4)(c).

For a benefit to be paid "in respect of" an accident, injury or disease, the accident, injury or disease must be an effective cause of the payment of benefit and an accident may cease to be an effective cause of disablement if its effects have worn off and been replaced by the effects of a worsening pre-accident condition (*R(CR) 1/01*). In *R(CR) 3/03*, it was held that only benefits the payment of which was caused by the relevant disease were paid "in respect of" the disease and that ordinary principles of causation applied, having regard to the conditions of entitlement to each benefit. A relevant accident, injury or disease could therefore cease to be an effective cause of the payment of benefit even if its effects had not worn off. It was enough merely for it to be shown that the benefit would have been paid due to a pre-existing condition even if the relevant disease had not been developed. In that case, the claimant was paid compensation in respect of asbestos–induced disease but the evidence was that the claimant was suffering from other, longer-standing, conditions that contributed to his disablement and were getting worse. The Commissioner found the claimant would have become incapable of work from a certain date even if he had not suffered from the asbestos-induced disease and therefore that the asbestos-induced disease

157

ceased to be a cause of the payment of benefits paid in respect of incapacity from that date, although it had accelerated the onset of incapacity. In relation to disability living allowance, he found that the asbestos-related disease had been a contributory factor in the claimant's entitlement to the mobility component throughout that part of the "relevant period" for which it had been paid but that it had never been a contributory factor in the claimant's entitlement to the care component. Thus, part of the incapacity benefits listed in the original certificate of recoverable benefits and all of the care component of disability living allowance were not recoverable but the rest of the incapacity benefits and all of the mobility component were recoverable.

Conversely, where the other cause of disablement arises *after* the relevant accident, benefit that would have been paid as a result of the relevant accident if the other cause had not arisen is attributable to the relevant accident, whereas benefit that would not have been paid but for the other cause of disablement is attributable to that other cause. In *R(CR) 2/04*, the claimant had returned to work for another employer after the relevant accident, even though he was still suffering from some minor disablement, and then suffered a second industrial accident, following which he was incapable of work again. The Commissioner found that the incapacity was initially attributable to the second accident because the claimant would have been able to continue working but for that accident. However, the effects of that accident then wore off and the effects of the relevant accident worsened and the Commissioner found that there came a time when the claimant would have been incapable of work due to the relevant accident even if the second accident had not occurred so that the payment of benefits became attributable to the relevant accident again.

Where a claimant undergoes a medical operation as a result of an accident, injury or disease and the operation causes further disablement, benefits paid in consequence of that further disablement will have been paid "in respect of" the accident (*CCR/2046/2002*). The same applied where the claimant suffered a psychological reaction due to stress caused by a misdiagnosis due to the misreading of an X-ray that was required by the relevant accident, although it was suggested that the result might have been different if it had been proved that the misdiagnosis had been due to negligence (*CCR/4307/2000*).

Where there has been medical negligence, compensation may be paid in respect of any injury or disease caused by the negligence. In *CCR/1022/2006*, it was pointed out that it is important to distinguish between the effects of the accident, injury or disease that led to the claimant being admitted to hospital and the effects of the medical negligence that occurred while he was a patient there. "The question for the tribunal was whether, had there not been the delay in arranging the MRI scan and therefore a delay in surgery, the appellant would have qualified for disability living allowance at the rate at which it was awarded or at a lower rate. If the answer was 'yes', the benefit was to that extent not recoverable."

However, where a claimant had accepted £50,000 in respect of a claim that injuries from a particular date were due solely to medical negligence, it was necessary to adopt a consistent approach and the claimant was not entitled to argue that the injuries he had suffered after that date were entirely due to the accident that had led him to be hospitalised rather than to the medical negligence (*CCR/2232/2006*).

The need for consistency between the approach taken by a party to court proceedings and the approach taken by the same party in proceedings under this Act is not confined to medical negligence cases and such consistency is expected from compensators as well as from claimants. In *R(CR) 1/07*, where a compensator settled a claim made on the basis that psychiatric injury was due to a particular cause, the compensator was not entitled to argue that the injury was due to a cause not covered by the claim and that the compensator was therefore not in fact liable in respect of the injury in consequence of which the compensation was paid. Attention was drawn to the word "alleged" in s.1(2)(a). Compensators must therefore pay careful attention to the certificate of recoverable benefits when deciding whether to compromise a case that could be defended. It is important to note that the principal issue in both *CCR/2232/2006* and *R(CR) 1/07* was whether the compensation had been paid in respect of a particular injury (in circumstances where it could not plausibly be claimed to have been paid in respect of some other injury or damage), rather than whether the benefits listed in the certificate of recoverable benefits were paid in respect of the injury. The issue therefore did not fall within the scope of the right of appeal conferred by s.11.

Benefits that ought not to have been paid at all—because they were paid under a mistake of fact or medical opinion or law, whether deliberately induced by the claimant or not—cannot be said to have been paid "in respect of " an accident, injury or disease *(R(CR) 1/02*, a decision of a Tribunal of Commissioners, and *Eagle Star Insurance v Department for Social Development*, a decision of the Court of Appeal in Northern Ireland reported as *R1/01(CRS)*). It follows that, if it is shown that benefit was paid at too high a rate, only that part of the benefit properly paid was paid "in respect of " the accident, injury or disease *(R(CR) 1/03*). See further the note to s.11.

However, in *R1/05(CRS)*, it was held that benefits paid as a result of bureaucratic delay between the date of a medical examination and a consequent supersession decision do not necessarily cease to be recoverable.

There is no provision for reducing the amount of recoverable benefit because some other benefit would have been paid to the claimant if the relevant accident or injury had not occurred or the relevant disease had not been developed. Furthermore, income support is paid "in respect of " an accident if it is paid on the basis of the claimant being incapable of work due to the accident, even if the claimant would have been paid income support on some other basis if the accident had not happened *(Hassall v Secretary of State for Social Security* [1995] 1 W.L.R. 812 (also reported as *R(CR) 1/95*)). Where a claimant might be at risk of having compensation reduced under s.8 in respect of post-accident benefits paid in place of pre-accident benefits, he or she may need to include a claim for the loss of the pre-accident benefits in the claim for compensation (*ibid.* and *Neal v Bingle* [1998] Q.B. 466), although this is less of a problem under this Act than it was under the legislation it replaced. In *R1/06 (CRS)*, the Commissioner followed *Hassall* when deciding that the whole of income support awarded during the relevant period on the grounds of incapacity caused by the accident was recoverable notwithstanding that part of it was attributable to dependants acquired by the claimant after the relevant accident. It would not have been necessary for benefit to be paid in respect of the dependants if the accident had not occurred. In *R(CR) 1/96*, the claimant was a hairdresser injured in a road accident. She was awarded income support on the basis of incapacity for work and later, after she became capable of light work, on the basis that she was available for work, although she was still unfit for work as a hairdresser. The Commissioner held that the income support paid on the basis of the claimant's availability for work was paid "otherwise than in consequence of the accident". It is suggested that this part of the decision is based on a misreading of *Hassall* and would probably not be followed by the Upper Tribunal if the issue were to arise again. *Hassall* was concerned with income support paid on the basis of availability for work *before* the accident but there seems no reason why such a benefit should not be recoverable when a claimant has lost employment as the result of an accident, particularly as jobseeker's allowance, which has replaced income support when a claimant is capable of, and available for, work is clearly listed in Sch.2. However, the issue may not arise for determination because, in practice, the Secretary of State seldom seeks recovery of jobseeker's allowance (see *R(CR) 2/04* at para.19).

There may be a question as to whether benefit paid in consequence of a disease for a period before the beginning of the "relevant period" is recoverable (see the note to s.3).

[¹Lump sum payments: regulation-making power

1A.—(1) The Secretary of State may by regulations make provision about the recovery of the amount of a payment to which subsection (2) applies (a "lump sum payment") where—

1.249

(a) a compensation payment in consequence of a disease is made to or in respect of a person ("P") to whom, or in respect of whom, a lump sum payment has been, or is likely to be, made, and

(b) the compensation payment is made in consequence of the same disease as the lump sum payment.

(2) This subsection applies to—

(a) a payment made in accordance with the Pneumoconiosis etc. (Workers' Compensation) Act 1979 ("the 1979 Act"),

(b) a payment made in accordance with Part 4 of the Child Maintenance and Other Payments Act 2008, and

(c) an extra-statutory payment (within the meaning given by subsection (5)(d) below).

(3) Regulations under this section may, in particular—

(a) make provision about the recovery of the amount of a lump sum payment made to or in respect of a dependant of P;

(b) make provision enabling the recovery of the amount of a lump sum payment from a compensation payment (including provision enabling the recovery of an amount which reduces the compensation payment to nil);

(c) enable the amount of a lump sum payment made before commencement to be recovered from a compensation payment made after commencement;

(d) make provision about certificates in respect of lump sum payments;

(e) apply any provision of this Act, with or without modifications.

(4) References in subsection (1) to a payment made in consequence of a disease—

(a) are references to a payment made by or on behalf of a person who is, or is alleged to be, liable to any extent in respect of the disease, but

(b) do not include references to a payment mentioned in Part 1 of Schedule 1.

(5) In this section—

(a) "commencement" means the date on which this section comes into force,

(b) "compensation payment" means a payment within section 1(1)(a) above,

(c) "dependant" has the meaning given by section 3 of the 1979 Act, and

(d) "extra-statutory payment" means a payment made by the Secretary of State to or in respect of a person following the rejection by the Secretary of State of a claim under the 1979 Act.]

AMENDMENT

1. Child Maintenance and Other Payments Act 2008, s.54 (June 10, 2008 for the purpose only of making regulations and October 1, 2008 for other purposes).

DEFINITIONS

"commencement"—see subs.(5).
"compensation payment"—*ibid.*
"dependant"—*ibid.*
"extra-statutory payment"—*ibid.*
"lump sum payment"—see subs.(1).
"payment"—see s.29.
"regulations"—*ibid.*

GENERAL NOTE

The Social Security (Recovery of Benefits) (Lump Sum Payments) Regulations 2008 are made under this section (and other provisions of this Act). They provide a scheme for the recovery of payments within the scope of subs.(2) that have been made by the Secretary of State in respect of death or disablement due to pneumoconiosis or mesothelioma from a person making a compensation payment on or after October 1, 2008 in respect of the relevant disease. The main differences between the scheme created by the Regulations and the scheme under the Act are that there is no five-year "relevant period" as there is under s.3 of the Act and that the Regulations also apply where the lump sum payment and compensation payment have been made to a dependant of the person who was suffering from the disease. Regulations 4 and 5 define the scope of the scheme, and s.1(3) of the Act applies with "Section 1A(1)(a)" substituted for "Subsection (1)(a)". Regulations 8 to 13 are broadly equivalent to ss.4 to 9 of the Act and reg.2 applies ss.10 to 34 (except ss.16, 24, 25, 32 and 34(2)) of, and Sch.1 to, the Act, with modifications. Most of the modifications are minor, but s.15 is completely substituted. Regulations 7 and 14 to 19 make provision equivalent to regs 2, 9, 3, 4, 6, 10 and 11, respectively, of the Social Security (Recovery of Benefits) Regulations 1997.

1.250

Compensation payments to which this Act applies

2. This Act applies in relation to compensation payments made on or after the day on which this section comes into force, unless they are made in pursuance of a court order or agreement made before that day.

1.251

DEFINITION

"compensation payment"—see s.1(4)(b).

GENERAL NOTE

By virtue of the Social Security (Recovery of Benefits) Act 1997 (Commencement Order) 1997 (SI 1997/2085), this section came into force on October 6, 1997. Where a court order or agreement was made before that date, the recovery provisions of Pt IV of the Social Security Administration Act 1992 continue to apply, unless the accident or injury occurred before January 1, 1989 (or, in the case of a disease, benefit was claimed before January 1, 1989), in which case benefits will not be recoverable by the Secretary of State at all (see s.81(7) of the 1992 Act). Regulation 12 of the Social Security (Recovery of Benefits) Regulations 1997 makes transitional provision for cases arising under the 1992 Act.

Lump sum payments within the scope of s.1A(2) may be recovered only where the compensation payment was made on or after October 1, 2008 (see reg.6 of the Social Security (Recovery of Benefits) Lump Sum Payments) Regulations 2008).

1.252

"The relevant period"

3.—(1) In relation to a person ("the claimant") who has suffered any accident, injury or disease, "the relevant period" has the meaning given by the following subsections.

(2) Subject to subsection (4), if it is a case of accident or injury, the relevant period is the period of five years immediately following the day on which the accident or injury in question occurred.

(3) Subject to subsection (4), if it is a case of disease, the relevant period is the period of five years beginning with the date on which the claimant first claims a listed benefit in consequence of the disease.

(4) If at any time before the end of the period referred to in subsection (2) or (3)—

1.253

(a) a person makes a compensation payment in final discharge of any claim made by or in respect of the claimant and arising out of the accident, injury or disease, or

(b) an agreement is made under which an earlier compensation payment is treated as having been made in final discharge of any such claim,

the relevant period ends at that time.

DEFINITIONS

"claimant"—see subs.(1).
"compensation payment"—see s.1(4)(b).
"listed benefit"—see s.29.

GENERAL NOTE

1.254   Subsection (2) identifies the beginning of the "relevant period" if the compensation is paid in consequence of an accident or injury and subs.(3) identifies the beginning of the "relevant period" if compensation is paid in consequence of a disease.

It was observed in *R(CR) 4/03* that this section implies that "accident" and "injury" are indistinguishable in this Act in cases where the injury is due to an accident, because subs.(2) clearly envisages them occurring on the same specific date, rather than contemplating the injury being the, possibly long-standing and possibly delayed, result of an accident. It was also observed that this section requires a distinction to be drawn between an "injury" and a "disease" and that that might not always be straightforward. It may be noted that the Social Security (Industrial Injuries) (Prescribed Diseases) Regulations 1985 in fact include prescribed injuries as well as diseases (see also s.108(1)(b) of the Social Security Contributions and Benefits Act 1992). It is unclear when the "relevant period" begins if a disease is caused by an accident and benefit in respect of the disease is not claimed until some time after the date of the accident.

If s.1(1)(b) and (4)(c) and subs.(3) of this section are all read literally, it appears that there is a possibility of more than five years' worth of benefit being recovered where compensation is paid in consequence of a disease. That is because the "relevant period" appears to run from the date of claim, rather than the date from which benefit is awarded. Typically, arrears of disablement benefit in respect of a prescribed disease are paid in respect of a period of three months before the date of claim, although the payment of those arrears is obviously made after that date and within the "relevant period". It may be arguable that one or more of the provisions should not be read literally on the basis that it is unlikely that it was intended that more than five years' worth of benefit should be recoverable, although the counter-argument is that the possibility of arrears being caught should have been obvious to the draftsman and could easily have been avoided if it was unintended.

Subsections (2) and (3) provide for a "relevant period" of five years but subs. (4) shortens it if compensation is paid sooner. As benefits payable after the "relevant period" are not recoverable (s.1(1)(b) and (4)(c)) and are ignored in the calculation of damages (s.17), it is likely to be in the interests of a compensator and, usually, a claimant to settle a claim for compensation as soon as possible.

Certificates of recoverable benefits

Applications for certificates of recoverable benefits

1.255   **4.**—(1) Before a person ("the compensator") makes a compensation payment he must apply to the Secretary of State for a certificate of recoverable benefits.

(2) Where the compensator applies for a certificate of recoverable benefits, the Secretary of State must—

(a) send to him a written acknowledgement of receipt of his application, and

(b) subject to subsection (7), issue the certificate before the end of the following period

(3) The period is—

(a) the prescribed period, or

(b) if there is no prescribed period, the period of four weeks,

which begins with the day following the day on which the application is received.

(4) The certificate is to remain in force until the date specified in it for that purpose.

(5) The compensator may apply for fresh certificates from time to time.

(6) Where a certificate of recoverable benefits ceases to be in force, the Secretary of State may issue a fresh certificate without an application for one being made.

(7) Where the compensator applies for a fresh certificate while a certificate ("the existing certificate") remains in force, the Secretary of State must issue the fresh certificate before the end of the following period.

(8) The period is—

(a) the prescribed period, or

(b) if there is no prescribed period, the period of four weeks,

which begins with the day following the day on which the existing certificate ceases to be in force.

(9) For the purposes of this Act, regulations may provide for the day on which an application for a certificate of recoverable benefits is to be treated as received.

DEFINITIONS

"compensator—see subs.(1).
"compensation payment"—see s.1(4)(b).
"existing certificate"—see subs.(7).
"prescribed—see s.29.
"recoverable benefit"—see s.1(4)(c).
"regulations"—see s.29.

GENERAL NOTE

No period has yet been prescribed for the purposes of subss.(3)(a) or (8)(a). By virtue of s.21, the consequence of the Secretary of State failing to issue a certificate of recoverable benefits within the specified period is that no benefits are recoverable and the victim is entitled to the full compensation without deduction. However, for s.21 to apply, the application for the certificate of recoverable benefits must have been accurate and it must have been acknowledged. The Compensation Recovery Unit asks compensators to tell them if an acknowledgement has not been received within 10 days.

In practice, potential compensators are asked to notify the Compensation Recovery Unit of any *claim* for compensation by sending form CRU1 within 14 days of the claim being received. This enables the Unit to start collecting the relevant information from the offices responsible for the payment of benefits. The Unit sends to the potential compensator a form CRU4 which is the form the compensator must use to obtain the certificate of recoverable benefits. Form CRU4 can also be used by a compensator to obtain, for the purposes of negotiation with the victim,

1.256

an informal indication of the benefits that have been paid, although the Unit stresses that the accuracy of such an indication depends on how much information they have to hand at that time and a formal certificate of recoverable benefits issued later may be based on more up-to-date information. The victim is, of course, entitled to that information as well and can obtain it directly from the office or offices responsible for payment.

This section does not apply in respect of the recovery of lump sum payments within the scope of s.1A(2). See, instead, reg.8 of the Social Security (Recovery of Benefits) Lump Sum Payments) Regulations 2008.

Subs. (9)

1.257   See reg.7(2) of the Social Security (Recovery of Benefits) Regulations 1997.

Information contained in certificates

1.258   **5.**—(1) A certificate of recoverable benefits must specify, for each recoverable benefit—

(a) the amount which has been or is likely to have been paid on or before a specified date, and

(b) if the benefit is paid or likely to be paid after the specified date, the rate and period for which, and the intervals at which, it is or is likely to be paid.

(2) In a case where the relevant period has ended before the day on which the Secretary of State receives the application for the certificate, the date specified in the certificate for the purposes of subsection (1) must be the day on which the relevant period ended.

(3) In any other case, the date specified for those purposes must not be earlier than the day on which the Secretary of State received the application.

(4) The Secretary of State may estimate, in such manner as he thinks fit, any of the amounts, rates or periods specified in the certificate.

(5) Where the Secretary of State issues a certificate of recoverable benefits, he must provide the information contained in the certificate to—

(a) the person who appears to him to be the injured person, or

(b) any person who he thinks will receive a compensation payment in respect of the injured person.

(6) A person to whom a certificate of recoverable benefits is issued or who is provided with information under subsection (5) is entitled to particulars of the manner in which any amount, rate or period specified in the certificate has been determined, if he applies to the Secretary of State for those particulars.

DEFINITIONS

"benefit"—see s.29.
"compensation payment"—see s.1(4)(b).
"injured person"—see s.1(4)(a).
"recoverable benefit"—see s.1(4)(c).
"the relevant period"—see s.3.

GENERAL NOTE

1.259   Note that only "recoverable" benefits should be specified on the certificate and, by virtue of s.1(1)(b) and (4)(c), that means benefits listed in col.2 of Sch.2 that have been, or are likely to be, paid to or for the victim during the relevant period *in respect of* the accident, injury or disease. Thus, not all benefits paid, or to be paid, during the relevant period should be specified in the certificate; only those that are attributable to the accident, injury or disease are recoverable. See the note to s.1.

For reviews of, and appeals against, certificates of recoverable benefits, see ss.10–14.

This section does not apply in respect of the recovery of lump sum payments within the scope of s.1A(2). See, instead, reg.9 of the Social Security (Recovery of Benefits) Lump Sum Payments) Regulations 2008.

Liability of person paying compensation

Liability to pay Secretary of State amount of benefits

6.—(1) A person who makes a compensation payment in any case is liable to pay to the Secretary of State an amount equal to the total amount of the recoverable benefits.

(2) The liability referred to in subsection (1) arises immediately before the compensation payment or, if there is more than one, the first of them is made.

(3) No amount becomes payable under this section before the end of the period of 14 days following the day on which the liability arises.

(4) Subject to subsection (3), an amount becomes payable under this section at the end of the period of 14 days beginning with the day on which a certificate of recoverable benefits is first issued showing that the amount of recoverable benefit to which it relates has been or is likely to have been paid before a specified date.

1.260

DEFINITIONS

"amount of the recoverable benefits"—see s.9(4)(b).
"compensation payment"—see s.1(4)(b).
"recoverable benefit"—see s.1(4)(c).

GENERAL NOTE

The compensator may recoup some of the payment by reducing under s.8 the amount of compensation paid to the victim. However, the additional cost of benefits paid to the victim during the relevant period falls on the compensator. The compensator may not appeal against the certificate of recoverable benefits until the compensation has been paid (s.11(3)).

This section does not apply in respect of the recovery of lump sum payments within the scope of s.1A(2). See, instead, reg.10 of the Social Security (Recovery of Benefits) Lump Sum Payments) Regulations 2008.

1.261

Recovery of payments due under section 6

7.—(1) This section applies where a person has made a compensation payment but—
(a) has not applied for a certificate of recoverable benefits, or
(b) has not made a payment to the Secretary of State under section 6 before the end of the period allowed under that section.

(2) The Secretary of State may—

1.262

(a) issue the person who made the compensation payment with a certificate of recoverable benefits, if none has been issued, or

(b) issue him with a copy of the certificate of recoverable benefits or (if more than one has been issued) the most recent one,

and (in either case) issue him with a demand that payment of any amount due under section 6 be made immediately.

(3) The Secretary of State may, in accordance with subsections (4) and (5), recover the amount for which a demand for payment is made under subsection (2) from the person who made the compensation payment.

(4) If the person who made the compensation payment resides or carries on business in England and Wales and a county court so orders, any amount recoverable under subsection (3) is recoverable by execution issued from the county court or otherwise as if it were payable under an order of that court.

(5) If the person who made the payment resides or carries on business in Scotland, any amount recoverable under subsection (3) may be enforced in like manner as an extract registered decree arbitral bearing a warrant for execution issued by the sheriff court of any sheriffdom in Scotland.

(6) A document bearing a certificate which—

(a) is signed by a person authorised to do so by the Secretary of State, and

(b) states that the document, apart from the certificate, is a record of the amount recoverable under subsection (3),

is conclusive evidence that that amount is so recoverable.

(7) A certificate under subsection (6) purporting to be signed by a person authorised to do so by the Secretary of State is to be treated as so signed unless the contrary is proved.

DEFINITIONS

"compensation payment"—see s.1(4)(b).
"payment"—see s.29.
"recoverable benefit"—see s.1(4)(c).

GENERAL NOTE

1.263   This section provides a simple way of recovering not only sums due under s.6 from compensators who have followed the proper procedures but also sums due from those who have failed to apply for a certificate of recoverable benefits at all. For reviews of, and appeals against, certificates issued under s.7(2)(a), see ss.10–14.

This section does not apply in respect of the recovery of lump sum payments within the scope of s.1A(2). See, instead, reg.11 of the Social Security (Recovery of Benefits) Lump Sum Payments) Regulations 2008.

Reduction of compensation payment

Reduction of compensation payment

1.264   **8.**—(1) This section applies in a case where, in relation to any head of compensation listed in column 1 of Schedule 2—

(a) any of the compensation payment is attributable to that head, and

(b) any recoverable benefit is shown against that head in column 2 of the Schedule.

(2) In such a case, any claim of a person to receive the compensation payment is to be treated for all purposes as discharged if—

(a) he is paid the amount (if any) of the compensation payment calculated in accordance with this section, and

(b) if the amount of the compensation payment so calculated is nil, he is given a statement saying so by the person who (apart from this section) would have paid the gross amount of the compensation payment.

(3) For each head of compensation listed in column 1 of the Schedule for which paragraphs (a) and (b) of subsection (1) are met, so much of the gross amount of the compensation payment as is attributable to that head is to be reduced (to nil, if necessary) by deducting the amount of the recoverable benefit or, as the case may be, the aggregate amount of the recoverable benefits shown against it.

(4) Subsection (3) is to have effect as if a requirement to reduce a payment by deducting an amount which exceeds that payment were a requirement to reduce that payment to nil.

(5) The amount of the compensation payment calculated in accordance with this section is—

(a) the gross amount of the compensation payment, and

(b) the sum of the reductions made under subsection (3),

(and, accordingly, the amount may be nil).

DEFINITIONS

"amount of the recoverable benefit"—see s.9(4)(b).
"compensation payment"—see s.1(4)(b).
"gross amount of the compensation payment"—see s.9(4)(a).
"payment"—see s.29.
"recoverable benefit"—see s.1(4)(c).

GENERAL NOTE

Under the scheme replaced by this Act, the compensation payment was reduced by the whole amount of benefits paid within the relevant period in respect of the accident, injury or disease, even if the compensation had been awarded solely in respect of pain and suffering (*CSS/36/1992*). The effect was that the compensator almost always passed the entire cost of the recovery of benefits on to the injured person. This could produce unfair results, because the claimant's compensation for pain and suffering was eroded, particularly in two types of cases. The first was where the benefits were paid in respect of, say, a need for personal care (i.e. where the care component of disability living allowance was paid) for which the claimant had not claimed compensation because, say, the care was provided by a spouse free of charge. To some extent this could be avoided by claimants inventing new and cumbersome claims for loss based on the effects of the legislation for recovery of benefits. The second was a less tractable problem, which arose because most claims for compensation are settled and there is likely to be an element of compromise. If a claim for loss of earnings was settled on the basis that was inconsistent with the basis of a claim for benefits, the recovery of benefits from the claimant could appear disproportionate (*CCR/8023/1995*). Whether that was unfair or not depended on whether or not the basis of settlement more accurately reflected the truth than the basis of the claim for benefit, but there could obviously be unfairness where there was a genuine compromise of the claim for compensation but the real burden of repaying the Secretary of State fell wholly on the claimant, rather than being shared by the compensator.

1.265

Under the new scheme, the compensator bears the cost of the alleged wrong-doing, being able to pass the cost on to the claimant only to the extent that he has paid relevant compensation to the claimant. Schedule 2 sets out three relevant heads of compensation (lost earnings, cost of care and loss of mobility) and sets out beside each of them the benefits in respect of which a deduction may be made under this section. Where a court makes an award of damages, it must quantify the amount allowed in respect of each of the heads of compensation set out in Sch.2 (s.15(2)). It is then for the compensator to make the appropriate deduction under s.8. Disputes as to the proper amount to be deducted under s.8 are not unusual. The legislation does not make explicit provision for the resolution of such disputes. Presumably, if the parties have become aware in the course of pre-trial negotiations that there is an issue as to the operation of s.8, the court can be asked to deal with that issue at the same time as assessing damages. What is quite clear is that the issue is to be determined by a court and not on an appeal to a tribunal under s.11. See *R(CR) 2/03* and *R(CR) 2/04*. In those decisions it was suggested that the issue could be determined in enforcement proceedings if it had not been dealt with by the judge at trial. Most cases, of course, are settled. Amendments to the Civil Procedure Rules have since made it clearer that the question whether a deduction is being properly made needs to be considered *before* a defendant's offer of settlement is accepted (see the note to s.16).

1.266   Where a payment into court is made, the compensator must state whether any deduction has been made under this section (see the note to s.16). Where a case is settled without there being a payment into court, the parties will no doubt have had regard to the operation of this section in reaching the settlement but it will usually be presumed that there was no reduction under this section unless the agreement expressly records such a reduction. It is important to the parties to record such a reduction if it is intended that the claimant should bring an appeal before a tribunal challenging the recoverability of benefits, because a claimant has a right of appeal only if there has been a reduction (see s.11(2)(b)). Otherwise only the compensator has a right of appeal. The question of who should bear the cost or risk of such an appeal can be a matter to be taken into account in negotiating a settlement but the settlement must be worded appropriately if it is to have the intended effect. Section 11(3) provides that an appeal may be brought only after the claim giving rise to the compensation payment has been disposed of, so that the Secretary of State does not get caught up in arguments between the claimant and the compensator as to the amount of compensation and the proper application of s.8. Where an application for review or an appeal by either party is successful in a case where there was a reduction of the compensation payment under this section, the refund is made to the compensator who must make a new calculation under this section (reg.11(4) and (5) of the Social Security (Recovery of Benefits) Regulations 1997). This has the effect that a compensator has no practical interest in appealing where the compensation payment has been reduced by the whole amount of recoverable benefits (*R(CR) 2/03*). The compensator has an interest only to the extent to which the amount of recoverable benefits *has not* been reflected in a reduction under this section, just as a claimant has an interest only to the extent to which the amount of recoverable benefits *has* been reflected in a reduction. Where, following a review or appeal, a compensator is obliged to make a further payment to the Secretary of State in a case where there was a reduction under this section, there are limited circumstances in which the reduction may be recalculated and the claimant may be required to make a refund to the compensator (*ibid.*, reg.11(6) and (7)).

Although neither s.8 nor Sch.2 refers to the period in respect of which recoverable benefits may be taken into account, it was suggested in *R(CR) 2/04* that benefits should be deducted under s.8 only in so far as they are payable in respect of the period for which compensation in respect of the relevant head of damages has been paid. The Commissioner also suggested that the calculation under s.8 should be made *before* the amount of compensation is reduced to take account of contributory negligence. However, as he also held that the proper operation of s.8 was a matter for the courts and not for tribunals or Commissioners, those suggestions are obiter dicta.

This section does not apply in respect of the recovery of lump sum payments within the scope of s.1A(2). See, instead, reg.12 of the Social Security (Recovery of Benefits) Lump Sum Payments) Regulations 2008.

Section 8: supplementary

9.—(1) A person who makes a compensation payment calculated in accordance with section 8 must inform the person to whom the payment is made—

1.267

(a) that the payment has been so calculated, and

(b) of the date for payment by reference to which the calculation has been made.

(2) If the amount of a compensation payment calculated in accordance with section 8 is nil, a person giving a statement saying so is to be treated for the purposes of this Act as making a payment within section 1(1)(a) on the day on which he gives the statement.

(3) Where a person—

(a) makes a compensation payment calculated in accordance with section 8, and

(b) if the amount of the compensation payment so calculated is nil, gives a statement saying so,

he is to be treated, for the purpose of determining any rights and liabilities in respect of contribution or indemnity, as having paid the gross amount of the compensation payment.

(4) For the purposes of this Act—

(a) the gross amount of the compensation payment is the amount of the compensation payment apart from section 8, and

(b) the amount of any recoverable benefit is the amount determined in accordance with the certificate of recoverable benefits.

DEFINITIONS

"compensation payment"—see s.1(4)(b).
"gross amount of the compensation payment"—see subs.(4)(a).
"payment"—see s.29.
"recoverable benefit"—see s.1(4)(c).

GENERAL NOTE

This section does not apply in respect of the recovery of lump sum payments within the scope of s.1A(2). See, instead, reg.13 of the Social Security (Recovery of Benefits) Lump Sum Payments) Regulations 2008.

1.268

Reviews and appeals

Review of certificates of recoverable benefits

10.—[¹(1) Any certificate of recoverable benefits may be reviewed by the Secretary of State—

1.269

(a) either within the prescribed period or in prescribed circumstances; and

(b) either on an application made for the purpose or on his own initiative.]

(2) On a review under this section the Secretary of State may either—

(a) confirm the certificate, or

(b) (subject to subsection (3)) issue a fresh certificate containing such variations as he considers appropriate[1 or

(c) revoke the certificate.]

(3) The Secretary of State may not vary the certificate so as to increase the total amount of the recoverable benefits unless it appears to him that the variation is required as a result of the person who applied for the certificate supplying him with incorrect or insufficient information.

AMENDMENT

1. Social Security Act 1998, Sch.7, para.149 (March 4, 1999 for the making of regulations, November 29, 1999 for other purposes).

DEFINITIONS

"amount of the recoverable benefits"—see s.9(4)(b).
"prescribed"—see s.29.
"recoverable benefit"—see s.1(4)(c).
"regulations"—see s.29.

GENERAL NOTE

This section is applied with modifications to cases concerned with the recovery of payments within the scope of s.1A(2) (see the Social Security (Recovery of Benefits) (Lump Sum Payments) Regulations 2008, reg.2 and Sch.1, para.3).

Subs. (1)

1.270   Note that the Social Security Act 1998 does not abolish the concept of review in this context. No period has been prescribed, so an application for review may be made at any time. The circumstances in which a decision may be reviewed are prescribed by regs 9 and 9ZA of the Social Security and Child Support (Decisions and Appeals) Regulations 1999 and are very broad. However, there is no right of appeal against a refusal to review a certificate of recoverable benefits so that it may be unwise to apply for a review instead of appealing if that might cause the time for appealing to expire, although pursuing that alternative course of action might be regarded as a reason for admitting a late appeal and subs.(3) provides protection on a review that is lacking on an appeal. Moreover, it is unnecessary to make a separate application for review before appealing because reg.9(d) of the 1999 Regulations provides that a decision may be reviewed if "a ground of appeal is satisfied under section 11 of the 1997 Act". In *CCR/3391/2005*, it was said that the Secretary of State should always consider reviewing a decision against which an appeal has been brought, so as to prevent unnecessary appeals reaching tribunals. "In effect, a submission to a tribunal should be an explanation for the Secretary of State not reviewing the decision in the light of the grounds of appeal." That approach is particularly necessary where the appellant has provided on the appeal evidence that was not before the Secretary of State either when the certificate of recoverable benefits was issued or when the benefits concerned were awarded so that there is a factual issue upon which the Secretary of State has not previously made a decision.

Subs. (3)

1.271   This is an important provision. Once a certificate has been issued, it cannot be varied on review so as to increase the amount of recoverable benefits unless the person who applied for the certificate (the compensator) caused the error. Where the compensator has provided incorrect or insufficient information as a result of being given incorrect or insufficient information by a claimant who knew it to be incorrect or insufficient and who provided it with intent to limit the amount of a reduction under s.8, the compensator may be able to recover from the claimant some or all of the additional money due to the Secretary of State (reg.11(6) and (7) of the Social Security (Recovery of Benefits) Regulations 1997). As the Secretary of State has only four weeks in which to issue the certificate (s.4(3)(b) and (8)(b)), it may occasionally be impossible to obtain accurate information and resort may be had to estimation (s.5(4)). If lack of information or an inaccurate estimate results in a calculation that turns out to be unfavourable to the Secretary of State, he is nevertheless bound by it until the certificate expires under s.4(4). However, any new certificate issued in respect of a later period may list the benefit omitted from the earlier one. Furthermore, subs.(3) does not prevent the amount of recoverable benefits from being increased on an appeal *(CSCS/1/1995)*.

Appeals against certificates of recoverable benefits

11.—(1) An appeal against a certificate of recoverable benefits may be made on the ground—   1.272
  (a) that any amount, rate or period specified in the certificate is incorrect, or
  (b) that listed benefits which have been, or are likely to be, paid otherwise than in respect of the accident, injury or disease in question have been brought into account [¹ or
  (c) that listed benefits which have not been, and are not likely to be, paid to the injured person during the relevant period have been brought into account, or
  (d) that the payment on the basis of which the certificate was issued is not a payment within section 1(1)(a)].
  (2) An appeal under this section may be made by—
  (a) the person who applied for the certificate of recoverable benefits, or
[¹(aa) (in a case where the certificate was issued under section 7(2)(a)) the person to whom it was so issued, or]
  (b) (in a case where the amount of the compensation payment has been calculated under section 8) the injured person or other person to whom the payment is made.
  (3) No appeal may be made under this section until—
  (a) the claim giving rise to the compensation payment has been finally disposed of, and
  (b) the liability under section 6 has been discharged.
  (4) For the purposes of subsection (3)(a), if an award of damages in respect of a claim has been made under or by virtue of—
  (a) section 32A(2)(a) of the Supreme Court Act 1981,
  (b) section 12(2)(a) of the Administration of Justice Act 1982, or
  (c) section 51(2)(a) of the County Courts Act 1984,
(orders for provisional damages in personal injury cases), the claim is to be treated as having been finally disposed of.
  (5) Regulations may make provision—
  (a) as to the manner in which, and the time within which, appeals under this section may be made,
  (b) [² . . .] and
  (c) for the purpose of enabling any such appeal to be treated as an application for review under section 10.
  (6) [¹ . . .]

AMENDMENTS

1. Social Security Act 1998, Sch.7, para.150 and Sch.8 (November 29, 1999).
2. Transfer of Tribunal Functions Order 2008 (SI 2008/2833), Sch.3 paras 138 and 139 (November 3, 2008).

DEFINITIONS

"compensation payment"—see s.1(4)(b).
"injured person"—see s.1(4)(a).
"listed benefit"—see s.29.
"payment"—*ibid*.
"recoverable benefit"—see s.1(4)(c).
"regulations"—see s.29.

GENERAL NOTE

This section is applied with modifications to cases concerned with the recovery of payments within the scope of s.1A(2) (see the Social Security (Recovery of Benefits) (Lump Sum Payments) Regulations 2008, reg.2 and Sch.1, para.4).

Subs.(1)

1.273   Any appeal is heard by the First-tier Tribunal (See s.12).

It is not easy to see the distinction between paras (a) and (c), save perhaps that para.(a) more clearly allows a challenge to the Secretary of State's view as to the appropriate "relevant period". Both paragraphs appear to permit an appeal based on a dispute as to the amount of benefit actually paid to the claimant.

Paragraph (b) permits an appeal where there is a dispute as to whether benefit was paid "in respect of " the relevant accident, injury or disease (see the note to s.1). This is the ground on which most appeals are brought. The burden of proving that benefit was paid otherwise than in respect of the relevant accident, injury or disease is placed on the appellant but the Secretary of State can be expected to provide a prima facie justification for the inclusion of the benefits in the certificate in the first place (*CCR/4307/2000*) and an adverse inference may be drawn if he fails to do so. A tribunal considering an appeal under this section is entitled to reach a decision that is inconsistent with the decision awarding benefit because benefit that ought not to have been awarded cannot be said to have been awarded "in respect of " the relevant accident, injury or disease (*R(CR) 1/02*, a decision of a Tribunal of Commissioners, and *Eagle Star Insurance v Department for Social Development* (reported as *R1/01 (CRS)*), a decision of the Court of Appeal in Northern Ireland). Similarly, a tribunal is entitled to find that benefit was paid at too high a rate (*R(CR) 1/03*). In *C2/01–02(CRS)*, a Commissioner in Northern Ireland held that it was not the tribunal's function to substitute their judgment for the authority who awarded benefit and that the question was whether benefit had reasonably been awarded. Thus, if the awarding authority could properly have awarded benefit in respect of the relevant accident, injury or disease on the evidence before them and there is no new evidence, it will be impossible to show that benefit was awarded otherwise than in respect of the accident, injury or disease. However, in many cases a tribunal considering an appeal under s.11 will have before them evidence that was not before the authority awarding benefit and in those circumstances the tribunal's judgment will be the only one that can be applied. Where benefit may be awarded on a number of different bases and it is being alleged that benefit ought not to have been awarded or that the disablement justifying the award was not caused by the relevant accident, injury or disease, it is important for the tribunal to be able to infer from the evidence on which basis the benefit in question was actually awarded because only then is it possible to determine whether the claimant's circumstances justified that award. For instance, it is a gross over-simplification to believe that incapacity benefit is paid because a person is actually incapable of work. Establishing that the claimant was in fact capable of work may not demonstrate a lack of entitlement. The personal capability assessment is applicable to most claimants of incapacity benefit and an argument that a claimant ought not to have been treated as satisfying that assessment on account of the relevant accident, injury or disease requires evidence focused on the activities considered in such an assessment. Before a personal capability assessment is actually made, a claimant is usually treated as incapable of work under reg.28 of the Social Security (Incapacity for Work) (General) Regulations 1995 (see Vol.I of this work) on the basis of medical certificates provided by a doctor. In *R(CR) 2/02*, it was suggested by the Tribunal of Commissioners that as long as a claimant was providing such certificates referring to the relevant disease, benefit was properly awarded in respect of that disease whether or not the claimant was actually incapable of work or would actually have satisfied a personal capability assessment. Doubtless, there would be exceptions where, for instance, a claimant was working and so was required to be treated as capable of work under reg.16 of the 1995 Regulations. It may also be arguable that, where a claimant had obtained the medical certificate by misleading his doctor as to the severity of his or her condition or, perhaps, where the doctor plainly ought not to have given a certificate, benefit can be said not to have been properly paid in respect of the relevant accident, injury or disease but, given that a medical certificate merely certifies that the claimant was advised not to work and is not actually a certificate that the person is incapable of work (see Sch.1 to the Social Security (Medical Evidence) Regulations 1976), it will not be easy to demonstrate that a certificate was inappropriate. However, *R(CR) 2/02* was distinguished in *R(CR) 1/04*. In the latter case, incapacity benefit had been awarded pending the carrying out of a personal capability assessment on the basis of medical certificates supplied by the claimant's doctor, which referred to an eye injury sustained when a fire extinguisher had gone off accidentally. The Commissioner found that the eye injury caused by the fire extinguisher had in fact had no disabling effect on the claimant after a week and that the disablement was the result of a pre-existing condition in the claimant's eye and, later, from both that cause and a depressive illness. In those circumstances, he held that the incapacity benefit had not been paid "in respect of" the relevant accident, notwithstanding that the claimant had been deemed to be incapable of work on the strength of the medical certificates. Some claimants are not required to satisfy the personal capability assessment and are treated as being incapable of work under reg.10 or reg.27 of the 1995 Regulations. Again, a submission that benefit was not properly awarded would have to focus on the terms of those regulations.

Paragraph (d) permits an appeal where there is a dispute as to whether the Act applies at all because, for instance, it is claimed that compensation was not paid "in consequence of any accident, injury or disease" (see the note to s.1). If this paragraph is read with para. (b), it is plain that a claimant or compensator is also entitled to argue that a payment of compensation was not paid in respect of a particular injury and that benefits paid in respect of that injury should not have been brought into account. However, such an argument can be advanced only where it can be shown that the compensation was in fact paid in respect of some other injury or damage. Thus, in *CCR/2232/2006*, where the claimant had received £50,000 damages on the basis that injuries after a particular date were due solely to medical negligence, he was not entitled to argue on an appeal under this section that the injury was due to the accident that led to him being hospitalised rather then to the medical negligence and, in *R(CR) 1/07*, where a compensator settled a claim made on the basis that psychiatric injury was due to a particular cause, the compensator was not entitled to argue that the injury was due wholly to a cause not covered by the claim for compensation.

Note that no appeal lies under this section against a compensator's decision to make a reduction under s.8. Any dispute about such a reduction must be determined by the court seised of the claim for compensation, either when compensation is assessed or in enforcement proceedings. A claimant should not accept a payment into court or an offer of settlement if he or she is not prepared to accept that s.8 has been applied reasonably or at least that the net award of compensation is adequate (see *R(CR) 2/03* and *R(CR) 2/04*).

Subs. (2)

1.274   A compensator always has a right of appeal but in fact has no interest in appealing insofar as the amount of compensation was reduced under s.8, due to the effect of reg.11(5) of the Social Security (Recovery of Benefits) Regulations 1997 which requires the recalculation of the s.8 reduction if the appeal is successful (*R(CR) 2/03*). An injured person has a right of appeal only if there has been a s.8 reduction. In any appeal under this section, any other person who could have appealed is made a party to the proceedings (see the definition of "respondent" in the Tribunal Procedure (First-tier Tribunal) (Social Entitlement Chamber) Rules 2008). In *CCR/3425/2003*, the Commissioner said that, as a claimant was entitled to be a party to a compensator's appeal only where there had been a deduction under s.8, it was to be inferred that the right to respond arose because the claimant might be entitled to a refund from the compensator under reg.11(5) of the 1997 Regulations, rather than because the Secretary of State might decide to revise or supersede an award of benefit, if the compensator was successful. Accordingly, as the claimant did not support the compensator's appeal and did not seek a refund, he had suffered no material loss when he had been misled by a letter from the Department suggesting that he need not attend the hearing. If both the claimant and the compensator appeal, the Compensation Recovery Unit should inform the tribunal and ask for the appeals to be heard together (*CCR/2231/2003*).

Subs. (3)

1.275   An appeal cannot be brought until after the compensation claim has been fully disposed of and the s.6 payment has been paid to the Secretary of State. A claim is not finally disposed of until any appeal against a court's order or judgment is determined (*Williams v Devon CC* [2003] EWCA Civ. 365 (*The Times*, March 26, 2003)) and so presumably the reference to the s.6 payment having been made must include any further payments required under reg.9 of the Social Security (Recovery of Benefits) Regulations 1997 in the event of a claimant's appeal being successful and requiring a further payment of compensation to be made. Generally, payment of compensation is made following the settlement of a claim, which implies agreement by the claimant as to the net amount of compensation to be paid after any reduction under s.8. However, where a court assesses compensation, it is not obliged at that stage to assess the appropriate amount of any reduction under s.8. That is left to the compensator. It was suggested in *R(CR) 2/04* that if the claimant wishes to challenge the amount of a s.8 reduction, he or she can do so in enforcement proceedings brought on the basis that the compensator has not fully satisfied the court's judgment.

    See Sch.1 to the Tribunal Procedure (First-tier Tribunal) (Social Entitlement Chamber) Rules 2008 for the time within which an appeal to a tribunal must be brought.

Subs. (5)

1.276   See regs 29, 31(3) and (4) and 32–34 of the Social Security and Child Support (Decisions and Appeals) Regulations 1999. Note that reg.29(6) has been made under subs.(5)(c). Note also that a tribunal considering an appeal under this section has no express power either to refer the victim for examination or to examine him themselves because the primary legislation contains no power equivalent to s.20 of the Social Security Act 1998 under which r.25 of the Tribunal Procedure (First-tier Tribunal) (Social Entitlement Chamber) Rules 2008 is made.

Reference of questions to [² the First-tier Tribunal]

1.277   **12.**—[¹(1) The Secretary of State must refer an appeal under section 11 to an [² the First-tier Tribunal].]

    (2) [¹. . .]

    (3) In determining [¹ any appeal under section 11], the tribunal must

take into account any decision of a court relating to the same, or any similar, issue arising in connection with the accident, injury or disease in question.

(4) On [¹ an appeal under section 11 [² the First-tier Tribunal]] may either—

(a) confirm the amounts, rates and periods specified in the certificate of recoverable benefits, or

(b) specify any variations which are to be made on the issue of a fresh certificate under subsection (5) [¹ or

(c) declare that the certificate of recoverable benefits is to be revoked.]

(5) When the Secretary of State has received [¹the decision of the tribunal on the appeal under section 11, he must in accordance with that decision] either—

(a) confirm the certificate against which the appeal was brought, or

(b) issue a fresh certificate [¹ or

(c) revoke the certificate.]

(6) [¹. . .]

(7) Regulations [¹. . .] may (among other things) provide for the nondis-closure of medical advice or medical evidence given or submitted following a reference under subsection (1).

(8) [¹. . .]

AMENDMENTS

1. Social Security Act 1998, Sch.7, para.151 and Sch.8 (November 29, 1999).
2. Transfer of Tribunal Functions Order 2008 (SI 2008/2833), Sch.3 paras 138 and 140 (November 3, 2008).

DEFINITIONS

"recoverable benefit"—see s.1(4)(c).
"regulations"—see s.29.

GENERAL NOTE

This section is applied with modifications to cases concerned with the recovery of payments within the scope of s.1A(2) (see the Social Security (Recovery of Benefits) (Lump Sum Payments) Regulations 2008, reg.2 and Sch.1 para.5).   1.278

Subs.(1)

The primary legislation includes no provision equivalent to s.20 of the Social Security Act 1998. Therefore, even when the tribunal includes a medically qualified panel member, the tribunal has no express power to examine the victim, although there is also no express prohibition on such an examination. Presumably the victim could consent to an examination. There is not even any express power to refer a victim for examination but it is difficult to see any objection to there being such a reference, provided the victim were to consent and some arrangement could be made for the payment of an examining doctor.   1.279

Subs. (3)

Note that the tribunal need only "take into account" any decision of a court; it is not bound by such a decision. This is partly because it would be unfair on the Secretary of State to be bound by a decision in proceedings to which he was not a party *(R(CR) 1/02)*. Most proceedings before courts are settled and do not result in reasoned decisions but claimants and compensators are expected to act before a tribunal in a manner that is consistent with the way they have settled a case or, in the case of a claimant, have claimed benefits. Thus a tribunal should   1.280

be slow to accept an argument advanced by a compensator that is inconsistent with a section 8 deduction that it has made, unless the claimant agrees that the deduction should not have been made, and, equally, a tribunal should be slow to accept an argument advanced by a claimant that is inconsistent with the basis on which compensation was obtained or benefits were claimed (*R(CR) 2/03*). Where a claimant had accepted £50,000 in respect of a claim that injury in respect of which benefits had been paid was due solely to medical negligence, he was not entitled to argue that the benefits were paid otherwise than in respect of that injury (*CCR/2232/2006*).

Similarly, where a compensator had settled a claim made on the basis that psychiatric injury was due to a particular cause, the compensator was not entitled to argue that the injury was due wholly to a cause not covered by the claim for compensation (*R(CR) 1/07*).

Subs. (4)

1.281   In *CCR/4/1993* and *CSCR/1/1995*, Commissioners held that, on appeals, the Secretary of State was entitled to refer to the tribunal questions which related to benefits that were not on the original "certificates of total benefit" (the forerunners of certificates of recoverable benefits). In the first case the Commissioner held that, on an appeal, all matters were at large. In the second case, the Commissioner took a narrower approach and held that a tribunal were strictly confined to the issues referred to them by the Secretary of State but that, in that case, the new benefits were within the scope of the reference. The Commissioner noted the contrast between the position on appeal and the limitation, now contained in s.10(3), with respect to reviews and warned of the perils of appealing.

Under the new legislation as amended, what are before the tribunal by virtue of subs.(1) are the "appeal" under s.11 and all matters that can fairly be said to arise within that appeal—and within the jurisdiction of the tribunal bearing in mind its constitution (see the note to subs.(1) above). There is no provision in this Act equivalent to s.12(8)(a) of the Social Security Act 1998, but it is suggested that the approach should be the same: the tribunal may deal with issues not expressly raised by the notice of appeal but are not bound to do so, provided they exercise that discretion judicially.

Subs. (7)

1.282   Since Tribunal Procedure Rules have replaced regulations made by the Secretary of State, this provision has fallen into disuse. See now r.14(2) to (6) of the Tribunal Procedure (First-tier Tribunal) (Social Entitlement Chamber) Rules 2008.

Appeal to [²Upper Tribunal]

1.283   **13.**—(1) [². . .]

(2) An appeal [² to the Upper Tribunal under section 11 of the Tribunals, Courts and Enforcement Act 2007 which arises from any decision of the First-tier Tribunal under section 12 of this Act] may be made by—

    (a) the Secretary of State,

    (b) the person who applied for the certificate of recoverable benefits,

 [¹(bb) (in a case where that certificate was issued under section 7(2)(a)) the person to whom it was issued, or]

    (c) (in a case where the amount of the compensation payment has been calculated in accordance with section 8) the injured person or other person to whom the payment is made.

    (3) [². . .]

    (4) [¹. . .]

AMENDMENTS

1. Social Security Act 1998, Sch.7, para.152 and Sch.8 (November 29, 1999).
2. Transfer of Tribunal Functions Order 2008 (SI 2008/2833), Sch.3 paras 138 and 141 (November 3, 2008).

DEFINITIONS

"compensation payment"—see s.1(4)(b).
"injured person"—see s.1(4)(a).

GENERAL NOTE

This section is applied with modifications to cases concerned with the recovery of   **1.284**
payments within the scope of s.1A(2) (see the Social Security (Recovery of Benefits) (Lump Sum Payments) Regulations 2008, reg.2 and Sch.1, para.6).

Reviews and appeals: supplementary

14.—(1) This section applies in cases where a fresh certificate of recover-   **1.285**
able benefits is issued as a result of a review under section 10 or an appeal under section 11.

(2) If—
(a) a person has made one or more payments to the Secretary of State under section 6, and
(b) in consequence of the review or appeal, it appears that the total amount paid is more than the amount that ought to have been paid,
regulations may provide for the Secretary of State to pay the difference to that person, or to the person to whom the compensation payment is made, or partly to one and partly to the other.

(3) If—
(a) a person has made one or more payments to the Secretary of State under section 6, and
(b) in consequence of the review or appeal, it appears that the total amount paid is less than the amount that ought to have been paid,
regulations may provide for that person to pay the difference to the Secretary of State.

(4) Regulations under this section may provide—
(a) for the re-calculation in accordance with section 8 of the amount of any compensation payment,
(b) for giving credit for amounts already paid, and
(c) for the payment by any person of any balance or the recovery from any person of any excess,
and may provide for any matter by modifying this Act.

DEFINITIONS

"compensation payment"—see s.1(4)(b).
"payment"—see s.29.
"recoverable benefit"—see s.1(4)(c).
"regulations"—see s.29.

GENERAL NOTE

See reg.11 of the Social Security (Recovery of Benefits) Regulations 1997.   **1.286**
This section is applied with modifications to cases concerned with the recovery of payments within the scope of s.1A(2) (see the Social Security (Recovery

of Benefits) (Lump Sum Payments) Regulations 2008, reg.2 and Sch.1, para.7). Regulation 19 of the 2008 Regulations makes provision equivalent to reg.11 of the 1997 Regulations.

Courts

Court orders

1.287   **15.**—(1) This section applies where a court makes an order for a compensation payment to be made in any case, unless the order is made with the consent of the injured person and the person by whom the payment is to be made.

(2) The court must, in the case of each head of compensation listed in column 1 of Schedule 2 to which any of the compensation payment is attributable, specify in the order the amount of the compensation payment which is attributable to that head.

DEFINITIONS

"compensation payment"—see s.1(4)(b).
"injured person"—see s.1(4)(a).

GENERAL NOTE

A substituted version of this section is applied to cases concerned with the recovery of payments within the scope of s.1A(2) (see the Social Security (Recovery of Benefits) (Lump Sum Payments) Regulations 2008, reg.2 and Sch.1, para.8).

Subs.(2)
1.288   A court hearing a case within five years of a relevant accident must specify the amount of the compensation awarded that was attributable to any particular head in col.1 of Sch.2 in respect of the whole five-year period, because the court cannot know when payment of the sum awarded will actually be made (*Mitchell v Laing*, 1998 S.C. 342). Nonetheless, the compensator was to deduct only those benefits that had been paid or were due to be paid up until the date of the payment of the sum awarded by the court.

The court's view must be taken into account by any tribunal considering an appeal against a certificate of recoverable benefits (see s.12(3)) and, presumably, also by the Secretary of State considering a review (see reg.9(d) of the Social Security and Child Support (Decisions and Appeals) Regulations 1999). However, the principal purpose of s.15(2) is to enable s.8 to be operated properly. There is no express requirement to state the period in respect of which each head of the compensation is paid (which, it has been suggested in *R(CR) 2/04*, is a material fact limiting the amount of any deduction under s.8) but that information will usually be clear from the court's reasoning.

Payments into court

1.289   **16.**—(1) Regulations may make provision (including provision modifying this Act) for any case in which a payment into court is made.

(2) The regulations may (among other things) provide—
  (a) for the making of a payment into court to be treated in prescribed circumstances as the making of a compensation payment,
  (b) for application for, and issue of, certificates of recoverable benefits, and

(c) for the relevant period to be treated as ending on a date determined in accordance with the regulations.

(3) Rules of court may make provision governing practice and procedure in such cases.

(4) This section does not extend to Scotland.

DEFINITIONS

"compensation payment"—see s.1(4)(b).
"recoverable benefit"—see s.1(4)(c).
"payment"—see s.29.
"prescribed"—*ibid.*
"regulations"—*ibid.*
"relevant period"—see s.3.

GENERAL NOTE

Subss.(1) and (2)

Regulation 8 of the Social Security (Recovery of Benefits) Regulations 1997 provides that a payment into court is treated as a compensation payment under the Social Security (Recovery of Benefits) Act 1997 and a current certificate of recoverable benefits must be lodged with it (reg.8(1)). However, the liability of the compensator under s.6 of the Act to pay the Secretary of State the recoverable benefits does not arise until notice has been given that all or part of the payment into court has been paid to the victim (reg.8(2)). If the payment into court is accepted by the victim within 21 days, the "relevant period" under s.3 is taken to have ended on the date the money, or the last part of it, was paid into court (reg.8(3)). If, however, the case is settled after that 21 days have expired and the money is paid to the victim by consent in satisfaction of the claim, the "relevant period" is taken to have ended on the date on which the application to the court for the payment is made (reg.8(4)). If all or part of the money in court is paid to the victim following an order of the court, the "relevant period" is taken to have ended on the date of the order (reg.8(5)). If the whole of the payment into court is returned to the defendant, the making of the payment into court ceases to be treated as the making of a compensation payment and there is no liability to pay anything to the Secretary of State (reg.8(7)).

1.290

Subs.(3)

Part 36 of the Civil Procedure Rules deals with offers to settle cases in England and Wales. Rule 36.15 provides—

1.291

"(1) In this rule and rule 36.9—
   (a) "the 1997 Act" means the Social Security (Recovery of Benefits) Act 1997;
   (b) "the 2008 Regulations" means the Social Security (Recovery of Benefits) (Lump Sum Payments) Regulations 2008;
   (c) "recoverable amount" means—
      (i) "recoverable benefits" as defined in section 1(4)(c) of the 1997 Act; and
      (ii) "recoverable lump sum payments" as defined in regulation 4 of the 2008 Regulations;
   (d) "deductible amount" means—
      (i) any benefits by the amount of which damages are to be reduced in accordance with section 8 of, and Schedule 2 to, the 1997 Act ("deductible benefits"); and
      (ii) any lump sum payment by the amount of which damages are to be reduced in accordance with regulation 12 of the 2008 Regulations ("deductible lump sum payments"); and
   (e) "certificate"—

     (i) in relation to recoverable benefits is construed in accordance with the provisions of the 1997 Act; and

    (ii) in relation to recoverable lump sum payments has the meaning given in section 29 of the 1997 Act as applied by regulation 2 of, and modified by Schedule 1 to, the 2008 Regulations.

(2) This rule applies where a payment to a claimant following acceptance of a Part 36 offer would be a compensation payment as defined in section 1(4)(b) or 1A(5)(b) of the 1997 Act.

(3) A defendant who makes a Part 36 offer should state either—

  (a) that the offer is made without regard to any liability for recoverable amounts; or

  (b) that it is intended to include any deductible amounts.

(4) Where paragraph (3)(b) applies, paragraphs (5) to (9) of this rule will apply to the Part 36 offer.

(5) Before making the Part 36 offer, the offeror must apply for a certificate.

(6) Subject to paragraph (7), the Part 36 offer must state—

  (a) the amount of gross compensation;

  (b) the name and amount of any deductible amount by which the gross amount is reduced; and

  (c) the net amount of compensation.

(7) If at the time the offeror makes the Part 36 offer, the offeror has applied for, but has not received a certificate, the offeror must clarify the offer by stating the matters referred to in paragraphs (6)(b) and (6)(c) not more than 7 days after receipt of the certificate.

(8) For the purposes of rule 36.14(1)(a), a claimant fails to recover more than any sum offered (including a lump sum offered under rule 36.5) if the claimant fails upon judgment being entered to recover a sum, once deductible amounts identified in the judgment have been deducted, greater than the net amount stated under paragraph (6)(c).

(Section 15(2) of the 1997 Act provides that the court must specify the compensation payment attributable to each head of damage. Schedule 1 to the 2008 Regulations modifies section 15 of the 1997 Act in relation to lump sum payments and provides that the court must specify the compensation payment attributable to each or any dependant who has received a lump sum payment.)

(9) Where—

  (a) further deductible amounts have accrued since the Part 36 offer was made; and

  (b) the court gives permission to accept the Part 36 offer,

the court may direct that the amount of the offer payable to the offeree shall be reduced by a sum equivalent to the deductible amounts paid to the claimant since the date of the offer.

(Rule 36.9(3)(b) states that permission is required to accept an offer where the relevant period has expired and further deductible amounts have been paid to the claimant)"

The effect of CPR r.36.14 is that a failure to recover a sum greater than the amount offered under Pt.36 is usually that the claimant has to pay any costs incurred by the defendant after the latest date the offer could have been accepted without the permission of the court. Rule 36.15(8), which makes it clear that the relevant sum is the net amount after deductions have been made under s.8, is therefore an improvement on the previous r.36.23(4) and (4A) in force before April 6, 2007, which referred to the gross amount offered and caused problems when a deduction had been made that was more than properly allowed under s.8.

Benefits irrelevant to assessment of damages

1.292   **17.** In assessing damages in respect of any accident, injury or disease, the amount of any listed benefits paid or likely to be paid is to be disregarded.

DEFINITION

"listed benefit"—see s.29.

GENERAL NOTE

Benefits are disregarded not only when assessing damages but also when calculating interest on the damages, so that recoverable benefits are not to be deducted from damages for loss of earnings before calculating the interest due (*Wisely v John Fulton (Plumbers) Ltd, Wadey v Surrey CC* [2000] 1 W.L.R. 820 (HL)). **1.293**

This section is applied with modifications to cases concerned with the recovery of payments within the scope of s.1A(2) (see the Social Security (Recovery of Benefits) (Lump Sum Payments) Regulations 2008, reg.2 and Sch.1, para.9).

Reduction of compensation: complex cases

Lump sum and periodical payments

18.—(1) Regulations may make provision (including provision modifying this Act) for any case in which two or more compensation payments in the form of lump sums are made by the same person to or in respect of the injured person in consequence of the same accident, injury or disease. **1.294**

(2) The regulations may (among other things) provide—

(a) for the re-calculation in accordance with section 8 of the amount of any compensation payment,

(b) for giving credit for amounts already paid, and

(c) for the payment by any person of any balance or the recovery from any person of any excess.

(3) For the purposes of subsection (2), the regulations may provide for the gross amounts of the compensation payments to be aggregated and for—

(a) the aggregate amount to be taken to be the gross amount of the compensation payment for the purposes of section 8,

(b) so much of the aggregate amount as is attributable to a head of compensation listed in column 1 of Schedule 2 to be taken to be the part of the gross amount which is attributable to that head;

and for the amount of any recoverable benefit shown against any head in column 2 of that Schedule to be taken to be the amount determined in accordance with the most recent certificate of recoverable benefits.

(4) Regulations may make provision (including provision modifying this Act) for any case in which, in final settlement of the injured person's claim, an agreement is entered into for the making of—

(a) periodical compensation payments (whether of an income or capital nature), or

(b) periodical compensation payments and lump sum compensation payments.

(5) Regulations made by virtue of subsection (4) may (among other things) provide—

(a) for the relevant period to be treated as ending at a prescribed time,

(b) for the person who is to make the payments under the agreement to be treated for the purposes of this Act as if he had made a single compensation payment on a prescribed date.

(6) A periodical payment may be a compensation payment for the purposes of this section even though it is a small payment (as defined in Part II of Schedule 1).

DEFINITIONS

"amount of any recoverable benefit"—see s.9(4)(b).
"compensation payment"—see.1(4)(b).
"gross amount of the compensation payment"—see s.9(4)(a).
"injured person"—see s.29.
"recoverable benefit"—see s.1(4)(c).
"payment"—see s.29.
"prescribed"—*ibid.*
"regulations"—*ibid.*
"the relevant period"—see s.3.

GENERAL NOTE

1.295   Regulation 9 of the Social Security (Recovery of Benefits) Regulations 1997 is made under subss.(1) to (3) and reg.10 is made under subss (4) and (5).

This section is applied with modifications to cases concerned with the recovery of payments within the scope of s.1A(2) (see the Social Security (Recovery of Benefits) (Lump Sum Payments) Regulations 2008, reg.2 and Sch.1, para.10). Regulations 14 and 18 of the 2008 Regulations make provision equivalent to regs.9 and 10 of the 1997 Regulations.

Payments by more than one person

1.296   **19.**—(1) Regulations may make provision (including provision modifying this Act) for any case in which two or more persons ("the compensators") make compensation payments to or in respect of the same injured person in consequence of the same accident, injury or disease.

(2) In such a case, the sum of the liabilities of the compensators under section 6 is not to exceed the total amount of the recoverable benefits, and the regulations may provide for determining the respective liabilities under that section of each of the compensators.

(3) The regulations may (among other things) provide in the case of each compensator—

(a) for determining or re-determining the part of the recoverable benefits which may be taken into account in his case,
(b) for calculating or re-calculating in accordance with section 8 the amount of any compensation payment,
(c) for giving credit for amounts already paid, and
(d) for the payment by any person of any balance or the recovery from any person of any excess.

DEFINITIONS

"amount of any recoverable benefit"—see s.9(4)(b).
"compensation payment"—see s.1(4)(b).
"compensator"—see subs.(1).
"injured person"—see s.1(4)(a).
"recoverable benefit"—see s.1(4)(c).
"payment"—see s.29.
"regulations"—*ibid.*
"the relevant period"—see s.3.

GENERAL NOTE

See reg.9 of the Social Security (Recovery of Benefits) Regulations 1997. Note that the liability for benefits paid before the making of the first compensation payment generally falls on the compensator who makes that payment and there is no provision for apportionment as such. Compensators therefore need to co-operate among themselves to ensure that the burden of making payments to the Secretary of State is shared appropriately. Note also that no provision can be made for cases where a claimant's disablement is attributable to two successive accidents caused by the negligence or breach of statutory duty of different compensators. The payment of benefits in consequence of the disablement must therefore be attributed solely to one accident or the other so that only one of the compensators is liable to make payments to the Secretary of State *(R(CR) 2/04* and see the note to s.1 for how the attribution is to be made).

This section is applied with modifications to cases concerned with the recovery of payments within the scope of s.1A(2) (see the Social Security (Recovery of Benefits) (Lump Sum Payments) Regulations 2008, reg.2 and Sch.1, para.11). Regulation 14 of the 2008 Regulations makes provision equivalent to reg.9 of the 1997 Regulations.

1.297

Miscellaneous

Amounts overpaid under section 6

20.—(1) Regulations may make provision (including provision modifying this Act) for cases where a person has paid to the Secretary of State under section 6 any amount ("the amount of the overpayment") which he was not liable to pay.

1.298

(2) The regulations may provide—

(a) for the Secretary of State to pay the amount of the overpayment to that person, or to the person to whom the compensation payment is made, or partly to one and partly to the other, or

(b) for the receipt by the Secretary of State of the amount of the overpayment to be treated as the recovery of that amount.

(3) Regulations made by virtue of subsection (2)(b) are to have effect in spite of anything in section 71 of the Social Security Administration Act 1992 (overpayments—general).

(4) The regulations may also (among other things) provide—

(a) for the re-calculation in accordance with section 8 of the amount of any compensation payment,

(b) for giving credit for amounts already paid, and

(c) for the payment by any person of any balance or the recovery from any person of any excess.

(5) This section does not apply in a case where section 14 applies.

DEFINITIONS

"compensation payment"—see s.1(4)(b).
"payment"—see s.29.
"regulations"—*ibid.*
"the amount of the overpayment"—see subs.(1).

GENERAL NOTE

No regulations have been made under this section.

1.299

The section is nonetheless applied with modifications to cases concerned with the recovery of payments within the scope of s.1A(2) (see the Social Security (Recovery of Benefits) (Lump Sum Payments) Regulations 2008, reg.2 and Sch.1, para.12).

Compensation payments to be disregarded

1.300 **21.**—(1) If, when a compensation payment is made, the first and second conditions are met, the payment is to be disregarded for the purposes of sections 6 and 8.

(2) The first condition is that the person making the payment—

(a) has made an application for a certificate of recoverable benefits which complies with subsection (3), and

(b) has in his possession a written acknowledgement of the receipt of his application.

(3) An application complies with this subsection if it—

(a) accurately states the prescribed particulars relating to the injured person and the accident, injury or disease in question, and

(b) specifies the name and address of the person to whom the certificate is to be sent.

(4) The second condition is that the Secretary of State has not sent the certificate to the person, at the address, specified in the application, before the end of the period allowed under section 4.

(5) In any case where—

(a) by virtue of subsection (1), a compensation payment is disregarded for the purposes of sections 6 and 8, but

(b) the person who made the compensation payment nevertheless makes a payment to the Secretary of State for which (but for subsection (1)) he would be liable under section 6,

subsection (1) is to cease to apply in relation to the compensation payment.

(6) If, in the opinion of the Secretary of State, circumstances have arisen which adversely affect normal methods of communication—

(a) he may by order provide that subsection (1) is not to apply during a specified period not exceeding three months, and

(b) he may continue any such order in force for further periods not exceeding three months at a time.

DEFINITIONS

"compensation payment"—see s.1(4)(b).
"injured person"—see s.29.
"payment"—see s.29.
"prescribed—*ibid.*
"recoverable benefit"—see s.1(4)(c).

GENERAL NOTE

1.301   If a certificate of recoverable benefits is not issued within four weeks (subject to subs.(6)) following receipt and acknowledgement of a full and accurate application, the Secretary of State loses his right of recovery. It is clear from subs.(4) that the late issue of a certificate will not do. However, if the compensator makes a payment to the Secretary of State in error—perhaps in reliance on an expired certificate—the Secretary of State is not obliged to pay it back because the dispensation under this

184

section ceases to apply (subs.(5)). For the date on which an application is treated as received, see reg.7(2) of the Social Security (Recovery of Benefits) Regulations 1997 which is made under s.4(9).

This section is applied with modifications to cases concerned with the recovery of payments within the scope of s.1A(2) (see the Social Security (Recovery of Benefits) (Lump Sum Payments) Regulations 2008, reg.2 and Sch.1, para.13).

Subs.(3)

For the prescribed particulars, see reg.7(1) of the Social Security (Recovery of Benefits) Regulations 1997. **1.302**

Subs.(4)

The period allowed under s.4(3) and (8) is four weeks, but see s.21(6). **1.303**

Subs.(5)

It is not clear whether the Secretary of State can, by issuing an out of time certificate, insist on obtaining more than the payment made by the compensator or whether he is confined to accepting what has been sent, which is likely to have been based on an earlier certificate. **1.304**

22. *Omitted.* **1.305**

Provision of information

23.—(1) Where compensation is sought in respect of any accident, injury or disease suffered by any person ("the injured person"), the following persons must give the Secretary of State the prescribed information about the injured person— **1.306**

  (a) anyone who is, or is alleged to be, liable in respect of the accident, injury or disease, and

  (b) anyone acting on behalf of such a person.

(2) A person who receives or claims a listed benefit which is or is likely to be paid in respect of an accident, injury or disease suffered by him, must give the Secretary of State the prescribed information about the accident, injury or disease.

(3) Where a person who has received a listed benefit dies, the duty in subsection (2) is imposed on his personal representative.

(4) Any person who makes a payment (whether on his own behalf or not)—

  (a) in consequence of, or

  (b) which is referable to any costs (in Scotland, expenses) incurred by reason of,

any accident, injury or disease, or any damage to property, must, if the Secretary of State requests him in writing to do so, give the Secretary of State such particulars relating to the size and composition of the payment as are specified in the request.

(5) The employer of a person who suffers or has suffered an accident, injury or disease, and anyone who has been the employer of such a person at any time during the relevant period, must give the Secretary of State the prescribed information about the payment of statutory sick pay in respect of that person.

(6) In subsection (5) "employer" has the same meaning as it has in Part XI of the Social Security Contributions and Benefits Act 1992.

(7) A person who is required to give information under this section must do so in the prescribed manner, at the prescribed place and within the prescribed time.

(8) Section 1 does not apply in relation to this section.

DEFINITIONS

"employer"—see subs.(6).
"injured person"—see subs.(1) (and subs.(8), disapplying s.1).
"listed benefit"—see s.29.
"payment"—*ibid.*
"prescribed"—*ibid.*
"the relevant period"—see s.3.

GENERAL NOTE

1.307   Regulations 3, 4, 5 and 6 of the Social Security (Recovery of Benefits) Regulations 1997 are made under subss (1), (2), (5) and (7) respectively.

This section is applied with modifications (which, among other things, disapply subss (5), (6) and (8)) to cases concerned with the recovery of payments within the scope of s.1A(2). See the Social Security (Recovery of Benefits) (Lump Sum Payments) Regulations 2008, reg. 2 and Sch.1, para.15. Regulations 15, 16 and 17 of the 2008 Regulations respectively make provision equivalent to regs 3, 4 and 6 of the 1997 Regulations.

Power to amend Schedule 2

1.308   **24.**—(1) The Secretary of State may by regulations amend Schedule 2.

(2) A statutory instrument which contains such regulations shall not be made unless a draft of the instrument has been laid before and approved by resolution of each House of Parliament.

DEFINITION

"regulations"—see s.29.

Provisions relating to Northern Ireland

1.309   **25.–27.** *Omitted.*

General

The Crown

1.310   **28.** This Act applies to the Crown.

GENERAL NOTE

1.311   This is effectively a new provision because s.104 of the Social Security Administration Act 1992 was never brought into force (see Social Security (Consequential Provisions) Act 1992, Sch.4, para.3). It is applied to cases concerned with the recovery of payments within the scope of s.1A(2) (see the Social Security (Recovery of Benefits) (Lump Sum Payments) Regulations 2008, reg.2).

General interpretation

29. In this Act—   1.312
[².. .]
"benefit" means any benefit under the Social Security Contributions and Benefits Act 1992, a jobseeker's allowance [¹, an employment and support allowance] or mobility allowance,
[².. .]
"compensation scheme for motor accidents" means any scheme or arrangement under which funds are available for the payment of compensation in respect of motor accidents caused, or alleged to have been caused, by uninsured or unidentified persons,
"listed benefit" means a benefit listed in column 2 of Schedule 2,
"payment" means payment in money or money's worth, and related expressions are to be interpreted accordingly,
"prescribed" means prescribed by regulations, and
"regulations" means regulations made by the Secretary of State.

AMENDMENTS

1. Employment and Support Allowance (Consequential Provisions) (No. 2) Regulations 2008 (SI 2008/1554), reg.50(1) and (2) (October 27, 2008).
2. Transfer of Tribunal Functions Order (SI 2008/2833), Sch.3, paras 138 and 142 (November 3, 2008).

GENERAL NOTE

This section is applied with modifications to cases concerned with the recovery of   1.313
payments within the scope of s.1A(2) (see the Social Security (Recovery of Benefits) (Lump Sum Payments) Regulations 2008, reg.2 and Sch.1, para.18). In particular, "certificate" is defined as meaning "a certificate which includes amounts in respect of recoverable benefits and of recoverable lump sum payments, including where any of those amounts are nil".

Regulations and orders

30.—(1) Any power under this Act to make regulations or an order is   1.314
exercisable by statutory instrument.
(2) A statutory instrument containing regulations or an order under this Act (other than regulations under section 24 or an order under section 34) shall be subject to annulment in pursuance of a resolution of either House of Parliament.
(3) Regulations under section 20, under section 24 amending the list of benefits in column 2 of Schedule 2 or under paragraph 9 of Schedule 1 may not be made without the consent of the Treasury.
(4) Subsections (4), (5), (6) and (9) of section 189 of the Social Security Administration Act 1992 (regulations and orders—general) apply for the purposes of this Act as they apply for the purposes of that.

DEFINITIONS

"benefit"—see s.29.
"regulations"—*ibid.*

1.315   This section is applied to cases concerned with the recovery of payments within the scope of s.1A(2) (see the Social Security (Recovery of Benefits) (Lump Sum Payments) Regulations 2008, reg.2).

1.316   **31.** *Omitted.*

Power to make transitional, consequential etc. provisions

1.317   **32.**—(1) Regulations may make such transitional and consequential provisions, and such savings, as the Secretary of State considers necessary or expedient in preparation for, in connection with, or in consequence of—

(a) the coming into force of any provision of this Act, or

(b) the operation of any enactment repealed or amended by a provision of this Act during any period when the repeal or amendment is not wholly in force.

(2) Regulations under this section may (among other things) provide—

(a) for compensation payments in relation to which, by virtue of section 2, this Act does not apply to be treated as payments in relation to which this Act applies,

(b) for compensation payments in relation to which, by virtue of section 2, this Act applies to be treated as payments in relation to which this Act does not apply, and

(c) for the modification of any enactment contained in this Act or referred to in subsection (1)(b) in its application to any compensation payment.

DEFINITIONS

"compensation payment"—see s.1(4)(b).
"payment"—see s.29.
"regulations"—*ibid.*

GENERAL NOTE

1.318   See reg.12 of the Social Security (Recovery of Benefits) Regulations 1997.

1.319   **33.** *Omitted.*

Short title, commencement and extent

1.320   **34.**—(1) This Act may be cited as the Social Security (Recovery of Benefits) Act 1997.

(2) Sections 1 to 24, 26 to 28 and 33 are to come into force on such day as the Secretary of State may by order appoint, and different days may be appointed for different purposes.

(3) Apart from sections 25 to 27, section 33 so far as it relates to any enactment which extends to Northern Ireland, and this section this Act does not extend to Northern Ireland.

GENERAL NOTE

1.321   Some regulation-making powers were brought into force on September 3, 1997 but the main provisions of the Act came into force on October 6, 1997 (see the Social Security (Recovery of Benefits) Act 1997 (Commencement Order) 1997 (SI 1997/2085)).

Subss.(1) and (3) are applied to cases concerned with the recovery of payments within the scope of s.1A(2) (see the Social Security (Recovery of Benefits) (Lump Sum Payments) Regulations 2008, reg.2).

SCHEDULES

SCHEDULE 1

COMPENSATION PAYMENTS

PART I

Exempted payments

1. Any small payment (defined in Part II of this Schedule).

2. Any payment made to or for the injured person under section 35 of the Powers of Criminal Courts Act 1973 or section 249 of the Criminal Procedure (Scotland) Act 1995 (compensation orders against convicted persons).

3. Any payment made in the exercise of a discretion out of property held subject to a trust in a case where no more than 50 per cent. by value of the capital contributed to the trust was directly or indirectly provided by persons who are, or are alleged to be, liable in respect of—

  (a) the accident, injury or disease suffered by the injured person, or

  (b) the same or any connected accident, injury or disease suffered by another.

4. Any payment made out of property held for the purposes of any prescribed trust (whether the payment also falls within paragraph 3 or not).

5. Any payment made to the injured person by an insurance company within the meaning of the Insurance Companies Act 1982 under the terms of any contract of insurance entered into between the injured person and the company before—

  (a) the date on which the injured person first claims a listed benefit in consequence of the disease in question, or

  (b) the occurrence of the accident or injury in question.

6. Any redundancy payment falling to be taken into account in the assessment of damages in respect of an accident, injury or disease.

7. So much of any payment as is referable to costs.

8. Any prescribed payment.

PART II

Power to disregard small payments

9.—(1) Regulations may make provision for compensation payments to be disregarded for the purposes of sections 6 and 8 in prescribed cases where the amount of the compensation payment, or the aggregate amount of two or more connected compensation payments, does not exceed the prescribed sum.

(2) A compensation payment disregarded by virtue of this paragraph is referred to in paragraph 1 as a "small payment".

(3) For the purposes of this paragraph—

  (a) two or more compensation payments are "connected" if each is made to or in respect of the same injured person and in respect of the same accident, injury or disease, and

  (b) any reference to a compensation payment is a reference to a payment which would be such a payment apart from paragraph 1.

DEFINITIONS

"compensation payment"—see s.1(4)(b) and para.9(3)(b).

"connected"—see para.9(3)(a).

"injured person"—see s.1(4)(a).

"listed benefit" –see s.29.

"payment"—*ibid.*

"prescribed"—*ibid.*

1.322

1.323

"regulations"—*ibid.*
"small payment"—see para.9.

GENERAL NOTE

1.324   For exempted trusts and payments prescribed for the purposes of paras 4 and 8, see reg.2 of the Social Security (Recovery of Benefits) Regulations 1997.

No regulations have been made under para.9. Under the former legislation, payments not exceeding £2,500 were disregarded. Now, general damages for pain and suffering are protected, because benefits can be recovered only from compensation for loss of earnings, care or loss of mobility, and so there is not considered to be a need for a general exemption for small claims.

This Schedule is applied with modifications to cases concerned with the recovery of payments within the scope of s.1A(2). See the Social Security (Recovery of Benefits) (Lump Sum Payments) Regulations 2008, reg.2 and Sch.1, paras 19 and 20. Regulation 7 of the 2008 Regulations makes provision equivalent to reg.2 of the 1997 Regulations.

SCHEDULE 2

CALCULATION OF COMPENSATION PAYMENT

(1) Head of compensation	(2) Benefit
1. Compensation for earnings lost during the relevant period	Disability working allowance Disablement pension payable under section 103 of the 1992 Act [¹Employment and support allowance] Incapacity benefit Income support Invalidity pension and allowance Jobseeker's allowance Reduced earnings allowance Severe disablement allowance Sickness benefit Statutory sick pay Unemployability supplement Unemployment benefit
2. Compensation for cost of care incurred during the relevant period	Attendance allowance Care component of disability living allowance Disablement pension increase payable under section 104 or 105 of the 1992 Act
3. Compensation for loss of mobility during the relevant period.	Mobility allowance Mobility component of disability living allowance

Notes

1.326   **1.**—(1) References to incapacity benefit, invalidity pension and allowance, severe disablement allowance, sickness benefit and unemployment benefit also include any income support paid with each of those benefits on the same instrument of payment or paid concurrently with each of those benefits by means of an instrument for benefit payment.

(2) For the purpose of this Note, income support includes personal expenses addition, special transitional additions and transitional addition as defined in the Income Support (Transitional) Regulations 1987.

2. Any reference to statutory sick pay—
    (a) includes only 80 per cent. of payments made between 6th April 1991 and 5th April 1994, and
    (b) does not include payments made on or after 6th April 1994.

190

3. In this Schedule "the 1992 Act" means the Social Security Contributions and Benefits Act 1992.

AMENDMENT

1. Employment and Support Allowance (Consequential Provisions) (No. 2) Regulations 2008 (SI 2008/1554), reg.50(1) and (3) (October 27, 2008).

DEFINITIONS

"compensation payment"—see s.1(4)(b).
"payment"—*ibid.*
"the relevant period"—see s.3.

GENERAL NOTE

In *R(CR) 2/04*, the Commissioner commented that disablement pension was not, strictly speaking, paid in respect of loss of earnings.   1.327

In *Lowther v Chatwin* [2003] EWCA Civ 729, the claimant had to close her business due to injuries sustained in an accident. She had been trading at a loss but had been able to pay 5/7ths of her business rent from the income of the business. She claimed damages in respect of her continuing liability to her landlord. The judge awarded her 5/7ths of the rent settlement and he held that that compensation was not for loss of earnings but for the destruction of the business. The Court of Appeal held that it was "compensation for earnings lost" and that the compensator was therefore entitled to deduct from that compensation the amount of relevant benefits paid to the claimant.

"Compensation for earnings lost" includes interest on damages for loss of earnings (*Griffiths v British Coal Corp* [2001] EWCA Civ 336 (*The Times*, March 13, 2001).

Given the way that ss.6 and 8 operate together, compensation for lost earnings presumably includes compensation for loss of *potential* earnings in the case of a person who was not employed at the time of a relevant accident or who was in temporary employment only. A benefit is recoverable only if it was paid "in respect of" the relevant accident, injury or disease (see the note to s.1).

"Compensation for cost of care" includes damages for services in the nature of care and domestic assistance given gratuitously, because the object of the legislation is to avoid double recovery as well as avoiding loss to the Secretary of State who had become liable to pay the benefits (*Griffiths v British Coal Corp* [2001] EWCA Civ 336; [2001] 1 W.L.R. 1493).

"Compensation for loss of mobility" in para.3, col.1 refers only to compensation for patrimonial (i.e. financial) loss, such as the cost of fares for journeys by bus or taxi, and does not refer to any element of solatium (i.e. compensation for pain and suffering or loss of amenity) (*Mitchell v Laing*, 1998 S.C. 342).

Schedules 3 and 4: Omitted.

Social Security Act 1998

(1998 C.14)

ARRANGEMENT OF SECTIONS

PART I

DECISIONS AND APPEALS

CHAPTER I

GENERAL

Decisions

CHAPTER II

SOCIAL SECURITY DECISIONS AND APPEALS

Decisions

Appeals

Social fund payment

36. to 38.   *Omitted.*

Supplemental

39.   Interpretation etc. of Chapter II.

CHAPTER III

OTHER DECISIONS AND APPEALS

40. to 47.   *Omitted.*

PART II

CONTRIBUTIONS

48. to 66.   *Omitted.*

PART III

BENEFITS

67. to 76.   *Omitted.*

PART IV

MISCELLANEOUS AND SUPPLEMENTAL

77.   Pilot schemes.
78.   *Omitted.*
79.   Regulations and orders.
80.   Parliamentary control of regulations.
81.   Reports by Secretary of State.
82.   *Omitted.*
83.   *Omitted.*
84.   Interpretation: general.
85.   *Omitted.*
86.   *Omitted.*
87.   Short title, commencement and extent.

SCHEDULES:

Schedule 1—*Repealed.*
Schedule 2—Decisions against which no appeal lies.

An Act to make provision as to the making of decisions and the determination of appeals under enactments relating to social security, child support, vaccine damage payments and war pensions; to make further provision with respect to social security; and for connected purposes.

[21st May 1998]

PART I

DECISIONS AND APPEALS

CHAPTER I

GENERAL

Decisions

Transfer of functions to Secretary of State

1. *Omitted*

1.329

Use of computers

2.—(1) Any decision, determination or assessment falling to be made or certificate falling to be issued by the Secretary of State under or by virtue of a relevant enactment, or in relation to a war pension, may be made or issued not only by an officer of his acting under his authority but also—

1.330

  (a) by a computer for whose operation such an officer is responsible; and

  (b) in the case of a decision, determination or assessment that may be made or a certificate that may be issued by a person providing services to the Secretary of State, by a computer for whose operation such a person is responsible.

(2) In this section "relevant enactment" means any enactment contained in—

  (a) Chapter II of this Part;

  (b) the Social Security Contributions and Benefits Act 1992 ("the Contributions and Benefits Act");

  (c) the Administration Act;

  (d) the Child Support Act;

  (e) the Social Security (Incapacity for Work) Act 1994;

  (f) the Jobseekers Act 1995 ("the Jobseekers Act");

(g) the Child Support Act 1995; [¹ . . .]
(h) the Social Security (Recovery of Benefits) Act 1997 [¹ or
(i) the State Pension Credit Act 2002;]
[²(j) Part 1 of the Welfare Reform Act 2007.]
(3) In this section and section 3 below "war pension" has the same meaning as in section 25 of the Social Security Act 1989 (establishment and functions of war pensions committees).

AMENDMENTS

1. State Pension Credit Act 2002, Sch.1, para.5 and Sch.3 (July 2, 2002 for the purpose of exercising any power to make regulations or orders and April 7, 2003 for other purposes).
2. Welfare Reform Act 2007, Sch.3, para.17(1) and (2) (July 27, 2008).

DEFINITIONS

"the Administration Act"—see s.84.
"the Child Support Act"—*ibid.*
"relevant enactment"—see subs.(2).
"war pension"—see subs.(3).

GENERAL NOTE

1.331   This section applies as though the Pension Schemes Act 1993 were a relevant enactment (Pension Schemes Act 1993, s.170(1)).
In *C3/07-08(IS)*, a Deputy Commissioner in Northern Ireland was highly critical of the failure of computer-generated letters issued in Northern Ireland to reflect the statutory provisions for decision-making in the Northern Ireland equivalent to this Act. He held a decision that failed adequately to inform the recipient of her rights to seek reasons or to appeal to be so defective as to be invalid.

Use of information

1.332   **3.**—(1) Subsection (2) below applies to information relating to [² any of the matters specified in subsection (1A) below] which is held—
(a) by the Secretary of State or the Northern Ireland Department; or
(b) by a person providing services to the Secretary of State or the Northern Ireland Department in connection with the provision of those services.
[² (1A) The matters are—
(a) social security, child support or war pensions;
(b) employment or training;
(c) private pensions policy;
(d) retirement planning.]
(2) Information to which this subsection applies—
(a) may be used for the purposes of, or for any purposes connected with, the exercise of functions in relation to [² any of the matters specified in subsection (1A) above]; and
(b) may be supplied to, or to a person providing services to, the Secretary of State or the Northern Ireland Department for use for those purposes.
(3) [¹ . . .]
(4) In this section "the Northern Ireland Department" means the Department of Health and Social Services for Northern Ireland [¹ the Department for Employment and learning in Northern Ireland].

[² (5) In this section—

"private pensions policy" means policy relating to occupational pension schemes for personal pension schemes (within the meaning given by section 1 of the Pension Schemes Act 1993);

"retirement planning" means promoting financial planning for retirement.]

AMENDMENT

1. Employment Act 2002, Sch.6, paras 1 and 4 (September 9, 2002).
2. Pensions Act 2004, Sch.10, para.1 (November 18, 2004).

DEFINITIONS

"the Administration Act"—see s.84.
"the Northern Ireland Department"—see subs.(4).
"private pensions policy"—see subs.(5).
"retirement planning"—ibid.
"war pension"—see s.2(3).

Appeals

4. [¹ ...]   1.333

AMENDMENT

1. Transfer of Tribunal Functions Order 2008 (SI 2008/2833), Sch.3, paras 143 and 144 (November 3, 2008).

5.–7. [¹ ...]

AMENDMENT

1. Transfer of Tribunal Functions Order 2008 (SI 2008/2833), Sch.3, paras 143 and 145 to 147 (November 3, 2008), subject to a saving under art.1(5).

GENERAL NOTE

These sections made provision for appeal tribunals, to whom appeals lay under   1.334
s.12 and from whom appeals lay to Social Security Commissioners under s.14. Both the appeal tribunals and Commissioners also had functions under other legislation. Subject to one exception, the functions of appeal tribunals constituted under this Act and Commissioners have been transferred respectively to the First-tier Tribunal and the Upper Tribunal. The exception is the determination by appeal tribunals of appeals referred by Scottish Ministers under s.158 of the Health and Social Care (Community Health and Standards) Act 2003 and the determination by Commissioners of appeals against such determinations under s.159. Those functions relate to the recovery of National Health Service charges in Scotland and could not be transferred because health is a devolved function in Scotland. Therefore, although ss. 5 to 7 are repealed for all other purposes, art.1(5) of the Transfer of Tribunal Functions Order 2008 has the effect that those provisions, and a number of other provisions relating to the appointment of appeal tribunals and Commissioners and their procedural rules, remain in force in Scotland for the purposes of the 2003 Act. In England and Wales, s.158 of the 2003 Act has been

amended by the 2008 Order and now provides for the Secretary of State to refer appeals to the First-tier Tribunal.

CHAPTER II

SOCIAL SECURITY DECISIONS AND APPEALS

Decisions

Decisions by Secretary of State

1.335
8.—(1) Subject to the provisions of this Chapter, it shall be for the Secretary of State—
  (a) to decide any claim for a relevant benefit;
  (b) to decide any claim for a social fund payment mentioned in section 138(1)(b) of the Contributions and Benefits Act; [¹ and]
  (c) subject to subsection (5) below, to make any decision that falls to be made under or by virtue of a relevant enactment; [¹ . . .]
  (d) [¹ . . .]
  (2) Where at any time a claim for a relevant benefit is decided by the Secretary of State—
  (a) the claim shall not be regarded as subsisting after that time; and
  (b) accordingly, the claimant shall not (without making a further claim) be entitled to the benefit on the basis of circumstances not obtaining at that time.
  (3) In this Chapter "relevant benefit" [² . . .] means any of the following, namely—
  (a) benefit under Parts II to V of the Contributions and Benefits Act;
  (b) a jobseeker's allowance;
[⁵(ba) an employment and support allowance]
[³(bb) state pension credit;]
  (c) income support;
  (d) [⁴ . . .];
  (e) [⁴ . . .];
  (f) a social fund payment mentioned in section 138(1)(a) or (2) of the Contributions and Benefits Act;
  (g) child benefit;
  (h) such other benefit as may be prescribed.
  (4) In this section "relevant enactment" means any enactment contained in this Chapter, the Contributions and Benefits Act, the Administration Act, the Social Security (Consequential Provisions) Act 1992 [³, the Jobseekers Act [⁵, the State Pension Credit Act 2002 or Part 1 of the Welfare Reform Act 2007], other than one contained in—
  (a) Part VII of the Contributions and Benefits Act so far as relating to housing benefit and council tax benefit;
  (b) Part VIII of the Administration Act (arrangements for housing benefit and council tax benefit and related subsidies).

(5) [¹ Subsection (1)(c) above does not include any decision which under section 8 of the Social Security Contributions (Transfer of Functions, etc.) Act 1999 falls to be made by an officer of the Inland Revenue.]

AMENDMENTS

1. Social Security Contributions (Transfer of Functions, etc.) Act 1999, Sch.7, para.22 (April 1, 1999).
2. Welfare Reform and Pensions Act 1999, s.88 and Sch.13 (April 6, 2000).
3. State Pension Credit Act 2002, Sch.1, para.6 (July 2, 2002 for the purpose of exercising any power to make regulations or orders and April 7, 2003 for other purposes).
4. Tax Credits Act 2002, Sch.6 (April 8, 2003, subject to a saving in respect of outstanding questions concerning work families' tax credit and disabled person's tax credit—see Tax Credits Act 2002 (Commencement No.4, Transitional Provisions and Savings) Order 2003 (SI 2003/962), art.3(1)–(3)).
5. Welfare Reform Act 2007, Sch.3, para.17(1) and (3) of (July 27, 2008 (March 18, 2008 for regulation-making purposes)).

DEFINITIONS

"the Administration Act"—see s.84.
"claim"—by virtue of s.39(2), see s.191 of the Social Security Administration Act 1992.
"claimant"—see s.39(1) and, by virtue of s.39(2), see s.191 of the Social Security Administration Act 1992.
"the Contributions and Benefits Act"—see s.84.
"Inland Revenue"—by virtue of s.39(2), see s.191 of the Social Security Administration Act 1992 but note that the Inland Revenue has been merged into Her Majesty's Revenue and Customs by the Commissioners for Revenue and Customs Act 2005.
"the Jobseekers Act"—see s.84.
"prescribed"—*ibid.*
"relevant enactment"—see subs.(4).
"relevant benefit"—see subs.(3).

GENERAL NOTE

This section makes general provision for initial decisions by the Secretary of State. However, by Tax Credits Act 1999, s.2(1)(b) and Sch.2, para.5(b)(i), the functions of making initial decisions in respect of working families' tax credit and disabled person's tax credit (both now abolished) were transferred to officers of the Inland Revenue. By s.50(2)(e) of the Tax Credits Act 2002, the Secretary of State's functions under this Act relating to child benefit and guardian's allowance were transferred to the Board of Inland Revenue with effect from April 7, 2003. The Inland Revenue has now been merged into Her Majesty's Revenue and Customs, by the Commissioners for Revenue and Customs Act 2005. 1.336

Subs.(1)
Where another body has made a decision on a question relevant to a claim for benefit, it is not necessary for the Secretary of State to consider that question from scratch as though the other decision did not exist, provided the other body made a considered decision on the point. He is entitled, in the absence of anything to compel a contrary conclusion, to regard the existence of that decision as satisfactory evidence *(R(H) 9/04)* of the facts found by that body. However, he is not bound to reach the same conclusion as the other body and must take account of any new evidence or any contrary submission made by the claimant. Thus, an immigration adjudicator's 1.337

decision accepting, contrary to the argument of the Home Secretary, that the claimant was validly married, was persuasive but not binding on the Secretary of State for Work and Pensions or a tribunal or a Commissioner determining a claim for widow's pension (*R. (Nahar) v Social Security Commissioners* [2001] EWHC 1049 (Admin). Although there was an appeal, the decision of the adjudicator had by then been set aside by the immigration appeal tribunal and so the point did not arise before the Court of Appeal [2002] EWCA Civ 859.) The same approach applies in relation to decisions of tax inspectors (*R(FC) 1/91*).

Subs. (2)

1.338   This subsection is disapplied in industrial disease cases where there has been recrudescence (see reg.12A of the Social Security and Child Support (Decisions and Appeals) Regulations 1999).

Paragraph (a) refers to a "claim" but in this context that is not to be read as being in contradistinction to, say, a supersession. The purpose of para.(a), read with s.12(8)(b) is to reverse the effect of *R(S) 1/83* and *R(S) 2/98*, in which it was held that a tribunal was entitled to take account of changes of circumstances occurring after the decision under appeal, on the basis that the claim made by the claimant subsisted until finally disposed of by the decision of the tribunal.

Paragraph (b) is not well drafted. The point being made in para.(a) is that a claim is effective only until it is decided *by the Secretary of State* (although benefit may then be awarded indefinitely or for a specified period in the future) and para.(b) is intended to make it clear that the consequence is that a change of circumstances taking place after the date of decision cannot give rise to entitlement under the original claim. This means that if a claimant appeals against the Secretary of State's decision, the tribunal cannot award benefit on the basis of a change of circumstances that has taken place between the Secretary of State's decision and its own decision. If no benefit was awarded on the initial claim, a new claim must, as para.(b) makes clear, be made if the claimant wishes to take advantage of the change of circumstances. That a decision refusing benefit cannot be superseded on the ground of a change of circumstances has been confirmed by a Tribunal of Commissioners in *R(I) 5/02*.

An assessment of disablement is a freestanding decision made under s.8(1)(c) and is appealable by virtue of reg.26 of the Social Security (Decisions and Appeals) Regulations 1999. In *R(I) 5/02*, the Tribunal of Commissioners held that a final assessment of disablement that had originally been made under s.47 of the Social Security Administration Act 1992 for a period that had come to an end could be superseded (having regard to para.4(1) of Sch.12 to the Social Security Act 1998 (Commencement No.8 and Savings and Consequential and Transitional Provisions) Order 1999) because it had continuing effect. However, they expressly declined to say whether the same approach would apply to an assessment originally made under s.8(1)(c). It is suggested that it would not, because such an assessment has no effect after the period for which it has been made comes to an end. What is required is an entirely new assessment made on a new claim for disablement benefit.

However, para.(b) overlooks the possibility that a claim may be decided some while after the date of claim and may be made in respect of a period beginning before the date of claim. In some cases a claimant will have been entitled to benefit in respect of the early part of the period for which it is claimed but, by reason of a change of circumstances, will have ceased to be entitled to benefit by the time the Secretary of State gives his decision. Read literally, para.(b) would require the claimant to be refused benefit altogether in such a case because, on the basis of circumstances obtaining at the date of decision, he or she would not qualify. However, it is suggested that the word "accordingly" shows that para.(b) merely makes provision for the natural consequence of para.(a) and should be read to the effect that the claimant shall not be entitled to the benefit on the basis of circumstances not obtaining at *or before* the date of decision. This approach is consistent with that taken in *CIS/2428/1999* in the context of s.12(8)(b). In that case, it was pointed out that a literal interpretation of s.12(8)(b) would prevent a tribunal from taking account of a cause for a late claim which existed before the claim was made and had ceased to exist before the Secretary of State's decision on the claim. The Commissioner considered that that would be absurd and would prevent adjudication on a case falling within reg.19(5) of the Social Security (Claims and Payments) Regulations 1987. He held that a circumstance "obtains" at the date of decision if it is a circumstance, whenever it occurred, that is relied on by a claimant in justifying a late claim.

In *R(DLA) 4/05*, a Tribunal of Commissioners held that para.(b) precluded the Secretary of State from taking account of an anticipated change of circumstances, even on a claim made in advance. However, they held that it did not preclude the Secretary of State from having regard to the effect on entitlement to benefit on the mere passage of time. Therefore, he can make an advance decision on a renewal claim taking into account the fact that by the renewal date the qualifying period for a particular rate of benefit will have elapsed or the claimant will have attained a certain age. Prediction is also permitted where entitlement to benefit at the date of decision depends on what is "likely" to happen in the future *(R(DLA) 3/01)*. Otherwise, where the Secretary of State anticipates a change of circumstances, he must either defer making a decision or make a decision ignoring the expected change but possibly marking the case for future consideration of revision or supersession. *R(DLA) 4/05* has been followed by a Tribunal of Commissioners in Northern Ireland *(R 2/05 (DLA))*. In *Secretary of State for Work and Pensions v Bhakta* [2006] EWCA Civ 65 (reported as *R(IS) 7/06*), the Court of Appeal approved *R(DLA) 4/05*. *Bhakta* was a case where the claimant intended to reside in the United Kingdom but had not become habitually resident in the United Kingdom at the date of the Secretary of State's decision only because a sufficient period of residence had not yet elapsed. The Court held that the Secretary of State could, under reg.13 of the Social Security (Claims and Payments) Regulations 1987, have made an advance award of income support from the date on which habitual residence had been likely to be established on the assumption that there would be no change in the claimant's circumstances. Regulation 13 has been amended with effect from May 23, 2007 so as to exclude that class of case (and all claims by "persons from abroad") from the scope of the regulation (see reg.2(2)(c) of the Social Security, Housing Benefit and Council Tax Benefit (Miscellaneous Amendments) Regulations 2007 (SI 2007/1331)), but the principle confirmed in *Bhakta* remains good in other contexts.

Subs.(3)

It having been pointed out that the lack of any reference in subs.(3) to mobility allowance meant that there was no power to revise or supersede a decision relating to mobility allowance so as to be able to recover an overpayment *(CDLA/2999/2004)*, the Social Security Act 1998 (Prescribed Benefits) Regulations 2006 prescribe a number of benefits payable under the Social Security Act 1995 and the Supplementary Benefits Act 1976. The benefits prescribed were all abolished before the 1998 Act came into force and are unemployment benefit, sickness benefit, invalidity benefit, attendance allowance (as paid to those under 65), mobility allowance and supplementary benefit.

The provisions of Chapter II of Part I of the 1998 Act are applied to decisions under ss.2 and 3 of the Age-Related Payments Act 2004, not by virtue of regulations made under this subsection but by s.5(5) of the 2004 Act. The same effect is achieved in relation to health in pregnancy grants by treating them as a relevant benefit (see s.132(8) of the Health and Social Care Act 2008).

1.339

Subs.(5)

Under s.8(1)(e) of the Social Security Contributions (Transfer of Functions, etc.) Act 1999 and the Commissioners for Revenue and Customs Act 2005, it is for Her Majesty's Revenue and Customs to determine whether contributions of a particular class have been paid in respect of any period. Thus, it is for Her Majesty's Revenue and Customs to determine the amount of contributions paid but it is for

1.340

the Secretary of State to decide any question about the interpretation or application of the Social Security (Earnings Factor) Regulations 1979 (*R(IB)1/09*).

However, any question as to the amount of contributions paid for graduated retirement benefit remains a matter for Secretary of State (*R(P)1/08*) as are the questions whether a person is entitled to "credits" (Sch.3, para.17 to the Social Security Act 1998, *CIB/2338/2000*) or is entitled to home responsibilities protection (Sch.3, para.16). It also appears that any dispute as to which is the relevant contribution year in respect of any claim is a matter for the Secretary of State, so that the effect of *Secretary of State for Social Security v Scully* [1992] 1 W.L.R. 927 (reported also as *R(S) 5/93*) is reversed and the effect of *R(G) 1/82* is restored. The Secretary of State's decisions are appealable under s.12.

Revision of decisions

1.341

9.—(1) Subject to section 36(3) below, any decision of the Secretary of State under section 8 above or section 10 below may be revised by the Secretary of State—

    (a) either within the prescribed period or in prescribed cases or circumstances; and

    (b) either on an application made for the purpose or on his own initiative;

and regulations may prescribe the procedure by which a decision of the Secretary of State may be so revised.

(2) In making a decision under subsection (1) above, the Secretary of State need not consider any issue that is not raised by the application or, as the case may be, did not cause him to act on his own initiative.

(3) Subject to subsections (4) and (5) and section 27 below, a revision under this section shall take effect as from the date on which the original decision took (or was to take) effect.

(4) Regulations may provide that, in prescribed cases or circumstances, a revision under this section shall take effect as from such other date as may be prescribed.

(5) Where a decision is revised under this section, for the purpose of any rule as to the time allowed for bringing an appeal, the decision shall be regarded as made on the date on which it is so revised.

(6) Except in prescribed circumstances, an appeal against a decision of the Secretary of State shall lapse if the decision is revised under this section before the appeal is determined.

DEFINITION

    "prescribed"—see s.84.

GENERAL NOTE

1.342

    This section applies to decisions under ss.2 and 3 of the Age-Related Payments Act 2004 (see s.5(5) of the 2004 Act). In relation to child benefit and guardian's allowance, the functions of the Secretary of State under this section were transferred with effect from April 7, 2003 to the Board of Inland Revenue (Tax Credits Act 2002, s.50(2)(e)). The functions of the Secretary of State in relation to the former working families' tax credit and disabled person's tax credit were similarly transferred to officers of the Inland Revenue from October 5, 1999 (Tax Credit Act 1999, s.2(1)(b) and Sch.2). The Inland Revenue has now been merged into Her Majesty's Revenue and Customs, by the Commissioners for Revenue and Customs Act 2005.

This section also applies to most decisions of Her Majesty's Revenue and Customs made under s.170(2) of the Pensions Schemes Act 1993, by virtue of s.170(4), and to decisions in relation to health in pregnancy grants, by virtue of s.132(8) of the Health and Social Care Act 2008.

Provision is made within the Social Security and Child Support (Decisions and Appeals) Regulations 1999 for decisions under the 1993 and 1999 Acts but separate regulations have been made in respect of child benefit and guardian's allowance (see the Child Benefit and Guardian's Allowance (Decisions and Appeals) Regulations 2003) and in respect of health in pregnancy grants (see the Health in Pregnancy Grant (Notices, Revisions and Appeals) (No.2) Regulations 2009).

Subs. (1)

Under the Social Security Administration Act 1992, provision was made for the "review" of decisions. Such reviews are replaced by "revisions" under s.9 and "supersessions" under s.10. Note that only a decision of the Secretary of State may be revised whereas a decision of the Secretary of State *or* of a tribunal or a Commissioner may be superseded. Apart from that, there is little that can be gleaned from the primary legislation as to the difference between revision and supersession. The most obvious distinction between the two concepts probably lies in the date from which the new decision takes effect. Where a decision is revised, the revised decision has effect from the effective date (or what should have been the effective date) of the original decision (see s.9(3)). On a supersession, the new decision takes effect from the date on which it is made and does not affect any past period, subject to limited provision for backdating in some cases (s.10(5)). A related distinction is that there is no appeal under s.12 against a refusal to revise under s.9. Formally, there is only a right of appeal against the original decision but s.9(5) extends the time for appealing against the original decision if it is revised, although not always if there is a refusal to revise (see the annotation to subs.(5)). By contrast, an appeal may be brought under s.12 against any decision under s.10. Beyond all that, no indication is given by the primary legislation as to the circumstances in which a revision of a decision is more appropriate than a supersession or vice versa. For that information, one must look at regs 3 and 4 of the Social Security and Child Support (Decisions and Appeals) Regulations 1999 and regs 5–11 of the Child Benefit and Guardian's Allowance (Decisions and Appeals) Regulations 2003 relating to revisions and at reg.6 of the 1999 Regulations and reg.13 of the 2003 Regulations relating to supersession. There would still be some overlap between the two procedures if it were not for reg.3(9) of the 1999 Regulations and reg.5(3) of the 2003 Regulations, which have the effect that supersession is always the appropriate procedure where there has been a change of circumstances since the Secretary of State's decision, and for reg.6(3) of the 1999 Regulations and reg.15 of the 2003 Regulations, which provide that a decision that may be revised cannot be superseded (save in limited circumstances where the revision could not take into account a further ground of supersession).

Happily, an application for supersession may be treated as an application for revision and vice versa (regs 3(10) and 6(5) of the 1999 Regulations and regs 7(1)(a) and 14(1)(a) of the 2003 Regulations), so that it is not fatal if claimants or their advisors do not fully understand the difference when making the application.

Despite, or perhaps because of, this flexibility, experience shows that decisions are not always issued in the correct form. Indeed, it is often Departmental practice to issue decisions that state the outcome without stating whether the decision is a revision or supersession. It has been suggested that that is not necessarily improper when the decision is first issued to the claimant but that the decision ought nonetheless to have been made in the appropriate form so that, if there is a request for reasons or an appeal, the true basis of the decision can be explained (*CIB/313/2002*). However, strong criticisms have been made of the Secretary of State's failure in many circumstances to record any decision at all in the proper form (see *CPC/3891/2004* and *R(IS) 13/05*). Even where a decision is made in terms of a revi-

1.343

sion or supersession, there are occasions when the wrong type of decision is issued. This is unfortunate because the distinction between revision and supersession is very important when an appeal is lodged. While an appeal following a revision or refusal to revise lies against the original decision, an appeal following a supersession or refusal to supersede lies against the later decision. It is particularly important for a decision terminating an award to be issued in the correct form if the Secretary of State or Her Majesty's Revenue and Customs intends subsequently to make a decision to the effect that there has been a recoverable overpayment, because s.71(5A) of the Social Security Administration Act 1992 generally requires there to have been a revision or supersession before an overpayment can be recovered (*CIS/3228/2003*, *R(IS) 13/05*). Section 71(5A) recognises that, unless an award is either revised or else superseded on a ground that makes the supersession retrospective by virtue of reg.7 of the 1999 Regulations or reg.16 of the 2003 Regulations, the original award still governs entitlement in respect of the period before the decision terminating it was made and it cannot be shown that any benefit was overpaid.

For the circumstances in which a tribunal may give a decision in terms of supersession on an appeal following a revision or refusal to revise and vice versa, see the note to s.12(2). It is suggested that many of the difficulties identified would be removed if grounds for revision under reg.3(4) and (5) to (8) of the Social Security and Child Support (Decisions and Appeals) Regulations 1999 and regs 8 to 11 of the Child Benefit and Guardian's Allowance (Decisions and Appeals) Regulations 2003 were instead grounds for supersession. In deciding whether revision or supersession was the more appropriate remedy, the draftsmen of the Regulations appear to have placed too much emphasis on the date from which a decision is effective and too little on the lack of an appropriate right of appeal against a decision given in terms of revision and the lack of any express provision for correcting on appeal a decision-maker's mistaken choice as to the appropriate procedure for making a change to an earlier decision.

Section 9(1) provides that "any decision . . . under section 8 above or section 10 below" may be revised. However, in s.12(1) there is reference to "any decision . . . under section 8 or 10 above (whether as originally made or as revised under section 9 above)" and similar words referring to section 9 are to be found in s.10(1)(a). Do those references to s.9 in ss.10 and 12 suggest that references to decisions under ss 8 and 10 normally include decisions that have been revised? Or does the fact that there are references to s.9 in ss.10 and 12 but none in s.9 itself suggest that a decision that has already been revised cannot be revised again? In *CIS/3535/2003*, the Deputy Commissioner preferred the former approach and said, obiter, that a decision that has already been revised may be revised again and that the time for bringing an application under reg.3(1) of the Social Security and Child Support (Decisions and Appeals) Regulations 1999 starts again from the date the revision is notified.

Subs.(2)

1.344
Note that the Secretary of State "need not", but nonetheless may, consider additional issues. On an appeal following a revision or refusal to revise, the decision under appeal is the original decision (see subs.(5) read with s.12(1)). The tribunal's duty to consider issues is determined by the issues raised by the appeal (see s.12(8)(a)) rather than by the issues raised by the earlier application for revision because it is not obliged to consider independently the merits of the revisions or refusal to revise, at any rate where the revision or application for revision was made under reg.3(1) or (3) of the Social Security and Child Support (Decisions and Appeals) Regulations 1999.

Subs.(4)

1.345
See reg.5 of the Social Security and Child Support (Decisions and Appeals) Regulations 1999 and reg.12 of the Child Benefit and Guardian's Allowance (Decisions and Appeals) Regulations 2003 which provide that the principal excep-

tion to the general rule is where a ground for the revision is that the original decision was made effective from the wrong date in the first place.

Subs. (5)

This allows a claimant to appeal against a revised decision. Note, however, that an application for a revision of a decision of the Secretary of State has the effect of automatically extending the time for appealing only where the application is brought under reg.3(1) or (3) of the Social Security and Child Support (Decisions and Appeals) Regulations 1999 (see reg.31(2)(a)). In other cases, it will generally be wise for any person asking for a revision to lodge an appeal at the same time so that, if the decision is not revised, the claimant will not have to bring a late appeal. The fact that a claimant was waiting for a decision on an application for revision may be regarded as a compelling reason for admitting an appeal late, but a claimant would be unwise to take that for granted. If, the claimant having lodged both an application for revision and an appeal, the decision is not revised, the appeal will proceed. If the decision is revised, the appeal will lapse under subs.(6) only if the revised decision is more advantageous to the claimant that the original decision. This subsection then applies to such a case, enabling the claimant to appeal against the decision as revised. If the original decision is revised otherwise than to the advantage of the claimant, the appeal will not lapse but the claimant will be given another month to make representations in the light of the revision.

In a case where an application for revision is made otherwise than under reg.3(1) and (3) of the Social Security and Child Support (Decisions and Appeals) Regulations 1999 and more than 13 months has elapsed since the original decision, so that no appeal may be brought against it, there is no way of challenging by way of an appeal a refusal to revise the decision (see *R(IS) 15/04* and *Beltekian v Westminster CC* [2004] EWCA Civ 1784 (reported as *R(H) 8/05*), in which no attempt appears to have been made to argue that subs.(5) should be read as including a refusal to revise in the same way that s.12(9) must be read as referring to a refusal to supersede). Recourse must be had to judicial review. See the note to reg.31 of the 1999 Regulations for further discussion of the problems caused by the lack of any reference in the primary legislation to refusals to revise.

Subs. (6)

See reg.30 of the Social Security and Child Support (Decisions and Appeals) Regulations 1999 and reg.27 of the Child Benefit and Guardian's Allowance (Decisions and Appeals) Regulations 2003.

Decisions superseding earlier decisions

10.—(1) Subject to [¹ subsection (3)] and section 36(3) below, the following, namely—

(a) any decision of the Secretary of State under section 8 above or this section, whether as originally made or as revised under section 9 above; and

(b) any decision under this Chapter [² of the First-tier Tribunal or any decision of the Upper Tribunal which relates to any such decision]

may be superseded by a decision made by the Secretary of State, either on an application made for the purpose or on his own initiative.

(2) In making a decision under subsection (1) above, the Secretary of State need not consider any issue that is not raised by the application or, as the case may be, did not cause him to act on his own initiative.

(3) Regulations may prescribe the cases and circumstances in which, and the procedure by which, a decision may be made under this section.

(4) [¹ . . .]

1.346

1.347

1.348

(5) Subject to subsection (6) and section 27 below, a decision under this section shall take effect as from the date on which it is made or, where applicable, the date on which the application was made.

(6) Regulations may provide that, in prescribed cases or circumstances, a decision under this section shall take effect as from such other date as may be prescribed.

AMENDMENT

1. Social Security Contributions (Transfer of Functions, etc.) Act 1999, Sch.7, para.23 (April 1, 1999).

2. Transfer of Tribunal Functions Order 2008 (SI 2008/2833), Sch.3, paras 143 and 148 (November 3, 2008).

DEFINITION

"prescribed"—see s.84.

GENERAL NOTE

1.349   Transitional provisions in the various commencement orders bringing this Act into force (see the note to s.87), provide for the supersession under this section of decisions made by the various adjudicating authorities that existed under earlier legislation and, in *CI/1800/01*, the Commissioner construed a reference to adjudicating medical authorities as including medical appeal tribunals so as to enable a claimant to apply for supersession of a decision of a medical appeal tribunal that had continuing effect. However, in *CDLA/2999/2004*, the Commissioner declined to find any power to supersede an award of mobility allowance (which was a benefit that was replaced by the mobility component of disability living allowance in April 1992) made by an adjudication officer in 1986.

The practical effect of *CDLA/2999/2004* has now substantially been reversed by the Social Security Act 1998 (Prescribed Benefits) Regulations 2006, which prescribes mobility allowance (and certain other benefits) for the purposes of s.8(3)(h) of this Act, and by the Social Security Act 1998 (Commencement Nos. 9 and 11) (Amendment) Order 2006 (SI 2006/2540), which amends transitional provisions relating to the replacement of sickness and invalidity benefit by incapacity benefit and to the replacement of attendance allowance for people under 65 and mobility allowance by disability living allowance.

This section applies to decisions under ss.2 and 3 of the Age-Related Payments Act 2004 (see s.5(5) of the 2004 Act).

In relation to child benefit and guardian's allowance, the functions of the Secretary of State under this section were transferred with effect from April 7, 2003 to the Board of Inland Revenue (Tax Credits Act 2002, s.50(2)(e)). The functions of the Secretary of State in relation to the former working families' tax credit and disabled person's tax credit were similarly transferred to officers of the Inland Revenue from October 5, 1999 (Tax Credit Act 1999, s.2(1)(b) and Sch.2). The Inland Revenue has now been merged into Her Majesty's Revenue and Customs, by the Commissioners for Revenue and Customs Act 2005.

This section also applies to most decisions of Her Majesty's Revenue and Customs made under s.170(2) of the Pensions Schemes Act 1993, by virtue of s.170(4).

Provision is made within the Social Security and Child Support (Decisions and Appeals) Regulations 1999 for decisions under the 1993 and 1999 Acts but separate regulations have been made in respect of child benefit and guardian's allowance.

Subs. (1)

1.350   For the distinction between revision and supersession, see the note to s.9(1). Note that an application for supersession may be treated as an application for revision and vice versa (regs 3(10) and 6(5) of the Social Security and Child Support (Decisions and Appeals) Regulations 1999 and regs 7(1)(a) and 14(1)(a) of the Child Benefit and Guardian's Allowance (Decisions and Appeals) Regulations 2003).

Also, under reg.6(5), the provision of information to the Secretary of State may be treated as an application for supersession. There are no other provisions specifying what constitutes an application for supersession. In *CI/954/2006*, the Commissioner doubted that giving information to a medical adviser during an examination was to be treated as an application for supersession, although the Secretary of State could have superseded on his own motion in the light of the information.

Often departmental procedures require a claimant to complete a claim form for what is really a supersession rather than a claim. This can lead to confusion. One example is the practice of requiring claimants of income support who move to a new address to complete a new claim. If this is not done promptly, a claimant may find that there is a gap in benefit payments that is not subsequently made up. The grounds upon which benefit is withheld in those circumstances may be somewhat dubious. In *CI/954/2006*, it was pointed out that where a claimant is in receipt of disablement benefit and suffers another industrial accident, a claim in respect of the subsequent accident may have to be treated in the alternative as an application for supersession of the original award, because, following *R(I) 4/03*, aggregation of assessments of disablement is an alternative to the making of two separate awards. One practical difference is that claims may be backdated but supersessions in those circumstances cannot, which the Commissioner suggested is anomalous. The Commissioner also pointed out that an application for supersession of an assessment of disablement needed to be treated also as an application for supersession of the underlying award if proper effect was to be given to any supersession of the assessment of disablement (see the annotations to regs 6 and 26 of the 1999 Regulations, below).

Subs. (2)

On an appeal against a supersession or refusal to supersede, it is doubtful that a tribunal may refuse to consider an issue raised by the appeal merely because it was not raised on the original application for supersession or, as the case may be, did not cause the Secretary of State to act on his own initiative. However, where an issue is not raised by an appeal, the fact that it was not raised before the Secretary of State either may be a factor the tribunal should take into account when deciding whether to consider the issue on the appeal (see s.12(8)(a)).

1.351

Subs. (3)

See regs 6 and 8 of the Social Security and Child Support (Decisions and Appeals) Regulations 1999 and regs 13 and 14 of the Child Benefit and Guardian's Allowance (Decisions and Appeals) Regulations 2003.

1.352

Where a person applies for supersession and the Secretary of State decides that the case and circumstances are not among those prescribed by reg.6 of the 1999 Regulations (or, equally, reg.13 of the 2003 Regulations), it has now been established that the Secretary of State may issue a decision refusing to supersede the original decision, rather than superseding it but without making any change (see *Wood v Secretary of State for Work and Pensions* [2003] EWCA Civ 53 (reported as *R(DLA) 1/03)*). It is not entirely clear whether he may still, as an alternative approach, supersede the original decision without making any change, but the distinction is of little practical importance. See the note to reg.6 of the 1999 Regulations.

Subs. (5)

In *R(IB)2/04*, the Tribunal of Commissioners decided that where a claimant has applied for supersession in order to obtain an increase of benefit but the Secretary of State supersedes the award so as to reduce entitlement, the supersession is made on the Secretary of State's own initiative and not on the claimant's applica-

1.353

tion. Therefore, subject to the effect of any regulations made under subs.(6), it is effective from the date of the decision and not the date of the claimant's application. Similarly, where the Secretary of State's supersession decision is not less favourable than the original decision but the claimant appeals and the tribunal not only does not allow the appeal but also makes a decision even less favourable than the original decision, the tribunal's decision is usually effective from the date of the Secretary of State's supersession decision. See paras 95 to 97 of the Tribunal's decision.

Where a decision has been made that invalid care allowance is not payable because incapacity benefit is in payment and reg.4 of the Social Security (Overlapping Benefits) Regulations 1977 precluded the payment of both benefits, a decision to resume payment of invalid care allowance after payment of incapacity benefit ceases is a decision under s.8 and not a supersession under s.10 (*Secretary of State for Work and Pensions v Adams* [2003] EWCA Civ 796 (reported as *R(G) 1/03*)). This means that, where there has been a delay in reinstating payment of invalid care allowance, the decision is nonetheless automatically effective from the date when payment of incapacity benefit ceased, rather than from a later date determined by s.10(5).

Subs.(6)

1.354   See reg.7 of, and Sch.3A to, the Social Security and Child Support (Decisions and Appeals) Regulations 1999 and reg.16 of the Child Benefit and Guardian's Allowance (Decisions and Appeals) Regulations 2003.

[¹*Reference of issues by Secretary of State to Inland Revenue*

References of issues by Secretary of State to Inland Revenue

1.355   **10A.**—(1) Regulations may make provision requiring the Secretary of State, where on consideration of any claim or other matter he is of the opinion that there arises any issue which under section 8 of the Social Security Contributions (Transfer of Functions, etc.) Act 1999 falls to be decided by an officer of the Inland Revenue, to refer the issue to the Inland Revenue.

Regulations under this section may—
(a) provide for the Inland Revenue to give the Secretary of State a pre-liminary opinion on any issue referred to them,
(b) specify the circumstances in which an officer of the Inland Revenue is to make a decision under section 8 of the Social Security Contributions (Transfer of Functions, etc.) Act 1999 on a reference by the Secretary of State,
(c) enable or require the Secretary of State, in specified circumstances to deal with any other issue arising on consideration of the claim or other matter pending the decision of the referred issue, and
(d) require the Secretary of State to decide the claim or other matter in accordance with the decision of an officer of the Inland Revenue on the issue referred to them, or in accordance with any determination of the [² First-tier Tribunal or Upper Tribunal] made on appeal from [² the tribunal's decision].]

AMENDMENT

1. Social Security Contributions (Transfer of Functions, etc.) Act 1999, Sch.7, para.24 (July 5, 1999).
2. Transfer of Tribunal Functions and Revenue and Customs Appeals Order 2009 (SI 2009/56), Sch.1, paras 247 and 248 (April 1, 2009).

DEFINITIONS

"claim"—by virtue of s.39(2), see s.191 of the Social Security Administration Act 1992.

"Inland Revenue"—*ibid*, but note that the Inland Revenue has been merged into Her Majesty's Revenue and Customs by the Commissioners for Revenue and Customs Act 2005.

"tax appeal Commissioners"—see s.39(1).

"prescribed"—see s.84.

GENERAL NOTE

See reg.11A of the Social Security and Child Support (Decisions and Appeals) Regulations 1999.

1.356

Some decisions fall to be made by Her Majesty's Revenue and Customs by virtue of s.170 of the Pensions Schemes Act 1993 (rather than by virtue of s.8 of the Social Security Contributions (Transfer of Functions, etc.) Act 1999) but the Secretary of State may nevertheless refer to Her Majesty's Revenue and Customs issues for determination under the 1993 Act notwithstanding that regulations under this section do not apply *(R(P) 1/04)*.

Regulations with respect to decisions

11.—(1) Subject to the provisions of this Chapter and the Administration Act, provision may be made by regulations for the making of any decision by the Secretary of State under or in connection with the current legislation, or the former legislation, including a decision on a claim for benefit.

1.357

(2) Where it appears to the Secretary of State that a matter before him involves a question of fact requiring special expertise, he may direct that in dealing with that matter he shall have the assistance of one or more experts.

(3) In this section—

"the current legislation" means the Contributions and Benefits Act, the Jobseekers Act [¹, the Social Security (Recovery of Benefits) Act 1997 [², the State Pension Credit Act 2002 and Part 1 of the Welfare Reform Act 2007]]

"expert" means a person appearing to the Secretary of State to have knowledge or experience which would be relevant in determining the question of fact requiring special expertise;

"the former legislation" means the National Insurance Acts 1965 to 1974, the National Insurance (Industrial Injuries) Acts 1965 to 1974, the Social Security Act 1975 and Part II of the Social Security Act 1986.

AMENDMENT

1. State Pension Credit Act 2002, ss.11 and 21 and Sch.1, para.7 and Sch.3 (July 2, 2002 for the purpose of exercising any power to make regulations or orders and April 7, 2003 for other purposes).

2. Welfare Reform Act 2007, Sch.3, para.17(1) and (4) (October 27, 2008).

DEFINITIONS

"the Administration Act"—see s.84.

"benefit"—by virtue of s.39(2), see s.191 of the Social Security Administration Act 1992.

"claim"—*ibid.*
"Contributions and Benefits Act"—see s.84.
"the current legislation"—see subs.(3).
"expert"—*ibid.*
"the former legislation"—*ibid.*
"the Jobseeker's Act"—see s.84.

GENERAL NOTE

1.358   In relation to the former working families' tax credit and disabled person's tax credit, the power to make regulations was transferred to the Commissioners of Inland Revenue and the other functions of the Secretary of State were transferred to officers of the Inland Revenue, with effect from October 5, 1999 (Tax Credits Act 1999, s.2(1)(b) and Sch.2, paras 5(b)(iii) and 8(a)). In relation to child benefit and guardian's allowance, powers and functions were similarly transferred to the Inland Revenue by the Tax Credits Act 2002 (see s.50(2)(e)). The Inland Revenue has now been merged into Her Majesty's Revenue and Customs, by the Commissioners for Revenue and Customs Act 2005.

Subs. (1)

See reg.28 of the Social Security and Child Support (Decisions and Appeals) Regulations 1999.

Appeals

Appeal to [² First-tier Tribunal]

1.359   **12.**—(1) This section applies to any decision of the Secretary of State under section 8 or 10 above (whether as originally made or as revised under section 9 above) which—

(a) is made on a claim for, or on an award of, a relevant benefit, and does not fall within Schedule 2 to this Act; [¹ or]

(b) is made otherwise than on such a claim or award, and falls within Schedule 3 to this Act; [¹ . . .]

(c) [¹ . . .]

[¹ (2) In the case of a decision to which this section applies, the claimant and such other person as may be prescribed shall have a right to appeal to [² First-tier Tribunal], but nothing in this subsection shall confer a right of appeal in relation to a prescribed decision, or a prescribed determination embodied in or necessary to a decision.]

(3) Regulations under subsection (2) above shall not prescribe any decision or determination that relates to the conditions of entitlement to a relevant benefit for which a claim has been validly made or for which no claim is required.

(4) Where the Secretary of State has determined that any amount is recoverable under or by virtue of section 71 or 74 of the Administration Act, any person from whom he has determined that it is recoverable shall have the same right of appeal to [² First-tier Tribunal] as a claimant.

(5) In any case where—

(a) the Secretary of State has made a decision in relation to a claim under Part V of the Contributions and Benefits Act; and

(b) the entitlement to benefit under that Part of that Act of any person

other than the claimant is or may be, under Part VI of Schedule 7 to
that Act, affected by that decision,
that other person shall have the same right of appeal to [² First-tier Tribunal]
as the claimant.

(6) A person with a right of appeal under this section shall be given such
notice of a decision to which this section applies and of that right as may
be prescribed.

(7) Regulations may make provision as to the manner in which, and the
time within which, appeals are to be brought.

(8) In deciding an appeal under this section, [² First-tier Tribunal]—

(a) need not consider any issue that is not raised by the appeal; and

(b) shall not take into account any circumstances not obtaining at the
time when the decision appealed against was made.

(9) The reference in subsection (1) above to a decision under section 10
above is a reference to a decision superseding any such decision as is mentioned in paragraph (a) or (b) of subsection (1) of that section.

AMENDMENTS

1. Social Security Contributions (Transfer of Functions, etc.) Act 1999, Sch.7,
para.25 (April 1, 1999).
2. Transfer of Tribunal Functions Order 2008 (SI 2008/2833), Sch.3, paras 143
and 149 (November 3, 2008).

DEFINITIONS

"the administration Act"—see s.84.
"claim"—by virtue of s.39(2), see s.191 of the Social Security Administration Act
1992.
"claimant"—see s.39(1) and, by virtue of s.39(2), see s.191 of the Social Security
Administration Act 1992.
"the Contributions and Benefits Act"—see s.84.
"prescribed"—*ibid.*
"relevant benefit"—see s.8(3).

GENERAL NOTE

This section provides only for appeals against decisions made by the Secretary   1.360
of State under ss.8 and 10 of this Act. However, it applies to decisions under ss.2
and 3 of the Age-Related Payments Act 2004 by virtue of s.5(5) of the 2004 Act)
and is also applied to other decisions of the Secretary of State by reg.9 of the
Social Security (Work-focused Interviews for Lone Parents) and Miscellaneous
Amendments Regulations 2000, reg.15 of the Social Security (Jobcentre Plus
Interviews) Regulations 2002, reg.14 of the Social Security (Jobcentre Plus
Interviews for Partners) Regulations 2003, reg.15 of the Social Security (Working
Neighbourhoods) Regulations 2004 and, reg.10 of the Social Security (Incapacity
Benefit Work-focused Interviews) Regulations 2008, all of which are concerned with
decisions that claimants have failed without good cause to attend interviews.

It also applies—with only the modification that references to the Secretary of
State are to be construed as references to the Board of Inland Revenue or to an
officer of the Inland Revenue—so as to provide for appeals against decisions relating to child benefit and guardian's allowance (by virtue of the Tax Credits Act 2002,
Sch.4, para.50), against decisions relating to the former working families' tax credit
and disabled person's tax credit (by virtue of the Tax Credits Act 1999, Sch.2,
para.21), against penalties imposed under s.9(1), (3)(a) or (5)(a) of the 1999 Act
(by virtue of Sch.4, para.3(2) of the 1999 Act), against decisions given under s.170
of the Pension Schemes Act 1993 in respect of retirement pensions (by virtue of

s.170(6) of the 1993 Act) and against decisions in relation to health in pregnancy grants (by virtue of s.132(8) of the Health and Social Care Act 2008). The Inland Revenue has now been merged into Her Majesty's Revenue and Customs, by the Commissioners for Revenue and Customs Act 2005.

Quite separate rights of appeal to the First-tier Tribunal are given under s.4 of the Vaccine Damage Payments Act 1979 (in respect of vaccine damage payments—see Volume I of this work), under ss.11 and 12 of the Social Security (Recovery of Benefits) Act 1997 (in respect of the recovery of benefits from those making compensation payments in respect of personal injury), under reg.10(2B) of the Employment Protection (Recoupment of Jobseeker's Allowance and Income Support) Regulations 1996 (in respect of the recovery of benefits from those making compensation payments in employment tribunal proceedings).

Separate rights of appeal to the First-tier Tribunal are also conferred by ss.21(9) and 22 of the Child Trust Funds Act 2004, but subss.(7) and (8)(b) of this section are applied in modified form to such appeals by reg.6 of the Child Trust Funds (Non-tax Appeals) Regulations 2005 (SI 2005/191) (which were originally made under s.24(5) of the 2004 Act and remain valid under the new s.23(6)). See Vol. IV for the 2004 Act and the Child Trust Funds (Appeals) Regulations 2005, made under subs.(7) as so applied.

Until April 1, 2009, a version of subs.(1) of this section, substituted for subs (1) and (2), and modified versions of subss.(7) and (8)(b) were applied to appeals under the Tax Credits Act 2002 by reg.4 of the Tax Credits (Appeals) Regulations 2002 (SI 2002/2926). However, s.63(8) of the 2002 Act, which conferred the power to make those Regulations, has been amended so as to apply only in Northern Ireland (see Vol.IV) and so those Regulations, together with the Tax Credits (Appeals) (No.2) Regulations 2002 (SI 2002/3196) which were made under subs.(7) and other provisions of this Act as similarly applied, have presumably lapsed in relation to cases in Great Britain.

Numerous statutes and regulations outside the scope of this work also provide rights of appeal to the First-tier Tribunal in classes of case allocated to the Social Entitlement Chamber.

Subs.(1)

1.361
This section provides only for appeals against decisions under ss.8 and 10 of this Act (but see the note above). Challenges to decisions under s.9 are brought by appealing against the original decision rather than the s.9 decision. The phrase "decision . . . under section . . . 10" includes a decision to refuse to supersede (*Wood v Secretary of State for Work and Pensions* [2003] EWCA Civ 53 (reported as *R(DLA) 1/03)*), notwithstanding the terms of subs.(9).

There cannot be an appeal unless there has been a decision under s.8 or s.10 and so a tribunal had no jurisdiction to consider a challenge to the Secretary of State's failure to exercise his power to make a winter fuel payment without a claim (*R(IS) 12/05*). In *CIS/4088/2004*, the Commissioner considered that there must have been a decision refusing to make a payment in circumstances where the claimant had previously received a winter fuel payment and it was erroneously believed within the Department for Work and Pensions that no further payment could be made in the absence of a claim after the claimant had ceased to be entitled to incapacity benefit but that decision was doubted in *CIS/840/2005*.

The scope of a tribunal's jurisdiction must depend on the scope of the decision which is the subject of the appeal. Paragraph (a) provides for an appeal against any decision made *on* a claim or award. Section 20(1)(a) and (b) of the Social Security Administration Act 1992 drew a distinction between a "claim" and a "question" and s.36 expressly enabled a tribunal to deal with any question first arising before them and not previously considered by an adjudication officer. The new legislation does not use the terms "claim" and "question" and there is no provision similar to the old s.36. However, it is suggested that this may not make much difference. In *CIB/2338/2000*, the Commissioner held that the only type of "decision" that could be appealed was an "outcome" decision which is "a useful expression to refer to decisions that have, in crude terms, an impact on a claimant's pocket". He pointed out that an appeal lay only against decisions under ss.8 and 10. Section 8(1)(a) and (b) provides only that the Secretary of State shall "decide any claim". Section 8(1)(c) provides for the making of "any decision that falls to be made under or by virtue of any enactment" but the Commissioner did not construe that as referring to the individual determinations that are the building blocks of a decision on a claim for benefit. He understood it to refer to the making of decisions in relation to, say, crediting of earnings for contributions purposes. Section 10 refers to the supersession of decisions under s.8 or decisions of tribunals or Commissioners on appeal against from s.8 decisions. Therefore, there is no appeal against a decision on what used to be called a "question". In *CIB/2338/2000*, that meant that there was no appeal solely against the determination that the claimant was incapable of work; the appeal was against the consequential decision that he was not entitled to a "credit". This approach, which was endorsed by a Tribunal of Commissioners in *R(IB) 2/04*, makes it unnecessary for there to be a provision equivalent to the old s.36 expressly providing for a tribunal to deal with an issue that has not been considered by a decision-maker, because it is implicit that, if a tribunal has rejected a ground upon which the decision-maker has made an "outcome decision", it is necessary (subject to s.12(8)(a)) for the tribunal to consider such other issues as are necessary in order to substitute its own "outcome decision" for the decision-maker's. However, this is all subject to two qualifications. First, Sch. 3 to the Act and reg.26 of the Social Security and Child Support (Decisions and Appeals) Regulations 1999 make provision for appeals to be brought against certain freestanding decisions that are not "outcome decisions". Secondly, there are circumstances in which a tribunal is not obliged to substitute an "outcome decision" for one under appeal but may, in effect, remit the case to the Secretary of State or Her Majesty's Revenue and Customs (*R(IS) 2/08*, discussed in more detail in the annotation to subs.(2) below).

Accurately identifying the scope of the appeal may be very important in some cases. For instance, where a person is in receipt of income support on the basis that he or she is incapable of work, that person will usually be in receipt also of incapacity benefit or "credits". A decision to the effect that he or she is not incapable of work will usually be made for the purposes of an "outcome decision" in relation to incapacity benefit or "credits". By virtue of reg.10 of the Social Security and Child Support (Decisions and Appeals) Regulations 1999, that determination will be conclusive for the purposes of the income support claim. If the claimant wishes both to challenge the determination that he or she is not incapable work and to suggest that the entitlement to income support should continue on another ground, it will be necessary for there to be an appeal against both "outcome decisions". In order to determine the scope of an appeal, it may be necessary to consider the terms of the form or letter of appeal as well as the notice of decision because, if another decision-maker has dealt with the consequences of the first decision, a claimant may have appealed against both decisions in the same letter of appeal.

By virtue of s.12(1)(b) there is a right of appeal against an assessment of disablement for industrial disablement benefit, as a freestanding decision (see para.9 of Sch.3 to the Act and reg.26 of the Social Security and Child Support (Decisions and Appeals) Regulations 1999). In *R(I) 5/02*, the Tribunal of Commissioners held that a tribunal considering such an appeal had no jurisdiction to consider a refusal of benefit consequent upon the assessment of disablement. It is not clear how the two decisions were notified to the claimant in that case but it has been suggested that an appeal against an assessment of disablement should be treated as being also an appeal against the refusal of benefit, unless the Secretary of State is prepared to treat it as an application for revision of the refusal of benefit (*CI/1547/2001*). This is because, if there is no appeal against the refusal of benefit, it would have to be revised or superseded to give effect to a successful appeal in respect of the assessment of disablement. It does not appear that any such revision or supersession could be effective from the beginning of the period of assessment if action for revision or supersession is taken only after the tribunal's decision. There are other circumstances where a decision against one decision should be taken to be also an appeal against another decision, even where the other decision is implicit and has not actually been recorded. Thus, in *R(JSA) 2/04*, it was held that, where a claimant seeks benefit for the period between the end of one award and a new claim, an appeal against a refusal to backdate the new claim must sometimes be treated as being also an appeal against the termination of that previous award, because the latter may be the decision that is really being challenged. In *Abbas v Secretary of State for Work and Pensions* [2005] EWCA Civ 652, where the claimant had made a continuation claim for disability living allowance and the Secretary of State's response was to supersede the existing award and terminate it before it had originally been due to end, it was necessary for the appeal against the supersession decision to be treated also as an appeal against a disallowance of the continuation claim because otherwise, if the claimant showed that she satisfied the conditions for entitlement to disability living allowance, benefit could not be awarded in respect of any period after the original renewal date.

A *lacuna* in subs.(1) was explored in *R(IS) 14/04*, where the claimant had purported to appeal to an appeal tribunal against a decision to the effect that benefit was recoverable from him under s.74 of the Social Security Administration Act 1992. The Commissioner agreed with the tribunal that a right of appeal could not arise under subs.(1)(b) because there was no reference in Sch.3 to decisions under s.74 of the 1992 Act, although paras 5 and 6 of the Schedule refer to recoverability decisions made under s.71 of the 1992 Act and subs.(4) shows that it is intended that claimants should be entitled to appeal against decisions under either s.71 or s.74. He concluded that the right of appeal arose under subs.(1)(a) because the decision under s.74 "is sufficiently related to the award of income support on which the excess payment has been made".

Subs. (2)

1.362
For regulations made under this subsection, see regs 25 and 27 of the Social Security and Child Support (Decisions and Appeals) Regulations 1999, reg.3 of the Tax Credits (Appeals) (No. 2) Regulations 2002 and regs 24 and 25 of the Child Benefit and Guardian's Allowance (Decisions and Appeal) Regulations 2003.

Although an appeal to the First-tier Tribunal must be lodged at an "appropriate office" administered by the Secretary of State or other body from whom the appeal is to be brought (see reg.33 of the 1999 Regulations and reg.31 of the 2003 Regulations), the Secretary of State is not entitled to refuse to refer the case to a tribunal if he considers that the tribunal has no jurisdiction to hear it. It is for the tribunal to determine whether it has jurisdiction to hear a case *(R(I) 7/94)* and, if the Secretary of State were to refuse to refer an appeal lodged at an office of the Department for Work and Pensions to the tribunal, it would be open to the tribunal to consider whether it had jurisdiction and, if it had, to determine the appeal without the appeal having been passed to it by the Secretary of State *(R(H) 1/07)*.

The nature of an appeal to the First-tier Tribunal

For the investigatory approach of the First-tier Tribunal and its approach to evidence, see the note to s.3(1) of the Tribunals, Courts and Enforcement Act 2007.

1.363
An appeal to a tribunal is a rehearing *(R(F) 1/72)*; it is not just a review of the decision under appeal. The tribunal stands in the shoes of the decision-maker and has the power to consider any issue and make any decision the decision-maker could have made *(R(IB) 2/04)*. Therefore, where the Secretary of State has a broad discretion, e.g. as to the period of disqualification for jobseeker's allowance to be imposed when a person leaves his employment voluntarily without just cause, the tribunal has to substitute its own judgment for that of the Secretary of State, rather than merely considering whether the Secretary of State has acted reasonably *(CJSA/1703/2006, R(AF) 3/07)*.

In *R(H) 6/06*, it was said that "a right of appeal against an exercise of discretion that is non-justiciable because the relevant considerations cannot be discerned must be limited to points of law". In other words, it would be a review rather than a true appeal. A discretion is non-justiciable only if the relevant considerations are policy matters requiring "essentially non-legal judgments" *(R(H) 3/04)* and legislation does not normally confer a right of appeal to a tribunal against such a decision unless it expressly limits the right to points of law. If legislation appears to confer such a right in respect of a non-justiciable decsion, there may arise questions as to the construction or validity of the legislation, as in *R(H) 6/06*. In *R(H) 1/08*, the Commissioner pointed out that the mere fact that different people might legitimately exercise their judgment differently on the same facts does not make the judgment a discretion and, if there is a discretion, does not make it non-justiciable. It has not been suggested that any appeal under s.12 is capable of raising a non-justiciable issue.

The powers of the First-tier Tribunal

There is nothing in s.12 to indicate what powers a tribunal has when it allows an appeal, and it is therefore open to a tribunal to set aside a decision and, in effect, to remit the case to the original decision-maker where that appears to be more appropriate than substituting its own decision. Examples are where the decision under appeal was made without jurisdiction or where a recoverability decision should have been made against a person who is not a party to the appeal *(R(H) 6/06)* or where issues first arise in the course of an appeal *(R(IS) 2/08*, where it was made clear that the tribunal must nonetheless deal with the issues originally raised in the appeal). Thus, although an appeal to a tribunal normally lies only against an "outcome decision" *(R(IB) 2/04)*, a tribunal hearing an appeal against an "outcome decision" is not always obliged to substitute another such decision. The Tribunal of Commissioners said, at para.48 of *R(IS) 2/08*—

"When an appeal against an outcome decision raises one issue on which the appeal is allowed but it is necessary to deal with a further issue before another outcome decision is substituted, a tribunal may set aside the original outcome decision without substituting another outcome decision, provided it deals with the original issue raised by the appeal and substitutes a decision on that issue. The Secretary of State must then consider the new issue and decide what outcome decision to give. In that outcome decision, he must give effect to the tribunal's decision on the original issue unless, at the time he makes the outcome decision, he is satisfied that there are grounds on which to supersede the tribunal's decision so as, for instance, to take account of any changes of circumstances that have occurred since he made the decision that was the subject of the appeal to the tribunal. Because his decision is an outcome decision, the claimant will have a right of appeal against it."

The Tribunal of Commissioners gave the following additional guidance at para. 55(2)—

"Where a tribunal, having dealt with the issues originally raised in an appeal, is not able immediately to give an outcome decision, it must decide whether to adjourn or whether to remit the question of entitlement to the Secretary of State. The technical difficulty of the outstanding issues and the likelihood of a further appeal if the entitlement question is remitted will be relevant considerations. The tribunal should consider whether the Secretary of State would be in a better position to decide the issue and to seek further information from the claimant. It may have to balance the desirability of a decision being made as quickly as possible against the desirability of it being made as accurately as possible, given that an appeal on a point of fact will not lie against a decision of the tribunal on any fresh issue. The wishes of the parties should be taken into account."

Correcting procedural errors by the Secretary of State

1.363.1   In *R(IB)2/04*, a Tribunal of Commissioners considered in depth the jurisdiction of tribunals and the extent to which tribunals are limited, or not limited, by the terms of the decision against which an appeal has been brought. They noted that s.12 makes no positive provision at all as to a tribunal's powers so that those powers must be found by a process of implication. They therefore considered the case law on adjudication before the 1998 Act came into force (in particular, *R(F) 1/72, R(P) 1/55, R(SB) 1/82* and *R(SB) 42/83*). That led to the conclusion that an appeal to an appeal tribunal under s.12 is by way of rehearing. At paragraph 24, the Tribunal said:

> "As a matter of principle, on such an appeal the tribunal may make any decision which the officer below could have made on the legal questions before that officer. That principle encompasses dealing with new questions so as to reach the right result on an appeal, within the limit that the appeal tribunal has no jurisdiction (in the absence of express legislation to that effect) to determine questions which fall outside the scope of that which the officer below could have done on the proper legal view of the issues before him, by way of a claim or an application or otherwise."

They pointed out, at para.31, that s.12(8)(a) reinforces that approach because it is implicit in that provision that an appeal tribunal is not limited to considering issues actually raised by the parties.

Against that background, the Tribunal considered three issues concerning the powers of tribunals: whether supersession decisions can be substituted for revision decisions and vice versa, whether defects in supersession decisions can be remedied, and whether a tribunal can make a decision less favourable to a claimant than the decision under appeal. (Other issues considered by the Tribunal are noted in the annotations to regs 3 and 6 of the Social Security and Child Support (Decisions and Appeals) Regulations 1999).

Can supersession decisions be substituted for revision decisions and vice versa?

1.364   The Tribunal's decision on this issue is based on their view of the nature of appeals following supersession decisions under s.10 and revision decisions under s.9. In the former case, the appeal is, both in form and in substance, an appeal against the decision to supersede or not to supersede. Where there has been a revision or a refusal to revise, any appeal is, in form, against the original decision because s.12(1) does not provide for an appeal against the decision under s.9 but reg.31(2) of the Social Security and Child Support (Decisions and Appeals) Regulations 1999 extends the time for appealing against the earlier decision as revised or, where the revision or non-revision was under regs 3(1) or (3), not revised. If there is a refusal to revise under, say, reg.3(5)(a) on the ground of "official error", the time for appealing is not extended which may have the consequence that the refusal to revise cannot be challenged save by way of judicial review (*R(IS)15/04* , approved by the Court of Appeal in *Beltekian v Westminster CC* [2004] EWCA Civ 1784 (reported as *R(H) 8/05*)). However, where a claimant is entitled to appeal following a refusal to revise a decision on the ground of "official error", he or she must show that the original decision did arise from an official error if the appeal is to be allowed. Therefore, the Tribunal held at para.40 of *R(IB)2/04*, an appeal following a revision or refusal to revise is, in substance, an appeal against the decision under s.9, even if in form it is an appeal against the original decision.

The parties nonetheless argued that the legislation did not allow a tribunal to give a supersession decision on appeal from a revision decision and vice versa, although counsel for the claimants submitted that it should readily be implied that a revision decision included a refusal to supersede and that a supersession decision included a refusal to revise. However, the Tribunal considered that the result of taking the approach advocated by the parties had too often been absurd. At para.50, they said:

"The meaning of a statutory provision which is so clear that it admits only one possible construction cannot be altered or departed from by reference to the consequences, however inconvenient or anomalous. However, in our judgement the statutory provisions relevant to this issue fail by some margin to reach the degree of clarity which would bring that principle into play. In these circumstances, in ascertaining the legislature's intention, it is quite proper to have regard to the potential consequences of possible alternative constructions, in the context of the statutory scheme as a whole. In the field of benefit decisions and appeals procedure, we consider it proper, in construing the relevant provisions, to assume that the legislature did not intend to create a scheme which would be likely to lead to impracticable or indeed absurd results in a significant number of cases. On the contrary, we proceed on the basis that the legislature intended the provisions relating to decisions and appeals (and in particular those relating to provisions changing the effect of a previous decision) to form at least a reasonably workable scheme."

Having given examples of some of the more absurd consequences of the parties' submissions, the Tribunal held, at para.55:

"In our judgment, if an appeal tribunal decides that the Secretary of State's decision under Section 9 or Section 10 changing or refusing to change a previous decision was wrong then (subject to the restriction in Section 12(8)(b), if relevant) it has jurisdiction to make the revision or supersession decision which it considers the Secretary of State ought to have made, even if that means making a decision under Section 9 when the Secretary of State acted only under Section 10, and vice versa."

They rejected the need to resort to the theory of implied decisions on the ground that "the 1998 legislation could not have been intended to involve consideration of such arid technicalities and complications" (para.59). However, in *R(IS)15/04*, the same Tribunal, sitting a few weeks later resiled somewhat from what they had said in both para.55 and para.59 of *R(IB)2/04*. In *R(IS)15/04* (subsequently approved by the Court of Appeal in *Beltekian v Westminster CC* [2004] EWCA Civ 1784 (reported as *R(H) 8/05*)), the Secretary of State had expressly both superseded and refused to revise a decision. The claimant appealed but was out of time for appealing against the original decision and so was unable to challenge the refusal to revise although he could challenge the supersession. The Tribunal of Commissioners held that the appeal tribunal had had no jurisdiction to substitute a revision for the supersession, saying, at para.78:

"It seems to us, in those circumstances, if an appeal tribunal were permitted to substitute a revision decision for the supersession decision, that would in effect be to permit by the back door what is not permitted by the front door, namely an appeal against the refusal to revise."

Obscurely, they added that "[i]t would have been a different matter if the Secretary of State had not made a decision (whether express or implied) on the issue of revision for official error". It is not clear why they took that view, which, strictly speaking, is obiter, particularly as it is not clear what they meant by an implied decision, given their rejection of the theory in *R(IB)2/04*. It is suggested that the theory of implied decisions would always treat a decision in terms of supersession as an implied refusal to revise, even if the issue of official error had not expressly been considered, because it is a precondition of any supersession decision that there are no grounds for revision (see reg.6(3) of the Social Security and Child Support (Decisions and Appeals) Regulations 1999, which allows only a technical exception to that general rule). However, in *CDLA/1707/2005*, the Deputy Commissioner applied the approach of the Tribunal of Commissioners and substituted for a refusal to supersede an award of benefit a decision revising the award on the ground of "official error".

Can defects in supersession decisions be remedied?

1.365   The Tribunal of Commissioners in *R(IB)2/04* held that an appeal tribunal can remedy defects in a decision such as failing to acknowledge that an existing decision needed superseding, failing to state the grounds of supersession or relying on the wrong grounds of supersession.

> "72. . . . there may be some decisions made by the Secretary of State which have so little coherence or connection to legal powers that they do not amount to decisions under Section 10 at all. . . .
> 73. If, however, the Secretary of State's decision was made under Section 10 (as to which, see paragraph 76 below), . . . the appeal tribunal has jurisdiction, on appeal, to decide whether the outcome arrived at by that decision (i.e. either to change or not to change the original decision) was correct. . . .
> 76. In our judgment a decision should generally be regarded as having been made under Section 10, regardless of the form in which it may be expressed, if it has the effect of terminating an existing entitlement from the date of the decision (or from some later date than the effective date of the original decision). . . . Similarly, a decision should generally be regarded as having been made under Section 9 if it changes the original decision with effect from the effective date of that decision."

The implication of the Tribunal's decision appears to be that an appeal tribunal should limit its decision to holding that the Secretary of State's decision was invalid only in cases where the Secretary of State's decision is completely incoherent and the nature of the decision cannot be implied or where the Secretary of State had no power to make any decision at all. Another implication of a tribunal being entitled to correct defects in decisions of the Secretary of State is that it will often be unnecessary for a tribunal to consider the exact nature of the decision of the Secretary of State that is under appeal; it will usually be enough to consider what he *should* have decided (*R(IS) 2/08*).

The Tribunal went on to say, at para.82, that it is necessary for an appeal tribunal chairman to "perfect" or "recast" a defective decision in the tribunal's decision notice only "if either (i) the decision as expressed is wrong in some material respect (e.g. states an incorrect ground of appeal) or (ii) there is likely to be some particular practical benefit to the claimant or to the adjudication process in future in reformulating the decision". However, if a statement of reasons is requested, giving reasons for the tribunal's decision is likely to involve explaining how any defects in the Secretary of State's decision were approached.

The ability of a tribunal to correct defects in a decision of the Secretary of State means that, where the Secretary of State wrongly applied the personal capability assessment as amended by regulations that had been held to be ultra vires, the tribunal was entitled to substitute a decision by applying the unamended test (*R(IB)5/05*).

Can a tribunal make a decision less favourable to a claimant than a supersession decision under appeal?

1.366   The Tribunal held that an appeal tribunal could make a decision less favourable to a claimant than a supersession decision under appeal. This followed both from the Tribunal's view as to the nature of an appeal to an appeal tribunal and from the terms of s.12(8)(a), implicitly providing that a tribunal may consider issues not raised by the parties. However, the Tribunal made two important comments at paras 94 and 97 of their decision.

Firstly, a tribunal must consciously exercise the discretion in s.12(8)(a) to consider a point not raised by the parties and, if a statement of reasons is requested, must explain in that statement why the discretion was exercised in the manner it was. For the points to be taken into account when exercising the discretion, see the annotation to s.12(8)(a) below.

Secondly, where the tribunal's decision is even less favourable to the claimant than the original decision that was the subject of the supersession decision under appeal, the tribunal's decision is "effectively the exercise by the tribunal of the Secretary of State's power to supersede 'on his own initiative" and so, by virtue of s.10(5), the decision is usually effective from the date of the Secretary of State's decision under appeal rather than from the date of the claimant's application for supersession.

Although the First-tier Tribunal is therefore entitled to make a decision less favourable to a claimant than the one under appeal, a Commissioner discouraged tribunals from doing so in borderline cases. In *CDLA/2738/2007*, it was said –

"The tribunal was entitled to take the view that the claimant was not virtually unable to walk but the Secretary of State was equally entitled to take the opposite view. Where a tribunal's findings are not materially different from the Secretary of State's and the Secretary of State's conclusion in favour of the claimant is not perverse, a tribunal should be slow to interfere and must, in accordance with *R(IB) 2/04*, give reasons for considering it necessary to do so."

In *CDLA/884/2008*, he said –

"8. An increasing number of appeals before Commissioners seem to be cases where a tribunal has made a decision less favourable to the claimant than the one the claimant was challenging before the tribunal. It is not surprising that appeals should be brought before Commissioners in such cases, particularly as the consequence of any such decision is that there will have been an over-payment, the recoverability of which will have been left undetermined by the tribunal. Tribunals need to be aware of the dangers of being both prosecutor and judge, one of which is the risk of making errors unprompted by the parties. Such errors are too common and are contributing significantly to the caseload of Commissioners. It is particularly unfortunate that two of the several errors made by the tribunal in the present case were on points in respect of which a Tribunal of Commissioners had relatively recently given clear guidance.
9. There are other risks in being both prosecutor and judge. The most obvious is that there can be a perception that the tribunal has prejudged the case. Of course a tribunal has an inquisitorial or investigative role but here it is noteworthy that the tribunal, having apparently formed the (not unreasonable) view on the papers that the claimant's entitlement to any disability living allowance was doubtful, started the proceedings by warning the claimant that his existing award was at risk and advising him that he could withdraw his appeal. The claimant having declined to withdraw his appeal, the tribunal then launched straight into the question of the claimant's entitlement to the mobility component, by question-ing him about how he had got to the hearing, without first listening to what the claimant had to say about his needs for care which was the issue upon which he had brought his appeal. It is little wonder that the claimant says, in effect, that he formed an early view that the tribunal was more interested in its own agenda than in what he had to say."

He pointed out that it was not necessarily enough to give a claimant an opportu-nity to withdraw his appeal; it had been said in *R(IB) 2/04* that the claimant had to be given sufficient notice to enable him to prepare his case on the new issue, which meant being given notice of the case against him where that would not be obvious to him.

"10. . . . A tribunal is in a difficult position. If it gives the claimant too robust a warning at the beginning of a hearing, it runs the risk of giving the impression of having prejudged the case. If it does not give such a robust warning, the warning may not adequately convey to the claimant the case he or she needs to consider resisting with the consequence that a decision not to withdraw the appeal, or not to ask for an adjournment, is not fully informed. This is a powerful reason for tribunals refraining from making decisions less favourable to claimants than the decisions being challenged, except in the most obvious cases (e.g., where the evi-dence is overwhelming or the facts are not in dispute and no element of judgment is involved or where the law has been misapplied by the Secretary of State) or after an appropriate adjournment. In such obvious cases, a failure expressly to state why a tribunal has considered a point not in issue between the parties will not necessarily render the tribunal's decision erroneous in point of law; in less obvious cases, the absence of a reason for considering the point may suggest that the discretion to do so has not been exercised properly.

11. If a tribunal does not consider the correctness of an award that is not directly in issue before it, it does not follow that it should do nothing if it has doubts about the award. The chairman is at liberty to draw the doubts to the Secretary of State's attention in the decision notice and can arrange for the parties to be sent a copy of the record of proceedings (including his or her note of evidence) without them having to request it. That would enable the Secretary of State to consider a supersession or revision and, in disability living allowance cases, would often avoid the possibility of there having been an overpayment, which is often a consequence of a tribunal considering the issue and which often worries claimants more than the mere cessation of entitlement."

In both cases, the Commissioner restored the Secretary of State's decision. In practice, cases often turn on the claimant's own oral evidence which, if unfavourable to the claimant, is unlikely to be in dispute and, provided the findings of fact are such as to make it clear why the claimant could not be entitled to benefit in the light of that evidence, a tribunal is unlikely then to be found to have erred in not expressly stating why it took the point on its own initiative. An adjournment is also unlikely to be necessary where a case can be determined on the basis of the claimant's own oral evidence and where it could not reasonably be argued that the claimant was entitled to benefit in the light of that evidence. The cases where most care is needed are those truly on a borderline and those where a claimant might be able to provide further evidence if given an opportunity to do so.

Subs. (3)

1.367   See the note to Sch.2 to the Social Security and Child Support (Decisions and Appeals) Regulations 1999 in which it is suggested that either much of that schedule is ultra vires or else this subsection is of no practical effect.

Subs. (4)

1.368   Although this subsection assumes that a claimant has a right of appeal against a decision under either s.71 or s.74 of the 1992 Act, only decisions under s.71 are mentioned in Sch.3. However, in *R(IS) 14/04*, the Commissioner held that a claimant was entitled to appeal against a decision under s.74 by virtue of subs.(1)(a) of this section, rather than subs.(1)(b).

Subs. (7)

1.369   See regs 32 and 33 of the Social Security and Child Support (Decisions and Appeals) Regulations 1999, regs 28–32 of the Child Benefit and Guardian's Allowance (Decisions and Appeals) Regulations 2003 and regs 7–9 of the Health in Pregnancy Grant (Notices, Revisions and Appeals) (No.2) Regulations 2009.

Subs. (8) (a)

1.370   In *CDLA/1000/2001*, it was held that the question whether an issue is "raised by the appeal" is to be determined by reference to the substance of the appeal and not just the wording of the letter of appeal. The claimant was in receipt of the mobility component of disability living allowance and was seeking the care component. The Commissioner decided that, as the claimant had attributed some of his care needs to the arthritis that caused his mobility difficulties, it was impossible for the tribunal to consider the care component without also considering the basis of the award of the mobility component. Therefore, the claimant's entitlement to the mobility component was raised by his appeal in respect of the care component. The

Commissioner also held that the claimant had no preserved right to the protection formerly accorded to life awards of one component when a claimant had sought the other. That protection had been swept away when Pt II of the Social Security Administration Act 1992 was repealed by the Social Security Act 1998.

Paragraph (a) confers a discretion. In *CI/531/2000*, the Commissioner considered a standard submission by the Secretary of State in appeals relating to the diagnosis of industrial diseases in which it was said that the only issue before the tribunal was the diagnosis question and that, if the tribunal decided that question in the claimant's favour, it was not possible for them to go on and consider whether to award benefit. The Commissioner held the submission to be wrong in law but that the discretion to consider other issues must be exercised judicially. He pointed out that it was often desirable to deal with disablement at the same time as diagnosis but he said that natural justice required that the claimant (and, it can be added, the Secretary of State) be warned that disablement would also be considered and that when a tribunal dealt with a factual issue that had not previously been considered, the result was that the claimant was deprived of any appeal on the facts (and, it may be added, any application for revision under reg.3(1)(b) of the Social Security and Child Support (Decisions and Appeals) Regulations 1999). However, as already noted in relation to subs.(1), it was held in *CIB/2338/2000* that appeals lie only against "outcome decisions" and not against determinations of mere "questions". It follows that, in any case where a claimant has claimed disablement benefit, a determination that he or she is not suffering from a prescribed disease will be a determination made for the purpose of deciding that disablement benefit is not payable and any challenge to the determination will be made in an appeal against the refusal of benefit. If, on such an appeal, a tribunal decides that the claimant *was* suffering from the prescribed disease at the date the Secretary of State's decision was given, can the tribunal refuse to go on and determine all the other issues that must be determined if a decision is to be made as to whether or not to award benefit? In the light of *R(IS) 2/08*, the answer is now clearly "yes" and, in situations like that arising in *CI/531/2000*, it is often very much easier for everyone if the tribunal leaves the Secretary of State to make a new "outcome decision" than it would be if it does so itself. Thus, it may be that the only error in the Secretary of State's submission in *CI/531/2000* was that it was written in terms of what the tribunal could legally do rather than in terms of what it could do as a matter of practicality without obtaining further submissions.

The approach taken in *R(IS) 2/08* gives greater effect to subs.(8)(a) than the alternative approach would, but the provision would in any event apply where a tribunal could give an "outcome decision" without considering any new issue. In some instances considering a new issue may be to the considerable disadvantage of the claimant who has appealed to the tribunal.

In *R(IB)2/04* at paras 93 and 94, the Tribunal of Commissioners held that, where an appeal tribunal is minded to make a decision less favourable to the claimant than the one under appeal and the respondent has not invited them to make such a decision, the appeal tribunal must address their minds to the power conferred by subs.(8)(a) not to consider the issue. The discretion is one to be exercised judicially, taking into account all the circumstances of the particular case. Furthermore, the tribunal's decision is likely to be held to be erroneous in point of law if the statement of reasons does not show that there has been a conscious exercise of the discretion.

"In exercising the discretion, the appeal tribunal must of course have in mind, in particular, two factors. First, it must bear in mind the need to comply with Article 6 of the Convention and the rules of natural justice. This will involve, at the very least, ensuring that the claimant has had sufficient notice of the tribunal's intention to consider superseding adversely to him to enable him properly to prepare his case. The fact that the claimant is entitled to withdraw his appeal any time before the appeal tribunal's decision may also be material to what Article 6 and the rules of natural justice demand. Second, the appeal tribunal may consider it more appropriate to leave the question whether the original decision should be superseded adversely to the claimant to be decided subsequently by the Secretary of State. This might be so if, for example, deciding that question would involve factual issues which do not overlap those raised by the appeal, or if it would necessitate an adjournment of the hearing."

The same approach is required where a tribunal takes a new point against the Secretary of State. In *CH/3009/2002*, a decision had been made on a claim that could have been treated also as an application for the revision of a decision terminating an earlier award. The Commissioner held that, although it followed from *R(IB)2/04* that the tribunal had the power to give a decision in terms of revision, the question of revision could be left to the Secretary of State. Thus, subs.(8)(a) can be seen as providing an alternative course of action to the adjournment that will sometimes be required where a new point is taken, although the Commissioner deciding *CH/3009/2002* did comment that, depending on the terms of the Secretary of State's decision, it might not be possible for a claimant to get the case back before a tribunal given the decision of the Tribunal of Commissioners in *R(IS)15/04* (subsequently approved by the Court of Appeal in *Beltekian v Westminster CC* [2004] EWCA Civ 1784 (reported as *R(H) 8/05*)). It is suggested that the position might be no different if there were an adjournment because the Secretary of State could presumably make a decision before the tribunal was reconvened.

In considering how the discretion conferred by para.(a) should be exercised, a tribunal ought to have regard (among other things) to the adequacy of any alternative action that the claimant or Secretary of State might take to have the new issue taken into account and, if it is not obvious, ought to draw attention to that alternative action (*CDLA/15961/1996*). If an entirely new point is being taken at a hearing, it is necessary for the parties to have the opportunity of dealing with it but that does not necessarily mean there must be an adjournment because it ought to be possible for most points to be adequately considered immediately. If a party has deliberately chosen not to attend, the question whether there should be an adjournment so that he or she may consider the new point may be more complicated. There are three options: to refuse to consider the new point, to consider it immediately or to adjourn. A lot will depend on the nature of the issue and whether any advance notice was given of it, as well as the possibility of applying for a revision or supersession on the new ground. A wise appellant who wishes to raise a new point will give both the tribunal and the Secretary of State notice as soon as possible. However, if the Secretary of State chooses not to be represented at a hearing, it may be thought that he can hardly complain about not being allowed to comment on any evidence the claimant may give.

Subs.(8)(a) implies a power to consider new issues but makes it clear that there are limits to the extent to which the inquisitorial role of a tribunal imposes a duty to consider such issues. As was said by a Tribunal of Commissioners in *R(SB) 2/83*,

> "Everything will depend on the circumstances in any given instance. We would be slow to convict a tribunal of failure to identify an uncanvassed factual point in favour of the claimant in the absence of the most obvious and clear cut circumstances."

In particular, where a claimant has an apparently competent representative, it is not always necessary for a tribunal to explore matters not raised by the representative (see *CSDLA/336/2000*, in which the Commissioner reviews the authorities and emphasises the summary nature of proceedings before tribunals). Thus, in *CSIB/160/2000*, the representative identified the descriptors in issue on the all work test and the tribunal were entitled to assume that the representative knew the claimant's case and so therefore the tribunal did not err in not considering other descriptors. In *CH/2484/2006*, the Deputy Commissioner said that "it would be unrealistic—especially in a case like this where both parties were represented—to expect tribunals to read every clause of a tenancy agreement in case a representative fails to rely on a clause which might be helpful to his case". He also said—

"To the extent that the local authority is dissatisfied with the outcome of this case, that perhaps highlights the need for thorough preparation of a local authority's factual case in advance of tribunal hearings, so that all the points can be raised there. Even the most thoroughly prepared appeal to a Commissioner is not an adequate substitute for doing so, for the reason that, however strongly a Commissioner might doubt the factual correctness of a tribunal decision . . ., the Commissioner's doubts are irrelevant in the absence of an error of law. And it will seldom be an error of law for a tribunal to fail to deal with a point that a local authority representative has not raised before it."

Even less is a tribunal required to investigate issues when a representative has declined to make submissions on them having been given a specific opportunity to do so (*CSIB/588/1998*).

However, sometimes issues raised by the evidence but overlooked by otherwise competent professional representatives are so fundamental that a tribunal will err in not dealing with them. That was the case in *R4/01(IS)*, a decision of a Tribunal of Commissioners in Northern Ireland. The claimant's executor had appealed to a tribunal against a decision that £63,735.31 had been overpaid to the claimant and was recoverable from her estate because the claimant had failed to disclose capital assets in the form of land. The executor was represented by counsel. The case was argued on the basis that there had been disclosure but it was stated that, although the legal interest in the land was vested in the claimant, the land had been regarded as belonging to her brother. The Tribunal of Commissioners held that that clearly raised the question whether the claimant had any beneficial interest in the land and that the appeal tribunal had erred in failing to consider that issue notwithstanding that it had not been raised by counsel representing the executor. The issue had been fundamental to the appeal. However, the Tribunal of Commissioners also said that an appeal tribunal must have a reasonable expectation that important and fundamental issues will be brought to its attention by professional representatives. Given the professional representation, if the issue of the property being regarded as belonging to the brother had not been mentioned by a witness at the hearing itself, the appeal tribunal would have been entitled to conclude it had been dropped.

The Court of Appeal in Northern Ireland has, in *Mongan v Department for Social Development* [2005] NICA 16 (reported as *R3/05 (DLA)*), taken a similar approach to that taken by Commissioners and the approach taken in *Mongan* has been expressly endorsed by the Court of Appeal in England and Wales (*Secretary of State for Work and Pensions v Hooper* [2007] EWCA Civ 495 (reported as *R(IB) 4/07*). In *Mongan*, the Court held that the identical wording of the Northern Ireland equivalent of s.12(8)(a) suggests "that the tribunal would not be absolved of the duty to consider relevant issues simply because they have been neglected by the appellant or her legal representatives and that it has a role to identify what issues are at stake on the appeal even if they have not been clearly or expressly articulated by the appellant." There is no duty "to exhaustively trawl the evidence to see if there is any remote possibility of an issue being raised by it" but issues "clearly apparent from the evidence" must be considered.

"[17] Whether an issue is sufficiently apparent from the evidence will depend on the particular circumstances of each case. Likewise, the question of how far the tribunal must go in exploring such an issue will depend on the specific facts of the case. The more obviously relevant an issue, the greater will be the need to investigate it. An extensive enquiry into an issue will not invariably be required. Indeed, a perfunctory examination of the issue may often suffice. It appears to us, however, that where a higher rate of benefit is claimed and the facts presented to the tribunal suggest that an appellant might well be entitled to a lower rate, it will normally be necessary to examine the issue, whether or not it has been raised by the appellant or her legal representatives.

[18] In carrying out their inquisitorial function, the tribunal should have regard to whether the party has the benefit of legal representation. It need hardly be said that close attention should be paid to the possibility that relevant issues might be overlooked where the appellant does not have legal representation. Where an appellant is legally represented the tribunal is entitled to look to the legal representative for elucidation of the issues that arise. But this does not relieve them of the obligation to enquire into potentially relevant matters. A poorly represented party should not be placed at any greater disadvantage than an unrepresented party."

In that case, the claimant had sought the higher rate of the mobility component of disability living allowance but the Court held that the arguments and evidence presented to the tribunal were such that it should have been alert to the need to investigate entitlement to the lower rate of the mobility component, whether or not that question was raised by the claimant's solicitor.

On the other hand, in *CDLA/4099/2004*, the Commissioner held that a tribunal had not erred in law in failing to deal with an issue when the claimant had an adequate alternative remedy. The claimant had applied for supersession of an award of disability living allowance. The application was treated as effective from the date it was received and, on appeal, the case was argued before the tribunal on that basis because the claimant's representative wrongly considered that an award of benefit for a period before the application could be considered on a subsequent application for revision. In fact, the tribunal could, by virtue of s.12(8)(a), have considered entitlement to benefit during that earlier period (because reg.7(6) of the Social Security and Child Support (Decisions and Appeals) Regulations 1999 would have applied if the claimant's proposed argument in respect of that earlier period had been accepted). However, the Commissioner held that the tribunal had not been *bound* to consider entitlement during that earlier period because the claimant still had an adequate alternative remedy in a further application for supersession.

Subs. (8) (b)

By contrast with para.(a), para.(b) confers no discretion. In the light of reg.3(9) of the Social Security and Child Support (Decisions and Appeals) Regulations 1999 and s.9(5) of the Act, when a decision has been revised under s.9, "the time when the decision appealed against was made" must refer to the date on which the original decision was made. Paragraph (b) is therefore consistent with the approach that any change of circumstances requires a new claim or a supersession under s.10 and it reverses the effect of *R(S)2/98*. Paragraph (b) did not apply where the appeal was brought before May 21, 1998 when this Act received the Royal Assent and Sch.6, para.3 (which made transitory provision preventing social security appeal tribunals and disability appeal tribunals from taking account of circumstances not obtaining at the date of the decision under appeal) came into force. In such a case, a tribunal had still to consider the claimant's entitlement to benefit throughout the period to the date of its decision or down to the date from which another decision was effective (*CIB/213/1999*).

It is important to note that para.(b) does not prevent a tribunal having regard to evidence that was not before the Secretary of State and came into existence after the decision was made or to evidence of events after the decision under appeal was made for the purpose of drawing inferences as to the circumstances obtaining when, or before, the decision was made (*R(DLA) 2/01*, *R(DLA) 3/01*). This creates particular difficulties where entitlement to benefit depends on a prognosis. Thus, in *R(DLA) 3/01*, the claimant would be entitled to disability living allowance only if she was likely to satisfy the relevant conditions for six months. She was recovering from an operation. The Commissioner held that, in such a case, a tribunal was entitled to take account of the actual rate of recovery, even though the evidence of that arose after the date of the decision under appeal, provided that the fact that the claimant had not recovered as quickly as originally expected merely reflected

1.371

the natural vagaries of an uncertain recovery process. Untoward circumstances arising after the date of the decision had to be disregarded, whether that operated to the claimant's advantage or to her disadvantage. Thus the fact that a claimant recovering from a heart attack developed pneumonia after the Secretary of State's decision was made would have to be ignored. So too would a dramatic improvement in a claimant's condition due to the use of a new drug. A similar case came before a Commissioner in *CDLA/2878/2000*. The claimant was a nurse who became incapacitated due to a slipped disc. She claimed disability living allowance on August 31, 1999, had a successful operation on December 17, 1999 and was able to return to work on February 14, 2000. The tribunal said simply that disability living allowance could not be awarded because there was no evidence that the claimant could have satisfied the conditions of entitlement from February 14, 2000, which was less than six months from the date of claim. The Commissioner set aside the tribunal's decision on the ground that the tribunal had not considered whether, at the date of claim, it had been likely that she would cease to satisfy the conditions of entitlement within six months. He directed the new tribunal to determine that likelihood on the basis of what was known at the date of claim.

A contention that subs.(8)(b) did not apply to changes of circumstances occurring between the date of a decision made in advance and the date from which the decision was effective was rejected by a Tribunal of Commissioners in *R(DLA) 4/05* who pointed out that s.8(2)(b) precluded the Secretary of State from taking account of any such change of circumstances that he might anticipate. However, they stressed that they were not disagreeing with the approach taken in *R(DLA) 3/01* and also that the Secretary of State (when making an advance award) could take account of the effects of the mere passage of time, such as the claimant attaining a certain age or the qualifying period for a benefit being completed. Consequently, a tribunal may take account of the effect of the mere passage of time after the date of the Secretary of State's decision in any case where the Secretary of State could have made an advance award of disability allowance under reg.13A of the Social Security (Claims and Payments) Regulations 1987. In *Secretary of State for Work and Pensions v Bhakta* [2006] EWCA Civ 65 (reported as *R(IS) 7/06*), the Court of Appeal approved *R(DLA) 4/05* and applied it to an income support case where an advance award could have been made under reg.13. The case was one where the only reason that the claimant had not been found by the Commissioner to be habitually resident at the date of the Secretary of State's decision was that a sufficient period of residence had not elapsed by that date. Reg.13 has been amended with effect from May 23, 2007 so as to exclude that class of case (and all claims by "persons from abroad") from the scope of the regulation (see reg.2(2)(c) of the Social Security, Housing Benefit and Council Tax Benefit (Miscellaneous Amendments) Regulations 2007 (SI 2007/1331)), but the principle confirmed in *Bhakta* remains good in other contexts. *R(DLA) 4/05* has also been followed by a Tribunal of Commissioners in Northern Ireland (*R3/05 (DLA)*).

In *CDLA/3293/2000*, a case where the claimant had appealed against a decision of the Secretary of State to make no award of disability living allowance, the Commissioner held that s.12(8)(b) did not preclude a tribunal from using hindsight to fix the length of an award that they considered should be made. However, in *CDLA/3722/2000*, a tribunal was held not entitled to do that where the award would be for less than the minimum period of six months. At the time of the Secretary of State's decision she was likely to satisfy the conditions for disability living allowance for six months. In fact, she had a course of treatment and got better much earlier than had been expected. The Commissioner held that the tribunal were obliged to turn a blind eye to the improvement and the Secretary of State would not be able to supersede the decision so as to prevent benefit being paid for longer than the claimant's condition merited. The Commissioner deciding *R(DLA) 3/01* observed that s.12(8)(b) required tribunals to indulge in the sort of artificial exercise that is frowned upon in modern courts where judges are not expected to close their eyes to reality and he referred to *Charles v Hugh James Jones and Jenkins (a firm)* [2000] 1 All E.R. 289, 299–301. Section 12(8)(b) is of particular importance in disablement benefit cases where tribunals can usually themselves examine the claimant (see reg.52 of the Social Security and Child Support (Decisions and Appeals) Regulations 1999) and must be careful to distinguish between those of their findings that are relevant to circumstances obtaining at the time of the decision under appeal and those that are not.

In *CIS/2428/1999*, it was pointed out that a literal interpretation of s.12(8)(b) would prevent a tribunal from taking account of a cause for a late claim which existed before the claim was made and had ceased to exist before the Secretary of State's decision on the claim. The Commissioner considered that that would be absurd and would prevent adjudication on a case falling within reg.19(5) of the Social Security (Claims and Payments) Regulations 1987. He extended the principle behind *R(DLA) 3/01* and held that a circumstance "obtains" at the date of decision if it is a circumstance, whenever it occurred, that is relied on by a claimant in justifying a late claim. The principle has been further extended in *CJSA/2375/00*. In that case, the claimant had failed to attend two courses and had been disqualified from jobseeker's allowance for two weeks in respect of the first failure and four weeks in respect of the second failure. The disqualification for four weeks was permitted only because there had been a previous disqualification. The claimant appealed against both disqualifications and the appeals came before two different tribunals. The appeal against the first disqualification was allowed. The second appeal was dismissed and the claimant appealed to the Commissioner. The Commissioner said that, following the decision of the first tribunal, the Secretary of State should have revised the second disqualification under reg.3(6) of the Social Security and Child Support (Decisions and Appeals) Regulations 1999, so as to reduce the period to two weeks. However, as the Secretary of State had not done so, the second tribunal should have reduced the period, notwithstanding that the decision of the first tribunal had been given after the Secretary of State's decision on the second disqualification. The Commissioner said:

> "In a case like this, an appeal tribunal is entitled to take account of any factor known to it that relates to a past period or past event that was relevant to the decision under appeal, even if the position at the date of the hearing is different from that at the date of the decision. This gives section 12(8)(b) a sensible operation. It allows an appeal tribunal to substitute a decision on factors relevant to the period the Secretary of State had considered. But it prevents the tribunal from trespassing into the period after that date by taking account of factors that are only relevant to that later period.

> I repeat that I have not defined the words used in section 12(8)(b). I have simply tried to give them a sensible operation in circumstances like those involved in this case. I emphasise that I have been concerned in this decision with past periods or events. I have not been concerned with cases where the Secretary of State has had to speculate on the likely future course of events, such as the qualifying period for a disability living allowance, which I considered in [*R(DLA) 3/01*]".

Similar contortions were required in *CJSA/2472/2005*. In this case, entitlement to jobseeker's allowance had been terminated on the ground that the claimant had to be treated as not being available for work because the restrictions he had put on his availability were more restrictive than those recorded in his jobseeker's agreement. He had already, before the termination of his entitlement to benefit, applied for a variation of his jobseeker's agreement. That application had been only partially successful and the claimant had appealed against both the variation of his jobseeker's agreement and the termination of his entitlement to jobseeker's allowance. The Commissioner held that the Secretary of State, a tribunal or a Commissioner may direct that a varied jobseeker's agreement be given retrospective effect so that it has effect from the date of the application for variation. The consequence of the Commissioner allowing the claimant's appeal in respect of the jobseeker's agreement and making such a direction in that case was that, if the claimant signed the varied agreement, the circumstances obtaining at the date of the decision in respect of entitlement to jobseeker's allowance would be changed, affecting the operation of s.12(8)(b). He therefore adjourned the appeal in respect of entitlement to jobseeker's allowance in order to give the claimant the opportunity to sign the varied jobseeker's agreement, pointing out that the Secretary of State would be able to revise the termination of entitlement if the agreement were signed.

Section 12(8)(b) would be unobjectionable if, like s.12(8)(a), it said "need not" instead of "shall not". As it is, it introduces an unwelcome element of technicality into appeals to tribunals that are generally supposed to be user-friendly. As the cases demonstrate, this is particularly so where "outcome decisions" in respect of entitlement are dependent on other decisions. In less complex cases, the remedy for a claimant is to make a new claim, or application for supersession, whenever there is an event that might be regarded as a new circumstance. There may be some cases where the wise claimant will make such claims or applications at regular intervals while an appeal is pending. The Secretary of State would then be obliged to make separate decisions on each claim or application (because the power to refer claims or applications to a tribunal so that they can be considered with a pending appeal has been abolished) and there would be a separate right of appeal against each decision. However, experience suggests that claimants do not consider new claims or applications to be necessary while an appeal is pending, even though some of the literature provided to them makes the suggestion, and so the reality may be that claimants lose benefit that they would undoubtedly have been entitled to but for s.12(8)(b).

Note that where a claimant does make a new claim or application for supersession pending an appeal, the Secretary of State is now empowered to revise the decision made on that claim or application in the light of the decision given on appeal (reg.3(5A) of the Social Security and Child Support (Decisions and Appeals) Regulations 1999). This makes it unnecessary for claimants to lodge repeated appeals based on the same grounds, but it remains necessary to lodge a further appeal if the point in issue arises out of a change of circumstances since the decision that was the subject of the original appeal.

Of course, s.12(8)(b) can work in a claimant's favour if there has been a new circumstance since the decision under appeal that would have reduced his or her entitlement to benefit. It may well be that the Secretary of State could not supersede the tribunal's decision (see the note to reg.6(2)(a) of the Social Security and Child Support (Decisions and Appeals) Regulations 1999). See *CDLA/3722/2000*, mentioned above. Giving effect to the tribunal's decision in the claimant's favour might, in some cases, give rise to an overpayment that was recoverable under s.71 of the Social Security Administration Act 1992 on the basis that the change of circumstances should have been disclosed to the Secretary of State so that the decision under appeal could have been superseded before the appeal was heard. However, in a case where the Secretary of State had refused benefit altogether in the decision under appeal and benefit had then been awarded by the tribunal on the basis of their findings as to the circumstances obtaining at the date of the Secretary of State's decision, it seems unlikely that there would have been any duty on the claimant to disclose any changes of circumstances while the appeal was pending. Even if the Secretary of State does have power to supersede a tribunal's decision in the light of a change of circumstances arising before the decision was given, another problem facing the Secretary of State may be continued ignorance of the new circumstance. He does not always send a representative to tribunal hearings and he does not usually ask for a copy of the record of proceedings or a full statement of the tribunal's findings and reasoning. Unless a tribunal refers in the short decision notice, recorded under r.33(2)(a) of the Tribunal Procedure (First-tier Tribunal) (Social Entitlement Chamber) Rules 2008, to a change of circumstances mentioned at the hearing, the Secretary of State may remain ignorant of it for ever and, of course, the tribunal will have been obliged by s.12(8)(b) to ignore the change when awarding benefit.

Although an element of discretion in s.12(8)(b) might make it much easier to do justice, a provision similar to s.12(8)(b) has been held not to be incompatible with the European Convention on Human Rights even in the context of asylum claims (*AS (Somalia) v Secretary of State for the Home Department* [2009] UKHL 32; [2009] 1 W.L.R. 1385).

Subs.(9)

1.372   In *Wood v Secretary of State for Work and Pensions* [2003] EWCA Civ 53 (reported as *R(DLA) 1/03*), the Court of Appeal overruled *R(DLA) 6/02* and held that the phrase "a decision superseding" should be read as "a decision taken pursuant to the power to supersede", so as to permit an appeal against a refusal to supersede. Rix LJ conceded that that left this subsection as "a fairly redundant provision".

Redetermination etc. of appeals by tribunal

1.373   **13.**—(1) This section applies where an application is made [² to the First-tier Tribunal for permission to appeal to the Upper Tribunal from any decision of the First-tier Tribunal under section 12 or this section].

(2) [² . . .]

(3) If each of the principal parties to the case expresses the view that the decision was erroneous in point of law, [²the First-tier Tribunal] shall set aside the decision and refer the case for determination by a differently constituted [²the First-tier Tribunal].

[¹(4) In this section and section 14 below "the principal parties" means—

(a) the persons mentioned in subsection (3)(a) and (b) of that section, and

(b) where applicable, the person mentioned in subsection (3)(d) and such a person as is first mentioned in subsection (4) of that section.]

AMENDMENT

1. Social Security Contributions (Transfer of Functions, etc.) Act 1999, Sch.7, para.26 (April 1, 1999).

2. Transfer of Tribunal Functions Order 2008 (SI 2008/2833), Sch.3, paras 143 and 150 (November 3, 2008), subject to a saving under art.1(5).

DEFINITION

"the principal parties"—see subs.(4).

GENERAL NOTE

1.374   By reg.7 of the Child Trust Funds (Non-tax Appeals) Regulations 2005 (SI 2005/191), this section is applied in a modified form to appeals under ss.21(9) and 22 of the Child Trust Funds Act 2004 (see Vol.IV) but, as the modifications involve the omission of subs.(3), which is now the only operative part of the section, and as the only reference to "principal parties" in s.14 has been repealed, the continued application of this section to those cases seems entirely pointless. Until April 1, 2009, this section was also applied in a similarly modified form to appeals under the Tax Credits Act 2002 but, for reasons explained in the note to s.12, the regulation applying it appears to have lapsed in relation to cases in Great Britain.

Indeed, it is not easy to see why this section has not been completely repealed for ordinary social security cases as well. Subsection (2) provided a power to set aside a decision where a tribunal chairman considering an application for leave to appeal against a decision of the tribunal considered that the decision was erroneous in point of law. That was obviously a useful power, enabling unnecessary appeals to be avoided, and it has been extended to all decisions of the First-tier Tribunal against which there is a right of appeal by s.9 of the Tribunals, Courts and Enforcement Act 2007. Subsection (2) has been repealed (subject to a saving for reasons explained in the note to ss.5 to 7) because it would add nothing to s.9 of the 2007 Act.

Now, subs.(3) is the only operative part of the section. It is a strange provision, *requiring* a judge to set aside a decision of the First-tier Tribunal if the principal parties express the view that it was erroneous in point of law, whether or not he or she agrees. It would be unobjectionable if it conferred a *power* to set aside a decision with which all the parties were dissatisfied but it is the duty to do so that creates the difficulty. The First-tier Tribunal will always have included a judge, whereas it is very rare for any party to be represented by a lawyer. Yet, if the parties express the view, no matter how unreasonably, that the decision is erroneous in point of law, their view prevails and the judge must set the decision aside. It is not even necessary for the parties to agree on the error of law. It might, perhaps, be arguable that, in some cases, different parts of a decision of a tribunal are different decisions for the purposes of this section but that will not always be possible. The First-tier Tribunal may have steered carefully between two extreme views advanced by the parties, all to no avail. If re-determining tribunals took the same approach and the parties remained stubborn, the litigation could go on for ever unless action were taken to avoid subs. (3) coming into play. There is no scope for a judge to take the view that the case would be better determined by the Upper Tribunal than by the First-tier Tribunal differently constituted.

Happily, the necessity of applying subs.(3) seldom arises because it is comparatively rare for all parties to assert that there is an error of law in a tribunal's decision. This is largely because it is unnecessary to ascertain the views of a respondent to an application for permission to appeal, since granting permission is not a final determination of the parties' rights and refusing permission is a decision in favour of the respondent. Most applications for permission are made by claimants. However, for some reason that may owe more to history rather than principle, where the Secretary of State applies for permission to appeal, it is the practice of the Social Entitlement Chamber of the First-tier Tribunal always to seek the view of the claimant before determining the application. That might be necessary if the judge were contemplating reviewing the decision instead of granting permission but is unnecessary otherwise. If, in those circumstances, the claimant asserts that the tribunal's decision is erroneous in point of law the judge will be bound to set the decision aside.

The other circumstance where this section may be brought into play is where both parties seek permission to appeal against a decision. However, a decision may not be set aside under this section once one such application for permission to appeal has been determined and permission has been either granted or refused (*CF/6923/1999*, but see *CIB/2949/2005*, where the Commissioner suggested that this might have been too broadly expressed).

It seems unlikely that this section will be found to apply where the First-tier Tribunal has refused to admit an application for permission because it was late (see r.38(5)(b) of the Tribunal Procedure (First-tier Tribunal) (Social Entitlement Chamber) Rules 2008).

Note that, where a decision is set aside, the case must be referred to a differently constituted tribunal. It is usual for the decision that has been set aside to be included in the papers before the new tribunal.

That is not inappropriate. Even if their findings of fact cannot be relied upon, issues identified by the first tribunal may well be of assistance to the new tribunal, although it must be careful not to be influenced by the discredited findings (*Swash v Secretary of State for the Home Department* [2006] EWCA Civ 1093; [2007] 1 W.L.R. 1264). There may, however, be special circumstances in which the legally qualified panel member setting the first decision aside considers that the interests of justice require the case to be heard by a tribunal that has not seen that decision and he or she will be able to issue appropriate directions to ensure that that happens (*ibid.*).

In *CIB/4193/2003*, a decision made on a consideration of the papers was set aside and a new paper consideration was arranged without that being made clear to the claimant who had decided that she wanted to attend a hearing. The Commissioner set aside the second decision and suggested that claimants should be given an opportunity to ask for a hearing when a decision is set aside under this section.

In *CIS/4533/2001*, it was held that there was no appeal against a setting aside under this section but that was because a decision under this section was then made by a legally qualified panel member whereas the right of appeal was expressed as being against a decision of an appeal tribunal. Since the coming into force of the Tribunals, Courts and Enforcement Act 2007, different considerations would apply.

Appeal from [²First-tier Tribunal to Upper Tribunal]

1.375   **14.**—(1) [² . . .]

(2) [¹ . . .]

(3) [¹ . . .] An appeal [² to the Upper Tribunal under section 11 of the Tribunals, Courts and Enforcement Act 2007 from any decision of the First-tier Tribunal under section 12 or 13 above lies] at the instance of any of the following—

(a) the Secretary of State;

(b) the claimant and such other person as may be prescribed;

(c) in any of the cases mentioned in subsection (5) below, a trade union; and

(d) a person from whom it is determined that any amount is recoverable under or by virtue of section 71 or 74 of the Administration Act.

(4) In a case relating to industrial injuries benefit an appeal [² to the Upper Tribunal under section 11 of the Tribunals, Courts and Enforcement Act 2007 from any decision of the First-tier Tribunal under section 12 or 13 above lies] at the instance of a person whose entitlement to benefit is, or may be, under Part VI of Schedule 7 to the Contributions and Benefits Act, affected by the decision appealed against, as well as at the instance of any person or body such as is mentioned in subsection (3) above.

(5) The following are the cases in which an appeal lies at the instance of a trade union—

(a) where the claimant is a member of the union at the time of the appeal and was so immediately before the matter in question arose;

(b) where that matter in any way relates to a deceased person who was a member of the union at the time of his death;

(c) where the case relates to industrial injuries benefit and the claimant or, in relation to industrial death benefit, the deceased, was a member of the union at the time of the relevant accident.

(6) Subsections [¹ . . .] (3) and (5) above, as they apply to a trade union, apply also to any other association which exists to promote the interests and welfare of its members.

(7) [² ...]

(8) [² ...]

(9) [² ...]

(10) [² ...]

(11) [² ...]

(12) [² ...]

AMENDMENTS

1. Social Security Contributions (Transfer of Functions, etc.) Act 1999, Sch.7, para.27 (April 1, 1999).
2. Transfer of Tribunal Functions Order 2008 (SI 2008/2833), Sch.3, paras 143 and 151 (November 3, 2008), subject to a saving under art.1(5).

DEFINITIONS

"the Administration Act"—see s.84.
"claimant"—see s.39(1) and, by virtue of s.39(2), see s.191 of the Social Security Administration Act 1992.
"the Contributions and Benefits Act"—*ibid.*
"industrial injuries benefit"—by virtue of s.39(2), see s.191 of the Social Security Administration Act 1992.
"prescribed"—see s.84.

GENERAL NOTE

Originally, this section provided for a right of appeal to a Social Security Commissioner from a decision of an appeal tribunal and it also introduced Sch.4, providing for the appointment of Commissioners. The right of appeal has now been replaced by the right of appeal to the Upper Tribunal under s.11 of the Tribunals, Courts and Enforcement Act 2007. However, the repeals of subsections (7) to (12) are subject to a saving for the reason given in the note to ss. 5 to 7.

Now this section merely makes provision as to who may appeal in social security cases. Subsections (3) and (4) probably add little to s.11(2) of the 2007 Act, which provides that "any party" has a right of appeal. Section 11(2) certainly means that the failure to exercise the power to make regulations under subs.(3)(b) to the same extent as the equivalent power in s.12(2) of this Act no longer creates any substantial difficulty. Subsections (5) and (6) reproduce provisions in earlier legislation which fell into disuse about thirty years ago. The modern approach of trade unions and other organisations is to act as a representative of a member rather than appealing in their own right.

In relation to cases where the original decision was made by Her Majesty's Revenue and Customs (i.e. cases under s.170 of the Pension Schemes Act 1993 or cases concerning the former working families' tax credit or disabled person's tax credit or, now child benefit or guardian's allowance), this section applies with the modification that the reference to the Secretary of State are to be read as a reference to Her Majesty's Revenue and Customs (Pensions Schemes Act 1993, s.170(7), Tax Credits Act 1999, Sch.2, para.21 and Sch.4, para.3(2), Tax Credits Act 2002, Sch.4, para.15 and Commissioners for Revenue and Customs Act 2005, s.4(1)).

By reg.8 of the Child Trust Funds (Non-tax Appeals) Regulations 2005 (SI 2005/191), this section is applied in a rather more modified form to appeals under ss.21(9) and 22 of the Child Trust Funds Act 2004 (see Vol.IV). Until April 1, 2009, this section was also applied, with similar modifications, to appeals under the Tax Credits Act 2002 but, for reasons explained in the note to s.12, the regulation applying it appears to have lapsed in relation to cases in Great Britain.

Application for permission to appeal against a decision of the Upper Tribunal

15.—(1) [¹ ...]
(2) [¹ ...]
(3) [¹ An application for permission to appeal from a decision of the Upper Tribunal in respect of a decision of the First-tier Tribunal under section 12 or 13] may only be made by—
(a) a person who, before the proceedings before the [¹ Upper Tribunal]

1.376

1.377

were begun, was entitled to appeal to the [¹ Upper Tribunal] from the decision to which the [¹ Upper Tribunal's] decision relates;

(b) any other person who was a party to the proceedings in which the first decision mentioned in paragraph (a) above was given;

(c) any other person who is authorised by regulations to apply for [¹
· permission];

[¹ ...]

(4) [¹ ...]

(5) [¹ ...]

AMENDMENTS

1. Transfer of Tribunal Functions Order 2008 (SI 2008/2833), Sch.3, paras 143 and 152 (November 3, 2008), subject to a saving under art.1(5).

GENERAL NOTE

1.378   Originally, this section provided for a right of appeal to an appellate court from a decision of a Social Security Commissioner. The equivalent right of appeal from a decision of the Upper Tribunal is now provided by s.13 of the Tribunals, Courts and Enforcement Act 2007. Now this section merely makes provision as to who may appeal in social security cases. It will seldom be necessary for a person to rely on this section rather than section 13(2) of the 2007 Act, which provides that "any party" has a right of appeal and therefore the continued application of this section to appeals under ss.21(9) and 22 of the Child Trust Funds Act 2004, by reg.10 of the Child Trust Funds (Non-tax Appeals) Regulations 2005 (SI 2005/191), seems unnecessary. Until April 1, 2009, this section was also applied to appeals under the Tax Credits Act 2002 but, for reasons explained in the note to s.12, the regulation applying it appears to have lapsed in relation to cases in Great Britain. The repeal of most of this section and the amendments to subs.(3) are subject to a saving so as to enable a person to appeal to the Court of Session against a decision of a Social Security Commissioner under s.159 of the Health and Social Care (Community Health and Standards) Act 2003 (see the note to ss.5 to 7).

[¹ Functions of Senior President of Tribunals

1.379   **15A.**—(1) The Senior President of Tribunals shall ensure that appropriate steps are taken by the First-tier Tribunal to secure the confidentiality, in such circumstances as may be prescribed, of any prescribed material, or any prescribed classes or categories of material.

(2) Each year the Senior President of Tribunals shall make to the Secretary of State and the Child Maintenance and Enforcement Commission a written report, based on the cases coming before the First-tier Tribunal, on the standards achieved by the Secretary of State and the Child Maintenance and Enforcement Commission in the making of decisions against which an appeal lies to the First-tier Tribunal.

(3) The Lord Chancellor shall publish the report.]

AMENDMENT

1. Transfer of Tribunal Functions Order 2008 (SI 2008/2833), Sch.3, paras 143 and 153 (November 3, 2008).

GENERAL NOTE

1.380   This section replaces paras.7 and 10 of Sch.1, the whole of that Schedule having been repealed. The Senior President may delegate his functions under this section to another judge, e.g., the President of the Social Entitlement Chamber of the First-tier Tribunal (see s.8 of the Tribunals, Courts and Enforcement Act 2008).

Procedure etc.

Procedure

16.—(1) Regulations ("procedure regulations") may make any such pro-   **1.381**
vision as is specified in Schedule 5 to this Act.

(2) [¹ . . .]

(3) It is hereby declared—

(a) [¹ . . .]

(b) that the power to provide for the procedure to be followed in connection with the making of decisions by the Secretary of State includes power to make provision with respect to the formulation of the matters to be decided, whether on a reference under section 117 of the Administration Act or otherwise.

(4) *Omitted.*

(5) *Omitted.*

(6) [¹ . . .]

(7) [¹ . . .]

(8) [. . .]

(9) [. . .]

AMENDMENTS

1. Transfer of Tribunal Functions Order 2008 (SI 2008/2833), Sch.3, paras 143 and 154 (November 3, 2008), subject to a saving under art.1(5).

DEFINITIONS

"the Administration Act"—see s.84.
"procedure regulations"—see subs.(1).

GENERAL NOTE

The repeal of most of this section is subject to a saving for reasons explained in   **1.382**
the note to ss. 5 to 7.

Subs.(1)
See the Social Security and Child Support (Decisions and Appeals) Regulations   **1.383**
1999 and the Child Benefit and Guardian's Allowance (Decisions and Appeals) Regulations 2003. By reg.11 of the Child Trust Funds (Non-tax Appeals) Regulations 2005 (SI 2005/191), this subsection is applied to appeals under ss. 21(9) and 22 of the Child Trust Funds Act 2004. See Vol.IV for that Act and the Child Trust Funds (Appeals) Regulations 2005 which are made under this subsection as so applied. Until April 1, 2009, it was also applied to appeals under the Tax Credits Act 2002 but, for reasons explained in the note to s.12, the regulation applying it appears to have lapsed in relation to cases in Great Britain.

Subss.(4) and (5)
These subsections are to be repealed by the Social Security Contributions   **1.384**
(Transfer of Functions, etc.) Act 1999, Sch.7, para.28, presumably at the same time as the only provisions that would have given them practical effect and which have never been brought into force.

Finality of decisions

1.385   17.—(1) Subject to the provisions of this Chapter [¹ and to any provision made by or under Chapter 2 of Part 1 of the Tribunals, Courts and Enforcement Act 2007], any decision made in accordance with the foregoing provisions of this Chapter shall be final; and subject to the provisions of any regulations under section 11 above, any decision made in accordance with those regulations shall be final.

(2) If and to the extent that regulations so provide, any finding of fact or other determination embodied in or necessary to such a decision, or on which such a decision is based, shall be conclusive for the purposes of—

(a) further such decisions;

(b) decisions made under the Child Support Act; and

(c) decisions made under the Vaccine Damage Payments Act.

AMENDMENT

1. Transfer of Tribunal Functions Order 2008 (SI 2008/2833), Sch.3, paras 143 and 155 (November 3, 2008).

DEFINITIONS

"the Child Support Act"—see s.84.
"the Vaccine Damage Payments Act"—see s.84.

GENERAL NOTE

1.386   By reg.12 of the Child Trust Funds (Non-tax Appeals) Regulations 2005 (SI 2005/191), this subsection is applied with substantial modifications to appeals under ss.21(9) and 22 of the Child Trust Funds Act 2004 (see Vol.IV). Until April 1, 2009, it was also applied in modified form to appeals under the Tax Credits Act 2002 but, for reasons explained in the note to s.12, the regulation applying it appears to have lapsed in relation to cases in Great Britain.

Subs. (1)

1.387   This re-enacts s.60(1) of the Social Security Administration Act 1992. Decisions are "final" subject to appeals and revisions or supersesssions. Therefore, it is not possible to sue the Secretary of State in negligence in respect of a decision (*Jones v Department of Employment* [1989] Q.B. 1) although an action could lie in misfeasance. That does not prevent the Department for Work and Pensions being sued in respect of bad advice. The finality of decisions does not prevent decisions being challenged by way of judicial review (*R. v Medical Appeal Tribunal, Ex p. Gilmore* [1957] 1 Q.B. 574, a decision made before there was a right of appeal from a medical appeal tribunal to a Commissioner) although the reluctance of the High Court to allow such challenges when there is a statutory right of appeal means that they are confined to exceptional cases.

Subs. (2)

1.388   See reg.10 of the Social Security and Child Support (Decisions and Appeals) Regulations 1999 (in relation to decisions as to whether or not a person is incapable of work) and reg.5(2) and 6(1) of the Social Security (Industrial Diseases) (Prescribed Diseases) Regulations 1985 (in relation to whether or not a person has been suffering from a prescribed disease). Note that there is no express provision re-enacting s.60(2) of the 1992 Act which provided that, as a general rule, a finding in one decision was *not* conclusive for the purpose of any other decision. However, it is suggested that such an express provision is not necessary and that, in the absence of any rule of evidence to the contrary, a person or body making a decision is entitled to rely on an earlier finding but is not bound to do so. If that were not the approach to be taken in the absence of any express provision, subs. (2) would be unnecessary. Thus, as was pointed out in *CIB/3327/2004*, although a decision as to whether or not a person is incapable of work that is made on a claim for incapacity benefit is conclusive for the purposes of credits in respect of incapacity for work (by virtue of reg.10 of the 1999 Regulations), a decision as to whether or not a person is engaged in remunerative work made on a claim for jobseeker's allowance is not conclusive for the purposes of credits in respect of involuntary unemployment.

There is no power to make decisions under this Act conclusive for the purpose of decisions under the Social Security (Recovery of Benefits) Act 1997. Therefore, a tribunal considering an appeal under s.11 of that Act is entitled to find that benefit was not paid in respect of an accident, even if that conclusion is inconsistent with the benefit having been awarded at all (*R(CR) 1/02*). Similarly, *CIS/1330/2002* holds that a finding of fact within a decision as to a claimant's entitlement to benefit is not conclusive for the purposes of a decision as to whether an overpayment has been made and is recoverable. Again, it was held in *CIS/3605/2005* that an erroneous decision on entitlement was a valid revision or supersession decision for the purposes of s. 71(5A) of the Social Security Administration Act 1992, so as to enable the Secretary of State to recover an overpayment, but was not conclusive as to the amount of the overpayment, with the result that only the amount actually overpaid was recoverable. This approach was applied in *CA/2650/2006*, where a tribunal had found a claimant not to be ordinarily resident in Great Britain from October 27, 2003, when she had moved abroad, and had upheld a decision superseding her award of attendance allowance from that date. On an appeal against a second tribunal decision to the effect that an overpayment from October 27, 2003 to January 4, 2004 was recoverable from the claimant, the Commissioner found that she had ceased to be ordinarily resident in Great Britain only from January 4, 2004 (even though she was also resident abroad) and so she had not been overpaid benefit as a result of any failure to disclose a material fact. Accordingly, he allowed her appeal. However, under the law as it then stood, the first tribunal ought to have superseded her award only from the date of supersession in February 2004. The Commissioner pointed out that, even if the claimant had in fact ceased to be ordinarily resident in Great Britain on October 27, 2003, the first tribunal would have wrongly decided that she had not been entitled to attendance allowance from then until January 4, 2004, but that decision was final by virtue of s.17(1) of the Social Security Act 1998. Moreover, if she had ceased to be ordinarily resident, she would have actually been overpaid during that period because, had she reported the fact that she had moved overseas straightaway, her award would have been terminated immediately. He considered that, in those circumstances, he would have been bound to find that there had been an overpayment and that it was recoverable, despite the first tribunal's error. That suggestion is, strictly speaking, obiter dicta. However, the same Commissioner returned to the point in *CIB/2762/2007* in circumstances where a supersession had been made effective from a date before it was made, when, under the defective legislation then in force, that was not permissible even though the claimant had been overpaid and it was arguable that she had failed to disclose a material fact. The claimant had appealed against a later decision that the overpayment was recoverable and the Commissioner held that the tribunal considering the appeal against the recoverability was bound to find that there had been an overpayment but he said that the appropriate course of action would have been to adjourn and allow the Secretary of State to revise the supersession decision on the ground of official error and then revise the overpayment decision in the claimant's favour, causing the appeal to lapse.

Note that s.29(2) makes an industrial accident declaration conclusive for the purposes of any claim for industrial injuries benefit in respect of that accident. That provision is not applied in respect of the onset of industrial diseases. However, in

Secretary of State for Work and Pensions v Whalley [2002] EWCA Civ 166 (reported as *R(I) 2/03*), the Court of Appeal held that a finding as to the date of onset of an industrial disease made in the context of a claim for disablement benefit was binding in respect of a later claim for reduced earnings allowance. The Court appears to have accepted an argument advanced by the Secretary of State that s.60(1) of the 1992 Act made the finding binding and that s.60(2) was concerned only with "preliminary matters such as the precise symptoms displayed at any particular time". This is, in effect, an argument that was rejected by the Tribunal of Commissioners in *R(CR) 1/02*. *Whalley* was considered in *R(I) 2/04*, in which it was held that the reason that a finding as to a date of onset of an industrial disease is conclusive lies in reg.6(1) of the Social Security (Industrial Injuries) (Prescribed Diseases) Regulations 1985 rather than in s.17. It was pointed out that in *Whalley* the issue had been whether a finding that the claimant was *not* suffering from a prescribed disease so that there was *no* date of onset was conclusive and that that had turned on the finality of a decision on a diagnosis question under the pre-1998 Act system of adjudication, which in turn had precluded a finding in a later claim for disablement pension that there had been an earlier date of onset. In *R(I) 5/04*, it was held that, while a finding that a claimant had suffered from a prescribed disease from a particular date was conclusive as to the date of onset by virtue of reg.6(1) of the 1985 Regulations, a finding that the claimant had *not* been suffering from a prescribed disease was not conclusive under the new system of adjudication in the context of the legislation then in force, but was merely final in respect of the period up to the date of the decision of the Secretary of State in which the finding was made. However, reg.5(2) of the 1985 Regulations was introduced with effect from March 18, 2005 to reverse *R(I) 5/04* by providing that a negative finding is now also conclusive.

Matters arising as respects decisions

1.389   **18.**—(1) Regulations may make provision as respects matters arising—

(a) pending any decision under this Chapter of the Secretary of State, [¹ or the First-tier Tribunal or any decision of the Upper Tribunal which relates to any decision of this Chapter of the First-tier Tribunal] which relates to—

(i) any claim for a relevant benefit; [¹ or]

(ii) any person's entitlement to such a benefit or its receipt; [¹ or]

(iii) [¹ . . .]

(iv) [¹ . . .]

(b) out of the revision under section 9 above or on appeal of any such decision.

(2) Regulations under subsection (1) above as it applies to child benefit may include provision as to the date from which child benefit is to be payable to a person in respect of a child [² or qualifying young person] in a case where, before the benefit was awarded to that person, child benefit in respect of the child [² or qualifying young person] was awarded to another person.

AMENDMENTS

1. Social Security Contributions (Transfer of Functions, etc.) Act 1999, Sch.7, para.29 (April 1, 1999).

2. Child Benefit Act 2005, Sch.1, para.26 (April 10, 2006).

3. Transfer of Tribunal Functions Order 2008 (SI 2008/2833), Sch.3, paras 143 and 156 (November 3, 2008).

DEFINITIONS

"claim"—by virtue of s.39(2), see s.191 of the Social Security Administration Act 1992.
"relevant benefit"—see s.8(3).

Medical examinations

Medical examination required by Secretary of State

19.—(1) Before making a decision on a claim for a relevant benefit, or   **1.390**
as to a person's entitlement to such a benefit [¹ . . .], the Secretary of State
may refer the person—

(a) in respect of whom the claim is made; or

(b) whose entitlement is at issue,

to a [² health care professional approved by the Secretary of State] for such
examination and report as appears to the Secretary of State to be necessary
for the purpose of providing him with information for use in making the
decision.

(2) Subsection (3) below applies where—

(a) the Secretary of State has exercised the power conferred on him by
subsection (1) above; and

(b) the [² health care professional approved by the Secretary of State]
requests the person referred to him to attend for or submit himself
to medical examination.

(3) If the person fails without good cause to comply with the request, the
Secretary of State shall make the decision against him.

AMENDMENTS

1. Social Security Contributions (Transfer of Functions, etc.) Act 1999, Sch.7,
para.30 (April 1, 1999).
2. Welfare Reform Act 2007, s.62(1) and (2) (July 3, 2007).

DEFINITIONS

"claim"—by virtue of s.39(2), see s.191 of the Social Security Administration Act
1992.
"health care professional"—see s.39(1).
"medical examination"—by virtue of s.39(2), see s.191 of the Social Security
Administration Act 1992
"relevant benefit"—see s.8(3).

GENERAL NOTE

Subss.(1) and (2)
This section must be distinguished from reg.19 of the Social Security and   **1.391**
Child Support (Decisions and Appeals) Regulations 1999. Under this section, the
Secretary of State refers the claimant for examination and report but it is the *health
care professional* who requests attendance for, or submission to, a medical examination. The penalty imposed by subs.(3) is imposed for failing to comply with
that person's request. Under reg.19, it is the Secretary of State who requires the
claimant to attend the examination and the penalty for failure to do so is different.
These distinctions reflect the different purposes of the two provisions. Section 19
makes provision for the obtaining of a report for the purpose of determining a claim
whereas reg.19 makes provision for obtaining a report for the purpose of determining whether an award should be revised or superseded.

If it is necessary for a tribunal to consider a report obtained under this section, it will usually also be necessary for the tribunal to know the professional qualification and areas of expertise of the health care professional providing the opinion (*CDLA/2466/2007*).

In *CDLA/4127/2003*, the Secretary of State conceded that a full-time medical practitioner had gone too far in not only drawing the attention of a part-time examining medical practitioner to apparent contradictions and other failings in his report, which was originally favourable to the claimant in certain respects, but also in suggesting alterations that made the report unfavourable. The Commissioner further observed that di culties were created by the fact that the examining medical practitioner had declared his original findings and opinions to be correct to the best of his knowledge but he had not made any such declaration in respect of his amendments or explained why the particular amendments made were justified despite the original declaration. On the claimant's appeal, the tribunal relied on the corrected report on the ground that it was "objective", without making any comment on the significance of the amendments. It was held that they had erred in law in exercising their inquisitorial role selectively, asking probing question of the claimant but not, even rhetorically, of the Secretary of State. Submissions to tribunals sometimes referred to s.19 when the decision was made under reg.19, with the consequence that the submissions have not addressed the correct issues and relevant evidence has not been before tribunals. See *CDLA/5167/2001* for an example. The Social Security (Incapacity for Work) (General) Regulations 1995 and the Employment and Support Allowance Regulations 2008 contain similar powers to require claimants to attend medical examinations and associated penalties for failure to comply. Note also that this section applies only to references by the Secretary of State: separate provision is made under s.20 for references required to assist tribunals.

A health care professional is entitled to decline to examine a person in the absence of a chaperon but, in such a case, even if a report is completed on the basis of informal observations and a lengthy conversation with the claimant, there has been no examination within the terms of this section. However, even where a health care professional has not examined a claimant, his or her opinion may be taken into account as evidence, provided the decision-maker or tribunal can identify the factual basis on which the opinion was given (*CDLA/2466/2007*), although, in *CDLA/4208/2004*, the Commissioner criticised a tribunal for referring to opinions formed by a doctor in those circumstances as "clinical findings".

For the recovery of expenses incurred in attending an examination, see s.20A.

Subs. (3)

1.392   What the decision is, depends on what the question was. It may be a decision to reject a whole claim but it may be a decision to award benefit but on a basis less favourable to the claimant than would otherwise have been the case. The claimant will usually be able to appeal against the decision (and apply for revision under s.9) and will be entitled to argue that he did have good cause for failing to comply with the request. He or she would also be entitled to argue that the decision was less favourable than was required by subs.(3), having regard to what was really in issue. The other remedy open to a claimant is to make a new claim (if benefit was not awarded) or make a new application for a supersession (if there is some continuing entitlement). The consequence will be to raise the question again and the Secretary of State will be obliged to make a new decision, which he will not be able to make under subs.(3) unless the claimant has failed without good cause to comply with a new request to attend for, or submit to, a medical examination.

It is suggested that what amounts to "good cause" under this provision is the same as under all similar provisions where benefit claimants are required to attend medical examinations. A number of decisions on the meaning of "good cause" were considered in *AF v SSWP* [2009] UKUT 56 (AAC) in the context of reg.8(2) of the Social Security (Incapacity for Work) (General) Regulations 1995 (see Vol.I). It was emphasised that the integrity of the social security scheme depends on there being appropriate tests in place, so that, in the absence of "good cause" a person who decides as a matter of principle not to attend an examination must be taken to accept the consequence that benefit is likely to be refused. On the other hand, reference was made to *R(S) 9/51* where the claimant was a Christian Scientist and the Commissioner accepted that an objection based on a firm religious conviction, rather than mere prejudice or distaste for the process, would amount to "good cause".

Medical examination required by appeal tribunal

20.—(1) This section applies where an appeal has been brought under section 12 above against a decision on a claim for a relevant benefit, or as to a person's entitlement to such a benefit [¹ . . .].

1.393

(2) [³ The First-tier Tribunal may, if conditions prescribed by Tribunal Procedure Rules] are satisfied, refer the person—

  (a) in respect of whom the claim is made; or

  (b) whose entitlement is at issue,

to a [² health care professional approved by the Secretary of State] for such examination and report as appears to [³ the First-tier Tribunal] to be necessary for the purpose of providing [³it] with information for use in determining the appeal.

[³ . . .]

[² (2A) The power under subsection (2) to refer a person to a healthcare professional approved by the Secretary of State includes power to specify the description of health care professional to whom the person is to be referred.]

(3) At a hearing before [³ the First-tier Tribunal, except in cases or circumstances prescribed by Tribunal Procedure Rules,] the tribunal—

  (a) may not carry out a physical examination of the person mentioned in subsection (2) above; and

  (b) may not require that person to undergo any physical test for the purpose of determining whether he satisfies the condition mentioned in section 73(1)(a) of the Contributions and Benefits Act.

AMENDMENTS

1. Social Security Contributions (Transfer of Functions, etc.) Act 1999, Sch.7, para.31 (April 1, 1999).

2. Welfare Reform Act 2007, s.62(1), (3) and (4) (July 3, 2007).

3. Transfer of Tribunal Functions Order 2008 (SI 2008/2833), Sch.3, paras 143 and 157 (November 3, 2008).

DEFINITIONS

"claim"—by virtue of s.39(2), see s.191 of the Social Security Administration Act 1992.

"the Contributions and Benefits Act"—see s.84.

"health care professional"—see s.39(1).

"medical examination"—by virtue of s.39(2), see s.191 of the Social Security Administration Act 1992.

"relevant benefit"—see s.8(3).

GENERAL NOTE

Subss. (2) and (2A)

A reference may be made only if there arises one or more of the issues listed in Sch.2 to the Tribunal Procedure (First-tier Tribunal (Social Entitlement Chamber)

1.394

Rules 2008 (see r.25(3)). For the recovery of expenses incurred in attending an examination, see s.20A. Note that this section and the rules made under it apply only to cases under s.12 of this Act and not to other cases before the First-tier Tribunal. Note also, that the examination may not require a person to undergo a physical test for the purpose of determining whether that person is unable to walk or virtually unable to do so (see r.25(4)). There is no statutory penalty for failing to attend for, or submit to, a medical examination required by an "eligible person" or requested by a health care professional making a report under this section. Such a penalty is unnecessary as it is open to the tribunal to draw such inferences from the failure as appear proper when deciding the medical issues arising before them.

It is not the practice for tribunals to obtain reports from the claimant's own doctors as a matter of course. However, claimants sometimes expect that that will be done. In *R(M) 2/80*, the claimant's consultant wrote suggesting that the Mobility Allowance Unit obtain medical evidence from his department. They did not do so. The Commissioner held that the claimant should have been told that her consultant's suggestion would not be followed up and that it would be up to her to obtain any further evidence if she so wished. Similar approaches were taken in *CI/13/1986* and *CA/133/1988*. These decisions were applied in *CIB/16604/1996* where the claimant wrote in his letter of appeal that "you are quite free to check my hospital and [doctor's] records". Neither the claimant nor the adjudication officer attended the hearing before the tribunal. The Commissioner held that there had been a breach of the rules of natural justice because the claimant reasonably believed that the tribunal would have before them his medical records and he was therefore prevented from providing relevant evidence in the sense that he could not reasonably be expected to produce evidence he thought the tribunal already had. That case was distinguished in *CIB/5030/1998* because there was evidence before the Commissioner that the Independent Tribunal Service issued a leaflet making it clear that claimants' doctors would not automatically be approached by the Benefits Agency, the Department of Social Security or the tribunal. The Commissioner held that it was not reasonable for the claimant to believe that the tribunal would have before them evidence from his doctors. That was so even though the claimant said that he had misunderstood the leaflet and thought he had only to give his consent. The Commissioner considered that there was no basis for that misunderstanding.

Subs. (3)

1.395   See r.25(2) and (4) of the Tribunal Procedure (First-tier Tribunal (Social Entitlement Chamber) Rules 2008. In *CDLA/433/1999*, it was held that carrying out a physical examination in breach of the forerunner of this subsection was not an error of law rendering a decision liable to be set aside but relying on evidence from the examination would have been. Observing a claimant during a hearing is not a physical examination or test (*R(DLA) 1/95*). In *R4/99(IB)*, the Commissioner in Northern Ireland said that a tribunal were entitled to use all their senses, including sight, in assessing evidence before them. In *R1/01(IB)*, a Tribunal of Commissioners in Northern Ireland adopted both those views. They held that the phrase "may not carry out a physical examination" suggests some formal process beyond mere observing and that a tribunal is not prohibited from looking at an injury if it is either readily visible or if the claimant wishes them to see it. They said that the tribunal had erred in simply rejecting the claimant's request to look at his knee. The tribunal should either have acceded to the request or else they should have given the claimant the opportunity of obtaining alternative evidence. A tribunal should not simply refuse such a request, unless they consider the evidence unnecessary or irrelevant. The Tribunal of Commissioners said that the legislation prohibits a tribunal from asking to see a part of the claimant's body but it does not prevent the claimant from asking the tribunal to look. Nor does it prevent the tribunal from looking at what they can see without making any request. However, they are not entitled to do more than observe and, except in a case within the scope of r.25(2), a tribunal member ought not to accede to a request to feel a lump or manipulate a limb. If such evidence is necessary, the tribunal should adjourn in order to obtain a report. However, in *R(DLA) 5/03*, the Commissioner noted the distinction between a "physical examination" and a "physical test" and held that the prohibition on tests for the purpose of determining whether a claimant is unable, or virtually unable, to walk did not prevent a tribunal from asking a claimant to demonstrate activities for other purposes. He further said that a tribunal might be entitled to draw inferences from a refusal to comply with such a request, depending on the reasonableness of the request and any reasons given by the claimant for not complying. In *GL v SSWP* [2008] UKUT 36 (AAC), it was suggested that testing a claimant's ability to estimate time by asking him for how long he had been sitting in the tribunal hearing was "approaching, if not crossing," the line between observing a claimant and conducting a physical examination, but that seems inconsistent with *R(DLA) 5/03* and to overlook the word "physical" used in both subparagraphs. In *R(IB) 2/06*, it was held that examining x-rays is not a "physical examination" but that a tribunal was entitled to decline to look at x-rays on the ground that it did not have the expertise to analyse them. However, in such a case, the tribunal was obliged to consider whether to adjourn to obtain a report, which would involve considering whether it was likely that such a report would assist the tribunal in determining the point in issue before it.

[¹ Travelling and other allowances

20A.—(1) The Lord Chancellor may pay to any person required under this Part (whether for the purposes of this Part or otherwise) to attend for or to submit to medical or other examination or treatment such travelling and other allowances as the Lord Chancellor may determine.

(2) In subsection (1) the reference to travelling and other allowances includes compensation for loss of remunerative time but such compensation shall not be paid to any person in respect of any time during which the person is in receipt of remuneration under section 28 of, or paragraph 5 of Schedule 2 to, the Tribunals, Courts and Enforcement Act 2007 (assessors and judges of First-Tier Tribunal).]

1.396

AMENDMENT

1. Transfer of Tribunal Functions Order 2008 (SI 2008/2833), Sch.3, paras 143 and 158 (November 3, 2008).

GENERAL NOTE

This section replaces para.4(1)(b) (and para.4(2) so far as relevant) of Sch.1 of this Act, which has been repealed.

1.397

Suspension and termination of benefit

Suspension in prescribed circumstances

21.—(1) Regulations may provide for—
(a) Suspending payments of a relevant benefit, in whole or in part, in prescribed circumstances;
(b) the subsequent making in prescribed circumstances of any or all of the payments so suspended.

(2) Regulations made under subsection (1) above may, in particular, make provision for any case where—

1.398

(a) it appears to the Secretary of State that an issue arises whether the conditions for entitlement to a relevant benefit are or were fulfilled;

(b) it appears to the Secretary of State that an issue arises whether a decision as to an award of a relevant benefit should be revised (under section 9 above) or superseded (under section 10 above);

(c) an appeal is pending against a decision of [² the First-tier Tribunal, the Upper tribunal] or a court; or

(d) an appeal is pending against the decision given in a different case by a [² the Upper tribunal] or a court, and it appears to the Secretary of State that if the appeal were to be determined in a particular way an issue would arise whether the award of a relevant benefit (whether the same benefit or not) in the case itself ought to be revised or superseded.

(3) For the purposes of subsection (2) above, an appeal against a decision is pending if—

(a) an appeal against the decision has been brought but not determined;

(b) an application for [² permission] to appeal against the decision has been made but not determined; or

(c) in such circumstances as may be prescribed, an appeal against the decision has not been brought (or, as the case may be, an application for [² permission] to appeal against the decision has not been made) but the time for doing so has not yet expired.

(4) [¹ . . .]

AMENDMENTS

1. Social Security Contributions (Transfer of Functions, etc.) Act 1999, Sch.7, para.32 (April 1, 1999).

2. Transfer of Tribunal Functions Order 2008 (SI 2008/2833), Sch.3, paras 143 and 159 (November 3, 2008).

DEFINITIONS

"prescribed"—s.84.
"relevant benefit"—see s.8(3).

GENERAL NOTE

1.399   See regs 16 and 20 of the Social Security and Child Support (Decisions and Appeals) Regulations 1999 and regs 18 and 21 of the Child Benefit and Guardian's Allowance (Decisions and Appeals) Regulations 2003.

Suspension for failure to furnish information etc.

1.400   **22.**—(1) The powers conferred by this section are exercisable in relation to persons who fail to comply with information requirements.

(2) Regulations may provide for—

(a) suspending payments of a relevant benefit, in whole or in part;

(b) the subsequent making in prescribed circumstances of any or all of the payments so suspended.

(3) In this section and section 23 below "information requirement" means a requirement, made in pursuance of regulations under subsection (1)(hh) of section 5 of the Administration Act, to furnish information or evidence needed for a determination whether a decision on an award of

benefit to which that section applies should be revised under section 9 or superseded under section 10 above.

[¹ (4) Subsection (3A) of section 5 of the Administration Act (which glosses paragraph (hh) in the case of state pension credit) shall apply in relation to subsection (3) above as it applies in relation to paragraph (hh) of subsection (1) of that section.]

AMENDMENT

1. State Pension Credit Act 2002, Sch.1, para.8 (July 2, 2002 for the purpose of exercising any power to make regulations or orders and October 6, 2003 for other purposes).

DEFINITIONS

"the Administration Act"—see s.84.
"information requirement"—see subs.(3).
"prescribed"—see s.84.
"relevant benefit"—see s.8(3).

GENERAL NOTE

See reg.17 of the Social Security and Child Support (Decisions and Appeals) Regulations 1999 and reg.19 of the Child Benefit and Guardian's Allowance (Decisions and Appeals) Regulations 2003.

1.401

Termination in cases of failure to furnish information

23. Regulations may provide that, except in prescribed cases or circumstances, a person—

(a) whose benefit has been suspended in accordance with regulations under section 21 above and who subsequently fails to comply with an information requirement; or

(b) whose benefit has been suspended in accordance with regulations under section 22 above for failing to comply with such a requirement,

shall cease to be entitled to the benefit from a date not earlier than the date on which payments were suspended.

1.402

DEFINITIONS

"information requirement"—see s.22(3).
"prescribed"—see s.84.

GENERAL NOTE

See reg.18 of the Social Security and Child Support (Decisions and Appeals) Regulations 1999 and reg.20 of the Child Benefit and Guardian's Allowance (Decisions and Appeals) Regulations 2003.

1.403

Suspension and termination for failure to submit to medical examination

24. Regulations may make provision—

(a) enabling the Secretary of State to require a person to whom a relevant benefit has been awarded to submit to medical examination;

(b) for suspending payments of benefit, in whole or in part, in a case of a person who fails to submit himself to a medical examination to which he is required to submit in accordance with regulations under paragraph(a) above;

1.404

(c) for the subsequent making in prescribed circumstances of any or all of the payments so suspended;

(d) for entitlement to the benefit to cease, except in prescribed cases or circumstances, from a date not earlier than the date on which payments were suspended.

DEFINITIONS

"medical examination"—by virtue of s.39(2), see s.191 of the Social Security Administration Act 1992.
"prescribed"—see s.84.
"relevant benefit"—see s.8(3).

GENERAL NOTE

1.405   See reg.19 of the Social Security and Child Support (Decisions and Appeals) Regulations 1999.

[*¹Appeals dependent on issues falling to be decided by Inland Revenue*

Appeals dependent on issues falling to be decided by Inland Revenue

1.406   **24A.**—(1) Regulations may make provision for [² the First-tier Tribunal or Upper Tribunal], where on any appeal there arises any issue which under section 8 of the Social Security Contributions (Transfer of Functions, etc.) Act 1999 falls to be decided by an officer of the Inland Revenue, to require the Secretary of State to refer the issue to the Inland Revenue.

(2) Regulations under this section may—

(a) provide for the appeal to be referred to the Secretary of State pending the decision of the Inland Revenue,

(b) enable or require the Secretary of State, in specified circumstances, to deal with any other issue arising on the appeal pending the decision on the referred issue, and

(c) enable the Secretary of State, on receiving the decision of an officer of the Inland Revenue, or any determination of the [³ First-tier Tribunal or Upper Tribunal] made on appeal from his decision—

    (i) to revise his decision,

    (ii) to make a decision superseding his decision, or

    (iii) to refer the appeal to the [² First-tier Tribunal or Upper Tribunal] for determination.]

AMENDMENTS

1. Social Security Contributions (Transfer of Functions, etc.) Act 1999, Sch.7, para.33 (July 5, 1999).

2. Transfer of Tribunal Functions Order 2008 (SI 2008/2833), Sch.3, paras 143 and 160 (November 3, 2008).

3. Transfer of Tribunal Functions and Revenue and Customs Appeals Order 2009 (SI 2009/56), Sch.1, paras 247 and 249 (April 1, 2009).

DEFINITIONS

"Inland Revenue"—by virtue of s.39(2), see s.191 of the Social Security Administration Act 1992 but note that the Inland Revenue has been merged into Her Majesty's Revenue and Customs by the Commissioners for Revenue and Customs Act 2005.

GENERAL NOTE

See reg.38A of the Social Security and Child Support (Decisions and Appeals)   1.407
Regulations 1999.

Decisions and appeals dependent on other cases

Decisions involving issues that arise on appeal in other cases

25.—(1) This section applies where—   1.408
   (a) a decision by the Secretary of State falls to be made under section 8,
       9 or 10 above in relation to a particular case; and
   (b) an appeal is pending against the decision given in another case by
       [¹the Upper Tribunal] or a court (whether or not the two cases
       concern the same benefit).

(2) In a case relating to a relevant benefit, the Secretary of State need not
make the decision while the appeal is pending if he considers it possible that
the result of the appeal will be such that, if it were already determined, there
would be no entitlement to benefit.

(3) If the Secretary of State considers it possible that the result of the
appeal will be such that, if it were already determined, it would affect the
decision in some other way—
   (a) he need not, except in such cases or circumstances as may be pre-
       scribed, make the decision while the appeal is pending;
   (b) he may, in such cases or circumstances as may be prescribed, make
       the decision on such basis as may be prescribed.

(4) Where the Secretary of State acts in accordance with subsection (3)
(b) above, following the determination of the appeal he shall if appropriate
revise his decision (under section 9 above) in accordance with that determination.

(5) For the purposes of this section, an appeal against a decision is
pending if—
   (a) an appeal against the decision has been brought but not deter-
       mined;
   (b) an application for leave to appeal against the decision has been made
       but not determined; or
   (c) in such circumstances as may be prescribed, an appeal against
       the decision has not been brought (or, as the case may be, an
       application for leave to appeal against the decision has not been
       made) but the time for doing so has not yet expired.

(6) In paragraphs (a), (b) and (c) of subsection (5) above, any reference to an appeal, or an application for leave to appeal, against a decision
includes a reference to—
   (a) an application for, or for leave to apply for judicial review of the deci-
       sion under section 31 of the Supreme Court Act 1981; or
   (b) an application to the supervisory jurisdiction of the Court of Session
       in respect of the decision.

AMENDMENT

1. Transfer of Tribunal Functions Order 2008 (SI 2008/2833), Sch.3, paras 143
and 161 (November 3, 2008).

DEFINITIONS
"prescribed"—see s.84.
"relevant benefit"—see s.8(3).

GENERAL NOTE

Subs. (1)

1.409   This section applies only where a decision falls to be made by the Secretary of State (or, in relation to decisions under s.170 of the Pension Schemes Act 1993 or in respect of child benefit or guardian's allowance, Her Majesty's Revenue and Customs—see s.170(7) of the 1993 Act (if it is not construed too literally) and ss.50(2)(e) and 51 of, and Sch.4, para.15 to, the Tax Credits Act 2002). See s.26 where a decision falls to be made by a tribunal. No appeal lies against a decision under this section (see Social Security and Child Support (Decisions and Appeals) Regulations 1999, Sch.2, para.7 and Child Benefit and Guardian's Allowance (Decisions and Appeals) Regulations 2003 Sch.2, para.4).

"Court" is not defined for the purposes of this section (compare s.27(7)) but the context in which the word appears limits its scope. There must be an appeal pending against a decision "in another case" of the Upper Tribunal or a court. This includes an application for judicial review of a tribunal decision (see subs.(6)) but not an application for judicial review of a decision of the Secretary of State or Her Majesty's Revenue and Customs or, in a housing benefit case, a local authority. However, an appeal to the Court of Appeal against a decision of the High Court, or to the Inner House of the Court of Session from a decision of the Outer House, on judicial review of the Secretary of State, Her Majesty's Revenue and Customs or a local authority would appear to be caught. A reference to the European Court of Justice by a Commissioner is certainly not caught. The words in parenthesis tend to suggest that the court must be concerned with some sort of social security benefit as does the general context of the provision and the need to have some sort of practical boundary. Otherwise, it might be suggested that, say, an appeal to the House of Lords from a decision of the Court of Appeal dealing with the meaning of the word "misrepresentation" in a marine insurance policy was a relevant appeal (because it might possibly assist with the understanding of that word in s.71 of the Social Security Administration Act 1992).

Subss. (2) and (3)

1.410   The Secretary of State (or Her Majesty's Revenue and Customs) must consider two separate issues. The first is whether a possible result of the appeal would affect the decision before him. The Secretary of State would be a party to most such appeals and it is to be hoped that he does not indulge in too much wishful thinking. The word "possible" is broad. And what is the meaning of "result of the appeal"? Is it confined to the ratio decidendi or is it sufficient that the Secretary of State considers that there might be some useful obiter dicta? The second issue the Secretary of State (or Her Majesty's Revenue and Customs) must consider is whether he should not make the decision or should decide it in accordance with subs.(3)(b) or whether he should ignore the fact that there is an appeal pending. He has a broad discretion and much will depend on such circumstances as the number of cases, the amount of money at stake, hardship to the claimants and the degree of probability that the court's decision will provide significant assistance with the determination of the cases before him.

For regulations under subs.(3)(b), see reg.21(1)–(3) of the Social Security and Child Support (Decisions and Appeals) Regulations 1999 and reg.22(1)–(3) of the Child Benefit and Guardian's Allowance (Decisions and Appeals) Regulations 2003.

Subs. (4)

1.411   The revision usually has effect from the same date as the original decision (see s.9(3)).

Subs. (5)
See reg.21(4) of the Social Security and Child Support (Decisions and Appeals)   **1.412**
Regulations 1999 and reg.22(4) of the Child Benefit and Guardian's Allowance
(Decisions and Appeals) Regulations 2003.

Appeals involving issues that arise on appeal in other cases

26.—(1) This section applies where—   **1.413**
   (a) an appeal ("appeal A") in relation to a decision under section 8, 9
       or 10 above is made to an appeal tribunal, or from [¹ the First-tier
       Tribunal, or from the First-tier Tribunal to the Upper Tribunal]
       and
   (b) an appeal ("appeal B") is pending against a decision given in a differ-
       ent case by [¹ the Upper Tribunal] or a court (whether or not the two
       appeals concern the same benefit).
   (2) If the Secretary of State considers it possible that the result of appeal
B will be such that, if it were already determined, it would affect the determination of appeal A, he may serve notice requiring [¹ First-tier Tribunal or
Upper Tribunal]—
   (a) not to determine appeal A but to refer it to him; or
   (b) to deal withthe appeal in accordance with subsection (4) below.
   (3) Where appeal A is referred to the Secretary of State under subsection
(2)(a) above, following the determination of appeal B and in accordance
with that determination, he shall if appropriate—
   (a) in a case where appeal A has not been determined by the [¹ First-tier
       Tribunal], revise (under section 9 above) his decision which gave rise
       to that appeal; or
   (b) in a case where appeal A has been determined by the [¹ First-tier
       Tribunal], make a decision (under section 10 above) superseding the
       tribunal's decision.
   (4) Where appeal A is to be dealt with in accordance with this subsection,
the [¹ First-tier Tribunal or Upper Tribunal] shall either—
   (a) stay appeal A until appeal B is determined; or
   (b) if the [¹ First-tier Tribunal or Upper Tribunal] considers it to be in
       the interests of the appellant to do so, determine appeal A as if—
       (i) appeal B had already been determined; and
       (ii) the issues arising on appeal B had been decided in the way that
            was most unfavourable to the appellant.
   In this subsection "the appellant" means the person who appealed or, as
the case may be, first appealed against the decision mentioned in subsection
(1)(a) above.
   (5) Where the [¹ First-tier Tribunal or Upper Tribunal] acts in accordance with subsection (4)(b) above, following the determination of appeal
B the Secretary of State shall, if appropriate, make a decision (under section
10 above) superseding the decision of the [¹ First-tier Tribunal or Upper
Tribunal] in accordance withthat determination.
   (6) For the purposes of this section, an appeal against a decision is
pending if—
   (a) an appeal against the decision has been brought but not deter-
       mined;
   (b) an application for leave to appeal against the decision has been made
       but not determined; or

(c) in such circumstances as may be prescribed, an appeal against the decision has not been brought (or, as the case may be, an application for leave to appeal against the decision has not been made) but the time for doing so has not yet expired.

(7) In this section—

(a) the reference in subsection (1)(a) above to an appeal to [¹ the Upper Tribunal] includes a reference to an application for leave to appeal to [¹ the Upper Tribunal]; and

(b) any reference in paragraph (a), (b) or (c) of subsection (6) above to an appeal, or to an application for leave to appeal, against a decision includes a reference to—

 (i) an application for, or for leave to apply for, judicial review of the decision under section 31 of the Supreme Court Act

 (ii) an application to the supervisory jurisdiction of the Court of Session in respect of the decision.

(8) Regulations may make provision supplementing that made by this section.

Amendments

1. Transfer of Tribunal Functions Order 2008 (SI 2008/2833), Sch.3, paras 143 and 162 (November 3, 2008).

Definition

"prescribed"—see s.84.

General Note

Subs. (1)

1.414 See the note to s.25(1) for the meaning of "court". See also subss.(6) and (7).

Subs. (2)

1.415 It is for the Secretary of State (or, in relation to decisions under s.170 of the Pension Schemes Act 1993 or in respect of child benefit or guardian's allowance, Her Majesty's Revenue and Customs—see s.170(7) of the 1993 Act (if it is not construed too literally) and ss.50(2)(e) and 51 of, and Sch.4, para.15 to, the Tax Credits Act 2002) to identify both appeal B and appeal A although there is no reason why one notice may not be issued in respect of several appeals A. As in s.25(2) and (3), the Secretary of State (or Her Majesty's Revenue and Customs) must first make a judgment as to the possible effects of the decision in appeal B and must then consider whether to serve notice under this subsection. It will not always be appropriate to do so. If the Secretary of State does decide to issue the notice, he must go on to decide whether the tribunal should be required to refer appeal A to him under para. (a) or to deal with the appeal in accordance with subs.(4) under para.(b). Which option is appropriate will depend on the circumstances of the case.

It may be thought to be unobjectionable that there be specific provision as to the way appeals should be handled while the decision in a "test case" is awaited, but to be highly objectionable that the decision as to the appropriate procedure should lie wholly in the hands of the Secretary of State who is a party in appeal A and is usually a party in appeal B. The perception that this provision was desirable appears to have arisen out of an occasion when the then President of social security appeal tribunals directed tribunals to determine a vast number of appeals notwithstanding the fact that an appeal against a Social Security Commissioner's decision was pending in the courts. This resulted in some thousands of extra appeals being brought before the Commissioners. It may be thought that this is unlikely to be repeated. In practice the Secretary of State is very often content to allow tribunals to manage blocks of "lookalike" cases without resorting to serving a notice under this section and where a notice is served it is usually after consultation with the relevant Chamber President. There can be an advantage to a claimant in having a notice served under this section where a tribunal might award some benefit on appeal A even if that appeal is determined on the basis that appeal B is determined adversely to the claimant. The claimant is then not deprived of that benefit while appeal B is awaiting final determination. It might be better if the legislation merely allowed the Secretary of State to seek a general direction in respect of a block of similar cases from the relevant Chamber President. As it is, any challenge to the Secretary of State's judgment must be by way of an application for judicial review.

Subs. (3)

Presumably para.(b) exists in case appeal A was decided in ignorance of the notice requiring it not to be determined. The decision is not rendered ineffective and so operates until it is superseded. It is not clear what happens if either party appeals against it.

1.416

Subs. (4)

It is for the tribunal to decide whether para.(a) or para.(b) should apply in any particular case. Paragraph (b) is unlikely to be used a great deal unless either the claimant asks for it to be used or else the tribunal is fairly sure that the decision on appeal B is unlikely to assist the claimant. A judgment as to what is the most unfavourable way in which the issues arising on appeal B might be decided requires that the tribunal be given considerable information about the appeal, including pleadings, so that it can be established what the issues really are.

1.417

Subs. (5)

The supersession is effective from the date from which the tribunals decision would have been effective had it been decided in accordance with the decision in "Appeal B", the test case (reg.7(33) of the Social Security and Child Support (Decisions and Appeals) Regulations 1999).

1.418

Subs. (6)

See reg.22 of the Social Security and Child Support (Decisions and Appeals) Regulations 1999 and reg.23 of the Child Benefit and Guardian's Allowance (Decisions and Appeals) Regulations 2003.

1.419

Cases of error

Restrictions on entitlement to benefit in certain cases of error

27.—(1) Subject to subsection (2) below, this section applies where—

1.420

(a) the effect of the determination, whenever made, of an appeal to [³the Upper Tribunal] or the court ("the relevant determination") is that the adjudicating authority's decision out of which the appeal arose was erroneous in point of law; and

(b) after the date of the relevant determination a decision falls to be made by the Secretary of State in accordance with that determination (or would, apart from this section, fall to be so made)—

  (i) in relation to a claim for benefit;

  (ii) as to whether to revise, under section 9 above, a decision as to a person's entitlement to benefit; or

  (iii) on an application made under section 10 above for a decision as to a person's entitlement to benefit to be superseded.

(2) This section does not apply where the decision of the Secretary of State mentioned in subsection (1)(b) above—

    (a) is one which, but for section 25(2) or (3)(a) above, would have been made before the date of the relevant determination; or

    (b) is one made in pursuance of section 26(3) or (5) above.

(3) In so far as the decision relates to a person's entitlement to a benefit in respect of—

    (a) a period before the date of the relevant determination; or

    (b) in the case of a widow's payment, a death occurring before that date,

it shall be made as if the adjudicating authority's decision had been found by [³the Upper Tribunal] or court not to have been erroneous in point of law.

(4) In deciding whether a person is entitled to benefit in a case where his entitlement depends on his having been entitled to the same or some other benefit before attaining a particular age, subsection (3) above shall be disregarded for the purpose only of deciding whether he was so entitled before attaining that age.

(5) Subsection (1)(a) above shall be read as including a case where—

    (a) the effect of the relevant determination is that part or all of a purported regulation or order is invalid; and

    (b) the error of law made by the adjudicating authority was to act on the basis that the purported regulation or order (or the part held to be invalid) was valid.

(6) It is immaterial for the purposes of subsection (1) above—

    (a) where such a decision as is mentioned in paragraph (b)(i) falls to be made, whether the claim was made before or after the date of the relevant determination;

    (b) where such a decision as is mentioned in paragraph (b)(ii) or (iii) falls to be made on an application under section 9 or (as the case may be) 10 above, whether the application was made before or after that date.

(7) In this section—

"adjudicating authority" means—

    (a) the Secretary of State;

    (b) any former officer, tribunal or body; or

    (c) any officer, tribunal or body in Northern Ireland corresponding to a former officer, tribunal or body;

"benefit" means—

    (a) benefit under Parts II to V of the Contributions and Benefits Act, other than Old Cases payments;

    (b) benefit under Part II of the Social Security Act 1975 (in respect of a period before July 1, 1992 but not before April 6, 1975);

    (c) benefit under the National Insurance Act 1946 or 1965, or the National Insurance (Industrial Injuries) Act 1946 or 1965 (in respect of a period before April 6, 1975);

    (d) a jobseeker's allowance;

[¹ (dd) state pension credit;]

[²(de) an employment and support allowance;]

    (e) any benefit corresponding to a benefit mentioned in [¹ paragraphs (a) to (dd) above]; and

    (f) any income-related benefit;

"the court" means the High Court, the Court of Appeal, the Court of Session, the High Court or Court of Appeal in Northern Ireland, the House of Lords or the Court of Justice in the European Community;

"former officer, tribunal or body" means any of the following, that is to say—

(a) an adjudication officer or, in the case of a decision given on a reference under section 21(2) or 25(1) of the Administration Act, a social security appeal tribunal, a disability appeal tribunal or a medical appeal tribunal;

(b) an adjudicating medical practitioner appointed under section 49 of that Act or a specially qualified adjudicating medical practitioner appointed in accordance with regulations under section 62(2) of that Act; or

(c) the National Assistance Board, the Supplementary Benefits Commission, the Attendance Allowance Board, a benefit officer, an insurance officer or a supplement officer.

(8) For the purposes of this section, any reference to entitlement to benefit includes a reference to entitlement—

(a) to any increase in the rate of a benefit; or

(b) to a benefit, or increase of benefit, at a particular rate.

(9) The date of the relevant determination shall, in prescribed cases, be determined for the purposes of this section in accordance with any regulations made for that purpose.

(10) Regulations made under subsection (9) above may include provision—

(a) for a determination of a higher court to be treated as if it had been made on the date of a determination of a lower court or a Commissioner; or

(b) for a determination of a lower court or a Commissioner to be treated as if it had been made on the date of a determination of a higher court.

AMENDMENTS

1. State Pension Credit Act 2002, Sch.1, para.9 (July 2, 2002 for the purposes of exercising any power to make regulations or orders and October 6, 2003 for other purposes).

2. Welfare Reform Act 2007, Sch.3, para.17(1) and (5) (October 27, 2008).

3. Transfer of Tribunal Functions Order 2008 (SI 2008/2833), Sch.3, paras 143 and 163 (November 3, 2008).

DEFINITIONS

"adjudicating authority"—see subs.(7).

"the Administration Act"—see s.84.

"benefit"—see subs.(7).

"claim"—by virtue of s.39(2), see s.191 of the Social Security Administration Act 1992.

"the Contributions and Benefits Act"—see s.84.

"the court"—see subs.(7).

"former officer, tribunal or body"—*ibid.*

"income-related benefit"—by virtue of s.39(2), see s.191 of the Social Security Administration Act 1992.

"Old Cases payments"—*ibid.*

"prescribed"—see s.84.

"the relevant determination"—see subs.(1).

GENERAL NOTE

1.421   In so far as they apply to child benefit and guardian's allowance, the Secretary of State's functions under this section were transferred to the Board of Inland Revenue (Tax Credit Act 2002, s.50(2)(e)) and are now exercised by Her Majesty's Revenue and Customs (Commissioners for Revenue and Customs Act 2005).

Subs. (1)

1.422   The Secretary of State is an adjudicating authority but an appeal tribunal is not (see subs.(7)). As the question for the Upper Tribunal or court is whether the *First-tier Tribunal* has erred in law, it may not always be easy to tell whether the effect of the Upper Tribunal's or court's determination is that the Secretary of State's decision was erroneous in point of law. See also subss.(5) and (6).

Paragraph (b) is in broad terms but it is suggested that, although s.27 would apply to revision under reg.3(5)(b) of the Social Security and Child Support (Decisions and Appeals) Regulations 1999 (mistake of fact too favourable to the claimant), it would not apply to the related decisions under s.71 of the Social Security Administration Act 1992 as to the amount of the overpayment or the Secretary of State's entitlement to recover the overpayment. Nor does it apply to decisions under the Social Security (Recovery of Benefits) Act 1997. Where successive Commissioners' decisions had held a departmental practice to be wrong, it was the first such decision that was "the relevant determination", even where Commissioners have differed as to their reasoning (*R(I) 1/03*, a decision of a Tribunal of Commissioners).

Subs. (3)

1.423   This subsection has the effect that any decision of a the Upper Tribunal or court that is unfavourable to the Secretary of State is only prospective in its effect in other cases. Such a provision is not necessarily unreasonable to the extent that it does not require existing decisions in respect of earlier periods to be reversed but this one takes the principle to extremes by requiring the Secretary of State to continue giving erroneous decisions in respect of the period before the Upper Tribunal's or court's decision after the error has been discovered. This is done so that all claimants are treated equally unfavourably in respect of that period. The perceived need for the provision may arise from the general power to revise at any time a decision arising from an official error (reg.3(5)(a) of the Social Security and Child Support (Decisions and Appeals) Regulations 1999). The corollary is that any supersession as a result of the Upper Tribunal's or court's determination is effective from the date of that determination (reg.7(6)) which tends to operate to the advantage of claimants although it is not entirely clear when supersession would be appropriate rather than revision on the ground of official error in this context. Most, if not all, of the objections to s.27 would be removed if it operated only in relation to the power to revise decisions on the ground of official error and did not catch other claims and applications where the conventional time limits (much more restrictive than when the forerunner of s.27 was first introduced in 1990) adequately limit the extent to which an unexpected decision could apply retrospectively.

Subs. (5)

1.424   This is logical but may be thought to reinforce the view that subs.(3) is objectionable. Parliament has here not only ratified in advance decisions made, presumably in good faith, in excess of powers; it has also enabled (and required) the Secretary of State to continue making decisions (in respect of past periods) in excess of those powers once he knows the limits of the powers. This is despite the fact that Parliament could not have known the extent to which the powers would be exceeded. Henry VIII could hardly have asked for more.

Subs. (7)

1.425   Note that the First-tier Tribunal is not an "adjudicating authority". Quite why a social security appeal tribunal giving a decision on a reference should have been included as a "former tribunal" is unclear because there was no reason to suppose that their view of the law would necessarily be consistent with that held by the Department of Social Security. Perhaps the draftsman had a particular case in mind. The inclusion of disability appeal tribunals and medical appeal tribunals is even more obscure as there was no power to refer cases to them under the provisions cited. The inclusion of the Court of Appeal in Northern Ireland in the definition of "court" is interesting as a decision of that court is not, strictly speaking, binding in Great Britain. Such a decision is, however, highly persuasive and should usually be followed. The implication is that, if the Secretary of State does decide to follow a decision of the Court of Appeal in Northern Ireland, the decision before him "falls to be made . . . in accordance with" the decision of the court for the purpose of subs.(1).

Subss. (9) and (10)
No regulations have yet been made under these powers.   1.426

Correction of errors and setting aside of decisions

28.—(1) Regulations may make provision with respect to—   1.427
  (a) the correction of accidental errors in any decision [⁴ of the Secretary of State] or record of a decision [⁴ of the Secretary of State] made under any relevant enactment;
  (b) [⁴. . .]
        [⁴. . .]
  [¹ (1A) In subsection (1) "decision" does not include [⁴ any decision of the First-tier Tribunal or] any decision made by an officer of the Inland Revenue, other than a decision under or by virtue of Part III of the Pensions Schemes Act 1993.]
  (2) Nothing in subsection (1) above shall be construed as derogating from any power to correct errors [⁴. . .] which is exercisable apart from regulations made by virtue of that subsection.
  (3) In this section "relevant enactment" means any enactment contained in—
  (a) this Chapter;
  (b) the Contributions and Benefits Act;
  (c) the Pension Schemes Act 1993;
  (d) the Jobseekers Act; [². . .]
  (e) the Social Security (Recovery of Benefits) Act 1997; [² or
  (f) the State Pension Credit Act 2002 [³ ; or
  (g) Part 1 of the Welfare Reform Act 2007.]

AMENDMENTS

1. Social Security Contributions (Transfer of Functions, etc.) Act 1999, Sch.7, para.34 (July 5, 1999).
2. State Pension Credit Act 2002, Sch.1, para.10 and Sch.3 (July 2, 2002 for regulation-making purposes and April 7, 2003 for other purposes).
3. Welfare Reform Act 2007, Sch.3, para.17(1) and (6) (March 18, 2008 for regulation-making purposes and July 27, 2008 for other purposes).
4. Transfer of Tribunal Functions Order 2008 (SI 2008/2833), Sch.3, paras 143 and 164 (November 3, 2008).

DEFINITIONS

"Contributions and Benefits Act"—see s.84.
"Inland Revenue"—by virtue of s.39(2), see s.191 of the Social Security Administration Act 1992 but note that the Inland Revenue has been merged into

Her Majesty's Revenue and Customs by the Commissioners for Revenue and Customs Act 2005.

"the Jobseekers Act"—see s.84.

"prescribed"—see s.84.

"relevant enactment"—see subs.(3).

GENERAL NOTE

1.428   See reg.9A of the Social Security and Child Support (Decisions and Appeals) Regulations 1999. This section is no longer concerned with the correction and setting aside of tribunal decisions, for which see now para.15 of Sch.5 to the Tribunals, Courts and Enforcement Act 2007.

Industrial accidents

Decision that accident is an industrial accident

1.429   **29.**—(1) Where, in connection with any claim for industrial injuries benefit, it is decided that the relevant accident was or was not an industrial accident—

(a) an express declaration of that fact shall be made and recorded; and

(b) subject to subsection (3) below, a claimant shall be entitled to have the issue whether the relevant accident was an industrial accident decided, notwithstanding that his claim is disallowed on other grounds.

(2) Subject to subsection (3) and section 30 below, any person suffering personal injury by accident shall be entitled, if he claims the accident was an industrial accident—

(a) to have that issue decided; and

(b) to have a declaration made and recorded accordingly,

notwithstanding that no claim for benefit has been made in connection with which the issue arises; and this Chapter shall apply for that purpose as if the issue had arisen in connection with a claim for benefit.

(3) The Secretary of State, [¹the First-tier Tribunal or the Upper Tribunal] (as the case may be) may refuse to decide the issue whether an accident was an industrial accident, if satisfied that it is unlikely to be necessary to decide the issue for the purposes of any claim for benefit and this Chapter shall apply as if any such refusal were a decision on the issue.

(4) Subject to sections 9 to 15 above, any declaration under this section that an accident was or was not an industrial accident shall be conclusive for the purposes of any claim for industrial injuries benefit in respect of that accident.

(5) Where subsection (4) above applies—

(a) in relation to a death occurring before April 11, 1988; or

(b) for the purposes of section 60(2) of the Contributions and Benefits Act,

it shall have effect as if at the end there were added the words "whether or not the claimant is the person at whose instance the declaration was made".

(6) For the purposes of this section (but subject to section 30 below), an accident whereby a person suffers personal injury shall be deemed, in relation to him, to be an industrial accident if—

(a) it arises out of and in the course of his employment;

(b) that employment is employed earner's employment for the purposes of Part V of the Contributions and Benefits Act; and

(c) payment of benefit is not under section 94(5) of that Act precluded because the accident happened while he was outside Great Britain.

(7) A decision under this section shall be final except that sections 9 and 10 above apply to a decision under this section that an accident was or was not an industrial accident as they apply to a decision under section 8 above if, but only if, the Secretary of State is satisfied that the decision under this section was given in consequence of any wilful non-disclosure or misrepresentation of a material fact.

AMENDMENT

1. Transfer of Tribunal Functions Order 2008 (SI 2008/2833), Sch.3, paras 143 and 165 (November 3, 2008).

DEFINITIONS

"benefit—by virtue of s.39(2), see s.191 of the Social Security Administration Act 1992.

"claim"—*ibid.*

"claimant"—see s.39(1) and, by virtue of s.39(2), see s.191 of the Social Security Administration Act 1992.

"Contributions and Benefits Act"—see s.84.

"industrial injuries benefit"—by virtue of s.39(2), see s.191 of the Social Security Administration Act 1992.

GENERAL NOTE

This section re-enacts s.44 of the Social Security Administration Act 1992 with only minor changes. It provides for the Secretary of State to make a declaration that a person has suffered an industrial accident, whether or not there has been a claim for benefit and whether or not any claim has any prospects of success on other grounds, although, under subs.(3), the Secretary of State (or a tribunal) may refuse to determine that question if it is unlikely there will ever be a claim for benefit.

A determination that there was or was not an industrial accident is conclusive for the purposes of later claims for benefit (unless it is set aside on appeal or is revised or superseded). However, it is important to note that this section is expressed to be subject to s.30, so that a decision under this section which implies that a person has suffered personal injury as a result of an accident does not require anyone to find that the claimant has suffered disablement as a result of the injury even though the two decisions may appear, in the circumstances of the case, to contradict one another.

The usual rights of appeal apply to declarations under this section, but the power to revise or supersede such decisions is strictly limited, by subs.(7), to cases of *wilful* non-disclosure or misrepresentation of a material fact.

The First-tier Tribunal hearing an appeal from a decision given under subs.(2) is constituted by a judge sitting alone (see the note to art.2 of the First-tier Tribunal and Upper Tribunal (Composition of Tribunal) Order 2008).

Where the Secretary of State has decided that a claimant has not suffered an industrial accident and the claimant appeals against that decision, a tribunal may exercise the power conferred by subs.(3) to refuse to decide the issue on the ground that it is unlikely to be relevant to any claim to benefit (*CI/1297/2002*). That refusal to decide the issue must replace the Secretary of State's decision, and will make an important difference if the tribunal is wrong and there ever is a claim for benefit, because the Secretary of State's decision would have been conclusive by virtue of subs.(4) and the scope for revision or supersession would have been limited by virtue of subs.(7). In *CI/732/2007*, the Commissioner accepted a submission by the

1.430

Secretary of State to the effect that it was also open to a tribunal to refuse to make a declaration where a claimant had suffered a vaccination reaction as the result of a vaccination in the course of her employment. A vaccination reaction is normal and so the claimant had not suffered an industrial accident, because there had been no unexpected or untoward event. The Secretary of State's submission was in the claimant's favour because its acceptance meant the claimant was not precluded from advancing new medical evidence in the future to show that other ill health was attributable to the vaccination, which would lead to a finding that she had suffered an industrial accident.

Effect of decision

30.—(1) A decision (given under subsection (2) of section 29 above or otherwise) that an accident was an industrial accident is to be taken as determining only that paragraphs (a), (b) and (c) of subsection (6) of that section are satisfied in relation to the accident.

(2) Subject to subsections (3) and (4) below, no such decision is to be taken as importing a decision as to the origin of any injury or disability suffered by the claimant, whether or not there is an event identifiable as an accident apart from any injury that may have been received.

(3) A decision that, on a particular occasion when there was no event so identifiable, a person had an industrial accident by reason of an injury shall be treated as a decision that, if the injury was suffered by accident on that occasion, the accident was an industrial accident.

(4) A decision that an accident was an industrial accident may be given, and a declaration to that effect be made and recorded in accordance with section 29 above, without its having been found that personal injury resulted from the accident.

(5) Subsection (4) above has effect, subject to the discretion under section 29(3) above, to refuse to decide the issue if it is unlikely to be necessary for the purposes of a claim for benefit.

DEFINITIONS

"benefit"—by virtue of s.39(2), see s.191 of the Social Security Administration Act 1992.

"claim"—*ibid*.

"claimant"—see s.39(1) and, by virtue of s.39(2), see s.191 of the Social Security Administration Act 1992.

GENERAL NOTE

This section replaces s.60(3) of the Social Security Administration Act 1992. The drafting of the new provision is a great improvement. The overall effect is the same. A finding that there has been an industrial accident does not prevent it from being found that there has been no loss of faculty resulting from the accident even if the two decisions appear to be inconsistent. This is so even in a case where a person suffers a heart attack and the only "accident" found was the heart attack itself. Another decision-maker is still entitled to hold that the heart attack was not the result of an accident. This provision was first introduced by the National Insurance Act 1972 to reverse the effect of *Jones v Secretary of State for Social Services* [1972] A.C. 944 (also reported as an appendix to *R(I) 3/69*). It is less important than it used to be now that all material decisions are made by the Secretary of State and there is no longer the old division of jurisdiction between adjudication officers and adjudicating medical authorities. However, it still has significance where a declaration is made under s.29(2) (i.e. otherwise than in the course of determining a claim to benefit) or where different decision-makers deal with the question whether there was an industrial accident and the question whether the claimant suffers a loss of faculty as a result of the accident (e.g. where a tribunal reverses a decision to the effect that there was no industrial accident but does not go on and deal with the other questions arising on the claim). In *CI/105/1998*, it was pointed out that, quite apart from cases where the accident is indistinguishable from the injury suffered, there are cases where an indication that an accident was one giving rise to personal injury is a necessary part of a decision-maker's reasoning because it may help to explain why a declaration is made in respect of that alleged cause of the injury rather than another. However, it was also made clear that the effect of the forerunner of this section was that any view as to causation expressed when making the decision that an accident was an industrial accident could be only provisional.

Other special cases

Incapacity for work

31.—(1) Regulations may provide that a determination that a person is disqualified for any period in accordance with regulations under section 171E of the Contributions and Benefits Act shall have effect for such purposes as may be prescribed as a determination that he is to be treated as capable of work for that period, and vice versa.

[[1] (1A) Regulations may provide that a determination that a person is disqualified for any period in accordance with regulations under section 18(1) to (3) of the Welfare Reform Act 2007 shall have effect for such purposes as may be prescribed as a determination that he is to be treated as not having limited capability for work for that period, and vice versa.]

(2) Provision may be made by regulations for matters of such descriptions as may be prescribed to be determined by the Secretary of State, notwithstanding that other matters fall to be determined by another authority.

(3) Nothing in this section shall be taken to prejudice the generality of the power conferred by section 17(2) above.

1.431

AMENDMENT

1. Welfare Reform Act 2007, Sch.3, para.17(1) and (7) (March 18, 2008 for regulation-making purposes and October 27, 2008 for other purposes).

DEFINITIONS

"Contributions and Benefits Act"—see s.84.
"prescribed"—*ibid.*

GENERAL NOTE

Subss. (1) and (1a)
See reg.10 of the Social Security and Child Support (Decisions and Appeals) Regulations 1999.

1.432

Subs. (2)
See reg.11 of the Social Security and Child Support (Decisions and Appeals) Regulations 1999.

1.433

Industrial diseases

32. Regulations shall provide for applying the provisions of this Chapter, subject to any prescribed additions or modifications, in relation to decisions

1.434

made or falling to be made under sections 108 to 110 of the Contributions and Benefits Act.

DEFINITIONS

"Contributions and Benefits Act"—see s.84.
"prescribed"—*ibid.*

GENERAL NOTE

1.435   See the Social Security (Industrial Injuries) (Prescribed Diseases) Regulations 1985 as amended by Art.4(8) of and Sch.8 to the Social Security Act 1998 (Commencement No.8 and Savings and Consequential and Transitional Provisions) Order 1999 in Vol.I of this book.

Christmas bonus

1.436   **33.**—(1) A decision by the Secretary of State that a person is entitled or not entitled to payment of a qualifying benefit in respect of a period which includes a day in the relevant week shall be conclusive for the purposes of section 148 of the Contributions and Benefits Act.

(2) In this section, expressions to which a meaning is assigned by section 150 of that Act have that meaning.

DEFINITIONS

"Contributions and Benefits Act"—see s.84.
"qualifying benefit"—by virtue of subs.(2), see s.150 of the Social Security Contributions and Benefits Act 1992.
"relevant week"—*ibid.*

GENERAL NOTE

1.437   This replaces s.67 of the Social Security Administration Act 1992.

Housing benefit and council tax benefit

1.438   **34.–35.** *Omitted.*

Social fund payments

1.439   **36.–38.** *Omitted.*

Supplemental

[¹ Certificates

1.440   **39ZA.** A document bearing a certificate which—
    (a) is signed by a person authorised in that behalf by the Secretary of State, and
    (b) states that the document, apart from the certificate, is a record of a decision of an officer of the Secretary of State,

shall be conclusive evidence of the decision; and a certificate purporting to be so signed shall be deemed to be so signed unless the contrary is proved.]

AMENDMENT

1. Transfer of Tribunal Functions Order 2008 (SI 2008/2833), Sch.3, paras 143 and 166 (November 3, 2008).

GENERAL NOTE

This section partially replaces para.13 of Sch.1 to this Act, which has been repealed. However, there is no longer any provision for certifying decisions of tribunals.

Computer records often need some interpretation in order to make them intelligible. However, a certificate is conclusive only to the extent that it authenticates the record of the decision. This section does not make the certificate conclusive to the extent that the certificate purports also to interpret the record of the decision.

Interpretation etc. of Chapter II

39.—(1) In this Chapter—
[⁴. . .]
[² "claimant", in relation to a joint-claim couple claiming a joint-claim jobseeker's allowance (within the meaning of the Jobseekers Act 1995), means the couple or either member of the couple;]
[⁴. . .]
[³ "health care professional" means—
(a) a registered medical practitioner,
(b) a registered nurse,
(c) an occupational therapist or physiotherapist registered with a regulatory body established by an Order in Council under section 60 of the Health Act 1999, or
(d) a member of such other profession regulated by a body mentioned in section 25(3) of the National Health Service Reform and Health Care Professions Act 2002 as the Secretary of State may prescribe;]
"relevant benefit" has the meaning given by section 8(3) above;
[⁵. . .]
(2) Expressions used in this Chapter to which a meaning is assigned by section 191 of the Administration Act have that meaning in this Chapter.
(3) Part II of the Administration Act, which is superseded by the foregoing provisions of this Chapter, shall cease to have effect.

AMENDMENTS

1. Social Security Contributions (Transfer of Functions, etc.) Act 1999, Sch.7, para.35 (April 1, 1999).
2. Welfare Reform and Pensions Act 1999, Sch.7, para.17 (March 19, 2001).
3. Welfare Reform Act 2007, s.62(1) and (5) (July 3, 2007).
4. Transfer of Tribunal Functions Order 2008 (SI 2008/2833), Sch.3, paras 143 and 167 (November 3, 2008), subject to a saving under art.1(5).
5. Transfer of Tribunal Functions and Revenue and Customs Appeals Order 2009 (SI 2009/56), Sch.1, paras 247 and 250 (April 1, 2009).

1.441

1.442

DEFINITION
"the Administration Act"—see s.84.

GENERAL NOTE

1.443   By reg.14 of the Child Trust Funds (Non-tax Appeals) Regulations 2005 (SI 2005/191), this subsection is applied with some modifications to appeals under ss 21(9) and 22 of the Child Trust Funds Act 2004 (see Vol.IV). Until April 1, 2009, it was also applied in modified form to appeals under the Tax Credits Act 2002 but, for reasons explained in the note to s.12, the regulation applying it appears to have lapsed in relation to cases in Great Britain.

Definitions omitted by virtue of the Transfer of Tribunal Functions Order 2008 remain in force for the purpose explained in the note to ss. 5 to 7.

No other professions have been prescribed for the purposes of the definition of "health care professional".

CHAPTER III

OTHER DECISIONS AND APPEALS

1.444   **40.–47.** *Omitted.*

PART II

CONTRIBUTIONS

1.445   **48.–66.** *Omitted.*

PART III

BENEFITS

1.446   **67.–76.** *Omitted.*

PART IV

MISCELLANEOUS AND SUPPLEMENTAL

Pilot schemes

77.—(1) Any regulations to which this subsection applies may be made so as to have effect for a specified period not exceeding 12 months.

(2) Any regulations which, by virtue of subsection (1) above, are to have effect for a limited period are referred to in this section as "a pilot scheme".

(3) A pilot scheme may provide that its provisions are to apply only in relation to—

(a) one or more specified areas of localities;

(b) one or more specified classes of person;

(c) persons selected—

    (i) by reference to prescribed criteria; or

    (ii) on a sampling basis,

(4) A pilot scheme may make consequential or transitional provision with respect to the cessation of the scheme on the expiry of the specified period.

(5) A pilot scheme ("the previous scheme") may be replaced by a further pilot scheme making the same, or similar, provision (apart from the specified period) to that made by the previous scheme.

(6) In so far as a pilot scheme would, apart from this subsection, have the effect of—

(a) treating as capable of work any person who would not otherwise be so treated; or

(b) reducing the total amount of benefit that would otherwise be payable to any person,

it shall not apply in relation to that person.

(7) Subsection (1) above applies to—

(a) regulations made under section 171D of the Contributions and Benefits Act (incapacity for work: persons treated as incapable of work); and

(b) in so far as they are consequential on or supplementary to any such regulations, regulations made under any of the provisions mentioned in subsection (8) below.

(8) The provisions are—

(a) subsection (5)(a) of section 22 of the Contributions and Benefits Act (earnings factors);

(b) section 30C of that Act (incapacity benefit);

(c) [¹ . . .];

(d) subsection (1)(e) of section 124 of that Act (income support) and, so far as relating to income support, subsection (1) of section 135 of that Act (the applicable amount);

(e) Part XIIA of that Act (incapacity for work);

(f) section 61A of the Administration Act and section 31 above (incapacity for work).

(9) A statutory instrument containing (whether alone or with other provisions) a pilot scheme shall not be made unless a draft of the instrument has been laid before Parliament and approved by a resolution of each House of Parliament.

AMENDMENT

1. Welfare Reform and Pensions Act 1999, Sch.13, Pt IV (April 6, 2001).

DEFINITIONS

"the Administration Act"—see s.84.
"the Contributions and Benefits Act"—*ibid.*
"prescribed"—*ibid.*

1.447 **78.** *Omitted.*

Regulations and orders

1.448   **79.**—(1) [²Subject to subsection 2A below] regulations under this Act shall be made by the Secretary of State.

(2) [². . .]

[¹ (2A) Subsection (1) has effect subject to any provision providing for regulations to be made by the Treasury or the Commissioners of Inland Revenue.]

(3) Powers under this Act to make regulations or orders are exercisable by statutory instrument.

(4) Any power conferred by this Act to make regulations or orders may be exercised—

(a) either in relation to all cases to which the power extends, or in relation to those cases subject to specified exceptions, or in relation to any specified cases or classes of case;

(b) so as to make, as respects the cases in relation to which it is exercised—

(i) the full provision to which the power extends or any less provision (whether by way of exception or otherwise);

(ii) the same provision for all cases in relation to which the power is exercised, or different provision for different cases or different classes of case or different provision as respects the same case or class of case for different purposes of this Act;

(iii) any such provision either unconditionally or subject to any specified condition;

and where such a power is expressed to be exercisable for alternative purposes it may be exercised in relation to the same case for any or all of those purposes.

(5) Powers to make regulations for the purposes of any one provision of this Act are without prejudice to powers to make regulations for the purposes of any other provision.

(6) Without prejudice to any specific provision in this Act, a power conferred by this Act to make regulations includes power to make thereby such incidental, supplementary, consequential or transitional provision as appears to the authority making the regulations to be expedient for the purposes of those regulations.

(7) Without prejudice to any specific provisions in this Act, a power conferred by any provision of this Act to make regulations includes power to provide for a person to exercise a discretion in dealing with any matter.

(8) Any power conferred by this Act to make regulations relating to housing benefit or council tax benefit shall include power to make different provision for different areas or different authorities.

(9) [². . .]

AMENDMENTS

1. Tax Credits Act 2002, Sch.4, para.13 (February 26, 2003).
2. Transfer of Tribunal Functions Order 2008 (SI 2008/2833), Sch.3, paras 143 and 168 (November 3, 2008), subject to a saving under art.1(5).

GENERAL NOTE

Subsections (2) and (9) remain in force for the purpose explained in the note to ss. 5 to 7. **1.449**

Subs. (2A)

The functions of the Commissioners of Inland Revenue have been transferred to the Commissioners for Her Majesty's Revenue and Customs (Commissioners for Revenue and Customs Act 2005, s.5(2)(a)). **1.450**

Parliamentary control of regulations

80.—(1) Subject to the provisions of this section, a statutory instrument containing (whether alone or with other provisions) regulations under— **1.451**

(a) section [³. . .] 12(2) or 72 above; or

(b) [³. . .] paragraph 9 of Schedule 2 [³. . .]

shall not be made unless a draft of the instrument has been laid before Parliament and been approved by a resolution of each House of Parliament.

(2) A statutory instrument—

(a) which contains (whether alone or with other provisions) regulations made under this Act by the Secretary of State [¹, the Treasury or the Commissioners of Inland Revenue]; and

(b) which is not subject to any requirement that a draft of the instrument be laid before and approved by a resolution of each House of Parliament,

shall be subject to annulment in pursuance of a resolution of either House of Parliament.

(3) [³. . .]

[²(4) [³. . .]]

AMENDMENTS

1. Tax Credits Act 2002, Sch.4, para.14 (February 26, 2003).

2. Tribunals, Courts and Enforcement Act 2007, Sch.10, para.29(5) (July 21, 2008).

3. Transfer of Tribunal Functions Order 2008 (SI 2008/2833), Sch.3, paras 143 and 169 (November 3, 2008), subject to a saving under art.1(5).

GENERAL NOTE

The omitted provisions remain in force for the purpose explained in the note to ss. 5 to 7. **1.452**

Reports by Secretary of State

81.—(1) The Secretary of State shall prepare, either annually or at such times or intervals as may be prescribed, a report on the standards achieved by the Secretary of State in the making of decisions against which an appeal lies to [¹the First-tier Tribunal]. **1.453**

(2) A copy of every such report shall be laid before each House of Parliament.

AMENDMENT

1. Transfer of Tribunal Functions Order 2008 (SI 2008/2833), Sch.3, paras 143 and 170 (November 3, 2008), subject to a saving under art.1(5).

DEFINITION

"prescribed"—see s.84.

1.454   **82.** *Omitted.*

1.455   **83.** *Omitted.*

Interpretation: general

1.456   **84.** In this Act—
"the Administration Act" means the Social Security Administration Act
   1992;
"the Child Support Act" means the Child Support Act 1991;
"the Contributions and Benefits Act" means the Social Security
   Contributions and Benefits Act 1992;
"the Jobseekers Act" means the Jobseekers Act 1995;
"the Vaccine Damage Payments Act" means the Vaccine Damage
   Payments Act 1979;
"prescribe" means prescribe by regulations.

1.457   **85.** *Omitted.*

1.458   **86.** *Omitted.*

Short title, commencement and extent

1.459   **87.**—(1) This Act may be cited as the Social Security Act 1998.
(2) This Act, except—
(a) sections 66, 69, 72 and 77 to 85, this section and Schedule 6 to this
   Act; and
(b) subsection (1) of section 50 so far as relating to a sum which
   is chargeable to tax by virtue of section 313 of the Income and
   Corporation Taxes Act 1988, and subsections (2) to (4) of that
   section,
shall come into force on such day as may be appointed by order made by
the Secretary of State; and different days may be appointed for different
provisions and for different purposes.
(3) An order under subsection (2) above may make such savings, or such
transitional or consequential provision, as the Secretary of State considers
necessary or expedient—
(a) in preparation for or in connection with the coming into force of any
   provision of this Act; or
(b) in connection with the operation of any enactment repealed or
   amended by a provision of this Act during any period when the
   repeal or amendment is not wholly in force.
(4) This Act, except—
(a) section 2 so far as relating to war pensions;
(b) sections 3, 15, 45 to 47, 59, 78 and 85 and this section; and
(c) section 86 and Schedules 7 and 8 so far as relating to enactments
   which extend to Northern Ireland,
does not extend to Northern Ireland.

(5) The following provisions of this Act extend to the Isle of Man, namely—

(a) in section 4, subsections (1)(c) and (2)(c);

(b) sections 6 and 7 and Schedule 1 so far as relating to appeals under the Vaccine Damage Payments Act;

(c) sections 45 to 47 and this section;

(d) paragraphs 5 to 10 of Schedule 7 and section 86(1) so far as relating to those paragraphs; and

(e) section 86(2) and Schedule 8 so far as relating to the Vaccine Damage Payments Act.

DEFINITION

"Vaccine Damage Payments Act"—see s.84.

GENERAL NOTE

Subss. (2) and (3)
The following commencement orders have been made: SI 1998/2209, SI 1998/2708, SI 1999/418, SI 1999/526, SI 1999/528, SI 1999/1055, SI 1999/1510, SI 1999/1958, SI 1999/2422, SI 1999/2739, SI 1999/2860 and SI 1999/3178. The main provisions relating to social security adjudication were brought into effect at different times, depending on the benefit in issue, according to the following timetable:

Industrial injuries benefit; Guardian's allowance; Child benefit; Pension Schemes Act 1993—July 5, 1999 (see, primarily, SI 1999/1958).

Retirement pension; Widow's benefit; Incapacity benefit; Severe disablement allowance; Maternity allowance—September 6, 1999 (see, primarily, SI 1999/2422).

Working families' tax credit; Disabled person's tax credit—October 5, 1999 (see, primarily, SI 1999/2739).

Attendance allowance; Disability living allowance; Invalid care allowance; Jobseeker's allowance; Credits of contributions or earnings; Home responsibilities protection; Vaccine damage payments—October 18, 1999 (see, primarily, SI 1999/2860).

All other purposes (including income support)—November 29, 1999 (see, primarily, SI 1999/3178).

1.460

SCHEDULES

SCHEDULE 1

[¹. . .]

1.461

AMENDMENT

1. Transfer of Tribunal Functions Order 2008 (SI 2008/2833), Sch.3, paras 143 and 171 (November 3, 2008), subject to a saving under art.1(5).

GENERAL NOTE

This Schedule remains in force for the limited purpose explained in the note to ss.5 to 7.

1.462

Decisions Against Which No Appeal Lies

Jobseeker's allowance for persons under 18

1.463   **1.** In relation to a person who has reached the age of 16 but not the age of 18, a decision—
(a) whether section 16 of the Jobseekers Act is to apply to him; or
(b) whether to issue a certificate under section 17(4) of that Act.

Christmas bonus

1.464   **2.** A decision whether a person is entitled to payment under section 148 of the Contributions and Benefits Act.

Priority between persons entitled to [³ carer's allowance]

1.465   **3.** A decision as to the exercise of the discretion under section 70(7) of the Contributions and Benefits Act.

Priority between persons entitled to child benefit

1.466   **4.** A decision as to the exercise of the discretion under paragraph 5 of Schedule 10 to the Contributions and Benefits Act.

Persons treated as if present in Great Britain

1.467   **5.** A decision whether to certify, in accordance with regulations made under section 64(1), 71(6), 113(1) or 119 of the Contributions and Benefits Act, that it is consistent with the proper administration of that Act to treat a person as though he were present in Great Britain.

[¹ *Work-focused interviews*

1.468   **5A.** A decision terminating or reducing the amount of a person's benefit made in consequence of any decision made under regulations under section 2A [⁴ or 2AA] of the Administration Act (work-focused interviews).]

Alteration of rates of benefit

1.469   **6.** A decision as to the amount of benefit to which a person is entitled, where it appears to the Secretary of State that the amount is determined by—
(a) the rate of benefit provided for by law; or
(b) an alteration of a kind referred to in—
(i)   section 159(1)(b) of the Administration Act (income support); [² . . .]
(ii) section 159A(1)(b) of that Act (jobseeker's allowance) [² or
(iii) section 129B(1)(b) of that Act (state pension credit)]][⁵ , or
(iv) section 159C(1)(b) of that Act (employment and support allowance).]

Increases in income support due to attainment of particular ages

1.470   **7.** A decision as to the amount of benefit to which a person is entitled, where it appears to the Secretary of State that the amount is determined by the recipient's entitlement to an increased amount of income support or income-based jobseeker's allowance in the circumstances referred to in section 160(2) or 160A(2) of the Administration Act.

Reduction in accordance with reduced benefit direction

1.471   **8.** A decision to reduce the amount of a person's benefit in accordance with a reduced benefit direction (within the meaning of section 46 of the Child Support Act).

Power to prescribe other decisions

1.472   **9.** Such other decisions as may be prescribed.

Amendments

1. Welfare Reform and Pensions Act 1999, s.81 and Sch.11, para.87 (November 11, 1999).

2. State Pension Credit Act 2002, s.11 and Sch.1, para.11 (July 2, 2002 for the purpose of exercising any power to make regulations or orders and October 6, 2003 for all other purposes).

3. Regulatory Reform (Carer's Allowance) Order 2002 (SI 2002/1457), art.2(1) and Sch., para.3(b) September 2002 for the purposes of exercising powers to make subordinate legislation and October 28, 2002 for all other purposes).

4. Employment Act 2002. s.53 and Sch.7, para.51 (July 5, 2003).

5. Welfare Reform Act 2007, Sch.3, para.17(1) and (8) (October 27, 2008).

DEFINITIONS

"the Administration Act"—see s.84.
"benefit"—by virtue of reg.39(2), see s.191 of the Social Security Administration Act 1992.
"the Child Support Act"—see s.84.
"the Contributions and benefits Act"—*ibid.*
"the Jobseekers Act"—*ibid.*
"prescribed"—*ibid.*

GENERAL NOTE

Para. 6
A decision under reg.22A of the Income Support (General) Regulations 1987, reducing the amount of income support payable to a person while an appeal against a decision that the claimant is capable of work is pending, is not a decision on the "rate of benefit" within para.6(a). Therefore, there is a right of appeal against such a decision (*Re Smyth's Application* [2001] N.I. 393, QBD (NI), in which Kerr J. considered the equivalent provision in the Social Security (Northern Ireland) Order 1998).

1.473

Para. 9
See Sch.2 to the Social Security and Child Support (Decisions and Appeals) Regulations 1999 and Sch.2 to the Child Benefit and Guardian's Allowance (Decisions and Appeals) Regulations 2003.

1.474

SCHEDULE 3

DECISIONS AGAINST WHICH AN APPEAL LIES

PART I

BENEFIT DECISIONS

Entitlement to benefit without a claim

1. In such cases or circumstances as may be prescribed, a decision whether a person is entitled to a relevant benefit for which no claim is required.
2. If so, a decision as to the amount to which he is entitled.

1.475

Payability of benefit

3. A decision whether a relevant benefit (or a component of a relevant benefit) to which a person is entitled is not payable by reason of—
   (a) any provision of the Contributions and Benefits Act by which the person is disqualified for receiving benefit;
   (b) regulations made under section 72(8) of that Act (disability living allowance);
   (c) regulations made under section 113(2) of that Act (suspension of payment); [¹ . . .]
   (d) section 19 of the Jobseekers Act (jobseeker's allowance);
   [¹(e) section 62 or 63 of the Child Support, Pensions and Social Security Act 2000;] [² or
   (f) section 7, 8 or 9 of the Social Security Fraud Act 2001][⁴ ; or
   (g) section 18 of the Welfare Reform Act 2007.]

1.476

Payments to third parties

1.477   **4.** Except in such cases or circumstances as may be prescribed, a decision whether the whole or part of a benefit to which a person is entitled is, by virtue of regulations, to be paid to a person other than him.

Recovery of benefits

1.478   **5.** A decision whether payment is recoverable under section 71 or 71A of the Administration Act.
6. If so, a decision as to the amount of payment recoverable.

Industrial injuries benefit

1.479   **7.** A decision whether an accident was an industrial accident for the purposes of industrial injuries benefit.

Jobseekers' agreements

1.480   **8.** A decision in relation to a jobseeker's agreement as proposed to be made under section 9 of the Jobseekers Act, or as proposed to be varied under section 10 of that Act.

[³ *State pension credit*

1.481   **8A.** A decision whether to specify a period as an assessed income period under section 6 of the State Pension Credit Act 2002.
8B. If so, a decision as to the period to be so specified.
8C. A decision whether an assessed income period comes to an end by virtue of section 9(4) or (5) of that Act.
8D. If so, a decision as to when the assessed income period so ends.]

Power to prescribe other decisions

1.482   **9.** Such other decisions relating to a relevant benefit as may be prescribed.

PART II

CONTRIBUTIONS DECISIONS

1.483   **10.–15.** *Omitted.*
16. A decision whether a person was (within the meaning of regulations) precluded from regular employment by responsibilities at home.
17. A decision whether a person is entitled to be credited with earnings or contributions in accordance with regulations made under section 22(5) of the Contributions and Benefits Act.
1.484   **18.–29.** *Omitted.*

AMENDMENTS

1. Child Support, Pensions and Social Security Act 2000, s.66 and Sch.9, Pt V (October 15, 2001).

2. Social Security Fraud Act 2001, s.12(2).

3. State Pension Credit Act 2002, Sch.1, para.12 (July 2, 2002 for the purpose of exercising any power to make regulations or orders and October 6, 2003 for other purposes).

4. Welfare Reform Act 2007, Sch.3, para.17(1) and (9) (October 27, 2008).

DEFINITIONS

"the Administration Act"—see s.84.
"benefit"—by virtue of reg.39(2), see s.191 of the Social Security Administration Act 1992.
"claim"—*ibid.*
"the Child Support Act"—see s.84.
"the Contributions and benefits Act"—*ibid.*
"industrial injuries benefit"—by virtue of s.39(2), see s.191 of the Social Security Administration Act 1992.

"the Jobseekers Act"—s.84.
"prescribed"—*ibid.*
"relevant benefit"—see s.8(3).

GENERAL NOTE

Para.3
A decision under art.13(2) of the Convention on Social Security between Great   **1.485**
Britain and Jamaica that a person is not permanently incapacitated for work is not
a decision under s.113 of the Social Security Contributions and Benefits Act 1992
disqualifying a person from benefit, even though it may lead to such a decision, and
therefore it does not fall within para.3(a) (*Campbell v Secretary of State for Work and
Pensions* [2005] EWCA Civ 989).

Para.5
Notwithstanding the omission from para.5 of any reference to s.74 of the   **1.486**
Administration Act, an appeal lies against a decision that benefit is recoverable
under that section (*R(IS)14/04*).

Para.9
Regulation 26 of the Social Security and Child Support (Decisions and Appeals)   **1.487**
Regulations 1999 is made under para.9.

Paras 10 to 29
Paragraphs 10–15 and 18–29 have never been brought into force and are all to be   **1.488**
repealed by the Social Security Contributions (Transfer of Functions, etc.,) Act 1999,
Sch.7, para.36 but so far the repealing provision has been brought into effect only in
respect of para.23 (twice! See SI 1999/527 and SI 1999/1662). The jurisdictions which
would have been conferred on appeal tribunals are instead transferred to the tax commissioners. Paragraphs 16 and 17, on the other hand, introduce new rights of appeal to
tribunals where none existed before 1999. In *CIB/3327/2004*, the Commissioner commented on the lack of arrangements within the Department for Work and Pensions for
proper decisions to be made in respect of the crediting of earnings or contributions. In
particular, it appeared that such decisions as were made did not include information
about the new right of appeal conferred by para.17. Arrangements have been made
under s.17 of the Social Security Contributions (Transfer of Functions, etc.) Act 1999
for Her Majesty's Revenue and Customs to make decisions on behalf of the Secretary
of State in respect of matters falling within the scope of para.16 and in respect of some
matters falling within the scope of para.17. These arrangements appear not to cover
decisions relating to the crediting of earnings or contributions in respect of unemployment or incapacity for work, although *CIB/3327/2004* reveals some confusion
among staff as to the division of responsibility between the Department for Work and
Pensions and Her Majesty's Revenue and Customs. Further criticism of the handling
of credits cases has been voiced in *CIB/1602/2006*. In particular, the Commissioner
criticised instructions to staff causing them to make undisclosed assumptions about
contributions and credits issues instead of issuing decisions in respect of such issues
informing claimants of their rights of appeal.

SCHEDULE 4

[¹...]

AMENDMENT

1. Transfer of Tribunal Functions Order 2008 (SI 2008/2833), Sch.3, paras 143
and 172 (November 3, 2008), subject to a saving under art.1(5).

1.489 This Schedule remains in force for the limited purpose explained in the note to ss.5 to 7.

SCHEDULE 5

REGULATIONS AS TO PROCEDURE: PROVISION WHICH MAY BE MADE

1.490 **1.** Provision prescribing the procedure to be followed in connection with—
    (a) the making of decisions or determinations by the Secretary of State, [¹. . .] and
    (b) the withdrawal of claims, applications, appeals or references falling to be decided or determined by the Secretary of State, [¹. . .].
  2. [¹. . .]
  3. Provision as to the form which is to be used for any document, the evidence which is to be required and the circumstances in which any official record or certificate is to be sufficient or conclusive evidence.
  4. Provision as to the time within which, or the manner in which—
    (a) any evidence is to be produced; or
    (b) any application, reference or appeal is to be made.
  5. [¹. . .]
  6. [¹. . .]
  7. [¹. . .]
  8. [¹. . .]
  9. Provision for the non-disclosure to a person of the particulars of any medical advice or medical evidence given or submitted for the purposes of a determination.

AMENDMENT

1. Transfer of Tribunal Functions Order 2008 (SI 2008/2833), Sch.3, paras 143 and 173 (November 3, 2008), subject to a saving under art.1(5).

GENERAL NOTE

1.491 This Schedule no longer enables regulations to be made in respect of the procedure before tribunals, having been replaced by Sch.5 to the Tribunals, Courts and Enforcement Act 2007, but the omitted provisions remain in force for the purpose explained in the note to ss.5 to 7. By reg.11(5) of the Child Trust Funds (Non-tax Appeals) Regulations 2005 (SI 2005/191), this Schedule is applied to appeals under ss.21(9) and 22 of the Child Trust Funds Act 2004 with the modification that "the Secretary of State" is omitted from both places where it occurs in para.1, which makes that paragraph redundant. Until April 1, 2009, it was also applied in similarly modified form to appeals under the Tax Credits Act 2002 but, for reasons explained in the note to s.12, the regulation applying it appears to have lapsed in relation to cases in Great Britain. It is still applied, with references to the Board substituted for references to the Secretary of State, to child benefit and guardian's allowance decisions and appeals (Tax Credits Act 2002, Sch.4, para.15).

See the Social Security and Child Support (Decisions and Appeals) Regulations 1999, the Child Benefit and Guardian's Allowance (Decisions and Appeals) Regulations 2003 and, in Vol.IV, the Child Trust Funds (Appeals) Regulations 2005.

Schedules 6 to 8

1.492 *Omitted.*

Social Security Contributions (Transfer of Functions, etc.) Act 1999

(1999 c.2)

ARRANGEMENT OF SECTIONS

PART I

GENERAL

1.–7. *Omitted.*   **1.493**

PART II

DECISIONS AND APPEALS

8.   Decisions by officers of Board.
9.–16. *Omitted.*
17.   Arrangement for discharge of decision-making functions.
18. and 19. *Omitted.*

PART III

MISCELLANEOUS AND SUPPLEMENTAL

20.–26. *Omitted.*
27.   Interpretation.
28.   Short title, commencement and extent.

SCHEDULES

Omitted.

An Act to transfer from the Secretary of State to the Commissioners of
Inland Revenue or the Treasury certain functions relating to national insurance contributions, the National Insurance Fund, statutory sick pay, statutory maternity pay or person schemes and certain associated functions
relating to benefits; to enable functions relating to any of those matters in
respect of Northern Ireland to be transferred to the Secretary of State, the
Commissioners of Inland Revenue or the Treasury; to make further provision, in connection with the functions transferred, as to the powers of the
Commissioners of Inland Revenue, the making of decisions and appeals;
to provide that rebates payable in respect of members of money purchase
contracted-out pension schemes are to be payable out of the National
Insurance Fund; and for connected purposes.

                                                             [25th February 1999]

PART I

GENERAL

1.–7. *Omitted.*   **1.494**

271

PART II

DECISIONS AND APPEALS

Decisions by officers of Board

1.495   **8.**—(1) Subject to the provisions of the Part, it shall be for an officer of the Board—

(a) to decide whether for the purposes of Parts I to V of the Social Security Contributions and Benefits Act 1992 a person is or was an earner and, if so, the category of earners in which he is or was to be included,

(b) to decide whether a person is or was employed in employed earner's employment for the purposes of Part V of the Social Security Contributions and Benefits Act 1992 (industrial injuries),

(c) to decide whether a person is or was liable to pay contributions of any particular class and, if so, the amount that he is or was liable to pay,

(d) to decide whether a person is or was entitled to pay contributions of any particular class that he is or was not liable to pay and, if so, the amount that he is or was entitled to pay,

(e) to decide whether contributions of a particular class have been paid in respect of any period,

(f) subject to and in accordance withregulations made for the purposes of this paragraph by the Secretary of State with the concurrence of the Board, to decide any issue arising as to, or in connection with, entitlement to statutory sick pay or statutory maternity pay,

(g) to make any other decision that falls to be made under Part XI of the Social Security Contributions and Benefits Act 1992 (statutory sick pay) or Part XII of that Act (statutory maternity pay),

(h) to decide any question as to the issue and content of a notice under subsection (2) of section 121C of the Social Security Administration Act 1992 (liability of directors etc. for company's contributions),

(i) to decide any issue arising under section 27 of the Jobseekers Act 1995 (employment of long-term unemployed; deductions by employers), or under any provision of regulations under that section, as to—

(i) whether a person is or was an employee or employer of another,

(ii) whether an employer is or was entitled to make any deduction from his contributions payments in accordance with regulations under section 27 of that Act,

(iii) whether a payment falls to be made to an employer in accordance with those regulations,

(iv) the amount that falls to be so deducted or paid, or

(v) whether two or more employers are, by virtue of regulations under section 27 of that Act, to be treated as one,

(j) [¹ . . .],

(k) to decide whether a person is liable to a penalty under—

(i) paragraph 7A(2) or 7B(2)(h) of Schedule 1 to the Social Security Contributions and Benefits Act 1992, or

(ii) section 113(1)(a) of the Social Security Administration Act 1992,

(l) to decide the [¹ . . .] or penalty payable under any of the provisions mentioned in [¹ paragraph k] above, and

(m) to decide such issues relating to contributions, other than the issues specified in paragraphs (a) to (l) above or in paragraphs 16 and 17 of Schedule 3 to the Social Security Act 1998, as may be prescribed by regulations made by the Board.

(2) *Omitted.*

(3) *Omitted.*

(4) *Omitted.*

AMENDMENT

1. Child Support, Pensions and Social Security Act 2000, s.76(6) and Sch.9, Pt VIII.

DEFINITIONS

"the Board"—see s.27, but note that the functions of the Board have been transferred to Her Majesty's Revenue and Customs by the Commissioners for Revenue and Customs Act 2005.

"contributions"—see s.27.

GENERAL NOTE

This section provides for a number of matters previously determined by the Secretary of State for Social Security to be determined by the Board of Inland Revenue (see s.27), whose functions have now been transferred to the Commissioners for Her Majesty's Revenue and Customs by s.5(2) of the Commissioners for Revenue and Customs Act 2005. They are mainly concerned with contributions and employment status (which is important for entitlement to industrial injuries benefits (see para.(b)), but also include statutory sick pay and statutory maternity pay (see paras (f) and (g)). Entitlement to statutory sick pay and statutory maternity pay had been determined by adjudication officers, until the Social Security Act 1998 transferred that function to the Secretary of State by provisions that never came fully into force because they were overtaken by this Act. Sections 9–14 of this Act make provision for decisions by Her Majesty's Revenue and Customs and appeals to the Tax Chamber of the First-tier Tribunal which are beyond the scope of this volume, but see Vol.IV.

The questions listed in s.8(1) are *not* to be decided by the Secretary of State (see s.8(5) of the Social Security Act 1998) and do not fall within the jurisdiction of the Social Entitlement Chamber of the First-tier Tribunal. However, although it was for the Inland Revenue to consider whether a person is or was in employed earner's employment, the Commissioner in *CI/7507/1999* accepted a submission by the Secretary of State that the question whether a person was to be *treated* as having been an employed earner for the purposes of the industrial injuries scheme was a matter for the Secretary of State and, on appeal, for an appeal tribunal. If that is the construction to be given to s.8(1)(b), presumably the same approach must be taken to s.8(1)(a), although questions relating to the payment of contributions will be matters for Her Majesty's Revenue and Customs by virtue of s.8(1)(c)–(e) and regulations made under s.8(1)(m). *CI/7507/1999* was distinguished in *R(JSA)8/02*, where the Commissioner held that the question whether a person was to be *treated* as having paid contributions (where contributions had been deducted from her salary but not passed on to the Inland Revenue) was a question to be determined by the Inland Revenue. Where, following a claim for retirement pension, there is a dispute between the Secretary of State and a claimant as to whether employment he had been in was contracted-out or contracted-in employment, it arises as part

1.496

of a question as to his liability to pay contributions or as to what contributions have been paid and so is a question falling within the jurisdiction of Her Majesty's Revenue and Customs by virtue of s.8(1)(c) or (e) (*CP/3833/2003*). Therefore any appeal lies to the Tax Chamber of the First-tier Tribunal and not to the Social Entitlement Chamber, notwithstanding that appeals against refusals of contracting-out certificates lie to the Social Entitlement Chamber by virtue of s.170 of the Pension Schemes Act 1993 (see the note to art.3 of the First-tier Tribunal and Upper Tribunal (Chambers) Order 2008). On the other hand, while Her Majesty's Revenue and Customs are responsible for determining the amount of contributions paid, it is for the Secretary of State to determine any question as to which contribution year is relevant to a claim for benefit (because it would appear from the language of s.8(1)(e) that the effect of *Secretary of State for Social Security v Scully* [1992] 1 W.L.R. 927 (reported as *R(S) 5/93*) has been reversed and the effect of *R(G) 1/82* has been restored) and also any question as to the application of the Social Security (Earnings Factor) Regulations 1979 (*R(IB) 1/09*).

Questions relating to "home responsibilities protection" and the crediting of contributions or earnings remain matters for the Secretary of State by virtue of the combined effect of s.8(1)(m) of this Act and s.8(1)(c) of the Social Security Act 1998. So too do matters relating to the payment of contributions for graduated retirement benefit, which were not contributions of a "class" and so do not fall within the scope of s.8(1)(c) of this Act with the result that they remain within the scope of s.8(1)(c) of the 1998 Act (*R(P) 1/08*). Note, however, that s.17 permits the Secretary of State to make arrangements for Her Majesty's Revenue and Customs to discharge his decision-making functions in relation to those matters.

1.497   **9.–16.** *Omitted.*

Arrangements for discharge of decision-making functions

1.498   **17.**—(1) The Secretary of State may make arrangements with the Board for any his functions under Chapter II of Part I of the Social Security Act 1998 in relation to—

 (a) a decision whether a person was (within the meaning of regulations) precluded from regular employment by responsibilities at home, or

 (b) a decision whether a person is entitled to be credited with earnings or contributions in accordance with regulations made under section 22(5) of the Social Security Contributions and Benefits Act 1992,

to be discharged by the Board or by officers of the Board.

 (2) No such arrangements shall effect the responsibility of the Secretary of State or the application of Chapter II of Part I of the Social Security Act 1998 in relation to any decision.

 (3) *Omitted.*

DEFINITIONS

"the Board"—see s.27, but note that the functions of the Board have been transferred to Her Majesty's Revenue and Customs by the Commissioners for Revenue and Customs Act 2005.

"contributions"—see s.27.

GENERAL NOTE

1.499   Questions about home responsibilities protection and the crediting of earnings or contributions are questions that are relevant to a person's contributions record, but they are nonetheless decisions within the jurisdiction of the Secretary of State and there are rights of appeal to the Social Entitlement Chamber of the First-tier Tribunal (see the Social Security Act 1998, Sch.3, paras 16 and 17). Despite this, decisions about home responsibilities protection are made by Her Majesty's Revenue and Customs under an arrangement under this section. So too are most decisions about "credits" other than those related to incapacity for work or availability for work, which are made by the Secretary of State because a person claiming benefit on the ground of incapacity for work or availability for work is usually treated also as claiming "credits". It appears that there is also an arrangement under this section in respect of questions concerning records of payment of contributions for graduated retirement benefit *(R(P)1/08)*.

18.–19. *Omitted.*   1.500

PART III

MISCELLANEOUS AND SUPPLEMENTAL

20.–26. *Omitted.*   1.501

Interpretation

27. In this Act, unless a contrary intention appears—   1.502
"the Board" means the Commissioners of Inland Revenue;
"contributions" means contributions under Part I of the Social Security
   Contributions and Benefits Act 1992.

GENERAL NOTE

"the Board"   1.503
The functions of the Commissioners of Inland Revenue have now been transferred to the Commissioners for Her Majesty's Revenue and Customs by s.5(2) of the Commissioners for Revenue and Customs Act 2005.

Short title, commencement and extent

28.—(1) This Act may be cited as the Social Security Contributions   1.504
(Transfer of Functions, etc.) Act 1999.
   (2) *Omitted.*
   (3) *Omitted.*

Welfare Reform and Pensions Act 1999

(1999 c.30)

ARRANGEMENT OF SECTIONS

PART I TO IV (*OMITTED*)

PART V

WELFARE

CHAPTER I

SOCIAL SECURITY BENEFITS

1.505   **52.–67.** *Omitted.*

Miscellaneous

1.506   **68.** Certain overpayments of benefit not to be recoverable.
69.–70. *Omitted.*

Supplementary

71. *Omitted.*
72. Supply of information for certain purposes.
73.–91. *Omitted.*

Certain overpayments of benefit not to be recoverable

1.507   **68.**—(1) An overpayment to which this section applies shall not be recoverable from the payee, whether by the Secretary of State or a local authority, under any provision made by or under Part III of the Administration Act (overpayments and adjustments of benefit).

(2) This section applies to an overpayment if—

(a) it is in respect of a qualifying benefit;

(b) it is referable to a decision given on a review that there has been an alteration in the relevant person's condition, being a decision to which effect is required to be given as from a date earlier than that on which it was given;

(c) the decision was given before June 1, 1999; and

(d) the overpayment is not excluded by virtue subsection (6).

(3) In subsection (2)(b) the reference to a decision on a review that there has been an alteration in the relevant person's condition is a reference to a decision so given that that person's physical or mental condition either was at the time when the original decision was given, or has subsequently become, different from that on which that decision was based, with the result—

(a) that he did not at that time, or (as the case may be) has subsequently ceased to, meet any of the conditions contained in the following provisions of the Contributions and Benefits Act, namely—

(i) section 64 (attendance allowance),

(ii) section 72(1) or (2) (care component of disability living allowance), and

(iii) section 73(1) or (2) (mobility component of that allowance); or

(b) that he was at that time, or (as the case may be) has subsequently become, capable of work in accordance with regulations made under section 171C(2) of that Act (the all work test).

(4) For the purposes of this section "qualifying benefit" means—

(a) attendance allowance;

(b) disability living allowance;

(c) any benefit awarded wholly or partly by reason of a person being (or being treated as being) in receipt of a component of disability living allowance or in receipt of attendance allowance;

(d) incapacity benefit;

(e) any benefit (other than incapacity benefit) awarded wholly or partly by reason of a person being (or being treated as being) in receipt of any benefit falling within paragraph (c), (d) or (e).

(5) For the purposes of this section—

(a) "review" means a review taking place by virtue of section 25(1) (a) or (b), 30(2)(a) or (b) or 35(1)(a) or (b) of the Administration Act;

(b) "the relevant person", in relation to a review, means the person to whose entitlement to a qualifying benefit or to whose incapacity for work the review related; and

(c) "the original decision", in relation to a review, means the decision as to any such entitlement or incapacity to which the review related.

(6) An overpayment is excluded by virtue of this subsection if (before or after the passing of this Act)—

(a) the payee has agreed to pay a penalty in respect of the overpayment under section 115A of the Administration Act,

(b) the payee has been convicted of any offence (under section 111A or 112(1) or (1A) of that Act or otherwise) in connection with the overpayment, or

(c) proceedings have been instituted against the payee for such an offence and the proceedings have not been determined or abandoned.

(7) Nothing in this section applies to an overpayment to the extent that it was recovered from the payee (by any means) before February 26, 1999.

(8) In this section—

"benefit" includes any amount included in—

(a) the applicable amount in relation to an income-related benefit (as defined by section 135(1) of the Contributions and Benefits Act), or

(b) the applicable amount in relation to a jobseeker's allowance (as defined by section 4(5) of the Jobseekers Act 1995);

"income-related benefit" has the meaning given by section 123(1) of the Contributions and Benefits Act;

"overpayment" means an amount of benefit paid in excess of entitlement;

"the payee", in relation to an overpayment, means the person to whom that amount was paid.

COMMENCEMENT

November 11, 1999.

GENERAL NOTE

1.508   The purpose of this provision is to give an amnesty to certain benefit holders held to have been overpaid benefit in the circumstances set out in subs.(2). The section is replete with difficulty. Subsection (1) says that the overpayment is not to be recoverable; quite what this means in the context of the section is not clear. Subsection (6) refers to circumstances which take the overpayment out of the scope of subs.(2). There are both issues of timing and of culpability in the section which it is difficult to understand. Clearly subs.(6) is intended to exempt culpable overpayments from the amnesty, but the drafting is obscure.

Supply of information for certain purposes

1.509   **72.**—(1) The Secretary of State may by regulations make such provision for or in connection with any of the following matters, namely—
   (a) the use by a person within subsection (2) of social security information held by that person,
   (b) the supply (whether to a person within subsection (2) or otherwise) of social security information held by a person within that subsection,
   (c) the relevant purposes for which a person to whom such information is supplied under the regulations may use it, and
   (d) the circumstances and extent (if any) in and to which a person to whom such information is supplied under the regulations may supply it to another person (whether within subsection (2) or not),
as the secretary of State considers appropriate in connection with any provision to which subsection (3) applies or in connection with any scheme or arrangements to which subsection (4) applies.
   (2) The persons within this subsection are—
   (a) a Minister of the crown,
   (b) a person providing services to, or designated for the purposes of this section by an order of, a Minister of the Crown;
   (c) a local authority (within the meaning of the Administration Act); and
   (d) a person providing services to, or authorised to exercise any function of, any such authority.
   (3) This subsection applies to any provision made by or under—
   (a) any of the sections of the Administration Act inserted by section 57, 58 or 71 of this Act,
   [¹ (aa) section 2AA of the Administration Act,]
   (b) section 60 of this Act
   (c) the Jobseekers Act 1995; or
   [²(d) Part 1 of the Welfare Reform Act 2007.]
   (4) This subsection applies to—
   (a) any scheme designated by regulations under subsection (1), being a scheme operated by the Secretary of State (whether under arrangements with any other person or not) for any purposes connected withemployment or training in the case of persons of a particular category or description;
   (b) any arrangements of a description specified in such regulations, being arrangements made by the Secretary of State for any such purposes.
   (5) Regulations under subsection (1) may, in particular, authorise information supplies to a person under the regulations—

(a) to be used for the purpose of amending or supplementing other information held by that person; and

(b) if it is so used, to be supplied to any other person, and used for any purpose, to whom or for whom that other information could be supplied or used.

(6) In this section—

"relevant provisions" means purposes connected with—

(a) social security, child support or war pensions, or

(b) employment or training;

"social security information" means information relating to social security, child support or war pensions;

and in this subsection "war pensions" means war pensions within the meaning of section 25 of the Social Security Act 1989 (establishment and functions of war pensions committees).

(7) Any reference in this section to purposes connected with employment or training includes purposes connected with the existing or future employment or training prospects or needs of persons, and (in particular) assisting or encouraging persons to enhance their employment prospects."

COMMENCEMENT

November 11, 1999.

AMENDMENTS

1. Employment Act 2002, s.53 and Sch.7 (July 5, 2003).
2. Welfare Reform Act 2007, Sch.3 para.18 (March 18, 2008 for the purpose of conferring the power to make regulations; October 27, 2008 otherwise).

GENERAL NOTE

Subs. (3)

Sections 57 and 58 inserted ss.2A–2C into the Administration Act. Section 71 inserted s.7A into the Administration Act. Section 60 concerns special schemes for claimants for jobseeker's allowance.

1.510

Child Support, Pensions and Social Security Act 2000

(2000 C.19)

ARRANGEMENT OF SECTIONS

PART III

SOCIAL SECURITY

Loss of benefit

1.511

An Act to amend the law relating to child support; to amend the law relating to occupational and personal pensions and war pensions; to amend the law relating to social security benefits and social security administration; to amend the law relating to national insurance contributions; to amend Part III of the Family Law Reform Act 1969 and Part III of the Family Law Act 1986; and for connected purposes.

[28th July 2000]

GENERAL NOTE TO SECTIONS 62–66

1.512   Except as set out below, ss.62–66 of the Child Support, Pensions and Social Security Act 2000 ("CSPSSA 2000") were brought into effect for certain pilot areas of England on October 15, 2001 by the Child Support, Pensions and Social Security Act 2000 (Commencement No.10) Order 2001 (SI 2001/2619). As there is at present no pilot area in Scotland, s.62(11) and subss.(3), (4)(b), 7(d), (9) and (11) of s.64 (which are included in the text below for the sake of completeness) have yet to be brought into force. In fact, it is now unlikely that those provisions will ever be brought into force because it has been announced that the Government will shortly propose that the current pilot scheme should be wound up on the ground that, "once all costs have been factored in, the overall sum for continuing the scheme would be in the region of £652,000, or £5.60p for every £1 of savings made under the scheme" (H.C., February 27, 2009: col 36WS to 38WS).

For an analysis of ss.62–66, see the General Note to Social Security (Breach of Community Order) Regulations 2001 (SI 2001/1395), below.

Sections 7–12 of the Social Security (Fraud) Act 2001 contain similar "loss of benefit" provisions for people convicted of two separate benefit offences within three years.

PART III

SOCIAL SECURITY

Loss of benefit

Loss of benefit for breach of community order

1.513   **62.**—(1) If—

(a) a court makes a determination that a person ("the offender") has failed without reasonable excuse to comply with the requirements of a relevant community order made in respect of him,

(b) the Secretary of State is notified in accordance with regulations under section 64 of the determination, and

(c) the offender is a person with respect to whom the conditions for any entitlement to a relevant benefit are or become satisfied,

then, even though those conditions are satisfied, the following restrictions shall apply in relation to the payment of that benefit in the offender's case.

(2) Subject to subsections (3) to (5), the relevant benefit shall not be payable in the offender's case for the prescribed period.

(3) Where the relevant benefit is income support, the benefit shall be payable in the offender's case for the prescribed period as if the appli-

cable amount used for the determination under section 124(4) of the Social Security Contributions and Benefits Act 1992 of the amount of the offender's entitlement for that period were reduced in such manner as may be prescribed.

(4) The Secretary of State may by regulations provide that, where the relevant benefit is jobseeker's allowance, any income-based jobseeker's allowance shall be payable, during the whole or a part of the prescribed period, as if one or more of the following applied—

(a) the rate of the allowance were such reduced rate as may be prescribed;

(b) the allowance were payable only if there is compliance by the offender with such obligations with respect to the provision of information as may be imposed by the regulations;

(c) the allowance were payable only if the circumstances are otherwise such as may be prescribed.

[² (4A) The Secretary of State may by regulations provide that, where the relevant benefit is an employment and support allowance, any income-related allowance (within the meaning of Part 1 of the Welfare Reform Act 2007) shall be payable, during the whole or part of the prescribed period, as if one or more of the following applied—

(a) the rate of the allowance were such reduced rate as may be prescribed;

(b) the allowance were payable only if there is compliance by the offender with such obligations with respect to the provision of information as may be imposed by the regulations;

(c) the allowance were payable only if the circumstances are otherwise such as may be prescribed.]

(5) Where the relevant benefit is a payment under section 2 of the Employment and Training Act 1973 (under which training allowances are payable), that benefit shall not be payable for the prescribed period except to such extent (if any) as may be prescribed.

(6) Where the determination by a court that was made in the offender's case is quashed or otherwise set aside by the decision of that or any other court, all such payments and other adjustments shall be made in his case as would be necessary if the restrictions imposed by or under this section in respect of that determination had not been imposed.

(7) The length of any period prescribed for the purposes of any of subsections (2) to (5) shall not exceed twenty-six weeks.

(8) In this section—

"income-based jobseeker's allowance" and "joint-claim jobseeker's allowance" have the same meanings as in the Jobseekers Act 1995;

"relevant benefit" means—

(a) income support;

(b) any jobseeker's allowance other than joint-claim jobseeker's allowance;

[² (ba) an employment and support allowance;]

(c) any benefit under the Social Security Contributions and Benefits Act 1992 (other than income support) which is prescribed for the purposes of this section; or

(d) any prescribed payment under section 2 of the Employment and Training Act 1973 (under which training allowances are payable);

"relevant community order" means—

[1(a) a community punishment order;
(b) a community rehabilitation order;
(c) a community punishment and rehabilitation order;]
(d) such other description of community order within the meaning of the Powers of Criminal Courts (Sentencing) Act 2000 as may be prescribed for the purposes of this section; or
(e) any order falling in England and Wales to be treated as an order specified in paragraphs (a) to (d).

(9) In relation to a relevant benefit falling within paragraph (d) of the definition of that expression in subsection (8), references in this section to the conditions for entitlement to that benefit being or becoming satisfied with respect to any person are references to there having been or, as the case may be, the taking of a decision to make a payment of such benefit to that person.

(10) In relation to any time before the coming into force of the Powers of Criminal Courts (Sentencing) Act 2000, the reference to that Act in sub-section (8) shall be taken to be a reference to Part I of the Criminal Justice Act 1991.

(11) In the application to Scotland of this section—

(a) in subsection (1) after the word "excuse" insert "(or, in the case of a probation order, failed)";
(b) for paragraph (b) of that subsection substitute—

"(b) the Secretary of State is notified in accordance with an Act of Adjournal made under section 64 of the determination"; and

(c) in subsection (8)—

(i) in the definition of relevant benefit, paragraph (d) does not apply in the case of any payment made by or on behalf of the Scottish Ministers; and
(ii) in the definition of relevant community order, for paragraphs (c) to (e) substitute—

[1(ii) in the definition of relevant community order, for paragraphs (a) to (e) substitute—

"(a) a community service order;
(b) a probation order;
(c) such other description of order made under the Criminal Procedure (Scotland) Act 1995 as may be prescribed for the purposes of this section; or
(d) any order falling in Scotland to be treated as an order specified in paragraphs (a) to (c)."]

AMENDMENTS

1. Criminal Justice and Courts Act 2000, Sch.7, paras 205 and 206 (April 1, 2001).

2. Welfare Reform Act 2007, Sch.3, para.20(1) to (3) (March 18, 2008 for regulation-making purposes and October 27, 2008 for other purposes).

DEFINITIONS

"income-based jobseeker's allowance"—by virtue of subs.(8), see Jobseeker's Act 1995, s.1(4).

"joint-claim jobseeker's allowance"—*ibid.*
"offender"—see subs.(1).
"prescribed"—see s.65(1).
"relevant benefit" see subs.(8)
"relevant community order" *ibid.*

GENERAL NOTE

See the General Note to the Social Security (Beach of Community Order)   1.514
Regulations 2001 below.

Subs.(8) and (11) were amended by the Criminal Courts and Justice Act 2000 on
April 1, 2001 (i.e. before they were in force) (see the Criminal Courts and Justice
Act 2000 (Commencement No.4) Order 2001 (SI 2001/919)). Subs.(11) is not yet
in force (see the General Note to Sections 62–66 above).

The Powers of Criminal Courts (Sentencing) Act 2000 came into force on August
25, 2000 (three months after it received Royal Assent (see s.168(1) of that Act).
Therefore although subs.(10) was brought into force on October 15, 2001 it has no
practical effect.

Loss of joint-claim jobseeker's allowance

63.—(1) Subsections (2) and (3) shall have effect, subject to the other   1.515
provisions of this section, where—
  (a) the conditions for the entitlement of any joint-claim couple to a joint-
      claim jobseeker's allowance are or become satisfied at any time; and
  (b) the restriction in subsection (2) of section 62 would apply in the case
      of at least one of the members of the couple if the entitlement were
      an entitlement of that member to a relevant benefit.
  (2) The allowance shall not be payable in the couple's case for so much of
the prescribed period as is a period for which—
  (a) in the case of each of the members of the couple, the restriction in
      subsection (2) of section 62 would apply if the entitlement were an
      entitlement of that member to a relevant benefit; or
  [¹(b) that restriction would apply in the case of one of the members of the
      couple and the other member of the couple—
    (i) is subject to sanctions for the purposes of section 20A of the
        Jobseekers Act 1995 (denial or reduction of joint-claim job-
        seeker's allowance); or
    (ii) is a person in whose case the restriction in subsection (2) of
        section 8 of the Social Security Fraud Act 2001 (loss of benefit
        for offenders) would apply if the entitlement were an entitlement
        to a sanctionable benefit (within the meaning of that section).]
  (3) For any part of the period for which subsection (2) does not apply,
the allowance—
  (a) shall be payable in the couple's case as if the amount of the allowance
      were reduced to an amount calculated using the method prescribed
      for the purposes of this subsection; but
  (b) shall be payable only to the member of the couple who is not the
      person in relation to whom the court has made a determination.
  (4) The Secretary of State may by regulations provide in relation to cases
to which subsection (2) would otherwise apply that joint-claim jobseeker's
allowance shall be payable in a couple's case, during the whole or a part of
so much of the prescribed period as falls within paragraph (a) or (b) of that
subsection, as if one or more of the following applied—

    (a) the rate of the allowance were such reduced rate as may be prescribed;

    (b) the allowance were payable only if there is compliance by each of the members of the couple with such obligations with respect to the provision of information as may be imposed by the regulations;

    (c) the allowance were payable only if the circumstances are otherwise such as may be prescribed.

(5) Subsection (6) of section 20A of the Jobseekers Act 1995 (calculation of reduced amount) shall apply for the purposes of subsection (3) above as it applies for the purposes of subsection (5) of that section.

(6) Subsection (6) of section 62 shall apply for the purposes of this section in relation to any determination relating to one or both members of the joint-claim couple as it applies for the purposes of that section in relation to the determination relating to the offender.

(7) The length of any period prescribed for the purposes of subsection (2) or (3) shall not exceed twenty-six weeks.

(8) In this section—

"joint-claim couple" and "joint-claim jobseeker's allowance" have the same meanings as in the Jobseekers Act 1995; and

"relevant benefit" has the same meaning as in section 62.

AMENDMENT

1. Social Security Fraud Act 2001, s.12(1) (April 1, 2002).

DEFINITIONS

"joint-claim couple"—by virtue of subs.(8), see Jobseeker's Act 1995, s.(4).
"joint-claim jobseeker's allowance"—*ibid.*
"prescribed—see s.65(1).
"relevant benefit"—by virtue of subs.(8), see s.62(8).

Information provision

1.516   **64.**—(1) A court in Great Britain shall, before making a relevant community order in relation to any person, explain to that person in ordinary language the consequences by virtue of sections 62 and 63 of a failure to comply with the order.

(2) The Secretary of State may by regulations require the [¹chief officer of a local probation board], or such other person as may be prescribed, to notify the Secretary of State at the prescribed time and in the prescribed manner—

    (a) of the laying by [² an officer of a local probation board] of any information that a person has failed to comply with the requirements of a relevant community order;

    (b) of any such determination as is mentioned in section 62(1);

    (c) of such information about the offender, and in the possession of the person giving the notification, as may be prescribed; and

    (d) of any circumstances by virtue of which any payment or adjustment might fall to be made by virtue of section 62(6) or 63(6).

(3) The High Court of Justiciary may, by Act of Adjournal, make provision requiring the clerk of the court in which any proceedings are commenced that could result in a determination of a failure to comply with a relevant community order to notify the Secretary of State at such time and in such manner as may be specified in the Act of Adjournal of—

(a) the commencement of the proceedings;

(b) any such determination made in the proceedings;

(c) such information about the offender as may be so specified; and

(d) any circumstances by virtue of which any payment or adjustment might fall to be made by virtue of section 62(6) or 63(6).

(4) Where it appears to the Secretary of State that—

(a) the laying of any information that has been laid in England and Wales, or

(b) the commencement of any proceedings that have been commenced in Scotland,

could result in a determination the making of which would result in the imposition by or under one or both of sections 62 and 63 of any restrictions, it shall be the duty of the Secretary of State to notify the person in whose case those restrictions would be imposed, or (as the case may be) the members of any joint-claim couple in whose case they would be imposed, of the consequences under those sections of such a determination in the case of that person, or couple.

(5) A notification required to be given by the Secretary of State under subsection (4) must be given as soon as reasonably practicable after it first appears to the Secretary of State as mentioned in that subsection.

(6) The Secretary of State may by regulations make such provision as he thinks fit for the purposes of sections 62 to 65 of this Act about—

(a) the use by a person within subsection (7) of information relating to community orders or social security;

(b) the supply of such information by a person within that subsection to any other person (whether or not within that subsection); and

(c) the purposes for which a person to whom such information is supplied under the regulations may use it.

(7) The persons within this subsection are—

(a) the Secretary of State;

(b) a person providing services to the Secretary of State;

(c) a person employed or appointed by a probation committee;

(d) a person employed by a council constituted under section 2 of the Local Government etc. (Scotland) Act 1994.

(8) Regulations under subsection (6) may, in particular, authorise information supplied to a person under the regulations—

(a) to be used for the purpose of amending or supplementing other information held by that person; and

(b) where so used, to be supplied to any other person to whom, and used for any purpose for which, the information amended or supplemented could be supplied or used.

(9) The explanation given to the offender by the court in pursuance of subsection (1) shall be treated as part of the explanation required to be given to the offender for the purposes of section 228(5) or 238(4) of the Criminal Procedure (Scotland) Act 1995.

(10) In this section "relevant community order" has the same meaning as in section 62.

(11) For the purposes of this section proceedings that could result in such a determination as is mentioned in subsection (3) are commenced in Scotland when, and only when, a warrant to arrest the offender or to cite the offender to appear before a court is issued under section 232(1) or 239(4) of the Criminal Procedure (Scotland) Act 1995.

AMENDMENTS

1. Criminal Justice and Courts Act 2000, Sch.7, paras 205 and 207(a) (April 1, 2001).
2. Criminal Justice and Courts Act 2000, Sch.7, paras 205 and 207(b) (April 1, 2001).
3. Criminal Justice and Courts Act 2000, Sch.7, paras 205 and 207(c) (April 1, 2001).

DEFINITIONS

"prescribed"—see s.65(1).
"relevant community order"—by virtue of subs.(10), see s.62(8).

GENERAL NOTE

1.517   Subss.(2) (7)(c) and (10) were amended by the Criminal Courts and Justice Act 2000 on April 1, 2001 (i.e. before they were in force) (see the Criminal Courts and Justice Act 2000 (Commencement No.4) Order 2001 (SI 2001/919). Subss.(3), (4) (b), 7(d), (9) and (11) are not yet in force (see the General Note to Sections 62–66).

For a discussion of "local probation boards" see the General Note to reg.1 of the Social Security (Breach of Community Order) Regulations 2001 (SI 2001/1395) below.

Loss of benefit regulations

1.518   **65.**—(1) In the loss of benefit provisions "prescribed" means prescribed by or determined in accordance with regulations made by the Secretary of State.

(2) Regulations prescribing a period for the purposes of any of the loss of benefit provisions may contain provision for determining the time from which the period is to run.

(3) Regulations under any of the loss of benefit provisions shall be made by statutory instrument which (except in the case of regulations to which subsection (4) applies) shall be subject to annulment in pursuance of a resolution of either House of Parliament.

(4) A statutory instrument containing (whether alone or with other provisions)—

(a) a provision prescribing the manner in which the applicable amount is to be reduced for the purposes of section 62(3),

(b) a provision prescribing the manner in which an amount of jointclaim jobseeker's allowance is to be reduced for the purposes of section 63(3)(a),

(c) a provision the making of which is authorised by section 62(4) [¹or (4A)] or 63(4),

(d) a provision prescribing benefits under the Social Security Contributions and Benefits Act 1992 as benefits that are to be relevant benefits for the purposes of section 62, or

(e) a provision that any description of order is to be a relevant community order for the purposes of that section,

shall not be made unless a draft of the instrument has been laid before, and approved by a resolution of, each House of Parliament.

(5) Subsections (4) to (6) of section 189 of the Social Security Administration Act 1992 (supplemental and incidental powers etc.) shall apply in relation to any power to make regulations that is conferred by the

loss of benefit provisions as they apply in relation to the powers to make regulations that are conferred by that Act.

(6) The provision that may be made in exercise of the powers to make regulations that are conferred by the loss of benefit provisions shall include different provision for different areas.

(7) Where regulations made under section 62(8) prescribe a description of order made under the Criminal Procedure (Scotland) Act 1995 as a relevant community order for the purposes of that section, the regulations may make such modifications of that section as appear to the Secretary of State to be necessary in consequence of so prescribing.

(8) In this section "the loss of benefit provisions" means sections 62 to 64 of this Act.

AMENDMENT

1. Welfare Reform Act 2007, Sch.3, para.20(1) and (4) (March 18, 2008 for regulation-making purposes and October 27, 2008 for other purposes).

DEFINITION

"the loss of benefit provisions"—see subs.(8).

Appeals relating to loss of benefit

66. *Omitted.*

1.519

Social Security Fraud Act 2001

(2001 C.11)

ARRANGEMENT OF SECTIONS

Loss of benefit provisions

Loss of benefit provisions

Loss of benefit for commission of benefit offences

7.—(1) If—   1.521

(a) a person ("the offender") is convicted of one or more benefit offences in each of two separate sets of proceedings,

(b) the benefit offence, or more of the benefit offences, of which he is convicted in the later proceedings is one committed within the period of [² five years] after the date, or any of the dates, on which he was convicted of a benefit offence in the earlier proceedings,

(c) the later set of proceedings has not been taken into account for the purposes of any previous application of this section or section 8 or 9 in relation to the offender or any person who was then a member of his family,

(d) the earlier set of proceedings has not been taken into account as the earlier set of proceedings for the purposes of any previous application of this section or either of those sections in relation to the offender or any person who was then a member of his family, and

(e) the offender is a person with respect to whom the conditions for an entitlement to a sanctionable benefit are or become satisfied at any time within the disqualification period,

then, even though those conditions are satisfied, the following restrictions shall apply in relation to the payment of that benefit in the offender's case.

(2) Subject to subsections (3) to (5), the sanctionable benefit shall not be payable in the offender's case for any period comprised in the disqualification period.

(3) Where the sanctionable benefit is income support, the benefit shall be payable in the offender's case for any period comprised in the disqualification period as if the applicable amount used for the determination under section 124(4) of the Social Security Contributions and Benefits Act 1992 (c. 4) of the amount of the offender's entitlement for that period were reduced in such a manner as may be prescribed.

(4) The Secretary of State may by regulations provide that, where the sanctionable benefit is jobseeker's allowance, any income-based jobseeker's allowance shall be payable, during the whole or a part of any period comprised in the disqualification period, as if one or more of the following applied—

(a) the rate of the allowance were such reduced rate as may be prescribed;

(b) the allowance were payable only if there is compliance by the offender with such obligations with respect to the provision of information as may be imposed by the regulations;

(c) the allowance were payable only if the circumstances are otherwise such as may be prescribed.

[¹ (4A) The Secretary of State may be regulations provide that, where the sanctionable benefit is state pension credit, the benefit shall be payable in the offender's case for any period comprised in the disqualification period as if the rate of benefit were reduced in such manner as may be prescribed.]

[³ (4B) The Secretary of State may by regulations provide that, where the sanctionable benefit is employment and support allowance, any income-related allowance shall be payable, during the whole or a part of any period comprised in the disqualification period, as if one or more of the following applied—

(a) the rate of the allowance were such reduced rate as may be prescribed;

(b) the allowance were payable only if there is compliance by the offender with such obligations with respect to the provision of information as may be imposed by the regulations;

(c) the allowance were payable only if the circumstances are otherwise such as may be prescribed.]

(5) The Secretary of State may by regulations provide that, where the sanctionable benefit is housing benefit or council tax benefit, the benefit shall be payable, during the whole or a part of any period comprised in the disqualification period, as if one or both of the following applied—

(a) the rate of the benefit were reduced in such manner as may be prescribed;

(b) the benefit were payable only if the circumstances are such as may be prescribed.

(6) For the purposes of this section the disqualification period, in relation to the conviction of a person of one or more benefit offences in each of two separate sets of proceedings, means the period of thirteen weeks beginning with such date, falling after the date of the conviction in the later set of proceedings, as may be determined by or in accordance withregulations made by the Secretary of State.

(7) Where—

(a) the conviction of any person of any offence is taken into account for the purposes of the application of this section in relation to that person, and

(b) that conviction is subsequently quashed,

all such payments and other adjustments shall be made as would be necessary if no restriction had been imposed by or under this section that could not have been imposed if the conviction had not taken place.

(8) In this section—

"benefit offence" means—

(a) any post-commencement offence in connection with a claim for a disqualifying benefit;

(b) any post-commencement offence in connection with the receipt or payment of any amount by way of such a benefit;

(c) any post-commencement offence committed for the purpose of facilitating the commission (whether or not by the same person) of a benefit offence;

(d) any post-commencement offence consisting in an attempt or conspiracy to commit a benefit offence;

"disqualifying benefit" means (subject to any regulations under section 10(1)—

(a) any benefit under the Jobseekers Act 1995 (c. 18) or the Jobseekers (Northern Ireland) Order 1995 (S.I. 1995/2705 (N.I. 15));

[¹ (aa) any benefit under the State Pension Credit Act 2002 or under any provision having effect in Northern Ireland corresponding to that Act;]

[³ (ab) any benefit under Part 1 of the Welfare Reform Act 2007 (employment and support allowance) or under any provision having effect in Northern Ireland corresponding to that Part;]

(b) any benefit under the Social Security Contributions and Benefits Act 1992 (c. 4) or the Social Security Contributions and Benefits (Northern Ireland) Act 1992 (c. 7) other than—

(i) maternity allowance;

(ii) working families' tax credit;

(iii) disabled person's tax credit; and

(iv) statutory sick pay and statutory maternity pay;

   (c) any war pension;

"sanctionable benefit" means (subject to subsection (11) and to any regulations under section 10(1)) any disqualifying benefit other than—

   (a) joint-claim jobseeker's allowance;

   (b) any retirement pension;

   (c) graduated retirement benefit;

   (d) disability living allowance;

   (e) attendance allowance;

   (f) child benefit;

   (g) guardian's allowance;

   (h) a payment out of the social fund in accordance with Part 8 of the Social Security Contributions and Benefits Act 1992;

   (i) a payment under Part X of that Act (Christmas bonuses).

(9) For the purposes of this section—

   (a) the date of a person's conviction in any proceedings of a benefit offence shall be taken to be the date on which he was found guilty of that offence in those proceedings (whenever he was sentenced); and

   (b) references to a conviction include references to a conviction in relation to which the court makes an order for a conditional discharge or a court in Scotland makes a probation order and to a conviction in Nothern Ireland.

(10) In this section references to any previous application of this section or section 8 or 9—

   (a) include references to any previous application of a provision having an effect in Northern Ireland corresponding to provision made by this section, or either of those sections; but

   (b) do not include references to any previous application of this section, or of either of those sections, the effect of which was to impose a restriction for a period comprised in the same disqualification period.

(11) In its application to Northern Ireland this section shall have effect as if references to a sanctionable benefit were references only to a war pension.

AMENDMENTS

1. State Pension Credit Act 2002, Sch.2, para.45 (July 2, 2002 for the purpose of exercising any power to make regulations or orders and October 6, 2003 for other purposes).

2. Welfare Reform Act 2007, s.49(1) (April 1, 2008, subject to a saving (see note below)).

3. Welfare Reform Act 2007, Sch., para.23(1) to (3) (March 18, 2008 for regulation-making purposes and October 27, 2008 for other purposes).

DEFINITIONS

"benefit offence"—see subs.(8).

"benefit"—see s.13.

"disqualification period"—see subs.(6).

"disqualifying benefit"—see subs.(8).

"family"—by virtue of s.13, see s.137(1) of the Social Security Contributions and Benefits Act 1992.

"income-based jobseeker's allowance"—by virtue of s.13, see s.1(4) of the Jobseekers Act 1995.

"joint-claim jobseeker's allowance"—*ibid.*

"offender"—see subs.(1).

"post-commencement offence"—see s.13.
"prescribed"—see s.11(1).
"sanctionable benefit"—see subs.(8).
"state pension credit"—see s.13.
"war pension"—by virtue of s.13, see s.25 of the Social Security Act 1989.

GENERAL NOTE

This section provides for the loss of a "sanctionable benefit" benefit for 13 weeks   1.522
by people who, having been convicted of a benefit offence, are subsequently convicted of another benefit offence that was committed within five years of the date
of the earlier conviction (i.e. the date he or she was found guilty, even if sentence
was passed much later—see subs.(9)(a)). The period of five years was substituted
for a period of three years on April 1, 2008 but the amendment is to be disregarded
"insofar as the application of section 7(1)(b) of [the 2001] Act involves considering whether an offence committed before [April 1, 2008] was committed within
the relevant period" (Welfare Reform Act 2007, s.49(2)). In other words, if the
second offence was committed before April 1, 2008 (even if the conviction was
later), the conviction for the first offence must have been within the preceding three
years. Section 8 makes provision in respect of joint-claim jobseeker's allowance
and s.9 allows the penalty to fall on another member of the offender's family where
that other person is claiming an income-related benefit that takes account of the
offender's membership of the family. Benefit offences are offences in connection
withthe obtaining of almost any social security benefit (including housing benefit
and council tax benefit), other than maternity allowance, tax credits or statutory
sick pay or statutory maternity pay. However, the term "sanctionable benefit" does
not include retirement pensions or certain benefits for the disabled or for children.
Further details are set out in regulations (see the Social Security (Loss of Benefit)
Regulations 2001).

Effect of offence on joint-claim jobseeker's allowance

8.—(1) Subsections (2) and (3) shall have effect, subject to the other   1.523
provisions of this section, where—
  (a) the conditions for the entitlement of any joint-claim couple to a
      joint-claim jobseeker's allowance are or become satisfied at any time;
      and
  (b) the restriction in subsection (2) of section 7 would apply in the case
      of at least one of the members of the couple if the entitlement were
      an entitlement of that member to a sanctionable benefit.
  (2) The allowance shall not be payable in the couple's case for so much
of any period comprised in the disqualification period as is a period for
which—
  (a) in the case of each of the members of the couple, the restriction in
      subsection (2) of section 7 would apply if the entitlement were an
      entitlement of that member to a sanctionable benefit; or
  (b) that restriction would so apply in the case of one of the members of
      the couple and the other member of the couple—
      (i) is subject to sanctions for the purposes of section 20A of the
          Jobseekers Act 1995 (c. 18) (denial or reduction of joint-claim
          jobseeker's allowance); or
      (ii) is a person in whose case the restriction in subsection (2) of
           section 62 of the Child Support, Pensions and Social Security
           Act 2000 (c. 19) would apply if the entitlement were an
           entitlement to a relevant benefit (within the meaning of that
           section).

(3) For any part of any period comprised in the disqualification period for which subsection (2) does not apply, the allowance—

    (a) shall be payable in the couple's case as if the amount of the allowance were reduced to an amount calculated using the method prescribed for the purposes of this subsection; but

    (b) shall be payable only to the member of the couple who is not the person by reference to whose convictions section 7 would apply.

(4) The Secretary of State may by regulations provide in relation to cases to which subsection (2) would otherwise apply that joint-claim jobseeker's allowance shall be payable in a couple's case, during the whole or a part of so much of any period comprised in the disqualification period as falls within paragraph (a) or (b) of that subsection, as if one or more of the following applied—

    (a) the rate of the allowance were such reduced rate as may be prescribed;

    (b) the allowance were payable only if there is compliance by each of the members of the couple with such obligations with respect to the provision of information as may be imposed by the regulations;

    (c) the allowance were payable only if the circumstances were otherwise such as may be prescribed.

(5) Subsection (6) of section 20A of the Jobseekers Act 1995 (c. 18) (calculation of reduced amount) shall apply for the purposes of subsection (3) above as it applies for the purposes of subsection (5) of that section.

(6) Where—

    (a) the conviction of any member of a couple for any offence is taken into account for the purposes of the application of this section in relation to that couple, and

    (b) that conviction is subsequently quashed,

all such payments and other adjustments shall be made as would be necessary if no restriction had been imposed by or under this section that could not have been imposed had the conviction not taken place.

DEFINITIONS

    "disqualification period"—by virtue of s.13, see s.7(6).
    "joint-claim couple"—by virtue of s.13, see s.1(4) of the Jobseekers Act 1995.
    "joint-claim jobseeker's allowance"—*ibid*.
    "prescribed"—see s.11(1).
    "sanctionable benefit"—by virtue of s.13, see s.7(8).

Effect of offence on benefits for members of offender's family

1.524   **9.**—(1) This section applies to—

    (a) income support;

    (b) jobseeker's allowance;

[¹ (bb) state pension credit;]

[²(bc) employment and support allowance]

    (c) housing benefit; and

    (d) council tax benefit.

(2) The Secretary of State may by regulations make provision in accordance with the following provisions of this section in relation to any case in which—

    (a) the conditions for entitlement to any benefit to which this section applies are or become satisfied in the case of any person ("the offender's family member");

(b) that benefit falls to be paid in that person's case for the whole or any part of a period comprised in a period ("the relevant period") which is the disqualification period in relation to restrictions imposed under section 7 in the case of a member of that person's family; or

(c) that member of that family ("the offender") is a person by reference to whom—

   (i) the conditions for the entitlement of the offender's family member to the benefit in question are satisfied; or

   (ii) the amount of benefit payable in the case of the offender's family member would fall (apart from any provision made under this section) to be determined.

(3) In relation to cases in which the benefit is income support, the provision that may be made by virtue of subsection (2) is provision that, in the case of the offender's family member, the benefit shall be payable for the whole or any part of any period comprised in the relevant period as if the applicable amount used for the determination under section 124(4) of the Social Security Contributions and Benefits Act 1992 (c.4) of the amount of the offender's entitlement for that period were reduced in such manner as may be prescribed.

(4) In relation to cases in which the benefit is jobseeker's allowance, the provision that may be made by virtue of subsection (2) is provision that, in the case of the offender's family member, any income-based jobseeker's allowance shall be payable, during the whole or a part of any period comprised in the relevant period, as if one or more of the following applied—

(a) the rate of the allowance were such reduced rate as may be prescribed;

(b) the allowance were payable only if there is compliance by the offender or the offender's family member, or both of them, with such obligations with respect to the provision of information as may be imposed by the regulations;

(c) the allowance were payable only if the circumstances are otherwise such as may be prescribed.

[¹ (4A) In relation to cases in which the benefit is state pension credit, the provision that may be made by virtue of subsection (2) is provision that, in the case of the offender's family member, the benefit shall be payable for the whole or any part of any period comprised in the relevant period as if the rate of the benefit were reduced in such manner as may be prescribed.]

[² (4B) In relation to cases in which the benefit is employment and support allowance, the provision that may be made by virtue of subsection (2) is provision that, in the case of the offender's family member, any income-related allowance shall be payable, during the whole or a part of any period comprised in the relevant period, as if one or more of the following applied—

(a) the rate of the allowance were such reduced rate as may be prescribed;

(b) the allowance were payable only if there is compliance by the offender or the offender's family member, or both of them, with such obligations with respect to the provision of information as may be imposed by the regulations;

(c) the allowance were payable only if circumstances are otherwise such as may be prescribed.]

(5) In relation to cases in which the benefit is housing benefit or council tax benefit, the provision that may be made by virtue of subsection (2) is provision that, in the case of the offender's family member, the benefit shall be payable, during the whole or a part of any period comprised in the relevant period, as if one or both of the following applied—

(a) the rate of the benefit were reduced in such manner as may be prescribed;

(b) the benefit were payable only if the circumstances are such as may be prescribed.

(6) Where—

(a) the conviction of any member of a person's family for any offence is taken into account for the purposes of any restriction imposed by virtue of any regulations under this section, and

(b) that conviction is subsequently quashed,

all such payments and other adjustments shall be made in that person's case as would be necessary if no restriction had been imposed that could not have been imposed had the conviction not taken place.

AMENDMENTS

1. State Pension Credit Act 2002, Sch.2, para.46 (July 2, 2002 for the purpose of exercising any power to make regulations or orders and October 6, 2003 for other purposes).

2. Welfare Reform Act 2007, Sch.3, para.23(1), (4) and (5) (March 18, 2008 for regulation-making purposes and October 27, 2008 for other purposes).

DEFINITIONS

"benefit"—see s.13.

"disqualifying benefit"—see subs.(8).

"family"—by virtue of s.13, see s.137(1) of the Social Security Contributions and Benefits Act 1992.

"income-based jobseeker's allowance"—by virtue of s.13, see s.1(4) of the Jobseekers Act 1995.

"the offender"—see subs.(2)(c).

"the offender's family member"—see subs.(2)(a).

"prescribed"—see s.11(1).

"the relevant period"—see subs.(2)(b).

"state pension credit"—see s.13.

Power to supplement and mitigate loss of benefit provisions

1.525   **10.**—(1) The Secretary of State may by regulations provide for any social security benefit to be treated for the purposes of sections 7 to 9—

(a) as a disqualifying benefit but not a sanctionable benefit; or

(b) as neither a sanctionable benefit nor a disqualifying benefit.

(2) The Secretary of State may by regulations provide for any restriction in section 7, 8 or 9 not to apply in relation to payments of benefit to the extent of any deduction that (if any payment were made) would fall, in pursuance of provision made by or under any enactment, to be made from the

payments and paid to a person other than the offender or, as the case may be, a member of his family.

(3) In this section "social security benefit" means—

(a) any benefit under the Social Security Contributions and Benefits Act 1992 (c.4) or the Social Security Contributions and Benefits (Northern Ireland) Act 1992 (c.7); [[1] . . .]

(b) any benefit under the Jobseekers Act 1995 (c. 18) or the Jobseekers (Northern Ireland) Order 1995 (S.I. 1995/2705 (N.I. 15));

[[1] (bb) any benefit under the State Pension Credit Act 2002 or under any provision having effect in Northern Ireland corresponding to that Act; or]

[[2] (bc) any benefit under Part 1 of the Welfare Reform Act 2007 (employment and support allowance) or under any provision having effect in Northern Ireland corresponding to that Part;]

(c) any war pension.

AMENDMENTS

1. State Pension Credit Act 2002, Sch.2, para.47 and Sch.3 (July 2, 2002 for the purpose of exercising any power to make regulations or orders and October 6, 2003 for other purposes).

2. Welfare Reform Act 2007, Sch., para.23(1) and (6) (March 18, 2008 for regulation-making purposes and October 27, 2008 for other purposes).

DEFINITIONS

"benefit"—see s.13.

"disqualifying benefit"—see s.7(8).

"family"—by virtue of s.13, see s.137(1) of the Social Security Contributions and Benefits Act 1992.

"sanctionable benefit"—by virtue of s.13, see s.7(8).

"war pension"—by virtue of s.13, see s.25 of the Social Security Act 1989.

Loss of benefit regulations

11.—(1) In sections 7 to 10 "prescribed" means prescribed by or determined in accordance with regulations made by the Secretary of State.   **1.526**

(2) Regulations under any of the provisions of sections 7 to 10 small be made by statutory instrument which (except in the case of regulations to which subsection (3) applies) shall be subject to annulment in pursuance of a resolution of either House of Parliament.

(3) A statutory instrument containing (whether alone or with other provisions)—

(a) a provision by virtue of which anything is to be treated for the purposes of section 7 as a disqualifying benefit but not a sanctionable benefit,

(b) a provision prescribing the manner in which the applicable amount is to be reduced for the purposes of section 7(3) or 9(3),

(c) a provision the making of which is authorised by section 7(4) [[1], (4A)] [[2],(4B)] or (5), 8(4) or 9(4) [[1], (4A)] [[2],(4B)] or (5), or

(d) a provision prescribing the manner in which the amount of joint-claim jobseeker's allowance is to be reduced for the purposes of section 8(3)(a),

shall not be made unless a draft of the instrument has been laid before, and approved by a resolution of, each House of Parliament.

(4) Subsections (4) to (6) of section 189 of the Administration Act (supplemental and incidental powers etc.) shall apply in relation to a power to make regulations that is conferred by any of the provisions of sections 7 to 10 as they apply in relation to the powers to make regulations that are conferred by that Act.

(5) The provision that may be made in exercise of the powers to make regulations that are conferred by sections 7 to 10 shall include different provision for different areas.

AMENDMENTS

1. State Pension Credit Act 2002, Sch.2, para.48 (July 2, 2002 for the purpose of exercising any power to make regulations or orders and October 6, 2003 for other purposes).
2. Welfare Reform Act 2007, Sch., para.23(1) and (7) (March 18, 2008 for regulation-making purposes and October 27, 2008 for other purposes).

DEFINITION

"the Administration Act", by virtue of s.18, means the Social Security Administration Act 1992.

Consequential amendments

1.527   **12.** *Omitted.*

Interpretation of Sections 7 to 12

1.528   **13.**—In this section and sections 7 to 12—
"benefit" includes any allowance, payment, credit or loan;
"disqualification period" has the meaning given by section 7(6);
"family" has the same meaning as in Part 7 of the Social Security Contributions and Benefits Act 1992 (c. 4);
"income-based jobseeker's allowance", "joint-claim jobseeker's allowance" and "joint-claim couple" have the same meanings as in the Jobseekers Act 1995 (c. 18);
[2 "income-related allowance" has the same meaning as in Part 1 of the Welfare Reform Act 2007 (employment and support allowance);]
"post-commencement offence" means any criminal offence committed after the commencement of section 7;
"sanctionable benefit" has the meaning given by section 7(8);
[1 "state pension credit" means state pension credit under the State Pension Credit Act 2002;]
"war pension" has the same meaning as in section 25 of the Social Security Act 1989 (c. 24) (establishment and functions of war pensions committees).

AMENDMENTS

1. State Pension Credit Act 2002, Sch.2, para.49 (July 2, 2002 for the purpose of exercising any power to make regulations or orders and October 6, 2003 for other purposes).
2. Welfare Reform Act 2007, Sch., para.23(1) and (8) (March 18, 2008 for regulation-making purposes and October 27, 2008 for other purposes).

(2002 c.21)

Tax Credits Act 2002

(2002 C. 21)

An Act to make provision for tax credits; to amend the law about child benefit and guardian's allowance; and for connected purposes.

[8th July 2002]

GENERAL NOTE

1.530   Part 1 of the Act provides for child tax credit and working tax credit which are dealt within Vol.IV of this work.

Part 2 of the Act transfers functions relating to child benefit and guardian's allowance from the Department for Work and Pensions to the Treasury and the Board of Inland Revenue which has now been merged into Her Majesty's Revenue and Customs. Those benefits remain social security benefits despite the change in responsibility for them and administration and adjudication remain under the Social Security Administration Act 1992 and the Social Security Act 1998, although new secondary legislation has been made.

1.531   **1.–48.** *Omitted.*

PART 2

CHILD BENEFIT AND GUARDIAN'S ALLOWANCE

Transfer of functions etc.

Functions transferred to Treasury

1.532   **49.**—(1) The functions of the Secretary of State under—
(a) section 77 of the Social Security Contributions and Benefits Act 1992 (c.4) (guardian's allowance: Great Britain),
(b) Part 9 of that Act (child benefit: Great Britain), except section 142(1)(c) and (2) and paragraphs 5 and 6(1) of Schedule 10,
(c) section 80 of the Social Security Administration Act 1992 (c.5) (overlap with benefits under legislation of other member States: Great Britain), and
(d) section 72 of the Social Security Act 1998 (c.14) (power to reduce child benefit for lone parents: Great Britain),
are transferred to the Treasury.
(2) The functions of the Northern Ireland Department under—
(a) section 77 of the Social Security Contributions and Benefits (Northern Ireland) Act 1992 (c.7) (guardian's allowance: Northern Ireland),
(b) Part 9 of that Act (child benefit: Northern Ireland), except section 138(1)(c) and (2) and paragraphs 5 and 6(1) of Schedule 10,
(c) section 76 of the Social Security Administration (Northern Ireland) Act 1992 (c.8) (overlap with benefits under legislation of other member States: Northern Ireland), and
(d) Article 68 of the Social Security (Northern Ireland) Order 1998 (1998/1506 (N.I. 10)) (power to reduce child benefit for lone parents: Northern Ireland),

are transferred to the Treasury.

(3) The functions of the Secretary of State under Part 10 of the Social Security Administration Act 1992 (c.5) (review and alteration of benefits: Great Britain) so far as relating to child benefit and guardian's allowance are transferred to the Treasury.

(4) The functions of the Northern Ireland Department under sections 132 to 134 of the Social Security Administration (Northern Ireland) Act 1992 (c. 8) (review and alteration of benefits: Northern Ireland) so far as relating to child benefit and guardian's allowance are transferred to the Treasury.

AMENDMENT

1. Child Benefit Act 2005, s.3 and Sch.2, Pt. 1 (April 10, 2006).

DEFINITION

"the Northern Ireland Department": see s.67.

GENERAL NOTE

This section transfers policy responsibility for child benefit and guardian's allow-ance (i.e. making the regulations as to entitlement and fixing the rates) from the Secretary of State for Work and Pensions to the Treasury.

1.533

Functions transferred to Board

50.—(1) The functions of the Secretary of State and the Northern Ireland Department under the provisions specified in subsection (2), so far as relating to child benefit and guardian's allowance, are transferred to the Board.

1.534

(2) The provisions referred to in subsection (1) are—

(a) the Social Security Contributions and Benefits Act 1992 (c.4),

(b) the Social Security Administration Act 1992, except Part 13 (advisory bodies and consultation: Great Britain),

(c) the Social Security Contributions and Benefits (Northern Ireland) Act 1992 (c. 7),

(d) the Social Security Administration (Northern Ireland) Act 1992, except Part 12 (advisory bodies and consultation: Northern Ireland),

(e) Chapter 2 of Part 1 of the Social Security Act 1998 (c.14) (social security decisions and appeals: Great Britain),

(f) Chapter 2 of Part 2 of the Social Security (Northern Ireland) Order 1998 (1998/1506 (N.I. 10)) (social security decisions and appeals: Northern Ireland), and

(g) any subordinate legislation made under any of the provisions specified in section 49 or any of the preceding provisions of this sub-section.

(3) This section has effect subject to section 49.

DEFINITIONS

"the Board": see s.67, but note that the functions of the Board have been trans-ferred to Her Majesty's Revenue and Customs by the Commissioners for Revenue and Customs Act 2005.

"the Northern Ireland Department": *ibid*.

GENERAL NOTE

1.535   While s.49 transfers policy responsibility for child benefit and guardian's allowance to the Treasury, this section transfers operational responsibility (i.e. administration and adjudication) from the Secretary of State for Work and Pensions to the Board of Inland Revenue, whose functions have now been transferred to Her Majesty's Revenue and Customs by the Commissioners for Revenue and Customs Act 2005. The primary legislation governing administration and adjudication remains the same (subject to consequential amendments made by s.51 and Sch.4 and repeals under s.60 and Sch.6) but the Board made new subordinate legislation (see the Child Benefit and Guardian's Allowance (Administrative Arrangements) Regulations 2003, the Child Benefit and Guardian's Allowance (Administration) Regulations 2003 and the Child Benefit and Guardian's Allowance (Decisions and Appeals) Regulations 2003).

Consequential amendments

1.536   **51.** *Omitted.*

1.537   **52.** *Omitted*

[¹ General functions of Commissioners for Revenue and Customs

1.538   **53.**—The Commissioners for Her Majesty's Revenue and Customs shall be responsible for the payment and management of child benefit and guardian's allowance.]

AMENDMENT

1. Commissioners for Revenue and Customs Act 2005, s.50 and para.90 of Sch.4 (April 18, 2005).

Transitional provisions

1.539   **54.**—(1) Any function covered by section 49 which is a function of making subordinate legislation may be exercised by the Treasury at any time after the passing of this Act if the subordinate legislation made in the exercise of the function comes into force after the commencement of that section.

(2) Any function covered by section 50 which is a function of making subordinate legislation may be exercised by the Board at any time after the passing of this Act if the subordinate legislation made in the exercise of the function comes into force after the commencement of that section.

(3) Nothing in section 49 or 50 affects the validity of anything done by or in relation to the Secretary of State or the Northern Ireland Department before its commencement.

(4) Anything (including legal proceedings) relating to any functions transferred by section 49, or any property, rights or liabilities transferred by section 52(1), which is in the course of being done or carried on by or in relation to the Secretary of State or the Northern Ireland Department immediately before the transfer may be continued by or in relation to the Treasury.

(5) Anything (including legal proceedings) relating to any functions transferred by section 50, or any property, rights or liabilities transferred by section 52(2), which is in the course of being done or carried on by or in relation to the Secretary of State or the Northern Ireland Department

immediately before the transfer may be continued by or in relation to the Board.

(6) Anything done by the Secretary of State or the Northern Ireland Department for the purposes of or in connection with any functions transferred by section 49, or any property, rights or liabilities transferred by section 52(1), which is in effect immediately before the transfer has effect afterwards as if done by the Treasury.

(7) Anything done by the Secretary of State or the Northern Ireland Department for the purposes of or in connection with any functions transferred by section 50, or any property, rights or liabilities transferred by section 52(2), which is in effect immediately before the transfer has effect afterwards as if done by the Board.

(8) The Treasury is substituted for the Secretary of State or the Northern Ireland Department in any subordinate legislation, any contracts or other documents and any legal proceedings relating to any functions transferred by section 49, or any property, rights or liabilities transferred by section 52(1), made or commenced before the transfer.

(9) The Board are substituted for the Secretary of State or the Northern Ireland Department in any subordinate legislation, any contracts or other documents and any legal proceedings relating to any functions transferred by section 50, or any property, rights or liabilities transferred by section 52(2), made or commenced before the transfer.

(10) Any order made under section 8 of the Electronic Communications Act 2000 (c.7) which—

(a) modifies provisions relating to child benefit or guardian's allowance, and

(b) is in force immediately before the commencement of this sub-section,

is to continue to have effect for the purposes of child benefit and guardian's allowance, despite subsection (7) of that section, until regulations made by the Board under section 132 of the Finance Act 1999 (c.16) which are expressed to supersede that order come into force.

DEFINITIONS

"the Board": see s.67, but note that the functions of the Board have been transferred to Her Majesty's Revenue and Customs by the Commissioners for Revenue and Customs Act 2005.

"the Northern Ireland Department": *ibid.*

GENERAL NOTE

Subsections (1) and (2) came into force on the passing of the Act (s.61), but the remaining provisions of this Part came into force for the purpose of making subordinate legislation on February 26, 2003, for the purpose of the transfer of functions on April 1, 2003 and for the purpose of entitlement to payment of child benefit and guardian's allowance on April 7, 2003 (Tax Credits Act 2002 (Commencement No.2) Order 2003).   **1.540**

Subs. 10

The Social Security (Electronic Communications) (Child Benefit) Order 2002 remains in force.   **1.541**

55.–57. *Omitted.*   **1.542**

PART 3

SUPPLEMENTARY

Information etc.

Administrative arrangements

1.543   **58.**—(1) This section applies where regulations under—

    (a) section 4 or 6 of this Act,

    (b) section 5 of the Social Security Administration Act 1992 (c.5), or

    (c) section 5 of the Social Security Administration (Northern Ireland) Act 1992 (c.8),

permit or require a claim or notification relating to a tax credit, child benefit or guardian's allowance to be made or given to a relevant authority.

    (2) Where this section applies, regulations may make provision—

    (a) for information or evidence relating to tax credits, child benefit or guardian's allowance to be provided to the relevant authority (whether by persons by whom such claims and notifications are or have been made or given, by the Board or by other persons),

    (b) for the giving of information or advice by a relevant authority to persons by whom such claims or notifications are or have been made or given, and

    (c) for the recording, verification and holding, and the forwarding to the Board or a person providing services to the Board, of claims and notifications received by virtue of the regulations referred to in subsection (1) and information or evidence received by virtue of paragraph (a),

    (3) "Relevant authority" means—

    (a) the Secretary of State,

    (b) the Northern Ireland Department, or

    (c) a person providing services to the Secretary of State or the Northern Ireland Department.

DEFINITIONS

    "the Board"—see s.67, but note that the functions of the Board have been transferred to Her Majesty's Revenue and Customs by the Commissioners for Revenue and Customs Act 2005.

    "relevant authority"—see subs.(3).

    "tax credit"—by virtue of s.67, see s.1(2).

GENERAL NOTE

1.544   See the Child Benefit and Guardian's Allowance (Administrative Arrangements) Regulations 2003.

1.545   **59.** *Omitted.*

Other supplementary provisions

60.–64. *Omitted.*   1.546

Regulations, orders and schemes

65.—(1) Any power to make regulations under sections 3, 7 to 13, 42 and   1.547
43, and any power to make regulations under this Act prescribing a rate of
interest, is exercisable by the Treasury.

(2) Any other power to make regulations under this Act is exercisable by
the Board.

(3) Subject to subsection (4), any power to make regulations, orders or
schemes under this Act is exercisable by statutory instrument.

(4) The power—

(a) of the Department of Health, Social Services and Public Safety to
make schemes under section 12(5), and

(b) of the Northern Ireland Department to make orders under section
62(1),

is exercisable by statutory rule for the purposes of the Statutory Rules
(Northern Ireland) Order 1979 (S.I. 1979/1573 (N.I. 12)).

(5) Regulations may not be made under section 25 or 26 in relation to
appeals in Scotland without the consent of the Scottish Ministers.

(6) Regulations may not be made under section 39(6) or 63(8) without
the consent of the Lord Chancellor and the Scottish Ministers.

(7) Any power to make regulations under this Act may be exercised—

(a) in relation to all cases to which it extends, to all those cases with prescribed exceptions or to prescribed cases or classes of case,

(b) so as to make as respects the cases in relation to which it is exercised
the full provision to which it extends or any less provision (whether
by way of exception or otherwise),

(c) so as to make the same provision for all cases in relation to which it
is exercised or different provision for different cases or classes of case
or different provision as respects the same case or class of case for
different purposes,

(d) so as to make provision unconditionally or subject to any prescribed
condition,

(e) so as to provide for a person to exercise a discretion in dealing with
any matter.

(8) Any regulations made under a power under this Act to prescribe a rate
of interest may—

(a) either themselves specify a rate of interest or make provision for any
such rate to be determined by reference to such rate or the average
of such rates as may be referred to in the regulations,

(b) provide for rates to be reduced below, or increased above, what they
otherwise would be by specified amounts or by reference to specified
formulae,

(c) provide for rates arrived at by reference to averages to be rounded up
or down,

(d) provide for circumstances in which alteration of a rate of interest is
or is not to take place, and

(e) provide that alterations of rates are to have effect for periods beginning on or after a day determined in accordance with the regulations

in relation to interest running from before that day as well as from or from after that day.

(9) Any power to make regulations or a scheme under this Act includes power to make any incidental, supplementary, consequential or transitional provision which appears appropriate for the purposes of, or in connection with, the regulations or scheme.

DEFINITIONS

"the Board"—see s.67, but note that the functions of the Board have been transferred to Her Majesty's Revenue and Customs by the Commissioners for Revenue and Customs Act 2005.
"prescribe"—see s.67.

Parliamentary etc. control of instruments

1.548   **66.**—(1) No regulations to which this subsection applies may be made unless a draft of the instrument containing them (whether or not together with other provisions) has been laid before, and approved by a resolution of, each House of Parliament.

(2) Subsection (1) applies to—
(a) regulations prescribing monetary amounts that are required to be reviewed under section 41,
(b) regulations made by virtue of subsection (2) of section 12 prescribing the amount in excess of which charges are not taken into account for the purposes of that subsection, and
(c) the first regulations made under sections 7(8) and (9), 9, 11, 12 and 13(2).

(3) A statutory instrument containing—
(a) regulations under this Act,
(b) a scheme made by the Secretary of State under section 12(5), or
(c) an Order in Council under section 52(7),
is (unless a draft of the instrument has been laid before, and approved by a resolution of, each House of Parliament) subject to annulment in pursuance of a resolution of either House of Parliament.

(4) A statutory instrument containing a scheme made by the Scottish Ministers under section 12(5) is subject to annulment in pursuance of a resolution of the Scottish Parliament.

(5) A statutory rule containing a scheme made by the Department of Health, Social Services and Public Safety under section 12(5) is subject to negative resolution within the meaning of section 41(6) of the Interpretation Act (Northern Ireland) 1954 (c. 33 (N.I.)).

Interpretation

1.549   **67.**—In this Act—
"the Board" means the Commissioners of Inland Revenue,
"modifications" includes alterations, additions and omissions, and "modifies" is to be construed accordingly,
"the Northern Ireland Department" means the Department for Social Development in Northern Ireland,
"prescribed" means prescribed by regulations, and

"tax credit" and "tax credits" have the meanings given by section 1(2).

GENERAL NOTE

"the Board"   1.550

The functions of the Commissioners of Inland Revenue have now been transferred to the Commissioners for Her Majesty's Revenue and Customs by s.5(2) of the Commissioners for Revenue and Customs Act 2005.

68.–70. *Omitted.*   1.551

Schedules 1.–6. *Omitted.*   1.552

Civil Partnership Act 2004

(2004 c.33)

An Act to make provision for and in connection with civil partnership.

PART 1

INTRODUCTION

Civil partnership

1.—(1) A civil partnership is a relationship between two people of the   1.553
same sex ("civil partners")—
  (a) which is formed when they register as civil partners of each other—
      (i)   in England or Wales (under Part 2),
      (ii) in Scotland (under Part 3),
      (iii) in Northern Ireland (under Part 4), or
      (iv) outside the United Kingdom under an Order in Council made
            under Chapter 1 of Part 5 (registration at British consulates etc.
            or by armed forces personnel), or
  (b) which they are treated under Chapter 2 of Part 5 as having formed
      (at the time determined under that Chapter) by virtue of having registered an overseas relationship.

(2) Subsection (1) is subject to the provisions of this Act under or by virtue of which a civil partnership is void.

(3) A civil partnership ends only on death, dissolution or annulment.

(4) The references in subsection (3) to dissolution and annulment are to dissolution and annulment having effect under or recognised in accordance with this Act.

(5) *Omitted.*

GENERAL NOTE

The Civil Partnership Act 2004 entered into force on December 5, 2005, and   1.554
received widespread publicity. The Act applies to the whole of the United Kingdom,

though there are different legislative provisions in the Act relating to England and Wales (Pt 2), Scotland (Pt 3) and Northern Ireland (Pt 4). The purpose of the Act is to enable same sex-couples to secure legal recognition of their relationship through the formal status of civil partnership. This is obtained through a process of registration. The conditions for entering a civil partnership are fourfold: (1) the parties are of the same sex; (2) neither party is already lawfully married or a member of a civil partnership; (3) the parties are not within the prohibited degrees of relationship; and (4) both parties are aged 16 or more. The fourth condition is subject to some regional variations since in England and Wales, and Northern Ireland additional consent is needed for a civil partnership if the parties are aged 16 but under 18.

Unsurprisingly, many amendments to social security law are required to accommodate recognition of this new relationship. These amendments are recorded in in the relevant substantive provisions.

There is a helpful explanatory memorandum to the new legislation at *http://www. opsi.gov.uk/acts/en2004/2004en33.htm.*

See also Jones, S, *The Civil Partnership Act 2004 and Social Security Law* [2005] JSSL 119.

246.—Interpretation of statutory references to stepchildren etc.

1.555

(1) In any provision to which this section applies, references to a stepchild or step-parent of a person (here, "A"), and cognate expressions, are to be read as follows—

A's stepchild includes a person who is the child of A's civil partner (but is not A's child);

A's step-parent includes a person who is the civil partner of A's parent (but is not A's parent);

A's stepdaughter includes a person who is the daughter of A's civil partner (but is not A's daughter);

A's stepson includes a person who is the son of A's civil partner (but is not A's son);

A's stepfather includes a person who is the civil partner of A's father (but is not A's parent);

A's stepmother includes a person who is the civil partner of A's mother (but is not A's parent);

A's stepbrother includes a person who is the son of the civil partner of A's parent (but is not the son of either of A's parents);

A's stepsister includes a person who is the daughter of the civil partner of A's parent (but is not the daughter of either of A's parents).

(2) For the purposes of any provision to which this section applies—

"brother-in-law" includes civil partner's brother,

"daughter-in-law" includes daughter's civil partner,

"father-in-law" includes civil partner's father,

"mother-in-law" includes civil partner's mother,

"parent-in-law" includes civil partner's parent,

"sister-in-law" includes civil partner's sister, and

"son-in-law" includes son's civil partner.

GENERAL NOTE

With effect from May 11, 2006 The Civil Partnership Act 2004 (Relationships   **1.556**
Arising Through Civil Partnership) Order 2006 (SI 2006/1121) applies s.246 to the
entry in column (A) of para. 7 of Pt 3 of Sch. 1(employment by father etc.) to the
Social Security Categorisation of Earners) Regulations 1978.

Welfare Reform Act 2007

(2007 c.5)

An Act to make provision about social security, to amend the Vaccine
Damage Payments Act 1979; and for connected purposes.

PART 3

SOCIAL SECURITY ADMINISTRATION: GENERAL

Sharing of social security information

Information relating to certain benefits

42.—(1) Information falling within subsection (3) may be supplied by the   **1.557**
person who holds it to a person falling within subsection (4) for purposes
connected with the application of grant paid under a relevant enactment
towards expenditure incurred by the recipient of the grant—
  (a) in providing, or contributing to the provision of, welfare services,
      or
  (b) in connection with such welfare services.
  (2) Information falling within subsection (3) which is held for a prescribed purpose by a person falling within any of paragraphs (c) to (h) of
subsection (4) may be—
  (a) used by that person for another prescribed purpose;
  (b) provided to another such person for use in relation to the same or
      another prescribed purpose.
  (3) The information is any information which is held by a person falling
within subsection (4) relating to—
  (a) income support;
  (b) income-based jobseeker's allowance;
  (c) income-related employment and support allowance;
  (d) state pension credit;
  (e) housing benefit;

(f) welfare services.

(4) The persons are—

(a) the Secretary of State;

(b) a person providing services to the Secretary of State;

(c) an authority administering housing benefit;

(d) a person authorised to exercise any function of such an authority relating to housing benefit;

(e) a person providing to such an authority services relating to housing benefit;

(f) a local authority to which any grant is or will be paid as mentioned in subsection (1);

(g) a person authorised to exercise any function of such an authority relating to the grant;

(h) a person providing to such an authority services relating to any such function.

(5) Information which is supplied under subsection (1) to an authority or other person falling within subsection (4)(f), (g) or (h) may be supplied by the authority or person to a person who provides qualifying welfare services for purposes connected with the provision of those services.

(6) A person provides qualifying welfare services if—

(a) he provides welfare services,

(b) a local authority contribute or will contribute to the expenditure incurred by him in providing those services, and

(c) that contribution is or will be derived (in whole or in part) from any grant which is or will be paid to the authority as mentioned in subsection (1).

(7) A relevant enactment is an enactment specified by order made by the Secretary of State; and the power to make an order under this subsection is exercisable by statutory instrument subject to annulment in pursuance of a resolution of either House of Parliament.

(8) In subsection (2) a prescribed purpose is a purpose relating to housing benefit or welfare services which is prescribed by regulations made by the Secretary of State by statutory instrument subject to annulment in pursuance of a resolution of either House of Parliament.

(9) The power to make an order or regulations under this section includes power—

(a) to make different provision for different purposes;

(b) to make such incidental, supplementary, consequential, transitional or saving provision as the Secretary of State thinks necessary or expedient.

(10) In this section—

"income-based jobseeker's allowance" has the same meaning as in the Jobseekers Act 1995 (c. 18);

"income-related employment and support allowance" means an income-related allowance under Part 1;

"local authority" means—

(a) in relation to England, a county council, a district council, a London borough council, the Common Council of the City of London or the Council of the Isles of Scilly;

(b) in relation to Wales, a county council or a county borough council;

"welfare services" includes services which provide support, assistance, advice or counselling to individuals with particular needs.

(11) In the Local Government Act 2000 (c. 22), sections 94 (disclosure of information) and 95 (unauthorised disclosure of information) are omitted.

COMMENCEMENT

This section entered into force on August 5, 2008.

Unlawful disclosure of certain information

43.—(1) A person to whom subsection (2) applies is guilty of an offence if he discloses without lawful authority any information—   **1.558**
   (a) which comes to him by virtue of section 42(1), (2) or (5), and
   (b) which relates to a particular person.
(2) This subsection applies to—
   (a) a person mentioned in section 42(4)(f) to (h);
   (b) a person who provides qualifying welfare services (within the meaning of section 42(6));
   (c) a person who is or has been a director, member of the committee of management, manager, secretary or other similar officer of a person mentioned in paragraph (a) or (b);
   (d) a person who is or has been an employee of a person mentioned in paragraph (a) or (b).
(3) A person guilty of an offence under this section shall be liable—
   (a) on conviction on indictment, to imprisonment for a term not exceeding 2 years or a fine or both, or
   (b) on summary conviction, to imprisonment for a term not exceeding 12 months or a fine not exceeding the statutory maximum or both.
(4) It is not an offence under this section—
   (a) to disclose information in the form of a summary or collection of information so framed as not to enable information relating to any particular person to be ascertained from it;
   (b) to disclose information which has previously been disclosed to the public with lawful authority.
(5) It is a defence for a person charged with an offence under this section to prove that at the time of the alleged offence—
   (a) he believed that he was making the disclosure in question with lawful authority and had no reasonable cause to believe otherwise, or
   (b) he believed that the information in question had previously been disclosed to the public with lawful authority and had no reasonable cause to believe otherwise.
(6) A disclosure is made with lawful authority if it is so made for the purposes of section 123 of the Administration Act.
(7) This section does not affect that section.
(8) Until the commencement of section 282 of the Criminal Justice Act 2003 (c. 44) (increase in maximum term that may be imposed on summary conviction of offence triable either way) the reference in subsection (3)(b) to 12 months must be taken to be a reference to 6 months.

COMMENCEMENT

This section entered into force on September 1, 2008.

Health and Social Care Act 2008

(2008 c.14)

PART 4

HEALTH IN PREGNANCY GRANT

England, Wales and Scotland

1.559   **131.** *Omitted.*

Administration: Great Britain

132.—(1) In section 5 of the Social Security Administration Act 1992 (claims and payments regulations), in subsection (2), after paragraph (f), insert—

"(fa) health in pregnancy grant;".

(2) The power to make regulations under that section in relation to health in pregnancy grant is exercisable by the Commissioners for Her Majesty's Revenue and Customs.

(3) *Omitted.*

(4) In section 71 of that Act (benefits in relation to which overpayments may be recovered), in subsection (11), after paragraph (e), insert—

"(ea) health in pregnancy grant; and".

(5) In the application of that section in relation to health in pregnancy grant, references to the Secretary of State are to be read as references to the Commissioners for Her Majesty's Revenue and Customs.

(6) *Omitted.*

(7) *Omitted.*

(8) Chapter 2 of Part 1 of the Social Security Act 1998 (decisions and appeals) is to have effect as if health in pregnancy grant were a relevant benefit for the purposes of that Chapter; and the functions of the Secretary of State under that Act are, in relation to that grant, exercisable by the Commissioners for Her Majesty's Revenue and Customs.

1.560   **133.** *Omitted.*

Northern Ireland

1.561   **134. – 137.** *Omitted.*

General and supplementary

138.—(1) The Commissioners for Her Majesty's Revenue and Customs are responsible for the payment and management of health in pregnancy grant.

(2) – (4) *Omitted.*

1.562

PART II

REGULATIONS

SECTION A

DWP-ADMINISTERED BENEFITS

NOTE

References to 1992 Acts in pre-1992 Regulations

Some regulations made before the consolidation of social security legislation in 1992 still refer to provisions in the earlier legislation even though they have been replaced by provisions of the Social Security Contributions and Benefits Act 1992 or Social Security Administration Act 1992. This is technically acceptable because those references are deemed to be references to that have replaced them but is apt to be confusing.

In order to be as helpful as possible to users of this volume, the authors have, wherever practicable, inserted in square brackets reference to the relevant provisions of the 1992 legislation.

However, some of the older regulations contain many references to legislation which has either been repealed or is only of significance to those able to retain an entitlement to a defunct benefit. In these cases, reference has generally been left to the earlier legislation. Equally, in some regulations, it was considered that it might mislead if the interpretation regulation was amended.

Readers should therefore note that the material appearing in square brackets is the authors' amendment to include reference to the 1992 legislation. Such amendments have no official standing. All other references to legislation are as they appear in the current version of the regulations printed in this volume.

The Social Security (Breach of Community Order) Regulations 2001

(SI 2001/1395)

Made   *5th April 2001*
Coming into force   *15th October 2001*

Whereas a draft of this instrument was laid before Parliament in accordance with   **2.1**
section 65(4) of the Child Support, Pensions and Social Security Act 2000 and
approved by resolution of each House of Parliament.

Now therefore, the Secretary of State for Social Security, in exercise of the
powers conferred upon him by sections 62(2) to (5) and (8), 63(2) to (4), 64(2),
(6) and (8) and 65(1) and (2) of the Child Support, Pensions and Social Security
Act 2000 and section 189(4) of the Social Security Administration Act 1992, and
of all other powers enabling him in that behalf, which is made before the end of a
period of 6 months beginning with the coming into force of sections 62 to 65 of the
Child Support, Pensions and Social Security Act, by this Instrument, hereby makes
the following Regulations:

GENERAL NOTE

These regulations implement the "loss of benefit provisions", which are defined   **2.2**
in s.65(8) of CSPSSA 2000 as meaning in ss.62–64 of that Act. Under the Child
Support, Pensions and Social Security Act 2000 (Commencement No.10) Order
2001 (SI 2001/2619), the provisions are being implemented progressively. At
present they only apply to "any person who, as a result of a relevant community
order . . . being made in relation to him, falls to be supervised by an officer of the
local probation board for any of the probation areas of Derbyshire, Hertfordshire,
Teesside and West Midlands" (see art.2(2)(a) of the Commencement Order).
Note that, by art.2(2)(b) of the Commencement Order it is also necessary for
a relevant community order to have been made under s.64(1) (which requires
offenders to have been warned before the order is made of the loss of benefit consequences of failing to comply with it—see below). The loss of benefit provisions
therefore do not apply where the community order was made before October 15,
2001—the date on which s.64(1) came into force—even if the failure to comply
occurred after that date. Note also that it has been announced that the Government
will shortly propose that these Regulations be revoked, rather than extended, on the
ground that, "once all costs have been factored in, the overall sum for continuing
the scheme would be in the region of £652,000, or £5.60p for every £1 of savings
made under the scheme" (H.C., February 27, 2009: col 36WS to 38WS).

The scheme established by the loss of benefit provisions is as follows:

The rules apply to people who have been convicted of a criminal offence and
sentenced to a *relevant community order*. Under s.62(1)(a) and (b), loss of benefit is
a sanction applied to a person where a court decides that s/he has failed, without
reasonable excuse, to comply with the requirements of a relevant community order
and the Secretary of State is notified of that determination under s.64. Such person
is referred to as "the offender".

"Relevant community order" is defined by s.62(8) as meaning a community punishment order (formerly a community service order), a community rehabilitation
order (formerly a probation order), a community punishment and rehabilitation
order (formerly a combination order), and "any order falling in England and Wales
to be treated as" such an order. There is power to prescribe any other community
order within the Powers of Criminal Courts (Sentencing) Act 2000 as being a

relevant community order but no such prescription has yet been made. Therefore, at least at present, failure to comply with the requirements of an exclusion order, a curfew order, a drug treatment and testing order, an attendance centre order, a supervision order, an action plan order or a drug abstinence order does not incur a community sentence sanction. Regulations under s.62(8) which add to the definition of "relevant community order" require an affirmative resolution of both Houses of Parliament—see s.65(4)(e).

Under s.62(1)(c) the loss of benefit provisions apply where the conditions of entitlement to a *relevant benefit* "are or become satisfied" by the offender. Subject to the provisions of reg.3 below, it therefore does not seem to matter whether the offender first becomes entitled to such a benefit before or after the court determines that s/he has failed to comply with the community order. Where the "relevant benefit" is a training allowance (see below), the reference in s.62(1) to satisfying the conditions of entitlement are to be read as references to "there having been or, as the case may be, the taking of a decision to make payment of such benefit" (see s.62(9)). This is because training allowances are discretionary in nature and there is therefore no "entitlement" to them.

Relevant benefit is defined in s.62(8) as being income support and "any jobseeker's allowance other than joint-claim jobseeker's allowance" (for which equivalent provision is made in s.63). The reference to *any* jobseeker's allowance demonstrates that both contribution-based and income-based jobseeker's allowance are included. Contribution-based jobseeker's allowance is the only contributory benefit currently affected by the provisions, although head (c) of the definition contains a power—as yet unexercised—for the Secretary of State to prescribe any benefit under SSCBA 1992 (other than income support) as a relevant benefit. There is also power—in head (d) of the definition—to prescribe as a relevant benefit any type of training allowance under s.2 of the Employment and Training Act 1973. That power has been exercised to make reg.2(1) below. Regulations under s.62(8) which prescribe benefits under SSCBA 1992 as relevant benefits require an affirmative resolution of both Houses of Parliament—see s.65(4)(d).

The effect of the loss of benefit provisions is, by virtue of s.62(1), that even though the conditions of entitlement to the relevant benefit are satisfied, restrictions apply "in relation to the payment of that benefit in the offender's case". It may be important in some contexts to note that the provisions are therefore concerned with the payability of benefit and (other than in the case of a training allowance—see above) do not appear to affect the underlying entitlement to the benefit concerned.

Official guidance refers to the restriction on payability imposed by s.62(1) (and also by s.63(2) and (3)—see below) as a "community sentence sanction". Although the phrase does not appear in the legislation, it will be convenient to use it in this Note and the Notes to the individual regulations.

The precise nature of the community sentence sanction is dealt with in subss. (2)–(5). The general rule, in subs.(2), is that for a *prescribed period* (which, under subs.(7) cannot exceed 26 weeks but is otherwise defined in reg.3 below) the relevant benefit is not payable. However:

(a) under subs.(3), if the relevant benefit is income support, it is payable at a reduced rate (see reg.4 below);

(b) under subs.(4), if the relevant benefit is *income-based* (i.e. not contribution-based) jobseeker's allowance, the Secretary of State has power to prescribe that payment should only be made in certain circumstances and/or at a reduced rate and/or only if the offender complies with requirements as to the provision of information. This power has been used to make the rules on hardship in Pt III of the regulations;

(c) under subs.(5), if the relevant benefit is a training allowance, the Secretary of State has power to make regulations allowing payment "to such extent (as any) as may be prescribed". This power has been used to make reg.2(2) below.

Section 63 makes similar provision in the case of a joint-claim jobseeker's allowance. For this benefit, the rules have to take into account the possibilities that, at any given time:

(a) both members have failed to comply with a relevant community order;

(b) one member of a joint-claim couple has failed to comply with a relevant community order and the other is subject to a labour market sanction under s.20A of the Jobseekers Act 1995;

(c) one member of a joint-claim couple has failed to comply with a relevant community order but the order is not subject to any type of sanction.

The effect of s.63 is to modify the rules in s.62 so that (subject to the regulations on "hardship" made under s.63(4)):

(a) where both members of the couple are subject to a sanction (whether community sentence or labour-market) joint-claim jobseeker's allowance is not payable during the prescribed period (see s.63(2));

(b) where one member of the couple is subject to a community sentence sanction and the other is not subject to any sanction, benefit is paid at a reduced rate to the member who is not subject to the sanction (see s.63(3)). By s.63(5) the Secretary of State's regulation-making powers are the same as under s.20A(6) of the Jobseekers Act 1995 (see Vol.II) in relation to labour-market sanctions. Reg.5 below, made under those powers, is identical in effect to reg.74B of the Jobseeker's Allowance Regulations (see Vol.II): if the non-sanctioned member is entitled to contribution-based jobseeker's allowance, benefit is paid to her/him at the appropriate "personal rate" under s.4(1) of the Jobseekers Act 1995. Otherwise, benefit is paid as if the non-sanctioned member were a single claimant.

Note finally that if the determination that the offender has failed to comply with the relevant community order without reasonable excuse is quashed or set aside, arrears of relevant benefit are to be paid so as to put the claimant (or, in the case of a joint claim for jobseeker's allowance, claimants) in the same position as if the community sentence sanction had not been imposed (see s.62(6) and s.63(6)).

Sections 62–63 are supplemented by ss.64–66.

Section 64 is headed "information provision". It imposes different obligations on the people and institutions involved in the process of criminal justice to notify one another, and the claimant, of information which might be relevant to the imposition of a community sentence sanction. Thus:

(a) under subs.(1) the court which makes the relevant community order must explain to the claimant "in ordinary language" the consequence by virtue of ss.62 and 63 of a failure to comply with it;

(b) under subs.(2) the Secretary of State may make regulations requiring chief officers of local probation boards to notify him when a probation officer refers an offender to court for failure to comply with a relevant community order, of a determination by the court that the offender has so failed to comply, of any circumstances which might give rise to a payment of arrears under ss.62(6) or 63(6) and such other information about the offender "as may be prescribed";

(c) under subss.(4) and (5), if the Secretary of State becomes aware that proceedings are being taken which could lead to a determination that the offender has failed to comply with a relevant community order, he must notify the offender (or in a case of a joint-claim couple, both members of that couple even if only one of them is an offender) as soon as reasonable practicable, that a community sentence sanction will be imposed if such a determination is made;

There are also powers to regulate the exchange of information between the Secretary of State, his contractors and local probation boards and the use to which such information is put.

Section 65 makes supplementary provision relating to the regulation-making powers of the Secretary of State.

Section 66 establishes a right to appeal to an Appeal Tribunal by adding ss.62 and 63 to the list in para.3 of Sch.3 to the Social Security Act 1998.

For the sake of completeness, it will also be convenient to note here the amendments to the Social Security and Child Support (Decisions and Appeals) Regulations 1999 ("the Decisions and Appeals Regulations") made by reg.2(2) of the Social Security (Breach of Community Order) (Consequential Amendments) Regulations 2001 (SI 2001/1711). They are to the following effect:

(a) reg.2(2)(b) of SI 2001/1711 inserts a new para.(i) into reg.6(2) of the Decisions and Appeals Regulations providing that the making by a court of an order within s.62(1) of CSPSSA is a ground for the supersession of a decision to award income support or jobseeker's allowance. By reg.2(2)(c), reg.7 of the Decisions and Appeals Regulations is amended to ensure that the superseding decision takes effect in accordance with reg.3 below.

(b) reg.2(2)(a) of SI 2001/1711 inserts a new para.(8A) in reg.3 of the Decisions and Appeals Regulations. This provides that the quashing or setting aside of an order within s.62(1) is a ground for revision of the decision to impose the community sentence sanction.

PART I

GENERAL

Citation, commencement and interpretation

2.3   **1.**—(1) These Regulations shall be cited as the Social Security (Breach of Community Order) Regulations 2001 and shall come into force on 15th October 2001.

(2) In these Regulations, unless the context otherwise requires—

"the Act" means the Child Support, Pensions and Social Security Act 2000;

"the Benefits Act" means the Social Security Contributions and Benefits Act 1992;

"the Jobseekers Act" means the Jobseekers Act 1995;

"the Income Support Regulations" means the Income Support (General) Regulations 1987;

"the Jobseeker's Allowance Regulations" means the Jobseeker's Allowance Regulations 1996;

"local probation board" means a local probation board established under section 4 of the Criminal Justice and Court Services Act 2000;

"offender" means the person in respect of whom a court has made a determination in accordance with section 62(1)(a) of the Act;

"prescribed period" means the period in respect of which the restrictions on payment of a relevant benefit apply in accordance with sections 62 and 63 of the Act and shall be interpreted in accordance with regulation 3.

(3) Expressions used in these Regulations which are defined either for

the purposes of the Jobseekers Act or for the purposes of the Jobseeker's Allowance Regulations shall, except where the context otherwise requires, have the same meaning as for the purposes of that Act or, as the case may be, those Regulations.

(4) In these Regulations, unless the context otherwise requires, a reference—

(a) to a numbered regulation is to the regulation in these Regulations bearing that number;

(b) in a regulation to a numbered paragraph is to the paragraph in that regulation bearing that number.

GENERAL NOTE

This regulation establishes a number of definitions for the purposes of the regulations which follow. Most of these are self explanatory.

2.4

Local probation boards are corporate bodies established under s.4 of, and Sch.1 to, the Criminal Justice and Court Services Act 2000 with effect from April 1, 2001 (see the Criminal Justice and Court Services Act 2000 (Commencement No.4 Order) 2001 (SI 2001/919)). They are part of the National Probation Service for England and Wales which, under s.1, exists for the purposes of ensuring that courts are given assistance in sentencing and of the supervision and rehabilitation of people charged with or convicted of offences. This latter purpose includes giving effect to community orders, supervising those released from prison on licence and providing approved accommodation. There are 42 local areas each with its own board. With one exception, these areas are the same as police areas. The exception is the London area which covers both the Metropolitan Police District and City of London Police Area. Under s.5 the function of a local probation board is to arrange for sufficient provision to be made in its area for the purposes listed in s.1 and, under s.5(1)(b), "to make arrangements for ensuring the performance of any functions conferred by virtue of . . . any enactment on officers of the board. The wording in s.5(1)(b) is clearly apt to include the obligations imposed on officers of local probation boards by s.64 of CSPSSA 2000.

Description of a prescribed payment for the purposes of section 62(8) of the Act and the extent to which it is payable in accordance with section 62(5) of the Act

2.—(1) A prescribed payment for the purposes of paragraph (d) of the definition of "relevant benefit" in section 62(8) of the Act is a payment of a training allowance made to an individual pursuant to arrangements under section 2 of the Employment and Training Act 1973 in respect of that individual's participation in—

2.5

(a) the programme known as Work-Based Learning for Adults;

(b) one of the employment programmes specified in regulation 75(1) (a)(ii) of the Jobseeker's Allowance Regulations or the training scheme specified in regulation 75(1)(b)(ii) of those Regulations;

(c) the Intensive Activity Period within the meaning of regulation 75(1) (a)(iv) of those Regulations; or

(d) the Intensive Activity Period for 50 plus as defined in regulation 1(3) of those Regulations.

(2) In accordance with section 62(5) of the Act, where section 62(2) of the Act applies, the payment prescribed in paragraph (1) shall be payable for the prescribed period only to the extent of any part of that payment that is within the meaning of—

(a) sub-paragraph (a), (b), (c) or (d) of paragraph 14 of Schedule 7 to the Jobseeker's Allowance Regulations; or

(b) paragraph 60 of Schedule 7 to those Regulations.

GENERAL NOTE

2.6   Regulation 2(1) lists the types of training allowance under s.2 of the Employment and Training Act 1973 which are to count as relevant benefits under head (d) of the definition in s.62(8). Other payments under s.2 cannot be restricted as part of a community sentence sanction.

Regulation 2(2) is made under s.62(5). The effect is that where the recipient of one of the types of training allowance listed in reg.2(1) is subject to a community sentence sanction to the element of the payment which reflects the underlying JSA entitlement is not paid. However, the elements of the allowance which are listed in paras 14 or 60 of Sch.17 to the Jobseeker's Allowance Regulations (see Vol.II) remain in payment. Those elements are travelling expenses, living away from home allowances, training premiums, certain child care expenses and certain mandatory top-up payments.

Prescribed period

2.7   **3.**—(1) Subject to paragraphs (5) and (6), in relation to a restriction under section 62(2) of the Act applying in respect of a jobseeker's allowance, the prescribed period shall be—

(a) where the offender was entitled to a jobseeker's allowance on the examination day, the period of four weeks commencing on the operative day;

(b) where the offender claims a jobseeker's allowance after the examination day but before the final day, the period commencing on the first day of the first benefit week after the examination day on which the offender is entitled to a jobseeker's allowance and ending on the last day of the benefit week which ends on, or immediately before, the final day.

(2) Subject to paragraphs (5) and (6), in relation to a restriction under section 62(2) of the Act applying in respect of a payment prescribed in regulation 2, the prescribed period shall be the period of four weeks commencing on the operative day.

(3) Subject to paragraphs [¹ (5), (6) and (6A)], in relation to a restriction under section 62(3) of the Act (income support), the prescribed period shall be—

(a) where the offender was entitled to income support on the examination day, the period of four weeks commencing on the operative day;

(b) where the offender claims income support after the examination day but before the final day, the period commencing on the first day of the first benefit week after the examination day on which the offender is entitled to income support and ending on the last day of the benefit week which ends on, or immediately before, the final day.

(4) Subject to paragraphs (5) and (6), in relation to a restriction under section 63(1) of the Act (joint-claim jobseeker's allowance), the prescribed period shall be—

(a) where a joint-claim couple of which at least one member is an offender is entitled to a joint-claim jobseeker's allowance on the examination day, the period of four weeks commencing on the operative day;

(b) where an offender is a member of a joint-claim couple which claims a joint-claim jobseeker's allowance after the examination day but before the final day, the period commencing on the first day of the first benefit week after the examination day on which the joint-claim couple is entitled to a joint-claim jobseeker's allowance and ending on the last day of the benefit week which ends on, or immediately before, the final day.

(5) Where the offender is aged 17 on the examination day but attains the age of 18 before the last day of the period prescribed in paragraphs (1) to (4), the prescribed period shall be the period commencing on the first day of the benefit week commencing immediately after the day on which the offender attains the age of 18 and ending on the last day of the period pre-scribed in paragraphs (1) to (4).

(6) Where the offender is aged 59 on the examination day but attains the age of 60 before the final day, the prescribed period shall be the period com-mencing on the first day of the period prescribed in paragraphs (1) to (4) and ending on the last day of the benefit week ending immediately before the day on which the offender attains the age of 60.

[[1] (6A) For the purposes of paragraph (3), the prescribed period shall not include any week in respect of which a payment of income support is subject to a restriction imposed pursuant to section 7 or 9 of the Social Security Fraud Act 2001.]

(7) In this regulation—

"benefit week"—

(a) in relation to income support, shall have the same meaning as in regulation 2(1) of the Income Support Regulations;

(b) in relation to a jobseeker's allowance, shall have the same meaning as in regulation 1(3) of the Jobseeker's Allowance Regulations;

(c) in relation to a payment referred to in regulation 2, means—

   (i) where the offender is also entitled to income support on the examination day, the relevant benefit week under (a) above;

   (ii) where the offender is also entitled to a jobseeker's allowance on the examination day, the relevant benefit week under (b) above;

   (iii) where the offender is in receipt of such a payment on the examination day but is not entitled to, or in receipt of, income support or jobseeker's allowance on that day, the period of seven days ending on the day which corresponds with the day of the week which is the last day of the period in respect of which that payment is made;

"the examination day" means the day on which the Secretary of State, pursuant to a notification made to him that a determination has been made as mentioned in section 62(1)(a) of the Act, examines his records to ascertain whether the offender is, on that day, entitled to a relevant benefit or whether he is a member of a joint-claim couple who are, on that day, entitled to a joint-claim jobseeker's allowance;

"the final day" means the day before the day which is four weeks after the examination day;

"the operative day" means the first day of the first benefit week following the date of the Secretary of State's decision—

(a) in relation to a relevant benefit, that that benefit shall not be payable or that it shall be reduced pursuant to section 62 of the Act;

(b) in relation to a joint-claim jobseeker's allowance, that that allowance shall not be payable or that it shall be reduced pursuant to section 63 of the Act.

AMENDMENT

1. Social Security (Loss of Benefit) (Consequential Amendments) Regulations 2002 (SI 2002/490), reg.11 (April 1, 2002).

GENERAL NOTE

2.8 This regulation defines the length of the *prescribed period* under s.62(2), i.e. the period during which the community sentence sanction is to apply.

The starting point is the concept of the *examination day* which is defined in reg.3(7). This is the day on which an officer acting on behalf of the Secretary of State examines the Department's records following a notification from the local probation board under reg.19 in order to determine whether the offender is entitled to a relevant benefit (or is one of a couple entitled to a joint-claim jobseeker's allowance). If the answer to that question is yes, the prescribed period is a period of *four weeks* beginning on the *operative day*—see regs 3(1)(a), (2) and (3)(a).

The "operative day" is the first day of the benefit week immediately following the Secretary of State's decision to impose a community sentence sanction. Where the offender is entitled to IS or JSA, "benefit week" has the same meaning as in the Income Support Regulations or, as the case may be, the Jobseeker's Allowance Regulations. However, if the offender is in receipt of one of the prescribed types of training allowance and is not also entitled to either IS or JSA "benefit week" means (in effect) the seven day period in respect of which that allowance is normally paid.

In most cases, the day of the Secretary of State's decision will, presumably, be the same as the examination day but there is no requirement that the two must necessarily be the same nor does there appear to be requirement that the decision to impose a sanction must be taken within a certain number of days or weeks of, or within a reasonable time of, the examination day.

Regs 3(1)(b), and (3)(b) deal with the position where an offender is not entitled to IS or JSA on the examination day but subsequently claims one of those benefits. In such a case, the prescribed period—and therefore also the sanction—begins on the first day of first benefit week for which the offender becomes entitled to benefit and ends on the last day of the benefit week which ends on, or immediately before the *final day*. The "final day" is defined by reg.3(7) as the day before the day which is four weeks after the examination day. An offender who does not become entitled to a relevant benefit until after the final day is not subject to a community sentence sanction.

Appeals concerning the application of regs 3(1)(b), and (3)(b) may present particular practical difficulties for tribunals. The correct sanction period will depend on when the Department first examined its records following notification by the local probation board that an order within s.62(1) has been made. However, by definition, the claimant will not have been entitled to either IS or JSA on that date and therefore no decision will have been made following that examination. It is unclear at present what records will be kept of the carrying out of an examination which does not lead to a decision. It is suggested that as the issue in such an appeal will be whether someone who is *Ex hypothesi* entitled to benefit should be disqualified for payment, the burden of proof is on the Secretary of State to establish on a balance of probabilities the length of the prescribed period which he asserts to be appropriate. In a case where the examination day for which the Secretary of State contends is substantially after the Department would ordinarily have received notice under reg.19 (see below) from the local probation board, the tribunal may—at least in the absence of an explanation for the delay—conclude it is more likely that the records were first examined reasonably quickly after the reg.19 notification would have been received in the ordinary course of the post.

All the above rules are subject to the exceptions established by paras (5) and (6) which affect, respectively, 17-year-olds who turn 18 and 59-year-olds who turn 60 in the four weeks between the examination day and the final day. In the former case, the sanction begins at the beginning of the first benefit week immediately following the 18th birthday and ends on the day when it would have ended if the offender had at all material times been 18. In the latter, the sanction begins under the usual rules but ends on the last day of the benefit week immediately before the 60th birthday.

Part II

Reduced Amounts

Reduction of income support

4.—(1) Subject to paragraphs (3) and (4), any payment of income support which falls to be made to an offender in respect of any week in the prescribed period shall be reduced—

  (a) where the offender or any other member of his family is pregnant or seriously ill, by a sum equal to 20%;

  (b) in any other case, by a sum equal to 40%,

      of the relevant amount applicable on the first day of the prescribed period under paragraph 1(1) of Schedule 2 to the Income Support Regulations in respect of a single claimant for income support.

(2) For the purposes of paragraph (1)(a), whether or not a person is a member of the offender's family shall be determined in accordance with section 137(1) of the Benefits Act and Part III of the Income Support Regulations.

(3) Payment shall not be reduced under paragraph (1) below 10 pence per week.

(4) A reduction under paragraph (1) shall, if it is not a multiple of 5p, be rounded to the nearest such multiple or, if it is a multiple of 2.5p but not of 5p, to the next lower multiple of 5p.

(5) Where the rate of income support payable to an offender changes, the rules set out above for a reduction in the benefit payable shall be applied to the new rates and any adjustment to the reduction shall take effect from the beginning of the first benefit week to commence for the offender following the change.

2.9

GENERAL NOTE

Reg.4 is broadly self-explanatory. Where the relevant benefit is IS, it is normally reduced by 40 per cent but if the offender or a member of his family is pregnant or seriously ill the reduction is 20 per cent. The reduction is applied to "any payment of income support" and therefore, it would seem, to premiums, housing costs and, in an appropriate case, residential allowances as well as the basic personal allowance. Note also that what is reduced is the payment "which falls to be made *to the offender*" (emphasis added) which means that the personal allowances paid in respect of other members of the claimant's family will also be reduced where the offender is the claimant. However, the regulation does not state that a reduction should be made in income support which is payable to someone else *in respect of* of the offender and there may therefore be some scope for certain couples (e.g, where both are retired, or incapable of work or otherwise within the categories listed in Sch.1B to the

2.10

Income Support Regulations) to "swap" claimants to that payment of benefit "falls to be made to" the offender's partner. This is particularly so, given that the offender is bound to have some notice of the possibility that a court order within s.62(1) will be made. Claimants considering this course (and advisers suggesting it to them) should ensure that the termination of the existing claim by the offender will not lead to the loss of transitional protection which would have been of greater value than the avoidance of the sanction.

As with reg.145 of the Jobseeker's Allowance Regulations, the circumstances in which a person is "seriously ill" for the purposes of eligibility for the lower, 20 per cent, reduction are not defined.

Reduction of joint-claim jobseeker's allowance

2.11
5.—(1) In respect of any part of the prescribed period for which section 63(2) of the Act does not apply but subject to paragraph (2), the reduced rate of joint-claim jobseeker's allowance payable to the member of that couple who is not the offender for the prescribed period shall be—

(a) in any case in which the member of the couple who is not the offender satisfies the conditions set out in section 2 of the Jobseekers Act (contribution-based conditions), a rate equal to the amount calculated in accordance with section 4(1) of that Act;

(b) in any case where the couple are a couple in hardship for the purposes of regulation 12, a rate equal to the amount calculated in accordance with regulation 17;

(c) in any other case, a rate calculated in accordance with section 4(3A) of the Jobseekers Act save that the applicable amount shall be the amount determined by reference to paragraph 1(1) of Schedule 1 to the Jobseeker's Allowance Regulations which would have been the applicable amount had the member of the couple who is not the offender been a single claimant.

(2) Paragraph (1) shall only apply to the extent that the member of the joint-claim couple who is not the offender is not also subject to sanctions for the purposes of section 20A of the Jobseekers Act.

GENERAL NOTE

2.12
The effect of reg.5 is noted in the General Note at the beginning of these Regulations. Its effect is equivalent to the effect of reg.74B of the Jobseeker's Allowance Regulations in relation to labour market sanctions (see Vol.II).

PART III

HARDSHIP

Meaning of "person in hardship"

2.13
6.—(1) In this Part of these Regulations, a "person in hardship" means, for the purposes of regulation 7, an offender, other than an offender to whom paragraph (3) or (4) applies where—

(a) she is a single woman who is pregnant and in respect of whom the Secretary of State is satisfied that, unless a jobseeker's allowance is paid, she will suffer hardship;

(b) he is a single person who is responsible for a young person, and the Secretary of State is satisfied that, unless a jobseeker's allowance is paid, the young person will suffer hardship;

(c) he is a member of [² a couple] where—
  [² (i) at least one member of the couple is a woman who is pregnant; and]
  (ii) the Secretary of State is satisfied that, unless a jobseeker's allowance is paid, she will suffer hardship;

(d) he is a member of a polygamous marriage and—
  (i) one member of the marriage is pregnant; and
  (ii) the Secretary of State is satisfied that, unless a jobseeker's allowance is paid, she will suffer hardship;

(e) he is a member of [² a couple] or of a polygamous marriage where—
  (i) one or both members of the couple, or one or more members of the polygamous marriage, are responsible for a child or young person; and
  (ii) the Secretary of State is satisfied that, unless a jobseeker's allowance is paid, the child or young person will suffer hardship;

(f) he has an award of a jobseeker's allowance which includes or would, if a claim for a jobseeker's allowance from him were to succeed, have included in his applicable amount a disability premium and the Secretary of State is satisfied that, unless a jobseeker's allowance is paid, the person who would satisfy the conditions of entitlement to that premium would suffer hardship;

(g) he suffers, or his partner suffers, from a chronic medical condition which results in functional capacity being limited or restricted by physical impairment and the Secretary of State is satisfied that—
  (i) the suffering has already lasted, or is likely to last, for not less than 26 weeks; and
  (ii) unless a jobseeker's allowance is paid to the offender, the probability is that the health of the person suffering would, within 2 weeks of the Secretary of State making his decision, decline further than that of a normally healthy adult and that person would suffer hardship;

(h) he does, or his partner does, or in the case of an offender who is married to more than one person under a law which permits polygamy, at least one of those persons does, devote a considerable portion of each week to caring for another person who—
  (i) is in receipt of an attendance allowance or the care component of disability living allowance at one of the two higher rates prescribed under section 72(4) of the Benefits Act;
  (ii) has claimed either attendance allowance or disability living allowance, but only for so long as the claim has not been determined, or for 26 weeks from the date of claiming, whichever is the earlier; or
  (iii) has claimed either attendance allowance or disability living allowance and has an award of either attendance allowance or the care component of disability living allowance at one of the two higher rates prescribed under section 72(4) of the Benefits Act for a period commencing after the date on which

that claim was made, and the Secretary of State is satisfied, after taking account of the factors set out in paragraph (5), in so far as they are appropriate to the particular circumstances of the case, that the person providing the care will not be able to continue doing so unless a jobseeker's allowance is paid to the offender;

(i) he is a person or is the partner of a person to whom section 16 of the Jobseekers Act applies by virtue of a direction issued by the Secretary of State, except where the person to whom the direction applies does not satisfy the requirements of section 1(2)(a) to (c) of that Act;

(j) he is a person—
   (i) to whom section 3(1)(f)(iii) of the Jobseekers Act (persons under the age of 18) applies, or is the partner of such a person; and
   (ii) in respect of whom the Secretary of State is satisfied that the person will, unless a jobseeker's allowance is paid, suffer hardship; or

(k) he is a person—
   (i) who, pursuant to the Children Act 1989, was being looked after by a local authority;
   (ii) with whom the local authority had a duty, pursuant to that Act, to take reasonable steps to keep in touch; or
   (iii) who, pursuant to that Act, qualified for advice and assistance from a local authority,
   but in respect of whom head (i), (ii) or, as the case may be, (iii) above had not applied for a period of three years or less as at the date on which he complies with the requirements of regulation 9; and
   (iv) as at the date on which he complies with the requirements of regulation 9, is under the age of 21.

(2) Except in a case to which paragraph (3) or (4) applies, an offender shall, for the purposes of regulation 8, be deemed to be a person in hardship where, after taking account of the factors set out in paragraph (5) in so far as they are appropriate to the particular circumstances of the case, the Secretary of State is satisfied that he or his partner will suffer hardship unless a jobseeker's allowance is paid to him.

(3) In paragraphs (1) and (2), the offender shall not be deemed to be a person in hardship—
   (a) where he is entitled, or his partner is entitled, to income support or where he or his partner fall within a category of persons prescribed for the purpose of section 124(1)(e) of the Benefits Act; or
   (b) during any period in respect of which it has been determined that a jobseeker's allowance is not payable to him pursuant to section 19 of the Jobseekers Act (circumstances in which a jobseeker's allowance is not payable).

(4) Paragraph (1)(h) shall not apply in a case where the person being cared for resides in a [¹ care home, an Abbeyfield Home or an independent hospital].

(5) Factors which, for the purposes of paragraphs (1) and (2), the Secretary of State is to take into account in determining whether the offender is a person in hardship are—
   (a) the presence in the offender's family of a person who satisfies the requirements for a disability premium specified in paragraphs 13 and

14 of Schedule 1 to the Jobseeker's Allowance Regulations or for a disabled child premium specified in paragraph 16 of that Schedule to those Regulations;

(b) the resources which, without a jobseeker's allowance, are likely to be available to the offender's family, the amount by which these resources fall short of the amount applicable in his case in accordance with regulation 11 (applicable amount in hardship cases), the amount of any resources which may be available to members of the offender's family from any person in the offender's household who is not a member of his family, and the length of time for which those factors are likely to persist;

(c) whether there is a substantial risk that essential items, including food, clothing, heating and accommodation, will cease to be available to the claimant or to a member of the offender's family, or will be available at considerably reduced levels and the length of time those factors are likely to persist.

(6) In determining the resources available to the offender's family under paragraph (5)(b), any training premium or top-up payment paid pursuant to the Employment and Training Act 1973 shall be disregarded.

AMENDMENTS

1. Social Security (Care Homes and Independent Hospitals) Regulations 2005 (SI 2005/2687), reg.14(2) (October 24, 2005).

2. Civil Partnership (Pensions, Social Security and Child Support) (Consequential, etc. Provisions) Order 2005 (SI 2005/2877), Sch.3, para.33(2) (December 5, 2005).

GENERAL NOTE

Regulation 6 defines the phrase "person in hardship" for the purposes of regs 7 and 8. The definition is almost identical to the definition in reg.140 of the Jobseeker's Allowance Regulations for the purposes of that benefit. Readers are referred to the commentary to that regulation in Vol.II.   **2.14**

Circumstances in which an income-based jobseeker's allowance is payable to an offender who is a person in hardship

7.—(1) This regulation applies to a person in hardship within the meaning of regulation 6(1) and is subject to the provisions of regulations 9 and 10.   **2.15**

(2) An income-based jobseeker's allowance shall be payable to a person in hardship even though section 62(2) of the Act prevents payment of a jobseeker's allowance to him but the allowance shall be payable only if and for so long as he satisfies the conditions for entitlement to an income-based jobseeker's allowance.

GENERAL NOTE

Where the offender satisfies the conditions of entitlement of an income-based jobseeker's allowance and s/he, or a member of her/his family is a "person in hardship" as defined in reg.6(1), that allowance remains payable despite the community sentence sanction. However, payment is at the reduced rates set out in reg.11. Payment is also subject to the offender's applying for the hardship payment on a (signed) approved form (reg.9) and providing information as to the circumstances of the person who is claimed to be "in hardship". Where the offender or family member is a "person in hardship" as defined by reg.6(2), reg.8 below applies.   **2.16**

Further circumstances in which an income-based jobseeker's allowance is payable to an offender who is a person in hardship

2.17   **8.**—(1) This regulation applies to a person in hardship within the meaning of regulation 6(2) and is subject to the provisions of regulations 9 and 10.

(2) An income-based jobseeker's allowance shall be payable to a person in hardship even though section 62(2) of the Act prevents payment of a jobseeker's allowance to him but the allowance—

(a) shall not be payable under this paragraph in respect of the first 14 days of the prescribed period; and

(b) shall be payable thereafter only if and for so long as he satisfies the conditions for entitlement to an income-based jobseeker's allowance.

GENERAL NOTE

2.18   Offenders who are entitled to income-based jobseeker's allowance and who are, or who have a family member who is, a "person in hardship" as defined in reg.6(2) are not entitled to a hardship payment for the first two weeks of the sanction period. Thereafter benefit is paid on the same basis as in reg.7.

Conditions for payment of income-based jobseeker's allowance

2.19   **9.**—(1) An income-based jobseeker's allowance shall not be payable in accordance with regulation 7 or 8 except where the offender has—

(a) furnished on a form approved for the purpose by the Secretary of State or in such other form as he may in any particular case approve, a statement of the circumstances he relies upon to establish entitlement under regulation 6(1), or, as the case may be 6(2); and

(b) signed the statement.

(2) The completed and signed form shall be delivered by the offender to such office as the Secretary of State may specify.

GENERAL NOTE

2.20   See the General Note to reg.7 above.

Provision of information

2.21   **10.** For the purposes of section 62(4)(b) of the Act, the offender shall provide to the Secretary of State information as to the circumstances of the person alleged to be in hardship.

GENERAL NOTE

2.22   See the General Note to reg.7 above.

Applicable amount in hardship cases

2.23   **11.**—(1) The weekly applicable amount of a person to whom an income-based jobseeker's allowance is payable in accordance with this Part shall be reduced by a sum equivalent to 40% or, in a case where the offender or any other member of his family is either pregnant or seriously ill, 20% of the following amount—

(a) where the offender is a single claimant aged not less than 18 but less than 25 or a member of a couple or polygamous marriage where one member is aged not less than 18 but less than 25 and the other member or, in the case of a polygamous marriage each other member, is a person under 18 who is not eligible for an income-based jobseeker's allowance under section 3(1)(f)(iii) of the Jobseekers Act or is not subject to a direction under section 16 of that Act, the amount specified in paragraph 1(1)(d) of Schedule 1 to the Jobseeker's Allowance Regulations;

(b) where the offender is a single claimant aged not less than 25 or a member of a couple or a polygamous marriage (other than a member of a couple or polygamous marriage to whom subparagraph (a) applies) at least one of whom is aged not less than 18, the amount specified in paragraph 1(1)(e) of Schedule 1 to the Jobseeker's Allowance Regulations.

(2) A reduction under paragraph (1) shall, if it is not a multiple of 5p, be rounded to the nearest such multiple or, if it is a multiple of 2.5p but not of 5p, to the next lower multiple of 5p.

GENERAL NOTE

This is the equivalent of reg.145 of the Jobseeker's Allowance Regulations 1996 (see Vol.II). Benefit is reduced by 40 per cent of the basic personal allowance for a single claimant or by 20 per cent of that amount if the offender or a member of her/his family is pregnant or seriously ill. The latter phrase is, again, undefined.

2.24

PART IV

HARDSHIP FOR JOINT-CLAIM COUPLES

Meaning of "couple in hardship"

12.—(1) In this Part of these Regulations, a "couple in hardship" means, for the purposes of regulation 13, a joint-claim couple, other than a couple to whom paragraph (3) or (4) applies, who are claiming a joint-claim jobseeker's allowance jointly where at least one member of that couple is an offender and where—

(a) [² at least one member of the couple is a woman who is pregnant] and the Secretary of State is satisfied that, unless a joint-claim jobseeker's allowance is paid, she will suffer hardship;

(b) one or both members of the couple are members of a polygamous marriage, one member of the marriage is pregnant and the Secretary of State is satisfied that, unless a joint-claim jobseeker's allowance is paid, she will suffer hardship;

(c) the award of a joint-claim jobseeker's allowance includes, or would, if a claim for a jobseeker's allowance from the couple were to succeed, have included in their applicable amount a disability premium and the Secretary of State is satisfied that, unless a jointclaim jobseeker's allowance is paid, the member of the couple who would have caused the disability premium to be applicable to the couple would suffer hardship;

(d) either member of the couple suffers from a chronic medical condition which results in functional capacity being limited or restricted

2.25

331

by physical impairment and the Secretary of State is satisfied that—
  (i) the suffering has already lasted or is likely to last, for not less than 26 weeks; and
  (ii) unless a joint-claim jobseeker's allowance is paid, the probability is that the health of the person suffering would, within two weeks of the Secretary of State making his decision, decline further than that of a normally healthy adult and the member of the couple who suffers from that condition would suffer hardship;
(e) either member of the couple, or where a member of that couple is married to more than one person under a law which permits polygamy, one member of that marriage, devotes a considerable portion of each week to caring for another person who—
  (i) is in receipt of an attendance allowance or the care component of disability living allowance at one of the two higher rates prescribed under section 72(4) of the Benefits Act;
  (ii) has claimed either attendance allowance or disability living allowance, but only for so long as the claim has not been determined, or for 26 weeks from the date of claiming, whichever is the earlier; or
  (iii) has claimed either attendance allowance or disability living allowance and has an award of either attendance allowance or the care component of disability living allowance at one of the two higher rates prescribed under section 72(4) of the Benefits Act for a period commencing after the date on which that claim was made, and the Secretary of State is satisfied, after taking account of the factors set out in paragraph (5) in so far as they are appropriate to the particular circumstances of the case, that the person providing the care will not be able to continue doing so unless a joint-claim jobseeker's allowance is paid; or
(f) section 16 of the Jobseekers Act applies to either member of the couple by virtue of a direction issued by the Secretary of State, except where the member of the joint-claim couple to whom the direction applies does not satisfy the requirements of section 1(2)(a) to (c) of that Act;
(g) section 3A(1)(e)(ii) of the Jobseekers Act (member of joint-claim couple under the age of 18) applies to either member of the couple and the Secretary of State is satisfied that unless a joint-claim jobseeker's allowance is paid, the couple will suffer hardship; or
(h) one or both members of the couple is a person—
  (i) who, pursuant to the Children Act 1989, was being looked after by a local authority;
  (ii) with whom the local authority had a duty, pursuant to that Act, to take reasonable steps to keep in touch; or
  (iii) who, pursuant to that Act, qualified for advice or assistance from a local authority,
  but in respect of whom head (i), (ii) or, as the case may be, (iii) above had not applied for a period of three years or less as at the date on which the requirements of regulation 16 are complied with; and
  (iv) as at the date on which the requirements of regulation 16 are complied with, that member is, or both of those members are, under the age of 21.

(2) Except in a case to which paragraph (3) or (4) applies, a joint-claim couple shall, for the purposes of regulation 14, be deemed to be a couple in hardship where the Secretary of State is satisfied, after taking account of the factors set out in paragraph (5) in so far as they are appropriate to the particular circumstances of the case, that the couple will suffer hardship unless a joint-claim jobseeker's allowance is paid.

(3) In paragraph (1) and (2), a joint-claim couple shall not be deemed to be a couple in hardship—

(a) where one member of the couple is entitled to income support or falls within a category of persons prescribed for the purposes of section 124(1)(e) of the Benefits Act; or

(b) during a period in respect of which it has been determined that both members of the couple are subject to sanctions for the purposes of section 20A of the Jobseekers Act (denial or reduction of joint-claim jobseeker's allowance).

(4) Paragraph (1)(e) shall not apply in a case where the person being cared for resides in a [¹ care home, an Abbeyfield Home or an independent hospital].

(5) Factors which, for the purposes of paragraphs (1) and (2), the Secretary of State is to take into account in determining whether a joint-claim couple will suffer hardship are—

(a) the presence in the joint-claim couple of a person who satisfies the requirements for a disability premium specified in paragraphs 20H and 20I of Schedule 1 to the Jobseeker's Allowance Regulations;

(b) the resources which, without a joint-claim jobseeker's allowance, are likely to be available to the joint-claim couple, the amount by which these resources fall short of the amount applicable in their case in accordance with regulation 17 (applicable amount in hardship cases for joint-claim couples), the amount of any resources which may be available to the joint-claim couple from any person in the couple's household who is not a member of the family and the length of time for which those factors are likely to persist;

(c) whether there is a substantial risk that essential items, including food, clothing, heating and accommodation, will cease to be available to the joint-claim couple, or will be available at considerably reduced levels, the hardship that will result and the length of time those factors are likely to persist.

(6) In determining the resources available to the offender's family under paragraph (5)(b), any training premium or top-up payment paid pursuant to the Employment and Training Act 1973 shall be disregarded.

Amendments

1. Social Security (Care Homes and Independent Hospitals) Regulations 2005 (SI 2005/2687), reg.14(3) (October 24, 2005).

2. Civil Partnership (Pensions, Social Security and Child Support) (Consequential, etc. Provisions) Order 2005 (SI 2005/2877), Sch.3, para.33(3) (December 5, 2005).

General Note

This regulation makes provision corresponding to reg.6 for joint-claim couples. See also the commentary to reg.140 of the Jobseeker's Allowance Regulations 1996. **2.26**

Circumstances in which a joint-claim jobseeker's allowance is payable where a joint-claim couple is a couple in hardship

2.27   **13.**—(1) This regulation applies where a joint-claim couple is a couple in hardship within the meaning of regulation 12(1) and is subject to the provisions of regulations 15 and 16.

(2) A joint-claim jobseeker's allowance shall be payable to a couple in hardship even though section 63(2) of the Act prevents payment of a joint-claim jobseeker's allowance to the couple or section 63(3) of the Act reduces the amount of a joint-claim jobseeker's allowance payable to the couple but the allowance shall be payable only if and for so long as—

    (a) the joint-claim couple satisfy the other conditions of entitlement to a joint-claim jobseeker's allowance; or

    (b) one member satisfies those conditions and the other member comes within any paragraph in Schedule A1 to the Jobseeker's Allowance Regulations (categories of members not required to satisfy conditions in section 1(2B)(b) of the Jobseekers Act).

GENERAL NOTE

2.28   This regulation makes provision corresponding to reg.7 for joint-claim couples.

Further circumstances in which a joint-claim jobseeker's allowance is payable to a couple in hardship

2.29   **14.**—(1) This regulation applies to a couple in hardship falling within regulation 12(2) and is subject to the provisions of regulations 15 and 16.

(2) A joint-claim jobseeker's allowance shall be payable to a couple in hardship even though section 63(2) of the Act prevents payment of a joint-claim jobseeker's allowance to them or section 63(3) of the Act reduces the amount of a joint-claim jobseeker's allowance payable to them but the allowance—

    (a) shall not be payable under this paragraph in respect of the first 14 days of the prescribed period; and

    (b) shall be payable thereafter only if and for so long as the conditions of entitlement to a joint-claim jobseeker's allowance are satisfied or where one member satisfies those conditions and the other member comes within any paragraph in Schedule A1 to the Jobseeker's Allowance Regulations (categories of members not required to satisfy conditions in section 1(2B)(b) of the Jobseekers Act).

GENERAL NOTE

2.30   This regulation makes provision corresponding to reg.8 for joint-claim couples.

Conditions for payment of a joint-claim jobseeker's allowance

2.31   **15.**—(1) A joint-claim jobseeker's allowance shall not be payable in accordance with regulation 13 or 14 except where either member of the couple has—

    (a) furnished on a form approved for the purpose by the Secretary of State or in such other form as he may in any particular case approve, a statement of the circumstances he relies upon to establish entitlement under regulation 12(1) or, as the case may be 12(2); and

    (b) signed the statement.

(2) The completed and signed form shall be delivered by a member of the couple to such office as the Secretary of State may specify.

GENERAL NOTE

This regulation makes provision corresponding to reg.9 for joint-claim couples.   **2.32**

Provision of information

16. For the purposes of section 63(4)(b) of the Act, a member of the   **2.33**
couple shall provide to the Secretary of State information as to the circumstances of the alleged hardship of the couple.

GENERAL NOTE

This regulation makes provision corresponding to reg.10 for joint-claim couples.   **2.34**

Applicable amount of joint-claim couple in hardship cases

17.—(1) The weekly applicable amount of a couple to whom a joint-   **2.35**
claim jobseeker's allowance is payable in accordance with this Part shall
be reduced by a sum equivalent to 40% or, in a case where a member of
the joint-claim couple is either pregnant or seriously ill or where a member
of the joint-claim couple is a member of a polygamous marriage and one
of those members is either pregnant or seriously ill, 20% of the following
amount—
  (a) where one member of the joint-claim couple or of the polygamous marriage is aged not less than 18 but less than 25 and the
      other member or, in the case of a polygamous marriage, each other
      member, is a person under 18 to whom section 3A(1)(e)(ii) of the
      Jobseekers Act applies or is not subject to a direction under section
      16 of that Act, the amount specified in paragraph 1(1)(d) of Schedule
      1 to the Jobseeker's Allowance Regulations;
  (b) where one member of the joint-claim couple or of the polygamous marriage (other than a member of a couple or polygamous
      marriage to whom sub-paragraph (a) applies) at least one of whom
      is aged not less than 18, the amount specified in paragraph 1(1)(e)
      of Schedule 1 to the Jobseeker's Allowance Regulations.
  (2) A reduction under paragraph (1) shall, if it is not a multiple of 5p, be
rounded to the nearest such multiple or, if it is a multiple of 2.5p but not of
5p, to the next lower multiple of 5p.

GENERAL NOTE

This regulation makes provision corresponding to reg.11 for joint-claim couples.   **2.36**

PART V

INFORMATION

Notification at the time of the laying of the information

18. As soon as practicable after an information has been laid in England   **2.37**
and Wales which could result in a determination the making of which would
result in the imposition by or under one or both of sections 62 and 63 of

the Act of any restrictions, the chief officer of the local probation board or other person acting on his behalf shall notify the Secretary of State in writing of—

   (a) the full name, address and date of birth of the person to whom the information relates;

   (b) the Probation Service Offender Reference Number relating to that person;

   (c) the date on which a court imposed the requirement to comply with the requirements of the relevant community order in respect of which the information was laid; and

   (d) the court at which it will be determined whether or not there has been a failure, without reasonable excuse, to comply with the requirements of a relevant community order.

GENERAL NOTE

2.38   Regulation 18 is made under s.64(2)(a) of CSPSSA 2000. In England and Wales, the laying of an information by an officer of the local parole board is the first stage in the process which might lead to a court making an order that the offender has failed, without reasonable excuse, to comply with the requirements of a relevant community order. Notification to the Secretary of State is required at this stage so that he may comply with his duty to notify the claimant (or the claimant and her/his partner in the case of a joint claim couple) under s.64(4).

Notification at the time of making the determination

2.39   **19.** As soon as practicable after a court has determined that there has been a failure, without reasonable excuse, to comply with the requirements of a relevant community order, the chief officer of the local probation board or other person acting on his behalf shall notify the Secretary of State in writing of—

   (a) the full name, address and date of birth of the person to whom the determination relates;

   (b) the Probation Service Offender Reference Number relating to that person; and

   (c) the date on which, and the place at which, the court determined that there had been a failure, without reasonable excuse, to comply with the requirements of a relevant community order.

GENERAL NOTE

2.40   Reg.19 is made under s.64(2)(b) of CSPSSA 2000. Its purpose is self-evident: if the Secretary of State is not notified that an order within s.62 has been made, he cannot arrange for the imposition of the sanction required by that section.

Notification where determination is set aside

2.41   **20.** As soon as practicable after a court has quashed or set aside a determination by that or any other court that there has been a failure, without reasonable excuse, to comply with the requirements of a relevant community order, the chief officer of the local probation board or other person acting on his behalf shall notify the Secretary of State in writing of—

   (a) the full name, address and date of birth of the person to whom the determination relates;

(b) the date on which, and the place at which, a court had determined that there had been a failure, without reasonable excuse, to comply with the requirements of a relevant community order;

(c) the Probation Service Offender Reference Number relating to that person; and

(d) the date on which, and the place at which, that or any other court quashed or set aside the determination that there had been a failure, without reasonable excuse, to comply with the requirements of a relevant community order.

GENERAL NOTE

Regulation 20 is made under s.64(2)(c) of CSPSSA 2000. Again its purpose is self-evident: if the court decision which led to the imposition of the sanction is quashed or set aside, the Secretary of State needs to know that fact so that payment of benefit may, in an appropriate case, be reinstated in full and so that the payment of arrears required by ss.62(6) and 63(6) can be made. **2.42**

Use or supply of information for other purposes

21. Information relating to community orders or social security which is either held by the Secretary of State as at the date on which these Regulations come into force or which subsequently comes into existence, may be used or supplied by the Secretary of State, in so far as it relates to sections 62 to 65 of the Act, for the purposes of research, monitoring or evaluation or for the purpose of maintaining statistics. **2.43**

GENERAL NOTE

Regulation 21 is made under s.64(6) to (8) of CSPSSA 2000. It confirms that information held by the Secretary of State in relation to the operation of the loss of benefit provisions may be used for research, for monitoring and evaluation of the operation of those provisions and for statistical purposes. **2.44**

The Social Security (Claims and Information) Regulations 1999

(SI 1999/3108)

ARRANGEMENT OF REGULATIONS

SCHEDULES (*OMITTED*)

The Secretary of State for Social Security, in exercise of the powers conferred upon him by sections 2C, 7A, 189(1), (4) and (5) and 1919 of the Social Security Administration Act 1992 and sections 72 and 83(1) and (4) to (8) of the Welfare Reform and Pensions Act 1999 and of all other powers enabling him in that behalf, after consultation in respect of provisions in these Regulations relating to housing benefit and council tax benefit with organisations appearing to him to be representative of the authorities concerned, by this instrument, which contains only regulations made by virtue of or consequential upon sections 58, 71 and 72 of the Welfare Reform and Pensions Act 1999 and which is made before the end of a period of 6 months beginning with the coming into force of those provisions, hereby makes the following Regulations:

Citation and commencement

2.46 **1.** These Regulations may be cited as the Social Security (Claims and Information) Regulations 1999 and shall come into force on 29th November 1999.

Interpretation

2.47 **2.** In these Regulations,—
"the Act" means the Welfare Reform and Pensions Act 1999;
"the Child Support Acts" means the Child Support Act 1991 and the Child Support Act 1995;
"the Council Tax Benefit Regulations" means the Council Tax Benefit (General) Regulations 1992;
"the Housing Benefit Regulations" means the Housing Benefit (General) Regulations 1987;
"relevant authority" means a person within section 72(2) of the Act.

Work-focused interview

2.48 **3.** A work-focused interview is an interview conducted for any or all of the following purposes—
(a) assessing a person's prospects for existing or future employment (whether paid or voluntary);
(b) assisting or encouraging a person to enhance his prospects of such employment;
(c) identifying activities which the person may undertake to strengthen his existing or future prospects of such employment;
(d) identifying current or future employment or training opportunities suitable to the person's needs; and
(e) identifying educational opportunities connected with the existing or future employment prospects or needs of the person.

Additional functions of local authorities

4.—(1) A local authority to whom Part I of Schedule I to these Regulations applies may conduct a work-focused interview with, or provide assistance to, a person to whom paragraphs (2) and (3) apply, where the interview or assistance is requested or consented to by that person.

(2) This paragraph applies to a person who resides in a postcode district identified in Part I of Schedule 2 to these Regulations.

(3) This paragraph applies to any person making a claim for, or entitled to, any benefit specified in paragraph (4) and applies whether or not a person has had an interview in accordance with regulations made under section 2A of the Administration Act(d).

(4) The benefits specified in this paragraph are—

(a) income support;
(b) housing benefit;
(c) council tax benefit;
(d) widow's benefit;
(e) bereavement benefits;
(f) incapacity benefit;
(g) severe disablement allowance;
(h) [² carer's allowance];
(i) a jobseeker's allowance;
(j) disability living allowance.

(5) For the purposes of paragraph (1), the request or consent may be made or given to—

(a) the local authority conducting the interview or giving the assistance;
(b) any person who, or authority which, may be specified as a designated authority for the purposes of section 2A(8) of the Administration Act; or
(c) a person designated an employment officer for the purposes of section 9 of the Jobseekers Act 1995.

(6) For the purposes of carrying out functions under paragraph (1), a local authority may in particular—

(a) obtain and receive information or evidence for the purpose of any work-focused interview to be conducted with that person;
(b) arrange for the work-focused interview to be conducted by one of the following—
  (i) the Secretary of State;
  (ii) a person providing services to the Secretary of State; or
  (iii) a person providing services to, or authorised to exercise any function of, the local authority;
(c) forward information supplied for the purpose of a work-focused interview to any person or authority conducting that interview;
(d) take steps to identify potential employment or training opportunities for persons taking part in work-focused interviews;
(e) [¹ . . .];
(f) take steps to identify—
  (i) obstacles which may hinder a person in taking up employment or training opportunities;
  (ii) educational opportunities which may assist in reducing or removing such obstacles; and
(g) record information supplied at a work-focused interview.

AMENDMENTS

1. The Social Security (Work-focused Interviews for Lone Parents) and Miscellaneous Amendments Regulations 2000 (SI 2000/1926), Sch.2 (August 14, 2000).

2. The Social Security Amendment (Carer's Allowance) Regulations 2002 (SI 2002/2497), Sch.2 (October 28, 2002).

Further provisions as to claims

2.50 *Amends Claims as Payments Regulations 1987; the changes are incorporated in these regulations.*

War Pensions and Child Support

2.51 **6.**—(1) Where a person resides in the area of an authority to which Part I or II of Schedule 1 to these Regulations refers, he may make a claim for a war pension, or submit an application under the Child Support Acts to any office [¹ of a relevant authority] displaying the **one** logo (whether or not that office is situated within the area of the local authority in which the person resides).

(2) Any change of circumstances arising since a claim or application was made in accordance with paragraph (1) may be reported to the office to which that claim or application was made.

(3) The areas to which this paragraph refers are those areas which are within both—

(a) the area of a local authority identified in Part I or II of Schedule1 to these Regulations, and

(b) a postcode area identified in Part I or II of Schedule 2 to these Regulations.

(4) A person making a claim or application to a participating authority in accordance with paragraph (1) shall comply with any requirements for the time being in force in relation to—

(a) claims for war pensions or applications under the Child Support Acts;

(b) the provision of information and evidence in support of such claims or applications,

as if those requirements also applied to the participating authority.

(5) A participating authority shall forward to the Secretary of State—

(a) any claim for a war pension or application under the Child Support Acts made in accordance with this regulation;

(b) details of changes of circumstances reported to the authority in accordance with this regulation; and

(c) any information or evidence—

(i) given to the authority by the person making a claim or application or reporting the change of circumstances; or

(ii) which is relevant to the claim or application or the change reported and which is held by the authority.

(6) For the purpose of this regulation, a "participating authority" means any authority or person to whom a claim or application may be made or change of circumstances reported in accordance with paragraphs (1) and (2).

AMENDMENT

1. The Social Security (Work-focused Interviews for Lone Parents) and Miscellaneous Amendments Regulations 2000 (SI 2000/1926), Sch.2 (August 14, 2000).

Holding information

7. A relevant authority to whom information or evidence relating to social security matters is supplied or by whom such information or evidence is obtained, including information obtained under regulation 8(2), may—   2.52
(a) make a record of that information or evidence; and
(b) hold the information or evidence, whether as supplied or as recorded.

Provision of information

8.—(1) A relevant authority may give information or advice to any person, or to a person acting on his behalf, concerning—   2.53
(a) a claim he made, or a decision given on a claim he made, for a social security benefit or a war pension;
(b) an application he made, or a decision given on an application he made, under the Child Support Acts.
(2) For the purpose of giving information or advice in accordance with paragraph (1), a relevant authority may obtain information held by any other relevant authority.

9. Claims for Housing Benefit

Amends the Housing Benefit Regulations   2.54

10. Consequential Amendments to the Housing Benefit Regulations

Further amends the Housing Benefit Regulations   2.55

11. Claims for Council Tax Benefit

Amends the Council Tax Benefit Regulations   2.56

12. Consequential Amendments to the Council Tax Benefit Regulations

Further amends to the Council Tax Benefit Regulations   2.57

Information

13.—(1) A relevant authority which holds social security information may—   2.58
(a) use that information—
    (i) in connection with arrangements known as the New Deal and made under section 2 of the Employment and Training Act 1973(**a**);
    (ii) for any purpose to which regulations 3, 4 and 6 of these Regulations, or any regulations inserted by these Regulations, apply; or

      (iii) for purposes connected with the employment or training of the persons to whom it relates;

   (b) supply the information—

      (i) to any other relevant authority to enable that authority to carry out a work-focused interview or any function conferred upon it by these Regulations or by regulations inserted by these Regulations;

      (ii) in so far as relevant for the purpose for which it is being provided, to any person in respect of whom the person undertaking the work-focused interview is notified has a vacancy or is about to have a vacancy in his employment or at his place of employment;

      (iii) to any person (an "employment zone provider") to whom payments are made by the Secretary of State in accordance with section 60(5)(c)(i) of the Act (special schemes for claimants for jobseeker's allowance);

      (iv) to any other relevant authority in connection with any scheme operated by, or any arrangements made by, the authority for purposes connected with employment or training;

      (v) to any other relevant authority in connection with arrangements made under section 2 of the Employment and Training Act 1973 and known as the New Deal.

(2) An employment zone provider may supply to any other relevant authority information relating to any person participating in a scheme for which he receives a payment under section 60(5)(c)(i) of the Act where the information may be relevant to the person's benefit entitlement.

(3) Where the work-focused interview is undertaken by a relevant authority other than the authority which obtained the information, then the authority supplying the information shall, for the purposes of that interview, supply any other social security information held by them.

(4) A relevant authority which holds social security information may supply that information to any other relevant authority for the purposes of research, monitoring or evaluation in so far as it relates to any purpose specified in paragraph (5).

(5) The purposes specified in this paragraph are—

   (a) work-focused interviews;

   (b) any purpose for which regulations 3, 4 and 6 of these Regulations, or any regulations inserted by these Regulations, applies;

   (c) any scheme or arrangements made by the Secretary of State connected with employment or training; and

   (d) section 60 of the Act.

Purposes for which information may be used

2.59   **14.**—(1) The purposes for which information supplied in connection with matters referred to in paragraph (2) may be used are for—

   (a) the processing of any claim for a social security benefit or a war pension or for an application for a maintenance assessment under the Child Support Act 1991;

   (b) the consideration of any application for employment by a person to whom information is supplied in connection with any employment opportunity;

(c) the consideration of the training needs of the person who supplied the information;

(d) any purpose for which a work-focused interview may be conducted;

(e) the prevention, detection, investigation or prosecution of offences relating to social security matters.

(2) The matters referred to in this paragraph are—

(a) work-focused interviews; or

(b) any other provision in or introduced by these Regulations.

Information supplied

15. Information supplied to a person or authority under these Regulations—

(a) may be used for the purposes of amending or supplementing information held by the person or authority to whom it is supplied; and

(b) if it is so used, may be supplied to another person or authority, and used by him or it for any purpose, to whom or for which that other information could be supplied or used.

2.60

Partners of claimants on jobseeker's allowance

16.—(1) The social security information specified in paragraph (2) may be supplied by a relevant authority to the partner of a claimant for a jobseeker's allowance where—

(a) the allowance has been in payment to the claimant, or would have been in payment to him but for section 19 of the Jobseekers Act 1995 (circumstances in which jobseeker's allowance is not payable) for a period of six months or more;

(b) the allowance remains in payment or would be in payment but for that section; and

(c) the partner is being invited to attend the office of the relevant authority for purposes connected with employment or training.

(2) The information which may be supplied is—

(a) that jobseeker's allowance is in payment to the claimant or would be in payment to him but for section 19 of the Jobseekers Act; and

(b) that payment has been made to the claimant or would have been so made but for section 19, for a period of at least six months.

(3) In this regulation, "partner" has the same meaning as in the Jobseeker's Allowance Regulations 1996 by virtue of section 1(3) of those Regulations.

2.61

Partners of claimants

17.—(1) The social security information specified in paragraph (4) may be supplied by a relevant authority to the partner of a claimant for a qualifying benefit where [¹...] [¹ one or more of the qualifying benefits has been payable to the claimant for at least six months.]

(2) The qualifying benefits are—

(a) a jobseeker's allowance;

(b) income support;

(c) incapacity benefit;

(d) severe disablement allowance;

(e) [² carer's allowance]

2.62

(3) [¹ . . .]

(4) The information which may be supplied is—

(a) that a qualifying benefit is or has been payable to the claimant;

(b) the period for which the qualifying benefit has been payable.

(5) In this regulation, [³ "partner"] means one member of [³ a couple] of which the claimant is also a member [³, and "couple" has the same meaning as in regulation 1(3) of the Jobseeker's Allowance Regulations 1996"].

AMENDMENTS

1. The Social Security (Claims and Information and Work-focused Interviews for Lone Parents) Amendment Regulations 2001 (SI 2001/1189), reg.2 (April 23, 2001).

2. The Social Security Amendment (Carer's Allowance) Regulations 2002 (SI 2002/2497), Sch.2 (October 28, 2002).

3. The Civil Partnership (Pensions, Social Security and Child Support) (Consequential etc. Provisions) Order 2005 (SI 2005/2877) (December 5, 2005).

Consequentials

2.63   **18.** *Omitted.*

The Social Security (Claims and Information) Regulations 2007

(SI 2007/2911)

IN FORCE OCTOBER 31, 2007

ARRANGEMENT OF REGULATIONS

2.64
1.	Citation, commencement and interpretation
2.	Use of social security information: local authorities
3.	Use of social security information: Secretary of State
4.	Social security information verified by local authorities.
5.	Specified benefits for the purpose of section 7B(3) of the Administration Act.
6–10	*Omitted*

The Secretary of State for Work and Pensions makes the following Regulations in exercise of the powers conferred by sections 5(1)(a), 7A(1), (2) and (6)(d), 7B(2) and (5), 189(1) and (4) to (6) and 191 of the Social Security Administration Act 1992.

In accordance with section 176(1)(a) of that Act, as regards provisions in the Regulations relating to housing benefit and council tax benefit, he has consulted organisations appearing to him to be representative of the authorities concerned.

The Social Security Advisory Committee has agreed that proposals in respect of these Regulations should not be referred to it.

Citation, commencement and interpretation

2.65   **1.**—(1) These Regulations may be cited as the Social Security (Claims and Information) Regulations 2007 and shall come into force on 31st October 2007.

(2) In regulations 4 and 5 "the Administration Act" means the Social Security Administration Act 1992.

(3) In regulations 2 to 4—

"specified benefit" means one or more of the following benefits—

(a) attendance allowance;
(b) bereavement allowance;
(c) bereavement payment;
(d) carer's allowance;
(e) disability living allowance;
(f) incapacity benefit;
(g) income support;
(h) jobseeker's allowance;
(i) retirement pension;
(j) state pension credit;
(k) widowed parent's allowance;
(l) winter fuel payment;

"the Secretary of State" includes persons providing services to the Secretary of State;

"local authority" includes persons providing services to a local authority and persons authorised to exercise any function of a local authority relating to housing benefit or council tax benefit.

Use of social security information: local authorities

2.—(1) This regulation applies where social security information held by a local authority was supplied by the Secretary of State to the local authority and this information—

   2.65.1

(a) was used by the Secretary of State in connection with a person's claim for, or award of, a specified benefit; and
(b) is relevant to that person's claim for, or award of, council tax benefit or housing benefit.

(2) The local authority must, for the purposes of the person's claim for, or award of, council tax benefit or housing benefit, use that information without verifying its accuracy.

(3) Paragraph (2) does not apply where—

(a) the information is supplied more than twelve months after it was used by the Secretary of State in connection with a claim for, or an award of, a specified benefit; or
(b) the information is supplied within twelve months of its use by the Secretary of State but the local authority has reasonable grounds for believing the information has changed in the period between its use by the Secretary of State and its supply to the local authority; or
(c) the date on which the information was used by the Secretary of State cannot be determined.

Use of social security information: Secretary of State

3.—(1) This regulation applies where social security information held by the Secretary of State was supplied by a local authority to the Secretary of State and this information—

   2.66

(a) was used by the local authority in connection with a person's claim for, or award of, council tax benefit or housing benefit; and

345

(b) is relevant to that person's claim for, or award of, a specified benefit.

(2) The Secretary of State must, for the purposes of the person's claim for, or award of, a specified benefit, use that information without verifying its accuracy.

(3) Paragraph (2) does not apply where—

(a) the information is supplied more than twelve months after it was used by a local authority in connection with a claim for, or an award of, council tax benefit or housing benefit; or

(b) the information is supplied within twelve months of its use by the local authority but the Secretary of State has reasonable grounds for believing the information has changed in the period between its use by the local authority and its supply to the Secretary of State; or

(c) the date on which the information was used by the local authority cannot be determined.

Social security information verified by local authorities

2.67   **4.**—(1) This regulation applies where social security information is verified by a local authority by virtue of regulations made under section 7A(2) (e) of the Administration Act and forwarded by that local authority to the Secretary of State.

(2) The Secretary of State must, for the purposes of a person's claim for, or award of, a specified benefit, use this information without verifying its accuracy.

(3) Paragraph (2) does not apply where—

(a) the Secretary of State has reasonable grounds for believing the social security information received from the local authority is inaccurate; or

(b) the Secretary of State receives the information more than four weeks after it was verified by the local authority.

Specified benefits for the purpose of section 7B(3) of the Administration Act

2.68   **5.** The benefits specified for the purpose of section 7B(3) of the Administration Act are—

(a) a "specified benefit" within the meaning given in regulation 1(3);

(b) housing benefit; and

(c) council tax benefit.

Regs 6–10 amend other legislation and the amendments are incorporated in the relevant regulations.

The Social Security (Claims and Payments) Regulations 1987

(SI 1987/1968) (AS AMENDED)

ARRANGEMENTS OF REGULATIONS

PART I

General

2.69

PART II

Claims

PART III

Payments

PART IV

Third Parties

PART V

Extinguishment

PART VI

Mobility Component of Disability Living Allowance and Disability Living Allowance for Children

PART VII

Miscellaneous

SCHEDULES

Whereas a draft of this instrument was laid before Parliament and approved by resolution of each House of Parliament:

Now therefore, the Secretary of State for Social Services, in exercise of the powers conferred by sections 165A and 166(2) of the Social Security Act 1975, section 6(1) of the Child Benefit Act 1975, sections 21(7), 51(1)(a) to (s), 54(1) and 84(1) of the Social Security Act 1986 and, as regards the revocations set out in Schedule 10 to this instrument, the powers specified in that Schedule, and all other powers enabling him in that behalf by this instrument which contains only regulations made under the sections of the Social Security Act 1986 specified above and provisions consequential on those sections and which is made before the end of a period of 12 months from the commencement of those sections, makes the following Regulations:

PART I

GENERAL

Citation and commencement

2.70   **1.** These Regulations may be cited as the Social Security (Claims and Payments) Regulations 1987 and shall come into operation on 11th April 1988.

Interpretation

2.71   **2.**—(1) In these Regulations, unless the context otherwise requires—

[20 . . .];

[27 "the 1992 Act" means the Social Security Administration Act 1992;]

[23 "the 2000 Act" means the Electronic Communications Act 2000;]

[22 "the 2002 Act" means the State Pension Credit Act 2002;]

[22 "advance period" means the period specified in regulation 4E(2);]

[17 "appropriate office" means an office of the Department for Work and Pensions [or, in the case of a Crown servant posted overseas or his partner, a Regimental Administrative Office, Unit Personnel Office, Personnel Management Squadron Office, British Embassy, High Commission or Consulate;]

[15 "bereavement allowance" means an allowance referred to in section 39B) of the Contributions and Benefits Act;

"bereavement benefit" means a benefit referred to in section 20(1)(ea) of the Contributions and Benefits Act;]

[21 "the Board means the Commissioners of Inland Revenue; and references to "the Board" in these regulations have effect only with respect to working families tax credit;]

[11 "claim for asylum" has the same meaning as in the Asylum and Immigration Appeals Act 1993;]

"claim for benefit" includes—

(a) an application for a declaration that an accident was an industrial accident;

(b) [3 . . .]

(c) an application for [14a revision under section 9 of the Social Security Act 1998 or a supersession under section 10 of that Act of] a decision for the purpose of obtaining any increase of benefit [6in respect of a child or adult dependant under the Social Security

Act 1975 or an increase in disablement benefit under section 60 (special hardship), 61 (constant attendance), 62 (hospital treatment allowance) or 63 (exceptionally severe disablement) of the Social Security Act 1975], but does not include any other application for [14 a revision under section 9 of the Social Security Act 1998 or a supersession under section 10 of that Act] of a decision;

[15 "Contributions and Benefits Act" means the Social Security Contributions and Benefits Act 1992;]

[25 "couple" means—
(a) a man and woman who are married to each other and are members of the same household;
(b) a man and woman who are not married to each other but are living together as husband and wife;
(c) two people of the same sex who are civil partners of each other and are members of the same household; or
(d) two people of the same sex who are not civil partners of each other but are living together as if they were civil partners, and for the purposes of paragraph (d), two people of the same sex are to be regarded as living together as if they were civil partners if, but only if, they would be regarded as living together as husband and wife were they instead two people of the opposite sex;]

[17 "Crown servant posted overseas" means a person performing the duties of any office or employment under the Crown in right of the United Kingdom who is, or was prior to his posting, ordinarily resident in the United Kingdom;]

[13 "'disabled person's tax credit' and 'working families' tax credit" shall be construed in accordance with section 1(1) of the Tax Credits Act 1999]

[23 "electronic communication" has the same meaning as in section 15(1) of the 2000 Act;]

[29 "'the Employment and Support Allowance Regulations'" means the Employment and Support Allowance Regulations 2008;]

[22 "guarantee credit" is to be construed in accordance with sections 1 and 2 of the 2002 Act;]

[26 . . .]

[10 "the Jobseekers Act" means the Jobseekers Act 1995;

"jobseeker's allowance" means an allowance payable under Part I of the Jobseekers Act;

"the Jobseeker's Allowance Regulations" means the Jobseeker's Allowance Regulations 1996;]

[16 "joint-claim couple" and "joint-claim jobseeker's allowance" have the same meaning in these Regulations as they have in the Jobseekers Act by virtue of section 1(4) of that Act;]

[29 "'limited capability for work'" has the same meaning as in section 1(4) of the Welfare Reform Act";]

"long-term benefits" means any retirement pension, [24 a shared additional pension] a widowed mother's allowance, a widow's pension, [15widowed parent's allowance, bereavement allowance,] attendance allowance, [5disability living allowance], [19 carer's allowance], [12. . .], any pension or allowance for industrial injury or disease and any increase in any such benefit;

[25 . . .];

"partner" means one of a [25 couple]; [4. . .]

[9 "pension fund holder" means with respect to a personal pension scheme or retirement annuity contract, the trustees, managers or scheme administrators, as the case may be, of the scheme or contract concerned;]

[9 "personal pension scheme" has the same meaning as in section 1 of the Pension Schemes Act 1993 in respect of employed earners and in the case of self-employed earners, includes a scheme approved by the Board of Inland Revenue under Chapter IV of Part XIV of the Income and Corporation Taxes Act 1988;]

[22 "qualifying age" has the same meaning as in the 2002 Act by virtue of section 1(6) of that Act;]

[11 "refugee" means a person recorded by the Secretary of State as a refugee within the definition in Article 1 of the Convention relating to the Status of Refugees done at Geneva on 28th July 1951 as extended by Article 1(2) of the Protocol relating to the Status of Refugees done at New York on 31st January 1967;]

[20 "relevant authority" means a person within section 72(2) of the Welfare Reform and Pensions Act 1999;]

[9 "retirement annuity contract" means a contract or trust scheme approved under Chapter III of Part XIV of the Income and Corporation Taxes Act 1988;]

[24 "shared additional pension" means a shared additional pension under section 55A of the Contributions and Benefits Act;]

[22 "state pension credit" means state pension credit under the 2002 Act;]

[25 . . .]

"week" means a period of 7 days beginning with midnight between Saturday and Sunday.

[29 "'the Welfare Reform Act'" means the Welfare Reform Act 2007;]

[15 "widowed parent's allowance" means an allowance referred to in section 39A of the Contributions and Benefits Act;]

(2) Unless the context otherwise requires, any reference in these Regulations to—

(a) a numbered regulation, Part or Schedule is a reference to the regulation, Part or Schedule bearing that number in these Regulations and any reference in a regulation to a numbered paragraph is a reference to the paragraph of that regulation having that number;

(b) a benefit includes any benefit under the Social Security Act 1975 [SSCBA], child benefit under Part I of the Child Benefit Act 1975, income support [22 state pension credit] [7, family credit and disability working allowance under the Social Security Act 1986 [SSCBA] and any social fund payments such as are mentioned in section 32(2) (a) [1and section 32(2A)] of that Act [SSCBA, s.138(1)(a) and (2)] [10and a jobseeker's allowance under Part I of the Jobseekers Act].

[10(2A) References in regulations 20, 21 (except paragraphs (3) and (3A)), 29, 30, 32 to 34, 37 (except paragraph (1A)), 37A, 37AA (except paragraph (3)), 37AB, 37B, 38 and 47 to "benefit", "income support" or "a jobseeker's allowance", include a reference to a back to work bonus which, by virtue of regulation 25 of the Social Security (Back to Work Bonus) Regulations 1996, is to be treated as payable as income support or, as the case may be, as a jobseeker's allowance [²⁴ . . .] [²⁹ , a shared additional pension or an employment and support allowance under Part 1 of the Welfare Reform Act].]

(3) For the purposes of the provisions of these Regulations relating to the making of claims every increase of benefit under the Social Security Act 1975 [SSCBA] shall be treated as a separate benefit [¹². . .].

[²² (4) In these Regulations references to "beneficiaries" include any person entitled to state pension credit.]

AMENDMENTS

1. The Social Security (Common Provisions) Miscellaneous Amendments Regulations 1988 (SI 1988/1725), reg.3 (November 7, 1988).

2. Transfer of Functions (Health and Social Security) Order 1988 (SI 1988/1843), art.3(4) (November 28, 1988).

3. The Social Security (Medical Evidence, Claims and Payments) Amendment Regulations 1989 (SI 1989/1686), reg.3 (October 9, 1989).

4. The Social Security (Miscellaneous Provisions) Amendment Regulations 1991 (SI 1991/2284), reg.5 (November 1, 1991).

5. The Social Security (Claims and Payments) Amendment Regulations 1991 (SI 1991/2741), reg.2(a) (February 3, 1992).

6. The Social Security (Miscellaneous Provisions) Amendment Regulations 1992 (SI 1992/247), reg.9 (March 9, 1992).

7. The Social Security (Claims and Payments) Amendment Regulations 1991 (SI 1991/2741), reg.2(b) (March 10, 1992).

8. The Social Security (Claims and Payments) Amendment (No.4) Regulations 1994 (SI 1994/3196), reg.2 (January 10, 1995).

9. Income-related benefit Schemes and Social Security (Claims and Payments) (Miscellaneous Amendments) Regulations 1995 (SI 1995/2303), reg.10(2) (October 2, 1995).

10. The Social Security (Claims and Payments) (Jobseeker's Allowance Consequential Amendments) Regulations 1996 (SI 1996/1460), reg.2(2) (October 7, 1996).

11. The Income Support and Social Security (Claims and Payments) (Miscellaneous Amendments) Regulations 1996 (SI 1996/2431), reg.7(a) (October 15, 1996).

12. The Social Security (Claims and Payments) Amendment Regulations 1999 (SI 1999/2358), reg.2 (September 20, 1999) and The Child Benefit, Child Support and Social Security (Miscellaneous Amendments) Regulations 1996 (SI 1996/1803), reg.18 (April 7, 1997).

13. The Tax Credits (Claims and Payments) (Amendment) Regulations 1999 (SI 1999/2572), reg.3 (October 5, 1999).

14. The Social Security Act 1998 (Commencement No.9 and Savings and Consequential and Transitional Provisions) Order 1999 (SI 1999/2422), Sch.7 (September 6, 1999).

15. The Social Security (Benefits for Widows and Widowers) (Consequential Amendments) Regulations 2000, reg.9 (SI 2000/1483) (April 9, 2001).

16. The Social Security (Joint Claims: Consequential Amendments) Regulations 2000 (SI 2000/1982), reg.2(2) (March 19, 2001).

17. Tax Credits (Miscellaneous Amendments No.4) Regulations 2002 (SI 2002/696), reg.2 (July 23, 2002).

18. Social Security (Electronic Communications) (Child Benefit) Order 2002 (SI 2002/1789), art.2 (October 28, 2002); revoked with effect from December 1, 2003.

19. The Social Security Amendment (Carer's Allowance) Regulations 2002 (SI 2002/2497), Sch.2 (October 28, 2002).

20. Social Security Act 1998, Sch.6 (November 29, 1999).

21. Tax Credits (Claims and Payments) (Amendment) Regulations 1999 (SI 1999/2572), reg.3 (October 5, 1999).

22. State Pension Credit (Consequential, Transitional and Miscellaneous Provisions) Regulations 2002, SI 2002/3019, reg.3 (April 7, 2003).

23. The Social Security (Electronic Communications) (Carer's Allowance) Order 2003 (SI 2003/2800), reg.2 (December 1, 2003).

24. The Social Security (Shared Additional Pension) (Miscellaneous Amendments) Regulations 2005 (SI 2005/1551) (July 6, 2005).

25. The Civil Partnership (Pensions, Social Security and Child Support) (Consequential etc. Provisions) Order 2005 (SI 2005/2887) (December 5, 2005).

26. The Social Security (Miscellaneous Amendments) (No.2) Regulations 2006 (SI 2006/832), reg.2 (April 10, 2006).

27. The Social Security (Claims and Payments) Amendment (No.2) Regulations 2006 (SI 2006/3188) (December 27, 2006).

28. The Social Security (Miscellaneous Amendments) (No.2) Regulations 2007 (SI 2007/1626) (July 3, 2007).

29. The Employment and Support Allowance (Consequential Provisions) (No. 2) Regulations 2008 (SI 2008/1554), reg.10 (October 27, 2008).

GENERAL NOTE

2.72   Section 15(1) of the Electronic Communications Act 2000 defines "electronic communication" as follows:

" 'electronic communication' means a communication transmitted (whether from one person to another, from one device to another or from a person to a device or vice versa)—
   (a) by means of a telecommunication system (within the meaning of the Telecommunications Act 1984); or
   (b) by other means but while in an electronic form;"

PART II

CLAIMS

Claims not required for entitlement to benefit in certain cases

2.73   **3.** It shall not be a condition of entitlement to benefit that a claim be made for it in the following cases—
   (a) In the case of a Category C retirement pension where the beneficiary is in receipt of—
      (i) another retirement pension under the Social Security Act 1975; or
      (ii) widow's benefit under Chapter 1 of Part II of that Act; or
      (iii) benefit by virtue of section 39(4) of that Act corresponding to a widow's pension or a widowed mother's allowance;
      (iv) bereavement benefit under Part II of the Contributions and Benefits Act;]
   (b) in the case of a Category D retirement pension where the beneficiary—
      (i) was ordinarily resident in great Britain on the day on which he attained 80 years of age; and
      (ii) is in receipt of another retirement pension under the Social Security Act 1975;

(c) age addition in any case;

[¹⁰ (ca) in the case of a Category A retirement pension where the beneficiary—

(i) is entitled to any category of retirement pension other than a Category A retirement pension; and

(ii) becomes divorced or the beneficiary's civil partnership is dissolved;]

[¹¹ (cb) in the case of a Category B retirement pension where the beneficiary is entitled to either a Category A retirement pensions or to a graduated retirement benefit or to both and

(i) the spouse or civil partner of the beneficiary becomes entitled to a Category A retirement pension; or

(ii) the beneficiary marries or enters into a civil partnership with a person who is entitled to a Category A retirement pension;]

(d) in the case of a Category A or B retirement pension—

(i) where the beneficiary is a woman over the age of 65 and entitled to a widowed mother's allowance [⁶ or widowed parent's allowance], on her ceasing to be so entitled; or

(ii) where the beneficiary is a woman under the age of 65 and in receipt of widow's pension [⁶ or bereavement allowance], on her attaining that age

[¹⁰ . . .]

[¹³ (da) in the case of a bereavement payment where the beneficiary is in receipt of a retirement pension at the date of death of the beneficiary's spouse or civil partner and satisfies the conditions of entitlement under section 36(1) of the Contributions and Benefits Act;]

(e) [¹in the case of retirement allowance]

(f) [². . .]

(g) [³ in the case of a jobseeker's allowance where—

(i) payment of benefit has been suspended in the circumstances described in regulation 16(2) of the Social Security and Child Support (Decisions and Appeals) Regulations 1999; and

(ii) the claimant whose benefit has been suspended satisfies the conditions of entitlement (apart from the requirement to claim) to that benefit immediately before the suspension ends.]

(h) [⁵ in the case of income support where the beneficiary—

(i) is a person to whom regulation [⁸ . . .] [⁷ or 6(5)] of the Income Support (General) Regulations 1987 (persons not treated as engaged in remunerative work) applies;

(ii) was in receipt of an income-based jobseeker's allowance [¹² or an income-related employment and support allowance] on the day before the day on which he was first engaged in the work referred to in sub-paragraph (a) of [⁷ those paragraphs] and

(iii) would satisfy the conditions of entitlement to income support (apart from the condition of making a claim would apply in the absence of this paragraph) only by virtue of regulation [⁸ . . . [⁷ . . .] regulation 6(6)] of those regulations.]

[⁹ (i) in the case of a shared additional pension where the beneficiary is in receipt of a retirement pension of any category.]

[¹² (j) in the case of an employment and support allowance where the beneficiary has made and is pursuing an appeal against the decision of the Secretary of State that he does not have limited capability for work.]

AMENDMENTS

1. The Social Security (Claims and Payments on Account, Overpayments and Recovery) Amendment Regulations 1989 (SI 1989/136), reg.3 (April 10, 1989).

2. The Social Security (Claims and Payments) Amendment (No.2) Regulations 1994 (SI 1994/2943), reg.2 (April 13, 1995).

3. The Social Security Act 1998 (Commencement No. 12 and Consequential and Transitional Provisions) Order 1999 (SI 1999/3178), Sch.6, para. 3 (November 29, 1999).

4. The Social Security Act 1998 (Commencement No.11 and Transitional Provisions) Order 1989 (SI 1999/2860), Sch.3 (October 18, 1999).

5. The Social Security (Miscellaneous Amendments) (No.2) Regulations 1999 (SI 1999/2556), reg.7, (October 4, 1999).

6. The Social Security (Benefits for Widows and Widowers) (Consequential Amendments) Regulations 2000 (SI 2000/1483), reg.9 (April 9, 2001).

7. The Social Security (Miscellaneous Amendments) Regulations 2001 (SI 2001/488), reg.11 (April 9, 2001).

8. Social Security (Back to Work Bonus and Lone Parent Run-on) (Amendment and Revocation) Regulations 2003 (SI 2003/1589), reg.5 (October 25, 2004).

9. The Social Security (Shared Additional Pension) (Miscellaneous Amendments) Regulations 2005 (SI 2005/1551) (July 6, 2005).

10. The Social Security (Miscellaneous Amendments) (No.4) Regulations 2007 (SI 2007/2470) (September 24, 2007).

11. The Social Security (Claims and Payments) Amendment Regulations 2008 (SI 2008/441) reg.2 (March 17, 2008).

12. The Employment and Support Allowance (Consequential Provisions) (No.2) Regulations 2008 (SI 2008/1554), reg.11 (October 27, 2008).

13. The Social Security (Miscellaneous Amendments) (No.5) Regulations 2008 (SI 2008/2667), reg.2 (October 30, 2008).

GENERAL NOTE

2.74   On the meaning of "ordinarily resident" see annotation to reg.5 of the Persons Abroad Regulations in Vol.1

The Training for Work (Scottish Enterprise and Highlands and Islands Enterprise Programmes) Order 1993 (SI 1993/498) provides that for the purpose of these regulations, a person using facilities under the training programmes to which the Order refers are treated as participating in arrangments for training under s.2(3) of the Enterprise and New Towns (Scotland) Act 1990 and payments made to persons on those programmes are treated as payments in respect of training. See also, to the same effect, the Training for Work (Miscellaneous Provisions) October 1993 (SI 1993/348).

Making a claim for benefit

2.75   **4.**—(1) [¹³ Subject to [²¹ paragraphs (10) to (11B)], every] claim for benefit [⁷other than a claim for income support or jobseeker's allowance] shall be made in writing on a form approved by the Secretary of State [³for the purpose of the benefit for which the claim is made], or in such other manner, being in writing, as the Secretary of State [⁸ or the Board] may accept as sufficient in the circumstances of any particular case.

[⁷ (1A) [²¹ Subject to paragraph (11A), in the case of] a claim for income support or jobseeker's allowance, the claim shall—

    (a) be made in writing on a form approved by the Secretary of State for the purpose of the benefit for which the claim is made;

(b) unless any of the reasons specified in paragraph (1B) applies, be made in accordance with the instructions on the form; and

(c) unless any of the reasons specified in paragraph (1B) applies, include such information and evidence as the form may require in connection with the claim.

(1B) The reasons referred to in paragraph (1A) are—

(a) [¹⁰ subject paragraph (IBA)—

    (i) the person making the claim is unable to complete the form in accordance with the instructions or to obtain the information or evidence it requires because he has a physical, learning, mental or communication difficulty; and

    (ii) it is not reasonably practicable for the claimant to obtain assistance from another person to complete the form or obtain the information or evidence; or

(b) the information or evidence required by the form does not exist; or

(c) the information or evidence required by the form can only be obtained at serious risk of physical or mental harm to the claimant, and it is not reasonably practicable for the claimant to obtain the information or evidence by other means; or

(d) the information or evidence required by the form can only be obtained from a third party, and it is not reasonably practicable for the claimant to obtain such information or evidence from such third party; or

(e) the Secretary of State is of the opinion that the person making the claim [¹⁰or, in the case of claim for a jobseeker's allowance by a joint-claim couple, either member of that couple,] has provided sufficient information or evidence to show that he is not entitled to the benefit for which the claim is made, and that it would be inappropriate to require the form to be completed or further information or evidence to be supplied.

[¹⁰ (1BA) In the case of a joint-claim couple claiming a jobseeker's allowance jointly, paragraph (1B)(a) shall not apply to the extent that it is reasonably practicable for a member of a joint-claim couple to whom that sub-paragraph applies to obtain assistance from the other member of that couple.]

(1C) If a person making a claim is unable to complete the claim form or supply the evidence or information it requires because one of the reasons specified in sub-paragraphs (a) to (d) of paragraph (1B) applies, he may so notify an appropriate office by whatever means.]

[¹⁸ (1D) In calculating any period of one month for the purposes of paragraph (7) and regulation 6(1A)(b), there shall be disregarded any period commencing on a day on which a person is first notified of a decision that he failed to take part in a work-focused interview and ending on a day on which he was notified that that decision has been revised so that the decision as revised is that he did take part.]

(2) [⁸In the case of a claim for working families' tax credit, where a married or unmarried couple is included in the family, the claim shall be made by whichever partner they agree should so claim.

(2A) Where, in a case to which paragraph (2) applies, the partners are unable to agree which of them should make the claim, the Board may in their discretion determine that the claim shall be made by the partner who, on the information available to the Board at the time of their determination, is in their opinion mainly caring for the children.]

(3) [⁵Subject to paragraph (3C),] in the case of a [¹⁶ couple], a claim for income support shall be made by whichever partner they agree should so claim or, in default of agreement, by such one of them as the Secretary of State shall in his discretion determine.

[²(3A) In the case of a married or unmarried couple where both partners satisfy the conditions set out in [⁸ section 129(1) of the Social Security Contributions and Benefits Act 1992], a claim for [⁸ disabled persons tax credit] shall be made by whichever partner they agree should so claim, or in default of agreement, by such one of them as [⁸ the Board] shall determine.]

[⁴(3B) For the purposes of income-based jobseeker's allowance—

(a) in the case of a [¹⁶ couple], a claim shall be made by whichever partner they agree should so claim or, in default of agreement, by such one of them as the Secretary of State shall in his discretion determine;

(b) [¹⁰ (b) where there is no entitlement to a contribution-based job-seeker's allowance on a claim made—

(i) by a member of a joint-claim couple, he subsequently claims a joint-claim jobseeker's allowance with the other member of that couple, the claim made by the couple shall be treated as having been made on the date on which the member of that couple made the claim for a jobseeker's allowance in respect of which there was no entitlement to contribution-based jobseeker's allowance;

(ii) by one partner and the other partner wishes to claim inco-mebased jobseeker's allowance, the claim made by that other partner shall be treated as having been made on the date on which the first partner made his claim;]

(c) where entitlement to income-based jobseeker's allowance arises on the expiry of entitlement to contribution-based jobseeker's allowance consequent on a claim made by one partner and the other partner then makes a claim—

(i) the claim of the first partner shall be terminated; and

(ii) the claim of the second partner shall be treated as having been made on the day after the entitlement to contribution-based jobseeker's allowance expired.]

[⁵(3C) In the case of a claim for income support for a period to which [⁹ regulation 21ZB(2)] of the Income Support (General) Regulations 1987 (treatment of refugees) refers, the claim shall be made by the refugee or in the case of a [¹⁶ couple] both of whom are refugees, by either of them.]

(4) Where one of a [¹⁶ couple] is entitled to income support under an award and, with his agreement, his partner claims income support that entitlement shall terminate on the day before that claim is made or treated as made.

[⁶(5) Where a person who wishes to make a claim for benefit and who has not been supplied with an approved form of claim notifies an appropriate office (by whatever means) of his intention to make a claim, he [¹⁰or if he is a member of a joint-claim couple, either member of that couple] shall be supplied, without charge, with such form of claim by such person as the Secretary of State [⁸ or the Board] may appoint or authorise for that purpose.]

[⁴(6) [¹² Subject to paragraphs (6A) to (6D),] A person wishing to make a claim for benefit shall—

(a) if it is a claim for a jobseeker's allowance, unless the Secretary of State otherwise directs, attend in person at an appropriate office or such other place, and at such time, as the Secretary of State may specify in his case in a [¹⁰notification under regulation 23 or 23A] of the Jobseeker's Allowance Regulations;

(b) if it is a claim for any other benefit, deliver or send the claim to an appropriate office.]

[¹² (6A) [¹⁹This paragraph applies to a person]—

(a) who has attained the qualifying age and makes a claim for—

(i) an attendance allowance, a bereavement benefit, a carer's allowance, a disability living allowance or incapacity benefit; or

(ii) a retirement pension of any category [¹⁵ or a shared additional pension] for which a claim is required or a winter fuel payment for which a claim is required under regulation 3(1)(b) of the Social Fund Winter Fuel Payment Regulations 2000;

(b) who has not yet attained the qualifying age and makes a claim for a retirement pension [¹⁵ or a shared additional pension] in advance in accordance with regulation 15(1); [¹⁷ . . .]

[¹⁹ (c) who makes a claim for income support; or

(d) who has not attained the qualifying age and who makes a claim for a carer's allowance, disability living allowance or incapacity benefit.]]

(6B) A person to whom paragraph (6A) applies may make a claim by sending or delivering it to, or by making it in person at—

(a) an office designated by the Secretary of State for accepting such claims; [¹⁷ . . .]

[¹⁹ (b) the offices of—

(i) a local authority administering housing benefit or council tax benefit,

(ii) a county council in England,

(iii) a person providing services to a person mentioned in head (i) or (ii),

(iv) a person authorised to exercise any function of a local authority relating to housing benefit or council tax benefit, or

(v) a person authorised to exercise any function a county council in England has under section 7A of the Social Security Administration Act 1992,

if the Secretary of State has arranged with the local authority, county council or other person for them to receive claims in accordance with this sub-paragraph.]

(6C) Where a person to whom paragraph (6A) applies makes a claim in accordance with paragraph (6B)(b), on receipt of the claim the local authority or other person specified in that sub-paragraph—

(a) shall forward the claim to the Secretary of State as soon as reasonably practicable;

(b) may receive information or evidence relating to the claim supplied by—

(i) the person making, or who has made, the claim; or

(ii) other persons in connection with the claim,

and shall forward it to the Secretary of State as soon as reasonably practicable;

(c) may obtain information or evidence relating to the claim from the person who has made the claim, but not any medical information or evidence except for that which the claimant must provide in accordance with instructions on the form, and shall forward the information or evidence to the Secretary of State as soon as reasonably practicable;

[¹⁹(cc) may verify any non-medical information or evidence supplied or obtained in accordance with sub-paragraph (b) or (c) and shall forward it to the Secretary of State as soon as reasonably practicable;]

(d) may record information or evidence relating to the claim supplied or obtained in accordance with sub-paragraphs (b) or (c) and may hold the information or evidence (whether as supplied or obtained or as recorded) for the purpose of forwarding it to the Secretary of State; and

(e) may give information and advice with respect to the claim to the person who makes, or who has made, the claim.

[¹⁴ (6CC) Paragraphs (6C)(b) to (e) apply in respect of information, evidence and advice relating to any claim by a person to whom paragraph (6A) applies, whether the claim is made in accordance with paragraph (6B) (b) or otherwise.]

(6D) The benefits specified in paragraph (6A) are relevant benefits for the purposes of section 7A of the Social Security Administration Act 1992.]

(7) If a claim [⁷ other than a claim for income support or jobseeker's allowance,] is defective at the date when it is received [¹² in an appropriate office, or other office specified in paragraph (6B) where that paragraph applies,] or has been made in writing but not on the form approved for the time being, the Secretary of State [⁸ or the Board] may refer the claim to the person making it or, as the case may be, supply him with the approved form, and if the form is received properly completed within one month, or such longer period as the Secretary of State [⁸ or the Board] may consider reasonable, from the date on which it is so referred or supplied, the Secretary of State shall treat the claim as if it has been duly made in the first instance.

[¹⁰ (7A) In the case of a claim for income support, if a defective claim is received, the Secretary of State shall advise the person making the claim of the defect and of the relevant provisions of regulation 6(1A) relating to the date of claim.

(7B) In the case of a claim for a jobseeker's allowance, if a defective claim is received, the Secretary of State shall advise—

(a) in the case of a claim made by a joint-claim couple, each member of the couple of the defect and of the relevant provisions of regulation 6(4ZA) relating to the date of that claim;

(b) in any other case, the person making the claim of the defect and of the relevant provisions of regulation 6(4A) relating to the date of claim.]

(8) A claim, other than a claim for income support or jobseeker's allowance, which is made on the form approved for the time being is, for the purposes of these Regulations, properly completed if completed in accordance with the instructions on the form and defective if not so completed.

[⁸(8A) Where—

(a) the Board determine under paragraph (2A) that a claim for working families' tax credit shall be made by the partner who in their opinion is mainly caring for the children,

(b) a claim for working families' tax credit is made by that partner on the form approved for the time being, and

(c) the claim is not completed in accordance with the instructions on the form by reason only that, in consequence of the other partner not agreeing which of them should make the claim, it has not been signed by the other partner

the Board may in their discretion treat that claim as completed in accordance with the instructions on the form for the purposes of paragraph (8), notwithstanding that it has not been signed by the other partner in accordance with those instructions.]

(9) In the case of a claim for income support or jobseeker's allowance, a properly completed claim is a claim which meets the requirements of paragraph (1A) and a defective claim is a claim which does not meet those requirements.]

[[11] (10) This regulation shall not apply to a claim for state pension credit [[20] or an employment and support allowance.]

[[13] (11) A claim for graduated retirement benefit [[15], or a shared additional pension] or retirement pension may be made by telephone call to the telephone number specified by the Secretary of State, unless the Secretary of State directs, in any particular case, that the claim must be made in writing.

[[21] (11A) A claim for income support or jobseeker's allowance may be made by telephone call to the telephone number specified by the Secretary of State where such a claim falls within a category of case which the Secretary of State accepts for the purposes of making a telephone claim.

(11B) Paragraph (11A) shall apply unless in any particular case the Secretary of State directs that the claim must be made in writing.]

(12) A claim made by telephone in accordance with [[21] paragraph (11) or (11A)] is defective unless the Secretary of State is provided, during that telephone call, with all the information he requires to determine the claim.

(13) Where a claim made by telephone is defective, the Secretary of State may refer the claim to the person making it.

(14) If the person corrects the defect within one month, or such longer period as the Secretary of State considers reasonable, of the date he referred the claim to the person, the Secretary of State shall treat the claim as if it have been duly made in the first instance.]

AMENDMENTS

1. The Social Security (Miscellaneous Provisions) Amendment Regulations 1990 (SI 1990/2208), reg.8 (December 5, 1990).

2. The Social Security (Claims and Payments) Amendment Regulations 1991 (SI 1991/2741), reg.3 (February 3, 1992).

3. The Social Security (Miscellaneous Provisions) Amendment Regulations 1992 (SI 1992/247), reg.10 (March 9, 1992).

4. The Social Security (Claims and Payments) (Jobseeker's Allowance Consequential Amendments) Regulations 1996 (SI 1996/1460), reg.2(4) (October 7, 1996).

5. The Income Support and Social Security (Claims and Payments) (Miscellaneous Amendments) Regulations 1996 (SI 1996/2431), reg.7(b) (October 15, 1996).

6. The Social Security (Miscellaneous Amendments) (No.2) Regulations 1997 (SI 1997/793), reg.2(4) (April 7, 1997).

7. The Social Security (Miscellaneous Amendments) (No.2) Regulations 1997 (SI 1997/793), reg.2 (October 6, 1997).

8. The Tax Credits (Claims and Payments) (Amendment) Regulations 1999 (SI 1999/2572), reg.4 (October 5, 1999).

9. The Social Security (Immigration and Asylum) Consequential Amendments Regulations 2000 (SI 2000/636), (April 3, 2000).

10. The Social Security (Joint Claims: Consequential Amendments) Regulations 2000 (SI 2000/1982), reg.2(3) (March 19, 2001).

11. State Pension Credit (Consequential, Transitional and Miscellaneous Provisions) Regulations 2002 (SI 2002/3019), reg.4 (April 7, 2003).

12. The Social Security (Claims and Payments and Miscellaneous Amendments) Regulations 2003 (SI 2003/1632), reg.2(2) (July 21, 2003).

13. The Social Security (Claims and Payments and Payments on account, Overpayments and Recovery) Amendment Regulations 2005 (SI 2005/34), reg.2 (May 2, 2005).

14. The Social Security, Child Support and Tax Credits (Miscellaneous Amendments) Regulations 2005 (SI 2005/337), reg.7 (March 18, 2005).

15. The Social Security (Shared Additional Pension) (Miscellaneous Amendments) Regulations 2005 (SI 2005/1551) (July 6, 2005).

16. The Civil Partnership (Pensions, Social Security and Child Support) (Consequential etc. Provisions) Order 2005 (SI 2005/2887) (December 5, 2005).

17. The Social Security (Miscellaneous Amendments) (No.2) Regulations 2006 (SI 2006/832) (April 10, 2006).

18. The Social Security (Work-focused Interviews) Regulations 2000 (SI 2000/897), (April 3, 2000).

19. The Social Security (Claims and Information) Regulations 2007 (SI 2007/2911) (October 31, 2007).

20. The Employment and Support Allowance (Consequential Provisions) (No.2) Regulations 2008 (SI 2008/1554), reg.12 (October 27, 2008).

21. The Social Security (Miscellaneous Amendments) (No. 5) Regulations 2008 (SI 2008/2667), reg.2 (October 30, 2008).

DEFINITIONS

"appropriate office"—see reg.2(1).
"benefit"—see reg.2(2).
"claim for benefit"—see reg.2(1).
"jobseeker's allowance"—*ibid.*
"married couple"—*ibid.*
"partner"—*ibid.*
"refugee"—*ibid.*
"unmarried couple"—*ibid.*

GENERAL NOTE

Introduction

2.76   Note that this regulation does not apply to claims for state pension credit, or for an employment and support allowance: para.(10).

Section 1 of the Administration Act requires a claim to be submitted for any benefit to which the section applies except where regulations otherwise prescribe (see reg.3), as a condition of entitlement to benefit. This largely removes the effect of the decision of the House of Lords in *Insurance Officer v McCaffrey* [1984] 1 W.L.R. 1353, though some doubt remained in relation to entitlement prior to September 2, 1985, when the first version of s.1 was implemented. This is now resolved by s.2 of the Administrative Act.

The claims system is largely predicated on a system of written claims, but recent amendments now make provision for telephone claims.

A fine line used to be drawn between the responsibilities of the Secretary of State and the adjudicating authorities under this regulation. It has been consistently held that it is for the Secretary of State to say whether a document (not in the prescribed form) is acceptable as "sufficient in the circumstances of the particular case," but the duty lies on the adjudicating authorities to decide whether such a document is a claim for benefit: *R(U)9/60* and *R(S)1/63*. It may be significant that in both these cases the Commissioner concluded that a document accepted by the Secretary of State did not constitute a claim for benefit. It is sometimes argued that the Secretary of State's authority under para.(1) extends to determining the date of the claim. This is not so. The sole issue reserved for the Secretary of State under para. (1) is whether the *form* of the claim (if not on a prescribed form) is acceptable as a claim. It is left for decision makers and tribunals to determine the date of the claim and what has been claimed once the Secretary of State has determined that it is in acceptable form: *R(SB)5/89* confirmed in *CU/94/1994*. This distinction now largely disappears with the abolition of adjudication officers.

The issue of whether tribunals have jurisdiction to consider the decision of the Secretary of State as to when a claim was validly made where it is initially defective has been considered in cases *R(IS) 6/04* and *CIS/758/2002*. The Commissioner, in *R(IS) 6/04*, ruled that the absence of a right of appeal was incompatible with Art.6 of the European Convention, and so disapplied the provision in Schedule 2 to the Decisions and Appeals Regulations in so far as it was necessary to do so in order to ensure that the claimant was entitled to appeal against a decision as to whether or when a claim had been validly made in accordance with this regulation. This has restored the position to that which previously applied before the SSA 1998 entered into force: see *R(U)9/60*.

On the substance of what is required for a valid claim, the Commissioner has this to say:

"I do not think an over-literal approach should be taken in this context: if, for example, all the figures required to determine entitlement are supplied and identified sufficiently clearly when the claimant submits his claim, either in answers recorded on the claim form itself or in annexed documents to which those answers expressly or impliedly refer, then it would in my judgment be open to a tribunal to hold on the facts that there has been no *material* failure such as to render the claim and the information supplied with it incomplete, even if admittedly the claimant has not complied with the instructions to the letter by repeating the actual figures in the boxes on the form itself. In addition, it seems to have been regarded as a defect fatal to the *claim* that he only gave details of his bank, and not of a Post Office, in the part of the form that asked him about the method of *payment* he preferred if benefit was in due course awarded." (para.54.)

and:

"I direct the tribunal that for this purpose they should concern themselves only with the matters and information necessary to determine entitlement to the benefit claimed. It seems to me that both sides are right in saying, as Mr Wright submits and Mr Spencer very fairly agrees in the most recent written submissions, that the requirements in regulation 4(1A)(b)–(c) strictly concern the information and evidence required in connection with the *claim* so as to enable it to be determined; not such things as the administrative arrangements for payment of any benefit that may subsequently be awarded on that claim. Thus even though it is of course convenient and sensible for the claimant to be asked about these at the same time and to put them on the same form, the omission of such additional details as the Post Office, needed (if at all) only for payment purposes (and as Mr Spencer points out, not in any event crucial or binding so far as the Secretary of State is concerned, under regulation 20 of the Claims and Payments regulations) does not render an otherwise complete claim defective." (para.56.)

CIS/758/2002 added a gloss on this case in relation to defective claims for income support or a jobseeker's allowance, namely that the mandatory four week time limit for correcting defects on the claim form is not contrary to Convention rights protected by the Human Rights Act 1998 when compared with the longer discretionary time limit allowed for correcting defects in claims for other benefits. This is said to be because income support and income-based jobseeker's allowance are not possessions for the purposes of the protection of property rights under Art.1 of Protocol 1 of the European Convention, although that proposition is almost certainly no longer good law following the decision of the Grand Chamber in the *Stec* case: see annotations to Article 1 of Protocol 1 at para 4.90.

Once a claim has been made, it may only be withdrawn before it has been adjudicated upon by an adjudication officer (now decision maker): *R(U)2/79* and *R(U)7/83* and see reg.5(2).

Para. (1)

2.77 Unless provision is made for telephone claims, para.(1) provides that claims must be made in writing, normally on an official form, although the Secretary of State may accept some other kind of written claim. In such a case, under para.(7), the Secretary of State may require the claimant to fill in the proper form. If this is done in the proper time the claim is treated as duly made in the first instance. It no longer seems possible for an oral claim to be accepted, but see below on telephone claims. However, see reg.6(1)(aa) for the position when a claimant contacts an office with a view to making a claim.

Note also *R(SB) 9/84* where a Tribunal of Commissioners holds that where a claim has been determined, the Secretary of State must be deemed, in the absence of any challenge at the time, to have accepted that the claim was made in sufficient manner. See the notes to reg.33. See also *CDLA/1596/1996* in which the Commissioner set aside the tribunal's decision because they had failed to consider whether they should refer to the Secretary of State the question whether the claimant's application for review should be treated as a claim under para. (1).

Paras (1A)–(1C)

2.78 These provisions, together with the new reg.6(1A) and (4A)–(4AB), introduce the so-called "onus of proof" changes for claims for income support and JSA from October 6, 1997. The aim is to place more responsibility on claimants for these benefits to provide information and evidence to support their claim (see the DSS's Memorandum to the Social Security Advisory Committee (SSAC) annexed to the Committee's report (Cm. 3586) on the proposals). SSAC supported this principle but considered that it was "premature to introduce penalties for failure to provide information when it is more likely that the current problems lie more with the forms and procedures than with dilatory or obstructive claimants". As the Committee pointed out, the current claim forms are lengthy, complex and difficult for many people to understand, and moreover in the past told claimants not to delay sending in the claim form even if they had not got all the required information. Furthermore, since income support and income-based JSA are basic subsistence benefits, claimants have every incentive to cooperate in providing all the information needed to get an early payment. Thus SSAC's main recommendation was that the claim forms and guidance to claimants should first be revised and tested "before introducing new penalties, which together with the proposed changes to backdating rules [see reg.19], will only serve to complicate the social security system and penalise the most disadvantaged claimants". But this recommendation was rejected by the Government, although the final form of the regulations did take limited account of some of SSAC's other recommendations.

Under the rules, in order for a claim for income support or JSA to be validly made, it must be in writing (unless telephone claims are permitted) on a properly completed approved form (there is no longer any provision for the Secretary of State to accept any other kind of written claim) and all the information and evidence required by the form must have been provided (para.(1A)). However, the requirement to complete the form fully or to provide the required evidence does not apply in the circumstances set out in para.(1B). The list in para.(1B) is exhaustive and there is no category of analogous circumstances. If any of sub-paras (a)–(d) of para. (1B) do apply, the person can inform an appropriate office (defined in reg.2(1)) "by whatever means" (e.g. verbally or through a third party) (para.(1C)). Note that the obligation to provide information and evidence only relates to that required by the claim form; if a claim is accepted as validly made it will still be open to the Department to seek further information if this is required in order to decide the claim, but this will not alter the date of claim.

See reg.6(1A) for the date of claim for an income support claim and reg.6(4A)–(4AB) for the date of claim for JSA claims (and note the differences).

Thus the major effect of these new rules is that there is now a requirement to produce the specified information and evidence *before* a claim is treated as having been made (although see reg.6(1A) and (4A)–(4AB) for the date of claim). Whether the necessary evidence has been produced or whether a claimant is exempt under para.(1B) will, however, now be subject to appeal to a tribunal, on the application, by analogy, of the principle established in *R(IS) 6/04*. The contrary position which has been set out in earlier editions and was approved by the Commissioner in *CJSA/ 69/2001* would seem to be inconsistent with the approach adopted in *R(IS) 6/04*.

Note also s.1(1A) of the Administration Act, under which claimants will not be entitled to benefit unless they satisfy requirements relating to the provision of national insurance numbers.

Paras (2) and (2A)

In working families' tax credit cases, if a couple is involved, the claim may be made by either partner.

2.79

Para.(3)

In income support cases, where a couple is involved, either partner can be the claimant, except in the case of a refugee under para.(3C). There is a free choice. If the couple cannot jointly agree who should claim, the Secretary of State is to break the tie. There are still some differences in entitlement according to which partner is the claimant, particularly since only the claimant is required to be available for work. In addition, head (b) of para.12(1) of Sch.2 to the Income Support Regulations (disability and higher pensioner premium) can only be satisfied by the claimant. But there is now no long-term rate and the full-time employment of either partner excludes entitlement to income support. See reg.7(2). Under the Income Support (Transitional) Regulations transitional protection is lost if the claimant for the couple changes. *CIS 8/1990* and *CIS 375/1990* challenged this rule on the grounds that it was indirectly discriminatory against women (since in 98 per cent of couples (at that time) the man was the claimant). Following the European Court of Justice's decision in the *Cresswell* case that income support is not covered by EC Directive 79/7 on equal treatment for men and women in social security (see the notes to reg.36 of the Income Support Regulations), the claimants could not rely on European law. The Commissioner also rejects a submission that the Sex Discrimination Act 1975 prevented the discriminatory effect of regs 2 and 10 of the Transitional Regulations. Paragraph (4) below deals with changes of partner.

2.80

Para.(3A)

Under para.(3A), if both partners in a couple satisfy the conditions of entitlement for a disabled person's tax credit, they may choose which one of them is to claim. If they cannot choose, the Secretary of State makes the decision.

2.81

Para. (3B)

2.82   Sub-paragraph (a) applies the normal income support rule for couples to income-based JSA. Sub-paragraphs (b) and (c) make provision about the deemed date of the claim for income-based JSA by one partner when a claim for contribution-based JSA by the other partner fails or entitlement comes to an end.

Para. (3C)

2.83   Where one of a couple is a refugee, the claim for income support must be made by that partner. If both are refugees, there is a free choice.

CIS/3438/2004 concerned a claim for income support by a Turkish woman admitted to the United Kingdom as a refugee. She claimed income support on August 6, 2003 enclosing a letter from the Home Office dated July 16, 2003 acknowledging her refugee status. She had also been instructed to provide the Department with details of any support provided to her as an asylum seeker by the Home Office. She did not include such a letter with her claim form because she did not have such a letter. It did not exist because it had not at that time been provided by the Home Office. The required information was subsequently obtained and provided to the Department. The claim for income support made on August 6, 2003 was rejected on the ground that the claimant had failed to comply with the requirement in reg.4(1A) to "include such information and evidence as the form may require in connection with the claim." The tribunal upheld the decision refusing the claim. The Commissioner concludes that there was no proper basis for finding a claimant, in these circumstances, to be in breach of reg.4(1A) by not submitting a document which she did not have at the time with the claim form. While it would be proper to require submission of the information, it was an error of law to treat the claim which had been made as a nullity.

Para. (4)

2.84   If there is a change of claimant within a couple in the middle of a continuing income support claim, the claims are not to overlap. The change is a matter of a new claim for benefit, not review as it was for supplementary benefit (*R(SB) 1/93*). In *CSIS 66/1992* the Commissioner rejects the argument that para.(4) combined with s.20(9) of the Social Security Act 1986 (SSCBA s.134(2)) meant that a change of claimant could not be backdated. If the claimant could show good cause for her delay in claiming, regs 19(2) and 6(3) enabled her claim to be backdated to the date from which she had good cause (subject to the then what was then a 12-month limit in reg.19(4)). Duplication of payment could be avoided by the AO reviewing the claimant's husband's entitlement for any past period in respect of which the claimant was held to be entitled to benefit and applying reg.5(1) and (2), Case 1, of the Payments Regulations. By becoming the claimant the wife qualified for a disability premium. There is a specific provision in para.19 of Sch.7 to the Income Support Regulations for arrears of a disability premium in these circumstances.

Para. (5)

2.85   Reg. 4(5) imposes a duty on the Department to provide a claim form in the circumstances set out there. The effect of a failure by the Department to comply with that duty is considered in *R (IS) 4/07*, which also reviews the earlier authorities on the point. The specific issue raised was whether a breach of reg.4(5) results in suspension of the operation of the time limits for claiming. The Commissioner concludes that it does not. However, the provisions of reg.19 on backdating would be available to a claimant who sought to have a claim backdated in such circumstances.

Para. (6)

2.86   The claim, except in the case of JSA, must be delivered or sent to the appropriate office, though increasing provision is now being made for telephone or electronic claims.

In *CSIS 48/1992* the Commissioner considered the effect of para.(6) in the light of s.7 and s.23 of the Interpretation Act 1978. He concludes that the effect of these provisions is that a claim for a social security benefit is a document authorised by an Act to be served by post, which is presumed to have been delivered in the ordinary course of post unless this is proved not to have been the case. The tribunal should therefore have considered whether it accepted that the claim had been posted, and, if so, whether the presumption of delivery had been rebutted by the adjudication officer. *CSIS 48/1992* has been followed in *CIS 759/1992*.

In *CIB/2805/2003* the Deputy Commissioner rules that, having regard to s.7 of the Interpretation Act 1978, the onus is on the Secretary of State to prove that a letter arrives at a date later than the date it should have been received in the ordinary course of post. This would involve producing some evidence of practice in the Department about date stamping incoming post. This was particularly important in this case since the letter in issue had been posted during the Easter holiday period. In such cases, the use of reg.19(7)(c), which deals with adverse postal conditions may be relevant: see annotations to that provision.

For JSA, a claimant wishing to make an initial claim must normally go in person to the nearest Job Centre to obtain a claim pack from the new jobseeker receptionist. An appointment will then be made for the claimant to return, usually within five days, for a new jobseeker interview. This is all part of the concept of "active signing". The claim will be treated as made on the date of the first attendance, if it is received properly completed within a month (reg.6(1)(aa) and (4A)).

Paras (6A) to (6D)

Note the rules in these paragraphs which relate to claims for the named benefits by those who have attained "the qualifying age". This is defined in reg. 2 by reference to s.1(6) of the State Pension Credit Act 2002, which provides:

In this Act "'the qualifying age'" means—
(a) in the case of a woman, pensionable age; or
(b) in the case of a man, the age which is pensionable age in the case of a woman born on the same day as the man.

Pensionable age for women is currently 60, but between 2010 and 2020 will rise gradually until it reaches 65 in line with men: see s.126 and Sch.4 to the Pensions Act 1995 for the detail.

2.87

Paras (7) and (8)

Paragraph (7), which does not apply to claims for income support or JSA (for which see para.(7A)), deals with written claims not made on the proper form (for which, see para.(1)), and situations where the proper form is not completed according to the instructions (see para.8)). The Secretary of State may simply treat this as an ineffective attempt to claim, but also has power to refer the form back to the claimant. Then there is one month (extendable by the Secretary of State) to complete the form properly, in which case the claim is treated as made on the date of the original attempt to claim (see reg.6(1)(b)). Note also *R(SB) 9/84*; see the note to para.(1).

CP/3447/2003 concerned a claim for an adult dependency increase to a retirement pension for the claimant's wife. The claimant had made his claim for retirement pension at the proper time in advance of his 65th birthday indicating on the claim form that he wished to claim the increase for his wife. Adult dependency increase is, by virtue of reg.2(3) of the Claims and Payments Regulations, treated as a separate benefit requiring a separate claim. The Department failed to pick up the statement in the retirement pension claim form and did not send the claimant a further form to complete. In the following year, the claimant wrote to ask whether he was getting the increase after a query on his tax return. The required form was then issued to him. He completed it and it was clear that he should have been receiving the increase all along. The Secretary of State refused to pay it back to the start of the retirement pension on the grounds that the claim was received following the enquiry and could only be backdated three months from that date. By the time the appeal came before the tribunal, the Secretary of State accepted that the decision was wrong. The issue

2.88

turned on the proper interpretation of reg.4(7). In particular, what was the date on which the claim was made 'in the first instance' in this case. Was it the date on which the claimant wrote his letter asking about his entitlement to the increase of his wife, or was it the indication in his original claim form for retirement pension indicating that he wanted the increase for his wife?

The Commissioner concluded,

"In those circumstances, given that (a) a claim in writing for the increase is now accepted as having been made in the first instance by the claimant in early 1999 as part of the original claim for his pension, and (b) the Secretary of State did in fact exercise his powers in regulation 4(7) to supply the claimant with the approved form which was returned duly completed well within the month stipulated, the conditions under which the Secretary of State is bound to treat the claim as if it had been duly made "in the first instance" are in my judgment satisfied in reference to the *original* date of claim in 1999, not just the enquiry letter the following year. Since the requirement to treat the claim as duly made "in the first instance" is mandatory once the conditions are met, there is no further exercise of discretionary or administrative judgment for the Secretary of State to make under regulation 4(7) before the effect in terms of entitlement to benefit can be properly determined. Although it was only in response to the further enquiry that the form was eventually supplied the Secretary of State could not in my judgment possibly rely on that as an argument for saying that the existence of the first claim should be ignored, when the failure to supply the form in the first instance was admittedly an administrative error by his own local officials and should never have happened at all." (para.15).

The Commissioner does, however, note that in so finding in the particular circumstances of this case, he is not to be taken as pronouncing as a matter of general principle that ticking boxes on a form in the expectation of receiving a further form ought in every case to constitute making a claim in writing for the benefit in question. (para.14).

Para. (7A)

2.89 There are special rules in reg.4 where the benefit claimed is income support. In *CIS/3173/2003*, the claimant had contacted an office of the Department with a view to making a claim for income support on October 14, 2002, and she had subsequently completed an income support claim form on October 24, 2002, but did not include payslips with that form. These were required since she declared that she was doing "therapeutic work" (actually work accepted as permitted for the purposes of incapacity benefit). The Department contacted the claimant on December 18, 2002 regarding the missing payslips. These were provided on December 19, 2002. The decision maker awarded income support only from December 19, 2002. The tribunal upheld that decision. The Commissioner also concludes that there was no entitlement until December 19, 2002. He concludes that the claim form sent in without the accompanying payslips was a defective claim under sub-para.(7A) with the consequences stated there, but that reg.6(1A) makes provision only for one month's leeway in providing the information or evidence required to cure the defect. More than one month had passed here, and accordingly no claim which complied with the requirement of reg.4(1A) was made until December 19, 2002. It did not matter that the Department had not requested the payslips earlier. The Commissioner has granted leave to appeal in this case.

Paras (7A), (7B) and (9)

2.90 If a claim for income support or JSA is defective (on which see para.(9)), the Secretary of State will simply advise the claimant of the defect and of the rules in reg.6(1A) (for income support claims) or reg.6(4A) (for JSA claims) as appropriate. It will then be up to the claimant to comply with those provisions if he is in a position to do so.

Paras (11) to (14)

2.91

These paragraphs make provision, in a system which has previously been based upon a requirement for written claims, for telephone claims for retirement pension and graduated retirement pension. Telephone claims will take the form of an interview between an officer of the Department and the claimant whose answers will be input directly into the Department's computer system. A decision on the claim may be made on the spot, since entitlement to pensions can very often be determined easily by reference to information already held in Departmental records. These paragraphs make provision for telephone claims, but reserve the Secretary of State's power to insist upon a written claim. Provision is also made for treating a telephone claim as a defective claim and allowing a period for the defect to be remedied.

[¹ Further provisions as to claims

2.92

4A.—(1) Where a claimant resides in both—

(a) the area of a local authority specified in Part I or II of Schedule 1 to the Social Security (Claims and Information) Regulations 1999; and

(b) a postcode district identified in Part I or II of Schedule 2 to the Social Security (Claims and Information) Regulations 1999,

any claim for a benefit to which paragraph (2) applies may be made to any office displaying the **one** logo(a) (whether or not that office is situated within the area of the local authority in which the claimant resides).

(2) The benefits to which this paragraph applies are—

(a) a jobseeker's allowance;

(b) income support;

(c) incapacity benefit;

(d) [² carer's allowance];

(e) severe disablement allowance;

(f) widow's benefit;

(g) bereavement benefits;

(h) disability living allowance.

(3) A claim made in accordance with paragraph (1), other than a claim for income support or a jobseeker's allowance, shall be made in writing on a form approved by the Secretary of State for the purpose of the benefit to which the claim is made, or in such other manner, being in writing, as the person to whom the claim is made may accept as sufficient in the circumstances of the particular case.

(4) In the case of a claim for income support or a jobseeker's allowance, the provisions of regulation 4(1A) to (1C) shall apply.

(5) In its application to the area of any authority specified in Part I or II of Schedule 1 to the Social Security (Claims and Information) Regulations 1999, the "appropriate office" in these Regulations includes also an office of an authority or person to whom claims may be made in accordance with paragraph (1).

(6) In these Regulations, a "participating authority" means any local authority or person to whom claims may be made in accordance with paragraph (1).

AMENDMENTS

1. This regulation inserted by The Social Security (Claims and Information) Regulations 1999 (SI 1999/3108), reg.5 (November 29, 1999).

2. The Social Security Amendment (Carer's Allowance) Regulations 2002 (SI 2002/2497), Sch.2 (October 23, 2002).

Forwarding claims and information

2.93   **4B.**—(1) A participating authority may—

(a) record information or evidence relating to any social security matter supplied by or obtained from a person at an office displaying the ▉one▉ logo, whether or not the information or evidence is supplied or obtained in connection with the making of a claim for benefit;

(b) give information or advice with respect to any social security matter to persons who are making, or have made, claims for any benefit to which regulation 4A(2) applies [² or for state pension credit.]

(2) A participating authority shall forward to the Secretary of State—

(a) any claim for benefit, other than a claim for housing benefit or council tax benefit, together with any information or evidence supplied to the authority in connection with that claim; and

(b) any information or evidence relating to any other social security matter, except where the information or evidence relates solely to housing benefit or council tax benefit given to the authority by a person making a claim for, or who has claimed, a benefit to which regulation 4A(2) applies.]

AMENDMENTS

1. This regulation inserted by The Social Security (Claims and Information) Regulations 1999 (SI 1999/3108), reg.5 (November 29, 1999)

2. State Pension Credit (Consequential, Transitional and Miscellaneous) Regulations 2002 (SI 2002/3019), reg.4 (April 7, 2003).

[¹ Electronic claims for benefit

2.94   **4ZC.**—(1) Any claim for benefit in relation to which this regulation applies, and any certificate, notice, information or evidence given in connection with that claim, may be made or given by means of an electronic communication, in accordance with the provisions set out in Schedule 9ZC.

(2) This regulation applies in relation to carer's allowance [², attendance allowance, disability living allowance, graduated retirement benefit, retirement pension and shared additional pension].]

AMENDMENTS

1. The Social Security (Electronic Communications) (Carer's Allowance) Order 2003 (SI 2003/2800), reg.2 (December 1, 2003).

2. The Social Security (Electronic Communications) (Miscellaneous Benefits) Order 2005 (SI 2005/3321) (January 30, 2006).

[¹ Electronic claims for benefit

2.95   **4C.**—(1) Any claim for benefit in relation to which this regulation applies, and any certificate, notice, information or evidence given in connection with that claim, may be made or given by means of an electronic communication, in accordance with the provisions set out in Schedule 9C.

(2) This regulation applies in relation to child benefit.]

AMENDMENT

1. Inserted by the Social Security (Electronic Communications) (Child Benefit) Order 2002 (SI 2002/1789), art.3 (October 28, 2002).

[¹ **Making a claim for state pension credit**

4D.—(1) A claim for state pension credit need only be made in writing if   2.96
the Secretary of State so directs in any particular case.

(2) A claim is made in writing either—

(a) by completing and returning in accordance with the instructions printed on it a form approved or provided by the Secretary of State for the purpose; or

(b) in such other written form as the Secretary of State accepts as sufficient in the circumstances of the case.

(3) A claim for state pension credit may be made in writing whether or not a direction is issued under paragraph (1) and may also be made [⁵ . . .] in person at an appropriate office [³ . . .].

[³ (3A) A claim made in writing may also be made at an office designated by the Secretary of State for accepting claims for state pension credit.]

[⁷ (4) A claim made in writing may also be made at the offices of—

(a) a local authority administering housing benefit or council tax benefit;

(b) a county council in England;

(c) a person providing services to a person mentioned in sub-paragraph (a) or (b);

(d) a person authorised to exercise any functions of a local authority relating to housing benefit or council tax benefit; or

(e) a person authorised to exercise any function a county council in England has under section 7A of the Social Security Administration Act 1992,

if the Secretary of State has arranged with the local authority, county council or other person for them to receive claims in accordance with this paragraph.]

[³ (5) Where a claim is made in accordance with paragraph (4), the local authority or other specified person—

(a) shall forward the claim to the Secretary of State as soon as reasonably practicable;

(b) may receive information or evidence relating to the claim supplied by the person making, or who has made, the claim to another person, and shall forward it to the Secretary of State as soon as reasonably practicable;

(c) may obtain information or evidence relating to the claim from the person who has made the claim and shall forward it to the Secretary of State as soon as reasonably practicable;

[⁷(cc) may verify any non-medical information or evidence supplied or obtained in accordance with sub-paragraph (b) or (c) and shall forward it to the Secretary of State as soon as reasonably practicable;]

(d) may record information or evidence relating to the claim supplied or obtained in accordance with sub-paragraph (b) or (c) and may hold the information or evidence (whether as supplied or obtained or as recorded) for the purpose of forwarding it to the Secretary of State; and

(e) may give information and advice with respect to the claim to the person who makes, or has made, the claim.]

[³ (5A) Paragraph (5)(b) to (e) applies in respect of information, evidence

371

and advice relating to any claim for state pension credit, whether it is made in accordance with paragraph (4) or otherwise.]

(6) A claim for state pension credit made in person [5 . . .] is not a valid claim unless a written statement of the claimant's circumstances, provided for the purpose by the Secretary of State, is approved by the person making the claim.

[5 (6A) A claim for state pension credit may be made by telephone call to the telephone number specified by the Secretary of State.

(6B) Where the Secretary of State, in any particular case, directs that the person making the claim approves a written statement of his circumstances, provided for the purpose by the Secretary of State, a claim made by telephone is not a valid claim unless the person complies with the direction.

(6C) A claim made by telephone in accordance with paragraph (6A) is defective unless the Secretary of State is provided, during that telephone call, with all the information he requires to determine the claim.

(6D) Where a claim made by telephone in accordance with paragraph (6A) is defective, the Secretary of State is to provide the person making it with an opportunity to correct the defect.

(6E) If the person corrects the defect within one month, or such longer period as the Secretary of State considers reasonable, of the date the Secretary of State last drew attention to the defect, the Secretary of State shall treat the claim as if it had been duly made in the first instance.]

(7) A [4 couple] may agree between them as to which partner is to make a claim for state pension credit, but in the absence of an agreement, the Secretary of State shall decide which of them is to make the claim.

(8) Where one member of a [4 couple] ("the former claimant") is entitled to state pension credit under an award but a claim for state pension credit is made by the other member of the couple, then, if both members of the couple confirm in writing that they wish the claimant to be the other member, the former claimant's entitlement shall terminate on the last day of the benefit week specified in paragraph (9).

(9) That benefit week is the benefit week of the former claimant which includes the day immediately preceding the day the partner's claim is actually made or, if earlier, is treated as made.

(10) If a claim for state pension credit is defective when first received, the Secretary of State is to provide the person making it with an opportunity to correct the defect.

(11) If that person corrects the defect so that the claim then satisfies the requirements of paragraph (2) and does so within 1 month [6 or such longer period as the Secretary of State considers reasonable] of the date the Secretary of State last drew attention to the defect, the claim shall be treated as having been properly made on the date—

(a) the defective claim was first received by the Secretary of State or the person acting on his behalf; or

(b) if regulation 4F(3) applies, the person informed an appropriate office [1 or other office specified in regulation 4F(3)] of his intention to claim state pension credit.

(12) [5 Paragraph (6E) and (11) do] not apply in a case to which regulation 4E(3) applies.

(13) State pension credit is a relevant benefit for the purposes of section 7A of the Social Security Administration Act 1992.]

AMENDMENTS

1. Inserted by The State Pension Credit (Consequential, Transitional and Miscellaneous) Regulations 2002 (SI 2002/3019), reg.4 (April 7, 2003).

2. The Social Security (Claims and Payments and Miscellaneous Amendments) Regulations 2003 (SI 2003/1632) reg.2 (July 21, 2003).

3. The Social Security, Child Support and Tax Credits (Miscellaneous Amendments) Regulations 2005 (SI 2005/337) reg.7 (March 18, 2005).

4. The Civil Partnership (Pensions, Social Security and Child Support) (Consequential etc. Provisions) Order 2005 (SI 2005/2887) (December 5, 2005).

5. The Social Security (Miscellaneous Amendments) (No. 2) Regulations 2006 (SI 2006/832) (July 24, 2006).

6. The Social Security (Miscellaneous Amendments) (No.3) Regulations 2006 (SI 2006/2377) (October 2, 2006).

7. The Social Security (Claims and Information) Regulations 2007 (SI 2007/2911) (October 31, 2007).

[¹ Making a claim before attaining the qualifying age

4E.—(1) A claim for state pension credit may be made, and any claim made may be determined, at any time within the advance period.

2.97

(2) The advance period begins on the date which falls 4 months before the day on which the claimant attains the qualifying age and ends on the day before he attains that age.

(3) A person who makes a claim within the advance period which is defective may correct the defect at any time before the end of the advance period.]

AMENDMENT

1. Inserted by the State Pension Credit (Consequential, Transitional and Miscellaneous) Regulations 2002 (SI 2002/3019), reg.4 (April 7, 2003).

[¹ Making a claim after attaining the qualifying age: date of claim

4F.—(1) This regulation applies in the case of a person who claims state pension credit on or after attaining the qualifying age.

2.98

(2) The date on which a claim is made shall, subject to paragraph (3), be—
  (a) where the claim is made in writing and is not defective, the date on which the claim is first received—
    (i) by the Secretary of State or the person acting on his behalf; or
    (ii) in a case to which regulation 4D(4) relates, in the office of a person specified therein;
  (b) where the claim is not made in writing but is otherwise made in accordance with regulation 4D(3) [⁴ or (6A)] and is not defective, the date the claimant provides details of his circumstances by telephone to, or in person at, the appropriate office or other office designated by the Secretary of State to accept claims for state pension credit; or
  (c) where a claim is initially defective but the defect is corrected under regulation [⁴ 4D(6E) or (11)], the date the claim is treated as having been made under that regulation.

(3) If a [³ person wishing to make a claim]—

(a) informs [³ (by whatever means) an appropriate office [², or other office designated by the Secretary of State for accepting claims for state pension credit or the office of the person specified in regulation 4(D)] of his intention to claim state pension credit; and

(b) subsequently makes the claim in accordance with regulation 4D within 1 month of complying with sub-paragraph (a), or within such longer period as the Secretary of State may allow,

the claim may, where in the circumstances of the particular case it is appropriate to do so, be treated as made on the day the claimant first informed [² an office specified in subparagraph (a)] of his intention to claim the credit.]

AMENDMENTS

1. Inserted by the State Pension Credit (Consequential, Transitional and Miscellaneous) Regulations 2002 (SI 2002/3019), reg.4 (April 7, 2003).

2. The Social Security (Claims and Payments and Miscellaneous Amendments) Regulations 2003 (SI 2003/1632), reg.2 (July 21, 2003).

3. Social Security (Housing Benefit, Council Tax Benefit, State Pension Credit and Miscellaneous Amendments) Regulations 2004 (SI 2004/2327), reg.8 (October 6, 2004).

4. The Social Security (Miscellaneous Amendments) (No. 2) Regulations 2006 (SI 2006/832) (July 24, 2006).

GENERAL NOTE

2.99   The amendments to reg.4 of the Claims and Payments Regulations are significant in that they may provision for much greater co-operation between the Department and local authorities in relation to the receipt of claims for benefits administered by these agencies.

Claims under these provisions may be directed to an office designated by the Secretary of State for accepting such claims. In relation to benefits administered by the Department, the party receiving the claim is under a duty to forward the claim to the Department as soon as reasonably practicable.

[¹ Making a claim for employment and support allowance by telephone

2.100   **4G.**—(1) A claim ("'a telephone claim'") for an employment and support allowance may be made by telephone call to the telephone number specified by the Secretary of State.

(2) Where the Secretary of State, in any particular case, directs that the person making the claim approves a written statement of his circumstances, provided for the purpose by the Secretary of State, a telephone claim is not a valid claim unless the person complies with the direction.

(3) A telephone claim is defective unless the Secretary of State is provided, during that telephone call, with all the information he requires to determine the claim.

(4) Where a telephone claim is defective, the Secretary of State is to advise the person making it of the defect and of the relevant provisions of regulation 6(1F) relating to the date of claim.

(5) If the person corrects the defect within one month, or such longer period as the Secretary of State considers reasonable, of the date the Secretary of State last drew attention to the defect, the Secretary of State must treat the claim as if it had been properly made in the first instance.]

AMENDMENT

1. The Employment and Support Allowance (Consequential Provisions) (No. 2) Regulations 2008, (SI 2008/1554), reg. 13 (October 27, 2008).

[¹ Making a claim for employment and support allowance in writing

4H.—(1) A claim ("a written claim") for employment and support allow-   2.101
ance need only be made in writing if the Secretary of State so directs in any particular case but a written claim may be made whether or not a direction is issued.

(2) A written claim must be made on a form approved for the purpose by the Secretary of State and be made in accordance with the instructions on the form.

(3) A claim in writing may also be made at the offices of—

(a) a local authority administering housing benefit or council tax benefit;

(b) a person providing to such an authority services relating to housing benefit or council tax benefit; or

(c) a person authorised to exercise the function of a local authority relating to housing benefit or council tax benefit,

if the Secretary of State has arranged with the local authority or person specified in sub-paragraph (b) or (c) for them to receive claims in accordance with this paragraph.

(4) Where a written claim is made in accordance with paragraph (3), on receipt of that claim the local authority or other person specified in that paragraph—

(a) must forward the claim to the Secretary of State as soon as reasonably practicable;

(b) may receive information or evidence relating to the claim supplied by—

(i) the person making, or who has made, the claim; or

(ii) other persons in connection with the claim,

and shall forward it to the Secretary of State as soon as reasonably practicable;

(c) may obtain information or evidence relating to the claim from the person who has made the claim, but not any medical information or evidence except for that which the claimant must provide in accordance with instructions on the form, and must forward the information or evidence to the Secretary of State as soon as reasonably practicable;

(d) may record information or evidence relating to the claim supplied or obtained in accordance with sub-paragraph (b) or (c) and may hold the information or evidence (whether as supplied or obtained or as recorded) for the purpose of forwarding it to the Secretary of State; and

(e) may give information and advice with respect to the claim to the person who makes, or who has made, the claim.

(5) Paragraphs (4)(b) to (e) apply in respect of information, evidence and advice relating to any claim whether the claim is made in accordance with paragraph (3) or otherwise.

(6) If a written claim is defective when first received, the Secretary of

State is to advise the person making it of the defect and of the provisions of regulation 6(1F) relating to the date of claim.

(7) If that person corrects the defect so that the claim then satisfies the requirements of paragraph (2) and does so within one month, or such longer period as the Secretary of State considers reasonable, of the date the Secretary of State last drew attention to the defect, the claim must be treated as having been properly made in the first instance.]

AMENDMENT

1. The Employment and Support Allowance (Consequential Provisions) (No. 2) Regulations 2008 (SI 2008/1554), reg.13 (October 27, 2008).

[¹Claims for employment and support allowance: supplemental

2.102   **4I.**—(1) Where a person who is a member of a couple may be entitled to an income-related employment and support allowance the claim for an employment and support allowance must be made by whichever member of the couple they agree should claim or, in default of agreement, by such one of them as the Secretary of State may choose.

(2) Where one member of a couple ("'the former claimant'") is entitled to an income-related employment and support allowance under an award but a claim for an employment and support allowance is made by the other member of the couple and the Secretary of State considers that the other member is entitled to an income-related employment and support allowance, then, if both members of the couple confirm in writing that they wish the claimant to be the other member, the former claimant's entitlement terminates on the day the partner's claim is actually made or, if earlier, is treated as made.

(3) In calculating any period of one month for the purposes of regulations 4G and 4H, any period commencing on a day on which a person is first notified of a decision in connection with his failure to take part in a work-focused interview and ending on a day on which he was notified that that decision has been revised so that the decision as revised is that he did take part is to be disregarded.

(4) Employment and support allowance is a relevant benefit for the purposes of section 7A of the 1992 Act.]

AMENDMENT

1. The Employment and Support Allowance (Consequential Provisions) (No. 2) Regulations 2008 (SI 2008/1554), reg.13 (October 27, 2008).

Amendment and withdrawal of claim

2.103   **5.**—(1) A person who has made a claim may amend it at any time by notice in writing received in an appropriate office [¹ except where the claim was made by telephone, in accordance with regulation 4(11)[² or 4D(6A)], where the amendment may be made by telephone,] before a determination has been made on the claim, and any claim so amended may be treated as if it had been so amended in the first instance.

(2) A person who has made a claim may withdraw it at any time before a determination has been made on it, by notice to an appropriate office, and any such notice of withdrawal shall have effect when it is received.

AMENDMENTS

1. The Social Security (Claims and Payments and Payments on account, Over-payments and Recovery) Amendment Regulations 2005 (SI 2005/34), reg.2 (May 2, 2005).
2. The Social Security (Miscellaneous Amendments) (No. 2) Regulations 2006 (SI 2006/832) (July 24, 2006).

DEFINITION

"appropriate office"—see reg.2(1).

GENERAL NOTE

Para. (1)

An issue arose in *CTC/1061/2001* on the meaning of reg.5. The claimant had **2.104** claimed a disabled person's tax credit, reporting that he worked as a private hire driver. He answered a question about the amount of usage of the car for private purpose and responded that he used it 50 per cent for private purposes; he later said he had intended to indicate that he used the car for 50 per cent of the time and five per cent or less was for private purposes. The Secretary of State argued that this was irrelevant since a claim could not be altered after it had been determined. The tribunal accepted the argument. The Commissioner notes that there is nothing in reg.5 which prevents a claimant from seeking to explain an answer in a way which is different from how the decision-maker interpreted it. He goes on to raise the question whether there might be a difference for the purpose of reg.5(1) between a claim and evidence on a claim, but does not seek to answer the question.

Regulation 5(1) would appear to be drafted sufficiently widely that it would encompass an amendment not only to the claim, but also to the evidence on which the claim is based. The underlying purpose of the regulation appears to be to ensure that the decision is based on full circumstances obtaining when the claim is determined. So, for example, a claimant might wish to include new members of his family to the claim, or correct an error on the claim form which has just been notices. Both would appear to be within reg.5(1).

Para. (2)

In *CJSA/3979/1999* the Commissioner explores the possibility of a claimant's **2.105** being able to withdraw a claim where there has been an award of benefit for an indefinite period. The Commissioner concludes,

> "If the original claim is for an indefinite period, so that the award is for an indefinite period, I do not think that the claim can later be converted into one for a definite period. The original claim cannot be unmade or amended. . . . However, it does not necessarily follow from that that a claim cannot be withdraw for a prospective period even though there is a current indefinite award. In a sense there has already been an adjudication on that period through the making of an indefinite award, but only in a fairly technical sense. If a claimant unequivocally says that he wishes his claim to stop at the current date or that he wishes to withdraw his claim for the future, why should that not be given effect? Some regard should be had for the autonomy of claimants. . . . I conclude that even where there is a current award of benefit, a claimant may with-draw a claim on a prospective basis." (para.24.)

But the Commissioner goes on to indicate that the termination of the indefinite award should be the subject of adjudication in order to ensure that the withdrawal is properly made and not, for example, the result of coercion or improper inducement. In the case before the Commissioner, one issue raised was whether the claimant had been coerced into withdrawing a claim to JSA by threats to investigate whether he had been working for certain periods prior to those in respect of which he was interviewed.

R(H) 2/06 concerned the interpretation of a provision of the Housing Benefit (General) Regulations 1987 (SI 1987/1971) in identical terms to reg.5(2). The Commissioner ruled that, although in some cases it may be possible to make a fresh claim which can be backdated to cover the period of a claim which has been withdrawn, the consequence of a genuine and effective withdrawal is, in the absence of any provision permitting reinstatement, to prevent any award from being made on the claim after the withdrawal took effect. Although different considerations might apply to claimants who are not fully able to manage their affairs or to understand the consequences of their actions, claimants who are not subject to any such disability would normally have to establish that the withdrawal of the claim was induced by some factor such as threatening or overbearing behaviour, deception or similar improper conduct in order to show that the notice of withdrawal of a claim was not a genuine expression of the claimant's intention at the time when the notice was given.

Date of claim

2.106

6.—(1) [³Subject to the following provisions of this regulation] [²⁹ or regulation 6A (claims by persons subject to work-focused interviews)] the date on which a claim is made shall be—

  (a) in the case of a claim which meets the requirements of regulation 4(1), the date on which it is received in an appropriate office;

[¹²(aa) in the case of a claim for—

    [³⁰ . . .]

    [³⁰ . . .]

    jobseeker's allowance if first notification is received before 6th October 1997; or

    income support if first notification is received before 6th October 1997;

which meets the requirements of regulation 4(1) and which is received in an appropriate office within one month of first notification in accordance with regulation 4(5), whichever is the later of—

    (i) the date on which that notification is received; and

    (ii) the first date on which that claim could have been made in accordance with these Regulations;]

  (b) in the case of a claim which does not meet the requirements of regulation 4(1) but which is treated, under regulation 4(7) as having been duly made, the date on which the claim was received in an appropriate office in the first instance.

[²³ (c) in the case of a claim made by telephone in accordance with [³⁴ regulation 4(11) or (11A), the date of that telephone call;

  (d) in the case of a claim made by telephone which is defective but which is treated, under regulation 4(14) as having been duly made, the date of that telephone call.]

[²¹ (1ZA) In the case of a claim made in accordance with regulation 4(6B)—

  (a) paragraph (1) shall apply in relation to a claim received at an office specified in that regulation as it applies in relation to a claim received at an appropriate office; and

  (b) paragraph (1A) shall apply in relation to an office specified in that regulation as it applies in relation to an appropriate office.]

[¹³ (1A) In the case of claim for income support—

(a) subject to the following sub-paragraphs, the date on which a claim is made shall be the date on which a properly completed claim is received in an appropriate office or the first day in respect of which the claim is made if later;

(b) where a properly completed claim is received in an appropriate office within one month of first notification of intention to make that claim, the date of claim shall be the date on which that notification is deemed to be made or the first day in respect of which the claim is made if later;

(c) a notification of intention to make a claim will be deemed to be made on the date when an appropriate office receives—

(i) a notification in accordance with regulation 4(5); or

(ii) a defective claim.]

[18a (1B) Subject to paragraph (1C), in the case of a claim for working families' tax credit or disabled person's tax credit which meets the requirements of regulation 4(1) and which is received in an appropriate office within one month of first notification in accordance with regulation 4(5)—

(a) where the claimant is entitled to that credit on the date on which that notification is received ("the notification date") and the first day of the period in respect of which that claim is made is on or before the notification date, the date on which a claim is made shall be the notification date; or

(b) where the claimant is not entitled to that credit on the notification date but becomes so entitled before the date on which the claim is received, the date on which the claim is received, the date on which a claim is made shall be—

(i) the date on which the claimant becomes so entitled, or

(ii) if later, the first day of the period in respect of which the claim is made provided that it is not later than the date on which the claim is received.

(1C) Paragraph (1B) shall not apply in the case of a claim which is received in an appropriate office—

(a) in the case of working families' tax credit, within the period specified opposite that credit at paragraphs (a) or (aa) in column (2) of Schedule 4(a); or

(b) in the case of disabled person's tax credit, within the period specified opposite that credit in paragraphs (a) or (b) in column (2) of Schedule 4.]

[18b unless the previous award of working families' tax credit or disabled person's tax credit was terminated by virtue of regulation 49ZA of the Family Credit (General) Regulations 1987 or regulation 54A of the Disability Working Allowance (General) Regulations 1991.]

[27 (1D) Subject to paragraph (1E) and without prejudice to the generality of paragraph (1), where a properly completed claim for incapacity benefit is received in an appropriate office within one month of the claimant first notifying such an office, by whatever means, of his intention to make that claim, the date of claim shall be the date on which that notification is made or the first day in respect of which the claim is made if later.

(1E) For the purposes of paragraph (1D), a person [32 . . .] may notify his intention and may send or deliver his claim to an office specified in regulation 4(6B)]

[33 (1F) For employment and support allowance—

  (a) in the case of a telephone claim made in accordance with regulation 4G(1) the date of claim is the date of the telephone call or the first day in respect of which the claim is made, if later;

  (b) subject to sub-paragraph (c) in the case of a written claim which meets the requirements of regulation 4H(2) the date of claim is the date the claim form was received in an appropriate office or office mentioned in regulation 4H(3) or the first day in respect of which the claim is made, if later;

  (c) where the claimant notifies the Secretary of State (by whatever means) of his intention of making a claim and, within one month or such longer period as the Secretary of State considers reasonable of first notification, a claim mentioned in sub-paragraph (b) is received, in an office mentioned in that sub-paragraph, the date of claim is the date notification was made or the first day in respect of which the claim is made, if later.]

(2) [¹. . .]

[¹(3) In the case of a claim for income support, [¹⁴ working families' tax credit, disabled person's tax credit] [¹²or jobseeker's allowance][⁵. . .], where the time for claiming is extended under regulation 19 the claim shall be treated as made on the first day of the period in respect of which the claim is, by reason of the operation of that regulation, timeously made.

(4) Paragraph (3) shall not apply when the time for claiming income support [¹⁴ working families' tax credit, disabled person's tax credit] or jobseeker's allowance]] has been extended under regulation 19 and the failure to claim within the prescribed time for the purposes of that regulation is for the reason only that the claim has been sent by post.]

[¹⁸ (4ZA) Where a member of a joint-claim couple notifies the employment officer (by whatever means) that he wishes to claim a jobseeker's allowance jointly with the other member of that couple, the claim shall be treated as made on the relevant date specified in accordance with paragraphs (4ZB) to (4ZD).

(4ZB) Where each member of a joint-claim couple is required to attend under regulation 4(6)(a)—

  (a) if each member subsequently attends for the purpose of jointly claiming a jobseeker's allowance at the time and place specified by the employment officer and complies with the requirements of paragraph (4AA)(a), the claim shall be treated as made on whichever is the later of the first notification of intention to make that claim and the first day in respect of which the claim is made;

  (b) if, without good cause, either member fails to attend for the purpose of jointly claiming a jobseeker's allowance at either the time or the place so specified or does not comply with the requirements of paragraph (4AA)(a), the claim shall be treated as made on the first day on which a member of the couple attends at the specified place and complies with the requirements of paragraph (4AA)(a).

(4ZC) Where only one member of the couple is required to attend under regulation 4(6)(a)—

  (a) subject to the following sub-paragraphs, the date on which the claim is made shall be the date on which a properly completed claim is received in an appropriate office or the first day in respect of which the claim is made, if later, provided that the member of the couple who is required to attend under regulation 4(6)(a) does so attend;

(b) where a properly completed form is received in an appropriate office within one month of first notification of intention to make that claim, the date of claim shall be the date of that notification;

(c) if, without good cause, the member of the couple who is required to attend under regulation 4(6)(a) fails to attend for the purpose of making a claim at either the time or place so specified or does not comply with the requirements of paragraph (4AA), the claim shall be treated as made on the first day on which that member does attend at that place and does provide a properly completed claim.

(4ZD) Where, as at the day on which a member of a joint-claim couple ("the first member") notifies the employment officer in accordance with paragraph (4ZA), the other member of that couple is temporarily absent from Great Britain in the circumstances specified in regulation 50(6B) of the Jobseeker's Allowance Regulations, the date on which the claim is made shall be the relevant date specified in paragraph (4ZB) or (4ZC) but nothing in this paragraph shall treat the claim as having been made on a day which is more than three months after the day on which the first member notified the employment officer in accordance with paragraph (4ZA).

[[13](4A) Where a person [[18]who is not a member of a joint-claim couple] notifies the Secretary of State (by whatever means) that he wishes to claim a jobseeker's allowance—

(a) if he is required to attend under regulation 4(6)(a)—

(i) if he subsequently attends for the purpose of making a claim for that benefit at the time and place specified by the Secretary of State and complies with the requirements of paragraph (4AA) [[18](b)], the claim shall be treated as made on whichever is the later of first notification of intention to make that claim and the first day in respect of which the claim is made;

(ii) if, without good cause, he fails to attend for the purpose of making a claim for that benefit at either the time or place so specified, or does not comply with the requirements of paragraph (4AA) [[18](b)], the claim shall be treated as made on the first day on which he does attend at that place and does provide a properly completed claim;

(b) if under regulation 4(6)(a) the Secretary of State directs that he is not required to attend—

(i) subject to the following sub-paragraph, the date on which the claim is made shall be the date on which a properly completed claim is received in an appropriate office or the first day in respect of which the claim is made if later;

(ii) where a properly completed claim is received in an appropriate office within one month of first notification of intention to make that claim, the date of claim shall be the date of that notification.

[[18] (4AA) Unless the Secretary of State otherwise directs, a properly completed claim for shall be provided—

(a) in a case to which paragraph (4ZA) applies, at or before the time when a member of the joint-claim couple is first required to attend for the purpose of making a claim for a jobseeker's allowance;

(b) in any other case, at or before the time when the person making the claim for a jobseeker's allowance is required to attend for the purpose of making a claim.]

(4AB) The Secretary of State may direct that the time for providing a properly completed claim may be extended to a date no later than the date one month after the date of first notification of intention to make that claim.]

(4B) Where a person's entitlement to a jobseeker's allowance has ceased in any of the circumstances specified in regulation 25(1)(a), (b) or (c) of the Jobseeker's Allowance Regulations (entitlement ceasing on a failure to comply) and—

    (a) where he had normally been required to attend in person, he shows that the failure to comply which caused the cessation of his previous entitlement was due to any of the circumstances mentioned in regulation 30(c) or (d) of those Regulations, and no later than the day immediately following the date when those circumstances cease to apply he makes a further claim for jobseeker's allowance; or

    (b) where he had not normally been required to attend in person, he shows that he did not receive the notice to attend and he immediately makes a further claim for jobseeker's allowance,

that further claim shall be treated as having been made on the day following that cessation of entitlement.

(4C) Where a person's entitlement to a jobseeker's allowance ceases in the circumstances specified in regulation 25(1)(b) of the Jobseeker's Allowance Regulations (failure to attend at time specified) and that person makes a further claim for that allowance on the day on which he failed to attend at the time specified, that claim shall be treated as having been made on the following day.]

[[11](4D) In the case of a claim for income support to which regulation 4(3C) (claim by refugee) refers, the claim shall be treated as made [[15] on the date on which his claim for asylum was recorded by the Secretary of State as having been made.]

[[2](5) Where a person submits a claim for attendance allowance [[6]or disability living allowance or a request under paragraph (8)] by post and the arrival of that [[6]claim or request] at an appropriate office is delayed by postal disruption caused by industrial action, whether within the postal service or elsewhere, the [[6]claim or request] shall be treated as received on the day on which it would have been received if it had been delivered in the ordinary course of post.]

[[3](6) Where—

    (a) on or after 9th April 1990 a person satisfies the capital condition in section 22(6) of the Social Security Act 1986 [SSCBA, s.134(1)] for income support and he would not have satisfied that condition had the amount prescribed under regulation 45 of the Income Support (General) Regulation 1987 been £6,000; and

    (b) a claim for that benefit is received from him in an appropriate office not later than 27th May 1990;

the claim shall be treated as made on the date [[4]not later than 5th December 1990] determined in accordance with paragraph (7).

(7) For the purpose of paragraph (6), where—

    (a) the claimant satisfies the other conditions of entitlement to income support on the date on which he satisfies the capital condition, the date shall be the date on which he satisfies that condition;

    (b) the claimant does not satisfy the other conditions of entitlement to income support on the date on which he satisfies the capital condition, the date shall be the date on which he satisfies the conditions of entitlement to that benefit.]

[⁶(8) [⁸Subject to paragraph (8A [²¹ and (8B)])],] where—

(a) a request is received in an appropriate office for a claim form for disability living allowance or attendance allowance; and

(b) in response to the request a claim form for disability living allowance or attendance is issued from an appropriate office; and

(c) within the time specified the claim form properly completed is received in an appropriate office,

the date on which the claim is made shall be the date on which the request was received in the appropriate office.

[⁸(8A) Where, in a case which would otherwise fall within paragraph (8), it is not possible to determine the date when the request for a claim form was received in an appropriate office because of a failure to record that date, the claim shall be treated as having been made on the date 6 weeks before the date on which the properly completed claim form is received in an appropriate office.]

[²¹ (8B) In the case of a claim for disability living allowance or attendance allowance made in accordance with regulation 4(6B), paragraphs (8) and (8A) shall apply in relation to an office specified in that regulation as they apply in relation to an appropriate office.]

(9) [⁹In paragraph (8) and (8A)]—

"a claim form" means a form approved by the Secretary of State under regulation 4(1); "properly completed" has the meaning assigned by regulation 4(8);

"the time specified" means 6 weeks from the date on which the request was received or such longer period as the Secretary of State may consider reasonable.]

[⁷(10) Where a person starts a job on a Monday or Tuesday in any week and he makes a claim for [¹⁴ disabled person's tax credit] in that week the claim shall be treated as made on the Tuesday of that week.

(11) [¹⁴ . . .]

[¹² (12) [¹⁴ . . .] Where a person has claimed [¹⁴ disabled person's tax credit] and that claim ("the original claim") has been refused, and a further claim is made in the circumstances specified in paragraph (13), that further claim shall be treated as made—

(a) on the date of the original claim; or

(b) on the first date in respect of which the qualifying benefit was payable, whichever is the later.

(13) The circumstances referred to in paragraph (12) are that—

(a) the original claim was refused on the ground that the claimant did not qualify under section 129(2) of the Contributions and Benefits Act;

(b) at the date of the original claim the claimant had made a claim for a qualifying benefit and that claim had not been determined;

(c) after the original claim had been determined, the claim for the qualifying benefit was determined in the claimant's favour; and

(d) the further claim for [¹⁴ disabled person's tax credit] was made within three months of the date that the claim for the qualifying benefit was determined.

(14) [¹⁴ . . .]

(15) In paragraphs (12) and (13) "qualifying benefit" means any of the benefits referred to in section 129(2) of the Contributions and Benefits Act.

[31 (15A) Paragraphs (16) to (34) shall not apply in any case where it would be advantageous to the claimant to apply the provisions of regulation 19 (time for claiming benefit.)]

[16 (16) Where a person has claimed a relevant benefit and that claim ("the original claim") has been refused in the circumstances specified in paragraph (17), and a further claim is made in the additional circumstances specified in paragraph (18), that further claim shall be treated as made—

    (a) on the date of the original claim; or

    (b) on the first date in respect of which the qualifying benefit was payable,

whichever is the later.

(17) The circumstances referred to in paragraph (16) are that the ground for refusal was—

    (a) in the case of severe disablement allowance, that the claimant's disablement was less than 80 per cent;

    (b) [27 . . .];

    (c) in any case, that the claimant [19, a member of his family or the disabled person] had not been awarded a qualifying benefit.

(18) The additional circumstances referred to in paragraph (16) are that—

[19(a) a claim for the qualifying benefit was made not later than 10 working days after the date of the original claim and the claim for the qualifying benefit had not been decided;

    (b) after the original claim had been decided the claim for the qualifying benefit had been decided in favour of the claimant, a member or his family or the disabled person; and]

    (c) the further claim was made within three months of the date on which the claim for the qualifying benefit was decided.

(19) Where a person has been awarded a relevant benefit and that award ("the [31 "original award"]) has been terminated or reduced or payment under that award ceases in the circumstances] specified in paragraph (20), and a further claim is made in the additional circumstances specified in paragraph (21), that further claim shall be treated as made—

    (a) on the date of termination of the original award; or

    (b) on the first date in respect of which the qualifying benefit [19 is [28 awarded or] [31 re-awarded or becomes payable again]],

whichever is the later.

[28 (20) The circumstances referred to in paragraph (19) are—

    (a) that the award of the qualifying benefit has itself been terminated or reduced by means of a revision, supersession, appeal or termination of an award for a fixed period in such a way as to affect the original award; [31 . . .]

    (b) at the date the original award was terminated the claimant's claim for a qualifying benefit had not been decided] [31 or]

[31 (c) that the qualifying benefit has ceased to be payable in accordance with—

        (i) regulation 6(1) of the Social Security (Attendance Allowance) Regulations 1991 or regulation 8(1) of the Social Security (Disability Living Allowance) Regulations 1991 because the claimant is undergoing treatment as an in-patient in a hospital or similar institution, or

        (ii) regulation 7 of the Social Security (Attendance Allowance)

Regulations 1991 or regulation 9 of the Social Security (Disability Living Allowance) Regulations 1991 because the claimant is resident in certain accommodation other than a hospital.]

(21) [³¹ Subject to paragraph (21A), the additional] referred to in paragraph (19) are that—

(a) after the original award has been terminated the claim for the qualifying benefit is decided in [¹⁹ favour of the claimant, a member of his family or the disabled person]; [³¹ or]

[³¹ (b) the qualifying benefit is re-awarded following revision, supersession or appeal; or

(c) the qualifying benefit is re-awarded on a renewal claim when an award for a fixed period expires; or

(d) the cessation of payment ends when the claimant leaves the hospital or similar institution or accommodation referred to in paragraph (20) (c); and

the further claim [³⁴ for a relevant benefit] referred to in paragraph (19), is made within three months of the date [³⁴ of the decision to award, re-award, or recommence payment of the qualifying benefit on the grounds that sub-paragraph (a), (b), (c) or (d) was satisfied.]]

[³¹ (21A) Paragraph (21) applies whether the benefit is re-awarded when the further claim is decided or following a revision of, or an appeal against, such a decision.]

(22) In paragraphs (16) to (21) [¹⁹ . . .] [²⁷, (30) and (33)]—

"relevant benefit" means any of the following, namely—

(a) benefits under Parts II to V of the Contributions and Benefits Act except incapacity benefit;

(b) income support;

(c) a jobseeker's allowance;

(d) a social fund payment mentioned in section 138(1)(a) or (2) of the Contributions and Benefits Act;

(e) child benefit;

[²⁴ (f) state pension credit]

"qualifying benefit" means—

(a) in relation to severe disablement allowance, the highest rate of the care component of disability living allowance;

(b) in relation to invalid care allowance, any benefit referred to in section 70(2) of the Contributions and Benefits Act;

(c) in relation to a social fund payment in respect of maternity or funeral expenses, any benefit referred to in regulation 5(1)(a) or 7(1)(a) of the Social Fund Maternity and Funeral Expenses (General) Regulations 1987;

(d) any other relevant benefit which [¹⁹, when it is awarded or reawarded,] has the effect of making another relevant benefit payable or payable at an increased rate;

"the disabled person" means the person for whom the invalid care allowanced claimant is caring in accordance with section 70(1)(a) of the Contributions and Benefits Act.

[¹⁹ "family" has the same meaning as in section 137(1) of the Contributions and Benefits Act or, as the case may be, section 35(1) of the Jobseekers Act [²⁴, and in the case of state pension credit "member of his family" means the other member of a couple where the claimant is a member of a [²⁵ . . .] couple].]

(23) Where a person has ceased to be entitled to incapacity benefit, and a further claim for that benefit is made in the circumstances specified in paragraph (24), that further claim shall be treated as made—

(a) on the date on which entitlement to incapacity benefit ceased; or

(b) on the first date in respect of which the qualifying benefit was payable,

whichever is the later.

(24) The circumstances referred to in paragraph (23) are that—

(a) entitlement to incapacity benefit ceased on the ground that the claimant was not incapable of work;

(b) at the date that entitlement ceased the claimant had made a claim for a qualifying benefit and that claim had not been decided;

(c) after entitlement had ceased, the claim for the qualifying benefit was decided in the claimant's favour; and

(d) the further claim for incapacity benefit was made within three months of the date on which the claim for the qualifying benefit was decided.

(25) In paragraphs (23) and (24) "qualifying benefit" means any of the payments referred to in regulation 10(2)(a) of the Social Security (Incapacity for Work) (General) Regulations 1995.

(26) In paragraph [27 (18)(a) and (c), 21(a), (24) and (30) and in paragraph (18)(b)] where the word appears for the second time, "decided" includes the making of a decision following a revision, supersession or an appeal, whether by the Secretary of State, [35 the First-tier Tribunal, the Upper Tribunal] or the court.]

(27) Where a claim is made for [14 working families' tax credit or disabled person's tax credit], and—

(a) the claimant had previously made a claim for income support or jobseeker's allowance ("the original claim");

(b) the original claim was refused on the ground that the claimant or his partner was in remunerative work; and

(c) the claim for [14 working families' tax credit or disabled person's tax credit] was made within 14 days of the date that the original claim was determined,

that claim shall be treated as made on the date of the original claim, or, if the claimant so requests, on a later date specified by the claimant.

(28) Where a claim is made for income support or jobseeker's allowance, and—

(a) the claimant had previously made a claim for [20 working tax credit] ("the original claim");

(b) the original claim was refused on the ground that the claimant or his partner was not in remunerative work [20 for the purposes of that tax credit]; and

(c) the claim for income support or jobseeker's allowance was made within 14 days of the date that the original claim was determined,

that claim shall be treated as made on the date of the original claim, or, if the claimant so requests, on a later date specified by the claimant.]

(29) In the case of a claim for an increase of severe disablement allowance or of invalid care allowance in respect of a child or adult dependant, [17 paragraph (16) and (19)] shall apply to the claim as if it were a claim for severe disablement allowance or, as the case may be, invalid care allowance.

[19 (30) Where—

(a) a claimant was awarded income support or income-based jobseeker's allowance ("the original award");

(b) the original award was termination and [[31] . . .], the claimant, a member of his family or the disabled person claimed a qualifying benefit; and

(c) the claimant makes a further claim for income support or income-based jobseeker's allowance within 3 months of the date on which the claim for the qualifying benefit was decided,

the further claim shall be treated as made on the date of termination of the original award or the first date in respect of which the qualifying benefit is awarded, whichever is the later.]

[[22] (31) Subject to paragraph (32), where—

(a) a person—
  (i) has attained pensionable age, but for the time being makes no claim for a Category A retirement pension; or
  (ii) has attained pensionable age and has a spouse [[26] or civil partner] who has attained pensionable age, but for the time being makes no claim for a Category B retirement pension;

(b) in accordance with regulation 50A of the Social Security (Contributions) Regulations 2001, (Class 3 contributions: tax years 1996–97 to 2001–02) the Commissioners of Inland Revenue subsequently accept Class 3 contributions paid after the due date by the person or, in the case of a Category B retirement pension, the spouse [[26] or civil partner];

(c) in accordance with regulation 6A of the Social Security (Crediting and Treatment of Contributions, and National Insurance Numbers) Regulations 2001 the contributions are treated as paid on a date earlier than the date on which they were paid; and

(d) the person claims a Category A or, as the case may be, a Category B retirement pension,

the claim shall be treated as made on—
  (i) 1st October 1998; or
  (ii) the date on which the person attained pensionable age in the case of a Category A retirement pension, or, in the case of a Category B retirement pension, the date on which the person's spouse [[26] or civil partner] attained pensionable age,
whichever is later.

(32) Paragraph (31) shall not apply where—

(a) the person's entitlement to a Category A or B retirement pension has been deferred by virtue of section 55(2)(a) of the Contributions and Benefits Act (increase of retirement pension where entitlement is deferred); or

(b) the person's nominal entitlement to a Category A or B retirement pension is deferred in pursuance of section 36(4) and (7) of the National Insurance Act 1965 (increase of graduated retirement benefit where entitlement is deferred),

nor where sub-paragraph (a) and (b) both apply.]

[[27] (33) [[31] Subject to paragraph 34, where] a person makes a claim for a carer's allowance [[34] or for an increase in carer's allowance in respect of an adult or child dependent] within 3 months of a decision made—

(a) on a claim;

(b) on revision or supersession; or

(c) on appeal whether by [[35] the First-tier Tribunal, the Upper Tribunal] or the court,

awarding a qualifying benefit to the disabled person, the date of claim [[34] shall be treated as the first day of the benefit week in which the award of the qualifying benefit became payable.]

[[31]. . . .]

[[34] (34) Where the decision awarding a qualifying benefit is made in respect of a renewal claim where a fixed period award of that benefit has expired, or is due to expire, the date of claim for carer's allowance shall be treated as the first day of the benefit week in which the renewal award of qualifying benefit became payable.]

AMENDMENTS

1. The Social Security (Claims and Payments) Amendment Regulations 1988 (SI 1988/522), reg.2 (April 11, 1988).

2. The Social Security (Medical Evidence, Claims and Payments) Amendment Regulations 1989 (SI 1989/1686), reg.4 (October 9, 1989).

3. The Social Security (Claims and Payments) Amendment Regulations 1990 (SI 1990/725), reg.2 (April 9, 1990).

4. The Social Security (Miscellaneous Provisions) Amendment Regulations 1990 (SI 1990/2208), reg.9 (December 5, 1990).

5. The Social Security (Miscellaneous Provisions) Amendment Regulations 1991 (SI 1991/2284), reg.6 (November 1, 1991).

6. The Social Security (Claims and Payments) Amendment Regulations 1991 (SI 1991/2741), reg.4 (February 3, 1992).

7. The Social Security (Claims and Payments) Amendment Regulations 1991 (SI 1991/2741), reg.4 (March 10, 1992).

8. The Social Security (Claims and Payments) Amendment (No.3) Regulations 1993 (SI 1993/2113), reg.3 (September 27, 1993).

9. The Social Security (Claims and Payments) Amendment Regulations 1994 (SI 1994/2319), reg.2 (October 3, 1994).

10. The Social Security (Claims and Payments) (Jobseeker's Allowance Consequential Amendments) Regulations 1996 (SI 1996/1460), reg.2(5) (October 7, 1996).

11. The Income Support and Social Security (Claims and Payments) (Miscellaneous Amendments) Regulations 1996 (SI 1996/2431), reg.7(c) (October 15, 1996).

12. The Social Security (Miscellaneous Amendments) (No.2) Regulations 1997 (SI 1997/793), reg.3 (April 7, 1997).

13. The Social Security (Miscellaneous Amendments) (No.2) Regulations 1997 (SI 1997/793), reg.3(3) and (5) (October 6, 1997).

14. The Tax Credits (Claims and Payments) (Amendment) Regulations 1999 (SI 1999/2572), reg.5 (October 5, 1999).

15. The Social Security (Immigration and Asylum) Consequential Amendments Regulations 2000 (SI 2000/636), reg.5 (April 3, 2000).

16. The Social Security and Child Support (Miscellaneous Amendments) Regulations 2000 (SI 2000/1596), reg.3(a) (June 19, 2000).

17. The Social Security and Child Support (Miscellaneous Amendments) Regulations 2000 (SI 2000/1596), reg.3(b) (June 19, 2000).

18. The Social Security (Joint Claims: Consequential Amendments) Regulations 2000 (SI 2000/1982), reg.2(4) (March 19, 2001).

18a. The Tax Credits (Claims and Payments) (Amendment) Regulations 2001 (SI 2001/567) (April 10, 2001)

18b. The Tax Credits (Claims and Payments) Amendment (No.3) Regulations 2001 (SI 2001/892) (April 10, 2001)

19. The Social Security (Claims and Payments and Miscellaneous Amendments) Regulations 2002 (SI 2002/428), reg.2 (April 2, 2002).

20. The Social Security (Working Tax Credit and Child Tax Credit) (Consequential Amendments) Regulations 2003 (SI 2003/455), Sch.4 (April 1, 2003).

21. The Social Security (Claims and Payments and Miscellaneous Amendments) Regulations 2003 (SI 2003/1632), reg.2 (July 21, 2003).

22. Social Security (Retirement Pensions) Amendment Regulations 2004 (SI 2004/2283), reg.2 (September 27, 2004).

23. The Social Security (Claims and Payments and Payments on account, Overpayments and Recovery) Amendment Regulations 2005 (SI 2005/34), reg.2 (May 2, 2005).

24. The Social Security, Child Support and Tax Credits (Miscellaneous Amendments) Regulations 2005 (SI 2005/337), reg.7 (March 19, 2005).

25. The Social Security (Civil Partnerships) (Consequential Amendments) Regulations 2005 (SI 2005/2878) (December 5, 2005).

26. The Civil Partnership (Pensions, Social Security and Child Support) (Consequential etc. Provisions) Order 2005 (SI 2005/2877) (December 5, 2005).

27. The Social Security (Miscellaneous Amendments) (No.2) Regulations 2006 (SI 2006/832) (April 10, 2006).

28. The Social Security (Miscellaneous Amendments) (No.3) Regulations 2006 (SI 2006/2377) (October 2, 2006).

29. The Social Security (Work-focused Interviews) Regulations 2000 (SI 2000/897) (April 3, 2000).

30. The Tax Credits (Claims and Payments) (Amendment) Regulations 2001 (SI 2001/567) (April 10, 2001).

31. The Social Security (Miscellaneous Amendments) (No.4) Regulations 2007 (SI 2007/2470) (September 24, 2007).

32. The Social Security (Claims and Information) Regulations 2007 (SI 2007/2911) (October 31, 2007).

33. The Employment and Support Allowance (Consequential Provisions) (No.2) Regulations 2008 (SI 2008/1554), reg.13 (October 27, 2008).

34. The Social Security (Miscellaneous Amendments) (No.5) Regulations 2008 (SI 2008/2667), reg.2 (October 30, 2008).

35. The Tribunals, Courts and Enforcement Act 2007 (Transitional and Consequential Provisions) Order 2008 (SI 2008/2683), reg.43 (November 3, 2008).

DEFINITIONS

"appropriate office"—see reg.2(1).
"claim for asylum"—*ibid.*
"claim for benefit"—*ibid.*
"jobseeker's allowance"—*ibid.*

GENERAL NOTE

Introduction

Claims are generally not made until received in any appropriate office.   2.107

R(SB)8/89 concerns the date of a claim for a single payment of supplementary benefit, but, since the date of claims for most benefits is also the date of receipt in the office of the Department, the decision is directly in point in relation to these benefits. The Commissioner's comments are worth quoting at length since the determination of the date of claim is often an issue arising on appeals:

"In order for the claim to be made it is not alone necessary for the claimant to despatch the form but it is also necessary for the office of the Department to receive it. In my judgment if the office of the Department puts it out of its power to receive the claim by closing its offices and also arranging with the Post Office not to deliver mail on the days upon which the office is closed, then it put it out of its power to receive the claim. It may be that the claim can be received by the office of the Department whether such office is open or closed, but it cannot be received in circumstances where the Department arranges that mail should not be delivered. In her submission to me the adjudication officer now concerned refers to no deliveries being made by the Post Office on days upon which the office of the Department are [*sic*] closed. It will be a question of fact for the new tribunal to find whether such is by arrangement between the Department and Post Office and then to consider whether the Department has put it out of its power to receive claims on a Saturday. If they come to the conclusion that it did and find that in the normal course of delivery on that day then such is the date of claim." (para.7.)

Where claim packs are sent out for disability living allowance and attendance allowance, it is not the practice of the Department (in contrast to the position where enquiries are made about other benefits) to follow the matter up if no completed claim is returned. The Claims and Payments Regulations clearly do not require such action, but it is understood that a number of welfare rights units are concerned that the variation in practice may operate to the disadvantage of claimants. It is, of course, the receipt of a completed claim (or at least some document which can be regarded as a claim under reg.4) which constitutes a claim under the regulations.

Establishing whether a person has claimed, and, if so, the date of a claim can arise with some frequency before tribunals. In *CP/4104/2004* the Commissioner reminds tribunals of the need to check on both departmental policies of destruction of documents and available computer records in assessing whether a claimant has made a claim. It may be necessary to receive evidence as to what a computer printout actually means. The core advice is not to accept unquestioningly assertions by the Department that it has no record of a claim or enquiry. In the case before the Commissioner that assertion was made to the tribunal, but on further enquiry turned out not to be the correct position.

Regulation 6 is one of the longest social security regulations, and is full of twists and turns. Great care should be taken in reading the regulation in any case raising questions concerning the date of claim.

Para. (1)

2.108   A properly completed claim on the proper form is made on the date that it is received in a benefit office.

There are now many complications around this basic rule following the introduction of JSA and the severe restriction on the backdating of claims under reg.19 from April 1997.

R(SB) 8/89 holds that if the Department puts it out of its power to receive a claim, as by closing its office and arranging with the Post Office not to deliver mail, e.g. on a Saturday, then if that day is the day on which the claim would have been delivered, it is the date of claim. It can be said that by making the arrangement with the Post Office the Department constitute the Post Office bailees of the mail (see *Hodgson v Armstrong* [1967] Q.B. 299 and *Lang v Devon General Ltd* [1987] I.C.R. 4). The Commissioner does not deal expressly with the situation where the office is closed, but there is no arrangement about the mail, e.g. if an office is closed on a Saturday and the Saturday and Monday mail is all stamped with the Monday date in the office. Here, principle would suggest that if it can be shown that in the normal course of the post delivery would have been on the Saturday, then the Saturday is the date of receipt and the date of claim. If a claimant proves a delivery by hand when the office is closed, the date of delivery is the date of receipt.

Note also *CIS/4901/2002* relating to arrangements between the Department and the Post Office for the handling of mail, which is reported in more detail in the annotations to reg.19.

Levy v Secretary of State for Work and Pensions [2006] EWCA Civ 890, reported as *R(G) 2/06* considered the applicability to social security claims of the rebuttable presumption in s.7 of the Interpretation Act 1978 that a letter put in the post is delivered to its addressee. The Court of Appeal ruled that reg.6(1) was not ultra vires. The next question was whether s.7 of the Interpretation Act 1978 applied. Dyson LJ (with whom Hallett and Pill LJJ agreed) concluded that the provision has no application in this context. Even if s.7 did apply, its application would appear to be excluded by the words "unless the contrary intention appears" in s.7 of the Interpretation Act. The Court of Appeal concludes that "It is plain that regulation 6(1) requires that the claim be received in fact and not merely that it be sent." (para. 32 of the judgment). It follows that *CIS/306/2003* and *CG/2973/2004* correctly analyse the legal position and that *CSIS/48/1992* and *CIS/759/1992* are wrong in so far as they suggest otherwise.

Para. (1A)

2.109

This provides that the date of claim for an income support claim will be the date a properly completed claim (i.e. one that complies with reg.4(1A)) is received (or the first day claimed for, if later). But if such a claim is received within one month of the date that the person first contacted the Department with a view to making a claim, or a previous defective claim (i.e. one that does not comply with reg.4(1A)), the date of claim will be the date of that initial contact or defective claim (or the first day claimed for, if later). Thus if more than a month elapses before the claimant complies with the requirements of reg.4(1A), the date of claim will be the date of that compliance (unless the rules on backdating apply: see reg.19(4)–(7)). See further the note to reg.4(1A)–(1C).

In *R(IS) 10/06* the Commissioner considers whether there is any priority in the claims covered by reg.6(1A)(c). He concludes:

"16. On further consideration, I now realise that I was wrong to be concerned about the absence of any specified priority between the two heads of reg.6(1A) (c).
17. This only appears puzzling if the heads in that provisions are read in isolation from subparagraph (b). Subparagraph (c) is expressed as a deeming provision. Its function, though, is more akin to a definition. It sets out the circumstances in which a person is tread as notifying an intention to make a claim. If heads (i) and (ii) are read into paragraph (b), it reads:

'where a properly completed claim is received in an appropriate office within one month of first notification of intention to make that clauim, *which may be shown by (i) a notification in accordance with regulation 4(5) or (ii) a defective claim*, the date of claim shall be the date on which that notification is deemed to be made or the first day in respect of which the claim is made if later.'

Set out like that, no issue of priority arises. The claimant is given a choice to rely on one month from the date of notification or from the date of defective claim."

It is worth noting that the view of the Department is that this decision conflicts with *R(IS)14/04* (which, the Department contends, holds that the one-month period runs from the *first* point of contact; that is, the request for the claim form or the submission of the defective claim form), and argues that the *R(IS)14/04* should be followed in preference to *R(IS) 10/06*.

In *R(IS) 3/04* the Commissioner rules that it is not possible for a valid claim to income support to be made where a claimant dies having given notification of intention to make a claim but not having perfected the claim before his death by completing and submitting a claim form. The case concerned a situation in which the claim was completed and submitted by the executor of the claimant's will.

Para. (3)

2.110

For these benefits, if the time for claiming is extended under reg.19, the claim is treated as made at the beginning of the period for which the claim is deemed to be in time. Initial claims for working families tax credit and disabled person's tax credit and claims for income support and JSA have to be made on the first day of the period claimed for (Sch.4, paras 6, 7 and 11).

Para. (4)

2.111   The interaction of this provision with others is far from clear. It does not look as though it can apply directly in a case where the decision maker has extended the time for claiming by up to a month under reg.19(6). If the claim is not actually made (i.e. received: para.(1)) within the extended period, the claim is not timeously made and para.(3) above does not apply anyway. Postal delay is not a circumstance listed in reg.19(5) (replacing the old good cause rule), but may be relevant to the reasonableness of the delay in claiming. See also reg.19(7).

Paras (4A)–(4AB)

2.112   In the case of JSA, if the person attends the Job Centre for the purpose of making a claim when required to do so and provides a properly completed claim (i.e. with all the necessary information: see reg.4(1A) and (9)), the date of claim will be the date the person first contacted the Job Centre (or the first day claimed for, if later) (para.(4)(a)(i) and (4AA)). Note the *discretion* to extend the time for delivery of a properly completed claim form under para.(4AB); unlike income support (and JSA postal signers) the month's allowance to return the fully completed claim form is not automatic. Note also para.(4A)(a)(ii) which provides that if the person fails to comply with these requirements without good cause the date of claim will be the date that he does comply. Thus if the person does have good cause for not so complying, presumably para.(4A)(a)(i) will apply when he does attend and does provide a fully completed claim form (and note the discretion in relation to the claim form under para.(4AB)). For claimants who are not required to attend the Job Centre in person (i.e. who are allowed to apply by post), their claim will be treated as made on the day they first contacted the Job Centre with a view to making a claim (or on the first day claimed for, if later) if a properly completed claim is received within one month, or the date the properly completed claim is received if more than one month has elapsed (para.(4A)(b)). See further the note to reg.4(1A)–(1C)).

In *CG/4060/2005* the Commissioner decided that reg.6(4AB) applied only to claims for a jobseeker's allowance, and so was of no assistance to persons claiming carer's allowance.

Paras (4B) and (4C)

2.113   These paragraphs deal with certain cases where entitlement to JSA has ceased because of a failure to attend the Job Centre or to provide a signed declaration of availability and active search for employment, so that a new claim is necessary.

Para. (4D)

2.114   These are special rules for claims by refugees.

Paras (6) and (7)

2.115   These provisions create a special rule on the increase of the capital limit for income support to £8,000. Where, from April 9, 1990, a claimant has capital of more than £6,000 but not more than £8,000, a claim made before May 28, 1990, can be backdated to the date on which all the conditions of entitlement are satisfied.

Para. (10)

2.116   Where a claimant starts work on a Monday or Tuesday and makes a claim for disability working allowance at any time in that week (i.e. Sunday to Saturday), the claim is treated as made on the Tuesday.

Paras (12)–(15)

2.117   Where a claim for disabled persons tax credit is disallowed on the ground that a qualifying benefit is not payable, although a claim for that benefit has been made, and later the qualifying benefit is awarded, a fresh claim for the tax credit made within three months of the award of the qualifying benefit is to be treated as made on the date of the original claim (or the date from which the qualifying benefit is awarded, if later). This rule is made necessary by the restrictions from April 1997 on the backdating of claims under reg. 19 and on the effect of reviews.

Paras (31) and (32)

These provisions 'get around' the twelve month limitation on back-dating set out   **2.118**
in s. 1(2) of the Administration Act in relation to claims for retirement pension. They enable claimants to go back as far as October 1, 1998 in certain circumstances. The Explanatory Memorandum to the regulations indicates that the intended benefici-aries of the provisions are those who did not receive notice that their contribution records were deficient for the tax years 1996/97 to 2002/02 because the annual Deficiency Notice procedure which identifies such cases and advises customers of the need to consider making voluntary contributions to make good the shortfall did not take place in those years.

Claims by persons subject to work-focused interviews

[¹**6A.**—[² (1) This regulation applies to any person who is required to   **2.119**
take part in a work-focused interview in accordance with regulations made under section 2A(1)(a) of the Social Security Administration Act 1992.]

(2) Subject to the following provisions of this regulation, where a person takes part in a work-focused interview, the date on which the claim is made shall be—

(a) in a case where—
    (i) the claim made by the claimant meets the requirements of regu-lation 4(1), or
    (ii) the claim made by the claimant is for income support and meets the requirements of regulation 4(1A),
the date on which the claim is received in the appropriate office.

(b) in a case where a claim does not meet the requirements of regulation 4(a) but is treated, under regulation 4(7), as having been duly made, the date on which the claim was treated as received in the appropri-ate office in the first instance;

(c) in a case where—
    (i) first notification of intention to claim income support is made to an appropriate office, or
    (ii) a claim for income support is received in an appropriate office which does not meet the requirements of regulation 4(1A),

[⁵ (d) without prejudice to sub-paragraphs (a) and (b), where a properly completed claim for incapacity benefit is received in an appropriate office within one month of the claimant first notifying such an office, by whatever means, of his intention to make that claim, the date of claim shall be the date on which that notification is made or the first day in respect of which the claim is made if later.]

the date of notification of, as the case may be, the date the claim is first received where the properly complete claim form is received within 1 month of notification or the date the claim is first received, or the day on which a properly completed claim form is received where these require-ments are not met.

(3) In a case where a decision is made that a person is regarded as not having made a claim for any benefit because he failed to take part in a

work-focused interview but subsequently claims such a benefit, in applying paragraph (2) to that claim no regard shall be had to any claim regarded as not having been made in consequence of that decision.

(4) Paragraph (2) shall not apply in any case where a decision has been made that the claimant has failed to take part in a work-focused interview.

[⁴ (5) In regulation 4 and this regulation, "work-focused interview" means an interview which [. . .] [is conducted for such purposes connected with employment or training as are specified under section 2A of the Social Security Administration Act 1992.]

AMENDMENTS

1. Regulation inserted by The Social Security (Work-focused Interviews) Regulations 2000 (SI 2000/897) (April 3, 2000).
2. The Social Security (Jobcentre Plus Interviews) Regulations 2001 (SI 2001/3210) (October 22, 2001).
3. Social Security (Jobcentre Plus Interviews) Regulations 2002 (SI 2002/1703), Sch.2, (September 30, 2002).
4. Social Security (Working Neighbourhoods) Regulations 2004 (SI 2004/959), reg.22 (April 26, 2004).
5. The Social Security (Miscellaneous Amendments) (No.2) Regulations 2006 (SI 2006/832) (April 10, 2006).

Evidence and information

2.120   7.—(1) [³Subject to paragraph (7),] every person who makes a claim for benefit shall furnish such certificates, documents, information and evidence in connection with the claim, or any question arising out of it, as may be required by the Secretary of State [⁴ or the Board] and shall do so within one month of being required to do so or such longer period as the Secretary of State [⁵Board] may consider reasonable.

[⁶ (1A) A claimant shall furnish such information and evidence as the Secretary of State may require as to the likelihood of future changes in his circumstances which is needed to determine—

(a) whether a period should be specified as an assessed income period under section 6 of the 2002 Act in relation to any decision; and

(b) if so, the length of the period to be so specified.

(1B) The information and evidence required under paragraph (1A) shall be furnished within 1 month of the Secretary of State notifying the claimant of the requirement, or within such longer period as the Secretary of State considers reasonable in the claimant's case.

(1C) In the case of a claimant making a claim for state pension credit in the advance period, time begins to run for the purposes of paragraphs (1) and (1B) on the day following the end of that period.]

(2) [³Subject to paragraph (7),] where a benefit may be claimed by either of two partners or where entitlement to or the amount of any benefit is or may be affected by the circumstances of a partner, the Secretary of State may require the partner other than the [⁵claimant to do either or both of the following, within one month of being required to do so or such longer period as the Board may consider reasonable—

(a) to certify in writing whether he agrees to the claimant making or, as the case may be, that he confirms the information given about his circumstances;

(b) to furnish such certificates, documents, information and evidence in

connection with the claim, or any question arising out of it, as the Board may require.]
claimant to certify in writing whether he agrees to the claimant making the claim or, as the case may be, that he confirms the information given about his circumstances [⁴working families tax credit or disabled persons tax credit].

(3) In the case of a claim for [⁴working families' tax credit] or [⁴disabled person's tax credit], the employer of the claimant or, as the case may be, of the partner shall [⁴within one month of being required to do so or such longer period as the Board may consider reasonable] furnish such certificates, documents, information and evidence in connection with the claim or any question arising out of it as may be required by the Secretary of State [⁴Board].

[² (4) In the case of a person who is claiming [⁴ disabled person's tax credit, working families' tax credit], [⁶ jobseeker's allowance [⁷ state pension credit or employment and support allowance.] where that person or any partner is aged not less than 60 and is a member of, or a person deriving entitlement to a pension under, a personal pension scheme, or is a party to, or a person deriving entitlement to a pension under, a retirement annuity contract, he shall where the [⁵ Board so require, within one month of being required to do so or such longer period as the Board may consider reasonable] Secretary of State so requires furnish the following information—

(a) the name and address of the pension fund holder;
(b) such other information including any reference or policy number as is needed to enable the personal pension scheme or retirement annuity contract to be identified.

(5) Where the pension fund holder receives from the Secretary of State [⁵Board] a request for details concerning the personal pension scheme or retirement annuity contract relating to a person or any partner to whom paragraph (4) refers, the pension fund holder shall [⁵, within one month of the request or such longer period as the Board may consider reasonable] provide the Secretary of State [⁵Board] with any information to which paragraph (6) refers.

(6) The information to which this paragraph refers is—

(a) where the purchase of an annuity under a personal pension scheme has been deferred, the amount of any income which is being withdrawn from the personal pension scheme;
(b) in the case of—
   (i) a personal pension scheme where income withdrawal is available, the maximum amount of income which may be withdrawn from the scheme; or
   (ii) a personal pension scheme where income withdrawal is not available, or a retirement annuity contract, the maximum amount of income which might be withdrawn from the fund if the fund were held under a personal pension scheme where income withdrawal was available,

calculated by or on behalf of the pension fund holder by means of tables prepared from time to time by the Government Actuary which are appropriate for this purpose.]

[³(7) Paragraphs (1) and (2) do not apply in the case of jobseeker's allowance.]

[⁴(8) Every person providing childcare in respect of which a claimant to whom regulation 46A of the Family Credit (General) Regulations 1987 applies is incurring relevant childcare charges, including a person providing childcare on behalf of a school, local authority, childcare scheme or establishment within paragraph (2)(b), (c) or (d) of that regulation, shall furnish such certificates, documents, information and evidence in connection with the claim made by the claimant, or any question arising out of it, as may required by the Board, and shall do so within one month of being required to do so or such longer period as the Board may consider reasonable.

(9) In paragraph (8) "relevant childcare charges" has the meaning given by regulation 46A(2) of the Family Credit (General) Regulations 1987.]

AMENDMENTS

1. The Social Security (Claims and Payments) Amendment Regulations 1991 (SI 1991/2741), reg.5 (March 10, 1992).

2. Income-related Benefit Schemes and Social Security (Claims and Payments) (Miscellaneous Amendments) Regulations 1995 (SI 1995/2303), reg.10(3) (October 2, 1995).

3. The Social Security (Claims and Payments) (Jobseeker's Allowance Consequential Amendments) Regulations 1996 (SI 1996/1460), reg.2(6) (October 7, 1996).

4. The Tax Credits (Claims and Payments) (Amendment) Regulations 1999 (SI 1999/2572), reg.6 (October 5, 1999).

5. For tax credits purposes only: The Tax Credits (Claims and Payments) (Amendment) Regulations 1999 (SI 1999/2572), reg.6 (October 5, 1999).

6. State Pension Credit (Consequential, Transitional and Miscellaneous) Regulations 2002 (SI 2002/3019), reg.4 (April 7, 2003).

7. The Employment and Support Allowance (Consequential Provisions) (No.2) Regulations 2008 (SI 2008/1554), reg.15 (October 27, 2008).

DEFINITIONS

"benefit"—see reg.2(2).
"claim for benefit"—see reg.2(1).
"jobseeker's allowance"—*ibid.*
"partner"—*ibid.*
"pension fund holder"—*ibid.*
"personal pension scheme"—*ibid.*
"retirement annuity contract"—*ibid.*

GENERAL NOTE

2.121   From time to time, decision makers have suggested that a person is not entitled to benefit because they have failed to furnish the Secretary of State with information within the one month referred to in reg.7(1). *R(IS)4/93* was just such a case. The adjudication officer decided that the claimant was not entitled to income support because the claimant had failed—inter alia to provide sufficient evidence as to the amount of capital held. The tribunal confirmed the adjudication officer's decision and the claimant appealed to the Commissioner.

Deputy Commissioner Mesher (as he then was) concluded that both the adjudication officer and the tribunal had misunderstood the operation of reg.7(1). Drawing on the reasoning of the Court of Appeal in *R. v Secretary of State for Social Services Ex p. Child Poverty Action Group* [1990] 2 Q.B. 540, the Deputy Commissioner explains that reg.7(1) is concerned with the responsibilities of the Secretary of State to collect information so that the Secretary of State can submit a claim to an adjudication officer for determination:

"Once such a submission is made, it is simply irrelevant whether or not the claimant has satisfied the Secretary of State under reg. 7(1) of the Claims and Payments Regulations or whether or not the claimant has furnished sufficient information for the Secretary of State to refer the claim to the adjudication officer. Those matters are entirely for the Secretary of State [see para. 11 of *R(SB) 29/83*]. Once the claim is submitted to him under section 98(1) [now s.20(1) of the Administration Act], the adjudication officer's duty is to take it into consideration and, so far as practicable, dispose of it within 14 days of its submission (Social Security Act 1975, s.99(1)) [now s.21(1) of the Administration Act]. As decided by the Court of Appeal in the passage quoted above, the adjudication officer has the power to make further investigations or call for further evidence before determining the claim. Or he may determine the claim on the evidence currently available, especially if he considers that the claimant has already had a reasonable opportunity of producing the required information or evidence." (para. 13.)

The Deputy Commissioner goes on to advise that adjudication officers and tribunals when presented with a claim for determination (whether initially or on appeal) must focus on the "essential elements of entitlement directly" in the light of the evidence available. Since claimants generally have the burden of showing on the balance of probabilities that they meet the conditions of entitlement, the absence of information from the claimant will often result in a finding against them.

The Deputy Commissioner does not spell out how tribunals should proceed if the absence of information means that the tribunal cannot make any findings of fact. There will be cases where there is insufficient information to find positively some fact which results in there being no entitlement. In these rare cases where a claimant's reluctance to participate defeats the inquisitorial jurisdiction of tribunals, it is open to the tribunal to decide the matter purely on the burden of proof. In such cases the proper approach is for the tribunal:

— to record no findings of fact, or perhaps only those that are proved, *avoiding* the inclusion of reference to those issues on which facts cannot be found

— to record in the decision that the claimant is not entitled to the benefit on the claim made on such and such a day because they have not proved on the balance of probabilities that they meet the conditions of entitlement for the benefit

— to explain fully in the reasons for the decision what the relevant conditions of entitlement are and why the tribunal is unable to make findings of fact on all the material issues.

R(IS) 4/93 has been referred to and disapproved by the Court of Appeal in Northern Ireland in *Kerr v Department for Social Development* [2002] N.I.C.A. 32, Judgment of July 4, 2002. That decision went an appeal to the House of Lords. The decision of the House of Lords in *Kerr v Department for Social Development,* [2004] UKHL 23; [2004] 1 W.L.R. 1372 (appendix to *R1/04(SF)*) was handed down on May 6, 2004. The discussion in the House of Lords broadened from the considerations which had taken place in the courts below. The comments, in particular of Baroness Hale, on the decision-making process are discussed in detail in the annotations to s.3(1) of the Tribunals, Courts and Enforcement Act 2007. The House of Lords dismissed the appeal. In their opinions, no mention is made of *R(IS) 4/93* which had been disapproved in the reasons of the Court of Appeal. Notwithstanding the absence of any comment, its authority must be considerably weakened by the dismissal of the appeal. However, it is suggested that it will still provide some useful guidance in those cases where, despite the best endeavours of the adjudicating authorities to collect all the evidence needed to determine a claim for benefit, they remain short of evidence on key matters. For a discussion of the similar provisions in relation to the adjudication of housing benefit and council tax benefit claims see the decision of the Tribunal of Commissioners in *R(H) 3/05*.

In *CIS/51/2007* and *CIB/52/2007* the Commissioner comments on the relationship between regs 4–6A, and reg.7. The context was a claim which left some uncertainty about the claimant's identity (the national insurance number provided did not correspond to the identity of the claimant) and the correctness of his address (enquiries to the address given had resulted in denials that the claimant had ever lived there). The Commissioner notes that there are requirements for making a claim under the regulations, which are a matter of form and procedure, and that these should be distinguished from "the obvious and universal necessity for any person making such a claim to substantiate it by showing he meets the qualifying conditions for entitlement". This is a matter of fact and evidence (para. 8). The provisions of reg.7(1) apply only to those who have made something that can be identified as a procedurally effective claim. That is determined by applying the rules in reg.4 to 6A. A claim which raises questions about the identity of the claimant may be a claim. Establishing identity is a matter of fact and evidence. If claimants cannot establish these matters, then they have failed to comply with the reasonable evidence requirements, and it will be appropriate to determine that they have not met the conditions of entitlement.

Attendance in person

2.122   **8.**—(1) [[1] ...]

(2) Every person who makes a claim for benefit [[1] (other than a jobseeker's allowance)] shall attend at such office or place and on such days and at such times as the Secretary of State [[2] or the Board] may direct, for the purpose of furnishing certificates, documents, information and evidence under regulation 7, if reasonably so required by the Secretary of State [[2] or the Board].

AMENDMENTS

1. The Social Security (Claims and Payments) (Jobseeker's Allowance Consequential Amendments) Regulations 1996 (SI 1996/1460), reg.2(7) (October 7, 1996).

2. The Tax Credits (Claims and Payments) (Amendment) Regulations 1999 (SI 1999/2572), reg.20 (October 5, 1999).

DEFINITIONS

"benefit"—see reg.2(2).
"claim for benefit"—see reg.2(1).

GENERAL NOTE

2.123   There seems now to be no direct sanction for a failure to comply with reg.8(2) in relation to benefits other than JSA. For JSA obligations, see reg.23 of the Jobseeker's Allowance Regulations.

Interchange with claims for other benefits

2.124   **9.**—(1) Where it appears that a person who has made a claim for benefit specified in column (1) of Part I of Schedule 1 may be entitled to the benefit specified opposite to it in column (2) of that Part, any such claim may be treated by the Secretary of State [[1] or the Board] as a claim alternatively, or in addition, to the benefit specified opposite to it in that column.

(2) Where it appears that a person who has claimed any benefit specified in Part II of Schedule 1 in respect of a child may be entitled to child benefit

in respect of the same child, the Secretary of State may t
natively, or in addition, for the benefit in question as a c
for child benefit.

(3) Where it appears that a person who has claim
respect of a child may be entitled to any benefit spe
Schedule 1 [². . .] in respect of the same child, the Se
treat the claim for child benefit as a claim alternativel
that person for the benefit in question specified in that

(4) Where it appears that a person who has made a cla....
than child benefit is not entitled to it, but that some other person may be
entitled to an increase of benefit in respect of him, the Secretary of State
may treat the claim as if it were a claim by such other person for an increase
of benefit in respect of the claimant.

(5) Where it appears that a person who has made a claim for an increase
of benefit other than child benefit in respect of a child or adult dependant
is not entitled to it but that some other person may be entitled to such an
increase of benefit in respect of that child or adult dependant, the Secretary
of State may treat the claim as if it were a claim by that other person for
such an increase.

(6) Where it appears that a person who has made a claim for a guardian's
allowance in respect of any child is not entitled to it, but that the claimant
or the wife or husband of the claimant, may be entitled to an increase of
benefit for that child, the Secretary of State may treat the claim as if it
were a claim by the claimant or the wife or husband of the claimant for an
increase of benefit for that child.

[³ (7) In determining whether he [¹ or they] should treat a claim
alternatively or in addition to another claim (the original claim) under this
regulation the Secretary of State shall treat the alternative or additional
claim, whenever made, as having been made at the same time as the original claim.]

AMENDMENTS

1. The Tax Credits (Claims and Payments) (Amendment) Regulations 1999 (SI
1999/2572), regs 20 and 22 (October 5, 1999).

2. The Child Benefit, Child Support and Social Security (Miscellaneous
Amendments) Regulations 1996 (SI 1996/1803), reg.19 (April 7, 1997).

3. The Social Security (Miscellaneous Provisions) Amendment Regulations 1992
(SI 1992/247), reg.12 (March 9, 1992).

GENERAL NOTE

This invaluable provision removes some of the rigour of ensuring that a clai-   2.125
mant chooses the right benefit to claim and is not prejudiced by making a mistaken
choice. The regulation now also covers interchange of claims for child benefit with
claims for other benefits. There was originally some doubt over whether a decision
to treat a claim as one in the alternative was for the adjudicating authorities or
the Secretary of State. Note that, with the introduction of incapacity benefit, the
arrangement whereby claims for unemployment benefit may be treated as claims for
one of the sickness benefits has been ended.

In *R. v Secretary of State for Social Security Ex p. Cullen and Nelson* (*The Times*,
May 16, 1997 reported as *R(A) 1/97*), the Court of Appeal confirmed the decision of Harrison J. in *Cullen* (November 16, 1996) and reversed the decision of
the Commissioner in *Nelson* (*CA 171/1993*). In both cases, unsuccessful claims for

mentary benefit had been made prior to April 11, 1988. At that time, the 1979
ms and Payments Regulations allowed the Secretary of State to treat a claim for
pplementary benefit as in the alternative a claim for attendance allowance. The
Claims and Payments Regulations 1987, which came into effect on April 11, 1988,
contained no such power. In 1991 (*Cullen*) and 1993 (*Nelson*) claims for attendance
allowance were made and it was sought to have the supplementary benefit claims
treated as claims for attendance allowance. The Court of Appeal held that the
Secretary of State had no power to do so, so that the Commissioner in *CA/171/1993*
was wrong to refer the question to the Secretary of State for determination. Once
the 1979 Regulations were revoked, the Secretary of State could no longer exercise
a power which no longer existed. As the Secretary of State had only had a discretion
under the 1979 Regulations whether or not to treat a supplementary benefit claim
as in the alternative a claim for attendance allowance, the claimants had no accrued
rights which were preserved on the revocation of the 1979 Regulations under s.16
of the Interpretation Act 1978.

[¹ Claim for incapacity benefit [³ , severe disablement allowance or employment and support allowance] where no entitlement to statutory sick pay or statutory maternity pay]

2.126   **10.**—(1) Paragraph (2) applies to a claim for incapacity benefit or severe]
disablement allowance for a period of incapacity for work of which the
claimant gave his employer a notice of incapacity under regulation 7 of the
Statutory Sick Pay (General) Regulations 1982, and for which he has been
informed in writing by his employer that there is no entitlement to statutory
sick pay.

[³ (1A) Paragraph (2) also applies to a claim for an employment and
support allowance for a period of limited capability for work in relation to
which the claimant gave his employer a notice of incapacity under regulation 7 of the Statutory Sick Pay (General) Regulations 1982, and for which
he has been informed in writing by his employer that there is no entitlement
to statutory sick pay.]

(2) A claim to which this paragraph applies shall be treated as made on
the date accepted by the claimant's employer as the first day of incapacity,
provided that he makes the claim—

  (a) within the appropriate time specified in paragraph 2 of Schedule 4
      beginning with the day on which he is informed in writing that he
      was not entitled to statutory sick pay; or
  (b) [² . . .]

(3) Paragraph (4) applies to a claim for maternity allowance for a pregnancy or confinement by reason of which the claimant gave her employer
notice of absence from work under [section 164(4) of the Social Security
Contributions and Benefits Act 1992] and regulation 23 of the Statutory
Maternity Pay (General) Regulations 1986 and in respect of which she has
been informed in writing by her employer that there is no entitlement to
statutory maternity pay.

(4) A claim to which this paragraph applies shall be treated as made on
the date when the claimant gave her employer notice of absence from work
or at the beginning of the 14th week before the expected week of confinement, whichever is later, provided that she makes the claim—

  (a) within three months of being informed in writing that she was not
      entitled to statutory maternity pay; or
  (b) [² . . .]

AMENDMENTS

1. The Social Security (Claims and Payments) Amendment (No.2) Regulations 1994 (SI 1994/2943), reg.3 (April 13, 1995).

2. The Social Security (Miscellaneous Amendments) (No.2) Regulations 1997 (SI 1997/793), reg.4 (April 7, 1997).

3. The Employment and Support Allowance (Consequential Provisions) (No.2) Regulations 2008 (SI 2008/1554), reg.16 (October 27, 2008).

Special provisions where it is certified that a woman is expected to be confined or where she has been confined

11.—(1) Where in a certificate issued or having effect as issued under the Social Security (Medical Evidence) Regulations 1976 it has been certified that it is to be expected that a woman will be confined, and she makes a claim for maternity allowance in expectation of that confinement any such claim may, unless the Secretary of State otherwise directs, be treated as a claim for [¹ incapacity city benefit] [³, severe disablement allowance or employment and support allowance] made in respect of any days in the period beginning with either—

2.127

(a) the beginning of the 6th week before the expected week of confinement; or

(b) the actual date of confinement, whichever is the earlier, and ending in either case on the 14th day after the actual date of confinement.

(2) Where, in a certificate issued under the Social Security (Medical Evidence) Regulations 1976 it has been certified that a woman has been confined and she claims maternity allowance within [² three months] of that date, her claim may be treated in the alternative or in addition as a claim for incapacity benefit [³, severe disablement allowance or employment and support allowance] for the period beginning with the date of her confinement and ending 14 days after that date.

AMENDMENTS

1. The Social Security (Claims and Payments) Amendment (No.2) Regulations 1994 (SI 1994/2943), reg.4 (April 13, 1995).

2. The Social Security (Miscellaneous Amendments) (No.2) Regulations 1997 (SI 1997/793), reg.5 (April 7, 1997).

3. The Employment and Support Allowance (Consequential Provisions) (No.2) Regulations 2008, (SI 2008/1554), reg.17 (October 27, 2008).

GENERAL NOTE

In *R(S)1/74* the Commissioner held that a similarly worded predecessor to this regulation which made similar, though not identical, provision neither confers title to sickness benefit nor restricts the right to it. The regulation does no more than define the period for which, having made an unsuccessful claim to maternity allowance, a woman may be treated as having made a claim to incapacity benefit. There is nothing to prevent her seeking to prove incapacity for some period or periods additional to that to which her claim is taken to relate.

2.128

Regulation 12 revoked by The Social Security (Claims and Payments on account, Overpayments and Recovery) Amendment Regulations 1989 (SI 1989/136) (February 27, 1989).

2.129

Advance claims and awards

2.130   **13.**—(1) Where, although a person does not satisfy the requirements of entitlement to benefit on the date on which a claim is made, the [³ Secretary of State] is of the opinion that unless there is a change of circumstances he will satisfy those requirements for a period beginning on a day (the relevant day") not more than 3 months after the date on which the claim is made, then [³ the Secretary of State] may—

    (a) treat the claim as if made for a period beginning with the relevant day; and

    (b) award benefit accordingly, subject to the condition that the person satisfies the requirements for entitlement when benefit becomes payable under the award.

    (2) [³ A decision pursuant to paragraph (1)(b) to award benefit may be revised under section 9 of the Social Security Act 1998] if the requirements for entitlement are found not to have been satisfied on the relevant day.

    (3) [² [⁶...] Paragraphs (1) and (2) do not apply] to any claim for maternity allowance, [⁶...], [⁴ state pension credit] retirement pension or increase, [⁵ a shared additional pension] [⁶...] [¹ disability living allowance], or any claim within regulations 11(1)(a) or (b).

    (4)–(8) [⁶...]

    [⁶ (9) Paragraphs (1) and (2) do not apply to—

    (a) a claim for income support made by a person from abroad as defined in regulation 21AA of the Income Support (General) Regulations 1987 (special cases: supplemental—persons from abroad); [⁷...]

    (b) a claim for a jobseeker's allowance made by a person from abroad as defined in regulation 85A of the Jobseeker's Allowance Regulations (special cases: supplemental—persons from abroad).] [⁷ and

    (c) a claim for an employment and support allowance made by a person from abroad as defined in regulation 70 of the Employment and Support Allowance Regulations (special cases: supplemental—persons from abroad).]

AMENDMENTS

1. The Social Security (Claims and Payments) Amendments Regulations 1991 (SI 1991/2741), reg.13 (March 9, 1992).

2. The Social Security (Claims and Payments) Amendment Regulations 1994 (SI 1994/2319), reg.3 (October 3, 1994).

3. The Social Security Act 1998 (Commencement No 9, and Savings and Consequential and Transitional Provisions) Order 1999 (SI 1999/2422), Sch.7 (September 6, 1999).

4. State Pension Credit (Consequential, Transitional and Miscellaneous) Regulations 2002 (SI 2002/3019), reg.6 (April 7, 2003).

5. The Social Security (Shared Additional Pension) (Miscellaneous Amendments) Regulations 2005 (SI 2005/1551) reg.2 (July 2, 2005).

6. The Social Security, Housing Benefit and Council Tax Benefit (Miscellaneous Amendments) Regulations 2007 (SI 2007/1331) (May 23, 2007)

7. The Employment and Support Allowance (Consequential Provisions) (No. 2) Regulations 2008 (SI 2008/1554), reg.18 (October 27, 2008).

GENERAL NOTE

2.131   This regulation contains a useful power in the case of the specified benefits to make awards in advance, subject to revision if the conditions of entitlement are found not to be satisfied as at the date the award takes effect. But amendments following the Court of Appeal's decision in *Secretary of State for Work and Pensions* v. *Bhakta*, [2006] EWCA Civ. 65 exclude advance awards for persons from abroad in relation to the habitual residence test.

Advance award of disability living allowance

[¹ **13A.**—(1) Where, although a person does not satisfy the requirements for entitlement to disability living allowance on the date on which the claim is made, the [² Secretary of State] is of the opinion that unless there is a change of circumstances he will satisfy those requirements for a period beginning on a day ("the relevant day" not more than 3 months after the date on which the claim is made, then [² the Secretary of State] may award disability living allowance from the relevant day subject to the condition that the person satisfies the requirements for entitlement on the relevant day.

(2) Where a person makes a claim for disability living allowance on or after 3rd February 1992 and before 6th April 1992 the adjudicating authority may award benefit for a period beginning on or after 5th April 1992 being a day not more than three months after the date on which the claim was made, subject to the condition that the person satisfies the requirements for entitlement when disability living allowance becomes payable under the award.

(3) [² A decision pursuant to paragraph (1) or (2) to award benefit may be revised under section 9 of the Social Security Act 1998] if the requirements for entitlement are found not to have been satisfied when disability living allowance becomes payable under the award.]

2.132

AMENDMENTS

1. The Social Security (Claims and Payments) Amendment Regulations 1991 (SI 1991/2741), reg.7 (February 3, 1992).
2. The Social Security Act 1998 (Commencement No.11 and Transitional Provisions) Order 1999 (SI 1999/2860), Sch.3 (October 18, 1999).

GENERAL NOTE

In *CSDLA/852/2002*, and repeated in *CSDLA/553/2005* the Commissioner explains:

"4. Regulation 13A thus permits an award of DLA where a claim is made no more than three months before the date from which the award takes effect, if the DM considers that by that date the claimant will satisfy the three months qualifying period for DLA and is then likely so to satisfy the qualifying conditions for a further six-month period. The claim subsists until the matter is determined by the DM (s.8(2)(a) of the Social Security Act 1998).
5. A claim is to be treated as being continuously made until it is determined. Therefore, although Regulation 13A only benefits the claimant if the claim is made within the relevant three-month period, it applies provided that the DLA conditions in question are satisfied by the date of the Secretary of State's decision under appeal and seemed likely to continue for both the three-month qualifying period and the six-month prospective period, so that the Secretary of State could then have made an advance award.
6. The issue for the tribunal was, therefore, whether . . . when the claim was decided by the Secretary of State (and beyond which circumstances could not be taken because of section 12(8)(b) of the Social Security Act 1998), circumstances existed, (even if proved by later evidence not available to the DM at the time) which justified an award under regulation 13A."

2.133

A different Commissioner had come to the same conclusion in *CDLA/3071/2005*. In *KH v SSWP* [2009] UKUT 54 (AAC), the Judge also came to the same conclusion by slightly different reasoning. Regulation 6(8) of the Claims and Payments Regulations did not require the date of claim to be regarded as the date a claim form was requested (provided that it was returned within six weeks or such longer period as the Secretary of State chooses to accept), since this would deprive Regulation 13A of much of its significance. The Judge says:

> 12. As I have said, there is no reason to give effect to regulation 6(8) beyond its context and purpose. Regulation 13A, in contrast to regulation 6(8), is concerned with the future, not the past. There is no need or reason to allow that provision to control the power to make an advance award. The natural meaning of 'the date on which the claim is made' in the context of regulation 13A is the date on which it is received. If the Secretary of State's argument is correct, the effectiveness of regulation 13A is significantly reduced. Potentially six weeks (or longer at the Secretary of State's discretion) may have past before the claim is even received and further weeks may pass while the Secretary of State obtains medical evidence and decides the claim. In that context, there may be little or no scope for an advance award if the 3 months begins on the date the claimant asked for a claim pack.

[¹ Advance claim for and award of disability working allowance

2.134   **13B.**—(1) Where a person makes a claim for disability working allowance on or after 10th March 1992 and before 7th April 1992 the adjudicating authority may—

(a) treat the claim as if it were made for a period beginning on 7th April 1992; and

(b) An award benefit accordingly, subject to the condition that the person satisfies the requirements for entitlement on 7th April 1992.

(2) An award under paragraph (1)(b) shall be reviewed by the adjudicating authority if the requirements for entitlement are found not to have been satisfied on 7th April 1992.]

AMENDMENT

The Social Security (Claims and Payments) Amendment Regulations 1991 (SI 1991/2741), reg.7(2) (March 10, 1992).

DEFINITION

"adjudicating authority"—see reg.2(1).

GENERAL NOTE

2.135   This allowed an advance claim in the few weeks immediately before the start of the scheme on April 7, 1992.

[¹ [² Further claim for and award of disability living allowance or attendance allowance

2.136   **13C.**—(1) A person entitled to an award of disability living allowance or attendance allowance may make a further claim for disability living allowance or attendance allowance, as the case may be, during the period of 6 months immediately before the existing award expires.]

(2) Where a person makes a claim in accordance with paragraph (1) the [³ Secretary of State] may—

(a) treat the claim as if made on the first day after the expiry of the existing award ("the renewal date"); and

(b) award benefit accordingly, subject to the condition that the person satisfies the requirements for entitlement on the renewal date.

(3) [⁴ A decision pursuant to paragraph (2)(b) to award benefit may be revised under section 9 of the Social Security Act 1998] if the requirements for entitlement are found not to have been satisfied on the renewal date.]

AMENDMENTS

1. The Social Security (Claims and Payments) Amendment Regulations 1991 (SI 1991/2741), reg.8, (February 3, 1992).
2. The Social Security, Child Support and Tax Credits (Miscellaneous Amendments) Regulations 2005 (SI 2005/337), reg.7 (March 18, 2005).
3. The Social Security Act 1998 (Commencement No.11, and Savings and Consequential and Transitional Provisions) Order 1999 (SI 1999/2860) Sch.3, para.2 (October 18, 1999).

GENERAL NOTE

This permits a continuation claim for disability living allowance to be made during the last six months of an existing award.

2.137

In *CDLA/14895/1996*, it was held that reg.13C(2) should not be applied until it has been considered whether, if the claim were treated as an application for review under s.30(13) of the Social Security Administration Act 1992, there would be grounds for review. If there are grounds for review, the existing award should be reviewed. Otherwise, the claim should be treated as a renewal claim, effective only from the end of the existing award.

The relationship of this regulation and the prohibition on tribunals of considering circumstances obtaining after the date of claim under s.12(8)(b) of the Social Security Act 1998 was considered in *CDLA/3848/2001*, where the Commissioner said,

"In my judgment it is implicit in Reg.13C of the 1987 Regulations that circumstances occurring between the date of a decision on a renewal claim and the renewal date can (and therefore must) be taken into account by an appeal tribunal.
. . .
Regulation 13C(2), having stated that the Secretary of State may treat the claim as if made on the renewal date, goes on to provide that he may 'award benefit accordingly.' That means that the task of a decision maker (and appeal tribunal on appeal) is to determine whether the conditions for disability living allowance will be (or were) satisfied *on the renewal date*. It is in my view implicit that circumstances which occur between the date of the decision maker's decision and the renewal date can be taken into account by an appeal tribunal. It cannot have been the intention of s.12(8)(b) and Reg.13C, read together, that an appeal tribunal is prevented from taking into account changes in circumstances relevant to the very issue which it has to decide. If it were to ignore such changes, the effect of its decision would not be to 'award benefit accordingly' (i.e. on the basis of a claim treated as made on the renewal date)."

A Scottish Commissioner agreed with this reasoning in deciding an appeal relating to a claim for an attendance allowance, where there is no corresponding provision. Though disability living allowance and attendance allowance are separate benefits, there is no logical reason why there should not be similar provision in relation to renewal claims. However, there is not. The Commissioner in *CSA/248/2002* had to decide the effect of a tribunal's only deciding matters down to the date of the decision, and whether this had constituted an error of law. The Commissioner concluded that the renewal claim could be competently made in advance of the

2.138

expiry of the existing award (paras 12–13). But the Commissioner found himself compelled to conclude that s.12(8)(b) did apply to the renewal of an attendance allowance claim (para.19).

In *CDLA/4331/2002*, it was held that, when hearing an appeal from a decision on a renewal claim effective from the claimant's 16th birthday, a tribunal is required to determine the appeal on the basis that that the claimant was 16, even if she was only 15 at the date of the Secretary of State's decision. The approach taken was different from that in *CDLA/3848/2001*, but the result was the same on the facts of the case. In *C12/2003–04 (DLA)*, a Commissioner in Northern Ireland expressly disagreed with *CDLA/3848/2001* and concluded that the Secretary of State was not entitled to refuse benefit at all until the date from which the renewal claim would have been effective. A tribunal, faced with an appeal against a disallowance of a renewal claim made before the date from which a new award would have been effective, therefore had no power to do more than set aside the Secretary of State's decision as having been made without jurisdiction, leaving the Secretary of State to make a new decision.

This conflict of authority has now been resolved in a decision of a Tribunal of Commissioners in *R(DLA)4/05*. The Tribunal of Commissioners departs from the reasoning in both *CDLA/3848/2001* and *C12/2003–04 (DLA)*. *CDLA/3848/2001* had failed to take into account that effect had to be given to the provisions of ss.8(2) (b) and 12(8)(b) of the Social Security Act 1998 in the context of renewal claims. This precluded the Secretary of State from taking into account any circumstances not obtaining at the date of the decision. This meant that the Secretary of State had to determine the renewal claim on the basis of circumstances existing at the time the decision was made. In so doing they dissent from paras 106–107 of another decision of a Tribunal of Commissioners in *R(IB)2/04* (see below) which had indicated that renewal claims required prediction. The later Tribunal of Commissioners concludes that this part of the earlier decision was made without full argument and consideration of the implications of s.8(2)(b). They consider that, if a change of circumstances before the renewal date is anticipated, best practice would be to defer the making of the decision until closer to the renewal date in order to know whether the anticipated change had indeed materialised. The Tribunal's disagreement with the Northern Ireland decision in that reg.13C(2)(b) only permits the imposition of a condition in the case of an advance award that all the conditions of entitlement exist as at the renewal date. So the Secretary of State did have power to disallow a renewal claim before the renewal date.

The earlier decision of the Tribunal of Commissioners in *R(IB)2/04* had, in its third issue, addressed the question of whether the power to revise in reg.13C(3) is a freestanding one, or whether reg.3 of the Decisions and Appeals Regulations needs to be established before a decision on a renewal claim can be altered under reg.13C(3). The Tribunal of Commissioners concludes that there is no need for a ground for revision under reg.3 of the Decisions and Appeals Regulations to exist to trigger a reg.13C(3) revision. However, in the usual case where the issue concerns the condition of the claimant at the renewal date, "it can be exercised only on the ground that the claimant's condition has either improved between the date of decision and the renewal date to a greater extent than anticipated by the decision maker or has not deteriorated during that period to the extent anticipated by the decision maker." (para.13 of the summary of conclusions on issues of law.' This conclusion must, however, now be read in the light of the decision of the Tribunal of Commissioners in the later decision referred to above.

[¹ Advance claims for an award of state pension credit

2.139   **13D.**—(1) Paragraph (2) applies if—
          (a) a person does not satisfy the requirements for entitlement to state pension credit on the date on which the claim is made; and

(b) the Secretary of State is of the opinion that unless there is a change of circumstances he will satisfy those requirements—
  (i) where the claim is made in the advance period, when he attains the qualifying age; or
  (ii) in any other case, within 4 months of the date on which the claim is made.

(2) Where this paragraph applies, the Secretary of State may—

(a) treat the claim as made for a period beginning on the day ("the relevant day") the claimant—
  (i) attains the qualifying age, where the claim is made in the advance period; or
  (ii) is likely to satisfy the requirements for entitlement in any other case; and

(b) if appropriate, award state pension credit accordingly, subject to the condition that the person satisfies the requirements for entitlement on the relevant day.

(3) An award under paragraph (2) may be revised under section 9 of the Social Security Act 1998 if the claimant fails to satisfy the conditions for entitlement to state pension credit on the relevant day.]

[² (4) This regulation does not apply to a claim made by a person not in Great Britain as defined in regulation 2 of the State Pension Credit Regulations (persons not in Great Britain).]

AMENDMENT

1. Inserted by the State Pension Credit (Consequential, Transitional and Miscellaneous Provisions) Regulations 2002 (SI 2002/3019), reg.6 (April 7, 2003).

2. The Social Security, Housing Benefit and Council Tax benefit (Miscellaneous Amendments) Regulations 2007 (SI 2007/1331) (May 23, 2007).

Advance claim for and award of maternity allowance

14.—(1) Subject to the following provisions of this regulation, a claim for maternity allowance in expectation of confinement, or for an increase in such an allowance in respect of an adult dependent, and an award on such a claim, may be made not earlier than 14 weeks before the beginning of the expected week of confinement.   2.140

(2) A claim for an increase of maternity allowance in respect of an adult dependant may not be made in advance unless, on the date when made, the circumstances relating to the adult dependant concerned are such as would qualify the claimant for such an increase if they occurred in a period for which she was entitled to a maternity allowance.

Advance notice of retirement and claim for and award of pension

15.—(1) A claim for a retirement pension of any category, and for any increase in any such pension, [⁶ or a shared additional pension] and an award on such a claim, may be made at any time not more than 4 months before the date on which the claimant will, subject to the fulfilment of the necessary conditions, become entitled to such a pension.   2.141

(2) [¹. . .]

(3) [¹. . .]

(4) [¹. . .]

[² (5) Where a person claims a Category A or Category B retirement pension and is, or but for that claim would be, in receipt of [³ incapacity benefit] [⁴. . .] for a period which includes the first day to which the claim relates, then if that day is not the appropriate day for the payment of retirement pension in his case, the claim shall be treated as if the first day of the claim was instead the next following such pay day.

(6) Where the spouse of such a person as is mentioned in paragraph (5) above claims a Category A or Category B retirement pension and the first day of that claim is the same as the first day of the claim made by that person, the provisions of that paragraph shall apply also to the claim made by the spouse [⁷ or civil partner].]

(7) For the purposes of facilitating the determination of a subsequent claim for a Category A, B or C retirement pension, a person may at any time not more than 4 months before the date on which he will attain pensionable age, and notwithstanding that he [⁵ intends to defer his entitlement to a Category A or Category B retirement pension] at that date, submit particulars in writing to the Secretary of State in a form approved by him for that purpose with a view to the determination (in advance of the claim) of any question under the Act relating to that person's title to such a retirement pension [⁵. . .] and subject to the necessary modifications, the provisions of these regulations shall apply to any such particulars.

AMENDMENTS

1. Social Security Act 1986 (October 1, 1989).
2. The Social Security (Abolition of Earnings Rule) (Consequential) Regulations 1989 (SI 1989/1642), reg.2(2) (October 1, 1989).
3. The Social Security (Claims and Payments) Amendment (No.2) Regulations 1994 (SI 1994/2943), reg.5 (April 13, 1995).
4. The Social Security (Claims and Payments) (Jobseeker's Allowance Consequential Amendments) Regulations 1996 (SI 1996/1460), reg.2 (October 7, 1996).
5. The Social Security (Abolition of Earnings Rule) (Consequential) Regulations 1989 (SI 1989/1642), reg.2(3) (October 1, 1989).
6. The Social Security (Shared Additional Pension) (Miscellaneous Amendments) Regulations 2005 (SI 2005/1551) (July 6, 2005).
7. The Civil Partnership (Pensions, Social Security and Child Support) (Consequential etc. Provisions) Order 2005 (SI 2005/2877) (December 5, 2005).

GENERAL NOTE

2.142   In *CP/1074/1997* a Commissioner had to consider the proper approach to be taken to the determination of a date of birth in relation to a claim for retirement pension. The claimant had been born in the Punjab, and his year of birth had been consistently stated on a number of documents as 1931, but there was no clear evidence of the day he was born in that year. On September 13, 1995 he made a claim for retirement pension, but the adjudication officer treated his date of birth as December 31, 1931 and concluded that the claim made on September 13, 1995 could not be accepted. This would have required the claimant to have been born no later than January 13, 1931 in order to be within the four months provided for in reg.15(1). The claimant adduced evidence that he had been born on December 18, 1930, but his was not accepted by the tribunal. In dealing with the appeal the Commissioner addresses a number of arguments put forward on behalf of the claimant. The Commissioner accepted that the claimant did not need to prove a particular date of birth, merely that he had reached retirement age by a particular date. He did not, however, accept a second argument which was based on the application of a mathematical approach to the evidential test of the balance of probabilities. The claimant argued that as each day passed in the year in which it was accepted that a person was born, it became more probable that the person had been born by that day in the year. By the beginning of July it could therefore be said that it was more probable than not that the claimant had been born by that date. In such circumstances, the practice of the adjudication officer in using the last day of the year as the date of birth was an error of law. The Commissioner rejects this argument, citing *Re JS (a minor)* [1980] 1 All E.R. 1061, for the proposition that the concept of evidential probability is not the same as the mathematical concept. The Commissioner approves the proposition in that case that the civil burden of proof requires the party on whom the burden falls to "satisfy the court that it is reasonably safe in all the circumstances of the case to act on the evidence before the court, bearing in mind the consequences which will follow". The Commissioner finally notes that this may not, in every case where a date of birth in the year is not known, result in the choice of the last day in the year. Regard must be had to all the evidence available at the time the decision is made in determining which date in the year is to be selected as the date by which the person was born.

In *CP/3017/2004* the Commissioner held, applying *R(DLA) 4/05* by analogy, that there is a power to disallow an advance claim made under reg. 15(1) for an increase of retirement pension for a wife up to four months before a claimant might become entitled to the pension (para. 7). However, the Commissioner considers,

" . . . in some cases where there was likely to be a significant change of circumstances before the start date of the period covered by a claim, it might well be good practice to defer making a decision until it was known whether that change had actually materialised. It seems to me that the present case is one where that course should have been taken. It was plain from the evidence provided that the claimant's wife's earnings fluctuated a great deal from one pay period to another. And the nature of the case is different from that of a person suffering some potentially disabling or incapacitating condition, where in most cases there can be a sensible prediction about how the condition might progress in the future. It was simply unknown on 3 March 2004 what the claimant's wife's earnings might be in the week prior to 31 May 2004. Quite apart from the doubts that I explain below about the averaging process carried out by the officer, it would have been better to have waited until close to 28 May 2004 and then considered the current evidence about the wife's earnings. I do not think that there would have been any difficulty in making an advance decision on the claimant's own retirement pension entitlement, but deferring the decision on the increase. However, that did not happen."

Cold weather payments

15A. [¹. . .]   2.143

AMENDMENT

1. Social Security (Miscellaneous Provisions) Amendment Regulations 1991 (SI 1991/2284), reg. 8 (November 1, 1991).

GENERAL NOTE

Claims for cold weather payments are no longer necessary or possible.   2.144

[¹ [²Advance claim for pension following deferment

15B. Where a person's entitlement to a Category A or Category B retire-   2.145
ment pension or a shared additional pension is deferred in accordance with

section 55(3) of the Contributions and Benefits Act (pension increase or lump sum where entitlement to retirement pension is deferred) or section 55C(3) (pension increase or lump sum where entitlement to shared additional pension is deferred) thereof (as the case may be) a claim for—

(a) a Category A or Category B retirement pension;
(b) any increase in that pension;
(c) a shared additional pension,

may be made at any time not more than 4 months before the day on which the period of deferment, within the meaning of section 55(3) or section 55C(3) (as the case may be), ends.]]

AMENDMENTS

1. Orginally marked by the Social Security (Claims and Payments) Amendment Regulations 2005 (SI 2005/455), reg.2 (April 6, 2005).
2. The Social Security (Shared Additional Pension) (Miscellaneous Amendments) Regulations 2005 (SI 2005/1551) (July 6, 2005).

GENERAL NOTE

2.146   This additional regulation regularises what has been operational practice in allowing those who claim a deferred retirement pension to do so four months in advance of the date on which they wish to claim their pension. The purpose of the advance claims provisions is to ensure that the retirement pension is put into payment on the due date without any delays.

There are further amendments to deal with the administrative arrangements needed to support the ability to take a lump sum rather than an increase in pension, and to extend the time limit for claiming but these changes do not take effect until 2006, though certain transition provisions come into effect in July 2005.

Date of entitlement under an award for the purpose of payability of benefit and effective date of change of rate

2.147   **16.**—(1) For the purpose only of determining the day from which benefit is to become payable, where a benefit other than one of those specified in paragraph (4) is awarded for a period of a week, or weeks, and the earliest date on which entitlement would otherwise commence is not the first day of a benefit week entitlement shall begin on the first day of the benefit week next following.

[1 (1A) Where a claim for [6 working families' tax credit] is made in accordance with paragraph 7(a) [2 or (aa)] of Schedule 4 for a period following the expiration of an existing award of family credit [6 or disabled person's tax credit], entitlement shall begin on the day after the expiration of that award.

(1B) Where a claim for [6 working families' tax credit or disabled person's tax credit] is made on or after the date when an up-rating order is made under [6 section 150 of the Social Security Administration Act 1992], but before the date when that order comes into force, and—

(a) an award cannot be made on that claim as at the date it is made but could have been made if that order were then in force, and
(b) the period beginning with the date of claim and ending immediately before the date when the order came into force does not exceed 28 days,

entitlement shall begin from the date the up-rating order comes into force.]

[² (1C) Where a claim for [⁶ disabled person's tax credit] is made in accordance with paragraph 11(a) or (b) of Schedule 4 for a period following the expiration of an existing award of [⁶ disabled person's tax credit or working families' tax credit], entitlement shall begin on the day after the expiration of that award.]

(2) Where there is a change in the rate of any benefit to which paragraph (1) applies [⁸ (other than widowed mother's allowance and widow's pension)] the change, if it would otherwise take effect on a day which is not the [⁸ first day of the benefit week] for that benefit, shall take effect from the [⁸ first day of the benefit week] next following.

[⁸ 2A) Subject to paragraph (2B), where there is a change in the rate of bereavement allowance, widowed mother's allowance, widowed parent's allowance or widow's pension, the change, if it would otherwise take effect on a day which is not the first day of the benefit week, shall take effect from the first day of the benefit week next following.

(2B) Paragraph (2A) shall not apply in a case where an award of benefit is terminated and benefit is paid in arrears.

(2C) Where a benefit specified in paragraph (2A) is paid in advance and the award is terminated, the termination, if it would otherwise take effect on a day which is not the first day of a benefit week, shall take effect on the first day of the benefit week next following.]

[¹ (3) For the purposes of this regulation the first day of the benefit week—

(a) in the case of child benefit [⁵ and guardian's allowance] is Monday,

(b) in the case of [⁶ disabled person's tax credit or working families' tax credit] is Tuesday, and

(c) in any other case is the day of the week on which the benefit is payable in accordance with regulation 22 (long-term benefits).]

(4) The benefits specified for exclusion from the scope of paragraph (1) are [⁴ jobseeker's allowance], [³ incapacity benefit], [⁷,employment and support allowance] maternity allowance, [¹. . .], severe disablement allowance, income support [⁶, state pension credit] [⁸ , bereavement allowance, widowed parent's allowance] [¹. . .] and any increase of those benefits.

AMENDMENTS

1. The Social Security (Claims and Payments) Amendment Regulations 1988 (SI 1988/522), reg.3 (April 11, 1988).

2. The Social Security (Claims and Payments) Amendment Regulations 1991 (SI 1991/2741), reg.9 (March 10, 1992).

3. The Social Security (Claims and Payments) Amendment (No.2) Regulations 1994 (SI 1994/2943), reg.6 (April 13, 1995).

4. The Social Security (Claims and Payments) (Jobseeker's Allowance Consequential Amendments) Regulations 1996 (SI 1996/1460), reg.2(9) (October 7, 1996).

5. The Social Security (Claims and Payments) Amendment Regulations 1999 (S.I. 1999, No.2358), reg.2 (September 20, 1999).

6. State Pension Credit (Consequential, Transitional and Miscellaneous Provisions) Regulations 2002, (SI 2002/3019), reg.7 (April 7, 2003).

7. The Employment and Support Allowance (Consequential Provisions) (No.2) Regulations 2008 (SI 2008/1554), reg.19 (October 27, 2008).

8. The Social Security (Claims and Payments) Amendment Regulations 2009 (SI 2009/604), reg.2 (April 6, 2009).

DEFINITIONS

"benefit"—see reg.2(2).
"jobseeker's allowance"—see reg.2(1).
"week"—*ibid.*

GENERAL NOTE

2.148   This regulation restates in part the rules formerly contained in reg.16(10) of the Claims and Payments Regulations 1979. In *R(P)2/73* it was held that the effect of a similarly worded predecessor to reg.16(10) was not just to make benefit payable from the next pay day but to make it begin on that day. The Commissioner made clear, though, that the regulation was concerned with "payability not title". The new wording does not appear wholly to resolve the difficulty, since para.(1) is prefaced by the intention only to concern itself with payability, though later the word "entitlement" is used. Presumably that means "entitlement to payment of benefit" and not title to the benefit itself. There are occasions where title to the benefit arising on an earlier date than the first date of payment has significant consequences.

[¹ Date of entitlement under an award of state pension credit for the purpose of payability and effective date of change of rate

2.149   **16A.**—(1) For the purpose only of determining the day from which state pension credit is to become payable, where the credit is awarded from a day which is not the first day of the claimant's benefit week, entitlement shall begin on the first day of the benefit week next following.

(2) In the case of a claimant who—

(a) immediately before attaining the qualifying age was entitled to income support [², income-based jobseekers allowance or income-related employment and support allowance] and is awarded state pension credit from the day on which he attains the qualifying age; or

(b) was entitled to an income-based jobseeker's allowance after attaining the qualifying age and is awarded state pension credit from the day which falls after the date that entitlement ends,

entitlement to the guarantee credit shall, notwithstanding paragraph (1), begin on the first day of the award.

(3) Where a change in the rate of state pension credit would otherwise take effect on a day which is not the first day of the claimant's benefit week, the change shall take effect from the first day of the benefit week next following.

(4) For the purpose of this regulation, "benefit week" means the period of 7 days beginning on the day on which, in the claimant's case, state pension credit is payable in accordance with regulation 26B.]

AMENDMENTS

1. State Pension Credit (Consequential, Transitional and Miscellaneous Provisions) Regulations 2002 (SI 2002/3019), reg.7 (April 7, 2003).

2. The Employment and Support Allowance (Consequential Provisions) (No.2) Regulations 2008 (SI 2008/1554), reg.20 (October 27, 2008).

Duration of awards

2.150   **17.**—(1) Subject to the provisions of this regulation and of section [¹37ZA(3) of the Social Security Act 1975 (disability living allowance) and section] 20(6) [² and (6F)] of the Social Security Act 1986 [⁴working families' tax credit and disabled person's tax credit] [SSCBA, ss.71(3), 128(3) and 129(6)] a claim for benefit shall be treated as made for an indefinite period and any award of benefit on that claim shall be made for an indefinite period.

[³ (1A) Where an award of income support or an income-based jobseeker's allowance is made in respect of [⁷ a couple] and one member of the couple is, at the date of claim, a person to whom section 126 of the Contributions and Benefits Act or, as the case may be, section 14 of the Jobseekers Act applies, the award of benefit shall cease when the person to whom section 126 or, as the case may be, section 14 applies returns to work with the same employer.]

(2) [³. . .]

(3) [⁶ Except in the case of claims for and awards of state pension credit,] if [³. . .] it would be inappropriate to treat a claim as made and to make an award for an indefinite period (for example where a relevant change of circumstances is reasonably to be expected in the near future) the claim shall be treated as made and the award shall be for a definite period which is appropriate in the circumstances.

(4) In any case where benefit is awarded in respect of days subsequent to the date of claim the award shall be subject to the condition that the claimant satisfies the requirements for entitlement [⁵. . .]

(5) The provisions of Schedule 2 shall have effect in relation to claims for [³ᵃ jobseeker's allowance] made during periods connected with public holidays.

AMENDMENTS

1. The Social Security (Claims and Payments) Amendment Regulations 1991 (SI 1991/2741), reg.10 (February 3, 1992).

2. The Social Security (Claims and Payments) Amendment Regulations 1991 (SI 1991/2741), reg.10 (March 10, 1992).

3. The Social Security (Claims and Payments) (Jobseeker's Allowance Consequential Amendments) Regulations 1996 (SI 1996/1460), reg.2(10) (October 7, 1996).

4. The Tax Credits (Claims and Payments) (Amendment) Regulations 1999 (SI 1999/2572), regs 24 & 25 (October 5, 1999).

5. The Social Security Act 1998 (Commencement No.12 and Consequential and Transitional Provisions) Order 1999 (SI 1999/3178), Sch.6 (November 29, 1999).

6. State Pension Credit (Consequential, Transitional and Miscellaneous Provisions) Regulations 2002 (SI 2002/3019), reg.8 (April 7, 2003).

7. The Civil Partnership (Pensions, Social Security and Child Support) (Consequential etc. Provisions) Order 2005 (SI 2005/2877) (December 5, 2005).

DEFINITIONS

"benefit"—see reg.2(2).
"claim for benefit"—see reg.2(1).
"jobseeker's allowance"—*ibid.*
"the Jobseekers Act"—*ibid.*

GENERAL NOTE

In general awards are to be made for an indefinite period (para.1), subject to revision or supersession where the claimant's circumstances change such that the entitlement is reduced or removed. An award of benefit can only be terminated by

2.151

supersession. In *CIS/4167/2003* the Commissioner queries whether terminations of indefinite awards have always been accompanied by the required supersession decision. In the case before him an award had been closed without the making of a supersession decision in circumstances where this suggested possible standard practice.

Paragraph (3) deals with short-term situations and allows awards for a fixed period, except in the case of state pension credit.

The effect of para.(1) is that awards of most benefits are now made for an indefinite period. Entitlement only ceases where there has been a revision or supersession which establishes that the conditions of entitlement are no longer met. In earlier times, there was a distinct tendency on reviews for adjudication officers to argue that it was for the claimant to establish continuing entitlement to the benefit, whereas the true position was that, where an indefinite award had been made, it was for the decision maker to show that there were good grounds to revise or supersede the award: see generally *R(S) 3/90*.

In *CIS/620/1990*, the Commissioner stressed that the requirements of reg.17 were not a mere technicality. An indefinite award of benefit can only be terminated on review if it its shown on review (under the earlier legislation) that the conditions of entitlement cease to be met. In any other circumstances the original award continues. Any purported subsequent award of benefit cannot overlap with the earlier award. Indeed there would be no jurisdiction to make a subsequent award since the matter is *res judicata:* see paras 8 and 11 of *CIS/620/1990*.

The power to review or supersede an award of benefit will arise under s.9 (revision, which takes effect from the operative date of the decision being revised) or s.10 (supersession, which takes effect from the date of the supersession decision) of the Social Security Act 1998. There must be grounds on which the decision maker can determine that the conditions of entitlement have ceased to exist. Some are specific to certain benefits while others are more general in application. Reference should be made to the annotations to ss.9 and 10 of the 1998 Act, as well as to Pt II of the Decisions and Appeals Regulations and the commentary on these regulations, if any issue under reg.17 arises.

2.152   *Regulation 18 revoked by The Social Security (Claims and Payments) (Jobseeker's Allowance Consequential Amendments) Regulations 1996 (SI 1996/1460) (October 7, 1996).*

[¹ Time for claiming benefit

2.153   **19.**—(1) Subject to the following provisions of this regulation, the prescribed time for claiming any benefit specified in column (1) of Schedule 4 is the appropriate time specified opposite that benefit in column (2) of that Schedule.

(2) The prescribed time for claiming the benefits specified in paragraph (3) is three months beginning with any day on which, apart from satisfying the condition of making a claim, the claimant is entitled to the benefit concerned.

(3) The benefits to which paragraph (2) applies are—

(a) child benefit;
(b) guardian's allowance;
(c) [¹³ . . .];
(d) invalid care allowance or carer's allowance;
(e) maternity allowance;
(f) [¹³ . . .];
[¹⁰ (ff) . . .]
(g) widow's benefit;

[[11] (ga) subject to paragraphs (3A) and (3B), bereavement benefit;]
  (h) [[11] . . .] any increase in any benefit (other than income support or jobseeker's allowance) in respect of a child or adult dependant.
[[16] (i) state pension credit]
  [[8] (3A) The prescribed time for claiming a bereavement payment [[11] within the meaning of section 36 of the Contributions and Benefits Act] is 12 months beginning with the day on which, apart from satisfying the condition of making a claim, the claimant is entitled to such a payment.]
  [[11] (3B) The time prescribed for claiming a bereavement benefit in respect of the day on which the claimant's spouse [[12] or civil partner] has died or may be presumed to have died where—
  (a) less than 12 months have elapsed since the day of the death; and
  (b) the circumstances are as specified in section 3(1)(b) of the Social Security Administration Act 1992 (death is difficult to establish),
is that day and the period of 12 months immediately following that day if the other conditions of entitlement are satisfied.]
  [[15] (3C) In any case where the application of paragraphs (16) to (34) of regulation 6 would be advantageous to the claimant, this regulation shall apply subject to those provisions.]
  (4) Subject to paragraph (8), in the case of a claim for income support, jobseeker's allowance, [[3] working families' tax credit or disabled persons' tax credit], where the claim is not made within the time specified for that benefit in Schedule 4, the prescribed time for claiming the benefit shall be extended, subject to a maximum extension of three months, to the date on which the claim is made, where—
  (a) any [[7] one or more] of the circumstances specified in paragraph (5) applies or has applied to the claimant; and
  (b) as a result of that circumstance or those circumstances the claimant could not reasonably have been expected to make the claim earlier.
  (5) The circumstances referred to in paragraph (4) are—
  (a) the claimant has difficulty communicating because—
    (i) he has learning, language or literacy difficulties; or
    (ii) he is deaf or blind,
  and it was not reasonably practicable for the claimant to obtain assistance from another person to make his claim;
  (b) except in the case of a claim for jobseeker's allowance, the claimant was ill or disabled, and it was not reasonably practicable for the claimant to obtain assistance from another person to make his claim;
  (c) the claimant was caring for a person who is ill or disabled, and it was not reasonably practicable for the claimant to obtain assistance from another person to make his claim;
  (d) the claimant was given information by an officer of the [[3] Department for Work and Pensions] [or in a case to which regulation 4A applies, a representative of a relevant authority] or the Board which led the claimant to believe that a claim for benefit would not succeed;
  (e) the claimant was given written advice by a solicitor or other professional adviser, a medical practitioner, a local authority, or a person working in a Citizens Advice Bureau or a similar advice agency, which led the claimant to believe that a claim for benefit would not succeed;
  (f) the claimant or his partner was given written information about his income or capital by his employer or former employer, or by a bank

or building society, which led the claimant to believe that a claim for benefit would not succeed;

(g) the claimant was required to deal with a domestic emergency affecting him and it was not reasonably practicable for him to obtain assistance from another person to make his claim; or

(h) the claimant was prevented by adverse weather conditions from attending the appropriate office.

(6) In the case of a claim for income support jobseeker's allowance, [³working families' tax credit or disabled person's tax credit] [⁷ where the claim is not made within the time specified for that benefit in Schedule 4, the prescribed time for claiming the benefit shall be extended, subject to a maximum extension of one month, to the date on which the claim is made, where—

(a) any one or more of the circumstances specified in paragraph (7) applies or has applied to the claimant; and

(b) as a result of that circumstance or those circumstances the claimant could not reasonably have been expected to make the claim earlier.]

(7) The circumstances referred to in paragraph (6) are—

(a) the appropriate office where the claimant would be expected to make a claim was closed and alternative arrangements were not available;

(b) the claimant was unable to attend the appropriate office due to difficulties with his normal mode of transport and there was no reasonable alternative available;

(c) there were adverse postal conditions;

(d) the claimant [⁷ or, in the case of income support jobseeker's allowance, the claimant or his partner] was previously in receipt of another benefit, and notification of expiry of entitlement to that benefit was not sent to the claimant [⁷ or his partner, as the case may be,] before the date that his entitlement expired;

[⁹ (e) in the case of a claim for working families' tax credit, the claimant had previously been entitled, or the partner of the claimant had previously been entitled in relation to the claimant, to income support or jobseeker's allowance and the claim for working families' tax credit was made within one month of—

　(i) the expiry of entitlement to income support ignoring any period in which entitlement resulted from the person entitled not being treated as engaged in remunerative work by virtue of regulation 6(2) and (3) of the Income Support (General) Regulations 1987; or

　(ii) the expiry of entitlement to jobseeker's allowance;]

(f) except in the case of a claim for family credit or disability working allowance, the claimant had ceased to be a member of a married or unmarried couple within the period of one month before the claim was made; [² . . .]

(g) during the period of one month before the claim was made a close relative of the claimant had died, and for this purpose "close relative" means partner, parent, son, daughter, brother or [² sister; or]

[⁹ (h) in the case of a claim for disabled person's tax credit, the claimant had previously been entitled to income support, jobseeker's allowance, incapacity benefit or severe disablement allowance and the claim for disabled person's tax credit was made within one month of—

    (i) the expiry of entitlement to income support ignoring any period in which entitlement resulted from the claimant being treated as engaged in remunerative work by virtue of paragraphs (2) and (3) or paragraph (5) and (6) of the Income Support (General) Regulations 1987; or

    (ii) the expiry of entitlement to jobseeker's allowance, incapacity benefit or severe disablement allowance;

(ha) in the case of a claim for disabled person's tax credit, the partner of the claimant had previously been entitled in relation to the claimant to income support or jobseeker's allowance, and the claim for disabled person's tax credit was made within one month of—

    (i) the expiry of entitlement to income support ignoring any period in which entitlement resulted from the partner of the claimant not being treated as engaged in remunerative work by virtue of paragraphs (2) and (3) or paragraph (5) and (6) of the Income Support (General) Regulations 1987; or

    (ii) the expiry of entitlement to jobseeker's allowance;]

[6 (i) in the case of a claim for a jobseeker's allowance by a member of a joint-claim couple where the other member of that couple failed to attend at the time and place specified by the Secretary of State for the purposes of regulation 6.]

[14 (j) the claimant was unable to make telephone contact with the appropriate office where he would be expected to notify his intention of making a claim because the telephone lines to that office were busy or inoperative.]

(8) This regulation shall not have effect with respect to a claim to which [4 regulation 21ZB] of the Income Support (General) Regulations 1987 (treatment of refugees) applies.]

AMENDMENTS

1. The Social Security (Miscellaenous Amendments) (No.2) Regulations 1997 (SI 1997/793), reg.6 (April 7, 1997).

2. The Social Security (Claims and Payments and Adjudication) Amendment (No.2) Regulations 1997 (SI 1997/2290), reg.6 (October 13, 1997).

3. The Secretaries of State for Education and Skills and for Work and Pensions Order 2002 (SI 2002/1397), art.18, (September 30, 2002).

4. The Social Security (Immigration and Asylum) Consequential Amendments Regulations 2000 (SI 2000/636), reg 5 (April 3, 2000).

5. The Social Security (Benefits for Widows and Widowers) (Consequential Amendments) Regulations 2000 (SI 2000/1483), reg.9 (April 9, 2001).

6. The Social Security (Joint Claims: Consequential Amendments) Regulations 2000 (SI 2000/1982), reg.2(5) (March 19, 2001).

7. The Social Security (Claims and Payments and Miscellaneous Amendments) Regulations 2002 (SI 2002/428), reg.3 (April 2, 2002).

8. The Social Security (Claims and Payments and Miscellaneous Amendments) (No.3) Regulations 2002 (SI 2002/2660), reg.2 (April 1, 2003).

9. The Tax Credits Schemes (Miscellaneous Amendments No.4) Regulations 2000 (SI 2000/2978), reg.10 (November 28, 2000).

10. Social Security (Claims and Payments) Amendment (No.2) Regulations 2004 (SI 2004/1821), reg.2(a) (October 6, 2004).

11. Social Security (Claims and Payments) Amendment (No.2) Regulations 2005 (SI 2005/777), reg.2 (April 11, 2005).

12. The Social Security (Civil Partnerships) (Consequential Amendments) Regulations 2005 (SI 2005/2878) (December 5, 2005).

13. The Social Security (Claims and Payment) Regulations 2005 (SI 2005/455), reg.3 (April 6, 2006).

14. The Social Security (Miscellaneous Amendments) (No.3) Regulations 2006 (SI 2006/2377) (October 2, 2006).

15. The Social Security (Miscellaneous Amendments) (No.4) Regulations 2007 (SI 2007/2470) (September 24, 2007).

16. The Social Security (Miscellaneous Amendments) (No. 4) Regulations 2008 (SI 2008/2424), reg.2 (October 6, 2008).

DEFINITIONS

"appropriate office"—see reg.2(1).
"jobseeker's allowance"—*ibid.*
"married couple"—*ibid.*
"partner"—*ibid.*
"unmarried couple"—*ibid.*

GENERAL NOTE

Introduction

2.154　　Regulation 19 was completely re-drafted in April 1997 to remove references to good cause and with it decades of case law. Administrative complexity in dealing with back-dated claims was said to justify the new approach introduced in 1997. New case law is now emerging which suggests that the more limited grounds for back-dating may not be quite as restrictive as appears at first sight. It remains true that appeals concerning back-dating require a meticulous attention to fact-finding and careful attention to the words of reg.19 as interpreted in Commissioners' decisions.

There are now broadly two groups of benefits: those which must be claimed on the day in respect of which the situation giving rise to the claim first occurs, and those where a three months time limit is allowed for claiming. There are also two groups of benefits where issues of backdating arise.

The first group of benefits is income support, jobseeker's allowance whether income-based or contribution-based, working families' tax credit, and disabled person's tax credit. For this first group, there are two possible extensions available. They may be backdated for up to three months if the conditions set out in paras (4) and (5) are met. If the conditions are met, the backdating is mandatory. There is also the possibility of an extension of the time limit for claiming for up to one month if a different set of conditions set out in paras (6) and (7) are met.

The second group of benefits is child benefit, guardian's allowance, carer's allowance, maternity allowance, bereavement benefit, certain widowhood benefits (see para.(3)(h)), and increases of benefit (other than income support and jobseeker's allowance) in respect of a child or adult dependent. Those benefits listed in Sch. 4 for which the time limit is three months can also be included in this second group: incapacity benefit; disablement benefit and increases; reduced earnings allowance; and social fund payment for funeral expenses. For these benefits there is a three month time limit for claiming, which means that whatever the reasons for any delay in claiming, they can be backdated for up to three months.

The regulation does not apply to claims within reg.21ZB of the Income Support General Regulations. These set out special rules for claims for income support for a person who has submitted a claim for asylum on or after April 3, 2000 and is treated as a refugee. See commentary on the regulation in Vol.II.

Regulation 19 can only apply where there is a claim which is properly constituted for the purposes of reg.4: *CIS/157/2001*.

Note that reg.19 does not apply to claims for winter fuel payments: *CIS/2337/2004*, para.19.

Para.(1): the time limits

2.155　　Paragraph (1) sets out the time limits for those benefits listed in Sch.4 to the regulations. These include income support.

418

If a claimant signs an ordinary income support claim form which contains no question asking from what date benefit is claimed, the claim will be interpreted as a claim for an indefinite period from the date on which the claim is made. If claimants wish to claim for a past period, that must be expressly stated: *R(SB)9/84*, para.11. But note that in *CIS/2057/1998* the Commissioner accepted that a claimant who had put on her claim form "disabled—aged 16" had indicated an intention to claim income support from her 16th birthday. If, before a decision is made on an ordinary claim, a claimant indicates a wish to claim for a past period, that can operate as an amendment of the original claim taking effect on the original date. But if, after there has been a decision on the claim, the claimant indicates such a wish (as often happens when the original claim has been successful), it is generally assumed that such a claim can only be treated as a fresh claim on the date on which it is made, and that any question of back-dating under reg.19(4) has to be assessed according to that date of claim.

Paras (2) and (3): benefits for which the time limit for claiming is three months

2.156

The prescribed time for claiming the benefits listed in para.(3) is three months beginning the any day of potential entitlement. The contrast between this formulation of backdating and the technique adopted for income-related benefits may be important. If the claimant was entitled to the benefit (apart from the requirement to make a claim for the benefit) where the three-month time limit applies, the payment of benefit can be backdated for three months without any reason being shown for the delay in claiming.

Paras (4) and (5): claims for income support, jobseeker's allowance, working families' tax credit and disabled person's tax credit

2.157

(1) Introduction: Although it is common to speak of the backdating of claims, it should be appreciated that the technique adopted in para.(4) is to extend the time for claiming for a past period forward from the first day of that period. There is an immediate problem in the working of the three month time limit. If, on May 31 in any year, a claim is made for income support for the period from February 1 to May 30 in that year, it appears that the time for claiming for the whole period cannot be extended under para.(4) because to do so would go beyond the maximum period of three months permitted under the regulation. It does not matter that one of the listed circumstances has made it reasonable for the claim not to have been made earlier. The claim could be amended before a decision is made on it so as to make it a claim from March 1 to May 30, that is, the maximum permitted period of back-dating.

It follows that it would be good practice for decision-makers in dealing with a claim which inevitably breaks the maximum period of backdating not to decide the claim, but to invite the claimant to amend the period claimed for.

An alternative approach would be for a decision-maker to treat a claim for an extension of the time limit for claiming beyond three months as being a claim for the maximum permitted period. It seems likely that most claimants, if asked, would say that they would prefer this approach if the alternative was the total rejection of the claim for an extension of the time limit for claiming.

Although reg.5(1) only provides for a claim to be amended before a determination of it, it does not explicitly state that a claim may not be amended after a determination has been made. Thus if an amendment is made before, or even at, an appeal hearing, it is suggested that a tribunal would be able to deal with the claim for an extension, as amended. Since the tribunal is conducting a complete rehearing of all the issues under appeal, it may also wish to consider whether to treat the claim as simply being a claim for the maximum period allowed for an extension whatever period was initially requested by the claimant. It certainly seems doubtful that the intention was that only claims for extensions of up to three months could be considered under para.(4). This view is supported by *CJSA/3994/1998* where the Deputy Commissioner held that a claimant who had asked for his claim to be backdated for nearly a year should be treated as asking for the time for his making his claim to be extended to the maximum permitted by the regulations.

In *R(IS) 16/04*, the Commissioner follows the approach adopted in *CIS/849/1998* and *CJSA/3994/1998* (the correctness of which was conceded by the Secretary of State) to the effect that a claim can be taken as including a claim for a period starting with the earliest date which would make the claim in time.

Note too that *R(IS) 3/01* holds that the maximum period of extension should be calculated backwards from the date of actual claim, not forwards from the first day of the period expressly claimed for.

In *R(IS) 16/04*, the Commissioner rules that the question of reasonableness under regs 19(4)(b) and 19(6)(b) can only be asked in relation to each particular period of claim, and not the totality of any delay. The Commissioner gives as an example the position of a claimant who delays making a claim for income support for several months, but who then makes a claim. Just after he posts the claim form, there is a strike by postal workers which holds up delivery of the claim for some weeks. The fact that the claimant could have claimed earlier than he did should not defeat his reliance on adverse postal conditions in relation to the claim he actually made.

For an interesting case concerning the position of jurors and benefits, see *CIS/1010/2003*.

2.158   *(2) The test to be satisfied under paras (4) and (5):* There are two questions which must be answered before there can be an extension of the time for claiming. The first is that one of the circumstances listed in para.(5) has applied to the claimant. There is no condition that the circumstances must have applied *throughout* the period claimed for or continues to apply at the date of claim. Such considerations may come in under the second question, which is whether as a result of the circumstances or a combination of them, the claimant could not reasonably have been expected to make the claim earlier. This approach is explicitly set out in the reported Northern Ireland decision *R002/01 (IS)*. Thus, if a claimant who has been affected, for example, by illness delays unreasonably after recovery from the illness in making the claim, the request for an extension of the time limit for claiming will fail on the second ground. Such a claim could also fail if there has been unreasonable delay at some earlier stage before one of the listed circumstances applies.

Just as careful findings of fact were the secret of good decision-making under the old good cause rules, so too similar attention to detail will be required under the rules introduced in 1997. This will include findings of fact on key dates, and precision in making findings about what a claimant has been told and by whom.

Note that the list of circumstances set out in para.(5) is exhaustive, and there is no category of analogous circumstances to deal with meritorious cases which were not foreseen by the draftsman: *CJSA/3121/1998*, para.9. Ignorance of one's rights or of the procedure for claiming, whether reasonable or otherwise, does not feature in the circumstances listed in para.(5).

Finally, since the maximum period of backdating is now three months (previously it was 12 months), will this change the qualitative nature of the decision-making? Perhaps not, when the restrictive grounds on which the Secretary of State can extend the period to one month as set out in paras (6) and (7) are considered.

2.159   *(3) Paras (5)(a), (b), (c) and (g): reasonable practicability of obtaining assistance:* Several of the paragraphs provide, in addition to a primary set of circumstances, a further requirement, namely that "it was not reasonably practicable for the claimant to obtain assistance from another person to make his claim". In *CIS/2057/1998*, the Commissioner points out that the question is whether it is reasonable practicable for the claimant to seek assistance from another person to make the claim, not whether it is reasonable practicable for another person to take the initiative in offering assistance.

The corresponding words of the Northern Ireland regulations have been considered by the Chief Commissioner in Northern Ireland. In *C12/98 (IS)* the

Chief Commissioner notes, having regard to the two-stage test set out in para. (4), that:

> "'reasonably practicable for him to obtain assistance' . . . must mean something other than 'can reasonably have been expected to make the claim earlier', otherwise there would be no need for the two sub-paragraphs to consist of different terminology in qualifying reasonableness." (para.11.)

The Chief Commissioner adds:

> " . . . I accept that [the adjudication officer] is correct in submitting that regulation 19(5)(b) places an obligation on a sick or disabled person to seek assistance with his or her claim unless it is not practicable for him to obtain it; but while it might be more likely that someone who suffers a mental health problem could satisfy the provisions of regulation 19(4) and (5), it is necessary for the Adjudicating Authorities to look at the circumstances of each case and they are not entitled to make an assumption that a person suffering from a mental health problem would automatically be unable to seek assistance from another person to make a claim."

The circumstances in which it will and will not be reasonably practicable to obtain assistance from another person are so varied that, once again, full and careful findings or fact are the key to good decision making in all claims involving consideration of this issue.

(4) Para. (5)(a): difficulty communicating: This sub-para. concerns difficulties of communication arising because a person has learning, language or literacy difficulties, or because a person is deaf or blind. The words "deaf" or "blind" are not defined and so should be given their ordinary meaning, namely and respectively a person without hearing and a person without sight. Those who are hearing impaired or visually impaired may not be properly described as deaf or blind, but might well fall within the scope of someone who has difficulty communicating because of learning, language or literacy difficulties. Note that those who are deaf and blind must have difficulty communicating as a result of that disability and, additionally, must show that it was not reasonably practicable to obtain assistance from another person to make the claim. This is certainly an area where the qualification of *reasonable* practicability will be important.   **2.160**

In *CIS/2057/1998* the claimant had learning difficulties. She made a claim for income support which was awarded. Later her mother requested on her behalf that benefit be backdated to her sixteenth birthday (no-one had been appointed to act on behalf of the claimant). The tribunal erred in taking the view that the claimant had a supportive family who should have taken the initiative in finding out about her benefit entitlement. The proper approach was to determine (and the Commissioner so found) whether the claimant came within sub-para.(a)(i) and then to ask whether it was reasonably practicable for her to obtain assistance, not whether it was reasonably practicable for her family to provide it.

(5) Para. (5)(b): illness and disability: This sub-paragraph does not apply to claims for jobseeker's allowance. It deals with those many situations in which a person's delay is caused by illness or disability. In *CIS/610/1998* (discussed below in relation to sub-para.(d)) the Commissioner noted that the tribunal should have investigated the nature of the claimant's illness and whether this prevented him from queuing.   **2.161**

The first determination is the nature and dates of the person's illness or disability. The illness or disability must be compounded by its not being reasonably practicable for the claimant to obtain assistance from another person to make the claim.

(6) Para. (5)(c): caring responsibilities: This sub-para. offers an escape route for those with caring responsibilities. The situation in which the sub-para. applies are likely   **2.162**

to be (but not expressed exclusively to be) situations where a period of intensive caring arises, or perhaps where another carer becomes unavailable and the claimant has stepped in to help. It is easy to think of circumstances where the circumstances will be satisfied, but also easy to think of rather more marginal cases. The sub-para. also requires the claimant to show that it was not reasonably practicable to obtain assistance from another person to make the claim.

2.163   *(7) Para. (5) (d): information from an officer of the Department leading a claimant to believe that a claim for benefit would not succeed:* This has proved to be a troublesome provision which the Department sought to argue was much narrower in its scope than its interpretation by the Commissioners. Note that there is no requirement that the claimant's belief that a claim would not succeed was reasonable in all the circumstances. But an unreasonably held belief might result in the claimant's failing the test in para. (4)(b).

Note that in paragraphs 13 and 14 of *R(IS) 4/07* the Commissioner ruled that a breach of reg. 4(5) of the Claims and Payments Regulations (duty to provide a claim form) does not suspend time limits for making a claim.

A very common problem is the gap in benefit which often occurs when claimants transfer from jobseeker's allowance to income support because they have become incapable of work. It was thus perhaps predictable that the first Commissioners' decisions on the 1997 backdating rules would stem from this issue.

In *CIS/610/1998* the claimant, who had been claiming a jobseeker's allowance, took a Form Med. 3 issued by his GP to the Benefits Agency. There was a queue so he approached a security guard. The guard advised him that he did not need to fill in any forms, took his medical certificate, and wrote his national insurance number in a logging-in book. A week later the claimant received an incapacity benefit claim form through the post. He completed it and took it to the Benefits Agency. While in the queue, he was advised by another claimant that he needed to complete an income support claim form with his incapacity benefit claim form. He checked this advice when he reached the counter and then submitted claims for both benefits. The adjudication officer refused to backdate the claim for income support. The matter came before the Commissioner for consideration.

The Commissioner concluded on the facts of this case that the security guard was an "officer of the Department". The information supplied by the guard to the claimant could have left the claimant with the impression that he did not need to make another claim in connection with his transfer from a jobseeker's allowance to income support, and that in that sense any new claim would not succeed.

In *CIS/1721/1998* the claimant was given an incapacity benefit claim form when she went to the Job Centre with a medical certificate after fracturing her wrist. Two weeks later her claim for incapacity benefit was refused and she was advised to claim income support. The adjudication officer refused to backdate the claim.

The Commissioner accepts that the implication of the advice to claim incapacity benefit was that the claimant would be entitled to that benefit and not to income support. He considered that this was a reasonable belief on her part (incapacity benefit, if payable, would have exceeded her income support applicable amount). The Commissioner also took account of reg. 4(5). The official to whom she produced the medical certificate should have supplied her with an income support claim form. A failure to supply this form would also have led her to believe that there was no entitlement to income support.

CIS/3749/1998 expands on this point. The Commissioner states that claimants were entitled by reason of reg. 4(5) to assume that they had been given the right forms for the benefits they requested, and, if they were not, sub-para. (d) should clearly be considered. The claimant in this case had been receiving an income-based jobseeker's allowance, so there was at least a reasonable possibility that a claim for incapacity benefit would fail for lack of contributions. The Commissioner also drew attention to the fact that a failure to provide the right form bought reg. 4(7A) into effect which would give the Secretary of State a discretion at accept a late claim.

In *CIS/3994/1998* (followed in *CSIS/815/2004*) the claimant had received advice that he was not entitled to income support on making two enquiries of the Department. That advice seemed to be correct in the light of the evidence of what the claimant had told the Department when he telephoned. The tribunal had ruled that this was not enough to bring the claimant within sub-para.(5)(d) in that the information he had received was reasonable. The Deputy Commissioner could find no such qualification in the sub-para.; the claimant had made an enquiry and had received information which caused him not to make a claim for income support sooner than he did. He was entitled to have the time limit for claiming extended.

In a Northern Ireland decision of a Tribunal of Commissioners in *R1/01(IS)(T)* (unreported reference *C3/00–01 (IS)(T)*), the tribunal had to decide whether a New Deal adviser was an "officer of the Department". The claimant was a 59-year old married man who had been claiming income-based JSA for a number of years, when he was told he was being sent on the New Deal scheme. The claimant obtained a medical certificate that he was incapable of work. He presented this at the Jobseekers Section, his claim to JSA was terminated, but he was not advised to claim income support. The claimant later claimed income support and sought to have the claim back-dated. The tribunal notes that the Northern Ireland legislation refers to "an officer of the Department" whereas the Great Britain legislation refers to "an officer of the Department of Social Security or of the Department for Education and Employment". In Northern Ireland New Deal advisers are not officers of the Department of Social Development. Thus, they are covered by the legislation applicable in Great Britain, but not that in Northern Ireland. The tribunal doubted whether this distinction was intended.

The second question was whether a failure to give advice can be said to come within these provisions. The tribunal concluded that the giving of information required "the transfer of factual data from an officer to a claimant" (para.35). The regulation requires the giving of information to lead the claimant to believe that a claim for benefit will not succeed; it is not enough that the information left the claimant in ignorance of the possibility of claiming a different benefit. The tribunal says it must actually have led him to believe that a claim would not succeed.

The tribunal goes on to find that the information referred to in sub-para.(d) does not need to relate in some way to the benefit that is claimed late. Information about one claim or benefit could lead a claimant to believe that a claim for another benefit would not succeed.

The fourth issue addressed by the tribunal was whether the test is an objective or subjective one. The tribunal agreed with the conclusions of a Great Britain Commissioner in *R(IS)3/01* (the report of *CIS/4354/1999*) that adjudicating authorities,

"may legitimately test whether or not it believes a claimant's evidence about what he was led to believe by what reason a person in the claimant's circumstances might have been led to believe." (para.18).

In *R(IS)3/01* the Commissioner had held that the words of reg.19(5)(d) "are not to be given any artificially restricted meaning" (para.14). The information to which the regulation refers is not limited to information given in respect of the claim in question, but could include information concerning the ending of entitlement to some other benefit (paras 13–18).

2.164

In *CIS/4884/2002* the Commissioner was considering a tribunal's decision following a paper hearing in which they had concluded that the claimant, who had been told to apply for incapacity benefit which had delayed his claim for income support to which he was actually entitled, had not received "advice that a claim for income support would not succeed." In concluding that the tribunal had erred in law, the Commissioner warns of the need to take care to avoid looseness of language, since the receipt of advice is different from the receipt of information. Indeed the Commissioner doubts the correctness of the Northern Ireland Commissioners as expressed in this regard in *C3/00–01 (IS)* The Commissioner goes on to advise,

"In my judgment the correct approach to regulation 19(5)(d) is that adopted by the Commissioner in report decision *R(IS)3/01*. The wording that 'the claimant was given information . . . which led the claimant to believe' needs to be given a practical, not an artificially restricted meaning, and it is not necessary for this purpose that what the claim was told by a departmental official should have referred *expressly* to the benefit afterwards sought to be claimed, if for example the information was that some different benefit was available which, if correct, would have made such a claim beside the point. Whether the claimant was given such information, and what he was or was not actually led to believe about the possibility of putting in a concurrent claim just in case, are matters of fact that need to be determined by the tribunal on the actual evidence; tested if necessary by cross-examination to resolve any doubt or dispute about what actually took place, or what the claimant afterwards says he believed at the time. Only when those facts have been clearly identified can a tribunal say if the condition in regulation 19(5)(d) has been met, and (if it has) then go on to assess as a matter of objective reasonableness whether the claimant also meets the further condition in regulation 19(4)(b) that he could not reasonably have been expected to make the claim earlier (not even one day earlier) than the date he did." (para.7.)

The Commissioner in *CJSA/580/2003* also followed the approach which had been adopted by Commissioners in Great Britain.

A rather unusual set of circumstances arose in *CJSA/3084/2004*. The claimant attended at an office of the Department to claim a jobseeker's allowance. He completed a form. This transpired to be not a claim form but a locally-used preliminary questionnaire (whose format frequently changed) which the Secretary of State conceded before the Commissioner gave the impression that a claim was being made. In allowing the backdating of a claim for a jobseeker's allowance, the Commissioner says:

"9. The point of law that emerged during the hearing before me of the application for leave to appeal, and which the tribunal did not consider is as follows. Regulation 19(5)(d) refers, not to advice, but to information. Reference was made to decisions by Commissioners in *R(IS) 3/01* and *CIS 4884 2002*. If a claimant has been led to believe that he has made a claim, but he has not in fact made a claim, and because no decision has been received therefore believes that the claim has not succeeded, that seems to me to amount to having been given information which led him to believe that a subsequent real or effective claim would also not succeed."

2.165   *(8) Para. (5) (e) and (f): written advice or information leading the claimant to believe that a claim to benefit would not succeed:* Sub-paragraph (e) is concerned with written advice given by knowledgeable advisers other than officers of the Department which also leads that claimant to believe that a claim for benefit would not succeed, while sub-para. (f) is concerned with written information from an employer or former employer, or a bank or a building society about income or capital which leads claimant to believe that a claim for benefit would not succeed. The additional requirement here is that the claimant must have received "written advice" or "written information". There may be significance in the use of the words "advice" and "information"; sub-para. (e) requires the advice to have led the claimant to believe that a claim for benefit would not succeed, whereas sub-para. (f) simply requires "information". So in the latter case, a bank statement may suffice. Quite what the limits of written advice and information are remains to be tested. Would oral advice backed up by a written file note setting out the advice be sufficient? That would appear to be a forced interpretation of the sub-para., which appears to suggest that the advice has been reduced to writing and given to the claimant. But it is suggested that a claimant should be able to rely on the sub-para. if they were given a document which they have lost. Here the issue will be whether the decision-maker accepts their account of the contents of the written advice. That is a matter of the claimant's credibility rather than substance. Not every advice agency keeps file copies of written advice to their clients.

CJSA/1136/1998 considers the requirement that the advice must be in writing. The claimant had been dismissed and was advised by his trade union official not to claim any benefit until the reasons for his dismissal had been investigated through his employer's appeal procedures. This advice was confirmed in writing in a letter produced by the tribunal hearing in January 1998. The Commissioner states that the reason the sub-para. required the advice to be in writing was to avoid any doubt or argument as to the contents of that advice. If before the decision made by the decision-maker or tribunal, the advice was confirmed in writing, these difficulties were avoided and the advice amounted to written advice for the purposes of the sub-para. The reasoning is questionable since the wording of the provision appears to require the written advice to be what leads the claimant to believe that a claim will not succeed. The Commissioners' approach could also raise difficulties now that tribunals cannot take account of any circumstances not obtaining at the time when the decision appealed against was made: s.12(8)(b), SSA 1998.

The group of advisers within the sub-paragraph is drawn widely, and covers a wide range of agencies.

In *CIS/1107/2008* the Commissioner ruled that reg.19(5)(e) was broad enough to include advice given by officials in the visa section of the British Embassy in Addis Ababa. The appellant had, incorrectly, been issued with a two year visa with a restriction on recourse to public funds. This resulted in his not claiming income support until he had received the correct visa which was for indefinite leave to remain with no restriction in relation to recourse to public funds.

As with sub-para.(5)(d), there is no requirement that the claimant's belief that a claim would not succeed was reasonable in all the circumstances. But an unreasonably held belief might result in the claimant's failing the test in para.(4)(b).

(9) Para.(5)(g): domestic emergencies: These circumstances are rather surprisingly included in para.(5) when they might more appropriately be included within the Secretary of State's discretion, since it is difficult to think of circumstances which would meet the requirements of the sub-para. which would last more than a month. Perhaps the distinction originally lay in the mandatory nature of the extension where para.(5) is satisfied compared with the discretionary nature of the extension in para.(7), but if that is the distinction, there are circumstances listed in para.(7) which should also be in para.(5). The extension in para.(6) is mandatory following the April 2002 amendment.

2.166

(10) Para.(5)(h): adverse weather conditions: Again these circumstances will usually be of very limited duration save in the more remote parts of the country, and the circumstances seem more appropriate for determination under the Secretary of State's decision-making under para.(6).

2.167

(11) Paras (6) and (7): the decision-maker's one-month decision: As originally drafted, this was the Secretary of State's discretion to extend the time limit for claiming up to one month and applies to claims for income support, jobseeker's allowance, working families' tax credit and disabled person's tax credit. The Secretary of State could extend the time limit for claiming for any period up to a maximum of one month,

2.168

- if the Secretary of State considered that to do so would be consistent with the proper administration of benefit, and

- any of the circumstances in para.(7) applied.

The April 2002 amendment makes this a mandatory list of special circumstances which justify a one month extension to the time limit for claiming. The reference to consistency with the proper administration of benefit happily disappears. Once again the list is exhaustive and has no category of analogous circumstances.

In *CJSA/3659/2001* the Commissioner notes that decisions under reg.19(6) and (7), which contain the requirement that the Secretary of State in the circumstances set out in these paragraphs extend the time limit for claiming to one month, are within the jurisdiction of tribunals. This flows from the provision in para.5(a) of Sch.2 to the Decisions and Appeals Regulations which excludes from the list of Secretary of State's decisions against which no appeal lies a decision under reg.19 as to the time for claiming benefit. This is drafted widely enough to bring within the tribunal's jurisdiction not only the matters in reg.19(4) and (5), but also those in reg.19(6) and (7). It follows that tribunals must consider both sets of rules relating to extension of the time limit for claiming.

Note in relation to these provisions, reg.6(1)(aa) and (1A) for the automatic allowance of one month to return the claim forms in the cases mentioned there, and note the discretionary rule in reg.6(4B) in relation to claims for a jobseeker's allowance.

It would seem that the principle of *CSIS/61/1992* still applies that in every case where a claim is made outside the time limit specified in Sch.4, the Secretary of State should consider the use of the operation of the extension under para.(6) before the claim is referred to a decision-maker for decision. If this has not been done, a tribunal may decide to adjourn for the matter to be considered. There may also be cases where information comes to light in the hearing which makes it appropriate to adjourn to enable the decision maker to re-consider the matter.

It is sometimes argued that the circumstances envisaged in sub-para.(7)(a) are exceptional, as when an office closes unexpectedly due to flooding or industrial action. It is submitted that this is to apply too narrow an interpretation to the words. The sub-para. surely covers situations where a claim would need to be made on a Saturday, but the office is closed and the claim is submitted on the following Monday.

There has been a decision on reg.19(7)(b), which may be limited to some rather special facts: *CSJSA/0811/2006*. It concerned a claimant's lack of funds to pay the ferry fare from Islay to the mainland. He argued that this meant that he was unable to attend the appropriate office due to difficulties with his normal mode of transport and there was no reasonable alternative available. The Deputy Commissioner, in remitting the appeal for determination a new tribunal, considered that "difficulties" in this context could include an inability to pay. He then addressed the issue of whether there was any reasonable alternative, and interpreted the regulation here as referring to reasonable alternative transport. Finally, it was necessary to consider whether the claimant could reasonably have been expected to make the claim earlier than he did. Here the issue was whether earlier claim by telephone was a reasonable course of action for the claimant to have taken. This would require consideration of any enquiry made by the claimant about telephone claims, and whether the claimant did as much as could reasonably be expected of him. If, having done that, he remained ignorant of the possibility of a telephone claim, then he would not fall foul of the provision in reg.19(6)(b).

In *CIS/4901/2002* the Commissioner considered what is meant by the term "adverse postal conditions" as used in reg.19(7)(c), but ultimately decided the case on different grounds. The circumstances of the case were that the claimant had received some claim forms in the post but no reply paid envelope had been provided. The forms were completed and mailed to the Department in an envelope provided by the claimant to which he affixed a single first class stamp. However, the correct postage was more than this. It was not received by the Department. A second claim was made and benefit paid from a later date; the claimant sought to have this claim backdated to the date of an enquiry made of the Jobcentre about his benefit entitlement which had resulted in his being advised to claim income support or incapacity benefit, and in his being sent the first set of forms. Eventually, the first set of forms was returned to the claimant by the Post Office endorsed by the Revenue Protection Section indicating that insufficient postage had been attached to the letter. Some £0.77 needed to be paid for the forms to be delivered.

A second endorsement was to the effect that the package had "not [been] called for." It was established that there was, in relation to the Benefit Office to which the claimant had sent the first set of forms, an arrangement under which the Post Office adopted a different policy from that which normally applies in relation to under-stamped mail. The normal practice is to advise the addressee that mail awaits them and is available on payment of the amount of the underpayment plus handling fee. The practice which it was accepted should have been adopted in this case was for the forms to have been delivered and for the amount of the under-payment to be included in a bulk surcharge arrangement with the Department. It would seem to flow from the detailed reasoning of the Commissioner in the case that he would accept that there might be an argument to bring the failure of such arrangements within the ambit of the phrase "adverse postal conditions." However, he decided the case on the basis that the Post Office in holding the first set of claim forms was the bailee for the Department and so the original forms are to be treated as being in the hands of the Department between the date of its receipt until they were returned to the claimant. This was sufficient to ground entitlement to the benefit from the earlier date.

In *R(IS) 16/04*, the Commissioner accepts that delays in post arriving over the Christmas period constitute adverse postal conditions within para.(7)(c).

In *CJSA/3960/2006*, the Deputy Commissioner ruled that a delay of two working days beyond the maximum period within which a letter should have been delivered constituted "adverse postal conditions". The mere fact of the delay established that there were adverse postal conditions. A second issue arose in the case on the inter-pretation of the words "before the date that his entitlement expired" in reg.19(7)(d). The Deputy Commissioner ruled that a decision that a person was not entitled to income support from February 4, 2006 meant that the claimant's entitlement ended on February 3, 2006, since "her entitlement expired on the very last moment of the Friday but before the very first moment of the Saturday." (para. 20).

In *CJSA/0743/2006* the Commissioner ruled that the words "another benefit" in reg.19(7)(d) referred to a different benefit. He said, "I consider that the natural meaning of the work in that context is 'different'" (para. 9).

(12) para.(8) CJSA/4383/2003 concerns the relationship of the 28 day time limit   **2.169** for claiming income support by asylum seekers who have received notification that they have been accepted as having refugee status under reg.21ZB(2) of the Income Support General Regulations. Provided income support is claimed within this time limit, the award can be backdated to the date of the asylum application. Because of delays inherent in the determination of such claims, this can be a very substan-tial period. In the appeal before the Commissioner, the issue arose as to whether a person within the ambit of reg.21ZB(2) lost all ability to use the provisions of reg.19(4) and (5) to seek backdating of a claim for income support. The Secretary of State had argued that the reg.19(8) had this effect. The Commissioner disagreed for the following reasons:

"17.... In my view this is to misunderstand the legislative framework. The start-ing point is section 1 of the Social Security Administration Act 1992, which (in virtually all cases) requires a claim to be made as a precondition of entitlement to benefit. Section 5 of the 1992 Act then grants the Secretary of State various regulation-making powers in relation to claims. In the exercise of these powers, the Social Security (Claims and Payments) Regulations 1987 have been made. Regulation 19(1) of, and Schedule 4 to, those Regulations sets out the basic rules for claiming various benefits and the time limits that apply. Thus the general rule is that claims for income support or jobseeker's allowance must be made on 'the first day of the period in respect of which the claim is made'. Regulation 19(4) and (5) then provide, by way of exception to this general principle, that the pre-scribed period for claiming these benefits can be extended for up to three months if 'good cause', as defined by the Regulations, can be established.

18. However, regulation 19(4) is expressly stated to be subject to regulation 19(8). The purpose of regulation 19(8) is to provide that those claimants who can avail themselves of regulation 21ZB are not to be caught by the standard limit of three months on backdating entitlement to income support. A successful applicant for asylum, who claims arrears of income support within 28 days of receiving the Home Office's notification, is a person who makes 'a claim to which regulation 21ZB [. . .] of the Income Support (General) Regulations 1987 (treatment of refugees) applies'. In that situation regulation 19(8) then provides that 'this regulation' (i.e. the normal three month rule) 'shall not have effect'. In other words, the claim for arrears of benefit, if made within the 28 day time limit, may be backdated by many more than three months and indeed right back to the date of the asylum application. This is supported by regulation 6(4D) of the 1987 Regulations, which deems the claim so made to have been made actually at the much earlier date when asylum was applied for—see the obiter opinion of Mrs Deputy Commissioner Rowley in *CIS/579/2004* (at paragraph 43.4).

19. In my view, therefore, there are not two entirely separate and mutually exclusive regimes, which appears to be the Secretary of State's contention. The correct position in law is that a person in the claimant's situation may be able to make a claim for backdated benefit in accordance with regulation 19(4) and (5). Just because he is a successful applicant for asylum does not take him out of that regime. However, if he had made his claim within 28 days of the Home Office letter, he might have his entitlement to benefit backdated to the date of his original application for asylum, by virtue of regulation 21ZB, regardless of the normal three month rule in regulation 19(4)."

PART III

PAYMENTS

[¹ Time of payment: general provision

2.170   20. Subject to regulations 21 to 26B, benefit shall be paid in accordance with an award as soon as is reasonably practicable after the award has been made.]

AMENDMENT

1. Inserted by The Social Security (Miscellaneous Amendments) (No.2) Regulations 2006 (SI 2006/832), reg.2 (April 10, 2006).

DEFINITION

"benefit"—see reg.2(2).

2.171   20A.—[¹ . . .]

AMENDMENT

1. The Social Security (Miscellaneous Amendments) (No.2) Regulations 2006 (SI 2006/832), reg.2 (April 10, 2006).

Direct credit transfer

2.172   21.—[⁹ (1) Subject to the provisions of this regulation, benefit may, by an arrangement between the Secretary of State and the person claiming or entitled to it [¹⁰ or person appointed under regulation 33 or specified in regulation 33(1)(c) or (d)], be paid by way of direct credit transfer into a bank or other account—

(a) In the name of the person entitled to benefit, or his spouse or partner, or a person acting on his behalf, or

(b) In the joint names of the person entitled to benefit and his spouse or partner, or the person entitled to benefit and a person acting on his behalf.]

(2) [⁹ . . .]

(3) [²Subject to paragraph (3A)] benefit shall be paid in accordance with paragraph (1) within seven days of the last day of each successive period of entitlement [⁹ . . .] [⁷or, so far as concerns working familiar tax credit, within such time as the Board may direct]

[²(3A) Income Support shall be paid in accordance with paragraph (1) within 7 days of the time determined for the payment of income support in accordance with Schedule 7.]

[⁶(3B) Where child benefit is payable in accordance with paragraph (1), [⁹ an arrangement under that paragraph] shall also have effect for any guardian's allowance to which the claimant is entitled and that allowance shall be paid in the same manner as the child benefit due in his case.

(3C) Where guardian's allowance is payable in accordance with paragraph (1), [⁹ an arrangement under that paragraph] shall also have effect for the child benefit to which the claimant is entitled and that child benefit shall be paid in the same manner as the guardian's allowance which is due in his case.]

(4) In respect of benefit which is the subject of an arrangement for payment under this regulation, the Secretary of State [⁷or the Board] may make a particular payment by credit transfer otherwise than is provided by paragraph (3) [²or (3A)] if it appears to him [⁷or them] appropriate to do so for the purpose of—

(a) paying any arrears of benefit, or

(b) making a payment in respect of a terminal period of an award or for any similar purpose.

(5) The arrangement for benefit to be payable in accordance with this regulation may be terminated—

(a) by the person entitled to benefit or a person acting on his behalf by notice in writing delivered or sent to an appropriate office or

(b) by the Secretary of State [⁷or the Board] if the arrangement seems to him [⁷or them] to be no longer appropriate to the circumstances of the particular case.

[⁸ (5A) In relation to payment of a joint-claim jobseeker's allowance, references in this regulation to the person entitled to benefit shall be construed as references to the member of the joint-claim couple who is the nominated member for the purposes of section 3B of the Jobseekers Act.]

(6) [⁵. . .]

AMENDMENTS

1. The Social Security (Miscellaneous Provisions) Amendment Regulations 1992 (SI 1992/247), reg.15 (March 9, 1992).

2. The Social Security (Claims and Payments) Amendment (No.2) Regulations 1993 (SI 1993/1113), reg.2 (May 12, 1993).

3. The Social Security (Claims and Payments) Amendment Regulations 1994 (SI 1994/2319), reg.4 (October 3, 1994).

4. The Social Security (Claims and Payments) Amendment Regulations 1994 (SI 1994/2319), reg.8 (April 13, 1995).

5. The Social Security (Claims and Payments) Amendment Regulations 1996 (SI 1996/672), reg.2(3) (April 4, 1996).

6. The Social Security (Claims and Payments) Amendment Regulations 1999 (SI 1999/2358), reg.2 (September 20, 1999).

7. The Tax Credits (Claims and Payments) (Amendment) Regulations 1999 (SI 1999/2572), regs 20, 23 & 24 (October 5, 1999).

8. The Social Security (Joint Claims: Consequential Amendments) Regulations 2000 (SI 2000/1982), reg.2(6) (March 19, 2001).

9. The Social Security (Claims and Payments and Miscellaneous Amendments) (No.2) Regulations 2002 (SI 2002/2441), reg.2 (April 6, 2003).

10. The Social Security (Miscellaneous Amendments) (No.2) Regulations 2006 (SI 2006/832), reg.2 (April 10, 2006).

DEFINITIONS

"appropriate office"—see reg.2(1).
"partner"—*ibid.*

GENERAL NOTE

2.173   Until May 12, 1993, it was not possible for income support to be paid by direct credit transfer.

[¹ Delayed payment of lump sum

2.174   **21A.**—(1) The regulation applies where—
(a) a person ("P") is entitled to a lump sum under, as the case may be—
   (i) Schedule 5 to the Contributions and Benefits Act (pensions increase or lump sum where entitlement to retirement pension is deferred);
   (ii) Schedule 5A to that Act (pension increase or lump sum where entitlement to share additional pension is deferred); or
   (iii) Schedule 1 to the Social Security (Graduated Retirement Benefit) Regulations 2005 (further provisions replacing section 36(4) of the National Insurance Act 1965: increases of graduated retirement benefit and lump sums);
or
(b) the Secretary of State decides to make a payment on account of such a lump sum.

(2) Subject to paragraph (3), for the purposes of section 7 of the Finance (No. 2) Act 2005 (charge to income tax of lump sum), P may elect to be paid the lump sum in the tax year ("the later year of assessment") next following the tax year which would otherwise be the applicable year of assessment by virtue of section 8 of that Act (meaning of "applicable year of assessment" in section 7).

(3) P may not elect in accordance with paragraph (2) ("a tax election") unless he elects on the same day as he chooses a lump sum in accordance with, as the case may be—
(a) paragraph A1 or 3C of Schedule 5 to the Contributions and Benefits Act;
(b) paragraph 1 of Schedule 5A to that Act;
(c) paragraph 12 or 17 of Schedule 1 to the Social Security (Graduated Retirement Benefit) Regulations 2005,

or within a month of that day.

(4) A tax election may be made in writing to an office specified by the Secretary of state for accepting such elections or, except where in any particular case the Secretary of State directs that the election must be made in writing, it may be made by telephone call to the number specified by the Secretary of State.

(5) If P makes a tax election, payment of the lump sum, or any payment on account of the lump sum, shall be made in the first month of the later year of assessment or as soon as reasonably practicable after that month, unless P revokes the tax election before the payment is made.

(6) If P makes no tax elections in accordance with paragraph (2) and (3), or revokes a tax election, payment of the lump sum or any payment on account of the lump sum shall be made as soon as reasonably practicable after P—

(a) elected for a lump sum, or was treated as having so elected; or

(b) revoked a tax election.

(7) If P dies before the beginning of the later year of assessment—

(a) any tax election in respect of P's lump sum shall cease to have effect; and

(b) no person appointed under regulation 30 to act on P's behalf may make a tax election.

(8) In this regulation "the later year of assessment" has the meaning given by section 8(5) of the Finance (No. 2) Act 2005.]

AMENDMENT

1. The Social Security (Deferral of Retirement Pensions, Shared Additional Pension and Graduated Retirement Benefit) (Miscellaneous Provisions) Regulations 2005 (SI 2005/2677) (April 6, 2006).

Long term benefits

22.—[5 (1) Subject to the provisions of this regulation and [7 regulations 22A and 25(1)], long term benefits may be paid at intervals of [6 four weekly in arrears, weekly in advance or, where the beneficiary agrees, at intervals not exceeding 13 weeks in arrears.]

(1A) Disability living allowance shall be paid at intervals of four weeks.]

(2) Where the amount of long-term benefit payable is less than[4 £5.00] a week the Secretary of State may direct that it shall be paid (whether in advance or in arrears) at such intervals as may be specified not exceeding 12 months.

(3) Schedule 6 specifies the days of the week on which the various long term benefits are payable.

2.175

AMENDMENTS

1. The Social Security (Claims and Payments) Amendment Regulations 1991 (SI 1991/2741), reg.12(a) (February 3, 1992).

2. The Social Security (Claims and Payments) Amendment Regulations 1991 (SI 1991/2741), reg.12(b) (February 3, 1992).

3. The Social Security (Claims and Payments) Amendment (No.4) Regulations 1994 (SI 1994/3196), reg.5 (January 10, 1995).

4. The Social Security (Claims and Payments and Adjudication) Amendment Regulations 1996 (SI 1996/2306), reg.22(2) (October 7, 1996).

5. The Social Security (Claims and Payments and Miscellaneous Amendments) (No.2) Regulations 2002 (SI 2002/2441), reg.2 (April 6, 2003).

6. The Social Security (Miscellaneous Amendments) (No.5) Regulations 2008 (SI 2008/2667), reg.2 (October 30, 2008).

7. The Social Security (Claims and Payments) Amendment Regulations 2009 (SI 2009/604) reg.2 (April 6, 2009).

[¹ Bereavement allowance, widowed mother's allowance, widowed parent's allowance and widow's pension

2.176

22A.—(1) Subject to paragraphs (2) and (4), bereavement allowance, widowed mother's allowance, widowed parent's allowance and widow's pension shall be paid fortnightly in arrears on the day of the week specified in paragraph (3).

(2) The Secretary of State may, in any particular case or class of case, arrange that a benefit specified in paragraph (1) be paid on any other day of the week.

(3) The day specified for the purposes of paragraph (1) is the day in column (2) which corresponds to the series of numbers in column (1) which includes the last 2 digits of the person's national insurance number—

(1)	(2)
00 to 19	Monday
20 to 39	Tuesday
40 to 59	Wednesday
60 to 79	Thursday
80 to 99	Friday.

(4) The Secretary of State may, in any particular case or class of case, arrange that the beneficiary be paid weekly in advance or in arrears or, where the beneficiary agrees to be paid in such manner, at intervals of four or 13 weeks in arrears.

Payment of bereavement allowance, widowed mother's allowance, widowed parent's allowance and widow's pension at a daily rate

22B.—(1) Where entitlement to a bereavement allowance or widowed parent's allowance begins on a day which is not the first day of the benefit week, it shall be paid at a daily rate in respect of the period beginning with the day on which entitlement begins and ending on the day before the first day of the following benefit week.

(2) Where the Secretary of State changes the day on which a benefit mentioned in paragraph (5) is payable, the benefit shall be paid at a daily rate in respect of any day for which payment would have been made but for that change.

(3) An award of benefit mentioned in paragraph (5) shall be paid at a daily rate where—

(a) the award is terminated;

(b) entitlement ends on a day other than the last day of the benefit week; and

(c) the benefit is paid in arrears.

(4) Where benefit is paid at a daily rate in the circumstances mentioned in paragraph (3), it shall be so paid in respect of the period beginning with

the first day of the final benefit week and ending on the last day for which there is an entitlement to the benefit.

(5) Paragraphs (2) and (3) apply to—

(a) bereavement allowance;
(b) widowed mother's allowance;
(c) widowed parent's allowance; and
(d) widow's pension.

(6) Where benefit is payable at a daily rate in the circumstances mentioned in this regulation, the daily rate shall be $1/7^{th}$ of the weekly rate.]

AMENDMENTS

1. Inserted byThe Social Security (Claims and Payments) Amendment Regulations 2009 (SI 2009/604) reg.2 (April 6, 2009).

GENERAL NOTE

Note that the Social Security (Transitional Payments) Regulations 2009 (SI 2009/609) make provision for the payment of a one-off transitional payment and an adjusting payment of benefit. Regulation 2 provides for a one-off transitional payment to be made where payments to persons in receipt of income support, widowed mother's allowance, widowed parent's allowance and widow's pension are changed from weekly in advance to weekly in arrears. Regulation 3 makes provision for an adjusting payment of benefit to be made where payments to persons in receipt of incapacity benefit, income support, severe disablement allowance, widowed mother's allowance, widowed parent's allowance and widow's pension are changed from weekly in arrears to fortnightly in arrears. Regulation 4 makes provision for the recovery of an adjusting payment of benefit.

[¹ Child benefit and guardian's allowance.]

23.—(1) Subject to the provisions of this regulation [³ . . .], child benefit shall be payable as follows:—

(a) in a case where a person entitled to child benefit elects to receive payment weekly in accordance with the provisions of Schedule 8, child benefit shall be payable weekly from the first convenient date after the election has been made;
(b) in any other case child benefit shall be payable in the last week of each successive period of four weeks of the period of entitlement.

(2) Subject to paragraph (3) and regulation 21, child benefit payable weekly or four-weekly shall be payable on Mondays or Tuesdays (as the Secretary of State may in any case determine) [² by means of serial orders or on presentation of an instrument for benefit payment]

(3) In such cases as the Secretary of State may determine, child benefit shall be payable otherwise than—

(a) by means of serial order [²or on presentation of an instrument for benefit payment,]
(b) on Mondays or Tuesdays, or
(c) at weekly or four-weekly intervals,

and where child benefit is paid at four-weekly intervals in accordance with paragraph (1)(b) the Secretary of State shall arrange for it to be paid weekly if satisfied that payment at intervals of four weeks is causing hardship.

[¹ (3A) Where a claimant for child benefit is also entitled to guardian's allowance, that allowance shall be payable in the same manner and at the same intervals as the claimant's child benefit under this regulation.]

2.177

2.178

(4) The Secretary of State shall take steps to notify persons to whom child benefit is payable of the arrangements he has made for payment so far as those arrangements affect such persons.

AMENDMENTS

1. The Social Security (Claims and Payments) Amendment Regulations 1999 (SI 1999/2358), reg.2(5) (September 20, 1999).
2. The Social Security (Claims and Payments) Amendment (No.4) Regulations 1994 (SI 1994/3196), reg.6 (January 10, 1995).
3. The Social Security (Claims and Payments and Miscellaneous Amendments) (No.2) Regulations 2002 (SI 2002/2441), reg.2 (April 1, 2003).

[¹ Incapacity benefit, maternity allowance and severe disablement allowance

2.179

24.—(1) Subject to [³ . . .] [⁴ paragraphs (3) and (3A)], incapacity benefit [⁴ , maternity allowance] and severe disablement allowance shall be paid fortnightly in arrears unless [⁴ in any particular case or class of case], the Secretary of State arranges otherwise.

[⁴ "(1A) Subject to paragraph (1B), the benefits specified in paragraph (1) shall be paid on the day of the week specified in paragraph (1C).

(1B) The Secretary of State may, in any particular case or class of case, arrange that a benefit specified in paragraph (1) be paid on any other day of the week.

(1C) The day specified for the purposes of paragraph (1A) is the day in column (2) which corresponds to the series of numbers in column (1) which includes the last 2 digits of the person's national insurance number—

(1)	(2)
00 to 19	Monday
20 to 39	Tuesday
40 to 59	Wednesday
60 to 79	Thursday
80 to 99	Friday.

]
(2) [⁴ . . .]
(3) If the weekly amount of incapacity benefit or severe disablement allowance is less than £1.00 it may be paid in arrears at intervals of 4 weeks.

[² (3A) Where the amount of incapacity benefit payable after reduction for pension payments under section 30DD of the Social Security Contributions and Benefits Act 1992 (including any reduction for other purposes) is less than £5.00 per week, the Secretary of State may direct that it shall be paid [⁴ in arrears] at such intervals as may be specified not exceeding 12 months.]
(4) [⁴ . . .]]

AMENDMENTS

1. Reg.24 substituted by The Social Security (Claims and Payments) Amendment (No.2) Regulations 1994 (SI 1994/2943), reg.9 (April 13, 1995); words in heading to and certain words in regulation deleted by The Social Security (Claims and Payments) (Jobseeker's Allowance Consequential Amendments) Regulations 1996 (SI 1996/1460), reg.2(13) (October 7, 1996).

2. The Social Security (Incapacity Benefit) Miscellaneous Amendments Regulations 2000 (SI 2000/3210), reg.3 (April 6, 2001).

3. The Social Security (Claims and Payments and Miscellaneous Amendments) (No.2) Regulations 2002 (SI 2002/2441), reg.2 (April 8, 2003).

4. The Social Security (Claims and Payments) Amendments Regulations 2009 (SI 2009/604), reg.2 (April 6, 2009).

Payment of attendance allowance and constant attendance allowance at a daily rate

25.—(1) Attendance allowance [¹or disability living allowance] [². . .] shall be paid in respect of any person, for any day falling within a period to which paragraph (2) applies, at the daily rate (which shall be equal to ⅐th of the weekly rate) and attendance allowance [¹ or disability living allowance] [². . .] payable in pursuance of this regulation shall be paid weekly or as the Secretary of State may direct in any case.

(2) This paragraph applies to any period which—

(a) begins on the day immediately following the last day of the period during which a person was living in [³ a hospital specified in or other accommodation provided as specified in regulations made under [section 72(8) of the Social Security Contributions and Benefits Act 1992] ("specified hospital or other accommodation")]; and

(b) ends—

   (i) if the first day of the period was a day of payment, at midnight on the day preceding the [³ 4th] following day of payment, or

   (ii) if that day was not a day of payment, at midnight on the day preceding the [³ 5th] following day of payment, or

   (iii) if earlier, on the day immediately preceding the day on which [³ he next lives in specified hospital or other accommodation],

if on the first day of the period it is expected that, before the expiry of the period of [³ 28 days] beginning with that day, he will return to [³ specified hospital or other accommodation].

(3) An increase of disablement pension under [section 104 of the Social Security Contributions and Benefits Act 1992] where constant attendance is needed ("constant attendance allowance") shall be paid at a daily rate of 1/7th of the weekly rate in any case where it becomes payable for a period of less than a week which is immediately preceded and immediately succeeded by periods during which the constant attendance allowance was not payable because regulation 21(1) of the Social Security (General Benefit) Regulations 1982 applied.

AMENDMENTS

1. The Social Security (Claims and Payments) Amendment Regulations 1991 (SI 1991/2741), reg.13(a) (April 6, 1992).

2. The Social Security (Disability Living Allowance and Claims and Payments) Amendment Regulations 1996 (SI 1996/1436), reg.3 (July 31, 1996).

3. The Social Security (Claims and Payments) Amendment Regulations 1991 (SI 1991/2741), reg.13(b)–(f) (April 6, 1992).

Income support

26.—(1) [³ Subject to regulation 21 (direct credit transfer), Schedule 7] shall have effect for determining the [⁶ . . .] time at which income support is to be paid, [. . .⁵] and the day when entitlement to income support is to begin.

2.180

2.181

(2) [⁶ . . .]

[² (3) [⁶ . . .].]

(4) Where the entitlement to income support is less than 10 pence or, in the case of a beneficiary to whom [¹ section 23(a)] of the Social Security Act 1986 [SSCBA, s.126] applies, £5, that amount shall not be payable unless the claimant is also entitled to payment of any other benefit with which income support [²may be paid] under arrangements made by the Secretary of State.

AMENDMENTS

1. The Social Security (Claims and Payments) Amendment Regulations 1988 (SI 1988/522), reg.6 (April 11, 1988).

2. The Social Security (Claims and Payments and Payments on account, Overpayments and Recovery) Amendment Regulations 1989 (SI 1989/136), reg.2 (February 27, 1989).

3. The Social Security (Claims and Payments) Amendment (No.2) Regulations 1993 (SI 1993/1113), reg.3 (May 12, 1993).

4. The Social Security Act 1998 (Commencment No.12 and Consequential and Transitional Provisions) Order 1999 (SI 1999/3178), Sch.6 (November 29, 1999).

5. The Social Security and Child Support (Miscellaneous Amendments) Regulations 2000 (SI 2000/1596), reg.4(1) (June 19, 2000).

6. The Social Security (Miscellaneous Amendments) (No.2) Regulations 2006 (SI 2006/832), reg.2 (April 10, 2006).

[¹ Jobseeker's allowance

2.182

26A.—(1) Subject to the following provisions of this regulation, jobseeker's allowance shall be paid fortnightly in arrears unless in any particular case or class of case the Secretary of State arranges otherwise.

(2) The provisions of paragraph 2A of Schedule 7 (payment of income support at times of office closure) shall apply for the purposes of payment of a jobseeker's allowance as they apply for the purposes of payment of income support [⁵ . . .]

(3) Where the amount of a jobseeker's allowance is less than £1.00 a week the Secretary of State may direct that it shall be paid at such intervals, not exceeding 13 weeks, as may be specified in the direction.

(4)–(8) [. . .⁴].

AMENDMENTS

1. The Social Security (Claims and Payments) (Jobseeker's Allowance Consequential Amendments) Regulations 1996 (SI 1996/1460), reg.2(14) (October 7, 1996).

2. The Social Security (Miscellaneous Amendments) (No.4) Regulations 1998 (SI 1998/1174), reg.8(3)(a) (June 1, 1998).

3. The Social Security Act 1998 (Commencement No.12 and Consequential and Transitional Provisions) Order 1999 (SI 1999/3178), Sch.6 (November 29, 1999).

4. The Social Security and Child Support (Miscellaneous Amendments) Regulations 2000 (SI 2000/1596), reg.4(2) (June 19, 2000).

5. The Secretaries of State for Education and Skills and for Work and Pensions Order 2002 (SI 2002/1397), art.18 (June 27, 2002).

DEFINITIONS

"jobseeker's allowance"—see reg.2(1).
"the Jobseeker's Allowance Regulations"—*ibid.*

"partner"—*ibid.*
"week"—*ibid.*

[¹ State pension credit

26B.—(1) Except where paragraph (2) applies, state pension credit shall   2.183
be payable on Mondays, but subject, [² to regulation 21 where payment is
by direct credit transfer].

(2) State pension credit shall be payable—

(a) if retirement pension is payable to the claimant, on the same day as
the retirement pension is payable; or

(b) on such other day of the week as the Secretary of State may, in the
particular circumstances of the case, determine.

(3) [² . . .]

(4) State pension credit paid [² otherwise than in accordance with regulation 21] shall be paid weekly in advance.

(5) Where the amount of state pension credit payable is less than £1.00
per week, the Secretary of State may direct that it shall be paid at such intervals, not exceeding 13 weeks, as may be specified in the direction.

(6) [² . . .]

(7) [² . . .].]

AMENDMENTS

1. Inserted by State Pension Credit (Consequential, Transitional and Miscellaneous
Provisions) Regulations 2002 (SI 2002/3019), reg.9 (April 7, 2003).

2. The Social Security (Miscellaneous Amendments) (No.2) Regulations 2006
(SI 2006/832), reg.2 (April 10, 2006).

[¹ Employment and support allowance

26C.—(1) Subject to paragraphs (3) to (7), employment and support   2.184
allowance is to be paid fortnightly in arrears on the day of the week determined in accordance with paragraph (2).

(2) The day specified for the purposes of paragraph (1) is the day in
column (2) which corresponds to the series of numbers in column (1) which
includes the last 2 digits of the claimant's national insurance number—

(1)	(2)
00 to 19	Monday
20 to 39	Tuesday
40 to 59	Wednesday
60 to 79	Thursday
80 to 99	Friday

(3) The Secretary of State may, in any particular case or class of case,
arrange that the claimant be paid otherwise than fortnightly.

(4) The Secretary of State may, in any particular case or class of case,
arrange that employment and support allowance be paid on any day of the
week and where it is in payment to any person and the day on which it is
payable is changed, it must be paid at a daily rate of 1/7th of the weekly rate
in respect of any of the days for which payment would have been made but
for that change.

(5) Where the weekly amount of employment and support allowance is less than £1.00 it may be paid in arrears at intervals of not more than 13 weeks.

(6) Where the weekly amount of an employment and support allowance is less than 10 pence that allowance is not payable.

(7) The provisions of paragraph 2A of Schedule 7 (payment of income support at time of office closure) apply for the purposes of payment of employment and support allowance as they apply for the purposes of payment of income support.]

AMENDMENT

1. The Employment and Support Allowance (Consequential provisions) (No.2) Regulations 2008 (SI 2008/1554), reg.21 (October 27, 2008).

[¹ [²Working families' tax credit and disabled persons' tax credit]]

2.185   **27.**—(1) Subject to regulation 21 [³and paragraph (1A)] [²working families' tax credit] and [²disabled persons' tax credit] shall be payable in respect of any benefit week on the Tuesday next following the end of that week by means of a book of serial orders [³or on presentation of an instrument for benefit payment] unless in any case the Secretary of State arranges [⁴ Board arrange] otherwise.

[⁵ (1A) Subject to paragraph (2), where an amount of [² working families' tax credit] and [² disabled persons' tax credit] becomes payable which is at a weekly rate of note more than £4.00, that amount shall, if the Secretary of State so directs [⁴ Board so direct], be payable as soon as practicable by means of a single payment; except that if that amount represents an increase in the amount of either of those benefits which has previously been paid in respect of the same period, this paragraph shall apply only if that previous payment was made by means of a single payment.]

(2) Where the entitlement to [²working families' tax credit] and [² disabled persons' tax credit] is less than 50 pence a week that amount shall not be payable.]

AMENDMENTS

1. Reg.27 substituted by The Social Security (Claims and Payments) Amendment Regulations 1991 (SI 1991/2741), reg.14 (April 6, 1992).
2. The Tax Credits (Claims and Payments) (Amendment) Regulations 1999 (SI 1999/2752), regs 24 and 25 (October 5, 1999).
3. The Social Security (Claims and Payments) Amendment (No.3) Regulations 1993 (SI 1993/2113), reg.3(4) (October 25, 1993).
4. For tax credits purposes only, these words are substitue for the words "Secretary of State arranges": The Tax Credits (Claims and Payments) (Amendment) Regulations 1999 (SI 1999/2572), reg.12(a) (October 5, 1999).
5. The Social Security (Claims and Payments) Amendment (No.3) Regulations 1993 (SI 1993/2113), reg.3(4) (October 25, 1993).

Fractional amounts of benefit

2.186   [¹ **28.**—(1) Subject to paragraph (2),] where the amount of any benefit payable would, but for this regulation, include a fraction of a penny, that fraction shall be disregarded if it is less than half a penny and shall otherwise be treated as a penny.

[¹ (2) Where the amount of any maternity allowance payable would, but for this regulation, include a fraction of a penny, that fraction shall be treated as a penny.]

AMENDMENT

1. Social Security (Claims and Payments) Amendment (No.2) Regulations 2002 (SI 2002/1950), reg.2 (September 2, 2002).

DEFINITION

"benefit"—see reg.2(2).

[¹ Payments to persons under age 18

29.—Where benefit is paid to a person under the age of 18 (whether on his own behalf or on behalf of another) [² . . .] [² a direct credit transfer under regulation 21 into any such person's account, or the receipt by him of a payment made by some other means] shall be sufficient discharge to the Secretary of State [³ or the Board].]

2.187

AMENDMENTS

1. The Social Security (Claims and Payments etc.) Amendment Regulations 1996 (SI 1996/672), reg.2(4) (April 4, 1996).
2. Social Security (Claims and Payments and Miscellaneous Amendments) (No.2) Regulations 2002 (SI 2002/2441), reg.6 (October 23, 2002).
3. The Tax Credits (Claims and Payments) (Amendment) Regulations 1999 (SI 1999/2572), reg.30 (October 5, 1999).

DEFINITION

"benefit"—see reg.2(2).

Payments on death

30.—(1) On the death of a person who has made a claim for benefit, the Secretary of State [¹or the Board] may appoint such person as he [¹or they] may think fit to proceed with the claim [¹⁵ and any related issue of revision, supersession or appeal].

2.188

(2) Subject to [¹² paragraphs (4) and (4A)], any sum payable by way of benefit which is payable under an award on a claim proceeded with under paragraph (1) may be paid or distributed by the Secretary of State to or amongst persons over the age of 16 claiming as personal representatives, legatees, next of kin, or creditors of the deceased (or, where the deceased was illegitimate, to or amongst other persons over the age of 16), and the provisions of regulation 38 (extinguishment of right) shall apply to any such payment or distribution; and—

(a) [¹³ a direct credit transfer under regulation 21 into any such person's account, or the receipt by him of a payment made by some other means,] shall be a good discharge to the Secretary of State [¹or the Board] for any sum so paid; and

(b) where the Secretary of State is satisfied [¹or the Board is satisfied] that any such sum or part thereof is needed for the benefit of any person under the age of 16, he [¹or they] may obtain a good discharge therefor by paying the sum or part thereof to a person over that age who satisfies the Secretary of State [¹or the Board] that he will apply the sum so paid for the benefit of the person under the age of 16.

(3) Subject to paragraph (2), any sum payable by way of benefit to the deceased, payment of which he had not obtained at the date of his death, may, unless the right thereto was already extinguished at that date, be paid or distributed to or amongst such persons as are mentioned in paragraph (2), and regulation 38 shall apply to any such payment or distribution, except that, for the purpose of that regulation, the period of 12 months shall be calculated from the date on which the right to payment of any sum is treated as having arisen in relation to any such person and not from the date on which that right is treated as having arisen in relation to the deceased.

(4) [¹⁹ Subject to paragraph (4B), paragraphs] (2) and (3) shall not apply in any case unless written application for the payment of any such sum is made to the Secretary of State [¹or the Board] within 12 months from the date of the deceased's death or within such longer period as the Secretary of State [¹or the Board] may allow in any particular case.

[¹² (4A) In a case where a joint-claim jobseeker's allowance has been awarded to a joint-claim couple and one member of the couple dies, the amount payable under that award shall be payable to the other member of that couple.]

[¹⁹ (4B) A written application is not required where—
(a) an executor or administrator has not been appointed;
(b) the deceased was in receipt of a retirement pension of any category or state pension credit including where any other benefit was combined for payment purposes with either of those benefits at the time of death;
(c) the sum payable by way of benefit to the deceased is payable to a person who was the spouse or civil partner of the deceased at the time of death; and
(d) either—
    (i) the spouse or civil partner and the deceased were living together at the time of death; or
    (ii) they would have been living together at the time of death but for the fact that either or both of them were in a residential care or a nursing home or in a hospital.]

(5) [¹⁶ Subject to paragraphs (5A) to [¹⁸ (5G),] where the conditions specified in paragraph (6) are satisfied, a claim may be made on behalf of the deceased to any benefit other than [²jobseeker's allowance,] income support, [¹⁴, state pension credit] [³working families' tax credit or disabled person's tax credit] or a social fund payment such as is mentioned in section 32(2)(a) [⁴and section 32(2A)] of the Social security Act 1986 [⁵, or reduced earnings allowance or disablement benefit], to which he would have been entitled if he had claimed it in the prescribed manner and within the prescribed time.

[¹⁸ (5A) Subject to paragraphs (5B) to (5G), a claim may be made in accordance with paragraph (5) on behalf of the deceased for a Category A or Category B retirement pension or graduated retirement benefit provided that the deceased was not married or in a civil partnership on the date of his death.

(5B) But, subject to paragraphs (5C) to (5G), a claim may be made in accordance with paragraph (5) on behalf of the deceased for a Category

A or Category B retirement pension or graduated retirement benefit where the deceased was a married woman or a civil partner on the date of death if the deceased's widower or surviving civil partner was under pensionable age on that date and due to attain pensionable age before 6th April 2010.

(5C) Where a claim is made for a shared additional pension under paragraph (5) or for a retirement pension or graduated retirement benefit under paragraphs (5) and (5A) or (5B), in determining the benefit to which the deceased would have been entitled if he had claimed within the prescribed time, the prescribed time shall be the period of three months ending on the date of his death and beginning with any day on which, apart from satisfying the condition of making a claim, he would have been entitled to the pension or benefit.

(5D) Paragraph (5E) applies where, throughout the period of 12 months ending with the day before the death of the deceased person, his entitlement to a Category A or a Category B retirement pension, shared additional pension or graduated retirement benefit was deferred in accordance with, as the case may be—

(a) section 55 of the Contributions and Benefits Act (pension increase or lump sum where entitlement to retirement pension is deferred);

(b) section 55C of that Act (pension increase or lump sum where entitlement to shared additional pension is deferred); or

(c) section 36(4A) of the National Insurance Act 1965(**c**) (deferment of graduated retirement benefit).

(5E) Where a person claims under paragraph (5) or under paragraphs (5) and (5A) or (5B) the deceased shall be treated as having made an election in accordance with, as the case may be—

(a) paragraph A1(1)(a) of Schedule 5 to the Contributions and Benefits Act (electing to have an increase of pension), where paragraph (5D) (a) applies;

(b) paragraph 1(1)(a) of Schedule 5A to that Act (electing to have an increase of a shared additional pension) where paragraph (5D)(b) applies; or

(c) paragraph 12(1)(a) of Schedule 1 to the Social Security (Graduated Retirement Benefit) Regulations 2005 (electing to have an increase of benefit), where paragraph (5D)(c) applies.

(5F) Paragraph (5G) applies where—

(a) the deceased person was a widow, widower or surviving civil partner ("W") who was married to, or in a civil partnership with, the other party of the marriage or civil partnership ("S") when S died;

(b) throughout the period of 12 months ending with the day before S's death, S's entitlement to a Category A or a Category B retirement pension or graduated retirement benefit was deferred in accordance with, as the case may be, paragraph (5D)(a) or (c); and

(c) W made no statutory election in consequence of the deferral.

(5G) Where a person claims under paragraphs (5) and (5A) the deceased ("W") shall be treated as having made an election in accordance with, as the case may be—

(a) paragraph 3C(2)(a) of Schedule 5 to the Contributions and Benefits Act (electing to have an increase of pension), where paragraph (5D) (a) applies; or

(b) paragraph 17(2)(a) of Schedule 1 to the Social Security (Graduated Retirement Benefit) Regulations 2005 (electing to have an increase in benefit), where paragraph (5D)(c) applies.]

(6) [⁶Subject to the following provisions of this regulation,] the following conditions are specified for the purposes of paragraph (5)—

  (a) Within six months of the death an application must have been made in writing to the Secretary of State for a person, whom the Secretary of State thinks fit to be appointed to make the claim, to be so appointed;

  (b) a person must have been appointed by the Secretary of State to make the claim;

  (c) there must have been no longer period than six months between the appointment and the making of the claim.

[⁷(6A) Where the conditions specified in paragraph (6B) are satisfied, a person may make a claim for reduced earnings or disablement benefit, including any increase under [section 104 or 105 of the Social Security Contributions and Benefits Act 1992], in the name of a person who had died.

(6B)[⁸Subject to the following provisions of this regulation,] the conditions specified for the purposes of paragraph (6A) are—

  (a) that the person who had died would have been entitled to the benefit claimed if he had made a claim for it in the prescribed manner and within the prescribed time;

  (b) that within 6 months of a death certificate being issued in respect of the person who has died, the person making the claim has applied to the Secretary of State to be made an appointee of the person who has died

[⁹(ba) that person has been appointed by the Secretary of State to make the claim]

  (c) the claim is made within six months of the appointment.]

[¹⁰(6C) Subject to paragraph (6D), where the Secretary of State certifies that to do so would be consistent with the proper administration of the Social Security Contributions and Benefits Act 1992 the period specified in paragraphs (6)(a) and (c) and (6B)(b) and (c) shall be extended to such period, not exceeding 6 months, as may be specified in the certificate.

(6D)(a) Where a certificate is given under paragraph (6C) extending the period specified in paragraph (6)(a) or (6B)(b), the period specified in paragraph (6)(c) or (6B)(c) shall be shortened by a period corresponding to the period specified in the certificate;

  (b) no certificate shall be given under paragraph (6C) which would enable a claim to be made more than 12 months after the date of death (in a case falling within paragraph (6)) or the date of a death certificate being issued in respect of the person who has died (in a case falling within paragraph (6B)); and

  (c) in the application of sub-paragraph (b) any period between the date when an application for a person to be appointed to make a claim is made and the date when that appointment is made shall be disregarded.]

(7) A claim made in accordance with paragraph (5) [¹¹or paragraph (6A)] shall be treated, for the purposes of these regulations, as if made by the deceased on the date of his death.

(8) The Secretary of State [¹or the Board] may dispense with strict proof of the title of any person claiming in accordance with the provisions of this regulation.

(9) In paragraph (2) "next of kin" means—

(a) in England and Wales, the persons who would take beneficially on an intestacy; and

(b) in Scotland, the persons entitled to the moveable estate of the deceased on intestacy.

AMENDMENTS

1. The Tax Credits (Claims and Payments) (Amendment) Regulations 1999 (SI 1999/2572), regs 13, 20 and 22 (October 5, 1999).

2. The Social Security (Claims and Payments) (Jobseeker's Allowance Consequential Amendments) Regulations 1996 (SI 1996/1460), reg.2(15) (October 7, 1996).

3. The Tax Credits (Claims and Payments) (Amendments) Regulations 1999 (SI 1999/2572), regs 24 and 25 (October 5, 1999).

4. The Social Security (Claims and Payments) Amendment Regulations 1991 (SI 1991/2741), reg.15 (March 10, 1992).

5. The Social Security (Common Provisions) Miscellaneous Amendments Regulations 1988 (SI 1988/1725), reg.3(6) (November 7, 1988).

6. The Social Security (Claims and Payments) Amendment (No.3) Regulations 1993 (SI 1993/2113), reg.3(5)(a) (September 27, 1993).

7. Paras (6A) and (6B) inserted by The Social Security (Miscellaneous Provisions) Amendment Regulations 1990 (SI 1990/2208), reg.11(3) (December 5, 1990).

8. The Social Security (Claims and Payments) Amendment (No.3) Regulations 1993 (SI 1993/2113), reg.3(5)(a) (September 29, 1993).

9. The Social Security (Claims and Payments) Amendment Regulations 1994 (SI 1994/2319), reg.5 (October 3, 1994).

10. Paras (6C) and (6D) inserted by The Social Security (Claims and Payments) Amendment (No.3) Regulations 1993 (SI 1993/2113), reg.3(5)(b) (September 27, 1993).

11. The Social Security (Miscellaneous Provisions) Amendment Regulations 1990 (SI 1990/2208), reg.11(4) (December 5, 1990).

12. The Social Security (Joint Claims: Consequential Amendments) Regulations 2000 (SI 2000/1982), reg.2(7) (March 19, 2001).

13. Social Security (Claims and Payments and Miscellaneous Amendments) (No.2) Regulations 2002 (SI 2002/2441), reg.7, (October 23, 2002).

14. State Pension Credit (Consequential, Transitional and Miscellaneous Provisions) Regulations 2002 (SI 2002/3019), reg.10 (April 7, 2003).

15. The Social Security, Child Support and Tax Credits (Miscellaneous Amendments) Regulations 2005 (SI 2005/337), reg.7 (March 18, 2005).

16. The Social Security (Claims and Payments) Amendment Regulations 2005 (SI 2005/455), reg.4 (April 6, 2006).

17. The Social Security (Shared Additional Pension) (Miscellaneous Amendments) Regulations 2005 (SI 2005/1551), reg.3 (April 6, 2006).

18. The Social Security (Retirement Pensions and Graduated Retirement Benefit) (Widowers and Civil Partnership) Regulations 2005 (SI 2005/3078), reg.4 (April 6, 2006).

19. The Social Security (Miscellaneous Amendments) (No.4) Regulations 2007 (SI 2007/2470) (September 24, 2007).

GENERAL NOTE

Note the decisions referred to in the annotations to reg.33.

It would seem that the power of appointment in reg.30(1) on the death of the claimant is a separate appointment from that under reg.33. It would follow that where a claimant has an appointee under reg.33 and dies, there should at least be confirmation of continuation of the appointment under reg.33 to enable the appointee to act under reg.30. The better course, since there are specific requirements in the regulation, would be for a separate appointment to be made.

In *CIS/1423/1997* the Commissioner holds, at para.21 of his decision, that the plain words of reg.30 do not allow the Secretary of State to appoint a person to represent the claimant or their estate in the context of a decision for the recoverability of an overpayment from the claimant's estate.

Note that paras (4)–(7) contain a special power of appointment to enable *a claim* to be made after a person's death.

R(IS)3/04 discusses aspects of reg.30 at paras 14–17 of the decision. The Commissioner notes that reg.30(5) is the only provision permitting claims to be made in respect of deceased persons, and reg.30(5) expressly does not apply to income support.

Death of claimant pending appeal to the Commissioner

2.189   It sometimes happens that the claimant dies while the appeal is pending before the Commissioner. In such cases the surviving partner may not wish to take on an appointment enabling the matter to continue, and there may be no personal representatives because there is no estate. The result is that, where there is a claimant's appeal, there is no one who can withdraw the appeal. In such circumstances, the practice of the Commissioners is to treat the appeal as abated: see *R(S)7/56*, *R(1)2/83* and *R(SB)25/84*. For all practical purposes the matter is then closed, though the possibility remains that the matter could be revived on application. This could happen if, for example, the Secretary of State chose to appoint someone to act for the deceased claimant. The most likely appointee would be the Official Solicitor, but is difficult to imagine circumstances in which it would be appropriate to take such action. In overpayment cases, care should be taken to ensure that the Benefits Agency has given an assurance that it will not seek recovery from the estate before treating an appeal as abated, since abatement of a claimant's appeal without such an assurance would not preclude recovery against the estate.

The use of the abatement procedure is not appropriate where the appellant is the adjudication officer. In such cases, the proper course of action is for the adjudication officer to withdraw the appeal: *R(1)2/83*, para.6.

In *CIS/1340/1999* the Commissioner was considering an appeal involving a substantial overpayment of benefit in which the claimant had died since filing the appeal. No executors or administrators were appointed, and the claimant's husband did not respond to an invitation by the Department to consider applying to be the claimant's appointee. The Commissioner comments on the reference in these annotations that care should be taken to obtain an assurance that the Benefits Agency will not seek to recover the overpayment from the estate before treating the appeal as abated. He states that he does not consider that proposition to flow from the cases, and that *R(I)2/83* is merely authority for the proposition that, where such an assurance is available in an overpayment case, it may be appropriate to dismiss the appeal rather than merely declare it abated. At para.20, he says,

"But I see no reason why, before declaring the appeal abated or indeed striking it out, I should require an assurance to be sought from the Secretary of State that recovery of the overpayment will not be pursued. So long as the original decision of the adjudication officer stands the Secretary of State should be entitled to recover the overpayment. If he does so and there is anyone who has an interest in ensuring that it is not recovered, that person will be able to take steps to have the appeal reinstated." (para.20)

The appeal was declared abated.

[¹ Payment of arrears of joint-claim jobseeker's allowance where the nominated person can no longer be traced

30A. Where—

(a) an award of joint-claim jobseeker's allowance has been awarded to a joint-claim couple;

(b) that couple ceases to be a joint-claim couple; and

(c) the member of the joint-claim couple nominated for the purposes of section 3B of the Jobseekers Act cannot be traced,

arrears on the award of joint-claim jobseeker's allowance shall be paid to the other member of the former joint-claim couple.]

2.190

AMENDMENT

1. The Social Security Amendment (Joint Claims) Regulations 2001 (SI 2001/518), reg.5 (March 19, 2001).

Time and manner of payments of industrial injuries gratuities

31.—(1) This regulation applies to any gratuity payable under [Part V of the Social Security Contributions and Benefits Act 1992].

2.191

[² (1A) In the case of a person who made a claim for benefit in accordance with regulation 4A(1), a change of circumstances may be notified to a relevant authority at any office to which the claim for benefit could be made in accordance with that provision.]

(2) Subject to the following provisions of this regulation, every gratuity shall be payable in one sum.

(3) A gratuity may be payable by instalments of such amounts and at such times as appear reasonable in the circumstances of the case to the adjudicating authority awarding the gratuity if—

(a) the beneficiary to whom the gratuity has been awarded is, at the date of the award, under the age of 18 years, or

(b) in any other case, the amount of the gratuity so awarded (not being a gratuity payable to the widow of a deceased person on her remarriage) exceeds £52 and the beneficiary requests that payments should be made by instalments.

(4) An appeal shall not be brought against any decision that a gratuity should be payable by instalments or as to the amounts of any such instalments or the time of payment.

(5) Subject to the provisions of regulation 37 (suspension), a gratuity shall—

(a) if it is payable by equal weekly instalments, be paid in accordance with the provisions of regulation 22 insofar as they are applicable; or

(b) in any case, be paid by such means as may appear to the Secretary of State to be appropriate in the circumstances.

AMENDMENTS

1. The Social Security Act 1998 (Commencement No.12 and Consequential and Transitional Provisions) Order 1999 (SI 1999/3178), Sch.6 (November 29, 1999).

2. The Social Security (Claims and Information) Regulations 1999 (SI 1999/3108) (November 29, 1999).

[⁵ Information to be given and changes to be notified

2.192   **32.**—(1) Except in the case of a jobseeker's allowance, every beneficiary and every person by whom or on whose behalf, sums by way of benefit are receivable shall furnish in such manner and at such times as the Secretary of State may determine such information or evidence as the Secretary of State may require for determining whether a decision on the award of benefit should be revised under section 9 of the Social Security Act 1998 or superseded under section 10 of that Act.

(1A) Every beneficiary and every person by whom, or on whose behalf, sums by way of benefit are receivable shall furnish in such manner and at such times as the Secretary of State may determine such information or evidence as the Secretary of State may require in connection with payment of the benefit claimed or awarded.

(1B) Except in the case of a jobseeker's allowance, every beneficiary and every person by whom or on whose behalf sums by way of benefit are receivable shall notify the Secretary of State of any change of circumstances which he might reasonably be expected to know might affect—

(a) the continuance of entitlement to benefit; or

(b) the payment of benefit

as soon as reasonably practicable after the change occurs by giving notice [⁸ of the change to the appropriate office—

(i) in writing or by telephone (unless the Secretary of State determines in any particular case that notice must be in writing or may be given otherwise than in writing or by telephone; or

(ii) in writing if in any class of class he requires written notice (unless he determines in any particular case to accept notice given otherwise than in writing)]]

[⁷ (1C) In the case of a person who made a claim for benefit in accordance with regulation 4A(1), a change of circumstances may be notified to a relevant authority at any office to which the claim for benefit could be made in accordance with that provision.]

(2) Where any sum is receivable on account of an increase of benefit in respect of an adult dependant, the Secretary of State may require the beneficiary to furnish a declaration signed by such dependant confirming the particulars respecting him, which have been given by the claimant.

[²(3) In the case of a person who is claiming income support, state pension credit . . . [¹¹, a jobseekers allowance or an employment and support allowance], where that person or any partner is aged not less than 60 and is a member of, or a person deriving entitlement to a pension under, a personal pension scheme, or is a party to, or a person deriving entitlement to a pension under, a retirement annuity contract, he shall where the Secretary of State so requires furnish the following information—

(a) the name and address of the pension fund holder;

(b) such other information including any reference or policy number as is needed to enable the personal pension scheme or retirement annuity contract to be identified.

(4) Where the pension fund holder receives from the Secretary of State a request for details concerning a personal pension scheme or retirement annuity contract relating to a person or any partner to whom paragraph (3) refers, the pension fund holder shall provide the Secretary of State with any information to which paragraph (5) refers.

(5) The information to which this paragraph refers is—

(a) where the purchase of an annuity under a personal pension scheme has been deferred, the amount of any income which is being withdrawn from the personal pension scheme;

(b) in the case of—

   (i) a personal pension scheme where income withdrawal is available, the maximum amount of income which may be withdrawn from the scheme; or

   (ii) a personal pension scheme where income withdrawal is not available, or a retirement annuity contract, the maximum amount of income which might be withdrawn from the fund if the fund were held under a personal pension scheme where income withdrawal was available,

calculated by or on behalf of the pension fund holder by means of tables prepared from time to time by the Government Actuary which are appropriate for this purpose.]

[⁶ (6) This regulation shall apply in the case of state pension credit subject to the following modifications—

(a) [¹⁰ in connection with the setting of a new assessed income period], the information and evidence [¹⁰ which the Secretary of State may require] to be notified in accordance with this regulation includes information and evidence as to the likelihood of future changes in the claimant's circumstances needed to determine—

   (i) whether a period should be specified as an assessed income period under section 6 of the 2002 Act in relation to any decision; and

   (ii) if so, the length of the period to be so specified; and

[⁹ (b) except to the extent that sub-paragraph (a) applies, changes to an element of the claimant's retirement provision need not be notified if—

   (i) an assessed income period is current in his case;

   (ii) the time limit set out in sub-paragraph (c) has not expired; or

   (iii) the Secretary of State grants, or has granted, such longer period as he considers reasonable under sub-paragraph (c) and that period has not expired; and

(c) [¹⁰ any information] and evidence [¹⁰ to be notified] under sub-paragraph (a) shall be furnished within one month of the date on which the Secretary of State notifies the claimant of the requirement or within such longer period as the Secretary of State considers reasonable.]

AMENDMENTS

1. The Social Security (Miscellaneous Provisions) Amendment (No.2) Regulations 1992 (SI 1992/2595), reg.4 (November 16, 1992).

2. Income-related benefit Schemes and Social Security (Claims and Payments) (Miscellaneous Amendments) Regulations 1995 (SI 1995/2303), reg.10(4) (October 2, 1995).

3. The Social Security (Claims and Payments) (Jobseeker's Allowance Consequential Amendments) Regulations 1996 (SI 1996/1460), reg.2(16) (October 7, 1996).

4. The Tax Credits (Claims and Payments) (Amendment) Regulations 1999 (SI 1999/2572), reg.14 (October 5, 1999).

5. The Social Security and Child Support (Miscellaneous Amendments) Regulations 2003 (SI 2003/1050), reg.2 (May 5, 2003).

6. State Pension Credit (Consequential, Transitional and Miscellaneous Provisions) Regulations 2002 (SI 2002/3019), reg.11 (April 7, 2003).

7. The Social Security (Claims and Payments and Miscellaneous Amendments) Regulations 2003 (SI 2003/1632), reg.2 (July 21, 2003).

8. The Social Security (Notification of Change of Circumstances) Regulations 2003, SI 2003/3209, reg.2 (January 6, 2004).

9. The State Pension Credit (Transitional and Miscellaneous Provisions) Amendment Regulations 2003 (SI 2003/2274) (October 6, 2003).

10. The Social Security (Students and Miscellaneous Amendments) Regulations 2008 (SI 2008/1599), reg.3 (August 25, 2008).

11. The Employment and Support Allowance (Consequential provisions) (No.2) Regulations 2008 (SI 2008/1554), reg.22 (October 27, 2008).

DEFINITIONS

"appropriate office"—see reg.2(1).
"beneficiary"—see Social Security Act 1975, Sch.20.
"benefit"—see reg.2(2).
"jobseeker's allowance"—see reg.2(1).
"pension fund holder"—*ibid.*
"personal pension scheme"—*ibid.*
"retirement annuity contract"—*ibid.*

GENERAL NOTE

2.193   A Tribunal of Commissioners in *CIS/4348/2003* ruled that the duty to disclose under s.71 of the Administration Act flowed from the provisions of reg.32. Note that the duty applies to beneficiaries and "every person by whom or on whose behalf, sums by way of benefit are receivable". The latter group includes appointees under reg.33.

The Tribunal of Commissioners draws a clear distinction between the two duties set out in reg.32. There is a duty in regs 32(1) and (1A) to notify the Secretary of State or Board of Inland Revenue of any matter where the Secretary of State or the Board has given unambiguous directions for the disclosure of the matter. There is no question of deciding in such cases whether disclosure was reasonably to be expected to the claimant. Any failure to disclose such information will render any overpayment of benefit resulting from the failure to disclose recoverable.

By contrast the duty in reg.32(1B) is to notify changes of circumstances which e benefit recipient might reasonably be expected to know might affect the continuance of entitlement to benefit or the payment of benefit. The Tribunal of Commissioners concludes that it is only in these cases that it is necessary to consider whether disclosure by the claimant was in all the circumstances reasonably to be expected.

The distinction may be easier to make in theory than in practice, but, given the different consequences of failure to disclose under the two separate duties, it will be necessary to consider very carefully the source of any obligation to provide the Secretary of State or Her Majesty's Revenue and Customs with information and the specificity of that information. So, a requirement to disclose that children are no longer living with the claimant but had been taken into care (as was the case in *CIS/4348/2003*) which is clearly set out in documentation given to the claimant, will give rise to the duty to disclose under the first duty. Arguments about the claimant's capacity are not relevant. By contrast, failure to disclose some unspecified set of circumstances which might affect benefit entitlement will fall under the second duty, and will require consideration of whether disclosure in all the circumstances of the case could reasonably be expected of the claimant.

In *CDLA/2328/2006* the Commissioner said,

" . . . There is nothing wrong in a tribunal relying on one paragraph rather than the other. The duties under paragraphs (1A) and (1B) are cumulative. The tribunal was entitled to rely on either duty. A finding that a claimant was in breach of paragraph (1B) is not rendered wrong in law just because the claimant was also in breach of paragraph (1A). What the tribunal must do is to rely on one or the other and make clear which." (para.20)

In interpreting the duty under paragraph (1A), the Commissioner stresses the distinction between information gathering and decision making. The claimant is required to report facts which might show that entitlement is affected. It is then for the decision maker to decide whether to investigate further, if necessary, and to make a decision on whether entitlement is in fact affected by the change in circumstances. The Commissioner says,

"23. The interpretation of the duties must reflect their nature and purpose. So the duty to report 'if things get easier for you' is not a duty to report 'if you believe that you are no longer virtually unable to walk'. Nor does this duty necessarily require a comparison between the claimant's abilities and disabilities at the time of the original award and those current at the time when the Secretary of State says a change should have been reported. That comparison does not arise until the later decision-making stage. The notes deal only with the earlier information-gathering stage. It is important not to confuse the issue whether the claimant failed to report a change of circumstances (an information-gathering question) and the issue whether that change was material to his entitlement (a decision-making question).
24. The duty does not set the focus of comparison on the time of the original award. If it did, it would become increasingly burdensome as time passes. In this case it would require the claimant to remember precisely how disabled he had been 18 years previously. The duty, like all the duties, is continuously speaking. It is to report if at any time things are easier for the claimant. That means easier by reference to the preceding period. Obviously that has to be applied in a reasonable time frame. It would not be necessary to report if a claimant were feeling a bit better today than yesterday. The test has to be applied over a period that is sufficient to show overall a sustained improvement or deterioration, taking account of any usual variation. This is not precise, but that is because it is a matter of judgment for each case."

On the interpretation of paragraph (1B) the Commissioner says,

"28. . . . If the Secretary of State has issued an instruction to the claimant or to claimants generally, that will found a duty under paragraph (1A) and there should be no need to rely on paragraph (1B). There may be circumstances in which the Secretary of State could not rely on paragraph (1A) and could only rely on the instructions under paragraph (1B), but I have not been able to imagine one. But, assuming that this is possible, I accept that the notes issued by the Secretary of State are relevant under paragraph (1B). The instructions they contain may inform what is reasonable to expect a claimant to know. It would usually be reasonable for a claimant to know the contents of those instructions. (I do not exclude the possibility that it may not be reasonable for the claimant to know everything that is in the Secretary of State's notes. For example, this may, perhaps, not be reasonable on account of the claimant's mental state.) And the notes may be so comprehensive that, in a particular case, there is no need to consider anything else. But the duty under paragraph (1B) is defined by the terms of that paragraph. The instructions given to claimants do not define that duty. They are merely evidence of what it was reasonable to expect the claimant to know. And the duty to report may be wider than any instructions given by the Secretary of State. For example, it may be reasonable for the claimant to realise from questions in a claim pack that a particular matter is relevant to entitlement, even if the notes issued by the Secretary of State do not specifically refer to them.
29. For completeness, I will mention that the focus under paragraph (1B) is

different from that under paragraph (1A). There the duty refers to entitlement, but only whether the claimant might reasonably be expected to know a change of circumstances *might* affect entitlement. It is not necessary for the claimant to understand the actual impact that a change will have, but the focus is different from that appropriate to the duty imposed under paragraph (1A). A comparison with his disablement at the time of the award may be justified. But it is also possible to envisage cases in which a claimant ought reasonably to realise that a change of circumstances might affect entitlement without undertaking a comparison with the time of the award. For example, a claimant's mobility may improve to such an extent that no reasonable person would consider that the claimant was virtually unable to walk."

Note that there is no general requirement that the form of disclosure must be in writing, though any disclosure will often be reduced to writing and signed by the claimant.

In *CSDLA/1282/2001* the Deputy Commissioner held that, where there was no appointment by the Secretary of State under reg.33, but there was a Power of Attorney, then benefit was not receivable by the person holding the Power of Attorney, and accordingly that person was under no duty to provide information under reg.32.

[¹ Information given electronically

2.194   **32ZA.**—(1) Where this regulation applies a person may given any certificate, notice, information or evidence required to be given and in particular may give notice or any change of circumstances required to be notified under regulation 32 by means of an electronic communication, in accordance with the provisions set out in Schedule 9ZC.

(2) This regulation applies in relation to carer's allowance.]

AMENDMENT

1. The Social Security (Electronic Communications) (Carer's Allowance) Order 2003 SI 2003/2800, reg.2 (December 1, 2003).

[¹ Information given electronically

2.195   **32A.**—(1) Where this regulation applies a person may give any certificate, notice, information or evidence required to be given and in particular may give notice of any change of circumstances required to be notified under regulation 32 by means of an electronic communication, in accordance with the provisions set out in Schedule 9C.

(2) This regulation applies in relation to child benefit.]

AMENDMENT

1. Social Security (Electronic Communications) (Child Benefit) Order 2002 (SI 2002/1789), art.4 (October 28, 2002).

[¹ Information relating to awards of benefit

2.196   **32B.** —(1) Where an authority or person to whom paragraph (2) applies has arranged with the Secretary of State for the authority or person to receive claims for a specified benefit or obtain information or evidence relating to claims for a specified benefit in accordance with regulation 4 or 4D, the authority or person may—

(a) receive information or evidence which relates to an award of that benefit and which is supplied by—
   (i) the person to whom the award has been made; or
   (ii) other persons in connection with the award,
      and shall forward it to the Secretary of State as soon as reasonably practicable;
(b) verify any information or evidence supplied; and
(c) record the information or evidence supplied and hold it (whether as supplied or recorded) for the purpose of forwarding it to the Secretary of State.

(2) This paragraph applies to—
(a) a local authority administering housing benefit or council tax benefit;
(b) a county council in England;
(c) a person providing services to a person mentioned in sub-paragraph (a) or (b);
(d) a person authorised to exercise any function of a local authority relating to housing benefit or council tax benefit;
(e) a person authorised to exercise any function a county council in England has under section 7A of the Social Security Administration Act 1992.

(3) In paragraph (1), "specified benefit" means one or more of the following benefits—
(a) attendance allowance;
(b) bereavement allowance;
(c) bereavement payment;
(d) carer's allowance;
(e) disability living allowance;
(f) incapacity benefit;
(g) income support;
(h) jobseeker's allowance;
(i) retirement pension;
(j) state pension credit;
(k) widowed parent's allowance;
(l) winter fuel payment.]

AMENDMENT

1. The Social Security (Claims and Information) Regulations 2007 (SI 2007/2911) (October 31, 2007).

PART IV

THIRD PARTIES

Persons unable to act

33.—(1) Where—   2.197
(a) a person is, or is alleged to be, entitled to benefit, whether or not a claim for benefit has been made by him or on his behalf; and

    (b) that person is unable for the time being to act; and either

    (c) no [6 deputy] has been appointed by the Court of Protection [6 under Part 1 of the Mental Capacity Act 2005 or receiver appointed under Part 7 of the Mental Health Act 1983 but treated as a deputy by virtue of the Mental Capacity Act 2005] with power to claim, or as the case may be, receive benefit on his behalf; or

    (d) in Scotland, his estate is not being administered by [4 a judicial factor or any guardian acting or appointed under the Adults with Incapacity (Scotland) Act 2004 who has power to claim or, as the case may be, receive benefit on his behalf],

the Secretary of State [2 or the Board] may, upon written application made to him by a person who, if a natural person, is over the age of 18, appoint that person to exercise, on behalf of the person who is unable to act, any right to which that person may be entitled and to receive and deal on his behalf with any sums payable to him.

    [4 (1A) Where a person has been appointed under [5 regulation 82(3) of the Housing benefit Regulations 2006, regulation 63(3) of the Housing benefit (Persons who have attained the qualifying age for state pension credit) Regulations 2006, regulation 68(3) of the Council Tax Benefit Regulations 2006, or regulation 52(3) of the Council Tax benefit (Persons who have attained the qualifying age for state pension credit) Regulations 2006] by a relevant authority within the meaning of those Regulations to act on behalf of another in relation to a benefit claim or award, the Secretary of State may, if the person agrees, treat him as if he had appointed him under paragraph (1).]

    (2) Where the Secretary of State has made [2 or the Board have made] an appointment [4, or treated an appointment as made,] under paragraph (1)—

    (a) he [2 or they] may at any time revoke it;

    (b) the person appointed may resign his office after having given one month's notice in writing to the Secretary of State [2 or the Board] of his intention to do so;

    (c) any such appointment shall terminate when the Secretary of State is notified [2 or the Board are notified] that a receiver or other person to whom paragraph (1)(c) or (d) applies has been appointed.

    (3) Anything required by these regulations to be done by or to any person who is for the time being unable to act may be done by or to the receiver, [4 judicial factor or] guardian, if any, or by or to the person appointed under this regulation or regulation 43 [1(disability living allowance for a child)] and [3 . . .] [3 a direct credit transfer under regulation 21 into the account of any person so appointed, or the receipt by him of a payment made by some other means] shall be a good discharge to the Secretary of State [2 or the Board] for any sum paid.

AMENDMENTS

    1. The Social Security (Claims and Payments) Amendment Regulations 1991 (SI 1991/2741), reg.16 (February 3, 1992).

    2. The Tax Credits (Claims and Payments) (Amendment) Regulations 1999 (SI 1999/2572), regs 15, 20, 22 and 23 (October 5, 1999).

    3. Social Security (Claims and Payments and Miscellaneous Amendments) (No.2) Regulations 2002 (SI 2002/2441), reg.8 (October 23, 2002).

    4. The Social Security, Child Support and Tax Credits (Miscellaneous Amendments) Regulations 2005 (SI 2005/337), reg.7 (March 18, 2005).

5. The Housing Benefit and Council Tax Benefit (Consequential Provisions) Regulations 2006 (SI 2006/217), Sch.2, para.2 (March 6, 2006).

6. The Social Security (Miscellaneous Amendments) (No.4) Regulations 2007 (SI 2007/2470) (September 24, 2007).

DEFINITIONS

"benefit"—see reg.2(2).

"claim for benefit"—see reg.2(1).

GENERAL NOTE

Appointment under the powers contained in regulation 33 should be carefully distinguished from situations in which a person is appointed under a private arrangement as an adviser to a claimant: see *Tkachuk* v. *Secretary of State for Work and Pensions*, reported as *R(IS) 3/07*, and *VB v SSWP* [2008] UKUT 15 (AAC).

2.198

Even if no appointment has been made, a claim made by a person unable to act, or by an "unauthorised person" on their behalf, is still valid (*CIS/812/1992*, applying para.8 of *R(SB) 9/84* where a Tribunal of Commissioners holds that in the absence of any challenge at the time the Secretary of State must be deemed to have accepted that the claim was made in sufficient manner). In *Walsh v CAO* (Consent Order, January 19, 1995) the Court of Appeal also applied *R(SB)9/84* when setting aside *CIS/638/1991* in which the Commissioner had held that a claim made on behalf of a person unable to act by a person who had not been formally appointed was a nullity.

Note that any subsequent appointment has retrospective effect (*R(SB)5/90*).

In *CIS/642/1994* the claimant's husband was her appointee under reg.33. She died before the tribunal hearing. The Commissioner holds that the tribunal decision was a nullity because there had been no appointment under reg.30 (deceased persons). Appointments under reg.30 were a distinct and different form of appointment from reg.33 appointments. He dissents from para.8 of *R(SB)9/84* and repeats his view (see *CIS/638/1991*) that it is open to adjudication officers and tribunals (and Commissioners) to determine that a claim is a nullity in cases where a person is unable to act and there has been no valid appointment. This is out of step with the current weight of authority.

CIS/812/1992 also confirms that, in relation to the pre-April 1997 form of the rules for backdating claims, if there has been no appointment it is only necessary to decide whether the claimant has good cause for a late claim; it is not necessary to consider the reasonableness of the failure to claim of a person who has been acting informally on his behalf. The Commissioner declines to follow paras 12 and 13 of *R(IS)5/91* since this could not be reconciled with paras 9 and 10 of *R(SB)9/84* (which was a Tribunal of Commissioners' decision). See also *CSB/168/1993* which takes a similar view and contains a useful summary of the authorities on this issue.

Under the current form of reg.19(5) the test is also of the claimant's personal circumstances, if there is no appointee, but those circumstances sometimes expressly include whether there is anyone who could help the claimant.

The Secretary of State's normal practice in making appointments is not to make an appointment generally but to limit it to a specific benefit: see *R(IS)5/91*. *R(IS)5/91* concerned the effect of an appointment for supplementary benefit purposes on a subsequent income support claim following the 1988 changes. There is some doubt whether such a limited appointment has survived the changes brought about then. There is now a single regulation governing appointments, and some argue that, at a consequence appointments are for all benefits. Tribunals do, however, continue to see appointments limited to certain benefits. The message is that the scope of the appointment needs to be considered in every case where it is relevant, though in the absence of any limiting conditions, there is a strong case for considering that it applies to all benefits.

Where a claimant has died, the Secretary of State may appoint a person to act: *R(SB)8/88*. Unless the Secretary of State does so, the tribunal has no jurisdiction to proceed in the absence of action by a personal representative under a grant of probate or letters of administration.

In *CSDLA/1282/2001*, the Deputy Commissioner concludes, following *CA/1014/1999*, that a person holding a Power of Attorney is not a person made an appointee under reg.33: see para.18.

In *R(SB)5/90*, Commissioner Goodman clarifies the decision in *R(SB)8/88* in holding that the appointment of a person to act by the Secretary of State operates retrospectively. Thus, so far as tribunals are concerned, an appointment after the date of the appeal but before the date of the hearing will be sufficient to ground jurisdiction. The power of appointment is to be found in reg.30(1).

Note that the power of appointment under this regulation is a separate power of appointment from that under reg.30 which arises on the death of the claimant, or where a claim is made after death, a potential claimant.

On the liability of appointees in respect of overpayments of benefit, see the discussion in the notes to s.71 of the Administration Act.

The practice of the Secretary of State in making appointments under reg.33 appears to vary. Since April 1988 there has been a single regulation governing appointments and the regulation is drafted in sufficiently wide terms to encompass a single appointment to cover all social security benefits; it covers "any sums payable to him". Previously there were separate sets of regulations covering means-tested and non-means-tested benefits, and it was the interaction of the sets of regulations which was primarily in issue in *R(IS)5/91*. The experience of tribunals appears to be that in some cases the appointment is for all benefits, and in other cases it is limited to particular benefits. Indeed, in some cases it is not clear what the scope of the appointment is, as when a claimant asks for an appointment in relation to a particular benefit and the appointment is made in general terms. The nature of the appointment seldom seems to be an issue upon which the appeal turns.

See also annotation to reg.30.

Payment to another person on the beneficiary's behalf

2.199

34.—[³ (1) Except in a case to which paragraph (2) applies,] the Secretary of State [² or the Board] may direct that benefit may be paid, wholly or in part, to [¹ another natural person] on the beneficiary's behalf if such a direction as to payment appears to the Secretary of State [² or the Board] to be necessary for protecting the interests of the beneficiary, or any child or dependant in respect of whom benefit is payable.

[³ (2) The Secretary of State may direct that a joint-claim jobseeker's allowance shall be paid wholly or in part to a natural person who is not a member of the joint-claim couple who is the nominated member for the purposes of section 3B of the Jobseekers Act if such a direction as to payment appears to the Secretary of State to be necessary for protecting the interests of the other member of that couple or, as the case may be, both members of that couple.]

AMENDMENTS

1. The Social Security (Miscellaneous Provisions) Amendment (No.2) Regulations 1992 (SI 1992/2595), reg.5 (January 4, 1993).

2. The Tax Credits (Claims and Payments) (Amendment) Regulations 1999 (SI 1999/2572), reg.20 (October 5, 1999).

3. The Social Security (Joint Claims: Consequential Amendments) Regulations 2000 (SI 2000/1982), reg.2(8) (March 19, 2001).

DEFINITIONS

"beneficiary"—see Social Security Act 1975, Sch.20.
"benefit"—see reg.2(2).
"child"—see 1986 Act, s.20(11).

[¹ Deductions of mortgage interest which shall be made from benefit and paid to qualifying lenders

34A.—(1) [² In relation to cases to which section 15A(1) or (1A) of the Social Security Administration Act 1992] (payment out of benefit of sums in respect of mortgage interest etc.) applies and in the circumstances specified in Schedule 9A, such part of any relevant benefits to which a relevant beneficiary is entitled as may be specified in that Schedule shall be paid by the Secretary of State directly to the qualifying lender and shall be applied by that lender towards the discharge of the liability in respect of that mortgage interest.

[³ (1A) Paragraph (1) shall only apply in relation to a relevant beneficiary who is entitled to state pension credit where he is entitled to a guarantee credit.]

(2) The provisions of Schedule 9A shall have effect in relation to mortgage interest payments.]

2.200

AMENDMENTS

1. The Social Security (Claims and Payments) Amendment Regulations 1992 (SI 1992/1026), reg.3 (May 25, 1992).
2. State Pension Credit (Consequential, Transitional and Miscellaneous Provisions) Regulations 2002 (SI 2002/3019), reg.12 (April 7, 2003).
3. The State Pension Credit (Consequential, Transitional and Miscellaneous Provisions) (No. 2) Regulations 2002 (SI 2002/3197) (April 7, 2003).

DEFINITIONS

"qualifying lender"—see Administration Act, s.15A(3).
"relevant beneficiary"—see Administration Act, s.15A(1).
"relevant benefits"—see Administration Act, s.15A(4).

[¹ Deductions of mortgage interest which may be made from benefits and paid to qualifying lenders in other cases

34B.—(1) In relation to cases to which section 151A(1A) of the Social Security Administration Act 1992 applied (others than those referred to in regulation 34A(1A))—

(a) in the circumstances specified in paragraph 2A(1) of Schedule 9A; and
(b) in either of the further circumstances specified in paragrpag 2A(2) of that Schedule,

such part of any relevant benefits to which a relevant beneficiary is entitled as may be paid by the Secretary of State directly to the qualifying lender and shall be applied by that lender towards the discharge of the liabilityn in respect of that interest.

(2) The provisions of Schedule 9A shall have effect in relation to mortgage interest payments made under this regulation.]

2.201

AMENDMENT

1. The State Pension Credit (Consequential, Transitional and Miscellaneous Provisions) (No. 2) Regulations 2002 (SI 2002/3197) (April 7, 2003).

[¹ [³Deductions which may be made from benefit and paid to third parties

2.202   **35.**—(1) Except as provided for in regulation 34A and Schedule 9A, deductions] may be made from benefit and direct payments may be made to third parties on behalf of a beneficiary in accordance with the provisions of Schedule 9 [⁴ and Schedule 9B].

(2) Where a social fund payment for maternity or funeral expenses [²or expenses for heating which appear to the Secretary of State to have been or to be likely to be incurred in cold weather] is made, wholly or in part, in respect of a debt which is, or will be, due to a third person, [⁵ . . .] [⁵ payment may be, and in the case of funeral expenses shall be, made to that person and where an instrument of payment is made to that person it may be sent to the beneficiary].

AMENDMENTS

1. The Social Security (Claims and Payments) Amendment Regulations 1988 (SI 1988/522), reg.7 (April 11, 1988).
2. The Social Security (Common Provisions) Miscellaneous Amendments Regulations 1988 (SI 1988/1725), reg.3 (November 7, 1988).
3. The Social Security (Claims and Payments) Amendment Regulations 1992 (SI 1992/1026), reg.4 (May 25, 1992).
4. The Social Security (Claims and Payments) Amendment Regulations 2001 (SI 2001/18), reg.2 (January 31, 2001).
5. Social Security (Claims and Payments and Miscellaneous Amendments) (No.2) Regulations 2002 (SI 2002/2441), reg.9 (April 8, 2003).

DEFINITIONS

"beneficiary"—see Social Security Act 1975, Sch.20.
"benefit"—see reg.2(2).

GENERAL NOTE

Child support payments
2.203   Regulation 35 and Sch.9 make provision for various deductions from benefit to be paid to third parties. These include payments in lieu of child support payments, which are at the bottom of the list of priorities. A new Sch.9B was introduced dealing specifically with child support maintenance and payments to persons with care. But the relationship between Sch.9B deductions and those arising under Sch.9 is not spelled out, so that it is unclear whether flat rate child support liabilities take precedence over other deductions from benefit under Sch.9.

The policy response appears to be that child support deductions from a range of benefits will set apart from the rest of the direct payments scheme rather than take precedence over them. So child support deductions will, as a matter of policy rather than law, be taken without regard to other Sch.9 deductions. Administrative arrangements will ensure that where only one of a child support deduction and another deduction can be taken, priority will be given to the child support deduction. The provisions of Sch.9B kick in in April 2002, although Sch.9B was inserted in January 2001. It is said to be the intention that existing child support cases will continue to be dealt with under the provisions of Sch.9 with conversion to the new scheme at some later common date.

This is all a most unsatisfactory way of sorting out deficiencies in the clarity of the legislative scheme.

Regulation 35A revoked by The Social Security (Care Homes and Independent   2.204
Hospitals) Regulations 2005 (SI 2005/2687) (October 24, 2005).

Payment to a partner as alternative payee

36.—[³(1)] [¹ Except where a wife has elected in accordance with regu-   2.205
lation 6A of the Social Security (Guardian's Allowances) Regulation 1975 (prescribed manner of making an election under section 77(9) of the Social Security Contributions and Benefits Act 1992) that guardian's allowance is not to be paid to her husband,] where one of a married or unmarried couple residing together is entitled to child benefit [² working families' tax credit, disabled person's tax credit][¹ or guardian's allowance] the Secretary of State [² or the Board] may make arrangements whereby that benefit as well as being payable to the person entitled to it, may, in the alternative, be paid to that person's partner on behalf of the person entitled.

[³ (2) Where a person is entitled to a winter fuel payment within the meaning of the Social Fund Winter Fuel Payment Regulations 2000 and—

(a) that person is one [⁴ member of a] couple of a member of a polyga-mous marriage;

(b) the other member of that couple or another member of that marriage ("the other person") is in receipt of income support [⁵, an income-based jobseeker's allowance or an income-related employment and support allowance] and

(c) both members of the couple or marriage are living together within the meaning of regulation 1(3)(b) of those Regulations,

the Secretary of State may pay the winter fuel payment to the other person on behalf of the person entitled notwithstanding that the other person has not yet attained the ago of 60 in the qualifying week.]

AMENDMENTS

1. The Social Security (Claims and Payments) Amendment Regulations1999 (SI 1999/2358), reg.2(6) (September 20, 1999).

2. The Tax Credits (Claims and Payments) (Amendment) Regulations 1999(SI 1999/2752), regs 20, 24 and 25 (October 5, 1999).

3. The Social Security (Claims and Payments and Miscellaneous Amendments) (No.3) Regulations 2002 (SI 2002/2660), reg.2 (November 2, 2002).

4. The Civil Partnership (Pensions, Social Security and Child Support) (Consequential etc. Provisions) Order 2005 (SI 2005/2877) (December 5, 2005).

5. The Employment and Support Allowance (Consequential provisions) (No.2) Regulations 2008 (SI 2008/1554), reg.23 (October 27, 2008).

Regulation 36A revoked by The Social Security (Claims and Payments)   2.206
Amendment Regulations 1991 (SI1991/2741), reg.18 (April 6, 1992).

PART V

[¹ . . .] EXTINGUISHMENT

AMENDMENT

1. Words in heading omitted by The Social Security Act 1998 (Commencement No.8, and Savings and Consequential and Transitional Provisions) Order 1999 (SI 1999/1958), Sch.9 (July 5, 1999).

2.207   *Regulations 37–37B revoked by The Social Security Act 1998 (Commencement No.8, and Savings and Consequential and Transitional Provisions) Order 1999 (SI1999/1958), Sch.9 (July 5, 1999).*

Extinguishment of right to payment of sums by way of benefit where payment is not obtained within the prescribed period

2.208   **38.**—(1) [¹Subject to paragraph (2A), the right to payment of any sum by way of benefit shall be extinguished] where payment of that sum is not obtained within the period of 12 months from the date on which the right is to be treated as having arisen; and for the purposes of this regulation the right shall be treated as having arisen—

(a) in relation to any such sum contained in an instrument of payment which has been given or sent to the person to whom it is payable, or to a place approved by the Secretary of State [⁴ or the Board] for collection by him (whether or not received or collected as the case may be)—

    (i) on the date of the said instrument of payment, or

    (ii) if a further instrument of payment has been so given or sent as a replacement, on the date of the last such instrument of payment;

[³(aa) [⁸ . . .];]

(b) in relation to any such sum to which sub-paragraph (a) does not apply, where notice is given (whether orally or in writing) or is sent that the sum contained in the notice is ready for collection on the date of the notice or, if more than one such notice is given or sent, the date of the first such notice;

[⁷ (bb) in relation to any such sum which the person entitled to it and the Secretary of State have arranged to be paid by means of direct credit transfer into a bank or other account, on the due date for payment of the sum;]

(c) in relation to any such sum to which [³none of (a), [⁸ . . .] or [⁷ (b) or (bb) apply], on such date as the Secretary of State determines [⁴ or the Board determine].

(2) The giving or sending of an instrument of payment under paragraph (1)(a), or of a notice under paragraph (1)(b), shall be effective for the purposes of that paragraph, even where the sum contained in that instrument, or notice, is more or less than the sum which the person concerned has the right to receive.

[¹(2A) Where a question arises whether the right to payment of any sum by way of benefit has been extinguished by the operation of this regulation and the [⁵ Secretary of State] is satisfied that—

    (a) [5 he] first received [4 or the Board first received] written notice requesting payment of that sum after the expiration of 12 months; and

    (b) from a day within that period of 12 months and continuing until the day the written notice was given, there was good cause for not giving the notice; and

[2(c) [5. . .] either—

    (i) [5. . .] no instrument of payment has been given or sent to the person to whom it is payable and [5. . .] no payment has been made under the provisions of regulation 21 ([6 direct] credit transfer); or

    (ii) that such instrument has been produced to [5 the Secretary of State] and [5. . .] no further instrument has been issued as a replacement,]

the period of 12 months shall be extended to the date on which the [5 Secretary of State] decides that question, and this regulation shall accordingly apply as though the right to payment had arisen on that date.]

(3) For the purposes of paragraph (1) the date of an instrument of payment is the date of issue of that instrument or, if the instrument specifies a date which is the earliest date on which payment can be obtained on the instrument and which is later than the date of issue, that date.(4) This regulation shall apply to a person authorised or appointed to act on behalf of a beneficiary as it applies to a beneficiary.(5) This regulation shall not apply to the right to a single payment of any industrial injuries gratuity or in satisfaction of a person's right to graduated retirement benefit.

AMENDMENTS

1. The Social Security (Medical Evidence, Claims and Payments) Amendment Regulations 1989 (SI 1989/1686), reg.7 (October 9, 1989).

2. Social Security (Claims and Payments) Amendment (No.3) Regulations 1993 (SI 1993/2113), reg.3(8) (September 27, 1993).

3. Social Security (Claims and Payments Etc.) Amendment Regulations 1996 (SI 1996/672), reg.2(5) (April 4, 1996).

4. The Tax Credits (Claims and Payments) (Amendment) Regulations 1999 (SI 1999/2572), reg.20 (October 5, 1999).

5. The Social Security Act 1998 (Commencement No.9, and Savings and Consequential and Transitional Provisions) Order 1999 (SI 1999/2422), Sch.7 (September 6, 1999).

6. Social Security (Claims and Payments and Miscellaneous Amendments) (No.2) Regulations 2002 (SI 2002/2441), reg.10 (April 8, 2003).

7. The Social Security, Child Support and Tax Credits (Miscellaneous Amendments) Regulations 2005 (SI 2005/337), reg.7 (March 18, 2005).

8. The Social Security (Miscellaneous Amendments) (No.2) Regulations 2006 (SI 2006/832), reg.2 (April 10, 2006).

DEFINITIONS

"beneficiary"—see Social Security Act 1975, Sch.20.
"benefit"—see reg.2(2).
"instrument for benefit payment"—see reg.2(1).

GENERAL NOTE

In *CDLA/2807/2003* the Commissioner said,

2.209

"It seems to me quite impossible to say in circumstances where the operative decision is that no benefit is payable that any right to payment, let alone a right to payment of any amount that has been quantified, is in existence. There could be no right to payment until that decision has been altered in some way. Regulation 38 simply cannot have any operation in such circumstances."

In *CU/2604/1999*, the Commissioner said,

"The subject of regulation 38 is the 'right to payment of any sum'. The regulation sets out various rules for ascertaining the date on which that right is to be treated as having arisen. This includes the rule in regulation 38(1)(c). However, there must *first* be a right to payment of a *sum*. The word 'sum' means something otherwise it could have been omitted and left the provision meaning something slightly different. . . . In my view, if the amount has not been quantified, there is no 'sum', even if there has been identified a basis for quantifying it. Contrary to what has been argued on behalf of the Secretary of State, the fact that the tribunal later quantified the amount does not affect the fact it had not bee quantified at the time when the adjudication officer sought to extinguish the right to payment. If there is no sum, then the right to payment of it cannot arise, and cannot be extinguished under regulation 38." (para.17.)

In *CDLA/2609/2002*, the Commissioner offers a helpful overview of reg.38:

"15. I start with the overall scheme of regulation 38 of the Claims and Payments Regulations. It is concerned not with payment of benefit in a general sense, but with the extinguishment of a 'right to payment of any sum by way of benefit' (regulation 38(1)). The basic condition for such extinguishment is that 'payment of that sum is not obtained within the period of 12 months from the date on which the right is to be treated as having arisen'. Mr Commissioner Levenson has in decision *CU/2604/1999* (in the papers under that reference, but now reported as *R(U)1/02*) stressed that some meaning must be given to the word 'sum'. So he held there that where a Commissioner had decided that unemployment benefit was payable to a claimant for a specified period, without quantifying the amount of benefit, there was no sum identified to which a right of payment attached which could be extinguished. Likewise, it seems to me that some weight must be attached to the use of the term 'any sum by way of benefit' and to the test being in terms of 'obtaining' payment of such a sum. The use of language does not point towards a situation where benefit of a sufficiently ascertainable amount has been merely been awarded by a decision on entitlement and payability, so that the Secretary of State is under an obligation to pay the benefit as soon as reasonably practicable (Claims and Payments Regulations, regulation 20). It points towards a situation where a particular sum has been allocated to the claimant and some steps along the administrative process of making payment have been taken, leaving the claimant with some relatively mechanical steps to take to 'obtain' payment.

16. That view is also consistent with the provisions of subparagraphs (a) to (b) of regulation 38(1), which define the dates on which the right to payment of a sum by way of benefit is to be treated as having arisen in certain circumstances. The rules are that: where the claimant has been given or sent an instrument of payment or an instrument has been made available for collection, the right arises on the date of the instrument or any replacement instrument (subparagraph (a)); where a sum is payable by means of an instrument for benefit payment (see regulation 20A), the right arises on the first date on which payment could be obtained by that means (subparagraph (aa)); and, where subparagraph (a) does not apply and notice is given or sent that the sum is available for collection, the right arises on the date that the notice is sent (subparagraph (b)). It makes perfect sense to say in all those situations that a right to payment of the particular sum by way of benefit had arisen and that, if the claimant does not take the other necessary steps to get paid (even in a situation, for instance, where a letter gets lost in

the post), payment has not been obtained. The final provision in regulation 38(1), the crucial provision in this case, is subparagraph (c), under which the right to payment is to be treated as having arisen:

'(c) in relation to any such sum to which none of (a), (aa) or (b) apply, on such date as the Secretary of State determines or the [Board of Inland Revenue] determine.'

17. It is plainly arguable that subparagraph (c) does not give the Secretary of State an unfettered discretion to choose any date whatsoever, but must be interpreted in accordance with the overall scheme and scope of regulation 38(1) and by reference to the circumstances of subparagraphs (a) to (b). It is true that regulation 38(2A) on good cause is drafted on the assumption that regulation 38(1) can apply in a case where no instrument of payment was given or sent to the claimant, but I do not think that that undermines what I have said above. Miss Topping submitted that, although subparagraph (c) might exclude irrational or completely unreasonable choices, it certainly allowed the Secretary of State to determine that a right to payment of a sum by way of benefit arose on the date on which a weekly payment of benefit would have been made in the ordinary course of things, even though no administrative steps at all had actually been taken towards making payment."

It is a common feature of social security benefit that the right to payment of benefit does not survive a delay of more than twelve months in obtaining payment of it. The determination of the date on which the right to payment is treated as arising may be crucial and is a matter for the Secretary of State (or Board of the Inland Revenue as appropriate).

Only where reg.38(2A) applies does any issue for the adjudicating authorities arise. Then it is only whether the right to payment has been extinguished, but it will still be for the Secretary of State to determine "whether there should be a replacement instrument." (para.7.)

Cases in which the claimant says that no giro was received are governed by *R(IS) 7/91* under which questions of payment were held not to be questions relating to the award of benefit.

Unravelling those matters which are for the adjudicating authorities and those matters which do not attract a right of appeal will become more complicated under the new system under which there adjudication officers have been abolished and all decisions are taken by the Secretary of State with some attracting a right of appeal and others not.

Note that *R(P)3/93* was concerned with the version of this regulation in force until September 27, 1993, and has no application to the present version of the regulation.

Good cause

The test of good cause is the test which formerly existed under the replaced reg.19 of the Claims and Payments Regulations. Reference to the 1996 edition of *Non Means Tested Benefits: The Legislation* contains a detailed account of the case law, but the classic definition of good cause is that found in *R(S)2/63*:

2.210

"In Decision *CS371/49* the Commissioner said "'Good cause'" means, in my opinion, some fact which, having regard to all the circumstances (including the claimant's state of health and the information which he had received and that which he might have obtained) would probably have caused a reasonable person of his age and experience to act (or fail to act) as the claimant did.' This description of good cause has been quoted in countless cases. It has stood the test of time. In our judgment it is correct. The word 'fact' of course includes a combination of events happening either simultaneously or in succession."

PART VI

[¹MOBILITY COMPONENT OF DISABILITY LIVING ALLOWANCE AND
DISABILITY LIVING ALLOWANCE FOR CHILDREN]

AMENDMENT

1. The Social Security (Claims and Payments) Amendment Regulations 1991 (SI 1991/2741), reg.19(a) (February 3, 1992).

2.211   *Regulations 39–41 revoked by The Social Security (Claims and Payments) Amendment Regulations 1991 (SI 1991/2741), reg.19(b) (February 3, 1992).*

Cases where allowance not to be payable

2.212   **42.**—(1) Subject to the provisions of this regulation, [¹disability living allowance by virtue of entitlement to the mobility component] shall not be payable to any person who would otherwise be entitled to it in respect of any period—

    (a) during which that person has the use of an invalid carriage or other vehicle provided by the Secretary of State under section 5(2) of and Schedule 2 to the National Health Service Act 1977 or section 46 of the National Health Service (Scotland) Act 1978 which is a vehicle propelled by petrol engine or by electric power supplied for use on the road and to be controlled by the occupant; or

    (b) in respect of which that person has received, or is receiving, any payment—

      (i) by way of grant under the said section 5(2) and Schedule 2 or section 46 towards the costs of running a private car, or

      (ii) of mobility supplement under the Naval, Military and Air Forces etc., (Disablement and Death) Service Pensions Order 1983 or the Personal Injuries (Civilians) Scheme 1983 or under the said Order by virtue of the War Pensions (Naval Auxiliary Personnel) Scheme 1964, the Pensions (Polish Forces) Scheme 1964, the War Pensions (Mercantile Marine) Scheme 1964 or an Order of Her Majesty in relation to the Home Guard dated 21st December, 1964 or 22nd December, 1964 or in relation to the Ulster Defence Regiment dated 4th January, 1971,

or any payment out of public funds which the Secretary of State is satisfied is analogous thereto.

(2) A person who has notified the Secretary of State that he no longer wishes to use such an invalid carriage or other vehicle as if referred to in paragraph (1)(a) and has signed an undertaking that he will not use it while it remains in his possession awaiting collection, shall be treated, for the purposes of this regulation, as not having the use of that invalid carriage or other vehicle.

(3) Where a person in respect of whom [¹disability living allowance] is claimed for any period has received any such payment as referred to in paragraph (1)(b) for a period which, in whole or in part, covers the period for which the allowance is claimed, such payment shall be treated as an aggregate of equal weekly amounts in respect of each week in the period for which it is made and, where in respect of any such week a person is treated

as having a weekly amount so calculated which is less than the weekly rate of [¹ mobility component of disability living allowance to which, apart from paragraph (1), he would be entitled], any allowance to which that person may be entitled for that week shall be payable at a weekly rate reduced by the weekly amount so calculated.

(4) In a case where the Secretary of State has issued a certificate to the effect that he is satisfied—

(a) that the person in question either—

    (i) has purchased or taken on hire or hire-purchase; or

    (ii) intends to purchase or take on hire or hire-purchase a private car or similar vehicle ("the car") for a consideration which is more than nominal, on or about a date (not being earlier than 13th January, 1982) specified in the certificate ("the said date");

(b) that that person intends to retain possession of the car at least during, and to learn to drive it within, the period of 6 months or greater or lesser length of time as may be specified in the certificate ("the said period") beginning on the said date; and

(c) that the person will use [¹ disability living allowance by virtue of entitlement to the mobility component] in whole or in part during the said period towards meeting the expense of acquiring the car, paragraph (1)(a) shall not apply, and shall be treated as having never applied, during a period beginning on the said date and ending at the end of the said period or (if earlier) the date on which the Secretary of State cancels the certificate because that person has parted with possession of the car or for any other reason.

AMENDMENT

1. The Social Security (Claims and Payments) Amendment Regulations 1991 (SI 1991/2741), reg.20 (February 3, 1992).

Children

43.—(1) In any case where a claim for [¹disability living allowance] for a child is received by the Secretary of State, he shall, in accordance with the following provisions of this regulation, appoint a person to exercise, on behalf of the child, any right to which he may be entitled under the [Social Security Contributions and Benefits Act 1992] in connection with [¹disability living allowance] and to receive and deal on his behalf with any sums payable by way of [¹that allowance].

(2) Subject to the following provisions of this regulation, a person appointed by the Secretary of State under this regulation to act on behalf of the child shall—

(a) be a person with whom the child is living; and

(b) be over the age of 18 [² or, if the person is a parent of the child and living with him, be over the age of 16]; and

(c) be either the father or mother of the child, or, if the child is not living with either parent, be such other person as the Secretary of State may determine; and

(d) have given such undertaking as may be required by the Secretary of State as to the use, for the child's benefit, of any allowance paid.

(3) For the purpose of paragraph (2)(a), a person with whom a child has

2.213

been living shall, subject to paragraph (4) and to the power of the Secretary of State to determine in any case that the provisions of this paragraph should not apply, be treated as continuing to live with that child during any period—

    (a) during which that person and the child are separated but such separation has not lasted for a continuous period exceeding [¹12 weeks]; or

    (b) during which the child is absent by reason only of the fact that he is receiving full-time education at a school; or

    (c) during which the child is absent and undergoing medical or other treatment as an in-patient in a hospital or similar institution; or

    (d) during such other period as the Secretary of State may in any particular case determine:

Provided that where the absence of the child under (b) has lasted for a continuous period of 26 weeks or the child is absent under (c), that person shall only be treated as continuing to live with that child if he satisfies the Secretary of State that he has incurred, or has undertaken to incur, expenditure for the benefit of the child of an amount not less than the allowance payable in respect of such period of absence.

    (4) Where a child in respect of whom an allowance is payable, is, by virtue of any provision of an Act of Parliament—

    (a) committed to, or received into the care of, a local authority; or

    (b) subject to a supervision requirement and residing in a residential establishment under arrangements made by a local authority in Scotland;

any appointment made under the foregoing provisions of this regulation shall terminate forthwith:

Provided that, when a child is committed to, or received into, care or is made subject to a supervision requirement for a period which is, and when it began was, not intended to last for more than [¹12 weeks] the appointment shall not terminate by virtue of this paragraph until such period has lasted for 8 weeks.

    (5) In any case where an appointment on behalf of any child in the care of, or subject to a supervision requirement under arrangements made by, a local authority is terminated in accordance with paragraph (4), the Secretary of State may, upon application made to him by that local authority or by an officer of such authority nominated for the purpose by that authority, appoint the local authority or nominated officer thereof or appoint such other person as he may, after consultation with the local authority, determine, to exercise on behalf of the child any right to which that child may be entitled under the Act in connection with the allowance and to receive and deal on his behalf with any sums payable to him by way of [¹disability living allowance] for any period during which he is in the care of, or, as the case may be, subject to a supervision requirement under arrangements made by, that authority.

    (6) Where a child is undergoing medical or other treatment as an inpatient in a hospital or similar institution and there is no other person to whom [¹disability living allowance] may be payable by virtue of an appointment under this regulation, the Secretary of State may, upon application made to him by the district health authority [¹ National Health Service Trust] [³ NHS Foundation Trust] or, as the case may be, social services authority, controlling the hospital or similar institution in which the child

is an in-patient, or by an officer of that authority [¹ or Trust] nominated for the purpose by the authority, appoint that authority [¹ or Trust] or the nominated officer thereof or such other person as the Secretary of State may, after consultation with that authority [¹ or Trust], determine, to exercise on behalf of the child any right to which that child may be entitled in connection with the allowance and to receive and deal on his behalf with any sums payable to him by way of [¹ disability living allowance] for any period during which he is an in-patient in a hospital or similar institution under the control of that authority [¹ or Trust].

(7) For the purpose of this regulation—

"district health authority" means, in relation to England and Wales a District Health Authority within the meaning of the National Health Service Act 1977 and, in relation to Scotland, a Health Board within the meaning of the National Health Services (Scotland) Act 1978;

[² "child" means a person under the age of 16;]

"child's father" and "child's mother" include a person who is a child's father or mother by adoption or would be such a relative if an illegitimate child had been borne legitimate;

"hospital or similar institution" means any premises for the reception of and treatment of person suffering from any illness, including any mental disorder, or of persons suffering from physical disability and any premises used for providing treatment during convalescence or for medical rehabilitation;

"local authority" means, in relation to England and Wales, a local authority as defined in the Local Government Act 1972 and, in relation to Scotland, a local authority as defined in the Local Government (Scotland) Act 1973;

"social services authority" means—

(a) in relation to England and Wales, the social services committee established by a local authority under section 2 of the Local Authority Social Services Act 1970; and

(b) in relation to Scotland, the social work committee established by a local authority under section 2 of the Social Work (Scotland) Act 1968.

AMENDMENTS

1. The Social Security (Claims and Payments) Amendment Regulations 1991 (SI 1991/2741), reg.21 (February 3, 1992).

2. The Social Security, Child Support and Tax Credits (Miscellaneous Amendments) Regulations 2005 (SI 2005/337), reg.7 (March 18, 2005).

3. The Health and Social Care (Community Health and Standards) Act 2003 (Suplementary and Consequential Provisions) (NHS Foundation Trusts) Order 2004 (SI 2004/696), Art.3 and Sch.3 (March 11, 2004).

Payment of [¹ disability living allowance] on behalf of a beneficiary

44.—(1) Where, under arrangements made or negotiated by Motability, an agreement has been entered into by or on behalf of a beneficiary in respect of whom [¹ disability living allowance is payable by virtue of entitlement to the mobility component at the higher rate] for the hire or hire-purchase of a vehicle, the Secretary of State may arrange that any

2.214

[¹ disability living allowance by virtue of entitlement to the mobility component at the higher rate payable] to the beneficiary shall be paid in whole or in part on behalf of the beneficiary in settlement of liability for payments due under that agreement.

(2) Subject to regulations 45 and 46 an arrangement made by the Secretary of State under paragraph (1) shall terminate at the end of whichever is the relevant period specified in paragraph (3), in the case of hire, or paragraph (4), in the case of a hire-purchase agreement.

(3) In the case of hire the relevant period shall be—

    (a) where the vehicle is returned to the owner at or before the expiration of the [³ . . .] term of hire, the period of the [³ . . .] term; or

    (b) where the vehicle is retained by or on behalf of the beneficiary with the owner's consent after the expiration of the original term of hire [³, other than where sub-paragraph (d) applies,], the period of the original term; or

    (c) where the vehicle is retained by or on behalf of the beneficiary otherwise than with the owner's consent after the expiration of the original term of hire or its earlier termination, whichever is the longer of the following periods—

        (i) the period ending with the return of the vehicle to the owner; or

        (ii) the period of the original term of hire.

[³; or

    (d) where the original term of hire is extended by an agreed variation of the agreement, the period of the extended term.]

(4) In the case of a hire-purchase agreement, the relevant period shall be—

    (a) the period ending with the purchase of the vehicle; or

    (b) where the vehicle is returned to the owner or is repossessed by the owner under the terms of the agreement before the completion of the purchase, the original period of the agreement.

[²(5) In this regulation "Motability" means the company, set up under that name as a charity and originally incorporated under the Companies Act 1985 and subsequently incorporated by Royal Charter].

AMENDMENTS

1. The Social Security (Claims and Payments) Amendment Regulations 1991 (SI 1991/2741), reg.22 (February 3, 1992).

2. The Social Security (Miscellaneous Provisions) Amendment Regulations 1990 (SI 1990/2208), reg.13 (December 5, 1990).

3. The Social Security, Child Support and Tax Credits (Miscellaneous Amendments) Regulations 2005 (SI 2005/337), reg.7 (March 18, 2005).

Power for the Secretary of State to terminate an arrangement

2.215   **45.** The Secretary of State may terminate an arrangement for the payment of [¹disability living allowance by virtue of entitlement to the mobility component at the higher rate] on behalf of a beneficiary under regulation 44 on such date as he shall decide—

    (a) if requested to do so by the owner of the vehicle to which the arrangement relates, or

(b) where it appears to him that the arrangement is causing undue hard-ship to the beneficiary and that it should be terminated before the end of any of the periods specified in regulation 44(3) or 44(4).

AMENDMENT

1. The Social Security (Claims and Payments) Amendment Regulations 1991 (SI 1991/2741), reg.23 (February 3, 1992).

Restriction on duration of arrangements by the Secretary of State

46. The Secretary of State shall end an arrangement for the payment of [¹ disability living allowance by virtue of entitlement to the mobility component at the higher rate] on behalf of a beneficiary made under regulation 44, where he is satisfied that the vehicle to which the arrangement relates has been returned to the owner, and that the expenses of the owner arising out of the hire or hire-purchase agreement have been recovered following the return of the vehicle.

2.216

PART VII

MISCELLANEOUS

[¹ Instruments of payment

47.—(1) Instruments of payment issued by the Secretary of State shall remain his property.

(2) Any person having an instrument of payment shall, on ceasing to be entitled to the benefit to which the instrument relates, or when so required by the Secretary of State, deliver it to the Secretary of State or such other person as he may direct.]

2.217

AMENDMENT

1. Inserted by The Social Security (Miscellaneous Amendments) (No.2) Regulations 2006 (SI 2006/832), reg.2 (April 10, 2006).

Revocations

48. The regulations specified in column (1) of Schedule 10 to these regulations are hereby revoked to the extent mentioned in column (2) of that Schedule, in exercise of the powers specified in column (3).

2.218

Savings

49. [¹. . .]

2.219

AMENDMENT

1. The Social Security (Miscellaneous Provisions) Amendment (No.2) Regulations 1992 (SI 1992/2595), reg.6 (November 16, 1992).

GENERAL NOTE

2.220   Regulation 49 maintained in force regulations about claims and reviews relating to supplementary benefit and family income support. See *CIS/465/1991*. Because its terms led to the mistaken impression that the substantive terms of the schemes survived the repeal of the Supplementary Benefits Act 1976 and the Family Income Supplements Act 1970 by the Social Security Act 1986, reg.49 has been revoked from November 16, 1992. See *R(SB) 1/94*. It is not immediately apparent that reg.49 was necessary in order to allow claims to be made for supplementary benefit for periods prior to April 11, 1988, and reviews of entitlement for such periods to be carried out. Therefore its revocation may have no effect on such matters. See Sch.10 to the Administration Act. However, *CSB 168/1993* is to the contrary.

In *CIS/12016/1996* a Commissioner, after a detailed review of the legal issues, concluded that from November 16, 1992, it has been impossible for an effective claim to be made for supplementary benefit. This was in spite of the powerful argument that an underlying entitlement to supplementary benefit for a period before April 11, 1988, and the right to pursue a remedy in respect of that entitlement could be preserved by s.16(1) of the Interpretation Act 1978 on the revocation of the supplementary benefit legislation. The reason was that any remedy protected would be under reg.3(1) of the Supplementary Benefit (Claims and Payments) Regulations 1981, which required a claim for weekly supplementary benefit to be made in writing on a form approved by the Secretary of State or in such other manner as the Secretary of State accepted as sufficient. In *CIS/12016/1996* the claim was made in a letter in July 1993. By that date, the Secretary of State had no power to accept the manner of claim as sufficient, because the 1981 Regulations no longer existed. Since the Secretary of State's power was discretionary, the claimant had no accrued right which could be preserved by s.16(1). It had been held in *R. v Secretary of State for Social Security Ex p. Cullen* (November 21, 1996), now confirmed by the Court of Appeal (*The Times*, May 16, 1997, and see the notes to reg.9) that the hope of having a discretion to treat a claim for supplementary benefit as in the alternative a claim for attendance allowance was not preserved by s.16(1) as an accrued right. The same had to apply to the power to accept claims as made in sufficient manner.

Note also *CIS/7009/1995* which confirms that it was not possible to make a late claim for National Assistance after the start of the supplementary benefit scheme on November 24, 1966. There were no savings provisions to enable claims for National Assistance to succeed after that date (see *CSB 61/1995*).

SCHEDULE 1

PART I

BENEFIT CLAIMED AND OTHER BENEFIT WHICH MAY BE TREATED AS IF CLAIMED IN ADDITION OR IN THE ALTERNATIVE

2.221

Benefit claimed (1)	Alternative benefit (2)
[¹ Incapacity benefit]	[¹ Severe disablement allowance]
[² . . .]	[² . . .]
Severe disablement allowance	[¹ Incapacity benefit]
[² . . .]	[² . . .]
[¹ Incapacity benefit for a woman]	[¹ Maternity allowance]
Severe disablement allowance for a woman	Maternity allowance

[¹¹ Employment and support allowance for a women]	[¹¹ Maternity allowance]
Maternity allowance	[¹ Incapacity benefit [¹¹, severe disablement allowance or employment and support allowance]
A retirement pension of any category	Widow's benefit [⁹ or bereavement benefit]
A retirement pension of any category	A retirement pension of any other category a shared additional pension [³ or graduated retirement benefit]
[¹ An increase of incapacity benefit]	An increase of severe disablement allowance
Attendance allowance	An increase of disablement pension where constant attendance is needed
An increase of disablement pension where constant attendance is needed	Attendance allowance [⁴ or disability living allowance]
An increase of severe disablement allowance	[¹ An increase of incapacity benefit]
Income support	[⁵ . . .] [⁴ . . .] or [¹⁰ carer's allowance]
[⁶ Widow's benefit [⁹ or bereavement benefit]]	[⁶ A retirement pension of any category or graduated retirement benefit]
[⁴ Disability living allowance]	[⁴ Attendance allowance or an increase of disablement pension where constant attendance is needed]
[⁴ Attendance allowance or an increase of disablement pension where constant attendance is needed]	[⁴ Disability living allowance]
[⁷ Disabled person's tax credit]	[⁷ Working families' tax credit]
[⁷ Working families' tax credit]	[⁷ Disabled person's tax credit]

In this part of this Schedule—
- (a) Reference to an increase of any benefit (other than an increase of disablement pension where constant attendance is needed) are to an increase of that benefit in respect of a child or adult dependant;
- (b) "widow's benefit" means widow's benefit under [Part II of the Social Security Contributions and Benefits Act 1992] and benefit by virtue of section [78(9)] of that Act corresponding to a widow's pension or a widowed mother's allowance.

PART II

INTERCHANGE OF CLAIMS FOR CHILD BENEFIT WITH CLAIMS FOR OTHER BENEFITS

[⁸ . . .]

2.222

Guardian's allowance
Maternity allowance claimed after confinement
Increase of child dependant by virtue of [sections 80 and 90 of the Social Security Contributions and Benefits Act 1992], or regulations made under [section 78(9)] of that Act.

AMENDMENTS

1. The Social Security (Claims and Payments) Amendment (No.2) Regulations 1994 (SI 1994/2943), reg.10 (April 13, 1995).

2. The Social Security (Claims and Payments) (Jobseeker's Allowance Consequential Amendments) Regulations 1996 (SI 1996/1460), reg.2 (October 7, 1996).

3. The Social Security (Claims and Payments) Amendment Regulations 1988 (SI 1988/522), reg.8 (April 11, 1988).

4. The Social Security (Claims and Payments) Amendment Regulations 1991 (SI 1991/2741), reg.25 (February 3, 1992).

5. The Social Security (Miscellaneous Provisions) Amendment (No.2) Regulations 1992 (SI 1992/2595), reg.7 (November 16, 1992).

6. The Social Security (Miscellaneous Provisions) Amendment Regulations 1990 (SI 1990/2208), reg.14 (December 5, 1990).

7. The Tax Credits (Claims and Payments) (Amendment) Regulations 1999 (SI 1999/2572), regs 24 and 25 (October 5, 1999).

8. The Child Benefit, Child Support and Social Security (Miscellaneous Amendments) Regulations 1996 (SI 1996/1803), reg.20 (April 7, 1997).

9. The Social Security (Benefits for Widows and Widowers) (Consequential Amendments) Regulations 2000 (SI 2000/1483), reg.9 (April 9, 2001).

10. The Social Security Amendment (Carer's Allowance) Regulations 2002 (SI 2002/2497), Sch.2 (October 28, 2002).

11. The Employment and Support Allowance (Consequential provisions) (No.2) Regulations 2008 (SI 2008/1554), reg.24 (October 27, 2008).

SCHEDULE 2   **Regulation 17(5)**

SPECIAL PROVISIONS RELATING TO CLAIMS FOR [¹JOBSEEKER'S ALLOWANCE] DURING PERIODS CONNECTED WITH PUBLIC HOLIDAYS

2.223   **1.**—(1) In this Schedule—

(a) "public holiday" means, as the case may be, Christmas Day, Good Friday or a Bank Holiday under the Banking and Financial Dealings Act 1971 or in Scotland local holidays; and "Christmas and New Year holidays" and "Good Friday and Easter Monday" shall be construed accordingly and shall in each case be treated as one period;

(b) "office closure" means a period during which an [¹ office of the Department for Education an Employment] or associated office is closed in connection with a public holiday;

(c) in computing any period of time Sundays shall not be disregarded.

(2) Where any claim for [¹a jobseeker's allowance] is made during one of the periods set out in paragraph (3), the following provisions shall apply—

(a) a claim for [¹a jobseeker's allowance] may be treated by [² the Secretary of State as a claim for that benefit for period, to be specified in his decision, not exceeding 35 days after the date of the claim where that claim is made during the period specified in sub-paragraph (a) of paragraph (3), or 21 days after the date of claim where the claim is made during the period specified in either sub-paragraph (b) or (c) of paragraph (3);

(b) on any claim so treated, benefit may be awarded as if the provisions of paragraph (4) of regulation 17 applied.

(3) For the purposes of paragraph (2) the periods are—

(a) in the case of Christmas and New Year holidays, a period beginning with the start of the 35th day before the first day of office closure and ending at midnight between the last day of office closure and the following day;

(b) in the case of Good Friday and Easter Monday, a period beginning with the start of the 16th day before the first day of the office closure and ending at midnight between the last day of office closure and the following day;

(c) in the case of any public holiday, a period beginning with the start of the 14th day before the first day of office closure and ending at midnight between the last day of office closure and the following day.

AMENDMENTS

1. The Social Security (Claims and Payments) (Jobseeker's Allowance Consequential Amendments) Regulations 1996 (SI 1996/1460), reg.2 (October 7, 1996).

2. The Social Security Act 1998 (Commencement No.11 and Transitional Provisions) Order 1999 (SI 1999/2860), Sch.3 (October 18, 1999).

Schedule 3 revoked by The Social Security (Claims and Payments) (Jobseeker's Allowance Consequential Amendments) Regulations 1996 (SI 1996/1460), reg.2 (October 7, 1996).

SCHEDULE 4

PRESCRIBED TIME FOR CLAIMING BENEFIT

Description of benefit (1)	Prescribed time for claiming benefit (2)
1. [¹ Jobseeker's allowance]	[¹ The first day of the period in respect of which the claim is made]
[² 2. Incapacity benefit or severe disablement allowance]	[² The day in respect of which the claim is made and period of [³ 3 months] immediately following it.]
3. Disablement benefit (not being an increase of benefit)	As regards any day on which, apart from satisfying the condition of making a claim, the claimant is entitled to benefit, that day and the period of 3 months immediately following it.
4. Increase of disablement benefit under section 61 (constant attendance), or 63 (exceptionally severe disablement) of the Social Security Act 1975.	As regards any day which apart form satisfying the conditions that there is a current award of disablement benefit and the making of a claim, the claimant is entitled to benefit, that day and the period of 3 months immediately following it.
5. Reduced earnings allowance	As regards any day on which apart from satisfying the conditions that there is an assessment of disablement of not less than one percent. and the making of a claim, the claim is entitled to the allowance, that day and the period of 3 months immediately following it.
6. Income support	The first day of the period in respect of which the claim is made.
7. [⁴ Working families' tax credit]	(a) Where [⁴ working families' tax credit] has previously been claimed and awarded the period beginning 28 days before and ending 14 days after the last day of that award;
	[⁵ (aa) where [⁴ disabled person's tax credit] has previously been claimed and awarded the period beginning 42 days before and ending 14 days after the last day of that award of [⁴ disabled person's tax credit]]
	(b) Subject to [⁵ (a) and (aa)], the first day of the period in respect of which the claim is made;
	(c) where a claim for [⁴ working families' tax credit] is treated as if made for a period beginning with the relevant day by virtue of regulation 13 of these Regulations, the period beginning on 10th March 1992 and ending on 6th April 1992]
8. Social fund payment in respect of maternity expenses	[⁷ The period beginning 11 weeks before the first day of the expected week of confinement and ending three months after—
	(a) the actual date of confinement; or

471

9. Social fund payment in respect of funeral expenses

(b) in the case of an adopted child, the date of the adoption order; or

(c) in the case of a child in respect of whom an order has been granted pursuant to section 30 of the Human Fertilisation and Embryology Act, the date of that Order.]

[⁸ The period beginning with the date of death and ending 3 months after the date of the funeral.]

9A. [⁹ . . .]

10. Increase of disablement benefit under [¹⁰ section 60 of the Social Security Act 1975 on grounds of special hardship or] section 62 of the Social Security Act 1975 on the grounds of receipt of hospital treatment.

A regards any day on which, apart form satisfying the conditions that there is a current award of disablement benefit and the making of a claim, the claimant is entitled to benefit, that day and the period 3 months immediately following it.

[¹¹ **11.** [¹² Disabled person's tax credit]

(a) Where [¹² disabled person's tax credit] has previously been claimed and awarded the period beginning 42 days before and ending 14 days after the last day of that award;

(b) where [¹² working families' tax credit] has previously been claimed and awarded the period beginning 28 days before and ending 14 days after the last day of that award of [¹² working families' tax credit];

(c) subject to (a) and (b), the first day of the period in respect of which the claim is made;

(d) where a claim for [¹² disabled person's tax credit] is made by virtue of regulation 13B(1), the period beginning on 10th March 1992 and ending on 6th April 1992.]

[¹³ **12.** State pension credit.

As regards any day on which, apart from satisfying the condition of making a claim, the claimant is entitled to benefit, that day and the period of 12 months immediately following it.]

[¹⁴ **13.** Retirement pension of any category

As regards any day on which apart from satisfying the condition of making a claim, the claimant is entitled to the pension, that day and the period of 12 months immediately following it.]

[¹⁴ **14.** Graduated retirement benefit

As regards any day on which, apart from satisfying the condition of making a claim, the claimant is entitled to benefit, that day and the period of 12 months immediately following it.]

[¹⁵ **15.** Shared additional pension

As regards any day on which, apart from satisfying the condition of making a claim, the claimant is entitled to the pension, that day and the period of 12 months immediately following it.]

[¹⁶ **16.** Employment and support allowance

The day in respect of which the claim is made and the period of three months immediately following it.]

472

For the purposes of this Schedule—

"actual date of confinement" means the date of the issue of the child or, if the woman is confined of twins or a greater number of children, the date of the issue of the last of them; and

"confinement" means labour resulting in the issue of a living child, or labour after 28 weeks of pregnancy resulting in the issue of a child whether alive or dead.

AMENDMENTS

1. The Social Security (Claims and Payments) (Jobseeker's Allowance Consequential Amendments) Regulations 1996 (SI 1996/460), reg.2 (October 7, 1996).

2. The Social Security (Claims and Payments) Amendment (No.2) Regulations 1994 (SI 1994/2943), reg.12 (April 13, 1995).

3. The Social Security (Miscellaneous Provisions) (No.2) Regulations 1997 (SI 1997/793), reg.7 (April 7, 1997).

4. The Tax Credits (Claims and Payments) (Amendment) Regulations 1999 (SI 1999/2572), regs 24 and 25 (October 5, 1999).

5. The Social Security (Claims and Payments) Amendment Regulations 1991 (SI 1991/2741), reg.26 (March 10, 1992).

6. The Social Security (Miscellaneous Provisions) Amendment Regulations 1991 (SI 1991/2284), reg.10 (November 1, 1991).

7. The Social Security (Social Fund and Claims and Payments) (Miscellaneous Amendments) Regulations 1997 (SI 1997/792), reg.8 (April 7, 1997).

8. The Social Security (Claims and Payments and Adjudication) Amendment Regulations 1996 (SI 1996/2306), reg.6 (October 7, 1996).

9. The Social Security (Miscellaneous Provisions) Amendment Regulations 1991 (SI 1991/2284), reg.11 (November 1, 1991).

10. The Social Security (Claims and Payments) Amendment Regulations 1988 (SI 1988/522), reg.9 (April 11, 1988).

11. The Social Security (Claims and Payments) Amendment Regulations 1991 (SI 1991/2741), reg 26(b) (March 10, 1992).

12. The Tax Credits (Claims and Payments) (Amendment) Regulations 1999 (SI 1999/2572), regs 24 and 25 (October 5, 1999).

13. Social Security (Claims and Payments) Amendment (No.2) Regulations 2004 (SI 2004/1821), reg.2(a) (October 6, 2004).

14. The Social Security (Claims and Payments) Amendment Regulations 2005 (SI 2005/455), reg.5 (April 6, 2006).

15. The Social Security (Shared Additional Pension (Miscellaneous Amendments) Regulations 2005 (SI 2005/1551), reg.3 (April 6, 2006).

16. The Employment and Support Allowance (Consequential provisions) (No.2) Regulations 2008 (SI 2008/1554), reg.24 (October 27, 2008).

GENERAL NOTE

Sometimes there is a need to be very precise about dates. *CIB/2805/2003* was just such a case. The Deputy Commissioner notes that the formulation used in relation to incapacity benefit (and, it should be noted, in relation to several other benefits) is to specify the time limit by reference to the day of claim and a period of three months immediately following it. The Deputy Commissioner rules that this means that the claimant gets the day of claim and a full three months immediately following the date in respect of which the claim is made. This gave the claimant two more days than the Secretary of State had calculated.

2.226

Schedule 5 revoked by The Social Security (Claims and Payments and Adjudication) Amendment Regulations 1996 (SI 1996/2306), reg.7 (October 7, 1996).

2.227

SCHEDULE 6 **Regulation 22(3)**

DAYS FOR PAYMENT OF LONG TERM BENEFITS

[¹ Attendance allowance and disability living allowance

2.228   **1.** Subject to the provisions of regulation 25 (payment of attendance allowance, constant attendance allowance and the care component of a disability living allowance at a daily rate) attendance allowance shall be payable on Wednesdays, except that the Secretary of State may in a particular case arrange for either allowance to be payable on any other day of the week and where it is in payment to any person and the day on which it is payable is changed, it shall be paid at a daily rate of 1/7th of the weekly rate in respect of any of the days for which payment would have been made but for that change.]

    2. [²...]

Industrial injuries benefit

2.229   **3.** Any pension or allowance under [Part V of the Social Security Contributions and Benefits Act 1992], including any increase, shall be payable on Wednesdays.

[⁵Carer's allowance]

2.230   **4.** [⁵carer's allowance] shall be payable on Mondays, except that where a person is entitled to that allowance in respect of a severely disabled person by virtue of regulation 3 of the Social Security (Invalid Care Allowance) Regulations 1976 the [⁵carer's allowance] shall be payable on Wednesdays.

Retirement pension

2.231   **5.** Retirement pension shall be payable on Mondays, except that—
    (a) where a person became entitled to a retirement pension before September 28, 1984, that pension shall be payable on Thursdays;
    [³(b) where—
        (i) a woman was entitled to a widow's benefit, or
        (ii) a man or a woman was entitled to a bereavement benefit,
    immediately before becoming entitled to a retirement pension, that pension shall be payable on [⁴ . . .] [⁴ the day of the week which has become the appropriate day for payment of such a benefit to him in accordance with paragraph 6];]
    (c) where a woman becomes entitled to a retirement pension immediately following the payment to her husband of an increase of retirement pension in respect of her, the retirement pension to which she becomes entitled shall be payable on the same days as those upon which the retirement pension of the husband is payable;
    (d) the Secretary of State may, notwithstanding anything contained in the foregoing provisions of this paragraph, arrange for retirement pension to be payable on such other day of the week as he may [⁴ . . .] [⁴ where payment is by credit transfer, or in the circumstances of any particular case, determine];
    (e) where, in relation to any person, any particular day of the week has become the appropriate day of the week for the payment of retirement pension, that day shall thereafter remain the appropriate day in his case for such payment.

Shared additional pension

2.232   [⁶ **5A.** Shared additional pension shall be payable on Mondays, except that—
    (a) where a retirement pension is payable to the claimant, it shall be payable on the same day as the retirement pension; or
    (b) the Secretary of State may, notwithstanding the provisions of sub-paragraph (a), arrange for a shared additional pension to be payable on such other day of the week as he may, in the circumstances of any particular case, determine.]

Widowed mother's allowance and widow's pension

2.233   **6.** Widowed mother's allowance [⁷ . . .]
    7. [¹...]

AMENDMENTS

1. The Social Security (Claims and Payments) Amendment Regulations 1991 (SI 1991/2741), reg.27 (April 6, 1992).

2. The Social Security (Claims and Payments) Amendment Regulations 1999 (SI 1999/2358), reg.2 (September 20, 1999).

3. The Social Security (Benefits for Widows and Widowers) (Consequential Amendments) Regulations 2000 (SI 2000/1483), reg.9 (April 9, 2001).

4. Social Security (Claims and Payments and Miscellaneous Amendments) (No.2) Regulations 2002 (SI 2002/2441), reg.11 (October 23, 2002).

5. The Social Security Amendment (Carer's Allowance) Regulations 2002 (SI 2002/2497), Sch.2 (October 28, 2002).

6. The Social Security (Shared Additional Pension) (Miscellaneous Amendments) Regulations 2005 (SI 2005/1551) (July 6, 2005).

7. The Social Security (Claims and Payments) Amendments Regulations 2009 (SI 2009/604), reg.2 (April 6, 2009).

SCHEDULE 7   **Regulation 26**

[¹⁵ TIME OF PAYMENT AND COMMENCEMENT OF ENTITLEMENT IN INCOME SUPPORT CASES]

Manner of payment
1. Except as otherwise provided in these Regulations income support shall be paid in arrears in accordance with the award.]   2.234

Time of payment
2. Income support shall be paid in advance where the claimant is—   2.235
  (a) in receipt of retirement pension; or
  (b) over pensionable age and not in receipt of [⁹. . .] [⁷incapacity benefit or severe disablement allowance and is not a person to whom section 126 of the Social Security Contributions and Benefits Act 1992 (trade disputes) applies] unless he was in receipt of income support immediately before the trade dispute began; or
  (c) [¹⁶ subject to paragraph 2ZA] in receipt of widow's benefit [¹³or bereavement benefit] and is not [¹⁴ . . .] providing or required to provide medical evidence of incapacity for work; or
  (d) a person to whom [¹section 23(a)] of the Social Security Act 1986 [SSCBA, s.127] applies, but only for the period of 15 days mentioned in that subsection.
  [¹⁶ 2ZA. Paragraph 2(c) shall only apply where a widow's benefit or a bereavement benefit is paid in advance.]
  [²2A.—(1) For the purposes of this paragraph—
  (a) "public holiday" means, as the case may be, Christmas Day, Good Friday or a Bank Holiday under the Banking and Financial Dealings Act 1971 or in Scotland local holidays, and
  (b) "office closure" means a period during which an office of the Department of Social Security or associated office is closed in connection with a public holiday.
  (2) Where income support is normally paid in arrears and the day on which the benefit is payable by reason of paragraph 3 is affected by office closure it may for that benefit week be paid wholly in advance or partly in advance and partly in arrears and on such a day as the Secretary of State may direct.
  (3) Where under this paragraph income support is paid either in advance or partly in advance and partly in arrears it shall for any other purposes be treated as if it was paid in arrears.]
  [³3. (1) Subject to [⁷sub-paragraph (1A) and to] any direction given by the Secretary of State in accordance with sub-paragraph (2), income support in respect of any benefit week shall, if the beneficiary is entitled to a relevant social security benefit or would be so entitled but for failure to satisfy the contribution conditions or had not exhausted his entitlement, be paid on the day and at the intervals appropriate to payment of that benefit.
  [⁷(1A) Subject to sub-paragraph (2), where income support is paid to a person on the grounds of incapacity for work, that entitlement commenced on or after 13th April 1995, and no relevant social security benefit is paid to that person, the income support shall be paid fortnightly in arrears.]

(2) The Secretary of State may direct that income support in respect of any benefit week shall be paid at such intervals and on such days as he may in any particular case or class of case determine.

2.236

3A.—(1) Income support for any part-week shall be paid in accordance with an award on such day as the Secretary of State may in any particular case direct.

(2) In this paragraph, "part-week" has the same meaning as it has in Part VII of the Income Support (General) Regulations 1987.]

4. [¹In this Schedule]—

"benefit week" means, if the beneficiary is entitled to a relevant social security benefit or would be so entitled but for failure to satisfy the contribution conditions or had not exhausted his entitlement, the week corresponding to the week in respect of which that benefit is paid, and in any other case a period of 7 days beginning or ending with such day as the Secretary of State may direct;

[¹"Income Support Regulations" means the Income Support (General) Regulations 1987;] and

"relevant social security benefit" means [⁹. . .] [⁷incapacity benefit], severe disablement allowance, retirement pension [¹² bereavement benefit] or widow's benefit.

Payment of small amounts of income support

2.237

5. Where the amount of income support is less than £1.00 a week the Secretary of State may direct that it shall be paid at such intervals as may be specified not exceeding 13 weeks.

Commencement of entitlement to income support

2.238

6.—(1) Subject to sub-paragraphs (3) and (4), in a case where income support is payable in arrears entitlement shall commence on the date of claim.

(2) [¹Subject to sub-paragraphs (2A) and (3)], in a case where, under paragraph 2, income support is payable in advance entitlement shall commence on the date of claim if that day is a day for payment of income support as determined under paragraph 3 but otherwise on the first such day after the date of claim.

[¹(2A) Where income support is awarded under regulation 17(3) for a definite period which is not a benefit week or a multiple of such a week entitlement shall commence on the date of claim.

(3) In a case where regulation 13 applies, entitlement shall commence on the day which is the relevant day for the purposes of that regulation [⁵ except where income support is paid in advance, when entitlement shall commence on the relevant day, if that day is a day for payment as determined under paragraph 3 but otherwise on the first day for payment after the relevant day].]

(4) [¹. . .]

[⁹(5) If a claim is made by a claimant within 3 days of the date on which he became resident in a resettlement place provided pursuant to section 30 of the Jobseekers Act or at a centre providing facilities for the rehabilitation of alcoholics or drug addicts, and the claimant is so resident for the purposes of that rehabilitation, then the claim shall be treated as having been made on the day the claimant became so resident.]

(6) Where, in consequence of a further claim for income support such as is mentioned in sub-paragraph 4(7) of Schedule 3 to the Income Support (General) Regulations 1987, a claimant is treated as occupying a dwelling as his home for a period before moving in, that further claim shall be treated as having been made on the date from which he is treated as so occupying the dwelling or the date of the claim made before he moved in to the dwelling and referred to in that sub-paragraph, whichever is the later.

7. [. . .¹²].

AMENDMENTS

1. The Social Security (Claims and Payments) Amendment Regulations 1988 (SI 1988/522), reg.10 (April 11, 1988).

2. Transfer of Functions (Health and Social Security) Order 1988 (SI 1988/1843); The Social Security (Claims and Payments and Payments on account, Overpayments and Recovery) Amendment Regulations 1989 (SI 1989/136), reg.2(b) (February 27, 1989).

3. The Social Security (Medical Evidence, Claims and Payments) Amendment Regulations 1989 (SI 1989/1686), reg.8 (October 9, 1989).

4. The Social Security (Miscellaneous Provisions) Amendment Regulations 1990 (SI 1990/2208), reg.15 (December 5, 1990).

5. The Enterprise (Scotland) Consequential Amendments Order 1991 (SI 1991/387), art.2 and Sch.(April 1, 1991).

6. The Social Security (Miscellaneous Provisions) Amendment Regulations 1992 (SI 1992/247), reg.17 (March 9, 1992).

7. The Social Security (Claims and Payments) Amendment (No.2) Regulations 1994 (SI 1994/2943), reg.14 (April 13, 1995).

8. The Social Security (Claims and Payments etc.) Amendment Regulations 1996 (SI 1996/672), reg.2(6) (April 4, 1996).

9. The Social Security (Claims and Payments) (Jobseeker's Allowance Consequential Amendments) Regulations 1996 (SI 1996/1460), reg.2(24) (October 7, 1996).

10. The Social Security (Miscellaneous) Amendment (No.4) Regulations 1998 (SI 1998/1174), reg.8(3)(b) (June 1, 1998).

11. The Social Security Act 1998 (Commencement No.12 and Consequential and Transitional Provisions) Order 1999 (SI 1999/3178), Sch.6 (November 29, 1999).

12. The Social Security and Child Support (Miscellaneous Amendments) Regulations 2000 (SI 2000/1596), reg.5 (June 19, 2000).

13. The Social Security (Benefits for Widows and Widowers) (Consequential Amendments) Regulations 2000 (SI 2000/1483), reg.9 (April 9, 2001).

14. The Social Security, Child Support and Tax Credits (Miscellaneous Amendments) Regulations 2005 (SI 2005/337), reg.7 (March 18, 2005).

15. The Social Security (Miscellaneous Amendments) (No.2) Regulations 2006 (SI 2006/832), reg.2 (April 10, 2006).

16. The Social Security (Claims and Payments) Amendments Regulations 2009 (SI 2009/604), reg.2 (April 6, 2009).

GENERAL NOTE

Para.2
These categories of claimant are paid income support in advance. Apart from pensioners and most widows, those returning to work after a trade dispute are covered.

2.239

Paras 3 and 4
Where a claimant meets the conditions of entitlement for one of the benefits listed as a "relevant social security benefit," the income support benefit week, pay-day and interval of payment is the same as for that benefit. Thus, those incapable of work are paid fortnightly in arrears (reg.24(1)), although under reg.24 the Secretary of State can arrange payment of incapacity benefit at other intervals (e.g. weekly), in which case income support follows suit. Otherwise the benefit week is to be defined by the Secretary of State. Income support paid for a definite period under reg.17(3) need not be in terms of benefit weeks. Paragraph 3A provides that payments for part-weeks may be made as the Secretary of State directs.

2.240

Para.6
The general rule for income support paid in arrears is that entitlement begins on the date of claim. The first payment on the pay day at the end of the first benefit week (or the second benefit week in the case of the unemployed) can thus be precisely calculated to include the right number of days. Payments can then continue on a weekly basis.

2.241

If income support is paid in advance, then, as for supplementary benefit, entitlement begins on the next pay day following the claim or coinciding with the date of claim.

Where the award is for a definite period under reg.17(3) entitlement begins with the date of claim (sub-para.(2A)). Sub-paragraph (3) deals with the special case of advance awards. Sub-paragraphs (5) and (6) cover other special cases.

SCHEDULE 8   **Regulation 23(1)(a)**

ELECTION TO HAVE CHILD BENEFIT PAID WEEKLY

2.242

1. A person to whom benefit is payable for an uninterrupted period beginning before and ending after March 15, 1982 may make an election, in accordance with paragraph 3, that benefit be payable weekly after that date, if either—

    (a) he makes the election before the end of the 26th week from the day on which benefit was payable for the first four weeks in respect of which the Secretary of State made arrangements for four-weekly payment to the person entitled in accordance with regulation 21 or regulation 23(1)(b); or

    (b) he was absent from Great Britain on the March 15, 1982 for one of the reasons specified in paragraph 4 and he makes the election before the end of the 26th week of the period beginning with the first week in respect of which benefit became payable to him in Great Britain on his return.

2. Subject to paragraph 5, a person entitled to benefit may make an election, in accordance with paragraph 3, that benefit be paid weekly if he satisfies either of the following conditions—

    (a) he is a lone parent within the meaning set out in regulation 2(2) of the Child Benefit and Social Security (Fixing and Adjustment of Rates) Regulations 1976, or]

    (b) he, or his spouse residing with him or the person with whom he is living as husband and wife, is receiving income support, [²an incomed-based jobseeker's allowance], [³ or payment in accordance with an award of family credit or disability working allowance which was awarded with effect for a date falling before 5th October 1999.]

3. An election for benefit to be payable weekly under paragraphs 1 or 2 shall be effected by giving notice in writing to the Secretary of State delivered or sent to the appropriate office and shall be made when it is received.

2.243

4. An election may not be made under paragraph 1(b) unless the person's absence abroad on the March 15, 1982 was by reason of his being—

    (a) a serving member of the forces, as defined by regulation 1(2) of the Social Security (Contributions) Regulations 1979, or

    (b) the spouse of such a member, or

    (c) a person living with such a member as husband and wife.

5. Every person making an election for benefit to be paid weekly under paragraph 2 shall furnish such certificates, documents and such other information of facts as the Secretary of State may, in his discretion, require, affecting his right to receive payment of benefit weekly and in particular shall notify the Secretary of State in writing of any change of circumstances which he might reasonably be expected to know might affect the right to receive payment of benefit weekly, as soon as reasonably practicable after the occurrence thereof.

6. Where a person makes an election, in accordance with this regulation, for benefit to be paid weekly, it shall continue to be so payable—

    (a) in the case of an election under paragraph 1, so long as that person remains continually entitled to benefit, or

    (b) in the case of an election under paragraph 2, so long as that person remains continually entitled to benefit and the conditions specified in that paragraph continue to be satisfied.

7. A person who has made an election that benefit be payable weekly may cancel it at any time by a notice in writing delivered or sent to the appropriate office; and effect shall be given to such a notice as soon as is convenient.

AMENDMENTS

1. The Child Benefit, Child Support and Social Security (Miscellaneous Amendments) Regulations 1996 (SI 1996/1803), reg.21 (April 7, 1997).

2. The Social Security (Claims and Payments) (Jobseeker's Allowance Consequential Amendments) Regulations 1996 (SI 1996/1460), reg.2 (October 7, 1996).

3. The Social Security and Child Support (Tax Credits) Consequential Amendments Regulations 1999 (SI 1999/2566), Sch.8 (September 5, 1999).

SCHEDULE 9   **Regulation 35**

DEDUCTIONS FROM BENEFIT AND DIRECT PAYMENT TO THIRD PARTIES

Interpretation

1. [[20]—(1)] In this Schedule—   2.244

[[11]"the Community Charges Regulations" means the Community Charges (Deductions from Income Support (No.2) Regulations 1990;

"the Community Charges (Scotland) Regulations" means the Community Charges (Deductions from Income Support) (Scotland) Regulations 1989;]

[[21]"contribution-based jobseeker's allowance" means any contribution-based jobseeker's allowance which does not fall within the definition of "specified benefit";]

[[43] "contributory employment and support allowance" means any contributory employment and support allowance which does not fall within the definition of "specified benefit"]

["the Council Tax Regulations" mean the Council Tax (Deductions from Income Support) Regulations 1993;]

"family" in the case of a claimant who is not a member of a family means that claimant [[31] and for the purposes of state pension credit "a family" comprises the claimant, his partner, any additional partner to whom section 12(1)(c) of the 2002 Act applies and any person who has not attained the age of 19, is treated as a child for the purposes of section 142 of the Contributions and Benefits Act and lives with the claimant or the claimant's partner;]];

[[11]"the Fines Regulations" means the Fines (Deductions from Income Support) Regulations 1992;]

[[6]"5 per cent of the personal allowance for the single claimant aged not less than 25" means where the percentage is not a multiple of 5 pence the sum obtained by rounding that 5 per cent to the next higher such multiple;

[[35] "hostel" means a building—

  (a) in which there is provided for persons generally, or for a class of persons, accommodation, otherwise than in separate and self-contained premises, and either board or facilities of a kind set out in paragraph 4A(1)(d) below adequate to the needs of those persons and—

  (b) which is—

     (i) managed by or owned by a housing association registered with the Housing Corporation established by the Housing Act 1964;

    [[44] (ii) managed or owned by a registered social landlord which is registered in accordance with Part 3 of the Housing (Scotland) Act 2001;]

     (iii) operated other than on a commercial basis and in respect of which funds are provided wholly or in part by a government department or a local authority; or

     (iv) managed by a voluntary organisation or charity and provides care, support or supervision with a view to assisting those persons to be rehabilitated or resettled within the community, and

  (c) which is not—

     (i) a care home;

     (ii) an independent hospital; or

     (iii) an establishment run by the Abbeyfield Society including all bodies corporate or incorporated which are affiliated to that Society, and

  (d) in sub-paragraph (b)(iv) above, "voluntary organisation" shall mean a body the activities of which are carried out otherwise than for profit, but shall not include any public or local authority;]

"housing authority" means a local authority, a new town corporation, [[44]. . .] or the Rural Development Board for Rural Wales;]

[[36] "the Housing Benefit Regulations" mean the Housing Benefit Regulations 2006;

"the Housing Benefit (State Pension Credit) Regulations" mean the Housing benefit (Persons who have attained the qualifying age for state pension credit) Regulations 2006;]

[[20]"housing costs" means any housing costs met under—

  (a) Schedule 3 to the Income Support Regulations but—

     (i) excludes costs under paragraph 17(1)(f) of that Schedule (tents and tent sites); and

479

        (ii) includes costs under paragraphs 17(1)(a) (ground rent [34 . . .]) and 17(1)(c) (rentcharges) of that Schedule but only when they are paid with costs under paragraph 17(1)(b) of that Schedule (service charges); or

   (b) Schedule 2 to the Jobseeker's Allowance Regulations but—
        (i) excludes costs under paragraph 16(1)(f) of that Schedule (tents and tent sites); and
        (ii) includes costs under paragraphs 16(1)(a) (ground rent and feu duty) and 16(1)(c) (rentcharges) of that Schedule but only when they are paid with costs under paragraph 16(1)(b) of that Schedule (service charges);]

[31 (c) Schedule II to the State Pension Credit Regulations but—
        (i) excludes costs under paragraph 13(1)(f) of that Schedule (tents and sites); and
        (ii) includes costs under paragraphs 13(1)(a) (ground rent and feu duty) and 13(1)(c) (rent charges) of that Schedule but only when they are paid with costs under paragraph 13(1)(b) of that Schedule (service charges);] [43 or

   (d) Schedule 6 to the Employment and Support Allowance Regulations but—
        (i) excludes costs under paragraph 18(1)(f) of that Schedule (tents and tent sites); and
        (ii) includes costs under paragraph 18(1)(a) (ground rent) and 18(1)(c) (rent charges) of that Schedule but only where they are paid with costs under paragraph 18(1)(b) of that Schedule (service charges);]

[34 . . .]

"the Income Support Regulations" means the Income Support (General) Regulations 1987;

[41 "integration loan which is recoverable by deductions" means an integration loan which is made under the Integration Loans for Refugees and Others Regulations 2007 and which is recoverable from the recipient by deductions from a specified benefit under regulation 9 of those Regulations;]

"miscellaneous accommodation costs" has the meaning assigned by paragraph 4(1);

[20"mortgage payment" means the aggregate of any payments which fall to be met under—

   (a) Schedule 3 to the Income Support Regulations in accordance with paragraphs 6 to 10 of that Schedule (housing costs to be met in income support) on a loan which qualifies under paragraph 15 or 16 of that Schedule, but less any amount deducted under paragraph 18 of that Schedule (non-dependant deductions); or

   (b) Schedule 2 to the Jobseeker's Allowance Regulations in accordance with paragraphs 6 to 9 of that Schedule (housing costs to be met in jobseeker's allowance) on a loan which qualifies under paragraph 14 or 15 of that Schedule, but less any amount deducted under paragraph 17 of that Schedule (non-dependant deductions),

[31

   (c) Schedule II to the State Pension Credit Regulations in accordance with paragraph 7 of that Schedule (housing costs to be met in state pension credit) on a loan which qualifies under paragraph 11 or 12 of that Schedule, but less any amount deducted under paragraph 14 of that Schedule (non-dependant deductions),] [43 or

   (d) Schedule 6 to the Employment and Support Allowance Regulations in accordance with paragraphs 8 to 11 of that Schedule (housing costs to be met in employment and support allowance) on a loan which qualifies under paragraph 16 or 17 of that Schedule, but less any amount deducted under paragraph 19 of that Schedule (non- dependant deductions),]

as the case may be.]

"personal allowance for a single claimant aged not less than 25 years" means the amount specified [31 in connection with income support and state pension credit] in [6paragraph 1(1)(e)] of column 2 of Schedule 2 to the Income Support Regulations [20or, [31 in connection with jobseeker's allowance], paragraph 1(1)(e) of Schedule 1 to the Jobseeker's Allowance Regulations]; [43 or, in connection with employment and support allowance, paragraph 1(1)(b) of Schedule 4 to the Employment and Support Allowance Regulations]

[2. . .]

"rent" has the meaning assigned to it in the Housing Benefit Regulations and, for the purposes of this Schedule
   (a) includes any water charges which are paid with or as part of the rent;
   (b) where in any particular case a claimant's rent includes elements which would not otherwise fall to be treated as rent, references to rent shall include those elements; and

    (c) references to "rent" include references to part only of the rent; and

[17"specified benefit" means—

    [34 (a) income support or, where in respect of any period it is paid together with any incapacity benefit or severe disablement allowance—

        (i) in a combined payment;

        (ii) in part to the beneficiary and in part to another person in accordance with regulation 34; or

        (iii) by means of two or more instruments of payment,

    income support and incapacity benefit or severe disablement allowance if the income support alone is insufficient for the purposes of this Schedule;]

    (b) [30 . . . .]

    (c) subject to sub-paragraph (2), jobseeker's allowance;]

    [34 (d) state pension credit or, where in respect of any period it is paid together with any retirement pension, incapacity benefit or severe disablement allowance—

        (i) in a combined payment; or

        (ii) in part to the beneficiary and in part to another person in accordance with regulation 34; or

        (iii) by means of two or more instruments of payment,

    state pension credit and retirement pension, incapacity benefit or severe disablement allowance if the state pension credit alone is insufficient for the purposes of this Schedule;] [43 (e) subject to sub-paragraph (3), employment and support allowance;]

[23but does not include any sum payable by way of child maintenance bonus in accordance with section 10 of the Child Support Act 1995) and the [24Social Security (Child Maintenance Bonus)] Regulations 1996;]]

[8"water charges" means charges for water or sewerage under Chapter I of Part V of the Water Industry Act 1991;]

[6"water undertaker" means a company which has been appointed under section 11(1) of the Water Act 1989 to be the water or sewerage undertaker for any area in England and Wales.]

[20(2) For the purposes of the definition of "specified benefit" in sub-paragraph (1), "jobseeker's allowance" means—

    (a) income-based jobseeker's allowance; and

    (b) in a case where, if there was no entitlement to contribution-based jobseeker's allowance, there would be entitlement to income-based jobseeker's allowance at the same rate, contribution-based jobseeker's allowance.]

[43 (3) For the purposes of the definition of "specified benefit" in sub-paragraph (1) "employment and support allowance" means—

    (a) income-related employment and support allowance; and

    (b) in a case where, if there was no entitlement to a contributory employment and support allowance, there would be entitlement to income-related employment and support allowance at the same rate, contributory employment and support allowance.]

General

2.—(1) The specified benefit may be paid direct to a third party in accordance with the following provisions of this Schedule in discharge of a liability of the beneficiary or his partner to that third party in respect of—

    (a) housing costs;

    (b) miscellaneous accommodation costs;

[6(bb) hostel payments;]

    (c) service charges for fuel, and rent not falling within head (a) above;

    (d) fuel costs; [10 . . .]

    (e) water charges; [10 and

    (f) payments in place of payments of child support maintenance under section 43(1) of the Child Support Act 1991 and regulation 28 of the Child Support (Maintenance Assessments and Special Cases) Regulations 1992.]

(2) No payment to a third party may be made under this Schedule unless the amount of the beneficiary's award of the specified benefit is not less than the total of the amount otherwise authorised to be so paid under this Schedule plus 10 pence.

(3) A payment to be made to a third party under this Schedule shall be made, at such intervals as the Secretary of State may direct, on behalf of and in discharge (in whole or in part) of the obligation of the beneficiary or, as the case may be, of his partner, in respect of which the payment is made.

2.245

Housing costs

2.246   **3.**—(1) Subject to [⁷sub-paragraphs (4) to (6)] and paragraph 8, where a beneficiary who has been awarded the specified benefit or his partner is in debt for any item of housing costs which continues to be applicable to the beneficiary in the determination of his applicable amount [³¹ or appropriate minimum guarantee], the [²⁵Secretary of State] may, if in [²⁷ his] opinion it would be in the interests of the family to do so, determine that the amount of the award of the specified benefit ("the amount deductible") calculated in accordance with the following sub-paragraphs shall be paid in accordance with sub-paragraph 2(3).

(2) [⁷Subject to sub-paragraphs (2A) and (3)], the amount deductible shall be such weekly aggregate of the following as is appropriate:—

(a)   in respect of any debt to which sub-paragraph (1) applies, or where the debt owed is in respect of an amount which includes more than one item of housing costs, a weekly amount equal to 5 per cent. of the personal allowance for a single claimant aged not less than 25 [¹. . .] for such period as it is necessary to discharge the debt, so however that in aggregate the weekly amount calculated under this sub-paragraph shall not exceed 3 times that 5 per cent;

(b)   for each such debt—

(i)   in respect of mortgage payments, the weekly amount of the mortgage payment in that case; and

(ii)   for any other housing item, the actual weekly cost necessary in respect of continuing needs for the relevant items,

and the [²⁵Secretary State] may direct that, when the debt is discharged, the amount determined under sub-paragraph (b) shall be the amount deductible.

[⁷(2A) Where a payment falls to be made to a third party in accordance with this Schedule, and—

(a)   more than one item of housing costs falls to be taken into account in determining the beneficiary's applicable amount; and

(b)   in accordance with [¹⁶paragraph 4(8) or (11) or] [¹⁵paragraph 18] of Schedule 3 to the Income Support Regulations [²⁰or, as the case may be, paragraph 4(8) or (11) or paragraph 17 of Schedule 2 to the Jobseeker's Allowance Regulations] [⁴³ or paragraph 6(10) or (13) or paragraph 19 of Schedule 6 to the Employment and Support Allowance Regulations] [³¹ or paragraph 5(9) or (12) or paragraph 14 of Schedule II to the State Pension Credit Regulations] an amount is not allowed or a deduction falls to be made from the amount to be met by way of housing costs,

then in calculating the amount deductible, the weekly aggregate amount ascertained in accordance with sub-paragraph (2) shall be reduced by an amount determined by applying the formula—

$$C \times \frac{B}{A}$$

where—

A =   housing costs;

B =   the item of housing costs which falls to be paid to a third party under this Schedule;

C =   the sum which is not allowed or falls to be deducted in accordance with [¹⁵paragraph 4(8) or (11) or paragraph 18] of Schedule 3 to the Income Support Regulations. [²⁰or, as the case may be, paragraph 4(8) or (11) or paragraph 17 of Schedule 2 to the Jobseeker's Allowance Regulations][³¹ or paragraph 5(9) or (12) or paragraph 14 of Schedule II to the State Pension Credit Regulations]] [⁴³ or paragraph 6(10) or (13) or paragraph 19 of Schedule 6 to the Employment and Support Allowance Regulations]

(3) Where the aggregate amount calculated under sub-paragraph (2) is such that paragraph 2(2) would operate to prevent any payment under this paragraph being made that aggregate amount shall be adjusted so that 10 pence of the award is payable to the beneficiary.

(4) Sub-paragraph (1) shall not apply to any debt which is either—

(a)   in respect of mortgage payments and the beneficiary or his partner has in the preceding 12 weeks paid sums equal to [⁸or greater than] 8 week's mortgage payments due in that period; or

(b)   for any other item of housing costs and is less than half the annual amount due to be paid by the beneficiary or his partner in respect of that item,

unless, in either case, in the opinion of the adjudicating authority it is in the overriding interests of the family that paragraph (1) should apply.

[⁷(5) No amount shall be paid pursuant to this paragraph in respect of mortgage interest in any case where a specified part of relevant benefits—

(a)   is required to be paid directly to a qualifying lender under regulation 34A and Schedule 9A; or

(b) would have been required to be paid to a body which, or a person who, would otherwise have been a qualifying lender but for an election given under paragraph 9 of Schedule 9A not to be regarded as such.

(6) In sub-paragraph (5), "specified part" and "relevant benefits" have the meanings given to them in paragraph 1 of Schedule 9A.]

Miscellaneous accommodation costs

[⁹**4.**—(1) Where an award of income support [³², jobseeker's allowance or [⁴³, state pension credit or employment and support allowance]]—   **2.247**

  (a) [³² in the case of income support] is made to a person [³⁵ residing in a care home, an Abbeyfield Home or an independent hospital] as defined in regulation [²⁸ 2(1)] of the Income Support Regulations [²⁰ or [³² in the case of jobseeker's allowance], regulation 1(3) of the Jobseeker's Allowance Regulations], [⁴³ or in the case of employment and support allowance, regulation 2(1) of the Employment and Support Allowance Regulations] or]

[³² (b) is made—

    (i) [³⁵ . . .]

    (ii) to person who is in accommodation provided under section 3(1) of, and Part II of the Schedule to, the Polish Resettlement Act 1947 (provision by the Secretary of State of accommodation in camps) except where that person is in receipt of state pension credit; [⁴³ or in the case of employment and support allowance, regulation 2(1) of the Employment and Support Allowance Regulations] or

    (iii) [³⁵ . . .]

    (iv) in the case of an award of state pension credit, to a person who is in accommodation provided within the meaning of regulation 15(7) of the State Pension Credit Regulations,]

[³² or to a person who is only temporarily absent from such accommodation] the [²⁵ Secretary of State] may determine that an amount of the specified benefit shall be paid direct to the person or body to whom the charges in respect of that accommodation are payable, [³² or to a person who is only temporarily absent from such accommodation] but, [³² except in a case where accommodation is provided under section 3(1) of, and Part II of the Schedule to, the Polish Resettlement Act 1947] or where the accommodation is [²run by a voluntary organisation either for purposes similar to the purposes for which resettlement units are provided] or which provides facilities for alcoholics or drug addicts, only if the adjudicating authority is satisfied that the beneficiary has failed to budget for the charges and that it is in the interests of the family.

[³² (2) Subject to sub-paragraphs (3) and (3A), the amount of any payment of income support, jobseeker's allowance [⁴³, state pension credit or employment and support allowance] to a third party determined under sub-paragraph (1) shall be—

  (a) in a case where the beneficiary is not in accommodation [³⁵ . . .] as specified in regulation 15(7)(d) of the State Pension Credit Regulations, an amount equal to the award of income support, jobseeker's allowance, [⁴³, guarantee credit or employment and support allowance] payable to the claimant but excluding an amount, if any, which when added to any other income of the beneficiary as determined in accordance with regulation 28 of the Income Support Regulations, regulation 93 of the Jobseeker's Allowance Regulations [⁴³, regulation 90 of the Employment and Support Allowance Regulations] or regulation 17 of the State Pension Credit Regulations will equal the amount prescribed in respect of personal expenses in sub-paragraph (2A); and

  (b) in any other case, the amount of the award of income support, jobseeker's allowance [⁴³, guarantee credit or employment and support allowance], excluding the amount allowed by sub-paragraph (2A) in respect of personal expenses.

(2A) The amount in respect of personal expenses where a beneficiary is in accommodation referred to in paragraphs 4(1)(a) or (b) shall be—

  (a) for a single person the sum of [⁴⁰ £21.90];

  (b) for a couple where both members of the couple are in such accommodation, [⁴⁰ £21.90]; for each member;

  (c) for a member of a polygamous marriage where more than one member is in such accommodation, [⁴⁰ £21.90]; for each member in such accommodation.

(3) This sub-paragraph shall apply where an award is made of—

  (a) income support calculated in accordance with Part VII of the Income Support Regulations (calculation of income support for part-weeks); or

  (b) jobseeker's allowance calculated in accordance with Part XI of the Jobseeker's Allowance Regulations (part-weeks);

  (c) state pension credit for a period of less than a week calculated under regulation 13A of the State Pension Credit Regulations (part-weeks), or a part week payment of state pension credit calculated otherwise. [⁴³ or

    (d) employment and support allowance for a period of less than a week calculated in accordance with Part 14 of the Employment and Support Allowance Regulations (periods of less than a week).]

(3A) Where sub-paragraph (3) applies then the amount of any payment to a third party determined under sub-paragraph (1) shall be an amount calculated in accordance with sub-paragraph (2)(a) or (b) as appropriate except that in respect of—

    (a) the income of the beneficiary, if any; and

    (b) the amount allowed for personal expenses by sub-paragraph (2A) above,

the amount shall be the amount used in the calculation under the provisions listed in sub-paragraph (3)(a), (b) or (c), divided by 7 and multiplied by the number of days in the part-week and no payment shall be made to a third party where the Secretary of State certifies it would be impracticable to do so in that particular case.]

(4) Where the amount calculated under sub-paragraph [³² (2) or (3A) is such that paragraph 2(2) would operate to prevent any payment under this paragraph being made the amount shall be adjusted so that 10 pence of the award is payable to the beneficiary.]

[⁶Hostel payments

2.248

4A.—(1) This paragraph applies to a beneficiary if—

    (a) he has been awarded specified benefit; and

    (b) he or his partner has claimed housing benefit in the form of a rent rebate or rent allowance; and

    (c) he or his partner is resident in a hostel; and

    (d) the charge for that hostel includes a payment, whether direct or indirect, for one or more of the following services—

        (i) water;

        (ii) a service charge for fuel;

        (iii) meals;

        (iv) laundry;

        (v) cleaning (other than communal areas).

(2) Subject to sub-paragraph (3) below, where a beneficiary [⁸ . . .] has been awarded specified benefit the [²⁵ Secretary of State] may determine that an amount of specified benefit shall be paid to the person or body to whom the charges referred to in subparagraph (1)(d) above are or would be payable.

(3) The amount of any payment to a third party under this paragraph shall be either—

    (a) the aggregate of the amounts determined by a housing authority in accordance with the provisions specified in sub-paragraph (4); or

    (b) if no amount has been determined under paragraph (a) of this sub-paragraph, an amount which the adjudicating authority estimates to be the amount which is likely to be so determined.

[³⁶ (4) The provisions referred to in sub-paragraph (3)(a) above are regulation 12(6) of, and paragraphs 1(a)(ii) and (iv), 2, 3, 4 and either 6(1)(b) or 6(2) or 6(3) or 6(4) of Schedule 1 to, the Housing Benefit Regulations or, as the case may be, the Housing Benefit (State Pension Credit) Regulations;]

(5) [³⁶ . . .]

[²⁰(6) Where—

    (a) an award of income support is calculated in accordance with regulation 73(1) of the Income Support Regulations (calculation of income support for part-weeks);

    (b) an award of jobseeker's allowance is calculated in accordance with regulation 150(1) of the Jobseeker's Allowance Regulations (amount of a jobseeker's allowance payable), [⁴³ or

    (c) an award of employment and support allowance is calculated in accordance with regulation 165 of the Employment and Support Allowance Regulations (entitlement of less than a week etc.),]

the amount of any payment of income support or, as the case may be, jobseeker's allowance [⁴³ or employment and support allowance] payable to a third party determined under sub-paragraph (2) above shall be an amount calculated in accordance with sub-paragraph (3)(a) or (b) above divided by 7 and multiplied by the number of days in the part-week, and no payment shall be made to a third party under this sub-paragraph where the Secretary of State certifies that it would be impracticable to do so in that particular case.]]

Service charges for fuel, and rent not falling within paragraph 2(1)(a)

5.—(1) Subject to paragraph 8, this paragraph applies to a beneficiary if— 2.249

(a) he has been awarded the specified benefit; and

(b) he or his partner is entitled to housing benefit in the form of a rent rebate or rent allowance; and

(c) [unless sup-paragraph (1A) applies] he or his partner has arrears of rent which equal or exceed four times the full weekly rent payable and—

    (i) there are arrears of rent in respect of at least 8 weeks and the landlord has requested the Secretary of State to make payments in accordance with this paragraph; or

    (ii) there are arrears of rent in respect of less than 8 weeks and in the opinion of the [25 Secretary of State] it is in the overriding interests of the family that payments shall be made in accordance with this paragraph.

[42 (1A) This sub-paragraph applies where the rent includes charges for services included under paragraph 4A(1)(d) and the arrears for these services exceeds £100.00.]

(2) For the purposes of sub-paragraph (1) arrears of rent do not include—

(a) the 20 per cent of eligible rates excluded from a rent allowance under [36 regulation 70 of the Housing Benefit Regulations or, as the case may be, regulation 50 of the Housing benefit (State Pension Credit) Regulations] (maximum housing benefit); or

(b) any amount falls to be deducted when assessing a person's rent rebate or rent allowance under regulation 63 of those Regulations (non-dependants).

(3) Subject to sub-paragraph (4), the adjudicating authority shall determine that a weekly amount of the specified benefit awarded to the beneficiary shall be paid to his or his partner's landlord if—

(a) he or his partner is entitled to housing benefit and in calculating that benefit a deduction is made under [36 regulation 12(3) of the Housing Benefit Regulations or, as the case may be, the Housing Benefit (State Pension Credit) Regulations] in respect of either or both of water charges or service charges for fuel; and

(b) the amount of the beneficiary's award is not less than the amount of the deduction, and the amount to be paid shall be equal to the amount of the deduction.

(4) [36. . .].

[20(5) A determination under this paragraph shall not be made without the consent of the beneficiary if the aggregate amount calculated in accordance with sub-paragraphs (3) and (6) exceeds [38 a sum calculated in accordance with paragraph 8(4);]

[31 (5A) [38 . . .]]

(6) In a case to which sub-paragraph (1) [42 or (1A)] applies the adjudicating authority may determine that a weekly amount of the specified benefit awarded to that beneficiary equal to 5 per cent. of the personal allowance for a single claimant aged not less than 25 [6 . . .] shall be paid to his landlord until the debt is discharged.

[8(7) Immediately after the discharge of any arrears of rent to which sub-paragraph (1) [42 or (1A)] applies and in respect of which a determination has been made under sub-paragraph (6) the adjudicating authority may, if satisfied that it would be in the interests of the family to do so, direct that an amount, equal to the amount by which the eligible rent is to be reduced by virtue of [36 regulation 12(3) of the Housing Benefit Regulations or, as the case may be, the Housing Benefit (State Pension Credit) Regulations] in respect of charges for water or service charges for fuel or both, shall be deductible.]

Fuel costs

6.—(1) [31 Subject to sub-paragraphs (6) and (6A)] and paragraph 8, where a beneficiary 2.250 who has been awarded the specified benefit or his partner is in debt for any item of mains gas or mains electricity [13including any charges for the reconnection of gas or disconnection or reconnection of electricity] ("fuel item") to an amount not less than the rate of personal allowance for a single claimant aged not less than 25 and continues to require that fuel, the [5 Secretary of State], if in its opinion it would be in the interests of the family to do so, may determine that the amount of the award of the specified benefit ("the amount deductible") calculated in accordance with the following paragraphs shall be paid to the person or body to whom payment is due in accordance with paragraph 2(3).

(2) The amount deductible shall, in respect of any fuel item, be such weekly aggregate of the following as is appropriate:—

[6(a) in respect of each debt to which sub-paragraph (1) applies ("the original debt"), a weekly amount equal to 5 per cent of the personal allowance for a person aged not less than 25 for such period as is necessary to discharge the original debt, but the aggregate of the amounts, calculated under this paragraph shall not exceed twice 5 per cent of the personal allowance for a single claimant aged not less than 25;]

    (b) except where current consumption is paid for by other means (for example prepayment meter), an amount equal to the estimated average weekly cost necessary to meet the continuing needs for that fuel item, varied, where appropriate, in accordance with sub-paragraph (4)(a).

(3) [⁶ . . .]

(4) Where an amount is being paid direct to a person or body on behalf of the beneficiary or his partner in accordance with a determination under sub-paragraph (1) and [²⁷ a decision which enbodies that determination falls to be reviewed]—

    (a) where since the date of that determination the average weekly cost estimated for the purpose of sub-paragraph (2)(b) has either exceeded or proved insufficient to meet the actual cost of continuing consumption so that in respect of the continuing needs for that fuel item the beneficiary or his partner is in credit or, as the case may be, a further debt has accrued, the adjudicating authority may determine that the weekly amount calculated under that paragraph shall, for a period of 26 weeks [⁸or such longer period as may be reasonable in the circumstances of the case], be adjusted so as to take account of that credit or further debt;

    (b) where an original debt in respect of any fuel item has been discharged the adjudicating authority may determine that the amount deductible in respect of that fuel item shall be the amount determined under sub-paragraph (2)(b).

(5) [⁶ . . .]

[²⁰(6) Subject to paragraph 8, a determination under this paragraph shall not be made without the consent of the beneficiary if the aggregate amount calculated in accordance with sub-paragraph (2) exceeds [³⁸ a sum calculated in accordance with paragraph 8(4).]

[³¹ [³⁸ . . .]]

(7) [⁶ . . .]

[⁶ Water charges

2.251
    7.—(1) This paragraph does not apply where water charges are paid with rent; and in this paragraph "original debt" means the debt to which sub-paragraph (2) applies, [¹³ including any disconnection or reconnection charges and any other costs (including legal costs) arising out of that debt].

(2) Where a beneficiary or his partner is liable, whether directly or indirectly, for water charges and is in debt for those charges, the [²⁵ Secretary of State] may determine, subject to paragraph 8, that a weekly amount of the specified benefit shall be paid either to a water undertaker to whom that debt is owed, or to the person or body authorised to collect water charges for that undertaker, [⁸ but only if [²⁷ the Secretary of State] is satisfied that the beneficiary or his partner has failed to budget for those charges, and that it would be in the interests of the family to make the determination.]

(3) Where water charges are determined by means of a water meter, the weekly amount to be paid under sub-paragraph (2) shall be the aggregate of—

    (a) in respect of the original debt, an amount equal to 5 per cent of the personal allowance for a single claimant aged not less than 25 years; and

    (b) the amount which the [²⁵ Secretary of State] estimates to be the average weekly cost necessary to meet the continuing need for water consumption.

(4) Where the sum estimated in accordance with sub-paragraph (3)(b) proves to be greater or less than the average weekly cost necessary to meet continuing need for water consumption so that a beneficiary or his partner accrues a credit, or as the case may be a further debt, the adjudicating authority may determine that the sum so estimated shall be adjusted for a period of 26 weeks [⁸ or such longer period as may be reasonable in the circumstances of the case] to take account of that credit or further debt.

(5) Where water charges are determined other than by means of a water meter the weekly amount to be paid under sub-paragraph (2) shall be the aggregate of—

    (a) the amount referred to in sub-paragraph (3)(a); and

    (b) an amount equal to the weekly cost necessary to meet the continuing need for water consumption.

(6) Where the original debt in respect of water charges is discharged, the [²⁵ Secretary of State] may direct that the amount deductible shall be—

    (a) where water charges are determined by means of a water meter, the amount determined under sub-paragraph (3)(b) taking into account any adjustment that may have been made in accordance with sub-paragraph (4); an

    (b) in any other case, the amount determined under sub-paragraph (5)(b).

(7) Where the beneficiary or his partner is in debt to two water undertakers—

    (a) only one weekly amount under sub-paragraph (3)(a) or (5)(a) shall be deducted; and

(b) a deduction in respect of an original debt for sewerage shall only be made after the whole debt in respect of an original debt for water has been paid; and

(c) deductions in respect of continuing charges for both water and for sewerage may be made at the same time.

[²⁰ (8) Subject to paragraph 8 (maximum amount of payments to third parties), a determination under this paragraph shall not be made without the consent of the beneficiary if the aggregate amount calculated in accordance with sub-paragraphs (3), (4), (5) and (6) exceeds [³⁸ a sum calculated in accordance with paragraph 8(4).]

[³¹ [³⁸ . . .]]

[¹⁰ Payments in place of payments of child support maintenance

7A.—[¹²(1) Subject to paragraph (2), where [²⁶ the Secretary of State] (within the meaning of section 13 of the Child Support Act 1991) has determined that section 43 of that Act and regulation 28 of the Child Support (Maintenance Assessments and Special Cases) Regulations 1992 (contribution to maintenance by deduction from benefit) apply in relation to a beneficiary or his partner, the [²⁵ Secretary of State] shall (subject to paragraph 8), if it is satisfied that there is sufficient specified benefit in payment, determine that a weekly amount of that benefit shall be deducted by the Secretary of State for transmission to the person or persons entitled to it.]

(2) Not more than one deduction shall be made under [¹²sub-paragraph (1)] in any one benefit week as defined in paragraph 4 of Schedule 7.

(3) [¹⁸Subject to sub-paragraph (4),] the amount of specified benefit to be paid under this paragraph shall be the amount prescribed by regulation 28(2) of the Child Support (Maintenance Assessments and Special Cases) Regulations 1992 for the purposes of section 43(2)(a) of the Child Support Act 1991 [¹⁸ . . .].]

[¹⁸(4) Where, apart from the provisions of this sub-paragraph, the provisions of paragraphs 8(1) and 9 would result in the maximum aggregate amount payable equalling 2 times 5 per cent of the personal allowance for a single claimant aged not less than 25 years, the amount of specified benefit to be paid under this paragraph shall be one half of the amount specified in sub-paragraph (3).]

2.252

[²¹Arrears of child support maintenance

7B.—(1) Where a beneficiary is entitled to contribution-based jobseeker's allowance [⁴³ or contributory employment and support allowance] and an arrears notice has been served on the beneficiary, the Secretary of State may request in writing that an amount in respect of arrears of child support maintenance be deducted from the beneficiary's jobseeker's allowance [⁴³ or contributory employment and support allowance].

(2) Where a request is made in accordance with sub-paragraph (1), the [²⁵ Secretary of State] shall determine that an amount in respect of the arrears of child support maintenance shall be deducted from the beneficiary's jobseeker's allowance [⁴³ or contributory employment and support allowance] for transmission to the person entitled to it.

(3) Subject to sub-paragraphs (4) and (5), the amount to be deducted under subparagraph (2) shall be the weekly amount requested by the Secretary of State, subject to a maximum of one-third of the age-related amount applicable to the beneficiary under section 4(1)(a) of the Jobseekers Act.

[⁴³ (3A) Subject to sub-paragraphs (4) and (5), the amount to be deducted from the beneficiary's employment and support allowance under sub-paragraph (2) is the weekly amount requested from the beneficiary's employment and support allowance by the Secretary of State, subject to a maximum of one-third of the amount applicable to the beneficiary under regulation 67(2) of the Employment and Support Allowance Regulations (prescribed amounts).]

(4) No deduction shall be made under this paragraph where a deduction is being made from the beneficiary's contribution-based jobseeker's allowance [⁴³ or contributory employment and support allowance] under the Community Charges Regulations, the Community Charges (Scotland) Regulations, the Fines Regulations or the Council Tax Regulations.

(5) Where the sum that would otherwise fall to be deducted under this paragraph includes a fraction of a penny, the sum to be deducted shall be rounded down to the next whole penny.

(6) In this paragraph—

"arrears notice" means a notice served in accordance with regulation 2(2) of the Child Support (Arrears, Interest and Adjustment of Maintenance Assessments) Regulations 1992; and

"child support maintenance" means such periodical payments as are referred to in section 3(6) of the Child Support Act 1991.]

2.253

[³⁹ Eligible loans

2.254   **7C.** —(1) In this paragraph—

"borrower" means a person who has, either solely or jointly, entered into a loan agreement with an eligible lender in respect of an eligible loan and who is, for the time being, entitled to an eligible benefit;

"eligible lender" means—

(a) a body registered under section 1 of the Industrial and Provident Societies Act 1965 (societies which may be registered);

(b) a credit union within the meaning of section 1 of the Credit Unions Act 1979 (registration under the Industrial and Provident Societies Act 1965);

(c) a charitable institution within the meaning of section 58(1) of the Charities Act 1992 (interpretation of Part II);

(d) a body entered on the Scottish Charity Register under section 3 of the Charities and Trustee Investment (Scotland) Act 2005 (Scottish Charities Register),which, except for a credit union, is licensed under the Consumer Credit Act 1974 and which may be determined by the Secretary of State as an appropriate body to which payments on behalf of the borrower may be made in respect of loans made by that body;

[⁴² (e)a community interest company within the meaning of Part 2 of the Companies (Audit, Investigations and Community Enterprise) Act 2004,]

"eligible loan" means a loan made by a lender, who is at that time an eligible lender, to a borrower except a loan—

(a) which is secured by a charge or pledge;

(b) which is for the purpose of business or self-employment; or

(c) which was made by means of a credit card;

"loan agreement" means an agreement between the eligible lender and the borrower in respect of an eligible loan.

(2) In this paragraph "eligible benefit" means—

(a) carer's allowance;

(b) the following contributory benefits—

    (i) incapacity benefit;

    (ii) retirement pension; or

(c) the following benefits—

    (i) income support;

    (ii) jobseeker's allowance;

    (iii) state pension credit.

    [⁴³ (iv) employment and support allowance.]

(3) Where the conditions set out in sub-paragraph (4) are met the Secretary of State may deduct a sum from an eligible benefit to which the borrower is entitled equal to 5 per cent. of the personal allowance for a single [⁴² claimant] aged not less than 25 and pay that sum to the eligible lender towards discharge of the sum owing under the loan agreement at the date of the application.

(4) The conditions referred to in sub-paragraph (3) are—

(a) the borrower has failed to make payments as agreed with the eligible lender for a period of 13 weeks before the date of the application and has not resumed making payments;

(b) the borrower has given his written permission to the eligible lender to provide to the Secretary of State personal data within the meaning of section 1 of the Data Protection Act 1998 (basic interpretive provisions);

(c) the eligible lender has agreed that no interest or other charge will be added to the amount owed at the date of the application;

(d) no sum is being deducted under this paragraph;

(e) no sum is being deducted from the borrower's eligible benefit under section 71(8) of the 1992 Act (overpayments-general) at the date of the application; and

(f) no sum is being deducted from the borrower's eligible benefit under section 78 of the 1992 Act (recovery of social fund awards) at the date of the application.

(5) The Secretary of State shall notify the borrower and the eligible lender in writing of a decision to make a deduction under this paragraph.

(6) The Secretary of State may make deductions under this paragraph only if the borrower is entitled to an eligible benefit throughout any benefit week.

(7) The Secretary of State shall not make deductions from a benefit mentioned in sub-paragraph (2)(a) where the borrower is in receipt of another eligible benefit unless that benefit is one mentioned in sub-paragraph (2)(b) and is insufficient to enable the deduction to be

made or is a benefit mentioned in sub-paragraph (2)(c) and the amount is insufficient to meet the deduction plus 10 pence.

(8) The Secretary of State shall not make deductions from a benefit mentioned in sub-paragraph (2)(b) where the borrower is in receipt of a benefit mentioned in sub-paragraph (2)(c) unless the amount of that benefit is insufficient to meet the deduction plus 10 pence.

(9) The Secretary of State shall cease making deductions from an eligible benefit if—

(a) there is no longer sufficient entitlement to an eligible benefit to enable him to make the deduction;

(b) entitlement to all eligible benefits has ceased;

(c) a sum is deducted from the borrower's eligible benefit under section 71(8) of the 1992 Act;

(d) an eligible lender notifies the Secretary of State that he no longer wishes to accept payments by deductions;

(e) the borrower's liability to make payment in respect of the eligible loan has ceased;

(f) the lender has ceased to be an eligible lender; or

(g) the borrower no longer resides in Great Britain.

(10) The sums deducted from an eligible benefit by the Secretary of State under this paragraph shall be paid to the eligible lender.

(11) The Secretary of State shall notify the borrower in writing of the total of sums deducted by him under any application—

(a) on receipt of a written request for such information from the borrower; or

(b) on the termination of deductions.

(12) Where a deduction is made under this paragraph from a specified benefit, paragraph 8 (maximum amount of payment to third parties) is to have effect as if—

(a) in sub-paragraph (1) for "and 7A" there were substituted", 7A and 7C"; and

(b) in sub-paragraph (2) for "and 7"there were substituted", 7 and 7C.]

[⁴¹ **Integration loans**

7D. Subject to paragraphs 2(2), 8 and 9, where a person has an integration loan which is recoverable by deductions, any weekly amount payable shall be equal to 5 per cent of the personal allowance of a single claimant aged not less than 25 years, including where the loan is a joint loan.]

2.255

Maximum amount of payments to third parties

8.—(1) The maximum aggregate amount payable under [¹⁹paragraphs] 3(2)(a), 5(6), 6(2)(a)[⁶, 7(3)(a)[¹¹, 7(5)(a) and 7A]] [²². . .] [¹¹, and [³⁴ regulation 5 of the Council Tax Regulations and regulation 4 of the Fines Regulations] [⁴¹, and in respect of an integration loan which is recoverable by deductions] shall not exceed an amount equal to 3 times 5 per cent of the personal allowance for a single claimant aged not less than 25 years.

2.256

(2) The maximum [⁵aggregate] amount payable under [⁶ paragraphs 3(2)(a), 5, 6 [⁴¹, 7 and 7D]] shall not without the consent of the beneficiary, exceed [³⁸ a sum calculated in accordance with sub-paragraph (4).]

[³¹ (2A) In the case of state pension credit, the maximum aggregate amount payable under paragraphs 3(2)(a), 5, 6, and 7 shall not, without the consent of the beneficiary, exceed a sum equal to 25 per cent. of the appropriate minimum guarantee less any housing costs under Schedule II to the State Pension Credit Regulations which may be applicable in the particular case.]

(3) [²². . .]

[³⁸ (4) The sum referred to in sub-paragraph (2) is—

(a) where the claimant or partner does not receive child tax credit, 25 per cent of—

(i) in the case of income support, the applicable amount for the family as is awarded under sub-paragraphs (a) to (d) of regulation 17(1) (applicable amounts) or sub-paragraphs (a) to (e) of regulation 18(1) (polygamous marriages) of the Income Support Regulations;

(ii) in the case of jobseeker's allowance, the applicable amount for the family as is awarded under paragraphs (a) to (e) of regulation 83 (applicable amounts) or sub-paragraphs (a) to (f) of regulation 84(1) (polygamous marriages) of the Jobseeker's Allowance Regulations; or

(iii) in the case of state pension credit, the appropriate minimum guarantee less any housing costs under Schedule 2 to the State Pension Credit Regulations 2002 which may be applicable in the particular case;

[⁴³ (iv) in the case of employment and support allowance, the applicable amount for the family as is awarded under paragraphs (a) to (d) of regulation 67 (prescribed amounts) or regulation 68 (polygamous marriages) of the Employment and Support Allowance Regulations; or]

(b) where the claimant or his partner receives child tax credit, 25 per cent of the sum of—

    (i) the amount mentioned in sub-paragraphs (a)(i) to (iii), which applies to the claimant;

    (ii) the amount of child benefit awarded to him or his partner by the Board under Part 2 of the Tax Credits Act 2002; and

    (iii) the amount of child tax credit awarded to him or his partner by the Board under section 8 of that Act.]

Priority as between certain debts

2.257

[[11]9.—(1A) Where in any one week—

(a) more than one of the paragraphs 3 to 7A [[39] or 7C] are applicable to the beneficiary; or

(b) one or more of those paragraphs are applicable to the beneficiary and one or more of the following provisions, namely, [[22]. . .] [[34] regulation 3 of the Community Charges Regulations, regulation 3 of the Community Charges (Scotland) Regulations, regulation 4 of the Fines Regulations [[41], regulation 5 of the Council Tax Regulations and regulation 9 of the Integration Loans for Refugees and Others Regulations 2007] also applies; and

(c) the amount of the specified benefit which may be made to third parties is insufficient to meet the whole of the liabilities for which provision is made;

the order of priorities specified in sub-paragraph (1)(B) shall apply.

(1B) The order of priorities which shall apply in sub-paragraph (1)(A) is—

(za) [[22]. . .]

(a) any liability mentioned in paragraph 3 (housing costs) [[44] paragraph 4 (miscellaneous accomodation costs) or paragraph 4A (hostel payments)];

(b) any liability mentioned in paragraph 5 (service charges for fuel and rent not falling within paragraph 2(1)(a));

(c) any liability mentioned in paragraph 6 (fuel costs);

(d) any liability mentioned in paragraph 7 (water charges);

(e) any liability mentioned in [[34] regulation 3 of the Community Charges Regulations (deductions from income support etc.), regulation 3 of the Community Charges (Scotland) Regulations (deductions from income support etc.) or any liability mentioned in regulation 5 of the Council Tax Regulations (deduction from debtor's income support etc.)];

(f) any liability mentioned in [[34] regulation 4 of the Fines Regulations (deductions from offender's income support etc.)];

(g) any liability mentioned in paragraph 7A (payments in place of payments of child support maintenance).]

[[41] (ga) any liability to repay an integration loan which is recoverable by deductions.]

[[39] (h) any liability mentioned in paragraph 7C (liability in respect of loans).]

(2) As between liability for items of housing costs liabilities in respect of mortgage payments shall have priority over all other items.

(3) As between liabilities for items of gas or electricity the [[25] Secretary of State] shall give priority to whichever liability it considers it would, having regard to the circumstances and to any requests of the beneficiary, be appropriate to discharge.

(4) [[6]. . .]

AMENDMENTS

1. The Social Security (Claims and Payments) Amendment Regulations 1988 (SI 1988/522), reg.11 (April 11, 1988).

2. The Social Security (Claims and Payments and Payments on account, Overpayments and Recovery) Amendment Regulations 1989 (SI 1989/136), reg.2(7) (February 27, 1989).

3. The Social Security (Claims and Payments and Payments on account, Overpayments and Recovery) Amendment Regulations 1989 (SI 1989/136), reg.2(7) (April 10, 1989).

4. The Social Security (Medical Evidence, Claims and Payments) Amendment Regulations 1989 (SI 1989/1686), reg.9 (October 9, 1989).

5. The Social Security (Miscellaneous Provisions) Amendment Regulations 1990 (SI 1990/2208), reg.16 (December 5, 1990).

6. The Social Security (Miscellaneous Provisions) Amendment Regulations 1991 (SI 1991/2284), regs 12 to 20 (November 1, 1991).

7. The Social Security (Claims and Payments) Amendment Regulations 1992 (SI 1992/1026), reg.5 (May 25, 1992).

8. The Social Security (Miscellaneous Provisions) Amendment (No.2) Regulations 1992 (SI 1992/2595), reg.8 (November 16, 1992).

9. The Social Security (Miscellaneous Provisions) Amendment (No.2) Regulations 1992 (SI 1992/2595), Sch.1, para.8 (April 1, 1993).

10. The Social Security (Claims and Payments) Amendment Regulations 1993 (SI 1993/478), reg.2 (April 1, 1993).

11. The Deductions from Income Support (Miscellaneous Amendments) Regulations 1993 (SI 1993/495), reg.2 (April 1, 1993).

12. The Social Security (Claims and Payments) Amendment (No.3) Regulations 1993 (SI 1993/2113), reg.3 (September 27, 1993).

13. The Social Security (Claims and Payments) Amendment Regulations 1994 (SI 1994/2319), reg.7 (October 3, 1994).

14. The Social Security (Claims and Payments) Amendment (No.2) Regulations 1994 (SI 1994/2943), reg.15 (April 13, 1995).

15. The Social Security (Income Support and Claims and Payments) Amendment Regulations 1995 (SI 1995/1613), reg.3 and Sch.2 (October 2, 1995).

16. The Social Security (Income Support, Claims and Payments and Adjudication) Amendment Regulations 1995 (SI 1995/2927), reg.3 (December 12, 1995).

17. The Social Security (Claims and Payments etc.) Amendment Regulations 1996 (SI 1996/672), reg.2(7) (April 4, 1996).

18. The Child Support (Maintenance Assessments and Special Cases) and Social Security (Claims and Payments) Amendment Regulations 1996 (SI 1996/481), reg.5 (April 8, 1996).

19. The Child Support (Maintenance Assessments and Special Cases) and Social Security (Claims and Payments) Amendment Regulations 1996 (SI 1996/481), reg.6 (April 8, 1996).

20. The Social Security (Claims and Payments) (Jobseeker's Allowance Consequential Amendments) Regulations 1996 (SI 1996/1460), reg.2(26) (October 7, 1996).

21. The Social Security (Jobseeker's Allowance Consequential Amendments) (Deductions) Regulations 1996 (SI 1996/2344), reg.25 (October 7, 1996).

22. The Social Security and Child Support (Miscellaneous Amendments) Regulations 1997 (SI 1997/827), reg.7(2) (April 7, 1997).

23. The Social Security (Child Maintenance Bonus) Regulations 1996 (SI 1996/3195), reg.16(2) (April 7, 1997).

24. The Social Security (Miscellaneous Amendments) Regulations 1997 (SI 1997/454), reg.8(10) (April 6, 1997).

25. The Social Security Act 1998 (Commencement No.11 and Transitional Provisions) Order 1999 (SI 1999/2860), Sch.3 (October 18, 1999).

26. The Social Security Act 1998 (Commencement No.7 and Consequential and Transitional Provisions) Order 1999 (SI 1999/1510), Sch.4 (June 1, 1999).

27. The Social Security Act 1998 (Commencement No.12 and Consequential and Transitional Provisions) Order 1999 (SI 1999/3178), Sch.6 (November 29, 1999).

28. The Social Security Amendment (Residential Care and Nursing Homes) Regulations 2002 (SI 2002/398), reg.2(2) (April 8, 2002).

29. The Social Security Amendment (Residential Care and Nursing Homes) Regulations 2002 (SI 2002/398), reg.2(3) (April 8, 2002).

30. Social Security (Claims and Payments and Miscellaneous Amendments) (No.2) Regulations 2002 (SI 2002/2441), reg.12 (October 23, 2002).

31. State Pension Credit (Consequential, Transitional and Miscellaneous Provisions) Regulations 2002 (SI 2002/3019), reg.14 (April 7, 2003).

32. The Social Security (Third Party Deductions and Miscellaneous Amendments) Regulations 2003 (SI 2003/2325), reg.2 (October 6, 2003).

33. The Social Security (Claims and Payments) Amendment Regulations 2004 (SI 2004/576), (April 12, 2004 of first benefit pay day thereafter).

34. Social Security (Claims and Payments) Amendment (No.2) Regulations 2005 (SI 2005/777), reg.3 (April 11, 2005).

35. The Social Security (Care Homes and Independent Hospitals) Regulations 2005 (SI 2005/2687) (October 24, 2005).

36. The Housing Benefit and Council Tax Benefit (Consequential Provisions) Regulations 2006 (SI 2006/217), Sch.2, para.2 (March 6, 2006).

37. The Social Security (Miscellaneous Amendments) (No.2) Regulations 2006 (SI 2006/832), reg.2 (April 10, 2006).

38. The Social Security (Miscellaneous Amendments) (No.3) Regulations 2006 (SI 2006/2377) (October 2, 2006).

39. The Social Security (Claims and Payments) Amendment (No. 2) Regulations 2006 (SI 2006/3188) (December 27, 2006).

40. The Social Security Benefits Up-rating Regulations 2009 (SI 2009/607) (April 6, 2009).

41. The Social Security (Claims and Payments) Amendment (No.2) Regulations 2007 (SI 2007/1866) (July 31, 2007).

42. The Social Security (Miscellaneous Amendments) Regulations 2008 (SI 2008/698), reg.3 (April 14, 2008).

43. The Employment and Support Allowance (Consequential provisions) (No.2) Regulations 2008 (SI 2008/1554), reg.26 (October 27, 2008).

44. The Social Security (Miscellaneous Amendments) (No.6) Regulations 2008 (SI 2008/2767), reg.3 (November 17, 2008).

DEFINITIONS

"adjudicating authority"—see reg.2(1).
"beneficiary"—see Social Security Act 1975, Sch.20.
"family"—see 1986 Act, s.20(11) (SSCBA, s.137(1)).
"instrument for benefit payment"—see reg.2(1).
"jobseeker's allowance"—*ibid.*
"partner"—*ibid.*
"qualifying lender"—see Administration Act, s.15A(3).

Note that these references are only to phrases defined outside Sch.9 itself. See para.1 for definitions special to Sch.9.

GENERAL NOTE

2.258   The provisions for part of weekly benefit to be diverted direct to a third party are of great importance in determining the actual weekly incomes of claimants. There have been changes in the provisions on fuel and water charges and Sch.9A now deals specifically with payments of mortgage interest.

On deductions in respect of rent arrears under para.5(6), *R(IS) 14/95* holds that the arrears must be proved, at least where these are disputed. In addition, the existence of an arguable counterclaim in possession proceedings is a matter that an adjudicating authority might properly take into account in deciding whether to exercise the discretionary power to make deductions under para.5(6).

See annotations to reg.35 for comment on the precedence to be accorded to child support payments and the relationship between Sch.9 and Sch.9B.

[¹ SCHEDULE 9A

DEDUCTIONS OF MORTGAGE INTEREST FROM BENEFIT AND PAYMENT TO QUALIFYING LENDERS

Interpretation
1. In this Schedule—   2.259
[⁹. . .]

"Income Support Regulations" means the Income Support (General) Regulations 1987;
[⁷"relevant benefits" means—
  [¹⁹ (a) income support, or income support and any incapacity benefit or severe disablement allowance where—
      (i) either benefit is paid with income support in a combined payment in respect of any period; and
      (ii) the income support alone is insufficient for the purpose of this Schedule;]
  (b) [¹⁶ . . . .]
  (c) income-based jobseeker's allowance;] [¹⁷
  [¹⁹ (d) state pension credit, or state pension credit and any retirement pension, incapacity benefit or severe disablement allowance where—
      (i) one of those benefits is paid with state pension credit in a combined payment in respect of any period; and
      (ii) the state pension credit alone is insufficient for the purpose of this Schedule;]
  [²⁶ (e) income-related employment and support allowance;]
[¹⁰but does not include any sum payable by way of child maintenance bonus in accordance with section 10 of the Child Support Act 1995 and the [¹¹Social Security (Child Maintenance Bonus)] Regulations 1996;]]
"specified part" shall be construed in accordance with paragraph 3.

Specified circumstances for the purposes of Regulation 34A
[⁵2. The circumstances referred to in regulation 34A are that—   2.260
[⁸(a) [¹⁷ the amount to be met under—
    (i) Schedule 3 to the Income Support Regulations; or
    (ii) Schedule 2 to the Jobseeker's Allowance Regulations; or
    (iii) Schedule II to the State Pension Credit Regulations,] or
    [²⁶ (iv) Schedule 6 to the Employment and Support Allowance Regulations,]
by reference to the standard rate [²¹ . . .] and, in the case of income support, to any amount payable in accordance with paragraph 7 of Schedule 3 to the Income Support Regulations;] and
  (b) the relevant benefits to which a relevant beneficiary is entitled are payable in respect of a period of 7 days or a multiple of such a period.]

[²³ Specified circumstances for the purposes of Regulation 34B
2A.—(1) The circumstances referred to in regulation 34B are that—   2.261
  (a) the relevant beneficiary is entitled to a savings credit as construed in accordance with sections 1 and 3 of the 2002 Act and not to a guarantee credit; and
  (b) sub-paragraphs (a) and (b) of paragraph 2 apply.
(2) The further circumstances referred to in that regulation are that —
  (a) the relevant beneficiary has requested the Secretary of State in writing to make such payments to the qualifying lender; or
  (b) the Secretary of State has determined that it would be in the relevant beneficiary's interests, or in the interests of his family to make such payment to the qualifying lender.
(3) In making the determination referred to in sub-paragraph (2)(b), the Secretary of State shall have regard to whether or not the relevant beneficiary is in arrears with his payments to the qualifying lender.
(4) For the purposes of sub-paragraph (2)(b), "a family" comprises the relevant beneficiary, his partner, any additional partner to whom section 12(1)(c) of the 2002 Act applies and any person who has not attained the age of [²⁵ 20], is treated as a child for the purposes of section 142 of the Contributions and Benefits Act and lives with the relevant beneficiary or the relevant beneficiary's partner.]

SPECIFIED PART OF RELEVANT BENEFIT

2.262

3. [5(1) Subject to the following provisions of this paragraph, the part of any relevant benefits which, as determined by the [14 Secretary of State in accordance with regulation 34A, shall be paid] directly to the qualifying lender ("the specified part") is[8, in the case of income support,] a sum equal to the amount of mortgage interest to be met in accordance with paragraphs 6 and 8 to 10 of Schedule 3 to the Income Support Regulations (housing costs) together with an amount (if any) determined under paragraph 7 of that Schedule (transitional protection) [8or, in the case of jobseeker's allowance, a sum equal to the amount of mortgage interest to be met in accordance with paragraphs 6 to 9 of Schedule 2 to the Jobseeker's Allowance Regulations] [26 or, in the case of employment and support allowance, a sum equal to the amount of mortgage interest to be met in accordance with paragraphs 8 to 11 of Schedule 6 to the Employment and Support Allowance Regulations].]

[17 (1A) Subject to the following provisions of this paragraph, the part of state pension credit which, as determined by the Secretary of State in accordance with regulation 34A, shall be paid directly to the qualifying lender, is a sum equal to the amount of mortgage interest to be met under paragraph 7 of Schedule II to the State Pension Credit Regulations.]

(2) [5...]

(3) Where, in determining a relevant beneficiary's applicable amount for the purposes of income support [[26 income-based jobseeker's allowance or income-related employment and support allowance] [17 or a relevant beneficiary's appropriate minimum guarantee in state pension credit]]—

    (a) a sum in respect of housing costs is brought into account in addition to a sum in respect of mortgage interest; and

    (b) in accordance with [5paragraph 4(8) or (11) or paragraph 18] of Schedule 3 to the Income Support Regulations [8or, as the case may be, [17 paragraph 5(9) or (12) or paragraph 14 of Schedule II to the State Pension Credit Regulations or] paragraph 4(8) or (11) or paragraph 17 of Schedule 2 to the Jobseeker's Allowance Regulations] [26 or paragraph 6(10) or (13) or 19 of Schedule 6 to the Employment and Support Allowance Regulations] an amount is not allowed or a deduction falls to be made from the amount to be met under [8either of those Schedules],

then the specified part referred to in [17 sub-paragraph (1) or (1A)] of this paragraph is the mortgage interest minus a sum calculated by applying the formula—

$$C \times \frac{B}{A}$$

[5where—

A = housing costs within the meaning of paragraph 1 of Schedule 3 to the Income Support Regulations [8or, as the case may be, [17 paragraph 1 of Schedule II to the State Pension Credit Regulations or] paragraph 1 of Schedule 2 to the Jobseeker's Allowance Regulations] [26 or paragraph 1 of Schedule 6 to the Employment and Support Allowance Regulations];

B = the housing costs to be met in accordance with paragraphs 6 and 8 to 10 of Schedule 3 to the Income Support Regulations (housing costs) together with an amount (if any) determined under paragraph 7 of that Schedule (transitional protection) [8or, as the case may be, [17 paragraph 7 of Schedule II to the State Pension Credit Regulations or] paragraphs 6 to 9 of Schedule 2 to the Jobseeker's Allowance Regulations] [26 or paragraphs 8 to 11 of Schedule 6 to the Employment and Support Allowance Regulations]; and

C = the sum which is not allowed or falls to be deducted in accordance with paragraph 18 of Schedule 3 to the Income Support Regulations [8or, as the case may be, [17 paragraph 5(9) or (12) or paragraph 14 of Schedule II to the State Pension Credit Regulations or] paragraph 4(8) or (11) or paragraph 17 of Schedule 2 to the Jobseeker's Allowance Regulations] [26 or paragraph 19 of Schedule 6 to the Employment and Support Allowance Regulations].]

(4) [17 Except where the relevant benefit is state pension credit,] Where a payment is being made under a policy of insurance taken out by a beneficiary to insure against the risk of his being unable to maintain repayments of mortgage interest to a qualifying lender, then the amount of any relevant benefits payable to that lender shall be reduced by a sum equivalent to so much of the amount payable under the policy of insurance as represents payments in respect of mortgage interest.

(5) [9...]

(6) [⁹...]

(7) [⁵...]

(8) Where the amount of any relevant benefits to which a relevant beneficiary is entitled is less than the sum which would, but for this sub-paragraph, have been the specified part, then the specified part shall be the amount of any relevant benefits to which the relevant beneficiary is entitled less 10p.

[¹⁵ (9) In the case of a person to whom regulation 6(5) of the Income Support Regulations applies, no part of any relevant benefit shall be paid directly by the Secretary of State to a qualifying lender.]

[¹⁷ (10) In sub-paragraph (1), the relevant benefits do not include in the case of state pension credit so much of any additional amount which is applicable in the claimant's case under Schedule II to the State Pension Credit Regulations (housing costs) in respect of a period before the decision awarding state pension credit was made.]

Direct payment: more than one loan

4.—(1) This paragraph applies where the borrower is liable to pay mortgage interest in respect of two or more different loans.

[⁵(2) Subject to the following provisions of this paragraph, the Secretary of State shall pay to the qualifying lender or, if there is more than one qualifying lender, to each qualifying lender—

    (a) a sum equal to the mortgage interest determined by reference to paragraph 12 of Schedule 3 to the Income Support Regulations [⁸or, as the case may be, paragraph 11 of Schedule 2 to the Jobseeker's Allowance Regulations] [²⁶ or paragraph 13 of Schedule 6 to the Employment and Support Allowance Regulations] (standard rate) in respect of each loan made by that lender, plus

    (b) any amount payable in accordance with paragraph 7 of Schedule 3 to the Income Support Regulations (transitional protection) attributable to the particular loan;
    [⁹...]

    (c) any additional amount attributable to a particular loan which may, under paragraph 3(5), have been taken into account in calculating the specified part.]

(3) If, by virtue of deductions made under either paragraph 3(2) or 3(3), the specified part is less than the amount payable by the borrower in respect of mortgage interest, then the sum payable under sub-paragraph (2)(a) shall be minus such proportion of the sum subtracted under those sub-paragraphs as is attributable to the particular loan.

(4) Paragraph 3(4) shall apply to reduce the amount payable to a qualifying lender mentioned in sub-paragraph (2) above as it applies to reduce the amount of any relevant benefits payable to a qualifying lender under paragraph 3.

(5) Where the specified part is the part referred to in paragraph 3(8), the Secretary of State shall pay the specified part directly to the qualifying lenders to whom mortgage interest is payable by the borrower in order of the priority of mortgages or (in Scotland) in accordance with the preference in ranking of heritable securities.

Relevant benefits

5. [⁷...]

Time and manner of payments

6. Payments to qualifying lenders under regulation 34A and this Schedule shall be made in arrears at intervals of 4 weeks.

Fees payable by qualifying lenders

7. For the purposes of defraying the expenses of the Secretary of State in administering the making of payments under regulation 34A and this Schedule a qualifying lender shall pay to the Secretary of State a fee of [¹⁷... [²⁴ £0.55]] in respect of each payment made under regulation 34A and this Schedule.

Qualifying lenders

8. The following bodies and persons shall be qualifying lenders—

    (a) the Housing Corporation;

    (b) Housing for Wales;

    (c) [²² Communities Scotland]

    (d) the Development Board for Rural Wales; and

    (e) any body incorporated under the Companies Act 1985 whose main objects include the making of loans secured by a mortgage of or a charge over land or (in Scotland) by a heritable security.

2.263

2.264

2.265

2.266

2.267

Election not to be regarded as a qualifying lender

2.268   **9.**—(1) A body which, or a person who, would otherwise be a qualifying lender may elect not to be regarded as such for the purposes of these Regulations by giving notice of election under this paragraph to the Secretary of State in accordance with sub-paragraphs (2) and (3).

(2) Subject to sub-paragraph (3), notice of election shall be given in writing—

(a) in the case of the financial year 1992 to 1993, before 23rd May 1992 and shall take effect on that date; and

(b) in the case of any other financial year, before 1st February in the preceding year and shall take effect on 1st April following the giving of the notice.

(3) A body which, or a person who, becomes a qualifying lender during a financial year and who wishes to elect not to be regarded as such for the purposes of these Regulations shall give notice of election in writing within a period of six weeks from the date on which the person or body becomes a qualifying lender.

(4) Regulation 34A shall not apply to a body which, or a person who, becomes a qualifying lender during a financial year for a period of six weeks from the date on which the person or body became a qualifying lender unless, either before the start of that period or at any time during that period, the person or body notifies the Secretary of State in writing that this sub-paragraph should not apply.

(5) A body which, or a person who, has made an election under this paragraph may revoke that election by giving notice in writing to the Secretary of State before 1st February in any financial year and the revocation shall take effect on the 1st April following the giving of the notice.

(6) Where a notice under this paragraph is sent by post it shall be treated as having been given on the day it was posted.

Provision of information

2.269   **10.**—(1) A qualifying lender shall provide the Secretary of State with information relating to—

(a) the mortgage interest payable by a borrower;

(b) the amount of the loan;

(c) the purpose for which the loan is made;

(d) the amount outstanding on the loan on which the mortgage interest is payable;

(e) any change in the amount of interest payable by the borrower;

at the times specified in sub-paragraphs (2) and (3).

[[17] (2) Subject to sub-paragraph (4), the information referred to in heads (a), (b), (c) and (d) of sub-paragraph (1) shall be provided at the request of the Secretary of State when a claim for—

(a) income support [[26], employment and support allowance] or income-based jobseeker's allowance is made and a sum in respect of mortgage interest is to be brought into account in determining the applicable amount; or

(b) state pension credit is made and a sum in respect of housing costs is applicable in the claimant's case in accordance with regulation 6(6)(c) of the State Pension Credit Regulations.]

(3) [[12]Subject to sub-paragraph (4),] the information referred to in heads (d) and (e) of sub-paragraph (1) shall be provided at the request of the Secretary of State—

(a) when a claim for income support [[26], employment and support allowance] [[17] state pension credit] [[8]or income-based jobseeker's allowance] ceases to be paid to a relevant beneficiary; and

(b) once every 12 months notwithstanding that, in relation to head (d), the information may already have been provided during the period of 12 months preceding the date of the Secretary of State's request.

[[12](4) Where a claimant or his partner is a person to whom either paragraph 1A of Schedule 3 to the Income Support (General) Regulations 1987 (housing costs) [[26], paragraph 3 of schedule 6 to the Employment and Support Allowance Regulation (housing costs)] or paragraph 1A of Schedule 2 to the Jobseeker's Allowance Regulations 1996 (housing costs) refers, the information to which sub-paragraphs (2) and (3)(b) refer shall be provided at the request of the Secretary of State on the anniversary of the date on which the housing costs in respect of mortgage interest were first brought into account in determining the applicable amount of the person concerned.]

Recovery of sums wrongly paid

11.—(1) Where sums have been paid to a qualifying lender under regulation 34A which ought not to have been paid for one or both of the reasons mentioned in sub-paragraph (2) of this paragraph, the qualifying lender shall, at the request of the Secretary of State, repay the sum overpaid.

(2) The reasons referred to in sub-paragraph (1) of this paragraph are—
  (a) that—
    (i) the rate at which the borrower pays mortgage interest has been reduced [5 or the rate [18 determined in accordance with] paragraph 12 of Schedule 3 to the Income Support Regulations [8or, as the case may be, paragraph 11 of Schedule 2 to the Jobseeker's Allowance Regulations] [26 or paragraph 13 of Schedule 6 to the Employment and Support Allowance Regulation] (standard rate) has been reduced] or the amount outstanding on the loan has been reduced, and
    (ii) as a result of this reduction the applicable amount of the relevant beneficiary has also been reduced, but
    (iii) no corresponding reduction was made to the specified part; or
  (b) subject to paragraph (3), that the relevant beneficiary has ceased to be entitled to any relevant benefits.

(3) A qualifying lender shall only repay sums which ought not to have been paid for the reason mentioned in sub-paragraph (2)(b) of this paragraph if the Secretary of State has requested that lender to repay the sums within a period of 4 weeks starting with the last day on which the relevant beneficiary was entitled to any relevant benefits.]

AMENDMENTS

1. The Social Security (Claims and Payments) Amendment Regulations 1992 (SI 1992/1026), reg.6 and Sch. (May 25, 1992).

2. The Social Security (Claims and Payments) Amendment (No.3) Regulations 1993 (SI 1993/2113), reg.3 (September 27, 1993).

3. The Social Security (Claims and Payments) Amendment (No.3) Regulations 1994 (SI 1994/2944), reg.2 (April 1, 1995).

4. The Social Security (Claims and Payments) Amendment (No.2) Regulations 1994 (SI 1994/2943), reg.16 (April 13, 1995).

5. The Social Security (Income Support and Claims and Payments) Amendment Regulations 1995 (SI 1995/1613), reg.3 and Sch.2 (October 2, 1995).

6. The Social Security (Claims and Payments) Amendment (No.2) Amendment Regulations 1996 (SI 1996/2988), reg.2 (April 1, 1997).

7. The Social Security (Claims and Payments etc.) Amendment Regulations 1996 (SI 1996/672), reg.2(8) (April 4, 1996).

8. The Social Security (Claims and Payments) (Jobseeker's Allowance Consequential Amendments) Regulations 1996 (SI 1996/1460), reg.2(27) (October 7, 1996).

9. The Social Security and Child Support (Miscellaneous Amendments) Regulations 1997 (SI 1997/827), reg.7(3) (April 7, 1997).

10. The Social Security (Child Maintenance Bonus) Regulations 1996 (SI 1996/3195), reg.16(2) (April 7, 1997).

11. The Social Security (Miscellaneous Amendments) Regulations 1997 (SI 1997/454), reg.8(10) (April 6, 1997).

12. The Social Security (Miscellaneous Amendments) (No.4) Regulations 1997 (SI 1997/2305), reg.5 (October 22, 1997).

13. The Social Security (Claims and Payments) Amendment Regulations 2002 (SI 2002/355), reg.2 (April 1, 2002).

14. The Social Security (Claims and Payments) Amendment Regulations 2000 (SI 2000/1366), reg.2, (June 14, 2000).

15. The Social security (Miscellaneous Amendments) Regulations 2001 (SI 2001/488), reg.11 (April 9, 2001).

16. Social Security (Claims and Payments and Miscellaneous Amendments) (No.2) Regulations 2002 (SI 2002/2441), reg.13 (October 23, 2002).

17. The Social Security (Claims and Payments) Amendment Regulations 2004 (SI 2004/576), (April 12, 2004 or first benefit pay day thereafter).

18. Social Security (Housing Costs Amendments) Regulations 2004 (SI 2004/2825), reg.3(b), (November 28, 2004).
19. Social Security (Claims and Payments) Amendment (No.2) Regulations 2005 (SI 2005/777), reg.4 (April 11, 2005).
20. The Social Security (Claims and Payments) Regulations 2006 (SI 2006/551) (April 1, 2006).
21. The Social Security (Housing Costs Amendments) Regulations 2004 (SI 2004/2825) (November 28, 2005).
22. The Social Security (Miscellaneous Amendments) (No.4) Regulations 2006, (SI 2006/2378) (October 1, 2006).
23. The State Pension Credit (Consequential, Transitional and Miscellaneous Provisions) (No. 2) Regulations 2002 (SI 2002/3197) (April 7, 2003).
24. The Social Security (Miscellaneous Amendments) Regulations 2009 (SI 2009/583), reg.3 (April 1, 2009).
25. The Social Security (Housing Costs and Miscellaneous Amendments) Regulations 2007 (SI 2007/3183) (December 17, 2007).
26. The Employment and Support Allowance (Consequential provisions) (No.2) Regulations 2008 (SI 2008/1554), reg.27 (October 27, 2008).

DEFINITIONS

"instrument for benefit payment"—see reg.2(1).
"jobseeker's allowance"—*ibid.*
"mortgage interest"—see Administration Act, s.15A(4).
"qualifying lender"—see Administration Act, s.15A(3).
"relevant beneficiary"—see Administration Act, s.15A(1).

GENERAL NOTE

2.270   Paragraph 11 only authorises recovery of overpaid interest in the circumstances specified in sub-paras (2) and (3).
In previous editions of this book it was suggested that it was not clear who decides that the interest has been overpaid, and that it was certainly arguable that this is the type of decision that should be made by an adjudication officer, now decision maker. *CIS 288/1994* and *CSIS 98/1994* hold that any decision regarding the recovery of any overpayment of mortgage interest from a qualifying lender is a matter for the Secretary of State, not the adjudication officer. The mortgage interest payment provisions are outside the scope of s.71 of the Administration Act (*CSIS 98/1994*). But in *CIS 5206/1995* the Commissioner reaches the opposite conclusion. He points out that under s.20 of the Administration Act all questions arising on claims or awards of benefit are to be determined by adjudication officers, unless reserved to the Secretary of State (or other bodies). The question of whether the Secretary of State was *entitled to* recover a payment under para.11 (which required consideration of whether the conditions in para.11(2) were satisified and also required calculation of the amount of the overpayment) was not reserved by para.11 (or any other provision) to the Secretary of State. It therefore fell to be determined by an adjudication officer. Once it had been determined that an overpayment was recoverable, the Secretary of State then had the discretion as to whether to request the lender to repay the sum to him. The process of adjudication was thus the same as that under s.71 of the Act, even though the circumstances in which recovery could be sought were different. Furthermore, where any question of recovery under para.11 arose, the claimant's award must first be reviewed and revised under s.25 (as had been accepted by the Court of Appeal in *Golding*, see below). If not, the Secretary of State would be bound to pay any overpayment recovered from the lender to the claimant, since the money recovered represented part of the benefit due to the claimant. There is thus a conflict between these decisions but *CIS 5206/1995* is cogently argued and it is suggested

that it is to be preferred.

Note also that under para.3(1) the amount that will be paid to the qualifying lender by the Secretary of State under reg.34A (the "specified part") is defined by reference to the amount of mortgage interest met in the income support or JSA assessment. Thus, if the claimant disputes the amount that has been awarded for mortgage interest, or maintains that there are no grounds for reviewing the amount of an existing award, he will have a right of appeal to a tribunal in the normal way.

In *R. v Secretary of State for Social Security Ex p. Golding, The Times*, March 15, 1996, there had been an overpayment of mortgage interest because the claimant's interest rate had reduced. Recovery of the overpayment was implemented by withholding current payments due to the claimant's building society. Brooke J. accepted the claimant's contention that the effect of sub-para.(2)(iii) was that the Secretary of State could only recover an overpayment where an adjudication officer had decided under sub-para.(2)(ii) that a claimant's applicable amount should be reduced but the amount paid to the lender had not changed. Thus the Secretary of State could not recover the overpayment from the lender under para.11 in respect of the period before the adjudication officer's decision. Paragraph 11 only applied to overpayments made after that decision (i.e. as a result of the decision not being implemented). The result of this decision would have been that in effect recovery of any overpayment would be governed by s.71 of the Administration Act (since it would normally be the period between the reduction in the interest rate and the adjudication officer's review decision that would be in issue, assuming the adjudication officer's decision was implemented promptly).

The Court of Appeal on July 1, 1996 reversed Brooke J.'s decision. It was held that in sub-para.(2)(ii), the applicable amount means the amount as determined by the adjudication officer's assessment current at the date when the question is asked. Thus, once there had been a review with retrospective effect of Mr Golding's entitlement to take account of the reduction in interest rates, there was a reduction for that retrospective period in his applicable amount, so that sub-para.(2)(ii) was met. Sub-paragraph (2)(iii) was also met, because the "specified part" actually paid to the lender in that past period could not be reduced. Therefore the overpayment was repayable by the lender. The Court of Appeal rejected Mr Golding's argument that the condition in sub-para. (1) that the sums "ought not to have been paid" was not met, because the sums were paid under the current adjudication officer's assessment. The provisions were to be interpreted so as to be consistent with the clear statutory intention of dealing with the built-in problem under the direct payment scheme of annual retrospective notification of interest rate changes under para.10. Note the circumstances in which there can be no review on a reduction in interest rates where the claimant's liability remains constant (Adjudication Regulations, reg.63(7)).

The Court of Appeal did express concern over the method of recovery adopted by the Secretary of State, who had not asked the lender to repay the overpayment, but had made deductions from the amounts of mortgage interest currently being paid direct to the lender. The concern was that that might put the claimant into arrears. The Secretary of State accepted that he could only use the set-off method if it did not adversely affect the position of the claimant. The Court of Appeal considered that that would only be so if each deduction was accompanied in the lender's accounting system by a corresponding credit to the claimant's interest account. The Department has apparently carried out a review of the arrangements for recovery of overpayments from lenders.

It should be noted that para.11 only applies where the overpayment has occurred for the reasons specified in sub-para.(2) and not, for example, where it is due to an incorrect amount of capital being taken into account.

Until April 1997, deductions could be made from a claimant's benefit in respect of mortgage interest arrears under para.3(5) (the April 1996 rate was £2.40). This is no longer possible if the lender is covered by the mortgage payments direct scheme.

CIS 15146/1996 holds that it was for the adjudication officer to decide whether such deductions were to be made and that a decision to alter the amount of a deduction had to be made by way of review, as this was not one of the up-rating changes which took effect automatically under s.159 of the Act without the need for a review decision. Furthermore, it was necessary to investigate whether there were in fact mortgage arrears, as the existence of arrears had to be proved in order to justify the deduction (see *R(IS) 14/95* which had adopted the same approach in relation to deductions under para.5 of Sch.9). Adjudication officers and tribunals were not limited to determining whether there was sufficient income support in payment to sustain the direct payment.

SCHEDULE 9B

DEDUCTIONS FROM BENEFIT IN RESPECT OF CHILD SUPPORT MAINTENANCE AND PAYMENT TO PERSONS WITH CARE

Interpretation

2.271   **1.** In this Schedule—

"the Act" means the Child Support Act 1991,

"beneficiary" means a person who has been awarded a specified benefit and includes each member of a joint-claim couple awarded joint-claim jobseeker's allowance,

"maintenance" [2, except in paragraph 3,] means maintenance which a non-resident parent is liable to pay under the Act at a flat rate of child support maintenance (or would be so liable but for a variation having been agreed to), and that rate applies (or would have applied) because he falls within paragraph 4(1)(b) or (c) or 4(2) of Schedule 1 to the Act, and includes such maintenance payable at a transitional rate in accordance with Regulations made under section 29(3)(a) of the Child Support, Pensions and Social Security Act 2000,

"specified benefit" means either a benefit, pension or allowance mentioned in section 5(2) of the Social Security Administration Act 1992 and which is prescribed for the purpose of paragraph 4(1)(b) or (c) of Schedule 1 to the Act or a war disablement pension or a war widow's pension within the meaning of section 150(2) of the Social Security Contributions and Benefits Act 1992.

Deductions

2.272   **2.**—(1) Subject to paragraphs 5 and 6, the Secretary of State may deduct from a specified benefit awarded to a beneficiary, an amount equal to the amount of maintenance which is payable by the beneficiary (or in the case of income support [3, state pension credit [4, income-based jobseekers allowance or income-related employment and support allowance] payable either by the beneficiary or his partner) and pay the amount deducted to or among the person or persons with care in discharge (in whole or in part) of the liability to pay maintenance.

(2) A deduction may only be made from one of the specified benefits in any one week.

(3) No deduction may be made unless the amount of the relevant specified benefit is not less than the total of the amounts to be deducted under this Schedule plus 10 pence.

Arrears

3.—(1) Except where income support [3, state pension credit] [4, income-based jobseekers allowance or income-related employment and support allowance] is payable to the beneficiary or his partner, the Secretary of State may deduct the sum of £1 per week from a specified benefit which the beneficiary has been awarded and, subject to sub-paragraph (2), pay the amount deducted to or among the person or persons with care in discharge (in whole or in part) of the beneficiary's liability to pay arrears of maintenance.

(2) Deductions made under sub-paragraph (1) may be retained by the Secretary of State in the circumstances set out in regulation 8 of the Child Support (Arrears, Interest and Adjustment of Maintenance Assessments) Regulations 1992.

[2 (3) In sub-paragraph (1) "maintenance" means child support maintenance as defined by section 3(6) of the Act—

(a) before the amendment of the definition of such maintenance by section 1(2)(a) of the Child Support, Pensions and Social Security Act 2000;

(b) after the amendment of the definition; or
(c) both before and after the amendment of the definition,
and includes maintenance payable at a transitional rate in accordance with regulations made under section 29(3)(a) of that Act.]

Apportionment
4. Where maintenance is payable to more than one person with care, the amount deducted shall be apportioned between the persons with care in accordance with paragraphs 6, 7 and 8 of Schedule 1 to the Act.

2.273

Flat rate maintenance
5.—(1) This sub-paragraph applies where the beneficiary and his partner are each liable to pay maintenance at a flat rate in accordance with paragraph 4(2) of Schedule 1 to the Act and either of them has been awarded income support [³, state pension credit] [⁴, income-based jobseekers allowance or income-related employment and support allowance].

(2) Where sub-paragraph (1) applies, an amount not exceeding £5 may be deducted in respect of the sum of both partners' liability to pay maintenance, in the proportions described in regulation 4(3) of the Child Support (Maintenance Calculations and Special Cases) Regulations 2000 and shall be paid in discharge (in whole or in part) of the respective liabilities to pay maintenance.

2.274

Flat rate maintenance (polygamous marriage)
6.—(1) This sub-paragraph applies where two or more members of a polygamous marriage are each liable to pay maintenance at a flat rate in accordance with paragraph 4(2) of Schedule 1 to the Act and any member of the polygamous marriage has been awarded income support [³, state pension credit] [⁴, income-based jobseekers allowance or income-related employment and support allowance].

(2) Where sub-paragraph (1) applies, an amount not exceeding £5 may be deducted in respect of the sum of all the members' liability to pay maintenance, in the proportions described in regulation 4(3) of the Child Support (Maintenance Calculations and Special Cases) Regulations 2000 and shall be paid in discharge (in whole or in part) of the respective liabilities to pay maintenance.

(3) In this paragraph "polygamous marriage" means any marriage during the subsistence of which a party to it is married to more than one person and the ceremony of marriage took place under the law of a country which permits polygamy.

2.275

Notice
7. When the Secretary of State commences making deductions, he shall notify the beneficiary in writing of the amount and frequency of the deduction and the benefit from which the deduction is made and shall give further such notice when there is a change to any of the particulars specified in the notice.

2.276

General
8. A deduction made in accordance with this Schedule is a deduction by way of recovery for the purposes of regulation 40(3) of the Income Support (General) Regulations 1987 [⁴, regulation 104 of the Employment and Support Allowance Regulation] and regulation 103(3) of the Jobseeker's Allowance Regulations 1996."

2.277

AMENDMENTS

1. The Social Security (Claims and Payments) Amendment Regulations 2001 (SI 2001/18), reg.2 (January 31, 2001).

2. Social Security (Claims and Payments) Amendment (No.2) Regulations 2002 (SI 2002/1950), reg.3 (entry into force tied to entry into force of s.43 of the Child Support Act 1991 as substituted by s.21 of the Child Support, Pensions and Social Security Act 2000: March 3, 2003 in relation to certain cases, see SI 2003/192; date to be appointed for remaining cases: see Child Support, Pensions and Social Security Act 2000, s.86(2)).

3. State Pension Credit (Consequential, Transitional and Miscellaneous Provisions) Regulations 2002, SI 2002/3019, reg.14 (April 7, 2003).

4. The Employment and Support Allowance (Consequential provisions) (No.2) Regulations 2008 (SI 2008/1554), reg.28 (October 27, 2008).

GENERAL NOTE

2.278   This schedule empowers the Secretary of State to deduct an amount in respect of certain child support maintenance liabilities from certain social security benefits where the person in receipt of the benefit is a non-resident parent. That sum is than paid to the person with the care of the child.

Regulation 3 of the amending regulations (SI 2001/18) contain a transitional provision as follows:

"No deductions shall be made under paragraph 7A or 7B of Schedule 9 to the Claims and Payments Regulations in respect of maintenance to which Schedule 9B applies."

See annotations to reg.35 for comment on the precedence to be accorded to child support payments and the relationship between Sch.9 and Sch.9B.

[¹ SCHEDULE 9ZC   **Regulations 4ZC and 32ZA**

ELECTRONIC COMMUNICATION

PART 1

INTRODUCTION

Interpretation
2.279   **1.** In this Schedule "official computer system" means a computer system maintained by or on behalf of the Secretary of State for the sending, receiving, processing or storing of any claim, certificate, notice, information or evidence.

PART 2

ELECTRONIC COMMUNICATION—GENERAL PROVISIONS

Conditions for the use of electronic communication
2.280   **2.**—(1) The Secretary of State may use an electronic communication in connection with claims for, and awards of, carer's allowance [² attendance allowance, disability living allowance, graduated retirement benefit, retirement pension and shared additional pension.].

(2) A person other than the Secretary of State may use an electronic communication in connection with the matters referred to in sub-paragraph (1) if the conditions specified in sub-paragraphs (3) to (6) are satisfied.

(3) The first condition is that the person is for the time being permitted to use an electronic communication by an authorisation given by means of a direction of the Secretary of State.

(4) The second condition is that the person uses an approved method of—
(a) authenticating the identity of the sender of the communication;
(b) electronic communication;
(c) authenticating any claim, certificate, notice, information or evidence delivered by means of an electronic communication; and
(d) subject to sub-paragraph (7), submitting to the Secretary of State any claim, certificate, notice, information or evidence.

(5) The third condition is that any claim, certificate, notice, information or evidence sent by means of an electronic communication is in a form approved for the purpose of this Schedule.

(6) The fourth condition is that the person maintains such records in written or electronic form as may be specified in a direction given by the Secretary of State.

(7) Where the person uses any method other than the method approved by the Secretary of State, of submitting any claim, certificate, notice, information or evidence, that claim, certificate, notice, information or evidence shall be treated as not having been submitted.

(8) In this paragraph "approved" means approved by means of a direction given by the Secretary of State for the purposes of this Schedule.

Use of intermediaries

3. The Secretary of State may use intermediaries in connection with—

    (a) the delivery of any claim, certificate, notice, information or evidence by means of an electronic communication; and

    (b) the authentication or security of anything transmitted by such means,

and may require other persons to use intermediaries in connection with those matters.

2.281

PART 3

ELECTRONIC COMMUNICATION—EVIDENTAL PROVISIONS

Effect of delivering information by means of electronic communication

4.—(1) Any claim, certificate, notice, information or evidence which is delivered by means of an electronic communication shall be treated as having been delivered, in the manner or form required by any provision of these Regulations, on the day the conditions imposed—

    (a) by this Schedule; and

    (b) by or under an applicable enactment,

are satisfied.

(2) The Secretary of State may, by a direction, determine that any claim, certificate, notice, information or evidence is to be treated as delivered on a different day (whether earlier or later) from the day provided for in sub-paragraph (1).

(3) Information shall not be taken to have been delivered to an official computer system by means of an electronic communication unless it is accepted by the system to which it is delivered.

2.282

Proof of identify of sender or recipient of information

5. If it is necessary to prove, for the purpose of any legal proceedings, the identity of—

    (a) the sender of any claim, certificate, notice, information or evidence delivered by means of an electronic communication to an official computer system; or

    (b) the recipient of any such claim, certificate, notice, information or evidence delivered by means of an electronic communication from an official computer system,

the sender or recipient, as the case may be, shall be presumed to be the person whose name is recorded as such on that official computer system.

2.283

Proof of delivery of information

6.—(1) If it is necessary to prove, for the purpose of any legal proceedings, that the use of an electronic communication has resulted in the delivery of any claim, certificate, notice, information or evidence this shall be presumed to have been the case where—

    (a) any such claim, certificate, notice, information or evidence has been delivered to the Secretary of State, if the delivery of that claim, certificate, notice, information or evidence has been recorded on an official computer system; or

    (b) any such certificate, notice, information or evidence has been delivered by the Secretary of State, if the delivery of that certificate, notice, information or evidence has been recorded on an official computer system.

(2) If it is necessary to prove, for the purpose of any legal proceedings, that the use of an electronic communication has resulted in the delivery of any such claim, certificate, notice, information or evidence, this shall be presumed not to be the case, if that claim, certificate, notice, information or evidence delivered to the Secretary of State has not been recorded on an official computer system.

(3) If it is necessary to prove, for the purpose of any legal proceedings, when any such claim, certificate, notice, information or evidence sent by means of an electronic communication has been received, the time and date of receipt shall be presumed to be that recorded on an official computer system.

2.284

Proof of content of information

2.285   7. If it is necessary to prove, for the purpose of any legal proceedings, the content of any claim, certificate, notice, information or evidence sent by means of an electronic communication, the content shall be presumed to be that recorded on an official computer system.]

AMENDMENTS

    1. The Social Security (Electronic Communications) (Carer's Allowance) Order 2003 SI 2003/2800, reg.2 (December 1, 2003).

    2. The Social Security (Electronic Communications) (Miscellaneous Benefits) Order 2005 (SI 2005/3321) (January 30, 2006).

[¹ SCHEDULE 9C   **Regulations 4C and 32A**

ELECTRONIC COMMUNICATION

PART 1

INTRODUCTION

Interpretation

2.286   1. In this Schedule "official computer system" means a computer system maintained by or on behalf of the Secretary of State for the–
    (a) sending or receiving of any claim, certificate, notice, information or evidence;
    or
    (b) processing or storing of any claim, certificate, notice, information or evidence.

PART 2

ELECTRONIC COMMUNICATION—GENERAL PROVISIONS

Conditions for the use of electronic communication

2.287   2.—(1) The Secretary of State may use an electronic communication in connection with claims for, and awards of, child benefit and elections under regulation 6A of the Social Security (Guardian's Allowances) Regulations 1975 (prescribed manner of making an election).

    (2) A person other than the Secretary of State may use an electronic communication in connection with the matters referred to in sub-paragraph (1) if the conditions specified in sub-paragraphs (3) to (6) are satisfied.

    (3) The first condition is that the person is for the time being permitted to use an electronic communication by an authorisation given by means of a direction of the Secretary of State.

    (4) The second condition is that the person uses an approved method of–
    (a) authenticating the identity of the sender of the communication;
    (b) electronic communication;
    (c) authenticating any claim, certificate, notice, information or evidence delivered by means of an electronic communication; and
    (d) subject to sub-paragraph (7), submitting to the Secretary of State any claim, certificate, notice, information or evidence.

    (5) The third condition is that any claim, certificate, notice, information or evidence sent by means of an electronic communication is in a form approved for the purpose of this Schedule.

    (6) The fourth condition is that the person maintains such records in written or electronic form as may be specified in a direction given by the Secretary of State.

    (7) Where the person uses any method other than the method approved by the Secretary of State, of submitting any claim, certificate, notice, information or evidence, that claim, certificate, notice, information or evidence shall be treated as not having been submitted.

    (8) In this paragraph "approved" means approved by means of a direction given by the Secretary of State for the purposes of this Schedule.

Use of intermediaries

3. The Secretary of State may use intermediaries in connection with–   2.288
   (a) the delivery of any claim, certificate, notice, information or evidence by means of an electronic communication; and
   (b) the authentication or security of anything transmitted by such means, and may require other persons to use intermediaries in connection with those matters.

PART 3

ELECTRONIC COMMUNICATION—EVIDENTIAL PROVISIONS

Effect of delivering information by means of electronic communication

4. —(1) Any claim, certificate, notice, information or evidence which is delivered by means   2.289
of an electronic communication shall be treated as having been delivered, in the manner or form required by any provision of these Regulations, on the day the conditions imposed–
   (a) by this Schedule; and
   (b) by or under an applicable enactment,
are satisfied.

(2) The Secretary of State may, by a direction, determine that any claim, certificate, notice, information or evidence is to be treated as delivered on a different day (whether earlier or later) from the day provided for in sub-paragraph (1).

Proof of identity of sender or recipient of information

5. If it is necessary to prove, for the purpose of any legal proceedings, the identity of–   2.290
   (a) the sender of any claim, certificate, notice, information or evidence delivered by means of an electronic communication to an official computer system; or
   (b) the recipient of any such claim, certificate, notice, information or evidence delivered by means of an electronic communication from an official computer system, the sender or recipient, as the case may be, shall be presumed to be the person recorded as such on that official computer system.

Proof of delivery of information

6. —(1) If it is necessary to prove, for the purpose of any legal proceedings, that the use   2.291
of an electronic communication has resulted in the delivery of any claim, certificate, notice, information or evidence this shall be presumed to have been the case where–
   (a) any such claim, certificate, notice, information or evidence has been delivered to the Secretary of State, if the delivery of that claim, certificate, notice, information or evidence has been recorded on an official computer system; or
   (b) any such certificate, notice, information or evidence has been delivered by the Secretary of State, if the delivery of that certificate, notice, information or evidence has been recorded on an official computer system.

(2) If it is necessary to prove, for the purpose of any legal proceedings, that the use of an electronic communication has resulted in the delivery of any such claim, certificate, notice, information or evidence, this shall be presumed not to be the case, if that claim, certificate, notice, information or evidence delivered to the Secretary of State has not been recorded on an official computer system.

(3) If it is necessary to prove, for the purpose of any legal proceedings, when any such claim, certificate, notice, information or evidence sent by means of an electronic communication has been received, the time of receipt shall be presumed to be that recorded on an official computer system.

Proof of content of information

7. If it is necessary to prove, for the purpose of any legal proceedings, the content of any   2.292
claim, certificate, notice, information or evidence sent by means of an electronic communication, the content shall be presumed to be that recorded on an official computer system.]

AMENDMENT

1. Inserted by The Social Security (Electronic Communications) (Child Benefit)   2.293
Order 2002 (SI 2002/1789) (October 28, 2002).

Social Security and Child Support (Decisions and Appeals) Regulations 1999

(SI 1999/991)

ARRANGEMENT OF REGULATIONS

PART I

GENERAL

PART II

REVISIONS, SUPERSESSIONS AND OTHER MATTERS (SOCIAL SECURITY
AND CHILD SUPPORT)

CHAPTER I

REVISIONS

CHAPTER II

SUPERSESSIONS

CHAPTER III

OTHER MATTERS

PART III

SUSPENSION, TERMINATION AND OTHER MATTERS

CHAPTER I

SUSPENSION AND TERMINATION

CHAPTER II

OTHER MATTERS

PART IV

RIGHTS OF APPEAL AND PROCEDURE FOR BRINGING APPEALS

CHAPTER I

GENERAL

General appeals matters not including child support appeals

PART V

APPEAL TRIBUNALS FOR SOCIAL SECURITY CONTRACTING OUT OF PENSIONS, VACCINE DAMAGE AND CHILD SUPPORT

PART VI

REVOCATIONS

SCHEDULES

2.295

Whereas a draft of this Instrument was laid before Parliament in accordance with section 80(1) of the Social Security Act 1998 and approved by resolution of each House of Parliament;

Now, therefore, the Secretary of State for Social Security, in exercise of powers set out in Schedule 1 to this Instrument and of all other powers enabling him in that behalf, with the concurrence of the Lord Chancellor in so far as the Regulations are made under section 6(3) of the Social Security Act 1998, by this Instrument, which contains only regulations made by virtue of, or consequential upon, those provisions of the Social Security Act 1998 and which is made before the end of the period of six months beginning with the coming into force of those provisions, after consultation with the Council on Tribunals in accordance with section 8 of the Tribunals and Inquiries Act 1992, hereby makes the following Regulations:

PART I

GENERAL

Citation, commencement and interpretation

2.296

1.—(1) These Regulations may be cited as the Social Security and Child Support (Decisions and Appeals) Regulations 1999.

(2) These Regulations shall come into force—

(a) in so far as they relate to child support and for the purposes of this regulation and regulation 2 on 1st June, 1999;

(b) in so far as they relate to—

    (i) industrial injuries benefit, guardian's allowance and child benefit; and

    (ii) a decision made under the Pension Schemes Act 1993 by virtue of section 170(2) of that Act;

on 5th July, 1999;

(c) in so far as they relate to retirement pension, widow's benefit, incapacity benefit, severe disablement allowance and maternity allowance, on 6th September, 1999;

(d) in so far as they relate to [³ working families' tax credit and disabled person's tax credit], on 5th October, 1999;

(e) in so far as they relate to attendance allowance, disability living allowance, invalid care allowance, jobseeker's allowance, credits of contributions or earnings, home responsibilities protection and vaccine damage payments, on 18th October, 1999; and

(f) for all remaining purposes, on 29th November, 1999.

(3) In these Regulations, unless the context otherwise requires—

"the Act" means the Social Security Act 1998;

"the 1997 Act" means the Social Security (Recovery of Benefits) Act 1997;

[⁶ "the Arrears, Interest and Adjustment of Maintenance Assessments Regulations" means the Child Support (Arrears, Interest and Adjustment of Maintenance Assessments) Regulations 1992;]

[¹⁰ "assessed income period" is to be construed in accordance with sections 6 and 9 of the State Pension Credit Act;]

"the Claims and Payments Regulations" means the Social Security (Claims and Payments) Regulations 1987;

"appeal" means an appeal to [²² the First-tier Tribunal];

[¹ "the Board" means the Commissioners of Inland Revenue;]

"claimant" means—

(a) any person who is a claimant for the purposes of section 191 of the Administration Act [¹⁰ section 35(1) of the Jobseekers Act or [¹⁸, section 17(1) of the State Pension Credit Act or section 24(1) of the Welfare Reform Act]] or any other person from whom benefit is alleged to be recoverable; and

(b) any person subject to a decision of [¹ an officer of the Board] under the Pension Schemes Act 1993;

[²² . . .]

[²¹ "'the Commission'" means the Child Maintenance and Enforcement Commission;]

[¹⁸ "'contributory employment and support allowance'" means a contributory allowance under Part 1 of the Welfare Reform Act;]

[¹⁶ "couple" means—

(a) a man and a woman who are married to each other and are members of the same household;

(b) a man and a woman who are not married to each other but are living together as husband and wife;

(c) two people of the same sex who are civil partners of each other and are members of the same household; or

(d) two people of the same sex who are not civil partners of each other but are living together as if they were single partners,

and for the purposes of paragraph (d), two people of the same sex are to be regarded as living together as if they were single partners if, but only if, they would be regarded as living together as husband and wife were they instead two people of the opposite sex.]

"the date of notification" means—

(a) the date that notification of a decision of the Secretary of State [³ or an officer of the Board] is treated as having been given or sent in accordance with regulation 2(b); or

(b) in the case of a social fund payment arising in accordance with regulations made under section 138(2) of the Contributions and Benefits Act—

(i) the date seven days after the date on which the Secretary of State makes his decision to make a payment to a person to meet expenses for heating;

(ii) where a person collects the instrument of payment at a post office, the date the instrument is collected;

(iii) where an instrument of payment is sent to a post office for collection but is not collected and a replacement instrument is issued, the date on which the replacement instrument is issued; or

(iv) where a person questions his failure to be awarded a payment for expenses for heating, the date on which the notification of the Secretary of State's decision given in response to that question is issued;

[¹⁷ "the Deferral of Retirement Pensions etc. Regulations" means the Social Security (Deferral of Retirement Pensions, Shared Additional Pension and Graduated Retirement Benefit) (Miscellaneous Provisions) Regulations 2005;]

[⁹ "designated authority" means—
  (a) the Secretary of State;
  (b) a person providing services to the Secretary of State;
  (c) a local authority;
  (d) a person providing services to, or authorised to exercise any functions of, any such authority.]

[¹⁸ "the Employment and Support Allowance Regulations" means the Employment and Support Allowance Regulations 2008;

"failure determination" means a determination by the Secretary of State under regulation 63(1) of the Employment and Support Allowance Regulations that a claimant has failed to satisfy the requirement of regulation 47 or 54 of those Regulations (requirement to take part in a work-focused health related assessment or a work-focused interview);]

[⁴ "family" has the same meaning as in section 137 of the Contributions and Benefits Act;]

[²² . . .]

[¹⁷ "the Graduated Retirement Benefit Regulations" means the Social Security (Graduated Retirement Benefit) Regulations 2005;]

[¹⁸ "income-related employment and support allowance" means an income-related allowance under Part 1 of the Welfare Reform Act;

"the Income Support Regulations" means the Income Support (General) Regulations 1987;

"the Jobseeker's Allowance Regulations" means the Jobseeker's Allowance Regulations 1996;

[⁶ "a joint-claim couple" has the same meaning as in section 1(4) of the Jobseekers Act 1995;

"a joint-claim jobseeker's allowance" has the same meaning as in section 1(4) of the Jobseekers Act 1995;]

[²² . . .]

[¹⁸ "'limited capability for work'" has the same meaning as in section 1(4) of the Welfare Reform Act;

[¹⁹ "the Lump Sum Payments Regulations" means the Social Security (Recovery of Benefits) (Lump Sum Payments) Regulations 2008;]

[⁷ "the Breach of Community Order Regulations" means the Social Security (Breach of Community Order) (Consequential Amendments) Regulations 2001;]

[⁵ "the Maintenance Calculation Procedure Regulations" means the Child Support (Maintenance Calculation Procedure) Regulations 2000;

"the Maintenance Calculations and Special Cases Regulations" means the Child Support (Maintenance Calculations and Special Cases) Regulations 2000;]

[²² . . .]

[¹⁵ . . .]

[⁸ "official error" means an error made by—
  (a) an officer of the Department for Work [²¹ , the Commission] and Pensions or the Board acting as such which no person outside the Department or the [²¹ , the Commission] Inland Revenue caused or to which no person outside the Department [²¹ , the Commission] or the Inland Revenue materially contributed;
  (b) a person employed by a designated authority acting on behalf

of the authority, which no person outside that authority caused or to which no person outside that authority materially contributed,

but excludes any error of law which is shown to have been an error by virtue of a subsequent decision of [22 the Upper Tribunal] or the court;]

[22 . . .]

[22 . . .]

[22 . . .]

[22 . . .]

[8 "partner" means—

(a) where a person is a member of [16 a couple] the other member of that couple; or

(b) where a person is polygamously married to two or more members of his household, any such member;]

"party to the proceedings" means the Secretary of State [21 or where the proceedings relate to child support, the Commission] [3 or, as the case may be, the Board or an officer of the Board,] and any other person—

(a) who is one of the principal parties for the purposes of sections 13 and 14;

(b) who has a right of appeal to [22 the First-tier Tribunal] under section 11(2) of the 1997 Act, section 20 of the Child Support Act [6 . . .] [13, section 2B(6) of the Administration Act] or section 12(2);

[22 . . .]

"referral" means a referral of an application for a departure direction to [22 the First-tier Tribunal] under section 28D(1)(b) of the Child Support Act;

[5 "relevant credit" means a credit of contributions or earnings resulting from a decision in accordance with regulations made under section 22(5) of the Contributions and Benefits Act;]

[6 except where otherwise provided "relevant person" means—

(a) a person with care;

(b) a non-resident parent;

(c) a parent who is treated as a non-resident parent under regulation 8 of the Maintenance Calculations and Special Cases Regulations;

(d) a child, where the application for a maintenance calculation is made by that child under section 7 of the Child Support Act,

in respect of whom a maintenance calculation has been applied for, [22 ...], or is or has been in force;]

[10 "state pension credit" means the benefit payable under the State Pension Credit Act;

"State Pension Credit Act" means the State Pension Credit Act 2002;

"State Pension Credit Regulations" means the State Pension Credit Regulations 2002;]

[3 "tax credit" means working families' tax credit or disabled person's tax credit, construing those terms in accordance with section 1(1) of the Tax Credits Act 1999;]

[2 "the Transfer Act" means the Social Security Contributions (Transfer of Functions, etc.) Act 1999.]

[7 "the Variations Regulations" means the Child Support (Variations) Regulations 2000;]

[18 " 'the Welfare Reform Act' " means the Welfare Reform Act 2007;]

[14 "work focused-interview" means an interview in which a person is required to take part in accordance with regulations made under section 2A or 2AA of the Administration Act;]

[¹ (3A) In these Regulations as they relate to any decision made under the Pension Schemes Act 1993 by virtue of section 170(2) of that Act, any reference to the Secretary of State is to be construed as if it were a reference to an officer of the Board.]

(4) In these Regulations, unless the context otherwise requires, a reference—

(a) to a numbered section is to the section of the Act bearing that number;

(b) to a numbered Part is to the Part of these Regulations bearing that number;

(c) to a numbered regulation or Schedule is to the regulation in, or Schedule to, these Regulations bearing that number;

(d) in a regulation or Schedule to a numbered paragraph is to the paragraph in that regulation or Schedule bearing that number;

(e) in a paragraph to a lettered or numbered sub-paragraph is to the sub-paragraph in that paragraph bearing that letter or number.

AMENDMENTS

1. Social Security Contributions (Transfer of Functions, etc.) Act 1999 (Commencement No.2 and Consequential and Transitional Provisions) Order 1999 (SI 1999/1662), art.3(2) (July 5, 1999).

2.297

2. Social Security and Child Support (Decisions and Appeals) Amendment (No.3) Regulations 1999 (SI 1999/1670), reg.2(2) (July 5, 1999).

3. Tax Credits (Decisions and Appeals) (Amendment) Regulations 1999 (SI 1999/2570), regs 3 and 4 (October 5, 1999). Note that amendments made by these regulations only have effect with respect to tax credit under the Tax Credits Act 1999 (reg.1(2) of the Amendment Regulations).

4. Social Security and Child Support (Miscellaneous Amendments) Regulations 2000 (SI 2000/1596), reg.14 (June 19, 2000).

5. Social Security Amendment (Joint Claims) Regulations 2001 (SI 2001/518), reg.4(a) (March 19, 2001).

6. Child Support (Decisions and Appeals) (Amendment) Regulations 2000 (SI 2000/3185), reg.2 (various dates as provided in reg.1(1)).

7. Social Security (Breach of Community Order) (Consequential Amendments) Regulations 2001 (SI 2001/1711), reg.2(2)(a) (October 15, 2001).

8. Social Security and Child Support (Decisions and Appeals) (Miscellaneous Amendments) Regulations 2002 (SI 2002/1379), reg.2 (May 20, 2002).

9. Social Security (Jobcentre Plus Interviews) Regulations 2002 (SI 2002/1703), Sch.2, para.6(a) (September 30, 2002).

10. State Pension Credit (Consequential, Transitional and Miscellaneous Provisions) Regulations 2002 (SI 2002/3019), reg.16 (April 7, 2003).

11. Child Benefit and Guardian's Allowance (Decisions and Appeals) Regulations 2003 (SI 2003/916), reg.36 (April 7, 2003). Note that this amendment replaces the words "regulation 27" only so far as the definition relates to child benefit and guardian's allowance. See the annotation to this definition.

12. Social Security and Child Support (Miscellaneous Amendments) Regulations 2003 (SI 2003/1050), reg.3(1) (May 5, 2003).

13. Social Security (Jobcentre Plus Interviews for Partners) Regulations 2003 (SI 2003/1886), reg.15(2) (April 12, 2004).

14. Social Security (Working Neighbourhoods) Regulations 2004 (SI 2004/959), reg.24(2) (April 26, 2004).

15. Social Security, Child Support, and Tax Credits (Decisions and Appeals)

Amendment Regulations 2004 (SI 2004/3368), reg.2(2) (December 21, 2004).

16. Civil Partnership (Consequential Amendments) Regulations 2005 (SI 2005/2878), reg.8(2) (December 5, 2005).

17. Social Security (Deferral of Retirement Pensions, Shared Additional Pension and Graduated Retirement Benefit) (Miscellaneous Provisions) Regulations 2005 (SI 2005/2677), reg.9(2) (April 6, 2006).

2.298   18. Employment and Support Allowance (Consequential Provisions) (No. 2) Regulations 2008 (SI 2008/1554), regs 29 and 30 (July 27, 2008).

19. Social Security (Recovery of Benefits) (Lump Sum Payments) Regulations 2008 (SI 2008/1596), Sch.2, para.1(a) (October 1, 2008).

20. Child Support (Consequential Provisions) Regulations 2008 (SI 2008/2543), reg. 4(1) and (2) (October 27, 2008).

21. Child Support (Consequential Provisions) (No. 2) Regulations 2008 (SI 2008/2656), reg. 4 (November 1, 2008).

22. Tribunals, Courts and Enforcement Act 2007 (Transitional and Consequential Provisions) Order 2008 (SI 2008/2683), Sch.1, paras 95 and 96 (November 3, 2008), subject to a saving under art.3 for reasons explained in the note to ss. 5 to 7 of the Social Security Act 1998.

DEFINITIONS

"the Child Support Act"—see s.84 of the Social Security Act 1998.
"the Contributions and Benefits Act"—see s.84 of the Social Security Act 1998.

GENERAL NOTE

Para. (3)
2.299   The definitions of "the Claims and Payments Regulations" and the "Breach of Community Order Regulations" are out of sequence due to drafting errors.

"the Board"
2.300   The definition of "the Board" must be read in the light of the Commissioners for Revenue and Customs Act 2005. Section 5(2)(a) vests all the functions of the former Commissioners of Inland Revenue in the Commissioners for Her Majesty's Revenue and Customs and s.4(1) provides that the Commissioners and the officers of Revenue and Customs may together be referred to as Her Majesty's Revenue and Customs.

"official error"
2.301   The definition of "official error" is important because it is a ground for revision under reg.3, whereas a mistake of fact or law that is not an "official error" is a ground of supersession under reg.6 and a supersession is usually effective from a later date than a revision.

Only clear and obvious mistakes amount to errors in this context and a failure to elucidate facts not disclosed by a claimant is unlikely to suffice *(R(SB) 10/91* and *R(SB) 2/93)*. There is also no "official error" where a decision is made without investigating a possible discrepancy in the evidence or on incomplete evidence, partly because in such cases a claimant is likely to have contributed to any error *(R(H) 1/04, R(H) 2/04)*. Adjudication officers under the pre-1998 Act system of adjudication were "officers of the Department . . . acting as such" and so an error by an adjudication officer can constitute an "official error" *(R(CS) 3/04*, not following *R(I) 5/02)*.

Since it was decided in *CDLA/1707/2005* that a tribunal is entitled to substitute a revision for a supersession or refusal to supersede (see the annotation to s.12(2) of the Social Security Act 1998, above), there have been a number of new decisions on the meaning of "official error". In *CDLA/393/2006*, the Commissioner regarded the adjudication officer's reliance on the claim form without obtaining further evidence

514

as "a failure in the proper standards of administration" but found that the claimant's mother had contributed to the error by the way in which she had completed the claim form. There was therefore no "official error". He said that "in judging what was a material contribution a common sense approach should be taken, rather than a highly refined analysis of causation" and that the way the claim form had been completed should not be seen as merely the setting for the adjudication officer's error. In *CH/687/2006*, the claimant was overpaid housing benefit because the amount of her partner's incapacity benefit changed due to the length of time he had been incapable of work. The Deputy Commissioner reviewed the cases and held that there was no official error. Although the local authority had known that the incapacity benefit in payment when the award was made was only short-term incapacity benefit, which would inevitably be replaced by a higher rate if the claimant's partner continued to be incapable of work, the local authority had been entitled to presume that any change in the rate of incapacity benefit would be reported to it. This can therefore be seen as another case where the claimant contributed to the error. In *CPC/206/2005*, the Commissioner stated that the term "official error" is not confined to errors of law but said that it "involves more than merely taking a decision that another decision-maker with the same information would not take". He considered that it would not be helpful further to explain what the term meant. However, he found an official error in the case because "no Secretary of State or decision-maker acting reasonably could have [made the decision under appeal]". That would have been an error of law and it is perhaps difficult to envisage an official error that would not be an error of law in its public law sense (see the annotation to s.11 of the Tribunals Courts and Enforcement Act 2007). An "official error" is not revealed merely because a decision made some time ago in the light of current medical opinion is shown to have been wrong as a result of a change in medical opinion (*R(AF) 5/07*). There will merely have been a mistake of fact justifying supersession.

Generally, notification of a change of circumstances must be made to the office dealing with the relevant benefit and so, if information is not acted on because it has been sent to another office, a claimant will generally have contributed to the error. However, that will not inevitably be the case. In *CH/2567/2007*, the Commissioner had regard to confusing nomenclature (such that even officials got it wrong and the tribunal was confused), the proliferation of correspondence, the repeated notification of the relevant facts to one department that ought to have passed the information to another and the complication of the benefit position (such that the claimant could not reasonably have been expected to realise there had been an overpayment) and he concluded that the claimant had not contributed to the official error involved in one department failing to pass information on to another.

The concluding words of the amended definition are imprecise but it is now fairly clear that they apply where the official was acting in accordance with a general Departmental misunderstanding of the law that has been shown to be wrong by a decision of the Upper Tribunal or court that need not itself have directly involved the particular claimant in respect of whom the error was made. The jurisprudential difficulties arising because the Upper Tribunal and courts only declare the law to be as it has always been and because the misunderstanding may not have been shared by anyone outside the Department are familiar ones. However, in *CP/1425/2007*, a Tribunal of Commissioners did not dwell on those theoretical problems and gave the words their practical meaning, deciding that there had been no official error where the Department had been shown by a decision of the European Court of Justice to have been misapplying European Community law. The consequence was that the claimant, who had made an application for revision or supersession shortly after the Court's decision, was entitled to have it treated only as an application for supersession effective from the date it was made, insofar as she needed to rely on the decision of the Court but could have it treated as an application for revision insofar as she could rely upon domestic legislation. An order made by a Court by consent is not a "decision" for these purposes (*R(FC) 3/98*).

"party to the proceedings"

2.302 In *CA/1014/1999*, it was held that, where the Secretary of State had decided that an overpayment was recoverable from a claimant but had made no decision in respect of the claimant's appointee, the claimant's appointee was not a "party to the proceedings" against whom the tribunal could make a recoverability decision, even though the appointee had brought the proceedings on behalf of the claimant (and had an express right of appeal under reg.25). However, in *CTC/3543/2004*, the same Commissioner held that, where Her Majesty's Revenue and Customs had made a decision to the effect that a tax credit was recoverable from both the husband and the wife, the husband was a "party to the proceedings" before the tribunal even though only his wife had appealed (although acting through her husband).

Where the Secretary of State has made a decision that an overpayment is recoverable from both a claimant and the claimant's appointee, an appeal brought by the appointee should be treated as an appeal brought on behalf of both the claimant and the appointee unless it is clear that an appeal on behalf of only one of them was intended (*R(A) 2/06*). Even if an appeal by only one of them is intended, *CA/1014/1999* is clearly distinguishable and whichever has not appealed will be a "party to the proceedings", as in *CTC/3543/2004*.

Service of notices or documents

2.303 **2.** Where, by any provision of the Act [³, of the Child Support Act] or of these Regulations—

    (a) any notice or other document is required to be given or sent [⁴. . .] to an officer authorised by the Secretary of State [¹ or to an officer of the Board], that notice or document shall be treated as having been so given or sent on the day that it is received [⁴. . .] by an officer authorised by the Secretary of State [¹ or by an officer of the Board], as the case may be, and

    (b) any notice (including notification of a decision of the Secretary of State [² or of an officer of the Board] or other document is required to be given or sent to any person other than [⁴. . .] [¹ [⁴. . .] an officer] authorised by the Secretary of State [¹ or an officer of the Board], as the case may be, that notice or document shall, if sent by post to that person's last known address, be treated as having been given or sent on the day that it was posted.

2.304 AMENDMENTS

1. Tax Credits (Decisions and Appeals) (Amendment) Regulations 1999 (SI 1999/2570), reg.5 (October 5, 1999). Note that amendments made by these regulations only have effect with respect to tax credit (reg.1(2) of the Amendment Regulations).

2. Tax Credits (Decisions and Appeals) (Amendment) Regulations 2000 (SI 2000/127), reg.2 (February 14, 2000). This amendment has effect with respect only to tax credit (reg.1(2) of the amending Regulations).

3. Child Support (Decisions and Appeals) (Amendment) Regulations 2000 (SI 2000/3185), reg.3 (various dates as provided by reg.1(1)).

4. Tribunals, Courts and Enforcement Act 2007 (Transitional and Consequential Provisions) Order 2008 (SI 2008/2683), Sch.1, paras 95 and 97 (November 3, 2008), subject to a saving under art.3 for reasons explained in the note to ss.5 to 7 of the Social Security Act 1998.

DEFINITIONS

2.305 "the Act"—see reg.1(3).
"the Board"—*ibid.*
"the Child Support Act"—see s.39(1) of the Social Security Act 1998.

GENERAL NOTE

This regulation re-enacts reg.1(3) of the Social Security (Adjudication)   2.306
Regulations 1995.

In *R(IB)4/02*, it was held that, where a document had, under reg.53(4) as then
in force, to be sent to a chairman or member of a tribunal, para.(a) did not apply.
Paragraph (b) applied instead so that the document was sent when posted and not
when it was received. Regulation 53(4) has been revoked but the reasoning still
holds good when a document must be sent to anyone not mentioned in para.(a).
A document may be sent by fax and is received for the purposes of reg.2(a) when it
is successfully transmitted to, and received by, a fax machine, irrespective of when it
is actually collected from the fax machine *(R(DLA)3/05)*.

In *CG/2973/2004*, the Commissioner had to consider whether the claimant had
made a claim for benefit on a certain date. A claim is generally effective only when
received. The position is therefore similar to that under reg.2(a), relating to documents to be sent to the Secretary of State. The Commissioner accepted that the
claimant had posted a claim form but found that it was more likely to have been
lost in the post before it reached the building where it was to be opened than lost
in that building or subsequently. Strictly speaking, it was therefore unnecessary for
him to consider whether, the claimant having succeeded in showing that the form
had been posted, the burden of proving that the letter was lost after arrival at that
building rested on her or whether the burden of proving that it was lost before then
rested on the Secretary of State. However, having heard full legal argument, he
said that the burden would have lain on the claimant to prove delivery so that, if it
had been impossible to say where the letter was more likely to have been lost, the
claimant would still have failed. He preferred *CIS/306/2003* to *CSIS/48/1992* and
CIS/759/1992. An appeal against the Commissioner's decision was dismissed (*Levy
v Secretary of State for Work and Pensions* [2006] EWCA Civ 890 (reported as *R(G)
2/06)*).

The "last known address" to which documents must be sent for para.(b) to
apply need not be the person's last known *residence* because the concepts are different. Moreover, the sender must consider the address to be reliable and, if he
does not, should take reasonable steps to see whether a more reliable one exists
(*CCS/2288/2005*). This approach exists to aid the innocent claimant and not the
one who has failed to take reasonable steps to keep the relevant authority aware of
his whereabouts. Generally, an authority is entitled to rely on a claimant to inform
it of any move.

PART II

REVISIONS, SUPERSESSIONS AND OTHER MATTERS SOCIAL SECURITY AND
CHILD SUPPORT

CHAPTER I

REVISIONS

Revision of decisions

3.—(1) Subject to the following provisions of this regulation, any deci-   2.307
sion of the Secretary of State [³ or the Board or an officer of the Board]
under section 8 or 10 ("the original decision") may be revised by him [³ or
them] if—

[¹⁰(a) he or they commence action leading to revision within one month of the date of notification of the original decision; or

(b) an application for a revision is received by the Secretary of State or the Board or an officer of the Board at the appropriate office—

(i) subject to regulation 9A(3), within one month of the date of notification of the original decision;

(ii) where a written statement is requested under paragraph(1)(b) of regulation 28 and is provided within the period specified in head (i), within 14 days of the expiry of that period;

(iii) where a written statement is requested under paragraph(1)(b) of regulation 28 and is provided after the period specified in head (i), within 14 days of the date on which the statement is provided; or

(iv) within such longer period as may be allowed under regulation 4.]

(2) Where the Secretary of State [3 or the Board or an officer of the Board] requires further evidence or information from the applicant in order to consider all the issues raised by an application under paragraph (1)(b) ("the original application"), he [³ or they] shall notify the applicant that further evidence or information is required and the decision may be revised—

(a) where the applicant provides further relevant evidence or information within one month of the date of notification or such longer period of time as the Secretary of State [³ or the Board or an officer of the Board] may allow; or

(b) where the applicant does not provide such evidence or information within the time allowed under sub-paragraph (a), on the basis of the original application.

(3) In the case of a payment out of the social fund in respect of maternity or funeral expenses, a decision under section 8 may be revised where the application is made—

(a) within one month of the date of notification of the decision, or if later

(b) within the time prescribed for claiming such a payment under regulation 19 of, and Schedule 4 to, the Claims and Payments Regulations, or

(c) within such longer period of time as may be allowed under regulation 4.

(4) In the case of a decision made under the Pension Schemes Act 1993 by virtue of section 170(2) of that Act, the decision may be revised at any time by [² an officer of the Board] where it contains an error.

[¹⁰ (4A) Where there is an appeal against an original decision (within the meaning of paragraph (1)) within the time prescribed [²¹ by Tribunal Procedure Rules], but the appeal has not been determined, the original decision may be revised at any time.]

(5) A decision of the Secretary of State [³ *Board or an officer of the Board*] under section 8 or 10—

(a) [¹⁸ except where paragraph (5ZA) applies] which arose from an official error; or

(b) [¹⁷ except in a case to which sub-paragraph (c) or (d) applies,] where the decision was made in ignorance of, or was based upon a mistake as to, some material fact and as a result of that ignorance of or mistake as to that fact, the decision was more advantageous to the claimant than it would otherwise have been but for that ignorance or mistake,

[³ *(bb) which was made in ignorance of, or was based on a mistake as to some material fact,*]

(c) [¹ [¹⁷ subject to subparagraph (d),] where the decision is a disability benefit decision, or is an incapacity benefit decision where there has been an incapacity determination [¹⁹ or is an employment and support allowance decision where there has been a limited capability for work determination] (whether before or after the decision), which was made in ignorance of, or was based upon a mistake as to, some material fact in relation to a disability determination embodies in or necessary to the disability benefit decision, [¹⁹ , the incapacity determination or the limited capability for work determination], and—

   (i) as a result of that ignorance or mistake as to that fact the decision was more advantageous to the claimant than it would otherwise have been but for that ignorance or mistake and,

   (ii) the Secretary of State is satisfied that at the time the decision was made the claimant or payee knew or could reasonably have been expected to know of the fact in question and that it was relevant to the decision,]

[¹⁷ (d) where the decision [¹⁹ is an employment and support allowance decision,] is a disability benefit decision, or is an incapacity benefit decision, which was made in ignorance of, or was based upon a mistake as to, some material fact not in relation to the [¹⁹ limited capability for work determination,] incapacity or disability determination embodied in or necessary to [¹⁹ the employment and support allowance decision,] the incapacity benefit decision or disability benefit decision, and as a result of that ignorance of, or mistake as to that fact, the decision was more advantageous to the claimant than it would otherwise have been but for the ignorance or mistake,]

may be revised at any time by the Secretary of State [³ *by the Board or an officer of the Board at any time not later than the end of the period of six years immediately following the date of the decision or, where ignorance of the material fact referred to in sub-paragraph (b) was caused by the fraudulent or negligent conduct of the claimant, not later than the end of the period of twenty years immediately following the date of the decision.*]

[¹⁸ (5ZA) This paragraph applies where—

(a) the decision which would otherwise fall to be revised is a decision to award a benefit specified in paragraph (5ZB), whether or not the award has already been put in payment;

(b) that award was based on the satisfaction by a person of the contribution conditions, in whole or in part, by virtue of credits of earnings for incapacity for work or approved training in the tax years from 1993–94 to 2007–08;

(c) the official error derives from the failure to transpose correctly information relating to those credits from the Department for Work and Pensions' Pension Strategy Computer System to Her Majesty's Revenue and Customs' computer system (NIRS2) or from related clerical procedures; and

(d) that error has resulted in an award to the claimant which is more advantageous to him than if the error had not been made.

(5ZB) The specified benefits are—
(a) bereavement allowance;
(b) contribution-based jobseeker's allowance;
(c) incapacity benefit;
(d) retirement pension;
(e) widowed mother's allowance;
(f) widowed parent's allowance; [19 ...]
(g) widow's pension. [19 and
(h) contributory employment and support allowance].

(5ZC) In paragraph (5ZA)(b), "tax year" has the meaning ascribed to it by section 122(1) of the Contributions and Benefits Act.]

[10 (5A) Where—
(a) the Secretary of State or the Board or an officer of the Board, as the case may be, makes a decision under section 8 or 10, or that decision is revised under section 9, in respect of a claim or award ("decision A") and the claimant appeals against decision A;
(b) decision A is superseded or the claimant makes a further claim which is decided ("decision B") after the claimant made the appeal but before the appeal results in a decision by [21 the First-tier Tribunal] ("decision C"); and
(c) the Secretary of State or the Board or an officer of the board, as the case may be, would have made decision B differently if he or they had been aware of decision C at the time he or they made decision B,
decision B may be revised at any time.]

[17 (5B) A decision by the Secretary of State under section 8 or 10 awarding incapacity benefit may be revised at any time if—
(a) it incorporates a determination that the condition in regulation 28(2)(b) of the Social Security (Incapacity for Work) (General) Regulations 1995 (conditions for treating a person as incapable of work until the personal capability assessment is carried out) is satisfied;
(b) the condition referred to in sub-paragraph (a) was not satisfied at the time when the further claim was first determined; and
(c) there is a period before the award which falls to be decided.]

[19 (5C) A decision of the Secretary of State under section 10 made in consequence of a failure determination may be revised at any time if it contained an error to which the claimant did not materially contribute;

(5D) A decision by the Secretary of State under section 8 or 10 awarding employment and support allowance may be revised at any time if—
(a) it incorporates a determination that the condition in regulation 30 of the Employment and Support Allowance Regulations is satisfied;
(b) the condition referred to in sub-paragraph (a) was not satisfied at the time when the claim was first determined; and
(c) there is a period before the award which falls to be decided.]

(6) A decision of the Secretary of State under section 8 or 10 that a jobseeker's allowance is not payable to a claimant for any period in accordance with section 19 [6 or 20A] of the Jobseekers Act may be revised at any time by the Secretary of State.

[5 (6A) A relevant decision within the meaning of section 2B (2) [13 or (2A)] of the Administration Act may be revised at any time if it contains an error.]

[⁹ (7) Where—

(a) the Secretary of State or an officer of the Board makes a decision under section 8 or 10 awarding benefit to a claimant ("the original award"); and

(b) an award of another relevant benefit or an increase in the rate of another relevant benefit is made to the claimant or a member of his family for a period which includes the date on which the original award took effect,

the Secretary of State or an officer of the Board, as the case may require, may revise the original award.]

[¹⁴ (7ZA) Where—

(a) the Secretary of State makes a decision under section 8 or 10 awarding income support [¹⁹, state pension credit or an income-related employment and support allowance] to a claimant ("the original award");

(b) the claimant has a non-dependant within the meaning of regulation 3 of the Income Support Regulations [¹⁹ or regulation 71 of the Employment and Support Allowance Regulations] or a person residing with him within the meaning of paragraph 1(1)(a)(ii), (b)(ii) or (c)(iii) of Schedule I to the State Pension Credit Regulations ("the non-dependant");

(c) but for the non-dependant—

  (i) a severe disability premium would be applicable to the claimant under regulation 17(1)(d) of the Income Support Regulations [¹⁹ or regulation 67 of the Employment and Support Allowance Regulations]; or

  (ii) an additional amount would be applicable to the claimant as a severe disabled person under regulation 6(4) of the State Pension Credit Regulations; and

(d) after the original award the non-dependant is awarded benefit which—

  (i) is for a period which includes the date on which the original award took effect; and

  (ii) is such that a severe disability premium becomes applicable to the claimant under paragraph 13(3)(a) of Schedule 2 to the Income Support Regulations [¹⁹, paragraph 6(4)(a) of Schedule 4 to the Employment and Support Allowance Regulations] or an additional amount for severe disability becomes applicable to him under paragraph 2(2)(a) of Schedule I to the State Pension Credit Regulations,

the Secretary of State may revise the original award.]

[¹⁰ (7A) Where a decision as to a claimant's entitlement to a disablement pension under section 103 of the Contributions and Benefits Act is revised by the Secretary of State, or changed on appeal, a decision of the Secretary of State as to the claimant's entitlement to reduced earnings allowance under paragraph 11 or 12 of Schedule 7 to that Act may be revised at any time provided that the revised decision is more advantageous to the claimant than the original decision.]

[¹⁴ (7B) A decision under regulation 22A of the Income Support Regulations (reduction in applicable amount where the claimant is appealing against a decision which embodies a determination that he is not incapable of work) may be revised if the appeal is successful [¹⁶ or lapses].

(7C) Where a person's entitlement to income support is terminated because of a determination that he is not incapable of work and [^{16} the decision which embodies that determination is revised or] he subsequently appeals the decision [^{16} which embodies] that determination and is entitled to income support under regulation 22A of the Income Support Regulations, the decision to terminate entitlement may be revised.]

[^{15} (7D) Where—

(a) a person elects for an increase of—
  (i) a Category A or Category B retirement pension in accordance with paragraph A1 or 3C of Schedule 5 to the Contributions and Benefits Act (pension increase or lump sum where entitlement to retirement pension is deferred);
  (ii) a shared additional pension in accordance with paragraph 1 of Schedule 5A to that Act (pension increase or lump sum where entitlement to shared additional pension is deferred); or, as the case may be,
  (iii) graduated retirement benefit in accordance with paragraph 12 or 17 of Schedule 1 to the Graduated Retirement Benefit Regulations (further provisions replacing section 36(4) of the National Insurance Act 1965: increases of graduated retirement benefit and lump sums);

(b) the Secretary of State decides that the person or his partner is entitled to state pension credit and takes into account the increase of pension or benefit in making or superseding that decision; and

(c) the person's election for an increase is subsequently changed in favour of a lump sum in accordance with regulation 5 of the Deferral of Retirement Pensions etc. Regulations or, as the case may be, paragraph 20D of Schedule 1 to the Graduated Retirement Benefit Regulations,

the Secretary of State may revise the state pension credit decision.

(7E) Where—

(a) a person is awarded a Category A or Category B retirement pension, shared additional pension or, as the case may be, graduated retirement benefit;

(b) an election is made, or treated as made, in respect of the award in accordance with paragraph A1 or 3C of Schedule 5 or paragraph 1 of Schedule 5A to the Contributions and Benefits Act or, as the case may be, in accordance with paragraph 12 or 17 of Schedule 1 to the Graduated Retirement Benefit Regulations; and

(c) the election is subsequently changed in accordance with regulation 5 of the Deferral of Retirement Pensions etc. Regulations or, as the case may be, paragraph 20D of Schedule 1 to the Graduated Retirement Benefit Regulations,

the Secretary of State may revise the award.]

[^{16} (7F) A decision under regulation 17(1)(d) of the Income Support Regulations that a person is no longer entitled to a disability premium because of a determination that he is not incapable of work may be revised where the decision which embodies that determination is revised or his appeal against the decision is successful.]

(8) A decision of the Secretary of State [^{3} or the Board of an officer of the Board] which is specified in Schedule 2 to the Act or is prescribed in regulation 27 (decisions against which no appeal lies) may be revised at any time.

[⁷ (8A) Where a court makes a determination which results in a restriction being imposed pursuant to section 62 or 63 of the Child Support, Pensions and Social Security Act 2000 (loss of benefit provisions) and that determination is quashed or set aside by that or any other court, a decision of the Secretary of State under section 8(1)(a) or 10 made in accordance with regulation 6(2)(i) may be revised at any time.]

[⁸ (8B) Where a court convicts a person of an offence, that conviction results in a restriction being imposed under section 7, 8 or 9 of the Social Security Fraud Act 2001 (loss of benefit provisions) and that conviction is quashed or set aside by that or any other court, a decision of the Secretary of State under section 8(1)(a) or 10 made in accordance with regulation 6(2)(j) or (k) may be revised at any time.]

[²⁰ (8C) A decision made under section 8 or 10 ("the original decision") may be revised at any time—

    (a) where, on or after the date of the original decision—

        (i) a late paid contribution is treated as paid under regulation 5 of the Social Security (Crediting and Treatment of Contributions and National Insurance Numbers) Regulations 2001 (treatment of late paid contributions where no consent, connivance or negligence by the primary contributor) on a date which falls on or before the date on which the original decision was made;

        (ii) a direction is given under regulation 6 of those Regulations (treatment of contributions paid late through ignorance or error) that a late contribution shall be treated as paid on a date which falls on or before the date on which the original decision was made; or

        (iii) an unpaid contribution is treated as paid under regulation 60 of the Social Security (Contributions) Regulations 2001 (treatment of unpaid contributions where no consent, connivance or negligence by the primary contributor) on a date which falls on or before the date on which the original decision was made; and

    (b) where any of paragraphs (i), (ii) or (iii) apply, either an award of benefit would have been made or the amount of benefit awarded would have been different.]

[²² (8D) A decision made under section 8 or 10 may be revised at any time where, by virtue of regulation 6C (treatment of Class 3 contributions paid under section 13A of the Act) of the Social Security (Crediting and Treatment of Contributions, and National Insurance Numbers) Regulations 2001, a contribution is treated as paid on a date which falls on or before the date on which the decision was made.]

[⁴ (9) Paragraph (1) shall not apply in respect of—

    (a) a relevant change of circumstances which occurred since the decision [¹² had effect] [¹⁴ or, in the case of an advance award under regulation 13, 13A or 13C of the Claims and Payments Regulations, since the decision was made,]or where the Secretary of State has evidence or information which indicates that a relevant change of circumstances will occur; [¹⁹ ...]

    (b) a decision which relates to an attendance allowance or a disability living allowance where the person is terminally ill, within the meaning of section 66(2)(a) of the Contributions and Benefit Act,

523

unless an application for revision which contains an express statement that the person is terminally ill is made either by—

(i) the person himself; or

(ii) any other person purporting to act on his behalf whether or not that other person is acting with his knowledge or authority,

but where such an application is received a decision may be so revised notwithstanding that no claim under section 66(1) or, as the case may be, 72(5) or 73(12) of that Act has been made;] [[19] nor

(c) a decision which relates to an employment and support allowance where the claimant is terminally ill, within the meaning of regulation 2(1) of the Employment and Support Allowance Regulations unless the claimant makes an application which contains an express statement that he is terminally ill and where such an application is made, the decision may be revised.".

(10) The Secretary of State [[3] or the Board] may treat an application for a supersession as an application for a revision.

(11) In this regulation and regulation 7, "appropriate office" means

(a) the office of the [[10] Department for Work and Pensions] the address of which is indicated on the notification of the original decision; or

(b) in the case of a person who has claimed jobseeker's allowance, the office specified by the Secretary of State in accordance with regulation 23 of the Jobseeker's Allowance Regulations [[2]; or

(c) in the case of a contributions decision which falls within Part II of Schedule 3 to the Act, any National Insurance Contributions office of the Board or any office of the [[10] Department for Work and Pensions]; or

(d) in the case of a decision made under the Pension Schemes Act 1993 by virtue of section 170(2) of that Act, any National Insurance Contributions office of the Board;] [[3] or

(e) in the case of a person who has claimed working families' tax credit or disabled person's tax credit, a Tax Credits Office, the address of which is indicated on the notification of the original decision;] [[5] or

[[11](f) in the case of a person who is, or would be, required to take part in a work-focused interview, an office of the Department for Work and Pensions which is designated by the Secretary of State as a Jobcentre Plus Office or an office of a designated authority which displays the **one** logo.]

AMENDMENTS

2.308

1. Social Security and Child Support (Decisions and Appeals) Amendment (No.2) Regulations 1999 (SI 1999/1623), reg.2 (July 5, 1999).

2. Social Security Contributions (Transfer of Functions, etc.) Act 1999 (Commencement No.2 and Consequential and Transitional Provisions) Order 1999 (SI 1999/1662), art.3(3) (July 5, 1999).

3. Tax Credits (Decisions and Appeals) (Amendment) Regulations 1999 (SI 1999/2570), reg.6 (October 5, 1999). Note that amendments made by these regulations only have effect with respect to tax credit (reg.1(2) of the Amendment Regulations). In the case of para.(5) the amendments are substituted in relation to tax credit; for this reason the substituted words in relation to tax credit are shown in italics.

4. Social Security and Child Support (Decisions and Appeals), Vaccine Damage Payments and Jobseeker's Allowance (Amendment) Regulations 1999 (SI 1999/2677), reg.6 (October 18, 1999).

5. Social Security (Work-focused Interviews) Regulations 2000 (SI 2000/897), reg.16(5) and Sch.6, para.3 (April 3, 2000).

6. Social Security (Joint Claims: Consequential Amendments) Regulations 2000 (SI 2000/1982), reg.5(a) (March 19, 2001).

7. Social Security (Breach of Community Order) (Consequential Amendments) Regulations 2001 (SI 2001/1711), reg.2(2)(b) (October 15, 2001).

8. Social Security (Loss of Benefit) (Consequential Amendments) Regulations 2002 (SI 2002/490), reg.8(a) (April 1, 2002).

9. Social Security (Claims and Payments and Miscellaneous Amendments) Regulations 2002 (SI 2002/428), reg.4(2) (April 2, 2002).

10. Social Security and Child Support (Decisions and Appeals) (Miscellaneous Amendments) Regulations 2002 (SI 2002/1379), reg.3(e), (May 20, 2002).

11. Social Security (Jobcentre Plus Interviews) Regulations 2002 (SI 2002/1703), Sch.2, para.6(b) (September 30, 2002).

12. Social Security and Child Support (Miscellaneous Amendments) Regulations 2003 (SI 2003/1050), reg.3(2) (May 5, 2003).

13. Social Security (Jobcentre Plus Interviews for Partners) Regulations 2003 (SI 2003/1886, reg.15(3) (April 12, 2004).

14. Social Security, Child Support and Tax Credits (Miscellaneous Amendments) Regulations 2005 (SI 2005/337), reg.2(2) (March 18, 2005).

15. Social Security (Deferral of Retirement Pensions, Shared Additional Pension and Graduated Retirement Benefit) (Miscellaneous Provisions) Regulations 2005 (SI 2005/2677), reg.9(3) (April 6, 2006).

16. Social Security (Miscellaneous Amendments) (No.2) Regulations 2006 (SI 2006/832), reg.5(2) (April 10, 2006).

17. Social Security (Miscellaneous Amendments) (No.4) Regulations 2007 (SI 2007/2470), reg.3(2) to (5) (September 24, 2007).

18. Social Security (National Insurance Credits) Amendment Regulations 2007 (SI 2007/2582), reg.3 (October 1, 2007).

19. Employment and Support Allowance (Consequential Provisions) (No. 2) Regulations 2008 (SI 2008/1554), regs 29 and 31 (July 27, 2008).

20. Social Security (Miscellaneous Amendments) (No. 5) Regulations 2008 (SI 2008/2667), reg.3(1) and (2) (October 30, 2008).

21. Tribunals, Courts and Enforcement Act 2007 (Transitional and Consequential Provisions) Order 2008 (SI 2008/2683) Sch.1., paras 95 and 98 (November 3, 2008).

22. Social Security (Additional Class 3 National Insurance Contributions) Amendment Regulations 2009 (SI 2009/659), reg.2 (April 6, 2009).

DEFINITIONS

"the Administration Act"—see s.84 of the Social Security Act 1998.　　　　**2.309**
"appeal"—see reg.1(3).
"appropriate office"—see para.(11).
"the Board"—see reg.1(3).
"claimant"—*ibid.*
"the Claims and Payments Regulations"—*ibid.*
"the Contributions and Benefits Act"—see s.84 of the Social Security Act 1998.
"contributory employment and support allowance"—see reg.1(3).
"the date of notification"—*ibid.*
"the Deferral of Retirement Pensions etc. Regulations"—*ibid.*
"designated authority"—*ibid.*
"disability benefit decision"—see reg.7A(1).
"disability determination"—*ibid.*
"employment and support allowance decision"—*ibid.*
"the Employment and Support Allowance Regulations"—see reg.1(3).
"family"—*ibid.*
"the Graduated Retirement Benefit Regulations"—*ibid.*

"incapacity benefit decision"—see reg.7A(1).
"incapacity determination"—*ibid.*
"income-related employment and support allowance"—see reg.1(3).
"the Jobseekers Act"—see s.84 of the Social Security Act 1998.
"the Jobseeker's Allowance Regulations"—see reg.1(3).
"limited capability for work determination"—see reg.7A(1).
"official error"—*See reg.1(3).*
"original decision"—see para.(1).
"payee"—see reg.7A(1).
"relevant benefit"—see s.39(1) of the Social Security Act 1998.
"tax credit"—see reg.1(3).
"tax year"–see para.(ZC).
"work-focused interview"—see reg.1(3).

GENERAL NOTE

2.310   This regulation provides for the circumstances in which a decision may be revised under s.9 of the Social Security Act 1998, whereas reg.6 provides for the circumstances in which a decision may be superseded under s.10. There are three main distinctions between revision and supersession. Firstly, only decisions of the Secretary of State may be revised, whereas not only decisions of the Secretary of State but also decisions of tribunals may be superseded. Secondly, revisions have effect from the date from which the decision being revised was effective (see s.9(3) of the Social Security Act 1998) unless a mistake was made in respect of that date, in which case the correct date is used (reg.5). Supersessions are usually effective from a later date (s.10(5) or reg.7). Thirdly, there is no right of appeal to a tribunal against a decision to revise or not to revise, whereas there is a right of appeal under s.12 against a decision to supersede or not to supersede. Instead, a decision to revise and, in limited circumstances, a decision not to revise, extends the time for appealing against the decision that has been revised (see s.9(5) of the 1998 Act and para.(c) in the second column of the first row of the table in Sch.1 to the Tribunal Procedure (First-tier Tribunal) (Social Entitlement Chamber) Rules 2008).

2.311   The first and third of these distinctions give rise to considerable problems where there is an appeal to a tribunal and the tribunal considers that a decision expressed as a revision should have been expressed as a supersession or vice versa. These problems were explored by a Tribunal of Commissioners in *R(IB)2/04* and *R(IS)15/04* (see the annotations to s.12 of the 1998 Act and para.(c) in the second column of the first row of the table in Sch.1 to the Tribunal Procedure (First-tier Tribunal) (Social Entitlement Chamber) Rules 2008). It is arguable that many of the problems are caused by the wide scope of reg.3, which appears to be based on the premise that if it is intended that a new decision should take place from the same date as the decision that is being reconsidered, the new decision must be expressed as a revision rather than a supersession. That approach is unnecessary, as appears to be accepted where it is desired that a new decision given on reconsideration of a decision of a tribunal should take effect from the same date as the original decision, because provision can be made by regulations under s.10(6) for a supersession to take effect from the same date as the decision that has been superseded (see reg.7(5)). If the grounds for revision contained in paras (4) and (5) to (8C) were instead grounds for supersession, many of the problems identified by the Tribunal of Commissioners would be removed. That would leave revision available only for cases where a decision is looked at again within a month or so of its being made or pending an appeal. It is only in those circumstances that the first and third of the distinctions drawn above suggest that revision is more appropriate than supersession.

In addition to the circumstances outlined in this regulation, decisions in respect of advance claims may be revised under regs 13(2), 13A(3) and 13C(3) of the Social Security (Claims and Payments) Regulations 1987 (*R(IB)2/04* at paras 106 and 107). A further power to revise is conferred by s.25(4) of the Social Security Act

1998 in respect of decisions made while a test case is pending before the Upper Tribunal or court.

Paras (1)–(3)

These allow a decision to be put right "on any ground" where the claimant applies for a revision within one month of the original decision being notified (but note the extension of time permitted where there has been a correction or request for reasons (see para.(1)(b)) or under para.(3)(b) in the case of a social fund payment or under reg.4). They also allow revision where the Secretary of State notices the error within that time. Note that the time for appealing against the original decision runs from the date the decision is revised *or is not revised* following an application under these paragraphs (s.9(5) of the Social Security Act 1998 and para.(c) in the second column of the first row of the table in Sch.1 to the Tribunal Procedure (First-tier Tribunal) (Social Entitlement Chamber) Rules 2008), so that a claimant is not prejudiced by seeking a revision before appealing.

A decision may now be revised under para.(4A) at any time while an appeal is pending against it. This makes it possible to avoid a tribunal hearing altogether where the Secretary of State is prepared to concede the case in its entirety.

2.312

Para.(4A)

This allows the Secretary of State to revise any decision while an appeal is pending in circumstances where it has not been, or could not be, revised under para.(1) or (3). The effect is that the appeal lapses under s.9(6) unless the revised decision is no more advantageous to the appellant than the decision that has been revised (see reg.30).

2.313

Para.(5)

Normally, a decision based on a mistake of law or fact made by the Secretary of State can only be superseded under reg.6(2)(b) unless the error is detected in time to allow revision under paras (1)–(3). Supersession will be effective only from the date the application was made (see s.10(5) of the Social Security Act 1998)'. Paragraph (5) provides for such a decision to be revised rather than superseded where either there has been an official error or else there has been an overpayment (which might be recoverable under s.71 of the Social Security Administration Act 1992) due to a mistake of fact). In effect, the time limit is removed because revisions generally take effect from the same date as the original decision (see s.9(3) of the Social Security Act 1998).

"Official error" is defined in reg.1. In *R(IS)15/04* (subsequently approved by the Court of Appeal in *Beltekian v Westminster CC* [2004] EWCA Civ 1784 (reported as *R(H)8/05*)), the Tribunal of Commissioners noted that a claimant might wish to assert that there were grounds for revision for "official error", whereas a claimant would not wish to rely on para.(5)(b) or (c). Consequently, a claimant might wish to challenge a refusal to revise under para.(5)(a) but, due to the limitations of what is now para.(c) in the second column of the first row of the table in Sch.1 to the Tribunal Procedure (First-tier Tribunal) (Social Entitlement Chamber) Rules 2008, might be unable to do so save by way of an application for judicial review. The burden of proving that there was an "official error" lies on the claimant where it is he who is applying for revision, but it is for the Secretary of State to produce evidence of the supersession or revision that is in issue before the tribunal (*CH/3439/2004*).

Note that para.(5)(c) protects claimants of disability benefits or incapacity benefits from the full rigour of para.(b) in most cases and effectively prevents there from being a recoverable overpayment where a claimant could not reasonably have known a fact of which the Secretary of State was ignorant, or as to which he made a mistake, or could not reasonably have known that it was relevant. It does not protect the claimant who reasonably did not know that the Secretary of State was ignorant of, or had made a mistake as to, an obviously relevant fact of which he was

2.314

aware, but that is presumably because in such cases any overpayment is unlikely to be recoverable anyway due to the lack of any misrepresentation or failure to disclose a material fact. More importantly, para.(5)(d) limits the effect of para.(5)(c) so that, where the ignorance or mistake relates to an issue other than the extent of the claimant's incapacity or disability, the general rule in para.(5)(b) applies.

Paras (5ZA) to (5ZC)

2.315 The amendment to para.(5)(a) and the insertion of paras (5ZA) to (5ZC) make it unnecessary to revise decisions awarding the benefits listed in para.(5ZB) made as a result of errors in claimants' favour in transposing information on the Department for Work and Pensions' computer system to Her Majesty's Revenue and Customs computer system. The claimants continue to receive the benefits.

Para. (5A)

2.316 This enables the Secretary of State to apply a tribunal's decision to any decision made while the appeal was pending, thus making it unnecessary for the claimant to appeal against the further decisions. The paragraph was required because, since the Social Security Act 1998 came into force, it has not been possible to refer to the tribunal questions arising while an appeal is pending or simply not to determine the questions on the basis that the tribunal could deal with all issues down to the date of decision. Although the Tribunal of Commissioners in *R(IS)15/04*, considered that para.(5)(a) was the only part of reg.3, other than paras. (1) to (3) upon which a claimant might wish to rely, it was suggested in *CDLA/3323/2003* that para.(5A) is another provision. The Commissioner held that he was not precluded by "decision B" from making a decision on an appeal from "decision C" that covered the same period as "decision B", in case the Secretary of State declined to revise "decision B" and the claimant was left without any remedy because the time for appealing had expired. He held that "decision B" lapsed in the light of his new award.

Para. (5B)

2.317 Regulation 28 of the Social Security (Incapacity for Work) (General) Regulations 1995 provides that a person is to be deemed to satisfy the personal capability assessment before the assessment is carried out if a medical certificate is provided and he or she has not failed a personal capability assessment in the last six months (subject to certain exceptions). In *R(IB) 1/01*, it was held that, where those conditions are not satisfied, the claimant is still entitled to benefit in respect of the claim if he or she subsequently passes the personal capability assessment and, in *R(IB) 8/04*, it was held that a new claim is not necessary once the six months have elapsed. Paragraph (5B) enables the Secretary of State to revise a decision awarding benefit from a date later than the date of claim (presumably because the claimant had failed a personal capability assessment less than six months before the date of claim but six months before the date from which the award was made) if the claimant subsequently satisfies the personal capability assessment.

Para. (6)

2.318 In *CJSA/2375/2000*, the claimant was twice disqualified for failing to attend training courses. The second disqualification was for four weeks because there had been the previous disqualification. An appeal against the first disqualification was allowed by a tribunal. The Commissioner, hearing an appeal against a decision by a tribunal dismissing an appeal against the second disqualification said that the Secretary of State should have revised the second disqualification under para.(6) following the first tribunal's decision, in order to reduce the period to two weeks.

Para. (7)

2.319 There are many instances where an award of benefit affects entitlement to another benefit awarded earlier. If the second award is made in respect of a period which includes the date from which a decision in respect of the first benefit took effect, that earlier decision is revised under this paragraph. If entitlement under the second award arises only after that date, the earlier decision is superseded under reg.6(2)(e) instead. Note that the earlier decision must have resulted in an "award" of benefit. It is suggested that that does not include a refusal of benefit, because the same term is used in sub-para.(b) in relation to the second decision and it is fairly clear that only an increase in entitlement under the second decision, and not a decrease in entitlement, gives rise to a revision under this paragraph. Where a decision in respect of one benefit is affected by a decision in respect of another benefit that is *less* favourable to a claimant, neither this paragraph nor reg.6(2)(e) applies and any consequent revision or supersession must be made under some other provision.

Para.(7ZA)

This enables an award of income support, employment and support allowance or state pension credit to be revised in circumstances where the award was made while a non-dependant was awaiting determination of a claim for benefit and, as a result of a favourable decision on the non-dependant's claim, the first claimant becomes entitled to a severe disability premium.   **2.320**

Para.(7A)

This enables a decision as to entitlement to reduced earnings allowance to be revised in favour of the claimant following a favourable revision of, or a successful appeal against, a decision in respect of disablement benefit.   **2.321**

Paras (7B) and (7C)

Decisions about capacity for work are, in practice, always made in the context of entitlement to incapacity benefit or credits. A person who has been entitled to income support on the ground of incapacity for work and is then found not to be incapable of work for the purposes of incapacity benefit or credits is likely to have the award of income support terminated but, if he or she appeals against the incapacity determination, a fresh award of income support will be made at a reduced rate until the appeal is determined. These paragraphs have the effect that, if the appeal is successful or lapses because the incapacity determination is revised, the income support decisions may be revised. Paragraph (7F) has the same effect in a case where a claimant in receipt of income support has been found not to be incapable of work but remains entitled to income support on other grounds (e.g. being a single parent) at a lower rate due to the loss of the disability premium.   **2.322**

Paras (7D) and (7E)

Where entitlement to certain pensions has been deferred, the claimant may elect to have either an increase in the pension or a lump sum. These paragraphs enable awards of state pension credit and the relevant pensions to be revised following a change in such an election.   **2.323**

Para.(7F)

See the note to paras (7B) and (7C).   **2.324**

Para.(8)

See the note to reg.6(2)(d).   **2.325**

Paras (8A) and (8B)

These paragraphs enable a decision based upon a determination of a court to be revised if the determination of the court is quashed or set aside.   **2.326**

Paras (8C) and (8D)

These paragraphs enable a decision to be revised if it is subsequently determined that a late or unpaid national insurance contribution is to be treated as having been   **2.327** paid from a date on or before the date on which the original decision was made. See regs. 6(2)(s) and 7(8A), which enable a decision to be superseded with effect from the date on which a late or unpaid contribution is treated as paid if that is later than the date of the original decision.

Para. (9)

2.328   On an appeal against a decision as revised, it is not possible for the appeal tribunal to have regard to any change of circumstances arising between the date of the original decision and the date of revision (*R(CS) 1/03*).

Para. (10)

2.329   An application for supersession may be treated as an application for revision. Regulation 6(5) provides that an application for revision may be treated as an application for supersession.

For the powers of the First-tier Tribunal to treat a revision as a refusal to supersede and vice versa, see the note to s.12 of the Social Security Act 1998.

2.330   **3A.** *Omitted*

Late application for a revision

2.331   **4.**—(1) The time limit for making an application for a revision specified in regulation 3(1) or (3) [² or 3A(1)(a)] may be extended where the conditions specified in the following provisions of this regulation are satisfied.

(2) An application for an extension of time shall be made by [² the relevant person,] the claimant or a person acting on his behalf.

(3) An application shall—

(a) contain particulars of the grounds on which the extension of time is sought and shall contain sufficient details of the decision which it is sought to have revised to enable that decision to be identified; and

(b) be made within 13 months of the date of notification of the decision which it is sought to have revised [³, but if the applicant has requested a statement of the reasons in accordance with regulation 28(1)(b) the 13 month period shall be extended by—

(i) if the statement is provided within one month of the notification, an additional 14 days; or

(ii) if it is provided after the elapse of a period after the one month ends, the length of that period and an additional 14 days.]

(4) An application for an extension of time shall not be granted unless the applicant satisfies the Secretary of State [¹ or the Board or an officer of the Board] that—

(a) it is reasonable to grant the application;

(b) the application for revision has merit; and

(c) special circumstances are relevant to the application and as a result of those special circumstances it was not practicable for the application to be made within the time limit specified in regulation 3 [² or 3A].

(5) In determining whether it is reasonable to grant an application, the Secretary of State [¹ or the Board or an officer of the Board] shall have regard to the principle that the greater the amount of time that has elapsed between the expiration of the time specified in regulation 3(1) and (3) [² and regulation 3A(1)(a)] for applying for a revision and the making of the application for an extension of time, the more compelling should be the special circumstances on which the application is based.

(6) In determining whether it is reasonable to grant the application for an extension of time, no account shall be taken of the following—

(a) that the applicant or any person acting for him was unaware of or misunderstood the law applicable to his case (including ignorance or misunderstanding of the time limits imposed by these Regulations); or

(b) that [⁴ the Upper Tribunal] or a court has taken a different view of the law from that previously understood and applied.

(7) An application under this regulation for an extension of time which has been refused may not be renewed.

AMENDMENTS

1. Tax Credits (Decisions and Appeals) (Amendment) Regulations 1999 (SI 1999/2570), reg.7 (October 5, 1999). Note that amendments made by these regulations only have effect with respect to tax credit (reg.1(2) of the Amendment Regulations).

2. Child Support (Decisions and Appeals) (Amendment) Regulations 2000 (SI 2000/3185), reg.6 (various dates as provided by reg.1(1)).

3. Social Security, Child Support and Tax Credits (Miscellaneous Amendments) Regulations 2005 (SI 2005/337), reg.2(3) (March 18, 2005).

4. Tribunals, Courts and Enforcement Act 2007 (Transitional and Consequential Provisions) Order 2008 (SI 2008/2683), Sch.1, paras 95 and 100 (November 3, 2008).

DEFINITIONS

"the Board"—see reg.1(3).   2.332
"claimant"—*ibid.*
"the date of notification"—see reg.1(3).
"relevant person"—*ibid.*

GENERAL NOTE

Para.(1)
It was held in *R(TC)1/05* that a tribunal did not have jurisdiction to consider   2.333
whether the Inland Revenue ought, under reg.4, to have extended the time for
applying for revision. In that case, the relevant decision was made on April 22,
2002, the claimant sought reconsideration on November 11, 2002 and the Inland
Revenue refused to extend the time for applying for revision and therefore refused
to revise the decision on November 25, 2002. The claimant appealed. There is no
right of appeal against a revision or refusal to revise and so the appeal had to be
treated as an appeal against the decision of April 22, 2002. The time for appealing
against a decision is not extended under reg.31 when the application for revision
is made late and time is not extended under reg.4. In those circumstances (and
subject to the possibility that the decision of April 22, 2002 had not been sent
to the claimant), the appeal should have been treated as having been late and
therefore invalid, unless the tribunal extended the time for appealing. On the facts
of *R(TC)1/05*, it made no difference whether the time for applying for revision
was extended under reg.4 or whether the time for appealing was extended under
reg.31, but the Commissioner pointed out that the test for extending the time for
applying for revision is now different from that for extending the time for appealing. He also pointed out that the thirteen-month absolute time limit for appeals
now to be found in r.23(5) of the Tribunal Procedure (First-tier Tribunal) (Social
Entitlement Chamber) Rules 2008 means that in some cases an appeal could be
valid only if the time for applying for revision had been extended. It seems regret-
table that a tribunal should not have the power to determine whether the Secretary
of State ought to have extended time under reg.4, especially as the exercise the
Secretary of State is required to perform is not all that simple and a considerable
amount of money may turn on it.

Para. (6) (b)

2.334   See the note to reg.32(8)(b) which is in similar terms.

Date from which a decision revised under section 9 takes effect

2.335   **5.**—[² (1)] Where, on a revision under section 9, the Secretary of State [¹ or the Board or an officer of the Board] decides that the date from which the decision under section 8 or 10 ("the original decision") took effect was erroneous, the decision under section 9 shall take effect on the date from which the original decision would have taken effect had the error not been made.

[² (2) Where—

(a) a person attains pensionable age, claims a retirement pension after the prescribed time for claiming and the Secretary of State decides ("the original decision") that he is not entitled because—

  (i) in the case of a Category A retirement pension, the person has not satisfied the contribution conditions; or

  (ii) in the case of a Category B retirement pension, the person's spouse [³ or civil partner] has not satisfied the contribution conditions;

(b) in accordance with regulation 50A of the Social Security (Contributions) Regulations 2001 (Class 3 contributions: tax years 1996–97 to 2001–02) the Board subsequently accepts Class 3 contributions paid after the due date by the claimant or, as the case may be, the spouse [³ or civil partner];

(c) in accordance with regulation 6A of the Social Security (Crediting and Treatment of Contributions, and National Insurance Numbers) Regulations 2001 the contributions are treated as paid on a date earlier than the date on which they were paid; and

(d) the Secretary of State revises the original decision in accordance with regulation 11A(4)(a),

the revised decision shall take effect from—

  (i) 1st October 1998; or

  (ii) the date on which the claimant attained pensionable age in the case of a Category A pension, or, in the case of a Category B pension, the date on which the claimant's spouse [³ or civil partner] attained pensionable age,

whichever is later."

AMENDMENTS

1. Tax Credits (Decisions and Appeals) (Amendment) Regulations 1999 (SI 1999/2570), reg.8 (October 5, 1999). Note that amendments made by these regulations only have effect with respect to tax credit (reg.1(2) of the Amendment Regulations).

2. Social Security (Retirement Pensions) Amendment Regulations 2004 (SI 2004/2283), reg.3 (September 27, 2004).

3. Civil Partnership (Consequential Amendments) Regulations 2005 (SI 2005/2878), reg.8(3) (December 5, 2005).

DEFINITION

"the Board"—see reg.1(3).

GENERAL NOTE

2.336   These paragraphs provide the exceptions to the general rule in s.9(3) of the Social Security Act 1998 that a revision takes effect from the same date as the original decision that has been revised.

Para. (1) deals with the obvious case where the effective date of the original decision was wrong.

Para. (2) is linked to reg.6(31) and (32) of the Social Security (Claims and Payments) Regulations 1987 and deals with a problem caused by the failure from 1996 to 2003 to inform contributors of deficiencies in their contribution records so that they could pay voluntary Class 3 contributions to make up the deficit. By regulation 50A of the Social Security (Contributions) Regulations 2001, claimants are being allowed to pay their contributions very late. Regulation 6(31) of the 1987 Regulations enables a late claim based on those contributions to be made and this amendment allows an earlier decision disallowing a claim to be revised with effect from October 1, 1998 or the date the claimant or, where appropriate, the claimant's spouse [or civil partner] reached pensionable age. Without these amendments, the new claim or the revision might be effective from a much later date and that might be unfair because, having discovered about the deficiency, the claimant might have delayed claiming on what was then a correct understanding that there was nothing that could be done about it.

5A. *Omitted*

2.337

CHAPTER II

SUPERSESSIONS

Supersession of decisions

6.—(1) Subject to the following provisions of this regulation, for the purposes of section 10, the cases and circumstances in which a decision may be superseded under that section are set out in paragraphs (2) to (4).

2.338

(2) A decision under section 10 may be made on the Secretary of State's [² or the Board's] own initiative or on an application made for the purpose on the basis that the decision to be superseded—

(a) is one in respect of which—

  (i) there has been a relevant change of circumstances since the decision [¹¹ had effect [¹⁵ or, in the case of an advance award under regulation 13, 13A or 13C of the Claims and Payments Regulations [¹⁷ or regulation 146 of the Employment and Support Allowance Regulations], since the decision was made]; or

  (ii) it is anticipated that a relevant change of circumstances will occur;

(b) is a decision of the Secretary of State [² or the Board or an officer of the Board] other than a decision to which sub-paragraph (d) refers and—

  (i) the decision was erroneous in point of law, or it was made in ignorance of, or was based upon a mistake as to, some material fact; and

  (ii) an application for a supersession was received by the Secretary of State [² or the Board], or the decision by the Secretary of State [² or the Board] to act on his [² or their] own initiative was taken, more than one month after the date of notification of the decision which is to be superseded or after the expiry of such longer period of time as may have been allowed under regulation 4;

[¹¹ (c) is a decision of [¹⁹ the First-tier Tribunal or of the Upper Tribunal" for "an appeal tribunal or of a Commissioner]—

    (i) that was made in ignorance of, or was based upon a mistake as to, some material fact; or

    (ii) that was made in accordance with section 26(4)(b), in a case where section 26(5) applies;]

  (d) is a decision which is specified in Schedule 2 to the Act or is prescribed in regulation 27 (decisions against which no appeal lies); [¹¹ . . .]

[⁵ (e) is a decision where—

    (i) the claimant has been awarded entitlement to a relevant benefit; and

    (ii) [⁹ subsequent to the first day of the period to which that entitlement relates], the claimant or a member of his family becomes entitled to [⁹ . . .] another relevant benefit or an increase in the rate of another relevant benefit;]

[¹⁵ (ee) is an original award within the meaning of regulation 3(7ZA) and sub-paragraphs (a) to (c) and (d)(ii) of regulation 3(7ZA) apply but not sub-paragraph (d)(i);]

[³ (f) is a decision that a jobseeker's allowance is payable to a claimant where that allowance ceases to be payable by virtue of section 19(1) of the Jobseekers Act [⁶ or ceases to be payable or is reduced by virtue of section 20A(5) of that Act];]

[¹ (g) is an incapacity benefit decision where there has been an incapacity determination (whether before or after the decision) and where, since the decision was made, the Secretary of State has received medical evidence following an examination in accordance with regulation 8 of the Social Security (Incapacity for Work) (General) Regulations 1995 from a [¹⁸ health care professional] referred to in paragraph (1) of that regulation;] [⁴ [¹¹ . . .]

  (h) is one in respect of a person who—

    (i) is subsequently the subject of a separate decision or determination as to whether or not he took part in a work-focused interview;

    (ii) had been held not to have taken part in a work-focused interview but who had, subsequent to the decision to be superseded, attained the age of 60 or ceased to reside in an area in which there is a requirement to take part in a work-focused interview [¹³ or, in the case of a partner who was required to take part in a work-focused interview [¹⁴ in accordance with regulations made under section 2AA of the Administration Act, ceased to be a partner for the purposes of those regulations or is no longer a partner to whom the requirement to take part in a work-focused interview under those regulations applies];]

[⁷ (i) is a decision of the Secretary of State that a jobseeker's allowance [¹⁷ or regulation 146 of the Employment and Support Allowance Regulations] is payable to a claimant where the Secretary of State is notified that a court has made a determination which results in a restriction being imposed pursuant to section 62 or 63 of the Child Support, Pensions and Social Security Act 2000;]

[8 (j) is a decision of the Secretary of State that a sanctionable benefit is payable to a claimant where that benefit ceases to be payable or falls to be reduced under section 7 or 9 of the Social Security Fraud Act 2001 and for this purpose "sanctionable benefit" has the same meaning as in section 7 of that Act;

(k) is a decision of the Secretary of State that a joint-claim jobseeker's allowance is payable where that allowance ceases to be payable or falls to be reduced under section 8 of the Social Security Fraud Act 2001;]

[10 (l) is a relevant decision for the purposes of section 6 of the State Pension Credit Act and—

(i) on making that decision, the Secretary of State specified a period as the assessed income period; and

(ii) that period has ended or is about to end;]

[12 (m) is a relevant decision for the purposes of section 6 of the State Pension Credit Act in a case where—

(i) the information and evidence required under regulation 32(6) (a) of the Claims and Payments Regulations has not been provided in accordance with the time limits set out in regulation 32(6)(c) of those Regulations;

(ii) the Secretary of State was prevented from specifying a new assessed income period under regulation 10(1) of the State Pension Credit Regulations; and

(iii) the information and evidence required under regulation 32(6) (a) of the Claims and Payments Regulations has since been provided;]

[15 (n) is a decision by [19 the First-tier Tribunal] confirming a decision by the Secretary of State terminating a claimant's entitlement to income support because he no longer falls within the category of person specified in paragraph 7 of Schedule 1B to the Income Support Regulations (persons incapable of work) and a further [19 decision of the First-tier Tribunal] subsequently determines that he is incapable of work;]

[16 (o) is a decision that a person is entitled to state pension credit and—

(i) the person or his partner makes, or is treated as having made, an election for a lump sum in accordance with—

(aa) paragraph A1 or 3C of Schedule 5 to the Contributions and Benefits Act;

(bb) paragraph 1 of Schedule 5A to that Act; or, as the case may be,

(cc) paragraph 12 or 17 of Schedule 1 to the Graduated Retirement Benefit Regulations;

or

(ii) such a lump sum is repaid in consequence of an application to change an election for a lump sum in accordance with regulation 5 of the Deferral of Retirement Pensions etc. Regulations or, as the case may be, paragraph 20D of Schedule 1 to the Graduated Retirement Benefit Regulations;]

[17 (p) is a decision awarding employment and support allowance where there has been a failure determination;

(q) is a decision made in consequence of a failure determination where the reduction ceases to have effect under of regulation 64 of the Employment and Support Allowance Regulations;

(r) is an employment and support allowance decision where, since the decision was made, the Secretary of State has received medical evidence from a health care professional approved by the Secretary of State for the purposes of regulation 23 or 38 of the Employment and Support Allowance Regulations.]

[18 (s) is a decision where on or after the date on which the decision was made, a late or unpaid contribution is treated as paid under—

    (i) regulation 5 of the Social Security (Crediting and Treatment of Contributions and National Insurance Numbers) Regulations 2001 (treatment of late paid contributions where no consent, connivance or negligence by the primary contributor) on a date which falls on or before the date on which the original decision was made;

    (ii) regulation 6 of those Regulations (treatment of contributions paid late through ignorance or error) on a date which falls on or before the date on which the original decision was made; or

    (iii) regulation 60 of the Social Security (Contributions) Regulations 2001 (treatment of unpaid contributions where no consent, connivance or negligence by the primary contributor) on a date which falls on or before the date on which the original decision was made.]

(3) A decision which may be revised under regulation 3 may not be superseded under this regulation except where—

    (a) circumstances arise in which the Secretary of State [2 or the Board or an officer of the Board] may revise that decision under regulation 3; and

    (b) further circumstances arise in relation to that decision which are not specified in regulation 3 but are specified in paragraph (2) or (4).

(4) Where the Secretary of State requires [2 or the Board require] further evidence or information from the applicant in order to consider all the issues raised by an application under paragraph (2) ("the original application"), he [2 or they] shall notify the applicant that further evidence or information is required and the decision may be superseded—

    (a) where the applicant provides further relevant evidence or information within one month of the date of notification or such longer period of time as the Secretary of State [2 or the Board] may allow; or

    (b) where the applicant does not provide such evidence or information within the time allowed under sub-paragraph (a), on the basis of the original application.

(5) The Secretary of State [2 or the Board] may treat an application for a revision or a notification of a change of circumstances as an application for a supersession.

(6) The following events are not relevant changes of circumstances for the purposes of paragraph (2)—

    (a) the repayment of a loan to which regulation 66A of the Income Support Regulations or regulation 136 of the Jobseeker's Allowance Regulations applies; [17 , regulation 137 of the Employment and Support Allowance Regulations]

    (b) [15 . . .]

[3 (c) the fact that a person has become terminally ill, within the meaning of section 66(2)(a) of the Contributions and Benefits Act, unless an

application for supersession which contains an express statement that the person is terminally ill is made either by—
   (i) the person himself; or
   (ii) any other person purporting to act on his behalf whether or not that other person is acting with his knowledge or authority;
and where such an application is received a decision may be so superseded notwithstanding that no claim under section 66(1) or, as the case may be, 72(5) or 73(12) of that Act has been made.]

(7) In paragraph (6)(b), "nursing home" and "residential care home" have the same meanings as they have in regulation 19 of the Income Support Regulations.

[[10] (8) In relation to the assessed income period, the only change of circumstances relevant for the purposes of paragraph (2)(a) is that the assessed income period ends in accordance with section 9(4) of the State Credit Pension Act or the regulations made under section 9(5) of that Act.]

AMENDMENTS

1. Social Security and Child Support (Decisions and Appeals) Amendment (No.2) Regulations 1999 (SI 1999/1623), reg.2 (July 5, 1999).

2. Tax Credits (Decisions and Appeals) (Amendment) Regulations 1999 (SI 1999/2570), reg.9 (October 5, 1999). Note that amendments made by these regulations only have effect with respect to tax credit (reg.1(2) of the Amendment Regulations).

3. Social Security and Child Support (Decisions and Appeals), Vaccine Damage Payments and Jobseeker's Allowance (Amendment) Regulations 1999 (SI 1999/2677), reg.7 (October 18, 1999).

4. Social Security (Work-focused Interviews) Regulations 2000 (SI 2000/897), reg.16(5) and Sch.6, para.4 (April 3, 2000).

5. Social Security and Child Support (Miscellaneous Amendments) Regulations 2000 (SI 2000/1596), reg.16 (June 19, 2000).

6. Social Security (Joint Claims: Consequential Amendments) Regulations 2000 (SI 2000/1982), reg.5(b) (March 19, 2001).

7. Social Security (Breach of Community Order) (Consequential Amendments) Regulations 2001 (SI 2001/1711), reg.2(2)(c) (October 15, 2001).

8. Social Security (Loss of Benefit) (Consequential Amendments) Regulations 2002 (SI 2002/490), reg.8(b) (April 1, 2002).

9. Social Security (Claims and Payments and Miscellaneous Amendments) Regulations 2002 (SI 2002/428), reg.4(3) (April 2, 2002).

10. State Pension Credit (Consequential, Transitional and Miscellaneous Provisions) Regulations 2002 (SI 2002/3019), reg.17 (April 7, 2003).

11. Social Security and Child Support (Miscellaneous Amendments) Regulations 2003 (SI 2003/1050), reg.3(3) (May 5, 2003).

12. State Pension Credit (Transitional and Miscellaneous Provisions) Amendment Regulations 2003 (SI 2003/2274), reg.5(2) (October 6, 2003).

13. Social Security (Jobcentre Plus Interviews for Partners) Regulations 2003 (SI 2003/1886), reg.15(4) (April 12, 2004).

14. Social Security (Working Neighbourhoods) Regulations 2004 (SI 2004/959), reg.24(3) (April 26, 2004).

15. Social Security, Child Support and Tax Credits (Miscellaneous Amendments) Regulations 2005 (SI 2005/337), reg.2(4) (March 18, 2005).

16. Social Security (Deferral of Retirement Pensions, Shared Additional Pension and Graduated Retirement Benefit) (Miscellaneous Provisions) Regulations 2005 (SI 2005/2677), reg.9(4) (April 6, 2006).

17. Employment and Support Allowance (Consequential Provisions) (No. 2) Regulations 2008 (SI 2008/1554), regs 29 and 32 (July 27, 2008).

18. Social Security (Miscellaneous Amendments) (No. 5) Regulations 2008 (SI 2008/2667), reg.3(1) and (3) (October 30, 2008).

19. Tribunals, Courts and Enforcement Act 2007 (Transitional and Consequential Provisions) Order 2008 (SI 2008/2683), Sch.1, paras 95 and 101 (November 3, 2008).

DEFINITIONS

"the Act"—see reg.1(3).
"assessed income period"—*ibid.*
"the Board"—*ibid.*
"claimant"—*ibid.*
"the Contributions and Benefits Act"—see s.84 of the Social Security Act 1998.
"the date of notification"—see reg.1(3).
"the Deferral of Retirement Pensions etc. Regulations"—*ibid.*
"employment and support allowance decision"—see reg.7A(1).
"the Employment and Support Allowance Regulations"—see reg.1(3).
"failure determination"—*ibid.*
"family"—*ibid.*
"the Graduated Retirement Benefit Regulations"—*ibid.*
"health care professional"—see s.39(2) of the Social Security Act 1998.
"incapacity benefit decision"—see reg.7A(1).
"incapacity determination"—*ibid.*
"the Income Support Regulations"—see reg.1(3).
"the Jobseekers Act"—see s.84 of the Social Security Act 1998.
"the Jobseeker's Allowance Regulations"—see reg.1(3).
"a joint-claim jobseeker's allowance"—*ibid.*
"nursing home"—see para.(7).
"payee"—see reg.7A(1).
"relevant benefit"—see s.39(1) of the Social Security Act 1998.
"residential care home"—see para.(7).
"State Pension Credit Act"—see reg.1(3).
"work-focused interview"—*ibid.*

GENERAL NOTE

Para. (1)

2.339   This regulation is made under s.10(3) of the Social Security Act 1998.

In *Wood v Secretary of State for Work and Pensions* [2003] EWCA Civ 53 (reported as *R(DLA) 1/03*), the Court of Appeal overruled *R(DLA) 6/02* and held that a decision may be superseded only if one of the conditions in paras (2)–(4) is satisfied. If a claimant has applied for supersession and the conditions are not met, the Secretary of State must refuse to supersede. That is the natural meaning of the provisions but the Tribunal of Commissioners deciding *R(DLA) 6/02* had thought it necessary to give a strained construction to reg.6 because they understood s.12(9) of the 1998 Act precluded an appeal against a refusal to supersede, which would have been unfair. The majority of the Court of Appeal acknowledged that it was difficult to give both reg.6 and s.12(9) a literal construction but they preferred to give an extended construction to s.12(9), holding that there is an appeal against a refusal to supersede, and to take a more literal approach to reg.6, which certainly makes it easier to apply reg.6.

Where a decision is superseded and then the superseding decision is itself superseded, the body making that third decision must be satisfied that there are grounds for superseding the first decision as well as the second decision if the outcome is to be different from that of the first decision (*R(DLA) 1/06*).

It was held by a Tribunal of Commissioners in *R(IB)2/04*, adopting at para.10(4) a suggestion made by Rix L.J. in *Wood*, that the ground of supersession which is found to exist must form the basis of the supersession in the sense that the original decision can only be altered in a way which follows from that ground. This over-rules *R(A)1/90*, although no reference was made to that decision by the Tribunal of Commissioners.

However, there is still a question whether the use of the word "may" in paras (1) and (2) means that the Secretary of State need not supersede even if he finds that one of the conditions in paras (2) to (4) is satisfied. In *Wood*, Rix L.J. regarded a superseded decision as an altered decision, which might imply that supersession of an award necessarily implied a change in the claimant's entitlement so that there was no scope for supersession without there being a different outcome. Such an approach would be rather different from that taken in the context of reviews under earlier legislation (see the note to para.(2)(a)(i) below). But, now that it has been established that there is a right of appeal against a refusal to supersede, there is no practical difference between a refusal to supersede and a decision to supersede "at the same rate", at least at the time the decision is given. There may be a difference later to the extent that, if there is a later supersession, the nature of an earlier decision may determine which decision must be superseded but, even then, it is difficult to see how the outcome in terms of entitlement to benefit could be affected. It may well be that there are two or more perfectly acceptable legal analyses, each producing the same practical result and any one of which can properly be applied without the decision-maker erring in law.

There may be no practical difference between a refusal to supersede and a supersession "at the same rate" but, in *CIS/6249/1999*, the Commissioner decided that the Secretary of State had a limited discretion to refuse to supersede even where grounds of supersession existed and any supersession would result in a change in entitlement. Although a power may appear discretionary, there is often a duty to exercise it in a particular way in order that the purpose for which the power is given is not frustrated (*Julius v Lord Bishop of Oxford* (1880) L.R. 5 App. Cas. 214) and therefore the Secretary of State is for practical purposes normally bound to supersede a decision if the conditions for supersession are met and would result in a change of entitlement. However, in *CIS/6249/1999*, there was a competing duty not to abuse power by reviewing an award of income support in respect of a period in the past in circumstances where the claimant would have been unfairly prejudiced. The facts of the case illustrate the operation of the principle. The claimant was an asylum seeker entitled to "urgent cases" payments of income support to which he was not entitled if he had any capital in the form of liquid assets. In October 1995, he had been paid almost £900, representing about 11 weeks' arrears of income support, which he paid into a bank. As long as it remained in his bank, that sum should have disentitled him from income support. In October 1996, he told a visiting officer that he still had £787 but benefit continued in payment until 1998, when a decision was made disentitling him from February 25, 1998. In principle, the claimant had not been entitled to income support from October 1995, but there was no question of the overpayment being recoverable as the Benefits Agency had known he had the money in October 1995. On the other hand, deciding that the claimant had not been entitled to income support throughout the period from October 1995 to February 1998 would have prevented the claimant from being paid any benefit in the future because the claimant would have been unable to show he was entitled to benefit immediately before February 5, 1996 and would have been deprived of the transitional protection given to asylum seekers in receipt of benefit at that date. Had benefit been stopped in October 1995, when it should have been, the claimant would undoubtedly have qualified for benefit again before February 5, 1996. The Commissioner considered that reviewing entitlement before February 25, 1998 would have been so unfair as to be an abuse of power. The same approach would presumably be appropriate in respect of supersession.

CIS/6249/1999 was distinguished (and to some extent its correctness was doubted) in *R1/07 (IB)*, where it was held that it was not an abuse of power for a decision to be superseded retrospectively in a case where the claimant had sought advice from the Department for Social Development about working while claiming incapacity benefit but had not been advised that he was required to give notice of any work in writing. The claimant had acted honestly at all times but, as the Commissioner observed, there was no question of the recovery of any overpaid benefit and she considered that any unfairness to the claimant did not outweigh the public interest in ensuring that a correct decision as to entitlement was made. It is not clear from the decision whether the claimant had in fact lost anything to which he would have been entitled had he not received the wrong advice except, presumably, credited contributions during the material period in the past. If a loss of entitlement in the past meant a loss of current entitlement because different contribution years had to be taken into account, that was not recorded. However, the Commissioner did point out that the claimant might have a remedy in the courts if he had suffered any loss.

Although it appears necessary first to determine whether one of the cases in para. (2) applies and then determine what the outcome should be, the two stages need not be kept rigidly apart. In *CDLA/5469/1999*, the Deputy Commissioner pointed out that the fact that a tribunal must, as a first step *in their deliberations*, ask themselves whether there are grounds for supersession does not translate into a rule of practice that the question whether grounds for supersession exist must be treated as a preliminary issue *in the hearing*. In most cases involving ignorance or mistake as to a material fact, he suggests, the tribunal should, after the hearing, first ask itself simply what the facts are that are material to the issue to be decided. Only then should it ask whether the original decision was made in ignorance of any of those facts. If the answer is yes, it can then give its own decision on the basis of the facts found. In *CSDLA/765/2004*, the Commissioner took the opposite approach and suggested that a hearing should initially be restricted to taking evidence relevant to a ground of supersession, but that was not followed in *CSDLA/637/2006*, where the Commissioner said:

> "It is sensible rather that a tribunal hears all the evidence, including what is potentially relevant to current entitlement, but without yet making a final determination with respect to that, in order to compare present circumstances with those which surrounded the original award."

Indeed, it may be a legitimate inference from a finding that the claimant does not satisfy the conditions of entitlement to benefit that an earlier award was based on a mistake of law or fact or that that there has been a change of circumstances so that the earlier award may be superseded (*CDLA/1820/1998*), although that applies only where no reasonable person could find the conditions of entitlement currently to be satisfied. It is then appropriate to presume that the ground of supersession is the one least unfavourable to the claimant (*Cooke v Secretary of State for Social Security* [2001] EWCA Civ 734 (reported as *R(DLA) 6/01*)). In *CSDLA/637/2006*, however, the Commissioner pointed out that drawing such an inference did not imply that an original award made by a tribunal, as opposed to the Secretary of State, could be superseded, because an error of law is not a ground for superseding a tribunal's decision. She rejected the Secretary of State's contention that it should be presumed that the earlier tribunal had not erred in law and she consequently upheld a decision to the effect that grounds for supersession had not been made out.

The Secretary of State may supersede a decision either on an application or on his own initiative. Where he considers a claimant's application for supersession but reduces entitlement rather than increasing it, he must be treated as having superseded the original decision on his own initiative, rather than on the claimant's application (*R(IB)2/04* at para.95). That is necessary to avoid the claimant being unfairly prejudiced in respect of the date from which the decision is effective under s.10(5) of the 1998 Act. For the same reason, where a claimant appeals against a decision made on his or her application for supersession and a tribunal makes a decision that is less favourable to the claimant than the decision that is being superseded, the decision will be effective from the date on which it would have been effective if the Secretary of State had acted on his own initiative *(R(IB)2/04* at para.97). It has been held that if the Secretary of State considers a case on his own motion but decides not to change the award, he is bound nonetheless to issue a decision refusing to revise or supersede the decision, or revising or superseding it "at the same rate" *(CTC/2979/2001)*. However, that was doubted in *CDLA/705/2002* and, in *CI/1547/2001*, it was said that the Secretary of State was nearly always bound to issue a decision on a claimant's application but need not do so when considering a case on his own motion. If a decision is given simply in terms of a new award without supersession being mentioned but in circumstances where the new award could be made only on supersession, the defect can be cured by a tribunal giving the decision in the correct form *(R(IB)2/04* at para.76). However, if the tribunal never discover that the decision should have been a supersession, because they are unaware that there was an award current when the decision was made, the tribunal's decision may well be set aside because it is impossible to infer that circumstances justifying a different outcome on supersession were made out *(CDLA/9/2001)*.

Section 10(3) permits regulations to be made prescribing the procedure by which a supersession may be made, but no regulation has been made prescribing the form of an application and the question whether a letter amounts to an application for supersession does not fall within the exclusive jurisdiction of the Secretary of State. A letter providing information about a change of circumstances will often imply a request for supersession (see para.(5)) but not all letters to the Department carry a clear implication to that effect and it may sometimes be difficult to determine whether, in reconsidering a decision, the Secretary of State is acting on his own initiative or in response to an application. This would not matter were it not for the impact the distinction may have on the date from which the application is effective (see s.10(5) of the Social Security Act 1998). It is doubtful whether giving information to a medical advisor during a medical examination amounts to an application for supersession, even though a notification of a change of circumstances may be treated as an application for supersession under para. (5), but the Secretary of State can made a supersession decision of his own motion when the information is passed to him *(CI/954/2006)*.

A final assessment of disablement made under the legislation replaced by the 1998 Act implies that there was no disablement after the end of the award, and so has ongoing effect and requires supersession as well as a new claim for benefit *(R(I) 5/02)*, whereas an assessment under the 1998 Act carries no such implication and, after it expires, requires just a new claim.

Save in the many instances where reg.7 or Schs 3A to 3C provide otherwise, a supersession is effective from the date on which it was made, if the supersession was made on the Secretary of State's own initiative, or on the date of application when the suppression was made on the application of a claimant or other interested person (s.10(5) of the 1998 Act). In *CI/1547/2001*, it was suggested that all appeals against assessment decisions should also be treated as appeals against the consequent entitlement decisions because the provisions for supersession and revision, are too limited, having regard to the dates from which they are effective, to deal satisfactorily with the consequences of a successful appeal on assessment alone. In *CI/954/2006*, the Commissioner made the same point in respect of an application to supersede an assessment of disablement. He also held that, where a person who had been awarded disablement benefit suffered another industrial accident, a claim for disablement benefit in respect of the second accident might have to be treated in the alternative as an application for supersession of the first award and he pointed out that there is an anomolous difference in the extent to which a claim and an application for supersession can be backdated.

Note that payment of benefit may be suspended under reg.16 while consideration is being given to supserseding an award. In a case where payment of attendance allowance was terminated on supersession, because a local authority was paying care home fees, but the claimant was in dispute with a financial adviser and it was possible that money to pay the fees retrospectively would be forthcoming, payment ought merely to have been suspended (*CA/3800/2006*). It made a difference because, if payments were superseded, it was not possible to reinstate them from the date they were terminated by way of a further supersession.

Even if an award of benefit is a possession within Art.1 of Protocol 1 to the European Convention on Human Rights, its removal under the provisions for supersession is not in breach of the Convention (*CDLA/3908/2001*).

Para. (2)

2.340   There is some degree of overlap between the sub-paras (e.g. (a)(i) and (e)) but this is not of particular significance. It is suggested that where two sub-paras apply, the person applying for, or initiating, the supersession is entitled to have the benefit of the more advantageous of the two as determined under reg.7 or Schs 3A to 3C (which provide numerous exceptions to the general rule under s.10(5) that a supersession is effective from the date it is made or the application for it was made). However, the Secretary of State is often content to have a decision in his favour that is effective only from the date of the decision rather than an earlier date unless the circumstances are such that he wishes the decision to reveal a recoverable overpayment. It is suggested that the assumption apparently made in *TW v SSWP* [2009] UKUT 91 (AAC) to the effect that equivalent provisions of reg.6A (which applies to child support and is therefore omitted from this book) are mutually exclusive is not correct.

Para. (2) (a) (i)

2.341   In *R(I) 56/54*, the Commissioner said: "A relevant change of circumstances postulates that the decision has ceased to be correct". This means that only an award may be superseded on the ground of change of circumstances. A decision that a claimant is not entitled to benefit at all may not be superseded on that ground. Instead, the claimant must make a new claim. *R(I) 56/54* also suggests that a change of circumstances is relevant only if it would result in a different "outcome decision". The same approach was taken in *Wood v Secretary of State for Work and Pensions* [2003] EWCA Civ 53 (reported as *R(DLA) 1/03*) but the Court did not refer to *Saker v Secretary of State for Social Services, The Times*, January 16, 1988 (reported as an appendix to *R(I) 2/88*) in which Nicholls L.J. considered what might amount to a "material" fact for the purposes of a provision similar to para.(2)(b)(i) and said that a fact was material "if it was one which, had it been known to the medical board, would have called for serious consideration by the board and might well have affected its decision". On the other hand, in *CIB/2338/2000*, the Commissioner said that the "subtleties based on the *Saker* decision, under which a change maybe relevant without justifying a different outcome, have no place in the scheme of adjudication under the 1998 Act" and in *CIS/3655/2007*, he effectively held that *Saker* no longer applied because the effect of *Wood* is that reg.6 prescribes "outcome criteria" rather than "threshold criteria". In practical terms there is probably nothing to choose between the *Wood* approach and the *Saker* approach because a refusal to supersede has the same effect as a supersession "at the same rate". In other words, properly applied, either approach produces the same outcome, a point acknowledged in *CIS/3655/2007*.

A new medical opinion is not itself a change of circumstances but a new medical report may reveal not only a new opinion but also new clinical findings which would show a change of circumstances (*R(IS) 2/97* and *Cooke v Secretary of State for Social Security* [2001] EWCA Civ 734 (reported as *R(DLA) 6/01*)). A lessening of care needs is itself a change of circumstances (*R1/05(DLA)*). A change in legislation is a change of circumstances (*R(A) 4/81*) but an unexpected decision of a court (or a Commissioner) is not (*Chief Adjudication Officer v McKiernon*, reported as *R(I)2/94*). Paragraph (6) makes further provision as to matters that are not relevant changes of circumstances. It is suggested that, at least in some contexts, the passage of time may be a material change of circumstances for the purposes of permitting supersession, e.g. the passing of the end of a qualifying period, and that in other cases it may be reasonable to presume there to have been a change of circumstances where time has passed, e.g. in some cases involving mental health factors.

Although reg.6(2)(a)(i) enables the Secretary of State to supersede a decision on the ground that there has been a change of circumstances "since the decision had effect", a Tribunal of Commissioners has suggested that it would be improper for the Secretary of State to supersede on that ground where the decision being superseded was that of a tribunal and, because the change of circumstances occurred before the decision under appeal and the tribunal was well aware of it, the tribunal could have taken it into account notwithstanding section 12(8)(b) of the Social Security Act 1998 but did not do so *(R(IS) 2/08)*. "The Secretary of State should abide by a tribunal's decision in such circumstances." If he considers that the change of circumstances has not properly been taken into account, his remedy is to appeal.

See reg.7(2) for the date from which the supersession is effective.

Para. (2) (a) (ii)

Section 8(2) of the Social Security Act 1998 provides that, when the Secretary of   2.342
State makes a decision on a claim, he is precluded from taking account of circumstances not obtaining at the date of his decision. There is no equivalent provision in s.10 in respect of supersessions and this head expressly permits the Secretary of State to anticipate a change of circumstances. This is obviously a useful provision allowing the Secretary of State to act immediately to make the appropriate adjustment when a claimant informs him that his circumstances are about to change. However, it raises some interesting questions. For instance, what ground of supersession would there be if the anticipated change of circumstances did not take place? Perhaps supersession or revision on the ground of mistake of fact would be appropriate? More problematic is that a tribunal is precluded by s.12(8)(b) from having regard to any change of circumstances not obtaining at the date of the Secretary of State's decision and would therefore apparently be bound to ignore the change of circumstances that the Secretary of State had anticipated, even if the tribunal found that the change of circumstances had occurred. It must presumably be inferred that the passage of time is a change of circumstances for the purpose of reg.6(2)(a) even though it is not for the purpose of s.12(8)(b) *(R(DLA) 4/05)*. Also, the amendment to this head made in respect of advance awards does not apply to an award made on supersession under this very head so that it might be difficult to supersede a decision in the light of an unanticipated change of circumstances occurring between the date of supersession and the date from which the supersession was effective.

Para. (2) (b) and (c)

Paragraph (2)(b)(ii) exists to prevent there from being any overlap between   2.343
supersession under para.(b) and revision under reg.3(1). A decision ought not to be superseded under sub-paras (b) or (c) so as to produce a different outcome if correcting the error of fact does not itself justify a different decision *(R(IB)2/04)*, although, as in cases where para (a)(i) might apply, it would probably make no practical difference in the long run whether a decision was superseded at the same rate or was not superseded at all. Ignorance or mistake must be as to a primary fact and not merely as to an inference or conclusion of fact. Thus, a decision cannot be superseded simply on the ground that the Secretary of State now takes a different view of the case. "He must go further and assert and prove that the inference might not have been drawn, if the determining authority had not been ignorant of some specific fact of which it could have been aware, or had not been mistaken as to some specific fact which it took into consideration" *(R(I) 3/75)*. It may be particularly difficult to show that a tribunal made a mistake of fact if neither party obtained a full statement of reasons and it may be equally difficult to show that a tribunal was

ignorant of a material fact if neither party obtained a record of proceedings which would include a note of evidence. In *CDLA/3875/2001* and *CDLA/2115/2003*, the Commissioners commented on the consequence of keeping inadequate records of Secretary of State's decisions. Lack of evidence as to the basis on which an adjudication officer's decision was made had made it impossible for the Secretary of State to point to an error in the decision that he wished to supersede.

A tribunal should hesitate before superseding the decision of an earlier tribunal for error of fact, where the issue must have been considered by the earlier tribunal if it was doing its job properly (*CDLA/3364/2001*). The tribunal should consider what the consequences may be and should obtain the parties' views. A copy of the statement of the earlier tribunal's reasons should also be obtained if one was issued.

Para. (2) (d)

2.344   This appears to overlap with reg.3(8) and therefore to be of no effect by virtue of para.(3).

Para. (2) (e)

2.345   The new decision has effect from the date on which entitlement arises to the other benefit or to an increase in the rate of that other benefit (reg.7(7)). If entitlement to the other benefit, or to an increase in the rate of that other benefit, arises on or before the date from which the decision being reconsidered was effective, the decision is revised under reg.3(7) instead of being superseded.

Para. (2) (g)

2.346   For the meaning of "incapacity benefit decision" and "incapacity determination", see reg.7A.

In *R(IB) 2/05*, the claimant had twice been referred for medical examinations after being awarded incapacity benefit. On the first occasion he satisfied the personal capability assessment and on the second occasion he did not. Following the second examination, the Secretary of State issued a decision purporting to supersede the original award. The Commissioner declined to rule on a submission that there should have been a supersession decision after the first medical examination because the grounds for supersession under reg.6(2)(g) are such that it made no difference whether there should already have been a supersession of the original award or even whether there had been a supersession of that award. On any view, there must have been a decision that could properly be superseded under reg.6(2)(g) and it was unnecessary further to identify the decision.

It has long been held that the obtaining of a new medical opinion does not itself amount to a change of circumstances justifying supersession under para.(2)(a)(i) (formerly a review) although a new medical report might include clinical findings revealing that there had been a change of circumstances (*R(IS) 2/97*, *Cooke v Secretary of State for Social Security* [2001] EWCA Civ 734 (reported as *R(DLA) 6/01*)). This sub-para. provides that obtaining a report is in itself grounds for supersession. In *CIB/2338/2000*, it was said that this sub-para. was unnecessary because, on a proper understanding of para.(2)(a)(i), it was always possible to identify a relevant change of circumstances in those cases where there was justification for terminating an award. However, it is suggested that there is a clear purpose underlying this sub-para. In *Cooke v Secretary of State for Social Security*, it was pointed out that, in the absence of a provision like para.(2)(g), a decision terminating an award following receipt of a medical report could be based either on the ground that there had been a change of circumstances (see para.(2)(a)(i)) or on the ground that benefit should never have been awarded in the first place (see para.(2)(b)). It was at least theoretically necessary to decide which of those grounds applied and, if there had been a change of circumstances, determine the date of the change, because that would determine the date from which the new decision would be effective which in turn would determine whether there had been any potentially reoverable overpayment, although the necessity was avoided if the Secretary of State made it clear that there was no intention to recover any payment. The advantage of superseding a decision under para.(2)(g) is that it is unnecessary to identify a change of circumstances since, or an error in, the decision being superseded because, in the absence of any specific provision in reg.7, the new decision is effective from the date it is made (s.10(5) of the Social Security Act 1998). It is to be noted that para.(2)(g) does not oust the power to supersede under, say, para.(2)(a)(i) in an incapacity benefit or credit case. Regulation 7(2)(c), which was amended at the same time as reg.6(2)(g) was introduced, makes specific provision as to the date from which decisions under para.(2)(a)(i) are effective in such cases.

One consequence of it being unnecessary to find a specific change of circumstances since, or error in, an earlier decision is that it may be less important to consider the evidence lying behind the decision being superseded. However, where a claimant submits that his or her condition is unchanged since an earlier personal capability assessment, the findings made an earlier assessment may well be relevant (*R(S)1/55*) as evidence of the claimant's present condition, particularly if the condition is variable and any examination is likely to be only a snapshot (*CIB/2338/2000*). Commissioners were therefore highly critical of a rumoured proposal to destroy all records of personal capability assessments so that they were not available to decision-makers or tribunals concerned with subsequent supersessions (*CIB/1972/2000*, *CIB/3667/2000*, *CIB/378/2001*, *CIB/3179/2000*). In *CIB/3985/2001*, it was held that, where a claimant had stated that his condition had not changed since he had previously satisfied a personal capability assessment, the Secretary of State ought to make the report on that assessment available because the claimant had identified that as relevant evidence and was unable to produce it himself. Where the Secretary of State had not produced that evidence, the tribunal had to proceed on the basis that they had before them an implied request for an adjournment. That meant they had to consider whether the evidence was potentially relevant, in the light of the other evidence before them and, in the circumstances of the case under consideration, the tribunal erred in law in failing to adjourn and direct the Secretary of State to produce the evidence. There was nothing to suggest that the earlier assessments had ceased to be relevant because, for instance, there had been a supervening operation or injury. In those circumstances, it was not sufficient for the tribunal to rely on the new assessment when the claimant's argument was that earlier assessments would show it to be incomplete and insufficient. The need to provide a tribunal with proper information about the adjudication history behind a decision, explaining the basis of previous awards and the grounds upon which the last award has been superseded, has again been emphasised by a Tribunal of Commissioners in Northern Ireland in *R1/04(IB)*.

Another consequence of it being unnecessary to find a change of circumstances since, or error in, an earlier decision is that a decision-maker is entitled to make a different judgement on the same facts so that, even if a tribunal accept that a claimant's condition has not changed since an earlier favourable assessment and they cannot identify an error of fact or law in that earlier decision, they may decide that the claimant is not entitled to benefit. Nonetheless, the burden of proving grounds for supersession always lies on the person seeking supersession so that, where a claimant has been entitled to incapacity benefit, it is for the Secretary of State to justify terminating the award by superseding it under reg.6(2)(g). However, it is pointed out in *CIB/1509/2004* that the burden of proof must be considered in two stages. For reg.6(2)(g) to apply at all, the Secretary of State must have received the necessary medical evidence following an appropriate medical examination. On an appeal to a tribunal, it is plainly for the Secretary of State to produce that evidence but he invariably does so and therefore that is not usually a live issue. The second stage is considering whether the claimant still satisfies the conditions for entitlement to benefit and so continues to be entitled to benefit notwithstanding that the requirements of reg.6(2)(g) are met. The Commissioner referred to *Kerr v Department for Social Development* [2004] UKHL 23; [2004] 1 W.L.R. 1372 (also reported as an appendix to *R1/04(SF)* (see the annotation to s.3(1) of the

Tribunals, Courts and Enforcement Act 2007, where Baroness Hale talked of "a co-operative process of investigation" (para.62) and said that "it will rarely be necessary to resort to concepts taken from adversarial litigation such as the burden of proof" (para.63). A tribunal must have regard to all the evidence produced in the investigation and decide the case on the balance of probabilities. The Commissioner followed *CIS/427/1991* in holding that the burden of proof is relevant only (a) if there is no relevant evidence on an issue (despite an adequate investigation) or (b) if the evidence on the issue is so evenly balanced that it is impossible to determine where the balance of probabilities lies. When superseding a decision on his own initiative, the burden of proof lies on the Secretary of State at both stages so that, in the few cases when it is relevant at the second stage, the case should be decided in favour of the claimant. Normally there is sufficient evidence to enable a tribunal to form a clear view one way or the other. That evidence includes the earlier decision and so, where it is decided to supersede it to the disadvantage of the claimant, it may be necessary for a tribunal's reasons to refer to the earlier decision *(R(M) 1/96)*. Decisions that appear inconsistent and are not adequately explained tend to bring the adjudication system into disrepute *(R(A) 2/83)*.

In *CIB/313/2002* and *R(IB)2/04* at para.125, Commissioners have suggested that reg.6(2)(g) is applicable only where the award to be superseded was based on a personal capability assessment (see the definition of "incapacity determination" in reg.7A) and that where, for instance, an award was based on deemed incapacity under reg.28 of the Social Security (Incapacity for Work) (General) Regulations 1995, the proper basis for supersession was reg.6(2)(a)(i). However, in neither case was the point determined because the result would have been the same whichever provision was applied. In *CSIB/501/2003* (subsequently approved by the Court of Appeal in *Hooper v Secretary of State for Work and Pensions* [2007] EWCA Civ 495 (reported as *R(IB) 4/07*)), it was held that a decision to award invalidity benefit could not be "an incapacity benefit decision" and therefore could not be superseded under reg.6(2)(g). Presumably it could have been superseded under reg.6(2)(a)(i) but the Deputy Commissioner left such issues to be considered by the Secretary of State.

Para.2(r)

2.347   See the note to para.(2)(g), which makes equivalent provision in respect of incapacity benefit decisions.

Para.(5)

2.348   An application for revision may be treated as an application for supersession. Regulation 3(10) provides that an application for supersession may be treated as an application for revision. For the power of an appeal tribunal to treat a supersession as a refusal to revise and vice versa, see the note to s.12 of the Social Security Act 1998.

2.349   **6A.** *Omitted.*
2.350   **6B.** *Omitted.*

Date from which a decision superseded under section 10 takes effect

2.351   7.—[⁴ (1) This regulation—
[¹² (a) is, except for [¹⁴ paragraphs (2)(b) [²⁷ , (bb)] [²⁶ or (be)], (29) and (30)], subject to Schedules3A [²⁶ , 3B and 3C]; and]
(b) contains exceptions to the provisions of section 10(5) as to the date from which a decision under section 10 which supersedes an earlier decision is to take effect.]
(2) Where a decision under section 10 is made on the ground that there has been, or it is anticipated that there will be, a relevant change of circum-

stances since the decision [[14] had effect] [[19] or, in the case of an advance award, since the decision was made], the decision under section 10 shall take effect—

[[4] (a) from the date the change occurred or, where the change does not have effect until a later date, from the first date on which such effect occurs where—
    (i) the decision is advantageous to the claimant; and
    (ii) the change was notified to an appropriate office within one month of the change occurring or within such longer period as may be allowed under regulation 8 for the claimant's failure to notify the change on an earlier date;]

(b) where the decision is advantageous to the claimant and the change was notified to an appropriate office more than one month after the change occurred or after the expiry of any such longer period as may have been allowed under regulation 8—
    (i) in the case of a claimant who is in receipt of income support [[12], jobseeker's allowance [[26], state pension credit or an employment and support allowance] and benefit is paid in arrears, from the beginning of the benefit week in which the notification was made;
    (ii) in the case of a claimant who is in receipt of income support [[12], jobseeker's allowance [[26] , state pension credit or an employment and support allowance]] and benefit is paid in advance and the date of notification is the first day of a benefit week from that date and otherwise, from the beginning of the benefit week following the week in which the notification was made; or
    (iii) in any other case, the date of notification of the relevant change of circumstances; or

[[27] (bb) where the decision is advantageous to the claimant and is made on the Secretary of State's own initiative—
    (i) except where paragraph (ii) applies, from the beginning of the benefit week in which the Secretary of State commenced action with a view to supersession; or
    (ii) in the case of a claimant who is in receipt of income support, jobseeker's allowance or state pension credit where benefit is paid in advance and the Secretary of State commenced action with a view to supersession on a day which was not the first day of the benefit week, from the beginning of the benefit week following the week in which the Secretary of State commenced such action;

(bc) where—
    (i) the claimant is a disabled person or a disabled person's partner;
    (ii) the decision is advantageous to the claimant; and
    (iii) the decision is made in connection with the cessation of payment of a carer's allowance relating to that disabled person, the day after the last day for which carer's allowance was paid to a person other than the claimant or the claimant's partner;]

[[24] (bd) [[25] . . .]]

[[26] (be) in the case of a claimant who is in receipt of an employment and support allowance and the claimant makes an application which contains an express statement that he is terminally ill within the meaning

of regulation 2(1) of the Employment and Support Allowance Regulations, from the date the claimant became terminally ill;]
  (c) where the decision is not advantageous to the claimant—
    (i) [⁴ ...]
    [¹(ii) in the case of a disability benefit decision, or an incapacity benefit decision where there has been an incapacity determination (whether before or after the decision), where the Secretary of State is satisfied that in relation to a disability determination embodied in or necessary to the disability benefit decision, or the incapacity determination, the claimant or payee failed to notify an appropriate office of a change of circumstances which regulations under the Administration Act required him to notify, and the claimant or payee, as the case may be, knew or could reasonably have been expected to know that the change of circumstances should have been notified,
      (aa) from the date on which the claimant or payee, as the case may be, ought to have notified the change of circumstances, or
      (bb) if more than one change has taken place between the date from which the decision to be superseded took effect and the date of the superseding decision, from the date on which the first change ought to have been notified, or
    (iii) [²² ...]
    [²²(iv) in the case of a disability benefit decision, where the change of circumstances is not in relation to the disability determination embodied in or necessary to the disability benefit decision, from the date of the change; or
    (v) in any other case, except in the case of a decision which supersedes a disability benefit decision, from the date of the change.]
  [²⁵ (2A) [²⁷ ...]]
  [²⁶ (3) For the purposes of paragraphs (2) and (8) "benefit week" has the same meaning, as the case may be, as in—
  (a) regulation 2(1) of the Income Support Regulations;
  (b) regulation 1(3) of the Jobseeker's Allowance Regulations;
  (c) regulation 1(2) of the State Pension Credit Regulations; or
  (d) regulation 2(1) of the Employment and Support Allowance Regulations.]
  (4) In paragraph (2) a decision which is to the advantage of the claimant includes a decision specified in regulation 30(2)(a) to (f).
  [⁷ (5) Where the Secretary of State supersedes a decision made by [²⁸ the First-tier Tribunal or the Upper Tribunal] on the grounds specified in regulation 6(2)(c) [¹⁴ (i)] (ignorance of, or mistake as to, a material fact), the decision under section 10 shall take effect, in a case where, as a result of that ignorance of or mistake as to material fact, the decision to be superseded was more advantageous to the claimant than it would otherwise have been and which either—
  (a) does not relate to a disability benefit decision or an incapacity benefit decision where there has been an incapacity determination; or
  (b) relates to a disability decision or an incapacity benefit decision where there has been an incapacity determination, and the Secretary of State is satisfied that at the time the decision was made the claimant

or payee knew or could reasonably have been expected to know of the fact in question and that it was relevant to the decision.
from the date on which the decision of [²⁸ the First-tier Tribunal or the Upper Tribunal] took, or was to take, effect.]

(6) Any decision made under section 10 in consequence of a decision which is a relevant determination for the purposes of section 27 shall take effect as from the date of the relevant determination.

[¹⁹ (6A) Where—

(a) there is a decision which is a relevant determination for the purposes of section 27 and the Secretary of State makes a benefit decision of the kind specified in section 27(1)(b);

(b) there is an appeal against the determination;

(c) after the benefit decision payment is suspended in accordance with regulation 16(1) and (3)(b)(ii); and

(d) on appeal a court, within the meaning of section 27, reverses the determination in whole or in part,

a consequential decision by the Secretary of State under section 10 which supersedes his earlier decision under sub-paragraph (a) shall take effect from the date on which the earlier decision took effect.]

[²² (7) A decision which is superseded in accordance with regulation 6(2)(e) or (ee) shall be superseded—

(a) subject to sub-paragraph (b), from the date on which entitlement arises to the other relevant benefit referred to in regulation 6(2)(e)(ii) or (ee) or to an increase in the rate of that other relevant benefit; or

(b) where the claimant or his partner—

(i) is not a severely disabled person for the purposes of section 135(5) of the Contributions and Benefits Act (the applicable amount) or section 2(7) of the State Pension Credit Act (guarantee credit) [²⁶ or paragraph 6 of Schedule 4 to the Employment and Support Allowance Regulations;]

(ii) by virtue of his having—

(aa) a non-dependant as defined by regulation 3 of the Income Support Regulations [²⁶ or regulation 71 of the Employment and Support Allowance Regulations]; or

(bb) a person residing with him for the purposes of paragraph 1 of Schedule 1 to the State Pension Credit Regulations whose presence may not be ignored in accordance with paragraph 2 of that Schedule,

at the date the superseded decision would, but for this sub-paragraph, have had effect,

from the date on which the claimant or his partner ceased to have a non-dependant or person residing with him or from the date on which the presence of that person was first ignored.]

[²¹ (7A) Where a decision is superseded in accordance with regulation 6(2)(o), the superseding decision shall take effect from the day on which a lump sum, or a payment on account of a lump sum, is paid or repaid if that day is the first day of the benefit week but, if it is not, from the next following such day.]

[³ (8) A decision to which regulation 6(2)(f) applies shall take effect—

(a) where section 19(2) [⁸ or 20A(3)] of the Jobseekers Act applies, as from the beginning of the period specified in regulation 69 of the Jobseeker's Allowance Regulations; or

 (b) where section 19(3) [⁸ or 20A(4)] of the Jobseekers Act applies, as from the beginning of the period determined in accordance with that subsection.]

[²⁷ (8A) Where a decision is superseded in accordance with regulation 6(2)(s), the superseding decision shall take effect from the date on which the late or unpaid contribution is treated as paid]

[⁴ (9) A decision relating to attendance allowance or disability living allowance which is advantageous to the claimant and which is made under section 10 on the basis of a relevant change of circumstances shall take effect from—

[¹⁴ (a) where the decision is made on the Secretary of State's own initiative—

  (i) the date on which the Secretary of State commenced action with a view to supersession; or

  (ii) subject to paragraph (30), in a case where the relevant circumstances are that there has been a change in the legislation in relation to attendance allowance or disability living allowance, the date on which that change in the legislation had effect;]

 (b) where—

  (i) the change is relevant to the question of entitlement to a particular rate of benefit; and

  (ii) the claimant notifies the change before a date one month after the satisfied the conditions of entitlement to that rate or within such longer period as may be allowed under regulation 8,

  the [²⁷ date on which] he satisfied those conditions;

 (c) where—

  (i) the change is relevant to the question of whether benefit is payable; and

  (ii) the claimant notifies the change before a date one month after the change or within such longer period as may be allowed under regulation 8,

  the [²⁷ date on which] the change occurred; or

 (d) in any other case, the date of the application for the superseding decision.]

(10) A decision as to an award of incapacity benefit, which is made under section 10 because section 30B(4) of the Contributions and Benefits Act applies to the claimant, shall take effect as from the date on which he became entitled to the highest rate of the care component of disability living allowance.

(11) A decision as to an award of incapacity benefit or severe disablement allowance, which is made under section 10 because the claimant is to be treated as incapable of work under regulation 10 of the Social Security (Incapacity for Work) (General) Regulations 1995 (certain persons with a severe condition to be treated as incapable of work), shall take effect as from the date he is to be treated as incapable of work.

(12) Where this paragraph applies, a decision under section 10 may be made so as to take effect as from such date not more than eight weeks before—

 (a) the application for supersession; or

 (b) where no application is made, the date on which the decision under section 10 is made,

as is reasonable in the particular circumstances of the case.

(13) Paragraph (12) applies where—

(a) the effect of a decision under section 10 is that there is to be included in a claimant's applicable amount an amount in respect of a loan which qualifies under—
   (i) paragraph 15 or 16 of Schedule 3 to the Income Support Regulations; or
   (ii) paragraph 14 or 15 of Schedule 2 to the Jobseeker's Allowance Regulations; [¹² or
   (iii) paragraph 11 or 12 of Schedule II to the State Pension Credit Regulations; [²⁶ or]]
[²⁶ (iv) paragraph 16 or 17 of Schedule 6 to the Employment and Support Allowance Regulations; and]
(b) that decision could not have been made earlier because information necessary to make that decision, requested otherwise than in accordance with paragraph 10(3)(b) of Schedule 9A to the Claims and Payments Regulations (annual requests for information), had not been supplied to the Secretary of State by the lender.

(14) Subject to paragraph (23), where a claimant is in receipt of income support and his applicable amount includes an amount determined in accordance with Schedule 3 to the Income Support Regulations (housing costs), and there is a reduction in the amount of eligible capital owing in connection with a loan which qualifies under paragraph 15 or 16 of that Schedule, a decision made under section 10 shall take effect—
(a) on the first anniversary of the date on which the claimant's housing costs were first met under that Schedule; or
(b) where the reduction in eligible capital occurred after the first anniversary of the date referred to in sub-paragraph (a), on the next anniversary of that date following the date of the reduction.

(15) Where a claimant is in receipt of income support and payments made to that claimant which fall within paragraph 29 or 30(1)(a) to (c) of Schedule 9 to the Income Support Regulations have been disregarded in relation to any decision under section 8 or 10 and there is a change in the amount of interest payable—
(a) on a loan qualifying under paragraph 15 or 16 of Schedule 3 to those Regulations to which those payments relate; or
(b) on a loan not so qualifying which is secured on the dwelling occupied as the home to which those payments relate,
a decision under section 10 which is made as a result of that change in the amount of interest payable shall take effect on whichever of the dates referred to in paragraph (16) is appropriate in the claimant's case.

(16) The date on which a decision under section 10 takes effect for the purposes of paragraph (15) is—
(a) the date on which the claimant's housing costs are first met under paragraph 6(1)(a), 8(1)(a) or 9(2)(a) of Schedule 3 to the Income Support Regulations; or
(b) where the change in the amount of interest payable occurred after the date referred to in sub-paragraph (a), on the date of the next alteration in the standard rate following the date of that change.

(17) In paragraph (16), "standard rate" has the same meaning as it has in paragraph 1(2) of Schedule 3 to the Income Support Regulations.

[¹² (17A) For the purposes of state pension credit—
(a) paragraph (14) shall apply as if the reference to—
   (i) "income support and his applicable amount" was a reference

to "state pension credit and his appropriate minimum guarantee";
- (ii) "Schedule 3 to the Income Support Regulations" was a reference to "Schedule II to the State Pension Credit Regulations"; and
- (iii) "paragraph 15 or 16" was a reference to "paragraph 11 or 12";
- (b) paragraphs (15) to (17) shall not apply.]

[[16] (17B) Paragraph 17C applies where—
- (a) a claimant is awarded state pension credit;
- (b) the claimant or his partner is aged 65 or over;
- (c) his appropriate minimum guarantee (as defined by the State Pension Credit Act) includes housing costs determined in accordance with Schedule II to the State Pension Credit Regulations; and
- (d) after the date from which sub-paragraph (c) applies—
    - (i) a non-dependant (as defined in that Schedule) begins to reside with the claimant; or
    - (ii) a non-dependant's income increases and this affects the applicable amount of the claimant's housing costs.

(17C) In the circumstances specified in paragraph (17B) a decision made under section 10 shall take effect—
- (a) where there is more than one change of the kind specified in paragraph (17B)(d) in respect of the same non-dependant within the same 26 week period, 26 weeks after the date on which the first such change occurred; and
- (b) in any other circumstances, 26 weeks after the date on which a change specified in paragraph (17B)(d) occurred.]

[[26] (17D) Except in a case where paragraph (23) applies, where a claimant is in receipt of an employment and support allowance and his applicable amount includes an amount determined in accordance with Schedule 6 to the Employment and Support Allowance Regulations (housing costs), and there is a reduction in the amount of eligible capital owing in connection with a loan which qualifies under paragraph 16 or 17 of that Schedule, a decision made under section 10 shall take effect—
- (a) on the first anniversary of the date on which the claimant's housing costs were first met under that Schedule; or
- (b) where the reduction in eligible capital occurred after the first anniversary of the date referred to in sub-paragraph (a), on the next anniversary of that date following the date of the reduction.

(17E) Where a claimant is in receipt of an employment and support allowance and payments made to that claimant which fall within paragraph 31 or 32(1)(a) to (c) of Schedule 8 to the Employment and Support Allowance Regulations have been disregarded in relation to any decision under section 8 or 10 and there is a change in the amount of interest payable—
- (a) on a loan qualifying under paragraph 16 or 17 of Schedule 6 to those Regulations to which those payments relate; or
- (b) on a loan not so qualifying which is secured on the dwelling occupied as the home to which those payments relate,
a decision under section 10 which is made as a result of that change in the amount of interest payable shall take effect on whichever of the dates referred to in paragraph (17F) is appropriate in the claimant's case.

(17F) The date on which a decision under section 10 takes effect for the purposes of paragraph (17E) is—

(a) the date on which the claimant's housing costs are first met under paragraph 8(1)(a), 9(1)(a) or 10(2)(a) of Schedule 6 to the Employment and Support Allowance Regulations; or

(b) where the change in the amount of interest payable occurred after the date referred to in sub-paragraph (a), on the date of the next alteration in the standard rate following the date of that change.

(17G) In paragraph (17F) "standard rate" has the same meaning as it has in paragraph 13(2) of Schedule 6 to the Employment and Support Allowance Regulations.

(17H) Where the decision is superseded in accordance with regulation 6(2)(a)(i) and the relevant circumstances are that the claimant has a non-dependant who has become entitled to main phase employment and support allowance, the superseding decision shall take effect from the date the main phase employment and support allowance is first paid to the non-dependant.]

(18) Subject to paragraph (24) and, except in a case to which paragraph (23) applies, where a claimant is in receipt of a jobseeker's allowance and his applicable amount includes an amount determined in accordance with Schedule 2 to the Jobseeker's Allowance Regulations (housing costs), and there is a reduction in the amount of eligible capital owing in connection with a loan which qualifies under paragraph 14 or 15 of that Schedule, a decision under section 10 made as a result of that reduction shall take effect—

(a) on the first anniversary of the date on which the claimant's housing costs were first met under that Schedule; or

(b) where the reduction in eligible capital occurred after the first anniversary of the date referred to in sub-paragraph (a), on the next anniversary of that date following the date of the reduction.

(19) Where a claimant is in receipt of a jobseeker's allowance and payments made to that claimant which fall within paragraph 30 or 31(1)(a) to (c) of Schedule 7 to the Jobseeker's Allowance Regulations have been disregarded in relation to any decision under section 8 or 10 and there is a change in the amount of interest payable—

(a) on a loan qualifying under paragraph 14 or 15 of Schedule 2 to those Regulations to which those payments relate; or

(b) on a loan not so qualifying which is secured on the dwelling occupied as the home to which those payments relate,

any decision under section 10 which is made as a result of that change in the amount of interest payable shall take effect on whichever of the dates referred to in paragraph (20) is appropriate in the claimant's case.

(20) The date on which a decision under section 10 takes effect for the purposes of paragraph (19) is—

(a) the date on which the claimant's housing costs are first met under paragraph 6(1)(a), 7(1)(a) or 8(2)(a) of Schedule 2 to the Jobseeker's Allowance Regulations; or

(b) where the changes in the amount of interest payable occurred after the date referred to in sub-paragraph (a), on the date of the next alteration in the standard rate following the date of that change.

(21) In paragraph (20), "standard rate" has the same meaning as it has in paragraph 1(2) of Schedule 2 to the Jobseeker's Allowance Regulations.

(22) Where—

(a) a claimant was paid benefit in respect of October 6, 1996 in accordance with an award of income support;

   (b) that claimant's applicable amount includes an amount determined in accordance with Schedule 3 to the Income Support Regulations (housing costs);

   (c) that claimant is treated as having been awarded a jobseeker's allowance by virtue of regulation 7 of the Jobseeker's Allowance (Transitional Provisions) Regulations 1996 (jobseeker's allowance to replace income support and unemployment benefit); and

   (d) a decision is made under section 10 in consequence of a reduction in the amount of eligible capital owing in connection with a loan which qualifies under paragraph 15 or 16 of Schedule 3 to the Income Support Regulations,

the decision under section 10 referred to in sub-paragraph (d) shall take effect on the next anniversary of the date on which housing costs were first met which occurs after the reduction.

[^{13} (23) Where, in any case to which paragraph (14), (17A) [^{16} . . .] [^{26}, 17D] or (18) applies, a claimant has been continuously in receipt of, or treated as having been continuously in receipt of income support, a jobseeker's allowance [^{26} , an employment and support allowance] or state pension credit, or one of those benefits followed by the other, and he or his partner continues to receive any of those benefits, the anniversary to which those paragraphs refer shall be—

   (a) in the case of income support [^{26} , jobseeker's allowance or employment and support allowance], the anniversary of the earliest date on which benefit in respect of those mortgage interest costs became payable;

   (b) in the case of state pension credit, the relevant anniversary date determined in accordance with paragraph 7 of Schedule II to the State Pension Credit Regulations.]

(24) Where—

   (a) it has been determined that the amount of a jobseeker's allowance payable to a young person is to be reduced under regulation 63 of the Jobseeker's Allowance Regulations because paragraph (1)(b)(iii), (c), (d), (e) or (f) of that regulation (reduced payments under section 17 of the Jobseekers Act) applied in his case; and

   (b) the decision made in consequence of sub-paragraph (a) falls to be superseded by a decision under section 10 because the Secretary of State has subsequently issued a certificate under section 17(4) of the Jobseekers Act with respect to the failure in question,

the decision under section 10 shall take effect as from the same date as the decision made in consequence of sub-paragraph (a) has effect.

[^{5} [^{17} (25) In a case where a decision ("the first decision") has been made that a person failed without good cause to take part in a work-focused interview, the decision under section 10 shall take effect as from—

   (a) the first day of the benefit week to commence for that person following the date of the first decision; or

   (b) in a case where a partner has failed without good cause to take part in a work-focused interview [^{18} in accordance with regulations made under section 2AA of the Administration Act]—

      (i) the first day of the benefit week to commence for the claimant [^{18} (meaning the person who has been awarded benefit within section 2AA(2) of the Administration Act at a higher rate referable to that partner)] following the date of the first decision; or

(ii) if that date arises five days or less after the day on which the first decision was made, as from the first day of the second benefit week to commence for the claimant following the date of the first decision.]

(26) In paragraph (25), "benefit week" means any period of 7 days corresponding to the week in respect of which the relevant social security benefit is due to be paid.]

[⁹ (27) A decision to which regulation 6(2)(i) applies shall take effect from the beginning of the period specified—

(a) subject to sub-paragraphs (d) and (e), in relation to jobseeker's allowance—
    (i) in regulation 3(1)(a) of the Breach of Community Order Regulations;
    (ii) in regulation 3(1)(b) of those regulations;
(b) subject to sub-paragraphs (d) and (e), in relation to income support—
    (i) in regulation 3(3)(a) of the Breach of Community Order Regulations;
    (ii) in regulation 3(3)(b) of those regulations;
(c) subject to sub-paragraphs (d) and (e), in relation to a joint-claim jobseeker's allowance—
    (i) in regulation 3(4)(a) of the Breach of Community Order Regulations;
    (ii) in regulation 3(4)(b) of those regulations;
(d) in regulation 3(5) of the Breach of Community Order Regulations;
(e) in regulation 3(6) of the Breach of Community Order Regulations.]

[¹⁰ (28) A decision to which regulation 6(2)(j) or (k) applies shall take effect from the first day of the disqualification period prescribed for the purposes of section 7 of the Social Security Fraud Act 2001.]

[¹² (29) [¹⁵ Subject to paragraphs (29A) and (29B), a] decision to which regulation 6(2)(1) (state pension credit) refers shall take effect from the day following the day on which the assessed income period ends if that day is the first day of the claimant's benefit week, but if it is not, from the next following such day.]

[¹⁵ (29A) A decision to which regulation 6(2)(l) applies, where—

(a) the decision is advantageous to the claimant; and
(b) the information and evidence required under regulation 32(1) of the Claims and Payments Regulations has not been provided within the period allowed under that regulation,

shall take effect from the day the information and evidence required under that regulation is provided if that day is the first day of the claimant's benefit week, but, if it is not, from the next following such day.

(29B) A decision to which regulation 6(2)(l) applies, where—

(a) the decision is disadvantageous to the claimant; and
(b) the information and evidence required under regulation 32(1) of the Claims and Payments Regulations has not been provided within the period allowed under that regulation,

shall take effect from the day after the period allowed under that regulation expired.

(29C) Except where there is a change of circumstances during the period in which the Secretary of State was prevented from specifying a new assessed income period under regulation 10(1) of the State Pension Credit Regulations, a decision to which regulation 6(2)(m) applies shall take effect from the day on which the information and evidence required under regulation 32(6)(a) of the Claims and Payments Regulations was provided.]

[14 (30) Where a decision is superseded in accordance with regulation 6(2)(a)(i) and the relevant circumstances are that there has been a change in the legislation in relation to a relevant benefit, the decision under section 10 shall take effect from the date on which that change in the legislation had effect.

(31) Where a decision is superseded in accordance with regulation 6(2)(a)(ii) and the relevant circumstances are that—

- (a) a personal capability assessment has been carried out in the case of a person to whom section 171C(4) of the Contributions and Benefits Act applies; and
- (b) the own occupation test remains applicable to him under section 171B(3) of that Act,

the decision under section 10 shall take effect on the day [27 . . .] on which the own occupation test is no longer applicable to that person.

(32) For the purposes of paragraph (31)—

- (a) "personal capability assessment" has the same meaning as in regulation 24 of the Social Security (Incapacity for Work) (General) Regulations 1995;
- (b) "own occupation test" has the same meaning as in section 171B(2) of the Contributions and Benefits Act.

(33) A decision to which regulation 6(2)(c)(ii) applies shall take effect from the date on which [28 the First-tier Tribunal or the Upper Tribunal's] decision would have taken effect had it been decided in accordance with the determination of the [28 Upper Tribunal] or the court in the appeal referred to in section 26(1)(b).]

[19 (34) A decision which supersedes a decision specified in regulation 6(2)(n) shall take effect from the effective date of the Secretary of State's decision to terminate income support which was confirmed by the decision specified in regulation 6(2)(n).]

[26 (35) A decision made in accordance with regulation 6(2)(p), where the failure determination was made before the 13th week of entitlement, shall take effect from the first day of the benefit week following that week.

(36) A decision made in accordance with regulation 6(2)(p) where paragraph (35) does not apply shall take effect from the first day of the benefit week in which the failure determination was made.

(37) A decision made in accordance with regulation 6(2)(q) shall take effect from the first day of the benefit week in which the reduction mentioned in that sub-paragraph ceased to have effect.

(38) A decision made in accordance with regulation 6(2)(r) that embodies a determination that the claimant has limited capability for work which is the first such determination shall take effect from the beginning of the 14th week of entitlement.

(39) A decision made in accordance with regulation 6(2)(r), following an application by the claimant, that embodies a determination that the claimant has limited capability for work-related activity shall take effect from the date of the application.]

AMENDMENTS

1. Social Security and Child Support (Decisions and Appeals) Amendment (No.2) Regulations 1999 (SI 1999/1623), reg.4 (July 5, 1999).

2. Tax Credits (Decisions and Appeals) (Amendment) Regulations 1999 (SI 1999/2570), reg.10 (October 5, 1999). Note that amendments made by these regulations only have effect with respect to tax credit (reg.1(2) of the Amendment Regulations).

3. Social Security and Child Support (Decisions and Appeals), Vaccine Damage Payments and Jobseeker's Allowance (Amendment) Regulations 1999 (SI 1999/2677), reg.8 (October 18, 1999).

4. Social Security Act 1998 (Commencement No.12 and Consequential and Transitional Provisions) Order 1999 (SI 1999/3178), art.3(19) and Sch.19, para.1 (November 29, 1999).

5. Social Security and Child Support (Decisions and Appeals) Amendment Regulations 2000 (SI 2000/119), reg.2 (February 17, 2000).

6. Social Security (Work-focused Interviews) Regulations 2000 (SI 2000/897), reg.16(5) and Sch.6, para.5 (April 3, 2000).

7. Social Security and Child Support (Miscellaneous Amendments) Regulations 2000 (SI 2000/1596), reg.17 (June 19, 2000).

8. Social Security (Joint Claims: Consequential Amendments) Regulations 2000 (SI 2000/1982), reg.5(c) (March 19, 2001).

9. Social Security (Breach of Community Order) (Consequential Amendments) Regulations 2001 (SI 2001/1711), reg.2(2)(d) (October 15, 2001).

10. Social Security (Loss of Benefit) (Consequential Amendments) Regulations 2002 (SI 2002/490), reg.8(c) (April 1, 2002).

11. Social Security (Claims and Payments and Miscellaneous Amendments) Regulations 2002 (SI 2002/428), reg.4(4) (April 2, 2002).

12. State Pension Credit (Consequential, Transitional and Miscellaneous Provisions) Regulations 2002 (SI 2002/3019), reg.18 (April 7, 2003).

13. State Pension Credit (Consequential, Transitional and Miscellaneous Provisions) (No.2) Regulations 2002 (SI 2002/3197), reg.6 (April 7, 2003).

14. Social Security and Child Support (Miscellaneous Amendments) Regulations 2003 (SI 2003/1050), reg.3(5) (May 5, 2003).

15. State Pension Credit (Transitional and Miscellaneous Provisions) Amendment Regulations 2003 (SI 2003/2274), reg.5(3) (October 6, 2003).

16. State Pension Credit (Miscellaneous Amendments) Regulations 2004 (SI 2004/647), reg.2 (April 5, 2004).

17. Social Security (Jobcentre Plus Interviews for Partners) Regulations 2003 (SI 2003/1886), reg.15(5) (April 12, 2004).

18. Social Security (Working Neighbourhoods) Regulations 2004 (SI 2004/959), reg.24(4) (April 26, 2004).

19. Social Security, Child Support and Tax Credits (Miscellaneous Amendments) Regulations 2005 (SI 2005/337), reg.2(5) (March 18, 2005).

20. Social Security (Housing Benefit, Council Tax Benefit, State Pension Credit and Miscellaneous Amendments) Regulations 2004 (SI 2004/2327), reg.4 (April 4, 2005).

21. Social Security (Deferral of Retirement Pensions, Shared Additional Pension and Graduated Retirement Benefit) (Miscellaneous Provisions) Regulations 2005 (SI 2005/2677), reg.9(5) (April 6, 2006).

22. Social Security (Miscellaneous Amendments) (No.2) Regulations 2006 (SI 2006/832), reg.5(3) (April 10, 2006).

23. Social Security (Miscellaneous Amendments) (No.3) Regulations 2006 (SI 2006/2377), reg.3(2) (October 2, 2006).

24. Social Security (Miscellaneous Amendments) (No.4) Regulations 2007 (SI 2007/2470), reg.3(6) and (7) (September 24, 2007).

25. Social Security (Miscellaneous Amendments) (No.2) Regulations 2008 (SI 2008/1042), reg.2 (May 19, 2008).

26. Employment and Support Allowance (Consequential Provisions) (No.2) Regulations 2008 (SI 2008/1554), regs 29 and 33 (July 27, 2008).

27. Social Security (Miscellaneous Amendments) (No.5) Regulations 2008 (SI 2008/2667), reg 3(1) and (4) (October 30, 2008).

28. Tribunals, Courts and Enforcement Act 2007 (Transitional and Consequential Provisions) Order 2008 (SI 2008/2683), Sch.1, paras 95 and 104 (November 3, 2008).

DEFINITIONS

"appropriate office"—see reg.3(11).
"assessed income period"—see reg.1(3).
"benefit week"—see para.(3).
"the Board"—see reg.1(3).
"the Breach of Community Order Regulations"—*ibid.*
"claimant"—*ibid.*
"the Claims and Payments Regulations"—*ibid.*
"the Contributions and Benefits Act"—see s.84 of the Social Security Act 1998.
"disability benefit decision"—see reg.7A(1).
"disability determination"—*ibid.*
"the Employment and Support Allowance Regulations"—see reg.1(3).
"failure determination"—*ibid.*
"incapacity benefit decision"—See reg.7A(1).
"incapacity determination"—*ibid.*
"the Income Support Regulations"—see reg.1(3).
"the Jobseekers Act"—see s.84 of the Social Security Act 1998.
"the Jobseeker's Allowance Regulations"—see reg.1(3).
"a joint-claim jobseeker's allowance"—*ibid.*
"limited capability for work"—*ibid.*
"payee"—see reg.7A(1).
"standard rate"—see paras(17) and (21).
"state pension credit"—see reg.1(3).
"State Pension Credit Regulations"—*ibid.*
"work-focused interview"—*ibid.*

GENERAL NOTE

2.352   This regulation is not quite as complicated as it looks at first sight. As is explained in para.(1), the regulation provides exceptions to the general rule that a supersession decision takes effect from the date it is made or, where applicable, the date the application for supersession was made (s.10(5) of the Social Security Act 1998). The structure of the regulations is as follows:

Para.(1):	Introductory.
Paras (2)–(4):	Supersession for change of circumstances.
Para.(5):	Supersession of a tribunal or Commissioner's decision for error of fact.
Para.(6) and 6(A):	Supersession following a test case.
Para.(7):	Supersession following an award of another relevant benefit.
Para.(7A):	Supersession following a change in election whether to receive an increase in pension or a lump sum following a deferral of pension.
Para.(8):	Supersession of an award of jobseeker's allowance following a finding of voluntary unemployment.
Para.(8A)	Supersession where a late or unpaid contribution has been treated as paid.
Para.(9):	Supersession advantageous to claimant of an award of attendance allowance or disability living allowance.
Para.(10):	Supersession of an award of short-term incapacity benefit to increase the rate following an award of the highest rate of the care component of disability living allowance.

Para.(11):	Supersession of an award of incapacity benefit following a determination that the claimant is to be treated as incapable of work because he or she is suffering from a severe condition.
Paras (12) and (13):	Supersession in an income support or jobseeker's allowance case where information about housing costs was not supplied to the Secretary of State by a lender.
Para.(14):	Supersession in an income support case where there has been a reduction in the amount of eligible capital owing in respect of a loan.
Paras (15)–(17):	Supersession in an income support case where the claimant has been receiving payments under an insurance policy in respect of housing costs and there has been a change in the amount of interest payable.
Para.(17A):	Supersession in a state pension credit case where there has been a reduction in the amount of eligible capital owing in respect of a loan.
Paras (17B) and (17C):	Supersession in a state pension credit case where a non-dependant commences residing with the claimant or has an increase in income.
Para (17D)	Supersession in an employment and support allowance case where there has been a reduction in the amount of capital owing on a loan.
Paras (17E) to (17G)	Supersession in an employment and support allowance case where the claiamant has been receiving payments under an insurance policy in respect of housing costs and there has been a change in the amount of interest payable.
Para.(17H)	Supersession in an employment and support allowance case where a non-dependant becomes entitled to main phase employment and support allowance.
Para.(18):	Supersession in a jobseeker's allowance case where there has been a reduction in the amount of eligible capital owing in respect of a loan.
Paras (19)–(21):	Supersession in a jobseeker's allowance case where the claimant has been receiving payments under an insurance costs in respect of housing costs and there has been a change in the amount of interest payable.
Para.(22):	Supersession in case where a claimant was transferred from income support to jobseeker's allowance on October 6, 1996 and there has been a reduction in the amount of eligible capital owing in respect of a loan.
Para.(23):	Supplementary to paras (14)–(18) in a case where a person has been in receipt of more than one of income support, jobseeker's allowance and state pension credit.
Para.(24):	Supersession in a case where the claimant is a young person and was receiving a reduced amount of jobseeker's allowance on account of failing to complete a course and the Secretary of State has issued a certificate stating that the claimant had good cause for failing to complete the course.
Paras (25)–(26):	Supersession following a determination that the claimant has failed without good cause to take part in a work-focused interview.
Para.(27):	Supersession in order to reduce benefit because an offender has breached a community order.
Para.(28):	Supersession in order to remove benefit because a person has been convicted of benefit offences.
Paras (29)–(29B):	Supersession in a state pension credit case on the ending of an assessed income period.

Para. (29C):	Supersession where late provision of information or evidence has delayed the specification of a new assessed income period.
Para. (30):	Supersession following a change in relevant legislation.
Paras (31)–(32):	Supersession following a personal capability assessment carried out before the all work test becomes applicable.
Para. (33):	Supersession of a decision determined by a tribunal or Commissioner under s.26 of the Social Security Act 1998 while a test case was pending.
Para. (34):	Supersession of a decision of a tribunal in relation to income support where another tribunal has subsequently decided that the claimant is incapable of work.
Paras (35) to (37)	Supersession in an employment and support allowance case where there has been a failure determination.
Para (38)	Supersession in an employment and support allowance case following receipt of a new medical opinion.

Note that Schs. 3A, 3B and 3C make further provision in respect of income-related benefits.

Para. (1)

2.353   Section 10(5) of the Social Security Act 1998 provides that a supersession decision takes effect from the date it is made or, where applicable, the date the application for supersession was made. Schedule 3A provides further refinement for income support and jobseeker's allowance cases as do Sch.3B for state pension credit cases and Sch.3C for employment and support allowance cases. Where a case is not covered by this regulation or by those schedules, s.10(5) applies.

Para. (2)

2.354   A supersession on the ground of change of circumstances advantageous to the claimant is effective from the date of the change if the change is notified within a month (or such longer period as is allowed under reg.8) but is otherwise effective only from the date of notification. Where the change is not advantageous to the claimant, the supersession is generally effective from the date of change or, in the case of incapacity and disability cases, from the date when the change should have been reported. See reg.7A for definitions material to para.(2)(c). Presumably, para. (2) does not apply to those attendance allowance and disability living allowance cases where para.(9) applies or, indeed, to any cases where any of paras (10)–(34) applies.

The inclusion of a reference to a disabled person's partner in head (i) of the new version of reg.7(2)(bc) reverses the effect of *SSWP v JJ* [2009] UKUT 2 (AAC).

Regulation 7(2)(c) is concerned to ensure that an appropriate effective date is fixed where the effect of a supersession due to a change of circumstances is that benefit has been overpaid and the overpayment is likely to be recoverable under s.71 of the Social Security Administration Act 1992. (Regulation 3(5)(b) and (c) makes similar provision by way of revision where the original decision was made in ignorance of, or on a mistake as to, a material fact). Section 71(5A) of the 1992 Act provides that an overpayment can generally be recovered only if a decision has properly been given in terms of revision or supersession, a point reiterated in *CIS/4434/2004*. If the decision is in terms of supersession, there will only be an overpayment if the date from which the supersession is effective is before the date on which payment ceased. It is therefore not surprising that the question whether a claimant has "failed to notify" a change of circumstances for the purposes of reg.7(2)(c)(ii) was found in *CDLA/1823/2004* to be similar to the familiar question whether a person has "failed to disclose" a change of circumstances for the purposes of s.71. The Commissioner noted that the phrase "regulations under the Administration Act" refers to regulation 32 of the Social Security (Claims and Payments) Regulations 1987, which was considered in some detail in the context of s.71 by the Court of Appeal in *B v Secretary of State for Work and Pensions* [2005] EWCA Civ 929; [2005] 1 W.L.R. 3796 (also reported as *R(IS) 9/06*). He suggested that there will be a failure to notify a change of circumstances if there is a breach of clear and unambiguous instructions, as was the position in *R(IS) 9/06* but that otherwise the issue is likely to be whether the Secretary of State could reasonably have expected the claimant to notify him of the material fact. Determining the question whether reg.7(2)(c)(ii) applies may, therefore, require some evidence as to the instructions given to the claimant. See also *R(A) 2/06*. The practice of dealing with the recovery of overpayments separately from decisions as to entitlement may lead to the same complex issues of fact being considered twice.

The application of head (ii) is particularly important in relation to attendance allowance, disability living allowance, severe disablement allowance and industrial injuries disablement benefit because heads (ii), (iv) and (v) have the combined effect that supersessions are not retrospective where the change of circumstances relates to a "disability determination" as defined in reg.7A, except where the claimant both was required to notify the change of circumstances and knew or could reasonably have been expected to know that the change of circumstances should be notified. This means that, except where the claimant has clearly been at fault, there is no overpayment and so any question of the recoverability of an overpayment simply does not arise.

The revocation of reg.7(2)(c)(iii) and its replacement with heads (iv) and (v), which contain no exceptions in respect of incapacity determinations, deals with the anomalies revealed in such incapacity benefit cases as *R(IB) 1/05* and *CIB/763/2004*, where there had been changes of circumstances but no failure by the claimant to disclose them (so that head (ii) did not apply) but the Commissioner found that head (iii) did not apply either. Now, any supersession will be effective from the date of the change of circumstances by virtue of head (v). That, of course, will be at least as early as the date applicable under head (ii) and it might seem odd at first sight that a supersession may be effective from an earlier date when there has been no failure to disclose a change of circumstances than where there has been. However, this only acts to the disadvantage of a claimant where a payment of benefit has not already been made. If it has already been made, it will not be recoverable due to the lack of a failure to disclose the change of circumstances. If the payment has not already been made, there are obvious reasons why the supersession should take effect from the date of the change so that only the benefit to which the claimant is properly entitled is paid.

However, there may still be some difficulties in incapacity cases due to the practice of determining that a person is incapable of work in the contest of "credits" and then relying on that determination when determining entitlement to income support (see reg.10). In *CIB/1599/2005*, the claimant was in receipt of income support on the basis of a decision, made for the purposes of incapacity credits, that he was incapable of work. He failed to inform the social security office that he had taken some casual employment. The Commissioner held that reg.7(2)(c)(ii) did not apply because the claimant was not required by "regulations under the Administration Act" to notify his change of circumstances. Regulation 32 of the Social Security (Claims and Payments) Regulations 1987 applies only to benefit cases and not to "credits" cases. That meant that the "credits" decision could not be superseded with effect from a date before it was made. Given the terms of reg.10, that in turn presumably also limited the scope for superseding the award of income support retrospectively, although the Commissioner expressed no view on that issue.

Para. (5)

This provides consistency between, on the one hand, revision and supersession of decisions of the Secretary of State on the ground of error of fact (under regs 3(5) and 6(2)(b)) and, on the other hand, supersession of decisions of tribunals on the ground of error of fact (under reg.6(2)(c)).

2.355

Para. (9)

2.356   Supersessions of decisions concerning attendance allowance and disability living allowance on the ground of changes of circumstances which are disadvantageous to claimants are dealt with under para.(2)(c). This paragraph deals with supersessions on the grounds of changes of circumstances that are advantageous to the claimant. It is difficult to envisage a situation in which para.(9)(c) can operate because if the claimant was not entitled to any benefit before the change occurred, a claim would have been appropriate rather than a supersession (*R(I) 56/54*). Perhaps its use is envisaged in cases where a claimant becomes terminally ill during the qualifying period, although it is arguable that, even then, a new claim would be appropriate. Paragraph (9)(b) is in terms similar to para.(2)(b) with variations that seem designed merely to take account of the qualifying periods for attendance allowance and disability living allowance and to require the supersession to be effective from the first pay day after the claimant qualifies for the new rate.

Paras (12)–(23)

2.357   These are all concerned with changes in housing costs and contain provisions similar to those previously found in regs 63 and 63A of the Social Security (Adjudication) Regulations 1995.

Paras (31) and (32)

2.358   Para (31) enables a personal capability assessment to be carried out while the own occupation test is still applicable to a person claiming to be incapable of work. It provides that the decision on the personal capability assessment will be effective only from when the own occupation test ceases to be applicable. In *CIB/586/2008*, the Deputy Commissioner commented that the tribunal would have been greatly assisted had the Secretary of State drawn attention to the provision.

[1 [4 Definitions for the purposes of Chapters I and II]

2.359   **7A.**—(1) For the purposes of regulations 3(5)(c), 6(2)(g) [2, 7(2)(c) and (5)]—

"disability benefit decision" means a decision to award a relevant benefit embodied in or necessary to which is a disability determination,

"disability determination" means—

(a) in the case of a decision as to an award of an attendance allowance or a disability living allowance, whether the person satisfies any of the conditions in section 64, 72(1) or 73(1) to (3), as the case may be, of the Contributions and Benefits Act,

(b) in the case of a decision as to an award of severe disablement allowance, whether the person is disabled for the purpose of section 68 of the Contributions and Benefits Act, or

(c) in the case of a decision as to an award of industrial injuries benefit, whether the existence or extent of any disablement is sufficient for the purposes of section 103 or 108 of the Contributions and Benefits Act or for the benefit to be paid at the rate which was in payment immediately prior to that decision;

[4 "employment and support allowance decision" means a decision to award a relevant benefit or relevant credit embodied in or necessary to which is a determination that a person has or is to be treated as having limited capability for work under Part 1 of the Welfare Reform Act;]

"incapacity benefit decision" means a decision to award a relevant benefit [2 or relevant credit] embodied in or necessary to which is a determination that a person is or is to be treated as incapable of work under Part XIIA of the Contributions and Benefits Act [3 or an award of long term incapacity benefit under regulation 17(1) (transitional awards of long-term incapacity benefit) of the Social Security (Incapacity Benefit) (Transitional) Regulations 1995],

"incapacity determination" means a determination whether a person is incapable of work by applying the [² personal capability assessment] in regulation 24 of the Social Security (Incapacity for Work) (General) Regulations 1995 or whether a person is to be treated as incapable of work in accordance with regulation 10 (certain persons with a severe condition to be treated as incapable of work) or 27 (exceptional circumstances) of those Regulations, and

[⁴ or "employment and support allowance decision"

"payee" means a person to whom a benefit referred to in paragraph (a), (b) or (c) of the definition of "disability determination", or a benefit referred to in the definition of "incapacity benefit decision" [⁴ "limited capability for work determination" means a determination whether a person has limited capability for work by applying the test of limited capability for work or whether a person is to be treated as having limited capability for work in accordance with regulation 20 of the Employment and Support Allowance Regulations;] is payable.

(2) Where a person's receipt of or entitlement to a benefit ("the first benefit") is a condition of his being entitled to any other benefit, allowance or advantage ("a second benefit") and a decision is revised under regulation 3(5)(c) or a superseding decision is made under regulation 6(2) to which regulation 7(2)(c)(ii) applies, the effect of which is that the first benefit ceases to be payable, or becomes payable at a lower rate than was in payment immediately prior to that revision or supersession, a consequent decision as to his entitlement to the second benefit shall take effect from the date of the change in his entitlement to the first benefit.]

AMENDMENTS

1. Social Security and Child Support (Decisions and Appeals) Amendment (No.2) Regulations 1999 (SI 1999/1623), reg.5 (July 5, 1999).

2. Social Security and Child Support (Miscellaneous Amendments) Regulations 2000 (SI 2000/1596), reg.18 (June 19, 2000).

3. Social Security (Miscellaneous Amendments) (No.4) Regulations 2007 (SI 2007/2470), reg.3(8) (September 24, 2007).

4. Employment and Support Allowance (Consequential Provisions) (No. 2) Regulations 2008 (SI 2008/1554), regs 29 and 34 (July 27, 2008).

DEFINITIONS

"the Contributions and Benefits Act"—see s.84 of the Social Security Act 1998.
"the Employment and Support Allowance Regulations"—see reg.1(3)
"limited capability for work"—*ibid*.
"relevant benefit"—see s.39(1) of the Social Security Act 1998.
"relevant credit"—see reg.1(3).
"the Welfare Reform Act"—*ibid*.

GENERAL NOTE

"disability determination"

In *CA/2650/2006*, the Commissioner held that the reference to s.64 of the Contributions and Benefits Act (which has a different structure from that in ss. 72 and 73) in head (a) of the definition of "disability determination" refers only to

2.360

"determinations whether the conditions set out in section 64(2) and (3) were satisfied (and possibly extending to age and non-entitlement to DLA)" and so does not extend to determinations as to residence or presence.

"incapacity benefit decision"

The amendment to this definition fills the lacuna revealed in *Hooper v Secretary of State for Work and Pensions* [2007] EWCA Civ 495 (reported as *R(IB) 4/07*).

"incapacity determination"

In *CIB/313/2002* and *R(IB) 2/04* (at para.125), a single Commissioner and then a Tribunal of Commissioners left open the question whether there was an "incapacity determination" when it was determined that a person should be treated as having satisfied the personal capability assessment under reg.28 of the 1995 Regulations. In *R(IB)1/05*, a single Commissioner decided that such a determination was an "incapacity determination", but his decision on that point did not make any difference to the ultimate result of the appeal before him. Although *R(IB)1/05* is likely to be followed, the point may therefore still be arguable. However, as illustrated by all three of those decisions, it is seldom, if ever, of any practical significance.

2.361   **7B.** *Omitted.*
2.362   **7C.** *Omitted.*

Effective date for late notifications of change of circumstances

2.363   **8.**—(1) For the purposes of regulation 7(2) [² and (9)], a longer period of time may be allowed for the notification of a change of circumstances in so far as it affects the effective date of the change where the conditions specified in the following provisions of this regulation are satisfied.

(2) An application for the purposes of regulation 7(2) [² or (9)] shall be made by the claimant or a person acting on his behalf.

(3) The application referred to in paragraph (2) shall—

(a) contain particulars of the relevant change of circumstances and the reasons for the failure to notify the change of circumstances on an earlier date; and

(b) be made within 13 months of the date the change occurred.

(4) An application under this regulation shall not be granted unless the Secretary of State is satisfied [¹ or the Board are satisfied] that—

(a) it is reasonable to grant the application;

(b) the change of circumstances notified by the applicant is relevant to the decision which is to be superseded; and

(c) special circumstances are relevant to the application and as a result of those special circumstances it was not practicable for the applicant to notify the change of circumstances within one month of the change occurring.

(5) In determining whether it is reasonable to grant the application, the Secretary of State [¹ or the Board] shall have regard to the principle that the greater the amount of time that has elapsed between the date one month after the change of circumstances occurred and the date the application for the purposes of regulation 7(2) [² or (9)] is made, the more compelling should be the special circumstances on which the application is based.

(6) In determining whether it is reasonable to grant an application, no account shall be taken of the following—

(a) that the applicant or any person acting for him was unaware of, or misunderstood, the law applicable to his case (including ignorance or misunderstanding of the time limits imposed by these Regulations); or

(b) that a [³ the Upper Tribunal] or a court has taken a different view of the law from that previously understood and applied.

(7) An application under this regulation which has been refused may not be renewed.

AMENDMENTS

1. Tax Credits (Decisions and Appeals) (Amendment) Regulations 1999 (SI 1999/2570), reg.11 (October 5, 1999). Note that amendments made by these regulations only have effect with respect to tax credit (reg.1(2) of the Amendment Regulations).

2. Social Security and Child Support (Decisions and Appeals) Amendment Regulations 2000 (SI 2000/119), reg.3 (February 17, 2000).

3. Tribunals, Courts and Enforcement Act 2007 (Transitional and Consequential Provisions) Order 2008 (SI 2008/2683), Sch.1, paras 95 and 106 (November 3, 2008).

DEFINITIONS

"the Board"—see reg.1(3).
"claimant"—*ibid.*

GENERAL NOTE

Para. (6) (b)
See the note to reg.32(8)(b) which is in similar terms.   2.364

CHAPTER III

OTHER MATTERS

Certificates of recoverable benefits

9. A certificate of recoverable benefits may be reviewed under section 10   2.365
of the 1997 Act where the Secretary of State is satisfied that—
  (a) a mistake (whether in computation of the amount specified or otherwise) occurred in the preparation of the certificate;
  (b) the benefit recovered from a person who makes a compensation payment (as defined in section 1 of the 1997 Act) is in excess of the amount due to the Secretary of State;
  (c) incorrect or insufficient information was supplied to the Secretary of State by the person who applied for the certificate and in consequence the amount of benefit specified in the certificate was less than it would have been had the information supplied been correct or sufficient; or
  (d) a ground for appeal is satisfied under section 11 of the 1997 Act.

DEFINITIONS

"the 1997 Act"—see reg.1(3).
"appeal"—*ibid.*

GENERAL NOTE

These grounds of review are very wide. In *CCR/3391/2005*, the Commissioner   2.366
suggested that the Secretary of State should always consider reviewing a decision

against which an appeal has been brought, so that unnecessary cases do not reach tribunals. Regulation 9(d) may have been drafted with such an approach in mind. A submission to a tribunal would then, in effect, be an explanation for the Secretary of State not reviewing the decision in the light of the grounds of appeal. Where the appellant is the compensator, grounds of appeal are often accompanied by a considerable amount of new evidence obtained in the course of defending the compensation proceedings. Considering a review is, in such circumstances, the first opportunity the Secretary of State has to take such evidence into account.

[¹ Review of certificates

2.367   **9ZA.**—(1) A certificate may be reviewed under section 10 of the 1997 Act where the Secretary of State is satisfied that—
   (a) a mistake (whether in the computation of the amount specified or otherwise) occurred in the preparation of the certificate;
   (b) the lump sum payment recovered from a compensator who makes a compensation payment (as defined in section 1A(5) of the 1997 Act) is in excess of the amount due to the Secretary of State;
   (c) incorrect or insufficient information was supplied to the Secretary of State by the compensator who applied for the certificate and in consequence the amount of lump sum payment specified in the certificate was less than it would have been had the information supplied been correct or sufficient;
   (d) a ground for appeal is satisfied under section 11 of the 1997 Act or an appeal has been made under that section; or
   (e) a certificate has been issued and, for any reason, a recoverable lump sum payment was not included in that certificate.

(2) In this regulation and regulations 1(3) in paragraph (b) of the definition of "party to the proceedings", [³ 29 and 33], where applicable—
   (a) any reference to the 1997 Act is to be construed so as to include a reference to that Act as applied by regulation 2 of the Lump Sum Payments Regulations and, where applicable, as modified by Schedule 1 to those Regulations;
   (b) [² "certificate" means a certificate of recoverable lump sum payments, including where any of the amounts is nil;]
   (c) "lump sum payment" is a payment to which section 1A(2) of the 1997 Act applies;
   (d) "P" is to be construed in accordance with regulations 4(1)(a)(i) and 5 of the Lump Sum Payments Regulations.]

AMENDMENTS

1. Social Security (Recovery of Benefits) (Lump Sum Payments) Regulations 2008 (SI 2008/1596), Sch.2 , para.1(b) (October 1, 2008).

2. Social Security (Miscellaneous Amendments) (No.3) Regulations 2008 (SI 2008/2365), reg. 6(1) and (4) (October 1, 2008).

3. Tribunals, Courts and Enforcement Act 2007 (Transitional and Consequential Provisions) Order 2008 (SI 2008/2683), Sch.1, paras 95 and 107 (November 3, 2008).

DEFINITIONS

"the 1997 Act"—see reg.1(3) and para. (2)(a).
"certificate"—see para. (2)(b).
"lump sum payment"—see para. (2)(c).
"P"—see para. (2)(d).

[¹ Correction of accidental errors

9A.—(1) Accidental errors in a decision of the Secretary of State or an officer of the Board under a relevant enactment within the meaning of section 28(3), or in any record of such a decision, may be corrected by the Secretary of State or an officer of the Board, as the case may be, at any time.

(2) A correction made to, or to the record of, a decision shall be deemed to be part of the decision, or of that record, and the Secretary of State or an officer of the Board shall give a written notice of the correction as soon as practicable to the claimant.

(3) In calculating the time within which an application can be made under regulation 3(1)(b) for a decision to be revised [². . .] there shall be disregarded any day falling before the day on which notice was given of the decision or to the record thereof under paragraph (2).]

2.368

AMENDMENTS

1. Social Security and Child Support (Decisions and Appeals) (Miscellaneous Amendments) Regulations 2002 (SI 2002/1379), reg.4 (May 20, 2002).

2. Tribunals, Courts and Enforcement Act 2007 (Transitional and Consequential Provisions) Order 2008 (SI 2008/2683) Sch.1, paras 95 and 108 (November 3, 2008).

DEFINITIONS

"appeal"—see reg.1(3).
"the Board"—*ibid.*
"claimant"—*ibid.*

[¹ Effect of determination as to capacity or capability for work

10.—(1) This regulation applies to a determination whether a person—
(a) is capable or incapable of work;
(b) is to be treated as capable or incapable of work;
(c) has or does not have limited capability for work; or
(d) is to be treated as having or not having limited capability for work.

(2) A determination (including a determination made following a change of circumstances) as set out in paragraph (1) which is embodied in or necessary to a decision under Chapter II of Part I of the Act or on which such a decision is based shall be conclusive for the purposes of any further decision.]

2.369

AMENDMENT

1. Employment and Support Allowance (Consequential Provisions) (No. 2) Regulations 2008 (SI 2008/1554), regs 29 and 36 (July 27, 2008).

DEFINITIONS

"the Act"—see reg.1(3)
"limited capability for work"—*ibid.*

GENERAL NOTE

Note that a decision that a person is *not*, or is not to be treated as, incapable of work is not of continuing effect. Consequently, it operates to allow supersession of any award of benefit current at the time it is made but it does not operate so as to prevent a person from making a new claim or a further application for supersession,

2.370

although reg.28 of the 1995 Regulations may not apply while a new assessment is arranged (*R(IB)1/01* and *R(IB)2/01*).

Secretary of State to determine certain matters

2.371 **11.** Where, in relation to a determination for any purpose to which Part XIIA of the Contributions and Benefits Act [¹ or Part 1 of the Welfare Reform Act] applies, an issue arises as to—

(a) whether a person is, or is to be treated as, capable or incapable of work in respect of any period; or

[¹ (aa) whether a person is, or is to be treated as, having or not having limited capability for work; or]

(b) whether a person is terminally ill,

that issue shall be determined by the Secretary of State, notwithstanding that other matters fall to be determined by another authority.

AMENDMENTS

1. Employment and Support Allowance (Consequential Provisions) (No. 2) Regulations 2008 (SI 2008/1554), regs 29 and 37 (July 27, 2008).

DEFINITIONS

"the Contributions and Benefits Act"—see s.84 of the Social Security Act 1998. "limited capability for work"—see reg.1(3).

[¹ Issues for decision by officers of Inland Revenue

2.372 **11A.**—(1) Where, on consideration of any claim or other matter, it appears to the Secretary of State that an issue arises which, by virtue of section 8 of the Transfer Act, falls to be decided by an officer of the Board, he shall refer that issue to the Board.

(2) Where—

(a) the Secretary of State has decided any claim or other matter on an assumption of facts—

(i) as to which there appeared to him to be no dispute, but

(ii) concerning which, had an issue arisen, that issue would have fallen, by virtue of section 8 of the Transfer Act, to be decided by an officer of the Board; and

(b) an application for revision or an application for supersession [² or an appeal] is made in relation to the decision of that claim or other matter; and

(c) it appears to the Secretary of State on [² receipt of the application or appeal] that such an issue arises,

he shall refer that issue to the Board.

(3) Pending the final decision of any issue which has been referred to the Board in accordance with paragraph (1) or (2) above, the Secretary of State may—

(a) determine any other issue arising on consideration of the claim or other matter or, as the case may be, of the application,

(b) seek a preliminary opinion of the Board on the issue referred and decide the claim or other matter or, as the case may be, the application in accordance with that opinion on that issue; or

(c) defer making any decision on the claim or other matter or, as the case may be, the application.

(4) On receipt by the Secretary of State of the final decision of an issue which has been referred to the Board in accordance with paragraph (1) or (2) above, the Secretary of State that—

    (a) in a case to which paragraph (3)(b) above applies—

        (i) consider whether the decision ought to be revised under section 9 or superseded under section 10, and

        (ii) if so, revise it, or, as the case may be, make a further decision which supersedes it; or

    (b) in a case to which paragraph (3)(a) or (c) above applies, decide the claim or other matter or, as the case may be, the application,

in accordance with the final decision of the issue so referred.

(5) In paragraphs (3) and (4) above "final decision" means the decision of an officer of the Board under section 8 of the Transfer Act or the determination of any appeal in relation to that decision.]

AMENDMENTS

1. Social Security and Child Support (Decisions and Appeals) Amendment (No.3) Regulations 1999 (SI 1999/1623), reg.2(3) (July 5, 1999).

2. Social Security and Child Support (Decisions and Appeals) (Miscellaneous Amendments) Regulations 2002 (SI 2002/1379), reg.5 (May 20, 2002).

DEFINITIONS

    "appeal"—see reg.1(3).

    "the Board"—*ibid.*

    "claim"—by virtue of s.39(2) of the Social Security Act 1998, see s.191 of the Social Security Administration Act 1992.

    "final decision"—see para.(5).

    "the Transfer Act"—see reg.1(3).

GENERAL NOTE

The Inland Revenue has been merged into Her Majesty's Revenue and Customs (HMRC). See the note to the definition of "the Board" in reg.1(3). Some decisions fall to be made by officers of the Inland Revenue by virtue of s.170 of the Pensions Schemes Act 1993 (rather than by virtue of s.8 of the Social Security Contributions (Transfer of Functions, etc.) Act 1999) but the Secretary of State may refer to officers of the Inland Revenue issues for determination under the 1993 Act notwithstanding that this regulation does not apply *(R(P)1/04)*.

Decision of the Secretary of State relating to industrial injuries benefit

12.—(1) This regulation applies where, for the purpose of a decision of the Secretary of State relating to a claim for industrial injuries benefit under Part V of the Contributions and Benefits Act an issue to be decided is—

    (a) the extent of a personal injury for the purposes of section 94 of that Act;

    (b) whether the claimant has a disease prescribed for the purposes of section 108 of that Act or the extent of any disablement resulting from such a disease; or

    (c) whether the claimant has a disablement for the purposes of section 103 of that Act or the extent of any such disablement.

(2) In connection with making a decision to which this regulation applies, the Secretary of State may refer an issue, together with any relevant evidence or information available to him, including any evidence or information provided by or on behalf of the claimant, to a [1 health care professional

2.373

approved by the Secretary of State] who has experience in such of the issues specified in paragraph (1) as are relevant to the decision, for such report as appears to the Secretary of State to be necessary for the purpose of providing him with information for use in making the decision.

(3) In making a decision to which this regulation applies, the Secretary of State shall have regard to (among other factors)—

    (a) all relevant medical reports provided to him in connection with that decision; and

    (b) the experience, in such of the issues specified in paragraph (1) as are relevant to the decision, of any [1 health care professional] who has provided a report, including a [1 health care professional approved by the Secretary of State] who has provided a report following an examination required by the Secretary of State under section 19.

AMENDMENT

1. Social Security (Miscellaneous Amendments) (No.2) Regulations 2007 (SI 2007/1626), reg.4(2) (July 3, 2007).

DEFINITIONS

    "claimant"—see reg.1(3).
    "health care professional"—see s.39(2) of the Social Security Act 1998
    "industrial injuries benefit"—by virtue of s.39(2) of the Social Security Act 1998, see s.191 of the Social Security Administration Act 1992.
    "medical practitioner"—*ibid.*

GENERAL NOTE

2.374   Adjudicating medical authorities have been abolished and so all decisions which an adjudication officer would, or might, have referred to such authorities under the Social Security Administration Act 1992 are now decided by the Secretary of State on the basis of medical advice which, since 2007, may be given by a health care professional other than a doctor. Approved health care professionals receive special training to make an assessment of the disabling effects of an impairment and relate this to the relevant legislation in order to provide advice or reports for those making decisions on behalf of the Secretary of State. Even where a health care professional has not examined a claimant, his or her opinion may be taken into account as evidence, provided the tribunal can identify the factual basis on which the opinion was given. On appeal, para (3)(b) makes it necessary for a tribunal to know the health care professional's professional qualification and area of expertise (see also *CDLA/2466/2007*).

See s.30 of the Social Security Act 1998 for the effect of an earlier declaration that the claimant has suffered personal injury by accident.

[1 Recrudescence of a prescribed disease

2.375   **12A.**—(1) This regulation applies to a decision made under sections 108 to 110 of the Contributions and Benefits Act where a disease is subsequently treated as a recrudescence under regulation 7 of the Social Security (Industrial Injuries) (Prescribed Diseases) Regulations 1985.

(2) Where this regulation applies Chapter II of Part I of the Act shall apply as if section 8(2) did not apply.]

AMENDMENT

1. Social Security and Child Support (Miscellaneous Amendments) Regulations 2000 (SI 2000/1596), reg.19 (June 19, 2000).

"the Contributions and Benefits Act"—see s.84 of the Social Security Act 1998.

Income support and social fund determinations on incomplete evidence

13.—(1) Where, for the purpose of a decision under section 8 or 10—   2.376
[¹ (a)   a determination falls to be made by the Secretary of State as to what housing costs are to be included in—
    (i)   a claimant's applicable amount by virtue of regulation 17(1)(e) or 18(1)(f) of, and Schedule 3 to, the Income Support Regulations; [² . . .]
    (ii)   a claimant's appropriate minimum guarantee by virtue of regulation 6(6)(c) and Schedule II to the State Pension Credit Regulations; [² or]]
    [² (iii)   a claimant's applicable amount under regulation 67(1)(c) or 68(1)(d) of the Employment and Support Allowance Regulations; and]
  (b)   it appears to the Secretary of State that he is not in possession of all of the evidence or information which is relevant for the purposes of such a determination,
he shall make the determination on the assumption that the housing costs to be included in the claimant's [¹ applicable amount or, as the case may be, appropriate minimum guarantee are those] that can be immediately determined.

(2) Where, for the purpose of a decision under section 8 or 10—
  (a)   a determination falls to be made by the Secretary of State as to whether—
    (i)   in relation to any person, the applicable amount falls to be reduced or disregarded to any extent by virtue of section 126(3) of the Contributions and Benefits Act (persons affected by trade disputes);
    (ii)   for the purposes of regulation 12 of the Income Support Regulations, a person is by virtue of that regulation to be treated as receiving relevant education; [² . . .]
    (iii)   in relation to any claimant, the applicable amount includes severe disability premium by virtue of regulation 17(1)(d) or 18(1)(e), and paragraph 13 of Schedule 2 to, the Income Support Regulations; [² or
    (iv)   in relation to any claimant, the applicable amount includes the severe disability premium by virtue of regulation 67(1) or 68(1) of, and paragraph 6 of Schedule 4 to, the Employment and Support Allowance Regulations; and]
  (b)   it appears to the Secretary of State that he is not in possession of all of the evidence or information which is relevant for the purposes of such a determination,
he shall make the determination on the assumption that the relevant evidence or information which is not in his possession is adverse to the claimant.

[¹ (3) Where, for the purposes of a decision under section 8 or 10—
  (a)   a determination falls to be made by the Secretary of State as to whether a claimant's appropriate minimum guarantee includes an

additional amount in accordance with regulation 6(4) of, and paragraph 1 of Schedule I to, the State Pension Credit Regulations; and

(b) it appears to the Secretary of State that he is not in possession of all the evidence or information which is relevant for the purpose of such a determination,

he shall make the determination on the assumption that the relevant evidence or information which is not in his possession is adverse to the claimant.]

AMENDMENTS

1. State Pension Credit (ConsequentialTransitional and Miscellaneous Provisions) Regulations 2002 (SI 2002/3019), reg.19 (April 7, 2003).
2. Employment and Support Allowance (Consequential Provisions) (No.2) Regulations 2008 (SI 2008/1554), regs 29 and 38 (July 27, 2008).

DEFINITIONS

"claimant"—see reg.1(3).
"the Contributions and Benefits Act"—see s.84 of the Social Security Act 1998.
"the Employment and Support Allowance Regulations"—see reg.1(3).
"the Income Support Regulations"—*ibid*.
"State Pension Credit Regulations"—*ibid*.

[¹ Retirement pension after period of deferment

2.377   **13A.**—(1) This regulation applies where—

(a) a person claims a Category A or Category B retirement pension, shared additional pension or, as the case may be, graduated retirement benefit;

(b) an election is required by, as the case may be—

(i) paragraph A1 or 3C of Schedule 5 to the Contributions and Benefits Act (pension increase or lump sum where entitlement to retirement pension is deferred);

(ii) paragraph 1 of Schedule 5A to that Act (pension increase or lump sum where entitlement to shared additional pension is deferred); or, as the case may be,

(iii) paragraph 12 or 17 of Schedule 1 to the Graduated Retirement Benefit Regulations (further provisions replacing section 36(4) of the National Insurance Act 1965: increases of graduated retirement benefit and lump sums); and

(c) no election is made when the claim is made.

(2) In the cicumstances specified in paragraph (1) the Secretary of State may decide the claim before any election is made, or is treated as made, for an increase or lump sum.

(3) When an election is made, or is treated as made, the Secretary of State shall revise the decision which he made in pursuance of paragraph (2).]

AMENDMENT

1. Social Security (Deferral of Retirement Pensions, Shared Additional Pension and Graduated Retirement Benefit) (Miscellaneous Provisions) Regulations 2005 (SI 2005/2677), reg.9(6) (April 6, 2006).

DEFINITIONS

"the Contributions and Benefits Act"—see s.84 of the Social Security Act 1998.
"the Graduated Retirement Benefit Regulations"—see reg.1(3).

Effect of alteration in the component rates of income support and jobseeker's allowance

14.—(1) Section 159 of the Administration Act (effect of alteration in the component rates of income support) shall not apply to any award of income support in force in favour of a person where there is applicable to that person—

2.378

(a) any amount determined in accordance with regulation 17(2) to (7) of the Income Support Regulations; or

(b) any protected sum determined in accordance with Schedule 3A or 3B of those Regulations; or

(c) any transitional addition, personal expenses addition or special transitional addition applicable under Part II of the Income Support (Transitional) Regulations 1987 (transitional protection).

(2) Where section 159 of the Administration Act does not apply to an award of income support by virtue of paragraph (1), a decision under section 10 may be made in respect of that award for the sole purpose of giving effect to any change made by an order under section 150 of the Administration Act.

(3) Section 159A of the Administration Act (effect of alterations in the component rates of jobseeker's allowance) shall not apply to any award of a jobseeker's allowance in force in favour of a person where there is applicable to that person any amount determined in accordance with regulations 87 of the Jobseeker's Allowance Regulations.

(4) Where section 159A of the Administration Act does not apply to an award of a jobseeker's allowance by virtue of paragraph (3), a decision under section 10 may be made in respect of that award for the sole purpose of giving effect to any change made by an order under section 150 of the Administration Act.

[¹ (5) Section 159B of the Administration Act (effect of alterations affecting state pension credit) shall not apply to any award of state pension credit in favour of a person where in relation to that person the appropriate minimum guarantee includes an amount determined under paragraph 6 of Part III of Schedule I to the State Pension Credit Regulations.

(6) Where section 159B of the Administration Act does not apply to an award of state pension credit by virtue of paragraph (5), a decision under section 10 may be made in respect of that award for the sole purpose of giving effect to any change made to an award under section 150 of the Administration Act.]

AMENDMENT

1. State Pension Credit (Consequential Transitional and Miscellaneous Provisions) Regulations 2002 (SI 2002/3019), reg.20 (April 7, 2003).

DEFINITIONS

"the Administration Act"—see s.84 of the Social Security Act 1998.
"the Income Support Regulations"—see reg.1(3).
"the Jobseeker's Allowance Regulations"—*ibid.*
"state pension credit"—*ibid.*
"State Pension Credit Regulations"—*ibid.*

[¹ Termination of award of income support [² , jobseeker's allowance or employment and support allowance]

2.379   **14A.**—(1) This regulation applies in a case where an award of income support [² , a jobseeker's allowance or an employment and support allowance] ("the existing benefit") exists in favour of a person and, if that award did not exist and a claim was made by that person or his partner for [² an employment and support allowance,] a jobseeker's allowance or, as the case may be, income support ("the alternative benefit"), an award of the alternative benefit would be made on that claim.

(2) In a case to which this regulation applies, if a claim for the alternative benefit is made the Secretary of State may bring to an end the award of the existing benefit if he is satisfied that an alternative benefit will be made on that claim.

(3) Where, under paragraph (2), the Secretary of State brings an award of the existing benefit to an end he shall do so with effect from the day immediately preceding the first day on which an award of the alternative benefit takes effect.

(4) Where an award of a jobseeker's allowance is made in accordance with the provisions of this regulation, paragraph 4 of Schedule 1 to the Jobseeker's Act (waiting days) shall not apply.]

[² (5) Where an award of an employment and support allowance is made in accordance with the provisions of this regulation, paragraph 2 of Schedule 2 to the Welfare Reform Act (waiting days) shall not apply.]

AMENDMENTS

1. Social Security and Child Support (Decisions and Appeals) (Miscellaneous Amendments) Regulations 2002 (SI 2002/1379), reg.6 (May 20, 2002).
2. Employment and Support Allowance (Consequential Provisions) (No.2) Regulations 2008 (SI 2008/1554), regs 29 and 39 (July 27, 2008).

DEFINITIONS

"the alternative benefit"—see para.(1).
"the Jobseekers Act"—see s.84 of the Social Security Act 1998.
"the Welfare Reform Act"—see reg.1(3).

Jobseeker's allowance determinations on incomplete evidence

2.380   **15.** Where, for the purpose of a decision under section 8 or 10—
(a) a determination falls to be made by the Secretary of State as to whether—
  (i) in relation to any person, the applicable amount falls to be reduced or disregarded to any extent by virtue of section 15 of the Jobseekers Act (persons affected by trade disputes); or
  (ii) for the purposes of regulation 54(2) to (4) of the Jobseeker's Allowance Regulations (relevant education), a person is by virtue of that regulation, to be treated as receiving relevant education; and
(b) it appears to the Secretary of State that he is not in possession of all of the evidence or information which is relevant for the purposes of such a determination.
he shall make the determination on the assumption that the relevant

evidence or information which is not in his possession is adverse to the claimant.

DEFINITIONS

"claimant"—see reg.1(3).
"the Jobseekers Act"—see s.84 of the Social Security Act 1998.
"the Jobseeker's Allowance Regulations"—see reg.1(3).

15A.–15D. *Omitted.*   2.381

PART III

SUSPENSION, TERMINATION AND OTHER MATTERS

CHAPTER I

SUSPENSION AND TERMINATION

Suspension in prescribed cases

16.—(1) Subject to paragraph (2), the Secretary of State [¹ or the Board]   2.382
may suspend payment of a relevant benefit, in whole or in part, in the
circumstances prescribed in paragraph (3).

(2) The Secretary of State shall suspend payment of a jobseeker's allowance in the circumstances prescribed in paragraph (3)(a)(i) or (ii) where
the issue or one of the issues is whether a person, who has claimed a jobseeker's allowance, is or was available for employment or whether he is or
was actively seeking employment.

(3) The prescribed circumstances are that—

(a) it appears to the Secretary of State [¹ or the Board] that—
   (i)   an issue arises whether the conditions for entitlement to a rele-
         vant benefit are or were fulfilled;
   (ii) an issue arises whether a decision as to an award of a relevant
         benefit should be revised under section 9 or superseded under
         section 10;
   (iii) an issue arises whether any amount paid or payable to a person
         by way of, or in connection with a claim for, a relevant benefit
         is recoverable under section 71(overpayments), 71A (recovery
         of jobseeker's allowance: severe hardship cases) or 74 (income
         support and other payments) of the Administration Act or regu-
         lations made under any of those sections; or
   (iv) the last address notified to him [¹ or them] of a person who is
         in receipt of a relevant benefit is not the address at which that
         person is residing; or

(b) an appeal is pending against—
   (i)   a decision of an [³ the First-tier Tribunal, the Upper Tribunal\
         or a court;
   (ii) a decision given in a different case by [³ the Upper Tribunal] or
         a court, and it appears to the Secretary of State [¹ or the Board]

575

that, if the appeal were to be determined in a particular way, an issue would arise as to whether the award of a relevant benefit (whether the same benefit or not) in the case itself ought to be revised or superseded.

[²(4) For the purposes of section 21(3)(c) an appeal is pending where a decision of [³ the First-tier Tribunal, the Upper Tribunal] or a court has been made and the Secretary of State—

(a) is awaiting receipt of that decision or (in the case of [³ a decision of the First-tier Tribunal]) is considering whether to apply for a statement of the reasons for it, or has applied for such a statement and is awaiting receipt thereof; or

(b) has received that decision or (in the case [³ a decision of the First-tier Tribunal]) the statement of the reasons for it, and is considering whether to apply for [³ permission] to appeal, or where [³ permission] to appeal has been granted, is considering whether to appeal;

and the Secretary of State shall give written notice of his proposal to make a request for a statement of the reasons for a tribunal decision, to apply for leave to appeal, or to appeal, as soon as reasonably practicable.]

AMENDMENTS

1. Tax Credits (Decisions and Appeals) (Amendment) Regulations 1999 (SI 1999/2570), reg.12 (October 5, 1999). Note that amendments made by these regulations only have effect with respect to tax credit (reg.1(2) of the Amendment Regulations).

2. Social Security and Child Support (Miscellaneous Amendments) Regulations 2000 (SI 2000/1596), reg.20 (June 19, 2000).

3. Tribunals, Courts and Enforcement Act 2007 (Transitional and Consequential Provisions) Order 2008 (SI 2008/2683), Sch.1, paras 95 and 109 (November 3, 2008).

DEFINITIONS

"the Administration Act"—see s.84 of the Social Security Act 1998.
"the Board"—see reg.1(3).
"relevant benefit"—see s.39(1) of the Social Security Act 1998.

GENERAL NOTE

2.383   There is no appeal against a decision under reg.16 (see Sch.2, para.24). The claimant must wait until a decision is made as to entitlement. Regulation 18 makes proision for the termination of entitlement if information is not provided and reg.20 makes provision for the reinstatement of payments.

In *CA/3800/2006*, a claimant entitled to attendance allowance had been paying her own nursing home fees. However, she got into financial difficulties because her money had been badly invested by a financial adviser and the local authority started paying the fees. The claimant was in dispute with her financial adviser and eventually recovered a substantial sum that required her to reimburse the local authority for the fees it had paid. It was held that it had been inappropriate to supersede the award of attendance allowance so as to terminate payment when the local authority started paying the fees because it was impossible to reinstate the payments with effect from the date they had been terminated on a supersession following the reimbursement of the local authority. Instead, because the claimant had been in dispute with her financial adviser, the Secretary of State should merely have suspended payment on the ground that an issue within the scope of reg.16(3)(a)(ii) had arisen. The Commissioner revised the first supersession on the ground of "official error" so that payments could be reinstated from the date they had been stopped.

Provision of information or evidence

17.—(1) This regulation applies where the Secretary of State requires   **2.384** information or evidence for a determination whether a decision awarding a relevant benefit should be—

(a) revised under section 9; or

(b) superseded under section 10.

(2) For the purposes of paragraph (1), the following persons must satisfy the requirements of paragraph (4)—

(a) a person in respect of whom payment of a benefit has been suspended in the circumstances prescribed in regulation 16(3)(a);

(b) a person who has made an application for a decision of the Secretary of State to be revised or superseded;

(c) a person who fails to comply with the provisions of regulation 32(1) of the Claims and Payments Regulations in so far as they relate to documents, information or facts required by the Secretary of State;

(d) a person who qualifies for income support by virtue of paragraph 7 of Schedule 1B to the Income Support Regulations;

(e) a person whose entitlement to benefit is conditional upon his being, or being treated as, incapable of work;

[[1] (f) a person whose entitlement to an employment and support allowance is conditional on his having, or being treated as having, limited capability for work.]

(3) The Secretary of State shall notify any person to whom paragraph (2) refers of the requirements of this regulation.

(4) A person to whom paragraph (2) refers must either—

(a) supply the information or evidence within—

    (i) a period of one month beginning with the date on which the notification under paragraph (3) was sent to him; or

    (ii) such longer period as he satisfies the Secretary of State is necessary in order to enable him to comply with the requirement; or

(b) satisfy the Secretary of State within the period of time specified in sub-paragraph (a)(i) that either—

    (i) the information or evidence required of him does not exist; or

    (ii) that it is not possible for him to obtain it.

(5) The Secretary of State may suspend the payment of a relevant benefit, in whole or in part, to any person to whom paragraph (2)(b) to (e) applies who fails to satisfy the requirements of paragraph (4).

(6) In this regulation, "evidence" includes evidence which a person is required to provide in accordance with regulation 2 of the Social Security (Medical Evidence) Regulations 1976.

AMENDMENT

1. Employment and Support Allowance (Consequential Provisions) (No.2) Regulations 2008 (SI 2008/1554), regs 29 and 40 (July 27, 2008).

DEFINITIONS

"the Claims and Payments Regulations"—see reg.1(3).

"evidence"—see para.(6).

"the Income Support Regulations"—see reg.1(3).

"limited capability for work"—*ibid.*

"relevant benefit"—see s.39(1) of the Social Security Act 1998.

GENERAL NOTE

2.385   A different version of this regulation (reproduced in editions of this work up to 2005) was enacted by reg.13 of the Tax Credits (Decisions and Appeals) (Amendment) Regulations 1999 (SI 1999/2570) with effect from October 5, 1999 in respect of working families' tax credit and disabled person's tax credit, payable under the Tax Credits Act 1999 until 2003.

Termination in cases of failure to furnish information or evidence

2.386   **18.**—(1) Subject to paragraphs (2), (3) and (4), the Secretary of State shall decide that where a person—

(a) whose benefit has been suspended in accordance with regulation 16 and who subsequently fails to comply with an information requirement made in pursuance of regulation 17; or

(b) whose benefit has been suspended in accordance with regulation 17(5),

that person shall cease to be entitled to that benefit from the date on which payment was suspended except where entitlement to benefit ceases on an earlier date other than under this regulation.

(2) Paragraph (1)(a) shall not apply where not more than one month has elapsed since the information requirement was made in pursuance of regulation 17.

(3) Paragraph (1)(b) shall not apply where not more than one month has elapsed since the first payment was suspended in accordance with regulation 17.

(4) Paragraph (1) shall not apply where benefit has been suspended in part under regulation 16 or, as the case may be, regulation 17.

GENERAL NOTE

2.387   A different version of this regulation (reproduced in editions of this work up to 2005) was enacted by reg.13 of the Tax Credits (Decisions and Appeals) (Amendment) Regulations 1999 (SI 1999/2570) with effect from October 5, 1999 in respect of working families' tax credit and disabled person's tax credit, payable under the Tax Credits Act 1999 until 2003.

A decision that entitlement has ceased under reg.18(1) will usually be a supersession decision against which an appeal lies (*R(H) 4/08*). A refusal to allow a home visit is not, in itself, a refusal to provide information and there can usually be no termination if the claimant has not been given a deadline under reg.17(3) and (4) by which the information must be provided (*CH/2995/2006*).

In *R(H)1/09*, a claimant of council tax benefit had an annual turnover below £15,000 and so was not required to produce a profit and loss account for tax purposes and had not done so. The local authority had no reason not to believe that he had no such account. It failed to inform the claimant of the council tax benefit provision equivalent to reg.17(4)(b) and did not ask for any alternative evidence when informed by the claimant that he did not have any accounts and that his expenses were simply the same as the previous year. The Deputy Commissioner held that there were no grounds for terminating the award of benefit under the equivalent of reg.18. If the local authority or tribunal had considered that the amount claimed for expenses was unrealistic, they could have asked for further evidence or simply recalculated the claimant's entitlement to council tax benefit on the basis that he had no, or a smaller amount of, expenses.

Suspension and termination for failure to submit to medical examination

19.—(1) Except where regulation 8 of the Social Security (Incapacity for Work) (General) Regulations 1995 [³ . . .] (where a question arises as to whether a person is capable of work) [³ or regulation 23 of the Employment and Support Allowance Regulations (where a question arises whether a person has limited capability for work) applies], the Secretary of State [¹or the Board] may require a person to submit to a medical examination by a [² health care professional approved by the Secretary of State] where that person is in receipt of a relevant benefit, and either—

(a) the Secretary of State considers [¹or the Board consider] it necessary to satisfy himself [¹or themselves] as to the correctness of the award of the benefit, or of the rate at which it was awarded; or

(b) that person applies for a revision or supersession of the award and the Secretary of State considers [¹ or the Board consider] that the examination is necessary for the purpose of making his [¹ or their] decision.

(2) The Secretary of State [¹ or the Board] may suspend payment of a relevant benefit in whole or in part, to a person who fails, without good cause, on two consecutive occasions to submit to a medical examination in accordance with requirements under paragraph (1) except where entitlement to benefit is suspended on an earlier date other than under this regulation.

(3) Subject to paragraph (4), the Secretary of State [¹ or the Board] may determine that the entitlement to a relevant benefit of a person, in respect of whom payment of such a benefit has been suspended under paragraph (2), shall cease from a date not earlier than the date on which payment was suspended except where entitlement to benefit ceases on an earlier date other than under this regulation.

(4) Paragraph (3) shall not apply where not more than one month has elapsed since the first payment was suspended under paragraph (2).

2.388

AMENDMENTS

1. Tax Credits (Decisions and Appeals) (Amendment) Regulations 1999 (SI 1999/2570), reg.14 (October 5, 1999). Note that amendments made by these regulations have effect only with respect to tax credit under the Tax Credit Act 1999 (reg.1(2) of the Amendment Regulations).

2. Social Security (Miscellaneous Amendments) (No.2) Regulations 2007 (S.I. 2007/1626), reg.4(3) (July 3, 2007).

3. Employment and Support Allowance (Consequential Provisions) (No.2) Regulations 2008 (SI 2008/1554), regs 29 and 41 (July 27, 2008)

DEFINITIONS

"the Board"—see reg.1(3).
"the Employment and Support Allowance Regulations"—*ibid.*
"health care professional"—see s.39 of the Social Security Act 1998.
"limited capability for work"—see reg.1(3).
"medical examination"—by virtue of s.39(2) of the Social Security Act 1998, see s.191 of the Social Security Administration Act 1992.
"medical practitioner"—*ibid.*
"relevant benefit"—see s.39(1) of the Social Security Act 1998.

GENERAL NOTE

Whereas s.19 of the Social Security Act 1998 provides for the obtaining of a report for the purpose of determining a claim, this regulation provides for the obtaining of a

2.389

report for the purpose of deciding whether an award should be revised or superseded. In *CDLA/2335/2001*, the claimant's award of disability living allowance was terminated because he had failed to attend two consecutive appointments for medical examinations. The claimant's appeal to a tribunal was dismissed and he appealed to a Commissioner. The Commissioner criticised the submission provided to the tribunal on behalf of the decision-maker, which had failed to include any reference to the statutory provision under which the award had been terminated. The Secretary of State conceded that the relevant provision was reg.19 and that the conditions for terminating an award of benefit under para.(3) were not met because, contrary to para.(2), benefit had been suspended before there had been any suggestion that the claimant should attend an appointment for an examination and, contrary to para.(4), more than a month had elapsed since the suspension. The Secretary of State's representative explained that the automated system used to generate decisions was unable to generate a decision in conformity with reg.19 and the decision-maker had used the "least inappropriate" code available. The claimant had said that, following the termination of the award of benefit, he had offered to attend a medical examination but that offer had been rebuffed. The Commissioner observed that a termination under reg.19(3) is effective only until the claimant makes a new claim and that, if the claimant had made such an offer, he should have been told he could make a new claim and that a medical examination would then be arranged.

A decision that entitlement has ceased under reg.19(3) will usually be a supersession decision against which an appeal lies (*R(H) 4/08* and see also paragraph 22 of *CH/2995/2006*). A decision under reg.19(3) cannot be justified merely because there has been a purported suspension under reg.19(2). The conditions for such a suspension must actually have been satisfied (*CDLA/5167/2001*). This will usually involve consideration of whether the claimant had "good cause" for failing to submit to a medical examination. It is suggested that what amounts to "good cause" under this provision is the same as under all similar provisions where benefit claimants are required to attend medical examinations. A number of decisions on the meaning of "good cause" were considered in *AF v SSWP* [2009] UKUT 56 (AAC) in the context of reg.8(2) of the Social Security (Incapacity for Work) (General) Regulations 1995 (see Vol.I). It was emphasised that the integrity of the social security scheme depends on there being appropriate tests in place, so that, in the absence of "good cause" a person who decides as a matter of principle not to attend an examination must be taken to accept the consequence that benefit is likely to be refused. On the other hand, reference was made to *R(S) 9/51* where the claimant was a Christian Scientist and the Commissioner accepted that an objection based on a firm religious conviction, rather than mere prejudice or distaste for the process, would amount to "good cause".

Making of payments which have been suspended

2.390   **20.**—(1) Subject to paragraphs (2) and (3), payment of a benefit suspended in accordance with regulation 16 [¹ or 17] shall be made where—

  (a) in a case to which regulation 16(2) or (3)(a)(i) to (iii) applies, the Secretary of State is satisfied [² or the Board are satisfied] that the benefit suspended is properly payable and no outstanding issues remain to be resolved;

  (b) in a case to which regulation 16(3)(a)(iv) applies, the Secretary of State is satisfied [² or the Board are satisfied] that the has [² or they have] been notified of the address at which the person is residing;

  (c) [³ . . .];

  (d) [¹ in a case to which regulation 17(5) applies, the Secretary of State is satisfied that the benefit is properly payable and the requirements of regulation 17(4) have been satisfied.]

[² (d) *in a case to which regulation 18(1) applies, the Board are satisfied that the benefit suspended is properly payable and the requirements of regulation 17(2), (4), (5) or (7) have been satisfied.*]

[³ (2) Where regulation 16(3)(b)(i) applies, payment of a benefit suspended shall be made if the Secretary of State—

(a) does not, in the case of a decision of [⁴ the First-tier Tribunal], apply for a statement of the reasons for that decision within the period [⁴ specified under Tribunal Procedure Rules];

(b) does not, in the case of a decision of [⁴ the First-tier Tribunal, the Upper Tribunal] or a court, make an application for [⁴ permission] to appeal and (where [⁴ the Upper Tribunal] to appeal is granted) make the appeal within the time prescribed for the making of such applications and appeals;

(c) withdraws an application for [⁴ permission] to appeal or the appeal; or

(d) is refused [⁴ permission]to appeal, in circumstances where it is not open to him to renew the application for leave or to make a further application for leave to appeal.

(3) Where regulation 16(3)(b)(ii) applies, payment of a benefit suspended shall be made if the Secretary of State, in relation to the decision of [⁴ the Upper Tribunal] or the court in a different case—

(a) does not make an application for [⁴ permission] to appeal and (where [⁴ permission] to appeal is granted) make the appeal within the time prescribed for the making of such applications and appeals;

(b) withdraws an application for [⁴ permission] to appeal or the appeal; or

(c) is refused [⁴ permission] to appeal, in circumstances where it is not open to him to renew the application for [⁴ permission] or to make a further application for [⁴ permission] to appeal.]

(4) Payment of benefit which has been suspended in accordance with regulation 19 for failure to submit to a medical examination shall be made where the Secretary of State is satisfied [² or the Board are satisfied] that it is no longer necessary for the person referred to in that regulation to submit to a medical examination.

AMENDMENTS

1. Social Security and Child Support (Decisions and Appeals) Amendment (No.2) Regulations 1999 (SI 1999/1623), reg.6 (July 5, 1999).

2. Tax Credits (Decisions and Appeals) (Amendment) Regulations 1999 (SI 1999/2570), reg.15 (October 5, 1999). Note that amendments made by these Regulations have effect only with respect to tax credit under the Tax Credit Act 1999 (reg.1(2) of the Amendment Regulations). There are thus two forms of para.(1)(d) as the second form is only substituted for the purposes of tax credit.

3. Social Security and Child Support (Miscellaneous Amendments) Regulations 2000 (SI 2000/1596), reg.21 (June 19, 2000).

4. Tribunals, Courts and Enforcement Act 2007 (Transitional and Consequential Provisions) Order 2008 (SI 2008/2683), Sch.1, paras 95 and 110 (November 3, 2008).

DEFINITIONS

"the Board"—see reg.1(3).

"medical examination"—by virtue of s.39(2) of the Social Security Act 1998, see s.191 of the Social Security Administration Act 1992.

CHAPTER II

OTHER MATTERS

Decisions involving issues that arise on appeal in other cases

2.391
21.—(1) For the purposes of section 25(3)(b) (prescribed cases and circumstances in which a decision may be made on a prescribed basis) a case which satisfies the condition in paragraph (2) is a prescribed case.

(2) The condition is that the claimant would be entitled to the benefit to which the decision which falls to be made relates, even if the appeal in the other case referred to in section 25(1)(b) were decided in a way which is the most unfavourable to him.

(3) For the purposes of section 25(3)(b), the prescribed basis on which the Secretary of State [¹ or the Board] may make the decision is as if—

(a) the appeal in the other case which is referred to in section 25(1)(b) had already been determined; and

(b) that appeal had been decided in a way which is the most unfavourable to the claimant.

(4) The circumstance prescribed under section 25(5)(c), where an appeal is pending against a decision for the purposes of that section, even though an appeal against the decision has not been brought (or, as the case may be, an application for [² permission] to appeal against the decision has not been made) but the time for doing so has not yet expired, is where the Secretary of State [¹ or the Board—

(a) certifies in writing that he is [¹, or certify in writing that they are,] considering appealing against that decision; and

(b) considers [¹, or consider,] that, if such an appeal were to be determined in a particular way—

(i) there would be no entitlement to benefit in a case to which section 25(1)(a) refers; or

(ii) the appeal would affect the decision in that case in some other way.

AMENDMENTS

1. Tax Credits (Decisions and Appeals) (Amendment) Regulations 1999 (SI 1999/2570), reg.16 (October 5, 1999). Note that amendments made by these regulations only have effect with respect to tax credit under the Tax Credit Act 1999 (reg.1(2) of the Amendment Regulations).

2. Tribunals, Courts and Enforcement Act 2007 (Transitional and Consequential Provisions) Order 2008 (SI 2008/2683), Sch.1, paras 95 and 111 (November 3, 2008).

DEFINITIONS

"the Board"—see reg.1(3).
"claimant"—*ibid.*

Appeals involving issues that arise in other cases

22. The circumstance prescribed under section 26(6)(c), where an appeal is pending against a decision in the case described in section 26(1)(b) even though an appeal against the decision has not been brought (or, as the case may be, an application for [² permission] to appeal against the decision has not been made) but the time for doing so has not yet expired, is where the Secretary of State [¹ or the Board—

    (a) certifies in writing that he is [¹, or certify in writing that they are,] considering appealing against that decision; and

    (b) considers [¹, or consider,] that, if such an appeal were already determined, it would affect the determination of the appeal described in section 26(1)(a).

2.392

AMENDMENTS

1. Tax Credits (Decisions and Appeals) (Amendment) Regulations 1999 (SI 1999/2570), reg.17 (October 5, 1999). Note that amendments made by these regulations only have effect with respect to tax credit under the Tax Credit Act 1999 (reg.1(2) of the Amendment Regulations).

2. Tribunals, Courts and Enforcement Act 2007 (Transitional and Consequential Provisions) Order 2008 (SI 2008/2683), Sch.1, paras 95 and 112 (November 3, 2008).

DEFINITION

"the Board"—see reg.1(3).

23. *Omitted.*

2.393

24. *Omitted.*

2.394

PART IV

RIGHTS OF APPEAL AND PROCEDURE FOR BRINGING APPEALS

CHAPTER I

GENERAL

General appeals matters not including child support appeals

Other persons with a right of appeal

25. For the purposes of [³ section 12(2)], the following other persons have a right to appeal to [⁴ the First-tier Tribunal]—

    [² (ai) any person who has been appointed by the Secretary of State or the Board under regulation 30(1) of the Claims and Payments Regulations (payments on death) to proceed with the claim of a person who has made a claim for benefit and subsequently died;

    (aii) any person who is appointed by the Secretary of State to claim benefit on behalf of a deceased person and who claims the benefit under regulation 30(5) and (6) of the Claims and Payments Regulations;

2.395

(aiii) any person who is appointed by the Secretary of State to make a claim for reduced earnings allowance or disablement benefit in the name of a person who has died and who claims under regulation 30(6A) and (6B) of the Claims and Payments Regulations;]

(a) any person appointed by the Secretary of State [¹ or the Board] under regulation 33(1) of the Claims and Payments Regulations (persons unable to act) to act on behalf of another;

(b) any person claiming attendance allowance or disability living allowance on behalf of another under section 66(2)(b) of the Contributions and Benefits Act or, as the case may be, section 76(3) of that Act (claims on behalf of terminally ill persons);

(c) in relation to a pension scheme, any person who, for the purposes of Part X of the Pension Schemes Act 1993, is an employer, member, trustee or manager by virtue of section 146(8) of that Act.

AMENDMENTS

1. Tax Credits (Decisions and Appeals) (Amendment) Regulations 1999 (SI 1999/2570), reg.18 (October 5, 1999). Note that amendments made by these regulations only have effect with respect to tax credit under the Tax Credit Act 1999 (reg.1(2) of the Amendment Regulations).

2. Social Security and Child Support (Decisions and Appeals) (Miscellaneous Amendments) Regulations 2002 (SI 2002/1379), reg.7 (May 20, 2002).

3. Social Security, Child Support and Tax Credits (Decisions and Appeals) Regulations 2004 (SI 2004/3368), reg.2(3) (December 21, 2004).

4. Tribunals, Courts and Enforcement Act 2007 (Transitional and Consequential Provisions) Order 2008 (SI 2008/2683), Sch.1, paras 95 and 115 (November 3, 2008).

DEFINITIONS

"appeal"—see reg.1(3).
"the Board"—see reg.1(3).
"the Claims and Payments Regulations"—*ibid.*
"the Contributions and Benefits Act"—see s.84 of the Social Security Act 1998.

GENERAL NOTE

2.396   In *CA/1014/1999*, an appointee appealed on behalf of a claimant against a decision that an overpayment was recoverable from the claimant. It was held that the tribunal were not entitled to consider whether it was recoverable from the appointee, who was not a "party to the proceedings" as that term is defined in reg.1. However, where an appeal is brought against a decision that an overpayment is recoverable from both the claimant and the appointee, the appeal will generally be regarded as having been brought on behalf of both of them and, even if it is not, both will be parties to the proceedings (*R(A) 2/06*).

Decisions against which an appeal lies

2.397   **26.** An appeal shall lie to [⁴ the First-tier Tribunal] against a decision made by the Secretary of State [¹ or an officer of the Board]—

(a) as to whether a person is entitled to a relevant benefit for which no claim is required by virtue of regulation 3 of the Claims and Payments Regulations; or

(b) as to whether a payment be made out of the social fund to a person to meet expenses for heating by virtue of regulations made under section 138(2) of the Contributions and Benefits Act (payments out of the social fund); [² or

(c) under Schedule 6 to the Contributions and Benefits Act (assessment of extent of disablement) in relation to sections 103 (disablement benefit) and 108 (prescribed diseases) of that Act for the purposes of industrial injuries benefit under Part V of that Act;] [³ or

(d) under section 59 of, and Schedule 7 to, the Welfare Reform and Pensions Act 1999 (couples to make joint-claim for jobseeker's allowance) where one member of the couple is working and the Secretary of State has decided that both members of the couple are not engaged in remunerative work].

AMENDMENTS

1. Tax Credits (Decisions and Appeals) (Amendment) Regulations 1999 (SI 1999/2570), reg.19 (October 5, 1999). Note that amendments made by these regulations only have effect with respect to tax credit under the Tax Credit Act 1999 (reg.1(2) of the Amendment Regulations).

2. Social Security and Child Support (Miscellaneous Amendments) Regulations 2000 (SI 2000/1596), reg.22 (June 19, 2000).

3. Social Security Amendment (Joint Claims) Regulations 2001 (SI 2001/518), reg.4(b) (March 19, 2001).

4. Tribunals, Courts and Enforcement Act 2007 (Transitional and Consequential Provisions) Order 2008 (SI 2008/2683), Sch.1, paras 95 and 116 (November 3, 2008).

DEFINITIONS

"appeal"—see reg.1(3).
"the Board"—see reg.1(3).
"the Claims and Payments Regulations"—*ibid.*
"the Contributions and Benefits Act"—see s.84 of the Social Security Act 1998.
"relevant benefit"—see s.89(1) of the Social Security Act 1998.

GENERAL NOTE

Paragraph (c) enables there to be an appeal against an assessment of disablement 2.398 independently of any appeal against a decision awarding, or refusing to award, benefit. This creates difficulties. In *CI/1547/2001*, it was suggested that all appeals against assessment decisions should also be treated as appeals against the consequent entitlement decisions because the provisions for supersession and revision are too limited, having regard to the dates from which they are effective, to deal satisfactorily with the consequences of a successful appeal on assessment alone. For the same reason, an application to supersede an assessment of disablement should generally be treated as also an application to supersede the underlying award (*CI/954/2006*).

A final assessment of disablement made under the legislation replaced by the Social Security Act 1998 Act implies that there was no disablement after the end of the award, and so has ongoing effect and requires supersession of the assessment as well as a new claim for benefit (*R(I) 5/02*), whereas an assessment under the 1998 Act carries no such implication and, after it expires, requires just a new claim.

Decisions against which no appeal lies

27.—(1) No appeal lies to [¹ the First-tier Tribunal] against a decision set 2.399 out in Schedule 2.

(2) In paragraph (1) and Schedule 2, "decision" includes determinations embodied in or necessary to a decision.

(3) [¹ . . .].

AMENDMENTS

1. Tribunals, Courts and Enforcement Act 2007 (Transitional and Consequential Provisions) Order 2008 (SI 2008/2683), Sch.1, paras 95 and 117 (November 3, 2008).

DEFINITIONS

"appeal"—see reg.1(3).
"decision"—see para.(2).

GENERAL NOTE

2.400   See note to Sch.2.

Notice of decision against which appeal lies

2.401   **28.**—(1) A person with a right of appeal under the Act or these Regulations against any decision of the Secretary of State [¹ or the Board or an officer of the Board] shall—

(a) be given written notice of the decision against which the appeal lies;

(b) be informed that, in a case where that written notice does not include a statement of the reasons for that decision, he may, within one month of the date of notification of that decision, request that the Secretary of State [¹ or the Board or an officer of the Board] provide him with a written statement of the reasons for that decision; and

(c) be given written notice of his right of appeal against that decision.

(2) Where a written statement of the reasons for the decision is not included in the written notice of the decision and is requested under paragraph (1)(b), the Secretary of State [¹ or the Board or an officer of the Board] shall provide that statement within 14 days of receipt of the request [² or as soon as practicable afterwards].

AMENDMENTS

1. Tax Credits (Decisions and Appeals) (Amendment) Regulations 1999 (SI 1999/2570), reg.20 (October 5, 1999). Note that amendments made by these regulations only have effect with respect to tax credit under the Tax Credit Act 1999 (reg.1(2) of the Amendment Regulations).

2. Social Security, Child Support and Tax Credits (Miscellaneous Amendments) Regulations 2005 (SI 2005/337), reg.2(6) (March 18, 2005).

DEFINITIONS

"the Act"—see reg.1(3).
"appeal"—*ibid.*
"the Board"—*ibid.*
"the date of notification"—*ibid.*

GENERAL NOTE

Para. (1)

2.402   There may be circumstances in which a failure to comply with the duties imposed by this regulation may invalidate the decision altogether (see *C3/07–08(IS)*, in which the Deputy Commissioner considered that computer-generated letters could not be reconciled with the statutory provisions for decision-making). However, in *R(P) 1/04*, it was held that a failure to issue notice of a decision simply had the effect that the time for appealing against the decision did not start to run. The same is true where a decision is issued but it incorrectly tells the claimant that benefit has been awarded for life when it has been awarded only for a limited period. The decision is valid but time for appealing runs from when the claimant is informed of the true nature of the decision (*CDLA/3440/2003*). It is suggested that, where a decision is issued, a failure to provide the information required by sub-para.(c) also has the effect that the decision is valid but that the time for appealing against it does not start to run. If that is so, the time for appealing would run from when the claimant does become aware of his rights. This is a necessary approach because reg.32(8)(a) makes it impossible to obtain from the Secretary of State an extension of time for appealing on the ground of ignorance of the time limits for appealing. Any dispute as to whether an appeal is in time should be resolved by a ruling by the First-tier Tribunal under reg.32(1). A different approach has been taken in child support cases where the interests of a third party entitled to rely on the decision have to be taken into account and time has been held to run from the date of a decision even though the parties have been misled into thinking they had no right of appeal (*CCS/5515/2002*). However, even though time for appealing does not start to run, the decision itself is not invalidated by a failure to give proper notice of it in the correct form. It is arguable that a statement of reasons only counts as such for the purposes of sub-para.(b) if it is adequate but the adequacy of a statement of reasons is very much a matter of judgment and depends on the issues arising in the particular case. However, a request made under para.(1)(b) extends the time for appealing but, presumably, only if it is properly made and the notice really does not include an adequate statement of reasons. Accordingly, the cautious claimant will treat any purported statement of reasons as being adequate for the purpose and will ensure that the appeal is lodged within the usual one month time limit, even if a fuller explanation is expected in the Secretary of State's submission to the tribunal.

A failure to refer to the fact that a decision is a supersession can, like most other defects, be cured by a tribunal giving a decision in the proper form (*R(IB)2/04*). On the other hand, if a tribunal does not realise that a decision under appeal was, or should have been, a supersession rather than a decision on a new claim, the tribunal's decision is liable to be set aside if it is impossible to infer that any ground for altering the decision on supersession was made out (*CDLA/9/2001*).

Further particulars required relating to certificate of recoverable benefits [³ or, as the case may be, recoverable lump sum payments] appeals

29.—(1) [⁴ . . .]

(2) [⁴ . . .]

(3) [⁴ Where it appears to the Secretary of State that a notice of appeal under the 1997 Act relating to a certificate of recoverable benefits or, as the case may be, recoverable lump sum payments does not contain the particulars required, the Secretary of State may direct the appellant to provide such particulars.]

(4) Where paragraph (3) applies, the time specified for making the appeal [⁴ ...] may be extended by such period, not exceeding 14 days from the date of the Secretary of State's direction under paragraph (3), as the Secretary of State may determine.

(5) Where further particulars [⁴ ...] are required under paragraph (3) they shall be sent to or delivered to the Compensation Recovery Unit of the [² Department for Work and Pensions] at [¹Durham House, Washington, Tyne and Wear, NE38 7SF] within such period as the Secretary of State may direct.

2.403

(6) The Secretary of State may treat any appeal relating to the certificate of recoverable benefits [³ or, as the case may be, recoverable lump sum payments] as an application for review under section 10 of the 1997 Act.

AMENDMENTS

1. (Social Security (Recovery of Benefits) (Miscellaneous Amendments) Regulations 2000 (SI 2000/3030), reg.3 (December 4, 2000)).

2. Social Security and Child Support (Decisions and Appeals) (Miscellaneous Amendments) Regulations 2002 (SI 2002/1379), reg.8 (May 20, 2002).

3. Social Security (Recovery of Benefits) (Lump Sum Payments) Regulations 2008 (SI 2008/1596), Sch.2, para.1(c), as amended by reg.6(1) and (5) of the Social Security (Miscellaneous Amendments) (No.3) Regulations 2008 (SI 2008/2365) (which erroneously refers to para.1(2)(c)(ii), rather than para.1(c)(ii)) (October 1, 2008).

4. Tribunals, Courts and Enforcement Act 2007 (Transitional and Consequential Provisions) Order 2008 (SI 2008/2683), Sch.1, paras 95 and 118 (November 3, 2008).

DEFINITIONS

2.404   "the 1997 Act"—see reg.1(3).
"appeal"—*ibid.*

General appeals matters including child support appeals

Appeal against a decision which has been [² replaced or] revised

2.405   **30.**—(1) An appeal against a decision of the Secretary of State [¹ or the Board or an officer of the Board] shall not lapse where the decision [² is treated as replaced by a decision under section 11 of the Child Support Act by section 28F(5) of that Act, or is revised under section 16 of that Act] or section 9 before the appeal is determined and the decision as [² replaced or] revised is not more advantageous to the appellant than the decision before it was [² replaced or] revised.

(2) Decisions which are more advantageous for the purposes of this regulation include decisions where—

(a) any relevant benefit paid to the appellant is greater or is awarded for a longer period in consequence of the decision made under section 9;

(b) it would have resulted in the amount of relevant benefit in payment being greater but for the operation of any provision of the Administration Act or the Contributions and Benefits Act restricting or suspending the payment of, or disqualifying a claimant from receiving, some or all of the benefit;

(c) as a result of the decision, a denial or disqualification for the receiving of any relevant benefit, is lifted, wholly or in part;

(d) it reverses a decision to pay benefit to a third party;

[³(dd) it reverses a decision under section 29(2) that an accident is not an industrial accident;]

(e) in consequence of the revised decision, benefit paid is not recoverable under section 71, 71A or 74 of the Administration Act or regulations made under any of those sections, or the amount so recoverable is reduced; or

(f) a financial gain accrued or will accrue to the appellant in consequence of the decision.

(3) Where a decision as [² replaced under section 28F(5) of the Child Support Act, or as revised under section 16 of that Act] or under section 9 is not more advantageous to the appellant than the decision before it was [² replaced or] revised, the appeal shall be treated as though it had been brought against the decision as [² replaced or] revised.

(4) The appellant shall have a period of one month from the date of notification of the decision as [² replaced or] revised to make further representations as to the appeal.

(5) After the expiration of the period specified in paragraph (4), or within that period if the appellant consents in writing, the appeal to the [⁴ First-tier Tribunal] shall proceed except where, in the light of the further representations from the appellant, the Secretary of State [¹ or the Board or an officer of the Board] further revises his [¹, or revise their,] decision and that decision is more advantageous to the appellant than the decision before it was [² replaced or] revised.

AMENDMENTS

1. Tax Credits (Decisions and Appeals) (Amendment) Regulations 1999 (SI 1999/2570), reg.21 (October 5, 1999). Note that amendments made by these regulations only have effect with respect to tax credit under the Tax Credit Act 1999 (reg.1(2) of the Amendment Regulations).
2. Child Support (Decisions and Appeals) (Amendment) Regulations 2000 (SI 2000/3185), reg.11 (various dates as provided by reg.1(1)).
3. Social Security, Child Support and Tax Credits (Miscellaneous Amendments) Regulations 2005 (SI 2005/337), reg.2(7) (March 18, 2005).
4. Tribunals, Courts and Enforcement Act 2007 (Transitional and Consequential Provisions) Order 2008 (SI 2008/2683), Sch.1, paras 95 and 119 (November 3, 2008).

DEFINITIONS

"the Administration Act"—see s.84 of the Social Security Act 1998.
"appeal"—see reg.1(3).
"the Board"—*ibid.*
"the Child Support Act"—see s.84 of the Social Security Act 1998.
"the Contributions and Benefits Act"—*ibid.*
"the date of notification"—see reg.1(3).
"relevant benefit"—see s.39(1) of the Social Security Act 1998.

GENERAL NOTE

Paragraph (1) provides an exception to the general rule that an appeal lapses when the decision under appeal is revised (see s.9(6) of the Social Security Act 1998). It makes it unnecessary for the claimant to submit a fresh appeal where the decision under appeal is replaced by a decision that is no more favourable to the claimant. Paragraph (2), however, makes it clear that a fresh appeal will be required where the new decision is only partially favourable to a claimant as well as when it is wholly favourable. In *R(IS) 2/08*, a decision was made in 2003 to the effect that the claimant was not entitled to income support from 17 May 2002. When the claimant appealed, the decision was revised and income support was paid in respect of the period from 17 May 2002 to 31 July 2002. It was held that reg.30(2)(a) did not require the appeal to be treated as having lapsed in respect of the period from 1 August 2002. The Tribunal of Commissioners said —

"... where a period before the date of the original decision is in issue and a revision affects only part of that period, it seems to us that there are many

2.406

circumstances in which it can be appropriate to regard the decision as being more advantageous to the appellant only in respect of that part of the period and not the remainder of the period. This is particularly so where the Secretary of State knows very well that the revision does not deal with the main issue raise by the appeal and that it would be a waste of time to treat the appeal as having lapsed and to require the appellant to start all over again."

The new subpara.(dd) appears to have effect only in relation to industrial accident declarations made otherwise than in the course of a claim for benefit. It is probably meant to apply not only to cases where the reversed decision was to the effect that an accident was not an industrial accident but also to cases where it was to the effect that an alleged industrial accident was not an accident at all or did not even take place.

2.407   **30A.** *Omitted.*

2.408   **31.** [¹ ...]

AMENDMENT

1. Tribunals, Courts and Enforcement Act 2007 (Transitional and Consequential Provisions) Order 2008 (SI 2008/2683), Sch.1, paras 95 and 121 (November 3, 2008).

Late appeals

2.409   **32.**—(1) [² Where a dispute arises as to whether an appeal was brought within the time specified under Tribunal Procedure Rules the dispute shall be referred to, and determined by, the First-tier Tribunal.]

(2) [² The Secretary of State, the Commission or the Board, as the case may be, may treat a late appeal as made in time in accordance with Tribunal Procedure Rules if the conditions in paragraphs (4) to (8) are satisfied.]

(3) [² . . .]

(4) [² An appeal may be treated as made in time if the Secretary of State, the Commission or the Board, as the case may be, is satisfied that it is in the interests of justice.]

(5) For the purposes of paragraph (4), it is not in the interests of justice to [² treat the appeal as made in time unless] [¹ the Secretary of State or the Board, as the case may be,] is satisfied that –

   (a) the special circumstances specified in paragraph (6) are relevant [² . . .]; or

   (b) some other special circumstances exist which are wholly exceptional and relevant [² . . .]

and as a result of those special circumstances, it was not pracable for the application to be made within the time specified in [² Tribunal Procedure Rules].

(6) For the purposes of paragraph (5)(a), the special circumstances are that –

   (a) the [² appellant] or a [¹ partner] or dependant of the [² appellant] has died or suffered serious illness;

   (b) the [² appellant] is not resident in the United Kingdom; or

   (c) normal postal services were disrupted.

(7) In determining whether it is in the interests of justice to [² treat the appeal as made in time], [¹ regard shall be had] to the principle that the greater the amount of time that has elapsed between the expiration of the time [² limit under Tribunal Procedure Rules and the submission of

the notice of appeal, the more compelling should be the special circumstances.]

(8) In determining whether it is in the interests of justice to [² treat the appeal as made in time], no account shall be taken of the following –

(a) that the applicant or any person acting for him was unaware of or misunderstood the law applicant to his case (including ignorance or misunderstanding the time limits imposed by [² Tribunal Procedure Rules]); or

(b) that [² the Upper Tribunal] or a court has taken a different view of the law from that previously understood and applied.

(9)   [² . . .]

(10) [² . . .]

(11) [² . . .]

AMENDMENTS

1. Social Security and Child Support (Decisions and Appeals) (Miscellaneous Amendments) Regulations 2002 (SI 2002/1379), reg.10 (May 20, 2002).

2. Tribunals, Courts and Enforcement Act 2007 (Transitional and Consequential Provisions) Order 2008 (SI 2008/2683), Sch.1, paras 95 and 122 (November 3, 2008).

DEFINITIONS

"appeal"—see reg.1(3).
"the Board"—*ibid.*
"partner"—*ibid.*
"party to the proceedings"—*ibid.*

GENERAL NOTE

The absolute time limit of 12 months, formerly in reg.32(1), is now to be found   2.410
in r.23(5) of the Tribunal Procedure (First-tier Tribunal) (Social Entitlement
Chamber) Rules 2008. Rule 23(2) of, and Sch. 1 to, the Rules provide the basic
time limit, generally one month in social security cases, and a broad discretion in the
Tribunal to extend it, subject to that absolute time limit. Rule 23(4) provides that,
subject to the absolute time limit, a late appeal will be treated as made in tiem if the
respondent does not object. It seems very odd that the Secretary of State should
restrict his own power not to object in the way he has done in paras. (4) to (8) of
this regulation, especially as, if he does object, he is bound by r.23(7)(a) to refer the
case to the Tribunal whose discretion to admit the appeal is not limited in the same
way at all.

Para. (8)(a)
If a claimant is ignorant of the time limit for appealing because the Secretary of   2.411
State failed to provide the information required by reg.28(1)(c), it is arguable that
time for appealing has not started to run. Section 12(6) of the Social Security Act
1998 requires that information to be given. If this is correct, it is unnecessary for the
claimant to apply for an extension of time for appealing (which might be difficult in
the light of para.(8)(a)) and, instead, should apply for a ruling under reg.31(4). Not
replacing "applicant" with "appellant" is probably a drafting slip.

Para. (8)(b)
Understood by whom? Presumably not the appellant because the view must   2.412
also be different from that previously applied. But is it the understanding of the
Department for Work and Pensions as a whole that matters or of the particular

local office? Whatever the answer, it is not easy to see what sub-para.(b) adds to sub-para.(a).

Notice of Appeal

2.413   **33.**—(1) [¹⁰ . . .]

(2) [¹⁰ A notice of appeal made in accordance with Tribunal Procedure Rules and on a form approved by the Secretary of State, the Commission or the Board, as the case may be, or in such other format as the Secretary of State, the Commission or the Board, as the case may be, accepts, is to be sent or delivered to the following appropriate office]—

   (a) in the case of an appeal under the 1997 Act against a certificate of recoverable benefits [⁹ or, as the case may be, recoverable lump sum payments], the Compensation Recovery Unit of the [⁸ Department for Work and Pensions] at [⁶ Durham House, Washington, Tyne and Wear, NE38 7SF];

   (b) in the case of an appeal against a decision relating to a jobseeker's allowance, an office of the [⁸ Department for Work and Pensions the address of which was indicated on the notification of the decision which is subject to appeal];

   (c) in the case of a contributions decision which falls within Part II of Schedule 3 to the Act, any National Insurance Contributions office [¹ of the Board, or any office of the [⁸ Department for Work and Pensions];

[¹(cc) in the case of a decision made under the Pension Schemes Act 1993 by virtue of section 170(2) of that Act, any National Insurance Contributions office of the Board;]

   (d) in the case of an appeal under section 20 of the Child Support Act [⁷. . .] an office of the Child Support Agency; [². . .]

[²(dd) in the case of an appeal against a decision relating to working families' tax credit or disabled person's tax crdit, a Tax Credits Office of the Board;]

[⁴(ddd) in a case where the decision appealed against was a decision arising from a claim to a designated office, an office of a designated authority;] and

   (e) in any other case, an office of the [⁸ Department for Work and Pensions the address of which was indicated on the notification of the decision which is subject to appeal].

(3) [¹⁰ Except where paragraph (4) applies, where a form does not contain the information required under Tribunal Procedure Rules the form may be returned by the Secretary of State, the Commission or the Board to the sender for completion in accordance with the Tribunal Procedure Rules.]

(4) Where the Secretary of State is satisfied [² or the Board are satisfied] that the form, although not completed in accordance with the instructions on it, includes sufficient information to enable the appeal [¹⁰ ...] to proceed, he [² or they] may treat the form as satisfying the requirements of [¹⁰ Tribunal Procedure Rules].

(5) Where [⁹ a notice of appeal] is made in writing otherwise than on the approved form ("the letter"), and the letter includes sufficient information to enable the appeal [⁹ . . .] to proceed, the Secretary of State [² or the Board] may treat the letter as satisfying the requirements of [⁹ Tribunal Procedure Rules].

(6) Where the letter does not include sufficient information to enable the appeal [⁹ . . .] to proceed, the Secretary of State [² or the Board] may request further information in writing ("further particulars") from the person who wrote the letter.

[⁸ (7) Where a person to whom a form is returned, or from whom further particulars are requested, duly completes and returns the form or sends the further particulars, if the form or particulars, as the case may be, are received by the Secretary of State or the Board within—

(a) 14 days of the date on which the form was returned to him by the Secretary of State or the Board, the time for making the appeal shall be extended by 14 days from the date on which the form was returned;

(b) 14 days of the date on which the Secretary of State's or the Board's request was made, the time for making the appeal shall be extended by 14 days from the date of the request; or

(c) such longer period as the Secretary of State or the Board may direct, the time for making the appeal shall be extended by a period equal to that longer period directed by the Secretary of State or the Board.]

(8) Where a person to whom a form is returned or from whom further particulars are requested does not complete and return the form or send further particulars within the period of time specified in paragraph (7)—

(a) the Secretary of State [² or the Board] shall forward a copy of the form, or as the case may be, the letter, together with any other relevant documents or evidence to [⁹ the First-tier Tribunal], and

(b) the [⁹ First-tier Tribunal] shall determine whether the form or the letter satisfies the requirement of [⁹ Tribunal Procedure Rules].

(9) Where—

(a) a form is duly completed and returned or further particulars are sent after the expiry of the period of time allowed in accordance with paragraph (7), and

(b) no decision has been made under paragraph (8) at the time the form or the further particulars are received by the Secretary of State [² or the Board],

that form or further particulars shall also be forwarded to the [⁹ First-tier Tribunal which] shall take into account any further information or evidence set out in the form or further particulars.

[⁸ (10) The Secretary of State or the Board may discontinue action on an appeal where the [⁹ notice of] appeal has not been forwarded to the [⁹ First-tier Tribunal] and the appellant or an authorised representative of the appellant has given written notice that he does not wish the appeal to continue.]

AMENDMENTS

1. Social Security Contributions (Transfer of Functions, etc.) Act 1999 (Commencement No.2 and Consequential and Transitional Provisions) Order 1999 (SI 1999/1662), art.3(4) (July 5, 1999).

2. Tax Credits (Decisions and Appeals) (Amendment) Regulations 1999 (SI 1999/2570), reg.23 (October 5, 1999). Note that amendments made by these regulations only have effect with respect to tax credit under the Tax Credit Act 1999 (reg.1(2) of the Amendment Regulations).

3. Social Security and Child Support (Decisions and Appeals), Vaccine Damage Payments and Jobseeker's Allowance (Amendment) Regulations 1999 (SI 1999/2677), reg.9 (October 18, 1999).

4. Social Security (Work-focused Interviews) Regulations 2000 (SI 2000/897), reg.16(5) and Sch.6, para.6 (April 3, 2000).

5. Social Security and Child Support (Miscellaneous Amendments) Regulations 2000 (SI 2000/1596), reg.23 (June 19, 2000).

6. Social Security (Recovery of Benefits) (Miscellaneous Amendments) Regulations 2000 (SI 2000/3030), reg.4 (December 4, 2000).

7. Child Support (Consequential Amendments and Transitional Provisions) Regulations 2001 (SI 2001/158), reg.4(4) (various dates as provided in reg.1(3)).

8. Social Security and Child Support (Decisions and Appeals) (Miscellaneous Amendments) Regulations 2002 (SI 2002/1379), reg.11 (May 20, 2002).

9. Social Security (Recovery of Benefits) (Lump Sum Payments) Regulations 2008 (SI 2008/1596), Sch.2, para.1(e) (October 1, 2008).

10. Tribunals, Courts and Enforcement Act 2007 (Transitional and Consequential Provisions) Order 2008 (SI 2008/2683), Sch.1, paras 95 and 123 (November 3, 2008).

DEFINITIONS

"the Act"—see reg.1(3).
"the 1997 Act"—*ibid*.
"appeal"—*ibid*.
"an appropriate office"—see para.(2).
"the Board"—see reg.1(3).
"the Child Support Act"—see s.84 of the Social Security Act 1998.
"designated authority"—see reg.1(3).
"tax credit"—*ibid*.
"the Vaccine Damage Payments Act"—see s.84 of the Social Security Act 1998.

GENERAL NOTE

This regulation is applied to an appeal against a determination by the Secretary of State on a claim, or on reconsideration of a determination on a claim, under the Mesothelioma Lump Sum Payments (Claims and Reconsiderations) Regulations 2008 (see reg.6 of those Regulations in Vol.I).

Para. (2)

2.414   At first sight it is surprising that it should be the Secretary of State who decides whether the appeal is in a sufficient format, but it is implicit in paras (4) and (5) that a technically deficient appeal should be allowed to proceed provided that it includes sufficient information to make that possible and the final decision not to admit an appeal is made by the First-tier Tribunal under para.(8).

Death of a party to an appeal

2.415   **34.**—(1) In any proceedings, on the death of a party to those proceedings (other than the Secretary of State [¹ or the Board]), the Secretary of State [¹ or the Board] may appoint such person as he thinks [¹ or they think] fit to proceed with the appeal in the place of such deceased party.

(2) A grant of probate, confirmation or letters of administration to the estate of the deceased party, whenever taken out, shall have no effect on an appointment made under paragraph (1).

(3) Where a person appointed under paragraph (1) has, prior to the date of such appointment, taken any action in relation to the appeal on behalf of the deceased party, the effective date of appointment by the Secretary of State [¹ or the Board] shall be the day immediately prior to the first day on which such action was taken.

AMENDMENT

1. Tax Credits (Decisions and Appeals) (Amendment) Regulations 1999 (SI 1999/2570), reg.24 (October 5, 1999). Note that amendments made by these regulations only have effect with respect to tax credit under the Tax Credit Act 1999 (reg.1(2) of the Amendment Regulations).

DEFINITIONS

"appeal"—see reg.1(3).
"the Board"—*ibid.*

PART V

APPEAL TRIBUNALS FOR SOCIAL SECURITY CONTRACTING OUT OF PENSIONS, VACCINE DAMAGE AND CHILD SUPPORT

35. to 38. [¹ . . .]

AMENDMENT

1. Tribunals, Courts and Enforcement Act 2007 (Transitional and Consequential Provisions) Order 2008 (SI 2008/2683), Sch.1, paras 95 and 124 (November 3, 2008), subject to a saving under art.1(3).

GENERAL NOTE

Except for parts of reg.36, these regulations remain in force in Scotland for the limited purpose explained in the note to ss. 5 to 7 of the Social Security Act 1998.

2.416

[¹Appeals raising issues for decision by officers of Inland Revenue

38A.—(1) Where, [² a person has appealed to [³ the First-tier Tribunal and it appears to the First-tier Tribunal,] that an issue arises which, by virtue of section 8 of the Transfer Act, falls to be decided by an officer of the Board, that tribunal [² [³ ...] shall—

2.417

(a) refer the appeal to the Secretary of State pending the decision of that issue by an officer of the Board; and

(b) require the Secretary of State to refer that issue to the Board;

and the Secretary of State shall refer that issue accordingly.

(2) Pending the final decision of any issue which has been referred to the Board in accordance with paragraph (1) above, the Secretary of State may revise the decision under appeal, or make a further decision superseding that decision, in accordance with his determination of any issue other than one which has been so referred.

(3) On receipt by the Secretary of State of the final decision of an issue which has been referred in accordance with paragraph (1) above, he shall consider whether the decision under appeal ought to be revised under section 9 or superseded under section 10, and—

(a) if so, revise it or, as the case may be, make a further decision which supersedes it; or

(b) if not, forward the appeal to the [³ First-tier Tribunal] which shall determine the appeal in accordance with the final decision of the issue so referred.

(4) In paragraphs (2) and (3) above, "final decision" has the same meaning as in regulation 11A(3) and (4).]

AMENDMENTS

1. Social Security and Child Support (Decisions and Appeals) Amendment (No.3) Regulations 1999 (SI 1999/1670), reg.2(4) (July 5, 1999).

2. Social Security and Child Support (Decisions and Appeals) (Miscellaneous Amendments) Regulations 2002 (SI 2002/1379), reg.12 (May 20, 2002).

3. Tribunals, Courts and Enforcement Act 2007 (Transitional and Consequential Provisions) Order 2008 (SI 2008/2683), Sch.1, paras 95 and 125 (November 3, 2008).

DEFINITIONS

"appeal"—see reg.1(3).
"the Board"—*ibid.*
"final decision"—by virtue of para.(4), see reg.11A(5).
"the Transfer Act"—see reg.1(3).

GENERAL NOTE

2.418   The Inland Revenue has been merged into Her Majesty's Revenue and Customs (HMRC). See the note to the definition of "the Board" in reg.1(3). Some decisions fall to be made by HMRC by virtue of s.170 of the Pensions Schemes Act 1993 (rather than by virtue of s.8 of the Social Security Contributions (Transfer of Functions, etc.) Act 1999) but the Tribunal may refer to HMRC issues for determination under the 1993 Act notwithstanding that this regulation does not apply (*R(P) 1/04*). It might be necessary to adjourn the hearing before the Tribunal while the question was being decided and procedures akin to those laid down in paras (2) and (3) could be followed.

2.419   **39. to 47.** [[1] ...]

AMENDMENT

1. Tribunals, Courts and Enforcement Act 2007 (Transitional and Consequential Provisions) Order 2008 (SI 2008/2683), Sch.1, paras 95 and 126 (November 3, 2008), subject to a saving under art.1(3).

GENERAL NOTE

2.420   Except for regs. 41, 44 and 45, these regulations remain in force in Scotland for the limited purpose explained in the note to ss. 5 to 7 of the Social Security Act 1998.

2.421   **48.** [[1] . . .]

AMENDMENT

1. Social Security, Child Support and Tax Credits (Decisions and Appeals) Regulations 2004 (SI 2004/3368), reg.2(8) (December 21, 2004).

2.422   **49. to 58.** [[1] . . .]

AMENDMENT

1. Tribunals, Courts and Enforcement Act 2007 (Transitional and Consequential Provisions) Order 2008 (SI 2008/2683), Sch.1, paras 95 and 126 (November 3, 2008), subject to a saving under art.1(3).

Except for regs. 50 and 52, these regulations remain in force in Scotland for the limited purpose explained in the note to ss.5 to 7 of the Social Security Act 1998.

2.423

[¹ Appeal to [² the Upper Tribunal] by a partner

58A. A partner within the meaning of section 2AA(7) of the Administration Act (full entitlement to certain benefits conditional on work-focused interview for partner) may appeal to [² the Upper Tribunal] under section 14 from a decision of [² the First-tier Tribunal] in respect of a decision specified in section 2B(2A) and (6) of the Administration Act.]

2.424

AMENDMENTS

1. Social Security, Child Support and Tax Credits (Miscellaneous Amendments) Regulations 2005 (SI 2005/337), reg.2(19) (March 19, 2005).
2. Tribunals, Courts and Enforcement Act 2007 (Transitional and Consequential Provisions) Order 2008 (SI 2008/2683), Sch.1, paras 95 and 127 (November 3, 2008).

DEFINITION

"the Administration Act"—see reg.1(3).

GENERAL NOTE

This regulation, made under s.14(3)(b) of the Social Security Act 1998, was necessary because a partner does not fall within the term "claimant" in s.14(3)(b). It has presumably been retained lest there be a case where a partner did not have a right of appeal under s.11 of the Tribunals, Courts and Enforcement Act 2007 as a "party".

2.425

PART VI

REVOCATIONS

59.—*Omitted*

2.426

SCHEDULE 1

PROVISIONS CONFERRING POWERS EXERCISED IN MAKING THESE REGULATIONS

2.427

Column (1) Provision		Column (2) Relevant Amendments
Vaccine Damage Payments Act 1979	Section 4(2) and (3)	The Act, Section 46
Child Support Act 1991	Section 7A(1)	The Act, Section 47
	Section 16(6)	The Act, Section 40
	Section 20(5) and (6)	The Act, Section 42
	Section 28ZA(2)(b) and (4)(c)	The Act, Section 43
	Section 28ZB(6)(c)	The Act, Section 43
	Section 28ZC(7)	The Act, Section 44

Column (1) Provision		Column (2) Relevant Amendments
	Section 28ZD(1) and (2)	The Act, Section 44
	Section 46B	The Act, Schedule 7, paragraph 44
	Section 51(2)	The Act, Schedule 7, paragraph 46
	Schedule 4A, paragraph 8	The Act, Schedule 7, paragraph 53
Social Security Administration Act 1992	Section 5(1)(hh)	The Act, Section 74
	Section 159	The Act, Schedule 7, paragraph 95
	Section 159A	The Act, Schedule 7, paragraph 96
Pension Schemes Act 1993	Section 170(3)	The Act, Schedule 7, paragraph 131
Social Security (Recovery of Benefits) Act 1997	Section 10	The Act, Schedule 7, paragraph 149
	Section 11(5)	
Social Security Act 1998	Section 6(3)	
	Section 7(6)	
	Section 9(1), (4) and (6)	
	Section 10(3) and (6)	
	Section 11(1)	
	Section 12(2) and (3), (6) and (7)	
	Section 14(10)(a) and (11)	
	Section 16(1) and Schedule 5	
	Section 17	
	Section 18(1)	
	Section 20	
	Section 21(1) to (3)	
	Section 22	
	Section 23	
	Section 24	
	Section 25(3)(b) and (5)(c)	
	Section 26(6)(c)	
	Section 28(1)	
	Section 31(2)	
	Section 79(1) and (3) to (7)	
	Section 84	
	Schedule 1, paragraphs 7, 11 and 12	
	Schedule 2, paragraph 9	
	Schedule 3, paragraphs 1, 4 and 9	

SCHEDULE 2

Regulation 27

DECISIONS AGAINST WHICH NO APPEAL LIES

Child benefit

2.428
    1. A decision of the Secretary of State as to whether an educational establishment be recognised for the purposes of Part IX of the Contributions and Benefits Act.

    2. A decision of the Secretary of State to recognise education provided otherwise than at a recognised educational establishment.

    3. A decision of the Secretary of State made in accordance with the discretion conferred upon him by the following provisions of the Child Benefit (Residence and Persons Abroad) Regulations 1976—

      (a) regulation 2(2)(c)(iii) (decision relating to a child's temporary absence abroad);

      (b) regulation 7(3) (certain days of absence abroad disregarded).

4. A decision of the Secretary of State made in accordance with the discretion conferred upon him by regulation 2(1) or (3) of the Child Benefit (General) Regulations 1976 (provisions relating to contributions and expenses in respect of a child).

Claims and payments

[⁵ **5.** A decision, being a decision of the Secretary of State unless specified below as a decision of the Board, under the following provisions of the Claims and Payments Regulations—

[⁸ (a) regulation 4(3) or (3B) (which partner should make a claim for income support or jobseeker's allowance);]

[⁹ (aa) regulation 4I (which partner should make a claim for an employment and support allowance);]

(b) [⁸ . . .];

[⁸ (bb) regulation 4D(7) (which partner should make a claim for state pension credit);]

(c) [⁸ . . .];

(d) [⁸ . . .];

(e) [⁸ . . .];

(f) regulation 7 (decision by the Secretary of State or the Board as to evidence and information required);

(g) regulation 9 and Schedule 1 (decision by the Secretary of State or the board as to interchange of claims with claims for other benefits);

(h) regulation 11 (treating claim for maternity allowance as claim for incapacity benefit [⁹ or employment and support allowance]);

(i) regulation 15(7) (approving form of particulars required for determination of retirement pension questions in advance of claim);

(j) regulations 20 to 24 (decisions by the Secretary of State or the Board as to the time and manner of payments);

(k) regulation 25(1) (intervals of payment of attendance allowance and disability living allowance where claimant is expected to return to hospital);

(l) regulation 26 (manner and time of payment of income support);

(m) regulation 26A (time and intervals of payment of jobseeker's allowance);

[⁷ (mm) regulation 26B (payment of state pension credit);]

[⁹ (mn) regulation 26C (manner and time of payment of employment and support allowance);]

(n) regulation 27(1) and (1A) (decision by the Board as to manner and time of payment of tax credits);

(o) regulation 30 (decision by the Secretary of State or the Board as to claims or payments after death of claimant);

(p) regulation 30A (payment of arrears of joint-claim jobseeker's allowance where nominated person can no longer be traced);

(q) regulation 31 (time and manner of payment of industrial injuries gratuities);

(r) regulation 32 (decision by the Secretary of State or the Board where person unable to act);

(s) regulation 33 (appointments by the Secretary of State or the Board where person unable to act);

(t) regulation 34 (decision by the Secretary of State or the Board as to paying another person on a beneficiaries behalf);

(u) regulation 34A(1) (payment, out of benefit, of mortgage interest to qualifying lender);

(v) regulation 35(2) (payment to third person of maternity expenses or expenses for heating in cold weather);

(w) regulation 36 (decision by the Secretary of State or the Board to pay partner as alternative payee);

(x) regulation 38 (decision by the Secretary of State or the Board as to the extinguishment of right to payment of sums by way of benefit where payment not obtained within the prescribed period, except a decision under paragraph (2A) (payment requested after expiration of prescribed period));

(y) regulations 42 to 46 (mobility component of disability living allowance and disability living allowance for children;

(z) regulation 47(2) and (3) (return of instruments of payment etc. to the Secretary of State or the Board).]

Contracted out pension schemes

6. A decision of the Secretary of State under section 109 of the Pension Schemes Act 1993 or any Order made under it (annual increase of guaranteed minimum pensions).

2.429

Decisions depending on other cases

2.430   7. A decision of the Secretary of State under section 25 or 26 (decisions and appeals depending on other cases).

Deductions

2.431   8. A decision which falls to be made by the Secretary of State under the Fines (Deductions from Income Support) Regulations 1992, other than [¹ a decision whether benefit is sufficient for a deduction to be made].

9.—(1) Except in relation to a decision to which sub-paragraph (2) applies, any decision of the Secretary of State under the Community Charges (Deductions from Income Support) (No.2) Regulations 1990, the Community Charges (Deductions from Income Support) (Scotland) Regulations 1989 or the Council Tax (Deductions from Income Support) Regulations 1993.

(2) This sub-paragraph applies to a decision—

  (a) whether there is an outstanding sum due of the amount sought to be deducted;
  (b) whether benefit is sufficient for a deduction to be made; and
  (c) on the priority to be given to any deduction.

European Community regulations

2.432   10. An authorization given by the Secretary of State in accordance with article 22(1) or (1) of Council Regulation (EEC) No.1408/71 on the application of social security schemes to employed persons, to self-employed persons and to members of their families moving within the Community.

Expenses

2.433   11. A decision of the Secretary of State whether to pay expenses to any person under section 180 of the Administration Act.

Guardian's allowance

2.434   12. A decision of the Secretary of State relating to the giving of a notice under regulation 5(8) of the Social Security (Guardian's Allowance) Regulations 1975 (children whose surviving parents are in prison or legal custody).

Income support

2.435   13. A decision of the Secretary of State [³ . . .] made in accordance with paragraph (1) or (2) of regulation 13 (income support and social fund determinations on incomplete evidence).

[⁶ State pension credit

2.436   13A. A decision of the Secretary of State made in accordance with paragraph (1) or (3) of regulation 13 in relation to state pension credit (determination on incomplete evidence).]

Industrial injuries benefit

2.437   14. A decision of the Secretary of State relating to the question whether—

  (a) disablement pension be increased under section 104 of the Contributions and Benefits Act (constant attendance); or
  (b) disablement pension be further increased under section 105 of the Contributions and Benefits Act (exceptionally severe disablement);

and if an increase is to be granted or renewed, the period for which and the amount at which it is payable.

15. A decision of the Secretary of State under regulation 2(2) of the Social Security (Industrial Injuries and Diseases) Miscellaneous Provisions Regulations 1986 as to the length of any period of interruption of education which is to be disregarded.

16. A decision of the Secretary of State to approve or not to approve a person undertaking work for the purposes of regulation 17 of the Social Security (General Benefit) Regulations 1982.

17. A decision of the Secretary of State as to how the limitations under Part VI of Schedule 7 to the Contributions and Benefits Act on the benefit payable in respect of any death are to be applied in the circumstances of any case.

Invalid vehicle scheme

18. A decision of the Secretary of State relating to the issue of certificates under regulation 13 of, and Schedule 2 to, the Social Security (Disability Living Allowance) Regulations 1991.

2.438

Jobseeker's allowance

19.—(1) A decision of the Secretary of State under Chapter IV of Part II of the Jobseeker's Allowance Regulations as to the day and the time a claimant is to attend at a job centre.

2.439

(2) A decision of the Secretary of State as to the day of the week on which a claimant is required to provide a signed declaration under regulation 24(10) of the Jobseeker's Allowance Regulations.

(3) A decision of the Secretary of State [³ . . .] made in accordance with regulation 15 (Jobseeker's allowance determinations on incomplete evidence).

[⁵ Loss of Benefit for Breach of Community Order

19A. A decision of the Secretary of State that a relevant benefit shall not be payable or shall be reduced in accordance with a determination of a court made under section 62(1) of the Child Support, Pensions and Social Security Act 2000 where the only ground of appeal is that the court's determination was made in error.]

2.440

Payments on account, overpayments and recovery

20. A decision of the Secretary of State under the Social Security (Payments on account, Overpayments and Recovery) Regulations 1988, except a decision of the Secretary of State under the following provisions of those Regulations—

2.441

  (a) regulation 3(1)(a) to offset any interim payment made in anticipation of an award of benefit;
  (b) regulation 4(1) as to the overpayment of an interim payment;
  (c) regulation 5 as to the offsetting of a prior payment against a subsequent award;
  (d) regulation 11(1) as to whether a payment in excess of entitlement has been credited to a bank or other account;
  (e) regulation 13 as to the sums to be deducted in calculating recoverable amounts;
  (f) regulation 14(1) as to the treatment of capital to be reduced;
  (g) regulation 19 determining a claimant's protected earnings; and
  (h) regulation 24 whether a determination as to a claimant's protected earnings is revised or superseded.

Persons abroad

21. A decision of the Secretary of State made under—

2.442

  (a) regulation 2(1)(a) of the Social Security Benefit (Persons Abroad) Regulations 1975 whether to certify that it is consistent with the proper administration of the Contributions and Benefits Act that a disqualification under section 113(1)(a) of that Act should not apply;
  (b) regulation 9(4) or (5) of those Regulations whether to allow a person to avoid disqualification for receiving benefit during a period of temporary absence from Great Britain longer than that specified in the regulation.

Reciprocal Agreements

22. A decision of the Secretary of State made in accordance with an Order made under section 179 of the Administration Act (reciprocal agreements with countries outside the United Kingdom).

2.443

Social fund awards

23. A decision of the Secretary of State under section 78 of the Administration Act relating to the recovery of social fund awards.

2.444

Suspension

24. A decision of the Secretary of State relating to the suspension of a relevant benefit or to the payment of such a benefit which has been suspended under Part III.

2.445

Up-rating

25. A decision of the Secretary of State relating to the up-rating of benefits under Part X of the Administration Act.

2.446

[²**26.** Any decision treated as a decision of the Secretary of State whether or not to waive or defer a work-focused interview.]

Loss of Benefit

2.447   [⁴ **27.** A decision of the Secretary of State that a sanctionable benefit as defined in section 7(8) of the Social Security Fraud Act 2001 is not payable, or is to be reduced, pursuant to section 7, 8 or 9 of that Act as a result of convictions for one or more benefit offences in each of two sets of proceedings, one offence being committed within 3 years of conviction for another, where the only ground of appeal is that any of the convictions was erroneous.]

AMENDMENTS

1. Social Security Act 1998 (Commencement No.12 and Consequential and Transitional Provisions) Order 1999 (SI 1999/3178), art.3(19) and Sch.19, para.2 (November 29, 1999).
2. Social Security (Work-focused Interviews) Regulations 2000 (SI 2000/897), reg.16(5) and Sch.6, para.7 (April 3, 2000).
3. Social Security and Child Support (Miscellaneous Amendments) Regulations 2000 (SI 2000/1596), reg.34 (June 19, 2000).
4. Social Security (Loss of Benefit) Regulations 2001 (SI 2001/4022), reg.21 (April 1, 2002).
5. Social Security and Child Support (Decisions and Appeals) (Miscellaneous Amendments) Regulations 2002 (SI 2002/1379), reg.21 (May 20, 2002).
6. State Pension Credit (Consequential, Transitional and Miscellaneous Provisions) Regulations 2002 (SI 2002/3019), reg.21 (April 7, 2003).
7. State Pension Credit (Decisions and Appeals—Amendments) Regulations 2003 (SI 2003/1581), reg.2 (June 18, 2003).
8. Social Security, Child Support and Tax Credits (Decisions and Appeals) Regulations 2004 (SI 2004/3368), reg.2(9) (December 21, 2004).
9. Employment and Support Allowance (Consequential Provisions) (No.2) Regulations 2008 (SI 2008/1554), regs 29 and 41 (July 27, 2008).

DEFINITIONS

"the Administration Act"—see s.84 of the Social Security Act 1998.
"the Claims and Payments Regulations"—see reg.1(3).
"the Contributions and Benefits Act"—see s.84 of the Social Security Act 1998.
"decision"—see reg.27(2).
"the Jobseeker's Allowance Regulations"—see reg.1(3).
"relevant benefit"—see s.39(1) of the Social Security Act 1998.
"state pension credit"—see reg.1(3).
"work-focused interview"—*ibid.*

GENERAL NOTE

2.448   Before December 21, 2004, para.5(a) to (e) had the effect that decisions under regs 4, 4A, 4D and 6 of the Social Security (Claims and Payments) Regulations 1987 as to whether a claim had been properly made were unappealable and that was also the effect of the original form of para.5 that was replaced from May 20, 2002. Now the only decisions under those regulations that are not appealable are decisions as to which of two partners should make claims where the partners do not agree.

If reg.27 is made under s.12(2) of the Social Security Act 1998, it is arguable that much of Sch.2 to the Regulations is ultra vires, having regard to s.12(3). It is not easy to see why, for instance, a decision of the Secretary of State that an educational establishment be recognised for the purposes of child benefit or to recognise education provided otherwise than at such a recognised establishment (paras 1 and 2 of Sch.2) is not a decision "that relates to the conditions of entitlement" to child benefit. The fact that a large element of discretion is involved is not material. There is no reason in principle why such a discretion should not be exercised by a tribunal. There may be sound reasons for restricting the rights of appeal in cases where there is a large element of pure discretion, so that any challenge has to be by way of application for revision under s.9 or for judicial review, and, of course, there was no right of appeal under the old legislation, but it is arguable that neither of those considerations carries much weight against the clear language of s.12(3). On the other hand, it is arguable that reg.27 is made under para.9 of Sch.2 to the Act, which is in much broader terms than s.12. Both regulation-making powers are to be found in Sch.1 to the Regulations. What the point is in having s.12(2) qualified by s.12(3) when there is the broader unqualified power in the same Act is unclear but an argument that a broad power should be regarded as qualified by the scope of the narrower power found little sympathy in *R. v Secretary of State for Social Security, Ex p. Moore, The Times,* March 9, 1993 (but see now *R. (BAPIO Action Ltd) v Secretary of State for the Home Department* [2008] UKHL 27; [2008] 2 W.L.R. 1073).

The question of the validity of this Schedule has been considered in four Commissioners' decisions without any very clear resolution of these issues. In the first two cases, the Schedule was held to be valid as far as it affected the individual cases, but different grounds were given. In *CJSA/69/2001,* the Commissioner considered that this Schedule was made under s.12(2) of the 1998 Act but held that para.5 was intra vires insofar as it then prohibited any appeal against a decision by the Secretary of State under reg.4 of the Social Security (Claims and Payments) Regulations 1987 that a claim was to be treated as not made until the claimant provided his P45. He pointed out that s.12(3) applies only in respect of a benefit for which a claim has been validly made. However, he declined to determine whether or not the claim *had* been validly made, accepting the submission of the Secretary of State that a right of appeal could arise only after the Secretary of State had decided that a claim had been validly made and that it was beyond the power of a tribunal to consider whether the condition of reg.4(1B)(b) of the 1987 Regulations (or reg.4(1B)(d) which might have been more relevant) was met. It is suggested that an alternative construction of s.12(3) would be that it is necessary for there to be a right of appeal against any decision as to whether or not a claim was valid. *CF/3565/2001,* decided a few days later by a different Commissioner who was apparently unaware of the approach taken in *CJSA/69/2001,* concerned a decision of the Secretary of State not to recognise education provided otherwise than at a recognised educational establishment, which the Commissioner held to fall within para.2 of this Schedule. The Commissioner held that this Schedule was validly made under s.12(1)(a) of, and para.9 of Sch.2 to, the 1998 Act. In fact, as was noted in *CJSA/69/2001,* s.12(1) is not listed in Sch.1 to the Regulations as being a power under which the Regulations were made, doubtless because it does not independently confer any power to make regulations. Curiously, the Commissioner in *CJSA/69/2001* stated that Sch.3 was also not listed in Sch.1 to the Regulations when it is, although it is not clear why the Commissioner mentioned it at all as it is irrelevant. Even more curiously, he did not mention para.9 of Sch.2, which *does* confer the relevant power to make regulations relied upon in *CF/3565/2001* and is also listed in Sch.1 to the Regulations. Equally, the Commissioner deciding *CF/3565/2001* did not consider the argument that the Schedule might have been made under s.12(2) of the 1998 Act. He did however reject a broader argument that the Schedule was ultra vires because it was inconsistent with the European Convention on Human Rights. He held, applying *R. (Alconbury Developments Ltd) v Secretary of State for the Environment, Transport and the Regions* [2001] UKHL 23; [2001] 2 W.L.R. 1389, that judicial review was an adequate remedy in the case before him, although he left open the question whether the Schedule would be ultra vires for the purposes of other cases.

In *R(IS) 6/04,* the Commissioner again had a challenge to para.5 in its first form and the question was whether an appeal lay against the Secretary of State's decision that the claimant had not complied with the prescribed requirements for making a valid claim. The Commissioner considered it unnecessary to say how the regulation-making power in para.9 of Sch.2 to the Act should be construed or whether para.5 of Sch.2 to the Regulations had been made under that power because he agreed with the construction of s.12 applied in *CJSA/69/2001* so that, even applying the approach more favourable to the claimant, he considered that para.5 was validly made when the Regulations first came into force. However, he held the absence of a right of appeal to be incompatible with Art.6 of the European Convention on Human Rights and so disapplied the paragraph insofar as it was necessary to do so to ensure that a claimant was entitled to appeal against a decision as to whether or when a claim had been validly made in accordance with the prescribed requirements. This restored the position to what it had been before the Social Security Act 1998 had come into force (*R(U) 9/60*). The Secretary of State withdrew an appeal to the Court of Appeal and subsequently amended para.5(a) in order to provide a right of appeal against a decision that a claim had not been validly made. It does not necessarily follow, however, that he accepted that the Commissioner's decision as to the application of Art. 6 of the Convention was correct. Indeed, in *R(H)3/05*, leading counsel for one of the claimants acknowledged that the reasoning in *R(IS)6/04* had been overtaken by that in *Runa Begum v Tower Hamlets London* (*First Secretary of State intervening*) [2003] UKHL 5; [2003] 2 A.C. 430 in which it was held by the House of Lords that there was no breach of Art. 6 of the Convention where an appeal from a local authority's decision in respect of their duties to homeless people lay only on a point of law. One possible inference to be drawn from the House of Lords' decision is that judicial review of the unappealable decisions listed in Sch.2 of these Regulations, or the similar provisions relating to housing benefit and council tax benefit in issue in *R(H)3/05*, is an adequate remedy under the Convention. However, counsel submitted that the House of Lords' conclusion in *Runa Begum*, that there was no unfairness in not having an appeal on a point of fact, was reached against the background of a system of internal review by a different officer of appropriate seniority, whereas, in housing benefit and council tax cases, such system of internal review as there had formerly been had been replaced by an appeal to a tribunal, which is the procedure available in other social security cases. In the absence of as sophisticated a system of review as there was in *Runa Begum*, he argued, there had to be a right of appeal on questions of fact. It was unnecessary for the Tribunal of Commissioners to express a view on that argument and they did not do so. Now that judicial review has adapted so as to be able to include a review of the merits of a decision as well as its legality, where that is required (see *Secretary of State for the Home Department v MB* [2006] EWCA Civ 1140; [2007] Q.B. 415), arguments that it does not provide an adequate remedy for the purposes of the Convention are more difficult to run and they may have become even more so now that is has become possible for judicial review cases to be transferred to the Upper Tribunal (see the note to s.15 of the Tribunals, Courts and Enforcement Act 2007)..

The fourth case in which an ultra vires challenge to Sch.2 was raised is *Campbell v Secretary of State for Work and Pensions* [2005] EWCA Civ 989, where the Court of Appeal agreed with a Tribunal of Commissioners that a decision under the Convention on Social Security between Great Britain and Jamaica was a decision on payability rather than entitlement, because the convention was given force by the Social Security (Jamaica) Order 1997 which was made under s.179 of the Social Security Administration Act 1992. Section 12(3) of the Social Security Act 1998 therefore did not come into play and the decision was unappealable by virtue of para.22 of Sch.2 to the Regulations, read with para.9 of Sch.2 to the Act.

In this Schedule, "decision" includes determinations embodied in or necessary to a decision (see reg.27(2)).

2.449   **Schedule 3.** *Revoked.*

[¹SCHEDULE 3A **Regulation 7(1)(a)**

DATE FROM WHICH SUPERSEDING DECISION TAKES EFFECT WHERE A CLAIMANT IS IN
RECEIPT OF INCOME SUPPORT OR JOBSEEKER'S ALLOWANCE.

Income Support

1. Subject to paragraphs 2 to 6, where the amount of income support payable under an   **2.450**
award is changed by a superseding decision made on the ground of a change of circumstances,
that superseding decision shall take effect—

(a) where income support is paid in arrears, from the first day of the benefit week in which
the relevant change of circumstances occurs or is expected to occur; or

(b) where income support is paid in advance, from the date of the relevant change of
circumstances, or the day on which the relevant change of circumstances is expected
to occur, if either of those days is the first day of the benefit week and otherwise from
the next following such day, and

for the purposes of this paragraph any period of residence in temporary accommodation under
arrangements for training made under section 2 of the Employment and Training Act 1973 or
section 2 of the Enterprise and New Towns (Scotland) Act 1990 for a period which is expected
to last for seven days or less shall not be regarded as a change of circumstances.

2. In the cases set out in paragraph 3, the superseding decision shall take effect from the day
on which the relevant change of circumstances occurs or is expected to occur.

3. The cases referred to in paragraph 2 are where—

(a) income support is paid in arrears and entitlement ends, or is expected to end, for a
reason other than that the claimant no longer satisfies the provisions of section 124(1)
(b) of the Contributions and Benefits Act;

[²(aa) income support is being paid from 8th April 2002 to persons who, immediately
before that day, had a preserved right for the purposes of the Income Support
Regulations;]

(b) a child or young person referred to in regulation 16(6) of the Income Support
Regulations (child in care of local authority or detained in custody) lives, or is
expected to live, with the claimant for part only of the benefit week;

(c) [⁵ . . .]

(d) a person referred to in paragraph 1, 2, 3 or 18 of Schedule 7 to the Income Support
Regulations—

(i) ceases, or is expected to cease, to be a patient; or

(ii) a member of his family ceases, or is expected to cease, to be a patient, in either
case for a period of less than a week;

(e) a person referred to in paragraph 8 of Schedule 7 to the Income Support
Regulations—

(i) ceases to be a prisoner; or

(ii) becomes a prisoner;

(f) a person to whom section 126 of the Contributions and Benefits Act (trade disputes)
applies—

(i) becomes incapable of work by reason of disease or bodily or mental disablement; or

(ii) enters the maternity period (as defined in section 126(2) of that Act) or the day
is known on which that person is expected to enter the maternity period;

(g) during the currency of the claim, a claimant makes a claim for a relevant social
security benefit—

(i) the result of which is that his benefit week changes; or

(ii) under regulation 13 of the Claims and Payment Regulations and an award of
that benefit on the relevant day for the purposes of that regulation means that
his benefit week is expected to change;

[⁷ (h) regulation 9 of the Social Security (Disability Living Allowance) Regulations 1991
(persons in certain accommodation other than hospitals) applies, or ceases to apply,
to the claimant for a period of less than one week.]

4. A superseding decision made in consequence of a payment of income being treated as
paid on a particular day under regulation 31(1)(b) [⁴ (2) or (3)] or 39C(3) of the Income
Support Regulations (date on which income is treated as paid) shall take effect from the day
on which that payment is treated as paid.

5. Where—

(a) it is decided upon supersession on the ground of a relevant change of circumstances

[⁵ or change specified in paragraph 12 and 13] that the amount of income support is, or is to be, reduced; and

(b) the Secretary of State certifies that it is impracticable for a superseding decision to take effect from the day prescribed in the preceding paragraphs of this Schedule (other than where paragraph 3(g) or 4 applies),

that superseding decision shall take effect—

    (i) where the relevant change has occurred, from the first day of the benefit week following that in which that superseding decision is made; or

    (ii) where the relevant change is expected to occur, from the first day of the benefit week following that in which that change of circumstances is expected to occur.

6. Where—

(a) a superseding decision ("the former supersession") was made on the ground of a relevant change of circumstances in the cases set out in paragraphs 3(b) to (g); and

(b) that superseding decision is itself superseded by a subsequent decision because the circumstances which gave rise to the former supersession cease to apply ("the second change"),

that subsequent decision shall take effect from the date of the second change.

Jobseeker's Allowance

2.451

7. Subject to paragraphs 8 to 11, where a decision in respect of a claim for jobseeker's allowance is superseded on the ground that there has been or there is expected to be, a relevant change of circumstances, the supersession shall take effect from the first day of the benefit week (as defined in regulation 1(3) of the Jobseeker's Allowance Regulations) in which that relevant change of circumstances occurs or is expected to occur.

8. Where the relevant change of circumstances giving rise to the supersession is that—

(a) entitlement to jobseeker's allowance ends, or is expected to end, for a reason other than that the claimant no longer satisfies the provisions of section 3(1)(a) [² or 3A(1) (a)] of the Jobseekers Act; or

[³ (aa) jobseeker's allowance is being paid from 8th April 2002 to persons who, immediately before that day, had a preserved right for the purposes of the Jobseeker's Allowance Regulations;]

(b) a child or young person who is normally in the care of a local authority or who is detained in custody lives, or is expected to live, with the claimant for a part only of the benefit week; or

(c) [⁵ . . .]

(d) the partner of the claimant or a member of his family ceases, or is expected to cease, to be a hospital in-patient for a period of less than a week; [² or,

(e) a joint-claim couple ceases to be [⁶ couple]],

the supersession shall take effect from the date that the relevant change of circumstances occurs or is expected to occur.

9. Where the relevant change of circumstances giving rise to a supersession is any of those specified in paragraph 8, and, in consequences those circumstances ceasing to apply, a further superseding decision is made, that further superseding decision shall take effect from the date that those circumstances ceased to apply.

10. Where, under the provisions of regulation 96 or 102C(3) of the Jobseeker's Allowance Regulations, income is treated as paid on a certain date and that payment gives rise, or is expected to give rise, to a relevant change of circumstance resulting in a supersession, that supersession shall take effect from that date.

11. Where a relevant change of circumstances [⁵ or change specified in paragraphs 12 and 13] occurs which results, or is expected to result, in a reduced award of jobseeker's allowance then, if the Secretary of State is of the opinion that it is impracticable for a supersession to take effect in accordance with [⁵ paragraph 12 or] the preceding paragraphs of this Schedule, the supersession shall take effect from the first day of the benefit week following that in which the relevant change of circumstances occurs.]

[⁵*Changes other than changes of circumstances*

2.452

12. Where an amount of income support or jobseeker's allowance payable under an award is changed by a superseding decision specified in paragraph 13 the superseding decision shall take effect—

(a) in the case of a change in respect of income support, from the day specified in paragraph 1(a) or (b) for a change of circumstances; and

(b) in the case of a change in respect of jobseeker's allowance, from the day specified in paragraph 7 for a change of circumstances.

13. The following are superseding decisions for the purposes of paragraph 12—

(a) a decision which supersedes a decision specified in regulation 6(2)(b) to (ee); and

(b) a superseding decision which would, but for paragraph 12, take effect from a date specified in regulation 7(5) to (7), (12) to (16), (18) to (20), (22), (24) and (33).]

AMENDMENTS

1. Social Security and Child Support (Miscellaneous Amendments) Regulations 2000 (SI 2000/1596), reg.35 (June 19, 2000).

2. Social Security Amendment (Joint Claim) Regulations 2001 (SI 2001/518), reg.4(c) (March 19, 2001).

3. Social Security Amendment (Residential Care and Nursing Homes) Regulations 2002 (SI 2002/398), reg.3 (April 8, 2002).

4. Social Security (Working Tax Credit and Child Tax Credit) (Consequential Amendments) (No.3) Regulations 2003 (SI 2003/1731), reg.5 (August 8, 2003).

5. Social Security, Child Support and Tax Credits (Miscellaneous Amendments) Regulations 2005 (SI 2005/337), reg.2(21) (March 19, 2005).

6. Civil Partnership (Consequential Amendments) Regulations 2005 (SI 2005/2878), reg.8(4) (December 5, 2005).

7. Social Security (Miscellaneous Amendments) (No. 3) Regulations 2006 (SI 2006/2377), reg.3(3) (October 2, 2006).

DEFINITIONS

"the Claims and Payments Regulations"—see reg.1(3).
"the Contributions and Benefits Act"—see s.84 of the Social Security Act 1998.
"the Income Support Regulations"—see reg.1(3).
"the Jobseekers Act"—see s.84 of the Social Security Act 1998.
"the Jobseeker's Allowance Regulations"—see reg.1(3).
"a joint-claim couple"—*ibid.*
"superseding decision"—see para.13.

GENERAL NOTE

Paragraphs 12 and 13 have the effect that any change to an existing award of income support or jobseeker's allowance takes place from the start of a benefit week. **2.453**

[¹ SCHEDULE 3B

DATE ON WHICH CHANGE OF CIRCUMSTANCES TAKES EFFECT WHERE CLAIMANT ENTITLED TO STATE PENSION CREDIT

1. Where the amount of state pension credit payable under an award is changed by a superseding decision made on the ground that there has been a relevant change of circumstances, that superseding decision shall take effect from the following days— **2.454**

(a) for the purpose only of determining the day on which an assessed income period begins under section 9 of the State Pension Credit Act, from the day following the day on which the last previous assessed income period ended; and

(b) except as provided in the following paragraphs, from the day that change occurs or is expected to occur if either of those days is the first day of a benefit week but if it is not from the next following such day.

2. Subject to paragraph 3, where the relevant change is that the claimant's income (other than deemed income from capital) has changed, the superseding decision shall take effect on the first day of the benefit week in which that change occurs or if that is not practicable in the circumstances of the case, on the first day of the next following benefit week. **2.455**

3. Paragraph 2 shall not apply where the only relevant change is that working tax credit under the Tax Credits Act 2002 becomes payable or becomes payable at a higher rate. **2.456**

4. A superseding decision shall take effect from the day the change of circumstances occurs or is expected to occur if— **2.457**

(a) the person ceases to be or becomes a prisoner, and for this purpose "prisoner" has the same meaning as in regulation 1(2) of the State Pension Credit Regulations; or

(b) whilst entitled to state pension credit a claimant is awarded another social security benefit and in consequence of that award his benefit week changes or is expected to change.

2.458   [² 5. In a case where the relevant circumstance is that the claimant ceased to be a patient, if he becomes a patient again in the same benefit week, the superseding decision in respect of ceasing to be a patient shall take effect from the first day of the week in which the change occured.]

2.459   6. In paragraph 5, "patient" means a person (other than a prisoner) who is regarded as receiving free in-patient treatment within the meaning of the [⁴ Social Security (Hospital In-Patients) Regulations 2005.]

2.460   [³ 7. Where an amount of state pension credit payable under an award is changed by a superseding decision specified in paragraph 8 the superseding decision shall take effect from the day specified in paragraph 1(b).

2.461   8. The following are superseding decisions for the purposes of paragraph 7—

(a) a decision which supersedes a decision specified in regulation 6(2)(b) to (ee) and (m); and

(b) a superseding decision which would, but for paragraphs 2 and 7, take effect from a date specified in regulation 7(5) to (7), (12) to (16) and (29C).]

AMENDMENTS

1. State Pension Credit (Consequential, Transitional and Miscellaneous Provisions) Regulations 2002 (SI 2002/3019), reg.22 (April 7, 2003).

2. State Pension Credit (Transitional and Miscellaneous Provisions) Amendment Regulations 2003 (SI 2003/2274), reg.5(4) (October 6, 2003).

3. Social Security (Miscellaneous Amendments) (No.2) Regulations 2006 (SI 2006/832), reg.5(4) (April 10, 2006).

4. Social Security (Miscellaneous Amendments) (No.4) Regulations 2007 (SI 2007/2470), reg.3(9) (September 24, 2007).

DEFINITIONS

"assessed income period"—see reg.1(3).
"patient"—see para.6.
"state pension credit"—*ibid.*
"State Pension Credit Act"—*ibid.*
"State Pension Credit Regulations"—*ibid.*

GENERAL NOTE

2.462   The misspelling of what should read as "occurred" in para.5 occurs in the Queen's Printer's copy of the statutory instrument.

[¹ SCHEDULE 3C

DATE FROM WHICH CHANGE OF CIRCUMSTANCES TAKES EFFECT WHERE CLAIMANT ENTITLED TO EMPLOYMENT AND SUPPORT ALLOWANCE

2.463   1. Subject to paragraphs 2 to 7, where the amount of an employment and support allowance payable under an award is changed by a superseding decision made on the ground of a change of circumstances, that superseding decision shall take effect from the first day of the benefit week in which the relevant change of circumstances occurs or is expected to occur.

2. In the cases set out in paragraph 3, the superseding decision shall take effect from the day on which the relevant change of circumstances occurs or is expected to occur.

3. The cases referred to in paragraph 2 are where—

(a) entitlement ends, or is expected to end, for a reason other than that the claimant no longer satisfies the provisions of paragraph 6(1)(a) of Schedule 1 to the Welfare Reform Act;

(b) a child or young person referred to in regulation 156(6)(d) or (h) of the Employment and Support Allowance Regulations (child in care of local authority or detained in custody) lives, or is expected to live, with the claimant for part only of the benefit week;

(c) a person referred to in paragraph 12 of Schedule 5 to the Employment and Support Allowance Regulations—

    (i) ceases, or is expected to cease, to be a patient; or

    (ii) a member of the person's family ceases, or is expected to cease, to be a patient,

    in either case for a period of less than a week;

(d) a person referred to in paragraph 3 of Schedule 5 to the Employment and Support Allowance Regulations—

    (i) ceases to be a prisoner; or

    (ii) becomes a prisoner;

(e) during the currency of the claim a claimant makes a claim for a relevant social security benefit—

    (i) the result of which is that his benefit week changes; or

    (ii) in accordance with regulation 13 of the Claims and Payments Regulations and an award of that benefit on the relevant day for the purposes of that regulation means that his benefit week is expected to change.

4. A superseding decision made in consequence of a payment of income being treated as paid on a particular day under regulation 93 of the Employment and Support Allowance Regulations (date on which income is treated as paid) shall take effect from the day on which that payment is treated as paid.

5. Where—

(a) it is decided upon supersession on the ground of a relevant change of circumstances or change specified in paragraphs 9 and 10 that the amount of an employment and support allowance is, or is to be, reduced; and

(b) the Secretary of State certifies that it is impracticable for a superseding decision to take effect from the day prescribed in paragraph 9 or the preceding paragraphs of this Schedule (other than where paragraph 3(e) or 4 applies),

that superseding decision shall take effect—

    (i) where the relevant change has occurred, from the first day of the benefit week following that in which that superseding decision is made; or

    (ii) where the relevant change is expected to occur, from the first day of the benefit week following that in which that change of circumstances is expected to occur.

6. Where—

(a) a superseding decision ("the former supersession") was made on the ground of a relevant change of circumstances in the cases set out in paragraph 3(b) to (e); and

(b) that superseding decision is itself superseded by a subsequent decision because the circumstances which gave rise to the former supersession cease to apply ("the second change"),

that subsequent decision shall take effect from the date of the second change.

7. In the case of an employment and support allowance decision where there has been a limited capability for work determination, where—

(a) the Secretary of State is satisfied that, in relation to a limited capability for work determination, the claimant or payee failed to notify an appropriate office of a change of circumstances which regulations under the Administration Act required him to notify; and

(b) the claimant or payee, as the case may be, could reasonably have been expected to know that the change of circumstances should have been notified,

the superseding decision shall take effect—

    (i) from the date on which the claimant or payee, as the case may be, ought to have notified the change of circumstances; or

    (ii) if more than one change has taken place between the date from which the decision to be superseded took effect and the date of the superseding decision, from the date on which the first change ought to have been notified.

Changes other than changes of circumstances

8. Where—

(a) the Secretary of State supersedes a decision made by an appeal tribunal or a Commissioner on the grounds specified in regulation 6(2)(c)(i) (ignorance of, or mistake as to, a material fact);

    (b) the decision to be superseded was more advantageous to the claimant because of the ignorance or mistake than it would otherwise have been; and

    (c) the material fact—

        (i) does not relate to the limited capability for work determination embodied in or necessary to the decision; or

        (ii) relates to a limited capability for work determination embodied in or necessary to the decision and the Secretary of State is satisfied that at the time the decision was made the claimant or payee, as the case may be, knew or could reasonably have been expected to know of it and that it was relevant,

the superseding decision shall take effect from the first day of the benefit week in which the decision of the appeal tribunal or the Commissioner took effect or was to take effect.

9. Where an amount of an employment and support allowance payable under an award is changed by a superseding decision specified in paragraph 10 the superseding decision shall take effect from the day specified in paragraph 1 for a change of circumstances.

10. The following are superseding decisions for the purposes of paragraph 9—

    (a) a decision which supersedes a decision specified in regulation 6(2)(b) and (d) to (ee); and

    (b) a superseding decision which would, but for paragraph 9, take effect from a date specified in regulation 7(6), (7), (12), (13), (17D) to (17F), and (33).]

AMENDMENT

1. Employment and Support Allowance (Consequential Provisions) (No. 2) Regulations 2008 (SI 2008/1554), regs 29 and 41 (July 27, 2008).

2.464   **Schedule 4.** *Omitted.*

The Social Security (General Benefit) Regulations 1982

(SI 1982/1408) (AS AMENDED)

ARRANGEMENT OF REGULATIONS

PART I

General

The Secretary of State for Social Services, in exercise of the powers conferred upon him by sections 50(4), 56(7), 57(5), 58(3), 60(4) and (7), 61(1), 62(2), 67(1), 68(2), 70(2), 72(1) and (8), 74(1), 81(6), 82(5) and (6), 83(1), 85(1), 86(2) and (5), 90(2), 91(1), 119(3) and (4) and 159(3) of, and paragraphs 2, 3 and 6 of Schedule 8, paragraphs 1 and 8 of Schedule 9 and Schedule 14 of the Social Security Act 1975 and of all other powers enabling him in that behalf, hereby makes the following regulations, which only consolidate the regulation hereby revoked, and which accordingly, by virtue of paragraph 20 of Schedule 3 to the Social Security Act 1980, are not subject to the requirements of section 10 of that Act for prior reference to the Social Security Advisory Committee and, by virtue of section 141(2) and paragraph 12 of Schedule 16 of the Social Security Act 1975, do not require prior reference to the Industrial Injuries Advisory Council:—

PART I

GENERAL

Citation, commencement and interpretation

1.—(1) These regulations may be cited as the Social Security (General   2.466
Benefit) Regulations 1982 and shall come into operation on 4th November,
1982.

(2) In these regulations, unless the context otherwise requires—

"the Act" means the Social Security Act 1975;

[³ 'bereavement benefit' means a benefit referred to in section 20(1)(ea)
of the Social Security Contributions and Benefits Act 1992;]

"the Child Benefit Act" means the Child Benefit Act 1975;

"child benefit" means benefit under Part I of the Child Benefit Act;

[¹ "determining authority" means, as the case may require, the Secretary
of State, [⁵ the First-tier Tribunal or the Upper Tribunal]

"entitled to child benefit" includes treated as so entitled;

"industrial injuries benefit" means [². . .] disablement benefit and industrial death benefit payable under section 50 of the Act;

"parent" has the meaning assigned to it by section 24(3) of the Child
Benefit Act;

[⁴ "shared additional pension" means a shared additional pension under
section 55A of the Social Security Contributions and Benefits Act
1992;]

"standard rate of increase" means the amount specified in Part IV or Part
V of Schedule 4 to the Act as the amount of an increase of the benefit
in question for an adult dependant;

"the Workmen's Compensation Act" means the Workmen's Compen-
sation Acts 1925 to 1945, or the enactments repealed by the Workmen's
Compensation Act 1925 or the enactments repealed by the Workmen's
Compensation Act 1906;

and other expressions have the same meanings as in the Act.

(3) Unless the context otherwise requires, any reference in these
regulation—

(a) to a numbered section is to the section of the Act bearing that
number;

(b) to a numbered regulation is a reference to the regulation bearing that
number in these regulations and any reference in a regulation to a
numbered paragraph is a reference to the paragraph of that regulation bearing that number.

AMENDMENTS

1. The Social Security Act 1998 (Commencement No.8, and Savings and
Consequential and Transitional Provisions) Order 1999 (SI 1999/1958), Sch.5 (July
4, 1999).

2. The Social Security (Abolition of Injury Benefit) (Consequential) Regulations
1983 (SI 1983/186), reg.13 (April 6, 1983).

3. The Social Security (Benefits for Widows and Widowers) (Consequential
Amendments) Regulations 2000 (SI 2000/1483), reg.8 (April 9, 2001).

4. The Social Security (Shared Additional Pension) (Miscellaneous Amendments)
Regulations 2005 (SI 2005/1551) (July 6, 2005).

5. The Tribunals, Courts and Enforcement Act 2007 (Transitional and
Consequential Provisions) Order 2008 (SI 2008/2683), reg.24 (November 3, 2008).

Exceptions from disqualification for imprisonment etc.

2.467
2.—(1) The following provisions of this regulation shall have effect to except benefit from the operation of [section 113(1)(b) of the Social Security Contributions and Benefits Act 1992] which provides that (except where regulations otherwise provide) a person shall be disqualified for receiving any benefit and an increase of benefit shall not be payable in respect of any person as the beneficiary's [⁸ spouse or civil partner], for any period during which that person is undergoing imprisonment or detention in legal custody (hereinafter in this regulation referred to as "the said provisions").

(2) The said provisions shall not operate to disqualify a person for receiving [¹incapacity benefit], [²attendance allowance, disability living allowance], widow's benefit, [⁶ bereavement benefit,] child's special allowance, maternity allowance, [⁷ a shared additional pension] retirement pension of any category, age addition, [³severe disablement allowance], [⁴. . .disablement benefit], [⁵. . .reduced earnings allowance, retirement allowance] or industrial death benefit or to make an increase of benefit not payable in respect of a person as the beneficiary's [⁸ spouse or civil partner], for any period during which that person is undergoing imprisonment or detention in legal custody in connection with a charge brought or intended to be brought against him in criminal proceedings, or pursuant to any sentence or order for detention made by a court in such proceedings, unless, in relation to him, a penalty is imposed at the conclusion of those proceedings or, in the case of default of payment of a sum adjudged to be paid on conviction, a penalty is imposed in respect of such default.

(3) The said provisions shall not operate to disqualify a person for receiving any benefit (not being a guardian's allowance or death grant), or to make an increase of benefit not payable in respect of a person as the beneficiary's [⁸ spouse or civil partner], for any period during which that person is undergoing detention in legal custody after the conclusion of criminal proceedings if it is a period during which he is liable to be detained in a hospital or similar institution in Great Britain as a person suffering from mental disorder unless—

[⁹ (a) he is detained or liable to be detained under section 45A of the Mental Health Act 1983 (hospital and limitation directions) or section 59A of the Criminal Procedure (Scotland) Act 1995 (hospital direction); or

(b) he is detained or liable to be detained under section 47 of the Mental Health Act 1983 (removal to hospital of persons serving sentences of imprisonment, etc.) or section 136 of the Mental Health (Care and Treatment) (Scotland) Act 2003 (transfer of prisoners for treatment for mental disorder).]

(4) Where, as respects a person in relation to whom [⁹ paragraph (3)(a) or (b)] is satisfied, a certificate given by or on behalf of the Secretary of State [⁹ or Scottish Ministers] shows the earliest date on which that person would have been expected to be discharged from the detention pursuant to the said sentence or order if he had not been transferred to a hospital or similar institution, the said conditions shall be deemed not to be satisfied in relation to that person as from the day next following that date.

(5) The said provisions shall not operate to disqualify a person for receiving a guardian's allowance or death grant.

[⁵(6) Subject to paragraph (7), the said provisions shall not operate to disqualify a person for receiving disablement benefit, other than any increase of that benefit, for any period during which he is undergoing imprisonment or detention in legal custody.]

(7) The amount payable by virtue of the last preceding paragraph by way of any disablement pension or pensions in respect of any period, other than a period in respect of which that person is excepted from disqualification by virtue of the provisions of paragraph (3) of this regulation, during which that person is and has continuously been undergoing imprisonment or detention in legal custody, shall not exceed the total amount payable by way of such pension or all such pensions for a period of one year.

(8) For the purposes of this regulation—

(a) "court" means any court in the United Kingdom, the Channel Islands or the Isle of Man or in any place to which the Colonial Prisoners Removal Act 1884 applies or any naval court-martial, army court-martial or air force court-martial within the meaning of the Courts-Martial (Appeals) Act 1968, or the Courts-Martial Appeal Court;

(b) "hospital or similar institution" means any place (not being a prison, a detention centre, a Borstal institution, a young offenders institution or a remand centre, and not being at or in any such place) in which persons suffering from mental disorder are or may be received for care or treatment;

(c) "penalty" means a sentence of imprisonment, Borstal training or detention under section 53 of the Children and Young Persons Act 1933 or under section 57(3) of the Children and Young Persons (Scotland) Act 1937 or under section 208(3) and 416(4) of the Criminal Proceedings (Scotland) Act 1975 or an order for detention in a detention centre;

(d) in relation to a person who is liable to be detained in Great Britain as a result of any order made under the Colonial Prisoners Removal Act 1884, references to a prison shall be construed as including references to a prison within the meaning of that Act;

(e) [⁹. . .]

(f) [⁹. . .]

(g) criminal proceedings against any person shall be deemed to be concluded upon his being found insane in those proceedings so that he cannot be tried or his trial cannot proceed.

(9) Where a person outside Great Britain is undergoing imprisonment or detention in legal custody and, in similar circumstances in Great Britain, he would have been excepted, by the operation of any of the preceding paragraphs of this regulation, from disqualification under the said provisions (referred to in paragraph (1)) for receiving the benefit claimed, he shall not be disqualified for receiving that benefit by reason only of his said imprisonment or detention.

(10) Paragraph (9) applies to increases of benefit not payable under the said provisions as it applied to disqualification for receiving benefit.

AMENDMENTS

1. The Social Security (Incapacity Benefit) (Consequential and Transitional Amendments and Savings) Regulations 1995 (SI 1995/829), reg. 16 (April 13, 1995).

2. The Disability Living Allowance and Disability Working Allowance (Consequential Provisions) Regulations 1991 (SI 1991/2742), reg. 11 (April 6, 1992).

3. The Social Security (Severe Disablement Allowance) Regulations 1984 (SI 1984/1303), reg.11 (November 29, 1984).

4. The Social Security (Abolition of Injury benefit) (Consequential) Regulations 1983 (SI 1983/186), reg.13 (April 6, 1983).

5. The Social Security (Industrial Injuries and Diseases) (Miscellaneous Amendments) Regulations 1996 (SI 1996/425), reg.4 (March 24, 1996).

6. The Social Security (Benefits for Widows and Widowers) (Consequential Amendments) Regulations 2000 (SI 2000/1483), reg.6 (April 9, 2001).

7. The Social Security (Shared Additional Pension) (Miscellaneous Amendments) Regulations 2005 (SI 2005/1551) (July 6, 2005).

8. The Social Security (Civil Partnership) (Consequential Amendments) Regulations 2005 (SI 2005/2878) (December 5, 2005).

9. The Social Security (Hospital In-Patients) Regulations 2005 (SI 2005/3360), reg.3 (April 10, 2006).

DEFINITIONS

"the Act"—reg.1.
"benefit"—C & BA 1992, s.122.
"court"—para.(8)(a).
"Great Britain"—by art.1 of the Union with Scotland Act 1706, this means England, Scotland and Wales.
"hospital or similar institution"—para.(8)(b).
"penalty"—para.(8)(c).
"the said provisions"—para.(1).

GENERAL NOTE

2.468

Persons who can bring themselves within the terms of this regulation can escape the disqualification from benefit provided for in s.113(1)(b) of the Contributions and Benefits Act. Different rules apply to different benefits.

Under para.(2) the disqualification applies in cases of imprisonment in connection with criminal proceedings where such penalty is imposed at the conclusion of proceedings. Imprisonment outside the exercise of criminal jurisdiction does not disqualify from benefit: *R(S)8/79*. It is now established that "penalty" in this paragraph includes the imposition of a suspended sentence and that a suspended sentence amounts to a sentence of imprisonment: *R(S)1/71*.

Paragraph (3) deals with the transfer of offenders from prison to hospital as mental patients under the mental health legislation. The disqualification in such circumstances exists only for the length of the original sentence: *R(P)2/57* reversing *R(S)9/56*. Provision is made for the Secretary of State to issue a certificate which is conclusive as to the earliest date on which the original sentence would come to an end had the person not been transferred to hospital.

References to the Mental Health Act 1959 should now be read as references to the Mental Health Act 1983.

A Commissioner has ruled in *CSS/239/2007* that, without a certificate of the type referred to in reg.2(4) of the General Benefit Regulations, an appellant could not obtain the advantage of the regulation. Paragraphs 8 to 10 of the decision address questions arising in relation to devolved government in Scotland.

A challenge relating to the exclusion from benefits of prisoners transferred to mental hospital under these regulations as being in breach of art.14 of the European Convention when read with Article 1 of Protocol No. 1 has failed with one exception: see *R. (on the application of EM and others) v Secretary of State for Work and Pensions*, [2009] EWHC 454 (Admin). The excepted class is a small group (there were 45 such persons in detention when the case was decided) of what are described as "technical lifers", namely those, although sentenced to life imprisonment, are treated by the Secretary of State after transfer to hospital as though they had been made the subject of a hospital order under s.37 of the Mental Health Act 1983 and to a restriction order under s.41 of that Act.

Suspension of payment of benefit during imprisonment etc.

3.—(1) Subject to the following provisions of this regulation, the payment   2.469
to any person of any benefit—

(a) which is excepted from the operation of [section 113(1)(b) of the
Social Security Contributions and Benefits Act 1992] by virtue of
the provisions of regulation 2(2), (5) and (6) or by any of those paragraphs as applied by regulation 2(9); or

(b) which is payable otherwise than in respect of a period during which
he is undergoing imprisonment or detention in legal custody;

shall be suspended while that person is undergoing imprisonment or detention in legal custody.

(2) Paragraph (1) shall not operate to require the payment of any benefit
to be suspended while the beneficiary is liable to be detained in a hospital or
similar institution as defined in regulation 2(8)(b) during a period for which
in his case, benefit to which regulation 2(3) applies is or would be excepted
from the operation of the said [section 113(1)] by virtue of the provision of
regulation 2(3).

(3) A guardian's allowance or death grant, or any benefit to which
paragraph (1)(b) applies may nevertheless be paid while the beneficiary
is undergoing imprisonment or detention in legal custody to any person
appointed for the purpose by the Secretary of State to receive and deal
with any sums payable on behalf of the beneficiary on account of that
benefit, and the receipt of any person so appointed shall be a good discharge to the Secretary of State and the National Insurance Fund for any
sum so paid.

(4) Where, by virtue of this regulation, payment of benefit under [Part V
of the Social Security Contribution and Benefits Act 1992] is suspended
for any period, the period of suspension shall not be taken into account in
calculating any period under the provisions of regulation 22 of the Social
Security (Claims and Payments) Regulations 1979 (extinguishment of
right to sums payable by way of benefit which are not obtained within the
prescribed time).

Interim payments by way of benefit under the Act

4.—(1) Where, under arrangements made by the Secretary of State   2.470
with the consent of the Treasury, payment by way of benefit has been
made pending determination of a claim for it without due proof of the
fulfilment of the relevant conditions or otherwise than in accordance with
the provisions of the Act and orders and regulations made under it, the
payment so made shall, for the purposes of those provisions, but subject to
the following provisions of this regulation, be deemed to be a payment of
benefit duly made.

(2) When a claim for benefit in connection with which a payment has
been made under arrangements such as are referred to in paragraph (1)
above is determined by a determining authority—

(a) if that authority decides that nothing was properly payable by way
of the benefit in respect of which the payment was made or that the
amount properly payable by way of that benefit was less than the
amount of the payment, it may, if appropriate, direct that the whole
or part of the overpayment be treated as paid on account of benefit
(whether benefit under the Act or the Supplementary Benefits

615

Act 1976) which is properly payable, but subject as aforesaid shall require repayment of the overpayment; and

(b) if that authority decides that the amount properly payable by way of the benefit in respect of which the payment was made equals or exceeds the amount of that payment, it shall treat that payment as paid on account of the benefit properly payable.

(3) Unless before a payment made under arrangements such as are mentioned in paragraph (1) above has been made to a person that person had been informed of the effect of sub-paragraph (a) of paragraph (2) above as it relates to repayment of an overpayment, repayment of an overpayment shall not be required except where the determining authority is satisfied that[1] he, or any person acting for him, has, whether fraudulently or otherwise, misrepresented or failed to disclose any material fact and that the interim payment has been made in consequence of the misrepresentation or failure.]

(4) An overpayment required to be repaid under the provisions of this regulation shall, without prejudice to any other method of recovery, be recoverable by deduction from any benefit then or thereafter payable to the person by whom it is to be repaid or any persons entitled to receive his benefit on his death.

AMENDMENT

1. The Social Security (Payments on account, Overpayment and Recovery) Regulations 1987 (SI 1987/491), reg.19 (April 6, 1987).

GENERAL NOTE

2.471   This regulation has not been repealed by the Overpayments Regulations because its provisions will still be needed for cases where the relevant determination was made before April 6, 1987. As time passes the provision will fall into disuse, and will in due course be revoked.

The Social Security (Incapacity Benefit Work-focused Interviews) Regulations 2008

(SI 2008/2928)

In force from December 15, 2008

2.472   The Secretary of State for Work and Pensions makes the following Regulations, in exercise of the powers conferred upon him by sections 2A(1), (3) to (6) and (8), 2B(2), (6) and (7), 189(4) to (6) and (7A) and 191 of the Social Security Administration Act 1992.

The Social Security Advisory Committee has agreed that proposals in respect of these Regulations should not be referred to it.

ARRANGEMENT OF REGULATIONS

1.   Citation and commencement
2.   Interpretation

616

Citation and commencement

1. These Regulations may be cited as the Social Security (Incapacity Benefit Work-focused Interviews) Regulations 2008 and come into force on 15th December 2008.

2.473

Interpretation

2.—(1) In these Regulations—

2.474

"the 1998 Act" means the Social Security Act 1998;

"the 2000 Regulations" means the Social Security (Work-focused Interviews) Regulations 2000;

"the 2001 Regulations" means the Social Security (Jobcentre Plus Interviews) Regulations 2001;

"the 2002 Regulations" means the Social Security (Jobcentre Plus Interviews) Regulations 2002;

"the 2003 Regulations" means the Social Security (Incapacity Benefit Work-focused Interviews) Regulations 2003;

"action plan" has the meaning given by regulation 7;

"benefit week" means any period of seven days corresponding to the week in respect of which the relevant specified benefit is due to be paid;

"relevant claimant" has the meaning given by regulation 3;

"relevant decision" has the meaning given by section 2B(2) of the Social Security Administration Act 1992 (supplementary provisions relating to work-focused interviews);

"specified benefit" means—

(a) incapacity benefit;

(b) income support, if any of the following paragraphs of Schedule 1B (prescribed categories of person) to the Income Support (General) Regulations 1987 applies—

(i) paragraph 7 (persons incapable of work);

(ii) paragraph 24 or 25 (persons appealing against a decision which embodies a determination that they are not capable of work);

(c) severe disablement allowance;

"work-focused interview" means an interview conducted under regulation 6 for the purposes described in regulation 4.

(2) Any notification under these Regulations that is sent by post is to be taken to have been received on the second working day after posting.

Relevant claimant

3.—(1) A relevant claimant is a person who satisfies all of the following conditions.

2.475

617

(2) The first condition is that the person is entitled to a specified benefit.

(3) The second condition is that, immediately before these Regulations came into force, the person—

    (a) was a "relevant person" within the meaning of the 2003 Regulations; or

    (b) would have been a "relevant person" within the meaning of the 2003 Regulations if not for the person being 16 or 17 years of age; or

    (c) was a "relevant person" within the meaning of the 2000 Regulations or the 2001 Regulations, as saved by regulation 16(2) of the 2002 Regulations.

(4) The third condition is that the person has not attained the age of 60 years.

(5) The fourth condition is that, on the day on which the requirement to take part in a work-focused interview would have arisen, the person is not treated as incapable of work in accordance with regulation 10 of the Social Security (Incapacity for Work) (General) Regulations 1995 (certain persons with a severe condition to be treated as incapable of work).

Purposes of a work-focused interview

2.476   **4.** A work-focused interview is an interview with a relevant claimant that is conducted for any or all of the following purposes—

    (a) assessing the relevant claimant's prospects of remaining in or obtaining work;

    (b) assisting or encouraging the relevant claimant to remain in or obtain work;

    (c) identifying activities that the relevant claimant may undertake that will make remaining in or obtaining work more likely;

    (d) identifying training, educational or rehabilitation opportunities for the relevant claimant which may make it more likely that the relevant claimant will remain in or obtain work or be able to do so;

    (e) identifying current or future work opportunities, including self-employment opportunities, for the relevant claimant, which are relevant to that person's needs and abilities.

Requirement for a relevant claimant to take part in a work-focused interview

2.477   **5.**—(1) Subject to the following provisions of this regulation, a relevant claimant may be required by the Secretary of State to take part in one or more work-focused interviews as a condition of continuing to be entitled to the full amount of the specified benefit which is payable to that claimant.

(2) The Secretary of State may determine that a requirement that a relevant claimant take part in a work-focused interview is not to apply, or is treated as not having applied, if that interview would not be, or would not have been, of assistance because the claimant is or was likely to be starting or returning to work.

(3) A relevant claimant in relation to whom a requirement to take part in a work-focused interview has been determined not to apply under paragraph (2) must be treated as having complied with that requirement in respect of that interview for the purposes of—

    (a) paragraph (1); and

    (b) entitlement to a specified benefit.

(4) A requirement to take part in a work-focused interview may be

deferred or treated as having been deferred by the Secretary of State if at the time the work-focused interview is to take place, or was due to take place, such an interview would not at that time be or have been—

(a) of assistance to that relevant claimant; or

(b) appropriate in the circumstances.

(5) A deferral under paragraph (4) may be made at any time after the requirement to take part in the work-focused interview is imposed, including after the time that the work-focused interview was due to take place or took place.

(6) If a requirement to take part in a work-focused interview is deferred, or treated as having been deferred, then the time that the work-focused interview is to take place must be re-determined and notified to the relevant claimant.

(7) Any requirement to take part in a work-focused interview ceases to have effect if the relevant claimant ceases to satisfy the conditions in regulation 3.

The work-focused interview

6.—(1) The Secretary of State must notify, in writing or otherwise, a relevant claimant who is required to take part in a work-focused interview of the date, time and place of that interview.

(2) A work-focused interview may take place at a relevant claimant's home if the Secretary of State determines that requiring the relevant claimant to attend elsewhere would cause undue inconvenience to, or endanger the health of, the relevant claimant.

(3) A relevant claimant is to be regarded as having taken part in a work-focused interview if the claimant—

(a) attends for the work-focused interview at the place and on the date and time notified under paragraph (1);

(b) provides information, if requested by the Secretary of State, about any or all of the matters set out in paragraph (4);

(c) participates in discussions to the extent the Secretary of State considers necessary, about any or all of the matters set out in paragraph (5);

(d) assists the Secretary of State in the completion of an action plan in accordance with regulation 7.

(4) The matters referred to in paragraph (3)(b) are—

(a) the relevant claimant's educational qualifications and vocational training;

(b) the relevant claimant's work history;

(c) the relevant claimant's aspirations for future work;

(d) the relevant claimant's skills that are relevant to work;

(e) the relevant claimant's work-related abilities;

(f) the relevant claimant's caring or childcare responsibilities;

(g) any paid or unpaid work that the relevant claimant is undertaking.

(5) The matters referred to in paragraph (3)(c) are—

(a) any activity the relevant claimant is willing to undertake which may make obtaining or remaining in work more likely;

(b) any such activity that the relevant claimant may have previously undertaken;

(c) any progress the relevant claimant may have made towards remaining in or obtaining work;

(d) the relevant claimant's opinion as to the extent to which the ability

2.478

to remain in or obtain work is restricted by the relevant claimant's physical or mental condition.

Action plan

2.479   7.—(1) An action plan is a written document completed by the Secretary of State, which contains a record of the discussions a relevant claimant has participated in with the Secretary of State in relation to the relevant claimant's employability, including any action the relevant claimant and the Secretary of State agree is reasonable and the relevant claimant is willing to take in order to help that relevant claimant enhance his or her employment prospects.

(2) The Secretary of State must provide the relevant claimant with a copy of the action plan completed under paragraph (1) at the end of the work-focused interview.

Failure to take part in a work-focused interview

2.480   8.—(1) A relevant claimant who is required to take part in a work-focused interview but fails to do so must show good cause for that failure within five working days of the date on which the Secretary of State gives notification of that failure.

(2) In determining whether a relevant claimant has shown good cause for a failure to take part in a work-focused interview, the matters to be taken into account include—

  (a) that the relevant claimant misunderstood the requirement to take part in the work-focused interview due to any learning, language or literacy difficulties of the relevant claimant or any misleading information given to the relevant claimant by the Secretary of State;

  (b) that the relevant claimant had transport difficulties and that no reasonable alternative was available;

  (c) that the relevant claimant was attending an interview with an employer with a view to remaining in or obtaining employment;

  (d) that the relevant claimant was pursuing employment opportunities as a self-employed earner;

  (e) that the relevant claimant was attending a medical or dental appointment and that it would have been unreasonable in the circumstances to re-arrange the appointment;

  (f) that the relevant claimant was accompanying another person for whom the claimant has caring responsibilities to a medical or dental appointment and that it would have been unreasonable for that other person to re-arrange the appointment;

  (g) that the relevant claimant, a dependant or another person for whom the relevant claimant provides care suffered an accident, sudden illness or relapse of a physical or mental health condition;

  (h) that the relevant claimant was attending the funeral of a relative or close friend on the day fixed for the work-focused interview;

  (i) that the physical or mental condition of the relevant claimant made it impracticable to attend at the time and place fixed for the interview;

  (j) that the established customs and practices of the religion to which the relevant claimant belongs prevented attendance on the day or at the time fixed for the work-focused interview;

  (k) any other matter that the Secretary of State considers appropriate.

(3) If the Secretary of State determines that a relevant claimant has failed to take part in a work-focused interview and good cause has not been shown for that failure within five working days of the day on which the interview was to take place, the Secretary of State shall make a relevant decision for the purposes of section 2B of the Social Security Administration Act 1992.

Consequences of failure to take part in a work-focused interview

9.—(1) A relevant claimant in respect of whom a relevant decision has been made in accordance with regulation 8(3) shall, in accordance with this regulation, have his or her benefit reduced—

    (a) by 50% of the "work-related activity component" in each of the first four benefit weeks to which, by virtue of section 10(5) of the 1998 Act or regulations made under section 10(6) of that Act, the reduction applies;

    (b) by 100% of that component for each subsequent benefit week.

2.481

(2) If two or more specified benefits are in payment to a relevant claimant, a reduction made in accordance with paragraph (1) shall be applied, subject to paragraphs (3) to (6), to the specified benefits in the following order of priority—

    (a) income support;

    (b) incapacity benefit;

    (c) severe disablement allowance.

(3) If the amount of the reduction is greater than some, but not all, of the specified benefits listed in paragraph (2), the reduction shall be made against the first benefit in that list that is the same as, or greater than, the amount of the reduction.

(4) For the purpose of determining whether a specified benefit is the same as, or greater than, the amount of the reduction for the purposes of paragraph (3), ten pence shall be added to the amount of the reduction.

(5) In a case where the whole of the reduction cannot be applied against any one specified benefit because the amount of no one benefit is the same as, or greater than, the amount of the reduction, the reduction shall be applied against the first benefit in payment in the list of priorities in paragraph (2) and so on against each benefit in turn until the whole of the reduction is exhausted or, if this is not possible, the whole of the specified benefits are exhausted.

(6) If the rate of any specified benefit payable to a relevant claimant changes, the rules set out in this regulation for a reduction in the benefit payable shall be applied to the new rates and any adjustments to the benefits against which the reductions are made shall take effect from the beginning of the first benefit week to commence for that relevant claimant following the change.

(7) Paragraph (1) applies to a relevant claimant each time a relevant decision is made in accordance with regulation 8(3) in respect of that person.

(8) In the case of a relevant claimant whose benefit has been reduced in accordance with paragraph (1) and who subsequently takes part in a work-focused interview, the whole of the reduction shall cease to have effect on the first day of the benefit week in which the requirement to take part in a work-focused interview was met.

(9) In the case of a relevant claimant whose benefit has been reduced in accordance with paragraph (1) and who subsequently fails to meet the

conditions specified in regulation 3(4) or (5), the whole of the reduction shall cease to have effect on the first day of the benefit week in which those conditions are no longer satisfied.

(10) For the purposes of determining the amount of any benefit payable, a relevant claimant shall be treated as receiving the amount of any specified benefit which would have been payable but for a reduction made in accordance with paragraph (1).

(11) Despite regulation 8(3), the consequences specified in paragraph (1) do not apply to a person who—

(a) brings new facts to the notice of the Secretary of State within one month of the date on which the initial determination was notified to that person and—

  (i) those facts could not reasonably have been brought to the Secretary of State's notice within five working days of the date on which the notification of the initial determination was received; and

  (ii) those facts show that there is good cause for the person's failure to take part in the work-focused interview;

(b) is no longer required to take part in a work-focused interview as a condition of continuing to be entitled to the full amount of the specified benefit that is payable to that person apart from these Regulations; or

(c) attains the age of 60.

(12) Despite anything to the contrary in this regulation, no benefit is to be reduced in any benefit week—

(a) below 10 pence;

(b) in relation to more than one relevant decision relating to a particular work-focused interview;

(c) by more than 100% of the work-related activity component.

(13) For the purposes of this regulation, "work-related activity component" is the amount specified in Part 4 of Schedule 4 to the Employment and Support Allowance Regulations 2008.

Appeals

2.482   **10.**—(1) This regulation applies to any relevant decision under regulation 8(3) or any decision made under section 10 of the 1998 Act (decisions superseding earlier decisions) superseding such a relevant decision.

(2) This regulation applies whether the decision is as originally made or as revised under section 9 of the 1998 Act (revision of decisions).

(3) In the case of a decision to which this regulation applies, the relevant claimant in respect of whom the decision was made shall have a right of appeal under section 12 of the 1998 Act (appeal to first-tier tribunal) to the First-tier tribunal.

Exercise of certain functions relating to work-focused interviews

2.483   **11.**—(1) Any function of the Secretary of State specified in paragraph (2) may be exercised by a person providing services to the Secretary of State (including the employees of such a person) as may be authorised by the Secretary of State.

(2) The functions are any function under—

(a) regulation 5(1), (2) and (4) (requirement to take part in a work-focused interview);

(b) regulation 6(1), (2) and (3)(b), (c) and (d) (the work-focused interview);

(c) regulation 7 (action plan).

Revocations, consequential amendments, savings and transitional provisions

12.—(1) The following Regulations are revoked—   2.484

(a) the 2003 Regulations;

(b) The Social Security (Incapacity Benefit Work-focused Interviews) Amendment Regulations 2005;

(c) The Social Security (Incapacity Benefit Work-focused Interviews) Amendment (No. 2) Regulations 2005;

(d) The Social Security (Incapacity Benefit Work-focused Interviews) Amendment Regulations 2006;

(e) The Social Security (Incapacity Benefit Work-focused Interviews) Amendment (No. 2) Regulations 2006.

(2) *Omitted*

(3) *Omitted*

(4) Despite paragraph (1)(a)—

(a) regulation 10(2) of the 2003 Regulations continues to have effect in respect of a person who immediately before these Regulations come into force is subject to the consequences specified in that provision; and

(b) any other provision of the 2003 Regulations continues to have effect insofar as is necessary to give full effect to sub-paragraph (a) above.

(5) For the purposes of regulation 9(8), (9) and (11) (ending of a sanction), a person referred to in paragraph (4)(a) above is deemed to be subject to the consequences under regulation 9(1) (a sanction imposed under these Regulations) and from that date regulation 10(2) of the 2003 Regulations will cease to apply to that person.

The Social Security (Jobcentre Plus Interviews) Regulations 2002

(SI 2002/1703) (AS AMENDED)

ARRANGEMENT OF REGULATIONS

The Secretary of State for Work and Pensions, in exercise of the powers conferred upon him by sections 2A(1), (3) to (6) and (8), 2B(6) and (7), 5(1)(a) and (b), 6(1)(a) and (b), 7A, 189(1), (4) and (5) and 191 of the Social Security Administration Act 1992 and section 68 of, and paragraphs 3(1), 4(4), 6(8), 20(3) and 23(1) of Schedule 7 to, the Child Support, Pensions and Social Security Act 2000, and of all other powers enabling him in that behalf, after consultation with the Council on Tribunals in accordance with section 8(1) of the Tribunals and Inquiries Act 1992 and in respect of provisions in these Regulations relating to housing benefit and council tax benefit with organisations appearing to him to be representative of the authorities concerned, and after agreement by the Social Security Advisory Committee that proposals in respect of these Regulations should not be referred to it, hereby makes the following Regulations:

Citation and commencement

2.486   **1.** These Regulations may be cited as the Social Security (Jobcentre Plus Interviews) Regulations 2002 and shall come into force on 30th September 2002.

Interpretation and application

2.487   **2.**—(1) In these Regulations, unless the context otherwise requires—
"the 1998 Act" means the Social Security Act 1998;
"benefit week" means any period of seven days corresponding to the week in respect of which the relevant specified benefit is due to be paid;
[³ . . .]
"the Careers Service" means—
>   (a) in England and Wales, a person with whom the Secretary of State or, as the case may be, the National Assembly for Wales, have made arrangements under section 10(1) of the Employment and Training Act 1973 or a local education authority to whom a direction has been given by the Secretary of State or the National Assembly for Wales under section 10(2) of that Act;
>   (b) in Scotland, a person with whom the Scottish Ministers have made arrangements under section 10(1) of the Employment and Training Act 1973 or any education authority to whom a direction has been given by the Scottish Ministers under section 10(2) of that Act;

"the Connexions Service" means a person of any description with whom the Secretary of State has made an arrangement under section 114(2)(a) of the Learning and Skills Act 2000 and section 10(1) of the Employment and Training Act 1973 and any person to whom he has given a direction under section 114(2)(b) of the Learning and Skills Act 2000 and section 10(2) of the Employment and Training Act 1973;
"interview" means a work-focused interview with a person who has claimed a specified benefit and which is conducted for any or all of the following purposes—

(a) assessing that person's prospects for existing or future employment (whether paid or voluntary);

(b) assisting or encouraging that person to enhance his prospects of such employment;

(c) identifying activities which that person may undertake to strengthen his existing or future prospects of employment;

(d) identifying current or future employment or training opportunities suitable to that person's needs; and

(e) identifying educational opportunities connected with the existing or future employment prospects or needs of that person;

[³ "lone parent" has the meaning it bears in regulation 2(1) of the Income Support (General) Regulations 1987;]

"officer" means a person who is an officer of, or who is providing services to or exercising functions of, the Secretary of State;

[³ "relevant benefit" means income support other than income support where one of the following paragraphs of Schedule 1B to the Income Support (General) Regulations 1987 applies—

(a) paragraph 7 (persons incapable of work), or

(b) paragraph 24 or 25 (persons appealing against a decision which embodies a determination that they are not incapable of work);]

[³ "specified benefit" means income support, incapacity benefit and severe disablement allowance;]

[³ "specified person" means—

(a) a lone parent, or

(b) a person who claims—

    (i) incapacity benefit,

    (ii) income support where paragraph 7 (persons incapable of work) of Schedule 1B to the Income Support (General) Regulations 1987 applies,

    (iii) income support where paragraph 24 or 25 (persons appealing against a decision which embodies a determination that they are not incapable of work) of Schedule 1B to the Income Support (General) Regulations 1987 applies, or

    (iv) severe disablement allowance.]

(2) For the purposes of these Regulations—

(a) a person shall be deemed to be in remunerative work where he is in remunerative work within the meaning prescribed in [⁴ regulation 6 of the Housing Benefit Regulations 2006]; but

(b) a person shall be deemed not to be in remunerative work where—

    (i) he is not in remunerative work in accordance with subparagraph (a) above; or

    (ii) he is in remunerative work in accordance with sub-paragraph (a) above and is not entitled to income support but would not be prevented from being entitled to income support solely by being in such work; and

(c) a person shall be deemed to be engaged in part-time work where he is engaged in work for which payment is made but he is not engaged or deemed to be engaged in remunerative work.

(3) Except in a case where regulation 16(2) applies [⁵ . . .] regulations 3 to 15 apply in respect of a person who makes a claim for a specified benefit on or after 30th September 2002 at an office of the Department for Work and Pensions which is designated by the Secretary of State as a Jobcentre Plus Office or at an

office of a relevant authority (being a person within section 72(2) of the Welfare Reform and Pensions Act 1999) which displays the **one** logo.

(4) Where a claim for benefit is made by a person ("the appointee") on behalf of another, references in these Regulations to a person claiming benefit shall be treated as a reference to the person on whose behalf the claim is made and not to the appointee.

(5) In these Regulations, unless the context otherwise requires, a reference—

   (a) to a numbered regulation is to a regulation in these Regulations bearing that number;

   (b) in a regulation to a numbered paragraph or sub-paragraph is to the paragraph or sub-paragraph in that regulation bearing that number;

   (c) to a numbered Schedule is to the Schedule to these Regulations bearing that number.

AMENDMENTS

1. The Social Security Amendment (Carer's Allowance) Regulations 2002 (SI 2002/2497), Sch.2 (October 28, 2002).

2. Social Security (Working Neighbourhoods) Regulations 2004 (SI 2004/959), reg.26(2) (April 26, 2004).

3. The Social Security (Work-focused Interviews) Amendment Regulations 2005 (SI 2005/2727) (October 31, 2005).

4. The Housing Benefit and Council Tax Benefit (Consequential Provisions) Regulations 2006 (SI 2006/217), Sch.2, para.21 (March 6, 2006).

5. The Social Security (Working Neighbourhoods) Miscellaneous Amendment Regulations 2006, (SI 2006/909) (April 24, 2006).

Requirement for person claiming a specified benefit to take part in an interview

2.488   **3.**—(1) Subject to regulations 6 to 9, a person who—

[¹ (a) either—

   (i) makes a claim for a relevant benefit, or

   (ii) is entitled to a specified benefit other than a relevant benefit;]

[¹ (b) on the day on which he [claims a specified benefit], has attained the age of 16 but has not attained the age of 60; and]

   (c) is not in remunerative work,

is required to take part in an interview.

(2) An officer shall, except where paragraph (3) applies, conduct the interview.

(3) An officer may, if he considers it appropriate in all the circumstances, arrange for a person who has not attained the age of 18 to attend an interview with the Careers Service or with the Connexions Service.

AMENDMENT

1. The Social Security (Work-focused Interviews) Amendment Regulations 2005 (SI 2005/2727) (October 31, 2005).

Continuing entitlement to specified benefit dependent on an interview

2.489   **4.**—(1) Subject to regulations [⁵ 4A and 6 to 9], a person who has not attained the age of 60 and who is entitled to a specified benefit, shall be required to take part in an interview as a condition of his continuing to be entitled to the full amount of benefit which is payable apart from these Regulations where paragraph (2) applies and—

(a) in the case of a lone parent who has attained the age of 18 and who is neither claiming incapacity benefit nor severe disablement allowance, [⁴ paragraph (3), (38), (3D), (3F), or (3H)] applies; or

(b) in any other case, any of the circumstances specified in paragraph (4) apply or where paragraph (5) applies.

(2) This paragraph applies in the case of a person who has taken part in an interview under regulation 3 or who would have taken part in such an interview [⁴ but for—

(i) the requirement being waived in accordance with regulation 6;

(ii) the requirement being deferred in accordance with regulation 7;

(iii) the requirement not arising because the person was at the time of the claim for the specified benefit subject to provisions within the Social Security (Working Neighbourhoods) Regulations 2004[13] by virtue of regulation 2(3) of those Regulations; or

(iv) the person being required to take part in an interview under the Social Security (Quarterly Work-focused Interviews for Certain Lone Parents) Regulations 2004.]

(3) This paragraph applies at the times specified in paragraph (3A) where the young child condition is not satisfied (see paragraph (5B)) and where the lone parent—

(a) last took part,

(b) last failed to take part, or

(c) was last treated as having taken part,

in a relevant interview on a date or after 30th April 2006 but before 30th October 2006.

(3A) Paragraph (3) first applies one year after that date, and it applies again every six months after the day on which it first applies.

(3B) This paragraph applies at the times specified in paragraph (3C) where the young child condition is not satisfied and where the lone parent—

(a) last took part,

(b) last failed to take part, or

(c) was last treated as having taken part,

in a relevant interview on a date that was not on or after 30th April 2006 but before 30th October 2006.

(3C) Paragraph (3B) first applies six months after that date, and it applies again every six months after the day on which it first applies.

(3D) This paragraph applies at the times specified in paragraph (3E) where the young child condition is satisfied and where the interview that the lone parent—

(a) last took part in,

(b) last failed to take part in, or

(c) was last treated as having taken part in,

was the first relevant interview.

(3E) Paragraph (3D) first applies six months after the date of that first interview, and it applies again upon each anniversary of the date of that first interview.

(3F) This paragraph applies at the times specified in paragraph (3G) where the young child condition is satisfied and where the interview that the lone parent—

(a) last took part in,

(b) last failed to take part in, or

(c) was last treated as having taken part in,

was the second relevant interview.

(3G) Paragraph (3F) first applies six months after the date of that second interview, and it applies again upon each anniversary of the date on which it first applies.

(3H) This paragraph applies at the times specified in paragraph (3I) where the young child condition is satisfied and where the interview that the lone parent—

(a) last took part in,

(b) last failed to take part in, or

(c) was last treated as having taken part in,

was not the first or second relevant interview.

(3I) Paragraph (3H) first applies one year after the date of that interview, and it applies again upon each subsequent anniversary of that date.]

(4) The circumstances specified in this paragraph are those where—

(a) it is determined in accordance with a personal capability assessment that a person is incapable of work and therefore, continues to be entitled to a specified benefit;

(b) a person's entitlement to an [1 carer's allowance] ceases whilst entitlement to [3a] specified benefit continues;

(c) a person becomes engaged or ceases to be engaged in part-time work;

(d) a person has been undergoing education or training arranged by the officer and that education or training comes to an end; and

(e) a person who has not attained the age of 18 and who has previously taken part in an interview, attains the age of 18.

(5) A requirement to take part in an interview arises under this paragraph where a person has not been required to take part in an interview by virtue of paragraph (4) for at least 36 months.

[4 (5A) In this regulation, "relevant interview" means an interview under—

(a) the Social Security (Working Neighbourhoods) Regulations 2004,

(b) the Social Security (Quarterly Work-focused Interviews for Certain Lone Parents) Regulations 2004, or

(c) these Regulations,

in relation to the lone parent's current claim.

(5B) For the purposes of this regulation, the young child condition is satisfied where the lone parent is responsible for and living in the same household as—

(a) a single child aged under 5, or

(b) more than one child where the youngest is aged under 5.]

(6) [3 . . .].

AMENDMENTS

1. The Social Security Amendment (Carer's Allowance) Regulations 2002 (SI 2002/2497), Sch.2 (October 28, 2002).

2. Social Security (Working Neighbourhoods) Regulations 2004 (SI 2004/959), reg.26 (April 26, 2004).

3. The Social Security (Work-focused Interviews) Amendment Regulations 2005 (SI 2005/2727) (October 31, 2005).

4. The Social Security (Work-focused Interviews for Lone Parents) Amendment Regulations 2007 (SI 2007/1034) (April 30, 2007).

5. The Social Security (Lone Parents and Miscellaneous Amendments) Regulations 2008 (SI 2008/3051), reg.8 (November 24, 2008).

[¹ Requirement for certain lone parents to take part in an interview

4A.—(1) This regulation applies to a lone parent who—

2.490

(a) is entitled to income support and is a person to whom paragraph 1 (lone parents) of Schedule 1B to the Income Support (General) Regulations 1987 applies;

(b) does not fall within any other paragraph of that Schedule; and

(c) is responsible for and living in the same household as—
(i) a single child aged 9, 10 or 11, or
(ii) more than one child where the youngest is aged 9, 10 or 11.

(2) Subject to regulations 6 to 9, a lone parent to whom this regulation applies is required to take part in an interview every 13 weeks after he—

(a) last took part,

(b) last failed to take part, or

(c) was last treated as having taken part,
in an interview.

(3) A lone parent who—

(a) is required to take part in an interview under this regulation, or

(b) has had a requirement to take part in an interview under this regulation waived or deferred,

is not required to take part in an interview under regulation 4 unless this regulation ceases to apply to him.]

AMENDMENT

1. The Social Security (Lone Parents and Miscellaneous Amendments) Regulations 2008 (SI 2008/3051), reg.8 (November 24, 2008).

GENERAL NOTE

Note that Part 1 of the Schedule to the Social Security (Lone Parents and Miscellaneous Amendments) Regulations 2008 (SI 2008/3051) contains special commencement provision for certain existing claimants.

2.491

Time when interview is to take place

5. An officer shall arrange for an interview to take place as soon as reasonably practicable after—

2.492

[¹ (a) the expiry of eight weeks after the date the claim for a specified benefit, other than a relevant benefit, is made;

(aa) the claim for a relevant benefit is made;]

(b) the requirement under regulation 4(1) arises; or,

(c) in a case where regulation 7(1) applies, the time when that requirement is to apply by virtue of regulation 7(2).

AMENDMENTS

1. The Social Security (Work-focused Interviews) Amendment Regulations 2005 (SI 2005/2727) (October 31, 2005).

2. The Social Security (Lone Parents and Miscellaneous Amendments) Regulations 2008 (SI 2008/3051), reg.8 (November 24, 2008).

Waiver of requirement to take part in an interview

6.—(1) A requirement imposed by these Regulations to take part in an interview shall not apply where an officer determines that an interview would not—

2.493

(a) be of assistance to the person concerned; or

(b) be appropriate in the circumstances.

(2) A person in relation to whom a requirement to take part in an interview has been waived under paragraph (1) shall be treated for the purposes of—

(a) regulation 3 or 4; and

(b) any claim for, or entitlement to, a specified benefit,

as having complied with that requirement.

Deferment of requirement to take part in an interview

2.494　　**7.**—(1) An officer may determine, in the case of any particular person, that the requirement to take part in an interview shall be deferred at the time the claim is made or the requirement to take part in an interview arises or applies because an interview would not at that time—

(a) be of assistance to that person; or

(b) be appropriate in the circumstances.

(2) Where the officer determines in accordance with paragraph (1) that the requirement to take part in an interview shall be deferred, he shall also determine when that determination is made, the time when the requirement to take part in an interview is to apply in the person's case.

(3) Where a requirement to take part in an interview has been deferred in accordance with paragraph (1), then until—

(a) a determination is made under regulation 6(1);

(b) the person takes part in an interview; or

(c) a relevant decision has been made in relation to that person in accordance with regulation 11(4),

that person shall be treated for the purposes of any claim for, or entitlement to, a specified benefit as having complied with that requirement.

Exemptions

2.495　　**8.**—(1) Subject to paragraph (2), persons who, on the day on which the claim for a specified benefit is made or the requirement to take part in an interview under regulation [⁵ 4 or 4A or 7(2)] arises or applies—

(a) are engaged in remunerative work; or

(b) are claiming, or are entitled to, a jobseeker's allowance, shall be exempt from the requirement to take part in an interview.

(2) Paragraph (1)(b) shall not apply where—

(a) a joint-claim couple (as defined for the purposes of section 1(4) of the Jobseekers Act 1995) have claimed a jobseeker's allowance; and

(b) a member of that couple is a person to whom regulation 3D(1)(c) of the Jobseeker's Allowance Regulations 1996 (further circumstances in which a joint-claim couple may be entitled to a jointclaim jobseeker's allowance) applies.

[¹ (3) A person who, on the day on which the claim for a specified benefit is made or the requirement to take part in an interview under regulation 4 or 7(2) arises or applies is—

(a) required to take part in an interview; or

(b) not required to take part in an interview by virtue of—

(i) a waiver of a requirement; or

(ii) a deferment of an interview,

under the [⁴ Social Security (Incapacity Benefit Work-focused Interviews) Regulations 2008.] [² or regulation 2A [³ or 2B] of the Social Security (Work-focused Interviews for Lone Parents) and Miscellaneous Amendments Regulations 2000] shall be exempt from the requirement to take part in an interview.]

AMENDMENTS

1. The Social Security (Incapacity Benefit Work-focused Interviews) Regulations 2003 (SI 2003/2439) (October 27, 2003).   2.496
2. The Social Security (Work-focused Interviews) Amendment Regulations 2005 (SI 2005/2727) (October 31, 2005).
3. The Social Security (Work-focused Interviews for Lone Parents) Amendment Regulations 2007 (SI 2007/1034) (April 30, 2007).
4. The Social Security (Incapacity Benefit Work-focused Interviews) Regulations 2008 (SI 2008/2928), reg.12 (December 15, 2008).
5. The Social Security (Lone Parents and Miscellaneous Amendments) Regulations 2008 (SI 2008/3051), reg.8 (November 24, 2008).

Claims for two or more specified benefits

9. A person who would otherwise be required under these Regulations to take part in interviews relating to more than one specified benefit—   2.497
  (a) is only required to take part in one interview; and
  (b) that interview counts for the purposes of all those benefits.

The interview

10.—(1) The officer shall inform a person who is required to take part in an interview of the place and time of the interview.   2.498
  (2) The officer may determine that an interview is to take place in the person's home where it would, in his opinion, be unreasonable to expect that person to attend elsewhere because that person's personal circumstances are such that attending elsewhere would cause him undue inconvenience or endanger his health.

Taking part in an interview

11.—(1) The officer shall determine whether a person has taken part in an interview.   2.499
  [² (2) A person who has not taken part in an interview under these Regulations before 31st October 2005 shall be regarded as having taken part in his first interview under these Regulations if—
  (a) he attends for the interview at the place and time notified to him by the officer;
  (b) where he is a specified person, he participates in discussions with the officer in relation to the specified person's employability, including any action the specified person and the officer agree is reasonable and they are willing to take in order to help the specified person enhance his employment prospects;
  (c) he provides answers (where asked) to questions and appropriate information about—
    (i)   the level to which he has pursued any educational qualifications;
    (ii) his employment history;
    (iii) any vocational training he has undertaken;

     (iv) any skills he has acquired which fit him for employment;

     (v) any paid or unpaid employment he is engaged in;

     (vi) any medical condition which, in his opinion, puts him at a disadvantage in obtaining employment;

     (vii) any caring or childcare responsibilities he has;

     (viii) his aspirations for future employment;

     (ix) any vocational training or skills which he wishes to undertake or acquire; and

     (x) his work related abilities; and

  (d) where he is a specified person, he assists the officer in the completion of an action plan which records the matters discussed in relation to sub-paragraph (b) above.

(2A) A person who has taken part in an interview under these Regulations before 31st October 2005 shall be regarded as having taken part in his first interview under these Regulations after 30th October 2005 if—

  (a) he attends for the interview at the place and time notified to him by the officer;

  (b) where he is a specified person, he participates in discussions with the officer in relation to the specified person's employability, including any action the specified person and the officer agree is reasonable and they are willing to take in order to help the specified person enhance his employment prospects;

  (c) he participates in discussions with the officer—

     (i) in relation to the person's employability or any progress he might have made towards obtaining employment; and

     (ii) in order to consider any of the programmes and support available to help the person obtain employment;

  (d) he provides answers (where asked) to questions and appropriate information about—

     (i) the content of any report made following his personal capability assessment, insofar as that report relates to the person's capabilities and employability;

    and

     (ii) his opinion as to the extent to which his medical condition restricts his ability to obtain employment; and

  (e) where he is a specified person, he assists the officer in the completion of an action plan which records the matters discussed in relation to sub-paragraph (b) above.

(2B) A person shall be regarded as having taken part in any subsequent interview under these Regulations if—

  (a) he attends for the interview at the place and time notified to him by the officer;

  (b) he participates in discussions with the officer—

     (i) in relation to the person's employability or any progress he might have made towards obtaining employment; and

     (ii) in order to consider any of the programmes and support available to help the person obtain employment;

  (c) where he is a specified person, he participates in discussions with the officer—

     (i) about any action the specified person or the officer might have taken as a result of the matters discussed in relation to paragraphs (2)(b) or (2A)(b) above; and

     (ii) about how, if at all, the action plan referred to in paragraphs (2)
         (d) or (2A)(e) above should be amended;

  (d) he provides answers (where asked) to questions and appropriate
     information about—

     (i) the content of any report made following his personal capability
        assessment, insofar as that report relates to the person's capa-
        bilities and employability;
     and
     (ii) his opinion as to the extent to which his medical condition
        restricts his ability to obtain employment; and

  (e) where he is a specified person, he assists the officer in the completion
     of any amendment of the action plan referred to in paragraphs (2)
     (d) or (2A)(e) above in light of the matters discussed in relation to
     sub-paragraphs (b) and (c) above and the information provided in
     relation to sub-paragraph (d) above.]

[¹ (3) A person who, on the day on which the claim for a specified benefit
is made or the requirement to take part in an interview under regulation 4
or 7(2) arises or applies is—

  (a) required to take part in an interview; or
  (b) not required to take part in an interview by virtue of—
     (i) a waiver of a requirement; or
     (ii) a deferment of an interview,

under the Social Security (Incapacity Benefit Work-focused Interviews
Regulations 2003 shall be exempt from the requirement to take part in an
interview.]

(4) Where an officer determines that a person has failed to take part in
an interview and good cause has not been shown for that failure within five
working days of the day on which the interview was to take place, a relevant
decision shall be made for the purposes of section 2B of the Social Security
Administration Act 1992.

AMENDMENTS

1. The Social Security (Incapacity Benefit Work-Focused Interviews) Regulations
2003 (SI 2003/2439), reg. 17 (October 27, 2003).

2. The Social Security (Work-focused Interviews) Amendment Regulations 2005
(SI 2005/2727) (October 31, 2005).

Failure to take part in an interview

12.—(1) A person in respect of whom a relevant decision has been made   **2.500**
in accordance with regulation 11(4) shall, subject to paragraph (12), suffer
the consequences set out below.

(2) Those consequences are—

  (a) where the interview arose in connection with a claim for a [² relevant
     benefit], that the person to whom the claim relates is to be regarded
     as not having made a claim for a [² relevant benefit];

  (b) where an interview which arose in connection with a claim for a
     [² relevant benefit] was deferred and benefit became payable by
     virtue of regulation 7(3), that the person's entitlement to that benefit
     shall terminate from the first day of the next benefit week following
     the date on which the relevant decision was made;

  (c) where the claimant has an award of benefit and the requirement for
     the interview arose under regulation [³ 4 or 4A], [² or by virtue of the

claimant falling within regulation 3(1)(a)(ii),] the claimant's benefit shall be reduced as from the first day of the next benefit week following the day the relevant decision was made, by a sum equal (but subject to paragraphs (3) and (4)) to 20 per cent. of the amount applicable on the date the deduction commences in respect of a single claimant for income support aged not less than 25.

(3) Benefit reduced in accordance with paragraph (2)(c) shall not be reduced below ten pence per week.

(4) Where two or more specified benefits are in payment to a claimant, a deduction made in accordance with this regulation shall be applied, except in a case to which paragraph (5) applies, to the specified benefits in the following order of priority—

(a) income support;

(b) incapacity benefit;

(c) [². . .];

(d) [². . .];

(e) severe disablement allowance.

(5) Where the amount of the reduction is greater than some (but not all) of the specified benefits listed in paragraph (4), the reduction shall be made against the first benefit in that list which is the same as, or greater than, the amount of the reduction.

(6) For the purpose of determining whether a specified benefit is the same as, or greater than, the amount of the reduction for the purposes of paragraph (5), ten pence shall be added to the amount of the reduction.

(7) In a case where the whole of the reduction cannot be applied against any one specified benefit because no one benefit is the same as, or greater than, the amount of the reduction, the reduction shall be applied against the first benefit in payment in the list of priorities at paragraph (4) and so on against each benefit in turn until the whole of the reduction is exhausted or, if this is not possible, the whole of the specified benefits are exhausted, subject in each case to ten pence remaining in payment.

(8) Where the rate of any specified benefit payable to a claimant changes, the rules set out above for a reduction in the benefit payable shall be applied to the new rates and any adjustments to the benefits against which the reductions are made shall take effect from the beginning of the first benefit week to commence for that claimant following the change.

(9) Where a claimant whose benefit has been reduced in accordance with this regulation subsequently takes part in an interview, the reduction shall cease to have effect on the first day of the benefit week in which the requirement to take part in an interview was met.

(10) For the avoidance of doubt, a person who is regarded as not having made a claim for any benefit because he failed to take part in an interview shall be required to make a new claim in order to establish entitlement to any specified benefit.

(11) For the purposes of determining the amount of any benefit payable, a claimant shall be treated as receiving the amount of any specified benefit which would have been payable but for a reduction made in accordance with this regulation.

(12) The consequences set out in this regulation shall not apply in the case of a person who brings new facts to the notice of the Secretary of State within one month of the date on which the decision was notified and—

(a) those facts could not reasonably have been brought to the Secretary of State's notice within five working days of the day on which the interview was to take place; and

(b) those facts show that he had good cause for his failure to take part in the interview.

(13) In paragraphs (2) and (12), the "decision" means the decision that the person failed without good cause to take part in an interview.

AMENDMENTS

1. The Social Security Amendment (Carer's Allowance) Regulations 2002 (SI 2002/2497), Sch.2 (October 28, 2002).

2. The Social Security (Work-focused Interviews) Amendment Regulations 2005 (SI 2005/2727) (October 31, 2005).

3. The Social Security (Lone Parents and Miscellaneous Amendments) Regulations 2008 (SI 2008/3051), reg.8 (November 24, 2008).

Circumstances where regulation 12 does not apply

13. The consequences of a failure to take part in an interview set out in regulation 12 shall not apply where—

    2.501

(a) he is no longer required to take part in an interview as a condition for continuing to be entitled to the full amount of benefit which is payable apart from these Regulations; or

(b) the person attains the age of 60.

Good cause

14. Matters to be taken into account in determining whether a person has shown good cause for his failure to take part in an interview include—

    2.502

(a) that the person misunderstood the requirement to take part in the interview due to any learning, language or literacy difficulties of the person or any misleading information given to the person by the officer;

(b) that the person was attending a medical or dental appointment, or accompanying a person for whom the claimant has caring responsibilities to such an appointment, and that it would have been unreasonable, in the circumstances, to rearrange the appointment;

(c) that the person had difficulties with his normal mode of transport and that no reasonable alternative was available;

(d) that the established customs and practices of the religion to which the person belongs prevented him attending on that day or at that time;

(e) that the person was attending an interview with an employer with a view to obtaining employment;

(f) that the person was actually pursuing employment opportunities as a self-employed earner;

(g) that the person or a dependant of his or a person for whom he provides care suffered an accident, sudden illness or relapse of [1 a physical or mental health condition];

(h) that he was attending the funeral of a close friend or relative on the day fixed for the interview;

(i) that a disability from which the person suffers made it impracticable for him to attend at the time fixed for the interview.

AMENDMENT

1. The Social Security (Work-focused Interviews) Amendment Regulations 2005 (SI 2005/2727) (October 31, 2005).

Appeals

2.503   **15.**—(1) This regulation applies to any relevant decision made under regulation 11(4) or any decision under section 10 of the 1998 Act superseding such a decision.

(2) This regulation applies whether the decision is as originally made or as revised under section 9 of the 1998 Act.

(3) In the case of a decision to which this regulation applies, the person in respect of whom the decision was made shall have a right of appeal under section 12 of the 1998 Act to [¹ the First-tier Tribunal]

AMENDMENT

1. The Tribunals, Courts and Enforcement Act 2007 (Transitional and Consequential Provisions) Order 2008 (SI 2008/2683), reg.178 (November 3, 2008).

Revocations and transitional provision

2.504   **16.**—(1) Subject to paragraph (2), the Social Security (Work-focused Interviews) Regulations 2000 ("the 2000 Regulations") and the Social Security (Jobcentre Plus Interviews) Regulations 2001 ("the 2001 Regulations") are hereby revoked to the extent specified in Schedule 1.

(2) Notwithstanding paragraph (1), both the 2000 Regulations (except for regulations 4, 5 and 12(2)(a) and (b)) and the 2001 Regulations (except for regulations 3 and 11(2)(a) and (b)) [² . . .] shall continue to apply as if these Regulations had not come into force for the period specified in paragraph (3) in the case of a person who, on the day before the day on which these Regulations come into force, is both a relevant person and entitled to a specified benefit for the purposes of those Regulations.

(3) The period specified for the purposes of paragraph (2) shall be the period beginning on the day on which these Regulations come to force and ending on the day on which the person—

(a) ceases to be a relevant person for the purposes of the 2000 Regulations or, as the case may be, the 2001 Regulations;

(b) is not entitled to any specified benefit for the purposes of those Regulations; or

(c) attains the age of 60,

whichever shall first occur.

AMENDMENTS

1. Social Security (Working Neighbourhoods) Regulations 2004 (SI 2004/959), reg.26(4) (April 26, 2004).

2. The Social Security (Working Neighbourhoods) Miscellaneous Amendment Regulations 2006, (SI 2006/909) (April 24, 2006).

Amendments to regulations

2.505   *Omitted*

2.506   *Schedules 1 and 2 omitted.*

(SI 2003/1886)

The Social Security (Jobcentre Plus Interviews for Partners) Regulations 2003

(SI 2003/1886)

ARRANGEMENT OF REGULATIONS

2.507

GENERAL NOTE

These controversial regulations extend the scheme of work-focused interviews to the partners of claimants, and cover five benefits: income support, income-based jobseeker's allowance, incapacity benefit, severe disablement allowance and carer's allowance. The pattern follows that to be found in the earlier regulations relating to work-focused interviews in other contexts. But those regulations apply only where the claim was made after the commencement date of the regulations where both the partners are between the ages of 18 and 60; these regulations apply whenever benefit is in payment and whenever the claim is through a Jobcentre Plus office. A further distinction is that the interview under these regulations is a once and for all interview without there being provisions for follow-up interviews. Failure to participate results in a deduction equal to 20 per cent of the single adult applicable amount for income support. Both partners have an independent right of appeal, so that both can, in principle, appeal against the same decision.

2.508

Whereas a draft of this instrument was laid before Parliament in accordance with s.190(1) of the Social Security Administration Act 1992 and approved by resolution of each House of Parliament;

Now, therefore, the Secretary of State for Work and Pensions, in exercise of the powers conferred upon him by ss.2AA(1) and (4) to (7), 2B(6), 189(1) and (4) to (6) and 191 of the Social Security Administration Act 1992 and of all other powers enabling him in that behalf, after consultation with the Council on Tribunals in accordance with s.8(1) of the Tribunals and Inquiries Act 1992, by this instrument, which contains only regulations made by virtue of, or consequential upon, section 2AA of the Social Security Administration Act 1992 and which is made before the end of the period of 6 months beginning with the coming into force of that provision, hereby makes the following Regulations:

Citation and commencement

2.509   **1.** These Regulations may be cited as the Social Security (Jobcentre Plus Interviews for Partners) Regulations 2003 and shall come into force on 12th April 2004.

Interpretation [⁴ . . .]

2.510   **2.**—(1) In these Regulations—

"the 1998 Act" means the Social Security Act 1998;

"benefit week" means any period of seven days corresponding to the week in respect of which the relevant specified benefit is due to be paid;

"claimant" means a claimant of a specified benefit who has a partner to whom these Regulations apply;

[² "couple" means—

(a) a man and woman who are married to each other and are members of the same household;

(b) a man and woman who are not married to each other but are living together as husband and wife;

(c) two people of the same sex who are civil partners of each other and are members of the same household; or

(d) two people of the same sex who are not civil partners of each other but are living together as if they were civil partners,

and for the purposes of paragraph (d), two people of the same sex are to be regarded as living together as if they were civil partners if, but only if, they would be regarded as living together as husband and wife were they instead two people of the opposite sex;]

"interview" means a work-focused interview with a partner which is conducted for any or all of the following purposes—

(a) assessing the partner's prospects for existing or future employment (whether paid or voluntary);

(b) assisting or encouraging the partner to enhance his prospects of such employment;

(c) identifying activities which the partner may undertake to strengthen his existing or future prospects of employment;

(d) identifying current or future employment or training opportunities suitable to the partner's needs; and

(e) identifying educational opportunities connected with the existing or future employment prospects or needs of the partner;

"officer" means a person who is an officer of, or who is providing services to or exercising functions of, the Secretary of State;

"partner" means a person who is a member of the same couple as the claimant, or, in a case where the claimant has more than one partner, a person who is a partner of the claimant by reason of a polygamous marriage, but only where—

(a) [⁴ . . .]

(b) both the partner and the claimant have attained the age of 18 but have not attained the age of 60;

"polygamous marriage" means any marriage during the subsistence of which a party to it is married to more than one person and the ceremony of marriage took place under the law of a country which permits polygamy;

"specified benefit" means a benefit to which section 2AA applies.

(2) [⁴ . . .]

AMENDMENTS

1. Social Security (Working Neighbourhoods) Regulations 2004 (SI 2004/959), reg.27(2) (April 26, 2004).
2. The Civil Partnership (Pensions, Social Security and Child Support) (Consequential etc. Provisions) Order 2005 (SI 2005/2877) (December 5, 2005).
3. The Social Security (Working Neighbourhoods) Miscellaneous Amendment Regulations 2006, (SI 2006/909) (April 24, 2006).
4. The Social Security (Jobcentre Plus Interviews for Partners) Amendment Regulations 2008 (SI 2008/759) (April 28, 2008).

[¹ Partner of a person claiming a specified benefit to take part in an interview

3.—(1) Subject to regulations 5 to 8, a partner to whom this regulation applies is required to take part in an interview as a condition of the claimant continuing to be paid the full amount of a specified benefit which is payable apart from these Regulations.

2.511

(2) This regulation applies to a partner of a person claiming a specified benefit where—

(a) the claimant has been continuously entitled to a specified benefit for at least 26 weeks;

(b) the claimant has been awarded the benefit at a higher rate referable to the partner;

(c) the benefit is administered from a designated Jobcentre Plus Office(4); and

(d) the partner has not taken part or been required to take part in an interview under these Regulations.

(3) Where a requirement to take part in an interview arises under this regulation in relation to a particular specified benefit, the requirement also applies in relation to any other specified benefit in payment to the claimant at a higher rate referable to his partner on the date set for the interview and notified to the partner in accordance with regulation 9(1).]

AMENDMENT

1. The Social Security (Jobcentre Plus Interviews for Partners) Amendment Regulations 2008 (SI 2008/759) (April 28, 2008).

[¹ Partner of a person claiming jobseeker's allowance to take part in an interview where child or qualifying young person in household

3A.—(1) Subject to regulations 5 to 8, a partner to whom this regulation applies is required to take part in an interview as a condition of the claimant continuing to be paid the full amount of a jobseeker's allowance which is payable apart from these Regulations.

2.512

(2) This regulation applies to a partner of a person claiming a jobseeker's allowance where—

(a) the claimant or the partner is responsible for a child or qualifying young person who is a member of that person's household;

(b) the claimant has been continuously entitled to a jobseeker's allowance for at least 26 weeks;

    (c) the claimant has been awarded that benefit at a higher rate referable to the partner;

    (d) the benefit is administered at a designated Jobcentre Plus Office; and

    (e) the partner has taken part or failed to take part in an interview under these Regulations.

(3) The requirement to take part in an interview under this regulation arises every six months, on a date to be determined in accordance with paragraphs (4) and (5).

(4) Where the interview referred to in paragraph (2)(e) was on a date before 28th October 2007—

    (a) the requirement arises for the first time on 28th April 2008; and

    (b) it then arises again every six months after the date on which the partner last took part or failed to take part in an interview.

(5) Where the interview referred to in paragraph (2)(e) was on a date on or after 28th October 2007, the requirement arises every six months after the date on which the partner last took part or failed to take part in an interview.

(6) For the purposes of paragraph (2)(a), "child" and "qualifying young person" are to be construed in accordance with section 142 of the Social Security Contributions and Benefits Act 1992(5).

(7) References in paragraphs (2)(e), (4) and (5) to a partner having taken part in an interview are to be construed as including cases where the partner is treated as having taken part in an interview under regulation 5 or 6.]

AMENDMENT

1. The Social Security (Jobcentre Plus Interviews for Partners) Amendment Regulations 2008 (SI 2008/759) (April 28, 2008).

Time when interview is to take place

2.513   **4.** An officer shall arrange for an interview to take place as soon as reasonably practicable after—

    (a) the requirement under regulation [¹ 3 or 3A] arises; or

    (b) in a case where regulation 6(1) applies, the time when that requirement is to apply by virtue of regulation 6(2).

AMENDMENT

1. The Social Security (Jobcentre Plus Interviews for Partners) Amendment Regulations 2008 (SI 2008/759) (April 28, 2008).

Waiver of requirement to take part in an interview

2.514   **5.**—(1) A requirement imposed by these Regulations to take part in an interview shall not apply where an officer determines that an interview would not—

    (a) be of assistance to the partner concerned; or

    (b) be appropriate in the circumstances.

(2) A partner in relation to whom a requirement to take part in an interview has been waived under paragraph (1) shall be treated [¹ . . .] as having complied with that requirement.

AMENDMENT

1. The Social Security (Jobcentre Plus Interviews for Partners) Amendment Regulations 2008 (SI 2008/759) (April 28, 2008).

Deferment of requirement to take part in an interview

6.—(1) An officer may determine, in the case of any particular partner,   2.515
that the requirement to take part in an interview shall be deferred at the
time that the requirement to take part in it arises or applies because an
interview would not at that time—
 (a) be of assistance to the partner concerned; or
 (b) be appropriate in the circumstances.
 (2) Where the officer determines in accordance with paragraph (1) that
the requirement to take part in an interview shall be deferred, he shall also,
when that determination is made, determine the time when the requirement to take part in an interview is to apply in the partner's case.
 (3) Where a requirement to take part in an interview has been deferred in
accordance with paragraph (1), then until—
 (a) a determination is made under regulation 5(1);
 (b) the partner takes part in an interview; or
 (c) a relevant decision has been made in accordance with regulation
     10(3),
the partner shall be treated for the purposes of regulation 3 as having complied with that requirement.

Exemption

7. A partner who, on the day on which the requirement to take part in an   2.516
interview arises or applies under regulation [¹ 3, 3A or 6(2)], is in receipt of
a specified benefit as a claimant in his own right shall be exempt from the
requirement to take part in an interview under these Regulations.

AMENDMENT

1. The Social Security (Jobcentre Plus Interviews for Partners) Amendment
Regulations 2008 (SI 2008/759) (April 28, 2008).

Claims for two or more specified benefits

8. A partner who would otherwise be required under these Regulations to   2.517
take part in interviews relating to more than one specified benefit—
 (a) is only required to take part in one interview during any period
     where the claimant is in receipt of two or more specified benefits
     concurrently; and
 (b) that interview counts for the purposes of each of those benefits.

The interview

9.—(1) An officer shall inform a partner who is required to take part in   2.518
an interview of the date, place and time of the interview.
 (2) The officer may determine that an interview is to take place in the
partner's home where it would, in his opinion, be unreasonable to expect
the partner to attend elsewhere because the partner's personal circumstances are such that attending elsewhere would cause him undue inconvenience or endanger his health.
 (3) An officer shall conduct the interview.

Taking part in an interview

10.—(1) The officer shall determine whether a partner has taken part in   2.519
an interview.

641

(2) A partner shall be regarded as having taken part in an interview if and only if—

  (a) he attends for the interview at the place and time notified to him by the officer; and

  (b) he provides answers (where asked) to questions and appropriate information about—

      (i) the level to which he has pursued any educational qualifications;

     (ii) his employment history;

    (iii) any vocational training he has undertaken;

    (iv) any skills he has acquired which fit him for employment;

     (v) any paid or unpaid employment he is engaged in;

    (vi) any medical condition which, in his opinion, puts him at a disadvantage in obtaining employment; and

    (vii) any caring or childcare responsibilities he has.

(3) Where an officer determines that a partner has failed to take part in an interview and good cause has not been shown either by the partner or by the claimant for that failure within five working days of the day on which the interview was to take place, a relevant decision shall be made for the purposes of section 2B of the Social Security Administration Act 1992 and the partner and the claimant shall be notified accordingly.

Failure to take part in an interview

2.520   **11.**—(1) Where a relevant decision has been made in accordance with regulation 10(3), subject to paragraph (11), the specified benefit payable to the claimant in respect of which the requirement for the partner to take part in an interview under regulation [¹ 3 or 3A] arose shall be reduced, either as from the first day of the next benefit week following the day on which the relevant decision was made, or, if that date arises five days or less after the day on which the relevant decision was made, as from the first day of the second benefit week following the date of the relevant decision.

(2) The deduction made to benefit in accordance with paragraph (1) shall be by a sum equal (but subject to paragraphs (3) and (4)) to 20 per cent. of the amount applicable on the date the deduction commences in respect of a single claimant for income support aged not less than 25.

(3) Benefit reduced in accordance with paragraph (1) shall not be reduced below ten pence per week.

(4) Where two or more specified benefits are in payment to a claimant, in relation to each of which a requirement for the partner to take part in an interview had arisen under [¹ these Regulations], a deduction made in accordance with this regulation shall be applied, except in a case to which paragraph (5) applies, to those benefits in the following order of priority—

  (a) an income-based jobseeker's allowance;

[² (aa) an income-related employment and support allowance under Part 1 of the Welfare Reform Act 2007 (employment and support allowance);]

  (b) income support;

  (c) incapacity benefit;

  (d) severe disablement allowance;

  (e) carer's allowance.

(5) Where the amount of the reduction is greater than some (but not all) of those benefits, the reduction shall be made against the first benefit in the list in paragraph (4) which is the same as, or greater than, the amount of the reduction.

(6) For the purpose of determining whether a benefit is the same as, or greater than, the amount of the reduction for the purposes of paragraph (5), ten pence shall be added to the amount of the reduction.

(7) In a case where the whole of the reduction cannot be applied against any one benefit because no one benefit is the same as, or greater than, the amount of the reduction, the reduction shall be applied against the first benefit in the list of priorities at paragraph (4) and so on against each benefit in turn until the whole of the reduction is exhausted or, if this is not possible, the whole of those benefits are exhausted, subject in each case to ten pence remaining in payment.

(8) Where the rate of any specified benefit payable to a claimant changes, the rules set out above for a reduction in the benefit payable shall be applied to the new rates and any adjustments to the benefits against which the reductions are made shall take effect from the beginning of the first benefit week to commence for that claimant following the change.

(9) Where the partner of a claimant whose benefit has been reduced in accordance with this regulation subsequently takes part in an interview, the reduction shall cease to have effect on the first day of the benefit week in which the requirement to take part in an interview was met.

(10) For the purposes of determining the amount of any benefit payable, a claimant shall be treated as receiving the amount of any specified benefit which would have been payable but for a reduction made in accordance with this regulation.

(11) Benefit shall not be reduced in accordance with this regulation where the partner or the claimant brings new facts to the notice of the Secretary of State within one month of the date on which the decision that the partner failed without good cause to take part in an interview was notified and—

(a) those facts could not reasonably have been brought to the Secretary of State's notice within five working days of the day on which the interview was to take place; and

(b) those facts show that he had good cause for his failure to take part in the interview.

AMENDMENTS

1. The Social Security (Jobcentre Plus Interviews for Partners) Amendment Regulations 2008 (SI 2008/759) (April 28, 2008).

2. The Employment and Support Allowance (Consequential Provisions) (No. 2) Regulations 2008 (SI 2008/1554), reg.71 (October 27, 2008).

Circumstances where regulation 11 does not apply

12. The reduction of benefit to be made under regulation 11 shall not apply as from the date when a partner who failed to take part in an interview ceases to be a partner for the purposes of these Regulations or is no longer a partner to whom [¹ regulation 3 or 3A applies]

2.521

AMENDMENT

1. The Social Security (Jobcentre Plus Interviews for Partners) Amendment Regulations 2008 (SI 2008/759) (April 28, 2008).

Good cause

2.522   **13.** Matters to be taken into account in determining whether the partner or the claimant has shown good cause for the partner's failure to take part in an interview include—

(a) that the partner misunderstood the requirement to take part in an interview due to any learning, language or literacy difficulties of the partner or any misleading information given to the partner by the officer;

(b) that the partner was attending a medical or dental appointment, or accompanying a person for whom the partner had caring responsibilities to such an appointment, and that it would have been unreasonable, in the circumstances, to rearrange the appointment;

(c) that the partner had difficulties with his normal mode of transport and that no reasonable alternative was available;

(d) that the established customs and practices of the religion to which the partner belongs prevented him attending on that day or at that time;

(e) that the partner was attending an interview with an employer with a view to obtaining employment;

(f) that the partner was actually pursuing employment opportunities as a self-employed earner;

(g) that the partner, claimant or a dependant or a person for whom the partner provides care suffered an accident, sudden illness or relapse of a chronic condition;

(h) that he was attending the funeral of a close friend or relative on the day fixed for the interview;

(i) that a disability from which the partner suffers made it impracticable for him to attend at the time fixed for the interview.

Appeals

2.523   **14.**—(1) This regulation applies to any relevant decision made under regulation 10(3) or any decision under section 10 of the 1998 Act superseding such a decision.

(2) This regulation applies whether the decision is as originally made or as revised under section 9 of the 1998 Act.

(3) In the case of a decision to which this regulation applies, the partner in respect of whom the decision was made and the claimant shall each have a right of appeal under section 12 of the 1998 Act to [¹ the First-tier Tribunal]

AMENDMENT

1. The Tribunals, Courts and Enforcement Act 2007 (Transitional and Consequential Provisions) Order 2008 (SI 2008/2683), reg.237 (November 3, 2008).

Amendments to the Social Security and Child Support (Decisions and Appeals) Regulations 1999

2.524   **15.** *Omitted*

The Social Security (Loss of Benefit) Regulations 2001

(SI 2001/4022)

Made   *18th December 2001*   2.525
Coming into force   *1st April 2002*

Whereas a draft of this instrument was laid before Parliament in accordance with section 11(3) of the Social Security Fraud Act 2001, section 80(1) of the Social Security Act 1998 and section 5A(3) of the Pensions Appeal Tribunals Act 1943 and approved by resolution of each House of Parliament.

Now, therefore, the Secretary of State, in exercise of the powers conferred by sections 7(3) to (6), 8(3) and (4), 9(2) to (5), 10(1) and (2) and 11(1) of the Social Security Fraud Act 2001, section 189(4) of the Social Security Administration Act 1992, sections 79(4) and 84 of, and paragraph 9 of Schedule 2 to, the Social Security Act 1998 and section 5A(2) of the Pensions Appeal Tribunals Act 1943, and of all other powers enabling him in that behalf, by this Instrument, which is made before the end of the period of 6 months beginning with the coming into force of sections 7 to 13 of the Social Security Fraud Act 2001 and which contains only regulations made by virtue of, or consequential upon, those sections, hereby makes the following Regulations:

PART I

GENERAL

Citation, commencement and interpretation

1.—(1) These Regulations may be cited as the Social Security (Loss of   2.526
Benefit) Regulations 2001 and shall come into force on 1st April 2002.

(2) In these Regulations, unless the context otherwise requires—

"the Act" means the Social Security Fraud Act 2001;

"the Benefits Act" means the Social Security Contributions and Benefits Act 1992;

"the Council Tax Benefit Regulations" means the Council Tax Benefit Regulations 2006;

[¹ "the Council Tax Benefit (State Pension Credit) Regulations" means the Council Tax Benefit (Persons who have attained pensionable age for state pension credit) Regulations 2006;

"the Housing Benefit Regulations" means the Housing Benefit Regulations 2006;

"the Housing Benefit (State Pension Credit) Regulations" means the Housing Benefit (Persons who have attained pensionable age for state pension credit) Regulations 2006;]

"the Income Support Regulations" means the Income Support (General) Regulations 1987;

"the Jobseekers Act" means the Jobseekers Act 1995;
"the Jobseeker's Allowance Regulations" means the Jobseeker's Allowance
Regulations 1996;
"claimant" in a regulation means the person claiming the sanctionable
benefit referred to in that regulation;
"disqualification period" means the period in respect of which the restrictions on payment of a relevant benefit apply in respect of an offender
in accordance with section 7(6) of the Act and shall be interpreted in
accordance with regulation 2; and
"offender" means the person who is subject to the restriction in the
payment of his benefit in accordance with section 7 of the Act.

(3) Expressions used in these Regulations which are defined either for
the purposes of the Jobseekers Act or for the purposes of the Jobseeker's
Allowance Regulations shall, except where the context otherwise requires,
have the same meaning as for the purposes of that Act or, as the case may
be, those Regulations.

(4) In these Regulations, unless the context otherwise requires, a
reference—
  (a) to a numbered regulation is to the regulation in these Regulations
      bearing that number;
  (b) in a regulation to a numbered paragraph is to the paragraph in that
      regulation bearing that number.

AMENDMENT

2.527   1. Housing Benefit and Council Tax Benefit (Consequential Provisions)
Regulations 2006 (SI 2006/217), Sch.2, para.20(2) (March 6, 2006).

Disqualification period

2.528   **2.**—(1) Subject to paragraph (2), the first day of the disqualification
period for the purpose of section 7(6) of the Act shall be—
  (a) [¹ subject to sub-paragraph (c),] where, on the determination day—
      (i) the offender is in receipt of a sanctionable benefit;
      (ii) the offender is a member of a joint-claim couple which is in
          receipt of a joint-claim jobseeker's allowance; or
      (iii) the offender's family member is in receipt of income support,
          jobseeker's allowance [², state pension credit] [³ , employment
          and support allowance], housing benefit or council tax benefit,
      the day which is 28 days after the determination day;
  (b) where sub-paragraph (a) does not apply, the day which is 28 days
      after the first day after the determination day on which the Secretary
      of State decides to award—
      (i) a sanctionable benefit to the offender;
      (ii) a joint-claim jobseeker's allowance to a joint-claim couple of
          which the offender is a member; or
      (iii) [¹ income support [² jobseeker's allowance [³ , state pension
          credit or employment and support allowance]] to an offender's
          family member.
  [¹(c) where the only sanctionable benefits which the offender or, as the
      case may be, the offender's family member, is in receipt of are
      housing benefit or council tax benefit or both of them, the day
      which is 28 days after the first day after the determination day on

which the Secretary of State is notified by the relevant authority that the offender or an offender's family member is in receipt of either or both of those benefits or, as the case may be, has been awarded either or both of those benefits and in this sub-paragraph, "relevant authority" means the relevant authority administering the offender's or the offender's family member's housing benefit or council tax benefit.]

(2) For the purposes of [¹ paragraph] (1), the first day of the disqualification period shall be no later than 3 years and 28 days after the date of the conviction of the offender for the benefit offence in the later proceedings referred to in section 7(1) of the Act and section 7(9) of the Act (date of conviction and references to conviction) shall apply for the purposes of this paragraph as it applies for the purposes of section 7 of the Act.

(3) In this regulation, "the determination day" means the day on which the Secretary of State determines that a restriction under—

    (a) section 7 of the Act would be applicable to the offender were he in receipt of a sanctionable benefit;

    (b) section 8 of the Act would be applicable to the offender were he a member of a joint-claim couple which is in receipt of a joint-claim jobseeker's allowance; or

    (c) section 9 of the Act would be applicable to the offender's family member were that member in receipt of income support, jobseeker's allowance [², state pension credit] [³ , employment and support allowance], housing benefit or council tax benefit.

AMENDMENTS

1. Social Security (Loss of Benefit) Amendment Regulations 2002 (SI 2002/486), reg.2 (April 1, 2002).

2. State Pension Credit Regulations 2002 (SI 2002/1792), regs 25(2) and 26(2)(i) (October 6, 2003).

3. Employment and Support Allowance (Consequential Provisions) (No. 2) Regulations 2008 (SI 2008/1554), reg.56(1) and (2) (October 27, 2008).

2.529

PART II

REDUCTIONS

Reduction of income support [¹ and income-related employment and support allowance]

3.—(1) Subject to paragraphs (2) to (4), any payment of income support [¹ or an income-related employment and support allowance] which falls to be made to an offender in respect of any week in the disqualification period, or to an offender's family member in respect of any week in the relevant period, shall be reduced—

    (a) where the claimant or a member of his family is pregnant or seriously ill, by a sum equivalent to 20 per cent.;

    (b) where the applicable amount of the offender used to calculate that payment of income support has been reduced pursuant to regulation

2.530

22A of the Income Support Regulations (appeal against a decision embodying an incapacity for work determination), whether or not the appeal referred to in that regulation is successful, by a sum equivalent to 20 per cent;

(c) in any other case, by a sum equivalent to 40 per cent.,

of the applicable amount of the offender in respect of a single claimant for income support on the first day of the disqualification period or, as the case may be, on the first day of the relevant period, and specified in paragraph 1(1) of Schedule 2 to the Income Support Regulations.

(2) Payment shall not be reduced under paragraph (1) to below 10 pence per week.

(3) A reduction under paragraph (1) shall, if it is not a multiple of 5p, be rounded to the nearest such multiple or, if it is a multiple of 2.5p but not of 5p, to the next lower multiple of 5p.

(4) A payment of income support [¹ or an income-related employment and support allowance] shall not be reduced as provided in paragraph (1) in respect of any week in the disqualification period in respect of which that payment of income support [¹ or an income-related employment and support allowance] is subject to a restriction imposed pursuant to section 62 or 63 of the Child Support, Pensions and Social Security Act 2000 (loss of benefit provisions).

(5) Where the rate of income support [¹ or an income-related employment and support allowance] payable to an offender or an offender's family member changes, the rules set out above for a reduction in the benefit payable shall be applied to the new rate and any adjustment to the reduction shall take effect from the first day of the first benefit week to start after the date of the change.

(6) In this regulation, "benefit week" shall have the same meaning as in regulation of 2(1) of the Income Support Regulations. [¹ or, as the case may be, regulation 2(1) of the Employment and Support Allowance Regulations 2008]

AMENDMENTS

1. Employment and Support Allowance (Consequential Provisions) (No. 2) Regulations 2008 (SI 2008/1554), reg.56(1) and (3) (October 27, 2008).

[¹ Reduction in state pension credit

2.531   **3A.**—(1) Subject to the following provisions of this regulation, state pension credit shall be payable in the case of an offender for any week comprised in the disqualification period or in the case of an offender's family member for any week comprised in the relevant period, as if the rate of benefit were reduced—

(a) where the offender or the offender's family member is pregnant or seriously ill, by 20 per cent. of the relevant sum; or

(b) where sub-paragraph (a) does not apply, by 40 per cent. of the relevant sum.

(2) In paragraph (1), the "relevant sum" is the amount applicable—

(a) except where sub-paragraph (b) applies, in respect of a single claimant aged not less than 25 under paragraph 1(1) of Schedule 2 to the Income Support Regulations; or

(b) if the claimant's family member is the offender and the offender has not attained the age of 25, the amount applicable in respect of a person of the offender's age under paragraph 1(1) of Part I of that Schedule,

on the first day of the disqualification period or, as the case may be, on the first day of the relevant period.

(3) Payment of state pension credit shall not be reduced under this regulation to less than 10 pence per week.

(4) A reduction under paragraph (1) shall, if it is not a multiple of 5 pence, be rounded to the nearest such multiple or, if it is a multiple of 2.5 pence but not of 5 pence, to the next lower multiple of 5 pence.

(5) Where the rate of state pension credit payable to an offender or an offender's family member changes, the rules set out above for a reduction in the credit payable shall be applied to the new rate and any adjustment to the reduction shall take effect from the first day of the first benefit week to start after the date of change.

(6) In paragraph (5), "benefit week" has the same meaning as in regulation 1(2) of the State Pension Credit Regulations 2002.

(7) A person of a prescribed description for the purposes of the definition of "family" in section 137(1) of the Benefits Act as it applies for the purpose of this regulation is—

(a) a person who is an additional spouse for the purposes of section 12(1) of the State Pension Credit Act 2002 (additional spouse in the case of polygamous marriages);

(b) a person aged 16 or over who is treated as a child for the purposes of section 142 of the Benefits Act.]

AMENDMENT

1. State Pension Credit Regulations 2002 (SI 2002/1792), reg. 25(3) (October 6, 2003).

Reduction of joint-claim jobseeker's allowance

4. In respect of any part of the disqualification period when section 8(2) of the Act does not apply, the reduced rate of joint-claim jobseeker's allowance payable to the member of that couple who is not the offender shall be—

2.532

(a) in any case in which the member of the couple who is not the offender satisfies the conditions set out in section 2 of the Jobseekers Act (contribution-based conditions), a rate equal to the amount calculated in accordance with section 4(1) of that Act;

(b) in any case where the couple are a couple in hardship for the purposes of regulation 11, a rate equal to the amount calculated in accordance with regulation 16;

(c) in any other case, a rate calculated in accordance with section 4(3A) of the Jobseekers Act save that the applicable amount shall be the amount determined by reference to paragraph 1(1) of Schedule 1 to the Jobseeker's Allowance Regulations as if the member of the couple who is not the offender were a single claimant.

PART III

HARDSHIP

Meaning of "person in hardship"

2.533   **5.**—(1) In this Part of these Regulations, a "person in hardship" means, for the purposes of regulation 6, a person, other than a person to whom paragraph (3) or (4) applies, where—

(a) she is a single woman who is pregnant and in respect of whom the Secretary of State is satisfied that, unless a jobseeker's allowance is paid, she will suffer hardship;

(b) he is a single person who is responsible for a young person and the Secretary of State is satisfied that, unless a jobseeker's allowance is paid, the young person will suffer hardship;

(c) he is a member of [² a couple] where—

[² (i) at least one member of the couple is a woman who is pregnant; and]

(ii) the Secretary of State is satisfied that, unless a jobseeker's allowance is paid, the woman will suffer hardship;

(d) he is a member of a polygamous marriage and—

(i) one member of the marriage is pregnant; and

(ii) the Secretary of State is satisfied that, unless a jobseeker's allowance is paid, that woman will suffer hardship;

(e) he is a member of [² a couple] or of a polygamous marriage where—

(i) one or both members of the couple, or one or more members of the polygamous marriage, are responsible for a child or young person; and

(ii) the Secretary of State is satisfied that, unless a jobseeker's allowance is paid, the child or young person will suffer hardship;

(f) he has an award of a jobseeker's allowance which includes or would, if a claim for a jobseeker's allowance from him were to succeed, have included in his applicable amount a disability premium and the Secretary of State is satisfied that, unless a jobseeker's allowance is paid, the person who would satisfy the conditions of entitlement to that premium would suffer hardship;

(g) he suffers, or his partner suffers, from a chronic medical condition which results in functional capacity being limited or restricted by physical impairment and the Secretary of State is satisfied that—

(i) the suffering has already lasted, or is likely to last, for not less than 26 weeks; and

(ii) unless a jobseeker's allowance is paid to that person, the probability is that the health of the person suffering would, within 2 weeks of the Secretary of State making his decision, decline further than that of a normally healthy adult and that person would suffer hardship;

(h) he does, or his partner does, or in the case of a person who is married to more than one person under a law which permits polygamy, at least one of those persons does, devote a considerable portion of each week to caring for another person who—

   (i) is in receipt of an attendance allowance or the care component of disability living allowance at one of the two higher rates prescribed under section 72(4) of the Benefits Act;

   (ii) has claimed either attendance allowance or disability living allowance, but only for so long as the claim has not been determined, or for 26 weeks from the date of claiming, whichever is the earlier; or

   (iii) has claimed either attendance allowance or disability living allowance and has an award of either attendance allowance or the care component of disability living allowance at one of the two higher rates prescribed under section 72(4) of the Benefits Act for a period commencing after the date on which that claim was made,

and the Secretary of State is satisfied, after taking account of the factors set out in paragraph (5), in so far as they are appropriate to the particular circumstances of the case, that the person providing the care will not be able to continue doing so unless a jobseeker's allowance is paid to the offender;

  (i) he is a person or is the partner of a person to whom section 16 of the Jobseekers Act applies by virtue of a direction issued by the Secretary of State, except where the person to whom the direction applies does not satisfy the requirements of section 1(2)(a) to (c) of that Act;

  (j) he is a person—

   (i) to whom section 3(1)(f)(iii) of the Jobseekers Act (persons under the age of 18) applies, or is the partner of such a person; and

   (ii) in respect of whom the Secretary of State is satisfied that the person will, unless a jobseeker's allowance is paid, suffer hardship; or

  (k) he is a person—

   (i) who, pursuant to the Children Act 1989, was being looked after by a local authority;

   (ii) with whom the local authority had a duty, pursuant to that Act, to take reasonable steps to keep in touch; or

   (iii) who, pursuant to that Act, qualified for advice and assistance from a local authority,

but in respect of whom head (i), (ii) or (iii) above, as the case may be, had not applied for a period of 3 years or less as at the date on which he complies with the requirements of regulation 9; and

   (iv) who, as at the date on which he complies with the requirements of regulation 9, is under the age of 21.

(2) Except in a case to which paragraph (3) or (4) applies, a person shall, for the purposes of regulation 7, be deemed to be a person in hardship where, after taking account of the factors set out in paragraph (5) in so far as they are appropriate to the particular circumstances of the case, the Secretary of State is satisfied that he or his partner will suffer hardship unless a jobseeker's allowance is paid to him.

(3) In paragraphs (1) and (2), a person shall not be deemed to be a person in hardship—

  (a) where he is entitled, or his partner is entitled, to income support or where he or his partner fall within a category of persons prescribed for the purpose of section 124(1)(e) of the Benefits Act;

(b) during any period in respect of which it has been determined that a jobseeker's allowance is not payable to him pursuant to section 19 of the Jobseekers Act (circumstances in which a jobseeker's allowance is not payable); or

(c) during any week in the disqualification period in respect of which he is subject to a restriction imposed pursuant to section 62 or 63 of the Child Support, Pensions and Social Security Act 2000 (loss of benefit provisions).

(4) Paragraph (1)(h) shall not apply in a case where the person being cared for resides in a [¹ care home, an Abbeyfield Home or an independent hospital].

(5) Factors which, for the purposes of paragraphs (1) and (2), the Secretary of State is to take into account in determining whether the person is a person in hardship are—

(a) the presence in that person's family of a person who satisfies the requirements for a disability premium specified in paragraphs 13 and 14 of Schedule 1 to the Jobseeker's Allowance Regulations or for a disabled child premium specified in paragraph 16 of that Schedule to those Regulations;

(b) the resources which, without a jobseeker's allowance, are likely to be available to the offender's family, the amount by which these resources fall short of the amount applicable in his case in accordance with regulation 10 (applicable amount in hardship cases), the amount of any resources which may be available to members of the offender's family from any person in the offender's household who is not a member of his family and the length of time for which those factors are likely to persist;

(c) whether there is a substantial risk that essential items, including food, clothing, heating and accommodation, will cease to be available to that person or a member of his family, or will be available at considerably reduced levels and the length of time those factors are likely to persist.

(6) In determining the resources available to that person's family under paragraph (5)(b), any training premium or top-up payment paid pursuant to the Employment and Training Act 1973 shall be disregarded.

Amendments

1. Social Security (Care Homes and Independent Hospitals) Regulations 2005 (SI 2005/2687), reg.15(2) (October 24, 2005).

2. Civil parnership (Pensions, Social Security and Child Support) (Consequential etc. Provisions) Order 2005 (SI 2005/2877), Sch.3, para.34(2) (December 5, 2005).

Circumstances in which an income-based jobseeker's allowance is payable to a person who is a person in hardship

2.534 **6.**—(1) This regulation applies to a person in hardship within the meaning of regulation 5(1) and is subject to the provisions of regulations 8 and 9.

(2) An income-based jobseeker's allowance shall be payable to a person in hardship even though section 7(2) of the Act prevents payment of a jobseeker's allowance to the offender or section 9 of the Act prevents payment

of a jobseeker's allowance to an offender's family member but the allowance shall be payable under this paragraph only if and so long as the claimant satisfies the conditions for entitlement to an income-based jobseeker's allowance.

Further circumstances in which an income-based jobseeker's allowance is payable to a person who is a person in hardship

7.—(1) This regulation applies to a person in hardship within the meaning of regulation 5(2) and is subject to the provisions of regulations 8 and 9.

   2.535

(2) An income-based jobseeker's allowance shall be payable to a person in hardship even though section 7(2) of the Act prevents payment of a job-seeker's allowance to the offender or section 9 of the Act prevents payment of a jobseeker's allowance to an offender's family member but the allowance shall not be payable under this paragraph—

(a) where the offender is the claimant, in respect of the first 14 days of the disqualification period;

(b) where the offender's family member is the claimant, in respect of the first 14 days of the relevant period,

and shall be payable thereafter only if and so long as the claimant satisfies the conditions for entitlement to an income-based jobseeker's allowance.

Conditions for payment of income-based jobseeker's allowance

8.—(1) An income-based jobseeker's allowance shall not be payable in accordance with regulation 6 or 7 except where the claimant has—

   2.536

(a) furnished on a form approved for the purpose by the Secretary of State or in such other form as he may in any particular case approve, a statement of the circumstances he relies upon to establish entitlement under regulation 5(1) or, as the case may be, 5(2); and

(b) signed the statement.

(2) The completed and signed form shall be delivered by the claimant to such office as the Secretary of State may specify.

Provision of information

9. For the purpose of section 7(4)(b) of the Act, the offender, and for the purpose of section 9(4)(b) of the Act, the offender or any member of his family, shall provide to the Secretary of State information as to the circumstances of the person alleged to be in hardship.

   2.537

Applicable amount in hardship cases

10.—(1) The weekly applicable amount of a person to whom an income-based jobseeker's allowance is payable in accordance with this Part shall be reduced by a sum equivalent to 40 per cent. or, in a case where the claimant or any other member of his family is either pregnant or seriously ill, 20 per cent. of the following amount—

   2.538

(a) where the claimant is a single claimant aged not less than 18 but less than 25 or a member of a couple or polygamous marriage where one member is aged not less than 18 but less than 25 and the other member or, in the case of a polygamous marriage each other member, is a person under 18 who is not eligible for an income-based jobseeker's allowance under section 3(1)(f)(iii) of the

Jobseekers Act or is not subject to a direction under section 16 of that Act, the amount specified in paragraph 1(1)(d) of Schedule 1 to the Jobseeker's Allowance Regulations;

(b) where the claimant is a single claimant aged not less than 25 or a member of a couple or a polygamous marriage (other than a member of a couple or polygamous marriage to whom sub-paragraph (a) applies) at least one of whom is aged not less than 18, the amount specified in paragraph 1(1)(e) of Schedule 1 to the Jobseeker's Allowance Regulations.

(2) A reduction under paragraph (1) shall, if it is not a multiple of 5p, be rounded to the nearest such multiple or, if it is a multiple of 2.5p but not of 5p, to the next lower multiple of 5p.

PART IV

HARDSHIP FOR JOINT-CLAIM COUPLES

Application of Part and meaning of "couple in hardship"

2.539
11.—(1) This Part of these Regulations applies in respect of any part of the disqualification period when section 8(2) of the Act would otherwise apply.

(2) In this Part of these Regulations, a "couple in hardship" means, for the purposes of regulation 13, a joint-claim couple, other than a couple to whom paragraph (4) or (5) applies, who are claiming a jointclaim jobseeker's allowance jointly where at least one member of that couple is an offender and where—

(a) [¹ care home, an Abbeyfield Home or an independent hospital] and the Secretary of State is satisfied that, unless a joint-claim jobseeker's allowance is paid, she will suffer hardship;

(b) one or both members of the couple are members of a polygamous marriage, one member of the marriage is pregnant and the Secretary of State is satisfied that, unless a joint-claim jobseeker's allowance is paid, she will suffer hardship;

(c) the award of a joint-claim jobseeker's allowance includes, or would, if a claim for a jobseeker's allowance from the couple were to succeed, have included in their applicable amount a disability premium and the Secretary of State is satisfied that, unless a joint-claim jobseeker's allowance is paid, the member of the couple who would have caused the disability premium to be applicable to the couple would suffer hardship;

(d) either member of the couple suffers from a chronic medical condition which results in functional capacity being limited or restricted by physical impairment and the Secretary of State is satisfied that—

(i) the suffering has already lasted or is likely to last, for not less than 26 weeks; and

(ii) unless a joint-claim jobseeker's allowance is paid, the probability is that the health of the person suffering would, within two weeks of the Secretary of State making his decision, decline further than that of a normally healthy adult and the member of the couple who suffers from that condition would suffer hardship;

(e) either member of the couple, or where a member of that couple is married to more than one person under a law which permits polygamy, one member of that marriage, devotes a considerable portion of each week to caring for another person who—

  (i) is in receipt of an attendance allowance or the care component of disability living allowance at one of the two higher rates prescribed under section 72(4) of the Benefits Act;

  (ii) has claimed either attendance allowance or disability living allowance, but only for so long as the claim has not been determined, or for 26 weeks from the date of claiming, whichever is the earlier; or

  (iii) has claimed either attendance allowance or disability living allowance and has an award of either attendance allowance or the care component of disability living allowance at one of the two higher rates prescribed under section 72(4) of the Benefits Act for a period commencing after the date on which that claim was made,

and the Secretary of State is satisfied, after taking account of the factors set out in paragraph (6) in so far as they are appropriate to the particular circumstances of the case, that the person providing the care will not be able to continue doing so unless a joint-claim jobseeker's allowance is paid; or

(f) section 16 of the Jobseekers Act applies to either member of the couple by virtue of a direction issued by the Secretary of State, except where the member of the joint-claim couple to whom the direction applies does not satisfy the requirements of section 1(2)(a) to (c) of that Act;

(g) section 3A(1)(e)(ii) of the Jobseekers Act (member of joint-claim couple under the age of 18) applies to either member of the couple and the Secretary of State is satisfied that unless a jointclaim jobseeker's allowance is paid, the couple will suffer hardship; or

(h) one or both members of the couple is a person—

  (i) who, pursuant to the Children Act 1989, was being looked after by a local authority;

  (ii) with whom the local authority had a duty, pursuant to that Act, to take reasonable steps to keep in touch; or

  (iii) who, pursuant to that Act, qualified for advice or assistance from a local authority,

but in respect of whom head (i), (ii) or (iii) above, as the case may be, had not applied for a period of 3 years or less as at the date on which the requirements of regulation 15 are complied with; and

  (iv) who, as at the date on which the requirements of regulation 15 are complied with, is under the age of 21.

(3) Except in a case to which paragraph (4) or (5) applies, a joint-claim couple shall, for the purposes of regulation 14, be deemed to be a couple in hardship where the Secretary of State is satisfied, after taking account of the factors set out in paragraph (6) in so far as they are appropriate to the particular circumstances of the case, that the couple will suffer hardship unless a joint-claim jobseeker's allowance is paid.

(4) In paragraphs (2) and (3), a joint-claim couple shall not be deemed to be a "couple in hardship"—

(a) where one member of the couple is entitled to income support or falls within a category of persons prescribed for the purposes of section 124(1)(e) of the Benefits Act; or

(b) during a period in respect of which it has been determined that both members of the couple are subject to sanctions for the purposes of section 20A of the Jobseekers Act (denial or reduction of joint-claim jobseeker's allowance).

(5) Paragraph (2)(e) shall not apply in a case where the person being cared for resides in a [² care home, an Abbeyfield Home or an independent hospital].

(6) Factors which, for the purposes of paragraphs (2) and (3), the Secretary of State is to take into account in determining whether a joint-claim couple will suffer hardship are—

(a) the presence in the joint-claim couple of a person who satisfies the requirements for a disability premium specified in paragraphs 20H and 20I of Schedule 1 to the Jobseeker's Allowance Regulations;

(b) the resources which, without a joint-claim jobseeker's allowance, are likely to be available to the joint-claim couple, the amount by which these resources fall short of the amount applicable in their case in accordance with regulation 16 (applicable amount of joint-claim couple in hardship cases), the amount of any resources which may be available to the joint-claim couple from any person in the couple's household who is not a member of the family and the length of time for which those factors are likely to persist;

(c) whether there is a substantial risk that essential items, including food, clothing, heating and accommodation, will cease to be available to the joint-claim couple, or will be available at considerably reduced levels, the hardship that will result and the length of time those factors are likely to persist.

(7) In determining the resources available to the offender's family under paragraph (6)(b), any training premium or top-up payment paid pursuant to the Employment and Training Act 1973 shall be disregarded.

AMENDMENTS

1. Social Security (Care Homes and Independent Hospitals) Regulations 2005 (SI 2005/2687), reg.15(3) (October 24, 2005).

2. Civil Partnership (Pensions, Social Security and Child Support) (Consequential etc. Provisions) Order 2005 (SI 2005/2877), Sch.3, para.34(3) (December 5, 2005).

Circumstances in which a joint-claim jobseeker's allowance is payable where a joint-claim couple is a couple in hardship

2.540   **12.**—(1) This regulation applies where a joint-claim couple is a couple in hardship within the meaning of regulation 11(2) and is subject to the provisions of regulations 14 and 15.

(2) A joint-claim jobseeker's allowance shall be payable to a couple in hardship even though section 8(2) of the Act prevents payment of a joint-claim jobseeker's allowance to the couple or section 8(3) of the Act reduces

the amount of a joint-claim jobseeker's allowance payable to the couple but the allowance shall be payable under this paragraph only if and for so long as—

    (a) the joint-claim couple satisfy the other conditions of entitlement to a joint-claim jobseeker's allowance; or

    (b) one member satisfies those conditions and the other member comes within any paragraph in Schedule A1 to the Jobseeker's Allowance Regulations (categories of members not required to satisfy conditions in section 1(2B)(b) of the Jobseekers Act).

Further circumstances in which a joint-claim jobseeker's allowance is payable to a couple in hardship

13.—(1) This regulation applies to a couple in hardship falling within regulation 11(3) and is subject to the provisions of regulations 14 and 15.

    (2) A joint-claim jobseeker's allowance shall be payable to a couple in hardship even though section 8(2) of the Act prevents payment of a joint-claim jobseeker's allowance to the couple or section 8(3) of the Act reduces the amount of a joint-claim jobseeker's allowance payable to the couple but the allowance—

    (a) shall not be payable under this paragraph in respect of the first 14 days of the prescribed period; and

    (b) shall be payable thereafter only where the conditions of entitlement to a joint-claim jobseeker's allowance are satisfied or where one member satisfies those conditions and the other member comes within any paragraph in Schedule A1 to the Jobseeker's Allowance Regulations (categories of members not required to satisfy conditions in section 1(2B)(b) of the Jobseekers Act).

2.541

Conditions for payment of a joint-claim jobseeker's allowance

14.—(1) A joint-claim jobseeker's allowance shall not be payable in accordance with regulation 12 or 13 except where either member of the couple has—

    (a) furnished on a form approved for the purpose by the Secretary of State or in such other form as he may in any particular case approve, a statement of the circumstances he relies upon to establish entitlement under regulation 11(2) or, as the case may be, 11(3); and

    (b) signed the statement.

    (2) The completed and signed form shall be delivered by a member of the couple to such office as the Secretary of State may specify.

2.542

Provision of information

15. For the purposes of section 8(4)(b) of the Act, a member of the couple shall provide to the Secretary of State information as to the circumstances of the alleged hardship of the couple.

2.543

Applicable amount of joint-claim couple in hardship cases

16.—(1) The weekly applicable amount of a couple to whom a joint-claim jobseeker's allowance is payable in accordance with this Part shall be reduced by a sum equivalent to 40 per cent. or, in a case where a member of the joint-claim couple is either pregnant or seriously ill or where a member of the joint-claim couple is a member of a polygamous marriage and one of

2.544

those members is either pregnant or seriously ill, 20 per cent of the following amount—

    (a) where one member of the joint-claim couple or of the polygamous marriage is aged not less than 18 but less than 25 and the other member or, in the case of a polygamous marriage, each other member, is a person under 18 to whom section 3A(1)(e)(ii) of the Jobseekers Act applies or is not subject to a direction under section 16 of that Act, the amount specified in paragraph 1(1)(d) of Schedule 1 to the Jobseeker's Allowance Regulations;

    (b) where one member of the joint-claim couple or at least one member of the polygamous marriage (other than a member of a couple or polygamous marriage to whom sub-paragraph (a) applies) is aged not less than 18, the amount specified in paragraph 1(1)(e) of Schedule 1 to the Jobseeker's Allowance Regulations.

    (2) A reduction under paragraph (1) shall, if it is not a multiple of 5p, be rounded to the nearest such multiple or, if it is a multiple of 2.5p but not of 5p, to the next lower multiple of 5p.

PART V

HOUSING BENEFIT AND COUNCIL TAX BENEFIT

2.545   **17.** *Omitted.*
2.546   **18.** *Omitted.*

PART VI

DEDUCTIONS FROM BENEFITS AND DISQUALIFYING BENEFITS

Social security benefits not to be sanctionable benefits

2.547   **19.** The following social security benefits are to be treated as a disqualifying benefit but not a sanctionable benefit—

    (a) constant attendance allowance payable under article 14 of the Naval, Military and Air Forces Etc. (Disablement and Death) Service Pensions Order 1983 ("the Order") or article 14 or 43 of the Personal Injuries (Civilians) Scheme 1983 ("the Scheme");

    (b) exceptionally severe disablement allowance payable under article 15 of the Order or article 15 or 44 of the Scheme;

    (c) mobility supplement payable under article 26A of the Order or article 25A or 48A of the Scheme;

    (d) constant attendance allowance and exceptionally severe disablement allowance, payable under sections 104 and 105 respectively of the Benefits Act where a disablement pension is payable under section 103 of that Act; and

    (e) a bereavement payment payable under section 36 of the Benefits Act.

Deductions from benefits

20. Any restriction in section 7, 8 or 9 of the Act shall not apply in relation to payments of benefit to the extent of any deduction from the payments which falls to be made under regulations made under section 5(1)(p) of the Social Security Administration Act 1992 for, or in place of, child support maintenance and for this purpose, "child support maintenance" means such maintenance which is payable under the Child Support Act 1991.

2.548

PART VII

OTHER AMENDMENTS

21. *Omitted.* 2.549
22. *Omitted.* 2.550

Social Security (Medical Evidence) Regulations 1976

(SI 1976/615) (AS AMENDED)

ARRANGEMENT OF REGULATIONS

The Secretary of State for Social Services, in exercise of powers conferred upon him by section 115(1) of, and Schedule 13 to, the Social Security Act 1975 and of all other powers enabling him in that behalf, after reference to the National Insurance Advisory Committee hereby makes the following regulations:

Citation, commencement, and interpretation

2.552   **1.** (1) These regulations may be cited as the Social Security (Medical Evidence) Regulations 1976, and shall come into operation on 4th October 1976.

(2) In these regulations, unless the context otherwise requires—

"the Act" means the Social Security Act 1975;

[² "the Contributions and Benefits Act" means the Social Security Contributions and Benefits Act 1992;]

[⁴ "the Employment and Support Allowance Regulations" means the Employment and Support Allowance Regulations 2008;]

[⁴ "limited capability for work" has the meaning given in section 1(4) of the Welfare Reform Act 2007;]

[⁴ "limited capability for work assessment" means the assessment of whether a person has limited capability for work as set out in regulation 19(2) of, and in Schedule 2 to, the Employment and Support Allowance Regulations']

[³ "personal capability assessment" means the assessment provided for in section 171C of the Contributions and Benefits Act;]

[¹ "registered midwife" means a midwife who is registered as a midwife with the United Kingdom Central Council for Nursing, Midwifery and Health Visiting under the Nurses, Midwives and Health Visitors Act 1979;]

"doctor" means a registered medical practitioner;

"signature" means, in relation to any statement or certificate given in accordance with these regulations, the name by which the person giving that statement or certificate, as the case may be, is usually known (any name other than the surname being either in full or otherwise indicated) written by that person in his own handwriting; and "signed" shall be construed accordingly.

(3) Any reference in these regulations to any provisions made by or contained in any enactment or instrument shall, except in so far as the context otherwise requires, be construed as a reference to that provision as amended or extended by any enactment or instrument and as including a reference to any provision which it re-enacts or replaces, or which may re-enact or replace it, with or without modification.

(4) The rules for the construction of Acts of Parliament contained in the Interpretation Act 1889 shall apply in relation to this instrument and in relation to the revocation effected by it as if this instrument, the regulations revoked by it and regulations revoked by the regulations so revoked were Acts of Parliament, and as if each revocation were a repeal.

AMENDMENTS

1. The Social Security (Medical Evidence) Amendment Regulations 1987 (SI 1987/409), reg. 2 (April 6, 1987).

2. The Social Security (Medical Evidence) Amendment Regulations 1994 (SI 1994/2975), reg.2 (April 13, 1995).

3. The Social Security (Incapacity for Work) Miscellaneous Amendments Regulations 1999 (SI 1999/3109), reg.5(a) (April 3, 2000).

4. The Employment and Support Allowance (Consequential provisions) (No.2) Regulations 2008 (SI 2008/1554), reg.68 (October 27, 2008).

Evidence of incapacity for work [⁸ , limited capability for work] and confinement

2.553

2.—(1) [¹ Subject to regulation 5] [³ where a person claims he is entitled to any benefit, allowance or advantage (other than industrial injuries benefit or statutory sick pay), and his entitlement to that benefit, allowance or advantage depends on his being incapable of work, [⁸ or having limited capability for work] then in respect of each day until he has been assessed for the purposes of the [⁵ personal capability assessment] [⁸ or the limited capability for work assessment], he shall provide evidence of such incapacity] [⁸ or limited capability for work]—

[³(a) by means of a certificate in the form of a statement in writing given by a doctor in accordance with the rules set out in Part I of Schedule 1 to these Regulations on the form set out in Part II of that Schedule; or

(b) where a doctor—

    (i) has not given a statement under sub-paragraph (a) of this paragraph since the patient was examined and wishes to give such a statement but more than one day has passed since the examination; or

    (ii) advises that the patient should refrain from work on the basis of a written report from another doctor,

by means of a special statement given in accordance with the rules set out in Part I of Schedule 1A to these Regulations on the form set out in Part II of that Schedule;] or

[²](c) [⁵ where the question of whether a person is capable or incapable of work [⁸ or whether a person has or does not have limited capability for work] fulls to be determined in accordance with the personal capability assessment] [⁸ or the limited capability for work assessment] and the Secretary of State so requests, a statement in writing given by a doctor in accordance with the rules set out in Part I of Schedule 1B to these Regulations on the form set out in Part II of that Schedule; or

(d) where it would be unreasonable to require a person to provide a statement [⁴ in accordance with sub-paragraphs (a) to (c),] such other evidence as may be sufficient to show that he should refrain [⁴ (or should have refrained)] from work by reason of some specific disease or bodily or mental disablement.]

(2) Every person to whom paragraph (1) applies [² who has not been assessed for the purposes of the [⁶ personal capability assessment]] [⁸ or the limited capability for work assessment] shall, before he returns to work, furnish evidence of the date on which he became fit for work either in accordance with rule 10 og Part 1 of Schedule 1 to these regulations, or by such other means as may be sufficient in the circumstances of the case.

[⁷ (3) Every woman who claims maternity benefit shall furnish evidence—

(a) where the claims is made in respect of expectation of confinement, that she is pregnant and as to the stage which she has reached in her pregnancy; or

(b) where the claim is made by virtue of the fact of confinement, that she has been confined;

and shall furnish such evidence by means of a maternity certificate given by a doctor or by as registered midwife [not earlier than the beginning of the 20th week before the week in which she is expected to be confined] in accordance with the rules set out in Part I of Schedule 2 to these regulations in the appropriate form set out in Part II of that Schedule or by such other means as may be sufficient in the circumstances of any particular case.]

AMENDMENTS

2.554 1. The Social Security (Medical Evidence, Claims and Payments) Amendments Regulations 1982 (SI 1982/699), reg.2 (June 14, 1982).
2. The Social Security (Medical Evidence) Amendment Regulations 1994 (SI 1994/2975), reg.2 (April 13, 1995).
3. The Social Security (Medical Evidence) Amendment Regulations 1992 (SI 1992/2471), reg.3 (March 9, 1992).
4. The Social Security (Incapacity for Work) Miscellaneous Amendments Regulations 1995 (SI 1995/987), reg.4 (April 13, 1995.)
5. The Social Security (Incapacity) Miscellaneous Amendments Regulations 2000 (SI 2000/590), reg.6 (April 3, 2000).
6. The Social Security (Incapacity for Work) Miscellaneous Amendments Regulations 1999 (SI 1999/3109), reg.5(b) (April 3, 2000).
7. The Social Security (Medical Evidence) and Statutory Maternity Pay (Medical Evidence) (Amendment) Regulations 2001 (SI 2001/2931), reg.2 (September 28, 2001).
8. The Employment and Support Allowance (Consequential provisions) (No.2) Regulations 2008 (SI 2008/1554), reg.68 (October 27, 2008).

GENERAL NOTE

2.555 In *R(15) 8/93*, the Commissioner ruled that the reference in the regulation to "such other means as may be sufficient in the particular circumstances of any particular case" meant that evidence of incapacity need not be in the form of a medical certificate. This means that medical certificates other than in the form set out in the Schedule may be acceptable as well as evidence from the claimant himself or herself (para.14). Whether such evidence is sufficient is a matter for determination by the decision-maker or tribunal. Failure to consider this issue will be an error of law.
In *CIB/17533/1996* the Commissioner addressed an issue which was being argued by a number of representatives, namely that there was no jurisdiction to make an all work test determination where the adjudication officer had requested the claimant to obtain the special Form Med. 4 and this form was not available to the adjudication officer when the decision was made. Form Med. 4 is the special form which specifically directs doctors to consider capacity for *all* work in certifying incapacity for work. The Commissioner concludes that "the somewhat legalistic proposition that a decision by an adjudication officer made without a form MED4 is a nullity or is erroneous in law cannot in my view be sustained" (para.8 of Common Appendix).

2.556 *Regulation 3 revoked by The Social Security (Claims and Payments) Regulations 1979 (SI1979/628), reg.32 (July 9, 1979).*

2.557 *Regulation 4 revoked by The Social Security (Medical Evidence, Claims and Payments) Amendments Regulations 1982 (SI1982/699), reg.2 (June 14, 1982).*

[¹ Self-certificate for first 7 days of a spell of incapacity for work [⁴ or limited capability for work]

5.—[² (1) [³ The evidence of incapacity [⁴ or limited capability for work] required for the purposes of determining entitlement to a benefit, allowance or advantage referred to in regulation 2(1)]—

(a) for a spell of incapacity which lasts for less than 8 days,

(b) in respect of any of the first 7 days of a longer spell of incapacity;
may consist of a self certificate instead of a certificate in the form of a statement in writing given by a doctor in accordance with regulation 2(1).]

[⁴ (c) for a period of limited capability for work which lasts less than 8 days; or

(d) in respect of any of the first 7 days of a longer period of limited capability for work.]

(2) For the purpose of this regulation:—

[⁴ "self-certificate means either—

(i) a declaration made by the claimant in writing, on a form approved for the purpose by the Secretary of State; or

(ii) where the claim has made a claim for employment and support allowance in accordance with regulation 4G of the Social Security (Claims and Payments) Regulations 1987, an oral declaration by the claimant,

that the claimant has been unfit for work from a date or for a period specified in the declaration and may include a statement that the claimant expects to continue to be unfit for work on days subsequent to the date on which it is made;]

[³ "spell of incapacity" has the meaning given to it by section 171B(3) of the Contributions and benefits Act.]]

2.558

AMENDMENTS

1. The Social Security (Medical Evidence, Claims and Payments) Amendments Regulations 1982 (SI 1982/699), reg.2 (June 14, 1982).

2. The Social Security (Medical Evidence, Claims and Payments) Amendment Regulations 1989 (SI 1989/1686), reg.2 (October 9, 1989).

3. The Social Security (Medical Evidence) Amendment Regulations 1994 (SI 1994/2975), reg.2 (April 13, 1995).

4. The Employment and Support Allowance (Consequential Provisions) (No. 2) Regulations 2008 (SI 2008/1554), reg.68 (October 27, 2008).

SCHEDULE 1   **Regulation 2(1)**

PART I

RULES

1. In these rules, unless the context otherwise requires— 2.559

"claimant" means the person in respect of whom a statement is given in accordance with these rules;

"doctor" means a registered medical practitioner not being the claimant;

"doctor's statement" means a statement given in accordance with these rules;

"2 weeks" means any period of 14 consecutive days.

2. The doctor's statement shall be in the form set out in Part II of this Schedule.

[¹**3.** Where the claimant—

    (a) is on the list of a person providing primary medical services under the National Health Service Act 1977 or the National Health Service (Scotland) Act 1978 and is being attended by a doctor performing such services; or

    (b) is on the list of a doctor, or list held jointly by two or more doctors performing personal medical services in connection with a pilot scheme under the National Health Service (Primary Care) Act 1997 and is being attended by such a doctor,

the doctor's statement shall be on the form provided by the Secretary of State for he purpose and shall be signed by the attending doctor.]

4. In any other case, the doctor's statement shall be either on a form provided by the Secretary of State for the purpose or in a form substantially to the like effect, and shall be signed by the doctor attending the claimant.

5. Every doctor's statement shall be completed in ink or other indelible substance, and shall contain the following particulars—

    (a) the claimant's name;

    (b) the date of the examination on which the doctor's statement is based;

    (c) the diagnosis of the claimant's disorder in respect of which the doctor is advising the claimant to refrain from work or, as the case may be, which has caused the claimant's absence from work;

    (d) the date on which the doctor's statement is given;

    (e) the address of the doctor.

and shall bear, opposite the words "Doctor's signature," the signature of the doctor making the statement written after there have been entered the claimant's name and the doctor's diagnosis.

6. Subject to rules 7 and 8 below, the diagnosis of the claimant's disorder in respect of which the doctor is advising the claimant to refrain from work or, as the case may be, which has caused the claimant's absence from work shall be specified as precisely as the doctor's knowledge of the claimant's condition at the time of the examination permits.

7. Where, in the doctor's opinion, a disclosure to the claimant of the precise disorder would be prejudicial to his well-being, the diagnosis may be specified less precisely.

8. In the case of an initial examination by a doctor in respect of a disorder stated by the claimant to have caused incapacity for work, where—

    (a) there are no clinical signs of that disorder, and

    (b) in the doctor's opinion, the claimant need not refrain from work,

instead of specifying a diagnosis "unspecified" may be entered.

9. A doctor's statement must be given on a date not later than one day after the date of the examination on which it is based, and no further doctor's statement based on the same examination shall be furnished other than a doctor's statement by way of replacement of an original which has been lost or mislaid, in which case it shall be clearly marked "duplicate."

10. Where, in the doctor's opinion, the claimant will become fit to resume work on a day not later than 2 weeks after the date of the examination on which the doctor's statement is based, the doctor's statement shall specify that day.

11. Subject to rules 12 and 13 below, the doctor's statement shall specify the minimum period during which, in the doctor's opinion, the claimant should, by reason of his disorder, refrain from work.

12. The period specified shall begin on the date of the examination on which the doctor's statement is based and shall not exceed 6 months unless the claimant has, on the advice of a doctor, refrained from work for at least 6 months immediately preceding that date.

13. Where—

    (a) the claimant has, on the advice of a doctor, refrained from work for at least 6 months immediately preceding the date of the examination on which the doctor's statement is based, and

    (b) in the doctor's opinion, it will be necessary for the claimant to refrain from work for the foreseeable future, instead of specifying a period, the doctor may, having regard to the circumstances of the particular case, enter the words "until further notice."

14. The Notes set out in Part III of this Schedule shall accompany the form of doctor's statement provided by the Secretary of State.

15. A doctor may, having regard to the circumstances of the particular case, indicate on the doctor's statement that the claimant should be considered for vocational rehabilitation.

PART II

FORM OF DOCTOR'S STATEMENT

2.560

DOCTOR'S STATEMENT

In confidence to

Mr./Mrs./Miss ....

I examined you today/yesterday and advised you that:

(a) you need not   (b) you should refrain from work
    refrain from work

                        for ....

                  OR until ....

Diagnosis of your disorder
causing absence from work ....
Doctor's remarks

Doctor's   Date of
signature   signing

Recommendation
for vocational
rehabilitation

PART III

THE NOTES

The following notes shall accompany the form of doctor's statement provided by the Secretary of State—

2.561

On the doctor's statement—

(1) After the words "you should refrain from work for", the period entered must not exceed 6 months unless the patient has, on the advice of a doctor, already refrained from work for a continuous period of 6 months.

(2) After the words "you should refrain from work until"—

    (a) if the patient is being given a date when he can return to work the date entered should not be more than 2 weeks after the date of the examination;

    (b) if the patient has already been incapable of work for at least 6 months and recovery of capacity for work in the foreseeable future is not expected "further notice" may be entered.

AMENDMENT

1. General Medical Services and Personal Medical Services Transition and Consequential Provisions Order 2004 (SI 2004/865), Sch.1 (April 1, 2004).

SCHEDULE 1A   **Regulation 2(1)**

PART I

RULES

1. In these rules, unless the context otherwise requires—

2.562

"claimant" means the person in respect of whom a statement is given in accordance with these rules;

"doctor" means a registered medical practitioner not being the claimant;

"special statement" means the form prescribed in Part II of this Schedule.

2. Where a doctor advises a claimant to refrain from work on the basis of a written report which he has received from another doctor or where a doctor has not issued a statement since the claimant was examined and he wishes to issue a statement more than a day after the examination he shall use the special statement.

3. The special statement shall be completed in the manner described in paragraph 5 of Part I to Schedule 1.

4. Subject to rules 5 and 6 below, the diagnosis of the claimant's disorder in respect of which the doctor is advising the claimant to refrain from work or as the case may be, which has caused the claimant's absence from work shall be specified as precisely as the doctor's knowledge of the claimant's condition permits.

5. Where, in the doctor's opinion, a disclosure to the claimant of the precise disorder would be prejudicial to his well being, the diagnosis may be specified less precisely.

6. In a case of a disorder stated by the claimant to have caused incapacity for work, where—

    (a) no clinical signs have been found of that disorder, and

    (b) in the doctor's opinion, the claimant need not refrain from work, instead of specifying a diagnosis "unspecified" may be entered.

7. Part B of the special statement must only be given on a date not later than one month after the date of the written report on which the special statement is based and that part shall only be used where the claimant is being advised to refrain from work for a specified period of not more than one month.

PART II

FORM OF SPECIAL STATEMENT

2.563   FOR SOCIAL SECURITY AND   Special Statement
            STATUTORY SICK PAY   by the Doctor
            PURPOSES ONLY

In confidence to

Mr./Mrs./Miss/Ms ....

(A) I have examined you on the   (B) I have not examined you but, on the
                                       basis of a recent written report from—
following dates ....   Doctor ....(Name if known)
....   of ....
....
and advised you that you should   .... (Address)
refrain from work   I have advised you that should refrain

From .... to ....   from work for/until ....

Diagnosis of your disorder
causing absence from work ....
Doctor's remarks

Doctor's   Date of
signature   signing

The special circumstances in which this form may be used are described in the handbook "Medical Evidence for Social Security and Statutory Sick Pay purposes".

AMENDMENT

1. The Social Security (Miscellaneous Provisions) Amendments Regulations 1992 (SI 1992/247), reg.3 (March 9, 1992).

SCHEDULE 1B   **Regulation 2(1)(c)**

PART I

RULES

1. In these rules, unless the context otherwise requires—   2.564

 "claimant" means the person in respect of whom a statement is given in accordance with these rules;
 "doctor" means a registered medical practitioner not being the claimant;
 [⁴ "personal capability assesment"] means a statement given by a doctor in accordance with these rules.

2. Where the Secretary of State has requested that the claimant provide an all work test statement, that statement shall be provided in the form prescribed in Part II of this Schedule notwithstanding that the claimant has already provided a statement in accordance with Schedule 1 or 1A.
3. The all work test statement shall be completed in accordance with rules 3, 4, 5 [² and 9 to 13] of Part I to Schedule 1.
4. Subject to rule 5 below, the diagnosis of—
 (a) the disorder in respect of which the doctor is advising the claimant to refrain from work or, as the case may be, which has caused the claimant's absence from work; and
 (b) any other condition which could affect the claimant's capacity for work, shall be specified as precisely as the doctor's knowledge of the claimant's condition at the time of the examination permits.
5. Where, in the doctor's opinion, a disclosure to the claimant of the precise disorder would be prejudicial to his well being, the diagnosis may be specified less precisely.
6. The notes set out in Part III of this Schedule shall accompany the form of doctor's statement provided by the Secretary of State.

PART II

FORM OF DOCTOR'S STATEMENT

                        2.565

THIS STATEMENT SHOULD <u>NOT</u> BE USED FOR PEOPLE CLAIMING STATUTORY SICK PAY FROM THEIR EMPLOYER.

Doctor's Statement

In confidence to
Mr/Mrs/Miss/Ms ....

 Note for Doctor—We are making an assessment of your patient's eligibility for incapacity Benefit and other state benefits under the terms [⁴personal capability assesment]. Please complete the following boxes.

Main diagnosis (*be as precise as possible*) ....

Other diagnoses ....

<u>Doctor's remarks</u>
(Including comments on the disabling effects of the condition, treatment and progress—accuracy and detail will avoid requests for completion of a medical report).
 Note for Doctor—While the all work test is being carried out, we need evidence that your patient should refrain from <u>his usual occupation</u>. Please provide the following information (which will not be part of the [³ perpetual capability assessment).

667

I am issuing the following statement based upon the current guidance to certifying medical practitioners. I examined you today/yesterday and advised you that:

(a) You need not refrain from your usual occupation	(b) You should refrain from your usual occupation

for (*insert period*) ....

OR until ....

Doctor's signature	Date of signing

Form
Med 4

PART III

THE NOTES

The following notes shall accompany the form of doctor's statement provided by the Secretary of State:

2.566   1. After the words on the doctor's statement "you should refrain from your usual occupation"—

  (i)   if the patient is being given a date when he can return to work, the date entered should not be more than 2 weeks after the date on which the statement is issued;

  (ii) if recovery of capacity for work in the foreseeable future is not expected, "further notice" may be entered.

2. The "remarks" box should be used to provide additional information; including further details of diagnosed conditions, the disabling effect of such conditions, and notes on the patient's treatment and progress. Accuracy and detail will avoid requests for completion of a medical report.

3. The "remarks" box should also be used to state whether or not the patient is able to travel a reasonable distance to a medical examination as a result of his condition. If no entry is made, it will be assumed that the patient can travel.

4. This form of doctor's statement should not be used where the patient is claiming statutory sick pay from their employer. Form Med 3 should be used for that purpose.

AMENDMENTS

1. The Social Security (Medical Evidence) Amendment Regulations 1994 (SI 1994/2975), reg.3 (April 13, 1995).

2. The Social Security (Incapacity for Work) Miscellaneous Amendments Regulations 1995 (SI 1995/987), reg.4 (April 13, 1995).

3. The Social Security (Incapacity) Miscellaneous Amendments Regulations 2000 (SI 2000/590), reg.6 (April 3, 2000).

4. The Social Security (Incapacity for Work) Miscellaneous Amendments Regulations 1999 (SI 1999/3109), reg.5(b) (April 3, 2000).

[¹]SCHEDULE 2   **Regulation 2(3)**

PART I

RULES

1. In these rules any reference to a woman is a reference to the woman in respect of whom   **2.567**
a maternity certificate is given in accordance with these rules.
    2. A maternity certificate shall be given by a doctor or registered midwife attending the
woman and shall not be given by the woman herself.
    3. The maternity certificate shall be on a form provided by the Secretary of State for the
purpose and the wording shall be that set out in the appropriate part of the form specified in
Part II of this Schedule.
    4. Every maternity certificate shall be completed in ink or other indelible substance and shall   **2.568**
contain the following particulars—
    (a)   the woman's name;
    (b)   the week in which the woman is expected to be confined or, if the maternity certificate
         is given after confinement, the date of that confinement and the date the confinement
         was expected to take place [² . . .];
    (c)   the date of the examination on which the maternity certificate is based;
    (d)   the date on which the maternity certificate is signed; and
    (e)   the address of the doctor or where the maternity certificate is signed by a registered
         midwife the personal identification number given to her by the United Kingdom
         Central Council for Nursing, Midwifery and Health Visiting ("UKCC") on her regis-
         tration in Part 10 of the register maintained under section 10 of the Nurses, Midwives
         and Health Visitors Act 1979 and the expiry date of that registration,
and shall bear opposite the word "Signature", the signature of the person giving the maternity
certificate written after there has been entered on the maternity certificate the woman's name
and the expected date or, as the case may be, the date of the confinement.
    5. After a maternity certificate has been given, no further maternity certificate based on
the same examination shall be furnished other than a maternity certificate by way of replacement of an original which has been lost or mislaid, in which case it shall be clearly marked
"duplicate".

[²]PART II

FORM OF CERTIFICATE

MATERNITY CERTIFICATE   **2.569**

Please fill in this form in ink

Name of patient

Fill in this part if you are giving the certificate before the confinement. *Do not fill this in more [³ than 20 weeks] before the week the baby is expected.*	*Fill in this part if you are giving the certificate after the confinement.* I certify that I attended you in connection with the birth which took place on
I certify that I examined you on the date given below. In my opinion you can expect to have your baby in the week that includes ..../.........../........ *Week means a period of 7 days starting on a Sunday and ending on a Saturday.*	......./.........../........ when you were delivered of a child [ ] children. In my opinion your baby was expected in the week that includes ..../.........../........

Date of examination ..../........./........

Registered midwives

Date of signing ..../........./........

Please give your UKCC Personal
Identification Number and the expiry
date of your registration with the UKCC.

Signature

Doctors
Please stamp your name and address here
if the form has not been stamped by the [³
Primary Care Trust or Local Health Board
in whose medical performers list you are
included (or, in Scotland, by the Health Board
in whose primary medical services performers
list you are included)] in whose medical list
you are included.

AMENDMENTS

1. The Social Security (Medical Evidence) Amendment Regulations 1987 (SI 1987/409), reg.4 (April 6, 1987)
2. The Social Security (Miscellaneous Provisions) Amendment Regulations 1991 (SI 1991/2284), reg.21 (November 1, 1991)
3. General Medical Services and Personal Medical Services Transition and Consequential Provisions Order 2004 (SI 2004/865), Sch.1 (April 1, 2004).

The Social Security (Notification of Change of Circumstances) Regulations 2001

(SI 2001/3252)

Made   26th September 2001
Laid before Parliament   2nd October 2001
Coming into force   18th October 2001

ARRANGEMENT OF REGULATIONS

2.570   1.   Citation and commencement
           2.   Notification for purpose of sections 111A and 112 of the Social Security
                   Administration Act 1992
           3.   Change affecting jobseeker's allowance
           4.   Change affecting housing benefit or council tax benefit
           5.   Change affecting other benefit payment or advantage.

GENERAL NOTE

2.571   Section 16 of the Social Security Fraud Act 2001 (c.11), which came fully into force on October 18, 2001, amends the Administration Act 1992 to create new offences relating to failure to notify a change of circumstances, which affects entitlement to benefit. The requirements of the offences under the amended provisions of the Administration Act (which are not reproduced in Vol.III) are, broadly, fourfold (1) there has been a change of circumstances affecting entitlement to benefit, (2) the change is not excluded by regulations from changes which are required to be notified, (3) the person knows that the change affects entitlement to benefit, and (4) the person dishonestly fails to give a prompt notification in the prescribed manner to the prescribed person. These regulations set out the matter prescribed by the statute for the purposes of the criminal offences. The explanatory note to the regulations indicates that they are intended to mirror the existing requirements prescribed for the purposes of claims and payments under ss.5 and 6 of the Administration Act. The regulations are reproduced here so that those dealing with questions arising in the appeal tribunals and elsewhere in relation to claims for benefit are aware of the existence of these requirements under the criminal law. They may be referred to in overpayment cases.

The Secretary of State for Work and Pensions, in exercise of the powers conferred on him by ss.111A(1A), (1B), (1D) and (1E), 112(1A) to (1D), 189(1), (3) and (4) and 191 of the Social Security Administration Act 1992 and of all other powers enabling him in that behalf, and after consultation in respect of provisions of these Regulations relating to housing benefit and council tax benefit with organisations appearing to him to be representative of the authorities concerned, by this Instrument, which is made before the end of the period of 6 months from the coming into force of s.16 of the Social Security Fraud Act 2001, hereby makes the following Regulations:

Citation and commencement

1. These Regulations may be cited as the Social Security (Notification of Change of Circumstances) Regulations 2001 and shall come into force on 18th October 2001.

    2.572

Notification for purposes of sections 111A and 112 of the Social Security Administration Act 1992

2. Regulations 3 to 5 below prescribe the person to whom, and manner in which, a change of circumstances must be notified for the purposes of sections 111A(1A) to (1G) and 112(1A) to (1F) of the Social Security Administration Act 1992 (offences relating to failure to notify a change of circumstances).

    2.573

Change affecting jobseeker's allowance

3.—(1) Where the benefit affected by the change of circumstances is a jobseeker's allowance, notice must be given [¹ . . .] to the Secretary of State [¹ . . .] at the office that the claimant is required to attend in accordance with a notification given to him under regulation 23 of the Jobseeker's Allowance Regulations 1996—

    2.574

[¹ (a) in writing or by telephone (unless the Secretary of State determines in any particular case that notice must be in writing or may be given otherwise than in writing or by telephone); or

(b) in writing if in any class of case he requires written notice (unless he determines in any particular case to accept notice given otherwise than in writing).]

(2) In this regulation "Secretary of State" includes a person designated

as an employment officer by an order made by the Secretary of State under section 8(3) of the Jobseekers Act 1995.

AMENDMENT

1. The Social Security (Miscellaneous Amendments) (No.2) Regulations 2006 (SI 2006/832), reg.2 (April 10, 2006).

Change affecting housing benefit or council tax benefit

2.575   **4.**—(1) Where the benefit affected by the change of circumstances is housing benefit or council tax benefit, notice must be given or sent in writing to the relevant authority at—

(a) the designated office; or

(b) in a case where notification at another office is permitted under [¹ regulation 88 of the Housing Benefit Regulations 2006, regulation 69 of the Housing Benefit (Persons who have attained the qualifying age for state pension credit) Regulations 2006, regulation 74 of the Council Tax benefit Regulations 2006 or regulation 59 of the Council Tax benefit (persons who have attained the qualifying age for state pension credit) Regulations 2006] (duty to notify changes for claims and payments purposes), that other office.

(2) In this regulation "designated office" and "relevant authority" have the same meaning as in the [¹ Housing Benefit Regulations 2006, Housing Benefit (Persons who have attained the qualifying age for state pension credit) Regulations 2006, Council Tax benefit regulations 2006, and Council Tax benefit (Persons who have attained the qualifying age for state pension credit) Regulations 2006].

AMENDMENT

1. The Housing Benefit and Council Tax Benefit (Consequential Provisions) Regulation 2006 (SI 2006/217), Sch.2, para.19 (March 6, 2006).

Change affecting other benefit payment or advantage

2.576   **5.**—(1) Where the benefit or other payment or advantage affected by the change of circumstances is not a jobseeker's allowance, housing benefit or council tax benefit, notice must be given [³ . . .] to the Secretary of State [³ at the appropriate office—

(a) in writing or by telephone (unless the Secretary of State determines in any particular case that notice must be in writing or may be given otherwise than in writing or by telephone); or

(b) in writing if in any class of case he requires written notice (unless he determine in any particular case to accept notice given otherwise than in writing)]

[² (1ZA) Where this paragraph applies, where the notice in writing referred to in paragraph (1) is given or sent by an electronic communication that notice must be given or sent in accordance with the provisions set out in Schedule 9ZC to the Social Security (Claims and Payments) Regulations 1987 (electronic communication). (1ZB) Paragraph (1ZA) applies in relation to carer's allowance.]

[¹ (1A) The reference in paragraph (1) to notice "in writing" includes where that notice relates to child benefit, notice given or sent in accordance with Schedule 9C to the Social Security (Claims and Payments) Regulations 1987 (electronic communication).]

(2) In this regulation "the appropriate office" has the same meaning as in the Social Security (Claims and Payments) Regulations 1987.

AMENDMENTS

1. The Social Security (Electronic Communications) (Child Benefit) Order 2002 (SI 2002/1789), art.8 (October 28, 2002). These regulations are revoked with effect from December 1, 2003 by the Social Security (Electronic Communications) (Carer's Allowance) Order 2003, SI 2003/2800, reg.4.

2. The Social Security (Electronic Communications) (Carer's Allowance) Order 2003, SI 2003/2800, reg.3, (December 1, 2003).

3. The Social Security (Notification of Change of Circumstances) Regulations 2003, SI 2003/3209, reg.3 (January 6, 2004).

Social Security (Payments on Account, Overpayments and Recovery) Regulations 1988

(SI 1988/664) (AS AMENDED)

ARRANGEMENT OF REGULATIONS

PART I

GENERAL

PART II

INTERIM PAYMENTS

PART III

OFFSETTING

PART IV

PREVENTION OF DUPLICATION OF PAYMENTS

PART V

DIRECT CREDIT TRANSFER OVERPAYMENTS

PART VI

REVISION OF DETERMINATION AND CALCULATION OF AMOUNT RECOVERABLE

PART VII

THE PROCESS OF RECOVERY

PART VIII

RECOVERY BY DEDUCTIONS FROM EARNINGS FOLLOWING TRADE DISPUTE

PART IX

REVOCATIONS, TRANSITIONAL PROVISIONS AND SAVINGS

30.   Revocations.
31.   Transitional provisions and savings.

Whereas a draft of the following Regulations was laid before Parliament in accordance with the provisions of section 83(3)(b) of the Social Security Act 1986 and approved by resolution of each House of Parliament.

Now, therefore, the Secretary of State for Social services, in exercise of the powers conferred upon him by sections 23(8), 27, 51(1)(t) and (u), 55, 83(1), 84(1) and 89 of that Act and all other powers enabling him in that behalf, by this instrument, which contains only regulations made under the sections of the Social Security Act 1986 specified above and provisions consequential on those sections and which is made before the end of a period of 12 months from the commencement of those sections, makes the following Regulations:

PART I

GENERAL

Citation, commencement and interpretation

1.—(1) These regulations may be cited as the Social Security (Payments on account, Overpayments and Recovery) Regulations 1988 and shall come into force on 6th April 1988.

2.578

(2) In these Regulations, unless the context otherwise requires—

"the Act" means the Social Security Act 1986;

[¹⁰ "the Administration Act" means the Social Security Administration Act 1992;]

[⁵ "adjudicating authority" means, as the case may require, the Secretary of State, [¹² the First-tier Tribunal or the Upper Tribunal;]]

"benefit" means [⁹ a jobseeker's allowance, state pension credit [¹¹ , an employment and support allowance] and] any benefit under the Social Security Act 1975 [SSCBA, Parts II to V], child benefit, family credit, income support and [¹any social fund payment under sections 32(2)(a) and 32(2A) of the Act [SSCBA, s.138(1)(a) and (2)] [³and any incapacity benefit under sections 30A(1) and (5) of the Contributions and Benefits Act]];

[⁸ "bereavement benefit" means a benefit referred to in section 20(1)(ea) of the Contributions and Benefits Act;

"bereavement payment" means the sum specified in Part II of Schedule 4 to the Contributions and Benefits Act and referred to in section 36 of that Act;]

[⁶"the Board" means the Commissioners of Inland Revenue]

"child benefit" means benefit under Part I of the Child Benefit Act 1975 [SSCBA, Part IX];

"the Claims and Payments Regulations" means the Social Security (Claims and Payments) Regulations 1987;

675

[³"the Contributions and Benefits Act" means the Social Security Contributions and Benefits Act 1992;]

[²"disability living allowance" means a disability living allowance under section 37ZA of the Social Security Act 1975 [SSCBA, s.71];

[⁷ "disabled person's tax credit" means a disabled person's tax credit under section 129 of the Contributions and Benefits Act and, in relation to things done, or falling to be done, prior to 5th October 1999, shall include a reference to disability working allowance;] [⁷. . .]

[¹¹ "the Employment and Support Allowance Regulations" means the Employment and Support Allowance Regulations 2008;]

"guardian's allowance" means an allowance under section 38 of the Social Security Act 1975 [SSCBA, s.77];

"income support" means income support under Part II of the Act [SSCBA, Part VII] and includes personal expenses addition, special transitional addition and transitional addition as defined in the Income Support (Transitional) Regulations 1987;

"Income Support Regulations" means the Income Support (General) Regulations 1987;

[⁴ "Jobseeker's Allowance Regulations" means the Jobseeker's Allowance Regulations 1996;]

"severe disablement allowance" means an allowance under section 36 of the Social Security Act 1975 [SSCBA, s.68].

[⁹ "state pension credit" means the benefit payable under the State Pension Credit Act 2002;

"the State Pension Credit Regulations" means the State Pension Credit Regulations 2002]

[⁷ "start notification" means a notification of entitlement to tax credit furnished to an employer by the Board, referred to in section 6(2)(a) of the Tax Credits Act 1999;

"tax credit" means working families' tax credit or disabled person's tax credit;

[¹¹ "the Welfare Reform Act means the Welfare Reform Act 2007;]

"working families' tax credit" means working families' tax credit under section 128 of the Contributions and Benefits Act and, in relation to things done, or falling to be done, prior to 5th October 1999 shall include a reference to family credit.]

(3) Unless the context otherwise requires, any reference in these regulations to a numbered Part or regulation is a reference to the Part or regulation bearing that number in these Regulations and any reference in a regulation to a numbered paragraph is a reference to the paragraph of that regulation bearing that number.

<small>AMENDMENTS</small>

1. The Social Security (Payments on account, Overpayments and Recovery) Amendments Regulations 1989 (SI 1989/136), reg.3 (February 27, 1989).

2. The Disability Living Allowance and Disability Working Allowance (Consequential Provisions) Regulations 1991 (SI 1991/2742), reg.15 (April 6, 1992).

3. The Social Security (Incapacity Benefit) (Consequential and Transitional Amendments and Savings) Regulations 1995 (SI 1995/829), reg.21(2) (April 13, 1995).

4. The Social Security and Child Support (Jobseeker's Allowance) (Consequential Amendments) Regulations 1996 (SI 1996/1345), reg.23(2) (October 7, 1996).

5. The Social Security Act 1998 (Commencement No.12 and Consequential and Transitional Provisions) Order 1999 (SI 1999/3178), Sch.9, para.1, (November 29, 1999).

6. For tax credits purposes only these words substituted by The Tax Credits (Payments on Account, Overpayments and Recovery) (Amendment) Regulations 1999 (SI 1999/2571), reg.3 (October 5, 1999).

7. The Tax Credits (Payments on Account, Overpayments and Recovery) (Amendment) Regulations 1999 (SI 1999/2571), reg.3 (October 5, 1999).

8. The Social Security (Benefits for Widows and Widowers) (Consequential Amendments) Regulations 2000 (SI 2000/1483), reg.10 (April 9, 2001).

9. State Pension Credit (Consequential, Transitional and Miscellaneous Provisions) Regulations 2002 (SI 2002/3019), reg.24 (October 6, 2003).

10. The Social Security, Child Support and Tax Credits (Miscellaneous Amendments) Regulations 2005 (SI 2005/337), reg.10 (March 18, 2005).

11. The Employment and Support Allowance (Consequential Provisions) (No. 2) Regulations 2008 (SI 2008/1554), reg.52 (October 27, 2008).

12. The Tribunals, Courts and Enforcement Act 2007 (Transitional and Consequential Provisions) Order 2008 (SI 2008/2683) Sch.1, para.44 (November 3, 2008).

PART II

INTERIM PAYMENTS

Making of interim payments

2.—(1) [³Subject to paragraph (1A),] the Secretary of State may, in his discretion, [⁴ the Board may in their discretion] make an interim payment, that is to say a payment on account of any benefit to which it appears to him [⁴ them] that a person is or may be entitled [⁶ (or, where subparagraph (a) applies, entitled apart from satisfying the condition of making a claim)], in the following circumstances—

2.579

(a) a claim for that benefit has not been made in accordance with the Claims and Payments Regulations and it is impracticable for such a claim to be made immediately [⁶, including where it is impracticable to satisfy immediately the national insurance number requirements in section 1(1A) and (1B) of the Administration Act]; or

(b) a claim for that benefit has been so made, but it is impracticable for it or [⁵ an] application or appeal which relates to it to be determined immediately; or

(c) an award of that benefit has been made but it is impracticable for the beneficiary to be paid immediately, except by means of an interim payment.

[⁶ (1A) Paragraph (1) shall not apply pending the determination of an appeal.]

(2) [¹Subject to paragraph (3)] on or before the making of an interim payment the recipient shall be given notice in writing of his liability under this Part to have it brought into account and to repay any over-payment.

(3) Where the recipient of an interim payment of disability living allowance—

(a) is terminally ill within the meaning of [section 66(2) of the Social Security Contributions and Benefits Act 1992]; or

(b) had an invalid carriage or other vehicle provided by the Secretary of State under section 5(2)(a) of the National Health Service Act 1977 and Schedule 2 to that Act or under section 46 of the National Health Service (Scotland) Act 1978,

the requirement to give notice in paragraph (2) of this regulation shall be omitted.

[²(4) Where an interim payment of income support [⁷ or income-related employment and support allowance] is made because a payment to which the recipient is entitled by way of child support maintenance under the Child Support Act 1991, or periodical payments under a maintenance agreement within the meaning of section 9(1) of that Act or under a maintenance order within the meaning of section 107(15) of the Social Security Administration Act 1992, has not been made, the requirement in paragraph (2) of this regulation to give notice shall be omitted.]

AMENDMENTS

1. The Disability Living Allowance and Disability Working Allowance (Consequential Provisions) Regulations 1991 (SI 1991/2742), reg.15 (April 6, 1992).

2. The Social Security (Payments on account, Overpayments and Recovery) Amendment Regulations 1993 (SI 1993/650), reg.2 (April 5, 1993).

3. The Social Security (Persons from Abroad) Miscellaneous Amendments Regulations 1996 (SI 1996/30), reg.10 (February 5, 1996).

4. For tax credits purposes only The Tax Credits (Payments on Account, Overpayments and Recovery) (Amendment) Regulations 1999 (SI 1999/2571), reg.4 (October 5, 1999).

5. The Social Security Act 1998 (Commencement No.9, and Savings and Consequential and Transitional Provisions) Order 1999 (SI 1999/2422), Sch.8 (September 6, 1999).

6. The Social Security, Child Support and Tax Credits (Miscellaneous Amendments) Regulations 2005 (SI 2005/337), reg.10 (March 18, 2005).

7. The Employment and Support Allowance (Consequential Provisions) (No. 2) Regulations 2008 (SI 2008/1554), reg.52 (October 27, 2008).

GENERAL NOTE

2.580 Interim payments are made at the discretion of the Secretary of State. Thus there is no right of appeal and any refusal can only be challenged (other than by making further representations) by judicial review. The test under para.(1) is not whether it is "clear" that the person will qualify for a particular benefit, but whether it appears to the Secretary of State that he "is or may be entitled" to that benefit (*R. v Secretary of State for Social Security Ex p. Sarwar, Getachew and Urbanek* (1995) 7 Admin. L.R. 781). Thus the Secretary of State can decide to make interim payments even where entitlement to, for example, income support is not certain. Interim payments are recoverable if the person is subsequently found not to be entitled to the benefit claimed (see reg.4).

The introduction of an habitual residence rule for income support from August 1, 1994 (see the additional definition of "person from abroad" in reg.21(3) of the Income Support Regulations) focussed fresh attention on this regulation. Most claimants who fail the test were not eligible for urgent cases payments under reg.70(3) of the Income Support Regulations, even before the February 1996 changes, and so face a delay of what can be several months until their appeal is heard without any benefit. This led to many claimants asking for interim payments pending the hearing of their appeals which in a few cases at least were paid. But this in turn precipitated the introduction of para.(1A).

Under para.(1A), in force from February 5, 1996, an interim payment will not be made if an appeal is pending unless the Secretary of State considers that there *is* entitlement to benefit. (See *R. v Secretary of State for Social Security Ex p. Grant* (High Court, July 31, 1997.)) This change is apparently to restore the original policy intention that interim payments could be made where entitlement was clear but the amount of benefit due was not (para.46 of the DSS Explanatory Memorandum to the Social Security Advisory Committee (Cm.3062/1996)). But the wording of para.(1)(b) and the first part of reg.4(3)(ii) somewhat belies this. Moreover, if the case involves a point of Community law (as, e.g. an appeal concerning the habitual residence test may do), para.(1A) could be in breach of Community law in so far as it prevents the Secretary of State from having the power to grant interim relief (see *Factortame Ltd v Secretary of State for Transport (No.2)* [1991] 1 A.C. 603, [1991] 1 All E.R. 70).

In a ruling made in the appeal *CDLA/913/1994*, reported as *R(DLA) 4/99* and *R(DLA)5/99* the Commissioner held that he had no jurisdiction to order interim payment of benefit where a question had been referred to the European Court of Justice for a preliminary ruling. The case in which the question arose was concerned with entitlement, not payment, and to make such an order would go beyond what was required by Community law. The Commissioner left it open whether there was jurisdiction to make an interim or provisional award of benefit in such circumstances, since he was satisfied that, even if such a power exists, he would not exercise his discretion to make an award.

That ruling was challenged by way of judicial review. In *R. v Social Security Commisioner Ex p. Snares* [1997] C.O.D. 403, Popplewell J. rejected the challenge. He decided that the exercise of discretion by the Commissioner could not be impugned. Unfortunately, however, Popplewell J. did not adopt the distinction made by the Commissioner between an award of entitlement and an order for payment and tended to run the two issues together. If it had been necessary to the determination, he would have regarded the question of the interim remedies available pending a ruling by the Court of Justice as not *acte claire* and would have made a further reference to the Court of Justice.

Bringing interim payments into account

[¹3. [²Subject to paragraph (2)] where it is practicable to do so and, where notice is required to be given under regulation 2(2), such notice has been given—
    (a) any interim payment, other than an interim payment made in the circumstances mentioned in regulation 2(4),—
        (i) which was made in anticipation of an award of benefit shall be offset by the adjudicating authority in reduction of the benefit to be awarded; and
        (ii) whether or not made in anticipation of an award, which is not offset under sub-paragraph (i) shall be deducted by the Secretary of State from—
           (a) the sum payable under the award of benefit on account of which the interim payment was made; or
           (b) any sum payable under any subsequent award of the same benefit to the same person; and
    (b) any interim payment made in the circumstances mentioned in regulation 2(4) shall be offset by the Secretary of State against any sum received by him in respect of arrears of child support maintenance payable to the person to whom the interim payment was made.]

[²(2) Where the interim payment in paragraph (1)(a) is a payment on account of tax credit, paragraph (1)(a), but not paragraph (1)(b), shall

2.581

679

apply with the modification that, for the words "Secretary of State" there is substituted the word "Board".]

AMENDMENTS

1. The Social Security (Payments on account, Overpayments and Recovery) Amendment Regulations 1993 (SI 1993/650), reg.2 (April 5, 1993).
2. The Tax Credits (Payments on Account, Overpayments and Recovery) (Amendment) Regulations 1999 (SI 1999/2571), reg.5 (October 5, 1999).

Recovery of overpaid interim payments

2.582   **4.**—(1) Where the adjudicating authority has determined that an interim payment has been overpaid in circumstances which fall within paragraph (3) and [¹where notice is required to be given under regulation 2(2), such notice has been given], that authority shall determine the amount of the overpayment.

(2) The amount of the overpayment shall be recoverable by the Secretary of State, by the same procedures and subject to the same conditions as if it were recoverable under section 53(1) of the Act [SSAA, s.71(1)].

(3) The circumstances in which an interim payment may be determined to have been overpaid are as follows—

(a) an interim payment has been made under regulation 2(1)(a) or (b) but—
  (i) the recipient has failed to make a claim in accordance with the Claims and Payments Regulations as soon as practicable, or has made a claim which is either defective or is not made on the form approved for the time being by the Secretary of State and the Secretary of State has not treated the claim as duly made under regulation 4(7) of the Claims and Payments Regulations; or
  (ii) it has been determined that there is no entitlement on the claim, or that the entitlement is less than the amount of the interim payment or that benefit is not payable; or
  (iii) the claim has been withdrawn under regulation 5(2) of the Claims and Payments Regulations; or

(b) an interim payment has been made under regulation 2(1)(c) which exceeds the entitlement under the award of benefit on account of which the interim payment was made[¹; or

(c) an interim payment of income support [³ or an income-related employment and support allowance] has been made under regulation 2(1)(b) in the circumstances mentioned in regulation 2(4).]

(4) For the purposes of this regulation a claim is defective if it is made on the form approved for the time being by the Secretary of State but is not completed in accordance with the instructions on the form.

[²(5) Where the interim payment in paragraph (1)(a) is a payment on account of tax credit, paragraph (1)(a), but not paragraph (1)(b), shall apply with the modification that, for the words "Secretary of State" there is substituted the word "Board".]

AMENDMENTS

1. The Social Security (Payments on account, Overpayments and Recovery) Amendment Regulations 1993 (SI 1993/650), reg.2 (April 5, 1993).

2. The Tax Credits (Payments on Account, Overpayments and Recovery) (Amendment) Regulations 1999 (SI 1999/2571), reg.5 (October 5, 1999).

3. The Employment and Support Allowance (Consequential Provisions) (No. 2) Regulations 2008 (SI 2008/1554), reg.52 (October 27, 2008).

PART III

OFFSETTING

Offsetting prior payment against subsequent award

5.—(1) Subject to [² paragraphs (1A) [⁷, (2A) and (6)] and] regulation 6 (exception from offset of recoverable overpayment), any sum paid in respect of a period covered by a subsequent determination in any of the cases set out in paragraph (2) shall be offset against arrears of entitlement under the subsequent determination and, except to the extent that the sum exceeds the arrears, shall be treated as properly paid on account of them.

[²(1A) In paragraph (1) the reference to "any sum paid" shall, in relation to tax credit, include a reference to any amount or calculation of tax credit payable in respect of a period to the date of subsequent determination, which is included in a start notification given by the Board to an employer, and for the payment of which the employer remains responsible.]

(2) Paragraph (1) applies in the following cases—

[⁶ *Case 1: Payment pursuant to a decision which is revised or superseded, or overturned on appeal*

Where a person has been paid a sum by way of benefit [or by way of a shared additional pension under section 55A of the Social Security Contributions and Benefits Act 1992] pursuant to a decision which is subsequently revised under section 9 of the Social Security Act 1998, superseded under Section 10 of that Act or overturned on appeal.]

Case 2: Award or payment of benefit in lieu
Where a person has been paid a sum by way benefit under the original award and it is subsequently determined, . . ., that another benefit should be awarded or is payable in lieu of the first.

Case 3: Child benefit and severe disablement allowance
Where either—

(a) a person has been awarded and paid child benefit for a period in respect of which severe disablement allowance [⁴ or incapacity benefit for persons incapacitated in youth in accordance with section 30(A)(1)(b) and (2A) of the Contributions and Benefits Act] is subsequently determined to be payable to the child concerned, or

(b) severe disablement allowance [⁴ or incapacity benefit for persons incapacitated in youth in accordance with section 30(A)(1)(b) and (2A) of the Contributions and Benefits Act] is awarded and paid for a period in respect of which child benefit is subsequently awarded to someone else, the child concerned in the subsequent determination being the beneficiary of the original award.

Case 4: Increase of benefit for dependant
Where a person has been paid a sum by way of an increase in respect of a dependent person under the original award and it is subsequently determined that that other person is entitled to benefit for that period, or

2.583

that a third person is entitled to the increase for that period in priority to the beneficiary of the original award.

Case 5: Increase of benefit for partner

Where a person has been paid a sum by way of an increase in respect of a partner (as defined in regulation 2 of the Income Support Regulations) and it is subsequently determined that that other person is entitled to benefit for that period.

[[2] (2A) In paragraph (2), Case 2 shall not apply where either—

(a) the sum paid under the original award, or

(b) the subsequent decision on the revision, supersession or appeal,

referred to in the Case (but not both) is or relates to tax credit.]

(3) Where an amount has been deducted under regulation 13(b) (sums to be deducted in calculating recoverable amounts) an equivalent sum shall be offset against any arrears of entitlement of that person under a subsequent award of [[5] income support, state pension credit and] [[1], or income-based jobseeker's allowance] [[8] or an income related employment and support allowance] [[8] or an income-related employment and support allowance] for the period to which the deducted amount relates.

(4) Where child benefit which has been paid under an award in favour of a person (the original beneficiary) is subsequently awarded to someone else for any week, the benefit shall nevertheless be treated as properly paid if it was received by someone other than the original beneficiary, who—

(a) either had the child living with him or was contributing towards the cost of providing for the child at a weekly rate which was not less than the weekly rate under the original award, and

(b) could have been entitled to child benefit in respect of that child for that week had a claim been made in time.

(5) Any amount which is treated, under paragraph (4), as properly paid shall be deducted from the amount payable to the beneficiary under the subsequent award.

[[7] (6) Subject to regulation 6, any sums under—

(a) Schedule 5 or 5A to the Contributions and Benefits Act (pension increases or lump sum where entitlement to retirement pension or shared additional pension is deferred); or

(b) Schedule 1 to the Social Security (Graduated Retirement Benefit) Regulations 2005 (increases or lump sum where entitlement to greaduate retirement benefit is deferred),

Paid pursuant to a decision which is subsequently revised under section 9 of the Social Security Act 1998, superseded under section 10 of that Act or overturned on appeal, shall be offset against any sums due under the subsequent determination and, except to the extent that the sum exceeds the amount now due, shall be treated as properly paid on account of it.]

AMENDMENTS

1. The Social Security and Child Support (Jobseeker's Allowance) (Consequential Amendments) Regulations 1996 (SI 1996/1345), reg.23(5) and (6) (October 7, 1996).

2. The Tax Credits (Payments on Account, Overpayments and Recovery) (Amendment) Regulations 1999 (SI 1999/2571), reg.7 (October 5, 1999).

3. The Social Security Act 1998 (Commencement No.11 and Transitional Provisions) Order 1999 (SI 1999/2860), Sch.4 (October 18, 1999).

4. The Social Security (Incapacity Benefits) Miscellaneous Amendments Regulations 2000 (SI 2000/3120), reg.5 (April 6, 2001).

5. State Pension Credit (Consequential, Transitional and Miscellaneous Provisions) Regulations 2002 (SI 2002/3019), reg.24 (October 6, 2003).

6. The Social Security (Shared Additional Pension) (Miscellaneous Amendments) Regulations 2005 (SI 2005/1551) (July 6, 2005).

7. The Social Security (Deferral of Retirement Pensions etc.) Regulations 2006 (SI 2006/516) (April 6, 2006).

8. The Employment and Support Allowance (Consequential Provisions) (No. 2) Regulations 2008 (SI 2008/1554), reg.52 (October 27, 2008).

GENERAL NOTE

This regulation contains important powers to deal with cases where a subsequent award of one benefit replaces an earlier award of a different benefit. It enables the benefit originally awarded to be treated as paid on account of the benefit subsequently awarded. The circumstances in which the power is available are spelled out in the five cases listed in the regulation. Tribunals may need to refer to this power when the result of their decision is to substitute one benefit for another which has already been awarded.

In *Brown v Secretary of State for Work and Pensions* [2006] EWCA Civ 89, reported as *R(DLA) 2/07*, the Court of appeal, interpreting reg.5(1) ruled that where payments of disability living allowance had been suspended because there has been an overpayment, and a new decision made, payments subsequently awarded could not be offset against the irrecoverable overpayment, since the amount of payments would vary depending on how long it took for the new decision to be reached.

The Department has issued fresh guidance following this case, which can be found at Memo DMG 17/07.

2.584

Exception from offset of recoverable overpayment

6. No amount may be offset under regulation 5(1) which has been determined to be a recoverable overpayment for the purposes of section 53(1) of the Act [SSAA, s.71(1)].

2.585

PART IV

PREVENTION OF DUPLICATION OF PAYMENTS

Duplication and prescribed income

7.—[¹ (1) For the purposes of section 74(1) of the Social Security Administration Act 1992 (⁴ income support, state pension credit and] [⁶, income-based jobseeker's allowance, income-related employment and support allowance] and other payments), a person's prescribed income is—

(a) income required to be taken into account in accordance with Part V of the Income Support Regulations [³or, as the case may be, Part VIII of the Jobseeker's Allowance Regulations] [⁴ or Part III of the State Pension Credit Regulations] [⁵ or Part 10 of the Employment and Support Allowance Regulations], except for the income specified in sub-paragraph (b); and]

[²(b) income which, if it were actually paid, would be required to be taken into account in accordance with Chapter VIIA of Part V of the Income Support Regulations [³or, as the case may be, Chapter VIII of Part VIII of the Jobseeker's Allowance Regulations] (child support maintenance); [⁵ or Chapter 9 of Part 10 to the Employment and Support Allowance Regulations (child support)] but only in so

2.586

far as it relates to the period beginning with the effective date of the maintenance assessment under which it is payable, as determined in accordance with regulation 30 of the Child Support (Maintenance Assessment Procedure) Regulations 1992, and ending with the first day which is a day specified by the Secretary of State under regulation 4(1) of the Child Support (Collection and Enforcement) Regulations 1992 as being a day on which payment of child support maintenance under that maintenance assessment is due.]

(2) The prescribed date in relation to any payment of income prescribed by [¹paragraph (1)(a)] is—

(a) where it is made in respect of a specific day or period, that day or the first day of the period;

(b) where it is not so made, the day or the first day of the period to which it is fairly attributable.

[²(3) Subject to paragraph (4), the prescribed date in relation to any payment of income prescribed by paragraph (1)(b) is the last day of the maintenance period, determined in accordance with regulation 33 of the Child Support (Maintenance Assessment Procedure) Regulations 1992, to which it relates.

(4) Where the period referred to in paragraph (1)(b) does not consist of a number of complete maintenance periods the prescribed date in relation to income prescribed by that sub-paragraph which relates to any part of that period which is not a complete maintenance period is the last day of that period.]

AMENDMENTS

1. The Social Security (Payments on account, Overpayments and Recovery) Amendment Regulations 1993 (SI 1993/650), reg.2, as amended by The Social Security (Miscellaneous Provisions) Amendment Regulations 1993 (SI 1993/846), reg.4 (April 5, 1993).

2. The Social Security (Payments on account, Overpayments and Recovery) Amendment Regulations 1993 (SI 1993/650), reg.2, as amended by The Social Security (Miscellaneous Provisions) Amendment Regulations 1993 (SI 1993/846), reg.4 (April 5, 1993).

3. The Social Security and Child Support (Jobseeker's Allowance) (Consequential Amendments) Regulations 1996 (SI 1996/1345), reg.23(3) (October 7, 1996).

4. State Pension Credit (Consequential, Transitional and Miscellaneous Provisions) Regulations 2002 (SI 2002/3019), reg.24 (October 6, 2003).

5. The Employment and Support Allowance (Consequential Provisions) (No. 2) Regulations 2008 (SI 2008/1554), reg.52 (October 27, 2008).

6. The Employment and Support Allowance (Miscellaneous Amendments) Regulations 2008 (SI 2008/2428), reg.22 (October 27, 2008).

GENERAL NOTE

2.587 See the notes to s.74(1) of the Administration Act.

Under s.54 of the Child Support Act 1991 "maintenance assessment" means an assessment of maintenance made under that Act, including, except where regulations prescribe otherwise, an interim assessment. Under reg.30 of the Child Support (Maintenance Assessment Procedure) Regulations 1992, the effective date of a new assessment is usually, when the application was made by the person with care of the child, the date on which a maintenance enquiry form was sent to the absent parent or, where the application was made by the absent parent, the date on which an effective maintenance form was received by the Secretary of State. Arrears will inevitably accrue while the assessment is being made. In the meantime income support or income-based JSA can be paid in full to the parent with care. When the arrears are paid, the amount of "overpaid" income support or JSA is recoverable under s.74(1) of the Administration Act.

See the notes to reg.60C of the Income Support (General) Regulations for the interaction with payments of other arrears of child support maintenance, which are excluded from the operation of s.74(1). Note also s.74A of the Administration Act and regs 55A and 60E of the Income Support Regulations and regs 119 and 127 of the Jobseeker's Allowance Regulations.

Duplication and prescribed payments

8.—(1) For the purposes of section [⁸ 74(2) of the Administration Act] (recovery of amount of benefit awarded because prescribed payment not made on prescribed date), the payment of any of the following is a prescribed payment—

2.588

(a) any benefit under the Social Security Act 1975 [SSCBA, Parts II to V] other than any grant or gratuity or a widow's payment;

(b) any child benefit;

(c) any family credit;

(d) any war disablement pension or war widow's pension which is not in the form of a gratuity and any payment which the Secretary of State accepts as analogous to any such pension;

(e) any allowance paid under the Job Release Act 1977;

(f) any allowance payable by or on behalf of [²Scottish Enterprise Highlands and Islands Enterprise or] [¹the Secretary of State] to or in respect of a person for his maintenance for any period during which he is following a course of training or instruction provided or approved by [²Scottish Enterprise Highlands and Islands Enterprise or] [¹the Secretary of State]

(g) any payment of benefit under the legislation of any member State other than the United Kingdom concerning the branches of social security mentioned in Article 4(1) of Regulation (EEC) No.1408/71 on the application of social security schemes to employed persons, to self-employed persons and to members of their families moving within the Community, whether or not the benefit has been acquired by virtue of the provisions of that Regulation;

[³. . .]

[⁶ (i) any bereavement benefit other than a bereavement payment.]

[⁸ (j) any contribution-based jobseeker's allowance within the meaning of section 1(4) of the Jobseekers Act.]

[⁹ (k) payments under the Financial Assistance Scheme Regulations 2005.]

(2) The prescribed date, in relation to any payment prescribed by paragraph (1) is the date by which receipt of or entitlement to that benefit would have to be notified to the Secretary of State if it were to be taken into account in determining, whether [⁵by way of revision or supersession], the amount of or entitlement to [⁷income support, a state pension credit] [⁴, or income-based jobseeker's allowance] [¹⁰ or income-related employment and support allowance].

AMENDMENTS

1. Employment Act 1989, Sch.5, paras 1 and 4 (November 16, 1989).

2. The Enterprise (Scotland) Consequential Amendments Order 1991 (SI 1991/387), art.14 (April 1, 1991).

3. The Tax Credits (Payments on Account, Overpayments and Recovery) (Amendment) Regulations 1999 (SI 1999/2571), reg.8 (October 5, 1999).

4. The Social Security and Child Support (Jobseeker's Allowance) (Consequential Amendments) Regulations 1996 (SI 1996/1345), reg.23(5) and (6) (October 7, 1996).

5. The Social Security Act 1998 (Commencement No.11 and Transitional Provisions) Order 1999 (SI 1999/2680), Sch.4 (October 18, 1999).

6. The Social Security (Benefits for Widows and Widowers) (Consequential Amendments) Regulations 2000 (SI 2000/1483), reg.10 (April 9, 2001).

7. State Pension Credit (Consequential, Transitional and Miscellaneous Provisions) Regulations 2002 (SI 2002/3019), reg.24 (October 6, 2003).

8. The Social Security, Child Support and Tax Credits (Miscellaneous Amendments) Regulations 2005 (SI 2005/337), reg.10 (March 18, 2005).

9. The Social Security (Payments on account, Overpayments and Recovery) Amendment Regulations 2005 (SI 2005/3476) (January 19, 2006).

10. The Employment and Support Allowance (Consequential Provisions) (No. 2) Regulations 2008 (SI 2008/1554), reg.52 (October 27, 2008).

GENERAL NOTE

2.589   See the notes to s.74(2) of the Administration Act.

R(IS) 14/94 concerned an overpayment of income support which arose from the award of invalid care allowance. The claimant was an elderly widow, whose daughter was her appointee. Income support was paid to the widow. The daughter was in receipt of invalid care allowance in respect of her mother. Recovery was sought under s.27 of the Social Security Act 1986 (now s.74 of the Administration Act) from the widow.

The claimant argued that the words in reg.8(2) "taken into account" meant that only the claimant's resources and requirements were to be considered. The Commissioner rejects such a narrow reading of the words and says that "the words 'into account' should be given a wide interpretation and in the context include 'take notice of'."

Duplication and maintenance payments

2.590   **9.** For the purposes of section 27(3) of the Act [SSAA, s.74(3)] (recovery of amount of benefit awarded because maintenance payments not made), the following benefits are prescribed—

(a) child benefit;

(b) increase for dependants of any benefit under the Social Security Act 1975 [SSCBA, Parts II to V];

(c) child's special allowance under section 31 of the Social Security Act 1975 [SSCBA, s.56]; and

(d) guardian's allowance.

GENERAL NOTE

2.591   See the notes to s.74(3) of the Administration Act.

Conversion of payments made in a foreign currency

2.592   **10.** Where a payment of income prescribed by regulation 7(1), or a payment prescribed by regulation 8(1), is made in a currency other than sterling, its value in sterling, for the purposes of section 27 of the Act [SSAA, s.74] and this Part, shall be determined, after conversion by the Bank of England, or by [¹any institution which is authorised under the Banking Act 1987], as the net sterling sum into which it is converted, after any banking charge or commission on the transaction has been deducted.

AMENDMENT

1. The Social Security (Payments on Account, Overpayments and Recovery) (Amendment) Regulations 1988 (SI 1988/688), reg.2(2) (April 11, 1988).

PART V

DIRECT CREDIT TRANSFER OVERPAYMENTS

Recovery of overpayments by automated or other direct credit transfer

11.—(1) [¹ Subject to paragraph (4)] where it is determined by the adjudicating authority that a payment in excess of entitlement has been credited to a bank or other account under an arrangement for automated or other direct credit transfer made in accordance with regulation 21 of the Claims and Payments Regulations and that the conditions prescribed by paragraph (2) are satisfied, the excess, or the specified part of it to which the Secretary of State's certificate relates, shall be recoverable under this regulation.

(2) The prescribed conditions for recoverability under paragraph (1) are as follows—

  (a) the Secretary of State has certified that the payment in excess of entitlement, or a specified part of it, is materially due to the arrangements for payments to be made by automated or other direct credit transfer; and

[² (b) notice of the effect to which this regulation would have, in the event of an overpayment, was given to the beneficiary or to a person acting form his—

    (i) in writing, where the claim was made in writing; or

    (ii) either orally or in writing, where the claim was made by telephone

before he agreed to the arrangement.]

(3) Where the arrangement was agreed to before April 6, 1987 the condition prescribed by paragraph (2)(b) need not be satisfied in any case where the application for benefit to be paid by automated or other direct credit transfer contained a statement, or was accompanied by a written statement made by the applicant, which complied with the provisions of regulation 16A(3)(b) and (8) of the Social Security (Claims and Payments) Regulations 1979 or, as the case may be, regulation 7(2)(b) and (6) of the Child Benefit (Claims and Payments) Regulations 1984.

[¹Where the payment mention in paragraph (1) is a payment of tax credit, paragraphs (1) and (2) shall apply with the modifications that—

  (a) in paragraph (1) for the words "Secretary of State" there is substituted the words "Board's", and

  (b) in paragraph (2) for the words "Secretary of State" there is substituted the word "Board".]

AMENDMENTS

1. The Tax Credits (Payments on Account, Overpayments and Recovery) (Amendment) Regulations 1999 (SI 1999/2571), reg.9 (October 5, 1999).

2.593

2. The Social Security (Claims and Payments and Payments on account, Overpayments and Recovery) Amendment Regulations 2005 (SI 2005/34), reg.3 (May 2, 2005).

PART VI

CALCULATION OF AMOUNT RECOVERABLE

Circumstances in which determination need not be revised

2.594   **12.** [² Section 71(5) or (5A) of the Administration Act] (recoverability dependent on reversal, variation, revision [¹ or supersession] of determination) shall not apply where the fact and circumstances of the misrepresentation or non-disclosure do not provide a basis for [¹ the decision pursuant to which the payment was made to be revised under section 9 of the Social Security Act 1998 or superseded under section 10 of that Act.]

AMENDMENTS

1. The Social Security Act 1998 (Commencement No.9, and Savings and Consequential and Transitional Provisions) Order 1999 (SI 1999/2422), Sch.8 (September 6, 1999).
2. The Social Security, Child Support and Tax Credits (Miscellaneous Amendments) Regulations 2005 (SI 2005/337), reg.10 (March 18, 2005).

GENERAL NOTE

2.595   See the notes to s.71(5A) of the Administration Act.

Sums to be deducted in calculating recoverable amounts

2.596   **13.**—[² Subject to paragraph (2)] in calculating the amounts recoverable under section 53(1) of the Act [SSAA, s.71(1)] or regulation 11, where there has been an overpayment of benefit, the adjudicating authority shall deduct—
    (a) any amount which has been offset under Part III;
    (b) any additional amount of income support [³ or state pension credit] [¹, or income-based jobseeker's allowance] which was not payable under the original, or any other, determination, but which should have been determined to be payable—
        (i) on the basis of the claim as presented to the adjudicating authority, or
        (ii) on the basis of the claim as it would have appeared had the misrepresentation or non-disclosure been remedied before the determination;
but no other deduction shall be made in respect of any other entitlement to benefit which may be, or might have been, determined to exist.
    [² (2) Paragraph (1) shall apply to tax credit only where both—
    (a) The overpayment of benefit referred to in paragraph (1), and
    (b) The amount referred to in sub-paragraph (a) of that paragraph,
Are tax credit, and with the modification that sub-paragraph (b) of that paragraph is omitted.]

AMENDMENTS

1. The Social Security and Child Support (Jobseeker's Allowance) (Consequential Amendments) Regulations 1996 (SI 1996/1345), reg.23(5) and (6) (October 7, 1996).

2. The Tax Credits (Payments on Account, Overpayments and Recovery) (Amendment) Regulations 1999 (SI 1999/2571), reg.11 (October 5, 1999).

3. State Pension Credit (Consequential, Transitional and Miscellaneous Provisions) Regulations 2002 (SI 2002/3019), reg.24 (October 6, 2003).

GENERAL NOTE

See the notes to s.71(1) and (2) of the Administration Act, 1992 for important case law affecting this provision.

2.597

In *CP/5257/1999* the Commissioner interpreted the poorly drafted reg.13 by holding that:

(a) the regulation is not limited to overpayments of income support or income-based jobseeker's allowance, but covers overpaid benefit other than these two benefits; and

(b) the regulation only applies where the benefit sought to be offset is income support or income-based jobseeker's allowance.

In *CIS/1777/2000* a different Commissioner said:

"[Regulation 13] was amended to include a reference to income-based jobseeker's allowance when that benefit was introduced in 1996. I do not read the provision as authorising the deduction from an overpayment of jobseeker's allowance that would have been paid if a claim for that benefit has been made rather than a claim for income support. Head (i) refers to the claim as presented—the claim as presented was for income support. Head (ii) refers to the claim as it would have appeared if the facts had been correctly represented—if the facts had been correctly known, the claim would have appeared as a claim for income support to which the claimant was not entitled. The claimant might have been advised by the Department of Social Security to make a claim for an income based jobseeker's allowance, but that would have been a different claim—there is no power for the Secretary of State to treat a claim for income support as a claim for income based jobseeker's allowance in the alternative under Schedule 1 to the Social Security (Claims and Payments) Regulations 1987." (para.9)

The interpretation of the regulation was revisited in *CIS/2291/2001* following the 1999 amendments. The Commissioner concludes:

"17. Although the wording is particularly obscure for such an important and potentially severe rule, the effect is clear. Anyone who is working or capable of work so as to exclude them from income support must claim jobseeker's allowance. If they do not, and they continue to receive income support, they risk losing both the income support actually received and the jobseeker's allowance they might have received.

18. Regulation 13 does not contain any discretion. That rests with the Secretary of State in deciding whether and how to collect any overpayment. No doubt the Secretary of State will take into account whether the public purse has in reality lost the sum claimed as overpaid or some other amount."

In *CDLA/3768/2002,* the Commissioner said:

"15. . . . the decision maker acting for the Secretary of State [in presenting the case to the tribunal] should first consider whether any amount has been offset under Part III (regulations 5 and 6 of the Social Security (Payments on Account, Overpayments and Recoveries) Regulations 1988. This may call for further enquiry, bearing in mind always that it is for the Secretary of State to meet any problems arising from conflicts of evidence or absence of proof of any relevant issue . . .

16. The other issues that regulation 13(1) requires the decision maker and tribunal to identify and deduct is:

'any additional amount of income support or income-based jobseeker's allowance which was not payable under the original or any other determination, but which should have been determined to be payable on the basis of the claim as presented to the adjudicating authority or on the basis of the claim as it would have appeared had the misrepresentation or nondisclosure been remedied before the determination'.

I have removed the punctuation for the reasons given in *CIS/2291/2001*. Regulation 13(1) then emphasises that no other deduction shall be made for any other actual or hypothetical entitlement."

In the particular circumstances of the case in *CIS/0546/2008*, a Deputy Commissioner decided that the appellant was entitled to the application of the set off provisions in reg.13 in the context of a claim for income support. Benefit had been stopped when it was established that the appellant and her partner were living together as husband and wife. It appeared that the appellant had not been given the opportunity to elect to make a claim for income support for herself, her partner and the children. In this case, there was a claim for income support affecting the appellant. There was an issue which 'should have been determined'. This meant that the appellant was entitled to have reg.13 applied to offset all or part of the overpayment which was recoverable from her.

The Administrative Court in *Larusai v Secretary of State for Work and Pensions*, [2003] EWHC 371 (Admin) was called upon to consider the relationship of benefits administered by the Department and tax credits administered by the Board of Inland Revenue in relation to the offsetting of benefits where there are recoverable overpayments of benefits administered by the Department. The claimant had been overpaid income support which was recoverable, but argued that a notional entitlement to working families tax credit should be set off against the overpayment notwithstanding the absence of such a provision in reg.13. The claimant argued that the Secretary of State in exercising his discretion as to the amount of the recoverable overpayment had acted unlawfully in failing to deduct a notional amount of working families tax credit from the overpayment. The decision was never likely to require the Secretary of State to exercise his discretion in the way for which the claimant argued, but the decision is interesting for the way in which the Administrative Court responded to the claimant's arguments:

(1) The claimant argued that the Secretary of State's approach in treating tax credits as different from benefits administered by the Department and so precluding any discretionary offset of working families tax credit was irrational. The Court did not accept this, seeing nothing irrational in attempts to change the perception of claimants about the difference between benefits which required a person to be out of work and those which were payable to people in work.

(2) The claimant argued that the policy of the Secretary of State had departed from its own guidelines in pursuing a policy of exercising its discretion only in "exceptional circumstances". The Court concluded that this was a matter of phraseology and did not render the policy unlawful.

(3) The claimant argued that the decision to recover the whole of the overpaid income support without deduction of a notional entitlement to working families tax credit constituted a penal sanction (it appears that the claimant would have been entitled to something in the order of £2,000 by way of working families tax credit). Since the policy in reg.13 was to secure full recovery subject to the specified offsets and since the notional amount of working families tax credit did not constitute a debt by the Department to the claimant, it could not be said that there was anything which could be characterised as a penal sanction; there was no basis for the claimant's argument.

(4) The Court said that an argument based on the Government securing a windfall equal to the notional amount of the working families tax credit was misconceived. It "misrepresents the structural position, as well as the law, to describe this as 'a windfall to the State.'" (para.30).

(5) The claimant raised the question of hardship resulting from the requirement to repay overpaid benefit. The Court simply notes that the Secretary of State has been provided with full details of the claimant's circumstances, that there is inevitably an element of hardship when overpaid benefit is recovered, but that it "is not for this court, unless it is satisfied that there has been an unlawful exercise of discretion, to form a view about the financial margins with which this case, or any case, might give rise to." (para.32)

See also *Department for Work and Pensions v Richards*, [2005] EWCA Crim 491.

Public Records Act 1958

R(IS) 1/05 gives guidance on the significance of the Public Records Act 1958 **2.598** to the retention of documents by the Department, and the onus of proof where a claimant asserts that there has been an underpayment of benefit in the past which reduces the amount of a recoverable overpayment. The overpayment at issue in this case had arisen as a result of admitted false statements made by the claimant which resulted in the award of income support. The point of contention was whether the claimant could offset the substantial overpayment by underpayments of benefit in circumstances where many of the relevant documents had long since been destroyed by the Department under its document retention policy.

The requirements of the Public Records Act 1958 were seen as something of a red herring, and the Commissioner has little time for them, noting, "It is difficult to believe that these elaborate procedures [in the 1958 Act] were ever intended to apply to social security claim forms". In fairness, the claimant's representative had abandoned this point in arguing the case before the Commissioner.

The onus of proof in cases such as this was a rather more substantial point, particularly in the light of the House of Lords in *Kerr v Department for Social Development* [2004] UKHL 23 (see para.1.373.1 of Vol.III). The Commissioner sees no real difference in the views expressed by Lady Hale in *Kerr* and the long-established wisdom that "if a particular matter relates to the qualifying conditions of entitlement it is a claimant who must bear the consequences of ignorance; however, if what is in issue constitute an exception to such conditions, then the Department bears the burden of establishing that factor which operates to disentitled the claimant". (para.43). The issue which arises under reg.13 is distinct from the recovery of the overpayment; it is not necessarily related to the period which is covered by the s.71 revision or supersession nor to the same benefit the subject of recovery. The Commissioner concludes:

"If, as is trite law, one who submits an initial claim for benefit has the burden of showing that its qualifying conditions are met, it can hardly be the case that one who must pay benefit back because it has been demonstrated that she should never have had it, has an easier task in establishing a similar entitlement to offset against the proven debt. In my judgement, nothing in principle or on account of the statutory language or from the structure of the overpayment scheme or to further its consistency can justify such a departure from what is usual and right." (para.47.)

Quarterly diminution of capital

14.—(1) For the purposes of section 53(1) of the Act [SSAA, s.71(1)], **2.599** where income support, [⁴ or state pension credit] [², or income-based job-seeker's allowance] [⁵ , or income-related employment and support allowance] [¹, working families' tax credit or disabled person's tax credit] has been overpaid in consequence of a misrepresentation as to the capital a claimant possesses or a failure to disclose its existence, the adjudicating authority shall treat that capital as having been reduced at the end of each quarter from the start of the overpayment period by the amount overpaid by way of income support, [⁴ or state pension credit] [², or income based jobseeker's allowance] [⁵ , or income-related employment and support allowance] [¹ working families' tax credit or disabled person's tax credit] within that quarter.

(2) Capital shall not be treated as reduced over any period other than a quarter or in any circumstances other than those for which paragraph (1) provides.

(3) In this regulation—

"a quarter" means a period of 13 weeks starting with the first day on which the overpayment period began and ending on the 90th consecutive day thereafter;

"overpayment period" is a period during which income support [³ or an income based jobseeker's allowance,] [⁵ , or income-related employment and support allowance] [¹ working families' tax credit or disabled person's tax credit] is overpaid in consequence of a misrepresentation as to capital or a failure to disclose its existence.

AMENDMENTS

1. The Tax Credits (Payments on Account, Overpayments and Recovery) (Amendment) Regulations 1999 (SI 1999/2571), reg.12 (October 5, 1999).

2. The Tax Credits (Payments on Account, Overpayments and Recovery) (Amendment) Regulations 1999 (SI 1996/2571), reg.23(5) and (6) (October 7, 1996).

3. The Social Security (Jobseeker's Allowance and Payments on account) (Miscellaneous Amendments) Regulations 1996 (SI 1996/2519), reg.3(2) (October 7, 1996).

4. State Pension Credit (Consequential, Transitional and Miscellaneous Provisions) Regulations 2002 (SI 2002/3019), reg.24 (October 6, 2003).

5. The Employment and Support Allowance (Consequential Provisions) (No. 2) Regulations 2008 (SI 2008/1554), reg.52 (October 27, 2008).

GENERAL NOTE

2.600   See the notes to s.71(1) and (2) of the Administration Act.

On the proper interpretation of the rule in reg.14, see *CIS/2570/2007* and *CIS/2365/2007*.

In *R(IS) 10/08*, the Commissioner effectively holds that capital held by a child should be subject to the diminishing capital rules if an overpayment arises as a result of capital held by a child of the family unit seeking entitlement to income support.

PART VII

THE PROCESS OF RECOVERY

Recovery by deduction from benefits

2.601   **15.**—(1) Subject to regulation 16, where any amount is recoverable under sections 27 or 53(1) of the Act [SSAA, ss.74 or 71(1)], or under these Regulations, that amount shall be recoverable by the Secretary of State from any of the benefits prescribed by the next paragraph, to which the person from whom [¹the amount is determined] to be recoverable is entitled.

(2) The following benefits are prescribed for the purposes of this regulation—

(a) subject to paragraphs (1) and (2) of regulation 16, any benefit under the Social Security Act 1975 [SSCBA, Parts II to V];

(b) subject to paragraphs (1) and (2) of regulation 16, any child benefit;

(c) [⁵. . .]

(d) subject to regulation 16, any income support [⁷ an employment and support allowance] [⁶ or state pension credit], [⁴or a jobseeker's allowance].

[²(e) [⁵. . .];

[³(f) any incapacity benefit.]

AMENDMENTS

1. The Social Security (Payments on account, Overpayments and Recovery) Amendments Regulations 1988 (SI 1988/688), reg.2(3) (April 11, 1988).

2. The Disability Living Allowance and Disability Working Allowance (Consequential Provisions) Regulations 1991 (SI 1991/2742), reg.15 (April 6, 1992).

3. The Social Security (Incapacity Benefit) (Consequential and Transitional Amendments and Savings) Regulations 1991 (SI 1995/829), reg.21(3) (April 13, 1995).

4. The Social Security (Jobseeker's Allowance and Payments on account) (Miscellaneous Amendments) Regulations 1996 (SI 1996/2519), reg.3(3) (October 7, 1996).

5. The Social Security (Jobseeker's Allowance and Payments on account) (Miscellaneous Amendments) Regulations 1996 (SI 1996/2519), reg.13 (October 5, 1999).

6. State Pension Credit (Consequential, Transitional and Miscellaneous Provisions) Regulations 2002 (SI 2002/3019), reg.24 (October 6, 2003).

7. The Employment and Support Allowance (Consequential Provisions) (No. 2) Regulations 2008 (SI 2008/1554), reg.52 (October 27, 2008).

Limitations on deductions from prescribed benefits

16.—(1) Deductions may not be made from entitlement to the benefits prescribed by paragraph (2) except as a means of recovering an overpayment of the benefit from which the deduction is to be made.

(2) The benefits [¹prescribed] for the purposes of paragraph (1) are guardian's allowance, [². . .] and child benefit.

(3) Regulation 15 shall apply without limitation to any payment of arrears of benefit other than any arrears caused by the operation of [¹² regulation 20 of the Social Security and Child Support (Decisions and Appeals) Regulations 1999 (making of payments which have been suspended)]

(4) Regulation 15 shall apply to the amount of [⁵benefit] to which a person is presently entitled only to the extent that there may, subject to paragraphs 8 and 9 of Schedule 9 to the Claims and Payments Regulations, be recovered in respect of any one benefit week—

(a) in a case to which paragraph (5) applies, not more than the amount there specified; and

(b) in any other case, 3 times 5 per cent of the personal allowance for a single claimant aged not less than 25, that 5 per cent being, where it is not a multiple of 5 pence, rounded to the next higher such multiple.

[⁶(4A) Paragraph (4) shall apply to the following benefits—

(a) income support;

2.602

693

    (b) an income-based jobseeker's allowance;

    (c) where, if there was no entitlement to a contribution-based jobseeker's allowance, there would be entitlement to an income-based jobseeker's allowance at the same rate, a contribution-based jobseeker's allowance.]

[¹¹ (d) state pension credit.]

[¹³ (e) an income-related employment and support allowance;

    (f) where, if there was no entitlement to a contributory employment and support allowance, there would be entitlement to an income-related employment and support allowance at the same rate, a contributory employment and support allowance.]

[⁹ (5) Where a person responsible for the misrepresentation or failure to disclose a material fact has, by reason thereof—

    (a) been found guilty of an offence whether under statute or otherwise; or

    (b) made an admission after caution of deception or fraud for the purpose of obtaining benefit; or

    (c) agreed to pay a penalty under section 115A of the Social Security Administration Act 1992 and the agreement has not been withdrawn,

the amount mentioned in paragraph (4)(a) shall be 4 times 5 per cent. of the personal allowance for a single claimant aged not less than 25, that 5 per cent. being, where it is not a multiple of 10 pence, rounded to the nearest 10 pence or, if it is a multiple of 5 pence but not of 10 pence, the next higher multiple of 10 pence.]

[⁶(5A) Regulation 15 shall apply to an amount of a contribution-based jobseeker's allowance, other than a contribution-based jobseeker's allowance to which paragraph (4) applies in accordance with paragraph (4A)(c), to which a person is presently entitled only to the extent that there may, subject to paragraphs 8 and 9 of Schedule 9 to the Claims and Payments Regulations be recovered in respect of any one benefit week a sum equal to one third of the age-related amount applicable to the claimant under section 4(1)(a) of the Jobseekers Act 1995.

(5B) For the purposes of paragraph (5A) where the sum that would otherwise fall to be deducted includes a fraction of a penny, the sum to be deducted shall be rounded down to the nearest whole penny.]

    (6) [⁵ Where—

    (a) in the calculation of the income of a person to whom income support is payable, the amount of earnings or other income falling to be taken into account is reduced by paragraphs 4 to 9 of Schedule 8 to the Income Support Regulations (sums to be disregarded in the calculation of earnings) or paragraphs 15 and 16 of Schedule 9 to those Regulations (sums to be disregarded in the calculation of income other than earnings); or

    (b) in the calculation of the income of a person to whom income-based jobseeker's allowance is payable, the amount of earnings or other income falling to be taken into account is reduced by paragraphs 5 to 12 of Schedule 6 to the Jobseeker's Allowance Regulations (sums to be disregarded in the calculation of earnings) or paragraphs 15 and 17 of Schedule 7 to those Regulations (sums to be disregarded in the calculation of income other than earnings),

[¹¹ or

    (c) in the calculation of the income of a person to whom state pension credit is payable, the amount of earnings or other income falling to be taken into account is reduced in accordance with paragraph 1 of Schedule 4 (sums to be disregarded in the calculation of income other than capital), or Schedule 6 (sums disregarded from claimant's earnings) to the State Pension Credit Regulations,] [[13] or

(d) in the calculation of the income of a person to whom income-related employment and support allowance is payable, the amount of earnings or other income falling to be taken into account is reduced by paragraph 7 of Schedule 7 to the Employment and Support Allowance Regulations (sums to be disregarded in the calculation of earnings) or paragraphs 16 and 17 of Schedule 8 to those Regulations (sums to be disregarded in the calculation of income other than earnings),]

the weekly amount] applicable under paragraph (4) may be increased by not more than half the amount of the reduction, and any increase under this paragraph has priority over any increase which would, but for this paragraph, be made under paragraph 6(5) of Schedule 9 to the Claims and Payments Regulations.

(7) Regulation 15 shall not be applied to a specified benefit so as to reduce the benefit in any one benefit week to less than 10 pence.

(8) In this regulation—

[[9] 'admission after caution' means—

(i) in England and Wales, an admission after a caution has been administered in accordance with a Code issued under the Police and Criminal Evidence Act 1984;

in Scotland, an admission after a caution has been administered, such admission being duly witnessed by two persons;]

"benefit week" means the week corresponding to the week in respect of which the benefit is paid;

[[11] "personal allowance for a single claimant aged not less than 25" means—

(a) in the case of a person who is entitled to [[13] an employment and support allowance,] income support or state pension credit, the amount for the time being specified in paragraph 1(1)(e) of column (2) of Schedule 2 to the Income Support Regulations; or

(b) in the case of a person who is entitled to income-based jobseeker's allowance, the amount for the time being specified in paragraph 1(1)(e) of column (2) of Schedule 1 to the Jobseeker's Allowance Regulations;]

"specified benefit" means—

(a) a jobseeker's allowance;

(b) income support when paid alone or together with any incapacity benefit, retirement pension or severe disablement allowance in a combined payment in respect of any period;

(c) if incapacity benefit, retirement pension or severe disablement allowance is paid concurrently with income support in respect of any period but not in a combined payment, income support and such of those benefits as are paid concurrently;

(d) state pension credit when paid alone or together with any retirement pension, incapacity benefit or severe disablement allowance in a combined payment in respect of any period;

(e) if retirement pension, incapacity benefit or severe disablement allowance is paid concurrently with state pension credit in respect of any period but not in a combined payment, state pension credit and such of those benefits as are paid concurrently, but does not include any sum payable by way of child maintenance bonus in accordance with section 10 of the Child Support Act 1995 and the Social Security (Child Maintenance Bonus) Regulations 1996.] [13 and

(f) an employment and support allowance,]

but does not include any sum payable by way of child maintenance bonus in accordance with section 10 of the Child Support Act 1995 and the Social Security (Child Maintenance Bonus) Regulations 1996.]

AMENDMENTS

1. The Social Security (Payments on account, Overpayments and Recovery) Amendments Regulations 1988 (SI 1988/688), reg.2(4) (April 11, 1988).

2. The Disability Living Allowance and Disability Working Allowance (Consequential Provisions) Regulations 1991 (SI 1991/2742), reg.15 (April 6, 1992).

3. The Social Security (Incapacity Benefit) (Consequential and Transitional Amendments and Savings) Regulations 1995 (SI 1995/829), reg.21(4) (April 13, 1995).

4. The Social Security (Claims and Payments, etc.) Amendment Regulations 1996 (SI 1996/672), reg.4 (April 4, 1996).

5. The Social Security and Child Support (Jobseeker's Allowance) (Consequential Amendments) Regulations 1996 (SI 1996/1345), reg.23(4) (October 7, 1996).

6. The Social Security (Jobseeker's Allowance and Payments on account) (Miscellaneous Amendments) Regulations 1996 (SI 1996/2519), reg.3(4) (October 7, 1996).

7. The Social Security (Child Maintenance Bonus) Regulations 1996 (SI 1996/3195), reg.16(3) (April 7, 1997).

8. The Social Security (Miscellaneous Amendments) Regulations 1997 (SI 1997/454), reg.8(10) (April 6, 1997).

9. The Social Security (Payments on Account, Overpayment and Recovery) Amendment Regulations 2000 (SI 2000/2336), reg.2, (October 2, 2000).

10. The Social Security (Claims and Payments and Miscellaneous Amendments) (No.2) Regulations 2002 (SI 2002/2441), reg.134, (October 23, 2002).

11. State Pension Credit (Consequential, Transitional and Miscellaneous Provisions) Regulations 2002 (SI 2002/3019), reg.24 (October 6, 2003).

12. The Social Security, Child Support and Tax Credits (Miscellaneous Amendments) Regulations 2005 (SI 2005/337) reg.10 (March 18, 2005).

13. The Employment and Support Allowance (Consequential Provisions) (No. 2) Regulations 2008 (SI 2008/1554), reg.52 (October 27, 2008).

Recovery from couples

2.603   **17.** In the case of an overpayment of income support [3 or state pension credit] [2, or income-based jobseeker's allowance] [5 or income-related employment and support allowance] [1, family credit or disability working allowance] to one of [4 a couple], the amount recoverable by deduction, in accordance with regulation 15, may be recovered by deduction from income support [3 or state pension credit] [2, or income-based jobseeker's allowance] [5 or income-related employment and support allowance] [1, family credit or disability working allowance] payable to either of them, provided that the two of them are [4 a couple] at the date of the deduction.

AMENDMENTS

1. The Disability Living Allowance and Disability Working Allowance (Consequential Provisions) Regulations 1991 (SI 1991/2742), reg.15 (April 6, 1992).

2. The Social Security and Child Support (Jobseeker's Allowance) (Consequential Amendments) Regulations 1996 (SI 1996/1345), reg.23(5) and (6) (October 7, 1996).

3. State Pension Credit (Consequential, Transitional and Miscellaneous Provisions) Regulations 2002 (SI 2002/3019), reg.24 (October 6, 2003).

4. The Civil Partnership (Pensions, Social Security and Child Support) (Consequential etc. Provisions) Order 2005 (SI 2005/2877) (December 5, 2005).

5. The Employment and Support Allowance (Consequential Provisions) (No. 2) Regulations 2008 (SI 2008/1554), reg.52 (October 27, 2008).

PART VIII

RECOVERY BY DEDUCTIONS FROM EARNINGS FOLLOWING TRADE DISPUTE

Recovery by deductions from earnings

18.—(1) Any sum paid to a person on an award of income support made to him by virtue of section 23(8) of the Act [SSCBA, s.127] (effect of return to work after a trade dispute) shall be recoverable from him in accordance with this Part of these Regulations.

    2.604

(2) In this Part, unless the context otherwise requires—

"available earnings" means the earnings, including any remuneration paid by or on behalf of an employer to an employee who is for the time being unable to work owing to sickness, which remain payable to a claimant on any pay-day after deduction by his employer of all amounts lawfully deductible by the employer otherwise than by virtue of a deduction notice;

"claimant" means a person to whom an award is made by virtue of section 23(8) of the Act [SSCBA, s.127];

"deduction notice" means a notice under regulation 20 or 25;

"employment" means employment (including employment which has been suspended but not terminated) in remunerative work, and related expressions shall be construed accordingly;

"pay-day" means an occasion on which earnings are paid to a claimant;

"protected earnings" means protected earnings as determined by an adjudicating authority, in accordance with regulation 19(2), under regulation 19(1)(a) or 24;

"recoverable amount" means the amount (determined in accordance with regulation 20(3) or (5) or regulation 25(2)(a)) by reference to which deductions are to be made by an employer from a claimant's earnings by virtue of a deduction notice;

"repaid by the claimant" means paid by the claimant directly to the Secretary of State by way of repayment of income support otherwise recoverable under this Part of these Regulations.

(3) Any notice or other document required or authorised to be given or sent to any person under the provisions of this Part shall be deemed to have been given or sent if it was sent by post to that person in accordance with

paragraph (6) of regulation 27 where that regulation applies and, in any other case, at his ordinary or last known address or in the case of an employer at the last place of business where the claimant to which it relates is employed, and if so sent to have been given or sent on the day on which it was posted.

Award and protected earnings

2.605   **19.**—(1) Where an adjudicating authority determines that a person claiming income support is entitled by virtue of section 23(8) of the Act [SSCBA, s.127] (effect of return to work after a trade dispute) and makes an award to him accordingly he shall determine the claimant's protected earnings (that is to say the amount below which his actual earnings must not be reduced by any deduction made under this Part).

(2) The adjudicating authority shall include in his decision—

(a) the amount of income support awarded together with a statement that the claimant is a person entitled by virtue of section 23(8) of the Act [SSCBA, s.127] and that accordingly any sum paid to him on that award will be recoverable from him as provided in this Part;

(b) the amount of the claimant's protected earnings, and

(c) a statement of the claimant's duty under regulation 28 (duty to give notice of cessation or resumption of employment).

[¹(3) The protected earnings of the claimant shall be the sum determined by—

(a) taking the sum specified in paragraph (4),

(b) adding the sum specified in paragraph (5), and

(c) subtracting from the result any child benefit which falls to be taken into account in calculating his income for the purposes of Part V of the Income Support Regulations.]

(4) The sum referred to in paragraph (3)(a) shall be the aggregate of the amounts calculated under regulation 17(a) to (d), 18(a) to (e), 20 or 21, as the case may be, of the Income Support Regulations.

(5) The sum referred to in paragraph (3)(b) shall be £27 except where the sum referred to in paragraph (3)(a) includes an amount calculated under regulation 20 in which case the sum shall be £8.00.

AMENDMENT

1. The Social Security (Payments on account, Overpayments and Recovery) Amendments Regulations 1988 (SI 1988/688), reg.2(5) (April 11, 1988).

Service and contents of deduction notices

2.606   **20.**—(1) Where the amount of income support has not already been repaid by the claimant, the Secretary of State shall serve a deduction notice on the employer of the claimant.

(2) A deduction notice shall contain the following particulars—

(a) particulars enabling the employer to identify the claimant;

(b) the recoverable amount;

(c) the claimant's protected earnings as specified in the notification of award.

(3) Subject to paragraph (5) the recoverable amount shall be—

(a) the amount specified in the decision as having been awarded to the claimant by way of income support; reduced by

(b) the amount (if any) which has been repaid by the claimant before the date of the deduction notice.

(4) If a further award relating to the claimant is made the Secretary of State shall cancel the deduction notice (giving written notice of the cancellation to the employer and the claimant) and serve on the employer a further deduction notice.

(5) The recoverable amount to be specified in the further deduction notice shall be the sum of—

(a) the amount determined by applying paragraph (3) to the further award; and

(b) the recoverable amount specified in the cancelled deduction notice less any part of that amount which before the date of the further notice has already been deducted by virtue of the cancelled notice or repaid by the claimant.

Period for which deduction notice has effect

21.—(1) A deduction notice shall come into force when it is served on the employer of the claimant to whom it relates and shall cease to have effect as soon as any of the following conditions is fulfilled—

2.607

(a) the notice is cancelled by virtue of regulation 20(4) or paragraph (2) of this regulation;

(b) the claimant ceases to be in the employment of the person on whom the notice was served;

(c) the aggregate of—

(i) any part of the recoverable amount repaid by the claimant on or after the date of the deduction notice, and

(ii) the total amount deducted by virtue of the notice,

reaches the recoverable amount;

(d) there has elapsed a period of 26 weeks beginning with the date of the notice.

(2) The Secretary of State may at any time give a direction in writing cancelling a deduction notice and—

(a) he shall cause a copy of the direction to be served on the employer concerned and on the claimant;

(b) the direction shall take effect when a copy of it is served on the employer concerned.

Effect of deduction notice

22.—(1) Where a deduction notice is in force the following provisions of this regulation shall apply as regards any relevant pay-day.

2.608

(2) Where a claimant's earnings include any bonus, commission or other similar payment which is paid other than on a day on which the remainder of his earnings is paid, then in order to calculate his available earnings for the purposes of this regulation any such bonus, commission or other similar payment shall be treated as being paid to him on the next day of payment of the remainder of his earnings instead of on the day of actual payment.

(3) If on a relevant pay-day a claimant's available earnings—

(a) do not exceed his protected earnings by at least £1, no deduction shall be made;

(b) do exceed his protected earnings by at least £1, his employer shall deduct from the claimant's available earnings one half of the excess over his protected earnings, so however that where earnings are paid other than weekly the amount of the protected earnings and the figure of £1 shall be adjusted accordingly, in particular—

   (c) where earnings are paid monthly, they shall for this purpose be treated as paid every five weeks (and the protected earnings and the figure of £1 accordingly multiplied by five);

   (d) where earnings are paid daily, the protected earnings and the figure of £1 shall be divided by five,

and if, in any case to which sub-paragraph (c) or (d) does not apply, there is doubt as to the adjustment to be made this shall be determined by the Secretary of State on the application of the employer or the claimant.

(4) Where on a relevant pay-day earnings are payable to the claimant in respect of more than one pay-day the amount of the protected earnings and the figure of £1 referred to in the preceding paragraph, adjusted where appropriate in accordance with the provisions of that paragraph, shall be multiplied by the number of pay-days to which the earnings relate.

(5) Notwithstanding anything in paragraph (3)—

   (a) the employer shall not make a deduction on a relevant pay-day if the claimant satisfies him that up to that day he has not obtained payment of the income support to which the deduction notice relates;

   (b) the employer shall not on any relevant pay-day deduct from the claimant's earnings by virtue of the deduction notice an amount greater than the excess of the recoverable amount over the aggregate of all such amounts as, in relation to that notice, are mentioned in regulation 21(1)(c)(i) and (ii); and

   (c) where the amount of any deduction which by this regulation the employer is required to make would otherwise include a fraction of 1p, that amount shall be reduced by that fraction.

(6) For the purpose of this regulation "relevant pay-day" means any pay-day beginning with—

   (a) the first pay-day falling after the expiration of the period of one month from the date on which the deduction notice comes into force; or

   (b) if the employer so chooses, any earlier pay-day after the notice has come into force.

Increase of amount of award on appeal or [¹ otherwise]

2.609   **23.** If the amount of the award is increased, whether on appeal or [¹ otherwise], this Part shall have effect as if on the date on which the amount of the award was increased—

   (a) the amount of the increase was the recoverable amount; and

   (b) the claimant's protected earnings [¹, where a notice of variation of protected earnings is given under regulation 24, were the earnings stated in the notice]

AMENDMENT

1. The Social Security Act 1998 (Commencement No.12, and Consequential and Transitional Provisions) Order 1999 (SI 1999/3178), Sch.9 (November 29, 1999).

[¹ Notice of variation] of protected earnings

2.610   [¹ . . .] **24.**—(1) [¹ . . .]

[¹ (2) The Secretary of State shall give a claimant's employer written notice varying the deduction notice where a decision as to a claimant's protected earnings is revised or superseded.]

(3) Variation of a deduction notice under paragraph (2) shall take effect either from the end of the period of 10 working days beginning with the day on which notice of the variation is given to the employer or, if the employer so chooses, at any earlier time after notice is given.

AMENDMENT

1. The Social Security Act 1998 (Commencement No. 12 and Consequential and Transitional Provisions) Order 1999 (SI 1999/3178), Sch. 9 (November 29, 1999).

Power to serve further deduction notice on resumption of employment

25.—(1) Where a deduction notice has ceased to have effect by reason of the claimant ceasing to be in the employment of the person on whom the notice was served, the Secretary of State may, if he thinks fit, serve a further deduction notice on any person by whom the claimant is for the time being employed.

(2) Notwithstanding anything in the foregoing provisions of these Regulations, in any such deduction notice—

(a) the recoverable amount shall be equal to the recoverable amount as specified in the previous deduction notice less the aggregate of—

   (i) the total of any amounts required to be deducted by virtue of that notice, and

   (ii) any additional part of that recoverable amount repaid by the claimant on or after the date of that notice,

or, where this regulation applies in respect of more than one such previous notice, the aggregate of the amounts as so calculated in respect of each such notice;

(b) the amount specified as the claimant's protected earnings shall be the same as that so specified in the last deduction notice relating to him which was previously in force or as subsequently [¹ varied].

2.611

AMENDMENT

1. The Social Security Act 1998 (Commencement No. 12 and Consequential and Transitional Provisions) Order 1999 (SI 1999/3178), Sch. 9 (November 29, 1999).

Right of Secretary of State to recover direct from claimant

26. Where [¹, at any time, it is not practicable for the Secretary of State] by means of a deduction notice, to effect recovery of the recoverable amount or of so much of that amount as remains to be recovered from the claimant, the amount which remains to be recovered shall, by virtue of this regulation, be recoverable from the claimant by the Secretary of State.

2.612

AMENDMENT

1. The Social Security Act 1998 (Commencement No. 12 and Consequential and Transitional Provisions) Order 1999 (SI 1999/3178), Sch. 9 (November 29, 1999).

Duties and liabilities of employers

27.—(1) An employer shall keep a record of the available earnings of each claimant who is an employee in respect of whom a deduction notice is in

2.613

force and of the payments which he makes in pursuance of the notice.

(2) A record of every deduction made by an employer under a deduction notice on any pay-day shall be given or sent by him to the Secretary of State, together with payment of the amount deduced, by not later than the 19th day of the following month.

(3) Where by reason only of the circumstances mentioned in regulation 22(5)(a) the employer makes no deduction from a claimant's weekly earnings on any pay-day he shall within 10 working days after that pay-day give notice of that fact to the Secretary of State.

(4) Where a deduction notice is cancelled by virtue of regulation 20(4) or 21(2) or ceases to have effect by virtue of regulation 21(1) the employer shall within 10 working days after the date on which the notice is cancelled or, as the case may be, ceases to have effect—

(a) return the notice to the Secretary of State and, where regulation 21(1) applies, give notice of the reason for its return;

(b) give notice, in relation to each relevant pay-day (as defined in regulation 22(6)), of the available earnings of the claimant and of any deduction made from those earnings.

(5) If on any pay-day to which regulation 22(3)(b) applies the employer makes no deduction from a claimant's available earnings, or makes a smaller deduction than he was thereby required to make, and in consequence any amount is not deducted while the deduction notice, or any further notice which under regulation 20(4) cancels that notice, has effect—

(a) the amount which is not deducted shall, without prejudice to any other method of recovery from the claimant or otherwise, be recoverable from the employer by the Secretary of State; and

(b) any amount so recovered shall, for the purposes of these Regulations, be deemed to have been repaid by the claimant.

(6) All records and notices to which this regulation applies shall given or sent to the Secretary of State, on a form approved by him, at such office of the [1Department of Social Security] as he may direct.

AMENDMENT

1. The Transfer of Functions (Health and Social Security) Order 1988 (SI 1988/1843), art.3(4) (November 28, 1988).

Claimants to give notice of cessation or resumption of employment

2.614   **28.**—(1) Where a claimant ceases to be in the employment of a person on whom a deduction notice relating to him has been duly served knowing that the full amount of the recoverable amount has not been deducted from his earnings or otherwise recovered by the Secretary of State, he shall give notice within 10 working days to the Secretary of State of his address and of the date of such cessation of employment.

(2) Where on or after such cessation the claimant resumes employment (whether with the same or some other employer) he shall within 10 working days give notice to the Secretary of State of the name of the employer and of the address of his place of employment.

Failure to notify

2.615   **29.** If a person fails to comply with any requirement under regulation 27 or 28 to give notice of any matter to the Secretary of State he shall be guilty of an offence and liable on summary conviction to a fine not exceeding—

    (a) for any one offence, level 3 on the standard scale; or

    (b) for an offence of continuing any such contravention, £40 for each day on which it is so continued.

The Social Security Act 1998 (Prescribed Benefits) Regulations 2006

(SI 2006/2529)

Made	*14th September 2006*
Laid before Parliament	*21st September 2006*
Coming into force	*16th October 2006*

The Secretary of State for Work and Pensions makes the following Regulations in exercise of the powers conferred by sections 8(3)(h), 79(1) and 84 of the Social Security Act 1998.

    2.616

In accordance with section 173(1)(b) of the Social Security Administration Act 1992, the Secretary of State has obtained the agreement of the Social Security Advisory Committee that proposals in respect of these Regulations need not be referred to it.

Citation and commencement

1. —(1) These Regulations may be cited as the Social Security Act 1998 (Prescribed Benefits) Regulations 2006 and shall come into force on 16th October 2006.

    2.617

Prescribed benefits

2. The benefits prescribed for the purposes of section 8(3)(h) of the Social Security Act 1998 (decisions by Secretary of State) are—

    2.618

    (a) the following benefits under the Social Security Act 1975—

        (i) sickness benefit under section 14;

       (ii) unemployment benefit under section 14;

      (iii) invalidity pension under section 15;

      (iv) invalidity allowance under section 16;

       (v) attendance allowance under section 35; and

      (vi) mobility allowance under section 37A;

    (b) supplementary benefit under the Supplementary Benefit Act 1976.

GENERAL NOTE

Except for attendance allowance, the benefits listed are benefits that had been abolished before the Social Security Act 1998 Act came into force and are therefore not within the scope of s.8(3)(a) to (g) of that Act. Attendance allowance has presumably been included from an abundance of caution because it is now payable only to people over the age of 65, whereas until 1992 it was payable to younger people. The need for this provision was revealed by *CDLA/2999/2004*, in which it was held that, because the transitional provision made when the 1998 Act came into force relies on the concept of a "relevant benefit" as defined by s.8(3), there was no power

    2.619–2

to make a supersession decision under s.10 of the 1998 Act in respect of mobility allowance, with the consequence that an overpayment of mobility allowance could not be recovered under s.71 of the Social Security Administration Act 1992. It is not entirely clear why the scope of s.8(3) of the 1998 Act has not been made precisely the same as the scope of s.71 of the 1992 Act (see para.4(1) of Sch.10 to the 1992 Act) but perhaps it was thought unlikely that any wider prescription would be required in practice. It is doubtful that the omission of the second "s" from the short title of the Supplementary Benefits Act 1976 is significant.

The Employment Protection (Recoupment of Jobseeker's Allowance and Income Support) Regulations 1996

(SI 1996/2349)

Made	*10th September 1996*
Laid before Parliament	*11th September 1996*
Coming into force	*7th October 1996*

2.631   The Secretary of State in exercise of the powers conferred on him by section 16 and section 41(4) of the Industrial Tribunals Act 1996, section 58(1) of the Social Security Administration Act 1992, and of all other powers enabling him in that behalf, and after reference to the Social Security Advisory Committee in so far as is required by section 172 of the Social Security Administration Act 1992, and after consultation with the Council on Tribunals, in so far as is required by section 8 of the Tribunals and Inquiries Act 1992, hereby makes the following Regulations:—

PART I

INTRODUCTORY

Citation and Commencement

2.632   **1.** These Regulations may be cited as the Employment Protection (Recoupment of Jobseeker's Allowance and Income Support) Regulations 1996 and shall come into force on 7th October 1996.

Interpretation

2.633   **2.**—(1) In these Regulations, unless the context otherwise requires, the following expressions have the meanings hereby assigned to them respectively, that is to say—

"the 1992 Act" means the Trade Union and Labour Relations (Consolidation) Act 1992;

"the 1996 Act" means the Employment Rights Act 1996;

"prescribed element" has the meaning assigned to it in Regulation 3 below and the Schedule to these Regulations;

"protected period" has the same meaning as in section 189(5) of the 1992 Act;

"protective award" has the same meaning as in section 189(3) of the 1992 Act;

"recoupable benefit" means any jobseeker's allowance or income support as the case may be, which is recoupable under these Regulations;

"recoupment notice" means a notice under these Regulations;

"Secretary of the Tribunals" means the Secretary of the Central Office of the [¹ Employment] Tribunals (England and Wales) or, as the case may require, the Secretary of the Central Office of the [¹ Employment] Tribunals (Scotland) for the time being;

(2) In the Schedule to these Regulations references to sections are references to sections of the 1996 Act unless otherwise indicated and references in column 3 of the table to the conclusion of the tribunal proceedings are references to the conclusion of the proceedings mentioned in the corresponding entry in column 2.

(3) For the purposes of these Regulations (and in particular for the purposes of any calculations to be made by an [¹ employment tribunal] as respects the prescribed element) the conclusion of the tribunal proceedings shall be taken to occur—

(a) where the [¹ employment tribunal] at the hearing announces the effect of its decision to the parties, on the date on which that announcement is made;

(b) in any other case, on the date on which the decision of the tribunal is sent to the parties.

(4) References to parties in relevant [¹ employment tribunal] proceedings shall be taken to include references to persons appearing on behalf of parties in a representative capacity.

(5) References in these Regulations to anything done, or to be done, in, or in consequence of, any tribunal proceedings include references to anything done, or to be done, in, or in consequence of any such proceedings as are in the nature of a review, or re-hearing or a further hearing consequent on an appeal.

AMENDMENT

1. Employment Rights (Dispute Resolution) Act 1998, s.1(2)(a) (August 1, 1998).

PART II

INDUSTRIAL TRIBUNAL PROCEEDINGS

Application to payments and proceedings

3.—(1) Subject to paragraph (2) below these Regulations apply— 2.634

(a) to the payments described in column 1 of the table contained in the Schedule to these Regulations, being, in each case, payments which are the subject of [¹ employment tribunal] proceedings of the kind described in the corresponding entry in column 2 and the prescribed element in relation to each such payment is so much of the relevant monetary award as is attributable to the matter described in the corresponding entry in column 3; and

(b) to payments of remuneration in pursuance of a protective award.

(2) The payments to which these Regulations apply by virtue of paragraph (1)(a) above include payments in proceedings under section 192 of the 1992 Act and, accordingly, where an order is made on an employee's complaint under that section, the relevant protective award shall, as respects that employee and to the appropriate extent, be taken to be subsumed in the order made under section 192 so that the provisions of these Regulations relating to monetary awards shall apply to payments under that order to the exclusion of the provisions relating to protective awards, but without prejudice to anything done under the latter in connection with the relevant protective award before the making of the order under section 192.

AMENDMENT

2.635   1. Employment Rights (Dispute Resolution) Act 1998, s.1(2)(a) (August 1, 1998).

Duties of the [¹ employment tribunals] and of the Secretary of the Tribunals in respect of monetary awards

2.636   **4.**—(1) Where these Regulations apply, no regard shall be had, in assessing the amount of a monetary award, to the amount of any jobseeker's allowance or any income support which may have been paid to or claimed by the employee for a period which coincides with any part of a period to which the prescribed element is attributable.

(2) Where the [¹ employment tribunal] in arriving at a monetary award makes a reduction on account of the employee's contributory fault or on account of any limit imposed by or under the 1992 Act or 1996 Act, a proportionate reduction shall be made in arriving at the amount of the prescribed element.

(3) Subject to the following provisions of this Regulation it shall be the duty of the [¹ employment tribunal] to set out in any decision which includes a monetary award the following particulars—

(a) the monetary award;

(b) the amount of the prescribed element, if any;

(c) the dates of the period to which the prescribed element is attributable;

(d) the amount, if any, by which the monetary award exceeds the prescribed element.

(4) Where the [¹ employment tribunal] at the hearing announces to the parties the effect of a decision which includes a monetary award it shall inform those parties at the same time of the amount of any prescribed element included in the monetary award and shall explain the effect of Regulations 7 and 8 below in relation to the prescribed element.

(5) Where the [¹ employment tribunal] has made such an announcement as is described in paragraph (4) above the Secretary of the Tribunals shall forthwith notify the Secretary of State that the tribunal has decided to make a monetary award including a prescribed element and shall notify him of the particulars set out in paragraph (3) above.

(6) As soon as reasonably practicable after the Secretary of the Tribunals has sent a copy of a decision containing the particulars set out in paragraph (3) above to the parties he shall send a copy of that decision to the Secretary of State.

(7) In addition to containing the particulars required under paragraph (3) above, any such decision as is mentioned in that paragraph shall contain

a statement explaining the effect of Regulations 7 and 8 below in relation to the prescribed element.

(8) The requirements of paragraphs (3) to (7) above do not apply where the tribunal is satisfied that in respect of each day falling within the period to which the prescribed element relates the employee has neither received nor claimed jobseeker's allowance or income support.

AMENDMENT

1. Employment Rights (Dispute Resolution) Act 1998, s.1(2)(a) (August 1, 1998).

Duties of the [¹ employment tribunals] and of the Secretary of the Tribunals in respect of protective awards

5. (1) Where, on a complaint under section 189 of the 1992 Act, an [¹ employment tribunal]—   2.637
  (a) at the hearing announces to the parties the effect of a decision to make a protective award; or
  (b) (where it has made no such announcement) sends a decision to make such an award to the parties; the Secretary of the Tribunals shall forthwith notify the Secretary of State of the following particulars relating to the award—
      (i) where the [¹ employment tribunal] has made such an announcement as is described in paragraph (1)(a) above, the date of the hearing or where it has made no such announcement, the date on which the decision was sent to the parties;
      (ii) the location of the tribunal;
      (iii) the name and address of the employer;
      (iv) the description of the employees to whom the award relates; and
      (v) the dates of the protected period.
(2)(a) Where an [¹ employment tribunal] makes such an announcement as is described in paragraph (1)(a) above in the presence of the employer or his representative it shall advise him of his duties under Regulation 6 below and shall explain the effect of Regulations 7 and 8 below in relation to remuneration under the protective award.
  (b) Without prejudice to (a) above any decision of an [¹ employment tribunal] to make a protective award under section 189 of the 1992 Act shall contain a statement advising the employer of his duties under Regulation 6 below and an explanation of the effect of Regulations 7 and 8 below in relation to remuneration under the protective award.

AMENDMENT

1. Employment Rights (Dispute Resolution) Act 1998, s.1(2)(a) (August 1, 1998).

Duties of the employer to give information about protective awards

6.—(1) Where an [¹ employment tribunal] makes a protective award   2.638
under section 189 of the 1992 Act against an employer, the employer shall give to the Secretary of State the following information in writing—
  (a) the name, address and national insurance number of every employee to whom the award relates; and

(b) the date of termination (or proposed termination) of the employment of each such employee.

(2) Subject to paragraph (3) below the employer shall comply with paragraph (1) above within the period of ten days commencing on the day on which the [¹ employment tribunal] at the hearing announces to the parties the effect of a decision to make a protective award or (in the case where no such announcement is made) on the day on which the relevant decision is sent to the parties.

(3) Where, in any case, it is not reasonably practicable for the employer to comply with paragraph (1) above within the period applicable under paragraph (2) above he shall comply as soon as reasonably practicable after the expiration of that period.

AMENDMENT

1. Employment Rights (Dispute Resolution) Act 1998, s.1(2)(a) (August 1, 1998).

PART III

RECOUPMENT OF BENEFIT

Postponement of Awards

2.639   7.—(1) This Regulation shall have effect for the purpose of postponing relevant awards in order to enable the Secretary of State to initiate recoupment under Regulation 8 below.

(2) Accordingly—

(a) so much of the monetary award as consists of the prescribed element;

(b) payment of any remuneration to which an employee would otherwise be entitled under a protective award, shall be treated as stayed (in Scotland, sisted) as respects the relevant employee until—

   (i) the Secretary of State has served a recoupment notice on the employer; or

   (ii) the Secretary of State has notified the employer in writing that he does not intend to serve a recoupment notice.

(3) The stay or sist under paragraph (2) above is without prejudice to the right of an employee under section 192 of the 1992 Act to present a complaint to an [¹ employment tribunal] of his employer's failure to pay remuneration under a protective award and Regulation 3(2) above has effect as respects any such complaint and as respects any order made under section 192(3) of that Act.

AMENDMENT

1. Employment Rights (Dispute Resolution) Act 1998, s.1(2)(a) (August 1, 1998).

Recoupment of Benefit

2.640   8.—(1) Recoupment shall be initiated by the Secretary of State serving on the employer a recoupment notice claiming by way of total or partial recoupment of jobseeker's allowance or income support the appropriate amount, computed, as the case may require, under paragraph (2) or (3) below.

(2) In the case of monetary awards the appropriate amount shall be whichever is the less of the following two sums—

    (a) the amount of the prescribed element (less any tax or social security contributions which fall to be deducted therefrom by the employer); or

    (b) the amount paid by way of or paid as on account of jobseeker's allowance or income support to the employee for any period which coincides with any part of the period to which the prescribed element is attributable.

(3) In the case of remuneration under a protective award the appropriate amount shall be whichever is the less of the following two sums—

    (a) the amount (less any tax or social security contributions which fall to be deducted therefrom by the employer) accrued due to the employee in respect of so much of the protected period as falls before the date on which the Secretary of State receives from the employer the information required under Regulation 6 above; or

    (b) the amount paid by way of or paid as on account of jobseeker's allowance or income support to the employee for any period which coincides with any part of the protected period falling before the date described in (a) above.

(4) A recoupment notice shall be served on the employer by post or otherwise and copies shall likewise be sent to the employee and, if requested, to the Secretary of the Tribunals.

(5) The Secretary of State shall serve a recoupment notice on the employer, or notify the employer that he does not intend to serve such a notice, within the period applicable, as the case may require, under paragraph (6) or (7) below, or as soon as practicable thereafter.

(6) In the case of a monetary award the period shall be—

    (a) in any case in which the tribunal at the hearing announces to the parties the effect of its decision as described in Regulation 4(4) above, the period ending 21 days after the conclusion of the hearing or the period ending 9 days after the decision has been sent to the parties, whichever is the later; or

    (b) in any other case, the period ending 21 days after the decision has been sent to the parties.

(7) In the case of a protective award the period shall be the period ending 21 days after the Secretary of State has received from the employer the information required under Regulation 6 above.

(8) A recoupment notice served on an employer shall operate as an instruction to the employer to pay, by way of deduction out of the sum due under the award, the recoupable amount to the Secretary of State and it shall be the duty of the employer to comply with the notice. The employer's duty under this paragraph shall not affect his obligation to pay any balance that may be due to the employee under the relevant award.

(9) The duty imposed on the employer by service of the recoupment notice shall not be discharged by payment of the recoupable amount to the employee during the postponement period or thereafter if a recoupment notice is served on the employer during the said period.

(10) Payment by the employer to the Secretary of State under this Regulation shall be a complete discharge in favour of the employer as against the employee in respect of any sum so paid but without prejudice to any rights of the employee under Regulation 10 below.

(11) The recoupable amount shall be recoverable by the Secretary of State from the employer as a debt.

GENERAL NOTE

2.641   When assessing compensation, an employment tribunal must make a gross award, ignoring any jobseeker's allowance or income support paid to the employee during the relevant period, (reg.4(1)) and must give the Secretary of State details of the award (regs 4 and 5). The award is then postponed under reg.7 to allow the Secretary of State to recoup under reg.8 from the employer the amount of jobseeker's allowance and income support paid to the employee during the relevant period. The relevant period is the period in respect of which compensation for loss of pay or arrears of pay is awarded but ends at the date of the employment tribunal's decision if the award covers a period in the future (reg.3 and Sch. and see *Homan v A1 Bacon Co Ltd* [1996] I.C.R. 721). The Secretary of State serves a recoupment notice on the employer who must pay the recoupable amount to the Secretary of State, by way of deduction out of the sum due under the award, and then pay the balance of the award to the employee (reg.8(8)). An employee may give notice to the Secretary of State that he does not accept the amount specified in the recoupment notice (reg.10(1)) and may appeal to the First-tier Tribunal against any decision of the Secretary of State in response to such a notice (reg.10(2B)).

Order made in secondary proceedings

2.642   **9.**—(1) In the application of any of the above provisions in the case of—
    (a) proceedings for an award under section 192 of the 1992 Act; or
    (b) proceedings in the nature of a review, a re-hearing or a further hearing consequent on an appeal,
it shall be the duty of the [1 employment tribunal] or, as the case may require, the Secretary of State, to take the appropriate account of anything done under or in consequence of these Regulations in relation to any award made in the original proceedings.
    (2) For the purposes of this Regulation the original proceedings are—
    (a) where paragraph (1)(a) above applies the proceedings under section 189 of the 1992 Act; or
    (b) where paragraph (1)(b) above applies the proceedings in respect of which the re-hearing, the review or the further hearing consequent on an appeal takes place.

AMENDMENT

1. Employment Rights (Dispute Resolution) Act 1998, s.1(2)(a) (August 1, 1998).

PART IV

DETERMINATION [2 . . .] OF BENEFIT RECOUPED

Provisions relating to determination of amount paid by way of or paid as on account of benefit

10.—(1) Without prejudice to the right of the Secretary of State to recover from an employer the recoupable benefit, an employee on whom a copy of a recoupment notice has been served in accordance with Regulation 8 above may, within 21 days of the date on which such notice was served on him or within such further time as the Secretary of State may for special reasons allow, give notice in writing to the Secretary of State that he does not accept that the amount specified in the recoupment notice in respect of jobseeker's allowance or income support is correct.

[² (2) Where an employee has given notice in writing to the Secretary of State under paragraph (1) above that he does not accept that an amount specified in the recoupment notice is correct, the Secretary of State shall make a decision as to the amount of jobseeker's allowance or, as the case may be, income support paid in respect of the period to which the prescribed element is attributable or, as appropriate, in respect of so much of the protected period as falls before the date on which the employer complies with Regulation 6 above.

(2A) The Secretary of State may revise either upon application made for the purpose or on his own initiative a decision under paragraph (2) above.

(2B) The employee shall have a right of appeal to [³ the First-tier Tribunal] against a decision of the Secretary of State whether as originally made under paragraph (2) or as revised under paragraph (2A) above.

(2C) The Social Security and Child Support (Decisions and Appeals) Regulations 1999 shall apply for the purposes of paragraphs (2A) and (2B) above as though a decision of the Secretary of State under paragraph (2A) above were made under section 9 of the 1998 Act and any appeal from such a decision were made under section 12 of that Act.

(2D) In this Regulation "the 1998 Act" means the Social Security Act 1998.

(3) Where the Secretary of State recovers too much money from an employer under these Regulations the Secretary of State shall pay to the employee an amount equal to the excess.]

(4) In any case where, after the Secretary of State has recovered from an employer any amount by way of recoupment of benefit, the decision given by the [¹ employment tribunal] in consequence of which such recoupment took place is set aside or varied on appeal or on a re-hearing by the industrial tribunal, the Secretary of State shall make such repayment to the employer or payment to the employee of the whole or part of the amount recovered as he is satisfied should properly be made having regard to the decision given on appeal or re-hearing.

AMENDMENTS

1. Employment Rights (Dispute Resolution) Act 1998, s.1(2)(a) (August 1, 1998).

2. The Social Security Act 1998 (Commencement No.12 and Consequential and Transitional Provisions) Order 1999 (SI 1999/3178) (November 29, 1999).

3. Tribunals, Courts and Enforcement Act 2007 (Transitional and Consequential Provisions Order 2008 (SI 2008/2683), Sch.1, para.73 (November 3, 2008).

GENERAL NOTE

The jurisdiction of the Secretary of State and the tribunal is confined to the question of the amount of jobseeker's allowance or income support paid in respect of the relevant period. In *R(JSA) 3/03*, it was held that no reduction could be made to the recoupable amount to take account of the loss of tax credits caused by the loss of employment. Presumably the loss of such benefits can be claimed from the employer as a head of compensation (see *Neal v Bingle* [1998] Q.B. 466).

Revocation and Transition Provision

2.645   **11.** *Omitted.*

SCHEDULE	**Regulation 3**

2.646   TABLE RELATING TO MONETARY AWARDS

Column 1	Column 2	Column 3
Payment	**Proceedings**	**Matter to which prescribed element is attributable**
1. Guarantee payments under section 28.	1. Complaint under section 34.	1. Any amount found to be due to the employee and ordered to be paid under section 34(3) for a period before the conclusion of the tribunal proceedings.
2. Payments under any collective agreement having regard to which the appropriate Minister has made an exemption order under section 35.	2. Complaint under section 35(4).	2. Any amount found to be due to the employee and ordered to be paid under section 34(3), as applied by section 35(4), for a period before the conclusion of the tribunal proceedings.
3. Payments of remuneration in respect of a period of suspension on medical grounds under section 64 and section 108(2).	3. Complaint under section 70.	3. Any amount found to be due to the employee and ordered to be paid under section 70(3) for a period before the conclusion of the tribunal proceedings.
4. Payments of remuneration in respect of a period of suspension on maternity grounds under section 68.	4. Complaint under section 70.	4. Any amount found to be due to the employee and ordered to be paid under section 70(3) for a period before the conclusion of the tribunal proceedings.
5. Payments under an order for reinstatement under section 114(1).	5. Complaint of unfair dismissal under section 111(1).	5. Any amount ordered to be paid under section 114(2)(a) in respect of arrears of pay for a period before the conclusion of the tribunal proceedings.
6. Payments under an order for re-engagement under section 117(8).	6. Complaint of unfair dismissal under section 111(1).	6. Any amount ordered to be paid under section 115(2)(d) in respect of arrears of pay for a period before the conclusion of the tribunal proceedings.
7. Payments under an award of compensation for unfair dismissal in cases falling under section 112(4) (cases where no	7. Complaint of unfair dismissal under section 111(1).	7. Any amount ordered to be paid and calculated under section 123 in respect of compensation for loss of wages for a

712

Column 1	Column 2	Column 3
Payment	**Proceedings**	**Matter to which prescribed element is attributable**
order for reinstatement or re-engagement has been made).		period before the conclusion of the tribunal proceedings.
8. Payments under an award of compensation for unfair dismissal under section 117(3) where reinstatement order not complied with.	8. Proceedings in respect of non-compliance with order.	8. Any amount ordered to be paid and calculated under section 123 in respect of compensation for loss of wages for a period before the conclusion of the tribunal proceedings.
9. Payments under an award of compensation for unfair dismissal under section 117(3) where re-engagement order not complied with.	9. Proceedings in respect of non-compliance with order.	9. Any amount ordered to be paid and calculated under section 123 in respect of compensation for loss of wages for a period before the conclusion of the tribunal proceedings.
10. Payments under an interim order for reinstatement under section 163(4) of the 1992 Act.	10. Proceedings on an application for an order for interim relief under section 161(1) of the 1992 Act.	10. Any amount found to be due to the complainant and ordered to be paid in respect of arrears of pay for the period between the date of termination of employment and the conclusion of the tribunal proceedings.
11. Payments under an interim order for re-engagement under section 163(5)(a) of the 1992 Act.	11. Proceedings on an application for an order for interim relief under section 161(1) of the 1992 Act.	11. Any amount found to be due to the complainant and ordered to be paid in respect of arrears of pay for the period between the date of termination of employment and the conclusion of the tribunal proceedings.
12. Payments under an order for the continuation of a contract of employment under section 163(5)(b) of the 1992 Act where employee reasonably refuses re-engagement.	12. Proceedings on an application for an order for interim relief under section 161(1) of the 1992 Act.	12. Any amount found to be due to the complainant and ordered to be paid in respect of arrears of pay for the period between the date of termination of employment and the conclusion of the tribunal proceedings.
13. Payments under an order for the continuation of a contract of employment under section 163(6) of the 1992 Act where employer fails to attend or is unwilling to reinstate or re-engage.	13. Proceedings on an application for an order for interim relief under section 161(1) of the 1992 Act.	13. Any amount found to be due to the complainant and ordered to be paid in respect of arrears of pay for the period between the date of termination of employment and the conclusion of the tribunal proceedings.
14. Payments under an order for the continuation of a contract of employment under sections 166(1) and (2) of the 1992 Act where reinstatement or	14. Proceedings in respect of non-compliance with order.	14. Any amount ordered to be paid to the employee by way of compensation under section 166(1)(b) of the 1992 Act for loss of wages for the period between the date of

713

Column 1	Column 2	Column 3
Payment	**Proceedings**	**Matter to which prescribed element is attributable**
re-engagement order not complied with.		termination of employment and the conclusion of the tribunal proceedings.
15. Payments under an order for compensation under sections 166(3)–(5) of the 1992 Act where order for the continuation of contract of employment not complied with.	15. Proceedings in respect of non-compliance with order.	15. Any amount ordered to be paid to the employee by way of compensation under section 166(3)–(4) of the 1992 Act for loss of wages for the period between the date of termination of employment and the conclusion of the tribunal proceedings.
16. Payments under an order under section 192(3) of the 1992 Act on employer's default in respect of remuneration due to employee under protective award. proceedings.	16. Complaint under section 192(1) of the 1992 Act.	16. Any amount ordered to be paid to the employee in respect of so much of the relevant protected period as falls before the date of the conclusion of the tribunal

The Social Security (Recovery of Benefits) Regulations 1997

(SI 1997/2205)

ARRANGEMENT OF REGULATIONS

The Secretary of State for Social Security, in exercise of the powers conferred by section 189(4), (5) and (6) of the Social Security Administration Act 1992 and sections 4(9), 14(2), (3) and (4), 16(1) and (2), 18, 19, 21(3), 23(1), (2), (5) and (7), 29 and 32 of, and paragraphs 4 and 8 of Schedule 1 to, the Social Security (Recovery of Benefits) Act 1997, and of all other powers enabling her in that behalf, hereby makes the following Regulations:

Citation, commencement and interpretation

2.648   **1.**—(1) These Regulations may be cited as the Social Security (Recovery of Benefits) Regulations 1997 and shall come into force on 6th October 1997.

(2) In these Regulations—

"the 1992 Act" means the Social Security Administration Act 1992;

"the 1997 Act" means the Social Security (Recovery of Benefits) Act 1997;

"commencement day" means the day these Regulations come into force;

"compensator" means a person making a compensation payment;

"Compensation Recovery Unit" means the Compensation Recovery Unit of the Department of Social Security at [¹ Durham House, Washington, Tyne and Wear, NE38 7SP].

(3) A reference in these Regulations to a numbered section or Schedule is a reference, unless the context otherwise requires, to that section of or Schedule to the 1997 Act.

AMENDMENT

1. Social Security (Recovery of Benefits) (Miscellaneous Amendments) Regulations 2000 (SI 2000/3030), reg.2 (December 4, 2000).

DEFINITION

"compensation payment"—see s.1(4) of the Social Security (Recovery of Benefits) Act 1997.

Exempted trusts and payments

2.—(1) The following trusts are prescribed for the purposes of paragraph 4 of Schedule 1—

(a) the Macfarlane Trust established on 10th March 1988 partly out of funds provided by the Secretary of State to the Haemophilia Society for the relief of poverty or distress among those suffering from haemophilia;

(b) the Macfarlane (Special Payments) Trust established on 29th January 1990 partly out of funds provided by the Secretary of State, for the benefit of certain persons suffering from haemophilia;

(c) the Macfarlane (Special Payments) (No.2) Trust established on 3rd May 1991 partly out of funds provided by the Secretary of State, for the benefit of certain persons suffering from haemophilia and other beneficiaries;

(d) the Eileen Trust established on 29th March 1993 out of funds provided by the Secretary of State for the benefit of persons eligible for payment in accordance with its provisions;

[¹(e) a trust established out of funds provided by the Secretary of State in respect of persons who suffered, or who are suffering, from variant Creutzfelt-Jakob disease for the benefit of persons eligible for interim payments in accordance with its provisions;

(f) a trust established out of funds provided by the Secretary of State in respect of persons who suffered, or who are suffering, from variant Creutzfelt-Jakob disease for the benefit of persons eligible for payments, other than interim payments, in accordance with its provisions;]

[⁴ (g) the UK Asbestos Trust established on 10th October 2006, for the benefit of certain persons suffering from asbestos-related diseases;

(h) the EL Scheme Trust established on 23rd November 2006, for the benefit of certain persons suffering from asbestos-related diseases.]

2.649

(2) The following payments are prescribed for the purposes of paragraph 8 of Schedule 1—

  (a) any payment to the extent that it is made—
- (i) in consequence of an action under the Fatal Accidents Act 1976; or
- (ii) in circumstances where, had an action been brought, it would have been brought under that Act;

  (b) any payment to the extent that it is made in respect of a liability arising by virtue of section 1 of the Damages (Scotland) Act 1976;

  (c) any payment made under the Vaccine Damage Payments Act 1979 to or in respect of the injured person;

  (d) any award of compensation made to or in respect of the injured person under the Criminal Injuries Compensation Act 1995 or by the Criminal Injuries Compensation Board under the Criminal Injuries Compensation Scheme 1990 or any earlier scheme;

  (e) any compensation payment made by British Coal in accordance with the NCB Pneumoconiosis Compensation Scheme set out in the Schedule to an agreement made on the 13th September 1974 between the National Coal Board, the National Union of Mine Workers, the National Association of Colliery Overmen Deputies and Shot-firers and the British Association of Colliery Management;

  (f) any payment made to the injured person in respect of sensorineural hearing loss where the loss is less than than 50 dB in one or both ears;

  (g) any contractual amount paid to an employee by an employer of his in respect of a period of incapacity for work;

  (h) any payment made under the National Health Service (Injury Benefits) Regulations 1995 or the National Health Service (Scotland) (Injury Benefits) Regulations 1974;

  (i) any payment made by or on behalf of the Secretary of State for the benefit of persons eligible for payment in accordance with the provisions of a scheme established by him on 24th April 1992 or, in Scotland, on 10th April 1992.

[2 (j) any payment made from the Skipton Fund, the ex-gratia payment scheme administered by the Skipton Fund Limited, incorporated on 25th March 2004, for the benefit of certain persons suffering from hepatitis C and other persons eligible for payments in accordance with the scheme's provisions.]

[3 (k) any payment made from the London Bombings Relief Charitable Fund, the company limited by guarantee (number 5505072) and registered charity of that name established on 11th July for the purpose of (amongst other things) relieving sickness, disability or financial need of victims (including families or dependants of victims) of the terrorist attacks carried out in London on 7th July 2005.]

AMENDMENTS

1. Social Security Amendment (Capital Disregards and Recovery of Benefits) Regulations 2001 (SI 2001/1118), reg.4 (April 12, 2001).

2. Social Security (Miscellaneous Amendments) (No.2) Regulations 2004 (SI 2004/1141), reg.7 (May 12, 2004).

3. Income-related Benefits (Amendment) (No.2) Regulations 2005 (SI 2005/3391), reg.6 (December 12, 2005).

4. Social Security (Recovery of Benefits) Amendment) Regulations 2007 (SI 2007/357, reg.2 (March 12, 2007).

DEFINITIONS

"compensation payment"—see s.1(4) of the Social Security (Recovery of Benefits) Act 1997.

"payment"—see s.29 of the Social Security (Recovery of Benefits) Act 1997.

Information to be provided by the compensator

3.—The following information is prescribed for the purposes of section 23(1):

   2.650

(a) the full name and address of the injured person;
(b) where known, the date of birth or national insurance number of that person, or both if both are known;
(c) where the liability arises, or is alleged to arise, in respect of an accident or injury, the date of the accident or injury;
(d) the nature of the accident, injury or disease; and
(e) where known, and where the relevant period may include a period prior to 6th April 1994, whether, at the time of the accident or injury or diagnosis of the disease, the person was employed under a contract of service, and, if he was, the name and address of his employer at that time and the person's payroll number.

DEFINITION

"injured person"—see s.1(4) of the Social Security (Recovery of Benefits) Act 1997.

Information to be provided by the injured person

4. The following information is prescribed for the purposes of section 23(2):

   2.651

(a) whether the accident, injury or disease resulted from any action taken by another person, or from any failure of another person to act, and, if so, the full name and address of that other person;
(b) whether the injured person has claimed or may claim a compensation payment, and, if so, the full name and address of the person against whom the claim was or may be made;
(c) the amount of any compensation payment and the date on which it was made;
(d) the listed benefits claimed, and for each benefit the date from which it was first claimed and the amount received in the period beginning with that date and ending with the date the information is sent;
(e) in the case of a person who has received statutory sick pay during the relevant period and prior to 6th April 1994, the name and address of any employer who made those payments to him during the relevant period and the dates the employment with that employer began and ended; and
(f) any changes in the medical diagnosis relating to the condition arising from the accident, injury or disease.

DEFINITIONS

"compensation payment"—see s.1(4) of the Social Security (Recovery of Benefits) Act 1997.

"injured person"—*ibid.*

"listed benefit"—see s.29 of the Social Security (Recovery of Benefits) Act 1997.

Information to be provided by the employer

2.652　　**5.** The following information is prescribed for the purposes of section 23(5):

 (a) the amount of any statutory sick pay the employer has paid to the injured person since the first day of the relevant period and before 6th April 1994;

 (b) the date the liability to pay such statutory sick pay first arose and the rate at which it was payable;

 (c) the date on which such liability terminated; and

 (d) the causes of incapacity for work during any period of entitlement to statutory sick pay during the relevant period and prior to 6th April 1994.

DEFINITION

"injured person"—see s.1(4) of the Social Security (Recovery of Benefits) Act 1997.

Provision of information

2.653　　**6.** A person required to give information to the Secretary of State under regulations 3 to 5 shall do so by sending it to the Compensation Recovery Unit not later than 14 days after—

 (a) where he is a person to whom regulation 3 applies, the date on which he receives a claim for compensation from the injured person in respect of the accident, injury or disease;

 (b) where he is a person to whom regulation 4 or 5 applies, the date on which the Secretary of State requests the information from him.

DEFINITIONS

"Compensation Recovery Unit"—see reg.1(2).

Application for a certificate of recoverable benefits

2.654　　**7.**—(1) The following particulars are prescribed for the purposes of section 21(3)(a) (particulars to be included in an application for a certificate of recoverable benefits):

 (a) the full name and address of the injured person;

 (b) the date of birth and, where known, the national insurance number of that person;

 (c) where the liability arises or is alleged to arise in respect of an accident or injury, the date of the accident or injury;

 (d) the nature of the accident, injury or disease;

 (e) where the person liable, or alleged to be liable, in respect of the accident, injury or disease, is the employer of the injured person, or has been such an employer, the information prescribed by regulation 5.

(2) An application for a certificate of recoverable benefits is to be treated for the purposes of the 1997 Act as received by the Secretary of State on the day on which it is received by the Compensation Recovery Unit, or if the application is received after normal business hours, or on a day which is not a normal business day at that office, on the next such day.

DEFINITIONS

"the 1997 Act"—see reg.1(2).
"Compensation Recovery Unit"—*ibid*.
"injured person"—see s.1(4) of the Social Security (Recovery of Benefits) Act 1997.
"recoverable benefit"—*ibid*.

Payments into court

8.—(1) Subject to the provisions of this regulation, where a party to an action makes a payment into court which, had it been paid directly to another party to the action ("the relevant party"), would have constituted a compensation payment—
2.655

- (a) the making of that payment shall be treated for the purposes of the 1997 Act as the making of a compensation payment;
- (b) a current certificate of recoverable benefits shall be lodged with the payment; and
- (c) where the payment is calculated under section 8, the compensator must give the relevant party the information specified in section 9(1), instead of the person to whom the payment is made.

(2) The liability under section 6(1) to pay an amount equal to the total amount of the recoverable benefits shall not arise until the person making the payment into court has been notified that the whole or any part of the payment into court has been paid out of court to or for the relevant party.

(3) Where a payment into court in satisfaction of his claim is accepted by the relevant party in the initial period, then as respects the compensator in question, the relevant period shall be taken to have ended, if it has not done so already, on the day on which the payment into court (or if there were two or more such payments, the last of them) was made.

(4) Where, after the expiry of the initial period, the payment into court is accepted in satisfaction of the relevant party's claim by consent between the parties, the relevant period shall end, if it has not done so already, on the date on which application to the court for the payment is made.

(5) Where, after the expiry of the initial period, payment out of court is made wholly or partly to or for the relevant party in accordance with an order of the court and in satisfaction of his claim, the relevant period shall end, if it has not done so already, on the date of that order.

(6) In paragraphs (3), (4) and (5), "the initial period" means the period of 21 days after the receipt by the relevant party to the action of notice of the payment into court having been made.

(7) Where a payment into court is paid out wholly to or for the party who made the payment (otherwise than to or for the relevant party to the action) the making of the payment into court shall cease to be regarded as the making of a compensation payment.

(8) A current certificate of recoverable benefits in paragraph (1) means one that is in force as described in section 4(4).

GENERAL NOTE

2.656   See the note to s.16(1) and (2) of the Social Security (Recovery of Benefits) Act 1997, under which this regulation is made.

Reduction of compensation: complex cases

2.657   **9.**—(1) This regulation applies where—

(a) a compensation payment in the form of a lump sum (an "earlier payment") has been made to or in respect of the injured person; and

(b) subsequently another such payment (a "later payment") is made to or in respect of the same injured person in consequence of the same accident, injury or disease.

(2) In determining the liability under section 6(1) arising in connection with the making of the later payment, the amount referred to in that subsection shall be reduced by any amount paid in satisfaction of that liability as it arose in connection with the earlier payment.

(3) Where—

(a) a payment made in satisfaction of the liability under section 6(1) arising in connection with an earlier payment is not reflected in the certificate of recoverable benefits in force at the time of a later payment, and

(b) in consequence, the aggregate of payments made in satisfaction of the liability exceeds what it would have been had that payment been so reflected,

the Secretary of State shall pay the compensator who made the later payment an amount equal to the excess.

(4) Where—

(a) a compensator receives a payment under paragraph (3), and

(b) the amount of the compensation payment made by him was calculated under section 8,

then the compensation payment shall be recalculated under section 8, and the compensator shall pay the amount of the increase (if any) to the person to whom the compensation payment was made.

(5) Where both the earlier payment and the later payment are made by the same compensator, he may—

(a) aggregate the gross amounts of the payments made by him;

(b) calculate what would have been the reduction made under section 8(3) if that aggregate amount had been paid at the date of the last payment on the basis that—

(i) so much of the aggregate amount as is attributable to a head of compensation listed in column (1) of Schedule 2 shall be taken to be the part of the gross amount which attributable to that head, and

(ii) the amount of any recoverable benefits shown against any head in column (2) of that Schedule shall be taken to be the amount determined in accordance with the most recent certificate of recoverable benefits;

(c) deduct from that reduction calculated under sub-paragraph (b) the amount of the reduction under section 8(3) from any earlier payment; and

(d) deduct from the latest gross payment the net reduction calculated under sub-paragraph (c) (and accordingly the latest payment may be nil).

(6) Where the Secretary of State is making a refund under paragraph (3), he shall send to the compensator (with the refund) and to the person to whom the compensation payment was made a statement showing—

(a) the total amount that has already been paid by that compensator to the Secretary of State;

(b) the amount that ought to have been paid by that compensator; and

(c) the amount to be repaid to that compensator by the Secretary of State.

(7) Where the reduction of a compensation payment is recalculated by virtue of paragraph (4) or (5) the compensator shall give notice of the calculation to the injured person.

GENERAL NOTE

This regulation is made under ss.18(1) to (3) and 19 of the Social Security   2.658
(Recovery of Benefits) Act 1997 and is concerned with cases where more than one lump-sum compensation payment is made to a victim in respect of a single accident, injury or disease. (Structured settlements involving periodical payments are dealt with in reg.10). Regulation 9 covers cases where the same compensator makes more than one lump-sum payment and also cases where different compensators make payments because they all contributed to the accident, injury or disease. However, it makes no attempt at apportionment of liability for recoverable benefits between different compensators. It is concerned only to ensure that there is not double recovery and it does not even attempt that in a case where benefit has been paid as a result of two different injuries each attributable to a different accident. See *R(CR)2/04* and the note to s.1 of the Act for the way that liability is attributed in such a case. Where two compensators are liable in respect of the same accident, injury or disease, the one making the first compensation payment is likely to have the greater liability to the Secretary of State and must seek a contribution from the other so that they each bear a fair share of the liability for benefits.

Paragraph (2) simply provides that when a second compensation payment is made, the Secretary of State should not recover benefits that were recovered when the earlier payment was made. Paragraph (3) provides for a refund to the compensator if benefits are erroneously recovered for a second time. Paragraph (4) provides that, where the compensator has reduced under s.8 of the Act the amount of compensation paid to the victim (in effect recovering from the victim the benefits that the victim had received and the compensator had to pay to the Secretary of State), he must recalculate the s.8 reduction in the light of a refund under para.(3) and pay the appropriate amount, if any, to the victim. Where the same compensator made both the compensation payments, he may aggregate them for the purpose of recalculating the appropriate s.8 reduction under para.(4) (para.(5)). Paragraphs (6) and (7) require the victim to be told by the Secretary of State about any refund under para.(3) and by the compensator about any recalculation under paras (4) and (5).

Structured settlements

10.—(1) This regulation applies where—   2.659

(a) in final settlement of an injured person's claim, an agreement is entered into—

(i) for the making of periodical payments (whether of an income or capital nature); or

(ii) for the making of such payments and lump sum payments; and

    (b) apart from the provisions of this regulation, those payments would fall to be treated for the purposes of the 1997 Act as compensation payments.

    (2) Where this regulation applies, the provisions of the 1997 Act and these Regulations shall be modified in the following way—

    (a) the compensator in question shall be taken to have made on that day a single compensation payment;

    (b) the relevant period in the case of the compensator in question shall be taken to end (if it has not done so already) on the day of settlement;

    (c) payments under the agreement referred to in paragraph (1)(a) shall be taken not to be compensation payments;

    (d) paragraphs (5) and (7) of regulation 11 shall not apply.

    (3) Where any further payment falls to be made to or in respect of the injured person otherwise than under the agreement in question, paragraph (2) shall be disregarded for the purpose of determining the end of the relevant period in relation to that further payment.

    (4) In any case where—

    (a) the person making the periodical payments ("the secondary party") does so in pursuance of arrangements entered into with another ("primary party") (as in a case where the primary party purchases an annuity for the injured person from the secondary party), and

    (b) apart from those arrangements, the primary party would have been regarded as the compensator,

then for the purposes of the 1997 Act, the primary party shall be regarded as the compensator and the secondary party shall not be so regarded.

    (5) In this regulation "the day of settlement" means—

    (a) if the agreement referred to in paragraph (1)(a) is approved by a court, the day on which that approval is given; and

    (b) in any other case, the day on which the agreement is entered into.

GENERAL NOTE

2.660   This regulation is made under s.8(4) to (6) of the Social Security (Recovery of Benefits) Act 1997.

    Where a final settlement is reached in the form of an agreement that involves the making of periodical payments (whether of a capital or income nature and whether or not they are combined with sum lump sums), the compensator is treated as having made a compensation payment on the day the agreement is reached. That is when the "relevant period" under s.3 of the Act is taken to have ended and when the compensator becomes liable to make a payment to the Secretary of State under s.6. Further payments under the agreement (by whomever they are made (see para.(4)) do not count as compensation payments (para.(2)(c)) but any payments outside it will (para.(3)) and reg.9 will apply to them.

Adjustments

2.661   **11.**—(1) Where the conditions specified in subsection (1) and paragraphs (a) and (b) of subsection (2) of section 14 are satisfied, the Secretary of State shall pay the difference between the amount that has been paid and the amount that ought to have been paid to the compensator.

    (2) Where the conditions specified in subsection (1) and paragraphs (a)

and (b) of subsection (3) of section 14 are satisfied, the compensator shall pay the difference between the total amounts paid and the amount that ought to have been paid to the Secretary of State.

(3) Where the Secretary of State is making a refund under paragraph (1), or demanding payment of a further amount under paragraph (2), he shall send to the compensator (with the refund or demand) and to the person to whom the compensation payment was made a statement showing—

(a) the total amount that has already been paid to the Secretary of State;

(b) the amount that ought to have been paid; and

(c) the difference, and whether a repayment by the Secretary of State or a further payment to him is required.

(4) This paragraph applies where—

(a) the amount of the compensation payment made by the compensator was calculated under section 8; and

(b) the Secretary of State has made a payment under paragraph (1).

(5) Where paragraph (4) applies, the amount of the compensation payment shall be recalculated under section 8 to take account of the fresh certificate of recoverable benefits and the compensator shall pay the amount of the increase (if any) to the person to whom the compensation payment was made.

(6) This paragraph applies where—

(a) the amount of the compensation payment made by the compensator was calculated under section 8;

(b) the compensator has made a payment under paragraph (2); and

(c) the fresh certificate of recoverable benefits issued after the review or appeal was required as a result of the injured person or other person to whom the compensation payment was made supplying to the compensator information knowing it to be incorrect or insufficient with the intent of enhancing the compensation payment calculated under section 8, and the compensator supplying that information to the Secretary of State without knowing it to be incorrect or insufficient.

(7) Where paragraph (6) applies, the compensator may recalculate the compensation payment under section 8 to take account of the fresh certificate of recoverable benefits and may require the repayment to him by the person to whom he made the compensation payment of the difference (if any) between the payment made and the payment as so recalculated.

GENERAL NOTE

This is a key provision. Paragraphs (1) to (3) simply provide for the appropriate refund or demand for further payment to be made by the Secretary of State following a review or appeal. Of more practical importance are paras (4) and (5) requiring that, where there is a refund, the compensator must recalculate any reduction in a compensation payment made under s.8 of the Social Security (Recovery of Benefits) Act 1997 and pay the amount of any increase in the compensation payment to the claimant. That means that a compensator does not have any practical interest in challenging a certificate for recoverable benefits insofar as he has reduced the claimant's compensation to take account of the benefits (*R(CR) 2/03*). Unfortunately, it appears that these paragraphs are sometimes

2.662

overlooked even by experienced insurance companies with the result that they retain money due to claimants. Paragraphs (6) and (7) make similar provision for cases where there is a demand for a further payment, only in those circumstances they have the effect that the claimant may have to make a further payment to the compensator. They operate only if the claimant knowingly supplied incorrect, or insufficient, information to the compensator and the compensator innocently passed it on to the Secretary of State.

Transitional provisions

2.663

12.—(1) In relation to a compensation payment to which by virtue of section 2 the 1997 Act applies and subject to paragraph (2), a certificate of total benefit issued under Part IV of the 1992 Act shall be treated on or after the commencement date as a certificate of recoverable benefits issued under the 1997 Act and the amount of total benefit treated as that of recoverable benefits.

(2) Paragraph (1) shall not apply to a certificate of total benefit which specifies an amount in respect of disability living allowance without specifying whether that amount was, or is likely to be, paid wholly by way of the care component or the mobility component or (if not wholly one of them) specifying the relevant amount for each component.

[¹(3) Any appeal under section 98 of the 1992 Act made on or after 6th October 1997 which has not been determined before 29th November 1999 shall be referred to an appeal tribunal constituted in accordance with paragraph (3I) below.

(3A) Any appeal duly made before 6th October 1997 which has not been referred to a medical appeal tribunal or a social security appeal tribunal shall be referred to and determined by an appeal tribunal constituted in accordance with paragraph (3I) below.

(3B) Any appeal duly made before 6th October 1997 and referred to a medical appeal tribunal shall be determined by an appeal tribunal constituted in accordance with paragraph (3I) below which shall determine all issues.

(3C) Any appeal duly made before 6th October 1997 and referred to a social security appeal tribunal shall be determined by an appeal tribunal which shall consist of a legally qualified panel member and in making its determination, the appeal tribunal shall be bound by any decision of a medical appeal tribunal to which a question under section 98(5) of the 1992 Act was referred.

(3D) An appeal tribunal constituted in accordance with paragraph (3I) below shall completely rehear any appeal made under section 98 of the 1992 Act which stands adjourned immediately before 29th November 1999.

(3E) Where a Commissioner holds that the decision of a medical appeal tribunal or a social security appeal tribunal on an appeal made before 6th October 1997 was erroneous in law and refers the case to an appeal tribunal, that appeal tribunal shall be constituted in accordance with paragraph (3I) below and shall determine all issues in accordance with the Commissioner's direction.

(3F) Regulation 11 of the Social Security (Recoupment) Regulations 1990 ("the 1990 Regulations") and regulation 12 of those Regulations shall have effect in relation to any appeal under section 98 of the 1992 Act made on or after 6th October 1997 with the modification that for the word "chairman" in each place in which it occurs there were substituted the words "legally qualified panel member".

(3G) Regulation 13 of the 1990 Regulations shall have effect in relation to any appeal under section 98 of the 1992 Act made on or after 6th October 1997.

(3H) Any other transitional question arising from an appeal made under section 98 of the 1992 Act in consequence of the coming into force of the Social Security and Child Support (Decisions and Appeals) Regulations 1999 ("the 1999 Regulations") shall be determined by a legally qualified panel member who may for this purpose give such directions consistent with these regulations as are necessary.

(3I) For the purposes of paragraphs (3) to (3B) and (3E) above an appeal tribunal shall be constituted under Chapter I of Part I of the Social Security Act 1998 as though the appeal were made under section 11(1)(b) of the 1997 Act.

(3J) In this regulation, "legally qualified panel member" has the meaning it bears in regulation 1(3) of the 1999 Regulations.]

(4) Paragraph (5) applies where—

(a) an amount has been paid to the Secretary of State under section 82(1)(b) of the 1992 Act,

(b) liability arises on or after the commencement day to make a payment under section 6(1), and

(c) the compensation payments which give rise to the liability to make both payments are to or in respect of the same injured person in consequence of the same accident, injury or disease.

(5) Where this paragraph applies, the liability under section 6 shall be reduced by the payment (or aggregate of the payments, if more than one) described in paragraph (4)(a).

(6) Where—

(a) a payment into court has been made on a date prior to the commencement day but the initial period, as defined in section 93(6) of the 1992 Act, in relation to that payment, expires on or after the commencement day; and

(b) the payment into court is accepted by the other party to the action in the initial period,

that payment into court shall be treated as a compensation payment to which the 1992 Act, and not the 1997 Act, applies.

(7) Where a payment into court has been made prior to the commencement day, remains in court on that day and paragraph (6) does not apply, that payment into court shall be treated as a payment to which the 1997 Act applies, but paragraph (1) (b) and (c) of regulation 8 shall not apply.

AMENDMENT

1. Social Security Act 1998 (Commencement No.12 and Consequential and Transitional Provisions) Order 1999 (SI 1999/3178), art.3(17) and Sch.17 (November 29, 1999).

GENERAL NOTE

This regulation has been amended in such a way that it now makes transitional provision not only for the coming into force of the Social Security (Recovery of Benefits) Act 1997 but also for the coming into force of the Social Security Act 1998.

2.664

Social Security (Recovery of Benefits) (Lump Sum Payments) Regulations 2008

(SI 2008/1596)

<table>
<tr><td>2.665</td><td>*Made*</td><td align="right">*18ᵗʰ June 2008*</td></tr>
<tr><td></td><td>*Laid before Parliament*</td><td align="right">*25ᵗʰ June 2008*</td></tr>
<tr><td></td><td>*Coming into force*</td><td align="right">*1ˢᵗ October 2008*</td></tr>
</table>

2.666   The Secretary of State for Work and Pensions makes the following Regulations in exercise of the powers conferred by section 189(4) and (6) of the Social Security Administration Act 1992, sections 1A, 14(2), (3) and (4), 18, 19, 21(3), 23(1), (2) and (7) and 29 of, and paragraphs 4 and 8 of Schedule 1 to, the Social Security (Recovery of Benefits) Act 1997, section 79(6) of the Social Security Act 1998 and section 53 of the Child Maintenance and Other Payments Act 2008, which contains only regulations made by virtue of, or consequential on sections 54 and 57(2) of the Child Maintenance and Other Payments Act 2008 and which are made before the end of a period of 6 months beginning with the coming into force of those sections:

PART 1

GENERAL

Citation, commencement and interpretation

2.667   1.—(1) These Regulations may be cited as the Social Security (Recovery of Benefits) (Lump Sum Payments) Regulations 2008 and shall come into force on 1st October 2008.

(2) In these Regulations—

"the Act" means the Social Security (Recovery of Benefits) Act 1997;

"compensator" means a person making a compensation payment;

"Compensation Recovery Unit" means the Compensation Recovery Unit of the Department for Work and Pensions at Durham House, Washington, Tyne and Wear, NE38 7SF;

"lump sum payments" are payments to which section 1A(2) of the Act applies, except in relation to regulation 18(1)(b);

"recoverable benefits" has the same meaning as in section 1(4)(c) of the Act;

"recoverable lump sum payments" means any lump sum payments which are recoverable by virtue of regulation 4.

Application of the Act

2.668   2.—(1) The provisions of the Act specified in paragraph (2) apply for the purposes of these Regulations with the modifications, where appropriate, prescribed in Schedule 1.

(2) The specified provisions are—
  (a) section 1(3) (cases in which this Act applies);
  (b) sections 10 to 14 (reviews and appeals);
  (c) sections 15 and 17 (courts);
  (d) sections 18 and 19 (reduction of compensation: complex cases);
  (e) sections 20 to 23 (miscellaneous);
  (f) sections 26 and 27 (provisions relating to Northern Ireland);
  (g) sections 28 to 31 (general);
  (h) section 33 (consequential amendments and repeals);
  (i) section 34(1) and (3) (short title and extent);
  (j) Schedule 1 (compensation payments—exempted payments and power to disregard small payments).

3. *Omitted.*

Recovery of lump sum payments

4.—(1) The Secretary of State may recover the amount of a payment to   **2.669**
which section 1A(2) of the Act applies ("a lump sum payment") where—
  (a) a compensation payment in consequence of a disease is made to or in respect of—
      (i) a person ("P"); or
      (ii) a dependant of P,
    to whom, or in respect of whom, a lump sum payment has been, or is likely to be, made; and
  (b) the compensation payment is made in consequence of the same disease as the lump sum payment.

(2) In paragraph (1), references to a payment made in consequence of a disease—
  (a) are references to a payment made by or on behalf of a person who is, or is alleged to be, liable to any extent in respect of the disease; but
  (b) do not include references to a payment mentioned in Part 1 of Schedule 1 to the Act.

Application of these Regulations to a dependant of P

5.—(1) Subject to paragraph (2), in these Regulations and any provision   **2.670**
of the Act as modified any reference to P is to be construed as if it included
a reference to a dependant of P where that dependant is the person to
whom, or in respect of whom, a lump sum payment is made.

(2) Paragraph (1) does not apply in relation to regulations 4, 10(7) and
12(7) and sections 15 and 23(2) of, and paragraphs 3(a) and 5(1) of Part 1
of Schedule 1 to, the Act.

Compensation payments to which these Regulations apply

6. These Regulations apply in relation to compensation payments made   **2.671**
on or after the day on which section 54 of the Child Maintenance and
Other Payments Act 2008 comes into force.

Exempted trusts and payments

7.—(1) The following trusts are prescribed for the purposes of paragraph   **2.672**
4 of Schedule 1 to the Act—

(a) the Macfarlane Trust established on 10th March 1988 partly out of funds provided by the Secretary of State to the Haemophilia Society for the relief of poverty or distress among those suffering from hae-mophilia;

(b) the Macfarlane (Special Payments) Trust established on 29th January 1990 partly out of funds provided by the Secretary of State, for the benefit of certain persons suffering from haemophilia;

(c) the Macfarlane (Special Payments) (No. 2) Trust established on 3rd May 1991 partly out of funds provided by the Secretary of State, for the benefit of certain persons suffering from haemophilia and other beneficiaries;

(d) the Eileen Trust established on 29th March 1993 out of funds pro-vided by the Secretary of State, for the benefit of persons eligible for payment in accordance with its provisions;

(e) a trust established out of funds provided by the Secretary of State in respect of persons who suffered, or who are suffering, from variant Creutzfeldt-Jakob disease for the benefit of persons eligible for interim payments in accordance with its provisions;

(f) a trust established out of funds provided by the Secretary of State in respect of persons who suffered, or who are suffering, from variant Creutzfeldt-Jakob disease for the benefit of persons eligible for payments, other than interim payments, in accordance with its provisions.

(2) The following payments are prescribed for the purposes of paragraph 8 of Schedule 1 to the Act—

(a) any payment made under the Vaccine Damage Payments Act 1979 to or in respect of P;

(b) any award of compensation made to or in respect of P under the Criminal Injuries Compensation Act 1995 or by the Criminal Injuries Compensation Board under the Criminal Injuries Compensation Scheme 1990 or any earlier scheme or under the Criminal Injuries Compensation (Northern Ireland) Order 2002;

(c) any payment made to P in respect of sensorineural hearing loss where the loss is less than 50 decibels in one or both ears;

(d) any contractual amount paid to P by an employer of P in respect of a period of incapacity for work;

(e) any payment made under the National Health Service (Injury Benefits) Regulations 1995, the National Health Service (Scotland) (Injury Benefits) Regulations 1998 or the Health and Personal Social Services (Injury Benefits) Regulations (Northern Ireland) 2001;

(f) any payment made by or on behalf of the Secretary of State for the benefit of persons eligible for payment in accordance with the provi-sions of a scheme established by the Secretary of State on 24th April 1992 or, in Scotland, on 10th April 1992;

(g) any payment made from the Skipton Fund, the ex-gratia payment scheme administered by the Skipton Fund Limited, incorporated on 25th March 2004, for the benefit of certain persons suffering from hepatitis C and other persons eligible for payment in accordance with the scheme's provisions;

(h) any payment made from the London Bombings Relief Charitable Fund, the company limited by guarantee (number 5505072) and registered charity of that name established on 11th July 2005 for the purpose of (amongst other things) relieving sickness, disability or financial need of victims (including families or dependants of victims) of the terrorist attacks carried out in London on 7th July 2005.

PART 2

CERTIFICATES

Applications for certificates

8.—(1) Before making a compensation payment the compensator must apply to the Secretary of State for a certificate.

(2) Where the compensator applies for a certificate, the Secretary of State must—

    (a) send to the compensator a written acknowledgment of receipt of the application; and

    (b) issue the certificate before the end of the period of 4 weeks.

(3) An application for a certificate is to be treated for the purposes of the Act as received by the Secretary of State on the day on which it is received by the Compensation Recovery Unit, or if the application is received after normal business hours, or on a day which is not a normal business day at that office, on the next such day.

2.673

Information contained in certificates

9.—(1) Subject to paragraph (2), a certificate must specify—

    (a) the amounts;

    (b) which of the type of payments referred to in section 1A(2) of the Act applies; and

    (c) the dates,

of any lump sum payments which have been, or are likely to have been paid.

(2) Where the type of payment is an extra-statutory payment the certificate may specify that type of payment as if it were a payment to which section 1A(2)(a) applies.

(3) The Secretary of State may estimate, in such manner as the Secretary of State thinks fit the amount of the lump sum payments specified in the certificate.

(4) Where the Secretary of State issues a certificate, the information contained in that certificate must be provided to—

    (a) the person who appears to the Secretary of State to be P; or

    (b) any person who the Secretary of State thinks will receive a compensation payment in respect of P.

(5) A person to whom a certificate is issued or who is provided with information under [¹ paragraph (4)] is entitled to particulars of the manner in which any amount, type of payment or date specified in the certificate has been determined, if that person applies to the Secretary of State for those particulars.

2.674

PART 3

LIABILITY OF PERSON PAYING COMPENSATION

Liability to pay Secretary of State amount of lump sum payments

2.675   **10.**—(1) A person who makes a compensation payment in any case is liable to pay the Secretary of State an amount equal to the total amount of—

(a) in a case to which paragraph (2) applies, the recoverable lump sum payments; or

(b) in a case to which paragraph (3) applies, the compensation payment.

(2) Paragraph (1)(a) applies to a case where—

(a) the compensation payment is equal to, or more than, any recoverable lump sum payments; or

(b) a dependant is a beneficiary of part of a compensation payment made in respect of P, that part of the compensation payment is equal to, or more than, any recoverable lump sum payments which have been made to that dependant.

(3) Paragraph 1(b) applies to a case where—

(a) the compensation payment; or

(b) a dependant is a beneficiary of part of a compensation payment made in respect of P, and recoverable lump sum payments have been made to that dependant, the share of the compensation payment,

is less than the lump sum payments.

(4) The liability referred to in paragraph (1) arises—

(a) immediately before the compensation payment or, if there is more than one, the first of them is made;

(b) prior to any liability to pay the Secretary of State an amount equal to the total amount of the recoverable benefits payable under section 6 of the Act.

(5) No amount becomes payable under this regulation before the end of the period of 14 days following the day on which the liability arises.

(6) Subject to paragraph (4), an amount becomes payable under this regulation at the end of the period of 14 days beginning with the day on which a certificate is first issued showing that the amount of recoverable lump sum payment to which it relates has been or is likely to have been paid.

(7) In the case of a lump sum payment which has been made to a dependant of P, this regulation applies only to the extent to which the compensator is making any payment—

(a) (i) under the Fatal Accidents Act 1976;

(ii) to the extent that it is made in respect of a liability arising by virtue of section 1 of the Damages (Scotland) Act 1976; or

(iii) under the Fatal Accidents (Northern Ireland) Order 1977, to that dependant; or

(b) in respect of P, and that dependant is an intended beneficiary of part or all of that payment.

Recovery of payment due under regulation 10

11.—(1) This regulation applies where a compensator has made a compensation payment but—

2.676

(a) has not applied for a certificate; or

(b) has not made a payment to the Secretary of State under regulation 10 before the end of the period allowed under that regulation.

(2) The Secretary of State may—

(a) issue the compensator who made the compensation payment with a certificate, if none has been issued; or

(b) issue that compensator with a copy of the certificate or (if more than one has been issued) the most recent one,

and (in either case) issue that compensator with a demand that payment of any amount due under regulation 10 be made immediately.

(3) The Secretary of State may, in accordance with paragraphs (4) and (5), recover the amount for which a demand for payment is made under paragraph (2) from the compensator who made the compensation payment.

(4) If the compensator who made the compensation payment resides or carries on business in England and Wales and a county court so orders, any amount recoverable under paragraph (3) is recoverable by execution issued from the county court or otherwise as if it were payable under an order of that court.

(5) If the compensator who made the payment resides or carries on business in Scotland, any amount recoverable under paragraph (3) may be enforced in like manner as an extract registered decree arbitral bearing a warrant for execution issued by the sheriff court of any sheriffdom in Scotland.

(6) A document bearing a certificate which—

(a) is signed by a person authorised to do so by the Secretary of State; and

(b) states that the document, apart from the certificate, is a record of the amount recoverable under paragraph (3),

is conclusive evidence that that amount is so recoverable.

(7) A certificate under paragraph (6) purporting to be signed by a person authorised to do so by the Secretary of State is to be treated as so signed unless the contrary is proved.

PART 4

REDUCTION OF COMPENSATION PAYMENT

Reduction of compensation payment

12.—(1) This regulation applies in a case where, in relation to any compensation payment in consequence of a disease made to, or in respect of P, a lump sum payment has been, or is likely to be made to, or in respect of P.

2.677

(2) In such a case, any claim of a person to receive the compensation payment is to be treated for all purposes as discharged if—

(a) that person is paid the amount (if any) of the compensation payment calculated in accordance with this regulation; and

(b) if the amount of the compensation payment so calculated is nil, that person is given a statement saying so by the compensator who (apart from this regulation) would have paid the gross amount of the compensation payment.

(3) For an award of compensation for which paragraph (1) is satisfied, so much of the gross amount of the compensation payment as is equal to the amount of the lump sum payment is to be reduced (to nil, if necessary) by deducting the amount of the recoverable lump sum payment.

(4) Paragraph (3) is to have effect as if a requirement to reduce a payment by deducting an amount which exceeds that payment were a requirement to reduce that payment to nil.

(5) The amount of the compensation payment calculated in accordance with this regulation is—

(a) the gross amount of the compensation payment;

less

(b) the reductions made under paragraph (3),

(and, accordingly, the amount may be nil).

(6) The reduction specified in paragraph (3) is to be attributed to the heads of compensation in the following order—

(a) damages for non-pecuniary loss;

(b) damages for pecuniary loss,

and, the reduction is to be made before any reduction in respect of recoverable benefits under section 8 of the Act.

(7) Where the lump sum payment has been made to a dependant of P, the reduction specified in paragraph (3) may be attributed—

(a) to any damages awarded to that dependant—

(i) under the Fatal Accidents Act 1976;

(ii) to the extent that they are made in respect of a liability arising by virtue of section 1 of the Damages (Scotland) Act 1976; or

(iii) under the Fatal Accidents (Northern Ireland) Order 1977,

other than those paid for funeral expenses;

(b) to any part of a compensation payment paid in respect of P, where that dependant is an intended beneficiary of part or all of that compensation.

Regulation 12: supplementary

2.678   **13.**—(1) A compensator who makes a compensation payment calculated in accordance with regulation 12 must inform the person to whom the payment is made—

(a) that the payment has been so calculated; and

(b) of the date for payment by reference to which the calculation has been made.

(2) If the amount of a compensation payment calculated in accordance with regulation 12 is nil, a compensator giving a statement saying so is to be treated for the purposes of these Regulations as making a payment within regulation 4(1)(a) on the day on which the statement is given.

(3) Where a compensator—

(a) makes a compensation payment calculated in accordance with regulation 12; and

(b) if the amount of the compensation payment so calculated is nil, gives a statement saying so,

the compensator is to be treated, for the purpose of determining any rights and liabilities in respect of contribution or indemnity, as having paid the gross amount of the compensation payment.

(4) For the purposes of these Regulations—

(a) the gross amount of the compensation payment is the amount of the compensation payment apart from regulation 12; and

(b) the amount of any recoverable lump sum payment is the amount determined in accordance with the certificate.

Reduction of compensation: complex cases

14.—(1) This regulation applies where—

(a) a compensation payment in the form of a lump sum (an "earlier payment") has been made to or in respect of P; and

(b) subsequently another such payment (a "later payment") is made to or in respect of the same P in consequence of the same disease.

(2) In determining the liability under regulation 10(1) arising in connection with the making of the later payment, the amount referred to in that regulation is to be reduced by any amount paid in satisfaction of that liability as it arose in connection with the earlier payment.

(3) Where—

(a) a payment made in satisfaction of the liability under regulation 10(1) arising in connection with an earlier payment is not reflected in the certificate in force at the time of a later payment; and

(b) in consequence, the aggregate of payments made in satisfaction of the liability exceeds what it would have been had that payment been so reflected,

the Secretary of State is to pay the compensator who made the later payment an amount equal to the excess.

(4) Where—

(a) a compensator receives a payment under paragraph (3); and

(b) the amount of the compensation payment made by that compensator was calculated under regulation 12,

then the compensation payment is to be recalculated under regulation 12, and the compensator must pay the amount of the increase (if any) to the person to whom the compensation payment was made.

(5) Where both the earlier payment and the later payment are made by the same compensator, that compensator may—

(a) aggregate the gross amounts of the payments made;

(b) calculate what would have been the reduction made under regulation 12(3) if that aggregate amount had been paid at the date of the last payment on the basis that—

(i) the aggregate amount is to be taken to be the gross amount; and

(ii) the amount of any recoverable lump sum payment is to be taken to be the amount determined in accordance with the most recent certificate;

(c) deduct from that reduction calculated under sub-paragraph (b) the amount of the reduction under regulation 12(3) from any earlier payment; and

    (d) deduct from the latest gross payment the net reduction calculated under sub-paragraph (c) (and accordingly the latest payment may be nil).

(6) Where a refund is made under paragraph (3), the Secretary of State is to send the compensator (with the refund) and the person to whom the compensation payment was made a statement showing—

    (a) the total amount that has already been paid by that compensator to the Secretary of State;

    (b) the amount that ought to have been paid by that compensator; and

    (c) the amount to be repaid to that compensator by the Secretary of State.

(7) Where the reduction of a compensation payment is recalculated by virtue of paragraph (4) or (5) the compensator must give notice of the calculation to P.

PART 5

MISCELLANEOUS

Information to be provided by the compensator

2.680   **15.** The following information is prescribed for the purposes of sections 21(3)(a) and 23(1) of the Act—

    (a) the full name and address of P;

    (b) where known, the date of birth or national insurance number of P, or both if both are known; and

    (c) the nature of the disease.

Information to be provided by P

2.681   **16.** The following information is prescribed for the purposes of section 23(2) of the Act—

    (a) whether P has claimed or may claim a compensation payment, and if so, the full name and address of the person against whom the claim was or may be made;

    (b) the amount of any compensation payment and the date on which it was made;

    (c) the amount of the lump sum payment claimed, the type of that payment and the date on which it was paid.

Provision of information

2.682   **17.** A person required to give information to the Secretary of State under regulation 15 or 16 is to do so by sending it to the Compensation Recovery Unit not later than 14 days after—

    (a) where the person is one to whom regulation 15 applies, the date on which the compensator receives a claim for compensation from P in respect of the disease;

    (b) where the person is one to whom regulation 16 applies, the date on which the Secretary of State requests the information from P.

Periodical payments

18.—(1) This regulation applies where in final settlement of P's claim, an agreement is entered into—   2.683

   (a) for the making of periodical payments (whether of an income or capital nature); or

   (b) for the making of such payments and lump sum payments,

and, those payments would fall to be treated for the purposes of the Act as compensation payments.

(2) Where this regulation applies—

   (a) the compensator in question is to be taken to have made a single compensation payment on the day of settlement;

   (b) the total of the payments due to be made under the agreement referred to in paragraph (1) are to be taken to be a compensation payment for the purposes of the Act; and

   (c) that single compensation payment is a payment from which lump sum payments may be recovered under these Regulations.

(3) In any case where—

   (a) the person making the periodical payments ("the secondary party") does so in pursuance of arrangements entered into with another ("the primary party") (as in a case where the primary party purchases an annuity for P from the secondary party); and

   (b) apart from those arrangements, the primary party would have been regarded as the compensator,

then for the purposes of the Act, the primary party is to be regarded as the compensator and the secondary party is not to be so regarded.

(4) In this regulation—

"the day of settlement" means—

   (a) if the agreement referred to in paragraph (1) is approved by a court, the day on which that approval is given; and

   (b) in any other case, the day on which the agreement is entered into;

"a single compensation payment" means the total amount of the payments due to be made under the agreement referred to in paragraph (1).

Adjustments

19.—(1) Where the conditions specified in subsection (1) and paragraphs (a) and (b) of subsection (2) of section 14 of the Act are satisfied,   2.684
the Secretary of State is to pay the difference between the amount that has been paid and the amount that ought to have been paid to the compensator.

(2) Where the conditions specified in subsection (1) and paragraphs (a) and (b) of subsection (3) of section 14 of the Act are satisfied, the compensator is to pay the difference between the amount that has been paid and the amount that ought to have been paid to the Secretary of State.

(3) Where the Secretary of State is making a refund under paragraph (1), or demanding a payment of a further amount under paragraph (2), the Secretary of State is to send to the compensator (with the refund or demand) and to the person to whom the compensation payment was made a statement showing—

(a) the total amount that has already been paid to the Secretary of State;

(b) the amount that ought to have been paid; and

(c) the difference, and whether a repayment by the Secretary of State or a further payment by the compensator to the Secretary of State is required.

(4) This paragraph applies where—

(a) the amount of the compensation payment by the compensator was calculated under regulation 12; and

(b) the Secretary of State has made a payment under paragraph (1).

(5) Where paragraph (4) applies, the amount of the compensation payment is to be recalculated under regulation 12 to take account of the fresh certificate and the compensator must pay the amount of the increase (if any) to the person to whom the compensation payment was made.

(6) This paragraph applies where—

(a) the amount of the compensation payment made by the compensator was calculated under regulation 12;

(b) the compensator has made a payment under paragraph (2); and

(c) the fresh certificate issued after the review or appeal was required as a result of P or such other person to whom the compensation payment was made supplying to the compensator information, knowing it to be incorrect or insufficient, with the intent of enhancing the compensation payment calculated under regulation 12, and the compensator supplying that information to the Secretary of State without knowing it to be incorrect or insufficient.

(7) Where paragraph (6) applies, the compensator may recalculate the compensation payment under regulation 12 to take account of the fresh certificate and may require the repayment of the difference (if any) between the payment made and the payment as so recalculated by the person to whom the compensator made the compensation payment.

SCHEDULE 1

MODIFICATION OF CERTAIN PROVISIONS OF THE ACT

2.685   1. This Schedule applies to any case to which regulation 4 applies.

2. Where this Schedule applies, section 1 (cases in which this Act applies) is to apply as if in subsection (3), for "Subsection (1)(a)" there were substituted "Section 1A(1)(a)".

3. Where this Schedule applies, section 10 (review of certificates of recoverable benefits) is to apply as if in—

(a) the heading and in subsection (1), there were omitted "of recoverable benefits" in each place it occurs;

(b) subsection (3), for "benefits" there were substituted "lump sum payments, except where that certificate has been reviewed under regulation 9ZA(1)(e) of the Social Security and Child Support (Decisions and Appeals) Regulations 1999 (review of certificates),".

4. Where this Schedule applies, section 11 (appeals against certificates of recoverable benefits) is to apply as if in—

(a) the heading and in subsections (1) and (2)(a), there were omitted "of recoverable benefits" in each place it occurs;

(b) subsection (1)(a), there were omitted ", rate or period";

(c) subsection (1)(b)—

  (i) for "listed benefits" there were substituted "lump sum payments";

  (ii) there were omitted "accident, injury or";

(d) subsection (1)(c)—

    (i) for "listed benefits" there were substituted "lump sum payments";

    (ii) for "the injured person during the relevant period" there were substituted "P";

  (e) subsection (1)(d), for "1(1)(a)" there were substituted "1A(1)(a)";

  (f) subsection (2)(aa) for "section 7(2)(a)" there were substituted "regulation 11(2)(a) of the Lump Sum Payments Regulations";

  (g) subsection (2)(b), for "section 8) the injured person" there were substituted "regulation 12 of the Lump Sum Payments Regulations) P";

  (h) subsection (3), for "section 6" there were substituted "regulation 10 of the Lump Sum Payments Regulations".

  5. Where this Schedule applies, section 12 (reference of questions to [² First-tier Tribunal]) is to apply as if in—

  (a) [² ...]

  (b) subsection (3), there were omitted "accident, injury or";

  (c) subsection (4)(a), for "amounts, rates and periods" there were substituted "amount, type and date of payments";

  (d) subsections (4)(a) and (c), there were omitted "of recoverable benefits" in each place it occurs.

  6. [¹ Where this Schedule applies, section 13 (appeal to [² Upper Tribunal]) is to apply as if in—

  (a) subsection (2)(b) there were omitted "of recoverable benefits" ;

  (b) subsection (2)(bb) for "section 7(2)(a)" there were substituted "regulation 11(2)(a) of the Lump Sum Payment Regulations"; and

  (c) subsection (2)(c) for "section 8) the injured person" there were substituted "regulation 12 of the Lump Sum Payments Regulations).]

  7. Where this Schedule applies, section 14 (reviews and appeals: supplementary) is to apply as if in—

  (a) subsection (1), there were omitted "of recoverable benefits";

  (b) subsections (2) and (3), for "section 6" there were substituted "regulation 10 of the Lump Sum Payments Regulations" in each place it occurs;

  (c) subsection (4), for "section 8" there were substituted "regulation 12 of the Lump Sum Payments Regulations".

  8. Where this Schedule applies, for section 15 (court orders) is to apply as if there were substituted—

"**15.**—(1) This section applies where a court makes an order for a compensation payment to be made in a case where a compensation payment is to be made to a dependant of P—

  (a) under the Fatal Accidents Act 1976 (c. 30);

  (b) to the extent that it is made in respect of a liability arising by virtue of section 1 of the Damages (Scotland) Act 1976 (c. 13);

  (c) under the Fatal Accidents (Northern Ireland) Order 1977 (S.I. 1977/1251 (N.I. 18)); or

  (d) in respect of P, where that dependant is an intended beneficiary of part or all of that compensation,

and a lump sum payment has been made to that dependant, unless the order is made with the consent of that dependant and the person by whom the payment is to be made.

(2) The court must specify in the order the amount of the payment made—

  (a) under the Fatal Accidents Act 1976;

  (b) to the extent that it is made in respect of a liability arising by virtue of section 1 of the Damages (Scotland) Act 1976;

  (c) under the Fatal Accidents (Northern Ireland) Order 1977; or

  (d) in respect of P, where a dependant of P is an intended beneficiary of part or all of that compensation,

which is attributable to each or any dependant of P who has received a lump sum payment.".

  9. Where this Schedule applies, section 17 (benefits irrelevant to assessment of damages) is to apply as if—

  (a) in the heading for "benefits" there were substituted "lump sum payments";

  (b) there were omitted "accident, injury or";

  (c) for "listed benefits" there were substituted "lump sum payments".

  10. Where this Schedule applies, section 18 (lump sum and periodical payments) is to apply as if—

  (a) in subsection (1)—

      (i) for "the injured person" there were substituted "P";

      (ii) there were omitted "accident, injury or";

  (b) in subsection (2), for "section 8" there were substituted "regulation 12 of the Lump Sum Payments Regulations";

  (c) for subsection (3) there were substituted—

"(3) For the purposes of subsection (2), the regulations may provide for—

  (a) the gross amounts of the compensation payments to be aggregated and for the aggregate amount to be the gross amount of the compensation payment for the purposes of regulation 12 of the Lump Sum Payments Regulations; and

  (b) for the amount of any lump sum payment to be taken to be the amount determined in accordance with the most recent certificate.";

  (d) in subsection (4), for "the injured person's" there were substituted "P's";

  (e) in subsection (5), there were omitted paragraph (a).

    11. Where this Schedule applies, section 19 (payments by more than one person) is to apply as if in—

  (a) subsection (1)—

      (i) for "injured person" there were substituted "P";

      (ii) there were omitted "accident, injury or";

  (b) subsection (2)—

      (i) for "section 6" there were substituted "regulation 10 of the Lump Sum Payments Regulations";

      (ii) for "benefits" there were substituted "lump sum payments";

  (c) subsection (3)—

      (i) in paragraph (a), for "benefits" there were substituted "lump sum payments";

      (ii) in paragraph (b), for "section 8" there were substituted "regulation 12 of the Lump Sum Payments Regulations".

    12. Where this Schedule applies, section 20 (amounts overpaid under section 6) is to apply as if in—

  (a) the heading and in subsection (1), for "section 6" there were substituted "regulation 10 of Lump Sum Payments Regulations" in each place it occurs;

  (b) subsection (4)(a), for "section 8" there were substituted "regulation 12 of the Lump Sum Payments Regulations".

    13. Where this Schedule applies, section 21 (compensation payments to be disregarded) is to apply as if in—

  (a) subsections (1) and (5)(a), for "sections 6 and 8" there were substituted "regulations 10 and 12 of the Lump Sum Payments Regulations" in each place it occurs;

  (b) subsection (2)(a), there were omitted "of recoverable benefits";

  (c) subsection (3)(a)—

      (i) for "the injured person" there were substituted "P";

      (ii) there were omitted "accident, injury or";

  (d) subsection (4), for "section 4" there were substituted "regulation 8 of the Lump Sum Payments Regulations";

  (e) subsection (5)(b), for "section 6" there were substituted "regulation 10 of the Lump Sum Payments Regulations".

    14. Where this Schedule applies, section 22(1) (liability of insurers) is to apply as if —

  (a) in paragraph (a), there were omitted "accident, injury or";

  (b) for "section 6" there were substituted "regulation 10 of the Lump Sum Payments Regulations".

    15. Where this Schedule applies, section 23 (provision of information) is to apply as if—

  (a) in subsection (1), for—

      (i) "any accident, injury or" there were substituted "a";

      (ii) "any person ("the injured person")" there were substituted "P";

      (iii) "the injured person" there were substituted "P";

  (b) in subsection (1)(a), there were omitted "accident, injury or";

  (c) for subsection (2), there were substituted—

"(2) Where P or a dependant of P, receives or claims a lump sum payment which is or is likely to be paid in respect of the disease suffered by P, the prescribed information about the disease must be given to the Secretary of State by P or a dependant of P, as the case may be.";

  (d) in subsection (3), for "listed benefit" there were substituted "lump sum payment";

  (e) in subsection (4)—

      (i) for "any accident, injury or" there were substituted "a";

      (ii) there were omitted ", or any damage to property,";

  (f) there were omitted subsections (5), (6) and (8).

16. Where this Schedule applies, section 26 (residence of the injured person—Northern Ireland) is to apply as if—

  (a) in subsections (1)(a) and (b)(i), (2)(a), (b) and (c) and (3)(d)(ii), there were omitted "of recoverable benefits" in each place it occurs;

  (b) in subsections (1)(c)(ii) and (2)(c)(i), for "section 6" there were substituted "regulation 10 of the Lump Sum Payments Regulations";

  (c) in subsections (1) and (2), for "injured person's address" there were substituted "address of P";

  (d) for subsection (3)(a), there were substituted—

    "(a) "the address of P" is the address first notified in writing to the person making the payment by or on behalf of P as the residence of P (or if P had died, by or on behalf of the person entitled to receive the compensation payment as the last residence of P),";

  (e) in subsection (3)(d)(i) and the heading to this section, for "the injured person" there were substituted "P" in each place it occurs.

17. Where this Schedule applies, section 27 (jurisdiction of courts—Northern Ireland) is to apply as if in—

  (a) subsections (1) and (2), for "section 7" there were substituted "regulation 11 of the Lump Sum Payments Regulations" in each place it occurs;

  (b) subsection (3)(a)(i), for—

    (i) "the injured person" the first time it occurs, there were substituted "P";

    (ii) "the injured person or, if he" there were substituted "P or, if P".

18. Where this Schedule applies, section 29 (general interpretation) is to apply as if—

  (a) there were omitted the following definitions—

    (i) "benefit";

    (ii) "compensation scheme for motor accidents";

    (iii) "listed benefit";

  (b) in the appropriate place, there were inserted the following definitions—

    (i) "certificate" means a certificate which includes amounts in respect of recoverable benefits and of recoverable lump sum payments, including where any of those amounts are nil;

    (ii) "P" is to be construed in accordance with regulation 5 of the Lump Sum Payments Regulations;

    (iii) "recoverable lump sum payments" means any lump sum payments which are recoverable by virtue of regulation 4 of the Lump Sum Payments Regulations;

    (iv) "the Lump Sum Payments Regulations" means the Social Security (Recovery of Benefits) (Lump Sum Payments) Regulations 2008.

19. Where this Schedule applies, Part 1 of Schedule 1 (compensation payments—exempted payments) is to apply as if—

  (a) in paragraph 2 and 3(a), for "the injured person" there were substituted "P" in each place it occurs;

  (b) in paragraph 3(a) and (b) there were omitted "accident, injury or" in each place it occurs;

  (c) for paragraph 5(1) there were substituted—

    "(1) Any payment made to P or a dependant of P by an insurer under the terms of any contract of insurance entered into between P and the insurer before the date on which P or a dependant of P first claims a lump sum payment in consequence of the disease in question suffered by P.";

  (d) in paragraph 6 for "an accident, injury or" there were substituted "a".

20. Where this Schedule applies, paragraph 9 of Part 2 of Schedule 1 (compensation payments—power to disregard small payments) is to apply as if in—

  (a) sub-paragraph (1), for "sections 6 and 8" there were substituted "regulations 10 and 12 of the Lump Sum Payments Regulations";

  (b) sub-paragraph (3)(a)—

    (i) for "injured person" there were substituted "P";

    (ii) there were omitted "accident, injury or".

AMENDMENTS

1. Social Security (Miscellaneous Amendments) (No.3) Regulations 2008 (SI 2008/2365), reg.6 (October 1, 2008).

2. Tribunals, Courts and Enforcement Act 2007 (Transitional and Consequential Provisions Order 2008 (SI 2008/2683), Sch.1, para.344 (November 3, 2008).

The Social Security (Work-focused Interviews for Lone Parents) and Miscellaneous Amendments Regulations 2000

(SI 2000/1926)

ARRANGEMENT OF REGULATIONS

The Secretary of State for Social Security, in exercise of the powers conferred upon him by sections 123(1)(d) and (e) and 137(1) of the Social Security Contributions and Benefits Act 1992 and sectons 2A(1), (3)(b) to (f), (4), (5)(a) and (b), (6), (7) and (8), 2B(2), (6) and (7), 2C, 189(4) to (7A) and 191 of the Social Security Administration Act 1992 and of all other powers enabling him in that behalf, after consultation with the Council on Tribunals in accordance with section 8(1) of the Tribunals and Inquiries Act 1992 and in respect of provisions in these Regulations relating to housing benefit and council tax benefit with organisations appearing to him to be representative of the authorities concerned and after agreement by the Social Security Advisory Committee that proposals in respect of these Regulations should not be referred to it, hereby makes the following Regulations:

Citation, commencement and interpretation

2.687   1.—(1) These Regulations may be cited as the Social Security (Work-focused Interviews for Lone Parents) and Miscellaneous Amendments Regulations 2000.

(2) This Regulation and paragraphs 2 to 5 of Schedule 2 and regulation 10 in so far as it relates to those paragraphs shall come into force on 14th August 2000.

(3) Regulations 2 to 9, paragraph 1 of Schedule 2 and regulation 10 in so far as it relates to that paragraph shall—

   (a) come into force on 30th October 2000 in respect of lone parents who on that date—
       (i) live in an area identified in Schedule 1: and
      (ii) are not entitled to income support;
   (b) subject to sub-paragraph (a), come into force on 30th April 2001 in respect of lone parents who on that date—
       (i) are not entitled to income support; or
      (ii) are entitled to income support and are not—
          (aa) responsible for; and
          (bb) living in the same household as,
     a child under the age of 13;
   (c) subject to the preceding sub-paragraphs, come into force on 1st April 2002 in respect of lone parents who on that date are entitled to income support and are not—
       (i) responsible for; and
      (ii) living in the same household as,
     a child under the age of 9;
   (d) subject to the preceding sub-paragraphs, where a lone parent—
       (i) is responsible for and living in the same household as a child whose 13th birthday occurs in the period beginning on 1st May 2001 and ending on 31st March 2002; and
      (ii) is not on the date of the 13th birthday responsible for and living in the same household as a younger child,
     come into force in respect of that lone parent on the date of that child's 13th birthday;
   (e) subject to the preceding sub-paragraphs, where a loneparent—
       (i) is responsible for and living in the same household as a child whose 9th birthday occurs in the period beginning on 2nd April 2002 and ending on 6th April 2003; and
      (ii) is not on the date of the 9th birthday responsible for and living in the same household as a younger child,
     come into force in respect of that lone parent on the date of that child's 9th birthday; and
[¹ (f) subject to the preceding sub-paragraphs, come into force on 7th April 2003 in respect of lone parents who on that date are entitled to income support and are not responsible for and living in the same household as a child under the age of 5 years and 3 months;
[³ (g) subject to the preceding sub-paragraphs, come into force on 5th April 2004 in respect of a lone parent who on that date is entitled to income support and is responsible for an living in the same household as a child.]
     come into force in respect of that lone parent on the date that child reaches the age of 5 years and 3 months.]

(4) In these Regulations, unless the context otherwise requires—

"the 1998 Act" means the Social Security Act 1998;

"benefit week" means any period of seven days corresponding to the week in respect of which income support is due to be paid;

"lone parent" has the meaning it bears in regulation 2(1) of the Income Support (General) Regulations 1987;

"interview" means a work-focused interview with a lone parent conducted for any or all of the following purposes—

(a) assessing that person's prospects for existing or future employment (whether paid or voluntary);

(b) assisting or encouraging that person to enhance his prospects of such employment;

(c) identifying activities which that person may undertake to strengthen his existing or future prospects of employment;

(d) identifying current or future employment or training opportunities suitable to that person's needs; and

(e) identifying educational opportunities connected with the existing or future employment prospects or needs of that person; and

"officer" means an officer of, or providing services to, the Secretary of State.

(5) In these Regulations, unless the context otherwise requires, a reference—

(a) to a numbered regulation is to a regulation in these Regulations bearing that number;

(b) in a regulation to a numbered paragraph or sub-paragraph is to the paragraph or sub-paragraph in that regulation bearing that number;

(c) to a numbered Schedule is to the Schedule to these Regulations bearing that number.

AMENDMENTS

1. The Social Security (Work-focused Interviews for Lone Parents) Amendment Regulations 2002 (SI 2002/670), reg.2 (April 8, 2002).

2. The Social Security (Work-focused Interviews for Lone Parents) Amendment Regulations 2003 (SI 2003/400), reg.2 (April 7, 2003).

3. The Social Security (Miscellaneous Amendments) Regulations 2004 (SI 2004/565), reg.7 (April 5, 2004).

[¹ General requirement for lone parents claiming or entitled to income support to take part in an interview

2.688 **2.**—(1) Subject to this regulation and regulations [² 2ZA] 2A, 2B and 4 to 6, a lone parent is required to take part in an interview if he falls within any of paragraphs to (4).

(2) A lone parent falls within this paragraph if he makes a claim for income support in respect of himself.

(3) A lone parent falls within this paragraph if he is entitled to income support and has not taken part or been required to take part in a relevant interview.

(4) A lone parent falls within this paragraph if he is entitled to income support and has—

(a) taken part,

(b) failed to take part, or

(c) been treated as having taken part,

in a relevant interview.

(5) Where a lone parent falls within paragraph (4) the requirement to take part in an interview arises at the times set out in paragraph (6), except where the young child condition is satisfied (see paragraph (9)) in which case the requirement arises at the times set out in paragraph (7).

(6) The requirement arises (where the young child condition is not satisfied)—

(a) where the lone parent—
    (i) last took part,
    (ii) last failed to take part, or
    (iii) was last treated as having taken part,

in a relevant interview on a date on or after 30th April 2006 but before 30th October 2006, one year after that date, and it arises again every six months after it first arises; or

(b) where the lone parent does not fall within sub-paragraph (a), every six months after the date on which he—
    (i) last took part,
    (ii) last failed to take part, or
    (iii) was last treated as having taken part,

in a relevant interview.

(7) The requirement arises (where the young child condition is satisfied)—

(a) here the interview that the lone parent—
    (i) last took part in,
    (ii) last failed to take part in, or
    (iii) was last treated as having taken part in,

was the first relevant interview, six months after the date of that first interview, and it arises again upon each anniversary of that date;

(b) here the interview that the lone parent—
    (i) last took part in,
    (ii) last failed to take part in, or
    (iii) was last treated as having taken part in,

was the second relevant interview, six months after the date of that second interview, and it arises again upon each anniversary of the day on which it first arises;

(c) in any other case, on each anniversary of the date of the interview that the lone parent—
    (i) last took part in,
    (ii) last failed to take part in, or
    (iii) was last treated as having taken part in.

(8) In this regulation, "elevant interview"means an interview under—

(a) the Social Security (Working Neighbourhoods) Regulations 2004
(b) the Social Security (Quarterly Work-focused Interviews for Certain Lone Parents) Regulations 2004, or
(c) these Regulations,

in relation to the lone parent's current claim.

(9) For the purposes of this regulation, the young child condition is satisfied where the lone parent is responsible for and living in the same household as—

(a) a single child aged under 5, or
(b) more than one child where the youngest is aged under 5.

(10) Where a determination has been made in relation to a lone parent under regulation 6(1) (waiver) or (as the case may be) under a corresponding provision of the Regulations referred to in paragraph (8)(a) or (b), he is to be treated for the purposes of paragraph (3) as if he has not taken part or been required to take part in a relevant interview.

AMENDMENT

1. Inserted by The Social Security (Work-focused Interviews for Lone Parents) Amendment Regulations 2007, (SI 2007/1034) (April 30, 2007).

2. The Social Security (Lone Parents and Miscellaneous Amendments) Regulations 2008 (SI 2008/3051), reg.5 (November 23, 2008).

[¹ Requirement for certain lone parents to take part in an interview

2.689

2ZA.—(1) This regulation applies to a lone parent if—

(a) he is entitled to income support and is a person to whom paragraph 1 (lone parents) of Schedule 1B to the Income Support (General) Regulations 1987 applies;

(b) no other paragraph of that Schedule applies to him; and

(c) he is responsible for and living in the same household as—

(i) a single child aged 9, 10 or 11, or

(ii) more than one child where the youngest is aged 9, 10 or 11.

(2) Subject to regulations 4 to 6, a lone parent to whom this regulation applies is required to take part in an interview every 13 weeks after he—

(a) last took part,

(b) last failed to take part, or

(c) was last treated as having taken part,

in an interview.

(3) A lone parent who—

(a) is required to take part in an interview under this regulation, or

(b) has had a requirement to take part in an interview under this regulation waived or deferred,

is not required to take part in an interview under regulation 2 unless this regulation ceases to apply to him.

AMENDMENT

1. Inserted by The Social Security (Lone Parents and Miscellaneous Amendments) Regulations 2008 (SI 2008/3051), reg.5 (November 23, 2008).

GENERAL NOTE

2.690

Note that Pt 1 of the Schedule to the Social Security (Lone Parents and Miscellaneous Amendments) Regulations 2008 (SI 2008/3051) contains special commencement provision for certain existing claimants.

[¹ Requirement for specified lone parents to take part in an interview

2.691

2A.—(1) In this regulation, "specified lone parent" means a lone parent who—

(a) is responsible for and living in the same household as—

(i) a single child aged 14 or 15, or

(ii) more than one child where the youngest is aged 14 or 15, and

(b) has been continuously entitled for at least 12 months to income support other than—

(i) income support where paragraph 7 (persons incapable of work) of Schedule 1B to the Income Support (General) Regulations 1987(a) applies, or

(ii) income support where paragraph 24 or 25 (persons appealing against a decision which embodies a determination that they are not incapable of work) of Schedule 1B to the Income Support (General) Regulations 1987(b) applies.

(2) Subject to paragraph (3) and regulations 4 to 6, a specified lone parent is required to take part in an interview.

(3) Where a lone parent has taken part in an interview under regulation 2 [² or 2B], a requirement shall not arise under paragraph (2) until the expiry of 13 weeks from the day of that interview.

(4) Subject to regulations 4 to 6, a specified lone parent is required to take part in a further interview after the expiry of 13 weeks from the day on which—

(a) he last took part in an interview;

(b) he last failed to take part in an interview; or

(c) a determination was made under regulation 6 with effect that he is to be treated as having taken part in an interview.

(5) [² . . .]

(6) A specified lone parent who—

(a) is required to take part in an interview under this regulation, or

(b) has had a requirement to take part in an interview under this regulation waived or deferred,

is not required to take part in an interview under regulation 2 unless he ceases to be a specified lone parent.

(7) For the avoidance of doubt, the words "lone parent" in the other provisions of these Regulations includes specified lone parents.]

AMENDMENTS

1. The Social Security (Work-focused Interviews) Amendment Regulations 2005 (SI 2005/2727) (October 31, 2005).

2. The Social Security (Work-focused Interviews for Lone Parents) Amendment Regulations 2007, (SI 2007/1034) (April 30, 2007).

[¹ Requirement for certain lone parents in certain areas to take part in an interview

2B. —(1) This regulation applies to a lone parent who—   2.692

(a) is responsible for and living in the same household as—

(i) a single child aged 11, 12 or 13, or

(ii) more than one child where the youngest is aged 11, 12 or 13;

(b) has been continuously entitled to income support for at least 12 months; and

(c) resides in an area specified in Schedule 3 to these Regulations.

(2) Subject to regulations 4 to 6, a lone parent to whom this regulation applies is required to take part in an interview every 13 weeks after he—

(a) last took part in an interview,

(b) last failed to take part in an interview, or

(c) was last treated as having taken part in an interview.

(3) A lone parent who—

(a) is required to take part in an interview under this regulation, or

(b) has had a requirement to take part in an interview under this regulation waived or deferred,

is not required to take part in an interview under regulation 2 unless he ceases to fall within this regulation.]

AMENDMENT

1. Inserted by The Social Security (Work-focused Interviews for Lone Parents) Amendment Regulations 2007, (SI 2007/1034) (April 30, 2007).

[¹ The interview

2.693

2C. —(1) An interview under these Regulations shall take place as soon as is reasonably practicable after the date on which the requirement to take part in the interview arises.

(2) An officer shall inform the lone parent of the place and time of the interview.

(3) An officer may determine that an interview is to take place in the lone parent's home where it would, in the opinion of the officer, be unreasonable to expect that lone parent to attend elsewhere because that lone parent's personal circumstances are such that attending elsewhere would—

(a) cause him undue inconvenience, or

(b) endanger his health.

AMENDMENT

1. Inserted by The Social Security (Work-focused Interviews for Lone Parents) Amendment Regulations 2007, (SI 2007/1034) (April 30, 2007).

Taking part in an interview

2.694

3.—(1) An officer shall determine whether a lone parent has taken part in an interview.

[¹ (2) Subject to regulations 5(2) and 6(2), a lone parent who has not taken part in an interview under these Regulations before 31st October 2005 shall be regarded as having taken part in his first interview under these Regulations if—

(a) he attends for the interview at the place and time notified to him by the officer;

(b) he participates in discussions with the officer in relation to the lone parent's employability, including any action the lone parent and the officer agree is reasonable and they are willing to take in order to help the lone parent enhance his employment prospects;

(c) he provides answers (where asked) to questions and appropriate information about—

(i) the level to which he has pursued any educational qualifications;

(ii) his employment history;

(iii) any vocational training he has undertaken;

(iv) any skills he has acquired which fit him for employment;

(v) any paid or unpaid employment he is engaged in;

(vi) any medical condition which, in his opinion, puts him at a disadvantage in obtaining employment;

(vii) any caring or childcare responsibilities he has;

(viii) his aspirations for future employment;

(ix) any vocational training or skills which he wishes to undertake or acquire; and

(x) his work related abilities; and

(d) he assists the officer in the completion of an action plan which records the matters discussed in relation to sub-paragraph (b) above.

(2A) Subject to regulations 5(2) and 6(2), a lone parent who has taken part in an interview under these Regulations before 31st October 2005 shall be regarded as having taken part in his first interview under these Regulations after 30th October 2005 if—

(a) he attends for the interview at the place and time notified to him by the officer;

(b) he participates in discussions with the officer in relation to the lone parent's employability, including any action the lone parent and the officer agree is reasonable and they are willing to take in order to help the lone parent enhance his employment prospects;

(c) he participates in discussions with the officer—

    (i) in relation to the lone parent's employability or any progress he might have made towards obtaining employment; and

    (ii) in order to consider any of the programmes and support available to help the lone parent obtain employment;

(d) he provides answers (where asked) to questions and appropriate information about—

    (i) the content of any report made following his personal capability assessment, insofar as that report relates to the lone parent's capabilities and employability; and

    (ii) his opinion as to the extent to which his medical condition restricts his ability to obtain employment; and

(e) he assists the officer in the completion of an action plan which records the matters discussed in relation to sub-paragraph (b) above.

(2B) Subject to regulations 5(2) and 6(2), a lone parent shall be regarded as having taken part in any subsequent interview under these Regulations if—

(a) he attends for the interview at the place and time notified to him by the officer;

(b) he participates in discussions with the officer—

    (i) in relation to the lone parent's employability or any progress he might have made towards obtaining employment;

    (ii) about any action the lone parent or the officer might have taken as a result of the matters discussed in relation to paragraph (2) (b) or (2A)(b) above;

    (iii) about how, if at all, the action plan referred to in paragraphs (2) (d) or (2A)(e) above should be amended; and

    (iv) in order to consider any of the programmes and support available to help the lone parent obtain employment;

(c) he provides answers (where asked) to questions and appropriate information about—

    (i) the content of any report made following his personal capability assessment, insofar as that report relates to the lone parent's capabilities and employability; and

    (ii) his opinion as to the extent to which his medical condition restricts his ability to obtain employment; and

(d) he assists the officer in the completion of any amendment of the action plan referred to in paragraphs (2)(d) or (2A)(e) above in light of the matters discussed in relation to sub-paragraph (b) above and the information provided in relation to sub-paragraph (c) above.]

AMENDMENT

1. The Social Security (Work-focused Interviews) Amendment Regulations 2005 (SI 2005/2727) (October 31, 2005).

[¹ **Circumstances where requirement to take part in an interview does not apply**

2.695   **4.**—(1) Regulation 2 shall not apply where the lone parent—

(a) has attained the age of 60;

(b) has not attained the age of 18; or

(c) is—

    (i) required to take part in an interview, or

    (ii) not required to take part in an interview by virtue of—

        (aa) a waiver of a requirement, or

        (bb) a deferment of an interview, under the Social Security (Work-focused Interviews) Regulations 2000, the Social Security (Jobcentre Plus Interviews) Regulations 2001, the Social Security (Jobcentre Plus Interviews) Regulations 2002, [³ or the Social Security (Incapacity Benefit Work-focused Interviews) Regulations 2003.]

(2) [²...]

[³ (3) Regulations [⁵ 2ZA, 2A and 2B] shall not apply where the lone parent—

(a) has attained the age of 60, or

(b) has not attained the age of 18.

(4) Regulation 2B shall not apply where the lone parent is—

(a) required to take part in an interview, or

(b) not required to take part in an interview by virtue of—

    (i) a waiver of a requirement, or

    (ii) a deferment of an interview,

under the [⁴ Social Security (Incapacity Benefit Work-focused Interviews) Regulations 2008] [⁵, under regulation 2ZA of these Regulations or regulation 4A of the Social Security (Jobcentre Plus Interviews) Regulations 2002.]

AMENDMENTS

1. The Social Security (Work-focused Interviews) Amendment Regulations 2005 (SI 2005/2727) (October 31, 2005).

2. The Social Security (Working Neighbourhoods) Miscellaneous Amendment Regulations 2006, (SI 2006/909) (April 24, 2006).

3. The Social Security (Work-focused Interviews for Lone Parents) Amendment Regulations 2007, (SI 2007/1034) (April 30, 2007).

4. The Social Security (Incapacity Benefit Work-focused Interviews) Regulations 2008 (SI 2008/2928), reg.12 (December 15, 2008).

5. The Social Security (Lone Parents and Miscellaneous Amendments) Regulations 2008 (SI 2008/3051), reg.5 (November 23, 2008).

Deferment of requirement to take part in an interview

2.696   **5.**—(1) A requirement by virtue of these Regulations to take part in an interview shall not apply to a person until a date determined by an officer where he determines that an interview would not [¹ until] that time be—

(a) of assistance to that person; or

(b) appropriate in the circumstances.

(2) Except for the purpose of [² regulations [³ 2, 2ZA, 2A and 2B]], where an officer has made a decision under paragraph (1), the person to whom that decision relates shall be treated for the purposes of any claim for, or entitlement to, income suppport as having complied with the requirement

to take part in an interview until an officer decides whether that person took part in the interview which had been deferred under paragraph (1).

AMENDMENTS

1. The Social Security (Claims and Information and Work-focused Interviews for Lone Parents) Amendment Regulations 2001 (SI 2001/1189), reg.3 (April 23, 2001).
2. The Social Security (Work-focused Interviews) Amendment Regulations 2005 (SI 2005/2727) (October 31, 2005).
3. The Social Security (Lone Parents and Miscellaneous Amendments) Regulations 2008 (SI 2008/3051), reg.5 (November 23, 2008).

Waiver

6.—(1) A requirement imposed by these Regulations to take part in an interview shall not apply if an officer determines that an interview would not be—

   (a) of assistance to the lone parent; or

   (b) appropriate in the circumstances.

(2) A person in relation to whom a requirement to take part in an interview has been waived under paragraph (1) shall be treated for the purposes of—

   (a) [¹ regulations 2 and 2A]; and

   (b) any claim for, or entitlement to, income support,

as having complied with that requirement.

2.697

AMENDMENT

1. The Social Security (Work-focused Interviews) Amendment Regulations 2005 (SI 2005/2727) (October 31, 2005).

Consequence of failure to take part in an interview

7.—(1) Subject to paragraphs (2) and (5) and regulations 5 and 6, the consequences specified in paragraphs (3) and (4) ensue if a person does not—

   (a) take part in any interview when required to do so; and

   (b) show good cause for not taking part in an interview before the end of five working days following the day on which the interview was to take place.

(2) In a case where within one month of the date on which the decision was notified to a lone parent that he failed without good cause to take part in an interview—

   (a) he brings new facts to the notice of an officer which could not reasonably have been brought to an officer's notice within five working days of the day on which the interview was to take place; and

   (b) those facts show that he had good cause for his failure to take part in the interview

paragraph (1)(b) shall apply with the modification that for the words "five working days following" there were substituted the words "one month of".

(3) A person to whom paragraph (1) and—

   (a) regulation [² 2(2)] applies shall be regarded as not having made a claim for income support; or

2.698

(b) regulation [² 2(3) or (4), [³ 2ZA] 2A or 2B] applies shall have his income support reduced in accordance wtih regulation 8.

(4) Where an interview which arose in connection with a claim was deferred and benefit became payable in accordance with regulation 5(2), the person's entitlement to income support shall terminate as from the first day of the next benefit week following the date the decision was made that the person failed without good cause to take part in an interview.

(5) For the purposes of this regulation and regulation 8(1), matters to be taken into account in determining whether a person has shown good cause for his failure to take part in an interview include—

(a) that the lone parent misunderstood the requirement to take part in the interview due to any learning, language or literacy difficulties of the lone parent or any misleading information given to him by an officer;

(b) that the lone parent was attending a medical or dental appointment, or accompanying someone for whom he has caring responsibilities to such an appointment, and that it would be unreasonable, in the circumstances, to have rearranged that appointment;

(c) that the lone parent had difficulties with his normal mode of transport and that no reasonable alternative was available;

(d) that the established customs and practices of the religion to which that lone parent belongs prevented him attending at the time and place for the interview notified to him by an officer;

(e) that the lone parent was attending an interview with an employer with a view to obtaining employment;

(f) that the lone parent was pursuing employment opportunities as a self-employed earner;

(g) that a dependant of the lone parent or someone for whom the lone parent provides care suffered an accident, sudden illness or relapse of [¹ a physical or mental health condition];

(h) that the lone parent was attending a funeral of a close friend or relative on the day fixed for the interview; and

(i) that a disability from which the lone parent suffers made it impracticable for him to attend at the time fixed for the interview.

(6) For the avoidance of doubt, a person who is regarded as not having made a claim for income support because he failed to take part in an interview shall be required to make a new claim for income support in order to establish entitlement to that benefit.

AMENDMENTS

1. The Social Security (Work-focused Interviews) Amendment Regulations 2005 (SI 2005/2727) (October 31, 2005).
2. The Social Security (Work-focused Interviews for Lone Parents) Amendment Regulations 2007, (SI 2007/1034) (April 30, 2007).
3. The Social Security (Lone Parents and Miscellaneous Amendments) Regulations 2008 (SI 2008/3051), reg.5 (November 23, 2008).

Reduction of income support

2.699   **8.**—(1) Subject to paragraphs (2) and (3), any payment of income support which falls to be made to a person after the date on which an officer decided under these Regulations that that person had not—

(a) taken part; and

(b) shown good cause for not taking part,

in an interview shall be reduced as from the first day of the next benefit week following the date the decision was made, by a sum equal to 20 per cent of the income applicable (specified in Part I of Schedule 2 to the Income Support (General) Regulations 1987) on the date the deduction commences in respect of a single claimant for income support aged not less than 25.

(2) Payment shall not be reduced under paragraph (1) below 10 pence per week.

(3) A reduction under this regulation shall cease to have effect as regards a person from whichever is the earlier of—

(a) the date on which that person attains the age of 60;

(b) the date on which that person ceased to be a lone parent; and

(c) the first day of the benefit week in which that person meets the requirement to take part in an interview.

(4) Where the rate of income support payable to a person changes, the rules set out above for a reduction in the benefit payable shall be applied to the new rates and any adjustments to the reduction shall take effect from the beginning of the first benefit week to commence for that person following the change.

Appeals

9.—(1) This regulation applies to any relevant decision made under these Regulations or any decision under section 10 of the 1998 Act (decisions superseding earlier decisions) superseding such a decision.   2.700

(2) This regulation applies—

(a) whether the decision is as originally made or as revised under section 9 of the 1998 Act (revision of decisions); and

(b) as if any decision made, superseded or revised otherwise than by the Secretary of State was a decision made, superseded or revised by him.

(3) In the case of a decision to which this regulation applies, the person in respect of whom the decision was made shall have a right of appeal under section 12 of the 1998 Act [¹ (appeal to First-tier Tribunal) to the First-tier Tribunal]

AMENDMENT

1. The Tribunals, Courts and Enforcement Act 2007 (Transitional and Consequential Provisions) Order 2008 (SI 2008/2683), reg.140 (November 3, 2008).

SCHEDULE 1   **Regulation 1(3)(a)**

AREAS WHERE THESE REGULATIONS COME INTO FORCE ON 30TH OCTOBER 2000 IN   2.701
RESPECT OF LONE PARENTS WHO ARE NOT ENTITLED TO INCOME SUPPORT

For the purposes of regulation 1(3)(a), the areas are—

(a) the areas of Shropshire County Council and Telford Wrekin District Council; and

(b) the following postcode districts—

DH2 1AA to DH2 1BO

DH2 1XA to DH2 1XQ

DH3 1 and DH3 2

NE8 and NE9
NE10 0
NE10 8 and NE10 9
NE11
NE16 3 to NE16 5
NE16 6NX to NE16 6PE
NE16 8
NE17 7AA to NE17 7HE
NE17 7HG to NE17 7LM
NE17 7TA to NE17 7ZZ
NE21 1
NE21 4 to NE21 6
NE31 1 to NE31 5
NE32 2 to NE32 4
NE33
NE34 0
NE34 6 to NE34 9
NE35 1 and NE35 9
NE36 0 and NE36 1
NE39
NE40 3 to NE40 4
NE42 5 to NE42 6
NE43 7
SR6 7.
(c) The area of Five Council excluding the following postcode districts—
DD 6 8 and DD 6 9
KY 14 6
KY 16 0
KY 16 9.

AMENDMENT

1. The Social Security (Work-focused Interviews for Lone Parents) Amendment
Regulations 2002 (SI 2002/670), reg.2 (April 8, 2002).

2.702   *Schedule 2 omitted.*

[¹ SCHEDULE 3]   **Regulation 2B(1)**

2.702.1   For the purposes of regulation 2B, the areas are the areas of—
Barnet London Borough Council;
Bexley London Borough Council;
Blaby District Council;
Cardiff Council;
Charnwood Borough Council;
City of Bradford Metropolitan District Council;
Dudley Metropolitan Borough Council;
East Lothian Council;
Edinburgh City Council;
Enfield London Borough Council;
Greenwich London Borough Council;
Harborough District Council;
Hinckley and Bosworth Borough Council;
Leicester City Council;
Leicestershire County Council;
Lewisham London Borough Council;
Melton Borough Council;
Midlothian Council;
North West Leicestershire District Council;
Oadby and Wigston Borough Council;
Sandwell Metropolitan Borough Council;

Scottish Borders Council;
Vale of Glamorgan Council;
West Lothian Council.]

AMENDMENT

1. Inserted by The Social Security (Work-focused Interviews for Lone Parents) Amendment Regulations 2007, (SI 2007/1034) (April 30, 2007).

SECTION B

HMRC-ADMINISTERED BENEFITS

Note

The administration and initial adjudication of claims for child benefit, guardian's allowance and health in pregnancy grants are the responsibility of Her Majesty's Revenue and Customs but are governed by the Social Security Administration Act 1992 and the Social Security Act 1998. Separate regulations have been made under those Acts for these benefits and they are reproduced in this section. They are naturally similar to, although they do not exactly replicate, the regulations made by the Secretary of State for Work and Pensions that are in Section A above. Where no specific annotation is provided to regulations reproduced in this section, readers are advised to check the annotation of the corresponding provision in Section A.

For equivalent legislation in respect of other HMRC-administered benefits, see Vol.IV.

The Child Benefit and Guardian's Allowance (Administration) Regulations 2003

(SI 2003/492)

Made	*5th March 2003*
Laid before Parliament	*5th March 2003*
Coming into force	*7th April 2003*

ARRANGEMENT OF REGULATIONS

PART I

GENERAL

2.703

PART II

CLAIMS AND AWARDS

PART III

PAYMENTS

PART IV

THIRD PARTIES

PART V

OVERPAYMENTS AND RECOVERY

PART VI

REVOCATIONS AND TRANSITIONAL PROVISIONS

SCHEDULE 1

POWERS EXERCISED IN MAKING THESE REGULATIONS

SCHEDULE 2

ELECTRONIC COMMUNICATIONS

PART I GENERAL

PART II GENERAL

PART III EVIDENTIAL PROVISIONS

SCHEDULE 3

REVOCATIONS

The Commissioners of Inland Revenue, in exercise of the powers conferred upon them by the provisions set out in Schedule 1, hereby make the following Regulations:

PART I

GENERAL

Citation, commencement and effect

1.—(1) These Regulations may be cited as the Child Benefit and Guardian's Allowance (Administration) Regulations 2003 and shall come into force on 7th April 2003 immediately after the commencement of section 50 of the Tax Credits Act 2002 for the purposes of entitlement to payment of child benefit and guardian's allowance.

(2) These Regulations have effect only in relation to—

(a) child benefit and guardian's allowance under the Contributions and Benefits Act; and

(b) child benefit and guardian's allowance under the Contributions and Benefits (NI) Act.

2.704

759

Interpretation

2.705   **2.** In these Regulations—

"the adjudicating authority" means—

(a) the Board;

(b) an appeal tribunal constituted under Chapter 1 of Part 1 of the Social Security Act 1998 or [² . . .]

(c) a Commissioner [² . . .] to whom an appeal lies under Article 15 of that Order;

[² (d) the First-tier Tribunal or the Upper Tribunal]

"the Administration Act" means the Social Security Administration Act 1992;

"the Administration (NI) Act" means the Social Security Administration (Northern Ireland) Act 1992;

"appropriate office" means—

(a) in relation to child benefit or guardian's allowance under the Contributions and Benefits Act—

(i) as regards the Board, the Child Benefit Office, Waterview Park, Washington, Tyne and Wear or [¹ any Enquiry Centre maintained by the Board];

(ii) as regards a relevant authority, any office of the Department for Work and Pensions which is designated by the Secretary of State as a Jobcentre Plus Office;

(b) in relation to child benefit or guardian's allowance under the Contributions and Benefits (NI) Act—

(i) as regards the Board, the Child Benefit Office (Northern Ireland), Windsor House, Bedford Street, Belfast or [¹ any Enquiry Centre maintained by the Board];

(ii) as regards a relevant authority, any office of the Social Security Agency of the Department for Social Development in Northern Ireland;

[¹ (c) in relation to child benefit or guardian's allowance under either of those Acts, as regards the Board, Comben House, Farriers Way, Netherton, Merseyside;]

"the approved form" has the meaning given by regulation 5(1)(a);

"the Board" means the [¹ Commissioners for Her Majesty's Revenue and Customs];

"the Contributions and Benefits Act" means the Social Security Contributions and Benefits Act 1992;

"the Contributions and Benefits (NI) Act" means the Social Security Contributions and Benefits (Northern Ireland) Act 1992;

"interim payment" has the meaning given by regulation 22(1);

"married couple" means a man and a woman who are married to each other and are neither—

(a) separated under a court order, nor

(b) separated in circumstances in which the separation is likely to be permanent;

"partner" means a member of a married or an unmarried couple;

"relevant authority" means—

(a) in relation to child benefit or guardian's allowance under the Contributions and Benefits Act, the Secretary of State or a person providing services to the Secretary of State;

(b) in relation to child benefit or guardian's allowance under the Contributions and Benefits (NI) Act, the Department for Social Development in Northern Ireland or a person providing services to that Department;

"unmarried couple" means a man and a woman who are not a married couple but are living together as husband and wife;

"writing" includes writing produced by electronic communications used in accordance with Schedule 2.

AMENDMENTS

1. The Child Benefit and Guardian's Allowance (Miscellaneous Amendments) Regulations 2006 (SI 2006/203) (April 10, 2006).

2. The Tribunals, Courts and Enforcement Act 2007 (Transitional and Consequential Provisions) Order 2008 (SI 2008/2683, reg.211 (November 3, 2008).

Use of electronic communications

3. Schedule 2 (the use of electronic communications) has effect.   2.706

Notification for purposes of sections 111A and 112 of the Administration Act and sections 105A and 106 of the Administration (NI) Act

4.—(1) This regulation prescribes the person to whom, and manner in which, a change of circumstances must be notified for the purposes of sections 111A(1A) to (1G) and 112(1A) to (1F) of the Administration Act and sections 105A(1A) to (1G) and 106(1A) to (1F) of the Administration (NI) Act (offences relating to failure to notify a change of circumstances).   2.707

(2) Notice of the change of circumstances must be given to the Board, or, where relevant, a relevant authority, in writing (except where they determine or it determines, in any particular case, that they or it will accept a notice other than in writing) by delivering or sending it to an appropriate office.

PART II

CLAIMS AND AWARDS

Making a claim

5.—(1) A claim for child benefit or guardian's allowance must be made to the Board or a relevant authority in writing—   2.708

(a) on a form for the time being approved by the Board ("the approved form") which has been completed in accordance with the instructions on it; or

(b) in such other manner as the Board may accept as sufficient in the circumstances of the particular case.

(2) The person making the claim must deliver or send it to an appropriate office.

(3) Subject to regulation 10, the claim is made on the date on which it is received by the appropriate office.

Time within which claims to be made

2.709   [¹ **6.**—(1) The time within which a claim for child benefit or guardian's allowance is to be made is 3 months beginning with any day on which, apart from satisfying the conditions for making the claim, the person making the claim is entitled to the benefit or allowance.

(2) Paragraph (1) shall not apply where—

(a) a person has been awarded child benefit or guardian's allowance while he was present and residing in great Britain, or Northern Ireland;

(b) at a time when payment of the award has not been suspended or terminated (under regulations 18 to 20 of the Child Benefit and Guardian's Allowance (Decisions and Appeals) Regulations 2003 or otherwise), he take up residence in Northern Ireland, or Great Britain as the case may be ("the new country of residence"); and

(c) a new claim for that benefit or allowance is made in the new country of residence, for a period commencing on the later of—

   (i) the date of the change of residence referred to in sub-paragraph (b), or

   (ii) the date on which, apart from satisfying the conditions for making the claim, the person became entitled to the benefit or allowance under the legislation of the new country of residence.]

[² (d) a person who has claimed asylum and, on or after 6th April 2004, makes a claim for that benefit or allowance and satisfies the following conditions—

   (i) the person is notified that he has been recorded as a refugee by the Secretary of State; and

   (ii) he claims that benefit or allowance within 3 months of receiving that notification.

(3) In a case falling within paragraph (2)(d) the person making the claim shall be treated as having made it on the date when he submitted his claim for asylum.]

AMENDMENTS

1. The Child Benefit and Guardian's Allowance) (Administration) (Amendment No.3) Regulations 2003 (SI 2003/2107), reg.6 (September 3, 2003).

2. The Child Benefit and Guardian's Allowance (Miscellaneous Amendments) Regulations 2004 (SI 2004/761), reg.2 (April 6, 2004).

GENERAL NOTE

2.710   The social security systems of Great Britain and Northern Ireland are formally separate, though in many respects—and certainly in relation to child benefit and guardian's allowance—identical. A problem arose that claimants moving from Great Britain to Northern Ireland (and the reverse) often continued to cash their Great Britain child benefit. This amendment replaces the three month limit on back-dating of benefit to an unlimited period where such a situation has arisen, so that entitlements can be "balanced out".

Evidence and information

7.—(1) A person making a claim for child benefit or guardian's allowance must furnish such certificates, documents, information and evidence in connection with the claim, or any question arising out of it, as may be required by the Board.

(2) A person required under paragraph (1) to furnish certificates, documents, information and evidence must do so—

(a) within one month of being required by the Board to do so; or

(b) within such longer period as the Board may consider reasonable.

[¹ (3) If a person is required, by virtue of paragraph (1) to furnish a certificate of a [² the birth or adoption of a child or qualifying young person], the certificate so produced must be either an original certificate or a copy authenticated in such manners as would render it admissible in proceedings in any court in the jurisdiction in which the copy was made.]

2.711

AMENDMENTS

1. Child Benefit and Guardian's Allowance (Administration) (Amendment) Regulations 2004 (SI 2004/1240) (May 1, 2004).
2. The Child Benefit and Guardian's Allowance (Miscellaneous Amendments) Regulations 2006 (SI 2006/203) (April 10, 2006).

GENERAL NOTE

This provision would appear to reflect the rather more legalistic approach the Board of Inland Revenue adopt to some issues, since the Department for Work and Pensions never seem to have felt the need for such a provision.

2.712

Amending claims

8.—(1) A person who has made a claim for child benefit or guardian's allowance may amend it by giving to the Board or a relevant authority notice in writing in accordance with paragraph (2).

(2) A notice under paragraph (1) must be delivered or sent to an appropriate office at any time before a determination has been made on the claim.

(3) The Board may treat a claim amended in accordance with this regulation as if it had been so amended when first made.

2.713

Withdrawing claims

9.—(1) A person who has made a claim for child benefit or guardian's allowance may withdraw it by giving notice in writing to the Board or a relevant authority.

(2) A notice of withdrawal given in accordance with paragraph (1) has effect when it is received by an appropriate office.

2.714

Defective applications

10.—(1) If an appropriate office receives a defective application, the Board or the relevant authority may refer it back to the person making it or supply him with the approved form for completion.

(2) Where—

(a) in accordance with paragraph (1), a defective application has been referred back, or an approved form supplied, to a person; and

2.715

(b) a claim is received by an appropriate office—
    (i) within the period of one month beginning with the date on which the defective application was referred back or the approved form was supplied; or
    (ii) within such longer period as the Board may consider reasonable,
        the claim shall be treated as having been made on the date on which the appropriate office received the defective application.

(3) "Defective application" means an intended claim which—

(a) is made on an approved form which has not been completed in accordance with the instructions on it; or

(b) is in writing but is not made on the approved form.

Claims for child benefit treated as claims for guardian's allowance and vice versa

2.716   **11.**—(1) Where it appears to the Board that a person who has made a claim for child benefit in respect of a child [¹ or qualifying young person] may be entitled to guardian's allowance in respect of the same child [¹ or qualifying young person], the Board may treat, either in the alternative or in addition, the claim as being a claim for guardian's allowance by that person.

(2) Where it appears to the Board that a person who has made a claim for guardian's allowance in respect of a child [¹ or qualifying young person] may be entitled to child benefit in respect of the same child [¹ or qualifying young person], the Board may treat, either in the alternative or in addition, the claim as being a claim for child benefit by that person.

AMENDMENT

1. The Child Benefit and Guardian's Allowance (Miscellaneous Amendments) Regulations 2006 (SI 2006/203) (April 10, 2006).

Advance claims and awards

2.717   **12.**—(1) This regulation applies where a person who has made a claim for child benefit or guardian's allowance does not satisfy the requirements for entitlement on the date on which the claim is made.

(2) If the Board are of the opinion that, unless there is a change of circumstances, the person will satisfy those requirements for a period beginning with a date ("the relevant date") not more than 3 months after the date on which the claim is made, they—

(a) may treat the claim as if made for a period beginning with the relevant date; and

(b) may award the benefit or allowance accordingly, subject to the condition that the person satisfies the requirements for entitlement when the benefit or allowance becomes payable under the award.

(3) If the requirements for entitlement are found not to have been satisfied on the relevant date, a decision under paragraph (2)(b) to award benefit may be revised under—

(a) in relation to child benefit and guardian's allowance under the Contributions and Benefits Act, section 9 of the Social Security Act 1998;

(b) in relation to child benefit and guardian's allowance under the Contributions and Benefits (NI) Act, Article 10 the Social Security (Northern Ireland) Order 1998.

Date of entitlement under an award for the purposes of payability

13.—(1) This regulation applies where child benefit or guardian's allowance is awarded for a period of a week or weeks and the earliest date on which entitlement would commence is not a Monday.

(2) For the purposes of determining the day from which the benefit or allowance is to become payable, entitlement shall be treated as beginning on the Monday next following the earliest date referred to in paragraph (1).

2.718

Effective date of change of rate

14. Where a change in the rate of child benefit or guardian's allowance would take effect, but for this regulation, on a day which would not be the appropriate pay day for the benefit or allowance, the change shall take effect from the appropriate pay day next following.

2.719

Duration of claims and awards

15.—(1) Subject to paragraphs (2) and (3), a claim for child benefit or guardian's allowance shall be treated as made for an indefinite period and any award shall be made for an indefinite period.

(2) If it would be inappropriate to treat a claim as made and to make an award for an indefinite period (for example, where a relevant change of circumstances is reasonably to be expected in the near future), the claim shall be treated as made for a definite period which is appropriate in the circumstances and any award shall be made for that period.

(3) In any case where benefit or allowance is awarded in respect of days subsequent to the date on which the claim was made, the award shall be subject to the condition that the person by whom the claim was made satisfies the requirements for entitlement.

2.720

Part III

Payments

Manner of payment

16.—(1) Subject to regulation 17, child benefit or guardian's allowance shall be paid by means of an instrument of payment or by such other means as appears to the Board to be appropriate in the circumstances of the particular case.

(2) If a person entitled to child benefit is also entitled to guardian's allowance, the allowance shall be paid in the same manner as that in which the child benefit is paid under this regulation.

(3) Instruments of payment which have been issued by the Board remain their property.

(4) A person who has an instrument of payment must on ceasing to be entitled to the benefit or allowance to which the instrument relates, or when required to do so by the Board, deliver it to the Board or such person as the Board may direct.

2.721

Direct credit transfers

2.722   **17.**—(1) The Board may make an arrangement with a person claiming, or entitled to, child benefit or guardian's allowance for the payment of the benefit or allowance by way of direct credit transfer in accordance with paragraphs (2) to (4).

(2) The direct credit transfer shall be into a bank account or other account—

(a) in the name of—

    (i) the person entitled to the benefit or allowance,

    (ii) that person's partner, or

    (iii) a person acting on behalf of that person; or

(b) in the joint names of the person entitled to benefit and—

    (i) that person's partner, or

    (ii) a person acting on that person's behalf.

(3) Subject to paragraph (4), the benefit or allowance shall be paid within seven days of the last day of each successive period of entitlement.

(4) The Board may make a particular payment by direct credit transfer otherwise than is provided by paragraph (3) if it appears to them appropriate to do so for the purpose of—

(a) paying any arrears of benefit or allowance, or

(b) making a payment in respect of a terminal period of an award for any similar purpose.

(5) Where an arrangement is made under paragraph (1)—

(a) in relation to child benefit, any guardian's allowance to which the person entitled to the child benefit is entitled shall be paid in the same manner as the child benefit;

(b) in relation to guardian's allowance, the child benefit to which the person entitled to the guardian's allowance is entitled shall be paid in the same manner as the guardian's allowance.

(6) An arrangement made under paragraph (1) may be terminated—

(a) by the person entitled to benefit, or by a person acting on behalf of that person, giving a notice in writing to the Board; or

(b) by the Board if the arrangement seems to them to be no longer appropriate to the circumstances of the particular case.

(7) A person giving a notice under paragraph (6)(a) must deliver or send it to an appropriate office as regards the Board.

Time of payment

2.723   **18.**—(1) Subject to paragraphs (2) to (4), child benefit and guardian's allowance shall be paid in accordance with an award as soon as reasonably practicable after the award has been made.

(2) Child benefit shall be paid—

(a) if a person entitled to it makes an election under regulation 19 or 20, weekly beginning with the first convenient date after the election has been made;

(b) in any other case, in the last week of each successive period of four weeks of the period of entitlement.

(3) Where benefit is paid at four-weekly intervals in accordance with paragraph (2)(b), the Board must arrange for it to be paid weekly if they are satisfied that payment at intervals of four weeks is causing hardship.

(4) If a person who has made a claim for child benefit is also entitled to guardian's allowance, the allowance shall be paid at the same intervals as the child benefit.

(5) The Board must take steps to notify persons to whom child benefit or guardian's allowance is payable of the arrangements they have made for payment in so far as those arrangements affect those persons.

Persons who may elect to have child benefit paid weekly

19.—(1) A person may make an election under this regulation to have child benefit paid weekly if—

2.724

(a) he is a lone parent; or

(b) he or his partner is receiving—

    (i) income support; or

    (ii) an income-based allowance payable under Part 1 of the Jobseekers Act 1995 or Part 2 of the Jobseekers (Northern Ireland) Order 1995.

(2) "Lone parent" means a person who has no partner and is entitled to child benefit in respect of a child [¹ or qualifying young person] for whom he is responsible.

(3) A person making an election under this regulation—

(a) must furnish, in such manner and at such times as the Board may determine, such certificates, documents, other information or facts as the Board may require which may affect his right to receive payment of the benefit weekly; and

(b) as soon as reasonably practicable after any change of circumstances which he might reasonably be expected to know might affect that right, must notify the Board in writing of that change in accordance with paragraph (4).

(4) A notification under paragraph (3)(b) must be delivered or sent to an appropriate office as regards the Board.

AMENDMENT

1. The Child Benefit and Guardian's Allowance (Miscellaneous Amendments) Regulations 2006 (SI 2006/203) (April 10, 2006).

Elections for weekly payment by persons to whom child benefit was payable for a period beginning before and ending after 15th March 1982

20.—(1) This regulation applies to a person to whom child benefit is payable for an uninterrupted period beginning before and ending after 15th March 1982.

2.725

(2) A person to whom this regulation applies may make an election to have the benefit paid weekly after 15th March 1982 if—

(a) he makes it before the end of the period of 26 weeks beginning with the day on which benefit was payable for the first four weeks in respect of which arrangements for four-weekly payment were made;

(b) in the case of benefit under the Contributions and Benefits Act, he was absent from Great Britain on 15th March 1982 for any of the reasons specified in paragraph (3) and he makes the election before the end of the period of 26 weeks beginning with the first week in respect of which benefit became payable to him in Great Britain on his return; or

(c) in the case of benefit under the Contributions and Benefits (NI) Act, he was absent from Northern Ireland on 15th March 1982 for any of the reasons specified in paragraph (3) and he makes the election before the end of the period of 26 weeks beginning with the first week in respect of which benefit became payable to him in Northern Ireland on his return.

(3) The reasons specified in this paragraph are that the person—

(a) was a serving member of the forces;

(b) was the spouse of such a serving member; or

(c) was living with such a serving member as husband or wife.

(4) "Serving member of the forces" means a person, other than one mentioned in Part 2 of Schedule 6 to the Social Security (Contributions) Regulations 2001, who, being over the age of 16 years, is a member of any establishment or organisation specified in Part 1 of that Schedule (being a member who gives full pay service) but does not include any such person while absent on desertion.

Manner of making elections under regulations 19 and 20

2.726   **21.**—(1) This regulation applies to elections under regulations 19 and 20.

(2) An election—

(a) must be made by notice in writing to the Board; and

(b) must be delivered or sent to an appropriate office as regards the Board.

(3) An election is made on the date on which it is received by the appropriate office.

(4) Where a person has made an election, child benefit is payable weekly so long as—

(a) he remains continually entitled to it; and

(b) in the case of an election under regulation 19, the conditions specified in paragraph (1)(a) or (b) of that regulation continue to be satisfied.

(5) A person who has made an election may cancel it at any time by giving to the Board a notice in writing which must be sent or delivered to an appropriate office as regards the Board.

(6) The Board must give effect to a notice given in accordance with paragraph (5) as soon as reasonably practicable after receiving it.

Interim payments

2.727   **22.**—[¹ (1) If the condition in any sub-paragraph of paragraph (1A) is satisfied, the Board may make a payment on account ("an interim payment") of any child benefit or guardian's allowance to which it appears to them that a person—

(a) is or may be entitled, were a claim made,

(b) where sub-paragraph (a) of paragraph (1A) applies, would or might be entitled, were a claim made,

(c) where sub-paragraph (b) of that paragraph applies, would or might be entitled, were the national insurance number condition satisfied.

(1A) The conditions are that—

(a) a claim for benefit or allowance has not been made in accordance with these Regulations and it is impracticable for such a claim to be made immediately;

(b) a claim has been made in accordance with these Regulations, the conditions of entitlement are satisfied other than the national insurance number condition, and it is impracticable for that condition to be satisfied immediately;

(c) a claim for the benefit or allowance has been so made but it is impracticable for it, or an application or appeal relating to it, to be determined immediately;

(d) an award of the benefit or allowance has been made but it is impracticable for the person entitled to it to be paid immediately other than by means of an interim payment.]

(2) Paragraph (1) does not apply pending the determination of an appeal [¹ ...]

(3) On or before the making of an interim payment, the Board must give the person to whom payment is to be made notice in writing of his liability under regulations 41 and 42 to have it brought into account and to repay any overpayment.

[¹ (4) In this regulation "the national insurance number condition" means the condition imposed—

(a) in Great Britain by section 13(1A) and (1B), of the Administration Act (requirement for claim to be accompanied by details of national insurance number);

(b) in Northern Ireland, by section 11(1A) and (1B) of the Administration (NI) Act.]

AMENDMENT

1. The Child Benefit and Guardian's Allowance (Miscellaneous Amendments) Regulations 2005 (SI 2005/343), reg.8 (March 18, 2005).

Information to be given and changes to be notified

23.—(1) This regulation applies to any person entitled to child benefit or guardian's allowance and any person by whom, or on whose behalf, payments of such benefit or allowance are receivable.

(2) A person to whom this regulation applies must furnish in such manner and at such times as the Board may determine such information or evidence as the Board may require for determining whether a decision on an award—

(a) in relation to benefit or allowance under the Contributions and Benefits Act, should be revised under section 9 or superseded under section 10 of the Social Security Act 1998;

(b) in relation to benefit or allowance under the Contributions and Benefits (NI) Act, should be revised under Article 10 or superseded under Article 11 of the Social Security (Northern Ireland) Order 1998.

(3) A person to whom this regulation applies must furnish in such manner and at such times as the Board may determine such information and evidence as the Board may require in connection with the payment of the benefit or allowance.

(4) A person to whom this regulation applies must notify the Board or a

2.728

769

relevant authority of any change of circumstances which he might reasonably be expected to know might affect—
- (a) the continuance of entitlement to the benefit or allowance; or
- (b) the payment of it,
  as soon as reasonably practicable after the change occurs.
- (5) A notification under paragraph (4)—
- (a) must be given by notice in writing or orally; and
- (b) must be sent, delivered or given to the appropriate office.

Fractional amounts of benefit or allowance

2.729   **24.** Where the amount of any child benefit or guardian's allowance payable includes a fraction of a penny, that fraction—
- (a) if it is less than a half, shall be disregarded;
- (b) if it is a half or more, shall be treated as a whole penny.

Payments to persons under the age of 18 years

2.730   **25.** Where a sum of child benefit or guardian's allowance is paid to a person under the age of 18 years (whether on his own behalf or on behalf of another), either of the following is a sufficient discharge to the Board for the sum paid—
- (a) a direct credit transfer under regulation 17 into the person's account;
- (b) the receipt by the person of a payment made by some other means.

Extinguishment of right to payment if payment is not obtained within the prescribed period

2.731   **26.**—(1) The right to payment of any sum of child benefit or guardian's allowance shall be extinguished if payment of that sum is not obtained within the period of 12 months from the date on which the right is treated as having arisen.

(2) Subject to paragraph (5), the right to payment of a sum is treated as having arisen—
- (a) if the Board have given or sent an instrument of payment in respect of the sum to the person to whom it is payable or have sent such an instrument to a place approved by them for collection by that person—
  - (i) on the date of the instrument, or
  - (ii) if a replacement instrument of payment has been so given or sent, on the date of the last such instrument;
- (b) in relation to any sum to which sub-paragraph (a) does not apply, if the Board have given or sent a notice (orally or in writing) that the sum is available for collection—
  - (i) on the date of the notice, or
  - (ii) if more than one such notice has been given or sent, on the date of the first notice;
- [¹ (bb) in relation to any sum which the person entitled to it and the Board have arranged to be paid by way of direct credit transfer into a bank or other account, on the due date for payment of such a sum;]
- (c) in relation to any sum to which [¹ none of the preceding sub-paragraphs applies], on such date as the Board may determine.

(3) The giving or sending by the Board of an instrument of payment under sub-paragraph (a) of paragraph (2), or a notice under sub-paragraph (b) of that paragraph, shall be effective even if the sum contained in the instrument, or the notice, is more or less than the sum which the person concerned has the right to receive.

(4) The date of an instrument of payment is—

(a) the date of issue of that instrument; or

(b) if later, the earliest date specified in the instrument on which payment may be obtained.

(5) Where a question arises as to whether a right to payment of a sum has been extinguished under this regulation, the period of 12 months referred to in paragraph (1) shall be extended to the date on which the Board decide the question, and the right shall be treated for the purposes of this regulation as having arisen on that date, if the Board are satisfied that—

(a) a notice in writing requesting payment of the sum was first received by them after the expiration of the period of 12 months from the date on which, ignoring this paragraph, the right would be treated as having arisen;

(b) from a day within that period until the date on which the notice in writing was given there was good cause for not giving the notice; and

(c) no payment of the sum has been made by way of direct credit transfer in accordance with regulation 17 and—

  (i) no instrument of payment has been given or sent to the person to whom the sum is payable; or

  (ii) any such instrument has been produced to them and no replacement instrument of payment has been given or sent to that person.

(6) This regulation has effect in relation to a person authorised or appointed to act on behalf of a person entitled to child benefit or guardian's allowance in the same manner as it has effect in relation to such a person.

AMENDMENT

1. The Child Benefit and Guardian's Allowance (Miscellaneous Amendments) Regulations 2005 (SI 2005/343), reg.9 (March 18, 2005).

PART IV

THIRD PARTIES

Persons who may act on behalf of those unable to act

27.—(1) Anything required by these regulations to be done by or to any person who is for the time being unable to act may be done by or to—   2.732

(a) in England and Wales, a receiver appointed by the Court of Protection with power to claim, or, as the case may be, receive, the benefit or allowance on behalf of the person;

(b) in Scotland, [¹ guardian acting or appointed under the Adults with Incapacity (Scotland) Act 2000] who is administering the estate of the person;

(c) in Northern Ireland, a controller appointed by the High Court, with power to claim, or, as the case may be, receive, the benefit or allowance on behalf of the person; or

(d) a person appointed under regulation 28(2) to act on behalf of the person.

(2) Where a sum of child benefit or guardian's allowance is paid to a receiver or other person mentioned in paragraph (1)(a), (b), (c) or (d), either of the following is a sufficient discharge to the Board for the sum paid—

(a) a direct credit transfer under regulation 17 into the person's account;

(b) the receipt by the person of a payment made by some other means.

AMENDMENT

1. The Child Benefit and Guardian's Allowance (Miscellaneous Amendments) Regulations 2005 (SI 2005/343), reg.10 (March 18, 2005).

Appointment of persons to act on behalf of those unable to act

2.733   **28.**—(1) This regulation applies where—

(a) a person is for the time being unable to act;

(b) the person is, or is alleged to be, entitled to child benefit or guardian's allowance (whether or not a claim for the benefit or allowance has been made by him or on his behalf); and

(c) no receiver or other person mentioned in regulation 27(1)(a), (b) or (c) has been appointed in relation to the person.

(2) The Board may appoint a person who—

(a) has applied in writing to them to act on behalf of the person who is unable to act, and

(b) if a natural person, is over the age of 18 years,

to exercise, on behalf of the person who is unable to act, any right relating to child benefit or guardian's allowance to which that person may be entitled and to receive and deal on his behalf with any sums payable to him in respect of the benefit or allowance.

(3) Where an appointment has been made under paragraph (2)—

(a) the Board may at any time revoke it; and

(b) the person appointed may resign from the appointment after having given one month's notice in writing to the Board of his intention to do so.

(4) An appointment made under paragraph (2) shall terminate when the Board are notified that a receiver or other person mentioned in regulation 27(1)(a), (b) or (c) has been appointed.

Persons who may proceed with a claim made by a person who has died

2.734   **29.**—(1) The Board may appoint such person as they think fit to proceed with a claim for child benefit or guardian's allowance [¹, and to deal with any issue related to the revision of, supersession of, or appeal in connection with a decision on, that claim] which has been made by a person who has died.

(2) Subject to regulation 32(2), the Board may pay or distribute any sum payable under an award on a claim proceeded with under paragraph (1) to or among—

(a) persons over the age of 16 years claiming as personal representatives, legatees, next of kin or creditors of the person who has died; and

(b) if the person who has died was illegitimate, any other persons over that age.

(3) "Next of kin" means—

(a) in England and Wales, and in Northern Ireland, the persons who would take beneficially on an intestacy;

(b) in Scotland, the persons entitled to the moveable estate of the deceased on intestacy.

(4) Where a sum is paid under paragraph (2) to a person, either of the following is a sufficient discharge to the Board for the sum paid—

(a) a direct credit transfer under regulation 17 into the person's account;

(b) the receipt by the person of a payment made by some other means.

(5) If the Board consider that a sum or part of a sum which may be paid or distributed under paragraph (2) is needed for the benefit of a person under the age of 16 years, they may obtain a good discharge for that sum by paying it to a person over that age whom they are satisfied will apply the sum for the benefit of the person under that age.

(6) Regulation 26 (extinguishment of right) applies to a payment or distribution made under paragraph (2).

AMENDMENT

1. The Child Benefit and Guardian's Allowance (Miscellaneous Amendments) Regulations 2005 (SI 2005/343), reg.11 (March 18, 2005).

Persons who may receive payments which a person who has died had not obtained

30.—(1) This regulation applies where a person who has died had not obtained at the date of his death a sum of child benefit or guardian's allowance which was payable to him.

(2) Subject to regulation 32(2), the Board may, unless the right to payment had already been extinguished at the date of death, pay or distribute the sum to or amongst the persons mentioned in regulation 29(2) (a) and (b).

(3) Regulation 26 (extinguishment of right) applies to a payment or distribution made under paragraph (2), except that, for the purposes of paragraph (1) of that regulation, the period of 12 months shall be calculated from the date on which the right to payment is treated as having arisen to the person to whom the payment or distribution is made (and not from the date on which that right is treated as having arisen in relation to the person who has died).

Person who may make a claim on behalf of a person who has died

31.—(1) If the conditions specified in paragraph (2) are satisfied, a claim may be made in the name of a person who has died for any child benefit or guardian's allowance to which he would have been entitled if he had claimed it in accordance with these Regulations.

(2) Subject to paragraph (3), the following conditions are specified in this paragraph—

2.735

2.736

   (a) within 6 months of the date of death an application must have been made in writing to the Board for a person, whom the Board think fit to be appointed to make the claim, to be so appointed;

   (b) a person must have been appointed by the Board to make the claim; and

   (c) the person so appointed must have made the claim not more than 6 months after the appointment.

(3) Subject to paragraphs (4) and (5), if the Board certify that to do so would be consistent with the proper administration of the Contributions and Benefits Act, the period of 6 months mentioned in paragraph (2)(a) or (c) shall be extended by such period (not exceeding 6 months) as may be specified in the certificate.

(4) If a certificate given under paragraph (3) specifies a period by which the period of 6 months mentioned in paragraph (2)(a) shall be extended, the period of 6 months mentioned in paragraph (2)(c) shall be shortened by a period corresponding to the period so specified.

(5) No certificate shall be given under paragraph (3) which would enable a claim to be made more than 12 months after the date of death. For the purposes of this paragraph, any period between the date on which the application for a person to be appointed to make the claim is made and the date on which that appointment is made shall be disregarded.

(6) A claim made in accordance with this regulation shall be treated for the purposes of these Regulations as if it had been made on the date of his death by the person who has died.

Regulations 29, 30 and 31: supplementary

2.737   **32.**—(1) The Board may dispense with strict proof of the title of a person claiming in accordance with regulation 29, 30 or 31.

(2) Neither paragraph (2) of regulation 29 nor paragraph (2) of regulation 30 applies unless written application for payment of the sum under that paragraph is made to the Board within 12 months from the date of death or such longer period as the Board may allow.

Payment to one person on behalf of another

2.738   **33.**—(1) Subject to paragraph (2), the Board may direct that child benefit or guardian's allowance shall be paid, wholly or in part, to another natural person on behalf of the person entitled to it.

(2) The Board may not make a direction under paragraph (1) unless they are satisfied that it is necessary for protecting the interests of—

   (a) the person entitled to the benefit or allowance; or

   (b) any child [¹ or qualifying young person] in respect of whom the benefit or allowance is payable.

AMENDMENT

1. The Child Benefit and Guardian's Allowance (Miscellaneous Amendments) Regulations 2006 (SI 2006/203) (April 10, 2006).

Payment to partner as alternative payee

2.739   **34.**—(1) Subject to paragraph (2), where a member of a married couple or an unmarried couple is entitled to child benefit or guardian's allowance, the Board may make arrangements whereby that benefit or allowance, as well as being payable to the person entitled to it, may, in the alternative, be paid to that person's partner on behalf of that person.

(2) Paragraph (1) does not apply to guardian's allowance where a wife has elected that the allowance is not to be paid to her husband in accordance with regulation 10 of the Guardian's Allowance (General) Regulations 2003 (prescribed manner of making an election under section 77(9) of the Contributions and Benefits Act and section 77(9) of the Contributions and Benefits (NI) Act).

PART V

OVERPAYMENTS AND RECOVERY

Recovery of overpayments by direct credit transfer

35.—(1) If the adjudicating authority determines that— 2.740

(a) a payment of child benefit or guardian's allowance in excess of entitlement has been credited to a bank account or other account under an arrangement for direct credit transfer made in accordance with regulation 17; and

(b) the conditions specified in paragraph (2) are satisfied,

the excess, or the specified part of it to which the certificate referred to in sub-paragraph (a) of that paragraph relates, shall be recoverable.

(2) The following conditions are specified in this paragraph—

(a) the Board must have certified that the payment in excess of entitlement, or a specified part of it, is materially due to the arrangement for payments to be made by direct credit transfer; and

(b) subject to paragraph (3), notice of the effect which this regulation would have, in the event of an overpayment, must have been given in writing to the person entitled to the benefit or allowance, or to a person acting in his behalf, before he agreed to the arrangement.

(3) In the case of an arrangement relating to child benefit which was agreed to before 6th April 1987, the condition specified in paragraph (2)(b) need not be satisfied in any case where the application for the benefit to be paid by direct credit transfer contained a statement, or was accompanied by a written statement made by the applicant, which complied with the provisions specified in paragraph (4).

(4) The provisions specified in this paragraph are—

(a) in relation to child benefit under the Contributions and Benefits Act, regulation 7(2)(b) and (6) of the Child Benefit (Claims and Payments) Regulations 1984;

(b) in relation to child benefit under the Contributions and Benefits (NI) Act, regulation 7(2)(b) and (6) of the Child Benefit (Claims and Payments) Regulations (Northern Ireland) 1985.

Circumstances in which determination need not be reversed, varied, revised or superseded

36.—(1) This regulation applies where, whether fraudulently or other- 2.741 wise, a person has misrepresented, or failed to disclose, material facts which do not provide a basis for the determination in pursuance of which an amount of child benefit or guardian's allowance was paid—

 (a) in relation to benefit or allowance under the Contributions and Benefits Act, to be revised under section 9 or superseded under section 10 of the Social Security Act 1998;

 (b) in relation to benefit or allowance under the Contributions and Benefits (NI) Act, to be revised under Article 10 or superseded under Article 11 of the Social Security (Northern Ireland) Order 1998.

(2) Where this regulation applies—

 (a) in relation to an amount mentioned in paragraph (1) relating to child benefit or guardian's allowance under the Contributions and Benefits Act, neither subsection (5) nor (5A) of section 71 of the Administration Act (recoverability dependent on reversal, variation, revision or supersession of determination) applies;

 (b) in relation to an amount mentioned in paragraph (1) relating to child benefit or guardian's allowance under the Contributions and Benefits (NI) Act, neither subsection (5) nor (5A) of section 69 of the Administration (NI) Act (recoverability dependent on reversal, variation, revision or supersession of determination) applies.

Calculating recoverable amounts

2.742   **37.** Where there has been an overpayment of child benefit or guardian's allowance, in calculating the amounts recoverable under section 71(1) of the Administration Act, section 69(1) of the Administration (NI) Act or regulation 35, the adjudicating authority must deduct any amount which is offset under regulation 38.

Offsetting prior payments of child benefit and guardian's allowance against arrears payable by virtue of a subsequent determination

2.743   **38.**—(1) Subject to regulation 40, in either of the cases specified in paragraphs (2) and (3)—

 (a) a sum of child benefit paid for a period covered by a subsequent determination shall be offset against any arrears of entitlement to the benefit payable for that period by virtue of the subsequent determination;

 (b) a sum of guardian's allowance paid for a period covered by a subsequent determination shall be offset against any arrears of entitlement to the allowance payable for that period by virtue of the subsequent determination, and, except to the extent that it exceeds them, the sum so paid shall be treated as properly paid on account of the arrears.

(2) The case specified in this paragraph is where a person has been paid a sum pursuant to a determination which subsequently—

 (a) is revised under section 9 or superseded under section 10 of the Social Security Act 1998;

 (b) is revised under Article 10 or superseded under Article 11 of the Social Security (Northern Ireland) Order 1998; or

 (c) is overturned on appeal.

(3) The case specified in this paragraph is where a person has been paid a sum for a period by way of an increase in respect of a dependent person and it is subsequently determined that—

(a) the dependent person is entitled to the benefit or allowance for that period; or

(b) a third person is entitled to the increase for that period in priority to the person who has been paid.

(4) Where child benefit which has been paid under an award in favour of a person ("the first claimant") is subsequently awarded to another ("the second claimant") for any week, the benefit shall nevertheless be treated as properly paid if it was received by someone (other than the first claimant) who—

(a) had [¹ the child or qualifying young person] living with him or was contributing towards the cost of providing for [¹ the child or qualifying young person] at a weekly rate which was not less than the weekly rate under the original award; and

(b) could have been entitled to child benefit in respect of [¹ that child or qualifying young person] for that week had a claim been made in time.

(5) Any amount which is treated under paragraph (4) as properly paid shall be deducted from the amount payable to the second claimant under the subsequent award.

AMENDMENT

1. The Child Benefit and Guardian's Allowance (Miscellaneous Amendments) Regulations 2006 (SI 2006/203) (April 10, 2006).

Offsetting prior payments of income support or jobseeker's allowance against arrears of child benefit or guardian's allowance payable by virtue of a subsequent determination

39.—(1) This regulation applies where—   2.744

(a) a person has been paid a sum by way of income support or jobseeker's allowance; and

(b) it is subsequently determined that—

(i) child benefit or guardian's allowance should be awarded or is payable in lieu of the income support or jobseeker's allowance; and

(ii) the income support or jobseeker's allowance was not payable.

(2) Subject to regulation 40, any sum of income support or jobseeker's allowance in respect of the period covered by the subsequent determination—

(a) shall be offset against any arrears of entitlement to the child benefit or guardian's allowance payable for that period by virtue of that determination; and

(b) except to the extent that it exceeds them, the sum so paid shall be treated as properly paid on account of the arrears.

Exception from offset of recoverable overpayment

40. No amount may be offset under regulation 38(1) or 39(2) which   2.745
has been determined to be a recoverable overpayment for the purposes

of section 71(1) of the Administration Act or section 69(1) of the Administration (NI) Act.

Bringing interim payments into account

2.746   **41.**—(1) Subject to paragraph (2), if it is practicable to do so—

(a) any interim payment made in anticipation of an award of child benefit or guardian's allowance shall be offset by the adjudicating authority in reduction of the benefit or allowance to be awarded;

(b) any interim payment (whether or not made in anticipation of an award) which is not offset under sub-paragraph (a) shall be deducted by the Board from—

(i) the sum payable under the award of benefit or allowance on account of which the interim payment was made; or

(ii) any sum payable under any subsequent award of the benefit or allowance to the same person.

(2) Paragraph (1) does not apply unless the Board have given the notice required by regulation 22(3).

Recovery of overpaid interim payments

2.747   **42.**—(1) Subject to paragraph (2), if the adjudicating authority, in the circumstances specified in either of paragraphs (3) and (4), has determined that an interim payment has been overpaid, it shall determine the amount of the overpayment.

(2) Paragraph (1) does not apply unless the Board have given the notice required by regulation 22(3).

(3) The circumstances specified in this paragraph are where an interim payment has been made under regulation 22(1)(a) and (b) and—

(a) the recipient has failed to make a claim in accordance with these Regulations as soon as practicable;

(b) the recipient has made a defective application and the Board have not treated the claim as duly made under regulation 10;

(c) it has been determined that—

(i) there is no entitlement on the claim;

(ii) the entitlement is less than the amount of the interim payment; or

(iii) the benefit or allowance on the claim is not payable; or

(d) the claim has been withdrawn.

(4) The circumstances specified in this paragraph are where an interim payment has been made under regulation 22(1)(c) which exceeds the entitlement under the award of benefit on account of which the interim payment was made.

(5) The amount of any overpayment determined under paragraph (1) shall be recoverable by the Board in the same manner as it would be if it were recoverable under—

(a) in relation to child benefit or guardian's allowance under the Contributions and Benefits Act, section 71(1) of the Administration Act;

(b) in relation to child benefit or guardian's allowance under the Contributions and Benefits (NI) Act, section 69(1) of the Administration (NI) Act.

PART VI

REVOCATIONS AND TRANSITIONAL PROVISIONS

Revocations

43. The subordinate legislation specified in column (1) of Parts 1 and 2 of Schedule 3, in so far as it relates to child benefit or guardian's allowance, is revoked to the extent mentioned in column (3) of that Schedule.

2.748

Transitional provisions

44.—(1) Anything done or commenced under any provision of the instruments revoked by regulation 43, so far as relating to child benefit or guardian's allowance, is to be treated as having been done or as being continued under the corresponding provision of these Regulations.

2.749

(2) The revocation by regulation 43 of an instrument which itself revoked an earlier instrument subject to savings does not prevent the continued operation of those savings, in so far as they are capable of continuing to have effect.

(3) "Instrument" includes a Statutory Rule of Northern Ireland.

SCHEDULE 1

Preamble

POWERS EXERCISED IN MAKING THESE REGULATIONS

1. The following provisions of the Administration Act—

2.750

  (a) section 5(1)(a), (b), (c), (d), (g), (h), (hh), (i), (j), (k), (l), (m), (p), (q) and (r) and (2) (a) and (g);
  (b) section 7(1), (2) and (3)(a);
  (c) section 71(4), (5), (5A), (6), (7) and (11)(a) and (f);
  (d) section 111A(1A), (1B), (1D) and (1E);
  (e) section 112(1A) to (1D);
  (f) section 189(1), (4), (5) and (6);
  (g) section 191.

2. The following provisions of the Administration (NI) Act—

  (a) section 5(1)(a), (b), (c), (d), (g), (h), (hh), (i), (j), (k), (l), (m), (n), (q), (r), (s) and (t) and (2)(a) and (g);
  (b) section 69(4), (5), (5A), (6), (7) and (11)(a) and (f);
  (c) section 105A(1A), (1B), (1D) and (1E);
  (d) section 106(1A) to (1D);
  (e) section 165(1), (4), (5), (6) and (11A);
  (f) section 167(1).

3. Sections 9(1) and 84 of the Social Security Act 1998.
4. Articles 2(2) and 10(1) of the Social Security (Northern Ireland) Order 1998.
5. Sections 132 and 133(1) and (2) of the Finance Act 1999.
6. Sections 50(1) and (2)(b) and (d) and 54(2) of the Tax Credits Act 2002.

<table>
<tr><td>**Regulation 3**</td><td>SCHEDULE 2</td></tr>
</table>

ELECTRONIC COMMUNICATIONS

PART I

GENERAL

Introduction

2.751   **1.** This Schedule supersedes the Social Security (Electronic Communications) (Child Benefit) Order 2002 which was made under section 8 of the Electronic Communications Act 2000.

Interpretation

2.752   **2.**—(1) In this Schedule—

"electronic communications" includes any communications by means of a telecommunication system (within the meaning of the Telecommunications Act 1984);

"official computer system" means a computer system maintained by or on behalf of the Board—

   (a) to send or receive information; or

   (b) to process or store information.

(2) References in this Schedule to the delivery of information and to information shall be construed in accordance with section 132(8) of the Finance Act 1999.

Scope of this Schedule

2.753   **3.** This Schedule applies to the delivery of information to or by the Board, the delivery of which is authorised or required by these Regulations.

PART II

GENERAL

Use of electronic communications by the Board

2.754   **4.** The Board may only use electronic communications in connection with the matters referred to in paragraph 3 if—

   (a) the recipient has indicated that he consents to the Board using electronic communications in connection with those matters; and

   (b) the Board have not been informed that that consent has been withdrawn.

Restrictions on the use of electronic communications by persons other than the Board

2.755   **5.**—(1) A person other than the Board may only use electronic communications in connection with the matters referred to in paragraph 3 if the conditions specified in subparagraphs (2) to (5) are satisfied.

(2) The first condition is that the person is for the time being permitted to use electronic communications for the purpose in question by an authorisation given by means of a specific or general direction of the Board.

(3) The second condition is that the person uses—

   (a) an approved method for authenticating the identity of the sender of the communication;

   (b) an approved method of electronic communications; and

   (c) an approved method for authenticating any information delivered by means of electronic communications.

(4) The third condition is that any information sent by means of electronic communications is in an approved form (including the manner in which the information is presented).

(5) The fourth condition is that the person maintains such records in written or electronic form as may be specified in a specific or general direction given by the Board.

(6) "Approved" means approved for the purposes of this Schedule, and for the time being, by means of a specific or general direction given by the Board.

Use of intermediaries

2.756   **6.** The Board may use intermediaries in connection with—

   (a)   the delivery of information by means of electronic communications in connection with the matters referred to in paragraph 3; and

   (b) the authentication or security of anything transmitted by any such means, and may require other persons to use intermediaries in connection with those matters.

PART III

EVIDENTIAL PROVISIONS

Effect of delivering information by means of electronic communications

7.—(1) Information which is delivered by means of electronic communications shall be treated as having been delivered in the manner or form required by any provision of these Regulations if, but only if, all the conditions imposed by—

    (a) this Schedule,

    (b) any other applicable enactment (except to the extent that the condition thereby imposed is incompatible with this Schedule); and

    (c) any specific or general direction given by the Board,
    are satisfied.

(2) Information delivered by means of electronic communications shall be treated as having been delivered on the day on which the last of the conditions imposed as mentioned in sub-paragraph (1) is satisfied.
This is subject to the following qualifications.

(3) The Board may by a general or specific direction provide for information to be treated as delivered upon a different date (whether earlier or later) than that given by sub-paragraph (2).

(4) Information shall not be taken to have been delivered to an official computer system by means of electronic communications unless it is accepted by the system to which it is delivered.

Proof of content

8.—(1) A document certified by an officer of the Board to be a printed-out version of any information delivered by means of electronic communications under this Schedule on any occasion shall be evidence, unless the contrary is proved, that that information—

    (a) was delivered by means of electronic communications on that occasion; and

    (b) constitutes the entirety of what was delivered on that occasion.

(2) A document purporting to be a certificate given in accordance with sub-paragraph (1) shall be presumed to be such a certificate unless the contrary is proved.

Proof of identity of sender or recipient

9. The identity of—

    (a) the sender of any information delivered to an official computer system by means of electronic communications under this Schedule, or

    (b) the recipient of any information delivered by means of electronic communications from an official computer system,

shall be presumed, unless the contrary is proved, to be the person recorded as such on an official computer system.

Information delivered electronically on another's behalf

10. Any information delivered by an approved method of electronic communications on behalf of any person shall be deemed to have been delivered by him unless he proves that it was delivered without his knowledge or connivance.

Proof of delivery of information

11.—(1) The use of an authorised method of electronic communications shall be presumed, unless the contrary is proved, to have resulted in the delivery of information—

    (a) in the case of information falling to be delivered to the Board, if the delivery of the information has been recorded on an official computer system;

    (b) in the case of information falling to be delivered by the Board, if the despatch of the information has been recorded on an official computer system.

(2) The use of an authorised method of electronic communications shall be presumed, unless the contrary is proved, not to have resulted in the delivery of information—

    (a) in the case of information falling to be delivered to the Board, if the delivery of the information has not been recorded on an official computer system;

    (b) in the case of information falling to be delivered by the Board, if the despatch of the information has not been recorded on an official computer system.

(3) The time of receipt of any information sent by an authorised means of electronic communications shall be presumed, unless the contrary is proved, to be that recorded on an official computer system.

2.757

2.758

2.759

2.760

2.761

Use of unauthorised means of electronic communications

2.762   **12.**—(1) Sub-paragraph (2) applies to information which is required to be delivered to the Board in connection with the matters mentioned in paragraph 3.

(2) The use of a means of electronic communications, for the purpose of delivering any information to which this paragraph applies, shall be conclusively presumed not to have resulted in the delivery of that information, unless—

(a) that means of electronic communications is for the time being approved for delivery of information of that kind; and

(b) the sender is approved for the use of that means of electronic communications in relation to information of that kind.

Regulation 43   SCHEDULE 3

REVOCATIONS

PART I

REVOCATIONS APPLICABLE TO GREAT BRITAIN

2.763   *Omitted*

PART II

REVOCATIONS APPLICABLE TO NORTHERN IRELAND

2.764   *Omitted*

The Child Benefit and Guardian's Allowance (Administrative Arrangements) Regulations 2003

(SI 2003/494)

Made   5th March 2003
Laid before Parliament   5th March 2003
Coming into force   7th April 2003

ARRANGEMENT OF REGULATIONS

2.765   1.   Citation and commencement
           2.   Interpretation
           3.   Provision of information or evidence to relevant authorities
           4.   Giving information or advice by relevant authorities
           5.   Recording, verification and holding, and forwarding, of claims etc. received
                   by relevant authorities

The Commissioners of Inland Revenue, in exercise of the powers conferred upon them by sections 58 and 65(1), (2), (7) and (9) of the Tax Credits Act 2002, hereby make the following Regulations:

Citation and commencement

1. These Regulations may be cited as the Child Benefit and Guardian's Allowance (Administrative Arrangements) Regulations 2003 and shall come into force on 7th April 2003 immediately after the Child Benefit and Guardian's Allowance (Administration) Regulations 2003.

2.766

Interpretation

2. In these Regulations—

2.767

"the Board" means the [¹ Commissioners for the Majesty's Revenue and Customs];

"defective application" has the meaning given by regulation 10(3) of the principal Regulations;

"the principal Regulations" means the Child Benefit and Guardian's Allowance (Administration) Regulations 2003;

"relevant authority" means—

(a) the Secretary of State;

(b) the Department for Social Development in Northern Ireland; or

(c) a person providing services to the Secretary of State or that Department.

AMENDMENT

1. The Child Benefit and Guardian's Allowance (Miscellaneous Amendments) Regulations 2006 (SI 2006/203) (April 10, 2006).

Provision of information or evidence to relevant authorities

3.—(1) Information or evidence relating to child benefit or guardian's allowance which is held—

2.768

(a) by the Board; or

(b) by a person providing services to the Board, in connection with the provision of those services,

may be provided to a relevant authority for the purposes of, or for any purposes connected with, the exercise of that relevant authority's functions under the principal Regulations.

(2) Information or evidence relating to child benefit and guardian's allowance may be provided to a relevant authority by persons other than the Board (whether or not persons by whom claims or notifications relating to child benefit or guardian's allowance are or have been made or given).

Giving of information or advice by relevant authorities

4. A relevant authority to which a claim or notification is or has been made or given by a person in accordance with the principal Regulations may give information or advice relating to child benefit and guardian's allowance to that person.

2.769

Recording, verification and holding, and forwarding, of claims etc. received by relevant authorities

5.—(1) A relevant authority may record and hold—

2.770

783

(a) claims and notifications received by virtue of the any of the principal Regulations; and

(b) information or evidence received by virtue of regulation 3(2).

(2) Subject to paragraphs (3) and (4), a relevant authority or a person providing services to the Board must forward to the Board such a claim or notification, or such information or evidence, as soon as reasonably practicable after being satisfied that it is complete.

(3) Before forwarding a claim or notification in accordance with paragraph (2), a relevant authority must verify whether the details of the claim or notification are consistent with any details held by it which have been provided in connection with a relevant claim for benefit that relates to—

(a) the person by whom the claim for child benefit or guardian's allowance is or has been made; or

(b) [¹ the child or qualifying young person in respect to whom] the child benefit or guardian's allowance is payable.

(4) Before forwarding a claim in accordance with paragraph (2), a relevant authority must verify that—

(a) any national insurance number provided in respect of the person by whom the claim is made exists and has been allocated to that person;

(b) the matters verified in accordance with sub-paragraph (a) accord with—

    (i) its own records; or

    (ii) in the case of a person providing services to the Secretary of State or the Department for Social Development in Northern Ireland, records held by the Secretary of State or that Department.

(5) Before forwarding a claim in accordance with paragraph (2), a relevant authority may verify the existence of any original document provided by the person making the claim which is required to be returned to him.

(6) If a relevant authority cannot locate any national insurance number in respect of a person by whom such a claim is made, it must forward to the Board or a person providing services to the Board the claim.

(7) "National insurance number" means the national insurance number allocated within the meaning of—

(a) regulation 9 of the Social Security (Crediting and Treatment of Contributions, and National Insurance Numbers) Regulations 2001; or

(b) regulation 9 of the Social Security (Crediting and Treatment of Contributions, and National Insurance Numbers) Regulations (Northern Ireland) 2001.

(8) "Claim for benefit" means a claim for—

(a) a benefit in relation to which—

    (i) the Secretary of State has functions under the Social Security Contributions and Benefits Act 1992; or

    (ii) the Department for Social Development in Northern Ireland has functions under the Social Security Contributions and Benefits (Northern Ireland) Act 1992; or

(b) a jobseeker's allowance under—

    (i) the Jobseekers Act 1995; or

    (ii) the Jobseekers (Northern Ireland) Order 1995.

AMENDMENT

1. The Child Benefit and Guardian's Allowance (Miscellaneous Amendments) Regulations 2006 (SI 2006/203) (April 10, 2006).

The Child Benefit and Guardian's Allowance (Decisions and Appeals) Regulations 2003

(SI 2003/916)

Made   *27th March 2003*
Coming into force   *7th April 2003*

ARRANGEMENT OF REGULATIONS

PART 1

GENERAL

PART 2

REVISION OF DECISIONS

PART 3

SUPERSEDING DECISIONS

Schedule 1 Powers Exercised in Making These Regulations

Schedule 2 Decisions Against Which No Appeal Lies

Part 1 Decisions Made Under Primary Legislation

Part 2 Decisions Made Under Secondary Legislation

Part 3 Other decisions

Whereas a draft of this instrument was laid before Parliament in accordance with section 80(1) of the Social Security Act 1998 and Article 75(1A) of the Social Security (Northern Ireland) Order 1998 and approved by resolution of each House of Parliament;

Now, therefore, the Commissioners of Inland Revenue, in exercise of the powers conferred upon them by the provisions set out in Schedule 1 and, in accordance with section 8 of the Tribunals and Inquiries Act 1992, after consultation with the Council on Tribunals, hereby make the following Regulations:

Part 1

General

Citation, commencement and effect

1.—(1) These Regulations may be cited as the Child Benefit and Guardian's Allowance (Decisions and Appeals) Regulations 2003 and shall come into force on 7th April 2003 immediately after the commencement of section 50 of the Tax Credits Act 2002 for the purposes of entitlement to payment of child benefit and guardian's allowance.

(2) These Regulations have effect only in relation to—
(a) child benefit and guardian's allowance under the Contributions and Benefits Act; and
(b) child benefit and guardian's allowance under the Contributions and Benefits (NI) Act.

Interpretation

2.—(1) In these Regulations—
"the 1998 Act" means the Social Security Act 1998;
"the Administration Act" means the Social Security Administration Act 1992;
"the Administration (NI) Act" means the Social Security Administration (Northern Ireland) Act 1992;
"the Administration Regulations" means the Child Benefit and Guardian's Allowance (Administration) Regulations 2003;

2.772

2.773

787

"appeal tribunal" means—

[¹ . . .]

in relation to child benefit or guardian's allowance under the Contributions and Benefits (NI) Act, an appeal tribunal constituted under Chapter 1 of Part 2 of the 1998 Order;

"the appropriate office" means—

(a) in relation to child benefit or guardian's allowance under the Contributions and Benefits Act, the Child Benefit Office, Waterview Park, Washington, Tyne and Wear;

(b) in relation to child benefit or guardian's allowance under the Contributions and Benefits (NI) Act, the Child Benefit Office (Northern Ireland), Windsor House, Bedford Street, Belfast;

(c) any Inland Revenue Enquiry Centre;

"the Board" means the Commissioners of Inland Revenue;

"claimant" means a person who has claimed child benefit or guardian's allowance and includes, in relation to an award or decision, a beneficiary under the award or a person affected by the decision;

"clerk to the appeal tribunal" means—

[¹ . . .]

in relation to child benefit or guardian's allowance under the Contributions and Benefits (NI) Act, a clerk assigned to the appeal tribunal in accordance with regulation 37 of the Decisions and Appeals Regulations (NI);

"Commissioner" means—

[¹ . . .]

in relation to child benefit or guardian's allowance under the Contributions and Benefits (NI) Act, the Chief Social Security Commissioner or any other Social Security Commissioner appointed under the 1998 Order and includes a tribunal of two or more Commissioners constituted under Article 16(7);

"the Contributions and Benefits Act" means the Social Security Contributions and Benefits Act 1992;

"the Contributions and Benefits (NI) Act" means the Social Security Contributions and Benefits (Northern Ireland) Act 1992;

"the Decisions and Appeals Regulations" means the Social Security and Child Support (Decisions and Appeals) Regulations 1999;

"the Decisions and Appeals Regulations (NI)" means the Social Security and Child Support (Decisions and Appeals) Regulations (Northern Ireland) 1999;

"family" has—

(a) in relation to child benefit and guardian's allowance under the Contributions and Benefits Act, the meaning given by section 137 of that Act;

(b) in relation to child benefit and guardian's allowance under the Contributions and Benefits (NI) Act, the meaning given by section 133 of that Act;

"legally qualified panel member" means—

[¹ . . .]

in relation to child benefit or guardian's allowance under the Contributions and Benefits (NI) Act, a panel member who satisfies the requirements of paragraph 1 of Schedule 2 to the Decisions and Appeals Regulations (NI);

"the Northern Ireland Department" means the Department for Social Development in Northern Ireland;

"the 1998 Order" means the Social Security (Northern Ireland) Order 1998;

"panel" means the panel constituted under [¹ . . .] or Article 7;

"panel member" means a person appointed to the panel;

"party to the proceedings" means the Board and any other person who—

(a) is one of the principal parties for the purposes of sections 13 and 14 or Articles 14 and 15; or

(b) has a right of appeal to an appeal tribunal under section 12(2) or Article 13(2);

"relevant benefit" means child tax credit under the Tax Credits Act 2002 and—

(a) in relation to child benefit or guardian's allowance under the Contributions and Benefits Act, any of the benefits mentioned in section 8(3);

(b) in relation to child benefit or guardian's allowance under the Contributions and Benefits (NI) Act, any of the benefits mentioned in Article 9(3);

"superseding decision" has the meaning given by regulation 13(1);

"writing" includes writing produced by electronic communications used in accordance with regulation 4.

(2) In these Regulations—

(a) a reference to a numbered section without more is a reference to the section of the 1998 Act bearing that number;

(b) a reference to a numbered Article without more is a reference to the Article of the 1998 Order bearing that number.

AMENDMENTS

1. Tribunals, Courts and Enforcement Act 2007 (Transitional and Consequential Provisions) Order 2008 (SI 2008/2683) Sch.1, paras 212 and 213 (November 3, 2008).

GENERAL NOTE

"the Board"

The definition of "the Board" must be read in the light of the Commissioners for Revenue and Customs Act 2005. Section 5(2)(a) vests all the functions of the former Commissioners of Inland Revenue in the Commissioners for Her Majesty's Revenue and Customs and s.4(1) provides that the Commissioners and the officers of Revenue and Customs may together be referred to as Her Majesty's Revenue and Customs.

Service of notices or documents

3.—(1) Where, under any provision of these Regulations—

    2.774

(a) a notice or other document is required to be given or sent to the clerk to the appeal tribunal or the Board, the notice or document is to be treated as having been so given or sent on the day that it is received by the clerk or the Board;

(b) a notice (including notification of a decision of the Board) or other document is required to be given or sent to any person other than clerk to the appeal tribunal or the Board, the notice or document is, if sent by post to that person's last known address, to be treated as having been given or sent on the day that it was posted.

(2) In these Regulations, "the date of notification", in relation to a decision of the Board, means the date on which notification of the decision is treated under paragraph (1)(b) as having been given or sent.

DEFINITIONS

"the Board"—see reg.2(1).
"clerk to the appeal tribunal"—*ibid.*

GENERAL NOTE

Para.(1)
2.775   See the note to reg.2 of the Social Security and Child Support (Decisions and Appeals) Regulations 1999 to which this is equivalent.

Para.(2)
2.776   This has the effect that whenever the phrase "the date of notification" is used in subsequent provisions in these Regulations, it refers to the date on which notification of a decision of the Board is treated under para.(1)(b) as having been given or sent.

Use of electronic communications

2.777   **4.**—(1) Schedule 2 to the Administration Regulations (the use of electronic communications) applies to the delivery of information to or by the Board which is authorised or required by these Regulations in the same manner as it applies to the delivery of information to or by the Board which is authorised or required by the Administration Regulations.

(2) References in paragraph (1) to the delivery of information shall be construed in accordance with section 132(8) of the Finance Act 1999.

DEFINITIONS

"the Administration Regulations"—see reg.2(1).
"the Board"—*ibid.*

PART 2

REVISION OF DECISIONS

Revision of decisions within a prescribed period or on an application

2.778   **5.**—(1) Subject to paragraph (3), if the conditions specified in paragraph (2) are satisfied—

(a) a decision under section 8 or 10 may be revised by the Board under section 9; and

(b) a decision under Article 9 or 11 may be revised by them under Article 10.

(2) The conditions specified in this paragraph are that—

(a) the Board commence action leading to the revision within one month of the date of notification of the decision; or

(b) subject to regulation 6, an application for the revision was received by the Board at the appropriate office—

    (i) within one month of the date of notification of the decision;

    (ii) if a written statement of the reasons for the decision requested under regulation 26(1)(b) was provided within the period specified in paragraph (i), within 14 days of the expiry of that period; or

    (iii) if such a statement was provided after the period specified in paragraph (i), within 14 days of the date on which the statement was provided.

(3) Paragraph (1) does not apply in respect of a relevant change of circumstances which occurred since the decision [1 had effect (or, in the case of an advance award under regulation 12 of the Child Benefit and Guardian's Allowance (Administration) Regulations 2003 (advance claims and awards), was made)] or where the Board have evidence or information which indicates that a relevant change of circumstances will occur.

AMENDMENT

1. Child Benefit and Guardian's Allowance (Miscellaneous Amendments) Regulations 2005 (SI 2005/343), reg.3 (March 18, 2005).

DEFINITIONS

"the appropriate office"—see reg.2(1).
"the Board"—*ibid*.
"the date of notification"—see reg.3(2).

GENERAL NOTE

This regulation provides for revision of a decision where the Board or the claimant takes action within one month of the date of notification of the decision. It is equivalent to reg.3(1) and (9)(a) of the Social Security and Child Support (Decisions and Appeals) Regulations 1999. The time for making an application may be extended if a request for reasons has been made promptly (para.(2)(b)(ii) and (iii)) or where the conditions of reg.6 are met. The time for appealing against a decision is extended if an application is made for revision, so that the claimant is not prejudiced by first having sought a revision (see reg.28(2)).

2.779

Late applications for revision of decisions

6.—(1) The Board may extend the time limits specified in regulation 5(2) (b)(i) to (iii) if the first and second conditions are satisfied.

2.780

(2) The first condition is that an application for an extension of time must be made to the Board by the claimant or a person acting on his behalf.

(3) The second condition is that the application for the extension of time must—

(a) contain particulars of the grounds on which the extension is sought;

(b) contain sufficient details of the decision which it is sought to have revised so as to enable it to be identified; and

(c) be made within 13 months of the latest date by which the application for revision should have been received by the Board in accordance with regulation 5(2)(b).

(4) An application for an extension of time must not be granted unless the Board are satisfied that—

(a) it is reasonable to grant it;

(b) the application for revision has merit; and

(c) special circumstances are relevant to the application for an extension of time as a result of which it was not practicable for the application for revision to be made within the time limits specified in regulation 5(2)(b)(i) to (iii).

(5) In determining whether it is reasonable to grant an application for an extension of time, the Board must have regard to the principle that the greater the amount of time that has elapsed between the expiration of the time limits specified in regulation 5(2)(b)(i) to (iii) and the making of the application, the more compelling the special circumstances mentioned in paragraph (4)(c) should be.

(6) In determining whether it is reasonable to grant an application for an extension of time, the Board must take no account of the following—

(a) that the applicant or any person acting for him was unaware of, or misunderstood, the law applicable to his case (including being unaware of, or misunderstanding, the time limits imposed by these Regulations); or

(b) that a Commissioner [¹ , the Upper Tribunal] or a court has taken a different view of the law from that previously understood and applied.

(7) An application for an extension of time which has been refused may not be renewed.

AMENDMENT

1. Tribunals, Courts and Enforcement Act 2007 (Transitional and Consequential Provisions) Order 2008 (SI 2008/2683) Sch.1, paras 212 and 214 (November 3, 2008).

DEFINITIONS

"the Board"—see reg.2(1).
"claimant"—*ibid.*
"Commissioner"—*ibid.*

GENERAL NOTE

2.781   This is equivalent to reg.4 of the Social Security and Child Support (Decisions and Appeals) Regulations 1999.

Procedure for revision of decisions on an application

2.782   7.—(1) The Board may treat—

(a) an application for a decision under section 10 as an application for a revision under section 9;

(b) an application for a decision under Article 11 as an application for a revision under Article 10.

(2) Paragraph (3) applies where, in order to consider all the issues raised by an application for such a revision, the Board require further evidence or information from the applicant.

(3) Where this paragraph applies, the Board must notify the applicant that further evidence or information is required and—

(a) if the applicant provides relevant further evidence or information within one month of the date of notification or such longer period of time as the Board may allow, the decision may be revised;

(b) if the applicant does not provide such evidence or information within that time, the decision may be revised on the basis of the application.

DEFINITIONS

"the Board"—see reg.2(1).
"the date of notification"—see reg.3(2).

GENERAL NOTE

Para.(1)
This is equivalent to reg.3(10) of the Social Security and Child Support   2.783
(Decisions and Appeals) Regulations 1999 and provides for an application for a superseding decision to be treated as an an application for revision. Regulation 14(1) makes provision for an application for a revision to be treated as an application for superseding decision.

Para.(2) and (3)
These are equivalent to reg.3(2) of the Social Security and Child Support   2.784
(Decisions and Appeals) Regulations 1999.

Revision of decisions against which there has been an appeal

8.—(1) In the circumstances prescribed by paragraph (2), any of the   2.785
following decisions may be revised by the Board at any time—

(a) a decision under section 8 or 10;

(b) a decision under Article 9 or 11.

(2) The circumstances prescribed by this paragraph are circumstances where there is an appeal to an appeal tribunal [¹ or the First-tier Tribunal] against the decision within the time prescribed by regulation 28, or in a case to which [¹ regulations 29 and 29A apply within the time prescribed by those regulations] but the appeal has not been determined.

(3) If—

(a) the Board make one of the following decisions ("the original decision")—

  (i) a decision under section 8 or 10 or one under section 9(1) revising such a decision; or

  (ii) a decision under Article 9 or 11 or one under Article 10(1) revising such a decision;

(b) the claimant appeals to an appeal tribunal against the original decision;

(c) after the appeal has been made, but before it results in a decision by the appeal tribunal, the Board make a second decision which—

  (i) supersedes the original decision in accordance with section 10 or Article 11; or

  (ii) decides a further claim for child benefit or guardian's allowance by the claimant; and

(d) the Board would have made their second decision differently if, at the time they made it, they had been aware of the decision subsequently made by the appeal tribunal,

the second decision may be revised by the Board at any time.

AMENDMENTS

1. Tribunals, Courts and Enforcement Act 2007 (Transitional and Consequential Provisions) Order 2008 (SI 2008/2683) Sch.1, paras 212 and 215 (November 3, 2008).

DEFINITIONS

"appeal tribunal"—see reg.2(1).
"the Board"—*ibid.*
"claimant"—*ibid.*

GENERAL NOTE

2.786   This is equivalent to reg.3(5A) of the Social Security and Child Support (Decisions and Appeals) Regulations 1999 and enables a decision made while an appeal to a tribunal is pending to be revised in the light of the tribunal's decision.

Revision of decisions against which no appeal lies

2.787   **9.**—(1) In the case prescribed by paragraph (2), any of the following decisions may be revised by the Board at any time—
    (a) a decision under section 8 or 10;
    (b) a decision under Article 9 or 11.
    (2) The case prescribed by this paragraph is the case of decisions which—
    (a) are specified in—
        (i) Schedule 2 to the 1998 Act; or
        (ii) Schedule 2 to the 1998 Order; or
    (b) are prescribed by regulation 25 (decisions against which no appeal lies).

DEFINITION

"the Board"—see reg.2(1).

GENERAL NOTE

2.788   This is equivalent to reg.3(8) of the Social Security and Child Support (Decisions and Appeals) Regulations 1999.

Revision of decisions arising from official error etc.

2.789   **10.**—(1) In the circumstances prescribed by paragraph (2), any of the following decisions may be revised by the Board at any time—
    (a) a decision under section 8 or 10;
    (b) a decision under Article 9 or 11.
    (2) The circumstances prescribed by this paragraph are circumstances where the decision—
    (a) arose from an official error; or
    (b) was made in ignorance of, or was based upon a mistake as to, some material fact and, as a result of that ignorance of, or mistake as to,

that fact, is more advantageous to the claimant than it would otherwise have been.

(3) "Official error" means an error made by—

(a) an officer of the Board acting as such, which no person outside
the Inland Revenue caused or to which no such person materially
contributed; or

(b) a person employed by a person providing services to the Board
and acting as such which no other person who was not so
employed caused or to which no such other person materially
contributed,

but does not include an error of law which is shown to have been an error by
virtue of a subsequent decision of a Commissioner [¹ , the Upper Tribunal]
or the court.

AMENDMENT

1. Tribunals, Courts and Enforcement Act 2007 (Transitional and Consequential
Provisions) Order 2008 (SI 2008/2683) Sch.1, paras 212 and 216 (November 3,
2008).

DEFINITIONS

"the Board"—see reg.2(1).
"claimant"—*ibid.*
"Commissioner"—*ibid.*
"Inland Revenue", by virtue of s.39(2) of the Social Security Act 1998, see s.191
of the Social Security Administration Act 1992.
"official error"—see para.(3).

GENERAL NOTE

This is equivalent to reg.3(5) of the Social Security and Child Support (Decisions   2.790
and Appeals) Regulations 1999. For the interpretation of the definition of "official
error", see the note to reg.1(3) of the 1999 Regulations.

Revision of decisions following the award of another relevant benefit

11.—(1) In the circumstances prescribed by paragraph (2), any of the   2.791
following decisions may be revised by the Board at any time—

(a) a decision under section 8 or 10;

(b) a decision under Article 9 or 11.

(2) The circumstances prescribed by this paragraph are circumstances
where—

(a) the decision awards child benefit or guardian's allowance to a person;
and

(b) an award of another relevant benefit, or of an increase in the rate of
another relevant benefit, is made to that person or a member of his
family for a period which includes the date on which the decision
took effect.

DEFINITIONS

"the Board"—see reg.2(1).
"family"—*ibid.*
"relevant benefit"—*ibid.*

2.792   This is equivalent to reg.3(7) of the Social Security and Child Support (Decisions and Appeals) Regulations 1999. A decision may be revised where a later decision in respect of a relevant benefit affects entitlement under the earlier decision from the date it took effect. If the later decision affects entitlement under the earlier decision from a later date, the earlier decision is superseded under reg.13(2)(e) instead of being revised.

Date as from which revised decisions take effect

2.793   **12.** If the Board decide that—

   (a) on a revision under section 9, the date as from which the decision under section 8 or 10 took effect was erroneous; or

   (b) on a revision under Article 10, the date as from which the decision under Article 9 or 11 took effect was erroneous,

the revision shall take effect as from the date from which the decision would have taken effect had the error not been made.

DEFINITION

   "the Board"—see reg.2(1).

GENERAL NOTE

2.794   This is equivalent to reg.5 of the Social Security and Child Support (Decisions and Appeals) Regulations 1999 and provides the exception to the general rule imposed by s.9(3) of the Social Security Act 1998 that a revision is effective from the same date as the decision being revised. The exception is where a ground for the revision is that the effective date of the original decision was wrong.

PART 3

SUPERSEDING DECISIONS

Cases and circumstances in which superseding decisions may be made

2.795   **13.**—(1) Subject to regulation 15, the Board may make a decision under section 10 or Article 11 ("a superseding decision"), either on their own initiative or on an application received by them at an appropriate office, in any of the cases and circumstances prescribed by paragraph (2).

   (2) The cases and circumstances prescribed by this paragraph are cases and circumstances where the decision to be superseded is—

   (a) a decision in respect of which—

      (i) there has been a relevant change of circumstances since it [1 had effect (or, in the case of an advance award under regulation 12 of the Child Benefit and Guardian's Allowance (Administration) Regulations 2003 (advance claims and awards), was made)]; or

      (ii) it is anticipated that there will be such a change;

   (b) a decision (other than one to which sub-paragraph (d) refers)—

      (i) which was erroneous in point of law, or was made in ignorance of, or was based upon a mistake as to, some material fact; and

> (ii) in relation to which an application for a superseding decision was received by the Board, or a decision by the Board to act on their own initiative was taken, more than one month after the date of notification of the decision to be superseded or after the expiry of such longer period of time as may have been allowed under regulation 6;
>
> (c) a decision of an appeal tribunal [² the First-tier Tribunal, the Upper Tribunal] or a Commissioner which—
> (i) was made in ignorance of, or was based upon a mistake as to, some material fact;
> (ii) in a case to which subsection (5) of section 26 applies, was dealt with in accordance with subsection (4)(b) of that section; or
> (iii) in a case to which paragraph (5) of Article 26 applies, was dealt with in accordance with paragraph (4)(b) of that Article;
>
> (d) a decision—
> (i) specified in Schedule 2 to the 1998 Act;
> (ii) specified in Schedule 2 to the 1998 Order; or
> (iii) prescribed by regulation 25 (decisions against which no appeal lies); or
>
> (e) a decision where—
> (i) the claimant has been awarded entitlement to child benefit or guardian's allowance; and
> (ii) subsequent to the first day of the period to which that entitlement relates, the claimant or a member of his family becomes entitled to, or to an increase in the rate of, another relevant benefit.

AMENDMENTS

1. Child Benefit and Guardian's Allowance (Miscellaneous Amendments) Regulations 2005 (SI 2005/343), reg.4 (March 18, 2005).
2. Tribunals, Courts and Enforcement Act 2007 (Transitional and Consequential Provisions) Order 2008 (SI 2008/2683) Sch.1, paras 212 and 217 (November 3, 2008).

DEFINITIONS

"appeal tribunal"—see reg.2(1).
"appropriate office"—*ibid.*
"the Board"—*ibid.*
"claimant"—*ibid.*
"Commissioner"—*ibid.*
"the date of notification"—see reg.3(2).
"family"—see reg.2(1).
"relevant benefit"—*ibid.*
"superseding decision"—see para.(1).

GENERAL NOTE

Para.(1)
    This is equivalent to reg.6(1) of the Social Security and Child Support (Decisions and Appeals) Regulations 1999. See the note to that provision. One difference is the use of the phrase "superseding decision" instead of "supersession" but this seems to be only a matter of style.

2.796

Para. (2)

2.797   This is equivalent to reg.6(2)(a) to (e) of the 1999 Regulations, the other sub-paragraphs of reg.6(2) of the 1999 regulations not being relevant to child benefit or guardian's allowance.

The context, as well as a comparison with the 1999 Regulations, makes it clear that the "decision" in subpara.(b) refers only to decisions of the Board. Decisions of tribunals and Commissioners fall to be superseded on the ground of ignorance of, or mistake as to, a material fact only under subpara.(c). Subpara.(b)(ii) prevents any overlap with reg.5. In subpara.(d) "decision" also refers only to decisions of the Board, because the relevant decisions do not fall within the jurisdiction of tribunals or Commissioners but, in subparas (a) and (e), "decision" includes decisions of tribunals and Commissioners.

Subparagraph (e) provides for supersession only where the later decision affects entitlement under the earlier decision from a date later than the date from which the earlier decision was effective. If the later decision has effect from the date from which the earlier decision was effective, revision under reg.11 is appropriate if the earlier decision was a decision of the Board. If the earlier decision was a decision of a tribunal or Commissioner, it is not clear that there will always be grounds for supersession, save under subpara.(a)(i), which is unlikely to produce the appropriate degree of backdating.

A superseding decision is effective from the date it is made (s.10(5) of the Social Security Act 1998), save where reg.16 provides otherwise.

See further the note to reg.6 of the 1999 Regulations.

Procedure for making superseding decisions on an application

2.798   **14.**—(1) The Board may treat—

(a) an application for a revision under section 9 as an application for a decision under section 10;

(b) an application for a revision under Article 10 as an application for a decision under Article 11.

(2) Paragraph (3) applies where, in order to consider all the issues raised by an application for a superseding decision, the Board require further evidence or information from the applicant.

(3) Where this paragraph applies, the Board must notify the applicant that further evidence or information is required and—

(a) if the applicant provides further relevant evidence or information within one month of the date of notification or such longer period of time as the Board may allow, the decision to be superseded may be superseded;

(b) if the applicant does not provide such evidence or information within that period, the decision to be superseded may be superseded on the basis of the application.

DEFINITIONS

"the Board"—see reg.2(1).
"the date of notification"—see reg.3(2).
"superseding decision"—by virtue of reg.2(1), see reg.13(1).

GENERAL NOTE

Para.(1)

2.799   This is equivalent to reg.6(5) of the Social Security and Child Support (Decisions and Appeals) Regulations 1999. It permits an application for revision to be treated as an application for supersession. Regulation 7(1) permits an application for super-session to be treated as an application for revision. See the note to s.12 of the Social Security Act 1998 for a discussion of the question whether, on appeal, a tribunal may treat a superseding decision as a refusal to revise or a revision as a refusal to supersede.

Paras (2) and (3)

These are equivalent to reg.6(4) of the 1999 Regulations. **2.800**

Interaction of revisions and superseding decisions

15.—(1) This regulation applies to any decision in relation to which **2.801** circumstances arise in which the decision may be revised under section 9 or Article 10.

(2) A decision to which this regulation applies may not be superseded by a superseding decision unless—

(a) circumstances arise in which the Board may revise the decision in accordance with Part 2; and

(b) further circumstances arise in relation to the decision which—

    (i) are not specified in any of the regulations in Part 2; but

    (ii) are prescribed by regulation 13(2) or are ones where a superseding decision may be made in accordance with regulation 14(3).

DEFINITIONS

"the Board"—see reg.2(1).
"superseding decision"—by virtue of reg.2(1), see reg.13(1).

GENERAL NOTE

This is equivalent to reg.6(3) of the Social Security and Child Support (Decisions **2.802** and Appeals) Regulations 1999.

Date as from which superseding decisions take effect

16.—(1) This regulation prescribes cases or circumstances in which a **2.803** superseding decision shall take effect as from a prescribed date other than the date on which it was made or, where applicable, the date on which the application for it was made.

(2) If a superseding decision is made on the basis that—

(a) there has been a relevant change of circumstances since the decision to be superseded had effect [¹ (or, in the case of an advance award, was made)]; or

(b) it is anticipated there will be such a change,

it shall take effect as from the earliest date prescribed by paragraphs (3) to (8).

(3) In any case where the superseding decision is advantageous to the claimant and notification of the change was given in accordance with any enactment or subordinate legislation under which that notification was required, the date prescribed by this paragraph is—

(a) if the notification was given within one month of the change occurring or such longer period as may be allowed under regulation 17, the date the change occurred or, if later, the first date on which the change has effect; or

(b) if the notification was given after the period mentioned in subparagraph (a), the date of notification of the change.

(4) In any case where the superseding decision is advantageous to the claimant and is made on the Board's own initiative, the date prescribed by this paragraph is the date on which the Board commenced action with a view to the supersession.

(5) In any case where the superseding decision is not advantageous to the claimant, the date prescribed by this paragraph is the date of the change.

(6) Decisions which are advantageous to claimants include those mentioned in regulation 27(5).

(7) If—

(a) the Board supersede a decision made by an appeal tribunal [² the First-tier Tribunal, the Upper Tribunal] or a Commissioner in accordance with paragraph (i) of regulation 13(2)(c); and

(b) as a result of the ignorance or mistake referred to in that paragraph, the decision to be superseded was more advantageous to the claimant than it would otherwise have been,

the superseding decision shall take effect as from the date on which the decision of the appeal tribunal or the Commissioner took, or was to take, effect.

(8) If the Board supersede a decision made by an appeal tribunal [² the First-tier Tribunal, the Upper Tribunal] or a Commissioner in accordance with paragraph (ii) or (iii) of regulation 13(2)(c), the superseding decision shall take effect as from the date on which it would have taken effect had it been decided in accordance with the determination of [² the Upper Tribunal,] the Commissioner or the court in the appeal referred to in section 26(1)(b) or Article 26(1)(b).

(9) If a superseding decision is made in consequence of a decision which is a relevant determination for the purposes of section 27 or Article 27, it shall take effect as from the date of the relevant determination.

[¹ (9A) Where—

(a) a Commissioner [², the Upper Tribunal] or the court determines an appeal as mentioned in section 27(1)(a) or Article 27(1)(a) ("the relevant determination") and the Board make a decision of the kind specified in section 27(1)(b) or Article 27(1)(b);

(b) there is an appeal against the relevant determination;

(c) after the Board's decision, payment is suspended in accordance with regulation 18(1) and (3)(b); and

(d) on appeal the court reverses the relevant determination in whole or in part,

a consequential decision by the Board under section 10 or Article 11 which supersedes the earlier decision referred to in sub-paragraph (a) above shall take effect from the date on which that earlier decision took effect.

In this paragraph "the court" has the meaning given in section 27 or Article 27 (as the case requires).]

(10) If the Board supersede a decision in accordance with subparagraph (e) of regulation 13(2), the superseding decision shall take effect as from the date on which entitlement arises—

(a) to the other relevant benefit referred to in paragraph (ii) of that subparagraph; or

(b) to an increase in the rate of that benefit.

AMENDMENTS

1. Child Benefit and Guardian's Allowance (Miscellaneous Amendments) Regulations 2005 (SI 2005/343), reg.5 (March 18, 2005).

2. Tribunals, Courts and Enforcement Act 2007 (Transitional and Consequential Provisions) Order 2008 (SI 2008/2683), Sch.1, paras 212 and 218 (November 3, 2008).

DEFINITIONS

"appeal tribunal"—see reg.2(1).
"the Board"—*ibid.*
"claimant"—*ibid.*
"Commissioner"—*ibid.*
"prescribed"—see s.84 of the Social Security Act 1998.
"relevant benefit"—see reg.2(1).
"superseding decision"—by virtue of reg.2(1), see reg.13(1).

GENERAL NOTE

This is equivalent to reg.7(1) to (7) and (33) of the Social Security and Child Support (Decisions and Appeals) Regulations 1999. See the notes to reg.7 of the 1999 Regulations. (The other provisions of reg.7 of the 1999 Regulations have no relevance to child benefit or guardian's allowance.) **2.804**

Effective date for late notifications of change of circumstances

17.—(1) For the purposes of paragraph (3) of regulation 16, the Board **2.805**
may allow a longer period of time than the period of one month mentioned in sub-paragraph (a) of that paragraph for the notification of a change of circumstances if the first and second conditions are satisfied.

(2) The first condition is that an application for the purposes of regulation 16(3) must be made by the claimant or a person acting on his behalf.

(3) The second condition is that the application for the purposes of regulation 16(3) must—
 (a) contain particulars of the relevant change of circumstances and the reasons for the failure to notify the change on an earlier date; and
 (b) be made within 13 months of the date on which the change occurred.

(4) An application under this regulation must not be granted unless the Board are satisfied that—
 (a) it is reasonable to grant it;
 (b) the change of circumstances notified by the applicant is relevant to the decision which is to be superseded; and
 (c) special circumstances are relevant to the application as a result of which it was not practicable for the applicant to notify the change of circumstances within one month of the change occurring.

(5) In determining whether it is reasonable to grant an application for the purposes of regulation 16(3), the Board must have regard to the principle that the greater the amount of time that has elapsed between the date one month after the change of circumstances occurred and the date the application is made, the more compelling the special circumstances mentioned in paragraph (4)(c) should be.

(6) In determining whether it is reasonable to grant an application for

the purposes of regulation 16(3), the Board must take no account of the following—

    (a) that the applicant or any person acting for him was unaware of, or misunderstood, the law applicable to his case (including being unaware of, or misunderstanding, the time limits imposed by these Regulations); or

    (b) that a Commissioner [¹, the Upper Tribunal] or a court has taken a different view of the law from that previously understood and applied.

(7) An application for the purposes of regulation 16(3) which has been refused may not be renewed.

AMENDMENT

1. Tribunals, Courts and Enforcement Act 2007 (Transitional and Consequential Provisions) Order 2008 (SI 2008/2683), Sch.1, paras 212 and 219 (November 3, 2008).

DEFINITIONS

"the Board"—see reg.2(1).
"claimant"—*ibid*.
"Commissioner"—*ibid*.

GENERAL NOTE

2.806   This is equivalent to reg.8 of the Social Security and Child Support (Decisions and Appeals) Regulations 1999.

PART 4

SUSPENSION AND TERMINATION

Suspension in prescribed cases

2.807   **18.**—(1) The Board may suspend payment of child benefit or guardian's allowance, in whole or in part, in the circumstances prescribed by paragraph (2) or (3).

(2) The circumstances prescribed by this paragraph are circumstances where it appears to the Board that—

    (a) an issue arises as to whether the conditions for entitlement to the benefit or allowance are or were fulfilled;

    (b) an issue arises as to whether a decision relating to an award of the benefit or allowance should be—

        (i) revised under section 9 or Article 10; or

        (ii) superseded under section 10 or Article 11;

    (c) an issue arises as to whether any amount paid or payable to a person by way of, or in connection with a claim for, the benefit or allowance is recoverable under—

        (i) section 71 of the Administration Act;

        (ii) section 69 of the Administration (NI) Act; or

        (iii) regulations made under either of those sections;

(d) the last address notified to them of a person who is in receipt of the benefit or allowance is not the address at which that person is residing; or

(e) the details of a bank account or other account which has been notified to them and to which payment of the benefit or allowance by way of a credit is to be made to a person are incorrect.

(3) The circumstances prescribed by this paragraph are where—

(a) an appeal is pending against a decision of an appeal tribunal, [¹ the First-tier Tribunal, the Upper Tribunal,] a Commissioner or a court; or

(b) an appeal is pending against a decision given in a different case by a Commissioner [¹ , the Upper Tribunal] or a court (whether or not relating to child benefit or guardian's allowance) and it appears to the Board that, if the appeal were to be determined in a particular way, an issue would arise as to whether the award of child benefit or guardian's allowance should be revised or superseded.

(4) For the purposes of section 21(3)(c) and Article 21(3)(c), the prescribed circumstances are circumstances where an appeal tribunal, [¹ the First-tier Tribunal, the Upper Tribunal,] a Commissioner or a court has made a decision and the Board—

(a) are awaiting receipt of the decision or, in the case of an appeal tribunal [¹ or First-tier Tribunal] decision, are considering whether to apply for a statement of the reasons for it;

(b) in the case of an appeal tribunal decision, [¹ or First-tier Tribunal] have applied for, and are awaiting receipt of, such a statement; or

(c) have received the decision, or, in the case of an appeal tribunal [¹ or First-tier Tribunal] decision, such a statement, and are considering—

    (i) whether to apply for leave [¹ or permission] to appeal; or

    (ii) where leave [¹ or permission] to appeal has been granted, whether to appeal.

(5) In the circumstances prescribed by paragraph (4), the Board must give written notice, as soon as reasonably practicable, to the person in respect of whom payment has been or is to be suspended of their proposal—

(a) to make a request for a statement of the reasons for an appeal tribunal [¹ or First-tier Tribunal] decision;

(b) to apply for leave [¹ or permission] to appeal; or

(c) to appeal.

AMENDMENTS

1. Tribunals, Courts and Enforcement Act 2007 (Transitional and Consequential Provisions) Order 2008 (SI 2008/2683), Sch.1, paras 212 and 220 (November 3, 2008).

DEFINITIONS

"the Administration Act"—see reg.2(1).
"the Administration (NI) Act"—*ibid*.
"appeal tribunal"—*ibid*.
"the Board"—*ibid*.
"Commissioner"—*ibid*.
"prescribed"—see s.84 of the Social Security Act 1998.

Provision of information or evidence

2.808   **19.**—(1) This regulation applies where the Board require information or evidence for a determination whether a decision awarding child benefit or guardian's allowance should be—

(a) revised under section 9 or Article 10; or

(b) superseded under section 10 or Article 11.

(2) A person to whom this paragraph applies must—

(a) supply the information or evidence within—

  (i) the period of one month beginning with the date on which the notification under paragraph (4) was sent to him; or

  (ii) such longer period as he satisfies the Board is necessary in order to enable him to comply with the requirement; or

(b) satisfy the Board within the period of time specified in subparagraph (a)(i) that—

  (i) the information or evidence required of him does not exist; or

  (ii) it is not possible for him to obtain it.

(3) A person to whom paragraph (2) applies is any of the following—

(a) a person in respect of whom payment of the benefit or allowance has been suspended in the circumstances prescribed by regulation 18(2);

(b) a person who has made an application for the decision to be revised or superseded;

(c) a person who fails to comply with the provisions of regulation 23 of the Administration Regulations in so far as they relate to information, facts or evidence required by the Board.

(4) The Board must notify a person to whom paragraph (2) applies of the requirements of that paragraph.

(5) The Board may suspend the payment of benefit or allowance, in whole or in part, to a person falling within paragraph (3)(b) or (c) who fails to satisfy the requirements of paragraph (2).

DEFINITIONS

"the Administration Regulations"—see reg.2(1).
"the Board"—*ibid.*

Termination in cases of failure to furnish information or evidence

2.809   **20.**—(1) Subject to paragraph (3), this regulation applies where—

(a) a person whose benefit or allowance has been suspended under regulation 18 subsequently fails to comply with a requirement for information or evidence under regulation 19 and more than one month has elapsed since the requirement was made; or

(b) a person's benefit or allowance has been suspended under regulation 19(5) and more than one month has elapsed since the first payment was so suspended.

(2) The Board must decide that the person ceases to be entitled to the benefit or allowance from the date on which payment was suspended except where entitlement to the benefit or allowance ceases on an earlier date.

(3) This regulation does not apply where benefit or allowance has been suspended in part under regulation 18 or 19.

DEFINITION

"the Board"—see reg.2(1).

Making of payments which have been suspended

21.—(1) Payment of benefit or allowance suspended in accordance with   **2.810**
regulation 18 or 19 must be made in any of the circumstances prescribed
by paragraphs (2) to (5).

(2) The circumstances prescribed by this paragraph are circumstances
where—

- (a) in a case to which regulation 18(2)(a), (b) or (c) applies, the Board
  are satisfied that—
    - (i) the benefit or allowance suspended is properly payable; and
    - (ii) no outstanding issues remain to be resolved;
- (b) in a case to which regulation 18(2)(d) applies, the Board are satisfied
  that they have been notified of the address at which the person is
  residing;
- (c) in a case to which regulation 18(2)(e) applies, the Board are satisfied
  that they have been notified of the correct details of the bank account
  or other account to which payment of the benefit or allowance by
  way of a credit is to be made to the person.

(3) The circumstances prescribed by this paragraph are circumstances
where, in a case to which regulation 18(3)(a) applies, the Board—

- (a) in the case of a decision of an appeal tribunal, [¹ or the First-tier
  Tribunal] do not apply for a statement of the reasons for that decision within the period of one month specified in—
    - (i) in relation to child benefit and guardian's allowance under
      the Contributions and Benefits Act, regulation 53(4) of the
      Decisions and Appeals Regulations;
    - (ii) in relation to child benefit and guardian's allowance under the
      Contributions and Benefits (NI) Act, regulation 53(4) of the
      Decisions and Appeals Regulations (NI);
- (b) in the case of a decision of an appeal tribunal, [¹ First-tier Tribunal,
  the Upper Tribunal] a Commissioner or a court—
    - (i) do not make an application for leave [¹ or permission] to appeal
      within the time prescribed for the making of such an application;
      or
    - (ii) where leave [¹ or permission] to appeal is granted, do not make
      the appeal within the time prescribed for the making of it;
- (c) withdraw an application for leave [¹ or permission] to appeal or the
  appeal; or
- (d) are refused leave [¹ or permission] to appeal in circumstances where
  it is not open to them to renew the application, or to make a further
  application, for such leave [¹ or permission].

(4) The circumstances prescribed by this paragraph are circumstances
where, in a case to which regulation 18(3)(b) applies, the Board, in relation
to the decision of the Commissioner [¹ , the Upper Tribunal] or the court
in the different case—

- (a) do not make an application for leave [¹ or permission] to appeal
  within the time prescribed for the making of such an application;
- (b) where leave [¹ or permission] to appeal is granted, do not make the
  appeal within the time prescribed for the making of it;

    (c) withdraw an application for leave [¹ or permission] to appeal or the appeal; or

    (d) are refused leave [¹ or permission] to appeal in circumstances where it is not open to them to renew the application, or to make a further application, for such leave [¹ or permission].

(5) The circumstances prescribed by this paragraph are circumstances where, in a case to which paragraph (5) of regulation 19 applies, the Board are satisfied that—

    (a) the benefit or allowance suspended is properly payable; and

    (b) the requirements of paragraph (2) of that regulation have been satisfied.

AMENDMENTS

1. Tribunals, Courts and Enforcement Act 2007 (Transitional and Consequential Provisions) Order 2008 (SI 2008/2683), Sch.1, paras 212 and 221 (November 3, 2008).

DEFINITIONS

    "appeal tribunal"—see reg.2(1).
    "the Board"—*ibid.*
    "Commissioner"—*ibid.*
    "the Contributions and Benefits Act"—*ibid.*
    "the Contributions and Benefits (NI) Act"—*ibid.*
    "the Decisions and Appeals Regulations"—*ibid.*
    "the Decisions and Appeals (NI) Regulations"—*ibid.*

PART 5

OTHER MATTERS

Decisions involving issues that arise on appeal in other cases

2.811   **22.**—(1) A case which satisfies the condition specified in paragraph (2) is a prescribed case for the purposes of section 25(3)(b) and Article 25(3) (b) (prescribed cases and circumstances in which a decision may be made on a prescribed basis).

(2) The condition specified in this paragraph is that the claimant would be entitled to the benefit or allowance to which the decision which falls to be made relates, even if the appeal in the other case referred to in section 25(1) (b) or Article 25(1)(b) were decided in a way which is the most unfavourable to him.

(3) For the purposes of subsection (3)(b) of section 25 and paragraph (3)(b) of Article 25, the prescribed basis on which the Board may make the decision is as if—

    (a) the appeal in the other case which is referred to in subsection (1)(b) of that section, or paragraph (1)(b) of that Article, had already been determined; and

    (b) that appeal had been decided in a way which is the most unfavourable to the claimant.

(4) For the purposes of subsection (5)(c) of section 25 and paragraph

(5)(c) of Article 25 (prescribed circumstances in which, for the purposes of the section or the Article, an appeal is pending against a decision), the prescribed circumstances are circumstances where the Board—

(a) certify in writing that they are considering appealing against that decision; and

(b) consider that, if such an appeal were to be determined in a particular way—

    (i) there would be no entitlement to the benefit or allowance in a case to which subsection (1)(a) of that section, or paragraph (1)(a) of that Article, refers; or

    (ii) the appeal would affect the decision in that case in some other way.

DEFINITIONS

"the Board"—see reg.2(1).
"claimant"—*ibid.*
"prescribed"—see s.84 of the Social Security Act 1998.

Appeals involving issues that arise on appeal in other cases

23. For the purposes of subsection (6)(c) of section 26 and paragraph (6)(c) of Article 26 (prescribed circumstances in which an appeal against a decision which has not been brought, or an application for leave [¹ or permission] to appeal has not been made, but the time for so doing has not yet expired, is pending for the purposes of the section or the Article), the prescribed circumstances are circumstances where the Board—   2.812

(a) certify in writing that they are considering appealing against that decision; and

(b) consider that, if such an appeal were already determined, it would affect the determination of the appeal described in subsection (1)(a) of that section or paragraph (1)(a) of that Article.

AMENDMENT

1. Tribunals, Courts and Enforcement Act 2007 (Transitional and Consequential Provisions) Order 2008 (SI 2008/2683), Sch.1, paras 212 and 222 (November 3, 2008).

DEFINITION

"the Board"—see reg.2(1).

PART 6

RIGHTS OF APPEAL AND PROCEDURE FOR BRINGING APPEALS

Other persons with a right of appeal

24. For the purposes of section 12(2) and Article 13(2), the following persons are prescribed—   2.813

(a) any person appointed by the Board under regulation 28(1) of the

Administration Regulations to act on behalf of another who is unable to act;

(b) any person appointed by the Board under regulation 29(1) of those regulations to proceed with the claim of a person who has made a claim for benefit or allowance and subsequently died;

(c) any person who, having been appointed by the Board under paragraph (2) of regulation 31 of those regulations to claim on behalf of a deceased person, makes a claim in accordance with that regulation.

DEFINITIONS

"the Administration Regulations"—see reg.2(1).
"prescribed"—see s.84 of the Social Security Act 1998.

GENERAL NOTE

2.814   See the note to reg.25 of the Social Security and Child Support (Decisions and Appeals) Regulations 1999.

Decisions against which no appeal lies

2.815   **25.**—(1) Subject to paragraph (2), for the purposes of section 12(2) and Article 13(2), the decisions set out in Schedule 2 are prescribed as decisions against which no appeal lies to an appeal tribunal [¹ or to the First-tier Tribunal].

(2) Paragraph (1) shall not have the effect of prescribing any decision that relates to the conditions of entitlement to child benefit or guardian's allowance for which a claim has been validly made or for which no claim is required.

(3) In this regulation and Schedule 2, "decision" includes any determination embodied in or necessary to a decision.

AMENDMENT

1. Tribunals, Courts and Enforcement Act 2007 (Transitional and Consequential Provisions) Order 2008 (SI 2008/2683), Sch.1, paras 212 and 223 (November 3, 2008).

DEFINITIONS

"appeal tribunal"—see reg.2(1).
"prescribed"—see s.84 of the Social Security Act 1998.

GENERAL NOTE

2.816   Paragraph (2) reiterates what is said in s.12(3) of the Social Security Act 1998. As para.9 of Sch.2 to the Act is not listed among the powers exercised in making these Regulations (see Sch.1), Sch.2 to these Regulations must be made under s.12. For the implication of that, see the note to Sch.2 to the Social Security and Child Support (Decisions and Appeals) Regulations 1999.

Notice of decision against which appeal lies

2.817   **26.**—(1) A person with a right of appeal under the 1998 Act, the 1998 Order or these Regulations against a decision of the Board must—

(a) be given written notice of the decision against which the appeal lies;

(b) be informed that, in a case where that written notice does not include a statement of the reasons for that decision, he may, within one month of the date of notification of that decision, request that the Board provide him with a written statement of the reasons for that decision; and

(c) be given written notice of his right of appeal against that decision.

(2) If the Board are requested under paragraph (1)(b) to provide a written statement of the reasons for the decision, they [¹ shall provide the statement within 14 days of receipt of the request or as soon as practicable afterwards].

AMENDMENT

1. Child Benefit and Guardian's Allowance (Miscellaneous Amendments) Regulations 2005 (SI 2005/343), reg.6 (March 18, 2005).

DEFINITIONS

"the 1998 Act"—see reg.2(1).
"the Board"—*ibid.*
"the 1998 Order"—*ibid.*

GENERAL NOTE

See the note to reg.28 of the Social Security and Child Support (Decisions and Appeals) Regulations 1999.

2.818

Appeals against decisions which have been revised

27.—(1) This regulation applies where—

2.819

(a) a decision—

(i) under section 8 or 10 is revised under section 9; or

(ii) under Article 9 or 11 is revised under Article 10, before an appeal against that decision is determined; and

(b) the decision as revised is not more advantageous to the appellant than the decision before it was revised.

(2) The appeal shall not lapse and is to be treated as though it had been brought against the decision as revised.

(3) The appellant shall have a period of one month from the date of notification of the decision as revised to make further representations as to the appeal.

(4) After the expiration of the period specified in paragraph (3), or within that period if the appellant consents in writing, the appeal shall proceed unless, in the light of the further representations from the appellant, the Board further revise their decision and that decision is more advantageous to the appellant than the decision before it was revised.

(5) Decisions which are more advantageous to the appellant include those in consequence of which—

(a) child benefit or guardian's allowance paid to him is greater or is awarded for a longer period;

(b) the amount of benefit or allowance in payment would have been greater but for the operation of—

(i) any provision of the Administration Act or the Administration (NI) Act; or

(ii) any provision of the Contributions and Benefits Act, or any provision of the Contributions and Benefits (NI) Act, restricting or suspending the payment of, or disqualifying a claimant from receiving, some or all of the benefit or allowance;

(c) a denial or disqualification for the receiving of benefit or allowance is lifted wholly or in part;

(d) a decision to pay benefit or allowance to a third party is reversed;

(e) benefit or allowance paid is not recoverable under—

    (i) section 71 of the Administration Act or section 69 of the Administration (NI) Act; or

    (ii) regulations made under either of those sections;

(f) the amount of benefit or allowance paid which is recoverable as mentioned in sub-paragraph (e) is reduced; or

(g) a financial gain accrues or will accrue to the appellant in consequence of the decision.

DEFINITIONS

"the Administration Act"—see reg.2(1).
"the Administration (NI) Act"—*ibid*.
"the Board"—*ibid*.
"claimant"—*ibid*.
"the Contributions and Benefits Act"—*ibid*.
"the Contributions and Benefits (NI) Act"—*ibid*.
"the date of notification"—see reg.3(2).
"writing"—see reg.2(1).

GENERAL NOTE

2.820   Like reg.30 of the Social Security and Child Support (Decisions and Appeals) Regulations 1999, this provides an exception to the general rule that an appeal lapses when the decision under appeal is revised (see s.9(6) of the Social Security Act 1998 and the note to s.9(5)).

Time within which an appeal is to be brought.

2.821   **28.**—(1) Subject to the following provisions of this Part, where an appeal lies from a decision of the Board to an appeal tribunal [² or the First-tier Tribunal], the time within which that appeal must be brought is—

(a) within one month of the date of notification of the decision against which the appeal is brought;

(b) if a written statement of the reasons for that decision is requested and provided within the period mentioned in sub-paragraph (a), within 14 days of the expiry of that period; or

(c) if a written statement of the reasons for that decision is requested but is not provided within the period mentioned in sub-paragraph (a), within 14 days of the date on which the statement is provided.

(2) If the Board—

(a) revise a decision under section 9 or Article 10;

(b) make a superseding decision; or

(c) following an application for a revision [¹ under regulation 5], do not revise a decision under section 9 or Article 10,

the period of one month specified in paragraph (1) shall begin to run from the date of notification of the revision or supersession or the date the Board issue a notice that they are not revising the decision.

(3) If a dispute arises as to whether an appeal was brought within the time limit specified in this regulation, the dispute must be referred to, and be determined by, a legally qualified panel member [² or, as the case may be, the First-tier Tribunal].

(4) The time limit specified in this regulation for bringing an appeal may be extended in accordance with regulation 29 [² or, as the case may be, regulation 29A].

AMENDMENTS

1. Child Benefit and Guardian's Allowance (Decisions and Appeals) (Amendment) Regulations 2004 (SI 2004/3377), reg.2(2) (December 21, 2004).

2. Tribunals, Courts and Enforcement Act 2007 (Transitional and Consequential Provisions) Order 2008 (SI 2008/2683), Sch.1, paras 212 and 224 (November 3, 2008).

DEFINITIONS

"appeal tribunal"—see reg.2(1).
"the Board"—*ibid.*
"the date of notification"—see reg.3(2).
"legally qualified panel member"—see reg.2(1).
"superseding decision"—by virtue of reg.2(1), see reg.13(1).

GENERAL NOTE

In ordinary social security cases in Great Britain, these time limits are to be found in Sch.1 to the Tribunal Procedure (First-tier Tribunal (Social Entitlement Chamber) Rules 2008. A perceived need to ensure continued consistency with Northern Ireland may be the explanation for the time limits for child benefit and guardian's allowance cases being in these Regulations (to which Sch.1 to the Rules refers).

2.822

The 2004 amendment deliberately introduced the anomaly, identified in *R(IS) 15/04* (subsequently approved by the Court of Appeal in *Beltekian v Westminster City Council* [2004] EWCA Civ 1784 (reported as *R(H) 8/05*)) that a refusal to revise where the application for revision was made otherwise than under reg.5 is not appealable if the decision being revised was given more than thirteen months earlier. The justification that has been advanced is that the claimant will have had more than thirteen months in which to challenge the original decision. Consistency with that argument would suggest that, say, "official error" should be a ground of supersession with limited backdating. It is also odd that there is a right of appeal where it is said that a revision does not lead to a high enough award but there is no right of appeal if there is a refusal to revise at all.

29. *Omitted.*

[¹ **Late appeals to the First-tier Tribunal**

29A. In respect of an appeal to the First-tier Tribunal, the Board may treat a late appeal as made in time in accordance with Tribunal Procedure Rules if the Board is satisfied that it is in the interests of justice, but no appeal shall in any event be brought more than one year after the expiration of the last day for appealing under regulation 28.]

2.823

AMENDMENT

1. Tribunals, Courts and Enforcement Act 2007 (Transitional and Consequential Provisions) Order 2008 (SI 2008/2683), Sch.1, paras 212 and 226 (November 3, 2008).

GENERAL NOTE

2.824   This regulation duplicates the effect of r.23(5) of the Tribunal Procedure (First-tier Tribunal (Social Entitlement Chamber) Rules 2008. The interests of justice are given a narrow interpretation in reg.30.

Interests of justice

2.825   **30.**—(1) For the purposes of paragraph (5)(b) of regulation 29 [¹ 29A], it is not in the interests of justice to grant an application [¹ or, as the case may be, treat the appeal as made in time][...] unless the panel member is satisfied, or the Board are satisfied, that—

(a) the special circumstances specified in paragraph (2) are relevant [¹ ...]; or

(b) some other special circumstances exist which are wholly exceptional and relevant [¹ ...],

and, as a result of those special circumstances, it was not practicable for the appeal to be brought within the time limit specified in regulation 28.

(2) The special circumstances specified in this paragraph are that—

(a) the applicant or a partner or dependant of the applicant has died or suffered serious illness;

(b) the applicant is not resident in the United Kingdom; or

(c) normal postal services were disrupted.

(3) "Partner" means—

(a) where a person is a member of a married couple or an unmarried couple, the other member of that couple; or

(b) where a person is polygamously married to two or more members of his household, any such member.

(4) In determining whether it is in the interests of justice to grant an application under regulation 29 [¹ or, as the case may be, treat the appeal as made in time under regulation 29A], the panel member or the Board must have regard to the principle that the greater the amount of time that has elapsed between the expiration of the time within which the appeal is to be brought under regulation 28 and the making of the application [¹ or, as the case may be, submission of a notice of appeal] the more compelling the special circumstances mentioned in paragraph (1) should be.

(5) In determining whether it is in the interests of justice to grant an application under regulation 29 [¹ or, as the case may be, treat the appeal as made in time under regulation 29A], the panel member or the Board must take no account of the following—

(a) that the applicant or any person acting for him was unaware of or misunderstood the law applicable to his case (including ignorance or misunderstanding of the time limits imposed by these Regulations); or

(b) that a Commissioner [¹ , the Upper Tribunal] or a court has taken a different view of the law from that previously understood and applied.

AMENDMENTS

1. Tribunals, Courts and Enforcement Act 2007 (Transitional and Consequential Provisions) Order 2008 (SI 2008/2683), Sch.1, paras 212 and 227 (November 3, 2008).

DEFINITIONS

"the Board"—see reg.2(1).
"Commissioner"—*ibid.*
"partner"— see para.(3).

GENERAL NOTE

This is equivalent to reg.32(5) to (8) of the Social Security and Child Support (Decisions and Appeals) Regulations 1999.   **2.826**

Para.(5)
See the notes to reg.32(8) of the 1999 Regulations.   **2.827**

Making of appeals and applications

31.—(1) Subject to the following provisions of this regulation, an appeal,   **2.828**
or an application for an extension of time for making an appeal, to an appeal
tribunal must—
  (a) be in writing—
      (i) on a form approved for the purpose by the Board ("the
          approved form"); or
      (ii) in such other format as the Board may accept as sufficient for
          the purpose;
  (b) be signed by—
      (i) the person who has a right of appeal under section 12(2) or
          Article 13(2); or
      (ii) if that person has provided written authority to a representative
          to act on his behalf, that representative;
  (c) be sent or delivered to an appropriate office;
  (d) contain particulars of the grounds on which it is made; and
  (e) contain sufficient particulars of the decision or the subject of the
      application, to enable that decision or subject to be identified.
[¹ (1A) A notice of appeal to the First-tier Tribunal made in accordance
with Tribunal Procedure Rules must be made on a form approved by the
Board, or in such other format as the Board may accept.
  (1B) Except where paragraph (3) applies, in respect of an appeal to the
First-tier Tribunal, where a form does not contain the information required
under Tribunal Procedure Rules the form may be returned by the Board
to the sender for completion in accordance with the Tribunal Procedure
Rules.]
  (2) [¹ In respect of an appeal to the appeal tribunal an approved] form
which is not completed in accordance with the instructions on it—
  (a) subject to paragraph (3), does not satisfy the requirements of para-
      graph (1), and
  (b) may be returned by the Board to the sender for completion in
      accordance with those instructions.

(3) If the Board are satisfied that an approved form, although not completed in accordance with the instructions on it, includes sufficient information to enable the appeal or application to proceed, they may treat it as satisfying the requirements of paragraph (1). [¹ or, as the case may be, Tribunal Procedure Rules]

(4) If an appeal or application made in writing otherwise than on the approved form includes sufficient information to enable the appeal or application to proceed, the Board may treat it as satisfying the requirements of paragraph (1). [¹ or, as the case may be, Tribunal Procedure Rules]

(5) If an appeal or application made in writing otherwise than on the approved form does not include sufficient information to enable the appeal or application to proceed, the Board may request further information in writing from the appellant or applicant.

(6) If an appellant or applicant to whom an approved form is returned, or from whom further information is requested, duly completes and returns the form or sends the further information and that form or further information is received by the Board—

(a) within 14 days of the date on which the form was returned to him by them, the time for making the appeal shall be extended by 14 days from the date on which the form was returned;

(b) within 14 days of the date on which the further information was requested by them, the time for making the appeal shall be extended by 14 days from the date of the request;

(c) within such longer period as they may direct, the time for making the appeal shall be extended by a period equal to that longer period.

(7) If an appellant or applicant to whom an approved form is returned, or from whom further information is requested, does not complete and return the form or send further information within the period of time specified in paragraph (6), the Board must forward a copy of the appeal or application, together with any other relevant documents or evidence, to a legally qualified panel member who [¹ , or, as the case may be, the First-tier Tribunal which,] must—

(a) determine whether the appeal or application satisfies the requirement of paragraph (1) [¹ or, as the case may be, Tribunal Procedure Rules], and

(b) inform the appellant or applicant and the Board of his determination.

(8) If—

(a) an approved form is duly completed and returned or further information is sent after the expiry of the period of time specified in paragraph (6); and

(b) no determination has been made under paragraph (7) at the time the form or the further information is received by the Board,

the Board must forward the duly completed form or further information to the legally qualified panel member who [¹ , or, as the case may be, the First-tier Tribunal which,] must take into account any further information or evidence set out in that form or the further information.

AMENDMENTS

1. Tribunals, Courts and Enforcement Act 2007 (Transitional and Consequential Provisions) Order 2008 (SI 2008/2683), Sch.1, paras 212 and 228 (November 3, 2008).

DEFINITIONS

"appeal tribunal"—see reg.2(1).
"appropriate office"—*ibid.*
"the approved form"—see para.(1)(a)(i).
"the Board"—see reg.2(1).
"legally qualified panel member"—*ibid.*

GENERAL NOTE

This is equivalent to reg.33(1) to (9) of the Social Security and Child Support (Decisions and Appeals) Regulations 1999.   2.829

Discontinuing action on appeals

32. The Board may discontinue action on an appeal to an appeal tribunal   2.830
[¹ or to the First-tier Tribunal] if—

(a) the appeal has not been forwarded to the clerk to an appeal tribunal or to a legally qualified panel member [¹ or, as the case may be, the First-tier Tribunal]; and

(b) the appellant or an authorised representative of the appellant has given written notice that he does not wish the appeal to continue.

AMENDMENTS

1. Tribunals, Courts and Enforcement Act 2007 (Transitional and Consequential Provisions) Order 2008 (SI 2008/2683), Sch.1, paras 212 and 229 (November 3, 2008).

DEFINITIONS

"appeal tribunal"—see reg.2(1).
"the Board"—*ibid.*
"clerk to the appeal tribunal"—*ibid.*
"legally qualified panel member"—*ibid.*

GENERAL NOTE

This is equivalent to reg.33(10) of the Social Security and Child Support   2.831
(Decisions and Appeals) Regulations 1999.

Death of a party to an appeal

33.—(1) In any proceedings, on the death of a party to those proceedings   2.832
(other than a member of the Board), the Board may appoint such person as they think fit to proceed with the appeal in the place of such deceased party.

(2) A grant of probate, confirmation or letters of administration to the estate of the deceased party, whenever taken out, shall have no effect on an appointment made under paragraph (1).

(3) If a person appointed under paragraph (1) has, prior to the date of such appointment, taken any action in relation to the appeal on behalf of the deceased party, the effective date of appointment by the Board shall be the day immediately prior to the first day on which such action was taken.

DEFINITION

"the Board"—see reg.2(1).

GENERAL NOTE

2.833   This is equivalent to reg.34 of the Social Security and Child Support (Decisions and Appeals) Regulations 1999.

PART VII

REVOCATIONS, TRANSITIONAL PROVISIONS AND CONSEQUENTIAL AMENDMENTS

Revocations

2.834   **34.** The following provisions are hereby revoked—
(a) in so far as they relate to child benefit or guardian's allowance under the Contributions and Benefits Act, Parts 2, 3 and 4 of, and Schedule 2 to, the Decisions and Appeals Regulations;
(b) in so far as they relate to child benefit or guardian's allowance under the Contributions and Benefits (NI) Act, Parts 2, 3 and 4 of, and Schedule 1 to, the Decisions and Appeals Regulations (NI).

DEFINITIONS

"the Contributions and Benefits Act"—see reg.2(1).
"the Contributions and Benefits (NI) Act"—*ibid.*
"the Decisions and Appeals Regulations"—*ibid.*
"the decision and Appeals (NI) Regulations"—*ibid.*

Transitional provisions

2.835   **35.** Anything done or commenced under any provision revoked by regulation 34, so far as relating to child benefit or guardian's allowance, is to be treated as having been done or as being continued under the corresponding provision of these Regulations.

2.836   **36.** *Omitted.*
2.837   **37.** *Omitted.*

SCHEDULE 1   Preamble

POWERS EXERCISED IN MAKING THESE REGULATIONS

2.838   **1.** Section 5(1)(hh) of the Administration Act.
2. Section 5(1)(hh) of the Administration (NI) Act.
3. The following provisions of the 1998 Act—
(a)   section 9(1), (4) and (6);
(b)   section 10(3) and (6);
(c)   section 12(2), (3), (6) and (7);
(d)   section 16(1) and paragraphs 1 to 4 and 6 of Schedule 5;
(e)   section 21;

(f)   section 22;
(g)   section 23;
(h)   section 25(3)(b) and (5)(c);
(i)   section 26(6)(c);
(j)   section 79(1), (2A) and (4) to (7);
(k)   section 84.

4. The following provisions of the 1998 Order—
(a)   Article 2(2);
(b)   Article 10(1), (4) and (6);
(c)   Article 11(3) and (6);
(d)   Article 13(2), (3), (6) and (7);
(e)   Article 16(1) and paragraphs 1 to 4 and 6 of Schedule 4;
(f)   Article 21;
(g)   Article 22;
(h)   Article 23;
(i)   Article 25(3)(b) and (5)(c);
(j)   Article 26(6)(c);
(k)   Article 74(1) and (3) to (6).

5. Sections 132 and 133(1) and (2) of the Finance Act 1999.

6. The following provisions of the Tax Credits Act 2002—
(a)   section 50(1) and (2)(e) and (f);
(b)   section 54(2);
(c)   paragraphs 15 and 19 of Schedule 4.

DEFINITIONS

"the 1998 Act"—see reg.2(1).
"the Administration Act"—*ibid.*
"the Administration (NI) Act"—*ibid.*
"the 1998 Order"—*ibid.*

SCHEDULE 2   **Regulation 25**

DECISIONS AGAINST WHICH NO APPEAL LIES

PART I

DECISIONS MADE UNDER PRIMARY LEGISLATION

1. A decision of the Board whether to recognise, for the purposes of Part 9 of the   **2.839**
Contributions and Benefits Act or Part 10 of the Contributions and Benefits (NI) Act—
(a)   an educational establishment; or
(b)   education provided otherwise than at a recognised educational establishment.

2. A decision of the Board whether to pay expenses to any person under—
(a)   sections 180 and 180A of the Administration Act; or
(b)   section 156 of the Administration (NI) Act.

3. A decision of the Treasury relating to the up-rating of child benefit or guardian's allowance under—
(a)   Part 10 of the Administration Act; or
(b)   Part 9 of the Administration (NI) Act.

4. A decision of the Board under—
(a)   section 25 or 26; or
(b)   Article 25 or 26.

PART II

DECISIONS MADE UNDER SECONDARY LEGISLATION

5. A decision of the Board relating to—   **2.840**
(a)   the suspension of child benefit or allowance under Part 4; or
(b)   the payment of such a benefit or allowance which has been so suspended.

6. A decision of the Board under any of the following provisions of the Administration
Regulations—

(a) [¹ . . .]
(b) regulation 7 (decision as to evidence and information required);
(c) [¹ . . .]
(d) regulation 11 (decision as to claims for child benefit treated as claims for guardian's allowance and vice versa);
(e) regulation 18 (decision as to the time of payments);
(f) regulation 19 (decision as to elections to have child benefit paid weekly);
(g) regulation 23 (decision as to information to be given);
(h) regulation 26 (decision as to extinguishment of right to payment if payment is not obtained within the prescribed period) other than a decision under paragraph (5) (decision as to payment request after expiration of prescribed period);
(i) regulation 28 (decision as to appointments where person unable to act);
(j) regulations 29 to 32 (decisions as to claims or payments after death of claimant);
(k) regulation 33 (decision as to paying a person on behalf of another);
(l) regulation 34 (decision as to paying partner as alternative payee);
(m) Part 5 other than a decision under—
  (i) regulation 35(1) (decision as to whether a payment in excess of entitlement has been credited to a bank or other account);
  (ii) regulation 37 (decision as to the sums to be deducted in calculating recoverable amounts);
  (iii) regulation 38 (decision as to the offsetting of a prior payment of child benefit or guardian's allowance against arrears of child benefit or guardian's allowance payable by virtue of a subsequent determination);
  (iv) regulation 39 (decision as to the offsetting of a prior payment of income support or jobseeker's allowance against arrears of child benefit or guardian's allowance payable by virtue of a subsequent determination);
  (v) regulation 41(1) (decision as to bringing interim payments into account);
  (vi) regulation 42(1) (decision as to the overpayment of an interim payment).

7. A decision of the Board made in accordance with the discretion conferred upon them by the following regulations of the Child Benefit (General) Regulations 2003—
(a) regulation 4(1) or (4) (provisions relating to contributions and expenses in respect of a child);
(b) regulation 24(1)(c) or 28(1)(c) (decisions relating to a child's temporary absence abroad).

8. A decision of the Board relating to the giving of a notice under regulation 8(2) of the Guardian's Allowance (General) Regulations 2003 (children whose surviving parents are in prison or legal custody).

9. A decision of the Board made in accordance with an Order made under—
(a) section 179 of the Administration Act (reciprocal agreements with countries outside the United Kingdom); or
(b) section 155 of the Administration (NI) Act (reciprocal agreements with countries outside the United Kingdom).

PART III

OTHER DECISIONS

2.841

10. An authorization given by the Board in accordance with Article 22(1) or 55(1) of Council Regulation (EEC) No.1408/71 on the application of social security schemes to employed persons, to self-employed persons and to members of their families moving within the Community.

AMENDMENTS

1. Child Benefit and Guardian's Allowance (Decisions and Appeals) (Amendment) Regulations 2004 (SI 2004/3377), reg.2(3) (December 21, 2004).

DEFINITIONS

"the Administration Act"—see reg.2(1).
"the Administration (NI) Act"—*ibid.*
"the Administration Regulations"—*ibid.*
"the Board"—*ibid.*

"the Contributions and Benefits Act"—*ibid.*
"the Contributions and Benefits (NI) Act"—*ibid.*

GENERAL NOTE

See the notes to reg.25 of these Regulations and Sch.2 to the Social Security and   2.842
Child Support (Decisions and Appeals) Regulations 1999.

The Health in Pregnancy Grant (Administration) Regulations 2008   2.843

(SI 2008/3109)

Made	*9th December 2008*
Laid before Parliament	*10th December 2008*
Coming into force	*1st January 2009*

The Commissioners for Her Majesty's Revenue and Customs, in exercise
of the powers conferred by sections 5, 12A(1) and (5), 189 and 191 of the
Social Security Administration Act 1992, sections 5, 10A(1) and (5), 165
and 167 of the Social Security Administration (Northern Ireland) Act 1992
and sections 132(2) and 135(2) of the Health and Social Care Act 2008,
make the following Regulations:

Citation, commencement and interpretation

1.—(1) These Regulations may be cited as the Health in Pregnancy   2.844
Grant (Administration) Regulations 2008 and shall come into force on 1st
January 2009.

(2) In these Regulations—
"appropriate office" means Comben House, Farriers Way, Netherton,
    Merseyside or any other office specified by the Commissioners;
"the Commissioners" means the Commissioners for Her Majesty's
    Revenue and Customs;
"couple" means—
  (a) a man and woman who are married to each other;
  (b) a man and woman who are not married to each other but are living
      together as husband and wife;
  (c) two people of the same sex who are civil partners of each other; or
  (d) two people of the same sex who are not civil partners of each other
      but are living together as if they were civil partners;
"partner" means one of a couple;
"health professional" has the meaning in the Health in Pregnancy Grant
    (Entitlement and Amount) Regulations 2008;
"SSAA" means the Social Security Administration Act 1992.

Claims in writing

2.—(1) A claim for health in pregnancy grant must be—   2.845
  (a) in writing;
  (b) made to the Commissioners;
  (c) on a form prescribed by the Commissioners;

(d) completed in accordance with the instructions on the form; and

(e) delivered or sent to an appropriate office.

(2) The claim must include a certificate signed by a health professional in relation to the claimant's pregnancy.

(3) The certificate must include—

(a) the name and date of birth of the claimant;

(b) confirmation that advice has been given to the claimant on matters relating to her maternal health;

(c) the date on which the certificate is signed; and

(d) the name and personal identity number of the Nursing and Midwifery Council, or the General Medical Council reference number, of the health professional.

Time within which claims must be made

2.846   **3.** A claim for health in pregnancy grant must be made within 31 days of the date of the certificate signed by the health professional.

Evidence and information

2.847   **4.**—(1) A person making a claim for health in pregnancy grant must furnish such certificates, documents, information and evidence in connection with the claim, or any question arising out of it, as may be required by the Commissioners.

(2) A person required under paragraph (1) to furnish certificates, documents, information and evidence must do so—

(a) within one month of being required by the Commissioners to do so; or

(b) within such longer period as the Commissioners may consider reasonable.

Cases where no national insurance number is required

2.848   **5.** Section 12A(2) of SSAA (requirement to provide national insurance number) shall not apply to women who are under the age of 16 at the time they make a claim.

Withdrawing claims

2.849   **6.**—(1) A person who has made a claim may withdraw it by giving notice in writing to the Commissioners.

(2) A notice of withdrawal given in accordance with paragraph (1) has effect when it is received by an appropriate office.

Defective claims

2.850   **7.**—(1) If an appropriate office receives a defective claim, the Commissioners may refer it back to the person who made it.

(2) "Defective claim" means an intended claim which—

(a) is made on an approved form which has not been completed in accordance with the instructions on it;

(b) is in writing but is not made on the approved form;

(c) is illegible; or

(d) is incomprehensible.

Persons to whom grant is to be paid

8. Health in pregnancy grant shall be paid to the person entitled to the grant.

2.851

Manner of payment

9.—(1) Subject to paragraph (2), health in pregnancy grant shall be paid by way of a credit to a bank account or other account—

2.852

    (a) in the name of the person to whom payment is to be made; or

    (b) in the joint names of the person to whom payment is to be made and that person's partner; or

    (c) in the name of a person or body acting on behalf of the claimant under regulation 12 or 13;

such account to be notified to the Commissioners by the person to whom payment is made.

(2) Where the person to whom payment is to be made does not have a bank account or other account, payment shall be made by an instrument of payment.

(3) Instruments of payment which have been issued by the Commissioners remain their property.

Time of payment

10. Health in pregnancy grant shall be paid in one payment, as soon as reasonably practicable after the award has been made.

2.853

Extinguishment of right to payment from an instrument of payment

11. The right to health in pregnancy grant shall be extinguished if an instrument of payment has not been presented for payment within 12 months of the date on which it was issued by the Commissioners.

2.854

Persons or bodies who may act on behalf of claimants unable to act

12.—(1) A person or body may act on behalf of a claimant for health in pregnancy grant if the claimant, ("C"), is for the time being unable to act.

2.855

(2) Anything required by these regulations to be done by or to C may be done by or to—

    (a) in England and Wales, a receiver appointed by the Court of Protection with power to claim, or, as the case may be, receive, the grant on behalf of C;

    (b) in Scotland, a guardian acting or appointed under the Adults with Incapacity (Scotland) Act 2000 who is administering the estate of C;

    (c) in Northern Ireland, a controller appointed by the High Court, with power to claim, or, as the case may be, receive, the grant on behalf of C;

    (d) (where no person has been appointed as mentioned in subparagraphs (a) to (c)) a person or body acting on behalf of C where that person or body—

        (i) is, if a natural person, over the age of 18 years

        (ii) has applied to the Commissioners in writing to act on behalf of C.

(3) A person or body under (d)—

(i) will be permitted to act subject to the discretion of the Commissioners;

(ii) must give one month's notice in writing to the Commissioners prior to ceasing to act on behalf of C.

(4) Where health in pregnancy grant is paid to a person or body mentioned in paragraph (2), either of the following is a sufficient discharge to the Commissioners for the sum paid—

(a) a credit to a bank or other account in the name of the person or body; or

(b) the receipt by the person or body of an instrument of payment.

Persons who may receive payment which a person who has died had not obtained

2.856   **13.**—(1) This regulation applies where a person who has died had not obtained at the date of her death health in pregnancy grant to which she was entitled.

(2) The Commissioners may, unless the right to payment had already been extinguished at the date of death, pay the grant to persons over the age of 16 years who are the personal representatives of the person who has died, provided written application for payment of the grant is made to the Commissioners within 12 months from the date of death.

(3) The Commissioners may dispense with strict proof of the title of a person claiming as a personal representative.

2.857   **The Health in Pregnancy Grant (Notices, Revisions and Appeals) (No.2) Regulations 2009**

(SI 2009/751)

Made   *20th March 2009*
Laid before Parliament   *23rd March 2009*
Coming into force in accordance with regulation 1(1)

The Commissioners for Her Majesty's Revenue and Customs, in exercise of the powers conferred by sections 9(1), (4) and (6), 12(6) and (7), and 79 (2A), (4) and (7) of the Social Security Act 1998, articles 10(1), (4) and (6), 13(7), and 74(2A) and (6) of the Social Security (Northern Ireland) Order 1998 and sections 132(8) and 135(8) and (9) of the Health and Social Care Act 2008, make the following Regulations:

Citation, commencement and interpretation

2.858   **1.**—(1) These Regulations may be cited as the Health in Pregnancy Grant (Notices, Revisions and Appeals) (No. 2) Regulations 2009 and shall come into force—

(a) for the purposes of regulation 11, on 5th April 2009; and

(b) for all other purposes, on 6th April 2009.

(2) In these Regulations—

"the Administration Regulations" means the Health in Pregnancy Grant (Administration) Regulations 2008;

"appeal" means an appeal under section 12 of the 1998 Act or under Article 14 of the 1998 Order;

"appropriate office" means the Health in Pregnancy Grant Office, Waterview Park, Washington, Tyne and Wear, England;

"claimant" means a person who has claimed health in pregnancy grant;

"the Commissioners" means the Commissioners for Her Majesty's Revenue and Customs;

"the Entitlement Regulations" means the Health in Pregnancy Grant (Entitlement and Amount) Regulations 2008;

"health in pregnancy grant decision" means a decision in respect of health in pregnancy grant made under either section 8 of the 1998 Act or Article 9 of the 1998 Order;

"month" means calendar month;

"the 1998 Act" means the Social Security Act 1998;

"the 1998 Order" means the Social Security (Northern Ireland) Order 1998;

"official error" means an error made by an officer of Her Majesty's Revenue and Customs acting as such, or a person providing services to the Commissioners; but does not include an error of law which is shown to have been an error by virtue of a subsequent decision of any Tribunal or Court;

"partner" has the meaning under regulation 1(2) of the Administration Regulations;

"Tribunal" means an appeal tribunal constituted under the Tribunals, Courts and Enforcement Act 2007, or, in relation to Northern Ireland, a tribunal constituted under the 1998 Order;

"Tribunal Procedure Rules" means the Social Security and Child Support (Decisions and Appeals) Regulations (Northern Ireland) 1999.

GENERAL NOTE

In Great Britain, the provisions of ss 8 to 39 of the Social Security Act 1998 are applied as though health in pregnancy grant were a relevant benefit for the purposes of that Act (see s.132(8) of the Health and Social Care Act 2008). Therefore, the "Tribunal" must be the First-tier Tribunal because s.12 of the 1998 Act provides that the right of appeal shall be to that tribunal.

2.859

Notice of decision and right of appeal

2.—(1) A person with a right of appeal against a health in pregnancy grant decision must—

(a) be given written notice of the decision;

(b) be informed that, in a case where that written notice does not include a statement of the reasons for that decision, that person may, within one month of the notification of that decision, request that the Commissioners provide them with a written statement of the reasons for that decision; and

(c) be given written notice of the right of appeal against that decision.

(2) If the Commissioners are requested under paragraph (1)(b) to provide a written statement of the reasons for the decision, they shall provide the

2.860

statement within 14 days of notification of the request or as soon as practicable afterwards.

(3) Where—

(a) any notice or other document is required to be given or sent to the Commissioners, that notice or document shall be treated as having been so given or sent on the day that it is received by the Commissioners; and

(b) any notice, including notification of a health in pregnancy grant decision, or other document is required to be given or sent to any person other than the Commissioners, that notice or document shall, if sent by post to that person's last known address, be treated as having been given or sent on the day that it was posted.

Grounds for revision of decisions

2.861   **3.**—(1) A health in pregnancy grant decision may be revised by the Commissioners on any grounds if—

(a) the Commissioners commence action leading to the revision within one month of the date of notification of the decision; or

(b) a request for the revision was received by the Commissioners at an appropriate office—

(i) within one month of the date of notification of the decision; or,

(ii) if a written statement of the reasons for the decision was requested under regulation 2(1)(b), within one month of the date that it is sent.

(2) Paragraph (1)(b) is subject to regulation 5.

(3) Where the decision on health in pregnancy grant arose from official error, or ignorance of, or mistake as to a material fact, it may be revised by the Commissioners at any time.

In this paragraph, "decision" includes a revised decision.

GENERAL NOTE

2.862   Paragraph (3) makes ignorance of, or a mistake as to, a material fact a ground for revision under s.9 of the Social Security Act 1998, whereas it is a ground for supersession under s.10 in relation to other benefits. These Regulations provide no grounds for supersession and so supersession can never be used in respect of a decision concerning health in pregnancy grant. It would therefore be unwise for a person ever to apply for a revision rather than simply appealing because there is no right of appeal against a refusal to revise a decision and a refusal to revise does not result in the time for appealing against the original decision being automatically extended (see the note to s.9 of the 1998 Act), with the consequence that any appeal would be out of time. An appeal does not preclude a revision but an unsuccessful application for revision may result in the loss of a right of appeal, although the Tribunal might accept the late appeal (see the note to reg.7 below).

Procedure for revision of decisions

2.863   **4.**—(1) The Commissioners may request by notice to the claimant further evidence or information as regards any revision under regulation 3.

(2) On a request for further evidence or information in relation to a request for revision from a claimant—

(a) if the claimant provides relevant further evidence or information within one month of the date of notification or such longer period of time as the Commissioners may allow, the decision may be revised;

(b) if the claimant does not provide such evidence or information within that time, the decision may be revised on the basis of the request for revision.

(3) The date on which a revised decision is to take effect is the date on which the claimant is notified of the revised decision, and regulation 2(3) (b) applies to the notification of the revised decision.

Appeals against decisions which have been revised

5.—(1) Where a health in pregnancy grant decision has been appealed and is subsequently revised by the Commissioners, unless the revision resulted in an award of health in pregnancy grant—

    2.864

(a) the appeal shall be treated as though it had been brought against the decision as revised; and

(b) the claimant shall have a period of one month from the date of notification of the decision as revised to make further representations as to the appeal.

(2) After the expiration of the period specified in paragraph (1), or within that period if the claimant consents in writing, the appeal shall proceed unless, in the light of further representations from the claimant, the Commissioners further revise their decision, resulting in an award of health in pregnancy grant.

Late applications for revision of decisions

6.—(1) The Commissioners may extend the time limits specified in regulation 3(1)(b) if—

    2.865

(a) an application for an extension of time is made to the Commissioners by the claimant or a person acting on her behalf; and

(b) the application for the extension of time—

(i) contains particulars of the grounds on which the extension is sought;

(ii) contains sufficient details of the decision which it is sought to have revised so as to enable it to be identified; and

(iii) is made within 12 months of the latest date by which an application should have been received by the Commissioners in accordance with regulation 3(1)(b).

(2) An application for an extension of time shall not be granted unless the Commissioners are satisfied that—

(a) it is reasonable to grant it; and

(b) special circumstances apply.

(3) The special circumstances specified in paragraph (2) are that—

(a) the claimant or her partner or a dependant of the claimant has died or suffered serious illness;

(b) the claimant is not resident in the United Kingdom; or

(c) normal postal services were disrupted.

(4) In determining whether it is reasonable to grant an application for an extension of time, the Commissioners must have regard to the principle that the greater the amount of time that has elapsed between the expiration of the time limits specified in regulation 3(1)(b) and the making of the application the more compelling the special circumstances in (3) must be.

(5) In determining whether it is reasonable to grant an application for an extension of time, the Commissioners may take no account of the following—

   (a) that the claimant or any person acting for her was unaware of or misunderstood the law applicable to her case (including ignorance or misunderstanding of the time limits imposed by these Regulations); or

   (b) that any tribunal or Court has taken a different view of the law from that previously understood and applied.

(6) An application for an extension of time which has been refused may not be renewed.

Time within which an appeal is to be brought

2.866   **7.**—(1) The time within which that appeal must be brought is—

   (a) within one month of notification of the decision or revised decision; or

   (b) if a written statement of the reasons for the decision was requested under regulation 2(1)(b), within one month of the date of notification.

(2) If a dispute arises as to whether an appeal was brought within the time limit specified in this regulation, the dispute must be referred to, and be determined by, the Tribunal.

(3) The time limit specified in paragraph (1) for bringing an appeal may be extended—

   (a) by the Commissioners in accordance with regulation 8; or

   (b) in Northern Ireland, by the Tribunal in accordance with the Tribunal Procedural Rules.

GENERAL NOTE

2.867   In Great Britain, para. (3) must be read with r. 23 of the Tribunal Procedure (First-tier Tribunal) (Social Entitlement Chamber) Rules 2008, which also provides (through Sch. 1) a time limit of one month but permits the Tribunal to extend the time, subject to an absolute time limit of thirteen months. By r.23(7), the Commissioners must refer a late appeal to the First-tier Tribunal if not prepared to extend time under reg.8 and the Tribunal has a broad discretion to extend the time. It seems a little strange that the Commissioners should fetter their own discretion to extend time through the terms of reg.8, but this is the same approach as that taken in reg.32 of the Social Security and Child Support (Decisions and Appeals) Regulations 1999.

Late appeals to the Tribunal

2.868   **8.**—(1) The Commissioners may treat a late appeal as made in time if the conditions in paragraphs (2) to (6) are satisfied.

(2) An appeal may be treated as made in time if the Commissioners are satisfied that it is in the interests of justice to do so.

(3) For the purposes of paragraph (2) it is not in the interests of justice to treat the appeal as made in time unless the Commissioners are satisfied that—

   (a) the special circumstances specified in paragraph (4) are relevant; or

   (b) some other special circumstances exist which are wholly exceptional and relevant, and as a result of those special circumstances, it was not practicable for the appeal to be made within the time limit specified in regulation 7.

(4) For the purposes of paragraph (3), the special circumstances are that—

(a) the claimant or her partner or a dependant of the claimant has died or suffered serious illness;

(b) the claimant is not resident in the United Kingdom; or

(c) normal postal services were disrupted.

(5) In determining whether it is in the interests of justice to treat the appeal as made in time, regard shall be had to the principle that the greater the amount of time that has elapsed between the expiration of the time limit under regulation 7 and the submission of the notice of appeal, the more compelling should be the special circumstances.

(6) In determining whether it is in the interests of justice to treat the appeal as made in time, no account shall be taken of the following—

(a) that the claimant or any person acting for her was unaware of or misunderstood the law applicable to her case (including ignorance or misunderstanding of the time limits imposed by regulation 7); or

(b) that any Tribunal or a court has taken a different view of the law from that previously understood and applied.

GENERAL NOTE

See the note to reg. 7 above. 2.869

Appeals procedure

9.—(1) A notice of appeal shall be— 2.870

(a) made, in Northern Ireland, in accordance with Tribunal Procedure Rules;

(b) on a form approved by the Commissioners; and

(c) sent or delivered to an appropriate office.

(2) Where a form does not contain the information required under the Tribunal Procedure Rules, the form may be returned by Commissioners to the sender for completion in accordance with the Tribunal Procedure Rules.

(3) Where a notice of appeal made in writing otherwise than on the approved form does not include sufficient information to enable the appeal to continue, the Commissioners may request further information in writing ("further particulars") from the claimant.

(4) Where a claimant to whom a notice of appeal is returned, or from whom further particulars are requested, duly completes and returns the notice or sends the further particulars, if the notice or particulars, as the case may be, are received by the Commissioners within—

(a) 14 days of the date on which the notice was returned to her by the Commissioners, the time for making the appeal shall be extended by 14 days from the date on which the notice was returned;

(b) 14 days of the date on which the Commissioners' request was made, the time for making the appeal shall be extended by 14 days from the date of the request; or

(c) such longer period as the Commissioners may direct, the time for making the appeal shall be extended by a period equal to that longer period directed by the Commissioners.

(5) Where a claimant to whom a notice of appeal is returned or from whom further particulars are requested does not complete and return the notice or send further particulars within the period of time identified under paragraph (4)—

(a) the Commissioners shall forward a copy of the notice, together with any other relevant documents or evidence to the Tribunal, and

(b) the Tribunal, in Northern Ireland, shall determine whether the notice satisfies the requirements of Tribunal Procedure Rules.

(6) Where—

(a) a notice of appeal is duly completed and returned or further particulars are sent after the expiry of the period of time allowed in accordance with paragraph (4), and

(b) no determination has been made under paragraph (5) at the time the form or the further particulars are received by the Commissioners,

that notice or further particulars shall also be forwarded to the Tribunal which shall take into account any further information or evidence set out in the form or further particulars.

(7) The Commissioners may discontinue action on an appeal where—

(a) the notice of appeal has not been forwarded to the Tribunal and the claimant or an authorised representative of the claimant has given written notice that she does not wish the appeal to continue; or

(b) the decision against which the appeal was made has been revised by the Commissioners in favour of the claimant.

Death of a party to an appeal

2.871   **10.**—(1) On the death of the claimant, the Commissioners may appoint such person as they think fit to proceed with the appeal in her place.

(2) If a person appointed under paragraph (1) has, prior to the date of such appointment, taken any action in relation to the appeal on behalf of the deceased party, the effective date of appointment by the Commissioners shall be the day immediately prior to the first day on which such action was taken.

Revocation

2.872   **11.** The Health in Pregnancy (Notices, Revisions and Appeals) Regulations 2009 are revoked.

GENERAL NOTE

2.873   The revoked set of regulations purported to provide that there should be no right of appeal against decisions relating to a person's immigration status and decisions permitting a person to act on behalf of a claimant who is unable to act, or in respect of the amount of the health in pregnancy grant. In fact there were no *vires* for such provisions. As a result, that set of regulations was withdrawn and replaced by the current version. It is understood that there are no current plans to enact primary legislation giving the vires for such exclusions to be made.

PART III

EUROPEAN COMMUNITY LAW

European Communities Act 1972

(1972 c.68) (as amended)

Arrangement of Sections Reproduced

1. Short title and interpretation   3.1
2. General implementation of Treaties
3. Decisions on, and proof of, Treaties and Community instruments, etc.

Part I

General Provisions

Short title and interpretation

1.—(1) This Act may be cited as the European Communities Act 1972.   3.2
(2) In this Act [¹ . . .]—
"the Communities" means the European Economic Community, the European Coal and Steel Community and the European Atomic Energy Community;
"the Treaties" or "the Community Treaties" means, subject to subsection (3) below, the pre-accession treaties, that is to say, those described in Part I of Schedule 1 to this Act, taken with—
(a) the treaty relating to the accession of the United Kingdom to the European Economic Community and to the European Atomic Energy Community, signed at Brussels on the 22nd January 1972; and
(b) the decision, of the same date, of the Council of the European Communities relating to the accession of the United Kingdom to the European Coal and Steel Community; [² and]
[³ (c) the treaty relating to the accession of the Hellenic Republic to the European Economic Community and to the European Atomic Energy Community, signed at Athens on 28th May 1979; and
(d) the decision, of 24th May 1979, of the Council relating to the accession of the Hellenic Republic to the European Coal and Steel Community; [⁴ and]]
[⁵ (e) the decisions of the Council of 7th May 1985, 24th June 1988, 31st October 1994, 29th September 2000 and 7th June 2007 on the Communities' system of own resources;]
[⁶ (g) the treaty relating to the accession of the Kingdom of Spain and the Portuguese Republic to the European Economic Community and to the European Atomic Energy Community, signed at Lisbon and Madrid on 12th June 1985; and
(h) the decision, of 11th June 1985, of the Council relating to the accession of the Kingdom of Spain and the Portuguese Republic to the European Coal and Steel Community; [⁷ and]]

831

[⁸ (j) the following provisions of the Single European Act signed at Luxembourg and The Hague on 17th and 28th February 1986, namely Title II (amendment of the treaties establishing the Communities) and, so far as they relate to any of the Communities or any Community institution, the preamble and Titles I (common provisions) and IV (general and final provisions);[⁹ and]]

[⁹ (k) Titles II, III and IV of the Treaty on European Union signed at Maastricht on 7th February 1992, together with the other provisions of the Treaty so far as they relate to those Titles, and the Protocols adopted at Maastricht on that date and annexed to the Treaty establishing the European Community with the exception of the Protocol on Social Policy on page 117 of Cm 1934;[¹⁰ and]]

[¹⁰ (l) the decision, of 1st February 1993, of the Council amending the Act concerning the election of the representatives of the European Parliament by direct universal suffrage annexed to Council Decision 76/787/ECSC, EEC, Euratom of 20th September 1976;[¹¹ and]]

[¹¹ (m) the Agreement on the European Economic Area signed at Oporto on 2nd May 1992 together with the Protocol adjusting that Agreement signed at Brussels on 17th March 1993;[¹² and]]

[¹² (n) the treaty concerning the accession of the Kingdom of Norway, the Republic of Austria, the Republic of Finland and the Kingdom of Sweden to the European Union, signed at Corfu on 24th June 1994;[¹³ and]]

[¹³ (o) the following provisions of the Treaty signed at Amsterdam on 2nd October 1997 amending the Treaty on European Union, the Treaties establishing the European Communities and certain related Acts—
   (i) Articles 2 to 9,
   (ii) Article 12, and
   (iii) the other provisions of the Treaty so far as they relate to those Articles,
and the Protocols adopted on that occasion other than the Protocol on Article J.7 of the Treaty on European Union;[¹⁴ and]]

[¹⁴ (p) the following provisions of the Treaty signed at Nice on 26th February 2001 amending the Treaty on European Union, the Treaties establishing the European Communities and certain related Acts—
   (i) Articles 2 to 10, and
   (ii) the other provisions of the Treaty so far as they relate to those Articles,
and the Protocol adopted on that occasion;[¹⁵ . . .]]

[¹⁶ (q) the treaty concerning the accession of the Czech Republic, the Republic of Estonia, the Republic of Cyprus, the Republic of Latvia, the Republic of Lithuania, the Republic of Hungary, the Republic of Malta, the Republic of Poland, the Republic of Slovenia and the Slovak Republic to the European Union, signed at Athens on 16th April 2003;[¹⁵ and]]

[¹⁵ (r) the treaty concerning the accession of the Republic of Bulgaria and Romania to the European Union, signed at Luxembourg on 25th April 2005;]

[¹⁷ (s) the Treaty of Lisbon Amending the Treaty on European Union and the Treaty Establishing the European Community signed at Lisbon on 13th December 2007 (together with its Annex and protocol), excluding any provision that relates to, or in so far as it relates to or could be applied in relation to, the Common Foreign and Security Policy;]

and any other treaty entered into by any of the Communities, with or without any of the member States, or entered into, as a treaty ancillary to any of the Treaties, by the United Kingdom;

and any expression defined in Schedule 1 to this Act has the meaning there given to it.

(3) If Her Majesty by Order in Council declares that a treaty specified in the Order is to be regarded as one of the Community Treaties as herein defined, the Order shall be conclusive that it is to be so regarded; but a treaty entered into by the United Kingdom after the 22nd January 1972, other than a pre-accession treaty to which the United Kingdom accedes on terms settled on or before that date, shall not be so regarded unless it is so specified, nor be so specified unless a draft of the Order in Council has been approved by resolution of each House of Parliament.

(4) For purposes of subsections (2) and (3) above, "treaty" includes any international agreement, and any protocol or annex to a treaty or international agreement.

AMENDMENTS

1. Interpretation Act 1978, s.25, Sch. 3.
2. European Communities (Greek Accession) Act 1979, s.1
3. European Communities (Greek Accession) Act 1979, s.1
4. European Communities (Finance) Act 2001, s.1 (December 4, 2001).
5. European Communities (Finance) Act 2008, s.1 (February 19, 2008).
6. European Communities (Spanish and Portuguese Accession) Act 1985, s.1.
7. European Communities (Amendment) Act 1986, s.1.
8. European Communities (Amendment) Act 1986, s.1
9. European Communities (Amendment) Act 1993, s.1(1) (July 23, 1993).
10. European Parliamentary Elections Act 1993, s.3(2) (November 5, 1993).
11. European Economic Area Act 1993, s.1 (November 5, 1993).
12. European Union (Accessions) Act 1994, s.1 (November 3, 1994).
13. European Communities (Amendment) Act 1998, s.1 (June 11, 1998).
14. European Communities (Amendment) Act 2002, s.1(1) (February 26, 2002).
15. European Union (Accessions) Act 2006, s.1(1) (February 16, 2006).
16. European Union (Accessions) Act 2003, s.1(1) (November 13, 2003).
17. European Union (Amendment) Act 2008, s.2 (June 19, 2008).

GENERAL NOTE

The Member States

The Member States of the European Union (with the date of their entry) are as follows: 3.3

Austria (January 1, 1995)	Denmark (January 1, 1973)
Belgium (January 1, 1958)	Estonia (May 1, 2004)
Bulgaria (January 1, 2007)	Finland (January 1, 1995)
Cyprus (May 1, 2004)	France (January 1, 1958)
Czech Republic (May 1, 2004)	Germany (January 1, 1958)
Greece (January 1, 1981)	Poland (May 1, 2004)

Hungary (May 1, 2004)   Portugal (January 1, 1986)
Ireland (January 1, 1973)   Romania (January 1, 2007)
Italy (January 1, 1958)   Slovakia (May 1, 2004)
Latvia (May 1, 2004)   Slovenia (May 1, 2004)
Lithuania (May 1, 2004)   Spain (January 1, 1986)
Luxembourg (January 1, 1958)   Sweden (January 1, 1995)
Malta (May 1, 2004)   United Kingdom (January 1, 1973)
Netherlands (January 1, 1958)

There are three additional countries which, with the Member States, form the countries of the European Economic Area (EEA):

Iceland   (January 1, 1994)
Liechtenstein   (January 1, 1994)
Norway   (January 1, 1994)

Community social security law generally applies to nationals of the Member States and of the additional countries of the EEA, since the social security rules are extended to their nationals by the EEA Treaty. For this reason the term "EEA country" or countries is frequently used to describe those countries whose nationals are beneficiaries of the Community rules on social security.

In addition, nationals of Switzerland are covered by the rules in Reg.1408/71 with effect from June 1, 2002. From June 1, 2003, third country nationals who have been lawfully resident in two Member States are covered by the co-ordinating regulation under Regulation 859/2003/EC, which is reproduced later in this volume.

The treaties

3.4   There are two key treaties: the European Community Treaty (EC Treaty) and the Treaty on European Union (EU Treaty or Maastricht Treaty). Both the EC Treaty and the Maastricht Treaty have been amended on a number of occasions, most significantly by the Treaty of Amsterdam, which entered into force on May 1, 1999, and the Treaty of Nice, which entered into force on February 1, 2003.

General implementation of Treaties

3.5   **2.**—(1) All such rights, powers, liabilities, obligations and restrictions from time to time created or arising by or under the Treaties, and all such remedies and procedures from time to time provided for by or under the Treaties, as in accordance with the Treaties are without further enactment to be given legal effect or used in the United Kingdom shall be recognised and available in law, and be enforced, allowed and followed accordingly; and the expression "enforceable Community right" and similar expressions shall be read as referring to one to which this subsection applies.

(2) Subject to Schedule 2 to this Act, at any time after its passing Her Majesty may by Order in Council, and any designated Minister or department may by [² by order, rules, regulations or scheme], make provision—

(a) for the purpose of implementing any Community obligation of the United Kingdom, or enabling any such obligation to be implemented, or of enabling any rights enjoyed or to be enjoyed by the United Kingdom under or by virtue of the Treaties to be exercised; or

(b) for the purpose of dealing with matters arising out of or related to any such obligation or rights or the coming into force, or the operation from time to time, of subsection (1) above;

and in the exercise of any statutory power or duty, including any power to give directions or to legislate by means of orders, rules, regulations or other subordinate instrument, the person entrusted with the power or duty may have regard to the objects of the Communities and to any such obligation or rights as aforesaid.

In this subsection "designated Minister or department" means such Minister of the Crown or government department as may from time to time be designated by Order in Council in relation to any matter or for any purpose, but subject to such restrictions or conditions (if any) as may be specified by the Order in Council.

(3) There shall be charged on and issued out of the Consolidated Fund or, if so determined by the Treasury, the National Loans Fund the amounts required to meet any Community obligation to make payments to any of the Communities or member States, or any Community obligation in respect of contributions to the capital or reserves of the European Investment Bank or in respect of loans to the Bank, or to redeem any notes or obligations issued or created in respect of any such Community obligation; and, except as otherwise provided by or under any enactment—

(a) any other expenses incurred under or by virtue of the Treaties or this Act by any Minister of the Crown or government department may be paid out of moneys provided by Parliament; and

(b) any sums received under or by virtue of the Treaties or this Act by any Minister of the Crown or government department, save for such sums as may be required for disbursements permitted by any other enactment, shall be paid into the Consolidated Fund or, if so determined by the Treasury, the National Loans Fund.

(4) The provision that may be made under subsection (2) above includes, subject to Schedule 2 to this Act, any such provision (of any such extent) as might be made by Act of Parliament, and any enactment passed or to be passed, other than one contained in this Part of this Act, shall be construed and have effect subject to the foregoing provisions of this section; but, except as may be provided by any Act passed after this Act, Schedule 2 shall have effect in connection with the powers conferred by this and the following sections of this Act to make Orders in Council [2 or orders, rules, regulations or schemes].

(5) [1 . . .] and the references in that subsection to a Minister of the Crown or government department and to a statutory power or duty shall include a Minister or department of the Government of Northern Ireland and a power or duty arising under or by virtue of an Act of the Parliament of Northern Ireland.

(6) A law passed by the legislature of any of the Channel Islands or of the Isle of Man, or a colonial law (within the meaning of the Colonial Laws Validity Act 1865) passed or made for Gibraltar, if expressed to be passed or made in the implementation of the Treaties and of the obligations of the United Kingdom thereunder, shall not be void or inoperative by reason of any inconsistency with or repugnancy to an Act of Parliament, passed or to be passed, that extends to the Island or Gibraltar or any provision having the force and effect of an Act there (but not including this section), nor by reason of its having some operation outside the Island or Gibraltar; and any such Act or provision that extends to the Island or Gibraltar shall be construed and have effect subject to the provisions of any such law.

1. Northern Ireland Constitution Act 1973, s.41.
2. Legislative and Regulatory Reform Act 2006 c.51 Pt.3 s.27(1) (January 8, 2007).

MODIFICATION

The operation of this section is modified in relation to Scotland by the Scotland Act 1998, s.15 and Sch.8 and the Scotland Act 1998 (Transfer of Functions to the Scottish Ministers etc.) Order 1999, (SI 1999/1750), and in relation to Northern Ireland by the Northern Ireland Act 1998 and the Northern Ireland Assembly Act 1973.

GENERAL NOTE

The binding nature of Community law

3.6   European Community law is binding on United Kingdom courts and tribunals by virtue of this section. Any rule of law qualifying as "an enforceable Community right" is to be given legal effect in the law of the United Kingdom. Whenever there is a conflict between United Kingdom law and European Community law, the rule of European Community law is to prevail: see s.2(4).

Community legislation

3.7   European Community law takes a variety of forms but the forms most likely to be met in tribunals and before the Commissioners are *regulations* and *directives*. art.249 EC provides that regulations are to have the force of law in all the Member States without further implementation, whereas directives are addressed to Member States and require conversion (if necessary) into national law.

Regulations retain their Community character and are binding in all Member States in exactly the same way as that Member State's primary legislation. Individuals may rely on the provisions of regulations by citing them just as if they were statutory provisions emanating from the United Kingdom Parliament. Indeed, they may be regarded as superior to national legislation since no national legislature can alter the form of a Community regulation.

Directives are a form of legislation which is intended to enable Community law to be enacted in each Member State in the manner which best fits the legal traditions of that Member State. So the obligation is to achieve the result required by the directive, but the choice of form and method is for each Member State to select. There is a requirement that each Member State to whom a directive is addressed must notify the Commission of the national law which implements the requirements of the directive.

Every piece of secondary legislation must find its authority in a provision of the EC Treaty. This is known as the legal basis or legal base for the measure. Legal base is important because the provision of the EC Treaty under which it is made will set out the decision-making procedure to be followed. This has generated disputes between the institutions, where an institution takes the view that the secondary legislation should have been made under a Treaty provision which requires its greater involvement in that procedure than under the provision under which the Council has adopted it.

The two most important doctrines developed in the case law of the Court of Justice of the European Communities (hereafter "Court of Justice") are:

- the supremacy of Community law
- the direct effect of Community law.

Supremacy

3.8   The supremacy of Community law requires that any conflict between a rule of Community law and a rule of national law must be decided in favour of the rule of Community law. See Case C-213/89 *R. v Secretary of State for Transport Ex p. Factortame* [1990] E.C.R. I-2433; [1991] 3 C.M.L.R. 589. Note the requirements of the doctrine as re-affirmed in this case, which involved a procedural rule in English law which operated as a barrier to a remedy under Community law; significantly, it involved the non-application of a United Kingdom statute.

Direct effect

A helpful distinction drawn by some authorities is between direct applicability and direct effect. **3.9**

Direct applicability refers to the *status* of the source of a rule of Community law, and refers to those sources which are automatically law in the national legal orders of all the Member States. Treaty articles have this character, as do regulations. It is not open to a Member State to interfere with the direct application of a regulation in the national legal order. This preserves the Community nature of the source of obligation throughout all the Member States. If you know that an article of a particular regulation gives you a right in your own national legal order, you can be sure that the same right is provided in all the national legal orders under the same article of the same regulation. The only difference is that it will be in another official language of the Community.

The attribute of direct applicability is a feature of the supremacy of Community law.

Note that in some areas the Member States have transferred sole competence to legislate to the Community; one purpose for such transfers of sovereignty is to ensure the uniform application of law throughout the Community. This is sometimes called the doctrine of *pre-emption*. The effect is that once an area is occupied by Community law, Member States cannot legislate in that area.

Direct effect refers to the *content* of a rule, and describes its capacity to give rise to rights for individuals which they can plead before national courts, and which national courts must recognise.

Just as it is the case that not every provision of national law gives rise to rights for individuals, so too it is the case that not every provision of Community law gives rise to direct effect. It is necessary to consider the scope and wording of any provision in order to determine whether it is capable of giving rise to direct effect.

Where the status of the provision of Community law in issue is one which has the attribute of direct applicability, it is simply a matter of interpretation to determine whether direct effect arises. So, in the case of Treaty articles and regulations, the requirements for direct effect are that the rule in question:

● is sufficiently clear and precise; and

● is unconditional.

The direct effect of directives has given rise to particular problems, since Art.249 EC provides that directives are:

● addressed to the Member States; and

● are binding as to the result to be achieved; but

● leave the choice of form and methods to the national authorities of the Member States.

All directives give Member States a time limit within which to implement the requirements of the directive. They are obliged to inform the Commission of the action taken to implement the directive. Failure to implement a directive by the deadline is likely to result in action being taken by the Commission to bring the Member State before the Court of Justice under art.226 EC for failing to fulfil its obligations under the EC Treaty.

Proper and complete implementation of a directive results in individuals acquiring rights under the implementing national law.

It is now accepted that, where the deadline for implementation has passed without the directive's being implemented or without its being implemented properly, a directive can give rise to direct effect where it contains an obligation as to the result to be achieved which meets the requirements for direct effect set out above, *provided that* the party against whom the right is asserted is the State or "an emanation of the State". This is called a vertical relationship, and so vertical direct effect of directives is said to be permitted. Note particularly the definition of what constitutes an emanation of the State in Case C-188/89 *Foster v British Gas* [1990] E.C.R. I-3313; [1990] 2 C.M.L.R. 833.

However, the Court of Justice has ruled that the direct effect of directives does not arise where the right is being asserted against another private party. This is called a horizontal relationship, and so horizontal direct effect of directives is said not to be possible. There are a number of reasons for this:

1. To do so would impose an insuperable burden on private parties. Whereas it is justifiable to refuse to permit the State and its emanations from being able to plead the State's wrongdoing to avoid its liabilities, it would be wrong to impose a similar burden on a private party.

2. Directives are addressed to Member States. To allow the horizontal direct effect of directives would be to remove the distinction between regulations and directives. It would also provide an incentive for Member States not to implement directives, since they would take effect in any event after the expiry of the time for implementation.

The doctrine of indirect effect

3.10   To mitigate the harshness of a rule relating to the direct effect of directives as between private parties, the Court of Justice has imposed obligations on national authorities and national courts to interpret national law compatibly with the requirements of directives so far as it is possible to do so. This obligation flows from the duty of solidarity to be found in art.10 EC.

State liability for breaches of Community law

3.11   The Court of Justice has developed rules which ensure the effective enjoyment of Community rights for individuals. The Court has even fashioned the requirement for a remedy where a Member State has failed either wholly or in part to implement a directive, and the relationship between the parties is a horizontal one. However, the remedy is available wherever there has been a breach of Community law of sufficient seriousness to engage the remedy.

Under the *Francovich* line of cases, courts in the Member States are obliged to compensate individuals who have suffered loss as a result of infringements of Community law by Member States. Three conditions for liability are required:

● the rule of Community law grants rights to individuals and the content of those rights is clearly identifiable;

● the breach by the Member State is sufficiently serious to trigger liability for loss;

● there is a direct causal link between the breach of the rule by the Member State and the loss suffered by the individuals concerned.

This important remedy has been refined in subsequent case law. This is helpfully summarised in the decision of the House of Lords of October 28, 1999 in *R. v Secretary of State for Transport Ex p. Factortame Ltd (No.5)*, HL, [1999] 3 W. L. R. 1062; [1999] 4 All E.R. 906; [1999] 3 C. M. L. R. 597.

For guidance on the application of limitation periods to *Francovich* actions, see *Spencer v Secretary of State for Work and Pensions,* and *Moore v Secretary of State for Transport,* [2008] EWCA Civ 750.

The Community law doctrine of the effective enjoyment of Community rights

The case law has established that national law must afford the same remedies   3.12
in relation to the enforcement of Community law as are available for the enforcement of national law. This has come to be known as the doctrine of the effective
enjoyment of Community rights and operates on the basis of two principles: see for
example, Case C-312/93 *Peterbroeck* v *Belgium* [1995] ECR I-4599, para.12).

The principle of *equivalence* requires that the conditions laid down by national
law for the pursuit of Community rights are not discriminatory by comparison
with those relating to domestic claims. The principle of *effectiveness* requires that
any restrictions imposed must not be such as to render the reliance on Community
rights virtually impossible or excessively difficult. The doctrine applies regardless
of the course of the Community right on which the individual is relying: it may be
a Treaty provision, regulation or directive, or indeed any other instrument having
legal effect. The case law of the Court of Justice on the application of this doctrine
to national time limits has proved difficult.

The issue first arose in the context of Ireland's failure fully to implement Dir.79/7.
In Case 286/85 *McDermott v Minister for Social Welfare* [1987] E.C.R. 1453; [1987]
2 C.M.L.R. 607, the Court of Justice ruled that Art.4(1) of Dir.79/7 could be relied
on by individuals as from December 23, 1984. In Case 208/90 *Emmott* v *Minister
for Social Welfare and Attorney General* [1991] E.C.R. I-4269, the Court of Justice
ruled as incompatible with Community law a limitation period operative under
national law which had the effect of completely defeating the claimant's reliance on
Community law entitlements. The case arose in the context of failures by the Irish
Government to implement the requirements of Directive 79/7 on equal treatment
of men and women in matters pertaining to social security. Mrs Emmott sought
payment of her disability benefit at the same rate paid to married men. Ultimately
she began judicial review proceedings but the national authorities pleaded that her
application was time-barred since the time limit was three months from the date
when the grounds of the application first arose. This completely defeated her claim.
The Court of Justice ruled that where directives had not been properly implemented
by a Member State, that State could not rely on national rules on time limits to
defeat entirely a claim arising from the Member State failure.

The scope of that decision has been clarified in later case law. In Case C-338/91
Steenhorst Neerings [1993] E.C.R. I-5475, the Court of Justice ruled that national
provisions which simply limit the period prior to the date of claim for which benefit
entitlement may be claimed were not inconsistent with Community law.

In *Steenhorst Neerings*, the Court of Justice said:

"21. It should be noted first that, unlike the rule of domestic law fixing time-limits
for bringing actions, the rule described in the question referred for a preliminary
ruling in this case does not affect the right of individuals to rely on Directive 79/7
in proceedings before the national courts against a defaulting Member State. It
merely limits the retroactive effect of claims made for the purpose of obtaining
the relevant benefits.
22. The time-bar resulting from the expiry of the time-limit for bringing proceedings serves to ensure that the legality of administrative decisions cannot be
challenged indefinitely. The judgment in Emmott indicates that that requirement
cannot prevail over the need to protect the rights conferred on individuals by the
direct effect of provisions in a directive so long as the defaulting Member State
responsible for those decisions has not properly transposed the provisions into
national law.
23. On the other hand, the aim of the rule restricting the retroactive effect of
claims for benefits for incapacity for work is quite different from that of a rule
imposing mandatory time-limits for bringing proceedings. As the Government
of the Netherlands and the defendant in the main proceedings explained in
their written observations, the first type of rule, of which examples can be
found in other social security laws in the Netherlands, serves to ensure sound

administration, most importantly so that it may be ascertained whether the claimant satisfied the conditions for eligibility and so that the degree of incapacity, which may well vary over time, may be fixed. It also reflects the need to preserve financial balance in a scheme in which claims submitted by insured persons in the course of a year must in principle be covered by the contributions collected during that same year.

24. The reply to the first question must therefore be that Community law does not preclude the application of a national rule of law whereby benefits for incapacity for work are payable not earlier than one year before the date of claim, in the case where an individual seeks to rely on rights conferred directly by Article 4(1) of Directive 79/7 with effect from 23 December 1984 and where on the date the claim for benefit was made the Member State concerned had not yet properly transposed that provision into national law."

The ruling in *Steenhorst Neerings* was followed in Case C-410/92 *Johnson v Chief Adjudication Officer* [1994] E.C.R. I-5483, where the Court said:

"26. However, it is clear from the judgment in *Steenhorst-Neerings* that the solution adopted in *Emmott* was justified by the particular circumstances of that case, in which a time-bar had the result of depriving the applicant of any opportunity whatever to rely on her right to equal treatment under the directive.

27. The Court pointed out in *Steenhorst-Neerings* (paragraph 20) that in *Emmott* the applicant in the main proceedings had relied on the judgment of the Court in Case 286/85 *McDermott v Minister for Social Welfare* [1987] E.C.R. 1453 in order to claim entitlement by virtue of Article 4(1) of Directive 79/7, with effect from 23 December 1984, to invalidity benefits under the same conditions as those applicable to men in the same situation. The administrative authorities had then declined to adjudicate on her claim since Directive 79/7 was the subject of proceedings pending before a national court. Finally, even though Directive 79/7 had still not been correctly transposed into national law, it was claimed that the proceedings she had brought to obtain a ruling that her claim should have been accepted were out of time.

28. In contrast, the rule at issue in *Steenhorst-Neerings* did not affect the right of individuals to rely on Directive 79/7 in proceedings before the national courts against a defaulting Member State but merely limited to one year the retroactive effect of claims for benefits for incapacity for work.

29. The Court concluded (paragraph 24) that Community law did not preclude the application of a national rule of law whereby benefits for incapacity for work were payable not earlier than one year before the date of claim, in the case where an individual sought to rely on rights conferred directly by Article 4(1) of Directive 79/7 with effect from 23 December 1984 and where on the date the claim for benefit was made the Member State concerned had not yet properly transposed that provision into national law.

30. In the light of the foregoing, the national rule which adversely affects Mrs Johnson's action before the Court of Appeal is similar to that at issue in *Steenhorst-Neerings*. Neither rule constitutes a bar to proceedings; they merely limit the period prior to the bringing of the claim in respect of which arrears of benefit are payable."

Walker-Fox v Secretary of State for Work and Pensions [2005] EWCA Civ 1441, reported as *R(IS) 3/06* is the appeal against the decision in *CIS/0488/2004*. The judgment contains a detailed discussion of the authorities; in particular, the Court of Appeal was keen to limit the situations in which the *Emmott* case would apply to circumstances close to the situation which arose in that case. In allowing the Secretary of State's appeal the Court of Appeal considered that the Deputy Commissioner had erred in confusing "the *making* of a claim with the *outcome* of a claim. The real question is whether it was virtually impossible or excessively difficult to *make* the claim" (para.46 of the judgment). The Court of Appeal concluded that it was not.

Interim relief

A Commissioner has for the first time had to consider whether Community 3.13
law principles on effective enjoyment of Community rights requires the grant of
interim relief in a case where payments of disability living allowance were stopped
when the claimant moved to Spain and where a Commissioner had referred questions to the Court of Justice under Art.234 EC. In *R(DLA) 4/99* and *R(DLA)
5/99* the Commissioner does not directly answer the question since he proceeds on
the assumption that there might be such a power but does not consider that the
claimant's case met the necessary threshold of being "strongly arguable" as distinct from being merely "arguable". Despite this conclusion the decision raises many
of the difficult issues which would arise if the Commissioners (and now, the Upper
Tribunal) were to have such a power. It could well follow that First-tier Tribunals
enjoyed a similar power. A particular difficulty is that Tribunals and the Upper
Tribunal are concerned with entitlement, whereas the mechanics of payment are
matters for the Secretary of State alone. Such a distinction of role (which has, of
course, for many purposes been removed by the Social Security Act 1998 without
removing all the possible problems) might not be able to survive an onslaught relying
on European authority on remedies before national judicial bodies.

The appellant in the case sought a judicial review of the Commissioner's decision
in *R. v Social Security Commissioner Ex p. Snares* [1997] C.O.D. 403, Divisional
Court of QBD, March 24, 1997, reported as *R(DLA) 4/99*. The Divisional Court
concluded that the Commissioner could not be faulted in the way he had exercised any discretion he had in the case. The case does not advance matters beyond
what the Commissioner said. The trend of the case law of the Court of Justice
is, however, that European Community law requires national judicial authorities
to have the power to give legal effect to rights arising under Community law. An
example of where this might be problematic is the absence of any express power to
award interest on late benefit or costs: see *R(FC)2/90*.

Decisions on, and proof of, Treaties and Community instruments, etc

3.—(1) For the purposes of all legal proceedings any question as to the 3.14
meaning or effect of any of the Treaties, or as to the validity, meaning or
effect of any Community instrument, shall be treated as a question of law
(and, if not referred to the European Court, be for determination as such in
accordance with the principles laid down by and any relevant [¹ decision of
the European Court or any court attached thereto)].

(2) Judicial notice shall be taken of the Treaties, of the Official Journal
of the Communities and of any decision of, or expression of opinion by,
the European Court [¹ or any court attached thereto] on any such question
as aforesaid; and the Official Journal shall be admissible as evidence of any
instrument or other act thereby communicated of any of the Communities
or of any Community institution.

(3) Evidence of any instrument issued by a Community institution,
including any judgment or order of the European Court [¹ or any court
attached thereto], or of any document in the custody of a Community
institution, or any entry in or extract from such a document, may be given
in any legal proceedings by production of a copy certified as a true copy by
an official of that institution; and any document purporting to be such a
copy shall be received in evidence without proof of the official position or
handwriting of the person signing the certificate.

(4) Evidence of any Community instrument may also be given in any
legal proceedings—

(a) by production of a copy purporting to be printed by the Queen's Printer;

(b) where the instrument is in the custody of a government department (including a department of the Government of Northern Ireland), by production of a copy certified on behalf of the department to be a true copy by an officer of the department generally or specially authorised so to do;

and any document purporting to be such a copy as is mentioned in paragraph (b) above of an instrument in the custody of a department shall be received in evidence without proof of the official position or handwriting of the person signing the certificate, or of his authority to do so, or of the document being in the custody of the department.

(5) *Omitted.*

AMENDMENT

1. European Communities (Amendment) Act 1986, s.2.

GENERAL NOTE

3.15   Questions as to the meaning and effect of the treaties and of any Community legislation are questions of law. Where such questions are decided by national courts or tribunals, they are to be decided in accordance with principles laid down in any decision of the Court of Justice or Court of First Instance. In deciding such questions, judicial notice is to be taken of the treaties and secondary legislation as well as of decisions of the Community courts.

Extracts from the EC Treaty

PART I

PRINCIPLES

Article 2 EC

3.16   The Community shall have as its task, by establishing a common market and an economic and monetary union and by implementing common policies or activities referred to in Articles 3 and 4, to promote throughout the Community a harmonious, balanced and sustainable development of economic activities, a high level of employment and of social protection, equality between men and women, sustainable and non-inflationary growth, a high degree of competitiveness and convergence of economic performance, a high level of protection and improvement of the quality of the environment, the raising of the standard of living and quality of life, and economic and social cohesion and solidarity among Member States.

Article 3 EC

3.17   **1.** For the purposes set out in Article 2, the activities of the Community shall include, as provided in this Treaty and in accordance with the timetable set out therein:

Article 3

(a) the prohibition, as between Member States, of customs duties and quantitative restrictions on the import and export of goods, and of all other measures having equivalent effect;

(b) a common commercial policy;

(c) an internal market characterised by the abolition, as between Member States, of obstacles to the free movement of goods, persons, services and capital;

(d) measures concerning the entry and movement of persons as provided for in Title IV;

(e) a common policy in the sphere of agriculture and fisheries;

(f) a common policy in the sphere of transport;

(g) a system ensuring that competition in the internal market is not distorted;

(h) the approximation of the laws of Member States to the extent required for the functioning of the common market;

(i) the promotion of coordination between employment policies of the Member States with a view to enhancing their effectiveness by developing a coordinated strategy for employment;

(j) a policy in the social sphere comprising a European Social Fund;

(k) the strengthening of economic and social cohesion;

(l) a policy in the sphere of the environment;

(m) the strengthening of the competitiveness of Community industry;

(n) the promotion of research and technological development;

(o) encouragement for the establishment and development of trans-European networks;

(p) a contribution to the attainment of a high level of health protection;

(q) a contribution to education and training of quality and to the flowering of the cultures of the Member States;

(r) a policy in the sphere of development cooperation;

(s) the association of the overseas countries and territories in order to increase trade and promote jointly economic and social development;

(t) a contribution to the strengthening of consumer protection;

(u) measures in the spheres of energy, civil protection and tourism.

2. In all the activities referred to in this Article, the Community shall aim to eliminate inequalities, and to promote equality, between men and women.

GENERAL NOTE

3.18 The Court has frequently found its inspiration for an interpretation of a particular provision of the Treaty or of secondary legislation by reference to the objectives of the Community as set out in arts 2 and 3: for example, Case 53/81 *Levin v Staatssecretaris van Justitie* [1982] E.C.R. 1035 (para.15 of the judgment), though the terms of these articles are not sufficiently precise to give rise to direct effect: Case 126/86 *Giménez Zaera v Instituto Nacional de la Seguridad Social* [1987] E.C.R. 3697 (para.11 of judgment in relation to art.2).

Article 5 EC

3.19 The Community shall act within the limits of the powers conferred upon it by this Treaty and of the objectives assigned to it therein.

In areas which do not fall within its exclusive competence, the Community shall take action, in accordance with the principle of subsidiarity, only if and insofar as the objectives of the proposed action cannot be sufficiently achieved by the Member States and can therefore, by reason of the scale or effects of the proposed action, be better achieved by the Community.

GENERAL NOTE

3.20   Note that Community law on social security only seeks to co-ordinate the different social security systems of the Member States (plus the three EEA countries). There has been no attempt to date to harmonise social entitlements in the Member States, though there are provisions requiring that there be no discrimination on grounds of sex in the application of the social security rules of the Member States: see Dir.79/7 reproduced below.

Article 10 EC

3.21   Member States shall take all appropriate measures, whether general or particular, to ensure fulfilment of the obligations arising out of this Treaty or resulting from action taken by the institutions of the Community. They shall facilitate the achievement of the Community's tasks. They shall abstain from any measure which could jeopardise the attainment of the objectives of this Treaty.

GENERAL NOTE

3.22   This article is sometimes referred to as establishing the principle of "solidarity" under which Member States undertake a legal obligation to further Community objectives. It has been used as the basis for the obligation to interpret national law compatibly with Community law: see Case 14/83 *Von Colson and Kamann v Land Nordrhein Westfalen* [1984] E.C.R. 1891; [1986] 2 C.M.L.R. 430; Case C-106/89 *Marleasing SA* [1990] E.C.R. I-4135; [1992] 1 C.M.L.R. 305; and Case C-168/95 *Criminal Proceedings against Arcaro* [1996] E.C.R. I-4705.

Article 12 EC

3.23   Within the scope of application of this Treaty, and without prejudice to any special provisions contained therein, any discrimination on grounds of nationality shall be prohibited.

The Council, acting in accordance with the procedure referred to in Article 251, may adopt rules designed to prohibit such discrimination.

GENERAL NOTE

3.24   This is the general statement of non-discrimination on grounds of nationality, which applies wherever the provisions of the treaty apply. In Case C-85/96 *Martínez Sala v Freistaat Bayern* [1998] E.C.R. I-2691, it was held that a person lawfully resident in Germany could rely on the principle of non-discrimination to gain access to social security benefits in Germany notwithstanding that she was not a worker under Community law. A crucial aspect of the case which is not fully explained is what constitutes lawful residence in a Member State. See also the case law discussed in the annotations to art.18 EC below.

Article 13

Article 13 EC

[1 **1.**] Without prejudice to the other provisions of this Treaty and within   3.25
the limits of the powers conferred by it upon the Community, the Council,
acting unanimously on a proposal from the Commission and after consulting the European Parliament, may take appropriate action to combat
discrimination based on sex, racial or ethnic origin, religion or belief, disability, age or sexual orientation.

[1 **2.** By way of derogation from paragraph 1, when the Council adopts
Community incentive measures, excluding any harmonisation of the laws
and regulations of the Member States, to support action taken by the
Member States in order to contribute to the achievement of the objectives
referred to in paragraph 1, it shall act in accordance with the procedure
referred to in Article 251.]

AMENDMENT

1. Treaty of Nice, art.2(2) (February 1, 2003).

Article 14 EC

1. The Community shall adopt measures with the aim of progressively estab-   3.26
lishing the internal market over a period expiring on December 31 1992, in
accordance with the provisions of this Article and of Articles 15, 26, 47(2), 49,
80, 93 and 95 and without prejudice to the other provisions of this Treaty.

2. The internal market shall comprise an area without internal frontiers in which the free movement of goods, persons, services and capital is
ensured in accordance with the provisions of this Treaty.

3. The Council, acting by a qualified majority on a proposal from the
Commission, shall determine the guidelines and conditions necessary to
ensure balanced progress in all the sectors concerned.

PART II

CITIZENSHIP OF THE UNION

Article 17 EC

1. Citizenship of the Union is hereby established. Every person holding   3.27
the nationality of a Member State shall be a citizen of the Union. Citizenship
of the Union shall complement and not replace national citizenship.

2. Citizens of the Union shall enjoy the rights conferred by this Treaty
and shall be subject to the duties imposed thereby.

GENERAL NOTE

The allocation of nationality to individuals is a matter for each Member State   3.28
to determine, subject to very limited intervention by Community law. These
qualifications mean that it will not be open to a Member State to deny that an
individual has the nationality of a Member State even though certain rules of its

own civil justice system operate in a way which does not recognise the nationality. An example is the Case C-369/90 *Micheletti*, [1992] E.C.R. I-4239. Micheletti held both Argentinean and Italian nationality. Prior to moving to Spain, he had been resident in Argentina for some time. Under certain Spanish rules, this meant that he was treated as an Argentinian national and his Italian nationality was not recognised. He was refused a residence permit on this basis. The Court of Justice ruled that a Member State could not use its internal law on nationality to deny recognition to a dual national of the nationality of another Member State. Nor is it necessary to have a passport as evidence of the holding of the nationality of a Member State if the nationality can be established by other means: see Case C-376/89 *Giagounidis*, [1991] E.C.R. I-1069.

The laws of the Member States govern changes of nationality just as they govern the attribution of nationality.

Article 18 EC

3.29 [¹ **1.** Every citizen of the Union shall have the right to move and reside freely within the territory of the Member States, subject to the limitations and conditions laid down in this Treaty and by the measures adopted to give it effect.

2. If action by the Community should prove necessary to attain this objective and this Treaty has not provided the necessary powers, the Council may adopt provisions with a view to facilitating the exercise of the rights referred to in paragraph 1. The Council shall act in accordance with the procedure referred to in Article 251.

3. Paragraph 2 shall not apply to provisions on passports, identity cards, residence permits or any other such document or to provisions on social security or social protection.]

AMENDMENT

1. Treaty of Nice, art.2(3) (February 1, 2003).

GENERAL NOTE

Preliminary note on the scope of these annotations

3.30 This commentary seeks to set out the content of European Community law as established by decisions of the Court of Justice in Luxembourg, and the key authorities in the national legal order. It covers the case law in the national legal order on the "right to reside". But it does not purport to cover all the decisions of the Commissioners, and now, the Upper Tribunal on the "right to reside". For a useful overview of the European authorities and the United Kingdom legislation, see *SSWP v IA* [2009] UKUT 35 (AAC). Much more detail on the now numerous individual decisions in the national legal order on the right to reside can be found in the commentary to regulation 21AA of the Income Support (General) Regulations 1987 in Volume II of this work.

The key Luxembourg authorities

3.31 There is now a line of cases which suggests that entitlement to social benefits in a Member State may flow from the holding of citizenship of the Union coupled with lawful residence in a Member State. The Court is beginning to repeat, rather like a mantra, that citizenship of the Union is "destined to be the fundamental status of nationals of the Member States, enabling those who find themselves in the same situation to receive the same treatment in law irrespective of their nationality, subject to such exceptions as are expressly provided for": see, for example, Case C-209/03

Bidar [2005] Q.B. 812, ECJ, para.31 of the judgment.

In Case C-85/96 *Martínez Sala*, [1998] E.C.R. I-2691, Maria Martínez Sala, a Spanish national lawfully resident in Germany, found herself in need of financial support from the State. The Court of Justice ruled that the prohibition of discrimination on grounds of nationality applied in this case and that she was entitled to obtain social assistance on the same basis as German nationals. But a key point in the case was that the referring court had stated that the claimant's residence in Germany was lawful.

Case C-184/99 *Grzelczyk*, [2001] E.C.R. I-6193, concerned a French student undertaking higher education in Belgium. For the first three years of the course, he managed to maintain himself, but ran into financial difficulties in his fourth year of study and sought help from the State. The referring court did not regard Grzelczyk as a worker and so he could derive no help from the provisions applicable to workers. He appeared to be a student; the Directive on the free movement of students expressly provides that students are not entitled to maintenance grants from the State as a matter of Community law entitlement, though this was without prejudice to their entitlement to social security on the same basis as nationals of the State of residence. Nevertheless the Court of Justice ruled that Grzelczyk was lawfully resident in Belgium as a student by reason of being a citizen of the Union and was entitled to receive the same support that would be afforded to a Belgian student in the same circumstances by reason of the operation of Article 12 EC. The declaration made on entry to the Member State of residence was of an expectation, based on reasonable conclusions at the time, of an ability to be self-sufficient for the duration of the course.

Case C-138/02 *Collins* [2005] Q.B. 145, concerned a man who came to the United Kingdom to look for work. He held the nationality of the United States and Ireland. Though he had worked in the United Kingdom many years before, the gap meant that he could not be considered to be a worker. He was subject to the requirement, under national law, that he show habitual residence in the United Kingdom before he could become entitled to income-based jobseeker's allowance. The Court of Justice recognised that it was legitimate to impose a requirement that the person seeking the benefit had established a genuine link with the employment market of the State in which he was seeking an unemployment benefit. Furthermore, a residence-based test was not, of itself, inappropriate provided that its scope and application were clear and proportionate to establish the necessary link. See the commentary on Article 7 of Regulation 1612/68 below for a discussion of the decision of the Commissioner following the ruling of the Court of Justice, and the appeal against that decision in *Collins v Secretary of State for Work and Pensions*, reported as *R(JSA) 3/06*.

Case C-456/02 *Trojani* [2004] All E.R. (EC) 1065, takes this further. Trojani was a single man of French nationality. He clearly fell on hard times. He was living in a Salvation Army hostel in Belgium under an arrangement where he undertook various jobs for the hostel as part of a personal rehabilitation scheme, in exchange for which he received board and lodging and an allowance of 25.00 per week. He claimed the minimex (the minimum subsistence allowance in Belgium). His claim was refused on the grounds that he was not a Belgian national. Trojani brought proceedings before the Labour Court in Brussels to challenge this refusal. That Court referred questions to the Court of Justice. The Luxembourg Court advised that Trojani did not appear to be a worker by reason of the nature of his activities in the hostel where he lived. The second argument essentially concerned the possible entitlement of Trojani to the minimex as a person exercising his right to reside in Belgium as a citizen of the European Union. The Advocate General concluded that it was open to Belgium to deny Trojani a right of residence because he did not have the means to support himself. The Court was a little more circumspect. Referring to the ruling in the *Baumbast* case, the Court indicates that it would not be disproportionate to deny Trojani a right of residence on the basis that he did not have the means to be self sufficient. In other words, he had no *Community* right to reside. But the Court went on to note that he may have a right to reside under *national law*, since he had been issued with a residence permit under national law by the municipal authorities in Brussels. The Court made three points (at paras 41–6 of its judgment):

(1) Social assistance falls within the scope of the EC Treaty.

(2) A citizen of the Union who is not economically active may rely on the prohibition of discrimination on grounds of nationality where he has been "lawfully resident" in the host Member State "for a certain time or possesses a residence permit" (para.43).

(3) Restricting entitlement to social assistance to the nationals of the host Member State constitutes discrimination on grounds of nationality contrary to Article 12 EC.

It would follow that, if the national court concluded that Trojani was "lawfully resident" in Belgium under *national law*, then the prohibition of discrimination in Community law would be engaged, and the restriction of entitlement to the minimex to Belgian nationals in the circumstances of this case would breach the equality provisions of the EC Treaty. Some answer to the question of what constitutes lawful residence in Community law may be provided when the Luxembourg Court responds to the reference made by the House of Lords in *McCarthy v Secretary of State for the Home Department* (the appeal from [2008] EWCA Civ 641) asking for advice on the interpretation of the words "resided legally" in Article 16 of Directive 2004/38/EC. The questions referred in this case are:

"1. Is a person of dual Irish and United Kingdom nationality who has resided in the United Kingdom for her entire life a "beneficiary" within the meaning of Article 3 of Directive 2004/38/EC of the European Parliament and of the Council ("the Directive")?
2. Has such a person "resided legally" within the host Member State for the purpose of Article 16 of the Directive in circumstances where she was unable to satisfy the requirements of Article 7 of Directive 2004/38/EC?"

The dramatic impact of the citizenship provisions is also illustrated by the judgment of the Court of Justice in case C-209/03 *Bidar*, March 15, 2005, [2005] ECR I-2119. This case concerned a claim for a student loan by a French national who had come to the United Kingdom some years earlier and had completed his secondary education here. The Court of Justice recalled what it described as "settled case-law" (para.32 of the judgment) that a citizen of the European Union lawfully resident in the territory of the host Member State can rely on Article 12 EC in all situations which fall within the material scope of the EC Treaty. Prior to this case, the award of financial support to students for their living expenses, whether in the form of grants or loans, had been considered to be outside the material scope of the EC Treaty. But the Court says that developments in Community law, especially the introduction of citizenship of the Union called for a change in that position. Such matters are now to be treated as within the scope of the EC Treaty for all the reasons set out in the judgment. The Court of Justice went on to rule that the application of the prohibition of discrimination meant that a person lawfully resident in the host Member State who has received a substantial part of his secondary education in that Member State and so has established a genuine link with the society of that State must be treated in the same manner as a national of that State. See also Case C-158/07 *Jacqueline Förster v Hoofdirectie van de Informatie Beheer Groep*, Judgment of November 18, 2008.

Case C-499/06 *Nerkowska*, May 22, 2008, decides that Article 18 must be interpreted as precluding legislation of a Member State under which it refuses, generally and in all circumstances, to pay to its nationals a benefit granted to civilian victims of war or repression solely because they are not resident in the territory of that Member State throughout the period of payment of the benefit, but in the territory of another Member State.

In Case *C-406/04, De Cuyper*, [2006] ECR I-6947, the Court of Justice ruled that freedom of movement and residence, conferred on citizens of the Union under Article 18 EC, does not preclude a residence clause, which is imposed on an unemployed person over 50 years of age who is exempt from the requirement to establish that he was available for work, as a condition for the retention of his entitlement to unemployment benefit. De Cuyper, a Belgian national, was born in 1942. He was no longer required to 'submit to the local control procedures' in connection with his entitlement to unemployment benefit because he was over 50 years of age. Following a routine check, it was established that he spent considerable periods each year living in France. He was subsequently refused unemployment benefit. The Court of Justice concluded that the benefit in question was an unemployment benefit (as distinct from a pre-retirement benefit) and that, although the restriction on his right of movement if he was to remain entitled to unemployment benefit was a restriction on his right to free movement, the requirement for residence was objectively justifiable having regard to the need to monitor the employment and family situation of unemployed persons. There was no less restrictive measure capable of meeting the monitoring requirement.

Case C-520/04 *Turpeinen* [2006] ECR I-10685, ruled that Article 18 EC outlaws national legislation under which the income tax charged on a retirement pension paid by an institution of the Member State concerned to a person in another Member State exceeds the tax charged on a pension payable to a resident of the Member State concerned, where that pension constitutes all or nearly all of the person's income.

This line of cases has implications for the United Kingdom which has made entitlement to means-tested benefits conditional upon the claimant having (a) a right to reside, and (b) being habitually resident in the United Kingdom, the Channel islands, the Isle of Man or the Republic of Ireland (see, for example, reg.21AA Income Support General Regulations 1987). The "right to reside" is not defined in primary national legislation, but it is clear both from secondary legislation and from decisions of courts and tribunals that such a right may flow from European Community law.

Considerable substance is given to the citizenship approach to the right to move and reside in a Member State other than that of a person's own nationality in Directive 2004/38/EC, which is reproduced later in this Volume. Though the drafting of that Directive may be criticized, (and there is evidence that it has been implemented in an incomplete manner in *all* Member States), it constitutes both an immigration code for nationals of the Member States, and gives citizens substantive rights according to the length of their residence. It marks a significant de-coupling of entitlements from economic activity, rather attaching them to the status of citizen of the Union than to migrant workers and other economically active persons. Decisions of the Luxembourg Court on the interpretation of the Directive are dealt with in the commentary to the relevant provision of the Directive.

National authorities

Courts and tribunals in England and Wales seem to be taking a narrow view of the right to reside flowing from Article 18 EC. So in *Ali v Secretary of State for the Home Department* [2006] EWCA Civ 484, the Court of Appeal ruled that the right to reside under Article 18 EC was not an unfettered right, that a parent could not claim a derivative right to reside by reason of a five-year-old child of that person being in primary education in the United Kingdom, and that a spouse (a Dutch national residing in the United Kingdom) who has not worked in the United Kingdom was not a worker under Community law.

CIS/3573/2005, decided by a Tribunal of Commissioners, concerned a Swedish national born in Somalia who had come to live in the United Kingdom. She had not worked in the United Kingdom, and claimed income support. The Tribunal of Commissioners said,

3.32

"31. Both the Treaty of Rome, as amended, and EEC Directive 90/364 make it entirely clear that national governments are entitled to restrict the right to residence of European Union nationals and to restrict any social assistance to them, even if they are, in fact, resident under a lawful right of entrance and no steps have been taken for their removal. Mr Knafler submitted that the reality of the situation is that no steps will ever be taken to remove the claimant as, even if she were removed, she would have an immediate right of re-entry. However, in our view having a right of re-entry is somewhat different to fulfilling conditions for social assistance."

A series of cases decided by a Tribunal of Commissioners (*CIS/3573/2005; CPC/2920/2005; CIS/2559/2005; CIS/2680/2005; and CH/2484/2005*) has determined that non-economically active nationals of the Member States (and of the EEA countries) do not acquire a right to reside under Community law and any discrimination which arises as a consequence of such nationals being required to establish a right to reside is objectively justified and proportionate. A memorandum (Memo DMG Vol 2 01/06) from the Department for Work and Pensions indicates that the changes consequent upon the entry into force of Directive 2004/38/EC (the "Citizenship Directive") do not alter the position. That proposition may be questionable, since it is based on the (unspoken) premise that the Citizenship Directive is purely a consolidating measure, when it is at least arguable that it develops the rights attached to Citizenship of the Union, and introduces a new Community right of permanent residence.

The decisions of the Tribunal of Commissioners have been largely upheld by the Court of Appeal in *Abdirahman v Secretary of State for Work and Pensions, Abdirahman v Leicester City Council and Secretary of State for Work and Pensions*, and *Ullusow v Secretary of State for Work and Pensions* [2007] EWCA Civ 657, reported as *R(IS) 8/07*. On the European points raised in argument, the Court of Appeal concluded that the rights claimed by the claimants were not within the scope of application of the EC Treaty, and so the prohibition of discrimination in Article 12 EC did not apply. They further held that the claimants had no "right to reside" under national law, and so neatly side-stepped the possible consequences of the decision of the Court of Justice in *Trojani*, which had ruled that equal treatment was required where a person had a right to reside in the country under national law (in that case, Trojani held a residence permit—of course, there is no direct equivalent under United Kingdom law). Of particular significance is that the Court of Appeal considered that the relevant Directive was Directive 90/364/EEC, which has been repealed by the Citizenship Directive. The Court of Appeal also ruled that the requirement that a claimant has the "right to reside" as a precondition to entitlement to benefit was not incompatible with European Community Law.

In *Zalewska v Department of Social Development*, Judgment of Northern Ireland Court of Appeal of May 9, 2007, the Northern Ireland Court of Appeal has dismissed an appeal from the decision of the Commissioner in *C 6/05-06*, in essence, to similar effect, though this case concerned the rights of nationals from some of the new Member States which joined in May 2004. The Court concluded that the Acts of Accession by which the new Member States joined the European Union permitted Member States to derogate from the Community provisions in Article 39 EC. During the transitional period, the rights of nationals of the designated new Member States arose solely under national law. The steps taken by the United Kingdom were reasonable and proportionate under the permitted derogations and so did not go beyond what was permitted. The House of Lords has upheld this decision in *Zalewska v Department for Social Development*, [2008] UKHL 67, reported as *R1/09 (IS)*. In a 3-2 decision, the House of Lords decided that the United Kingdom regulations establishing the regime for A8 nationals (requiring them to register their work and to have an uninterrupted period of 12 months in employment before becoming assimilated with workers under Article 39 EC) were not inconsistent with obligations arising under the EC Treaty. The difference of opinion related to the issue of proportionality. Baroness Hale and Lord Neuberger considered that the scheme adopted was disproportionate in that the complete disenfranchisement from the protection of social security went beyond the scope of the permissible derogation in the Treaty of Accession.

In *CIS/3875/2005* the Commissioner found that a French national could not claim a right to reside in Community law based on his being a recipient of services. It may be significant that the Commissioner did not consider the *Carpenter* case (C- 60/00 *Carpenter v Secretary of State for the Home Department* [2002] ECR I-6279). See also *CIS/3182/2005* which concerned a Dutch national who had also worked for about six weeks before giving up work because she was pregnant. The Commissioner concluded that she had no right to reside under the United Kingdom regulations. See also *CH/3314/2005* and *CIS/3315/2005* which concerned a person who claimed to be seeking work, but who had worked from mid-July to mid-October 2004; the Commissioner ruled that she nevertheless had no "right to reside" in the United Kingdom.

CH/1400/2006 concerned a woman who was a Slovenian national. She had entered the United Kingdom with her three children in September 2003. She began a postgraduate course in contemporary cinema culture in September 2004. In July 2005 she applied for housing benefit, and had appealed against its refusal. The tribunal had held that she had a right to reside under Community law as a person receiving services, namely the education on the course on which she was enrolled at the time of her claim. The Commissioner allowed the local authority's appeal on the grounds that the claimant was a person from abroad. In coming to that conclusion, he relied on Case 263/86 *Humbel* [1988] ECR 5365, and Case C- 109/92, *Wirth*, [1993] ECR I-6447 in concluding that the provision of education was not the provision of services. It is certainly possible to read paragraphs 18 and 19 of the Luxembourg Court's ruling in *Wirth* as *not applying* to the provision of a course in a University where a student is paying (as in this case) full cost fees because she has the status of an overseas student (some of the circumstances appear to have related to a period prior to accession to the Union by Slovenia). The Commissioner went on to consider whether the claimant had a right to reside as a student under the terms of the Students Directive (Directive 93/96/EEC) but concluded that this Directive required a student to have "sufficient resources to avoid becoming a burden on the social assistance system of the host Member State". However, in coming to that conclusion the Commissioner does not refer to Case C-184/99 *Grzelczyk* where the Court accepted that, in the case of students, what was required was an assurance of sufficient resources, which may be frustrated by the passage of time, and which does not preclude access to national assistance. The Commissioner also rejected a final argument based on Regulation 1408/71. It seems that no argument was presented based upon Case C-456/02 *Trojani* on the grounds that the claimant was lawfully resident in the United Kingdom, and on these grounds alone was entitled to equal treatment.

The Court of Appeal has upheld the Commissioner's decision in *CIS/2358/2006* in *Kaczmarek v Secretary of State for Work and Pensions,* [2008] EWCA Civ 1310; R(IS) 5/09; this was a case concerning a Polish student who had worked in the United Kingdom but had ceased work following the birth of a daughter. Two key issues arose for the Court of Appeal. Having regard to Article 12, does the reference to lawful residence "for a certain time" in the *Trojani* case give rise to an eligibility based on residence of unspecified but significant duration and of a type which evidences a degree of social integration in the host Member State? Maurice Kay LJ, giving the judgment of the Court, ruled that it did not, stating that "eligibility is primarily and more appropriately a matter for normative regulation. . . ." (para. 16). It is suggested that this may not be the view taken by the Luxembourg Court were the matter to be raised before them. Although there is much debate about the significance of the Luxembourg Court's decision in the *Trojani* case, it can certainly be read as indicating that lawful residence for a certain, and unspecified, time which evidences a degree of social integration does give rise to the right to be treated equally with nationals. It is also true that the old system of residence permits (abandoned in Directive 2004/38/EC) did not require lawful presence for a significant period in order to obtain it. It was obtainable through employment which might then come to an end through no fault of the permit holder after very short duration without prejudice to the rights of the permit holder under the residence permit. The permit was always regarded as merely being evidence of rights arising under the EC Treaty and not as conferring those rights.

The second question was whether, under Article 18 EC, it was disproportion-ate to deny a right of residence to a person in the position of the appellant. Having regard to what might be regarded as corresponding provisions in Directive 2004/38/ EC, Maurice Kay LJ concluded that he was not dealing with a lacuna in the scheme in the EC Treaty. It was accordingly not disproportionate to deny the appellant a right to reside.

In *CIS/408/2006*, the Commissioner said that, in his view, Directive 2004/38/ EC "sets a standard by reference to which proportionality must be judged for the purpose of Article 18(1) in a case arising before the directive came into force." (para.33). This case is an important authority on when a burden on the public purse will be regarded as reasonable, though the decision may turn on its rather special facts (which involved the rights of a Cameroon national married to a French national). The Commissioner summarises the position as follows:

"54. In my judgment, having regard to all these considerations, the claimant's wife's right of free movement for the purpose of working, guaranteed to her by Article 39 of the Treaty, would be infringed if she and the claimant were not rec-ognised as having the right to reside in the United Kingdom in the circumstances of this case. There was a lacuna in the directives in force at the time of the claim-ant's claim for income support and there is now a lacuna in Directive 2004/38/ EC but I am satisfied that the claimant and his wife retained rights of residence by virtue of Article 18(1) of the Treaty. Where a worker exercising rights under Article 39 of the Treaty in the United Kingdom is obliged to cease work and cannot be available for alternative work due to a need to care for his or her spouse who is a not a citizen of the Union but who is temporarily seriously disabled, they both retain rights of residence in the United Kingdom in the circumstances that arise in this case. Among those circumstances are the facts that—

(a) the disabled person had been exercising his Community law right to work in the United Kingdom and had become temporarily incapable of work;
(b) the disability had first manifested itself some considerable time after the disabled person had arrived in the United Kingdom, after he had married and after he had started work;
(c) the disabled person had qualified for free National Health Service treat-ment by virtue of his period of residence in the United Kingdom, which was at least in part by virtue of his right of residence under Community law, and was continuing to undergo such treatment while being cared for by his wife;

the recognition of the claimant's right of residence under Community law when he married had led to him losing the opportunity of establishing a right of resi-dence in his own right as a refugee.

Whether any of those circumstances is determinative can be decided when the need arises. (If point (a) is not determinative, it may follow that a person retains a right of residence while temporarily unable to be available for work due to the need to care for a dependant child, although, I would suggest, only where the child's need for care is temporary and is wholly due to the seriousness of the dis-ability rather than the child's age.)"

In *CIS/4010/2006*, which concerned a French woman who had lived in the United Kingdom for just over a year and had become pregnant, the Commissioner noted:

"9. The claimant argues that it is enough that she had been living in the United Kingdom for just over a year. She refers to *CIS/3182/2005* and relies on Articles 12 and 18 of the EC Treaty. I do not agree that a year's residence is long enough. When considering Article 18, regard must be had to the standard set by Directive 2004/38/EC under which a right of permanent residence giving access to social assistance to people who are not economically active is not generally acquired until after five years' residence, although there are specified exceptions, and, in the light of *Abdirahman v. Secretary of State for Work and Pensions* [2007] EWCA Civ 657, it is clear that Article 12 cannot be relied upon independently."

However, the Commissioner makes no reference to Article 24(2) of Directive 2004/38/EC which provides that "the host Member State shall not be obliged to confer entitlement to social assistance during the first three months of residence"; it remains to be seen what this provision means in the light of the other provisions of the Directive. That same provision also makes reference to entitlement to grant maintenance aid for studies only after a period of residence of five years. See *CIS/419/2007* which considered the position of a Polish student whose studies were in suspense, and who was found not to have a right of residence.

For an example of a judgment exploring some of the issues raised in the line of cases referred to in these annotations, including issues of student status and entitlement to reside as the parent of a child born in the United Kingdom, see the decision of the Court of Appeal in *Jeleniewicz v Secretary of State for Work and Pensions*, [2008] EWCA Civ 1163, reported as *R(IS) 3/09*, upholding the Commissioner's decision in *CIS/1545/2007*. The Court of Appeal concluded that the Commissioner was right to rule that a claimant, a Polish national, could not rely on a claimed right to reside by a young child (without any independent means of support) whose father (with whom the claimant was no longer living) was said to have a right to reside in the United Kingdom as a student. The case before the Commissioner was characterised by a lack of clear evidence on a number of key issues. The Court of Appeal noted that the claimed right to reside was "doubly indirect in law".

In *CIS/185/2008*, the Commissioner relied on art.18 in finding that the claimant—a Portuguese national—had a right to reside. The claimant had come to the United Kingdom in January 1998; she appears to have worked almost continuously until the summer of 2002. She then took maternity leave until April 2003, when she chose not to return to work. She claimed are received income support until 26 April 2004. She then returned to work until March 2007, when she decided to give up work to spend more time with her children. Her claim for income support was refused on the grounds that she had no "right to reside". She held a residence permit valid from 13 May 2000 until 13 May 2005. Taking account of the effect of the residence permit, the Commissioner concluded that the claimant had become permanently resident under the national legislation implementing Directive 2004/38/EC. He went on to consider whether a right of permanent residence could have been acquired by reason of the claimant's having worked continuously for five years before her maternity leave had ended. The Commissioner accepted that a right of permanent residence under the Directive could *not* have been acquired prior to its entry into force (an issue covered by the reference to the Luxembourg Court made by the Court of Appeal in *Secretary of State for Work and Pensions v Lassal*, [2009] EWCA Civ 157), but, referring to his decisions in *CIS/2358/2006* and *CIS/408/2006*, concludes that the claimant had, in any event, acquired a right of residence under Article 18 EC during the earlier period. He goes on to observe:

> "It does appear inconsistent with the concept of citizenship of the Union to deny a right of residence in a Member State to a person who has lived in that State for nine years and been a worker for eight of those years, including a continuous period of over five years. On the other hand, applying the approach I have taken in CIS/2358/2006 and CIS/408/2006, the question would arise whether it could be said that there was a lacuna in the Directive, in which case a national court or tribunal could apply Article 18(1) of the EC Treaty, or whether the Directive had deliberately been given the effect it had despite it appearing to be inconsistent with the EC Treaty, in which case a national court or tribunal would be obliged to refer the case to the European Court of Justice. In view of the conclusions I have already reached in favour of the claimant, it is unnecessary for me to consider that question further" (para. 22).

In *W (China) and X (China) v Secretary of State for the Home Department* [2006] EWCA Civ 1494, rather surprisingly, distinguished the decision of the Court of Justice in the *Chen* case (Case C-200/02, *Zhu and Chen*, [2004] ECR I-9925) in which it had held that third country nationals who were the parents of a Union citizen—in this case a baby born in Northern Ireland who thereby became entitled to Irish citizenship—had a right to reside in a Member State since otherwise the entitled of the child to reside would be rendered nugatory. The Court of Appeal indicated disagreement with the decision in the *Chen* case on the grounds that certain matters were not argued. In approaching the case in the way it did, the Court of Appeal focused exclusively on the technical requirements of Directive 90/364, giving it a priority which the Court of Justice had not, and arguably failed to give sufficient weight to the growing case law on rights flowing from Union citizenship provided in the Treaty.

3.32.1 *European Convention on Social and Medical Assistance ETS 14 of December 11, 1953*

As a postscript to the commentary on the right to reside and Article 18 EC, it should be noted that the Court of Appeal has also ruled that escape from the exclusion of persons from abroad (with its requirements for a right to reside and habitual residence) cannot arise under the European Convention on Social and Medical Assistance (ECSMA). In *Gulhanim Yesoliz v London Borough of Camden abd Secretary of State for Work and Pensions*, [2009] EWCA Civ 415, Pill LJ, delivering the judgment of the Court, said:

> 31. Whether the appellant has a right to reside in the United Kingdom depends on the construction of the appropriate statute or statutory instrument, in this case regulation 10 of the 2006 [Housing Benefit] Regulations. The appellant must establish that she has a right to reside. Otherwise she is a "person from abroad" and not entitled to housing benefit. Regulation 10(3B) specifies many categories of persons who are not "persons from abroad". It was, and was intended to be, a comprehensive list. The need, in this context, for a clear and specific classification is obvious.
>
> 32. The categories do not include nationals of states party to ECSMA. In those circumstances, such persons cannot be said to have a right to reside either because of their position in the schedule to the 2000 Regulations [SI 2000/636], or because the introduction of the concept of right to reside was primarily aimed at nationals of A8 states, or because there is no powerful reason in public policy for depriving them of the right to reside, or by reason of any combination of those factors. The inclusion of paragraph 4 in part 1 to the schedule to the 2000 Regulations, whatever its purpose, does not, in my view, carry for paragraph 4 persons the implication of entitlement to a right to reside.

Article 19 EC

3.33 **1.** Every citizen of the Union residing in a Member State of which he is not a national shall have the right to vote and to stand as a candidate at municipal elections in the Member State in which he resides, under the same conditions as nationals of that State. This right shall be exercised subject to detailed arrangements adopted by the Council, acting unanimously on a proposal from the Commission and after consulting the European Parliament; these arrangements may provide for derogations where warranted by problems specific to a Member State.

2. Without prejudice to Article 190(4) and to the provisions adopted for its implementation, every citizen of the Union residing in a Member State of which he is not a national shall have the right to vote and to stand as a candidate in elections to the European Parliament in the Member State in which he resides, under the same conditions as nationals of that State. This right shall be exercised subject to detailed arrangements adopted by the Council, acting unanimously on a proposal from the Commission and after consulting the European Parliament; these arrangements may provide for derogations where warranted by problems specific to a Member State.

Article 20 EC

Every citizen of the Union shall, in the territory of a third country in which the Member State of which he is a national is not represented, be entitled to protection by the diplomatic or consular authorities of any Member State, on the same conditions as the nationals of that State. Member States shall establish the necessary rules among themselves and start the international negotiations required to secure this protection.

3.34

Article 21 EC

Every citizen of the Union shall have the right to petition the European Parliament in accordance with Article 194.

Every citizen of the Union may apply to the Ombudsman established in accordance with Article 195.

Every citizen of the Union may write to any of the institutions or bodies referred to in this Article or in Article 7 in one of the languages mentioned in Article 314 and have an answer in the same language.

3.35

Article 22 EC

The Commission shall report to the European Parliament, to the Council and to the Economic and Social Committee every three years on the application of the provisions of this Part. This report shall take account of the development of the Union.

On this basis, and without prejudice to the other provisions of this Treaty, the Council, acting unanimously on a proposal from the Commission and after consulting the European Parliament, may adopt provisions to strengthen or to add to the rights laid down in this Part, which it shall recommend to the Member States for adoption in accordance with their respective constitutional requirements.

3.36

TITLE III

FREE MOVEMENT OF PERSONS, SERVICES AND CAPITAL

CHAPTER I

WORKERS

Article 39 EC

1. Freedom of movement for workers shall be secured within the Community.

2. Such freedom of movement shall entail the abolition of any discrimination based on nationality between workers of the Member States as regards employment, remuneration and other conditions of work and employment.

3.37

3. It shall entail the right, subject to limitations justified on grounds of public policy, public security or public health:
  (a) to accept offers of employment actually made;
  (b) to move freely within the territory of Member States for this purpose;
  (c) to stay in a Member State for the purpose of employment in accordance with the provisions governing the employment of nationals of that State laid down by law, regulation or administrative action;
  (d) to remain in the territory of a Member State after having been employed in that State, subject to conditions which shall be embodied in implementing regulations to be drawn up by the Commission.
4. The provisions of this Article shall not apply to employment in the public service.

GENERAL NOTE

3.38   The activities of the Community include an internal market characterised by the abolition, as between Member States, of obstacles to the free movement of goods, persons, services and capital: art.3 EC. Free movement of persons is generally regarded as encompassing workers, establishment, and services under arts 39 to 55. EC Directives (now replaced by Directive 2004/38/EC: the "Citizenship Directive" set out below in this Volume) grant rights of free movement for students and retired persons, provided they are not a burden on the social assistance schemes of the Member State of residence, and for persons of independent means. Article 18 (ex 8a) EC recognises these rights as incidents of European citizenship.

Beneficiaries of the rules are nationals of the Member States. Companies or firms must meet both a nationality and "residence" test; they must, under art.48 EC be formed under the law of a Member State and have their registered office, central administration or principal place of business within the Community. To claim the rights accorded by Community law, there must generally be some activity which engages the Community rules: Case 175/78 *Saunders* [1979] E.C.R. 1129; Case C-41/90 *Höfner v Macrotron* [1991] E.C.R. I-1979. So-called reverse discrimination is permitted. But the rights deriving from Community law can be pleaded against the State of which the person is a national if there is some connecting factor to the situations contemplated by Community law: Cases C-332/90 & C-132/93 *Volker Steen* [1992] E.C.R. I-341 and [1994] E.C.R. I-2715.

Community law defines a worker as someone obliged to provide services for another, in return for reward, and subject to the direction and control of that other person: Case 66/85 *Lawrie-Blum* [1986] E.C.R. 2121. Workers include those in low-paid, part-time work, provided that their work is effective and genuine and not on such a small scale as to be regarded as purely marginal and ancillary: Case 53/81 *Levin* [1982] E.C.R. 1035, though in applying this test account need only be taken of the pattern of work in the Member State of residence: Case C-357/89 *Raulin* [1992] E.C.R. I-1027. For a consideration of this line of cases by a national court, see *Mohamed Barry v London Borough of Southwark*, [2008] EWCA Civ 1440.

A person does not cease to be a worker for the purposes of art.39 simply by ceasing to be employed. So a German worker whose employment ended not long after it had started when she suffered a back injury did not, by that reason alone, cease to be a worker: *CIS/3890/2005*. A period of maternity leave does not interrupt self-employment: *CIS/1042/2008*, nor prevent a person from continuing to be treated as a worker: *CIS/0185/2008*. The appeal against *CIS/0185/2008* to the Court of Appeal as *Secretary of State for Work and Pensions v Dias*, [2009] EWCA Civ 807 has resulted in a further reference to the Luxembourg Court. See below at para.3.76. The same is true of a period of sick leave where the person's contract of employment nevertheless subsists: *BS v SSWP* [2009] UKUT 16 (AAC). Note that art.7(3)(a) of the Citizenship Directive expressly provides that a person temporarily unable to work by reason of illness or accident retains the status of a worker. Furthermore, art.17(1)(b) affords a right of permanent residence to those who become permanently incapacitated for work after a continuous period of residence in the host Member State for two years.

In case C-258/04 *Ioannidis*, [2005] ECR I-8275, the Court avoided ruling on the interpretation of arts 12, 17 and 18 EC, but did rule that it is contrary to art.39 EC and art.7(2) of reg.1612/68 for a member state to refuse to grant a tideover allowance to a national of another Member State seeking their first employment, who is not the dependent child of a migrant worker residing in the Member State granting the allowance, solely on the ground that the claimant completed their secondary education in another Member State.

Work or employment should be distinguished from establishment (governed by arts 43–48 EC) which includes self-employment, the setting up of agencies, branches and subsidiaries, and activities by companies or firms. A modest continuing presence will constitute establishment: Case 205/84 *Commission v Germany* [1986] E.C.R. 3755. Freedom of movement (governed by arts 49–55 EC) also exists for both providers and recipients of services: Case 186/87 *Cowan* [1989] E.C.R. 195. Services are activities provided for remuneration. Education principally financed by public funds is not a service: Case C-109/93 *Wirth* [1993] E.C.R. I-6447.

Where Community law applies, there is a prohibition on any form of discrimination based on nationality. A breach of Community law could flow from a non-discriminatory provision which has the effect of hindering free movement: Case C-415/93 *Bosman* [1995] E.C.R. I-4921.

Those within the Community provisions have a right of entry and residence in the Member State which are elaborated in Dir.2004/38/EC, reproduced at para.3.72 of this Volume. There are rights for both the economic actor and members of their families. Non-national spouses are treated as if they were nationals of a Member State: Case 131/85 *Gül* [1986] E.C.R. 1573.

Note that certain persons whose circumstances do not bring themselves within the Treaty rules on free movement of workers may have an independent right to reside in a Member State other than that of their nationality under art.18 EC, which was held in Case C-413/99 *Baumbast and R v Secretary of State for the Home Department*, Judgment of September 17, 2002, [2002] E.C.R. I-7091, to be directly effective as regards Mr Baumbast.

Work seekers enjoy a limited right of entry and residence, but not other social rights accorded to those who have found work: Case 316/85 *Lebon* [1987] E.C.R. 2811. Note that the citizenship line of cases discussed in the annotations to art.18 may require some reconsideration of the law as stated in *Lebon*. Those now in the position of Lebon who are lawfully resident in the host Member State and have the necessary link with the host Member State are entitled to be treated equally with nationals of that State even though they are not workers.

Failure to recognise qualifications, and regulation of the activity by the host State have generated much case law in relation to establishment and services. Equality of treatment with nationals is required, but where there are harmonising directives, those prevail. But even in the absence of harmonising directives, the equal treatment provisions of the Treaty give rise to an obligation to consider the equivalence of qualifications and schemes of regulation. In all cases there is an obligation to give reasons for any refusal to recognise qualifications, which must be susceptible of challenge in the Member State to test the compatibility of the decision with the requirements of Community law: Case 226/86 *Heylens* [1987] E.C.R. 4097.

National rules regulating economic activity can only be applied where they can be justified by imperative reasons relating to the public interest, where they apply equally to all persons engaged in that activity in the Member State, where there are no applicable safeguards applied in the home State, where the controls are objectively necessary, and where the measures imposed are the least restrictive to secure the legitimate objective: Case C-106/91 *Ramrath* [1992] E.C.R. I-3351.

The rights are subject to exceptions and limitations. Limitations may be imposed on grounds of public policy, public health and public security under arts 39(3), 46(1) and 55 EC, spelled out in Dir.2004/38/EC. The public policy ground requires the presence of a genuine and sufficiently serious threat to the requirements of public policy affecting one of the fundamental interests of society: Case 30/77 *Bouchereau* [1977] E.C.R. 1999. The genuineness of the limitation is tested by looking at the regulation of the objectionable conduct within the State: Joined Cases 115 & 116/81 *Adoui and Cornuaille* [1982] E.C.R. 1665.

Article 39(4) EC excludes employment in the public service. A functional test has been adopted for identifying such employment: it must involve the exercise of powers conferred by public law, and responsibility for safeguarding the interests of either central and local government: Case 149/79 *Commission v Belgium* [1980] E.C.R. 3881 and [1982] E.C.R. 1845. Articles 45 and 55 EC exclude from the rights of establishment and services activities connected with the exercise of official authority. Again a functional approach is adopted: Case 2/74 *Reyners* [1974] E.C.R. 631.

Whenever adverse decisions are taken in respect of entry and residence, there are due process guarantees in Chapter VI at Dir.2004/38/EC.

Enlargement, free movement and access to social security benefits

3.39   Ten new States joined the European Union on May 1, 2004, but there are detailed Treaties of Accession with these ten new Member States. In relation to the law of the internal market relating to workers, establishment and services, there will be transitional periods over which the full application of the Treaty rules will be phased in. The Europe Agreements, which paved the way for membership, did not give a right of access to the labour markets of the Member States for nationals of the applicant countries. The result is that virtually all nationals from the new Member States who were, prior to May 1, 2004, workers in the territories of the 15 existing Member States were there as a result of the application national immigration rules or of the provisions of bilateral agreements between the countries in question. Those lawfully resident in one of the Member States acquired rights under the Europe Agreements, and from May 1, 2004 will acquire rights under the EC Treaty.

In the past, it has been common to have transitional periods for the implementation. These have been followed by, or coupled with, a period during which safeguard measures may be taken if there is serious or persistent disruption of the labour market as a result of the exercise of the free movement rights. In the case of the accession of Spain and Portugal, a transitional period of seven to ten years for the free movement of workers was agreed, though the full operation of the Treaty provisions was achieved after six years. Transitional periods for the right of establishment, and freedom of movement to provide services have not been applied on past enlargements. This is largely accounted for by provisions in agreements prior to accession which have paved the way for free movement in these sectors. There are, however, special rules in relation to posting of workers from Germany and Austria.

The 2004 enlargement has been accompanied by a very high level of concern about the potential of labour migration to disturb the labour markets of some Member States. Such concerns have flowed from geographic proximity, (leading to a prediction that labour migration will be concentrated in the so-called "frontline" Member States) considerable variations in earnings levels, differential levels of unemployment, and a concern that there will be a greater propensity for labour migration than with earlier enlargements.

It is important to realise that the transitional period covers only the right of movement for the purposes of employment. There will be an immediate right to move for the purposes of study or residence, or establishment.

The arrangements for the 2004 enlargement are as follows. Until May 1, 2006, the current Member States may choose to apply national rules to the admission of workers from the new Member States (except Cyprus and Malta, whose nationals will enjoy full Community law rights from May 1, 2004). After this two-year period, the Commission will report on migration patterns and the current Member States will be required to define their position from May 1, 2006. The expectation is that some of the alarmist talk about labour migration will not materialise and that it will be possible to move to the application of Community rules on the free movement of workers. Those countries which did so would be able to apply safeguard measures for a period of three years in the event of their experiencing serious and unexpected disturbances of the labour market. On previous enlargements, similar safeguard measures have been available, but they have never been invoked.

From May 1, 2009, those current Member States still applying national rules would be called upon to open up their labour markets subject to the possibility of seeking safeguard measures to address serious and unexpected disturbances of the labour market. From May 1, 2011, Community rules will apply to movement of workers to all current Member States.

Free movement of workers who are nationals of the current Member States to the new Member States will take effect under the same transitional arrangements, though it is likely that some Member States will choose to apply a very liberal regime from the date of enlargement. There is a seven-year safeguard provision written into the Treaty of Accession for Malta.

Finally, there is a standstill clause, under which no Member State may introduce measures more restrictive than those in place immediately prior to May 1, 2004. There will also be a Community preference in the labour market for nationals of the new Member States over nationals from countries which are not members of the EU.

What does this mean for entitlement to benefits under UK law? The position will be complex, since the first task will be to determine the status of the claimant under the EC Treaty. Government concerns about so-called "benefit tourism" ("safeguarding the UK's social security system from the possibility of exploitation") have led to the introduction of amendments to the habitual residence test in order to avoid this phenomenon. These are to be found in the Social Security (Habitual Residence) Amendment Regulations 2004 (SI 2004/1232), which were made on April 28, 2004, laid before Parliament on April 30, 2004, and entered into force on May 1, 2004), which will need to be read with the Accession (Immigration and Worker Registration) Regulations 2004 (SI 2004/1219) which also entered into force on May 1, 2004. The regulations provide that for the purposes of entitlement to income support, income-based jobseeker's allowance, council tax benefit, housing benefit, and State pension credit, a person will not be treated as habitually resident in the UK, the Channel Islands, the Isle of Man or the Republic of Ireland—a condition of entitlement to these benefits—unless they have a "right to reside" in the UK, the Channel Islands, the Isle of Man or the Republic of Ireland.

The position in relation to nationals of the new Member States who joined in May 2009 would accordingly appear to be as follows:

1. A distinction is made between nationals of Cyprus and Malta, who will enjoy full Treaty rights from May 1, 2004 and nationals of the remaining eight Member States. Nationals of Cyprus and Malta will accordingly be treated in exactly the same way as nationals of existing EEA countries.

2. Claims to disability living allowance and attendance allowance for those resident in the United Kingdom will not be restricted. There is already a residence test for entitlement to these benefits.

3. For the eight countries of central and eastern Europe who are joining (referred to in DWP jargon as "A8 nationals"), there will be a distinction between those in employment and those in self-employment. The Government has indicated if those admitted under the right of establishment cease their occupational activity, they will not be eligible for benefit. That is a controversial proposition under Community law.

4. Access to means-tested benefits will only be available for those who meet the new habitual residence test which includes a requirement that the person enjoys a "right to reside". Those who do not meet the habitual residence test are treated as "persons from abroad" under the various regulations regardless of their nationality.

5. Nationals of the eight affected new Member States who come to the United Kingdom to work will be required to register with the Home Office as soon as they take up employment. The requirement to register will cease once the person has been working (periods of self-employment will not count as working) in the United Kingdom while holding a valid worker's registration scheme certificate for a continuous period of 12 months.

6. The combined effect of the habitual residence test and the requirement for registration would seem to mean that a registered worker who becomes unemployed before they have accrued their 12 months registration will not be eligible for benefit.

7. Access to contribution-based benefits will not be affected and entitlement will arise once the requisite contribution record has been established.

8. Co-ordination of social security under Regulation 1408/71 applies to all new Member States with effect from May 1, 2004.

The following background documentation sets out the thoughts behind the new legislation and the response of the Social Security Advisory Committee to it:

— Note from the Social Security Advisory Committee, March 23, 2004 on the Social Security (Habitual Residence) Amendment Regulations.

— Consultation on the Social Security (Habitual Residence) Amendment Regulations 2004: Supplemental Information to Explanatory Memorandum: The Draft Accession (Immigration and Worker Registration) Regulations 2004.

— Press release: April 30, 2004, Department for Work and Pensions: "Regulations to protect benefit system and welcome workers".

— The Report of the Social Security Advisory Committee dated April 22, 2004 on the proposals referred to them in respect of these Regulations, Cm. 6181.

Very similar arrangements have been made following the accession of Bulgaria and Romania on January 1, 2007, sometimes referred to as A2 nationals. These are set out in the commentary to Regulation 21AA to the Income Support (General) Regulations 1987 in Volume II.

The workers registration scheme for A8 nationals has been continued in effect beyond the initial transitional period until the end of April 2011: see the Accession (Immigration and Worker Registration) (Amendment) Regulations 2009 (SI 2009/982).

In *Secretary of State for the Home Department v Limbuela, Tesema and Adam,* [2004] EWCA Civ 540, the Court of Appeal ruled that the refusal to provide State support for three asylum seekers who had not applied for asylum within three days of their arrival in the United Kingdom under s.55 of the Nationality, Immigration and Asylum Act 2002 engaged their Convention rights under Article 3. The appeal of the Secretary of State against the decision of the Court of Appeal has been dismissed by a unanimous House of Lords, [2005] UKHL 66. For a discussion of the potential impact of the new rules on A8 nationals and some issues relating to their compatibility with Community law, see *R. (on the application of H and D) v Secretary of State for Work and Pensions* [2004] EWHC 1097 Admin. This is the decision of Collins J on the application for judicial review of the new regulations. Collins J dismissed the application in so far as it related to compatibility with Community law since he regarded the matter as covered by the derogation from the full application of the provisions on the free movement of workers. Collins J refers to what was at the time the pending appeal in *Limbuela* as possibly being determinative of the human rights arguments raised in the application.

Note that the relevant current regulations relating to worker authorisation and worker registration are The Accession (Immigration and Worker Authorisation) Regulations 2006 (SI 2006/3317) as amended by SI 2007/475 and SI 2007/3012.

In *CJSA/1475/2006* the Commissioner addressed some important questions on a person's position as a worker and as a work seeker, and made the following statements in his decision:

"13. The Secretary of State also concedes that a claimant who satisfies the conditions of entitlement to jobseeker's allowance set out in section 1(1) of the Jobseekers Act 1995, which include being available for employment, entering into a jobseeker's agreement and actively seeking employment, will satisfy the *Antonissen* test of seeking employment and having genuine chances of being engaged in employment. Moreover, in this particular case, Mr Kolinsky conceded that the *Antonissen* test was satisfied in respect of the period from 9 September, 2005 and he supported the claimant's appeal in respect of that period.

14. I accept the Secretary of State's concessions. The "right to reside" test imposed by reg.85(4B) does not, in practice, provide an additional hurdle for citizens of the European Union claiming jobseeker's allowance, save where there is a derogation from the usual rules. . . ."

However, in *CIS/2364/2006* the same Commissioner said:

"6. I think I was wrong to state in paragraph 14 of *CJSA/1475/2006* that, in the light of *Antonissen*, "the 'right to reside' test . . . does not, in practice, provide an additional hurdle for citizens of the European Union claiming jobseeker's allowance, save where there is a derogation from the usual rules" and I may have inaccurately recorded the Secretary of State's concession in paragraph 13. I accept that some people may be available for work and be actively seeking employment but not have a genuine chance of being engaged because, for instance, they have an insufficient command of English or Welsh for the type of job they are seeking or, perhaps, they have settled in an area where there is a particularly high level of unemployment and a dearth of jobs, so that the requirement to have a genuine chance of being engaged can be an additional hurdle. However, that additional hurdle will not often be significant and I suggest that the proportion of cases in which it will be right to reject a claim for jobseeker's allowance on the ground that the claimant does not have a right of residence rather than on the ground that the claimant does not satisfy one or more of the conditions in section 1(2) of the Jobseekers Act 1995—because, for instance, he or she is not genuinely available for, or is not actively seeking, employment—may be relatively small. It is true that a person who is not genuinely available for, or is not actively seeking, employment may not have a right of residence, but, in such a case, it is not helpful to reject the claim solely on the ground of the lack of a right of residence without reference to the underlying ground that would apply to British citizens as well as other EEA nationals.

7. The present case, of course, arises on a claim for income support and there is no requirement that a claimant of income support be available for work. However, in the light of my decision in *CH/3314/2005*, the Secretary of State concedes that a person claiming income support is not precluded from seeking employment and therefore, until regulation 21 of the 1987 Regulations was amended with effect from 30 April 2006, was not precluded from establishing a right of residence as a workseeker. When granting leave, Mr Commissioner Jacobs said that, in the light of *CH/3314/2005*, he understood the issue in this case to be whether the claimant was seeking "genuine and effective" employment rather than work that was marginal and ancillary. The Secretary of State has submitted that that issue arises only in the context of deciding whether a person has obtained the status of "worker" and is not relevant where reliance is placed on *Antonissen*. I disagree. It seems obvious that the rationale behind *Antonissen* is that an EEA national must be given a proper opportunity to become a "worker" in the host state and the decision does not, in my view, require Member States to recognise a right of residence in a case where a person is not seeking work that would be "genuine and effective". However, this has probably ceased to be a live issue because, since 30 April 2006, a person claiming a right of residence as a jobseeker (the term used both in the amended 1987 Regulations and in the 2006 Regulations conferring rights of residence) is not entitled to income support and must claim jobseeker's allowance instead and, even when a jobseeker has responsibilities as a carer, he or she must be seeking employment amounting to at least 16 hours a week to qualify

for jobseeker's allowance. Employment to such an extent can generally be taken to be "effective". The somewhat complicated test I devised in *CH/3314/2005* was necessary only because the claimant had claimed income support, rather than jobseeker's allowance, and had declared that she was available to work for only 15 hours a week, although in the event I did find that the claimant's earning capacity was such that she could be taken to have been seeking effective employment.

8. As the present case also arises on a claim for income support made before 30 April 2006, I agree with Mr Commissioner Jacobs that the issues that arose in CH/3314/2005 potentially arise here too. However, the Secretary of State concedes on the facts that the claimant had a right of residence. In particular, the Secretary of State does not seek to challenge the tribunal's finding that the claimant was looking for work and, although there is some evidence that she had language difficulties, she had found work by the time the case came before the tribunal and, in the light of that evidence, the Secretary of State concedes that she also had a genuine chance of being engaged in employment at the time of her claim. The first job the claimant obtained was for only a few hours a week, but there is no evidence that she had not been looking for work for considerably more hours a week and, given the lengthy history of this case, I do not consider it necessary to go behind the Secretary of State's concession that the claimant had a right of residence."

Article 40 EC

3.40   The Council shall, acting in accordance with the procedure referred to in Article 251 and after consulting the Economic and Social Committee, issue directives or make regulations setting out the measures required to bring about freedom of movement for workers, as defined in Article 39, in particular:

(a) by ensuring close cooperation between national employment services;

(b) by abolishing those administrative procedures and practices and those qualifying periods in respect of eligibility for available employment, whether resulting from national legislation or from agreements previously concluded between Member States, the maintenance of which would form an obstacle to liberalisation of the movement of workers;

(c) by abolishing all such qualifying periods and other restrictions provided for either under national legislation or under agreements previously concluded between Member States as imposed on workers of other Member States conditions regarding the free choice of employment other than those imposed on workers of the State concerned;

(d) by setting up appropriate machinery to bring offers of employment into touch with applications for employment and to facilitate the achievement of a balance between supply and demand in the employment market in such a way as to avoid serious threats to the standard of living and level of employment in the various regions and industries.

Article 41 EC

3.41   Member States shall, within the framework of a joint programme, encourage the exchange of young workers.

Article 42 EC

3.42   The Council shall, acting in accordance with the procedure referred to in Article 251, adopt such measures in the field of social security as are necessary to provide freedom of movement for workers; to this end, it shall make arrangements to secure for migrant workers and their dependants:

  (a) aggregation, for the purpose of acquiring and retaining the right to benefit and of calculating the amount of benefit, of all periods taken into account under the laws of the several countries;

  (b) payment of benefits to persons resident in the territories of Member States.

The Council shall act unanimously throughout the procedure referred to in Article 251.

GENERAL NOTE

Article 42 EC provides for the co-ordination of social security rules in the Member   **3.43** States (extended to the EEA countries by the EEA Agreement, and to Switzerland under the Swiss Agreement) in order to minimise a potential barrier to the free movement of workers. Co-ordination requires co-operation between the Member States to provide interchange between different national social security systems. The Court of Justice has frequently drawn attention to the distinction between harmonisation and co-ordination and noted that the substantive and procedural differences between the social security systems of the Member States remain unaffected by art.42 and its secondary legislation: Case 41/84 *Pinna* [1986] E.C.R. 1 at 24–5. But it has also been established that those exercising the right of freedom of movement should not lose advantages in the field of social security; this has come to be known as the *Petroni* principle: Case 24/75 *Petroni* [1975] E.C.R. 1149, para.13 of judgment.

Three general principles emerge from the complex rules of co-ordination which can be found in reg.1408/71 and the case law:

1. A national of a Member State (or EEA country or Switzerland) is not to be disqualified from entitlement to benefits on the grounds of nationality or on a change of country or residence within the European Union (or EEA).

2. A national of a Member State (or EEA country or Switzerland) may become entitled to a benefit by having contributions or qualifying periods of employment in one Member State (or EEA country or Switzerland) aggregated with those arising in another Member State (or EEA country or Switzerland).

3. A national of a Member State (of EEA country or Switzerland) should not be better off in relation to entitlement to benefits by reason of his or her exercise of rights to move freely between Member States (or EEA countries or Switzerland).

Note that Regulation 1408/71 is due to be replaced by the "simplified" social security regulation, probably some time in 2010: see Regulation 883/2004/EC of April 29, 2004 on the coordination of social security systems [2004] OJ L200/1, correcting OJ L166/1.

SECTION 4

THE COURT OF JUSTICE

Article 220 EC

[[1]] The Court of Justice and the Court of First Instance, each within its   **3.44** jurisdiction, shall ensure that in the interpretation and application of this Treaty the law is observed.

In addition, judicial panels may be attached to the Court of First Instance under the conditions laid down in Article 225a in order to exercise, in certain specific areas, the judicial competence laid down in this Treaty.]

AMENDMENT

1. Treaty of Nice, art.2(26) (February 1, 2003).

Article 225 EC

3.45   [¹ **1.** The Court of First Instance shall have jurisdiction to hear and determine at first instance actions or proceedings referred to in Articles 230, 232, 235, 236 and 238, with the exception of those assigned to a judicial panel and those reserved in the Statute for the Court of Justice. The Statute may provide for the Court of First Instance to have jurisdiction for other classes of action or proceeding.

Decisions given by the Court of First Instance under this paragraph may be subject to a right of appeal to the Court of Justice on points of law only, under the conditions and within the limits laid down by the Statute.

2. The Court of First Instance shall have jurisdiction to hear and determine actions or proceedings brought against decisions of the judicial panels set up under Article 225a.

Decisions given by the Court of First Instance under this paragraph may exceptionally be subject to review by the Court of Justice, under the conditions and within the limits laid down by the Statute, where there is a serious risk of the unity or consistency of Community law being affected.

3. The Court of First Instance shall have jurisdiction to hear and determine questions referred for a preliminary ruling under Article 234, in specific areas laid down by the Statute.

Where the Court of First Instance considers that the case requires a decision of principle likely to affect the unity or consistency of Community law, it may refer the case to the Court of Justice for a ruling.

Decisions given by the Court of First Instance on questions referred for a preliminary ruling may exceptionally be subject to review by the Court of Justice, under the conditions and within the limits laid down by the Statute, where there is a serious risk of the unity or consistency of Community law being affected.]

AMENDMENT

1. Treaty of Nice, art.2(31), (February 1, 2003).

[¹*Article 225a EC*

3.46   The Council, acting unanimously on a proposal from the Commission and after consulting the European Parliament and the Court of Justice or at the request of the Court of Justice and after consulting the European Parliament and the Commission, may create judicial panels to hear and determine at first instance certain classes of action or proceeding brought in specific areas.

The decision establishing a judicial panel shall lay down the rules on the organisation of the panel and the extent of the jurisdiction conferred upon it.

Decisions given by judicial panels may be subject to a right of appeal on points of law only or, when provided for in the decision establishing the panel, a right of appeal also on matters of fact, before the Court of First Instance.

Article 225a

The members of the judicial panels shall be chosen from persons whose independence is beyond doubt and who possess the ability required for appointment to judicial office. They shall be appointed by the Council, acting unanimously.

The judicial panels shall establish their Rules of Procedure in agreement with the Court of Justice. Those Rules shall require the approval of the Council, acting by a qualified majority.

Unless the decision establishing the judicial panel provides otherwise, the provisions of this Treaty relating to the Court of Justice and the provisions of the Statute of the Court of Justice shall apply to the judicial panels.]

AMENDMENT

1. Inserted by the Treaty of Nice, art.2(32) (February 1, 2003).

Article 226 EC

If the Commission considers that a Member State has failed to fulfil an obligation under this Treaty, it shall deliver a reasoned opinion on the matter after giving the State concerned the opportunity to submit its observations.   3.47

If the State concerned does not comply with the opinion within the period laid down by the Commission, the latter may bring the matter before the Court of Justice.

Article 227 EC

A Member State which considers that another Member State has failed to fulfil an obligation under this Treaty may bring the matter before the Court of Justice.   3.48

Before a Member State brings an action against another Member State for an alleged infringement of an obligation under this Treaty, it shall bring the matter before the Commission.

The Commission shall deliver a reasoned opinion after each of the States concerned has been given the opportunity to submit its own case and its observations on the other party's case both orally and in writing.

If the Commission has not delivered an opinion within three months of the date on which the matter was brought before it, the absence of such opinion shall not prevent the matter from being brought before the Court of Justice.

Article 228 EC

1. If the Court of Justice finds that a Member State has failed to fulfil an obligation under this Treaty, the State shall be required to take the necessary measures to comply with the judgment of the Court of Justice.   3.49

2. If the Commission considers that the Member State concerned has not taken such measures it shall, after giving that State the opportunity to submit its observations, issue a reasoned opinion specifying the points on which the Member State concerned has not complied with the judgment of the Court of Justice.

If the Member State concerned fails to take the necessary measures to comply with the Court's judgment within the time limit laid down by the Commission, the latter may bring the case before the Court of Justice. In so doing it shall specify the amount of the lump sum or penalty payment to be paid by the Member State concerned which it considers appropriate in the circumstances.

If the Court of Justice finds that the Member State concerned has not complied with its judgment it may impose a lump sum or penalty payment on it.

This procedure shall be without prejudice to Article 227.

Article 230 EC

3.50

[¹ The Court of Justice shall review the legality of acts adopted jointly by the European Parliament and the Council, of acts of the Council, of the Commission and of the ECB, other than recommendations and opinions, and of acts of the European Parliament intended to produce legal effects vis-à-vis third parties.

It shall for this purpose have jurisdiction in actions brought by a Member State, the European Parliament, the Council or the Commission on grounds of lack of competence, infringement of an essential procedural requirement, infringement of this Treaty or of any rule of law relating to its application, or misuse of powers.

The Court of Justice shall have jurisdiction under the same conditions in actions brought by the Court of Auditors and by the ECB for the purpose of protecting their prerogatives.

Any natural or legal person may, under the same conditions, institute proceedings against a decision addressed to that person or against a decision which, although in the form of a regulation or a decision addressed to another person, is of direct and individual concern to the former.

The proceedings provided for in this article shall be instituted within two months of the publication of the measure, or of its notification to the plaintiff, or, in the absence thereof, of the day on which it came to the knowledge of the latter, as the case may be.]

AMENDMENT

1. Treaty of Nice, art.2(34) (February 1, 2003).

Article 231 EC

3.51

If the action is well founded, the Court of Justice shall declare the act concerned to be void.

In the case of a regulation, however, the Court of Justice shall, if it considers this necessary, state which of the effects of the regulation which it has declared void shall be considered as definitive.

Article 234 EC

The Court of Justice shall have jurisdiction to give preliminary rulings concerning:

(a) the interpretation of this Treaty;

(b) the validity and interpretation of acts of the institutions of the Community and of the ECB;

(c) the interpretation of the statutes of bodies established by an act of the Council, where those statutes so provide.

Where such a question is raised before any court or tribunal of a Member State, that court or tribunal may, if it considers that a decision on the question is necessary to enable it to give judgment, request the Court of Justice to give a ruling thereon.

Where any such question is raised in a case pending before a court or tribunal of a Member State against whose decisions there is no judicial remedy under national law, that court or tribunal shall bring the matter before the Court of Justice.

3.52

GENERAL NOTE

Any national court or tribunal can refer questions on the interpretation of the EC Treaty, and on the validity and interpretation of Community legislation to the Court of Justice under art.234 EC. The objective of the procedure is a partnership between national courts and tribunals and the Court of Justice to ensure the uniform application in all Member States of Community law.

3.53

Courts other than final appeal courts have a *discretion* to make a reference, whereas final appeal courts have a *duty* to refer questions for consideration by the Court of Justice where answers to those questions are necessary to enable the national court to determine the question before it.

The effect of a court or tribunal seeking a ruling is that the national proceedings stand adjourned pending the receipt of the ruling of the Court of Justice. The case is then relisted for determination before the national court or tribunal in the light of the ruling of the Court of Justice on the point of Community law. The Court of Justice is careful not to determine the point arising under national law.

It is an error of law for a tribunal to fail to address a point of European Community law raised in the course of an appeal: *R(SB)6/91*, para.5, and *R(S)2/93*.

Care should be taken whenever a tribunal is called upon to decide an issue involving a national of an EEA country. If a case involves a national of an EEA country, inquiry should be made to determine whether the provisions of European Community law apply to that person and assist in qualifying them for benefit. Failure to do so is an error of law: *CIS/771/1997*.

The Court of Justice has stressed in Case 166/73 *Rheinmühlen* [1974] E.C.R. 33 at 38, that the objective of the preliminary ruling procedure is a partnership between national courts and tribunals and the Court of Justice with a view to ensuring the uniform application of Community law in all the Member States.

Under the procedure, the Court of Justice advises on the meaning of Community law put to it by a national court or tribunal. The discretion as to whether a reference is made is a wide one, and may be exercised by the court or tribunal of its own notion or on application for the court or tribunal to consider doing so by the parties. The leading case of the Court of Justice on the exercise of the discretion to refer is Joined Cases 36 & 71/80 *Irish Creamery Milk Suppliers Association v Ireland* [1981] E.C.R. 735. The principles laid down in this case have been approved in Case 72/83 *Campus Oil v Minister for Industry and Energy* [1984] E.C.R. 2727; and Case 14/86 *Pretore di Salo v Persons Unknown* [1987] E.C.R. 2545. The following points emerge from this line of cases:

1. It is for the national court or tribunal to decide at what stage of proceedings it is appropriate for a preliminary ruling to be requested.

2. In order to assist the Court of Justice, it is essential for the national court or tribunal to define the legal context in which the reference is made.

3. This suggests that in some cases it might well be appropriate for the facts in the case to be established and for questions of purely national law to be settled at the time of the reference.

4. Attempts to fetter or limit the discretion of the national court or tribunal are inconsistent with Community law.

5. The discretion to refer is that of the national court or tribunal and not that of the parties.

Practice in English courts and tribunals has been influenced by the guidelines expressed by Lord Denning in *Bulmer v Bollinger (No.2)* [1974] Ch 401, but these are not binding on any court or tribunal and aspects of them are inconsistent with statements of the Court of Justice. Distilling a considerable body of case law and adding points specific to the social security jurisdictions, the following factors are relevant in the determination by a tribunal or Commissioner of the exercise of the discretion to refer questions to the Court of Justice, namely whether:

1. a serious point of Community law arises in the case which has been fully argued by the parties;

2. the relevant facts have been found or are substantially agreed;

3. the point of law will be substantially determinative of the case;

4. there is any Community authority precisely or closely in point;

5. there is any Commissioners' authority addressing the point of Community law; and

6. it seems certain that at some stage in the life of the case, it will have to be referred to the Court of Justice.

The expense and delay caused by an inappropriate reference will be issues every adjudicating body will consider. The factors set out above are consistent with Community law on the exercise of the discretion to refer. The absence of full argument on the Community point—from both the claimant and the Secretary of State—(and full argument is likely to be rare in tribunals) suggests that caution should be the order of the day before the First-tier tribunals. On the other hand, tribunals should not be inhibited from making a reference if the relevant facts have been found, if the point has been fully argued, if the tribunal concludes that the appeal turns on the proper interpretation of a point of Community law, if there is no relevant authority which suggests that the question of interpretation is free from doubt, and if it seems certain that at some stage a reference will need to be made to resolve the question. It is probably fair to say that such circumstances will not be common place in the First-tier tribunals.

The Court of Justice has itself issued guidance for national courts and tribunals on the making of references and this is reproduced at the end of the annotations to this Article.

Although there are prescribed forms of order for references from the High Court, the Court of Justice does not make any formal requirements as to form: see CPR r.68. The adjudicating body is responsible for drafting the questions it wishes to refer. The question should be couched in terms which pose a general question of law rather than the specific issues raised in the case. The questions should be self-contained and self-explanatory, since they will be notified to the Commission, Council and the Member States under art.20 of the Statute of the Court. These may choose within two months of the notification to submit written observations on the questions raised. Though the only requirement is the formulation of questions for the Court of Justice, it will be helpful to the Court to provide the following further information:

1. the facts of the case;

2. the relevant provisions of United Kingdom law;

3. the relevant provisions of Community law;

4. a summary of the contentions of the parties on the question or questions referred;

5. if necessary, the reasons why the answers to the questions referred are considered necessary to decide the case.

A ruling given by the Court of Justice is binding on the national court or tribunal as to the interpretation of the Community law in question. It will also bind future courts or tribunal determining similar questions: see s.3(1), European Communities Act 1972.

In *CIS/501/1993* the Commissioner had to consider whether he had jurisdiction to consider the validity of a reference to the Court of Justice made by a tribunal. The Commissioner, of course, only has jurisdiction when there is a "final" decision of a tribunal. The question was whether a reference could be regarded as a final decision. The Commissioner relied on RSC Ord.114, r.6 and *R. v International Stock Exchange of the United Kingdom and the Republic of Ireland Ltd Ex p. Else (1982) Ltd* [1993] Q.B. 534 in holding that an order referring questions to the Court of Justice is to be treated as a final decision against which appeal will lie. He then set aside the decision to refer since the answer to the question posed was clearly not "necessary" to enable the tribunal to resolve the issue before it. The Commissioner also makes reference to the guidelines set down by the Court of Appeal in *Bulmer*. Those guidelines are, as noted above, not wholly consistent with statements made by the Court of Justice and care should be taken in relying exclusively upon them without referring to the relevant decisions of the Court of Justice and subsequent decisions of the United Kingdom courts: see generally A. Arnull, "References to the European Court" (1990) 15 E.L.Rev. 375.

The Court of Justice's Information Note [2005] OJ C143/1 reads as follows:

Information note on references from national courts for a preliminary ruling

1. The preliminary ruling system is a fundamental mechanism of European Union law aimed at enabling national courts to ensure uniform nterpretation and application of that law in all the Member States.   **3.54**

2. The Court of Justice of the European Communities has jurisdiction to give preliminary rulings on the interpretation of the law of the European Union and on the validity of acts of secondary legislation. That general jurisdiction is conferred on it by Article 234 of the EC Treaty and, in certain specific cases, by other provisions.

3. The preliminary ruling procedure being based on cooperation between the Court and national courts, it may be helpful, in order to ensure that that cooperation is effective, to provide the national courts with the following information.

4. This practical information, which is in no way binding, is intended to provide guidance to national courts as to whether it is appropriate to make a reference for a preliminary ruling and, should they proceed, to help them formulate and submit questions to the Court.

The role of the Court in the preliminary ruling procedure

3.55   5. Under the preliminary ruling procedure, the Court's role is to give an interpretation of Community law or to rule on its validity, not to apply that law to the factual situation underlying the main proceedings, which is the task of the national court. It is not for the Court to decide issues of fact raised in the main proceedings or to resolve differences of opinion on the interpretation or application of rules of national law.

6. In ruling on the interpretation of validity of Community law, the Court makes every effort to give a reply which will be of assistance in resolving the dispute, but it is for the referring court to draw the appropriate conclusions from that reply, if necessary by disapplying the rule of national law in question.

The decision to submit a question to the Court

The originator of the question

3.56   7. Under Article 234 of the EC Treaty and Article 150 of the EAEC Treaty, any court or tribunal of a Member State, in so far as it is called upon to give a ruling in proceedings intended to arrive at a decision of a judicial nature, may as a rule refer a question to the Court for a preliminary ruling. The status of that court or tribunal is interpreted by the Court as a self-standing concept of Community law.

8. However, in the specific sphere of acts of the institutions in Title IV of Part Three of the EC Treaty on visa, asylum, immigration and other policies related to free movement of persons — in particular jurisdiction and the recognition and enforcement of judicial decisions — a reference may be made only by courts or tribunals against the decisions of which there is no appeal, in accordance with Article 68 of the EC Treaty.

9. Likewise, under Article 35 of the Treaty on European Union, acts of the institutions in the area of police and judicial cooperation in criminal matters may be the subject of a reference for a preliminary ruling only from courts in the Member States which have accepted the jurisdiction of the Court, each Member State specifying whether that right of referral to the Court applies to any court or tribunal of that State or only to those against the decisions of which there is no appeal.

10. It is not necessary for the parties in the case to raise the question; the national court may do so of its own motion.

References on interpretation

3.57   11. Any court or tribunal may refer a question to the Court on the interpretation of a rule of Community law if it considers it necessary to do so in order to resolve a dispute brought before it.

12. However, courts or tribunals against whose decisions there is no judicial remedy under national law must, as a rule, refer such a question to the Court, unless the Court has already ruled on the point (and there is no new context that raises any serious doubt as to whether that case-law may be applied), or unless the correct interpretation of the rule of Community law is obvious.

13. Thus, a court or tribunal against whose decisions there is a judicial remedy may, in particular when it considers that sufficient clarification is given by the case-law of the Court, itself decide on the correct interpretation of Community law and its application to the factual situation before it.

However, a reference for a preliminary ruling may prove particularly useful, at an appropriate stage of the proceedings, when there is a new question of interpretation of general interest for the uniform application of Community law throughout the Union, or where the existing case-law does not appear to be applicable to a new set of facts.

14. It is for the national court to explain why the interpretation sought is necessary to enable it to give judgment.

References on determination of validity

15. Although national courts may reject pleas raised before them challenging the validity of Community acts, the Court has exclusive jurisdiction to declare such acts invalid.

16. All national courts must therefore refer a question to the Court when they have doubts about the validity of a Community act, stating the reasons for which they consider that the Community act may be invalid.

17. If a national court has serious doubts about the validity of a Community act on which a national measure is based, it may exceptionally suspend application of that measure temporarily or grant other interim relief with respect to it. It must then refer the question of validity to the Court of Justice, stating the reasons for which it considers the Community act to be invalid.

The stage at which to submit a question for a preliminary ruling

18. A national court or tribunal may refer a question to the Court of Justice for a preliminary ruling as soon as it finds that a ruling on the point or points of interpretation or validity is necessary to enable it to give judgment; it is the national court which is in the best position to decide at what stage of the proceedings such a question should be referred.

19. It is, however, desirable that a decision to seek a preliminary ruling should be taken when the proceedings have reached a stage at which the national court is able to define the factual and legal context of the question, so that the Court has available to it all the information necessary to check, where appropriate, that Community law applies to the main proceedings. It may also be in the interests of justice to refer a question for a preliminary ruling only after both sides have been heard.

The form of the reference for a preliminary ruling

20. The decision by which a national court or tribunal refers a question to the Court of Justice for a preliminary ruling may be in any form allowed by national law as regards procedural steps. It must however be borne in mind that it is that document which serves as the basis of the proceedings before the Court and that it must therefore contain such information as will enable the latter to give a reply which is of assistance to the national court. Moreover, it is only the actual reference for a preliminary ruling which is notified to the parties entitled to submit observations to the Court, in particular the Member States and the institutions, and which is translated.

21. Owing to the need to translate the reference, it should be drafted simply, clearly and precisely, avoiding superfluous detail.

22. A maximum of about ten pages is often sufficient to set out in a proper manner the context of a reference for a preliminary ruling. The order for reference must be succinct but sufficiently complete and must contain all

3.58

3.59

3.60

the relevant information to give the Court and the parties entitled to submit observations a clear understanding of the factual and legal context of the main proceedings. In particular, the order for reference must:

— include a brief account of the subject-matter of the dispute and the relevant findings of fact, or, at least, set out the factual situation on which the question referred is based;

— set out the tenor of any applicable national provisions and identify, where necessary, the relevant national case-law, giving in each case precise references (e.g. page of an official journal or specific law report, with any internet reference);

— identify the Community provisions relevant to the case as accurately as possible;

— explain the reasons which prompted the national court to raise the question of the interpretation or validity of the Community provisions, and the relationship between those provisions and the national provisions applicable to the main proceedings;

— include, where appropriate, a summary of the main arguments of the parties.

In order to make it easier to read and refer to the document, it is helpful if the different points or paragraphs of the order for reference are numbered.

23. Finally, the referring court may, if it considers itself to be in a position to do so, briefly state its view on the answer to be given to the questions referred for a preliminary ruling.

24. The question or questions themselves should appear in a separate and clearly identified section of the order for reference, generally at the beginning or the end. It must be possible to understand them without referring to the statement of the grounds for the reference, which however provides the necessary background for a proper assessment.

The effects of the reference for a preliminary ruling on the national proceedings

3.61   25. A reference for a preliminary ruling in general calls for the national proceedings to be stayed until the Court has given its ruling.

26. However, the national court may still order protective measures, particularly in a reference on determination of validity (see point 17 above).

Costs and legal aid

3.62   27. Proceedings for a preliminary ruling before the Court are free of charge and the Court does not rule on the costs of the parties to the main proceedings; it is for the national court to rule on those costs.

28. If a party has insufficient means and where possible under national rules, the national court may grant that party legal aid to cover the costs, including those of lawyers' fees, which it incurs before the Court. The Court itself may also grant legal aid.

Communication between the national court and the Court of Justice

3.63   29. The order for reference and the relevant documents (including, where applicable, the case file or a copy of the case file) are to be sent by the national court directly to the Court of Justice, by registered post (addressed to the Registry of the Court of Justice of the European Communities, L-2925 Luxembourg, telephone + 352-4303-1).

30. The Court Registry will stay in contact with the national court until a ruling is given, and will send it copies of the procedural documents.

31. The Court will send its ruling to the national court. It would welcome information from the national court on the action taken upon its ruling in the national proceedings and, where appropriate, a copy of the national court's final decision.

PART VI

GENERAL AND FINAL PROVISIONS

Article 308 EC

If action by the Community should prove necessary to attain, in the course of the operation of the common market, one of the objectives of the Community and this Treaty has not provided the necessary powers, the Council shall, acting unanimously on a proposal from the Commission and after consulting the European Parliament, take the appropriate measures.

3.64

GENERAL NOTE

This provision is sometime referred to as the "reserve power", since it gives the Community a power to take action in the absence of a specific authority to do so in the Treaty where action is necessary to attain one of the objectives of the Community. The power has been used in relation to certain social security measures, for example, Dir.79/7 (see below).

3.65

Regulation (EEC) No 1612/68 of the Council of 15 October 1968 on Freedom of Movement for Workers within the Community

[1968] O.J. L257/2

TITLE I *OMITTED*

TITLE II:

EMPLOYMENT AND EQUALITY OF TREATMENT

Article 7

1. A worker who is a national of a Member State may not, in the territory of another Member State, be treated differently from national workers by reason of his nationality in respect of any conditions of employment and work, in particular as regards remuneration, dismissal, and should he become unemployed, reinstatement or reemployment;

3.66

2. He shall enjoy the same social and tax advantages as national workers.

3. He shall also, by virtue of the same right and under the same conditions as national workers, have access to training in vocational schools and retraining centres.

4. Any clause of a collective or individual agreement or of any other collective regulation concerning eligibility for employment, employment, remuneration and other conditions of work or dismissal shall be null and void in so far as it lays down or authorises discriminatory conditions in respect of workers who are nationals of the other Member States.

GENERAL NOTE

3.67   If a national of a Member State is a worker within the meaning of Title II of the Regulation, then art.7(2) may often be a better passport to entitlement to a social security benefit than the co-ordinating rules in Regulation 1408/71, or reliance on citizenship of the Union. There is no limitation in relation to the material scope of Regulation 1612/68; this provision covers social assistance as well as social security falling within Regulation 1408/71. The worker is entitled to be treated in exactly the same way as someone in a similar position who is a national of the Member State. See, for examples, *R(IS) 4/98* and *R(IS) 12/98,* which concerned, respectively, entitlement to a funeral payment, and entitlement to income support.

Defining workers for the purpose of Title II of Regulation 1612/68 was at the heart of the appeal in *CJSA/4065/1999,* in which the Commissioner referred questions to the Court of Justice. The ruling of the Court of Justice can be found in Case C-138/02 *Collins v Secretary of State for Work and Pensions,* [2004] ECR I-2703, annexed to *R(JSA) 3/06.*

Collins held both Irish and American nationality. He had been a student in the United Kingdom for a semester in 1978, and in 1980 and 1981 had spent about ten months working in part-time casual work in the United Kingdom. He subsequently worked in the United States and in South Africa. In 1998 he returned to the United Kingdom to look for work, and shortly afterwards claimed an income-based jobseeker's allowance. This was refused because he was not regarded as being habitually resident in the United Kingdom.

The Advocate General and the Court use different reasoning in reaching essentially the same conclusion. The Advocate General begins his Opinion by recalling the rights of citizens of the Union under Article 39 EC, but also notes that a person must have the status of actually being a "worker" (as distinct from a "work seeker") before he or she can rely on Article 7(2) of Regulation 1612/68. The Advocate General goes on to note that the habitual residence test is, in principle, indirectly discriminatory since it is easier for United Kingdom nationals to fulfil the requirement than nationals of other Member States. However, the Advocate General considers that a condition as to residence which makes it possible to ascertain the degree of connection with the host State and the links which the claimant has with the domestic employment market may be justified in order to avoid the movement of persons for the purpose of taking advantage of non-contributory benefits and to prevent abuses. The Advocate General accordingly proposes that the answer to the questions posed by the Commissioner should that Community law as it now stands does not require that an income-based social security benefit be provided to a citizen of the Union who seeks work in a Member State with whose employment market he lacks any connection or link.

The Court concludes that a person in Collins' situation is not a "worker" for the purposes of Title II of Regulation 1612/68, although it is for the national adjudicating authorities to determine whether the term 'worker', as used in the national legislation, is to be understood in the same sense. The link with the earlier employment is too remote to permit his classification as a worker in 1998. Furthermore, Collins did not have a right to reside in the United Kingdom solely on the basis of Council Directive 68/360. Finally, the Court concludes,

". . . the right to equal treatment laid down in Art.48(2) (now 39(2)) of the Treaty, read in conjunction with Arts 6 (now 12) and 8 (now 17) of the Treaty, does not preclude legislation which makes entitlement to a jobseeker's allowance conditional on a residence requirement, in so far as that requirement may be justified on the basis of objective considerations that are independent of nationality of the persons concerned and proportionate to the legitimate aim of the national provisions". (para.73).

CJSA/4065/1999, March 4, 2005, is the Commissioner's decision on the reference in *Collins*. On the status of Collins as a worker for the purposes of Regulation 1612/68 in the JSA Regulations, the Commissioner had this to say:

"In my judgment, the reference in regulation 85(4) of the JSA Regulations to a 'workers for the purposes of [Regulation 1612/68]' must have been intended to have a narrower effect than a reference to a person within the scope of application of the Regulation as a whole. By 'worker' is meant a person who falls within the Community concept of worker in relation to the parts of Regulation 1612/68 that expressly confer entitlements on people in their capacity as workers, rather than in their capacity as nationals of a Member State. That restricts the meaning on the reference in the JSA Regulations to persons who are workers for the purposes of Title II of Part I of Regulation 1612/68. The meaning does not extend to persons who are entitled to assistance under Title I of Part I (in particular Article 5) or who fall only within the broader sense of 'worker' mentioned in paragraph 32 of the ECJ's judgment." (para.16).

The Commissioner then turns to the Court of Justice's conclusions on Community law requirements in relation to justification for the requirement to establish habitual residence, and finds that the test of justification and proportionality is met by the habitual residence test as a condition of entitlement to a means tested jobseeker's allowance. However, he adds a proviso: for the application of the requirement for any day to be proportionate in any particular case, the answer to the question, "Has the point been reached that the relevant national authority has become satisfied of the genuineness of the claimant's search for work?" must be in the negative.

The Commissioner's decision is largely upheld by the Court of Appeal in *Collins v Secretary of State for Work and Pensions* [2006] EWCA Civ 376, annexed to *R(JSA) 3/06*. However, the Court of Appeal concludes that the Commissioner erred in concluding that in order to render the habitual residence test compatible with Community law it was necessary to introduce the proviso set out above. The result is that the habitual residence test alone is, in the view of the Court of Appeal, sufficient to secure compatibility with Community law on access to a jobseekers allowance.

The *Hartmann* case in the Court of Justice (C-212/05, *Hartmann v Freistaat Bayern*, [2007] ECR I-6303) also concerned the definition of "worker" for the purposes of Article 7(2). Mr and Mrs Hartmann are a married couple with three children. Before the couple married in 1990, Mr Hartmann lived and worked in Germany. Following the marriage he moved to Austria, but continued to work in Germany. Claims for a German child-raising allowance were refused on the grounds that the applicant, Mrs Hartmann, was not resident in Germany. Regulation 1408/71 was not applicable because Mr Hartmann was a civil servant, and at the material time, civil servants were not included within the personal scope of that regulation; they now are. Mr Hartmann became a frontier worker, living in Austria but working in Germany. The question was whether a person who had moved his residence, not in connection with his employment, but for other reasons, could be considered to be a worker for the purposes of Regulation 1612/68. The Advocate General came to a different conclusion from that reached by the Court, but his discussion of the issues provides helpful background to the judgment of the Court. The Court concluded that Mr Hartmann was a worker within the meaning of that term in art.7(2) of Regulation 1612/68; his motivation for moving his country of residence, unconnected as it was with his employment, did not justify refusing him the status of migrant worker.

The Court then moves on to consider whether the ability of Mrs Hartmann to claim a German child-raising allowance constitutes a social advantage for Mr Hartmann; in other words, does the indirect nature of the benefit of equal treatment extend to the spouse of a worker? The benefit claimed has as one of its conditions of entitlement that the person claiming it devotes herself to the raising of children and has no full-time employment. The Court considers that the benefit is a social advantage for the worker since the income contributes to the overall family expenses, which would otherwise fall exclusive on the parent who was working. A residence requirement is capable of discriminating against workers who do not reside in Germany, and would require objective justification and proportionality to be established. The Court reports that the German authorities exercised some discretion in relation to the residence requirement in the case of frontier workers. For the Court this meant that residence was not the only connecting link with Germany; and it followed that the allowance could not be refused on Mrs Hartmann's application.

The *Geven* case, decided on the same day, also concerned also concerned an application for a German child-raising allowance in rather difference circumstances. Ms Geven is a Dutch national. When her son was born she was living in the Netherlands with her husband. After the statutory maternity protection period and during her son's first year, she worked in Germany for between three and fourteen hours a week. Her claim for a child-raising allowance in Germany was refused on the grounds that she was neither resident in Germany nor in more than minor employment. The Court confirms that the allowance is a social advantage within the scope of Regulation 1612/68. But, contrary to its conclusion in the *Hartmann* case, the Court concludes that the requirement for a substantial link with the German labour market established by the nature of the employment is capable of constituting a legitimate justification for a refusal to grant the social advantage at issue.

In cases where a person is not currently working but has worked in the past in a period which is sufficiently closely connected in time to the claim for benefit, it will be important to recall that a person does not automatically lose worker status simply by reason of the employment ending. It is the circumstances in which the work ends which must be considered. In Case C-413/01 *Ninni-Orasche v Bundesminister für Wissenschaft,Verkehr und Kunst,* [2003] ECR I-13187, the Court of Justice was considering a reference from *Verwaltungsgerichthof* in Austria concerning an Italian national, Franca Ninni-Orasche, who had been married to an Austrian national since January 1993, and had been resident in Austria since November 1993. Ninni-Orasche had been employed as a waitress between July 6 and September 25, 1995; she also had some duties as a cashier and in relation to stock control. She was also undertaking part-time study and subsequently passed examinations qualifying her for admission to an Austrian university. She was refused financial support for her studies. The question was whether she was a worker for the purposes of Article 39 EC, and more particularly Regulation 1612/68, since she would then appear potentially to be entitled to financial support for her studies under Article 7(2) of the Regulation (provided other conditions were satisfied). The Court concluded that the short-term work Ninni-Orasche had undertaken qualified her as a worker under Article 39 EC "provided that the activity performed as an employed person is not purely marginal or ancillary" (para.32). This is an issue to be determined by the national courts. Furthermore, a person would not be treated as voluntarily unemployed merely because the initial contract of employment was for a fixed term which has expired. See also observations in *R(IS) 12/98.*

Article 12

3.68   The children of a national of a Member State who is or has been employed in the territory of another Member State shall be admitted to that State's general educational, apprenticeship and vocational training courses under the same conditions as the nationals of that State, if such children are residing in its territory.

Member States shall encourage all efforts to enable such children to attend these courses under the best possible conditions.

GENERAL NOTE

For an elaboration of the rights contained in this article, see Joined Cases 389 and 390/87 *Echternach and Moritz*, [1989] ECR 723. In Case C-413/99 *Baumbast and R*, [2002] ECR I-7091, the Luxembourg Court recognised the right of a parent, who was a third country national and the primary carer of children, to reside in the United Kingdom in order for the children to be able to exercise their right to education.   **3.69**

For the relationship of this provision with provisions of the Citizenship Directive, see commentary to art.12 of the Citizenship Directive.

Article 42

1. *Omitted.*   **3.70**
2. This regulation shall not affect measures taken in accordance with Article 51 of this Treaty.
3. *Omitted.*

GENERAL NOTE

Following the amendment of the EC Treaty, art.51 is now art.42 EC and refers to the adoption of measures in the field of social security.   **3.71**

In *C50/90-00 (DLA)* a Commissioner in Northern Ireland concluded that the effect of art.42(2) can be to preclude the application of art.7(2) where the matter is governed by Regulation 1408/71 (a regulation made under art.51 (now 42) EC). The case concerned a claimant for a disability living allowance on the basis of Community law; the claimant was at all relevant times resident in Ireland. She later claimed a disability living allowance in Northern Ireland where she worked, arguing that art.7(2) meant that the residence and presence conditions could not be applied to her. The Commissioner upholds the decision of the tribunal that she could not maintain the art.7(2) right since disability living allowance was a benefit falling within art.10a of Regulation 1408/71, which alone applied to her situation. She says:

"28. It does not appeal to me that Article 42(2) can be given anything other than its plain meaning, i.e. that Regulation (EEC)1612/68 is not to affect measures taken under Article 51. The provisions of that regulation cannot have any effect on such measures".

In *CIS/825/2001* a Commissioner in England, while not dissenting from the decision of the Commissioner in Northern Ireland, disagrees with the reasoning, since it is too wide. The Commissioner in England says:

"43. I conclude from both the specific comments of the Court in *EC Commission v French Republic* and from the absence of the point being taken by or to the Court in other cases that the 'plain meaning' attached to Article 42(2) in C 50/99-00 (DLA) is too wide. The right granted by Article 7(2) of Regulation 1612/68 is a fundamental aspect of the freedom of movement of workers—and, perhaps it should now be said, of European citizens. It is one of the essential aspects of the freedom granted by Article 39 (formerly Article 48) of the Treaty, securing the freedom of movement of workers. Regulation 1408/71 is about coordinating social security systems under Article 42 (formerly 51) of the Treaty by adopting 'such measures as are necessary to provide freedom of movement of workers'. Those Articles pursue parallel aims, and I do not readily read a final provision in Regulation 1612/68 as undercutting those parallel aims so as to reduce a worker's rights under Article 7 of that Regulation unless there is clear reason to do so. The reason to do so, as the European Court reflects, is that there is some provision of Regulation 1408/71 in application which provides a benefit to a worker in a different way to Regulation 1612/68 but, by reason of the purposes of those Regulations, to the same end. In other words, it is an example of what used to be given the Latin tag *specialia generalibus derogant*—a specific rule derogates from a general rule. But, in this context, both rules are concerned with granting rights and not restricting them".

In *Secretary of State for Work and Pensions v Bobezes* [2005] EWCA Civ 111, (the appeal against the Commissioner's decision in *CIS/825/2001*) reported as *R(IS) 6/05*, the Court of Appeal alluded to the question of whether art.42 precluded the application of art.7 of Regulation 1612/68 to the claimant's case. Lord Slynn said:

"15. Despite all these arguments based on the European Court's authorities the real point for the purpose of this case is that, when considering whether there is discrimination against Mr Bobezes in the application of . . . the United Kingdom Regulation, there is no difference between Article 3 [of Regulation 1408/71] and Article 7 [of Regulation 1612/68]. . . . Both unequivocally prohibit the different treatment of migrant workers and national workers in the grant and payment of the allowance. .. Despite the Secretary of State's argument [that it was essential for the court to decide under which of the two regulations the matter had to be resolved] I do not consider that it would be appropriate in the circumstances for the court to review all the authorities and to express an opinion on what is at best a theoretical question with no consequences for the parties to this appeal."

Directive 2004/38/EC of the European Parliament and of the Council of 29 April 2004 on the right of citizens of the Union and their family members to move and reside freely within the territory of the Member States amending Regulation (EEC) No 1612/68 and repealing Directives 64/221/EEC, 68/360/EEC, 72/194/EEC, 73/148/EEC, 75/34/EEC, 75/35/EEC, 90/364/EEC, 90/365/EEC and 93/96/EEC

[2004] OJ L229/35 Corrigendum [2005] OJ L197/34

Date for implementation: April 30, 2006

The European Parliament and the Council of the European Union

3.72 *Having regard* to the Treaty establishing the European Community, and in particular Articles 12, 18, 40, 44 and 52 thereof,

Having regard to the proposal from the Commission,

Having regard to the opinion of the European Economic and Social Committee,

Having regard to the opinion of the Committee of the Regions,

Acting in accordance with the procedure laid down in Article 251 of the Treaty,

Whereas:

(1) Citizenship of the Union confers on every citizen of the Union a primary and individual right to move and reside freely within the territory of the Member States, subject to the limitations and conditions laid down in the Treaty and to the measures adopted to give it effect.

(2) The free movement of persons constitutes one of the fundamental freedoms of the internal market, which comprises an area without internal frontiers, in which freedom is ensured in accordance with the provisions of the Treaty.

(3) Union citizenship should be the fundamental status of nationals of the Member States when they exercise their right of free movement and residence. It is therefore necessary to codify and review the existing Community instruments dealing separately with workers, self employed persons, as well as students and other inactive persons in order to simplify and strengthen the right of free movement and residence of all Union citizens.

(4) With a view to remedying this sector-by-sector, piecemeal approach to the right of free movement and residence and facilitating the exercise of this right, there needs to be a single legislative act to amend Council Regulation (EEC) No 1612/68 of 15 October 1968 on freedom of movement for workers within the Community, and to repeal the following acts: Council Directive 68/360/EEC of 15 October 1968 on the abolition of restrictions on movement and residence within the Community for workers of Member States and their families, Council Directive 73/148/EEC of 21 May 1973 on the abolition of restrictions on movement and residence within the Community for nationals of Member States with regard to establishment and the provision of services, Council Directive 90/364/EEC of 28 June 1990 on the right of residence (8), Council Directive 90/365/EEC of 28 June 1990 on the right of residence for employees and self-employed persons who have ceased their occupational activity (9) and Council Directive 93/96/EEC of 29 October 1993 on the right of residence for students.

(5) The right of all Union citizens to move and reside freely within the territory of the Member States should, if it is to be exercised under objective conditions of freedom and dignity, be also granted to their family members, irrespective of nationality. For the purposes of this Directive, the definition of "family member" should also include the registered partner if the legislation of the host Member State treats registered partnership as equivalent to marriage.

(6) In order to maintain the unity of the family in a broader sense and without prejudice to the prohibition of discrimination on grounds of nationality, the situation of those persons who are not included in the definition of family members under this Directive, and who therefore do not enjoy an automatic right of entry and residence in the host Member State, should be examined by the host Member State on the basis of its own national legislation, in order to decide whether entry and residence could be granted to such persons, taking into consideration their relationship with the Union citizen or any other circumstances, such as their financial or physical dependence on the Union citizen.

(7) The formalities connected with the free movement of Union citizens within the territory of Member States should be clearly defined, without prejudice to the provisions applicable to national border controls.

(8) With a view to facilitating the free movement of family members who are not nationals of a Member State, those who have already obtained a residence card should be exempted from the requirement to obtain an entry visa within the meaning of Council Regulation (EC) No 539/2001 of 15 March 2001 listing the third countries whose nationals must be in possession of visas when crossing the external borders and those whose nationals are exempt from that requirement (1) or, where appropriate, of the applicable national legislation.

(9) Union citizens should have the right of residence in the host Member State for a period not exceeding three months without being subject to any conditions or any formalities other than the requirement to hold a valid identity card or passport, without prejudice to a more favourable treatment applicable to job-seekers as recognised by the case-law of the Court of Justice.

(10) Persons exercising their right of residence should not, however, become an unreasonable burden on the social assistance system of the host Member State during an initial period of residence. Therefore, the right of residence for Union citizens and their family members for periods in excess of three months should be subject to conditions.

(11) The fundamental and personal right of residence in another Member State is conferred directly on Union citizens by the Treaty and is not dependent upon their having fulfilled administrative procedures.

(12) For periods of residence of longer than three months, Member States should have the possibility to require Union citizens to register with the competent authorities in the place of residence, attested by a registration certificate issued to that effect.

(13) The residence card requirement should be restricted to family members of Union citizens who are not nationals of a Member State for periods of residence of longer than three months.

(14) The supporting documents required by the competent authorities for the issuing of a registration certificate or of a residence card should be comprehensively specified in order to avoid divergent administrative practices or interpretations constituting an undue obstacle to the exercise of the right of residence by Union citizens and their family members.

(15) Family members should be legally safeguarded in the event of the death of the Union citizen, divorce, annulment of marriage or termination of a registered partnership. With due regard for family life and human dignity, and in certain conditions to guard against abuse, measures should therefore be taken to ensure that in such circumstances family members already residing within the territory of the host Member State retain their right of residence exclusively on a personal basis.

(16) As long as the beneficiaries of the right of residence do not become an unreasonable burden on the social assistance system of the host Member State they should not be expelled. Therefore, an expulsion measure should not be the automatic consequence of recourse to the social assistance system. The host Member State should examine whether it is a case of temporary difficulties and take into account the duration of residence, the personal circumstances and the amount of aid granted in order to consider whether the beneficiary has become an unreasonable burden on its social

assistance system and to proceed to his expulsion. In no case should an expulsion measure be adopted against workers, self-employed persons or job-seekers as defined by the Court of Justice save on grounds of public policy or public security.

(17) Enjoyment of permanent residence by Union citizens who have chosen to settle long term in the host Member State would strengthen the feeling of Union citizenship and is a key element in promoting social cohesion, which is one of the fundamental objectives of the Union. A right of permanent residence should therefore be laid down for all Union citizens and their family members who have resided in the host Member State in compliance with the conditions laid down in this Directive during a continuous period of five years without becoming subject to an expulsion measure.

(18) In order to be a genuine vehicle for integration into the society of the host Member State in which the Union citizen resides, the right of permanent residence, once obtained, should not be subject to any conditions.

(19) Certain advantages specific to Union citizens who are workers or self-employed persons and to their family members, which may allow these persons to acquire a right of permanent residence before they have resided five years in the host Member State, should be maintained, as these constitute acquired rights, conferred by Commission Regulation (EEC) No 1251/70 of 29 June 1970 on the right of workers to remain in the territory of a Member State after having been employed in that State (1) and Council Directive 75/34/EEC of 17 December 1974 concerning the right of nationals of a Member State to remain in the territory of another Member State after having pursued therein an activity in a self-employed capacity.

(20) In accordance with the prohibition of discrimination on grounds of nationality, all Union citizens and their family members residing in a Member State on the basis of this Directive should enjoy, in that Member State, equal treatment with nationals in areas covered by the Treaty, subject to such specific provisions as are expressly provided for in the Treaty and secondary law.

(21) However, it should be left to the host Member State to decide whether it will grant social assistance during the first three months of residence, or for a longer period in the case of job-seekers, to Union citizens other than those who are workers or self-employed persons or who retain that status or their family members, or maintenance assistance for studies, including vocational training, prior to acquisition of the right of permanent residence, to these same persons.

(22) The Treaty allows restrictions to be placed on the right of free movement and residence on grounds of public policy, public security or public health. In order to ensure a tighter definition of the circumstances and procedural safeguards subject to which Union citizens and their family members may be denied leave to enter or may be expelled, this Directive should replace Council Directive 64/221/EEC of 25 February 1964 on the coordination of special measures concerning the movement and residence of foreign nationals, which are justified on grounds of public policy, public security or public health.

(23) Expulsion of Union citizens and their family members on grounds of public policy or public security is a measure that can seriously harm persons who, having availed themselves of the rights and freedoms conferred

on them by the Treaty, have become genuinely integrated into the host Member State. The scope for such measures should therefore be limited in accordance with the principle of proportionality to take account of the degree of integration of the persons concerned, the length of their residence in the host Member State, their age, state of health, family and economic situation and the links with their country of origin.

(24) Accordingly, the greater the degree of integration of Union citizens and their family members in the host Member State, the greater the degree of protection against expulsion should be. Only in exceptional circumstances, where there are imperative grounds of public security, should an expulsion measure be taken against Union citizens who have resided for many years in the territory of the host Member State, in particular when they were born and have resided there throughout their life. In addition, such exceptional circumstances should also apply to an expulsion measure taken against minors, in order to protect their links with their family, in accordance with the United Nations Convention on the Rights of the Child, of 20 November 989.

(25) Procedural safeguards should also be specified in detail in order to ensure a high level of protection of the rights of Union citizens and their family members in the event of their being denied leave to enter or reside in another Member State, as well as to uphold the principle that any action taken by the authorities must be properly justified.

(26) In all events, judicial redress procedures should be available to Union citizens and their family members who have been refused leave to enter or reside in another Member State.

(27) In line with the case-law of the Court of Justice prohibiting Member States from issuing orders excluding for life persons covered by this Directive from their territory, the right of Union citizens and their family members who have been excluded from the territory of a Member State to submit a fresh application after a reasonable period, and in any event after a three year period from enforcement of the final exclusion order, should be confirmed.

(28) To guard against abuse of rights or fraud, notably marriages of convenience or any other form of relationships contracted for the sole purpose of enjoying the right of free movement and residence, Member States should have the possibility to adopt the necessary measures.

(29) This Directive should not affect more favourable national provisions.

(30) With a view to examining how further to facilitate the exercise of the right of free movement and residence, a report should be prepared by the Commission in order to evaluate the opportunity to present any necessary proposals to this effect, notably on the extension of the period of residence with no conditions.

(31) This Directive respects the fundamental rights and freedoms and observes the principles recognised in particular by the Charter of Fundamental Rights of the European Union. In accordance with the prohibition of discrimination contained in the Charter, Member States should implement this Directive without discrimination between the beneficiaries of this Directive on grounds such as sex, race, colour, ethnic or social origin, genetic characteristics, language, religion or beliefs, political or other opinion, membership of an ethnic minority, property, birth, disability, age or sexual orientation.

Have Adopted this Directive

GENERAL NOTE

The Citizenship Directive was a long time in the making. The initial proposal **3.73** was made in 2001 and the Directive entered into force on April 30, 2006. It repeals and re-enacts nine directives, and amends one regulation. Commission Regulation 1251/70/EEC on the right of worker to remain in the territory of a Member State after having been employed there has been repealed by the Commission.

There were more than two years of negotiations about the Directive before it was adopted in 2004, and a further two years was allowed for its implementation. This suggests that it is more than mere consolidation of the secondary legislation to be found in the repealed legislative measures.

Note that The Immigration (European Economic Area) Regulations 2006 (SI 2006/1003) implement in United Kingdom law the requirements of the Directive.

The thrust of the Citizenship Directive can explored under a number of headings.

Integrating the rules on free movement

The existing piecemeal approach to the regulation of rights of entry and residence **3.74** is replaced with a single instrument which sets out rights of exit and entry, the right to reside, and an elaboration of the circumstances in which a person can be removed from the territory of a Member State other than that of their nationality. There are two remaining regulations which are likely to be central to the movement of persons. First, Regulation 1612/68 remains which sets out specific arrangements to facilitate the free movement of workers. Secondly, Regulation 1408/71/EEC is unaffected. This seeks to co-ordinate the social security systems of the Member States so that they are not an obstacle to the free movement of persons.

Extending the concept of the family

Under the previous regime, the family of a worker for Community purposes **3.75** included the spouse, children under the age of 21, and children over the age of 21 together with relatives in the ascending line of the worker and spouse who are actually dependent on the worker. Family members need not be citizens of the Union, though many will be. This list is extended by Art.2(2) of the Citizenship Directive to include:

> "the partner with whom the Union citizen has contracted a registered partnership, on the basis of the legislation of a Member State, if the legislation of the host Member State treats registered partnerships as equivalent to marriage and in accordance with the conditions laid down in the relevant legislation of the host Member State;"

This extends the notion of spouse to include the recognition of unmarried partner status in the legislation of the Member States. The language is clearly broad enough to encompass same-sex relationships, but there is a requirement that the host Member State treats such partnerships as equivalent to marriage in the same circumstances. There is also the limitation that the registered partnership on which the mover is depending arises under the law of one of the Member States.

Article 3 of the Citizenship Directive which defines the beneficiaries of the rules in the Directive refers to the definitions in Art.2, but goes on to incorporate an obligation to "facilitate" entry and residence for other persons including "the partner with whom the Union citizen has a durable relationship, duly attested." Some substance is given to the concept of facilitation by the last sentence of art.3:

> "The host Member State shall undertake an extensive examination of the personal circumstances and shall justify denial of entry or residence to these people."

The outcome is a complex definition of family. The inclusion of registered partners is bound to give rise to difficulty.

There are sure to be references to the Court of Justice on the extended concept of the family for the purposes of rights of free movement.

A new right of permanent residence

3.76   A continuing right of residence under the old regime required repeated renewal of residence permits, or the completion of periods of economic activity which led to a right to remain after completion of a period of economic activity. The new regime is far simpler. A continuous period of five years residence entitles citizens of the Union and their families to a right of permanent residence under art.16 of the Citizenship Directive. This is not conditional on any particular activity or possession of a particular level of resources. The right of permanent residence is only lost after absence from the host Member State for "a period exceeding two consecutive years".

In *CIS/0185/2008* the Commissioner considers the relationship between art.18 EC and this Directive:

> For the purposes of this decision, I am quite content to accept the Secretary of State's submission that the claimant cannot have acquired a right of permanent residence under art.16 before Directive 2004/38/EC came into effect. However, in CIS/2358/2006 and CIS/408/2006, I have held that a claimant can rely instead on art.18(1) of the EC Treaty. In short, my reasoning has been that it is clear from *Baumbast v Secretary of State for the Home Department* (Case C-413/99) [2002] E.C.R. I-7091, having particular regard to what Mr Advocate General Geelhoed said at paras 19 to 36 and 120 to 122 of his Opinion about the inadequacy of existing Directives, that the Directives in force before 30 April 2006 could not be regarded as the sole source of rights of residence and that, once Council Directive 2004/38/2004 had been adopted, it provided a guide as to the scope of the rights conferred directly by art.18(1) of the EC Treaty, although not an exhaustive guide if it was possible to show a lacuna in that Directive. Thus, in CIS/408/2006, the claimant was successful even though his case would not have fallen within Directive 2004/38/EC had it been in force. In CIS/2358/2006, the claimant was unsuccessful (and now has an appeal pending before the Court of Appeal). Although Directive 2004/38/EC was not adopted until a few days after the claimant in the present case had returned to work in 2004, in my judgment it is still capable of providing a guide as to the scope of art.18(1) as at 18 April, 2003. Moreover, it is particularly appropriate to have regard to it when considering what is in effect a transitional case arising under art.16 of the Directive itself. (para.20).

The appeal against *CIS/0185/2008* to the Court of Appeal as *Secretary of State for Work and Pensions v Dias* [2009] EWCA Civ 807 has resulted in a further reference to the Luxembourg Court.

The Court of Appeal split its decision into a number of issues. (1) The question of whether the appellant could acquire the status of a permanent resident prior to the entry into force of Directive 2004/38 turned on the reference made in *Secretary of State for Work and Pensions v Lassal*. (2) The question of whether the appellant had retained worker status during the period of nearly a year when she was not working was rightly decided by the Commissioner. This broke the continuity of a period of residence which ended after Directive 2004/38 entered into force. (3) The question of the effect of the appellant's holding a residence permit under rules in force prior to Directive 2004/38 coupled with the application of art.16 of Directive 2004/38 turned on the proper interpretation of the words "resided legally" on which authoritative guidance would be forthcoming following the reference in *McCarthy v Secretary of State for the Home Department*, but also required a further question to be referred to the Luxembourg Court. (4) The question of whether the appellant had a right to reside flowing from art.18 EC required a question to be referred to the Luxembourg Court.

The two questions referred to the Luxembourg Court in the *Dias* case are:

"If a European Union citizen, present in a Member State of which she is not a national, was, prior to the transposition of Directive 2004/38/EC, the holder of a residence permit validly issued pursuant to Article 4(2) of Directive 68/360/EEC, but was for a period of time during the currency of the permit voluntarily unemployed, not self-sufficient and outside the qualifications for the issue of such a permit, did that person by reason only of her possession of the permit, remain during that time someone who "resided legally" in the host Member State for the purpose of later acquiring a permanent right of residence under Article 16(1) of Directive 2004/38/EC"

"If five years' continuous residence as a worker prior to 30 April 2006 does not qualify to give rise to the permanent right of residence created by Article 16(1) of Directive 2004/38/EC, does such continuous residence as a worker give rise to a permanent right of residence directly pursuant to Article 18(1) of the EU Treaty on the grounds that there is a lacuna in the Directive?"

Reducing bureaucracy

Citizens of the Union will no longer need to obtain residence permits. Simple registration (if required by the host Member State) is all that can be required. A registration certificate will be issued where registration is required. A residence card is introduced for family members who are not themselves citizens of the Union.   3.77

Tighter controls on deportation

The Commission considers that expulsion of citizens of the Union does not have a place in the area of freedom, security and justice, being built in Europe. So, the Citizenship Directive reduces the scope for Member States to rely on the derogations in the EC Treaty on grounds of public policy, public security and public health in deporting nationals of other Member States. Once a person has acquired a right of permanent residence, then *serious* grounds of public policy or public security will alone justify expulsion. Once a person has resided in the host Member State for a period of 10 years, then only *imperative* ground of public security will justify expulsion.   3.78

In any case where expulsion is contemplated on grounds of public policy or public security, the host Member State shall take account of considerations such as how long the individual concerned has resided on its territory, his/her age, state of health, family and economic situation, social and cultural integration into the host Member State and the extent of his/her links with the country of origin.

Equal treatment

The prohibition of discrimination on grounds of nationality in matters within the scope of the EC Treaty has always been a foundational principle of the Community and Union. In the early days of the Community, the prohibition of discrimination belonged to the market integration model, and was targeted at removing obstacles to economic activity. That approach had to develop organically as social integration became a stronger feature of the ever-closer union of peoples envisaged by the EC Treaty. Now the prohibition of discrimination has become attached to citizenship of the Union, and its constitutional status has been confirmed. Advocate General Jacobs said in his Opinion in Case C-274/96, *Bickel and Franz* [1998] E.C.R. I-7637:   3.79

"Freedom from discrimination on grounds of nationality is the most fundamental right conferred by the Treaty and must be seen as a basic ingredient of Union citizenship."

Taken without any qualifications, this would mean that any citizen of any Member State present in a state other than that of his or her own nationality must be treated in exactly the same manner as nationals of the host State in the same situation. Any difference of treatment would need to be objectively justified on grounds which did not relate to the nationality of the individual. Such a proposition concerns Member States particularly in relation to access to public benefits. While Member States are generally very welcoming of self-sufficient, healthy nationals of other Member States coming to work, study or live, concerns soon emerge with the prospect of the mover needing the support of the State for financial assistance or medical assistance.

Article 24(1) of the Citizenship Directive provides:

"Subject to such specific provisions as are expressly provided for in the Treaty and secondary law, all Union citizens residing on the basis of this Directive in the territory of the host Member State shall enjoy equal treatment with the nationals of that Member State within the scope of the Treaty. The benefit of this right shall be extended to family members who are not nationals of a Member State and who have the right of residence or permanent residence."

Article 24(2) excludes entitlement to equal treatment in access to social assistance for those with the right of residence for up to three months or longer period as work seekers. It also excludes from equal treatment in access to financial support for studies (other than for those who had and retain economically active status as workers, or self-employed persons) those present for less than five years.

Implementation of the Citizenship Directive

3.80   The Report from the Commission to the European Prliament and the Council on the application of Directive 2004/38/EC on the right of citizens of the Union and their family members to move and reside freely within the territory of the Member States, COM (2008) 840/3 of December 10, 2008, reports that no Member State has fully transposed the requirement of the Directive, and that there is no single provision of the Directive which has been fully implemented in all the Member States. The Report observes in relation to the United Kingdom that it "incorrectly takes no account of periods of residence acquired by EU citizens before their countries acceded to the EU." (para.3.7).

Questions referred to the Luxembourg Court

As at September 1, 2009, there were questions referred to the Luxembourg Court relevant to the interpretation of Directive 2004/38 and related EC material in five cases.

In *London Borough of Harrow v Ibrahim and Secretary of State for the Home Department* [2008] EWCA Civ 386, and *Teixeira v London Borough of Lambeth* [2008] EWCA Civ 1088 (see para.3.100 below), questions were raised concerning the right to reside for those caring for children in education. These are sometimes referred to as the *Baumbast* issues, since they flow from the Luxembourg Court's judgment in that case.

In *Secretary of State for Work and Pensions v Lassal* [2009] EWCA Civ 157, the Court of Appeal referred questions relating to the temporal effect of the right of permanent residence (see para.3.106 below).

In *McCarthy v Secretary of State for the Home Department,* the House of Lords has referred questions on the meaning of the words "resided legally" (see para.3.31 above and 3.106 below).

In *Secretary of State for Work and Pensions v Dias* [2009] EWCA Civ 807, the Court of Appeal has referred further questions relating to the interpretation of Directive 2004/38, as well as the interaction of the "old" residence permit provisions with the residence provisions of Directive 2004/38 (see para.3.76 above).

Article 1

CHAPTER I

GENERAL PROVISIONS

Article 1

Subject

This Directive lays down: 3.81

(a) the conditions governing the exercise of the right of free movement and residence within the territory of the Member States by Union citizens and their family members;

(b) the right of permanent residence in the territory of the Member States for Union citizens and their family members;

(c) the limits placed on the rights set out in (a) and (b) on grounds of public policy, public security or public health.

GENERAL NOTE

See discussion at para.3.30 to 3.32 above of a series of cases which considered the   3.82
requirement that person must have a "right to reside" in the United Kingdom as a condition of entitlement to certain benefits.

Article 2

Definitions

For the purposes of this Directive: 3.83

1. "Union citizen" means any person having the nationality of a Member State;

2. "family member" means:

(a) the spouse;

(b) the partner with whom the Union citizen has contracted a registered partnership, on the basis of the legislation of a Member State, if the legislation of the host Member State treats registered partnerships as equivalent to marriage and in accordance with the conditions laid down in the relevant legislation of the host Member State;

(c) the direct descendants who are under the age of 21 or are dependants and those of the spouse or partner as defined in point (b);

(d) the dependent direct relatives in the ascending line and those of the spouse or partner as defined in point (b);

3. "host Member State" means the Member State to which a Union citizen moves in order to exercise his/her right of free movement and residence.

GENERAL NOTE

Case C-291/05 *Eind*, Judgment of December 11, 2007, was decided under   3.84
provisions of Regulation 1612/68 which have been repealed and re-enacted in slightly different form in the Citizenship Directive. Article 10 of Regulation 1612/68 provided (so far as relevant):

887

1. The following shall, irrespective of their nationality, have the right to install themselves with a worker who is a national of one Member State and who is employed in the territory of another Member State:

    (a) his spouse and their descendants who are under the age of 21 or are dependants; . . . .

The case concerned the position of third country nationals who are relatives of a citizen of the Union. Mr Eind, a Dutch national, moved to the United Kingdom in February 2000 where he found work. In December 2000 he was joined by his eleven year old daughter, Rachel, who came direct to the United Kingdom from Surinam. The United Kingdom authorities accepted that Rachel was entitled to reside in the United Kingdom as the daughter of a worker.

In October 2001, Mr Eind and his daughter went to The Netherlands. Mr Eind did not work there because of ill-health. Rachel was refused a residence permit on the grounds that her father was not a worker for Community law purposes. When that decision was challenged, questions were referred to the Luxembourg Court. Relying in part on Case C-10/05 *Mattern and Cikotic*, [2006] ECR I-3145, the Court ruled that:

". . . the right of a third-country national who is a member of the family of a Community worker to install himself with that worker may be relied on only in the Member State where that worker resides." (para.24).

So it followed that the Dutch authorities were not bound by the grant of a right to reside by another Member State even where that decision is made under art.10 of Regulation 1612/68. However, that was not the end of the story. Any refusal to grant the family the possibility of returning to the Member State of origin would be an obstacle to free movement. Rachel Eind was entitled to reside in The Netherlands with her father by reason of art.10 of Regulation 1612/68.

Both the judgment of the Court and the Opinion of the Advocate General are silent on the Citizenship Directive, since they were concerned with events occurring before the entry into force of the Citizenship Directive. But it is worth noting one difference between the wording of Regulation 1612/68 and the Citizenship Directive. In the *Eind Case* the Court, following the *Mattern and Cikotic Case*, interpreted arts 10 and 11 of Regulation 1612/68 as meaning that the rights could only be relied on *in the State in which the person was a worker*. Though the line of reasoning covers a range of provisions of the Citizenship Directive, It is arguable that this limitation no longer applies.

For a discussion of the notion of being a dependant in the light of case law of the Court of Justice, see *CIS/2100/2007*.

Although it concerns the interpretation of an earlier Directive, some guidance on the approach to determining dependence can be found in Case C-1/05 *Yunying Jia v Migrationsverket*, January 9, 2007, [2007] ECR I-1,where the Court of Justice ruled:

"Article 1(1)(d) of Council Directive 73/148/EEC of 21 May 1973 on the abolition of restrictions on movement and residence within the Community for nationals of Member States with regard to establishment and the provision of services is to be interpreted to the effect that 'dependent on them' means that members of the family of a Community national established in another Member State within the meaning of Article 43 EC need the material support of that Community national or his or her spouse in order to meet their essential needs in the State of origin of those family members or the State from which they have come at the time when they apply to join that Community national. Article 6(b) of that directive must be interpreted as meaning that proof of the need for material support may be adduced by any appropriate means, while a mere undertaking from the Community national or his or her spouse to support the family members concerned need not be regarded as establishing the existence of the family members' situation of real dependence."

Beneficiaries

1. This Directive shall apply to all Union citizens who move to or reside in a Member State other than that of which they are a national, and to their family members as defined in point 2 of Article 2 who accompany or join them.

2. Without prejudice to any right to free movement and residence the persons concerned may have in their own right, the host Member State shall, in accordance with its national legislation, facilitate entry and residence for the following persons:

   (a) any other family members, irrespective of their nationality, not falling under the definition in point 2 of Article 2 who, in the country from which they have come, are dependants or members of the household of the Union citizen having the primary right of residence, or where serious health grounds strictly require the personal care of the family member by the Union citizen;

   (b) the partner with whom the Union citizen has a durable relationship, duly attested.

The host Member State shall undertake an extensive examination of the personal circumstances and shall justify any denial of entry or residence to these people.

GENERAL NOTE

3.85

KG and AK v Secretary of State for the Home Department, [2008] EWCA Civ 13 concerned the interpretation of art.3. KG is a national of Sri Lanka. In November 2000 he arrived "clandestinely" in the United Kingdom and claimed asylum, but that claim was refused. He nevertheless remained in the United Kingdom without leave to remain. He had a brother who had been granted refugee status in Germany and had acquired German nationality in 2001. In January 2006 the brother came to the United Kingdom and applied for a residence permit. KG then immediately applied to stay in the United Kingdom as the brother of a Union citizen.

3.86

Since KG was not an art.2 family member, (that is, spouse, partner under a registered partnership, son or daughter under the age of 21 or dependent on the citizen of the Union, or a dependent relative in the ascending line of the citizen or spouse/partner) his entitlement to reside in the United Kingdom turned on the art.3 provisions relating to "other family members". Here the obligation (so far as relevant to the circumstances of this case) of the Member State is "in accordance with its national legislation, [to] facilitate entry and residence" of other family members who "are dependants or members of the household of the Union citizen. . . ." Before denying entry or residence, the Member State is required to "undertake an extensive examination of the personal circumstances."

The national implementing legislation, The Immigration (European Economic Area) Regulations 2006, required other family members to arrive in the United Kingdom from *another Member State*. KG had arrived in the United Kingdom from Sri Lanka. Accordingly, it was argued that the national legislation did not correctly transpose the requirements of the Directive. KG argued that the expression in the Directive "who, in the country from which they have come, are dependants or members of the household of the Union citizen" had to be read as referring to any country and not just to a Member State. KG argued that he had been a member of the household of a Union citizen in Sri Lanka between 1968 and 1992.

It is inherent in the Court of Appeal's judgment that the Citizenship Directive is essentially a consolidation of the earlier law. Buxton LJ, giving the lead judgment, says:

". . . the assumptions and procedures of Directive 2004/38 do not mark a fundamental change from the previous state of the law. In particular . . . Directive 2004/38 proceeds not by replacing but by amending the workers' Regulation 1612/68." (para.17)

It was argued that the Directive placed considerable emphasis on family reunion and that its terms should be interpreted and transposed with due respect for this principle. But the Court said:

"Put shortly, Community law recognises rights of movement on the part of relations not in order to support family values as such, but in order to make real the right of movement of the Union citizen: who may be deterred from exercising that right if he cannot take his relevant family with him. That is the constant theme of the cases that we were shown in support of the attempt to assert the doctrine of family reunion." (para.33)

The Court concluded:

"The tight relationship between the exercise of rights by the Union citizen and the requirement that the [other family members] accompanying or joining him should have been his dependants or members of his household in the country from which they have come very strongly suggests that that relationship should have existed in the country from which the *Union citizen* has come, and thus have existed immediately before the Union citizen was accompanied or joined by the [other family member]. It seems wholly unlikely that when article 10(2) of Regulation 1612/68 and article 3(2)(a) of Directive 2004/38 introduce the requirement of dependence on and membership of the household of the Union citizen in the country from which the [other family member] has come, they can have had in mind anything other than dependence on the Union citizen in the country movement from which by the Union citizen is the whole basis of his rights and, thus of the rights of the [other family member]." (para.65)

That judgment now needs to be read in the light of the Luxembourg Court's judgment in Case C-127/08 *Metock and others,* July 25, 2008. This is a very significant case on the interpretation of art.3 on a reference from the Irish courts. It concerns national implementation of art.3 which has some similarities with implementation in the United Kingdom, and has important implications for the interpretation of the United Kingdom's national regulations implementing the Directive. This makes it worth setting out the circumstances of some of the individuals whose cases were the subject of this reference.

Metock is a national of Cameroon who arrived in Ireland in June 2006 and whose application for asylum failed. Ikeng, born a national of Cameroon acquired United Kingdom nationality and resided and worked in Ireland since late in 2006. Metock and Ikeng met in Cameroon in 1994 and have been in a stable relationship. There are two children. They were married in Ireland in October 2006. An application for a residence card for Metock was refused on the grounds that he did not satisfy the requirement of the Irish regulations that he had resided lawfully in another Member State prior to the application.

Mr Ikogho was also a failed asylum seeker; he was subject to a deportation order at the material time. Mrs Ikogho, a United Kingdom national, has lived and worked in Ireland since 1996. Mr and Mrs Ikogho met in Ireland in 2004 and were married in June 2006. An application for a residence card was refused on the grounds that Mr Ikogho was staying illegally in Ireland at the time of his marriage.

Chinedu, a national of Nigeria is also a failed asylum seeker. Babucke is a woman of German nationality lawfully resident in Ireland. Chinedu and Babucke married in July 2006. An application for a residence card was refused on the grounds that Chinedu did not meet the condition in the national regulations of lawful residence in another Member State prior to the application.

The applicants all argued that the Irish regulations implementing the Directive were incompatible with it. Their argument was that a national of a non-member country who becomes a family member of a Union citizen while that citizen is resident in a Member State other than that of which he is a national accompanies that citizen within the meaning of arts 3(1) and 7(2) of the Directive. The Irish Government argued that the Directive does not preclude the imposition of a condition of prior lawful residence in another Member State in the national implementing legislation.

The Court of Justice observed that nothing in the Directive makes the application of its provisions conditional on persons having previously resided in a Member State. The Court concludes:

. . . Directive 2004/38 confers on all nationals of non-member countries who are family members of a Union citizen within the meaning of part 2 of Article 2 of that directive, and accompany or join the Union citizen in a Member State other than that of which he is a national, rights of entry into and residence in the host Member State, regardless of whether the national of a non-member country has already been lawfully resident in another Member State (para.70).

The Court went on to consider cases where rights arose from marriage and concluded:

. . . Article 3(1) of Directive 2004/38 must be interpreted as meaning that a national of a non-member country who is the spouse of a Union citizen residing in a Member State whose nationality he does not possess and who accompanies or joins that Union citizen benefits from the provisions of that directive, irrespective of when and where their marriage took place and of how the national of a non-member country entered the host Member State. (para.99).

For some observations by the Court of Appeal on the propositions in *KG* in the light of the Luxembourg's judgments in *Metock,* see *Bigia and others v Entry Clearance Officer,* [2009] EWCA Civ 79.

In *CIS/2100/2007* the Commissioner analyses and discusses the European authorities on the notion of dependence under a regulation and two earlier directives of the European Community. He concludes that the case law is authority for the propositions: (1) a person is only dependent who actually receives support from another; (2) there need be no right to that support and it is irrelevant that there are alternative sources of support available; and (3) the support must be material, although not necessarily financial, and must provide for, or contribute towards, the basic necessities of life. (para.44).

Art.3(2)(b)

Article 3(2)(b) requires Member States to facilitate the entry and residence of the partner of a Union citizen, with whom that citizen has a "durable relationship". The provision has been implemented in the United Kingdom through reg.8(5) of the Immigration (European Economic Area) Regulation 2006, which provides:

3.87

A person satisfies the condition in this paragraph if the person is a partner of an EEA national (other than a civil partner) and can prove to the decision-maker that he is in a durable relationship with the EEA national.

In *CIS/0612/2008* the Commissioner ruled that the concept of a "durable relationship" must be given a Community meaning. He went on to say that the concepts in art.3(2)(b) are expressed "in ordinary words that do not require definition and can be left to the relevant fact-finding body" (para.30). However, he considered that there was an element of ambiguity in the notion of durability in that it "may mean that it has lasted or that it is capable of lasting" (para.36), although plainly it was the relationship with the partner rather than the partnership itself that had to display this quality. The relationship may have existed prior to the persons becoming partners. Subject to these considerations the question of the durability of the relationship was one of fact.

CHAPTER II

RIGHT OF EXIT AND ENTRY

Article 4

Right of exit

3.88   **1.** Without prejudice to the provisions on travel documents applicable to national border controls, all Union citizens with a valid identity card or passport and their family members who are not nationals of a Member State and who hold a valid passport shall have the right to leave the territory of a Member State to travel to another Member State.

2. No exit visa or equivalent formality may be imposed on the persons to whom paragraph 1 applies.

3. Member States shall, acting in accordance with their laws, issue to their own nationals, and renew, an identity card or passport stating their nationality.

4. The passport shall be valid at least for all Member States and for countries through which the holder must pass when travelling between Member States. Where the law of a Member State does not provide for identity cards to be issued, the period of validity of any passport on being issued or renewed shall be not less than five years.

Article 5

Right of entry

3.89   **1.** Without prejudice to the provisions on travel documents applicable to national border controls, Member States shall grant Union citizens leave to enter their territory with a valid identity card or passport and shall grant family members who are not nationals of a Member State leave to enter their territory with a valid passport.

No entry visa or equivalent formality may be imposed on Union citizens.

2. Family members who are not nationals of a Member State shall only be required to have an entry visa in accordance with Regulation (EC) No.539/2001 or, where appropriate, with national law. For the purposes of this Directive, possession of the valid residence card referred to in Article 10 shall exempt such family members from the visa requirement.

Member States shall grant such persons every facility to obtain the necessary visas. Such visas shall be issued free of charge as soon as possible and on the basis of an accelerated procedure.

3. The host Member State shall not place an entry or exit stamp in the passport of family members who are not nationals of a Member State provided that they present the residence card provided for in Article 10.

4. Where a Union citizen, or a family member who is not a national of a Member State, does not have the necessary travel documents or, if required, the necessary visas, the Member State concerned shall, before turning them back, give such persons every reasonable opportunity to obtain the necessary documents or have them brought to them within a reasonable period of time or to corroborate or prove by other means that they are covered by the right of free movement and residence.

5. The Member State may require the person concerned to report his/her presence within its territory within a reasonable and non-discriminatory period of time. Failure to comply with this requirement may make the person concerned liable to proportionate and non-discriminatory sanctions.

GENERAL NOTE

Regulation 539/2001/EC does not apply to the United Kingdom.   3.90

CHAPTER III

RIGHT OF RESIDENCE

Article 6

Right of residence for up to three months

1. Union citizens shall have the right of residence on the territory of   3.91 another Member State for a period of up to three months without any conditions or any formalities other than the requirement to hold a valid identity card or passport.

2. The provisions of paragraph 1 shall also apply to family members in possession of a valid passport who are not nationals of a Member State, accompanying or joining the Union citizen.

Article 7

Right of residence for more than three months

1. All Union citizens shall have the right of residence on the territory of   3.92 another Member State for a period of longer than three months if they:

(a) are workers or self-employed persons in the host Member State; or

(b) have sufficient resources for themselves and their family members not to become a burden on the social assistance system of the host Member State during their period of residence and have comprehensive sickness insurance cover in the host Member State; or

(c) — are enrolled at a private or public establishment, accredited or financed by the host Member State on the basis of its legislation or administrative practice, for the principal purpose of following a course of study, including vocational training; and

— have comprehensive sickness insurance cover in the host Member State and assure the relevant national authority, by means of a declaration or by such equivalent means as they may choose,

that they have sufficient resources for themselves and their family members not to become a burden on the social assistance system of the host Member State during their period of residence;
    or

(d) are family members accompanying or joining a Union citizen who satisfies the conditions referred to in points (a), (b) or (c).

2. The right of residence provided for in paragraph 1 shall extend to family members who are not nationals of a Member State, accompanying or joining the Union citizen in the host Member State, provided that such Union citizen satisfies the conditions referred to in paragraph 1(a), (b) or (c).

3. For the purposes of paragraph 1(a), a Union citizen who is no longer a worker or self-employed person shall retain the status of worker or self-employed person in the following circumstances:

(a) he/she is temporarily unable to work as the result of an illness or accident;

(b) he/she is in duly recorded involuntary unemployment after having been employed for more than one year and has registered as a job-seeker with the relevant employment office;

(c) he/she is in duly recorded involuntary unemployment after completing a fixed-term employment contract of less than a year or after having become involuntarily unemployed during the first twelve months and has registered as a jobseeker with the relevant employment office. In this case, the status of worker shall be retained for no less than six months;

(d) he/she embarks on vocational training. Unless he/she is involuntarily unemployed, the retention of the status of worker shall require the training to be related to the previous employment.

4. By way of derogation from paragraphs 1(d) and 2 above, only the spouse, the registered partner provided for in Article 2(2)(b) and dependent children shall have the right of residence as family members of a Union citizen meeting the conditions under 1(c) above. Article 3(2) shall apply to his/her dependent direct relatives in the ascending lines and those of his/her spouse or registered partner.

GENERAL NOTE

3.93   Courts and tribunals, in addressing the right to reside which has been introduced as a condition of entitlement to very many social benefits, are increasingly indicating that the right to reside must be residence construed strictly under the terms of the Directive read narrowly. So in *R(IS) 3/08* the Commissioner said:

"26. But there is a more fundamental objection to the tribunal's decision in this case, which arises irrespective of whether *GN* was correctly decided. For the reasons I have given, temporary admission does not confer a right of residence and so the domestic immigration authorities have never in fact recognised that the claimant has a right of residence in this case. In its context, it is quite clear that, in Article 16 of the Directive, the phrase "resided legally" means resided in accordance with rights of residence. That is apparent from paragraph (17) of the preamble and from the reference back to Chapter III in the second sentence of Article 16 itself. Chapter III is concerned with an initial right of residence for three months, not subject to any conditions, and to further rights of residence that are subject to conditions. A permanent right of residence is something that may be acquired after a person has had five years' residence in accordance with Chapter III or, as I have suggested may be arguable, analogous rights under

Article 18(1) of the EC Treaty or domestic law. Mere presence in exercise of the right of entry under Chapter II or rights under domestic law is not sufficient. This is why *Martinez-Sala* and *Trojani,* upon which Mr Tegg placed so much reliance, do not assist the claimant and, indeed, in paragraph [43] of *Abdirahman,* Lloyd LJ specifically made the point that "*Trojani* . . . shows that an EU citizen, lawfully present in another Member State, but not economically self-sufficient, does not, merely by virtue of lawful presence in the host State, acquire a Treaty-based right of residence". A person cannot acquire a permanent right of residence in the United Kingdom through Community law when he has not only never exercised any Community right of residence in the United Kingdom but he has also never had a right of residence under United Kingdom domestic law."

In *CIS/599/2007* the Commissioner (interpreting the corresponding provision in the Immigration (European Economic Area) Regulations 2006, which implement this Directive) agreed that the requirement in art.7(3)(a) related to the incapacity of the worker and would not apply where the incapacity in question was that of the claimant's child. That did not enable the claimant to retain the status of worker and so she did not have a right to reside as required by national law.

2W v SSWP [2009] UKUT 25 (AAC), concerned, in part, whether participation in a work-focused interview was or involved registration sufficient to satisfy art.7(3)(b) and (c) (implemented in national law as regulation 6(2)(b) of the Immigration (European Economic Area) Regulations 2006. The Judge concluded that the concept of registration in this Article should be interpreted as being evidence of remaining in contact with the labour market. But the concept in the Article is not an autonomous one: "What is required is that the Union citizen register in accordance with the particular arrangements in the host State." (para.24). It followed that a work-focused interview did not "provide an opportunity for claimants to register for work . . . the interview is not itself registration nor does it involve registration. It is at best a preliminary stage." (para.27).

In *1A v SSWP,* [2009] UKUT 35 (AAC), the Judge observes:

"The six months' limit in Article 7(3)(c) and the prohibition on expulsion in Article 14(4)(b) reflect the [Luxembourg] Court's answer in *Antonissen,* but the Directive does not translate the Court's reasoning in that case into a right to reside for those [who] are not in the labour market." (para.23).

Article 8

Administrative formalities for Union citizens

1. Without prejudice to Article 5(5), for periods of residence longer than three months, the host Member State may require Union citizens to register with the relevant authorities.   **3.94**

2. The deadline for registration may not be less than three months from the date of arrival. A registration certificate shall be issued immediately, stating the name and address of the person registering and the date of the registration. Failure to comply with the registration requirement may render the person concerned liable to proportionate and non-discriminatory sanctions.

3. For the registration certificate to be issued, Member States may only require that

— Union citizens to whom point (a) of Article 7(1) applies present a valid identity card or passport, a confirmation of engagement from the employer or a certificate of employment, or proof that they are self-employed persons,

— Union citizens to whom point (b) of Article 7(1) applies present a valid identity card or passport and provide proof that they satisfy the conditions laid down therein,

— Union citizens to whom point (c) of Article 7(1) applies present a valid identity card or passport, provide proof of enrolment at an accredited establishment and of comprehensive sickness insurance cover and the declaration or equivalent means referred to in point (c) of Article 7(1).

Member States may not require this declaration to refer to any specific amount of resources.

4. Member States may not lay down a fixed amount which they regard as "sufficient resources", but they must take into account the personal situation of the person concerned. In all cases this amount shall not be higher than the threshold below which nationals of the host Member State become eligible for social assistance, or, where this criterion is not applicable, higher than the minimum social security pension paid by the host Member State.

5. For the registration certificate to be issued to family members of Union citizens, who are themselves Union citizens, Member States may require the following documents to be presented:

(a) a valid identity card or passport;

(b) a document attesting to the existence of a family relationship or of a registered partnership;

(c) where appropriate, the registration certificate of the Union citizen whom they are accompanying or joining;

(d) in cases falling under points (c) and (d) of Article 2(2), documentary evidence that the conditions laid down therein are met;

(e) in cases falling under Article 3(2)(a), a document issued by the relevant authority in the country of origin or country from which they are arriving certifying that they are dependants or members of the household of the Union citizen, or proof of the existence of serious health grounds which strictly require the personal care of the family member by the Union citizen;

(f) in cases falling under Article 3(2)(b), proof of the existence of a durable relationship with the Union citizen.

GENERAL NOTE

3.95   In *SSWP v EM* [2009] UKUT 44 (AAC), the Judge considers the effect of the *permissive, not required*, registration scheme which a Member State may establish under art.8. The Judge observes:

13. The most important distinction between Article 8 of Directive 2004/38/EC and Directive 68/360/EEC, which was among the Directives that it replaced, is that, under the new Directive, there is no requirement to have a registration scheme and there is no requirement placed on a Member State to issue registration certificates if there is no scheme. Nor is anything said in Directive 2004/38/EC as to the effect of a registration certificate or as to the period for which it is valid. However, it may be inferred from paragraph (2) of Article 8 that the certificate operates, firstly, as evidence that the holder has complied with a requirement to register imposed by a Member State in conformity with paragraph (1) and is therefore not liable to the sanctions permitted under paragraph (2) and, secondly, as evidence that, at the date of issue, the applicant was a citizen of the European Union with a right of residence under Article 7(1). On that basis, there

is no reason to limit the period of a registration certificate's validity. The passing of time cannot logically affect its value as evidence of the position at the date of issue. Thus, there is nothing to suggest that a registration certificate has the same effect as a residence permit which, it could be inferred from the earlier Directives, had continuing effect until it expired or was withdrawn because otherwise it would not perform the designated function of proving a right of residence.

The Judge rejected arguments that the registration certificate had the same effect as the former residence permit. That must be right. The former residence permit was a document required to be provided under Community law as evidence of a person's entitlement in a Member State other than that of his or her nationality under the EC Treaty. The case law clearly established that it was merely evidence of Treaty rights and did not grant them. By contrast the scheme of registration under art.8 is a discretionary national scheme which a Member State may choose to set up as a matter of its own internal administration. It follows that the effect of the registration certificate will be determined under national law, although that national law must be applied consistently with Community law entitlements.

Article 9

Administrative formalities for family members who are not nationals of a Member State

1. Member States shall issue a residence card to family members of a Union citizen who are not nationals of a Member State, where the planned period of residence is for more than three months.

2. The deadline for submitting the residence card application may not be less than three months from the date of arrival.

3. Failure to comply with the requirement to apply for a residence card may make the person concerned liable to proportionate and non-discriminatory sanctions.

3.96

Article 10

Issue of residence cards

1. The right of residence of family members of a Union citizen who are not nationals of a Member State shall be evidenced by the issuing of a document called "Residence card of a family member of a Union citizen" no later than six months from the date on which they submit the application. A certificate of application for the residence card shall be issued immediately.

2. For the residence card to be issued, Member States shall require presentation of the following documents:
   (a) a valid passport;
   (b) a document attesting to the existence of a family relationship or of a registered partnership;
   (c) the registration certificate or, in the absence of a registration system, any other proof of residence in the host Member State of the Union citizen whom they are accompanying or joining;
   (d) in cases falling under points (c) and (d) of Article 2(2), documentary evidence that the conditions laid down therein are met;

3.97

(e) in cases falling under Article 3(2)(a), a document issued by the relevant authority in the country of origin or country from which they are arriving certifying that they are dependants or members of the household of the Union citizen, or proof of the existence of serious health grounds which strictly require the personal care of the family member by the Union citizen;

(f) in cases falling under Article 3(2)(b), proof of the existence of a durable relationship with the Union citizen.

Article 11

Validity of the residence card

3.98   **1.** The residence card provided for by Article 10(1) shall be valid for five years from the date of issue or for the envisaged period of residence of the Union citizen, if this period is less than five years.

2. The validity of the residence card shall not be affected by temporary absences not exceeding six months a year, or by absences of a longer duration for compulsory military service or by one absence of a maximum of 12 consecutive months for important reasons such as pregnancy and childbirth, serious illness, study or vocational training, or a posting in another Member State or a third country.

Article 12

Retention of the right of residence by family members in the event of death or departure of the Union citizen

3.99   **1.** Without prejudice to the second subparagraph, the Union citizen's death or departure from the host Member State shall not affect the right of residence of his/her family members who are nationals of a Member State.

Before acquiring the right of permanent residence, the persons concerned must meet the conditions laid down in points (a), (b), (c) or (d) of Article 7(1).

2. Without prejudice to the second subparagraph, the Union citizen's death shall not entail loss of the right of residence of his/her family members who are not nationals of a Member State and who have been residing in the host Member State as family members for at least one year before the Union citizen's death.

Before acquiring the right of permanent residence, the right of residence of the persons concerned shall remain subject to the requirement that they are able to show that they are workers or self-employed persons or that they have sufficient resources for themselves and their family members not to become a burden on the social assistance system of the host Member State during their period of residence and have comprehensive sickness insurance cover in the host Member State, or that they are members of the family, already constituted in the host Member State, of a person satisfying these requirements. "Sufficient resources" shall be as defined in Article 8(4).

Such family members shall retain their right of residence exclusively on a personal basis.

3. The Union citizen's departure from the host Member State or his/her death shall not entail loss of the right of residence of his/her children or of the parent who has actual custody of the children, irrespective of nationality, if the children reside in the host Member State and are enrolled at an educational establishment, for the purpose of studying there, until the completion of their studies.

GENERAL NOTE

In *London Borough of Harrow v Ibrahim and Secretary of State for the Home Department*, [2008] EWCA Civ 386, the Court of Appeal has, on April 21, 2008, made a reference to the Luxembourg Court which touches on the proper interpretation of the Citizenship Directive.

3.100

Ms Ibrahim is a Somali woman married to a Danish citizen, Mr Yusuf. There are four children in the family whose ages range from 1 up to 9 years. Yusuf came to the United Kingdom in 2002 where he worked. His wife and children then joined him. Yusuf then became unfit for wok and claimed and received social security benefits. But when he was subsequently declared fit, he moved to what is described as eastern Europe for a while. When Yusuf left the United Kingdom, he and Ms Ibrahim became estranged. By this time two of the children were in education in the United Kingdom. When Yusuf returned to the United Kingdom, the couple again lived together for a while, but things obviously did not work out and they again separated. They remain married. Ms Ibrahim then applied for social housing from the London Borough of Harrow. A condition of entitlement included a requirement that Ms Ibrahim had a right to reside, which would be satisfied if she had a right to reside under national law or Community Law.

Ms Ibrahim argued that she had a right to reside as the primary carer of children who were citizens of the Union and who were the children of a person who had been a worker. She relied on art.12 of Regulation 1612/68 coupled with the *Baumbast* Case.

It was conceded that Ms Ibrahim would not have a right to reside solely on the application of art.12 of the Citizenship Directive, because Yusuf had ceased to be a worker by the time she sought to rely on this provision. The parties appear to have accepted that there was a lacuna in art.12 in this regard.

The local authority and the Home Secretary argued that Ms Ibrahim's right to reside could only arise under the Citizenship Directive, which had replaced any earlier case law entitlement.

The Court of Appeal referred the following questions:

In circumstances where (i) a non-EU national spouse and her EU national children accompanied an EU national who came to the United Kingdom (ii) the EU national was in the United Kingdom as a worker (iii) the EU national then ceased to be a worker and subsequently left the United Kingdom (iv) the EU national, the non-EU national spouse and children are not self-sufficient and are dependent upon social assistance in the United Kingdom (v) the children commenced primary education in the United Kingdom shortly after their arrival there while the EU national was a worker:

(1) do the spouse and children only enjoy a right of residence in the United Kingdom if they satisfy the conditions set out in Directive 2004/38 of the European Parliament and of the Council of 29 April 2004?;

OR

(2) (i) do they enjoy a right to reside derived from Article 12 of Regulation (EEC) No 1612/68 of 15 October 1968, as interpreted by the Court of Justice,

without being required to satisfy the conditions set out in Directive 2004/38 of the European Parliament and of the Council of 29 April 2004; and

(ii) if so, must they have access to sufficient resources so as not to become a burden on the social assistance system of the host Member State during their proposed period of residence and have comprehensive sickness insurance cover in the host Member State?;

(3) if the answer to question 1 is yes, is the position different in circumstances such as the present case where the children commenced primary education and the EU-national worker ceased working prior to the date by which Directive 2004/38 of the European Parliament and of the Council of 29 April 2004 was to be implemented by the Member States?

A reference to the Luxembourg Court has been made in *Teixeira v London Borough of Lambeth,* [2008] EWCA Civ 1088 in a homelessness case in the following terms:

In circumstances where (i) an EU citizen came to the United Kingdom (ii) the EU citizen was for certain periods a worker in the United Kingdom (iii) the EU citizen ceased to be a worker but did not depart from the United Kingdom, (iv) the EU citizen has not retained her status as a worker and has no right to reside under Article 7 and has no right of permanent residence under Article 16 of Directive 2004/38 of the Council and the European Parliament (v) the EU citizen's child entered education at a time when the EU citizen was not a worker but the child remained in education in the United Kingdom during periods when the EU citizen was in work in the United Kingdom, (vi) the EU citizen is the primary carer of her child and (vii) the EU citizen and her child are not self-sufficient:

(1) does the EU citizen only enjoy a right of residence in the United Kingdom if she satisfies the conditions set out in Directive 2004/38 of the European Parliament and the Council of 29 April 2004?;

OR

(2)(i) does the EU citizen enjoy a right to reside derived from Article 12 of Regulation (EEC) No 1612/68 of 15 October 1968, as interpreted by the Court of Justice, without being required to satisfy the conditions set out in Directive 2004/38 of the European Parliament and of the Council of 29 April 2004; and

(ii) if so, must she have access to sufficient resources so as not to become a burden on the social assistance system of the host Member State during their proposed period of residence and have comprehensive sickness insurance cover in the host Member State?;

(iii) if so, must the child have first entered education at a time when the EU citizen was a worker in order to enjoy a right to reside derived from Article 12 of Regulation (EEC) No 1612/68 of 15 October 1968, as interpreted by the Court of Justice, or is it sufficient that the EU citizen has been a worker at some time after the child commenced education?;

(iv) does any right that the EU citizen has to reside, as the primary carer of a child in education, cease when her child attains the age of eighteen?

(3) if the answer to question 1 is yes, is the position different in circumstances such as the present case where the child commenced education prior to the date by which Directive 2004/38 of the European Parliament and of the Council of 29 April 2004 was to be implemented by the Member States but the mother did not become the primary carer and did not claim the right to reside on the basis that she was the primary carer of the child until March 2007, ie after the date by which the Directive was to be implemented?

Article 13

Retention of the right of residence by family members in the event of divorce, annulment of marriage or termination of registered partnership

1. Without prejudice to the second subparagraph, divorce, annulment of   3.101
the Union citizen's marriage or termination of his/her registered partnership,
as referred to in point 2(b) of Article 2 shall not affect the right of residence
of his/her family members who are nationals of a Member State. Before
acquiring the right of permanent residence, the persons concerned must
meet the conditions laid down in points (a), (b), (c) or (d) of Article 7(1).

2. Without prejudice to the second subparagraph, divorce, annulment of
marriage or termination of the registered partnership referred to in point
2(b) of Article 2 shall not entail loss of the right of residence of a Union
citizen's family members who are not nationals of a Member State where:

(a) prior to initiation of the divorce or annulment proceedings or ter-
    mination of the registered partnership referred to in point 2(b) of
    Article 2, the marriage or registered partnership has lasted at least
    three years, including one year in the host Member State; or

(b) by agreement between the spouses or the partners referred to in
    point 2(b) of Article 2 or by court order, the spouse or partner who is
    not a national of a Member State has custody of the Union citizen's
    children; or

(c) this is warranted by particularly difficult circumstances, such as
    having been a victim of domestic violence while the marriage or reg-
    istered partnership was subsisting; or

(d) by agreement between the spouses or partners referred to in point
    2(b) of Article 2 or by court order, the spouse or partner who is not
    a national of a Member State has the right of access to a minor child,
    provided that the court has ruled that such access must be in the host
    Member State, and for as long as is required.

Before acquiring the right of permanent residence, the right of residence of
the persons concerned shall remain subject to the requirement that they are
able to show that they are workers or self-employed persons or that they
have sufficient resources for themselves and their family members not to
become a burden on the social assistance system of the host Member State
during their period of residence and have comprehensive sickness insurance
cover in the host Member State, or that they are members of the family,
already constituted in the host Member State, of a person satisfying these
requirements. "Sufficient resources" shall be as defined in Article 8(4).

Such family members shall retain their right of residence exclusively on
personal basis.

Article 14

Retention of the right of residence

1. Union citizens and their family members shall have the right of   3.102
residence provided for in Article 6, as long as they do not become an

unreasonable burden on the social assistance system of the host Member State.

2. Union citizens and their family members shall have the right of residence provided for in Articles 7, 12 and 13 as long as they meet the conditions set out therein.

In specific cases where there is a reasonable doubt as to whether a Union citizen or his/her family members satisfies the conditions set out in Articles 7, 12 and 13, Member States may verify if these conditions are fulfilled. This verification shall not be carried out systematically.

3. An expulsion measure shall not be the automatic consequence of a Union citizen's or his or her family member's recourse to the social assistance system of the host Member State.

4. By way of derogation from paragraphs 1 and 2 and without prejudice to the provisions of Chapter VI, an expulsion measure may in no case be adopted against Union citizens or their family members if:

(a) the Union citizens are workers or self-employed persons, or

(b) the Union citizens entered the territory of the host Member State in order to seek employment. In this case, the Union citizens and their family members may not be expelled for as long as the Union citizens can provide evidence that they are continuing to seek employment and that they have a genuine chance of being engaged.

GENERAL NOTE

3.103   Article 14(4)(b) codifies the position established under Case C-292/89 *Antonissen*, [1991] ECR I-745 to the effect that work seekers have a right under art.39 EC to be in a Member State while looking for work provided that they have a genuine prospect of securing employment. This is also reflected in the Immigration (European Economic Area) Regulations 2006 which implement the Directive: see reg.6(1)(a) referring to jobseekers. This analysis of the legal position was accepted by the Commissioner in *R(IS) 8/08.*

Article 15

Procedural safeguards

3.104   **1.** The procedures provided for by Articles 30 and 31 shall apply by analogy to all decisions restricting free movement of Union citizens and their family members on grounds other than public policy, public security or public health.

2. Expiry of the identity card or passport on the basis of which the person concerned entered the host Member State and was issued with a registration certificate or residence card shall not constitute a ground for expulsion from the host Member State.

3. The host Member State may not impose a ban on entry in the context of an expulsion decision to which paragraph 1 applies.

CHAPTER IV

RIGHT OF PERMANENT RESIDENCE

Section I

Eligibility

Article 16

General rule for Union citizens and their family members

1. Union citizens who have resided legally for a continuous period of five years in the host Member State shall have the right of permanent residence there. This right shall not be subject to the conditions provided for in Chapter III.

2. Paragraph 1 shall apply also to family members who are not nationals of a Member State and have legally resided with the Union citizen in the host Member State for a continuous period of five years.

3. Continuity of residence shall not be affected by temporary absences not exceeding a total of six months a year, or by absences of a longer duration for compulsory military service, or by one absence of a maximum of 12 consecutive months for important reasons such as pregnancy and childbirth, serious illness, study or vocational training, or a posting in another Member State or a third country.

4. Once acquired, the right of permanent residence shall be lost only through absence from the host Member State for a period exceeding two consecutive years.

GENERAL NOTE

For comment on acquiring permanent residence, see paras 21–25 of *R(IS) 3/08*.

In *McCarthy v Secretary of State for the Home Department*, [2008] EWCA Civ 641, Pill LJ (with whom Arden and Wilson LJJ agreed) said:

The Directive creates and regulates rights of movement and residence for Union citizens. The lawful residence contemplated in article 16 is residence which complies with community law requirements specified in the Directive and does not cover residence lawful under domestic law by reason of United Kingdom nationality. Article 3 provides in terms that the Directive applies to Union citizens who reside in a Member State "other than that of which they are a national". The expression "resided legally" in article 16 should, in my view, be read consistently with, and in the sense of, preamble 17 of the Directive, that is residence "in compliance with the conditions laid down in this Directive". The repeated use in the Directive of the expression "host Member State" supports that conclusion. It indicates rights to be enjoyed in Member States other than that of nationality; the word "host" suggests that the Union citizen is a "guest", an inappropriate expression for persons in the state of their own nationality. (para.31)

3.105

3.106

This decision has gone on appeal to the House of Lords. It is understood that the House of Lords has referred questions concerning the interpretation of the Directive to the Luxembourg Court on the interpretation of the words "resided legally" in art.16. For the questions referred to the Luxembourg Court, see para.3.31 above.

In *CIS/4299/2007* the Commissioner ruled:

> . . . a claimant's period of residence as a jobseeker prior to 30 April 2006, when the 2006 [Immigration (European Economic Area] Regulations came into force, may be counted as part of legal residence for the purpose of the Directive, but not for the purpose of the 2000 [Immigration (European Economic Area] Regulations. (para.26).

In para. 25 the Commissioner had noted:

> The specific reason why the nature of the EEA legislation is significant concerns the position of jobseekers. Until Directive 2004/38, they had no express right to reside in EC law and they were not mentioned in the 2000 Regulations. However, in *R v Immigration Appeal Tribunal, ex parte Antonissen* (Case C-292/89) [1991] ECR 1-745, the European Court of Justice decided (at paragraphs 14 and 15 of its judgment) that the right of a jobseeker to reside in a host State was implicit both in what is now Article 39 of the EC Treaty and in Regulation 1612/68/EEC. Jobseekers are, therefore, an example of a category of person who have a right to reside that derives from EC law but is not contained in domestic legislation.

The decision is under appeal to the Court of Appeal as *Secretary of State for Work and Pensions v Lassal,* although it appears that the Secretary of State accepts that residence before Directive 2004/38/EC came into force is relevant for the purposes of acquiring permanent residence on or after April 30, 2006: see *CIS/0185/2008,* para.18. This decision has been appealed to the Court of Appeal as *Secretary of State for Work and Pensions v Dias* [2009] EWCA Civ 807. See para.3.76 above.

The Court of Appeal has made an order for reference to the Luxembourg Court. The question posed is as follows:

> 1.1 In circumstances where (i) an EU citizen came to the United Kingdom in September 1999 as a worker and remained as a worker until February 2005 (ii) the EU citizen then left the United Kingdom and returned to the Member State of which she is a national for a period of 10 months (iii) the EU citizen returned to the United Kingdom in December 2005 and resided there continuously until November 2006, when she made a claim for social security assistance:
>
> > Is Article 16(1) of Directive 2004/38 of the European Parliament and the Council of 29 April 2004 to be interpreted as entitling that EU citizen to a right of permanent residence by virtue of the fact that she had been legally resident, in accordance with earlier Community law instruments conferring rights of residence on workers, for a continuous period of five years which ended prior to 30 April 2006 (the date by which Member States had to transpose the Directive)?

In *CIS/2258/2008* the Commissioner was considering whether the appellant could claim to be permanently resident under art.16 in a case in which there were periods when the appellant had been absent abroad. The Commissioner ruled that the tribunal had erred in law by including in the period of residence the time when the appellant was abroad. The Commissioner says:

> 17. If Article 16(1) stood on its own, any gaps in the residence would prevent a right of permanent residence arising. However, Article 16(3) allows for periods of

absence. Provided that the claimant's absences comply with the conditions in that paragraph, continuity of residence is preserved. That does not affect the period of residence that is required. Continuity and the period of five years are separate, albeit related, conditions for the right to arise. This interpretation accords with the wording of the paragraph. Any other interpretation would produce a surprising result. If periods of absence were included in the period of residence, it is conceivable that a person might acquire a right of permanent residence after being resident here for a period considerably shorter than five years. It may be an extreme and unrealistic example, but a person could spend one year studying abroad, spend the next two or three years on compulsory military service abroad and then spend half of each year abroad. A person in those circumstances would surely not 'have chosen to settle long term in the host Member State', to quote recital 17 to the Directive.

It is suggested that, were the question to be raised in Luxembourg, the Court of Justice may not view the interpretation of art.16 in the same way as the Commissioner in separating the period of residence and its continuity. It is clearly more integrationist and more compatible with the concept of citizenship of the Union to *include* permitted periods of absence abroad as part of the period of residence required to acquire the status of permanent citizenship.

Article 17

Exemptions for persons no longer working in the host Member State and their family members

1. By way of derogation from Article 16, the right of permanent residence   **3.107** in the host Member State shall be enjoyed before completion of a continuous period of five years of residence by:
  (a) workers or self-employed persons who, at the time they stop working, have reached the age laid down by the law of that Member State for entitlement to an old age pension or workers who cease paid employment to take early retirement, provided that they have been working in that Member State for at least the preceding twelve months and have resided there continuously for more than three years. If the law of the host Member State does not grant the right to an old age pension to certain categories of self-employed persons, the age condition shall be deemed to have been met once the person concerned has reached the age of 60;
  (b) workers or self-employed persons who have resided continuously in the host Member State for more than two years and stop working there as a result of permanent incapacity to work. If such incapacity is the result of an accident at work or an occupational disease entitling the person concerned to a benefit payable in full or in part by an institution in the host Member State, no condition shall be imposed as to length of residence;
  (c) workers or self-employed persons who, after three years of continuous employment and residence in the host Member State, work in an employed or self-employed capacity in another Member State, while retaining their place of residence in the host Member State, to which they return, as a rule, each day or at least once a week.
    For the purposes of entitlement to the rights referred to in points (a) and (b), periods of employment spent in the Member State in

which the person concerned is working shall be regarded as having been spent in the host Member State.

Periods of involuntary unemployment duly recorded by the relevant employment office, periods not worked for reasons not of the person's own making and absences from work or cessation of work due to illness or accident shall be regarded as periods of employment.

2. The conditions as to length of residence and employment laid down in point (a) of paragraph 1 and the condition as to length of residence laid down in point (b) of paragraph 1 shall not apply if the worker's or the self-employed person's spouse or partner as referred to in point 2(b) of Article 2 is a national of the host Member State or has lost the nationality of that Member State by marriage to that worker or self-employed person.

3. Irrespective of nationality, the family members of a worker or a self-employed person who are residing with him in the territory of the host Member State shall have the right of permanent residence in that Member State, if the worker or self-employed person has acquired himself the right of permanent residence in that Member State on the basis of paragraph 1.

4. If, however, the worker or self-employed person dies while still working but before acquiring permanent residence status in the host Member State on the basis of paragraph 1, his family members who are residing with him in the host Member State shall acquire the right of permanent residence there, on condition that:

(a) the worker or self-employed person had, at the time of death, resided continuously on the territory of that Member State for two years; or

(b) the death resulted from an accident at work or an occupational disease; or

(c) the surviving spouse lost the nationality of that Member State following marriage to the worker or self-employed person.

Article 18

Acquisition of the right of permanent residence by certain family members who are not nationals of a Member State

3.108 Without prejudice to Article 17, the family members of a Union citizen to whom Articles 12(2) and 13(2) apply, who satisfy the conditions laid down therein, shall acquire the right of permanent residence after residing legally for a period of five consecutive years in the host Member State.

Section II

Administrative formalities

Article 19

Document certifying permanent residence for Union citizens

3.109 **1.** Upon application Member States shall issue Union citizens entitled to permanent residence, after having verified duration of residence, with a document certifying permanent residence.

2. The document certifying permanent residence shall be issued as soon as possible.

Article 20

Permanent residence card for family members who are not nationals of a Member State

1. Member States shall issue family members who are not nationals of a Member State entitled to permanent residence with a permanent residence card within six months of the submission of the application. The permanent residence card shall be renewable automatically every 10 years.

3.110

2. The application for a permanent residence card shall be submitted before the residence card expires. Failure to comply with the requirement to apply for a permanent residence card may render the person concerned liable to proportionate and non-discriminatory sanctions.

3. Interruption in residence not exceeding two consecutive years shall not affect the validity of the permanent residence card.

Article 21

Continuity of residence

For the purposes of this Directive, continuity of residence may be attested by any means of proof in use in the host Member State. Continuity of residence is broken by any expulsion decision duly enforced against the person concerned.

3.111

CHAPTER V

PROVISIONS COMMON TO THE RIGHT OF RESIDENCE AND THE RIGHT OF PERMANENT RESIDENCE

Article 22

Territorial scope

The right of residence and the right of permanent residence shall cover the whole territory of the host Member State. Member States may impose territorial restrictions on the right of residence and the right of permanent residence only where the same restrictions apply to their own nationals.

3.112

Article 23

Related rights

Irrespective of nationality, the family members of a Union citizen who have the right of residence or the right of permanent residence in a

3.113

Member State shall be entitled to take up employment or self-employment there.

Article 24

Equal treatment

3.114   **1.** Subject to such specific provisions as are expressly provided for in the Treaty and secondary law, all Union citizens residing on the basis of this Directive in the territory of the host Member State shall enjoy equal treatment with the nationals of that Member State within the scope of the Treaty. The benefit of this right shall be extended to family members who are not nationals of a Member State and who have the right of residence or permanent residence.

2. By way of derogation from paragraph 1, the host Member State shall not be obliged to confer entitlement to social assistance during the first three months of residence or, where appropriate, the longer period provided for in Article 14(4)(b), nor shall it be obliged, prior to acquisition of the right of permanent residence, to grant maintenance aid for studies, including vocational training, consisting in student grants or student loans to persons other than workers, self-employed persons, persons who retain such status and members of their families.

GENERAL NOTE

3.115   This provision reflects the EC Treaty obligation to treat people equally. The key proposition is that those enjoying the right of permanent residence (and their families regardless of their nationality) are entitled to be treated equally in very respect with nationals of the host Member State.

The difficult area is the obligation of equal treatment when a national of another Member State (and note that the Directive has been extended to nationals of the three EEA countries) has been resident for more than three months but less than five years. This is because there is no obligation (but equally no prohibition) to confer entitlement to social assistance in the first three months (or longer where a process of seeking work under Article 14(4)(b) is continuing) when there is an unconditional right to reside. Nor is there any entitlement to support for living expenses of students prior to attainment of permanent residence under the Directive. However, this does not mean that, during this period, claims to equal treatment are bound to fail. Any differential treatment during this period must be objectively and reasonably justified and also proportionate in the particular circumstances of the case.

The provision is also without prejudice to the provisions of Article 7(2) of Regulation 1612/68 which entitle those within the definition of "worker" under Title II of that Regulation to the same social and tax advantages as nationals of the host Member State.

Article 25

General provisions concerning residence documents

3.116   **1.** Possession of a registration certificate as referred to in Article 8, of a document certifying permanent residence, of a certificate attesting submission of an application for a family member residence card, of a residence card or of a permanent residence card, may under no circumstances be made a precondition for the exercise of a right or the completion of an administrative formality, as entitlement to rights may be attested by any other means of proof.

2. All documents mentioned in paragraph 1 shall be issued free of charge or for a charge not exceeding that imposed on nationals for the issuing of similar documents.

Article 26

Checks

Member States may carry out checks on compliance with any requirement deriving from their national legislation for non nationals always to carry their registration certificate or residence card, provided that the same requirement applies to their own nationals as regards their identity card. In the event of failure to comply with this requirement, Member States may impose the same sanctions as those imposed on their own nationals for failure to carry their identity card.

3.117

CHAPTER VI

RESTRICTIONS ON THE RIGHT OF ENTRY AND THE RIGHT OF RESIDENCE ON GROUNDS OF PUBLIC POLICY, PUBLIC SECURITY OR PUBLIC HEALTH

Article 27

General principles

1. Subject to the provisions of this Chapter, Member States may restrict the freedom of movement and residence of Union citizens and their family members, irrespective of nationality, on grounds of public policy, public security or public health. These grounds shall not be invoked to serve economic ends.

3.118

2. Measures taken on grounds of public policy or public security shall comply with the principle of proportionality and shall be based exclusively on the personal conduct of the individual concerned. Previous criminal convictions shall not in themselves constitute grounds for taking such measures. The personal conduct of the individual concerned must represent a genuine, present and sufficiently serious threat affecting one of the fundamental interests of society. Justifications that are isolated from the particulars of the case or that rely on considerations of general prevention shall not be accepted.

3. In order to ascertain whether the person concerned represents a danger for public policy or public security, when issuing the registration certificate or, in the absence of a registration system, not later than three months from the date of arrival of the person concerned on its territory or from the date of reporting his/her presence within the territory, as provided for in Article 5(5), or when issuing the residence card, the host Member State may, should it consider this essential, request the Member State of origin and, if need be, other Member States to provide information concerning any previous police record the person concerned may have. Such enquiries shall not be made as a matter of routine. The Member State consulted shall give its reply within two months.

4. The Member State which issued the passport or identity card shall allow the holder of the document who has been expelled on grounds of public policy, public security, or public health from another Member State to re-enter its territory without any formality even if the document is no longer valid or the nationality of the holder is in dispute.

Article 28

Protection against expulsion

3.119   **1.** Before taking an expulsion decision on grounds of public policy or public security, the host Member State shall take account of considerations such as how long the individual concerned has resided on its territory, his/her age, state of health, family and economic situation, social and cultural integration into the host Member State and the extent of his/her links with the country of origin.

2. The host Member State may not take an expulsion decision against Union citizens or their family members, irrespective of nationality, who have the right of permanent residence on its territory, except on serious grounds of public policy or public security.

3. An expulsion decision may not be taken against Union citizens, except if the decision is based on imperative grounds of public security, as defined by Member States, if they:

(a) have resided in the host Member State for the previous 10 years; or
(b) are a minor, except if the expulsion is necessary for the best interests of the child, as provided for in the United Nations Convention on the Rights of the Child of 20 November 1989.

Article 29

Public health

3.120   **1.** The only diseases justifying measures restricting freedom of movement shall be the diseases with epidemic potential as defined by the relevant instruments of the World Health Organisation and other infectious diseases or contagious parasitic diseases if they are the subject of protection provisions applying to nationals of the host Member State.

2. Diseases occurring after a three-month period from the date of arrival shall not constitute grounds for expulsion from the territory.

3. Where there are serious indications that it is necessary, Member States may, within three months of the date of arrival, require persons entitled to

Article 29

the right of residence to undergo, free of charge, a medical examination to certify that they are not suffering from any of the conditions referred to in paragraph 1. Such medical examinations may not be required as a matter of routine.

Article 30

Notification of decisions

1. The persons concerned shall be notified in writing of any decision taken under Article 27(1), in such a way that they are able to comprehend its content and the implications for them.

3.121

2. The persons concerned shall be informed, precisely and in full, of the public policy, public security or public health grounds on which the decision taken in their case is based, unless this is contrary to the interests of State security.

3. The notification shall specify the court or administrative authority with which the person concerned may lodge an appeal, the time limit for the appeal and, where applicable, the time allowed for the person to leave the territory of the Member State. Save in duly substantiated cases of urgency, the time allowed to leave the territory shall be not less than one month from the date of notification.

Article 31

Procedural safeguards

1. The persons concerned shall have access to judicial and, where appropriate, administrative redress procedures in the host Member State to appeal against or seek review of any decision taken against them on the grounds of public policy, public security or public health.

3.122

2. Where the application for appeal against or judicial review of the expulsion decision is accompanied by an application for an interim order to suspend enforcement of that decision, actual removal from the territory may not take place until such time as the decision on the interim order has been taken, except:

— where the expulsion decision is based on a previous judicial decision; or

— where the persons concerned have had previous access to judicial review; or

— where the expulsion decision is based on imperative grounds of public security under Article 28(3).

3. The redress procedures shall allow for an examination of the legality of the decision, as well as of the facts and circumstances on which the proposed measure is based. They shall ensure that the decision is not disproportionate, particularly in view of the requirements laid down in Article 28.

4. Member States may exclude the individual concerned from their territory pending the redress procedure, but they may not prevent the individual from submitting his/her defence in person, except when his/her appearance may cause serious troubles to public policy or public security or when the appeal or judicial review concerns a denial of entry to the territory.

Article 32

Duration of exclusion orders

3.123   **1.** Persons excluded on grounds of public policy or public security may submit an application for lifting of the exclusion order after a reasonable period, depending on the circumstances, and in any event after three years from enforcement of the final exclusion order which has been validly adopted in accordance with Community law, by putting forward arguments to establish that there has been a material change in the circumstances which justified the decision ordering their exclusion. The Member State concerned shall reach a decision on this application within six months of its submission.

2. The persons referred to in paragraph 1 shall have no right of entry to the territory of the Member State concerned while their application is being considered.

Article 33

Expulsion as a penalty or legal consequence

3.124   **1.** Expulsion orders may not be issued by the host Member State as a penalty or legal consequence of a custodial penalty, unless they conform to the requirements of Articles 27, 28 and 29.

2. If an expulsion order, as provided for in paragraph 1, is enforced more than two years after it was issued, the Member State shall check that the individual concerned is currently and genuinely a threat to public policy or public security and shall assess whether there has been any material change in the circumstances since the expulsion order was issued.

CHAPTER VII

FINAL PROVISIONS

Article 34

Publicity

3.125   Member States shall disseminate information concerning the rights and obligations of Union citizens and their family members on the subjects covered by this Directive, particularly by means of awareness-raising

Article 34

campaigns conducted through national and local media and other means of communication.

Article 35

Abuse of rights

Member States may adopt the necessary measures to refuse, terminate or withdraw any right conferred by this Directive in the case of abuse of rights or fraud, such as marriages of convenience.

Any such measure shall be proportionate and subject to the procedural safeguards provided for in Articles 30 and 31.

3.126

Article 36

Sanctions

Member States shall lay down provisions on the sanctions applicable to breaches of national rules adopted for the implementation of this Directive and shall take the measures required for their application. The sanctions laid down shall be effective and proportionate. Member States shall notify the Commission of these provisions not later than 30 April 2006 and as promptly as possible in the case of any subsequent changes.

3.127

Article 37

More favourable national provisions

The provisions of this Directive shall not affect any laws, regulations or administrative provisions laid down by a Member State which would be more favourable to the persons covered by this Directive.

3.128

Article 38

Repeals

1. Articles 10 and 11 of Regulation (EEC) No 1612/68 shall be repealed with effect from 30 April 2006.

2. Directives 64/221/EEC, 68/360/EEC, 72/194/EEC, 73/148/EEC, 75/34/EEC, 75/35/EEC, 90/364/EEC, 90/365/EEC and 93/96/EEC shall be repealed with effect from 30 April 2006.

3. References made to the repealed provisions and Directives shall be construed as being made to this Directive.

3.129

Article 39

Report

3.130   No later than 30 April 2008 the Commission shall submit a report on the application of this Directive to the European Parliament and the Council, together with any necessary proposals, notably on the opportunity to extend the period of time during which Union citizens and their family members may reside in the territory of the host Member State without any conditions. The Member States shall provide the Commission with the information needed to produce the report.

Article 40

Transposition

3.131   **1.** Member States shall bring into force the laws, regulations and administrative provisions necessary to comply with this Directive by 30 April 2006. When Member States adopt those measures, they shall contain a reference to this Directive or shall be accompanied by such a reference on the occasion of their official publication. The methods of making such reference shall be laid down by the Member States.

2. Member States shall communicate to the Commission the text of the provisions of national law which they adopt in the field covered by this Directive together with a table showing how the provisions of this Directive correspond to the national provisions adopted.

Article 41

Entry into force

3.132   This Directive shall enter into force on the day of its publication in the *Official Journal of the European Union*.

Article 42

Addresses

3.133   This Directive is addressed to the Member States.
         Done at Strasbourg, 29 April 2004.

Council Regulation (EEC) No 1408/71 on the application of social security schemes to employed persons, to self-employed persons and to members of their families moving within the Community

TEXT AS AMENDED BY COUNCIL REGULATION (EC) 118/97 OF
DECEMBER 2, 1996

[1997] OJ L28/4 (AS FURTHER AMENDED)

CONTENTS

Annex VI: Special procedures for applying the legislations of certain Member States

Annex VII: Instances in which a person shall be simultaneously subject to the legislation of two Member States

Annex VIII: Schemes that provide only for family allowances or supplementary or special allowances for orphans.

GENERAL NOTE

A consolidated version of reg.1408/71 was passed in December 1996. The version of the regulation printed here is based on that text. Amendments made prior to December 1996 are not noted, but the text has been updated to take account of subsequent amendments of the Regulation and annotated to show the source of those amendments in the same manner as for United Kingdom statutory material.

3.135

It is important to realize that the Regulation is concerned with the co-ordination of social security schemes and not with the harmonization of the social security laws of the Member States. The Court of Justice has consistently stressed this distinction in its judgments on provisions of Regulation 1408/71. So, for example, in Joined Cases C-393 and C-394/99 *Hervein and Lorthiois*, [2002] E.C.R. I-2829, the Court said:

". . . the system put in place by Regulation No 1408/71 is merely a system of coordination. . . .

. . . it . . . does not follow from [Articles 39 and 43 of the Treaty] that, in the absence of harmonisation of the social security legislation, neutrality as regard the complexity, for the persons concerned, of the administration of their social security cover will be guaranteed in all circumstances." (paras 52 and 58 of the judgment.)

In Case C-228/07, *Jörn Petersen*, September 11, 2008, the Luxembourg Court said:

. . . Regulation 1408/71 does not set up a common scheme of social security, but allows different social security schemes to exist and its sole objective is to ensure the coordination of those schemes (Case 21/87 *Borowitz* [1988] ECR 3715, paragraph 23, and Case C-331/06 *Chuck* [2008] ECR I-0000, paragraph 27). (para.41).

The purpose of the Regulation is to build bridges in order to connect different social security schemes so that those moving within the EEA are not disadvantaged as a result of exercising their rights of free movement. However, notwithstanding this important distinction between co-ordination and harmonisation, there are certainly adaptive pressures on Member States as a result of the requirements of co-ordination of benefit schemes which tend to pull Member State policy closer together.

See http://europa.eu.int/comm/employment_social/social_security_schemes/index_en.htm for useful information from the European Commission on the coordination of social security schemes.

The scheme of co-ordination applies to the Member States, to the three countries which together with the Member States form the European Economic Area (Iceland, Liechtenstein and Norway), and to Switzerland.

From April 1, 2006 a protocol entered into force which extends the Agreement on the Free Movement of Persons between the EU and Switzerland to the 10 Member States which joined the European Union on May 1, 2004.

Regulation 883/2004/EC—the "simplified" regulation

A new "simplified" regulation has been produced on the coordination of social security, which is expected to come into force some time in 2010: see Regulation 883/2004/EC of April 29, 2004 on the coordination of social security schemes, [2004] OJ L200/1, correcting OJ L166/1. Work is currently under way on the preparation of an updated version of the implementing regulation. The new regulation is not merely a consolidating measure, since it adds new benefits

3.136

(pre-retirement benefits) to those which are coordinated among the Member States. The new regulations were finalised at the end of July, and the new regulation is scheduled to come into force on March 1, 2010.

The Council of the European Union

3.137   *Having regard* to the Treaty establishing the European Community, and in particular Articles 51 and 235 thereof,

Having regard to the proposal from the Commission,

Having regard to the opinion of the European Parliament,

Having regard to the opinion of the Economic and Social Committee,

Whereas the provisions for co-ordination of national social security legislations fall within the framework of freedom of movement for workers who are nationals of Member States and should contribute towards the improvement of their standard of living and conditions of employment;

Whereas freedom of movement for persons, which is one of the cornerstones of the Community, is not confined to employed persons but also extends to self-employed persons in the framework of the freedom of establishment and the freedom to supply services;

Whereas the considerable differences existing between national legislations as regards the persons to whom they apply make it preferable to establish the principle that the Regulation applies to all persons insured under social security schemes for employed persons and for self-employed persons or by virtue of pursuing employment or self-employment;

Whereas it is necessary to respect the special characteristics of national social security legislations and to draw up only a system of coordination;

Whereas it is necessary, within the framework of that co-ordination, to guarantee within the Community equality of treatment under the various national legislations to workers living in the Member States and their dependants and their survivors;

Whereas the provisions for coordination must guarantee that workers moving within the Community and their dependants and their survivors retain the rights and the advantages acquired and in the course of being acquired;

Whereas these objectives must be attained in particular by aggregation of all the periods taken into account under the various national legislations for the purpose of acquiring and retaining the right to benefits and of calculating the amount of benefits, and by the provision of benefits for the various categories of persons covered by the Regulation regardless of their place of residence within the Community;

Whereas employed persons and self-employed persons moving within the Community should be subject to the social security scheme of only one single Member State in order to avoid overlapping of national legislations applicable and the complications which could result therefrom;

Whereas the instances in which a person should be subject simultaneously to the legislation of two Member States as an exception to the general rule should be as limited in number and scope as possible;

Whereas with a view to guaranteeing the equality of treatment of all workers occupied on the territory of a Member State as effectively as possible, it is appropriate to determine as the legislation applicable, as a general rule, that of the Member State in which the person concerned pursues employment of self-employment;

Whereas in certain situations which justify other criteria of applicability, it is possible to derogate from this general rule;

Whereas certain benefits foreseen under national laws may fall simultaneously within social security and social assistance, because of the personal scope of their application, their objectives and their manner of application, it is necessary to lay down a system of coordination, which takes into account the special characteristics of the benefits concerned, that should be included in the Regulation in order to protect the interests of migrant workers in accordance with the provisions of the Treaty;

Whereas such benefits should be granted, in respect of persons falling within the scope of this Regulation, solely in accordance with the legislation of the country of residence of the person concerned or of the members of his or her family, with such aggregation of periods of residence completed in any other Member State as is necessary and without discrimination on grounds of nationality;

Whereas it is necessary to lay down specific rules, in particular in the field of sickness and unemployment, for frontier workers and seasonal workers, taking account of the specific nature of their situation;

Whereas in the field of sickness and maternity benefits, it is necessary to guarantee the protection of persons living or staying in a Member State other than the competent Member State;

Whereas the specific position of pension claimants and pensioners and the members of their families calls for the provisions governing sickness insurance to adapted to their situation;

Whereas for invalidity benefits a system of coordination should be drawn up which respects the specific characteristics of national legislations; whereas it is therefore necessary to make a distinction between legislations under which the amount of invalidity benefit is independent of the length of insurance and legislations under which the amount depends on the aforementioned length;

Whereas the differences between the schemes in the Member States call for the adoption of rules of coordination which are applicable in the case of aggravation of invalidity;

Whereas it is expedient that a system for the award of old-age benefits and survivors benefits be worked out where the employed or self-employed person has been subject to the legislation of one or more Member States;

Whereas there is a need to determine the amount of a pension calculated in accordance with the method used for aggregation and pro rata calculation and guaranteed by Community law where the application of national legislation, including provisions concerning reduction, suspension or withdrawal, is less favourable than the aforementioned method;

Whereas, to protect migrant workers and their survivors against an excessively stringent application of the national provisions concerning reduction, suspension or withdrawal, it is necessary to include provisions laying down strict rules for the application of these provisions;

Whereas, in respect of benefits for accidents at work and occupational diseases, it is necessary, for the purpose of affording protection, that rules be laid down covering the situation of persons residing or staying in a Member State other than the competent Member State;

Whereas it is necessary to lay down specific provisions for death grants;

Whereas, in order to secure mobility of labour under improved conditions, it is necessary henceforth to ensure closer coordination between the unemployment insurance schemes and the unemployment assistance schemes of all the Member States;

Whereas it is therefore particularly appropriate, in order to facilitate search for employment in the various Member States, to grant to an unemployed worker, for a limited period, the unemployment benefits provided for by the legislation of the Member State to which he was last subject;

Whereas, with a view to determining the legislation applicable to family benefits, the criterion of employment ensures equal treatment between all workers subject to the same legislation;

Whereas, in order to avoid unwarranted overlapping of benefits, there is a need to provide for rules of priority in the case of overlapping of the right to family benefits under the legislation of the competent State and under the legislation of the country of residence of the members of the family;

Whereas the legislations of the Member States differ from each other and are specific in nature, it is considered necessary to draw up specific rules for the coordination of the national schemes providing benefits for dependent children of pensioners and for orphans;

Whereas it is necessary to establish an Administrative Commission consisting of a government representative from each of the Member States, charged in particular with dealing with all administrative questions or questions of interpretation arising from the provisions of this Regulation, and to further cooperation between the Member States;

Whereas it is desirable, within the framework of an Advisory Committee, to have the representatives of workers and employers examine the issues treated by the Administrative Commission;

Whereas it is necessary to lay down special provisions which correspond to the special characteristics of the national legislations in order to facilitate the application of the rules of co-ordination.

Has Adopted this Regulation

Title I

General Provisions

Article 1

Definitions

3.138 For the purpose of this Regulation:

(a) *employed person* and *self-employed person* mean respectively:

(i) [¹ any person who is insured, compulsorily or on an optional continued basis, for one or more of the contingencies covered by the branches of a social security scheme for employed or self-employed persons or by a special scheme for civil servants;]

(ii) any person who is compulsorily insured for one or more of the contingencies covered by the branches of social security dealt with in this Regulation, under a social security dealt with in this Regulation, under a social security scheme for all residents or for the whole working population, if such person:

— can be identified as an employed or self-employed person by virtue of the manner in which such scheme is administered or financed, or,

— failing such criteria, is insured for some other contingency specified in Annex I under a scheme for employed or self-employed persons, or under a scheme referred to in (iii), either compulsorily or on an optional continued basis, or, where no such scheme exists in the Member State concerned, complies with the definition given in Annex I;

(iii) any person who is compulsorily insured for several of the contingencies covered by the branches dealt with in this Regulation, under a standard social security scheme for the whole rural population in accordance with the criteria laid down in Annex I;

(iv) any person who is voluntarily insured for one or more of the contingencies covered by the branches dealt with in this Regulation, under a social security scheme of a Member State for employed or self-employed persons or for all residents or for certain categories of residents:

— if such person carries out an activity as an employed or self-employed person, or

— if such person has previously been compulsorily insured for the same contingency under a scheme for employed or self-employed persons for the same Member State;

(b) *frontier worker* means any employed or self-employed person who pursues his occupation in the territory of a Member State and resides in the territory of another Member State to which he returns as a rule daily or at least once a week; however, a frontier worker who is posted elsewhere in the territory of the same or another Member State by the undertaking to which he is normally attached, or who engages in the provision of services elsewhere in the territory of the same or another Member State, shall retain the status of frontier worker for a period not exceeding four month, even if he is prevented, during that period, from returning daily or at least once a week to the place where he resides;

(c) *seasonal worker* means any employed person who goes to the territory of a Member State other than the one in which he is resident to do work there of a seasonal nature for an undertaking or an employer of that State for a period which may on no account exceed eight month, and who stays in the territory of the said State for the duration of this work; work of a seasonal nature shall be taken to mean work which, being dependent on the succession of the seasons, automatically recurs each year;

[² (ca) *student* means any person other than an employed or self-employed person or a member of his family or survivor within the meaning of this Regulation who studies or receives vocational training leading to a qualification officially recognised by the authorities of a Member

921

State, and is insured under a general social security scheme or a special social security scheme applicable to students;]

(d) *refugee* shall have the meaning assigned to it in Article 1 of the Convention of the Status of Refugees, signed at Geneva on 28 July 1951;

(e) *stateless person* shall have the meaning assigned to it in Article 1 of the Convention on the Status of Stateless Persons, signed in New York on 28 September 1954;

(f) (i) *member of the family* means any person defined or recognized as a member of the family or designated as a member of the household by the legislation under which benefits are provided or, in the cases referred to in Articles 22(1)(a) and 31, by the legislation of the Member State in whose territory such person resides; where, however, the said legislations regard as a member of the family or a member of the household only a person living under the same roof as the [2 employed or self-employed person or student], this condition shall be considered satisfied if the person in question is mainly dependent on that person. [3 Where the legislation of a Member State does not enable members of the family to be distinguished from the other persons to whom it applies, the term 'member of the family' shall have the meaning given in Annex I.]

(ii) where, however, the benefits concerned are benefits for disabled persons granted under the legislation of a Member State to all nationals of that State who fulfil the prescribed conditions, the term "member of the family" means at least the spouse of an [2 employed or self-employed person or student] and the children of such person who are either minors or dependent upon such person;

(g) *survivor* means any person defined or recognized as such by the legislation under which the benefits are granted; where, however, the said legislation regards as a survivor only a person who was living under the same roof as the deceased, this condition shall be considered satisfied if such person was mainly dependent on the deceased;

(h) *residence* means habitual residence;

(i) *stay* means temporary residence;

(j) *legislation* means in respect of each Member State statutes, regulations and other provisions and all other implementing measures, present or future, relating to the branches and schemes of social security covered by Article 4(1) and (2) or those special non-contributory benefits covered by Article 4(2a).

The term excludes provisions of existing or future industrial agreements, whether or not they have been the subject of a decision by the authorities rendering them compulsory or extending their scope. However, in so far as such provisions:

(i) serve to put into effect compulsory insurance imposed by the laws and regulations referred to in the preceding subparagraph; or

(ii) set up a scheme administered by the same institution as that which administers the schemes set up by the laws and regulations referred to in the preceding subparagraph, the limitation on the term may at any time be lifted by a declaration of the Member State concerned specifying the schemes of such a kind to which this Regulation applies. Such a declaration shall be notified and published in accordance with the provisions of Article 97.

The provisions of the preceding subparagraph shall not have the effect of exempting from the application of this Regulation the schemes to which Regulation No 3 applied.

The term "legislation" also excludes provisions governing special schemes for self-employed persons the creation of which is left to the initiatives of those concerned or which apply only to a part of the territory of the Member State concerned, irrespective of whether or not the authorities decided to make them compulsory or extend their scope. The special schemes in question are specified in Annex II;

[¹ (ja) *special scheme of civil servants* means any social security scheme which is different from the general social security scheme applicable to employed persons in the Member States concerned and to which all, or certain categories of, civil servants or persons treated as such are directly subject;]

(k) *social security convention* means any bilateral or multilateral instrument which binds or will bind two or more Member States exclusively, and any other multilateral instrument which binds or will bind at least two Member States and one or more other States in the field of social security, for all or part of the branches and schemes set out in Article 4(1) and (2), together with agreements, of whatever kind, concluded pursuant to the said instruments;

(l) *competent authority* means, in respect of each Member State, the Minister, Ministers or other equivalent authority responsible for social security schemes throughout or in any part of the territory of the State in question;

(m) *Administrative Commission* means the commission referred to in Article 80;

(n) *institution* means, in respect of each Member State, the body or authority responsible for administering all or part of the legislation;

(o) *competent institution* means:

   (i) the institution with which the person concerned is insured at the time of the application for benefit;
     or

  (ii) the institution from which the person concerned is entitled or would be entitled to benefits if he or a member or members of his family were resident in the territory of the Member State in which the institution is situated; or

  (iii) the institution designated by the competent authority of the member State concerned; or

  (iv) in the case of a scheme relating to an employer's liability in respect of the benefits set out in Article 4(1), either the employer or the insurer involved or, in default thereof, a body or authority designated by the competent authority of the Member State concerned;

(p) *institution of the place of residence* and *institution of the place of stay* means respectively the institution which is competent to provide benefits in the place where the person concerned resides and the institution which is competent to provide benefits in the place where the person concerned is staying, under the legislation administered by that institution or, where no such institution exists, the institution designated by the competent authority of the Member State in question;

(q) *competent State* means the Member State in whose territory the competent institution is situated;

(r) *periods of insurance* means periods of contribution or period of employment or self-employment as defined or recognized as periods of insurance by the legislation under which they were completed or considered as completed, and all periods treated as such, where they are regarded by the said legislation as equivalent to periods of insurance; [[1] periods completed under a special scheme for civil servants are also considered as periods of insurance;]

(s) *periods of employment* and *periods of self-employment* means periods so defined or recognized by the legislation under which they were completed, and all periods treated as such, where they are regarded by the said legislation as equivalent to periods of employment or of self-employment; [[1] periods completed under a special scheme for civil servants are also considered as periods of insurance;]

(sa) *periods of residence* means periods as defined or recognized as such by the legislation under which they were completed or considered as completed;

(t) *benefits* and *pensions* mean all benefits and pensions, including all elements thereof payable out of public funds, revalorization increases and supplementary allowances, subject to the provisions of Title III, as also lump-sum benefits which may be paid in lieu of pensions, and payments made by way of reimbursement of contributions;

(u) (i) the term *family benefits* means all benefits in kind or in cash intended to meet family expenses under the legislation provided for in Article 4(1)(h), excluding the special childbirth or adoption allowances referred to in Annex II;

    (ii) *family allowances* means periodical cash benefits granted exclusively by reference to the number and, where appropriate, the age of members of the family;

(v) *death grants* means any once-for-all payment in the event of death exclusive of the lump-sum benefits referred to in subparagraph (t).

AMENDMENTS

1. Regulation 1606/98/EC, [1998] OJ L209/1 (October 25, 1998).
2. Regulation 307/99/EC, [1999] OJ L38/1 (May 1, 1999).
3. Regulation 1290/97/EC, [1997] OJ L176/1 (October 4, 1997).

GENERAL NOTE

3.139   Article 1 contains crucial definitions in the application of the co-ordinating rules it contains. These are autonomous concepts under Community law and are to be applied from a Community perspective.

Two particularly important definitions are those of "residence" and "stay". Residence is defined as habitual residence which is similar to but not necessarily identical to the concept adopted in United Kingdom regulations as a condition of entitlement to benefit. Residence is contrasted with stay which is temporary residence in a Member State; residence here probably means presence since holidays abroad constitute a stay in another Member State.

Article 1

For a discussion of the concept of "habitual residence" under Community law, see *Marinos v Marinos,* [2007] EWHC 2047 (Fam); [2007] 2 *Family Law Reports* 1018.

Definition of employed or self-employed person

In a closely reasoned decision, the Commissioner in *R(IS) 1/06* held that, in order to be within the personal scope of the Regulation in relation to a claim for a means-tested benefit, it was not enough to have been insured against some of the risks envisaged by the Regulation, there was a need to be an employed or self-employed person as defined by the Regulation. A claimant who had received benefits in another Member State on the basis of residence alone could not bring herself within the definition of being an employed or self-employed person. One way of establishing the status of an employed or self-employed person is to have made contributions as a person falling within such a category of contributors. In the case before the Commissioner there was, however, nothing to in the administration or financing of the Dutch social security scheme to identify the claimant as an employed or self-employed person.

For a discussion of the definitions, see *JR v HMRC* [2009] UKUT 18 (AAC), discussed in more detail in the commentary to art.73 of this Regulation.

3.140

[¹Article 2

Persons covered

1. This Regulation shall apply to employed and self-employed persons and to students who are or have been subject to the legislation of one or more Member States and who are nationals of one of the Member States or who are stateless persons or refugees residing within the territory of one of the Member States, as well as to members of their families and their survivors.

2. This Regulation shall apply to the survivors of employed or self-employed persons and of students who have been subject to the legislation of one or more Member States, irrespective of the nationality of such persons, where their survivors are nationals of one of the Member States, or stateless persons or refugees residing within the territory of one of the Member States.]

3.141

AMENDMENT

1. Regulation 307/99/EC, [1999] OJ L38/1 (May 1, 1999).

GENERAL NOTE

The latest amendment brings students into the framework of the Regulation, though they must have been subject to the legislation of one or more Member States in their own right in order to fall within the scope of the Regulation by reason of their student status.

Note that the Regulation applies to both employed and self-employed persons. It also covers their families who have rights as such and not simply derivative rights flowing from the work of another member of their family: Case C-308/93 *Cabanis-Issarte* [1996] E.C.R. I-2097. In order to be a beneficiary of the rules in the Regulation, a person must be a national of an EEA country.

3.142

Article 3

Equality of treatment

3.143   **1.** Subject to the special provisions of this Regulation, persons [¹ . . .] to whom this Regulation applies shall be subject to the same obligations and enjoy the same benefits under the legislation of any Member State as the nationals of the State.

2. The provisions of paragraph 1 shall apply to the right to elect members of the organs of social security institutions or to participate in their nomination, but shall not affect the legislative provisions of any Member State relating to eligibility or methods of nomination of persons concerned to those organs.

3. Save as provided in Annex III, the provisions of social security onventions which remain in force pursuant to Article 7.2(c) [¹ . . .], shall apply to all persons to whom this Regulation applies.

AMENDMENT

1. Regulation 647/2005/EC, [2005] OJ L117/1 (May 5, 2005).

GENERAL NOTE

3.144   The obligation in this article is central to the system of co-ordination established by the regulation. Equality of treatment is a foundational principle of the Community which is set out in art.12 EC. The prohibition is restated in art.39(2) EC on the free movement of workers; the co-ordination of social security is part of the chapter on the free movement of workers. The requirement of equal treatment has been given a broad interpretation by the Court of Justice, which has consistently stated that it covers not only overt forms of discrimination but also covert forms of discrimination under which certain requirements and conditions which are not on their face based on nationality in effect operate to discriminate between nationals of the EEA countries: see Case 237/78 *Toia* [1979] E.C.R. 2645.

In Case C-346/05 *Chateignier*, [2006] ECR I-10951, the Court of Justice ruled:

"Article 39(2) EC and Article 3(1) of Council Regulation (EEC) No 1408/71 of 14 June 1971 . . . are to be interpreted as precluding national legislation under which the competent institution of the Member State of residence denies unemployment benefits to a national of another Member State on the ground that, on the date when the benefit claim was submitted, the person concerned had not completed a specified period of employment in that Member State of residence, whereas there is no such requirement for nationals of that Member State."

Article 2 of reg.1408/71 brings refugees, as defined in art.1, within its personal scope. Article 3(1) provides that those within the personal scope of the Regulation are entitled to the same rights as nationals of the Member State in which they are resident. But note that "resident" is defined in art.1 as involving "habitual residence".

In *CF/3662/1999* a person seeking asylum sought to rely on this provision to obtain a right of entry and residence in the United Kingdom. The Commissioner dismissed the appeal on the authority of *Krasniqi v Chief Adjudication Officer* (reported as *R(IS) 15/99)*, to the effect that a claimant who has no connection with any Member State of the European Union other than the United Kingdom cannot rely on reg.1408/71. That decision is found to be entirely consistent with authority from the Court of Justice of the European Communities in Joined Cases C-95/99–C-98/99 *Khalil v Bundesanstalt für Arbeit* [2001] ECR I-7413.

The issue of discrimination prohibited by art.3 was discussed in *Secretary of State for Work and Pensions* v *Bobezes*, [2005] EWCA Civ 111, reported as *R(IS) 6/05*. The claimant was a Portuguese national who had been a worker in the United Kingdom who had become permanently incapable of work. He was in receipt of income support including an allowance for a child. When the child when to visit her grandmother in Portugal from August to November 1998, the decision maker concluded that there was no entitlement to the child allowance on the grounds of absence from Great Britain for more than four weeks. The claimant argued that he had been the victim of discrimination prohibited by Community law in that, had the child gone to stay with a grandparent in Great Britain, there would have been a continuing entitlement to the allowance. There was discussion in the Court of Appeal as to whether art.7(2) of reg.1612/68 applied or art.3 of reg.1408/71. The Court of Appeal declines to resolve the question of the relationship of these two provisions and proceeds on the basis that the claimant could rely on art.3 of reg.1408/71.

The key question then addressed concerned proof of discrimination. The Secretary of State argued that the claimant must produce statistical evidence to show the claimed discrimination, while the claimant argued that he had to do no more than show that the requirements of the United Kingdom legislation were intrinsically more likely to affect essentially migrant workers. The Court of Appeal concludes that adjudicating authorities should take a "broad approach and to find that indirect discrimination is liable to affect a significant number of migrant workers on the ground of nationality without statistical proof being available." (para.24 of judgment). Lord Slynn said that the proper approach was to compare the children of migrant workers with British children whose families are normally resident here.

CPC/1072/2006 was an attempt to use art.3 of Regulation 1408/71 as a means of challenging the requirement of a right to reside as a condition of entitlement to state pension credit. The Commissioner ruled that the Secretary of State's concession that state pension credit fell within the material scope of the regulation was plainly right. This meant that art.3 bit, even though the benefit was listed in Annex IIa as a special non-contributory benefit. The appellant argued that the requirement of a right to reside as a condition of entitlement constituted prohibited discrimination under art.3 which could not be justified. The Commissioner ruled:

> I have no doubt that a requirement that is always satisfied by citizens of the Member State but not necessarily by citizens of other Member States will rarely prove justifiable in practice, but I am not satisfied that there is any principle that forbids an attempt to justify such a requirement, particularly where the case touches upon an issue that is beyond the European Community's sphere of competence (para.17).

He went on to say:

> A condition that confines entitlement only to nationals of the Member State concerned is unlawful, but a condition designed to confer entitlement on all such nationals and some nationals of other member states may be justified to the extent that it is consistent with the Community's approach to social assistance (para.19).

The Community's approach was to require Member States to extend the protection of social assistance to nationals of other Member States with a sufficient connection with the host Member States. The condition of entitlement that a person has a right to reside "is justified because such a condition distinguishes between those guaranteed equal treatrment in relation to social assistance by Community law and those for whom Community law provides no such guarantee." (para.19). The Commissioner took the view that the first step is to determine whether a person has a right to reside under Art.18 EC. This determines the question of the right to be treated equally with nationals of the Member State. The Commissioner then says:

In effect, the approach that satisfied the Court of Appeal in *Abdirahman* that the claimed right was outside the scope of Article 12 of the EC Treaty satisfies me that the imposition of a right of residence in respect of state pension credit is justified and is not contrary to Article 3 of Regulation (EEC) 1408/71. (para.23).

The Court of Appeal has dismissed the claimant's appeal against the Commissioner's decision in *Patmalniece v Secretary of State for Work and Pensions*, [2009] EWCA Civ 621. It was accepted that State pension credit is a special noncontributory benefit within the material scope of art.3 of reg.1408/71, but that did not mean that it lost the characteristics of social assistance. Restrictions on entitlement to the benefit could be limited to those with a right to reside in the United Kingdom. That was a test of the level of social integration which was justified by reference to the need to protect the finances of the country of residence. Only those who were economically or socially integrated to a sufficient degree could become a burden on the United Kingdom's social assistance schemes.

Article 4

Matters covered

3.145   **1.** This Regulation shall apply to all legislation concerning the following branches of social security:
(a) sickness and maternity benefits;
(b) invalidity benefits, including those intended for the maintenance or improvement of earning capacity;
(c) old-age benefits;
(d) survivors' benefits;
(e) benefits in respect of accidents at work and occupational diseases;
(f) death grants;
(g) unemployment benefits;
(h) family benefits.
2. This Regulation shall apply to all general and special social security schemes, whether contributory or non-contributory, and to schemes concerning the liability of an employer or shipowner in respect of the benefits referred to in paragraph 1.
[² **2a.** This Article shall apply to special non-contributory cash benefits which are provided under legislation which, because of its personal scope, objectives and/or conditions for entitlement has characteristics both of the social security legislation referred to in paragraph 1 and of social assistance.
"Special non-contributory cash benefits" means those:
(a) which are intended to provide either:
(i) supplementary, substitute or ancillary cover against the risks covered by the branches of social security referred to in paragraph 1, and which guarantee the persons concerned a minimum subsistence income having regard to the economic and social situation in the Member State concerned;
or
(ii) solely specific protection for the disabled, closely linked to the said person's social environment in the Member State concerned,
and
(b) where the financing exclusively derives from compulsory taxation intended to cover general public expenditure and the conditions for

providing and for calculating the benefits are not dependent on any contribution in respect of the beneficiary. However, benefits provided to supplement a contributory benefit shall not be considered to be contributory benefits for this reason alone;
and

(c) which are listed in Annex IIa.]

2b. This Regulation shall not apply to the provisions in the legislation of a Member State concerning special non-contributory benefits, referred to in Annex II, Section III, the validity of which is confined to part of its territory.

3. The provisions of Title III of this Regulation shall not, however, affect the legislative provisions of any Member State concerning a shipowner's liability.

4. This Regulation shall not apply to social and medical assistance, to benefit schemes for victims of war or its consequences, [[1] . . .].

AMENDMENTS

1. Regulation 1606/98/EC, [1998] OJ L209/1 (October 25, 1998).
2. Regulation 647/2005/EC, [2005] OJ L117/1 (May 5, 2005).

GENERAL NOTE

The Regulation applies to all legislation governing benefits protecting against the eight named risks. These social risks are those identified in ILO Convention 102. It does not matter whether the specified benefits are provided under contributory or non-contributory schemes. Special non-contributory benefits are also covered where they provide supplementary, substitute or ancillary cover against the social risk set out in the article, or are specific protection for disabled people. The provision contains an exhaustive list of the branches of social security governed by the Regulation. It applies to all legislation concerning the specified branch of social security; legislation is defined in very broad terms in art.1, and the Court of Justice has described the definition as "remarkable for its breadth": Case 87/76 *Bozzone* [1977] E.C.R. 687.

3.146

Whether a particular benefit falls within the scope of these eight branches of social security as well as whether any of the exceptions applies is determined in accordance with Community law, and not simply the classification of a benefit under the national scheme. The Court of Justice has consistently said that whether a benefit is within the material scope of the Regulation "rests entirely on the factors relating to each benefit, in particular its purpose and the conditions for its grant": Case 9/78 *Gillard* [1978] E.C.R. 1661, para.12 of the judgment. The fact that the benefit has a dual purpose does not exclude it from the material scope of the Regulation.

In Case C-160/96 *Molenaar* [1998] E.C.R. I-843, the Court of Justice ruled that care insurance was a benefit intended to supplement sickness insurance and so constituted a sickness benefit for the purpose of reg.1408/71. This was taken further in Joned Cases C-502/01 and C-31/02 *Gaumain-Cerri* and *Barth*, [2004] ECR I-6483, where the Court ruled that the payment of old-age insurance in respect of carers of a person in receipt of care insurance also constituted a sickness benefit.

Case C-228/07 *Jörn Petersen*, September 11, 2008, illustrates the need for careful consideration of the classification of benefits. Petersen is a German national who was working in Austria. He claimed an incapacity pension, which was refused. While an appeal against this decision was pending, the Austrian authorities granted Petersen an advance of pension payments under provisions of Austrian law headed "advance pension payments." Petersen was considering returning to German and asked for the advance unemployment benefit to be continued after his change of residence. That application was refused. The first question before the Court was whether the benefit was an unemployment benefit or an invalidity benefit. Though the benefit had certain characteristics of both, the Court concluded that the benefit was an unemployment benefit within art.4(1)(g).

The second question concerned the exportability of the benefit, since Austrian law provided that the benefit was payable subject to a condition of residence in the national territory. The Court noted that the provisions of arts 69 and 71 were not applicable to the present case. However, in exercising their discretion to regulate the scheme, the Austrian authorities were required to exercise their choices having appropriate and proportionate regard to arts 39 to 42 EC. The Court concluded that the Austrian Government had not put forward any objective justification for the condition that recipients of the benefit to which Petersen was entitled must be residence on the national territory.

Note that the United Kingdom, after much argument, eventually conceded that winter fuel payments are an old-age benefit within the material scope of Regulation 1408/71. For background and discussion of the implications, see *Secretary of State for Work and Pensions v Walker-Fox* [2005] EWCA Civ. 1441, reported as *R(IS) 3/06*, and *R(IS) 8/06*.

It is possible that issues will arise as to whether child trust contributions under the Child Trust Funds Act 2004 constitute family benefits within reg.1408/71, since s.2 of the Act excludes payment of the contribution where child benefit is in payment under the coordination rules, but the child is not resident in the United Kingdom.

Social assistance is excluded from the scope of the Regulation together with medical assistance, and schemes for war victims.

The distinction between social insurance and social assistance used to be more clear cut than it is today. Social insurance as originally conceived related to insurance-based schemes in respect of certain risks against which workers or their employers would insure; it also included provision for what might be regarded as the certainties of life: birth, old age and death. By contrast social assistance is support provided by the State at its discretion on the basis of need. There is also a third group of benefits which are provided on the basis of need, but are a matter of legal entitlement and not discretion. Considerable debate still surrounds the true nature of benefits like income support in the United Kingdom which are means tested but are paid as a matter of legal right to those who meet closely specified conditions of entitlement and at a rate also set out in regulations. In *Perry v Chief Adjudication Officer*, [1999] 2 C.M.L.R. 439, reported as *R(IS) 4/99*, the Court of Appeal held that income support was not a special non contributory benefit (see art.10a below) within the meaning of the Regulation, but this decision must now be read in the light of Case C-90/97 *Swaddling v Adjudication Officer* [1999] E.C.R. I-1075; [1999] 2 C.M.L.R. 679, reported as *R(IS) 6/99*, in which the Court of Justice ruled that income support is a special non-contributory benefit within the meaning of the Regulation.

In *CIB/4243/1999*, the Commissioner held that short-term incapacity benefit whether paid at the lower or the higher rate is a sickness benefit for the purposes of reg.1408/71, while long-term incapacity benefit is an invalidity benefit for the purposes of the Regulation (para.17).

Certain United Kingdom benefits take the form of a contribution-based benefit and an income-related benefit within the same overall benefit: jobseeker's allowance, and employment and support allowance. The contribution-based component will fall within the scope of the regulation as, respectively, an unemployment benefit, and a sickness or invalidity benefit. The willingness of the Court of Justice to unravel national benefit structures became abundantly clear in Case C-299/05, *Commission v European Parliament and Council*, [2007] ECR I-8695, in which the Court split the care component and the mobility component of disability living allowance. Though not definitively established, it was accepted that the mobility component was a special non-contributory benefit, but the Court ruled that the care component is a form of sickness benefit, whose exportability could not be excluded: see also commentary on art.10a below.

Article 5

Declarations by the Member States on the scope of this Regulation

The Member States shall specify the legislation and schemes referred to in Article 4(1) and (2), the special non-contributory benefits referred to in Article 4(2a), the minimum benefits referred to in Article 50 and the benefits referred to in Articles 77 and 78 in declarations to be notified and published in accordance with Article 97.

3.147

GENERAL NOTE

Little assistance is provided by reference to declarations made by Member States, since they are not always kept up to date.

3.148

Article 6

Social security conventions replaced by this Regulation.

Subject to the provisions of Articles 7, 8 and 46(4) this Regulation shall, as regards persons and matters which it covers, replace the provisions of any social security convention binding either;

3.149

(a) two or more Member States exclusively, or
(b) at least two Member States and one or more other States, where settlement of the cases concerned does not involve any institution of one of the latter States.

RELEVANT PROVISIONS OF THE IMPLEMENTING REGULATION

Art.5, Reg. 574/72/EEC.

RELEVANT DECISIONS OF THE ADMINISTRATIVE COMMISSION

Recommendation No 22 of June, 18 2003 concerning the *Gottardo* judgment, according to which the advantages enjoyed by a state's own nationals under a bilateral convention on social security with a non-member country must also be granted to workers who are nationals of other Member States, [2003] OJ L326/35.

GENERAL NOTE

This article gives priority to the provisions of the Regulation over social security conventions concluded between the Member States. This has given rise to some complex and difficult case law. The essential question was whether advantages arising under the existing conventions were lost when the Regulation came into force, and whether this was compatible with the EC Treaty provisions. In its first decision on this issue in Case 82/72 *Walder*, [1973] E.C.R. 599, the Court ruled that the provisions of art.6 were mandatory and did not allow for exceptions which were not expressly set out in the Regulation. Case 227/89 *Rönfeldt*, [1991] E.C.R. I-323 concerned a German national who had from 1941 to 1957, and so prior to the entry into force of Regulation 1408/71 (or its predecessor), worked in Germany before moving to Denmark and working there until 1971 when he returned to Germany. Retirement pension ages were 65 in Germany and 67 in Denmark; in Germany an early retirement pension could be claimed at 63 provided that a

3.150

person had completed 35 years of insurance. Rönfeldt claimed an early retirement pension but was refused since the German authorities took the view that contributions paid in Denmark could not be taken into account in Germany until the claimant reached the Danish retirement age of 67. The Court noted that art.45 of the Regulation to take insurance periods completed in other Member States into account in determining whether a person has acquired, retained or recovered a right to benefit, but art.46 does not require contributions paid elsewhere to be taken into account in calculating the amount of a benefit. This was in contrast to the requirements of a convention between Germany and Denmark. The Court then ruled that it was incompatible with the provisions of the EC Treaty on free movement of workers to deprive a person of advantages which they had acquired under a convention.

The judgment presented very significant problems of administration for the Member States since it would mean that in very many cases multiple computations would be needed because of the number of bilateral and multilateral treaties in existence. The Court clarified its judgment in the *Rönfeldt* case in Case 475/93 *Thévenon and Speyer* [1995] E.C.R. I-3813. The Court explained that the rule in the *Rönfeldt* case only applied where a right to freedom of movement had been exercised prior to the entry into force; it did not apply where the right of free movement was first exercised after reg.1408/71 had replaced the provisions of the bilateral convention. The *Rönfeldt* exception applied only to those who had already accrued certain rights under the bilateral convention. It did not preserve the more beneficial rule in the convention for those first exercising their right of free movement under the regime set in place by reg.1408/71. The consequence is that it is not a requirement for institutions in the Member States to investigate in every claim whether a person might have a more advantageous position under a bilateral or multilateral convention. In Case C-113/96 *Gómez Rodríguez*, [1998] E.C.R. I-2482, ruled that a comparison of rights had to be made only once: at the first determination of benefit entitlement within the terms of Regulation 1408/71. In Case C-75/99 *Thelen*, [2000] E.C.R. I-9399 and Case C-277/99 *Kaske*, [2000] E.C.R. I-1261, the Court ruled that the only purpose of the *Rönfeldt* exception was to preserve entitlement to an established social right which was not part of Community law at the time when the national of a Member State relying on it had such an entitlement. The *Rönfeldt* exception was based on a person's legitimate expectation that accrued rights would not be lost.

Article 7

International provisions not affected by this Regulation

3.151   **1.** This Regulation shall not affect obligations arising from:

   (a) any convention adopted by the International Labour Conference which, after ratification by one or more Member States, has entered into force;

   (b) the European Interim Agreements on Social Security of 11 December 1953 concluded between the Member States of the Council of Europe.

2. The provisions of Article 6 notwithstanding, the following shall continue to apply:

   (a) the provision of the Agreements of 27 July 1950 and 30 November 1979 concerning social security for Rhine boatmen;

   (b) the provisions of the European Convention of 9 July 1956 concerning social security for workers in international transport;

Article 7

[[1] (c) certain provisions of social security conventions entered into by the Member States before the date of application of this Regulation provided that they are more favourable to the beneficiaries or if they arise from specific historical circumstances and their effect is limited in time if these provisions are listed in Annex III.]

AMENDMENT

1. Regulation 647/2005/EC, [2005] OJ L117/1 (May 5, 2005).

RELEVANT PROVISIONS OF THE IMPLEMENTING REGULATION

Art.5, reg.574/72/EEC.

GENERAL NOTE

Art.3(3) and Annex III provide exceptions to the operation of certain provisions of this article.

3.152

Article 8

Conclusion of conventions between Member States

1. Two or more Member States may, as need arises, conclude conventions with each other based on the principles and in the spirit of this Regulation.

2. Each Member State shall notify, in accordance with the provisions of Article 97(1), any convention concluded with another member State under the provisions of paragraph 1.

3.153

GENERAL NOTE

Art.3(3) and Annex III provide exceptions to the operation of certain provisions of this article.

3.154

Article 9

Admission to voluntary or optional continued insurance

1. The provisions of the legislation of any Member State which make admission to voluntary or optional continued insurance conditional upon residence in the territory of that State shall not apply to persons resident in the territory of another Member State, provided that at some time in their past working life they were subject to the legislation of the first State as employed or as self-employed persons.

2. Where under the legislation of a Member State, admission to voluntary or optional continued insurance is conditional upon completion of periods of insurance, the periods of insurance or residence completed under the legislation of another Member State shall be taken into account, to the extent required, as if they were completed under the legislation of the first State.

3.155

RELEVANT PROVISIONS OF THE IMPLEMENTING REGULATION

Art.6, reg.574/72/EEC.

Article 9a

[¹ Prolongation of the reference period

3.156   If the legislation of a Member State subordinates recognition of entitlement to a benefit to the completion of a minimum period of insurance during a determined period preceding the contingency insured against (reference period) and lays down that periods during which benefits were paid under the legislation of that Member State or periods devoted to child-rearing in the territory of that Member State shall extend this reference period, the periods during which invalidity or old age pensions or sickness, unemployment, industrial accidents at work or occupational disease benefits were paid under the legislation of another Member State and periods devoted to child-rearing in the territory of another Member State shall also extend this reference period.]

AMENDMENT

1. Regulation 647/2005/EC, [2005] OJ L117/1 (May 5, 2005).

Article 10

Waiving of residence clauses—Effect of compulsory insurance on reimbursement of contributions

3.157   **1.** Save as otherwise provided in this Regulation invalidity, old-age or survivors' cash benefits, pension for accidents at work or occupational diseases and death grants acquired under the legislation of one or more Member States shall not be subject to any reduction, modification, suspension, withdrawal or confiscation by reason of the fact that the recipient resides in the territory of a Member State other than that in which the institution responsible for payment is situated.

The first subparagraph shall also apply to lump-sum benefits granted in cases of remarriage of a surviving spouse who was entitled to a survivors' pension.

2. Where under the legislation of a Member State reimbursement of contributions is conditional upon the person concerned having ceased to be subject to compulsory insurance, this condition shall not be considered satisfied as long as the person concerned is subject to compulsory insurance [¹ . . .] under the legislation of another Member State.

AMENDMENT

1. Regulation 307/99/EC, [1999] OJ L38/1 (May 1, 1999).

GENERAL NOTE

3.158   This article and art.10a deal with the exportability of benefits. They set out the general rules on which a benefit acquired in one EEA country may continue

934

in payment where the beneficiary moves to another EEA country. Though issues remain as to the classification of certain benefits, those rules seem fairly clear. Member States tend to argue that benefits are social assistance and are not capable of exportation. So in Case 139/82 *Piscitello* [1983] E.C.R. 1427, the Italian Government argued that the *pensione sociale* was social assistance, but the Court concluded that it was a benefit analogous to an old age pension and so Paolo Piscitello could take it with her when she moved from Italy to Belgium to join members of her family living there.

The exportability of sickness and maternity, and unemployment benefits applies only to a very limited extent, since the Member States are extremely cautious about losing the ability to monitor the genuineness of the claim or the claimant's continuing job search activities. The putting together of sickness and maternity benefits is unfortunate in this regard.

The concern of the Member States that certain individuals would tour the Member States collecting the most favourable benefit entitlements and exporting them to where they wanted to live led to a new regime being introduced for what are called special non-contributory benefits. Such benefits are under art.10a payable only in the territory of the Member State to those resident there. Special non-contributory benefits must be listed in Annex IIa of the Regulation. Though payability is linked to residence, the process of acquisition is not tied to a single Member State.

Entitlement to export those benefits which were excluded from the exportability rules in art.10 continued for those who already had an entitlement as at the date art.10a was introduced into the Regulation, that is, June 1, 1992 (see Reg.1247/93/EEC[1992] O.J. L136/1). DLA is a single benefit, and so the addition of a care component where a mobility component is already in payment prior to the date of this change does not result in the loss of the protected exportability of the benefit: see *CDLA/402/2003.*

On the exportability of winter fuel payments, see *CIS/488/2004* and *CIS/1491/ 2004.* In *CIS/1491/2004* the Commissioner had to consider whether there was an entitlement to winter fuel payments by a person born in 1928 whose residence in Great Britain had ended before the introduction of winter fuel payments. The Commissioner concluded that the payments are not a supplement to retirement pension, but are a separate and free-standing form of old age benefit. It was not accordingly contrary to Community law to condition entitlement to such a benefit on residence in Great Britain. Since the claimant could not secure entitlement to a winter fuel payment, it followed that he could not export that to which he was not entitled. Article 10 only permits the export of a benefit to another Member State after entitlement to it has been acquired. That was not the case here.

Secretary of State for Work and Pensions v Burley, [2008] EWCA Civ 376, to be reported as *R(P) 2/08,* is the appeal against the decision in *CP/633/2006 and CP/634/2006.* It concerned the reduction in the payment of pension to a couple who had moved permanently to France. However, entitlement to the pension depended upon the operation of a bilateral agreement with Australia under which contributions paid in Australia were treated as paid in the United Kingdom. The Commissioner had ruled that reg.1408/71 applied, but the Secretary of State appealed arguing that the derogation to be found in Annex VI, Point Y, para.7 applied (see para.3.317 of the main Volume). The Court of Appeal considered that the Secretary of State was correct in that the operation of reg.1408/71 was ousted since the respondents entitlement to the retirement pension was governed by the provisions of the reciprocal agreements whose priority was preserved by the derogation. This case indicates just how important it will be to determine whether any entitlement which appears at first sight to be governed by reg.1408/71 is not affected by the operation of a reciprocal agreement.

Article 10a

Special non-contributory benefits

3.159 [[1] 1. The provisions of Article 10 and of Title III shall not apply to the special non-contributory cash benefits referred to in Article 4(2a). The persons to whom this Regulation applies shall receive these benefits exclusively in the territory of the Member State in which they reside and under the legislation of that State, in so far as these benefits are mentioned in Annex IIa. Benefits shall be paid by, and at the expense of, the institution of the place of residence.]

2. The institution of a Member State under whose legislation entitlement to benefits covered by paragraph 1 is subject to the completion of periods of employment, self-employment or residence shall regard, to the extent necessary, periods of employment, self-employment or residence completed in the territory of any other Member State as periods completed in the territory of the first Member State.

3. Where entitlement to a benefit covered by paragraph 1 but granted in the form of a supplement is subject, under the legislation of a Member State, to receipt of a benefit covered by Article 4 (1) (a) to (h), and no such benefit is due under that legislation, any corresponding benefit granted under the legislation of any other Member State shall be treated as a benefit granted under the legislation of the first Member State for the purposes of entitlement to the supplement.

4. Where the granting of a disability or invalidity benefit covered by paragraph 1 is subject, under the legislation of a Member State, to the condition that the disability or invalidity should be diagnosed for the first time in the territory of that Member State, this condition shall be deemed to be fulfilled where such diagnosis is made for the first time in the territory of another Member State.

AMENDMENT

1. Regulation 647/2005/EC, [2005] OJ L117/1 (May 5, 2005).

RELEVANT DECISIONS OF THE ADMINISTRATIVE COMMISSION

Decision No. 151 of 22 April, 1993 concerning the application of art.10a of reg.1408/71/EEC and of art.2 of reg.1247/92/EEC, [1994] OJ L244/1.

Decision No. 153 of 13 May, 1993 on the implementation of art.10a of reg.1408/71/EEC and of art.2 of reg.1247/92/EEC, [1994] OJ L244/19.

GENERAL NOTE

3.160 The concept of special non-contributory benefits was introduced into Regulation 1408/71 by reg.1247/92/EEC, [1992] OJ L/136/1 with effect from June 1, 1992. Such benefits are benefits which provide "supplementary, substitute or ancillary cover" in respect of the risks set out in art.4, or "solely as specific protection for the disabled" (see art.4(2a) above). By an amendment in 2005 additional qualifying words were added which refer to minimum subsistence income benefits and qualify the benefits for disabled people by referring to their being "closely linked to the said person's social environment in the Member State concerned."

The significance of the designation of a benefit as a special non-contributory benefit is *not* that it is taken outside the scope of reg.1408/71 completely, but that it is payable only on the territory of the competent State. The United Kingdom's list of benefits included in Annex IIa has always been among the longer lists of such benefits.

The nature of disability living allowance was considered in Case C-20/96 *Snares v The Adjudication Officer* [1997] E.C.R. I-6057, reported as *R(DLA)5/99*, and of attendance allowance in Case C-297/96 *Partridge v The Adjudication Officer* [1998] E.C.R. I-1467, reported as *R(A) 1/99*. The Court of Justice took the view that the listing of the benefit in Annex IIa must be accepted as establishing the nature of the benefit; the absence of a revised declaration under art.5 did not prejudice this position. The result was the same in *Partridge*.

It was accepted in the Court of Appeal in *Perry v Chief Adjudication Officer*, reported as *R(IS)4/99* that income support is a special non-contributory benefit. This was confirmed in a ruling from the Court of Justice in *Swaddling v Adjudication Officer*, reported as *R(IS)6/99*, but that ruling also indicated the effect of the benefit remaining one within the scope of reg.1408/71 for other purposes.

Though it is a precondition for claiming that a benefit is a special non-contributory benefit that it is listed in Annex IIa, that is not conclusive as to its status. It remains open to the Court of Justice to determine that the benefit is a supplement to one of the benefits within the material scope of the Regulation: Case C-215/99 *Jauch* [2001] E.C.R. I-1901, and Case C-43/99 *Leclere* [2001] E.C.R. I-4265. This case rather took the Member States by surprise, since they had assumed that inclusion in Annex IIa was conclusive. But the Court ruled that it must examine in cases where the issue arose whether a benefit genuinely qualified as a special non-contributory benefit; specification in Annex IIa was not conclusive. The fallout from the decision in *Jauch and Leclere* is that claims that benefits are special non-contributory benefits can now subject to more detailed enquiry if that matter comes before the Court of Justice.

In Case C-160/02 *Skalka*, [2004] ECR I-5613 the Court had to consider the status of a supplementary pension in Austria, which was listed in Annex IIa. In essence this is a topping up pension to bring a pensioner's income up to a certain level. It was, however, only payable to people habitually resident in Austria. Skalka was an Austrian national who had retired early and moved to Spain. The Court accepted that it was a special non-contributory benefit. There was clear evidence that the benefit was non-contributory. In para.22 the Court said:

"22. A special benefit within the meaning of Article 4(2a) of Regulation No 1408/71 is defined by its purpose. It must either replace or supplement a social security benefit and be by its nature social assistance justified on economic and social grounds and fixed by legislation setting objective criteria (see to that effect Case C-20/96 *Snares* [1997] ECR I-6057, paragraphs 33, 42 and 43, Case C-297/96 *Partridge* [1998] ECR I-3467, paragraph 34, and Case C-43/99 *Leclère and Deaconescu* [2001] ECR I-4265, paragraph 32).

26. As all the interveners have stated, the Austrian compensatory supplement tops up a retirement pension or an invalidity pension. It is by nature social assistance in so far as it is intended to ensure a minimum means of subsistence for its recipient where the pension is insufficient. Its grant is dependent on objective criteria defined by law. Consequently, it must be classified as a 'special benefit' within the meaning of Regulation No 1408/71."

In Case C-286/03 *Silvia Hosse*, [2006] ECR I-1771, the Grand Chamber of the Court of Justice was faced with a reference concerning a German care allowance. It was regional benefit, but that did not prove to be material to the Court's ruling. The Court noted that the Community institutions were entitled to legislate for certain exceptions to the principle of exportability of social security benefits, but recapitulated its earlier case law on the classification of benefits. The Court then explained why the German benefit was not a special non-contributory benefit:

"36. The scheme of Regulation No 1408/71 shows that the concept of 'social security benefit' within the meaning of Article 4(1) and the concept of 'special non-contributory benefit' within the meaning of Article 4(2a) and (2b) of the regulation are mutually exclusive. A benefit which satisfies the conditions of a 'social security benefit' within the meaning of Article 4(1) of Regulation No 1408/71 therefore cannot be analysed as a 'special non-contributory benefit".

37. A benefit may be regarded as a social security benefit in so far as it is granted to the recipients, without any individual and discretionary assessment of personal needs, on the basis of a legally defined position and relates to one of the risks expressly listed in Article 4(1) of Regulation No 1408/71 (see, inter alia, Case 249/83 *Hoeckx* [1985] ECR 973, paragraphs 12 to 14; Case C-78/91 *Hughes* [1992] ECR I-4839, paragraph 15; Case C-160/96 *Molenaar* [1998] ECR I-843, paragraph 20; and *Jauch*, paragraph 25).

38. It follows that benefits which are granted objectively on the basis of a legally defined position and are intended to improve the state of health and life of persons reliant on care have the essential purpose of supplementing sickness insurance benefits, and must be regarded as 'sickness benefits' within the meaning of Article 4(1)(a) of Regulation No 1408/71 (*Molenaar*, paragraphs 24 and 25, and *Jauch*, paragraph 28).

39. A care allowance such as that granted under the SPGG is intended to compensate, in the form of a flat-rate contribution, for the additional expenditure resulting from the recipients' condition of reliance on care, in particular the cost of the assistance it is necessary to provide them with.

40. The amount of such a care allowance depends of the degree of reliance on care. It corresponds to the time spent on care, expressed in terms of hours per month. Assessment of reliance on care is regulated in detail in a measure laying down a classification according to degrees of reliance. The other income of the person reliant on care has no effect on the amount of the care allowance.

41. The allowance is paid to persons who do not receive any pension under the Federal provisions. Those persons are essentially members of the families of socially insured persons, recipients of social assistance, disabled workers, and persons receiving pensions from the provinces and municipalities.

42. Consequently, while a care allowance such as that at issue in the main proceedings may have a different system from that applicable to the German benefits of insurance against reliance on care at issue in *Molenaar* and the Austrian federal care allowance at issue in *Jauch*, it none the less remains of the same kind as those benefits.

43. Moreover, as the Court observed in *Jauch*, the conditions for the grant of care allowance and the way in which it is financed cannot have the intention or the effect of changing the character of care allowance as analysed in the *Molenaar* and *Jauch* judgments. The fact that the grant of the benefit is not necessarily linked to payment of a sickness insurance benefit or a pension awarded on a basis other than sickness insurance cannot therefore change that analysis.

44. In those circumstances, even if they have their own particular characteristics, such benefits must be regarded as sickness benefits within the meaning of Article 4(1)(a) of Regulation No 1408/71.

45. In the light of the above factors, one of the conditions necessary for Article 4(2b) of Regulation No 1408/71 to apply, namely the classification of the benefit in question as a 'special benefit', is not satisfied. There is thus no longer any need to consider whether the other conditions laid down in that article are satisfied."

Case C-154/05 *Kersbergen-Lap and Dams-Schipper* [2006] ECR I-6249, raised the question of whether an incapacity benefit for disabled young people who had never worked constituted a special non-contributory benefit. Two recipients of the benefit had moved to France and Germany respectively, and the payment of the benefit had been stopped. It was again easy to conclude that the benefit was non-contributory, and as in the earlier cases the focus was on whether the benefit was special. The Third Chamber concluded:

"30. A special benefit within the meaning of Article 4(2a) of Regulation No 1408/71 is defined by its purpose. It must either replace or supplement a social security benefit and be by its nature social assistance justified on economic and social grounds and fixed by legislation setting objective criteria (see Case C-160/02 *Skalka* [2004] ECR I-5613, paragraph 25, and case-law cited).

31. As was pointed out by the Netherlands Government, the Wajong benefit is a replacement allowance intended for those who do not satisfy the conditions of insurance for obtaining invalidity benefit under Article 4(1)(b) of Regulation No 1408/71. By guaranteeing a minimum income to a socially disadvantaged group (disabled young people), the Wajong benefit is by its nature social assistance justified on economic and social grounds. Moreover, it is granted according to objective criteria defined by law.

32. With regard to the fact that the benefit at issue in the main proceedings is granted without any means test or needs assessment being carried out, as was pointed out by the Commission, the majority of disabled young people would not have sufficient means of subsistence if they did not receive that benefit.

33. Further, that benefit is closely linked to the socio-economic situation in the Netherlands since it is based on the minimum wage and the standard of living in that Member State. The Court has in the past accepted that the grant of benefits closely linked with the social environment may be made subject to a condition of residence in the State of the competent institution (see, to that effect, Case 313/86 *Lenoir* [1988] ECR 5391, paragraph 16; Case C-20/96 *Snares* [1997] ECR I-6057, paragraph 42; and Case C-43/99 *Leclerc and Deaconescu* [2001] ECR I-4265, paragraph 32).

34. It follows that a benefit under the Wajong must be classified as a special benefit within the meaning of Regulation No 1408/71."

Case C-265/05 *José Perez Naranjo*, [2007] ECR I-347, 2007, concerned a supplementary old-age allowance payable in France. Perez Naranjo was a Spanish national who had worked in France but then return to Spain. Since November 1991 he has been in receipt of a French old-age pension. His claim for the supplementary allowance was refused. In this case the Grand Chamber quickly concluded that the benefit was a special benefit; it was similar to both social security and social assistance, and so had a mixed character which meant it had to be regarded as a special benefit (para.35 of the Judgment). The question of whether it was contributory was rather more complex and required an examination of the financing of the benefit. It is acknowledged that this is an enquiry which might better be resolved following consideration in the national courts (para.36). In connection with this enquiry the Court observes that it is necessary to consider whether there is an identifiable link between the supplementary allowance and the general social contribution on earned income and substitute income. In a steer to the national court, the Grand Chamber says,

". . . even if the part of the general social contribution based on earned income and substitute income must be regarded as a contribution rather than financing from public resources, the link between that contribution and the supplementary allowance is not sufficiently identifiable for that allowance to be classified as a contributory benefit." (para.52).

In Case C-287/05 *Hendrix v Raad van Vestuur van het Uitvoeringsinstituut Werknemersversekeringen*, Judgment of September 11, 2007, the Grand Chamber ruled:

"1. A benefit such as that provided under the Law on provision of incapacity benefit to disabled young people (Wet arbeidsongeschiktheidsvoorziening jonggehandicapten) of 24 April 1997 must be regarded as a special non-contributory benefit within the meaning of Article 4(2a) of Council Regulation (EEC) No 1408/71 of 14 June 1971 on the application of social security schemes to employed persons, to self employed persons and to members of their families moving within the Community, as amended and updated by Council Regulation

(EC) No 118/97 of 2 December 1996, as amended by Council Regulation (EC) No 1223/98 of 4 June 1998, with the result that only the coordinating provision in Article 10a of that regulation must be applied to persons who are in the situation of the applicant in the main proceedings and that payment of that benefit may validly be reserved to persons who reside on the territory of the Member State which provides the benefit. The fact that the person concerned previously received a benefit for disabled young people which was exportable is of no relevance to the application of those provisions.

2. Article 39 EC and Article 7 of Regulation (EEC) No 1612/68 of the Council of 15 October 1968 on freedom of movement for workers within the Community must be interpreted as not precluding national legislation which applies Article 4(2a) and Article 10a of Regulation No 1408/71, as amended and updated by Regulation No 118/97, as amended by Regulation No 1223/98, and provides that a special non-contributory benefit listed in Annex IIa to Regulation No 1408/71 may be granted only to persons who are resident in the national territory. However, implementation of that legislation must not entail an infringement of the rights of a person in a situation such as that of the applicant in the main proceedings which goes beyond what is required to achieve the legitimate objective pursued by the national legislation. It is for the national court, which must, so far as possible, interpret the national legislation in conformity with Community law, to take account, in particular, of the fact that the worker in question has maintained all of his economic and social links to the Member State of origin."

3.161   The issue of what are genuinely special non-contributory benefits was raised in an action for annulment brought by the Commission against the European Parliament and Council, arguing that the legislators had acted beyond their powers in agreeing to the inclusion of certain benefit by three Member States in Annex IIa. The United Kingdom benefit in issue were attendance allowance, carer's allowance, and disability living allowance. In Case C-299/05, *Commission v European Parliament and Council,* [2007] ECR I-8695, the Court has ruled that attendance allowance, carer's allowance, and the care component of a disability living allowance constitute sickness benefits and not special non-contributory benefits. The problem of the care component being part of a single benefit, namely, disability living allowance, is acknowledged, with the possibility of severing the two components of the allowance. To give the United Kingdom an opportunity to reconstitute the two components of the disability living allowance as separate benefits, the Court attached a temporal limitation to its judgment in the following terms:

"74. It is necessary, however, for the Court to state that the straightforward annulment of the inclusion of the DLA in the list in Annex IIa as amended would lead to the United Kingdom being forced to grant the 'mobility' element of that benefit to an unspecified number of recipients throughout the European Union, although the fact that that part of the DLA is in the nature of a non-contributory benefit cannot be disputed and it could lawfully be included in that list as a non-exportable benefit.

75. That fact warrants the Court exercising the power expressly conferred on it by the second paragraph of Article 231 EC in the event of annulment of a regulation, provisionally to maintain the effects of inclusion of the DLA as regards solely the 'mobility' part so that, within a reasonable period, appropriate measures can be taken to include it in Annex IIa as amended."

The decision makes it clear that attendance allowance, carer's allowance and the care component of a disability living allowance (together referred to below as "the relevant benefits") are exportable from May 5, 2005 (the date reg.1408/71 was amended) where entitlement has been established and the only issue is termination of payment by reason of time spent outside Great Britain. Furthermore, no change to the structure of disability living allowance has yet been put in place, which leaves claimants and tribunals in some uncertainty as to how to proceed. There remains some uncertainty as to how far back the United Kingdom Government may need to go in order to divide disability living allowance into a component which is exportable and one which is (arguably) not.

In *JS v SSWP* [2009] UKUT 81 (AAC), Judge Mesher has indicated that questions relating to the status of the mobility component following the Luxembourg Court's decision will need to be the subject of a reference to the Luxembourg Court.

The following would seem to be the most likely scenarios and their outcomes:

(1) Appeals against refusals to pay the relevant benefits which relate to periods on or after May 5, 2005 should be allowed. Claims in relation to earlier periods (and indeed some new claims which seek to go back only to May 5, 2005) will almost certainly run into difficulties in relation to time limits.

(2) Appeals concerning disability living allowance which concern both components should be allowed in relation to the care component in relation to periods to which they apply on or after May 5, 2005.

(3) Appeals concerning only the mobility component or periods before May 5, 2005 are likely to be more complex. The mobility component issue is complicated because its status as a special non-contributory benefit was conceded rather than established before the Luxembourg Court. This leaves open a possible challenge to its status. Cases involving time limits raise the application of the anti-test case rule in s.27 of the Social Security Act 1998. That provision does not apply because the change in the law has not arisen in the context of an appeal, but in the context of an action under Article 230 EC taken by one Community institution against two other Community institutions seeking the annulment of parts of Community legislation. It is a direct action before the Luxembourg Court rather than a reference in appeal proceedings before the national courts.

For the latest guidance from the Department on the export of attendance allowance, the care component of disability living allowance, and carer's allowance, see Memo DMG 17/09 available on the Department's website.

Article 11

Revalorization of benefits

Rules for revalorization provided by the legislation of a Member State shall apply to benefits due under that legislation taking into account the provisions of this Regulation.

3.162

GENERAL NOTE

"Revalorization" would appear to refer to uprating of benefits.

3.163

Article 12

Prevention of overlapping of benefits

1. This Regulation can neither confer nor maintain the right to several benefits of the same kind for one and the same period of compulsory insurance. However, this provision shall not apply to benefits in respect of invalidity, old age, death (pensions) or occupational disease which are awarded by the institutions of two or more Member States, in accordance with the provisions of Articles 41, 43(2) and (3), 46, 50 and 51 or Article 60(1)(b).

3.164

2. Save as otherwise provided in this Regulation, the provisions of the legislations of a Member State governing the reduction, suspension or withdrawal of benefits in cases of overlapping with other social security benefits or any other form of income may be invoked even where such benefits were acquired under the legislation of another Member State or where such income was acquired in the territory of another Member State.

3. The provisions of the legislation of a Member State for reduction, suspension or withdrawal of benefit in the case of a person in receipt of invalidity benefits or anticipatory old-age benefits pursuing a professional or trade activity may be invoked against such person even though he is pursuing his activity in the territory of another Member State.

4. An invalidity pension payable under Netherlands legislation shall, in case where the Netherlands institution is bound under the provisions of Article 57(5) or 60(29)(b) to contribute also to the cost of benefits for occupational disease granted under the legislation of another Member State, be reduced by the amount payable to the institution of the other Member State which is responsible for granting the benefits for occupational disease.

RELEVANT PROVISIONS OF THE IMPLEMENTING REGULATION

Arts 7–10a, reg.574/72/EEC.

GENERAL NOTE

3.165   Article 12 contains the Community rules on overlapping benefits, which provide the authority for national systems to adjust national benefit by reason of entitlement to a benefit in another EEA country which is awarded by reason of the application of the Community co-ordination rules. Article 12 lays down a number principles relating to overlapping of benefits:

(1) Regulation 1408/71 can neither confer nor maintain the right to several benefits *of the same kind* for one and the same period of compulsory insurance.

(2) The rules apply only to short-term benefits since the rules on aggregation and apportionment which apply to long-term benefits achieve the same effect without the need for rules relating to the overlapping of benefits.

(3) The rules only apply where acquisition of a benefit arises through the application of the Community rules.

See also arts 7–10a of reg.574/72 reproduced below.

TITLE II

DETERMINATION OF THE LEGISLATION APPLICABLE

Article 13

General rules

3.166   [¹ **1.** Subject to Articles 14c and 14f, persons to whom this Regulation applies shall be subject to the legislation of a single Member State only. That legislation shall be determined in accordance with the provisions of this Title.]

2. Subject to Articles 14 to 17:

(a) a person employed in the territory of one Member State shall be subject to the legislation of that State even if he resides in the territory of another Member State or if the registered office or place of business of the undertaking or individual employing him is situated in the territory of another Member State;

(b) a person who is self-employed in the territory of one Member State shall be subjected to the legislation of that State even if he resides in the territory of another Member State;

(c) a person employed on board a vessel flying the flag of a Member State shall be subject to the legislation of the State;

(d) civil servants and persons treated as such shall be subject to the legislation of the Member State to which the administration employing them is subject;

(e) a person called up or recalled for service in the armed forces, or for civilian service, of a Member State shall be subject to the legislation of that State. If entitlement under that legislation is subject to the completion of periods of insurance before entry into or after release from such military or civilian service, periods of insurance completed under the legislation of any other Member State shall be taken into account, to the extent necessary, as if they were periods of insurance completed under the legislation of the first State. The employed or self-employed person called up or recalled for service in the armed forces or for civilian service shall retain the status of employed or self-employed person;

(f) a person to whom the legislation of a Member State ceases to be applicable, without the legislation of another Member State becoming applicable to him in accordance with one of the rules laid down in the aforegoing subparagraphs or in accordance with one of the exceptions or special provisions laid down in Articles 14 to 17 shall be subject to the legislation of the Member State in whose territory he resides in accordance with the provisions of that legislation alone.

AMENDMENTS

1. Regulation 1606/98/EC, [1998] OJ L209/1 (October 25, 1998).

RELEVANT PROVISIONS OF THE IMPLEMENTING REGULATION

Art.10b, reg.574/72/EEC.

GENERAL NOTE

Title II of Reg.1408/71 provides a complete system of the conflict of laws for answering questions concerning both jurisdiction and the choice of law to apply to any situation involving an international element between EEA countries. The basic proposition is that persons to whom the regulation applies are at any given time subject to the legislation of a single EEA country only, which will normally apply its own social security laws to the matter subject to the co-ordinating rules in the Regulation. The starting point to which there are exceptions is that priority is given to the place of employment or self-employment. There are, however, very many special situations where this rule is displaced.

CF/1727/2006 contains guidance on the procedure for obtaining a formal decision of the National Insurance Contributions Office as to a person's liability to pay national insurance contributions. That is important for reg.1408/71, since it will also determine which law is applicable to a claim for child benefit.

Both employed (art.13(2)(a)) and self-employed (art.13(2)(b)) persons who live in one EEA country but work in another EEA country are subject, for any

3.167

given claim, to the legislation of the EEA country in which they work. This rule applies even if the registered office of centre of administration of an employer is in a different EEA country. The Court of Justice has even applied the provisions of Title II by analogy where a situation arises which is not covered directly by its provisions. So in Case 60/93 *Aldewereld* [1994] E.C.R. I-2991, a question arose as to whether a Dutch national recruited by a company established in Germany and sent to work in Thailand was covered by the legislation of The Netherlands or Germany. The Court concluded that there was a sufficient link with Community law for Community law to apply, and that there was a real and substantial link with Germany in relation to the employment. Aldewereld should accordingly be treated as a person employed in Germany, and the provisions of German social security law would apply to his liability to pay social security contributions.

Determining the location of self employment may be more complex than determining the location of employment. Given the varied nature of self employment, careful enquiry may be needed in order to determine whether there is a separation of the place of residence and the place of the self employment, especially where the activity is conducted from him. For example, a person who moves to Spain to live there, but who continues his self-employment as a business adviser advising only clients in the United Kingdom may well continue to be self-employed in the United Kingdom.

The Court has interpreted the rules on the applicable legislation in order to ensure that practical effect is given to the scheme in the Regulation. The facts of Case 196/90 *De Paep* [1991] E.C.R. I-4815, were rather unusual. Mrs De Paep owned a vessel on which her husband and son were employed. Following damage to the vessel, it was declared unseaworthy. Despite this it was sailed across the Channel from Belgium to the United Kingdom. During this passage, the vessel was shipwrecked, and the husband and son were lost at sea. Under Belgian law on employment contracts for seamen, contracts of employment automatically terminate when a vessel is declared unseaworthy. The effect in law was that the husband and son were technically not employed on the vessel when it sank. Nor were they flying on a vessel carrying the flag of Belgium (the vessel was registered in the United Kingdom). The Court ruled that neither condition precluded the legislation of Belgium from applying to the claim made by Madeleine De Paep for an annuity by way of compensation for loss sustained as a result of accidents at work following the death of her son. The Court said:

> ". . . according to the case-law of the Court the provisions of Title II of Regulation No. 1408/71 . . . constitute a complete and uniform system of conflict rules . . . and that those provisions are intended not only to prevent the simultaneous application of a number of national legislative systems and the complications which might ensue, but also to ensure that the persons covered by Regulation No 1408/71 are not left without social security cover because there is no legislation applicable to them. In particular, the conditions concerning the right of a person to become affiliated to a social security scheme may not have the effect of excluding from the scope of the legislation at issue persons to whom it applies pursuant to Regulation No 1408/71 . . ." (para.18 of the judgment).

Art.13(2)(a)

3.168   Case C-352/06 *Bosmann*, May 20, 2008, concerns the interpretation of art.13(2)(a) which provides that the competent State is the State in which a person is employed even if they reside in another Member State. The main principle of art.13 is to ensure that there is only one competent State. But does that mean that there can be no entitlement to a benefit under the law of the Member State of residence? That was the question which arose in this case. Brigitte Bosmann, a Belgian national, worked in The Netherlands, but lived in Germany. When she undertook this employment, the German authorities terminated the award of child benefits for her two children. There was no comparable entitlement under Dutch law since the legislation of that country does not provide for the payment of child benefits for children over 18.

At first sight, it would seem that Bosmann was caught by art.13(2)(a) in that, when she became employed in Germany, that country was alone the competent State for the purpose of benefits falling within the scope of Regulation 1408/71. But the Court ruled that "the application of provisions from another system of legislation is not thereby always precluded" (para.20). While Community law does not *require* the German authorities to pay child benefit in respect of the two children, it does not *exclude* that possibility. How sweeping an exception to the single State rule in art.13 is that? That remains contentious. One view is that the possibility of dual State competence is limited to family benefit cases where there remain wide variations in both the conditions of entitlement and the level of benefits. The second is that the case establishes that a State other than the competent State *may* elect to pay benefits where a person meets the conditions of entitlement in that State through some linking factor, such as residence, on the basis of national law alone. It is worth observing that the Opinion of Advocate General Mazák came to the opposite view, namely that Bosmann was not entitled to the application of German law so as to receive child benefit.

Art. 13 (2) (f)
Article 13(2)(f) resolves an uncertainty that had arisen from the decision of the   **3.169**
Court of Justice in Case 302/84 *Ten Holder*, [1986] E.C.R. 1821, in which had suggested that the legislation of the place where a person last worked was applicable to them forever thereafter until such time as the person undertook further employment or self-employment. The Court, however, mitigated its decision in two subsequent cases: Case C-140/88 *Noij*, [1991] E.C.R. I-387, and Case C-245/88 *Daalmeijer*, [1991] ECR I-555, ruling that a person who had ceased all work and moved country became subject to the legislation of the State of residence.

The application of the principle in art.13(2)(f) appears to have become more sweeping than might first have been expected. One of the questions which arose in Case C-275/96 *Kuusijärvi*, [1998] E.C.R. I-3419, was whether the exception applied where a person had permanently ceased all occupational activity, or whether it also applied where a person had ceased occupational activity in circumstances where it might reasonably be expected that he or she would resume occupational activities at some time in the future. In its judgment the Court ruled that art.13(2)(f) also applied in the latter situation. This would appear to permit Member States to draft their social security legislation in such a way that they can impose a residence requirement for continued entitlement to benefit acquired in that State.

See art.89 and paras 18 to 20 of Annex VI for special provisions applicable in the United Kingdom on the application of the rule in art.13(2)(f).

Students
Note that there are no rules in Title II relating to the applicable legislation for students (who do not fall within any of the other rules). This suggests that, for the   **3.170**
purposes of the Regulation, they may be subject to the social security systems of two Member States, or fall outside the social security system of any Member State.

Article 14

Special rules applicable to persons, other than mariners, engaged in paid employment

Article 13(2)(a) shall apply subject to the following exceptions and   **3.171**
circumstances:
1. (a) A person employed in the territory of a Member State by an undertaking to which he is normally attached who is posted by that undertaking to the territory of another Member State to perform

work there for that undertaking shall continue to be subject to the legislation of the first Member State, provided that the anticipated duration of that work does not exceed 12 months and that he is not sent to replace another person who has completed his term of posting.

(b) if the duration of the work to be done extends beyond the duration originally anticipated, owing to unforeseeable circumstances, and exceeds 12 months, the legislation of the first Member State shall continue to apply until the completion of such work, provided that the competent authority of the Member State in whose territory the person concerned is posted or the body designated by that authority gives its consent; such consent must be requested before the end of the initial 12 month period. Such consent cannot, however, be given for a period exceeding 12 months.

2. A person normally employed in the territory of two or more Member States shall be subject to the legislation determined as follows:

(a) A person who is a member of the travelling or flying personnel of an undertaking which, for hire or reward or on its own account, operates international transport services for passengers or goods by rail, road, air or inland waterway and has its registered office or place of business in the territory of a Member State shall be subject to the legislation of the latter State, with the following restrictions:

(i) where the said undertaking has a branch or permanent representation in the territory of a Member State other than that in which it has its registered office or place of business, a person employed by such branch or permanent representation shall be subject to the legislation of the Member State in whose territory such branch or permanent representation is situated;

(ii) where a person is employed principally in the territory of the Member State in which he resides, he shall be subject to the legislation of that State, even if the undertaking which employs him has no registered office or place of business or branch or permanent representation in that territory.

(b) A person other than that referred to in (a) shall be subject:

(i) to the legislation of the Member State in whose territory he resides, if he pursues his activity partly in that territory or if he is attached to several undertakings or several employers who have their registered offices or places of business in the territory of different Member States;

(ii) to the legislation of the Member State in whose territory is situated the registered office or place of business of the undertaking or individual employing him, if he does not reside in the territory of any of the Member States where he is pursuing his activity.

3. A person who is employed in the territory of one Member State by an undertaking which has its registered office or place of business in the territory of another Member State and which straddles the common frontier of these States shall be subject to the legislation of the Member State in whose territory the undertaking has its registered office or place of business.

RELEVANT PROVISIONS OF THE IMPLEMENTING REGULATION

Arts 11 and 12a, reg.574/72/EEC.

Article 14

Decision No 126 of 17 October, 1985 concerning the application of Article 14(1)(a), 14a(1)(a), 14b(1) and (2) of Regulation (EEC) No 1408/71, [1986] OJ C141/3.

Decision No 148 of 25 June, 1992 concerning the use of the certificate concerning the applicable legislation (Form E101) where the period of posting does not exceed three months, [1993] OJ C22/124.

Decision No 181 of 13 December, 2000 concerning the interpretation of arts 14(1), 14a(1) and 14b(1) and (2) of Council Regulation (EEC) No 1408/71 on the legislation applicable to posted workers and self-employed workers temporarily working outside the competent State, [2001] OJ L329/73.

GENERAL NOTE

Article 14 deals with two very different sets of circumstances. The first concerns the posting of workers by an enterprise in circumstances where the affiliation to the home social security system is maintained. Similar rules also apply to self employed persons temporarily working in a Member State other than that to which they are affiliated for social security purposes under art.14a. The rules set out below are essentially applied by analogy to the situation of self employed persons. The second concerns the determination of the applicable legislation where a person has two or more employments in different Member States. There is also a third rule concerning enterprises which 'straddle' frontiers; this probably concerns only one or two agricultural enterprises on the borders of Member States. **3.172**

The rules on posted workers

On the posting of workers, see also Decision No 181 of the Administrative Commission of December 13, 2000, [2000] OJ L329/73, and *Practical Guide for the Posting of Workers in the Member States of the European Union and the European Economic Area and in Switzerland,* issued by the Administrative Commission: *http://europa.eu.int/comm/employment_social/social_security_schemes/docs/posting_en.pdf* **3.173**

There are four conditions which must be satisfied for the posting rules to apply: (1) affected workers must be sent to work abroad by an undertaking to which they are normally attached; (2) the workers must be performing work abroad for the undertaking that sent them abroad; (3) the anticipated duration of the posting must not initially exceed 12 months, though in the circumstances set out in the article, this can be extended to 24 months; and (4) the posting must not be for the purpose of replacing another posted worker. It is important that there is, throughout the posting, a direct relationship between the undertaking and the posted worker.

Such a direct relationship will be present when the following features will be present: (a) a contractual relationship continues to exist between employer and employee; (b) the power to terminate that contract remains with the posting undertaking; (c) the nature of the work undertaken by the posted worker must be determinable by the posting undertaking; and (d) the obligation with regard to the remuneration of the worker rests with the undertaking which concluded the contract, irrespective of who actually makes the payment of that remuneration.

Some of the guidance flows from the decision of the Court of Justice in Case C-202/97 *Fitzwilliam Executive Search Ltd,* [2002] ECR I-883. This case concerned the activities of Fitzwilliam in placing workers both in Ireland in the Netherlands in the agricultural and horticultural sectors. The company recruited workers in order for them to be posted. Its turnover in the Netherlands came to exceed that in Ireland. The Dutch authorities took the view that workers engaged by Fitzwilliam in order to be posted to the Netherlands were subject to Dutch law and required to pay Dutch social security contributions. The question which arose in the reference made by the Dutch courts was whether workers recruited for the purpose posting to another Member State were within the posting rules in art.14. The Court decided that, for art.14 to apply, the undertaking in question must normally carry on its activities in the sending State, which meant that it habitually carries on significant activities in that State. Performance of management activities which are purely internal in that State cannot justify the use of the posting provisions. The following are considered in Decision No 181 and the Guide to be helpful indicators of the significance of the activities carried out in the sending State: (a) the place where the undertaking has its registered office and administration; (b) the number and nature of its staff there; (c) the place of recruitment of the posted worker; (d) the place where the majority of contracts are concluded; (e) the law applicable to the contracts signed by the undertaking with its clients and with its workers; and (f) turnover in the sending State and in the Member State(s) to which the workers are sent. The Guide indicates that habitual performance of the activities will be met if the activity has been carried out for four months or more; in the case of lesser periods a case-by-case consideration having regard to all the circumstances is required.

A person's status as a posted worker is attested by the issue in the sending State of Form E101 which certifies that the holder is subject to the legislation of the issuing State and so is exempt from the application of the legislation of the receiving State. Case C-178/97 *Barry Banks*, [2000] ECR I-2005 concerned a refusal by the Belgian authorities to accept the validity of a Form E101 issued by the United Kingdom authorities (for which provision is made in Arts 11 and 11a of Regulation 574/72). Banks was an opera singer who undertook short term contracts singing in Brussels. The Belgian authorities took the view that Banks and his colleagues were employed in Belgium, but they held Forms E101 certifying that they were self-employed persons in the United Kingdom. The Court of Justice ruled that, as long as it had not been withdrawn or declared invalid, the Form E101 certificate is binding on the competent institution of the place where the worker or self employed person goes. That institution may refer the matter back to the certifying institution for investigation if it suspects fraud, but otherwise must accept the exemption from its own legislation.

These decisions have been affirmed in Case C-2/05 *Herbosch Kiere NV* [2006] ECR I-1079.

Note that longer periods of exemption may be secured by an agreement between two Member States under art.17.

The Commission has set up a Committee of Experts on Posting of Workers ([2009] OJ L8/26, January 13, 2009) to examine the practical difficulties in the operation of the posting rules in Directive 96/71/EC concerning the posting of workers in the framework of the provision of services. The topic is related to the issue of posting under reg.1408/71.

Article 14a

Special rules applicable to persons, other than mariners, who are self-employed

3.174   Article 13(2)(b) shall apply subject to the following exceptions and circumstances:

1. (a) A person normally self-employed in the territory of a Member State and who performs work in the territory of another Member State shall continue to be subject to the legislation of the first Member State, provided that the anticipated duration of the work does not exceed 12 months.

   (b) If the duration of the work to be done extends beyond the duration originally anticipated, owing to unforeseeable circumstances, and exceeds 12 months, the legislation of the first Member State shall continue to apply until the completion of such work, provided that the competent authority of the Member State in whose territory the person concerned has entered to perform the work in question or the body appointed by that authority gives its consent; such consent must be requested before the end of the initial 12-month period, Such consent cannot, however, be given for a period exceeding 12 months.

2. A person normally self-employed in the territory of two or more Member States shall be subject to the legislation of the Member State in whose territory he resides if he pursues any part of his activity in the territory of that Member State. If he does not pursue any activity in the territory of the Member State in which he resides, he shall be subject to the legislation of the Member State in whose territory he pursue his main activity. The criteria used to determine the principal activity are laid down in the Regulation referred to in Article 98.

3. A person who is self-employed in an undertaking which has its registered office or place of business in the territory of one Member State and which straddles the common frontier of two Member States shall be subject to the legislation of the Member State in whose territory the undertaking has its registered office or place of business.

4. If the legislation to which a person should be subject in accordance with paragraph 2 or 3 does not enable that person, even on a voluntary basis, to join a pension scheme, the person concerned shall be subject to the legislation of the other Member State which would apply apart from these particular provisions, or should the legislations of two or more Member States apply in this way, he shall be subject to the legislation decided on by common agreement amongst the Member States concerned or their competent authorities.

RELEVANT PROVISIONS OF THE IMPLEMENTING REGULATION

Arts 11a and 12a, reg.574/72/EEC.

RELEVANT DECISIONS OF THE ADMINISTRATIVE COMMISSION

Decision No 126 of 17 October, 1985 concerning the application of art.14(1)(a), 14a(1)(a), 14b(1) and (2) of reg.1408/71/EEC, [1986] OJ C141/3.

Decision No 181 of 13 December, 2000 concerning the interpretation of art.14(1), 14a(1) and 14b(1) and (2) of Council Regulation (EEC) No 1408/71 on the legislation applicable to posted workers and self-employed workers temporarily working outside the competent State, [2001] OJ L329/73.

GENERAL NOTE

See annotations to art.14 for comment on the provisions concerning "posting" of self employed persons. **3.175**

Article 14b

Special rules application to mariners

Article 13(2)(c) shall apply subject to the following exceptions and circumstances: **3.176**

1. A person employed by an undertaking to which he is normally attached, either in the territory of a Member State or on board a vessel flying the flag of a Member State, who is posted by that undertaking on board a vessel flying the flag of another Member State to perform work there for that undertaking shall, subject to the conditions provided in Article 14(1), continue to be subject to the legislation of the first Member State.

2. A person normally self-employed, either in the territory of a Member State or on board a vessel flying the flag of a Member State and who performs work on his own account on board a vessel flying the flag of another Member State shall, subject to the conditions provided in Article 14a(1), continue to be subject to the legislation of the first Member State.

3. A person who, while not being normally employed at sea, performs work in the territorial waters or in a port of a Member State on a vessel flying the flag of another Member State within those territorial waters or in that port, but is not a member of the crew of the vessel, shall be subject to the legislation of the first Member State.

4. A person employed on board a vessel flying the flag of a Member State and remunerated for such employment by an undertaking or a person whose registered office or place of business is in the territory of another Member State shall be subject to the legislation of the latter State if he is resident in the territory of that State; the undertaking or person paying the remuneration shall be considered as the employer for the purpose of the said legislation.

RELEVANT PROVISIONS OF THE IMPLEMENTING REGULATION

Art.11a, reg.574/72/EEC.

RELEVANT PROVISIONS OF THE ADMINISTRATIVE COMMISSION

Decision No 126 of 17 October, 1985 concerning the application of art.14(1)(a), 14a(1)(a), 14b(1) and (2) of reg.1408/71/EEC, [1986] OJ C141/3.

Decision No 181 of 13 December, 2000 concerning the interpretation of art.14(1), 14a(1) and 14b(1) and (2) of Council Regulation (EEC) No 1408/71 on the legislation applicable to posted workers and self-employed workers temporarily working outside the competent State, [2001] OJ L329/73.

Article 14c

Special rules applicable to persons who are simultaneously employed in the territory of one Member State and self-employed in the territory of another Member State

3.177   A person who is simultaneously employed in the territory of one Member State and self-employed in the territory of another Member State shall be subject:

    (a) save as otherwise provided in subparagraph (b) to the legislation of the Member State in the territory of which he is engaged in paid employment or, where he pursues such an activity in the territory of two or more Member States, to the legislation determined in accordance with Article 14(2) or (3);

(b) in the cases mentioned in Annex VII:
— to the legislation of the Member State in the territory of which he is engaged in paid employment, that legislation having been determined in accordance with the provisions of Article 14(2) or (3), where he pursues such an activity in the territory of two or more Member States,
and
— to the legislation of the Member State in the territory of which he is self-employed, that legislation having been determined in accordance with Article 14a(2), (3) or (4), where he pursues such an activity in the territory of two or more Member States.

RELEVANT PROVISIONS OF THE IMPLEMENTING REGULATION

Art.12a, reg.574/72/EEC.

Article 14d

Miscellaneous provisions

[¹ **1.** The person referred to in Article 14(2) and (3), Article 14a(2), (3) and (4), Article 14c(a) and Article 14e shall be treated, for the purposes of application of the legislation laid down in accordance with these provisions, as if he pursued all his professional activity or activities in the territory of the Member State concerned.]   3.178

2. The person referred to in Article 14c(b) shall be treated, for the purposes of determining the rates of contributions to be charged to self-employed workers under the legislation of the Member State in whose territory he is self-employed, as if he pursued his paid employment in the territory of the Member State concerned.

3. The provisions of the legislation of a Member State under which a pensioner who is pursuing a professional or trade activity is not subject to compulsory insurance in respect of such activity shall also apply to a pensioner whose pension was acquired under the legislation of another Member State, unless the person concerned expressly asks to be so subject by applying to the institution designated by the competent authority of the first Member State and named in Annex 10 to the Regulation referred to in Article 98.

AMENDMENT

1. Regulation 1606/98/EC, [1998] OJ L209/1 (October 25, 1998).

[¹*Article 14e*

Special rules applicable to persons insured in a special scheme for civil servants who are simultaneously employed and/or self-employed in the territory of one or more other Member States

A person who is simultaneously employed as a civil servant or a person treated as such and insured in a special scheme for civil servants in one   3.179

Member State and who is employed and/or self-employed in the territory of one or more other Member States shall be subject to the legislation of the Member State in which he is insured in a special scheme for civil servants.]

AMENDMENT

1. Regulation 1606/98/EC, [1998] OJ L209/1 (October 25, 1998).

RELEVANT PROVISIONS OF THE IMPLEMENTING REGULATION

Art.12b, reg.574/72/EEC.

[¹*Article 14f*

Special rules applicable to civil servants simultaneously employed in more than one Member State and insured in one of these States in a special scheme

3.180 A person who is simultaneously employed in two or more Member States as a civil servant or person treated as such and insured in at least one of those Member States in a special scheme for civil servants shall be subject to the legislation of each of these Member States.]

AMENDMENT

1. Regulation 1606/98/EC, [1998] OJ L209/1 (October 25, 1998).

RELEVANT PROVISIONS OF THE IMPLEMENTING REGULATION

Art.12b, reg.574/72/EEC.

Article 15

Rules concerning voluntary insurance or optional continued insurance

3.181 **1.** Articles 13 to 14d shall not apply to voluntary insurance or to optional continued insurance unless, in respect of one of the branches referred to in Article 4, there exists in any Member State only a voluntary scheme of insurance.

2. Where application of the legislations of two or more Member States entails overlapping of insurance:

— under a compulsory insurance scheme and one or more voluntary or optional continued insurance schemes, the person concerned shall be subject exclusively to the compulsory insurance scheme;

— under two or more voluntary or optional continued insurance schemes, the person concerned may join only the voluntary or optional continued insurance scheme for which he has opted.

3. However, in respect of invalidity, old age and death (pensions), the person concerned may join the voluntary or optional continued insurance scheme of a Member State, even if he is compulsorily subject to the legislation of another Member State, to the extent that such overlapping is explicitly or implicitly admitted in the first Member State.

Article 16

Special rules regarding persons employed by diplomatic missions and consular posts, and auxiliary staff of the European Communities

1. The provisions of Article 13 (2) (a) shall apply to persons employed by diplomatic missions and consular posts and to the private domestic staff of agents of such missions or posts.

2. However, employed persons covered by paragraph 1 who are nationals of the Member State which is the accrediting or sending State may opt to be subject to the legislation of that State. Such right of option may be renewed at the end of each calendar year and shall not have retrospective effect.

3. Auxiliary staff of the European Communities may opt to be subject to the legislation of the Member State in whose territory they are employed, to the legislation of the Member State to which they were last subject or to the legislation of the Member State whose nationals they are, in respect of provisions other than those relating to family allowances, the granting of which is governed by the conditions of employment applicable to such staff. This right of option, which may be exercised once only, shall take effect from the date of entry into employment.

3.182

RELEVANT PROVISIONS OF THE IMPLEMENTING REGULATION

Arts 13 and 14, reg.574/72/EEC.

RELEVANT DECISIONS OF THE ADMINISTRATIVE COMMISSION

Decision No 89 of 20 March, 1973 concerning the interpretation of art.16(1) and (2) of Council Regulation (EEC) No 1408/71 relating to persons employed by diplomatic missions and consular posts, [1974] OJ C86/7.

Article 17

Exceptions to Articles 13 to 16

Two or more Member States, the competent authorities of these States or the bodies designated by these authorities may by common agreement provide for exceptions to the provisions of Articles 13 to 16 in the interest of certain categories of persons or of certain persons.

3.183

RELEVANT PROVISIONS OF THE IMPLEMENTING REGULATION

Arts 11, 11a, reg.574/72/EEC.

RELEVANT DECISIONS OF THE ADMINISTRATIVE COMMISSION

Recommendation No 16 of 12 December, 1984 concerning the conclusion of Agreement pursuant to art.17 of Council Regulation (EEC) No 1408/71, [1985] OJ C273/3.

GENERAL NOTE

3.184 This provision was used in Case 101/83 *Brusse* [1984] E.C.R. 2223 to "rescue" a claimant from a long gap in his contribution record in the United Kingdom. The terms of the agreement covered a period before the UK was a Member State of the European Community but was expressly made under art.17 in relation to the period from January 1, 1973 (when the UK acceded). The Court of Justice ruled that agreements under art.17 could be retrospective; the test was whether the agreement was in the interests of the worker concerned. This approach was confirmed in Case C-454/93 *van Gestel* [1995] E.C.R. I-1707. The scope of agreements under art.17 is accordingly very wide, provided that the parties are satisfied that the terms of the agreement are in the interests of certain persons or categories of persons.

Article 17a

Special rules concerning recipients of pensions due under the legislation of one or more Member State

3.185 The recipient of a pension due under the legislation of a Member State or of pensions due under the legislation of several Member States who resides in the territory of another Member State may at his request be exempted from the legislation of the latter State provided that he is not subject to that legislation because of the pursuit of an occupation.

GENERAL NOTE

3.186 This provision requires the pensioner to trigger the exemption by applying for it.

TITLE III

SPECIAL PROVISIONS RELATING TO THE VARIOUS CATEGORIES OF BENEFITS

CHAPTER 1

SICKNESS AND MATERNITY

SECTION 1

COMMON PROVISIONS

Article 18

Aggregation of periods of insurance, employment or residence

3.187 **1.** The competent institution of a Member State whose legislation makes the acquisition, retention or recovery of the right to benefits conditional upon the completion of periods of insurance, employment or residence shall, to the extent necessary, take account of periods of insurance, employment or residence completed under the legislation of any other Member State as if they were periods completed under the legislation which it administers.

2. The provisions of paragraph 1 shall apply to seasonal workers, even in respect of periods prior to any break in insurance exceeding the period allowed by the legislation of the competent State, provided, however, that the person concerned has not ceased to be insured for a period exceeding four months.

RELEVANT PROVISIONS OF THE IMPLEMENTING REGULATION

Arts 15 and 16, reg.574/72/EEC.

GENERAL NOTE

Where the person claiming a sickness benefit has been employed or self-employed **3.188** and falls ill in a Member State while not working, then the competent State will be the Member State in which that person was last insured as an employed or self employed person.

The determination of the applicable legislation in relation to entitlement to sickness benefits was considered by the Court of Justice of the European Communities in Case 150/82 *Coppola v Insurance Officer*, [1983] E.C.R. 43. The Court ruled:

"11. By virtue of [Article 13(2)(a)], and in the absence of contrary provisions referring to the particular type of benefit in question, only the legislation of the State in whose territory the worker is employed is therefore applicable. Although that provision does not expressly mention the case of a worker who is not employed when he seeks sickness benefit, it is appropriate to interpret it as meaning that, where necessary, it refers to the legislation of the State in whose territory the worker was last employed.

12. It follows from the fact that, by virtue of Article 13(2)(a), the legislation of only one Member State is applicable, that the institution or institutions of a single Member State, namely the State in whose territory the worker is or was last employed, must be considered competent for the purpose of the application of Article 18(1). . . ."

Note that art.89 and Annex VI contains special rules relating to the determination of the applicable law where there has been a change of the applicable law arising under art.13(2)(f): see para.20 of Section Y of Annex VI reproduced below.

See *R(IB)1/02* for an example of the application of the aggregation principles. Periods of receipt of sickness benefit in another Member State assisted the claimant in qualifying for entitlement to long-term incapacity benefit.

SECTION 2

EMPLOYED OR SELF-EMPLOYED PERSONS AND MEMBERS OF THEIR FAMILIES

Article 19

Residence in a Member State other than the competent State— General rules

1. An employed or self-employed person residing in the territory of a **3.189** Member State other than the competent State, who satisfies the conditions

of the legislation of the competent State for entitlement to benefits, taking account where appropriate of the provisions of Article 18, shall receive in the State in which he is resident:

    (a) benefits in kind provided on behalf of the competent institution by the institution of the place of residence in accordance with the provisions of the legislation administered by that institution as though he were insured with it;

    (b) cash benefits provided by the competent institution in accordance with the legislation which it administers. However, by agreement between the competent institution and the institution of the place of residence, such benefits may be provided by the latter institution on behalf of the former, in accordance with the legislation of the competent State.

    2. The provisions of paragraph 1 shall apply by analogy to members of the family who reside in the territory of a Member State other than the competent State in so far as they are not entitled to such benefits under the legislation of the State in whose territory they reside.

Where the members of the family reside in the territory of a Member State under whose legislation the right to receive benefits in kind is not subject to condition of insurance or employment, benefits in kind which they receive shall be considered as being on behalf of the institution with which the employed or self-employed person is insured, unless the spouse or the person looking after the children pursues a professional or trade activity in the territory of the said Member State.

RELEVANT PROVISIONS OF THE IMPLEMENTING REGULATION

    Arts 17 and 18, reg.574/72/EEC.

GENERAL NOTE

3.190   Chapter 1 of Title III applies both to benefits in kind (medical treatment, provision of medication and the such like) as well as to benefits in cash (sums to offset the loss of income which usually accompanies sickness). Benefits in kind are the responsibility of the Department of Health and are outside the scope of this work, though there is an exceptionally lively and topical case law on these matters. Much of the case law relating to sickness benefits relates to benefits in kind.

The provisions of Chapter 1 need to be read carefully to ensure that the correct rules are applied where benefits in cash are in issue.

Case C-215/90 *Chief Adjudication Officer* v *Twomey* [1992] E.C.R. I-1823, reported as *R(S) 3/92*, determined that art.19 applies to nationals of a Member State who, after being in paid employment in one Member State, go to live in another Member State where they fall ill, even though they have not worked there before falling ill.

Article 20

Frontier workers and members of their families—Special rules

3.191   A frontier worker may also obtain benefits in the territory of the competent State. Such benefits shall be provided by the competent institution in accordance with the provisions of the legislation of that State, as though the person concerned where resident in that State. Members of his family may receive benefits under the same conditions; however, receipt of such benefits shall, except in urgent cases, be conditional upon an agreement between the States concerned or between the competent authorities of those States or, in its absence, on prior authorization by the competent institution.

RELEVANT PROVISIONS OF THE IMPLEMENTING REGULATION

Art.19, reg.574/72/EEC.

RELEVANT DECISIONS OF THE ADMINISTRATIVE COMMISSION

Decision No 116 of 15 December, 1982 concerning the granting of benefits in kind provided for in art.17(7) and art.60(6) of reg.574/72 and the concepts of urgency within the meaning of art.20 of reg.1408/71 and of extreme urgency within the meaning of arts 17(7) and 60(6) of reg.574/72, [1983] OJ C193/8. Decision No 135 of July 1, 1987 concerning the granting of benefits in kind provided for in art.17(7) and art.60(6) of reg.574/72 and the concepts of urgency within the meaning of art.20 of reg.1408/71 and of extreme urgency within the meaning of arts 17(7) and 60(6) of reg.574/72, [1988] OJ C64/5.

Article 21

Stay in or transfer of residence to the competent State

1. The employed or self-employed person referred to in Article 19 (1) who is staying in the territory of the competent State shall receive benefits in accordance with the provisions of the legislation of that State as though he were resident there, even if he has already received benefits for the same case of sickness or maternity before his stay.

2. Paragraph 1 shall apply by analogy to the members of the family referred to in Article 19 (2).

However, where the latter reside in the territory of a Member State other than the one in whose territory the employed or self-employed person resides, benefits in kind shall be provided by the institution of the place of stay on behalf of the institution of the place of residence of the persons concerned.

3. Paragraphs 1 and 2 shall not apply to frontier workers and the members of their families.

4. An employed or self-employed person and members of his family referred to in Article 19 who transfer their residence to the territory of the competent State shall receive benefits in accordance with the provisions of the legislation of that State even if they have already received benefits for the same case of sickness or maternity before transferring their residence.

RELEVANT PROVISIONS OF THE IMPLEMENTING REGULATION

Art.19a, reg.574/72/EEC.

3.192

Article 22

Stay outside the competent State—Return to or transfer of residence to another Member State during sickness or maternity—Need to go to another Member State in order to receive appropriate treatment

3.193   **1.** An employed or self-employed person who satisfies the conditions of the legislation of the competent State for entitlement to benefits, taking account where appropriate of the provisions of Article 18, and:

[¹ (a) whose condition requires benefits in kind which become necessary on medical grounds during a stay in the territory of another Member State, taking into account the nature of the benefits and the expected length of the stay;]

or

(b) who, having become entitled to benefits chargeable to the competent institution, is authorized by that institution to return to the territory of the Member State where he resides, or to transfer his residence to the territory of another Member State;

or

(c) who is authorized by the competent institution to go to the territory of another Member State to receive there the treatment appropriate to his condition,

shall be entitled:

(i) to benefits in kind provided on behalf of the competent institution by the institution of the place of stay or residence in accordance with the provisions of the legislation which it administers, as though he were insured with it; the length of the period during which benefits are provided shall be governed, however, by the legislation of the competent State;

(ii) to cash benefits provided by the competent institution in accordance with the provisions of the legislation which it administers. However, by agreement between the competent institution and the institution of the place of stay or residence, such benefits may be provided by the latter institution on behalf of the former, in accordance with the provisions of the legislation of the competent State.

[¹ **1a.** The Administrative Commission shall establish a list of benefits in kind which, in order to be provided during a stay in another Member State, require, for practical reasons, a prior agreement between the person concerned and the institution providing the care;]

2. The authorization required under paragraph 1 (b) may be refused only if it is established that movement of the person concerned would be prejudicial to his state of health or the receipt of medical treatment.

The authorization required under paragraph 1 (c) may not be refused where the treatment in question is among the benefits provided for by the legislation of the Member State on whose territory the person concerned resided and where he cannot be given such treatment within the time normally necessary for obtaining the treatment in question in the Member State of residence taking account of his current state of health and the probable course of the disease.

[¹ **3.** Paragraphs 1, 1a and 2 shall apply by analogy to members of the family of an employed or self-employed person.]

However, for the purpose of applying paragraph 1 (a) and (c) (i) to the members of the family referred to in Article 19 (2) who reside in the territory of a Member State other than the one in whose territory the employed or self-employed person resides:

(a) benefits in kind shall be provided on behalf of the institution of the Member State in whose territory the members of the family are residing by the institution of the place of stay in accordance with the provisions of the legislation which it administers as if the employed or self-employed person were insured there. The period during which benefits are provided shall, however, be that laid down under the legislation of the Member State in whose territory the members of the family are residing;

(b) the authorization required under paragraph 1 (c) shall be issued by the institution of the Member State in whose territory the members of the family are residing.

4. The fact that the provisions of paragraph 1 apply to an employed or self-employed person shall not affect the right to benefit of members of his family.

AMENDMENT

1. Regulation 631/2004/EC, [2004] OJ L100/1 (June 1, 2004).

RELEVANT PROVISIONS OF THE IMPLEMENTING REGULATION

Arts 21–24, reg.574/72/EEC.

RELEVANT DECISIONS OF THE ADMINISTRATIVE COMMISSION

Decision No 74 of 22 February, 1973 concerning the provision of medical care in cases of temporary stay under art.22(1)(a)(i) of reg.1408/71 and art.21 of reg.574/72, [1973] OJ C75/4.

Decision No 138 of 17 February, 1989 concerning the interpretation of art.22(1) (c)(i) of reg.1408/71 in the case of organ transplants or other forms of surgery requiring tests on biological samples while the person concerned is not present in the Member State where the tests are carried out, [1989] OJ C287/3.

Decision No 175 of 23 June, 1999 on interpretation of the concept of "benefits in kind" in the event of sickness or maternity pursuant to art.19(1) and (2), art.22, art.22a, art.22b, art.25(1), (3) and (4), art.26, art.28(1), art.28a, art.29, art.31, art.34a and art.34b of Council Regulation (EEC) No 1408/71 and on calculation of the amounts to be refunded under arts 93, 94 and 95 of reg.574/72 as well as the advances to be paid pursuant to art.102(4) of the same Regulation, [2000] OJ L47/32.

Decision No 194 of 17 December, 2003 conerning the uniform application of Article 22(1)(a)(i) of Council Regulation (EEC) No 1408/71 in the Member State of stay, [2004] OJ L104/127.

Decision No 195 of 23 March, 2004 on the uniform application of art.22(1)(a)(i) of reg.1408/71 as regards health care in conjunction with pregnancy and childbirth, [2004] OJ L160/134.

Decision No 196 of 23 March, 2004 pursuant top art.22(1a), [2004] OJ L160/136.

GENERAL NOTE

3.194   Where cash benefits are in issue, they are to be awarded by the competent institution in the competent State in accordance with its own legislation, subject to any agreement for them to be paid in the State of stay or residence on behalf of the institution of the competent State.

R(S) 2/94 concerned an earlier form of wording in this Article, but the proposition for which it stands remains pertinent. Although a person is entitled to cash benefits for the period during which that person's condition necessitates benefits in kind, that period is to be interpreted as meaning the period of medical treatment at hospital and not the subsequent period during which the person is not at hospital but is taking prescribed medication. Since the claimant was only at the hospital for one day, that day fell within the first three days of an interruption of employment and so sickness benefit was not payable for that day.

Article 22a

Special rules for certain categories of persons

3.195   Notwithstanding Article 2 of the Regulation, Article 22(1)(a) and (c) shall also apply to persons who are nationals of a Member State and are insured under the legislation of a Member State and to the members of their families residing with them.

RELEVANT DECISIONS OF THE ADMINISTRATIVE COMMISSION

Decision No 174 of 20 April, 1999 concerning the interpretation of Article 22a of Regulation (EEC) No 1408/71, [2000] OJ L47/30.

Decision No 175 of 23 June, 1999 on interpretation of the concept of "benefits in kind" in the event of sickness or maternity pursuant to Article 19(1) and (2), Article 22, Article 22a, Article 22b, Article 25(1), (3) and (4), Article 26, Article 28(1), Article 28a, Article 29, Article 31, Article 34a and Article 34b of Council Regulation (EEC) No 1408/71 and on calculation of the amounts to be refunded under Articles 93, 94 and 95 of Regulation (EEC) No 574/72 as well as the advances to be paid pursuant to Article 102(4) of the same Regulation, [2000] OJ L47/32.

Article 22b

Employment in a Member State other than the competent State— Stay in the State of employment

3.196   [¹ . . .]

AMENDMENT

1. Regulation 631/2004/EC, [2004] OJ L100/1 (June 1, 2004).

Article 22c

Studies in a Member State other than the competent State—stay in the State where the studies are pursued

3.197   [¹ . . .]

Article 22c

AMENDMENT

1. Regulation 307/99/EC, [1999] OJ L38/1 (May 1, 1999).

Article 23

Calculation of cash benefits

1. The competent institution of a Member State whose legislation provides that the calculation of cash benefits shall be based on average earnings
or on average contributions, shall determine such average earnings or contributions exclusively by reference to earnings or contributions completed
under the said legislation.

3.198

2. The competent institution of a Member State whose legislation
provides that the calculation of cash benefits shall be based on standard
earnings, shall take account exclusively of the standard earnings or, where
appropriate, of the average of standard earnings for the periods completed
under the said legislation.

[¹ **2a.** The provisions of paragraphs 1 and 2 shall also apply where the
legislation applied by the competent institution provides for a specific reference period and this period coincides, where appropriate, with the whole or
part of the periods completed by the person concerned under the legislation
of one or more other Member States.]

3. The competent institution of a Member State under whose legislation the amount of cash benefits varies with the number of members
of the family, shall also take into account the members of the family
of the person concerned who are resident in the territory of another
Member State as if they were resident in the territory of the competent
State.

AMENDMENT

1. Regulation 647/2005/EC, [2005] OJ L117/1 (May 5, 2005).

RELEVANT PROVISIONS OF THE IMPLEMENTING REGULATION

Art.25, reg.574/72/EEC.

Article 24

Substantial benefits in kind

1. Where the right of an employed or self-employed person or a member
of his family to a prosthesis, a major appliance or other substantial benefits
in kind has been recognized by the institution of a Member State before
he becomes insured with the institution of another Member State, the said
employed of self-employed person shall receive such benefits at the expense
of the first institution, even if they are granted after he becomes insured
with the second institution.

3.199

2. The Administrative Commission shall draw up the list of benefits to
which the provisions of paragraph 1 apply.

Decision No 115 of 15 December, 1982 concerning the granting of prostheses, major appliances and other substantial benefits in kind provided for in art.24(2) of regulation (EEC) No 1408/71 of the Council, [1983] OJ C193/7.

SECTION 3

UNEMPLOYED PERSONS AND MEMBERS OF THEIR FAMILIES

Article 25

3.200

[¹ 1. An unemployed person who was formerly employed or self-employed and to whom the provisions of Article 69(1) of Article 71(1)(b)(ii), second sentence apply and who satisfies the conditions laid down in the legislation of the competent State for entitlement to benefits in kind and cash benefits, taking account where necessary of the provisions of Article 18, shall receive for the period of time referred to in Article 69(1)(c):

    (a) benefits in kind which become necessary on medical grounds for this person during his stay in the territory of the Member State where he is seeking employment, taking account of the nature of the benefits and the expected length of the stay. These benefits in kind shall be provided on behalf of the competent institution by the institution of the Member State in which the person is seeking employment, in accordance with the provisions of the legislation which the latter institution administers, as if he were insured with it;

    (b) cash benefits provided by the competent institution in accordance with the provisions of the legislation which it administers. However, by agreement between the competent institution and the institution of the Member State in which the unemployed person seeks employment, benefits may be provided by the latter institution on behalf of the former institution in accordance with the provisions of the legislation of the competent State. Unemployment benefits under Article 69(1) shall not be granted for the period during which cash benefits are received.

    1a. Article 22(1a) shall apply by analogy.]

    2. A totally unemployed person who was formerly employed and to whom the provisions of Article 71(1)(a)(ii) or the first sentence of Article 71(1)(b) (ii) apply, shall receive benefits in kind and in cash in accordance with the provisions of the legislation of the Member State in whose territory he resides, as though he had been subject to that legislation during his last employment, taking account where appropriate of the provisions of Article 18; the cost of such benefits shall be met by the institution of the country of residence.

    3. Where an unemployed person satisfies the conditions of the legislation of the Member State which is responsible for the cost of unemployment benefits for entitlement to sickness and maternity benefits, taking account where appropriate of the provisions of Article 18, the members of his family shall receive these benefits, irrespective of the Member State in whose territory they reside or are staying. Such benefits shall be provided:

    (a) with regard to the benefits in kind, by the institution of the place of residence or stay in accordance with the provisions of the legislation which it administers, on behalf of the competent institution of the

Article 25

Member State which is responsible for the cost of unemployment benefits;

(b) with regard to cash benefits, by the competent institution of the Member State which is responsible for the cost of unemployment benefits, in accordance with the legislation which it administers.

4. Without prejudice to any provisions of the legislation of a Member State which permit an extension of the period during which sickness benefits may be granted, the period provided for in paragraph 1 may, in cases of force majeure, be extended by the competent institution within the limit fixed by the legislation administered by that institution.

AMENDMENT

1. Reg.631/2004/EC, [2004] OJ 100/1 (June 1, 2004).

RELEVANT PROVISIONS OF THE IMPLEMENTING REGULATION

Arts 26 and 27, reg.574/72/EEC.

RELEVANT DECISIONS OF THE ADMINISTRATIVE COMMISSION

Decision No 175 of 23 June, 1999 on interpretation of the concept of "benefits in kind" in the event of sickness or maternity pursuant to art.19(1) and (2), art.22, art.22a, art.22b, art.25(1), (3) and (4), art.26, art.28(1), art.28a, art.29, art.31, art.34a and art.34b of Council Regulation (EEC) No 1408/71 and on calculation of the amounts to be refunded under arts 93, 94 and 95 of reg.574/72 as well as the advances to be paid pursuant to art.102(4) of the same Regulation, [2000] OJ L47/32.

Article 25a

Contributions payable by wholly unemployed persons

The institution which is responsible for granting benefits in kind and cash benefits to the unemployed persons referred to in Article 25(2) and which belongs to a Member State whose legislation provides for deduction of contributions payable by unemployed persons to cover sickness and maternity benefits shall be authorized to make such deductions in accordance with the provisions of its legislation.

3.201

SECTION 4

PENSION CLAIMANTS AND MEMBERS OF THEIR FAMILIES

Article 26

Right to benefits in kind in cases of cessation of the right to benefits from the institution which was last competent

1. An employed or self-employed person, members of his family or his survivors who, during the investigation of a claim for pension, cease to be

3.202

entitled to benefits in kind under the legislation of the Member State last competent, shall nevertheless receive such benefits under the following conditions: benefits in kind shall be provided in accordance with the provisions of the legislation of the Member State in whose territory the person or persons concerned reside, provided that they are entitled to such benefits under that legislation or would be entitled to them under the legislation of another Member State if they were residing in the territory of that State, taking account where appropriate of the provisions of Article 18.

2. A pension claimant who is entitled to benefits in kind under the legislation of a Member State which obliges the person concerned to pay sickness insurance contributions himself during the investigation of his pension claim shall cease to be entitled to benefits in kind at the end of the second month for which he has not paid the contributions due.

3. Benefits in kind provided in accordance with the provisions of paragraph 1 shall be chargeable to the institution which has collected contributions in accordance with the provisions of paragraph 2; where no contributions are payable under the provisions of paragraph 2, the institution responsible for the cost of the benefits in kind after awarding the pension in accordance with the provisions of Article 28 shall refund the amount of the benefits provided to the institution of the place of residence.

RELEVANT PROVISIONS OF THE IMPLEMENTING REGULATION

Art.28, Reg.574/72/EEC.

RELEVANT DECISIONS OF THE ADMINISTRATIVE COMMISSION

Decision No 175 of 23 June, 1999 on interpretation of the concept of "benefits in kind" in the event of sickness or maternity pursuant to art.19(1) and (2), art.22, art.22a, art.22b, art.25(1), (3) and (4), art.26, art.28, art.28(1), art.28a, art.29, art.31, art.34a and art.34b of Council Regulation (EEC) No 1408/71 and on calculation of the amounts to be refunded under arts 93, 94 and 95 of reg.574/72 as well as the advances to be paid pursuant to Article 102(4) of the same Regulation, [2000] OJ L47/32.

SECTION 5

PENSIONERS AND MEMBERS OF THEIR FAMILIES

Article 27

Pensions payable under the legislation of several State where there is a right to benefits in the country of residence

3.203   A pensioner who is entitled to draw pensions under the legislation of two or more Member States, of which one is that of the Member State in whose territory he resides, and who is entitled to benefits under the legislation of the latter Member State, taking account where appropriate of the provisions of Article 18 and Annex VI, shall, with the members of his family, receive such benefits from the institution of the place of residence and at the expense of that institution as though the person concerned were a pensioner whose pension was payable solely under the legislation of the latter Member State.

Article 28

Pensions payable under the legislation of one or more States, in cases where there is no right to benefits in the country of residence

1. A pensioner who is entitled to a pension under the legislation of one Member State or to pensions under the legislation of two or more Member States and who is not entitled to benefits under the legislation of the Member State in whose territory he resides shall nevertheless receive such benefits for himself and for members of his family, in so far as he would, taking account where appropriate of the provisions of Article 18 and Annex VI, be entitled thereto under the legislation of the Member State or of at least one of the Member States competent in respect of pensions if he were resident in the territory of such State. The benefits shall be provided under the following conditions:

    (a) benefits in kind shall be provided on behalf of the institution referred to in paragraph 2 by the institution of the place of residence as though the person concerned were a pensioner under the legislation of the State in whose territory he resides and were entitled to such benefits;

    (b) cash benefits shall, where appropriate, be provided by the competent institution as determined by the rules of paragraph 2, in accordance with the legislation which it administers. However, upon agreement between the competent institution and the institution of the place of residence, such benefits may be provided by the latter institution on behalf of the former, in accordance with the legislation of the competent State.

2. In the cases covered by paragraph 1, the cost of benefits in kind shall be borne by the institution as determined according to the following rules:

    (a) where the pensioner is entitled to the said benefits under the legislation of a single Member State, the cost shall be borne by the competent institution of that State;

    (b) where the pensioner is entitled to the said benefits under the legislation of two or more Member States, the cost thereof shall be borne by the competent institution of the Member State to whose legislation the pensioner has been subject for the longest period of time; should the application of this rule result in several institutions being responsible for the cost of benefits the cost shall be borne by the institution administering the legislation to which the pensioner was last subject.

RELEVANT PROVISIONS OF THE IMPLEMENTING REGULATION

Art.29, reg.574/72/EEC.

3.204

RELEVANT DECISIONS OF THE ADMINISTRATIVE COMMISSION

Decision No 175 of 23 June, 1999 on interpretation of the concept of "benefits in kind" in the event of sickness or maternity pursuant to art.19(1) and (2), art.22, art.22a, art.22b, art.25(1), (3) and (4), art.26, art.28(1), art.28a, art.29, art.31, art.34a and art.34b of Council Regulation (EEC) No 1408/71 and on calculation of the amounts to be refunded under arts 93, 94 and 95 of reg.574/72 as well as the advances to be paid pursuant to art.102(4) of the same Regulation, [2000] OJ L47/32.

GENERAL NOTE

For a discussion of the operation of art.28 in the context of the export of the care component of a disability living allowance as a sickness benefit, see *JS v SSWP* [2009] UKUT 81 (AAC).

Article 28a

Pensions payable under the legislation of one or more of the Member States other than the country of residence where there is a right to benefits in the latter country

3.205   Where the pensioner entitled to a pension under the legislation of one Member State, or to pensions under the legislations of two or more Member States, resides in the territory of a Member State under whose legislation the right to receive benefits in kind is not subject to conditions of insurance or employment, nor is any pension payable, the cost of benefits in kind provided to him and to members of his family shall be borne by the institution of one of the Member States competent in respect of pensions, determined according to the rules laid down in Article 28(2), to the extent that the pensioner and members of his family would have been entitled to such benefits under the legislation administered by the said institution if they resided in the territory of the Member State where that institution is situated.

RELEVANT PROVISIONS OF THE IMPLEMENTING REGULATION

Art.29, reg.574/72/EEC.

RELEVANT DECISIONS OF THE ADMINISTRATIVE COMMISSION

Decision No 175 of 23 June, 1999 on interpretation of the concept of "benefits in kind" in the event of sickness or maternity pursuant to art.19(1) and (2), art.22, art.22a, art.22b, art.25(1), (3) and (4), art.26, art.28(1), art.28a, art.29, art.31, art.34a and art.34b of Council Regulation (EEC) No 1408/71 and on calculation of the amounts to be refunded under arts 93, 94 and 95 of reg.574/72 as well as the advances to be paid pursuant to art.102(4) of the same Regulation, [2000] OJ L47/32.

Article 29

Residence of members of the family in a State other than the one in which the pensioner resides—Transfer of residence to the State where the pensioner resides

3.206   **1.** Members of the family of a pensioner entitled to a pension under the legislation of one Member State or to pensions under the legislation of two or more Member States who reside in the territory of a Member State other than the one in which the pensioner resides shall, where he is entitled to benefits under the legislation of one Member State, receive benefits as though the pensioner were resident in the same territory as themselves. Benefit shall be provided under the following conditions:

[¹ (a) benefits in kind shall be provided by the institution of the place of residence of the members of the family in accordance with the provisions of the legislation which that institution administers, the cost being borne by the institution determined in accordance with the provisions of Article 27 or Article 28(2); if the place of residence is situated in the competent Member State, benefits in kind shall be provided, and the cost borne, by the competent institution;]

(b) cash benefits shall, where appropriate, be provided by the competent institution as determined by the provisions of Article 27 or 28(2), in accordance with the provisions of the legislation which it administers. However, upon agreement between the competent institution and the institution of the place of residence of the members of the family, such benefits may be provided by the latter institution on behalf of the former, in accordance with the provisions of the legislation of the competent State.

2. Members of the family referred to in paragraph 1 who transfer their residence to the territory of the Member State where the pensioner resides, shall receive:

(a) benefits in kind under the provisions of the legislation of that State, even if they have already received benefits for the same case of sickness or maternity before transferring their residence;

(b) cash benefits provided where appropriate by the competent institution determined by the provisions of Article 27 or 28(2), in accordance with the legislation which it administers. However, upon agreement between the competent institution and the institution of the place of residence of the pensioner, such benefits may be provided by the latter institution on behalf of the former, in accordance with the provisions of the legislation of the competent State.

AMENDMENT

1. Regulation 1223/98/EC, [1998] OJ L168/1 (January 1, 1998, but in relation to France January 1, 2002).

RELEVANT PROVISIONS OF THE IMPLEMENTING REGULATION

Art.30, Reg.574/72/EEC.

RELEVANT DECISIONS OF THE ADMINISTRATIVE COMMISSION

Decision No 175 of 23 June, 1999 on interpretation of the concept of "benefits in kind" in the event of sickness or maternity pursuant to art.19(1) and (2), art.22, art.22a, art.22b, art.25(1), (3) and (4), art.26, art.28(1), art.28a, art.29, art.31, art.34a and art.34b of Council Regulation (EEC) No 1408/71 and on calculation of the amounts to be refunded under Articles 93, 94 and 95 of Regulation (EEC) No 574/72 as well as the advances to be paid pursuant to Article 102(4) of the same Regulation, [2000] OJ L47/32.

Article 30

Substantial benefits in kind

3.207   The provisions of Article 24 shall apply by analogy to pensioners.

[¹ *Article 31*

Stay of the pensioner and/or members of his family in a State other than the State in which they reside

3.208   **1.** A pensioner entitled to a pension or pensions under the legislation of one Member State or to pensions under the legislation of to or more Member States who is entitled to benefits under the legislation of one of those States shall, with members of his family who are staying in the territory of a Member State other than the State in which they reside, receive:

(a) benefits in kind which become necessary on medical grounds during a stay in the territory of the Member State other than the State of residence, taking into account the nature of the benefits and the expected length of the stay. These benefits in kind shall be provided by the institution of the place of stay, in accordance with the provisions of the legislation which it administers, on behalf of the institution of the place of residence of the pensions or of the members of his family;

(b) cash benefits provided, where appropriate, by the competent institution as determined by Article 27 or 28(2), in accordance with the provisions of the legislation which it administers. However, upon agreement between the competent institution and the institution of the place of stay, these benefits may be provided by the latter institution on behalf of the former, in accordance with the provisions of the legislation of the competent State.

2. Article 22(1a) shall apply by analogy.]

AMENDMENT

1. Regulation 631/2004/EC, [2004] OJ L100/1 (June 1, 2004).

RELEVANT PROVISIONS OF THE IMPLEMENTING REGULATION

Art.31, reg.574/72/EEC.

RELEVANT PROVISIONS OF THE ADMINISTRATIVE COMMISSION

Decision No 175 of 23 June, 1999 on interpretation of the concept of "benefits in kind" in the event of sickness or maternity pursuant to art.19(1) and (2), art.22, art.22a, art.22b, art.25(1), (3) and (4), art.26, art.28(1), art.28a, art.29, art.31, art.34a and art.34b of Council Regulation (EEC) No 1408/71 and on calculation of the amounts to be refunded under arts 93, 94 and 95 of Regulation (EEC) No 574/72 as well as the advances to be paid pursuant to art.102(4) of the same Regulation, [2000] OJ L47/32.

Article 32

[. . .]   3.209

Article 33

Contributions payable by pensioners

1. The institution of a Member State which is responsible for payment   3.210
of a pension and which administers legislation providing for deductions
from pensions in respect of contributions for sickness and maternity shall
be authorized to make such deductions, calculated in accordance with the
legislation concerned, from the pension payable by such institution, to the
extent that the cost of the benefits under Article 27, 28, 28a, 29, 31 and 32
is to be borne by an institution of the said Member State.
2. Where, in the cases referred to in Article 28a, the acquisition of
benefits in respect of sickness and maternity is subject to the payment of
contributions or similar payments under the legislation of a Member State
in whose territory the pensioner in question resides, by virtue of such residence, these contributions shall not be payable.

GENERAL NOTE

In Case C-50/05 *Nikula* [2006] ECR I-7029, the Court of Justice ruled that   3.211
art.33(1) does not preclude the inclusion, in the basis of calculation in determining
sickness insurance contributions in the Member State of residence, of pensions paid
by the institutions of another Member State, provided that the sickness insurance
contributions do not exceed the amount of pension paid in then Member State
of residence. But art.39 EC does preclude the amount of pensions received from
institutions of another Member State being taken into account if contributions have
already been paid in the other State out of the income from work received in that
State. It is for the person concerned to prove that the earlier contributions were in
fact paid.

Article 34

General provisions

1. For the purposes of Articles 28, 28a, 29 and 31, a pensioner who is   3.212
in receipt of two or more pensions due under the legislation of a single
Member State shall be regarded as a pensioner entitled to draw a pension
under the legislation of one Member State, within the meaning of these
provisions.
2. Articles 27 to 33 shall not apply to a pensioner or to members of his
family who are entitled to benefits under the legislation of a Member State
as a result of pursuing a professional or trade activity. In such a case, the
person concerned shall, for the purposes of the implementation of this
chapter, be considered as an employed or self-employed person or as a
member of an employed or self-employed person's family.

[¹ SECTION 5A

PERSONS WHO STUDY OR RECEIVE VOCATIONAL TRAINING AND MEMBERS
OF THEIR FAMILIES

Article 34a

Special provisions for students and members of their families

3.213   [² Articles 18, 19, 22(1)(a) and (c) and (1a), 22(2), second subparagraph, 22(3), 23, and 24 and Sections 6 and 7 shall apply by analogy to
students and to members of their families, as required.]

AMENDMENTS

1. Regulation 307/99/EC, [1999] OJ L38/1 (May 1, 1999).
2. Regulation 631/2004/EC, [2004] OJ L100/1.

RELEVANT DECISIONS OF THE ADMINISTRATIVE COMMISSION

Decision No 175 of 23 June 1999 on interpretation of the concept of "benefits in
kind" in the event of sickness or maternity pursuant to Article 19(1) and (2), Article
22, Article 22a, Article 22b, Article 25(1), (3) and (4), Article 26, Article 28(1),
Article 28a, Article 29, Article 31, Article 34a and Article 34b of Council Regulation
(EEC) No 1408/71 and on calculation of the amounts to be refunded under Articles
93, 94 and 95 of Regulation (EEC) No 574/72 as well as the advances to be paid
pursuant to Article 102(4) of the same Regulation, [2000] OJ L47/32.

Article 34b

Common provisions

3.214   [¹ . . .]

AMENDMENT

1. Regulation 631/2004/EC, [2004] OJ L100/1.

SECTION 6

MISCELLANEOUS PROVISIONS

Article 35

**Scheme applicable where there are a number of schemes in the
country of residence or stay—Previous illness—Maximum
period during which benefits are granted**

3.215   **1.** Subject to paragraph 2, where the legislation of the country of stay
or residence contains several sickness or maternity insurance schemes,

the provisions applicable under Article 19, 21(1), 22, 25, 26, 28(1), 29(1) or 31 shall be those of the scheme covering manual workers in the steel industry. Where, however, the said legislation includes a special scheme for workers in mines and similar undertakings, the provisions of such scheme shall apply to that category of workers and members of their families provided the institution of the place of stay or residence to which application is made is competent to administer such scheme.

2. [² . . .].

3. Where, under the legislation of a Member State, the granting of benefits is conditional upon the origin of the illness, that conditions [¹ shall not apply to persons] to whom this Regulation applies, regardless of the Member State in whose territory they reside.

4. Where the legislation of a Member State fixes a maximum period for the granting of benefits, the institution which administers that legislation may, where appropriate, take account of the period during which the benefits have already been provided by the institution of another Member State for the same case of sickness or maternity.

AMENDMENTS

1. Regulation 307/99/EC, [1999] OJ L38/1 (May 1, 1999).
2. Regulation 647/2005/EC, [2005] OJ L117/1 (May 5, 2005).

RELEVANT PROVISIONS OF THE IMPLEMENTING REGULATION

Arts 32–24, reg.574/72/EEC.

SECTION 7

REIMBURSEMENT BETWEEN INSTITUTIONS

Article 36

1. Benefits in kind provided in accordance with the provisions of this chapter by the institution of one Member State on behalf of the institution of another Member State shall be fully refunded.

2. The refunds referred to in paragraph 1 shall be determined and made in accordance with the procedure provided for by the implementing Regulation referred to in Article 98, either on production of proof of actual expenditure or on the basis of lump-sum payments.

In the latter case, the lump-sum payments shall be such as to ensure that the refund is as close as possible to actual expenditure.

3. Two or more Member States, or the competent authorities of those States, may provide for other methods of reimbursement or may waive all reimbursement between institutions under their jurisdiction.

3.216

CHAPTER 2

INVALIDITY

RELEVANT PROVISIONS OF THE IMPLEMENTING REGULATION

Provisions relating to administrative checks and medical examinations can be found in arts 51–2, and on payment of benefits in arts 53–59, reg.574/72/EEC.

GENERAL NOTE

3.217   Whereas the Regulation adopts an approach to short-term benefits which results generally in one Member State being responsible for the payment of such benefits, such an approach is applied less easily to long-term benefits, since, under such a system, a Member State may become liable to pay a long-term benefit for a substantial period without having received contributions to support that benefit. The general approach to long-term benefits is that each Member State pays its proportionate share of the pension. The position becomes more complicated in the case of invalidity pensions, since the Member States take two fundamentally different approaches to invalidity benefits. Some Member States operate invalidity benefits in much the same way as they operate old age benefits. These are known as Type B schemes. Other Member States have schemes under which invalidity benefit is paid on fixed scales (which may be related to the level of previous earnings) which are not tied to periods of insurance, though there may be a requirement for a minimum period of insurance. These schemes are known as Type A schemes. The United Kingdom scheme is a Type A scheme. Co-ordination of Type A and Type B schemes presents particular difficulties. The effect of the provisions of the Regulation can be summarised as follows:

1. Claimant insured in a single country.	Entitled to invalidity benefits calculated in accordance with the legislation of that country.
2. Claimant insured in more than one country where the amount of the invalidity benefit is determined by reference to the length of insurance periods.	Entitled to invalidity benefits from each country in accordance with the periods of insurance. The calculation is as for retirement pensions.
3. Claimant insured in more than one country where the amount of the invalidity benefit is independent of the length of insurance periods.	Entitled to invalidity benefits from the country in which the claimant became an invalid (even if this is lower than the benefits paid in any of the other countries where the claimant has been insured).
4. Claimant first insured in a country where the amount of the invalidity benefit depends on the length of insurance periods and then in a country where the amount of invalidity benefit is independent of the length of insurance periods.	Entitled to invalidity benefit from the first country in accordance with periods of insurance, and an invalidity benefit from the second country which may be reduced to take account of the benefit received from the first country.
5. Claimant first insured in a country where the amount of the pension is independent of the length of	Entitled to invalidity benefit from the first country and an invalidity benefit from the second country in

insurance periods and then in a country where the amount of invalidity benefit depends on the length of insurance periods. accordance with the periods of insurance.

SECTION 1

EMPLOYED PERSONS OR SELF-EMPLOYED PERSONS SUBJECT ONLY TO LEGISLATION UNDER WHICH THE AMOUNT OF INVALIDITY BENEFITS ITS INDEPENDENT OF THE DURATION OF THE PERIODS OF INSURANCE

Article 37

General provisions

1. An employed person or a self-employed person who has been succes- 3.218
sively or alternately subject to the legislation of two or more Member States and who has completed periods of insurance exclusively under legislation according to which the amount of invalidity benefits is independent of the duration of periods of insurance shall receive benefits in accordance with Article 39. This Article shall not affect pension increases or supplements in respect of children, granted in accordance with Chapter 8.

2. Annex IV, part A, lists legislations of the kind mentioned in paragraph 1 which are in force in the territory of each of the Member States concerned.

RELEVANT PROVISIONS OF THE IMPLEMENTING REGULATION

Arts 35, 39, 40, and 41–50 of reg.5764/72/EEC.

Article 38

Consideration of periods of insurance or of residence completed under the legislation to which an employed person or a self-employed person was subject for the acquisition, retention or recovery of the right to benefits

1. Where the legislation of a Member State makes the acquisition, reten- 3.219
tion or recovery of the right to benefits, under a scheme which is not a special scheme within the meaning of paragraph 2 or 3, subject to the completion of periods of insurance or of residence, the competent institution of that Member State shall take account, where necessary, of the periods of insurance or of residence completed under the legislation of any other Member State, be it under a general scheme or under a special scheme and either as an employed person or as a self-employed person. For that purpose, it shall take account of these periods as if they had been completed under its own legislation.

2. Where the legislation of a Member State makes the granting of certain benefits conditional upon the periods of insurance having been completed only in a occupation which is subject to a special scheme for employed persons or, where appropriate, in a specific employment, periods completed under the legislation of other Member States shall be taken into account for the granting of these benefits only if completed under a corresponding scheme or, failing that, in the same occupation or, where appropriate, in the same employment.

If, account having been taken of the periods thus completed, the person concerned does not satisfy the conditions for receipt of these benefits, these periods shall be taken into account for the granting of the benefits under the general scheme or, failing that, under the scheme applicable to manual or clerical workers, as the case may be, subject to the condition that the person concerned has been affiliated to one or other of these schemes.

3. Where the legislation of a Member State makes the granting of certain benefits conditional upon the period of insurance having been completed only in a occupation subject to a special scheme for self-employed persons, periods completed under the legislation of other Member States shall be taken into account for the granting of these benefits only if completed under a corresponding scheme or, failing that, in the same occupation. The special schemes for self-employed persons referred to in this paragraph are listed in Annex IV, part B, for each Member State concerned.

If, account having been taken of the periods thus completed, the person concerned does not satisfy the conditions for receipt of these benefits, these periods shall be taken into account for the granting of the benefits under the general scheme or, failing that, under the scheme applicable to manual or clerical workers, as the case may be, subject to the condition that the person concerned has been affiliated to one or other of these schemes.

RELEVANT PROVISIONS OF THE IMPLEMENTING REGULATION

Arts 15, and 35, reg.574/72/EEC.

Article 39

Award of benefits

3.220   **1.** The institution of a Member State whose legislation was applicable at the time when incapacity for work followed by invalidity occurred shall determine, in accordance with that legislation, whether the person concerned satisfies the conditions for entitlement to benefits, taking account, where appropriate, of Article 38.

2. A person who satisfies the conditions referred to in paragraph 1 shall receive the benefits only from the said institution, in accordance with the provisions of the legislation which it administers.

3. A person who is not entitled to benefits under paragraph 1 shall receive the benefits to which he is still entitled under the legislation of another Member State taking account, where appropriate, of Article 38.

4. If the legislation referred to in paragraph 2 or 3 provides that the amount of the benefits shall be determined taking into account the existence of members of the family other than the children, the competent institution shall also take into consideration those members of the family of the person concerned who are residing in the territory of another Member State, as if they were residing in the territory of the competent State.

5. If the legislation referred to in paragraph 2 or 3 lays down provisions for the reduction, suspension or withdrawal of benefits in the case of overlapping with other income or with benefits of a different kind within the meaning of Article 461(2), Article 46a(3) and Article 46c(5) shall apply *mutatis mutandis*.

6. A wholly unemployed employee to whom Article 71(1)(a)(ii) or the first sentence of Article 71(1)(b)(ii) applies shall receive the invalidity benefits provided by the competent institution of the Member State in whose territory he resides, in accordance with the legislation which it administers, as though he had been subject to that legislation during his last employment, account being taken, where appropriate, of Article 38 and/or Article 25(2). The institution of the country of residence shall be responsible for paying these benefits.

Where that institution applies legislation providing for deduction of contributions payable by unemployed persons to cover invalidity benefits, it shall be authorized to make such deductions in accordance with the provisions of its legislation.

If the legislation which that institution administers provides for the calculation of benefits to be based on wages or salaries, the institution shall take into account the wages or salaries received in the last country of employment and in the country of residence in accordance with the legislation which it administers. Where no wage or salary has been received in the country of residence, the competent institution shall refer, as necessary and in accordance with the rules laid down in its legislation, to the salaries received in the last country of employment.

RELEVANT PROVISIONS OF THE IMPLEMENTING REGULATION

Arts 35, and 38 of reg.5764/72/EEC.

SECTION 2

EMPLOYED PERSONS OR SELF-EMPLOYED PERSONS SUBJECT EITHER ONLY TO LEGISLATION UNDER WHICH THE AMOUNT OF INVALIDITY BENEFIT DEPENDS ON THE DURATION OF PERIODS OF INSURANCE OR RESIDENCE OR THE LEGISLATION OF THIS TYPE AND OF THE TYPE REFERRED TO IN SECTION 1

Article 40

General provisions

1. An employed person or a self-employed person who has been successively or alternately subject to the legislation of two or more Member States, of which at least one is not of the type referred to in Article 37(1), shall receive benefits under the provisions of Chapter 3, which shall apply *mutatis mutandis*, taking into account the provisions of paragraph 4.

2. However, an employed or self-employed person who suffers incapacity for work leading to invalidity while subject to a legislation listed in Annex

3.221

IV, part A, shall receive benefits in accordance with the provisions of Article 37 (1) on the following conditions:

— that he satisfies the conditions of that legislation or other legislations of the same type, taking account where appropriate of Article 38, but without having recourse to periods of insurance completed under legislations not listed in Annex IV, part A, and

— that he does not satisfy the conditions required for the acquisition of the right to invalidity benefits under a legislation not listed in Annex IV, part A, and

— that he does not assert any claims to old-age benefits, account being taken of the second sentence of Article 44(2).

3.(a) For the purpose of determining the right to benefits under the legislation of a Member State, listed in Annex IV, part A, which makes the granting of invalidity benefits conditional upon the person concerned having received cash sickness benefits or having been incapable or work during a specified period, where an employed person or a self-employed person who has been subject to that legislation suffers incapacity for work leading to invalidity while subject to the legislation of another Member State, account shall be taken of the following, without prejudice to Article 37(1):

(i) any period during which, in respect of that incapacity for work, he has, under the legislation of the second Member State, received cash sickness benefits, or, in lieu thereof, continued to receive a wage or salary;

(ii) any period during which, in respect of the invalidity which followed that incapacity for work, he has received benefits within the meaning of this Chapter 2 and of Chapter 3 that follows, of the Regulation granted in respect of invalidity under the legislation of the second Member State.

as if it were a period during which cash sickness benefits were paid to him under the legislation of the first Member State or during which he was incapable or working within the meaning of that legislation.

(b) The right to invalidity benefits under the legislation of the first Member State shall be acquired either upon expiry of the preliminary period of compensation for sickness, as required by that legislation, or upon expiry of the preliminary period of incapacity of work as required by that legislation, but not before:

(i) the date of acquisition of the right to invalidity benefits referred to in subparagraph (a)(ii) under the legislation of the second Member State,

or

(ii) the day following the last day on which the person concerned is entitled to cash sickness benefits under the legislation of the second Member State.

4. A decision taken by an institution of a Member State concerning the degree of invalidity of a claimant shall be binding on the institution of any other Member State concerned, provided that the concordance between the legislation of these States on conditions relating to the degree of invalidity is acknowledged in Annex V.

Article 40

RELEVANT PROVISIONS OF THE IMPLEMENTING REGULATION

Arts 35, 36, 37, 40, and 41–50 of reg.5764/72/EEC.

RELEVANT DECISIONS OF THE ADMINISTRATIVE COMMISSION

Decision No 132 of 23 April, 1987 concerning the interpretation of art.40(3)(a) (ii) of Council Regulation (EEC) No 1408/71 of 14 June, 1971.

GENERAL NOTE

In *R(IB) 1/02* the Commissioner ruled that short-term incapacity benefit (whether paid at the lower or higher rate) is a sickness benefit within the meaning of art.4, and long-term incapacity benefit is an invalidity benefit which is not subject to contribution requirements but to the receipt for the specified period of short-term incapacity benefit. The Commissioner notes that the provision of the Regulation on invalidity benefit do not use the concept of the competent State; entitlement to invalidity benefit in the United Kingdom can arise where the claimant has received sickness benefit for 364 days in another Member State, since the claimant's entitlement to sickness benefit in another Member State is to be treated as entitlement in the United Kingdom. The facts of *CIB/4471/2000* were much more complex. The claimant had worked and paid social security contributions successively in the United Kingdom, Belgium and Italy. Following an injury suffered at work in Italy, the claimant had moved to Belgium. He sought to claim invalidity benefits in Belgium and the United Kingdom. There appears to have been considerable difficulty in obtaining official information about the benefit position in Italy and Belgium. The Commission again notes that the claimant would become entitled to invalidity benefit in the United Kingdom (his claim pre-dated the introduction of incapacity benefit) if he could establish that he had received sickness benefit for 168 days in another Member State. It transpired that he was paid the equivalent of statutory sick pay by his employer in Italy for less than the requisite period, and so his claim for United Kingdom invalidity benefit could not succeed. Note that an employer paying sickness benefit under a statutory scheme can be the competent institution within the meaning of the Regulation: Case C-45/90 *Paletta* [1992] E.C.R. I-3423, paras 19–24 of the judgment).

3.222

SECTION 3

AGGRAVATION OF INVALIDITY

Article 41

1. In the case of aggravation of an invalidity for which an employed person or a self-employed person is receiving benefits under the legislation of a single Member State, the following provisions shall apply:

3.223

(a) if the person concerned has not been subject to the legislation of another Member State since receiving benefits, the competent institution of the first State shall grant the benefits, taking the aggravation into account, in accordance with the provisions of the legislation which it administers;

(b) if the person concerned has been subject to the legislation of one or more of the other Member States since receiving benefits, the benefits shall be granted to him, taking the aggravation into account, in accordance with Article 37(1) or 40(1) or (2), as appropriate;

(c) if the total number of the benefit or benefits payable under subparagraph (b) is lower than the amount of the benefit which the person concerned was receiving at the expense of the institution previously liable for payment, such institution shall pay him a supplement equal to the difference between the two amounts;

(d) if, in the case referred to in subparagraph (b), the institution responsible for the initial incapacity is a Dutch institution, and if:

    (i) the illness which caused the aggravation is the same as the one which gave rise to the granting of benefits under Dutch legislation,

    (ii) this illness is an occupational disease within the meaning of the legislation of the Member State to which the person concerned was last subject and entitles him to payment of the supplement referred to in Article 60(1)(b), and

    (iii) the legislation or legislations to which the person concerned has been subject since receiving benefits is or are listed in Annex IV, part A,

the Dutch institution shall continue to provide the initial benefit after the aggravation occurs, and the benefit due under the legislation of the last Member State to which the person concerned was subject shall be reduced by the amount of the Dutch benefit;

(e) if, in the case referred to in subparagraph (b), the person concerned is not entitled to benefits at the expense of an institution of another Member State, the competent institution of the first State shall grant the benefits, according to the provisions of the legislation of the State, taking into account the aggravation and, where appropriate, Article 38.

2. In the case of aggravation of an invalidity for which an employed person or a self-employed person is receiving benefits under the legislation of two or more Member States, the benefits shall be granted to him, taking the aggravation into account, in accordance with Article 40(1).

RELEVANT PROVISIONS OF THE IMPLEMENTING REGULATION

Arts 35, 36, and 37 of reg.5764/72/EEC.

SECTION 4

RESUMPTION OF PROVISION OF BENEFITS AFTER SUSPENSION OR
WITHDRAWAL—CONVERSION OF INVALIDITY BENEFITS INTO OLD-AGE
BENEFITS—RECALCULATION OF BENEFITS GRANTED UNDER ARTICLE 39

Article 42

Determination of the institution responsible for the provision of benefits where provision of invalidity benefits is resumed

3.224   **1.** If provision of benefits is to be resumed after suspension, such provision shall, without prejudice to Article 43, be the responsibility of the institution or institutions which were responsible for provision of the benefits at the time of their suspension.

2. If, after withdrawal of benefits, the condition of the person concerned warrants the granting of further benefits, they shall be granted in accordance with Article 37(1) or Article 40(1) or (2), as appropriate.

RELEVANT PROVISIONS OF THE IMPLEMENTING REGULATION

Arts 35, 36, and 37 of reg.5764/72/EEC.

Article 43

Conversion of invalidity benefits into old-age benefits—Recalculation of benefits granted under Article 39

1. Invalidity benefits shall be converted into old-age benefits, where appropriate, under the condition laid down by the legislation or legislations under which they were granted, and in accordance with Chapter 3.   3.225

2. Where a person receiving invalidity benefits can establish a claim to old-age benefits under the legislation of one or more Member States, in accordance with Article 49, any institution which is responsible for providing invalidity benefits under the legislation of a Member State shall continue to provide such a person with the invalidity benefits to which he is entitled under the legislation which it administers until the provisions of paragraph 1 become applicable as regards that institution or so long as the person concerned fulfils the conditions for such benefits.

3. Where invalidity benefits granted in accordance with Article 39 under the legislation of a Member State are converted into old-age benefits and where the person concerned does not yet satisfy the conditions required by one or more national legislations to receive these benefits, the person concerned shall receive, from this or these Member States, from the date of the conversion, invalidity benefits granted in accordance with Chapter 3 as if that Chapter had been applicable at the time when his incapacity for work leading to invalidity occurred, until the person concerned satisfies the qualifying conditions for old-age benefit laid down by the national legislations concerned or, where such conversion is not provided for, as long as he has a right to invalidity benefits under the legislation or legislations concerned.

4. The invalidity benefits provided under Article 39 shall be recalculated pursuant to Chapter 3 as soon as the beneficiary satisfies the qualifying conditions for invalidity benefits laid down by a legislation not listed in Annex IV, part A, or as soon as he receives old-age benefits under the legislation of another Member State.

RELEVANT PROVISIONS OF THE IMPLEMENTING REGULATION

Arts 36 and 37 of reg.5764/72/EEC.

[¹ SECTION 5

PERSONS COVERED BY A SPECIAL SCHEME FOR CIVIL SERVANTS

Article 43a

1. The provisions of Articles 37, 38(1), 39 and Sections 2, 3 and 4 shall apply by analogy to persons covered by a special scheme for civil servants.   3.226

2. However, if the legislation of a Member State makes the acquisition, liquidation, retention or recovery of the rights to benefit under a special scheme for civil servants subject to the condition that all periods of insurance have been completed under one or more special schemes for civil servants in that Member State, or are regarded by the legislation of that Member State as equivalent to such periods, account shall be taken only of the periods which can be recognised under the legislation in that Member State.

If, account having been taken of the periods thus completed, the person concerned does not satisfy the conditions for the receipt of these benefits, these periods shall be taken into account for the granting of the benefits under the general scheme or, failing that, the scheme applicable to manual or clerical workers, as the case may be.

3. Were, under the legislation of a Member State, benefits are calculated on the basis of the last salary or salaries received during a reference period, the competent institution of that State shall take into account for the purposes of the calculation only those salaries, duly revalued, received during the period for which the person concerned was subject to that legislation.]

AMENDMENT

1. Regulation1606/98/EC, [1998] OJ L209/1 (October 25, 1998).

RELEVANT PROVISIONS OF THE IMPLEMENTING REGULATION

Arts 36 and 37 of reg.5764/72/EEC.

CHAPTER 3

RELEVANT PROVISIONS OF THE IMPLEMENTING REGULATION

Provisions relating to administrative checks and medical examinations can be found in Arts 51–2, and on payment of benefits in Arts 53–59, Reg.574/72/EEC.

OLD AGE AND DEATH (PENSIONS)

Article 44

General provisions for the award of benefits where an employed or self-employed person has been subject to the legislation of two or more Member States

3.227 **1.** The rights to benefits of an employed or self-employed person who has been subject to the legislation of two or more Member States, or of his survivors, shall be determined in accordance with the provisions of this Chapter.

2. Save as otherwise provided in Article 49, the processing of a claim for an award submitted by the person concerned shall have regard to all the legislations to which the employed or self-employed person has been subject. Exception shall be made to this rule if the person concerned expressly asks for postponement of the award of old-age benefits to which he would be entitled under the legislation of one or more Member States.

[¹ **3.** This chapter shall not apply to increases in or supplements to pensions in respect of children or to orphans' pensions to be granted in accordance with the provisions of Chapter 8.]

AMENDMENT

1. Regulation 1399/99/EC, [1999] OJ L164/1 (September 1, 1999).

RELEVANT PROVISIONS OF THE IMPLEMENTING REGULATION

Arts 36 and 37 of reg.5764/72/EEC.

RELEVANT DECISIONS OF THE ADMINISTRATIVE COMMISSION

Recommendation No 23 of 29 October, 2003 on the processing of pension claims, [2004] OJ L104/125.

Article 45

Consideration of periods of insurance or of residence completed under the legislations to which an employed person or self-employed person was subject, for the acquisition, retention or recovery of the right to benefits

1. Where the legislation of a Member State makes the acquisition, retention or recovery of the right to benefits, under a scheme which is not a special scheme within the meaning of paragraph 2 or 3, subject to the completion of periods of insurance or of residence, the competent institution of that Member State shall take account, where necessary, of the periods of insurance or of residence completed under the legislation of any other Member State, be it under a general scheme or under a special scheme and either as an employed person or a self-employed person. For that purpose, it shall take account of these periods as if they had completed under its own legislation.

2. Where the legislation of a Member State makes the granting of certain benefits conditional upon the periods of insurance having been completed only in an occupation which is subject to a special scheme for employed persons or, where appropriate, in a specific employment, periods completed under the legislation of other Member States shall be taken into account for the granting of these benefits only if completed under a corresponding scheme or, failing that, in the same occupation or, where appropriate, in the same employment. If, account having been taken of the periods thus completed, the person concerned does not satisfy the conditions for receipt of these benefits, these periods shall be taken into account for the granting of the benefits under the general scheme or, failing that, under the scheme applicable to manual or clerical workers, as the case may be, subject to the condition that the person has been affiliated to one or other of these schemes.

3.228

3. Where the legislation of a Member State makes the granting of certain benefits conditional upon the periods of insurance having been completed only in an occupation subject to a special scheme for self-employed persons, periods completed under the legislations of other Member States shall be taken into account for the granting of these benefits only if completed under a corresponding scheme or, failing that, in the same occupation. The special schemes for self-employed persons referred to in this paragraph are listed in Annex IV, part B, for each Member State concerned. If, account having been taken of the periods referred to in this paragraph, the person concerned does not satisfy the conditions for receipt of these benefits, these periods shall be taken into account for the granting of the benefits under the general scheme or, failing this, under the scheme applicable to manual or clerical workers, as the case may be, subject to the condition that the person concerned has been affiliated to one or other of these schemes.

4. The periods of insurance completed under a special scheme of a Member State shall be taken into account under the general scheme or, failing that, under the scheme applicable to manual or clerical workers, as the case may be, of another Member State for the acquisition, retention or recovery of the right to benefits, subject to the condition that the person concerned has been affiliated to one or other of these schemes, even if these periods have already been taken into account in the latter State under a scheme referred to in paragraph 2 or in the first sentence of paragraph 3.

5. Where the legislation of a Member State makes the acquisition, retention or recovery of the right to benefits conditional upon the person concerned being insured at the time of the materialization of the risk, this condition shall be regarded as having been satisfied in the case of insurance under the legislation of another Member State, in accordance with the procedures provided in Annex VI for each Member State concerned.

6. A period of full employment of a worker to whom Article 81(1)(a) (ii) or (b)(ii), first sentence, applies shall be taken into account by the competent institution of the Member State in whose territory the worker concerned resides in accordance with the legislation administered by that institution, as if that legislation applied to him during his last employment.

Where that institution applies legislation providing for deduction of contributions payable by unemployed persons to cover old age pensions and death, it shall be authorized to make such deductions in accordance with the provisions of its legislation.

If the period of full unemployment in the country of residence of the person concerned can be taken into account only if contribution periods have been completed in that country, this condition shall be deemed to be fulfilled if the contribution periods have been completed in another Member State.

RELEVANT PROVISIONS OF THE IMPLEMENTING REGULATION

Arts 15, 36 and 37 of reg.574/72/EEC.

RELEVANT DECISIONS OF THE ADMINISTRATIVE COMMISSION

Decision No 81 of 22 February, 1973 concerning aggregation of insurance periods completed in a given occupation in application of art.45(2) of Regulation (EEC) No 1408/71, [1973] OJ C 75/11.

Article 45

Decision No 134 of 1 July, 1987 concerning the interpretation of art.45(2) of Regulation (EEC) No 1408/71 relating to aggregation of insurance periods completed in an occupation subject to a special scheme in one or more Member States, [1988] OJ C64/4.

Decision No 136 of 1 July, 1987 concerning the interpretation of art.45(1) to (3) of Council Regulation (EEC) No 1408/71 with regard to the taking into account of insurance periods completed under the legislations of other Member States for the acquisition, retention or recovery of the right to benefits, [1988] OJ C64/7.

Article 46

Award of benefits

1. Where the conditions required by the legislation of a Member State for entitlement to benefits have been satisfied without having to apply Article 45 or Article 40(3), the following rules shall apply:

3.229

(a) the competent institution shall calculate the amount of the benefit that would be due:
   (i) on the one hand, only under the provisions of the legislation which it administers;
   (ii) on the other hand, pursuant to paragraph 2;
(b) the competent institution may, however, waive the calculation to be carried out in accordance with (a)(ii) if the result of this calculation, apart from differences arising from the use of round figures, is equal to or lower than the result of the calculation carried out in accordance with (a)(i), in so far as that institution does not apply any legislation containing rules against overlapping as referred to in Articles 46b and 46c or if the aforementioned institution applies a legislation containing rules against overlapping in the case referred to in Article 46c, provided that the said legislation lays down that benefits of a different kind shall be taken into consideration only on the basis of the relation of the periods of insurance or of residence completed under that legislation alone to the periods of insurance or of residence required by that legislation in order to qualify for full benefit entitlement.
   Annex IV, part C, lists for each Member State concerned the cases where the two calculations would lead to a result of this kind.

2. Where the conditions required by the legislation of a Member State for entitlement to benefits are satisfied only after application of Article 45 and or Article 40(3), the following rules shall apply:

(a) the competent institution shall calculate the theoretical amount of the benefit to which the person concerned could lay claim provided all periods of insurance and/or of residence, which have been completed under the legislation of the Member States to which the employed person or self-employed person was subject, have been completed in the State in question under the legislation which it administers on the date of the award of the benefit. If, under this legislation, the amount of the benefit is independent of the duration of the periods completed, the amount shall be regarded as being the theoretical amount referred to in this paragraph;
(b) the competent institution shall subsequently determine the actual amount of the benefit on the basis of the theoretical amount referred

983

to in the preceding paragraph in accordance with the ratio of the duration of the periods of insurance or of residence completed before the materialization of the risk under the legislation which it administers to the total duration of the periods of insurance and of residence completed before the materialization of the risk under the legislations of all the Member States concerned.

3. The person concerned shall be entitled to the highest amount calculated in accordance with paragraphs 1 and 2 from the competent institution of each Member State without prejudice to any application of the provisions concerning reduction, suspension or withdrawal provided for by the legislation under which this benefit is due.

Where that is the case, the comparison to be carried out shall relate to the amounts determined after the application of the said provisions.

4. When, in the case of invalidity, old-age or survivor's pensions, the total of the benefits due from the competent institutions of two or more Member States under the provisions of a multilateral social security convention referred to in Article 6 (b) does not exceed the total which would be due from such Member States under paragraphs 1 to 3, the person concerned shall benefit from the provisions of this Chapter.

RELEVANT PROVISIONS OF THE IMPLEMENTING REGULATION

Arts 36 and 37 of reg.5764/72/EEC.

RELEVANT DECISIONS OF THE ADMINISTRATIVE COMMISSION

Decision No 91 of 12 July, 1973 concerning the interpretation of art.46(3) of Council Regulation (EEC) No 1408/71 relating to the award of benefits due under para.1 of the said Article.

GENERAL NOTE

3.230
This article is at the heart of the treatment of entitlement to old age pensions where a person has contribution records in more than one Member State. Article 45 contains the basic aggregation rule requiring the competent institution of a Member State to take account of periods of insurance, employment or self-employment completed in another Member State as if they had been completed there. In Case 2/72 *Murru* [1972] E.C.R. 333, the Court of Justice ruled that a period of unemployment could be assimilated to a period of employment under Community rules if the legislation of the country under which the period of unemployment had been completed so provided. Periods are aggregated under Community rules even where they would not be aggregated under the legislation of the State of the competent institution: Joined Cases 113–114/92 and 156/92 *Fabrizii* [1993] E.C.R. I-6707.

Article 46 sets out the basis for determining the award of benefits. Each Member State to whose legislation the claimant has been subject must undertake the following computation. Periods of less than one year are generally ignored: art.48. First it calculates the pension entitlement to which claimant would be entitled if that country applies only its own legislation.

Next, the first step in the second calculation is taken: regard is had to the total period to be taken into account under the legislation of all the relevant countries. Each country then determines the amount of pension to which that would give entitlement: this is known as the "theoretical amount". The second step in the second calculation is to calculate what proportion of the theoretical amount the ratio of years completed in the country doing the calculation to the total years bears. This is called the "actual amount". So in the case of a claim who had spent ten years out of 40 years taken into account under the legislation of the country in question, the actual amount would be one quarter of the theoretical amount. But the actual amount is not what the claimant necessarily receives since this must first be compared with the amount calculated solely under the legislation of the country of claim. The higher of these two amounts is awarded. Each country to whose legislation the claimant has been subject makes this calculation and awards a pension on the basis of the calculation. So the pensioner will receive a pension made up of contributions from each of the Member State's to whose legislation he has been subject.

See art.50 for a provision guaranteeing a minimum pension. The purpose is to ensure a basic standard of living where a person has a series of relatively short periods of employment of self employment in several Member States.

The specific rules on the overlapping of benefits in arts 46a, 46b and 46c display characteristics of technicality and complexity, and are not always easy to understand. But note that they do not apply to benefits calculated in accordance with art.46(2). This means that the individual pro rata pensions calculated in accordance with the formula in art.46 are protected against the rules on the overlapping of benefits.

Article 46a

General provisions relating to reduction, suspension or withdrawal applicable to benefits in respect of invalidity, old age or survivors under the legislations of the Member States

1. For the purposes of the Chapter, overlapping of benefits of the same kind shall have the following meaning: all overlapping of benefits in respect of invalidity, old age and survivors calculated or provided on the basis of periods of insurance and/or residence completed by one and the same person.

3.231

2. For the purposes of this Chapter, overlapping of benefits of different kinds means all overlapping of benefits that cannot be regarded as being of the same kind within the meaning of paragraph 1.

3. The following rules shall be applicable for the application of provisions on reduction, suspension or withdrawal laid down by the legislation of a Member State in the case of overlapping of a benefit in respect of invalidity, old age or survivors with a benefit of the same kind or a benefit of a different kind or with other income:

  (a) account shall be taken of the benefits acquired under the legislation of another Member State or of other income acquired in another Member State only where the legislation of the first Member State provides for the taking into account of benefits or income acquired abroad;

  (b) account shall be taken of the amount of benefits to be granted by another Member State before deductions of taxes, social security contributions and other individual levies or deductions;

  (c) no account shall be taken of the amount of benefits acquired under the legislation of another Member State which are awarded on the basis of voluntary insurance or continued optional insurance;

  (d) where provisions on reduction, suspension or withdrawal are applicable under the legislation of only one Member State on account of the fact that the person concerned receives benefits of a similar or different kind payable under the legislation of other Member States or other income acquired within the territory of other Member

States, the benefit payable under the legislation of the first Member State may be reduced only within the limit of the amount of the benefits payable under the legislation or the income acquired within the territory of other Member States.

RELEVANT PROVISIONS OF THE IMPLEMENTING REGULATION

Arts 36 and 37 of reg.5764/72/EEC.

Article 46b

Special provisions applicable in the case of overlapping of benefits of the same kind under the legislation of two or more Member States

3.232   **1.** The provisions on reduction, suspension or withdrawal laid down by the legislation of a Member State shall not be applicable to a benefit calculated in accordance with Article 46(2).

2. The provisions on reduction, suspension or withdrawal laid down by the legislation of a Member State shall apply to a benefit calculated in accordance with Article 46(1)(a)(i) only if the benefit concerned is:

(a) either a benefit, which is referred to in Annex IV, part D, the amount of which does not depend on the length of the periods of insurance of residence completed,

or

(b) a benefit, the amount of which is determined on the basis of a credited period deemed to have been completed between the date on which the risk materialized and a later date. In the latter case, the said provisions shall apply in the case of overlapping of such a benefit:

(i) either with a benefit of the same kind, except where an agreement has been concluded between two or more Member States providing that one and the same credited period may not be taken into account two or more times;

(ii) or with a benefit of the type referred to in (a).

The benefits referred to in (a) and (b) and agreements are mentioned in Annex IV, part D.

RELEVANT PROVISIONS OF THE IMPLEMENTING REGULATION

Arts 36 and 37 of reg.5764/72/EEC.

Article 46c

Special provisions applicable in the case of overlapping of one or more benefits referred to in Article 46a(1) with one or more benefits of a different kind or with other income, where two or more Member States are concerned

3.233   **1.** If the receipt of benefits of a different kind or other income entails the reduction, suspension or withdrawal of two or more benefits referred to in Article 46(1)(a)(i), the amounts which would not be paid in strict application of the provisions concerning reduction, suspension or withdrawal provided for by the legislation of the Member States concerned shall be divided by the number of benefits subject to reduction, suspension or withdrawal.

2. Where the benefit in question is calculated in accordance with Article 46(2), the benefit or benefits of a different kind from other Member States or other income and all other elements provided for by the legislation of the Member State for the application of the provisions in the respect of reduction, suspension or withdrawal shall be taken into account in proportion to the periods of insurance and/or residence referred to in Article 46(2)(b), and shall be used for the calculation of the said benefit.

3. If the receipt of benefits of a different kind or of other income entails the reduction, suspension or withdrawal of one or more benefits referred to in Article 46(1)(a)(i), and of one or more benefits referred to in Article 46(2), the following rules shall apply:

(a) where in a case of a benefit or benefits referred to in Article 46(1)(a)(i), the amounts which would not be paid in strict application of the provisions concerning reduction, suspension or withdrawal provided for by the legislation of the Member States concerned shall be divided by the number of benefits subject to reduction, suspension or withdrawal;

(b) where in a case of a benefit or benefits calculated in accordance with Article 46(2), the reduction suspension or withdrawal shall be carried out in accordance with paragraph 2.

4. Where, in the case referred to in paragraphs 1 and 3(a), the legislation of a Member State provides that, for the application of provisions concerning reduction, suspension or withdrawal, account shall be taken of benefits of a different kind and/or other income and all other elements in proportion to the periods of insurance referred to in Article 46(2)(b), the division provided for in the said paragraphs shall not apply in respect of that Member State.

5. All the above mentioned provisions shall apply *mutatis mutandis* where the legislation of one or more Member States provides that the right to a benefit cannot be acquired in the case where the person concerned is in receipt of a benefit of a different kind, payable under the legislation of another Member State, or of other income.

RELEVANT PROVISIONS OF THE IMPLEMENTING REGULATION

Arts 36 and 37 of reg.5764/72/EEC.

Article 47

Additional provisions for the calculation of benefits

1. For the calculation of the theoretical and pro rata amounts referred to in Article 46 (2), the following rules shall apply:

(a) where the total length of the periods of insurance and of residence completed before the risk materialized under the legislations of all the Member States concerned is longer than the maximum period

3.234

required by the legislation of one of these States for receipt of full benefit, the competent institution of that State shall take into consideration this maximum period instead of the total length of the periods completed; this method of calculation must not result in the imposition on that institution of the cost of a benefit greater than the full benefit provided for by the legislation which it administers. This provisions shall not apply to benefits, the amount of which does not depend on the length of insurance;

(b) the procedure for taking account of overlapping periods is laid down in the implementing Regulation referred to in Article 98;

(c) where, under the legislation of a Member State, benefits are calculated on the basis of average earnings, an average contribution, an average increase or on the relation which existed, during the periods of insurance, between the claimant's gross earnings and the average gross earnings of all insured persons other than apprentices, such average figures or relations shall be determined by the competent institution of that State solely on the basis of the periods of insurance completed under the legislation of the said State, or the gross earnings received by the person concerned during those periods only;

(d) where, under the legislation of a Member State, benefits are calculated on the basis of the amount of earnings, contributions or increases, the competent institution of the State shall determine the earnings, contributions and increases to be taken into account in respect of the periods of insurance or residence completed under the legislation of other Member States on the basis of the average earnings, contributions or increases recorded in respect of the periods of insurance completed under the legislation which it administers;

(e) where, under the legislation of a Member State, benefits are calculated on the basis of standard earnings or a fixed amount, the competent institutions of that State shall consider the standard earnings or the fixed amount to be taken into account by it in respect of periods of insurance or residence completed under the legislations of other Member States as being equal to the standard earnings or fixed amount or, where appropriate, to the average of the standard earnings or the fixed amount corresponding to the periods of insurance completed under the legislation which it administers;

(f) where, under the legislation of a Member State, benefits are calculated for some periods on the basis of the amount of earnings and, for other periods, on the basis of standard earnings or a fixed amount, the competent institution of that State shall, in respect of periods of insurance or residence completed under the legislations of other Member States, take into account the earnings or fixed amounts determined in accordance with the provisions referred to in (d) or (e) or, as appropriate, the average of these earnings or fixed amounts, where benefits are calculated on the basis of standard earnings or a fixed amount for all the periods completed under the legislation which it administers, the competent institution shall consider the earnings to be taken into account in respect of the periods of insurance or residence completed under the legislations of other Member States as being equal to the national earnings corresponding to the standard earnings or fixed amounts;

(g) where, under the legislation of a Member State, benefits are calculated on the basis of average contributions, the competent institution shall determine that average by reference only to those periods of insurance completed under the legislation of the said State.

2. The provisions of the legislation of a Member State concerning the revalorization of the factors taken into account for the calculation of benefits shall apply, as appropriate, to the factors to be taken into account by the competent institution of that state, in accordance with paragraph 1, in respect of the periods of insurance or residence completed under the legislation of other Member States.

3. If, under the legislation of a Member State, the amount of benefits is determined taking into account the existence of members of the family other than children, the competent institution of that State shall also take into consideration those members of the family of the person concerned who are residing in the territory of another Member State as if they were residing in the territory of the competent State.

4. If the legislation which the competent institution of a Member State administers requires a salary to be taken into account for the calculation of benefits, where the first and second subparagraphs of Article 45(6) have been applied, and if, in this Member State, only periods of full unemployment with benefit in accordance with Article 71(1)(a)(ii) or the first sentence of Article 71(1)(b)(ii) are taken into consideration for the payment of pensions, the competent institution of that Member State shall pay the pension on the basis of the salary it used as the reference for providing that unemployment benefit in accordance with the legislation which it administers.

RELEVANT PROVISIONS OF THE IMPLEMENTING REGULATION

Arts 36, 37, and 38 of reg.5764/72/EEC.

Article 48

Periods of insurance or of residence of less than one year

1. Notwithstanding Article 46(2), the institution of a Member State shall not be required to award benefits in respect of periods completed under the legislation it administers which are taken into account when the risk materializes, if:

— the duration of the said periods does not amount to one year,

and

— taking only these periods into consideration, no right to benefit is acquired by virtue of the provisions of that legislation.

2. The competent institution of each of the Member States concerned shall take into account the periods referred to in paragraph 1, for the purposes of applying Article 46(2) excepting subparagraph (b).

3. If the effect of applying paragraph 1 would be to relieve all the institutions of the Member States concerned of their obligations, benefits shall be awarded exclusively under the legislation of the last of those States whose conditions are satisfied, as if all the periods of insurance and residence

3.235

completed and taken into account in accordance with Article 45(1) to (4) had been completed under the legislation of that State.

RELEVANT PROVISIONS OF THE IMPLEMENTING REGULATION

Arts 36 and 37 of reg.5764/72/EEC.

RELEVANT DECISIONS OF THE ADMINISTRATIVE COMMISSION

Decision No 79 of 22 February, 1973 concerning the interpretation of art.48(2) of Regulation (EEC) No 1408/71 relating to the aggregation of insurance periods and periods treated as such for the purposes of invalidity, old age and death, [1973] OJ C75/9.

GENERAL NOTE

3.236   In Case C-331/06 *Chuck*, Judgment of April 3, 2008, the Luxembourg Court decided that art.48(2) required the competent institution of the last Member State in which a worker who is a national of a Member State resided to take into account, in calculating the old-age pension of that worker, who, when he submitted his pension claim, was resident in a non-Member State, of the periods worked in another Member State under the same conditions as if that worker still resided in the European Community.

Article 49

Calculation of benefits where the person concerned does not simultaneously satisfy the conditions laid down by all the legislations under which periods of insurance or of residence have been completed or when he has expressly requested a postponement of the award of old-age benefits

3.237   **1.** If, at a given time, the person concerned does not satisfy the conditions laid down for the provisions of benefits by all the legislations of the Member States to which he has been subject, taking into account where appropriate Article 45 and/or Article 40(3), but satisfies the conditions or one or more of them only, the following provisions shall apply:

(a)   each of the competent institutions administering a legislation whose conditions are satisfied shall calculate the amount of the benefit due, in accordance with Article 46;

(b)   however:

(i)   if the person concerned satisfies the conditions of at least two legislations without having recourse to periods of insurance or residence completed under the legislations whose conditions are not satisfied, these periods shall not be taken into account for the purposes of Article 46(2) unless taking account of the said periods makes it possible to determine a higher amount of benefit;

(ii)   if the person concerned satisfies the conditions of one legislation only without having recourse to periods of insurance or residence completed under the legislations whose conditions are not satisfied, the amount of the benefit due shall, in accordance with Article 46(1)(a)(i), be calculated only in accordance with the provisions of the legislation whose conditions are satisfied,

Article 49

taking account of the periods completed under that legislation only, unless taking account of the periods completed under the legislations whose conditions are not satisfied makes it possible, in accordance with Article 46(1)(a)(ii), to determine a higher amount of benefit.

The provisions of this paragraph shall apply mutatis mutandis where the person concerned has expressly requested the postponement of the award of old-age benefits, in accordance with the second sentence of Article 44(2).

2. The benefit or benefits awarded under one or more of the legislations in question, in the case referred to in paragraph 1, shall be recalculated automatically in accordance with Article 46, as and when the conditions required by one or more of the other legislations to which the person concerned has been subject are satisfied, taking into account, where appropriate, Article 45 and taking into account once again, where appropriate, paragraph 1. This paragraph shall apply mutatis mutandis where a person requests the award of old-age benefits acquired under the legislation of one or more Member States which had until than been postponed in accordance with the second sentence of Article 44(2).

3. A recalculation shall automatically be made in accordance with paragraph 1, without prejudice to Article 40(2), where the conditions required by one or more of the legislations concerned are no longer satisfied.

RELEVANT PROVISIONS OF THE IMPLEMENTING REGULATION

Arts 36 and 37 of reg.5764/72/EEC.

RELEVANT DECISIONS OF THE ADMINISTRATIVE COMMISSION

Decision No 96 of 15 March, 1974 concerning the revision of rights to benefit pursuant to art.49(2) of Council Regulation (EEC) No 1408/71.

Article 50

Award of a supplement where the total of benefits payable under the legislations of the various Member States does not amount to the minimum laid down by the legislation of the State in whose territory the recipient resides

A recipient of benefits to whom this Chapter applies may not, in the State in whose territory he resides and under whose legislation a benefit is payable to him, be awarded a benefit which is less than the minimum benefit fixed by that legislation for a period of insurance or residence equal to all the periods of insurance or residence equal to all the periods of insurance taken into account for the payment in accordance with the preceding Articles. The competent institution of that State shall, if necessary, pay him throughout the period of his residence in its territory a supplement equal to the difference between the total of the benefits payable under this Chapter and the amount of the minimum benefit.

3.238

RELEVANT PROVISIONS OF THE IMPLEMENTING REGULATION

Arts 36 and 37 of reg.5764/72/EEC.

Decision No 105 of 19 December, 1975 on the implementation of Article 50 of Regulation (EEC) No 1408/71, [1976] OJ C117/3.

Article 51

Revalorization and recalculation of benefits

3.239   **1.** If, by reason of an increase in the cost of living or changes in the level of wages or salaries or other reasons for adjustment, the benefits of the States concerned are altered by a fixed percentage or amount, such percentage or amount must be applied directly to the benefits determined under Article 46, without the need for a recalculation in accordance with that Article.

2. On the other hand, if the method of determining benefits or the rules for calculating benefits should be altered, a recalculation shall be carried out in accordance with Article 46.

RELEVANT PROVISIONS OF THE IMPLEMENTING REGULATION

Arts 36 and 37 of reg.5764/72/EEC.

[Article 51a

Persons covered by a special scheme for civil servants

3.240   **1.** The provisions of Article 44, 45(1), (5) and (6) and Articles 46 to 51 shall apply by analogy to persons covered by a special scheme for civil servants.

2. However, if the legislation of a Member State makes the acquisition, liquidation, retention or recovery of the rights to benefits under a special scheme for civil servants subject to the condition that all periods of insurance have been completed under one or more special schemes for civil servants in that Member State, or are regarded by the legislation of that Member State as equivalent to such periods, account shall be taken only of the periods which can be recognised under the legislation in that Member State.

If, account having been taken of the periods thus completed, the person concerned does not satisfy the conditions for the receipt of these benefits, these periods shall be taken into account for the granting of the benefits under the general scheme or, failing that, the scheme applicable to manual or clerical workers, as the case may be.

3. Where, under the legislation of a Member State, benefits are calculated on the basis of the last salary or salaries received during a reference period, the competent institution of that State shall take into account for the purposes of the calculation only those salaries, duly revalued, received during the period or periods for which the person concerned was subject to that legislation.

AMENDMENT

1. Regulation 1606/98/EC, [1998] OJ L209/1 (October 25, 1998).

CHAPTER 4

ACCIDENTS AT WORK AND OCCUPATIONAL DISEASES

RELEVANT PROVISIONS OF THE IMPLEMENTING REGULATION

Provisions relating to administrative checks and medical examinations can be found at Art.76, and on payment of pensions at Art.77, Reg.574/72/EEC.   **3.241**

GENERAL NOTE

Chapter 4 of Title III contains provisions covering accidents at work and occupational diseases. Though these provisions are detailed and substantial, they appear to give rise to fewer difficulties than certain other types of benefit. This may, in part, be because the EEA countries do not make entitlement to benefits for accidents at work and occupational diseases conditional upon the completion of particular periods of insurance. So, the provisions of Chapter 4 do not need to deal with rules of aggregation.   **3.242**

It will be recalled that under Title II the competent State is normally the State in which the claimant is working. Articles 52 to 56 provide modifications to that rule. Article 52, reflecting the approach adopted in relation to sickness benefits, provides that persons habitually resident in a country other than that in which they work are to receive benefits in the State in which they reside. The distinction familiar from the sickness benefit rules between benefits in kind and cash benefits is repeated. Benefits in kind are provided on behalf of the competent State in accordance with the legislation of the country of residence as if the beneficiary were insured there. They are re-imbursed by the competent State. Cash benefits are, however, provided by the competent institution in accordance with the legislation of the competent State.

Frontier workers, presumably by reason of their likely proximity to the country in which they work, may also obtain benefits in the territory of the competent State: Art.53. Article 54 provides for generous treatment of those who are temporarily residing in the competent State or who transfer their permanent residence to the competent State. Article 55 contains provisions which apply to those who sustain an accident at work or contract an occupational disease:

- who are staying in the territory of an EEA country other than the competent State; or

- who have become entitled to benefits chargeable to the competent institution and are authorised to return to the country of their residence or to transfer their residence to another EEA country; or

- who are authorised by the competent institution to go to another EEA country for treatment appropriate to their condition.

These groups are entitled to benefits in kind in accordance with the legislation of the country of stay or residence, and cash benefits in accordance with the legislation of the competent State. There are limitations on the refusal of authority to move in Article 55(2). Finally, Article 56 provides that an accident while travelling which occurs in the territory of a State other than the competent State is deemed to have occurred in the territory of the competent State.

It is in the nature of some occupational diseases that they develop as a result of prolonged exposure to a particular environment. Article 57 deals with situations where the claimant has been exposed to the same risk in several EEA countries. In such cases, the starting point is that benefits are to be awarded exclusively under the legislation of the last of those countries whose conditions of entitlement are satisfied. So, if a claimant does not meet the conditions of entitlement in the last country, that country is required to forward to application to the next country in line to see whether the conditions of entitlement are met there. Paragraphs (2) to (5) add glosses to this rule. Any condition that the disease was first diagnosed on the territory of that country are to be read as a condition that the disease first arose in any EEA country: Case 28/85 *Deghillage* [1986] E.C.R. 991.

Similarly time limits are liberated from any territorial constraints; activities pursued in other EEA countries are to be treated as activities pursued in the country of claim. Article 57(5) contains a special rule where the occupational disease is sclerogenic pneumoconiosis, under which the costs of the benefits are to be shared between the countries where the claimant pursued an activity likely to have caused the disease.

Article 58 deals with the calculation of cash benefits. If the national scheme meets the cost of taking the injured or sick persons to hospital or to their home, Article 59(1) contains provisions for authorising the cost of taking persons sustaining an accident at work or suffering an occupational disease to hospital or to the place of residence in their country of residence. The provision presumably refers to a move either home or to a hospital near home after initial treatment; otherwise the provision produces the odd result that initial hospitalisation which is likely to be required in an emergency would require prior authorisation. No authorisation is needed if the person is a frontier worker. Article 59(2) contains corresponding provisions for the transport of a body of a person killed in an accident at work to 'the place of burial' in the country of residence. Presumably this provision would also apply where the method of disposal of the body was cremation, though the article refers only to burial.

Where there is a subsequent aggravation of the injury or disease, little difficult arises if the person has not been engaged in an occupation likely to cause aggravation of the disease in another country. The first country continues to have jurisdiction over the matter: Art.60(1)(a). But where there has been some engagement in an occupation likely to cause an aggravation in another country, the first country continues to be liable for the benefits under its own legislation for the disease ignoring the aggravation, while the second country is required to pay a supplement which is the difference between the amount it would have awarded if the disease had first occurred under its own legislation and the amount of benefit to which there is entitlement under its own legislation having regard to the aggravation: Art.60(1)(b). The two awards from different countries do not overlap: Art.60(1)(c).

Section 3 of Chapter 4 contains a number of detailed rules which accommodate a variety of special features which exist in the legislation of some EEA countries. The provisions are detailed and specific.

SECTION 1

RIGHT TO BENEFITS

Article 52

Residence in a Member State other than the competent State—General rules

3.243   An employed or self-employed person who sustains an accident at work or contracts an occupational disease, and who is residing in the territory of a Member State other than the competent State, shall receive in the State in which he is residing:

(a) benefits in kind, provided on behalf of the competent institution by the institutions of his place of residence in accordance with the provisions of the legislation which it administers as if he were insured with it;

(b) cash benefits provided by the competent institution in accordance with the provisions of the legislation which it administers. However, by agreement between the competent institution and the institution of the place of residence, these benefits may be provided by the latter institution on behalf of the former in accordance with the legislation of the competent State.

RELEVANT PROVISIONS OF THE IMPLEMENTING REGULATION

Arts 60–61, and 65–66, reg.574/72/EEC.

Article 53

Frontier workers—Special rule

A frontier worker may also obtain benefits in the territory of the competent State. Such benefits shall be provided by the competent institution in accordance with the provisions of the legislation of that State, as if the person concerned were residing there.

3.244

RELEVANT PROVISIONS OF THE IMPLEMENTING REGULATION

Arts 60–61, and 65–66, reg.574/72/EEC.

Article 54

Stay in or transfer of residence to the competent State

1. An employed or self-employed person covered by Article 52 who is staying in the territory of the competent State shall receive benefits in accordance with the provisions of the legislation of that State, even if he has already received benefits before his stay. This provision shall not, however, apply to frontier workers.

3.245

2. An employed or self-employed person covered by Article 52 who transfers his place of residence to the territory of the competent State shall receive benefits in accordance with the provisions of the legislation of that State, even if he has already received benefits before transferring his residence.

RELEVANT PROVISIONS OF THE IMPLEMENTING REGULATION

Arts 65–66, reg.574/72/EEC.

Article 55

Stay outside the competent State—Return to or transfer of residence to another Member State after sustaining an accident or contracting an occupational disease—Need to go to another Member State in order to receive appropriate treatment

3.246   **1.** An employed or self-employed person who sustains an accident at work or contracts an occupational disease and:

(a) who is staying in the territory of a Member State other than the competent State;

or

(b) who, after having become entitled to benefits chargeable to the competent institution, is authorized by that institution to return to the territory of the Member State where he is resident, or to transfer his place of residence to the territory of another Member State;

or

(c) who is authorized by the competent institution to go to the territory of another Member State in order to receive there the treatment appropriate to his condition;

shall be entitled:

(i) to benefits in kind provided on behalf of the competent institution by the institution of the place of stay or residence in accordance with the provisions of the legislation administered by that institution as though he were insured with it, the period during which benefits are provided shall, however, be governed by the legislation of the competent State;

(ii) to cash benefits provided by the competent institution in accordance with the legislation which it administers. However, by agreement between the competent institution and the institution of the place of say or residence, those benefits may be provided by the latter institution on behalf of the former institution, in accordance with the legislation of the competent State.

2. The authorization required under paragraph 1(b) may be refused only if it is established that movement of the person concerned would be prejudicial to his state of health or to the medical treatment being given.

The authorization required under paragraph 1(c) may not be refused where the treatment in question cannot be given to the person concerned in the territory of the Member State in which he resides.

RELEVANT PROVISIONS OF THE IMPLEMENTING REGULATION

Arts 62–66, reg.574/72/EEC.

Article 56

Accidents while travelling

3.247   An accident while travelling which occurs in the territory of a Member State other than the competent State shall be deemed to have occurred in the territory of the competent State.

Article 56

RELEVANT PROVISIONS OF THE IMPLEMENTING REGULATION

Arts 65–66, reg.574/72/EEC.

Article 57

Benefits for an occupational disease where the person concerned has been exposed to the same risk in several Member States

1. When a person who has contracted an occupational disease has, under the legislation of two or more Member States, pursued an activity which by its nature is likely to cause that disease, the benefits that he or his survivors may claim shall be awarded exclusively under the legislation of the last of those States whose conditions are satisfied, taking into account, where appropriate, paragraphs 2 to 5.

3.248

2. If, under the legislation of a Member State, the granting of benefits in respect of an occupational disease is subject to the condition that the disease in question was first diagnosed within its territory, such condition shall be deemed to be satisfied if the disease was first diagnosed in the territory of another Member State.

3. If, under the legislation of a Member State, the granting of benefits in respect of an occupational disease is subject to the condition that the disease in question was diagnosed within a specific time limit following cessation of the last activity which was likely to cause such a disease, the competent institution of that State, when checking the time at which such activity was pursued, shall take into account, to the extent necessary, similar activities pursued under the legislation of any other Member State, as if they had been pursued under the legislation of the first State.

4. If, under the legislation of a Member State, the granting of benefits in respect of an occupational disease is subject to the condition that an activity likely to cause the disease in question was pursued for a certain length of time, the competent institution of the State shall take into account, to the extent necessary, periods during which such activity was pursued under the legislation of any other Member State, as if it had been pursued under the legislation of the first State.

5. In cases of sclerogenic pneumoconiosis, the cost of cash benefits, including pensions, shall be divided among the competent institutions of the Member States in whose territory the person concerned pursued an activity likely to cause the disease. This division shall be carried out on the basis of the ratio which the length of the periods of old-age insurance or residence referred to in Article 45(1) completed under the legislation of each of the States bears to the total length of the periods of old-age insurance or residence completed under the legislation of all the States at the dates on which the benefits commenced.

6. The Council shall determine unanimously, on a proposal from the Commission, the occupational diseases to which the provisions of paragraph 5 shall be extended.

RELEVANT PROVISIONS OF THE IMPLEMENTING REGULATION

Arts 67–69, and 75, reg.574/72/EEC.

Decision No 85 of 22 February, 1973 concerning the interpretation of art.57(1) of Regulation (EEC) No 1408/71 and art.67(3) of Regulation (EEC) No 574/72 relating to the determination of the applicable legislation and the institution competent for the award of benefits in respect of occupation diseases, [1973] OJ C75/17.

Article 58

Calculation of cash benefits

3.249   **1.** The competent institution of a Member State whose legislation provides that the calculation of cash benefits shall be based on average earnings shall determine such average earnings exclusively by reference to earnings confirmed as having been paid during the periods completed under the said legislation.

2. The competent institution of a Member State whose legislation provides that the calculation of cash benefits shall be based on standard earnings shall take account exclusively of the standard earnings, or where appropriate, of the average of standard earnings for the periods completed under the said legislation.

3. The competent institution of a Member State whose legislation provides that the amount of cash benefits shall vary with the number of members in the family shall take into account also the members of the family of the person concerned who are residing in the territory of another Member State, as if they were residing in the territory of the competent State.

RELEVANT PROVISIONS OF THE IMPLEMENTING REGULATION

Art.70, reg.574/72/EEC.

GENERAL NOTE

3.250   In Case C-205/05 *Nemec,* [2006] ECR I-10745, the Court of Justice ruled:

"Article 58(1) of Regulation (EEC) No 1408/71 . . . interpreted in accordance with the objective set out in Article 42 EC, requires that, in a situation such as that in the main proceedings, calculation of the 'average wage or salary', within the meaning of the first of those two provisions, takes into account the pay that the person concerned could reasonably have earned, given his subsequent employment record, had he continued to work in the Member State in which the competent institution is situated."

Article 59

Costs of transporting a person who has sustained an accident at work or is suffering from an occupational disease

3.251   **1.** The competent institution of a Member State whose legislation provides for meeting the costs of transporting a person who has sustained an accident at work or is suffering from an occupational disease, either to his place of residence or to a hospital, shall meet such costs to the corresponding place in the territory of another Member State where the person resides, provided that that institution gives prior authorization for such transport, duly taking into account the reasons justifying it. Such authorization shall not be required in the case of a frontier worker.

2. The competent institution of a Member State whose legislation provides for the costs of transporting the body of a person killed in an accident at work to the place of burial shall, in accordance with the provisions of the legislation which it administers, meet such costs to the corresponding place in the territory of another Member State, where the person was residing at the time of the accident.

SECTION 2

AGGRAVATION OF AN OCCUPATIONAL DISEASE FOR WHICH THE BENEFIT
HAS BEEN AWARDED

Article 60

1. In the event of aggravation of an occupational disease for which an   3.252
employed or self-employed person has received or is receiving benefit under the legislation of a Member State, the following rules shall apply:

(a) if the person concerned has not, while in receipt of benefits, been engaged in an occupation under the legislation of another Member State likely to cause or aggravate the disease in question, the competent institution of the first Member State shall be bound to meet the cost of the benefits under the provisions of the legislation which it administers taking into account the aggravation;

(b) if the person concerned, while in receipt of benefits, has pursued such an activity under the legislation of another Member State, the competent institution of the first Member State shall be bound to meet the cost of the benefits under the legislation which it administers without taking the aggravation into account. The competent institution of the second Member State shall grant a supplement to the person concerned, the amount of which shall be equal to the difference between the amount of benefits due after the aggravation and the amount which would have been due prior to the aggravation under the legislation which it administers if the disease in question had occurred under the legislation of that Member State;

(c) if, in the case covered by subparagraph (b), an employed or self-employed person suffering from sclerogenic pneumoconiosis or from a disease determined under Article 57(6) is not entitled to benefits under the legislation of the second Member State, the competent institution of the first Member State shall be bound to provide benefits under the legislation which it administers, taking the aggravation into account. The competent institution of the second Member State shall, however, meet the cost of the difference between the amount of cash benefits, including pensions, due from the competent institution of the first Member State, taking the aggravation into account, and the amount of the corresponding benefits which were due prior to the aggravation;

(d) the provisions for reduction, suspension or withdrawal laid down by the legislation of a Member State shall not apply to persons receiving benefits awarded by institutions of two Member States in accordance with subparagraph (b).

2. In the event of aggravation of an occupational disease giving rise to the application of the provisions of Article 57(5), the following provisions shall apply:

(a) the competent institution which granted the benefits in accordance with the provisions of Article 57(1) shall be bound to provide benefits under the legislation which it administers taking the aggravation into account;

(b) the cost of cash benefits, including pensions, shall continue to be divided between the institutions which shared the costs of former benefits in accordance with the provisions of Article 57(5). Where, however, the person has again pursued an activity likely to cause or to aggravate the occupational disease in question, either under the legislation of one of the Member States in which he had already pursued an activity of the same nature or under the legislation of another Member State, the competent institution of such State shall meet the cost of the difference between the amount of benefits due, taking account of the aggravation, and the amount of benefits due prior to the aggravation.

RELEVANT PROVISIONS OF THE IMPLEMENTING REGULATION

Art.71, reg.574/72/EEC.

SECTION 3

MISCELLANEOUS PROVISIONS

Article 61

Rules for taking into account the special features of certain legislations

3.253   **1.** If there is no insurance against accidents at work or occupational diseases in the territory of the Member State in which the person concerned happens to be, or if such insurance exists but there is no institution responsible for providing benefits in kind, those benefits shall be provided by the institution of the place of stay or residence responsible for providing benefit in kind in the event of sickness.

2. Where the legislation of the competent State makes wholly cost-free benefits in kind conditional upon use of the medical service organized by the employer, benefits in kind provided in the cases referred to in Articles 52 and 55(1) shall be deemed to have been provided by such a medical service.

3. Where the legislation of the competent State includes a scheme relating to the obligations of the employer, benefits in kind provided in the case referred to in Articles 52 and 55(1) shall be deemed to have been provided at the request of the competent institution.

4. Where the nature of the scheme of the competent State relating to compensation for accidents at work is not that of compulsory insurance, the provision of benefits in kind shall be made directly by the employer or by the insurer involved.

5. Where the legislation of a Member State provides expressly or by implication that accidents at work or occupational diseases which have occurred or have been confirmed previously shall be taken into consideration in order to assess the degree of incapacity, to establish a right to any benefit, or to determine the amount of benefit, the competent institution of that Member State shall also take into consideration accidents at work or occupational diseases which have occurred or have been confirmed previously under the legislation of another Member State as if they had occurred or had been confirmed under the legislation which it administers.

6. Where the legislation of a Member State provides expressly or by implication that accidents at work or occupational diseases which have occurred or have been confirmed subsequently shall be taken into consideration in order to assess the degree of incapacity, to establish the right to any benefit, or to determine the amount of such benefit, the competent institution of that Member State shall also take into consideration accidents at work or occupational diseases which have occurred or have been confirmed subsequently under the legislation of another Member State, as if they had occurred or had been confirmed under the legislation which it administers, but only where:

(a) no compensation is due in respect of the accident at work or the occupational disease which had occurred or had been confirmed previously under the legislation which it administers; and

(b) no compensation is due by virtue of the legislation of the other Member State under which the accident at work or the occupational disease occurred or was confirmed subsequently, account having been taken of the provisions of paragraph 5, in respect of that accident at work or that occupational disease.

RELEVANT PROVISIONS OF THE IMPLEMENTING REGULATION

Arts 72–3, reg.574/72/EEC.

Article 62

Scheme applicable where there are several schemes in the country of stay or residence—Maximum duration of benefits

1. If the legislation of the country of stay or residence has several insurance schemes, the provisions applicable to employed or self-employed

3.254

persons covered by Article 52 or 55(1) shall be those of the scheme for manual workers in the steel industry. However, if that legislation includes a special scheme for workers in mines and similar undertakings, the provisions of that scheme shall apply to that category of workers where the institution of the place of stay or residence to which they submit their claim is competent to administer that scheme.

2. If the legislation of a Member State fixes a maximum period during which benefits may be granted, the institution which administers that legislation may take into account any period during which the benefits have already been provided by the institution of another Member State.

RELEVANT PROVISIONS OF THE IMPLEMENTING REGULATION

Art.74, reg.574/72/EEC.

SECTION 4

REIMBURSEMENTS BETWEEN INSTITUTIONS

Article 63

3.255   **1.** The competent institution shall be obliged to reimburse the amount of benefits in kind provided on its behalf in accordance with the provisions of Articles 52 and 55(1).

2. The reimbursements referred to in paragraph 1 shall be determined and made in accordance with the procedures laid down by the implementing Regulation referred to in Article 98, on proof of actual expenditure.

3. Two or more Member States, or the competent authorities of such States, may provide for other methods of reimbursement or waive reimbursement between the institutions coming under their jurisdiction.

[¹ SECTION 5

STUDENTS

Article 63a

3.256   The provisions of Sections 1 to 4 shall apply by analogy to students.]

AMENDMENT

1. Regulation 307/99/EC, [1999] OJ L38/1 (May 1, 1999).

Article 63a

CHAPTER 5

DEATH GRANTS

Article 64

Aggregation of periods of insurance or residence

The competent institution of a Member State whose legislation makes   3.257
the acquisition, retention or recovery of the right to death grants subject to
the completion of periods of insurance or residence shall take account, to
the extent necessary, of periods of insurance or residence completed under
the legislation of any other Member State as though they had been completed under the legislation which it administers.

RELEVANT PROVISIONS OF THE IMPLEMENTING REGULATION

Arts 15, and 78–9, reg.574/72/EEC.

Article 65

Right to grants where death occurs in, or where the person entitled resides in, a Member State other than the competent State

1. When an employed or self-employed person, a pensioner or a pension   3.258
claimant, or a member of his family, dies in the territory of a Member State
other than the competent State, the death shall be deemed to have occurred
in the territory of the competent State.
2. The competent institution shall be obliged to award death grants
payable under the legislation which it administers, even if the person entitled
resides in the territory of a Member State other than the competent State.
3. The provisions of paragraphs 1 and 2 shall also apply when the death
is the result of an accident at work or an occupational disease.

RELEVANT PROVISIONS OF THE IMPLEMENTING REGULATION

Arts 78–79, reg.574/72/EEC.

Article 66

Provision of benefits in the event of the death of a pensioner who had resided in a Member State other than the one whose institution was responsible for providing benefits in kind

In the event of the death of a pensioner who was entitled to a pension   3.259
under the legislation of one Member State, or to pensions under the legislations of two or more Member States, when such pensioner was residing in
the territory of a Member State other than the one whose institution was
responsible for providing him with benefits in kind under the provisions of
Article 28, the death grants payable under the legislation administered by

that institution shall be provided by that institution at its own expense as though the pensioner had been residing in the territory of the Member State of that institution at the time of his death.

The provisions of the preceding paragraph shall apply by analogy to the members of the family of a pensioner.

[¹*Article 66a*

Students

3.260 The provisions of Articles 64 to 66 shall apply by analogy to students and to the members of their family.]

AMENDMENT

1. Regulation 307/99/EC, [1999] OJ L38/1 (May 1, 1999).

CHAPTER 6

UNEMPLOYMENT BENEFITS

SECTION 1

COMMON PROVISIONS

Article 67

Aggregation of periods of insurance or employment

3.261 1. The competent institution of a Member State whose legislation makes the acquisition, retention or recovery of the right to benefits subject to the completion of periods of insurance shall take into account, to the extent necessary, periods of insurance or employment completed as an employed person under the legislation of any other Member State, as though they were periods of insurance completed under the legislation which it administers, provided, however, that the periods of employment would have been counted as periods of insurance had they been completed under that legislation.

2. The competent institution of a Member State whose legislation makes the acquisition, retention or recovery of the right to benefits subject to the completion of periods of employment shall take into account, to the extent necessary, periods of insurance or employment completed as an employed person under the legislation of any other Member State, as though they were periods of employment completed under the legislation which it administers.

3. Except in the cases referred to in Article 71(1)(a)(ii) and (b)(ii), application of the provisions of paragraphs 1 and 2 shall be subject to the condition that the person concerned should have completed lastly:

— in the case of paragraph 1, periods of insurance,

— in the case of paragraph 2, periods of employment,

in accordance with the provisions of the legislation under which the benefits are claimed.

4. Where the length of the period during which benefits may be granted depends on the length of periods of insurance or employment, the provisions of paragraph 1 or 2 shall apply, as appropriate.

RELEVANT PROVISIONS OF THE IMPLEMENTING REGULATION

Arts 15, and 80, reg.574/72/EEC.

GENERAL NOTE

The provisions of reg.1408/71 dealing specifically with unemployment benefit demonstrate an overly cautious view by the Member States of the motives of unemployed persons moving between the Member States. Provision is made in Art.67 for periods of employment or insurance to be aggregated in order to determine entitlement to unemployment benefits. But there is a sting in the tail of the provision. Aggregation is only possible under the legislation of the country in which the person claiming "lastly" completed periods of insurance or employment. The result is, for example, that a British national living and working in Germany who becomes unemployed cannot return to the United Kingdom and claim jobseeker's allowance on the basis of contributions to the German scheme, because he or she will not have lastly completed a period of insurance in the United Kingdom unless he or she came within the scope of art.71: see below. This territorial limitation on aggregation seems unnecessarily restrictive, and has been the subject of criticism: See, for example, Wikeley, N., *"Migrant Workers and Unemployment Benefit in the European Community"* [1988] J.S.W.L. 300.

3.262

The severity of the rule is illustrated in Case C-62/91 *Gray* v *Adjudication Officer* [1992] E.C.R. I-2737. Gray, a British national, had lived and worked in Spain running a restaurant from 1971 to 1990. He returned to the United Kingdom after selling the business without having registered as unemployed in Spain. He claimed unemployment benefit in the United Kingdom, and appealed the refusal to award him the benefit to the Bognor Regis social security appeal tribunal. It was argued by the adjudication officer that there was no entitlement in the United Kingdom because the claimant was last insured in Spain. Furthermore since he had not registered as unemployed in Spain, no question could arise as to any entitlement under Art.69. The tribunal also concluded that the claimant had been habitually resident in Spain and so could not take the benefit of the rules in art.71. The lay members of the tribunal (the lawyer chairman of the tribunal considered that the provisions were consistent with the Treaty rules) clearly saw an injustice and felt that certain provisions of arts 67 and 69 militated against the Treaty rules on free movement of persons. They clearly insisted (as they were entitled to) that a reference be made concerning the validity of the provisions in question. The Court, however, concluded that there was no factor of such a kind as to affect the validity of the provisions in issue. Both conferred on workers rights which they would not otherwise enjoy.

Article 68

Calculation of benefits

1. The competent institution of a Member State whose legislation provides that the calculation of benefits should be based on the amount of

3.263

the previous wage or salary shall take into account exclusively the wage or salary received by the person concerned in respect of his last employment in the territory of that State.

However, if the person concerned had been in his last employment in that territory for less than four weeks, the benefits shall be calculated on the basis of the normal wage or salary corresponding, in the place where the unemployed person is residing or staying, to an equivalent or similar employment to his last employment in the territory of another Member State.

2. The competent institution of a Member State whose legislation provides that the amount of benefits varies with the number of members of the family, shall take into account also members of the family of the person concerned who are residing in the territory of another Member State, as though they were residing in the territory of the competent State. This provision shall not apply if, in the country of residence of the members of the family, another person is entitled to unemployment benefits for the calculation of which the members of the family are taken into consideration.

RELEVANT PROVISIONS OF THE IMPLEMENTING REGULATION

Arts 81–82, reg.574/72/EEC.

RELEVANT DECISIONS OF THE ADMINISTRATIVE COMMISSION

Decision No 83 of 22 February 1973 concerning the interpretation of art.68(2) of reg.1408/71 and of art.82 of reg.574/72 relating to increases in unemployment benefit for dependent members of the family, [1973] OJ C75/14.

GENERAL NOTE

3.264   Article 68(1) provides that where unemployment benefit is linked to a previous wage or salary, the salary or wages to be taken into account are those in respect of the last employment in that State: Case 67/79 *Fellinger* [1980] E.C.R. 535. However, where the amount of benefit varies with the number of members of the family, members of the family residing in another EEA country are to be treated as residing in the competent State.

SECTION 2

UNEMPLOYED PERSONS GOING TO A MEMBER STATE OTHER THAN THE COMPETENT STATE

Article 69

Conditions and limits for the retention of the right to benefits

3.265   **1.** An employed or self-employed person who is wholly unemployed and who satisfies the conditions of the legislation of a Member State for entitlement to benefits and who goes to one or more other Member States in order to seek employment there shall retain his entitlement to such benefits under the following conditions and within the following limits:

(a) Before his departure, he must have been registered as a person seeking work and have remained available to the employment services of the competent State for at least four weeks after becoming unemployed, However, the competent services or institutions may authorize his departure before such time has expired.

(b) He must register as a person seeking work with the employment services of each of the Member States to which he goes and be subject to the control procedure organized therein. This condition shall be considered satisfied for the period before registration if the person concerned registered within seven days of the date when he ceased to be available to the employment services of the State he left. In exceptional cases, this period may be extended by the competent services or institutions.

(c) Entitlement to benefits shall continue for a maximum period of three months from the date when the person concerned ceased to be available to the employment services of the State which he left, provided that the total duration of the benefits does not exceed the duration of the period of benefits he was entitled to under the legislation of that State. In the case of a seasonal worker such duration shall, moreover, be limited to the period remaining until the end of the season for which he was engaged.

2. If the person concerned returns to the competent State before the expiry of the period during which he is entitled to benefits under the provisions of paragraph 1(c), he shall continue to be entitled to benefits under the legislation of that State; he shall lose all entitlement to benefits under the legislation of the competent State if he does not return there before the expiry of that period. In exceptional cases, this time limit may be extended by the competent services or institutions.

3. The provisions of paragraph 1 may be invoked only once between two periods of employment.

4. [¹ . . .]

AMENDMENT

1. Regulation 647/2005/EC, [2005] OJ L117/1 (May 5, 2005).

RELEVANT PROVISIONS OF THE IMPLEMENTING REGULATION

Art.83, reg.574/72/EEC.

RELEVANT DECISIONS OF THE ADMINISTRATIVE COMMISSION

Recommendation No 21 of 28 November 1996 concerning the application of art.69(1)(a) of reg.1408/71 to unemployed persons accompanying their spouses employed in a Member State other than the competent State, [1997] OJ C67/3.

GENERAL NOTE

Article 69 provides a limited right to export unemployment benefit for up to three months where the person goes to another EEA country for the purpose of seeking work. Strict conditions surround the right to export the benefit, and failure to return to the competent State within the three-month period normally results in the loss of all entitlement to benefits under the legislation of the competent State. The right

3.266

to export unemployment benefit can only be exercised once in any period of unemployment. Under art.70 benefits are paid by the unemployment benefit institution in the place to which the person goes but are to be reimbursed by the competent State. Because of the limitation on aggregation, the rules in art.71 take on extra significance and have been the subject of many references to the Court of Justice. They provide exceptions to the rule that the competent State is that in which the claimant lastly worked, and permit claims in the EEA country in which persons are habitually resident where that country is different from that in which they worked. There are separate rules for frontier workers and others.

In Joined Cases 41, 121 & 796/79 *Testa, Maggio and Vitale* [1980] E.C.R. 1979, the validity of art.69(2) of Reg.1408/71 was questioned in circumstances where each of three Italian nationals lost the residual entitlement to unemployment benefit in Germany when they did not return within three months to Germany from an authorised stay in Italy in order to look for work there. In two of the cases, the later return was explained by an intervening illness. The Court had little difficulty in concluding that there was nothing to impugn the validity of the provisions of art.69(2) which provided that all entitlement to unemployment benefit would cease if the beneficiary did not return to the competent State before the expiry of the authorised period of absence. There was, according to the Court, a clear advantage to the person in that they were, during their period of absence abroad, exempt from the controls applicable in the competent State (even though they would be subject to the controls in the country to which they went). The only glimmer of hope related to the Court's advice on how the discretion to extend the period in exceptional cases should be applied: see also Case 139/78 *Coccioli* [1979] E.C.R. 991. First, retrospective applications for extensions of the period are admissible. Secondly, the competent institution in exercising its discretion must take account of the principle of proportionality in Community law. In each case, the institution must consider the extent to which the three-month period has been exceeded, the reasons for the delay in returning, and the seriousness of the legal consequences arising from the delay. This would, presumably, include consideration of the residual amount of benefit which might be forfeit if all entitlement were to cease.

The Commission's Proposal for a Council Regulation amending, for the benefit of unemployed workers, reg.1408/71 on the application of social security schemes to employed persons and their families moving within the Community, 18 June 1980, [1980] O.J. C169/22, contained amendments which would not deprive workers of entitlement to any residual period of entitlement in the territory of the Member State they left. The proposals have not been implemented.

Art. 69(1)(a)

3.267   In C-215/00 *Rydergård* [2002] E.C.R. I–1817, the Court ruled that the period of four weeks referred to in Art.69(1)(a) need not be completed without a break. Short breaks—for example, where the claimant moved to a child caring benefit because her child was ill for just a few days—would not cause the four week qualifying period to start to run all over again.

Article 70

Provision of benefits and reimbursements

3.268   1. In the cases referred to in Article 69 (1), benefits shall be provided by the institution of each of the States to which an unemployed person goes to seek employment.

The competent institution of the Member State to whose legislation an employed or self-employed person was subject at the time of his last employment shall he obliged to reimburse the amount of such benefits.

2. The reimbursements referred to in paragraph 1 shall be determined and made in accordance with the procedure laid down by the implementing Regulation referred to in Article 98, on proof of actual expenditure, or by lump sum payments.

3. Two or more Member States, or the competent authorities of those States, may provide for other methods of reimbursement or payment, or may waive all reimbursement between the institutions coming under their jurisdiction.

SECTION 3

UNEMPLOYED PERSONS WHO, DURING THEIR LAST EMPLOYMENT, WERE RESIDING IN A MEMBER STATE OTHER THAN THE COMPETENT STATE

Article 71

1. An unemployed person who was formerly employed and who, during   3.269
his last employment, was residing in the territory of a Member State other than the competent State shall receive benefits in accordance with the following provisions:

(a)(i) A frontier worker who is partially or intermittently unemployed in the undertaking which employs him, shall receive benefits in accordance with the provisions of the legislation of the competent State as if he were residing in the territory of that State; these benefits shall be provided by the competent institution.

  (ii) A frontier worker who is wholly unemployed shall receive benefits in accordance with the provisions of the legislation of the Member State in whose territory he resides as though he had been subject to that legislation while last employed; these benefits shall be provided by the institution of the place of residence at its own expense.

(b)(i) An employed person, other than a frontier worker, who is partially, intermittently or wholly unemployed and who remains available to his employer or to the employment services in the territory of the competent State shall receive benefits in accordance with the provisions of the legislation of that State as though he were residing in its territory; these benefits shall be provided by the competent institution.

  (ii) An employed person, other than a frontier worker, who is wholly unemployed and who makes himself available for work to the employment services in the territory of the Member State in which he resides, or who returns to that territory, shall receive benefits in accordance with the legislation of that State as if he had last been employed there; the institution of the place of residence shall provide such benefits at its own expense. However, if such an employed person has become entitled to benefits at the expense of the competent institution of the Member State to whose legislation he was last subject, he shall receive benefits under the provisions of Article

69. Receipt of benefits under the legislation of the State in which he resides shall be suspended for any period during which the unemployed person may, under the provisions of Article 69, make a claim for benefits under the legislation to which he was last subject.

2. An unemployed person may not claim benefits under the legislation of the Member State in whose territory he resides while he is entitled to benefits under the provisions of paragraph 1(a)(i) or (b)(i).

RELEVANT PROVISIONS OF THE IMPLEMENTING REGULATION

Art.84, reg.574/72/EEC.

RELEVANT DECISIONS OF THE ADMINISTRATIVE COMMISSION

Decision No 160 of 28 November 1995 concerning the scope of art.71(1)(b)(ii) of Council regulation (EEC) No 1408/71 relating to the right to unemployment benefits of workers, other than frontier workers, who, during their last employment, were residing in the territory of a Member State other than the competent State, [1996] OJ L49/31.

GENERAL NOTE

3.270 Some of the rigours of the limited aggregation and exportability rules is moderated by the provisions of art.71, which concern situations in which the claimant was residing, during their last period of work, in a country other than the competent State. Since the provisions of art.71 are exceptions to the rules in arts 67 and 69, the Court of Justice has said that they must be strictly interpreted: Case 76/76 *di Paolo* [1977] E.C.R. 315, paras 12 and 13 of the judgment.

The rules in art.71(1)(a) concern *frontier workers*, who are defined by art.1(b) as persons who work in one Member State and reside in a different Member State to which they return "as a rule daily or at least once a week." Note that there is specific provision made in art.1(b) for posted frontier workers enabling them to retain the status of frontier worker for four months even where the posting prevents them from returning home at least once a week.

Under art.71(1)(a)(i), frontier workers who are "partially or intermittently unemployed" receive unemployment benefits in accordance with the legislation of the competent State as though they were residing there. Under art.71(1)(a)(ii), frontier workers who are "wholly unemployed" receive unemployment benefits in accordance with the legislation of the country in which they reside as though they had been subject to that legislation while working.

Article 71(1)(b) deals with *workers other than frontier workers*, and is rather more complex, since it permits a wholly unemployed worker to choose whether unemployment benefits are paid in the country of last employment or in the country of residence. Article 71(1)(b)(i) provides that workers who are "partially, intermittently or wholly unemployed" and who remain available for work in the territory of the competent State receive unemployment benefits in accordance with the provisions of the legislation of the competent State as though they resided there. Article 71(1)(b)(ii) provides that wholly unemployed workers may make themselves available to the employment office in the country of residence and receive unemployment benefits there as though they had been last employed there.

The references to residence in art.71 refer to the concept of "habitual residence" which has a specific meaning in Community law. Workers, other than frontier workers, will only be able to take advantage of the more favourable rules on entitlement to unemployment benefit if they can show that they were habitually resident in a country other than that in which they worked. For a decision of a Social Security Commissioner holding that a determination by the Inland Revenue that a person is "ordinarily resident" in the United Kingdom for tax purposes "has no relevant whatsoever" in assessing whether a person is habitually resident here, see

R(U)4/86. It may be putting it too strongly to say that it has no relevance whatsoever, but it is clearly not determinative of the question. It is not difficult to imagine
the complexity of the circumstances presented in many cases, where, for example,
the employment is of comparatively short duration, or where a family is split with
certain family members remaining in one country while others live with the worker
in the place of work. For a useful survey of the case-law on art.71(1)(b)(ii), see the
Advocate General's Opinion in Case 388/87 *Warmerdam-Steggerda* [1989] E.C.R.
1203. Article 71(2) contains anti-overlapping provisions precluding the payment of
unemployment benefits in the country of residence alongside payment of benefits
under the legislation of the country of last employment.

The Court in *di Paolo* had indicated that the special rules in art.71 were justified
for certain categories of workers who retain close ties, in particular of a personal
and vocational nature, with the country where they have settled and are habitually
resident. There is in such cases the best possibility of finding new employment in
that country. It is consistent with this principle to permit a person to change their
habitual residence from the country of work to another country during the course
of their employment.

In Case 236/87 *Bergemann* [1988] E.C.R. 5125 Anna Bergemann, a Dutch
national living and working in the Netherlands, married and during a period of leave
moved to Germany with her husband. She remained on leave from her employment until it ended and did not return to the Netherlands. The question arose as
to whether art.71(1)(b)(ii) applied to someone in her situation. Having regard to
the justification set out above, the Court concluded that her move during a period
of leave and the fact that she had not returned to work in the Netherlands did not
preclude her being regarded as within the terms of the article.

Similarly, the Court had little difficulty in regarding a university employee
who had undertaken a fixed term two year exchange with a university in another
Member State and who returned home in the vacations as falling within the ambit
of the provision: Case C-216/89 *Reibold* [1990] E.C.R. I-4163.

In such cases account should be taken of the duration and continuity of the
residence of the persons concerned before they moved, of the length and purpose
of their absence, of the nature of the work in the other EEA country, and of their
intentions as ascertained from all the surrounding circumstances.

The circumstances presented in Case C-102/91 *Knoch* [1991] E.C.R. I-4341,
were a little more complex. Doris Knoch was employed at the University of Bath as
a language assistant for two years. At the end of her contract she claimed and was
awarded unemployment benefit in England for the best part of July and August.
She subsequently returned to Germany where she claimed unemployment benefit in
December. The question arose as to whether she could claim in Germany after having
claimed in England, and, if so, how the German authorities should deal with any
unemployment benefit paid in England. The Court ruled that, provided that Knoch
was habitually resident in Germany during her employment in England, she was
entitled to the benefit of the rules in art.71. There was nothing in those rules which
precluded a person first claiming under the legislation of the country where they were
employed and subsequently in the country in which they were habitually resident.
However, the benefits received would almost certainly overlap under the provisions
of art.12 of reg.1408/71. It followed that in determining entitlement under the legislation of the country of residence, a deduction should be made of the benefit received in
respect of the days for which unemployment benefit had been paid in the country of
employment. Entitlement to unemployment benefit would, of course, be suspended
for any period in which such a person exported their unemployment benefit entitlement in accordance with the rules in art.69. Case C-287/92 *Toosey* [1994] E.C.R.
I-279, reported as *R(S) 7/94*, concerned a British national who had last worked in
the United Kingdom in 1964–65. She then moved to Belgium where she worked
until 1982, when she became disabled. She subsequently moved back to the United
Kingdom. She claimed severe disablement allowance, but was refused on the basis
that she had not been resident in Great Britain for ten of the twenty years preceding

her claim. The Court of Justice ruled that the determining factor as to whether Art.71 applied at all is the residence of the person concerned in a Member State other than that to whose legislation she was subject during her last employment. This meant that the first sentence of Art.71(1)(b)(ii) did not apply to a worker in the position of the claimant who was resident in the State of employment, that is, Belgium, when the incapacity for work followed by invalidity occurred.

[¹ SECTION 4

PERSONS COVERED BY A SPECIAL SCHEME FOR CIVIL SERVANTS

Article 71a

3.271   **1.** The provisions of Sections 1 and 2 shall apply to persons covered by a special unemployment scheme for civil servants.

2. The provisions of Section 3 shall not apply to persons covered by a special unemployment scheme for civil servants. An unemployed person who is covered by a special scheme for civil servants, who is partially or wholly unemployed, and who, during his last employment, was residing in the territory of a Member State other than the competent State, shall receive benefits in accordance with the provisions of the legislation of the competent State as if he were residing in the territory of that State; these benefits shall be provided by the competent institution at its expense.]

AMENDMENT

1. Regulation 1606/98/EC, [1998] OJ L209/1 (October 25, 1998).

CHAPTER 7

FAMILY BENEFITS

GENERAL NOTE

3.272   Where entitlement to benefits is conditional on the completion of periods of insurance, employment or self-employment, there is the usual requirement that such periods completed in the territory of an EEA country other than the competent State are to be treated as completed under the legislation of the competent State: art.72. The normal rule is that entitlement to family benefits is determined in accordance with the law of the EEA country in which the claimant is employed or self-employed. Where the children reside in a different country, they are treated as residing in the EEA country where the claimant is in work: art.73. Those who are wholly unemployed and come within the provisions of art.71(1)(a)(ii) or 71(1)(b)(ii) are, however, entitled to benefits under the legislation of the country of their residence for the family members residing with them: art.72a. Other unemployed persons are entitled to family benefits from the country responsible for their unemployment benefits: art.74. There are a number of special situations which may need to be considered. Where entitlement arises under arts 73 or 74, this is made subject to the provisions of the substantial Annex VI which sets out special procedures for applying the legislation of certain countries. Provision is made in art.75 for payment to an institution or person actually maintaining the members of the family rather than to the claimant "if the family benefits are not used by the person to whom they should be provided for the maintenance of the members of the family."

The above rules are easy to understand. Complications, however, arise where entitlement to family benefits arises in more than one country. In the United Kingdom child benefit is normally payable to the mother (provided that she is responsible for the maintenance of the children, which is presumed where the children are living with her), but this is not universally the case. Equally family benefits may be payable on the basis of residence rather than the completion of insurance periods. Finally, both parents may be working in different countries and have an entitlement by reason of their occupation. This situation can be illustrated by the facts of Case C-119/91 *McMenamin* [1992] E.C.R. I-6393. The family lived in Ireland, where the father worked. The mother was a frontier worker crossing into Northern Ireland each working day to teach there. The family claimed and received child benefits in Ireland. The mother claimed child benefits in Northern Ireland on the basis of her employment there. Since the effect of the provisions of ch.7 of Title II was that her children were treated as residing in Northern Ireland, she met the conditions of entitlement to child benefits in Northern Ireland. Much of the case-law of the Court of Justice has been concerned with the application of provisions for dealing with the overlap of such benefits in such cases as this. The provisions of reg.1408/71 have been modified in this regard on many occasions.

The current position is governed by art.76 of reg.1408/71 and art.10 and 10a of reg.574/72. Article 76 deals with overlapping benefits where family benefits are provided by the country of residence in addition to the legislation of some other country. Where the benefits in the country of residence of the family members are provided:

- during the same period, and
- for the same family members, and
- by reason of the claimant carrying on an occupation,

benefits payable under the legislation of another country are suspended "up to the amount provided for in the legislation of the country of residence of the family members." In this way, the family gets the higher of the family benefits in the two countries, but the payment of those benefits may be apportioned between them. Article 76(2) effectively requires a claim to be made in the country where the family members resides, since the other country may suspend the benefits up to the amount provided in the legislation of the country of residence even if a claim for benefit there is not made. But it is clear that the provision will only apply where entitlement to the benefit exists: Case 134/77 *Ragazzoni* [1978] E.C.R. 963.

Article 10(1)(a) of reg.574/72 makes corresponding provision where entitlement is not subject to conditions of insurance, employment or self-employment. Again the effect is either that the higher of two benefits is alone payable, or that the lower benefits are topped up in the other country by the difference between that amount and the higher amount which it pays. The possible permutations are considerable, but the overall effect of ch.7 of Title II is to produce a result which means that the family effectively gets the benefit of the most favourable regime among those countries to whose legislation it is subject.

Note also Case C-352/06 *Bosmann*, May 20, 2008, discussed in the commentary to art.13 above, which suggests that family benefits may be paid *wholly under national law* as an exception to the single State rule, where national conditions are met, and where the law of the Member State applicable under reg.1408/71 does not provide for the payment of such benefits.

Article 72

Aggregation of periods of insurance, employment or self-employment

3.273   Where the legislation of a Member State makes acquisition of the right to benefits conditional upon completion of periods of insurance, employment or self-employment, the competent institution of that State shall take into account for this purpose, to the extent necessary, periods of insurance, employment or self-employment completed in any other Member State, as if they were periods completed under the legislation which it administers.

RELEVANT PROVISIONS OF THE IMPLEMENTING REGULATION

Art.85, reg.574/72/EEC.

Article 72a

Employed persons who have become fully unemployed

3.274   An employed person who has become fully unemployed and to whom Article 71(1)(a)(ii) or (b)(ii), first sentence, apply shall, for the members of his family residing in the territory of the same Member State as he, receive family benefits in accordance with the legislation of the State, as if he had been subject to that legislation during his last employment, taking account, where appropriate, of the provisions of Article 72. These benefits shall be provided by, and at the expense of, the institution of the place of residence.

Where that institution applies legislation providing for deduction of contributions payable by unemployed persons to cover family benefits, it shall be authorized to make such deductions in accordance with the provisions of its legislation.

Article 73

Employed or self-employed persons the members of whose families reside in a Member State other than the competent State

3.275   An employed or self-employed person subject to the legislation of a Member State shall be entitled, in respect of the members of his family who are residing in another Member State, to the family benefits provided for by the legislation of the former State, as if they were residing in that State, subject to the provisions of Annex VI.

RELEVANT PROVISIONS OF THE IMPLEMENTING REGULATION

Art.86, reg.574/72/EEC.

RELEVANT DECISIONS OF THE ADMINISTRATIVE COMMISSION

Decision No 142 of 13 February 1990 concerning the application of arts 73, 74 and 75 of reg.1408/71, [1990] OJ C80/7.

Decision No 145 of 27 June 1990 concerning the payment of arrears of family benefits due to self-employed persons pursuant to arts 73 and 74 of reg.1408/71, [1991] OJ C235/1.

GENERAL NOTE

In *CF/667/1997* the Commissioner at paras 19–25 examines the question which needs to be considered in determining the entitlement of parents, resident in France, to child benefit under United Kingdom law under art.73 of the Regulation.

In *R(F) 1/94* the Commissioner had ruled that art.73 applies only to employed or self-employed persons whose families reside in a Member State other than the competent State. Where a person ceases to be employed or self-employed, the Article does not apply.

The Judge in *JR v HMRC*, [2009] UKUT 18 (AAC), has not followed *R(F) 1/94* on the grounds that he considers that it was wrong on a proper understanding of the authorities at the time, but also because it has been overtaken to some extent by later case law of the Luxembourg Court. The circumstances before the Upper Tribunal Judge were of a Portuguese family who had been living and working in the United Kingdom save for two of the daughters who had remained in Portugal with the mother of the claimant's wife. The claimant's capacity for work ended and he was awarded a disability living allowance and income support qualifying for national insurance credits on grounds of incapacity for work. The question arose as to whether child benefit was payable in respect of the two daughters in Portugal at that time. It seems that child benefit had only been paid in respect of the child residing with her parents in Great Britain. Section 146(1) provides that no child benefit is payable in respect of a child "unless he is in Great Britain in that week". In contrast, art.73 deems the children residing outside the competent State to be residing within the competent State.

The Judge had invited the parties to consider whether the term "employed or self-employed person" in art.73 should be read in accordance with the definition in art.1(a) of the Regulation. This was conceded by the parties, but counsel for the HMRC argued that when the definition was read in conjunction with the United Kingdom entry in Annex I, the meaning was restricted to those currently in employment or self-employment. Following a careful analysis of the definitions in art.1(a), the Judge concludes that the appellant fell within the definition in art.1(a)(ii): he had been compulsorily insured and continued to be insured for many braches of social security within the material scope of the Regulation. Furthermore, he was clearly within the scope of art.2(1). Support for this approach was found in Case C-85/96) *Martínez Sala*, [1998] ECR I-2691, and Case C-292/96) *Sürül*, [1999] ECR I-2685.

The Judge then turned to the interpretation of art.73, finding no difficulty in regarding the two daughters residing in Portugal as members of the appellant's family. He was also satisfied on the evidence that it could be argued that they were members of the appellant's family for whom he was responsible (as required by national legislation: s.143 of the Contributions and Benefits Act). The Judge could find no basis for considering the term "employed or self-employed person" having a meaning other than that attributed through art.1(a) or art.2(1). The effect of art.73 was that the provisions in s.146 of the Contributions and Benefits Act must be disapplied where the provisions of art.73 were met.

Article 74

Unemployed persons the members of whose families reside in a Member State other than the competent State

An unemployed person who was formerly employed or self-employed and who draws unemployment benefits under the legislation of a Member

3.276

3.277

State shall be entitled, in respect of the members of his family residing in another Member State, to the family benefits provided for by the legislation of the former State, as if they were residing in that State, subject to the provisions of Annex VI.

RELEVANT PROVISIONS OF THE IMPLEMENTING REGULATION

Art.88, reg.574/72/EEC.

RELEVANT DECISIONS OF THE ADMINISTRATIVE COMMISSION

Decision No 142 of 13 February 1990 concerning the application of arts 73, 74 and 75 of reg.1408/71, [1990] OJ C80/7.

Decision No 145 of 27 June 1990 concerning the payment of arrears of family benefits due to self-employed persons pursuant to arts 73 and 74 of reg.1408/71, [1991] OJ C235/1.

Article 75

Provisions of benefits

3.278   **1.** Family benefits shall be provided, in the cases referred to in Article 73, by the competent institution of the State to the legislation of which the employed or self-employed person is subject and, in the cases referred to in Article 74, by the competent institution of the State under the legislation of which an unemployed person who was formerly employed or self-employed receives unemployment benefits. They shall be provided in accordance with the provisions administered by such institutions, whether or not the natural or legal person to whom such benefits are payable is residing or staying in the territory of the competent State or in that of another Member State.

2. However, if the family benefits are not used by the person to whom they should be provided for the maintenance of the members of the family, the competent institution shall discharge its legal obligations by providing the said benefits to the natural or legal person actually maintaining the members of the family, at the request of, and through the agency of, the institution of their place of residence or of the designated institution or body appointed for this purpose by the competent authority of the country of their residence.

3. Two or more Member States may agree, in accordance with the provisions of Article 8, that the competent institution shall provide the family benefits due under the legislation of those States or of one of those States to the natural or legal person actually maintaining the members of the family, either directly or through the agency of the institution of their place of residence.

RELEVANT PROVISIONS OF THE IMPLEMENTING REGULATION

Art.86, reg.574/72/EEC.

RELEVANT DECISIONS OF THE ADMINISTRATIVE COMMISSION

Decision No 142 of 13 February 1990 concerning the application of arts 73, 74 and 75 of reg.1408/71, [1990] OJ C80/7.

Article 76

Rules or priority in cases of overlapping entitlement to family benefits under the legislation of the competent State and under the legislation of the Member State of residence of the members of the family

1. Where, during the same period, for the same family member and by reason of carrying on an occupation, family benefits are provided for by the legislation of the Member State in whose territory the members of the family are residing, entitlement to the family benefits due in accordance with the legislation of another Member State, if appropriate under Article 73 or 74, shall be suspended up to the amount provided for in the legislation of the first Member State.

2. If an application for benefits is not made in the Member States in whose territory the members of the family are residing, the competent institution of the other Member State may apply the provisions of paragraph 1 as if benefits were granted in the first Member State.

RELEVANT DECISIONS OF THE ADMINISTRATIVE COMMISSION

Decision No 119 of 24 February 1983 concerning the interpretation of Article 76 and Article 79(3) of regulation (EEC) No 1408/71 and of Article 10(1) of Regulation (EEC) No 574/72 relating to the overlapping of family benefits and allowances, [1983] OJ C295/3.

Decision No 147 of 10 October 1990 concerning the application of Article 76 of regulation (EEC) No 1408/71, [1991] OJ C235/21.

[¹ *Article 76a*

Students

The provisions of Article 72 shall apply by analogy to students.]

AMENDMENT

1. Regulation 307/99/EC, [1999] OJ L38/1 (May 1, 1999).

CHAPTER 8

BENEFITS FOR DEPENDENT CHILDREN OF PENSIONERS AND FOR ORPHANS

Article 77

Dependent children of pensioners

1. The term "benefits", for the purposes of this Article, shall mean family allowances for persons receiving pensions for old age, invalidity or an accident at work or occupational disease, and increases or supplements to such pensions in respect of the children of such pensioners, with the exception of supplements granted under insurance schemes for accidents at work and occupational diseases.

3.279

3.280

3.281

2. Benefits shall be granted in accordance with the following rules, irrespective of the Member State in whose territory the pensioner or the children are residing:

    (a) to a pensioner who draws a pension under the legislation of one Member State only, in accordance with the legislation of the Member State responsible for the pension;

    (b) to a pensioner who draws pensions under the legislation of more than one Member State:

        (i) in accordance with the legislation of whichever of these States he resides in provided that, taking into account, where appropriate, the provisions of Article 79(1)(a), a right to one of the benefits referred to in paragraph 1 is acquired under the legislation of that State;

        or

       (ii) in other cases in accordance with the legislation of the Member State to which he has been subject for the longest period of time, provided that, taking into account, where appropriate, the provisions of Article 79(1)(a), a right to one of the benefits referred to in paragraph 1 is acquired under such legislation; if no right to benefit is acquired under that legislation, the conditions for the acquisition of such right under the legislations of the other Member States concerned shall be examined in decreasing order of the length of periods of insurance or residence completed under the legislation of those Member States.

RELEVANT PROVISIONS OF THE IMPLEMENTING REGULATION

Arts 90–92, reg.574/72/EEC.

RELEVANT DECISIONS OF THE ADMINISTRATIVE COMMISSION

Decision No 150 of 26 June 1992 concerning the application of arts 77, 78 and 79(3) of Regulation (EEC) No 1408/71 and of art.10 of regulation (EEC) No 574/72, [1993] OJ C229/5.

GENERAL NOTE

3.282   In *R(F) 1/94* the Commissioner ruled that the pension which the pensioners must be in receipt of has to be a pension awarded on the grounds of old age, invalidity, industrial accident or occupational disease. It did not cover a Fire Brigade Medical Discharge pension. In *R(F) 1/98* the Commissioner concluded that war or service pensions are also generally outside the scope of pensions which bring art.77 into play. The claimant was in receipt of a service pension and an invalidity pension, but the latter was not payable because it was wholly offset by the higher service pension that was in payment. The Commissioner added the following important rider to the proposition that war or service pensions are generally outside art.77:

"22. In my judgment therefore, a person 'draws a pension for invalidity' for the purposes of Art.77 so long as he has a present entitlement to it and in fact receives payment equal to or exceeding the amount of that entitlement, **either** by means of the general arrangements for payment of such benefit under the national social security scheme, **or** by receiving payment out of public funds under some other scheme which the terms of the social security scheme integrate with itself *pro tanto* by making the other payment in effect satisfy the social security entitlement. Whether this is viewed in strict analysis as the person 'drawing' the social security pension by another means or as the scheme that actually pays him being brought within the scope *ratione materiae of* the EEC Regulation to the limited extent to which it thus becomes integrated with the national social security scheme, does not seem to me greatly to matter."

Article 78

Orphans

[¹ 1. The term "benefits", for the purposes of this Article, means family allowances and, where appropriate, supplementary or special allowances for orphans.]   3.283

2. Orphans' benefits shall be granted in accordance with the following rules, irrespective of the Member State in whose territory the orphan or the natural or legal person actually maintaining him is resident:

(a) for the orphan of a deceased employed or self-employed person who was subject to the legislation of one Member State only in accordance with the legislation of that State;

(b) for the orphan of a deceased employed or self-employed person who was subject to the legislation of several Member States:

   (i) in accordance with the legislation of the Member State in whose territory the orphan resides provided that, taking into account, where appropriate, the provisions of Article 79(1)(a), a right to one of the benefits referred to in paragraph 1 is acquired under the legislation of that State;

   (ii) in other cases in accordance with the legislation of the Member State to which the deceased had been subject for the longest period of time, provided that, taking into account, where appropriate, the provisions of Article 79(1)(a), the right to one of the benefits referred to in paragraph 1 is acquired under the legislation of that State; if no right is acquired under that legislation, the conditions for the acquisition of such right under the legislations of the other Member States shall be examined in decreasing order of the length of periods of insurance or residence completed under the legislation of those Member States.

However, the legislation of the Member State applicable in respect of provisions of the benefits referred to in Article 77 for a pensioner's children shall remain applicable after the death of the said pensioner in respect of the provisions of the benefits to his orphans.

AMENDMENT

1. Regulation 1399/99/EC, [1999] OJ L164/1 (September 1, 1999).

RELEVANT PROVISIONS OF THE IMPLEMENTING REGULATION

Arts 90–92, reg.574/72/EEC.

RELEVANT DECISIONS OF THE ADMINISTRATIVE COMMISSION

Decision No 150 of 26 June 1992 concerning the application of arts 77, 78 and 79(3) of Regulation (EEC) No 1408/71 and of art.10 of regulation (EEC) No 574/72, [1993] OJ C229/5.

[¹ Article 78a

3.284   Orphans' pensions, except those granted under insurance schemes for accidents at work and occupational diseases, shall be treated as 'benefits' within the scope of Article 78(1) if the deceased was at any time covered by a scheme which provides only family allowances or supplementary or special allowances for orphans. These schemes are listed in Annex VIII.]

AMENDMENT

1. Regulation 1399/99/EC, [1999] OJ L164/1 (September 1, 1999).

Article 79

Provisions common to benefits for dependent children of pensioners and for orphans

3.285   **1.** Benefits, within the meaning of [¹ Articles 77, 78 and 78a], shall be provided in accordance with the legislation determined by applying the provisions of those Articles by the institution responsible for administering such legislation and at its expense as if the pensioner or the deceased had been subject only to the legislation of the competent State.

However:

(a) if that legislation provides that the acquisition, retention or recovery of the right to benefits shall be dependent on the length of periods of insurance, employment, self-employment or residence such length shall be determined taking into account, where appropriate, the provisions of Article 45 or, as the case may be, Article 72;

(b) if that legislation provides that the amount of benefits shall be calculated on the basis of the amount of the pension, or shall depend on the length of periods of insurance the amount of these benefits shall be calculated on the basis of the theoretical amount determined in accordance with the provisions of Article 46(2).

2. In a case where the effect of applying the rule laid down in Articles 77(2)(b)(ii) and 78(2)(b)(ii) would be to make several Member States competent, the length of the periods being equal, benefits within the meaning of Article [¹ 77, 78 or 78a], as the case may be, shall be granted in accordance with the legislation of the Member States to which the pensioner or the deceased was last subject.

3. The right to benefits due only under the national legislation or under the provisions of paragraph 2 and under [1 Articles 77, 78 and 78a] shall be suspended if the children become entitled to family benefits or family allowances under the legislation of a Member State by virtue of the pursuit of a professional or trade activity. In such a case, the persons concerned shall be considered as members of the family of an employed or self-employed person.

AMENDMENT

1. Regulation 1399/99/EC, [1999] OJ L164/1 (September 1, 1999).

RELEVANT PROVISIONS OF THE IMPLEMENTING REGULATION

Arts 90–92, reg.574/72/EEC.

RELEVANT DECISIONS OF THE ADMINISTRATIVE COMMISSION

Decision No 119 of 24 February 1983 concerning the interpretation of art.76 and art.79(3) of regulation (EEC) No 1408/71 and of art.10(1) of Regulation (EEC) No 574/72 relating to the overlapping of family benefits and allowances, [1983] OJ C295/3.

Decision No 150 of 26 June 1992 concerning the application of arts 77, 78 and 79(3) of Regulation (EEC) No 1408/71 and of art.10 of regulation (EEC) No 574/72, [1993] OJ C229/5.

[¹ *Article 79a*

Provisions relating to benefits for orphans entitled to benefits under a special scheme for civil servants

1. Notwithstanding the provisions of [² Article 78a], orphans' pen-   3.286
sions drawn under a special scheme for civil servants shall be calculated in accordance with the provisions of Chapter 3.

2. Where, in a case provided for in paragraph 1, periods of insurance, employment, self-employment or residence have been completed under a general scheme, then benefits due under that general scheme shall be paid in accordance with the provisions of Chapter 8 [2 unless otherwise provided for in Article 44(3)]. Periods of insurance, self-employment or employment completed in accordance with the legislation of a special scheme for civil servants or periods which are regarded by the legislation of that Member State as equivalent to such periods, shall, where appropriate, be taken into account for the acquisition, retention or recovery of the rights to benefit in accordance with the legislation of the general scheme.]

AMENDMENTS

1. Regulation 1606/98/EC, [1998] OJ L209/1 (October 25, 1998).
2. Regulation 1399/99/EC, [1999] OJ L164/1 (September 1, 1999).

TITLE IV

ADMINISTRATIVE COMMISSION ON SOCIAL SECURITY FOR MIGRANT WORKERS

Article 80

Composition and working methods

1. There shall be attached to the Commission an Administrative   3.287
Commission on Social Security for Migrant Workers (hereinafter called

"the Administrative Commission") made up of a government representative of each of the Member States, assisted, where necessary, by expert advisers. A representative of the Commission shall attend the meetings of the Administrative Commission in an advisory capacity.

2. The Administrative Commission shall be assisted in technical matters by the International Labour Office under the terms of the agreements concluded to that end between the European Community and the International Labour Organization.

3. The rules of the Administrative Commission shall be drawn up by mutual agreement among its members.

Decisions on questions of interpretation referred to in Article 81 (a) shall be unanimous. They shall be given the necessary publicity.

4. Secretarial services shall be provided for the Administrative Commission by the Commission.

Article 81

Tasks of the Administrative Commission

3.288   The Administrative Commission shall have the following duties:

(a) to deal with all administrative questions and questions of interpretation arising from the provisions of this Regulation and subsequent Regulations, or from any agreement or arrangement concluded thereunder, without prejudice to the right of the authorities, institutions and persons concerned to have recourse to the procedures and tribunals provided for by the legislations of Member States, by this Regulation or by the Treaty;

(b) to carry out all translations of documents relating to the implementation of this Regulation at the request of the competent authorities, institutions and tribunals of the Member States, and in particular translations of claims submitted by persons who may be entitled to benefit under the provisions of this Regulation;

(c) to foster and develop cooperation between Member States in social security matters, particularly in respect of health and social measures of common interest;

(d) [1 to foster and develop co-operation between Member States by modernizing procedures for exchange of information, in particular by adapting the information flow between institutions for the purpose of telematic exchange, taking account of the development of data processing in each Member State. The main aim of such modernization shall be to expedite the award of benefits.]

(e) to assemble the factors to be taken into consideration for drawing up accounts relating to the costs to be borne by the institutions of the Member States under the provisions of this Regulation and to adopt the annual accounts between the said institutions;

(f) to undertake any other function coming within its competence under the provisions of this and of subsequent Regulations or any agreement or arrangement made thereunder;

(g) to submit proposals to the Commission for working out subsequent Regulations and for the revision of this and subsequent Regulations.

Article 81

AMENDMENT

1. Regulation 1290/97/EC, [1997] OJ L176/1 (October 4, 1997).

GENERAL NOTE

The Administrative Commission from time to time makes decisions on the   3.289
interpretation and application of provisions of Regulation 1408/71 and Regulation
574/72. These are for guidance, but often provide very helpful guidance; they also
often address concerns which have been expressed by Member States in the meetings of the Administrative Commission. The most important decisions are reported
in the *Official Journal*.

TITLE V

ADVISORY COMMITTEE ON SOCIAL SECURITY FOR MIGRANT WORKERS

Article 82

ESTABLISHMENT, COMPOSITION AND WORKING METHODS

1. An advisory Committee on Social Security for Migrant Workers (here-   3.290
inafter called "the Advisory Committee") is hereby established, with [1
150] members comprising, from each Member State:
  (a) two representatives of the government, of whom one at least must be
       a member of the Administrative Commission;
  (b) two representatives of trade unions;
  (c) two representatives of employers' organizations.
For each of the categories referred to above, an alternate member shall be
appointed for each Member State.
2. Members of the Advisory Committee and their alternates shall be
appointed by the Council which shall endeavour, when selecting representatives of trade unions and employers' organizations, to achieve an equitable
representation on the Committee of the various sectors concerned.
The list of members and their alternates shall be published by the Council
in the *Official Journal of the European Communities*.
3. The term of office for members and alternates shall be two years. Their
appointments may be renewed. On expiry of their term of office, members
and alternates shall remain in office until they are replaced or until their
appointments are renewed.
4. The Advisory Committee shall be chaired by a representative of the
Commission. The chairman shall not vote.
5. The Advisory Committee shall meet at least once each year. It shall be
convened by its chairman, either on his own initiative or on written application to him by at least one-third of the members. Such application must
include concrete proposals concerning the agenda.
6. Acting on a proposal from its chairman, the Advisory Committee
may decide, in exceptional circumstances, to take advice from any persons
or representatives of organizations with extensive experience in social
security matters. Furthermore, the Committee shall receive technical
assistance from the International Labour Office under the same conditions

as the Administrative Commission, under the terms of the agreement concluded between the European Community and the International Labour Organization.

7. The opinions and proposals of the Advisory Committee must state the reasons on which they are based. They shall be delivered by an absolute majority of the votes validly cast.

The Committee shall, by a majority of its members, draw up its rules of procedure which shall be approved by the Council, after receiving the opinion of the Commission.

8. Secretarial services shall be provided for the Advisory Committee by the Commission.

AMENDMENT

1. Regulation 1791/2006/EC, [2006] OJ L363/1 (January 1, 2007).

Article 83

Tasks of the Advisory Committee

3.291   The Advisory Committee shall be empowered, at the request of the Commission of the European Communities, of the Administrative Commission or on its own initiative:

(a) to examine general questions or questions of principle and problems arising from the implementation of the Regulations adopted within the framework of the provisions of Article 51 of the Treaty;

(b) to formulate opinions on the subject for the Administrative Commission and proposals for any revision of the Regulations.

TITLE VI

MISCELLANEOUS PROVISIONS

Article 84

Cooperation between competent authorities

3.292   **1.** The competent authorities of Member States shall communicate to each other all information regarding:

(a) measures taken to implement this Regulation:

(b) changes in their legislation which are likely to affect the implementation of this Regulation.

2. For the purposes of implementing this Regulation, the authorities and institutions of Member States shall lend their good offices and act as though implementing their own legislation. The administrative assistance furnished by the said authorities and institutions shall, as a rule, be free of charge. However, the competent authorities of the Member States may agree to certain expenses being reimbursed.

3. The authorities and institutions of Member States may, for the purpose of implementing this Regulation, communicate directly with one another and with the persons concerned or their representatives.

4. The authorities, institutions and tribunals of one Member State may not reject claims or other documents submitted to them on the grounds that they are written in an official language of another Member State. They shall have recourse where appropriate to the provisions of Article 81(b).

5. (a) Where, under this Regulation or under the implementing Regulation referred to in Article 98, the authorities or institutions of a Member State communicate personal data to the authorities or institutions of another Member State, that communication shall be subject to the legal provisions governing protection of data laid down by the Member State providing the data.

Any subsequent transmission as well as the storage, alteration and destruction of the data shall be subject to the provisions of the legislation on data protection of the receiving Member State.

(b) The use of personal data for purposes other than those of social security shall be subject to the approval of the person concerned or in accordance with the other guarantees provided for by national legislation.

[¹*Article 84a*]

Relations between the institutions and the persons covered by this Regulation

1. The institutions and persons covered by this Regulation shall have a duty of mutual information and cooperation to ensure the correct implementation of this Regulation.

The institutions, in accordance with the principle of good administration, shall respond to all queries within a reasonable period of time and shall in this connection provide the persons concerned with any information required for exercising the rights conferred on them by this Regulation.

The persons concerned shall inform the institution of the competent State and of the State of residence as soon as possible of any changes in their personal or family situation which affect their right to benefits under this Regulation.

2. Failure to respect the obligation of information referred to in paragraph 1, third subparagraph, may result in the application of proportionate measures in accordance with national law. Nevertheless, these measures shall be equivalent to those applicable to similar situations under domestic law and shall not make it impossible or excessively difficult in practice for claimants to exercise the rights conferred on them by this Regulation.

3. In the event of difficulties in the interpretation or application of this Regulation which could jeopardise the rights of a person covered by it, the institution of the competent State or of the State of residence of the person involved shall contact the institution(s) of the Member State(s) concerned. If a solution cannot be found within a reasonable period, the authorities concerned may call on the Administrative Commission to intervene.]

3.293

AMENDMENT

1. Regulation 631/2004/EC, [2004] OJ L100/1 (June 1, 2004).

Article 85

Exemptions from or reductions of taxes—Exemption from authentication

3.294   **1.** Any exemption from or reduction of taxes, stamp duty, notarial or registration fees provided for in the legislation of one Member State in respect of certificates or documents required to be produced for the purposes of the legislation of that State shall be extended to similar documents required to be produced for the purposes of the legislation of another Member State or of this Regulation.

2. All statements, documents and certificates of any kind whatsoever required to be produced for the purposes of this Regulation shall be exempt from authentication by diplomatic or consular authorities.

[¹ **3.** An electronic message sent by an institution in conformity with the provisions of this Regulation and the implementing Regulation may not be rejected by any authority or institution of another Member State on the grounds that it was received by electronic means, once the receiving institution has declared its ability to receive electronic messages. Reproduction and recording of such messages shall be presumed to be a correct and accurate reproduction of the original document or recording of the information it relates to, unless there is proof to the contrary.

An electronic message shall be considered valid if the computer system on which the message is recorded contains the safeguards necessary in order to avoid any alteration, disclosure or access to the recording. It shall at any time be possible to reproduce the information recorded in directly legible form. When an electronic message is transferred from one social security institution to another, appropriate security measures shall be taken in accordance with the relevant Community provisions.]

AMENDMENT

1. Regulation 1290/97/EC, [1997] OJ L176/1 (October 4, 1997).

Article 86

Claims, declarations or appeals submitted to an authority, institution or tribunal of a Member State other than the competent State

3.295   **1.** Any claim, declaration or appeal which should have been submitted, in order to comply with the legislation of one Member State, within a specified period to an authority, institution or tribunal of that State shall be admissible if it is submitted within the same period to a corresponding authority, institution or tribunal of another Member State. In such a case the authority, institution, or tribunal receiving the claim, declaration or appeal shall forward it without delay to the competent authority, institution or tribunal of the former State either directly or through the competent authorities of the Member State concerned. The date on which such claims, declarations or appeals were submitted to the authority, institution or tribunal of the Second State shall be considered as the date of their submission to the competent authority, institution or tribunal.

2. Where a person entitled to do so under the legislation of a Member State has submitted to that State a claim for family benefits even though that State is not competent by priority right, the date on which that first application was made shall be considered as the date on which it was submitted to the competent authority, institution or tribunal, provided that a new application is submitted in the Member State which is competent by priority right by a person entitled to do so under the legislation of that State. The second application must be submitted within a period of one year after notification of the rejection of the first application or the cessation of payment of benefits in the first Member State.

GENERAL NOTE

This Article contains the important provision that a claim made to a State other than the competent State is to be forwarded to the competent State without delay and is to be treated by that State as a claim made in time if it was received within the relevant time limit in the first State.

3.296

Article 87

Medical examinations

1. Medical examinations provided for by the legislation of one Member State may be carried out at the request of the competent institution, in the territory of another Member State, by the institution of the place of stay or residence of the person entitled to benefits, under conditions laid down in the implementing Regulation referred to in Article 98 or, failing these, under conditions agreed upon between the competent authorities of the Member States concerned.

2. Medical examinations carried out under the conditions laid down in paragraph 1 shall be considered as having been carried out in the territory of the competent State.

3.297

Article 88

Transfers from one Member State to another of sums of money payable pursuant to this Regulation

Where appropriate, money transfers effected in accordance with this Regulation shall be made in accordance with the relevant agreements in force between the Member States concerned at the time of transfer. Where no such agreements are in force between two Member States, the competent authorities of the said States or the authorities responsible for international payments shall, by mutual agreement, determine the measures necessary for effecting such transfers.

3.298

Article 89

Special procedures for implementing certain legislations

Special procedures for implementing the legislations of certain Member States are set out in Annex VI.

3.299

GENERAL NOTE

3.300   Note that there are special rules in Annex VI for determining the applicable legislation. So far as the United Kingdom is concerned, these contains multiple provisions including special rules where art.13(2)(f) comes into play.

Article 90

3.301   [. . .]

Article 91

Contributions chargeable to employers or undertakings not established in the competent State

3.302   An employer shall not be bound to pay increased contributions by reason of the fact that his place of business or the registered office or place of business of his undertaking is in the territory of a Member State other than the competent State.

Article 92

Collection of contributions

3.303   **1.** Contributions payable to an institution of one Member State may be collected in the territory of another Member State in accordance with the administrative procedure and with the guarantees and privileges applicable to the collection of contributions payable to the corresponding institution of the latter State.

2. The procedure for the implementation of the provisions of paragraph 1 shall be governed, in so far as is necessary, by the implementing Regulation referred to in Article 98 or by means of agreements between Member States. Such implementing procedures may also cover procedures for enforcing payment.

Article 93

Rights of institutions responsible for benefits against liable third parties

3.304   **1.** If a person receives benefits under the legislation of one Member State in respect of an injury resulting from an occurrence in the territory of another State, any rights of the institution responsible for benefits against a third party bound to compensate for the injury shall be governed by the following rules:

1028

Article 93

(a) Where the institution responsible for benefits is, by virtue of the legislation which it administers, subrogated to the rights which the recipient has against the third party, such subrogation shall be recognized by each Member State.

(b) Where the said institution has direct rights against the third party, such rights shall be recognized by each Member State.

2. If a person receives benefits under the legislation of one Member State in respect of an injury resulting from an occurrence in the territory of another Member State, the provisions of the said legislation which determine in which cases the civil liability of employers or of the persons employed by them is to be excluded shall apply with regard to the said person or to the competent institution.

The provisions of paragraph 1 shall also apply to any rights of the institution responsible for benefit against an employer or the persons employed by him in cases where their liability is not excluded.

3. Where, in accordance with the provisions of Article 36(3) and/or Article 63(3), two or more Member States or the competent authorities of those States have concluded an agreement to waive reimbursement between institutions under their jurisdiction, any rights arising against a liable third party shall be governed by the following rules:

(a) Where the institution of the Member State of stay or residence awards benefits to a person in respect of an injury which was sustained within its territory, that institution, in accordance with the legislation which it administers, shall exercise the right to subrogation or direct action against the third party liable to provide compensation for the injury.

(b) For the purpose of implementing (a):
   (i) the person receiving benefits shall be deemed to be insured with the institution of the place of stay or residence,
       and
   (ii) that institution shall be deemed to be the debtor institution.

(c) The provisions of paragraphs 1 and 2 shall remain applicable in respect of any benefits not covered by the waiver agreement referred to in this paragraph.

TITLE VII

TRANSITIONAL AND FINAL PROVISIONS

Article 94

Transitional provisions for employed persons

1. No right shall be acquired under this Regulation in respect of a period prior to 1 October, 1972 or to the date of its application in the territory of the Member State concerned or in a part of the territory of that State. 3.305

2. All periods of insurance and, where appropriate, all periods of employment or residence completed under the legislation of a Member State before 1 October, 1972 or before the date of its application in the territory of that Member State or in a part of the territory of that State shall be taken into consideration for the determination of rights acquired under the provisions of this Regulation.

3. Subject to the provisions of paragraph 1, a right shall be acquired under this Regulation even though it relates to a contingency which materialized prior to 1 October, 1972 or to the date of its application in the territory of the Member State concerned or in a part of the territory of that State.

4. Any benefit which has not been awarded or which has been suspended by reason of the nationality or place of residence of the person concerned shall, on the application of the person concerned, be awarded or resumed with effect from 1 October, 1972 or the date of its application in the territory of the Member State concerned or in a part of the territory of that State, provided that the rights previously determined have not given rise to a lump sum payment.

5. The rights of a person to whom a pension was awarded prior to 1 October, 1972 or to the date of its application in the territory of the Member State concerned or in a part of the territory of that State may, on the application of the person concerned, be reviewed, taking into account the provisions of this Regulation. This provision shall also apply to the other benefits referred to Article 78.

6. If an application referred to in paragraph 4 or 5 is submitted within two years from 1 October, 1972 or from the date of its application in the territory of the Member State concerned, the rights acquired under this Regulation shall have effect from that date, and the provisions of the legislation of any Member State concerning the forfeiture or limitation of rights may not be invoked against the persons concerned.

The same provisions shall apply as regards the application of this Regulation in those territories which became a part of the Federal Republic of Germany on 3 October, 1990 provided that the application referred to in paragraph 4 or 5 is submitted within two years of 1 June, 1992.

7. If an application referred to in paragraph 4 or 5 is submitted after the expiry of the two-year period after 1 October, 1972 or following the date of its application in the territory of the Member State concerned, rights which have not been forfeited or which are not time barred shall have effect from the date on which the application was submitted, except where more favourable provisions of the legislation of any Member state apply.

The same provisions shall apply as regards the application of this Regulation in those territories which became a part of the Federal Republic of Germany on 3 October, 1990 provided that the application referred to in paragraph 4 or 5 is submitted after two years have elapsed from 1 June, 1992.

8. In case of sclerogenic pneumoconiosis, the provision of Article 57(5) shall apply to cash benefits for an occupational disease the expense of which, in the absence of agreement between the institutions concerned, could not be divided between those institutions before 1 October, 1972.

9. The family allowances received by employed persons employed in France or unemployed workers receiving unemployment benefits under French legislation in respect of the members of their families residing in another Member State on the date of 15 November, 1989 shall continue to be paid at the rates, within the limits and according to the procedures applicable on that date as long as their amount exceeds that of the benefits that would be due as from the date of 16 November, 1989 and as long as the persons concerned are subject to French legislation. Account shall not be taken of interruptions lasting less than one month nor of periods during which unemployment or sickness is drawn.

The procedure for implementing this paragraph and in particular the sharing of the cost of these allowances shall be determined by mutual agreement between the Member States concerned or by their competent authorities after the Administrative Commission has delivered an opinion.

10. The rights of persons to whom a pension was awarded prior to the entry into force of Article 45 (6) may be reviewed at their request subject to the provisions of Article 45 (6).

RELEVANT DECISIONS OF THE ADMINISTRATIVE COMMISSION

Decision No 75 of 22 February 1973 concerning the investigation of applications for review made under art.94(5) of regulation (EEC) No 1408/71 by invalidity pensioners, [1973] OJ C75/5.

Decision No 146 of 10 October 1990 concerning the interpretation of art.94(9) of regulation (EEC) No 1408/71, [1991] OJ C235/9.

Article 95

Transitional provisions for self-employed persons

1. No right shall be acquired under this Regulation in respect of a period prior to 1 July, 1982 or to the date of its implementation in the territory of the Member State concerned or in a part of the territory of that State.

2. All insurance periods and, where appropriate, all periods of employments, of self-employment or of residence completed under the legislation of a Member State before 1 July, 1982 or before the date of implementation of this Regulation in the territory of that Member State or in a part of the territory of that State shall be taken into consideration for the determination of rights acquired under this Regulation.

3. Subject to paragraph 1, a right shall be acquired under this Regulation even though it relates to a contingency which materialized prior to 1 July, 1982 or to the date of implementation of this Regulation in the territory of the Member State concerned or in a part of the territory of that State.

4. Any benefit which has not been awarded or which has been suspended by reason of the nationality or place of residence of the person concerned shall, on the application of the person concerned, be awarded or resumed with effect from 1 July, 1982 or from the date of implementation of this Regulation in the territory of the Member State concerned or in a part of the territory of that State, provided that the rights previously determined have not given rise to a lump-sum payment.

5. The rights of a person to whom a pension was awarded prior to 1 July, 1982 or to the date of implementation of this Regulation in the territory of the Member State concerned or in a part of the territory of that State may, on the application of the person concerned, be reviewed, taking into account this Regulation. This provision shall also apply to the other benefits referred to in Article 78.

3.306

6. If an application referred to in paragraph 4 or 5 is submitted within two years of 1 July, 1982 or of the date of implementation of this Regulation in the territory of the Member State concerned, the rights acquired under this Regulation shall have effect from that date, and the provisions of the legislation of any Member State concerning the forfeiture or limitation of rights may not be invoked against the persons concerned.

The same provisions shall apply as regards the application of this Regulation in those territories which became a part of the Federal Republic of Germany on 4 October, 1990 provided that the application referred to in paragraph 4 or 5 is submitted within two years of 1 June, 1992.

7. If an application referred to in paragraph 4 or 5 is submitted after the expiry of the two-year period from 1 July, 1982 or following the date of implementation of this Regulation in the territory of the Member State concerned, rights which have not been forfeited or are not barred by limitation shall have effect from the date on which the application was submitted, except where more favourable provisions of the legislation of any Member State apply.

The same provisions shall apply as regards the application of this Regulation in those territories which became a part of the Federal Republic of Germany on 3 October, 1990 provided that the application referred to in paragraph 4 or 5 is submitted after two years have elapsed from 1 June, 1992.

Article 95a

Transitional provisions for application of Regulation (EEC) No 1248/92 [1992] OJ L136/7

3.307

1. Under Regulation (EEC) No 1248/92 no right shall be acquired for a period prior to 1 June 1992.

2. All insurance periods or periods of residence completed under the legislation of a Member State before 1 June 1992 shall be taken into consideration for the determination of rights to benefits pursuant to Regulation (EEC) No 1248/92.

3. Subject to paragraph 1, a right shall be acquired under Regulation (EEC) No 1248/92 even though relating to a contingency which materialized prior to 1 June 1992.

4. The rights of a person to whom a pension was awarded prior to 1 June 1992 may, on the application of the person concerned, be reviewed, taking into account the provisions of Regulation (EEC) No 1248/92.

5. If an application referred to in paragraph 4 is submitted within two years from 1 June 1992 the rights acquired under Regulation (EEC) No 1248/92 shall have effect from that date, and the provisions of the legislation of any Member State concerning the forfeiture of limitation of rights may not be invoked against the persons concerned.

6. If the application referred to in paragraph 4 is submitted after the expiry of the two-year period after 1 June 1992, rights which have not been forfeited or not barred by limitation shall have effect from the date on which the application was submitted, except where more favourable provisions of the legislation of any Member State apply.

Article 95b

Transitional provisions for application of Regulation (EEC) No 1247/92 [1992] OJ L136/1

1. Regulation (EEC) No 1247/92 shall not provide any entitlement for periods prior to 1 June 1992.

3.308

2. The periods of residence and periods of employment or of self-employment completed on the territory of a Member State before 1 June 1992 shall be taken into consideration for the determination of rights acquired under the provisions of Regulation (EEC) No 1247/92.

3. Subject to paragraph 1, a right shall be acquired pursuant to Regulation (EEC) No 1247/92 even where it relates to a contingency that occurred before 1 June 1992.

4. All special non-contributory benefits which have not been awarded or which have been suspended by reason of the nationality of the person concerned shall, on the application of the person concerned, be awarded or resumed with effect from 1 June 1992, provided that the rights previously determined have not given rise to a lump-sum payment.

5. The rights of persons to whom a pension was awarded prior to 1 June 1992, may, on the application of the persons concerned, be reviewed, taking account of the provisions of Regulation (EEC) No 1247/92.

6. If an application referred to in paragraph 4 or 5 is submitted within two years from 1 June 1992, the rights acquired pursuant to Regulation (EEC) No 1247/92 shall have effect from that date, and the provisions of the legislation of any Member State concerning the forfeiture or limitation of rights may not be invoked against the persons concerned.

7. If an application referred to in paragraph 4 or 5 is submitted after the expiry of the two-year period after 1 June 1992, rights which have not been forfeited or which are not time-barred shall have effect from the date on which the application was submitted, except where more favourable provisions of the legislation of any Member State apply.

8. The application of Article 1 of Regulation (EEC) No 1247/92 may not result in the withdrawal of benefits which are awarded before 1 June 1992 by the competent institutions of the Member State under Title III of Regulation (EEC) No 1408/71 to which Article 10 of the latter Regulation is applicable.

9. The application of Article 1 of Regulation (EEC) No 1247/92 may not result in the rejection of an application for a special non-contributory benefit awarded as a supplement to a pension, which was submitted by the person concerned who had satisfied the conditions for the award of this benefit before 1 June 1992, even where the person concerned resides on the territory of a Member State other than the competent Member State, provided that the application for the benefit is submitted within a period of five years starting from 1 June 1992.

10. Notwithstanding the provisions of paragraph 1, any special non-contributory benefit, granted as a supplement to a pension, which has not been awarded or which has been suspended by reason of the residence of the person concerned on the territory of a Member State other than the competent Member State shall, on the application of the person concerned, be awarded or resumed with effect from 1 June 1992, in the first case from the date on which the benefit should have been awarded, and in the second case on the date of suspension of the benefit.

11. Where special non-contributory benefits as referred to in Article 4 (2a) of Regulation (EEC) No 1408/71 may, during the same period and for the same person, be granted pursuant to Article 10a of that Regulation by the competent institution of the Member State in the territory of which that person is resident and pursuant to paragraphs 1 to 10 of this Article by the competent institution of another Member State, the person concerned may only aggregate those benefits up to the limit of the highest amount of the special benefit he could claim under one of the legislations in question.

12. The detailed rules of application of paragraph 11, and in particular the application, with regard to the benefits referred to in that paragraph, of the clauses for reduction, suspension or abolition provided for under the legislation of one or more Member States and the allocation of the differential additional amounts shall be set by decision of the Administrative Commission on Social Security for Migrant Workers and, where appropriate, by common accord of the Member States concerned or their competent authorities.

[¹Article 95c

Transitional provisions for application of Regulation (EC) 1606/98 [1998] OJ L209/1

3.309   **1.** No rights shall be acquired under Regulation (EC) No 1606/98 for any period prior to 25 October 1998.

2. Any period of insurance and, where appropriate, any period of employment, self-employment or residence completed under the legislation of a Member State before 25 October 1998 shall be taken into account for the determination of rights acquired in accordance with the provisions of Regulation (EC) No 1606/98.

3. Subject to the provisions of paragraph 1, a right shall be acquired under Regulation (EC) No 1606/98 even if it relates to a contingency arising prior to 25 October 1998.

4. Any benefit that has not been awarded or that has been suspended on account of the nationality or the residence of the person concerned shall, at the latter's request, be awarded or resumed from 25 October 1998, provided that the rights for which benefits were previously awarded did not give rise to a lump-sum payment.

5. The rights of persons who prior to 25 October 1998, obtained the award of a pension may be reviewed at their request, account being taken of the provisions of Regulation (EC) No 1606/98. The provision shall also apply to the other benefits referred to in Articles 78 and 79 insofar as it applies to Articles 78 and 79a.

6. If the request referred to in paragraph 4 or 5 is lodged within two years from 25 October 1998, rights deriving from Regulation (EC) No 1606/98 shall be acquired from that date and the provisions of the legislation of any Member State on the forfeiture or lapse of rights may not be applied to the persons concerned.

7. If the request referred to in paragraph 4 or 5 is lodged after expiry of the period of two years following 25 October 1998, rights not forfeited or lapsed shall be acquired from the date of such request, subject to any more favourable provision of the legislation of any Member State.]

AMENDMENT

1. Regulation 1606/98/EC, [1998] OJ L209/1.

[¹*Article 95d*

Transitional provisions applicable to students

1. No rights shall be acquired under this Regulation by students, members of their families or their survivors for any period prior to 1 May 1999.

2. Any period of insurance and, where appropriate, any period of employment, self-employment or residence completed under the legislation of a Member State before 1 May 1999 shall be taken into account for the determination of rights acquired in accordance with the provisions of this Regulation.

3. Subject to the provisions of paragraph 1, a right shall be acquired under this Regulation even if it relates to a contingency arising prior to 1 May 1999.

4. Any benefit that has not been awarded or that has been suspended on account of the nationality or the residence of the person concerned shall, at the latter's request, be awarded or resumed from 1 May 1999, provided that the rights for which benefits were previously awarded did not give rise to a lump-sum payment.

5. If the request referred to in paragraph 4 is lodged within two years of 1 May 1999, rights deriving from this Regulation in favour of students, members of their families and their survivors shall be acquired from that date and the provisions of the legislation of any Member State on the forfeiture or lapse of rights may not be applied to the persons concerned.

6. If the request referred to in paragraph 4 is lodged after the expiry of the period of two years following 1 May 1999, rights not forfeited or lapsed shall be acquired from the date of such request, subject to any more favourable provisions of the legislation of any Member State.]

3.310

AMENDMENT

1. Regulation 307/99/EC, [1999] OJ L38/1 (May 1, 1999).

[¹*Article 95e*

Transitional provisions for application of Regulation (EC) 1399/99 [1999] OJ L164/1

1. Regulation (EC) No 1399/1999 shall be applicable to rights of orphans where the parent under whom the orphan is entitled died after 1 September 1999.

2. Any period of insurance or residence completed under the legislation of a Member State before 1 September 1999 shall be taken into account for

3.311

the determination of rights acquired in accordance with Regulation (EC) No 1399/1999.

3. The rights of orphans where the parent under whom they are entitled died before 1 September 1999 may be reviewed at their request in accordance with Regulation (EC) 1399/1999.

4. If the request referred to in paragraph 3 is lodged within two years from 1 September 1999, rights deriving from Regulation (EC) No 1399/1999 shall be acquired from that date and the provisions of any Member State on the forfeiture or lapse of rights may not be applied to the persons concerned.

5. If the request referred to in paragraph 3 is lodged after the expiry of the period of two years following 1 September 1999, rights not forfeited or lapsed shall be acquired from the date of such request, subject to any more favourable provisions of the legislation of any Member State.]

AMENDMENT

1. Regulation 1399/99/EC, [1999] OJ L164/1 (September 1, 1999).

[¹*Article 95f*

Transitional provisions relating to Annex II, section I, under the headings "D. GERMANY" and "R. AUSTRIA"

3.312   **1.** Annex II, section I, under the headings "D. GERMANY" and "R. AUSTRIA", as amended by Regulation (EC) No 647/2005 of the European Parliament and of the Council of 13 April 2005 amending Council Regulations (EEC) No 1408/71 on the application of social security schemes to employed persons, to self-employed persons and to members of their families moving within the Community and (EEC) No 574/72 laying down the procedure for implementing Regulation (EEC) No 1408/71 (*), shall not establish any entitlement for the period prior to 1 January 2005.

2. Any period of insurance and, where appropriate, any period of employment, self-employment or residence under the legislation of a Member State prior to 1 January 2005 shall be taken into consideration in determining acquired rights in accordance with the provisions of this Regulation.

3. Subject to the provisions of paragraph 1, a right shall be acquired under this Regulation even where it relates to a contingency that occurred prior to 1 January 2005.

4. Any benefit that has not been awarded or that has been suspended on account of the nationality or the residence of the person concerned shall, at the latter's request, be awarded or resumed from 1 January 2005, provided that the rights for which benefits were previously awarded did not give rise to a lump-sum payment.

5. The rights of persons to whom a pension was awarded prior to 1 January 2005 may, on the application of the persons concerned, be reviewed, taking account of the provisions of this Regulation. This shall also apply to other benefits pursuant to Article 78.

6. If an application referred to in paragraph 4 or 5 is submitted within two years from 1 January 2005, the rights acquired under this Regulation shall have effect from that date and the provisions of the legislation of any Member State concerning the forfeiture or limitation of rights may not be invoked against the persons concerned.

7. If the application referred to in paragraph 4 or 5 is submitted after the expiry of the two-year period after 1 January 2005, rights which have not been forfeited or barred by limitation shall have effect from the date on which the application was submitted, except where more favourable provisions of the legislation of any Member State apply.]

AMENDMENT

1. Regulation 647/2005/EC, [2005] OJ L117/1 (May 5, 2005).

[¹*Article 95g*

Transitional provisions relating to the deletion, in Annex IIa, of the entry relating to the Austrian care allowance (Pflegegeld).

In the case of applications for care allowances under Austrian federal law (Bundespflegegeldgesetz) submitted not later than 8 March 2001 on the basis of Article 10a(3) of this Regulation, this provision shall continue to apply as long as the beneficiary of the care allowance continues to reside in Austria after 8 March 2001.]   3.313

AMENDMENT

1. Regulation 647/2005/EC, [2005] OJ L117/1 (May 5, 2005).

Article 96

Agreements relating to reimbursement between institutions

The Agreements concluded pursuant to Articles 36(3), 63(3) and 70(3) before 1 July 1982 shall apply likewise to persons to whom the scope of the present Regulation was extended on that date, except in the event of an objection by one of the contracting Member States to these Agreements.   3.314

This objection shall be taken into account if the competent authority of that Member State informs the competent authority of the other Member State(s) concerned in writing before 1 October 1983. A copy of this communication shall be forwarded to the Administrative Commission.

Article 97

Notification pursuant to certain provisions

1. The notifications referred to in Articles 1(j), 5 and 8(2) shall be addressed to the president of the Council. They shall indicate the date of entry into force of the laws and schemes in question or, in the case of the   3.315

notifications referred to in Article 1(j), the date from which this Regulation shall apply to the schemes mentioned in the declarations of the Member States.

2. Notifications received in accordance with the provisions of paragraph 1 shall be published in the *Official Journal of the European Communities*.

Article 98

Implementing Regulation

3.316   A furher Regulation shall lay down the procedure for implementing this Regulation.

GENERAL NOTE

3.317   The implementing regulation is reg.574/72 reproduced below.

ANNEX I

PERSONS COVERED BY THE REGULATION

*Sections marked ** reordered by part 2.1(b)(ii) of Annex II of the Treaty of Accession with effect from 1 May, 2004.*

I. Employed persons and/or self-employed persons (Article 1(a)(ii) and (iii) of the Regulation)

3.318   A. BELGIUM

Does not apply.

[⁵ B.]   BULGARIA

Any person working without an employment contract within the meaning of points 5 and 6 of art.4(3) of the Social Security Code shall be considered a self-employed person within the meaning of art.1(a)(ii) of the Regulation.]

[¹ [⁵C.] CZECH REPUBLIC

Does not apply.]

**[⁵D.] DENMARK

1. Any person who, from the fact of pursuing an activity as an employed person, is subject:
- (a) to the legislation on accidents at work and occupational diseases for the period prior to 1 September 1977;
- (b) to the legislation on supplementary pensions for employed persons (arbejdsmarkedets tillaegspension, ATP) for a period commencing on or after 1 September 1977, shall be considered as an employed person within the meaning of Article 1(a)(ii) of the Regulation.

2. Any person who, pursuant to the law on daily cash benefits in the event of sickness or maternity, is entitled to such benefits on the basis of an earned income other than a wage or salary shall be considered a self-employed person within the meaning of Article 1(a)(ii) of the Regulation.

**[⁵E.] GERMANY

If the competent institution for granting family benefits in accordance with Chapter 7 of Title III of the Regulation is a German institution, then within the meaning of Article 1(a)(ii) of the Regulation:

(a) "employed person" means compulsorily insured against unemployment or any person who, as a result of such insurance, obtains cash benefits under sickness insurance or comparable benefits [² or any established civil servant in receipt of a salary in respect of his/her civil servant status which is at least equal to that which, in the case of an employed person, would result in compulsory insurance against unemployment;]

(b) "self-employed person" means any person pursuing self-employment which is bound:
— to join, or pay contributions in respect of, an old-age insurance within a scheme for self-employed persons,
or
— to join a scheme within the framework of compulsory pension insurance.

[¹ [⁵F.] ESTONIA

Does not apply.]

**[⁵G.] GREECE

1. Persons insured under the OGA scheme who pursue exclusively activities as employed persons or who are or have been subject to the legislation of another Member State and who consequently are or have been "employed persons" within the meaning of Article 1(a) of the Regulation are considered as employed persons within the meaning of Article 1(a)(iii) of the Regulation.

2. For the purposes of granting the national family allowance, persons referred to in Article 1(a)(i) and (iii) of the Regulation are considered as employed persons within the meaning of Article 1(a)(ii) of the Regulation.

**[⁵H.] SPAIN

Does not apply.

**[⁵I.] FRANCE

If a French institution is the competent institution for the grant of family benefits in accordance with Title III, Chapter 7 of the Regulation:

1. "employed person" within the meaning of Article 1(a)(ii) of the Regulation shall be deemed to mean any person who is compulsorily insured under the social security scheme in accordance with Article L311-2 of the Social Security Code and who fulfils the minimum conditions regarding work or remuneration provided for in Article L313-1 of the Social

Security Code in order to benefit from cash benefits under sickness insurance, maternity and invalidity cover or the person who benefits from these cash benefits;

2. "self-employed person" within the meaning of Article 1(a)(ii) of the Regulation shall be deemed to mean any person who performs a self-employed activity and who is required to take out insurance and to pay old-age benefit contributions to a self-employed persons' scheme.

**[⁵J.] IRELAND

1. Any person who is compulsorily or voluntarily insured pursuant to the provisions of [³ Sections 9, 21 and 49 of the Social Welfare (Consolidation) Act 1993] shall be considered an employed person within the meaning of Article 1(a)(ii) of the Regulation.

2. Any person who is compulsorily or voluntarily insured pursuant to the provisions of [³ Sections 17 and 21 of the Social Welfare (Consolidation) Act 1993] shall be considered a self-employed person within the meaning of Article 1(a)(ii) of the Regulation.

**[⁵K.] ITALY

Does not apply.

[¹ [⁵L.] CYPRUS

Does not apply.]

[¹ [⁵M.] LATVIA

Does not apply.]

[¹ [⁵N.] LITHUANIA

Does not apply.]

**[⁵O.] LUXEMBOURG

Does not apply.

[¹ [⁵P.] HUNGARY

Does not apply.]

[¹ [⁵Q.] MALTA

Any person who is a self-employed person or a self-occupied person within the meaning of the Social Security Act (Cap. 318) 1987 shall be considered as a self-employed person within the meaning of Article 1(a)(ii) of the Regulation.]

**[⁵R.] NETHERLANDS

Any person pursuing an activity or occupation without a contract of employment shall be considered a self-employed person within the meaning of Article 1(a)(ii) of the Regulation.

**[⁵S.] AUSTRIA

Does not apply.

[¹ [⁵T.] POLAND

Does not apply.]

**[⁵U.] PORTUGAL

Does not apply.

[⁵ V. ROMANIA

Does not apply]

[¹ [⁵W.] SLOVENIA

Does not apply.]

[¹ [⁵X.] SLOVAKIA

Does not apply.]

**[⁵Y.] FINLAND

Any person who is an employed or self-employed person within the meaning of the legislation on the Employment Pensions Scheme shall be considered respectively as employed or self-employed with the meaning of Article 1(a)(ii) of the Regulation.

**[⁵Z.] SWEDEN

Any person who is an employed or self-employed person within the meaning of the legislation on work injury insurance shall be considered respectively as employed or self-employed with the meaning of Article 1(a)(ii) of the Regulation.

**[⁵AA.] UNITED KINGDOM

Any person who is an "employed earner" or a "self-employed earner" within the meaning of the legislation of Great Britain or of the legislation of Northern Ireland shall be regarded respectively as an employed person or a self-employed person within the meaning of Article 1(a)(ii) of the Regulation. Any person in respect of whom contributions are payable as an "employed person" or a "self-employed person" in accordance with the legislation of Gibraltar shall be regarded respectively as an employed person or a self-employed person within the meaning of Article 1(a)(ii) of the Regulation.

II. Members of the family (Second sentence of Article 1(f) of the Regulation)

A. BELGIUM

3.319

Does not apply.

[⁵ B. BULGARIA

Does not apply.]

[¹ [⁵C.] CZECH REPUBLIC

For the purpose of determining entitlement to benefits in kind pursuant to the provisions of Chapter 1 of Title III of the Regulation, the expression "member of the family" means a spouse and/or a dependent child as defined by the State Social Support Act No 117/1995 sb.]

★★[⁵D.] DENMARK

For the purpose of determining a right to sickness or maternity benefits in kind existing pursuant to Articles 22(1)(a) and 31 of the Regulation, the expression "member of the family" shall mean:

1. the spouse of an employed person, a self-employed person or other entitled persons under the terms of the Regulation, in so far as they are not themselves entitled persons under the terms of the Regulation; or

2. a child under 18 years of age in the care of someone who is an entitled person under the terms of the Regulation.

★★[⁵E.] GERMANY

Does not apply.

[¹ [⁵F.] ESTONIA

Does not apply.]

★★[⁵G.] GREECE

Does not apply.

★★[⁵H.] SPAIN

Does not apply.

★★[⁴ [⁵I.] FRANCE

For the purpose of determining entitlement to family allowances or family benefits, the term "member of the family" means any person mentioned in Article L 512-3 of the Social security Code.]

★★[⁵J.] IRELAND

In order to determine the right to benefits in kind for sickness and maternity in application of the Regulation, the term "member of the family" shall mean any person considered as being a dependent of an employed person or of a self-employed person for the application of the Health Acts of 1947 to 1970.

★★[⁵K.] ITALY

Does not apply.

[¹ [⁵L.] CYPRUS

Does not apply.]

[¹ [⁵M.] LATVIA

For the purpose of determining entitlement to benefits in kind pursuant to the provisions of Chapter 1 of Title III of the Regulation, "member of the family" means a spouse or a child under the age of 18.]

[¹ [⁵N.] LITHUANIA

For the purpose of determining entitlement to benefits in kind pursuant to the provisions of Chapter 1 of Title III of the Regulation, "member of the family" means a spouse or a child under the age of 18.]

**[⁵O.] LUXEMBOURG

Does not apply.

[¹ [⁵P.] HUNGARY

Does not apply.]

[¹ [⁵Q.] MALTA

Does not apply.]

**[⁵R.] NETHERLANDS

Does not apply.

**[⁵S.] AUSTRIA

Does not apply.

[¹ [⁵T.] POLAND

Does not apply.]

**[⁵U.] PORTUGAL

Does not apply.

[⁵V.] ROMANIA

For the purposes of determining entitlement to benefits in kind pursuant to the provisions of Chapter I of Title III of the Regulation, 'member of the family' means a spouse, a dependent parent, a child under the age of 18 (or under the age of 26 and dependent).]

[¹ [⁵W.] SLOVENIA

Does not apply.]

[¹ [⁵X.] SLOVAKIA

For the purpose of determining entitlement to benefits in kind pursuant to the provisions of Chapter 1 of Title III of the Regulation, "member of the family" means a spouse and/or a dependent child as defined by the Act on child allowances and additional child allowances.]

**[⁵Y.] FINLAND

For the purpose of determining entitlement to benefits in kind pursuant to the provisions of Chapter 1 of Title III of the Regulation, "member of the family" means a spouse or a child as defined by the Sickness Insurance Act.

**[⁵Z.] SWEDEN

For the purpose of determining entitlement to benefits in kind pursuant to the provisions of Chapter 1 of Title III of the Regulation, "member of the family" means a spouse or a child under the age of 18.

**[⁵AA.] UNITED KINGDOM

For the purpose of determining entitlement to benefits in kind the term "member of the family" means:

1. As regards the legislation of Great Britain and Northern Ireland:

(1) a spouse, provided that:

(a) that person, whether employed or self-employed, or another person entitled under the Regulation, is:
  (i) residing with the spouse; or
  (ii) contributing to the maintenance of the spouse;
  and

(b) the spouse does not:
  (i) have earnings as an employed or self-employed person or income as a person entitled under the Regulation; or
  (ii) receive a social security benefit or pension based on the spouse's own insurance;

(2) a person having care of a child, provided that:

(a) the employed or self-employed person or person entitled under the Regulation is:
  (i) living together with the person as though husband and wife; or
  (ii) contributing to the maintenance of the person;
  and

(b) the person does not:
  (i) have earnings as an employed or self-employed worker or income as a person entitled under the Regulation; or
  (ii) receive a social security benefit or pension based on that person's own insurance;

(3) a child in respect of whom that person, the employed or self-employed person, or another person entitled under the Regulation is or could be paid child-benefit.

2. As regard the legislation of Gibraltar:

any person regarded as a dependent within the meaning of the Group Practice Scheme Ordinance, 1973.

AMENDMENTS

1. Annex II of Treaty of Accession (May 1, 2004).
2. Regulation 1399/99/EC, [1999] OJ L164/1 (September 1, 1999).
3. Regulation 1223/98/EC, [1998] OJ L168/1 (July 1, 1998).
4. Regulation 1290/97/EC, [1997] OJ L176/1 (October 4, 1997).
5. Regulation 1791/2006/EC, [2006] OJ L363/1 (January 1, 2007).

ANNEX II

(Article 1(j) and (u) of the Regulation)

*Sections marked ** reordered by part 2.1(b)(ii) of Annex II of the Treaty of Accession with effect from 1 May, 2004.*
Only provisions relating to the United Kingdom have been reproduced.

I. Special schemes for self-employed persons excluded from the scope of the Regulation pursuant to the fourth subparagraph of Article 1(j)

**[¹AA.] UNITED KINGDOM

Does not apply.

3.320

II. Special childbirth or adoption allowances excluded from the scope of the Regulation under the terms of Article 1(u)(i)

**[¹AA.] UNITED KINGDOM

None.

3.321

III. Special non-contributory benefits within the meaning of Article 4(2b) which do not fall within the scope of the Regulation

**[¹AA.] UNITED KINGDOM

None.

3.322

AMENDMENT

1. Regulation 1791/2006/EC, [2006] OJ L363/1 (January 1, 2007).

ANNEX IIA

SPECIAL NON-CONTRIBUTORY BENEFITS

(Article 10a of the Regulation)

*Sections marked ** reordered by part 2.1(b)(ii) of Annex II of the Treaty of Accession with effect from 1 May, 2004.*
Only provisions relating to the United Kingdom have been reproduced.

**[³AA.] UNITED KINGDOM

[² (a) State Pension credit (State Pension Credit Act 2002)

3.323

    (b) Income-based allowances for jobseekers (Jobseekers Act 1995, 28 June 1995, Sections 1, (2)(d)(ii) and 3, and Jobseekers (Northern Ireland) Order 1995 of 18 October 1995, Articles 3(2)(d)(ii) and 5)

    (c) Income Support (Social Security Act 1986 of 25 July 1986, Section 20 to 22 and Section 23, and Social Security (Northern Ireland) Order 1986 of 5 November 1986, Articles 21 to 24)

    (d) Disability Living Allowance (Disability Living Allowance and Disability Working Allowance Act 1991 of 27 June 1991, Section 1, and Disability Living Allowance and Disability Working Allowance (Northern Ireland) Order 1991 of 24 July 1991, Article 3)

    (e) Attendance Allowance (Social Security Act 1975 of 20 March 1975, Section 35, and Social Security (Northern Ireland) Act 1975 of 20 March 1975, Section 35)

    (f) Carer's Allowance (Social Security Act 1975 of 20 March 1975, Section 37, and Social Security (Northern Ireland) Act 1975 of 20 March 1975, Section 37).]

AMENDMENTS

    1. Regulation 1386/2001/EC, [2001] OJ L187/1 (September 1, 2001) (*earlier replaced amendment*).

    2. Regulation 647/2005/EC, [2005] OJ L117/1 (May 5, 2005).

    3. Regulation 1791/2006/EC, [2006] OJ L363/1 (January 1, 2007).

GENERAL NOTE

3.324   See in particular Case C-299/05, *Commission v European Parliament and Council*, [2007] ECR I-8695, and other cases, discussed in the commentary to art.10a above.

    In Case C-299/05, the Court of Justice ruled that the following United Kingdom benefits had been unlawfully included in Annex IIa: attendance allowance, carer's allowance, and the care component of a disability living allowance.

ANNEX III

PROVISIONS OF SOCIAL SECURITY CONVENTIONS REMAINING APPLICABLE NOTWITHSTANDING ARTICLE 6 OF THE REGULATION—PROVISIONS OF SOCIAL SECURITY CONVENTIONS WHICH DO NOT APPLY TO ALL PERSONS TO WHOM THE REGULATION APPLIES

(Articles 7(2)(c) and 3(3) of the Regulation)

Only current provisions relating to the United Kingdom have been reproduced.

General comments

3.325   1. In so far as the provisions contained in this Annex provide for references to the provisions of other conventions, those references shall be replaced by references to the corresponding provisions of this Regulation, unless the provisions of the conventions in question are themselves contained in this Annex.

2. The termination clause provided for in a social security convention, some of whose provisions are contained in this Annex, shall continue to apply as regards those provisions.

[² **3.** Account being taken of the provisions of Article 6 of this Regulation, it is to be noted that the provisions of bilateral Conventions which do not fall within the scope of this Regulation and which remain in force between Member States are not listed in this Annex, inter alia, provisions providing for aggregation of insurance periods fulfilled in a third country.]

A. Provisions of social security conventions remaining applicable notwithstanding Article 6 of the Regulation. (Article 7(2)(c) of the Regulation)

23. GERMANY-UNITED KINGDOM

3.326

(a) Article 7(5) and (6) of the Convention on social security of 20 April 1960 (legislation applicable to civilians serving the military forces).
(b) Article 5(5) and (6) of the Convention on unemployment insurance of 20 April 1960 (legislation applicable to civilians serving the military forces).

25. IRELAND-UNITED KINGDOM

3.327

Article 8 of the Agreement of 14 September 1971 on social security (concerning the transfer and reckoning of certain disability credits).

30. PORTUGAL-UNITED KINGDOM

3.328

(a) Article 2(1) of the Protocol on medical treatment of 15 November 1978.
(b) As regards Portuguese employed persons, and for the period from 22 October 1987 to the end of the transitional period provided for in Article 220(1) of the Act relating to the conditions of accession of Spain and Portugal: Article 26 of the Social Security Convention of 15 November 1978, as amended by the Exchange of Letters of 28 September 1987.

B. Provisions of Conventions which do not apply to all persons to whom the Regulations applies (Article 3(3) of the Regulation)
None applicable

3.329

ANNEX IV

(Articles 37(2), 38(3), 45(3), 46(1)(b) and 46b(2) of the Regulation)

Only current provisions relating to the United Kingdom have been reproduced.

A. Legislations referred to in Article 37(1) of the Regulation under which the amount of invalidity benefits is independent of the length of periods of insurance

3.330   **[¹AA.] UNITED KINGDOM

(a) *Great Britain*
Sections 15 and 36 of the Social Security Act 1975.
Sections 14, 15 and 16 of the Social Security Pensions Act 1975.
(b) *Northern Ireland*
Sections 15 and 36 of the Social Security (Northern Ireland) Act 1975.
Articles 16, 17 and 18 of the Social security Pensions (Northern Ireland) Order 1975.

GENERAL NOTE

3.331   Sections 15 and 36 of the Social Security Act 1975 and sections 14, 15 and 16 of the Social Security Pensions Act 1975 have been repealed and re-enacted with effect from July 1, 1992 respectively in sections 33 and 68, and sections 33(3), 40 and 41 o the Social Security (Contributions and Benefits) Act 1992.

B. Special schemes for self-employed persons within the meaning of Articles 38(3) and 45(3) of Regulation No 1408/71

3.332   **[¹AA.] UNITED KINGDOM

None.

C. Cases referred to in Article 46(1)(b) of the Regulation where the calculation of benefit in accordance with Article 46(2) of the Regulation may be waived

**[¹AA.] UNITED KINGDOM

3.333   All applications for retirement and widow's pension determined pursuant to the provisions of Title III, Chapter 3 of the Regulation, with the exception of those for which:
  (a) during a tax year beginning on or after 6 April 1975:
      (i)   the party concerned had completed periods of insurance, employment or residence under the legislation of the United Kingdom and of another Member State; and
      (ii) one (or more) of the tax years referred to in (i) was not considered a qualifying year within the meaning of the legislation of the United Kingdom;
  (b) the periods of insurance completed under the legislation in force in the United Kingdom for the periods prior to 5 July 1948 would be taken into account for the purposes of Article 46(2) of the Regulation by application of the periods of insurance, employment or residence under the legislation of another Member State.

D. Benefits and agreements referred to in Article 46b(2) of the Regulation

3.334   **1.** Benefits referred to in Article 46b(2)(a) of the Regulation, the amount of which is independent of the length of periods of insurance or residence completed:

(a) The invalidity benefits provided for by the legislations referred to in part A of this Annex.

(b) The full Danish national old-age pension acquired after 10 years' residence by persons who will have been awarded a pension by 1 October 1989 at the latest.

(c) The Spanish death allowances and survivors' pensions granted under the general and special schemes.

(d) The widows' allowance under the widowhood insurance of the French general social security system or the agricultural workers' system.

(e) The widowers' or widows' invalidity pension under the French general social security system or the agricultural workers' system, when calculated on the basis of the invalidity pension of a deceased spouse, paid in accordance with Article 46(1)(a)(i).

(f) the Netherlands survivors' pension under the Law of 21 December 1995 on general insurance for surviving dependants.

(g) Finnish national pensions determined according to the National Pensions Act of 8 June 1956 and awarded under the transitional rules of the National Pensions Act (547/93) and the additional amount of the child's pension in accordance with the Survivors' pension Act of 17 January 1969.

(h) The full Swedish basic pension awarded under the basic pension legislation which applied before 1 January 1993 and the full basic pension awarded under the transitional rules to the legislation applying from that date.

(i) Swedish guarantee pension and guaranteed compensation which have replaced the full Swedish state pensions provided under the legislation on the state pension which applied before 1 January 1993, the full state pension awarded under the transitional rules of the legislation applying from that date and Swedish income-related sickness compensation and activity compensation.

2.   Benefits referred to in Article 46(2)(b) of the Regulation, the amount of which is determined by reference to a credited period deemed to have been completed bwteen the date on which the risk materialised and a later date:

(a) Danish early-retirement pension, the amount of shich is determined in accordance with legislation in force before 1 October 1984.

(b) German invalidity and survivors' pension, for which account is taken of a supplementary period, and German old-age pensions, for which account is taken of a supplementary period already acquired.

(c) Italian pensions for total incapacity for work (inabilità)

(d) Latvian invalidity and survivors' pensions for which account is taken of a credited period of insurance.

(e) Lithuanian social insurance invalidity and survivors' pensions.

(f) Luxembourg invalidity and survivors' pension.

(g) Slovak invalidity pension and survivors' pension derived therefrom.

(h) Finnish employment pensions for which account is taken of future periods according to national legislation.

(i) Swedish sickness compensation and activity compensation in the form of guaranteed compensation (Act 1962:381), as amended by Act 2001:489), survivor's pension, as calculated on the basis of reckonable periods (Acts 2000:461 and 2000:462) and Swedish old-age pension in the form of guarantee pension calculated on the basis of previously credited periods (Act 1998:702).

3. Agreements referred to in Article 46b(2)(b)(i) of the Regulation intended to prevent the same credited period being taken into account two or more times:

(a) Nordic Convention on Social Security of 18 August 2003.

(b) The Social Security Agreement of 28 April 1997 between the Federal Republic of Germany and Finland.

(c) Social Security Agreement of 10 November 2000 between the Republic of Finland and the Grand Duchy of Luxembourg.

ANNEX V

CONCORDANCE BETWEEN THE LEGISLLATIONS OF MEMBER STATES ON CONDITIONS RELATING TO THE DEGREE OF INVALIDITY

(Article 40(4) of the Regulation)

3.335   *Omitted.*

ANNEX VI

SPECIAL PROCEDURES FOR APPLYING THE LEGISLATIONS OF CERTAIN MEMBER STATES

(Article 89 of the Regulation)

*Sections marked ** reordered by part 2.1(b)(ii) of Annex II of the Treaty of Accession with effect from 1 May, 2004.*
Only the section concerning the United Kingdom has been reproduced.

**[5AA.] UNITED KINGDOM

3.336   **1.** When a person who is normally resident in Gibraltar, or who has been required, since he last arrived in Gibraltar, to pay contributions under the legislation of Gibraltar as an employed person, applies, as a result of incapacity to work, maternity or unemployment, for exemption from the payment of contributions over a certain period, and asks for contributions for that period to be credited to him, any period during which that person has been working in the territory of a Member State other than the United Kingdom shall, for the purposes of his application, be regarded as a period during which he has been employed in Gibraltar and for which he has paid contributions as an employed person in accordance with the legislation of Gibraltar.

2. Where, in accordance with United Kingdom legislation, a person may be entitled to a retirement pension if:

   (a) the contributions of a former spouse are taken into account as if they were that person's own contributions, or

   (b) the relevant contribution conditions are satisfied by that person's spouse or former spouse,

then provided, in each case, that the spouse or former spouse is or was an employed or self-employed person who had been subject to the legislation of two or more Member States, the provisions of Chapter 3 of Title III of the Regulation shall apply in order to determine entitlement under United Kingdom legislation. In this case, references in the said Chapter 3 to "periods of insurance" shall be construed as references to periods of insurance completed by:

   [⁴ (i) a spouse or former spouse where a claim is made by:
   — a married woman, or
   — a person whose marriage has terminated otherwise than by the death of the spouse,
   or

   (ii) a former spouse, where a claim is made by:
   — a widower who immediately before pensionable age is not entitled to widowed parent's allowance, or
   — a widow who immediately before pensionable age is not entitled to widowed mother's allowance, widowed parent's allowance or widow's pension, or who is only entitled to an age-related widow's pension calculated pursuant to Article 46(2) of the Regulation, and for this purpose "age-related widow's pension" means a widow's pension payable at a reduced rate in accordance with section 39(4) of the Social Security Contributions and Benefits Act 1992.]

3. (a) If unemployed benefit provided under United Kingdom legislation is paid to a person pursuant to Article 71(1)(a)(ii) or (b)(ii) of the Regulation, then for the purpose of satisfying the conditions imposed by United Kingdom legislation in relation to child benefit concerning a period of presence within Great Britain or, as the case may be, Northern Ireland, periods of insurance, employment or self-employment completed by that person under the legislation of another Member State shall be regarded as periods of presence in Great Britain or, as the case may be, Northern Ireland.

   (b) If, pursuant to Title II of the Regulation, excluding Article 13(2)(f), United Kingdom legislation is applicable in respect of an employment or self-employed person who does not satisfy the condition imposed by United Kingdom legislation in relation to child benefit concerning:

   (i) presence within Great Britain or, as the case may be, Northern Ireland, he shall be regarded, for the purpose of satisfying such condition, as being so present;

   (ii) a period of presence within Great Britain, or, as the case may be, Northern Ireland, periods of insurance, employment or self-employment completed by the said worker under the legislation of another Member State shall, for the purpose of satisfying such conditions, be regarded as periods of presence in Great Britain or, as the case may be, Northern Ireland.

(c) In respect of claims to family allowances under the legislation of Gibraltar the foregoing provisions of subparagraphs (a) and (b) shall apply by analogy.

4. The widow's payment provided under United Kingdom legislation shall be treated, for the purposes of Chapter 3 of the Regulation, as a survivor's pension.

5. For the purposes of applying Article 10a(2) to the provisions governing entitlement to attendance allowance, invalid care allowance and disability living allowance, a period of employment, self-employment or residence completed in the territory of a Member State other than the United Kingdom shall be taken into account insofar as is necessary to satisfy conditions as to presence in the United Kingdom, prior to the day on which entitlement to the benefit in question first arises.

6. In the event of an employed person subject to United Kingdom legislation being the victim of an accident after leaving the territory of one Member State while travelling, in the course of this employment, to the territory of another Member State, but before arriving there, his entitlement to benefits in respect of that accident shall be established:

(a) as if the accident had occurred within the territory of the United Kingdom,
   and

(b) for the purpose of determining whether he was an employed earner under the legislation of Great Britain or the legislation of Northern Ireland or an employed person under the legislation of Gibraltar, by disregarding his absence from those territories.

7. The Regulation does not apply to those provisions of United Kingdom legislation which are intended to bring into force any social security agreement concluded between the United Kingdom and a third State.

8. For the purposes of Chapter 3 of Title III of the Regulation no account shall be taken of graduated contributions paid by the insured person under United Kingdom legislation or of graduated retirement benefits payable under that legislation. The amount of the graduated benefits shall be added to the amount of the benefit due under the United Kingdom legislation as determined in accordance with the said chapter. The total of these two amounts shall constitute the benefit actually due to the person concerned.

9. [. . .]

10. For the purpose of applying the Non-Contributory Social Insurance Benefit and Unemployment Insurance Ordinance (Gibraltar), any person to whom this Regulation is applicable shall be deemed to be ordinarily resident in Gibraltar if he resides in a Member State.

11. [^{1} For the purposes of Articles 27, 28, 28a, 29, 30 and 31 of this Regulation, benefits payable outside the United Kingdom solely because of Article 95b(8) of the Regulation shall be considered as invalidity benefits.]

12. For the purpose of Article 10(1) of the Regulation any beneficiary under United Kingdom legislation who is staying in the territory of another Member State shall, during that stay, be considered as if he resided in the territory of that other Member State.

13.1. For the purpose of calculating an earnings factor with a view to determining the right to benefits under United Kingdom legislation, subject to point 15, each week during which an employed or self-employed person has been subject to the legislation of another Member State and which commenced during the relevant income tax year within the meaning of United Kingdom, legislation shall be taken into account in the following way:

(a) Periods between 6 April 1975 and 5 April 1987:
  (i) for each week of insurance, employment or residence as an employed person, the person concerned shall be deemed to have paid contributions as an employed earner on the basis of earnings equivalent to two-thirds of that year's upper earnings limit;
  (ii) for each week of insurance, self-employment or residence as a self-employed person the person concerned shall be deemed to have paid class 2 contributions as a self-employed earner.

(b) Periods from 6 April 1987 onwards:
  (i) for each week of insurance, employment or residence as an employed person, the person concerned shall be deemed to have received, and paid contributions as an employed earner, for, weekly earnings equivalent to two-thirds of that week's upper earnings limit;
  (ii) for each week of insurance, self-employment or residence as a self-employed person the person concerned shall be deemed to have paid class 2 contibutions as a self-employed earner.

(c) For each full week during which he has completed a period treated as a period of insurance, employment, self-employment or residence, the person concerned shall be deemed to have had contributions or earnings credited to him as appropriate, but only to the extent required to bring his total earnings factor for that tax year to the level required to make that tax year a reckonable year within the meaning of the United Kingdom legislation governing the crediting of contributions or earnings.

13.2. For the purposes of Article 46(2)(b) of the Regulation, where:

(a) if in any income tax year starting on or after 6 April 1975, an employed person has completed periods of insurance, employment or residence exclusively in a Member State other than the United Kingdom, and the application of paragraph 1(a)(i) or paragraph 1(b)(i) results in that year being counted as a qualifying year within the meaning of United Kingdom legislation for the purposes of Article 46(2)(a) of the Regulation, he shall be deemed to have been insured for 52 weeks in that year in that other Member State:

(b) any income tax year starting on or after 6 April 1975 does not count as a qualifying year within the meaning of United Kingdom legislation for the purposes of Article 46(2)(a) of the Regulation, any periods of insurance, employment or residence completed in that year shall be disregarded.

13.3. For the purpose of converting an earnings factor into periods of insurance the earnings factor achieved in the relevant income tax year within the meaning of United Kingdom legislation shall be divided by that year's lower earnings limit. The result shall be expressed as a whole number, any remaining fraction being ignored.

The figure so calculated shall be treated as representing the number of weeks of insurance completed under United Kingdom legislation during that year provided that such figure shall not exceed the number of weeks during which in that year that person was subject to that legislation.

14. In applying Article 40(3)(a)(ii), account shall only be taken of periods during which the employed or self-employed person was incapable of work within the meaning of United Kingdom legislation.

15.1. For the purpose of calculating, under Article 46(2)(a) of the Regulation, the theoretical amount of that part of the pension which consists of an additional component under United Kingdom legislation:

(a) the expression "earnings, contributions or increases" in Article 47(1)(b) of the Regulation shall be construed as meaning surpluses in earnings factors as defined in the Social Security Pensions Act 1975 or, as the case may be, the Social Security Pensions (Northern Ireland) Order 1975;

(b) an average of the surpluses in earnings factor shall be calculated in accordance with Article 47(1)(b) of the Regulation as construed in subparagraph (a) above by dividing the aggregated surpluses recorded under United Kingdom legislation by the number of income tax years within the meaning of United Kingdom legislation (including part income tax years) completed under that legislation since 6 April 1978 which occur within the relevant period of insurance.

15.2. The expression "periods of insurance or residence" in Article 46(2) of the Regulation shall be construed, for the purpose of assessing the amount of that part of the pension which consists of an additional component under United Kingdom legislation, as meaning periods of insurance or residence which have been completed since 6 April 1978.

16. An unemployed person returning to the United Kingdom after the end of the period of three months during which he continued to receive benefits under the legislation of the United Kingdom pursuant to Article 69(1) of the Regulation shall continue to be entitled to unemployment benefits by way of derogation from Article 69(2) if he satisfies the conditions in the aforementioned legislation.

17. For the purposes of entitlement to severe disablement allowance any employed or self-employed person who is, or has been, subject to United Kingdom legislation in accordance with Title II of the Regulation, excluding Article 13(2)(f):

(a) shall, for the entire period during which he was employed or self-employed and subject to United Kingdom legislation whilst present or resident in another Member State, be treated as having been present or resident in the United Kingdom;

(b) shall be entitled to have periods of insurance as an employed or self-employed person completed in the territory and under the legislation of another Member State treated as periods of presence or residence in the United Kingdom.

18. A period of subjection to United Kingdom legislation in accordance with Article 13(2)(f) of the Regulation may not:

(a) be taken into account under that provision as a period of subjection to United Kingdom legislation for the purposes of Title III of the Regulation,
nor

(b) make the United Kingdom the competent State for the provision of the benefits provided for in Article 18, 38 or 39(1) of the Regulation.

19. Subject to any conventions concluded with individual Member States, for the purposes of Article 13(2)(f) of the Regulation and Article 10b of the Implementing Regulation, United Kingdom legislation shall cease to apply at the end of the day on the latest of the following three days to any person previously subject to United Kingdom legislation as an employed or self-employed person:

(a) the day on which residence is transferred to the other Member State referred to in Article 13(2)(f);

(b) the day of cessation of the employment or self-employment, whether permanent or temporary, during which that person was subject to United Kingdom legislation;

(c) the last day of any period of receipt of United Kingdom sickness or maternity benefit (including benefits in kind for which the United Kingdom is the competent State) or unemployment benefit which

    (i) began before the date of transfer of residence to another Member State or, if later,

    (ii) immediately followed employment or self-employment in another Member State while that person was subject to United Kingdom legislation.

20. The fact that a person has become subject to the legislation of another Member State in accordance with Article 13(2)(f) of the Regulation, Article 10b of the Implementing Regulation and point 19 above, shall not prevent:

(a) the application to him by the United Kingdom as the competent State of the provisions relating to employed or self-employed persons of Title III, Chapter 1 and Chapter 2, Section 1 or Article 40(2) of the Regulation if he remains and employed or self-employed person for those purposes and was last so insured under the legislation of the United Kingdom;

(b) his treatment as an employed or self-employed person for the purposes of Chapter 7 and 8 of Title III of the Regulation or Articles 10 or 10a of the Implementing Regulation, provided United Kingdom benefit under Chapter 1 of Title III is payable to him in accordance with paragraph (a).

[² **21.** In the case of either students or members of their family or survivors of a student, Article 10a(2) of the Regulation shall not apply to benefits intended solely as specific protection for the disabled.]

22. [⁴ . . .]

AMENDMENTS

1. Regulation 1290/97/EC, [1997] OJ L176/1 (October 4, 1997).
2. Regulation 307/99/EC, [1999] OJ L307/99 (May 1, 1999).
3. Regulation 1399/99/EC, [1999] OJ L164/1 (September 1, 1999).
4. Regulation 647/2005/EC, [2005] OJ L117/1 (May 5, 2005).
5. Regulation 1791/2006/EC [2006] OJ L363/1 (JANUARY 1, 2007).

GENERAL NOTE

Note *Secretary of State for Work and Pensions v Burley,* [2008] EWCA Civ 376 **3.337**
referred to in para.3.158 above.

[¹ ANNEX VII

INSTANCES IN WHICH A PERSON SHALL BE SIMULTANEOUSLY SUBJECT TO THE LEGISLATION OF TWO MEMBER STATES

Annex reproduced as currently in force

(Article 14c(1)(b) of the Regulation)

3.338

1. Where he is self-employed in Belgium and gainfully employed in any other Member State.

2. Where a person is self-employed in Bulgaria and gainfully employed in any other Member State.

3. Where a person is self-employed in the Czech Republic and gainfully employed in any other Member State.

4. Where a person resident in Denmark is self-employed in Denmark and gainfully employed in any other Member State.

5. For the agricultural accident insurance scheme and the old-age insurance scheme for farmers: where he is self-employed in farming in Germany and gainfully employed in any other Member State.

6. Where a person resident in Estonia is self-employed in Estonia and gainfully employed in any other Member State.

7. For the pension insurance scheme for self-employed persons: where he is self-employed in Greece and gainfully employed in any other Member State.

8. Where a person resident in Spain is self-employed in Spain and gainfully employed in any other Member State.

9. Where he is self-employed in France and gainfully employed in any other Member State, except Luxembourg.

10. Where he is self-employed in farming in France and gainfully employed in Luxembourg.

11. Where he is self-employed in Italy and gainfully employed in any other Member State.

12. Where a person resident in Cyprus is self-employed in Cyprus and gainfully employed in any other Member State.

13. Where a person is self-employed in Malta and gainfully employed in any other Member State.

14. Where he is self-employed in Portugal and gainfully employed in any other Member State.

15. Where a person is self-employed in Romania and gainfully employed in any other Member State.

16. Where a person resident in Finland is self-employed in Finland and gainfully employed in any other Member State.

17. Where a person is self-employed in Slovakia and gainfully employed in any other Member State.

18. Where a person resident in Sweden is self-employed in Sweden and gainfully employed in any other Member State.

[1 Annex VIII

[¹ ANNEX VIII

SCHEMES THAT PROVIDE ONLY FOR FAMILY ALLOWANCES
OR SUPPLEMENTARY OR SPECIAL ALLOWANCES
FOR ORPHANS

(Article 78a of the Regulation)

*Sections marked ** reordered by part 2.1 (b) (ii) of Annex II of the Treaty of*   3.339
Accession with effect from 1 May, 2004.
Only provisions relating to the United Kingdom have been reproduced.

**[²AA.] UNITED KINGDOM

1. Great Britain and Northern Ireland
Provisions under the Social Security Contributions and Benefits Act
1992 and the Social Security Contributions and Benefits (Northern
Ireland) Act 1992, relating to child benefit (including any higher rates for
lone parents); child dependency allowances paid to pensioners and guardian's allowance.
2. Gibraltar
Provisions under the Social Security (Open Long-Term Benefits Scheme)
Ordinance 1997 and the Social Security (Closed Long-Term Benefits
Scheme) Ordinance 1996 relating to child dependency increased paid to
pensioners and guardian's allowance.

AMENDMENTS

1. Regulation 1399/99/EC, [1999] OJ L164/1 (September 1, 1999).
2. Regulation 1791/2006/EC [2006] OJ L363/1 (January 1, 2007).

**Council Regulation (EEC) No 574/72 of 21 March 1972 Laying
Down the Procedure for Implementing Regulation (EEC)
No 1408/71 on the Application of Social Security Schemes
to Employed Persons, to Self Employed Persons, to
Self-employed Persons and to Their Families Moving
within the Community**

GENERAL NOTE

This is the implementing regulation which lays down detailed rules, generally but   3.340
not exclusively, of an administrative nature. Reference is given in the annotations to
Reg.1408/71 to the applicable provisions of this regulation.

Council Regulation (EEC) No 574/72

CONTENTS

TITLE I: GENERAL PROVISIONS (ARTICLES 1 TO 4).

TITLE II: IMPLEMENTATION OF THE GENERAL PROVISIONS OF THE REGULATION (ARTICLES 5 TO 10A)

TITLE III: IMPLEMENTATION OF THE PROVISIONS OF THE REGULATION FOR DETERMINING THE LEGISLATION APPLICABLE (ARTICLES 10B TO 14).

TITLE IV: IMPLEMENTATION OF THE SPECIAL PROVISIONS OF THE REGULATION RELATING TO THE VARIOUS CATEGORIES OF BENEFITS

TITLE V: FINANCIAL PROVISIONS (ARTICLES 93 TO 107)

TITLE VI: MISCELLANEOUS PROVISIONS (ARTICLES 108 TO 117)

TITLE VII: TRANSITIONAL AND FINAL PROVISIONS (ARTICLES 118 TO 122)

ANNEXES

The Council of the European Union

3.341   *Having regard* to the Treaty establishing the European Community, and in particular Articles 51 and 235 thereof,

Having regard to Regulation (EEC) No 1408/71 on the application of social security schemes to employed persons, to self-employed persons and to members of their families moving within the Community, and in particular Article 98 thereof,

Having regard to the proposal from the Commission,

Having regard to the opinion of the European Parliament,

Having regard to the opinion of the Economic and Social Committee,

Whereas there is a need to lay down the procedure for implementing Regulation (EEC) No 1408/71 adapted to the basic rules and to the experience gained in applying these texts over the years;

Whereas it is necessary, in particular, to specify the competent authorities and institutions in each Member State as well as the liaison bodies entitled to exchange information directly between themselves;

Whereas it is necessary to specify the documents to be furnished and to be completed by the persons concerned in order to obtain benefits;

Whereas it is necessary to specify in detail the procedure for implementing the provisions of Regulation (EEC) No 1408/71 concerning the determination of the legislation applicable as well as the provisions concerning the different categories of benefits;

Whereas it is also necessary to specify the conditions for the refund of benefits provided by the institution of one Member State on behalf of the institution of another Member State, and the duties of the Audit Board;

Whereas it is necessary to lay down the methods of application for the procedure to be followed for currency conversion within the framework of the European Monetary System;

Whereas it is necessary, with a view to facilitating communication between the authorities and institutions of the Member State, to provide for the possibility of electronic data processing in connection with the application of Regulation (EEC) No 1408/71;

Whereas it should be made possible for Annexes 1, 4, 5, 6, 7 and 8 to Regulation (EEC) No 574/72 to be amended by means of a regulation adopted by the Commission at the request of the Member State or Member States concerned or their competent authorities and after consultation of the Administrative Commission; whereas the sole aim of amending these Annexes is to incorporate into a Community instrument decisions adopted by the Member State concerned or by their competent authorities,

Has Adopted this Regulation

Title I

General Provisions

Article 1

Definitions

For the purposes of this Regulation:

(a) "Regulation" means Regulation (EEC) No 1408/71;

(b) "implementing Regulation" means this Regulation;

3.342

1059

(c) the definitions in Article 1 of this Regulation have the meaning assigned to them in the said Article.

Article 2

Printed model forms—Information on legislations—Guides

3.343   [¹ **1.** Models of the documents necessary for the application of the Regulation and of the implementing Regulation shall be drawn up by the Administrative Commission.

These documents may be transferred between institutions either in paper or other form or by means of telematic services as standardised electronic messages in accordance with Title Via. The exchange of information by means of telematic services shall be subject to agreement between the competent authorities or the bodies designated by the competent authorities of the sending Member State and those of the receiving Member State.]

2. For the benefit of the competent authorities of each Member State, the Administrative Commission may assemble information on the provisions which come within the scope of this Regulation.

3. The Administrative Commission shall prepare guides for the purpose of advising persons concerned of their rights and of the administrative formalities to be completed for the exercise of those rights.

The Advisory Committee shall be consulted before such guides are drawn up.

AMENDMENT

1. Regulation 631/2004/EC, [2004] OJ L100/1 (June 1, 2004).

Article 3

Liaison bodies—Communications between institutions and between beneficiaries and institutions

3.344   **1.** The competent authorities may designate liaison bodies which may communicate directly with each other.

2. Any institution of a Member State, and any person residing or staying in the territory of a Member State, may make application to the institution of another Member State, either directly or through the liaison bodies.

3. Decisions and other documents emanating from an institution of a Member State and intended for persons residing or staying in the territory of another Member State may be communicated directly by registered letter with acknowledgement of receipt.

Article 4

Annexes

3.345   **1.** The competent authority or authorities of each Member State are listed in Annex I.

2. The competent institutions of each Member State are listed in Annex 2.

3. The institutions of the place of residence and the institutions of the place of stay of each Member State are listed in Annex 3.

4. The liaison bodies designated pursuant to Article 3(1) of the implementing Regulation are listed in Annex 4.

5. The provisions referred to in Articles 5, 53(3), 104, 105(2), 116 and 121 of the implementing Regulation are listed in Annex 5.

6. The procedure for the payment of benefits chosen by the institutions responsible for payment in each Member State, in accordance with Article 53(1) of the implementing Regulation, is listed in Annex 6.

7. The names and registered offices or place of business of the banks referred to in Article 55(1) of the implementing Regulation are listed in Annex 7.

8. The Member States to which the provisions of Article 10a(1)(d) of the implementing Regulation apply in their dealings with each other are listed in Annex 8.

9. The schemes to be taken into consideration when calculating the average annual cost of benefits in kind, in accordance with Articles 94(3)(a) and 95(3)(a) of the implementing Regulation, are listed in Annex 9.

10. Annex 10 lists the institutions or bodies designated by the competent authorities pursuant, in particular, to the following provisions:

(a) Regulation: Article 14c, Article 14d(3) and 17;

(b) implementing Regulation: Article 6(1), Article 8, Articles 10b, 11(1), 11a(1), 12a, 13(3) and (3), 14(1), (2) and (3), 38(1), 70(1), 80(2), 81, 82(2), 85(2), 86(2), 89(1), 91(2), 102(2), 109, 110, 113(2).

11. [^{1} . . .]

AMENDMENT

1. Regulation 647/2005/EC, [2005] OJ L117/1 (May 5, 2005).

TITLE II

IMPLEMENTATION OF THE GENERAL PROVISIONS OF THE REGULATION

IMPLEMENTATION OF ARTICLES 6 AND 7 OF THE REGULATION

Article 5

Replacement by the implementing Regulation of arrangements for implementing conventions

The provisions of the implementing Regulation shall replace those of the arrangements for implementing the conventions referred to in Article 6 of the Regulation; they shall also replace the provisions relating to the implementation of the provisions of the conventions referred to in Article 7(2)(c) of the Regulation in so far as they are not listed in Annex 5.

3.346

IMPLEMENTATION OF ARTICLE 9 OF THE REGULATION

Article 6

Admission to voluntary or optional continued insurance

3.347 **1.** If, by virtue of Articles 9 and 15(3) of the Regulation, a person satisfies the conditions for admission to a voluntary or optional continued insurance in respect of invalidity, old age and death (pensions) in several schemes under the legislation of one Member State, and if he has not been subject to compulsory insurance under one of those schemes by virtue of his last employment or self-employment he may, under the said Articles, join the voluntary or optional continued insurance scheme specified by the legislation of that Member State or, failing that, the scheme of his choice.

2. In order to invoke the provisions of Article 9(2) of the Regulation, a person shall submit to the institution of the Member State in question a certified statement relating to the insurance periods or periods of residence completed under the legislation of any other Member State. Such certified statement shall be issued, at the request of the person concerned, by the institution or institutions who administer the legislation under which he has completed those periods.

IMPLEMENTATION OF ARTICLE 12 OF THE REGULATION

Article 7

General rules on the application of the provisions designed to prevent overlapping

3.348 **1.** Where the benefits due under the legislation of two or more Member States are conditional upon mutual reductions, suspensions or withdrawals, the amounts which would not be paid in strict application of the provisions concerning reduction, suspension or withdrawal provided for by the legislation of the Member States concerned shall be divided by the number of benefits subject to reduction, suspension or withdrawal.

2. In order to implement Article 12(2), (3) and (4), Article 46a, Article 46b and Article 46c of the Regulation, the competent institutions concerned shall provide each other, at their own request, with all appropriate information.

Article 8

Rules applicable in the case of overlapping of rights to sickness or maternity benefits under the legislation of several Member States

3.349 **1.** If an employed or self-employed person or a member of his family is entitled to claim maternity benefits under the legislations of two or more

Member States, those benefits shall be granted exclusively under the legislation of the Member State in whose territory the confinement took place or, if the confinement did not take place in the territory of one of these Member States, exclusively under the legislation of the Member State to which the employed or self-employed person was last subject.

2. If an employed or self-employed person is entitled to claim sickness benefits under the legislation of Ireland and the United Kingdom for the same period of incapacity for work, those benefits shall be granted exclusively under the legislation of the Member State to which the person concerned was last subject.

3. In the cases referred to in Article 14c(b) [[1] and 14f] of the Regulation, where the person in question or a member of his family is entitled to claim benefits in kind in respect of sickness or maternity under the two legislations in questions, the following rules shall be applicable:

 (a) Where at least one of those legislations stipulates that the benefits shall be awarded in the form of a reimbursement to the person entitled to benefit, this shall be the exclusive responsibility of the institution of the Member State in whose territory they have been awarded.

 (b) If the benefits have been awarded in the territory of a Member State other than the two Member States in question, they shall be the exclusive responsibility of the institution of the Member State to whose legislation the person in question is subject by virtue of his paid employment.

AMENDMENT

 1. Regulation 1606/98/EC, [1998] OJ L209/1 (October 25, 1998).

Article 8a

Rules applicable in the case of overlapping of rights to sickness benefits, benefits with respect to accidents at work or occupational disease under Greek legislation and the legislation of one or more other Member States

If during the same period an employed or self-employed person or member of his family is entitled to claim sickness benefits, benefits with respect to accidents at work or occupational disease under Greek legislation and under the legislation of one or more Member States, these benefits shall be granted exclusively under the legislation to which the person concerned was last subject.

3.350

Article 9

Rules applicable in the case of overlapping of rights to death grants under the legislation of several Member States

1. Where the death occurs in the territory of a Member State, the right to a death grant acquired under the legislation of that Member State only shall

3.351

be maintained, whilst the right acquired under the legislation of any other Member State shall lapse.

2. Where the death occurs in the territory of one Member State when the right to a death grant has been acquired under the legislation of two or more other Member States, or where the death occurs outside the territory of the Member States and the said right has been acquired under the legislation of two or more Member States, only the right acquired under the legislation of the Member State to which the deceased person was last subject shall be maintained, whilst the right acquired under the legislation of any other Member State shall lapse.

[¹ **3.** By way of derogation from paragraphs 1 and 2, in the cases referred to in Articles 14c(b) or 14f of the Regulation, any entitlement to death grants acquired under the legislation of the Member States concerned shall be retained.

AMENDMENT

1. Regulation 1606/98/EC, [1998] OJ L209/1 (October 25, 1998).

Article 9a

Rules applicable in the case of overlapping of rights to unemployment benefits

3.352   If an employed or self-employed person, entitled to unemployment benefits under the legislation of a Member State to which he was subject during his last employment or self-employment pursuant to Article 69 of the Regulation, goes to Greece where he is also entitled to unemployment benefits by virtue of a period of insurance, employment or self-employment previously completed under Greek legislation, the right to benefits under Greek legislation shall be suspended for the period laid down in Article 69(1)(c) of the Regulation.

Article 10

Rules applicable in the case of overlapping of rights to family benefits or family allowances for employed or self-employed persons

3.353   **1.** (a) Entitlement to benefits or family allowances due under the legislation of a Member State, according to which acquisition of the right to those benefits or allowances is not subject to conditions of insurance, employment or self-employment, shall be suspended when, during the same period and for the same member of the family, benefits are due only in pursuance of the national legislation of another Member State or in application of Articles 73, 74, 77 or 78 of the Regulation, up to the sum of those benefits.

   (b) However, where a professional or trade activity is carried out in the territory of the first member State:

   (i) in the case of benefits due either only under national legislation of another Member State or under Articles 73 or 74 of the Regulation to the person entitled to family benefits or to the person to whom they are to be paid, the right to family benefits due either only under national legislation of that other Member State or under theses Articles shall be suspended up to the sum of family benefits provided for by the legislation of the Member State in whose territory the member of the family is residing. The cost of the benefits paid by the Member State in whose territory the member of the family is residing shall be borne by that Member State;

(ii) in the case of benefits due either only under national legislation of another Member State or under Articles 77 or 78 of the Regulation, to the person entitled to these benefits or to the person to whom they are payable, the right to these family benefits or family allowances due either only under the national legislation of that other Member State or in application of those Articles shall be suspended; where this is the case, the person concerned shall be entitled to the family benefits or family allowances of the Member State in whose territory the children reside, the cost to be borne by that Member State, and, where appropriate, to benefits other than the family allowances referred to in Article 77 or Article 78 of the Regulation, the cost to be borne by the competent State as defined by those Articles.

2. If an employed person subject to the legislation of a Member State is entitled to family allowances by virtue of periods of insurance or employment previously completed under Greek legislation, this right shall be suspended where, during the same period and for the same member of the family, family benefits or allowance are due under the legislation of the first Member State pursuant to Articles 73 and 74 of the Regulation, up to the sum of those benefits.

3. Where family benefits are due, over the same period and for the same member of the family, from two Member States pursuant to Articles 73 and/or 74 of the Regulation, the competent institution of the Member State with legislation providing for the highest levels of benefit shall pay the full amount of such benefit and be reimbursed half this sum by the competent institution of the other Member State up to the limit of the amount provided for in the legislation of the latter Member State.

RELEVANT DECISIONS OF THE ADMINISTRATIVE COMMISSION

Decision No 119 of 24 February 1983 concerning the interpretation of Article 76 and Article 79(3) of regulation (EEC) No 1408/71 and of Article 10(1) of Regulation (EEC) No 574/72 relating to the overlapping of family benefits and allowances, [1983] OJ C295/3.

Decision No 150 of 26 June 1992 concerning the application of Articles 77, 78 and 79(3) of Regulation (EEC) No 1408/71 and of Article 10 of regulation (EEC) No 574/72, [1993] OJ C229/5.

Article 10a

Rules applicable where an employed or self-employed person is subject successively to the legislation of several Member States during the same period or part of a period

Where an employed or self-employed person has been subject successively to the legislation of two Member States during the period separating

3.354

two dates for the payment of family benefits as provided for by the legislation of one or both of the Member States concerned, the following rules shall apply:

(a) The family benefits which the person concerned may claim by virtue of being subject to the legislation of each one of these States shall correspond to the number of daily benefits due under the relevant legislation. Where such legislation does not provide for daily benefits, the family benefits shall be granted in proportion to the length of time during which the person concerned has been subject to the legislation of each one of the Member States in relation to the period fixed by the legislation concerned.

(b) Where the family benefits have been provided by an institution during a period when they should have been provided by another institution, there shall be an adjustment of accounts between the said institutions.

(c) For the purposes of subparagraphs (a) and (b), where periods of employment or self-employment completed under the legislation of one Member State are expressed in units different from those which are used for the calculation of family benefits under the legislation of another Member State to which the person concerned has also been subject during the same period, the conversion shall be carried out in accordance with the provisions of Article 15 (3) of the implementing Regulation.

(d) Notwithstanding the provisions of subparagraph (a) in respect of dealings between the Member States listed in Annex 8 to the implementing regulation, the institution bearing the costs of the family benefits by reason of the first employment or self-employment during the period concerned shall bear such costs throughout the entire current period.

TITLE III

IMPLEMENTATION OF THE PROVISIONS OF THE REGULATIONS FOR DETERMINING THE LEGISLATION APPLICABLE

IMPLEMENTATION OF ARTICLES 13 TO 17 OF THE REGULATION

Article 10b

Formalities pursuant to Article 13(2)(f) of the Regulation

3.355   The date and conditions on which the legislation of a Member State ceases to be applicable to a person referred to in Article 13(2)(f) of the Regulation shall be determined in accordance with that legislation. The institution designated by the competent authority of the Member State whose legislation becomes applicable to the person shall apply to the institution designated by the competent authority of the former Member State with a request to specify this date.

[¹*Article 10c*

Formalities laid down in the event of the application of Article 13(2) (d) of the Regulation to civil servants and persons treated as such

For the application of Article 13(2)(d), the institution designated by the competent authority of the Member State whose legislation is applicable shall issue a certificate stating that the civil servant or the person treated as such is subject to its legislation.]

3.356

AMENDMENT

1. Regulation 647/2005/EC, [2005] OJ L117/1 (May 5, 2005).

Article 11

Formalities in the case of the posting elsewhere of an employed person pursuant to Articles 14(1) and 14b(1) of the Regulation and in the case of Agreements concluded under Article 17 of the Regulation

1. The institutions designated by the competent authority of the Member State whose legislation is to remain applicable shall issue a certificate stating that an employed person shall remain subject to that legislation up to a specific date:
(a) at the request of the employed person or his employer in cases referred to in Articles 14(1) and 14b(1) of the Regulation;
(b) in cases where article 17 of the Regulation applies.
2. The consent provided for in cases referred to in Articles 14(1)(b) and 14b(1) of the Regulation shall be requested by the employer.

3.357

Article 11a

Formalities pursuant to Articles 14a(1) and 14b(2) of the Regulation and in the case of Agreements concluded under Article 17 of the Regulation in the case of work carried out in the territory of a Member State other than that in which the person concerned is normally self-employed

1. The institution designated by the competent authority of the Member State whose legislation is to remain applicable shall issue a certificate stating that the self-employed person shall remain subject to that legislation up to a specified date:
(a) at the request of the self-employed person in cases referred to in Articles 14a(1) and 14b(2) of the Regulation;
(b) in cases where Article 17 of the Regulation applies.
2. The consent provided for in cases referred to in Articles 14a(1) and 14b(2) of the Regulation shall be requested by the self-employed person.

3.358

Article 12

Special provisions concerning insurance of employed persons under the German social security scheme

3.359 Where, under the terms of Articles 13(2)(a), 14(1) and (2) or 14b(1) of the Regulation, or under an agreement concluded pursuant to Article 17 of the Regulation, German legislation applies to a person employed by an undertaking or employer whose registered office or place of business is not situated on German territory, and the person concerned has no fixed job on German territory, this legislation shall apply as if the person concerned were employed in his place of residence on German territory.

If the employed person has no residence on German territory, German legislation shall apply as if he were employed in a place for which the Allgemeine Ortskrankenkasse Bonn (Local General Sickness Fund of Bonn), Bonn, is competent.

Article 12a

[¹ **Rules applicable in respect of the persons referred to in Article 14(2) and (3), Article 14a(2) to (4) and Article 14c of the Regulation who normally carry out an employed or self-employed activity in the territory of two or more Member States**

3.360 For the application of the provisions of Article 14(2) and (3), Article 14a(2) to (4) and Article 14c of the Regulation, the following rules shall apply:]

1. (a) A person who normally pursues his activity in the territory of two or more Member States or in an undertaking which has its registered office or place of business in the territory of one Member State and which straddles the common frontier of two Member States, or who is employed simultaneously in the territory of one Member State and self-employed in the territory of another Member State shall notify this situation to the institution designated by the competent authority of the Member State in the territory of which he resides.

    (b) Where the legislation of the Member State in the territory of which the person resides is not applicable to him, the institution designated by the competent authority of that Member State shall in turn notify the situation to the institution designated by the competent authority of the Member State whose legislation is applicable.

[¹ **1a.** Where, in accordance with Article 14(2)(a) of the Regulation, a person who is a member of the travelling or flying personnel of an international transport undertaking is subject to the legislation of the Member State in whose territory the registered office or place of business of the undertaking, or the branch or permanent establishment employing him, is located, or where he resides and is predominantly employed, the institution designated by the competent authority of that Member State shall issue to the person concerned a certificate stating that he is subject to its legislation.]

2. (a) Where, in accordance with Article 14(2)(b)(i) or the first sentence of paragraph 2 of Article 14a of the Regulation, a person who is normally employed or self-employed in the territory of two or more Member States and who pursues part of his activity in the Member State in whose territory he resides is subject to the legislation of that Member State,

the institution designated by the competent authority of that Member State shall issue to the person concerned a certificate stating that he is subject to its legislation and shall send a copy thereof to the institution designated by the competent authority of any other Member State:

    (i) in the territory of which the person concerned pursues a part of his activity,
       and/or

   (ii) if he is an employed person, in the territory of which an undertaking or an employer by whom he is employed has its registered office or place of business.

(b) The latter institution shall, where necessary, send to the institution designated by the competent authority of the Member State whose legislation is applicable the information necessary to assess the contributions for which the employer or employers and/or the person concerned are liable by virtue of that legislation.

3. (a) Where, in accordance with Article 14(3) or 14a(3) of the Regulation, a person who is employed in the territory of one Member State by an undertaking which has its registered office or place of business in the territory of another Member State and which straddles the common frontier of those States, or who is self-employed in such an undertaking, is subject to the legislation of the Member State in whose territory the undertaking has its registered office or place of business, the institution designated by the competent authority of the latter Member State shall issue to the person concerned a certificate stating that he is subject to its legislation and shall send a copy thereof to the institution designated by the competent authority of any other Member State:

    (i) in the territory of which the person concerned is employed or self-employed;

   (ii) in the territory of which the person concerned resides.

(b) Paragraph 2 (b) above shall apply by analogy.

4. (a) Where, in accordance with Article 14(2)(b)(ii) of the Regulation, an employed person who does not reside in the territory of any of the Member States in which he is pursuing his activity is subject to the legislation of the Member State in whose territory is situated the registered office or place of business of the undertaking or individual employing him, the institution designated by the competent authority of the latter Member State shall issue to the employed person a certificate stating that he is subject to its legislation and shall send a copy thereof to the institution designated by the competent authority of any other Member State:

    (i) in the territory of which the employed person pursues a part of his activity;

   (ii) in the territory of which the employed person resides.

(b) Paragraph 2(b) above shall apply by analogy.

5. (a) Where, in accordance with the provisions of the second sentence of paragraph 2 of Article 14a of the Regulation, a person who is normally self-employed in the territory of two or more Member States, but who does not pursue any part of his activity in the territory of the Member State in which he resides, is subject to the legislation of the Member State in whose territory he pursues his principal activity, the institution designated by the competent authority of the Member State in the territory of which he resides shall forthwith inform the institution designated by the competent authorities of the other Member States concerned.

(b) The competent authorities of the Member States concerned or the institutions designated by those competent authorities shall by common agreement determine the legislation applicable to the person concerned, account being taken of the provisions of subparagraph (d) and, where appropriate, of the provisions of Article 14a(4) of the Regulation, within a period of not more than six months counting from the day on which the situation of the person concerned was notified to one of the institutions concerned.

(c) The institution administering the legislation that has been determined as being applicable to the person concerned shall issue a certificate to that person showing that he is subject to that legislation and shall send a copy thereof to the other institutions concerned.

(d) For the purpose of determining, in pursuance of the third sentence of Article 14a(2) of the Regulation, the principal activity of the person concerned, account shall be taken first and foremost of the locality in which the fixed and permanent premises from which the person concerned pursues his activities is situated. Failing this, account shall be taken of criteria such as the usual nature or the duration of the activities pursued, the number of services rendered and the income arising from those activities.

(e) The institution concerned shall exchange all information necessary to determine both the principal activity of the person concerned and the contributions payable under the legislation that has been determined as being applicable to him.

6. (a) Without prejudice to paragraph 5, and in particular to subparagraph (b) thereof, if an institution designated by the competent authority of the Member State whose legislation would be applicable by virtue of Article 14a(2) or (3) of the Regulation establishes that the provisions of paragraph 4 of the said Article apply in the case of the person concerned, it shall notify the competent authorities of the other Member States concerned or the institutions designated by those authorities; where necessary, the legislation to be applicable to the person concerned shall be decided on by common agreement.

(b) The information referred to in paragraph 2(b) above shall be sent by the other institutions concerned to the institutions designated by the competent authority of the Member State whose legislation is determined to be applicable.

7. (a) Where, in accordance with Article 14c(a) of the Regulation, a person who is employed simultaneously in the territory of one Member State, and is self-employed in the territory of another Member State, is subject to the legislation of the Member State in whose territory he is engaged in paid employment, the institution designated by the competent authority of the latter Member State shall issue to the employed person a certificate stating that he is subject to its legislation and shall send a copy thereof to the institution designated by the competent authority of any other Member State:

(i) in the territory of which that person is self-employed;

(ii) in the territory of which that person resides.

(b) Paragraph 2(b) above shall apply by analogy.

8. Where, in accordance with the provisions of Article 14, 14c(b) of the

Article 12a

Regulation, a person who is simultaneously employed in the territory of one Member State and self-employed in the territory of another Member State is subject to the legislation of two Member States, the provisions of points 1, 2, 3 and 4 shall be applicable in respect of paid employment, and the provisions of points 1, 2, 3, 5 and 6 shall be applicable mutatis mutandis in respect of self-employment.

The institution designated by the competent authorities of the two Member States, whose legislation is determined to be applicable, shall inform each other accordingly.

AMENDMENT

1. Regulation 647/2005/EC, [2005] OJ L117/1 (May 5, 2005).

Article 12b

Rules applicable in respect of persons referred to in Article 14e or 14f of the Regulation

The provisions are Article 12a(1), (2), (3) and (4) shall apply by analogy to those persons covered by Articles 14e or 14f of the Regulation. In cases covered by Article 14f of the Regulation, the institution designated by the competent authorities of the Member States whose legislation is determined to be applicable shall inform each other accordingly.

AMENDMENT

1. Regulation 1606/98/EC, [1998] OJ L209/1 (October 25, 1998).

Article 13

Exercise of the right of option by persons employed by diplomatic missions and consular posts

1. The right of option provided for in Article 16(2) of the Regulation must be exercised in the first instance within the three months following the date on which the employed person was engaged by the diplomatic mission or consular post concerned, or on which he entered into the personal service of agents of such mission or post.

The option shall take effect on the date of entry into employment.

When the person concerned renews his right of option at the end of a calendar year, the option shall take effect on the first day of the following calendar year.

2. The person concerned who exercises his right of option shall inform the institution designated by the competent authority of the Member State for whose legislation he has opted, at the same time notifying his employer thereof. The said institution shall, where necessary, forward such information to all other institutions of the same Member State, in accordance with directives issued by the competent authority of that Member State.

3. The institution designated by the competent authority of the Member State for whose legislation the person concerned has opted shall issue to him a certificate testifying that he is subject to the legislation of that Member State while he is employed by the diplomatic mission or consular post in question or in the personal service of agents of such mission or post.

3.361

3.362

4. Where the person concerned has opted for German legislation to be applied, the provisions of that legislation shall be applied as though he were employed in the place where the German Government has its seat. The competent authority shall designate the competent sickness insurance institution.

Article 14

Exercise of right of option by auxiliary staff of the European Communities

3.363   **1.** The right of option provided for in Article 16(3) of the Regulation must be exercised at the time when the contract of employment is concluded. The authority empowered to conclude such contract shall inform the institution designated by the competent authority of the Member State for whose legislation the auxiliary sta member has opted. The said institution shall, where necessary, forward such information to all other institutions of the same Member State.

2. The institution designated by the competent authority of the Member State for whose legislation the auxiliary staff member has opted shall issue to him a certificate testifying that his is subject to the legislation of that Member State while he is employed by the European Communities as an auxiliary staff member.

3. The competent authorities of the Member States shall, where necessary, designate the competent institutions in respect of members of the auxiliary staff of the European Communities.

4. Where an auxiliary staff member, employed in the territory of a Member State other than Germany, has opted for German legislation to be applied, the provisions of that legislation shall be applied as though the auxiliary staff member were employed in the place where the German Government has its seat. The competent authority shall designate the competent sickness insurance institution.

TITLE IV

IMPLEMENTATION OF THE SPECIAL PROVISIONS OF THE REGULATION RELATING TO THE VARIOUS CATEGORIES OF BENEFITS

CHAPTER 1

GENERAL RULES FOR THE AGGREGATION OF PERIODS

Article 15

3.364   **1.** In the cases referred to in Articles 18(1), 38, 45(1) to (3), 64, and 67(1) and (2) of the Regulation, aggregation of periods shall be effected in accordance with the following rules:

Article 15

(a) To periods of insurance or residence completed under the legislation of one Member State shall be added periods of insurance or residence completed under the legislation of any other Member State, to the extent that this is necessary to have recourse thereto in order to supplement periods of insurance or residence completed under the legislation of the first Member State for the purpose of acquiring, retaining, or recovering the rights to benefits, provided that such periods of insurance or residence do not overlap. Where benefits in respect of invalidity, old age or death (pensions) are to be awarded by the institutions of two or more Member States in accordance with the provisions of Article 46(2) of the Regulation, each of the institutions concerned shall effect a separate aggregation, by taking into account the whole of the periods of insurance or residence completed by the employed or self-employed person under the legislations of all the Member States to which he has been subject, without prejudice, where appropriate, to the provisions of Article 45(2) and (3) and Article 47(1)(a) of the Regulation. Nevertheless, in the cases referred to in Article 14c(b) of the Regulation, the above mentioned institutions shall likewise take account, for the award of benefits, of the periods of insurance or of residence completed under an obligatory insurance scheme under the legislation of the two Member States in question which overlap each other.

[1 Nevertheless, in the cases referred to in Articles 14c(b) or 14f of the Regulation, the abovementioned institutions shall likewise take account, for the award of benefits, of the periods of insurance or of residence completed under an obligatory insurance scheme under the legislation of the Member States in question which overlap each other.]

(b) When a period of insurance or residence completed under compulsory insurance under the legislation of one Member State coincides with a period of insurance completed under voluntary or optional continued insurance under the legislation of another Member State, only the period completed under compulsory insurance shall be taken into account.

(c) When a period of insurance or residence, other than a period treated as such, completed under the legislation of one Member State coincides with a period treated as such under the legislation of another Member State, only the period other than a period treated as such shall be taken into account.

(d) Any period treated as such under the legislations of two or more Member States shall be taken into account only by the institution of the Member State under whose legislation the insured person was last compulsorily insured prior to the said period; where the insured person has not been compulsorily insured under the legislation of a Member State before the said period, the latter shall be taken into account by the institution of the Member State under whose legislation he was compulsorily insured for the first time after the said period.

(e) Where it is not possible to determine accurately the period of time in which certain periods of insurance or residence were completed under the legislation of one Member State, such periods shall be presumed not to overlap with periods of insurance or residence completed under the legislation of another Member State and shall, where advantageous, be taken into account.

(f) Where under the legislation of one Member State certain periods of insurance or residence are taken into account only if they have been completed within a specified time limit, the institution which administers such legislation shall:

    (i) only take into account periods of insurance or residence completed under the legislation of another Member State if they were completed within the said time limit,

    (ii) extend such a time limit for the duration of periods of insurance or residence completed wholly or partly within the said time limit under the legislation of another Member State, where the periods of insurance or residence involved under the legislation of the second Member State give rise only to the suspension of the time limit within which the periods of insurance or residence must be completed.

2. Periods of insurance or residence completed under the legislation of a Member State to which the Regulation does not apply, but which are taken into account under the legislation of that Member State to which the Regulation does apply, shall be considered as periods of insurance or residence to be taken into account for the purposes of aggregation.

3. When periods of insurance completed under the legislation of one Member State are expressed in units different from those used by the legislation of another Member State, the conversion necessary for the purposes of aggregation shall be carried out according to the following rules:

(a) Where the person concerned is an employed person who has been subject to a six-day week or if he is self-employed:

    (i) one day shall be equivalent to eight hours and vice versa;

    (ii) six days shall be equivalent to one week and vice versa;

    (iii) 26 days shall be equivalent to one month and vice versa;

    (iv) three months or 13 weeks or 78 days shall be equivalent to one quarter and vice versa;

    (v) for the conversion of weeks into months and vice versa the weeks and months shall be converted into days;

    (vi) the application of the preceding rules shall not have the effect of producing, for the sum total of the periods of insurance completed during one calendar year, a total exceeding 312 days or 52 weeks or 12 months or four quarters.

(b) If the person concerned is an employed person who has been subject to a five-day week:

    (i) one day shall be equivalent to nine hours and vice versa;

    (ii) five days shall be equivalent to one week and vice versa;

    (iii) 22 days shall be equivalent to one month and vice versa;

    (iv) three months or 13 weeks or 66 days shall be equivalent to one quarter and vice versa;

    (v) for the conversion of weeks into months and vice versa, the weeks and the months shall be converted into days;

    (vi) the application of the preceding rules shall not have the effect of producing, for the sum total of the periods of insurance completed during one calendar year, a total exceeding 264 days or 52 weeks or 12 months for four quarters.

(c) If the person concerned is an employed person who has been subject to a seven-day week:
 (i) one day shall be equivalent to six hours and vice versa;
 (ii) seven days shall be equivalent to one week and vice versa;
 (iii) thirty days shall be equivalent to one month and vice versa;
 (iv) three months or 13 weeks or 90 days shall be equivalent to one quarter and vice versa;
 (v) for the conversion of weeks into months and vice versa, the weeks and the months shall be converted into days;
 (vi) the application of the preceding rules shall not have the effect of producing, for the sum total of the periods of insurance completed during one calendar year, a total exceeding 360 days or 52 weeks or 12 months for four quarters.

Where the periods of insurance completed under the laws of a Member State are expressed in months, the days which correspond to a fraction of a month, in accordance with the conversion rules set out in this paragraph, are considered as an entire month.

AMENDMENT

1. Regulation 1606/98/EC, [1998] OJ L209/1 (October 25, 1998).

RELEVANT DECISIONS OF THE ADMINISTRATIVE COMMISSION

Decision No 137 of 15 December 1988 concerning the application of art.15(3) of regulation (EEC) No 574/72, [1989] OJ C140/3.

CHAPTER 2

SICKNESS AND MATERNITY

IMPLEMENTATION OF ARTICLE 18 OF THE REGULATION

Article 16

Certification of periods of insurance

1. In order to invoke the provisions of Article 18 of the Regulation, an employed or self-employed person shall submit to the competent institution a certified statement specifying the periods of insurance completed under the legislation to which he was last subject.

2. This certified statement shall be issued at the request of the employed or self-employed person by the institution or institutions of the Member State to whose legislation he was last subject. If he does not submit the said certified statement, the competent institution shall obtain it from the institution or institutions concerned.

3. The provisions of paragraph 1 and 2 shall apply by analogy if it is necessary to take into account periods of insurance previously completed under the legislation of any other Member State in order to satisfy the conditions of the legislation of the competent State.

3.365

IMPLEMENTATION OF ARTICLE 19 OF THE REGULATION

Article 17

Benefits in kind in the case of residence in a Member State other than the competent State

3.366

1. In order to receive benefits in kind under Article 19 of the Regulation, an employed or self-employed person must register himself and the members of his family with the institution of his place or residence by submitting a certified statement testifying that he and the members of his family are entitled to the said benefits. This certified statement, based upon information supplied by the employer, where appropriate, shall be issued by the competent institution. If the employed or self-employed person or the members of his family do not submit the said certified statement the institution of the place of residence shall obtain it from the competent institutions.

2. That certified statement shall remain valid until the institution of the place of residence receives notification of its cancellation.

However, where the said certified statement has been issued by a German, French, Italian or Portuguese institution, it shall be valid only for a period of one year following the date on which it was issued and must be renewed every year.

3. If the person concerned is a seasonal worker, the certified statement referred to in paragraph 1 shall be valid for the whole of the expected duration of the seasonal work, unless, in the meanwhile, the competent institution notifies the institution of the place of residence of its cancellation.

4. The institution of the place of residence shall inform the competent institution of every registration effected in accordance with the provisions of paragraph 1.

5. Upon each application for benefits in kind, the person concerned shall submit the supporting documents required for the granting of benefits in kind under the legislation of the Member State in whose territory he resides.

6. [^{1} . . .]

7. [^{1} . . .]

8. The employed or self-employed person or the members of his family shall inform the institution of the place of residence of any change in their situation which is likely to alter their entitlement to benefits in kind, in particular any cessation or change of the employment or self-employment of the person concerned or any transfer of residence or stay of the employed or self-employed person or of a member of his family. Likewise, should the employed or self-employed person cease to be insured or cease to be entitled to benefits in kind, the competent institution shall inform the institution of the place of residence accordingly. The institution of the place of residence may, at any time, request the competent institution to supply it with any information relating to the employed or self-employed person's insurance or to his entitlement to benefits in kind.

9. Two or more Member States or the competent authorities of those Member States may, having received the opinion of the Administrative Commission, agree on other implementing provisions.

Article 17

AMENDMENT

1. Regulation 631/2004/EC, [2004] OJ L100/1 (June 1, 2004).

Article 18

Cash benefits in the case of residence in a Member State other than the competent State

1. In order to receive cash benefits under Article 19(1)(b) of the Regulation an employed or self-employed person shall, within three days of commencement of the incapacity for work, apply to the institution of the place of residence by submitting a notification of having ceased work, or, if the legislation administered by the competent institution or by the institution of the place of residence so provides, a certificate of incapacity for work issued by the doctor providing treatment for the person concerned.

3.367

2. Where the doctors providing treatment in the country of residence do not issue certificates of incapacity for work, the person concerned shall apply directly to the institution of the place of residence within the time limit fixed by the legislation which it administers.

That institution shall immediately have the incapacity for work medically confirmed and the certificate referred to in paragraph 1 drawn up. Such certificate shall state the probable duration of the incapacity and shall be forwarded to the competent institution forthwith.

3. In cases where paragraph 2 does not apply, the institution of the place of residence shall, as soon as possible and in any event within the three days following the date on which the person concerned applied to it, have him medically examined as if he were insured with that institution. The report of the examining doctor shall indicate, in particular, the probable duration of the incapacity for work, and shall be forwarded to the competent institution by the institution of the place of residence within the three days following the date of the examination.

4. The institution of the place of residence shall subsequently carry out any necessary administrative checks or medical examination of the person concerned as if he were insured with that institution. As soon as it establishes that the person concerned is fit to resume work, it shall forthwith notify him and the competent institution accordingly, stating the date on which his incapacity for work ceased. Without prejudice to the provisions of paragraph 6, the notification to the person concerned shall be treated as a decision taken on behalf of the competent institution.

5. In all cases the competent institution shall reserve the right to have the person concerned examined by a doctor of its own choice.

6. If the competent institution decides to withhold the cash benefits because the person concerned has not completed the formalities laid down by the legislation of the country of residence, or if it establishes that the person concerned is fit to resume work, it shall notify the person concerned of its decision and shall simultaneously send a copy of such decision to the institution of the place of residence.

7. When the person concerned resumes work, he shall notify the competent institution accordingly, if such notification is required by the legislation administered by that institution.

8. The competent institution shall pay cash benefits by the appropriate method, in particular by international money order, and shall inform the institution of the place of residence and the person concerned accordingly. Where cash benefits are paid by the institution of the place of residence on behalf of the competent institution, the latter shall inform the person concerned of his rights and shall notify the institution of the place of residence of the amount of the cash benefits, the dates for payment, and the maximum period during which they should be granted, in accordance with the legislation of the competent State.

9. Two or more Member States, or the competent authorities of those Member States may, having received the opinion of the Administrative Commission, agree on other implementing provisions.

IMPLEMENTATION OF ARTICLE 20 OF THE REGULATION

Article 19

Special provisions for frontier workers and members of their families

3.368 In the case of frontier workers or members of their families, medicinal products, bandages, spectacles and small appliances may be issued, and laboratory analyses and tests carried out, only in the territory of the Member State in which they were prescribed, in accordance with the provisions of the legislation of that Member State, except where the legislation administered by the competent institution or an agreement concluded between the Member States concerned or the competent authorities of those Member States is more favourable.

APPLICATION OF THE SECOND INDENT OF ARTICLE 21(2) OF THE REGULATION

Article 19a

Benefits in kind in the event of a stay in the competent State—embers of the family resident in the Member State other than that in which the employed or self-employed person resides

3.369 **1.** In order to receive benefits in kind under the terms of Article 21 of the Regulation, members of the family shall present to the institution at the place of stay a certificate stating that they are entitled to the said benefits. This certificate, which shall be provided by the institution of the place of residence of the members of the family, if possible prior to their leaving the territory of the Member State on which they reside, shall, in particular, indicate where appropriate the maximum period for granting benefits in kind, as laid down by the legislation of that Member State. If the members of the family do not present the said certificate, the institution at the place of stay shall contact the institution of the place of residence in order to obtain it.

[¹ Article 17(9) of the implementing Regulation shall apply by analogy.]

Article 19a

AMENDMENT

1. Regulation 631/2004/EC, [2004] OJ L100/1 (June 1, 2004).

IMPLEMENTATION OF ARTICLE 22 OF THE REGULATION

Article 20

Benefits in kind in the case of a stay in a Member State other than the competent State—Special case of persons employed in international transport and members of their families

[¹ . . .]   3.370

AMENDMENT

1. Regulation 631/2004/EC, [2004] OJ L100/1 (June 1, 2004).

[¹Article 21

Benefits in kind in the case of a stay in a Member State other than the competent State

1. In order to receive benefits in kind under Article 22(1)(a)(i) of the   3.371
Regulation, an employed or self-employed person shall submit to the care
of the provider a document issued by the competent institution certifying
that he is entitled to benefits in kind. That document shall be drawn up in
accordance with Article 2. If the person concerned is not able to submit that
document, he shall contact the institution of the place of stay which shall
request from the competent institution a certified statement testifying that
the person concerned is entitled to benefits in kind.

A document issued by the competent institution for entitlement to
benefits in accordance with Article 22(1)(a)(i) of the Regulation, in each
individual case concerned, shall have the same effect with regard to the care
provider as national evidence of the entitlements of the person insured with
the institution of the place of stay.

2. Article 17(9) of the implementing Regulation shall apply by analogy.]

AMENDMENT

1. Regulation 631/2004/EC, [2004] OJ L100/1 (June 1, 2004).

Article 22

Benefits in kind for employed or self-employed persons who transfer their residence or return to their country of residence, and for employed or self-employed persons authorized to go to another Member State for medical treatment

1. In order to receive benefits in kind under Article 22(1)(b)(i) of the   3.372
Regulation, an employed or self-employed person shall submit to the

institution of the place of residence a certified statement testifying that he is entitled to continue receiving the said benefits. The certified statement, which shall be issued by the competent institution, shall specify in particular, where necessary, the maximum period during which such benefits may continue to be provided, in accordance with the provisions of the legislation of the competent State. The certified statement may, at the request of the person concerned, be issued after his departure if, for reasons of force majeure, it cannot be drawn up beforehand.

[¹ **2.** Article 17(9) of the implementing Regulation shall apply by analogy.]

3. Paragraphs 1 and 2 shall apply by analogy in respect of the provisions of benefits in kind in the case referred to in Article 22(1)(c)(i) of the Regulation.

AMENDMENT

1. Regulation 631/2004/EC, [2004] OJ L100/1 (June 1, 2004).

Article 23

Benefits in kind for members of the family

3.373   The provisions of Article 21 or 22 of the implementing Regulation, as appropriate, shall apply by analogy in respect of the granting of benefits in kind to members of the family as provided for in Article 22(3) of the Regulation.

[¹ However, in the cases referred to in the second subparagraph of Article 22(3) of the Regulation, the institution of the place of residence and the legislation of the country of residence of the members of the family shall be considered, respectively, as the competent institution and as the legislation of the competent State for the purposes of Article 17(9), 21 and 22 of the implementing Regulation.]

AMENDMENT

1. Regulation 631/2004/EC, [2004] OJ L100/1 (June 1, 2004).

Article 24

Cash benefits for employed or self-employed persons in the case of a stay in a Member State other than the competent State

3.374   The provisions of Article 18 of the implementing Regulation shall apply by analogy in respect of the receipt of cash benefits under Article 22(1)(a)(ii) of the Regulation. However, without prejudice to the obligation to submit a certificate of incapacity for work, an employed or self-employed person who is staying in the territory of a Member State without pursing any employment or self-employment there, shall not be required to submit the notification of having ceased work referred to in Article 18(1) of the implementing Regulation.

Article 24

Article 25

Certified statement relating to the members of the family to be taken into account in the calculation of cash benefits

1. In order to receive benefits under the provisions of Article 23(3) of the Regulation, an employed or self-employed person shall submit to the competent institution a certified statement relating to the members of his family who are resident in the territory of a Member State other than that wherein the said institution is situated.

2. This certified statement shall be issued by the institution of the place of residence of the members of the family.

It shall be valid for the 12 months following the date of its issue.

It may be renewed; in such a case, it shall be valid from the date of its renewal.

The person concerned shall immediately notify the competent institution of any occurrence necessitating an amendment to the said certified statement. Such amendment shall take effect from the date of such occurrence.

3. In place of the certified statement provided for in paragraph 1, the competent institution may require the person concerned to produce recent civil status documents relating to the members of his family who are resident in the territory of a Member State other than that wherein the said institutions is situated.

3.375

Article 26

Benefits for unemployed persons who go to a Member State other than the competent State in order to seek employment there

[¹ **1.** In order to receive benefits in cash and in kind under Article 25(1) (a) and (1a) of the Regulation, an unemployed person or a family member accompanying him shall submit to the care provider a document issued by the competent institution certifying that he is entitled to benefits in kind. That document shall be drawn up in accordance with the provisions of Article 2. If the person concerned is not able to submit that document, he shall contact the institution of the place of stay which shall request from the competent institution a certified statement testifying that the person concerned is entitled to benefits in kind.

A document issued by the competent institution for entitlement to benefits in accordance with Article 25(1)(a) of the Regulation, in each individual case concerned, shall have the same effect with regard to the care provider as national evidence of the entitlement of persons insured with the institution of the place to which the unemployed person has gone.

1a. In order to receive benefits in cash under Article 25(1)(b) of the

3.376

Regulation for himself and for members of his family, an unemployed person shall submit to the insurance institution of the place where he has gone a certified statement for which, prior to his departure, he shall have applied to the competent insurance institution. If the unemployed person does not submit that certified statement, the institution of the place to which he has gone shall obtain it from the competent institution. That certified statement must testify the existence of the right to the benefits in question under the conditions set out in Article 69(1)(a) of the Regulation, indicate the duration of such right taking into account the provisions of Article 69(1)(c) of the Regulation and, in the case of incapacity for work or hospitalisation, specify the amount of cash benefits to be provided, where appropriate, by way of sickness insurance during the abovementioned period.]

2. The unemployment insurance institution of the place where the unemployed person has gone shall testify, on a copy of the certified statement referred to in Article 83 of the implementing Regulation which shall be sent to the sickness insurance institution of that same place, that the conditions laid down in Article 69(1)(b) of the Regulation have been fulfilled and shall specify the date from which they were fulfilled, and the date from which the unemployed person shall receive unemployment insurance benefits at the expense of the competent institution.

[¹ **3.** Article 17(9) of the implementing Regulation shall apply by analogy.]

4. In order to receive the cash benefits provided for by the legislation of the competent State, the unemployed person shall, within three days, send a certificate of incapacity for him, to the sickness insurance institution of the place to which he has gone. He shall also state the date up to which he has received sickness insurance benefits and his address in the country where he is.

5. The sickness insurance institution of the place to which the unemployed person has gone shall, within three days, notify the competent sickness insurance institution, as well as the institution where the unemployed person is registered as seeking employment, of the date when the incapacity for work began and ended.

6. In the cases defined in Article 25(4) of the Regulation, the sickness insurance institution of the place to which the unemployed person has gone shall inform the competent sickness insurance institution and the competent unemployment insurance institution that it considers that the conditions justifying the extension of the period during which benefits in cash and in kind may be granted are satisfied, stating the grounds on which its opinion is based, and shall attach to the communication it sends to the competent sickness insurance institution a detailed report from the examining doctor on the condition of the patient, indicating the probable period during which the conditions for applying Article 25(4) of the Regulation will exist. The competent sickness insurance institution shall then take the decision as to the extension of the period during which benefits may be granted to the sick unemployed person.

7. The provisions of Article 18(2), (3), (4), (5), (6), (8) and (9) of the implementing Regulation shall apply by analogy.

AMENDMENT

1. Regulation 631/2004/EC, [2004] OJ L100/1 (June 1, 2004).

Article 27

Article 27

Benefits in kind for members of the family of unemployed persons in the case of residence in a Member State other than the competent State

The provisions of Article 17 of the implementing Regulation shall apply by analogy in respect of the granting of benefits in kind to the members of the family of unemployed persons when such members of the family are resident in the territory of a Member State other than the competent State.

3.377

At the time of the registration of the members of the family of unemployed persons receiving benefits under the provisions of Article 69(1) of the Regulation the certified statement referred to in Article 26(1) of the implementing Regulation must be produced. This certified statement shall be valid for the period of time during which the benefits may be granted under Article 69(1) of the Regulation.

Article 28

Benefits in kind for pension claimants and for members of their families

1. In order to receive benefits in kind in the territory of the Member State in which he resides, under Article 26(1) of the Regulation, a claimant and the members of his family shall register with the institution of the place of residence by submitting a certified statement testifying that he is entitled under the legislation of another Member State to the said benefits for himself and for the members of his family. This certified statement shall be issued by the institution of that other Member State which is responsible for benefits in kind.

3.378

2. The institution of the place of residence shall inform the institution which has issued the certified statement of every registration effected in accordance with paragraph 1.

Article 29

Benefits in kind for pensioners and members of their families who are not resident in a Member State under whose legislation they receive a pension and are entitled to benefits

1. In order to receive benefits in kind in the territory of the Member State in which he resides, under Articles 28(1) and 28a of the Regulation,

3.379

a pensioner and the members of his family [¹ residing in the same Member State] shall register with the institution of the place of residence by submitting a certified statement testifying that he is entitled to the said benefits for himself and for the members of his family, under the legislation or one of the legislations under which a pension is payable.

2. This certified statement shall be issued, at the request of the pensioner, by the institution or one of the institutions responsible for payment of the pension or, where appropriate, by the institution empowered to determine entitlement to benefits in kind, as soon as the pensioner satisfies the conditions for acquisition of the right to such benefits. If the pensioner does not submit the certified statement, the institution of the place of residence shall obtain it from the institution or institutions responsible for payment of the pension, or, where appropriate, from the institution empowered to issue such certified statement. Whilst awaiting the receipt of this certified statement the institution of the place of residence may, in the light of the documentary evidence accepted by it, register the pensioner and the members of his family [¹ residing in the same Member State] provisionally. This registration shall bind the institution responsible for the payment of benefits in kind only if this latter institution has issued the certified statement provided for in paragraph 1.

3. The institution of the place of residence shall inform the institution which has issued the certified statement provided for in paragraph 2 of every registration effected in accordance with the provisions of the said paragraph.

4. When an application is made for benefits in kind it must be proved to the institution of the place of residence, by means of the receipt or the counterfoil of the money order of the last payment made, that the pensioner is still entitled to a pension.

5. The pensioner or the members of his family [¹ residing in the same Member State] shall inform the institution of the place of residence of any entitlement to benefits in kind, in particular any suspension or withdrawal of the pension and any transfer of their residence. The institutions responsible for the pension shall also inform the institution of the pensioners place of residence of any such change.

6. The Administrative Commission shall, to the extent necessary, fix the procedure for determining the institution which shall bear the cost of the payment of benefits in kind, in the case referred to in Article 28(2)(b) of the Regulation.

AMENDMENT

1. Regulation 1223/98/EC, [1998] OJ L168/1 (January 1, 1998 but for France 1 January 2002).

IMPLEMENTATION OF ARTICLE 29 OF THE REGULATION

Article 30

Benefits in kind for members of the family who are resident [¹ outside the competent Member State] in a Member State other than the State in which the pensioner is resident

3.380   1. In order to receive benefits in kind, in the territory of the Member State in which they reside, under Article 29(1) of the Regulation, the members of the family shall register with the institution of their place of residence by submitting the documentary evidence required by the legislation which that institution administers for the granting of such benefits to members of the family of a pensioner, together with a certified statement testifying that the pensioner is entitled to benefits in kind for himself and for the members of his family. [¹ This certified statement, which shall be issued by the institution or by one of the institutions responsible for paying the pension, or, where applicable, the institution empowered to decide on entitlement to benefits in kind, shall remain valid as long as the institution of the place of residence of the members of the family has not been notified of its cancellation. However, where the said certified statement has been issued by a German, French, Italian or Portuguese institution, it shall be valid only for a period of one year following the date on which it was issued and must be renewed every year. If the members of the family do not present a certified statement, the institution of the place of residence shall, in order to obtain it, contact the institution or institutions responsible for paying the pension or, where applicable, the institution empowered to do so.]

2. When making an application for benefits in kind the members of the family shall submit to the institution of their place of residence the certified statement referred to in paragraph 1, if the legislation which that institution administers provides that such an application must be accompanied by evidence of entitlement to a pension.

[¹ **3.** The institution which has issued the certified statement, the institution of the place of residence shall, in order to obtain it, contact the institution or institutions responsible for paying the pension or, where applicable, the institution empowered to do so.]

4. The members of the family shall inform the institution of their place of residence of any change in their situation which is likely to alter their entitlement to benefits in kind, in particular any transfer of residence.

5. The institution of the place of residence shall inform the institution of which issued the statement referred to in paragraph 1 of any registration it has carried out, in accordance with the provisions of that paragraph.

AMENDMENT

1. Regulation 1223/98/EC, [1998] OJ L168/1 (January 1, 1998 but for France 1 January 2002).

IMPLEMENTATION OF ARTICLE 31 OF THE REGULATION

[¹*Article 31*

Benefits in kind for pensioners and members of their families staying in a Member State other than the one in which they reside

1. In order to receive benefits in kind under Article 31 of the Regulation, a pensioner shall submit to the care provider a document issued by the institution of the place of residence certifying that he is entitled to the benefits in kind. That document shall be drawn up in accordance with Article 2. If the person concerned is not able to submit that document, he shall contact

3.381

the institution of the place of stay shall request from the institution of the place of residence a certified statement testifying that the person concerned is entitled to benefits in kind.

A document issued by the competent institution for entitlement to benefits is accordance with Article 31 of the Regulation, in each individual case concerned, shall have the same effect with regard to the care provider as national evidence of the entitlements of persons insured with the institution of the place of stay.

2. Article 17(9) of the implementing Regulation shall apply by analogy.

3. Paragraphs 1 and 2 shall apply by analogy in respect of the granting of benefits in kind to the members of the family covered by Article 31 of the Regulation. If these family members reside in the territory of a Member State other than that of the pensioner, the document referred to in paragraph 1 shall be issued by the institution of their place of residence.]

AMENDMENT

1. Regulation 631/2004/EC, [2004] OHJ L100/1 (June 1, 2004).

IMPLEMENTATION OF ARTICLE 35(1) OF THE REGULATION

Article 32

Institution to which workers in mines and similar undertakings and members of their families may apply when staying or residing in a Member State other than the competent State

3.382

1. In the cases referred to in Article 35(1) of the Regulation and where, in the country of stay or residence, the benefits provided under the insurance scheme for sickness or maternity covering manual workers in the steel industry are equivalent to those provided under the special scheme for workers in mines and similar undertakings, workers belonging to the latter category and members of their families may apply to the nearest institution in the territory of the Member State in which they are staying or residing, specified in Annex 3 to the implementing Regulation, even if the latter is an institution of the scheme applicable to manual workers in the steel industry, which institution shall then provide such benefits.

2. Where the benefits provided under the special scheme for workers in mines and similar undertakings are more advantageous, such workers or the members of their families shall have the option of applying either to the institution responsible for the administration of that scheme, or to the nearest institution in the territory of the Member State in which they are staying or residing which administers the scheme for manual workers in the steel industry. In the latter case, the institution in question shall draw the attention of the person concerned to the fact that by applying to the institution responsible for the administration of the abovementioned special scheme, he will obtain more advantageous benefits; it must, furthermore, inform him of the name and address of such institution.

Article 32a

IMPLEMENTATION OF ARTICLE 35(2) OF THE REGULATION

Article 32a

[¹ . . .]   3.383

AMENDMENT

    1. Regulation 647/2005/EC, [2005] OJ L117/1 (May 5, 2005).

IMPLEMENTATION OF ARTICLE 35(4) OF THE REGULATION

Article 33

Taking account of the period during which benefits have already been provided by the institution of another Member State

For the purposes of implementing the provisions of Article 35(4) of   3.384
the Regulation, the institution of a Member State called upon to provide
benefits may request the institution of another Member State to supply it
with information relating to the period during which the latter institution
has already provided benefits for the same case of sickness or maternity.

Article 34

Refund by the competent institution of one Member State of expenses incurred during a stay in another Member State

1. If it is not possible during an employed or self-employed person's   3.385
stay in a Member State other than the competent State to complete the
formalities provided for in Articles 20(1) and (4) and 21, 23 and 31 of
the implementing Regulation, his expenses shall, upon his application, be
refunded by the competent institution in accordance with the refund rates
administered by the institution of the place of stay.

2. The institution of the place of stay shall, at the request of the competent institution, supply it with the necessary information about such rates.
If the institution of the place of stay and the competent institution are
bound by an agreement providing either that no refund, or that a lump-
sum refund of benefits provided, in pursuance of Articles 22(1)(a)(i) and
31 of the Regulation, be made, the institution of the place of stay shall, in
addition, be required to transfer to the competent institution the amount
to be refunded to the person concerned in pursuance of the provisions of
paragraph 1.

3. Where major expenses are involved, the competent institution may
pay an appropriate advance to the person concerned as soon as that person
submits to the said institution the claim for refund.

4. Notwithstanding paragraphs 1, 2 and 3, the competent institution may effect the reimbursement of expenses incurred in accordance with the rates it administers provided that it is possible to make a refund in accordance with these rates, that the expenses to be refunded do not exceed a level determined by the Administrative Commission and that the employed person or self-employed person or pensioner agrees to the application of this provision. In any case, the amount of reimbursement shall not exceed the amount of the expenses actually incurred.

[¹ **5.** If the legislation of the State of stay does not provide for rates of reimbursement, the competent institution may effect the reimbursement in accordance with the rates it administers, without the agreement of the person concerned being necessary. In no case shall the amount of reimbursement exceed the amount of the expenses actually incurred.]

AMENDMENT

1. Regulation 1386/2001/EC, [2001] OJ L187/1 (September 1, 2001).

CHAPTER 3

INVALIDITY, OLD-AGE AND DEATH (PENSIONS)

SUBMISSION AND INVESTIGATION OF CLAIMS FOR BENEFITS

Article 35

Applications for invalidity benefits where an employed person or a self-employed person has been subject only to the legislations mentioned in part A of Annex IV to the Regulation and also in the case referred to in Article 40(2) of the Regulation

3.386   **1.** In order to receive benefits under Articles 37, 38 and 39 of the Regulation, including the cases referred to in Articles 40(2), 41(1) and 42(2) of the Regulation, an employed or self-employed person shall submit a claim either to the institution of the Member State to whose legislation he was subject at the time of occurrence of the incapacity for work followed by invalidity or the aggravation of such invalidity, or to the institution of the place of residence, which shall then forward the claim to the first institution, indicating the date on which it was submitted; this date shall be regarded as the date of the submission of the claim to the first institution. However, if sickness insurance cash benefits have been granted, the date on which such cash benefits ceased to be granted must, where appropriate, be regarded as the date of submission of the pension claim.

2. In the case referred to in Article 41(1)(b) of the Regulation, the institution with which the employed or self-employed person was last insured shall notify the amount and the operative date of the benefits due under the legislation which it administers to the institution initially responsible for payment of the benefits. With effect from that date, the benefits due prior to the aggravation of the invalidity shall be cancelled or reduced to an amount not exceeding the supplement referred to in Article 41(1) of the Regulation.

3. The provisions of paragraph 2 shall not apply in the case referred to in Article 41(1)(d) of the Regulation. In this case, the institution with which the claimant was last insured shall apply to the Netherlands institution in order to ascertain the amount due from that institution.

Article 36

Claims for old-age and survivors' benefits (excluding orphans' benefits) and invalidity benefits in cases not referred to in Article 35 of the implementing Regulation

1. In order to receive benefits under Articles 40 to 51 of the Regulation, except in the cases referred to in Article 35 of the implementing Regulation, the person concerned shall submit a claim to the institution of the place of residence in accordance with the procedure provided for by the legislation administered by that institution. If the employed or self-employed person has not been subject to that legislation, the institution of the place of residence shall forward the claim to the institution of the Member State to whose legislation he was last subject, indicating the date on which the claim was submitted. That date shall be regarded as the date on which the claim was submitted to the latter institution.

2. Where a claimant resides in the territory of a Member State to whose legislation the employed or self-employed person has not been subject, he may submit his claim to the institution of the Member State to whose legislation the employed or self-employed person was last subject.

3. Where a claimant resides in the territory of a State which is not a Member State, he shall submit his claim to the competent institution of that Member State to whose legislation the employed or self-employed person was last subject.

Should the claimant submit his claim to the institution of the Member State of which he is a national, the latter shall forward such claim to the competent institution.

4. A claim for benefits sent to the institution of one Member State shall automatically involve the concurrent award of benefits under the legislation of all the Member States in question whose conditions the claimant satisfies except where, under Article 44(2) of the Regulation, the claimant asks for postponement of any old-age benefits to which he would be entitled under the legislation of one or more Member States.

3.387

Article 37

Documents and information which should accompany claims to the benefits referred to in article 36 of the implementing Regulation

The submission of the claims referred to in Article 36 of the implementing Regulation shall be subject to the following rules:

3.388

(a) the claim must be accompanied by the required supporting documents and must be made on the form provided for by the legislation:
   (i) of the Member State on whose territory the claimant resides, in the case referred to in Article 36(1);
   (ii) of the Member State to which the employed or self-employed person was last subject, in the cases referred to in Article 36(2) and (3);
(b) the accuracy of the information supplied by the claimant must be established by official documents attached to the claim form, or confirmed by the competent bodies of the Member State in whose territory the claimant resides;
(c) the claimant must indicate, in so far as is possible, either the institution or institutions administering insurance in respect of invalidity, old-age or death (pensions) of any Member State with which the employed or self-employed person has been insured, or in the case of an employed person the employer or employers for whom he has worked in the territory of any Member State, by producing any employment certificates which he may have in his possession;
(d) if, under Article 44(2) of the Regulation, the claimant asks for the postponement of the award of any old-age benefits to which he would be entitled under the legislation of one or more member States he must specify the legislation under which he is claiming benefits.

Article 38

Certified statements of the members of the family to be taken into account when establishing the amount of the benefit

3.389   **1.** In order to receive benefits under the provisions of Article 39(4) or 47(3) of the Regulation, the claimant shall submit a certified statement relating to the members of his family, his children excepted, who are residing in the territory of a Member State other than in which the institution responsible for the award of benefits is situated.

This certified statement shall be issued by the sickness insurance institution of the place of residence of the members of the family, or by another institution designated by the competent authority of the Member State in whose territory they are resident. The provisions of the second and third sub-paragraphs of Article 25(2) of the implementing Regulation shall apply by analogy.

In place of the certified statement provided for in the first sub-paragraph, the institution responsible for the award of benefits may require the claimant to supply recent civil status documents relating to the members of his family, his children excepted, who are residing in the territory of a Member State other than the State in which the said institution is situated.

2. In the case referred to in paragraph 1, if the legislation administered by the institution concerned requires that the members of the family should live under the same roof as the pensioner, the fact that the said members of the family who do not satisfy that condition are nevertheless mainly dependent on the claimant must be established by documents proving the regular transmission of part of the claimant's earnings.

Article 39

Investigation of applications for invalidity benefits where an employed person or a self-employed person has been subject only to the legislations mentioned in part A of Annex IV to the Regulation

1. If an employed or self-employed person has submitted a claim for invalidity benefits, and the institution establishes that the provisions of Article 37(1) of the Regulation apply, that institution shall, where necessary, obtain from the institution with which the person concerned was last insured a certified statement of the periods of insurance completed by him under the legislation administered by the last institution.

2. Where it is necessary to take into account periods of insurance previously completed under the legislation of any other Member State in order to satisfy the conditions of the legislation of the competent State, the provisions of paragraph 1 shall apply by analogy.

3. In the case referred to in Article 39(3) of the Regulation, the institution which has investigated the claimant's case shall forward his file to the institution with which the person concerned was last insured.

4. Articles 41 to 50 of the implementing Regulation shall not apply to the investigation of claims referred to in paragraphs 1, 2 and 3.

3.390

Article 40

Determination of the degree of invalidity

In order to determine the degree of invalidity, the institution of the Member State shall take into consideration the documents and medical reports and the information of an administrative nature obtained by the institution of any other Member State. Each institution shall, however, retain the right to have the claimant examined by a doctor of its own choice except where the provisions of Article 40(4) of the Regulation apply.

3.391

INVESTIGATION OF CLAIMS FOR BENEFITS IN RESPECT OF INVALIDITY, OLD AGE AND SURVIVORS IN THE CASES REFERRED TO IN ARTICLE 36 OF THE IMPLEMENTING REGULATION

Article 41

Determination of the investigating institutions

1. Claims for benefit shall be investigated by the institution to which they have been sent or forwarded in accordance with the provisions of Article 36 of the implementing Regulation. This institution is hereinafter referred to as the "investigating institution".

3.392

2. The investigating institution shall forthwith notify claims for benefits to all the institutions concerned on a special form, so that the claims may be investigated simultaneously and without delay by all these institutions.

Article 42

Forms to be used for the investigation of claims for benefits

3.393
1. When investigating claims for benefits the investigating institution shall use a form which will include, in particular, a statement and a summary of the periods of insurance or residence completed by the employed or self-employed person under the legislation of all the Member States concerned.

2. These forms, when forwarded to the institution of any other Member State, shall take the place of supporting documents.

Article 43

Procedure to be followed by the institution concerned in the investigation of a claim

3.394
1. The investigating institution shall enter on the form provided for in Article 42(1) of the implementing Regulation the periods of insurance or residence completed under the legislation which it administers and it shall forward a copy of that form to the institution administering insurance in respect of invalidity, old-age or death (pensions) of any Member State with which the employed or self-employed person has been insured enclosing, where appropriate, any employment certificates produced by the claimant.

2. Where only one other institution is involved, that institution shall complete the said form by indicating:

  (a) the periods of insurance or residence completed under the legislation which it administers;

  (b) the amount of benefit which the claimant could claim in respect of those periods of insurance or residence only;

  (c) the theoretical amount and the actual amount of benefits calculated in accordance with the provisions of Article 46(2) of the Regulation.

The form, thus completed, shall be returned to the investigating institution.

If a right to benefits is acquired taking into account only the periods of insurance or residence completed under the legislation administered by the institution of the second Member State, and if the amount of benefit corresponding to those periods can be determined without delay, whereas the calculation procedure referred to in subparagraph (c) requires an appreciably longer period of time, the form shall be returned to the investigating institution with the information referred to in subparagraphs (a) and (b); the information referred to in subparagraph (c) shall be forwarded to the investigating institution as soon as possible.

3. If two or more other institutions are involved, each one of those institutions shall complete the said form by indicating the periods of insurance or residence completed under the legislation which it administers, and shall return it to the investigating institution.

If a right to benefits is acquired taking into account only the periods of insurance or residence completed under the legislation administered by one or more of those institutions, and if the amount of benefit corresponding to those periods can be determined without delay, the investigating institution shall be simultaneously notified of that amount and of the periods of insurance or residence; if the determination of the said amount involves some delay, the investigating institution shall be notified of that amount as soon as it has been determined.

On receipt of all the forms giving information concerning periods of insurance or residence and, where appropriate, the amount or amounts due under the legislation of one or more of the Member States concerned, the investigating institution shall forward a copy of the forms thus completed to each of the institutions concerned which shall specify thereon the theoretical amount and the actual amount of the benefits, calculated in accordance with the provisions of Article 46(2) of the Regulation, and shall return the form to the investigating institution.

4. As soon as the investigating institution, upon receipt of the information referred to in paragraphs 2 or 3, establishes the fact that the provisions of Article 40(2) or 48(2) or (3) of the Regulation should be applied, it shall inform the other institutions concerned accordingly.

5. In the case provided for in Article 37(d) of the implementing Regulation, the institutions of the Member States to whose legislation the claimant has been subject but to which he has applied for postponement of the award of the benefits shall enter on the form provided for in Article 42(1) of the implementing Regulation only the periods of insurance or residence completed by the claimant under the legislation which they administer.

Article 44

Institution empowered to take a decision relating to the degree of invalidity

1. Subject to the provisions of paragraphs 2 and 3, only the investigating institution shall be empowered to take the decision referred to in Article 40(4) of the Regulation concerning the degree of invalidity of the claimant. It shall take such a decision as soon as it is in a position to determine whether, taking account, where appropriate, of the provisions of Article 45 of the Regulation, the conditions for entitlement fixed by the legislation which it administers are fulfilled. It shall notify such decision forthwith to the other institutions concerned.

3.395

2. If, taking account of the provisions of Article 45 of the Regulation, the conditions for entitlement, other than those relating to the degree of invalidity, laid down by the legislation administered by the investigating institution are not fulfilled, that institution shall immediately notify the competent institution in respect of invalidity of the other Member State to whose legislation the employed or self-employed person was last subject.

This institution shall, if the conditions for entitlement laid down by the legislation which it administers are fulfilled, be empowered to take the decision relating to the degree of invalidity of the claimant; it shall forthwith notify that decision to the other institutions concerned.

3. Where necessary, the matter may have to be referred back, under the same conditions, to the competent institution in respect of invalidity of the Member State to whose legislation the employed or self-employed person was first subject.

Article 45

Provisional payment of benefits and advance payments of benefits

3.396

1. If the investigating institution establishes that the claimant is entitled to benefits under the legislation which it administers without having recourse to periods of insurance or residence completed under the legislation of other Member States, it shall pay such benefits immediately on a provisional basis.

2. If the claimant is not entitled to benefits under paragraph 1 but, from information supplied to the investigating institution pursuant to Article 43(2) or (3) of the implementing Regulation, it transpires that a right to benefits is acquired under the legislation of another Member State taking into account only the periods of insurance or residence completed under that legislation, the institution which administers the said legislation shall pay such benefits on a provisional basis as soon as the investigating institution has informed it of its obligation to do so.

3. If, in the case referred to in paragraph 2, a right to benefits is acquired under the legislation of more than one Member State, taking into account only those periods of insurance or residence completed under each one of those legislations, the payment of benefits on a provisional basis shall be the responsibility of the institution which in the first place informed the investigating institution of the existence of such a right; it shall be the duty of the investigating institution to inform the other institutions concerned.

4. The institution required to pay benefits under paragraph 1, 2 or 3 shall forthwith inform the claimant of the fact, drawing his attention explicitly to the provisional nature of the measure taken and to the fact that is not open to appeal.

5. If no benefit is payable to the claimant on a provisional basis under paragraph 1, 2 or 3, but it transpires from information received that a right is acquired under Article 46(2) of the Regulation, the investigating institution shall pay him an appropriate recoverable advance, the amount of which shall be as close as possible to the amount he will probably be awarded under Article 46(2) of the Regulation.

6. Two Member States or the competent authorities or those member States may agree to apply other methods of payment of benefits on provisional basis in cases where only the institutions of those States are concerned. Any such agreements which are concluded on this subject shall be notified to the Administrative Commission.

Article 46

Amounts due for periods of voluntary insurance or optional continued insurance, which must not be taken into consideration under Article 15(1)(b) of the implementing Regulation.

For the calculation of the theoretical amount and of the actual amount of the benefit in accordance with Article 46(2)(a) and (b) of the Regulation, the rules laid down in Article 15(1)(b), (c) and (d) of the implementing Regulation shall be applicable.

3.397

The amount actually due, calculated in accordance with Article 46(2) of the Regulation, shall be increased by the amount which corresponds to the periods of voluntary or optional continued insurance, which have not been taken into account under Article 15(1)(b) of the implementing Regulation. This increase shall be calculated in accordance with the provisions of the Member State's legislation under which the periods of voluntary insurance or of optional continued insurance have been completed.

The comparison referred to in Article 46(3) of the Regulation must be made bearing the aforesaid increase in mind.

Article 47

Calculation of the amounts due corresponding to the periods of voluntary or optional continued insurance

In accordance with the legislation it applies, the institution of each Member State shall calculate the amount corresponding to the periods of voluntary or optional continued insurance which, under Article 46a(3)(c) of the Regulation, is not subject to the provisions for withdrawal, reduction or suspension of another Member State.

3.398

Article 48

Notification to the claimant of the decisions of the institutions

1. The final decision taken by each of the institutions concerned shall be notified to the investigating institution. Each of these decisions must specify the grounds and time-limits for appeal provided for by the legislation in question. When all these decisions have been received, the investigating institution shall communicate them to the claimant in his own language by means of a summarized statement to which the aforesaid decisions shall be appended. Periods allowed for appeals shall commence only on the date of receipt of the summarized statement by the claimant.

3.399

2. On dispatch to the claimant of the summarized statement provided for in paragraph 1, the investigating institution shall simultaneously forward a copy to each one of the institutions concerned, enclosing with it a copy of the decisions of the other institutions.

GENERAL NOTE

See *BH v SSWP* [2009] UKUT 95 (AAC).

Article 49

Recalculation of benefits

3.400   **1.** For the purpose of implementing Article 43(3) and (4), Article 49(2) and (3) and Article 51(2) of the Regulation, the provisions of Article 45 of the implementing Regulation shall apply mutatis mutandis.

2. In the event of recalculation, withdrawal or suspension of a benefit, the institution which has taken such a decision shall immediately notify the person concerned and each of the institutions on which the person concerned has a claim, if necessary through the good offices of the investigating institution. The decision must specify the grounds and time-limits for appeal provided for by the legislation in question. Periods allowed for appeals shall commence only on the date of receipt of the decision by the person concerned.

Article 50

Measures designed to accelerate the award of benefits

3.401   **1.** (a)   (i) Where an employed or self-employed person who is a national of one Member State becomes subject to the legislation of another Member State, the competent institution in respect of pensions of the latter Member State shall, using all the means at its disposal and at the time of registration of the person concerned, forward to the body designated by the competent authority of that same Member State, all information relating to the identification of the person concerned and the name of the said competent institution and the insurance number allotted by the latter.

(ii) Moreover, the competent institution referred to in subparagraph (i) shall also, as far as possible, forward to the body designated under the provisions of subparagraph (i) any other information which may facilitate and accelerate the award of the pensions.

(iii) Such information shall be forwarded, under conditions fixed by the Administrative Commission, to the body designated by the competent authority of the Member State concerned.

(iv) For the implementation of the provisions of subparagraphs (i), (ii) and (iii), stateless persons and refugees shall be deemed to be nationals of the member State to whose legislation they were first subject.

(b) The institutions concerned shall, at the request of the person concerned or of the institution with which he is currently insured, draw up his insurance history starting not later than one year before the date on which he will reach pensionable age.

2. The Administrative Commission shall fix the methods for implementing the provisions of paragraph 1.

RELEVANT DECISIONS OF THE ADMINISTRATIVE COMMISSION

Decision No 117 of 7 July 1982 concerning the conditions for implementing art.50(1)(a) of Council Regulation (EEC) No 574/72 of 21 March 1972, [1983] OJ C238/3.

Article 50

Decision No 118 of 20 April 1983 concerning the conditions for implementing Article 50(1)(b) of Council Regulation (EEC) No 574/72 of 21 March 1972, [1983] OJ 306/2.

Decision No 192 of 29 October 2003 concerning the conditions for implementing Article 50(1)(b) of Council Regulation (EEC) No 574/72, [2004] OJ L104/114.

ADMINISTRATIVE CHECKS AND MEDICAL EXAMINATIONS

Article 51

1. When a person in receipt of benefits, in particular:

(a) invalidity benefits;

(b) old-age benefits awarded in the event of unfitness for work;

(c) old-age benefits awarded to elderly unemployed persons;

(d) old-age benefits awarded in the event of cessation of a professional or trade activity;

(e) survivors' benefits awarded in the event of invalidity or unfitness for work;

(f) benefits awarded on condition that the means of the recipient do not exceed a prescribed limit,

is staying or residing in the territory of a Member State other than the State in which the institution responsible for payment is situated, administrative checks and medical examinations shall be carried out, at the request of that institution, by the institution of the place of stay or residence of the recipient in accordance with the procedures laid down by the legislation administered by the latter institution. The institution responsible for payment shall, however, reserve the right to have the recipient examined by a doctor of its own choice.

2. If it is established that the recipient referred to in paragraph 1 is employed or self-employed or has means in excess of the prescribed limit while receiving benefits, the institution of the place of stay or residence shall send a report to the institution responsible for payment which has requested the check or examination. This report shall indicate in particular the nature of the employment or self-employment pursued by the person concerned, the amount of earnings or means which he has had during the last complete quarter, the normal earnings obtained in the same area by an employed person or a self-employed person at the same level as the person concerned in the occupation which he followed before becoming an invalid over a reference period to be determined by the institution responsible for payment and, where appropriate, the opinion of a medical expert on the state of health of the person concerned.

3.402

Article 52

When, after suspension of the benefits which he was receiving, the person concerned recovers his right to benefits whilst residing in the territory of a Member State other than the competent State, the institutions concerned shall exchange all relevant information with a view to the resumption of the provision of the said benefits.

3.403

PAYMENT OF BENEFITS

Article 53

Method of payment of benefits

3.404   *Omitted*

Article 54

Notification to the paying body of the detailed schedule of payments to be made

3.405   *Omitted*

Article 55

Payment of amounts due into the account of the paying body

3.406   *Omitted*

Article 56

Payment of amounts due by the paying body to persons entitled to benefits

3.407   *Omitted*

Article 57

Settlement of accounts in respect of the payment referred to in Article 56 of the implementing Regulation

3.408   *Omitted*

Article 58

Recovery of expenses incurred in the payment of benefits

3.409   *Omitted*

Article 59

Notification of transfer of residence of the person entitled to benefits

3.410   When a person entitled to benefits due under the legislation of one or more Member States transfers his residence from the territory of one State to that of another State, he shall notify this fact to the institution or institutions responsible for the payment of such benefits and to the paying body.

CHAPTER 4

ACCIDENTS AT WORK AND OCCUPATIONAL DISEASES

IMPLEMENTATION OF ARTICLES 52 AND 53 OF THE REGULATION

Article 60

Benefits in kind in the case of residence in a Member State other than the competent State

1. In order to receive benefits in kind under Article 52(a) of the Regulation, 3.411 an employed or self-employed person shall submit to the institution of the place of residence a certified statement testifying that he is entitled to such benefits in kind. This certified statement, based upon information supplied by the employer, where appropriate, shall be issued by the competent institution. Moreover, if the legislation of the competent State so provides, the employed or self-employed person shall submit to the institution of the place of residence a receipt from the competent institution of notification of an accident at work or of an occupational disease. If the person concerned does not submit such documents, the institution of the place of residence shall obtain them from the competent institution and, pending their arrival, it shall grant him the benefits in kind under sickness insurance, provided that he satisfies the conditions for entitlement thereto.

2. That certified statement shall remain valid until the institution of the place of residence receives notification of its cancellation.

However, when the said certified statement has been issued by a French institution, it shall be valid only for a year following the date of its issue, and must be renewed every year.

3. If the person concerned is a seasonal worker, the certified statement referred to in paragraph 1 shall be valid for the whole of the expected duration of the seasonal work unless, in the meanwhile, the competent institution notifies the institution of the place of residence of its cancellation.

4. Upon each application for benefits in kind, the person concerned shall submit the supporting documents for the granting of benefits in kind under the legislation of the Member State in whose territory he resides.

5. In the event of hospitalization the institution of the place of residence shall, within three days of becoming aware of the fact, notify the competent institution of the date of entry into hospital, the probable duration of hospitalization and the date of leaving hospital.

6. The institution of the place of residence shall notify the competent institution in advance of any decision relating to the granting of benefits in kind where the likely or actual cost exceeds a lump sum which is fixed and periodically reviewed by the Administrative Commission.

The competent institution shall have 15 days from the day on which such information is sent within which to raise any objection and to state the reasons on which such objection is based; if, at the end of that period, no such objection has been raised, the institution of the place of residence shall grant the benefits in kind. Where such benefits in kind have to be granted in a case of extreme urgency, the institution of the place of residence shall forthwith inform the competent institution thereof.

7. The person concerned shall inform the institution of the place of residence of any change in his situation which is likely to alter his entitlement to benefits in kind, in particular any cessation or change of employment or self-employment or any transfer of residence or stay. Likewise, should the person concerned cease to be insured or cease to be entitled to benefits in kind, the competent institution shall inform the institution of the place of residence accordingly. The institution of the place of residence may, at any time, request the competent institution to supply it with any information relating to the insurance of the person concerned or to his entitlement to benefits in kind.

8. In the case of frontier workers, medicinal products, bandages, spectacles and small appliances may be issued, and laboratory analyses and tests carried out, only in the territory of the Member State in which they were prescribed in accordance with the provisions of the legislation of that Member State.

9. Two or more Member State or the competent authorities of these Member States may, having received the opinion of the Administrative Commission, agree on other implementing provisions.

RELEVANT DECISIONS OF THE ADMINISTRATIVE COMMISSION

Decision No 116 of 15 December 1982 concerning the granting of benefits in kind provided for in art.17(7) and art.60(6) of reg.574/72 and the concepts of urgency within the meaning of art.20 of reg.1408/71 and of extreme urgency within the meaning of arts 17(7) and 60(6) of reg.574/72, [1983] OJ C193/8.

Decision No 133 of 2 July 1987 concerning the application of art.17(7) and 60(6) of Council Regulation (EEC) No 574/72, [1987] OJ C284/3.

Decision No 135 of 1 July 1987 concerning the granting of benefits in kind provided for in art.17(7) and art.60(6) of reg.574/72 and the concepts of urgency within the meaning of art.20 of reg.1408/71 and of extreme urgency within the meaning of arts 17(7) and 60(6) of reg.574/72, [1988] OJ C64/5.

Article 61

Cash benefits other than pensions in the case of residence in a Member State other than the competent State

3.412   **1.** In order to receiver cash benefits other than pensions under Article 52(b) of the Regulation, an employed or self-employed person shall, within three days of commencement of the incapacity for work, apply to the institution of the place of residence by submitting a notification of having ceased work or, if the legislation administered by the competent institution or by the institution of the place of residence so provides, a certificate of incapacity for work issued by the doctor providing treatment for the person concerned.

2. If the doctors providing treatment in the country of residence do not issue certificates of incapacity for work, the person concerned shall apply directly to the institution of the place of residence within the time limit fixed by the legislation which it administers.

The institution shall immediately have the incapacity for work medically confirmed and the certificate referred to in paragraph 1 drawn up. Such certificate shall state the probable duration of the incapacity and shall be forwarded to the competent institution forthwith.

3. In case where paragraph 2 does not apply, the institution of the place of residence shall, as soon as possible and in any event within the three days following the date on which the person concerned applied to it, have him medically examined as if he were insured with that institution. The report of the examining doctor shall indicate, in particular, the probable duration of the incapacity for work, and shall be forwarded to the competent institution of the place of residence within the three days following the date of the examination.

4. The institution of the place of residence shall subsequently carry out any necessary administrative checks or medical examinations of the person concerned as if he were insured with that institution. As soon as it establishes that he is fit to resume work it shall forthwith notify the person concerned and the competent institution accordingly stating the date on which the incapacity for work ceased. Without prejudice to the provisions of paragraph 6, the notification to the person concerned shall be treated as a decision taken on behalf of the competent institution.

5. In all cases, the competent institution shall reserve the right to have the person concerned examined by a doctor of its own choice.

6. If the competent institution decides to withhold the cash benefits because the person concerned has not completed the formalities laid down by the legislation of the country of residence, or if it establishes that the person concerned is fit to resume work, it shall notify the person concerned of its decision and shall simultaneously send a copy of such decision to the institution of the place of residence.

7. When the person concerned resumes work, he shall notify the competent institution accordingly if such notification is required by the legislation administered by that institution.

8. The competent institution shall pay cash benefits by the appropriate method, in particular by international money order, and shall inform the institution of the place of residence and the person concerned accordingly. Where cash benefits are paid by the institution of the place of residence on behalf of the competent institution, the latter shall inform the person concerned of his rights and shall notify the institution of the place of residence of the amount of the cash benefits, the dates for payment and the maximum period during which they should be granted, in accordance with the legislation of the competent State.

9. Two or more Member States or the competent authorities of those Member States may, having received the opinion of the Administrative Commission, agree on other implementing provisions.

IMPLEMENTATION OF ARTICLE 55 OF THE REGULATION

Article 62

Benefits in kind in the case of a stay in a Member State other than the competent State

1. In order to receive benefits in kind, a person employed in international transport covered by Article 14(2)(a) of the Regulation who, in the course of his employment, goes to the territory of a Member State other than the competent State, shall, as soon as possible, submit to the institution of the place of stay a special certified statement issued by the employer or by

3.413

his agent during the current calendar month or during the two calendar months preceding its submission. Such certified statement shall state in particular the date from which the person concerned has been employed by the said employer and the name and address of the competent institution. If the person concerned has submitted such certified statement, he shall be presumed to have satisfied the conditions for acquisition of the right to benefits in kind. If the person concerned is unable to contact the institution of the place of stay before receiving medical treatment he shall nevertheless receive such treatment on presentation of the said certified statement as if he were insured with that institution.

2. The institution of the place of stay shall within three days inquire of the competent institution whether the person concerned satisfied the conditions for acquisition of the right to benefits in kind. The institution of the place of stay shall provide the benefits in kind until it receives a reply from the competent institution, but for not more than 30 days.

3. The competent institution shall send its reply to the institution of the place of stay within 10 days of the receipt of the request from that institution. If that reply is in the affirmative, the competent institution shall indicate, if necessary, the maximum period during which the benefits in kind may be granted, in accordance with the legislation which it administers, and the institution of the place of stay shall continue to provide the said benefits.

4. Benefits in kind provided by virtue of the presumption made in paragraph 1 shall be reimbursed as provided for in Article 36(1) of the Regulation.

5. In place of the certified statement provided for in paragraph 1 the employed person referred to in that paragraph may submit to the institution of the place of stay a certified statement as provided for in paragraph 6.

6. In order to receive benefits in kind under Article 55(1)(a)(i) of the Regulation, except in cases where a presumption is made under paragraph 1, the employed or self-employed person shall submit to the institution of the place of stay a certified statement stating that he is entitled to benefits in kind. Such certified statement, which shall be issued by the competent institution, if possible before the person concerned leaves the territory of the Member State in which he resides, shall specify in particular, where necessary, the maximum period during which benefits in kind may be granted, in accordance with the legislation of the competent State. If the person concerned does not submit the said certified statement, the institution of the place of stay shall obtain it from the competent institution.

7. The provisions of Article 60(5), (6) and (9) of the implementing Regulation shall apply by analogy.

Article 63

Benefits in kind for employed or self-employed persons who transfer their residence or return to their country of residence, and for employed or self-employed persons authorized to go to another Member State for medical treatment

3.414   **1.** In order to receive benefits in kind under Article 55(1)(b)(i) of the Regulation, an employed or self-employed person shall submit to the institution of the place of residence a certified statement testifying that he is entitled to continue receiving the said benefits. This certified statement, which shall be issued by the competent institution, shall specify in particular, where necessary, the maximum period during which such benefits may continue to be provided, in accordance with the provisions of the legislation of the competent State. The certified statement may, at the request of the person concerned, be issued after his departure if, for reasons of force majeure, it cannot be draw up beforehand.

2. The provisions of Article 60(5), (6) and (9) of the implementing Regulation shall apply by analogy.

3. Paragraphs 1 and 2 shall apply by analogy in respect of the provision of benefits in kind in the case referred to in Article 55(1)(c)(i) of the Regulation.

Article 64

Cash benefits other than pensions in the case of a stay in a Member State other than the competent State

The provisions of Article 61 of the implementing Regulation shall apply by analogy in respect of the receipt of cash benefits, other than pensions, under Article 55(1)(a)(ii) of the Regulation.

3.415

However, without prejudice to the obligation to submit a certificate of incapacity for work, an employed or self-employed person who is staying in the territory of a Member State without pursuing any professional or trade activity there shall not be required to submit the notification of having ceased work referred to in Article 61(1) of the implementing Regulation.

IMPLEMENTATION OF ARTICLES 52 TO 56 OF THE REGULATION

Article 65

Declarations, investigations and exchange of information between institutions to an accident at work sustained in, or an occupational disease contracted in, a Member State other than the competent State

1. When an accident at work is sustained in, or an occupational disease is diagnosed for the first time in, the territory of a Member State other than the competent State, a declaration of the accident at work or occupational disease must be made in accordance with the provisions of the legislation of the competent State without prejudice to any legal provisions in force in the territory of the Member State in which the accident at work was sustained or in which the occupational disease was first diagnosed, and which shall in such a case remain applicable. This declaration shall be sent to the competent institution and a copy shall be sent to the institution of the place of residence or to the institution of the place of stay.

3.416

2. The institution of the Member State in whose territory the accident at work was sustained or in which the occupational disease was first diagnosed, shall forward to the competent institution, in duplicate, the medical certificate drawn up in that territory and any relevant information which the latter institution may request.

3. If, in the case of an accident sustained while travelling in the territory of a Member State other than the competent State, there are grounds for holding an enquiry in the territory of the first Member State, an investigator may be appointed for that purpose by the competent institution, which shall so inform the authorities of that Member State. Those authorities shall assist the said investigator, in particular by appointing a person to assist him in the consultation of official reports and any other documents relating to the accident.

4. At the end of the treatment, a detailed report shall be forwarded to the competent institution together with medical certificates concerning the permanent consequences of the accident or disease, and in particular the present condition of the person concerned, and the recovery from the injuries or their consolidation. The relevant fees shall be paid by the institution of the place of residence or the institution of the place of stay, as the case may be, in accordance with the rate applied by the institution, but shall be chargeable to the competent institution.

5. The competent institution shall, on request, notify the institution of the place of residence or the institution of the place of stay, as the case may be, of the decision determining the date of recovery from the injuries or their consolidation and, where appropriate, the decision relating to the granting of a pension.

Article 66

Disputes concerning the occupational nature of the accident or disease

3.417   **1.** When, in the cases referred to in Article 52 or 55(1) of the Regulation, the competent institution disputes the application of the legislation relating to accidents at work or occupational diseases, it shall forthwith notify that fact to the institution of the place of residence or institution of the place of stay which provided the benefits in kind; those benefits shall then be considered as coming under sickness insurance and shall continue to be provided thereunder upon presentation of the certificates or certified statements referred to in Articles 20 and 21 of the implementing Regulation.

2. When a final decision has been reached on this subject, the competent institution shall forthwith notify the fact to the institution of the place of residence or to the institution of the place of stay which provided the benefits in kind. Where the case is not one of an accident at work or an occupational disease that institution shall continue to provide the said benefits in kind under sickness insurance if the employed or self-employed person is entitled thereto. In other cases, the benefits in kind received by the person concerned under sickness insurance shall be considered as benefits for an accident at work or an occupational disease.

IMPLEMENTATION OF ARTICLE 57 OF THE REGULATION

Article 67

Procedure in the case of exposure to the risk of an occupational disease in several Member States

1. In the case covered by Article 57(1) of the Regulation, notification of the occupational disease shall be forwarded either to the competent institution in respect of occupational diseases of the Member State under whose legislation the person suffering from the disease last pursued an activity likely to cause the disease in question, or to the institution of the place of residence, which shall forward the notification to the said competent institution. 3.418

2. If the competent institution referred to in paragraph 1 ascertains that an activity which might cause the occupational disease in question was last pursued under the legislation of another Member State, it shall forward the notification and the accompanying documents to the corresponding institution of that Member State.

3. When the institution of the Member State under whose legislation the person suffering from the disease last pursued an activity which might cause the occupational disease in question ascertains that such person or his survivors do not satisfy the conditions of that legislation, taking into account the provisions of Article 57(2), (3) and (4) of the Regulation, the said institution shall:

    (a) forward, without delay, to the institution of the Member State under whose legislation the person suffering from the disease previously pursued an activity which might cause the disease in question, the notification and all accompanying documents, including the findings and reports of the medical examinations arranged by the first institution, and a copy of the decision referred to under (b);

    (b) simultaneously notify the person concerned of its decision, indicating in particular the reasons for the refusal of benefits, the grounds and time limits for appeal, and the date on which the file was forwarded to the institution referred to under (a).

4. Where necessary the case should be referred back, in accordance with the same procedure, to the corresponding institution of the Member State under whose legislation the person suffering from the disease first pursued the activity which might cause the occupational disease in question.

Article 68

Exchange of information between institutions in the event of an appeal against a decision to reject a claim—Payment of advances in the event of such an appeal

1. Where an appeal its lodged against a decision to reject a claim taken by the institution of one of the Member States under whose legislation the person suffering from the disease pursued an activity which might cause the 3.419

occupational disease in question, that institution shall so inform the institution to which the notification has been forwarded in accordance with the procedure laid down in Article 67(3) of the implementing Regulation, and shall subsequently notify it of the final decision reached.

2. If the right to benefits was acquired under the legislation administered by the latter institution, taking into account the provisions of Article 57(2), (3) and (4) of the Regulation, that institution shall pay advances up to an amount to be determined, where necessary, after consultation with the institution against whose decision the appeal was lodged. The latter institution shall reimburse the amount of the advance paid if, as a result of the appeal, it is required to provide the benefits. That amount shall then be deducted from the total amount of the benefits due to the person concerned.

Article 69

Apportionment of the cost of cash benefits in cases of sclerogenic pneumoconiosis

3.420   The following rules shall apply for the implementation of Article 57(5) of the Regulation:

(a) the competent institution of the Member State under whose legislation cash benefits are granted pursuant to Article 57(1) of the Regulation (hereinafter called "the institution responsible for payment of cash benefits") shall use a form containing, in particular, a statement and summary of all periods of insurance (old-age insurance) or periods of residence completed by the person suffering from the disease under the legislation of each one of the Member States concerned;

(b) the institution responsible for payment of cash benefits shall forward that form to all old-age insurance institutions of those Member States with which the person suffering from the disease was insured; each one of the said institutions shall enter on the form the periods of insurance (old-age insurance) or periods of residence completed under the legislation which it administers and shall return the form to the institution responsible for payment of cash benefits;

(c) the institution responsible for payment of cash benefits shall then apportion the costs between itself and the other competent institutions concerned; it shall notify the latter of such apportionment for their approval together with appropriate supporting evidence in particular as regards the total amount of cash benefits granted and the calculation of the percentages of the apportionment;

(d) to the end of each calendar year, the institution responsible for payment of cash benefits shall forward to each of the other competent institutions concerned a statement of cash benefits paid during the financial year under consideration, showing the amount due from each of them according to the apportionment provided for under (c); each one of those institutions shall refund the amount due to the institution responsible for payment of cash benefits as soon as possible, and within three months at the latest.

IMPLEMENTATION OF ARTICLE 58(3) OF THE REGULATION

Article 70

Certified statement relating to the members of the family to be taken into consideration when calculating cash benefits including pensions

1. In order to receive benefits under the provisions of Article 58(3) of the Regulation the claimant shall submit a certified statement relating to the members of his family who are residing in the territory of a Member State other than that in which the institution responsible for the award of cash benefits is situated.

This certified statement shall be issued by the sickness insurance institution of the place of residence of the member of the family or by another institution designated by the competent authority of the Member State in whose territory they are resident. The provisions of the second and third subparagraphs of Article 25(2) of the implementing Regulation shall apply by analogy.

In place of the certified statement provided for in the first subparagraph, the institution responsible for the award of cash benefits may require the claimant to produce recent civil status documents relating to member of his family who are residing in the territory of a Member State other than that in which the said institution is situated.

2. In the case referred to in paragraph 1, if the legislation administered by the institution concerned requires that the members of the family should live under the same roof as the claimant, the fact that the said member of the family who do not satisfy that condition are nevertheless mainly dependent on the claimant must be established by documents proving the regular transmission of part of the claimant's earnings.

IMPLEMENTATION OF ARTICLE 60 OF THE REGULATION

Article 71

Aggravation of an occupational disease

1. In the cases covered by Article 60(1) of the Regulation, the claimant shall supply the institution of the Member State from which he is claiming rights to benefits with all information relating to benefits previously granted in respect of the occupational disease in question. That institution may apply to any other institution which has previously been competent in order to obtain any information which it considers necessary.

2. In the case covered by Article 60(1) of the Regulation, the competent institution required to pay the cash benefits shall notify the other institution concerned, for its approval, of the amount of costs to be borne by the latter institution as a result of the aggravation, together with appropriate support-

3.421

3.422

ing evidence. At the end of each calendar year, the first institution shall send the second institution a statement of the cash benefits paid during the financial year in question, showing the amount due from the latter institution which shall make the refund to the first institution as soon as possible, and within three months at the latest.

3. In the case referred to in the first sentence of Article 60(2)(b) of the Regulation, the institution responsible for payment of cash benefits shall notify the competent institutions concerned, for their approval, of the changes made in the previous apportionment of costs together with the appropriate supporting evidence.

4. In the case referred to in the second sentence of Article 60(2)(b) of the Regulation, the provisions of paragraph 2 shall apply by analogy.

IMPLEMENTATION OF ARTICLE 61(5) AND (6) OF THE REGULATION

Article 72

Assessment of the degree of incapacity in the case of an accident at work sustained previously or subsequently or an occupational disease diagnosed previously or subsequently

3.423

1. In order to asses the degrees of incapacity, to establish a right to any benefit, or to determine the amount of such benefit in the cases referred to in Article 61(5) and (6) of the Regulation, a claimant shall supply the competent institution of the Member State to whose legislation he was subject at the time when the accident at work was sustained or the occupational disease was first diagnosed, with all information on previous or subsequent accidents at work sustained or occupational diseases contracted by him when he was subject to the legislation of any other Member State, whatever the degree of incapacity caused by those previous or subsequent cases.

2. In accordance with the legislation which it administers in respect of the acquisition of the right to benefit, and the determination of the amount of benefit, the competent institution shall take into account the degree of incapacity caused by those previous or subsequent cases.

3. The competent institution may apply to any other institution which was previously or subsequently competent to obtain any information which it considers necessary.

When a previous or a subsequent incapacity for work was caused by an accident sustained while the person concerned was subject to the legislation of a Member State which makes no distinction as to the origin of the incapacity for work, the competent institution in respect of a previous or subsequent incapacity for work or the body designated by the competent authority of the Member State concerned shall, at the request of the competent institution of another Member State, supply information on the degree of the previous or subsequent incapacity for work and, as far as possible, any information which would make it possible to determine whether the incapacity was the result of an accident at work within the meaning of the legislation administered by the institution of the second Member State. Where such is the case, the provisions of paragraph 2 shall apply by analogy.

IMPLEMENTATION OF ARTICLE 61(1) OF THE REGULATION

Article 73

Institutions to which workers in mines and similar undertakings may apply when staying or residing in a Member State other than the competent State

1. In the cases referred to in Article 62(1) of the Regulation and where, in the country of stay or residence, the benefits provided under the insurance scheme for accidents at work and occupational disease covering manual workers in the steel industry are equivalent to those provided under the special scheme for workers in mines and similar undertakings, workers belonging to the latter category may apply to the nearest institution in the territory of the Member State in which they are staying or residing specified in Annex 3 of the implementing Regulation, even if the latter is an institution of the scheme applicable to manual workers in the steel industry, which institution shall then provide such benefits.

2. Where the benefits provided under the special scheme for workers in mines and similar undertakings are more advantageous, such workers shall have the option of applying either to the institution responsible for the administration of that scheme, or to the nearest institution in the territory of the Member State in which they are staying or residing, which administers the scheme for manual workers in the steel industry. In the latter case the institution in question shall draw the attention of the person concerned to the fact that by applying to the institution responsible for the administration of the abovementioned special scheme, he will obtain more advantageous benefits; it must, furthermore, inform him of the name and address of such institution.

IMPLEMENTATION OF ARTICLE 62(2) OF THE REGULATION

Article 74

Taking account of the period during which benefits have already been provided by the institution of another Member State

For the purpose of Article 61(2) of the Regulation, the institution of a Member State called upon to provide benefits may request the institution of another Member State to supply it with information relating to the period during which the latter institution has already provided benefits for the same case of accident at work or occupational disease.

3.424

3.425

SUBMISSION AND INVESTIGATION OF PENSION CLAIMS, EXCLUDING
PENSIONS IN RESPECT OF OCCUPATIONAL DISEASES COVERED BY ARTICLE
57 OF THE REGULATION

Article 75

3.426   **1.** In order to receive a pension or supplementary allowance under the
legislation of a Member State, an employed or self-employed person or his
survivors residing in the territory of another Member State shall make a
claim either to the competent institution, or to the institution of the place of
residence, which shall forward such claim to the competent institution. The
submission of the claim shall be subject to the following rules:

(a) the claim must be accompanied by the required supporting documents and made on the form provided for by the legislation administered by the competent institution;

(b) the accuracy of the information supplied by the claimant must be
established by official documents attached to the claim form, or
confirmed by the competent bodies of the Member State in whose
territory the claimant resides.

2. The competent institution shall notify the claimant of its decisions
directly or through the liaison body of the competent State; it shall send a
copy of that decision to the liaison body of the Member State in whose territory the claimant resides.

ADMINISTRATIVE CHECKS AND MEDICAL EXAMINATIONS

Article 76

3.427   **1.** Administrative checks and medical examinations, including medical
examinations provided for in the event of pensions being reviewed, shall
be carried out at the request of the competent institution by the institution of the Member State in whose territory the person entitled to benefits
happens to be, in accordance with the procedures laid down by the legislation administered by the latter institution. The competent institution shall,
however, reserve the right to have the person entitled to benefits examined
by a doctor of its own choice.

2. Any person drawing a pension for himself or for an orphan shall inform
the institution responsible for payment of any change in his situation or in
that of the orphan which is likely to modify the pension rights.

PAYMENT OF PENSIONS

Article 77

3.428   Payment of pensions due from the institution of one Member State to
pensioners resident in the territory of another Member State shall be made
in accordance with the provisions of Articles 53 to 58 of the implementing
Regulation.

CHAPTER 5

DEATH GRANTS

IMPLEMENTATION OF ARTICLES 64, 65 AND 66 OF THE REGULATION

Article 78

Submission of a claim for a grant

In order to receive a death grant under the legislation of a Member State   3.429
other than the State in whose territory he resides, the claimant shall submit
his claim either to the competent institution or to the institution of the place
of residence.

The claim must be accompanied by the supporting documents required
by the legislation which the competent institution administers.

The accuracy of the information supplied by the claimant must be established by official documents attached to the claim or confirmed by the competent bodies of the Member State in whose territory the claimant resides.

Article 79

Certified statement of periods

1. In order to invoke the provisions of Article 64 of the Regulation, a   3.430
claimant shall submit to the competent institution a certified statement
specifying the periods of insurance or residence completed by the employed
or self-employed person under the legislation to which he was last subject.

2. This certified statement shall be issued, at the request of the claimant,
by the sickness insurance or the old-age insurance institution, as the case may
be, with which the employed or self-employed person was last insured. If the
claimant does not submit the said certified statement, the competent institution shall obtain it from one or other of the aforementioned institutions.

3. The provisions of paragraphs 1 and 2 shall apply by analogy if, in
order to satisfy the conditions of the legislation of the competent State, it is
necessary to take into account periods of insurance or residence previously
completed under the legislation of any other Member State.

CHAPTER 6

UNEMPLOYMENT BENEFITS

IMPLEMENTATION OF ARTICLE 67 OF THE REGULATION

Article 80

Certified statement of periods of insurance or employment

1. In order to invoke the provisions of Article 67(1), (2) or (4) of the   3.431
Regulation, the person concerned shall submit to the competent institution

a certified statement specifying the periods of insurance or employment completed previously as an employed person under the legislation to which he was last subject, together with any further information required by the legislation administered by that institution.

2. This certified statement shall be issued, at the request of the person concerned, either by the competent institution in respect of unemployment of the Member State to whose legislation he was last subject, or by another institution designated by the competent authority of the said Member State. If he does not submit the said certified statement, the competent institution shall obtain it from one or other of the aforementioned institutions.

3. The provisions of paragraphs 1 and 2 shall apply by analogy if, in order to satisfy the conditions of the legislation of the competent State, it is necessary to take into account periods of insurance or employment completed previously as an employed person under the legislation of any other Member State.

IMPLEMENTATION OF ARTICLE 68 OF THE REGULATION

Article 81

Certified statement for the calculation of benefits

3.432   Where the responsibility for the calculation of benefits rests upon an institution covered by Article 68(1) of the Regulation, and where a person has not pursued his last employment for at least four weeks in the territory of the Member State in which that institution is situated, he shall submit to the said institution a certified statement indicating the nature of the last employment pursued for at least four weeks in the territory of another Member State, and the branch of the economy in which that employment was pursued. If the person concerned does not submit this certified statement, the said institution shall obtain it either from the competent institution in respect of unemployment of the latter Member State with which he was last insured, or from another institution designated by the competent authority of that Member State.

Article 82

Certified statement relating to the members of the family to be taken into consideration for the calculation of benefits

3.433   **1.** In order to invoke the provisions of Article 68(2) of the Regulation, the person concerned shall submit to the competent institution a certified statement relating to the members of his family who are resident in the territory of a Member State other than the one in which the said institution is situated.

2. This certified statement shall be issued by the institution designated by the competent authority of the Member State in whose territory those members of the family reside. It must certify that the members of the family are not taken into consideration for the calculation of unemployment benefits due to another person under the legislation of the said Member State.

The certified statement shall be valid for the 12 months following the date of its issue. It may be renewed; in such case, it shall be valid from the date of its renewal. The person concerned shall immediately notify the competent institution of any occurrence necessitating an amendment to the said certified statement. Such amendment shall take effect from the date of such occurrence.

3. Where the institution issuing the certified statement referred to in paragraph 1 is not in a position to certify that the members of the family are not taken into consideration for the calculation of unemployment benefits due to another person under the legislation of the Member State in whose territory they reside, the person concerned shall, when submitting the certified statement to the competent institution, supplement the said certified statement by a declaration to that effect.

The provisions of the second subparagraph of paragraph 2 shall apply by analogy to that declaration.

IMPLEMENTATION OF ARTICLE 69 OF THE REGULATION

Article 83

Conditions and limits for the retention of the right to benefits when an unemployed person goes to another Member State

1. In order to retain the right to benefits, an unemployed person covered by Article 69(1) of the Regulation shall submit to the institution of the place to which he has gone a certified statement in which the competent institution shall certify that he is still entitled to benefits under the conditions laid down in paragraph 1(b) of the said Article. The competent institution shall specify in particular in this certified statement:

3.434

(a) the amount of benefit to be paid to the unemployed person under the legislation of the competent State;
(b) the date on which the unemployed person ceased to be available to the employment services of the competent State;
(c) the time limit under Article 69(1)(b) of the Regulation for registration as a person seeking work in the Member State to which the unemployed person has gone;
(d) the maximum period, in accordance with Article 69(1)(c) of the Regulation, during which the right to benefit may be retained;
(e) facts which might alter entitlement to benefit.

2. An unemployed person who intends to go to another Member State in order to seek employment there shall before his departure, apply for the certified statement referred to in paragraph 1. If the unemployed person does not submit the said certified statement, the institution of the place to which he has gone shall obtain it from the competent institution. The employment services of the competent State must ensure that the unemployed person has been informed of his obligations under Article 69 of the Regulation and under this Article.

3. The institution of the place to which the unemployed person has gone shall notify the competent institution of the date on which the unemployed person registered and the date on which payment of benefits was commenced and shall pay out the benefits of the competent State in accordance with the procedure provided for by the legislation of the Member State to which the unemployed person has gone.

The institution of the place to which the unemployed person has gone shall carry out a check or arrange for one to be carried out as if it were dealing with an unemployed person entitled to benefits under the legislation which it administers. It shall inform the competent institution of any occurrence coming within paragraph 1(e) above as soon as the same comes to its knowledge and, in cases where the benefit has to be suspended or withdrawn, it shall immediately discontinue payment of the benefit. The competent institution shall forthwith inform it to what extent, and from what date, the unemployed person's entitlement to benefit is affected by that fact.

Payment of benefits may only be resumed, where appropriate, after receipt of such information. Where the benefit has to be reduced, the institution of the place to which the unemployed person has gone shall continue to pay him a reduced amount of benefit, subject to adjustment, after receipt of the reply from the competent institution.

4. Two or more Member States or the competent authorities of those Member States may, having received the opinion of the Administrative Commission, agree on other implementing provisions.

IMPLEMENTATION OF ARTICLE 71 OF THE REGULATION

Article 84

Unemployed persons who were formerly employed and who, during their last employment, were residing in a Member State other than the competent State

3.435   **1.** In the cases referred to in Article 71(1)(a)(ii) and in the first sentence of Article 71(1)(b)(ii) of the Regulation, the institution of the place of residence shall be considered to be the competent institution, for the purposes of implementing the provisions of Article 80 of the implementing Regulation.

2. In order to claim benefits under the provisions of Article 71(1)(b)(ii) of the Regulation, an unemployed person who was formerly employed shall submit to the institution of his place of residence, in addition to the certified statement provided for in Article 80 of the implementing Regulation, a certified statement from the institution of the Member State to whose legislation he was last subject, indicating that he has no right to benefits under Article 69 of the Regulation.

3. For the purposes of implementing the provisions of Article 71(2) of the Regulation, the institution of the place of residence shall ask the competent institution for any information relating to the entitlements, from the latter institution, of the unemployed person who was formerly an employed person.

CHAPTER 7

FAMILY BENEFITS

IMPLEMENTATION OF ARTICLE 72 OF THE REGULATION

Article 85

Certified statement of periods of employment or self-employment

1. In order to invoke the provisions of Article 72 of the Regulation, a person shall submit to the competent institution a certified statement specifying the period of insurance, employment or self-employment completed under the legislation to which he was last subject.

2. That certified statement shall be issued, at the request of the person concerned, either by the competent institution in respect of family benefits of the Member State with which he was last insured, or by another institution designated by the competent authority of the said Member State. If he does not submit the said certified statement, the competent institution shall obtain it from one or other of the abovementioned institution unless the sickness insurance institution is able to forward him a copy of the certified statement provided for in Article 16(1) of the implementing Regulation.

3. The provisions of paragraphs 1 and 2 shall apply by analogy if, in order to satisfy the conditions of the legislation of the competent State, it is necessary to take into account periods of insurance, employment or self-employment completed previously under the legislation of any other Member State.

3.436

IMPLEMENTATION OF ARTICLES 73 AND 75(1) AND (2) OF THE REGULATION

Article 86

1. In order to receive family benefits under Article 73 of the Regulation, an employed person shall submit a claim to the competent institution, where necessary through his employer.

2. In support of his claim, the employed person shall submit a certificate relating to members of his family residing in the territory of a Member State other than that in which the competent institution is situated. Such certificate shall be issued, either by the authorities competent in civil status matters in the country of residence of those members of the family, or by the competent institution in respect of sickness insurance in the place of residence of those members of the family, or by another institution desig-

3.437

nated by the competent authority of the Member State in whose territory those members of the family reside. Such a certificate must be renewed every year.

3. Where the legislation of the competent State provides that the family benefits may or must be paid to a person other than the employed person, the latter shall also submit in support of his claim, information identifying the individual to whom the family benefits are to be paid in the country of residence (name, forename, full address).

4. The competent authorities of two or more Member States may agree on special procedures for the payment of family benefits, in particular with a view to facilitating the implementation of Article 75(1) and (2) of the Regulation. Such agreements shall be communicated to the Administrative Commission.

5. An employed person shall inform the competent institution where necessary through his employer:

— of any change in the situation of the members of his family which might alter entitlement to family benefits,

— of any change in the number of members of his family for whom family benefits are due,

— of any transfer of residence or stay of such members of the family,

— of any pursuit of a professional or trade activity by virtue of which family benefits are also due under the legislation of the Member State in whose territory the members of the family are resident.

Article 87

3.438   [. . .]

IMPLEMENTATION OF ARTICLE 74 OF THE REGULATION

Article 88

3.439   The provisions of Article 86 of the implementing Regulation shall apply by analogy to unemployed persons who where formerly employed or self-employed and who are covered by Article 74 of the Regulation.

Article 89

3.440   [. . .]

CHAPTER 8

BENEFITS FOR DEPENDENT CHILDREN OF PENSIONERS AND FOR ORPHANS

IMPLEMENTATION OF ARTICLES 77, 78 AND 79 OF THE REGULATION

Article 90

1. In order to receive benefits under Article 77 or 78 of the Regulation, a claimant shall submit a claim to the institution of his place of residence, in accordance with the procedures laid down by the legislation administered by that institution.   3.441

2. If, however, the claimant does not reside in the territory of the Member State in which the competent institution is situated, he may submit his claim either to the competent institution or to the institution of his place of residence, which shall then forward the claim to the competent institution, indicating the date on which it was submitted. The date shall be considered as the date of submission of the claim to the competent institution.

3. If the competent institution referred to in paragraph 2 finds that there is no entitlement under the legislation which it administers, it shall forward the claim forthwith, together with all necessary documents and information, to the institution of the Member State to whose legislation the employed or self-employed person was subject for the longest period of time.

Where necessary the matter may have to be referred back, under the same conditions, to the institution of the Member State under whose legislation the person concerned completed the shortest of his periods of insurance or residence.

4. The Administrative Commission shall, where necessary, lay down any supplementary procedures required for the submission of claims for benefits.

Article 91

1. Payment of benefits due under Article 77 or 78 of the Regulation shall be made in accordance with the provisions of Articles 53 to 58 of the implementing Regulation.   3.442

2. The competent authorities of the Member States shall, where necessary, designate the competent institution for paying benefits due under Article 77 or 78 of the Regulation.

Article 92

Any person to whom benefits are paid under Article 77 or 78 of the Regulation for a pensioner's children or for orphans, shall inform the institution responsible for the payment of such benefits: 3.443

— any change in the situation of the children or orphans that is likely to alter the entitlement to benefits,

— any modification in the number of children or orphans in respect of whom benefits are due,

— any transfer of residence of the children or orphans,

— of any pursuit of a professional or trade activity giving entitlement to family benefits or family allowances for such children or orphans.

TITLE V

FINANCIAL PROVISIONS

3.444 *Title V omitted.*

TITLE VI

MISCELLANEOUS PROVISIONS

Article 108

Proof of status of seasonal worker

3.445 In order to prove that he is a seasonal worker, the employed person covered by Article 1(c) of the Regulation shall be required to submit his contract of employment stamped by the employment services of the Member State in whose territory he has gone to work or has worked. If no seasonal employment contract is concluded in that Member State, the institution of the country of employment shall, where appropriate, issue, in the case of a claim for benefits, a certificate attesting that, on the basis of information supplied by the person concerned, the work which he is doing or has done is of a seasonal nature.

Article 109

Arrangement for payment of contributions

3.446 The employer who has no place of business in the Member State in whose territory the employed person is employed may agree with the latter that he shall assume the obligations of the employer with regard to the payment of contributions.

The employer shall notify the competent institution or, where necessary, the institution designated by the competent authority of the said Member State of any such arrangement.

Article 110

Mutual administrative aid relating to the recovery of benefits which were not due

If the institution of a Member State which provided benefits intends to take action against a person who has received benefits which were not due to him, the institution of the place of residence of such person, or the institution designated by the competent authority of the Member State in whose territory that person resides, shall lend its good offices to the first institution.

3.447

Article 111

Recovery by social security institutions of payments not due, and claims by assistance bodies

1. If, when awarding or reviewing benefits in respect of invalidity, old-age or death (pensions) pursuant to Chapter 3 of Title III of the Regulation, the institution of a Member State has paid to a recipient of benefits a sum in excess of that to which he is entitled, that institution may request the institution of any other Member State responsible for the payment of corresponding benefits to that recipient to deduct the amount overpaid from the arrears which it pays to the said recipient. The latter institution shall transfer the amount deducted to the creditor institution. Where the amount overpaid cannot be deducted from the arrears, the provisions of paragraph 2 shall apply.

3.448

2. When the institution of a Member State has paid to a recipient of benefits a sum in excess of that to which he is entitled that institution may, within the conditions and limits laid down by the legislation which it administers, request the institution of any other Member State responsible for the payment of benefits to that recipient to deduct the amount overpaid from the amounts which it pays to the said recipient. The latter institution shall make the deduction under the conditions and within the limits provided for such setting-off by the legislation which it administers, as if the sums had been overpaid by itself, and shall transfer the amount deducted to the creditor institution.

3. When a person to whom the Regulation applies has received assistance in the territory of a Member State during a period in which he was entitled to benefits under the legislation of another Member State, the body which gave the assistance may, if it is legally entitled to reclaim the benefits due to the said person, request the institution of any other Member State responsible for the payment of benefits in favour of that person to deduct the amount of the assistance paid from the amounts which the latter pays to the said person.

When a member of the family of a person to whom the Regulation applies has received assistance in the territory of a Member State during a period in which the said person was entitled to benefits under the legislation of another Member State in respect of the member of the family concerned, the body which gave the assistance may, if it is legally entitled to reclaim the benefits due to the said person in respect of the member of the family concerned, request the institution of any other Member State responsible for the payment of such benefits in favour of that person to deduct the amount of assistance paid from the amounts which the latter pays to the said person in respect of the member of the family concerned.

The institution responsible for payment shall make the deduction under the conditions and within the limits provided for such setting-off by the legislation which it administers, and shall transfer the amount deducted to the creditor body.

GENERAL NOTE

3.449   This is the provision dealing with recovery of overpayments as between EEA countries. Perhaps unsurprisingly, it has given rise to a number of Commissioners' decisions.

In *R(SB) 3/91* the Commissioner ruled that for art.111 to apply, it was not necessary for the other State's benefit to have been awarded under Regulation 1408/71. It sufficed that the claimant was a person to whom the personal scope of Regulation 1408/71 applied. This did not require the person to have been a migrant worker.

In *R(IS) 6/02* the Commissioner ruled, confirming *CIS/12082/1996*, that nothing in reg.1408/71 or reg.574/72 precluded the application of s.74(2) of the Administration Act to the circumstances of the case. Furthermore supplementary benefit and income support were not to be regarded as supplements to old age pensions under Art.46 of reg.1408/71; in so holding the Commissioner found that the benefit at issue in Case C-132/96 *Stinco* [1998] E.C.R. I-5225 could be distinguished. The Commissioner ruled:

> "In my judgment, a 'supplementary allowance' within Article 1(t) is one which has the specific connections with a specific social security benefit, as exemplified by the Italian supplement in *Stinco and Panfilo*. It does not extend to a general social benefit which may provide a practical supplement to recipients of specific social security benefits, but which provides an income to others in many different circumstances whose resources are inadequate for their needs." (para.23 of decision.)

In *Scrivner v Chief Adjudication Officer* [1990] 1 C.M.L.R. 637 reported as *R(SB) 1/91*, the Court of Appeal upheld the decision of the Commissioner to the effect that art.111(3) only applies where a member of the claimant's family receives a benefit in their own right, and not where the claimant receives an additional amount of benefit because he has a family.

Article 112

3.450   When an institution has made payments which are not due, either directly or through another institution, and when their recovery has become impossible, the amounts in question shall remain finally chargeable to the first institution, save where the payment which was not due is the result of fraud.

Article 113

Recovery of benefits in kind provided but not due to persons employed in international transport

3.451   1. If the right to benefits in kind is not recognized by the competent institution, the benefits in kind which have been provided to a person employed in international transport by the institution of the place of stay by virtue of the presumption referred to in Article 20(1) or 62(1) of the implementing Regulation, shall be refunded by the competent institution.

2. Expenses incurred by the institution of the place of stay in respect of any person employed in international transport who has not previously applied to the institution of the place of stay and is not entitled to benefits in kind but has nevertheless received benefits in kind upon presentation of the certified statement referred to in Article 20(1) or 62(1) of the implementing Regulation, shall be refunded by the institution shown as competent in the said certified statement or by any other institution designated for that purpose by the competent authority of the Member State concerned.

3. The competent institution or, in the case referred to in paragraph 2, the institution shown as competent or the institution designated for that purpose shall debit the recipient of benefits with the value of the benefits in kind which were provided but were not due to him. The said institution shall notify these debits to the Audit Board referred to in Article 101(3) of the implementing Regulation which shall draw up a statement thereof.

Article 114

Provisional payments of benefits in cases of dispute over the legislation to be applied or the institution which should provide benefits

In the case of a dispute between the institutions or competent authorities of two or more Member States, either as to which legislation should apply under Title II of the Regulation, or as to which institution should provide the benefits, the person concerned who could claim benefits if there were no dispute shall provisionally receive the benefits provided for by the legislation administered by the institution of the place of residence or, if the person concerned does not reside in the territory of one of the Member States concerned, the benefits provided for by the legislation administered by the institution to which his claim was submitted in the first instance.

3.452

Article 115

Procedures for medical examinations carried out in a Member State other than the competent State

The institution of the place of stay or residence which is required under Article 87 of the Regulation to carry out a medical examination, shall act in accordance with the procedures laid down by the legislation which it administers.

In the absence of such procedures, it shall apply to the competent institution for information on the procedures to be applied.

3.453

Article 116

Agreements relating to the recovery of contributions

3.454   **1.** Agreements concluded pursuant to Article 92(2) of the Regulation shall be entered in Annex 5 to the implementing Regulation.

2. Agreements concluded for the implementation of Article 51 of the Regulation shall continue to apply provided they are included in Annex 5 to the implementing Regulation.

[¹ TITLE VIA

PROVISIONS GOVERNING ELECTRONIC DATA PROCESSING]

3.455   *Title VIa omitted.*

AMENDMENT

1. Regulation 1290/97/EC, [1997] OJ L176/1 (October 4, 1997).

TITLE VII

TRANSITIONAL AND FINAL PROVISIONS

Article 118

Transitional provisions relating to pensions for employed persons

3.456   **1.** Where the contingency arises before 1 October 1972 or before the date of implementation of the implementing Regulation in the territory of the Member State concerned and the claim for pension has not been awarded before that date, such claim shall give rise to a double award, in as much as benefits must be granted, pursuant to such contingency, for a period prior to that date:

    (a) for the period prior to 1 October 1972 or to the date of implementation of the implementing Regulation in the territory of the Member State concerned, in accordance with the Regulation or agreements in force between the Member States concerned.

    (b) for the period commencing on 1 October 1972 or on the date of implementation of the implementing Regulation in the territory of the Member State concerned, in accordance with the Regulation.

However, if the amount calculated pursuant to the provisions referred to under (a) is greater than that calculated pursuant to the provisions referred to under (b), the person concerned shall continue to be entitled to the amount calculated pursuant to the provisions referred to under (a).

Article 118

2. A claim for invalidity, old age or survivors' benefits submitted to an institution of a Member State from 1 October 1972 or from the date of implementation of the implementing Regulation in the territory of the Member State concerned, or in a part of the territory of that State, shall automatically necessitate the reassessment of the benefits which have been awarded for the same contingency prior to that date by the institution or institutions of one or more of the other Member States, in accordance with the Regulation; such reassessment may not give rise to any reduction in the amount of the benefit awarded.

Article 119

Transitional provisions relating to pensions for self-employed persons

1. Where the contingency arises before 1 July 1982 or before the date of implementation of the implementing Regulation in the territory of the Member State concerned and the claim for pension has not been awarded before that date, such claim shall give rise to a double award, in as much as benefits must be granted, pursuant to such contingency, for a period prior to that date:

3.457

  (a) for the period prior to 1 July 1982 or to the date of implementation of the implementing Regulation in the territory of the Member State concerned, in accordance with the Regulation or agreements in force between the Member States concerned before that date;

  (b) for the period commencing on 1 July 1982 or on the date of implementation of the implementing Regulation in the territory of the Member State concerned, in accordance with the Regulation.

However, if the amount calculated pursuant to the provisions referred to under (a) is greater than that calculated pursuant to the provisions referred to under (b), the person concerned shall continue to be entitled to the amount calculated pursuant to the provisions referred to under (a).

2. A claim for invalidity, old age or survivors' benefits submitted to the institution of a Member State from 1 July 1982 or from the date of implementation of the implementing Regulation in the territory of the Member State concerned, or in a part of the territory of that State, shall automatically necessitate the reassessment of the benefits that have already been awarded for the same contingency prior to that date by the institution or institutions of one or more of the other Member States, in accordance with the Regulation; such reassessment may not give rise to any reduction in the amount of benefit awarded.

Article 119a

Transitional provisions relating to pensions for the purpose of applying the last part of Article 15(1)(a) of the implementing Regulation

1. Where the date on which the contingency arises precedes 1 January 1987 and where the claim for a pension has not yet resulted in an award before that date, such claim shall, in as much as benefits must be granted,

3.458

pursuant to such contingency, for a period prior to the last-mentioned date, give rise to a double award:

    (a) for the period prior to 1 January 1987, in accordance with the provisions of the Regulation or of agreements in force between the Member States concerned;

    (b) for the period commencing on 1 January 1987, in accordance with the provisions of the Regulation.

If, however, the amount calculated in pursuance of the provisions referred to under (a) is greater than that calculated in pursuance of the provisions referred to under (b), the person concerned shall continue to be entitled to the amount calculated in pursuance of the provisions referred to under (a).

2. A claim for invalidity, old-age or survivors' benefits submitted to an institution of a Member State from 1 January 1987 shall automatically necessitate the reassessment, in accordance with the provisions of the Regulation, of the benefits which have been awarded for the same contingency prior to that date by the institution or institutions of one or more of the other Member States, without prejudice to the provisions of Article 3.

3. The rights of the persons concerned who obtained the award of pensions prior to 1 January 1987 in the territory of the Member State in question may be revised at their request in the light of the provisions of Council Regulation (EEC) No 3811/86.[1]

4. If the request referred to in paragraph 3 is submitted within one year following 1 January 1987, entitlement to rights under Regulation (EEC) No 3811/86 shall be acquired from 1 January 1987 or from the date of the entitlement to a pension where the last-mentioned date is subsequent to 1 January 1987; in such case the provisions of the legislation of any Member State with regard to the withdrawal or limitation of rights may not be relied upon as against the persons concerned.

5. If the request referred to in paragraph 3 is submitted after expiry of the period of one year following 1 January 1987, entitlement to rights acquired under Regulation (EEC) No 3811/86 which have not been withdrawn or in respect of which the period of limitation has not been exceeded shall be acquired from the date on which the request is submitted, unless more favourable provisions of the legislation of any of the Member States are applicable.

FOOTNOTE

    1. OJ NO L355, 16.12.1986, p.5.

[1*Article 120*

Persons who study or receive vocational training

3.459   The provisions of this Regulation, with the exception of Article 10 and 10a, shall apply, where appropriate, by analogy to students.]

AMENDMENT

    1. Regulation 307/99/EC, [1999] OJ L307/99 (May 1, 1999).

Article 121

Supplementary implementing agreements

1. Two or more Member States or the competent authorities of those   3.460
Member States may, where necessary, conclude agreements designed to
supplement the administrative procedure for implementing the Regulation.
Such agreements are listed in Annex 5 to the implementing Regulation.

2. Agreements similar to those referred to in paragraph 1, which are in
force on the day preceding 1 October 1972, shall continue to apply provided they are included in Annex 5 to the implementing Regulation.

[¹*Article 122*

Special provisions concerning amendment of the Annexes

The Annexes to the implementing Regulation may be amended by a   3.461
Commission Regulation at the request of the Member State or Member
States concerned or their competent authorities, and after the unanimous
opinion of the Administrative Commission has been obtained.]

AMENDMENT

1. Regulation 1399/99/EC, [1999] OJ L164/1.

ANNEX 1

COMPETENT AUTHORITIES

*(Article 1(1) of the Regulation, and Articles 4(1) and 122 of the implementing
Regulation)*

** *Section numbering re-ordered by Annex II of the Treaty of Accession with*   3.462
effect from May 1, 2004.
Only provisions concerning the United Kingdom have been reproduced.

**[³AA.] UNITED KINGDOM

[¹ 1. Secretary of State for Work and Pensions, London]

1a. Secretary of State for Health, London

[² 1b. The Commissioners of the Inland Revenue or their official representative, London]

2. Secretary of State for Scotland, Edinburgh

3. Secretary of State for Wales, Cardiff

[¹ 4. Department for Social Development, Belfast; Department of Health and Social Services and Public Safety, Belfast]

[² 5. Principal Secretary, Social Affairs, Gibraltar.]

[² 6. Chief Executive of the Gibraltar Health Authority.]

AMENDMENTS

1. Regulation 185/2003/EC, [2003] OJ L271/3 (November 11, 2003).
2. Regulation 89/2001/EC, [2001] OJ L14/16 (February 6, 2001).
3. Regulation 1791/2006/EC [2006] OJ L363/1 (January 1, 2007).

ANNEX 2

3.463   ** *Section numbering re-ordered by Annex II of the Treaty of Accession with effect from May 1, 2004.*
Only provisions concerning the United Kingdom have been reproduced.

COMPETENT INSTITUTIONS

(Article 1(o) of the Regulation and Article 4(2) of the implementing Regulation)

**[¹AA.] UNITED KINGDOM

1. Benefits in kind

—Great Britain and Northern Ireland	Authorities which grant National Health Service Benefits
—Gibraltar	Gibraltar Health Authority

2. Cash benefits

—Great Britain	Department for Work and Pensions, London
—Northern Ireland	Department for Social Development, Belfast
—Gibraltar	Principal Secretary, Social Affairs, Gibraltar

3. Family benefits

—Great Britain	Inland Revenue, Child Benefit Office, Newcastle upon Tyne
	Inland Revenue, Tax Credit Office, Preston
—Northern Ireland	Inland Revenue, Tax Credit Office, Belfast
	Inland Revenue, Child Benefit Office (NI), Belfast

—Gibraltar   Principal Secretary, Social Affairs,
                              Gibraltar

AMENDMENTS

1. Regulation 1791/2006/EC [2006] OJ L363/1 (January 1, 2007).

ANNEX 3

INSTITUTIONS OF THE PLACE OF RESIDENCE AND INSTITUTIONS OF THE
PLACE OF STAY

*(Article 1(p) of the Regulation and Article 4(3) of the implementing
Regulation)*

** *Section numbering re-ordered by Annex II of the Treaty of Accession with*   3.464
effect from May 1, 2004.
Only provisions concerning the United Kingdom have been reproduced.

**[¹AA.] UNITED KINGDOM

1. Benefits in kind

—Great Britain and   Authorities which grant National
  Northern Ireland   Health Service Benefits
—Gibraltar   Gibraltar Health Authority, 17 Johnstone's
                               Passage, Gibraltar

2. Cash benefits (except for family benefits)

—Great Britain   Department for Work and Pensions,
                               The Pension Service, International Pension
                               Centre, Tyneview Park, Newcastle upon
                               Tyne NE98 1BA
—Northern Ireland   Department for Social Development,
                               Northern Ireland Social Security Agency,
                               Network Support Branch, Overseas Benefit
                               Unit, Block 2, Stormont Estate, Belfast
                               BT4 3SJ
—Gibraltar   Department of Social Services,
                               23 Mackintosh Square, Gibraltar

3. Family benefits

For the purpose of applying Articles 73 and 74 of the Regulation:

—Great Britain   Inland Revenue, Child Benefit Office
                               of Great Britain, Newcastle upon Tyne
                               NE88 1AA
—Northern Ireland   Inland Revenue, Tax Credit Office,

Dorchester House, Great Victoria Street,
Belfast BT2 7WF
Inland Revenue, Child Benefit Office (NI),
Windsor House, 9-15 Bedford Street,
Belfast BT2 7UW

—Gibraltar

Department of Social Services,
23 Mackintosh Square, Gibraltar

AMENDMENT

1. Regulation 1791/2006/EC [2006] OJ L363/1 (January 1, 2007).

ANNEX 4

LIASION BODIES

(Articles 3(1), 4(4) and 122 of the implementing Regulation)

3.465   ** *Section numbering re-ordered by Annex II of the Treaty of Accession with effect from May 1, 2004.*
Only provisions concerning the United Kingdom have been reproduced.

**[1AA.] UNITED KINGDOM

Great Britain:

(a) contributions and benefits in kind for posted workers

Inland Revenue, Centre for Non Residents, Benton Park View, Newcastle upon Tyne NE98 1ZZ

(b) all other questions

Department for Work and Pensions, The Pension Service, International Pension Centre, Tyneview Park, Newcastle upon Tyne NE98 1BA

Northern Ireland:

(a) contributions and benefits in kind for posted workers

Inland Revenue, Centre for Non Residents, Benton Park View, Newcastle upon Tyne NE98 1ZZ

(b) all other questions

Department for Social Development, Northern Ireland Social Security Agency, Network Support Branch, Overseas Benefits Unit, Block 2, Stormont Estate, Belfast BT4 3SJ

Gibraltar:

Department for Work and Pensions, The Pension Centre, International Pensions Centre, Tyneview Park, Newcastle upon Tyne NE98 1BA

AMENDMENT

1. Regulation 1791/2006/EC [2006] OJ L363/1 (January 1, 2007).

ANNEX 5

IMPLEMENTING PROVISIONS OF BILATERAL CONVENTIONS WHICH REMAIN IN FORCE

(Articles 4(5), 5, 53(3), 104, 105(2), 116, 121 and 122 of the implementing Regulation)

** *Section numbering re-ordered by Annex II of the Treaty of Accession with effect from May 1, 2004.*
Only provisions concerning the United Kingdom have been reproduced.

General observations

I. Whenever the provisions set out in this Annex refer to the provisions of Conventions or of Regulations No 3, No 4 or No 36/63/EEC, those references shall be replaced by references to the corresponding provisions of the Regulation or of the implementing Regulation, unless the provisions of those Conventions remain in force by virtue of their inclusion in Annex II to the Regulation.

II. The denunciation clause contained in a Convention, certain provisions of which are included in this Annex, shall remain in force in respect of the said provisions.

3.466

**[³26.] BELGIUM-UNITED KINGDOM

(a) The exchange of letters of 4 May and 14 June 1976 regarding Article 105(2) of the implementing Regulation (waiving of reimbursement of the costs of administrative checks and medical examinations).
(b) The exchange of letters of 18 January and 14 March 1977 regarding Article 36(3) of the Regulation (arrangement for reimbursement or waiving of reimbursement of the costs of benefits in kind provided under the terms of Chapter 1 of Title III of the Regulation) as amended by the exchange of letters of 4 May and 23 July 1982 (agreement for reimbursement of costs incurred under Article 22(1) (a) of the Regulation).

[³ 51. BULGARIA-UNITED KINGDOM

None.]

[¹ [75.] CZECH REPUBLIC—UNITED KINGDOM

None.]

**[³98.] DENMARK—UNITED KINGDOM

1. The exchange of letters of 30 March and 19 April 1977 as modified by an exchange of letters of 8 November 1989 and of 10 January 1990 shall be added in point 1 after 19 April 1977 regarding Articles 36(3), 63(3) and 70(3) of the Regulation and Article 105(2) of the implementing Regulation (waiving of reimbursement of the costs of:

(a) benefits in kind provided under the terms of Chapter 1 or 4 of Title III of the Regulation;

(b) [. . .]

(c) administrative checks and medical examinations referred to in Article 105 of the implementing Regulation).

2. The exchange of letters of 5 March and 10 September 1984 relating to the non-application to self-employed persons of agreements regarding the waiver of reimbursement of unemployment benefits paid pursuant to Article 69 of the Regulation, in dealings with Gibraltar.

**[³120.] GERMANY—UNITED KINGDOM

(a) Articles 8, 9, 25 to 27 and 29 to 32 of the Arrangement of 10 December 1964 on the implementation of the Agreement of 20 April 1960.

(b) The Agreement of 29 April 1977 concerning the waiving of the reimbursement of costs of benefits in kind for sickness, maternity, accidents at work and occupational diseases, costs of unemployment benefit and costs of administrative checks and medical examinations.

(c) The exchange of letters of 18 July and 28 September 1983 relating to the non-application to self-employed persons of agreements concerning the waiver of reimbursement of unemployment benefits paid pursuant to Article 69 of the Regulation, in dealings with Gibraltar.

[¹ [³141.] ESTONIA—UNITED KINGDOM

No convention.]

**[³161.] GREECE—UNITED KINGDOM

No convention.

[² [³180.] SPAIN—UNITED KINGDOM

The exchange of letters of 30 July and 26 September 1980 concerning reciprocal waiver of the reimbursement of unemployment benefits (Article 70(3) of the Regulation.]

**[³198.] FRANCE—UNITED KINGDOM

[² (a) The Exchange of Letters of 25 March and 28 April 1997 regarding Article 105(2) of the implementing Regulation (waiving of reimbursement of the costs of administrative checks and medical examinations).

(b) The Agreement of 8 December 1998 on the specific methods of determining the amounts to be re-imbursed for benefits in kind pursuant to Regulation (EEC) No 1408/71 and (EEC) 574/72.

[³215.] IRELAND—UNITED KINGDOM

Agreement of 8 November 2000 on the waiving of reimbursement of the costs of benefits in kind of sickness, maternity, accidents at work and occupational diseases, and the costs of administrative and medical controls.

[³231.] ITALY—UNITED KINGDOM

The exchange of letters of 1 and 16 February 1995 concerning Articles 36(3) and 63(3) of the Regulation (reimbursement of waiving of reimbursement of expenditure for benefits in kind) and article 105(2) of the implementing Regulation (waiving of reimbursement of the costs of administrative checks and medical examinations).

[¹ [³246.] CYPRUS—UNITED KINGDOM

None.]

[¹ [³260.] LATVIA—UNITED KINGDOM

No convention.]

[¹ [³273.] LITHUANIA—UNITED KINGDOM

No convention.]

[³285.] LUXEMBOURG—UNITED KINGDOM

(a) The exchange of letters of 28 November and 18 December 1975 regarding Article 70(3) of the Regulation (waiving of reimbursement of benefits paid pursuant to Article 69 of the Regulation).
(b) The exchange of letters of 18 December 1975 and 20 January 1976 regarding Articles 36(3) and 63(3) of the Regulation and Article 105(2) of the implementing Regulation (waiving of reimbursement of costs of benefits in kind provided under the terms of Chapter 1 or 4 or Title III of the Regulation, and also of the costs entailed in administrative checks and medical examinations referred to in Article 105 of the implementing Regulation).
(c) The exchange of letters of 18 July and 27 October 1983 relating to the non-application of the agreement detailed at (a) to self-employed persons moving between Luxembourg and Gibraltar.

[¹ [³296.] HUNGARY—UNITED KINGDOM

None.]

[¹ [³306.] MALTA—UNITED KINGDOM

None.]

[³315.] NETHERLANDS—UNITED KINGDOM

(a) The second sentence of Article 3 of the Administrative Arrangement of 12 June 1956 on the implementation of the Convention of 11 August 1954.
(b) The exchange of letters of 25 April and 26 May 1986 concerning

Article 36(3) of the Regulation (reimbursement or waiver of reimbursement of expenditure for benefits in kind), as amended.

**[³323.] AUSTRIA—UNITED KINGDOM

(a) Article 18(1) and (2) of the Arrangement of 10 November 1980 for the implementation of the Convention on social security of 22 July 1980 as amended by Supplementary Arrangements No 1 of 26 March 1986 and No 2 of 4 June 1993 with regard to persons who cannot claim treatment under Chapter 1 of Title III of the Regulation.

(b) Article 18(1) of the said Arrangement with regard to persons who can claim treatment under Chapter 1 of Title III of the Regulation on the understanding that for Austrian nationals resident in the territory of Austria and for nationals of the United Kingdom resident in the territory of the United Kingdom (with the exception of Gibraltar) the relevant passport shall replace the form E 111 for all benefits covered by that form.

(c) Agreement of 30 November 1994 concerning the reimbursement of expenditure for social security benefits.

[¹ [³330.] POLAND—UNITED KINGDOM

None.]

[³ 336. PORTUGAL-UNITED KINGDOM

The arrangement of 8 June 2004 concerning Articles 36(3) and 63(3) of Regulation (EEC) No. 1408/71 establishing other methods of reimbursement of the costs of benefits in kind under the Regulation by both countries with effect from 1 January 2003.]

[³ 341. ROMANIA-UNITED KINGDOM

None.]

[¹ [³345.] SLOVENIA—UNITED KINGDOM

None.]

[¹ [³350.] SLOVAKIA—UNITED KINGDOM

None.]

**299. FINLAND—UNITED KINGDOM

The exchange of letters of 1 and 20 June 1995 concerning Articles 36(3) and 63(3) of Regulation (EEC) No 1408/71 (reimbursement or waiving of reimbursement of the cost of benefits in kind) and Article 105(2) of Regulation (EEC) No 574/72 (waiving of reimbursement of the cost of administrative checks an medical examinations).

**[³351.] SWEDEN—UNITED KINGDOM

The arrangement of 15 April 1997 concerning Article 36(3) and 63(3) of the Regulation (reimbursement or waiving of reimbursement of the cost of benefits in kind) and Article 105(2) of the implementing Regulation (waiving of refunds of the costs of administering checks and medical examinations).

AMENDMENTS

1. Annex II to the Treaty of Accession (May 1, 2004).
2. Regulation 89/2001/EC, [2001] OJ L14/16 (February 6, 2001).
3. Regulation 1791/2006/EC [2006] OJ L363/1 (January 1, 2007).

ANNEX 6

PROCEDURE FOR THE PAYMENT OF BENEFITS

(Articles 4(6), 53(1) and 122 of the Implementing Regulation)

** *Section numbering re-ordered by Annex II of the Treaty of Accession with effect from May 1, 2004.*
Only provisions concerning the United Kingdom have been reproduced.

General observation

Payments of arrears and other single payments shall in principle be made through the liaison bodies. Current and sundry payments shall be made in accordance with the procedure set out in this Annex.

3.467

**[¹AA.] UNITED KINGDOM

Direct payment.

AMENDMENT

1. Regulation 1791/2006/EC [2006] OJ L363/1 (January 1, 2007).

ANNEX 7

BANKS

(Articles 4(7), 55(3) and 122 of the implementing Regulation)

** *Section numbering re-ordered by Annex II of the Treaty of Accession with effect from May 1, 2004.*
Only provisions concerning the United Kingdom have been reproduced.

3.468

**[¹AA.] UNITED KINGDOM

Great Britain
  Bank of England, London
Northern Ireland
  Northern Bank Limited, Belfast

Gibraltar
Barclays Bank, Gibraltar

AMENDMENT

1. Regulation 1791/2006/EC [2006] OJ L363/1 (January 1, 2007).

[¹ ANNEX 8

GRANT OF FAMILY BENEFITS

(Articles 4(8), 10a(d) and 122 of the implementing Regulation)

3.469 *Only provisions concerning the United Kingdom have been reproduced.*
Article 10a (d) of the implementing Regulation is applicable to:

A. Employed and self-employed persons

(a) with a reference period of one calendar month in dealings between
— Belgium and the United Kingdom
[² Bulgaria and the United Kingdom]
— the Czech Republic and the United Kingdom
— Germany and the United Kingdom
— Lithuania and the United Kingdom
— Austria and the United Kingdom
— Poland and the United Kingdom
— Portugal and the United Kingdom
[² Romania and the United Kingdom]
— Slovenia and the United Kingdom
— Slovakia and the United Kingdom
— Finland and the United Kingdom
— Sweden and the United Kingdom
(b) with a reference period of a quarter of a calendar year in dealings
between:
[. . .]

B. Self-employed persons

With a reference period of a quarter of a calendar year in dealings
between:
[. . .]

C. Employed persons

With a reference period of one calendar month in dealing between:
[. . .]

AMENDMENTS

1. Annex II to the Treaty of Accession (May 1, 2004).
2. Regulation 1791/2006/EC [2006] OJ L363/1 (January 1, 2007).

ANNEX 9

CALCULATION OF THE AVERAGE ANNUAL COST OF BENEFITS IN KIND

(Articles 4(9), 94(3)(a) and 95(3)(a) of the implementing Regulation)

3.470

** *Section numbering re-ordered by Annex II of the Treaty of Accession with effect from May 1, 2004.*
Only provisions concerning the United Kingdom have been reproduced.

**[¹AA.] UNITED KINGDOM

The average annual cost of benefits in kind shall be calculated by taking into consideration the benefits provided by the National Health Service of the United Kingdom.

AMENDMENT

1. Regulation 1791/2006/EC [2006] OJ L363/1 (January 1, 2007).

ANNEX 10

INSTITUTIONS AND BODIES DESIGNATED BY THE COMPETETENT AUTHORITIES

(Article 4(10) of the implementing Regulation)

** *Section numbering re-ordered by Annex II of the Treaty of Accession with effect from May 1, 2004.*
Only current provisions concerning the United Kingdom have been reproduced.

3.471

AA. UNITED KINGDOM

1. For the purposes
of applying Articles
14c,14d(3) and 17 of the
Regulation and Articles
6(1), 11(1), 11a(1), 12a,
13(2) and (3), 14(1), (2)
and (3), 80(2), 81, 82(2)
and 109 of the imple-
menting Regulation:

Great Britain:
HM Revenue and Customs, Centre for Non-Residents, Benton Park View, Newcastle upon Tyne, NE98 1ZZ;

Northern Ireland:
Department for Social Development, Social Security Agency, Network Support Branch Overseas Benefits Unit, Level 2, James House, 2–4 Cromac Street, Belfast, BT7 2JA,

HM Revenue and Customs, Centre for Non-Residents, Benton Park View, Newcastle upon Tyne, NE98 1ZZ.

2. For the purposes of applying Articles 36 and 63 of the Regulation and Articles 8, 38(1), 70 (1), 91(2), 102(2), 110 and 113(2) of the implementing Regulation:

Great Britain:
Department for Work and Pensions, The Pension Service, International Pension Centre, Tyneview Park, Newcastle upon Tyne NE98 1BA.

Northern Ireland:
Department for Social Development, Northern Ireland Social Security Agency, Network Support Branch, Overseas Benefits Unit, Block 2, Stormont Estate, Belfast BT4 3SJ.

3. For the purposes of applying Articles 85(2), 86(2) and 89(1) of the implementing Regulation:

Great Britain:
HM Revenue and Customs, Child Benefit Office, Newcastle upon Tyne, NE88 1AA,

HM Revenue and Customs, Tax Credit Office, Preston, PR1 0SB;

Northern Ireland:
HM Revenue and Customs, Child Benefit Office (Belfast), Windsor House, 9-15 Bedford Street, Belfast, BT2 7UW,

HM Revenue and Customs, Tax Credit Office (Belfast), Dorchester House, 52-58 Great Victoria Street, Belfast, BT2 7WF.

ANNEX 11

[¹ . . .]

AMENDMENTS

1. Regulation 647/2005/EC, [2005] OJ L117/1 (May 5, 2005).
2. Regulation 1791/2006/EC [2006] OJ L363/1 (January 1, 2007).

Selected list of E-Forms

This is an unofficial list of the principal E Forms used in connection with the administration of social security benefits under Regulation 1408/71. It is drawn from the list on the European Commission website.

3.472

E Form	Description
	General
E001	Request for information, communication of information, request for forms, reminder of an employed person, self-employed person, a frontier work, a pensioner, an unemployed person, a dependant.
	Posting
E101	Certificate concerning the legislation applicable.
E101a	Certificate concerning the legislation applicable to unemployed persons engaged in part-time work in a Member State other than the State of residence.
E102	Extension of term of posting or of activity as a self-employed person.
	Healthcare sector
E103	Exercising the right of option.
E104	Certificate concerning the aggregation of periods of insurance, employment or residence.
E106	Certificate of entitlement to sickness and maternity insurance benefits in kind for persons residing in a country other than the competent country.
E107	Application for a certificate of entitlement to benefits in kind.
E108	Notification of suspension or withdrawal of the right to sickness and maternity insurance benefits in kind.
E109	Certificate for the registration of members of the employed or self-employed person's family and the updating of lists.
E112	Certificate concerning the retention of the right to sickness or maternity benefits currently being provide.
E115	Claim for cash benefits for incapacity for work.
E116	Medical report relating to incapacity for work (Sickness, maternity, accident at work, occupational disease).
E117	Granting of cash benefits in the case of maternity and incapacity for work.
E118	Notification of non-recognition or of end of incapacity for work.
E118 Annex	Legal remedies and periods allowed for appeals.
E119	Certificate concerning the entitlement of unemployed persons and members of their family to sickness and maternity insurance benefits.
E120	Certificate of entitlement to benefits in kind for pension claimants and members of their family.
E121	Certificate for the registration of pensioners and the updating of lists.
E123	Certificate of entitlement to benefits in kind under insurance against accidents at work and occupational diseases.

E124	Claim for death grant.
E125	Individual record of actual expenditure.
E126	Rates for refund of benefits in kind.

Pensions sector

E201	Certificate concerning the aggregation of perios of insurance or periods of residence.
E202	Investigation of a claim for old-age pension.
E203	Investigation of a claim for a survivor's pension.
E204	Investigation of a claim for an invalidity pension.
E207	Information concerning the insured person's insurance history.
E210	Notification of decision concerning a claim for pension.
E211	Summary of decisions.
E213	Detailed medical report.
E215	Administrative report on the position of a pensioner.
E501	Request for information on insurance history of a worker.
E502	Notification of registration.
E503	Request for information on insurance history of a worker.
E505	Certificate concerning the insurance history of a worker.
E551	Notification of amendment.

Unemployment sector

E301	Certificate concerning the periods to be taken into account for the granting of unemployment benefits.
E302	Certificate relating to members of the family of an unemployed person who must be taken into account for the calculation of benefits.

Family benefits

E401	Certificate concerning the composition of a family for the purpose of the granting of family benefits.
E402	Certificate of continuation of studies for the purposed of the granting of family benefits.
E403	Certificate of apprenticeship and/or vocational training for the purpose of the granting of family benefits.
E404	Medical certificate for the purpose of the granting of family benefits.
E405	Certificate concerning the aggregation of persionds of insurance, employment or self-employment or concerning successive employment in several Member States, between the date on which payment is due.
E407	medical certificate for the grant of a special family allowance or of increased family allowances for handicapped children.
E411	Request for information on entitlement to family benefits in the Member States of residence of the members of the family.

Non-contributory benefits

E601	Request for information concerning the amount of income received in a Member State other than the competent Member State.
E602	Certificate concerning the aggregation of periods of employment, or self-employment or of residence.

RELEVANT DECISIONS OF THE ADMINISTRATIVE COMMISSION

Decision No 76 of 22 February 1973 concerning the conditions for the use of Forms E402, E403 and E404, [1973] OJ C75/6

Council Regulation (EC) No 859/2003 of 14 May 2003 Extending the Provisions of Regulation (EEC) No 1408/71 and Regulation (EEC) No 574/72 to Nationals of Third Countries Who are not Already Covered by Those Provisions Solely on the Ground of Their Nationality

[2003] OJ L124/1

GENERAL NOTE

As the Preamble makes clear, for some years, there has been concern that nationals of countries other than EEA countries and Switzerland ("participating countries") were at a disadvantage in that there was no provision for the co-ordination of the social security rules of two or more participating countries for the benefit of third country nationals who had lawfully lived and worked in the EU. This regulation seeks to ameliorate their circumstances by extending, with effect from June 1, 2003, the provisions of Regulation 1408/71 to such third country nationals where they have had contact with two or more participating countries.

3.473

The Council of the European Union

Having regard to the Treaty establishing the European Community and in particular Article 63, point 4 thereof,

Having regard to the proposal from the Commission,[1]

Having regard to the opinion of the European Parliament,[2]

Whereas:

1. As its special meeting in Tampere on 15 and 16 October 1999, the European Council proclaimed that the European Union should ensure fair treatment of third-country nationals who reside legally in the territory of its Member States, grant them rights and obligations comparable to those of EU citizens, enhance non-discrimination in economic, social and cultural life and approximate their legal status to that of Member States' nationals.

2. In its resolution of 27 October 1999,[3] the European Parliament called for prompt action on promises of fair treatment for third-country nationals legally resident in the Member States and on the definition of their legal status, including uniform rights as close as possible to those enjoyed by the citizens of the European Union.

3. The European Economic and Social Committee has also appealed for equal treatment of Community nationals and third-country nationals in the social field, notably in its opinion of 26 September 1991 on the status of migrant workers from third countries.[4]

4. Article 6(2) of the Treaty on European Union provides that the Union shall respect fundamental rights, as guaranteed by the European Convention on the Protection of Human Rights and Fundamental Freedoms signed in Rome on 4 November 1950 and as they result from the consti-

3.474

tutional traditions common to the Member States, as general principles of Community law.

5. This Regulation respects the fundamental rights and observes the principles recognised in particular by the Charter of Fundamental Rights of the European Union, in particular the spirit of its Article 34(2).

6. The promotion of a high level of social protection and the raising of the standard of living and quality of life in the Member States are objectives of the Community.

7. As regards the conditions of social protection of third-country nationals, and in particular the social security scheme applicable to them, the Employment and Social Policy Council argued in its conclusions of 3 December 2001 that the coordination applicable to third-country nationals should grant them a set of uniform rights as near as possible to those enjoyed by EU citizens.

8. Currently, Council Regulation (EEC) No 1408/71 of 14 June 1971 on the application of social security schemes to employed persons and their families moving within the Community,[5] which is the basis for the coordination of the social security schemes of the different Member States, and Council Regulation (EEC) No 574/72 of 21 March 1972, laying down the procedure for implementing Regulation (EEC) No 1408/71,[6] apply only to certain third-country nationals. The number and diversity of legal instruments used in an effort to resolve problems in connection with the coordination of the Member States' social security schemes encountered by nationals of third countries who are in the same situation as Community nationals give rise to legal and administrative complexities. They create major difficulties for the individuals concerned, their employers, and the competent national social security bodies.

9. Hence, it is necessary to provide for the application of the coordination rules of Regulation (EEC) No 1408/71 and Regulation (EEC) No 574/72 to third-country nationals legally resident in the Community who are not currently covered by the provisions of these Regulations on grounds of their nationality and who satisfy the other conditions provided for in this Regulation; such an extension is in particular important with a view to the forthcoming enlargement of the European Union.

10. The application of Regulation (EEC) No 1408/71 and Regulation (EEC) No 574/72 to these persons does not give them any entitlement to enter, to stay or to reside in a Member State or to have access to its labour market.

11. The provisions of Regulation (EEC) No 1408/71 and Regulation (EEC) No 574/72 are, by virtue of this Regulation, applicable only in so far as the person concerned is already legally resident in the territory of a Member State. Being legally resident is therefore a prerequisite for the application of these provisions.

12. The provisions of Regulation (EEC) No 1408/71 and Regulation (EEC) No 574/72 are not applicable in a situation which is confined in all respects within a single Member State. This concerns, inter alia, the situation of a third country national who has links only with a third country and a single Member State.

13. The continued right to unemployment benefit, as laid down in Article 69 of Regulation (EEC) No 1408/71, is subject to the condition of registering as a job-seeker with the employment services of each Member State entered. Those provisions may therefore apply to a third-country national only provided he/she has the right, where appropriate pursuant to his/her residence permit, to register as a job-seeker with the employment services of the Member State entered and the right to work there legally.

14. Transitional provisions should be adopted to protect the persons covered by this Regulation and to ensure that they do not lose rights as a result of its entry into force.

15. To achieve these objectives it is necessary and appropriate to extend the scope of the rules coordinating the national social security schemes by adopting a Community legal instrument which is binding and directly applicable in every Member State which takes part in the adoption of this Regulation.

16. This Regulation is without prejudice to rights and obligations arising from international agreements with third countries to which the Community is a party and which afford advantages in terms of social security.

17. Since the objectives of the proposed action cannot be sufficiently achieved by the Member States and can therefore, by reason of the scale or effects of the proposed action, be better achieved at Community level, the Community may take measures in accordance with the principle of subsidiarity enshrined in Article 5 of the Treaty. In compliance with the principle of proportionality as set out in that Article, this Regulation does not go beyond what is necessary to achieve these objectives.

18. In accordance with Article 3 of the Protocol on the position of the United Kingdom and Ireland annexed to the Treaty on the European Union and to the Treaty establishing the European Community, Ireland and the United Kingdom gave notice, by letters of 19 and 23 April 2002, of their wish to take part in the adoption and application of this Regulation.

19. In accordance with Articles 1 and 2 of the Protocol on the position of Denmark annexed to the Treaty on the European Union and to the Treaty establishing the European Community, Denmark is not taking part in the adoption of this Regulation and is not therefore bound by or subject to it,

FOOTNOTES

1. OJ C 126 E, 28.5.2002, p.388.
2. Opinion of 21 November 2002.
3. OJ C 154, 5.6.2000, p.63.
4. OJ C 339, 231.12.1991, p.82.
5. OJ L 149, 5.7.1971, p.2; Regulation last amended by Regulation (EC) No 1386/2001 of the European parliament and of the Council (OJ L187, 10.7.2001, p.1).
6. OJ L 74, 27.3.1972, p.1; Regulation last amended by Commission Regulation (EC) No 410/2002 (OJ L 62, 5.3.2002, p.17).

Has Adopted this Regulation

Article 1

Subject to the provisions of the Annex to this Regulation, the provisions of Regulation (EEC) No 1408/71 and Regulation (EEC) No 574/72 shall apply to nationals of third countries who are not already covered by those provisions solely on the ground of their nationality, as well as to members of their families and to their survivors, provided they are legally resident in the territory of a Member State and are in a situation which is not confined in all respects within a single Member State.

3.475

GENERAL NOTE

3.476   This short article enfranchises third country nationals into the scheme for the co-ordination of social security found in the two principal regulations where they are not already within that scheme. Some third country nationals are already covered by the rules in reg.1408/71, namely, stateless persons, refugees and members of families and survivors of Community nationals in the circumstances set out in reg.1408/71.

The condition for third country nationals is that they are "lawfully resident" in the territory of a Member State. This phrase is not defined, but will have to be applied by national authorities in accordance with their immigration laws. The most likely way forward will be that Member States will regard as lawfully resident all those whose immigration status is compliant with national requirements. But see for discussion of the phrase in a different context, *Szoma v Secretary of State for Work and Pensions* [2005] UKHL 64, reported as *R(IS) 2/01*, in which the House of Lords ruled that, under UK social security regulations and in the context of asylum seekers, persons subject to immigration control are lawfully present in the United Kingdom.

Note too that the extension of Regulation 1408/71 to third country nationals only relates to the co-ordination of schemes within the participating countries, and so has no application where the third country national has only had contact with the social security system of one Member State. So, for example, the regulation does not apply where an Australian national is living and working in the UK, and has had no contact with the social security system of any other Member State.

Article 2

3.477   **1.** This Regulation shall not create any rights in respect of the period before 1 June 2003.

2. Any period of insurance and, where appropriate, any period of employment, self-employment or residence completed under the legislation of a Member State before 1 June 2003 shall be taken into account for the determination of rights acquired in accordance with the provisions of this Regulation.

3. Subject to the provisions of paragraph 1, a right shall be acquired under this Regulation even if it relates to a contingency arising prior to 1 June 2003.

4. Any benefit that has not been awarded or that has been suspended on account of the nationality or the residence of the person concerned shall, at the latter's request, be awarded or resumed from 1 June 2003, provided that the rights for which benefits were previously awarded did not give rise to a lump-sum payment.

5. The rights of persons who prior to 1 June 2003, obtained the award of a pension may be reviewed at their request, account being taken of the provisions of this Regulation.

6. If the request referred to in paragraph 4 or paragraph 5 is lodged within two years from 1 June 2003, rights deriving from this Regulation shall be acquired from that date and the provisions of the legislation of any Member State on the forfeiture or lapse of rights may not be applied to the persons concerned.

7. If the request referred to in paragraph 4 or paragraph 5 is lodged after expiry of the deadline referred to in paragraph 6, rights not forfeited or lapsed shall be acquired from the date of such request, subject to any more favourable provisions of the legislation of any Member State.

Article 2

GENERAL NOTE

This article deals with the temporal effect of the extension of the system of co-ordination to third country nationals. Rights may not be acquired prior to June 1, 2003, but periods of insurance or residence before that date may be taken into account in determining entitlement to a right accruing after June 1, 2003. So, periods of contribution prior to June 1, 2003 may be taken into account in determining whether there is entitlement to a benefit payable with effect from June 1, 2003 or later.

3.478

Article 3

This Regulation shall enter into force on the first day of the month following its publication in the Official Journal of the European Union.

This Regulation shall be binding in its entirety and directly applicable in the Member States in accordance with the Treaty establishing the European Community.

Done at Brussels, 14 May 2003.

3.479

ANNEX

SPECIAL PROVISIONS REFERRED TO IN ARTICLE 1

I. GERMANY

In the case of family benefits, this Regulation shall apply only to third-country nationals who are in possession of a residence permit meeting the definition in German law of the "Aufenthaltserlaubnis" or "Aufenthaltsberechtigung".

3.480

II. AUSTRIA

In the case of family benefits, this Regulation shall apply only to third-country nationals who fulfil the conditions laid down by Austrian legislation for permanent entitlement to family allowances.

3.481

Council Directive 79/7/EEC of December 19 1978 on the Progressive Implementation of the Principle of Equal Treatment for Men and Women in Matters of Social Security

[1979] OJ L6/24

THE COUNCIL OF THE EUROPEAN COMMUNITIES,

Having regard to the Treaty establishing the European Economic Community, and in particular Article 235 thereof,

3.482

Having regard to the proposal from the Commission,[1]

Having regard to the opinion of the European Parliament,[2]

Having regard to the opinion of the Economic and Social Committee,[3] whereas Article 1 (2) of Council Directive 76/207 of February 9 1976 on the implementation of the principle of equal treatment for men and women as regards access to employment, vocational training and promotion, and working conditions[4] provides that, with a view to ensuring the progressive implementation of the principle of equal treatment in matters of social security, the Council, acting on a proposal from the Commission, will adopt provisions defining its substance its scope and the arrangements for its application;

whereas the Treaty does not confer the specific powers required for this purpose;

whereas the principle of equal treatment in matters of social security should be implemented in the first place in the statutory schemes which provide protection against the risks of sickness, invalidity, old age, accidents at work, occupational diseases and unemployment, and in social assistance in so far as it is intended to supplement or replace the abovementioned schemes;

whereas the implementation of the principle of equal treatment in matters of social security does not prejudice the provisions relating to the protection of women on the ground of maternity;

whereas, in this respect, Member States may adopt specific provisions for women to remove existing instances of unequal treatment,

HAS ADOPTED THIS DIRECTIVE:

FOOTNOTES

1. [1977] O.J. C34/3.
2. [1977] O.J. C299/13.
3. [1977] O.J. C180/36.
4. [1976] O.J. L39/40.

GENERAL NOTE

3.483   The Community institutions recognised that moves to secure the principle of equal treatment for men and women would be incomplete without the inclusion of provisions dealing with social security. Directive 79/7 was made under art.235 EC, and was part of the programme of legislation flowing from the commitment to equal pay for equal work to be found in art.141 (ex 119) EC, rather than part of the programme for securing the free movement of workers.

Unfortunately a number of concepts in the directive have been interpreted slightly differently from what might be regarded as corresponding provisions of reg.1408/71. Furthermore, the coverage of Dir.79/7 is not the same as that of reg.1408/71 in terms of the benefits covered.

The Directive was required to be implemented in all the Member States from and including December 23, 1984.

Article 1

The purpose of this Directive is the progressive implementation, in the **3.484** field of social security and other elements of social protection provided for in Article 3, of the principle of equal treatment for men and women in matters of social security, hereinafter referred to as "the principle of equal treatment".

Article 2

This Directive shall apply to the working population—including self- **3.485** employed persons, workers and self-employed persons whose activity is interrupted by illness, accident or involuntary unemployment and persons seeking employment—and to retired or invalided workers and selfemployed persons.

GENERAL NOTE

Those within the personal scope of this Directive are not the same as those who **3.486** are within the personal scope of Reg.1408/71. The Directive applies to the "working population". There is a link with employment (which includes selfemployment) related social security benefits in the Directive which makes it more limited than the concept of insured persons under Reg.1408/71.

The Court of Justice has given a very wide meaning to the term "working population", holding that it covers any worker, including those who are seeking work: Case C-280/94 *Van Damme* [1996] E.C.R. I-179. It extends to include someone who gives up work to care for a sick relative: Case 150/85 *Drake v Chief Adjudication Officer* [1986] E.C.R. 1995. But it does not include those who have never worked in a paid capacity: Joined Cases 48/88, 106/88 & 107/88 *Achterberg te Riele* [1989] E.C.R. 1963. Nor does it cover someone who gives up work to look after healthy children, since this is not one of the risks covered in Art.3: Case C-31/90 *Johnson v Chief Adjudication Officer (Johnson I)*, [1991] E.C.R. 3723, reported as *R(S) 1/95*.

In *CG/5425/1995* the Commissioner held that the Directive did not apply to a woman who had last worked in 1949, and who claimed invalid care allowance to look after her mother in 1989. It is clear that there must be a causal link between giving up work and the incidence of one of the risks covered by Art.3.

Article 3

1. This Directive shall apply to: **3.487**
   (a) statutory schemes which provide protection against the following risks:
   — sickness,
   — invalidity,
   — old age,
   — accidents at work and occupational diseases,
   — unemployment;
   (b) social assistance, in so far as it is intended to supplement or replace the schemes referred to in (a).
2. This Directive shall not apply to the provisions concerning survivors' benefits nor to those concerning family benefits, except in the case of family

benefits granted by way of increases of benefits due in respect of the risks referred to in paragraph 1(a).

3. With a view to ensuring implementation of the principle of equal treatment in occupational schemes, the Council, acting on a proposal from the Commission, will adopt provisions defining its substance, its scope and the arrangements for its application.

GENERAL NOTE

3.488   In Case 150/85 *Drake v Chief Adjudication Officer* [1986] E.C.R. 1995, the Court of Justice said that:

"Article 3(1) must be interpreted as including any benefit which in a broad sense forms part of one of the statutory schemes referred to or a social assistance provision intended to supplement or replace such a scheme." (para.21)

In case C-243/90 *R. v Secretary of State for Social Security Ex p. Smithson* [1992] E.C.R. I-467, the Court explained,

"In order to fall within the scope of the Directive, the benefit must be directly and effectively linked to the protection against one of the risks specified in Article 3(1)." (para.14)

R(A)2/94 holds that attendance allowance is an "invalidity benefit" within the meaning of art.10 of reg.1408/71. It follows that it also falls within the scope of this directive, as will disability living allowance. The position is not changed by the categorisation of those benefits as special non-contributory benefits which are not exportable under reg.1408/71.

The Court of Justice has ruled that income support constitutes social assistance: Joined Cases C-63/91 & C-64/91 *Jackson and Cresswell v Chief Adjudication Officer* [1992] E.C.R. I-4737 (printed as appendix to *R(IS)10/91*). But discriminatory treatment may fall foul of Council Dir.76/207 on the implementation of the principle of equal treatment for men and women as regards access to employment, vocational training and promotion and working conditions, [1976] O.J. L39/40. A similar view has been taken in relation to family credit (now working families' tax credit), see Case C-116/94 *Meyers v Chief Adjudication Officer* [1995] E.C.R. I-2131, reported as *R(FC)2/98*.

The classification of family credit (now working families' tax credit) proved to be somewhat problematic. It was classified as a family benefit for the purposes of Reg.1408/71: Case C-78/91 *Hughes v Chief Adjudication Officer* [1992] E.C.R. I-4839. However, it could arguably be regarded as having provided protection against the risk of unemployment through its role in topping up low pay.

In Case C-137/94 *R. v Secretary of State for Health Ex p. Richardson* [1995] E.C.R. I-3407, the Court ruled that free prescription charges fell within the material scope of the directive; it did not matter that these were regarded as a health benefit in the United Kingdom. In Case C-382/98 *R. v Secretary of State for Social Security Ex p. Taylor* judgment of December 16, 1999 [1999] E.C.R. I-8955, the Court ruled that winter fuel payments under the social fund were also within the material scope of the Directive.

In *Hockenjos v Secretary of State for Social Security*, Court of Appeal, May 2, 2001 [2001] EWCA Civ. 624, the Court of Appeal ruled that there is one statutory scheme for a jobseeker's allowance and that the benefit is one which provides protection against the risk of unemployment. Accordingly the benefit falls within the scope of art.3 of the Directive.

In *CPC/4177/2005*, the Commissioner decided that state pension credit is a benefit falling within the scope of Directive 79/7.

See also *R(P) 1/95* and *R(P) 1/96*.

1. The principle of equal treatment means that there shall be no dis-   **3.489**
crimination whatsoever on ground of sex either directly, or indirectly by reference in particular to marital or family status, in particular as concerns:
— the scope of the schemes and the conditions of access thereto,
— the obligation to contribute and the calculation of contributions,
— the calculation of benefits including increases due in respect of a
  spouse and for dependants and the conditions governing the duration and retention of entitlement to benefits.

2. The principle of equal treatment shall be without prejudice to the provisions relating to the protection of women on the grounds of maternity.

GENERAL NOTE

The Court of Justice has ruled that art.4 outlaws both direct and indirect forms   **3.490**
of discrimination: Case 30/85 *Teuling* [1987] E.C.R. 2497, and Case C-226/91
Molenbroek [1992] E.C.R. I-5943.

The test to be applied was laid down in Case C-229/89 *Commission v Belgium*
[1991] E.C.R. I-2205:

"Article 4(1) of Directive 79/7 precludes less favourable treatment from being
accorded to a social group when it is shown to be made up of a much greater
number of person or one or other sex, unless the provision ins question is 'based
on objectively justified factors unrelated to any discrimination on grounds of
sex'." (para.13)

Note that in *Blaik v Chief Adjudication Officer*, reported as *R(SB) 6/91*, the Court
of Appeal decided that a difference of treatment accorded to a man and a woman
on the ground of differing marital or family status (in the context of supplementary benefit) was not indirect discrimination within art.4 and so did not breach
Dir.79/7.

In *CIB/230/2000*, the Commissioner had to consider whether the provisions of
regs 4 and 5 of the Overlapping Benefits Regulations resulted in discrimination
prohibited by the Directive. The claimant had been in receipt of widow's pension
since July 1995; she subsequently became entitled to incapacity benefit, but the
adjudication officer decided that the benefit was not payable to her because it over-
lapped with widow's pension on the application of regs 4 and 5 of the Overlapping
Benefits Regulations. The claimant argued that there was discrimination contrary
to Dir.79/7/EEC relying on Case C-337/91 *A M van Gemert-Derks v Bestuur van
de Nieuwe Industriële Bedrijfsvereniging* [1993] E.C.R. I-5435, which decided that,
although survivors' benefits are outside the scope of the Directive, Art.4 precludes
a national rule which withdraws from widows who are unfit for work the benefits
applicable to that risk on their being granted a widow's pension, if that withdrawal is
not the result of a voluntary renunciation by the beneficiary and is not applicable to
widowers who are entitled to benefits for incapacity to work.

The Secretary of State argued before the Commissioner that (1) there was a difference between a withdrawal of benefit and an adjustment of the amount payable,
and (2) it was essential that the withdrawl should involve a drop in income. The
Commissioner rejected both those arguments. The Commissioner says that "what
matters is the practical effect that the claimant was to receive nothing by way of
incapacity benefit" (para.12). On the second issue, the Commissioner notes,

"The principle was stated clearly and unequivocally in [*van Gemert-Derks*] that
there is discrimination whenever women are deprived of a right to claim a benefit
which men continue to receive in the same situation." (para.13.)

Addressing the issue in the case, the Commissioner says,

". . . if I had to, I would conclude that in the present case regulation 4(5) of the Overlapping Benefits Regulations, as applied to incapacity benefit and women in receipt or claiming widow's pension discriminated against women for the purposes of Directive 79/7. However, since below I have concluded that there is nevertheless objective justification for that discrimination, so that Article 4(1) of the Directive is not breached, I do not have to reach a final decision on this point." (para.20.)

Addressing the issue of objective justification, the Commissioner concluded that reg.4(5) of the Overlapping Benefits Regulations served the aim of co-ordinating the social security system, which is unrelated to any discrimination based on sex. So the Commissioner concludes that, if there was prima facie discrimination on grounds of sex contrary to Dir.79/7 in the application of reg.4(5) to the claimant, the discrimination was objectively justified (para.33).

In *Secretary of State for Social Security v Walter* [2001] EWCA Civ 1913; [2002] 1 C.M.L.R. 27 (reported as *R(JSA)3/02*) the Court of Appeal held that there was no breach of Dir.79/7 in the context of a claim by a student, whose studies were in suspense, and who had claimed a jobseeker's allowance. She challenged the regulations as directly discriminatory against pregnant women.

A Tribunal of Commissioners in *R(JSA)4/03* has held that the rule in reg.51(2) (c) of the Jobseeker's Allowance Regulations 1996 affects disproportionately more women than men and cannot be objectively justified. It is accordingly incompatible with art.4 of Dir.79/7 and has no effect. Regulation 51(2)(c) provides that the number of hours persons or their partners are engaged in remunerative work is to be determined by disregarding those periods in which they are not required to work where they work at a school or other educational establishment or some other place of employment and the cycle of work consists of one year but with school holidays or similar vacations during which they do not work.

In *CJSA/4890/1998* the Commissioner ruled that reg.77(1), (2) and (3)(b) of the JSA Regulations on child additions and family premium discriminates unlawfully on grounds of sex. Statistical information had been presented to the Commissioner which showed that 92 per cent of men who shared the care of their children for at least 104 nights a year could not get child additions in income-based JSA because they did not receive child benefit as compared with eight per cent of women sharing care who could not get the addition for that reason.

In *Hockenjos v Secretary of State for Social Security*, Judgment of December 21, 2004, [2004] EWCA Civ 1749, the Court of Appeal has allowed the claimant's appeal against the decision of the Commissioner in *CJSA/4890/2003* and dismissed the Department's cross appeal. It will be recalled that *Hockenjos v Secretary of State for Social Security* [2001] EWCA Civ 624 (and referred to in the annotations to art.3) was the decision of the Court of Appeal determining that jobseeker's allowance was a benefit falling within the material scope of the Directive. This decision of the Court of Appeal deals with the substance of the claimant's claim to entitlement to additional amounts in respect of his children (the child premium) and to the family premium. Though he had shared care of the children, child benefit was paid to the children's mother which precluded payment of the additions to the claimant.

All three judges in the Court of Appeal reach the same conclusion by somewhat different lines of reasoning on the detail of the case. The Department conceded that the conditions of entitlement for child additions to a jobseeker's allowance, which linked these to entitlement to child benefit, were indirectly discriminatory, but argued that the discrimination could be objectively justified. The claimant was a man with shared care of his children following his separation from his wife. The Department argued that the link with entitlement to child benefit ensured consistency of decision-making. Scott Baker LJ, delivering the first judgment said:

"45. According, in my judgment the position is this. The law is set out in the European Court's judgment in *Seymour-Smith*. The Secretary of State must first show that the discriminatory rule reflects a legitimate aim of social policy. Next he must show that the aim is unrelated to any discrimination based on sex and finally that he could reasonably consider that the means chosen are suitable for attaining that aim. Built into this final question is the balance between holding fast to the Community's fundamental principles on the one hand and the Member State's freedom to achieve its own social policy on the other."

Scott Baker L.J. concludes that regs 77(1), (2), (3) and (5) are discriminatory contrary to art.4 of the Directive and have not been justified by the Secretary of State.

The question of the remedy to be applied once this conclusion was reached clearly troubled the Court of Appeal, and there was an ultimately fruitless excursion into the possible impact of the Apportionment Act 1870. The conclusion reached is that the proper remedy is for the whole allowance to be paid to the claimant in respect of each child, since both children met the test of being members of the claimant's household for whom he was responsible. This is because there is no provision in the jobseeker's allowance scheme permitting the splitting of the additions for children.

The alleged unlawful discrimination in *CIB/3933/2001* arose in the context of claims to for an increase of incapacity benefit for children. The parents were separated, but the children lived with their father for part of the week. He was refused an increase in his incapacity benefit for the children because he was not in receipt of child benefit for the children. He argued that the requirement that a person be in receipt of child benefit in order to be entitled to the increased constituted unlawful discrimination between men and women. The Commissioner accepted that men were more likely to be adversely affected by this requirement but that it was objectively justified on the grounds that, in most cases where parents are separated, it is mothers who undertake the greater proportion of the practical responsibility for caring for children of the family.

The alleged unlawful discrimination in *R(IB)5/04* arose in the context of the age requirements in relation to entitlement to an incapacity benefit. The claimant, a woman, became incapable of work when she was 64. If she had been a man, she would have paid contribution and would have been eligible to claim incapacity benefit at that age. The Commissioner felt bound by the decision in *Graham* to rule that the alleged discrimination was not unlawful under the provisions of the Directive. However, he stayed the case on the basis that proceeding might be brought to enable the claimant to pay contributions, but in the absence of such proceedings the appeal is to be treated as dismissed. The appeal was definitively dismissed on March 26, 2004 since the claimant had indicated that no such proceedings were to be brought.

Issues arising under the Gender Recognition Act 2004

In Case C-423/04 *Richards v Secretary of State for Work and Pensions*, reported as **3.491** *R(P) 1/07*, the Court of Justice has ruled that art.4(1) of the Directive precludes legislation which denies a person, who has undergone male-to-female gender reassignment, entitlement to a retirement pension on the ground that she has not reached the age of 65, when she would have been entitled to such a pension at the age of 60 had she been held to be a woman as a matter of national law. This is the response to the Commissioner's reference in *CP/0428/2004*. Following the receipt of the opinion of the Luxembourg court, the Commissioner issued a short decision under file as *CP/0428/2004* in terms consented to by the parties, awarding the appellant retirement pension from her sixtieth birthday and stating simply that this was in the light of the judgment of the Luxembourg Court and for the reasons given by that court on what was seen to be a determinative issue in respect of the claim under appeal. See now new Departmental Guidance in Memo DMG 06/07.

On the application of the principle established in the *Richards* case to a case in which the claimant had not by the date of the decision under appeal undergone gender reassignment surgery, see *CP/3485/2003*.

CIB/2248/2006 concerned a claim to incapacity benefit by a female to male transsexual. The claimant, who was born on August 18,1942, and his gender at birth was registered as female. He began to live as a man from the age of 19, and underwent gender re-assignment surgery early in 2003. His assigned gender from that date was male, but his registered gender remained as female. The claimant reached the age of 60 in August 2002 (when his registered gender remained female). He had not option but to claim a retirement pension on the cessation of his entitlement to incapacity benefit on attaining the age of 60. On November 30, 2005 the claimant obtained a gender recognition certificate as a man. He was then 63. His entitlement to retirement pension ceased. He reclaimed incapacity benefit on December 2, 2005, but his claim was refused. The Commissioner first considered any issue arising under the European Convention on Human Rights, but could not conclude that it was possible to interpret s.30A of the Contributions and Benefits Act in such a way as to avoid the discrimination on grounds of sex which arose when art.8 was read together with art.14 of the European Convention.

The Commissioner then turned to the application of Directive 79/7/EEC to the circumstances presented by the appellant. The Commissioner concludes that there is a breach of the equal treatment requirement in art.4:

"37. Persons who are incapable of work and whose legal gender changes from female to male between the ages of 60 and 65 are entitled to incapacity benefit until the age of 60, then to a retirement pension until the change in their legal gender. Thereafter, depending on the time that has elapsed, they may be entitled to neither. That makes them unique in that the link between the loss of incapacity benefit and entitlement to a retirement pension is broken. And it is broken solely because of the change in legal gender between those ages. The claimant has not been treated equally with persons in the other categories because his legal gender changed as a result of having acquired an assigned gender. Unlike the persons in every other category, he is deprived of the opportunity of ensuring a continuity between entitlement to incapacity benefit and a retirement pension. . . .

38. That effect is a direct result of the change in the claimant's legal gender and prohibited by the wording of Article 4(1). Alternatively, it is attributable to the acquisition of the claimant's acquisition of an assigned gender and is prohibited on the authority of *Richards.*"

But once again the Commissioner finds, for the same reasons as in relation to the European Convention, that interpretation is of no assistance. But a remedy can be provided by disapplying the national law to the extent necessary to remove the prohibited discriminatory treatment:

"43. The 2004 Act fails to comply with Article 4, because it deprives the claimant of the link between entitlement to incapacity benefit and a retirement pension. I can remove that discrimination by disapplying the legislation to the extent necessary in order to allow that link to be maintained in the circumstances of his case. For practical purposes, that result can be achieved by deciding the claim for incapacity benefit as if it was made the day that his entitlement previously ceased. The claimant must, of course, be incapable of work, but for other purposes the gap in entitlement is to be disregarded."

The key points decided by the Tribunal of Commissioners in *R(P)2/09*, *CSP/503/2007* and *R(P)1/09* (which issued separate decisions in each of the cases before them) were as follows. The Gender Recognition Act 2004 had not removed the possibility of a direct effect claim based on art.4 of the Directive on the grounds that equal treatment was absent when the position of a transsexual of the acquired gender was compared with that of a non-transsexual member of the acquired gender. Such claims could apply to periods both prior and subsequent to the entry into force of the Gender Recognition Act 2004. In *CSP/503/2007* and *CP/1425/2007* the applicants were entitled from the date of their applications to be given the automatic increase in the weekly rate under s.55 of the Contributions and Benefits Act appropriate to a woman whose pension had started later than its earliest possible date, for a deferment period measured from when the appellants could first have insisted on their pension under the Directive as a woman down to its actual start at the age of 65. In this regard, the Tribunal of Commissioners concluded that the special provisions in Sch.5 of the Gender Recognition Act 2004 are over-ridden as they fall short of the achievement of equal treatment of two comparable groups.

However, whether a person's change of gender is to be recognised for the purposes of the right to equal treatment under the Directive is to be determined by applying the substantive provisions of the Gender Recognition Act 2004 even as regards periods prior to the entry into force of the recognition machinery in the national legal order. *CP/3485/2003* is followed and approved. The Tribunal of Commissioners indicates its view (not strictly necessary for the cases before them) that this means that there is no right to a pension as a single woman while still married as a man to another.

See also *CT v SSWP* [2009] UKUT 49 (AAC) for a decision dealing with a claim for a pension by a male-to-female transsexual relating to a period prior to the coming into force of the Gender Recognition Act 2004.

Article 5

Member States shall take the measures necessary to ensure that any laws, regulations and administrative provisions contrary to the principle of equal treatment are abolished.   3.492

Article 6

Member States shall introduce into their national legal systems such measures as art necessary to enable all persons who consider themselves wronged by failure to apply the principle of equal treatment to pursue their claims by judicial process, possibly after recourse to other competent authorities.   3.493

GENERAL NOTE

In Case C-66/95 *R. v Secretary of State for Social Security Ex p. Sutton* [1997]   3.494
E.C.R. I-2163, the Court of Justice ruled that art.6 required a judicial process which would ensure that those who had been wronged by discrimination prohibited by the directive could get the benefit to which they were entitled, but went on to rule that "the payment of interest on arrears of benefits cannot be regarded as an essential component of the right as so defined." (para.25.) Contrast certain decisions under the European Convention on Human Rights which seem to assume that just satisfaction under the Convention will require the payment of interest: see annotations to art.41 ECHR.

Article 7

1. This Directive shall be without prejudice to the right of Member   3.495
States to exclude from its scope:

    (a) the determination of pensionable age for the purposes of grant-
ing old-age and retirement pensions and the possible consequences
thereof for other benefits;

    (b) advantages in respect of old-age pension schemes granted to
persons who have brought up children; the acquisition of benefit
entitlements following periods of interruption of employment due to
the bringing up of children;

    (c) the granting of old-age or invalidity benefit entitlements by virtue of
the derived entitlements of a wife;

    (d) the granting of increases of long-term invalidity, old-age, accidents at
work and occupational disease benefits for a dependent wife;

    (e) the consequences of the exercise, before the adoption of this
Directive, of a right of option not to acquire rights or incur obligations under a statutory scheme.

2. Member States shall periodically examine matters excluded under
paragraph 1 in order to ascertain, in the light of social developments in
the matter concerned, whether there is justification for maintaining the
exclusions concerned.

GENERAL NOTE

3.496   Cases involving the Directive frequently raise issues of the scope of the derogations
to be found in this article. The Court of Justice always takes the view that exceptions
should be strictly construed, whereas freedoms are to be liberally construed.

Art.7(1)(a)

3.497   In Case C-9/91 *R. v Secretary of State for Social Security Ex p. Equal Opportunities
Commission* [1992] E.C.R. I-4297, the Court of Justice ruled that art.7(1)(a) permitted a Member State which retained differential pensionable ages for men and
women and in which pensions were funded from contributions to retain a system
under which men continued to be contribute for five years longer than women in
order to be entitled to the same basic pension and by requiring men who work until
the age of 65 to pay contributions whereas a woman who chooses to work beyond
the age of 60 is not required to continue to pay contributions. The difference in
treatment must, however, be necessarily linked to the difference in the statutory
pensionable age.

    In Case C-328/91 *Thomas v Secretary of State for Social Security* [1993] E.C.R.
I-1247, reported as *R(G) 2/94*, the Court of Justice was called upon to rule on
the nature of non-contributory invalidity benefits having regard to whether the
different entitlement of men and women were such as to have "possible consequences . . ." for the purposes of prescribing different pensionable ages within the
meaning of art.7(1)(a). The Court ruled that the situations envisaged by the words
"possible consequences thereof for other benefits" were limited to the forms of
discrimination which are necessarily and objectively linked to the difference in
retirement age.

    In Case C-92/94 *Secretary of State for Social Security v Graham* [1995] E.C.R.
I-2521, reported as *R(S)2/95*, concerned entitlement to invalidity benefit and the
differential requirements applied to men and women. Rose Graham was 58 when
she ceased work after several years in self-employment. As a person within five years
of pensionable age who was not entitled to the invalidity allowance component
of invalidity benefit; when she reached the age of 60 her entitlement to an invalidity pension was limited to the amount of her retirement pension (a condition
which does not apply to a man until the age of 65), and her retirement was taxable
whereas invalidity pension was tax-free. The claimant argued that the differential
treatment was neither necessarily nor objectively linked to the difference in retirement age. The Court is somewhat unsatisfactory reasoning holds that the differential

treatment is within the exception having regard to the coherence of the social security system. It is estimated that there were almost 40,000 look-alike cases affected by the decision. Where there are appeals on the grounds of links between invalidity benefit or unemployment benefit (by analogy), they seem certain to fail.

By contrast in Case C-137/94 *R. v Secretary of State for Health Ex p. Richardson* [1995] E.C.R. I-3407, it was held that the discriminatory treatment of men and women in relation to the restriction of entitlement to free prescriptions to those over retirement age unlawfully discriminated against men, since there was no necessary or objective link to pensionable age in the case of this social benefit. See also Case C-382/98 *R. v Secretary of State for Social Security Ex p. Taylor*, judgment of December 16, 1999, [1999] E.C.R. I-8955, in which the Court ruled that the different conditions of entitlement for man and women to winter fuel payments under the social fund could not be justified under the derogations in this article.

In Case C-303/02 *Haackert v Pensionsversicherungsanstalt der Angestellten*, Judgment of March 4, 2004, the Court of Justice ruled that the exception in art.7(1)(a) applied to early old-age pension schemes with different entitlement ages for men and women because of the close link with the age at which old-age pensions, which were not awarded early, would arise. In the circumstances of the case before the Court, the early old-age pension operated as a substitute for the old-age pension.

In *CIB/13368/1996* the Commissioner ruled that the claimant (and all women whose entitlement to incapacity benefit derives from industrial injury or prescribed disease) are entitled to continue to receive the benefit after the age of 60 and before reaching the age of 65 since there is a breach of the principle of equal treatment in the United Kingdom regulations which does not fall within the exemption in art.7(1)(a) but this decision was set aside, by consent, in the Court of Appeal on June 20, 2000 in *Chief Adjudication Officer v Rowlands*, because it was accepted that, in the light of the decision of the Court of Justice in Case C-196/98 *Hepple v Adjudication Officer* judgment of May 23, 2000, [2000] E.C.R. I-3701, the Commissioner's decision could not be upheld. In *Hepple*, the Court of Justice ruled that, in relation to reduced earnings allowance, the age conditions were held to fall within the exception in art.7(1)(a) in order to preserve coherence between the rules on reduced earnings allowance and the rules on old age pensions. The Court said that discrimination of the kind at issue in the main proceedings is objectively and necessarily linked to the difference between the retirement age for men and that for women, to that it is covered by the derogation for which art.7(1)(a) of the Directive provides (para.34 of the judgment). A key issue in the case had been the permissibility of introducing age conditions which differ according to sex *after* the date for implementation of the Directive.

Art.7(1)(c)

In *R(P) 1/96* the Commissioner held that the question of whether United **3.498** Kingdom contribution requirements breached the prohibition of discrimination in Dir.79/7 is a question of law and so was not be determined by the Secretary of State. The claimant, who had been married more than once, was arguing that the failure to take into account her first husband's contributions in determining her entitlement to a retirement pension constituted indirect discrimination against women. The Commissioner considered that such discrimination as there might be was permitted by Art.7(1)(c).

Art.7(1)(d)

In Case C-420/92 *Bramhill v Chief Adjudication Officer* [1994] E.C.R. I-3191, **3.499** reported as *R(P) 2/96*, the Court of Justice ruled that,

"Article 7(1)(d) of Council Directive 79/7 . . . does not preclude a Member State which provided for increases in long-term old-age benefits in respect of a dependent spouse to be granted only to me from abolishing that discrimination solely with regard to women who fulfil certain conditions."

Art. 7(2)

3.500   This would appear to be insufficiently precise to give rise to direct effect, since the term "periodically" is so open-ended. It is also difficult to see what right an individual could claim as a result of any such review.

Article 8

3.501   **1.** Member States shall bring into force the laws, regulations and administrative provisions necessary to comply with this Directive within six years of its notification. They shall immediately inform the Commission thereof.

2. Member States shall communicate to the Commission the text of laws, regulations and administrative provisions which they adopt in the field covered by this Directive, including measures adopted pursuant to Article 7(2).

They shall inform the Commission of their reasons for maintaining any existing provisions on the matters referred to in Article 7(1) and of the possibilities for reviewing them at a later date.

GENERAL NOTE

3.502   The Directive was required to be implemented from and including December 23, 1984. Those of its provisions that meet the requirements for direct effect have so operated since that date.

Article 9

3.503   Within seven years of notification of this Directive, Member States shall forward all information necessary to the Commission to enable it to draw up a report on the application of this Directive for submission to the Council and to propose such further measures as may be required for the implementation of the principle of equal treatment.

Article 10

3.504   This Directive is addressed to the Member States.

A Select Bibliography on European Social Security Law

Migration and Social Security Handbook (4th ed., CPAG, London, 2007)
European Commission, *Compendium of Community Provisions on Social Security 1995* (4th ed., Office for Official Publications of the European Communities, Luxembourg, 1995).

European Commission, *Judgments of the Court of Justice of the European Communities related to Social Security for Migrant Workers* (Office for Official Publications of the European Communities, Luxembourg, 1995).

European Commission, *Your Social Security Rights when Moving within the European Union. A Practical Guide* (Office for Official Publications of the European Communities, Luxembourg, 1997).

Pennings, F, *Introduction to European Social Security Law* (4th ed., Intersentia, Antwerp, 2003).

Pieters, D *The Social Security Systems of the Member States of the European Union,* (Intersentia, Antwerp, 2002).

White, R, *EC Social Security Law* (Longman, London, 1999).

Wikeley, N, *The Law of Social Security,* 5th ed. (London, Butterworths, 2002), ch.3.

PART IV

HUMAN RIGHTS LAW

Human Rights Act 1998

(1998 c.42)

ARRANGEMENT OF SECTIONS

Judges of the European Court of Human Rights

Parliamentary procedure

Supplemental

SCHEDULES

GENERAL NOTE

4.2   This Act has been described as "the first historic step . . . towards a constitutional Bill of Rights" (Lester, A and Pannick, D (ed.) *Human Rights Law and Practice* (Butterworths, London, 1999) at para.1.44. It followed a Labour consultation paper of December 1996 entitled *Bringing Rights Home*, a manifesto commitment by the Labour Party in 1997, and an October 1997 White Paper entitled *Rights Brought Home: The Human Rights Bill*, Cm.3782.

The Act entered into force on October 2, 2000: The Human Rights Act 1998 (Commencement No.2) Order 2000 (SI 2000/1851). The commencement of each section is noted in the annotation to each section.

The UK has been a party to the European Convention on Human Rights since September 23, 1953 and has recognised the right of individual petition under the Convention continuously since January 14, 1966. Until this Act come into force, rights accruing for individuals under the Convention could not be invoked directly to determine whether they have been victims of a violation of the rights protected by the Convention. Individuals within the jurisdiction could only use the "ordinary" law of the land to secure their rights. If they believed that these have been denied them by the State or a part of the State, and they have sought redress under the national legal order (exhausted domestic remedies in the language of the Convention), they have been able to make an application to the Commission of Human Rights (prior to November 1, 1998) and direct to the Court of Human Rights (from November 1, 1998) claiming to be victims of a violation of one of the rights protected. If the application is admitted, then the Court of Human Rights may adjudicate on the issue. The Convention organs, which are part of the Council of Europe, are located in Strasbourg; they should not be confused with the institutions of the European Union. The Court of Justice of the European Communities is located in Luxembourg.

Introduction

The Convention Rights

1.—(1) In this Act "the Convention rights" means the rights and funda-   4.3
mental freedoms set out in—
  (a) Articles 2 to 12 and 14 of the Convention,
  (b) Articles 1 to 3 of the First Protocol, and
  [2 (c) Article 1 of the Thirteenth Protocol,]
as read with Articles 16 to 18 of the Convention.
  (2) Those Articles are to have effect for the purposes of this Act subject to any designated derogation or reservation (as to which see sections 14 and 15).
  (3) The Articles are set out in Schedule 1.
  (4) The [¹ Secretary of State] may by order make such amendments to this Act as he considers appropriate to reflect the effect, in relation to the United Kingdom, of a protocol.
  (5) In subsection (4) "protocol" means a protocol to the Convention—
  (a) which the United Kingdom has ratified; or
  (b) which the United Kingdom has signed with a view to ratification.
  (6) No amendment may be made by an order under subsection (4) so as to come into force before the protocol concerned is in force in relation to the United Kingdom.

COMMENCEMENT

October 2, 2000: the Human Rights Act 1998 (Commencement No.2) Order 2000 (SI 2000/1851).

AMENDMENTS

1. The Secretary of State for Constitutional Affairs Order 2003 (SI 2003/1887) (August 19, 2003).
2. Human Rights Act 1998 (Amendment) Order 2004 (SI 2004/1574) (22 June, 2004)

GENERAL NOTE

The Preamble to the Act describes its objective as to give "further effect" to the   4.4
rights and freedoms guaranteed by the European Convention on Human Rights. The further effect given to the rights encompassed by the Act is their effect within the national legal order, so that they can be invoked directly in proceedings before United Kingdom courts and tribunals. This is the scheme of incorporation adopted for the United Kingdom. The late former President of the Court has expressed the advantages of incorporation as follows,

"It has in fact two advantages: it provides the national court with the possibility of taking account of the Convention and the Strasbourg case-law to resolve the dispute before it, and at the same time it gives the European organs an opportunity to discover the views of the national courts regarding the interpretation of the Convention and its application to a specific set of circumstances. The dialogue which thus develops between those who are called upon to apply the Convention on the domestic level and those who must do so on the European level is crucial for an effective protection of the rights guaranteed under the Convention." (Rolv Ryssdal, Speech at the ceremony for the 40th anniversary of the European Convention on Human Rights at Trieste, 18 December 1990, Council of Europe document Court (90) 318, 2.

Convention rights are defined in subs.(1) as arts 2–12 and 14 of the Convention itself, together with certain articles of the First and Sixth Protocols as read with arts 16–18 of the Convention. These articles are set out in Sch.1. Their effect is subject to the terms of any derogation under art.15 of the Convention or any reservation filed by the UK Government. Derogations are governed in more detail by s.14, and reservations by s.15; any current derogations and reservations are set out in Sch.3. The Secretary of State is given power to amend the Act to give effect to rights contained in protocols to the Convention which have not yet been ratified by the UK. For example, the UK Government has indicated that consideration is being given to ratification of certain provisions of the Seventh Protocol, but not of the Fourth Protocol.

Convention rights as defined in s.1 do not include art.1 which provides that parties to the Convention "shall secure to everyone within their jurisdiction the rights and freedoms" set out in arts 2–18 of the Convention. Nor do they include art.13 which gives a right to an effective remedy in the following terms:

> "Everyone whose rights and freedoms as set forth in this Convention are violated shall have an effective remedy before a national authority notwithstanding that the violation has been committed by persons acting in an official capacity."

The incorporation of art.1 among Convention rights named by the Act is probably not necessary since the purpose of the Act is to give effect to Convention rights within the national legal order. However, it should be noted that the rights given by the Convention are not linked in any way to the nationality of an individual; they are guaranteed to all within the UK's jurisdiction. This differs from many rights given by EU law where the beneficiaries are nationals of the Member States of the European Union.

The failure to include art.13 among the Convention rights may be more problematic, though the Lord Chancellor stoutly argued that its inclusion was not necessary because the Act gives effect "to Article 13 by establishing a scheme under which Convention rights can be raised before out domestic courts": HL Vol.583 col.475 (November 18, 1997). In the Commons, the Home Secretary made a similar point. There is apparently some concern that inclusion of the article might lead all manner of courts and tribunals to "invent" new remedies for violation of Convention rights. The Act is cautious on the issue of remedies where a violation is found: see commentary to s.8. However, both the Lord Chancellor and the Home Secretary conceded that in considering any question of remedies, courts or tribunals may have regard to the terms of art.13 under s.2 of the Act. However, situations may arise where the scheme of the Act arguably does not offer an effective remedy for the violation, though it should be noted that the nature and scope of the effectiveness of the remedy required under art.13 has hardly been touched on in the Strasbourg case law.

An example might help to illustrate the possible lacuna. Suppose a claimant before an appeal tribunal succeeds in persuading the tribunal that there has been an excessive delay in giving judgment on an appeal; This would constitute a violation of art.6(1), ECHR. In this type of case, the Court of Human Rights has often awarded some compensation for the delay, but an appeal tribunal has no power to award compensation, or interest on late benefit. This would leave the individual without a remedy unless the mere statement that there was a violation was considered sufficient in the circumstances of the case. Any claim for compensation would have to be the subject of separate (and wholly novel) proceedings in a different forum. It is at least arguable that making a person in this position go to two judicial bodies for a remedy for the same violation is a failure to provide an effective remedy.

Interpretation of Convention rights

2.—(1) A court or tribunal determining a question which has arisen in connection with a Convention right must take into account any— 4.5

(a) judgment, decision, declaration or advisory opinion of the European Court of Human Rights,

(b) opinion of the Commission given in a report adopted under Article 31 of the Convention,

(c) decision of the Commission in connection with Article 26 or 27(2) of the Convention, or

(d) decision of the Committee of Ministers taken under Article 46 of the Convention,

whenever made or given, so far as, in the opinion of the court or tribunal, it is relevant to the proceedings in which that question has arisen.

(2) Evidence of any judgment, decision, declaration or opinion of which account may have to be taken under this section is to be given in proceedings before any court or tribunal in such manner as may be provided by rules.

(3) In this section "rules" means rules of court or, in the case of proceedings before a tribunal, rules made for the purposes of this section—

(a) by [1 . . .] [2 the Lord Chancellor or] the Secretary of State, in relation to any proceedings outside Scotland;

(b) by the Secretary of State, in relation to proceedings in Scotland; or

(c) by a Northern Ireland department, in relation to proceedings before a tribunal in Northern Ireland—

    (i) which deals with transferred matters; and

    (ii) for which no rules made under paragraph (a) are in force.

COMMENCEMENT

October 2, 2000: The Human Rights Act 1998 (Commencement No.2) Order 2000 (SI 2000/1851).

AMENDMENTS

1. The Secretary of State for Constitutional Affairs Order 2003 (SI 2003/1887) (August 19, 2003).

2. The Transfer of Functions (Lord Chancellor and Secretary of State) Order 2005 (SI 2005/3429) (January 12, 2006).

GENERAL NOTE

Introduction

This section requires courts and tribunals to have regard to the Strasbourg case law, past, present and future, in deciding any question relating to a Convention right. Note that the Strasbourg case law is not binding. There are two reasons for this. First, it will not always be easy to transplant directly the point being made by the Strasbourg organ where the case involves the complexities of other legal systems. Secondly, the Convention sets a minimum standard; one possibly dramatic effect of incorporation is that the United Kingdom authorities will set a higher standard than the common European standard which is set by the Strasbourg organs. 4.6

The section refers to dispositions of three Strasbourg organs: the Commission, the Court and the Committee of Ministers. In order to understand the reasons for this, both the old and the new Strasbourg systems must be understood.

The "old" system of protection

4.7   The Convention, in its original form, created two organs "to ensure the observance of the engagements undertaken by the High Contracting Parties": the European Commission of Human Rights and the European Court of Human Rights. The main function of these two organs, sometimes collectively referred to as the Strasbourg organs, (together with the Committee of Ministers discussed later) was to deal with applications made by States and by individuals alleging violations of the Convention. Under old art.24, any State party to the Convention could refer to the Commission any alleged breach of the provisions of the Convention by another State party. Under old art.25, the Commission could receive applications from any person, non-governmental organization, or group of individuals claiming to be the victim of a violation by one of the Member States of the rights set forth in the Convention and any relevant Protocols. The procedure differed depending on whether the application is made under art.24 or 25; what follows describes the process in relation to individual applications under art.25.

Once an application was registered, the Commission first considered, and issued a *decision* on, whether the application met the admissibility requirements. If it did not, that was an end of the matter. If the application was declared admissible, the Commission went on to conduct an investigation into the merits of the complaint and to consider whether there had been a violation of the Convention. The result was a *report* from the Commission expressing an *opinion* (which is not legally binding) as to whether or not there has been a violation. The report was communicated on a confidential basis to the applicant and to the State concerned and was delivered to the Committee of Ministers, the political organ of the Council of Europe. Throughout this time, attempts would have been made to secure a friendly settlement "on the basis of respect for human rights".

Final decisions on cases on which the Commission had reported and which had not resulted in a friendly settlement were made by the Committee of Ministers, or the Court of Human Rights. Recognition of the jurisdiction of the Court was technically voluntary under old art.46 of the Convention. Within three months of the transmission of the Commission report to the Committee of Ministers, the application could be referred to the Court for determination by the Commission, the defendant State, or the State whose national was alleged to be the victim. The applicant had no standing to refer the application to the Court, unless the defendant State was a party to Protocol 9. Where this was so, the applicant could refer the matter to the Court, but (unless it was also referred to the Court by the Commission or a State) it first had to be submitted to a panel of three judges, who could decide unanimously that the application should not be considered by the Court because it did not raise a serious question affecting the interpretation or application of the Convention.

If the case was referred to the Court and heard by it, there was a full judicial procedure, and even where Protocol 9 had not been ratified, some accommodations were made which allowed limited participation by the applicant. The Courts at in plenary session or in Chambers of nine. Decisions were made by a majority of the judges present and voting, with the President enjoying a casting vote if this was necessary. Separate opinions could be attached to the judgment of the majority.

Those cases which were not referred to the Court within three months of transmission of the Commission's report to the Committee of Ministers were automatically referred to the Committee of Ministers for final decision. The practice of the Committee of Ministers in recent years was simply to endorse the Commission report without any further investigation of the merits of the case.

The use of a political organ was a compromise to ensure that all applications resulted in a final determination. In the early years, there were States which had not recognised the competence of the Court, and there have always been cases which no one has referred to the Court.

The "new" system of protection

Protocol 11 has amended the Convention to make provision for a new wholly judicial system of determination of applications. The Commission and the Court have been replaced from November 1, 1998 by a new permanent Court, which handles both the admissibility and merits phases of application. The Court is also charged with seeking to secure friendly settlement of matters before it.   **4.8**

Individual applications are made to the Court under art.34 and individuals have full standing before the Court. Complaints are initially considered by a three-judge committee which will consider whether the application meets the Convention's admissibility criteria, but it can only rule an application to be inadmissible if it is unanimous. These criteria have not changed and flow from the terms of arts 34 and 35 and involve the consideration of nine questions:

1. Can the applicant claim to be a victim?
2. Is the defendant State a party to the Convention?
3. Have domestic remedies been exhausted?
4. Is the application filed within the six-month time-limit?
5. Is the application signed?
6. Has the application been brought before?
7. Is the application compatible with the Convention?
8. Is the application manifestly ill-founded?
9. Is there an abuse of the right of petition?

Those cases which are not ruled inadmissible by the three judge committee are put before a seven judge chamber of the Court, which will include the judge sitting in respect of the defendant State. The chamber will consider the written arguments of the parties, investigate the material facts if these are in contention, and hear oral argument. This stage of the proceedings concludes with a decision whether the complaint is admissible and whether a friendly settlement is possible. There follows a consideration of the merits. In many cases, the admissibility and merits phases are now joined.

Certain cases of special difficulty may be relinquished by a chamber to a Grand Chamber of 17 judges: art.30. It is also possible for any party to a judgment of a chamber to request referral of the judgment to a Grand Chamber. In such cases, a panel of five judges of the Grand Chamber decides whether or not to accept the request. Many such requests are denied. In 2008, 295 such requests were made, of which 10 were accepted.

Which authorities are the most important?

Though the section requires courts and tribunals to have regard to authorities from all three Strasbourg organs, but there can be little doubt that the most important are the judgments of the Court of Human Rights.   **4.9**

Too great a reliance should not be placed on decisions on admissibility of any antiquity, since these have not always been fully reasoned and where the decision is to declare an application inadmissible are, by definition, not based on any comprehensive consideration of the merits. Furthermore the volume of such decisions has been such that the quality of the reasoning in admissibility decisions can be opaque. How much can be learned from a decision which outlines some facts as asserted in the application and then decides that the application is "manifestly ill-founded"? In many cases no observations had been sought from the respondent government.

Authorities on the interpretation of the concept of a "victim" of a violation of the Convention may be particularly persuasive, because of the drafting of s.7(7): see commentary to that section. The same view is taken of the concept of "just satisfaction" in s.8(3): see commentary to that section.

The relationship between Strasbourg judgments and national judgments

4.10   *Kay v Lambeth LBC, Leeds CC v Price* [2006] UKHL 10, [2006] 2 WLR 570 provides guidance for courts and tribunals when faced with a judgment of the Court of Human Rights which conflicts with an earlier binding authority of a national court. Both Justice and Liberty were permitted to intervene in the case. The Court rejected the argument that a lower court could depart from what would otherwise be a binding precedent of a higher court where there was a later judgment of the Court of Human Rights which was clearly inconsistent with the judgment of the higher court. The effect of the House of Lords ruling is that the development of case law will be influenced by the judgments of the Court of Human Rights, but that legal certainty can only be maintained if conflicts between decisions of the Court of Human Rights and those of national courts are determined within the hierarchy of courts in the national legal order.

There are aftershocks of this decision in the social security context in the context of whether non-contributory benefits are 'possessions' within art.1 of Protocol 1. So, for example, both *Couronne* and *CIS/1757/2006* (para.40) decide that they were bound to follow *Reynolds* and *Campbell R (H) 1/05* in the Court of Appeal to the effect that non-contributory benefits are not possessions, notwithstanding the decision of the Grand Chamber to the contrary in *Stec*. It is understood that CPAG are concerned about this approach and have raised the matter with the Department for Work and Pensions. There is certain to be further case law on this point in the social security context. In such litigation it would be argued that the special circumstances of the post-Court of Appeal litigation in *Reynolds* would provide grounds for *not* following the general rule laid down in *Kay*.

In *R. (on the application of RJM) v Secretary of State for Work and Pensions*, [2008] UKHL 63, the House of Lords addressed the questions touched on in *Kay*. Lord Neuberger said:

> 64. Where the Court of Appeal considers that an earlier decision of this House, which would otherwise be binding on it, may be, or even is clearly, inconsistent with a subsequent decision of the ECtHR, then (absent wholly exceptional circumstances) the court should faithfully follow the decision of the House, and leave it to your Lordships to decide whether to modify or reverse its earlier decision. To hold otherwise would be to go against what Lord Bingham decided. As a matter of principle, it should be for this House, not for the Court of Appeal, to determine whether one of its earlier decisions has been overtaken by a decision of the ECtHR. As a matter of practice, as the recent decision of this House in *Animal Defenders* [2008] 2 WLR 781 shows, decisions of the ECtHR are not always followed as literally as some might expect. As to what would constitute exceptional circumstances, I cannot do better than to refer back to the exceptional features which Lord Bingham identified as justifying the Court of Appeal's approach in *East Berkshire* [2004] QB 558: see *Kay* [2006] 2 AC 465, para 45.

But the position in relation to the Court of Appeal's respect for its own previous decisions is different:

> 65. When it comes to its own previous decisions, I consider that different considerations apply. It is clear from what was said in *Young* [1944] KB 718 that the Court of Appeal is freer to depart from its earlier decisions than from those of this House: a decision of this House could not, I think, be held by the Court of Appeal to have been arrived at per incuriam. Further, more recent jurisprudence suggests that the concept of per incuriam in this context has been interpreted rather generously—see the discussion in the judgment of Lloyd LJ in *Desnousse v Newham London Borough Council* [2006] EWCA Civ 547, [2006] QB 831, paras 71 to 75.
>
> 66. The principle promulgated in *Young* [1944] KB 718 was, of course, laid down at a time when there were no international courts whose decisions had the domestic force which decisions of the ECtHR now have, following the passing of

the 1998 Act, and in particular section 2(1)(a). In my judgment, the law in areas such as that of precedent should be free to develop, albeit in a principled and cautious fashion, to take into account such changes. Accordingly, I would hold that, where it concludes that one of its previous decisions is inconsistent with a subsequent decision of the ECtHR, the Court of Appeal should be free (but not obliged) to depart from that decision.

Legislation

Interpretation of legislation

3.—(1) So far as it is possible to do so, primary legislation and subordi-   4.11
nate legislation must be read and given effect in a way which is compatible
with the Convention rights.

(2) This section—

(a) applies to primary legislation and subordinate legislation whenever enacted;

(b) does not affect the validity, continuing operation or enforcement of any incompatible primary legislation; and

(c) does not affect the validity, continuing operation or enforcement of any incompatible subordinate legislation if (disregarding any possibility of revocation) primary legislation prevents removal of the incompatibility.

COMMENCEMENT

October 2, 2000: The Human Rights Act 1998 (Commencement No.2) Order 2000 (SI 2000/1851).

GENERAL NOTE

There is a powerful new principle of statutory interpretation here: so far as it   4.12
is *possible* to do so, primary and secondary legislation whenever enacted *must* be
read in a way which is compatible with Convention rights whenever a question of
Convention rights is in issue. The requirement applies to all users of the legislation;
it does not apply solely to courts and tribunals, nor does it require that a public
authority (see s.6) is a party to the issue raised.

The principle is clearly mandatory and strongly so. A judge writing in a journal has
said that the section creates a rebuttable presumption in favour of an interpretation
consistent with Convention rights: Lord Steyn, "Incorporation and Devolution—A
Few Reflections on the Changing Scene" [1998] E.H.R.L.R. 153, at 155.

However, where primary legislation cannot be read compatibly with Convention
rights, then a court or tribunal does not have the power to strike down or ignore
the incompatible primary legislation. Certain courts may, however, declare the
legislation incompatible with Convention rights. This preserves the sovereignty of
Parliament and is one of the clever features of the Act that have enabled it to fit into
the constitutional traditions of the UK.

Where secondary legislation cannot be read compatibly with Convention rights,
two possibilities will arise. First, if the incompatibility of the secondary legislation
is required by the primary legislation under which it is made, then the status of the
secondary legislation is the same as that of incompatible primary legislation. Its
validity, continuing operation and enforcement are unaffected. But if the incompatibility is not required by the primary legislation, then it cannot be said to be within
the powers of the primary legislation under which it is enacted, and any court or

tribunal (and seemingly anyone called on to interpret that legislation) can disregard it: its validity, continuing operation and enforcement will be affected.

To some extent, this obligation to force an interpretation from a statutory provision is not entirely new, since European Community law requires legislation implementing the requirements of Community law to be read, so far as it is possible to do so, in a manner which achieves the objectives of the EC Treaty: see the view taken in the House of Lords in *Webb v EMO Air Cargo (UK) Ltd* [1992] 2 All E.R. 929.

The application of the rule of interpretation in s.3 has now been the subject of comment in the highest courts of the United Kingdom.

The distinction between interpretation and legislation had been made by Lord Woolf C.J., in the Court of Appeal in *Poplar Housing and Regeneration Community Association Ltd v Donoghue* [2002] Q.B. 48,

> "It is difficult to overestimate the importance of section 3. It applies to legislation passed both before and after the Human Rights Act 1998 came into force. Subject to the section not requiring the court to go beyond what is possible, it is mandatory in its terms. . . . Now, when section 3 applies, the courts have to adjust their traditional role in relation to interpretation so as to give effect to the direction contained in section 3. It is as though legislation which predates the Human Rights Act 1998 and conflicts with the Convention has to be treated as being subsequently amended to incorporate the language of section 3. . . . Section 3 does not entitle the court to *legislate* (its task is still one of *interpretation*, but interpretation in accordance with the direction contained in section 3. . . .
>
> The most difficult task which courts face is distinguishing between legislation and interpretation. Here practical experience of seeking to apply section 3 will provide the best guide. However, if it is necessary in order to obtain compliance to radically alter the effect of the legislation this will be an indication that more than interpretation is involved."

In *R. v A (Complainant's Sexual History) (No. 2)* [2002] A.C. 45, the House of Lords has commented on the effect of the obligation in s.3 in the context of the interpretation of s.41 of the Youth Justice and Criminal Evidence Act 1999 in relation to the evidence which may be adduced in rape trials. Lord Steyn said,

> ". . . the interpretative obligation under section 3 is a strong one. It applies even if there is no ambiguity in the language in the sense of the language being capable of two different meanings. It is an emphatic adjuration by the legislature . . . Section 3 places a duty on the court to strive to find a possible interpretation compatible with Convention rights. Under ordinary methods of interpretation a court may depart from the language of the statute to avoid absurd consequences: section 3 goes much further. . . . Section 3 . . . requires a court to find an interpretation compatible with Convention rights if it is possible to do so. . . . In accordance with the will of Parliament as reflected in section 3 it will sometimes be necessary to adopt an interpretation which linguistically may appear strained. The techniques to be used will not only involve the reading down of express language in a statute but also the implication of provisions. A declaration of incompatibility is a measure of last resort. It must be avoided unless it is plainly impossible to do so."

Lord Hope of Craighead said,

> "The rule of construction which section 3 lays down is quite unlike any previous rule of statutory interpretation. There is no need to identify an ambiguity or absurdity. Compatibility with Convention rights is the sole guiding principle. That is the paramount object which the rule seeks to achieve. But the rule is only a rule of interpretation. It does not entitle the judges to act as legislators."

The Court also endorsed the distinction between interpretation and legislation identifed by Lord Woolf C.J. in the *Poplar Housing* case.

This point was also reiterated by the House of Lords in *Re S (FC); Re S and Re W* [2002] 2 All E.R. 192, where Lord Nicholls said,

"In applying section 3 courts must be ever mindful of this outer limit. The Human Rights Act reserves the amendment of primary legislation to Parliament. By this means the Act seeks to preserve parliamentary sovereignty. The Act maintains the constitutional boundary. Interpretation of statutes is a matter for the courts; the enactment of statutes, and the amendment of statutes, are matters for Parliament. . . . The area of real difficulty lies in identifying the limits of interpretation in a particular case. . . . For present purposes it is sufficient to say that a meaning which departs substantially from a fundamental feature of an Act of Parliament is likely to have crossed the boundary between interpretation and amendment. This is especially so where the departure has important practical repercussions which the court is not equipped to evaluate. In such a case the overall contextual setting may leave no scope for rendering the statutory provision Convention compliant by legitimate use of the process of interpretation."

In *Ghaidan v Godin-Mendoza*, [2004] UKHL 30, the House of Lords ruled that the policy reasons for giving a statutory tenancy to the survivor of a cohabiting heterosexual couple applied equally to the survivor of a cohabiting homosexual couple. In so holding, they interpreted para.2 and 3 of Sch.1 to the Rent Act 1977 to secure compatibility with Convention rights. This avoided less favourable treatment of homosexual couples in the enjoyment of their Convention rights under art.8 ECHR which could not be objectively justified.

The case is important for its re-affirmation of the approach which should be adopted in reading and giving effect to primary and subordinate legislation in a way which is compatible with Convention rights. Significantly, the judges in the House of Lords did not attempt to write words into or delete words from the statutory provisions in issue, preferring simply to indicate what the substantive effect of those provisions should be (see opinion of Lord Nicholls at para.35). The task of interpretation under s.3 required courts, if necessary, to depart from the unambiguous meaning of a legislative provision in order to ensure respect for Convention rights. Lord Steyn said that declarations of incompatibility under s.4 were remedies of last resort, and that s.3 represents the principal remedial measure. Lord Steyn also indicated that there had been a tendency to concentrate too much on linguistic features of particular legislative provisions; what was required was a broad purposive approach concentrating on the Convention right in issue. Lord Rodger said,

"123. Attaching decisive importance to the precise adjustments required to the language of any particular provision would reduce the exercise envisaged by s.3(1) to a game where the outcome would depend in part on the particular turn of phrase chosen by the draftsman and in part on the skill of the court in devising brief formulae to make the provision compatible with Convention rights. The statute book is the work of many different hands in different parliaments over hundreds of years and, even today, two different draftsmen might choose different language to express the same proposition. In enacting s.3(1), it cannot have been the intention of parliament to place those asserting their rights at the mercy of the linguistic choices of the individual who happened to draft the provision in question. What matters is not so much the particular phraseology chosen by the draftsman as the substance of the measure which Parliament has enacted in those words. Equally, it cannot have been the intention of Parliament to place a premium on the skill of those called on to think up a neat way round the draftsman's language. Parliament was not out to devise an entertaining parlour game for lawyers, but, so far as possible, to make legislation operate compatibly with Convention rights. This means concentrating on matters of substance, rather than on matters of mere language.

124. Sometimes it may be possible to isolate a particular phrase which causes the difficulty and to read in words that modify it so as to remove the incompatibility. Or else the court may read in words that qualify the provision as a whole. At other times the appropriate solution may be to read down the provision so that it falls to be given effect in a way that is compatible with the Convention rights in question. In other cases the easiest solution may be to put the offending part of the provision into different words which convey the meaning that will be compatible with those rights. The preferred technique will depend on the particular provision and also, in reality, on the person doing the interpreting. This does not matter since they are simply different means of achieving the same substantive result. However, precisely because s.3(1) is to be operated by many others besides the courts, and because it is concerned with interpreting and not with amending the offending provision, it respectfully seems to me that it would be going too far to insist that those using the section to interpret legislation should match the standards to be expected of a parliamentary draftsman amending the provision: *cf. R. v Lambert* [2002] 2 A.C. 545 at 585, para.80, *per* Lord Hope of Craighead. It is enough that the interpretation placed on the provision should be clear, however it may be expressed and whatever the precise means adopted to achieve it."

The proper approach to the application of s.3 would appear in the light of all the authorities to involve a number of steps. First, it is necessary to identify the legislative provision which it is argued breaches Convention rights: see *R. v A (No.2)* [2002] A.C. 45. Then consideration should be given to whether that provision involves a breach of Convention rights: see *Poplar Housing and Regeneration Community Association Ltd v Donoghue* [2002] Q.B. 48. If there is, then a s.3 interpretation is needed and the focus here should be on compatibility with the Convention right. This can be achieved by reading in Convention rights, that is, by implying words in the legislative provision to secure compatibility with Convention rights; or by reading down, that is, by applying a narrower interpretation in order to secure compatibility. But it is not necessary to specify the precise rewording of the provision: see *Ghaidan v Godin-Mendoza* above.

The limits of interpretation are reached where the required construction conflicts with the express words of a legislative provision: see *R. (Anderson) v Secretary of State for the Home Department* [2003] 1 A.C. 837. The same conclusion will be reached if there is a conflict with the legislative provision by necessary implication. Finally, the limits of construction are reached when the construction placed on the provision alters the statutory scheme in a fundamental way.

In *R(G) 2/04*, the reported decision in *CG/1467/2001*, the Commissioner, following the decision of the Court of Appeal in *R. (Hooper) v Secretary of State for Work and Pensions* [2003] 1 W.L.R 2623 in this respect—which was not in issue in the appeal to the House of Lords—that the words of the statute admitted of only one interpretation. The effect of this was to preclude a man from claiming widow's benefit in respect of a spouse who died before April 9, 2001. See annotations to art.14 ECHR for more detail on this line of cases.

Declaration of incompatibility

4.13

4.—(1) Subsection (2) applies in any proceedings in which a court determines whether a provision of primary legislation is compatible with a Convention right.

(2) If the court is satisfied that the provision is incompatible with a Convention right, it may make a declaration of that incompatibility.

(3) Subsection (4) applies in any proceedings in which a court determines whether a provision of subordinate legislation, made in the exercise of a power conferred by primary legislation, is compatible with a Convention right.

(4) If the court is satisfied—

(a) that the provision is incompatible with a Convention right, and

(b) that (disregarding any possibility of revocation) the primary legislation concerned prevents removal of the incompatibility,

it may make a declaration of that incompatibility.

(5) In this section "court" means—

(a) the House of Lords;

(b) the Judicial Committee of the Privy Council;

(c) the Courts-Martial Appeal Court;

(d) in Scotland, the High Court of Justiciary sitting otherwise than as a
trial court or the Court of Session;

(e) in England and Wales or Northern Ireland, the High Court or the
Court of Appeal.

[¹ (f) the Court of Protection, in any matter being dealt with by the
President of the Family Division, the Vice-Chancellor or a puisne
judge of the High Court.]

(6) A declaration under this section ("a declaration of incompatibility")—

(a) does not affect the validity, continuing operation or enforcement of
the provision in respect of which it is given; and

(b) is not binding on the parties to the proceedings in which it is made.

COMMENCEMENT

October 2, 2000: The Human Rights Act 1998 (Commencement No.2) Order
2000 (SI 2000/1851).

AMENDMENT

1. Mental Capacity Act 2005, Sch.6 para.43 (October 1, 2007).

GENERAL NOTE

This section gives certain courts power to make declarations of incompatibility   4.14
where primary or secondary legislation cannot be read compatibly with Convention
rights. It is a discretionary power available to the higher courts only. It arises in any
proceedings; there is again no requirement that one of the parties is a public authority. Neither First-tier tribunals nor the Upper Tribunal have the power to make
declarations of incompatibility.

It is perhaps unfortunate that the only routes to declarations of incompatibility in
the social security jurisdiction are appeal from the Upper Tribunal to the Court of
Appeal, or taking judicial review proceedings in the High Court against a decision of
a First-tier tribunal or the Upper Tribunal, assuming in the latter case that judicial
review lies against the Upper Tribunal.

The effect of a declaration of incompatibility is not to declare the legislation
invalid, inoperative or unenforceable, and so does not give rise to any claim for
damages for breach of the Human Rights Act: *Re K: A Child*, Court of Appeal,
November 15, 2000 [2001] 2 All E.R. 719. The impeached provision will continue in full force and effect pending any amendment. The effect of a declaration
of incompatibility is to put the Government on notice of the incompatibility. The
Government may then choose to take the remedial action provided for in s.10 of
and Sch.2 to the Act.

On July 10, 2003, the House of Lords ruled on the appeal in *Wilson v Secretary
of State for Trade and Industry*, [2003] UKHL 40. They reversed the decision of the
Court of Appeal to make a declaration of incompatibility in respect of s.127 of the
Consumer Credit Act 1974.

Wilson had borrowed £5,000 from First County Trust on the security of her BMW

318 convertible. The loan agreement added a £250 document fee to the £5,000 loan, thus mis-stating the amount of the loan as £5,250. In 1999 Wilson issued a claim in the county court, inter alia, for a declaration that the loan agreement was unenforceable because it did not contain all the prescribed terms. The county court ruled in the lender's favour, but this was reversed in the Court of Appeal, but adjourned to enable Convention rights arguments to be considered. The Secretary of State argued that the Court had no power to make a declaration of incompatibility because the agreement pre-dated October 2, 2000, the date the Human Rights Act 1998 entered into force. However, the Court said that the act which violated Convention rights was not the agreement but any order of the Court making the loan agreement unenforceable. They went on to make a declaration of incompatibility.

The House of Lords has ruled that the Human Rights Act 1998 is not to be applied retrospectively, and so there was no jurisdiction in the Court of Appeal to make the declaration of incompatibility. A statute concerned with Convention rights could not render acts unlawful which were lawful when they were undertaken, since this would impose retrospective liability.

Their Lordships did go on to consider whether the provisions of s.127 were compatible with Convention rights. The section imposed a mandatory sanction designed to ensure that lenders directed their minds to compliance with their obligations. It was a measure for the protection of the consumer, the weaker party in such transactions. This appeared to be in the view of the court not a violation of Convention rights in relation to the loans covered by the section (up to £25,000). In these circumstances there was no lack of proportionality in the sanction for failure to comply with the requirements of the legislation.

In *R(IS)12/04* the Commissioner concludes that a tribunal's lack of power to make a declaration of incompatibility is not a good reason for not dealing fully with human rights issues raised before tribunals. The Commissioner notes that in some circumstances, tribunals do have the power to declare subordinate legislation to have been invalidly made. The tribunal's reasons were found to be inadequate because they had dismissed detailed human rights arguments on the basis that they could not make a declaration of inadmissibility under s.4.

In its admissibility decision of June 18, 2002 in *Hobbs v United Kingdom (App.63684/00)*, the Court of Human Rights ruled that a declaration of incompatibility is not an effective remedy within the meaning of art.35 of the Convention for the purpose of the rule requiring an applicant to exhaust domestic remedies. The Court rejected the Government's invitation to reconsider this position in its admissibility decision of March 16, 2004 in *Walker v United Kingdom (App.37212/02)*. The Court was strongly influenced by the fact that a declaration of incompatibility was not binding on the parties.

This view has been confirmed by the Grand Chamber of the Strasbourg Court in *Burden v United Kingdom* (App. 13378/05), judgment of April 28, 2008, paras 40-4.

Right of Crown to intervene

4.15   **5.**—(1) Where a court is considering whether to make a declaration of incompatibility, the Crown is entitled to notice in accordance with rules of court.

(2) In any case to which subsection (1) applies—

(a) a Minister of the Crown (or a person nominated by him),

(b) a member of the Scottish Executive,

(c) a Northern Ireland Minister,

(d) a Northern Ireland department,

is entitled, on giving notice in accordance with rules of court, to be joined as a party to the proceedings.

(3) Notice under subsection (2) may be given at any time during the proceedings.

(4) A person who has been made a party to criminal proceedings (other than in Scotland) as the result of a notice under subsection (2) may, with leave, appeal to the House of Lords against any declaration of incompatibility made in the proceedings.

(5) In subsection (4)—

"criminal proceedings" includes all proceedings before the Courts-Martial Appeal Court; and

"leave" means leave granted by the court making the declaration of incompatibility or by the House of Lords.

COMMENCEMENT

October 2, 2000: The Human Rights Act 1998 (Commencement No.2) Order 2000 (SI 2000/1851).

Public authorities

Acts of public authorities

6.—(1) It is unlawful for a public authority to act in a way which is incompatible with a Convention right.   4.16

(2) Subsection (1) does not apply to an act if—

(a) as the result of one or more provisions of primary legislation, the authority could not have acted differently; or

(b) in the case of one or more provisions of, or made under, primary legislation which cannot be read or given effect in a way which is compatible with the Convention rights, the authority was acting so as to give effect to or enforce those provisions.

(3) In this section "public authority" includes—

(a) a court or tribunal, and

(b) any person certain of whose functions are functions of a public nature,

but does not include either House of Parliament or a person exercising functions in connection with proceedings in Parliament.

(4) In subsection (3) "Parliament" does not include the House of Lords in its judicial capacity.

(5) In relation to a particular act, a person is not a public authority by virtue only of subsection (3)(b) if the nature of the act is private.

(6) "An act" includes a failure to act but does not include a failure to—

(a) introduce in, or lay before, Parliament a proposal for legislation; or

(b) make any primary legislation or remedial order.

COMMENCEMENT

October 2, 2000: The Human Rights Act 1998 (Commencement No.2) Order 2000 (SI 2000/1851).

GENERAL NOTE

The obligation in s.6(1) is at the heart of the scheme of incorporation in the Act.   4.17
It could be said that all the other provisions flow from the requirement that public authorities of any kind act compatibly with Convention rights. Note that there is a

"defence" in s.6(2) where there was a statutory requirement to act in a particular manner. Here there will, of course, be an incompatibility between the statutory provision and Convention rights.

The key concept in the section is that of a public authority. This includes courts and tribunals, but not either House of Parliament, and is extended to "any person certain of whose functions are functions of a public nature" The difficult two words become very difficult 12 words. Only "certain" of the authority's functions need be of a public nature, and there is no liability in respect of the exercise of their functions of a private nature.

The question of what constitutes a public authority is reminiscent of the definitional problem of determining what are "emanations of the State" for the purposes of the horizontal application of EC Directives. The test is certainly not the same, but the same difficulties will arise in determining those institutions at the margins of State power which constitute public authorities. The definition will require judicial interpretation, but it is clearly a functional test.

There is, however, no doubt that the Department and all its constituent parts constitute public authorities, as, of course, do the tribunals and other judicial bodies. All must act compatibly with Convention rights. This means that they must take up obvious Convention points even if they are not raised by the parties, since otherwise they would be acting unlawfully by acting in a manner which is not compatible with Convention rights.

In *Poplar Housing and Regeneration Community Association Ltd v Donoghue* [2002] Q.B. 48, the Court of Appeal provided some useful guidance on the definition of the notion of a public authority as defined in the section. The definition is to be given a generous interpretation. Hybrid bodies which exercised both public and private functions were public authorities only in relation to acts of a public nature and not acts of a private nature. But the fact that a public regulatory body supervised a body did not necessarily indicate that any act subject to supervision was an act of a public nature.

On the concept of "public authority" for the purposes of this Act, see also *Parochial Church Council of the Parish of Aston Cantlow and Wilmcote with Billesley, Warwickshire v Wallbank* [2003] UKHL 37; [2003] 3 W.L.R. 283; and *Hampshire County Council v Beer t/a Hammer Trout Farm* [2003] EWCA Civ 1056; [2004] 1 W.L.R. 233.

In the *Aston Cantlow* case, Lord Nicholls said,

> "12. What, then, is the touchstone to be used in deciding whether a function is public for this purpose? Clearly there is no single test of universal application. There cannot be, given the diverse nature of governmental functions and the variety of means by which these functions are discharged today. Factors to be taken into account include the extent to which in carrying out the relevant function the body is publicly funded, or is exercising statutory powers, or is taking the place of central government or local authorities, or is providing a public service."

For a detailed consideration of the concept of "public authority" and the way in which the courts are approaching the determination of this issue, see generally *The Meaning of Public Authority under the Human Rights Act*. Seventh Report of the Joint Committee on Human Rights of Session 2003–04 HL Paper 39 HC 382, which can be found at http://www.publications.parliament.uk/pa/jt2003/04/jtselect/jtrights/39/39.pdf.

The Joint Committee expresses some concern about the way the courts are interpreting the concept, but commends the approach adopted by the House of Lords in the *Aston Cantlow* case.

The duty of courts to act compatibly and precedent

4.18   In *Leeds City Council v Price* [2006] UKHL 10, the House of Lords ruled that in almost all cases where there is a conflict between authorities of the Court of Human

Rights in Strasbourg and of a superior court in the United Kingdom, an inferior court or tribunal in the United Kingdom should follow the decision of the national court. That is a controversial proposition, but the rule may well not apply if the point at issue is not in dispute between the parties. So, for example, in *Esfandiari* [2006] EWCA Civ 282, reported as *R(IS) 11/06*, neither party contested the proposition that all benefits count as possessions following the decision of the Court of Human Rights in *Stec*, even though an earlier Court of Appeal decision has ruled that means-tested benefits cannot be treated as "possessions" for the purpose of art.1 of Protocol 1. This may simply be an illustration of the Court of Appeal not regarding the House of Lords ruling as applying to them, or, perhaps rather more likely, that there was recent and specific Strasbourg authority on the point. There is certainly authority that in such circumstances, any court or tribunal should not lightly depart from germane Strasbourg case law: see *Attorney General's reference No 4 of 2002* [2004] UKHL 43, at para.33; and *Anderson* [2002] UKHL 46, paras 17–18.

See further annotations to s.2 at para.4.09.

Section 6(2)
The proper interpretation of subs.(2) is discussed in the judgment of the House of Lords in *Hooper* [2005] UKHL 29: see paras 2–6, 41–52, 62–83, 91–96, and 101–126.   **4.19**

In July 2008, the House of Lords again considered this aspect of the Act in *Doherty and others v Birmingham City Council* [2008] UKHL 57 in a case which concerned the obtaining of a possession order against a traveller under a procedure which it was argued would breach art.8 of the Convention (on which see *Connors v United Kingdom,* (App.66746/01) May 24 2004, (2005) 40 EHRR 9; and *McCann v United Kingdom,* (App.19009/04) May 13, 2008). In the course of their deliberations, the House gives detailed consideration to the circumstances in which a breach of the Act will be avoided because of the operation of s.6(2)(b). The position adopted in earlier cases was re-affirmed. The House confirmed that three distinct situations can arise under the provision. The first is where a decision to exercise or not to exercise a power that is given in primary legislation would inevitably give rise to a violation of Convention rights. The second is at the opposite end of the spectrum where no statutory provision concerns the exercise of discretion by a public body which acts in violation of Convention rights; such action will be unlawful under s.6(1) because s.6(2)(b) cannot apply. The third situation is said to lie in the middle:

> This is where the act or omission takes place within the context of a scheme which primary legislation has laid down that gives general powers, such as powers of management, to a public authority. . . . The answer to the question whether or not s.6(2)(b) applies will depend on the extent to which the act or omission can be said to give effect to any of the provisions of the scheme that is to be found in the statutes. (para.39, per Lord Hope of Craighead).

The House has indicated that there are two possible gateways by which a violation of Convention rights might be addressed in such situations. The first gateway provides two possibilities. The first is that the use of the interpretative obligation in s.3 results in an interpretation which avoids the violation which is alleged. The second is that the interpretative obligation does not help, but that a court of sufficient seniority can give a declaration of incompatibility under s.4 which results in a remedial order under s.10. The second gateway involves an argument that the public authority whose decision is challenged has made an improper use of its powers; this route offers a procedural protection in that the court will consider whether the public authority acted unreasonably in the *Wednesbury* sense in taking the action that it did (paras 52–55).

Proceedings

4.20

7.—(1) A person who claims that a public authority has acted (or proposes to act) in a way which is made unlawful by section 6(1) may—

(a) bring proceedings against the authority under this Act in the appropriate court or tribunal, or

(b) rely on the Convention right or rights concerned in any legal proceedings,

but only if he is (or would be) a victim of the unlawful act.

(2) In subsection (1)(a) "appropriate court or tribunal" means such court or tribunal as may be determined in accordance with rules; and proceedings against an authority include a counterclaim or similar proceeding.

(3) If the proceedings are brought on an application for judicial review, the applicant is to be taken to have a sufficient interest in relation to the unlawful act only if he is, or would be, a victim of that act.

(4) If the proceedings are made by way of a petition for judicial review in Scotland, the applicant shall be taken to have title and interest to sue in relation to the unlawful act only if he is, or would be, a victim of that act.

(5) Proceedings under subsection (1)(a) must be brought before the end of—

(a) the period of one year beginning with the date on which the act complained of took place; or

(b) such longer period as the court or tribunal considers equitable having regard to all the circumstances,

but that is subject to any rule imposing a stricter time limit in relation to the procedure in question.

(6) In subsection (1)(b) "legal proceedings" includes—

(a) proceedings brought by or at the instigation of a public authority; and

(b) an appeal against the decision of a court or tribunal.

(7) For the purposes of this section, a person is a victim of an unlawful act only if he would be a victim for the purposes of Article 34 of the Convention if proceedings were brought in the European Court of Human Rights in respect of that act.

(8) Nothing in this Act creates a criminal offence.

(9) In this section "rules" means—

(a) in relation to proceedings before a court or tribunal outside Scotland, rules made by [1 . . .] [2 the Lord Chancellor or] the Secretary of State for the purposes of this section or rules of court,

(b) in relation to proceedings before a court or tribunal in Scotland, rules made by the Secretary of State for those purposes,

(c) in relation to proceedings before a tribunal in Northern Ireland—

(i) which deals with transferred matters; and

(ii) for which no rules made under paragraph (a) are in force, rules made by a Northern Ireland department for those purposes,

and includes provision made by order under section 1 of the Courts and Legal Services Act 1990.

(10) In making rules, regard must be had to section 9.

(11) The Minister who has power to make rules in relation to a particular tribunal may, to the extent he considers it necessary to ensure that the tribunal can provide an appropriate remedy in relation to an act (or proposed

act) of a public authority which is (or would be) unlawful as a result of section 6(1), by order add to—

(a) the relief or remedies which the tribunal may grant; or

(b) the grounds on which it may grant any of them.

(12) An order made under subsection (11) may contain such incidental, supplemental, consequential or transitional provision as the Minister making it considers appropriate.

(13) "The Minister" includes the Northern Ireland department concerned.

COMMENCEMENT

October 2, 2000: The Human Rights Act 1998 (Commencement No.2) Order 2000 (SI 2000/1851).

AMENDMENTS

1. The Secretary of State for Constitutional Affairs Order 2003 (SI 2003/1887) (August 19, 2003).

2. The Transfer of Functions (Lord Chancellor and Secretary of State) Order 2005 (SI 2005/3429) (January 12, 2006).

GENERAL NOTE

Introduction

This section is full of difficulty. A person who believes that a public authority has acted unlawfully by not acting in a manner compatible with Convention rights may bring proceedings under s.7. Such a person must under subs.(7) show that they would be a victim for the purposes of art.34 of the Convention if proceedings were brought before the Court of Human Rights in respect of the allegedly unlawful act.

The section refers to at least three different types of proceedings: (1) the so-called new "constitutional tort" under subs.(1)(a); (2) judicial review under subs.(3); and (3) "any legal proceedings" in subs.(1)(b).

Changes to the Civil Procedures Rules to accommodate these proceedings left a number of questions unanswered.

Standing to raise the complaint: the victim requirement

Under subs.(7) which applies to the whole section, only a person who can show that they would fall within the victim requirement under art.34 of the Convention has standing to complain of the unlawful act by the public authority. The concept of "victim" is a particular concept under Convention case law, and for this reason the interpretative requirement to have regard to Convention case law must be particularly strong since otherwise the specific reference to art.34 in subs.(7) would be otiose. Article 34 has replaced art.25 in the original version of the Convention prior to its amendment by Protocol 11.

Fortunately, the Strasbourg authorities—and here admissibility decisions of the Commission under the "old" system of protection (see commentary to s.2) will be particularly useful—have been generous in the matter of standing to make an application under the Convention.

The term "person" under the Convention (*personne physique* in the French text) clearly refers only to natural persons, but the Commission has accepted applications from corporate and unincorporated bodies whose rights under the Convention have been violated. So complaints have been accepted from companies, partnerships, trades unions, churches, political parties, and numerous other types of institution. It would seem that only public bodies themselves are excluded from the possibility of making an individual petition. Furthermore there are no restrictions on grounds of nationality, residence or any other status.

Standing has been extended to representative complaints, for example, by parents

4.21

4.22

on behalf of children where that is appropriate, though there is no age limit for making an application: App.10929/84 *Nielsen v Denmark* (1986) 46 D.R. 55 and App.22920/93 *MB v United Kingdom* (1994) 77-A D.R. 42. Equally, there is no bar to application by persons under a disability: App.1572/62 *X v Austria* (1962) 5 Yearbook 238.

Associations have no standing to bring actions in a representative capacity: App.10581/83 *Norris and National Gay Federation v Ireland* (1984) 44 D.R. 132, though if they provide evidence that they are acting on behalf of specified individuals, the application may be accepted: App.10983/84 *Confédération des Syndicats me´dicaúx franc¸ais et Fédération nationale des Infirmiers v France* (1986) 47 D.R. 225.

In some cases potential victims may make an application, such as in cases where covert surveillance might take place without any notification of the possibility to the individual: *Klass v Germany*, judgment of September 6, 1978, Series A No.28; (1979–80) 2 E.H.R.R. 214.

The Commission and the Court will not, however, countenance an application in the abstract as a means of testing the compatibility of provisions of a national legal order: App.9297/81 *X Association v Sweden* (1982) 28 D.R. 204. Drawing the distinction between potential victims and claims in the abstract is not always easy: see App.10039/82 *Leigh v United Kingdom* (1984) 38 D.R. 74.

In *Director General of Fair Trading v Proprietary Association of Great Britain*, Court of Appeal, July 26, 2001 [2001] EWCA Civ 1217 (sometimes referred to as *Re medicaments (No.4)*), the Court of Appeal made some passing, and inconclusive comments on the nature of the "victim requirement" under s.7. The Court expressly avoided dealing with the possible distinction between interest groups which are really associations of interested individuals which might be regarded as a group of individuals each of whom may be regarded as a victim and broader representative groups (examples given are Amnesty International or the Joint Council for the Welfare of Immigrants) which have special expertise but who cannot be classified as a collection of victims. The Court simply stated that each case must be decided in its own context.

Note the discussion of the victim requirement (particularly victim status and retrospectivity) in the judgment of the House of Lords in *Hooper* [2005] UKHL 29: see paras 53–9.

Subs.(1)(a): the new constitutional tort

4.23   A person who can show that they meet the victim test may bring proceedings against the authority "in the appropriate court or tribunal". This is to be determined in accordance with rules to be made, outside Scotland, by the Lord Chancellor or the Secretary of State. The Civil Procedure Rules simply map this action onto the existing division of responsibilities between the county courts and the High Court.

The time limits for such an action are, however, specified in subs.(5). The action is to be brought within one year of the date on which the act complained of took place or such longer period as the court or tribunal considers equitable having regard to all the circumstances. There is a proviso that both the one year time limit and any extension of it is to be without prejudice to any rule imposing a stricter time limit "in relation to the procedure in question." An example would be judicial review where the normal time limit is three months unless this is extended by the court. However, where an action is brought under a procedure with a longer limitation period, it would seem that the longer limitation period will apply; such proceedings would not, however, arise under subs.(1)(a) but presumably under subs.(1)(b).

Under s.9(1), where the unlawful act of which the applicant complains is a judicial act, it is stated that proceedings under s.7(1)(a) may be brought only by exercising a right of appeal, seeking judicial review against those bodies susceptible to judicial review, or "in such other forum as may be prescribed by rules."

Judicial review: subss (3) and (4)

4.24   Where the proceedings are by way of judicial review on the grounds that a public authority has acted unlawfully, the normal sufficient interest test of standing (which would permit action by a representative body or a pressure group) is replaced by a test that the applicant must satisfy the victim test in subs.(7).

Raising Convention rights in any legal proceedings: subs. (1) (b)

Convention rights may be raised in any legal proceedings, provided that the person can show that they would be a victim under art.34 of the Convention. So a person bringing proceedings on a well-established cause of action can raise his or her Convention rights at any time. Indeed, the court or tribunal is under a duty by virtue of s.6(1) to take obvious Convention points since they are under a duty to act in a manner compatible with the Convention.

4.25

Apart from judicial review claims (which may be important if a person is seeking the possibility of a money remedy), Convention rights are most likely to be raised in the course of appeals to the First-tier Tribunal and the Upper Tribunal. The commentary to the Convention rights set out in Sch.1 gives some indication of the sorts of issues which might be raised under them.

In *CSIB/973/1999* a Scottish Commissioner warns of the need for responsible resort to the taking of human rights points. He complains of a point which was "in the nature of a wrap up omnibus ground of appeal placed before the Commissioners no doubt in the hope that there was something in the point." The Commissioner regrets the absence of rules setting out the manner in which human rights points are to be taken before the Commissioners. He goes on to indicate the content of those rules; this might assist those contemplating raising human rights points before both tribunals and Commissioners. The provision of the Convention which it is argued has been breached should be identified, together with the remedy sought in respect of the breach. The legal principles and authorities relied on and any error of law by the tribunal which it is asserted were made consequent on the breach should also be identified. Such points should be taken on proper notice so that both parties can research them and focus on them in their arguments to the adjudicating body. That is, no doubt, good advice, but the duty in s.6(1) on public authorities to act compatibly with Convention rights means that adjudicating bodies must themselves consider obvious points arising under the Convention even if they are not raised by the parties.

In *R(IS) 12/04* the Commissioner reminds tribunals of the need to address fully arguments based on Convention rights in the following terms,

"13. Finally, it is necessary to consider the adequacy of the tribunal's reasons. I agree with the Secretary of State that a tribunal's lack of any power to make a declaration of incompatibility is not a good reason for not dealing fully with Human Rights issues, particularly since a tribunal may have power in some cases to declare subordinate legislation to have been invalidly made–see *Chief Adjudication Officer v Foster* [1993] 1 All ER 705. The claimant in this appeal clearly went to considerable trouble to set out his arguments under the Human Rights Act clearly and comprehensively in response to the chairman's direction, and I consider that he was entitled to a much fuller explanation of the tribunal's reasons for rejecting his arguments than the very short passage at the end of the statement of reasons set out above. The reasons for the tribunal's rejection of the claimant's discrimination arguments are not apparent from the statement, and I therefore consider that, in all the circumstances, the tribunal's reasons were inadequate."

The Court of Appeal in *R. (on the application of Hooper, Withey, Naylor and Martin v Secretary of State for Work and Pensions* [2003] EWCA Civ 813 addresses at paras 29–46 the question of when a person becomes a victim within the meaning of s.7, and did not find the application of Strasbourg case law to be satisfactory. The Strasbourg authorities appeared to provide that only when a man has made a claim to a benefit is he in a position to complain that he is not being treated in the same way as a woman, and so, only then, would become a victim for the purposes of art.34 of the Convention. The Court of Appeal describes as "unattractive" an argument raised by the United Kingdom Government before the Court of Human Rights in *White v United Kingdom* (App.53134/99), admissibility decision of June 7, 2001, that the claimant was not a victim because he had not claimed on the official form, notwithstanding that this was designed specifically for widows. Differing from the views expressed by Moses J in the court below, the Court of Appeal concludes that it is not necessary for the claim to be made in writing in order to constitute the applicant as a victim for the purpose of asserting his Convention rights. The Court of Appeal says, ". . . we can see no reason in principle why an oral claim, made and rejected, should not suffice to constitute a claim." Note, however, that the oral claim is not a perfected claim for the purposes of the Claims and Payments Regulations, simply for the purposes of giving a person standing to claim Convention rights as a victim of a violation of those rights. This aspect of the Court of Appeal's decision was accepted by the House of Lords, [2005] EWHL 29.

Judicial remedies

4.26   **8.**—(1) In relation to any act (or proposed act) of a public authority which the court finds is (or would be) unlawful, it may grant such relief or remedy, or make such order, within its powers as it considers just and appropriate.

(2) But damages may be awarded only by a court which has power to award damages, or to order the payment of compensation, in civil proceedings.

(3) No award of damages is to be made unless, taking account of all the circumstances of the case, including—

(a) any other relief or remedy granted, or order made, in relation to the act in question (by that or any other court), and

(b) the consequences of any decision (of that or any other court) in respect of that act,

the court is satisfied that the award is necessary to afford just satisfaction to the person in whose favour it is made.

(4) In determining—

(a) whether to award damages, or

(b) the amount of an award,

the court must take into account the principles applied by the European Court of Human Rights in relation to the award of compensation under Article 41 of the Convention.

(5) A public authority against which damages are awarded is to be treated—

(a) in Scotland, for the purposes of section 3 of the Law Reform (Miscellaneous Provisions) (Scotland) Act 1940 as if the award were made in an action of damages in which the authority has been found liable in respect of loss or damage to the person to whom the award is made;

(b) for the purposes of the Civil Liability (Contribution) Act 1978 as liable in respect of damage suffered by the person to whom the award is made.

(6) In this section—

"court" includes a tribunal;

"damages" means damages for an unlawful act of a public authority; and

"unlawful" means unlawful under section 6(1).

COMMENCEMENT

October 2, 2000: The Human Rights Act 1998 (Commencement No.2) Order 2000 (SI 2000/1851).

GENERAL NOTE

Section 8(1) grants a broad competence, but the nature of the remedies available will vary according to the forum. The relief, remedy or order open to the court or tribunal must be one already within its powers. So the Act gives no new competence to decision-making bodies to provide a remedy for a violation of a Convention right. The decision not to extend the powers of all courts and tribunals to include new remedies for violations of Convention rights was apparently motivated by a concern that there would be an explosion of damages awards in this area across a wide range of decision-making bodies. This was the same concern which led to the exclusion of art.13 of the Convention from the incorporated rights. There is, accordingly, a wide but not unlimited range of remedies available for breaches of Convention rights.

4.27

The drafting of s.8 reveals a concern that damages for violations of Convention rights should be contained. Section 8(2) provides that damages for an unlawful act of a public authority under the Act may be awarded only by a court (or tribunal) which has power to award damages, or to order the payment of compensation, in civil proceedings. Furthermore, damages, though not the remedy of last resort, are circumscribed since they are not to be made unless the court is satisfied that the award is necessary to afford just satisfaction to the person in whose favour the award is made, having regard to all the circumstances of the case, and in particular any other remedy or relief granted and the consequences of any decision in respect of the breach of Convention rights: subs.(3). As noted above, decisions about the award of damages and the amount of damages are to be informed by reference to the case law of the Court of Human Right in awarding just satisfaction.

A number of observations need to be made about the structure of s.8. It assumes that the range of remedies currently available to United Kingdom courts will be adequate to remedy breaches of Convention rights. It seeks to discourage an explosion of damages awards. The Lord Chancellor indicated that the intent was to match the awards victims would get if they received just satisfaction under art.41: HL Vol.582 col.1232, November 3, 1997. It establishes a system in which the luck of the forum will determine whether duplication of litigation will be needed to secure a money remedy. A good example would be an appeal heard by an appeal tribunal, which has no power to award damages, and it has been established that it has no power award interest on the late payment of benefit; This undoubtedly follows from the reasoning of the Social Security Commissioner in *R(FC)2/90*; see also the decision of the Court of Justice in *R. v Secretary of State for Social Security; Ex p. Sutton* [1997] E.C.R. I-2163; [1997] 2 C.M.L.R. 382. Nor it seems would any other court. Yet the Court of Human Rights has awarded interest on the late payment of benefit: *Schuler-Zgraggen v Switzerland*, judgment of June 24, 1993, Series A, No.263; (1993) 16 E.H.R.R. 405. In the early days of Community law, an action for a declaration was one means of securing a judicial statement of an entitlement under Community law. This would seem to be the only route open within the national legal order to a victim who had only received social security benefit to which he or she was entitled some years late and who wished to raise the claim for interest on the late payment. Otherwise, such a person would have to raise the complaint that no interest was available before the Court in Strasbourg.

Perhaps the most pertinent point to make is that the deference to the provisions of the Convention on just satisfaction in the national legislation is misplaced. The provisions in art.41 of the Convention on affording just satisfaction are a safety net where the national legal order does not offer full compensation for the breach of the Convention.

The starting point is that the national legal order should determine what remedies are appropriate for breaches of the Convention. Such an obligation flows from art.13 of the Convention. Indeed, it could be argued that the effect of s.8 replicates the failures of earlier years to recognise what was demanded by the Convention. It assumes that the current panoply of remedies available in the national legal order meets the requirements of the Convention. It also reveals a deep anxiety about damages as a remedy for breach of a Convention right.

The potential gap in remedies available can, however, be cured under the rule-making power in s.7(11) and (12) which enables additional powers to be given to tribunals to add to the remedies open to them, and to define the grounds on which any additional remedies may be granted.

Where the act complained of is a judicial act, damages as a remedy is limited to compensation for unlawful detention awarded in accordance with art.5(5): s.9(3).

In *CSIS/460/2002,* the Commissioner makes some comments on the nature of remedies for a violation of Convention rights in the context of an argument that one remedy could be to order a permanent stay of the proceedings. The Commissioner concludes,

> "A tribunal has no power to impose a permanent stay of an appeal. There is no express statutory provision nor can one be implied by virtue of necessity. Mr Orr drew an analogy with an appeal abating. However that derives from a principle of common law and is not a stay by a court or tribunal. Where an appellant dies before the determination of the appeal, the appeal is not terminated by that fact. However, unless and until there is an appointment of someone to proceed with the appeal or there is a personal representative, then no-one is legally competent to take the appeal forward. In such circumstances, the appeal is considered as auto-matically 'abated', by which is meant suspended. It can nevertheless be revived by the appropriate procedure. Any statement by a tribunal or a Commissioner that an appeal has been abated is thus for clarification only. Abatement is therefore very different from the power to grant a permanent stay. Such a concept could in any event give no advantage to the respondent as it would leave outstanding the adverse decision. The Secretary of State is not legally obliged to contine the cus-tomary suspension of recovery procedures and would have no reason to do so if the appeal is permanently stayed." (para.49.)

See also discussion of remedies in *Dyer v Watson* [2002] 4 All E.R. 1, especially the analysis by Lord Millett at paras 128–133.

Judicial acts

4.28   **9.**—(1) Proceedings under section 7(1)(a) in respect of a judicial act may be brought only

(a) by exercising a right of appeal;

(b) on an application (in Scotland a petition) for judicial review; or

(c) in such other forum as may be prescribed by rules.

(2) That does not affect any rule of law which prevents a court from being the subject of judicial review.

(3) In proceedings under this Act in respect of a judicial act done in good faith, damages may not be awarded otherwise than to compensate a person to the extent required by Article 5(5) of the Convention.

(4) An award of damages permitted by subsection (3) is to be made against the Crown; but no award may be made unless the appropriate person, if not a party to the proceedings, is joined.

(5) In this section—

"appropriate person" means the Minister responsible for the court concerned, or a person or government department nominated by him;

"court" includes a tribunal;

"judge" includes a member of a tribunal, a justice of the peace [[1] (or, in Northern Ireland, a lay magistrate)] and a clerk or other officer entitled to exercise the jurisdiction of a court;

"judicial act" means a judicial act of a court and includes an act done on the instructions, or on behalf, of a judge; and

"rules" has the same meaning as in section 7(9).

COMMENCEMENT

October 2, 2000: The Human Rights Act 1998 (Commencement No.2) Order 2000 (SI 2000/1851).

AMENDMENT

1. The Justice (Northern Ireland) Act 2002 (Commencement No.8) Order 2005 SR 2005/109, art.2, Sch. (April 1, 2005).

Remedial action

Power to take remedial action

10.—(1) This section applies if—

   (a) a provision of legislation has been declared under section 4 to be incompatible with a Convention right and, if an appeal lies—

      (i) all persons who may appeal have stated in writing that they do not intend to do so;

      (ii) the time for bringing an appeal has expired and no appeal has been brought within that time; or

      (iii) an appeal brought within that time has been determined or abandoned; or

   (b) it appears to a Minister of the Crown or Her Majesty in Council that, having regard to a finding of the European Court of Human Rights made after the coming into force of this section in proceedings against the United Kingdom, a provision of legislation is incompatible with an obligation of the United Kingdom arising from the Convention.

(2) If a Minister of the Crown considers that there are compelling reasons for proceeding under this section, he may by order make such amendments to the legislation as he considers necessary to remove the incompatibility.

(3) If, in the case of subordinate legislation, a Minister of the Crown considers—

   (a) that it is necessary to amend the primary legislation under which the subordinate legislation in question was made, in order to enable the incompatibility to be removed, and

   (b) that there are compelling reasons for proceeding under this section, he may by order make such amendments to the primary legislation as he considers necessary.

(4) This section also applies where the provision in question is in subordinate legislation and has been quashed, or declared invalid, by reason of incompatibility with a Convention right and the Minister proposes to proceed under paragraph 2(b) of Schedule 2.

(5) If the legislation is an Order in Council, the power conferred by subsection (2) or (3) is exercisable by Her Majesty in Council.

(6) In this section "legislation" does not include a Measure of the Church Assembly or of the General Synod of the Church of England.

(7) Schedule 2 makes further provision about remedial orders.

4.29

COMMENCEMENT

October 2, 2000: The Human Rights Act 1998 (Commencement No.2) Order 2000 (SI 2000/1851).

GENERAL NOTE

4.30   This section and Sch.2 make provision for a fast-track Parliamentary procedure to respond to a declaration of incompatibility by a court.

Other rights and proceedings

Safeguard for existing human rights

4.31   **11.**—A person's reliance on a Convention right does not restrict—

(a) any other right or freedom conferred on him by or under any law having effect in any part of the United Kingdom; or

(b) his right to make any claim or bring any proceedings which he could make or bring apart from sections 7 to 9.

COMMENCEMENT

October 2, 2000: The Human Rights Act 1998 (Commencement No.2) Order 2000 (SI 2000/1851).

GENERAL NOTE

4.32   The rights given to persons under s.7 to complain of unlawful acts by public authorities in acting in a manner incompatible with the Convention does not limit in any way existing rights under UK law. The new rights are additional to existing rights and not in substitution for them.

Freedom of expression

4.33   **12.**—(1) This section applies if a court is considering whether to grant any relief which, if granted, might affect the exercise of the Convention right to freedom of expression.

(2) If the person against whom the application for relief is made ("the respondent") is neither present nor represented, no such relief is to be granted unless the court is satisfied—

(a) that the applicant has taken all practicable steps to notify the respondent; or

(b) that there are compelling reasons why the respondent should not be notified.

(3) No such relief is to be granted so as to restrain publication before trial unless the court is satisfied that the applicant is likely to establish that publication should not be allowed.

(4) The court must have particular regard to the importance of the Convention right to freedom of expression and, where the proceedings relate to material which the respondent claims, or which appears to the court, to be journalistic, literary or artistic material (or to conduct connected with such material), to—

(a) the extent to which—

(i) the material has, or is about to, become available to the public; or

(ii) it is, or would be, in the public interest for the material to be published;

(b) any relevant privacy code.

(5) In this section—

"court" includes a tribunal; and

"relief " includes any remedy or order (other than in criminal proceedings).

COMMENCEMENT

October 2, 2000: The Human Rights Act 1998 (Commencement No.2) Order 2000 (SI 2000/1851).

GENERAL NOTE

This section is a response to concerns expressed by media interests that the Act would limit freedom of expression by giving priority to the development of privacy under art.8 of the Convention. The section is not needed, since the Strasbourg case law makes it clear that a balance has to be struck between the privacy of the individual and the freedom of the press.

Freedom of thought, conscience and religion

13.—(1) If a court's determination of any question arising under this Act might affect the exercise by a religious organisation (itself or its members collectively) of the Convention right to freedom of thought, conscience and religion, it must have particular regard to the importance of that right.

(2) In this section "court" includes a tribunal.

COMMENCEMENT

October 2, 2000: The Human Rights Act 1998 (Commencement No.2) Order 2000 (SI 2000/1851).

GENERAL NOTE

This section was included in response to concerns expressed on behalf of religious groups that priority would be given to other provisions of the Convention than the provision on freedom of religion in art.9 and that churches would find themselves being required in the name of human rights to do things contrary to their tenets. Like s.12, this section is not needed, since the Strasbourg case law makes it clear that a balance has to be struck between the pluralism of a modern democratic societies and respect for religious and personal beliefs.

Derogations and reservations

Derogations

14.—(1) In this Act "designated derogation" means—

[. . .¹] any derogation by the United Kingdom from an Article of the Convention, or of any protocol to the Convention, which is designated for the purposes of this Act in an order made by the Secretary of State.

(2) [. . .¹].

(3) If a designated derogation is amended or replaced it ceases to be a designated derogation.

(4) But subsection (3) does not prevent the [² Secretary of State] from

4.34

4.35

4.36

4.37

exercising his power under subsection (1)[. . .¹] to make a fresh designation order in respect of the Article concerned.

(5) The [² Secretary of State] must by order make such amendments to Schedule 3 as he considers appropriate to reflect—

(a) any designation order; or

(b) the effect of subsection (3).

(6) A designation order may be made in anticipation of the making by the United Kingdom of a proposed derogation.

COMMENCEMENT

October 2, 2000: The Human Rights Act 1998 (Commencement No.2) Order 2000 (SI 2000/1851).

AMENDMENTS

1. The Human Rights Act (Amendment) Order 2001 (SI 2001/1216), art.2 (April 1, 2001).

2. The Secretary of State for Constitutional Affairs Order 2003 (SI 2003/1887) (August 19, 2003).

Reservations

4.38
    15.—(1) In this Act "designated reservation" means—

(a) the United Kingdom's reservation to Article 2 of the First Protocol to the Convention; and

(b) any other reservation by the United Kingdom to an Article of the Convention, or of any protocol to the Convention, which is designated for the purposes of this Act in an order made by the Secretary of State.

(2) The text of the reservation referred to in subsection (1)(a) is set out in Part II of Schedule 3.

(3) If a designated reservation is withdrawn wholly or in part it ceases to be a designated reservation.

(4) But subsection (3) does not prevent the [¹ Secretary of State] from exercising his power under subsection (1)(b) to make a fresh designation order in respect of the Article concerned.

(5) The [¹ Secretary of State] must by order make such amendments to this Act as he considers appropriate to reflect—

(a) any designation order; or

(b) the effect of subsection (3).

COMMENCEMENT

October 2, 2000: The Human Rights Act 1998 (Commencement No.2) Order 2000 (SI 2000/1851).

AMENDMENT

1. The Secretary of State for Constitutional Affairs Order 2003 (SI 2003/1887) (August 19, 2003).

Period for which designated derogations have effect

4.39
    16.—(1) If it has not already been withdrawn by the United Kingdom, a designated derogation ceases to have effect for the purposes of this Act— [. . .¹] at the end of the period of five years beginning with the date on which the order designating it was made.

(2) At any time before the period—
(a) fixed by subsection (1) [. . .¹], or
(b) extended by an order under this subsection,
comes to an end, the [² Secretary of State] may by order extend it by a further period of five years.

(3) An order under section 14(1)[. . .¹] ceases to have effect at the end of the period for consideration, unless a resolution has been passed by each House approving the order.

(4) Subsection (3) does not affect—
(a) anything done in reliance on the order; or
(b) the power to make a fresh order under section 14(1)[. . .¹].

(5) In subsection (3) "period for consideration" means the period of forty days beginning with the day on which the order was made.

(6) In calculating the period for consideration, no account is to be taken of any time during which—
(a) Parliament is dissolved or prorogued; or
(b) both Houses are adjourned for more than four days.

(7) If a designated derogation is withdrawn by the United Kingdom, the [² Secretary of State] must by order make such amendments to this Act as he considers are required to reflect that withdrawal.

COMMENCEMENT

October 2, 2000: The Human Rights Act 1998 (Commencement No.2) Order 2000 (SI 2000/1851).

AMENDMENTS

1. The Human Rights Act (Amendment) Order 2001 (SI 2001/1216), art.3 (April 1, 2001).
2. The Secretary of State for Constitutional Affairs Order 2003 (SI 2003/1887) (August 19, 2003).

Periodic review of designated reservations

17.—(1) The appropriate Minister must review the designated reserva-   4.40
tion referred to in section 15(1)(a)—
(a) before the end of the period of five years beginning with the date on which section 1(2) came into force; and
(b) if that designation is still in force, before the end of the period of five years beginning with the date on which the last report relating to it was laid under subsection (3).

(2) The appropriate Minister must review each of the other designated reservations (if any)—
(a) before the end of the period of five years beginning with the date on which the order designating the reservation first came into force; and
(b) if the designation is still in force, before the end of the period of five years beginning with the date on which the last report relating to it was laid under subsection (3).

(3) The Minister conducting a review under this section must prepare a report on the result of the review and lay a copy of it before each House of Parliament.

COMMENCEMENT

October 2, 2000: The Human Rights Act 1998 (Commencement No.2) Order 2000 (SI 2000/1851).

Judges of the European Court of Human Rights

4.41   *Section 18 omitted.*

Parliamentary procedure

Statements of compatibility

4.42   **19.**—(1) A Minister of the Crown in charge of a Bill in either House of
Parliament must, before Second Reading of the Bill—
  (a) make a statement to the effect that in his view the provisions of the
      Bill are compatible with the Convention rights ("a statement of com-
      patibility"); or
  (b) make a statement to the effect that although he is unable to make a
      statement of compatibility the government nevertheless wishes the
      House to proceed with the Bill.
  (2) The statement must be in writing and be published in such manner as
the Minister making it considers appropriate.

COMMENCEMENT

Section 19 entered into force on November 24, 1998: (SI 1998/2882).

GENERAL NOTE

4.43   Part of the scheme of the Act is to require improved pre-legislative scrutiny of
legislation to ensure its compliance with Convention rights. The use of the section
to date has been disappointing, since no reasoning is publicly available to elaborate
a simple Ministerial statement that the provisions of a Bill are compatible with
Convention rights.
    Reviews carried out by the Parliamentary Joint Committee on Human Rights are
rather more rigorous.

Supplemental

4.44   *Section 20 omitted.*

Interpretation, etc.

4.45   **21.**—(1) In this Act—
    "amend" includes repeal and apply (with or without modifications);
    "the appropriate Minister" means the Minister of the Crown having
      charge of the appropriate authorised government department (within
      the meaning of the Crown Proceedings Act 1947);
    "the Commission" means the European Commission of Human Rights;
    "the Convention" means the Convention for the Protection of Human
      Rights and Fundamental Freedoms, agreed by the Council of Europe
      at Rome on 4th November 1950 as it has effect for the time being in
      relation to the United Kingdom;
    "declaration of incompatibility" means a declaration under section 4;
    "Minister of the Crown" has the same meaning as in the Ministers of the
      Crown Act 1975;
    "Northern Ireland Minister" includes the First Minister and the deputy
      First Minister in Northern Ireland;

"primary legislation" means any—
- (a) public general Act;
- (b) local and personal Act;
- (c) private Act;
- (d) Measure of the Church Assembly;
- (e) Measure of the General Synod of the Church of England;
- (f) Order in Council—
    - (i) made in exercise of Her Majesty's Royal Prerogative;
    - (ii) made under section 38(1)(a) of the Northern Ireland Constitution Act 1973 or the corresponding provision of the Northern Ireland Act 1998; or
    - (iii) amending an Act of a kind mentioned in paragraph (a), (b) or (c);

and includes an order or other instrument made under primary legislation (otherwise than by the National Assembly for Wales, a member of the Scottish Executive, a Northern Ireland Minister or a Northern Ireland department) to the extent to which it operates to bring one or more provisions of that legislation into force or amends any primary legislation;

"the First Protocol" means the protocol to the Convention agreed at Paris on March 20 1952;

[¹. . .]

"the Eleventh Protocol" means the protocol to the Convention (restructuring the control machinery established by the Convention) agreed at Strasbourg on May 11 1994;

[¹ "the Thirteenth Protocol" means the protocol to the Convention (concerning the abolition of the death penalty in all circumstances agreed at Vilnius on 3rd May 2002;]

"subordinate legislation" means any—
- (a) Order in Council other than one—
    - (i) made in exercise of Her Majesty's Royal Prerogative;
    - (ii) made under section 38(1)(a) of the Northern Ireland Constitution Act 1973 or the corresponding provision of the Northern Ireland Act 1998; or
    - (iii) amending an Act of a kind mentioned in the definition of primary legislation;
- (b) Act of the Scottish Parliament;
- [² (ba) Measure of the National Assembly for Wales;
- (bb) Act of the National Assembly for Wales;]
- (c) Act of the Parliament of Northern Ireland;
- (d) Measure of the Assembly established under section 1 of the Northern Ireland Assembly Act 1973;
- (e) Act of the Northern Ireland Assembly;
- (f) order, rules, regulations, scheme, warrant, byelaw or other instrument made under primary legislation (except to the extent to which it operates to bring one or more provisions of that legislation into force or amends any primary legislation);
- (g) order, rules, regulations, scheme, warrant, byelaw or other instrument made under legislation mentioned in paragraph (b), (c), (d) or (e) or made under an Order in Council applying only to Northern Ireland;
- (h) order, rules, regulations, scheme, warrant, byelaw or other instrument made by a member of the Scottish Executive, [² Welsh Ministers, the First Minister for Wales, the Counsel General to the Welsh Assembly

Government,] a Northern Ireland Minister or a Northern Ireland department in exercise of prerogative or other executive functions of Her Majesty which are exercisable by such a person on behalf of Her Majesty;

"transferred matters" has the same meaning as in the Northern Ireland Act 1998; and

"tribunal" means any tribunal in which legal proceedings may be brought.

(2) The references in paragraphs (b) and (c) of section 2(1) to Articles are to Articles of the Convention as they had effect immediately before the coming into force of the Eleventh Protocol.

(3) The reference in paragraph (d) of section 2(1) to Article 46 includes a reference to Articles 32 and 54 of the Convention as they had effect immediately before the coming into force of the Eleventh Protocol.

(4) The references in section 2(1) to a report or decision of the Commission or a decision of the Committee of Ministers include references to a report or decision made as provided by paragraphs 3, 4 and 6 of Article 5 of the Eleventh Protocol (transitional provisions).

(5) Any liability under the Army Act 1955, the Air Force Act 1955 or the Naval Discipline Act 1957 to suffer death for an offence is replaced by a liability to imprisonment for life or any less punishment authorised by those Acts; and those Acts shall accordingly have effect with the necessary modifications.

COMMENCEMENT

Section 21(5) entered into force on November 9, 1998. The remainder of the section entered into force on October 2, 2000: The Human Rights Act 1998 (Commencement No.2) Order 2000 (SI 2000/1851).

AMENDMENTS

1. Human Rights Act 1998 (Amendment) Order 2004 (SI 2004/1574), art.2(2) (June 22, 2004).

2. Government of Wales Act 2006, Sch.10 para.56(4) (May 3, 2007 immediately after the ordinary election as specified in 2006 c.32 s.161(1); May 25, 2007 immediately after the end of the initial period for purposes of functions of the Welsh Ministers, the First Minister, the Counsel General and the Assembly Commission and in relation to the Auditor General and the Comptroller and Auditor General as specified in 2006 c.32 s.161(4)-(5)).

Short title, commencement, application and extent

4.46   22.—(1) This Act may be cited as the Human Rights Act 1998.

(2) Sections 18, 20 and 21(5) and this section come into force on the passing of this Act.

(3) The other provisions of this Act come into force on such day as the Secretary of State may by order appoint; and different days may be appointed for different purposes.

(4) Paragraph (b) of subsection (1) of section 7 applies to proceedings brought by or at the instigation of a public authority whenever the act in question took place; but otherwise that subsection does not apply to an act taking place before the coming into force of that section.

(5) This Act binds the Crown.

(6) This Act extends to Northern Ireland.

(7) Section 21(5), so far as it relates to any provision contained in the

Army Act 1955, the Air Force Act 1955 or the Naval Discipline Act 1957, extends to any place to which that provision extends.

GENERAL NOTE

This section entered into force on November 9, 1998. 4.47

Subsection (4), which entered into force on November 9, 1998, provides that the lawfulness of an act of a public authority may be called into question in proceedings under s.7(1)(b) (any legal proceedings in which Convention rights are raised) whenever that act took place if those proceedings are begun by a public authority. In other words, it has a retrospective effect in this regard, but if the proceedings are brought other than by a public authority, no complaint can be made about an act of a public authority prior to the entry into force of s.7(1)(b).

The issue of the possible retrospective application of the Human Rights Act 1998 in the context of tribunal decisions would appear to have been laid to rest; the position is neatly summarised in *R(IS)3/02*, where the Commissioner concludes,

"The effect and interaction of sections 3, 6, 7 and 22 of the Human Rights Act in relation to appeals from inferior tribunal decisions given before 2 October 2000 was much debated before me but the argument that Mr Cox [of Counsel] sought to advance in this appeal, that the 1998 Act had a retrospective effect extending even to turning past lawful decisions of courts and tribunals into unlawful ones in United Kingdom law from 2 October 2000 and to obliging appellate courts to reverse the effect retrospectively from that date onwards, has now conclusively been shown to be untenable: see *R v Lambert* [2001] 3 WLR 206, affirming what was said by Sir Andrew Morritt V-C in *Wilson v First County Trust Ltd (No.2)* [2001] 3 WLR 42, 51; and cf also the recent decision of the Tribunal of Scots Commissioners in case *CSDLA 1019/99*." (para.15.)

A tribunal sitting on or after October 2, 2000 on an appeal against a decision made before October 2, 2000 cannot consider Convention points, since s.12(8)(b) of the SSA 1998 confines the tribunal to the state of United Kingdom law at the time the decision was given, and cannot be interpreted in any other way. It might be observed, however, that there may be circumstances in which the Convention provides assistance in the interpretation of existing UK law without there being a situation in which a claimant can be said to be relying on Convention rights as provided by s.7 of the HRA 1998 *(CDLA/1338/2001)*.

See also *R(IS)6/04*, *CSIS/460/2002*, and *CCS/1306/2001*. The latter summarises at para.22 the case law on the extent to which Convention rights can be relied upon prior to October 2, 2000.

SCHEDULES

SCHEDULE 1

THE ARTICLES

PART I

THE CONVENTION

RIGHTS AND FREEDOMS

Article 2—Right to life

1. Everyone's right to life shall be protected by law. No one shall be deprived of his life 4.48 intentionally save in the execution of a sentence of a court following his conviction of a crime for which this penalty is provided by law.

2. Deprivation of life shall not be regarded as inflicted in contravention of this Article when it results from the use of force which is no more than absolutely necessary:

> (a) in defence of any person from unlawful violence;
> (b) in order to effect a lawful arrest or to prevent the escape of a person lawfully detained;
> (c) in action lawfully taken for the purpose of quelling a riot or insurrection.

GENERAL NOTE

4.49   This article is unlikely to have much relevance in the social security jurisdiction. It is not a vehicle for arguing for a particular allocation of resources by the State. So arguments that without the payment of benefit, a person's life will be at risk and so the State cannot be said to be protecting by law everyone's right to life are destined to fail. This would appear to follow from those cases where the relatives of murder victims have sought to argue that the police failed to protect the victim: App.9837/82 *M v United Kingdom and Ireland* (1986) 47 D.R. 27.

Article 3—Prohibition of torture

4.50   No one shall be subjected to torture or to inhuman or degrading treatment or punishment.

GENERAL NOTE

4.51   This article is concerned with conduct which attains at least a minimum level of severity. It is not concerned with anything which a person might find degrading. See *Ireland v United Kingdom*, judgment of January 18, 1978, Series A No.25; (1979–80) 2 E.H.R.R. 25, para.162 of the judgment, and *Tyrer v United Kingdom*, judgment of April 25, 1978, Series A No.26; (1979–80) 2 E.H.R.R.1, para.30 of the judgment. The effect of setting a high threshold is that trivial complaints, and even activity which is considered undesirable or illegal, will not fall within the scope of the article unless they cause sufficiently serious suffering or humiliation to the victim. The assessment of seriousness is relative. In its judgment in *Ireland v United Kingdom*, the Court suggested that the following factors are relevant in determining the existence of inhuman treatment: the duration of the treatment, its physical and mental effects, and the sex, age, and state of health of the victim. But it should also be remembered that the Convention is a "living instrument" whose standards are not set in stone; it receives a living interpretation and must be considered in the light of present day circumstances.

It follows that arguments, for example, that a medical examination in connection with a benefit claim was felt to be degrading or inhuman by the claimant will fall well below the threshold required to engage this article even where the doctor behaves improperly.

In *R. (on the application of Joanne Reynolds) v Secretary of State for Work and Pensions*, judgment of March 7, 2002, [2002] EWHC 426, it was argued that a failure to pay the claimant more than £41.35 per week by way of social security constituted degrading treatment. Wilson J. gives this argument short shrift, pointing out that "Article 3 proscribes ill-treatment of a depth which the level of payment to Ms Reynolds wholly fails to reach."

In *Secretary of State for the Home Department v Limbuela, Tesema and Adam* [2004] EWCA Civ 540, the Court of Appeal ruled that the refusal to provide State support for three asylum seekers, who had not applied for asylum within three days of their arrival in the United Kingdom under s.55 of the Nationality, Immigration and Asylum Act 2002, engaged their Convention rights under art.3. Carnwath L.J. said that the case raised the question of the level of abject destitution to which such individuals must sink before their suffering reaches the minimum threshold for art.3 to bite. Shelter was regarded as a basic amenity and the threat of not having access to shelter in the future could come within the ambit of inhuman and degrading treatment under art.3. Laws L.J. dissented. Carnwath L.J. said,

> "118. . . . I acknowledge with gratitude the illumination provided by Laws L.J.'s powerful discussion of the scope of Art.3, and its application in the present

context. As he says, the legal reality is a spectrum. At one end is state-authorised violence. At the other are to be found executive decisions in exercise of lawful policy objectives, which have consequences for individuals so severe that 'the court is bound to limit the State's right to implement the policy on Art.3 grounds'. I agree also with much of his analysis of the consequences of that distinction, and of the correct approach to the task of drawing the line in an individual case.

119. Laws L.J. accepts that Art.3 may be engaged by a particular 'vulnerability' in the individual, or external circumstances which make it impossible for him to find food and other basic amenities. Where, with respect, I part company from him is in his view that, on the evidence available to us, the judges were not entitled to find that such circumstances existed in the present cases. I would add that I find it diΩcult not to regard shelter of some form from the elements at night (even if it is limited as it was in *T's* case) as a 'basic amenity', at least in winter and bad weather. . . ."

The appeal of the Secretary of State against the decision of the Court of Appeal has been dismissed by a unanimous House of Lords, [2005] UKHL 66.

The judgment is important because it sets out circumstances within the context of State support for individuals which fall within the ambit of inhuman and degrading treatment in art.3.

Article 4—Prohibition of slavery and forced labour

1. No one shall be held in slavery or servitude.　　　　　　　　　　　　　　　**4.52**

2. No one shall be required to perform forced or compulsory labour.

3. For the purpose of this Article the term "forced or compulsory labour" shall not include:

    (a) any work required to be done in the ordinary course of detention imposed according to the provisions of Article 5 of this Convention or during conditional release from such detention;

    (b) any service of a military character or, in case of conscientious objectors in countries where they are recognised, service exacted instead of compulsory military service;

    (c) any service exacted in case of an emergency or calamity threatening the life or well-being of the community;

    (d) any work or service which forms part of normal civic obligations.

GENERAL NOTE

Being required to be available for work as a condition of entitlement to benefit will not constitute forced or compulsory labour.　　　　　　　　　　　　　　　　　**4.53**

In joined decisions *CSJSA/495/2007* and *CJSA/505/2007*, the Commissioner dismissed as unarguable a complaint by an appellant that the requirements of the New Deal programme with its obligation to participate in an intensive activity period employment programme constituted a modern form of slavery.

Article 5—Right to liberty and security

1. Everyone has the right to liberty and security of person. No one shall be deprived of his liberty save in the following cases and in accordance with a procedure prescribed by law:　**4.54**

    (a) the lawful detention of a person after conviction by a competent court;

    (b) the lawful arrest or detention of a person for non-compliance with the lawful order of a court or in order to secure the fulfilment of any obligation prescribed by law;

    (c) the lawful arrest or detention of a person effected for the purpose of bringing him before the competent legal authority on reasonable suspicion of having committed an offence or when it is reasonably considered necessary to prevent his committing an offence or fleeing after having done so;

    (d) the detention of a minor by lawful order for the purpose of educational supervision or his lawful detention for the purpose of bringing him before the competent legal authority;

    (e) the lawful detention of persons for the prevention of the spreading of infectious diseases, of persons of unsound mind, alcoholics or drug addicts or vagrants;

    (f) the lawful arrest or detention of a person to prevent his effecting an unauthorised entry into the country or of a person against whom action is being taken with a view to deportation or extradition.

2. Everyone who is arrested shall be informed promptly, in a language which he understands, of the reasons for his arrest and of any charge against him.

3. Everyone arrested or detained in accordance with the provisions of paragraph 1 (c) of this Article shall be brought promptly before a judge or other officer authorised by law to exercise judicial power and shall be entitled to trial within a reasonable time or to release pending trial. Release may be conditioned by guarantees to appear for trial.

4. Everyone who is deprived of his liberty by arrest or detention shall be entitled to take proceedings by which the lawfulness of his detention shall be decided speedily by a court and his release ordered if the detention is not lawful.

5. Everyone who has been the victimof arrest or detention in contravention of the provisions of this Article shall have an enforceable right to compensation.

GENERAL NOTE

4.55   There are two parts to the protections afforded by art.5. First, it prohibits detention save in the exhaustive list of circumstances listed in para.(1). Secondly, it offers a set of procedural guarantees for those detained. Though the article refers to liberty and security of the person, the Strasbourg organs have not treated liberty and security as different concepts; there is no authority for arguing that security of the person refers to physical integrity independent of liberty. The article has little application in the field of social security.

Article 6—Right to a fair trial

4.56   1. In the determination of his civil rights and obligations or of any criminal charge against him, everyone is entitled to a fair and public hearing within a reasonable time by an independent and impartial tribunal established by law. Judgment shall be pronounced publicly but the press and public may be excluded from all or part of the trial in the interest of morals, public order or national security in a democratic society, where the interests of juveniles or the protection of the private life of the parties so require, or to the extent strictly necessary in the opinion of the court in special circumstances where publicity would prejudice the interests of justice.

2. Everyone charged with a criminal offence shall be presumed innocent until proved guilty according to law.

3. Everyone charged with a criminal offence has the following minimum rights:
   (a) to be informed promptly, in a language which he understands and in detail, of the nature and cause of the accusation against him;
   (b) to have adequate time and facilities for the preparation of his defence;
   (c) to defend himself in person or through legal assistance of his own choosing or, if he has not sufficient means to pay for legal assistance, to be given it free when the interests of justice so require;
   (d) to examine or have examined witnesses against him and to obtain the attendance and examination of witnesses on his behalf under the same conditions as witnesses against him;
   (e) to have the free assistance of an interpreter if he cannot understand or speak the language used in court.

GENERAL NOTE

4.57   Article 6 is central to the scheme of protection in the Convention, and has generated the largest number of applications and judgments. Article 6 is an omnibus provision which contains a blueprint for what constitutes a fair trial. Accordingly, it warrants extensive treatment.

There is a discernible trend among some Commissioners to use the fair trial requirements embedded in art.6 rather than the common law language of natural justice in deciding whether tribunal proceedings have been fair. A good example is *CJSA/5100/2001*, where the Commissioner said,

"5. I chose to explain my decision in term's of the claimant's Convention right to a fair hearing under article 6(1) of the European Convention on Human Rights and Fundamental Freedoms. In particular, I rely on the equality of arms principle that has developed in the jurisprudence of the Strasbourg authorities as part of that right. It requires that the procedure followed by the tribunal must strike a fair balance between the parties so that none is at a disadvantage as against the others. . .

6. I could, no doubt, have reached the same conclusion under domestic principles of natural justice. However, the Human Rights Act 1998 provides a convenient opportunity for Commissioners to rebase their decisions on procedural fairness in fresh terms. In my view, this would be desirable. I am sure that tribunals are familiar with the principles of natural justice. However, increasingly the cases that come to me suggest that they are not applying them. If there is a common theme in those cases, it is that the tribunal has not provided a procedural balance between the parties. The introduction of the language of balance would provide a touchstone for tribunals."

The Commissioner in *CIB/2751/2002* agreed with those sentiments in the context of a case which had involved the refusal of a domiciliary hearing in joined appeals concerning entitlement to an incapacity benefit and a severe disablement allowance.

Does the resolution of social security disputes involve the determination of civil rights and obligations?

The first question which must be addressed is whether decision-making in 4.58 social security constitutes "the determination of . . . civil rights and obligations". Answering this question requires detailed discussion of a line of Convention cases. The formulation in art.6 would seem to exclude the initial decisions by decision-makers since the article contemplates a situation in which there is a dispute. This is clearer from the French text, which refers to *contestations*. It cannot be said that there is a dispute when what is at issue is an initial determination of entitlement to benefit (see *Feldbrugge v The Netherlands*, judgment of May 29, 1986, Series A, No.99; (1986) 8 E.H.R.R. 425, para.25 of the judgment); the vast majority of such decisions are not the subject of appeal to a tribunal. But what of the tribunals? Are they determining civil rights and obligations? The essential question is whether art.6 covers only private law rights to the exclusion of public law matters: a distinction which is much more formal in continental systems of law than in the United Kingdom's common law system.

It was not long before the issue came before the Court of Human Rights in the *Ringeisen* case (*Ringeisen v Austria (No. 1)*, judgment of July 16, 1971, Series A, No.13; (1979–80) 1 E.H.R.R. 455) after the majority of the Commission had concluded that Art.6 should be construed restrictively as including only those proceedings which are typical of relations between private individuals and as excluding those proceedings in which the citizen is confronted by those who exercise public authority. The Court took a different view. Article 6 covers all proceedings the result of which is decisive for the private rights and obligations of individuals, and neither the character of the legislation (whether, for example civil, commercial or administrative) nor that of the authority with jurisdiction over the dispute (whether, for example, court, tribunal or administrative body) are of great consequence. Since the decision in this case, the Court has adopted a liberal interpretation of the concept of civil rights and obligations.

Several cases have considered whether social security disputes involve the determination of civil rights and obligations.

The *Feldbrugge* case (*Feldbrugge v The Netherlands*, judgment of May 29, 1986, Series A, No.99; (1986) 8 E.H.R.R. 425) concerned a dispute over entitlement to a sickness allowance in The Netherlands. Mrs Feldbrugge had been registered as unemployed, but then ceased to register because she had become ill and did not consider herself fit for work. The Occupational Association (the body responsible for administering sickness allowance in The Netherlands) arranged for her to be medically examined by their consulting doctor, who concluded that she was fit for work. The sickness allowance was stopped. The claimant appealed to the Appeals Board and the President of the Appeals Board arranged for her to be seen by a gynaecologist who was one of the permanent medical experts attached to the Appeals Board. That doctor examined her and gave her an opportunity to comment. The doctor consulted another gynaecologist and two general practitioners (one of whom was the claimant's GP). They all agreed with the decision that the claimant was fit for work, but the permanent medical expert considered that an orthopaedic specialist should also be consulted. An orthopaedic surgeon examined the claimant who was again given an opportunity to comment. The three practitioners consulted by the gynaecologist were also consulted following this examination. The orthopaedic surgeon concluded in the light of all the medical findings that the claimant was fit for work in accordance with the initial contested decision. The President of the Appeals Board then ruled against the claimant, who filed an objection which raised the matter before the Appeals Board itself, which found the objection lacking in substance. An appeal to the Central Appeals Board was unsuccessful. Mrs Feldbrugge complained that she had not had a fair trial before the President of the Appeals Board in violation of art.6(1). The Court had to face squarely the issue of whether the adjudication of the claimant's dispute was a matter concerning her civil rights and obligations. The Court weighed the features of the case which suggested that the matter was one of public law against the features which suggested that it was one of private law. The public law nature of the legislation on sickness allowances, the compulsory nature of insurance against illness, and the assumption by the State of responsibility for social protection had to be weighed against the personal and economic nature of the asserted right, its connection with the contract of employment, and affinities with insurance under the ordinary law. After weighing these interests, the Court ruled by a majority of ten votes to seven, that, taken together, the private law aspects of the sickness allowance scheme were "predominant" and the adjudication of Mrs Feldbrugge's claim was therefore covered by art.6(1).

The *Deumeland* case (*Deumeland v Germany*, judgment of May 29, 1986, Series A, No.20; (1986) 8 E.H.R.R. 448), decided on the same day as the *Feldbrugge* case, concerned industrial injury pensions in Germany. The proceedings in Germany were extraordinarily protracted, and this was the substance of the applicant's complaint. Gerhard Deumeland had in January 1970 slipped on a snow covered pavement as he was coming home from an appointment with an ear-nose-and-throat specialist whom he had consulted on leaving his workplace. He died in March 1970, and his widow claimed a widow's supplementary pension on the basis that the death of Gerhard had been the consequence of an industrial accident. The first set of proceedings before the Berlin Social Security Court of Appeal lasted from June 1970 to December 1972. The outcome of these proceedings was a decision that the accident in question was neither an industrial accident nor an accident on the way to or from work. There was accordingly no entitlement to a widow's supplementary pension. Mrs Deumeland appealed to the Berlin Social Security Court of Appeal, where the first set of proceedings lasted from November 1972 to September 1973. These were unsuccessful. An appeal on a point of law was pursued before the Bundessozialgericht (Federal Social Security Court) which lasted from October 1973 to May 1975. In the course of these proceedings, the claimant challenged a judge for bias accusing him of delaying the proceedings. That challenge was not successful and the appeal decision was taken by a panel which included the unsuccessfully challenged judge. The decision of the Bundessozialgericht was to set aside the decision of the Berlin Social Security Court of Appeal and to remit the case for a fresh hearing.

4.59   The second set of proceedings before the Berlin Social Security Court of Appeal lasted from May 1975 to March 1979. In December 1976 during the course of these proceedings, Mrs Deumeland died and her son, Klaus, was allowed to continue the proceedings. The outcome was a decision that the claim to the widow's pension was unfounded. Klaus Deumeland sought to appeal to the Bundessozialgericht. Leave to appeal was eventually refused. Leave for a further appeal to the Bundesverfassungsgericht (Federal Constitutional Court) was refused by that Court, and a subsequent application to the Berlin Social Security Court of Appeal by Klaus Deumeland to have the proceedings reopened was not only unsuccessful but also resulted in his being fined DM800 for bringing vexatious proceedings. For reasons which are very similar to those in the *Feldbrugge* case, the Court, by a majority of 9 votes to 8, concluded that the proceedings of which the applicant complained had been concerned with the determination of civil rights and obligations.

The *Feldbrugge* and *Deumeland* cases had involved benefits which flowed from an insurance principle, and this feature might be seen as critical in drawing a distinction between social insurance and social assistance. The latter term refers to those benefits which fall outside the sphere of social insurance and involve the State stepping in to provide benefits for those who have no entitlement to insurance-based benefits, or whose entitlement is such that their income is below subsistence level. The distinction came before the Court in the *Salesi* case (*Salesi v Italy*, judgment of February 26, 1993, Series A, No.257-E (1998) 26 E.H.R.R. 187). Enrica Salesi had claimed a monthly disability allowance in the Lazio social security department, which had been refused. In February 1986, she brought proceedings against the Minister of the Interior before the pretore del lavoro (magistrates' court exercising their labour jurisdiction) in Rome seeking payment of the benefit. The Minister appealed against the decision of the pretore awarding the benefit, and the Rome District Court dismissed the appeal in May 1989. A subsequent appeal to the Court of Cassation was also dismissed. Even though the claimant was ultimately the winning party, she complained to the Commission alleging a violation of art.6(1) by reason of the length of the proceedings.

The Court re-affirmed its decisions in *Feldbrugge* and *Deumeland* noting,

". . . the development in the law that was initiated by those judgments and the principle of equality of treatment warrant taking the view that today the general rule is that Article 6(1) does apply in the field of social insurance."

The Court went on,

"In the present case, however, the question arises in connection with welfare assistance and not . . . social insurance. Certainly there are differences between the two, but they cannot be regarded as fundamental at the present stage of development of social security law. This justifies following, in relation to the entitlement to welfare allowances, the opinion which emerges from [the judgments in *Feldbrugge* and *Deumeland*] as regards the classification of the right to social insurance benefits, namely that State intervention is not sufficient to establish that Article 6(1) is inapplicable." (para.19 of the judgment.)

The Court concluded that there were no convincing reasons for distinguishing welfare benefits from the rights to social insurance benefits asserted in the earlier cases. The decision of the Court may be criticised for its poverty of reasoning, but nevertheless remains an authority for the extension of art.6(1) to all disputes concerning social security benefits.

The *Schuler-Zgraggen* case (*Schuler-Zgraggen v Switzerland*, judgment of June 24, 1993, Series A, No.263; (1993) 16 E.H.R.R. 405) concerned a claim to an invalidity pension. The claimant had been employed and paid contributions into the federal invalidity insurance scheme. She contracted open pulmonary tuberculosis and applied for an invalidity pension. The Compensation Office awarded a half pension, which was subsequently increased to a full pension. In 1984 the applicant gave birth to a son. In 1985 she was required to undergo a medical examination by doctors appointed by the Invalidity Insurance Board. This resulted in a decision to terminate the award of the invalidity pension. The claimant appealed to the relevant Appeals Board. In the course of these proceedings she was refused a sight of her medical file which had been seen by the Appeals Board. The Board subsequently dismissed her appeal. The claimant lodged an appeal against this decision with the Federal

Insurance Court, whose decision was to remit the case to the Compensation Office, whose reconsideration did not result in the award of a pension. The Court followed its earlier decisions in concluding that the proceedings in issue were concerned with the determination of civil rights and obligations. The Court also followed the decision in *Salesi* in virtually identical language,

> ". . . the development in the law that was initiated by those judgments [in *Feldbrugge* and *Deumeland*] and the principle of equality of treatment warrant taking the view that today the general rule is that Article 6(1) does apply in the field of social insurance, including even welfare assistance." (para.46 of the judgment.)

The *Schouten and Meldrum* case (*Schouten and Meldrum v The Netherlands*, judgment of December 9, 1994, Series A, No.304; (1994) 19 E.H.R.R. 432) concerned the liability of persons in similar positions to employers to pay contributions to an occupational association in respect of physiotherapists who worked for them. This was the first case in which the Court had been called upon to determine an issue involving the payment of contributions under a social security scheme as distinct from disputes concerning entitlement to benefits. The Court took the view that the approach adopted in *Feldbrugge* and *Deumeland* was appropriate in the case of liability to pay contributions. The public law and private law aspects of the arrangements should be weighed to see whether one or the other were predominant. Using exactly the same factors as had been in issue in *Feldbrugge*, the Court concluded that the private law aspects were predominant and that art.6(1) applied.

A challenge to the system of recovering State benefits from personal injury awards has also failed at the admissibility stage (App.2877/95, *Graeme Knightley v United Kingdom*, decision of September 4, 1997). See also *Stevens and Knight v United Kingdom*, decision of September 9, 1998, in which the Commission simply ignored arguments that the determination of claims to sickness benefit, statutory sick pay and invalidity benefit did not constitute the determination of civil rights and obligations.

These cases establish beyond a peradventure that adjudication of social security disputes involves the determination of civil rights and obligations to which the procedural guarantees of art.6(1) apply: see also *CDLA/5413/1999*. They have been followed even in cases where the pensions of those employed in the public service were involved (*Lombardo v Italy*, judgment of November 26, 1992, Series A, No.249-B; (1996) 21 E.H.R.R. 188; and *Massa v Italy*, judgment of August 24, 1993, Series A, No.265-B; (1994) 18 E.H.R.R.266. It follows that the rules on what constitutes a fair trial apply to the proceedings of tribunals and the courts when dealing with social security questions.

The Secretary of State made a concession in *Wood v Secretary of State for Work and Pensions* [2003] EWCA Civ 53 (see para.24) (reported as *R(DLA) 1/03*) which would appear to mean that all social security appeals involve the determination of civil rights and obligations and so attract the protection of art.6. See also *R(IS)6/04*, but note para.68 of *R(H) 3/05*.

In a housing case, *Begum v Tower Hamlets LBC* [2003] UKHL 5, the House of Lords also took a broad view of what constitutes the determination of civil rights and obligations (without making any definitive ruling on what does and does not fall within this formulation in art.6) and went on to make a number of pertinent comments on what constitutes independence and impartiality for the purposes of the article. A decision by a rehousing manager employed by a local authority reviewing a decision to offer a particular property to the applicant was held not to constitute an "independent and impartial" tribunal' for the purposes of art.6, but a determination on review by the county court "on any point of law arising from the decision" which did not permit the making of fresh findings of fact did meet the requirements of art.6.

What is a fair trial under Article 6(1)?

The Strasbourg organs have indicated that art.6(1) demands not only an overall **4.60** requirement of a fair hearing but also the presence of specific features in order for there to be a fair trial. The overall requirement has been summarised as follows,

"The effect of Article 6(1) is, inter alia, to place the 'tribunal' under a duty to conduct a proper examination of the submissions, arguments and evidence adduced by the parties, without prejudice to its assessment of whether they are relevant to its decision." (*Kraska v Switzerland*, judgment of April 19, 1993, Series A, No.254-B; (1994) 18 E.H.R.R. 188, para.30 of the judgment.)

It is important that the general requirements for a fair trial are appreciated, since they continue to be developed in specific circumstances by the Strasbourg organs. Certain of the requirements are of a general nature, whereas others are more specifically stated in art.6.

Four features *inherent* in the concept of a fair trial appear to have flowed from this general notion of a fair trial.

The first and perhaps most important is the concept of *e'galite' des armes*, which translates inelegantly into English as "equality of arms". In English law, it is an aspect of the requirement of natural justice. It requires that each party has a broadly equal opportunity to present a case in circumstances which do not place one of the parties as a substantial disadvantage as regards the opposing party (see *Dombo Beheer BV v The Netherlands*, judgment of October 27, 1993, Series A, No.274-A; (1994) 18 E.H.R.R. 213, para.33 of the judgment). In *CDLA/5413/1999*, the Commissioner expresses concern that the principle of equality of arms may be breached by the provisions of the Adjudication Regulations on notice, which provide that notice required to be given or sent by the Department are, if sent by post, deemed to be given on the day of posting, whereas notice required to be given by a claimant is only treated as given when it reaches the Department.

In an expansive reading of the Strasbourg case law, the Commissioner in *CDLA/2748/2002* draws on specific case law relating to criminal proceedings in art.6(3)(e) on the provision of interpretation and translation to suggest that art.6 requires that effective and efficient interpretation and translation is a feature of tribunal adjudication where the claimant needs this. He says that "a failure of interpretation must therefore affect the fairness of the tribunal hearing." (para.11).

Secondly, there must be a judicial process, which requires each side to have the opportunity to have knowledge of and comment on the observations filed or evidence adduced by the opposing party (*Ruiz-Mateos v Spain*, judgment of June 23, 1993, Series A, No.262; (1993) 16 E.H.R.R. 505, para.63 of the judgment). Non-disclosure of material by one side to the other is likely to give rise to violations of this feature of a fair trial, as might issues of the circumstances in which evidence was acquired. In the *Feldbrugge* case, the applicant complained that she had not had a proper opportunity to present her case. The Court found that the proceedings before the President of the Appeals Board "were not attended to a sufficient degree, by one of the principal guarantees of a judicial procedure" (para.44 of the judgment) in that, although the applicant had been afforded the opportunity to comment on her condition during the medical examinations, she was neither able to present oral argument nor to file written pleadings before the President of the Appeals Board; nor was she able to consult the two reports of the consultants and to formulate objections to them.

Thirdly, there is a requirement for a reasoned decision, which is regarded as implicit in the notion of a fair trial. The level of reasoning need not be detailed. If a court gives reasons, then the requirement for a reasoned decision is prima facie met, but a decision which on its face shows that it was made on a basis not open to the judge cannot be said to be a reasoned decision (see *De Moor v Belgium*, judgment of June 23, 1994, Series A, No.292-A; (1994) 18 E.H.R.R. 372). For a case in which a violation of art.6 was found because of the inadequacy of the reasons for rejecting certain medical evidence in a social security context, see *H.A.L. v Finland*

(App.38267/97) Judgment of January 27, 2004. The introduction of short-form decisions in tribunals is unlikely to fall foul of this provision, since a party is entitled to a full statement of reasons on application within one month of the day on which the decision notice was notified to the parties. Decisions of the Commissioners are always given in full, except a decision made with the consent of the parties to set aside a tribunal decision and remit the case for a rehearing by the tribunal.

The final issue is whether a trial can be fair if there is no right of appearance in person. The law here remains in a state of development and the Court has yet to pronounce in detail on this in civil cases, but the Commission has held that in some cases a fair trial is only possible in the presence of the parties. An example would be a case where the personal character and manner of life of a party are directly relevant to the formation of the court's opinion on the point at issue. Custody disputes over children might be such cases (See App.434/58, *X v Sweden*, June 30, 1959, 2 Y.B. 354 at 370). Presence may need to be distinguished from participation. In the *Schuler-Zgraggen* case, the applicant had not availed herself of the opportunity to request a hearing, but nevertheless complained that the proceedings were unfair because the Federal Insurance Court had not ordered a hearing of its own motion. The Court accepted the arguments of the Government that purely written proceedings did not in the circumstances of this case prejudice the interests of the litigant. It was accepted that a written procedure would offer advantages of efficiency and speed which might be jeopardised if oral hearings became the rule. The Court concluded,

> "The Court reiterates that the public character of court hearings constitutes a fundamental principle enshrined in Article 6(1). Admittedly, neither the letter nor the spirit of this provision prevents a person from waiving of his own free will, either expressly or tacitly, the entitlement to have his case heard in public, but any such waiver must be made in an unequivocal manner and must not run counter to any important public interest." (para.58 of the judgment.)

These comments have relevance both for paper hearings before appeal tribunals and for procedure before the Commissioners (see below).

4.61   There are four *specific features* of a fair trial to be found on the face of art.6.

First, trial must be before "an independent and impartial tribunal established by law." This requirement includes a subjective and an objective element. The subjective test involves an enquiry into whether the particular judge in the case was actually biased, or lacking in independence or impartiality. Propriety will be presumed in the absence of specific evidence of bias. The objective test involves determination of whether the court or tribunal offers guarantees sufficient to exclude any legitimate doubt about its impartiality or independence. This can include both specific difficulties caused by certain persons being involved in particular decisions, as well as what might be called structural problems with the forum for the resolution of the dispute. A good example of structural problems can be found in the English courts-martial cases, which have determined that the role (at the time) of the convening officer in the management of the prosecution case conflicted with his role as convenor of the court-martial, in particular his appointment of its members (who were subordinate in rank to himself and fell within his chain of command) (see *Findlay v United Kingdom*, judgment of February 25, 1997; (1997) 24 E.H.R.R. 221; and *Coyne v United Kingdom*, judgment of September 24, 1997, *The Times*, October 24, 1997, E.C.H.R.).

Tsfayo v United Kingdom (App. 60860) Judgment of November 14, 2006, is now largely of historical interest, but a violation of Article 6 was found on the grounds that the Housing Benefit Review Board was not an independent and impartial tribunal. However, the comments in the case on the relationship between appeals and other remedies are of considerable significance, and it was suggested that, for this reason, the United Kingdom would seek to have the case referred to the Grand Chamber. That does not appear to have happened. Note in relation to the *Tsfayo* case, the admissibility decision of the Strasbourg Court in *BH v United Kingdom* (App. 59580/00), Decision of September 25, 2007).

Secondly, publicity is seen as one of the guarantees of the fairness of a trial, but the requirement for hearings to be in public is surrounded by a substantial list of circumstances in which the presumption of public hearings is displaced. It is now also clear that interlocutory matters do not have to be in public. So the Commission has rejected a complaint that interlocutory proceedings before a High Court Master in Chambers without elaborating its reasons violated art.6: App.3860/68, *X v United Kingdom* (1970) 30 C.D. 70). A similar view would almost certainly be taken of proceedings for leave to appeal. As already noted, a written procedure may suffice provided that there are proper opportunities for requesting or ordering an oral hearing.

Thirdly, art.6(1), on its face, requires that judgment is pronounced publicly, and this requirement is not expressed to be subject to the list of limitations which apply to a public trial. The leading case is *Pretto (Pretto and others v Italy*, judgment of December 8, 1983, Series A, No.71; (1984) 6 E.H.R.R. 182. The Court seems to have been very accommodating to a wide range of practice in this regard among the Contracting States, indicating that the form of publicity to be given to a judgment is to be assessed in the light of special features of particular proceedings. It certainly appears to be the case that nothing more than the formal disposition need be announced publicly, and it seems that the public availability of the outcome is as important as the matter being read out in open court. So in the *Pretto* case, the availability of the disposition in the court registry was considered to meet the requirements for public pronouncement of the judgment.

Lastly, under art.6(1), litigants are entitled to judgment in a reasonable time. Complaints of violations of this requirement have been the single most numerous sort of alleged violation of the Convention. Such cases have rarely involved the United Kingdom (but see *Robins v United Kingdom*, judgment of September 23, 1997; (1998) 26 E.H.R.R. 527). Though the case law is voluminous, the principles can be stated quite simply. The first task is to determine the period or periods in issue, before moving on to consider the reasonableness of the length of the proceedings. The period in issue will include any appellate proceedings. In forming judgments on the reasonableness of the length of the proceedings, the following factors are relevant: the complexity of the case, the behaviour of the applicant, the conduct of the judicial authorities, and what is at stake for the applicant. However, backlogs of judicial business are not a defence to unreasonable delays. In *Deumeland*, the period in issue was 10 years, seven months and three weeks from the application to the Berlin Social Security Court to the rejection of the application to the Bundesverfassungsgericht. The claim to benefit involved a straightforward factual issue involving no great legal complexity, but the behaviour of Klaus Deumeland had protracted the proceedings. Detailed examination of the progress of the case through the various courts showed that the case had lain dormant before the Berlin Social Security Court for significant periods, and the period taken to resolve the second set of proceedings before the appellate body was excessive. There was a violation of the right to judgment within a reasonable time, but it is significant that the Court also finds that the mere declaration of a violation was in the circumstances of the case considered to be adequate just satisfaction under what is now art.41 of the Convention. A delay of a little over six years in the *Salesi* case was also found to constitute a violation of art.6(1). The reasonableness of the time taken to give judgment must be determined in each case in the light of its own particular circumstances.

The issue of judgment within a reasonable time in the social security context was raised in *R(IS)1/04*, where the claimant argued that the (it should be said typical) lengthy period before an overpayment decision is taken meant that there was a breach of art.6. An overpayment decision was made on October 14, 2000 in respect of an overpayment which had arisen in 1994 and 1995. The Commissioner concludes that for the purposes of the measurement of time in the context of a complaint that judgment has not been given within a reasonable time, time started running on October 14, 2000, since it was at that point that a dispute arose; a different Commissioner in *R(IS)2/04* takes the same view at para.20. That was enough to dispose of the point since a tribunal determined the appeal in May 2001 which was manifestly within a reasonable time. The claimant had also sought to suggest that overpayment decisions were in the nature of criminal charges. The Commissioner, after careful consideration of the authorities, concludes that overpayment decisions involve the determination of civil rights and obligations and not the determination of a criminal charge (see paras 12–17).

See also *CIS/4220/2002*, which draws on the decision of the Court in *Dyer v Watson*, [2002] 4 All E.R. 1.

The Court of Human Rights has ruled, in *Bullerwell v United Kingdom* (App.48013/99), decision of December 12, 2002 (2003) 36 E.H.R.R. CD 76, ECHR, as inadmissible a complaint that judgment was not given in a reasonable time in an industrial injuries benefit case which involved four hearings by a medical appeal tribunal, three appeals to the Commissioner, and an application for judicial review which resulted in an unsuccessful appeal to the Court of Appeal. The outcome is unsurprising even though the first appeal was lodged in July 1991 and the trail of litigation ended in July 1998 when the House of Lords refused a petition for leave to appeal the refusal of leave to apply for judicial review. The Court applies its tried and tested methodology of considering the complexity of the case, the parties' conduct and that of the competent authorities, and the importance of what was at stake for the applicant in the litigation. There is nothing significant in the decision but it is an excellent example of the approach of the new Court to admissibility of complaints and contains a detailed and fair analysis of the course of these lengthy proceedings. There is one interesting comment on Commissioner's directions, as follows:

> "On 7 May 1996 the applicant applied to the Commissioner for leave to appeal against the MAT's decision of 26 April 1996. Less than a month later the Commissioner made directions for the filing of observations by the Secretary of State, and, on 21 August 1996, just over a month after these observations were filed, leave to appeal was granted. Thereafter the Commissioner made a number of further directions for the determination of the appeal itself, but it was not until 15 January 1997 that he decided that it was necessary for the Secretary of State to file a written submission on the mean of the word 'diffuse'. Although it cannot be said that the period between 21 August 1996 and 15 January 1997 was one of judicial inactivity, the Court considers that time would have been saved if the Commissioner had explicitly requested these observations from the Secretary of State at the outset." (p.13.)

This illustrates that the new Court is willing to look in considerable detail at the course of the proceedings as part of its examination of whether judgment has been given within a reasonable time. While it is important to remember that this is a decision on the admissibility of the complaint, it does suggest that a succession of small and unnecessary delays could accumulate into a sufficient lengthy period of delay for the Court to consider that there was a case to answer in relation to the length of proceedings.

The application of art. 6(1) to appeal proceedings

4.62   Article 6 does not require Contracting States to have a system of appeals from decisions at first instance in civil cases (*De Cubber v Belgium*, judgment of October 26, 1984, Series A, No.86; (1985) 7 E.H.R.R. 236, para.32 of the Judgment), but if the State does provide a system of appeals, it too must comply with the guarantees to be found in Art.6(1) (*Fejde v Sweden*, judgment of September 26, 1991, Series A, No.212-C; (1994) 17 E.H.R.R. 14, para.32 of the judgment). It follows that a defect at first instance might be corrected at the appellate stage of the proceedings. Where there is an appeal, the requirement to exhaust domestic remedies before a complaint can be made under the Convention means that it must be used, and it will then be the totality of the domestic proceedings which is considered by the Commission and Court. It will always be necessary to look at the character of the appellate proceedings to determine the extent to which they are able to remedy any deficiency at first instance. For example, the shortcoming identified in the *Feldbrugge* case could not be remedied on appeal, because the nature of the appeal was restricted to four very narrow grounds, none of which offered the opportunity for the applicant to participate to the extent required by Art.6 in the proceedings which determined her dispute.

A fair appeal is unlikely to be able to correct a defect arising from a structural problem in the first instance court or tribunal which results in its not being an independent and impartial tribunal (*De Cubber v Belgium*, judgment of October 26, 1984, Series A, No.86; (1985) 7 E.H.R.R. 236, para.33 of the judgment). There is a suggestion that the quashing by an appeal court on the specific ground that the first instance court or tribunal was not independent and impartial might have cured the defect, but this could amount to recognition that there was no right to a court in the particular instance. This is a right which the Court has read into art.6.

There has been an ongoing debate in English law concerning the adequacy of judicial review as a remedy for what might be regarded as an earlier breach of Convention rights. In *CTC/0031/2006* the Commissioner considered this question in the context of an appeal concerning the backdating of a claim to Child Tax Credit. The Commissioner dismissed the appeal on the grounds that the acceptance of a "manner" of claiming is an administrative act involving the exercise of discretion. Accordingly, judicial review was an adequate remedy and there was no basis for the argument that art.6 ECHR required the recognition of a right to appeal to a tribunal on this question.

The right to a court

The Court has recognised that art.6 must contain a right of access to a court for the determination of a particular issue. So the prohibition (at the time) in English Prison Rules on bringing a defamation action against a prison officer, who was alleged to have accused the prisoner wrongly of having assaulted him, violated this right (*Golder v United Kingdom*, judgment of February 21, 1975, Series A, No.18; (1979–80) 1 E.H.R.R. 524). A similar conclusion was reached in a case originating from Ireland where there was no procedure by which a father could challenge a decision of the authorities placing his daughter for adoption (*Keegan v Ireland*, judgment of May 26, 1994, Series A, No.290; (1994) 18 E.H.R.R. 342). The right might even include a right to some sort of representation in order to make the right effective. In the *Airey* case (*Airey v Ireland*, judgment of October 9, 1979, Series A, No.32; (1979–80) 2 E.H.R.R. 305), the applicant had been unable to find a lawyer to act for her because of her financial position and the absence of legal aid. She needed a separation order to protect her from her husband who was prone to violence towards her. The procedure was complex and not such as could be managed effectively by a litigant in person. The Court concluded that, in such circumstances, art.6 requires the provision of legal assistance where "such assistance proves indispensable for an effective access to court." (para.26 of the judgment). The case is sometimes wrongly read too sweepingly as imposing an obligation on State to have a legal aid scheme, at least for complex litigation. The judgment is rather more limited; it will be necessary to look at the nature of the right being protected by the litigation, what is at stake for the applicant, and the complexity of the procedure before the particular decision-making body in making a judgment as to whether art.6 requires a State to provide legal assistance.

In *CJSA/5101/2001* the claimant sought to rely on the *Airey* case to ground an entitlement to legal representation. The Commissioner stated:

"The claimant has no right to legal representation under British law in a social security case, and the European Convention on Human Rights does not give him

4.63

that right. I have no power under British law to grant him legal representation and the European Convention on Human Rights, again does not give me that power." (para.9).

Though undoubtedly correct in the circumstances of the case before him, it is not entirely inconceivable that a set of circumstances might arise in which the *Airey* test requiring legal assistance and possibly legal representation might arise in the future.

Legal aid for representation at oral hearings is now possible in England and Wales through the Community Legal Service established by the Access to Justice Act 1999. The Lord Chancellor has made directions which permit support to be provided for representation where one of four criteria is met:

1. The case must be of significant public interest.
2. The case must be of overwhelming importance for the claimant.
3. It is practically possible for the claimant to bring the proceedings.
4. A lack of public funding would lead to obvious unfairness.

It must follow that Commissioners should be alert to the need to consider the circumstances of claimants and should make directions which might lead to the grant of funded legal representation where one of the four criteria set out above is satisfied. The position in Scotland is more favourable; since December 2002, publicly-funded legal representation is available in all proceedings before the Commissioners sitting in Scotland.

Application to social security procedure

4.64   As noted above, initial decision-making on claims to benefit does not fall within art.6, though appeals to the First-tier tribunal and the Upper Tribunal do attract the due process guarantees of art.6.

There have now been a number of cases in which English courts have had to consider the application of the requirement for a fair trial under art.6 to proceedings arising in England. The state of the authorities is helpfully summarised by the Court of Appeal in *R. (on the application of Thompson) v The Law Society* [2002] EWCA Civ 167. Clarke L.J. delivering the judgment of the Court with which his colleagues agreed says,

> "The key point as a matter of principle is that the question whether the procedure satisfies article 6(1), where there is a determination of civil rights and obligations, must be answered by reference to the whole process. The question in each case is whether the process involves a court or courts having 'full jurisdiction to deal with the case as the nature of the decision requires'. There may be cases in which a public and oral hearing is required at first instances and other cases where it is not, just as there may be cases in which the potential availability of judicial review will not be sufficient to avoid a breach of article 6(1)".

Procedure before the tribunals is unlikely to raise any difficulties under art.6. It is just possible that an issue could arise from the introduction of paper hearings. However, paper hearings will only arise where the claimant does not ask for an oral hearing. There might be an arguable violation of art.6 where a paper hearing proceeds in a case which is for particular reasons more appropriate for an oral hearing. reg.39(5) of the Decisions and Appeals Regulations provides a power for the chairman of an appeal tribunal of his or her own motion to direct an oral hearing of an appeal. A good example of an appeal which might not be appropriate for a paper hearing might be a case involving a substantial overpayment of benefit where the claimant maintained that disclosure had taken place. Here issues of credibility are raised which can best be resolved by seeing and hearing the claimant.

In *CDLA/5413/1999* the Commissioner concluded that the claimant had been denied a fair hearing when she had asked for an oral hearing and an appeal proceeded in her absence because the deemed notice of the hearing had never reached her. The Commissioner says:

"49. Rehearsing again the salient features of this case in the light of the above analysis [of the requirements of Art.6 ECHR], it is one where the claimant asked, in accordance with regulations, for an oral hearing. The hearing was to be before the only tribunal or court competent to give her case a full hearing as to issues of fact. It was a case in which her presence and evidence were clearly relevant to the issue before the tribunal. She was unrepresented. She was not present at the hearing. The Secretary of State was not represented. There was no clerk present. The tribunal heard the case, and in doing so both assumed it had the capacity to do so and that it did not need to adjourn. It did that because the claimant was assumed to know about the hearing because of the deemed notice provision. But the claimant did not know about the hearing through no fault of her own.

50. The question for me on those facts is whether there was a fair hearing of this case before the decision of the tribunal was made, in the judicial sense of 'fair hearing'. In my view there was not. This is because the claimant asked for an oral hearing and did not receive it. This was through no fault of her own but because of the operation, against her interests, of a rule of procedure that was not a 'fair balance' as between her and the other party to the appeal, the Secretary of State.

51. It does not matter whether that unfairness was the result of the decision of the tribunal itself to continue with the case or whether it was the result of some failure in the method by which the claimant was supposed to be given notice and for which the tribunal itself had no direct responsibility. The essential matter is that the decision under appeal was reached without the tribunal hearing the claimant and without if having any of the permissible grounds for not hearing her."

In *C5/05-06 (IB)*, a Commissioner in Northern Ireland set aside the decision of a tribunal where the claimant had asked for an oral hearing but did not attend. The claimant subsequently indicated that he had not received notification of the hearing, nor had his solicitors. The Commissioner, following *CDLA/5413/1999*, appears to consider that in such circumstances there had been a breach of art.6.

Support for this view can now be found in the Strasbourg case law. In *Elo v Finland* (App. 30742/02) the Court of Human Rights was considering a complaint that the lack of an oral hearing before an Accident Board whose task was to determine the level of disability following an accident at work. The Court found no breach of art.6. It stated the general proposition:

". . . unless there are exceptional circumstances that justify dispensing with a hearing, the right to a public hearing under Article 6(1) implies a right to an oral hearing at least before one instance." (para.34).

The Court went on:

"36. The Court reiterates that the character of the circumstances that may justify dispensing with an oral hearing essentially comes down to the nature of the issues to be decided by the competent national court not to the frequency with which such issues come before the courts. This does not mean that refusing to hold an oral hearing may be justified only in rare cases (see *Miller v Sweden*, No. 55853/00, § 29, 8 February 2005). Thus, the Court has recognised that disputes concerning benefits under social-security schemes are generally rather technical and their outcome usually depends on the written opinions given by medical doctors. Many such disputes may accordingly be better dealt with in writing than in oral argument. Moreover, it is understandable that in this sphere the national authorities should have regard to the demands of efficiency and economy. Systematically holding hearings could be an obstacle to the particular diligence required in social-security cases (see *Schuler-Zgraggen v Switzerland*, cited above, pp. 19–20, § 58).

37. Turning to the particular circumstances of the present case, the Court observes that the jurisdiction of the Accident Board and the Insurance Court was not limited to matters of law but also extended to factual issues. The issue before

them was whether the applicant's injuries attained the category 7 disability on the scale of injuries and whether his injuries could have been assessed under the general title "the lower extremities as a whole" as alleged by the applicant. The question is whether hearing oral evidence from the applicant and the doctors treating him could have produced anything relevant and decisive which was not already encompassed in the written evidence and submissions. The Accident Board found an oral hearing manifestly unnecessary. Nor did the Insurance Court find an oral hearing necessary as the decisive factor for reaching a decision in the applicant's case was the medical opinions on the applicant's injuries.

38. The Court observes that under the Ministry's decision the personal circumstances of a claimant are not taken into account when assessing the disability category to be attributed. Thus the Accident's Board's and Insurance Court's assessments were entirely based on the medical evidence in the case, presented in the form of written medical certificates issued by the applicant's doctors. The medical certificates on which the applicant relied supported his claim. It does not appear that the doctors' opinions differed (see, *mutatis mutandis, Döry v Sweden*, cited above, § 42). The Court sees no reason to differ from the finding of the Insurance Court that the applicant's entitlement to compensation had to be based on the evaluation of the injuries sustained to his heels and ankles, which assessment could be made on the basis of the written medical evidence. Further, there is no indication that a hearing was needed in order to hear oral testimony (see *Ringel v Sweden* (dec.), No. 13599/03, 23 March 2004).

39. In these circumstances, it must be concluded that the dispute in the case concerned the correct interpretation of written medical evidence. The Court considers that the Accident Board and the Insurance Court could adequately resolve this issue on the basis of the medical certificates before them and the applicant's written submissions.

40. Having regard to the foregoing, the Court finds that there were circumstances which justified dispensing with a hearing in the applicant's case."

It will also be important to ensure that the requirements implicit in "e´galite´ des armes" are always met; this will mean that the claimant always has the opportunity to respond to the case put forward on behalf of the Secretary of State, and that new evidence is not put before the tribunal at such a late stage that the claimant has no opportunity to comment upon it.

It has long been held that a tribunal must give both sides the opportunity to consider authorities raised by the other side, and, where the introduction of a new and key authority is introduced at a late stage, to consider an adjournment to enable the significance of the authority to be fully considered in the argument put to the tribunal. That requirement flowed from the requirements of natural justice. A case relating to the employment tribunals now makes the same point in relation to the requirements for a fair hearing under art.6: see *Sheridan v Stanley Cole (Wainfleet) Ltd*, [2003] EWCA Civ 1046. The Court of Appeal stresses that the relevant authority must have a central role in shaping the decision for the requirement to bite. It had to have altered or affected the way the issues had been addressed to a significant extent. Again the notion of the fair-minded observer is called into play in that the authority will have had a major effect on the proceedings if a fair-minded observer would say that the case had been decided in a way which could not have been anticipated by a party fixed with such knowledge of the law and procedure as it would be reasonable to attribute to that party in all the circumstances.

It is possible that a claimant might take issue with the composition of a tribunal in which there is no guarantee that, for example, a medically qualified panel member is not also a member of the panel of examining medical practitioners used by the Benefits Agency. There would clearly be a breach of natural justice (and a violation of art.6(1)) if a doctor who had examined a claimant sat on the tribunal which heard the appeal, but it is clear that this would be obvious from the papers and that the normal expectation is that the doctor would not sit. The requirement that an applicant must exhaust all domestic remedies before complaining of a breach of the Convention would mean that an applicant would need to pursue an appeal to the Social Security Commissioner, who would, in the face of the circumstances described, have no hesitation in setting the tribunal decision aside for breach of natural justice and remitting the case for an oral hearing before a properly constituted tribunal. In this way, a remedy would be provided for the breach of Art. 6 in the domestic courts. However, where the objection related to the *possibility* of inclusion of a doctor on the tribunal who also conducted examinations for the Benefits Agency, it is difficult to see how a remedy could be provided by the tribunal. A claimant might find little sympathy given to the argument that he or she has no complaint about the impartiality of the specific member of the tribunal, but objects that a medical member might also be an examining medical practitioner for the Benefits Agency. There is something slightly odd about a tribunal holding in the abstract that it is not an independent and impartial tribunal. For this reason, it may well be that judicial review would be the proper route to raise such a challenge, although to be a victim for the purposes of the Convention, the claimant would of necessity also have an appeal to the tribunal.

The most significant decision applying art. 6 to tribunal practice and procedure is the decision of the Tribunal of Commissioners in *CSDLA/1019/1999*, (the *Gillies* case—reversed in the Court of Session, whose decision was upheld in the House of Lords, reported as *R(DLA) 5/06)* in which the practice of medical members of the tribunal also on occasion holding office as examining medical practitioners for the Department, though ultimately the decision is based upon common law tests of bias applying in Scotland. There is an indication that the present law in England and Wales would produce the same outcome. The decision of the Tribunal of Commissioners is that the presence on an appeal tribunal of a medical member of a disability appeal tribunal who regularly undertook work as an examining medical practitioner could give rise to a reasonable apprehension of bias on the part of an objective third party. This would taint the independence and impartiality of a tribunal on which that medical member sat.

4.65

In *CSDLA/91/2003* a Scottish Commissioner considered an argument that "the presence of an EMP on the tribunal compromised the appearance of independence of the tribunal." The Commissioner says,

"12. What was struck down in the *Gillies* case, was a situation where a medical member sitting on a tribunal is also an EMP and where the report of another EMP was part of the evidence in the case. As the Tribunal said, what raises objective bias is the concern that an EMP member of a tribunal (see paragraph 80 of *CSDLA/1019/1999:*—

'. . . because of the substantial current involvement in the same role as the reporting doctor, may start with an inclination to accept that evidence rather than objectively viewing the competing version.'

13. The Tribunal of Commissioners gave no support to an argument that EMPs are intrinsically not independent of the Department. The Tribunal did not therefore suggest that the mere presence on a tribunal of an EMP as a member compromised the appearance of the independence of a tribunal. I disagree with what is said at page 732 of Volume III of the Social Security Legislation 2002:—

'The decision of the Tribunal of Commissioners is that the presence on an appeal tribunal of a medical member of a disability appeal tribunal who regularlay undertook work as an examining medical practitioner could give rise to a reasonable apprehension of bias on the part of an objective third party. That would taint the independence and impartiality of a tribunal on which that medical member sat.'"

It is quite correct that the detailed factual circumstances presented in *CSDLA/ 1019/1999* are as stated by the Commissioner; it is suggested, however, that the

Commissioner's reading of the implications of the case is too narrow. It is at least arguable that *CSDLA/1019/1999* can be read as authority for the proposition cited (especially when the decision is read against the background of the approach of the Strasbourg organs to issues of bias). It is argued that it is difficult to see why objective bias might be present only where the report of another examining medical practitioner is before the tribunal. The reasonable apprehension of bias results from the presence on the tribunal of medical members who regularly provide reports for one of the parties to the proceedings. That seems to be intrinsic to the reasoning of the Tribunal in *CSDLA/1019/1999*. The Scottish Commissioner concludes,

> "14. In this appeal, there was no report by an EMP for consideration by the tribunal. Therefore, the presence on the tribunal of an EMP and the fact that, because this was a paper hearing the point could not be put to the claimant, is irrelevant. No issue arose of the member starting off with a prejudice in favour of any particular type of evidence which was before the tribunal."

The last sentence would seem to get close to confusing the distinction between subjective and objective bias which is at the heart of the Strasbourg approach to independence and impartiality under art.6 ECHR. Subjective bias would be present where an issue arose as to a member "starting off with a prejudice in favour of any type of evidence", whereas objective bias would arise if there was the reasonable prospect of an impartial observer concluding that there *might* be bias in such circumstances (for the decision of the House of Lords upholding the Court of Session reversing *CSDLA/1019/1999 (Gillies)* see below.)

Leave to appeal to the Court of Appeal was granted but not pursued in respect of *CI/4421/2000*, in which the Commissioner observes, having regard to various ways in which the Secretary of State might become involved in an appeal, "Taken together, those factors form a strong case that the appeal tribunal might appear not to be independent from the Secretary of State." (para.32.)

The formulation of the test of bias in United Kingdom law has been changed to take account of the case law of the European Court of Human Rights by the Court of Appeal in *Re Medicaments and Related Classes of Goods (No.2)* [2001] 1 W.L.R. 700. The key passage reads,

> "When the Strasbourg jurisprudence is taken into account, we believe that a modest adjustment of the test in *R v Gough* is called for, which makes it plain that it is, in effect, no different from the test applied in most of the Commonwealth and in Scotland. The court must first ascertain all the circumstances which have a bearing on the suggestion that the judge was biased. It must then ask itself whether those circumstances would lead a fair-minded and informed observer to conclude that there was a real possibility, or a real danger, the two being the same, that the tribunal was biased." (at 726–7.)

This formulation of the test of bias has now been approved by the House of Lords in *Magill v Weeks; Magill v Porter*, judgment of July 8, 2002, [2002] H.R.L.R. 16. *CI/5880/1999* and the Northern Ireland Tribunal of Commissioners' decision in *C28/001–01 (IB)(T)* establish that Art.6 of the European Convention does not require more in the way of reasons for decisions than well-established principles established over the year in Commissioners' decisions.

The discussion of bias has been advanced with the decision of the House of Lords in *Lawal v Northern Spirit Ltd*, [2003] UKHL 35, judgment of June 19, 2003. The House of Lords was considering the "systemic issue" of possible objective bias under a system which permitted counsel appointed as part-time judges of the Employment Appeal Tribunal (EAT) to appear on appeals before that court. Though the opinion of the House of Lords is couched very much in the context of the system of adjudication in employment cases, the broad approach is of more general application stressing the "indispensable requirement of public confidence in the administration of justice" which "requires higher standards today than was the case even a decade or two ago." (para.22.) The House of Lords re-affirms the test of bias set out in

Porter v Magill: "The question is whether the fair-minded and informed observer, having considered the facts, would conclude that there was a real possibility that the tribunal was biased" The House of Lords says that it is unnecessary to delve into the characteristics to be attributed to the fair-minded and informed observer save that such an observe "will adopt a balanced approach." The conclusion is that the practice of permitting counsel appointed as part-time judges of the EAT to appear before it should be discontinued.

This more robust approach to the issue of objective bias is certain to influence developments in social security adjudication.

The House of Lords has upheld the decision of the Court of Session reversing the decision of the Tribunal of Commissioners in *Gillies v Secretary of State for Work and Pensions* [2006] UKHL 2. The Court of Session had concluded:

> "Having considered the factual circumstances we are of the view that the fact that Dr A. carried out examinations and provided reports for the Benefits Agency as an EMP would not be sufficient to raise in the mind of a reasonable and well-informed observed an apprehension as to his or her impartiality as a member of a disability appeal tribunal. The mere fact that the tribunal would require to con-sider and assess report of other doctors who acted as EMPs would not be such as to raise such an apprehension." (para.38.)

In coming to this decision, the Court of Session considered the decision of the House of Lords in *Lawal v Northern Spirit Ltd*, but appears to have distinguished it on the grounds that the circumstances before the House of Lords were that, in the Employment Appeal Tribunal, lay members "look to the judge for guidance on the law and can be expected to develop a fairly close relationship of trust and con-fidence with the judge". The Court of Session did not consider that the case before them involved any likelihood of deference, there being "no relationship of law to professional or of subordinate to superior" (para.37). The Court of Session appear to accept that the Tribunal of Commissioners identified the right test, but applied it incorrectly—and this constituted an error of law. The Court of Session took a different view on the application of the test; they were influenced by the argument that, taken too widely, an objection could be based simply on membership of a par-ticular professional body: did pointing to a subset of certain professionals involve a distinction with real difference?

This leaves the authorities on bias in something of any unsatisfactory state. *Lawal v Northern Spirit Limited* would appear to be more in tune with the Strasbourg authorities in its approach to the issue of the possible perception of bias. It takes a broader view of the notion of the objective bystander; *Gillies* make distinctions which would probably be lost on the objective bystander. However, support for the approach adopted by the Court of Session can be found in the decision of the Administrative Court in *R. (on the application of PD) v Merseyside Care NHS Trust* [2003] EWHC 2469. This case concerned the possibility of objective bias resulting from the presence on a mental health review tribunal of a consultant psychiatrist employed by the health authority in a case where that authority had detained the patient. The consultant psychiatrist had had no contact with the patient or with the detaining hospital. There was absolutely no question of his having been *actually* biased. The Administrative Court considered that there were adequate safeguards to avoid any objective bystander apprehending the possibility of bias. The issue is not whether a professional is able to retain his or her independence in a particular set of circumstances, but whether an objective and fair-minded observer would be satisfied as to the independence and impartiality of that decision maker. The Administrative Court appears to have been partly influenced by the potential problems of finding a sufficient number of consultant psychiatrists to serve on the tribunals if consultant psychiatrists employed by the NHS Trust which had detained the patient whose appeal was being heard were excluded. That may be a less pressing issue in relation to medical members of the appeal tribunals. The decision of the Administrative

Court was upheld in the Court of Appeal in even more trenchant terms: [2004] EWCA Civ 311. It is questionable whether resourcing issues are a legitimate consideration under the Strasbourg case law which has always rejected arguments based on practicalities in Contracting Parties' fulfilling their obligations under art.6 (for example, in relation to the giving of judgment with a reasonable time where arguments about shortage of judicial resources have been given short shrift: see *Hentrich v France*, (1994) 18 E.H.R.R. 440, para.61 of the judgment).

The decision of the House of Lords in the *Gillies* case is considered in detail in the commentary on s.14 of the Social Security Act 1998, and that detail is not repeated here. The decision of the House of Lords is perhaps remarkable for the absence of a detailed focus on Art.6 of the Convention, preferring to root its decision in UK authorities on bias. The test which is applied is that of the "fair-minded and informed observer" who is neither complacent nor unduly sensitive or suspicious, and who is able to distinguish between what is relevant and what is not, and to be able to determine what weight should be given to those matters which are relevant.

The House of Lords did not consider the decision of the Court of Session on bias and medical members in *Secretary of State for Work and Pensions v Cunningham*, Court of Session, August 6, 2004, reported as *R(DLA) 7/04*. The Deputy Commissioner had ruled that a situation might well have arisen of a reasonable apprehension of bias in circumstances where an examining medical practitioner had sat as the medical member of a tribunal with the chairman at 22 tribunal sessions, with the disability member at 14 tribunal sessions, and with both the chairman and the disability member at three tribunal sessions. The Court of Session agreed. The facts before the Deputy Commissioner were said by the Court of Session to be "readily distinguishable" from those which arose in *Gillies*.

Counsel for the Secretary of State, were the Court to go against him (as it did), asked for clarification as to how far the decision depended on the frequency with which the doctor had sat with the other members of the tribunal. The Court of Session declined to go further than the obvious point that it might have made a difference if the doctor had sat only once with the other members some considerable time before the case in issue.

CDLA/2379/2005 concerned a claim that there was bias which would constitute a violation of art.6 where the doctor had sat with the chairman of the tribunal on three previous occasions in a two year period. The Commissioner concluded, with some reservations, that, though there was no actual bias, there was the perception of bias. He had resolved these in favour of setting aside the decision since the Court of Appeal in *Locabail* had indicated that doubts should be resolved in favour of recusal, or, as in this case, setting the decision aside.

In an unreported decision in *Secretary of State for Work and Pensions v McNab*, the Court of Session on March 20, 2007, by consent, allowed the Secretary of State's appeal against the decision in *CSDLA/0364/2005* insofar as the decision relates to the composition of the tribunal. The apparent effect of this decision is that, where there has only been one prior sitting of the tribunal chair or carer member with a medical member who is also an examining medical practitioner, there will be no appearance of bias in the absence of other circumstances.

In its admissibility decision of April 8, 2003 in *Wingrave v United Kingdom (App.40029/02)*, the Court of Human Rights had declared inadmissible part of the claim (relating (1) to a breach of contract claim, (2) to the requirement to make a new claim at age 65 for disability living allowance, and (3) concerning the quality of her representation) but adjourned the issue concerning the length of the proceedings. The appeal had been twice remitted for rehearing by the Commissioners and had taken nearly five years to conclude. The decision on the admissibility of that complaint was adjourned by the Court of Human Rights in its decision of April 8, 2003. By a decision of May 18, 2004, the Court of Human Rights has declared this aspect of the complaint admissible. A friendly settlement was subsequently reached in this case under which the applicant's executors received from the respondent State an *ex gratia* payment of £4,500: November 29, 2005.

Part of the decision of the Tribunal of Commissioners in *CIB/3645/2002* concerned an argument that the absence of a right of appeal in the social security legislation contravened the claimant's rights under art.6 of the Convention. The Tribunal of Commissioners decided the decision that the claimant was, on not permanently incapacitated for work at the time of leaving Great Britain for Jamaica concerned the payability of benefit while the claimant was in Jamaica rather his entitlement to the benefit. The decision was accordingly not within the scope of s.12(3) of the Social Security Act 1998. Furthermore art.6 was not relevant because art.6 had "no part to play in the ambit of substantive rights, as opposed to procedural rights." (para.43), since art.13(2) of the Social Security (Jamaica) Order 1997 (SI 1997/871) provided a subjective test, under which the Secretary of State determined whether benefit was to continue to be payable abroad if he considered the claimant likely to be permanently incapacitated for work when leaving Great Britain.

The Tribunal of Commissioners indicates that it has not come to this decision lightly and adds a rider in para.54 of its decision:

"Finally, we should make clear that our decision is limited to the issues before us. On the basis of the decision of Mr Commissioner Howell Q.C. *in CIB/3654/2002* [this appears to be an erroneous reference, which should be to *CIS/540/2002*, now reported as *R(IS) 6/04*], it may be arguable that that the Human Rights Act and Art.6 of the European Convention may require rights of appeal to be granted against decisions under reciprocal agreement provisions in respect of which rights of appeal had existed previously. There may also be other cases in which it may be arguable that para.22 of Sch.2 of the Decisions and Appeals Regulations does not restrict certain rights of appeal without deciding whether the provision is ultra vires (as found in CIB/3586/2000 (starred decision 15/00)). We express no view on the correctness of those decisions."

The claimant is appealing to the Court of Appeal under the name *Campbell v Secretary of State for Work and Pensions*. The appeal was dismissed on July 28, 2005, [2005] EWCA Civ. 989.

The presence on the adjudicating panel of a member who has drunk alcohol over lunch and falls asleep during the afternoon sitting and demonstrably fails to concentrate on the proceedings will render the proceedings unfair: see *Stansby v Datapulse* [2003] EWCA Civ 1951, an employment tribunal case. Arguments in multi-panel courts or tribunals that bias on the part of one of the members might be overlooked because they can be outvoted by the remaining members will not be regarded as sound: *Lodwick v London Borough of Southwark* [2004] EWCA Civ 306, a case in which alleged bias on the part of one member of an employment tribunal was in issue.

CSIB/85/2007 concerned an appellant whose appeal had been heard in her absence. An application to set that decision aside was successful on the grounds that a family emergency had prevented the appellant's attendance. The renewed hearing was before a tribunal with the same chairman. That chairman drew this fact to the appellant's attention and she did not object. An appeal against the decision of the tribunal raised the question of whether there had been a fair hearing. Applying the fair-minded and informed observe test, the Commissioner, somewhat reluctantly and clearly viewing the case as "exceedingly borderline", set aside the tribunal's decision and remitted the case for a further rehearing before an entirely differently composed tribunal. The Commissioner, having observed that the claimant in this case *might* not have had sufficient time to consider all the pros and cons of agreeing to a hearing before a tribunal chaired by the same chairman who had dealt with the case at an earlier stage, notes:

"22. . . . The very fact that an adjudicator offers a claimant an opportunity to object means that the adjudicator appreciates that justice must not only be done but be seen to be done . . . and judges that present appearances could seem to suggest the contrary even if this was not the actual position; if the adjudicator then gives inadequate scope to the claimant's freedom to object, if the latter so wishes, this is one factor which *could* support objective bias."

The tribunals are structured in such a way that claimants can appear in person. It is unlikely that the significant evidence that represented claimants do better than unrepresented ones (Genn, H. and Genn, Y., *The Effectiveness of Representation at Tribunals*, (Lord Chancellor's Department, London, 1989)) would persuade the Court of Human Rights that proceedings before the tribunals were such that the State was obliged to provide legal assistance.

Perhaps the tribunals are most at risk of complaints that judgment has not been given in a reasonable time, particularly where an appeal to the Commissioner has resulted in the setting aside of the decision and the remission of the case for a fresh hearing. Current delays both before the tribunals and the Commissioners can result in four or more years passing before a final decision is made. This could in a simple case be regarded as excessive under art.6, particularly if the case had lain dormant for some time either in the Commissioner's office after the papers were ready for determination, or within the appeals service awaiting listing for the rehearing. The existence of backlogs and excessive workloads on the judiciary are not accepted as justifications for unreasonable delays. The Court has consistently stated that the Contracting States must organise their judicial systems in such a way that their tribunals can meet the requirement to give judgment within a reasonable time (see, for example, *Massa v Italy*, judgment of August 24, 1993, Series A, No.265-B; (1994) 18 E.H.R.R. 266, para.28 of the judgment).

In *CDLA/1761/2002* the claimant raised an art.6 issue in relation to the delay (of about six months) in producing the written statement of reasons for the tribunal's decision. The Commissioner did not need to address the argument in full, but rightly notes that Art.6 is concerned with the overall length of the proceedings and not with delays in relation to specific parts of the process.

CJSA/5100/2001 was an overpayments case. The claimant argued that a witness the Secretary of State intended to have give evidence at the tribunal (but who declined to attend) would not have been able to identify his wife as the person who had undertaken remunerative work. No further attempts were made to secure this evidence. In remitting the case for a rehearing, the Commissioner indicates that the language of "equality of arms" under the case law of the Court of Human Rights may be more helpful than the language of natural justice in ensuring fairness between the parties in a tribunal hearing:

> "5. I chose to explain my decision in terms of the claimant's Convention right to a fair hearing under Article 6(1) of the European Convention on Human Rights and Fundamental Freedoms. In particular, I rely on the equality of arms principle that has been developed in the jurisprudence of the Strasbourg authorities as part of that right. It requires that the procedure followed by the tribunal must strike a fair balance between the parties so that none is at a disadvantage as against the others: see paragraph 33 of the judgment of the ECHR in *Dombo Beheer BV v The Netherlands* (1993) 18 EHRR 213.
>
> 6. I could, no doubt, have reached the same conclusion under domestic principles of natural justice. However, the Human Rights Act 1998 provides a convenient opportunity for Commissioners to rebase their decisions on procedural fairness in fresh terms. In my view, this would be desirable. I am sure that tribunals are familiar with the principles of natural justice. However, increasingly the cases that come before me suggest that they are not applying them. If there is a common theme in those cases, it is that the tribunal had not provided a procedural balance between the parties. The introduction of the language of balance would provide a touchstone for tribunals.

7. I detect at least three factors that have contributed to the trend that I have observed. One factor is that the language of natural justice may have become stale to tribunals from over familiarity. A second factor is that the time between an appeal being lodged and being heard is now much shorter than it was. That will often be to the claimant's advantage. However, it is not an advantage if a claimant does not have time to prepare a case. The final factor, for which there is clear evidence across all regions of the Appeals Service, is the concern to avoid adjournments. This has led some tribunals to take an approach to hearings that is robust at the expense of fairness.

8. The new language would help to counter any staleness with the traditional language of natural justice. That language is the language of procedural fairness. There is nothing wrong with that. But it has led to an emphasis on the disposal of the case, with less concern than is appropriate on the procedure. The language of balance would provide criteria by which appropriate cases for adjournments could be identified and distinguished from inappropriate cases.

9. There are decisions on which this new approach could be built. I have used the language of equality of arms and balance when dealing with adjournments to allow a claimant to obtain medical evidence (*CIB/3427/2001*) and with the provision of evidence by the Secretary of State relating to earlier personal capability assessments (*CIB/3985/2001*). And Mr Commissioner Williams has used the same language when dealing with deemed notice provisions and the exercise of discretions (*CDLA/5413/1999*)."

In *CJSA/5101/2001* the Commissioner concluded (relying on the Court of Human Rights decision in the *Airey* case: see para.4.60 above) that art.6 does not give any automatic entitlement to legal representation, though particular circumstances may result in the need for legal representation if there is to be a fair trial.

Article 6 does not require an appeal to the tribunal if there is another recognised remedy, such as judicial review, which provides the opportunity for a fair trial involving the determination of a person's civil rights and obligations: *CF/3565/2001*, paras 11–15.

CDLA/3432/2001 involved a challenge to the rules in regs 31 and 32 of the Social Security Commissioners Procedure Regulations limiting the grounds on which a Commissioner could set aside a decision of a Commissioner as being an interference with the rights in art.6. The Commissioner rightly give such arguments short shrift, noting that they contribute to the rights enshrined in art.6.

In *R. (on the application of Wall) v The Appeals Service and Benefits Agency* [2003] EWHC 465 Admin, the applicant raised three objections that proceedings before a tribunal had breached the requirements of art.6. First, no or no sufficient reasons had been given for the tribunal's decision. Secondly, there was no oral hearing. Thirdly, the District Chairman who had heard his appeal had previously been involved in other decisions concerning the applicant's case. All three objections were dismissed. The first and second were rejected because art.6 does not require that there is an oral hearing in every case, and that there were appropriate safeguards in striking out cases (this was such a case). In relation to the third objection, the Court observes that there needs to be something more than the mere involvement of a judge in a latter case where they have been involved in an earlier case in order to establish a lack of impartiality for art.6 to be breached.

It is clear that a judicial process in social security decision-making which constitute bargaining with the claimant will not meet the requirements of a fair hearing under art.6. As an illustration, see *CSDLA/606/2003* where the tribunal's record of proceedings tells it all:

Parties introduced.

Offer put to the appellant just to reinstate higher mobility

Told to think about it. 10 mins.

Put to appellant risk of losing all if goes ahead.

Told to think again. 5 mins later.

Has decided will accept offer (reproduced in para.7 of Commissioner's decision).

The Social Security Act 1998

4.66   A number of aspects of the Social Security Act 1998 would appear to leave open the possibility of challenge for compatibility with Convention rights.

One of the great achievements of the Office of the President of Social Security Appeal Tribunals (OPSSAT) and its successor, the Independent Tribunal Service (ITS), has been to emphasise the independence of the tribunals hearing appeals by claimants against decisions of adjudication officers in the Department of Social Security. That success has dramatically increased respect for the tribunals. Certain provisions of the Social Security Act 1998 at best undermine that independence, and at worst may leave the structure exposed to challenges under the Convention as not constituting independent and impartial tribunals. New "unified appeal tribunals" have replaced the tribunals which formed part of the ITS, which is itself abolished. Appointment to the panels is happily not a matter for the Secretary of State, but for the Lord Chancellor (or Lord Advocate in Scotland), though s.6 provides that the number of appointments and their terms and conditions are subject to the consent of the Secretary of State. Appeal tribunals may consist of one, two or three members and the requirements for a lawyer chairman of the tribunals goes.

The authority of the new tribunals is, however, undermined by the provision that the Secretary of State may supersede any decision of a tribunal or of a Social Security Commissioner (s.11(1)). That power is subject to provisions of the Decisions and Appeals Regulations, which broadly limit the exercise of the power to situations where there is a change of circumstances or new evidence comes to light. Formerly such limitations appeared in the primary legislation (s.35, Social Security Administration Act 1992), and it is disturbing to see that this practice has been discontinued.

Section 13(3) contains a bizarre provision (see commentary on it in this volume), which raises interesting questions about the relationship between the parties and the tribunal, but, for the reasons set out in the commentary to the provision, it is unlikely to have real significance.

Section 26 would appear to be objectionable in that it enables the Secretary of State who is one of the parties to the dispute to direct the tribunal on the determination of the appeal. Such a provision must result in the tribunal not being independent and impartial, since it is a characteristic of an independent and impartial tribunal that it is not susceptible to instructions concerning the exercise of its judicial function (*Ettl v Austria*, judgment of April 23, 1987, Series A, No.117; (1988) 10 E.H.R.R. 255, para.38 of the judgment).

The Council on Tribunals has suggested that the proposed new structure for the tribunals could resemble the unsatisfactory system which was abandoned many years ago, and has suggested that the new arrangements are a cause for concern (*Annual Report of the Council on Tribunals for 1996/97*, (1997–98) H.C. 376). There may, accordingly, be challenges to the compatibility of the new structure with the requirement that tribunals are independent and impartial. The Secretary of State, who is a party to proceedings before the tribunals is also the paymaster and, in certain circumstances, is able to overrule their decisions. Their independence certainly appears less clear cut than that of their predecessors, which may well also be relevant were the matter to be considered by the Court of Human Rights.

The issue which faced the Tribunal of Commissioners in *R(IS)15/04* was whether there is a right of appeal against a decision taken by the Secretary of State not to revise a previous decision under reg.3(5)(a) of the Decisions and Appeal Regulations. The parties accepted that there was no such right under the provisions of national law, so the issue was whether one or more provisions of the European Convention required that there be such an appeal. An argument based on art.6 failed. The Tribunal of Commissioners accepted that a decision whether or not to revise was a determination of a claimant's civil rights and obligations within art.6, but that the process of judicial review taken together with the right to an appeal in relation to the original decision produced a situation in which there was no denial of access to a court. The alternative argument was based on art.14 ECHR where the comparator was a person whom was within the scope of the Decisions and Appeal Regulations governing housing benefit and council tax benefit. Such a claimant, it was argued, would have a right of appeal. The Tribunal of Commissioners concluded that there was no right of appeal for a person in comparable circumstances under the housing benefit regime. Hence the claim to discrimination was not sustained.

Criminal charges

A question arises as to whether determinations of the Upper Tribunal under the Forfeiture Act of 1982, of proceedings for penalty additions to overpayments under the Social Security Administration (Fraud) Act 1997, and of possible penalty proceedings under the Tax Credits Act 1999 constitute the determination of criminal charges under art.6 and so attract the additional protections for such matters in the article. Though these matters are largely outside the ambit of these volumes, it may be helpful to express a view on this question.

The concept of a criminal charge is an autonomous one under the Convention, and so it is not the classification of the matter under national law which is determinative of the issue. National classification is not, however, wholly irrelevant since the Strasbourg organs have always regarded as a criminal charge something so considered by national law.

In other cases the following factors have been taken into account in making the determination: the nature of the "offence", the severity of the sanction imposed having regard in particular to any loss of liberty since this is a principal characteristic of criminal liability: see *Engel v The Netherlands*, judgment of June 8, 1976; Series A, No.22; (1979–80) 1 E.H.R.R. 647. Having regard to this case and to the judgment of the Court in *Ravnsborg v Sweden* (judgment of March 23, 1994, SeriesA, No.283-B; (1994) 18 E.H.R.R. 38), it is argued that such proceedings would not constitute the determination of a criminal charge. The essence of the penalty provision is civil rather than criminal in nature.

4.67

Article 7—No punishment without law

1. No one shall be held guilty of any criminal offence on account of any act or omission which did not constitute a criminal offence under national or international law at the time when it was committed. Nor shall a heavier penalty be imposed than the one that was applicable at the time the criminal offence was committed.

2. This Article shall not prejudice the trial and punishment of any person for any act or omission which, at the time when it was committed, was criminal according to the general principles of law recognised by civilised nations.

4.68

Article 8—Right to respect for private and family life

1. Everyone has the right to respect for his private and family life, his home and his correspondence.

2. There shall be no interference by a public authority with the exercise of this right except such as is in accordance with the law and is necessary in a democratic society in the interests of national security, public safety or the economic well-being of the country, for the prevention of disorder or crime, for the protection of health or morals, or for the protection of the rights and freedoms of others.

4.69

GENERAL NOTE

Introduction

4.70   Article 8 is one of the most open-ended provisions of the Convention and is not yet fully developed in its scope. The concept of private life is very wide and not easily contained within a single comprehensive definition. The protection of private life (as distinct from family life) under art.8 can now be organised under a number of headings:

- freedom from interference with physical and psychological integrity, which includes interference with the person, searches of property, surveillance and interception of communications, and the dissemination of images;

- the collection, storage and use of personal information;

- freedom to develop one's identity, which includes discovering information about childhood and parenthood, aspects of the use of names, transsexuality, and cultural identity;

- a right to personal autonomy, which includes sexual preference, and the establishment of a settled circle of friends, and respect for decisions in relation to health and medical treatment;

- the protection of one's living environment;

- protection of the home; and

- protection of correspondence.

Like the series of articles which follows, the rights given in para.(1) are limited by the exceptions listed in para.(2). If there is an interference with one of the rights protected in the first paragraph, then it will be necessary to see whether this is justified under the limitations in the second paragraph. Here the Strasbourg organs have consistently required the interference to be (1) for one of the specified reasons; (2) in accordance with law; (3) necessary in a democratic society; and (4) proportionate in the sense that there is no other way of protecting the recognised interest which constitutes a lesser interference with the right.

Benefit, family life and private life

4.71   Article 8 of the Convention guarantees respect private life, home and correspondence, for family life, subject to the limitation contained in the article. Family life encompasses ties between near relatives, which certainly extends to children, parents and grandparents, though it is unclear how far it includes relationships between siblings, aunts and uncles. In general the Strasbourg organs have preferred relationships in the vertical line to those in the horizontal line.

In the *CG v Austia* (1737/90) case, the applicant had complained that the refusal to award him the emergency assistance requested violated respect for his family life (presumably on the grounds that refusal of the assistance threatened the break up of, or hardship to, his family); the admissibility decision is not specific on the basis for declaring this part of his complaint admissible (see (1994) 18 E.H.R.R. CD51). Neither the Commission nor the Court found it necessary to consider this aspect of the complaint since they concluded that there was a violation of art.14 read in conjunction with art.1 of Protocol 1. Nevertheless, it remains open for the limits of the protection under art.8 to be explored in the context of entitlements to social security. But it would be fair to say that there are few indications that the Strasbourg organs regard the Convention right here as including an obligation on the State to make payments to families for their support.

In *CJSA/935/1999* the Commissioner made some *obiter* comments on the rights of transsexuals to respect for their identity. The issue had arisen in the context of a claim that the use of the national insurance number in a jobseeker's agreement enabled the claimant's gender at birth to be identified. The decision contains a useful overview of some leading decisions in this area both under European Community law and under the European Convention on Human Rights.

For the latest summary of the position of transsexuals in the light of recent decisions of the Strasbourg Court, see the opinions of the House of Lords in *Bellinger v Bellinger* [2003] UKHL 21 (April 10, 2003).

But note the decision of the Court of Human Rights in *Grant v United Kingdom (App. 32570/03)*, Judgment of May 23, 2006, which concerned a male-to-female transsexual who had been refused a pension on reaching the age of 60. Initial failures to secure the pension before reaching the age of 65 were re-opened following the grant of a gender recognition certificate under the Gender Recognition Act 2004. Grant succeeded in securing a judgment that the United Kingdom was in breach of art.8 E.C.H.R. from July 2002 when the Court of Human Rights handed down its decision in *Goodwin v United Kingdom* (2002) 35 E.H.R.R. 447.

It is clear from the decision of the Court of Appeal and House of Lords in *R. (on the application of Hooper, Withey, Naylor and Martin) v Secretary of State for Work and Pensions,* [2003] EWCA Civ 813, and [2005] UKHL 29, that benefits for widows and widowers fall within the ambit of art.8. However, income support and income-based jobseeker's allowance schemes do not, according to the Court of Appeal, *per se* engage art.8: see *Carson and Reynolds v The Secretary of State for Work and Pensions,* [2003] EWCA Civ 797.

In *R. (Smith) v Secretary of State for Defence and Secretary of State for Work and Pensions* [2004] EWHC 1797 (Admin), Wilson J. held that respect for private life under Art.8 encompasses respect for a person's need for financial support "when under as well as over the age of 60". The case concerned an argument by an ex-wife that she was entitled to payment of that part of a pension which was subject to a pension sharing order below the age of 60 since the pension was so payable to her former husband. The judge held that the provisions governing the payment to the ex-wife of the pension at the age of 60 did not breach her rights under art.8:

> "One cannot say that the impugned provision challenges the principle that the claimant needs financial support before as well as after the age of 60. In making the provision the state has decreed only that provision carved out of pension rights should not result in payment earlier than what is presently regarded, in the context of state provision, as normal pensionable age. In other words pension credits are conferred so as to address later, rather than earlier, need; and, because of the delay in payment suffered by some pension credit members, the real amount of their pension is correspondingly increased. The impugned provision does not derogate from the duty of the divorce court under [the matrimonial legislation] to have regard to a spouse's likely needs prior to the age of 60 in deciding what, of any, order to make for her or his benefit by way of financial provision or property adjustment in addition to the pension sharing order." (para.21(b).)

In *C1/05-06 (WB)*, *C2/05-06 (WB)*, and *C3/05-06 (WB)*, a Commissioner in Northern Ireland concluded that an absolute three months time limit for claiming widow's benefit does not violate art.8. She said,

> "17. . . . . . I am doubtful that the three month time limit for claiming a benefit can in any way be linked to or have a "meaningful connection" with an Article 8 right in the absence of any Article 14 discrimination. However, even if a link exists, it is too tenuous to be within the ambit of the right. The right is not to the benefit but to the respect set out in Article 8. The time limit in no way violates that respect."

In *CP/1183/2007* the Commissioner dismisses in short form the possibility of arguing that differential State retirement ages for men and women can constitute a violation of Article 8 when read in conjunction with art.14.

Surveillance in social security cases

4.72   In *R(DLA) 4/02* the claimant argued that covert filming of the claimant in public places by the Department violated her Convention rights under art.8. The Commissioner did not agree having regard to the balance which had to be struck between the interests of the individual and those of the community as a whole. In claiming benefit, the claimant had necessarily accepted a degree of interference with her private life. The covert filming had been limited to activities in public and was brief. The information gathered was used only for the purposes of considering the claimant's continuing entitlement to the benefit she had claimed.

In *CIS/1481/2006* which is excoriating about the behaviour of officers of the Department in the matter before him, and critical of the tribunal's approach to the case, a Commissioner has provided very useful guidance on issues concerning the use of surveillance techniques to support decision-making in the Department. In particular, there is the most helpful guidance about the application of the Regulation of Investigatory Powers Act 2000 (RIPA) to surveillance by the Department. Such action is, of course, frequently attacked as a violation of art.8 ECHR. The Commissioner summarises a detailed section of his decision as follows:

> 50. More generally, where there is a challenge under Article 8 of the European Convention against evidence produced by the Secretary of State, or the conduct or results of surveillance are otherwise challenged before an appeal tribunal, RIPA now provides effective answers. If the Secretary of State provides the tribunal and the claimant with a copy of the application and authorisation for the surveillance, and it is clear that the authorisation covers the surveillance, then the tribunal will usually need to take matters no further. The tribunal may properly take the view that the Secretary of State can rely fully on the evidence obtained from the surveillance without further investigation by itself. If the claimant has continuing or other concerns, then he or she may take them to the investigatory powers tribunal. With that in mind, I suggest that the Secretary of State should, in cases such as this, produce the proper documentation about surveillance to an appellant and the tribunal together with the evidence from the surveillance on which the Secretary of State seeks to rely.

For observations by the Court of Appeal on the issue of surveillance, see *Jones v University of Warwick*, [2003] 1 W.L.R. 954.

Article 9—Freedom of thought, conscience and religion

4.73   **1.** Everyone has the right to freedom of thought, conscience and religion; this right includes freedom to change his religion or belief and freedom, either alone or in community with others and in public or private, to manifest his religion or belief, in worship, teaching, practice and observance.

2. Freedom to manifest one's religion or beliefs shall be subject only to such limitations as are prescribed by law and are necessary in a democratic society in the interests of public safety, for the protection of public order, health or morals, or for the protection of the rights and freedoms of others.

GENERAL NOTE

4.74   Reliance on this article to avoid the normal requirements, for example, to pay national insurance contributions are most unlikely to succeed. The Commission has held that a Dutch system of old-age pension insurance, alleged to interfere with the religious duty of caring for old people, did not violate the article: App.1497/62, *Reformed Church of X v The Netherlands* (1962) 5 Y.B. 286; and App.2065/63, *X v The Netherlands* (1965) 8 Y.B. 266.

Article 10—Freedom of expression

4.75   **1.** Everyone has the right to freedom of expression. This right shall include freedom to hold opinions and to receive and impart information and ideas without interference by public authority and regardless of frontiers. This Article shall not prevent States from requiring the licensing of broadcasting, television or cinema enterprises.

2. The exercise of these freedoms, since it carries with it duties and responsibilities, may be subject to such formalities, conditions, restrictions or penalties as are prescribed by law and are necessary in a democratic society, in the interests of national security, territorial integrity or public safety, for the prevention of disorder or crime, for the protection of health or morals, for the protection of the reputation or rights of others, for preventing the disclosure of information received in confidence, or for maintaining the authority and impartiality of the judiciary.

Article 11—Freedom of assembly and association

1. Everyone has the right to freedom of peaceful assembly and to freedom of association with others, including the right to form and to join trade unions for the protection of his interests.

2. No restrictions shall be placed on the exercise of these rights other than such as are prescribed by law and are necessary in a democratic society in the interests of national security or public safety, for the prevention of disorder or crime, for the protection of health or morals or for the protection of the rights and freedoms of others. This Article shall not prevent the imposition of lawful restrictions on the exercise of these rights by members of the armed forces, of the police or of the administration of the State.

4.76

Article 12—Right to marry

Men and women of marriageable age have the right to marry and to found a family, according to the national laws governing the exercise of this right.

4.77

Article 14—Prohibition of discrimination

The enjoyment of the rights and freedoms set forth in this Convention shall be secured without discrimination on any ground such as sex, race, colour, language, religion, political or other opinion, national or social origin, association with a national minority, property, birth or other status.

4.78

GENERAL NOTE

Introduction

Article 14 prohibits discrimination on the grounds of sex, race, colour, language, religion, political or other opinion, national or social origin, association with a national minority, property, birth or other status. Discrimination can be either direct or indirect: *D.H. and others v Czech Republic,* (App.57325/00), November 13, 2007 [Grand Chamber]; see also *CP/518/2003; CH/5125, 5126, 5128, 5129 and 5130/2002,* upheld in *Campbell v South Northamptonshire DC and the Secretary of State for Work and Pensions* [2004] EWCA Civ 409. In *Esfandiari* [2006] EWCA Civ 282, the Court of Appeal was of the view that an indirect discrimination claim under art.14 should be treated with some care because the case law is limited in this area. The key test will be whether the effects on the disadvantaged group are disproportionately prejudicial. But this case was decided before the judgment of the Grand Chamber in the *D.H.* case, which establishes without doubt that art.14 does cover indirect discrimination.

The protection of art.14 is only applicable in relation to the enjoyment of the rights and freedoms set forth in the Convention. It is the linking of art.14 with another article of the Convention which gives it substance. In order to have effect, it does not have to be shown that there is a violation of the substantive article, merely that the alleged discrimination operates in a field which is covered by the protections afforded by those provisions. Indeed the practice of the Strasbourg Court has been to decline to consider art.14 in conjunction with another article if they find a violation of the article on its face, unless the essence of the complaint is discrimination. The article is a fruitful source of complaints in social security cases. Following the admissibility decision of the Grand Chamber in the *Stec* case (*Stec v United Kingdom* (Apps 65731/01 and 65900/01), September 5, 2005, (2005) 41 EHRR SE295),

4.79

which ruled that both contributory and non-contributory social security benefits fall within the ambit of art.1 of Protocol 1, it will be easy for claimants to establish that any claimed discrimination in the operation of the conditions of entitlement for benefit can be contested under art.14. Any lingering doubts about the comprehensiveness of this decision would seem to be resolved by the House of Lords in *R. (on the application of RJM) v Secretary of State for Work and Pensions,* [2008] UKHL 63, where Lord Neuberger says:

> 31. . . . I recognise that the admissibility decision in *Stec* represents a departure from the principle normally applied to claims which rely on A1P1. However, *Stec* . . . was a carefully considered decision, in which the relevant authorities and principles were fully canvassed, and where the Grand Chamber of the ECtHR came to a clear conclusion, which was expressly intended to be generally applied by national courts. Accordingly, it seems to me that it would require the most exceptional circumstances before any national court should refuse to apply the decision.

The Strasbourg approach to the determination of complaints raising art.14 issues is threefold. The first question is whether the complaint of discrimination falls within the sphere or ambit of a protected right. The second question is whether the applicants can properly compare themselves with a class of persons who are treated more favourably. The Strasbourg Court has not developed a single statement which it repeats in this regard. Over time, it has referred to the comparators being in "similar situations", (*Marckx v Belgium,* (App.6833/74), June 13, 1979, Series A, No. 31, (1979–80) 2 EHRR 330, para. 32) or in 'relevantly similar situations', (*Burden v United Kingdom,* (App. 13378/05), April 29, 2008 [Grand Chamber], para.60), or in "analogous situations" (*Stubbings and others v United Kingdom* (Apps 22083/93 and 22095/93), October 22, 1996, (1997) 23 EHRR 213, para.71). The phrase "relevantly similar situations" appears to be the currently favoured formulation. The third question is whether the difference in treatment can be justified. The Court has made it clear that art.14 is concerned with arbitrary discrimination, and so a difference of treatment will only be in breach art.14 if it has no objective or reasonable justification. art.14 enumerates certain grounds upon which different treatment may be based (such as sex, race, language and religion), but also leaves the list open by referring to "other status". Some of the enumerated grounds of discrimination in art.14, most notably sex, and race, enjoy special protection, whereas discrimination based on "other status" is likely to be somewhat easier to justify. The grounds enjoying special protection will require what the Strasbourg Court refers to as "very weighty reasons" to justify treating the protected group differently from the comparators.

Does the complaint of discrimination fall within the sphere of a protected right?

The Strasbourg Court formulated the requirement that the complaint fall within the sphere of a protected right as follows in *Stec v United Kingdom* (Apps 65731/01 and 65900/01), Decision of September 5, 2005, (2005) 41 EHRR SE295):

> 39. The Court recalls that art.14 complements the other substantive provisions of the Convention and the Protocols. It has no independent existence since it has effect solely in relation to 'the enjoyment of the rights and freedoms' safeguarded by those provisions. . . . The application of art.14 does not necessarily presuppose the violation of one of the substantive rights guaranteed by the Convention. It is necessary but it is also sufficient for the facts of the case to fall 'within the ambit' of one or more of the Convention Articles. . . .
>
> 40. The prohibition of discrimination in art.14 thus extends beyond the enjoyment of the rights and freedoms which the Convention and Protocols require each State to guarantee. It applies also to those additional rights, falling within the general scope of any Convention article, for which the State has voluntarily decided to provide. This principle is well entrenched in the Court's case-law.

In social security cases, art.14 ECHR is most frequently linked with art.8 and with art.1 of Protocol 1. Following the decision in the *Stec* case, most complaints of discrimination will be raised in conjunction with art.1 of Protocol 1. As in *Willis v United Kingdom*, (App. 36042/97), judgment of June 11, 2002, (2002) 35 EHRR 21, the Strasbourg Court is likely to address social security cases on the basis that art.1 of Protocol 1 is engaged, which will render it unnecessary to consider a complaint under art.14 taken together with art.8.

However, complaints under art.14 in conjunction with art.8 have been raised in relation to widow's benefits: the *Willis* case; *Runkee and White v United Kingdom*, (Apps 42949/98 and 53134/99), Judgments of May 10, 2007); *Thomas v United Kingdom*, (App. 63701/00), July 17, 2008; and to State pensions: *Carson and others v United Kingdom*, (App. 42184/05), November 4, 2008; note that the Chamber judgement has been referred to the Grand Chamber. In all these cases, the Strasbourg Court examined the case using the link to property rights rather than the link to private and family life in art.8.

In national proceedings, there have been cases arguing that the housing benefit scheme and child support falls within the sphere of application of art.8. But the complex discussions in both the Court of Appeal and the House of Lords which arose in *Secretary of State for Work and Pensions v M; Langley v Bradford Metropolitan District Council and Secretary of State for Work and Pensions* [2004] EWCA Civ 1343; and *Secretary of State for Work and Pensions v M* [2006] UKHL 11 would not now be necessary in relation to the housing benefit scheme, and probably also the child support system, since art.1 of Protocol 1 would be regarded as engaged following the *Stec* decision.

In *Francis v Secretary of State for Work and Pensions* [2005] EWCA Civ 1303 (the appeal against *CIS/1965/2003*, reported as *R(IS) 6/06*), the Court of Appeal found that the refusal to award a maternity grant constituted discrimination contrary to art.14 of the Convention. The Secretary of State had conceded that the circumstances presented by Ms Francis engaged art.8 of the Convention. Ms Francis argued that her situation as a person with a residence order in respect of a child born to her sister was analogous to that of an adopter under the Adoption Act 1976. There was no objective justification for the difference in treatment.

In *Douglas v North Tyneside MBC and Secretary of State for Education and Skills* [2003] EWCA Civ 1847, the Court of Appeal accepted that tertiary education, and the student loan system which provided access to it, fell within the Ambit of art2 of Protocol 1 and went on to consider the art.14 complaint in relation to the upper age limit for eligibility for a student loan.

Is there different treatment of persons in relevantly similar or analogous situations?

Those complaining of discrimination will compare themselves with others whom they argue are more favourably treated. The choice of comparator is often of considerable importance, and the broad drafting of art.14 raises problems. As noted above, the Strasbourg Court requires the comparator to be in a relevantly similar or analogous situation. The national authorities have been somewhat dogged by the question of whether the ground of differentiation must relate to a personal characteristic. An example of a personal characteristic would be differential treatment based on ethnic origin, whereas an example of something which is not would be differential treatment based on place of residence. The latter is said to be a matter of choice, whereas the former is not.

4.80

The Strasbourg Court has not determined the answer to this question definitively; it is one of the troublesome aspects of art.14. However, there is no direct authority which provides that the ground of differentiation must be based on a personal characteristic. The better view, therefore, is that there is no formal requirement flowing from the Strasbourg case law which requires that the party seeking to show discrimination falling within art.14 is based upon a personal characteristic: see *Stubbings v United Kingdom* (Apps 22083/93 and 22095/93), October 22, 1996, (1997) 23

EHRR 213, where the differential treatment related to the legal system's approach to providing a remedy for psychological harm resulting from child abuse and other types of actionable wrong; and *National & Provincial Building Society v United Kingdom* (Apps 21319/93, 21449/93 and 21675/93), October 23, 1997, (1998) 25 EHRR 127, which concerned recovery of tax paid under invalidated tax regulations. It will, however, be easier to establish a situation as falling within art.14 where the ground of differentiation is a personal characteristic. Differential treatment which is based other than on a personal characteristic will be easier for the State to justify.

The United Kingdom authorities contain a variety of messages. *R v Chief Constable of South Yorkshire Police, ex parte LS and ex parte Marper* [2004] UKHL 39, paras 48–9, followed in *Taylor v Lancashire County Council and Secretary of State for Environment Food and Rural Affairs as intervenor* [2005] EWCA Civ 284, para.49, suggests that 'other status' requires a person to establish that the ground of differentiation is a personal characteristic. The comparison is said to be 'to do with who people are, not what their problem is.'

In *Barber v Secretary of State for Work and Pensions* [2002] EWHC 1915 (Admin), it was also suggested that the difference in treatment must be based on a personal characteristic. This can be contrasted with *Wandsworth LBC v Michalak* [2002] EWCA Civ 271, (which concerned the arrangements for the assignment of, and succession to, tenancies), which suggest that the difference need not be based on personal characteristics in the strict sense. *Barber* has been followed by the Commissioner in *CIS/3280/2001*, where the differential treatment arose in relation to persons in local authority residential accommodation and persons in private residential accommodation in relation to entitlement to a funeral payment. The Commissioner ultimately concluded that the claimant was not able to show any discrimination based on her 'status' for the purposes of the application of art.14.

The opinions of the House of Lords in *Carson and Reynolds* [2005] UKHL 39, paras 13 and 53–4, confirmed the importance of identifying a personal characteristic, but also indicated that this is to be interpreted broadly so that it does not simply encompass something a person is born with. So in *Francis v Secretary of State for Work and Pensions* [2005] EWCA Civ 1303, reported as *R(IS) 6/06* the Court of Appeal affirmed the need to identify a personal characteristic but indicated that this need not be immutable and can be the result of the exercise of choice. The Strasbourg Court in *Carson and others v United Kingdom,* (App. 42184/05), November 4, 2008, accepted that residence can form the basis of comparison, and this is, in many cases, of course, a matter of choice. But note that the Chamber judgement has been referred to the Grand Chamber.

AL (Serbia) v Secretary of State for the Home Department; R. (on the application of Rudi) v Secretary of State for the Home Department, [2008] UKHL 42, contains a very helpful discussion by Baroness Hale of aspects of art.14 at paras 20-35. This stresses that Strasbourg case law does not place great emphasis on the identification of an exact comparator, rather asking whether differences in otherwise similar situations justify a different treatment. It is also hinted that too much attention has been focused on the notion of "personal characteristic" which is not central to the Strasbourg case law, although clearly differences based on such matters as sex, race or ethnic origin will require very weighty reasons if they are not to be condemned as violations of art.14.

The issue of what is required for art.14 to bite was also considered by the House of Lords in *R. (on the application of RJM) v Secretary of State for Work and Pensions,* [2008] UKHL 63 (summarised in the annotations to art.1 of Protocol 1 below). Lord Walker says:

> 5. The other point on which I would comment is the expression 'personal characteristics' used by the European Court of Human Rights in *Kjeldsen, Busk, Madsen and Pedersen v Denmark* (1976) 1 EHRR 711, and repeated in some later cases. 'Personal characteristics' is not a precise expression and to my mind a binary approach to its meaning is unhelpful. 'Personal characteristics' are more like a

series of concentric circles. The most personal characteristics are those which are innate, largely immutable, and closely connected with an individual's personality: gender, sexual orientation, pigmentation of skin, hair and eyes, congenital disabilities. Nationality, language, religion and politics may be almost innate (depending on a person's family circumstances at birth) or may be acquired (though some religions do not countenance either apostates or converts); but all are regarded as important to the development of an individual's personality (they reflect, it might be said, important values protected by articles 8, 9 and 10 of the Convention). Other acquired characteristics are further out in the concentric circles; they are more concerned with what people do, or with what happens to them, than with who they are; but they may still come within art.14 (Lord Neuberger instances military status, residence or domicile, and past employment in the KGB). Like him, I would include homelessness as falling within that range, whether or not it is regarded as a matter of choice (it is often the culmination of a series of misfortunes that overwhelm an individual so that he or she can no longer cope). The more peripheral or debateable any suggested personal characteristic is, the less likely it is to come within the most sensitive area where discrimination is particularly difficult to justify.

Lord Neuberger addresses paras 35-47 to this issue in reversing the Court of Appeal to hold that homelessness is a status within art.14. In para.45 he says:

45. Further, while reformulations are dangerous, I consider that the concept of *"personal* characteristic" (not surprisingly, like the concept of status) generally requires one to concentrate on what somebody is, rather than what he is doing or what is being done to him. Such a characterisation approach appears not only consistent with the natural meaning of the expression, but also with the approach of the ECtHR and of this House to the issue. Hence, in *Gerger v Turkey* (Application No 24919/94) (unreported) 8 July 1999, the ECtHR held there could be no breach of art.14 where the law concerned provided that 'people who commit terrorist offences . . . will be treated less favourably with regard to automatic parole than persons convicted under the ordinary law', because 'the distinction is made not between different groups of people, but between different types of offence' (para 69). It appears to me that, on this approach, homelessness is an 'other status'.

The currently favoured formulation by the Strasbourg Court requires the comparators to be in "relevantly similar situations". The result is that the purpose for which the distinction is made cannot be separated from the distinction itself. The comparator group may be relevant in relation to certain policy objectives of the State but not others. So, in *Shackell v United Kingdom,* (App.45851/99), Decision of April 27, 2000, the Strasbourg Court confirmed that the situations of married partners and unmarried cohabitees are not analogous in the context of benefit schemes for surviving spouses. By contrast, men and women who are surviving spouses are in relevantly similar situations in relation to such benefit schemes: *Willis v United Kingdom,* (App.36042/97), June 11, 2002, (2002) 35 EHRR 21.

(App.45851/99), Decision of April 27, 2000, the Strasbourg Court confirmed that the situations of married partners and unmarried cohabitees are not analogous. The Court said,

"The Court accepts that there may well now be increased social acceptance of stable personal relationships outside the traditional notion of marriage. However, marriage remains an institution which is widely accepted as conferring a particular status on those who enter it. The situation of the applicant [a woman whose partner had died] is therefore not comparable to that of a widow."

The Court went on to say that any distinctions would be within the State's margin of appreciation:

"The Court considers that the promotion of marriage, by way of limited benefits for surviving spouses, cannot be said to exceed the margin of appreciation afforded to the respondent Government."

The application was accordingly found to be manifestly ill-founded. The Commissioner in *R(G) 1/04* follows this decision. In *CG/1259/2002* the Commissioner refused to regard widows and the partners of deceased men as in a comparable situation for the purposes of entitlement to widow's benefits.

For a case arising under the war pensions legislation which includes provision for an "unmarried dependant living as a spouse", see *Secretary of State for Defence v Hopkins* [2004] EWHC 299 (Admin).

Is the difference of treatment capable of objective and reasonable justification?

4.81   In *Burden v United Kingdom*, (App.13378/05), April 29, 2008 [Grand Chamber], the Strasbourg Court said:

> . . . a difference of treatment is discriminatory if it has no objective and reasonable justification; in other words, if it does not pursue a legitimate aim or if there is not a reasonable relationship of proportionality between the means employed and the aim sought to be realised. The Contracting State enjoys a margin of appreciation in assessing whether and to what extent differences in otherwise similar situations justify a different treatment, and this margin is usually wide when it comes to general measures of economic or social strategy. . . . (para.60).

Where applicants can show that there is differential treatment of persons in relevantly similar situations, the respondent State is required to show that the underlying policy basis for the treatment in issue serves a legitimate aim and does not impose a disproportionate burden on the group claiming to be disadvantaged.

In asserting a legitimate aim for the differential treatment, the respondent State must not only show the nature of the legitimate aim it is pursuing, but must also show by convincing evidence the link between the legitimate aim pursued and the differential treatment challenged by the applicant. This is not generally a difficult hurdle for the respondent State to clear.

There is, however, a margin of appreciation accorded to Contracting Parties whose breadth will vary according to the circumstances. In *Stec and others v United Kingdom*, (App.65731/01), 12 April 2006, the Grand Chamber said:

> As a general rule, very weighty reasons would have to be put forward before the Court could regard a difference in treatment based exclusively on the ground of sex as compatible with the Convention. . . . On the other hand, a wide margin is usually allowed to the State under the Convention when it comes to general measures of economic or social strategy. . . . Because of their direct knowledge of their society and its needs, the national authorities are in principle better placed than the international judge to appreciate what is in the public interest on social or economic grounds, and the Court will generally respect the legislature's policy choice unless it is 'manifestly without reasonable foundation'. . . . (para.52).

Where the differential treatment is between men and women, (*Van Raalte v Netherlands* (App. 20060/92), February 21, 1997, (1997) 24 EHRR 503, para.39), on grounds of nationality, (*Gaygusuz v Austria* (App. 17371/90), September 16, 1996, (1997) 23 EHRR 364, para.42), on grounds of race (*Timishev v Russia*, (Apps. 55762/00 and 55974/00), 13 December 2005, (2007) 44 EHRR 776, para. 58.), on grounds of religion (*Hoffmann v Austria*, (App. 12875/87), June 23, 1993, Series A, No. 255–C, (1994) 17 EHRR 293, para.36), on grounds of legitimacy (*Inze v Austria*, (App. 8695/79), October 28, 1987, Series A, No. 126, (1988) 10 EHRR 394, para.41), and on grounds of sexual orientation (*E.B. v France*, (App. 43546/02), January 22, 2008 [Grand Chamber], para.93) very weighty reasons are required to justify the differential treatment.

Where the basis for the difference of treatment is grounds of sex or race, the Contracting Parties enjoy no margin of appreciation and will find it very difficult to establish objective and reasonable justification.

It follows that the nature of the justification presented will vary with the nature of the differential treatment in issue. While it will be reasonably easy for a Contracting Party to show that a difference of treatment pursues a legitimate aim, the case law suggests that meeting the test of objective and reasonable justification will vary according to the circumstances of each case. The test is tied in with the margin of appreciation.

The Michalak test: avoiding a rigidly formulaic approach

What came to be known as the *Michalak* test, from its adoption by the Court of Appeal in *Wandsworth London Borough Council v Michalak*, [2003] 1 W.L.R. 617, was a distillation of the questions it was said that the Convention organs ask themselves when examining a complaint under art.14 enunciated in S Grosz, J Beatson and P Duffy, *Human Rights. The 1998 Act and the European Convention* (London, 2000), para.C14–08. The original four questions were expanded to five:

(1) Do the facts fall within the ambit of one or more of the Convention rights?

(2) Was there a difference in treatment in respect of that right between the complainant and others put forward for comparison?

(3) If so, was the difference in treatment on one or more of the proscribed grounds under art.14?

(4) Were those others in an analogous situation?

(5) Was the difference in treatment objectively justified in the sense that it had a legitimate aim and bore a reasonable relationship of proportionality to that aim?

However, the framework questions did not seem to work in every situation and in *Ghaidan v Godin-Mendoza* [2004] UKHL 30; [2004] 3 W.L.R. 113, Baroness Hale sounded a warning:

". . . the *Michalak* questions are a useful tool of analysis but there is a considerable overlap between them: in particular between whether the situations to be compared were truly analogous, whether the difference in treatment was based on a proscribed ground and whether it had an objective justification. If the situations were not truly analogous it may be easier to conclude that the difference was based on something other than a proscribed ground. The reasons why their situations are analogous but their treatment different will be relevant to whether the treatment is objective justified. A rigidly formulaic approach is to be avoided". (para.134.)

Without offering an alternative test, Lord Hoffmann in his judgment in the House of Lords in *Carson and Reynolds* [2005] UKHL 37, paras 28–33 expresses reservations about the *Michalak* test, and does not apply it in coming to his conclusions on the claims of the applicants in the case. The influence of the *Michalak* test must be regarded as being considerably in decline, though it will remain 'a useful tool of analysis' for some time. But the so-called *Michalak* test can no longer be regarded as the definitive approach to the determination of questions arising under art.14 in the national courts and tribunals. A rigidly formulaic approach to questions arising under art.14 should be avoided.

Application in social security cases: bereavement benefits

In App. 365789/97, *Cornwell v United Kingdom* and App.38890/97, *Leary v United Kingdom*, two widowers complained that they were not entitled to benefits which would have been available to them had they been widows. The United Kingdom

4.82

Government did not contest the admissibility of either case (save in relation to one of the periods in respect of which Cornwell complained): see admissibility decisions of May 11, 1999 in both cases. The cases have been struck out of the Court's list on a friendly settlement being reached. The Government indicated that it would pay the applicants, on an extra-statutory basis, the amounts to which they would have been entitled had they been widows. The Government also drew attention to provisions in what are now ss.54–56 of the Welfare Reform and Pensions Act 1999 making provision for bereavement payments, allowances for bereaved spouses, and certain new pension arrangements, which avoid the discrimination which previously existed as between widows and widowers.

Willis v United Kingdom (App.36042/97), June 11, 2002, [2002] 35 E.H.R.R. 21 concerned a complaint by a man. The complainant argued that there was a breach art.14 taken in conjunction with art.8, and a branch of art.14 when taken in conjunction with art.1 of Protocol 1 of the Convention since, had he been a woman in a similar position, he would have been entitled to a widowed mother's allowance and widow's payment. He also complained in identical terms about his future non-entitlement to a widow's pension, and of a violation of art.13.

The Court ruled unanimously that a widow's payment and widowed mother's allowance, being contributory in nature, are capable of constituting a pecuniary right within the ambit of art.1 of Protocol 1. This was all that was necessary in order to open the door to complaints of discrimination under art.14. Consistently with its often stated case law, the Court said that 'very weighty' reasons would be necessary to ground objective justification where the grounds of discrimination were sex. The Government had not advanced any arguments which met the requirements of objective and reasonable justification. There was a violation of art.14 taken together with art.1 of Protocol 1 concerning entitlement to widow's payment and to a widowed mother's allowance. In relation to a widow's pension, the Court concluded that the claimant had not been treated any differently from a woman in an analogous situation. A widow in the claimant's position would not qualify for a widow's pension under the Contributions and Benefits Act 1992 until at least 2006 and might never qualify by reason of certain other statutory conditions. The Court accordingly concluded that no issue of discrimination as regards entitlement to a widow's pension arose on the facts of this case.

The Court sidesteps consideration of any violation of art.14 read in conjunction with art.8 in relation (a) to a widowed mother's allowance and widow's payment because it had concluded that there was a breach of art.14 read in conjunction with art.1 of Protocol 1, and (b) to a widow's pension because it had concluded that no issue of discrimination arose on the facts of the case. The Strasbourg Court did not consider that any separate issues were raised by the complaint or discrimination raised in relation to the claimant's late wife. Short shrift was given to the complaint of a violation of art.13 since the Court recalled its well established case law that art.13 does not go so far as to guarantee a remedy allowing a State's primary legislation to be challenged before a national authority on the grounds that it is contrary to the Convention.

The saga of the Government's response to the discrimination between men and women which occurred in relation to benefits for widows and widowers was considered by the House of Lords in *R v Secretary of State for Work and Pensions, ex parte Hooper* [2005] UKHL 29. The four claimants were widowers, whose circumstances were such that, had they been widows, they would have been able to claim widow's benefits. At issue were widow's payments (the lump sum benefit of £1,000); widowed mother's allowance; and widow's pension. They claimed that this differential treatment of men and women who had lost their spouses constituted discrimination contrary to art.14 when read with art.8 or art.1 of Protocol 1 with effect from 2 October 2000. The new scheme of bereavement benefits took effect in April 2001: widow's payment was replaced by a bereavement payment, widowed mother's allowance by a widowed parent's allowance, and widow's pension by a bereavement allowance. In both the Court of Appeal and the House of Lords, the Secretary of

State conceded that all widow's benefits fall within the ambit of one or both of the substantive Convention articles on which the claimants relied.

The Secretary of State argued that the payment of widow's pension to women only could be objectively justified, whereas the application of s.6(2) of the Human Rights Act 1998 meant that the payment of widow's payment and widowed mother's allowance was not unlawful under s.6(1) of the Act. Lord Hoffmann, giving the lead judgment of the House, first addressed objective justification for widow's pension. Lord Hoffman notes that widow's pension was never a means-tested benefit; it was predicated on the basis that older widows as a class were more likely to be in financial need than older widowers. Furthermore "there has never been any social or economic justification for extending widow's pension to men under pensionable age". Bearing these two considerations in mind, Lord Hoffmann offers a history of widow's pensions up to their abolition and replacement with a 52-week bereavement allowance for both men and women whose spouses had died. Lord Hoffmann notes:

"So the question in the case of WP is not so much whether there was justification for not paying it to men as whether there was justification for not having moved faster in abolishing its payment to women." (para.17.)

The essence of the conclusion that there was objective justification can be found in para.32:

"Once it is accepted that older widows were historically an economically disadvantaged class which merited special treatment but were gradually becoming less disadvantaged, the question of the precise moment at which such special treatment is no longer justified becomes a social and political question within the competence of Parliament."

The second argument put by the Secretary of State was that any unlawful discrimination arising from the non-payment of the equivalent of widow's payment and widowed mother's allowance to widowers was 'immunised' by the effect of s.6(2) of the 1998 Act. The argument of the widowers before the House of Lords was not that the payments to widows infringed their Convention rights; they also accepted that the Contributions and Benefits Act 1992 imposed no obligation on the Secretary of State to make payments to widowers, but they did argue that the Secretary of State "could have made such payments by exercising the common law powers of the Crown as a corporation sole to make discretionary payments of funds under its control" (para.43). The failure to do so constituted a breach of their Convention rights. Lord Hoffman concludes that s.6(2)(b) applies to the circumstances of the case. Section 6(2)(b) assumes that the Secretary of State could have acted differently but excludes liability if the Minister was giving effect to a statutory provision which could not be read as Convention-compatible. That was the situation here; in paying widows but not widowers, the Secretary of State was giving effect to ss 36 and 37 of the Contributions and Benefits Act 1992, which could not be read as requiring payments to widowers.

The final complaint made by the widowers related to the differential treatment by the Government of those who had petitioned the Court of Human Rights before the Human Rights Act 1998 came into force and themselves. The petitioners to the Strasbourg Court had received payments in the friendly settlement of their cases, but those making claims after the entry into force of the 1998 Act had not. Lord Hoffmann is unimpressed with this claim which he says fails for three reasons. First, there is doubt about whether being a person who has started legal proceedings is a personal characteristic. Secondly, any discrimination there might be does not appear to come within the scope of the Convention. Thirdly, there would be objective justification for the differential treatment even if the first two hurdles could be cleared.

Note that in *R(G) 2/04*, the Commissioner rules on a point of interpretation on which he regarded himself as bound by the decision of the Court of Appeal in the *Hooper* litigation (which was not in issue in the appeal to the House of Lords in that litigation) that "no man who claims widow's benefit in respect of a spouse who died before April 9, 2001 is entitled under British social security legislation to any payment of widow's benefit." (para.2).

The long-awaited judgment of the Court of Human Rights in *Runkee and White v United Kingdom* (Apps 42949/98 and 53134/99) was handed down on May 10, 2007. This finally resolved the position in relation to the litigation concerning widowers' entitlements under the legislation in force prior to April 9, 2001. The Court ruled that there was no violation of art.14 taken in conjunction with art.1 of Protocol 1 in connection with non-entitlement to a widow's pension, but that there was a violation of art.14 taken in conjunction with art.1 of Protocol 1 concerning non-entitlement to a widow's payment. The Court further ruled that it was not necessary to consider either complaint under art.14 taken in conjunction with art.8.

See *Hobbs, Richard, Walsh and Geen v United Kingdom* (Apps. 63684/00, 63475/00, 63484/00 and 63468/00), November 14, 2006, for the corresponding decision to that in *Runkee and White* in relation to widow's bereavement allowance in which a violation of art.14 taken with art.1 of Protocol 1 was found. There have been very many decisions and judgments in respect of applications against the United Kingdom in 2008 as the Strasbourg Court clears the decks of the backlog of applications concerning alleged discrimination in the sphere of bereavement benefits. The lead judgments on these benefits are (a) *Willis*, (b) *Runkee and White*, and (c) *Hobbs, Richard, Walsh and Geen*.

R(G) 1/06 concerned entitlement of an elderly widower to a bereavement payment. Section 36(1)(a) of the Contributions and Benefits Act provides that, even where the contribution conditions are met, there is no entitlement to a bereavement payment when the bereaved party is over pensionable age at the time of the relevant death, and the spouse who has died was getting their own Category A retirement pension. The Commissioner explains the historical origins of this limiting condition. It was argued on behalf of the claimant that the restrictive condition operated to discriminate between deceased spouses who had or had not opted for a Category B rather than a Category A retirement pension, and that this was contrary to art.14 when read with either art.8 or art.1 of Protocol 1. The Commissioner found that he could not interpret the relevant statutory provisions in a manner compatible with this interpretation. However, he was not persuaded that there was discrimination in breach of the Convention. He ruled,

> "28. . . . In a system as complicated and interlocking as the insured benefits scheme under the United Kingdom social security system it is inevitable that differences of treatment, even anomalies and incongruities, may arise at the boundaries between one set of facts and another. Such things are inherent in the system but it is clear on the authority of the House of Lords in *R (Carson) v Secretary of State* [2005] UKHL 37, [2006] 1 AC 173 that the mere existence of such dividing lines, not raising questions of differential treatment between categories of human beings on the "suspect" grounds, such as sex, race, and so forth or otherwise offensive to accepted notions of the respect due to the individual, does not constitute unlawful discrimination in the human rights context.
>
> 29. The dividing lines drawn in a contributory insurance system between the benefits for those who are themselves just under or over pensionable age, those whose deceased partners happen to have just under or over the 25% level of contributions to qualify them for a Category A retirement pension (or for that matter those whose deceased partners had a 100% contribution record, or 99% or something less, on the alternative construction put forward), or those whose partners had or had not happened to elect under section 43 to forgo their own contributory pension benefit on their own contributions and receive a Category B pension on their spouse's contributions instead, are all in my judgment squarely within the area that is left to be determined by the national legislation; and the same applies to deciding whether or in what way what may now be viewed largely as an historical anomaly in section 36(1)(a) should be eliminated. If the effect

of the condition is now "incongruous" as suggested in the tribunal chairman's statement of reasons at pages 42 to 43 of file CG 1614/05, that is a matter those concerned for claimants in this position must take up in some other forum than this."

Up rating of pensions for beneficiaries living abroad

A second art.14 battleground has related to the practice of the Government *not* to up rate retirement pensions payable to pensioners in some countries, while allowing up rating in relation to pensions payable in other countries. **4.83**

The House of Lords gave judgment in 2005 on the claim by Annette Carson that there is discrimination in breach of Convention rights in payment of contributory pensions to pensioners in some overseas countries without up rating of those pensions; and on the claim by Joanne Reynolds that the payment of jobseeker's allowance and income support to those under the age of 25 at a lower rate than those aged 25 or more constituted discrimination in breach of Convention rights: *R. v Secretary of State for Work and Pensions, ex parte Carson, R. v Secretary of State for Work and Pensions, ex parte Reynolds* [2005] UKHL 37. Lord Hoffmann and Lord Walker of Gestingthorpe gave the lead judgments in a 4–1 decision that there is no breach of Convention rights in the *Carson* case and a unanimous decision that there is no breach of Convention rights in the *Reynolds* case. Lord Hoffmann's judgment is intellectually seductive, but turns very much on the premise that "social security benefits are part of an intricate and interlocking system of social welfare which exists to ensure certain minimum standards of living for the people of this country" (para.18) which is, in turn linked to a certain extent to the tax system. Lord Hoffmann is "content to assume that Ms Carson's pension rights were a possession" (para.12). Likewise, he was content to accept that residence abroad constituted a personal characteristic and so constituted a 'status' for the purpose of the application of Article14. Because of the interlocking nature of the system, and its relationship with the tax system, Lord Hoffmann concludes that the position of non-residents is materially and relevantly different from that of United Kingdom residents. (para.25). Once this is accepted, it is a matter for Parliament to determine the amount, if any, which she receives. Lord Hoffmann continues:

". . . in deciding what expatriate pensioners should be paid, Parliament must be entitled to take into account competing claims on public funds." (para.25.)

Lord Hoffmann took a similarly robust view of the distinction between payments to expatriate pensioners where there is a treaty (which frequently makes provision for up rating of pensions) and those where there is no such treaty. Without determining whether income support constitutes a possession for the purposes of Article1 of Protocol 1, Lord Hoffmann concluded that the relative positions of those under and over the age of 25 are relevantly different. A line had to be drawn somewhere. So it followed that the claim of Ms Reynolds failed.

Lord Carswell dissented in relation to Ms Carson's appeal. Lord Carswell considers that contributors whose pensions are paid countries where pensions are up rated and contributors whose pensions are paid in countries where pensions are not up rated are in relevantly comparable situations. For Lord Carswell, some objective justification needs to be provided for the differential treatment of these groups. He was not persuaded that any of the arguments put forward constituted objective justification. He is clearly persuaded by the fact that all the pensioners have "duly paid the contributions required to qualify for their pensions" (para.98.)

Following the judgment in the House of Lords, application was made to the Strasbourg Court. That Court delivered judgment in *Carson and others v. United Kingdom,* (App.42184/05), on November 4, 2008. In a six to one majority decision, the Strasbourg Court, largely adopting the reasoning of the House of Lords, decided that there had been no violation of art.14 when taken in conjunction with art.1 of Protocol 1. Though it conceded that place of residence could constitute "other status" under art.14, the Chamber decided that persons subject to up rating and persons not entitled to up rating of their pensions were not in analogous situations. But even if art.14 applied, the differential treatment was justifiable. The Court declined to consider the complaint of a violation of art.14 taken in conjunctions with art.8.

Note that the Chamber judgement has been referred to the Grand Chamber.

Further Strasbourg authorities relating to the United Kingdom

4.84   The substantive issue in *Stec and others v United Kingdom*, (Apps 65731/01 and 65900/01) April 12, 2006 [Grand Chamber], (2006) 43 EHRR 1017, related to the impact of differential State pensionable ages on entitlement to a reduced earnings allowance. The Court concludes:

> 61. Differential pensionable ages were first introduced for men and women in the United Kingdom in 1940, well before the Convention had come into existence, although the disparity persists to the present day. . . . It would appear that the difference in treatment was adopted in order to mitigate financial inequality and hardship arising out of the woman's traditional unpaid role of caring for the family in the home rather than earning money in the workplace. At their origin, therefore, the differential pensionable ages were intended to correct "factual inequalities" between men and women and appear therefore to have been objectively justified under art.14 (see paragraph 51 above).
>
> 62. It follows that the difference in pensionable ages continued to be justified until such time that social conditions had changed so that women were no longer substantially prejudiced because of a shorter working life. This change, must, by its very nature, have been gradual, and it would be difficult or impossible to pinpoint any particular moment when the unfairness to men caused by differential pensionable ages began to outweigh the need to correct the disadvantaged position of women. Certain indications are available to the Court. Thus, in the 1993 White Paper, the Government asserted that the number of women in paid employment had increased significantly, so that whereas in 1967 only 37% of employees were women, the proportion had increased to 50% in 1992. In addition, various reforms to the way in which pension entitlement was assessed had been introduced in 1977 and 1978, to the benefit of women who spent long periods out of paid employment. As of 1986, it was unlawful for an employer to have different retirement ages for men and women (see paragraph 33 above).
>
> 63. According to the information before the Court, the Government made a first, concrete, move towards establishing the same pensionable age for both sexes with the publication of the Green Paper in December 1991. It would, no doubt, be possible to argue that this step could, or should, have been made earlier. However, as the Court has observed, the development of parity in the working lives of men and women has been a gradual process, and one which the national authorities are better placed to assess (see paragraph 52 above). Moreover, it is significant that many of the other Contracting States still maintain a difference in the ages at which men and women become eligible for the State retirement pension. . . . Within the European Union, this position is recognised by the exception contained in the Directive. . . .
>
> 64. In the light of the original justification for the measure as correcting financial inequality between the sexes, the slowly evolving nature of the change in women's working lives, and in the absence of a common standard amongst the Contracting States . . . the Court finds that the United Kingdom cannot be criticised for not having started earlier on the road towards a single pensionable age.
>
> 65. Having once begun the move towards equality, moreover, the Court does not consider it unreasonable of the Government to carry out a thorough process of consultation and review, nor can Parliament be condemned for deciding in 1995 to introduce the reform slowly and in stages. Given the extremely far-reaching and serious implications, for women and for the economy in general, these are matters which clearly fall within the State's margin of appreciation.

In *Pearson v United Kingdom,* (App.8374/03), August 22, 2006, the Strasbourg Court ruled that the differential age for entitlement to a State retirement pension of 65 for a man and 60 for a woman was objectively justifiable. The Court refers to its decision in the *Stec* case (citing paras 61-65) in finding that the differential State pensionable ages are within the State's margin of appreciation and that it cannot be criticised for not having moved earlier towards equalization of the pension age for men and women (which will be reached in 2020).

On the same day, the judgment in *Walker v United Kingdom,* (App. 37212/02) was delivered. This concerned the requirement for a man to pay national insurance contributions beyond the age of 60 when the liability of a woman ceases. For exactly the same reasons as given in *Pearson,* the Strasbourg Court finds that there is no violation of art.14 read in conjunction with art.1 of Protocol 1.

The same conclusion was also reached in *Barrow v United Kingdom,* (App. 42735/02), August 22, 2006, in a complaint concerning a woman who suffered a reduction in benefit at the age of 60 where her long-term incapacity benefit was replaced with the State retirement pension. She complained that such a reduction would not arise for a man, for whom the transition would not arise until he reached State pensionable age of 65.

Further United Kingdom authorities

In *Esfandiari v Secretary of State for Work and Pensions* [2006] EWCA Civ 282 (the appeals against *CIS/1870/2003; CIS/2302/2003; CIS/2305/2003* and *CIS/2624/2003*), reported as *R(IS) 11/06,* the Court of Appeal considered whether the funeral payments provisions which restrict the payment of funeral expenses where the funeral is held in the United Kingdom (or in certain cases another country within the European Economic Area) are compatible with the European Convention. The Court was unanimous in concluding that this was not a case of discrimination at all, but even if those migrants who wished to bury relatives in their country of origin were a group, then any differential treatment could easily be justified as matters where the State enjoyed a wide margin of appreciation is setting its policy. The Court of Appeal regards the different outcome in Community law as arising because of the special rights which migrant workers are accorded under the EC Treaty.

In *R(P) 2/06* a Tribunal of Commissioners concluded that the United Kingdom rules preventing the payment of widows' benefits to widows of polygamous marriages in the circumstances of the cases before them did not fall foul of the prohibition of discrimination in art.14 when read with art.8. The Tribunal of Commissioners was unanimous as to the outcome, but one Commissioner's line of reasoning differs from that of his two colleagues.

In *Couronne v Secretary of State for Work and Pensions, Bontemps v Secretary of State for Work and Pensions* [2006] EWHC 1514 (Admin), it was argued that the refusal to award jobseekers allowance to British Citizens arriving from Mauritius (whose parents had been displaced from the Chagos Islands) constituted discrimination in breach of art.14 when read with art.8 and/or art.1 of Protocol 1. It was argued, inter alia, that the comparator group (British Citizens of Irish ethnic origin are exempt from the habitual residence test, whereas the claimants were not. Bennett J. concluded:

> "96. In my judgment the aim of the habitual residence test is a legitimate one. Both the ECJ and the Court of Appeal have said so, at least in the context of community law. If the aim, as explained in the evidence, is to protect the British taxpayer from claims by persons who have no genuine or real intention of settling in the UK, if it has been the subject of wide debate and consultation, and if Parliament itself has debated the matter in 1999, it is a nonsense to suggest that the habitual residence test does not have a legitimate aim. The real complaint of the Claimants is, in my judgment, that the implementation of the habitual residence test in relation to the Chagossians, given their special history, is not a proportionate means of achieving the legitimate aim.

4.85

97. The word 'proportionate' to my mind imports the notion of a balanced response to a given situation. I do not see how it can be said that the inclusion of British citizens of Irish national or ethnic origin within the habitual residence test is not proportionate to the legitimate aim. The complaint of the Chagossians must be that they were not exempted from the scope of the habitual residence test, particularly in the light of their exile and being granted British citizenship. But that, with all due respect, is, as Mr Howell submitted, not the question. The question is whether the habitual residence test is a proportionate means of achieving a legitimate aim given the particular disadvantage to which it is said to put other British citizens not of Irish national or ethnic origin only if an exception is made for the Chagossians. I am afraid that the brutal reality is that the Chagossians are seeking to be treated better than their comparator group and thus seeking a complete exemption from the habitual residence test. The argument as to exile (particularly as British citizens) has no relevance, because it is an exemption that they would have to seek even if the habitual residence test was framed solely in terms of habitual residence in the United Kingdom; and, as is apparent, the Claimants could not (and do not) object to a habitual residence test framed solely in those terms. The distinction made by the UK Government between the plight of the people of Montserrat and of the Chagossians is one about which argument will rage. But hard and difficult decisions have to be made. There may be no 'right' answer, only a least wrong one. The question is whether the refusal of the UK Government to exempt them from the habitual residence is a proportionate response. In my judgment it is. . . ."

The decision of Bennett J. has been upheld on appeal to the Court of Appeal: [2007] EWCA Civ 1086. On the human rights issues the Court concluded that the judge at first instance had been correct in his analysis of the application of the Convention.

In *R. (on the application of RJM) v Secretary of State for Work and Pensions* [2008] UKHL 63, the House of Lords ruled that a question of entitlement to a disability premium as part of income support falls within the ambit of art.1 of Protocol 1 such that art.14 is engaged. The House went on to conclude that homelessness was a status within art.14, but that the differential treatment could be justified.

In *HMRC v DH,* [2009] UKUT 24 (AAC), the Judge decided that the payment of child tax credit to the principal carer does not breach art.14 when read with art.1 of Protocol No. 1, since any discrimination against the secondary carer is objectively justified. His decision is under appeal to the Court of Appeal as *Humphreys v HM Revenue and Customs.*

In *NT v SSWP* [2009] UKUT 37 (AAC), the Judge ruled that the age cut-off of 65 for entitlement to the mobility component of a disability living allowance was a matter within the margin of appreciation of the United Kingdom. Consideration of the justification for the choice to legislate an age cut-off date simply required the Secretary of State to provide a rational explanation for the policy of the law in this case. The Secretary of State had, in the consideration of the Judge, met that obligation.

In *CM v SSWP* [2009] UKUT 43 (AAC), the Judge ruled that denial of income support to a pregnant student nurse intercalating a period of study was objectively and reasonably justified.

A challenge relating to the exclusion from benefits of prisoners transferred to mental hospital under these regulations as being in breach of art.14 of the European Convention when read with art.1 of Protocol No. 1 has failed with one exception: see *R. (on the application of EM and others) v Secretary of State for Work and Pensions,* [2009] EWHC 454 (Admin). The excepted class is a small group (there were 45 such persons in detention when the case was decided) of what are described as "technical lifers", namely those, although sentenced to life imprisonment, are treated by the Secretary of State after transfer to hospital as though they had been made the subject of a hospital order under s.37 of the Mental Health Act 1983 and to a restriction order under s.41 of that Act.

For a useful discussion of art.14 in the social security context, see M Cousins, "The European Convention on Human Rights, Non-Discrimination and Social Security: Great Scope, Little Depth?" [2009] JSSL 120. For a more general discussion of art.14, see R O'Connell, "Cinderella comes to the Ball: Art 14 and the right to non-discrimination in the ECHR", (2009) 29 *Legal Studies* 211.

Article 16—Restrictions on political activity of aliens

Nothing in Articles 10, 11 and 14 shall be regarded as preventing the High Contracting Parties from imposing restrictions on the political activity of aliens.   **4.86**

Article 17—Prohibition of abuse of rights

Nothing in this Convention may be interpreted as implying for any State, group or person any right to engage in any activity or perform any act aimed at the destruction of any of the rights and freedoms set forth herein or at their limitation to a greater extent than is provided for in the Convention.   **4.87**

Article 18—Limitation on use of restrictions on rights

The restrictions permitted under this Convention to the said rights and freedoms shall not be applied for any purpose other than those for which they have been prescribed.   **4.88**

PART II

THE FIRST PROTOCOL

Article 1—Protection of property

Every natural or legal person is entitled to the peaceful enjoyment of his possessions. No one shall be deprived of his possessions except in the public interest and subject to the conditions provided for by law and by the general principles of international law. The preceding provisions shall not, however, in any way impair the right of a State to enforce such laws as it deems necessary to control the use of property in accordance with the general interest or to secure the payment of taxes or other contributions or penalties.   **4.89**

GENERAL NOTE

Introduction

The protection of property rights as human rights presents particular problems, and it is therefore not surprising that agreement could not be reached on their inclusion in the Convention as originally drafted. A right to property is included in art.1 of Protocol 1, but its content is broadly framed and the permissible restrictions are broad in scope.   **4.90**

Though drafted rather differently, the structure of the provision is similar to that found in arts 8–11. There is a general right to peaceful enjoyment of possessions. Interferences can, however, be justified on the conditions set out in the article which include references both to the "public interest" and the "general interest"; this is the test of proportionality that pervades the Convention's consideration of interferences and requires the balancing of the interests of the individual against the collective interest.

The Court has repeatedly said that the article comprises three distinct rules: *Sporrong and Lönnroth v Sweden*, (Apps 7151-2/75), 23 September 1982, Series A, No. 52, (1983) 5 EHRR 35, para.61. See, more recently, *Jahn and others v Germany*, (Apps 46720/99, 72203/01, and 72552/01), 30 June 2005 [Grand Chamber], (2006) 42 EHRR 1084, ECHR 2005-VI, para.78; and *Hutten-Czapska v Poland*, (App.35014/97), 19 June 2006 [Grand Chamber], (2007) 45 EHRR 52, ECHR

2006-VIII, para.157. Firstly, everyone is entitled to peaceful enjoyment of their possessions. Secondly, deprivation of possessions is subject to certain conditions. Finally, Contracting Parties are entitled to control the use of property where it is in the general interest. But these are not distinct rules, since the second and third rules relate to interferences with the peaceful enjoyment of possessions which may be justified in the general interest.

Once it has been established that the applicant has an interest which can be classified as a possession, the general approach of the Strasbourg Court is to consider first whether there has been a deprivation of possessions, followed by consideration of whether there has been a control of the use of possessions, since these are matters specifically dealt with by the article. Only if there has been neither deprivation of possessions nor a control of their use does the Court consider, as a separate issue, whether there has been some other interference with the peaceful enjoyment of possessions. Such interferences will, however, only be unlawful if they are not in the general interest. In its more recent case law, the Court has brought together the tests it applies in relation to deprivations, the control of the use of property, and to other interferences with property, so that the questions the Court will ask in each of these circumstances raise essentially the same issues.

Possessions have been defined in broad terms by both the Commission and the Court. In this context, it is worth noting that the French text of the Convention uses the term *"biens"* which connotes a very broad range of property rights. The term has an autonomous meaning; it extends beyond physical goods, and covers a wide range of rights and interests which may be classified as assets.

Social security payments and pensions

4.91   Entitlements arising under pension and social security schemes have proved difficult to classify; the position was for some time unclear. A distinction had been drawn in the case law between benefits which were paid on the basis of contributions, and those which were paid without reference to contributions. But the case law did not always seem to maintain this distinction. However, the admissibility decision of the Grand Chamber in the *Stec* case (*Stec and others v United Kingdom* (Apps 65731/01 and 65900/01), Decision of July 6, 2005 [Grand Chamber], (2005) 41 EHRR SE18) has clarified matters.

An example of the ambiguity caused by the earlier case law can be found in the *Gaygusuz* case (*Gaygusuz v Austria* (App. 17371/90), 16 September 1996, (1997) 23 EHRR 364). Gaygusuz was a Turkish national who had worked in Austria, where he had paid contributions under the Austrian social security scheme. He had experienced periods of unemployment and periods when he was unfit for work. He applied for an advance on his retirement pension as a form of emergency assistance, but was refused because he was not an Austrian national. He complained that there had been a violation of art.14 when read in conjunction with art.1 of Protocol 1. The first question was whether the substance of the claim was a matter within the scope of the article, since otherwise art.14 could not be brought into play. Both the Commission and the Court concluded that the article was applicable but for different reasons. The Commission concluded that the article was brought into play because the obligation to pay "taxes or other contributions" falls within its field of application. The Court, however, concluded that the link with the obligation to pay taxes or other contributions was not required. That was sufficient to engage the anti-discrimination provision in art.14 and to find a violation since the discrimination between nationals and non-nationals was blatant. The Court took the same approach in the *Koua Poirrez* case (*Koua Poirrez v France* (App.40892/98), 30 September 2003, (2005) 40 EHRR 34, para.37).

In the *Stec* case, the Grand Chamber accepted that the *Gaygusuz* case was ambiguous on the significance of contributions in bringing a claim within the scope of art.1 of Protocol 1 for the purpose of claiming discriminatory treatment which breached art.14 of the Convention. The Grand Chamber lays down a new approach which is to be applied in future cases, relying on an interpretation which renders the rights in the Convention practical and effective rather than theoretical and illusory. The Grand Chamber also referred to the Court's case law under art.6 which had brought disputes concerned all forms of social security within the scope of that article. The Court concluded that, whenever persons can assert a right to a welfare benefit under national law, art.1 of Protocol 1 applies. The Court goes on to note that the bringing of social security fairly and squarely within the scope of art.1 of Protocol 1 does not create any right to acquire property. However, if a Contracting Party does create rights to social security benefits, the benefit schemes must be operated in a manner which is compatible with the prohibition of discrimination set out in art.14.

Attempts have been made to argue that the suspension of retirement pension for those serving terms of imprisonment breached the property rights in art.1 of Protocol 1, but the applications were declared inadmissible (Apps.27004/95, *Josef Szrabjer v United Kingdom*, and 27011/95, *Walter Clarke v United Kingdom*, Decisions of October 23, 1997) and invalidity benefit (App.27537/95, *George Carlin v United Kingdom*, Decision of December 3, 1997). The public interest was served by avoiding a situation in which prisoners enjoyed the advantage of accumulating a lump sum by receiving a State benefit without any outgoing living expenses. Arguments based on discrimination between prisoners and non-prisoners were dismissed as a comparison of two different factual situations. Other comparisons were also found to be without merit. See also discussion of benefits for widowers in the commentary on art.14 above.

In *CP/4762/2001* the Commissioner found that the provisions under which a person became entitled to a retirement pension normally with effect from the Monday following their 65th birthday gives rise to no Convention issue either under art.1 of Protocol 1, nor under that provision when read in conjunctions with art.14

In *CP/0281/2002*, the Commissioner ruled that there was no breach of art.1 of Protocol 1 as a consequence of the requirement under the Pension Schemes Act 1993 that any additional pension is reduced by the amount of any guaranteed minimum pension payable to a person.

In *R. (Smith) v Secretary of State for Defence and Secretary of State for Work and Pensions* [2004] EWHC 1797 (Admin), Wilson J. held that a non-contributory pension under the Armed Forces Pension Scheme was a possession within the ambit of art.1 of Protocol 1. This extended to the spouse of the pension holder following the making of a pension-sharing order. However, art.1 of Protocol 1 does not guarantee a right to a pension of a particular amount, nor payment from a particular time.

In *R(P) 1/06*, the Commissioner ruled that the three months time limit on the backdating of a claim for retirement pension did not constitute a deprivation of property contrary to art.1 of Protocol 1. Nor was there any question of a claim based on discrimination by reading art.14 together with art.1 of Protocol 1.

In *C8/06-07(IB)* a Commissioner in Northern Ireland said,

"15. I consider there is no merit in the submission based on art.1 of Protocol 1. There is no inbuilt Convention right to any State benefit. A State is not obliged to provide benefit. The right to benefit only arises when the conditions therefore (which are provided under domestic legislation) are satisfied. In this case they were not so satisfied. The claimant was not entitled to the benefit because he worked and his work did not fall within the categories of exempt work. The basic rule in relation to IB is that those who work are not entitled to it. The benefit is, after all, an incapacity for work benefit. There are exceptions to this basic rule but they relate only to certain categories of work. The relevant category here includes that the work be work of which the required notice is given. Working on the assumption that the domestic law requirement of written notice within 42 days is valid, there is no entitlement to IB if work is done which does not come within an exempt category. art.1 of Protocol 1 is not therefore invoked, there being no property to enjoy. The claimant is not being asked to repay benefit incorrectly paid.

His benefit entitlement is merely being determined according to the applicable statutory conditions of entitlement."

Article 2—Right to education

4.92   No person shall be denied the right to education. In the exercise of any functions which it assumes in relation to education and to teaching, the State shall respect the right of parents to ensure such education and teaching in conformity with their own religious and philosophical convictions.

GENERAL NOTE

4.93   The full scope of this right is yet to be determined. The existing case law is mainly concerned with primary education, but the Commission has not ruled out the application of the provision to higher education (see, for example, *Sulak v Turkey* (1996) 84 D.R. 101). The confused state of the exclusion of students in full-time higher education from entitlement to most social security benefits might well leave the United Kingdom exposed to challenge under this provision. On the assumption that the provision applies to higher education, it could be argued that students are currently required to abandon their courses completely in order to become eligible for certain social security benefits with the result that they lose entitlement to the balance of finance to support their studies if they wish to return to their courses later on. This could be argued to operate to deny them the right to an education.

In *Douglas v North Tyneside MBC and Secretary of State for Education and Skills* [2003] EWCA Civ 1847, the Court of Appeal ruled that tertiary education falls within the ambit of art.2 of Protocol 1. The Court of Appeal held that, although there was no European or domestic authority establishing clearly that tertiary education falls within the ambit of art.2 of Protocol 1, the Convention was a living instrument and the number of adults in higher education had grown. There was no principle that the article applied only to earlier stages of education, and so tertiary education falls within the ambit of the article. The case turned on the application of art.14 when read in conjunction with art.2 of Protocol 1, and is discussed in the update to the annotations on art.14 above.

Article 3—Right to free elections

4.94   The High Contracting Parties undertake to hold free elections at reasonable intervals by secret ballot, under conditions which will ensure the free expression of the opinion of the people in the choice of the legislature.

PART III

ARTICLE 1 OF THE THIRTEENTH PROTOCOL

Omitted (concerns the abolition of the death penalty).

4.95   *Schedule 2 omitted.*

SCHEDULE 3

DEROGATION AND RESERVATION

4.96   [. . .]

PART II

RESERVATION

At the time of signing the present (First) Protocol, I declare that, in view of certain **4.97**
provisions of the Education Acts in the United Kingdom, the principle affirmed in the second
sentence of Article 2 is accepted by the United Kingdom only so far as it is compatible with
the provision of efficient instruction and training, and the avoidance of unreasonable public
expenditure.

Dated March 20, 1952. Made by the United Kingdom Permanent Representative to the
Council of Europe.

GENERAL NOTE

The derogations of 1988 and 1989 in respect of art.5(3) of the Convention were **4.98**
withdrawn by the Government on February 26, 2001. The amendments to the Act
were made by The Human Rights Act (Amendment) Order 2001 (SI 2001/1216)
which entered into force on April 1, 2001.

The derogation contained in the Human Rights Act (Designated Derogation)
Order 2001 (SI 2001/3644) in force from November 13, 2001 contained derogations from the provisions of art.5(1) to permit the detention of foreign nationals
in the United Kingdom under the Anti-terrorism, Crime and Security Act 2001.
That derogation has been withdrawn and effect is given to its withdrawal by the
repeal of P I of Sch.3 to the Human Rights Act 1998 by the Human Rights Act 1998
(Amendment) Order 2005 (SI 2005/1071) with effect from April 8, 2005.

Schedule 4 omitted. **4.99**

A Select Bibliography on Human Rights Law

The following material may be found to be helpful on the Human Rights Act
1998:

Baker, C. (ed.), *Human Rights Act 1998: A Practitioner's Guide* (Sweet & Maxwell,
London, 1998): see particularly Ch.12 entitled "Social Security".

Grosz, S., Beatson, J. and Duffy, P., *Human Rights. The 1998 Act and the European
Convention,* (Sweet & Maxwell, London, 2000).

Lester, A. and Pannick, D. (ed.) *Human Rights Law and Practice,* (Butterworths,
London, 1999).

Starmer, K., *European Human Rights Law/The Human Rights Act 1998 and the
European Convention on Human Rights* (Legal Action Group, London, 1999).

Wadham, J., Mountfield, H., Edmundson, A., and Gallagher, C., *Blackstone's
Guide to the Human Rights Act 1998* (4th ed., Oxford University Press, 2007).

Three useful texts on the European Convention on Human Rights are:

Harris, D. O'Boyle, M. and Warbrick, C., *Law of the European Convention on
Human Rights* (2nd ed., Oxford University Press, Oxford, 2009).

Ovey, C. and White, R., *The European Convention on Human Rights* (4th ed.,
Oxford University Press, Oxford, 2006).

Reid, K., *A Practitioner's Guide to the European Convention on Human Rights* (2nd
ed., Sweet & Maxwell, London, 2004).

PART V

TRIBUNALS

Tribunals, Courts and Enforcement Act 2007

(2007 c.15)

Contents

Part 1

Tribunal Judiciary: and Inquiries

Chapter 1

Tribunal Judiciary: Independence and Senior President

Chapter 2

First-Tier Tribunal and Upper Tribunal

Establishment

Members and composition of tribunals

Review of decisions and appeals

"Judicial review"

Part 4 — Power to amend legislation in connection with Tribunal Procedure Rules

Schedules 6 to 23 — *Omitted.*

An Act to make provision about tribunals and inquiries; to establish an Administrative Justice and Tribunals Council; to amend the law relating to judicial appointments and appointments to the Law Commission; to amend the law relating to the enforcement of judgments and debts; to make further provision about the management and relief of debt; to make provision protecting cultural objects from seizure or forfeiture in certain circumstances; to amend the law relating to the taking of possession of land affected by compulsory purchase; to alter the powers of the High Court in judicial review applications; and for connected purposes.

[19th July 2007]

PART 1

TRIBUNALS AND INQUIRIES

CHAPTER 1

TRIBUNAL JUDICIARY: INDEPENDENCE AND SENIOR PRESIDENT

1. *Omitted.*   5.2

Senior President of Tribunals

2.—(1) Her Majesty may, on the recommendation of the Lord Chancellor,   5.3
appoint a person to the office of Senior President of Tribunals.

(2) Schedule 1 makes further provision about the Senior President of Tribunals and about recommendations for appointment under subsection (1).

(3) A holder of the office of Senior President of Tribunals must, in carrying out the functions of that office, have regard to—

(a) the need for tribunals to be accessible,

(b) the need for proceedings before tribunals—

(i) to be fair, and

(ii) to be handled quickly and efficiently,

(c) the need for members of tribunals to be experts in the subject-matter of, or the law to be applied in, cases in which they decide matters, and

(d) the need to develop innovative methods of resolving disputes that are of a type that may be brought before tribunals.

(4) In subsection (3) "tribunals" means—

(a) the First-tier Tribunal,

(b) the Upper Tribunal,

    (c) employment tribunals,
    (d) the Employment Appeal Tribunal, and
    (e) the Asylum and Immigration Tribunal.

GENERAL NOTE

5.4   This section came into force on September 19, 2007 and Sir Robert Carnwath CVO, a Lord Justice of Appeal (i.e. a judge of the Court of Appeal) in England and Wales, has been appointed as the first Senior President of Tribunals. Part 4 of Sch.1, which is not reproduced in this work, confers on him certain functions in relation to judges and members of relevant tribunals (those listed in subs.(4) and also those tribunals listed in Pts 1 to 4 of Sch.6 that have not yet been abolished) that are equivalent to the functions the Lord Chief Justice of England and Wales has in relation to judges in the courts under the Constitutional Reform Act 2005. In addition, this Act, together with other provisions such as s.15A of the Social Security Act 1998, confers on him a wide number of functions, which (apart from the power to make orders under s.7(9)) he may delegate to other members of the judiciary or to staff (see s.8). By virtue of s.3(4), he presides over both the First-tier Tribunal and the Upper Tribunal.

CHAPTER 2

FIRST-TIER TRIBUNAL AND UPPER TRIBUNAL

Establishment

The First-tier Tribunal and the Upper Tribunal

5.5   **3.**—(1) There is to be a tribunal, known as the First-tier Tribunal, for the purpose of exercising the functions conferred on it under or by virtue of this Act or any other Act.

(2) There is to be a tribunal, known as the Upper Tribunal, for the purpose of exercising the functions conferred on it under or by virtue of this Act or any other Act.

(3) Each of the First-tier Tribunal, and the Upper Tribunal, is to consist of its judges and other members.

(4) The Senior President of Tribunals is to preside over both of the First-tier Tribunal and the Upper Tribunal.

(5) The Upper Tribunal is to be a superior court of record.

GENERAL NOTE

5.6   This section came into force on November 3, 2008 when the functions of the appeal tribunals constituted under the Social Security Act 1998 and the Social Security Commissioners appointed under that Act were, subject to one exception (see the note to ss.5 to 7 of the Social Security Act 1998), transferred to the two new tribunals established under this section. The functions of many other tribunals, outside the scope of this work, have also been transferred to these new tribunals and more will be transferred over the next year. It should, however, be noted that the relevant parts of the Social Security Act 1998 extended only to Great Britain and that, in Northern Ireland, appeal tribunals and Commissioners, constituted and appointed under different legislation, continue in existence. Consequently, so far as social security matters are concerned, the First-tier Tribunal and the Upper Tribunal have jurisdiction only in Great Britain.

As the panel members and Commissioners were transferred into the new tribunals as judges and members, the new tribunals function in much the same way as their predecessors, although they are now subject to different procedural rules.

Subs. (1)

The First-tier Tribunal was established with three chambers and a fourth was added from April 1, 2009 (see s.7). Further chambers are expected to be added as more functions are transferred. The functions of the appeal tribunals constituted under the Social Security Act 1998 were transferred to the Social Entitlement Chamber of the First-tier Tribunal, as were the functions of the Criminal Injuries Compensation Panel and the asylum support adjudicators. Although the Social Entitlement Chamber is a single entity in legal terms, its administration continues to reflect the old divisions, with the criminal injuries compensation and asylum support cases being administered separately in central offices and the social security cases being administered regionally. Hearings take place at a large number of venues around Great Britain. More details about the First-tier Tribunal may be found on the website of the Tribunals Service *(http://www.tribunals.gov.uk)* although, curiously, the page with information concerning social security cases remains at *http://www.appeals-service.gov.uk*.

The role of tribunals in a social security context has been the subject of a considerable amount of case law.

The inquisitorial role of the tribunal and the burden of proof

It has long been recognised that proceedings before tribunals are inquisitorial rather than adversarial and this has been confirmed by the House of Lords in *Kerr v Department for Social Development* [2004] UKHL 23; [2004] 1 W.L.R. 1372 (also reported as an appendix to *R1/04(SF)*), where some of the consequences of this approach were considered. Baroness Hale of Richmond said:

> "61. Ever since the decision of the Divisional Court in *R. v Medical Appeal Tribunal (North Midland Region), Ex p. Hubble* [1958] 2 Q.B. 228, it has been accepted that the process of benefits adjudication in inquisitorial rather than adversarial. Diplock J. as he then was said this of an industrial injury benefit claim at p.240:
>
>> 'A claim by an insured person to benefit under the Act is not truly analogous to a *lis inter partes*. A claim to benefit is a claim to receive money out of the insurance funds . . . Any such claim investigation to determine whether any, and if so, what amount of benefit is payable out of the fund. In such an investigation, the minister or insurance officer is not a party adverse to the claimant. If analogy be sought in the other branches of the law, it is to be found in an inquest rather than an action.'
>
> 62. What emerges from all this is a co-operative process of investigation in which both the claimant and the department play their part. The department is the one which knows what questions it needs to ask and what information it needs to have in order to determine whether the conditions of entitlement have been met. The claimant is the one who generally speaking can and must supply that information. But where the information is available to the department rather than the claimant, then the department must take the necessary steps to enable it to be traced.
>
> 63. If that sensible approach is taken, it will rarely be necessary to resort to concepts taken from adversarial litigation such as the burden of proof. The first question will be whether each partner in the process has played their part. If there is still ignorance about a relevant matter then generally speaking it should be determined against the one who has not done all that they reasonably could to discover it. As Mr Commissioner Henty put it in *CIS/5321/1998*: 'a claimant must to the best of his or her ability give such information to the AO as he reasonably can, in default of which a contrary inference can always be drawn.' The same should apply to information which the department can reasonably be expected to discover for itself."

5.7

5.8

In that particular case the claimant had been unable to tell the department whether either his brother or sister, with whom he had lost contact, was in receipt of relevant benefits. The department could have discovered that information had they had the brother's and sister's dates of birth, which the claimant could have given them but for which the department never asked. It was held that the department could not rely on their failure to ask questions which would have led to the right answer to defeat the claim.

Where all relevant questions have been asked and there are still things unknown, it was held in *Kerr* that it has to be decided who should bear the consequences of the collective ignorance. If the ignorance concerns a matter relevant to conditions of entitlement, the claimant has to bear the consequences but if the ignorance concerns an exception to those conditions, the department must bear the consequences. In *Kerr*, the claimant was prima facie entitled to a funeral payment but would not be entitled if his brother or sister was not receiving benefit or had capital. The ignorance as to whether they were receiving benefit or had capital was therefore ignorance concerning an exception to entitlement and the department had to bear the burden and pay the claim. Lord Hope of Craighead set out, at para.[16], the following basic principles to be applied where the information available to a decision-maker falls short of what is needed for a clear decision one way or the other.

> "(1) Facts which may reasonably be supposed to be within the claimant's own knowledge are for the claimant to supply at each stage in the inquiry.
> (2) But the claimant must be given a reasonable opportunity to supply them. Knowledge as to the information that is needed to deal with his claim lies with the department, not with him.
> (3) So it is for the department to ask the relevant questions. The claimant is not to be faulted if the relevant questions to show whether or not the claim is excluded by the Regulations were not asked.
> (4) The general rule is that it is for the party who alleges an affirmative to make good his allegation. It is also a general rule that he who desires to take advantage of an exception must bring himself within the provisions of the exception. As Lord Wilberforce observed, exceptions are to be set up by those who rely on them: *Nimmo v Alexander Cowan & Sons Ltd* [1968] A.C. 107, 130."

It is suggested that the tribunal in *Kerr* would not necessarily have been obliged to determine the case in the claimant's favour when the case first came before them. The inquisitorial role of tribunals obliges them to ask questions that the Secretary of State should have asked but has not *(R(IS) 11/99)*. It would have been open to the tribunal to ask the claimant whether he knew the dates of birth of his brother and sister and, if the answer was in the affirmative, to give the department the opportunity of investigating the matter further. However, the question whether to adjourn in those circumstances is a matter within the discretion of the tribunal and the department cannot expect always to be given a chance to do something it could perfectly well have done earlier. By the time *Kerr* reached the courts, it was doubtless felt to be a bit late for the department to be making further enquiries.

Kerr was decided in the context of a claim. It is suggested, however, that it is reasonably clear that, on an appeal against a supersession decision made on the Secretary of State's own initiative, it is the Secretary of State who must bear the burden of ignorance as to whether there are grounds for supersession because it is he who must assert that there are grounds for supersession.

In the light of *Kerr*, it was held in *CIS/213/2004* that, where a question of French law arose when considering a claimant's possible interest in a property in France, it was reasonable to require the Secretary of State to obtain the necessary evidence of French law. (Questions of foreign law are treated as question of fact as to which expert witnesses may give evidence.)

The effect of the tribunal having an inquisitorial role was considered by a Tribunal of Commissioners in *R(IS) 17/04*. In 2002, the Secretary of State had superseded awards of benefit from 1988, amounting to some £30,000. The claimant appealed and the Secretary of State made a written submission and produced a considerable amount of evidence. A tribunal chairman directed that a presenting officer attend the hearing to put the Secretary of State's case. In the event, two investigating officers attended as witnesses but there was no presenting officer and a short adjournment established that none would attend. On the basis that the burden of proof lay on the Secretary of State and that the written material was not sufficient in the light of the specific direction that there be a presenting officer, the tribunal allowed the claimant's appeal without putting to her the Secretary of State's case. The Tribunal of Commissioners held the tribunal to have erred. The written material had been sufficient to raise a case for the claimant to answer and the inquisitorial role of the tribunal required the tribunal "to ascertain and determine the true amount of social security benefit to which the claimant was properly entitled", which, once the tribunal had decided not to adjourn, entailed putting the case raised by the Secretary of State's written material to the claimant and enabling her representative to question the witnesses. The Tribunal of Commissioners rejected a submission that a tribunal could not act fairly if it "descended into the arena" and they referred to another decision of a Tribunal of Commissioners, *R(S) 4/82*, where it was said that it was legitimate for a tribunal to put questions, even probing questions, to a claimant to deal with the obvious points that arose on an appeal. However, questions from a tribunal have to be put carefully and phrased neutrally and a tribunal judge must avoid the risk described in *Southwark LBC v Kofi-Adu* [2006] EWCA Civ 281 that his descent into the arena "may so hamper his ability properly to evaluate and weigh the evidence before him as to impair his judgment, and may *for that reason* render the trial unfair" (emphasis of the Court of Appeal). Plainly it is better that the Secretary of State be represented in highly contentious or complex cases and the Tribunal of Commissioners recorded both the Secretary of State's declared policy "to appear by way of a presenting officer at every tribunal hearing where the tribunal had made a direction requiring a presenting officer to attend" and the Secretary of State's acceptance of a recommendation of the National Audit Office that he should himself identify complex cases where spending money on presenting officers might achieve greater financial savings.

The Tribunal of Commissioners cited with approval *CI/1021/2001*, where it was held that a tribunal is not entitled to rely upon a "failure to discharge the burden of proof as a substitute for a proper enquiry where there is evidence that there is something into which there needs to be an enquiry". A similar approach led a Tribunal of Commissioners in Northern Ireland to hold a tribunal to have erred when, at a "paper hearing", they had incomplete evidence that raised important issues it could not answer and they failed to adjourn in order to give the claimant the opportunity of attending (*R1/02(IB)*). However, it does not follow from *R(IS) 17/04* that decision-making bodies need make no effort to present evidence to a tribunal. In *CTC/2090/2004*, the Board of Inland Revenue failed to provide any evidence to a tribunal on the question whether the claimant or his ex-wife had the main responsibility for their daughter. That was important because it determined which of the parents was entitled to child tax credit. Both of the parents had claimed child tax credit and it had been awarded to the claimant's ex-wife. The Board did not ask for an adjournment and did not even send an officer to the hearing. The tribunal heard evidence from the claimant as to which parent had the main responsibility for the child and allowed his appeal. The Board appealed on the ground that its position was neutral and that as child tax credit could not be awarded to both parents, the tribunal's inquisitorial jurisdiction required it to summons the claimant's ex-wife to provide evidence against the claimant in her interest. The Commissioner gave that argument short shrift. Being neutral did not justify inactivity on the Board's part. In the light of *Kerr*, it had been the Board's duty to investigate the cases of both parents properly and avoid inconsistent decisions, which clearly meant enquiring themselves into the question of which parent had the main responsibility. However, the tribunal's decision would not be binding on the claimant's ex-wife and the tribunal had been entitled to assume that the Board was content for the claimant's appeal to be determined without information being obtained from his ex-wife. In other words, the tribunal's inquisitorial duty in respect of the father's claim had been satisfied by obtaining relevant evidence from him.

What, however, is made plain in *R(IS) 17/04* is that the inquisitorial role of the tribunal is not brought into play only for the purpose of assisting a claimant. A tribunal is part of the machinery for determining the true entitlement of a claimant. It follows that a tribunal is at liberty to follow its own view of a case even if that does not coincide with the view of either the claimant or the Secretary of State (*R. v Deputy Industrial Injuries Commissioner, Ex p. Moore* [1965] 1 Q.B. 456 (C.A.) (also reported as an appendix to *R(I) 4/65*)). Where medical issues arise in a case, a tribunal will often have a medically qualified practitioner among its members. It is entitled to rely on its own medical expertise and will not routinely obtain medical evidence from a claimant's doctor, even if a claimant asks it to do so, although it has power to obtain a medical report (see s.20).

However, there are limits to the inquisitorial rule of the First-tier Tribunal. In *JB v SSWP* [2009] UKUT 61 (AAC), the chairman of the appeal tribunal had personally telephoned a doctor's surgery to check the authenticity of documents that had been produced by a claimant. It was held that the chairman had "stopped being a judge and become both an investigator and a witness" and that, as the claimant had already been given an opportunity to prove the authenticity of the documents, the tribunal should either have proceeded on the basis that she had failed to prove their authenticity or have set in motion enquiries by a third person, possibly the tribunal's clerk.

Evidence

5.9 It may be arguable that the emphasis in *Kerr* on the duty of the department to cooperate in the investigation of cases has some implications for the standard of evidence that should be expected from the department so far as its own records are concerned. In *R(IS) 11/92*, the Commissioner held that no adverse inference was to be drawn against the department where it had destroyed documents in a general "weeding" programme rather with any specific intention of destroying evidence. However, it may be suggested that a tribunal should not be quick to disbelieve a claimant where the department's inability to produce contrary evidence is due to the reckless weeding of documents that should have been seen to be relevant to foreseeable proceedings. Even more is that true when documents have been destroyed while a case has been pending. In *Post Office Counters Ltd v Mahida* [2003] EWCA Civ 1583, the Court of Appeal held a judge to have erred in allowing the Post Office to rely on secondary evidence when the defendant's ability to challenge it had been undermined by the Post Office's own loss or destruction of original documents before proceedings were brought but when proceedings might have been contemplated. On the other hand, secondary evidence of the terms of a decision is acceptable where there were plainly grounds for a decision that produced the outcome that had been achieved, particularly as the law generally presumes, in the absence of evidence to the contrary, that that which ought to have been done has in fact been done (*CIB/3838/2003*). Similarly, it may be inferred from a record that a document has been "issued" that it was actually posted (*Secretary of State for Work and Pensions v Roach* [2007] EWCA Civ 1746 (reported as *R(CS) 4/07*)). In *CIB/62/2008*, the Commissioner refused leave to appeal because the claimant had delayed making an application for over six months, with the result that the tribunal's file, which would probably have contained evidence that would either have corroborated the claimant's claim that he had asked for an oral hearing and not been granted one or would have contradicted it, had been destroyed. As the claimant was largely to blame for the lack of evidence, the Commissioner held that he would be unable to overcome the presumption that procedures had been properly followed.

In *CCS/3757/2004*, the Commissioner points out that a failure to provide evidence does not necessarily justify the drawing of an adverse inference against the person who should have provided the evidence. All the circumstances and the other evidence that is available must be considered. It may be particularly relevant to consider whether the failure to produce evidence might have been due to it being unfavourable to the party concerned. In many cases, a failure to produce evidence merely justifies a conclusion that there is no, or no adequate, evidence on a particular point, which will then fall to be determined against the person who bears the "burden of collective ignorance" (see *Kerr*, above). That is not quite the same as drawing an adverse inference, which involves making a positive finding against the party concerned. However, the effect will be much the same in many cases and, where it is not, it will often be appropriate to draw an adverse inference, which *Kerr* makes clear is permissible. Thus, for instance, a claimant's failure to produce evidence of the amount of her income following a clear request may well justify a positive finding that she receives income at a level that makes her ineligible for benefit *(R(H) 3/05)*. *CCS/3757/2004*, however, emphasises the need to consider any other evidence in the case before going so far as to draw an adverse inference. Note, also, that providing evidence late is unlikely to justify the drawing of an adverse inference, unless it justifies ignoring the evidence altogether (see *CIB/4253/2004*).

Tribunals are not bound by the common law rules of evidence and so, in *CDLA/2014/2004*, a tribunal erred in refusing to allow a disability consultant to give evidence of his opinion. However, it does not follow that those rules of evidence have no relevance at all. Tribunals have no power to override any privilege of a witness not to give evidence, such as the privilege attaching to solicitor-client communications and the privilege against self-incrimination. Furthermore, the common law rules of evidence may be relevant in the evaluation of evidence because the considerations which have led to the evidence being inadmissible often mean that it has little weight. Thus, in *CDLA/2014/2004*, there might have been good reasons for treating the disability consultant's evidence with caution, but it was wrong to refuse to consider it at all. Similarly, in *R(IB) 7/05*, the Commissioner held that it was not necessary for the Secretary of State to follow the certification procedure under s.7 of the under the Electronic Communications Act 2000 when there was a challenge to the authenticity of an electronic signature. This approach has also been taken in relation to evidence gathered through surveillance. The conduct of surveillance is governed by the Regulation of Investigatory Powers Act 2000. Evidence gained by illegal surveillance is not inadmissible, although the circumstances in which evidence is obtained illegally may make it of little weight (*CIS/1481/2006*, in which the Commissioner criticised the Department for Work and Pensions for refusing to provide the evidence gathered in the surveillance upon which the reports of the surveillance were based). It is also not necessarily a breach of the rules of natural justice to admit a witness statement from an investigator where the investigator is not present at the hearing and so cannot be questioned, although, if contested, such evidence is clearly likely to be given less weight than evidence that has been tested through cross-examination (*CSIS/21/2008*) and, particularly where a great deal of money is at stake, the tribunal may require the witnesses to attend, as was done in *R(IS) 17/04*).

If a tribunal directs any body (including an agency of the Department for Work and Pensions) to disclose information in its possession, that body may not rely on the Data Protection Act 1998 to justify ignoring the direction, because s.35(1) provides that "[p]ersonal data are exempt from the non-disclosure proceedings where disclosure is required by or under any enactment, by any rule of law or by order of a court". If the body considers that the material should not be disclosed, its remedy lies in an application to the tribunal for a variation of the direction (*Regina (Davies) v The Commissioners Office and the Child Support Agency* [2008] EWHC 334 (Admin)).

Disability consultants are now relied upon not just by claimants but also by the Secretary of State. An "approved disability analyst" may be a doctor but alternatively may be another health care professional who has received special training to make an assessment of the disabling effects of an impairment and relate this to the relevant legislation in order to provide advice or reports for those making decisions on behalf of the Secretary of State (see ss.19 and 39). Even where such analysts have not examined a claimant, their opinions may be taken into account as evidence, provided the tribunal can identify the factual basis on which any opinion was given. It will usually also be necessary for the tribunal to know the professional qualification and areas of expertise of the analyst so that the weight to be attached to any particular aspect of the report may be assessed (*CDLA/2466/2007*).

In *CCS/3749/2003*, it was held that a tribunal should refuse to consider any information about proceedings relating to children of a court sitting in private (because use of the information by a party is potentially a contempt of court) but was entitled to hear evidence about ancillary relief proceedings that had taken in place in private. The distinction arises because it is not a contempt of court to disclose to a tribunal information about proceedings before a court sitting in private unless the case comes within one of the categories specified in s.12(1)(a) to (d) of the Administration of Justice Act 1960, or the court has expressly prohibited publication of the information under s.12(1)(e) of that Act (*AF Noonan Ltd v Bournemouth and Boscombe AFC* [2007] EWCA Civ 848; [2007] 1 W.L.R. 2614). However, evidence disclosed to a court sitting in private may be regarded as confidential and should not usually be disclosed without the permission of the court (*CCS/3749/2003*), although permission is not difficult to obtain if the relevant document really is relevant to an issue before a tribunal (*CCS/1495/2005*). Rule 10.21A(2) of the Family Proceedings Rules 1991, as amended, makes it unnecessary (subject to a court's direction) for the court's permission to be obtained if a party wishes to disclose information relating to ancillary relief proceedings held in private to a tribunal hearing a child support appeal. No similar provision has been made in respect of social security cases, where the issue is less likely to arise, but, in *CCR/3425/2003*, the Commissioner held that a tribunal did not err in considering medical reports that a compensator seeking to avoid liability under the Social Security (Recovery of Benefits) Act 1997 had obtained in civil proceedings brought by the claimant and had disclosed to the Secretary of State.

In *R(DLA) 3/99*, the Commissioner held that it was wrong for a tribunal to accept evidence of an examining medical practitioner on the basis that it must normally prevail over other evidence, even though in practice, once a proper weighing exercise had been carried out without giving an examining medical practitioner's evidence any special weight, the examining medical practitioner's evidence might be accepted in the majority of cases. Equally, a tribunal is not entitled to arrive at a view of the credibility of the claimant and then, as a separate exercise, consider whether that finding might be shifted by the expert evidence available; "The evidence has to be looked at as a whole" (*AJ (Cameroon) v Secretary of State for the Home Department* [2007] EWCA Civ 373). Even where an expert's evidence is found convincing, a tribunal is entitled to accept evidence from a blameless and honest witness that conflicts with it and conclude that, although it cannot identify an error in the expert's evidence, some such error must exist (*Armstrong v First York Ltd* [2005] EWCA Civ 277; [2005] 1 W.L.R. 2751). In *CIB/3074/2003*, the Commissioner suggested that a distinction could be drawn in some cases between the weight to be given to clinical findings of an examining medical officer and the weight to be given to his or her assessment as to the claimant's capabilities in the light of those findings.

"13. In *CIB/15663/1996*, deputy Commissioner Fellner (as she then was) stated that a tribunal was entitled to give full weight to an examining medical officer's findings. A tribunal should of course give full weight to all the evidence, but may often be justified in regarding clinical findings of an examining medical officer as reliable, although even clinical findings should not be regarded as conclusive and may in some cases be displaced by other evidence. However, the impact of any given degree of loss of function will vary from claimant to claimant. In some cases (such as incontinence) a clinical examination will often give very little indication of the extent of impairment of the activities which need to be considered in carrying out the personal capability assessment, although in such cases the examining medical practitioner will often be able to make an informed assessment of the degree of impairment on the basis of the claimant's medical history and other evidence of functional ability. The examining medical officer's choice of a descriptor will therefore generally require the exercise of judgment to a greater or lesser degree, and a tribunal may therefore not necessarily give the same weight to an examining medical officer's choice of descriptors as it does to clinical findings on examination."

In *R(DLA) 3/06*, the foster parent and appointee of the 12-year old claimant, who was alleged to have learning difficulties and behavioural problems, did not arrange for her to attend the hearing to give oral evidence, despite a summons. The Tribunal of Commissioners said:

"[W]e consider the approach of the tribunal to the child claimant—in summonsing the child to give evidence, and then in drawing an adverse inference from the fact that she did not attend (despite the view of the local authority, her carer and a clinical psychologist that her attendance might have an adverse effect upon her)—was inappropriate and unlawful as breaching the claimant's right to a fair hearing."

The Tribunal of Commissioners gave general guidance as to the circumstances in which a child's evidence should be heard (see the note r.27 of the Tribunal Procedure (First-tier Tribunal) (Social Entitlement Chamber) Rules 2008).

Use of the tribunal's own expertise or observations

Where a tribunal raises a new issue, fairness requires that the parties have the opportunity to comment on it. If the tribunal includes a doctor among its members and the doctor puts a different interpretation on the same clinical findings from that advanced in a report before the tribunal, it may be impossible for the parties or their representatives effectively to comment without seeking medical advice and, therefore, an adjournment may be necessary (*Evans v Secretary of State for Social Security* (reported as *R(I) 5/94*), *Butterfield v Secretary of State for Defence* [2002] EWHC 2247 (Admin)). However, in most other cases, it will be reasonable to expect the parties or their representatives to comment at the hearing on a point raised by the tribunal, without any adjournment. Where a tribunal observes a claimant acting in a way that seems inconsistent with a claimed level of disability, it has been said that "there is usually no excuse not to put observations to a party, as it can rarely be the case that the perceived inconsistency between a claimant's evidence and what is being observed does not strike any or all of the tribunal members at the time" (*CSDLA/288/2005*). However, in *R(DLA) 8/06*, the Commissioner held that there was not always a duty to put observations to a party where, for instance, the observation merely confirmed a view the tribunal would have formed anyway. In such circumstances, it can be argued that the observation does not really raise a new issue. He also held that it was not necessary to explain the legal significance of an observation before obtaining a comment. In any event, it does not follow that a tribunal necessarily errs in law in not putting observations to a claimant even where it would be good practice to do so. As has been pointed out in *CSDLA/463/2007*, if, on appeal, a claimant does not indicate that the opportunity to comment would have led to a comment that might have made a difference to the outcome of the case (whether a suggestion that the observation was inaccurate or a suggestion that the observation was not as significant as the tribunal thought), it is difficult to see that the claimant will have suffered any unfairness. Procedural irregularities do not amount to errors of law unless they result in unfairness or injustice (*R(DLA)3/08*). | **5.10**

Relying on decisions of other bodies

The First-tier Tribunal may rely upon, but is not bound by, findings of fact made, or inferentially made, by other bodies including other social security decision-makers (*R(H) 9/04*), tax inspectors (*R(FC) 1/91*), the asylum and immigration tribunal (*R (Nahar) v Social Security Commissioners* [2001] EWHC 1049 (Admin), affirmed on a different point [2002] EWCA Civ 859) and courts (*RC v SSWP* [2009] UKUT 62 (AAC)). In *RC v SSWP*, the Upper Tribunal said— | **5.10.1**

"Tribunals must make the best findings they can on the information and evidence available to them. The information may include findings made by previous tribunals and family courts. The significance of those findings will depend on their reliability and relevance. In assessing their reliability, tribunals must consider: (i) the evidence on which they were based; (ii) the nature of the fact-finding process (for example, whether the parent was subject to cross-examination); and (iii) the evidence now available. If there is no evidence to the contrary, tribunals may be entitled to conclude that the findings previously made are sufficient and reliable in the child support context. Whether or not this is so will depend on their relevance in the particular case. In assessing the relevance of previous findings, tribunals must consider: (iv) the facts that are relevant to the issue before the tribunal; (v) the precision with which they have to be found in order to apply the legislation; (vi) whether the previous findings relate, or can be related by other evidence, to the time now in issue; and (vii) the extent to which the issues in the previous proceedings affected the evidence that was obtained or the facts that were found."

Subs. (2)

5.11   The Upper Tribunal's principal function is hearing appeals on points of law brought under s.11 from decisions of the First-tier Tribunal. In the social security field, it also deals with references of questions arising under s.4 of the Forfeiture Act 1982 and it has a "'judicial review'" jurisdiction (see. ss.15 to 21 of this Act). From April 1, 2009, it has been divided into two Chambers (see s.7) and two more are expected to be added as more functions are transferred to it over the next year. Appeals from the Social Entitlement Chamber of the First-tier Tribunal (which includes most social security cases) are allocated to the Administrative Appeals Chamber, which has its main offices in London and Edinburgh, where the social security cases are administered, and other offices in Cardiff and Belfast. Many of its cases are dealt with on paper but hearings take place at its offices and also in Manchester, Leeds and, less often, in other venues.

Although most cases before the Upper Tribunal involve issues of law, legal aid is not generally available in social security cases in England and Wales, save where they are brought by way of judicial review. Only exceptional funding, usually granted in fewer than ten cases a year, is available. In Scotland, the position is different and legal aid is generally available, even if seldom applied for.

The Chamber's website is at http:// www.administrativeappeals.tribunals.gov.uk.

Precedent

5.12   An important function of the Upper Tribunal is the giving of guidance to the First-tier Tribunal and first-instance decision-makers. It was well established that decisions on matters of legal principle of Social Security Commissioners and Child Support Commissioners in Great Britain were binding on appeal tribunals and the Secretary of State (*R(I) 12/75*). The giving of opinions on matters of law was the reason that Commissioners, and their forerunner, the Umpire appointed under the National Insurance Act 1911, were established and the binding effect of their decisions has been implicitly recognised in statutory provisions (see now ss. 25 to 27 of the Social Security Act 1998). In *Dorset Healthcare NHS Foundation Trust v MH* [2009] UKUT 4 (AAC), a three-judge panel of the Administrative Appeals Chamber of the Upper Tribunal held that the principles laid down in *R(I) 12/75* should be applied to decisions of the Upper Tribunal. Thus, both decisions of the Upper Tribunal and decisions of Commissioners in Great Britain are binding on the First-tier Tribunal and on the Secretary of State, where the decisions are on matters of legal principle.

Decisions of Commissioners in Northern Ireland are not strictly binding on the First-tier Tribunal or the Secretary of State in Great Britain but are highly persuasive (*R(SB) 1/90*) and should usually be followed as a matter of comity. Decisions of superior courts on points of legal principle must be followed by the First-tier Tribunal and the Secretary of State (*R(I) 12/75*), although this may technically be a matter of comity where the decision was made in a different jurisdiction within the United Kingdom (*Clarke v Frank Staddon Ltd* [2004] EWCA Civ 422).

Where there are conflicting decisions of the Upper Tribunal or Commissioners, a decision of a three-judge panel of the Upper Tribunal or of a Tribunal of Commissioners (which consisted of three Commissioners) must be followed by the First-tier Tribunal or the Secretary of State in preference to a decision of a single judge or Commissioner (*Dorset Healthcare NHS Foundation Trust v MH* [2009] UKUT 4 (AAC)). Generally, a decision of the Upper Tribunal in a social security, child support, war pension or armed forces compensation case that has been reported in the official series of reports currently published by the Department for Work and Pensions and The Stationery Office or a reported decision of a Commissioner should be followed by the First-tier Tribunal or the Secretary of State in preference to an unreported decision, because decisions are reported only if they command the general assent of the majority of the permanent judges of the Administrative Appeals Chamber of the Upper Tribunal or, in the past, the majority of Commissioners (*R(I) 12/75.*). However, where a reported decision has been carefully considered in a later, unreported, decision and not followed, that presumption does not apply (*R1/00(FC)*), particularly if the later decision is too recent to have been considered for reporting (*CIB/1205/2005*). Different considerations apply to decisions of the Upper Tribunal in other subject areas because the judges themselves have no role in the reporting of the decisions.

Strictly speaking, it is only that part of a decision of the Upper Tribunal or a Commissioner that is both on a point of legal principle and vital to the decision that must be followed. Other comments are to be regarded as merely persuasive, although the weight to be attached to them depends, as a matter of common sense, on the extent to which the judge or Commissioner intended reliance to be placed on them and on the extent to which they were the subject of argument before the judge or Commissioner. In *Office of Communications v Floe Telecom Limited* [2009] EWCA Civ 47, the Court of Appeal sought to discourage the giving of unnecessary guidance and said, at [21]—

"Specialist tribunals seem to be more prone than ordinary courts to yield to the temptation of generous general advice and guidance. The wish to be helpful to users is understandable. It may even be commendable. But bodies established to adjudicate on disputes are not in the business of giving advisory opinions to litigants or potential litigants. They should take care not to be, or to feel, pressured by the parties or by interveners or by critics to do things which they are not intended, qualified or equipped to do. In general, more harm than good is likely to be done by deciding more than is necessary for the adjudication of the actual dispute".

However, a lot depends on the context and, in particular, the attitude of the party, usually a public body, at whom the guidance is principally aimed. Guidance that is not strictly necessary to a decision is likely to be mere *obiter dicta* and is not strictly binding. Indeed, it is often proffered as a suggestion rather than a requirement. Provided care is taken and a tribunal is appropriately "qualified or equipped", the giving of guidance may be valuable to all concerned. The problem in the *Ofcom* case seems to have been that the guidance was on matters that had been the subject of detailed argument and could not be ignored and yet was unwelcome to the public authority that was expected to apply it. Worse, much of it was wrong.

In one case, *CDLA/2288/2007*, it was held that, where a Commissioner has made a decision on a question of fact in the light of detailed medical evidence, that decision is binding on tribunals, unless it can be distinguished or has been overtaken by later medical research which at least casts significant doubt on its accuracy. In that case, a tribunal had found that arrested development or incomplete development of the brain had not occurred in a claimant with autism, contrary to the finding made in *CDLA/1678/1997*. Certainly tribunals are entitled to apply the Upper Tribunal approach to a question of fact to similar cases where the detailed evidence available to the the Upper Tribunal is not before them and, indeed, they may err in law if they fail to provide adequate reasons for reaching a different conclusion.. However, it is arguable that *CDLA/2288/2007* goes too far in stating that decisions on questions of fact can be said to be binding.

The Upper Tribunal itself generally follows its own decisions on matters of legal principle "in the interests of comity and to secure certainty and avoid confusion". However, it recognises that "a slavish adherence to this could lead to the perpetuation of error", in a jurisdiction where most decisions are given without the assistance of legal submissions by professional representatives acting for the parties, and so a single judge will not follow a decision of another single judge if satisfied that it was wrong (*Dorset Healthcare NHS Foundation Trust v MH* [2009] UKUT 4 (AAC)). Similarly, a three-judge panel will generally follow a decision of another three-judge panel or a decision of a Tribunal of Commissioners but will not do so if satisfied that it was wrong (*R(U) 4/88*). However, a single judge will always follow a decision of a three-judge panel (*Dorset Healthcare*). This has the effect that a serious difference of opinion can be resolved by a single judge referring a case to the Chamber President with a view to a three-judge panel being appointed to decide it.

Judges of the Administrative Appeal Chamber of the Upper Tribunal will take the same approach to decisions of judges of equivalent seniority as they take to each other's decisions (*R(IS) 3/08*, where a Commissioner considered a decision of the asylum and immigration tribunal presided over by a senior immigration judge to be of equal status).

High Court judges may sit in the Upper Tribunal but are of a higher status than most judges of the Upper Tribunal. Nonetheless, where the Upper Tribunal is exercising a jurisdiction formerly exercised by the High Court, any single judge is not bound to follow a decision of a High Court judge exercising that jurisdiction before its transfer (*Chief Supplementary Benefit Officer v Leary* [1985] 1 W.L.R. 84 (also reported as an appendix to *R(SB) 6/85*); *R(AF) 1/07*). In *R(SB) 52/83*, a Tribunal of Commissioners declined to follow a decision of a divisional court (i.e. a court of three High Court judges) exercising the court's supervisory role, in circumstances where that role had since been replaced, for all practical purposes, by an appeal to a Commissioner. In *R(IS) 15/99*, it was suggested that a single Commissioner would follow a decision of a divisional court as a matter of comity but that, save where the court had been exercising its supervisory role in relation to Commissioners, a single Commissioner was not strictly bound to follow a decision of a single High Court judge. In relation to Commissioners, the breadth of that approach might, perhaps, have been doubtful in the light of *Howard de Walden Estates v Aggio* [2007] EWCA Civ 499; [2008] Ch.26 (subsequently reversed by the House of Lords [2009] 1 A.C. 39, but without reference to this issue) where the Court of Appeal stressed that inferior courts and tribunals were always bound to follow decisions of superior courts (although it was not referred to *Leary*) but the Upper Tribunal is now a superior court of record (see subs.(5)) and so the approach taken in *R(IS) 15/99* now has a sounder basis. In any event, the point only matters if the Upper Tribunal is minded to disagree with the High Court, which is rare.

Judges of the Upper Tribunal in England and Wales applying the law of England and Wales are bound by decisions of the Court of Appeal and will always, as a matter of comity and practicality, follow decisions of the Court of Session or the Court of Appeal in Northern Ireland that are not in conflict with decisions of the Court of Appeal, although they are not strictly bound by them (*Clarke v Frank Staddon Ltd* [2004] EWCA Civ 422 and *R(IB)4/04*). Similarly, judges of the Upper Tribunal in Scotland applying the law of Scotland are bound by decisions of the Court of Session and, subject to that, will always follow decisions of the Court of

Appeal in England and Wales or the Court of Appeal in Northern Ireland. Should there ever be a conflict between decisions of the Court of Appeal and the Court of Session, judges in England and Wales would follow the Court of Appeal and judges in Scotland would follow the Court of Session and the Secretary of State's decision-makers would also have to make different decisions depending on which side of the border the cases arose. Presumably steps would be taken, by way of an appeal to the House of Lords or by legislation, to remove the conflict as rapidly as possible. All Upper Tribunal judges are bound by decisions of the House of Lords. (which in October 2009 will become the Supreme Court). However, even though the Judicial Committee of the Privy Council has generally been composed of Law Lords, its decisions on appeal from overseas courts are not binding in the United Kingdom and, in England and Wales, a decision of the Court of Appeal must be followed by the Upper Tribunal even if it has been criticised by the Privy Council (*Re Spectrim Plus Ltd* [2004] EWCA Civ 670; [2004] Ch. 337).

As with decisions of the Upper Tribunal, strictly speaking, only the reasoning vital to the decision of a court is binding and other comments are not but, where those other comments are made after full argument and expressly for the purpose of giving guidance, they should be followed by the Upper Tribunal except in quite exceptional circumstances *(R(IB)4/04)*. Similarly, a decision of the Court of Appeal refusing permission to appeal to that Court is not a full decision for these purposes and, while reasons given by the Court of Appeal for refusing permission are not to be disregarded lightly, their value as precedent must be assessed taking account of all relevant factors, in particular whether the Court heard substantial argument and whether the reasons were given fully *(CCS/2567/1998*, applying *Clark v University of Humberside and Lincolnshire* [2000] 1 W.L.R. 1988, and see also *R(IS)* 15/96).

Decisions of the European Court of Human Rights must be taken into account (Human Rights Act 1998, s.2) but do not take precedence over a binding decision of a domestic court unless the decision of the domestic court predates, and cannot survive, the coming into force of the Human Rights Act 1998 *(Kay v Lambeth LBC* [2006] UKHL 10; [2006] 2 A.C. 465 as explained in *R (RJM) v Secretary of State for Work and Pensions* [2008] UKHL 63; [2009] 1 A.C. 311). Decisions of the European Court of Justice determine European Union law, which takes precedence over domestic law (European Communities Act 1972, s.2(4)) and so such decisions are always binding. Where domestic legislation is inconsistent with European Union legislation or European Union directives having direct effect, tribunals must disapply the domestic legislation *(R. (Manson) v Ministry of Defence* [2005] EWCA Civ 1678; [2006] I.C.R. 355, *R(JSA) 4/03*).

Subs. (3)

The judges of the First-tier Tribunal include all the legally qualified chairmen of the tribunals whose functions have been transferred to the First-Tier Tribunal and the members of the First-tier Tribunal include all the other members of those tribunals. The judges of the Upper Tribunal include the former Social Security Commissioners and Child Support Commissioners and the deputy Commissioners and the former presidents of abolished tribunals. Members of the Upper Tribunal (who are former members of the care standards tribunal) sit with judges hearing appeals from the Independent Safeguarding Authority, which are beyond the scope of this work. There is also a broad power to nominate judges from the courts to sit in the First-tier Tribunal and Upper Tribunal and to assign judges and members of the employment tribunal, the Employment Appeal Tribunal and the asylum and immigration tribunal to chambers of the First-tier Tribunal and Upper Tribunal and *vice versa*. For the composition of a tribunal for the purpose of deciding individual cases, see the First-tier Tribunal and Upper Tribunal (Composition of Tribunal) Order 2008.

Quite a number of medically qualified tribunal members also work as examining medical practitioners providing reports for use by the Secretary of State when determining claims. In *Gillies v Secretary of State for Work and Pensions* [2006] UKHL 2; [2006] 1 W.L.R. 781 (also reported as *R(DLA) 5/06*), the House of Lords considered whether it was proper for a person who acted as an examining medical practitioner in some cases to sit as a member of a tribunal when reports of other examining medical practitioners were being challenged by claimants. Lord Hope of Craighead pointed out that the "fair-minded and informed observer" by whose standards fairness is to be judged must be taken to be neither complacent nor unduly sensitive or suspicious and to be able distinguish between what is relevant and what is irrelevant and decide what weight should be given to facts that are relevant. He then said:

> "18. . . . A fair-minded observer who had considered the facts properly would appreciate that professional detachment and the ability to exercise her own independent judgment on medical issues lay at the heart of [the examining medical practitioner's] relationship with the [Benefits] Agency. He would also appreciate that she was just as capable of exercising those qualities when sitting as a medical member of a disability appeal tribunal. So there is no basis for a finding that there was a reasonable apprehension of bias on the ground that Dr Armstrong had a predisposition to favour the interests of the Benefits Agency. . . .
>
> "20. . . . The fair-minded observer would understand that there was a crucial difference between approaching the issues which the tribunal had to decide with a predisposition in favour of the views of the EMP, and drawing upon her medical knowledge and experience when testing those views against the other evidence. He would appreciate, looking at the matter objectively, that he knowledge and experience could cut both ways as she would be just as well placed to spot the weaknesses in these reports as to spot their strengths. He would have no reason to think, in the absence of other facts indicating the contrary, that she would not apply her medical knowledge and experience in just the same impartial way when she was sitting as a tribunal member as she would when she was acting as an EMP.
>
> "21. . . . The observer would appreciate that Dr Armstrong's experience of working as an EMP would be likely to be of benefit to her, and through her to the other tribunal members, when she was evaluating the EMP report. The exercise of her independent judgment, after all, was the function that she was expected to perform as the tribunal's medical member. Her experience in the preparation of these reports was an asset which was available, through her, for the other tribunal members to draw upon when they were considering the whole of the evidence. . . .
>
> "23. The fact is that the bringing of experience to bear when examining evidence and reaching a decision upon it has nothing to do with bias. The purpose of disqualification on the ground of apparent bias is to preserve the administration of justice from anything that might detract from the basic rules of fairness. One guiding principle is to be found in the concept of independence. . . . There is no suggestion that that principle was breached in this case. The other principle is to be found in the concept of impartiality—that justice must not only be done but be seen to be done. This too has at its heart the need to maintain public confidence in the integrity of the administration of justice. Impartiality consists in the absence of a predisposition to favour the interests of either side in the dispute. Therein lies the integrity of the adjudication system. But its integrity is not compromised by the use of specialist knowledge or experience when the judge or tribunal member is examining the evidence."

Lord Rodger of Earlsferry pointed out that the approach adopted on behalf of the claimant in that case might lead to an argument that a member of a tribunal who was disabled should be disqualified on the ground that they would be likely to be partial to the disabled person claiming benefit. He also said that "the position might have been different if there had been any reason to suppose that the [examining medical practitioners] were a close-knit group sharing an esprit de corps". Baroness Hale made a similar point and emphasised that the Tribunal of Commissioners (CSDLA/1019/1999) had rejected the suggestion that an examining medical practitioner was a "Benefits Agency doctor" rather than an independent expert adviser. Doctors frequently have to review each others' decisions. She further observed that the Benefits Agency had no particular interest in the outcome of any individual case and was not realistically in a position to influence the doctor's decision one way or the other. Accordingly, the House of Lords held that there was no apparent bias.

There is, nonetheless, a difficulty that must arise if some examining medical practitioners sit also as members of tribunals. Inevitably, there will be cases where the report of such an examining medical practitioner has to be considered by a tribunal, the chairman or disability qualified panel member of which know the examining medical practitioner because he or she has been the medically qualified member of a tribunal on which they have sat on a previous occasion. In *Secretary of State for Work and Pensions v Cunningham*, 2004 S.L.T. 1007 (also reported as *R(DLA) 7/04*) the issue was whether there was apparent bias when a tribunal had to consider a report by an examining medical practitioner who had sat 22 times as a member of a tribunal with the chairman and 14 times with the member of the tribunal with a disability qualification. The Court of Session held that there was an apprehension of bias applying *Lawal v Northern Spirit Ltd* [2003] UKHL 35; [2003] I.C.R. 856, in which the House of Lords held there to have been apparent bias where one party to proceedings before the Employment Appeal Tribunal was represented by a barrister who had previously sat as a part-time judge of that tribunal with the lay members before whom he was appearing. *Cunningham* was cited in argument in *Gillies* but is not mentioned in the speeches of the House of Lords. It is suggested that a case like *Cunningham* turns not on whether examining medical practitioners are "a close-knit group sharing an esprit de corps" but on whether the tribunal is. As a tribunal must work together in a way that examining medical practitioners do not, *Cunningham* can be distinguished from *Gillies* and it is suggested that it is unaffected by the later case. In *Cunningham*, the Court of Session declined to give guidance as to how often a member of a tribunal has to have sat with an examining medical practitioner before there is apparent bias. In *CSDLA/364/2005*, decided before the House of Lords' decision in *Gillies*, it was held that a chairman was disqualified from hearing an appeal if he had sat with the examining medical practitioner only once. However, that decision was not followed in *R(DLA) 3/07* and was subsequently reversed by the Court of Session, without reasons, when the claimant withdrew her opposition to the Secretary of State's appeal. In *R(DLA) 3/07*, the Commissioner referred to *Locabail (UK) Ltd v Bayfield Properties Ltd* [1999] EWCA Civ 3004; [2000] Q.B. 451 in which it was suggested that each case had to be determined on its facts, that any doubts had to be resolved in favour of recusal and that "[t]he greater the passage of time between the event relied on as showing a danger of bias and the case in which the objection is raised, the weaker (other things being equal) the objection will be" but held that there was a reasonable apprehension of bias where the chairman of the tribunal had sat on a tribunal with the examining medical practitioner whose report was being considered on three occasions, the last being three and a half months before the relevant hearing. The practical answer to the problem revealed in these cases is for those responsible for tribunals to ensure that medically qualified tribunal members who are also examining medical practitioners do not sit in the areas where they usually act as examining medical practitioners, so that they only rarely sit with judges and other members who might subsequently have to consider their reports.

Subs. (5)

The precise significance of the Upper Tribunal being a "superior court of record" is uncertain. It may have some bearing on the extent to which judges of the Upper

Tribunal are bound to follow decisions of High Court judges (see the note to subs. (2) above). More important is the question whether the Upper Tribunal is subject to the supervisory jurisdiction of the High Court and the Court of Session: in other words, is it possible to bring judicial review proceedings against decisions of the Upper Tribunal? This is important because there is no right of appeal from a decision of the Upper Tribunal refusing permission to appeal from a decision of the First-tier Tribunal (see s.13(8)(c)). There was similarly no right of appeal against a decision of a Social Security Commissioner to refuse leave to appeal but judicial review did lie (*Bland v Chief Supplementary Benefit Officer* [1983] 1 W.L.R. 262 (also reported as *R(SB) 12/83*)). The Government itself has admitted that it does not know the answer to the question, which is ultimately a matter for the High Court and, in Scotland, the Court of Session to determine (see the Government's Response to the Consultation Paper CP 30/07, which was published on May 19, 2008). The competing approaches were identified by the Court of Appeal in *G v Secretary of State for the Home Department* [2004] EWCA Civ 265, without any conclusion being reached by the Court. One is that judicial review lies only against inferior courts and tribunals, save where legislation provides otherwise. That approach would preclude judicial review of a decision of the Upper Tribunal. The other is that judicial review lies against any court or tribunal with limited jurisdiction, which would include the Upper Tribunal, although that in turn raises the question whether judicial review would lie only on narrow "pre-*Anisminic*" (see *Anisminic v Foreign Compensation Commission* [1969] 2 A.C. 147) jurisdictional grounds. Perhaps the most telling argument will be that it is unlikely to have been intended that there should be no way of challenging in the higher courts a decision of the Upper Tribunal in relation to a national security certificate, which is an "excluded decision" by virtue of s.13(8)(a) or (b). On the other hand, it might be thought odd that judicial review should lie against a tribunal which itself exercises a "judicial review" jurisdiction (see ss.15 to 21) although it would in fact be unnecessary for there to be the possibility of there being a judicial review of a refusal of permission for judicial review in England and Wales if an unsuccessful application may be renewed in the Court of Appeal (as is the position when the Administrative Court refuses permission). The answer may be that judicial review will lie but only on narrow grounds and perhaps not when the Upper Tribunal is exercising its "judicial review" jurisdiction. As far as England and Wales are concerned, it is expected that this issue will be resolved by a ruling by the Administrative Court in October 2009.

Members and composition of tribunals

5.13   **4. to 6.** *Omitted.*

Chambers: jurisdiction and Presidents

5.14   7.—(1) The Lord Chancellor may, with the concurrence of the Senior President of Tribunals, by order make provision for the organisation of each of the First-tier Tribunal and the Upper Tribunal into a number of chambers.

(2) There is—

(a) for each chamber of the First-tier Tribunal, and

(b) for each chamber of the Upper Tribunal,

to be a person, or two persons, to preside over that chamber.

(3) A person may not at any particular time preside over more than one chamber of the First-tier Tribunal and may not at any particular time preside over more than one chamber of the Upper Tribunal (but may at the same time preside over one chamber of the First-tier Tribunal and over one chamber of the Upper Tribunal).

(4) A person appointed under this section to preside over a chamber is to be known as a Chamber President.

(5) Where two persons are appointed under this section to preside over the same chamber, any reference in an enactment to the Chamber President of the chamber is a reference to a person appointed under this section to preside over the chamber.

(6) The Senior President of Tribunals may (consistently with subsections (2) and (3)) appoint a person who is the Chamber President of a chamber to preside instead, or to preside also, over another chamber.

(7) The Lord Chancellor may (consistently with subsections (2) and (3)) appoint a person who is not a Chamber President to preside over a chamber.

(8) Schedule 4 (eligibility for appointment under subsection (7), appointment of Deputy Chamber Presidents and Acting Chamber Presidents, assignment of judges and other members of the First-tier Tribunal and Upper Tribunal, and further provision about Chamber Presidents and chambers) has effect.

(9) Each of the Lord Chancellor and the Senior President of Tribunals may, with the concurrence of the other, by order—

(a) make provision for the allocation of the First-tier Tribunal's functions between its chambers;

(b) make provision for the allocation of the Upper Tribunal's functions between its chambers;

(c) amend or revoke any order made under this subsection.

GENERAL NOTE

From April 1, 2009, the First-tier Tribunal is organised into four chambers by art.2 of the First-tier Tribunal and Upper Tribunal (Chambers) Order 2008 (SI 2008/2684, as amended by SI 2009/196)). By art.3, there are assigned to the Social Entitlement Chamber of the First-tier Tribunal—

"all functions relating to appeals—

(a) in cases regarding support for asylum seekers, failed asylum seekers, persons designated under section 130 of the Criminal Justice and Immigration Act 2008 or the dependants of any such persons;

(b) in criminal injuries compensation cases;

(c) regarding entitlement to, payments of, or recovery or recoupment of payments of, social security benefits, child support, vaccine damage payment, tax credits and child trust funds, with the exception of—

(i) appeals in respect of employer penalties or employer information penalties (as defined in section 63(11) and (12) of the Tax Credits Act 2002;

(ii) appeals under regulation 28(3) of the Child Trust Funds Regulations 2004;

(d) regarding payments in consequence of diffuse mesothelioma;

(e) regarding a certificate or waiver decision in relation to NHS charges;

(f) regarding entitlement to be credited with earnings or contributions;

(g) against a decision as to whether an accident was an industrial accident."

Paragraph (c) will be amended from September 1, 2009 to make it clear that appeals against decisions under s.8 of the Social Security Contributions (Transfer of Functions, etc.) Act 1999 are also excepted (First-tier Tribunal and Upper Tribunal (Chambers) Amendment No.3) Order 2009 (SI 2009/1590), art.4). The excepted appeals are assigned to the Tax Chamber under art.5A. The President of the Social Entitlement Chamber of the First-tier Tribunal is His Honour Judge

Robert Martin. His Honour Stephen Oliver QC is Acting President of the Tax Chamber.

The Upper Tribunal is organised into two chambers under art.6. By art.7, there are assigned to the Administrative Appeals Chamber of the Upper Tribunal, inter alia, all appeals against decisions of the Social Entitlement Chamber of the First-tier Tribunal, all references under s.9(5)(b) by that Chamber and all judicial review cases. The article will be amended from September 1, 2009 to include determinations and decisions under the Forfeiture Act 1982 and to exclude certain judicial reviews (SI 2009/1590, art.7(c) and (e)). Mr Justice Walker succeeded Mr Justice Hickinbottom as the President of the Administrative Appeals Chamber of the Upper Tribunal on April 21, 2009. Appeals from the Tax Chamber of the First-tier Tribunal are heard by the Finance and Tax Chamber (to be renamed as the Tax and Chancery Chamber) of the Upper Tribunal (art.8). Mr Justice Warren is the President of that Chamber.

Senior President of Tribunals: power to delegate

5.15
8.—(1) The Senior President of Tribunals may delegate any function he has in his capacity as Senior President of Tribunals—

(a) to any judge, or other member, of the Upper Tribunal or First-tier Tribunal;

(b) to staff appointed under section 40(1).

(2) Subsection (1) does not apply to functions of the Senior President of Tribunals under section 7(9).

(3) A delegation under subsection (1) is not revoked by the delegator's becoming incapacitated.

(4) Any delegation under subsection (1) that is in force immediately before a person ceases to be Senior President of Tribunals continues in force until varied or revoked by a subsequent holder of the office of Senior President of Tribunals.

(5) The delegation under this section of a function shall not prevent the exercise of the function by the Senior President of Tribunals.

GENERAL NOTE

5.15.1
Any function delegated to a Chamber President may be further delegated to another judge or a member of staff, under Sch.4, para.4.

Review of decisions and appeals

Review of decision of First-tier Tribunal

5.16
9.—(1) The First-tier Tribunal may review a decision made by it on a matter in a case, other than a decision that is an excluded decision for the purposes of section 11(1) (but see subsection (9)).

(2) The First-tier Tribunal's power under subsection (1) in relation to a decision is exercisable—

(a) of its own initiative, or

(b) on application by a person who for the purposes of section 11(2) has a right of appeal in respect of the decision.

(3) Tribunal Procedure Rules may—

(a) provide that the First-tier Tribunal may not under subsection (1) review (whether of its own initiative or on application under subsection (2)(b)) a decision of a description specified for the purposes of this paragraph in Tribunal Procedure Rules;

(b) provide that the First-tier Tribunal's power under subsection (1) to review a decision of a description specified for the purposes of this paragraph in Tribunal Procedure Rules is exercisable only of the tribunal's own initiative;

(c) provide that an application under subsection (2)(b) that is of a description specified for the purposes of this paragraph in Tribunal Procedure Rules may be made only on grounds specified for the purposes of this paragraph in Tribunal Procedure Rules;

(d) provide, in relation to a decision of a description specified for the purposes of this paragraph in Tribunal Procedure Rules, that the First-tier Tribunal's power under subsection (1) to review the decision of its own initiative is exercisable only on grounds specified for the purposes of this paragraph in Tribunal Procedure Rules.

(4) Where the First-tier Tribunal has under subsection (1) reviewed a decision, the First-tier Tribunal may in the light of the review do any of the following—

(a) correct accidental errors in the decision or in a record of the decision;

(b) amend reasons given for the decision;

(c) set the decision aside.

(5) Where under subsection (4)(c) the First-tier Tribunal sets a decision aside, the First-tier Tribunal must either—

(a) re-decide the matter concerned, or

(b) refer that matter to the Upper Tribunal.

(6) Where a matter is referred to the Upper Tribunal under subsection (5)(b), the Upper Tribunal must re-decide the matter.

(7) Where the Upper Tribunal is under subsection (6) re-deciding a matter, it may make any decision which the First-tier Tribunal could make if the First-tier Tribunal were re-deciding the matter.

(8) Where a tribunal is acting under subsection (5)(a) or (6), it may make such findings of fact as it considers appropriate.

(9) This section has effect as if a decision under subsection (4)(c) to set aside an earlier decision were not an excluded decision for the purposes of section 11(1), but the First-tier Tribunal's only power in the light of a review under subsection (1) of a decision under subsection (4)(c) is the power under subsection (4)(a).

(10) A decision of the First-tier Tribunal may not be reviewed under subsection (1) more than once, and once the First-tier Tribunal has decided that an earlier decision should not be reviewed under subsection (1) it may not then decide to review that earlier decision under that subsection.

(11) Where under this section a decision is set aside and the matter concerned is then re-decided, the decision set aside and the decision made in re-deciding the matter are for the purposes of subsection (10) to be taken to be different decisions.

GENERAL NOTE

This convoluted section replaces s.13(2) of the Social Security Act 1998. Note that, s.13(3) of the 1998 Act remains in place.   5.17

Subss. (1) to (3)

At first sight, this section provides a very broad power to review a decision. However, Tribunal Procedure Rules have the effect of restricting the grounds of   5.18

review in social security cases to errors of law and they provide for a combined application for review and application for permission for review, so that the circumstances in which there may be a review are similar to those that formerly existed is under s.13(2) of the 1998 Act. (As decisions in respect of criminal injuries compensation and asylum support are excluded decisions, there is no power of review in such cases.)

See rr.39 and 40 of the Tribunal Procedure (First-tier Tribunal) (Social Entitlement Chamber) Rules 2008.

Subs. (4)

5.19
Note that, upon a review, the tribunal is not limited to setting aside its decision but may instead correct its decision or amend its reasons.

The power to correct decisions overlaps with the power there will be in Tribunal Procedure Rules (see para.15(1) of Sch.5) and, in view of subs.(10), it may be important to identify which of the two powers is being exercised.

The power to amend reasons may be useful where the tribunal has simply failed to explain part of its reasoning but it is suggested that it would not be appropriate for a tribunal to use this power to reject a new point raised in the application for review when it had not originally considered it. It is suggested that the better approach in those circumstances would be to refuse to review the decision, and to refuse permission to appeal, on the ground that the new point would have made no difference. Presumably only the particular judge and members (if any) who made the original decision will be entitled to add anything substantial to the reasons.

Subss. (5) (b), (6) and (7)

5.20
It may be appropriate to set aside a decision and then refer the case to the Upper Tribunal if it is clear that the decision is wrong on one ground but the case raises another point that merits the attention of the Upper Tribunal and will arise whatever findings are made when re-deciding the case. However, it is suggested that it will generally be preferable for the First-tier Tribunal to re-decide a case and to leave the unsuccessful party to consider whether to appeal when reasons for the new decision have been given.

Subs. (8)

5.21
This tends to suggest that there need not be complete rehearing if the reason for a decision being set aside does not vitiate findings made as part of the original decision. If this is so, it may be appropriate in some cases (subject to the views of the parties) for a judge setting aside a decision on the papers to give a new decision straightaway on the basis that it is clear what decision the tribunal should have given on its findings of fact. However, this may be impossible where s.13(3) of the 1998 Act requires the case to be referred to a differently constituted First-tier Tribunal.

Subs. (9)

5.22
Presumably this subsection was included in case the power under para.15(1) of Sch.5 was not fully exercised. It enables a correction of a decision under subs.(4)(c) to set aside a decision.

Subss. (10) and (11)

5.23
If a decision is corrected under subs.(4)(a) or amended reasons are given under subs.(4)(b), there can be no further review of that decision, although there seems no reason why there should not be a correction under the separate power in r.36 of the Tribunal Procedure (First-tier Tribunal) (Social Entitlement Chamber) Rules 2008. The lack of any further power of review makes it particularly important for the tribunal to obtain the views of the other parties before amending the reasons for a decision.

There can also be no review once there has been a refusal to review. Rule 39(2) has the effect that a tribunal refusing to review a decision will automatically consider whether to grant permission to appeal. The restriction imposed by subs.(10) is unfortunate if two parties apply for a review and the less meritorious application is rejected before the second application is received.

However, where a decision is set aside under subs.(4)(c), a decision substituted for it under subs.(5)(a) is treated as a different decision and may itself be reviewed. It is also the substituted decision against which any appeal must be brought because the decision that has been set aside is an "excluded decision" under s.11(5)(e).

Review of decision of Upper Tribunal

10.—(1) The Upper Tribunal may review a decision made by it on a matter in a case, other than a decision that is an excluded decision for the purposes of section 13(1) (but see subsection (7)).

(2) The Upper Tribunal's power under subsection (1) in relation to a decision is exercisable—

(a) of its own initiative, or

(b) on application by a person who for the purposes of section 13(2) has a right of appeal in respect of the decision.

(3) Tribunal Procedure Rules may—

(a) provide that the Upper Tribunal may not under subsection (1) review (whether of its own initiative or on application under subsection (2)(b)) a decision of a description specified for the purposes of this paragraph in Tribunal Procedure Rules;

(b) provide that the Upper Tribunal's power under subsection (1) to review a decision of a description specified for the purposes of this paragraph in Tribunal Procedure Rules is exercisable only of the tribunal's own initiative;

(c) provide that an application under subsection (2)(b) that is of a description specified for the purposes of this paragraph in Tribunal Procedure Rules may be made only on grounds specified for the purposes of this paragraph in Tribunal Procedure Rules;

(d) provide, in relation to a decision of a description specified for the purposes of this paragraph in Tribunal Procedure Rules, that the Upper Tribunal's power under subsection (1) to review the decision of its own initiative is exercisable only on grounds specified for the purposes of this paragraph in Tribunal Procedure Rules.

(4) Where the Upper Tribunal has under subsection (1) reviewed a decision, the Upper Tribunal may in the light of the review do any of the following—

(a) correct accidental errors in the decision or in a record of the decision;

(b) amend reasons given for the decision;

(c) set the decision aside.

(5) Where under subsection (4)(c) the Upper Tribunal sets a decision aside, the Upper Tribunal must re-decide the matter concerned.

(6) Where the Upper Tribunal is acting under subsection (5), it may make such findings of fact as it considers appropriate.

(7) This section has effect as if a decision under subsection (4)(c) to set aside an earlier decision were not an excluded decision for the purposes of section 13(1), but the Upper Tribunal's only power in the light of a review under subsection (1) of a decision under subsection (4)(c) is the power under subsection (4)(a).

(8) A decision of the Upper Tribunal may not be reviewed under subsection (1) more than once, and once the Upper Tribunal has decided that an earlier decision should not be reviewed under subsection (1) it may not then decide to review that earlier decision under that subsection.

(9) Where under this section a decision is set aside and the matter concerned is then re-decided, the decision set aside and the decision made in re-deciding the matter are for the purposes of subsection (8) to be taken to be different decisions.

GENERAL NOTE

5.25   This section is in terms that are very similar to s.9, save that there is no equivalent of s.9(5)(b), (6) and (7). However, the power of review is even more severely curtailed, being limited to cases where the Upper Tribunal has overlooked a piece of legislation or a binding authority or there has been a binding decision of a superior court since the Upper Tribunal's decision was given (see rr.45(1) and 46 of the Tribunal Procedure (Upper Tribunal) Rules 2008). An exception is made in relation to decisions made under the Forfeiture Act 1982 where there is a much broader power of review (see r.47) because there is no power in anyone to supersede a decision of the Upper Tribunal under the 1982 Act on the ground of error of fact or change of circumstances.

Right to appeal to Upper Tribunal

5.26   **11.**—(1) For the purposes of subsection (2), the reference to a right of appeal is to a right to appeal to the Upper Tribunal on any point of law arising from a decision made by the First-tier Tribunal other than an excluded decision.

(2) Any party to a case has a right of appeal, subject to subsection (8).

(3) That right may be exercised only with permission (or, in Northern Ireland, leave).

(4) Permission (or leave) may be given by—

(a) the First-tier Tribunal, or

(b) the Upper Tribunal, on an application by the party.

(5) For the purposes of subsection (1), an "excluded decision" is—

(a) any decision of the First-tier Tribunal on an appeal made in exercise of a right conferred by the Criminal Injuries Compensation Scheme in compliance with section 5(1)(a) of the Criminal Injuries Compensation Act 1995 (appeals against decisions on reviews),

(b) any decision of the First-tier Tribunal on an appeal under section 28(4) or (6) of the Data Protection Act 1998 (appeals against national security certificate),

(c) any decision of the First-tier Tribunal on an appeal under section 60(1) or (4) of the Freedom of Information Act 2000 (appeals against national security certificate),

(d) a decision of the First-tier Tribunal under section 9—

(i) to review, or not to review, an earlier decision of the tribunal,

(ii) to take no action, or not to take any particular action, in the light of a review of an earlier decision of the tribunal,

(iii) to set aside an earlier decision of the tribunal, or

(iv) to refer, or not to refer, a matter to the Upper Tribunal,

(e) a decision of the First-tier Tribunal that is set aside under section 9 (including a decision set aside after proceedings on an appeal under this section have been begun), or

(f) any decision of the First-tier Tribunal that is of a description specified in an order made by the Lord Chancellor.

(6) A description may be specified under subsection (5)(f) only if—

(a) in the case of a decision of that description, there is a right to appeal to a court, the Upper Tribunal or any other tribunal from the decision and that right is, or includes, something other than a right (however expressed) to appeal on any point of law arising from the decision, or

(b) decisions of that description are made in carrying out a function transferred under section 30 and prior to the transfer of the function under section 30(1) there was no right to appeal from decisions of that description.

(7) Where—

(a) an order under subsection (5)(f) specifies a description of decisions, and

(b) decisions of that description are made in carrying out a function transferred under section 30, the order must be framed so as to come into force no later than the time when the transfer under section 30 of the function takes effect (but power to revoke the order continues to be exercisable after that time, and power to amend the order continues to be exercisable after that time for the purpose of narrowing the description for the time being specified).

(8) The Lord Chancellor may by order make provision for a person to be treated as being, or to be treated as not being, a party to a case for the purposes of subsection (2).

GENERAL NOTE

Subs. (1)

There is no right of appeal against an "excluded decision", for the meaning of which see subs.(5).

5.27

An appeal against any other decision lies only on a "point of law". Judges of the Upper Tribunal may therefore be expected to resist any attempt by an appellant to present an appeal on facts as raising questions of law, even if they have grave doubts about the decision under appeal. No appeal on a question of law should be allowed to be turned into a rehearing of parts of the evidence (*Yeboah v Crofton* [2002] I.R.L.R. 634). However, once a judge is satisfied that a decision is erroneous in point of law, he or she is entitled to determine any outstanding questions of fact (see s.12(2)(b)(ii) and (4)).

The meaning of "point of law" was considered by the Court of Appeal in *Nipa Begum v Tower Hamlets LBC* [2000] 1 W.L.R. 306 in a case where a homeless person appealed to the county court under s.204 of the Housing Act 1996 against a decision of a housing authority. An appeal lay "on any point of law arising from" such a decision and the Court of Appeal held that the county court had powers akin to those available on an application for judicial review in the High Court and so could quash a decision on the ground of procedural error, lack of vires, irrationality or inadequacy of reasons as well as for straightforward errors of legal interpretation.

In *R(A) 1/72* and *R(IS) 11/99*, Social Security Commissioners had made similar lists of errors that would amount to errors of law, rather than of fact. More recently, in *R(I) 2/06* and *R(DLA) 3/08*, Tribunals of Commissioners have referred to the judgment of the Court of Appeal in *R (Iran) v Secretary of State for the Home Department* [2005] EWCA Civ 982, offering a "brief summary of the points of law that will most often be encountered in practice". These were—

"(i) Making perverse or irrational findings on a matter or matters that were material to the outcome ('material matters');

(ii) Failing to give reasons or any adequate reasons for findings on material matters;

(iii) Failing to take into account and/or resolve conflicts of fact or opinion on material matters;

(iv) Giving weight to immaterial matters;

(v) Making a material misdirection of law on any material matter;

(vi) Committing or permitting a procedural or other irregularity capable of making a material difference to the outcome or the fairness of proceedings;

(vii) Making a mistake as to a material fact which could be established by objective and uncontentious evidence, where the appellant and/or his advisers were not responsible for the mistake, and where unfairness resulted from the fact that a mistake was made.

"Each of these grounds for detecting any error of law contains the word 'material' (or 'immaterial'). Errors of law of which it can be said that they would have made no difference to the outcome do not matter."

The seven points identified by the Court of Appeal and the issue of "materiality" are considered in more detail below.

Challenging findings of fact

5.28   The Court of Appeal's points (i), (iii), (iv) and (vii) show the limited grounds on which findings of fact may be challenged.

The Court emphasised what a demanding concept "perversity" was and so did the Tribunal of Commissioners in *R(I) 2/06*, citing *Murrell v Secretary of State for Social Services* (reported as an appendix to *R(I) 3/84*) in which it was said that an assessment of disablement is perverse only if it is "so wildly wrong that it can be set aside". A finding of fact is also perverse if it "was wholly unsupported by any evidence" (*Iran*) or it is based on a misunderstanding that "is plain and incontrovertible and where there is no room for difference about it" (*Braintree DC v Thompson* [2005] EWCA Civ 178, a housing benefit case in which the Court of Appeal said that a Deputy Commissioner had not been entitled to substitute his view of the facts for the view of the tribunal). It is particularly difficult to show that a decision is perverse where it required an element of judgment (such as, for instance, whether the claimant was virtually unable to walk). In *Moyna v Secretary of State for Work and Pensions* [2003] UKHL 44, [2003] 1 W.L.R. 1929 (also reported as *R(DLA) 7/03*), Lord Hoffmann, with whom the other members of the House of Lords agreed, said:

"In any case in which a tribunal has to apply a standard with a greater or lesser degree of imprecision and to take a number of factors into account, there are bound to be cases in which it will be impossible for a reviewing court to say that the tribunal must have erred in deciding the case either way: see *George Mitchell (Chesterhall) Ltd v Finney Lock Seeds Ltd* [1983] 2 A.C. 803, 815–816."

If perversity is not shown, it is usually necessary to show some flaw in the reasoning instead, either because a finding is irrational (i.e. there is something illogical in the reasoning leading to it) or because the tribunal has failed to take into account a relevant matter or has given weight to an irrelevant matter. In order to show that any of these errors has been made, it is necessary to analyse the tribunal's statement of reasons. On the other hand, merely pointing to a different analysis of the evidence from that adopted by the tribunal is not sufficient to show an error of law (*Secretary of State for Work and Pensions v Roach* [2007] EWCA Civ 1746 (reported as *R(CS) 4/07*)).

Although tribunals may be found to have erred in the way they have dealt with the evidence before them, Commissioners have pointed out that tribunals cannot be criticised for not taking account of evidence that was not before them at all. In *CDLA/7980/1995*, the Commissioner said that—

"Finality is another important principle. Parties cannot demand a rehearing simply because, at the original hearing, they failed to adduce the right evidence, failed to ask the right questions or failed to advance the right arguments."

However, the Court of Appeal's point (vii) in the *Iran* case is a limited exception to this approach, derived from *E v Secretary of State for the Home Department* [2004] EWCA Civ 49; [2004] Q.B. 1044. The strictness of the requirements listed in point (vii) for finding a mistake of fact to be an error of law has been emphasised in *Shehu v Secretary of State for the Home Department* [2004] EWCA Civ 854, where the material evidence could, with reasonable diligence, have been obtained and adduced before the tribunal and the lack of the evidence did not make the decision unfair. Where neither those conditions nor the traditional grounds identified in points (i), (iii) and (iv) are met, the only remedy for a mistake of fact made by a tribunal is an application for supersession under regulation 6(2)(c) of the Social Security and Child Support (Decisions and Appeals) Regulations 1999 or reg.13(2)(c) of the Child Benefit and Guardian's Allowance (Decisions and Appeals) Regulations 2003. The value of that remedy may be limited by the date from which any supersession can be effective.

Challenging misdirections of law

It is much more obvious that a misdirection of law (e.g. the tribunal misunderstanding or overlooking a regulation or making a mistake about the law of property), the Court of Appeal's point (v) in the *Iran* case, is an error of law. It is also a misdirection of law for a tribunal to rely upon a regulation that is ultra vires (*Foster v Chief Adjudication Officer* [1993] A.C. 754 (also reported as *R(IS) 22/93*)) or is inconsistent with European Community law (see s.2(4) of the European Communities Act 1972).

5.29

Inadequate reasons

The standard of reasoning required from tribunals by the Court of Appeal's point (ii) and the requirement to resolve conflicts (see point (iii)) is considered in detail in the note to r.34of the Tribunal Procedure (First-tier Tribunal) (Social Entitlement Chamber) Rules 2008. The reasons should be sufficient to avoid "substantial doubt as to whether the [tribunal] erred in law" on any of the other grounds identified in the *Iran* case, but they "need refer only to the main issues in the dispute, not to every consideration" (*South Bucks DC v Porter (No.2)* [2004] UKHL 33; [2004] 1 W.L.R. 1953 at [36]. In the *Iran* case itself, the Court of Appeal referred to *Eagil Trust Co Ltd v Pigott-Brown* [1985] 3 All E.R. 119, 122, where Griffiths L.J. said that, "if it be that the judge has not dealt with a particular argument but it can be seen that there are grounds on which he would have been entitled to reject it, this court should assume that he acted on those grounds unless the appellant can point to convincing reasons leading to a contrary conclusion."

5.30

Procedural and other irregularities

Whether a breach of procedural rules renders a decision invalid or erroneous in point of law is to be determined by considering whether the legislature intended that to be the effect of such a breach (*R(DLA) 3/08*, a decision of a Tribunal of Commissioners). Therefore, not every procedural error entitles a party to have a decision set aside on appeal. It largely depends on whether there was any unfairness as a result of the breach. This is point (vi) in the *Iran* case.

The old distinction between "mandatory" and "directory" requirements is no longer regarded as helpful. Instead, it is necessary to consider the language of the legislation and the legislator's intention against the factual situation and seek to do what is just in all the circumstances. This involves considering whether the procedural requirement is satisfied by "substantial" compliance with it and, if so, whether there has in fact been such substantial compliance or whether

5.31

non-compliance had been waived. If there has not been sufficient compliance and non-compliance has not been waived, consideration should also be given to the intended consequence of non-compliance because it does not necessarily follow from an applicant's failure to comply with a procedural requirement that the application is a nullity (*R. v Secretary of State for the Home Department, Ex p. Jeyeanthan* [2000] 1 W.L.R. 354).

Consideration must be given to whether the breach of procedural rules might have made any difference to the decision of the tribunal or whether a party to the proceedings has lost anything (such as the opportunity of advancing a particular argument on appeal) as a result of the breach, so that a rehearing is the only way of remedying the breach. For this reason, a breach of a requirement to keep a record of proceedings will render a decision of a tribunal erroneous in point of law if the lack of a record of proceedings makes it difficult to determine whether or not the tribunal has provided an adequate statement of reasons (*R(DLA) 3/08*). On the other hand, a failure to provide any summary of reasons in a decision notice will not render the decision erroneous in point of law because the remedy is to apply for a full statement of reasons (*CIB/4497/1998*). The most commonly relied upon breach is a breach of the statutory duty to give reasons for a decision (see the note to r.34 of the Tribunal Procedure (First-tier Tribunal) (Social Entitlement Chamber) Rules 2008), although this is considered in the *Iran* case to be an entirely separate type of error of law, perhaps because there would be a common law duty to give reasons even if the legislation imposed no duty.

When considering breaches of procedural rules, fairness is judged by reference to the three "rules of natural justice", which are that every party should have a proper opportunity to present his or her case, that there should be no bias and that a decision should be based on the evidence. Even where there is no breach of a statutory provision, breach of the rules of natural justice will amount to at least an irregularity. The scope of the rules is fairly broad but it has nonetheless been suggested that judges ought to express their decisions in terms of the parties' right to a fair hearing under Art.6(1) of the European Convention on Human Rights rather than in terms of the rules of natural justice which are apt to be misunderstood (*CJSA/5100/2001* and the linked cases *CIB/2751/2002 and CS/3202/2002*) even if the practical differences are not great. In *CSDLA/773/2004*, the judge disagreed and said that the issue was whether there had been a breach of the rules of natural justice and that any assertion that a convention right had been breached had to be raised as a separate issue. It is suggested that that goes too far in the opposite direction and that, while a Commissioner is entitled to focus on the questions whether a tribunal listened fairly to the contentions of both sides and whether it was biased, those questions must now be considered in the light of Art.6 of the Convention.

In *R. v Secretary of State for the Home Department, Ex p. Al-Mehdawi* [1990] 1 A.C. 876 it was said to be incorrect to state simply that a party to a dispute who has not been heard through no fault of his own has been denied justice. In that case, notice of the hearing had been given to the party's solicitors but they had wrongly addressed their letter telling the party of the hearing. Although the House of Lords accepted that a decision of a tribunal may be erroneous in point of law where the tribunal has been entirely blameless but there had been some fault on the part of the other party, they held that there was no error of law in that case because the solicitors had had notice. Service on a solicitor was also treated as service on a claimant in *Tkachuk v Secretary of State for Work and Pensions* [2007] EWCA Civ 515 (reported as *R(IS) 3/07*). However, in social security cases, notices of hearings and decisions are usually sent both to the claimant and any representative. In *CCS/6302/1999*, a decision was set aside because a party had not received notice of the appeal due to the Child Support Agency failing to tell the clerk to the tribunal of his change of address. In *CIB/5227/1999*, the claimant simply did not receive the letter from the clerk inviting him to seek an oral hearing and there was no fault on the part of either the tribunal or the Benefits Agency. The Commissioner distinguished *Al-Mehdawi* and did not base his decision to allow the appeal on there having been any fault of anyone (although presumably the failure of the letter to arrive was attributable to someone). He just said that there had been a fundamental unfairness about the proceedings before the tribunal. That was not so in *CIB/4533/1999*, where the claimant's representative had not been sent notice of the hearing but notice was sent to the claimant, who made a mistake about the date and appeared three days late. It was held that the claimant had not been denied a hearing, notwithstanding the lack of notice to his representative, and his appeal to the Commissioner was dismissed.

It is not necessarily a breach of the rules of natural justice for a tribunal to cite authoritative' decisions that were not mentioned during the course of the proceedings before the tribunal. The question is whether the proceedings were unfair and that depends on whether it might reasonably be considered that the case has been decided on a basis that could not have been anticipated by the parties so that they did not have a proper opportunity of addressing the tribunal on the relevant issues (*Sheridan v Stanley Cole (Wainfleet) Ltd* [2003] EWCA Civ 1046; [2003] 4 All E.R. 1181).

The rule against bias was considered in detail in *Locabail (UK) Ltd v Bayfield Properties Ltd* [1999] EWCA Civ 3004; [2000] Q.B. 451. It has the effect that, where a member of a tribunal has any direct personal interest, apart from the most trivial, in the outcome of proceedings, he or she is automatically disqualified from hearing the case, irrespective of his or her knowledge of the interest. In cases where there is no direct personal interest, the question is whether the circumstances would lead a fair-minded and informed observer to conclude that there was a real possibility that the tribunal was biased, in the sense that the tribunal member might unfairly regard with favour or disfavour a party in the proceedings (*Porter v Magill* [2001] UKHL 67; [2002] 2 A.C. 357) and, on appeal, it will be relevant whether the tribunal member knew of the connection with the party because, if he or she did not, no favour or disfavour would have been shown. It was stressed in *CS/1753/2000* that the issue was whether there was a likelihood of bias, not whether there was actual bias. Appearances are therefore important and a decision may be set aside if a tribunal member gives the appearance of having fallen asleep (*Stansby v Datapulse* [2003] EWCA Civ 1951; [2004] I.C.R. 523) but, in *Locobail* itself, it was stressed that "[t]he mere fact that a judge, earlier in the same case or in a previous case, had commented adversely on a party or witness, or found the evidence of a party or witness to be unreliable, would not without more found a sustainable objection". Judicial continuity may be positively desirable where the same factual issues arise in two separate cases and is permissible provided the tribunal approaches the second case with an open mind. Thus, it is not unlawful for the question whether an overpayment has arisen and is recoverable to be determined by a tribunal with the same constitution as one that has previously decided that the claimant was not entitled to benefit during the period in issue *(R(IS) 1/09)*, applying *AMEC Capital Projects Ltd v Whitefriars City Estates Ltd* [2004] EWCA 1535; [2005] 1 All E.R. 723). On the other hand, in *CCS/1876/2006*, the Commissioner made the point that the mere fact that a tribunal chairman is not bound to recuse himself when he has previously decided a case against a party before him does not mean that he is not entitled to arrange for the appeal to be heard by another chairman if he considers it desirable do so in order to strengthen the party's confidence in the fairness of the procedures and if undue expense will not be involved. See also *KU v Bradford MBC* [2009] UKUT 15 (AAC), where the authorities are considered in some detail.

In *Lawal v Northern Spirit Ltd* [2003] UKHL 35; [2003] I.C.R. 856, the House of Lords held there to have been apparent bias where a party was represented by a barrister who had previously sat as a part-time judge with lay members of the Employment Appeal Tribunal before whom he was appearing. *Lawal* was followed in *Secretary of State for Work and Pensions v Cunningham* [2004] S.L.T. 1007 (also reported as *R(DLA) 7/04)*, where a tribunal had relied on a medical report by an examining medical practitioner with whom two members of the tribunal had sat previously and the Court of Session held there had been apparent bias. On the other hand, in *Gillies v Secretary of State for Work and Pensions* [2006] UKHL 2; [2006] 1 W.L.R. 781, it was held by the House of Lords that there was no appearance of bias merely because a member of a tribunal also acted as an examining medical practitioner for the Secretary of State. (For further discussion of *Cunningham* and *Gillies*, see the note to s.3(3).) A long-standing personal friendship with a witness will also give rise to an appearance of bias and a judge was wrong to take into account the inconvenience to the parties in having to adjourn when he refused to recuse himself. "There was either a real possibility of bias, in which case the judge was disqualified by the principle of judicial impartiality, or there was not, in which case there was no valid objection to trial by him." (*AWG Group Ltd v Morrison* [2006] EWCA Civ 6; [2006] 1 W.L.R. 1163 at [20]). Friendship with an advocate will not give rise to an appearance of bias unless the advocate is "a domestic partner of the judge or any other person of either sex in a close personal relationship with the judge" or "a companion or employee of the judge and who lives in the judge's household" (*Guide to Judicial Conduct*, para.7.2.8, which also says that a judge should not try a case in which his or her spouse, children, children-in-law or other close relative living in the judge's household is an advocate). A judge is not normally assumed to endorse all the views expressed in publications of an organisation of which she or he is a member and so is not to be regarded as tainted by the views of other members of the organisation, provided the organisation's published aims and objectives are in themselves unobjectionable (*Helow v Secretary of State for the Home Department* [2008] UKHL 62; [2008] 1 W.L.R. 2416).

A party can waive the right to object to the lack of independence of a member of a tribunal but any such waiver must be voluntary, informed and unequivocal (*Millar v Dickson* [2001] UKPC D4; [2002] 1 W.L.R. 1615). However, in *CSDLA/ 444/2002*, it was pointed out, referring to *CS/343/1994* and *CDLA/2050/2002*, that, if objection to the constitution of a tribunal is not taken *before* a hearing, a party does run a substantial risk of being taken to have waived the right to object. It was held that the claimant in *CSDLA/444/2002* had not waived the right to object to the members of the tribunal. Although her lay representative had been aware of a relevant decision of a Tribunal of Commissioners on the point, she could not have been expected fully to understand the legal issues involved. The Court of Session did not consider the question of waiver when dismissing the appeal against the Commissioner's decision (*Cunningham* (see above)).

However, a similar point has been made by the Court of Appeal. A tribunal may legitimately give assistance to the parties by telling them what it thinks of the evidence it has heard so far, but it may not form, or give the impression of having formed, a firm view in favour of one side's credibility when the other side has not yet called its evidence on the relevant point. To do so suggests bias. However, where there is such a manifestation of bias, attention should be drawn to it straightaway, because the Upper Tribunal or a court may not look favourably on an allegation of bias if the dissatisfied party has taken his or her chance on the outcome of the case and found it unwelcome (*Amjad v Steadman-Byrne* [2007] EWCA Civ 625; [2007] 1 W.L.R. 2484).

The materiality of errors

5.32   In the *Iran* case, the Court of Appeal stressed the point that only "material" errors of law are important. An error is not material only if the tribunal "would have been *bound* to have reached the same conclusion, notwithstanding the error of law", given findings it made that are not tainted by the error (*Detamu v Secretary of State for the Home Department* [2006] EWCA Civ 604). Errors that would make no difference may be ignored and Commissioners and the Upper Tribunal have often simply dismissed an appeal despite identifying an error of law because the identified error would have made no difference. On the other hand, Commissioners and the Upper Tribunal have frequently set aside decisions on the ground of error of law only to substitute a decision to the same effect as the tribunal's. This is not necessarily inconsistent. It has to be borne in mind that, in social security cases, the Secretary of

State has wide, but not unlimited, powers to supersede a decision of a tribunal or a Commissioner on the ground of mistake of fact or change of circumstances and the way in which a decision is expressed may well affect those powers. It may therefore be important for a the Upper Tribunal to correct an error made by a tribunal even though the correction has no immediate effect on the amount of benefit payable to the claimant.

Subs. (2)

A "party" is presumably a person who was, or should have been, a party to the proceedings before the First-tier Tribunal. Note that s.13 of the Social Security (Recovery of Benefits) Act 1997 and s.14 of the Social Security Act 1998 make additional (and largely unnecessary) provision as to who may appeal to the Upper Tribunal under this section. Subsection (8) permits further provision to be made as to who may or may not exercise the right of appeal.

The scope of the right of appeal is largely defined by subs.(1). Note, however, that this right of appeal exists alongside a right of appeal on questions of fact in penalty appeals under paras 2(2) and 4(1) of Sch.2 to the Tax Credits Act 2002 and s.21(10) of the Child Trust Funds Act 2004.

It also needs to be borne in mind that, in *Morina v SSWP* [2007] EWCA Civ 749; [2007] 1 W.L.R. 3033 (also reported as *R(IS) 6/07*), it was held that a similarly broad provision conferring a right of appeal was to be construed so as to exclude appeals against certain types of decision. This approach has been taken where it has been considered that a certain type of decision is inherently unappealable (because allowing an appeal would defeat its purpose) or that an appeal is unnecessary (as in *Carpenter v SSWP* [2003] EWCA Civ 33 (reported as *R(IB) 6/03*) which was concerned with a refusal to adjourn). In the social security context, where hearings are usually very short, an appeal against a refusal to adjourn is unnecessary because, if it is unfair, it is likely to render the final decision erroneous in point of law and so a remedy lies in appealing against that final decision (see *R. v Medical Appeal Tribunal (Midland Region), ex parte Carrarini* [1966] 1 W.L.R. 883 (also reported as an appendix to *R(I) 13/65*)). However, in *Dorset Healthcare NHS Foundation Trust v MH* [2009] UKUT 4 (AAC), it was argued that the approach taken in *Morina* and *Carpenter* was not justified in relation to s.11 because specific provision has been made for the exclusion of decisions in subs.(5). It was unnecessary for the Upper Tribunal to rule on that point but it is at least possible that it will take the view that any decision of the First-tier Tribunal that is not an "excluded decision" is potentially appealable and that unnecessary appeals of the type arising in *Carpenter* can be prevented by the refusal of permission rather than on jurisdictional grounds.

Subss. (3) and (4)

Permission must first be sought from the First-tier Tribunal (r.21(2) of the Tribunal Procedure (Upper Tribunal) Rules 2008), which gives the First-tier Tribunal the opportunity to consider reviewing its decision under s.9 and so remove the necessity for an appeal. Therefore, although the Upper Tribunal may waive the requirement first to apply to the First-tier Tribunal, it will seldom do so unless already seised of the applicant's case and, in particular, will not do so as to enable the applicant to defeat an absolute time bar (*MA v SSD* [2009] UKUT 57 (AAC), disagreeing with *HM v SSWP* [2009] UKUT 40 (AAC) on the issue whether there was a power to waive the requirement).

Leave to appeal may be granted on grounds other than those raised by the parties (*Krasniqi v Secretary of State for the Home Department* [2006] EWCA Civ 391). Nonetheless, a Commissioner considering an application for leave to appeal is not bound to trawl through the papers looking for grounds of appeal that have not been advanced by the applicant (*R. (Anayet Begum) v Social Security Commissioner* [2002] EWHC 401 (Admin)). The same approach has been taken in the Court of Session in *Mooney v SSWP*, 2004 S.L.T. 1141 (also reported *sub. nom. Mooney v*

5.33

5.34

Social Security Commissioner as *R(DLA)5/04)*. In that case, it was unsuccessfully argued that a Commissioner should have granted leave to appeal on the ground that a tribunal had failed to ask a claimant certain questions. Lord Brodie regarded it as significant that the claimant had failed to aver that the questions would have elicited any favourable evidence and also that the claimant had been represented and his representative had failed to adduce the evidence).

There is no appeal against a refusal of permission to appeal. Where the First-tier Tribunal refuses permission, the remedy is to apply to the Upper Tribunal. It is not open to the First-tier Tribunal to reconsider its refusal of permission (*R(U) 10/55*) unless there are grounds for the refusal to be set aside under r.37 of the Tribunal Procedure (First-tier Tribunal) (Social Entitlement Chamber) Rules 2008. Where the Upper Tribunal refuses permission, there is no right of appeal because such a decision is an excluded decision under s.13(8)(c). It is unclear whether judicial review lies (see the note to s.3(5)). However, if the conditions of r.43 of the Tribunal Procedure (Upper Tribunal) Rules 2008 are satisfied, a refusal of permission by the Upper Tribunal may be set aside and reconsidered.

Subss. (5) to (7)

5.35   Subject to the point made in the note to subs.(2), there is a right of appeal to the Upper Tribunal against all decisions of the Social Entitlement Chamber of the First-tier Tribunal except decisions concerned with criminal injuries compensation (excluded under subs.(5)(a)), certain review decisions (excluded under subs.(5)(d)), decisions set aside on review (excluded under subs.(5)(e)) and decisions concerned with asylum support (excluded by art.2 of the Appeals (Excluded Decisions) Order 2009 (SI 2009/275), made under subs.(5)(f)).

Subs. (8)

5.36   No relevant order has been made but note that s.13 of the Social Security (Recovery of Benefits) Act 1997, s.14 of the Social Security Act 1998 and legislation concerning housing benefit, council tax benefit and child support maintenance (outside the scope of this work) make further provision as to who may appeal to the Upper Tribunal under this section.

Proceedings on appeal to Upper Tribunal

5.37   **12.**—(1) Subsection (2) applies if the Upper Tribunal, in deciding an appeal under section 11, finds that the making of the decision concerned involved the making of an error on a point of law.

(2) The Upper Tribunal—

(a) may (but need not) set aside the decision of the First-tier Tribunal, and

(b) if it does, must either—

(i) remit the case to the First-tier Tribunal with directions for its reconsideration, or

(ii) re-make the decision.

(3) In acting under subsection (2)(b)(i), the Upper Tribunal may also—

(a) direct that the members of the First-tier Tribunal who are chosen to reconsider the case are not to be the same as those who made the decision that has been set aside;

(b) give procedural directions in connection with the reconsideration of the case by the First-tier Tribunal.

(4) In acting under subsection (2)(b)(ii), the Upper Tribunal—

(a) may make any decision which the First-tier Tribunal could make if the First-tier Tribunal were re-making the decision, and

(b) may make such findings of fact as it considers appropriate.

GENERAL NOTE

Subsection (2) (a) expressly permits the Upper Tribunal to refuse to set aside a decision of the First-tier Tribunal even if it is erroneous in point of law. Certainly courts will generally dismiss an appeal on a point of law where satisfied that the result of decision under appeal was correct even if the decision was otherwise flawed. However, it can be important to substitute a decision based on correct reasoning if there is any possibility of there being a subsequent application for supersession and judges of the Upper Tribunal therefore often set aside a decision only to substitute a decision to the same effect makes explicit that an appeal need not be allowed if an error of law would not have made any difference to the outcome.

Subsection (2)(b) gives the Upper Tribunal a wide discretion as to whether it remits a case to the First-tier Tribunal or re-makes the decision itself. Relevant considerations are likely to be whether there will be a non-legal member of the First-tier Tribunal with relevant expertise and whether a further, or any, hearing is necessary. Thus, where it is unlikely that a claimant will be present or represented at a hearing before the First-tier Tribunal if the case is remitted to it and both parties have made full submissions in writing, the Upper Tribunal is likely to take the view that it should re-make the decision itself (*VB v SSWP* [2008] UKUT 15 (AAC)).

Subsection (3)(a) requires a positive direction to be made if is intended that a case that is remitted to the First-tier Tribunal is to be heard by a differently constituted tribunal. Subsection.(3)(b) makes it plain that other procedural directions may be given as well as directions under subs.(2)(b)(i) on the law and under subs.(3)(a) as to the constitution of the tribunal.

The Upper Tribunal should identify outstanding issues of fact or law before referring a case to another tribunal, because otherwise a tribunal is likely to find its role unclear (*Secretary of State for Work and Pensions v Menary-Smith* [2006] EWCA Civ 1689). To like effect, a Tribunal of Commissioners said in *R(IB) 2/07* that it was wrong to suggest that a Commissioner allowing an appeal necessarily had to refer a case to another tribunal, just because no witness had attended to give evidence before the Commissioner and there was a dispute between the parties as to the decision that should be substituted for one that had been set aside. Neither party in that case had suggested there was any material evidence not recorded in the papers or that anything turned on a dispute about that evidence. If the evidence was not in issue, the dispute between the parties was likely to be one of law that a Commissioner should resolve. Similarly, where a tribunal's findings of primary fact are adequate and the reasoning supporting those findings is also adequate, it is wrong to suggest that a the Upper Tribunal should refer the case to another tribunal to identify grounds for supersession. The Upper Tribunal can perform that exercise itself under subs.(2)(b)(ii) without making new findings of primary fact (*CDLA/4217/2001*). Moreover, a successful appellant cannot insist on a the Upper tribunal referring a case to another tribunal under para.(2)(b)(i) so that the tribunal can consider a factual case entirely different from the one presented to the tribunal whose decision has been set aside if the the Upper Tribunal is able, to give the decision the first tribunal should have given on the basis of its findings of fact, especially if the claimant was legally represented before the first tribunal (*CH/2484/2005*, a decision of a Tribunal of Commissioners subsequently upheld by the Court of Appeal, without reference to this point, in *Abdirahman v Secretary of State for Work and Pensions* [2007] EWCA Civ 657).

If a case is referred to a differently constituted tribunal, it is usual for the decision that has been set aside to be included in the papers. That is not inappropriate. Even if their findings of fact cannot be relied upon, issues identified by the first tribunal may well be of assistance to the new tribunal, although it must be careful not to be influenced by the discredited findings (*Swash v Secretary of State for the Home Department* [2006] EWCA Civ 1093; [2007] 1 W.L.R. 1264). There may, however, be special circumstances in which the Upper Tribunal setting the first decision aside considers that the interests of justice require the case to be heard by a tribunal that has not seen that decision and he or she will be able to issue appropriate directions to ensure that that happens (*ibid.*).

If a decision of a tribunal has been superseded while an appeal against it has been pending, it is necessary to consider the effect of the supersession on the appeal or vice versa. If the supersession was under reg.6(2)(c) of the Social Security and Child Support (Decisions and Appeals) Regulations 1999 (ignorance of, or mistake as to, fact), there may be circumstances in which the appeal to the the Upper Tribunal should be treated as having lapsed, particularly if the supersession has given the claimant all that he or she seeks on the appeal. If the appeal is not treated as having lapsed and is allowed, the supersession decision is generally allowed to stand, and the decision to be made by the Upper Tribunal or another tribunal following the setting aside of the first tribunal's decision is made in respect of a period ending immediately before the supersession took effect. This approach was held in *R(DLA)2/04* to be justifiable where the parties are content with the outcome of the supersession or where it is plain that supersession would have been appropriate whatever the outcome of the appeal because there had been an obvious change of circumstances or, perhaps, new medical evidence justifying supersession under reg.6(2)(g) of the Social Security and Child Support (Decisions and Appeals) Regulations 1999 in an incapacity benefit case. In *R(DLA)2/04* itself, the claimant had both appealed against and applied for supersession of a decision of a tribunal. The appeal was successful and a Commissioner had referred the case to another tribunal. The application for supersession had failed and the claimant's appeal came before the same tribunal as the remitted appeal. The new tribunal made an award on the remitted appeal and did not limit it on account of the failed supersession application. No award was made on the supersession appeal. On further appeals, the Commissioner held that that was the correct approach where, as in that case, the application for supersession had been under reg.6(2)(c) (error of fact). He advanced three rules:

"1. An application for supersession that results in a refusal to supersede the original decision does not terminate the period under consideration on an appeal against the original decision.
2. Live proceedings arising out of an application for supersession based on ignorance of, or a mistake as to, a material fact lapse when the decision to be superseded is set aside on appeal (provided that there is no further appeal in respect of the original decision).
3. Live proceedings arising out of an application for supersession based on a change of circumstances do not lapse when the decision to be superseded is set aside on appeal (but the application may have to be treated as an application for supersession of a different decision or, perhaps, as a new claim, depending on the circumstances)."

The second and third rules arise because a tribunal a hearing an appeal against the original decision must correct any error of fact in the original decision but, by virtue of s.12(8)(b) of the Social Security Act 1998, must not take account of any subsequent change of circumstances. In *CDLA/3948/2002*, a different Commissioner also held that a supersession of a tribunal's decision became ineffective when the Commissioner set the tribunal's decision aside. Latham L.J. considered that approach to be correct and refused leave to appeal (*Farrington v Secretary of State for Work and Pensions* [2004] EWCA Civ 435).

Where the Upper Tribunal sets aside a decision of a tribunal awarding benefit for a fixed period, the period in issue before the Commissioner or a tribunal to whom the case is remitted is not necessarily limited by the fact that there has been a decision on a renewal claim, although the award on the renewal claim must be treated as having lapsed if an award on the original claim is made in respect of the same period and any benefit paid as a result of the renewal claim must be treated as having been paid on account of the decision eventually made on the earlier claim (*CDLA 3323/2003*).

Right to appeal to Court of Appeal etc.

13.—(1) For the purposes of subsection (2), the reference to a right of   5.39
appeal is to a right to appeal to the relevant appellate court on any point
of law arising from a decision made by the Upper Tribunal other than an
excluded decision.

(2) Any party to a case has a right of appeal, subject to subsection (14).

(3) That right may be exercised only with permission (or, in Northern
Ireland, leave).

(4) Permission (or leave) may be given by—

(a) the Upper Tribunal, or

(b) the relevant appellate court, on an application by the party.

(5) An application may be made under subsection (4) to the relevant
appellate court only if permission (or leave) has been refused by the Upper
Tribunal.

(6) The Lord Chancellor may, as respects an application under subsection (4) that falls within subsection (7) and for which the relevant appellate
court is the Court of Appeal in England and Wales or the Court of Appeal
in Northern Ireland, by order make provision for permission (or leave) not
to be granted on the application unless the Upper Tribunal or (as the case
may be) the relevant appellate court considers—

(a) that the proposed appeal would raise some important point of principle or practice, or

(b) that there is some other compelling reason for the relevant appellate
court to hear the appeal.

(7) An application falls within this subsection if the application is for
permission (or leave) to appeal from any decision of the Upper Tribunal on
an appeal under section 11.

(8) For the purposes of subsection (1), an "excluded decision" is—

(a) any decision of the Upper Tribunal on an appeal under section 28(4)
or (6) of the Data Protection Act 1998 (appeals against national
security certificate),

(b) any decision of the Upper Tribunal on an appeal under section 60(1)
or (4) of the Freedom of Information Act 2000 (appeals against
national security certificate),

(c) any decision of the Upper Tribunal on an application under section
11(4)(b) (application for permission or leave to appeal),

(d) a decision of the Upper Tribunal under section 10—

   (i) to review, or not to review, an earlier decision of the tribunal,

   (ii) to take no action, or not to take any particular action, in the
   light of a review of an earlier decision of the tribunal, or

   (iii) to set aside an earlier decision of the tribunal,

(e) a decision of the Upper Tribunal that is set aside under section 10
(including a decision set aside after proceedings on an appeal under
this section have been begun), or

(f) any decision of the Upper Tribunal that is of a description specified
in an order made by the Lord Chancellor.

(9) A description may be specified under subsection (8)(f) only if—

(a) in the case of a decision of that description, there is a right to appeal
to a court from the decision and that right is, or includes, something
other than a right (however expressed) to appeal on any point of law
arising from the decision, or

(b) decisions of that description are made in carrying out a function transferred under section 30 and prior to the transfer of the function under section 30(1) there was no right to appeal from decisions of that description.

(10) Where—

(a) an order under subsection (8)(f) specifies a description of decisions, and

(b) decisions of that description are made in carrying out a function transferred under section 30,

the order must be framed so as to come into force no later than the time when the transfer under section 30 of the function takes effect (but power to revoke the order continues to be exercisable after that time, and power to amend the order continues to be exercisable after that time for the purpose of narrowing the description for the time being specified).

(11) Before the Upper Tribunal decides an application made to it under subsection (4), the Upper Tribunal must specify the court that is to be the relevant appellate court as respects the proposed appeal.

(12) The court to be specified under subsection (11) in relation to a proposed appeal is whichever of the following courts appears to the Upper Tribunal to be the most appropriate—

(a) the Court of Appeal in England and Wales;

(b) the Court of Session;

(c) the Court of Appeal in Northern Ireland.

(13) In this section except subsection (11), "the relevant appellate court", as respects an appeal, means the court specified as respects that appeal by the Upper Tribunal under subsection (11).

(14) The Lord Chancellor may by order make provision for a person to be treated as being, or to be treated as not being, a party to a case for the purposes of subsection (2).

(15) Rules of court may make provision as to the time within which an application under subsection (4) to the relevant appellate court must be made.

GENERAL NOTE

Subs. (1) and (2)

5.40   There is no right of appeal against an "excluded decision", for the meaning of which see subs.(8). For the "relevant appellate court", see subss.(11) to (13).

An appeal lies only on a point of law (for the meaning of which, see the note to s.11(1)) and, where the appeal is against a decision on an appeal under s.11, only if it would raise some important point of principle or practice or there is some other compelling reason for the relevant appellate court to hear the appeal (see the note to subs.(6)).

A "party" is presumably a person who was, or should have been, a party to the proceedings before the Upper Tribunal. Note that s.15 of the Social Security Act 1998 makes additional (and largely unnecessary) provision as to who may appeal to the Upper Tribunal under this section. Subsection (14) permits further provision to be made as to who may or may not exercise the right of appeal.

Where the claimant is the appellant in a social security case, the respondent will be either the Secretary of State for Work and Pensions or Her Majesty's Revenue and Customs (*not* the Upper Tribunal). Service should be effected on the Solicitor to the Department for Work and Pensions, Adelphi, 1-11 John Adam Street, London WC2N 6HT or on the Solicitor to Her Majesty's Revenue and Customs, Somerset House, The Strand, London WC2R 1LB, as appropriate.

For the powers of the relevant appellate court, see s.14.

Subss. (3) to (5)

Permission to appeal must first be sought from the Upper Tribunal, which gives   **5.41**
the Upper Tribunal the opportunity to consider reviewing its decision under s.10
and so remove the necessity for an appeal. If permission is refused by the Upper
Tribunal, permission may be sought from the relevant appellate court. In *Secretary
of State for Work and Pensions v Dias* [2009] EWCA CIV 807, the Secretary of State
had appealed to a Commissioner who found the appeal tribunal's decision to be
erroneous in point of law but substituted a decision to the same effect. On the
Secretary of State's appeal to the Court of Appeal, the respondent claimant wished
not only to support the Commissioner's decision but also, in the alternative, to
support the original decision of the appeal tribunal. It was not sufficient for her to
file a respondent's notice: she also had to seek permission to cross-appeal against
the Commissioner's decision to set aside the appeal tribunal's decision. Subsection
(5) required her first to seek permission from the Upper Tribunal (to which the
Commissioner's functions had by then been transferred), even though the case was
already pending in the Court of Appeal.

Where a case does not raise an important point of principle or practice, a party
is unlikely to be granted permission to appeal on grounds not advanced before the
Upper Tribunal if the Upper Tribunal gave a clear opportunity to argue the point
by indicating its provisional views (*Secretary of State for Work and Pensions v DH (a
child)* [2004] EWCA Civ 16 (reported as *R(DLA) 1/04)*). The Court said that it was
"of the utmost value, on an appeal from a specialist tribunal, to have the considered
views of the points at issue of that specialist tribunal before testing them on appeal".
They were not impressed by the argument that the Commissioner's decision would
remain an unfortunate precedent, saying that if the issue was that important it was
because there were many similar cases and therefore the Secretary of State would be
able to find another case in which to advance his arguments before a Commissioner
and, if necessary, the Court.

For the procedure for applying to the Upper Tribunal for permission to appeal,
see rr. 44 and 45 of the Tribunal Procedure (Upper Tribunal) Rules 2008. Note that
r.44(6)(b) provides that, where the Upper Tribunal refuses to extend the time for
applying for permission to appeal, it must refuse permission to appeal, thus satisfying the condition of subs.(5) and reversing the effect of *White v Chief Adjudication
Officer* [1986] 2 All E.R. 905 (also reported as an appendix to *R(S) 8/85*). In *White*,
it had been held that a Commissioner's refusal to extend time for applying for
leave to appeal to the Court of Appeal did not amount to a refusal of leave and was
challengeable only by way of a application for judicial review. Now, if permission is
refused by the Upper Tribunal on the ground of delay, it is possible for the applicant simply to make an application to the relevant appellant court for permission
to appeal, although that court will of course have regard to the delay in applying to
the Upper Tribunal.

For the procedure for applying to the Court of Appeal in England and Wales for
permission to appeal, see C.P.R. Pt 52. Note that a grant of permission may be set
aside by the Court of Appeal under C.P.R. r.52.9(1)(b), but such applications are
strongly discouraged.

Subss. (6) and (7)

The Appeals from the Upper Tribunal to the Court of Appeal Order 2008 (SI   **5.42**
2008/2834) provides that permission to appeal from a decision of the Upper
Tribunal to the Court of Appeal may not be given unless one of the conditions set
out in subs.(6)(a) and (b) applies. Although the Order does not say so, it can apply
only to appeals against decisions of the Upper Tribunal given on appeals under s.11,
because subs.(7) limits the order-making power in subs.(6) to such cases.

Subsection (6) and the Order do not apply to appeals to the Court of Session in

Scotland. However, the Rules of the Court of Session have been amended to have precisely the same effect, see r.41.59.

Subss. (8) to 10)

5.43   There is currently a right of appeal to an appellate court against all decisions of the Administrative Appeals Chamber of the Upper Tribunal except refusals of permission to appeal to the Upper Tribunal (excluded under subs.(8)(c)), certain review decisions (excluded under subs.(8)(d)) and decisions set aside on review (excluded under subs.(8)(e)). Insofar as it relates to the Upper Tribunal, the Appeals (Excluded Decisions) Order 2009 (SI 2009/275) made under subs.(8)(f) is concerned only with decisions made by the Finance and Tax Chamber.

Whether or not judicial review lies against the Upper Tribunal in respect of excluded decisions is a matter of some doubt (see the note to s.3(5)).

Subss. (11) to (13)

5.44   The Upper Tribunal must specify the relevant appellate court even if it refuses permission to appeal, so that the Applicant knows to which court to renew the application. In a social security case, the relevant appellate court will generally be where the claimant lives but there is a considerable element of discretion where there are more than two parties or where the claimant has moved. Relevant considerations are likely to be the convenience of the parties and whether the case raises a point of law where the law may not be the same in all parts of the United Kingdom.

Subs. (14)

5.45   No relevant order has been made but note that s.13 of the Social Security (Recovery of Benefits) Act 1997, s.14 of the Social Security Act 1998 and legislation concerning housing benefit, council tax benefit and child support maintenance (outside the scope of this work) make further provision as to who may appeal to an appellate court under this section.

Subs. (15)

5.46   In England and Wales, see C.P.R r.52.2 and PD 52, para.17.4A(1), under which "the appellant's notice must be filed within 42 days of the date on which the Upper Tribunal's decision on permission to appeal to the Court of Appeal is given", in appeals from the Administrative Appeals Chamber of the Upper Tribunal.

In Scotland, see R.C. rr. 41.2(3) and 41.20(2) to (2B) which provide a 42-day time limit from the date the refusal or grant of leave "was intimated to the appellant" in the case of decisions of the Upper Tribunal in the exercise of functions transferred from the Social Security Commissioners or where a decision of a Commissioner is to be treated as a decision of the Upper Tribunal.

Proceedings on appeal to Court of Appeal etc.

5.47   **14.**—(1) Subsection (2) applies if the relevant appellate court, in deciding an appeal under section 13, finds that the making of the decision concerned involved the making of an error on a point of law.

(2) The relevant appellate court—

(a) may (but need not) set aside the decision of the Upper Tribunal, and

(b) if it does, must either—

(i) remit the case to the Upper Tribunal or, where the decision of the Upper Tribunal was on an appeal or reference from another tribunal or some other person, to the Upper Tribunal or that other tribunal or person, with directions for its reconsideration, or

(ii) re-make the decision.

(3) In acting under subsection (2)(b)(i), the relevant appellate court may also—

(a) direct that the persons who are chosen to reconsider the case are not to be the same as those who—
  (i) where the case is remitted to the Upper Tribunal, made the decision of the Upper Tribunal that has been set aside, or
  (ii) where the case is remitted to another tribunal or person, made the decision in respect of which the appeal or reference to the Upper Tribunal was made;
(b) give procedural directions in connection with the reconsideration of the case by the Upper Tribunal or other tribunal or person.

(4) In acting under subsection (2)(b)(ii), the relevant appellate court—

(a) may make any decision which the Upper Tribunal could make if the Upper Tribunal were re-making the decision or (as the case may be) which the other tribunal or person could make if that other tribunal or person were re-making the decision, and
(b) may make such findings of fact as it considers appropriate.

(5) Where—

(a) under subsection (2)(b)(i) the relevant appellate court remits a case to the Upper Tribunal, and
(b) the decision set aside under subsection (2)(a) was made by the Upper Tribunal on an appeal or reference from another tribunal or some other person,

the Upper Tribunal may (instead of reconsidering the case itself) remit the case to that other tribunal or person, with the directions given by the relevant appellate court for its reconsideration.

(6) In acting under subsection (5), the Upper Tribunal may also—

(a) direct that the persons who are chosen to reconsider the case are not to be the same as those who made the decision in respect of which the appeal or reference to the Upper Tribunal was made;
(b) give procedural directions in connection with the reconsideration of the case by the other tribunal or person.

(7) In this section "the relevant appellate court", as respects an appeal under section 13, means the court specified as respects that appeal by the Upper Tribunal under section 13(11).

GENERAL NOTE

It was made plain in *McAllister v Secretary of State for Work and Pensions* (2003) S.L.T. 1195 that, before allowing an appeal against a decision of a person or body exercising statutory powers, the Court of Session in Scotland requires to be satisfied that there are proper grounds for doing so. Therefore a written argument must be submitted, on the basis of which the Court will decide whether the case should be listed for hearing. In England and Wales, the Court of Appeal readily allows appeals by consent, without considering their merits. It is arguable that that is not appropriate in public law cases and that the Court of Session's approach is preferable, but the contrary argument is that experience shows that decisions given when there is no real dispute between the parties are often unsatisfactory because the opposing points of view are not fully explored. There have been a small number of instances when Commissioners' decisions have been set aside by the Court of Appeal without the Court considering the merits of the appeal. Although such a decision given by the Court of Appeal is not binding on anyone other than for the purposes of that particular case (*R(FC) 1/97*), it can create difficulties because the fact that the

5.48

Commissioner's decision has been set aside plainly means that that too cannot be regarded as binding, although the Commissioner's reasoning may still be regarded as persuasive. The law is thus left uncertain.

"Judicial review"

Upper Tribunal's "judicial review" jurisdiction

5.49   **15.**—(1) The Upper Tribunal has power, in cases arising under the law of England and Wales or under the law of Northern Ireland, to grant the following kinds of relief—

(a) a mandatory order;

(b) a prohibiting order;

(c) a quashing order;

(d) a declaration;

(e) an injunction.

(2) The power under subsection (1) may be exercised by the Upper Tribunal if—

(a) certain conditions are met (see section 18), or

(b) the tribunal is authorised to proceed even though not all of those conditions are met (see section 19(3) and (4)).

(3) Relief under subsection (1) granted by the Upper Tribunal—

(a) has the same effect as the corresponding relief granted by the High Court on an application for judicial review, and

(b) is enforceable as if it were relief granted by the High Court on an application for judicial review.

(4) In deciding whether to grant relief under subsection (1)(a), (b) or (c), the Upper Tribunal must apply the principles that the High Court would apply in deciding whether to grant that relief on an application for judicial review.

(5) In deciding whether to grant relief under subsection (1)(d) or (e), the Upper Tribunal must—

(a) in cases arising under the law of England and Wales apply the principles that the High Court would apply in deciding whether to grant that relief under section 31(2) of the Supreme Court Act 1981 on an application for judicial review, and

(b) in cases arising under the law of Northern Ireland apply the principles that the High Court would apply in deciding whether to grant that relief on an application for judicial review.

(6) For the purposes of the application of subsection (3)(a) in relation to cases arising under the law of Northern Ireland—

(a) a mandatory order under subsection (1)(a) shall be taken to correspond to an order of mandamus,

(b) a prohibiting order under subsection (1)(b) shall be taken to correspond to an order of prohibition, and

(c) a quashing order under subsection (1)(c) shall be taken to correspond to an order of certiorari.

GENERAL NOTE

5.50   Sections 15 to 21 introduce the novel concept of a tribunal exercising "judicial review" powers. The provisions are set out in this work because "judicial review" proceedings in relation to the First-tier Tribunal (and perhaps some other "judicial review" proceedings in the social security sphere) are likely to find their way to the Upper Tribunal.

Section 18(6) enables the Lord Chief Justice of England and Wales or the Lord Chief Justice of Northern Ireland to issue a Practice Direction having the effect that cases falling within a specified class will be within the jurisdiction of the Upper Tribunal subject to the other conditions mentioned in s.18 being met. Such cases must be started by making an application for "judicial review" directly to the Upper Tribunal under s.16. If an application is made to the court in such a case, the court will be bound to transfer the case to the Upper Tribunal under s.31A of the Supreme Court Act 1981 or s.25A of the Judicature (Northern Ireland) Act 1978, as the case may be, both those provisions having been inserted into the relevant Acts by s.19 of this Act. Those provisions also permit any case that does not fall within a class specified in a Practice Direction but where other conditions are satisfied to be transferred to the Upper Tribunal on a case-by-case basis. Relevant considerations will include the expertise of the Upper Tribunal in those areas in which it exercises an appellate jurisdiction (including social security law), which might point towards a transfer, and the role and standing of the High Court, which might suggest refusing a transfer in a particularly novel, complex or important case. It is always possible for the High Court to transfer a case with a recommendation that it be heard in the Upper Tribunal by a High Court Judge, so as to achieve "the best of both worlds", but, even when a High Court Judge is sitting, the Upper Tribunal has no power to make a declaration of incompatibility under s.4 of the Human Rights Act 1998. Another consideration that may be particularly relevant where there is an unrepresented litigant, is the less formal procedure in the Upper Tribunal which permits, for instance, a decision to be made without a hearing. If a case that is not within a specified class is started in the Upper Tribunal in error, the Upper Tribunal must transfer it to the High Court in England and Wales (i.e. the Administrative Court) or the High Court in Northern Ireland, as the case requires, under s.18(3).

By virtue of ss.20 and 21, the position in Scotland is similar, the main difference being that cases cannot be started in the Upper Tribunal.

The main difference between "judicial review" proceedings seeking a "quashing order" or its equivalent in respect of a tribunal decision and an appeal is that the tribunal that made the decision will itself be the respondent in "judicial review" proceedings, although it will seldom take an active part and will usually leave any application to be contested by the "interested party" (who would be the respondent in an appeal). However, another major difference is that, in judicial review proceedings, the Upper Tribunal has a far more limited power to give a final decision rather than remitting the case to the lower tribunal (compare ss.12 and 17). An application for a "mandatory order" or its equivalent might be sought if it was claimed that a tribunal had failed or refused to make a decision and a "prohibiting order" or its equivalent might be sought if it was desired to prevent a tribunal from making a decision.

Application for relief under section 15(1)

16.—(1) This section applies in relation to an application to the Upper Tribunal for relief under section 15(1).

(2) The application may be made only if permission (or, in a case arising under the law of Northern Ireland, leave) to make it has been obtained from the tribunal.

(3) The tribunal may not grant permission (or leave) to make the application unless it considers that the applicant has a sufficient interest in the matter to which the application relates.

(4) Subsection (5) applies where the tribunal considers—

5.51

(a) that there has been undue delay in making the application, and

(b) that granting the relief sought on the application would be likely to cause substantial hardship to, or substantially prejudice the rights of, any person or would be detrimental to good administration.

(5) The tribunal may—

(a) refuse to grant permission (or leave) for the making of the application;

(b) refuse to grant any relief sought on the application.

(6) The tribunal may award to the applicant damages, restitution or the recovery of a sum due if—

(a) the application includes a claim for such an award arising from any matter to which the application relates, and

(b) the tribunal is satisfied that such an award would have been made by the High Court if the claim had been made in an action begun in the High Court by the applicant at the time of making the application.

(7) An award under subsection (6) may be enforced as if it were an award of the High Court.

(8) Where—

(a) the tribunal refuses to grant permission (or leave) to apply for relief under section 15(1),

(b) the applicant appeals against that refusal, and

(c) the Court of Appeal grants the permission (or leave),

the Court of Appeal may go on to decide the application for relief under section 15(1).

(9) Subsections (4) and (5) do not prevent Tribunal Procedure Rules from limiting the time within which applications may be made.

GENERAL NOTE

5.52   For the procedure for applying to the Upper Tribunal for judicial review, see rr.27 to 33 of the Tribunal Procedure (Upper Tribunal) Rules 2008. Those rules also apply to cases transferred to the Upper Tribunal under s.31A of the Supreme Court Act 1981, s.25A of the Judicature (Northern Ireland) Act 1978 or s.20 of this Act.

Quashing orders under section 15(1): supplementary provision

5.53   **17.**—(1) If the Upper Tribunal makes a quashing order under section 15(1)(c) in respect of a decision, it may in addition—

(a) remit the matter concerned to the court, tribunal or authority that made the decision, with a direction to reconsider the matter and reach a decision in accordance with the findings of the Upper Tribunal, or

(b) substitute its own decision for the decision in question.

(2) The power conferred by subsection (1)(b) is exercisable only if—

(a) the decision in question was made by a court or tribunal,

(b) the decision is quashed on the ground that there has been an error of law, and

(c) without the error, there would have been only one decision that the court or tribunal could have reached.

(3) Unless the Upper Tribunal otherwise directs, a decision substituted by it under subsection (1)(b) has effect as if it were a decision of the relevant court or tribunal.

GENERAL NOTE

Note that the Upper Tribunal has a far more limited power under s.17(1)(b) to 5.53.1
substitute a decision for a decision quashed in judicial review proceedings than it
does under s.12(2)(b)(ii) to re-make a decision set aside on an appeal. Compare
s.12(4) with s.17(2)(c).

Limits of jurisdiction under section 15(1)

18.—(1) This section applies where an application made to the Upper 5.54
Tribunal seeks (whether or not alone)—
  (a) relief under section 15(1), or
  (b) permission (or, in a case arising under the law of Northern Ireland,
    leave) to apply for relief under section 15(1).
(2) If Conditions 1 to 4 are met, the tribunal has the function of deciding
the application.
(3) If the tribunal does not have the function of deciding the application,
it must by order transfer the application to the High Court.
(4) Condition 1 is that the application does not seek anything other
than—
  (a) relief under section 15(1);
  (b) permission (or, in a case arising under the law of Northern Ireland,
    leave) to apply for relief under section 15(1);
  (c) an award under section 16(6);
  (d) interest;
  (e) costs.
(5) Condition 2 is that the application does not call into question anything done by the Crown Court.
(6) Condition 3 is that the application falls within a class specified for the
purposes of this subsection in a direction given in accordance with Part 1 of
Schedule 2 to the Constitutional Reform Act 2005.
(7) The power to give directions under subsection (6) includes—
  (a) power to vary or revoke directions made in exercise of the power, and
  (b) power to make different provision for different purposes.
(8) Condition 4 is that the judge presiding at the hearing of the application is either—
  (a) a judge of the High Court or the Court of Appeal in England
    and Wales or Northern Ireland, or a judge of the Court of Session, or
  (b) such other persons as may be agreed from time to time between the
    Lord Chief Justice, the Lord President, or the Lord Chief Justice of
    Northern Ireland, as the case may be, and the Senior President of
    Tribunals.
(9) Where the application is transferred to the High Court under subsection (3)—
  (a) the application is to be treated for all purposes as if it—
    (i) had been made to the High Court, and
    (ii) sought things corresponding to those sought from the tribunal,
      and
  (b) any steps taken, permission (or leave) given or orders made by the
    tribunal in relation to the application are to be treated as taken, given
    or made by the High Court.
(10) Rules of court may make provision for the purpose of supplementing subsection (9).

(11) The provision that may be made by Tribunal Procedure Rules about amendment of an application for relief under section 15(1) includes, in particular, provision about amendments that would cause the application to become transferrable under subsection (3).

(12) For the purposes of subsection (9)(a)(ii), in relation to an application transferred to the High Court in Northern Ireland—

- (a) an order of mandamus shall be taken to correspond to a mandatory order under section 15(1)(a),
- (b) an order of prohibition shall be taken to correspond to a prohibiting order under section 15(1)(b), and
- (c) an order of certiorari shall be taken to correspond to a quashing order under section 15(1)(c).

GENERAL NOTE

Subs. (6)

5.55   The Lord Chief Justice of England and Wales has issued *Practice Direction (Upper Tribunal: Judicial Review Jurisdiction)* [2009] 1 W.L.R. 327 specifying the following classes of case

"(a) Any decision of the First-tier Tribunal on an appeal made in the exercise of a right conferred by the Criminal Injuries Compensation Scheme in compliance with section 5(1) of the Criminal Injuries Compensation Act 1995 (appeals against decisions on review) and

(b) Any decision of the First-tier Tribunal made under Tribunal Procedure Rules or section 9 of the 2007 Act where there is no right of appeal to the Upper Tribunal and that decision is not an excluded decision within paragraph (b), (c), or (f) of section 11(5) of the 2007 Act."

The Practice Direction does not apply where the applicant seeks a declaration of incompatibility under s.4 of the Human Rights Act 1998.

Note that the class of case specified in Scotland under s.20(3) is more limited.

5.56   **19.**—*Omitted.*

Transfer of judicial review applications from the Court of Session

5.57   **20.**—(1) Where an application is made to the supervisory jurisdiction of the Court of Session, the Court—

- (a) must, if Conditions 1, 2 and 4 are met, and
- (b) may, if Conditions 1, 3 and 4 are met, but Condition 2 is not, by order transfer the application to the Upper Tribunal.

(2) Condition 1 is that the application does not seek anything other than an exercise of the supervisory jurisdiction of the Court of Session.

(3) Condition 2 is that the application falls within a class specified for the purposes of this subsection by act of sederunt made with the consent of the Lord Chancellor.

(4) Condition 3 is that the subject matter of the application is not a devolved Scottish matter.

(5) Condition 4 is that the application does not call into question any decision made under—

- (a) the Immigration Acts,
- (b) the British Nationality Act 1981,
- (c) any instrument having effect under an enactment within paragraph (a) or (b), or

(d) any other provision of law for the time being in force which determines British citizenship, British overseas territories citizenship, the status of a British National (Overseas) or British Overseas citizenship.

(6) There may not be specified under subsection (3) any class of application which includes an application the subject matter of which is a devolved Scottish matter.

(7) For the purposes of this section, the subject matter of an application is a devolved Scottish matter if it—

(a) concerns the exercise of functions in or as regards Scotland, and

(b) does not relate to a reserved matter within the meaning of the Scotland Act 1998.

(8) In subsection (2), the reference to the exercise of the supervisory jurisdiction of the Court of Session includes a reference to the making of any order in connection with or in consequence of the exercise of that jurisdiction.

GENERAL NOTE

Subs. (1)

For the procedure for transfer, see R.C. r.58.7A in relation to mandatory trans- **5.58**
fers under s.20(1)(a) and r.58(11) in relation to discretionary transfers under s.20(1)(b).

Subs. (3)

Cases within a class specified under this subsection must be transferred to the **5.59**
Upper Tribunal under s.20(1)(a) if the other two conditions are satisfied. The Act of Sederunt (Transfer of Judicial Review Applications from the Court of Session) 2008 (SSI 2008/357) specifies "an application which challenges a procedural decision or a procedural ruling of the First-tier Tribunal, established under section 3(1) of the Tribunals, Courts and Enforcement Act 2007". Note that criminal injuries cases, which are specified in England and Wales under s.18(6), are not specified in Scotland, although they may be transferred on a discretionary basis.

Note also that even cases within a specified class must be started in the Court of Session because, in relation to Scotland, s.20 does not admit to the possibility of cases being started in the Upper Tribunal as is done in ss.15 and 16 (see, in particular, s.16(1)). In *EF v SSWP* [2009] UKUT 92 (AAC), an application for judicial review made to the Upper Tribunal in Scotland was therefore held to be incompetent.

Upper Tribunal's "judicial review" jurisdiction: Scotland

21.—(1) The Upper Tribunal has the function of deciding applications **5.60**
transferred to it from the Court of Session under section 20(1).

(2) The powers of review of the Upper Tribunal in relation to such applications are the same as the powers of review of the Court of Session in an application to the supervisory jurisdiction of that Court.

(3) In deciding an application by virtue of subsection (1), the Upper Tribunal must apply principles that the Court of Session would apply in deciding an application to the supervisory jurisdiction of that Court.

(4) An order of the Upper Tribunal by virtue of subsection (1)—

(a) has the same effect as the corresponding order granted by the Court of Session on an application to the supervisory jurisdiction of that Court, and

(b) is enforceable as if it were an order so granted by that Court.

(5) Where an application is transferred to the Upper Tribunal by virtue of section 20(1), any steps taken or orders made by the Court of Session in relation to the application (other than the order to transfer the application under section 20(1)) are to be treated as taken or made by the tribunal.

(6) Tribunal Procedure Rules may make further provision for the purposes of supplementing subsection (5).

GENERAL NOTE

5.61   For the procedure in the Upper Tribunal, see rr.27, 30(2) to (5) and 31 to 33 of the Tribunal Procedure (Upper Tribunal) Rules 2008.

Miscellaneous

Tribunal Procedure Rules

5.62   **22.**—(1) There are to be rules, to be called "Tribunal Procedure Rules", governing—

   (a) the practice and procedure to be followed in the First-tier Tribunal, and

   (b) the practice and procedure to be followed in the Upper Tribunal.

(2) Tribunal Procedure Rules are to be made by the Tribunal Procedure Committee.

(3) In Schedule 5—

   (a) Part 1 makes further provision about the content of Tribunal Procedure Rules,

   (b) Part 2 makes provision about the membership of the Tribunal Procedure Committee,

   (c) Part 3 makes provision about the making of Tribunal Procedure Rules by the Committee, and

   (d) Part 4 confers power to amend legislation in connection with Tribunal Procedure Rules.

(4) Power to make Tribunal Procedure Rules is to be exercised with a view to securing—

   (a) that, in proceedings before the First-tier Tribunal and Upper Tribunal, justice is done,

   (b) that the tribunal system is accessible and fair,

   (c) that proceedings before the First-tier Tribunal or Upper Tribunal are handled quickly and efficiently,

   (d) that the rules are both simple and simply expressed, and

   (e) that the rules where appropriate confer on members of the First-tier Tribunal, or Upper Tribunal, responsibility for ensuring that proceedings before the tribunal are handled quickly and efficiently.

(5) In subsection (4)(b) "the tribunal system" means the system for deciding matters within the jurisdiction of the First-tier Tribunal or the Upper Tribunal.

GENERAL NOTE

5.63   This section, and Sch.5, came into force on May 19, 2008. The Tribunal Procedure Committee is similar to the committees that make rules for the courts, being composed mainly of judges and members of tribunals and representatives who appear before tribunals. It is to be hoped that the Committee will be able to keep the Tribunal Procedure Rules under constant review. In the past, some tribunals have found it very difficult to get changes made to their rules. Paragraphs 28 and 29 of Sch.5 enable to Lord Chancellor to disallow Rules or require Rules to be made.

There are a number of specific rule-making powers in this Act, not confined to Part 1 of Sch.5, and in other Acts but they are not to be taken to limit the generality of s.22(1) (see para.1 of Sch.5). The power to make Tribunal Procedure Rules is therefore very wide.

The approach that has been taken is to produce a set of rules for each chamber of the First-tier Tribunal and a single set of rules for the Upper Tribunal. The Tribunal Procedure (First-tier Tribunal) (Social Entitlement Chamber) Rules 2008 and the Tribunal Procedure (Upper Tribunal) Rules 2008 are set out in this volume.

Practice directions

23.—(1) The Senior President of Tribunals may give directions— **5.64**
(a) as to the practice and procedure of the First-tier Tribunal;
(b) as to the practice and procedure of the Upper Tribunal.

(2) A Chamber President may give directions as to the practice and procedure of the chamber over which he presides.

(3) A power under this section to give directions includes—
(a) power to vary or revoke directions made in exercise of the power, and
(b) power to make different provision for different purposes (including different provision for different areas).

(4) Directions under subsection (1) may not be given without the approval of the Lord Chancellor.

(5) Directions under subsection (2) may not be given without the approval of—
(a) the Senior President of Tribunals, and
(b) the Lord Chancellor.

(6) Subsections (4) and (5)(b) do not apply to directions to the extent that they consist of guidance about any of the following—
(a) the application or interpretation of the law;
(b) the making of decisions by members of the First-tier Tribunal or Upper Tribunal.

(7) Subsections (4) and (5)(b) do not apply to directions to the extent that they consist of criteria for determining which members of the First-tier Tribunal or Upper Tribunal may be chosen to decide particular categories of matter; but the directions may, to that extent, be given only after consulting the Lord Chancellor.

GENERAL NOTE

Practice Directions are a common feature in courts and have also been used in **5.65**
some tribunals. They may be directed at the parties appearing before the tribunals or to the judges and members of tribunals and the staff of tribunals. This section provides for Practice Directions to be issued by the Senior President of Tribunals (who may delegate that function under s.8) or by a Chamber President. The latter may issue a Practice Direction only with the approval of the Senior President of Tribunals.

Practice Directions may be used to supplement Tribunal Procedure Rules and a failure by a party to comply with a Practice Direction attracts the same consequences as a failure to comply with a direction given by a tribunal in a particular case (see r.7(2) of the Tribunal Procedure (First-tier Tribunal) (Social Entitlement Chamber) Rules 2008 and r.7(2) of the Tribunal Procedure (Upper Tribunal) Rules 2008.

Subss.(4) and (5)(b) provide that a Practice Direction may be issued only with the approval of the Lord Chancellor, but those subsections do not apply to the extent that a Practice Direction consists of guidance about the application or interpretation of the law or the making of decisions by judges and other members of tribunals. Practice Directions as to the criteria for deciding which judges and other members may be chosen to decide particular types of case do not require the approval of the Lord Chancellor but do require that he be consulted.

Practice Direction (First-tier and Upper Tribunals: Welsh Language) [2009] 1 W.L.R. 331, *Practice Direction (First-tier and Upper Tribunals: Witnesses)* [2009] 1 W.L.R. 332 and *Practice Direction (Upper Tribunal: Transcripts)* [2009] 1 W.L.R. 328 are set out in this volume. All practice directions are also published at http://www.tribunals.gov.uk/Tribunals/Rules/directions.htm.

Mediation

5.66
24.—(1) A person exercising power to make Tribunal Procedure Rules or give practice directions must, when making provision in relation to mediation, have regard to the following principles—

(a) mediation of matters in dispute between parties to proceedings is to take place only by agreement between those parties;

(b) where parties to proceedings fail to mediate, or where mediation between parties to proceedings fails to resolve disputed matters, the failure is not to affect the outcome of the proceedings.

(2) Practice directions may provide for members to act as mediators in relation to disputed matters in a case that is the subject of proceedings.

(3) The provision that may be made by virtue of subsection (2) includes provision for a member to act as a mediator in relation to disputed matters in a case even though the member has been chosen to decide matters in the case.

(4) Once a member has begun to act as a mediator in relation to a disputed matter in a case that is the subject of proceedings, the member may decide matters in the case only with the consent of the parties.

(5) Staff appointed under section 40(1) may, subject to their terms of appointment, act as mediators in relation to disputed matters in a case that is the subject of proceedings.

(6) In this section—

"member" means a judge or other member of the First-tier Tribunal or a judge or other member of the Upper Tribunal;

"practice direction" means a direction under section 23(1) or (2);

"proceedings" means proceedings before the First-tier Tribunal or proceedings before the Upper Tribunal.

Supplementary powers of Upper Tribunal

5.67
25.—(1) In relation to the matters mentioned in subsection (2), the Upper Tribunal—

(a) has, in England and Wales or in Northern Ireland, the same powers, rights, privileges and authority as the High Court, and

(b) has, in Scotland, the same powers, rights, privileges and authority as the Court of Session.

(2) The matters are—

(a) the attendance and examination of witnesses,

(b) the production and inspection of documents, and

(c) all other matters incidental to the Upper Tribunal's functions.

(3) Subsection (1) shall not be taken—

(a) to limit any power to make Tribunal Procedure Rules;

(b) to be limited by anything in Tribunal Procedure Rules other than an express limitation.

(4) A power, right, privilege or authority conferred in a territory by subsection (1) is available for purposes of proceedings in the Upper Tribunal that take place outside that territory (as well as for purposes of proceedings in the tribunal that take place within that territory).

GENERAL NOTE

The powers of the High Court and the Court of Session include the power to punish a person for contempt of court. Failure to comply with a direction, order, summons or citation issued by a tribunal is a contempt of court but is unlikely to be punishable unless accompanied by a warning (which is a specific requirement in respect of orders, summonses and citations issued under r.16 of either set of Rules).   **5.68**

This section gives the Upper Tribunal power to punish for contempt of court in relation to its own proceedings. Where a person has failed to comply with requirement to attend at any place for the purpose of giving evidence to the First-tier Tribunal or otherwise to make themselves available to give evidence to the First-tier Tribunal or to swear an oath for in connection with giving evidence in First-tier Tribunal proceedings, that tribunal may refer the case to the Upper Tribunal which may exercise its powers under this section as though the First-tier Tribunal had been the Upper Tribunal (see r.7(3) of the Tribunal Procedure (First-tier Tribunal) (Social Entitlement Chamber) Rules 2008 and r.7(3) and (4) of the Tribunal Procedure (Upper Tribunal) Rules 2008).

The maximum punishment that may be imposed is a sentence of two years' imprisonment or an unlimited fine (see ss.14 and 15 of the Contempt of Court Act 1981).

First-tier Tribunal and Upper Tribunal: sitting places

26.—Each of the First-tier Tribunal and the Upper Tribunal may decide a case—   **5.69**

(a) in England and Wales,

(b) in Scotland, or

(c) in Northern Ireland,

even though the case arises under the law of a territory other than the one in which the case is decided.

Enforcement

27.—(1) A sum payable in pursuance of a decision of the First-tier Tribunal or Upper Tribunal made in England and Wales—   **5.70**

(a) shall be recoverable as if it were payable under an order of a county court in England and Wales;

(b) shall be recoverable as if it were payable under an order of the High Court in England and Wales.

(2) An order for the payment of a sum payable in pursuance of a decision of the First-tier Tribunal or Upper Tribunal made in Scotland (or a copy of such an order certified in accordance with Tribunal Procedure Rules) may be enforced as if it were an extract registered decree arbitral bearing a warrant for execution issued by the sheriff court of any sheriffdom in Scotland.

(3) A sum payable in pursuance of a decision of the First-tier Tribunal or Upper Tribunal made in Northern Ireland—

(a) shall be recoverable as if it were payable under an order of a county court in Northern Ireland;

(b) shall be recoverable as if it were payable under an order of the High Court in Northern Ireland.

(4) This section does not apply to a sum payable in pursuance of—

(a) an award under section 16(6), or

(b) an order by virtue of section 21(1).

(5) The Lord Chancellor may by order make provision for subsection (1) or (3) to apply in relation to a sum of a description specified in the order with the omission of one (but not both) of paragraphs (a) and (b).

(6) Tribunal Procedure Rules—

(a) may make provision as to where, for purposes of this section, a decision is to be taken to be made;

(b) may provide for all or any of subsections (1) to (3) to apply only, or not to apply except, in relation to sums of a description specified in Tribunal Procedure Rules.

Assessors

5.71 **28.**—(1) If it appears to the First-tier Tribunal or the Upper Tribunal that a matter before it requires special expertise not otherwise available to it, it may direct that in dealing with that matter it shall have the assistance of a person or persons appearing to it to have relevant knowledge or experience.

(2) The remuneration of a person who gives assistance to either tribunal as mentioned in subsection (1) shall be determined and paid by the Lord Chancellor.

(3) The Lord Chancellor may—

(a) establish panels of persons from which either tribunal may (but need not) select persons to give it assistance as mentioned in subsection (1);

(b) under paragraph (a) establish different panels for different purposes;

(c) after carrying out such consultation as he considers appropriate, appoint persons to a panel established under paragraph (a);

(d) remove a person from such a panel.

Costs or expenses

5.72 **29.**—(1) The costs of and incidental to—

(a) all proceedings in the First-tier Tribunal, and

(b) all proceedings in the Upper Tribunal,

shall be in the discretion of the Tribunal in which the proceedings take place.

(2) The relevant Tribunal shall have full power to determine by whom and to what extent the costs are to be paid.

(3) Subsections (1) and (2) have effect subject to Tribunal Procedure Rules.

(4) In any proceedings mentioned in subsection (1), the relevant Tribunal may—

    (a) disallow, or

    (b) (as the case may be) order the legal or other representative con-
cerned to meet,

the whole of any wasted costs or such part of them as may be determined in
accordance with Tribunal Procedure Rules.

    (5) In subsection (4) "wasted costs" means any costs incurred by a
party—

    (a) as a result of any improper, unreasonable or negligent act or omis-
sion on the part of any legal or other representative or any employee
of such a representative, or

    (b) which, in the light of any such act or omission occurring after they
were incurred, the relevant Tribunal considers it is unreasonable to
expect that party to pay.

    (6) In this section "legal or other representative", in relation to a party
to proceedings, means any person exercising a right of audience or right to
conduct the proceedings on his behalf.

    (7) In the application of this section in relation to Scotland, any reference
in this section to costs is to be read as a reference to expenses.

GENERAL NOTE

Subss. (1) to (3)

    Rule 10 of the Tribunal Procedure (First-tier Tribunal) (Social Entitlement   **5.73**
Chamber) Rules 2008 provides that the tribunal "shall not make any order in
respect of costs (or, in Scotland, expenses)". By virtue of rr.10(1)(b) and (2) of
the Tribunal Procedure (Upper Tribunal) Rules 2008, the same approach applies
in the Upper Tribunal to appeals from the Social Entitlement Chamber of the
First-tier Tribunal and to cases under the Forfeiture Act 1982. However, from
April 1, 2009, the Upper Tribunal's power to award costs under subss.(1) and (2)
is not restricted in judicial review cases. It remains to be seen whether the Upper
Tribunal will take the same approach as the courts in such cases (see the note to
the Rules).

Subss. (4) to (6)

    These subsections provide for a "wasted costs" order to be made against a rep-   **5.74**
resentative (rather than a party) whose "improper, unreasonable or negligent act
or omission" makes it unreasonable for a party to pay costs he or she has incurred.
It is not entirely clear whether such orders may be made by the Social Entitlement
Chamber or by the Upper Tribunal on appeal from that chamber or in Forfeiture
Act cases. The doubt arises because Tribunal Procedure Rules made under subs.
(3) may qualify only subss.(1) and (2). If subs.(4) confers a free-standing power to
award costs, that power remains available notwithstanding the Tribunal Procedure
Rules. However, the better approach may be that subs.(4) merely defines the circumstances in which the broad power in subs.(2) to determine "by whom" costs are
to be paid is to be exercised against representatives. Even if the power is available, it
is suggested that it will rarely be appropriate to use it. So far as the representative's
own client is concerned, the question of who bears any costs may be thought to be
a matter between the representative and the client and, so far as any other party is
concerned, it needs to be borne in mind that equally improper, unreasonable or
negligent acts by an unrepresented party do not result in any award of costs. Making
a wasted costs order where there is no other power to award costs would arguably
be merely for punitive or deterrent purposes. Where many claimants rely on the
free services of representatives, too liberal a use of wasted costs order might unduly
affect that availability of representation.

CHAPTERS 3 TO 5

5.75   **30.–45.**—*Omitted.*

CHAPTER 6

SUPPLEMENTARY

5.76   **46.–48.**—*Omitted.*

Orders and regulations under Part 1: supplemental and procedural provisions

5.77   **49.**—(1) Power—

       (a) of the Lord Chancellor to make an order, or regulations, under this Part,

       (b) of the Senior President of Tribunals to make an order under section 7(9), or

       (c) of the Scottish Ministers, or the Welsh Ministers, to make an order under paragraph 25(2) of Schedule 7,

is exercisable by statutory instrument.

(2) The Statutory Instruments Act 1946 shall apply in relation to the power to make orders conferred on the Senior President of Tribunals by section 7(9) as if the Senior President of Tribunals were a Minister of the Crown.

(3) Any power mentioned in subsection (1) includes power to make different provision for different purposes.

(4) Without prejudice to the generality of subsection (3), power to make an order under section 30 or 31 includes power to make different provision in relation to England, Scotland, Wales and Northern Ireland respectively.

(5) No order mentioned in subsection (6) is to be made unless a draft of the statutory instrument containing it (whether alone or with other provision) has been laid before, and approved by a resolution of, each House of Parliament.

(6) Those orders are—

       (a) an order under section 11(8), 13(6) or (14), 30, 31(1), 32, 33, 34, 35, 36, 37 or 42(3);

       (b) an order under paragraph 15 of Schedule 4;

       (c) an order under section 42(1)(a) to (d) that provides for fees to be payable in respect of things for which fees have never been payable;

       (d) an order under section 31(2), (7) or (9), or paragraph 30(1) of Schedule 5, that contains provision taking the form of an amendment or repeal of an enactment comprised in an Act.

(7) A statutory instrument that—

       (a) contains—

          (i) an order mentioned in subsection (8), or

          ii) regulations under Part 3 of Schedule 9, and

       (b) is not subject to any requirement that a draft of the instrument be laid before, and approved by a resolution of, each House of Parliament, is subject to annulment in pursuance of a resolution of either House of Parliament.

(8) Those orders are—

(a) an order made by the Lord Chancellor under this Part;

b) an order made by the Senior President of Tribunals under section 7(9).

(9) A statutory instrument that contains an order made by the Scottish Ministers under paragraph 25(2) of Schedule 7 is subject to annulment in pursuance of a resolution of the Scottish Parliament.

(10) A statutory instrument that contains an order made by the Welsh Ministers under paragraph 25(2) of Schedule 7 is subject to annulment in pursuance of a resolution of the National Assembly for Wales.

PARTS 2 TO 7

50.–143.—*Omitted.*   5.78

PART 8

GENERAL

144.—*Omitted.*   5.79

Power to make supplementary or other provision

145.—(1) The Lord Chancellor (or, in relation to Chapter 3 of Part   5.80
5 only, the Secretary of State) may by order make any supplementary, incidental, consequential, transitory, transitional or saving provision which he considers necessary or expedient for the purposes of, in consequence of, or for giving full effect to, any provision of this Act.

(2) An order under this section may in particular—

(a) provide for any provision of this Act which comes into force before another to have effect, until that other provision has come into force, with modifications specified in the order;

(b) amend, repeal or revoke any enactment other than one contained in an Act or instrument passed or made after the Session in which this Act is passed.

(3) The amendments that may be made by an order under this section are in addition to those made by or under any other provision of this Act.

(4) An order under this section may make different provision for different purposes.

(5) The power to make an order under this section is exercisable by statutory instrument.

(6) A statutory instrument containing an order under this section, unless it is an order to which subsection (7) applies, is subject to annulment in pursuance of a resolution of either House of Parliament.

(7) No order amending or repealing an enactment contained in an Act may be made under this section unless a draft of the order has been laid before and approved by a resolution of each House of Parliament.

146.—*Omitted.*   5.81

Extent

5.82   **147.**—(1) Parts 1, 2 and 6 and this Part extend to England and Wales, Scotland and Northern Ireland.

(2) The other provisions of this Act extend only to England and Wales.

(3) Subsections (1) and (2) are subject to subsections (4) and (5).

(4) Unless provided otherwise, amendments, repeals and revocations in this Act extend to any part of the United Kingdom to which the provisions amended, repealed or revoked extend.

(5) The following extend also to the Isle of Man—

(a) section 143(1) and (2),

(b) the repeal by this Act of any provision specified in Part 6 of Schedule 23 that extends to the Isle of Man,

(c) sections 145 and 148(5) to (7) so far as relating to—

(i) section 143(1) and (2), and

(ii) the provisions of this Act by which the repeals mentioned in paragraph (b) are effected, and

(d) this section and section 149.

Commencement

5.83   **148.**—(1) Section 60 comes into force at the end of the period of two months beginning with the day on which this Act is passed.

(2) The provisions of Chapter 3 of Part 5 come into force in accordance with provision made by the Lord Chancellor or the Secretary of State by order.

(3) The provisions of Part 6 come into force, except as provided by subsection (4), in accordance with provision made by the Secretary of State by order.

(4) The provisions of Part 6 come into force, in so far as they extend to Scotland, in accordance with provision made by the Scottish Ministers by order.

(5) The remaining provisions of this Act, except sections 53, 55, 56, 57, 145, 147, 149, this section and Schedule 11, come into force in accordance with provision made by the Lord Chancellor by order.

(6) An order under this section may make different provision for different purposes.

(7) The power to make an order under this section is exercisable by statutory instrument.

Short title

5.84   **149.**—This Act may be cited as the Tribunals, Courts and Enforcement Act 2007.

5.85   **Schedules 1 to 3** *Omitted.*

SCHEDULE 4

CHAMBERS AND CHAMBER PRESIDENTS: FURTHER PROVISION

PART 1

CHAMBER PRESIDENTS: APPOINTMENT, DELEGATION, DEPUTIES AND FURTHER PROVISION

1. to 3. *Omittted.*   5.86

Delegation of functions by Chamber Presidents

4. (1) The Chamber President of a chamber of the First-tier Tribunal   5.87
or Upper Tribunal may delegate any function he has in his capacity as the
Chamber President of the chamber—
  (a) to any judge, or other member, of either of those tribunals;
  (b) to staff appointed under section 40(1).
(2) A delegation under sub-paragraph (1) is not revoked by the delegator's becoming incapacitated.
(3) Any delegation made by a person under sub-paragraph (1) that
is in force immediately before the person ceases to be the Chamber
President of a chamber continues in force until subsequently varied or
revoked by another holder of the office of Chamber President of that
chamber.
(4) The delegation under sub-paragraph (1) of a function shall not prevent
the exercise of the function by the Chamber President of the chamber concerned.
(5) In this paragraph "delegate" includes further delegate.

5. to 8. *Omitted.*   5.88

PART 2

JUDGES AND OTHER MEMBERS OF CHAMBERS: ASSIGNMENT AND JURISDICTION

9. to 14. *Omitted.*   5.89

Composition of tribunals

15. (1) The Lord Chancellor must by order make provision, in relation   5.90
to every matter that may fall to be decided by the First-tier Tribunal or the
Upper Tribunal, for determining the number of members of the tribunal
who are to decide the matter.

(2) Where an order under sub-paragraph (1) provides for a matter to be decided by a single member of a tribunal, the order—

    (a) must make provision for determining whether the matter is to be decided by one of the judges, or by one of the other members, of the tribunal, and

    (b) may make provision for determining, if the matter is to be decided by one of the other members of the tribunal, what qualifications (if any) that other member must have.

(3) Where an order under sub-paragraph (1) provides for a matter to be decided by two or more members of a tribunal, the order—

    (a) must make provision for determining how many (if any) of those members are to be judges of the tribunal and how many (if any) are to be other members of the tribunal, and

    (b) may make provision for determining—

        (i) if the matter is to be decided by persons who include one or more of the other members of the tribunal, or

        (ii) if the matter is to be decided by two or more of the other members of the tribunal,

    what qualifications (if any) that other member or any of those other members must have.

(4) A duty under sub-paragraph (1), (2) or (3) to provide for the determination of anything may be discharged by providing for the thing to be determined by the Senior President of Tribunals, or a Chamber President, in accordance with any provision made under that sub-paragraph.

(5) Power under paragraph (b) of sub-paragraph (2) or (3) to provide for the determination of anything may be exercised by giving, to the Senior President of Tribunals or a Chamber President, power to determine that thing in accordance with any provision made under that paragraph.

(6) Where under sub-paragraphs (1) to (4) a matter is to be decided by two or more members of a tribunal, the matter may, if the parties to the case agree, be decided in the absence of one or more (but not all) of the members chosen to decide the matter.

(7) Where the member, or any of the members, of a tribunal chosen to decide a matter does not have any qualification that he is required to have under sub-paragraphs (2)(b), or (3)(b), and (5), the matter may despite that, if the parties to the case agree, be decided by the chosen member or members.

(8) Before making an order under this paragraph, the Lord Chancellor must consult the Senior President of Tribunals.

(9) In this paragraph "qualification" includes experience.

GENERAL NOTE

Para.15

5.91   See the First-tier Tribunal and Upper Tribunal (Composition of Tribunal) Order 2008, below. The Order makes much use of the power in para.15(4) for an order to leave matters of composition to be determined by the Senior President of Tribunals who who has issued practice statements. The relevant practice statements are set out in the notes to the Order. Note that subpara.(6) provides for a case to be determined in the absence of some (but not all!) members of the tribunal, provided the parties agree. Subparagraph (7) also enables a tribunal to proceed if any of the members of the tribunal does not have the requisite qualifications, provided the parties agree. Thus, if one of the members does not have the relevant qualification, there is a choice between the proceedings being adjourned, the case proceeding without that member and the case proceeding with that member. In this context "member" clearly include a judge, so it would be possible for a hearing to take place without a judge by virtue of either of those paragraphs. However, not only must the parties agree that it is appropriate to proceed but so must the tribunal itself. There are likely to be cases where the lack of the relevant expertise obliges the tribunal to adjourn the proceedings in the interests of justice. Where no-one realises that a member lacks the relevant qualifications, including the member himself or herself, and the tribunal therefore hears the case, the decision of the tribunal is not invalid unless the member deliberately closed his or her eyes to the problem or the lack of relevant qualification has rendered the proceedings unfair (*Coppard v Customs and Excise Commissioners* [2003] EWCA Civ 511; [2003] Q.B. 118).

SCHEDULE 5

PROCEDURE IN FIRST-TIER TRIBUNAL AND UPPER TRIBUNAL

PART 1

TRIBUNAL PROCEDURE RULES

Introductory

1. (1) This Part of this Schedule makes further provision about the content of Tribunal Procedure Rules.

(2) The generality of section 22(1) is not to be taken to be prejudiced by—

(a) the following paragraphs of this Part of this Schedule, or

(b) any other provision (including future provision) authorising or requiring the making of provision by Tribunal Procedure Rules.

(3) In the following paragraphs of this Part of this Schedule "Rules" means Tribunal Procedure Rules.

5.92

Concurrent functions

2. Rules may make provision as to who is to decide, or as to how to decide, which of the First-tier Tribunal and Upper Tribunal is to exercise, in relation to any particular matter, a function that is exercisable by the two tribunals on the basis that the question as to which of them is to exercise the function is to be determined by, or under, Rules.

5.93

Delegation of functions to staff

3. (1) Rules may provide for functions—

(a) of the First-tier Tribunal, or

(b) of the Upper Tribunal,

to be exercised by staff appointed under section 40(1).

(2) In making provision of the kind mentioned in sub-paragraph (1) in relation to a function, Rules may (in particular)—

(a) provide for the function to be exercisable by a member of staff only

5.94

if the member of staff is, or is of a description, specified in exercise of a discretion conferred by Rules;

(b) provide for the function to be exercisable by a member of staff only if the member of staff is approved, or is of a description approved, for the purpose by a person specified in Rules.

Time limits

5.95   **4.** Rules may make provision for time limits as respects initiating, or taking any step in, proceedings before the First-tier Tribunal or the Upper Tribunal.

Repeat applications

5.96   **5.** Rules may make provision restricting the making of fresh applications where a previous application in relation to the same matter has been made.

Tribunal acting of its own initiative

5.97   **6.** Rules may make provision about the circumstances in which the First-tier Tribunal, or the Upper Tribunal, may exercise its powers of its own initiative.

Hearings

5.98   **7.** Rules may—

(a) make provision for dealing with matters without a hearing;

(b) make provision as respects allowing or requiring a hearing to be in private or as respects allowing or requiring a hearing to be in public.

Proceedings without notice

5.99   **8.** Rules may make provision for proceedings to take place, in circumstances described in Rules, at the request of one party even though the other, or another, party has had no notice.

Representation

5.100   **9.** Rules may make provision conferring additional rights of audience before the First-tier Tribunal or the Upper Tribunal.

Evidence, witnesses and attendance

10. (1) Rules may make provision about evidence (including evidence on oath and administration of oaths).

(2) Rules may modify any rules of evidence provided for elsewhere, so far as they would apply to proceedings before the First-tier Tribunal or Upper Tribunal.

(3) Rules may make provision, where the First-tier Tribunal has required a person—

    (a) to attend at any place for the purpose of giving evidence,

    (b) otherwise to make himself available to give evidence,

    (c) to swear an oath in connection with the giving of evidence,

    (d) to give evidence as a witness,

    (e) to produce a document, or

    (f) to facilitate the inspection of a document or any other thing (including any premises),

for the Upper Tribunal to deal with non-compliance with the requirement as though the requirement had been imposed by the Upper Tribunal.

(4) Rules may make provision for the payment of expenses and allowances to persons giving evidence, producing documents, attending proceedings or required to attend proceedings.

Use of information

11. (1) Rules may make provision for the disclosure or non-disclosure of information received during the course of proceedings before the First-tier Tribunal or Upper Tribunal.

(2) Rules may make provision for imposing reporting restrictions in circumstances described in Rules.

Costs and expenses

12. (1) Rules may make provision for regulating matters relating to costs, or (in Scotland) expenses, of proceedings before the First-tier Tribunal or Upper Tribunal.

(2) The provision mentioned in sub-paragraph (1) includes (in particular)—

    (a) provision prescribing scales of costs or expenses;

    (b) provision for enabling costs to undergo detailed assessment in England and Wales by a county court or the High Court;

    (c) provision for taxation in Scotland of accounts of expenses by an Auditor of Court;

    (d) provision for enabling costs to be taxed in Northern Ireland in a county court or the High Court;

    (e) provision for costs or expenses—

        (i) not to be allowed in respect of items of a description specified in Rules;

        (ii) not to be allowed in proceedings of a description so specified;

5.101

5.102

5.103

(f) provision for other exceptions to either or both of subsections (1) and (2) of section 29.

Set-off and interest

5.104   **13.** (1) Rules may make provision for a party to proceedings to deduct, from amounts payable by him, amounts payable to him.

(2) Rules may make provision for interest on sums awarded (including provision conferring a discretion or provision in accordance with which interest is to be calculated).

Arbitration

5.105   **14.** Rules may provide for Part 1 of the Arbitration Act 1996 (which extends to England and Wales, and Northern Ireland, but not Scotland) not to apply, or not to apply except so far as is specified in Rules, where the First-tier Tribunal, or Upper Tribunal, acts as arbitrator.

Correction of errors and setting-aside of decisions on procedural grounds

5.106   **15.** (1) Rules may make provision for the correction of accidental errors in a decision or record of a decision.

(2) Rules may make provision for the setting aside of a decision in proceedings before the First-tier Tribunal or Upper Tribunal—

(a) where a document relating to the proceedings was not sent to, or was not received at an appropriate time by, a party to the proceedings or a party's representative,

(b) where a document relating to the proceedings was not sent to the First-tier Tribunal or Upper Tribunal at an appropriate time,

(c) where a party to the proceedings, or a party's representative, was not present at a hearing related to the proceedings, or

(d) where there has been any other procedural irregularity in the proceedings.

(3) Sub-paragraphs (1) and (2) shall not be taken to prejudice, or to be prejudiced by, any power to correct errors or set aside decisions that is exercisable apart from rules made by virtue of those sub-paragraphs.

Ancillary powers

5.107   **16.** Rules may confer on the First-tier Tribunal, or the Upper Tribunal, such ancillary powers as are necessary for the proper discharge of its functions.

Rules may refer to practice directions

5.108   **17.** Rules may, instead of providing for any matter, refer to provision made or to be made about that matter by directions under section 23.

Presumptions

18. Rules may make provision in the form of presumptions (including, in particular, presumptions as to service or notification). **5.109**

Differential provision

19. Rules may make different provision for different purposes or different areas. **5.110**

PART 2

20. to **26.**—*Omitted.* **5.111**

PART 3

MAKING OF TRIBUNAL PROCEDURE RULES BY TRIBUNAL PROCEDURE COMMITTEE

Meaning of "Rules" and "the Committee"

27. In the following provisions of this Part of this Schedule— **5.112**
"the Committee" means the Tribunal Procedure Committee;
"Rules" means Tribunal Procedure Rules.

Process for making Rules

28. (1) Before the Committee makes Rules, the Committee must— **5.113**
(a) consult such persons (including such of the Chamber Presidents) as it considers appropriate,
(b) consult the Lord President of the Court of Session if the Rules contain provision relating to proceedings in Scotland, and
(c) meet (unless it is inexpedient to do so).
(2) Rules made by the Committee must be—
(a) signed by a majority of the members of the Committee, and
(b) submitted to the Lord Chancellor.
(3) The Lord Chancellor may allow or disallow Rules so made.
(4) If the Lord Chancellor disallows Rules so made, he must give the Committee written reasons for doing so.
(5) Rules so made and allowed—
(a) come into force on such day as the Lord Chancellor directs, and
(b) are to be contained in a statutory instrument to which the Statutory Instruments Act 1946 applies as if the instrument contained rules made by a Minister of the Crown.
(6) A statutory instrument containing Rules made by the Committee is subject to annulment in pursuance of a resolution of either House of Parliament.

(7) In the case of a member of the Committee appointed under paragraph 24, the terms of his appointment may (in particular) provide that, for the purposes of sub-paragraph (2)(a), he is to count as a member of the Committee only in relation to matters specified in those terms.

Power of Lord Chancellor to require Rules to be made

5.114   **29.** (1) This paragraph applies if the Lord Chancellor gives the Committee written notice that he thinks it is expedient for Rules to include provision that would achieve a purpose specified in the notice.

(2) The Committee must make such Rules, in accordance with paragraph 28, as it considers necessary to achieve the specified purpose.

(3) Those Rules must be made—

(a) within such period as may be specified by the Lord Chancellor in the notice, or

(b) if no period is so specified, within a reasonable period after the Lord Chancellor gives the notice to the Committee.

PART 4

POWER TO AMEND LEGISLATION IN CONNECTION WITH TRIBUNAL PROCEDURE RULES

Lord Chancellor's power

5.115   **30.** (1) The Lord Chancellor may by order amend, repeal or revoke any enactment to the extent he considers necessary or desirable—

(a) in order to facilitate the making of Tribunal Procedure Rules, or

(b) in consequence of—

(i) section 22,

(ii) Part 1 or 3 of this Schedule, or

(iii) Tribunal Procedure Rules.

(2) In this paragraph "enactment" means any enactment whenever passed or made, including an enactment comprised in subordinate legislation (within the meaning of the Interpretation Act 1978).

GENERAL NOTE

Para.1

5.116   The scope of the power to make Tribunal Procedure Rules in s.22(1) is very broad and is not to be treated as limited by any other rule-making power in this Act, including this Schedule, or indeed in any other Act.

Para.3

5.117   There is no need to make rules for the delegation of purely administrative functions and therefore this paragraph is concerned only with the delegation of judicial functions.

Para. 10

    See s.25 for the powers of the Upper Tribunal to which reference is made in sub-para.(3).

          5.118

Para. 15

    There is potentially some overlap between Tribunal Procedure Rules made under this paragraph and the power to correct or set aside a decision on a review under s.9 or s.10. However, the circumstances in which a decision may be reviewed are likely to be limited and it is likely to be fairly clear which power should be used.

          5.119

    Note that para.15(2) is broader than s.28(1) of the Social Security Act 1998, which it replaces, as it covers any procedural irregularity (which, at one time, some regulations purporting to be made under s.28 of the 1998 Act did).

Paras 27 to 29

    The Lord Chancellor may disallow Rules or require particular provision to be made in Rules.

          5.120

    Schedules 6 to 23 *Omitted.*

          5.121

The Transfer of Tribunal Functions Order 2008

(SI 2008/2833)

Made   *29th October 2008*
Coming into force   *3rd November 2008*

    The Lord Chancellor makes the following Order in exercise of the powers conferred by sections 30(1) and (4), 31(1), (2) and (9), 32(3) and (5), 33(2) and (3), 34(2) and (3), 37(1), 38 and 145 of, and paragraph 30 of Schedule 5 to, the Tribunals, Courts and Enforcement Act 2007. The Scottish Ministers have consented to the making of this order in so far as their consent is required by section 30(7) of that Act.

          5.122

    A draft of this Order was laid before Parliament and approved by a resolution of each House of Parliament in accordance with section 49(5) of that Act.

Citation, commencement, interpretation and extent

    1.—(1) This Order may be cited as the Transfer of Tribunal Functions Order 2008 and comes into force on 3rd November 2008.

          5.123

    (2) A reference in this Order to a Schedule by a number alone is a reference to the Schedule so numbered in this Order.

    (3) Subject as follows, this Order extends to England and Wales, Scotland and Northern Ireland.

    (4) Except as provided by paragraph (5) or (6), an amendment, repeal or revocation of any enactment by any provision of Schedule 3 extends to the part or parts of the United Kingdom to which the enactment extends.

    (5) For the purposes of article 3(3)(a) and (b) the following amendments, repeals and revocations made by the provisions of that Schedule do not extend to Scotland—

    (a) paragraphs 145 to 147;

    (b) paragraph 150;

    (c) paragraph 151(d);

(d) paragraph 152;

(e) paragraph 154;

(f) paragraphs 167 to 173; and

(g) paragraph 228(h), (l), (n) and (r).

(6) The amendments and repeals made by paragraphs 198 to 201 of Schedule 3 do not extend to Scotland.

GENERAL NOTE

5.123.1   The reason for paras (5) and (6) is explained in the note to ss.5 to 7 of the Social Security Act 1998.

5.124   **2.** *Omitted.*

Transfer of functions of certain tribunals

5.125   **3.**—(1) Subject to paragraph (3), the functions of the tribunals listed in Table 1 of Schedule 1 are transferred to the First-tier Tribunal.

(2) Subject to paragraph (3), the functions of the tribunals listed in Table 2 of Schedule 1 are transferred to the Upper Tribunal.

(3) The following functions are not transferred—

(a) the determination by an appeal tribunal constituted under Chapter 1 of Part 1 of the Social Security Act 1998 of an appeal which is referred to such tribunal by the Scottish Ministers, or the Secretary of State on their behalf, pursuant to section 158 (appeal tribunals) of the Health and Social Care (Community Health and Standards) Act 2003 ("the 2003 Act"); and

(b) the determination by a Social Security Commissioner of an appeal made under section 159 (appeal to social security commissioner) of the 2003 Act against a decision falling within sub-paragraph (a).

GENERAL NOTE

5.126   The reason for para.(3) is explained in the note to ss.5 to 7 of the Social Security Act 1998.

Abolition of tribunals transferred under section 30(1)

5.127   **4.** The tribunals listed in Table 1 and Table 2 of Schedule 1 are abolished except for—

(a) appeal tribunals constituted under Chapter 1 of Part 1 of the Social Security Act 1998 in respect of Scotland for the purposes of the function described in article 3(3)(a); and

(b) the Social Security Commissioners in respect of Scotland for the purposes of the function described in article 3(3)(b).

GENERAL NOTE

5.128   The reason for the saving is explained in the note to ss.5 to 7 of the Social Security Act 1998.

5.129   **5. to 8.** *Omitted.*

Minor, consequential and transitional provisions

5.130   **9.**—(1) Schedule 3 contains minor, consequential and supplemental amendments, and repeals and revocations as a consequence of those amendments.

(2) Schedule 4 contains transitional provisions.

SCHEDULE 1

FUNCTIONS TRANSFERRED TO THE FIRST-TIER TRIBUNAL AND UPPER TRIBUNAL

Table 1: Functions transferred to the First-tier Tribunal   5.131

Tribunal	Enactment
Adjudicator	Section 5 of the Criminal Injuries Compensation Act 1995
Appeal tribunal	Chapter 1 of Part 1 of the Social Security Act 1998
Asylum Support Adjudicators	Section 102 of the Immigration and Asylum Act 1999
Mental Health Review Tribunal for a region of England	Section 65(1) and (1A)(a) of the Mental Health Act 1983
Pensions Appeal Tribunal in England and Wales	Section 8(2) of the War Pensions (Administrative Provisions) Act 1919 and paragraph 1(1) of the Schedule to the Pensions Appeal Tribunals Act 1943
Special Educational Needs and Disability Tribunal	Section 28H of the Disability Discrimination Act 1995 and section 333 of the Education Act 1996
Tribunal, except in respect of its functions under section 4 of the Safeguarding Vulnerable Groups Act 2004	Section 9 of the Protection of Children Act 1999

Table 2: Functions transferred to the Upper Tribunal   5.132

Tribunal	Enactment
Child Support Commissioner	Section 22 of the Child Support Act 1991
Social Security Commissioner	Schedule 4 to the Social Security Act 1998
Tribunal, in respect of its functions under section 4 of the Safeguarding Vulnerable Groups Act 2006	Section 9 of the Protection of Children Act 1999

Schedules 2. and 3. *Omitted.*   5.133

SCHEDULE 4

TRANSITIONAL PROVISIONS

Transitional provisions

1. Subject to article 3(3)(a) any proceedings before a tribunal listed in Table 1 of Schedule 1 which are pending immediately before 3rd November 2008 shall continue on and after 3rd November 2008 as proceedings before the First-tier Tribunal.   5.134

2. Subject to article 3(3)(b) any proceedings before a tribunal listed in Table 2 of Schedule 1 which are pending immediately before 3rd November 2008 shall continue on and after 3rd November 2008 as proceedings before the Upper Tribunal.

3.—(1) The following sub-paragraphs apply where proceedings are continued in the First-tier Tribunal or Upper Tribunal by virtue of paragraph 1 or 2.

(2) Where a hearing began before 3rd November 2008 but was not completed by that date, the First-tier Tribunal or the Upper Tribunal, as the case may be, must be comprised for the continuation of that hearing of the person or persons who began it.

(3) The First-tier Tribunal or Upper Tribunal, as the case may be, may give any direction to ensure that proceedings are dealt with fairly and, in particular, may—

(a) apply any provision in procedural rules which applied to the proceedings before 3rd November 2008; or

(b) disapply provisions of Tribunal Procedure Rules.

(4) In sub-paragraph (3) "procedural rules" means provision (whether called rules or not) regulating practice or procedure before a tribunal.

(5) Any direction or order given or made in proceedings which is in force immediately before 3rd November 2008 remains in force on and after that date as if it were a direction or order of the First-tier Tribunal or Upper Tribunal, as the case may be.

(6) A time period which has started to run before 3rd November 2008 and which has not expired shall continue to apply.

(7) An order for costs may only be made if, and to the extent that, an order could have been made before 3rd November 2008.

4. Subject to article 3(3)(a) and (b) where an appeal lies to a Child Support or Social Security Commissioner from any decision made before 3rd November 2008 by a tribunal listed in Table 1 of Schedule 1, section 11 of the 2007 Act (right to appeal to Upper Tribunal) shall apply as if the decision were a decision made on or after 3rd November 2008 by the First-tier Tribunal.

5. Subject to article 3(3)(b) where an appeal lies to a court from any decision made before 3rd November 2008 by a Child Support or Social Security Commissioner, section 13 of the 2007 Act (right to appeal to Court of Appeal etc.) shall apply as if the decision were a decision made on or after 3rd November 2008 by the Upper Tribunal.

6. Subject to article 3(3)(a) and (b) any case to be remitted by a court on or after 3rd November 2008 in relation to a tribunal listed in Schedule 1 shall be remitted to the First-tier Tribunal or Upper Tribunal as the case may be.

7. *Omitted.*

GENERAL NOTE

Paras 1–4

5.135   Proceedings pending before November 3, 2008 continue as proceedings in the First-tier Tribunal or Upper Tribunal, as appropriate. A case that is part-heard must continue before the same person or persons. If necessary for reasons of fairness, the First-tier Tribunal or Upper Tribunal may apply the procedural regulations that were in force before November 3, 2008 instead of the new Tribunal Procedure Rules. Any direction made before November 3, 2008 remains effective after that date as though it had been made by the First-tier Tribunal or Upper Tribunal. Any time period that has started to run and has not expired continues to apply.

Paras 5–6

If a decision was made before November 3, 2008 and an appeal lay to a Social Security Commissioner but has not been brought until that date or later, the appeal must instead be brought to the Upper Tribunal under s.11 of the Tribunals, Courts and Enforcement Act 2007. Similarly, if a Commissioner gave a decision before November 3, 2008, any appeal to the Court of Appeal or Court of Session brought on or after that date must be brought under s.13 of the 2007 Act. Where an appeal against a Commissioner's decision brought before November 3, 2008 is allowed and the case is remitted on or after that date, it must be remitted to the First-tier Tribunal or Upper Tribunal. The references to art.3 in each of these paragraphs are a reminder that these provisions do not apply to cases in Scotland under the Health and Social Care (Community Health and Standards) Act 2003, because art.3 leaves such cases in the hands of appeal tribunals and Commissioners.

5.136

The First-tier Tribunal and Upper Tribunal (Composition of Tribunal) Order 2008

(SI 2008/2835)

Made	*29th October 2008*
Coming into force	*3rd November 2008*

The Lord Chancellor makes the following Order in exercise of the powers conferred by section 145(1) of, and paragraph 15 of Schedule 4 to, the Tribunals, Courts and Enforcement Act 2007.

5.137

In accordance with paragraph 15(8) of that Act the Lord Chancellor has consulted the Senior President of Tribunals.

In accordance with section 49(5) of that Act a draft of this instrument was laid before Parliament and approved by a resolution of each House of Parliament.

Citation and commencement

1. This Order may be cited as the First-tier Tribunal and Upper Tribunal (Composition of Tribunal) Order 2008 and comes into force on 3rd November 2008.

5.138

Number of members of the First-tier Tribunal

2.—(1) The number of members of the tribunal who are to decide any matter that falls to be decided by the First-tier Tribunal must be determined by the Senior President of Tribunals in accordance with paragraph (2).

5.139

(2) The Senior President of Tribunals must have regard to—

(a) where the matter which falls to be decided by the tribunal fell to a tribunal in a list in Schedule 6 to the Tribunals, Courts and Enforcement Act 2007 before its functions were transferred by order under section 30(1) of that Act, any provision made by or under any enactment for determining the number of members of that tribunal; and

(b) the need for members of tribunals to have particular expertise, skills or knowledge.

GENERAL NOTE

5.140   As is permitted by para.15(4) of Sch.4 to the Tribunals Courts and Enforcement Act 2007, this article leaves it to the Senior President of Tribunals to determine the number of members to determine any particular type of case and the qualifications they must have. He has issued practice statements. That for the "Composition of tribunals in social security and child support cases in the social entitlement chamber on or after 3 November 2008" is in the following terms—

"1. In this Practice Statement;
    a. "the 2008 Order" means the First-tier Tribunal and Upper Tribunal (Composition of Tribunal) Order 2008;
    b. "the Qualifications Order" means the Qualifications for Appointment of Members to the First-tier Tribunal and Upper Tribunal Order 2008;
    c. "the 2008 Rules" means the Tribunal Procedure (First-tier Tribunal) (Social Entitlement Chamber) Rules 2008;
    d. "social security and child support case" has the meaning given in rule 1(3) of the 2008 Rules.

2. In exercise of the powers conferred by the 2008 Order the Senior President of Tribunals makes the following determinations and supplementary provision:—
3. The number of members of the Tribunal must not exceed three.
4. Where the appeal relates to an attendance allowance or a disability living allowance under Part III of the Social Security Contributions and Benefits Act 1992, the Tribunal must, subject to paragraphs 8 to 13, consist of a Tribunal Judge, a Tribunal Member who is a registered medical practitioner, and a Tribunal Member who has a disability qualification as set out in article 2(3) of the Qualifications Order.
5. Where—
    a. the appeal involves the personal capability assessment, as defined in regulation 2(1) of the Social Security (Incapacity for Work)(General) Regulations 1995;
    b. the appeal involves the limited capability for work assessment, as defined in regulation 2(1) of the Employment and Support Allowance Regulations 2008;
    c. the appeal involves the determination of limited capability for work-related activity within the meaning of regulations 34 and 35 of the Employment and Support Allowance Regulations 2008;
    d. the appeal is made under section 11(1)(b) of the Social Security (Recovery of Benefits) Act 1997;
    e. the appeal raises issues relating to severe disablement allowance under section 68 of the Social Security Contributions and Benefits Act 1992 or industrial injuries benefit under Part V of that Act (except for an appeal where the only issue is whether there should be a declaration of an industrial accident under section 29(2) of the Social Security Act 1998);
    f. the appeal is made under section 4 of the Vaccine Damage Payments Act 1979;
    g. the appeal is against a certificate of NHS charges under section 157(1) of the Health and Social Care (Community Health and Standards) Act 2003;
    h. the appeal arises under Part IV of the Child Maintenance and Other Payments Act 2008;
    the Tribunal must, subject to paragraphs 7 to 14, consist of a Tribunal Judge and a Tribunal Member who is a registered medical practitioner.
6. In any other case the Tribunal must consist of a Tribunal Judge.
7. The Chamber President may determine that the Tribunal constituted under paragraph 5 or 6 must also include—

    a. a Tribunal Member who is an accountant within the meaning of Article 2(i) of the Qualifications Order, where the appeal may require the examination of financial accounts;

    b. an additional Member who is a registered medical practitioner, where the complexity of the medical issues in the appeal so demands;

    c. such an additional Tribunal Judge or Member as he considers appropriate for the purposes of providing further experience for that additional Judge or Member or for assisting the Chamber President in the monitoring of standards of decision-making.

8. Where the Chamber President considers, in a particular case, that a matter that would otherwise be decided in accordance with paragraphs 4 or 5 only raises questions of law and the expertise of any of the other members is not necessary to decide the matter, the Chamber President may direct that the Tribunal must consist of a Tribunal Judge, or a Tribunal Judge and any Tribunal Member whose experience and qualifications are necessary to decide the matter.

9. The powers of the Chamber President referred to in paragraphs 7, 8, 10 and 12 may be delegated to a Regional Tribunal Judge and those referred to in paragraphs 7, 8 and 12 may be delegated to a District Tribunal Judge.

10. A decision, including a decision to give a direction or make an order, made under, or in accordance with, rules 5 to 9, 11, 14 to 19, 25(3), 30, 32, 36, 37 or 41 of the 2008 Rules may be made by a Tribunal Judge, except that a decision made under, or in accordance, with rule 7(3) or rule 5(3)(b) to treat a case as a lead case (whether in accordance with rule 18 (lead cases) or otherwise) of the 2008 Rules must be made by the Chamber President.

11. The determination of an application for permission to appeal under rule 38 of the 2008 Rules and the exercise of the power of review under section 9 of the Tribunals, Courts and Enforcement Act 2007 must be carried out—

    a. where the Judge who constituted or was a member of the Tribunal that made the decision was a fee-paid Judge, by a salaried Tribunal Judge; or

    b. where the Judge who constituted or was a member of the Tribunal that made the decision was a salaried Judge, by that Judge or, if it would be impracticable or cause undue delay, by another salaried Tribunal Judge,

save that, where the decision is set aside under section 9(4)(c) of the Act, the matter may only be re-decided under section 9(5)(a) by a Tribunal composed in accordance with paragraph 4, 5 or 6 above.

12. Where the Tribunal consists of a Tribunal Judge and one or two Tribunal Members, the Tribunal Judge shall be the presiding member. Where the Tribunal comprises more than one Tribunal Judge, the Chamber President must select the presiding member. The presiding member may regulate the procedure of the Tribunal.

13. Under rule 34(2) of the 2008 Rules it will be for the presiding member to give any written statement of reasons.

14. In rule 25(2) (Medical and physical examination in appeals under section 12 of the Social Security Act 1998) of the 2008 Rules "an appropriate member" of the Tribunal is a Tribunal Member who is a registered medical practitioner."

This largely reproduces the previous practice in appeal tribunals constituted under the Social Security Act 1998 but paras 7(b) and 8 introduce an additional element of flexibility. Thus, for instance, it is now possible for there to be a doctor on an appeal against a refusal to make an industrial accident declaration under s.29(2) of the Social Security Act 1998 where there has been no claim for benefit. Equally, it is not necessary for there to be a doctor where only a point of law arises. It is possible to envisage challenges to the constitution of a tribunal.

However, there is no obligation on the Chamber President to ensure that a medically qualified tribunal member sitting in any particular case is a specialist in the field of medicine relevant to the case (*CSI/146/2003*). Even if a case is unusual any medical practitioner will ordinarily be able to deal adequately with competing views. If a specialist's report is necessary, it is open to the Tribunal to ask the parties to obtain a relevant opinion or to obtain one itself where s.20 of the Social Security Act 1998 applies.

It is not inappropriate for a doctor who acts as an examining medical practitioner for an agency of the Department for Work and Pensions also to sit as a tribunal member (*Gillies v Secretary of State for Work and Pensions* [2006] UKHL 2; [2006] 1 W.L.R. 781 (also reported as *R(DLA) 5/06*), but it may be inappropriate for a tribunal judge or a tribunal member with a disability qualification to sit on a tribunal considering a medical report compiled by a doctor with whom they have sat on previous occasions (*Secretary of State for Work and Pensions v Cunningham*, 2004 S.L.T. 1007 (also reported as *R(DLA) 7/04*)). In practice, therefore tribunal members do not sit in areas where they act as examining medical practitioners. See further the notes to ss. 3 and 11 of the Tribunals, Courts and Enforcement Act 2007.

Until 1999, there was a provision requiring that, where practical, at least one member of a tribunal should be of the same sex as the claimant. Notwithstanding the repeal of that provision, it was said in *CIB/2620/2000*

> "exceptional cases where the absence of a tribunal member of the same sex as the claimant may inhibit the presentation or understanding of the claimant's case to such an extent that there will be a breach of the requirements of natural justice and of Article 6 of the European Convention on Human Rights if the tribunal is not reconstituted. It is obviously sensible to have a female member of the tribunal, if possible, in a case such as this one; raising as it does sensitive issues relating to a female medical condition. If a claimant specifically raises as an issue the absence from the tribunal of a member of the same sex, it will also be necessary for the tribunal to consider whether there is a real possibility of an injustice if the tribunal is not reconstituted. The repeal of s.46(1) [of the Social Security Administration Act 1992] means that there is no longer a need for the tribunal to consider in every case whether it is practicable for the tribunal to include a member of the same sex as the claimant, but a tribunal will nevertheless be under a duty to raise the matter of its own motion if there is a genuine reason to believe that in the circumstances of the particular case the absence of such a member may lead to injustice."

However, in the case before him, no point had been taken before the tribunal as to the absence of a woman and, although the case was concerned with a female medical condition, the examining medical officer's report was not disputed and the tribunal was not required to investigate any further the effect on the claimant of that condition. Accordingly, a fair-minded and informed observer would not have concluded that there was a real possibility of the hearing having been unfair due to the lack of a woman member of the tribunal and the Commissioner rejected that particular ground of appeal.

Number of members of the Upper Tribunal

5.141　　**3.**—(1) The number of members of the tribunal who are to decide any matter that falls to be decided by the Upper Tribunal is one unless determined otherwise under paragraph (2).

(2) The tribunal may consist of two or three members if the Senior President of Tribunals so determines.

GENERAL NOTE

5.142　　As is permitted by para.15(4) of Sch.4 to the Tribunals Courts and Enforcement Act 2007, this article leaves it to the Senior President of Tribunals to determine the number of members to determine any particular type of case and the qualifications they must have. He has issued practice statements. The *Practice Statement (Upper Tribunal: Composition of Tribunal)* [2009] 1 W.L.R. 328 provides for the composition of the Upper Tribunal in relation to matters that fall to be decided by the Administrative Appeals Chamber on or after November 3, 2008 in the following terms—

"1.   In this Practice Statement;
    a. "the 2007 Act" means the Tribunals, Courts and Enforcement Act 2007;
    b. "the 2008 Order" means the First-tier Tribunal and Upper Tribunal (Composition of Tribunal) Order 2008;
    c. "the 2008 Rules" means the Upper Tribunal Rules 2008;
2. In exercise of the powers conferred by the 2008 Order the Senior President of Tribunals makes the following determinations and supplementary provision:-
3. In accordance with articles 3 and 4 of the 2008 Order, any matter that falls to be decided by the Administrative Appeals Chamber of the Upper Tribunal is to be decided by one judge of the Upper Tribunal (or by a Registrar if the Senior President of Tribunals has approved that they may decide the matter) except that—
    a. where the Senior President of Tribunals or the Chamber President considers that the matter involves a question of law of special difficulty or an important point of principle or practice, or that it is otherwise appropriate, the matter is to be decided by two or three judges of the Upper Tribunal; and
    b. where the matter is the determination of an appeal brought under section 4 of the Safeguarding Vulnerable Groups Act 2006 (otherwise than by the striking out of the appeal under rule 8(2) or (3)(a) or (b) of the 2008 Rules), the matter is to be decided by—
        i. one judge and two other members of the Upper Tribunal; or
        ii. where the Senior President of Tribunals or Chamber President considers that the matter involves a question of law of special difficulty or an important point of principle or practice, or that it is otherwise appropriate, two judges and one other member of the Upper Tribunal.
4. Other members of the Upper Tribunal may be chosen under paragraph 3(b) only if they satisfy the requirements of paragraph 5 or the requirements of paragraphs 6 and 7.
5. The requirements of this paragraph are—
    a. experience in the provision of services which must or may be provided by local authorities under the Adoption Act 1976 or the Children Act 1989 or which are similar to such services, and
    b. experience in relevant social work.
6. The requirements of this paragraph are—
    a. experience in the provision of services by a Health Authority, a Special Health Authority, a National Health Service trust, an NHS foundation trust or a Primary Care Trust;
    b. experience in the provision of education in a school or in an institution within the further education sector; or
    c. experience of being employed by a local education authority in connection with the exercise of its functions under Part I of the Education Act 1996.
7. The requirements of this paragraph are—
    a. experience in the conduct of disciplinary investigations;
    b. experience on an Area Child Protection Committee, or similar experience;
    c. experience of taking part in child protection conferences or in child protection review conferences, or similar experience; or

    d. experience in negotiation the conditions of service of employees.

8. Where more than one member of the Upper Tribunal is to decide a matter, the "presiding member" for the purposes of article 7 of the 2008 Order and the paragraphs below is—

    a. the senior judge, as determined by the Senior President of Tribunals or Chamber President, if the tribunal is composed under paragraph 3(a) of (b) (ii); or

    b. the judge if the tribunal is composed under paragraph 3(b)(i).

9. Where, under paragraph 3(a) or (b), two or three members of the Upper Tribunal have been chosen to give a decision that will, or may, dispose of proceedings, any ancillary matter that arises before that decision is given may be decided by—

    a. the presiding member; or

    b. by all the members so chosen; or

    c. otherwise than at a hearing, by a judge or Registrar (who the Senior President of Tribunals has approved may decide the matter) nominated by the Chamber President or presiding member.

10. Where the Upper Tribunal has given a decision that disposes of proceedings ("the substantive decision"), any matter decided under, or in accordance with, rule 5(3)(l) or Part 7 of the 2008 Rules or section 9 of the 2007 Act must be decided by the same member or members of the Upper Tribunal as gave the substantive decision.

11. Paragraph 10 does not apply where complying with it would be impractical or would cause undue delay and, in such a case, the matter decided under, or in accordance with, rule 5(3)(l) or Part 7 of the 2008 Rules or section 9 of the 2007 Act must be decided by—

    a. if the substantive decision was given by more than one member of the Upper Tribunal and the presiding member or any other judge from that constitution is available, the members of the Upper Tribunal who gave the substantive decision and are available to decide the matter;

    b. otherwise, another judge of the Upper Tribunal nominated by the Chamber President."

Paragraph 3(a) of the Practice Statement for the Upper Tribunal provides for the tribunal to be composed of more than one judge in circumstances where a Tribunal of Commissioners could formerly have been constituted under s.16(7) of the Social Security Act 1998, but there is more flexibility. Two or three judges (as opposed to three or more Commissioners, although the power to appoint more than three Commissioners that existed from 1999 was never exercised) may sit to consider a case raising an important point of principle or practice even if it does not involve a question of law of special difficulty. A three-judge panel may be appointed where there has been disagreement between single judges of the Upper Tribunal. The decision of the three-judge panel will resolve the disagreement because a single judge must always follow a three-judge panel (*Dorset Healthcare NHS Foundation Trust v MH* [2009] UKUT 4 (AAC)). A three-judge panel will generally follow a decision of another three-judge panel or a decision of a Tribunal of Commissioners but will not do so if satisfied that it was wrong (*R(U) 4/88*). The precise status of a decision of a two-judge panel has not yet been determined.

Tribunal consisting of single member

5.143   **4.**—(1) Where a matter is to be decided by a single member of a tribunal, it must be decided by a judge of the tribunal unless paragraph (2) applies.

(2) The matter may be decided by one of the other members of the tribunal if the Senior President of Tribunals so determines.

GENERAL NOTE

The power to provide for a case to be decided by a single member who is not a judge has not been exercised in relation to social security cases.

5.144

Tribunal consisting of two or more members

5. The following articles apply where a matter is to be decided by two or more members of a tribunal.

5.145

6. The number of members who are to be judges of the tribunal and the number of members who are to be other members of the tribunal must be determined by the Senior President of Tribunals.

GENERAL NOTE

See the practice statements set out in the notes to arts 2 and 3.

5.145.1

7. The Senior President of Tribunals must select one of the members (the "presiding member") to chair the tribunal.

GENERAL NOTE

The function of the Senior President of Tribunals may be delegated (see s.8 of the Tribunals, Courts and Enforcement Act 2007).

5.145.2

8. If the decision of the tribunal is not unanimous, the decision of the majority is the decision of the tribunal; and the presiding member has a casting vote if the votes are equally divided.

The Tribunal Procedure (First-tier Tribunal) (Social Entitlement Chamber) Rules 2008

(SI 2008/2685)

IN FORCE NOVEMBER 3, 2008

CONTENTS

PART 1

INTRODUCTION

5.146

PART 2

GENERAL POWERS AND PROVISIONS

PART 3

PROCEEDINGS BEFORE THE TRIBUNAL

CHAPTER 1

BEFORE THE HEARING

CHAPTER 2

HEARINGS

CHAPTER 3

DECISIONS

PART 4

CORRECTING, SETTING ASIDE, REVIEWING AND APPEALING TRIBUNAL DECISIONS

SCHEDULE 1

TIME LIMITS FOR PROVIDING NOTICES OF APPEAL TO THE DECISION MAKER

SCHEDULE 2

ISSUES IN RELATION TO WHICH THE TRIBUNAL MAY REFER A PERSON FOR MEDICAL
EXAMINATION UNDER SECTION 20(2) OF THE SOCIAL SECURITY ACT 1998

After consulting in accordance with paragraph 28(1) of Schedule 5 to, the Tribunals,
Courts and Enforcement Act 2007, the Tribunal Procedure Committee has made
the following Rules in exercise of the powers conferred by sections 20(2) and (3) of
the Social Security Act 1998 and sections 9(3), 22 and 29(3) of, and Schedule 5 to,
the Tribunals, Courts and Enforcement Act 2007. The Lord Chancellor has allowed
the Rules in accordance with paragraph 28(3) of Schedule 5 to the Tribunals,
Courts and Enforcement Act 2007.

PART 1

INTRODUCTION

Citation, commencement, application and interpretation

1.—(1) These Rules may be cited as the Tribunal Procedure (First-tier   5.147
Tribunal) (Social Entitlement Chamber) Rules 2008 and come into force
on 3rd November 2008.

(2) These Rules apply to proceedings before the Tribunal which have
been assigned to the Social Entitlement Chamber by the First-tier Tribunal
and Upper Tribunal (Chambers) Order 2008.

(3) In these Rules—

"the 2007 Act" means the Tribunals, Courts and Enforcement Act 2007;

"appeal" includes an application under section 19(9) of the Tax Credits Act 2002;

"appellant" means a person who makes an appeal to the Tribunal, or a person substituted as an appellant under rule 9(1) (substitution of parties);

"asylum support case" means proceedings concerning the provision of support for an asylum seeker [1 , a failed asylum seeker or a person designated under s.130 of the Criminal Justice and Immigration Act 2008, or the dependants of any such person]

"criminal injuries compensation case" means proceedings concerning the payment of compensation under a scheme made under the Criminal Injuries Compensation Act 1995;

"decision maker" means the maker of a decision against which an appeal has been brought;

"dispose of proceedings" includes, unless indicated otherwise, disposing of a part of the proceedings;

"document" means anything in which information is recorded in any form, and an obligation under these Rules to provide or allow access to a document or a copy of a document for any purpose means, unless the Tribunal directs otherwise, an obligation to provide or allow access to such document or copy in a legible form or in a form which can be readily made into a legible form;

"hearing" means an oral hearing and includes a hearing conducted in whole or in part by video link, telephone or other means of instantaneous two-way electronic communication;

"legal representative" means an authorised advocate or authorised litigator as defined by section 119(1) of the Courts and Legal Services Act 1990, an advocate or solicitor in Scotland or a barrister or solicitor in Northern Ireland;

"party" means—

(a) a person who is an appellant or respondent in proceedings before the Tribunal;

(b) a person who makes a reference to the Tribunal under section 28D of the Child Support Act 1991;

(c) a person who starts proceedings before the Tribunal under paragraph 3 of Schedule 2 to the Tax Credits Act 2002; or

(d) if the proceedings have been concluded, a person who was a party under paragraph (a), (b) or (c) when the Tribunal finally disposed of all issues in the proceedings;

"practice direction" means a direction given under section 23 of the 2007 Act;

"respondent" means—

(a) in an appeal against a decision, the decision maker and any person other than the appellant who had a right of appeal against the decision;

(b) in a reference under section 28D of the Child Support Act 1991—

(i) the absent parent or non-resident parent;

(ii) the person with care; and

(iii) in Scotland, the child if the child made the application for a departure direction or a variation;

(c) in proceedings under paragraph 3 of Schedule 2 to the Tax Credits Act 2002, a person on whom it is proposed that a penalty be imposed; or

(d) a person substituted or added as a respondent under rule 9 (substitution and addition of parties);

"Social Entitlement Chamber" means the Social Entitlement Chamber of the First-tier Tribunal established by the First-tier Tribunal and Upper Tribunal (Chambers) Order 2008;

"social security and child support case" means any case allocated to the Social Entitlement Chamber except an asylum support case or a criminal injuries compensation case;

"Tribunal" means the First-tier Tribunal.

AMENDMENT

1. Tribunal Procedure (Amendment) Rules 2009, r.2 (April 1, 2009).

DEFINITIONS

"the 2007 Act"—see para.(3).
"appellant"—*ibid.*
"asylum support case"—*ibid.*
"criminal injuries compensation case"—*ibid.*
"party"—*ibid.*
"respondent"—*ibid.*
"Social Entitlement Chamber"—*ibid.*
"Tribunal"—*ibid.*

GENERAL NOTE

By para.(2), these Rules apply to all cases within the Social Entitlement Chamber of the First-tier Tribunal which are those cases formerly dealt with by the appeal tribunals constituted under the Social Security Act 1998, by asylum support adjudicators (known collectively as the "asylum support tribunal") acting under ss.103 and 103A of the Immigration and Asylum Act 1999 and by the adjudicators of the Criminal Injuries Compensation Appeal Panel dealing with cases under schemes made under the Criminal Injuries Compensation Act 1995.

Although the appeal tribunals dealt with a wide variety of cases outside the scope of this work and some that could not properly be called either social security or child support cases, these Rules treat any case within the jurisdiction of the Chamber that is not an asylum support or criminal injuries compensation case as a "social security and child support case".

Note that a "hearing" means an "oral hearing" so that the term "paper hearing" is no longer appropriate for the consideration of a case on the papers. Perhaps "paper determination" will become the commonly used term.

Overriding objective and parties' obligation to co-operate with the Tribunal

2.—(1) The overriding objective of these Rules is to enable the Tribunal to deal with cases fairly and justly.

(2) Dealing with a case fairly and justly includes—

(a) dealing with the case in ways which are proportionate to the importance of the case, the complexity of the issues, the anticipated costs and the resources of the parties;

(b) avoiding unnecessary formality and seeking flexibility in the proceedings;

5.148

(c) ensuring, so far as practicable, that the parties are able to participate fully in the proceedings;

(d) using any special expertise of the Tribunal effectively; and

(e) avoiding delay, so far as compatible with proper consideration of the issues.

(3) The Tribunal must seek to give effect to the overriding objective when it—

(a) exercises any power under these Rules; or

(b) interprets any rule or practice direction.

(4) Parties must—

(a) help the Tribunal to further the overriding objective; and

(b) co-operate with the Tribunal generally.

DEFINITIONS

"party"—see r.1(3).
"practice direction"—*ibid.*
"Tribunal"—*ibid.*

GENERAL NOTE

5.149   It is nowadays conventional for procedural rules in England and Wales to set out clearly their overriding objective in this manner. The overriding objective of these Rules is rather different from that of the Civil Procedure Rules. There, one object is to ensure, so far as practical, that the parties are on an equal footing. It may be thought that that is not achievable in Citizen v State litigation before tribunals and these Rules do not require it. Instead, they emphasise the need to avoid "unnecessary formality" (see para.(2)(b)) and to promote the "enabling role" of tribunals (see para.(2)(c)) and they do not expressly refer to the resources of the tribunal in the way that the Civil Procedure Rules refer to the resources of the court as a matter to be taken into account when making procedural decisions. Perhaps, the key concept is "proportionality" (see para.(2)(a)) which is likely to be relevant in most cases where procedural decisions are being made.

By para.(3), the tribunal is required to "seek to give effect to" the overriding objective when exercising any power under the Rules or interpreting the Rules or a Practice Direction. Note that this does not extend to the exercise of powers under the Tribunal, Courts and Enforcement Act 2007 or other legislation but the principles of the overriding objective might anyway be relevant to the exercise of such powers. By para.(4), parties must help the tribunal to further the overriding objective and co-operate with the tribunal generally and a failure to do so may, in an extreme case, lead to proceedings being struck out under r.8(3)(b).

Courts have from time to time emphasised the importance of overriding objectives. A particularly striking example is in the judgment of Girvan L.J. in *Peifer v Castlederg High School* [2008] NICA 49, where he referred to reg.3 of the Industrial Tribunals (Constitutional Rules of Procedure) Regulations (Northern Ireland) 2005 and said –

"The provisions of . . . Regulation 3 were intended to be exactly what they are described as being, namely *overriding* objectives. The full implications of those rules identifying the overriding objectives have not been fully appreciated by courts, tribunals or practitioners. These overriding objectives should inform the court and the tribunals in the proper conduct of proceedings. Dealing with cases justly involves dealing with cases in ways which are proportionate to the complexity and importance of the issues ensuring that the case is dealt with expeditiously and fairly and the saving of expense. Parties and practitioners are bound to conduct themselves in a way which furthers those overriding objectives. Having regard to the imperative nature of the overriding objectives tribunals should strive to avoid time wasting and repetition. Parties should be required to concentrate on relevant issues and the pursuit of irrelevant issues and questions should be strongly discouraged. Our system of justice properly regards cross-examination as a valuable tool in the pursuit of justice but that tool must not be abused. Tribunals must ensure proper focus on the relevant issues and ensure that time taken in cross-examination is usefully spent. The overriding objectives, which are, of course, always intended to ensure that justice is done, impel a tribunal to exercise its control over the litigation before it robustly but fairly. Tribunals can expect the appellate and supervisory courts to give proper and due weight to the tribunals' decisions made in the fulfilment of their duty to ensure the overriding objectives. Tribunals should not be discouraged from exercising proper control of proceedings to secure those objectives through fear of being criticised by a higher court which must itself give proper respect to the tribunal's margin of appreciation in the exercise of its powers in relation to the proper management of the proceedings to ensure justice, expedition and the saving of cost."

Alternative dispute resolution and arbitration

3.—(1) The Tribunal should seek, where appropriate—

   (a) to bring to the attention of the parties the availability of any appropriate alternative procedure for the resolution of the dispute; and

   (b) if the parties wish and provided that it is compatible with the overriding objective, to facilitate the use of the procedure.

(2) Part 1 of the Arbitration Act 1996 does not apply to proceedings before the Tribunal.

5.150

DEFINITIONS

"party"—see r.1(3).
"Tribunal"—*ibid*.

GENERAL NOTE

Rule 3(1) applies only if there is an alternative procedure available. Apart from a pilot scheme in relation to disability living allowance and attendance allowance claims, there are currently no schemes available in relation to social security cases. The scope for such schemes is limited by the facts that tribunal proceedings in social security cases are relatively cheap, quick and informal and that the conditions of entitlement often allow for little compromise, which means that alternative methods of dispute resolution normally offer little advantage over tribunal proceedings. However, that is not to say that there are no cases that could be better dealt with outside the tribunal process.

5.151

PART 2

GENERAL POWERS AND PROVISIONS

Delegation to staff

4.—(1) Staff appointed under section 40(1) of the 2007 Act (tribunal staff and services) may, with the approval of the Senior President of Tribunals, carry out functions of a judicial nature permitted or required to be done by the Tribunal.

5.152

(2) The approval referred to at paragraph (1) may apply generally to the carrying out of specified functions by members of staff of a specified description in specified circumstances.

(3) Within 14 days after the date on which the Tribunal sends notice of a decision made by a member of staff under paragraph (1) to a party, that party may apply in writing to the Tribunal for that decision to be considered afresh by a judge.

DEFINITIONS

"the 2007 Act"—see r.1(3).
"party"—*ibid.*
"Tribunal"—*ibid.*

GENERAL NOTE

5.153   There is no need to make provision for the delegation of functions of a purely administrative nature and so this rule refers only to functions of a judicial nature. The Senior President of Tribunals has issued a Practice Statement (available at: http://www.tribunals.gov.uk/Tribunals/Rules/statements.htm) recording his approval of the delegation of functions in relation to asylum support cases and criminal injuries compensation cases but not in relation to any other type of case in the Social Entitlement Chamber. Thus, clerks lose the judicial functions they had before November 3, 2008 to strike out and reinstate cases under regs 46 and 47 of the Social Security and Child Support (Decisions and Appeals) Regs 1999, to correct decisions under reg.56 of those Regulations and to issue directions under reg.38(3). The loss of the last power may be of particular significance because it has the effect that a clerk cannot issue a warning that a failure to comply with an instruction will, or may, result in a case being struck out; such a warning must be in a direction (see r.8(1) and (3)).

Case management powers

5.154   **5.**—(1) Subject to the provisions of the 2007 Act and any other enactment, the Tribunal may regulate its own procedure.

(2) The Tribunal may give a direction in relation to the conduct or disposal of proceedings at any time, including a direction amending, suspending or setting aside an earlier direction.

(3) In particular, and without restricting the general powers in paragraphs (1) and (2), the Tribunal may—

  (a) extend or shorten the time for complying with any rule, practice direction or direction;
  (b) consolidate or hear together two or more sets of proceedings or parts of proceedings raising common issues, or treat a case as a lead case (whether in accordance with rule 18 (lead cases) or otherwise);
  (c) permit or require a party to amend a document;
  (d) permit or require a party or another person to provide documents, information, evidence or submissions to the Tribunal or a party;
  (e) deal with an issue in the proceedings as a preliminary issue;
  (f) hold a hearing to consider any matter, including a case management issue;
  (g) decide the form of any hearing;
  (h) adjourn or postpone a hearing;
  (i) require a party to produce a bundle for a hearing;

(j) stay (or, in Scotland, sist) proceedings;
(k) transfer proceedings to another court or tribunal if that other court
    or tribunal has jurisdiction in relation to the proceedings and—
      (i) because of a change of circumstances since the proceedings
          were started, the Tribunal no longer has jurisdiction in relation
          to the proceedings; or
     (ii) the Tribunal considers that the other court or tribunal is a more
          appropriate forum for the determination of the case; or
(l) suspend the effect of its own decision pending the determination by
    the Tribunal or the Upper Tribunal of an application for permission
    to appeal against, and any appeal or review of, that decision.

DEFINITIONS

"the 2007 Act"—see r.1(3).
"dispose of proceedings"—*ibid.*
"document"—*ibid.*
"hearing"—*ibid.*
"party"—*ibid.*
"practice direction"—*ibid.*
"Tribunal"—*ibid.*

GENERAL NOTE

Para. (1)

This paragraph, which is in conventional terms, permits the Tribunal to vary the   5.155
way it handles a case so that the procedure is appropriate to the issues that arise and
to the level of representation, if any.

Para. (2)

This is in very broad terms and, although para.(3) and r.15(1) set out examples   5.156
of directions the tribunal may give, they do not restrict the width of the power in
this paragraph. The power must, however, be exercised so as to give effect to the
overriding objective in r.2 (see r.2(3)). It must also be exercised judicially. A judge is
not generally entitled to subvert the decision of a Tribunal to adjourn for a medical
report by directing that the case be relisted without the report. On the other hand, if
the case is relisted and no point is taken about the absence of the report, the Upper
Tribunal may take the view that the final decision is not erroneous in point of law
(CSDLA/866/2002). For the consequences of failing to comply with a direction, see
r.7.
The procedure for applying for and giving directions is to be found in r.6. Note
that, where a direction requires something to be done by a particular day, it must
be done by 5pm on that day (r.12(1)) but, if that day is not a working day, the act is
done in time if it is done on the next working day (r.12(2)).

Para. (3)(c)

Sub-paragraph (c) presumably refers to grounds of appeal and other submissions,   5.157
rather than to evidence, despite the statutory definition.

Para. (3)(f), (g) and (h)

Sub-paragraphs (f), (g) and (h) must be read with rr.27 to 30.   5.158
In sub-para.(h), the distinction between a postponement and an adjournment is
that the former occurs before the beginning of the hearing and the latter occurs once
the hearing has begun, although an application for an adjournment may be made
right at the beginning of a hearing. In *CDLA/3680/1997*, the Commissioner said
that "[w]here an application for a postponement is refused—or no reply is received

to such an application—it is incumbent on the claimant to take all possible steps to appear, or to have someone appear on his or her behalf, before the tribunal in order to assist the tribunal in considering whether there should be an adjournment". A representative should be ready to argue the case as well as possible if the application for an adjournment is refused.

This regulation is concerned only with the postponement or adjournment of oral hearings. There is no express power to adjourn the paper consideration of a case but such a power is to be implied (see *CDLA/1552/1998*).

In *CSDLA/90/1998*, the Commissioner was highly critical of a local authority representative who had represented a claimant before a tribunal on an application for an adjournment. The claimant had had a prior engagement and the Commissioner found that the representative had indicated to her that she need not attend the tribunal hearing without asking her why the other engagement should take priority. When the tribunal refused to adjourn the hearing the representative had withdrawn. The Commissioner said that the nature of the other engagement should have been explained to the tribunal, that it was not for a representative to tell a claimant not to attend a hearing (because a tribunal were not bound to grant an adjournment merely because the claimant was not there) and that a representative who wished to withdraw should obtain the leave of the tribunal to do so. The claimant had been entitled to expect her representative to argue her case on the basis of the evidence available to him and doing so would not have prevented him from arguing on appeal that the tribunal had erred in refusing the adjournment.

The power to postpone or adjourn proceedings must not be used arbitrarily or capriciously and, in particular, must not be used in order to defeat the general purpose of the legislation, but otherwise there is a complete discretion so long as it is exercised judicially (*CIS/2292/2000*, citing *Jacobs v Norsalta Ltd* [1977] I.C.R. 189) and in accordance on the overriding objective in r.2(2). Nonetheless, in *CIS/2292/2000*, a tribunal erred in rejecting an application for an adjournment made by the representative of a claimant who was in prison, in circumstances where the claimant's oral evidence had an important part to play.

The overriding objective in r.2(2) may be particularly important where a power to postpone or adjourn a hearing is being considered. It requires a case to be dealt with "in ways that are proportionate to the importance of the case, the complexity of the issues, the anticipated costs and the resources of the parties" and also to the avoidance of delay but only "so far as compatible with proper consideration of the issues".

In both *CIB/1009/2004* and *CIB/2058/2004*, Commissioners have emphasised that the inquisitorial approach of tribunals is not a complete substitute for representation and have cited *R. v Social Security Commissioner, Ex p. Bibi* (unreported, May 23, 2000) in which Collins J said that, although there is no absolute right to representation, there is an absolute right to be dealt with fairly and that it was hardly unreasonable for a person to wish to be represented by the particular solicitor with whom she had been dealing. Therefore, a claimant's desire to be represented, or to be represented by a particular person, is a factor that ought to be given proper weight in considering whether or not to grant an adjournment. As to the balancing exercise itself, in *CIB/1009/2004* the Commissioner said—

"13.   A tribunal will always require to be persuaded that an adjournment is necessary—because there is always a potential disadvantage in adjourning a case—but the arguments against an adjournment in tribunal proceedings in a social security case may not be quite the same as those applicable in adversarial proceedings in the courts. In particular, the interests of the parties are not usually as closely balanced. In an ordinary social security case, where the Secretary of State does not provide a representative or have witnesses in attendance, there is very little disadvantage to the Secretary of State in granting the claimant an adjournment. It is usually the claimant himself who suffers the principal disadvantage of delay. If the claimant judges that disadvantage to be less than the disadvantage of proceeding without representation, a tribunal should not too readily substitute its own judgment on the relative weight of those two factors. The main consideration for the tribunal will therefore be whether the adjournment can be justified in the light of the substantial cost of a further hearing and the delay in the determination of another case whose place the adjourned hearing will take. Thus the interests of taxpayers and claimants in general need to be balanced against the interests of the particular appellant.

14.   If the claimant is to blame for need to request an adjournment, his interests are likely to be given correspondingly less weight. A claimant's interests may also be given less weight where his representative's fault has led to the request for an adjournment. By agreeing to act for a claimant, a representative takes some responsibility for the case and tribunals are entitled to exert pressure on representatives to behave properly. However, in an environment where most representatives are not qualified lawyers and where most claimants are not paying for the services of their representatives, some care must be taken not to cause injustice to a claimant by visiting upon him the sins of his representative. The tribunal's response must be proportionate, having regard to the consequences for the claimant of possibly losing his appeal."

In *CSDLA/90/1998*, the Commissioner also held that, when representation is undertaken by a local authority, the claimant is entitled to be fully represented by the authority until disposal of the appeal and the local authority must, if necessary, arrange representation through their legal department in order to avoid a postponement or an adjournment of a hearing. In *CIB/1009/2004*, the Commissioner disagreed with that approach and said that a local authority was entitled to limit the power of representatives to call upon other resources of the authority when a particular representative was unavailable due to illness. However, he went on to say that a representative should make reasonable efforts to secure alternative representation, even if that meant cancelling some other appointments, and that that implied that a request for an adjournment due to the non-availability of a representative should contain a clear indication that consideration had been given to the possibility of someone else representing the claimant. In the absence of such an explanation, the tribunal might be entitled to infer that the reasonable efforts had not been made to find alternative representation. However, a failure by a representing authority to make reasonable efforts to secure alternative representation should not have led to a refusal of an adjournment, when further efforts might not have made any difference, the claimant himself was blameless, a lot of money was at stake and the case was not straightforward so that an experienced representative might have assisted the tribunal to reach a conclusion favourable to the claimant.

In *Evans v Secretary of State for Social Security* (reported as *R(I)5/94*), a medical appeal tribunal disagreed with the opinions of two consultants. The Court of Appeal held that, where a tribunal proposed to put a different interpretation on the same clinical findings from that put by another expert, "fairness points to the need for an adjournment so that, where possible, the tribunal's provisional view can be brought to the attention of the claimant's own advisers". A similar approach has been taken by Park J when hearing an appeal from a Pensions Appeal Tribunal (*Butterfield v Secretary of State for Defence* [2002] EWHC 2247 (Admin)). He said that, when a medically qualified member of a tribunal is the only person present with specialist medical knowledge and he perceives a possible medical objection to the claimant's case that has not been pointed out before, he must draw it to the claimant's attention and it may be necessary to offer the claimant an adjournment so that he has a realistic opportunity to consider the point "however inconvenient and irksome that may be". This makes clear what was probably meant in *Evans*. There need not always be an adjournment but the tribunal's provisional view should be put to the claimant and the claimant should expressly be *offered* an adjournment.

There is no general rule that an appeal to a tribunal should be postponed while related criminal proceedings are pending (*Mote v Secretary of State for Work and Pensions* [2007] EWCA Civ 1324 (reported as *R(IS) 4/08*)). The wishes of the parties will be relevant but will not be determinative. Often a claimant will not wish an appeal to be heard while criminal proceedings are pending lest anything he says at the tribunal hearing is used against him in the criminal trial. However, another claimant may prefer an appeal to be heard first because a finding that he or she was entitled to benefit is likely to undermine a prosecution for obtaining the same benefit by deception.

Adjournments are sometimes necessary because a member of the tribunal is obliged to stand down to avoid an appearance of bias (see the annotation to s.11 of the Tribunals, Courts and Enforcement Act 2007). In *CCS/1876/2006*, the Commissioner suggested that there might be occasions when it was prudent for a member of a tribunal to stand down in order to strengthen a party's confidence in the fairness of the procedures, even if there was no strict legal duty to do so, but he did acknowledge that the expense of an adjournment had to be kept in mind.

At a hearing following an adjournment, the tribunal may be constituted by one or more members who sat on the earlier tribunal and one or more who did not, if no evidence was taken before the adjournment. If evidence was taken before the adjournment, the tribunal should generally be either entirely the same or entirely differently constituted and, in the latter case, must have a complete rehearing, although it is entitled to accept the recorded evidence of a witness who gave evidence at the first hearing provided the rules of natural justice are not infringed (*R(U) 3/88*).

In fact current practice requires a judge to indicate whether any evidence has been heard at an adjourned hearing and, if it has, the clerk will always arrange for the tribunal to consist either of entirely the same members or entirely different members. This avoids the risk of subconscious bias being carried over from one hearing to the other or of a member remembering evidence from the first hearing that does not appear in the record of proceedings (see *CDLA/2429/2004*).

A decision to adjourn is appealable only if it disposes of the substantive issues before the tribunal and either makes the outcome of the case before the tribunal inevitable or prevents a final decision from being made (*CDLA/557/2001*). Otherwise, the parties must wait until the final decision is made and appeal against that decision. A judge should not subvert a decision of a tribunal to adjourn for a medical report by immediately directing that the case be relisted without the report (*CSDLA/866/2002*). Even if a refusal to adjourn is not itself appealable (*Carpenter v Secretary of State for Work and Pensions* [2003] EWCA Civ 33 (reported as *R(IB) 6/03*) but see the note to s.11(2) of the Tribunals, Courts and Enforcement Act 2007), an unfair refusal to adjourn may make the final decision of the tribunal erroneous in point of law so that an appeal may be brought against that final decision (*R. v Medical Appeal Tribunal (Midland Region) Ex p. Carrarini* [1966] 1 W.L.R. 883 (also reported as an appendix to *R(I) 13/65*)).

That was the position in *CM/449/1990*, where the claim was made on behalf of a child with severe learning difficulties. His mother had written as soon as she was given notice of the hearing to apply for an adjournment on the ground that her son was away in short-term care. The tribunal refused the adjournment and dismissed the appeal, saying that they were not prepared to grant it "due to the high incidence of requests for adjournments". The Commissioner allowed the claimant's appeal on the ground that no reasonable tribunal could have refused the request for an adjournment and also on the ground that the tribunal had based their decision entirely on a wholly irrelevant consideration. It may be arguable that the Commissioner went too far in holding that the prevalence of requests for adjournments can never be a factor to be taken into account in considering such a request, but even if that is right, such a consideration cannot prevail without any regard at all being had to the particular facts and circumstances of the individual case.

A refusal to adjourn should be recorded in the record of proceedings (*R(DLA) 3/08*) and it is desirable for a brief reason for the refusal to be included either in the record of proceedings or in the statement of reasons for the tribunal's decision (*Carpenter*), although a failure in either of these respects will not necessarily render a tribunal's decision erroneous in point of law.

Para. (3) (k)

Sub-paragraph (k) applies only where the First-tier Tribunal had jurisdiction at the time the proceedings were begun. Otherwise, the Tribunal is required to strike the proceedings out under r.8(2). Rule 5(3)(k)(i) applies where the First-tier Tribunal loses jurisdiction and r.5(3)(k)(ii) applies only where the First-tier Tribunal and another tribunal have concurrent jurisdiction (which may be the case in some circumstances where a person moves to or from Northern Ireland).

Para. (3) (l)

Sub-paragraph (l) permits the effect of a decision to be suspended pending an appeal to the Upper Tribunal. It is usually unnecessary for the Tribunal to suspend a decision in a social security case concerned with entitlement, due to the Secretary of State's power to suspend payments under reg.16 of the Social Security and Child Support (Decisions and Appeals) Regs 1999 (see, in particular, reg.16(3)(b)(i) and (4)). In the past, the Secretary of State has generally not taken action to recover an overpayment while an appeal against a decision that the overpayment is recoverable is pending but he could now take the view that an appeal does not require him to stay his hand unless the Tribunal so directs under this provision, which would not necessarily be appropriate as a matter of course and could in any event presumably be limited to part of its decision. The power to suspend the effect of a decision may also be useful in appeals under the Social Security (Recovery of Benefits) Act 1997, because s.14 of that Act and the regulations made under it completely fail to deal with the consequences of a successful appeal to the Upper Tribunal.

Procedure for applying for and giving directions

6.—(1) The Tribunal may give a direction on the application of one or more of the parties or on its own initiative.   5.159

(2) An application for a direction may be made—

(a) by sending or delivering a written application to the Tribunal; or

(b) orally during the course of a hearing.

(3) An application for a direction must include the reason for making that application.

(4) Unless the Tribunal considers that there is good reason not to do so, the Tribunal must send written notice of any direction to every party and to any other person affected by the direction.

(5) If a party or any other person sent notice of the direction under paragraph (4) wishes to challenge a direction which the Tribunal has given, they may do so by applying for another direction which amends, suspends or sets aside the first direction.

DEFINITIONS

"hearing"—see r.1(3).
"party"—*ibid.*
"Tribunal"—*ibid.*

GENERAL NOTE

There is no requirement that a person be given the opportunity to make represen-   5.160
tations before a direction is given. Plainly it is to be expected that such an opportunity would be given where a direction is to be given at a hearing but in other cases, where an application is made in writing or the tribunal proposes to issue a direction on its own initiative, it is often simpler and more proportionate to make the direction and then see whether anyone objects. If a direction is given and a party or other

person affected objects to it, the remedy is to apply for another direction amending, suspending or setting aside the first direction (see para.(5)).

It is uncertain to what extent, if at all, there is any right of appeal against a direction or a refusal to give a direction. In *Dorset Healthcare NHS Foundation Trust v MH* [2009] UKUT 4 (AAC), the Upper Tribunal accepted that an appeal lay against a direction issued under r.5(3)(d) of the Tribunal Procedure (First-tier Tribunal) (Health, Education and Social Care Chamber) Rules 2008 (SI 2008/2699) (similar to r.5(3)(d) of these Rules), requiring one party to disclose documents to another. It was unnecessary for the Upper Tribunal to decide whether to accept a broad argument advanced by counsel for the Appellant, to the effect that the power to exclude a decision from the scope of the right of appeal under s.11(1) of the Tribunals, Courts and Enforcement Act 2007 means that the word "decision" in that provision must apply to *any* decision of a tribunal. The consequence of accepting that argument would be that a right of appeal under that Act lies against any decision of the First-tier Tribunal (including any decision to issue a direction) unless a decision is expressly "excluded" under s.11(8). However, it would remain open to the Upper Tribunal to refuse permission to appeal against interlocutory decisions where it would be more appropriate for the dissatisfied party to await the conclusion of proceedings in the First-tier Tribunal. The giving or refusal of a direction may provide a ground of appeal against a final decision in a case (see, in relation to adjournment, the note to r.5(3)(h)). In any event, in the *Dorset Healthcare* case, the Upper Tribunal emphasised the desirability of the Tribunal considering whether to vary a direction, either on its own initiative under r.5(3) or on an application under r.6(5), before contemplating granting permission to appeal, at least in a case where the original direction was made without the benefit of full argument.

Failure to comply with rules etc.

5.161   **7.**—(1) An irregularity resulting from a failure to comply with any requirement in these Rules, a practice direction or a direction, does not of itself render void the proceedings or any step taken in the proceedings.

(2) If a party has failed to comply with a requirement in these Rules, a practice direction or a direction, the Tribunal may take such action as it considers just, which may include—

(a) waiving the requirement;

(b) requiring the failure to be remedied;

(c) exercising its power under rule 8 (striking out a party's case); or

(d) exercising its power under paragraph (3).

(3) The Tribunal may refer to the Upper Tribunal, and ask the Upper Tribunal to exercise its power under section 25 of the 2007 Act in relation to, any failure by a person to comply with a requirement imposed by the Tribunal—

(a) to attend at any place for the purpose of giving evidence;

(b) otherwise to make themselves available to give evidence;

(c) to swear an oath in connection with the giving of evidence;

(d) to give evidence as a witness;

(e) to produce a document; or

(f) to facilitate the inspection of a document or any other thing (including any premises).

DEFINITIONS

"the 2007 Act"—see r.1(3).
"document"—*ibid.*
"party"—*ibid.*

"practice direction"—*ibid.*
"Tribunal"—*ibid.*

GENERAL NOTE

Paragraphs (1) and (2)(a) enable a tribunal to overlook a breach of a rule, prac- 5.162
tice direction or direction. On the other hand, under para.2(c), such a breach can
lead to a case being struck out under r.8, provided an appropriate warning has been
given. Alternatively, para.(3) enables a breach of a requirement to give evidence or
produce or make available a document to be referred to the Upper Tribunal with
a view to the Upper Tribunal punishing the person for contempt of court (with a
term of imprisonment of up to two years and an unlimited fine) under s.25 of the
Tribunals' Courts and Enforcement Act 2007, as applied by r.7(4) of the Tribunal
Procedure (Upper Tribunal) Rules 2008, although that should be a last resort.
Paragraph (3)(c) must be read subject to s.5 of the Oaths Act 1978, which permits a
person who objects to being sworn to make a solemn affirmation instead.

A failure to comply with a direction to provide evidence may simply lead to the
case being heard without the evidence, which will usually be to the disadvantage of
the person who has failed to provide the evidence. Whether it is appropriate to draw
an adverse inference from a failure to provide evidence will depend on the circumstances (*CCS/3757/2004*).

Striking out a party's case

8.—(1) The proceedings, or the appropriate part of them, will automati- 5.163
cally be struck out if the appellant has failed to comply with a direction that
stated that failure by a party to comply with the direction would lead to the
striking out of the proceedings or that part of them.

(2) The Tribunal must strike out the whole or a part of the proceedings
if the Tribunal—

(a) does not have jurisdiction in relation to the proceedings or that part
of them; and

(b) does not exercise its power under rule 5(3)(k)(i) (transfer to another
court or tribunal) in relation to the proceedings or that part of
them.

(3) The Tribunal may strike out the whole or a part of the proceedings
if—

(a) the appellant has failed to comply with a direction which stated that
failure by the appellant to comply with the direction could lead to the
striking out of the proceedings or part of them;

(b) the appellant has failed to co-operate with the Tribunal to such an
extent that the Tribunal cannot deal with the proceedings fairly and
justly; or

(c) the Tribunal considers there is no reasonable prospect of the appellant's case, or part of it, succeeding.

(4) The Tribunal may not strike out the whole or a part of the proceedings under paragraph (2) or (3)(b) or (c) without first giving the appellant
an opportunity to make representations in relation to the proposed striking
out.

(5) If the proceedings, or part of them, have been struck out under paragraph (1) or (3)(a), the appellant may apply for the proceedings, or part of
them, to be reinstated.

(6) An application under paragraph (5) must be made in writing and
received by the Tribunal within 1 month after the date on which the
Tribunal sent notification of the striking out to the appellant.

(7) This rule applies to a respondent as it applies to an appellant except that—

    (a) a reference to the striking out of the proceedings is to be read as a reference to the barring of the respondent from taking further part in the proceedings; and

    (b) a reference to an application for the reinstatement of proceedings which have been struck out is to be read as a reference to an application for the lifting of the bar on the respondent from taking further part in the proceedings.

(8) If a respondent has been barred from taking further part in proceedings under this rule and that bar has not been lifted, the Tribunal need not consider any response or other submission made by that respondent.

DEFINITIONS

    "appellant"—see r.1(3).
    "party"—*ibid.*
    "respondent"—*ibid.*
    "Tribunal"—*ibid.*

GENERAL NOTE

5.164   Note that, although paras (1) to (6) are expressed in terms of striking out proceedings brought by the appellant, by virtue of paras (7) and (8) they also provide for barring a respondent from taking further part in the proceedings.

Para.(1)

5.165   This provides for an automatic strike out where a person has failed to comply with a direction that carried a warning that, unless there was compliance, the case "will" be struck out. In theory, no further judicial act is required for the strike-out to take effect provided that it is clear that there has not been compliance. It is important to distinguish this paragraph from para.(3)(a), which provides for a case to be struck out for failure to comply with a direction that carried a warning that if there was no compliance the case "may" be struck out. In such a case, there needs to be a judicial decision exercising the power to strike out. However, proceedings struck out under this paragraph may be reinstated on an application under paras (5) and (6).

Para.(2)

5.166   This replaces reg.46(1)(a) of the Social Security and Child Support (Decisions and Appeals) Regs 1999. However, it is not limited to cases excluded from the scope of s.12 of the Social Security Act 1998 by virtue of Sch.2 to that Act or Sch.2 to the 1999 Regs. Moreover, unlike reg.46, its terms are mandatory, so that a final decision to the effect that the tribunal lacks jurisdiction must always be in the form of a decision to strike out the appeal. These differences suggest that the decision in *Morina v Secretary of State for Work and Pensions* [2007] EWCA Civ 749; [2007] 1 W.L.R. 3033 (also reported as *R(IS) 6/07*), in which the Court of Appeal held that that there was no right of appeal under s.14 of the Social Security Act 1998 against a decision under reg.46(1)(a), is distinguishable so that it is arguable that there is a right of appeal under s.11 of the Tribunals, Courts and Enforcement Act 2007 against a decision under this rule, even if the broader argument advanced mentioned in the annotation to r.6 above is not accepted.

     By virtue of para.(4), a party must be given an opportunity to make representations before his or her case is struck out and there will be some cases where justice requires there to be a hearing, notwithstanding r.27(3).

Para. (3)

Striking out is discretionary and must be proportionate (see r.2(2)(a) and (3)), having regard to the culpability of the party whose case is being struck out and the amount at stake on the appeal.

Sub-paragraph (c) reintroduces a power to strike a case out where it has no reasonable prospect of success. An equivalent power in reg.48 of the 1999 Regs was revoked in 2004.

Rule 27(3) permits the Tribunal to strike out a case without a hearing but, by virtue of para.(4), a party must be given an opportunity to make representations before his or her case is struck out under sub-para.(b) or (c). Where an effective opportunity to make representations would require a hearing, it is likely to be simpler and fairer to determine the appeal in the ordinary way instead of striking it out. Thus sub-paras (b) and (c) should probably be used only in clear and obvious cases.

There is no right to make representations before a case is struck out under sub-paragraph (a); instead there is a right to apply for reinstatement after the event, by virtue of paras (5) and (6).

Paras (5) and (6)

These paragraphs apply only to cases struck out under para.(1) or (3)(a). In other cases, the Tribunal must give the party an opportunity to make representations *before* a case is struck out. In *Synergy Child Services Ltd v Ofsted* [2009] UKUT 125 (AAC), the Upper Tribunal accepted that an appeal lay against a refusal to reinstate a struck-out appeal under the equivalent provisions in the Tribunal Procedure (First-tier Tribunal) (Health, Education and Social Care Chamber) Rules 2008 (SI 2008/2699) and held that, when considering whether to reinstate an appeal, "a Tribunal should have regard to the broad justice of the case, in the light of all the circumstances obtaining at the time the application for reinstatement is being considered". Nonetheless, it said that "[w]here there has been flagrant disobedience by a party, belated compliance or a change of circumstances making compliance irrelevant will not always require a Tribunal to reinstate an appeal".

Paras (7) and (8)

This rule does not work in an entirely even-handed manner. An appellant (which may in a few cases be the Secretary of State or HMRC) may find that the whole or part of the proceedings he or she has brought are struck out. The equivalent sanction in respect of a respondent is merely being barred from taking further part in proceedings, which has the effect that the Tribunal "need not consider any response or other submission made by that respondent". This appears to mean that the Tribunal need not consider any written response or other submission even if it was submitted before the respondent was barred, particularly as the bar might otherwise be ineffective. However, the language of both para.(8) and r.24(4) suggests that the term "response" does not include the evidence provided with it. If that is correct, the effect is that, although being barred from taking further part in proceedings presumably includes being barred from providing further evidence, the Tribunal is not entitled to ignore evidence provided before the bar was imposed, which may reduce the effectiveness of the bar. In any event, the implications of barring a respondent from taking further part in proceedings are likely to be far more serious in cases where the primary duty to provide evidence lies on the respondent than in cases where it lies on the appellant.

Judicial review provides an alternative remedy. In *R. (Davies) v The Commissioners' Office and the Child Support Agency* [2008] EWHC 334 (Admin), Black J declared irrational the Secretary of State's refusal to comply with a tribunal's directions to disclose evidence. She said that the only proper course for the Secretary of State, if he objected to directions, was to return to the tribunal and seek a variation. See now r.6(5), although there might now also be the possibility of appealing against the directions.

5.167

5.167.1

5.168

Substitution and addition of parties

5.169   **9.**—(1) The Tribunal may give a direction substituting a party if—

(a) the wrong person has been named as a party; or

(b) the substitution has become necessary because of a change in circumstances since the start of proceedings.

(2) The Tribunal may give a direction adding a person to the proceedings
as a respondent.

(3) If the Tribunal gives a direction under paragraph (1) or (2) it may give
such consequential directions as it considers appropriate.

DEFINITIONS

"party"—see r.1(3).
"respondent"—*ibid.*
"Tribunal"—*ibid.*

GENERAL NOTE

Para.(2)

5.170   A person joined as a respondent becomes a party and acquires all the rights of a
party, including the right to require there to be a hearing, the right to obtain a statement of reasons and the right to apply for permission to appeal.

Given the wide scope of the definition of "respondent" in r.1(3), it will seldom be
necessary to add a party as a respondent in a social security case because a person
with an interest in a decision under appeal will usually have had a right of appeal
against it and so will automatically be a respondent. In the past, there were at least
two types of cases where non-parties were invited to attend hearings. The injured
person would sometimes be invited to attend a hearing of an appeal under the Social
Security (Recovery of Benefits) Act 1997 brought by a compensator even though
there had been no deduction under s.8 of that Act so that the injured person had
no right of appeal and no direct interest in the case. A person in receipt of widow's
benefit would sometimes be invited to attend a hearing of an appeal against a refusal
to award another woman widow's benefit based on contributions paid by the same
man where there was a possibility that there might have been polygamous marriages.
In both cases, the reason for inviting the non-party was that success by the appellant might logically lead to an award of benefit to the non-party being revised or
superseded. The problem was, and remains, that, in the unfortunate absence of any
power in the Secretary of State to refer the question of revision or supersession to a
tribunal, any decision on the first appeal is not binding in relation to the revision or
supersession. It would be unfair for it to be binding without the question properly
being referred and the non-party being given a clear indication of the grounds upon
which there might be revision or supersession. It is suggested that, under the new
legislation, it will be preferable in these circumstances for a non-party to be invited
to attend as a witness rather than for him or her to be joined as a respondent and
thereby to become a party, although sometimes it might be desirable for him or her
to be able to make representations as well (see *CG/1164/2006*).

No power to award costs

5.171   **10.** The Tribunal may not make any order in respect of costs (or, in
Scotland, expenses).

DEFINITION

"Tribunal"—see r.1(3).

GENERAL NOTE

See the note to s.29 to the Tribunals, Courts and Enforcement Act 2007.　　5.172

Representatives

11.—(1) A party may appoint a representative (whether a legal repre-　5.173
sentative or not) to represent that party in the proceedings.

(2) Subject to paragraph (3), if a party appoints a representative, that
party (or the representative if the representative is a legal representative)
must send or deliver to the Tribunal written notice of the representative's
name and address.

(3) In a case to which rule 23 (cases in which the notice of appeal is
to be sent to the decision maker) applies, if the appellant (or the appellant's representative if the representative is a legal representative) provides
written notification of the appellant's representative's name and address to
the decision maker before the decision maker provides its response to the
Tribunal, the appellant need not take any further steps in order to comply
with paragraph (2).

(4) If the Tribunal receives notice that a party has appointed a representative under paragraph (2), it must send a copy of that notice to each other
party.

(5) Anything permitted or required to be done by a party under these
Rules, a practice direction or a direction may be done by the representative
of that party, except signing a witness statement.

(6) A person who receives due notice of the appointment of a representative—

(a) must provide to the representative any document which is required
to be provided to the represented party, and need not provide that
document to the represented party; and

(b) may assume that the representative is and remains authorised as such
until they receive written notification that this is not so from the representative or the represented party.

(7) At a hearing a party may be accompanied by another person whose
name and address has not been notified under paragraph (2) or (3) but
who, with the permission of the Tribunal, may act as a representative or
otherwise assist in presenting the party's case at the hearing.

(8) Paragraphs (2) to (6) do not apply to a person who accompanies a
party under paragraph (7).

DEFINITIONS

"appeal"—see r.1(3).
"appellant"—*ibid.*
"decision maker"—*ibid.*
"document"—*ibid.*
"hearing"—*ibid.*
"legal representative"—*ibid.*
"party"—*ibid.*
"practice direction"—*ibid.*
"Tribunal"—*ibid.*

GENERAL NOTE

Para. (1)

5.174
A party has a right to be represented by any person (subject to their proper behaviour). Thus, under earlier legislation, a chairman erred in refusing to hear submissions by what he described as a "McKenzie friend" and it was an error of law for him to insist that the claimant specify at the beginning of the hearing whether the person accompanying her was going to act as a representative in the conventional sense (*CS/1753/2000*). In *CDLA/2462/2003*, the Commissioner has reiterated the point that representatives may also be witnesses.

> "8. Tribunals operate less formally than courts. They do not operate rights of audience. They allow, of course, professional legal representation. But they also allow lay representation and assistance from anyone whom the claimant wishes to assist in presenting a case to a tribunal. Given that breadth of representation, it is inevitable that the roles of representative and witness cannot be separated in the way that they would in a court. The same person may wish to put the claimant's case and give evidence in support of that case. The tribunal must take care to distinguish evidence from representation so that the former's provenance is known and can be the subject of questioning by the tribunal and other parties. But, subject to the practicalities of the way in which the taking of evidence is handled, there is no objection in principle to the same person acting in different capacities as a witness and as a representative. Nor is there any reason in principle why the probative value of evidence should depend upon whether or not it came from a representative."
>
> . . .
>
> 13. I emphasise that I am concerned here with a representative who wanted to give evidence from his own knowledge. I am not concerned with the different circumstance of a representative who wants to make a statement of the claimant's evidence to the appeal tribunal. Some tribunals refuse a representative the chance to do this. They insist on hearing the evidence from the claimant, allowing the representative to supplement the tribunal's questions to ensure that all the evidence is elicited from the claimant. That is a matter that is within the chairman's control of the procedure under regulation 49(1) [now r.5(1)]. Nothing I have written above affects the use of that power by [a] chairman to control the way that the claimant's own evidence is presented."

The possible conflict of interest where a person employed by a local authority represents a claimant in a housing benefit case where the same local authority is a party was considered in *CSHC/729/2003*. The Commissioner commended the practice of the representative concerned in drawing claimants' attention to the potential conflict. The Commissioner reserved the question whether he or a tribunal had any power to prevent a representative chosen by a claimant from acting. It is suggested that, in the absence of misconduct by the representative, there is no such power, although the Tribunal could ensure that the claimant had made an informed choice.

Paras (2) to (6)

5.175
These paragraphs provide for the formal appointment of a representative. Notice must be given to the Tribunal (para.(2)) unless an appellant has already given notice to the decision-maker before the decision-maker has sent the response to the appeal to the Tribunal (para.(3)), in which case the decision-maker must inform the Tribunal of the name and address of the appellant's representative (see r.24(4)(c)). A formally appointed representative may act on behalf of the party in all respects (except to sign a witness statement) and should be sent any documents that would otherwise be sent to the party (paras (5) and (6)(a)). However, it is presumably possible for the Tribunal to exclude a representative from a hearing under r.30(5) without excluding the party.

Paras (7) and (8)

These paragraphs enable a party who is present at a hearing to be represented or
assisted at the hearing by any person, without there having been any formal notice
of appointment. Although the Tribunal's permission is required, it is suggested that,
unless r.30(5) applies, it will only exceptionally be appropriate for the Tribunal
to refuse permission, particularly as the party need only provide a written notice
under para.(2) in order to avoid the need for permission. Without a written notice
of appointment, a person who acts as a representative at a hearing has no rights as a
representative outside the hearing. Obviously, a written notice may be provided at the
hearing so that the person becomes entitled to act as a full representative thereafter.

Calculating time

12.—(1) Except in asylum support cases, an act required by these Rules,
a practice direction or a direction to be done on or by a particular day must
be done by 5pm on that day.

(2) If the time specified by these Rules, a practice direction or a direction
for doing any act ends on a day other than a working day, the act is done in
time if it is done on the next working day.

(3) In this rule "working day" means any day except a Saturday or
Sunday, Christmas Day, Good Friday or a bank holiday under section 1 of
the Banking and Financial Dealings Act 1971.

DEFINITIONS

"asylum support case"—see r.1(3).
"practice direction"—*ibid.*
"working day"—see para.(3).

GENERAL NOTE

Para.(3)

Christmas Day and Good Friday are holidays under the common law in England,
Wales and Northern Ireland, rather than being bank holidays, which is why they
are specifically mentioned in this paragraph. The following days are bank holidays
in England, Wales and Northern Ireland, either because they are mentioned in
Schedule 1 to the 1971 Act or by virtue of Royal proclamations under s.1(2) and
(3) of that Act: New Year's Day, Easter Monday, the first Monday in May, the last
Monday in May, the last Monday in August, and December 26. In Northern Ireland,
there are additional bank holidays on March 17 (St Patrick's Day), by virtue of Sch.1
to the 1971 Act, and July 12 (the anniversary of the Battle of the Boyne), by virtue
of a proclamation by the Secretary of State for Northern Ireland under s.1(5) of that
Act. Where a bank holiday would otherwise fall on a Saturday or Sunday, the following Monday (and Tuesday, where December 26 is on a Sunday) is substituted.

Scotland has different bank holidays under the 1971 Act but they are not always
observed as public holidays as there is a tradition of observing various local public
holidays or institutional holidays instead of, or occasionally as well as, bank holidays.
The statutory bank holidays, including those announced by Royal proclamation, are
New Year's Day, January 2, Good Friday, the first Monday in May, the last Monday
in May, the first Monday in August, November 30 (St Andrew's Day), Christmas
Day and December 26. Where a bank holiday would otherwise fall on a Saturday or
Sunday the following Monday (or Tuesday, where January 2 or December 26 is on
a Sunday), is substituted. These are the relevant days for the purposes of this rule
although Royal Mail does in fact operate on November 30. November 30 is a comparatively recent addition to the list and, where it is observed as a holiday, it is often

5.176

5.177

5.178

in place of one of the other bank holidays. Ironically, the clearing banks observe the English bank holidays so that they are open on January 2, the first Monday in August and November 30 but are closed on Easter Monday and the last Monday in August.

The relevant days to be treated as bank holidays will depend on the part of the United Kingdom in which the "act"—which will be the receipt of a document where the Rules provide that a document must be received by the Tribunal or a party within a specified time—must be performed. No specific provision is made in respect of local holidays or other causes of postal delays where a party lives outside the United Kingdom but the general power to extend time under r.5(3)(a) may be invoked.

Sending and delivery of documents

5.179

13.—(1) Any document to be provided to the Tribunal under these Rules, a practice direction or a direction must be—

  (a) sent by pre-paid post or delivered by hand to the address specified for the proceedings;
  (b) sent by fax to the number specified for the proceedings; or
  (c) sent or delivered by such other method as the Tribunal may permit or direct.

(2) Subject to paragraph (3), if a party provides a fax number, email address or other details for the electronic transmission of documents to them, that party must accept delivery of documents by that method.

(3) If a party informs the Tribunal and all other parties that a particular form of communication (other than pre-paid post or delivery by hand) should not be used to provide documents to that party, that form of communication must not be so used.

(4) If the Tribunal or a party sends a document to a party or the Tribunal by email or any other electronic means of communication, the recipient may request that the sender provide a hard copy of the document to the recipient. The recipient must make such a request as soon as reasonably practicable after receiving the document electronically.

(5) The Tribunal and each party may assume that the address provided by a party or its representative is and remains the address to which documents should be sent or delivered until receiving written notification to the contrary.

DEFINITIONS

"document"—see r.1(3).
"party"—*ibid*.
"practice direction"—*ibid*.
"Tribunal"—*ibid*.

GENERAL NOTE

5.180

In these Rules, a party is usually required to provide, or send, a document so that it is *received* by a certain date. See r.12 for the calculation of time. A document may be sent by fax and, in *R(DLA) 3/05*, it was held that a fax is received when it is successfully transmitted to, and received by, a fax machine, irrespective of whether anyone actually collects it from the machine.

Furthermore, the faxed request for a statement of reasons in that case was received by the clerk to the appeal tribunal when received at the tribunal venue, even though the clerk did not visit that venue until some days later. The Commissioner said that it would have been different if the venue had been a casual venue, such as local authority premises. Here, it was a dedicated venue and the fax number had been given to representatives precisely to enable them to communicate with the clerk. There was nothing in any document issued with the decision notice to indicate that the request for a statement of reasons had to be addressed to a different place. If it is accepted that a notice of hearing, or a direction, was not in fact received by a claimant even though it was properly posted. An application under r.37 is generally the appropriate procedure to be followed in such a case, rather than an appeal *(R(SB) 19/83)*.

A provision deeming a document to be received if sent was held to be invalid in *R. v Secretary of State for the Home Department Ex p. Saleem* [2001] 1 W.L.R. 443 but Commissioners distinguished that case on the ground that there was no remedy in the regulations under consideration in that case where a document was not in fact received *(CCS/6302/1999* and *CIB/303/1999)*. Rule 37 provides such a remedy here where documents relating to a hearing before a tribunal have gone astray and there are also provisions for extending the time for appealing when notices of decisions are not received.

In *R(SB) 55/83*, it was held that an application under what is now r.37 was the *only* remedy when a tribunal heard a case in a claimant's absence because he or she did not receive notice of the hearing. However, Commissioners have subsequently declined to follow that decision. In *CDLA/5413/1999*, the Commissioner referred to the European Convention on Human Rights. In *CIB/303/1999*, where there had been a refusal to set aside the tribunal decision, the Commissioner applied *Ex p. Saleem* and held that the right of appeal to a Commissioner could not be ousted by the provision of an alternative remedy in a case where the other remedy had proved ineffective. There was a breach of the rules of natural justice or an analogous error of law, notwithstanding that the tribunal had not been at fault, and the claimant was entitled to have the decision set aside on appeal. The Commissioner did, however, endorse what was said in *R(SB) 19/83* and repeated that an application under what is now r.37 was the procedure to be preferred where a party does not receive notice of a hearing.

Where documents are sent by the Tribunal to a party under these Rules, the important date is usually the date they are sent. However, a decision of the Tribunal may be set aside under r.37

Para. (1)

When sending documents to the Tribunal, fax may always be used if available but email may be used only if the Tribunal has specifically said so. **5.181**

Paras (2) and (3)

When sending documents to a party, any available method of communication may be used unless the party has specifically said that fax or email may not be used. Any address or number given may be assumed to be still in use until notice to the contrary is given (see para.(5)). **5.182**

Para. (4)

This paragraph enables a party or the Tribunal to require a hard copy of a faxed or emailed document to be provided even though the fax or email delivery may have been sufficient for the purpose of complying with a time limit. It might be used, for instance, where a fax is poorly reproduced or where printing a large email attachment would be unduly onerous. Note that it is not necessary to provide a hard copy of a fax or email unless requested to do so. However, where a time limit runs to the date a document is received, it might be wise to send a hard copy if there is any reason to doubt that the document will be received electronically even if sent. **5.183**

Use of documents and information

14.—(1) The Tribunal may make an order prohibiting the disclosure or publication of— **5.184**

(a) specified documents or information relating to the proceedings; or

(b) any matter likely to lead members of the public to identify any person whom the Tribunal considers should not be identified.

(2) The Tribunal may give a direction prohibiting the disclosure of a document or information to a person if—

(a) the Tribunal is satisfied that such disclosure would be likely to cause that person or some other person serious harm; and

(b) the Tribunal is satisfied, having regard to the interests of justice, that it is proportionate to give such a direction.

(3) If a party ("the first party") considers that the Tribunal should give a direction under paragraph (2) prohibiting the disclosure of a document or information to another party ("the second party"), the first party must—

(a) exclude the relevant document or information from any documents that will be provided to the second party; and

(b) provide to the Tribunal the excluded document or information, and the reason for its exclusion, so that the Tribunal may decide whether the document or information should be disclosed to the second party or should be the subject of a direction under paragraph (2).

(4) The Tribunal must conduct proceedings as appropriate in order to give effect to a direction given under paragraph (2).

(5) If the Tribunal gives a direction under paragraph (2) which prevents disclosure to a party who has appointed a representative, the Tribunal may give a direction that the documents or information be disclosed to that representative if the Tribunal is satisfied that—

(a) disclosure to the representative would be in the interests of the party; and

(b) the representative will act in accordance with paragraph (6).

(6) Documents or information disclosed to a representative in accordance with a direction under paragraph (5) must not be disclosed either directly or indirectly to any other person without the Tribunal's consent.

DEFINITIONS

"document"—see r.1(3).
"party"—*ibid.*
"Tribunal"—*ibid.*

GENERAL NOTE

Para. (1)

5.185   An order under this paragraph may be directed to an individual and be concerned only with an individual document (e.g. prohibiting an appellant from disclosing to someone else a document disclosed to the appellant by the respondent) or it may be directed to the public in general and effectively amount to a reporting restriction. Hearings of social security cases are usually attended only by those immediately interested in them but most hearings are, in principle, open to the public, including the press (see r.30). It is difficult to envisage it being appropriate to prohibit the publication of any information at all about a hearing held in public but it might often be appropriate to make an order prohibiting the publishing of information that may lead to a child or vulnerable adult being identified if there would otherwise be any serious risk of such publication. It will generally be necessary properly to balance the right of one person to respect of his or her private life under Art.8 of the European Convention on Human Rights and the right of another person to freedom of expression under art.10 (see *Re British Broadcasting Corporation* [2009] UKHL

34; [2009] 3 W.L.R. 142, where it is noteworthy that, although the House of Lords discharged an anonymity order so as to permit the BBC to broadcast an acquitted defendant's name, it saw no need to mention his name itself). The existence of the powers conferred by this paragraph is a factor to be borne in mind when deciding under r.30(3) whether a hearing should be in private or in public, which requires consideration of the terms of Art.6(1).

A breach of an order made under this paragraph is a contempt of court. However, it can be enforced only through an application for committal made to the High Court or, in Scotland, the Court of Session.

Paras (2) to (6)

These paragraphs replace reg.42 of the Social Security and Child Support (Decisions and Appeals) Regs 1999, although they are not limited to medical advice or evidence. It is suggested that "serious harm" merely means harm that would be sufficiently serious to justify what would otherwise be a breach of the right to a fair hearing guaranteed by Art.6 of the European Convention on Human Rights. In effect, the application of this rule requires a person's art.8 rights to be balanced against his or her art.6 rights. A similar balancing exercise was required under the former legislation even before the Human Rights Act 1998 came into effect (*CDLA/1347/1999*, disagreeing with the absolutist view expressed in *CSDLA/5/1995* that "no adverserial dispute should be decided against a party on the basis of evidence not disclosed to them unless that party has been given sufficient indication of the gist of that evidence to give them a proper opportunity to put forward their case"). Provided the risk of harm to the claimant is properly balanced against his or her right to a fair hearing, there is unlikely to be a breach of the European Convention on Human Rights, particularly if the claimant has a representative to whom disclosure has been made (see *R. (Roberts) v Parole Board* [2005] UKHL 45; [2005] 2 A.C. 738). Note the power in r.30(5)(c) to exclude a person from a hearing, and the power in r.33(2) not to provide a full statement of reasons, in order to give effect to a direction under para.(2).

In *CDLA/1347/1999*, it was suggested that, if a tribunal was minded to reveal evidence that had been withheld on medical advice, it might be prudent to give the medical advisor the opportunity of justifying the advice before revealing the evidence. The Commissioner also agreed with a suggestion that, if reasons for a decision were being given, withheld evidence should be referred to in a supplementary statement of reasons given to the Secretary of State (and the claimant's representative if the evidence had been revealed to him or her) but not given to the claimant. That would have the effect that, in the event of an appeal, the Upper Tribunal would know how the evidence had been approached.

In most cases concerning attendance allowance or disability living allowance, this rule will not give rise to great problems because evidence that a claimant is seriously ill, which is the sort of evidence that would normally be withheld, is evidence that is likely to assist the claimant rather than the reverse. It is in cases concerning disablement benefit, where causation is often in issue, that the problem arises most acutely. There, if a tribunal are satisifed that evidence should be withheld but would be likely to be contested by a claimant if he or she knew of it, it is suggested that they should take care to ensure that it is properly tested by, for example, obtaining a second opinion. If proceedings cannot properly be adversarial, they must be truly inquisitorial. Indeed, if there were contradictory evidence and the claimant would be likely to contest the withheld evidence, a tribunal might well be particularly slow to conclude that this rule should be applied and might choose either to disclose the evidence or else to disregard it.

In *Dorset Healthcare NHS Foundation Trust v MH* [2009] UKUT 4 (AAC), it was made clear that serious harm was not the only ground upon which disclosure of documents may be withheld. In that case, documents were withheld from a patient on the ground of confidentiality but it was not suggested that the tribunal should

5.186

see the withheld documents. It is doubtful that a tribunal could properly have regard to evidence that had not been disclosed to a party in any circumstances other than those contemplated in this rule unless, perhaps, a legally qualified representative acting for the party was prepared to consent to it doing so despite not being able to obtain the informed consent of the party.

Evidence and submissions

5.187   **15.**—(1) Without restriction on the general powers in rule 5(1) and (2) (case management powers), the Tribunal may give directions as to—

    (a) issues on which it requires evidence or submissions;

    (b) the nature of the evidence or submissions it requires;

    (c) whether the parties are permitted or required to provide expert evidence;

    (d) any limit on the number of witnesses whose evidence a party may put forward, whether in relation to a particular issue or generally;

    (e) the manner in which any evidence or submissions are to be provided, which may include a direction for them to be given—

        (i) orally at a hearing; or

        (ii) by written submissions or witness statement; and

    (f) the time at which any evidence or submissions are to be provided.

(2) The Tribunal may—

    (a) admit evidence whether or not—

        (i) the evidence would be admissible in a civil trial in the United Kingdom; or

        (ii) the evidence was available to a previous decision maker; or

    (b) exclude evidence that would otherwise be admissible where—

        (i) the evidence was not provided within the time allowed by a direction or a practice direction;

        (ii) the evidence was otherwise provided in a manner that did not comply with a direction or a practice direction; or

        (iii) it would otherwise be unfair to admit the evidence.

(3) The Tribunal may consent to a witness giving, or require any witness to give, evidence on oath, and may administer an oath for that purpose.

DEFINITIONS

    "decision maker"—see r.1(3).

    "hearing"—*ibid.*

    "party"—*ibid.*

    "practice direction"—*ibid.*

    "Tribunal"—*ibid.*

GENERAL NOTE

Para. (1)

5.188   Rule 6 makes the necessary procedural provision.

Para. (2)

5.189   Paragraph (2)(a) makes explicit powers to admit evidence that were formerly implicit. Note that the Tribunal merely has a power to admit evidence that would be inadmissible in a civil trial and it cannot override any privilege of a witness not to give evidence (see the note to s.(3)(1) of the Tribunal, Courts and Enforcement Act 2007). Beyond that, the main consideration will simply be whether the evidence is relevant.

Paragraph (2)(b) enables evidence to be excluded. This power, like all other powers under the Rules, must be exercised so as to give effect to the overriding objective in r.2 and it is suggested that it will rarely be proportionate to exclude relevant evidence simply because it is provided late, unless some prejudice would be suffered by another party or the delay makes it more difficult for the tribunal to consider the evidence. See *CIB/4253/2004*

Para. (3)

This makes explicit that the Tribunal may consent to evidence being given on   **5.190** oath where it is the witness or a party who wishes that to be done. In practice, it is fairly rare for evidence to be given on oath in social security cases.

By virtue of s.5 of the Oaths Act 1978, any person who objects to being sworn shall be permitted to make his or her solemn affirmation instead of taking an oath. In England, Wales and Northern Ireland, a Christian or Jew usually swears an oath with the New Testament, or, in the case of a Jew, the Old Testament, in his or her uplifted hand (*Ibid.*, s.1(1)) but if the person desires to swear without holding the Bible but "with uplifted hand in the form and manner in which an oath is usually administered in Scotland", he or she must be permitted to do so (s.3). In the case of a person who is neither a Christian not a Jew, the oath shall be administered in any lawful manner (*Ibid.*, s.1(3)), but such a person may prefer to affirm.

Summoning or citation of witnesses and orders to answer questions or produce documents

16.—(1) On the application of a party or on its own initiative, the   **5.191** Tribunal may—

   (a) by summons (or, in Scotland, citation) require any person to attend as a witness at a hearing at the time and place specified in the summons or citation; or

   (b) order any person to answer any questions or produce any documents in that person's possession or control which relate to any issue in the proceedings.

(2) A summons or citation under paragraph (1)(a) must—

   (a) give the person required to attend 14 days' notice of the hearing or such shorter period as the Tribunal may direct; and

   (b) where the person is not a party, make provision for the person's necessary expenses of attendance to be paid, and state who is to pay them.

(3) No person may be compelled to give any evidence or produce any document that the person could not be compelled to give or produce on a trial of an action in a court of law in the part of the United Kingdom where the proceedings are due to be determined.

(4) A summons, citation or order under this rule must—

   (a) state that the person on whom the requirement is imposed may apply to the Tribunal to vary or set aside the summons, citation or order, if they have not had an opportunity to object to it; and

   (b) state the consequences of failure to comply with the summons, citation or order.

DEFINITIONS

"document"—see r.1(3).
"hearing"—*ibid.*
"party"—*ibid.*
"Tribunal"—*ibid.*

5.192   This rule includes a power to order the production of documents without requiring attendance at a hearing. A failure to comply with a summons, citation or order under this rule is a contempt of court that may be referred to the Upper Tribunal under r.7(3). The Upper Tribunal has the power to impose a term of imprisonment not exceeding two years and an unlimited fine.

Withdrawal

5.193   **17.**—(1) Subject to paragraph (2), a party may give notice of the withdrawal of its case, or any part of it—

(a) at any time before a hearing to consider the disposal of the proceedings (or, if the Tribunal disposes of the proceedings without a hearing, before that disposal), by sending or delivering to the Tribunal a written notice of withdrawal; or

(b) orally at a hearing.

(2) In the circumstances described in paragraph (3), a notice of withdrawal will not take effect unless the Tribunal consents to the withdrawal.

(3) The circumstances referred to in paragraph (2) are where a party gives notice of withdrawal—

(a) under paragraph (1)(a) in a criminal injuries compensation case; or

(b) under paragraph (1)(b).

(4) A party who has withdrawn their case may apply to the Tribunal for the case to be reinstated.

(5) An application under paragraph (4) must be made in writing and be received by the Tribunal within 1 month after—

(a) the date on which the Tribunal received the notice under paragraph (1)(a); or

(b) the date of the hearing at which the case was withdrawn orally under paragraph (1)(b).

(6) The Tribunal must notify each party in writing of an withdrawal under this rule.

"criminal injuries compensation case"—see r.1(3).
"dispose of proceedings"—*ibid.*
"hearing"—*ibid.*
"party"—*ibid.*
"Tribunal"—*ibid.*

5.194   Paragraphs (1) and (6) replace reg.40 of the Social Security and Child Support (Decisions and Appeals) Regs 1999. However, there are differences. First, this applies to the withdrawal of a respondent's case as well as to an appeal or reference. Secondly, paras (2) and (3)(b) have the effect that a case cannot be withdrawn at a hearing without the consent of the Tribunal (although it apparently can be withdrawn during an adjournment). Thirdly, paras (4) and (5) allow a party who has withdrawn a case to apply for it to be reinstated, avoiding the difficulty that arose in *Rydqvist v Secretary of State for Work and Pensions* [2002] EWCA Civ 947; [2002] 1 W.L.R. 3343. Clearly any possible prejudice to the respondent will be highly relevant when the Tribunal is considering whether to permit the case to be reinstated. The existence of the one-month time limit for an application for reinstatement may suggest that an application should be granted if made within that period unless there is a clear reason for not doing so, such as the previous conduct of the party, obvious lack of merit in the case or prejudice to another party.

Lead cases

18.—(1) This rule applies if—

5.195

(a) two or more cases have been started before the Tribunal;

(b) in each such case the Tribunal has not made a decision disposing of the proceedings; and

(c) the cases give rise to common or related issues of fact or law.

(2) The Tribunal may give a direction—

(a) specifying one or more cases falling under paragraph (1) as a lead case or lead cases; and

(b) staying (or, in Scotland, sisting) the other cases falling under paragraph (1) ("the related cases").

(3) When the Tribunal makes a decision in respect of the common or related issues—

(a) the Tribunal must send a copy of that decision to each party in each of the related cases; and

(b) subject to paragraph (4), that decision shall be binding on each of those parties.

(4) Within 1 month after the date on which the Tribunal sent a copy of the decision to a party under paragraph (3)(a), that party may apply in writing for a direction that the decision does not apply to, and is not binding on the parties to, a particular related case.

(5) The Tribunal must give directions in respect of cases which are stayed or sisted under paragraph (2)(b), providing for the disposal of or further directions in those cases.

(6) If the lead case or cases lapse or are withdrawn before the Tribunal makes a decision in respect of the common or related issues, the Tribunal must give directions as to—

(a) whether another case or other cases are to be specified as a lead case or lead cases; and

(b) whether any direction affecting the related cases should be set aside or amended.

DEFINITIONS

"dispose of proceedings"—see r.1(3).
"party"—*ibid.*
"Tribunal"—*ibid.*

GENERAL NOTE

The effect of this rule could be achieved through case management directions under r.5 but the rule provides an off-the-peg process for dealing with cases raising common or related issues of fact or law. It need not be used if a different process appears more appropriate. If it is used, one or more lead cases are selected and are then treated as binding on the other cases unless, within one month of being sent a copy of the decision in the lead cases, a party in another case objects. Presumably "decision" in para.(3) must include the reasons for the decision. Paragraph (4) appears to allow an objection either on the ground that the lead case is distinguishable and does not apply for that reason or on the ground that the party simply wishes to challenge the decision in the lead case and have his or her case dealt with

5.196

separately, possibly with a view to appealing. The likelihood of objections on that latter ground may be a reason for not applying this rule in the first place but it would be unfair if parties who were separately represented could not elect to have their own cases decided individually.

Where common issues of law arise in social security cases, s.26 of the Social Security Act 1998 may provide an alternative procedure.

Confidentiality in child support or child trust fund cases

5.197   **19.**—(1) Paragraph (3) applies to proceedings under the Child Support Act 1991 in the circumstances described in paragraph (2), other than an appeal against a reduced benefit decision (as defined in section 46(10)(b) of the Child Support Act 1991, as that section had effect prior to the commencement of section 15(b) of the Child Maintenance and Other Payments Act 2008).

(2) The circumstances referred to in paragraph (1) are that the absent parent, non-resident parent or person with care would like their address or the address of the child to be kept confidential and has given notice to that effect—

    (a) to the Secretary of State or the Child Maintenance and Enforcement Commission in the notice of appeal or when notifying any subsequent change of address;

    (b) to the Secretary of State or the Child Maintenance and Enforcement Commission, whichever has made the enquiry, within 14 days after an enquiry is made; or

    (c) to the Tribunal when notifying any change of address.

(3) Where this paragraph applies, the Secretary of State, the Child Maintenance and Enforcement Commission and the Tribunal must take appropriate steps to secure the confidentiality of the address, and of any information which could reasonably be expected to enable a person to identify the address, to the extent that the address or that information is not already known to each other party.

(4) Paragraph (6) applies to proceedings under the Child Trust Funds Act 2004 in the circumstances described in paragraph (5).

(5) The circumstances referred to in paragraph (4) are that a relevant person would like their address or the address of the eligible child to be kept confidential and has given notice to that effect, or a local authority with parental responsibility in relation to the eligible child would like the address of the eligible child to be kept confidential and has given notice to that effect—

    (a) to HMRC in the notice of appeal or when notifying any subsequent change of address;

    (b) to HMRC within 14 days after an enquiry by HMRC; or

    (c) to the Tribunal when notifying any change of address.

(6) Where this paragraph applies, HMRC and the Tribunal must take appropriate steps to secure the confidentiality of the address, and of any information which could reasonably be expected to enable a person to identify the address, to the extent that the address or that information is not already known to each other party.

(7) In this rule—

"eligible child" has the meaning set out in section 2 of the Child Trust Funds Act 2004;

"HMRC" means Her Majesty's Revenue and Customs;
"non-resident parent" and "parent with care" have the meanings set out
in section 54 of the Child Support Act 1991;
"parental responsibility" has the meaning set out in section 3(9) of the
Child Trust Funds Act 2004; and
"relevant person" has the meaning set out in section 22(3) of the Child
Trust Funds Act 2004.

DEFINITIONS

"appeal"—see r.1(3).
"eligible child"—see para.(7).
"HMRC"—*ibid.*
"non-resident parent"—*ibid.*
"parent with care"—*ibid.*
"parental responsibility"—*ibid.*
"party"—see r.1(3).
"relevant person"—see para.(7).
"Tribunal"—see r.1(3).

20.—*Omitted.*   5.198

Expenses in social security and child support cases

21.—(1) This rule applies only to social security and child support   5.199
cases.
(2) The Secretary of State may pay such travelling and other allowances
(including compensation for loss of remunerative time) as the Secretary of
State may determine to any person required to attend a hearing in proceedings under section 20 of the Child Support Act 1991, section 12 of the
Social Security Act 1998 or paragraph 6 of Schedule 7 to the Child Support,
Pensions and Social Security Act 2000.

DEFINITIONS

"hearing"—see r.1(3).
"social security and child support case"—*ibid.*

GENERAL NOTE

This rule reproduces the effect of para.4(1)(a) of Sch.1 to the Social Security   5.200
Act 1998. (Paragraph 4(1)(b) is replaced by a new s.20A.) It suffers from the same
defect as the old provision, which is that it does not apply to all social security cases
in which claimants might be required to attend hearings, although in practice the
Tribunals Service seems never to have refused to pay expenses to those not within
the scope of the old provision (e.g. an injured person appealing under s.11 of the
Social Security (Recovery of Benefits) Act 1997).
The rule is in also unsatisfactory because it seems unlikely that para.10(4) of
Sch.5 to the Tribunals, Courts and Enforcement Act 2007 envisages Rules that
give the Secretary of State the power to determine what expenses are to be paid,
although it is perhaps more appropriate that the power should lie with the Secretary
of State rather than the Tribunal Procedure Committee.

PART 3

PROCEEDINGS BEFORE THE TRIBUNAL

CHAPTER 1

BEFORE THE HEARING

5.201   **22.**—*Omitted.*

Cases in which the notice of appeal is to be sent to the decision maker

5.202   **23.**—(1) This rule applies to social security and child support cases (except references under the Child Support Act 1991 and proceedings under paragraph 3 of Schedule 2 to the Tax Credits Act 2002).

(2) An appellant must start proceedings by sending or delivering a notice of appeal to the decision maker so that it is received within the time specified in Schedule 1 to these Rules (time limits for providing notices of appeal to the decision maker).

(3) If the appellant provides the notice of appeal to the decision maker later than the time required by paragraph (2) the notice of appeal must include the reason why the notice of appeal was not provided in time.

(4) Subject to paragraph (5), where an appeal is not made within the time specified in Schedule 1, it will be treated as having been made in time if the decision maker does not object.

(5) No appeal may be made more than 12 months after the time specified in Schedule 1.

(6) The notice of appeal must be in English or Welsh, must be signed by the appellant and must state—

(a) the name and address of the appellant;

(b) the name and address of the appellant's representative (if any);

(c) an address where documents for the appellant may be sent or delivered;

(d) details of the decision being appealed; and

(e) the grounds on which the appellant relies.

(7) The decision maker must refer the case to the Tribunal immediately if—

(a) the appeal has been made after the time specified in Schedule 1 and the decision maker objects to it being treated as having been made in time; or

(b) the decision maker considers that the appeal has been made more than 12 months after the time specified in Schedule 1.

DEFINITIONS

"appeal"—see r.1(3).
"appellant"—*ibid.*
"decision maker"—*ibid.*
"social security and child support case"—*ibid.*
"Tribunal"—*ibid.*

GENERAL NOTE

Para. (1)

The social security and child support cases not within the scope of this rule fall within the scope of r.26 instead.

5.203

Para. (3)

Giving the reason for delay assists the decision-maker in deciding whether or not to object to a late appeal being treated as made in time under para.(4). It seems unlikely that a failure to comply with this paragraph would be held to render a late appeal invalid; rather it merely increases the likelihood of the Secretary of State objecting so that the case must be sent to the tribunal under para.(7)(a).

5.204

Para. (4)

The amended reg.32 of the Social Security and Child Support (Decision and Appeals) Regulation 1999 sits uneasily with the broad discretion conferred on the decision-maker by this paragraph.

5.205

In *R(TC)1/05*, there was no evidence that anyone had considered whether there were grounds for admitting a late appeal, perhaps because the appeal had been proceeding on the basis that it was an in-time appeal against a supersession decision whereas, on a proper analysis, the supersession had been a refusal to revise so that the appeal was against an earlier decision and the circumstances were such that time had not been extended by virtue of reg.31(2). There was also a suggestion that notice of the original decision had not been sent to the claimant so that the appeal was not late at all. The Commissioner considered that the tribunal's brief reasons suggested that if the chairman had considered whether to extend the time for appealing, he would have refused. However, the Commissioner held the decision was invalid because, if the appeal had been late and there was no extension of time, the tribunal had had no jurisdiction to hear the appeal. The claimant was entitled to have the question of an extension of time properly considered. Had the chairman clearly refused an extension of time, the Commissioner said that it appeared that he would have had no jurisdiction to consider an appeal against that refusal, notwithstanding that there appeared to be no clear finding that notice of the decision under appeal had ever been issued. However, it is suggested that, if the tribunal had declined jurisdiction on the ground that time had not been extended, the refusal to accept jurisdictions would have been appealable and a failure to record a finding as to whether notice of the original decision had been issued might have led to the appeal being allowed. It is not clear whether, in a case where there is a respondent other than the decision-maker, that other respondent may object to the case being admitted if the decision-maker does not.

Para. (5)

The absolute time limit of 12 months, formerly found in reg.32(1) of the 1999 Regs, is retained. The fact that the Tribunal has erroneously admitted an appeal that ought not to have been admitted because it was too late does not oblige the tribunal to determine the appeal. Instead, it must decline jurisdiction *(R(AF)1/09)*, which, under these Rules, would require the Tribunal to strike the appeal out under r.8(2).

5.206

The absolute time limit prohibiting the bringing of appeals more than a year late is not incompatible with the European Convention on Human Rights (*Denson v Secretary of State for Work and Pensions* [2004] EWCA Civ 462 (reported as *R(CS) 4/04*). Nonetheless, it can work injustice, particularly in a case where an unrepresented claimant has been challenging the wrong decision and nobody tells him or her until it is too late which decision it is that must be challenged if he or she is to succeed in obtaining the benefit sought.

Para. (6)

5.207   The reference to the language is included for consistency with r.22 where a similar provision thought necessary in the former Asylum Support Rules has been reproduced (with the addition of a reference to Welsh).

A typed name can amount to a signature when it has been adopted by the person concerned through his or her signing another document or taking some other active step in an appeal (*R(DLA) 2/98*). In *CIB/460/2003*, the claimant's mother, who had not been appointed to act on behalf of the claimant, signed the appeal. No-one had objected and the claimant himself had signed form issued by the clerk, asking him, among other things, whether he wanted to withdraw his appeal. He had said "no". The Commissioner rejected a submission made on behalf of the Secretary of State to the effect that the appeal was not valid.

Para. (7)

5.208   Presumably the requirement imposed by para.(5) (that an appeal be brought not more than 12 months after the times specified in Sch.1) cannot be waived under r.7(2)(a), because to do so would entirely undermine the point of para.(5). In any event, from September 1, 2009, art.3 of the Tribunal Procedure (Amendment No.2) Rules 2009 (SI 2009/1975) will add a para.(8) making it clear that "the Tribunal must not extend the time limit in paragraph (5)". In other cases, an appeal that is late will be admitted if the time for bringing the appeal is extended by the Tribunal under r.5(3)(a).

Where the notice of appeal fails to comply with the rules in some other respect, the decision-maker must first give the appellant the opportunity of making good the defect and, if the defect is not remedied, must send the form to the Tribunal for a decision whether or not the form complies with the rules (see reg.33 of the 1999 Regs). There seems no reason why defects other than a failure to comply with para. (5) should not be waived under r.7(2)(a), provided that they do not in practice make it impossible to process the appeal.

Responses and replies

5.209   **24.**—(1) When a decision maker receives the notice of appeal or a copy of it, the decision maker must send or deliver a response to the Tribunal—

    (a) in asylum support cases, so that it is received within 3 days after the date on which the Tribunal received the notice of appeal; and

    (b) in other cases, as soon as reasonably practicable after the decision maker received the notice of appeal.

(2) The response must state—

    (a) the name and address of the decision maker;

    (b) the name and address of the decision maker's representative (if any);

    (c) an address where documents for the decision maker may be sent or delivered;

    (d) the names and addresses of any other respondents and their representatives (if any);

    (e) whether the decision maker opposes the appellant's case and, if so, any grounds for such opposition which are not set out in any documents which are before the Tribunal; and

    (f) any further information or documents required by a practice direction or direction.

(3) The response may include a submission as to whether it would be appropriate for the case to be disposed of without a hearing.

(4) The decision maker must provide with the response—

(a) a copy of any written record of the decision under challenge, and any statement of reasons for that decision, if they were not sent with the notice of appeal;

(b) copies of all documents relevant to the case in the decision maker's possession, unless a practice direction or direction states otherwise; and

(c) in cases to which rule 23 (cases in which the notice of appeal is to be sent to the decision maker) applies, a copy of the notice of appeal, any documents provided by the appellant with the notice of appeal and (if they have not otherwise been provided to the Tribunal) the name and address of the appellant's representative (if any).

(5) The decision maker must provide a copy of the response and any accompanying documents to each other party at the same time as it provides the response to the Tribunal.

(6) The appellant and any other respondent may make a written submission and supply further documents in reply to the decision maker's response.

(7) Any submission or further documents under paragraph (6) must be provided to the Tribunal within 1 month after the date on which the decision maker sent the response to the party providing the reply, and the Tribunal must send a copy to each other party.

DEFINITIONS

"appeal"—see r.1(3).
"appellant"—*ibid.*
"asylum support case"—*ibid.*
"decision maker"—*ibid.*
"document"—*ibid.*
"hearing"—*ibid.*
"party"—*ibid.*
"practice direction"—*ibid.*
"respondent"—*ibid.*
"Tribunal"—*ibid.*

GENERAL NOTE

Paras (1) to (5)

These paragraphs make express provision for the decision-maker's response to an appeal, as to which the Social Security and Child Support (Decisions and Appeals) Regs 1999 were curiously silent. They largely reproduce previous practice and make no provision for any precise time limit. In part this is because some time may be taken investigating points raised in the grounds of appeal and deciding whether to revise the decision being challenged under reg.3(4A) of the 1999 Regs, which would cause the appeal to lapse under s.9(6) of the Social Security Act 1998.   5.210

Paras (6) and (7)

These paragraphs make express provision for other parties to reply to the decision-makers response. Again, the 1999 Regs made no such provision but in practice parties were given the opportunity when asked whether they wanted a hearing. A one-month time limit is now provided, but that may be regarded as a minimum period that must be given to the parties before a case is determined and it will seldom be proportionate to refuse to accept a late submission or evidence unless   5.211

another party would be unduly affected by the delay, particularly where there is to be an oral hearing at which submissions and new evidence can be expected whether or not written notice has been given.

Medical and physical examination in appeals under section 12 of the Social Security Act 1998

5.212

25.—(1) This rule applies only to appeals under section 12 of the Social Security Act 1998.

(2) At a hearing an appropriate member of the Tribunal may carry out a physical examination of a person if the case relates to—

(a) the extent of that person's disablement and its assessment in accordance with section 68(6) of and Schedule 6 to, or section 103 of, the Social Security Contributions and Benefits Act 1992(**13**); or

(b) diseases or injuries prescribed for the purpose of section 108 of that Act.

(3) If an issue which falls within Schedule 2 to these Rules (issues in relation to which the Tribunal may refer a person for medical examination) is raised in an appeal, the Tribunal may exercise its power under section 20 of the Social Security Act 1998 to refer a person to a health care professional approved by the Secretary of State for—

(a) the examination of that person; and

(b) the production of a report on the condition of that person.

(4) Neither paragraph (2) nor paragraph (3) entitles the Tribunal to require a person to undergo a physical test for the purpose of determining whether that person is unable to walk or virtually unable to do so.

DEFINITIONS

"hearing"—see r.1(3).
"Tribunal"—*ibid.*

GENERAL NOTE

Para. (2)

5.213

For the meaning of "physical examination", see the note to s.20(3) of the Social Security Act 1998. The "appropriate member" will be a registered medical practitioner (see para.14 of the practice statement reproduced in the note to art.2 of the First-tier Tribunal and Upper Tribunal (Composition of Tribunal) Order 2008).

These are the *only* circumstances in which a person may be examined on an appeal under s.12 of the 1998 Act (see s.20(3)). However, the limitation does not apply in other cases, such as appeals under the Social Security (Recovery of Benefits) Act 1997.

Where the Tribunal has the power to examine a claimant it need not do so if it considers that an examination is unnecessary. It is not always necessary to carry out a physical examination in order to assess functional loss. It may be better in some cases simply to question the claimant about the practical effects of an injury. However, if not minded to conduct a physical examination, it is good practice for the Tribunal to state as much during the course of the hearing so that the claimant has an opportunity to make representation on the point (*R(I) 10/62, CI/3384/2006*). Whether a failure to do so renders a decision liable to be set aside on appeal is likely to depend on the circumstances and, in particular, whether the claimant can show that an examination might have led to a different outcome.

Para.(4)

This paragraph applies to examinations within para.(3) as well as those within para.(2). It must be presumed to do so by prescribing a "condition" under s.20(2) of the Social Security Act 1998 and thereby extending the limitation imposed by s.20(3)(b), which is otherwise confined to what may be done "at a hearing".

5.214

Social security and child support cases started by reference or information in writing

26.—(1) This rule applies to proceedings under section 28D of the Child Support Act 1991 and paragraph 3 of Schedule 2 to the Tax Credits Act 2002.

5.215

(2) A person starting proceedings under section 28D of the Child Support Act 1991 must send or deliver a written reference to the Tribunal.

(3) A person starting proceedings under paragraph 3 of Schedule 2 to the Tax Credits Act 2002 must send or deliver an information in writing to the Tribunal.

(4) The reference or the information in writing must include—
(a) an address where documents for the person starting proceedings may be sent or delivered;
(b) the names and addresses of the respondents and their representatives (if any); and
(c) a submission on the issues that arise for determination by the Tribunal.

(5) Unless a practice direction or direction states otherwise, the person starting proceedings must also provide a copy of each document in their possession which is relevant to the proceedings.

(6) Subject to any obligation under rule 19(3) (confidentiality in child support cases), the person starting proceedings must provide a copy of the written reference or the information in writing and any accompanying documents to each respondent at the same time as they provide the written reference or the information in writing to the Tribunal.

(7) Each respondent may send or deliver to the Tribunal a written submission and any further relevant documents within one month of the date on which the person starting proceedings sent a copy of the written reference or the information in writing to that respondent.

DEFINITIONS

"document"—see r.1(3).
"practice direction"—*ibid.*
"respondent"—*ibid.*
"social security and child support case"—*ibid.*
"Tribunal"—*ibid.*

GENERAL NOTE

This rule makes specific provision for certain child support cases initiated by the Secretary of State and tax credit penalty cases initiated by HMRC. Paragraph (7) provides for responses by respondents. A one-month time limit is provided, but that may be regarded as a minimum period that must be given to the respondents before a case is determined and it will seldom be proportionate to refuse to accept a late submission or evidence unless another party would be unduly

5.216

affected by the delay, particularly where there is to be an oral hearing at which submissions and new evidence can be expected whether or not written notice has been given.

CHAPTER 2

HEARINGS

Decision with or without a hearing

5.217   **27.**—(1) Subject to the following paragraphs, the Tribunal must hold a hearing before making a decision which disposes of proceedings unless—
  (a) each party has consented to, or has not objected to, the matter being decided without a hearing; and
  (b) the Tribunal considers that it is able to decide the matter without a hearing.
   (2) This rule does not apply to decisions under Part 4.
   (3) The Tribunal may in any event dispose of proceedings without a hearing under rule 8 (striking out a party's case).
   (4) In a criminal injuries compensation case—
  (a) the Tribunal may make a decision which disposes of proceedings without a hearing; and
  (b) subject to paragraph (5), if the Tribunal makes a decision which disposes of proceedings without a hearing, any party may make a written application to the Tribunal for the decision to be reconsidered at a hearing.
   (5) An application under paragraph (4)(b) may not be made in relation to a decision—
  (a) not to extend a time limit;
  (b) not to set aside a previous decision;
  (c) not to allow an appeal against a decision not to extend a time limit; or
  (d) not to allow an appeal against a decision not to reopen a case.
   (6) An application under paragraph (4)(b) must be received within 1 month after the date on which the Tribunal sent notice of the decision to the party making the application.

DEFINITIONS

  "criminal injuries compensation case"—see r.1(3).
  "dispose of proceedings"—*ibid.*
  "hearing"—*ibid.*
  "party"—*ibid.*
  "Tribunal"—*ibid.*

GENERAL NOTE

Paras (1) to (3)

5.218   Paragraph (1) applies where the decision to be made will be one "which disposes of proceedings". It is primarily concerned with the final substantive decision on an appeal or reference but, were it not for para.(3), it would also apply to decisions to strike out proceedings. Para.(2) makes it clear that it does not apply to decisions relating to reviews and permission to appeal to the Upper Tribunal. It is less clear whether it applies to a decision whether or not to extend the time for appealing to the First-tier Tribunal. On one view, a decision not to extend time disposes of proceedings but the better argument may be that it merely prevents the proceedings from being started. However, even where this rule does not require there to be a hearing, it may be appropriate for the Tribunal to direct one under r.5(3)(f).

The paragraph has the effect that, where it applies, there must be a hearing if any party wants one. The Secretary of State or HMRC will say whether or not they want a hearing when submitting a response (see r.24(3)), reference or information. The Tribunal asks the other parties whether or not they want a hearing by sending them a form to return. If there is no reply, the party may be taken to have "not objected to the matter being decided without a hearing." In effect, therefore, these paragraphs replace reg.39 of the Social Security and Child Support (Decisions and Appeals) Regs 1999. However, note that the legislation no longer refers to an approved form on which a party was required to indicate whether or not he wished to have a hearing, so that the basis for the decision in *R3/04(IB)* has been removed, and that the provision in reg.46(1)(d) for simply striking proceedings out if the approved form was not returned by a party has not been re-enacted. Now, a case cannot be struck out for failure to return a form unless the Tribunal (which currently means a judge, see the note to r.4) has directed the form be returned and has warned the party that being struck out will, or may, be the consequence of not complying with the direction (see r.8(1) and (3)(a)). In *R3/04(IB)*, the requirement to issue an approved form to a party was held to be the reason why a clerk to a tribunal could not rely on an indication in the appellant's letter of appeal that a hearing was not wanted. There may still be reasons why reliance should not be placed on such an indication, not the least of which is that the appellant is unlikely to have been aware of the precise case against him or her before receiving the response to the appeal.

Where a claimant asks for a paper determination and asks for it not to take place until a certain date because further evidence will be provided, the tribunal must either wait until that date or inform the claimant that it will not do so (*CDLA/792/2006*). It will seldom be appropriate not to wait for evidence unless the time requested is unreasonably long or there has been previous delay on the part of the claimant.

There are many cases where a claimant really has no realistic prospects of success unless he or she attends an oral hearing and gives evidence. Even though claimants are advised in general terms that the chances of success may be greater at an oral hearing, it may be thought that the mere fact that they are offered the choice will suggest to many that a paper hearing is a not a foolish option. In *CDLA/1347/1999*, it was said that, if a tribunal considering an appeal on the papers was wholly unable to do justice without there being an oral hearing, it ought to adjourn the proceedings, and direct that there be one but that, otherwise, a tribunal was generally entitled to take the view that a claimant who had rejected the option of an oral hearing having had notice of the issues in the case had had an adequate opportunity to put his case and had lost the chance of strengthening it by giving oral evidence. In *R1/02(IB)*, a Tribunal of Commissioners in Northern Ireland set aside a decision of a tribunal who did not adjourn in the face of incomplete evidence raising questions that they could not answer. In *CIS/4248/2001*, the Commissioner held that an oral hearing should have been directed in a case where an apparently unrepresented claimant had opted for a paper hearing of an appeal against a decision that income support amounting to some £10,000 had been overpaid and was recoverable from her, in circumstances where the claimant had put forward a case that was tenable if she was believed.

"A very great deal of money was at stake. Oral evidence would have assisted the tribunal's assessment of honesty, which was central to the case. She had not, as far as could be seen, had the benefit of advice from anyone with experience of tribunals. Those are all factors that suggest that justice required an oral hearing in this case."

On a paper determination, or indeed any hearing not attended by a claimant, it will always be an error of law for a tribunal to remove an award that has already been made unless the claimant has been given specific notice (in the sense of being focussed on their own particular case) that this is under consideration (*CDLA/1480/2006*).

When a decision is set aside by the Upper Tribunal and referred to another tribunal, it is the invariable practice to hold an oral hearing. However, in *CIB/4193/2003*, the Commissioner noted that that was not the practice where a decision was set aside by a legally qualified panel member under s.13 of the Social Security Act 1998 and he suggested that claimants should be given a fresh opportunity to ask for an oral hearing. He commented that some claimants might reassess their prospects of success "on a paper determination" once they had lost a case and had to apply for leave to appeal. On the facts of the case, he held that there had been a breach of the rules of natural justice because the claimant had been inadvertently misled into not asking for the oral hearing she wanted.

In *CIB/2751/2002 and CS/3202/2002*, the Commissioner considered the difficulties that arise on a request for a domiciliary hearing, where a refusal to allow such a hearing may require the determination of the very issues that arise on the appeal itself. He said that fairness may require that a claimant who is refused a domiciliary hearing is given a further opportunity to provide evidence, perhaps by being visited by an expert appointed under s.7(4) of the Social Security Act 1998, who could then give evidence to the tribunal under reg.50. It is suggested, however, that the reality may be that a domiciliary hearing would not be refused where the judge believed that the claimant might not be able to attend a hearing at an ordinary venue. Virtual inability to walk does not usually preclude travelling in a car, perhaps driven by a relative, or use of a taxi. The greater need may therefore be that, where a domiciliary hearing is refused, it should be made clear to the claimant that it is considered that he or she could attend a hearing at an ordinary venue and should speak to the clerk about any special arrangements that might be necessary to enable him or her to do so. If it becomes apparent to a clerk that the claimant's difficulties are greater than was originally understood, the issue can always be referred back to the judge.

The tribunal has considerable latitude in deciding how a hearing will be conducted but it must be fair. If the rules of natural justice (which effectively guarantee a fair hearing) are broken, the decision of the tribunal is liable to be set aside on appeal on the ground that it is erroneous in point of law. See further the annotation to s.11 of the Tribunals, Courts and Enforcement Act 2007.

A tribunal is entitled to take account of all that it sees and hears at a hearing but if it sees something that appears important, fairness generally requires that the party concerned should be given an opportunity of commenting on what the tribunal has seen. In *R(DLA) 2/06*, the Commissioner cautioned tribunals against giving too much weight to observations of a claimant's apparent well-being that might be unrepresentative and so be unreliable as evidence of his health generally. Giving a claimant an opportunity to comment enables the claimant to put the observation into a broader context. However, the Commissioner also pointed out that, where an observation merely confirms a conclusion that the tribunal would have reached anyway, a failure to invite the claimant to comment on it will not render the decision erroneous in point of law although, unless a judge makes clear what significance a recorded observation had in the tribunal's reasoning when he or she is writing the statement of reasons, it is likely to be assumed that it must have had an effect on the decision. The Commissioner also made clear that a judge does not have to ask precise questions amounting to a cross-examination of the claimant but can ask an open question that gives a claimant the opportunity to comment. He said—

"...the chairman did not point out to the claimant the significance of the observations that the tribunal had made. But the claimant must have realised this. He had presented his claim on the basis of pain and exhaustion and the observations were clearly directly relevant to that."

What is important is whether, taking the hearing as a whole, the claimant has an adequate opportunity to address the issues raised by any significant observations.

In *R(DLA) 3/06*, the Tribunal of Commissioners allowed an appeal against a decision of a tribunal who had drawn an adverse inference against a 12-year old claimant, alleged to have learning difficulties and behavioural problems, because her foster parent and appointee had failed to arrange for her to give evidence to the tribunal despite a summons. The Tribunal of Commissioners gave the following general guidance about child witnesses.

"(i)   A tribunal should have proper regard to the wishes of a child of sufficiently mature years and understanding who wishes to give evidence in a DLA claim made on his behalf. However, a tribunal should be very cautious before requiring any child to give evidence, and should only call for a child to give evidence if it is satisfied that a just decision cannot otherwise be made. Before reaching such a conclusion, the tribunal should consider first all the other available evidence, and then ask itself whether any necessary additional evidence can be obtained from another source, for example, a health visitor, social worker, teacher, family member or friend, to avoid the need for the child to be called at all.

"(ii)   In any event, a tribunal should be very slow to exercise its power to require a child to give evidence if that child's parent or carer takes the view that for the child to give evidence may be detrimental to the child's welfare, particularly if there is evidence from a competent professional that to do so might be harmful. It would be wholly exceptional for it to be appropriate for a tribunal to call a child in such circumstances.

"(iii)   Even if it is those representing the child, rather than the tribunal, who wish the child to give evidence, as *Brown v Secretary of State for the Home Department* (LTA 97/6885/J) indicates, a tribunal has power to disallow the child from giving evidence if it is against the child's interests to do so. If it is proposed that the child gives evidence, the tribunal must consider whether it is in that child's interests to do so.

"(iv)   The tribunal should bear in mind that the mere presence of a child at a hearing is unlikely to give a reliable indication of the effect of a child's disability in normal circumstances.

"(v)   Where a decision is taken to call a child to give evidence, after submissions from interested persons (including the parents or carers of the child) a tribunal should give consideration to precisely how that evidence will be taken, so that the interests and welfare of the child are maintained, giving any directions that are appropriate. In doing so the tribunal will bear in mind that a child may perceive what is said at a tribunal hearing very differently from an adult. It will be necessary for the tribunal to identify any matters that the child ought not to hear (e.g. it will not generally be appropriate for a child to hear criticism of those responsible for his or her care) and questions that the child ought not to be asked (e.g. it will not generally be appropriate to question a child about his or her own care needs).

"(vi)   In addition, where a child is to be called to give evidence, the tribunal will need to give consideration to practical matters such as the geography of the hearing room, having an appropriate adult in close attendance, whether any of the tribunal (including the chairman) should be selected because of experience in dealing with child witnesses and even (in appropriate cases) taking such steps as taking the child's evidence by video link if available, giving directions where appropriate."

See also the practice direction of the Senior President of Tribunals, below.

Record of proceedings

There is no statutory duty upon the presiding tribunal judge to keep a record of proceedings before the First-tier Tribunal. However, the Senior President of Tribunals has issued a Practice Statement dated 30 October 2008 which more

5.219

or less replaces reg.55 of the Social Security and Child Support (Decisions and Appeals) Regulations 1999. It is in the following terms—

5.220   "1. In this Practice Statement "social security and child support case" has the meaning given in rule 1(3) of the Tribunal Procedure (First-tier Tribunal) (Social Entitlement Chamber) Rules 2008.

2. A record of the proceedings at a hearing must be made by the presiding member, or in the case of a Tribunal composed of only one member, by that member.

3. The record must be sufficient to indicate any evidence taken and submissions made and any procedural applications, and may be in such medium as the member may determine.

4. The Tribunal must preserve—
   a. the record of proceedings;
   b. the decisions notice; and
   c. any written reasons for the Tribunal's decision for the period specified in paragraph 5.

5. The specified period is six months form the date of—
   a. the decision made by the Tribunal;
   b. any written reasons for the Tribunal's decision;
   c. any correction under Rule 36 of the above Rules;
   d. any refusal to set aside a decision under Rule 37; or
   e. any determination of an application for permission to appeal against decision, or until the date on which those documents are sent to the Upper Tribunal in connection with an appeal against the decision or an application for permission to appeal, if that occurs within the six months.

6. Any party to the proceedings may within the time specified in paragraph 5 apply in writing for a copy of the record of proceedings and a copy must be supplied to him."

The record of proceedings should be a record of what has happened at a hearing and therefore should include not only a note of evidence and submissions but also a record of any procedural application, such as an application for an adjournment, and the tribunal's decision on the application (*R(DLA)3/08*).

Where an appeal is based on what happened at a hearing, the Upper Tribunal will be slow to go behind a full record of proceedings (*CS/343/1994*) but will admit evidence if it is necessary to do so where a full and particularised allegation is made that the conduct of the hearing led to a breach of the rules of natural justice (*R(M)1/89*). The Upper Tribunal may obtain statements from those present at the hearing, including the members of the tribunal, but it will not be necessary to obtain statements from members of the tribunal if the appellant's case is supported by other evidence, such as the record of proceedings and the statement of reasons, unless the case involves an allegation of personal misconduct that it would be unfair to find proved without the person concerned having had the opportunity of commenting (*CDLA/5574/2002*).

However, it is not just in cases where procedural impropriety is alleged that a record of proceedings is an important document. Because a statement of reasons ought to deal with the principal points raised by the parties but a tribunal is not always required to consider points that have not been explicitly raised and because a tribunal may have an investigatory role, the record of proceedings may be an important document in a case where it is suggested that the statement of reasons is inadequate or that the tribunal failed to ask questions about a particular issue. It may, however, be supplemented. In *CH/2484/2006*, the Deputy Commissioner said—

"I appreciate that a record of proceedings is not a complete *verbatim* note and that it is possible for points to be omitted, but if an appellant to the Commissioner wishes to base a submission on the overlooking of evidence or submissions and the evidence or submission are not recorded in the record, it seems to me to be necessary as a general rule for it to equip itself with evidence (such as a statement by someone who was present) that that piece of evidence or submission was in fact made. It should also raise the matter with the other side in advance, so as to avoid surprise and facilitate agreement on the position if possible."

In that case, the local authority was the appellant. Where a claimant is an appellant and the Secretary of State was not present at the hearing before the tribunal, the Secretary of State will not be in a position to dispute a statement by the claimant as to what occurred at that hearing. As suggested above, it will be open to the Upper Tribunal to seek the views of the tribunal but it will not be obliged to do so.

Paragraph 3 of the Practice Statement shows that the "record of proceedings" is a note of the evidence and submissions received at the hearing. This is often taken to refer to the oral evidence and submissions but it probably extends to at least a record of what written evidence was before the tribunal which may in turn imply a duty on someone to keep a copy of that evidence. In practice, the Tribunals Service usually keeps the whole file for six months from the last action on the file, which complies with the duty imposed however the statement is construed.

Until 1999, a record of proceedings had to be kept for 18 months. The duty to keep the other documents was first introduced in 2005 and usually makes it unnecessary for a person seeking permission to appeal to the Upper Tribunal to supply copies with the application. All parties should have had copies of the decision notice and any statement of reasons and would have had six months in which to ask for a copy of the record of proceedings and, the effect of the six-month period is that it remains necessary for an applicant to provide the documents required to support a very late application for leave to appeal. In *CIB/62/2008*, a claimant who made an application to a tribunal chairman for leave to appeal more than six months late, with the consequence that the tribunal's file had been destroyed, was refused leave to appeal by both the chairman and a Commissioner. The latter held that the claimant's assertion that he had asked for an oral hearing of his appeal before the tribunal which had been refused would not be enough to overcome the presumption that the tribunal proceedings had been properly conducted, when the claimant's own delay had resulted in the probable destruction of the evidence that would either have supported or contradicted his assertion.

The duty to provide a record of proceedings is a duty to provide one that is intelligible or capable of being made intelligible to those to whom it is issued (*R(DLA)3/08*). Providing an illegible document is therefore not sufficient, although one obvious remedy is to ask the clerk to obtain and provide a legible copy. A failure to comply with this duty will not always render the tribunal's decision erroneous in point of law but it will do so if, in a particular case, the consequence is a real possibility of unfairness or injustice. The extent to which a lack of a record of proceedings results in unfairness or injustice may turn on the extent to which the deficiency can be made good by obtaining evidence as to what happened or was said at a hearing from the parties or the tribunal (ibid).

Entitlement to attend a hearing

28. Subject to rule 30(5) (exclusion of a person from a hearing), each party to proceedings is entitled to attend a hearing.

5.221

DEFINITIONS

"hearing"—see r.1(3).
"party"—*ibid.*

GENERAL NOTE

5.222   This makes it plain that, except where r.30(5) applies, a party may always attend a hearing even when the hearing is in private. By virtue of r.11(5) a properly appointed representative also has a right to attend a hearing, whether or not the party does so. By virtue of r.11(7), a party who attends hearing may be accompanied by a person acting as a representative or assistant.

Notice of hearings

5.223   **29.**—(1) The Tribunal must give each party entitled to attend a hearing reasonable notice of the time and place of the hearing (including any adjourned or postponed hearing) and any changes to the time and place of the hearing.

(2) The period of notice under paragraph (1) must be at least 14 days except that—

(a) in an asylum support case the Tribunal must give at least 1 day's and not more than 5 days' notice; and

(b) the Tribunal may give shorter notice—

(i) with the parties' consent; or

(ii) in urgent or exceptional circumstances.

DEFINITIONS

"asylum support case"—see r.1(3).
"hearing"—*ibid.*
"party"—*ibid.*
"Tribunal"—*ibid.*

Public and private hearings

5.224   **30.**—(1) Subject to the following paragraphs, all hearings must be held in public.

(2) A hearing in a criminal injuries compensation case must be held in private unless—

(a) the appellant has consented to the hearing being held in public; and

(b) the Tribunal considers that it is in the interests of justice for the hearing to be held in public.

(3) The Tribunal may give a direction that a hearing, or part of it, is to be held in private.

(4) Where a hearing, or part of it, is to be held in private, the Tribunal may determine who is permitted to attend the hearing or part of it.

(5) The Tribunal may give a direction excluding from any hearing, or part of it—

(a) any person whose conduct the Tribunal considers is disrupting or is likely to disrupt the hearing;

(b) any person whose presence the Tribunal considers is likely to prevent another person from giving evidence or making submissions freely;

(c) any person who the Tribunal considers should be excluded in order to give effect to a direction under rule 14(2) (withholding information likely to cause harm); or

(d) any person where the purpose of the hearing would be defeated by the attendance of that person.

(6) The Tribunal may give a direction excluding a witness from a hearing until that witness gives evidence.

DEFINITIONS

"appellant"—see r.1(3).
"criminal injuries compensation case"—*ibid.*
"hearing"—*ibid.*
"Tribunal"—*ibid.*

GENERAL NOTE

Paras (1) and (2)

Paragraph (1) expresses the general rule, which is that hearings should usually be in public. Paragraph (2), which applies only to criminal injuries compensation cases, is anomalous but continues the previous practice in such cases.

5.225

Para. (3)

Paragraph (3) enables the Tribunal to direct that a particular case be heard in private, either in whole or in part. In practice, this does not arise as a live issue very often because it is very rare for members of the general public to attend hearings. The issue perhaps arises primarily where one party is accompanied by a large number of people and there arises the question whether it is appropriate for them all to attend the hearing. Directing that a hearing be in private enables the numbers to be regulated under para.(4).

5.226

The Rules give no guidance as to how it is to be decided whether or not a hearing is to be in private. Regulation 49(6) of the Social Security and Child Support (Decisions and Appeals) Regs 1999 provided that a hearing could be in private only—

"(a) in the interests of national security, morals, public order or children;

(b) for the protection of the private or family life of one or more parties to the proceedings; or

(c) in special circumstances, because publicity would prejudice the interests of justice."

The language was based on Art.6(1) of the European Convention on Human Rights, but Art.6 is concerned with the right of *a party* to a public hearing. Consequently, as far as Art.6 is concerned, a party may waive that right (*Schuler-Zgraggen v Switzerland*, judgment of June 24, 1993, Series A, No.263; (1993) 16 E.H.R.R. 405, at para.58) and consent to a hearing being in private even if those grounds are not made out. Regulation 49(6) did not permit such a waiver. The reason for that may have been that there are other interests in there being a public hearing, not least of which is the right of the public to see how justice is administered, which includes the right of the press to comment on the administration of justice. That right, too, may require the approach formerly taken in reg.49(6), although the need to protect the private or family life of people other than the parties (e.g. witnesses and people who might be mentioned in evidence) may need to be taken into account so reg.49(6)(b) may have been too narrowly drawn.

However, where the press are not present and where the parties wish a hearing to be in private so that the number of people present may be limited to avoid a timid claimant from being overwhelmed and unable properly to present his or her case, it may be open to a Tribunal to direct that the hearing be in private even if the conditions of the former reg.49(6) are not met, simply on the ground that the interests of justice require that the claimant should be enabled to put his or her case effectively (see r.2(2)(c)).

In all of this, it should not be forgotten that concerns about publicity can be met by the imposition of appropriate reporting restrictions under r.14(1). Generally, it will be preferable for the Tribunal to impose reporting restrictions rather than holding a hearing in private if the reporting restrictions will achieve all that is necessary.

In *CIB/2751/2002 and CS/3202/2002*, the Commissioner considered how domiciliary hearings might be affected by the former reg.49(6). He suggested that it might be possible to hold a public hearing near a claimant's home rather than actually in it. Given that few people other than those invited by the parties ever watch tribunal hearings, the problems raised may be more theoretical than real but the legislation does require them to be addressed. The answer may be that, where a domiciliary hearing in a claimant's home is necessary, it will always be justifiable to hold the hearing in private in order to protect the claimant's private or family life. Presumably a claimant who has asked for a domiciliary hearing can be taken to have waived his rights to privacy to the extent necessary to allow the hearing to take place with other parties being present.

Para. (4)

5.227   If a case is to be heard in private, the tribunal has a broad power to determine who may attend it. However, certain people have a right to attend a hearing even if it is in private. By r.28, a party always has a right to be present (subject to r.30(5)) and, the consequence is that, by virtue of r.11(5), so does a properly appointed representative whether the party attends or not. Where a party does attend, he or she may be accompanied by a person acting either as a representative or merely as an assistant (see r.11(7)). Plainly relevant witnesses must be allowed to attend for the purpose of giving evidence. By virtue of para.22 of Sch.7 to the Tribunals, Courts and Enforcement Act 2007, a member of the Administrative Justice and Tribunals Council, or its Scottish Committee or Welsh Committee, also has a right to attend any hearing.

Beyond that, it is all a matter of discretion, there being no equivalent to reg.49(9) of the 1999 Regs. It is likely to be desirable for the clerk or usher to be present and also a judge or Chamber President or the Senior President of Tribunals monitoring the tribunal. It is also likely to be appropriate to allow a claimant to be accompanied by a friend or relative even if he or she is there only for moral support and is not providing any actual assistance. As to others, it is suggested that, where a person has a reason for attending other than mere curiosity, the views of the parties should be ascertained and taken into account. In practice, parties seldom object to a person being present if they are made aware of a good reason for his or her presence. It will therefore generally be appropriate to allow people undergoing training to attend, whether the person is a member of the decision-maker's staff, a new judge or member of the Tribunal or a trainee lawyer shadowing the judge.

Para. (5)

5.228   This paragraph allows any person who would otherwise be entitled to attend a hearing to be excluded, where that is necessary on one of the specified grounds. Plainly the power to exclude a party or representative should be exercised only where there is absolutely no practical alternative. In relation to sub-para.(b), it would be desirable to consider whether alternative methods of giving evidence (e.g. by videolink or from behind a screen) would achieve the necessary effect and be practical.

Para. (6)

5.229   Whether witnesses should be excluded from a hearing until they give evidence depends very much on the circumstances of the case. There is often a fear that dishonest witnesses will tailor their evidence so that it fits with other evidence in the case if they hear that evidence before giving their own. Evidence can often be stronger if it is consistent without the witnesses having had the opportunity of hearing each other's answers to questions. On the other hand, witnesses can often usefully comment on other evidence and can pick up points not mentioned by other witnesses, which is important in social security cases, where parties are seldom represented by lawyers and there is rarely any proper examination-in-chief or cross-examination. Indeed, a representative may often be a witness (see the note to r.11(1)). The Tribunal is given a broad discretion as to how to approach a case. If it intends to exclude witnesses from a hearing, it is suggested it should take the same approach to the witnesses of all parties lest it give the impression of having formed a view that the witnesses of one party only are suspected of dishonesty.

Hearings in a party's absence

31. If a party fails to attend a hearing the Tribunal may proceed with the hearing if the Tribunal—   5.230

    (a) is satisfied that the party has been notified of the hearing or that reasonable steps have been taken to notify the party of the hearing; and

    (b) considers that it is in the interests of justice to proceed with the hearing.

DEFINITIONS

    "hearing"—see r.1(3).
    "party"—*ibid.*
    "Tribunal"—*ibid.*

GENERAL NOTE

In *Cooke v Glenrose Fish Co* [2004] I.C.R. 1188, the Employment Appeal Tribunal   5.231
suggested that an employment tribunal should always at least consider telephoning an appellant who has failed to appear before proceeding in his absence and should ordinarily do so where there was an indication that the appellant had been intending to appear at the hearing because, for instance, solicitors were on the record. An oversight can then be rectified. However, the Employment Appeal Tribunal also held that employment tribunals were entitled to take a robust approach and generally to proceed to hear cases where there was an unexplained absence, because any injustice could be put right on review. The provision in these Rules equivalent to a review would be r.37, which permits the setting aside of a decision where a party or his representative was not present at a hearing. The Employment Appeal Tribunal remarked that "it would appear to be a necessary concomitant of the more stringent attitude encouraged by [the President] that there be the less stringent attitude on a review if a party who has not attended comes forward with a genuine and full explanation and shows that the original hearing was not one from which he deliberately absented himself".

Where a claimant sent a message to a representative to say she would not be attending a hearing and wished the tribunal to proceed in her absence and the representative made no application for an adjournment, a Commissioner declined to hold the tribunal to have erred in not adjourning (*CSIB/404/2005*). However, he set the tribunal's decision aside for failure to deal adequately with questions concerning the claimant's mental health, even though it was difficult to see how the tribunal could have allowed the claimant's appeal on the evidence before it. That may suggest that, where the claimant's presence is really required to establish the facts and the non-attendance might have been attributable, at least in part, to the claimant's mental health, a tribunal really should consider whether an adjournment would be in the interests of justice, just as they would if the claimant had not asked for a hearing (see the annotation to r.27). Of course, a tribunal is entitled to take into account the fact that the claimant has asked for a hearing and then failed to attend it in considering whether justice requires an adjournment and whether attendance in the future is likely.

CHAPTER 3

DECISIONS

Consent orders

5.232   **32.**—(1) The Tribunal may, at the request of the parties but only if it considers it appropriate, make a consent order disposing of the proceedings and making such other appropriate provision as the parties have agreed.

(2) Notwithstanding any other provision of these Rules, the Tribunal need not hold a hearing before making an order under paragraph (1), or provide reasons for the order.

DEFINITIONS

"hearing"—see r.1(3).
"party"—*ibid.*
"Tribunal"—*ibid.*

GENERAL NOTE

5.233   Consent orders have little place in social security cases before the First-tier Tribunal because decision-makers generally have the power to revise the decision under appeal, which causes the appeal to lapse (see, for instance, s.9(1) and (6) of the Social Security Act 1998 and reg.3(4A) of the Social Security and Child Support (Decisions and Appeals) Regs 1999).

Notice of decisions

5.234   **33.**—(1) The Tribunal may give a decision orally at a hearing.

(2) Subject to rule 14(2) (withholding information likely to cause harm), the Tribunal must provide to each party as soon as reasonably practicable after making a decision which finally disposes of all issues in the proceedings (except a decision under Part 4)—

(a) a decision notice stating the Tribunal's decision;

(b) where appropriate, notification of the right to apply for a written statement of reasons under rule 34(3); and

(c) notification of any right of appeal against the decision and the time within which, and the manner in which, such right of appeal may be exercised.

(3) In asylum support cases the notice and notifications required by paragraph (2) must be provided at the hearing or sent on the day that the decision is made.

DEFINITIONS

"asylum support case"—see r.1(3).
"hearing"—*ibid.*

"party"—*ibid.*
"Tribunal"—*ibid.*

GENERAL NOTE

Para. (1)

It is common practice to give a decision orally. Such a decision is not effective   **5.235**
until written notice of it is given *(SK (Sri Lanka) v Secretary of State for the Home
Department* [2008] EWCA Civ 495, *R(I) 14/71*), but as decision notices are usually
issued before the parties leave the hearing venue, there is not much opportunity
for a change of mind. If the tribunal does change its mind, it should invite further
submissions *(SK (Sri Lanka))*.

Para. (2)

It is not entirely clear whether "finally disposes of all issues in the proceedings"   **5.236**
means something different from "disposes of proceedings" (see the note to r.27
above).

Although a decision may be made by a majority where the Tribunal is composed
of more than one member (see art.8 of the First-tier Tribunal and Upper Tribunal
(Composition of Tribunal) Order 2008), there is no longer an express requirement
to state whether or not a decision has been made by a majority.

Where the Secretary of State's decision is defective in form but the tribunal
agrees with its substance, it is not necessary for the tribunal to reformulate the
Secretary of State's decision in the tribunal's decision notice unless the decision
as expressed by the Secretary of State is wrong in some *material* respect (e.g. it
states an incorrect ground of supersession) or there is likely to be some practical
benefit to the claimant or to the adjudication process in future in reformulating the
decision *(R(IB) 2/04* at para.82). On the other hand, attempting to reformulate the
decision may serve to focus the tribunal's mind on the correct issues and so it may
have a value. Where a statement of reasons is requested under r.34(3), the statement should explain what the decision under appeal should have been even if the
decision notice does not.

Where an appeal is against an "outcome decision" expressed in terms of a claimant's entitlement to benefit, a decision notice "should make it absolutely clear
whether the tribunal has made an outcome decision (subject, in some cases, to the
precise amount being calculated by the Secretary of State) or has remitted the final
decision on entitlement to the Secretary of State" *(R(IS) 2/08*, in which it was suggested that the President of appeal tribunals might wish to consider whether the
form of decision notice usually issued in income support and similar cases should
be altered to assist chairmen with that task).

The form of decision notice currently in use does not have a special space for
reasons to be given but there is nothing forbidding a chairman from including brief
reasons in the decision notice and it is suggested that it may often good practice
to do so (although differing views have been expressed by Commissioners on this
issue, see *CIB/4497/1998* and *CSDLA/551/1999*). Apart from anything else, an
unsuccessful party is more likely to ask for a statement of reasons under r.34 if no
reasons at all are given for a decision, especially if it arises at a paper determination.
There being no duty to include any reasons at all in a decision notice, where some
reasons are given but are inadequate, the consequence is not to render the tribunal's
decision erroneous in point of law. The remedy is to apply for a proper statement of
reasons under r.34(3) *(CIB/4497/1998)*. Such a statement cures any inadequacy in
reasons given in a decision notice *(CSDLA/531/2000, CIS/2345/2001)*. However, if
the reasons in the full statement are inconsistent with the reasons given in a decision notice, the decision of the tribunal will be set aside as erroneous in point of law
(CCR/3396/2000, CIS/2345/2001).

Reasons for decisions

5.237   **34.**—(1) In asylum support cases the Tribunal must send a written statement of reasons for a decision which disposes of proceedings (except a decision under Part 4) to each party—

(a) if the case is decided at a hearing, within 3 days after the hearing; or

(b) if the case is decided without a hearing, on the day that the decision is made.

(2) In all other cases the Tribunal may give reasons for a decision which disposes of proceedings (except a decision under Part 4)—

(a) orally at a hearing; or

(b) in a written statement of reasons to each party.

(3) Unless the Tribunal has already provided a written statement of reasons under paragraph (2)(b), a party may make a written application to the Tribunal for such statement following a decision which finally disposes of all issues in the proceedings.

(4) An application under paragraph (3) must be received within 1 month of the date on which the Tribunal sent or otherwise provided to the party a decision notice relating to the decision which finally disposes of all issues in the proceedings.

(5) If a party makes an application in accordance with paragraphs (3) and (4) the Tribunal must, subject to rule 14(2) (withholding information likely to cause harm), send a written statement of reasons to each party within 1 month of the date on which it received the application or as soon as reasonably practicable after the end of that period.

DEFINITIONS

"asylum support case"—see r.1(3).
"dispose of proceedings"—*ibid.*
"hearing"—*ibid.*
"party"—*ibid.*
"Tribunal"—*ibid.*

GENERAL NOTE

Paras (2) to (5)

5.238   These paragraphs replace reg.53(4) of the Social Security and Child Support (Decisions and Appeals) Regs 1999 but add two refinements. The first is to make it clear that reasons may be given orally but that a written statement (which could simply be a transcript) may subsequently be requested. The second is to impose a time limit, albeit not absolute, within which a tribunal must provide a statement of reasons. Whether a tribunal would be found to have erred in law because reasons were not provided "as soon as reasonably practicable" after the standard one month in circumstances where delay would not previously have been sufficient to vitiate the decision remains to be seen. Note also that reg.53(5) has not been re-enacted, so that there is no longer any express duty to record the reasons of the dissenting member of the Tribunal where a decision is made by a majority, or even to record that the decision was reached only by a majority.

A refusal to adjourn is not a "decision" for which a statement of reasons may be required under this rule, although an unexplained refusal to adjourn may make a final decision erroneous in point of law unless an explanation that is not perverse may be inferred from the circumstances (*Carpenter v Secretary of State for Work and Pensions* [2003] EWCA Civ 33 (reported as *R(IB) 6/03)*).

A judge's power to write a statement of reasons survives the termination of his or her appointment to the panel. The statement must at least be adopted by the judge (or possibly another member) of the tribunal who heard the appeal. Therefore a statement written by a regional chairman in the erroneous belief that it could not be written by the chairman who heard the appeal because her appointment had come to an end, was not valid (*CIS/2132/1998*).

In *R. (Sturton) v Social Security Commissioner* [2007] EWHC 2957 (Admin), the decision notice was not sent on the day of the hearing to a party who had not been present at the hearing, even though the notice stated that it had been sent then, so that, when that party subsequently obtained a copy and made an application for a statement of reasons within a month of the copy actually being sent to him, the application was in time.

It is usually an error of law to fail to issue a statement of reasons when a request is made within the prescribed time and there are occasions when an application for leave to appeal should be treated as such a request *(R(IS) 11/99)*. An application for leave to appeal received within the time allowed for asking for a statement of reasons is treated as a request for such a statement (r.38(7)). In both *R(IS) 11/99* and *R3/02(IB)*, it is stated that there are occasions when an error of law can be demonstrated without there being a statement of reasons and that a Commissioner could determine an appeal in those circumstances, although it is obviously not possible to challenge a tribunal's decision on the grounds of inadequacy of reasoning in circumstances where there is no written statement of reasons. Furthermore, a tribunal's decision will not be erroneous in law for breach of the duty to imposed by this rule if the decision notice issued under r.33(2)(a) in fact contains all that would be required in a full statement of reasons *(R(IS) 11/99)*, or if the two documents read together provide an adequate statement between them (*CIS/2345/2001*). The practice of some chairmen of stating that the summary reasons on a decision notice amount to a full statement of reasons has been frowned upon, on the basis that such summary reasons are more likely to contain errors than fuller statements produced in response to a request. In *CSDLA/551/1999*, the Commissioner went as far as to say that it was of no effect and that a separate statement of reasons was required in all cases, but that is not the conventional view and is inconsistent with what was said in *R(IS) 11/99*.

Long decisions need to be properly organised. In *Jasim v Secretary of State for the Home Department* [2006] EWCA Civ 342, the Court of Appeal commented on the "unmanageable length" of some paragraphs in a decision of the Asylum and Immigration Tribunal, one of which ran for almost three pages of single-spaced type. It was suggested that the use of shorter paragraphs, with sub-paragraphs and cross-headings where appropriate, was a useful aid not just to the reader but also to the writer.

This rule includes no express duty to record the tribunal's findings but it is necessary to record a tribunal's findings on any matters in dispute as part of the explanation for its decision *(R(I) 4/02* and also *R2/01(IB)*, a decision of a Tribunal of Commissioners in Northern Ireland). Indeed, it has been said in *Evans v Secretary of State for Social Services* (reported as *R(I) 5/94*) that there are occasions when a record of the tribunal's findings provides a complete explanation for the decision.

In *CDLA/1807/2003*, the tribunal chairman produced two statements of reasons for the tribunal's decision, the second because he had forgotten he had already written a statement. The reasons differed. The Commissioner commented that the reasons should be a statement of the *tribunal's* reasons and not the chairman's later rationalisation of the conclusion reached by the tribunal and that at least one of the statements plainly did not accurately reflect the tribunal's reasons. He set aside the tribunal's decision. Inexplicable inconsistency between the decision notice and the statement of reasons led to an appeal being allowed in *CCR/3396/2000*.

The inadequacy of statements of reasons is probably the most common ground upon which decsions are set aside by the Upper Tribunal. The superficiality of many submissions made by both claimants' representatives and the Secretary of

State's representatives on this issue has been the subject of adverse comment by Commissioners (see, for example, *CIB/4497/1998* in which it was said that there is no simple formula for writing reasons for a decision).

In *Re Poyser and Mills' Arbitration* [1964] 2 Q.B. 467, 478, Megaw J. said:

> "Parliament provided that reasons shall be given, and in my view that must be read as meaning that proper, adequate reasons must be given. The reasons that are set out must be reasons that will not only be intelligible, but which deal with the substantial points that have been raised."

In *R(A) 1/72*, the Chief Commissioner, considering an appeal from a delegated medical practioner acting on behalf of the Attendance Allowance Board, said:

> "The obligation to give reasons for the decision in [a case involving a conflict of evidence] imports a requirement to do more than only to state the conclusion, and for the determining authority to state that on the evidence the authority is not satisfied that the statutory conditions are met, does no more than this. It a ords no guide to the selective process by which the evidence has been accepted, rejected, weighed or considered, or the reasons for any of these things. It is not, of course, obligatory thus to deal with every piece of evidence or to over elaborate, but in an administrative quasi-judicial decision the minimum requirement must at least be that the claimant, looking at the decision should be able to discern on the face of it the reasons why the evidence has failed to satisfy the authority. For the purpose of the regulation which requires the reasons for the review decision to be set out, a decision based, and only based, on a conclusion that the total e ect of the evidence fails to satisfy, without reasons given for reaching that conclusion, will in many cases be no adequate decision at all."

In *R. (Asha Foundation) v Millennium Commission* [2003] EWCA Civ 66 (*The Times,* January 24, 2003), the Court of Appeal considered the approach Sedley J. had taken in *R. v Higher Education Funding Council Ex p. Institute of Dental Surgery* [1994] 1 W.L.R. 242 to the question of whether there was a duty to give any reasons at all and held that, where there is a duty to give reasons, the same approach should be taken to the question whether reasons were adequate. Sedley J.'s approach required the balancing of a number of considerations, which might vary from case to case. He said:

> "The giving of reasons may among other things concentrate the decision-maker's mind on the right questions; demonstrate to the recipient that this is so; show that the issues have been conscientiously addressed and how the result has been reached or alternatively alert the recipient to a justiciable flaw in the process.
>
> On the other side of the argument, it may place an undue burden on decision-makers; demand an appearance of unanimity where there is diversity; call for the articulation of sometimes inexpressible value judgments; and offer an invitation to the captious to comb the reasons for previously unsuspected grounds of challenge."

It was acknowledged in *Baron v Secretary of State for Social Services* (reported as an appendix to *R(M) 6/86*) that there are limits to the extent to which a tribunal can be expected to give reasons for decisions on matters of judgment, such as the distance a claimant could walk without having to stop or the extent of breathlessness and pain which caused him to stop. Assessments of disablement also give rise to difficult judgments. In *CI/636/1993*, the Commissioner said:

> "Whether or how far the duty in law to give reasons for their decision extends beyond saying that the particular percentage arrived at is in the medical judgment of the tribunal a fair one on these particular facts must depend on the nature of the individual case and the issues that have been raised in it. It seems to me that the position is correctly summarised by the Commissioner in *R(I) 30/61* at paragraph 8: there may well be cases where a mere statement that the tribunal

makes an assessment at a particular percentage is in itself a sufficient record, since it implies that they think that is a fair assessment; but in other cases findings of fact and an explanation of reasons will be needed to show that evidence they have accepted or rejected as justifying the making of a smaller or larger assessment, since otherwise the claimant will be left guessing as to the basis on which the decision has been arrived at. And in a case where specific submissions backed with expert medical evidence have been addressed to them on the basis of assessment to be used, it will normally be an error of law for the tribunal simply to state their conclusion in the form of a percentage without making it clear to what extent and for what reasons they are accepting or rejecting the suggested basis, since they will not have carried out the general duty to give reasons on a material issue raised before them: see *R(I) 18/61* para.13."

In many cases it will be obvious from a finding as to the claimant's loss of faculty what the resulting disablement must have been but in others it is necessary for a tribunal to make specific findings as to the resulting disabilities (*CI/343/1988*). In *CI/1802/2001*, it was again stressed that a decision assessing the extent of a claimant's disablement is likely to be inadequate if the tribunal have not explained the factual basis of their decision.

"This can often be simply expressed. In many cases it will be enough to say that the evidence given by the claimant about the effect of a particular accident or disease on his or her daily life has been accepted. In some cases, where the claimant's evidence is for some reason found to be unreliable, it may be that the tribunal will state that it felt able to accept only those disabilities which in its expert opinion were likely to flow from problems disclosed on clinical examination. Other cases may need more detail."

However, where a tribunal assesses disablement for the purpose of determining entitlement to disablement benefit and the claimant is not suffering from an injury specified in Sch.2 of the Social Security (General Benefit) Regulations 1982, it is not necessary for the statement of reasons to refer to the prescribed degrees of disablement set against the injuries in that Schedule even though reg.11(8) of those Regulations suggests that the Schedule may act as a general guide to the assessment of disablement (*R(I) 1/04*). See, also, the decision of the Tribunal of Commissioners in *R(I) 2/06*, where the same approach was taken and *CI/1802/2001* was approved.

Resorting to describing a Benefits Agency Medical Service doctor as "independent" as a reason for preferring his evidence to medical evidence obtained on behalf of the claimant was described as "irrational" in *CIB/563/2001*, given that the Benefits Agency Medical Service doctor was trained and paid by one of the parties to the proceedings. In any event, that reason was inadequate because the doctor acting on behalf of the claimant had recorded different clinical findings and there was no suggestion that he did not conduct a full examination or failed to take account of the claimant's history.

A Tribunal of Commissioners in Northern Ireland has held in *R 3/01 (IB)* that there is no universal obligation on a tribunal to explain an assessment of credibility. It will usually be sufficient to say that a witness is not believed or is exaggerating. It is the decision that has to be explained. A tribunal is not obliged to give reasons for its reasons. There may be situations when a further explanation will be required but the only standard is that the reasons should explain the decision. Much the same approach has been taken in Great Britain, the authorities being analysed in *CIS/4022/2007*.

In *R3/01(IB)*, the Tribunal of Commissioners also held that a tribunal must record their findings on every descriptor of the all work test that is in issue and those raised by clear implication but that there is no universal rule that individual reasons must be given for the selection of a particular descriptor. The reasons given must explain why the tribunal reached the decision they did but need not always explain why it did not reach any different conclusion. However, it is suggested that there *is* a need to explain why a *specific* contention advanced by a party has not been accepted, at least where the contention is a major part of that party's case. It was said in *Flannery v Halifax Estate Agencies Ltd* [2001] 1 W.L.R. 377, CA, that, where there is expert evidence and analysis advanced by both parties, a statement of reasons must "enter into the issues" in order to explain why the unsuccessful party's evidence has failed to prevail. However, in *English v Emery Reimbold & Strick Ltd.* [2002] ECWA Civ 605; [2002] 1 W.L.R. 2409, the Court of Appeal sought to discourage the "cottage industry" of applications inspired by *Flannery* and followed *Eagil Trust Co Ltd v Pigott-Brown* [1985] 3 All E.R. 119, 122 in which Griffiths L.J. had stressed that there was no duty on a judge in giving his reasons to deal with every argument presented to him. The Court also said that, while a judge will often need to refer to a piece of evidence or to a submission which he has accepted or rejected, provided the reference is clear, it may be unnecessary to detail, or even summarise, the evidence or submission in question.

> "The essential requirement is that the terms of the judgment should enable the parties and any appellate tribunal readily to analyse the reasoning that was essential to the Judge's decision."

Where a tribunal has rejected a claimant's account as to how he came by an injury, it is not bound to make any finding as to how he did come by it, where that would be no more than speculation (*AJ (Cameroon) v Secretary of State for the Home Department* [2007] EWCA Civ 373). However, there will, of course, be cases where a tribunal's finding that the injury was due to a different cause is the explanation for rejecting the claimant's case. In *CCS/1626/2002*, the Commissioner said that a person could hardly complain about the adequacy of findings of fact or reasoning lying behind an estimate of income when the need to make an estimate was due to that person's failure to provide better evidence. In *R(I) 3/03*, a Tribunal of Commissioners criticised the Secretary of State for supporting, by reference to an occasional infelicitous word in a statement of reasons, an unrealistic argument advanced by a claimant to the effect that a tribunal had overlooked a basic proposition of law. They said that there are some propositions of law, such as the nature of the civil burden and standard of proof, that are of such fundamental importance in the work of tribunals that it is almost inconceivable that tribunals will have overlooked them and that it should therefore be assumed that they have understood them unless there is something to show otherwise in the substance of what a tribunal has decided.

Specific guidance as to the approach to be taken in medical cases before tribunals has been given by the Court of Appeal in *Evans v Secretary of State for Social Services* (reported as *R(I) 5/94*) where it was said:

> "1. The decision should record the medical question or questions which the tribunal is required to answer. Provided the questions are set out and the answers are directed to the questions it should then be possible for the parties to know the issues to which the tribunal have addressed themselves.
> 2. In cases where the tribunal have medically examined the claimant they should record their findings. These findings by themselves may be sufficient to demonstrate the reason why they have reached a particular conclusion.
> 3. Where, however, the clinical findings do not point to some obvious diagnosis it may be necessary to give a short explanation as to why they have made one diagnosis rather than another. Such an explanation will be important in cases where the tribunal's diagnosis differs from a reasoned diagnosis of another qualified practitioner who has examined the claimant on an earlier occasion.
> 4. A decision on a question of causation may pose particular difficulties when one is examining the adequacy of the reasons for a decision. In some cases it may be sufficient for the tribunal to record that it was not satisfied that the present condition was caused by the relevant trauma. Where, however, a claimant has previously been in receipt of some benefit or allowance (particularly if paid over a long period of time) and there is no question of malingering or bad faith then . . . the

tribunal should go further than merely to state a conclusion. If one accepts that the underlying principle is fairness the claimant should be given some explanation, which may be very short, to enable him or his advisors to know where the break in causation has been found. Thus it may well be that the claimant will wish to reapply and for this purpose fairness requires that, if possible, he should be told why his claim has failed."

That was in the context of decisions of a medical appeal tribunal who had jurisdiction in respect of certain issues only, including the "medical questions" in respect of mobility allowance and the "disablement questions" in respect of disablement benefit. The reference to "the medical question or questions" must be read against that background and must therefore be taken to refer to the *legal* issues as much as the medical issues in a case.

In *CDLA/5419/1999*, it is pointed out that the fact that a claimant is unsuccessful does not always imply rejection of the medical evidence advanced by him or her. In that case, the claimant's doctor said that the claimant required attention but he did not specify how much. The tribunal accepted that the claimant required some attention but found that it was not sufficient to qualify for disability living allowance. The Commissioner said that the doctor's evidence had therefore not supported the element of the claimant's case upon which she failed and that, in the circumstances of the case, there had been no duty to refer to the doctor's evidence at all. A similar point has been made by a Tribunal of Commissioners in Northern Ireland (*R2/04(DLA)*) and by the Court of Appeal in Northern Ireland (*Quinn v Department for Social Development* [2004] NICA 22). In the former case, however, the Tribunal of Commissioners added that, "where it is evident that the claimant attaches great significance to a letter or report, it may be prudent for a tribunal to say, briefly, that it has read the document but derived no assistance from it" and it may be helpful to say why if the relevance or value of the evidence is likely to be controversial. In *R(M) 1/96*, the Commissioner held that the fact of a previous award does not raise any presumption in the claimant's favour or result in the need for consistency having to be treated as a separate issue on a renewal claim. However, he said that the requirement for a tribunal to give reasons for its decision means that it is usually necessary for a tribunal to explain why it is not renewing a previous award, unless that is obvious from their findings. That approach was applied by the Court of Appeal in Northern Ireland in *Quinn*. The Court also accepted that, in the circumstances of that particular case, there had been no need for the tribunal to refer to a medical report obtained for the purpose of determining the previous claim. Similarly, in *R. (Viggers) v Pensions Appeal Tribunal* [2006] EWHC 1066 (Admin), a Pensions Appeal Tribunal was held to have erred when it did not even mention that it was making a much lower assessment of disablement than the Veterans Agency Medical Services, let alone refer to any evidence in the papers including the reasoned opinion of the VAMS' medical adviser. "If they were going to differ, and differ so markedly, from the opinion of the VAMS, the basis of that disagreement required, in my judgment, to be spelt out."

In *Baron v Secretary of State for Social Services* (reported as an appendix to *R(M) 6/86*), it was said that:

"The overriding test must always be: is the tribunal providing both parties with the materials which will enable them to know that the tribunal has made no error of law in reaching its findings of fact?"

The approach taken in social security cases is not very different from that taken in other areas of public law. In the context of planning, Lord Brown of Eaton-under-Heywood summarised the effect of case law in *South Bucks DC v Porter* (No.2) [2004] UKHL 33 [2004] 1 W.L.R. 1953 at [36]:

"The reasons for a decision must be intelligible and they must be adequate. They must enable the reader to understand why the matter was decided as it was and what conclusions were reached on the 'principal important controversial issues', disclosing how any issue of law or fact was resolved. Reasons can be briefly stated, the degree of particularity required depending entirely on the nature of the issues falling for decision. The reasoning must not give rise to a substantial doubt as to whether the decision-maker erred in law, for example by misunderstanding some relevant policy or some other important matter or by failing to reach a rational decision on relevant grounds. But such adverse inference will not readily be drawn. The reasons need refer only to the main issues in the dispute, not to every material consideration. They should enable disappointed developers to assess their prospects of obtaining some alternative development permission, or, as the case may be, their unsuccessful opponents to understand how the policy or approach underlying the grant of permission may impact upon future such applications. Decision letters [which contain statements of reasons] must be read in a straightforward manner, recognising that they are addressed to parties well aware of the issues involved and the arguments advanced. A reasons challenge will only succeed if the party aggrieved can satisfy the court that he has genuinely been substantially prejudiced by the failure to provide an adequately reasoned decision".

In *R(DLA)3/08*, a Tribunal of Commissioners adopted that passage and said that it applied equally to social security cases.

However, in *SP v SSWP* [2009] UKUT 97 (AAC), a deputy judge of the Upper Tribunal held that, if a statement of reasons was inadequate, it was not necessary for the appellant also to show prejudice. He relied upon *Mirza v City of Glasgow Licensing Board* 1996 SC 450 (2nd Div) when distinguishing *South Bucks* on the ground that the latter was a planning case in which the High Court had power to quash a decision only if the applicant had been "substantially prejudiced" by a failure to comply with a duty to give reasons. However, in *Mirza*, the Court of Session had itself followed an earlier decision, *Wordie Property Co Ltd v Secretary of State for Scotland* 1984 SLT 345, where the Lord President, having considered the test of adequacy of reasons, said that "reasons which fail to pass the tests I have just discussed will demonstrate a failure to comply with statutory requirements which cannot have been other than prejudicial to the appellant". In other words, prejudice is part of the test of adequacy of reasons rather than a test to be applied in addition, although it may be observed that, as the Upper Tribunal has an explicit discretion to refuse to set aside a decision even if it is erroneous in point of law (see s.12(2)(a) of the Tribunals, Courts and Enforcement Act 2007), it could require prejudice to be shown at either stage.

Even when reasons are plainly flawed, a decision will not necessarily be set aside. Referring to a decision of a reviewing officer as to whether a homeless person had a priority need for housing, Lord Neuberger said in *Holmes-Moorhouse v London Borough of Richmond upon Thames* [2009] UKHL 7; [2009] 1 W.L.R. 413—

". . . a decision can often survive despite the existence of an error in the reasoning advanced to support it. For example, sometimes the error is irrelevant to the outcome; sometimes it is too trivial (objectively, or in the eyes of the decision-maker) to affect the outcome; sometimes it is obvious from the rest of the reasoning, read as a whole, that the decision would have been the same notwithstanding the error; sometimes, there is more than one reason for the conclusion, and the error only undermines one of the reasons; sometimes, the decision is the only one which could rationally have been reached. In all such cases, the error should not (save, perhaps, in wholly exceptional circumstances) justify the decision being quashed."

The European Court of Human Rights has taken much the same approach as the United Kingdom's courts. In *Hirvisari v Finland* 2001, it was said:

"Although Article 6(1) obliges courts to give reasons for their decisions, it cannot be understood as requiring a detailed answer to every argument. Thus, in dismissing an appeal, an appellate court may, in principle, simply endorse the reasons for the lower court's decision . . . A lower court or authority in turn must give such reasons as to enable the parties to make effective use of any existing rights of appeal."

Standard form decisions have been frowned upon in *CI/5199/1998* and *CIB/4497/1998*, not on grounds of principle but because they tend to be used not only when appropriate but also when the circumstances of the case make it inappropriate.

In *R(IS) 5/04*, it was held that a delay in providing reasons did not necessarily render a decision erroneous in point of law. The Commissioner said that a delay in providing reasons may itself amount to a breach of Article 6 of the European Convention on Human Rights (although, if the tribunal's decision was not flawed in any other respect, the remedy for such a breach would presumably be an award of damages by a court) and she also held that a delay may be relevant on an appeal because it may indicate that the reasons are unreliable. However, in the particular case before her, where the statement of reasons had been requested on July 1, 2002 and was not sent to the parties until October 29, 2002, the Commissioner found there to have been no error of law. In *R(DLA)3/08*, the Tribunal of Commissioners observed that *R(IS)5/04* appeared to be consistent with *Bangs v Connex South Eastern Ltd* [2005] EWCA Civ 14, in which it was held that there had been no error of law despite the fact that a decision of an employment tribunal was not promulgated until a year after the hearing ended. Delay may give rise to the state's liability to pay compensation to the victim of the delay but, where an appeal against the tribunal's decision lies only on a point of law, the Court of Appeal held that it was not enough to claim that the decision is "unsafe" because of the delay. However, that was before the time limit in para(5) was introduced and, in any event, there may be exceptional cases in which unreasonable delay in promulgating a decision can properly be treated as a serious procedural error or material irregularity giving rise to a question of law if there is a real risk that, due to the delayed decision, the party complaining was deprived of the substance of his right to a fair trial under art.6 of the Convention. It is necessary to consider whether the delay has caused the tribunal to reach a wrong finding or to overlook or forget evidence. Effectively, therefore, delay is merely a factor to be borne in mind when assessing the adequacy of a statement of reasons.

In *Barke v SEETEC Business Technology Centre Ltd* [2005] EWCA Civ 578, the Court of Appeal approved the practice in the Employment Appeal Tribunal of sifting appeals and inviting employment tribunals to supplement their reasons when the reasons appear to be inadequate. This is done to save the costs of an appeal and of a rehearing where the reasons can adequately be supplemented, although it was recognised in *Barke* that it will not always be appropriate if, for example "the inadequacy of reasoning is on its face so fundamental that there is a real risk that supplementary reasons will be reconstructions of proper reasons, rather than the unexplained actual reasons for the decision". It was also said that the Employment Appeal Tribunal "should always be alive to the danger that an employment tribunal might tailor its response to a request for explanations or further reasons (usually subconsciously rather than deliberately) so as to put the decision in the best possible light". In *Hatungimana v Secretary of State for the Home Department* [2006] EWCA Civ 231, the Court of Appeal declined to apply *Barke* on an appeal from the Asylum and Immigration Tribunal, stressing that the procedural rules of that tribunal were different from those governing employment tribunals. In *CA/4297/2004*, a Commissioner had already distinguished *Barke* and held that a salaried chairman, considering an application for leave to appeal under reg.58(6)(a), had been wrong to ask the fee-paid chairman of the tribunal to supplement his statement of reasons for the tribunal's decision and that the fee-paid chairman had had no power to do so. There are substantial practical arguments against the course taken by the salaried chairman in the case before the Commissioner because some substantial delay was caused as the claimant had to be given the opportunity to comment on the supplemented statement. The Commissioner pointed out that appeals to Commissioners were usually dealt with speedily without oral hearings and that the cost and length of rehearings before tribunals are relatively modest. That is quite apart from the danger referred to by the Commissioner of a fee-paid chairman being led into introducing reasoning on issues that were not in fact considered by the whole tribunal. However, it is arguable that the Commissioner went too far in suggesting that reasons can never be supplemented when an application is made for leave to appeal. What might have been permissible would have been for the salaried chairman to have referred the application to the fee-paid chairman for determination, with an indication that he might feel able to answer the grounds of appeal. A modest expansion of reasons when leave to appeal is being refused (or granted) may be acceptable in some cases (e.g. *R(M) 2/78*). It will be for the Upper Tribunal to consider whether the reasons are reliable against the background of the case. In *CAF/2150/2007*, the Commissioner suggested that additional reasons should be confined to comments on the grounds of appeal and pointed out that, where the tribunal consisted of more than one person, they had to reflect the views of the tribunal as a whole.

PART 4

CORRECTING, SETTING ASIDE, REVIEWING AND APPEALING TRIBUNAL
DECISIONS

Interpretation

5.239   **35.** In this Part—
"appeal" means the exercise of a right of appeal—
  (a) under paragraph 2(2) or 4(1) of Schedule 2 to the Tax Credits Act 2002;
  (b) under section 21(10) of the Child Trust Funds Act 2004; or
  (c) on a point of law under section 11 of the 2007 Act; and
"review" means the review of a decision by the Tribunal under section 9 of the 2007 Act.

DEFINITIONS

"the 2007 Act"—see r.1(3).
"'Tribunal"—*ibid.*

GENERAL NOTE

5.240   The references to the Tax Credits Act 2002 and the Child Trust Funds Act 2004 are to appeals against decisions in penalty cases, where rights of appeal, which are not confined to points of law, remain in force alongside the right of appeal under s.11 of the Tribunals, Courts and Enforcement Act 2007.

Clerical mistakes and accidental slips or omissions

5.241   **36.** The Tribunal may at any time correct any clerical mistake or other accidental slip or omission in a decision, direction or any document produced by it, by—
  (a) sending notification of the amended decision or direction, or a copy of the amended document, to all parties; and

(b) making any necessary amendment to any information published in relation to the decision, direction or document.

DEFINITIONS

"document"—see r.1(3).
"party"—*ibid.*
"Tribunal"—*ibid.*

GENERAL NOTE

Rule 36 allows correction only of accidental errors, "such as a typing mistake or misspelling of a name or an omission about which both sides if asked, would agree" (*CI/3887/1999*). It cannot be used to remove an error of law on an issue central to an appeal. If a judge realises, after a decision has been issued, that there is an obvious and fundamental error of law in the decision, a party may be invited to apply for permission to appeal so that the decision may be reviewed and a rehearing directed.

A correction is effective only when notice is given as required by para.(a). If notice is not given, the date from which time for appealing runs is left in abeyance (*CI/3887/1999*). It has been held that an application for leave to appeal against a decision lapses if the decision is corrected and a new application may be required, although a pending application may be treated as being an application against the new decision, at any rate by the Upper Tribunal (*CSI/74/1991*).

A decision is only effective when it is sent out ((*R(I) 14/74*), *SK (Sri Lanka) v Secretary of State for the Home Department* [2008] EWCA Civ 495). Until then, it may be altered informally. Even if an oral "decision" has been given, the case may be recalled by the tribunal before it is sent out, if it appears to them that they have made a serious mistake (*CI/141/1987*). Generally it would then be necessary to have a rehearing (*SK (Sri Lanka)*).

A correction no longer automatically extends time limits. Note that a separate power to correct a decision arises on review (see s.9(4)(a) of the Tribunals, Courts and Enforcement Act 2007.

5.242

Setting aside a decision which disposes of proceedings

37.—(1) The Tribunal may set aside a decision which disposes of proceedings, or part of such a decision, and re-make the decision, or the relevant part of it, if—

(a) the Tribunal considers that it is in the interests of justice to do so; and

(b) one or more of the conditions in paragraph (2) are satisfied.

(2) The conditions are—

(a) a document relating to the proceedings was not sent to, or was not received at an appropriate time by, a party or a party's representative;

(b) a document relating to the proceedings was not sent to the Tribunal at an appropriate time;

(c) a party, or a party's representative, was not present at a hearing related to the proceedings; or

(d) there has been some other procedural irregularity in the proceedings.

(3) A party applying for a decision, or part of a decision, to be set aside under paragraph (1) must make a written application to the Tribunal so that it is received no later than 1 month after the date on which the Tribunal sent notice of the decision to the party.

5.243

DEFINITIONS

"dispose of proceedings"—see r.1(3).
"document"—*ibid.*
"hearing"—*ibid.*
"party"—*ibid.*
"Tribunal"—*ibid.*

GENERAL NOTE

5.244   The one-month time limit for making an application may be extended under r.5(3)(a).

Note that a separate power to set aside a decision arises on review (see s.9(4)(c) of the Tribunals, Courts and Enforcement Act 2007).

Setting aside under r.37 is appropriate where a claimant has not received notice of a hearing that has been properly sent *(R(SB) 19/83)*. In *R(SB) 55/83*, it was held that that was the only remedy available to a claimant in those circumstances and that there was no basis upon which a Commissioner could allow an appeal. That approach has been rejected in *CDLA/5413/1999* where it is held that a decision of a tribunal is erroneous in law where notice of a hearing has not been received by a party even though there may have been no breach of the rules of natural justice by the tribunal. See also *CIB/303/1999*. In *CIB/5227/1999*, it was pointed out that it was necessary to explain fully the circumstances of the case when making an application for a decision to be set aside. In that case, as in *CDLA/5413/1999*, the reason that the claimant had not received notice of the hearing was that none had been sent because the claimant had not received the clerk's direction requiring him to state whether he wished there to be an oral hearing.

In *CSB/15394/1996* and *CSB/574/1997*, a tribunal refused to set aside a decision on the ground that the claimant's case for the setting aside amounted to an allegation that there had been a breach of the rules of natural justice which was an error of law so that an appeal to a Commissioner was the appropriate course for the claimant to take. The Commissioner hearing the appeal disagreed with that approach. He pointed out that most grounds for setting aside would also be proper grounds for appeal and that the forerunner of this rule existed to provide an expeditious alternative to an appeal. On the other hand, in *CSDLA/303/1998*, the Commissioner held that a claimant was not entitled to raise by way of appeal an issue of fact determined under the forerunner of this rule. The tribunal considering the application for setting aside had found as a fact that a fax allegedly sent to the Independent Tribunal Service had not in fact been sent. The Commissioner held that that question of fact could not be considered on an appeal because "there could be no question of unfairness arising as the claimant had been provided with the remedy of seeking set aside". It is not recorded whether or not the claimant was offered an oral hearing of the application for setting aside, which would have been unusual. It may still be arguable that a finding made on such an application without an oral hearing is not sufficient to remove the Upper Tribunal's jurisdiction to consider the same issue on an appeal.

In *CG/2973/2004*, the Commissioner held a tribunal decision to be erroneous in point of law because medical evidence sent by the claimant in support of an application for an adjournment had not been received by the tribunal. He also held that the fact that the claimant had unsuccessfully tried to have the decision set aside on the same ground did not prevent her from taking the point on appeal to a Commissioner. He observed that the chairman who had refused to set the decision aside had done so on the basis that her presence could not have made any difference to the outcome of her hearing. The case is therefore distinguishable from *CSDLA/303/1998*. The fact that the applicant's presence would not have made any difference is a matter that can legitimately be taken into account when considering whether "to set the decision aside is in the interests of justice" and it would also be relevant to the question whether there had been a breach of the rules of natural justice, but the Commissioner disagreed with the chairman's view of the possible importance of the claimant's evidence.

An appeal against *CG/2973/2004* was dismissed by the Court of Appeal (*Levy v Secretary of State for Work and Pensions* [2006] EWCA Civ 890 (reported as *R(G) 2/06)*), but the relevance of the claimant's application under the forerunner of r.37 was not the subject of argument in the Court of Appeal.

Tribunals are entitled to take a robust approach to the non-appearance of parties and to proceed to hear cases in their absence, but a necessary concomitant of such a robust approach must be a greater preparedness to set aside decisions under r.37(2)(c) (*Cooke v Glenrose Fish Co* [2004] I.C.R. 1188).

Paragraph (1)(a) specifically provides that, even where the conditions of para.2 are satisfied, a decision need be set aside only if it is "in the interests of justice to do so". This is consistent with the European Convention on Human Rights. Under the Convention, a person who did not receive notice of a hearing is not entitled as of right to have the decision set aside, unless he has a real prospect of success on a rehearing (*Akram v Adam* [2004] EWCA Civ 1601; [2005] 1 W.L.R. 2762).

Where there has been a breach of natural justice that does not fall within the scope of r.37 and an application under this rule has been rejected for that reason, the judge should consider reviewing the decision if an application for permission to appeal is submitted (*CDLA/792/2006*).

If a case is reheard by a differently constituted tribunal, it is usual for the decision that has been set aside to be included in the papers. That is not inappropriate. Even if their findings of fact cannot be relied upon, issues identified by the first tribunal may well be of assistance to the new tribunal, although it must be careful not to be influenced by the discredited findings (*Swash v Secretary of State for the Home Department* [2006] EWCA Civ 1093; [2007] 1 W.L.R. 1264). There may, however, be special circumstances in which the judge setting the first decision aside considers that the interests of justice require the case to be heard by a tribunal that has not seen that decision and he or she will be able to issue appropriate directions to ensure that that happens (*ibid*).

Application for permission to appeal

38.—(1) This rule does not apply to asylum support cases or criminal injuries compensation cases.

(2) A person seeking permission to appeal must make a written application to the Tribunal for permission to appeal.

(3) An application under paragraph (2) must be sent or delivered to the Tribunal so that it is received no later than 1 month after the latest of the dates that the Tribunal sends to the person making the application—

(a) written reasons for the decision;

(b) notification of amended reasons for, or correction of, the decision following a review; or

(c) notification that an application for the decision to be set aside has been unsuccessful.

(4) The date in paragraph (3)(c) applies only if the application for the decision to be set aside was made within the time stipulated in rule 37 (setting aside a decision which disposes of proceedings) or any extension of that time granted by the Tribunal.

(5) If the person seeking permission to appeal sends or delivers the application to the Tribunal later than the time required by paragraph (3) or by any extension of time under rule 5(3)(a) (power to extend time)—

5.245

(a) the application must include a request for an extension of time and the reason why the application was not provided in time; and

(b) unless the Tribunal extends time for the application under rule 5(3) (a) (power to extend time) the Tribunal must not admit the application.

(6) An application under paragraph (2) must—

(a) identify the decision of the Tribunal to which it relates;

(b) identify the alleged error or errors of law in the decision; and

(c) state the result the party making the application is seeking.

(7) If a person makes an application under paragraph (2) when the Tribunal has not given a written statement of reasons for its decision—

(a) if no application for a written statement of reasons has been made to the Tribunal, the application for permission must be treated as such an application;

(b) unless the Tribunal decides to give permission and directs that this sub-paragraph does not apply, the application is not to be treated as an application for permission to appeal; and

(c) if an application for a written statement of reasons has been, or is, refused because of a delay in making the application, the Tribunal must only admit the application for permission if the Tribunal considers that it is in the interests of justice to do so.

DEFINITIONS

"appeal"—see r.35.
"asylum support case"—see r.1(3).
"criminal injuries compensation case"—*ibid.*
"dispose of proceedings"—*ibid.*
"party"—*ibid.*
"Tribunal"—*ibid.*

GENERAL NOTE

Para. (5)

5.246   There is no longer an absolute time limit on applications. Previously an application could not be accepted if it was more than a year late. It is still unlikely that permission would be given where there had been such a delay but it is not inconceivable in, say, a case where an unrepresented claimant has been actively challenging some other decision and has not been told that success in that challenge depended on a successful appeal against the decision of the Tribunal.

Rule 5(3)(a) does not expressly require "special reasons" to be shown for an extension of time, as was the position under reg.58 of the Social Security and Child Support (Decisions and Appeals) Regulations 1999, but it is suggested that this may not make any difference because "[t]he concept of special reasons [was] a broad and flexible one" (*R. (Howes) v Social Security Commissioner* [2007] EWHC 559 (Admin)). The reasons for delay were never the only relevant factor (*R(M) 1/87*, applying the approach of the Court of Appeal in *R. v Secretary of State for the Home Department Ex p. Mehta* [1975] 1 W.L.R. 1087)

In *CCS/2064/1999*, it was suggested that relevant factors included the strength of the grounds of appeal, the amount of money involved, whether the decision affected current entitlement, whether there was an adequate alternative remedy, the difficulties that the lapse of time might create for making any further findings of fact and the way in which the parties had conducted the case, including their respective contributions to delay. However, in *R. (Howes) v Social Security Commissioner* [2007]

EWHC 559 (Admin), Black J., in rejecting an argument that deciding whether there were special reasons required consideration of the factors listed in C.P.R r.3.9, also disapproved of judge-made lists of relevant considerations and said that "the factors that are relevant will be dependent upon the circumstances of the individual case". The amount of delay is likely to be relevant in most cases but, in *CSDLA/71/1999*, the Commissioner made it plain that "special reasons" for admitting a late application for leave to appeal would not necessarily be found merely because the application was made only two or three days late, even if the applicant had an arguable case on the merits. In that case, the applicant was not helped by the fact that the original explanation for the delay advanced by his representative turned out not to be true and the Commissioner refused leave to appeal.

Para.(7)

Although the circumstances in which a person can demonstrate an error of law in the absence of a statement of reasons are limited, they are not negligible (see *R(IS) 11/99*). This paragraph makes provision for cases where there is no statement of reasons, either because no application has previously been made or because a statement of reasons has been refused. If there has not already been an application for a statement of reasons, the application for permission to appeal is treated as such an application either instead of, or if it so directs under sub-para.(b), as well as an application for permission to appeal. Sub-paragraph (b) applies only if the Tribunal decides to give permission to appeal either at the same time as issuing a statement of reasons or despite the refusal of such a statement. Where the Tribunal would refuse permission to appeal or would review its decision, it must give the applicant another opportunity to apply for permission to appeal in the light of its decision whether or not to issue a statement of reasons. However, it is arguable that sub-para.(b) does not prevent the Tribunal from treating the application as an application for a correction or setting aside (see r.41).   **5.247**

Sub-paragraph (c) (unlike sub-paras (a) and (b)) applies whether or not there has been a previous application for a statement of reasons. It has the effect of treating the delay in applying for a statement of reasons (which is the only ground upon which a statement of reasons may be refused) in the same way as delay in applying for permission to appeal. The application for permission will not be admitted unless the Tribunal is persuaded that it is in the interests of justice to admit it despite the delay, just as, under para.(5)(b), a late application for permission will not be admitted unless it is in the interests of justice to extend the time for making the application.

Tribunal's consideration of application for permission to appeal

39.—(1) On receiving an application for permission to appeal the Tribunal must first consider, taking into account the overriding objective in rule 2, whether to review the decision in accordance with rule 40 (review of a decision).   **5.248**

(2) If the Tribunal decides not to review the decision, or reviews the decision and decides to take no action in relation to the decision, or part of it, the Tribunal must consider whether to give permission to appeal in relation to the decision or that part of it.

(3) The Tribunal must send a record of its decision to the parties as soon as practicable.

(4) If the Tribunal refuses permission to appeal it must send with the record of its decision—

(a) a statement of its reasons for such refusal; and

(b) notification of the right to make an application to the Upper Tribunal for permission to appeal and the time within which, and the method by which, such application must be made.

(5) The Tribunal may give permission to appeal on limited grounds, but must comply with paragraph (4) in relation to any grounds on which it has refused permission.

DEFINITIONS

"appeal"—see r.35.
"party"—see r.1(3).
"review"—see r.35.
"Tribunal"—see r.1(3).

GENERAL NOTE

5.249   The Senior President of Tribunals has issued a Practice Statement which has the effect of replacing reg.58(6) of the Social Security and Child Support (Decisions and Appeals) Regs 1999 so that, as before, applications for permission to appeal are considered by salaried judges where the decision was made by, or by a tribunal presided over by, a fee-paid judge (see para.11 of the *Practice Statement on the composition of the tribunals in social security and child support cases in the Social Entitlement Chamber* set out in the note to art.2 of the First-tier Tribunal and Upper Tribunal (Composition of Tribunal) Order 2008, below).

There is no requirement to obtain observations from parties other than the applicant and it is suggested that it is unnecessary to do so unless the Tribunal is contemplating reviewing the decision that is being challenged and, even then, it will not always be necessary to do so because a dissatisfied party may apply for the new decision to be set aside (see r.40(4)).

Paras (1) and (2)

5.250   Before deciding whether or not to grant permission to appeal, the Tribunal must first decide whether or not to review the decision under s.9 of the Tribunals, Courts and Enforcement Act 2007, as limited by r.40. However, it does not follow from the fact that there may be grounds for review that the decision must be reviewed. For instance, although the Tribunal may take the view that its decision is erroneous in law, it is entitled to grant permission to appeal on the basis that, if the issue is a matter of contention between the parties and there would probably be an appeal against the review decision, the issue should be resolved by the Upper Tribunal sooner rather than later.

Para. (4)

5.251   Reasons for refusing permission to appeal can usually be very brief and will often simply be that the application does not raise any point of law. Reasons can be valuable in persuading an applicant not to make an application to the Upper Tribunal in a hopeless case or in alerting the applicant of the need to rewrite the grounds. If an application raises allegations about the conduct of the Tribunal, it is likely to be desirable to make it clear whether the Tribunal disputes the accuracy of the allegations.

Para. (5)

5.252   Except where some grounds advanced are completely misconceived, it may not be helpful to grant a party without a legal representative permission to appeal on limited grounds, because doing so can make an appeal to the Upper Tribunal more complicated and the Upper Tribunal itself generally makes observations and issues directions before any response to an appeal is required, thus focussing the parties' attention on the more important issues. Moreover, the Upper Tribunal exercises an investigatory approach to appeals and so is not confined by the grounds of appeal or the grounds of permission. Where a party is represented by a lawyer used to formal pleading, other considerations may apply.

Review of a decision

40.—(1) This rule does not apply to asylum support cases or criminal injuries compensation cases.

(2) The Tribunal may only undertake a review of a decision—

(a) pursuant to rule 39(1) (review on an application for permission to appeal); and

(b) if it is satisfied that there was an error of law in the decision.

(3) The Tribunal must notify the parties in writing of the outcome of any review, and of any right of appeal in relation to the outcome.

(4) If the Tribunal takes any action in relation to a decision following a review without first giving every party an opportunity to make representations, the notice under paragraph (3) must state that any party that did not have an opportunity to make representations may apply for such action to be set aside and for the decision to be reviewed again.

5.253

DEFINITIONS

"appeal"—see r.35.
"asylum support case"—see r.1(3).
"criminal injuries compensation case"—*ibid.*
"party"—*ibid.*
"review"—see r.35.
"Tribunal—see r.1(3).

GENERAL NOTE

Para. (2)

The power of review arises under s.9(1) of the Tribunals, Courts and Enforcement Act 2007.

Section 9(2) provides for the power of review to be exercised either on the tribunal's initiative or on an application, but s.9(3)(b) enables rules to provide that it is exercisable only on the Tribunal's own initiative. That is what para.(2)(a) of this rule does: a party may not make a freestanding application for a review (although if he or she does, it may be treated as an application for a correction, setting aside or permission to appeal (see r.41)) but the Tribunal may review a decision on its own initiative once there has been an application for permission to appeal. Paragraph (2)(b), made under s.9(3)(d), limits the ground of review to an error of law. Since appeals under s.11 lie only on points of law, a review therefore provides a way of avoiding an appeal where the appeal would plainly be allowed. See s.9(4), (5) and (8) for the powers of the Tribunal on review. These powers are wider than they were under s.13(2) of the Social Security Act 1998 and the similar provisions relating to housing benefit, council tax benefit and child support, which s.9, as limited by this rule, replaces. Note, however, that s.13(3) of the 1998 Act remains in place.

5.254

Para. (3)

Section 11(5)(d) of the 2007 Act has the effect that there is no right of appeal against a decision whether or not to review a decision, to take no action on a review, to set aside a decision on a review or to refer, or not refer, a matter to the Upper Tribunal on review. However, that is because there is always another decision that may be the subject of an appeal. Where the Tribunal refuses to review a decision or reviews it but takes no action, the Tribunal must consider whether to give permission to appeal against the original decision. Where the tribunal reviews a decision and either takes action itself or refers it to the Upper Tribunal to be redecided, there will be a right to apply for permission to appeal against the new decision.

5.255

Where a decision is reviewed without all the parties having had the opportunity to make representations, notice must also be given of the right to apply for the new decision to be set aside (see para.(4)).

Para.(4)

5.256   The clear implication of this paragraph is that the Tribunal may either obtain submissions from the parties other than the applicant before reviewing a case or review the case first and then wait to see whether any of the other parties objects. Plainly the second of those approaches may lead to a quicker decision and less work where there is no objection to the review. It is suggested, however, that that approach is appropriate only where the parties other than the applicant can reasonably be expected to be able to judge whether or not to object or where the ground of review and appropriate decision on review are both very clear. If submissions are obtained and all the parties assert that the decision is erroneous in point of law, the Tribunal will be obliged to set the decision aside in those cases where s.13(3) of the Social Security Act 1998 (or an equivalent provision in legislation beyond the scope of this work) applies.

Power to treat an application as a different type of application

5.257   **41.** The Tribunal may treat an application for a decision to be corrected, set aside or reviewed, or for permission to appeal against a decision, as an application for any other one of those things.

DEFINITIONS

"appeal"—see r.35.
"review"—*ibid.*
"Tribunal"—see r.1(3).

SCHEDULE 1

TIME LIMITS FOR PROVIDING NOTICES OF APPEAL TO THE DECISION MAKER

Type of proceedings	*Time for providing notice of appeal*
cases other than those listed below	the latest of— (a) one month after the date on which notice of the decision being challenged was sent to the appellant; (b) if a written statement of reasons for the decision is requested, 14 days after the later of (i) the date on which the period at (a) expires; and (ii) the date on which the written statement of reasons was provided; or (c) where the appellant made an application for revision of the decision under regulation 3(1) or (3) or 3A(1) of the Social Security and Child Support (Decision & Appeals) Regulations 1999 or regulation 17(1)(a) of the Child Support (Maintenance Assessment Procedure) Regulations 1992, and that application was unsuccessful, one month of the date on which notice that the decision would not be revised was sent to the appellant

5.258

Type of proceedings	Time for providing notice of appeal
appeal against a certificate of NHS charges under section 157(1) of the Health and Social Care (Community Health and Standards) Act 2003	(a) 3 months after the latest of— (i) the date on the certificate; (ii) the date on which the compensation payment was made; (iii) if the certificate has been reviewed, the date the certificate was confirmed or a fresh certificate was issued; or (iv) the date of any agreement to treat an earlier compensation payment as having been made in final discharge of a claim made by or in respect of an injured person and arising out of the injury or death; or (b) if the person to whom the certificate has been issued makes an application under section 157(4) of the Health and Social Care (Community Health and Standards) Act 2003, one month after— (i) the date of the decision on that application; or (ii) if the person appeals against that decision under section 157(6) of that Act, the date on which the appeal is decided or withdrawn
appeal against a waiver decision under section 157(6) of the Health and Social Care (Community Health and Standards) Act 2003	one month after the date of the decision
appeal against a certificate of NHS charges under section 7 of the Road Traffic (NHS Charges) Act 1999	3 months after the latest of— (a) the date on which the liability under section 1(2) of the Road Traffic (NHS Charges) Act 1999 was discharged; (b) if the certificate has been reviewed, the date the certificate was confirmed or a fresh certificate was issued; or (c) the date of any agreement to treat an earlier compensation payment as having been made in final discharge of a claim made by or in respect of a traffic casualty and arising out of the injury or death
appeal against a certificate of recoverable benefits under section 11 of the Social Security (Recovery of Benefits) Act 1997	one month after the latest of— (a) the date on which any payment to the Secretary of State required under section 6 of the Social Security (Recovery of Benefits) Act 1997 was made; (b) if the certificate has been reviewed, the date the certificate was confirmed or a fresh certificate was issued; or (c) the date of any agreement to treat an earlier compensation payment as having been made in final discharge of a claim made by or in respect of an injured person and arising out of the accident, injury or disease
appeal under the Vaccine Damage Payments Act 1979	no time limit

Type of proceedings	Time for providing notice of appeal
appeal under the Tax Credits Act 2002	as set out in the Tax Credits Act 2002
appeal under the Child Trust Funds Act 2004	as set out in the Child Trust Funds Act 2004
appeal against a decision in respect of a claim for child benefit or guardian's allowance under section 12 of the Social Security Act 1998	as set out in regulation 28 of the Child Benefit and Guardian's Allowance (Decisions and Appeals) Regulations 2003

DEFINITIONS

"appeal"—see r.1(3).
"appellant"—*ibid.*
"decision maker"—*ibid.*

GENERAL NOTE

Para.(1(c))

5.259   There is no right of appeal against a decision under s.9 of the Social Security Act 1998 to revise or not revise an earlier decision. This paragraph allows most s.9 decisions effectively to be challenged by extending the time for appealing against the decision that has been revised or not revised. However, it does not apply to refusals to revise, except where there was an application under regs 3(1) or (3) or 3A(1) of these Regulations or reg.17 of the Child Support (Maintenance Assessment Procedure Regulations 1992.

     The reference to reg.3A(1) (which is also concerned only with child support decisions and is therefore not reproduced in this work) is interesting because reg.3A(1) is much broader in its scope than reg.3(1) and includes revision for "official error" which, in social security cases, falls under reg.3(5)(a). The consequence is that, in child support cases to which reg.3A applies, the time limit for appealing against a decision that has not been revised for "official error" is extended under reg.31(2) but the same is not true in social security cases. In *R(IS)15/04* (subsequently approved by the Court of Appeal in *Beltekian v Westminster CC* [2004] EWCA Civ 1784 (reported as *R(H)8/05).* a Tribunal of Commissioners held that it followed that there was no way of challenging a refusal to revise in a social security case, if it was too late to appeal against the original decision, other than by way of an application for judicial review. This is most unsatisfactory. The Tribunal pointed out that claimants would not wish to apply for revision under reg.3(5) except on the ground of "official error" because the other grounds for revision result in decisions less favourable to the claimant than the decision that has been revised. However, claimants might well apply for supersession under other paragraphs in reg.3 and so the problem is not confined to "official error" cases.

     Where it is still possible to appeal against the original decision following a refusal to revise, the Tribunal held in *R(IB)2/04* at para.39 that the appeal can succeed only if it can be shown that the decision should have been revised. Otherwise, as was pointed out in *CCS/5515/2002*, late appeals could easily be brought by making entirely unmeritorious applications for revision.

Rule 25(3)

1B.43   SCHEDULE 2

ISSUES IN RELATION TO WHICH THE TRIBUNAL MAY REFER A PERSON FOR MEDICAL
EXAMINATION UNDER SECTION 20(2) OF THE SOCIAL SECURITY ACT 1998

An issue falls within this Schedule if the issue—   **5.260**
- (a) is whether the claimant satisfies the conditions for entitlement to—
  - (i) an attendance allowance specified in section 64 and 65(1) of the Social Security Contributions and Benefits Act 1992;
  - (ii) severe disablement allowance under section 68 of that Act;
  - (iii) the care component of a disability living allowance specified in section 72(1) and (2) of that Act;
  - (iv) the mobility component of a disability living allowance specified in section 73(1), (8) and (9) of that Act; or
  - (v) a disabled person's tax credit specified in section 129(1)(b) of that Act.
- (b) relates to the period throughout which the claimant is likely to satisfy the conditions for entitlement to an attendance allowance or a disability living allowance;
- (c) is the rate at which an attendance allowance is payable;
- (d) is the rate at which the care component or the mobility component of a disability living allowance is payable;
- (e) is whether a person is incapable of work for the purposes of the Social Security Contributions and Benefits Act 1992;
- (f) relates to the extent of a person's disablement and its assessment in accordance with Schedule 6 to the Social Security Contributions and Benefits Act 1992;
- (g) is whether the claimant suffers a loss of physical or mental faculty as a result of the relevant accident for the purposes of section 103 of the Social Security Contributions and Benefits Act 1992;
- (h) relates to any payment arising under, or by virtue of a scheme having effect under, section 111 of, and Schedule 8 to, the Social Security Contributions and Benefits Act 1992 (workmen's compensation);
- (i) is whether a person has limited capability for work or work-related activity for the purposes of the Welfare Reform Act 2007.

DEFINITIONS

"Tribunal"—see r.1(3).

Tribunal Procedure (Upper Tribunal) Rules 2008

(SI 2008/2698)

IN FORCE NOVEMBER 3, 2008

CONTENTS

PART 1

INTRODUCTION

PART 2

GENERAL POWERS AND PROVISIONS

PART 3

PROCEDURE FOR CASES IN THE UPPER TRIBUNAL

PART 4

JUDICIAL REVIEW PROCEEDINGS IN THE UPPER TRIBUNAL

PART 5

HEARINGS

PART 6

DECISIONS

PART 7

CORRECTING, SETTING ASIDE, REVIEWING AND APPEALING DECISIONS OF THE
UPPER TRIBUNAL

After consulting in accordance with paragraph 28(1) of Schedule 5 to, the Tribunals, Courts and Enforcement Act 2007 the Tribunal Procedure Committee has made the following Rules in exercise of the power conferred by sections 10(3), 16(9), 22 and 29(3) and (4) of, and Schedule 5 to, that Act.

The Lord Chancellor has allowed the Rules in accordance with paragraph 28(3) of Schedule 5 to the Tribunals, Courts and Enforcement Act 2007.

PART 1

INTRODUCTION

Citation, commencement, application and interpretation

1.—(1) These Rules may be cited as the Tribunal Procedure (Upper   5.262
Tribunal) Rules 2008 and come into force on 3rd November 2008.

(2) These Rules apply to proceedings before the Upper Tribunal.

(3) In these Rules—

"the 2007 Act" means the Tribunals, Courts and Enforcement Act 2007;

[¹ "appellant" means—

(a) a person who makes an appeal, or applies for permission to appeal, to the Upper Tribunal;

(b) in proceedings transferred or referred to the Upper Tribunal from the First-tier Tribunal, a person who started the proceedings in the First-tier Tribunal; or

(c) a person substituted as an appellant under rule 9(1) (substitution and addition of parties);]

"applicant" means a person who applies for permission to bring, or does bring, judicial review proceedings before the Upper Tribunal and, in judicial review proceedings transferred to the Upper Tribunal from a court, includes a person who was a claimant or petitioner in the proceedings immediately before they were transferred;

[¹ . . .]

"dispose of proceedings" includes, unless indicated otherwise, disposing of a part of the proceedings;

"document" means anything in which information is recorded in any form, and an obligation under these Rules or any practice direction or direction to provide or allow access to a document or a copy of a document for any purpose means, unless the Upper Tribunal directs otherwise, an obligation to provide or allow access to such document or copy in a legible form or in a form which can be readily made into a legible form;

"hearing" means an oral hearing and includes a hearing conducted in whole or in part by video link, telephone or other means of instantaneous two-way electronic communication;

"interested party" means—

(a) a person who is directly affected by the outcome sought in judicial review proceedings, and has been named as an interested party under rule 28 or 29 (judicial review), or has been substituted or added as an interested party under rule 9 (substitution and addition of parties); and

(b) in judicial review proceedings transferred to the Upper Tribunal under section 25A(2) or (3) of the Judicature (Northern Ireland) Act 1978 or section 31A(2) or (3) of the Supreme Court Act 1981, a person who was an interested party in the proceedings immediately before they were transferred to the Upper Tribunal;

"judicial review proceedings" means proceedings within the jurisdiction of the Upper Tribunal pursuant to section 15 or 21 of the 2007 Act, whether such proceedings are started in the Upper Tribunal or transferred to the Upper Tribunal;

[¹ . . .]

"mental health case" means proceedings before the Upper Tribunal on appeal against a decision in proceedings under the Mental Health Act 1983 or paragraph 5(2) of the Schedule to the Repatriation of Prisoners Act 1984;

"party" means a person who is an appellant, an applicant, a respondent or an interested party in proceedings before the Upper Tribunal, a person who has referred a question to the Upper Tribunal or, if the proceedings have been concluded, a person who was an appellant, an applicant, a respondent or an interested party when the Tribunal finally disposed of all issues in the proceedings;

"permission" includes leave in cases arising under the law of Northern Ireland;

"practice direction" means a direction given under section 23 of the 2007 Act;

"respondent" means—

(a) in an appeal, or application for permission to appeal, against a decision of another tribunal, any person other than the appellant who—

    (i) was a party before that other tribunal;

    (ii) [¹. . .] or

    (iii) otherwise has a right of appeal against the decision of the other tribunal and has given notice to the Upper Tribunal that they wish to be a party to the appeal;

(b) in an appeal against any other decision, the person who made the decision;

(c) in judicial review proceedings—

    (i) in proceedings started in the Upper Tribunal, the person named by the applicant as the respondent;

    (ii) in proceedings transferred to the Upper Tribunal under section 25A(2) or (3) of the Judicature (Northern Ireland) Act 1978 or section 31A(2) or (3) of the Supreme Court Act 1981, a person who was a defendant in the proceedings immediately before they were transferred;

    (iii) in proceedings transferred to the Upper Tribunal under section 20(1) of the 2007 Act, a person to whom intimation of the petition was made before the proceedings were transferred, or to whom the Upper Tribunal has required intimation to be made;

[¹ (ca) in proceedings transferred or referred to the Upper Tribunal from the First-tier Tribunal, a person who was a respondent in the proceedings in the First-tier Tribunal;]

(d) in a reference under the Forfeiture Act 1982, the person whose eligibility for a benefit or advantage is in issue; or

(e) a person substituted or added as a respondent under rule 9 (substitution and addition of parties);

[¹. . .]

"working day" means any day except a Saturday or Sunday, Christmas Day, Good Friday or a bank holiday under section 1 of the Banking and Financial Dealings Act 1971.

Amendments

1. Tribunal Procedure (Amendment) Rules 2009 (SI 2009/274), r.5 (April 1, 2009).

Definitions

"the 2007 Act"—see para.(3).
"appellant"—*ibid.*
"applicant"—*ibid.*
"interested party"—*ibid.*
"judicial review proceedings"—*ibid.*
"party"—*ibid.*
"permission"—*ibid.*

"practice direction"—*ibid.*
"respondent"—*ibid.*

GENERAL NOTE

5.263   The Upper Tribunal has jurisdiction in some "judicial review proceedings", by
virtue of ss.15 to 21 of the Tribunals, Courts and Enforcement Act 2007. Note that
the terms "applicant" and "interested party" are used only in relation to such cases.
A person applying for permission to appeal *to* the Upper Tribunal is included within
the term "appellant" and in all cases other than judicial review proceedings, every
party other than the appellant or person making a reference is a "respondent". A
person applying for a decision to be set aside or for permission to appeal *from* the
Upper Tribunal is referred to in the Rules merely as "a party applying for . . . " or "a
person seeking . . . ".

For the meaning of "bank holiday" in the definition of "working day", see the
note to r.12(3) of the Tribunal Procedure (First-tier Tribunal) (Social Entitlement
Chamber) Rules 2008, above.

Overriding objective and parties' obligation to co-operate with the Upper Tribunal

5.264   **2.**—(1) The overriding objective of these Rules is to enable the Upper
Tribunal to deal with cases fairly and justly.

(2) Dealing with a case fairly and justly includes—

(a) dealing with the case in ways which are proportionate to the importance of the case, the complexity of the issues, the anticipated costs
and the resources of the parties;

(b) avoiding unnecessary formality and seeking flexibility in the proceedings;

(c) ensuring, so far as practicable, that the parties are able to participate
fully in the proceedings;

(d) using any special expertise of the Upper Tribunal effectively; and

(e) avoiding delay, so far as compatible with proper consideration of the
issues.

(3) The Upper Tribunal must seek to give effect to the overriding objective when it—

(a) exercises any power under these Rules; or

(b) interprets any rule or practice direction.

(4) Parties must—

(a) help the Upper Tribunal to further the overriding objective; and

(b) co-operate with the Upper Tribunal generally.

DEFINITIONS

"party"—see r.1(3).
"practice direction"—*ibid.*

GENERAL NOTE

5.265   See the note to r.2 of the Tribunal Procedure (First-tier Tribunal) (Social
Entitlement Chamber) Rules 2008, above.

Alternative dispute resolution and arbitration

5.266   **3.**—(1) The Upper Tribunal should seek, where appropriate—

(a) to bring to the attention of the parties the availability of any appropriate alternative procedure for the resolution of the dispute; and

    (b) if the parties wish and provided that it is compatible with the overriding objective, to facilitate the use of the procedure.

(2) Part 1 of the Arbitration Act 1996 does not apply to proceedings before the Upper Tribunal.

DEFINITION

"party"—see r.1(3).

GENERAL NOTE

Rule 3(1) applies only if there is an alternative procedure available and none currently is. Such a procedure would be useful only where the Upper Tribunal was concerned with a complicated issue of fact, which is very seldom the position in a social security case.

        5.267

PART 2

GENERAL POWERS AND PROVISIONS

Delegation to staff

4.—(1) Staff appointed under section 40(1) of the 2007 Act (tribunal staff and services) may, with the approval of the Senior President of Tribunals, carry out functions of a judicial nature permitted or required to be done by the Upper Tribunal.

(2) The approval referred to at paragraph (1) may apply generally to the carrying out of specified functions by members of staff of a specified description in specified circumstances.

(3) Within 14 days after the date on which the Upper Tribunal sends notice of a decision made by a member of staff under paragraph (1) to a party, that party may apply in writing to the Upper Tribunal for that decision to be considered afresh by a judge.

        5.268

DEFINITIONS

"the 2007 Act"—see r.1(3).
"party"—*ibid.*

GENERAL NOTE

There is no need to make provision for the delegation of functions of a purely administrative nature and so this rule refers only to functions of a judicial nature. The Senior President of Tribunals has issued a Practice Statement (available at: http://www.tribunals.gov.uk/Tribunals/Rules/statements.htm) recording his approval of the delegation of certain functions to legally qualified members of staff of the Upper Tribunal, known as Registrars. The functions that are delegated are—

        5.269

    (a) exercising any case management powers under r.5 except—
        (i) extending time under r.5(3)(a) in relation to the time limits for appeals referred to in rr.21(3) and (6), 22(5), 23(2) and (5) and 44(3), (4) and (6) or in relation to the time limits for judicial review proceedings referred to in rr.28(2), (3) and (7) and 30(5);
        (ii) suspending a decision under r.5(3)(l) or (m);
        (iii) requiring a tribunal to provide reasons for its decision under r.5(3)(n);

(b) dealing with irregularities under r.7(2) (except taking action under r.7(2)(d) or (4));

(c) striking out under r.8(1) or (3)(a) and reinstating proceedings under r.8(5);

(d) giving directions substituting or adding parties under r.9;

(e) summarily assessing costs under r.10(8)(a);

(f) making orders prohibiting disclosure or publication of documents and information under r.14;

(g) giving directions in relation to evidence and submissions under r.15(1);

(h) summoning (or, in Scotland, citing) witnesses and issuing orders to persons to answer questions and produce documents under r.16;

(i) giving consent to withdraw a case and reinstating a case under r.17.

Case management powers

5.270   **5.**—(1) Subject to the provisions of the 2007 Act and any other enactment, the Upper Tribunal may regulate its own procedure.

(2) The Upper Tribunal may give a direction in relation to the conduct or disposal of proceedings at any time, including a direction amending, suspending or setting aside an earlier direction.

(3) In particular, and without restricting the general powers in paragraphs (1) and (2), the Upper Tribunal may—

(a) extend or shorten the time for complying with any rule, practice direction or direction;

(b) consolidate or hear together two or more sets of proceedings or parts of proceedings raising common issues, or treat a case as a lead case;

(c) permit or require a party to amend a document;

(d) permit or require a party or another person to provide documents, information, evidence or submissions to the Upper Tribunal or a party;

(e) deal with an issue in the proceedings as a preliminary issue;

(f) hold a hearing to consider any matter, including a case management issue;

(g) decide the form of any hearing;

(h) adjourn or postpone a hearing;

(i) require a party to produce a bundle for a hearing;

(j) stay (or, in Scotland, sist) proceedings;

(k) transfer proceedings to another court or tribunal if that other court or tribunal has jurisdiction in relation to the proceedings and—

   (i) because of a change of circumstances since the proceedings were started, the Upper Tribunal no longer has jurisdiction in relation to the proceedings; or

   (ii) the Upper Tribunal considers that the other court or tribunal is a more appropriate forum for the determination of the case;

(l) suspend the effect of its own decision pending an appeal or review of that decision;

(m) in an appeal, or an application for permission to appeal, against the decision of another tribunal, suspend the effect of that decision pending the determination of the application for permission to appeal, and any appeal;

(n) require any other tribunal whose decision is the subject of proceedings before the Upper Tribunal to provide reasons for the decision, or other information or documents in relation to the decision or the proceedings in that tribunal.

DEFINITIONS

"the 2007 Act"—see r.1(3).
"dispose of proceedings"—*ibid.*
"document"—*ibid.*
"hearing" *ibid.*
"party"—*ibid.*
"permission"—*ibid.*
"practice direction"—*ibid.*

GENERAL NOTE

Para. (2)

This is in very broad terms and, although para.(3) and r.15(1) set out examples of **5.271**
directions the Upper Tribunal may give, they do not restrict the width of the power
in this paragraph. The power must, however, be exercised so as to give effect to the
overriding objective in r.2 (see r.2(3)). The procedure for applying for and giving
directions is to be found in r.6. Note that, where a direction requires something to
be done by a particular day, it must be done by 5pm on that day (r.12(1)) but, if
that day is not a working day, the act is done in time if it is done on the next working
day (r.12(2)).

Para. (3)

Sub-paragraph (c) presumably refers to grounds of appeal and other submissions, **5.272**
rather than to evidence.

Sub-paragraphs (f), (g) and (h) must be read with rr.34 to 37. See also the note
to r.5(3)(h) of the Tribunal procedure (First-tier Tribunal) (Social Entitlement)
Chamber Rules 2008, above.

Sub-paragraph (k) applies only where the Upper Tribunal had jurisdiction at the
time the proceedings were begun. Otherwise, the Tribunal is required to strike the
proceedings out under r.8(2). Rule 5(3)(k)(i) applies where the Upper Tribunal
loses jurisdiction and r.5(3)(k)(ii) applies only where the Upper Tribunal and
another tribunal have concurrent jurisdiction (which may be the case in some circumstances where a person moves to or from Northern Ireland).

Sub-paragraphs (l) and (m) permit the effect of a decision to be suspended
pending an appeal from or to the Upper Tribunal. The power to suspend the effect
of its own decision conferred by sub-para.(l) does not extend to suspending its
precedential effect on other claims pending an appeal (*SSD v AD and MM (No.2)*
[2009] UKUT 69 (AAC)), but in social security cases such an extended power is
unnecessary in the light of s.25 (and s.26) of the Social Security Act 1998. The
First-tier Tribunal also has power to suspend the effect of its decision pending an
appeal to the Upper Tribunal (see r.5(3)(l) of the Tribunal Procedure (First-tier
Tribunal) (Social Entitlement Chamber) Rules 2008 and so the power in sub-
para.(m) is most likely to be invoked where the First-tier Tribunal has refused to
suspend the effect of its own decision. It is usually unnecessary to suspend a decision in a social security case concerned with entitlement, due to the Secretary of
State's power to suspend payments under reg.16 of the Social Security and Child
Support (Decisions and Appeals) Regs 1999 (see, in particular, reg.16(3)(b)(i) and
(4)). In the past, the Secretary of State has generally not taken action to recover an
overpayment while an appeal against a decision that the overpayment is recoverable
is pending but he could now take the view that an appeal does not require him to
stay his hand unless the tribunal so directs under this provision, which would not
necessarily be appropriate as a matter of course and could in any event presumably be limited to part of its decision. The power to suspend the effect of a decision
may also be useful in appeals against decisions under the Social Security (Recovery
of Benefits) Act 1997, because s.14 of that Act and the regulations made under it

completely fail to deal with the consequences of a successful appeal to the Upper Tribunal or an appellate court.

Sub-paragraph (n) enables the Upper Tribunal to direct the First-tier Tribunal to provide reasons for its decision. It remains to be seen how this power will be exercised. Given the speed with which the First-tier Tribunal hears and determines cases, it may often be simpler to allow an appeal and direct a rehearing rather than to obtain reasons for a previous decision.

Procedure for applying for and giving directions

5.273   **6.**—(1) The Upper Tribunal may give a direction on the application of one or more of the parties or on its own initiative.

(2) An application for a direction may be made—

(a) by sending or delivering a written application to the Upper Tribunal; or

(b) orally during the course of a hearing.

(3) An application for a direction must include the reason for making that application.

(4) Unless the Upper Tribunal considers that there is good reason not to do so, the Upper Tribunal must send written notice of any direction to every party and to any other person affected by the direction.

(5) If a party or any other person sent notice of the direction under paragraph (4) wishes to challenge a direction which the Upper Tribunal has given, they may do so by applying for another direction which amends, suspends or sets aside the first direction.

DEFINITIONS

"hearing"—see r.1(3).
"party"—*ibid*.

GENERAL NOTE

5.274   See the note to r.6 of the Tribunal Procedure (First-tier Tribunal) (Social Entitlement Chamber) Rules 2008, above.

Failure to comply with rules etc.

5.275   **7.**—(1) An irregularity resulting from a failure to comply with any requirement in these Rules, a practice direction or a direction, does not of itself render void the proceedings or any step taken in the proceedings.

(2) If a party has failed to comply with a requirement in these Rules, a practice direction or a direction, the Upper Tribunal may take such action as it considers just, which may include—

(a) waiving the requirement;

(b) requiring the failure to be remedied;

(c) exercising its power under rule 8 (striking out a party's case); or

(d) except in mental health cases, restricting a party's participation in the proceedings.

(3) Paragraph (4) applies where the First-tier Tribunal has referred to the Upper Tribunal a failure by a person to comply with a requirement imposed by the First-tier Tribunal—

(a) to attend at any place for the purpose of giving evidence;

(b) otherwise to make themselves available to give evidence;

(c) to swear an oath in connection with the giving of evidence;

(d) to give evidence as a witness;
(e) to produce a document; or
(f) to facilitate the inspection of a document or any other thing (including any premises).

(4) The Upper Tribunal may exercise its power under section 25 of the 2007 Act (supplementary powers of the Upper Tribunal) in relation to such non-compliance as if the requirement had been imposed by the Upper Tribunal.

DEFINITIONS

"the 2007 Act"—see r.1(3).
"document"—*ibid*.
"mental health case"—*ibid*.
"party"—*ibid*.
"practice direction"—*ibid*.

GENERAL NOTE

Paragraphs (1) and (2)(a) enable the Upper Tribunal to overlook a breach of a rule, practice direction or direction. On the other hand, under para.2(c), such a breach can lead to a case being struck out under r.8, provided an appropriate warning has been given. Alternatively, the Upper Tribunal may exercise its powers under s.25 of the Tribunals, Courts and Enforcement Act 2007 to punish the person for contempt of court (with a term of imprisonment of up to two years and an unlimited fine). Paragraphs (3) and (4) are concerned with cases where the First-tier Tribunal refers a case to the Upper Tribunal because there has been non-compliance with a summons, order or direction issued by that tribunal in connection with the attendance or examination of witnesses or the production or inspection of documents. They are made under para.10 of Sch.5 to the 2007 Act. A referral is necessary because the First-tier Tribunal does not have its own power to punish for contempt. Paragraph (3)(c) must be read subject to s.5 of the Oaths Act 1978, which permits a person who objects to being sworn to make a solemn affirmation instead.

Paragraph (1) may imply a greater power of waiver than exists in para.(2)(a), because an irregularity may be the fault of a lower tribunal (see the examples in the note to r.21(2)) or of the Upper Tribunal, rather than of a party, and it may be too late to remedy it.

5.276

Striking out a party's case

8.—(1) The proceedings, or the appropriate part of them, will automatically be struck out if the appellant or applicant has failed to comply with a direction that stated that failure by the appellant or applicant to comply with the direction would lead to the striking out of the proceedings or that part of them.

(2) The Upper Tribunal must strike out the whole or a part of the proceedings if the Upper Tribunal—
(a) does not have jurisdiction in relation to the proceedings or that part of them; and
(b) does not exercise its power under rule 5(3)(k)(i) (transfer to another court or tribunal) in relation to the proceedings or that part of them.

(3) The Upper Tribunal may strike out the whole or a part of the proceedings if—
(a) the appellant or applicant has failed to comply with a direction which stated that failure by the appellant or applicant to comply with the direction could lead to the striking out of the proceedings or part of them;

5.277

 (b) the appellant or applicant has failed to co-operate with the Upper Tribunal to such an extent that the Upper Tribunal cannot deal with the proceedings fairly and justly; or

 (c) in proceedings which are not an appeal from the decision of another tribunal or judicial review proceedings, the Upper Tribunal considers there is no reasonable prospect of the appellant's or the applicant's case, or part of it, succeeding.

(4) The Upper Tribunal may not strike out the whole or a part of the proceedings under paragraph (2) or (3)(b) or (c) without first giving the appellant or applicant an opportunity to make representations in relation to the proposed striking out.

(5) If the proceedings have been struck out under paragraph (1) or (3)(a), the appellant or applicant may apply for the proceedings, or part of them, to be reinstated.

(6) An application under paragraph (5) must be made in writing and received by the Upper Tribunal within 1 month after the date on which the Upper Tribunal sent notification of the striking out to the appellant or applicant.

(7) This rule applies to a respondent [¹ or an interested party] as it applies to an appellant or applicant except that—

 (a) a reference to the striking out of the proceedings is to be read as a reference to the barring of the respondent [¹ or an interested party] from taking further part in the proceedings; and

 (b) a reference to an application for the reinstatement of proceedings which have been struck out is to be read as a reference to an application for the lifting of the bar on the respondent [¹ or an interested party] from taking further part in the proceedings.

(8) If a respondent [¹ or an interested party] has been barred from taking further part in proceedings under this rule and that bar has not been lifted, the Upper Tribunal need not consider any response or other submission made by that respondent. [¹ or interested party, and may summarily determine any or all issues against that respondent or interested party].

AMENDMENTS

1. Tribunal Procedure (Amendment) Rules 2009 (SI 2009/274), r.6 (April 1, 2009).

DEFINITIONS

 "appellant"—see r.1(3).
 "applicant"—*ibid.*
 "interested party"—*ibid.*
 "party"—*ibid.*
 "respondent"—*ibid.*

GENERAL NOTE

5.278 Note that, although paras (1) to (6) are expressed in terms of striking out proceedings brought by the appellant, by virtue of paras (7) and (8) they also provide for barring a respondent from taking further part in the proceedings.

Para. (1)

5.279 This provides for an automatic strike out where a person has failed to comply with a direction that carried a warning that, unless there was compliance, the case "will" be struck out. In theory, no further judicial act is required for the strike-out to take effect provided that it is clear that there has not been compliance. It is important to distinguish this paragraph from para.(3)(a), which provides for a case to be struck out for failure to comply with a direction that carried a warning that if there was no compliance the case "may" be struck out. In such a case, there needs to be a judicial decision exercising the power to strike out. It is suggested that, unless there has been a previous history of non-compliance with directions and rules, warnings should be of the "may" variety rather than the "will" variety. Note that proceedings struck out under this paragraph may be reinstated on an application under paras (5) and (6).

Para. (2)

The terms of this paragraph are mandatory, so that a final decision to the effect that the tribunal lacks jurisdiction must always be in the form of a decision to strike out the appeal. By virtue of para.(4), a party must be given an opportunity to make representations before his or her case is struck out and there will be some cases where justice requires there to be a hearing.   **5.280**

Para. (3)

By virtue of para.(4), a party must be given an opportunity to make representa- **5.281**
tions before his or her case is struck out under sub-para.(b). There is no right to make representations before a case is struck out under sub-para.(a); instead there is a right to apply for reinstatement after the event, by virtue of paras (5) and (6). Striking out is discretionary and must presumably be proportionate, having regard to the culpability of the party whose case is being struck out and the amount at stake on the appeal.

Sub-paragraph (c) introduces a power to strike a case out where it has no reason-able prospect of success, but it is unlikely to have any application to social security cases because the permission requirement in respect of appeals or judicial review proceedings makes it unnecessary and it cannot apply to a reference.

Paras (5) and (6)

These paragraphs apply only to cases struck out under para.(1) or (3)(a). In **5.281.1**
other cases, the Tribunal must give the party an opportunity to make representa-tions *before* a case is struck out. In *Synergy Child Services Ltd v Ofsted* [2009] UKUT 125 (AAC), it was held that, when considering whether to reinstate an appeal, "a Tribunal should have regard to the broad justice of the case, in the light of all the circumstances obtaining at the time the application for reinstatement is being con-sidered". Nonetheless, "[w]here there has been flagrant disobedience by a party, belated compliance or a change of circumstances making compliance irrelevant will not always require a Tribunal to reinstate an appeal".

Paras (7) and (8)

The amendment to the end of para.(8) means that these provisions can be **5.282**
operated in a more even handed way than the equivalent provisions in r.8 of the Tribunal Procedure (First-tier Tribunal) (Social Entitlement Chamber) Rules 2008. The paragraph now provides for the summary determination of issues against the respondent or interested party, which is equivalent of striking out part, or the whole, of an appellant or applicant's case.

Substitution and addition of parties

9.—(1) The Upper Tribunal may give a direction substituting a party **5.283**
if—

  (a) the wrong person has been named as a party; or

(b) the substitution has become necessary because of a change in circumstances since the start of proceedings.

(2) The Upper Tribunal may give a direction adding a person to the proceedings as a respondent or, in judicial review proceedings, as an interested party.

(3) If the Upper Tribunal gives a direction under paragraph (1) or (2) it may give such consequential directions as it considers appropriate.

DEFINITIONS

"interested party"—see r.1(3).
"judicial review proceedings"—*ibid.*
"party"—*ibid.*
"respondent"—*ibid.*

GENERAL NOTE

5.284   See the note to r.9 of the Tribunal Procedure (First-tier Tribunal) (Social Entitlement Chamber) Rules 2008, above.

[¹ Orders for costs

5.285   **10.**—(1) The Upper Tribunal may not make an order in respect of costs (or, in Scotland, expenses) in proceedings referred by or on appeal from another tribunal except—

(a) in proceedings on appeal from the Tax Chamber of the First-tier Tribunal; or

(b) to the extent and in the circumstances that the other tribunal had the power to make an order in respect of costs (or, in Scotland, expenses).

(2) The Upper Tribunal may not make an order in respect of costs or expenses under section 4 of the Forfeiture Act 1982.

(3) In other proceedings, the Upper Tribunal may not make an order in respect of costs or expenses except—

(a) in judicial review proceedings;

(b) in proceedings transferred from the Tax Chamber of the First-tier Tribunal;

(c) under section 29(4) of the 2007 Act (wasted costs); or

(d) if the Upper Tribunal considers that a party or its representative has acted unreasonably in bringing, defending or conducting the proceedings.

(4) The Upper Tribunal may make an order for costs (or, in Scotland, expenses) on an application or on its own initiative.

(5) A person making an application for an order for costs or expenses must—

(a) send or deliver a written application to the Upper Tribunal and to the person against whom it is proposed that the order be made; and

(b) send or deliver with the application a schedule of the costs or expenses claimed sufficient to allow summary assessment of such costs or expenses by the Upper Tribunal.

(6) An application for an order for costs or expenses may be made at any time during the proceedings but may not be made later than 1 month after the date on which the Upper Tribunal sends—

(a) a decision notice recording the decision which finally disposes of all issues in the proceedings; or

(b) notice of a withdrawal under rule 17 which ends the proceedings.

(7) The Upper Tribunal may not make an order for costs or expenses against a person (the "paying person") without first—

(a) giving that person an opportunity to make representations; and

(b) if the paying person is an individual and the order is to be made under paragraph (3)(a), (b) or (d), considering that person's financial means.

(8) The amount of costs or expenses to be paid under an order under this rule may be ascertained by—

(a) summary assessment by the Upper Tribunal;

(b) agreement of a specified sum by the paying person and the person entitled to receive the costs or expenses ("the receiving person"); or

(c) assessment of the whole or a specified part of the costs or expenses incurred by the receiving person, if not agreed.

(9) Following an order for assessment under paragraph (8)(c), the paying person or the receiving person may apply—

(a) in England and Wales, to the High Court or the Costs Office of the Supreme Court (as specified in the order) for a detailed assessment of the costs on the standard basis or, if specified in the order, on the indemnity basis; and the Civil Procedure Rules 1998 shall apply, with necessary modifications, to that application and assessment as if the proceedings in the tribunal had been proceedings in a court to which the Civil Procedure Rules 1998 apply;

(b) in Scotland, to the Auditor of the Court of Session for the taxation of the expenses according to the fees payable in that court; or

(c) in Northern Ireland, to the Taxing Office of the High Court of Northern Ireland for taxation on the standard basis or, if specified in the order, on the indemnity basis.]

AMENDMENT

1. Tribunal Procedure (Amendment) Rules 2009 (SI 2009/274), r.7 (April 1, 2009).

DEFINITIONS

"the 2007 Act"—see r.1(3).
"party"—*ibid.*

GENERAL NOTE

The effect of para.(1) is that there is no power to award costs in social security cases on appeal from the First-tier Tribunal, because the First-tier Tribunal has no power to award costs in such cases (see r.10 of the Tribunal Procedure (First-tier Tribunal) (Social Entitlement Chamber) Rules 2008, above, and also the note to s.29 to the Tribunals, Courts and Enforcement Act 2007). Paragraph (2) has the effect that there is no power to award costs in cases under the Forfeiture Act 1982.

Paragraph (3) leaves the general discretion to award costs in judicial review proceedings entirely unfettered. It remains to be seen whether the Upper Tribunal adopts the same approach as the High Court and Court of Session. The whole issue of costs in court proceedings in England and Wales is, in any event, currently being reviewed by Lord Justice Jackson.

Currently, the general rule in the courts is that "that the unsuccessful party will be ordered to pay the costs of the successful party" although "the court may make

5.286

a different order" (C.P.R. r.44.3(2)). In judicial review cases at the permission stage, the general rule is that a successful respondent is entitled to recover the costs of filing an acknowledgment of service but not the costs of attending a hearing, unless there are exceptional circumstances such as the hopelessness of the claim (particularly if this has been drawn to the applicant's attention when permission was refused on the papers), abuse of the procedure for collateral ends or the effective obtaining of a substantive hearing through the deployment of full argument and documentary evidence by both sides at the permission stage (*R. (Mount Cook Land Limited) v Westminster City Council* [2003] EWCA Civ 1346). Arguments to the effect that a respondent has no need to attend to resist a hopeless application have been given short shrift in *R. (Starling) v Child Support Commissioners* [2008] EWHC 1319 (Admin) and *R. (Rew) v Secretary of State for Work and Pensions* [2008] EWHC 2120 (Admin). *Mount Cook* was decided on the basis that a respondent was bound to submit an acknowledgment of service but was not obliged to attend a hearing. In the Upper Tribunal, a respondent or interested party is, in practice, offered the opportunity to file an acknowledgment of service without a submission and so the question of costs in respect of an acknowledgment of service is likely to arise only if a submission is made.

Representatives

5.287   **11.**—(1) A party may appoint a representative (whether a legal representative or not) to represent that party in the proceedings.

(2) If a party appoints a representative, that party (or the representative if the representative is a legal representative) must send or deliver to the Upper Tribunal and [¹ . . .] written notice of the representative's name and address.

[¹ (2A) If the Upper Tribunal receives notice that a party has appointed a representative under paragraph (2), it must send a copy of that notice to each other party.]

(3) Anything permitted or required to be done by a party under these Rules, a practice direction or a direction may be done by the representative of that party, except signing a witness statement.

(4) A person who receives due notice of the appointment of a representative—

(a) must provide to the representative any document which is required to be provided to the represented party, and need not provide that document to the represented party; and

(b) may assume that the representative is and remains authorised as such until they receive written notification that this is not so from the representative or the represented party.

(5) At a hearing a party may be accompanied by another person whose name and address has not been notified under paragraph (2) but who, subject to paragraph (8) and with the permission of the Upper Tribunal, may act as a representative or otherwise assist in presenting the party's case at the hearing.

(6) Paragraphs (2) to (4) do not apply to a person who accompanies a party under paragraph (5).

(7) In a mental health case if the patient has not appointed a representative the Upper Tribunal may appoint a legal representative for the patient where—

(a) the patient has stated that they do not wish to conduct their own case or that they wish to be represented; or

(b) the patient lacks the capacity to appoint a representative but the Upper Tribunal believes that it is in the patient's best interests for the patient to be represented.

(8) In a mental health case a party may not appoint as a representative, or be represented or assisted at a hearing by—

(a) a person liable to be detained or subject to guardianship or after-care under supervision, or who is a community patient, under the Mental Health Act 1983; or

(b) a person receiving treatment for mental disorder at the same hospital home as the patient.

[[1] (9) In this rule "legal representative" means an authorised advocate or authorised litigator as defined by section 119(1) of the Courts and Legal Services Act 1990, an advocate or solicitor in Scotland or a barrister or solicitor in Northern Ireland.]

AMENDMENTS

1. Tribunal Procedure (Amendment) Rules 2009 (SI 2009/274), r.6 (April 1, 2009).

DEFINITIONS

"document"—see r.1(3).
"hearing"—*ibid.*
"legal representative"—see para.(9).
"mental health case"—see r.1(3).
"party"—*ibid.*
"permission"—*ibid.*
"practice direction"—*ibid.*

GENERAL NOTE

See the note to r.11(1) of the Tribunal Procedure (First-tier Tribunal) (Social Entitlement) Rules 2008.   **5.288**

Paras (2) to (4)

These paragraphs provide for the formal appointment of a representative who   **5.289** may then act on behalf of the party in all respects (except to sign a witness statement) and should be sent any documents that would otherwise be sent to the party. However, it is presumably possible for the Upper Tribunal to exclude a representative from a hearing under r.37(4) without excluding the party.

Note that representatives, other than solicitors, barristers and advocates, are expected to provide written authority to act, signed by the party. In *CSDLA/2/ 2001*, two different representatives, each purporting to act on behalf of the same claimant, lodge separate applications for leave to appeal. The Commissioner said that a representative should obtain a fresh mandate from a claimant before sending what would now be an application for permission to appeal to the Upper Tribunal, rather than relying on a mandate obtained before a hearing before a lower tribunal. That would show that the representative had discussed the case with the claimant and had obtained specific instructions to apply for permission to appeal.

Paras (5) and (6)

These paragraphs enable a party who is present at a hearing to be represented or   **5.290** assisted at the hearing by any person, without there having been any formal notice of appointment. Although the Tribunal's permission is required, it is suggested that, unless r.37(4) applies, it will only exceptionally be appropriate for the Upper Tribunal to refuse permission, particularly as the party need only provide a written notice under para.(2) in order to avoid the need for permission. Without a written notice of appointment, a person who acts as a representative at a hearing has no rights as a representative outside the hearing. Obviously, a written notice may be provided at the hearing so that the person becomes entitled to act as a full representative thereafter.

Paras (7) and (8)

5.291   These paragraphs do not apply to social security cases.

Calculating time

5.292   **12.**—(1) An act required by these Rules, a practice direction or a direction to be done on or by a particular day must be done by 5pm on that day.

(2) If the time specified by these Rules, a practice direction or a direction for doing any act ends on a day other than a working day, the act is done in time if it is done on the next working day.

(3) In a special educational needs case or a disability discrimination in schools case, the following days must not be counted when calculating the time by which an act must be done—

(a) 25th December to 1st January inclusive; and

(b) any day in August.

(4) Paragraph (3) does not apply where the Upper Tribunal directs that an act must be done by or on a specified date.

[¹ (5) In this rule—

"disability discrimination in schools case" means proceedings concerning disability discrimination in the education of a child or related matters; and

"special educational needs case" means proceedings concerning the education of a child who has or may have special educational needs.]

AMENDMENT

1. Tribunal Procedure (Amendment) Rules 2009 (SI 2009/274), r.9 (April 1, 2009).

DEFINITIONS

"disability discrimination in schools case"—see para.(5).
"practice direction"—see r.1(3).
"special educational needs case"—see para.(5).
"working day"—see r.1(3).

Sending and delivery of documents

5.293   **13.**—(1) Any document to be provided to the Upper Tribunal under these Rules, a practice direction or a direction must be—

(a) sent by pre-paid post or [¹ by document exchange, or delivered by hand] to the address specified for the proceedings;

(b) sent by fax to the number specified for the proceedings; or

(c) sent or delivered by such other method as the Upper Tribunal may permit or direct.

(2) Subject to paragraph (3), if a party provides a fax number, email

address or other details for the electronic transmission of documents to them, that party must accept delivery of documents by that method.

(3) If a party informs the Upper Tribunal and all other parties that a particular form of communication, other than pre-paid post or delivery by hand, should not be used to provide documents to that party, that form of communication must not be so used.

(4) If the Upper Tribunal or a party sends a document to a party or the Upper Tribunal by email or any other electronic means of communication, the recipient may request that the sender provide a hard copy of the document to the recipient. The recipient must make such a request as soon as reasonably practicable after receiving the document electronically.

(5) The Upper Tribunal and each party may assume that the address provided by a party or its representative is and remains the address to which documents should be sent or delivered until receiving written notification to the contrary.

AMENDMENT

1. Tribunal Procedure (Amendment) Rules 2009 (SI 2009/274), r.10 (April 1, 2009).

DEFINITIONS

"document"—see r.1(3).
"party"—*ibid*.
"practice direction"—*ibid*.

GENERAL NOTE

See the note to r.13 of the Tribunal Procedure (First-tier Tribunal) (Social **5.294** Entitlement Chamber) Rules 2008, above.

Use of documents and information

14.—(1) The Upper Tribunal may make an order prohibiting the disclo- **5.295** sure or publication of—
  (a) specified documents or information relating to the proceedings; or
  (b) any matter likely to lead members of the public to identify any person whom the Upper Tribunal considers should not be identified.

(2) The Upper Tribunal may give a direction prohibiting the disclosure of a document or information to a person if—
  (a) the Upper Tribunal is satisfied that such disclosure would be likely to cause that person or some other person serious harm; and
  (b) the Upper Tribunal is satisfied, having regard to the interests of justice, that it is proportionate to give such a direction.

(3) If a party ("the first party") considers that the Upper Tribunal should give a direction under paragraph (2) prohibiting the disclosure of a document or information to another party ("the second party"), the first party must—
  (a) exclude the relevant document or information from any documents that will be provided to the second party; and
  (b) provide to the Upper Tribunal the excluded document or information, and the reason for its exclusion, so that the Upper Tribunal may decide whether the document or information should be disclosed to the second party or should be the subject of a direction under paragraph (2).

(4) The Upper Tribunal must conduct proceedings as appropriate in order to give effect to a direction given under paragraph (2).

(5) If the Upper Tribunal gives a direction under paragraph (2) which prevents disclosure to a party who has appointed a representative, the Upper Tribunal may give a direction that the documents or information be disclosed to that representative if the Upper Tribunal is satisfied that—

(a) disclosure to the representative would be in the interests of the party; and

(b) the representative will act in accordance with paragraph (6).

(6) Documents or information disclosed to a representative in accordance with a direction under paragraph (5) must not be disclosed either directly or indirectly to any other person without the Upper Tribunal's consent.

(7) Unless the Upper Tribunal gives a direction to the contrary, information about mental health cases and the names of any persons concerned in such cases must not be made public.

DEFINITIONS

"document"—see r.1(3).
"mental health case"—*ibid.*
"party"—*ibid.*

GENERAL NOTE

Para. (1)

5.296   An order under this paragraph may be directed to an individual and be concerned only with an individual document (e.g. prohibiting an appellant from disclosing to someone else a document disclosed to the appellant by the respondent) or it may be directed to the public in general and effectively amount to a reporting restriction. Hearings of social security cases are usually attended only by those immediately interested with them but most hearings are, in principle, open to the public, including the press (see r.37). It is difficult to envisage it being appropriate to prohibit the publication of any information at all about a hearing held in public (despite para. (7)) but it might often be appropriate to make an order prohibiting the publishing of information that may lead to a child or vulnerable adult being identified if there would otherwise be any serious risk of such publication. It will generally be necessary properly to balance the right of one person to respect of his or her private life under art.8 of the European Convention on Human Rights and the right of another person to freedom of expression under art.10 (see *Re British Broadcasting Corporation* [2009] UKHL 34; [2009] 3 W.L.R. 142, where it is noteworthy that, although the House of Lords discharged an anonymity order so as to permit the BBC to broadcast an acquitted defendant's name, it saw no need to mention his name itself). The existence of the powers conferred by this paragraph is a factor to be borne in mind when deciding under r.37(2) whether a hearing should be in private or in public, which requires consideration of the terms of art.6(1).

A breach of an order made under this paragraph is a contempt of court and may be punished by the Upper Tribunal under s.25 of the Tribunals, Courts and Enforcement Act 2007 by a term of imprisonment not exceeding two years and an unlimited fine.

Paras (2) to (6)

5.297   See the note to r.14(2) to (6) of the Tribunal Procedure (First-tier Tribunal) (Social Entitlement Chamber) Rules 2008, above. Note the power in r.37(4)(c) to exclude a person from a hearing, and the power in r.40(2) not to provide a full decision, in order to give effect to a direction under para.(2).

Para. (7)

This paragraph does not apply to social security cases and, in applying to *all* information, appears anomalous.

Evidence and submissions

15.—(1) Without restriction on the general powers in rule 5(1) and (2)   **5.298**
(case management powers), the Upper Tribunal may give directions as
to—
  (a) issues on which it requires evidence or submissions;
  (b) the nature of the evidence or submissions it requires;
  (c) whether the parties are permitted or required to provide expert
     evidence, and if so whether the parties must jointly appoint a single
     expert to provide such evidence;
  (d) any limit on the number of witnesses whose evidence a party may put
     forward, whether in relation to a particular issue or generally;
  (e) the manner in which any evidence or submissions are to be provided,
     which may include a direction for them to be given—
      (i) orally at a hearing; or
      (ii) by written submissions or witness statement; and
  (f) the time at which any evidence or submissions are to be provided.
 (2) The Upper Tribunal may—
  (a) admit evidence whether or not—
      (i) the evidence would be admissible in a civil trial in the United
        Kingdom; or
      (ii) the evidence was available to a previous decision maker; or
  (b) exclude evidence that would otherwise be admissible where—
      (i) the evidence was not provided within the time allowed by a
        direction or a practice direction;
      (ii) the evidence was otherwise provided in a manner that did not
        comply with a direction or a practice direction; or
      (iii) it would otherwise be unfair to admit the evidence.
 (3) The Upper Tribunal may consent to a witness giving, or require any
witness to give, evidence on oath, and may administer an oath for that purpose.

DEFINITIONS

  "hearing"—see r.1(3).
  "party"—*ibid.*
  "practice direction"—*ibid.*

GENERAL NOTE

  See the note to r.15 of the Tribunal Procedure (First-tier Tribunal) (Social   **5.299**
Entitlement Chamber) Rules 2008, above.

Summoning or citation of witnesses and orders to answer questions or produce documents

16.—(1) On the application of a party or on its own initiative, the Upper   **5.300**
Tribunal may—
  (a) by summons (or, in Scotland, citation) require any person to attend
     as a witness at a hearing at the time and place specified in the
     summons or citation; or

(b) order any person to answer any questions or produce any documents in that person's possession or control which relate to any issue in the proceedings.

(2) A summons or citation under paragraph (1)(a) must—

(a) give the person required to attend 14 days' notice of the hearing or such shorter period as the Upper Tribunal may direct; and

(b) where the person is not a party, make provision for the person's necessary expenses of attendance to be paid, and state who is to pay them.

(3) No person may be compelled to give any evidence or produce any document that the person could not be compelled to give or produce on a trial of an action in a court of law in the part of the United Kingdom where the proceedings are due to be determined.

[¹ (4) A person who receives a summons, citation or order may apply to the Upper Tribunal for it to be varied or set aside if they did not have an opportunity to object to it before it was made or issued.

(5) A person making an application under paragraph (4) must do so as soon as reasonably practicable after receiving notice of the summons, citation or order.

(6) A summons, citation or order under this rule must—

(a) state that the person on whom the requirement is imposed may apply to the Upper Tribunal to vary or set aside the summons, citation or order, if they did not have an opportunity to object to it before it was made or issued; and

(b) state the consequences of failure to comply with the summons, citation or order.]

Amendment

1. Tribunal Procedure (Amendment) Rules 2009 (SI 2009/274), r.11 (April 1, 2009).

Definitions

"document"—see r.1(3).
"hearing"—*ibid.*
"party"—*ibid.*

General Note

5.301   This rule includes a power to order the production of documents without requiring attendance at a hearing. A failure to comply with a summons, citation or order under this rule is a contempt of court that may be punished by the Upper Tribunal with a term of imprisonment not exceeding two years and an unlimited fine under s.25 of the Tribunals, Courts and Enforcement Act 2007.

Withdrawal

5.302   **17.**—(1) Subject to paragraph (2), a party may give notice of the withdrawal of its case, or any part of it—

(a) at any time before a hearing to consider the disposal of the proceedings (or, if the Upper Tribunal disposes of the proceedings without a hearing, before that disposal), by sending or delivering to the Upper Tribunal a written notice of withdrawal; or

(b) orally at a hearing.

(2) Notice of withdrawal will not take effect unless the Upper Tribunal

consents to the withdrawal except in relation to an application for permission to appeal.

(3) A party which has withdrawn its case may apply to the Upper Tribunal for the case to be reinstated.

(4) An application under paragraph (3) must be made in writing and be received by the Upper Tribunal within 1 month after—

(a) the date on which the Upper Tribunal received the notice under paragraph (1)(a); or

(b) the date of the hearing at which the case was withdrawn orally under paragraph (1)(b).

(5) The Upper Tribunal must notify each party in writing of a withdrawal under this rule.

DEFINITIONS

"dispose of proceedings"—see r.1(3).
"hearing"—*ibid.*
"party"—*ibid.*
"permission"—*ibid.*

GENERAL NOTE

This rule replaces reg.26 of the Social Security Commissioners (Procedure) Regs 1999 but it applies to the withdrawal of a respondent's case as well as to the case of an appellant or person making a reference. The existence of the one-month time limit for an application for reinstatement, which did not exist in the old provision, may suggest that an application should be granted if made within that period unless there is a clear reason for not doing so, such as the previous conduct of the party, obvious lack of merit in the case or prejudice to another party.   5.303

Notice of funding of legal services

18. If a party is granted funding of legal services at any time, that party must as soon as practicable—   5.304

(a) (i) if funding is granted by the Legal Services Commission or the Northern Ireland Legal Services Commission, send a copy of the funding notice to the Upper Tribunal; or

(ii) if funding is granted by the Scottish Legal Aid Board, send a copy of the legal aid certificate to the Upper Tribunal; and

(b) notify every other party in writing that funding has been granted.

DEFINITION

"party"—see r.1(3).

GENERAL NOTE

Public funding is rare in social security cases but it is helpful for a judge to know whether a party is funded if he or she is considering directing the party to produce a submission or a bundle of documents.   5.305

It will also be relevant in judicial review proceedings and other proceedings where the Upper Tribunal has the power to award costs.

Confidentiality in child support or child trust fund cases

19.—(1) Paragraph (3) applies to an appeal against a decision of the First-tier Tribunal in proceedings under the Child Support Act 1991   5.306

in the circumstances described in paragraph (2), other than an appeal against a reduced benefit decision (as defined in section 46(10)(b) of the Child Support Act 1991, as that section had effect prior to the commencement of section 15(b) of the Child Maintenance and Other Payments Act 2008).

(2) The circumstances referred to in paragraph (1) are that—

(a) in the proceedings in the First-tier Tribunal in respect of which the appeal has been brought, there was an obligation to keep a person's address confidential; or

(b) a person whose circumstances are relevant to the proceedings would like their address (or, in the case of the person with care of the child, the child's address) to be kept confidential and has given notice to that effect—

    (i) to the Upper Tribunal in an application for permission to appeal or notice of appeal;

    (ii) to the Upper Tribunal within 1 month after an enquiry by the Upper Tribunal; or

    (iii) to the Secretary of State, the Child Maintenance and Enforcement Commission or the Upper Tribunal when notifying a change of address after proceedings have been started.

(3) Where this paragraph applies, the Secretary of State, the Child Maintenance and Enforcement Commission and the Upper Tribunal must take appropriate steps to secure the confidentiality of the address, and of any information which could reasonably be expected to enable a person to identify the address, to the extent that the address or that information is not already known to each other party.

(4) Paragraph (6) applies to an appeal against a decision of the First-tier Tribunal in proceedings under the Child Trust Funds Act 2004 in the circumstances described in paragraph (5).

(5) The circumstances referred to in paragraph (4) are that—

(a) in the proceedings in the First-tier Tribunal in respect of which the appeal has been brought, there was an obligation to keep a person's address confidential; or

(b) a person whose circumstances are relevant to the proceedings would like their address (or, in the case of the person with care of the eligible child, the child's address) to be kept confidential and has given notice to that effect—

    (i) to the Upper Tribunal in an application for permission to appeal or notice of appeal;

    (ii) to the Upper Tribunal within 1 month after an enquiry by the Upper Tribunal; or

    (iii) to HMRC or the Upper Tribunal when notifying a change of address after proceedings have been started.

(6) Where this paragraph applies, HMRC and the Upper Tribunal must take appropriate steps to secure the confidentiality of the address, and of any information which could reasonably be expected to enable a person to identify the address, to the extent that the address or that information is not already known to each other party.

(7) In this rule—

"eligible child" has the meaning set out in section 2 of the Child Trust Funds Act 2004; and

"HMRC" means Her Majesty's Revenue and Customs.

DEFINITIONS

"eligible child"—see para.(7).
"HMRC"—*ibid.*
"party"—see r.1(3).
"permission"—*ibid.*

Power to pay expenses and allowances

20.—(1) In proceedings brought under section 4 of the Safeguarding   5.307
Vulnerable Groups Act 2006 [1. . .], the Secretary of State may pay such
allowances for the purpose of or in connection with the attendance of
persons at hearings as the Secretary of State may, with the consent of the
Treasury, determine.

(2) Paragraph (3) applies to proceedings on appeal from a decision
of—

  (a) the First-tier Tribunal in proceedings under the Child Support Act
      1991, section 12 of the Social Security Act 1998 or paragraph 6 of
      Schedule 7 to the Child Support, Pensions and Social Security Act
      2000;
  (b) the First-tier Tribunal in a war pensions and armed forces case
      (as defined in the Tribunal Procedure (First-tier Tribunal) (War
      Pensions and Armed Forces Compensation Chamber) Rules 2008);
      or
  (c) a Pensions Appeal Tribunal for Scotland or Northern Ireland.

(3) The Lord Chancellor (or, in Scotland, the Secretary of State) may
pay to any person who attends any hearing such travelling and other allowances, including compensation for loss of remunerative time, as the Lord
Chancellor (or, in Scotland, the Secretary of State) may determine.

AMENDMENT

1. Tribunal Procedure (Amendment) Rules 2009 (SI 2009/274), r.12 (April 1,
2009).

DEFINITIONS

"hearing"—see r.1(3).
"judicial review proceedings"—*ibid.*

GENERAL NOTE

Paragraph (1) does not apply to social security cases. Paragraphs (2) and (3)   5.308
reproduce the effect of para.3 of Sch.4 to the Social Security Act 1998. Paragraph
(2) suffers from the same defect as the old provision, which is that it does not apply
to all social security cases in which claimants might be required to attend hearings, although in practice the Tribunals Service seems never to have refused to pay
expenses to those not within the scope of the old provision (e.g. an injured person
appealing against a decision under the Social Security (Recovery of Benefits) Act
1997).

The rule is in also unsatisfactory because it seems unlikely that para.10(4) of
Sch.5 to the Tribunals, Courts and Enforcement Act 2007 envisages Rules that
give the Secretary of State the power to determine what expenses are to be paid,
although it is perhaps more appropriate that the power should lie with the Secretary
of State than with the Tribunal Procedure Committee.

PART 3

[PROCEDURE FOR CASES IN] THE UPPER TRIBUNAL

Application to the Upper Tribunal for permission to appeal

5.309   **21.**—(1) This rule applies to an application for permission to appeal to the Upper Tribunal against any decision.

(2) A person may apply to the Upper Tribunal for permission to appeal to the Upper Tribunal against a decision of another tribunal only if—

(a) they have made an application for permission to appeal to the tribunal which made the decision challenged; and

(b) that application has been refused or has not been admitted.

(3) An application for permission to appeal must be made in writing and received by the Upper Tribunal no later than—

(a) in the case of an application under section 4 of the Safeguarding Vulnerable Groups Act 2006, 3 months after the date on which written notice of the decision being challenged was sent to the appellant; or

(b) otherwise, a month after the date on which the tribunal that made the decision under challenge sent notice of its refusal of permission to appeal, or refusal to admit the application for permission to appeal, to the appellant.

(4) The application must state—

(a) the name and address of the appellant;

(b) the name and address of the representative (if any) of the appellant;

(c) an address where documents for the appellant may be sent or delivered;

(d) details (including the full reference) of the decision challenged;

(e) the grounds on which the appellant relies; and

(f) whether the appellant wants the application to be dealt with at a hearing.

(5) The appellant must provide with the application a copy of—

(a) any written record of the decision being challenged;

(b) any separate written statement of reasons for that decision; and

(c) if the application is for permission to appeal against a decision of another tribunal, the notice of refusal of permission to appeal, or notice of refusal to admit the application for permission to appeal, from that other tribunal.

(6) If the appellant provides the application to the Upper Tribunal later than the time required by paragraph (3) or by an extension of time allowed under rule 5(3)(a) (power to extend time)—

(a) the application must include a request for an extension of time and the reason why the application was not provided in time; and

(b) unless the Upper Tribunal extends time for the application under rule 5(3)(a) (power to extend time) the Upper Tribunal must not admit the application.

(7) If the appellant makes an application to the Upper Tribunal for permission to appeal against the decision of another tribunal, and that other tribunal refused to admit the appellant's application for permission to

appeal because the application for permission or for a written statement of reasons was not made in time—

(a) the application to the Upper Tribunal for permission to appeal must include the reason why the application to the other tribunal for permission to appeal or for a written statement of reasons, as the case may be, was not made in time; and

(b) the Upper Tribunal must only admit the application if the Upper Tribunal considers that it is in the interests of justice for it to do so.

DEFINITIONS

"appellant"—see r.1(3).
"document"—*ibid.*
"hearing"—*ibid.*
"permission"—*ibid.*

GENERAL NOTE

This replaces regs 9 and 10 of the Social Security Commissioners (Procedure) Regs 1999 but without the absolute time limit of 13 months and without any express duty on a public authority to notify a claimant that it has made an application.

5.310

Para. (2)

Paragraph (2) has given rise to some difficulties. Generally, it will be enforced because an application to the First-tier Tribunal gives it the opportunity to review its decision but there are circumstances where the existence of an irregularity emerges only after a case has apparently been properly brought before the Upper Tribunal or where the Upper Tribunal wishes to give permission in a case related to another one already before it. In such cases waiving the requirement to apply to the lower tribunal for permission might be sensible but there is disagreement as to whether it is permissible.

5.310.1

In *HM v SSWP* [2009] UKUT 40 (AAC), the claimant applied to what was then an appeal tribunal for leave to appeal but was then wrongly told that leave had been granted when in fact no decision had been made. The Upper Tribunal held it had no jurisdiction to consider the appeal, referring to *CSCS/4/2008*, where a Commissioner had said that a breach of the similar requirement in reg.9(1) of the Social Security Commissioners (Procedure) Regulations 1999 had not been the sort of irregularity that could be waived. However, in *MA v SSD* [2009] UKUT 57 (AAC), another judge disagreed with that approach and held that, as the requirement to obtain permission was imposed by the Rules rather than by primary legislation, it could be waived under r.7(2)(a). He did not in fact waive it in that case, where a chairman of a Pensions Appeal Tribunal had purported to grant leave to appeal but had done so unlawfully because the application had been made more than 13 months late, in breach of the absolute time-limit that then applied. The Upper Tribunal judge took the view that the Secretary of State should not have the advantage of the time bar removed retrospectively. If the irregularity was on the part of the Pensions Appeal Tribunal rather then the appellant, it is arguable that the power of waiver arose by implication under r.7(1) rather than expressly under r.7(2)(a) (see the note to r.7), although it is also arguable both that the material irregularity lay in the applicant making her application late and that r.21(2) imposes on an appellant a duty to obtain a valid decision so that the appellant is in any event in breach if the decision is invalid.

Paras (3) to (7)

5.310.2   Note that, under para.(3), the application must now be *received* by the Upper
Tribunal within the time limit). The power to extend time is no longer limited to
cases where there are "special reasons" but that may not make much difference
in practice because the same considerations are likely to be relevant (see the note
to r.38(5) of the Tribunal Procedure (First-tier Tribunal) (Social Entitlement
Chamber) Rules 2008, above). Paragraph (7) makes it clear that, where an application for permission made to the First-tier Tribunal was made late but nonetheless
accepted, there is no need for the Upper Tribunal to consider that delay (giving
effect to *CIB/4791/2001*). Paragraph (7) also makes specific provision for cases
where there is no statement of the First-tier Tribunal's reasons due to delay in
applying for one. The word "any" in para.(5)(b) has the effect that there is no
longer an irregularity just because no statement of reasons is submitted in such a
case. However, it remains difficult to demonstrate an error of law without a statement of reasons and, in particular, the First-tier Tribunal's decision cannot be challenged on the ground of inadequacy of reasons in the absence of such a statement
or a duty to provide one (*R(IS) 11/99*).

Decision in relation to permission to appeal

5.311   **22.**—(1) If the Upper Tribunal refuses permission to appeal, it must send
written notice of the refusal and of the reasons for the refusal to the appellant.

(2) If the Upper Tribunal gives permission to appeal—

(a) the Upper Tribunal must send written notice of the permission, and
of the reasons for any limitations or conditions on such permission,
to each party;

(b) subject to any direction by the Upper Tribunal, the application for
permission to appeal stands as the notice of appeal and the Upper
Tribunal must send to each respondent a copy of the application
for permission to appeal and any documents provided with it by the
appellant; and

(c) the Upper Tribunal may, with the consent of the appellant and each
respondent, determine the appeal without obtaining any further
response.

[[1] (3) Paragraph (4) applies where the Upper Tribunal, without a hearing,
determines an application for permission to appeal—

(a) against a decision of—

    (i) the Tax Chamber of the First-tier Tribunal;

    (ii) the Health, Education and Social Care Chamber of the First-
tier Tribunal;

    (iii) the Mental Health Review Tribunal for Wales; or

    (iv) the Special Educational Needs Tribunal for Wales; or

(b) under section 4 of the Safeguarding Vulnerable Groups Act 2006.]

(4) In the circumstances set out at paragraph (3) the appellant may apply
for the decision to be reconsidered at a hearing if the Upper Tribunal—

(a) refuses permission to appeal; or

(b) gives permission to appeal on limited grounds or subject to conditions.

(5) An application under paragraph (4) must be made in writing and
received by the Upper Tribunal within 14 days after the date on which the
Upper Tribunal sent written notice of its decision regarding the application
to the appellant.

AMENDMENT

1. Tribunal Procedure (Amendment) Rules 2009 (SI 2009/274), r.14 (April 1, 2009).

DEFINITIONS

"appellant"—see r.1(3).
"document"—*ibid.*
"hearing"—*ibid.*
"party"—*ibid.*
"permission"—*ibid.*
"respondent"—*ibid.*

GENERAL NOTE

Para. (2)

Generally, applications for permission to appeal are considered without notice to the respondent and, when permission to appeal is granted by the Upper Tribunal, the application stands as the appeal and is sent to the respondent. In social security cases, the Upper Tribunal will have obtained the First-tier Tribunal's file to assist it determine the application and that will form the basis of the bundle of documents sent to the respondent (and to the appellant). The next stage in the proceedings will simply be for the respondent to submit a response under r.24. This is the effect of para.(2)(b).

However, where the respondent has had notice of the application and made submissions on it, it is possible to seek the consent of both parties to the appeal being determined without any further response. This is the effect of para.(2)(c).

5.312

Paras(3) to (5)

These paragraphs do not apply to social security cases on appeal from the Social Entitlement Chamber of the First-tier Tribunal. If the person applying for permission to appeal wants an oral hearing in a social security case, it is necessary to say so in the application for permission (see r.21(4)(f)).

5.313

Notice of appeal

23.—(1) This rule applies—
   (a) if another tribunal has given permission for a party to appeal to the Upper Tribunal; or
   (b) subject to any other direction by the Upper Tribunal, if the Upper Tribunal has given permission to appeal and has given a direction that the application for permission to appeal does not stand as the notice of appeal.

(2) The appellant must provide a notice of appeal to the Upper Tribunal so that it is received within 1 month after the tribunal that gave permission to appeal sent notice of such permission to the appellant.

(3) The notice of appeal must include the information listed in rule 21(4) (a) to (e) (content of the application for permission to appeal) and, where the Upper Tribunal has given permission to appeal, the Upper Tribunal's case reference.

(4) If another tribunal has granted permission to appeal, the appellant must provide with the notice of appeal a copy of—
   (a) any written record of the decision being challenged;
   (b) any separate written statement of reasons for that decision; and
   (c) the notice of permission to appeal.

5.314

(5) If the appellant provides the notice of appeal to the Upper Tribunal later than the time required by paragraph (2) or by an extension of time allowed under rule 5(3)(a) (power to extend time)—

    (a) the notice of appeal must include a request for an extension of time and the reason why the notice was not provided in time; and

    (b) unless the Upper Tribunal extends time for the notice of appeal under rule 5(3)(a) (power to extend time) the Upper Tribunal must not admit the notice of appeal.

(6) When the Upper Tribunal receives the notice of appeal it must send a copy of the notice and any accompanying documents to each respondent.

DEFINITIONS

    "appellant"—see r.1(3).
    "document"—*ibid.*
    "party"—*ibid.*
    "permission"—*ibid.*
    "respondent"—*ibid.*

GENERAL NOTE

Para. (1)

5.315   Because r.22(2)(b) has the effect that an application for permission to appeal in a social security case almost invariably stands as an appeal where the Upper Tribunal has granted permission, this rule generally applies only where the First-tier Tribunal has granted permission to appeal.

Para. (5)

5.316   See the note to r.38(5) of the Tribunal Procedure (First-tier Tribunal) (Social Entitlement Chamber) Rules 2008, above.

Para. (6)

5.317   In practice in social security cases, the Upper Tribunal obtains the First-tier Tribunal's file and constructs its own bundle of documents.

Response to the notice of appeal

5.318   **24.**—(1) Subject to any direction given by the Upper Tribunal, a respondent may provide a response to the notice of appeal.

(2) Any response provided under paragraph (1) must be in writing and must be sent or delivered to the Upper Tribunal so that it is received—

    (a) if the application for permission stands as the notice of appeal, no later than 1 month after the date on which the Upper Tribunal sent notice that it had granted permission to appeal to the respondent; or

    (b) in any other case, no later than 1 month after the date on which the Upper Tribunal sent a copy of the notice of appeal to the respondent.

(3) The response must state—

    (a) the name and address of the respondent;

    (b) the name and address of the representative (if any) of the respondent;

    (c) an address where documents for the respondent may be sent or delivered;

    (d) whether the respondent opposes the appeal;

   (e) the grounds on which the respondent relies, including any grounds on which the respondent was unsuccessful in the proceedings which are the subject of the appeal, but intends to rely in the appeal; and

   (f) whether the respondent wants the case to be dealt with at a hearing.

(4) If the respondent provides the response to the Upper Tribunal later than the time required by paragraph (2) or by an extension of time allowed under rule 5(3)(a) (power to extend time), the response must include a request for an extension of time and the reason why the [¹ response] was not provided in time.

(5) When the Upper Tribunal receives the response it must send a copy of the response and any accompanying documents to the appellant and each other party.

AMENDMENT

1. Tribunal Procedure (Amendment) Rules 2009 (SI 2009/274), r.15 (April 1, 2009).

DEFINITIONS

"appellant"—see r.1(3).
"document"—*ibid.*
"hearing"—*ibid.*
"party"—*ibid.*
"permission"—*ibid.*
"respondent"—*ibid.*

GENERAL NOTE

If there is more than one respondent, this rule has the effect that they must make 5.319 simultaneous responses unless the Upper Tribunal directs otherwise. In practice, it nearly always directs sequential responses from the respondents with the appellant replying after the last respondent has had an opportunity to respond to the appeal.

Appellant's reply

25.—(1) Subject to any direction given by the Upper Tribunal, the appel- 5.320 lant may provide a reply to any response provided under rule 24 (response to the notice of appeal).

(2) Any reply provided under paragraph (1) must be in writing and must be sent or delivered to the Upper Tribunal so that it is received within one month after the date on which the Upper Tribunal sent a copy of the response to the appellant.

(3) When the Upper Tribunal receives the reply it must send a copy of the reply and any accompanying documents to each respondent.

DEFINITIONS

"appellant"—see r.1(3).
"document"—*ibid.*
"respondent"—*ibid.*

GENERAL NOTE

This rule is expressly made subject to a direction by the Upper Tribunal. Where it 5.321 appears to a judge granting permission to appeal that there is an obvious error in a decision of the First-tier Tribunal, it is common for the judge to direct simultaneous observations from all parties in order to speed up the process.

References under the Forfeiture Act 1982

5.322   **26.**—(1) If a question arises which is required to be determined by the Upper Tribunal under section 4 of the Forfeiture Act 1982, the person to whom the application for the relevant benefit or advantage has been made must refer the question to the Upper Tribunal.

(2) The reference must be in writing and must include—

(a) a statement of the question for determination;

(b) a statement of the relevant facts;

(c) the grounds upon which the reference is made; and

(d) an address for sending documents to the person making the reference and each respondent.

(3) When the Upper Tribunal receives the reference it must send a copy of the reference and any accompanying documents to each respondent.

(4) Rules 24 (response to the notice of appeal) and 25 (appellant's reply) apply to a reference made under this rule as if it were a notice of appeal.

DEFINITIONS

"document"—see r.1(3).
"respondent"—*ibid.*

GENERAL NOTE

This rule is made under s.4(2) of the Forfeiture Act 1982.

[¹ Cases transferred or referred to the Upper Tribunal, applications made directly to the Upper Tribunal and proceedings without notice to a respondent

5.323   **26A.**—(1) Paragraphs (2) and (3) apply to a case which—

(a) has been transferred or referred to the Upper Tribunal from the First-tier Tribunal; or

(b) is a case, other than an appeal or a case to which rule 26 (references under the Forfeiture Act 1982) applies, which is started by an application made directly to the Upper Tribunal.

(2) In a case to which this paragraph applies—

(a) the Upper Tribunal must give directions as to the procedure to be followed in the consideration and disposal of the proceedings; and

(b) the preceding rules in this Part will only apply to the proceedings to the extent provided for by such directions.

(3) If a case or matter to which this paragraph applies is to be determined without notice to or the involvement of a respondent—

(a) any provision in these Rules requiring a document to be provided by or to a respondent; and

(b) any other provision in these Rules permitting a respondent to participate in the proceedings does not apply to that case or matter.]

AMENDMENT

1. Tribunal Procedure (Amendment) Rules 2009 (SI 2009/274), r.16 (April 1, 2009).

GENERAL NOTE

This rule makes provision for cases other than appeals and references within the scope of r.26 by effectively leaving it to the Upper Tribunal to give case management directions on a case-by-case basis. It has no application to social security cases, except where a case is referred to the Upper Tribunal under s.9(5)(b) of the Tribunals, Courts and Enforcement Act 2007 or r.7(3) of the Tribunal Procedure (First-tier Tribunal) (Social Entitlement Chamber) Rules 2008.

5.324

PART 4

JUDICIAL REVIEW PROCEEDINGS IN THE UPPER TRIBUNAL

Application of this Part to judicial review proceedings transferred to the Upper Tribunal

27.—(1) When a court transfers judicial review proceedings to the Upper Tribunal, the Upper Tribunal—

5.325

(a) must notify each party in writing that the proceedings have been transferred to the Upper Tribunal; and

(b) must give directions as to the future conduct of the proceedings.

(2) The directions given under paragraph (1)(b) may modify or disapply for the purposes of the proceedings any of the provisions of the following rules in this Part.

(3) In proceedings transferred from the Court of Session under section 20(1) of the 2007 Act, the directions given under paragraph (1)(b) must—

(a) if the Court of Session did not make a first order specifying the required intimation, service and advertisement of the petition, state the Upper Tribunal's requirements in relation to those matters;

(b) state whether the Upper Tribunal will consider summary dismissal of the proceedings; and

(c) where necessary, modify or disapply provisions relating to permission in the following rules in this Part.

DEFINITIONS

"the 2007 Act"—see r.1(3).
"judicial review proceedings"—*ibid.*
"party"—*ibid.*
"permission"—*ibid.*

GENERAL NOTE

This rule applies to judicial review proceedings transferred from a court, as opposed to proceedings started in the Upper Tribunal. Because cases may be transferred at any stage of the proceedings, the Upper Tribunal is given a broad power to give directions as to how the case will proceed and how much of rr.28 to 33 need apply to the case. Rules 28 and 29 cannot apply to cases transferred by the Court of Session, because there is no requirement to obtain permission to apply for judicial review in Scotland. Instead, the Upper Tribunal may hold a preliminary hearing to consider whether summary dismissal of the proceedings is appropriate, which would be equivalent to a first hearing in the Court of Session and has much the same effect as considering whether to refuse permission to apply for judicial review. Hence para. (3)(b) and r.30(2) and (3)(b).

Applications for permission to bring judicial review proceedings

5.326   **28.**—(1) A person seeking permission to bring judicial review proceedings before the Upper Tribunal under section 16 of the 2007 Act must make a written application to the Upper Tribunal for such permission.

(2) Subject to paragraph (3), an application under paragraph (1) must be made promptly and, unless any other enactment specifies a shorter time limit, must be sent or delivered to the Upper Tribunal so that it is received no later than 3 months after the date of the decision [[1], action or omission] to which the application relates.

(3) An application for permission to bring judicial review proceedings challenging a decision of the First-tier Tribunal may be made later than the time required by paragraph (2) if it is made within 1 month after the date on which the First-tier Tribunal sent—

(a) written reasons for the decision; or

(b) notification that an application for the decision to be set aside has been unsuccessful, provided that that application was made in time.

(4) The application must state—

(a) the name and address of the applicant, the respondent and any other person whom the applicant considers to be an interested party;

(b) the name and address of the applicant's representative (if any);

(c) an address where documents for the applicant may be sent or delivered;

(d) details of the decision challenged (including the date, the full reference and the identity of the decision maker);

(e) that the application is for permission to bring judicial review proceedings;

(f) the outcome that the applicant is seeking; and

(g) the facts and grounds on which the applicant relies.

(5) If the application relates to proceedings in a court or tribunal, the application must name as an interested party each party to those proceedings who is not the applicant or a respondent.

(6) The applicant must send with the application—

(a) a copy of any written record of the decision in the applicant's possession or control; and

(b) copies of any other documents in the applicant's possession or control on which the applicant intends to rely.

(7) If the applicant provides the application to the Upper Tribunal later than the time required by paragraph (2) or (3) or by an extension of time allowed under rule 5(3)(a) (power to extend time)—

(a) the application must include a request for an extension of time and the reason why the application was not provided in time; and

(b) unless the Upper Tribunal extends time for the application under rule 5(3)(a) (power to extend time) the Upper Tribunal must not admit the application.

(8) When the Upper Tribunal receives the application it must send a copy of the application and any accompanying documents to each person named in the application as a respondent or interested party.

AMENDMENT

1. Tribunal Procedure (Amendment) Rules 2009 (SI 2009/274), r.17 (April 1, 2009).

DEFINITIONS

"the 2007 Act"—see r.1(3).
"applicant"—*ibid.*
"document"—*ibid.*
"interested party"—*ibid.*
"judicial review proceedings"—*ibid.*
"party"—*ibid.*
"permission"—*ibid.*
"respondent"—*ibid.*

GENERAL NOTE

This rule applies to judicial review proceedings started in the Upper Tribunal   **5.327**
(see the notes to ss.15 and 18 of the Tribunals, Courts and Enforcement Act 2007)
Rule 9 gives the Upper Tribunal wide power to substitute the correct parties and
add additional parties where the applicant fails to identify the correct respondent
and interested party. Where, as will currently always be the case, the decision being
challenged is a decision of the First-tier Tribunal, the respondent will be the First-
tier Tribunal and the parties to the case before the First-tier Tribunal, other than the
applicant, will be interested parties.

Acknowledgment of service

29.—(1) A person who is sent a copy of an application for permission   **5.328**
under rule 28(8) (application for permission to bring judicial review proceedings) and wishes to take part in the proceedings must send or deliver to
the Upper Tribunal an acknowledgment of service so that it is received no
later than 21 days after the date on which the Upper Tribunal sent a copy of
the application to that person.

(2) An acknowledgment of service under paragraph (1) must be in
writing and state—

(a) whether the person intends to [¹ support or] oppose the application
for permission;

(b) their grounds for any [¹ support or] opposition under sub-paragraph
(a), or any other submission or information which it considers may
assist the Upper Tribunal; and

(c) the name and address of any other person not named in the application as a respondent or interested party whom the person providing
the acknowledgment considers to be an interested party.

(3) A person who is sent a copy of an application for permission under
rule 28(8) but does not provide an acknowledgment of service may not take
part in the application for permission, but may take part in the subsequent
proceedings if the application is successful.

AMENDMENTS

1. Tribunal Procedure (Amendment) Rules 2009 (SI 2009/274), r.18 (April 1,
2009).

DEFINITIONS

"interested party"—see r.1(3).
"judicial review proceedings"—*ibid.*
"party"—*ibid.*
"permission"—*ibid.*
"respondent"—*ibid.*

5.329 This rule, including the 21-day time limit, is based on the procedure in the Administrative Court in England and Wales under C.P.R. rr.54.8 and 54.9. The respondent, i.e. the First-tier Tribunal whose decision is being challenged, will only rarely take part in proceedings, so that it will fall to the interested parties to decide whether or not to oppose the application, just as it does on an appeal.

Decision on permission or summary dismissal, and reconsideration of permission or summary dismissal at a hearing

5.330 **30.**—(1) The Upper Tribunal must send to the applicant, each respondent and any other person who provided an acknowledgment of service to the Upper Tribunal, and may send to any other person who may have an interest in the proceedings, written notice of—

(a) its decision in relation to the application for permission; and

(b) the reasons for any refusal of the application, or any limitations or conditions on permission.

(2) In proceedings transferred from the Court of Session under section 20(1) of the 2007 Act, where the Upper Tribunal has considered whether summarily to dismiss of the proceedings, the Upper Tribunal must send to the applicant and each respondent, and may send to any other person who may have an interest in the proceedings, written notice of—

(a) its decision in relation to the summary dismissal of proceedings; and

(b) the reasons for any decision summarily to dismiss part or all of the proceedings, or any limitations or conditions on the continuation of such proceedings.

(3) Paragraph (4) applies where the Upper Tribunal, without a hearing—

(a) determines an application for permission to bring judicial review proceedings and either refuses permission, or gives permission on limited grounds or subject to conditions; or

(b) in proceedings transferred from the Court of Session, summarily dismisses part or all of the proceedings, or imposes any limitations or conditions on the continuation of such proceedings.

(4) In the circumstances specified in paragraph (3) the applicant may apply for the decision to be reconsidered at a hearing.

(5) An application under paragraph (4) must be made in writing and must be sent or delivered to the Upper Tribunal so that it is received within 14 days after the date on which the Upper Tribunal sent written notice of its decision regarding the application to the applicant.

DEFINITIONS

"the 2007 Act"—see r.1(3).
"applicant"—*ibid.*
"hearing"—*ibid.*
"judicial review proceedings"—*ibid.*
"permission"—*ibid.*
"respondent"—*ibid.*

GENERAL NOTE

5.331 This rule is based on the procedure in the Administrative Court in England and Wales under C.P.R. rr.54.10 to 54.12. An application for permission to apply for judicial review that is refused, or is only partially successful, on paper may be renewed at an oral hearing under paras (3)(a) and (4). Dismissal of judicial review proceedings at a first hearing under R.C. r.58.9 is the equivalent in Scotland of a refusal of permission to apply for judicial review in England and Wales or Northern Ireland and so equivalent provision for summary dismissal by the Upper Tribunal is made in paras (3)(b) and (4).

Responses

31.—(1) Any person to whom the Upper Tribunal has sent notice of the grant of permission under rule 30(1) (notification of decision on permission), and who wishes to contest the application or support it on additional grounds, must provide detailed grounds for contesting or supporting the application to the Upper Tribunal.

5.332

(2) Any detailed grounds must be provided in writing and must be sent or delivered to the Upper Tribunal so that they are received not more than 35 days after the Upper Tribunal sent notice of the grant of permission under rule 30(1).

DEFINITION

"permission"—see r.1(3).

GENERAL NOTE

This rule, including the 35-day time limit, is based on the procedure in the Administrative Court in England and Wales under C.P.R. r.54.14(a).

5.333

Applicant seeking to rely on additional grounds

32. The applicant may not rely on any grounds, other than those grounds on which the applicant obtained permission for the judicial review proceedings, without the consent of the Upper Tribunal.

5.334

DEFINITIONS

"applicant"—see r.1(3).
"judicial review proceedings"—*ibid.*
"permission"—*ibid.*

GENERAL NOTE

This rule is based on the procedure in the Administrative Court in England and Wales under C.P.R. r.54.15.

5.335

Right to make representations

33. Each party and, with the permission of the Upper Tribunal, any other person, may—

5.336

(a) submit evidence, except at the hearing of an application for permission;
(b) make representations at any hearing which they are entitled to attend; and
(c) make written representations in relation to a decision to be made without a hearing.

DEFINITIONS

"hearing"—see r.1(3).

"party"—*ibid.*
"permission"—*ibid.*

GENERAL NOTE

5.337   This rule is based on the procedure in the Administrative Court in England and Wales under C.P.R. rr.54.14(b) and 54, 17.

PART 5

HEARINGS

Decision with or without a hearing

5.338   **34.**—(1) Subject to paragraph (2), the Upper Tribunal may make any decision without a hearing.

(2) The Upper Tribunal must have regard to any view expressed by a party when deciding whether to hold a hearing to consider any matter, and the form of any such hearing.

DEFINITIONS

"hearing"—see r.1(3).
"party"—*ibid.*

GENERAL NOTE

5.339   The European Convention on Human Rights does not require a second-tier tribunal such as the Upper Tribunal to hold an oral hearing where there has been an opportunity to have an oral hearing before the First-Tier tribunal (*Hoppe v Germany* [2003] F.L.R. 384). At common law a case can be determined without an oral hearing unless that would be unfair because, for instance, oral evidence is required (*R. (O'Connell) v Parole Board* [2007] EWHC 2591 (Admin); [2008] 1 W.L.R 979) or the case is complex (*R. (Thompson) v Law Society* [2004] EWCA Civ 167 [2004] 1 W.L.R. 2522). It is suggested that the Upper Tribunal is entitled to refuse a request for an oral hearing where oral evidence would be irrelevant and there is no reason to suppose that oral argument could make any difference to the outcome.

A judge who is minded to reject a claimant's appeal despite the fact that it has been supported by the Secretary of State is not bound to direct an oral hearing if no request for a hearing has been made despite an opportunity having been given (*Miller v Secretary of State for Work and Pensions*, 2002 G.W.D. 25–861, IH).

This rule replaces reg.23 of the Social Security Commissioners (Procedure) Regs 1999. Regulation 23(2) specifically sated that, where a request for a hearing was made by a party, "the Commissioner shall grant the request unless he is satisfied that the proceedings can properly be determined without a hearing" but the absence of a similar provision in this rule may well make no difference because a refusal of a request for a hearing must be for a good reason. In practice, requests by unrepresented claimants are often refused because the judge is prepared to decide the case in favour of the claimant or because they are made specifically for the purpose of giving evidence in circumstances where the appeal lies on a point of law in respect of which it is clear the claimant will be unable to provide any assistance. It will normally be appropriate to give a written reason for refusing a request for an oral hearing (see r.40(4)). A direction as to whether there will be a hearing falls within the scope of r.5 (see r.5(3)(f)) and so the provisions of r.6 apply. A person applying for permission to appeal to the Upper Tribunal should indicate whether he or she wants the application to be determined at a hearing (see r.21(4)(f)), which is particularly important in social security cases where there is no right to renew orally an application refused on paper. A respondent should indicate whether or not he or she wishes there to be an oral hearing when submitting a response to an appeal or reference (see r.24(3)(f)) and the appellant is usually asked by the Upper Tribunal to do so when replying, although there is no specific provision to that effect in r.25.

Entitlement to attend a hearing

35. Subject to rule 37(4) (exclusion of a person from a hearing), each party is entitled to attend a hearing.   5.340

DEFINITIONS

"hearing"—see r.1(3).
"party"—*ibid*.

GENERAL NOTE

This rule makes it plain that, except where r.37(4) applies, a party may always   5.341
attend a hearing even when the hearing is in private. By virtue of r.11(3) a properly appointed representative also has a right to attend a hearing, whether or not the party does so. By virtue of r.11(5), a party who attends a hearing may be accompanied by a person acting as a representative or assistant.

Notice of hearings

36.—(1) The Upper Tribunal must give each party entitled to attend a   5.342
hearing reasonable notice of the time and place of the hearing (including any adjourned or postponed hearing) and any change to the time and place of the hearing.

(2) The period of notice under paragraph (1) must be at least 14 days except that—

    (a) in applications for permission to bring judicial review proceedings, the period of notice must be at least 2 working days; and

    (b) the Upper Tribunal may give shorter notice—

        (i) with the parties' consent; or

        (ii) in urgent or exceptional cases.

DEFINITIONS

"hearing"—see r.1(3).
"judicial review proceedings"—*ibid*.
"party"—*ibid*.
"permission"—*ibid*.
"working day"—*ibid*.

Public and private hearings

37.—(1) Subject to the following paragraphs, all hearings must be held   5.343
in public.

(2) The Upper Tribunal may give a direction that a hearing, or part of it, is to be held in private.

(3) Where a hearing, or part of it, is to be held in private, the Upper Tribunal may determine who is entitled to attend the hearing or part of it.

(4) The Upper Tribunal may give a direction excluding from any hearing, or part of it—

(a) any person whose conduct the Upper Tribunal considers is disrupting or is likely to disrupt the hearing;

(b) any person whose presence the Upper Tribunal considers is likely to prevent another person from giving evidence or making submissions freely;

(c) any person who the Upper Tribunal considers should be excluded in order to give effect to a direction under rule 14(2) (withholding information likely to cause harm); or

(d) any person where the purpose of the hearing would be defeated by the attendance of that person [[1]] ; or

(e) a person under the age of eighteen years.]

(5) The Upper Tribunal may give a direction excluding a witness from a hearing until that witness gives evidence.

AMENDMENT

1. Tribunal Procedure (Amendment) Rules 2009 (SI 2009/274), r.19 (April 1, 2009).

DEFINITION

"hearing"—see r.1(3).

GENERAL NOTE

Paras (1) and (2)

5.344   These paragraphs replace reg.24(5) of the Social Security Commissioners (Procedure) Regs 1999. Paragraph (1) expresses the general rule, which is that hearings should usually be in public. Paragraph (2) enables the Upper Tribunal to direct that a particular case be heard in private, either in whole or in part. Although it does not specifically provide that a hearing may take place in public only for "special reasons", as reg.24(5) did, the same considerations will still apply (see the note to r.30(3) of the Tribunal Procedure (First-tier Tribunal) (Social Entitlement Chamber) Rules 2008, above). As in the First-tier Tribunal, this does not arise as a live issue very often because it is very rare for members of the general public to attend hearings.

Where someone does attend, concerns raised by a party can often be met by the imposition of appropriate reporting restrictions under r.14(1).

Para. (3)

5.345   If a case is to be heard in private, the tribunal has a broad power to determine who may attend it. However, certain people have a right to attend a hearing even if it is in private. By r.35, a party always has a right to be present (subject to r.37(4)) and, the consequence is that, by virtue of r.11(3), so does a properly appointed representative whether the party attends or not. Where a party does attend, he or she may be accompanied by a person acting either as a representative or merely as an assistant (see r.11(5)). Plainly relevant witnesses must be allowed to attend for the purpose of giving evidence. By virtue of para.22 of Sch.7 to the Tribunals, Courts and Enforcement Act 2007, a member of the Administrative Justice and Tribunals Council, or its Scottish Committee or Welsh Committee, also has a right to attend any hearing.

Beyond that, it is all a matter of discretion, as it was under reg.24(6)(g) of the Social Security Commissioners (Procedure) Regs 1999. See the note to r.30(4) of the Tribunal Procedure (First-tier Tribunal) (Social Entitlement Chamber) Rules 2008, above.

Paras (4) and (5)

See the notes to r.30(5) and (6) of the Tribunal Procedure (First-tier Tribunal) (Social Entitlement Chamber) Rules 2008, above, but note that a power to exclude children has been added.

Hearings in a party's absence

38. If a party fails to attend a hearing, the Upper Tribunal may proceed with the hearing if the Upper Tribunal—

  (a) is satisfied that the party has been notified of the hearing or that reasonable steps have been taken to notify the party of the hearing; and

  (b) considers that it is in the interests of justice to proceed with the hearing.

5.346

DEFINITIONS

  "hearing"—see r.1(3).
  "party"—*ibid.*

GENERAL NOTE

See the note to r.31 of the Tribunal Procedure (First-tier Tribunal) (Social Entitlement Chamber) Rules 2008, above.

5.347

PART 6

DECISIONS

Consent orders

39.—(1) The Upper Tribunal may, at the request of the parties but only if it considers it appropriate, make a consent order disposing of the proceedings and making such other appropriate provision as the parties have agreed.

(2) Notwithstanding any other provision of these Rules, the Tribunal need not hold a hearing before making an order under paragraph (1)[¹ ...].

5.348

AMENDMENT

1. Tribunal Procedure (Amendment) Rules 2009 (SI 2009/274), r.20 (April 1, 2009).

DEFINITIONS

  "hearing"—see r.1(3).
  "party"—*ibid.*

GENERAL NOTE

This rule may not have a great deal of relevance to social security cases because it is concerned with cases where there needs to be an "order" and where "other appropriate provision" may need to be made and it applies only "at the request of the parties". Where the parties are agreed as to the outcome of a social security case before the Upper Tribunal, it is usually sufficient for the judge to give a decision to that effect under r.40, which may be given without reasons if the parties consent.

5.349

Decisions

5.350   **40.**—(1) The Upper Tribunal may give a decision orally at a hearing.

(2) [¹ ...] The Upper Tribunal must provide to each party as soon as reasonably practicable after making a decision which finally disposes of all issues in the proceedings (except a decision under Part 7)—

    (a) a decision notice stating the Tribunal's decision; and

    (b) notification of any rights of review or appeal against the decision and the time and manner in which such rights of review or appeal may be exercised.

(3) [¹ Subject to rule 14(2) (withholding harmful information,] the Upper Tribunal must provide written reasons for its decision with a decision notice provided under paragraph (2)(a) unless—

    (a) the decision was made with the consent of the parties; or

    (b) the parties have consented to the Upper Tribunal not giving written reasons.

(4) The Tribunal may provide written reasons for any decision to which paragraph (2) does not apply.

AMENDMENTS

1. Tribunal Procedure (Amendment) Rules 2009 (SI 2009/274), r.21 (April 1, 2009).

DEFINITIONS

"hearing"—see r.1(3).
"party"—*ibid.*

GENERAL NOTE

See the notes to rr.33 and 34 of the Tribunal Procedure (First-tier Tribunal) (Social Entitlement Chamber) Rules 2008, above. Presumably the clause "finally disposes of all issues in the proceedings" includes a decision to strike proceedings out under r.8 but does not include a refusal of permission to appeal, a refusal of permission to apply for judicial review or summary dismissal of judicial review proceedings, in respect of all of which specific provision is made (see rr.22(1), 30(1)(b) and 30(2)(b)). In any event, it is usually good practice to provide reasons for any decision (where they may not be obvious to the parties adversely affected by the decision) and para.(4) makes specific provision for that to be done.

A decision given by consent without reasons has effect in the particular proceedings in which it is made but is not binding authority in any other case. Therefore, the Secretary of State was wrong to rely upon directions given in such a case when making a written submission to a Social Security Commissioner (*CSDLA/101/2000*).

PART 7

CORRECTING, SETTING ASIDE, REVIEWING AND APPEALING DECISIONS OF THE
UPPER TRIBUNAL

Interpretation

5.351   **41.** In this Part—

"appeal" [¹ ,except in rule 44(2) (application for permission to appeal),] means the exercise of a right of appeal under section 13 of the 2007 Act; and

"review" means the review of a decision by the Upper Tribunal under section 10 of the 2007 Act.

AMENDMENT

1. Tribunal Procedure (Amendment) Rules 2009 (SI 2009/274), r.22 (April 1, 2009).

DEFINITION

"the 2007 Act"—see r.1(3).

Clerical mistakes and accidental slips or omissions

42. The Upper Tribunal may at any time correct any clerical mistake or other accidental slip or omission in a decision or record of a decision by—
  (a) sending notification of the amended decision, or a copy of the amended record, to all parties; and
  (b) making any necessary amendment to any information published in relation to the decision or record.

    5.352

DEFINITION

"party"—see r.1(3).

GENERAL NOTE

See the note to r.36 of the Tribunal Procedure (First-tier Tribunal) (Social Entitlement Chamber) Rules 2008, above. Note that a separate power to correct a decision arises on review (see s.10(4)(a) of the Tribunals, Courts and Enforcement Act 2007).

Setting aside a decision which disposes of proceedings

43.—(1) The Upper Tribunal may set aside a decision which disposes of proceedings, or part of such a decision, and re-make the decision or the relevant part of it, if—
  (a) the Upper Tribunal considers that it is in the interests of justice to do so; and
  (b) one or more of the conditions in paragraph (2) are satisfied.
(2) The conditions are—
  (a) a document relating to the proceedings was not sent to, or was not received at an appropriate time by, a party or a party's representative;
  (b) a document relating to the proceedings was not sent to the Upper Tribunal at an appropriate time;
  (c) a party, or a party's representative, was not present at a hearing related to the proceedings; or
  (d) there has been some other procedural irregularity in the proceedings.
(3) A party applying for a decision, or part of a decision, to be set aside under paragraph (1) must make a written application to the Upper Tribunal so that it is received no later than 1 month after the date on which the Tribunal sent notice of the decision to the party.

    5.353

DEFINITIONS

"dispose of proceedings"—see r.1(3).
"document"—*ibid.*
"hearing"—*ibid.*
"party"—*ibid.*

GENERAL NOTE

5.354   See the note to r.37 of the Tribunal Procedure (First-tier Tribunal) (Social Entitlement Chamber) Rules 2008, above. The one-month time limit for making an application may be extended under r.5(3)(a). Note that a separate power to set aside a decision arises on review (see s.10(4)(c) of the 2007 Act).

Application for permission to appeal

5.355   **44.**—(1) A person seeking permission to appeal must make a written application to the Upper Tribunal for permission to appeal.

(2) Paragraph (3) applies to an application under paragraph (1) in respect of a decision—

(a) on an appeal against a decision in a social security and child support case (as defined in the Tribunal Procedure (First-tier Tribunal) (Social Entitlement Chamber) Rules 2008);

(b) on an appeal against a decision in proceedings in the War Pensions and Armed Forces Compensation Chamber of the First-tier Tribunal); [¹ . . .]

[¹ (ba) on an appeal against a decision of a Pensions Appeal Tribunal for Scotland or Northern Ireland; or]

(c) in proceedings under the Forfeiture Act 1982.

(3) Where this paragraph applies, the application must be sent or delivered to the Upper Tribunal so that it is received within 3 months after the date on which the Upper Tribunal sent to the person making the application—

(a) written notice of the decision;

(b) notification of amended reasons for, or correction of, the decision following a review; or

(c) notification that an application for the decision to be set aside has been unsuccessful.

(4) Where paragraph (3) does not apply, an application under paragraph (1) must be sent or delivered to the Upper Tribunal so that it is received within 1 month after the latest of the dates on which the Upper Tribunal sent to the person making the application—

(a) written reasons for the decision;

(b) notification of amended reasons for, or correction of, the decision following a review; or

(c) notification that an application for the decision to be set aside has been unsuccessful.

(5) The date in paragraph (3)(c) or (4)(c) applies only if the application for the decision to be set aside was made within the time stipulated in rule 43 (setting aside a decision which disposes of proceedings) or any extension of that time granted by the Upper Tribunal.

(6) If the person seeking permission to appeal provides the application to the Upper Tribunal later than the time required by paragraph (3) or (4), or by any extension of time under rule 5(3)(a) (power to extend time)—

(a) the application must include a request for an extension of time and the reason why the application notice was not provided in time; and

(b) unless the Upper Tribunal extends time for the application under rule 5(3)(a) (power to extend time) the Upper Tribunal must refuse the application.

(7) An application under paragraph (1) must—

(a) identify the decision of the Tribunal to which it relates;

(b) identify the alleged error or errors of law in the decision; and

(c) state the result the party making the application is seeking.

AMENDMENTS

1. Tribunal Procedure (Amendment) Rules 2009 (SI 2009/274), r.23 (April 1, 2009).

DEFINITIONS

"appeal"—see r.41.
"dispose of proceedings"—see r.1(3).
"party"—*ibid.*
"permission"—*ibid.*

GENERAL NOTE

Paragraph (3), which prescribes a three-month time limit, applies to social security cases, rather than para.(4). This generous time-limit existed under the earlier legislation because it is commonly only at this stage that parties, including the Secretary of State, HMRC and local authorities, first seek legal advice.

Note that para.(6)(b) uses the word "refuse", from which it follows that a decision by the Upper Tribunal not to extend the time for applying for permission to appeal does not prevent the applicant from applying to the appellate court for permission, although the appellate court will, of course, have regard to the delay in applying to the Upper Tribunal. This is because the condition in s.13(5) of the Tribunals, Courts and Enforcement Act 2007 (that permission have been "refused" by the Upper Tribunal before an application may be made to the appellate court) will have been satisfied. Thus, the effect of *White v Chief Adjudication Officer* [1986] 2 All E.R. 905 (also reported as an appendix to *R(S) 8/85*) has at last been reversed. In *White*, it had been held that a Commissioner's refusal to extend time for applying for leave to appeal to the Court of Appeal did not amount to a refusal of leave to appeal and was challengeable only by way of an application for judicial review.

Upper Tribunal's consideration of application for permission to appeal

45.—(1) On receiving an application for permission to appeal the Upper Tribunal may review the decision in accordance with rule 46 (review of a decision), but may only do so if—

(a) when making the decision the Upper Tribunal overlooked a legislative provision or binding authority which could have had a material effect on the decision; or

(b) since the Upper Tribunal's decision, a court has made a decision which is binding on the Upper Tribunal and which, had it been made before the Upper Tribunal's decision, could have had a material effect on the decision.

5.356

(2) If the Upper Tribunal decides not to review the decision, or reviews the decision and decides to take no action in relation to the decision or part of it, the Upper Tribunal must consider whether to give permission to appeal in relation to the decision or that part of it.

(3) The Upper Tribunal must send a record of its decision to the parties as soon as practicable.

(4) If the Upper Tribunal refuses permission to appeal it must send with the record of its decision—

    (a) a statement of its reasons for such refusal; and

    (b) notification of the right to make an application to the relevant appellate court for permission to appeal and the time within which, and the method by which, such application must be made.

(5) The Upper Tribunal may give permission to appeal on limited grounds, but must comply with paragraph (4) in relation to any grounds on which it has refused permission.

DEFINITIONS

    "appeal"—see r.41.
    "permission"—see r.1(3).
    "party"—*ibid.*
    "review"—see r.41.

GENERAL NOTE

Paras (1) and (2)

5.357   Before deciding whether or not to grant permission to appeal, the Upper Tribunal must first decide whether or not to review the decision under s.10 of the Tribunals, Courts and Enforcement Act 2007, as limited by para.(1). A decision may be reviewed only if the judge overlooked an important piece of legislation or case law or superior court has since made a decision that suggests that the decision of the Upper Tribunal was wrong. The word "could" is used, which perhaps suggests that the Upper Tribunal might set aside a decision before hearing full argument rather than obtaining representations before deciding whether or not the decision should be reviewed.

Para.(4)

Reasons for refusing permission to appeal can usually be very brief and will often simply be that the application does not raise any point of law or does not raise an important point of principle and practice, as required by the Order made under s.13(6) of the 2007 Act (see the note to that provision), or that a new point of law would not have persuaded the judge to reach a different conclusion. Reasons can be valuable in persuading an applicant not to make an application to the appellate court in a hopeless case. If an application raises allegations about the conduct of the Upper Tribunal, it is likely to assist the court if the Upper Tribunal makes it clear whether it disputes the accuracy of the allegations.

Review of a decision

5.358   **46.**—(1) The Upper Tribunal may only undertake a review of a decision—

    (a) pursuant to rule 45(1) (review on an application for permission to appeal); or

(b) pursuant to rule 47 (reviews of decisions in proceedings under the Forfeiture Act 1982).

(2) The Upper Tribunal must notify the parties in writing of the outcome of any review and of any rights of review or appeal in relation to the outcome.

(3) If the Upper Tribunal decides to take any action in relation to a decision following a review without first giving every party an opportunity to make representations, the notice under paragraph (2) must state that any party that did not have an opportunity to make representations may apply for such action to be set aside and for the decision to be reviewed again.

DEFINITIONS

"appeal"—see r.41.
"party"—see r.1(3).
"review"—see r.41.

GENERAL NOTE

Para. (1)

The power of review arises under s.10(1) of the Tribunals, Courts and Enforcement Act 2007. Section 10(2) provides for the power to be exercised either on the tribunal's initiative or on an application but s.10(3)(b) enables rules to provide that it is exercisable only on the Upper Tribunal's own initiative. That is what para.(1)(a) of this rule does. Except in a forfeiture case falling within r.47, a party may not make a free-standing application for a review (although if he or she does, the Upper Tribunal could presumably treat it as an application permission to appeal, despite the absence of an equivalent to r.41 of the Tribunal Procedure (First-tier Tribunal) (Social Entitlement Chamber) Rules 2008) but the Upper Tribunal may review a decision on its own initiative once there has been an application for permission to appeal. Rule 45(1), made under s.10(3)(d), limits the ground of review to cases where the Upper Tribunal overlooked a legislative provision or binding authority or there has since been a new binding authority. Since appeals under s.13 lie only on points of law, a review therefore provides a way of avoiding an appeal where the appeal would plainly be allowed or where the Upper Tribunal ought to deal with an overlooked issue before the question of permission to appeal is considered. See s.10(4), (5) and (6) for the powers of the Upper Tribunal on review.

5.359

Para. (2)

Section 13(8)(d) has the effect that there is no right of appeal against a decision whether or not to review a decision, to take no action on a review, to set aside a decision on a review or to refer, or not refer, a matter to the Upper Tribunal on review. However, that is because there is always another decision that may be the subject of an appeal. Where the Upper Tribunal refuses to review a decision or reviews it but takes no action, the Upper Tribunal must consider whether to give permission to appeal against the original decision. Where the tribunal reviews a decision and either takes action itself or refers it to the Upper Tribunal to be redecided, there will be a right to apply for permission to appeal against the new decision.

Where a decision is reviewed without all the parties having had the opportunity to make representations, notice must also be given of the right to apply for the new decision to be set aside (see para.(3)).

5.360

Para. (3)

5.361   The clear implication of this paragraph is that the Upper Tribunal may either obtain submissions from the parties other than the applicant before reviewing a case or review the case first and then wait to see whether any of the other parties objects. Plainly the second of those approaches may lead to a quicker decision and less work where there is no objection to the review. However, it is suggested that that approach is appropriate only where both the ground of review and the appropriate decision are very clear.

Review of a decision in proceedings under the Forfeiture Act 1982

5.362   **47.**—(1) A person who referred a question to the Upper Tribunal under rule 26 (references under the Forfeiture Act 1982) must refer the Upper Tribunal's previous decision in relation to the question to the Upper Tribunal if they—

(a) consider that the decision should be reviewed; or

(b) have received a written application for the decision to be reviewed from the person to whom the decision related.

(2) The Upper Tribunal may review the decision if—

(a) the decision was erroneous in point of law;

(b) the decision was made in ignorance of, or was based on a mistake as to, some material fact; or

(c) there has been a relevant change in circumstances since the decision was made.

(3) When a person makes the reference to the Upper Tribunal, they must also notify the person to whom the question relates that the reference has been made.

(4) The Upper Tribunal must notify the person who made the reference and the person who to whom the question relates of the outcome of the reference.

(5) If the Upper Tribunal decides to take any action in relation to a decision following a review under this rule without first giving the person who made the reference and the person to whom the question relates an opportunity to make representations, the notice under paragraph (4) must state that either of those persons who did not have an opportunity to make representations may apply for such action to be set aside and for the decision to be reviewed.

DEFINITION

"review"—see r.41.

GENERAL NOTE

5.363   Wide grounds of review are provided for in cases under the Forfeiture Act 1982, where the Upper Tribunal is the primary fact-finding body and there is no other mechanism for dealing with errors of fact that might have been made. This rule largely reproduces the effect of reg.15(2) and (3) of the Social Security Commissioners (Procedure) Regs 1999. The effect of paragraph (4) of reg.15 has not been reproduced and it is therefore merely left implicit that the Upper Tribunal may determine the date from which the review takes effect. Note that, by virtue of s.13(8)(d) of the Tribunals, Courts and Enforcement Act 2007, there is no right of appeal against a refusal to review an earlier decision or to take no action on a review and in some cases there may be no effective right of appeal against the original decision either, since such appeals are limited to points of law.

Practice Direction (First-Tier And Upper Tribunals: Child, Vulnerable Adult And Sensitive Witnesses)

1. In this Practice Direction:
   a. "child" means a person who has not attained the age of 18;
   b. "vulnerable adult" has the same meaning as in the Safeguarding Vulnerable Groups Act 2006;
   c. "sensitive witness" means an adult witness where the quality of evidence given by the witness is likely to be diminished by reason of fear or distress on the part of the witness in connection with giving evidence in the case.

5.364

Circumstances under which a child, vulnerable adult or sensitive witness may give evidence

2. A child, vulnerable adult or sensitive witness will only be required to attend as a witness and give evidence at a hearing where the Tribunal determines that the evidence is necessary to enable the fair hearing of the case and their welfare would not be prejudiced by doing so.

5.365

3. In determining whether it is necessary for a child, vulnerable adult or sensitive witness to give evidence to enable the fair hearing of a case the Tribunal should have regard to all the available evidence and any representations made by the parties.
4. In determining whether the welfare of the child, vulnerable adult or sensitive witness would be prejudiced it may be appropriate for the Tribunal to invite submissions from interested persons, such as a child's parents.
5. The Tribunal may decline to issue a witness summons under the Tribunal Procedure Rules or to permit a child, vulnerable adult or sensitive witness to give evidence where it is satisfied that the evidence is not necessary to enable the fair hearing of the case and must decline to do so where the witness's welfare would be prejudiced by them giving evidence.

Manner in which evidence is given

6. The Tribunal must consider how to facilitate the giving of any evidence by a child, vulnerable adult or sensitive witness.

5.366

7. It may be appropriate for the Tribunal to direct that the evidence should be given by telephone, video link or other means directed by the Tribunal, or to direct that a person be appointed for the purpose of the hearing who has the appropriate skills or experience in facilitating the giving of evidence by a child, vulnerable adult or sensitive witness.
8. This Practice Direction is made by the Senior President of Tribunals with the agreement of the Lord Chancellor. It is made in the exercise of powers conferred by the Tribunals, Courts and Enforcement Act 2007.

LORD JUSTICE CARNWATH
Senior President of Tribunals
30 October 2008

Practice Direction (First-Tier And Upper Tribunals: Use Of The Welsh Language In Tribunals In Wales)

General

5.367

1. The purpose of this Practice Direction is to reflect the principle of the Welsh Language Act 1993 that in the administration of justice in Wales, the English and Welsh languages should be treated on a basis of equality.

2. In this Practice Direction "Welsh case" means a case which is before the Tribunal in which all "individual parties" are resident in Wales or which has been classified as a Welsh case by the Tribunal. An "individual party" is a party other than a Government Department or Agency. Where not all of the "individual parties" are resident in Wales the Tribunal will decide whether the case should be classified as a Welsh case or not.

Use of the Welsh language

5.368

3. In a Welsh case the Welsh language may be used by any party or witnesses or in any document placed before the Tribunal or (subject to the listing provisions below) at any hearing.

Listing

5.369

4. Unless it is not reasonably practicable to do so a party, or their representative, must inform the Tribunal 21 days before any hearing in a Welsh case that the Welsh language will be used by the party, their representative, any witness to be called by that party or in any document to be produced by the party.

5. Where the proceedings are on appeal to the Upper Tribunal and the Welsh language was used in the Tribunal below, the Tribunal Manager must make arrangements for the continued use of the Welsh language in the proceedings before the Upper Tribunal.

6. Where practicable, a hearing in which the Welsh language is to be used must be listed before a Welsh speaking Tribunal and, where translation facilities are needed, at a venue with simultaneous translation facilities.

Interpreters

5.370

7. Whenever an interpreter is needed to translate evidence from English into Welsh or from Welsh into English, the Tribunal Manager in whose tribunal the case is to be heard must ensure that the attendance is secured of an interpreter whose name is included in the list of approved interpreters.

Witnesses

5.371

8. When a witness in a case in which the Welsh language may be used is required to give evidence on oath or affirmation the Tribunal must inform the witness that they may be sworn or affirm in Welsh or English as they wish.

9. This Practice Direction is made by the Senior President of Tribunals with the agreement of the Lord Chancellor. It is made in the exercise of powers conferred by the Tribunals, Courts and Enforcement Act 2007.

LORD JUSTICE CARNWATH
Senior President of Tribunals
30 October 2008

Practice Direction (Upper Tribunal: Transcripts Of Proceedings)

1. At any hearing where the proceedings are recorded such recordings must be preserved by the Tribunal for six months from the date of the hearing to which the recording relates, and any party to the proceedings may, within that period, apply in writing for a transcript and a transcript must be supplied to that party.

2. If a transcript is supplied to a party under paragraph 1, that party must pay for the production and supply of the transcript unless they have applied in writing for, and the Tribunal has given, a direction that the transcript be produced and supplied at public expense.

3. The Tribunal may direct a transcript be supplied at public expense if satisfied that:
   a. a recording of the relevant proceedings is in existence; and
   b. the party making the application;
      i. has applied, or intends to apply, for permission to challenge the Upper Tribunal's decision in another court and has reasonable grounds for bringing or intending to challenge that decision; or
      ii. has been granted permission to challenge the Upper Tribunal's decision and has brought, or intends to bring, such proceedings; or
      iii. is a respondent to any such challenge to a decision of the Upper Tribunal in another court; and
   c. the transcript is necessary for the purpose of challenging the Upper Tribunal's decision; and
   d. the party's financial circumstances are such that that party cannot afford to pay for the transcript from their own income or funds.

4. Any transcript of proceedings directed to be supplied at public expense must be restricted to that part of the proceedings necessary for the purposes of any such challenge.

5. For the purposes of considering an application for a transcript at public expense, the Tribunal may give directions, for example, requiring the party to disclose details of their financial circumstances.

6. This Practice Direction is made by the Senior President of Tribunals with the agreement of the Lord Chancellor. It is made in the exercise of powers conferred by the Tribunals, Courts and Enforcement Act 2007.

LORD JUSTICE CARNWATH
Senior President of Tribunals
30 October 2008

5.372

INDEX

LEGAL TAXONOMY
FROM SWEET & MAXWELL

This index has been prepared using Sweet and Maxwell's Legal Taxonomy. Main index entries conform to keywords provided by the Legal Taxonomy except where references to specific documents or non-standard terms (denoted by quotation marks) have been included. These keywords provide a means of identifying similar concepts in other Sweet & Maxwell publications and online services to which keywords from the Legal Taxonomy have been applied. Readers may find some minor differences between terms used in the text and those which appear in the index. Suggestions to *sweetandmaxwell.taxonomy@thomson.com*.

(All references are to paragraph number)

Abuse of rights
generally, 4.87
Accidents
Council Regulation
aggravation, 3.251
general note, 3.240–3.241
implementing regulations, 3.411–3.428
miscellaneous, 3.252–3.253
reimbursement between institutions, 3.254
rights to benefits, 3.242–3.250
students, 3.255
industrial injuries benefits
notification, 1.47–1.49
"Accommodation costs"
payment of benefit, 2.247
Adjudication (benefits)
introduction, 1.75
Adjudication officers
transfer of functions, 1.329
Adjustment (benefits)
child benefit, 1.130–1.131
child maintenance, 1.120–1.121
income support, 1.113–1.119
overlapping benefits, 1.110–1.112
Administration
See **Social security administration**
Administrative Commission on Social Security for Migrant Workers
generally, 3.286
tasks, 3.287–3.288
Advance claims
disability living allowance, 2.132–2.133
disability working allowance, 2.134–2.135
generally, 2.130–2.131
maternity allowance, 2.140
pension following deferment, for, 2.145–2.146
retirement pensions, 2.141–2.142
state pension credit, 2.139
Advisory bodies
Administrative Commission on Social Security for Migrant Workers

generally, 3.286
tasks, 3.287–3.288
Advisory Committee on Social Security for Migrant Workers
generally, 3.289
tasks, 3.290
Industrial Injuries Advisory Council
cases where consultation not required, 1.205
functions, 1.204
generally, 1.203
Social Security Advisory Committee
cases where consultation not required, 1.205
functions, 1.204
generally, 1.201–1.202
Advisory Committee on Social Security for Migrant Workers
generally, 3.289
tasks, 3.290
Age
provision of information, 1.149–1.150
Age addition
claims for benefit, 2A.73–2A.74
imprisonment, 2.467–2.469
Age-related payments
employment and support allowance, 1.193
income support, 1.188–1.190
job-seeker's allowance, 1.191–1.192
Aggregation
accidents at work, 3.251
death grants, 3.256
family benefits, 3.272
general rules, 3.364
invalidity, 3.222
maternity, 3.186
sickness, 3.186
unemployment benefits, 3.260
Alienation (benefits)
generally, 1.219–1.221
Aliens
human rights, 4.86

1433